Georgia, North Carolina & South Carolina

Are we meeting your travel needs?
Send written comments to:

AAA Member Comments
1000 AAA Drive, Box 61
Heathrow, FL 32746-5063

Published by AAA Publishing
1000 AAA Drive
Heathrow, FL 32746-5063

Advertising Rate and Circulation Information: (407) 444-8280

Printed in the USA by Quebecor World, Buffalo, NY

Photo Credit: (Cover & Title Page)
Providence Canyon State Park, Lumpkin, GA
© James Randklev Photography

Printed on recyclable paper.
Please recycle whenever possible.

Mixed Sources
Product group from well-managed forests and other controlled sources
www.fsc.org Cert no. SW-COC-002550
© 1996 Forest Stewardship Council

Stock #4610

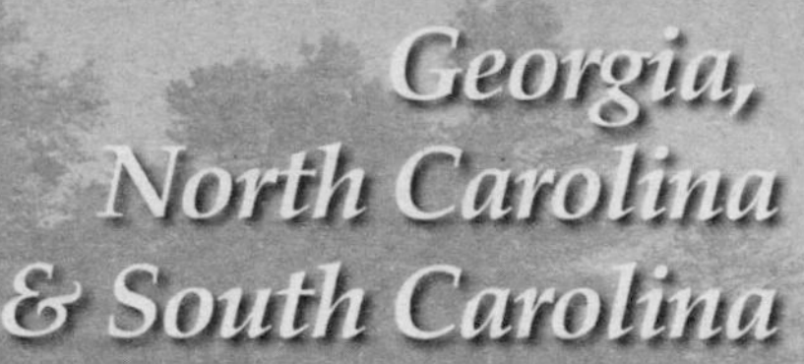

■ Georgia

■ North Carolina

■ *South Carolina*

Featured Information

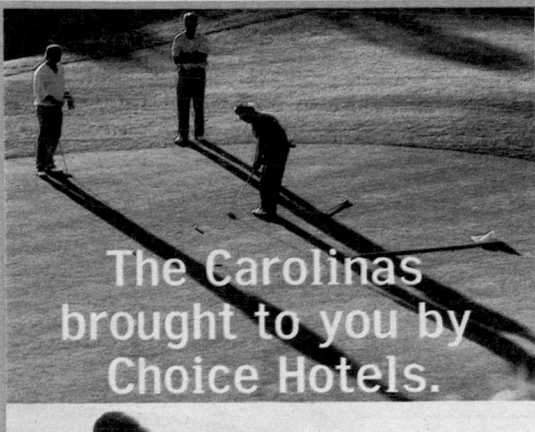

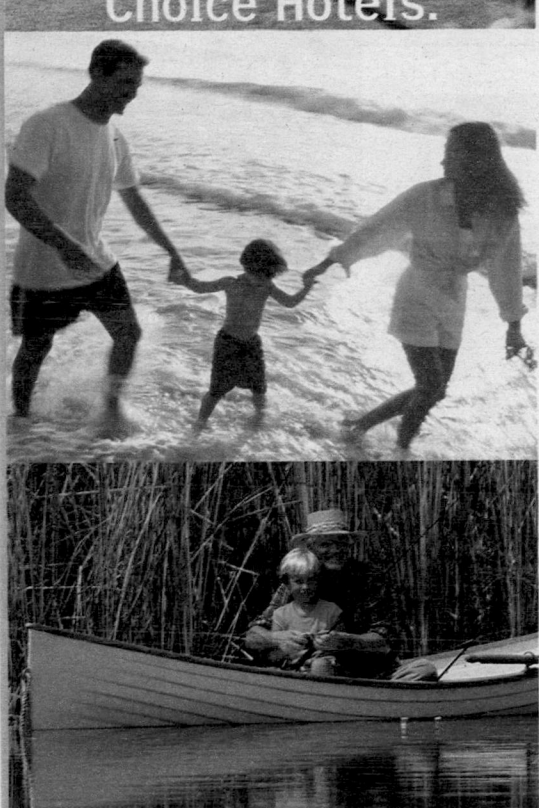

Tips for AAA.com's

Quick tips for using TripTik® Travel Planner's enhanced features.

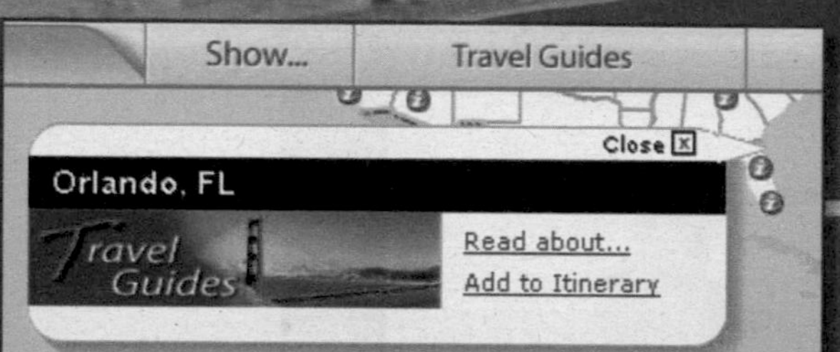

TRAVEL GUIDE
Select the 'Travel Guides' button to get AAA's exclusive travel information.

HOTEL BOOKING AT LOW RATES
Click to book partner hotels at low online rates.

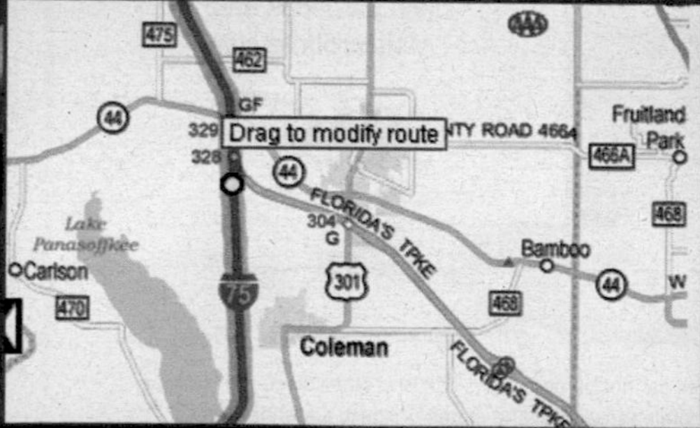

CLICK AND DRAG ROUTE MODIFICATION
Click and drag the route to the roads you prefer to travel.

USING YOUR GUIDE

Attractions, lodgings and restaurants are listed on the basis of merit alone after careful evaluation and approval by one of AAA/CAA's full-time, professionally trained inspectors. Evaluations are unannounced to ensure that we see an establishment just as you would see it.

An establishment's decision to advertise in the TourBook guide has no bearing on its evaluation or rating. Advertising for services or products does not imply AAA endorsement.

Information in this guide was believed accurate at the time of publication. However, since changes inevitably occur between annual editions, we suggest you work with your AAA travel professional or check on AAA.com to confirm prices and schedules.

How the TourBook Guide is Organized

The TourBook guide is organized into three distinct sections.

The **Points of Interest** section helps you plan daily activities and sightseeing excursions and provides details about the city or attraction you are visiting.

The **Lodgings and Restaurants** section helps you select AAA Approved accommodations and dining facilities meeting your specific needs and expectations.

The **Reference** section provides indexes for locating information within this guide and items to aid the trip planning process.

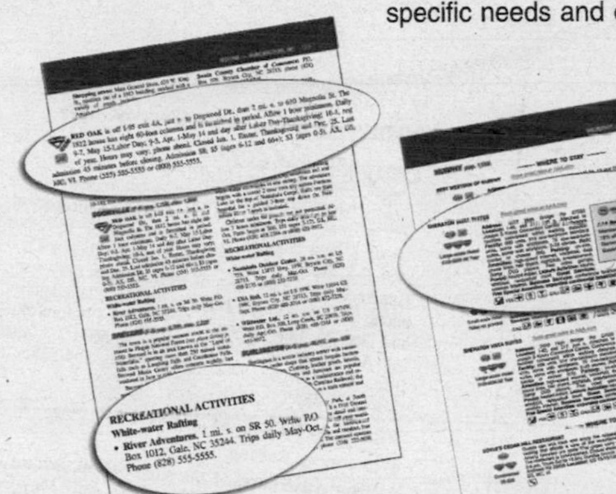

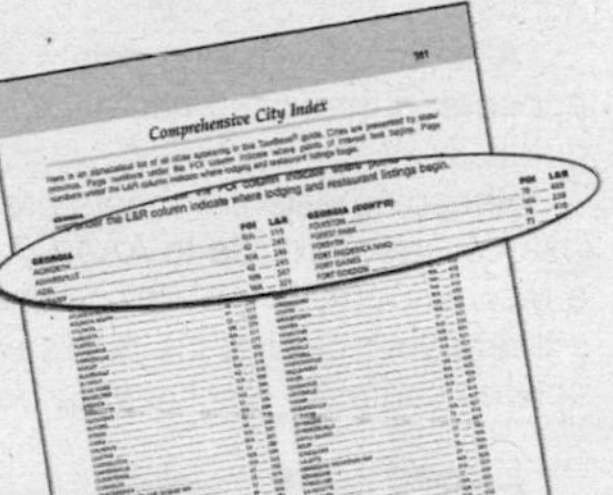

Locating the Attractions, Lodgings and Restaurants

Attractions, lodgings and restaurants are listed under the city in which they physically are located - or in some cases under the nearest recognized city. Most listings are alphabetically organized by state, province, region or island, then by city and establishment name.

A color is assigned to each state or province so that you can match the color bars at the top of the page to switch from the **Points of Interest** section to the **Lodgings and Restaurants** section.

Spotting maps help you physically locate points of interest, lodgings and restaurants in the major destinations.

The Comprehensive City Index located in the **Reference** section contains an A-to-Z list of cities.

Destination Cities and Destination Areas

Destination cities, established based on government models and local expertise, include metropolitan areas plus nearby vicinity cities. **Destination areas** are regions with broad tourist appeal; several cities will comprise the area.

If a city falls within a destination's vicinity, the city name will appear at its alphabetical location in the book, and a cross reference will give you the exact page on which listings for that city begin.

An orientation map appears at the beginning of each destination section to familiarize you with that destination.

Understanding the Points of Interest Listing

GEM Designation

A [GEM icon] indicates the attraction has been rated a AAA GEM, a "must see" point of interest that offers a *Great Experience for Members®*. These attractions have been judged to be of exceptional interest and quality by AAA Inspectors.

A GEM listing page with a brief description of individual GEM attractions follows the Orientation map near the beginning of each state or province Points of Interest section. Cross-references guide the reader to the attraction's listing page.

Discount Savings

The [SAVE] icon denotes those attractions offering AAA/CAA, AAA MasterCard, AAA VISA or international Show Your Card & Save discount cardholders a discount off the attraction's standard admission. Present your card at the attraction's admission desk.

A list of participating points of interest appears in the Reference section of this guide.

Shopping establishments preceded by a [SAVE] icon also provide to AAA/CAA members a discount and/or gift with purchase; present your card at the mall's customer service center to receive your benefit.

Exceptions

- Members should inquire in advance concerning the validity of the discount for special rates.
- The [SAVE] discount may not be used in conjunction with other discounts.
- Attractions that already provide a reduced senior or child rate may not honor the [SAVE] discount for those age groups.
- All offers are subject to change and may not apply during special events, particular days or seasons or for the entire validity period of the TourBook guide.

Adventure Travel

There are inherent risks with adventure travel activities like air tours, hiking, skiing and white-water rafting. For your own safety, please read and adhere to all safety instructions. Mentions of these activities are for information only and do **not** imply endorsement by AAA.

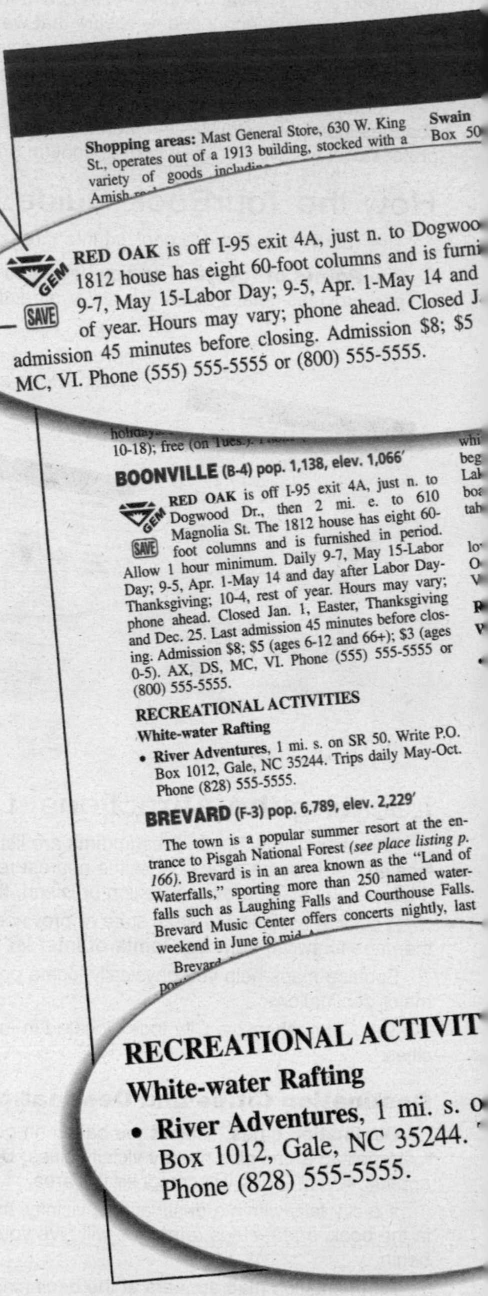

Shopping areas: Mast General Store, 630 W. King St., operates out of a 1913 building, stocked with a variety of goods including ... Amish ...

RED OAK is off I-95 exit 4A, just n. to Dogwoo... 1812 house has eight 60-foot columns and is furni... 9-7, May 15-Labor Day; 9-5, Apr. 1-May 14 and ... of year. Hours may vary; phone ahead. Closed J... admission 45 minutes before closing. Admission $8; $5 ... MC, VI. Phone (555) 555-5555 or (800) 555-5555.

10-18); free (on Tues.) ...

BOONVILLE (B-4) pop. 1,138, elev. 1,066'

RED OAK is off I-95 exit 4A, just n. to Dogwood Dr., then 2 mi. e. to 610 Magnolia St. The 1812 house has eight 60-foot columns and is furnished in period. Allow 1 hour minimum. Daily 9-7, May 15-Labor Day; 9-5, Apr. 1-May 14 and day after Labor Day-Thanksgiving; 10-4, rest of year. Hours may vary; phone ahead. Closed Jan. 1, Easter, Thanksgiving and Dec. 25. Last admission 45 minutes before closing. Admission $8; $5 (ages 6-12 and 66+); $3 (ages 0-5). AX, DS, MC, VI. Phone (555) 555-5555 or (800) 555-5555.

RECREATIONAL ACTIVITIES

White-water Rafting

- **River Adventures**, 1 mi. s. on SR 50. Write P.O. Box 1012, Gale, NC 35244. Trips daily May-Oct. Phone (828) 555-5555.

BREVARD (F-3) pop. 6,789, elev. 2,229'

The town is a popular summer resort at the entrance to Pisgah National Forest *(see place listing p. 166)*. Brevard is in an area known as the "Land of Waterfalls," sporting more than 250 named waterfalls such as Laughing Falls and Courthouse Falls. Brevard Music Center offers concerts nightly, last weekend in June to mid-...

RECREATIONAL ACTIVIT...

White-water Rafting

- **River Adventures,** 1 mi. s. o... Box 1012, Gale, NC 35244. ... Phone (828) 555-5555.

NE — BURLINGTON, NC 125

y Chamber of Commerce: P.O.
son City, NC 28713; phone (828)

, then 2 mi. e. to 610 Magnolia St. The
in period. Allow 1 hour minimum. Daily
after Labor Day-Thanksgiving; 10-4, rest
, Easter, Thanksgiving and Dec. 25. Last
6-12 and 66+); $3 (ages 0-5). AX, DS,

, departing
Bryson City, combines rail and
er excursions in one outing. The adventure
th a scenic 2-hour train trip across Fontana
he top of Nantahala Gorge. Rafts are then
for a guided 3-hour trip down the Nan-
ver. Lunch is included.
en under 60 pounds are not permitted. Al-
ours minimum. Trips daily mid-Apr. to late
es begin at $66; $51 (ages 3-12). DS, MC,
ne (828) 488-2384 or (800) 451-9972.

EATIONAL ACTIVITIES
water Rafting

tahala Outdoor Center, 26 mi. s.w. on US
. Write 13077 Hwy. 19W, Bryson City, NC
13. Trips daily Mar.-Oct. Phone (828)
-2175 or (800) 232-7238.

A Raft, 12 mi. s. on US 19W. Write 11044 US
W, Bryson City, NC 28713. Trips daily Mar.-
pt. Phone (828) 488-3316 or (800) 872-7238.

Vildwater Ltd., 12 mi. s.w. on US 19/74W.
Vrite P.O. Box 309, Long Creek, SC 29658. Trips
aily Apr.-Oct. Phone (828) 488-2384 or (800)
451-9972.

URLINGTON (A-5) pop. 44,917, elev. 656'
Burlington is a textile industry center with numer-
outlet shops that attract bargain hunters
. Clothing, leather goods, towels,
and furniture are popular
as a maintenance and re-
Carolina Railroad; the
as a train station and

S

SR 50. Write P.O.
ps daily May-Oct.

ty Park, at South
is a 1910 Dentzel
ir detail and intri-
s still exist world-
, the hand-carved
ffe and reindeer, four
. The carousel operates
, phone (336) 222-5030.

Directions

Unless otherwise specified, directions are given from the center of town, using the following highway designations:

I=interstate highway
SR=state route
FM=farm to market
Mex.=Mexican highway
US=federal highway
CR=county road
FR=forest road
Hwy.=Canadian or Caribbean highway

Prices and Dates of Operations

Admission prices are quoted without sales tax. Children under the lowest age specified are admitted free when accompanied by an adult. Days, months and age groups written with a hyphen are inclusive.

Prices pertaining to points of interest in the United States are quoted in U.S. dollars; points of interest in Canada are quoted in Canadian dollars; prices for points of interest in Mexico and the Caribbean are quoted as an approximate U.S. dollar equivalent.

Schedules and admission rates may change throughout the validity period of this guide. Check AAA.com for the most current information.

Credit Cards Accepted

AX=American Express
CB=Carte Blanche
DC=Diners Club
DS=Discover
JC=Japan Credit Bureau
MC=MasterCard
VI=VISA

Bulleted Listings

Gambling establishments within hotels are presented for member information regardless of whether the lodging is AAA Approved.

Recreational activities of a participatory nature (requiring physical exertion or special skills) are not inspected.

Wineries are inspected by AAA Inspectors to ensure they meet listing requirements and offer tours.

All are presented in an abbreviated bulleted format for informational purposes.

Understanding the Lodging Listing

Local Member Value

AAA or CAA and SAVE identify hotels that offer members a rate guarantee and up to two free special amenities as part of their Official Appointment partnership with AAA. Rate guarantee: Discounted standard room rate (usually based on last standard room availability) or the lowest public rate available at time of booking for dates of stay. Free special amenity options are included in the listing and could be either: breakfast, local telephone calls, newspaper, room upgrade, preferred room, or high-speed Internet.

Diamond Rating

The number of Diamonds informs you of the overall complexity of a lodging's amenities and service. Red indicates an Official Appointment lodging. An fyi in place of Diamonds indicates the property has not been rated but is included as an "information only" service. A detailed description of each rating level appears on page 20.

Classification

All Diamond Rated lodgings are classified using three key elements: style of operation, overall concept and service level. See pages 22-23 for details on our classifications.

Rates

The property's standard 2-person rates and effective dates are shown.

Rates are provided to AAA by each lodging and represent the publicly available rate or ranges for a standard room. Rates are rounded to the nearest dollar and do not include taxes. U.S., Mexican and Caribbean rates are in U.S. dollars; rates for Canadian lodgings are in Canadian dollars.

Information about cancellation and minimum stay policies is provided in the **Terms** section of the property's listing.

Online Reservations

This notation indicates AAA/CAA members can conveniently check room availability, validate room rates and make reservations for this property in a secure online environment at AAA.com.

Service Availability

Unit types, amenities and room features preceded by the word "Some" indicate the item is available on a limited basis, potentially within only one unit. The term "Fee" appearing to the left of an amenity icon indicates an extra charge applies.

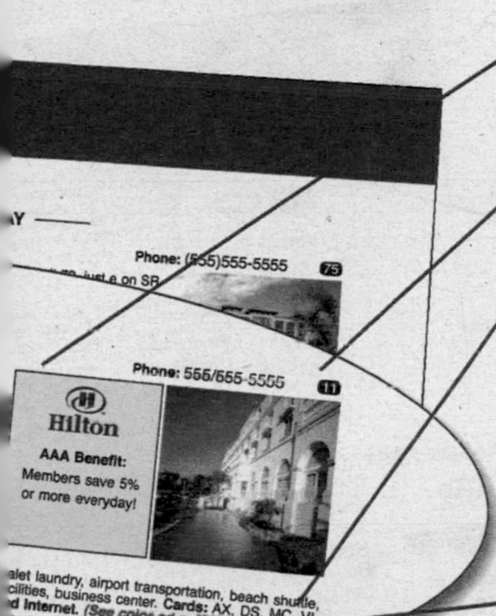

Nationwide Member Value

The blue box in the listing identifies hotel brands that offer an everyday member benefit at all AAA Approved locations. (See page 19 for additional program benefits.)

Spotting Symbol

Black ovals with white numbers are used to locate, or "spot," lodgings on maps we provide for larger cities.

Credit Cards Accepted

AX=American Express
CB=Carte Blanche
DC=Diners Club
DS=Discover
JC=Japan Credit Bureau
MC=MasterCard
VI=VISA

Some properties accept cash but require a credit card at registration. If you plan to pay in cash, call in advance for restrictions.

Icons

Lodging icons represent some of the member values, services and facilities offered.

Discounts

- ASK May offer discount

Member Services

- Airport transportation
- Pets allowed (call property for restrictions and fees)
- Restaurant on premises
- Restaurant off premises (walking distance)
- 24-hour room service
- Full bar
- Child care
- Accessible features (call property for available services and amenities)

Leisure Activities

- Full-service casino
- Pool
- Health club on premises
- Health club off premises
- Recreational activities

In-Room Amenities

- Designated non-smoking rooms
- VCR
- Movies
- Refrigerator
- Microwave
- Coffee maker
- No air conditioning
- No TV
- No cable TV
- No telephones

Safety Features

(see page 24)
(Mexico and Caribbean only)

- S Sprinklers
- D Smoke detectors

Understanding the Restaurant Listing

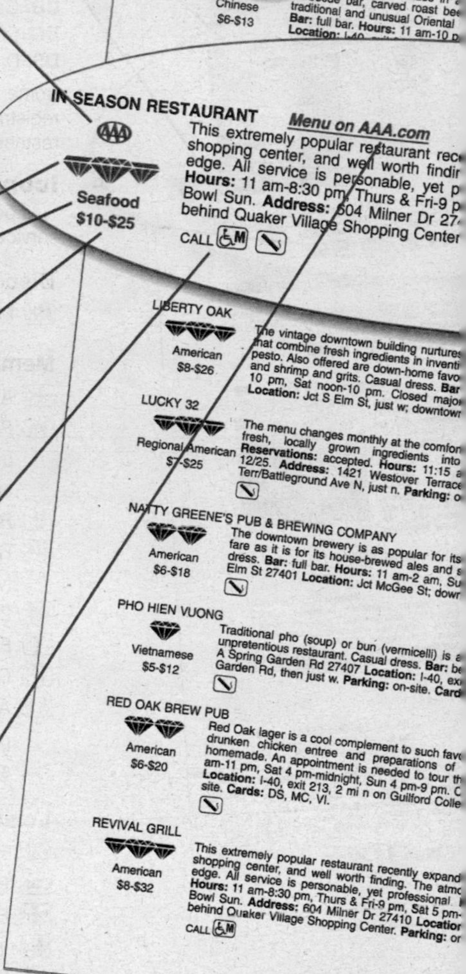

Official Appointment

(AAA) or (CAA) indicates Official Appointment (OA) restaurants. The OA program permits restaurants to display and advertise the AAA or CAA emblem. These establishments are highlighted in red to help you quickly identify them. The AAA or CAA Approved sign helps traveling members find restaurants that want member business.

Local Member Value

(SAVE) identifies restaurants that offer a Show Your Card & Save® discount to AAA/CAA members.

Diamond Rating

The number of Diamonds informs you of the overall complexity of food, presentation, service and ambience. Red indicates an Official Appointment restaurant. A detailed description of each Diamond level appears on page 21.

Cuisine Type

The cuisine type helps you select a dining facility that caters to your individual taste. AAA currently recognizes more than 120 different cuisine types.

Prices

Rates shown represent the minimum and maximum entree cost per person. Exceptions may include one-of-a-kind or special market priced items. Rates are rounded to the nearest dollar and do not include taxes. U.S., Mexican and Caribbean rates are in U.S. dollars; rates for Canadian restaurants are in Canadian dollars.

Icons

Icons provide additional information about services and facilities.

- (AC) No air-conditioning
- (&M) Accessible features offered (call property for available services and amenities)
- (smoking icon) Designated smoking section available

Menus

This notation indicates AAA/CAA members can conveniently view the restaurant's menu in a secure online environment at AAA.com.

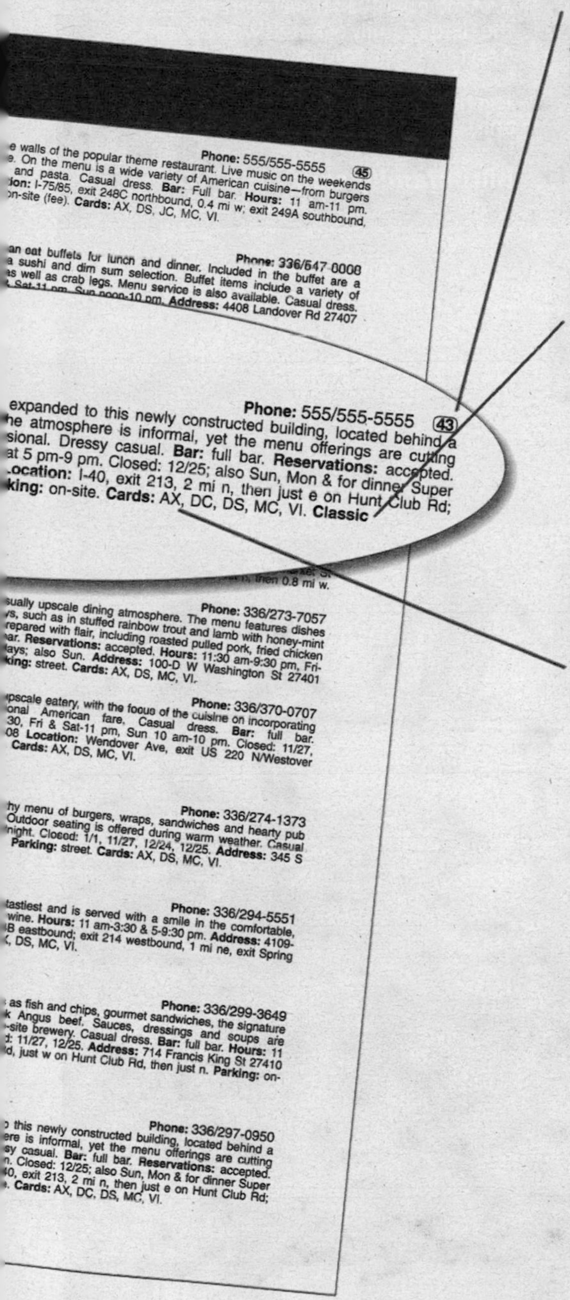
e walls of the popular theme restaurant. Live music on the weekends **Phone:** 555/555-5555 (45)
e. On the menu is a wide variety of American cuisine—from burgers
and pasta. Casual dress. **Bar:** Full bar. **Hours:** 11 am-11 pm.
ion: I-75/85, exit 248C northbound, 0.4 mi w; exit 249A southbound,
on-site (fee). **Cards:** AX, DS, JC, MC, VI.

an eat buffets for lunch and dinner. Included in the buffet are a **Phone:** 336/547-0008
a sushi and dim sum selection. Buffet items include a variety of
as well as crab legs. Menu service is also available. Casual dress.
Sat-11 pm, Sun noon-10 pm. **Address:** 4408 Landover Rd 27407

expanded to this newly constructed building, located behind a **Phone:** 555/555-5555 (43)
he atmosphere is informal, yet the menu offerings are cutting
sional. Dressy casual. **Bar:** full bar. **Reservations:** accepted.
at 5 pm-9 pm. Closed: 12/25; also Sun, Mon & for dinner Super
Location: I-40, exit 213, 2 mi n, then just e on Hunt Club Rd;
king: on-site. **Cards:** AX, DC, DS, MC, VI. **Classic**

n, then 0.8 mi w.

sually upscale dining atmosphere. The menu features dishes **Phone:** 336/273-7057
s, such as in stuffed rainbow trout and lamb with honey-mint
repared with flair, including roasted pulled pork, fried chicken
ar. **Reservations:** accepted. **Hours:** 11:30 am-9:30 pm, Fri-
ays; also Sun. **Address:** 100-D W Washington St 27401
king: street. **Cards:** AX, DS, MC, VI.

pscale eatery, with the focus of the cuisine on incorporating **Phone:** 336/370-0707
onal American fare. Casual dress. **Bar:** full bar.
30, Fri & Sat-11 pm, Sun 10 am-10 pm. Closed: 11/27,
08 **Location:** Wendover Ave, exit US 220 N/Westover
Cards: AX, DS, MC, VI.

hy menu of burgers, wraps, sandwiches and hearty pub **Phone:** 336/274-1373
Outdoor seating is offered during warm weather. Casual
night. Closed: 1/1, 11/27, 12/24, 12/25. **Address:** 345 S
Parking: street. **Cards:** AX, DS, MC, VI.

tastiest and is served with a smile in the comfortable, **Phone:** 336/294-5551
wine. **Hours:** 11 am-3:30 & 5-9:30 pm. **Address:** 4109-
B eastbound; exit 214 westbound, 1 mi ne, exit Spring
, DS, MC, VI.

as fish and chips, gourmet sandwiches, the signature **Phone:** 336/299-3649
k Angus beef. Sauces, dressings and soups are
-site brewery. Casual dress. **Bar:** full bar. **Hours:** 11
d: 11/27, 12/25. **Address:** 714 Francis King St 27410
d, just w on Hunt Club Rd, then just n. **Parking:** on-

this newly constructed building, located behind a **Phone:** 336/297-0950
ere is informal, yet the menu offerings are cutting
sy casual. **Bar:** full bar. **Reservations:** accepted.
n. Closed: 12/25; also Sun, Mon & for dinner Super
40, exit 213, 2 mi n, then just e on Hunt Club Rd;
. **Cards:** AX, DC, DS, MC, VI.

Spotting Symbol

White ovals with black numbers serve as restaurant locators and are used to locate, or "spot," restaurants on maps for larger cities.

Classifications

If applicable, a restaurant may be defined as:

Classic - renowned and/or landmark restaurant in business longer than 25 years, known for unique style and ambience.

Historic - establishments must meet one of the following criteria:

- Listed on the National Register of Historic Places
- Designated a National Historic Landmark
- Located in a National Register Historic District

Separate criteria designate historic properties in Canada, Mexico and the Caribbean.

Credit Cards Accepted

AX = American Express
CB = Carte Blanche
DC = Diners Club
DS = Discover
JC = Japan Credit Bureau
MC = MasterCard
VI = VISA

AAA/CAA members can generally expect to pay no more than the maximum regular rate printed in the TourBook guide in each rate range for a standard room. On rare occasions AAA receives or inadvertently publishes incorrect rates.

Obtain current AAA/CAA member rates and make reservations at AAA.com. Rates may vary within the range, depending on season and room type. Listed rates are usually based on last standard room availability.

Discounts

Member discounts, when offered, will apply to rates quoted within the rate range and are applicable at the time of booking. Special rates used in advertising, as well as special short-term promotional rates lower than the lowest listed rate in the range, are not subject to additional member discounts.

Exceptions

Rates for properties operating as concessionaires for the U.S. National Park Service are not guaranteed due to governing regulations. Rates in the Mexico TourBook are not guaranteed and may fluctuate based on the exchange rate of the peso.

Lodgings may temporarily increase room rates, not recognize discounts or modify pricing policies during special events. Examples of special events range from Mardi Gras and the Kentucky Derby (including pre-Derby events) to college football games, holidays, holiday periods and state fairs. Although some special events are listed in AAA/CAA TourBook guides and on AAA.com, it is always wise to check in advance with AAA travel professionals for specific dates.

Get the Room You Reserved

When making your reservation, identify yourself as a AAA or CAA member and request written confirmation to guarantee: type of room, rate, dates of stay, and cancellation and refund policies. At registration, show your membership card.

When you find your room is not as specified, and you have written confirmation of reservations for a certain type of accommodation, you should be given the option of choosing a different room or finding one elsewhere. Should you choose to go elsewhere and a refund is refused or resisted, submit the matter to AAA/CAA within 30 days, along with complete documentation, including your reasons for refusing the room and copies of your written confirmation and any receipts or canceled checks associated with this problem.

If you are charged more than the maximum rate listed in the TourBook guide for a standard room, question the additional charge. If management refuses to adhere to the published rate, pay for the room and submit your receipt and membership number to AAA/CAA within 30 days. Include all pertinent information: dates of stay, rate paid, itemized paid receipts, number of persons in your party and the room number you occupied, and list any extra room equipment used. A refund of the amount paid in excess of the stated maximum will be made if our investigation indicates that unjustified charging occurred.

Deposit, Refund and Cancellation Policies

Most establishments give full deposit refunds if they have been notified at least 48 hours before the normal check-in time. Listing prose will note if more than 48 hours' notice is required for cancellation. Some properties may charge a cancellation or handling fee. When this applies, "cancellation fee imposed" will appear in the listing. If you cancel too late, you have little recourse if a refund is denied.

When an establishment requires full or partial payment in advance and your trip is cut short, a refund may not be given.

When canceling a reservation, phone the lodging immediately. Make a note of the date and time you called, the cancellation number if there is one, and the name of the person who handled the cancellation. If your AAA/CAA club made your reservation, allow them to make the cancellation for you as well, so you will have proof of cancellation.

Check-in and Check-out Times

Check-in and check-out times are shown in the lodging listings, under Terms, only if they are before 3 p.m. or after 10 a.m. respectively.

Members Save With Our Partners

These National Show Your Card & Save® partners provide the listed member benefits. Visit AAA.com/Save to discover all the great Show Your Card & Save® discounts in your area. Admission tickets that offer greater discounts may be available for purchase at the local AAA/CAA club. A maximum of six attraction tickets is available at the discount price at the gate; six discounted tickets is also the maximum for Amtrak and Gray Line.

SeaWorld, Busch Gardens, Sesame Place
AAA.com/SeaWorld, AAA.com/BuschGardens, AAA.com/SesamePlace

- Save on admission at the gate, at participating offices, or online

- Save 10% on up-close dining; visit Guest Relations for details

Six Flags AAA.com/SixFlags

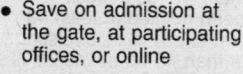

- Save on admission at the gate, at participating offices, or online
- Save 10% on merchandise purchases of $15 or more at in-park stores

Universal Orlando Resort and Universal Studios Hollywood
AAA.com/Universal

- Save on admission at the gate, at participating offices, or online

- Save 10% at select food and merchandise venues in-park and at Universal CityWalk®

Restaurant Partner
Savings applies to AAA/CAA members and up to five guests.

Joe's Crab Shack

- Save 10% on food, non-alcoholic beverages and merchandise

Landry's Seafood House, The Crab House, Chart House, Muer Seafood Restaurants, and Aquarium and Downtown Aquarium Restaurants

- Save 10% on food and non-alcoholic beverages at all of the above restaurants
- Save 10% on merchandise at Aquarium and Downtown Aquarium restaurants

Hard Rock Cafe

- Save 10% on food, non-alcoholic beverages and merchandise at all U.S. and select Canadian and international locations

Tanger Outlet Centers www.tangeroutlet.com

- Save up to 20% on total purchase at select merchants with AAA/CAA coupon booklet
- Member BONUS: FREE $5 gift card for each additional Tanger Outlet Center visited after first within same calendar year
- Show membership card and register at the AAA customer service desk when you visit

Amtrak

- 10% discount on rail fare when booked at least 3 days in advance of travel date

Grand Canyon Railway

- Save up to 20% on rail fare, hotel accommodations, restaurant and gift shop purchases sold outside of Grand Canyon National Park

Gray Line
AAA.com/GrayLine

- Save 10% on sightseeing tours of 1 day or less worldwide

AAA Preferred Lodging Partners

EXPECT SAVINGS, SELECTION, AND SATISFACTION

- **Best AAA/CAA member rates for your dates of stay.** Provide valid membership number when placing reservation and show your card at hotel check-in.
- **Satisfaction guarantee.** Notify the property if you are dissatisfied with any part of your stay. If the matter cannot be resolved, you may be entitled to compensation (see page 17).
- **Seasonal promotions and special member offers.** Visit AAA.com to view current offers.
- **Everyday member benefit.*** Look for the blue boxes in the TourBook listings for everyday values offered at all AAA Approved locations.

**Offer good at time of publication: Chains and offers may change without notice. Preferred Hotel Partner discounts may vary in Mexico and the Caribbean.*

10% Off Best Available Rates
Best Western International

5% or more Off Best Available Rates
Conrad, Doubletree, Embassy Suites, Hampton, Hilton, Hilton Garden Inn, Hilton Grand Vacations, Homewood Suites, and Waldorf=Astoria Collection

10% Off Best Available Rates
Andaz, Grand Hyatt, Hyatt Place, Hyatt Regency, Hyatt Summerfield Suites, and Park Hyatt

5% or more Off Best Available Rates
Courtyard, Fairfield Inn, JW Marriott, Marriott, Renaissance Hotels & Resorts, Residence Inn, SpringHill Suites, and TownePlace Suites

5-15% Off Best Available Rates
aloft, element, Four Points, Le Meridien, Sheraton, St. Regis, The Luxury Collection, Westin, and W Hotels

Understanding the Diamond Ratings

AAA/CAA inspectors have evaluated and rated each of the 58,000 lodging and restaurant establishments in the TourBook series to ensure quality travel information for our members. All properties must meet AAA's minimum requirements (for lodgings) concerning cleanliness, comfort and security - or - AAA's minimum requirements (for restaurants) pertaining to cleanliness, food preparation and service.

Eligible applicants receive an unannounced evaluation by a AAA/CAA inspector that includes two distinct components:

- **AAA Approval:** The inspector first must determine whether the property meets the criteria required to be AAA Approved. Every establishment that meets these strict guidelines offers AAA members the assurance that, regardless of the Diamond Rating, it provides acceptable quality, cleanliness, service and value.
- **AAA Diamond Rating:** Once an establishment becomes AAA Approved, it is then assigned a rating of one to five Diamonds, indicating the extensiveness of its facilities, amenities and services, from basic to moderate to luxury. These Diamond Ratings guide members in selecting establishments appropriately matched to their needs and expectations.

LODGINGS

1 Diamond

One Diamond lodgings typically appeal to the budget-minded traveler. They provide essential, no-frills accommodations and basic comfort and hospitality.

2 Diamond

Two Diamond lodgings appeal to family travelers seeking affordable yet more than the basic accommodations. Facilities, decor and amenities are modestly enhanced.

3 Diamond

Three Diamond lodgings offer a distinguished style. Properties are multi-faceted, with marked upgrades in physical attributes, amenities and guest comforts.

4 Diamond

Four Diamond lodgings are refined and stylish. Physical attributes are upscale. The fundamental hallmarks at this level include an extensive array of amenities combined with a high degree of hospitality, service and attention to detail.

5 Diamond

Five Diamond lodgings provide the ultimate in luxury and sophistication. Physical attributes are extraordinary in every manner. Service is meticulous, exceeding guest expectations and maintaining impeccable standards of excellence. Extensive personalized services and amenities provide first-class comfort.

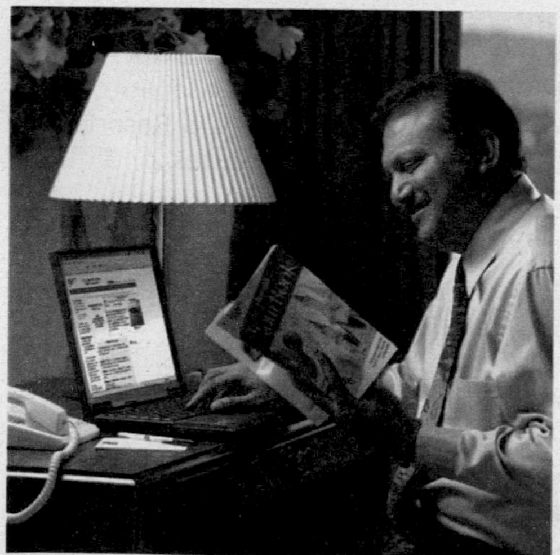

fyi The lodging listings with **fyi** in place of Diamonds are included as an *information only* service for members. The icon indicates that a property has not been rated for one or more of the following reasons: too new to rate, under construction, under major renovation, not evaluated, may not meet all AAA requirements.

A property not meeting all AAA requirements is included for either its member value or because it may be the only accommodation available in the area. Listing prose will give insight as to why the **fyi** designation was assigned.

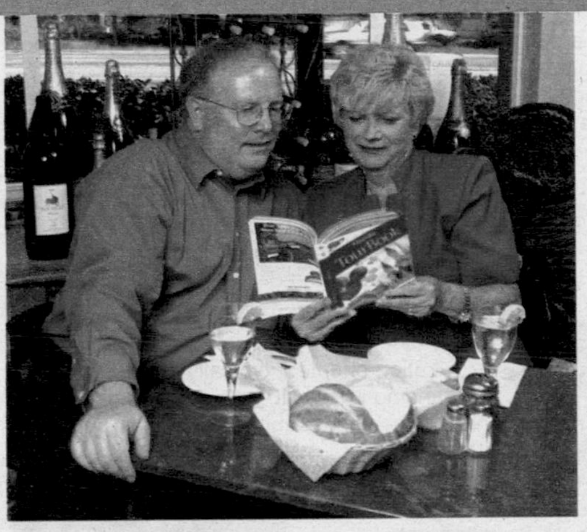

RESTAURANTS

1 Diamond

One Diamond restaurants provide simple, familiar specialty food (such as burgers, chicken, pizza or tacos) at an economical price. Often self-service, basic surroundings complement a no-nonsense approach.

2 Diamond

Two Diamond restaurants offer a familiar, family-oriented experience. Menu selection includes home-style foods and family favorites, often cooked to order, modestly enhanced and reasonably priced. Service is accommodating yet relaxed, a perfect complement to casual surroundings.

3 Diamond

Three Diamond restaurants convey an entry into fine dining and are often positioned as adult-oriented experiences. The atypical menu may feature the latest cooking trends and/or traditional cuisine. Expanded beverage offerings complement the menu. The ambience is well coordinated, comfortable and enhanced by a professional service staff.

4 Diamond

Four Diamond restaurants provide a distinctive fine-dining experience that is typically expensive. Surroundings are highly refined with upscale enhancements throughout. Highly creative chefs use imaginative presentations to augment fresh, top-quality ingredients. A proficient service staff meets or exceeds guest expectations. A wine steward may offer menu-specific knowledge to guide selection.

5 Diamond

Five Diamond restaurants are luxurious and renowned for consistently providing a world-class experience. Highly acclaimed chefs offer artistic menu selections that are imaginative and unique, using only the finest ingredients available. A maitre d' leads an expert service staff in exceeding guest expectations, attending to every detail in an effortless and unobtrusive manner.

fyi The restaurants with **fyi** in place of Diamonds are included as an *information only* service for members. These listings provide additional dining choices but have not yet been evaluated.

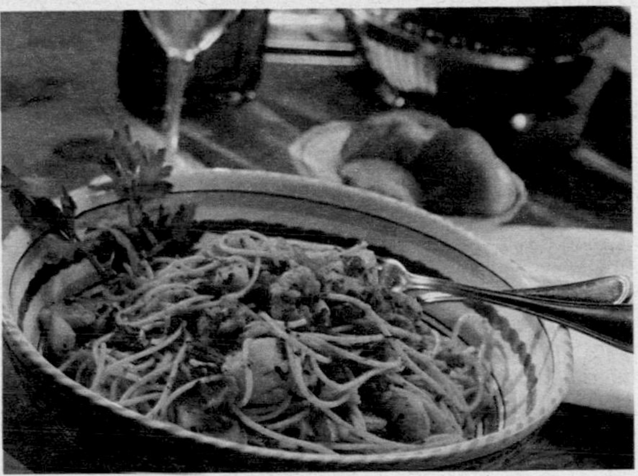

Understanding the Lodging Classifications

To ensure that your lodging needs and preferences are met, we recommend that you consider an establishment's classification when making your travel choices. While the quality and comfort at properties with the same Diamond Rating should be consistent (regardless of the classification), there are differences in typical decor/theme elements, range of facilities and service levels.

Lodging Classifications

Bed & Breakfast

Typically smaller scale properties emphasizing a high degree of personal touches that provide guests an "at home" feeling. Guest units tend to be individually decorated. Rooms may not include some modern amenities such as televisions and telephones, and may have a shared bathroom. Usually owner-operated with a common room or parlor separate from the innkeeper's living quarters, where guests and operators can interact during evening and breakfast hours. Evening office closures are normal. A continental or full, hot breakfast is served and is included in the room rate.

1884 Paxton House Inn
Thomasville, GA

Cabin

Vacation-oriented, typically smaller scale, freestanding units of simple construction—roughly finished logs or stone—and basic design or décor. Often located in wooded, rural, or waterfront locations. As a rule, basic cleaning supplies, kitchen utensils, and complete bed and bath linens are supplied. The guest registration area may be located off site.

Greenbrier Valley Resorts
Gatlinburg, TN

Condominium

Vacation-oriented—commonly for extended-stay purposes—apartment-style accommodations of varying design or décor. Routinely available for rent through a management company, units often contain one or more bedrooms, a living room, full kitchen, and an eating area. Studio-type models combine the sleeping and living areas into one room. As a rule, basic cleaning supplies, kitchen utensils, and complete bed and bath linens are supplied. The guest registration area may be located off site.

Sands of Kahana
Kahana, Maui, HI

Cottage

Vacation-oriented, typically smaller scale, freestanding units with home style enhancements in architectural design and interior décor. Often located in wooded, rural, or waterfront locations. Units may vary in design and décor. As a rule, basic cleaning supplies, kitchen utensils, and complete bed and bath linens are supplied. The guest registration area may be located off site.

Paradise Villas, Little Cayman Island

Country Inn

Although similar in definition to a bed and breakfast, country inns are usually larger in scale with spacious public areas and offer a dining facility that serves—at a minimum—breakfast and dinner.

Greenville Inn, Greenville, ME

Hotel

Commonly, a multistory establishment with interior room entrances offering a variety of guest unit styles. The magnitude of the public areas is determined by the overall theme, location and service level, but may include a variety of facilities such as a restaurant, shops, fitness center, spa, business center, and/or meeting rooms.

The Grand America Hotel
Salt Lake City, UT

Motel

Commonly, a one- or two-story establishment with exterior room entrances and drive up parking. Typically, guest units have one bedroom with a bathroom of similar décor and design. Public areas and facilities are often limited in size and/or availability.

Best Western Deltona Inn, Deltona, FL

Ranch

Typically a working ranch with an obvious rustic, Western theme featuring equestrian-related activities and a variety of guest unit styles.

Lost Valley Ranch, Deckers, CO

Vacation Rental House

Vacation-oriented—commonly for extended-stay purposes—typically larger scale, freestanding, and of varying design or décor. Routinely available for rent through a management company, houses often contain two or more bedrooms, a living room, full kitchen, dining room, and multiple bathrooms. As a rule, basic cleaning supplies, kitchen utensils, and complete bed and bath linens are supplied. The guest registration area may be located off site.

ResortQuest, Hilton Head Island, SC

Lodging Sub-classifications

The following are sub-classifications that may appear along with the classifications listed previously to provide a more specific description of the lodging.

Boutique

Often thematic and typically an informal, yet highly personalized experience; may have a luxurious or quirky style which is fashionable or unique.

Casino

Extensive gambling facilities are available, such as: blackjack, craps, keno, and slot machines. **Note:** This sub-classification will not appear beneath its Diamond Rating in the listing. It will be indicated by a icon and will be included in the row of icons immediately below the lodging listing.

Classic

Renowned and landmark properties, older than 50 years, well-known for their unique style and ambience.

Contemporary

Overall design and theme reflects characteristics of the present era's mainstream tastes and style.

Extended Stay

Offers a predominance of long-term accommodations with a designated full-service kitchen area within each unit.

Historic

These properties are typically over 75 years of age and exhibit many features of a historic nature with respect to architecture, design, furnishings, public record, or acclaim. Properties must meet one of the following criteria:

- Maintained the integrity of the historical nature
- Listed on the National Register of Historic Places
- National Historic Landmark or located in a National Register Historic District

Separate criteria designate historic properties in Canada, Mexico and the Caribbean.

Resort

Recreation-oriented, geared to vacation travelers seeking a specific destination experience. Travel packages, meal plans, themed entertainment, and social and recreational programs are typically available. Recreational facilities are extensive and may include spa treatments, golf, tennis, skiing, fishing, or water sports. Larger resorts may offer a variety of guest accommodations.

Retro

Overall design and theme reflect a contemporary design reinterpreting styles from a bygone era.

Vacation Rental

Typically houses, condos, cottages or cabins; these properties are a "home away from home" offering more room and greater value for the money. In general, they provide the conveniences of home, such as full kitchens and washers/dryers. Located in resort or popular destination areas within close proximity to major points of interest, attractions, or recreation areas, these properties may require a pre-arranged reservation and check-in at an off-site location. Housekeeping services may be limited or not included.

Vintage

Offers a window to the past and provides an experience reflecting a predominance of traits associated with the era of their origin.

Guest Safety

Room Security

In order to be approved for listing in AAA/CAA TourBook guides for the United States and Canada, accommodations must have dead bolt locks on all guest room entry doors and connecting room doors.

If the area outside the guest room door is not visible from inside the room through a window or door panel, viewports must be installed on all guest room entry doors. Bed and breakfast properties and country inns are not required to have viewports. Ground floor and easily accessible sliding doors must be equipped with some type of secondary security locks.

Even with those approval requirements, AAA cannot guarantee guest safety. AAA Inspectors view a percentage of rooms at each property since it is not feasible to evaluate every room in every lodging establishment. Therefore, AAA cannot guarantee that there are working locks on all doors and windows in all guest rooms.

Fire Safety

Because of the highly specialized skills needed to conduct professional fire safety inspections, AAA/CAA Inspectors cannot assess fire safety.

Properties must meet all federal, state/province and local fire codes. Each guest unit in all U.S. and Canadian lodging properties must be equipped with an operational, single-station smoke detector. A AAA/CAA Inspector has evaluated a sampling of the rooms to verify this equipment is in place.

Mexico and the Caribbean

Requirements for some features, such as door locks and smoke detectors/sprinkler systems, differ in Mexico and the Caribbean. If a property met AAA's security requirements at the time of the evaluation, the phrase "Meets AAA guest room security requirements" appears in the listing.

Service Animals

The Americans with Disabilities Act (ADA) prohibits U.S. businesses that serve the public from discriminating against persons with disabilities. Some businesses have mistakenly denied access to persons who use service animals. Businesses must permit entry to guests and their service animals, as well as allow service animals to accompany guests to all public areas of a property.

A property is permitted to ask whether the animal is a service animal or a pet, and whether the guest has a disability. The property may not, however, ask questions about the nature of the disability, the service provided by the animal, or require proof of a disability or certification that the animal is a service animal. These regulations may not apply in Canada, Mexico or the Caribbean.

No fees or deposits, even those normally charged for pets, may be charged for service animals. Service animals fulfill a critical need for their owners—they are not pets.

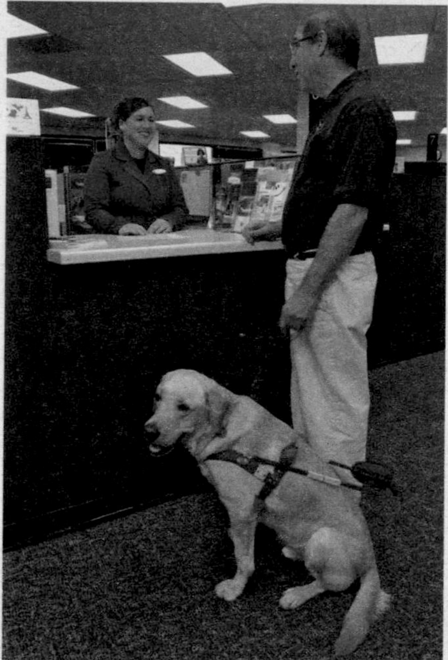

Frank Frand with his seeing eye dog, Cardinal.

Savings for all Seasons

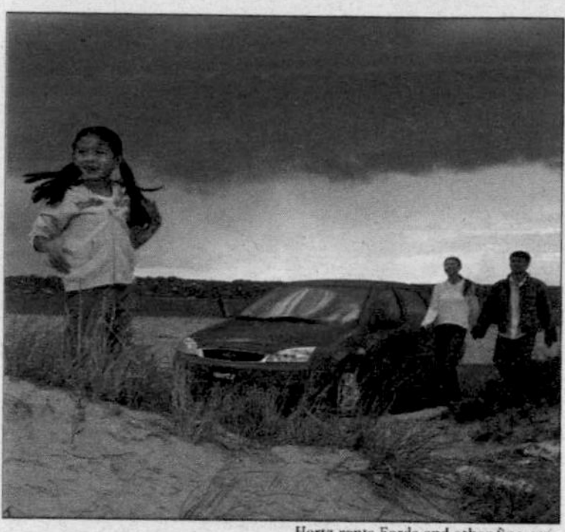

Hertz rents Fords and other fine cars.
® REG. U.S. PAT. OFF. © 2008 HERTZ SYSTEM INC.

No matter the season, Hertz offers AAA members exclusive discounts and benefits.

Operating in 145 countries at over 8,000 locations, Hertz makes traveling more convenient and efficient wherever and whenever you go. Hertz offers AAA members discounts up to 20% on car rentals worldwide.

To receive your exclusive AAA member discounts and benefits, mention your AAA membership card at time of reservation and present it at time of rental. **In addition**, to receive a free one car class upgrade on daily, weekly or weekend rental in the United States, Puerto Rico and Canada, mention PC# 969194 at the time of reservation. Offer is valid for vehicle pick-up on or before 12/15/09.

For reservations and program details, visit AAA.com/hertz, call your AAA Travel office or the Hertz/AAA Desk at **1-800-654-3080.**

Receive a free One Car Class Upgrade on a Hertz daily, weekend or weekly rental when reserving a Compact through Full-Size four-door car and take advantage of your AAA/CAA discount as well. Highest obtainable upgrade is to a Premium vehicle. Advance reservations are required. Your AAA CDP# and the applicable PC# must be included in the reservation. This offer is available at participating Hertz locations in the U.S., Canada and Puerto Rico and is subject to availability. Blackout periods may apply. If a blackout period does occur, you are still entitled to your member discount. Offer may be limited in some cities at some times, especially during periods of peak demand. Not all vehicles, vehicle equipment and services are available at all locations. This offer has no cash value, may not be used with Tour Rates or Insurance Replacement Rates and cannot be combined with any other certificate, voucher, offer or promotion. Hertz age, driver, credit and daily, weekend, and weekly rate qualifications for the renting location apply. Taxes, tax reimbursement, age differential charges, fees and optional service charges, such as refueling, are not included. Discounts apply to time and mileage charges only. Discounts in local currency on redemption. At the time of rental, present your AAA membership card or Hertz/AAA Discount card for identification. Offer is valid for vehicle pick-up on or before 12/15/2009. Call for details.

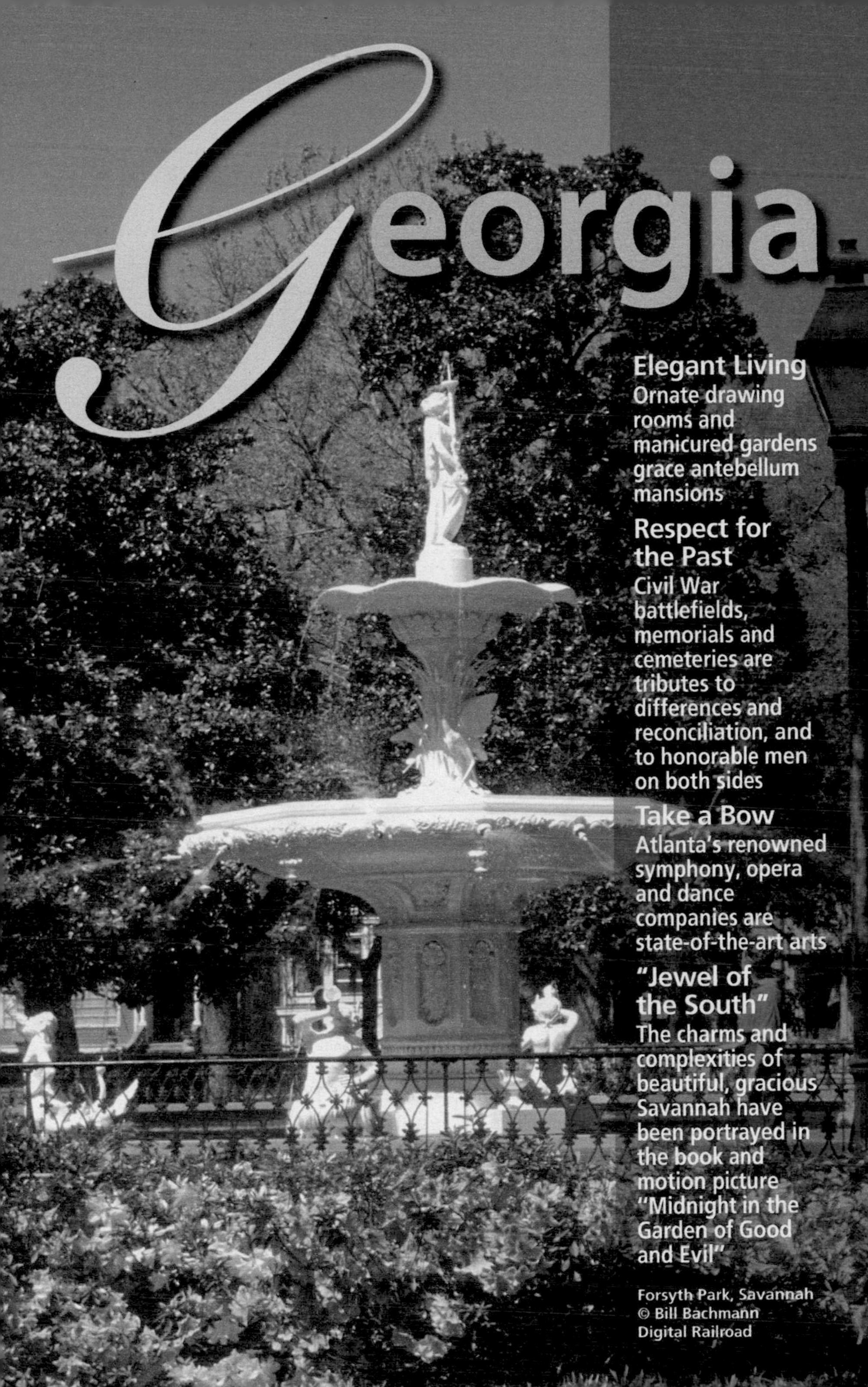

Georgia
Elegant Living
Ornate drawing rooms and manicured gardens grace antebellum mansions
Respect for the Past
Civil War battlefields, memorials and cemeteries are tributes to differences and reconciliation, and to honorable men on both sides
Take a Bow
Atlanta's renowned symphony, opera and dance companies are state-of-the-art arts
"Jewel of the South"
The charms and complexities of beautiful, gracious Savannah have been portrayed in the book and motion picture "Midnight in the Garden of Good and Evil"

Forsyth Park, Savannah
© Bill Bachmann
Digital Railroad

Callaway Gardens, Pine Mountain / © Nancy Rotenberg / Jaynes Gallery / Danita Delimont Stock Photography

Georgia is all about contrast and variety. Craggy Appalachian summits and gentle sandy shores. Mazelike swamps and manicured peach orchards. Unhurried small towns and fast-paced cities. Gleaming office towers and venerable old homes.

History hounds can stroll the 250-year-old streets of Savannah; recall the War of 1812 at Fort Jackson; walk the Civil War battlefields of Chickamauga and Chattanooga; or ponder Martin Luther King Jr.'s dream at his Atlanta birthplace.

Lovers of the outdoors can catch the waves and a tan at the beaches; stalk birdies on the golf courses; hike the trails of the Chattahoochee

National Forest; run the rapids of the Chattooga; or jig for bass and bream in the rivers.

Sightseers can view four states from atop Brasstown Bald; meander along the Chattahoochee-Flint Heritage Highway; gaze at 'gators from the safety of a boat in the Okefenokee Swamp; or check out the chrysanthemums at Callaway Gardens.

Spectators applaud with joy at the Atlanta Ballet; cry bravo at the Atlanta Symphony; or cheer the Braves, Bulldogs, Falcons, Hawks and Thrashers.

Georgia truly is a peach of a state.

How far can you travel in 1 day in Georgia? Try 4,874 feet down, from above the clouds to sea level. You could shiver on the summit of Brasstown Bald in the morning and toast your toes on sandy Atlantic beaches in the afternoon. You could leave behind Macon's pine needles and drumming woodpeckers for Savannah's acrid tang of sea salt and screeching sea gulls. You could catch the evening performance of the Atlanta Symphony Orchestra and easily make the next day's matinee concert of 'gators, birds and bugs in the swamps of the Okefenokee.

Here and Now, or There and Then

You can travel from Indian mounds built thousands of years before Christ to the 21st century in Atlanta.

A religious site near Eatonton built 2,000-4,000 years ago is—relatively speaking—one of the state's newer mounds. This striking quartz representation of a spread-winged eagle is composed of quartz rocks laid 125 feet wide and 102 feet long and piled up to 11 feet high. Arizona's thunderbirds pale by comparison with this New World Stonehenge.

In contrast, Atlanta's CNN Center uses chrome and glass buildings to pay homage to instant communication, immediate gratification and entertainment in the 21st century.

Even trivia buffs might not know where the first U.S. gold rush took place. The answer? Dahlonega. The 1828 strike here was so great that in 1838 a federal mint was opened. Building materials from this area still contain traces of gold, and after very heavy rains gold nuggets have washed up in Atlanta water-treatment plants.

There are many places where military historians will have a field day; Georgia provided troops and battlefields during the Revolution and the War between the States. The most infamous of these sites is the prisoner-of-war camp at Andersonville, where thousands died of diseases resulting from overcrowding and malnutrition. The oppressive silence hanging over the prison site and cemetery is regularly broken by owls asking the wrong question.

Although this is a state of contrasts, civility and hospitality are Georgia's bedrock. You still hear "Yes, Ma'am," and merchants have been known not to ask for identification when cashing a check. Georgia has roots in both the Old and the New South; it is not *newly* Southern.

Hernando de Soto's party of soldiers and of priests explores the Southeast.

1540

Library of Congress

On Jan. 2, Georgia becomes the fourth state.

1788

A mint opens in Dahlonega, site of the 1829 Gold Rush near tribal land, and the Cherokee are forced to resettle in the Oklahoma Territory via "The Trail of Tears."

1838

1863

General Sherman's Union troops loot and burn Georgia on their "March to the Sea."

Library of Congress

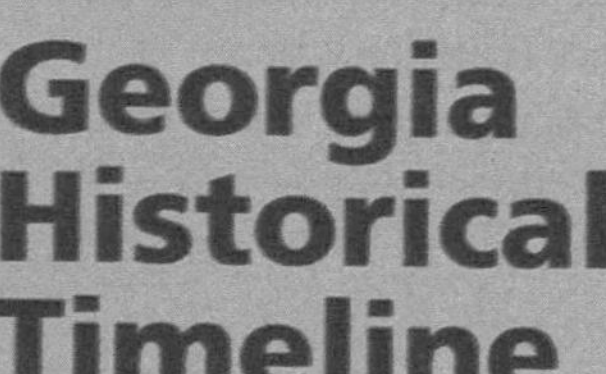

1961

Georgia becomes the first state in the Deep South to integrate without a major curtailment of its public school system.

If "Gone With the Wind" whetted your appetite for Southern architecture, you need to visit a mansion built when cotton was king. Many of these splendid homes have been scrupulously restored and opulently refurnished, and now welcome paying guests, some even overnight.

Architectural Digest described Savannah's 1819 Regency-style Owens-Thomas House as "...the most beautiful home in America." Among its stylistic delights is the pink drawing room, which has a ceiling that lends to its rectangularity the feel of a circular room. Mansions weren't the only buildings on plantations, however. The slave cabins and overseer's house at Stone Mountain's Antebellum Plantation are a good place to see how the other nine-tenths lived.

Sherman's Georgia

What is the distance between Atlanta and Savannah? Some 250 miles and more than 100 years.

Atlanta had existed scarcely more than 25 years when Gen. William Tecumseh Sherman's troops put the town to the torch during the Civil War. Sophisticated Savannah had accumulated more than 125 years of tradition and architecture when it was spared by Sherman. The difference in treatment by the Union general determined the futures of these two major cities.

Savannah continued undiverted along a well-trodden path. Its motto seems to have been "If it ain't broke don't fix it." Today she is the gracious *grande dame* who displays her charms with decorum, even in tell-all best sellers such as "Midnight in the Garden of Good and Evil."

Atlanta built anew, without preconceived notions of what it should be based upon what it had been. In the latter part of the 20th century the city became a financial and cultural mecca, the symbol for the contemporary South. The diverse population supports a World Series-winning baseball team and a world-class symphony orchestra, and its corporate headquarters include such home-grown yet worldwide enterprises as Coca-Cola® and CNN.

Atlanta is the state's superstar; it has an underlying charm, but is quite high-tech, fast-paced and slightly in-your-face.

Unlike most places, where you get to in this state can be noticeably different from where you started out. When you travel in Georgia you notice a difference!

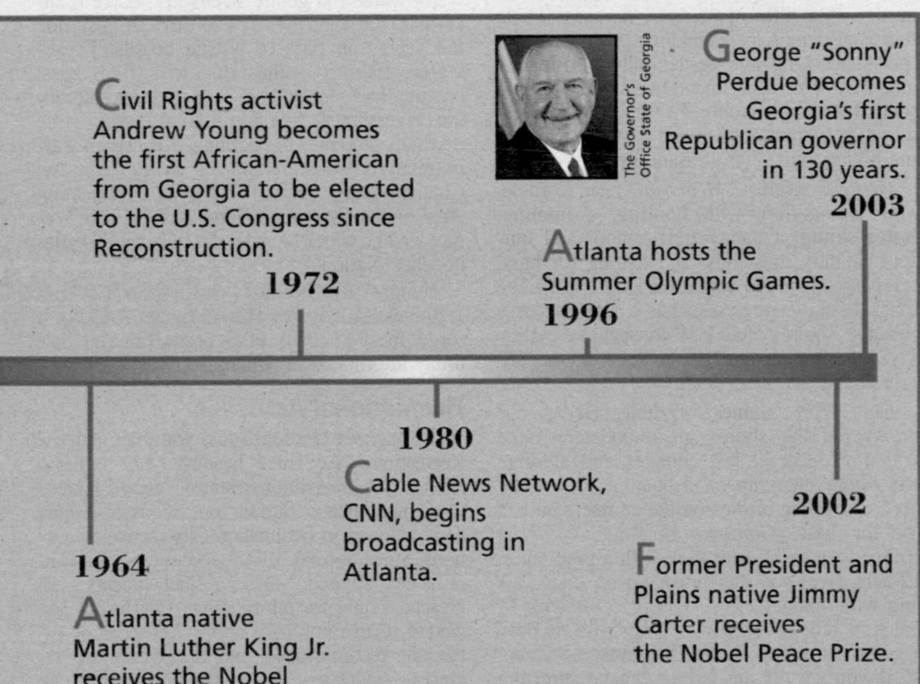

1964
Atlanta native Martin Luther King Jr. receives the Nobel Peace Prize.
1972
Civil Rights activist Andrew Young becomes the first African-American from Georgia to be elected to the U.S. Congress since Reconstruction.
1980
Cable News Network, CNN, begins broadcasting in Atlanta.
1996
Atlanta hosts the Summer Olympic Games.
2002
Former President and Plains native Jimmy Carter receives the Nobel Peace Prize.
2003
George "Sonny" Perdue becomes Georgia's first Republican governor in 130 years.
The Governor's Office State of Georgia

Recreation

Variety makes Georgia the South's playground. Within a day's drive you can hike in the Blue Ridge Mountains, or drop down 3,640 feet to slap the surf of the Atlantic Coast. You can sit in a box seat in Atlanta and snag a foul ball, or stand in a stream and fly-cast to snag a trout. You can watch the masters make eagles in Augusta or the eagles fly at the birds-of-prey center in Statesboro. Recreation in Georgia is a whole lot more than touring antebellum houses.

Stay and Play

Many a **golfing** vacation that starts out in Florida and doglegs its way up the seaboard to Virginia putts out in Georgia. Late afternoon thunderstorms keep the courses verdant and allow for lush plantings. Seven out of the 42 state parks that allow **camping** also have courses offering unlimited weekday play, generally for under $20, and 18 holes on the weekend for under $25. Senior citizen discounts are available at all the courses. All the parks mentioned below have campsites.

Hard Labor Creek's 18-hole course near Rutledge is part of a 5,800-acre complex with cottages, two lakes, a **swimming** beach, boat rentals and a bring-your-own-horse stable. The steep rolling hills of *Victoria Bryant's* 9-hole course just north of Franklin Springs make it both challenging and aesthetically pleasing. A June Civil War reenactment, two stocked fishing ponds (one for use only by the physically impaired), a swimming pool and 5 miles of **hiking** and **biking** trails offer pleasant diversions.

Georgia Veterans Memorial, near Cordele, woos non-golfers with **boating**, swimming, **water skiing**, a nature trail, indoor and outdoor military museums, and fishing for bass, crappie, catfish and bream on 7,000-acre Lake Blackshear. Veterans also has a stay-and-play package which includes 30 consecutive nights/days of camping and greens fees on the 18-hole course for under $400.

Near Fort Gaines, 18-hole *George T. Bagby*, on the shores of 48,000-acre Lake Walter F. George, has cottages and a lodge and offers swimming and boating; if you are tired of chasing birdies on the course, you can try for bass. *Gordonia-Alatamaha's* 9-hole course is in a 280-acre park with a pool and a 12-acre lake; you can brush up on your putting with miniature golf. *Laura S. Walker's* 18 holes, 9 miles southeast of Waycross, is only a gator's growl from the Okefenokee Swamp, so if you are off the fairway, make sure that log behind your ball isn't an alligator. Walker has a nature trail, boating and fishing and **canoe** rentals for a close encounter of a reptilian kind. Two miles north of McRae is one of the prettiest golf courses in the state, *Little Ocmulgee*, where the broad fairways are lined with pines and magnolias. Ocmulgee's 1,397 acres include cottages and a lodge, a beach and **tennis** courts where you can forget your hook and worry about your backhand.

Each April when the azaleas bloom the world's best golfers spring up at the Masters® Golf Tournament in Augusta. Don't expect to play here; Augusta National is a members-only course. Jekyll Island's three 18-hole courses are set in woods and marshes; the 9-hole course was built in the late 19th century. Hunger pangs may be a problem, because the aroma of the wild onions growing near a hole at one of them is reminiscent of juicy hamburgers. A marvelous sandy beach, tennis courts, miles of bike trails, tabby ruins of mid-18th-century buildings and the aroma of pine needles baking in the sun have made this footprint-shaped island a favorite Eastern Seaboard vacation spot.

Wet and Mild

The labyrinth of coastal channels and the surf off the fine beaches of the Sea Islands make for excellent **saltwater fishing**. The warm water and gentle swells also make it enjoyable for even novices to **surf** or just ride the waves on rafts or boogie boards. **Freshwater fishing** enthusiasts will find bass, bream, shad and catfish in the winding southern rivers and marshes. Trout inhabit the northern streams. If paddling a canoe or **raft** in relative isolation appeals to you, try the Chattahoochee River National Recreation Area or the Chattooga National Wild and Scenic River, which winds through the Chattahoochee National Forest.

Hungry? Try hot dogs and Atlanta's cola at a Braves, Falcons or Hawks game. And don't forget the University of Georgia Bulldogs Saturday afternoons in Athens.

Recreational Activities

Throughout the TourBook, you may notice a Recreational Activities heading with bulleted listings of recreation-oriented establishments listed underneath. Similar operations also may be mentioned in Destination City recreation sections. Since normal AAA inspection criteria cannot be applied, these establishments are presented only for information. Age, height and weight restrictions may apply. Reservations often are recommended and sometimes are required. Addresses and/or phone numbers are provided so visitors can contact the attraction for additional information.

Fast Facts

POPULATION: 8,186,453.

AREA: 58,876 square miles; ranks 21st.

CAPITAL: Atlanta.

HIGHEST POINT: 4,784 ft., Brasstown Bald.

LOWEST POINT: Sea level, Atlantic Ocean.

TIME ZONE(S): Eastern. DST.

TEEN DRIVING LAWS: No more than one passenger (parent/guardian) is permitted for the first six months. No more than four passengers (three passengers under age 21 plus a parent/guardian) for the remaining six months. Driving is not permitted midnight-6 a.m. The minimum age for unrestricted driver's license is 18.

SEAT BELT/CHILD RESTRAINT LAWS: Seat belts required for driver, front-seat passengers and ages 6 until 18. Child restraints required for under age 6 and less than 57 inches; must be in the rear seat if available.

HELMETS FOR MOTORCYCLISTS: Required.

RADAR DETECTORS: Permitted.

MOVE OVER LAW: Driver is required to slow down and vacate the lane nearest stopped police, fire, rescue and tow truck vehicles using audible or flashing signals.

FIREARMS LAWS: Vary by state and/or county. Contact the State Attorney General's Office, 40 Capitol Sq., Atlanta, GA 30334-1300; phone (404) 657-3981.

HOLIDAYS: Jan. 1; Martin Luther King Jr. Day, Jan. (third Mon.); Washington's Birthday, Feb. (3rd Mon.); Confederate Memorial Day, Apr. 26; Memorial Day, May (last Mon.); July 4; Labor Day; Columbus Day, Oct. (2nd Mon.); Veterans Day, Nov. 11; Robert E. Lee's Birthday,

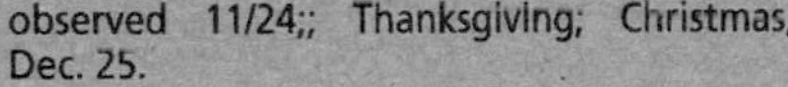

observed 11/24;; Thanksgiving; Christmas, Dec. 25.

TAXES: The statewide sales tax is 4 percent and most counties in Georgia levy a 6-7 percent tax on sales; in a few counties it may be slightly less.

INFORMATION CENTERS: State information centers are near Augusta, Columbus, Kingsland, Lavonia, Plains, Ringgold, Savannah, Sylvania, Tallapoosa, Valdosta and West Point; open daily 8:30-5:30.

FURTHER INFORMATION FOR VISITORS:

Georgia Department of Economic Development—Tourism Division
75 Fifth St. N.W., Suite 1200
Atlanta, GA 30308
(404) 962-4000 or
(800) 847-4842

See color ad on insert.

RECREATION INFORMATION:

Department of Natural Resources
Division of Parks, Recreation and Historic Sites
#2 Martin Luther King Jr. Dr. S.E., Suite 1352 East
Atlanta, GA 30334
(404) 656-2770 or (800) 864-7275 (reservations)

FISHING AND HUNTING REGULATIONS:

Department of Natural Resources
Wildlife Resources Division
2070 US 278 S.E.
Social Circle, GA 30025
(770) 918-6418 (fisheries) (770) 918-6416 (game management)

NATIONAL FOREST INFORMATION:

U.S. Forest Service
Chattahoochee & Oconee National Forests
1755 Cleveland Hwy.
Gainesville, GA 30501
(770) 297-3000
(877) 444-6777 (reservations)

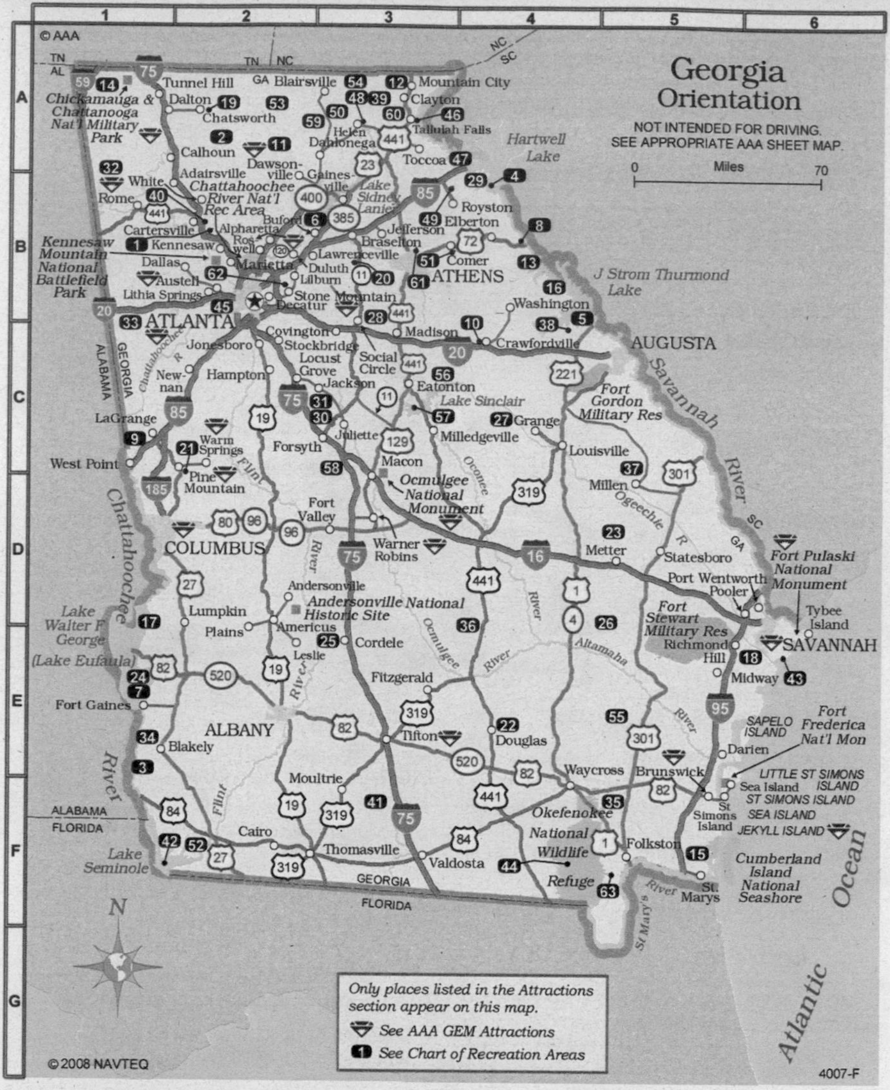

© AAA

Georgia Orientation

NOT INTENDED FOR DRIVING.
SEE APPROPRIATE AAA SHEET MAP.

Miles 0 70

Only places listed in the Attractions section appear on this map.

See AAA GEM Attractions

See Chart of Recreation Areas

© 2008 NAVTEQ

4007-F

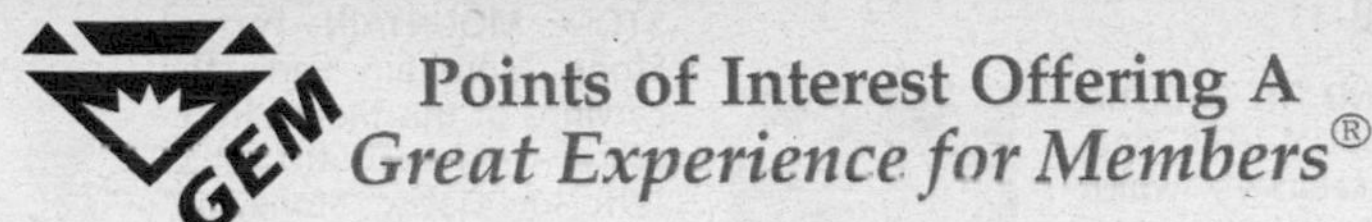

Points of Interest Offering A *Great Experience for Members*®

Atlanta (B-2)

ATLANTA HISTORY CENTER—The displays and buildings of the society's museum relate the horticultural and cultural history of the Atlanta area. See p. 50.

GEORGIA AQUARIUM—This state-of-the-art aquarium will transport you into the world of our finny friends and foes. See p. 53.

HIGH MUSEUM OF ART—Included in the museum's permanent collection are more than 11,000 works of European, American, African, folk, modern and contemporary art as well as photography and decorative arts. See p. 55.

MARTIN LUTHER KING JR. NATIONAL HISTORIC SITE—This site pays homage to a great man who chose non-violence as a means to convey his civil rights message and, as a result of his belief, paid with his life. See p. 54.

WOODRUFF ARTS CENTER—This cutting-edge facility harmoniously houses the Alliance Theatre Company, High Museum of Art, Atlanta College of Art, 14th Street Playhouse and the Atlanta Symphony Orchestra. See p. 55.

WORLD OF COCA-COLA ATLANTA—Pause here to refresh your memories and quench your thirst for knowledge about the world's first bottled soft drink. See p. 55.

ZOO ATLANTA—An extensive array of animals from all over the world, all within their natural habitats, are represented on the zoo's 37 acres. See p. 53.

Austell (B-2)

SIX FLAGS OVER GEORGIA—Hoist your spirits on one of the rides at this more than 100-acre theme park. See p. 58.

Brunswick (E-5)

HOFWYL-BROADFIELD PLANTATION—A thriving rice plantation in the 1850s, this plantation is now a 1,268-acre wildlife preserve with a museum. See p. 67.

Chickamauga and Chattanooga National Military Park (A-1)

CHICKAMAUGA AND CHATTANOOGA NATIONAL MILITARY PARK—Dedicated September 18-20, 1895, this is the first and most intact national military park; most of the monuments and historical markers were planned and placed by veterans of the battle. See p. 68.

Columbus (D-2)

NATIONAL CIVIL WAR NAVAL MUSEUM AT PORT COLUMBUS—Chronicling the history-making innovations in naval weaponry that characterized the Civil War, this museum's many exhibits include the recovered remnants of an ironclad that was sunk nearby. See p. 70.

Dawsonville (A-2)

KANGAROO CONSERVATION CENTER—Scenic trails, kangaroos, Australian plants and a kookaburra aviary comprise this 87-acre wildlife sanctuary. See p. 59.

Fort Pulaski National Monument (D-6)

FORT PULASKI NATIONAL MONUMENT—The supposedly impenetrable 7.5-foot-thick walls of this 1847 masonry fort proved unable to withstand Union bombardment by rifled cannon on April 11, 1862. See p. 74.

Jekyll Island (F-6)

JEKYLL ISLAND HISTORIC LANDMARK DISTRICT TOUR—You don't have to be a Rockefeller anymore to tour the elegant Gilded Age vacation "cottages" built by millionaires with such recognizable names as Goodyear, Morgan, Pulitzer and, of course, Rockefeller. See p. 79.

Ocmulgee National Monument (D-3)

OCMULGEE NATIONAL MONUMENT—Within the monument's 702 acres are some of the most impressive American Indian mounds and archeological remains in the Southeast. See p. 88.

Pine Mountain (D-2)

CALLAWAY GARDENS—Scenic woodland roads meander through the 14,000 acres of these gardens in the foothills of the Appalachians. See p. 89.

Rome (B-1)

OAK HILL AND THE MARTHA BERRY MUSEUM—The one-room log cabin in which Martha Berry, the mother of public education in Georgia, began teaching local children in 1902 has evolved into the 28,000-acre Berry College. See p. 91.

Roswell (B-2)

ARCHIBALD SMITH PLANTATION HOME—Surrounded by 12 original outbuildings, this 1845 plantation home was occupied by the Smiths until 1981. See p. 61.

Savannah (E-6)

SAVANNAH HISTORY MUSEUM—Although, as the song suggests, they don't all "Ac-Cent-Tchu-Ate The Positive" the exhibits in this restored 19th-century train shed relate the history of this genteel southern city, and include one of native son and lyricist Johnny Mercer's Oscars. See p. 98.

TELFAIR'S OWENS-THOMAS HOUSE —This 1819 house is considered by some to be this country's finest example of Regency architecture and contains many of the original furnishings. See p. 99.

Stone Mountain (B-2)

THE ANTEBELLUM PLANTATION—Part of Stone Mountain Park, this complex re-creates the atmosphere of the Old South. See p. 62.

STONE MOUNTAIN—Part of Stone Mountain Park, the carvings of this Mount Rushmore of the South depict Jefferson Davis, "Stonewall" Jackson and Robert E. Lee. See p. 62.

STONE MOUNTAIN PARK—Three popular ways to see portions of this scenic 3,300-acre park are by its aerial cable car, paddlewheel riverboat and railroad. See p. 62.

Tifton (E-3)

AGRIRAMA, GEORGIA'S MUSEUM OF AGRICULTURE & HISTORIC VILLAGE—What was life like in rural Georgia in the 1890s? This outdoor living-history village takes you there. See p. 102.

Warm Springs (C-2)

FDR'S LITTLE WHITE HOUSE STATE HISTORIC SITE—This house and its furnishings remain much as they were when President Franklin Delano Roosevelt died here April 12, 1945. See p. 105.

Warner Robins (D-3)

MUSEUM OF AVIATION—Four buildings on 51 acres offer aviation enthusiasts an impressive array of exhibits. See p. 105.

RECREATION AREAS	MAP LOCATION	CAMPING	PICNICKING	HIKING TRAILS	BOATING	BOAT RAMP	BOAT RENTAL	FISHING	SWIMMING	PETS ON LEASH	BICYCLE TRAILS	NATURE PROGS.	VISITOR CENTER	LODGE/CABINS	FOOD SERVICE
NATIONAL FORESTS *(See place listings)*															
Chattahoochee and Oconee 865,670 acres. Central and northern Georgia.		•	•	•	•	•		•	•	•	•	•	•		
NATIONAL RECREATION AREA *(See place listings)*															
Chattahoochee River (B-2) 4,100 acres n. of Atlanta.			•	•	•	•		•		•	•	•	•		
NATIONAL SEASHORE *(See place listings)*															
Cumberland Island (F-6) 36,415 acres 8 mi. e. of St. Marys.		•	•	•	•			•	•		•	•	•		
ARMY CORPS OF ENGINEERS															
Allatoona Lake (B-2) 25,806 acres 6 mi. s.e. of Cartersville off I-75. Historic. Water skiing; playground.	1	•	•	•	•	•	•	•	•	•	•	•	•	•	•

RECREATION AREAS

	MAP LOCATION	CAMPING	PICNICKING	HIKING TRAILS	BOATING	BOAT RAMP	BOAT RENTAL	FISHING	SWIMMING	PETS ON LEASH	BICYCLE TRAILS	NATURE PROGS.	VISITOR CENTER	LODGE/CABINS	FOOD SERVICE
Carters Lake (A-2) 3,442 acres 34 mi. n. of Cartersville off US 411 to Old US 411. Water skiing; playground.	2	•	•	•	•	•	•	•	•	•	•	•	•	•	•
George W. Andrews Lake (E-1) 1,540 acres 1 mi. e. of Columbia, Ala., on the state line.	3	•	•		•	•		•		•	•	•		•	
Hartwell Lake (A-4) 56,000 acres 6 mi. n. of Hartwell on US 29. Water skiing; bicycle trail, power plant tours in summer.	4	•	•	•	•	•	•	•	•	•			•		
J. Strom Thurmond Lake (B-4) 70,000 acres 20 mi. n.w. of Augusta on SR 28.	5	•	•	•	•	•		•	•	•	•	•	•		
Lake Sidney Lanier (B-3) 38,000 acres. Geocaching, golf (18 holes), horseback riding, miniature golf, tennis, water skiing; amphitheater, beach, waterslide, wave pool. *(See Buford p. 58 and Gainesville p. 75)*	6	•	•	•	•	•	•	•	•	•		•	•	•	•
Lake Walter F. George (E-1) 45,000 acres 2 mi. n. of Fort Gaines off SR 39. Skiing; playground.	7	•	•	•	•	•	•	•	•	•	•	•	•	•	•
Richard B. Russell Lake (B-4) 26,500 acres 20 mi. e. of Elberton on SR 72.	8	•	•	•	•	•	•	•	•	•		•	•	•	•
West Point Lake (C-1) 25,900 acres on the Alabama state line at West Point. Amphitheater, playground.	9	•	•	•	•	•	•	•	•	•		•	•	•	•
STATE															
A.H. Stephens State Historic Park (C-4) 1,177 acres at Crawfordville on US 278 and SR 22. Historic. Boat rentals, equestrian trails. Electric boat motors only. *(See Crawfordville p. 71)*	10	•	•	•	•	•	•	•	•	•	•	•	•	•	
Amicalola Falls (A-2) 829 acres 15 mi. w. of Dahlonega on SR 52 near jct. with SR 183. Scenic. Conference center, ropes course, waterfalls.	11	•	•	•				•		•		•	•	•	•
Black Rock Mountain (A-3) 1,738 acres 3 mi. n. of Clayton via US 23/441. Scenic.	12	•	•	•				•		•		•	•	•	
Bobby Brown (B-4) 665 acres 21 mi. s.e. of Elberton off SR 72. Water skiing.	13	•	•	•	•	•	•	•		•		•	•		•
Cloudland Canyon (A-1) 3,485 acres 25 mi. n.w. of La Fayette off SR 136. Scenic. Disc golf, tennis.	14	•	•	•					•	•			•	•	
Crooked River (F-5) 500 acres 12 mi. e. of Kingsland via SR 40. Birding, miniature golf; bicycle rental, playground.	15	•	•	•	•	•		•		•	•	•	•	•	
Elijah Clark (B-4) 447 acres 6 mi. n.e. of Lincolnton on US 378. Historic. Miniature golf, water skiing; museum.	16	•	•	•	•	•		•	•	•				•	
Florence Marina (D-1) 173 acres 4 mi. s. of Omaha on SR 39C. Birding, miniature golf, tennis; bicycle rentals, playground.	17	•	•	•	•	•	•	•	•	•		•	•	•	
Fort McAllister (E-6) 1,725 acres 10 mi. e. of I-95 on State Spur 144. Historic. Water skiing; playground. *(See Richmond Hill p. 90)*	18	•	•	•	•	•	•	•		•	•	•	•	•	
Fort Mountain (A-2) 1,930 acres 7 mi. e. of Chatsworth off SR 52. Historic. Miniature golf; horse rental, pedal boats.	19	•	•	•	•		•	•	•	•	•	•	•	•	
Fort Yargo (B-3) 1,814 acres 1 mi. s. of Winder on SR 81. Historic. Miniature golf, tennis.	20	•	•	•	•	•	•	•	•	•	•	•	•	•	•
Franklin D. Roosevelt (C-2) 9,049 acres 5 mi. s.e. of Pine Mountain off US 27. Horse rental, pool, scuba diving lessons. Note: Food service is seasonal.	21	•	•	•	•		•	•	•			•	•	•	
General Coffee (E-4) 1,511 acres 6 mi. e. of Douglas on SR 32. Amphitheater, heritage farm, nature programs. swimming pool. Note: Only park rental boats are permitted.	22	•	•	•	•		•	•	•	•	•	•	•	•	
George L. Smith II (D-5) 1,634 acres 4 mi. s.e. of Twin City off SR 23. Birding; mill tours.	23	•	•	•	•	•	•	•		•	•	•	•	•	
George T. Bagby (E-1) 700 acres 3 mi. n. of Fort Gaines off SR 39. Golf, tennis, water skiing; marina.	24		•	•	•	•	•	•	•	•		•		•	•
Georgia Veterans Memorial (E-3) 1,322 acres 9 mi. w. of Cordele on US 280. Historic. Golf (18 holes), water skiing; exhibits, pool. *(See Cordele p. 70)*	25	•	•	•	•	•	•	•	•	•	•	•	•	•	•

RECREATION AREAS

Recreation Area	MAP LOCATION	CAMPING	PICNICKING	HIKING TRAILS	BOATING	BOAT RAMP	BOAT RENTAL	FISHING	SWIMMING	PETS ON LEASH	BICYCLE TRAILS	NATURE PROGS.	VISITOR CENTER	LODGE/CABINS	FOOD SERVICE
Gordonia-Alatamaha (D-5) 462 acres on US 280 near Reidsville. Golf, miniature golf, tennis. Only park rental boats are allowed in the water.	26	•	•		•		•	•	•	•		•	•		
Hamburg (C-4) 750 acres 6 mi. n.e. of Warthen via Hamburg Rd. on SR 102. Grist mill, museum.	27	•	•	•	•	•	•	•		•	•		•		•
Hard Labor Creek (B-3) 5,805 acres 2 mi. n. of Rutledge off I-20. Golf (18 holes), horseback riding; equestrian campsites.	28	•	•	•	•	•	•	•	•	•			•	•	
Hart (B-4) 147 acres 3 mi. n.e. of Hartwell off US 29. Water skiing; Cricket Theater (music programs).	29	•	•	•	•	•	•	•	•	•	•	•	•	•	
High Falls (C-3) 1,050 acres 11 mi. n. of Forsyth just off I-75 at High Falls Rd. exit. Miniature golf.	30	•	•	•	•	•	•	•	•	•			•		•
Indian Springs (C-3) 528 acres 5 mi. s.e. of Jackson on SR 42. Historic. Miniature golf, pedal boats. *(See Jackson p. 82)*	31	•	•	•	•	•	•	•	•	•			•	•	
James H. "Sloppy" Floyd (A-1) 561 acres 3 mi. s.e. of Summerville off US 27. Playground.	32	•	•	•	•	•	•	•		•				•	
John Tanner (B-1) 136 acres 6 mi. w. of Carrollton off SR 16. Miniature golf.	33	•	•	•	•		•	•	•	•			•	•	
Kolomoki Mounds (E-1) 1,293 acres. Miniature golf; fishing boat and canoe and paddleboat rentals, museum, pool. *(See Blakely p. 66)*	34	•	•	•	•	•	•	•	•	•		•	•		•
Laura S. Walker (F-5) 626 acres 10 mi. s.e. of Waycross near US 84. Golf, water skiing; group lodge/cabins.	35	•	•	•	•	•	•	•	•	•		•	•		•
Little Ocmulgee (D-4) 1,397 acres 2 mi. n. of McRae on US 441. Scenic. Golf (18 holes), miniature golf, tennis, water skiing; amphitheater.	36	•	•	•	•	•	•	•	•	•	•	•	•	•	•
Magnolia Springs (C-5) 1,071 acres 5 mi. n. of Millen on US 25. Aquarium, playground, pool, springs.	37	•	•	•	•	•	•	•	•	•	•		•	•	
Mistletoe (C-4) 1,920 acres 10 mi. n. of Appling off SR 150. Water skiing.	38	•	•	•	•	•	•	•	•	•	•	•	•	•	•
Moccasin Creek (A-3) 32 acres 16 mi. s.w. of Clayton on SR 197. Water skiing; playground.	39	•	•	•	•	•	•	•		•			•		•
Red Top Mountain (B-1) 1,562 acres 2 mi. e. of I-75 Red Top exit. Miniature golf, tennis, water skiing; marina, playground.	40	•	•	•	•	•	•	•	•	•		•	•	•	•
Reed Bingham (F-3) 1,613 acres 6 mi. w. of Adel off SR 37. Miniature golf, water skiing; playground.	41	•	•	•	•	•	•	•	•	•		•	•		•
Seminole (F-1) 604 acres 16 mi. s. of Donalsonville off SR 39. Water skiing.	42	•	•	•	•	•	•	•	•	•	•		•	•	
Skidaway Island (E-6) 588 acres 6 mi. s.e. of Savannah; take I-16 to SR 21. Birding; playground, pool.	43	•	•	•					•	•	•	•	•		
Stephen C. Foster (F-4) 80 acres 18 mi. n.e. of Fargo on SR 177. Boat tours, museum, playground. Note: As of June 2007, boat tours were unavailable due to low water levels. Phone ahead to confirm availability.	44	•	•		•	•	•	•		•		•	•	•	•
Sweetwater Creek (B-2) 2,549 acres 15 mi. w. of Atlanta off I-20. Historic. Playground. NOTE: Due to the drought, the level of the lake is very low; boat and canoe rentals are currently unavailable.	45		•	•	•	•	•	•		•		•	•		
Tallulah Gorge (A-3) 2,689 acres at Tallulah Falls. Tennis; nature trails, playground. *(See Tallulah Falls p. 101)*	46	•	•	•	•			•	•	•	•	•	•		
Tugaloo (A-3) 393 acres 6 mi. n. of Lavonia off SR 328. Miniature golf, tennis, water skiing.	47	•	•	•	•	•	•	•	•	•		•		•	
Unicoi (A-3) 1,081 acres 2 mi. n.e. of Helen via SR 356. Tennis; playground, ropes course.	48	•	•	•	•		•	•	•	•	•	•	•	•	•
Victoria Bryant (B-3) 475 acres 4 mi. w. of Royston off US 29 and SR 327. Golf (18 holes); playground. Only campers or the physically impaired are permitted to fish.	49	•	•	•				•	•	•	•		•		
Vogel (A-3) 233 acres 11 mi. s. of Blairsville on US 19/129. Pedal boats only. *(See Blairsville p. 66)*	50	•	•	•	•		•	•	•	•	•	•	•	•	•

RECREATION AREAS

	MAP LOCATION	CAMPING	PICNICKING	HIKING TRAILS	BOATING	BOAT RAMP	BOAT RENTAL	FISHING	SWIMMING	PETS ON LEASH	BICYCLE TRAILS	NATURE PROGS.	VISITOR CENTER	LODGE/CABINS	FOOD SERVICE
Watson Mill Bridge (B-3) 1,018 acres. Historic. Scenic. Canoeing; paddleboats, horse trails and equestrian camping and stalls. *(See Comer p. 70)*	51	●	●	●	●		●	●		●	●		●	●	
OTHER															
Earl May Boat Basin and Park (F-2) 600 acres on W. Shotwell St. in Bainbridge. Tennis, water skiing; playground, train museum.	52	●	●	●	●	●		●	●	●			●		
Lake Blue Ridge (A-2) 3,290 acres 4 mi. e. of Blue Ridge via old US 76 and CR 23. Water skiing; marina.	53		●	●	●	●	●	●	●	●			●		
Lake Chatuge (A-3) 6,950 acres 3 mi. s.w. of Hiawassee via US 76 and SR 288.	54	●	●	●	●	●		●	●	●			●		
Lake Lindsay Grace (E-5) 250 acres 8 mi. w. of Jesup on SR 203. Birding, water skiing.	55	●	●		●	●		●			●				
Lake Oconee (C-3) 19,255 acres 7 mi. e. of Eatonton. Water skiing.	56	●	●	●	●	●	●	●	●	●				●	●
Lake Sinclair (C-3) 15,330 acres n.e. of Milledgeville on SR 441. Marinas.	57	●	●			●		●	●	●				●	●
Lake Tobesofkee (C-3) 1,750 acres 12 mi. w. of Macon off I-475 at SR 74 and Thomaston Rd. Tennis, water skiing.	58	●	●		●	●	●	●	●	●	●			●	
Lake Winfield Scott (A-2) 18 acres 4 mi. e. of Suches on SR 180.	59	●	●	●	●	●		●	●	●				●	
Rabun Beach (A-3) 934 acres 13 mi. s. of Clayton via US 23, SR 15 and CR 10.	60	●	●	●	●	●		●	●	●					
Sandy Creek Park (B-3) 634 acres 2.5 mi. n. of Athens bypass off US 441. Boats with electric motors only.	61	●	●	●	●	●	●	●	●	●			●		
Stone Mountain Park (B-2) 3,200 acres. Golf (36 holes), miniature golf, tennis; waterslides.	62	●	●	●	●	●	●	●	●	●			●		●
Suwannee Canal Recreation Area (F-5) 396,000 acres. *(See Folkston p. 74)*	63		●	●	●	●	●	●		●	●	●	●		●

Georgia Temperature Averages Maximum/Minimum

From the records of The Weather Channel Interactive, Inc.

	JAN	FEB	MAR	APR	MAY	JUNE	JULY	AUG	SEPT	OCT	NOV	DEC
Atlanta	52/33	57/37	65/44	73/50	80/59	87/67	89/71	88/70	82/64	73/53	63/44	55/36
Augusta	56/33	61/36	69/43	77/48	84/57	90/65	92/70	90/68	85/62	76/50	68/41	59/35
Columbus	57/37	62/39	69/46	77/52	83/61	90/69	92/72	91/71	86/66	77/55	68/46	59/39
Macon	57/34	61/37	69/44	76/50	83/59	90/67	92/71	91/70	85/64	77/51	68/43	59/36
Savannah	60/38	64/41	71/47	78/53	84/61	90/68	92/72	90/71	86/67	78/56	71/47	63/40

Points of Interest

ADAIRSVILLE (B-2) pop. 2,542, elev. 714'

BARNSLEY GARDENS RESORT is at 597 Barnsley Garden Rd. The 1,300-acre estate, built by Sir Godfrey Barnsley in the 1800s, features historic outbuildings, a cemetery, ruins of the original manor house and a museum containing Barnsley family memorabilia. The gardens have been restored to their 19th-century style; a variety of flowers and plants, water cascades and fountains are on view. A resort and a golf course also are on the property. Food is available. Garden open daily dawn-dusk. Museum open Mon.-Sat. 8-6, Sun. 8-5. Museum free. Garden tour $10; $8 (ages 55+); $5 (ages 0-11). AX, DS, MC, VI. Phone (770) 773-7480 or (877) 773-2447.

ALBANY (E-2) pop. 76,939, elev. 210'

The site that eventually became Albany was bought in 1836 by a Connecticut man who hired surveyors to plat a town. Later that year Nelson Tift and a group of companions brought supplies up the Flint River from Apalachicola, Fla., and began to construct log buildings. The town took its name from the city in New York that also was at a river's head of navigation.

The Parks at Chehaw are outside of town on Lake Chehaw on SR 91, 1.2 miles north of US 19/82/SR 50. Offering a Wild Animal Park and a petting zoo, the parks feature animals of the African savannah in surroundings resembling their natural habitat. There also are nature trails and camping facilities; phone (229) 430-5275.

A bronze statue of Albany native Ray Charles playing his piano sits in Ray Charles Plaza on Front Street.

Albany Convention and Visitors Bureau: 112 Front St., Albany, GA 31701; phone (229) 317-4760. *See color ad.*

ALBANY CIVIL RIGHTS MOVEMENT MUSEUM is at 326 Whitney Ave. Housed in the restored 1906 Mt. Zion Church, the museum commemorates the 1960s civil rights movement in southwest Georgia, emphasizing the role played by ordinary people in the struggle for civil rights. Exhibits, historic photographs and videotape footage recount the movement's history. Guided tours are available. Allow 1 hour minimum. Wed.-Sat. 10-4, Sun. 2-5. Admission $4; $3 (ages 6-17, ages 65+ and students with ID); $2 (ages 0-5). Phone (229) 432-1698.

SAVE **ALBANY MUSEUM OF ART,** 311 Meadowlark Dr., features six rotating galleries, a children's hands-on space and a collection of American, European and African art. Tues.-Sat. 10-5. Admission $4; $2 (ages 55+, military and students with ID); free (Thurs.). AX, MC, VI. Phone (229) 439-8400.

FLINT RIVERQUARIUM, at 101 Pine Ave., features a 175,000-gallon, blue-hole spring aquarium that is home to more than 100 varieties of aquatic life. The Flint River Gallery contains fresh- and saltwater tanks as well as a live fish hatchery. Discovery Caverns allows children to learn about nature through interactive exhibits. The World of Water draws comparisons between rivers around the globe and Flint River. The RiverQuarium Imagination Theater shows films, many in 3-D.

Allow 1 hour minimum. Mon.-Fri. 9-5, Sat. 10-6, Sun. 1-5; closed Thanksgiving and Dec. 25. Admission $9; $8 (ages 62+); $6.50 (ages 4-12). Theater $6; $4.50 (ages 4-12). Combination ticket $14; $12.50 (ages 62+); $10 (ages 4-12). AX, DS, MC, VI. Phone (229) 639-2650. *See color ad p. 40.*

THRONATEESKA HERITAGE CENTER AND WETHERBEE PLANETARIUM is at 100 W. Roosevelt Ave. The heritage center is housed on a historic plaza and includes a museum that recounts the history of southwest Georgia, a railroad museum, a planetarium and a science discovery center featuring hands-on exhibits. Allow 1 hour minimum. Museum open Thurs.-Sat. noon-4. Planetarium show times and discovery center Thurs.-Fri. at 2:45, Sat. at 12:30, 1:30 and 2:30. Heritage center admission free. Planetarium show $2. MC, VI. Phone (229) 432-6955. *See color ad p. 40.*

ALPHARETTA—*see Atlanta p. 58.*

AMERICUS (D-2) pop. 17,013, elev. 360'

Americus-Sumter Tourism Council: 123 W. Lamar St., Americus, GA 31709; phone (229) 928-6059.

Self-guiding tours: A brochure detailing a driving tour past more than 30 antebellum, Greek Revival and Victorian homes in the historic district may be obtained from the Americus-Sumter Tourism Council.

HABITAT FOR HUMANITY INTERNATIONAL GLOBAL VILLAGE & DISCOVERY CENTER is at 721 W. Church St. The six-acre site includes the Welcome Center, the Living in Poverty Area and 15 replicas of Habitat homes from around the world. Traditional household items also are displayed. Mon.-Fri. 9-5 (also Sat. 10-2, Mar.-Nov.); phone for holiday schedule. Donations. Phone (229) 924-6935, ext. 7663 or (229) 924-6935, ext. 7937, or (800) 422-4828, ext. 7937.

ANDERSONVILLE (D-2) pop. 331, elev. 394'

ANDERSONVILLE CIVIL WAR VILLAGE, .2 mi. e. on SR 49, is a restored village that once was the point of disembarkation for Civil War prisoners on their way to Andersonville, the Confederate prison. A numbered walking tour of the village begins at the welcome center. Highlights include a pioneer farm, a 1927 log church and the Drummer Boy Civil War Museum, which displays Civil War uniforms and an Andersonville diorama.

Food and picnic facilities are available. Allow 1 hour minimum. Daily 9-5; closed Dec. 25. Free. Phone (229) 924-2558.

ANDERSONVILLE NATIONAL HISTORIC SITE (D-3)

Andersonville National Historic Site is 10 miles northeast of Americus on SR 49. It encompasses the Andersonville National Cemetery and The National Prisoner of War Museum *(see attraction listing)* as well as the grounds of what was probably the Civil War's most infamous prisoner-of-war camp.

Opened in February 1864, the Andersonville prison was an almost impenetrable stockade encompassing 26.5 acres. Inside this enclosure was a line—called the "deadline"—that prisoners were not permitted to cross under penalty of death. A creek was the main water supply and eventually, because of contamination, a prime source of illness and death among the prisoners.

Although built to accommodate 10,000 prisoners, Andersonville at one time confined more than 32,000. The impoverished Confederate government was unable to supply prisoners with the bare necessities, and the mortality rate soared. Although prison commander Capt. Henry Wirz was powerless to prevent the overcrowding, after the war he was convicted by a military tribunal and hanged for conspiring to murder Union war prisoners.

A July 1864 excerpt from the diary of Sgt. David Kennedy of the 9th Ohio Cavalry describes the conditions of the site and its inhabitants as a "hell on Earth, where it takes seven of its occupants to make a shadow."

Andersonville commemorates those who have been prisoners of war in defense of this nation. More than 18,000 veterans and their dependents are buried at the site. On the grounds is Providence Spring, which reputedly gushed forth in answer to the prayers of thirsty prisoners. The remains of wells and escape tunnels still exist. One corner and the north gate of the prison stockade have been rebuilt. Picnicking is permitted in designated areas. Site open daily 8-5. Free. Phone (229) 924-0343.

THE NATIONAL PRISONER OF WAR MUSEUM, just e. of SR 49 adjacent to the prison, contains various types of exhibits about prisoners of war from the Revolutionary War through Operation Iraqi Freedom. Letters and videotapes give first-hand historical accounts by prisoners; displays contain personal items belonging to those who were confinedhere. The museum stands as a memorial to the 12,920 Union soldiers and civilians who died at Andersonville during the 14 months it existed 1864-65. Allow 1 hour minimum. Daily 8:30-5; closed Jan. 1, Thanksgiving and Dec. 25. Free. Phone (229) 924-0343.

ATHENS (B-3) pop. 101,489, elev. 800'

Athens, the largest city in the rolling piedmont of northeastern Georgia, has many buildings that exemplify the Federal and Greek Revival architectural style so popular in the Old South. The Athens Welcome Center, 280 E. Dougherty St., offers daily guided heritage tours featuring four house museums. In spring, home and garden tours also are available; phone (706) 357-4430 or (800) 653-0603.

The double-barreled cannon in City Hall Plaza was cast at the Athens Foundry during the Civil War. Probably the only one of its kind, this unusual

Civil War relic was intended to maximize damage to the enemy by firing two balls joined by a chain. Legend has it that the chain broke during the weapon's only firing and the cannonballs went their separate ways, destroying a cabin and a cow.

Athens' most unusual property owner must be the white oak that stands in a square at Dearing and Finley streets. The owner of the oak deeded the huge tree possession of itself and all the land within 8 feet in appreciation of its beauty and shade. The original tree was destroyed by a storm in 1942 and another was grown from one of its acorns on the same site. The legal rights of "The Tree That Owns Itself" have never been questioned.

Athens Convention and Visitors Bureau: 300 N. Thomas St., Athens, GA 30601; phone (706) 357-4430 or (800) 653-0603.

Self-guiding tours: Brochures and maps detailing a walking tour past historic homes as well as audio tours are available at the Athens Welcome Center, 280 E. Dougherty St.; phone (706) 353-1820 or (866) 455-1820. The center is in the Church-Waddel-Brumby House, a Federal-style house built in 1820. The Athens Welcome Center also operates an information kiosk downtown on Washington St., just outside of city hall.

TAYLOR-GRADY HOUSE is at 634 Prince Ave. The restored Greek Revival mansion was built in the mid-1840s by Gen. Robert Taylor, a planter and cotton merchant. In 1863 it was purchased by the family of Henry W. Grady, a newspaper editor considered by many to be the spokesman of the New South. An impressive orator, Grady stressed the importance of reconciliation between the North and South after the Civil War.

Allow 30 minutes minimum. Mon.-Fri. 9-1 and 2:30-5; closed holidays and during special events. Admission $3. Phone (706) 549-8688.

DID YOU KNOW

Actress Kim Basinger was born in Athens.

UNIVERSITY OF GEORGIA campus can be entered from Broad St. through a mid-19th-century arch that symbolizes the state seal of Georgia. Founded in 1785, it is said to be the nation's first state-chartered university. Visitors can stroll the 615-acre campus and view historic structures, many of which were built before 1850. The Collegiate Tennis Hall of Fame, at Henry Feild Tennis Stadium, pays tribute to collegiate tennis players and is open during tennis matches. Guided tours of the campus are offered Mon.-Fri. by reservation. Free. Phone (706) 542-0842 for the visitor center and tour reservations, or (706) 542-1231 for Georgia Bulldogs teams tickets.

Butts-Mehre Heritage Hall, at Pinecrest Dr. and Lumpkin St., is a modern athletic complex named for two former coaches of the Georgia Bulldogs, Wallace Butts and Harry Mehre. The Heritage Museum on the second, third and fourth floors contains exhibits honoring Georgia athletes. Displays include Heisman and National Championship trophies, the Circle of Honor and videotapes that replay great moments in the university's sports history.

Allow 30 minutes minimum. Mon.-Fri. 8-5; closed major holidays. Free. Phone (706) 542-9036.

Founders Memorial Garden, 325 S. Lumpkin St., honors the founders of the first garden club in America, begun in 1891. The 2.5-acre grounds, landscaped 1936-1946, include a formal boxwood garden, a perennial garden, an arboretum, two courtyards and a terrace, and are a museum of landscape design. Allow 30 minutes minimum. Daily dawn-dusk. Free. Phone (706) 542-1816.

The Georgia Museum of Art is at 90 Carlton St. on the East Campus. The museum was founded in 1945 when Alfred H. Holbrook donated his collection of 100 American paintings to the university.

Now the collection contains more than 10,000 works including 19th-century through contemporary American paintings, Italian Renaissance paintings and an extensive collection of prints and drawings by American, European and Oriental masters. Allow 1 hour minimum. Tues.-Sat. 10-5 (also Wed. 5-9), Sun. 1-5; closed major holidays. Free. Phone (706) 542-4662.

State Botanical Garden of Georgia, 2450 S. Milledge Ave., is a 313-acre cultural, educational and recreational facility on the Middle Oconee River. Five miles of nature trails extend into the natural areas typical of the habitats and plant communities found in Piedmont Georgia. A number of theme gardens and special collections display species from around the world.

The visitor center and conservatory contain a collection of tropical and semi-tropical plants providing a backdrop for concerts, lectures and art exhibitions. Food is available Tues.-Sun. Allow 30 minutes minimum. Grounds open daily 8-8, Apr.-Sept.; 8-6, rest of year. Visitor center open Tues.-Sat. 9-4:30, Sun. 11:30-4:30; closed major holidays. Free. Phone (706) 542-1244.

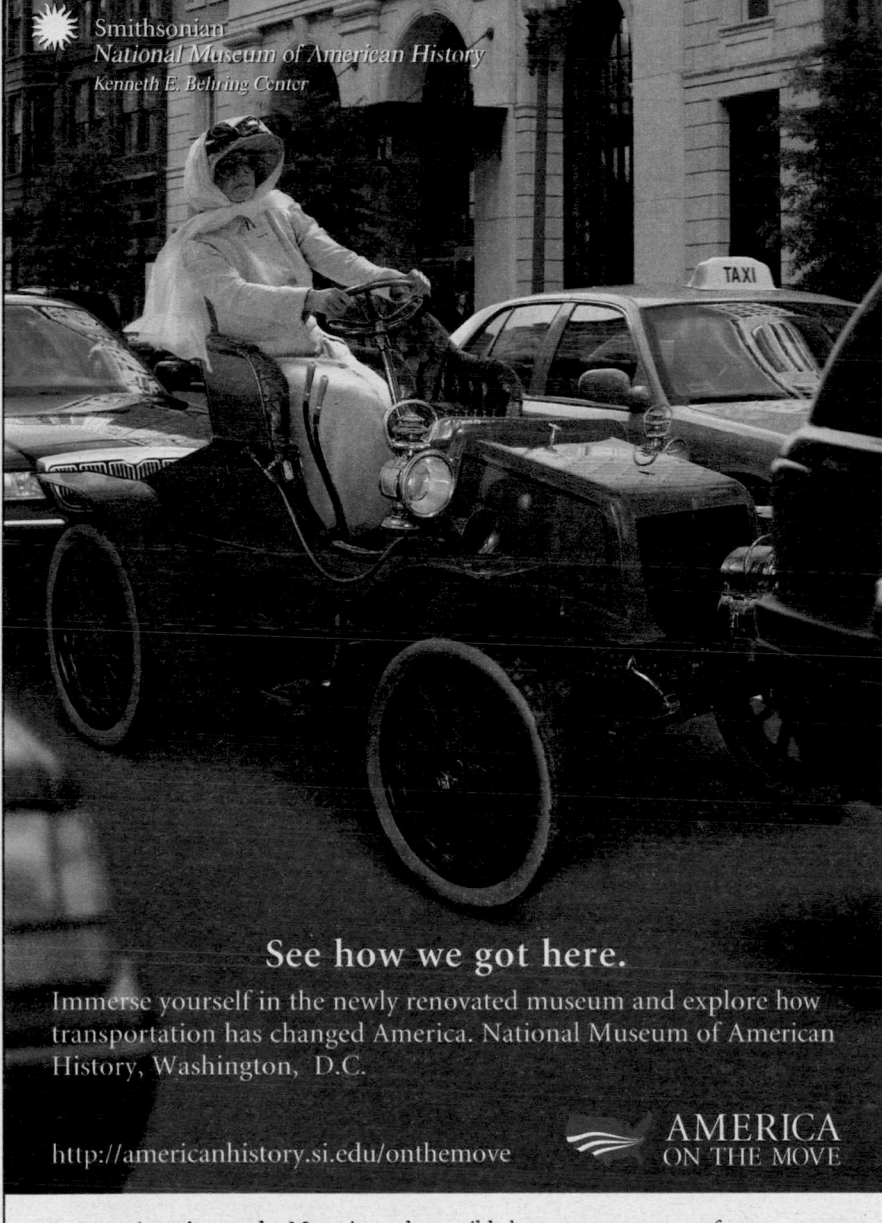

Atlanta

City Population: 416,474 **Elevation:** 1,050 ft.

Editor's Picks:

Atlanta History Center.............. *(see p. 50)*
High Museum of Art................ *(see p. 55)*
Zoo Atlanta........................... *(see p. 53)*

Find more AAA top picks at AAA.com

Centennial Olympic Park / © Gary Conner
Index Stock / Photolibrary

Atlanta, capital of Georgia, is the commercial, industrial and financial giant of the Southeast. It is crisscrossed with crowded expressways and throbs with teeming industry, yet manages to maintain a gracious air of Southern living. At its center towering skyscrapers rise along streets with names evocative of the Old South. Throughout the city many trees and shrubs lend an ever present note of green.

Atlanta began in 1837 as a railroad surveyor's stake in a pine clearing. The city rapidly grew into an important railway and manufacturing center, becoming the Confederate arsenal during the Civil War. Reduced to a smoking ruin by Gen. William Tecumseh Sherman's occupation in 1864, the city drew upon its unconquerable spirit and the wise use of carpetbagger money to again become a booming commercial center.

Rapid growth has continued unabated for more than a century. Due to active urban renewal and the fact that few of its buildings predate the Civil War, Atlanta has suffered less from urban blight than most U.S. cities. Evidence of this good fortune is reflected in the burgeoning skyline; however, there are still reminders of an earlier Atlanta and of a city closer to the Old South and its small towns. The 50-year-old Varsity, a drive-in restaurant near Georgia Tech., stands in stark contrast to the chrome and glass skyscrapers that now surround it.

The CNN Center at Marietta Street and Centennial Olympic Park houses the worldwide headquarters for the Cable News Network as well as broadcast studios, a behind-the-scenes tour, shops, restaurants and the Philips Arena. Just across Marietta Street is Centennial Olympic Park, a 21-acre landscaped green space that is the focal point of downtown Atlanta; sculptures, walkways and the Fountain of the Rings grace the park, which was the largest single facility of the 1996 Summer Olympics. Adjacent to Centennial Olympic Park is the Georgia Aquarium, which houses more than 100,000 fish and other animals in eight million gallons of water. The aquarium is reputed to be the largest in the world. The Georgia World Congress Center on Andrew Young International Boulevard is a huge exhibition hall and convention center. The mammoth AmericasMart sits across from a complex of skyscrapers comprising Peachtree Center.

Some 3,700 manufacturers produce a range of commodities including aircraft, automobiles, furniture, textiles, chemicals, food, paper, iron and steel. More than 750 Fortune 1000 companies have offices in Atlanta, including the headquarters of Coca-Cola, which was introduced in the city in 1886. Atlanta is the Southeastern headquarters for the U.S. Public Health Service and the national headquarters of the Centers for Disease Control, United Parcel Service and the American Cancer Society.

Atlanta also leads the South in social reform. Civil rights leader Dr. Martin Luther King Jr. worked to eliminate racial discrimination in the city

Getting There — *starting on p. 45*
Getting Around — *starting on p. 49*
What To See — *starting on p. 50*
What To Do — *starting on p. 56*
Where To Stay — *starting on p. 320*
Where To Dine — *starting on p. 331*
Essential Experiences — *visit AAA.com*
Editor's Event Picks — *visit AAA.com*

and throughout the nation, and Ralph McGill, publisher of the *Atlanta Constitution*, was a leading force for integration in the early 1960s. Dr. King's birthplace, church and tomb as well as other buildings are preserved in the Martin Luther King Jr. National Historic Site *(see attraction listing p. 54)*.

A tour of the suburbs is a must for any visitor, for the elegant houses and curving, wooded streets make up some of the country's most beautiful residential areas. They are especially stunning in April during the Dogwood Festival, when millions of dogwoods and azaleas burst into red, pink and white blooms.

The Atlanta University Center District is comprised of a group of distinguished African-American colleges and universities. Campus tours are offered Monday through Friday; phone (800) 251-1254 or (404) 681-2800 for Morehouse College; phone (800) 982-2411 for Spelman College; phone (404) 880-8000 for Clark Atlanta University; phone (404) 739-1000 for Morris Brown College; and phone (404) 527-7700 for the Interdenominational Theological Center.

Atlanta enjoys four definite seasons. Warm summers and mild winters permit nearly year-round golfing, fishing and outdoor living—happy distractions from the ambitions of a progressive, sophisticated city.

Kangaroo Conservation Center, Dawsonville
Georgia Department of Economic Development

Getting There

By Car

Major highways provide speedy access to Atlanta from nearly all directions. Three interstate highways cross the Perimeter (I-285), which circles the city. I-75 (the Northwest Expressway) joins I-85 (the Northeast Expressway) just north of downtown to become the Downtown Connector (I-75/85), which passes to the east of downtown.

From the southeast I-75 becomes the South Expressway to the point south of downtown near Turner Field, where it meets I-20 from the east (the East Expressway) and the west (the West Expressway).

Other roads also run from I-285 toward downtown. I-85 approaches the city from the southwest, joining the South Expressway within I-285. The Arthur Langford Parkway (SR 166) also connects the southwest portion of I-285 with the South Expressway. US 78 from the east passes Stone Mountain before crossing I-285, after which it runs into Scott Boulevard and Ponce de Leon Avenue.

Additional highways that approach the city include SR 400 (toll 50c) from the north, which crosses I-285 and ends on I-85 just north of the I-85 and I-75 connector; US 41 from the northwest, which runs into the Northside Parkway inside I-285; and US 19, which becomes Roswell Road, Peachtree Street and finally Spring Street as it moves

Destination Atlanta

Atlanta—or "Hotlanta," as locals like to say—embraces both sleek skyscrapers and stately Southern homes. This city is fast-paced and cosmopolitan: Cars vie for space on busy Spaghetti Junction, and cultural offerings include theater, ballet and symphonic performances. And all the while, a favorite pastime is sipping iced tea while relaxing under the shade of a peach tree.

The home of the 1996 Olympics and capital of Georgia certainly is a city to be reckoned with. But you and your pals will feel like locals when welcomed with a friendly "hey, y'all."

Georgia Department of Economic Development

Zoo Atlanta.
Giant pandas are only one of nearly 1,000 animals that call the zoo home. (See listing page 53)

© The Coca-Cola Company

World of Coca-Cola Atlanta
Commissioned for the 1996 Centennial Olympic Games, these folk art bottles represent the diverse cultural connection to the world's most recognized brand. (See listing page 55)

Places included in this AAA Destination City:

© Rainer Kiedrowski age fotostock

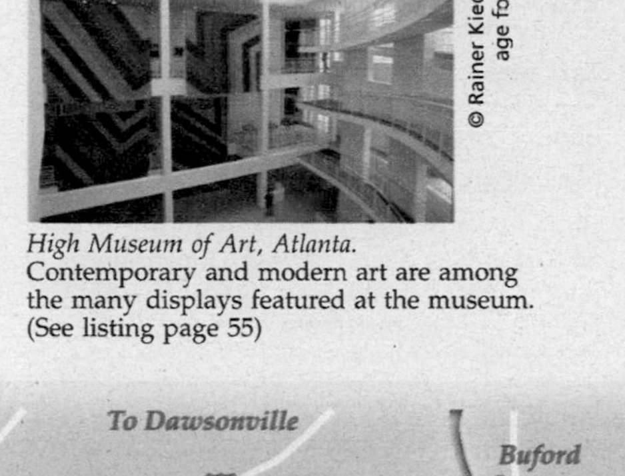

High Museum of Art, Atlanta.
Contemporary and modern art are among the many displays featured at the museum. (See listing page 55)

Georgia Department of Economic Development

Southern Museum of Civil War and Locomotive History, Kennesaw
Stolen in 1862 by Union spies, "The General" was at the center of what is known as the Great Locomotive Chase. (See listing page 59)

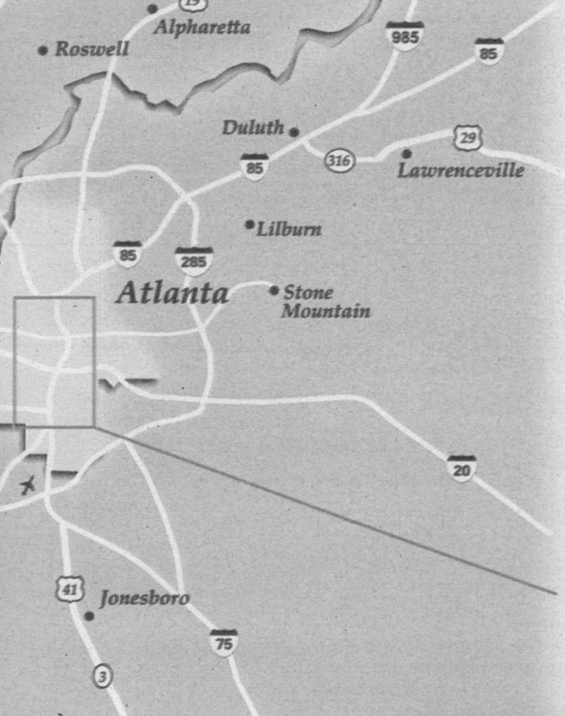

See Vicinity map page 51

© Georgia Aquarium

Georgia Aquarium, Atlanta
At least six galleries and areas provide visitors an opportunity to explore the universal wonders of the ocean. (See listing page 53)

The Informed Traveler

Sales Tax: The sales tax in the Atlanta metro area is 8 percent. An additional 7 percent is levied on hotel rooms, bringing the total tax on hotel stays to 15 percent.

WHOM TO CALL

Emergency: 911

Police (non-emergency): (404) 853-3434

Time and Temperature: (770) 455-7141

Hospitals: Emory Johns Creek Hospital, (678) 474-7000; Emory University Hospital, (404) 712-2000; Grady Memorial Hospital, (404) 616-1000; Northside Hospital, (404) 851-8000; Piedmont Hospital, (404) 605-5000; Saint Joseph's Hospital of Atlanta, (404) 851-7001.

WHERE TO LOOK

Newspapers

Metro Atlanta's newspapers include the *Atlanta Journal-Constitution* and the weekly *Atlanta Business Chronicle*.

Radio

WSB (750 AM) is a news/talk radio station; WABE (90.1 FM) is a member of National Public Radio.

Visitor Information

Atlanta Convention & Visitors Bureau: 233 Peachtree St. N.E., Suite 1400, Atlanta, GA 30303; phone (404) 521-6645.

TRANSPORTATION

Air Travel

Atlanta is served by Hartsfield-Jackson Atlanta International Airport nine miles southwest of the business district via the Southwest Expressway and I-85. Rapid rail transportation to downtown Atlanta and the metropolitan area is provided by the Metropolitan Atlanta Rapid Transit Authority (MARTA). The fare is $1.75.

Taxi fare to downtown Atlanta averages $30. Travel time to the business district is about 30 minutes.

Rental Cars

Hertz, with offices downtown and at the airport, offers discounts to AAA members; phone (404) 530-2925 or (800) 654-3131. For listings of other agencies check the telephone directory.

Rail Service

Amtrak train service is provided out of Southern Railway's Peachtree Station, known locally as Brookwood Station, at 1688 Peachtree St. N.W.; phone (800) 872-7245.

Buses

Greyhound Lines Inc., 232 Forsyth St. S.W., is the major bus line serving Atlanta; phone (404) 584-1728 for recorded information or (800) 231-2222. There is a location at the airport at 6000 N. Terminal Dr.; phone (404) 765-9598.

Taxis

Cab companies include Checker Cab, (404) 351-1111, and Yellow, (404) 521-0200. Taxis are metered. Base fare for Checker Cab and Yellow is $2.50, plus $2.50 for each additional mile. Other taxi companies are listed in the telephone directory.

Public Transport

Atlanta's public transportation consists of the Metropolitan Atlanta Rapid Transit Authority's (MARTA) bus, rail and subway systems. *See Public Transportation for details.*

Note: In the *Points of Interest* section, attraction listings often include the nearest MARTA Rapid Rail stop and, if applicable, the number of the connecting bus route.

south. Because of the profusion of expressways, be sure to use a detailed map of the city.

Getting Around

Try to time your arrival in Atlanta after rush hours when it is easier to navigate the high-speed expressways and meandering main streets. Rush hours in general are from 6:30 to 9 a.m. and from 3:30 to 7 p.m. during which expressway traffic in both the city and the suburbs is often bumper-to-bumper. Observe posted speed limit signs.

Interstate traffic in the Metro Atlanta area is monitored and managed by NAVIGATOR, the Georgia Department of Transportation's Intelligent Transportation System (ITS). NAVIGATOR's Traffic Management Center provides 24/7 information and alerts on traffic delays, incidents and road construction.

Street System

The center of the downtown area is the Five Points Intersection, where Peachtree, Marietta, Decatur, Edgewood and Whitehall converge near the site of the original surveyor's stake. It also is where the city's four geographical divisions—N.E., N.W., S.E. and S.W.—merge.

Atlanta is not laid out in the traditional grid, so there are few rectangular blocks and square intersections. The main street is Peachtree, extending north and south through the center of the city; North and Ponce de Leon avenues are the principal east-west links. The Downtown Connector (I-75/85) skirts the business district. The East and West expressways (I-20) carry traffic from the city center.

Though Peachtree Street is the main thoroughfare, there are more than 100 other streets, avenues and lanes in the metro area that include the name. Do not be misled by West Peachtree Street, Peachtree Memorial Drive, Peachtree View, Peachtree Circle, Peachtree Heights, Peachtree Place, Peachtree Battle Avenue, Peachtree Hills Avenue or a similar name.

Parking

On-street parking in the downtown business district is virtually nonexistent. However, garages and lots are plentiful throughout the city, with rates usually $1 for the first half-hour or $7-$8 per day. Rates downtown, especially near the CNN Center, the Georgia World Congress Center and the Philips Arena, exceed $7 per day. Many parking lots and decks now offer "early bird specials": Drivers parking before 9 or 10 a.m. and leaving after 2 or 3 p.m. pay $4-$5 per day. Metered parking is available in other areas, but it is usually strictly enforced during business hours and violators' cars are often towed.

Public Transportation

Atlanta's Metropolitan Atlanta Rapid Transit Authority (MARTA) has a 47-mile Rapid Rail transit system and extensive connector bus routes. Buses are available to Six Flags Over Georgia and Turner

CityPass

The Atlanta CityPass includes the Georgia Aquarium, the Inside CNN Studio Tour, New World of Coca-Cola, and Zoo Atlanta. Also included are two option tickets for either the Atlanta Botanical Garden or the Fernbank Museum of Natural History, and either the Atlanta History Center or the High Museum of Art.

The pass may be purchased at any participating attraction and is valid for 9 days once the first ticket is used. The price through March 2010 is $74; $54 (ages 3-12). Credit cards accepted vary with the vendor. Phone (707) 256-0490 for recorded information, or phone (888) 330-5008 for customer service.

See color ad p. 50.

Field. Minimum fare is $1.75. For information contact the route information center Mon.-Fri. 6 a.m.-11 p.m., Sat.-Sun. and most holidays 8 a.m.-10 p.m.; phone (404) 848-5000.

At the Five Points Station, the "A-to-Z" bus route connects visitors with the Georgia Aquarium and Zoo Atlanta. The fare is $1.75. The route is available Mon.-Fri. 8-5 and Sat.-Sun. and holidays 9-5.

The Peach, or MARTA Route 110, offers bus service with frequent stops, many at some of the city's most historic and popular locations. The $1.75 fare includes transfers to other MARTA bus and rail services. The Peach is available daily 6 a.m.-1 a.m. and departs every 30 minutes.

The Buckhead Uptown Connection (BUC), a free shuttle service offering two routes and connecting directly to MARTA's rail service, transports passengers to area attractions, hotels and restaurants, including Lenox Square and Phipps Plaza. Service is available Mon.-Fri. 7 a.m.-9 p.m. and Sat. 10-9; phone (404) 812-7433 to confirm route and schedule information.

The Tech Trolley bus service is provided by the Georgia Institute of Technology and offers access to Technology Square, the midtown MARTA station and the institute's campus. The trolley is available Mon.-Fri. 5:45 a.m.-11 p.m., Sat. 10-6:30 and Sun. 3-9:45 p.m.; the route does not run on Saturdays of Georgia Tech home football games. Phone (404) 894-9645 to confirm schedule.

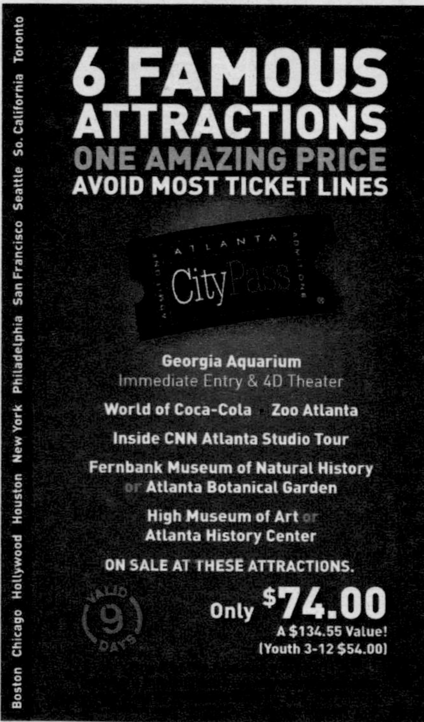

What To See

APEX MUSEUM, 135 Auburn Ave. S.E. at Piedmont Ave. S.E. (MARTA: Five Points Station to bus #113), celebrates African-Americans' contributions to history. Highlights include a reproduction of the 1923 Yates & Milton Drugstore, one of the first African-American-owned businesses in Atlanta, as well as interactive programs and art and photography exhibits.

Guided tours are available. Allow 1 hour minimum. Tues.-Sat. 10-5, Sun. 1-5, in Feb. and June-Aug.; Tues.-Sat. 10-5, rest of year. Admission $4; $3 (ages 55+ and students with ID); free (ages 0-3). AX, DS, MC, VI. Phone (404) 521-2739.

SAVE **ATLANTA BOTANICAL GARDEN** is adjacent to midtown's Piedmont Park at 1345 Piedmont Ave. N.E. (MARTA: Arts Center Station). The garden's 34 acres contain woodland shade, parterre, Japanese rock and rose gardens. The interactive Children's Garden has play areas designed to teach children about plants. The Fuqua Conservatory features tropical, Mediterranean, desert and endangered plants; the Fuqua Orchid Center houses rare orchids from around the world.

Allow 1 hour minimum. Tues.-Sun. (also Mon. holidays) 9-7, Apr.-Oct.; 9-5, rest of year. Closed Jan. 1, Thanksgiving and Dec. 25. Admission $12; $9 (ages 3-17, 65+ and students with ID). AX, MC, VI. Phone (404) 876-5859. *See color ad.*

GEM SAVE **ATLANTA HISTORY CENTER** is at 130 W. Paces Ferry Rd. N.W. (MARTA: Lenox Station to bus #23; also bus #38). The history center features a 30,000-square-foot museum housing exhibitions about the history of Atlanta, the Civil War and Southern folk arts. Some 33 acres of gardens and woodland trails relate the horticultural history of the area and are the setting for two historic houses: The Swan House, a 1928 classically styled mansion, and Tullie Smith Farm, a restored 1860 farmhouse complete with traditional outbuildings and antebellum activities.

The Centennial Olympic Games Museum at the center is a two-story exhibition capturing the spirit of the Olympic Games, especially the 1996 Atlanta Summer Games. The museum has an interactive sports lab.

Allow 3 hours minimum. Mon.-Sat. 10-5:30, Sun. noon-5:30; holiday hours vary. Last admission 1 hour before closing. Admission $15; $12 (ages 65+ and students with ID); $10 (ages 4-12). AX, MC, VI. Phone (404) 814-4000. *See color ad.*

THE BREMAN JEWISH HERITAGE MUSEUM is in the Selig Center at 1440 Spring St. N.W. (MARTA: Arts Center Station). The Blonder Heritage Gallery presents the exhibition "Creating Community: The Jews of Atlanta from 1845 to the

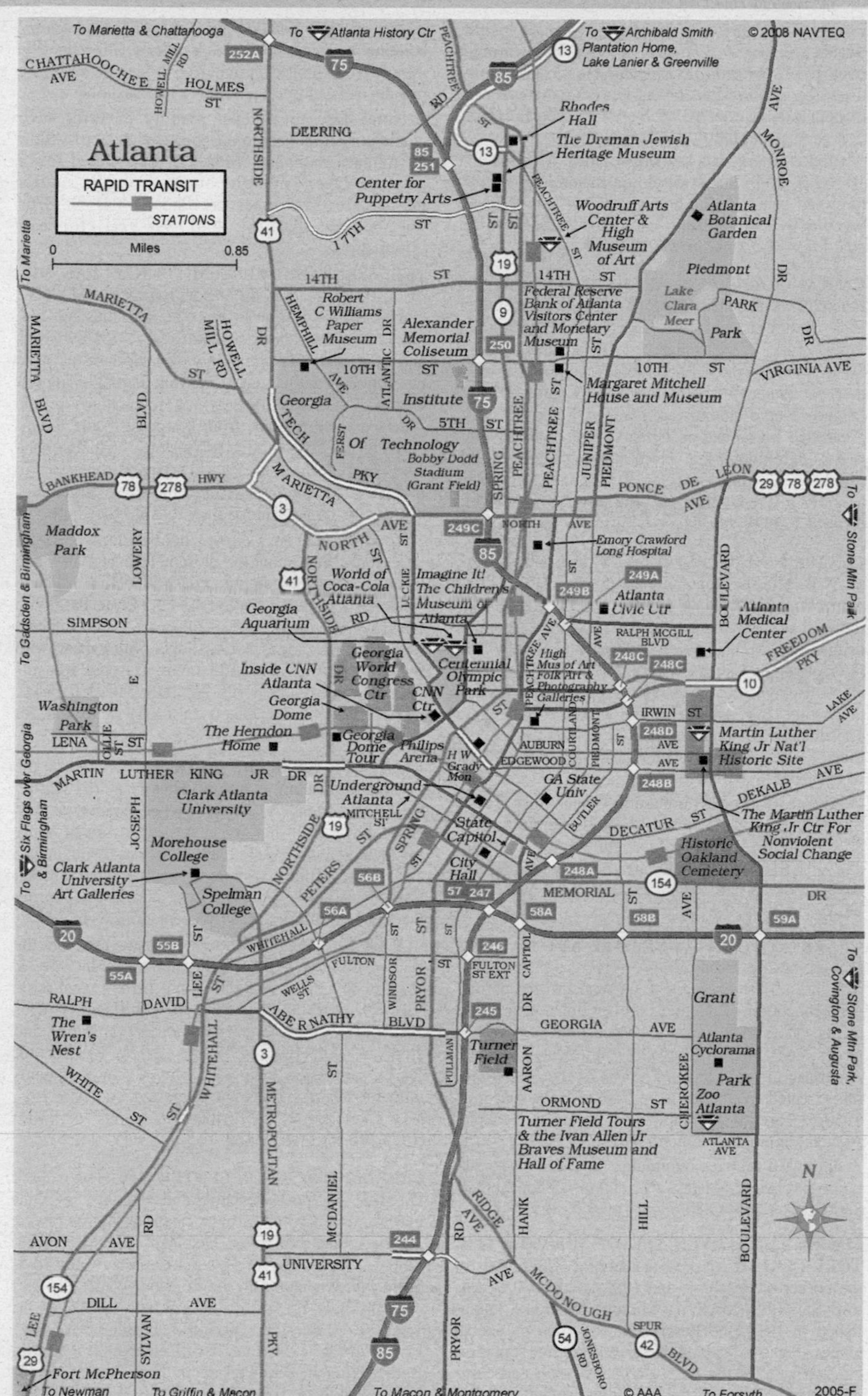
Atlanta
RAPID TRANSIT
STATIONS
Miles
0
0.85
To Marietta & Chattanooga
To Atlanta History Ctr
To Archibald Smith Plantation Home, Lake Lanier & Greenville
© 2008 NAVTEQ
Rhodes Hall
The Breman Jewish Heritage Museum
Center for Puppetry Arts
Woodruff Arts Center & High Museum of Art
Atlanta Botanical Garden
Piedmont Park
Lake Clara Meer
Robert C Williams Paper Museum
Alexander Memorial Coliseum
Federal Reserve Bank of Atlanta Visitors Center and Monetary Museum
Margaret Mitchell House and Museum
Georgia Institute Of Technology
Bobby Dodd Stadium (Grant Field)
Maddox Park
Emory Crawford Long Hospital
World of Coca-Cola Atlanta
Imagine It! The Children's Museum of Atlanta
Atlanta Civic Ctr
Georgia Aquarium
Atlanta Medical Center
Georgia World Congress Ctr
Centennial Olympic Park
High Mus of Art Folk Art & Photography Galleries
Inside CNN Atlanta
Georgia Dome
CNN Ctr
Washington Park
The Herndon Home
Georgia Dome Tour
Philips Arena
H W Grady Mon
Martin Luther King Jr Nat'l Historic Site
Underground Atlanta
GA State Univ
The Martin Luther King Jr Ctr For Nonviolent Social Change
Clark Atlanta University
Morehouse College
State Capitol
City Hall
Historic Oakland Cemetery
Clark Atlanta University Art Galleries
Spelman College
The Wren's Nest
Turner Field
Grant Park
Atlanta Cyclorama
Zoo Atlanta
Turner Field Tours & the Ivan Allen Jr Braves Museum and Hall of Fame
To Marietta
To Gadsden & Birmingham
To Six Flags over Georgia & Birmingham
To Stone Mtn Park
To Stone Mtn Park, Covington & Augusta
Fort McPherson
To Newman
To Griffin & Macon
To Macon & Montgomery
© AAA
To Forsyth
2005-F
N

Present." "Absence of Humanity: The Holocaust Years, 1933-1945" interprets the Holocaust through photographs, documents, memorabilia, family pictures and oral histories of survivors who rebuilt new lives in Atlanta after World War II. A special exhibition gallery and library also are available.

Guided tours are available. Open Mon.-Thurs. 10-5, Fri. 10-3, Sun. 1-5; closed major Jewish holidays and some federal holidays. Admission $10; $6 (ages 62+); $4 (students with ID); $2 (ages 3-6). AX, MC, VI. Phone (678) 222-3700.

CALLANWOLDE FINE ARTS CENTER is at 980 Briarcliff Rd. N.E. (MARTA: Edgewood/Candler Park Station to bus #6). This 1920, late Gothic-Tudor style, 27,000-square-foot mansion was built for Charles Howard Candler, eldest son of Asa Candler, the founder of the Coca-Cola Company. Also on the 12-acre grounds are gardens, a conservatory, a carriage house and an Oriental bath house. Workshops, exhibitions and performing arts events are regularly scheduled. Allow 30 minutes minimum. Mon.-Fri. 9 a.m.-10 p.m., Sat. 9-4. Free. Phone (404) 872-5338.

CENTER FOR PUPPETRY ARTS is at 1404 Spring St. N.W. at 18th. Reputedly the country's largest organization dedicated to puppetry, the center houses more than 1,000 puppets and regularly features original performances for children and adults. The interactive museum "Puppets: The Power of Wonder" displays more than 350 puppets from around the world and documents the history and artistic contributions of puppetry. Children may also create their own puppets in hands-on educational workshops.

Allow 30 minutes minimum. Center open Tues.-Sat. 9-5, Sun. 11-5; closed holidays. Admission $8; $6 (children). Admission for Family Series performances is $16 and includes the performance, workshop, museum and special exhibits. MC, VI. Phone (404) 873-3391.

CLARK ATLANTA UNIVERSITY ART GALLERIES are on the second floor of Trevor Arnett Hall at 223 James P. Brawley Dr. S.W. Works in the permanent collection of about 1,000 paintings, sculptures, prints, photographs and quilts constitute one of the larger and more historically significant African-American art collections. The Art of the Negro murals, created by former art professor Hale Woodruff 1950-51, are in the building's atrium and depict African-Americans' cultural past.

Allow 30 minutes minimum. Tues.-Fri. 11-4, Sat. noon-4; closed holidays. Donations. Phone (404) 880-6102 or (404) 880-6644.

FEDERAL RESERVE BANK OF ATLANTA VISITORS CENTER AND MONETARY MUSEUM is at the corner of Peachtree and 10th sts. at 1000 Peachtree St. N.E. (MARTA: Midtown Station). Established in 1914, the Reserve Bank is one of twelve composing the Federal Reserve System. Tours include a view of the site's automated vault and cash-processing procedures; multimedia displays focusing on the history and evolution of U.S. and global banking and currency; and Banker's Challenge, an interactive exhibit examining how banks earn profit, manage risk and provide security to customers.

Note: Due to national security concerns, tour availability is subject to change; phone ahead. Allow 45 minutes minimum. Mon.-Fri. 9-4; closed major holidays. Free. Parking is available at garages near the bank for $5-$10 per day. Phone (404) 498-8764 for the museum, or (404) 498-8777 for tour information.

SAVE **FERNBANK MUSEUM OF NATURAL HISTORY** is at 767 Clifton Rd. N.E. (MARTA: North Avenue Station to bus #2). The museum features dioramas, interactive displays, IMAX films and other exhibits pertaining to natural history, the environment and culture. "A Walk Through Time in Georgia" places visitors within re-creations of the state's diverse regions, from the coast to the mountains, to illustrate the Earth's history. "Giants of the Mesozoic" features the world's largest dinosaurs in a scene that highlights a 123-foot-long Argentinosaurus, the largest animal ever to walk the Earth.

Food is available. Allow 1 hour minimum. Mon.-Sat. 10-5, Sun. noon-5; closed Thanksgiving and Dec. 25. Museum admission $15; $14 (ages 62+ and students with ID); $13 (ages 3-12). Value Pass with one IMAX film $23; $21 (ages 62+ and students with ID); $19 (ages 3-12). Super Value Pass with two IMAX films $30; $27 (ages 62+ and students with ID); $24 (ages 3-12). AX, DS, MC, VI. Phone (404) 929-6400 for tickets or (404) 929-6300 for information. *See color ad p. 50.*

Rankin M. Smith Sr. IMAX Theater is in the Fernbank Museum of Natural History at 767 Clifton Rd. N.E. (MARTA: North Avenue Station to bus #2). The theater houses a five-story screen more than 70 feet wide and features a variety of nature and science films. Visitors may dine, view special screenings and experience live jazz music during weekly Martinis & IMAX presentations.

Food is available. Shows are presented on the hour Mon.-Sat. 10-5, Sun. noon-5; Martinis & IMAX Fri. 5:30-10, Jan.-Nov. IMAX admission $13; $12 (ages 62+ and students with ID); $11 (ages 3-12). IMAX double feature $21; $19 (ages 62+ and students with ID); $17 (ages 3-12). Martinis & IMAX admission $15; $14 (ages 62+ and students with ID). Reservations are suggested. AX, DS, MC, VI. Phone (404) 929-6400 for tickets or (404) 929-6300 for information.

FERNBANK SCIENCE CENTER, 156 Heaton Park Dr. N.E., offers science-related exhibits, a planetarium and a 65-acre forest featuring native plants. Allow 1 hour minimum. Displays open Mon.-Wed. 8:30-5, Thurs.-Fri. 8:30 a.m.-10 p.m., Sat. 10-5, Sun. 1-5. Planetarium shows Mon.-Wed. 11, 1:30 and 3, Thurs.-Fri. at 11, 1:30, 3 and 8, Sat. at 11, 1:30 and 3, Sun. at 1:30 and 3. Forest open Mon.-Fri. 2-5, Sat. 10-5, Sun. 1-5. Center closed Martin Luther King Jr. Day, Presidents' Day, Easter, Memorial Day, July 4, Labor Day, Thanksgiving and Dec.

24-25 and 31. Displays and forest free. Planetarium $4; $3 (ages 62+ and students with ID). AX, MC, VI. Phone (678) 874-7102.

GEM **GEORGIA AQUARIUM** is at 225 Baker St. in downtown across from Centennial Olympic Park and the Georgia World Congress Center. The building opened in 2005 and is one of the world's larger aquariums, with 8 million gallons of water housing a large collection of aquatic life. The aquarium showcases such exotic species as whale sharks, penguins, great hammerhead sharks and beluga whales.

The 4-D theater combines the 3-D film Deepo's Undersea 3D WonderShow with an actor and interactive seats to allow viewers to experience the world as denizens of the deep.

Note: All tickets are non-refundable. No outside food, beverage or gum is allowed. Guns, knives, fishing poles, lighters and matches are not allowed inside the aquarium. Food is available from 1 hour after the aquarium opens until 1 hour before it closes. Sun.-Fri. 10-5, Sat. 9-6. Hours may be extended in summer and vary during holidays; phone ahead. Daily theater times start 30 minutes after the aquarium opens. Last admission is 1 hour before closing. Admission $26; $21.50 (ages 55+); $19.50 (ages 3-12). 4-D theater $5.50; $4 (ages 3-12). Reservations are recommended. Parking fee is $10. AX, DS, MC, VI. Phone (404) 581-4000. *See color ad p. 50.*

GEORGIA DOME TOUR is at One Georgia Dome Dr. This behind-the-scenes guided tour includes a view of the dome from the coaches' level, the print media and luxury suites, broadcast media area, the locker room and a walk on the field. Tours of the dome are not offered during special events. Allow 1 hour minimum. Tours depart on the hour Tues.-Sat. 10-3; closed Jan. 1, July 4, Thanksgiving and Dec. 25. Last tour begins at 3. Phone ahead to confirm schedule. Admission $6; $4 (ages 55+ and students with ID). MC, VI. Phone (404) 223-8687.

GEORGIA STATE CAPITOL, 206 Washington St. between Mitchell St. and Martin Luther King Jr. Dr. (MARTA: Georgia State Station), was patterned after the national Capitol. Gold leaf mined in northern Georgia covers the exterior dome. Inside, the Capitol Museum contains exhibits about the building's architecture, history and purpose; displays include rocks, minerals, American Indian artifacts and colorful dioramas. On the first floor, the Hall of Valor showcases historic flags. The General Assembly is in session from early January to mid-April.

Allow 1 hour, 30 minutes minimum. Mon.-Fri. 8-5; closed holidays. Guided tours depart Mon.-Fri. at 10, 11, 1 and 2. Free. Phone (404) 656-2844.

GLOBAL HEALTH ODYSSEY/HARKIN CENTER is at 1600 Clifton Rd. (MARTA: Lindbergh Station to bus #6). Permanent and changing exhibits depict the history of diseases and the efforts toward their elimination as well as highlight the organization's history. Mon.-Fri. 9-5 (also Thurs. 5-7); closed major holidays. Free. Phone (404) 639-0830 or (800) 311-3435.

GRANT PARK is bounded by Atlanta Ave., Sydney St., Cherokee Ave. and the Boulevard S.E. The land for this 131-acre public park was donated in 1883 by Col. Lemuel Pratt Grant, a civil engineer with the railroads, who designed the defensive fortifications around Atlanta in anticipation of a Union siege during the Civil War. The park includes Fort Walker, walking trails, historic structures and native plantings as well as the Atlanta Cyclorama and Zoo Atlanta. A walking tour of the park and surrounding historic district is offered by the Atlanta Preservation Center *(see Walking Tours p. 56)*. Picnic facilities are available. Park open daily 6:30 a.m.-11 p.m. Guided tours are given Sun. at 10 for a nominal fee. Free. Phone (404) 521-0938, or (404) 688-3353 for tour information.

Atlanta Cyclorama is in the Civil War Museum at 800C Cherokee Ave. S.E. A 360-degree painting of the Battle of Atlanta, the cyclorama is 358 feet in circumference and 42 feet high. Visitors view the painting from a revolving platform as sound and light effects, narration and 3-D figures heighten the experience. Also in the building is the "Texas", a locomotive used in the pursuit of Maj. James Andrews and his Union soldiers during the 1862 Andrews Railroad Raid.

Allow 1 hour minimum. Tours offered every hour on the half-hour Tues.-Sun. 9-4:30; closed Jan. 1, Martin Luther King Jr. Day, Thanksgiving and Dec. 25. Admission $7; $6 (ages 60+); $5 (ages 6-12). MC, VI. Phone (404) 658-7625.

GEM SAVE **Zoo Atlanta,** 800 Cherokee Ave. S.E., exhibits nearly 1,000 animals in naturalistic habitats. Known for its extensive reptile collection, it is one of only four zoos in the U.S. that house giant pandas and holds one of the nation's largest collections of Western Lowland gorillas. The Living Tree House features 15 species of African birds as well as various species of smaller primates. Other animals from around the world include Asian small-clawed otters, red kangaroos, Bornean and Sumatran orangutans and a Komodo dragon.

Picnicking is permitted in the surrounding Grant Park. Food is available. Allow 4 hours minimum. Ticket office open daily 9:30-4:30. Grounds remain open 1 hour after ticket office closes. Closed Thanksgiving and Dec. 25. Admission $17.99; $13.99 (ages 55+); $12.99 (ages 3-11). Train or carousel $2 each. Parking is free. AX, DS, DC, MC, VI. Phone (404) 624-5600. *See color ad p. 50.*

HENRY W. GRADY MONUMENT, on Marietta St. near Forsyth St., is a bronze statue of the late-19th-century writer and newspaper publisher who coined the phrase "The New South." The sculpture, created by artist Alexander Doyle, depicts Grady facing the rising sun. His likeness is supported by two seated female virtues, one facing to the north and the other to the south.

THE HERNDON HOME, 587 University Pl. N.W., is a 15-room Beaux Arts Classical house built in 1910 by wealthy African-American businessman Alonzo Herndon, founder of the Atlanta Life Insurance Co. Guided tours are available by appointment. Allow 30 minutes minimum. Tues. and Thurs. 10-4; closed holidays. Admission $5; $3 (students with ID). MC, VI. Phone (404) 581-9813.

HISTORIC OAKLAND CEMETERY is at 248 Oakland Ave. S.E. (MARTA: King Memorial Station). Founded in 1850, this Victorian cemetery contains majestic oaks and some of the city's oldest magnolia trees. Gothic Revival and neoclassic tombs are found throughout 48-acre cemetery as well as the graves of 26 former Atlanta mayors, six Georgia governors, "Gone With the Wind" author Margaret Mitchell, golfing great Bobby Jones and approximately 6,900 Confederate soldiers. Self-guiding walking tour brochures are available at the visitor center.

Guided tours are available. Cemetery open daily dawn-dusk. Visitor center open Mon.-Fri. 9-5, Sat. 9-8, Sun. noon-8, during DST; Mon.-Sat. 9-5, Sun. noon-5, in Mar. and Nov.; daily noon-4, Dec.-Feb. (weather permitting). Guided tours are given Sat. at 10, 2 and 6:30, Sun. at 2 and 6:30, during DST; Sat. at 10 and 2, Sun. at 2, in Mar. and Nov. Admission free. Tour fee $10; $5 (ages 6-17 and students with ID); $5 (ages 65+). MC, VI. Phone (404) 688-2107.

SAVE **IMAGINE IT! THE CHILDREN'S MUSEUM OF ATLANTA** is at 275 Centennial Olympic Park Dr. N.W. (MARTA: Peachtree Center). The museum features ongoing displays, special daily programs and a variety of hands-on learning activities. Children may paint on walls, create sand sculptures, operate pulleys and levers of a giant ball machine and simulate the splashing of water underneath a make-believe waterfall.

Food is available. Allow 1 hour minimum. Mon.-Fri. 10-4, Sat.-Sun. 10-5; closed Thanksgiving and Dec. 25. Admission $11; free (ages 0-1). AX, DS, MC, VI. Phone (404) 659-5437.

INSIDE CNN ATLANTA is at One CNN Center/190 Marietta St. N.W. at Centennial Olympic Park Dr. (MARTA: Philips Arena/Georgia Dome). This 50- to 60-minute guided walking tour emphasizes network operations and technical aspects of CNN, Headline News, CNN International and CNN En Espanol. Special effects demonstrations show how weather maps are displayed behind news anchors during broadcasts; teleprompters are demonstrated as well. Viewers see newscasters prepare for an upcoming program and watch them in action from an overhead observation booth.

Note: The walking tour descends eight flights of stairs; comfortable attire and footwear are recommended. Allow 1 hour minimum. Tours, limited to 40 people, are offered every 10 minutes daily 9-5; closed Easter, Thanksgiving and Dec. 25. Tour $12; $11 (ages 65+); $9 (ages 4-18). Children under the age of 4 years are free but must have a ticket. A limited number of same-day tickets is available on a first-come, first-served basis daily starting at 8:30 a.m. Reservations can be made at least one day in advance and are highly recommended. AX, MC, VI. Phone (404) 827-2300 or (877) 426-6868. *See color ad p. 50.*

JIMMY CARTER PRESIDENTIAL LIBRARY & MUSEUM, at exit 248C (Freedom Pkwy.) and following signs to the Carter Center, contains more than 27 million documents, photographs and other objects detailing the Carter administration. Changing special-interest exhibits also are offered.

The library is open only to researchers. Food is available Mon.-Sat. Allow 1 hour, 30 minutes minimum. Museum open Mon.-Sat. 9-4:45, Sun. noon-4:45; closed Jan. 1, Thanksgiving and Dec. 25. Admission $8; $6 (ages 60+, military and students with ID); free (ages 0-16). AX, DS, MC, VI. Phone (404) 865-7100.

MARGARET MITCHELL HOUSE AND MUSEUM is at the corner of Peachtree and 10th sts. at 990 Peachtree St. N.E. (MARTA: Midtown Station). Visitors can tour the carefully restored home where Margaret Mitchell wrote her Pulitzer Prize-winning novel, "Gone With the Wind." A museum dedicated to the story behind the film houses a portrait of Scarlett in a blue dress along with the doorway to Tara that appeared in the movie version. Mon.-Sat. 9:30-5, Sun. noon-5; closed Jan. 1, Thanksgiving and Dec. 24-25. Admission $12; $9 (ages 65+ and students with ID); $5 (ages 4-12). AX, MC, VI. Phone (404) 249-7015.

GEM **MARTIN LUTHER KING JR. NATIONAL HISTORIC SITE** is at 450 Auburn Ave. N.E. (MARTA: King Memorial Station). The 39-acre site includes the birthplace, church and grave of Dr. Martin Luther King Jr., African-American civil rights leader and Nobel Peace Prize winner. Dr. King paid the ultimate price for the civil rights cause when he was assassinated by James Earl Ray on April 4, 1968, while lending his support to a sanitation workers' strike in Memphis, Tenn. In Jan. 2006, his wife, Coretta Scott King, died; she is buried beside her husband.

The years since his assassination have proven that King endures as a symbol of inspiration to everyone who believes in social and economic equality for all Americans. The visitor center contains exhibits and video presentations about King and the civil rights movement. The King Center features the final resting place of Dr. King, Jr. as well as exhibits about Coretta Scott King and Mahatma Gandhi. The surrounding district preserves sections of Sweet Auburn, the center of Atlanta's African-American community for most of the 20th century.

Visitors also may rent a GPS Ranger, a hand-held device which automatically provides relevant audio and video narration based on its user's location on the site. Units are available at the Eastern National Bookstore, inside of Fire Station No. 6 at the corner of Auburn Ave. and Boulevard.

Open daily 9-6, mid-June through mid-Aug.; 9-5, rest of year. Closed Jan. 1, Thanksgiving and Dec. 25. Guided 30-minute tours of Dr. King's birthplace are available. Free. GPS Ranger unit rental $9.95. Phone (404) 331-5190.

The Martin Luther King Jr. Center for Nonviolent Social Change, 449 Auburn Ave., includes the Freedom Hall Complex. Surrounding Rev. Dr. King's crypt are the Freedom Walkway, a reflecting pool, the Chapel of All Faiths and Freedom Hall. The archives are open to the public only by appointment. Self-guiding tours are available. Daily 9-5. Free. Phone (404) 526-8900.

MICHAEL C. CARLOS MUSEUM OF EMORY UNIVERSITY, 571 S. Kilgo Cir. on the Emory University campus, offers the art and artifacts of ancient Egypt, the Near East, Africa, Asia, Greece, Rome and the Americas, as well as prints and drawings from the Middle Ages to the present. Temporary and traveling exhibitions also are featured. Guided and MP3 audio tours are available. Open Tues.-Sat. 10-5, Sun. noon-5; closed university holidays. Free guided tour Sun. at 2:30. Admission $7. MP3 audio tour $3. DS, MC, VI. Phone (404) 727-4282.

SAVE **RHODES HALL,** 1516 Peachtree St. N.W., was constructed in 1904 for Atlanta businessman A.G. Rhodes. Inspired by European castles, the mansion is made primarily of granite from nearby Stone Mountain. A series of painted and stained-glass windows reflecting historic events of the Confederacy surrounds the carved mahogany staircase. Original pieces of furniture are displayed. The building also houses the Georgia Trust for Historic Preservation.

Allow 30 minutes minimum. Tours depart on the hour Tues.-Fri. 11-4, Sat. 10-2, Sun. noon-3; closed Thanksgiving and Dec. 25. Last tour begins 1 hour before closing. Tour of all four floors (including tower) $8. Tour of first floor $5; $4 (ages 6-12, students with ID and 60+). AX, MC, VI. Phone (404) 885-7800.

ROBERT C. WILLIAMS PAPER MUSEUM is at 500 10th Street N.W. in the Institute of Paper Science and Technology, part of the Georgia Institute of Technology. The museum houses more than 2,000 books and 10,000 items tracing the invention and evolution of paper. Global artifacts dating from as early as 200 B.C. to the technology of today focus on such devices as the paper machine, as well as efforts to conserve and recycle paper. Changing exhibits feature works by contemporary and worldwide papermaking artists.

Allow 1 hour minimum. Mon.-Fri. 9-5; closed holidays. Free. Phone (404) 894-7840.

SAVE **TURNER FIELD TOURS AND THE IVAN ALLEN JR. BRAVES MUSEUM AND HALL OF FAME** is at 755 Hank Aaron Dr. One-hour guided tours give Braves fans a glimpse into the clubhouse, dugout, press box, luxury suites and broadcast booth. The museum traces the team's history from 1871 to the present and contains more than 600 Braves-related memorabilia pieces. Photographs commemorate key members of the Milwaukee Braves' 1957 World Champion team as well as former Braves inducted into the National Baseball Hall of Fame in Cooperstown, N.Y.

Allow 1 hour, 30 minutes minimum. Mon.-Sat. 9-3, Sun. 1-3; Mon.-Sat. 10-2 during the off-season (Oct.-Mar.). No tours are offered on Sunday game days or when an afternoon home game is scheduled. Museum admission on game days $2; $5 (non-game days). Guided tour $12; $7 (ages 3-13). AX, MC, VI. Phone (404) 614-2311.

GEM **WOODRUFF ARTS CENTER** is at 1280 Peachtree St. N.E. (MARTA: Arts Center Station). The Woodruff combines performing and visual arts and is home to the Alliance Theatre, the Atlanta Symphony Orchestra, the High Museum of Art, Young Audiences and the 14th Street Playhouse. Food is available. Allow 2 hours minimum. Tues.-Wed. and Fri.-Sat. 10-5 (also third Fri. of each month 5-10 for Friday Jazz), Thurs. 10-8, Sun. noon-5. Schedule for each facility may vary; phone ahead to confirm hours or inquire about event and performance schedule. Closed Jan. 1, July 4, Thanksgiving and Dec. 25. Fee depends upon facilities visited. Phone (404) 733-5000 for ticket information.

GEM **High Museum of Art** is at 1280 Peachtree St. N.E. (MARTA: Arts Center Station). The 312,000-square-foot building has more than 11,000 works of art in its permanent collection including American and decorative art, European paintings and sculpture, modern and contemporary art, photography, folk art and African art.

Guided tours and food are available. Allow 2 hours minimum. Tues.-Wed. 10-5, Thurs. 10-8, Fri.-Sat. 10-5 (also third Fri. of the month 5-10 for Friday Jazz), Sun. noon-5; closed Jan. 1, July 4, Thanksgiving and Dec. 25. Admission $18; $15 (ages 65+ and students with ID); $11 (ages 6-17). AX, DS, MC, VI. Phone (404) 733-4444. *See color ad p. 50.*

GEM **WORLD OF COCA-COLA ATLANTA** is at 121 Baker St. N.W. (MARTA: Dome/GWCC/Philips Arena/CNN Center Station or Peachtree Center Station), adjacent to the Georgia Aquarium at Pemberton Place. The 92,000-square-foot building houses a collection of more than 1,200 articles of memorabilia tracing the rich heritage and global reach of Coca-Cola.

After learning about the company's history and future in a variety of exhibits including a 4-D cinematic presentation and a fully functioning bottling line, visitors take home a commemorative bottle. Almost 70 different domestic and international beverages produced by The Coca-Cola Company are available in several sampling areas. Four acres of outdoor space, a reflecting pool and a plaza paying tribute to John Pemberton, the beverage's inventor, are among the new site's highlights.

Food is available. Picnicking is permitted. Allow 1 hour minimum. Mon.-Sat. 9-6, Sun. 10-6, June-Aug.; Mon.-Sat. 9-5, Sun. 10-5, rest of year. Closed

Easter, Thanksgiving and Dec. 25. Last admission at closing. Admission $15; $13 (ages 55+); $9 (ages 3-12). Phone to verify prices and hours. Limited parking is available at New Coca-Cola's parking deck on Ivan Allen Jr. Blvd. for $10. AX, DS, MC, VI. Phone (404) 676-5151 or (800) 676-2653. *See color ad p. 50.*

SAVE **THE WREN'S NEST,** 1050 Ralph D. Abernathy Blvd. S.W. (MARTA: West End Station and bus #71), was the home of author and journalist Joel Chandler Harris from 1881 until his death in 1908. Best known as the creator of the "Uncle Remus Stories," Harris was a folklorist who preserved the Brer Rabbit stories that otherwise might have been lost. The original 1870 house was remodeled in 1884 to its current Victorian appearance and features original Harris family furnishings.

Picnicking is permitted. Allow 1 hour minimum. Tues.-Sat. 10-2:30; closed holidays. Storytelling sessions Sat. at 1 and by appointment. Guided tours daily; phone ahead for schedule. Admission $8; $7 (ages 13-18 and senior citizens); $5 (ages 3-12). MC, VI. Phone (404) 753-7735.

What To Do

Sightseeing

Bus Tours

American Sightseeing Tours, SAVE Gray Line and other companies offer a variety of excursions around downtown Atlanta, to Stone Mountain and through residential areas.

Walking Tours

House and garden tours of Druid Hills, Ansley Park and Midtown are conducted in mid-April. Further information can be obtained at your hotel or from the telephone directory.

Guided tours of Atlanta's historic districts are offered by the Atlanta Preservation Center throughout the year. Comfortable walking shoes should be worn; phone (404) 688-3353.

Free guided 20-minute tours of the 1967 Greek Revival-style Governor's Mansion are offered Tuesday through Thursday 10-11:30. The mansion is at 391 West Paces Ferry Rd. N.W. Phone (404) 656-1776.

Sports and Recreation

Atlanta's leisure activities are many. Visitors can go **fishing** in or **rafting** or **canoeing** down the Chattahoochee River, the focal point of the Chattahoochee River National Recreation Area *(see place listing p. 58)*. Affectionately known as "the Hooch" by natives, the river is usually no more than 5 feet deep and affords excellent opportunities for year-round fishing. Trout, bass, catfish and other species of fish frequent the river. For fishing license and regulation information phone (888) 748-6887. Canoes, rafts, life jackets and shuttle service back to the departure point are provided by the Chattahoochee Outdoor Center early May to mid-September; phone (770) 992-2055. **Jogging** trails border the river.

Golf can be played at six city courses. The BellSouth Atlanta Golf Classic and other tournaments attract many spectators each year. The municipal parks also provide **riding** and **hiking** trails, **tennis** courts and **swimming** pools. Piedmont Park, off Monroe Drive and 10th Street in midtown, is a popular spot for **bicycling** and jogging.

Fishing, boating and swimming off a sandy beach are available at Lake Sidney Lanier, about 35 miles northeast off US 23 *(see Buford p. 58 in the Vicinity section and Gainesville p. 75)*.

The National League's Atlanta Braves play **baseball** from early April to late September at Turner Field, off I-75/85 exits 246 or 248A (Martin Luther King Jr. Dr.). **Football** games are played in the Georgia Dome from early September to late December when the Atlanta Falcons of the National Football League take the field.

The National **Hockey** League's Atlanta Thrashers, the National **Basketball** Association's Atlanta Hawks and the Women's National Basketball Association's Atlanta Dream host opponents downtown at the Philips Arena, 1 Philips Dr. (next to CNN Center).

Racing in Atlanta focuses on horsepower. Fans of the checkered flag can see it waved almost all year at Atlanta Motor Speedway *(see attraction listing in Hampton p. 82)*, 20 miles south, and at Road Atlanta, 39 miles northeast near Braselton. The former is host to NASCAR racing; the latter offers sports car, Formula One, motorcycle and motocross events on its road circuit March through November.

Shopping

The area immediately surrounding the Five Points intersection downtown is a modern bazaar. To the north is the Peachtree Center. In between is a mix of old and new buildings housing retail stores and other commercial enterprises.

Atlantic Station, 1380 Atlantic Dr., is a 138-acre development providing office and residential space, hotels and entertainment. Dining and shopping opportunities also are provided. The site features such restaurants as California Pizza Kitchen and Geisha House. Ann Taylor, Banana Republic, Gap and Ikea are among the community's retailers.

The convenience of MARTA rapid rail and the addition of Peachtree Center's multilevel mall have further enhanced downtown shopping, blending modern elegance with the renovated romance of late 19th-century buildings.

One of the city's novelty shopping areas is somewhat of a misnomer—two of Underground Atlanta's three levels are actually above ground, offering the wares of more than 130 prominent national and local merchants. The underground portion of the nearly 12-acre urban marketplace has existed since before the Civil War, when streets were built above railroad tracks that converged at the heart of Terminus, as Atlanta was then called.

Storefronts and historic buildings below and above the streets have been carefully restored. Visitors can dine in one of eight varied restaurants, stroll down landscaped pedestrian promenades, or relax on park benches while being entertained by street performers.

At night the district is an entertainment center with nightclubs featuring bluegrass, comedy, Dixieland, rock and jazz. Lying between Peachtree Street and Central Avenue at Alabama Street, Underground Atlanta is next to the Five Points MARTA Station and has some 1,200 parking spaces.

Atlanta is not all big-city glitter; the sophistication of downtown's Five Points has a more casual counterpart in Little Five Points, 3 miles away in Inman Park at the intersection of Moreland and Euclid avenues. This residential Victorian enclave also has a mix of shops, boutiques, restaurants and clubs catering to the young and trendy.

Another shopping area worth exploring is fashionable Buckhead, noted for its antique shops and galleries as well as its malls, spacious Lenox Square and upscale Phipps Plaza.

Atlanta also has a number of malls studding its perimeter—Cumberland Mall, the Galleria, North Point Mall and Town Center to the northwest; Outlet Square and Perimeter Mall to the north; Gwinnett Place and Northlake Mall to the northeast; Southlake Mall to the southeast; and Arbor Place Mall to the west. An alternative to the mall environment is the 146-acre Atlanta State Farmers Market, popular for both its seasonal selection of fruits and vegetables and its cafeteria.

Bass Pro Shops in Discover Mills Mall in Lawrenceville features wildlife exhibits and sporting demonstrations.

Performing Arts

Atlanta's cultural offerings range from grand opera and fine symphony to summer stock and vintage films. Founded in 1929, the Atlanta Ballet is one of the oldest civic ballet companies in the country. The company performs from October through May at the Cobb Energy Performing Arts Centre, 2800 Cobb Galleria Pkwy. Highlights include a holiday presentation of The Nutcracker, which is performed at the Fox Theatre, 660 Peachtree St.; phone (404) 881-2100 Monday through Friday 10-6 for the ballet box office. Tickets for the ballet, the Broadway Series and other fine arts events may also be obtained by calling Ticketmaster Arts Line, (404) 817-8700.

During the fall-winter concert season several other ballet and modern-dance groups stage revues, which are usually presented in the Woodruff Arts Center, 1280 Peachtree St. N.E.; phone (404) 733-5000. *See attraction listing p. 55.*

The renowned Atlanta Symphony Orchestra has musical presentations September through May also in the Woodruff Arts Center. The series is supplemented by free concerts June through August. The orchestra performs in Chastain Memorial Park Amphitheatre June through August; most seats, except for lawn seats are reserved. The Chastain concert series features headliners performing with the ASO. For ticket information, phone (404) 733-5000.

The Atlanta Opera offers four productions from late September through May at Cobb Energy Performing Arts Centre at 2800 Cobb Galleria Pkwy. The 2008-09 schedule includes "Madama Butterfly" in October 2008, "La Cenerentola" (Cinderella) in November 2008, "Il Trovatore" in late February-early March 2009 and "Der Fliegende Hollander" in April-May 2009. For ticket information phone (770) 989-5035 or (404) 881-8801.

The Alliance Theatre Company, in the Woodruff Arts Center, presents performances that range from musicals to new and classic dramas.

Dinner theater productions at Agatha's—A Taste of Mystery, 161 Peachtree Center Ave., feature audience participation; phone (404) 584-2211. The city also is the home of numerous professional, experimental and community theater groups. Daily and weekly newspapers give details about theater and dance productions, concerts and film showings.

Special Events

Atlanta's Dogwood Festival each April features a parade, driving tours of residential areas and various other events; phone (404) 817-6642. The Atlanta Jazz Festival, May's monthlong celebration of jazz, features international artists and offers a range of activities in the metro area. Festivities in Piedmont Park during Memorial Day weekend provide a coda for the event; phone (404) 853-4234. The Peachtree Road Race, a 10-kilometer event in which 55,000 runners participate, takes place July 4 in downtown Atlanta. In late July the National Black Arts Festival celebrates the achievements of artists of African descent. Music, theater, film, literature, dance, visual, performing and folk arts are featured at various downtown locations; phone (404) 730-7315.

DID YOU KNOW

Georgia is the largest state east of the Mississippi River.

The Atlanta Vicinity

ALPHARETTA (B-2) pop. 34,854, elev. 1,138′

Alpharetta is home to the campus of DeVry Institute of Technology, as well as a campus of Georgia State University. The 1912 Queen Anne-style Mansell House and Gardens is furnished in period; phone (770) 475-4663 Monday or Friday 10-4.

Alpharetta Welcome Center: 20 North Main St., Alpharetta, GA 30004; phone (678) 297-0102 or (800) 294-0923.

Shopping areas: The 175 establishments of North Point Mall, at 1000 North Point Cir. off SR 400 between Encore Parkway and Haynes Bridge Road, are anchored by Dillard's, Macy's, JC Penney, Parisian and Sears.

AUSTELL (B-2) pop. 5,359, elev. 927′

GEM SAVE **SIX FLAGS OVER GEORGIA,** 7.4 mi. s.e. on I-20, has more than 100 acres where visitors of all ages can experience thrilling coasters, rides and live shows. Guests will want to be sure to bring a swimsuit and a towel to appreciate the interactive water play structure Skull Island; changing facilities are available.

Thrill-seekers won't want to miss Mind Bender, a triple-loop roller coaster, and Thunder River, a white-water rafting adventure. Also included among the park's 10 coasters are Superman Ultimate Flight, which turns riders upside down in a pretzel-shaped loop; Batman: The Ride, which carries visitors through loops and a corkscrew spin; The Georgia Scorcher, said to be one of the region's tallest and fastest stand-up roller coasters; and Goliath, more than 200 feet tall and traveling up to 70 miles per hour.

Bugs Bunny World is filled with attractions for small children, including the child-size Wile E. Coyote Canyon Blaster roller coaster. Thomas Town, a themed area just for children, features a Thomas the Tank Engine train ride and an interactive play structure. Other entertainment options are Broadway-style musical shows, summer concerts and chances to meet and greet characters.

Picnic facilities and kennels are available. Park open daily at 10, late May-early Aug.; Sat.-Sun. at 10:30, early Mar.-late May and early Aug.-late Sept. Closing time varies. The park also is open for Fright Fest late-Sept.-early Nov.; phone ahead for schedule. All-inclusive 1-day admission $39.99; $29.99 (children under 49 inches tall); free (ages 0-2). Parking $15. AAA members save on select services and merchandise. See Guest Relations for details. AX, DS, MC, VI. Phone (770) 948-9290.

BUFORD (B-2) pop. 10,668, elev. 1,205′

Buford Dam is on the Chattahoochee River 5 miles northwest. Above the dam Lake Sidney Lanier *(see Recreation Chart)* extends up both the Chattahoochee and Chestatee rivers, offering some 540 miles of shoreline.

Gwinnett Convention and Visitors Bureau: 6500 Sugarloaf Pkwy., Suite 200, Duluth, GA 30097; phone (770) 623-3600 or (888) 494-6638.

Shopping areas: Forum Shops, 5155 Peachtree Pkwy. in Buford, and The Avenue Webb Gin, 1350 Scenic Highway in nearby Snellville, each offer more than 60 boutiques, shops and stores. Mall of Georgia, on SR 20 between I-85 and I-985, features 225 stores including Belk, Dillard's, JCPenney, Macy's and Nordstrom.

LAKE LANIER ISLANDS, n.w. off SR 365, were formed when the waters of Lake Sidney Lanier failed to cover a cluster of forested hilltops. The four islands are connected to the mainland by causeways and each offers different recreational facilities. Facilities and amenities include a resort and rental units, campgrounds, tennis courts, boat and bicycle rentals, a beach, two golf courses, water parks and restaurants. Also available are horseback riding, fishing, sailing and hiking. Parking $8 daily. Phone (770) 945-8787.

CHATTAHOOCHEE RIVER NATIONAL RECREATION AREA (B-2)

Extending along a 48-mile stretch of the Chattahoochee River from Lake Sidney Lanier to Peachtree Creek in northwest Atlanta, 6,639-acre Chattahoochee River National Recreation Area has preserved the natural riverway within an extensive metropolitan area. Its day-use trails are popular with Atlantans and tourists alike.

Long scenic runs and gentle rapids offer excellent canoeing, rafting and kayaking. Small motorboats are permitted, but there is a limited number of boat ramps. The southernmost public take-out point is Paces Mill on US 41. Recreation area admission is free; parking is $3 per private vehicle or annual permit $25.

For information contact the Superintendent, Chattahoochee River National Recreation Area, 1978 Island Ford Pkwy., Atlanta, GA 30350-3400; phone (678) 538-1200. *See Recreation Chart.*

DAWSONVILLE (A-2) pop. 619, elev. 1,376′

AMICALOLA STATE PARK is at 418 Amicalola Falls State Park Rd. The 829-acre park features a cascading waterfall—said to be the tallest east of the Mississippi River. Recreational activities include hiking, picnicking and fishing. A visitor center provides nature displays and live exhibits. Interpretive programs also are offered. Allow 4 hours minimum.

Park open daily 7 a.m.-10 p.m. Visitor center open daily 8-5. Fee $3 per vehicle; free on Wednesdays. Phone (706) 265-4703 or (800) 864-7275.

GEM **KANGAROO CONSERVATION CENTER** is at 222 Bailey-Waters Rd. The center houses more than 300 kangaroos of nine species which are seen in a variety of exhibits and presentations. Conducted by trained guides, the 90-minute Aussie Adventure tour features a boomerang exhibition, a KangaRanger truck ride and an up-close encounter with the animals at the Wild Australia show. The Aussie Walkabout is a quarter-mile trail that is surrounded by kangaroo enclosures. Before or after the tour, visitors are welcome to stroll through the Billabong Encounter—an indoor/outdoor exhibit featuring Australian plants and reptiles. A kookaburra/parrot aviary and a butterfly picnic garden also are on the grounds. The trail through Fern Valley leads visitors to a native Appalachian forest.

Note: While no strenuous activity is required to participate in the tour, visitors should be capable of and expect a fair amount of walking. Some grassy, uneven slopes may be encountered; comfortable clothing and walking shoes are recommended. Walk-in ticket purchases are possible if the guided tours are not sold out. Reservations are highly recommended. Picnicking is permitted. Food is available. Smoking is not permitted.

Allow 2 hours minimum. Tues.-Sat. 10-5, Mar. 15-Nov. 30.; closed major holidays. Tours are given at 10:15 and 1:15. Guests should arrive a minimum of 30 minutes before the start of a tour. Schedule may vary; phone ahead to confirm. Admission (includes guided tour) $30; $28 (ages 65+); $25 (ages 6-17). Children under age 6 are not permitted. AX, DS, MC, VI. Phone (706) 265-6100 for tickets.

DULUTH (B-2) pop. 22,122, elev. 1,100'

SAVE **SOUTHEASTERN RAILWAY MUSEUM** is at 3595 Peachtree Rd. The 30-acre site features more than 80 items of rolling stock including Pullman cars, steam locomotives and restored cabooses. A 10-minute caboose train ride is included in the admission. Allow 1 hour minimum. Thurs.-Sat. 10-5, Apr.-Dec.; Sat. 10-5, rest of year. Admission $8; $6 (ages 65+); $4 (ages 2-12). DS, MC, VI. Phone (770) 476-2013.

JONESBORO (C-2) pop. 3,829, elev. 917'

Clayton County Convention and Visitors Bureau: 104 North Main St., Jonesboro, GA 30236; phone (770) 478-4800 or (800) 662-7829.

SAVE **ROAD TO TARA MUSEUM** is at 104 N. Main St. Housed on the second floor of the 1867 Jonesboro Depot, the majority of exhibits are dedicated to the novel and movie "Gone With the Wind." Memorabilia, reproduction garments, information about author Margaret Mitchell, collectors' items, copies of foreign translations and foreign movie posters are displayed. Also included is information about the fictional plantation Tara and the stars of the film, its premiere and awards.

Picnicking is permitted. Allow 30 minutes minimum. Mon.-Fri. 8:30-5:30, Sat. 10-4. Last admittance 45 minutes before closing. Admission $7; $6 (ages 55+, students with ID and ages 6-12). AX, DS, MC, VI. Phone (770) 478-4800 or (800) 662-7829.

SAVE **STATELY OAKS PLANTATION,** off Jodeco Rd. at 100 Carriage Ln., is an 1839 Greek Revival plantation house furnished with antiques. Also on-site are various outbuildings that include a one-room schoolhouse, original log kitchen and tenant house. Audio tours and historical interpreters add to the experience. Allow 1 hour minimum. Tours offered Mon.-Sat. 10-4; closed major holidays. Tour $12; $9 (ages 55+); $6 (ages 5-11). MC, VI. Phone (770) 473-0197.

KENNESAW (B-1) pop. 21,675, elev. 1,093'

The passengers aboard a train leaving Big Shanty—modern day Kennesaw—the morning of April 12, 1862, had no idea that a dramatic episode in the Civil War was about to begin before their breakfast coffee cooled. While the passengers and crew ate, civilian James Andrews and 21 Union soldiers, who had boarded in civilian clothes, stole the train and headed for Chattanooga, Tenn.

The conductor and crew chased the stolen train on foot, by handcar and with commandeered engines, catching Andrews just 5 miles from his goal. Andrews and seven of his "raiders" were returned to Atlanta and executed as spies. The Walt Disney movie "The Great Locomotive Chase" was based on the incident.

SAVE **SOUTHERN MUSEUM OF CIVIL WAR AND LOCOMOTIVE HISTORY** is at 2829 Cherokee St. This Smithsonian affiliate focuses on the history of railroads during the Civil War. The museum's exhibits tell the story of "The General", which was stolen during an incident known as "The Great Locomotive Chase." The museum also features a replica of the Glover Machine Works locomotive factory complete with restored belt-driven assembly line and several trains in various stages of completion. Changing exhibits also are offered.

Allow 30 minutes minimum. Mon.-Sat. 9:30-5, Sun. noon-5; closed Jan. 1, Easter, Thanksgiving and Dec. 24-25 and 31. Admission $7.50; $6.50 (ages 60+); $5.50 (ages 4-12). MC, VI. Phone (770) 427-2117.

KENNESAW MOUNTAIN NATIONAL BATTLEFIELD PARK (B-1)

Kennesaw Mountain National Battlefield Park occupies 2,923 acres 2.5 miles northwest of Marietta off I-75 exit 269, then 4 mi. w. on OLD US 41. In June 1864, Gen. Joseph E. Johnston's Confederate Army, retreating before Gen. William Tecumseh Sherman's march to Atlanta, took up a strong position on Kennesaw (KEN-uh saw) Mountain in the path of the invading forces. Sherman, however, ultimately forced Johnston and his troops to abandon the mountain and retreat south.

Earthworks from this battle are well preserved. A paved road to the crest of Kennesaw Mountain has fine views; around the crest is a trail with maps illustrating the conflict. The visitor center at the foot of the mountain on OLD US 41 offers audiovisual programs and exhibits. Living history demonstrations and temporary exhibits also are available.

Picnicking is permitted in designated areas. The mountain road is closed weekends and major holidays; a shuttle bus provides transportation to the mountaintop during these times.

Allow 2 hours minimum. Mon.-Fri. 8:30-5, Sat.-Sun. 8:30-6, during DST; daily 8:30-5, rest of year. Closed Jan. 1, Thanksgiving and Dec. 25. Free. Shuttle bus fare $2; $1 (ages 6-11). Phone (770) 427-4686.

LAWRENCEVILLE (B-3) pop. 22,397, elev. 1,066′

SAVE **MEDIEVAL TIMES DINNER AND TOURNAMENT** is .8 mi. n. of jct. Duluth Hwy. and Sugarloaf Pkwy. at 5900 Sugarloaf Pkwy. N.W. In a replica of a medieval-style castle, guests feast on a four-course meal and witness entertainment, grandeur and pageantry evocative of centuries ago. Knights contend in jousting tournaments, sword battles and equestrian competitions featuring Andalusian stallions.

Allow 2 hours minimum. Performances Wed.-Thurs. and Sat. at 7:30 (also Sat.-Sun. at 5), Fri. at 8. Times may vary; phone ahead. Admission $49.95; $37.95 (ages 0-12). Prices may vary; phone ahead. AX, CB, DC, DS, JC, MC, VI. Phone (770) 225-0230 or (888) 935-6878.

Shopping areas: Discover Mills, at I-85 exit 108, offers 200 outlet shops and movie theaters.

LILBURN (B-2) pop. 11,307, elev. 876′

SAVE **YELLOW RIVER GAME RANCH,** at 4525 US 78, is 2.5 mi. e. of Stone Mountain Park. The ranch is a wildlife preserve that contains more than 600 animals and birds native to Georgia including mountain lions, buffaloes and bears. Wild animals are enclosed, but docile, tame animals wander free. Opportunities for petting and feeding animals are available. A hiking trail almost a mile long provides a chance to see animals close up.

Picnicking is permitted. Food is available. Allow 1 hour minimum. Daily 9:30-6; closed Jan. 1, Easter, Thanksgiving and Dec. 24-25. Last admission is 1 hour before closing. Admission $8; $7 (ages 2-11). AX, MC, VI. Phone (770) 972-6643 or (877) 972-6643.

LITHIA SPRINGS (B-1) pop. 2,072

SWEETWATER CREEK STATE PARK is at 1750 Mt. Vernon Rd. This 2,549-acre park offers visitors an opportunity to explore the ruins of a textile mill that was burned during the Civil War. The visitor center features wildlife and historic exhibits. Recreational activities include hiking, fishing and picnicking. Ranger-led programs also are available. Allow 2 hours minimum. Daily 7 a.m.-10 p.m. Trails close at dusk. Park admission by donation. Parking $3. Phone (770) 732-5871.

MARIETTA (B-2) pop. 58,748, elev. 1,118′

Winners of the Cherokee lands lottery settled Marietta in 1834, and the location soon attracted a seasonal population of lowland planters. The town's leisurely serenity was shattered by the Civil War. During Gen. William Tecumseh Sherman's push toward nearby Atlanta, Union and Confederate forces fought a bloody battle just beyond Marietta's boundaries at what is now Kennesaw Mountain National Battlefield Park *(see place listing p. 59)*.

Although Marietta was spared, two of the city's cemeteries bear witness to the bitterness of the war. In 1866 Henry Cole, a local businessman, donated land for the Marietta National Cemetery as a gesture of peace so that the dead from each side could lie in the same ground. This was not to be as the Confederate Cemetery had already been established to bury soldiers killed in a nearby train wreck.

Downtown's Glover Park, complete with an ornate Victorian gazebo, recalls the late 19th century, of which few traces remain in this growing city northwest of Atlanta. Quiet walks among courtly old houses and picnics at Kennesaw Mountain National Battlefield Park are two of the area's recreational possibilities.

Marietta Welcome Center & Visitors Bureau: 4 Depot St., Marietta, GA 30060; phone (770) 429-1115 or (800) 835-0445.

Self-guiding tours: The Marietta Welcome Center, just off the square in the old train depot at Number 4 Depot St., provides brochures outlining a walking/driving tour of the historic district, which includes Sherman's former headquarters at Kennesaw House. Phone (770) 429-1115.

SAVE **MARIETTA/COBB MUSEUM OF ART,** 30 Atlanta St. S.E., features various collections of 19th- century to contemporary art housed in a 1909 Greek Revival building that was formerly a post office. Allow 30 minutes minimum. Tues.-Fri. 11-5, Sat. 11-4; closed major holidays, between exhibitions and for special events. Admission $5; $3 (ages 6-18 and 55+). MC, VI. Phone (770) 528-1444.

MARIETTA GONE WITH THE WIND MUSEUM: SCARLETT ON THE SQUARE is at 18 Whitlock Ave. The museum houses Dr. Christopher Sullivan's collection of "Gone With The Wind" memorabilia, which includes foreign editions of the book, as well as film costumes, contracts, original scripts, personal items that belonged to cast members, and an original gown worn by Vivien Leigh as Scarlett O'Hara. Allow 30 minutes minimum. Mon.-Sat. 10-5. Admission $7; $6 (ages 60+ and students with ID); free (ages 0-7). AX, DS, MC, VI. Phone (770) 794-5576.

MARIETTA MUSEUM OF HISTORY is at 1 Depot St., Suite 200, on the second floor of the 1845 Kennesaw House. The museum includes a series of galleries documenting the history of Marietta and Cobb

County. Exhibits relate the development of local railroads, businesses and industries, display Civil War artifacts and showcase a variety of 19th- and 20th-century clothing, furnishings and inventions. The history of former local courthouses and a printing shop are the focus of several displays.

Allow 30 minutes minimum. Mon.-Sat. 10-4; closed Jan. 1, Easter, Thanksgiving and Dec. 25. Admission $5; $3 (ages 55+ and students with ID); free (ages 0-5). AX, DS, MC, VI. Phone (770) 794-5710.

THE ROOT HOUSE is at 145 Denmead St. The furnishings of this two-story house reflect the life of a middle-class merchant in the mid-19th-century. The garden contains period plants. Tues.-Sat. 11-4; closed major holidays. Admission $4; $3 (senior citizens and children). MC, VI. Phone (770) 426-4982.

SAVE **SIX FLAGS WHITE WATER** is at 250 N. Cobb Pkwy. On a 50-acre site, the park has a wide array of water attractions, including the Little Hooch lazy river ride; Cliffhanger, a six-story thrill ride; the Atlanta Ocean wave pool; and Tornado, a 75-foot-tall superstructure that twists riders down into a 60-foot-tall, 130-foot-long giant funnel, accompanied by rushing water.

Food is available. Allow a full day. Park open daily at 10, Memorial Day weekend to mid-Aug.; Sat.-Sun. and Labor Day at 10, mid-Aug. to mid-Sept. Closing times vary; phone ahead. Admission $36.99; $26.99 (children under 49 inches tall). Parking $10. AX, DS, MC, VI. Phone (770) 948-9290.

ROSWELL (B-2) pop. 79,334, elev. 1,059'

Founded in 1839 by businessman Roswell King, Roswell was a leading supplier of cotton and woolen goods to the Confederacy during the Civil War. It was in Roswell that Union troops occupied the mansions as their headquarters and set up hospitals in the Presbyterian Church and "The Old Bricks"—apartments built in 1840 for the employees of the Roswell Mill. Roswell's historic district on Canton Street offers a variety of shops.

Hour-long guided walking tours sponsored by the Roswell Historical Society are offered by reservation and depart from the convention and visitors bureau. The cost is $5 per person; phone (770) 640-3253 or (770) 992-1665.

The Historic Roswell Convention and Visitors Bureau: 617 Atlanta St., Roswell, GA 30075; phone (770) 640-3253 or (800) 776-7935.

Self-guiding tours: A booklet outlining a tour of Roswell's historic district and a brochure highlighting local events and sites of the Civil War are available from the convention and visitor bureau. Also available is the Passport that offers discounted admission to three historic houses.

GEM SAVE **ARCHIBALD SMITH PLANTATION HOME,** 935 Alpharetta St., is the preserved former home of one of Roswell's founding families. The 1845 house features original furnishings, clothing and family possessions kept intact by descendants of the Smiths. An 1840s piano, a Civil War soldier's trunk and a walnut plantation desk are among the antiques and artifacts displayed.

The property also features several original buildings, including a barn, carriage house, greenhouse, corn crib, kitchen, slave cabin and spring house. Docents convey generations of history regarding the house and its inhabitants.

Allow 1 hour minimum. Guided tours Mon.-Sat. on the hour 10-3, Sun. 1-3; closed Jan. 1, Martin Luther King Jr. Day, Memorial Day, July 4, Thanksgiving and Dec. 25. Last tour leaves at closing. Phone to verify holidays. Fee $8; $7 (senior citizens); $6 (ages 6-12). Combination ticket with Barrington Hall and Bulloch Hall $18; $15 (ages 6-12). Phone (770) 641-3978.

SAVE **BARRINGTON HALL** is at jct. SRs 120 and 9 at 535 Barrington Dr. Constructed by Barrington King in 1842, the restored Greek Revival hall was the home of three King family generations. Prior to the Civil War, the King family left Roswell; Union troops occupied the seven-acre site as the war neared its end. The Kings later returned and regained ownership of the home, which now displays original family furniture and possessions.

Allow 1 hour minimum. Guided tours are given on the hour Mon.-Sat. 10-3, Sun. 1-3; closed major holidays. Last tour departs at 3. Fee $8; $7 (ages 65+); $6 (ages 6-12). Combination ticket with Archibald Smith Plantation Home and Bulloch Hall $18; $15 (ages 6-12). Phone (770) 640-3855.

BULLOCH HALL, 1 blk. w. of the Old Square at 180 Bulloch Ave., was the girlhood home of President Theodore Roosevelt's mother, Martha (Mittie) Bulloch. This 1839 Greek Revival house features restored rooms with period furnishings. Allow 1 hour minimum. Tours on the hour Mon.-Sat. 10-3, Sun. 1-3; closed major holidays. Last tour begins at closing. Phone to verify schedule. Fee $8; $6 (ages 6-12). Combination ticket with Archibald Smith Plantation Home and Barrington Hall $18; $15 (ages 6-12). AX, DS, MC, VI. Phone (770) 992-1731.

CHATTAHOOCHEE NATURE CENTER, off SR 120 at 9135 Willeo Rd., encompasses 127 acres and has native gardens, a river boardwalk and several nature trails that wind through wetlands and woodlands. The trails are self-guiding, with native flora well marked. Carnivorous plants can be seen in the wetland demonstration area. Live reptiles and birds are exhibited. Guided walks, canoe trips, entertainment and special events are offered every weekend. Bicycles, pets and smoking are not permitted. Allow 1 hour minimum. Mon.-Sat. 9-5, Sun. noon-5; closed Jan. 1, Thanksgiving and Dec. 25. Admission $5; $4 (senior citizens); $2 (ages 3-12). Phone (770) 992-2055.

STONE MOUNTAIN (B-2)

pop. 7,145, elev. 1,043'

STONE MOUNTAIN PARK is just e. of downtown Atlanta off I-285 exit 39B via US 78 exit 8. This 3,200-acre recreational and historic park surrounding Stone Mountain features Crossroads, a re-creation of an 1870s Southern town where skilled crafts workers and costumed interpreters portray 19th-century daily life. Crossroads also features Tall Tales of the South 4-D Theater where a 3-D film is combined with theatrical effects to create a multi-sensory experience.

The park also includes the Sky Hike family adventure course, The Great Barn interactive play areas for children, along with a paddlewheel riverboat, the Skyride to the mountain's top, a scenic railroad, miniature golf, seasonal live entertainment and amphibious sightseeing tours. Miles of nature trails allow visitors to hike up the mountain.

Discovering Stone Mountain Museum at Memorial Hall features displays detailing the geological and cultural history of the granite mountain. Large picture windows offer views of Stone Mountain's Confederate memorial carving.

"Lasershow Spectacular" is a laser light show that can be viewed from the Memorial Lawn Saturdays in spring and fall, and most evenings Memorial Day weekend through mid-August (weather permitting).

Park open daily 6 a.m.-midnight. Schedule for attractions varies seasonally; phone ahead. One-Day Adventure Pass $25; $22 (senior citizens and military with ID); $20 (ages 3-11). Daily parking $8 per private vehicle or annual permit $35; cash only accepted. AX, DS, MC, VI. Phone (770) 498-5690 or (800) 317-2006.

The Antebellum Plantation is at jct. John B. Gordon Dr. and Jefferson Davis Dr., in Stone Mountain Park just e. of downtown Atlanta off I-285 exit 39B via US 78 exit 8. This compound is a complex of early 19th-century houses and buildings relocated from throughout the state. The 19 buildings include the main house, overseer's house, slave cabins and a cookhouse, all furnished in period. Allow 1 hour minimum. Daily 10-8, late May to mid-Aug.; closing time varies Feb. 1-late May and mid-Aug. through Dec. 31. Closed Dec. 24-25. Admission included in the One-Day Adventure Pass. Individual ticket $9; $7 (ages 3-11). Phone (770) 498-5690 or (800) 317-2006.

Antique Car and Treasure Museum in Stone Mountain Park at jct. Old Hugh Howell Rd. and Robert E. Lee Rd., displays classic cars, brass automotive accessories, a large musical exhibit and toys. Allow 30 minutes minimum. Daily 10-8, late May to mid-Aug.; closing time varies Feb. 1-late May and mid-Aug. through Dec. 31. Closed Dec. 24-25. Admission included in the One-Day Adventure Pass. Phone (770) 498-5690 or (800) 317-2006.

The Carillon, in Stone Mountain Park at jct. John B. Gordon Dr. and Jefferson Davis Dr., is a 13-story spire rising from the lakeshore. This tower uses miniature bell-tone rods and amplification to create its 732 bell sounds. Live concerts are given on weekends. Free. Phone (770) 498-5690 or (800) 317-2006.

Ride the Ducks in Stone Mountain Park at Crossroads. Visitors learn about the park's history in an entertaining way while seated in a covered amphibious vehicle. Allow 30 minutes minimum. **Note:** Tours are not offered during cold weather. Daily 10-8, late May to mid-Aug.; closing time varies Feb. 1-late May and mid-Aug. through Dec. 31. Closed Dec. 24-25. Schedule varies; phone ahead. Tours are included in the One-Day Adventure Pass. Individual ticket $12.85. Children under 12 must be accompanied by an adult. AX, DS, MC, VI. Phone (770) 498-5690 or (800) 317-2006.

Riverboat Cruises depart from the jct. Robert E. Lee Blvd. and Marina Dr. in Stone Mountain Park. Trips aboard the side-wheeler *Scarlett O'Hara* feature views of the mountain and shoreline. The 150-passenger riverboat offers 30-minute lake cruises daily noon-8, late May to mid-Aug. (weather permitting); schedule varies Feb. 1-late May and mid-Aug. through Dec. 31. Closed Dec. 24-25. Fare included in the One-Day Adventure Pass. Individual ticket $9; $7 (ages 3-11). Phone (770) 498-5690 or (800) 317-2006.

Stone Mountain, at US Hwy. 78 exit 8 in Stone Mountain Park, is a massive dome of granite rising 825 feet above the surrounding plain. The 300-million-year-old mountain measures 5 miles in circumference and covers 583 acres. A 1.3-mile hiking trail leads up the western flank of the mountain to its summit, and the Cherokee Trail offers 5-mile hikes around the mountain.

Three colossal Civil War figures—Confederate president Jefferson Davis, Gen. Thomas "Stonewall" Jackson and Gen. Robert E. Lee—are sculpted on 3 acres of the mountain's sheer northern face. Even though the figure of Lee is the height of a nine-story building and the entire sculpture rests in a niche the size of a city block, the figures seem small compared to the mountain's bulk. The creation of this work of art spanned 57 years, including a 36-year hiatus. The figures are illuminated at night. Phone (770) 498-5690 or (800) 317-2006.

Stone Mountain Scenic Railroad departs Robert E. Lee Blvd. and Old Hugh Howell Rd. in Stone Mountain Park and runs along a 5-mile route around Stone Mountain. During the excursion, a detailed history of trains at Stone Mountain is presented through music. A live show is presented seasonally. Allow 30 minutes minimum. Trips daily 11-8, late May to mid-Aug.; operating schedule varies Feb. 1-late May and mid-Aug. through Dec. 31. Closed Dec. 24-25. Fare included in the One-Day Adventure Pass. Individual ticket $9; $7 (ages 3-11). Phone (770) 498-5690 or (800) 317-2006.

Summit Skyride leaves from Robert E. Lee Blvd. and John B. Gordon Dr. in Stone Mountain Park. This cable-car ride to the top of Stone Mountain provides spectacular views of the mountain's carving and the countryside. Guided tours are available in season on the mountaintop. Allow 30 minutes minimum. Rides daily (weather permitting) 10-8, late May to mid-Aug.; departure of last car varies rest of year. Closed Dec. 24-25. Fare included in One-Day Adventure Pass. Individual tickets $9; $7 (ages 3-11). Phone (770) 498-5690 or (800) 317-2006.

Stone Mountain Park, Stone Mountain / Georgia Department of Economic Development

This ends listings for the Atlanta Vicinity.
The following page resumes the alphabetical listings of cities in Georgia.

AUGUSTA (C-5) pop. 199,775, elev. 162'

Augusta, Georgia's second oldest city, was founded in 1736, 3 years after Savannah. Long a crossroads of American Indian territory, the city continued as a trading center from Colonial days until after the Revolution, becoming one of the main proponents of the New South during the post Civil War Reconstruction era.

The city served as the colony's temporary capital before and during the Revolution, as well as the state capital from 1786-95 after the war concluded. The Declaration of Independence was signed by three Georgians, each associated with the Augusta government: Button Gwinnett, Lyman Hall and George Walton.

Augusta assumed the role of manufacturing center after a canal was built in 1845. The 9-mile Augusta Canal, now a National Heritage Area, is open for tours and features an interpretive center *(see attraction listing)*.

After the Civil War, many residents opened their homes to paying guests from the North who were attracted by the region's mild winters. By the 1890s Augusta had become a major winter resort area.

During this period the owner of one resort hotel built a nine-hole golf course, introducing the game to his wealthy guests. The game was so popular that the following year an 18-hole course was built at what is now the Augusta Country Club. Each April the Masters Golf Tournament, played at the Augusta National Golf Course, attracts the country's best golfers and a number of international champions, as well as thousands of spectators.

Augusta also is home to world-class water-sports events including the Head of the South Rowing Regatta and the Augusta Southern Nationals drag boat races. The Augusta Futurity, a cutting horse competition and the NBHA World Championship Barrel Horse Show are two of the several equestrian events the city hosts.

The city has several neighborhoods on the National Register, including the Olde Towne Historic District and Summerville neighborhood. The former home of influential educator Lucy Craft Laney, at 1116 Phillips St., is now the Lucy Craft Laney Museum of Black History. A 10-minute video describes her life and legacy; phone (706) 724-3576.

Throughout the city are a number of historical sites and monuments commemorating prominent figures in Augusta history. The Monument to Georgia's Signers *(see attraction listing)* of the Declaration of Independence is on Greene Street between 5th and 6th streets. At the center of the Augusta Common, Broad Street between 8th and 9th streets, a statue of Augusta founder Gen. James E. Oglethorpe stands. In the 800 block of Broad Street, a life-size bronze statue of musician and singer James Brown pays tribute to his contributions to the music industry and the Augusta community. The Korean War Memorial, in the 400 block of Broad Street, honors Augusta-area Korean War soldiers.

The 2.5-acre Springfield Village Park is adjacent to the Springfield Baptist Church. The church, 114 12th St., is the oldest independently formed African-American Baptist church; the adjoining park features a reflecting pool, bronze plaques and African-American sculptor Richard Hunt's 45-foot-tall stainless steel sculpture "The Tower of Aspiration."

Riverwalk, between 5th and 13th streets, is eight blocks of landscaped lawns and gardens on two levels along the Savannah River. The area, which is the site of a variety of festivals and events, also features a marina, restaurants, shops, museums and the Jessye Norman Amphitheater, which plays host to a variety of performances. Phone (706) 821-1754 for events information.

Augusta Convention and Visitors Bureau: In the lobby of the Augusta Museum of History at 560B Reynolds St., Augusta, GA 30901; phone (706) 724-4067 or (800) 726-0243.

Self-guiding tours: Pamphlets describing walking and driving tours of Augusta's historic districts and its special events are available at the Augusta Visitor Information Center within the Augusta Museum of History *(see attraction listing)*.

AUGUSTA CANAL INTERPRETIVE CENTER is at 1450 Greene St., Suite 400. Part of the Augusta Canal National Heritage Area, the interpretive center, which is housed in a renovated 19th-century cotton mill, describes the canal's 160-year history through interactive exhibits and displays of working mill machinery. The Petersburg Boat Guided Tour departs several times daily and offers a variety of 1-hour and 3-hour canal excursions (weather permitting), passing natural and historic sites along the way.

Allow 1 hour minimum. One-hour boat tour departs Mon.-Sat. at 10, 11:30, 1:30 and 3, Sun. at 1:30, 3 and 4:30, Apr.-Nov.; Tues.-Sat. at 11:30, 1:30 and 3, rest of year. Three-hour boat tours are available on weekends Apr.-Nov.; phone ahead for schedule. Closed Jan. 1, Easter, Thanksgiving and Dec. 25. Hours may vary; phone ahead.

Interpretive center admission $6; $4 (ages 4-18, 65+, military and college students with ID); free (ages 0-3 with paid adult). One-hour tour fare (includes interpretive center admission) $12; $10 (ages 4-18, 65+, military and college students with ID); free (ages 0-3 with paid adult). Three-hour tour fare (includes interpretive center admission) $20; $18 (ages 4-18, 65+, military and college students with ID). Reservations are suggested. MC, VI. Phone (706) 823-0440 or (888) 659-8926.

AUGUSTA MUSEUM OF HISTORY, 560 Reynolds St., features Augusta's Story, an exhibit that focuses on the history of Augusta and the surrounding region. Other highlights include the Art of Healing, a restored 1914 steam locomotive and a 1930s gas station. Historical documentaries are shown continuously. An interactive children's gallery includes a dugout canoe, a space shuttle simulator and a 1920s airplane. Allow 1 hour minimum. Tues.-Sat. 10-5, Sun. 1-5; closed major holidays. Admission $4; $3 (ages 65+); $2 (ages 6-18). Phone (706) 722-8454.

THE BOYHOOD HOME OF PRESIDENT WOODROW WILSON is at 419 7th St.; entrance is at visitors center, 415 7th St. Built in 1859, the house was purchased by the First Presbyterian Church as the church's manse. The Rev. Dr. Joseph Ruggles Wilson lived here 1860-70 with his family, including his son Thomas Woodrow. "Tommy" was 3 when the family moved in, and would grow up to become the 28th president of the United States. Fourteen rooms feature Victorian furnishings, including 13 pieces that were used by the Wilson family.

Allow 1 hour minimum. Guided 45-minute tours begin on the hour Tues.-Sat. 10-4. Last tour departs at closing. Fee $5; $4 (ages 60+); $3 (grades K-12). AX, DS, MC, VI. Phone (706) 722-9828.

CONFEDERATE MONUMENT, Broad St. between 7th and 8th sts., is a 76-foot-high Italian marble shaft. The monument, dominated by a statue of Confederate Sgt. Barry Greenwood Benson, includes life-size figures of Gens. Robert E. Lee, Thomas J. "Stonewall" Jackson, W.H.T. Walker and Thomas R.R. Cobb. Phone (706) 821-2426.

GERTRUDE HERBERT INSTITUTE OF ART, 506 Telfair St., is a handsome three-story Federal-style house built by Georgia legislator Nicholas Ware in 1818. Because of its huge cost of $40,000, the structure was known as "Ware's Folly." Works by local and nationally known contemporary artists are displayed. Tues.-Fri. 10-5; closed holidays. Donations. Phone (706) 722-5495.

SAVE **MEADOW GARDEN** is at 1320 Independence Dr. (off 13th St. between Telfair and Walton Way), near the Augusta Canal. The 1792 home of George Walton, a signer of the Declaration of Independence, is furnished with 18th- and early 19th-century pieces. Guided 30-45-minute tours Mon.-Fri. 10-4, Sat. by appointment only. Last tour 1 hour before closing. Admission $4; $3.50 (senior citizens); $3 (college students with ID); $1 (grades K-12). Phone (706) 724-4174.

MONUMENT TO GEORGIA'S SIGNERS of the Declaration of Independence, on Greene St. between 5th and 6th sts., is an 1848 marble obelisk beneath which lie the remains of George Walton and Lyman Hall. Also honored by the monument is Button Gwinnett, whose remains are believed to be buried in Savannah.

MONUMENT TO THE POETS OF GEORGIA, in the 700 block of Greene St., is a marble monument honoring 19th-century Southern poets Sidney Lanier, a native of Macon, James R. Randall and Father Abram Ryan who each lived in Augusta for a while, and Paul Hamilton Hayne who lived in Grovetown and is buried in Augusta.

MORRIS MUSEUM OF ART is downtown on the Riverwalk at One 10th St. The museum's permanent collection of nearly 5,000 pieces of Southern art includes paintings, drawings, prints, photographs and sculptures dating from the late 18th-century to the present. Artworks are displayed in dedicated galleries: Antebellum Portraiture, Civil War, Genre, Still Life, Impressionism, and Landscapes.

Allow 1 hour minimum. Tues.-Sat. 10-5, Sun. noon-5; closed major holidays. Admission $5; $3 (senior citizens and military and students with ID); free (Sun. and ages 0-5). Phone (706) 724-7501.

SAVE **NATIONAL SCIENCE CENTER'S FORT DISCOVERY,** on the Riverwalk at One 7th St., offers more than 250 fun and educational hands-on exhibits including a high-wire bicycle, an indoor lightning storm and demonstrations in the Power Station. The Paul S. Simon Discovery Theater presents the "History of Communications."

Food is available. Allow 3 hours minimum. Mon.-Sat. 10-5, Sun. noon-5. Theater times vary; phone for schedule. Closed Jan. 1, Easter, Thanksgiving and Dec. 25. Admission $8; $6 (ages 4-17, ages 55+ and military with ID). Theater $2. Parking $1 per hour, $4 maximum per day. AX, MC, VI. Phone (706) 821-0200 or (800) 325-5445.

PHINIZY SWAMP NATURE PARK, 1 mi. s. of I-520 exit 10 at 1858 Lock and Dam Rd., contains 1,150 acres of natural and constructed wetlands, swamps and streams. Several nature trails, boardwalks and four observation decks offer views of wildlife. Information is available at the park's visitor center. Picnicking is permitted. Allow 1 hour, 30 minutes minimum. Mon.-Fri. noon-dusk, Sat.-Sun. dawn-dusk. Guided tour first Sat. of the month at 9:30. Visitor center open Sat.-Sun. 9-5. Free. Phone (706) 828-2109.

SACRED HEART CULTURAL CENTER, 1301 Greene St., was formerly Sacred Heart Catholic Church. The 1900 Romanesque and Byzantine building features intricate brickwork, a barrel-vaulted ceiling, 92 stained-glass windows, tall turrets and graceful arches and now serves as a cultural center, reception hall, concert hall and meeting place for local artists and cultural groups. Guided tours are available by appointment.

Allow 30 minutes minimum. Mon.-Fri. 9-5; closed holidays and during private functions. Free. Phone (706) 826-4700.

ST. PAUL'S EPISCOPAL CHURCH, 605 Reynolds St., was founded in 1750, but the original building was destroyed during the Revolution. A second structure, built in 1819, burned down almost a century later. The present church, a classic example of Colonial-style architecture, was completed in 1919. The exterior of the building closely resembles the 1819 structure. Interred in the church's cemetery is Col. William Few Jr., Georgia's signer of the U.S. Constitution.

Mon.-Thurs. 9-5, Fri.-Sat. 9-noon, day after Labor Day-Memorial Day; Mon.-Fri. 9-4, Sat. 9-noon, rest of year. Donations. Phone (706) 724-2485.

SITE OF FORT AUGUSTA, at 605 Reynolds St. between St. Paul's Church and the river, is marked by a Celtic cross in the churchyard. Near the cross is a historical marker commemorating a visit by President George Washington. The fort was built in 1736. At the foot of the cross is a cannon believed to date to the 1730s. Free.

AUSTELL—*see Atlanta p. 58.*

BLAIRSVILLE (A-2) pop. 659, elev. 1,926′

Blairsville is entirely within the Chattahoochee National Forest *(see place listing p. 68)* and provides easy access to numerous historic buildings, scenic spots and recreational facilities. The Old Court House in the center of town contains a historical museum. Brasstown Bald, Georgia's highest mountain, provides a panorama of four states, and the Richard Russell Scenic Highway offers 14 miles of overlooks, trails and peaks.

Blairsville-Union County Chamber of Commerce: 385 Welcome Center Ln., P.O. Box 789, Blairsville, GA 30514; phone (706) 745-5789 or (877) 745-5789.

VOGEL STATE PARK, 11 mi. s. on US 19/129, covers 233 acres adjacent to the Chattahoochee National Forest in the Blue Ridge Mountains. There are 17 miles of hiking trails, 1 mile of which is interpreted by signs, as well as cottages and facilities for camping, fishing and swimming. Organized programs during the summer include guided walks and campfire nights. Daily 8 a.m.-10 p.m., June-Oct.; 8-5, rest of year. Admission $3 per private vehicle; free (Wed.). Phone (706) 745-2628. *See Recreation Chart and the AAA Southeastern CampBook.*

BLAKELY (E-2) pop. 5,696, elev. 270′

Blakely and surrounding Early County constitute one of the largest peanut-producing areas in the country. The Peanut Monument on the Courthouse Square's northeast corner was donated by citizens of the town and county.

Other sites in and near Blakely are reminders of the past. In the northwest corner of the square stands the last known Confederate flagpole, erected in 1861. Nine miles southwest, a covered bridge on Old River Road spans picturesque Coheelee Creek. Built in 1883, it is one of the few covered bridges in the South.

Blakely-Early County Chamber of Commerce: 52 Court Sq., P.O. Box 189, Blakely, GA 39823; phone (229) 723-3741.

KOLOMOKI MOUNDS STATE HISTORIC PARK, 6 mi. n. off US 27 at 205 Indian Mounds Rd., is an important archeological site and a popular recreation area. This 1,293-acre park contains seven mounds built by the Swift Creek and Weeden Island Indians. A museum at the west entrance chronicles the area's American Indian cultures from 250 A.D. to 950 A.D. One exhibit shows the interior of a mound as archeologists left it.

Park open daily 7 a.m.-10 p.m. Museum open daily 8-5; closed Jan. 1, Thanksgiving and Dec. 25. Park admission $3 per private vehicle. Museum admission $3; $2.50 (ages 62+); $1.75 (ages 6-18). Phone (229) 724-2150 for the park or (229) 724-2151 for the museum. *See Recreation Chart and the AAA Southeastern CampBook.*

BRASELTON (B-3) pop. 1,206

MAYFIELD DAIRY FARM is at 1160 Broadway Ave. Since 1923, the farm has provided high-quality dairy products. Tours of the milk production facility give visitors a glimpse of the processes involved in getting a worthy product to market. Allow 30 minutes minimum. Tours are given Mon.-Fri. 9-5, Sat. 9-2. Last tour begins 1 hour before closing. Free. Phone (888) 298-0396.

WINERIES

- **Chateau Élan**, SR 211 off I-85 exit 126 to 100 Rue Charlemagne. Tours and tastings are given Mon.-Fri. at 11 and 3, Sat. on the hour noon-5, Sun. on the hour noon-4; closed holidays. Phone (678) 425-0900 or (800) 233-9463.

BRUNSWICK (E-5) pop. 15,600, elev. 14′

Brunswick was founded in 1771 on a peninsula that juts into the Brunswick River; the city was named for Braunschweig, Germany, the ancestral home of King George II. Streets and parks named after members of England's ruling family and English places help preserve the town's past. Victorian houses remain from the late 19th century, when Brunswick was a busy shipping center for lumber and naval stores.

Shrimp- and crabmeat-processing plants are concentrated along Bay Street from Gloucester to Prince streets. In season, boats unload shrimp onto the street's docks most weekdays in the late afternoon. Charter fishing trips leave from Brunswick, St. Simons Island and Jekyll Island.

Among Brunswick's landmarks are two oak trees. Lover's Oak, at Albany and Prince streets, is thought to date from the 12th century. Local legend tells of an American Indian and his love, who met beneath its branches. Lanier's Oak overlooks the marshes on US 17. It is said that under this tree the Georgia poet Sidney Lanier was inspired to write "The Marshes of Glynn." The James Oglethorpe Monument, on Newcastle Street in Queens Square, honors the founder of Georgia.

Brunswick-Golden Isles Convention and Visitors Bureau-Brunswick: 4 Glynn Ave., Brunswick, GA 31520; phone (912) 265-0620 or (800) 933-2627.

Self-guiding tours: Driving tour maps of Brunswick, St. Simons Island, Sea Island and Jekyll Island are available at the Golden Isles Welcome Center on I-95 off the southbound lanes between exits 42 and 38, at the area's visitor center on US 17 at the Torras Causeway to St. Simons Island and on St. Simons Island in the village area.

GEM **HOFWYL-BROADFIELD PLANTATION,** 10 mi. n. to 5556 US 17N, provides a glimpse of early 19th-century life on the Georgia rice coast as well as a chance to observe the vegetation and animal life native to this freshwater marsh country. In 1806 William Brailsford purchased a tract of land and named it Broadfield. Later generations built the present house, which they named Hofwyl, in the 1850s. The estate remained in the family until 1973.

The plantation is presently a 1,268-acre wildlife preserve with a museum where a videotape presentation details the history of Hofwyl and the rice industry. Exhibits show how slaves, many of them experienced in rice cultivation in Africa, carved a thriving rice plantation from the virgin cypress swamp along the Altamaha River. The house has family furnishings from different periods.

Picnicking is permitted. Guided 1-hour house tours depart on the hour Tues.-Sat. (also Mon. holidays) 9-5, Sun. 2-5:30; closed Tues. after Mon. holiday, Jan. 1, Thanksgiving and Dec. 25. Last tour departs one hour before closing. Admission $5; $4.50 (ages 62+); $2.50 (ages 6-18). AX, DS, MC, VI. Phone (912) 264-7333.

BUFORD—*see Atlanta p. 58.*

CAIRO (F-2) pop. 9,239, elev. 265′

Though the Cairo (KAY-ro) area was supposedly visited by Hernando de Soto in 1540, it was not settled until pioneers from North Carolina founded the Tired Creek Primitive Baptist Church in 1826. By 1870 the local Atlantic & Gulf Railroad station had grown large enough to support a town, and Cairo was born.

Cairo-Grady County Chamber of Commerce: 961 N. Broad St., P.O. Box 387, Cairo, GA 39828; phone (229) 377-3663.

RODDENBERY MEMORIAL LIBRARY, 320 N. Broad St., contains displays describing area history. Mon.-Tues. 9-7, Wed. 9-6, Thurs. 9-7, Fri. 9-6, Sat. 9-3. Free. Phone (229) 377-3632.

CALHOUN (A-2) pop. 10,667, elev. 716′

Calhoun and surrounding Gordon County were the home of the Cherokee Indians until 1838, when the Cherokees were forced to sell their land and move to Oklahoma. Local industry includes carpet and textile manufacturing. Resaca Confederate Cemetery, 5 miles north on I-75, was the site of the Civil War battle that opened the way to Atlanta for Gen. William Tecumseh Sherman.

Calhoun/Gordon Convention & Visitors Bureau: 300 S. Wall St., Calhoun, GA 30701; phone (706) 625-3200 or (800) 887-3811.

NEW ECHOTA STATE HISTORIC SITE is off I-75 exit 317, 1 mi. n. on SR 225 to 1211 Chatsworth Hwy. (SR 225). The site was the last capital of the Cherokee Nation in Georgia. The tribal nation adopted as the Cherokees' first written language the alphabet devised by the American Indian scholar Sequoyah. The *Cherokee Phoenix,* published in 1828, was the first newspaper to use this alphabet. The treaty that moved the Cherokee westward was signed at New Echota under the administration of President Andrew Jackson.

Tues.-Sat. (also Mon. holidays) 9-5, Sun. 2-5:30; closed Jan. 1, Thanksgiving and Dec. 25 and Tues. following Mon. holidays. Admission $4; $3.50 (ages 62+); $2.50 (ages 6-18). AX, DS, MC, VI. Phone (706) 624-1321.

CARTERSVILLE (B-1) pop. 15,925, elev. 787′

Only two of Cartersville's houses survived the Federal occupation of 1864, but the town's location in Bartow County's rich mineral belt led to its speedy reconstruction. Two miles east is Red Top Mountain State Park *(see Recreation Chart and the AAA Southeastern CampBook).*

Cartersville-Bartow Convention and Visitors Bureau: One Friendship Plaza, P.O. Box 200397, Cartersville, GA 30120; phone (770) 387-1357 or (800) 733-2280.

SAVE **BOOTH WESTERN ART MUSEUM** is 1 blk. n. of town square at 501 Museum Dr. The museum houses contemporary American western art along with illustrations and movie posters. Particular subjects highlighted by individual galleries within the museum include cowboys and the Civil War. One gallery features presidential photographs and memorabilia; another offers interactive, hands-on exhibits for children ages 2-12.

Free guided 45-minute tours are available. Food is available Tues.-Sat. Allow 1 hour minimum. Tues.-Sat. 10-5 (also Thurs. 5-8), Sun. 1-5; guided tours at 1:30. Closed Jan. 1, July 4, Thanksgiving and Dec. 25. Admission $8; $6 (ages 65+ and military with ID); $5 (students with ID); free (ages 0-12, active military with ID and to all on the first Thurs. of the month 4-7). AX, CB, JC, MC, VI. Phone (770) 387-1300.

ETOWAH INDIAN MOUNDS STATE HISTORICAL SITE, 6 mi. s. of I-75 exit 288 following signs to 813 Indian Mounds Rd., preserves the remains of an American Indian settlement occupied 950-1550 A.D. The 54-acre site includes six earthen mounds, a plaza, borrow pits, a fish trap in the Etowah River and a defense ditch. A museum displays artifacts excavated from the mounds and interprets religious and cultural practices of the site's former residents.

Museum open Tues.-Sat. 9-5, Sun. 2-5:30; grounds close 30 minutes before museum. Closed Jan. 1, Thanksgiving and Dec. 25. Admission $4; $3.50 (ages 62+); $2.50 (ages 6-18). Phone (770) 387-3747.

ROSELAWN MUSEUM is at 224 W. Cherokee Ave. This restored Victorian mansion was the home of late-19th-century evangelist Samuel Porter Jones. It houses his writings and memorabilia as well as those belonging to Rebecca Latimer Felton, who in 1922 became the first woman to serve in the U.S. Senate. The 3.5-acre grounds feature a one-room schoolhouse, a brick smokehouse and a carriage house. Allow 30 minutes minimum. Guided tours Tues.-Fri. 10-noon and 1-5. Admission $4; $2 (students with ID). Phone (770) 387-5162.

CHATSWORTH (A-2) pop. 3,531, elev. 752'

Chatsworth is noted for the Chief Vann House, the first brick home within the Cherokee Nation. Just east is Fort Mountain State Park; to the south is Carters Lake *(see Recreation Chart and the AAA Southeastern CampBook)*.

Chatsworth-Murray County Chamber of Commerce: 126 N. 3rd Ave., Chatsworth, GA 30705; phone (706) 695-6060 or (800) 969-9490.

CHIEF VANN HOUSE STATE HISTORIC SITE, Spring Pl. 1 mi. s. at 82 SR 225N, is the restored 1804 mansion of Chief James Vann, a Cherokee who sponsored the influential Moravian Mission next to his plantation. The house is part of a memorial to the Cherokee Nation.

Picnicking is permitted. Guided 45-minute tours Tues.-Sat. (and Mon. holidays) 9-5, Sun. 2-5:30; closed Jan. 1, Thanksgiving, Dec. 25 and Tues. when open on a Mon. holiday. Last tour begins 45 minutes before closing. Admission $4; $3.50 (ages 62+); $2.50 (ages 6-18). Phone (706) 695-2598.

CHATTAHOOCHEE AND OCONEE NATIONAL FORESTS

Elevations in the forests range from 500 ft. in Oconee National Forest to 4,784 ft. at Brasstown Bald in Chattahoochee National Forest. Refer to AAA maps for additional elevation information.

The 750,194 acres of the Chattahoochee National Forest are in northern Georgia, and the 115,476 acres of the Oconee National Forest are in central Georgia. Within the forests are campsites, picnic areas, wilderness areas, trails and the Chattooga National Wild and Scenic River.

The Chattahoochee National Forest includes the southern part of one of the world's most extensive and productive hardwood forests. Its Cohutta Wilderness, covering some 35,268 acres, is a popular area for fishing, hunting and hiking.

Also in the forest are the twin cascades of Anna Ruby Falls, where two creeks converge before running into Unicoi Lake and on into the Chattahoochee River. Anna Ruby Falls Scenic Area offers several hiking trails, including a quarter-mile-long paved trail and one with Braille signage, a visitor center and picnic areas. The Anna Ruby Falls Information Center has exhibits and information about the history and natural resources of the area as well as a trout-viewing pond and trails.

At 4,784 feet above sea level, Brasstown Bald is Georgia's highest mountain. The Brasstown Bald Visitor Center, off SR 180 near Blairsville, is open daily Memorial Day weekend through October and weekends in early spring and early November (weather permitting); phone (706) 745-6928. The center features a theater, a rooftop observation deck and exhibits about the relationship between people and mountains. The summit also has picnic facilities and three hiking trails, and on clear days affords views of four states.

The forest is open daily 24 hours. Forest admission free; some facilities within require a fee. Forest and area maps are sold at the Forest Supervisor's Office, 1755 Cleveland Hwy., Gainesville, GA 30501. Phone (770) 297-3000. *See Recreation Chart and the AAA Southeastern CampBook.*

CHATTAHOOCHEE RIVER NATIONAL RECREATION AREA—*see Atlanta p. 58.*

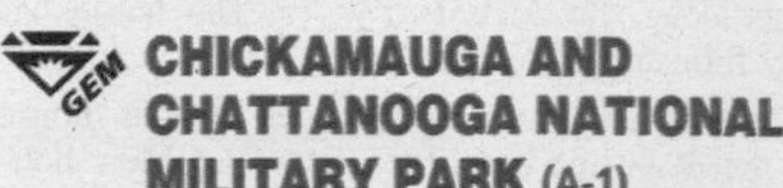

CHICKAMAUGA AND CHATTANOOGA NATIONAL MILITARY PARK (A-1)

The 9,000-acre Chickamauga and Chattanooga National Military Park's largest section is in northwest Georgia, with the remainder in Tennessee. It is the oldest national military park administered by the U.S. National Park Service. The park commemorates Civil War battles that were fought for control of Chattanooga, Tenn., a strategic railway center.

Early in September 1863, Gen. William S. Rosecrans and 58,000 Union soldiers crossed the Tennessee River southwest of Chattanooga, forcing the Confederate troops of Gen. Braxton Bragg to abandon the city and move south to protect their Atlanta supply lines. After obtaining reinforcements, Bragg moved back northward, hoping to retake Chattanooga. The two forces clashed at Chickamauga Creek near the Georgia-Tennessee line.

Although victorious, the Confederates suffered heavy losses: of the 66,000 engaged, about one-quarter were killed, wounded or missing in action. The Union forces withdrew to Chattanooga after suffering 16,000 casualties. The ensuing Confederate siege of the city almost subdued the Union army. However, bolstered by reinforcements and a new supply route, Union forces resumed the offensive by November.

The 3-day Battle of Chattanooga began Nov. 23, with Union forces driving the Confederates back to the base of Missionary Ridge and capturing Orchard Knob. When the Union troops assaulted the remaining Confederates in the Battle of Lookout Mountain the next day, the Confederates chose to evacuate the area rather than risk separation from their main line.

The decisive blow came a day later. Gen. Ulysses S. Grant directed the all-day Battle of Missionary Ridge, in which the Confederates were dislodged from strategic points and Union forces took the steep slopes above the city. The Confederates withdrew after dark; their defeat opened the way to Atlanta and the heart of the Confederacy.

The woods and fields of this beautiful park are maintained to some degree in their wartime condition. More than 1,600 markers, monuments, cannons and tablets indicate the battle lines of both sides and recount the story of the area. Self-guiding tours enable visitors to explore the battlefields of Chickamauga, Lookout Mountain and Missionary Ridge.

Among points of interest are Orchard Knob, Grant's headquarters during the Battle of Chattanooga; Crest Road, along Missionary Ridge; Wilder Brigade Monument, commanding a good view of the Chickamauga Battlefield and its surroundings; the Brotherton House, a prewar farmhouse marking the spot where the Union line was broken; Snodgrass Hill, the scene of the last fighting at Chickamauga; and Snodgrass House, which served as a Union field hospital during the battle.

The park is open daily dawn-dusk; closed Dec. 25. Free. Phone (706) 866-9241.

BATTLES FOR CHATTANOOGA ELECTRIC MAP AND MUSEUM is at 1110 E. Brow Rd., next to Point Park. A miniature battlefield display with more than 5,000 soldiers and cannons depicts the Battle of Chattanooga. Narration and music describe the historic conflict. Allow 1 hour minimum. Daily 9-6:30, Memorial Day weekend-Labor Day; 10-5, rest of year. Closed Dec. 25. Admission $6.95; $4.95 (ages 3-12). AX, DS, MC, VI. Phone (423) 821-2812.

CHICKAMAUGA VISITOR CENTER is 9 mi. s. of Chattanooga, Tenn., on US 27, near the n. end of the park on Chickamauga Battlefield. A museum has Civil War exhibits and the Fuller Gun Collection, a display of American military shoulder arms. Orientation programs are offered, including a multimedia presentation depicting the Battle of Chickamauga.

Daily 8:30-5, closed Dec. 25. Visitor center free. Audiotapes narrating a self-guiding tour of the park are available for purchase at the bookstore. Phone (706) 866-9241.

CRAVENS HOUSE is at 1040 Cravens Terrace Rd., off SR 148 on Lookout Mountain. Built by Robert Cravens in 1855, the house was occupied by both Confederate and Federal troops during the Civil War; it also served as a Confederate field hospital. Relics are displayed in the house and on the grounds. Guided 30-minute tours Sat.-Sun. 9-4:30, mid-June to mid-Aug. Hours may vary; phone ahead. Free. Phone (423) 821-7786.

POINT PARK is on Lookout Mountain at 110 Point Park Rd. The park overlooks Chattanooga and the Moccasin Bend of the Tennessee River. The Ochs Memorial Museum and Observatory, the New York Peace Monument, Cravens House and Umbrella Rock are in the park. The Lookout Mountain Battlefield Visitor Center at the north end of E. Brow Road contains the restored James Walker painting "Battle of Lookout Mountain."

Park open daily 8:30-dusk. Visitor center open daily 8:30-6, Memorial Day through mid-Aug.; 8:30-5, rest of year. Park and visitor center closed Dec. 25. Park admission $3; free (ages 0-15). AX, DS, MC, VI. Phone (423) 821-7786.

CLAYTON (A-3) pop. 2,019, elev. 1,925′

RECREATIONAL ACTIVITIES

White-water Rafting

- **Southeastern Expeditions**, 7 mi. e. on US 76E. Write 5637 Hwy. 411, Benton, TN 37307. Daily 9-5, mid-Mar. through Oct. 31. Phone for minimum age requirements. Phone (404) 329-0433 or (800) 868-7238.

COLUMBUS (D-2) pop. 186,291, elev. 261′

Columbus, once the site of a Creek Indian village on the Chattahoochee River on the western Georgia border, later became a trading post. On April 16, 1865, in one of the final battles of the Civil War, Union troops seized the important Confederate supply depot at Columbus. Remains of the breastworks are still visible.

The restored 1871 Springer Opera House, 103 10th St., is just outside Columbus' 26-block historic district. The opera house, which once featured such prominent figures as Edwin Booth, Oscar Wilde, Lily Langtry and Irving Berlin, now offers productions on a seasonal basis.

The Columbus Historic Riverfront Industrial District is the site of the remains of 19th-century mills and ironworks along the east bank of the Chattahoochee River, beginning at 800 Front Ave.

The Columbus, Georgia Convention & Trade Center, 801 Front Ave., operated 1853-1964 as an iron works. The breech-loading cannon, the first successful ice-making machine and the Confederate ironclad CSS *Jackson* were manufactured at the works, which is now a convention and trade center. The Chattahoochee Promenade on Front Avenue borders the river between Fifth and Ninth streets.

Noteworthy among Columbus' events is the Thunder in the Valley Air Show, held in mid-March and featuring a variety of military and civilian aircraft and vehicles. Christmas Made in the South, a holiday arts and crafts show, occurs the last weekend of October. The Steeplechase at Callaway Gardens *(see attraction listing p. 89)* attracts more than 10,000 admirers of equestrian skills each November.

Columbus Convention and Visitors Bureau: 900 Front Ave., P.O. Box 2768, Columbus, GA 31902; phone (706) 322-1613 or (800) 999-1613.

Self-guiding tours: Brochures detailing a walking and/or driving tour of the original city are available at the visitor bureau Mon.-Fri. 8:30-5:30, Sat., 10-4.

COCA-COLA SPACE SCIENCE CENTER is at 701 Front Ave. This facility features a Challenger Learning Center, the Omnisphere Theater and the Mead Observatory. Simulators and interactive displays give visitors a glimpse of the cosmos. Allow 1 hour minimum. Mon.-Thurs. 10-4, Fri. 10-8, Sat. 10:30-8;

closed July 4, Thanksgiving and Dec. 24-25. Admission, includes one Omnisphere Theater show, $6; $5 (ages 55+ and military with ID); $4 (ages 4-12). $3 for each additional show. AX, MC, VI. Phone (706) 649-1470 for recorded information or (706) 649-1477.

THE COLUMBUS MUSEUM is at 1251 Wynnton Rd. Among this museum's exhibits are 18th-century through contemporary works of American art, prehistoric American Indian artifacts, Yuchi Indian materials, a display of American decorative arts and regional historical items. Changing exhibits of American art and about history are presented. Allow 1 hour minimum. Tues.-Sat. 10-5 (also Thurs. 5-9), Sun. 1-5; closed holidays. Free. Phone (706) 748-2562.

FORT BENNING, s.e. of Columbus, in addition to being the only U.S. Army training center for infantry it also trains airborne troops. Monday through Wednesday visitors can go to the drop zone and watch the paratroopers land. Phone (706) 545-2238.

National Infantry Museum, at Fort Benning in Bldg. 396 on Baltzell Ave., is dedicated to the evolution of the infantry since the French and Indian Wars. Artifacts, weapons, uniforms, battle flags, medals and military vehicles are displayed. **Note:** The museum is moving to a new location and is scheduled to re-open in March 2009; visitors should phone the Fort Benning number to confirm hours. Due to security concerns, visitors must go through a military checkpoint and provide ID, proof of automobile insurance and vehicle registration. Allow 1 hour minimum.

Mon.-Fri. 10-4:30, Sat.-Sun. 12:30-4:30; open Memorial Day, July 4 and Veterans' Day with the hours of the day of the week on which the holiday falls. Closed Jan. 1, Thanksgiving, Dec. 25 and federal holidays celebrated on Mon. Free. Phone (706) 545-2958.

HERITAGE CORNER guided walking tours depart from the Historic Columbus Foundation farmhouse at 708 Broadway. The tour, ranging from 60 to 90 minutes, encompasses five dwellings dating 1800-70; only two are on their original foundations. All are furnished and decorated in period. The Walker-Peters-Langdon House, a simple Federal cottage, is believed to be the oldest residence in the original city of Columbus.

The Pemberton House was occupied by Dr. J.S. Pemberton, a druggist and originator of the formula for Coca-Cola. Allow 1 hour minimum. Tours depart daily at 2; closed Jan. 1, Easter, July 4, Thanksgiving and Dec. 25. Admission $5; $1 (students with ID). There is a two person minimum. Phone (706) 322-0756.

NATIONAL CIVIL WAR NAVAL MUSEUM AT PORT COLUMBUS is at 1002 Victory Dr. This 40,000-square-foot museum houses the remains of two Civil War vessels: the ironclad CSS *Jackson,* and the gunboat CSS *Chattahoochee,* a steam-powered sailing ship. The museum also contains re-created sections of the USS *Monitor,* the ironclad CSS *Albemarle,* and Adm. David Glasgow Farragut's flagship the USS *Hartford,* which visitors can enter to experience what shipboard life was like then. A multimedia show simulates a battle aboard an ironclad.

Murals depict the various craft designed for river, coastal and deep-water warfare. A chronology of the Civil War at sea is illustrated by eight wall panels. Historic items displayed include rare firearms, a uniform coat of the officer who commanded the CSS *Virginia (Merrimac)* when it fought the USS *Monitor,* and approximately 2,000 square feet of Civil War naval-related flags from ships and coastal forts throughout the South.

Allow 1 hour minimum. Daily 9-5; closed Dec. 25. Admission $6.50; $5.50 (ages 65+ and military with ID); $5 (students with ID). MC, VI. Phone (706) 327-9798.

COMER (B-3) pop. 1,052, elev. 573'

WATSON MILL BRIDGE STATE PARK is 3 mi. s. on SR 22 at 650 Watson Mill Rd. A 229-foot four-span covered bridge built in 1885 crosses the South Fork River. Picnicking, camping and fishing in the river are permitted; canoe and paddleboat rentals are available. Hiking, bicycle and horse trails also are in the park; horses are not available. Daily 7 a.m.-10 p.m. Parking $3 per private vehicle. Phone (706) 783-5349. *See Recreation Chart and the AAA Southeastern CampBook.*

CORDELE (E-3) pop. 11,608, elev. 336'

GEORGIA VETERANS MEMORIAL STATE PARK is 9 mi. w. on US 280. Established in 1946, the park honors Georgia's war veterans. The 1,322-acre park includes an 18-hole golf course, a military museum with outdoor exhibits of vintage aircraft and military equipment and an indoor collection of artifacts from various wars. A marina at 8,600-acre Lake Blackshear provides boat rentals.

Park open daily 7 a.m.-10 p.m. Museum daily 8-5; closed Dec. 25. Free. Parking $3; free (Wed.). Phone (229) 276-2371. *See Recreation Chart and the AAA Southeastern CampBook.*

COVINGTON (C-2) pop. 11,547

Scarcely 30 miles from the hustle and bustle of Atlanta, Covington boasts a wealth of carefully restored antebellum and Victorian-era manor homes that can be viewed on a self-guided driving or walking tour; maps are available at the welcome center.

The 1884 Newton County Courthouse is known to thousands from the TV series "In the Heat of the Night" that was filmed in Covington for eight seasons. The first five episodes of "The Dukes of Hazzard" also were filmed in Covington. The Covington Welcome Center offers a brochure detailing the location sites of these and other series as well as motion pictures filmed in Covington and Newton County.

Nearby is Hard Labor Creek State Park, a 5,800-acre complex with cottages, two lakes, a swimming beach, boat rentals, an 18-hole golf course and a bring-your-own-horse stable. *See Recreation Chart and Rutledge in the AAA Southeastern CampBook.*

Covington Welcome Center and Visitors Bureau: 2101 Clark St., Covington, GA 30015; phone (770) 787-3868.

CRAWFORDVILLE (C-4) pop. 572, elev. 589′

A.H. STEPHENS STATE HISTORIC PARK is 2 mi. n. of I-20 via SR 22 exit at 456 Alexander St. N. Named after the vice president of the Confederacy and governor of Georgia, the park has both natural and historic features. Liberty Hall, Stephens' home, has been renovated to its 1875 appearance; tours are available of the furnished interior. A Confederate museum houses a fine collection of Civil War artifacts, including uniforms and documents.

Park open daily 7 a.m.-10 p.m. Historic site open Tues.-Sat. 9-5 (also Mon. holidays), Sun. 2-5. Closed Jan. 1, Thanksgiving, Dec. 25 and the Tues. following Mon. holidays. Admission $3; $2 (ages 6-18 and 62+). Parking $3. Phone (706) 456-2602 for the park or (706) 456-2221 for the museum. *See Recreation Chart and the AAA Southeastern CampBook.*

CUMBERLAND ISLAND NATIONAL SEASHORE—*see Golden Isles p. 76.*

DAHLONEGA (A-2) pop. 3,638, elev. 1,875′

In 1828, nearly 3 centuries after Hernando de Soto sought gold in northeastern Georgia, the area around Dahlonega (dah-LON-a-gah) boomed with the discovery of the ore. A federal mint built in 1838 coined more than $6 million before it was closed at the outbreak of the Civil War. Gold coins minted in Dahlonega are highly prized by collectors.

Gold mining continued in Dahlonega until the early 20th century when the fixing of the metal's worth at $35 an ounce made mining unprofitable. Tourism and vineyards have replaced commercial gold mining. In 1958 and again in the mid-1970s, gold donated by residents was driven to Atlanta in a mule train and used to re-cover the dome of the Capitol with gold leaf.

The price of gold is no longer fixed, and visitors can pan for the metal at Consolidated Gold Mine and Crisson Gold Mine, where visitors also can take underground mine tours and see exhibits of mining equipment.

Dahlonega-Lumpkin County Chamber of Commerce: 13 S. Park St., Dahlonega, GA 30533; phone (706) 864-3711 or (800) 231-5543.

CONSOLIDATED GOLD MINES, 185 Consolidated Gold Mine Rd., offers guided 45-minute tours of a former gold mine. Demonstrations of drilling and gold-panning techniques are featured. The underground mine remains at a constant temperature of 60 F. Panning for gold and gemstones is offered.

Allow 1 hour, 30 minutes minimum. Tours depart as needed daily 10-5, Memorial Day-Labor Day; Mon.-Fri. 10-4, Sat.-Sun. 10-5, rest of year. Closed Easter, Thanksgiving and Dec. 25. Last tour begins at closing. Tour (includes sample panning) $14; $9 (ages 4-14). Gold panning $6 per pan. Children under 4 are not permitted. MC, VI. Phone (706) 864-8473.

DAHLONEGA GOLD MUSEUM STATE HISTORIC SITE, on the public square, depicts America's first major gold rush through exhibits of nuggets and gold dust, Dahlonega minted gold coins, mining apparatus and photographs of early mining activities. A 17-minute film titled "America's First Gold Rush" talks about the discovery of gold in the North Georgia mountains. Allow 1 hour minimum. Mon.-Sat. 9-5, Sun. 10-5; closed Jan. 1, Thanksgiving and Dec. 25. Admission $4; $3.50 (ages 62+); $2.50 (ages 6-18). Phone (706) 864-2257.

RECREATIONAL ACTIVITIES

Canoeing

- **Appalachian Outfitters** is on SR 60 S. at 2084 S. Chestatee, Dahlonega, GA 30533. Daily 10-3, June-Aug.; Thurs.-Sun. 10-3, Apr.-May and in Sept.; Sat.-Sun. 10-2, in Oct. Phone (706) 864-7117, or (800) 426-7117 for reservations.

WINERIES

- **Three Sisters Vineyards** is at 439 Vineyard Way. Thurs.-Sat. 11-5, Sun. 1-5, Mon.-Wed. by appointment, Feb. 1-Dec. 25. Phone (706) 865-9463.
- **Wolf Mountain Vineyards & Winery** is at 180 Wolf Mountain Tr. Mon. and Thurs.-Sat. noon-5, Sun. 12:30-5. Phone (706) 867-9862.

DALLAS (B-1) pop. 5,056, elev. 1,050′

PICKETT'S MILL BATTLEFIELD STATE HISTORIC SITE is 5 mi. n.e. on Dallas-Acworth Hwy. (SR 381), then 1 mi. w. on Due West Rd., then n. to 4432 Mt. Tabor Church Rd. At this site in 1864, Confederate troops defeated Union troops advancing toward Atlanta. Walking trails with explanatory signs cross the battlefield; living-history programs, a film, a videotape explanation of the battle and battle artifacts also are featured.

Picnicking is permitted. Allow 1 hour minimum. Tues.-Sat. and Mon. holidays 9-5, Sun. noon-5; closed Jan. 1, Thanksgiving and Dec. 25. Admission $3; $2.50 (ages 62+); $1.75 (ages 6-18). DS, MC, VI. Phone (770) 443-7850.

DALTON (A-2) pop. 27,912, elev. 767′

In the early 1900s a local farm girl sold a hand-tufted bedspread for $2.50 and unknowingly revived a century-old craft that was to become big business in Dalton. Although the bedspreads are now rare, the craft is perpetuated in the production of tufted floor coverings. Currently, Dalton supplies more than half of the world's tufted carpets.

Another craft is preserved 10 miles northeast of Dalton, off I-75 exit 341 on SR 2, at the restored Prater's Mill. Dating from the 1800s, the mill still grinds cornmeal during annual fairs held on the site; phone (706) 694-6455.

Dalton Convention and Visitors Bureau: Write P.O. Box 6177, Dalton, GA 30722; phone (706) 270-9960 or (800) 331-3258.

CROWN GARDENS AND ARCHIVES is at 715 Chattanooga Ave. The site features the 1855 Crown Cotton Mill, archives housing mill documents and genealogical research materials, and a museum with exhibits focusing on the chenille cottage and textile industries of north Georgia. Civil War and Cherokee artifacts and antiques also are displayed. Tues.-Fri. 10-5. Free. Phone (706) 278-0217.

DARIEN (E-5) pop. 1,719, elev. 30'

Established as a stronghold to protect England's rich Southern holdings from Spanish, French and Indian attacks in the 1720s, Darien was settled by Gen. James E. Oglethorpe's Scottish Highlanders. The town became a prosperous center of timber shipping and trade by the mid-1800s. The Darien River, which determined the town's location, is dotted with shrimp boats that now underpin the local economy. A 7-mile bicycle path connects the historic district with Fort King George; the path begins at the foot of the bridge at the intersection of US 17 and Fort King George Drive.

Recreational opportunities, including bird-watching, kayaking, fishing and deep-sea charter excursions, are available downtown and north on US 17 at Shellman Bluff and Harris Neck National Wildlife Refuge. Harris Neck's 2,856 acres are a mix of wooded areas, grassy plains and marshes and Spanish moss draped oaks, and offer a pleasant drive on a comfortable afternoon. In the summer the refuge is home to nesting egrets, herons and wood storks; in winter ducks take up residence. Pets are not permitted in the refuge, which is open dawn-dusk. To reach the refuge take exit 67 off I-95 and go south on U.S. 17 for about 1 mile and then go east on Harris Neck Road for about 7 miles.

Darien-McIntosh County Chamber of Commerce: 105 Fort King George Dr., P.O. Box 1497, Darien, GA 31305; phone (912) 437-6684.

Shopping areas: Georgia Islands Factory Shoppes off I-95 exit 49 at 1 Magnolia Bluff Way features more than 24 stores, including Gap, Polo Ralph Lauren and Tommy Hilfiger outlets.

FORT KING GEORGE STATE HISTORIC SITE is 1 mi. e. of US 17 on Fort King George Dr. Serving as the Southern outpost for the British Empire 1721-27, the fort was the first English settlement in what is now the state of Georgia. It was reconstructed based on documents from the British Public Records Office. The remains of sawmills and a tabby house are on the site. A museum interprets American Indian, Spanish and British occupation, as well as the history of coastal sawmills.

Allow 1 hour minimum. Tues.-Sat. and Mon. holidays 9-5, Sun. 2-5:30; closed Jan. 1, Thanksgiving, Dec. 25 and the Tues. following a Mon. holiday. Admission $5; $4.50 (ages 62+); $2.50 (ages 6-18). Phone (912) 437-4770.

HOFWYL-BROADFIELD PLANTATION—*see Brunswick p. 67.*

DAWSONVILLE—*see Atlanta p. 58.*

DOUGLAS (E-4) pop. 10,639, elev. 275'

Douglas was platted in 1858 on 50 acres of land donated by J. S. Pearson and named for Stephen A. Douglas, a presidential candidate running against Abraham Lincoln. Douglas, the seat of Coffee County, has a bustling downtown and a thriving economy with a strong industrial and agricultural influence. Recreational opportunities abound in nearby General Coffee State Park *(see Recreation Chart).*

More than 500 species of plants native to Georgia may be seen at Broxton Rocks Preserve. Guided hikes of the site are provided and require a reservation; phone (912) 384-4555.

Douglas Area Welcome Center: 211 S. Gaskin Ave., Douglas, GA 31533; phone (912) 384-4555 or (888) 426-3334.

DULUTH—*see Atlanta p. 59.*

EATONTON (C-3) pop. 6,764, elev. 578'

Eatonton was the birthplace in 1848 of Joel Chandler Harris, creator of the popular children's characters Uncle Remus, Brer Fox, Brer Bear and Brer Rabbit. A statue of Brer Rabbit on Courthouse Square commemorates Harris' works; many originals are displayed at the Uncle Remus Museum *(see attraction listing)*. Eatonton also was home to Alice Walker, author of the 1983 Pulitzer Prize-winning novel "The Color Purple."

Fifteen miles southeast, county-owned Oconee Springs Park provides recreational facilities on Lake Sinclair *(see Recreation Chart and the AAA Southeastern CampBook)*. Lake Oconee *(see Recreation Chart)*, suitable for water skiing and other water sports, is 7 miles east.

Eatonton-Putnam Chamber of Commerce: 305 N. Madison Ave., P.O. Box 4088, Eatonton, GA 31024; phone (706) 485-7701.

Self-guiding tours: Maps outlining historic home tours and a 6-loop scenic byway driving trail tour are available at the chamber of commerce.

ROCK EAGLE, 7 mi. n. on US 441 to 350 Rock Eagle Rd., is a 1,428-acre state 4-H center. On the center's grounds is an effigy mound topped by a huge representation of an open-winged bird, thought to be a buzzard or a hawk, made of milky quartz stones ranging from baseball-size to boulders. Archeologists believe the Moundbuilders created the effigy A.D. 100-300. A tower affords a complete view of the structure. Daily dawn-dusk. Free. Phone (706) 484-2899.

UNCLE REMUS MUSEUM is 3 blks. s. on US 441 at 214 Oak St. in Turner Park. Housed in a log cabin built from two slave cabins, the museum recreates the setting where the little boy in Joel Chandler Harris' tales heard the stories of Uncle Remus, thought to be a composite of two slaves who excelled at storytelling. Displays include woodcarvings and paintings of Harris' characters, first editions of many of his books and Civil War memorabilia.

Allow 30 minutes minimum. Mon.-Sat. 10-5, Sun. 2-5. Closed for lunch; phone ahead to confirm. Admission $1; 50c (ages 3-7). Phone (706) 485-6856.

ELBERTON (B-3) pop. 4,743, elev. 708′

ELBERTON GRANITE MUSEUM & EXHIBIT is on SR 17, .5 mi. w. of SR 77 at 1 Granite Plaza. With 45 quarries and more than 100 manufacturing plants, the Elberton area is thought to be the largest granite-producing region in the world. The museum displays interesting granite products of the past, antique working tools and a chart detailing quarrying procedures. Allow 30 minutes minimum. Mon.-Sat. 2-5; closed Dec. 25-Jan. 1. Free. Phone (706) 283-2551.

FITZGERALD (E-3) pop. 8,758, elev. 275′

Originally founded in 1896 as a colony for aging Union soldiers fleeing Midwestern droughts and frigid Northern winters, Fitzgerald features a historic downtown laid out in a perfect grid. Evidence of the city's Civil War heritage and early spirit of compromise can be seen in the street names here: seven are named for Confederate generals and seven for Union generals.

Fitzgerald Convention and Visitors Bureau: 115 S. Main St., Fitzgerald, GA 31750; phone (229) 426-5033 or (800) 386-4642.

SAVE **BLUE AND GRAY MUSEUM** is in the Municipal Building (former train Depot) at 116 N. Johnston St. The museum's centerpiece, the Hall of Honor, celebrates the Civil War veterans who founded Fitzgerald in the 1890s; veterans of other wars also are recognized. The videotape documentary "Marching as One" relates the city's history. The museum also features items from the estate of Confederate president Jefferson Davis as well as rare Civil War swords, guns, documents and quilts.

Allow 1 hour minimum. Tues.-Sat. 10-4, Sun. 1-5; closed holidays. Admission $3; $1 (students with ID). Phone (229) 426-5069 for events and special exhibits information.

JEFFERSON DAVIS MEMORIAL is at 338 Jeff Davis Park Rd. The 13-acre historic site contains a monument marking where Confederate President Jefferson Davis was captured by Union forces. A museum, nature trail and playground also are available. Picnicking is permitted. Allow 30 minutes minimum. Wed.-Sun. 9-5; closed Jan. 1, Thanksgiving and Dec. 25. Admission $3; $2.50 (senior citizens and students); $1.75 (children). AX, DS, MC, VI. Phone (229) 831-2335.

FOLKSTON (F-5) pop. 2,178, elev. 80′

Folkston is near the eastern entrance to Okefenokee Swamp, an area of more than 600 square miles. Most of the swamp was declared a wildlife refuge in 1937.

Thanks to a track configuration that funnels railroad traffic into and out of Florida through Folkston, more than 60 trains pass through the town each day. The Folkston Funnel Train Watching Platform, near the corner of Tower and Main streets, offers a covered area from which enthusiasts can watch the trains pass by.

Okefenokee Chamber of Commerce: 202 W. Main St., P.O. Box 756, Folkston, GA 31537; phone (912) 496-2536.

OKEFENOKEE ADVENTURES is 7 mi. s. on SR 121/23, then 4 mi. w. on SR 121 following signs to the Okefenokee National Wildlife Refuge east entrance. Within the wildlife refuge, this company offers 90-minute guided boat tours as well as a 2.5-hour sunset tour and extended day and overnight excursions. Naturalist guides teach about the area's cultural and natural history, flora and fauna. The refuge features walking trails, an interpretive center, observation tower and a swamper homestead.

Food is available. Motor boat, canoe, kayak and bicycle rentals are available. Allow 1 hour, 30 minutes minimum. Daily a half-hour before dawn-7:30 p.m., Mar.-Oct.; a half-hour before dawn-5:30 p.m., rest of year. Closed Dec. 25. Refuge admission $5 per private vehicle. Ninety-minute boat tour $16; $10 (ages 5-11). Sunset tour $25; $17 (ages 5-11). MC, VI. Phone (912) 496-7156 or (866) 843-7926.

OKEFENOKEE NATIONAL WILDLIFE REFUGE occupies 402,000 acres of the Okefenokee Swamp and surrounding uplands. The main entrance is 7 mi. s.w. on SR 121/23, then 3.5 mi. w. on SR 121 following signs. There also is a western entrance at Stephen C. Foster State Park *(see Recreation Chart and Fargo in the AAA Southeastern CampBook)* and a northern entrance at Okefenokee Swamp Park *(see Waycross p. 106)*.

The swamp's abundant plant and animal life can best be observed on overnight canoe trips lasting from 2 to 5 days. The trips require advance permits issued by the refuge office; reservations can be made up to 2 months prior. Contact the Refuge Manager, Route 2, Box 3330, Folkston, GA 31537.

A 7-day pass good for the east or west entrance to the refuge costs $5 per private vehicle. Fee at the north entrance near Waycross is $12 per person; $11 (ages 62+, active military with ID and ages 3-11).

Combination admission and boat tour (from Waycross entrance) $16-$30. Phone (912) 496-7836 (east entrance), (912) 283-0583 (north entrance), (912) 637-5274 (Stephen Foster entrance) or (912) 496-3331 for overnight wilderness canoe reservations through the Refuge Manager.

Suwannee Canal Recreation Area (east entrance), 7 mi. s.w. on SR 23/121, then 3.5 mi. w. on the Okefenokee National Wildlife Refuge entrance road, is the main or eastern entrance to the refuge. A visitor center offers exhibits, a 15-minute film and information about recreational activities. A wildlife drive provides access to more than 10 miles of walking trails, a restored swamp homestead and a .75-mile boardwalk leading to a 50-foot observation tower. A concessionaire offers guided boat trips as well as canoe, kayak and motorboat rentals, fishing supplies and food service.

Daily a half-hour before dawn-7:30 p.m., Mar.-Oct.; a half-hour before dawn-5:30 p.m., rest of year. Closed Dec. 25. Admission (valid for seven days) $5 per private vehicle. Phone (912) 496-7836. *See Recreation Chart.*

FORSYTH (C-2) pop. 3,776, elev. 704'

Forsyth is named for Gov. John Forsyth, who served as secretary of state to Presidents Andrew Jackson and Martin Van Buren. In 1834 the town became a regional transportation center when it was linked with the railroad. It also served as a distribution point when cotton planters brought their product to Forsyth for shipment to Macon and the southern United States.

The Monroe County Courthouse, in the center of Courthouse Square, was built in 1896 and is an example of Victorian architecture. The courthouse is in the middle of an eight-block historic district that preserves late 19th- and early 20th-century buildings. The Monroe County Museum and Genealogy Room, Tift College Drive, is a restored 1896 Victorian depot; phone (478) 994-5070. Its museum features railroad memorabilia and exhibits about local history.

The Rum Creek Wildlife Management Area, 7 miles east on SR 18, is 8,100 acres on Lake Juliette. High Falls State Park, 11 miles north on High Falls Road just off I-75, features a scenic waterfall *(see Recreation Chart and Jackson in the AAA Southeastern CampBook)*.

Forsyth-Monroe County Chamber of Commerce: 5 W. Adams St., P.O. Box 811, Forsyth, GA 31029; phone (478) 994-9239 or (888) 642-4628.

FORT FREDERICA NATIONAL MONUMENT—*see Golden Isles p. 77.*

FORT GAINES (E-1) pop. 1,110, elev. 163'

At 100 Bluff St. overlooking the Chattahoochee River is Fort Gaines Frontier Village, an open-air museum with log cabins, a cane mill, a smokehouse and a Civil War cannon. A partial replica of the 1814 frontier fort and a pioneer cemetery are nearby.

Also in the area is Lake Walter F. George *(see Recreation Chart and the AAA Southeastern CampBook)*. The 3-mile-long Walter George Dam has a lock with what is purported to be one of the highest lifts in the world.

Clay County Chamber of Commerce: P.O. Box 825, Fort Gaines, GA 39851; phone (229) 768-2247.

Self-guiding tours: A walking tour guide book is available from the Clay County Library, 208 Hancock St., (229) 768-2248.

FORT GORDON (C-5)

U.S. ARMY SIGNAL CORPS MUSEUM, in Conrad Hall (Bldg. 29807) on Chamberlain Ave., is both a research library and a museum for communications and military signal history since the corps' inception in 1860. Items displayed include signal devices from the Civil War to Desert Storm and an Oscar awarded to the movie, "Seeds of Destiny," a Signal Corps film made after World War II. Of special interest are items from Albert J. Myer, the father of the Signal Corps. Tues.-Fri. 8-4; closed federal holidays. Free. Phone (706) 791-2818 or (706) 791-3856.

GEM FORT PULASKI NATIONAL MONUMENT (D-6)

Fort Pulaski National Monument, 15 miles east of Savannah via US 80, occupies Cockspur and McQueens islands at the mouth of the Savannah River. Fort Pulaski, on the eastern end of Cockspur Island, was preceded by Fort George (1761-76) and Fort Greene (1794-1804).

When a British fleet approached in 1776, American patriots dismantled Fort George. A hurricane demolished Fort Greene in 1804. Construction of Fort Pulaski began in 1829 and required 18 years and 25 million bricks to complete. The fort, in the shape of a massive irregular pentagon and surrounded by a moat crossed by drawbridges, was a link in an impressive chain of coastal forts built to protect the United States from foreign invasion. The long galleries are distinguished by fine brick arches. Today, it survives as one of the nation's best-preserved fortifications.

The Battle for Fort Pulaski, fought Apr. 10-11, 1862, marked a turning point in military history and included the first significant use of rifled cannons. Union forces on Tybee Island bombarded the fort for 30 hours, eventually forcing the surrender of the Confederate garrison. Upon the bombardment's conclusion, the fort's southeast angle lay in ruins. The battle clearly demonstrated the improved power, range and accuracy of rifled cannons and also signaled the end of masonry fortifications.

The fort offers daily tours and soldier demonstrations of military arts and garrison life from the Civil War era. The visitor center features artillery exhibits, displays and a film presentation detailing the fort's past. Various daily programs are scheduled and self-guiding trails and picnic facilities are available. Allow 1 hour, 30 minutes minimum. Daily 9-7, Memorial Day-Labor Day; 9-5, rest of year. Closed Thanksgiving and Dec. 25. Admission $3; free (ages 0-15). Phone (912) 786-5787.

FORT STEWART MILITARY RESERVATION (D-5)

THE FORT STEWART MUSEUM, in Bldg. T904, 2022 Frank Cochran Dr., showcases coastal Georgia's military heritage. Exhibits include photographs, uniforms, weapons, equipment and artwork. Fort Stewart is home of the U.S. Army's 3rd Infantry Division, "The Rock of the Marne." Allow 1 hour minimum. Open Tues.-Sat. 10-4; closed federal holidays. Free. Phone (912) 767-7885.

FORT VALLEY (D-3) pop. 8,005, elev. 525'

Legend has it that the real name of the town was Fox Valley, but when submitted to the Post Office in 1825, illegible handwriting was read as "Fort" and so it has remained.

In 1875 a new peach variety, the Elberta, was introduced. The new peach and access to railroads made Fort Valley a peach-growing center in the Peach State. The area became so successful that a new county was formed—ultimately named Peach. The Georgia Peach Festival, home to what is purported to be the world's largest peach cobbler, is held in June; for information phone the festival office at (478) 825-4002 or (877) 322-4371.

Peach County Chamber of Commerce: 201 Oakland Heights Pkwy., P.O. Box 1238, Fort Valley, GA 31030; phone (478) 825-3733.

SAVE **MASSEE LANE GARDENS** is 5.5 mi. s. on SR 49 to 100 Massee Ln. Headquarters of the American Camellia Society, the 9-acre camellia collection contains hundreds of varieties that bloom November through March. Highlights include a greenhouse, a Japanese garden, a rose garden, an environmental garden and the Children's Garden. Two galleries house porcelains by Edward Marshall Boehm and other artists. A library has rare camellia books dating from 1699.

Guided tours are available. Allow 30 minutes minimum. Tues.-Sat. 10-4:30 (also Mon. in Feb.), Sun. 1-4:30. Admission $5; $4 (ages 62+); free (ages 0-11). Phone (478) 967-2358 to verify holiday schedule.

GAINESVILLE (B-3) pop. 25,578, elev. 1,227'

Gainesville is on the northeast shore of Lake Sidney Lanier *(see Recreation Chart)*. In the early 19th century the city was known as Mule Camp Springs.

The Green Street Historical District consists of late Victorian and neoclassical revival structures along a broad tree-lined street. The Quinlan Visual Art Center at 514 Green Street N.E. displays exhibits by state and local artists; phone (770) 536-2575. Road Atlanta, 10 miles south on SR 53 in Braselton, is an SCCA-sanctioned road-racing course and is home to the Petit Le Mans race; phone (770) 967-6143 or (800) 849-7223.

Lake Lanier County Convention and Visitors Bureau: 117 Jesse Jewell Pkwy., Suite 105, P.O. Box 2995, Gainesville, GA 30503; phone (770) 536-5209 or (888) 536-0005.

INTERACTIVE NEIGHBORHOOD FOR KIDS is at 999 Chestnut St. Several hands-on exhibits provide children with opportunities to experience adult professions and responsibilities within a fun environment. "Employees" get a taste of what it's like working in a beauty salon, dentist office and post office. Allow 45 minutes minimum. Mon.-Sat. 10-5, Sun. 1-5; closed major holidays. Admission $8; $6 on Sundays. DS, MC, VI. Phone (770) 536-1900.

SAVE **NORTHEAST GEORGIA HISTORY CENTER** is at 322 Academy St. The center's main exhibit covers 500 years of northeast Georgia history. Highlights include a simulation of the Gainesville Tornado of 1936 and the Sports Hall of Fame. Also featured is the collection of Ed Dodd, creator of the adventure strip "Mark Trail." A collection of works by regional folk pottery families is displayed, and the 1780 cabin of Chief Whitepath is on the grounds. The American Freedom Garden features a circle of 24 granite pillars engraved with veterans' names.

Allow 1 hour minimum. Tues.-Sat. 10-4; closed Jan. 1, Thanksgiving and Dec. 25. Admission $5; $4 (ages 65+); $3 (ages 6-18). MC, VI. Phone (770) 297-5900.

DID YOU KNOW

In 1943, Georgia became the first state to allow 18-year-olds to vote.

Golden Isles

When Spain claimed the lovely subtropical islands along the Georgia coast as the Golden Isles of Guale in the 16th century, habitation was not new to the land. Archeological evidence traces American Indian settlement to about 2500 B.C. Spain ceded the islands to Great Britain in 1763.

The term Golden Isles refers to St. Simons Island, Sea Island, Little St. Simons Island and Jekyll Island, all near the city of Brunswick. St. Simons Island is the largest of the four. St. Simons Island, Sea Island and Jekyll Island are the only islands accessible by car. Other islands in the area include Blackbeard, Cumberland, St. Catherines and Sapelo.

Just northeast of Sapelo is Blackbeard Island, where the pirate Edward Teach is said to have hidden his loot. St. Catherines Island is the former home of Button Gwinnett, one of Georgia's three signers of the Declaration of Independence. Southernmost in the chain and once the Carnegie family's private resort, Cumberland Island is now a national seashore.

Brunswick-Golden Isles Convention and Visitors Bureau: 4 Glynn Ave., Brunswick, GA 31520; phone (912) 265-0620 or (800) 933-2627. *See color ad p. 79.*

CUMBERLAND ISLAND NATIONAL SEASHORE (F-6)

The largest and southernmost of Georgia's barrier islands, Cumberland Island parallels the Georgia coast just north of the Florida border. The relatively flat island, 17.5 miles long by 3 miles wide, is separated from the mainland by several miles of salt marsh, river and sound. On its eastern side white sand beaches rise to dunes that give way to a forest of magnolias, oaks, palmettos and pines. More than 300 species of birds have been sighted on the island.

Although Cumberland Island exists in a relatively undisturbed state, American Indians inhabited it as early as 4,000 years ago. They called the island Missoe, which meant "sassafras." These American Indians were succeeded by the Spanish in 1566 and the English in 1736. At various times live oaks were cut for ships timbers, and land was cleared for the cultivation of fruits and sea island cotton.

The family of Revolutionary War officer Gen. Nathanael Greene built Dungeness plantation on the island in the late 18th century. Only a small building of tabby—a mixture of oyster shell, lime and sand—and a family cemetery remain, the latter the original burial site of Henry "Light-Horse Harry" Lee of Virginia, the father of Gen. Robert E. Lee and a friend of Greene.

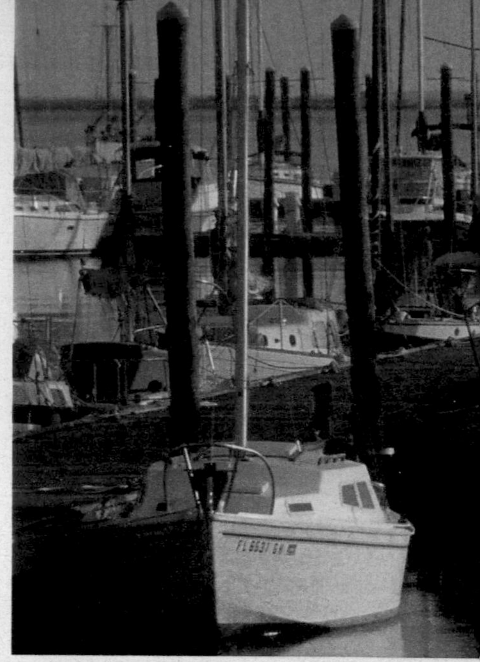

St. Simons Island
Georgia Department of Economic Development

A century later Thomas Carnegie built a lavish 30-room mansion called Dungeness as the centerpiece of an estate that covered 90 percent of Cumberland. Vegetation grows through the remains of the second Dungeness mansion, which burned in 1959. Wild horses and other wildlife roam along the beaches and throughout the ruins. Plum Orchard, another Carnegie house, survives on the banks of the Brick Hill River. A small percentage of the island is privately owned and not open to visitors.

Restricted camping is available at developed and back-country campsites; reservations are required. For further information contact Cumberland Island National Seashore, P.O. Box 806, St. Marys, GA 31558.

The island is open daily 24 hours and the ferry operates every day except Dec. 25. A 45-minute ferry ride provides the only access; just 300 visitors are permitted per day. Private vehicles, bicycles and pets are not permitted on the Island. The ferry departs from the St. Marys Visitor Center daily at 9 a.m. and 11:45 a.m. The ferry returns from the island daily at 10:15 a.m. and 4:45 p.m. (also Wed.-Sun. at 2:45, Mar.-Nov.). There are no scheduled ferry trips Tues.-Wed. Dec.-Feb. The visitor center is open daily 8-4:30. The museum at 129 Osborne St. is open daily 1-4; closed Dec. 25.

Admission to the island is $4 per person. Round-trip ferry fare $17; $15 (ages 65+); $12 (ages 0-12). Ferry reservations are required. Phone (877) 860-6787 for information or (912) 882-4335 for ferry reservations. *See Recreation Chart.*

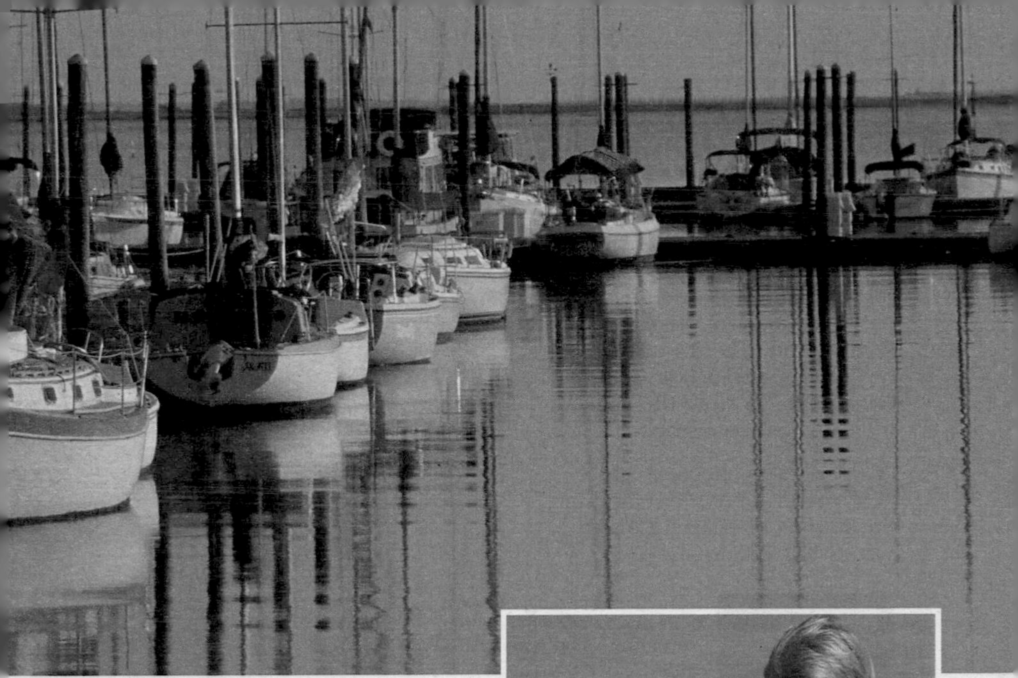

FORT FREDERICA NATIONAL MONUMENT (E-6)

Fort Frederica National Monument is on St. Simons Island, which is reached from the mainland via the F.J. Torras Causeway.

In 1736 Gen. James E. Oglethorpe began construction of an earthwork that became one of the most important British fortifications in America. Next to the fort he laid out the town of Frederica. The settlement and fort were vital in the defense of English interests in the conflict with Spain that erupted in 1739.

On July 7, 1742, the Battle of Bloody Marsh settled the fighting. The entire Colony of Georgia remained under English rule. The Bloody Marsh Memorial Site, a separate area 6 miles south, is open daily.

Oglethorpe's regiment disbanded in 1749, ruining Frederica's economy. A fire in 1758 destroyed most of the town, and the last soldiers left the fort in 1763. Ruins lie atop a bluff on the island's western shore overlooking the Frederica River, and foundations of original houses have been uncovered. Field exhibits explain features of the area.

A visitor center houses pictorial panels, a diorama and artifacts pertaining to Frederica. A historical film is shown every 30 minutes. Self-guiding and audio tours are available. Allow 1 hour, 30 minutes minimum. Daily 9-5; closed Dec. 25. Entrance fee $3; free (ages 0-15). Phone (912) 638-3639.

JEKYLL ISLAND (F-6)

The most crowded chapter in the history of Jekyll Island began in 1886 when prominent East Coast millionaires, including Frank Henry Goodyear, Edwin and George Gould, J.P. Morgan, Joseph Pulitzer and William Rockefeller bought the island for $125,000. Naming themselves the Jekyll Island Club, they built a large clubhouse and elaborate cottages for use as a hunting preserve and family getaway.

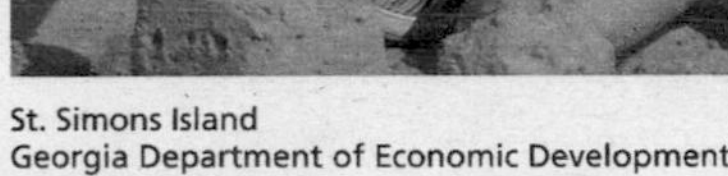

St. Simons Island
Georgia Department of Economic Development

The activities of some members while staying at this haven changed world events. In 1910 the first draft of the Federal Reserve Act, the foundation of the nation's monetary system, was drawn up. From Jekyll Island in 1915 the president of AT&T made the first transcontinental telephone call, speaking with President Woodrow Wilson in Washington, D.C., Alexander Graham Bell in New York and Bell's assistant Thomas Watson in San Francisco.

By the early 20th century Jekyll Island Club members were said to represent one-sixth of the world's wealth. By World War II, later generations had lost interest and had largely left the island, which was sold in 1947 to the state of Georgia for use as a state park.

Destination Golden Isles

On the Golden Isles, you can do a lot or do nothing at all. Tour a late 19th-century historic district. Go bird-watching on a national seashore. Visit a British fortification. Check out the beam on a 100-year-old working lighthouse. Explore the ruins of a once-lavish mansion.

Or simply choose a spot under a palm tree and let the sounds of peaceful ocean waves lull you to sleep.

Georgia Department of Economic Development

Christ Church, Frederica
Local writer Eugenia Price is buried in the cemetery of this circa 1736 church. (See listing page 80)

Georgia Department of Economic Development

Sapelo Lighthouse, Sapelo Island
Activated in 1820, the lighthouse is located within the island's National Estuarine Research Reserve. (See listing page 80)

Georgia Department of Economic Development

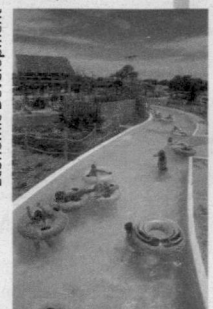

Summer Waves, Jekyll Island.
Numerous attractions, including a children's wading pool and waterslides, make this water park a popular choice to visit. (See listing page 79)

Sapelo Island
95
25
27
82
520
17
Little St. Simons Island
Sea Island
St. Simons Island
Jekyll Island
Golden Isles
95

Georgia Department of Economic Development

Jekyll Island Historic Landmark District Tour
For more than 4 decades, the prestigious Jekyll Island Club was the social hub of America's elite. (See listing page 79)

Places included in this AAA Destination Area:

Jekyll Island is now one of Georgia's major resort areas. The 10-mile beach offers surf fishing, swimming, bathhouses and a beach walk. The island's sand dunes form a natural buffer to protect land and buildings from tides, winds, waves and storms. Crossovers can be used for beach access. Golf, nature walks, tennis, miniature golf, sightseeing cruises and miles of bicycle trails are all available, plus picnic areas, campsites and a water park. Bicycles can be rented.

Visitors traveling by private vehicle to Jekyll Island are required to pay a $3 daily parking fee at the island's entrance at the end of the Jekyll Island Causeway.

Jekyll Island Welcome Center: 901 Downing Musgrove Causeway, Jekyll Island, GA 31527; phone (912) 635-3636 or (877) 453-5955.

GEORGIA SEA TURTLE CENTER is at 214 Stable Rd. in the Jekyll Island Historic Landmark District. The center is an educational, rehabilitation and research center for sick and wounded sea turtles. An interactive exhibit room features literature and video documenting the life cycle of a sea turtle. Rehabilitating turtles are displayed inside as well as outside in several aquatic tanks. Evening turtle walks and morning hatchling walks are offered in summer and focus on the natural history of sea turtles; a guided beach tour is included.

Allow 30 minutes minimum. Center open daily 10-7, May-Aug.; 10-6, rest of year. Closed Dec. 25. Turtle walks daily at 8:30 and 9:30 p.m., June-July (except July 4). Admission $6; $5 (ages 65+); $4 (ages 4-12). Children under 4 are not permitted on walks. Turtle walks $10; $5 (ages 4-12). AX, DS, MC, VI. Phone (912) 635-4444.

GEM **JEKYLL ISLAND HISTORIC LANDMARK DISTRICT TOUR,** a cluster of late 19th-century cottages along Riverview Dr., is a reminder of an era when social life revolved around the Jekyll Island Club. Tours begin at the Jekyll Island History Center in the old club stables on Stable Road, where permanent exhibits and a videotape presentation explain the island's history.

The 90-minute, narrated Passport to the Century open-air tram tour of the district includes entry to two restored historic homes. Tour departs daily at 10, 11, 1, 2 and 3, Memorial Day-Labor Day; at 11, 1 and 3, Jan. 2-day before Memorial Day and day after Labor Day-early Dec. History center open daily 9-5. Closed Jan. 1 and Dec. 25. Tour $16; $7 (ages 6-12). AX, DS, MC, VI. Phone (912) 635-4036 or (912) 635-2762.

SUMMER WAVES, 210 S. Riverview Dr., is an 11-acre water park. Featured attractions are six waterslides 30-50 feet high, a splash zone with a 750-gallon tipping bucket, a lazy river, a wave pool and a children's wading pool. Food is available. Mon.-Fri. 10-6, Sat. 10-8, Sun. 11-7, Memorial Day weekend through mid-Aug.; phone for off-season schedule. Admission $19.95; $15.95 (children under 48 inches tall); $10.95 (ages 60+); free (ages 0-3).

Night Splash, after 4 p.m. $10.95 (Sun.-Fri.); $12.95 (Sat.). Two-day ticket $24.95. AX, DS, MC, VI. Phone (912) 635-2074.

LITTLE ST. SIMONS ISLAND (E-6)

Accessible only by boat, Little St. Simons Island is a pristine hideaway off the northern shore of St. Simons Island that has been privately owned by the same family since 1908. What was once the exclusive retreat of a New York timber baron and his wealthy friends is now open on a limited basis to nature lovers and others who wish to enjoy the vast tracts of undeveloped tidal creeks, marshes, forests and seashell-strewn beaches. Day trips of the island are available by reservation; phone (912) 638-7472.

ST. SIMONS ISLAND (F-5)

St. Simons Island had an active Colonial period. The area around Gascoigne Bluff served as the headquarters for English ships after 1736. Land disputes between Spain and England exploded in 1742 with the Battle of Bloody Marsh *(see Fort Frederica National Monument p. 77)*. Timber cut on the island was used in the first ships of the U.S. Navy, including the USS *Constitution.*

Aaron Burr sought refuge along the shores of St. Simons Island after his duel with Alexander Hamilton. British actress Fanny Kemble Butler penned many of her anti-slavery letters at the Hampton Plantation. Near the remains of the moat that surrounded the town of Frederica stand ancient live oaks under which John and Charles Wesley, the Anglican ministers who founded Methodism, once preached.

The village, at the island's southern tip, includes an 1872 working lighthouse, coastal history museum and fishing pier. St. Simons Island provides an appropriate setting for such activities as golf, tennis, fishing and boating. Bicycle trails parallel many of the roads on the island.

St. Simons Island Visitors Center: 530B Beachview Dr., St. Simons Island, GA 31522; phone (912) 638-9014.

ARTHUR J. MOORE METHODIST MUSEUM is, from entrance to St. Simons Island via F.J. Torras Cswy., .2 mi. e. to Sea Island Rd., .4 mi. n.e. to Epworth Rd./Methodist Center Booth Gate and .2 mi. n. to 100 Arthur J. Moore Dr. The museum is part of the Epworth-by-the-Sea Methodist Center and displays an assortment of Methodist artifacts, a nativity collection and a history of St. Simons Island. It also houses a 6,000-volume library pertaining to Methodist and general church history. Videotape presentations relate to the work of leaders in Methodist ministry and missions.

Allow 1 hour minimum. Tues.-Sat. 10-4; closed Dec. 25-Jan. 1. Free. Phone (912) 638-4050.

CHRIST CHURCH, FREDERICA, just s. of Fort Frederica National Monument at 6329 Frederica Rd., was established in 1736. Charles Wesley, chaplain to Gen. James E. Oglethorpe's settlers at Fort Frederica, was the first priest. After building the present edifice in 1885 as a memorial to his wife, Anson Green Phelps Dodge Jr. took Holy Orders and served as rector until 1898. His life was the subject of the 1977 novel "Beloved Invader" by local writer Eugenia Price; Ms. Price is buried in the church cemetery. Daily 2-5; closed Thanksgiving, Dec. 24-25 and 31. Donations. Phone (912) 638-8683.

MARITIME MUSEUM AT THE HISTORIC COAST GUARD STATION is at 4201 First St. Seven galleries depict the station's history and the natural history of Georgia's barrier islands through interactive exhibits and activities. A 12-minute video presentation introduces visitors to the museum. Guided tours are available. Allow 1 hour minimum. Mon.-Sat. 10-5, Sun. 1:30-5; closed Jan. 1, Thanksgiving Day and Dec. 24-25. Admission $6; $3 (ages 6-12). MC, VI. Phone (912) 638-4666.

ST. SIMONS ISLAND LIGHTHOUSE MUSEUM AND A.W. JONES HERITAGE CENTER, 101 12th St., is in a restored 1872 lighthouse keeper's house. Exhibits depict local history and the life of a lighthouse keeper and his family. The adjacent lighthouse offers a fine view of the island. A lighthouse built here in 1810 was destroyed during the Civil War. Museum open Mon.-Sat. 10-5, Sun. 1:30-5. Light house open Mon.-Sat. 10-4:45, Sun. 1:30-4:45. Closed Jan. 1, Thanksgiving and Dec. 24-25. Last lighthouse admission 15 minutes before closing. Admission $6; $3 (ages 6-11). Phone (912) 638-4666.

ST. SIMONS ISLAND TROLLEY TOURS departs from various locations. A charming and humorous narrated tour that includes the St. Simons Island Lighthouse, Fort Frederica, Christ Church and Bloody Marsh. **Note:** It is important that visitors phone ahead to confirm departure times and locations. Allow 1 hour, 30 minutes minimum. Daily at 11. Fare $20; $10 (ages 4-12). Cash and traveler's checks only are accepted. Phone (912) 638-8954.

SAPELO ISLAND (E-6)

SAPELO ISLAND NATIONAL ESTUARINE RESEARCH RESERVE is reached by a 30-minute ferry ride. To reach the dock take I-95 exit 58, then SR 99 s. 9.1 mi. to Landing Rd. in Meridian, then left to the Sapelo Island Visitors Center. Private vehicles cannot access the island. The visitor center at the dock features exhibits and information about the area. A 3-hour bus tour of the island includes the Palladian-style R.J. Reynolds mansion, the Sapelo Lighthouse, the University of Georgia Marine Institute and Hog Hammock, a small community of Sapelo Plantation slave descendants.

Allow 4 hours minimum. Ferry departs Wed. at 8:30 and Sat. at 9, (also Fri. at 8:30, June 1-Labor

Day weekend) and returns 4 hours later. Extended tour departs at 8:30 and returns at 3 the last Tues. of the month, Mar.-Oct. Visitor center open Tues.-Fri. 7:30-5:30, Sat. 8-5:30, Sun. 1:30-5. Closed federal and state holidays. Visitor center free. Ferry $10; $6 (ages 6-18). Reservations are required. Credit cards are not accepted. Phone (912) 437-3224.

SEA ISLAND (F-6)

Seaward of St. Simons Island and accessible from there by causeway, Sea Island is an all-year resort in a lush garden setting of flowering shrubs, ancient oaks, palms and pines. The island lies between the Atlantic Ocean and the marshes of Glynn, the subject of Sidney Lanier's poem.

Sea Island has long been a favorite with heads of state. Presidents Calvin Coolidge, Herbert Hoover, Dwight Eisenhower, Richard Nixon, Gerald Ford, Jimmy Carter and George H.W. Bush all vacationed on the island. In addition to a smooth 5-mile beach and a spa, there are excellent facilities for golf, skeet shooting, horseback riding, tennis and fishing.

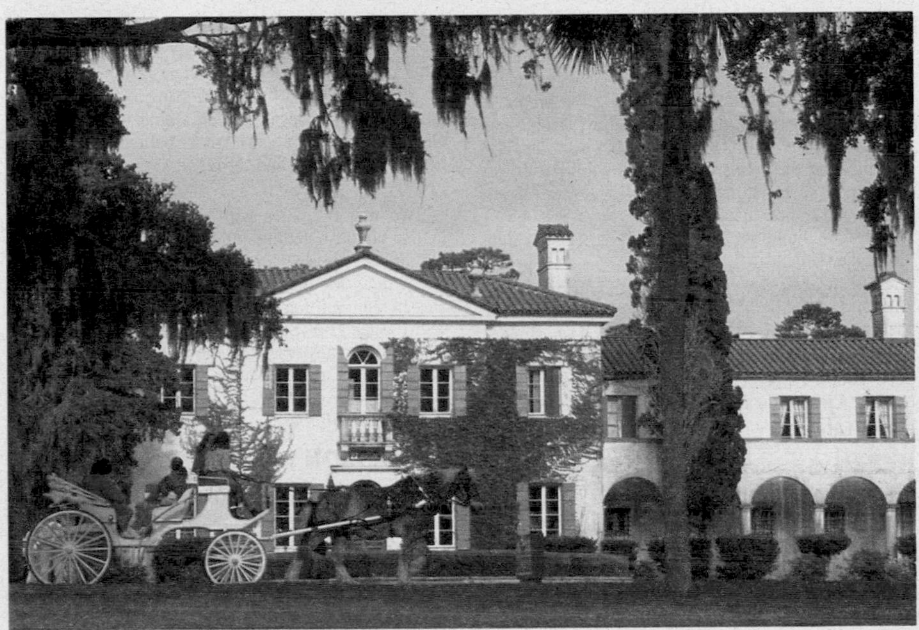

Jekyll Island / Georgia Department of Economic Development

This ends listings for the Golden Isles.
The following page resumes the alphabetical listings of cities in Georgia.

HAMPTON (C-2) pop. 3,857, elev. 890′

ATLANTA MOTOR SPEEDWAY is .2 mi. w. of jct. US 19/41. Tours of the motorsport facility allow visitors to ride on the track (dependent upon availability) as well as visit the NASCAR garage, victory lane and a VIP suite high above the grandstand. A small garden dedicated to Richard Petty contains a statue of the race car driver. Guided tours every half-hour Mon.-Sat. 9-4:30, Sun. 1-4:30; closed major holidays. No tours are conducted during race weeks. Last tour departs at closing. Tours $5; $2 (ages 7-18). DS, MC, VI. Phone (770) 707-7970.

MELVIN L. NEWMAN WETLANDS CENTER is 2.2 mi. e. of SR 3/US 19/41 at 2755 Freeman Rd. The center educates visitors about such issues as the conservation of natural resources and the preservation of the environment and its wildlife. The 32-acre site includes a .5-mile nature trail with displays documenting the area's ecology and wildlife; visitors may spot such animals as beavers, deer, foxes, turtles and more than 130 bird species. A 4,800-square-foot building features exhibits and videos about the wetlands.

Guided tours are available. Picnicking is permitted. Allow 1 hour minimum. Center open Mon.-Fri. 8:30-5, Sept.-May; Tues.-Sat. 8:30-5, rest of year. Nature trail open daily 7-7, Mar.-Oct.; 7-5, rest of year. Tours are given Mon.-Fri.; reservations are required. Closed major holidays. Free. Phone (770) 603-5603.

HELEN (A-3) pop. 430

After deteriorating from an 1829 Georgia Gold Rush hot spot turned lumber mill town abandoned by 1969, the rejuvenated Helen mirrors a whimsical Alpine village. Surrounded by mountains and intersected by the Chattahoochee River, the town boasts cobblestone walkways, kaleidoscopic buildings, a market square and more than 200 specialty shops.

Cast a line, hail a horse-drawn carriage, and pan for gold. Browse lines of shops filled with antiques, imported items and local crafts; or explore nearby Nacoochee Village, home to the 1876 Nora Mill and the 3-floor Nacoochee Antique Mall. If you're the outdoorsy type, several state parks and the surrounding Chattahoochee National Forest *(see place listing p. 68)* might entice you with sightseeing, hiking, camping, canoeing and rafting.

Offering two beaches along a 53-acre lake, Unicoi State Park *(see Recreation Chart and the AAA Southeastern CampBook)* is 2 miles northeast off SR 356. The Russell-Brasstown Scenic Byway (SR 348) traverses the Chattahoochee National Forest between Helen and Brasstown Bald—at 4,784 feet, the highest point in the state—and is particularly beautiful in autumn.

And you'll be certain autumn has arrived when you hear a chorus of *Prosts* (slang equivalent of *Cheers*) ringing through Helen during the 6-week Oktoberfest celebration, which begins in mid-September. Unwind with a beer-garden brewsky or flaunt your Chicken Dance moves as you soak up the sound of genuine German tunes and the aroma of fresh wurst.

In June, bid *Auf Wiedersehen* to your favorite balloon at the annual Helen-to-the-Atlantic Balloon Race. Reputed to be the only long-distance hot air balloon competition in the United States, the event is conquered by the first contestant who crosses I-95.

Alpine Helen/White County Convention & Visitors Bureau: 726 Bruckenstrasse, Helen, GA 30545; phone (706) 878-2181 or (800) 858-8027.

JACKSON (C-3) pop. 3,934, elev. 697′

INDIAN SPRINGS STATE PARK, 5 mi. s.e. on SR 42 off US 23, is on the site of mineral springs in use long before European settlers came to this part of Georgia. Creek Indians once believed the water healed their sick and brought extra vigor to the healthy.

Two major treaties with the Creeks were signed in the vicinity, ceding millions of acres of land to the federal government. Open to the public since 1825, the park includes a small museum that operates in summer. Park open daily 7 a.m.-10 p.m. Museum open Fri.-Sun. 10-6, Memorial Day-Labor Day. Hours may vary; phone ahead. Museum free. Parking $3 per private vehicle. Phone (770) 504-2277. *See Recreation Chart and the AAA Southeastern CampBook.*

JEFFERSON (B-3) pop. 3,825, elev. 850′

CRAWFORD W. LONG MUSEUM, off the public square at 28 College St., honors Dr. Long who in 1842 performed the first painless surgery using sulfuric ether as an anesthesia. The three-building museum occupies the original site of Dr. Long's discovery, emphasizing his life and the history of anesthesia. The museum includes an antebellum general store. A video presentation documenting Dr. Long's achievements also is offered.

Allow 30 minutes minimum. Tues.-Fri. 10-4; closed federal holidays. Admission $5; $3 (ages 3-12). Phone (706) 367-4340.

JEKYLL ISLAND—*see Golden Isles p. 77.*

JONESBORO—*see Atlanta p. 59.*

JULIETTE (C-3) elev. 376′

The nearly abandoned town of Juliette, a thriving mill town in the 1930s, was revived in the 1980s with the local filming of the movies "A Killing Affair" and then once again in the early 1990s with "Fried Green Tomatoes." Visitors can sample fried green tomatoes at the Whistle Stop Cafe next to the former train depot.

JARRELL PLANTATION STATE HISTORIC SITE is 7 mi. s.e. via Round Oak-Juliette Rd. and Jarrell Plantation Rd. to 711 Jarrell Plantation Rd. An example of a self-sufficient working cotton plantation, this 236-acre historic site was settled in the 1840s and belonged to the Jarrell family until 1974. Inside the two main residences are original 19th-century furnishings. Among the 20 historic buildings on the site are a mill complex with steam engines, a cotton gin, a blacksmith and woodworking shop, a syrup evaporator and a barn.

Comfortable shoes are advised. Picnicking is permitted. Allow 1 hour minimum. Tues.-Sat. 9-5, Sun. 2-5:30; closed Jan. 1, Thanksgiving and Dec. 25. Last tour begins 1 hour before closing Tues.-Sat. and 1 hour, 30 minutes before closing on Sun. Admission $4; $3.50 (ages 62+); $2.50 (ages 6-18). Phone (478) 986-5172.

KENNESAW—*see Atlanta p. 59.*

KENNESAW MOUNTAIN NATIONAL BATTLEFIELD PARK—*see Atlanta p. 59.*

LaGRANGE (C-1) pop. 25,998, elev. 786′

SAVE **BELLEVUE,** 204 Ben Hill St., was the home of Sen. Benjamin Harvey Hill. Built in the early 1850s, the house is a fine example of Greek Revival architecture, featuring Ionic columns, porticos and elaborate millwork and ceiling medallions. Tues.-Sat. 10-noon and 2-5; closed major holidays. The facility may be closed for private affairs. Admission $5; $3 (students with ID). Phone (706) 884-1832 to verify accessibility.

LaGRANGE ART MUSEUM, 112 Lafayette Pkwy., exhibits local and nationally acclaimed artwork. Major shows include the LaGrange National, an art competition held even-numbered years in March and April. Tues.-Fri. 9-5, Sat. 11-5; closed holidays. Free. Phone (706) 882-3267.

LAWRENCEVILLE—*see Atlanta p. 60.*

LESLIE (E-2) pop. 455, elev. 344′

GEORGIA RURAL TELEPHONE MUSEUM is .2 mi. s. off US 280 on SR 195. Guided tours of the museum showcase its vast collection of telephone memorabilia from the 19th and 20th centuries. Displays in a renovated 1920s cotton warehouse include early telephones, pay phones, phone booths, switchboards, a Model A Ford truck (much like those used by telephone companies in the 1920s) and a replica of Alexander Graham Bell's workshop.

Allow 1 hour minimum. Tours are given on the hour Mon.-Fri. 9-3:30; closed holidays. Admission $5; $4 (ages 60+); $2 (students with ID). Phone (229) 874-4786.

LILBURN—*see Atlanta p. 60.*

LITHIA SPRINGS—*see Atlanta p. 60.*

LITTLE ST. SIMONS ISLAND—*see Golden Isles p. 80.*

LOCUST GROVE (C-2) pop. 2,322, elev. 837′

Shopping areas: SAVE Tanger Outlet Center, off I-75 exit 212 to 1000 Tanger Dr., features more than 70 outlet shops including such retailers as Aéropostale, Liz Claiborne, Nautica and Old Navy.

NOAH'S ARK ANIMAL REHABILITATION CENTER, 1 blk. s. of the post office, then 2.8 mi. w. to 712 L.G. Griffin Rd., is a facility dedicated to the care of injured and orphaned animals. Rehabilitated wildlife is returned to its natural habitat; exotic animals that cannot be released are housed permanently. Rehabilitated domestic and farm animals become part of a therapy program for children. Picnicking is permitted. Tues.-Sat. noon-3 (weather permitting). Phone for weather updates. Donations. Phone (770) 957-0888 to verify schedule.

LOUISVILLE (C-4) pop. 2,712, elev. 310′

In the heart of the cotton belt, Louisville was founded in 1786 and served as Georgia's first permanent capital 1796-1807. Early settlers were reluctant to move away from the coast, so to encourage settlement of the interior an inland site was chosen as the new state capital.

A spot near Galphinton, a trading post older than some of the coastal settlements, was picked because it was in an area of friendly American Indians, had good drinking water and was on high ground above the unhealthy swamplands. Named in honor of King Louis XVI, the new town was modeled after Philadelphia; the Capitol, governor's mansion and some houses were built before it had any residents.

Jefferson County Chamber of Commerce: 302 E. Broad St., P.O. Box 630, Louisville, GA 30434; phone (478) 625-8134.

THE OLD MARKET HOUSE is at Broad and Mulberry sts. Built from great oak timbers in the mid-1790s before the town was laid out, the structure once served as a market. A tower houses a bell cast in France in 1772 for a New Orleans convent. Pirates plundered the ship carrying the bell; in turn, the pirate ship was captured near Savannah. The bell was sent to the new capital, where it was rung to celebrate the 13 Colonies' independence. Open daily 24 hours. Free. Phone (478) 625-3166.

LUMPKIN (D-2) pop. 1,369, elev. 593′

Incorporated in 1830, Lumpkin was named for Wilson Lumpkin, a 19th-century governor of Georgia. Although Lumpkin is in an agricultural region where peanuts are the major crop, the area has not always been suitable for farming. Severe erosion caused by water percolating into the layers of loose clay, sand and blue-marl limestone beneath the topsoil left much of the land unproductive by the mid-1950s. Terracing helped solve the problem.

Southwest Georgia Chamber of Commerce—Lumpkin: 201 N. Lumpkin St., Cuthbert, GA 39840; phone (229) 732-2683.

BEDINGFIELD INN is on the town square. A stagecoach stop during Lumpkin's frontier days, the inn was built in 1836 by Dr. Bryan Bedingfield and also served as his home. The restored inn is furnished as it would have been for a prosperous family in the 1840s. The unusually bright colors found in each room are reproductions of the originals. Guided tours of the house and grounds include the 1900 Hatchett Drug Store, which features more than 5,000 antique drugstore memorabilia. Mon.-Fri. 10-4, Sat. by appointment; closed major holidays. Admission $5; $2 (students with ID). Phone (229) 838-6419.

PROVIDENCE CANYON STATE PARK, 7 mi. w. on SR 39C at 8930 Canyon Rd., is known as "Georgia's Little Grand Canyon." The park preserves a 1,109-acre area containing 16 canyons eroded to a depth of 150 feet. The still-eroding walls of the winding gullies exhibit varicolored strata. A trail leads into the canyons from the visitor center, which has interpretive displays.

Pets must be on a leash. Picnicking is permitted. Park open daily 7 a.m.-9 p.m., Apr. 15-Sept. 14; 7-6, rest of year. Phone to confirm days of operation. Visitor center open daily 8-5. Free. Parking $3 per private vehicle; free (Wed.). Phone (229) 838-6202.

WESTVILLE, .5 mi. s. on Martin Luther King Dr., is a village of 32 relocated and restored buildings. This living-history museum, including a doctor's office, blacksmith shop, potter's shop, cotton gin, cotton-baling press, farm complex and mansion, depicts pioneer life in a west Georgia village in 1850. Costumed interpreters demonstrate crafts and trades from 1850.

Tues.-Sat. 10-5, closed first week in Jan., Thanksgiving and Dec. 24-25. Admission $10; $8 (ages 65+ and college students with ID); $4 (grades K-12). MC, VI. Phone (229) 838-6310 or (888) 733-1850.

MACON (C-3) pop. 97,255, elev. 335'

Macon is near Georgia's geographical center. Laid out in 1823 on the west side of the Ocmulgee River, Macon is said to be the only city in the Southeast that can trace its origin to a frontier fort. The remains of Fort Hawkins on Emery Highway include a replica of one of the original blockhouses.

At nearby Ocmulgee National Monument *(see place listing p. 88)*, more than 12,000 years of human habitation are celebrated and preserved. Visitors may enter a reconstructed earth lodge to see the original 1,000-year-old clay floor and seating as well as an eagle effigy.

Other city landmarks include Wesleyan College, founded in 1836 and the first college chartered specifically to grant degrees to women. Mercer University, founded in Penfield in 1833, has been in Macon since 1871.

A highlight among Macon's historic buildings is the 1836 City Hall. Originally built as a fireproof bank, the Classical Revival-style building also served as the temporary state capitol 1864-65.

The older residential sections are lined with antebellum mansions spared by Gen. William Tecumseh Sherman on his march to the sea. Many are open to the public on a regular basis, including the Sidney Lanier Cottage at 935 High St. and birthplace of Sidney Lanier, Georgia's foremost poet of the Old South; phone (478) 743-3851. *See color ad.*

Recreational opportunities are available at nearby Lake Tobesofkee *(see Recreation Chart)*.

Macon celebrates the blooming of some 300,000 Yoshino cherry trees in mid-March. The Macon International Cherry Blossom Festival features more than 500 events, including arts and children's festivals, hot air balloon events, an international food fair, concerts, evening torchlight walks, tours of historic houses and the downtown area, parades, ball and a grand finale of fireworks. A cherry blossom trail showcases the flowering trees.

Each April, Macon hosts the Tubman Pan-African Festival of Georgia, celebrating the rich cultural heritage of African art, music and story. Fired Works, a regional ceramics show featuring 50 artists and more than 4,000 works, presents a variety of demonstrations and workshops and also takes place in April. Visitors can tour private homes and hidden gardens in Macon's historic districts during Macon Gardens, Mansions and Moonlight in May.

Christmas in Olde Macon, which features tours of decorated historic houses, special museum programs including Festival of Trees and Kwanzaa and holiday activities and performances is held Thanksgiving through Dec. 31.

Macon-Bibb County Convention and Visitors Bureau: 450 Martin Luther King Jr. Blvd., P.O. Box 6354, Macon, GA 31201; phone (478) 743-3401 or (800) 768-3401. *See color ad p. 84.*

Self-guiding tours: Maps and brochures describing walking and driving tours are available from the convention and visitor bureau or the welcome center north on I-75; phone (478) 743-3401.

AROUND TOWN TOURS depart from the downtown visitors bureau at 450 Martin Luther King Jr. Blvd. Tours offered include walking and trolley historic tours; stops may include the Cannonball House, Douglass Theatre, Georgia Music Hall of Fame, Georgia Sports Hall of Fame, Hay House, St. Joseph's Catholic Church, Sidney Lanier Cottage and Tubman African-American Museum. Mon.-Sat. 9-5; closed major holidays. Fare $17-$32; $8.50-$16.50 (ages 0-17). AX, DS, MC, VI. Phone (478) 743-3401 or (800) 768-3401. *See color ad p. 84.*

SAVE **THE CANNONBALL HOUSE** is at 856 Mulberry St. This 1853 Greek Revival-style house was Macon's only home to sustain damage during the Civil War. The house contains the historic meeting parlors of the Alpha Delta Pi and Phi Mu societies, which were founded in Macon. The surrounding grounds feature a period English-style garden. The guided tour includes the original two-story brick kitchen and servants' quarters behind the house.

Allow 1 hour minimum. Guided tours leave every half-hour Mon.-Sat. 10-5, Mar.-Dec.; Mon.-Sat. 11-5, rest of year. Closed major holidays. Last tour begins 1 hour before closing. Tour $6; $5 (ages 62+ and military with ID); $2 (students with ID); free (ages 0-6). MC, VI. Phone (478) 745-5982. *See color ad p. 84.*

GEORGIA MUSIC HALL OF FAME, 200 Martin Luther King Jr. Blvd., features costumes, photographs, instruments and career memorabilia of nearly 400 Georgia musicians, including such legends as Ray Charles, Otis Redding, R.E.M. and the Allman Brothers Band. Tune Town, a 12,000-square-foot exhibit hall, resembles a Southern village, complete with winding streets and the Gospel Chapel. Interactive displays and videos focus on the state's musical origins.

Mon.-Sat. 9-5, Sun. 1-5; closed Jan. 1, Thanksgiving and Dec. 25-26. Admission $8; $6 (ages 55+, military and students with ID); $3.50 (ages 4-16). AX, DS, MC, VI. Phone (478) 751-3334 or (888) 427-6257. *See color ad p. 84.*

GEORGIA SPORTS HALL OF FAME is at 301 Cherry St. The museum comprises exhibits dedicated to the history of sports relating to Georgia. Picnicking is permitted. Allow 30 minutes minimum. Mon.-Sat. 9-5, Sun. 1-5; closed major holidays. Admission $8; $6 (senior citizens, students and military with ID); $4.50 (ages 0-16). AX, DS, MC, VI. Phone (478) 752-1585.

SAVE **HAY HOUSE** is at 934 Georgia Ave. This 24-room, 1860 Italian Renaissance Revival mansion boasted many new amenities for its time, including a plumbing system with hot and cold running water in several indoor bathrooms. Mr. and Mrs. Parks Lee Hay Sr. bought and redecorated the mansion in 1926 to reflect 20th-century living. Ornate plasterwork, 19th-century faux marble *trompe l'oeil* walls, crystal chandeliers and hand-carved front doors adorn the house. The decorative arts collection includes furniture and porcelains.

Allow 1 hour minimum. Guided tours on the hour Tues.-Sat. 10-4, Sun. 1-4, Mar.-June and Sept.-Dec.; Tues.-Sat. 10-4, rest of year. Closed Jan. 1, Easter, July 4, Thanksgiving and Dec. 25. Last tour begins 1 hour before closing. Fee $8; $7 (ages 55+ and military with ID); $4 (ages 6-18 and students with ID). Admission prices may vary seasonally or during special events. AX, MC, VI. Phone (478) 742-8155. *See color ad p. 84.*

SAVE **MUSEUM OF ARTS AND SCIENCES,** 7.5 mi. n. on US 41 at 4182 Forsyth Rd., features three galleries with frequently changing exhibitions. The Mark Smith Planetarium and the Mini-Zoo, a live animal habitat, present daily programs. The three-story Discovery House features hands-on activities for the family. There also are nature trails and an observatory that opens on clear Friday evenings.

Museum open Mon.-Sat. 10-5 (also 5-8 last Fri. of the month), Sun. 1-5; closed Jan. 1, Easter, Memorial Day, July 4, Labor Day, Thanksgiving and Dec. 24-25. Planetarium shows are presented Mon.-Thurs. at 4, Fri. at 4 and 8, Sat. at noon, 2 and 4, Sun. at 2 and 4. Mini-Zoo programs are presented daily at 3 (also Sat. at 1). Museum admission (including all daily programs) $8; $6 (ages 62+); $5 (ages 12-17 and students with ID); $4 (ages 2-11). AX, DS, MC, VI. Phone (478) 477-3232.

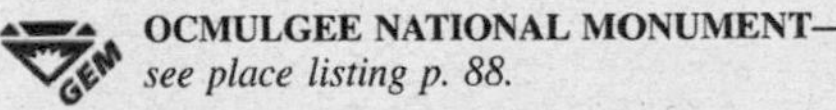

OCMULGEE NATIONAL MONUMENT— *see place listing p. 88.*

PIEDMONT NATIONAL WILDLIFE REFUGE, 25 mi. n. just e. of the Ocmulgee River, covers about

35,000 acres. The area offers three nature trails, a driving trail and a visitor center with exhibits about the refuge. Address inquiries to the Refuge Manager, 718 Juliette Rd., Round Oak, GA 31038. Refuge open daily dawn-dusk. Visitor center open Mon.-Fri. 7:30-5; closed federal holidays. Free. Phone (478) 986-5441.

TUBMAN AFRICAN AMERICAN MUSEUM, 340 Walnut St., presents the historic, artistic and cultural contributions of African-Americans. Included in the museum's 14 galleries is a mural chronicling the history of African-Americans. Allow 30 minutes minimum. Mon.-Sat. 9-5; closed major holidays. Admission $5; $3 (ages 0-12). AX, DS, MC, VI. Phone (478) 743-8544. *See color ad p. 84.*

MADISON (C-3) pop. 3,636, elev. 664′

Incorporated in 1809, Madison's antebellum houses remain virtually intact, possibly due to the efforts of Sen. Joshua Hill, an anti-secessionist who resigned his seat in Congress rather than vote on the issue of secession. When Gen. William Tecumseh Sherman's Union forces approached Madison in November 1864, Hill and two other men worked to spare the town from the torch. Only the train depot, a cotton gin and a cloth factory were burned.

The Morgan County Courthouse on the downtown square is a blend of formal and country architectural styles; it is open daily 8:30-5. Many of the historic houses are open during the Madison Tours in May and December.

Madison-Morgan Welcome Center: 115 E. Jefferson St., P.O. Box 826, Madison, GA 30650; phone (706) 342-4454 or (800) 709-7406.

Self-guiding tours: Walking tour maps and brochures are available at the welcome center.

MADISON-MORGAN CULTURAL CENTER is on US 441 at 434 S. Main St. This 1895 Romanesque Revival building was one of the first brick grade schools in the South. The center includes a museum with 19th-century regional artifacts and decorative arts, a restored early 20th-century classroom and three art galleries with changing exhibits. Permanently displayed, the Boxwood Parlor is an exact replica of an 1850 Rococo Renaissance parlor, complete with the original furnishings.

Allow 30 minutes minimum. Center open Tues.-Sat. 10-5, Sun. 2-5; closed Jan. 1, Memorial Day, July 4, Labor Day, Thanksgiving, and Dec. 24-25. Admission $3; $2.50 (ages 65+); $2 (students with ID). Phone (706) 342-4743 or (877) 233-0598.

DID YOU KNOW

Georgia was the last of the 13 original colonies to be established.

MARIETTA—*see Atlanta p. 60.*

METTER (D-4) pop. 3,879, elev. 200′

GUIDO GARDENS is off I-16 exit 104, 2.5 mi. n. on SR 121 to 600 N. Lewis St. This Christian-oriented garden features manicured grounds, splashing waterfalls, Biblical topiaries, a small chapel and several places to sit and relax. Hymns can be heard playing in the background. Guided tours are available. Allow 30 minutes minimum. Gardens open daily 24 hours. Office open Mon.-Fri. 8-noon and 1-5. Free. Phone (912) 685-2222.

MIDWAY (E-5) pop. 900, elev. 10′

FORT MORRIS STATE HISTORIC SITE is off I-95 exit 76, 7 mi. e. via Islands Hwy. (SR 38) and Fort Morris Rd., following brown Liberty Trail signs. The Continental Congress commissioned Fort Morris in 1776, and American patriots garrisoned the post to protect the port of Sunbury against British forces in the Revolutionary War and, as Fort Defiance, in the War of 1812. A video presentation and a museum interpret the history of the site. Special events are offered in July and November. A walking tour and picnic facilities also are available. Allow 1 hour minimum. Wed.-Sun. and Mon. federal holidays 9-5; closed Jan. 1, Thanksgiving and Dec. 25. Admission $3; $2.50 (ages 62+); $1.75 (ages 6-18). Phone (912) 884-5999.

MIDWAY CHURCH, next door to Midway Museum on US 17 at jct. US 84, was founded in 1752 by Puritans who moved to the area seeking land grants and religious freedom and became missionaries. This 1792 building is a replica of the original church, burned during the Revolution, complete with a slave gallery and high pulpit. From its congregation came Lyman Hall and Button Gwinnett, two signers of the Declaration of Independence; two Revolutionary War generals; and a U.S. senator.

The cemetery can be visited daily 24 hours. The keys for the church are available only at the Midway Museum Tues.-Sat. 10-4, Sun. 2-4; closed holidays. Free.

MIDWAY MUSEUM, next door to Midway Church on US 17 at jct. US 84, dating from 1957, was constructed in the 18th-century raised-cottage style. Displayed are furniture, artifacts and documents from the early 18th to the mid-19th centuries. Allow 30 minutes minimum. Tues.-Sat. 10-4, Sun. 2-4; closed holidays. Admission $5; $3 (students with ID); free (ages 0-5). Phone (912) 884-5837.

MILLEDGEVILLE (C-3)

pop. 18,757, elev. 276′

Milledgeville looks much as it did when it was laid out as the capital of Georgia in 1803. The city served as the state capital 1803-68. The Old Capitol Building, built in 1807, is considered the first example of Gothic architecture for a public building in the United States.

The Stetson-Sanford House, 601 W. Hancock St., is an 1825 two-story clapboard Federal house constructed by architect John Marlor. The house is open by request; phone (478) 453-1803.

Also historically significant is St. Stephen's Episcopal Church on S. Wayne Street. During Gen. William Tecumseh Sherman's November 1864 occupation, his troops, who stabled their horses in the church, poured sorghum syrup down the organ pipes to prevent the organ from being used to signal Confederate sympathizers.

One notable Milledgeville resident was author Flannery O'Connor who moved here with her family when she was 13 in 1938 and left in 1945 to attend the Iowa Writers' Workshop. She is buried in Memorial Hill Cemetery, along the fence. A museum on the campus of O'Connor's *alma mater,* Georgia College & State University, presents rotating exhibits in the Flannery O'Connor Room Monday through Saturday; phone (478) 445-4391.

Guided trolley tours that include alternating stops at Lockerly Hall, the Old Capitol Building, St. Stephens Episcopal Church and Stetson-Sanford House depart from the convention and visitors bureau Mon.-Fri. at 10 and Sat. at 2. The fare is $10; ages 6-16, $5.

Milledgeville-Baldwin County Convention and Visitors Bureau: 200 W. Hancock St., Milledgeville, GA 31061; phone (478) 452-4687 or (800) 653-1804. *See color ad.*

Self-guiding tours: A free walking-tour map of historic Milledgeville can be obtained from the convention and visitors bureau.

ANDALUSIA—HOME OF FLANNERY O'CONNOR is at 2628 N. Columbia St. Her family's dairy farm, Andalusia is where O'Connor found the source of many of the settings, situations and characters of her stories, writing and publishing several works. She lived at Andalusia from 1951 until her death in 1964. The interior of the main house is preserved and showcases the furnishings exactly as they were when the author occupied the home. Allow 45 minutes minimum. Mon.-Tues. and Sat. 10-4, Sun. and Wed.-Fri. by appointment only; closed Jan. 1, Martin Luther King Jr. Day, Memorial Day, July 4, Labor Day, Thanksgiving and Dec. 25. Donations. Phone (478) 454-4029.

GEORGIA'S OLD CAPITAL MUSEUM is at 201 E. Greene St., on the campus of the Georgia Military College. Located within a restored circa 1807 statehouse, the museum preserves the historical and cultural heritage of the area. Ten galleries interpret middle Georgia's timeline beginning with early American Indian cultures through exploration and colonization of Georgia and concludes with reconstruction efforts of the late 19th century. Guided tours are available. Allow 30 minutes minimum. Mon.-Fri. 10-4, Sat. noon-4; closed major holidays, the week after Thanksgiving and Dec. 25-early Jan. Admission $5; $4 (senior citizens); $3 (students). MC, VI. Phone (478) 453-1803.

GEORGIA'S OLD GOVERNORS MANSION is at 120 S. Clarke St. Guided tours share the mansion's history. Completed in 1839, the building was home to eight of Georgia's governors 1839-68 that included George Crawford, Howell Cobb and Joseph E. Brown. The house's interior is restored and furnished in period. Allow 45 minutes minimum. Tues.-Sat. 10-4, Sun. 2-4; closed major holidays. Admission $10; $6 (senior citizens); $2 (students). AX, DS, MC, VI. Phone (478) 445-4545.

LOCKERLY ARBORETUM is at 1534 Irwinton Rd. More than 3,000 plant varieties on 50 acres grace the site. Nature trails wind through the shaded woods with several bridges crossing over creeks. Also on the grounds is Lockerly Hall—an 1839

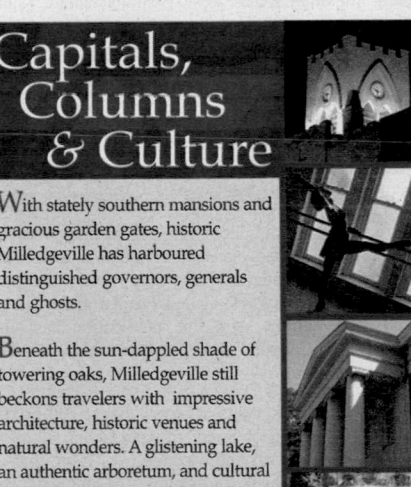

Greek Revival antebellum mansion. Allow 1 hour minimum. Mon.-Fri. 8:30-4:30; Sat. 1-5; closed major holidays. Guided tours of Lockerly Hall are offered Monday through Wednesday mornings. Gardens are free. Admission for Lockerly Hall $3. Phone (478) 452-2112 or (800) 653-1804 for guided tour reservations.

MILLEN (D-5) pop. 3,492, elev. 160′

BO GINN AQUARIUM AND AQUATIC EDUCATION CENTER is 4 mi. n. on US 25 at 1061 Hatchery Rd. in Magnolia Springs State Park *(see Recreation Chart and the AAA Southeastern CampBook)*. Approximately 70 species are displayed in 26 tanks and aquariums. The clear water of the adjacent springs allows viewing of native fish, turtles, alligators and other wildlife. Park open daily 7 a.m.-10 p.m. Aquarium open daily 9-4. Closed Thanksgiving and Dec. 25. Aquarium free. Park admission $3 per private vehicle. Phone (478) 982-1660 or (478) 982-4168.

MOULTRIE (F-2) pop. 14,387, elev. 319′

ELLEN PAYNE ODOM GENEALOGY LIBRARY, 204 5th St. S.E. in the Moultrie/Colquitt County Library, houses the archives of more than 130 Scottish clans. The collection also includes genealogical research materials about families who entered the United States from the Eastern Seaboard and traces their migration routes west. Exhibits feature Cherokee and Creek Indian documents and artifacts as well as a telecommunications display.

Allow 1 hour minimum. Mon.-Sat. 8:30-5:30; closed major holidays, last week of July and Dec. 20-Jan. 2. Free. Phone (229) 985-6540.

MOUNTAIN CITY (A-3)
pop. 829, elev. 2,168′

In 1966 a high school English teacher in nearby Rabun Gap helped his students publish a quarterly magazine dedicated to recording nearly forgotten Appalachian folkways. Called *Foxfire* after a lichen that glows in the dark, the publication has since grown into a popular series of books and an educational foundation.

FOXFIRE MUSEUM is off Cross St. at 200 Foxfire Ln. This museum of Southern Appalachia features a self-guiding tour around a complex of more than 20 log buildings, which are examples of authentic, replica and modern log construction. The museum includes a gristmill, a blacksmith's shop, a replica church, a wagon collection and several single- and multi-room cabins. Historic items are displayed throughout.

Allow 30 minutes minimum. Mon.-Sat. 8:30-4:30. Guided tours are offered Mon.-Fri. 9-4; phone ahead for availability. Closed major holidays. Admission $5; free (ages 0-10). Reservations are required for guided tours. MC, VI. Phone (706) 746-5828.

NEWNAN (C-1) pop. 16,242, elev. 957′

Newnan, 35 miles south of Atlanta, is proud of its architectural heritage. The 1904 Neo-Greek Revival County Courthouse is one of the most well-known in the United States because it appears in so many motion picture and television productions. Four of the historic districts surrounding downtown have fine examples of antebellum and Victorian houses.

Newnan is near the beginning of the scenic Chattahoochee-Flint Heritage Highway; a map is available at the Coweta County Welcome Center. This scenic route meanders through west-central Georgia from Roscoe in the north to **West Point,** Hamilton and **Warm Springs** in the south.

Coweta County Convention and Visitors Bureau Welcome Center: 100 Walt Sanders Memorial Dr., Newnan, GA 30265; phone (770) 254-2627 or (800) 826-9382.

MALE ACADEMY MUSEUM is at the corner of Temple Ave. and College St. The museum offers an extensive collection of clothing, arts and furnishings from the 19th and early 20th centuries. Featured are period photographs, a Confederate battle flag, a large collection of weapons and equipment and other artifacts. Guided tours are available. Allow 30 minutes minimum. Tues.-Thurs. 10-noon and 1-3. Admission $3; $1 (ages 0-11). Phone (770) 251-0207.

GEM OCMULGEE NATIONAL MONUMENT (D-3)

Ocmulgee (oak-MUL-gee) National Monument is on Macon's eastern limits; take US 80 east from I-16 exit 2 and follow signs. Within the monument's 702 acres are some of the most impressive American Indian mounds and archeological remains in the Southeast. Creeks, early and late Mississippi farmers and Paleo-Indian, Archaic and Woodland hunters and gatherers are known to have inhabited the area from around 10,000 B.C. through the early 19th century.

American Indian farmers migrated to central Georgia about A.D. 900 and built a large village and ceremonial center on the Macon Plateau. Six of their temple mounds, one burial mound and one ceremonial earth lodge remain. The restored earth lodge, which dates from about 1015, was a meeting chamber. The clay floor, benches around the walls, lower portion of the walls and raised bird-shaped platform have survived.

About 1350 a new village, which archeologists named Lamar, was built 2 miles down the river. Around 1690 the Creek Indians built a village, and the Ocmulgee River then marked the southwestern frontier of the Carolinas and Georgia for British colonists. Charleston supported a fur-trading post in the area 1690-1715.

Foot trails connect most of the park's features, and a drive approaches the large mounds. The Opelofa Nature Trail branches off the main walking trail and explores the lowlands of Walnut Creek.

The visitor center houses archeological displays and dioramas. The videotape "Ocmulgee: Mysteries of the Mounds" is shown upon request.

The annual Ocmulgee Indian Celebration, held at the monument the third weekend of September, attracts one of the largest gatherings of American Indians in the Southeast. Such activities as dancing and arts and crafts demonstrations are provided. Phone the monument office to confirm the schedule.

Events are held February through November. Picnic facilities are available. Daily 9-5; closed Jan. 1 and Dec. 25. Free. Phone (478) 752-8257.

OCONEE NATIONAL FOREST—

see Chattahoochee and Oconee national forests p. 68.

PINE MOUNTAIN (D-2)

pop. 1,141, elev. 1,052′

CALLAWAY GARDENS, 1 mi. w. at SRs 18 and 354, covers 13,000 acres in the foothills of the Appalachians. Founded in 1952 by industrialist Cason J. Callaway, the park features beautiful horticultural displays and miles of scenic woodland drives. Attractions include an early 1800s log cabin, the Ida Cason Callaway Memorial Chapel, Mr. Cason's Vegetable Garden and the Virginia Hand Callaway Discovery Center. The center offers a daily birds of prey show and serves as an information center for Callaway's recreational opportunities, which include golf, miniature golf, bicycling, walking, racquetball, swimming, fishing, boating, tennis and a gun club.

The gardens contain native azaleas, once plentiful in the natural woodlands of the Southeast. These rare varieties, usually more pure in color than cultivated shrubs, display brilliant reds, oranges and yellows.

Picnicking is permitted. Food is available. Allow 4 hours minimum. Gardens open daily 9-6, third Sat. in Mar.-Sun. before Labor Day; 9-5, rest of year. Admission $13; $10 (military and dependents with ID); $6.50 (ages 6-12); $5 (military dependents ages 6-12 with ID). AX, DS, MC, VI. Phone (706) 663-2281 or (800) 225-5292.

Cecil B. Day Butterfly Center occupies 4.5 acres within Callaway's Meadowlark Gardens. Tropical plants support and shelter macaws and more than 1,000 tropical butterflies of 50 species in the center's octagonal, dome-shaped conservatory. The grounds surrounding the conservatory include plantings designed to attract native butterflies and birds.

Admission is included in the Callaway Gardens entrance fee of $13; $10 (military and dependents with ID); $6.50 (ages 6-12); $5 (military dependents ages 6-12 with ID). AX, DS, MC, VI. Phone (706) 663-2281 or (800) 225-5292.

John A. Sibley Horticultural Center is within the Callaway Gardens. This five-acre greenhouse/garden complex features plants from various geographic regions in stylized garden designs that showcase a great diversity of tropical and subtropical plants. Colorful seasonal floral displays complement the permanent displays. The Outdoor Garden offers expansive lawns and flowerbeds displaying spring shrubs, summer annuals, fall chrysanthemums and poinsettias around the holidays.

Admission is included in the Callaway Gardens entrance fee of $13; $10 (military and dependents with ID); $6.50 (ages 6-12); $5 (military dependents ages 6-12 with ID). AX, DS, MC, VI. Phone (706) 663-2281 or (800) 225-5292.

SAVE **WILD ANIMAL SAFARI** is at 1300 Oak Grove Rd. The 200-acre park exhibits animals from six continents. The collection includes alligators, camels, deer, giraffes and zebras. Visitors may drive through the park in a private vehicle or tour the park in the Zebra Bus or Zebra Van. Food is available. Allow 2 hours minimum. Park open daily 10-7:30, Memorial Day through mid-Aug.; daily 10-6:30, Apr. 1-day before Memorial Day; Mon.-Fri. 10-5:30, Sat.-Sun. 10-6:30, in Mar. and Sept.-Oct.; Mon.-Fri. 10-5:30, Sat.-Sun. 10-7:30, mid-Aug to Aug. 31; daily 10-5:30, rest of year. Closed Dec. 25. Zebra Bus availability varies seasonally; phone ahead. Last admission 1 hour before closing. Admission $16.95; $13.95 (ages 3-12 and 60+). AX, DS, MC, VI. Phone (706) 663-8744 or (800) 367-2751.

PLAINS (E-2) pop. 637, elev. 499′

JIMMY CARTER NATIONAL HISTORIC SITE, 300 N. Bond St., consists of the restored former Plains High School, from which Jimmy and Rosalyn Carter graduated; the Plains Depot, campaign headquarters for Carter's 1976 Presidential Campaign; and the Jimmy Carter Boyhood Farm, 2 miles north of Plains. The high school now is a visitor center with a small museum and a 28-minute orientation film. Other landmarks around Plains include brother Billy Carter's service station and the Carter Peanut Warehouse.

Note: The Carters' current residence is not open to the public. Allow 1 hour minimum. High school museum open daily 9-5. Plains Depot open daily 9-4:30. Farm museum open daily 10-5. Closed Jan. 1, Thanksgiving and Dec. 25. Free. Phone (229) 824-4104.

POOLER (D-5) pop. 6,239, elev. 23′

MIGHTY EIGHTH AIR FORCE MUSEUM is just n.e. of I-95 exit 102 at 175 Bourne Ave. The 90,000-square-foot museum engages visitors in the story of American air power from World War II through today. Features include the Memorial Gardens and the Chapel of the Fallen Eagles, which honors the 26,000 Eighth Air Force members who died in battle during World War II. Also available are Escape and Evasion, a replica of an underground escape network for downed pilots, a 7,000-volume library and archives containing oral histories, period photographs and wartime journals.

Food is available 11-2. Allow 2 hours minimum. Daily 9-5; closed Jan. 1, Easter, Thanksgiving and Dec. 25. Admission $10; $9 (senior citizens); $6 (ages 6-12). AX, DS, MC, VI. Phone (912) 748-8888.

PORT WENTWORTH (D-5)

pop. 3,276, elev. 23′

Ten miles upstream from Savannah, Port Wentworth accesses the 29,175-acre Savannah National Wildlife Refuge, an area composed largely of marshes, tidal rivers and creeks in both Georgia and South Carolina. The refuge is home to such threatened and endangered species as bald eagles, wood storks and manatees, as well as less-exotic horned owls, ducks, wading and shorebirds, turkeys, wild hogs, deer and the omni-lurking American alligator. Bird watching is good all year, better October through March and best in April when birds who have wintered here are about to migrate and overlap with birds who already are migrating and stopover here.

A great way to experience the refuge is via Laurel Hill Wildlife Drive which is 1 mile north of Port Wentworth off SR 25. This scenic drive follows 4 miles of earthen dikes through freshwater pools; not only is this a pleasant drive, but fishing from the banks of the dikes is permissible year-round. Other fishing is seasonal, as is hunting waterfowl, turkeys, deer and wild hogs. Defined time periods are set aside for archery hunts. For two days in November, several areas are designated for use by "wheelchair-dependent hunters." The refuge does not have a visitor center.

Pets, including horses, are not permitted on the refuge grounds. There is no fee for entering the refuge. For more information contact the Savannah Coastal Refuges, Parkway Business Center, 1000 Business Center Dr., Suite 10 Savannah, Georgia 31405; phone (912) 652-4415 weekdays 8-4:30. *See attraction listing in Hardeeville, S.C., p. 261.*

Port Wentworth Chamber of Commerce/Welcome Center: 7532 SR 21, Port Wentworth, GA 31407; phone (912) 965-1999.

RICHMOND HILL (E-5) pop. 6,959, elev. 17′

A few miles north of Richmond Hill, US 17 crosses the Ogeechee River near the site of the Battle of Kings Ferry, an audacious 18th-century defeat of the British by a Colonial colonel, two other officers and three enlisted men. Using widely spaced watch fires and misleading shouts to imaginary sentinels, the Americans convinced the British commander that they vastly outnumbered the five ships and 130 men intended to capture Savannah.

Riding alone into the British camp the next morning, the American leader informed the British commander that the bloodthirsty Colonial soldiers would accept nothing but unconditional surrender. The erstwhile invader handed over his entire force, which was marched away by the lone American while the other five followed behind to restrain their nonexistent restless troops.

Richmond Hill Convention & Visitors Bureau: 165 Richard R. Davis Dr., Richmond Hill, GA 31324; phone (912) 756-2676.

FORT McALLISTER STATE HISTORIC PARK is 4.5 mi. s.e. on SR 144, then 4 mi. e. on SR 144 Spur to 3894 Fort McAllister Rd. On a bank of the Great Ogeechee River, the fort is an example of Confederate earthwork fortifications; it withstood bombardments by the Union navy on Mar. 3, 1863. The fort finally fell before Gen. William Tecumseh Sherman's army on Dec. 13, 1864. A museum contains exhibits and artifacts.

Park open daily 7 a.m.-10 p.m. Museum open daily 8-5. Closed Thanksgiving and Dec. 25. Admission $4; $3.50 (ages 62+); $2.50 (ages 6-18). Phone (912) 727-2339. *See Recreation Chart and the AAA Southeastern CampBook.*

ROME (B-1) pop. 34,980, elev. 603′

Rome's name is apt, for like its Italian counterpart it is built upon seven hills. The city was founded in 1834 when three men stopped to provide water for their horses where the Etowah and Oostanaula rivers become the Coosa River. The men laid out a townsite and drew a name for it from a hat.

Rome's importance to the Confederacy as a rail and manufacturing center led to the 1863 ride of John Wisdom. Wearing out five horses and a mule in 11 hours, Wisdom rode 67 miles from Alabama to Rome to warn of an impending Union attack. A giant cannon lathe atop Civic Center Hill survived even Gen. William Tecumseh Sherman. Marks made by the sledgehammers of Union soldiers who tried to destroy it can be seen on the lathe's sides.

There are other reminders of the past, including Boswell Cabin, a mid-19th-century log house; a cotton gin next to the lathe; and a cemetery on Myrtle Hill that contains 377 Confederate and Union graves and those of two of Rome's founders. Ellen Louise Axson Wilson, wife of President Woodrow Wilson, also is buried in this cemetery. Atop the water tower on another of the city's seven hills is the Old Town Clock, dating from 1871.

Early 20th-century houses and commercial buildings can be seen in downtown Rome along Broad Street. In front of City Hall is the Capitoline Wolf, a bronze replica of the Roman statue depicting a she-wolf nursing Romulus and Remus, the legendary founders of Rome, Italy. It was given to the city by the Italian government in 1929.

Greater Rome Convention and Visitors Bureau: 402 Civic Center Dr., P.O. Box 1837, Rome, GA 30162-1837; phone (706) 295-5576 or (800) 444-1834.

Self-guiding tours: Brochures and cassette tapes describing walking tours of the Between the Rivers Historic District are available from the convention and visitors bureau.

CHIEFTAINS MUSEUM/MAJOR RIDGE HOME, 501 Riverside Pkwy., is the early 19th-century home of Cherokee leader Major Ridge, who struggled to maintain his American Indian heritage while adapting to the white man's culture. Ridge is best known for his leadership of the Treaty Party in the years preceding the Cherokee removal from their homeland. Ridge was killed in 1839 by Cherokee who felt betrayed by the Treaty Party. The original early 19th-century log cabin remains at the center of this gracious mansion. Tues.-Fri. 9-3, Sat. 10-4; closed holidays. Admission $3; $2 (ages 62+); $1.50 (students with ID). MC, VI. Phone (706) 291-9494.

GEM SAVE **OAK HILL AND THE MARTHA BERRY MUSEUM** are 3 mi. n. on US 27 (Martha Berry Hwy.) to 24 Veterans Memorial Hwy. NE on the campus of Berry College. Oak Hill was the home of Martha Berry, a cotton broker's daughter who began teaching local children in a one-room log cabin in the late 19th century. Her school eventually developed into Berry College, and her former home is furnished and maintained as it was during her lifetime.

The Martha Berry Museum contains memorabilia of the school and its founder, including paintings, portraits of philanthropists and furniture made by students. Three exhibit rooms chronicle Miss Berry's life. Visitors can take a guided tour of Oak Hill and a tour of five gardens, including a sunken garden with Japanese cherry trees. The college's 28,000-acre campus, near Oak Hill on US 27, also features nature trails, buildings constructed by students and a gristmill with a 42-foot wheel, said to be one of the largest in the world.

Allow 2 hours minimum. Open Mon.-Sat. 10-5; closed holidays. Admission $5; $4 (senior citizens); $3 (ages 6-12). AX, DS, MC, VI. Phone (706) 368-6789 or (800) 220-5504.

ROME AREA HISTORY MUSEUM is at 305 Broad St. in the historic section. Organized in chronological order, the museum's exhibits form a historical timeline beginning with the area's original inhabitants, American Indians, and proceeding with the founding of Floyd County and Rome. Through original blueprints, maps and photographs, visitors can view how the town grew during the 1800s.

Guided tours are available. Tues.-Sat. 10-5; closed Jan. 1, July 4, Thanksgiving, day after Thanksgiving and Dec. 24-25. Admission $4; $3 (ages 60+); $2 (ages 6-12). Phone (706) 235-8051.

RECREATIONAL ACTIVITIES

Horseback Riding

- **Zion Farms Equestrian Center** is at 2979 Big Texas Valley Rd. N.W. Write P.O. Box 860, Armuchee, GA 30105. Guided 2- and 3-hour trail rides daily 10-5. Reservations are required. Phone (706) 235-8002.

ROSWELL—*see Atlanta p. 61.*

ROYSTON (B-4) pop. 2,493, elev. 898'

TY COBB MUSEUM is at 461 Cook St. The museum promotes education and understanding of baseball and professional baseball hitter Ty Cobb. Exhibits include rare photographs, memorabilia, books and archives. A video presentation also is featured. Allow 30 minutes minimum. Mon.-Fri. 9-4, Sat. 10-4; closed Jan. 1, July 4, Labor Day, Thanksgiving and Dec. 24 and 31. Phone to confirm schedule. Admission $5; $4 (ages 62+); $3 (students with ID); free (ages 0-5 and military with ID). MC, VI. Phone (706) 245-1825.

ST. MARYS (F-5) pop. 13,761, elev. 11′

From treasure-smuggling pirates to commercial fishermen, St. Marys' past blends into its present. Many shrimp and fishing boats line the docks along the St. Marys River. The town provides access to the Cumberland Island National Seashore Visitor Center and ferry dock *(see place listing p. 76)*. St. Marys also is home to the Kings Bay Naval Sub Base, the Atlantic Coast home base of Trident nuclear submarines.

McIntosh Sugar Mill Tabby Ruins, on Spur 40, is the largest tabby structure (a material made of oyster shells, sand and water) in the area. Built by John Houston McIntosh in the 18th century, the site was used for cane grinding and the boiling and processing of sugar products. Ten miles north on SR 40, Crooked River State Park offers year-round recreational opportunities *(see Recreation Chart and the AAA Southeastern CampBook)*.

The Howard Gilman Memorial Park is on the waterfront and hosts a variety of seasonal festivities, including fireworks during summer months. Near downtown, the St. Marys Aquatic Center, a water park featuring slides, pools and seasonal activities, opens in April; phone (912) 673-8118.

St. Marys Convention and Visitors Bureau: 406 Osborne St., St. Marys, GA 31558; phone (912) 882-4000 or (800) 868-8687. *See color ad.*

Self-guiding tours: Maps and brochures for a walking tour of the National Historic District featuring houses dating from 1801 are available at the welcome center. The Braille Trail, within the historic district, highlights 38 historically significant sites marked with raised letters and braille for visually impaired visitors.

ORANGE HALL HOUSE MUSEUM is just n. of the waterfront at 311 Osborne St. The stately house, with its white Doric columns and wide steps leading to a main entrance on the second floor, is considered a fine example of Greek Revival architecture. The house, believed to have undergone its last enlargement and remodeling in 1856, is furnished with 19th-century items. Allow 30 minutes minimum. Mon.-Sat. 9-4, Sun. 1-4; closed Jan. 1, Easter, Thanksgiving and Dec. 25. Admission $3; $1 (ages 0-12). Phone (912) 576-3644.

SAVE **ST. MARYS SUBMARINE MUSEUM,** 102 St. Marys St. W., displays items from both United States and foreign military submarines including a hands-on periscope and other major submarine shipboard components. Also on the premises are a reading library, photos, models and plaques. Open Tues.-Sat. 10-4, Sun. 1-5; closed Easter, Thanksgiving and Dec. 21-Jan. 3. Admission $4; $3 (ages 62+ and military with ID); $2 (ages 6-18). MC, VI. Phone (912) 882-2782.

ST. SIMONS ISLAND—

see Golden Isles p. 80.

SAPELO ISLAND—*see Golden Isles p. 80.*

SAVANNAH (E-6) pop. 131,510, elev. 43′

Gen. James E. Oglethorpe and his settlers founded Savannah, England's 13th and last colony, in February 1733. Forgoing the usual village grid system, Oglethorpe and Col. William Bull laid out their new settlement in a series of wards in which commercial and residential buildings centered on a public square. This visionary plan has survived as the city's blueprint because of Oglethorpe's choice of location.

On a bluff overlooking the Savannah River, the new settlement soon prospered as a crossroads of

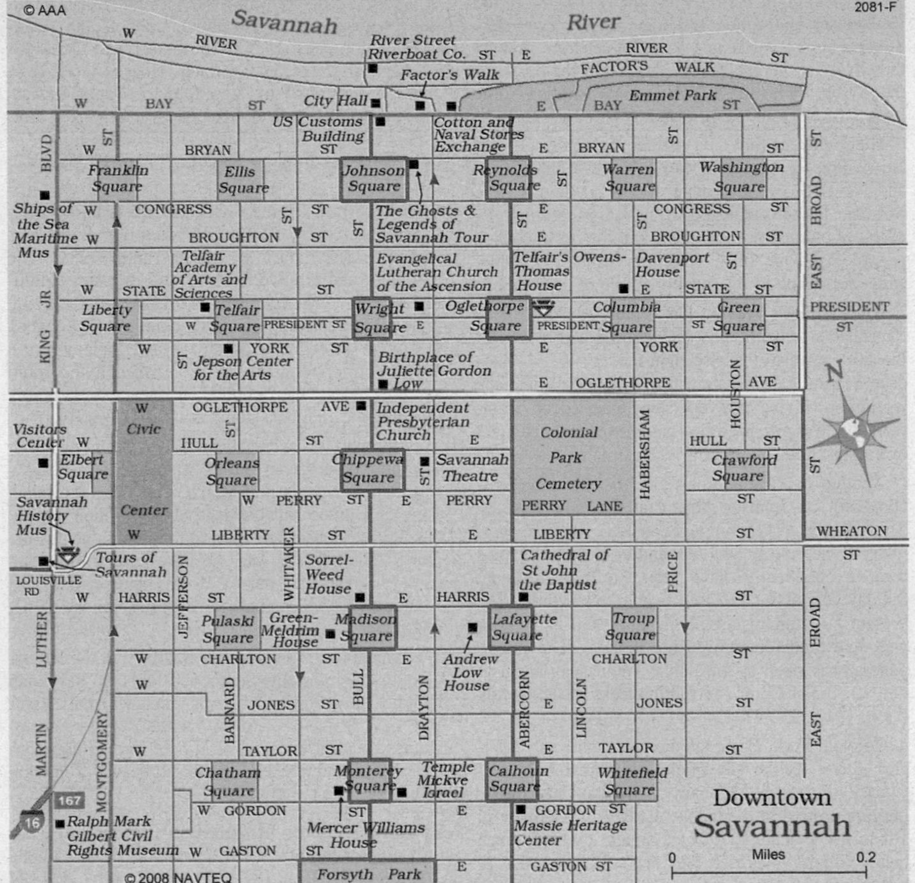

trade with England and the new communities of the interior. Port traffic, begun in 1744, experienced a steady increase along with the plantation economy of tobacco and cotton.

Residents eagerly embraced the revolt against England, and Savannah was garrisoned by some 900 Colonial troops under Gen. Robert Howe. British forces captured the city by surprise in December 1778 and made it a base for their operations against the Colonies until their departure in 1782.

Nineteenth-century Savannah grew and flourished with King Cotton, becoming a vital port. In 1862 Union forces closed the port to all but blockade runners when they captured Fort Pulaski *(see Fort Pulaski National Monument, p. 74)*.

Two years later Gen. William Tecumseh Sherman blazed a trail of destruction across Georgia to the city. Confederate forces fought stubbornly, but with the fall of Fort McAllister, Gen. William J. Hardee realized further resistance was futile and withdrew his troops to prevent the city's destruction. Sherman entered Savannah on Christmas Day 1864 and offered it to President Abraham Lincoln as a present.

Cotton again proved to be Savannah's salvation after the war as the city grew into a major trading center. The collapse of the cotton market at the beginning of the 20th century left Savannah languishing until just before World War II when other industries began to develop.

The city almost lost, however, what Sherman had spared some 100 years earlier: its squares, its houses and its heritage. In the drive to reshape the city's skyline, developers began to tear down historic structures. The proposed demolition of the Davenport House, now a Savannah museum *(see attraction listing)*, sparked the founding of the Historic Savannah Foundation. This dedicated group of women organized one of the country's first and most successful restoration programs, buying hundreds of properties and selling them to private parties with covenants to restore and repair them.

Presently, 21 of Oglethorpe's original 24 squares survive, bordered by handsome town houses and landscaped with live oaks, azaleas, fountains and statues. The success of Historic Savannah Foundation's early efforts has spawned other civic renewal projects.

The cleanup of the river and the restoration of the warehouses and cotton brokerage offices along Bay Street, Factor's Walk and River Street have revived the city's historic waterfront. Instead of the bustle of the cotton trade, these 19th-century buildings now house specialty shops, restaurants and nightspots.

Highlights in this area include Solomon's Lodge No. 1, Free & Accepted Masons, in the 1886 Cotton and Naval Stores Exchange at 100 E. Bay St. The Masonic lodge, organized in 1734, is the country's oldest in continuous operation, and the old exchange is said to be the first building to straddle a public street according to the legal principle of air rights.

River Street's Waving Girl statue is evocative of Savannah's romantic character. In the early years of the 20th century the city light-tender's sister, Florence Martus, became known to seamen all over the world for waving at every ship. One legend maintains that she promised her sailor sweetheart to greet every ship until his return.

Another historic building is Christ Church (Episcopalian), on Johnson Square at Bull and East St. Julian streets. The congregation was the first organized in the colony, in 1733, and in 1736 established what is believed to have been the first Protestant Sunday school for children in the New World. The present structure was built in 1838 and its interior was renovated following a fire in 1895. The church generally is open to the public Wednesday and Friday 10:30-3 the first and fourth weeks of the month. Phone (912) 232-4131 or (912) 238-0434.

Colonial Park, East Oglethorpe Avenue and Abercorn Street, is the site of the old Christ Episcopal Church cemetery, for many years the only public burying ground in the colony. Closed to interment in 1853, the cemetery suffered much damage when Gen. William Tecumseh Sherman's troops used it as a stabling ground.

Founded in 1755 by members of the Church of Scotland, Independent Presbyterian Church is at the corner of Bull Street and West Oglethorpe Avenue. This 1891 church building and steeple are a re-creation of the 1829 building that was destroyed by an 1889 fire; the original structure was modeled after St. Martin-in-the-Fields Church in London's Trafalgar Square. If volunteer staff is available, the Georgian interior is open for public viewing Monday 1-3 and Friday 10-noon. Phone (912) 236-3346.

First African Baptist Church, at 23 Montgomery St., was established in 1775. The church is housed in the 1859 brick sanctuary built by congregation members. It is reputedly North America's oldest African-American church, and its museum contains archives and memorabilia dating from the 18th century. The Sunday school, organized in 1826, is said to have been the first African-American Sunday school in North America. The church offers guided tours Monday through Saturday at 11, 1 and 3. Phone (912) 233-6597.

Since 1839, the Georgia Historical Society library and archives have preserved the history of the state of Georgia. The collection includes more than 4 million manuscripts, 90,000 photographs, 24,000 architectural drawings, 15,000 rare books, and thousands of maps, portraits, and artifacts. Housed in an 1876 structure designed by AIA founder Detlef Lienau, the Georgia Historical Society is across from Forsyth Park at 501 Whitaker Street. The library is open Tuesday through Saturday, 10-5. Phone (912) 651-2128.

Writer Mary Flannery O'Connor was born in Savannah March 25, 1925, and lived at 207 East Charlton St. on Lafayette Square until 1938. The basement and top two floors of this four-story building are privately occupied apartments, but it is being gradually restored to its configuration when O'Connor lived here. Saturdays and Sundays from 1-4, the first floor and its refurbished living room are open to the public. Phone the Flannery O'Connor Childhood Home at (912) 233-6014.

A number of events take place during the year. The city dons green during a festive St. Patrick's Day Parade held in mid-March. The 4-day Savannah Tour of Homes and Gardens, during which numerous private houses are open to the public, begins the fourth Thursday in March. For more information contact Savannah Tour of Homes and Gardens, 18 Abercorn St., Savannah, GA 31401; phone (912) 234-8054.

Savannah dresses for the holidays in December with the month-long Southern Lights, A Savannah Holiday Celebration. Events includes the River Street Christmas Festival & Parade, Holiday Tour of Homes musical events. For a more information contact the convention and visitors bureau information center.

Savannah Visitor Information Center: 301 Martin Luther King Blvd., Savannah, GA 31402; phone (912) 944-0455 or (877) 728-2662. *See color ad p. 95.*

Self-guiding tours: Information about Savannah's scenic tour route is available at the visitor information centers at 301 Martin Luther King Blvd. and 1 River St. Audio tours from Savannah Talking Tours can be purchased on cassette or CD for $18.99.

ANDREW LOW HOUSE, 329 Abercorn St. at Lafayette Sq., was built by Andrew Low, a wealthy cotton merchant. The 1848 stuccoed brick house, noted for its well-proportioned rooms with plaster cornices, carved woodwork and crystal chandeliers, was the home of Juliette Gordon Low, who founded America's first Girl Scout troop in 1912. Guests have included Gen. Robert E. Lee and novelist William Makepeace Thackeray.

Allow 30 minutes minimum. Guided 25-minute tours are given every half-hour Mon.-Wed. and Fri.-Sat. 10-4:30, Sun. noon-4:30; closed major holidays. Last tour begins 30 minutes before closing. Fee $8; $4.50 (ages 0-12). MC, VI. Phone (912) 233-6854.

BIRTHPLACE OF JULIETTE GORDON LOW is at 10 E. Oglethorpe Ave. Founder of the Girl Scouts of

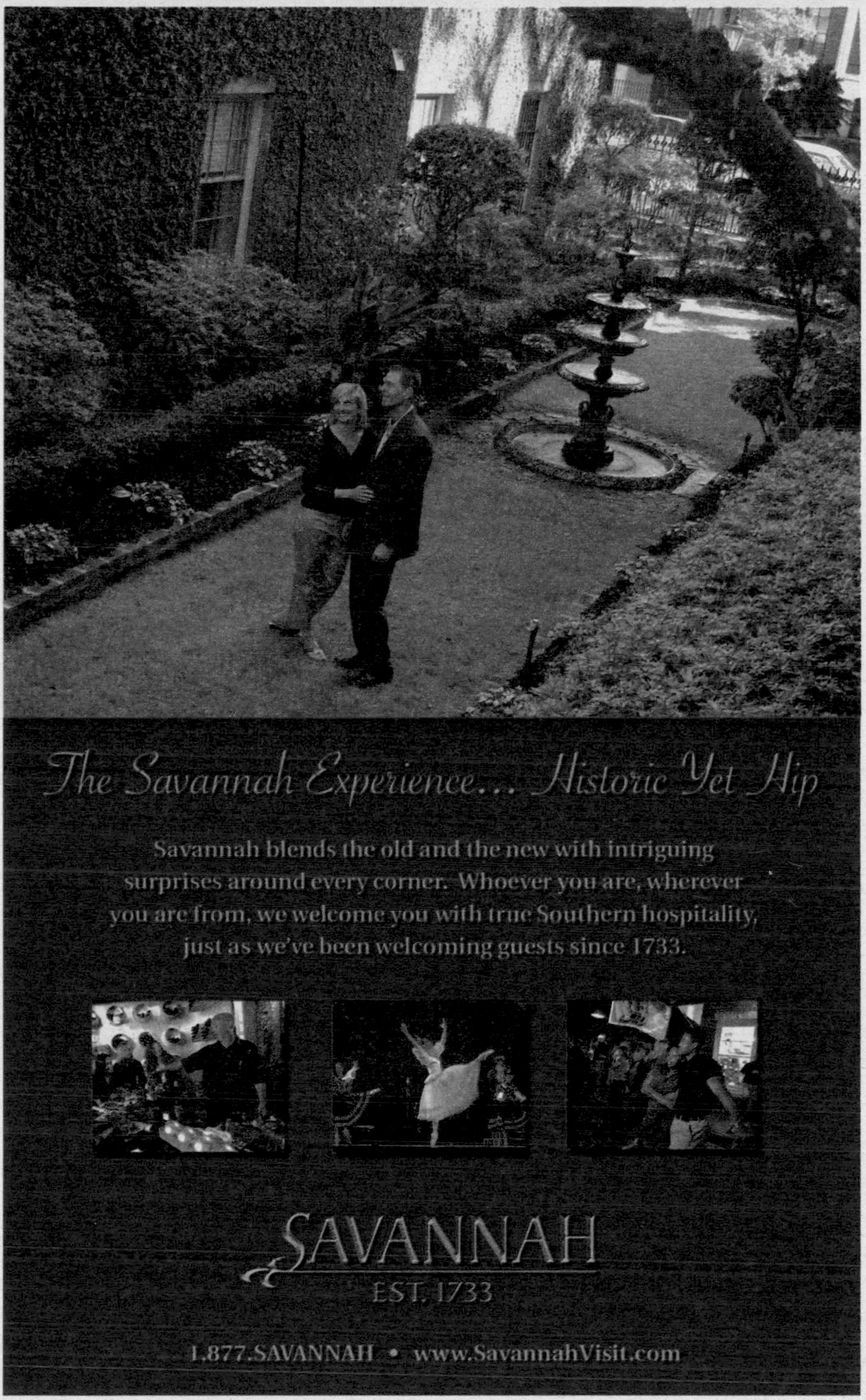
The Savannah Experience... Historic Yet Hip
Savannah blends the old and the new with intriguing surprises around every corner. Whoever you are, wherever you are from, we welcome you with true Southern hospitality, just as we've been welcoming guests since 1733.
SAVANNAH
EST. 1733
1.877.SAVANNAH • www.SavannahVisit.com

the USA, Juliette Gordon Low was born in this elegant 1821 English Regency house in 1860. The home has been restored to its appearance in 1886, the year of Juliette Low's marriage. Exhibits include period arrangements of original Gordon family furnishings, artwork by Low, a Victorian garden, a stable and a carriage house. Guided 40-minute tours offer insight into the lives of Low and her family.

Note: Restoration projects will cause brief closures in January through February 2009; phone ahead to confirm schedule. Tours every 15 minutes Mon.-Sat. 10-4, Sun. 11-4, Mar.-Oct.; Mon.-Tues. and Thurs.-Sat. 10-4, Sun. 11-4, rest of year. Closed Jan. 1-17, Mar. 17, Easter, July 4, Thanksgiving, day after Thanksgiving, the week of Dec. 25 and 31. Admission $8; $7 (students ages 5-20); $25 (family rate for two adults and four children). AX, DS, MC, VI. Phone (912) 233-4501.

BONAVENTURE CEMETERY is at 330 Bonaventure Rd. This former plantation has been a cemetery since the mid-19th century. The site, which encompasses 100 acres, overlooks the Wilmington River and has an abundance of live oak trees, some of which are 250 years old. Many of the graves incorporate beautiful statues and ornate carvings. Among the famous persons interred here are author Conrad Aiken and composer Johnny Mercer.

Note: Visitors should be aware of the potential for theft and are not advised to travel alone. Valuables should not be left in automobiles. Cemetery maps are available in the administrative building. Picnicking is permitted. Allow 1 hour minimum. Daily 8-5. Donations. Phone (912) 651-6843.

CATHEDRAL OF ST. JOHN THE BAPTIST, 222 E. Harris St. at Abercorn St., is a Gothic-style cathedral completed in 1896, then rebuilt in 1899 after a severe fire. One of the largest cathedrals in the South, it features marble railings, floors and altar. In addition there are murals, stained-glass windows, large carved-wood stations of the cross, and a solid white-oak 2,081-pipe Noack tracker organ. Allow 30 minutes minimum. Open Mon.-Sat. and holidays 9-5, Sun. 8-5; no tours available during church services. Donations. Phone (912) 233-4709.

CITY HALL, jct. Bull and Bay sts., was completed in 1906 on the site of the 1799 City Exchange. Bronze tablets attached to the building's front commemorate the 1834 launching of the SS *John Randolph,* the first iron ship seen in American waters, and the SS *Savannah,* the first steam-propelled ship to cross the Atlantic. Mon.-Fri. 8:30-5; closed holidays. Free. Phone (912) 651-6410 or (912) 651-6790.

SAVE **DAVENPORT HOUSE** is on Columbia Square at 324 E. State St. Master builder Isaiah Davenport finished his Federal-style home in 1820. The finely proportioned house is noted for its historically accurate interiors, delicate ironwork, elliptical stairway and handsome plasterwork. The building was saved from demolition in 1955 by seven women who went on to form the Historic Savannah Foundation—one of the earliest preservation movements in the United States.

Guided 30-minute tours depart every half-hour Mon.-Sat. 10-4, Sun. 1-4 (10-1 on day before Thanksgiving and Dec. 24 and 31); closed Jan. 1, Mar. 17, Easter, July 4, Thanksgiving and Dec. 25. Last tour leaves at closing. Fee $8; $5 (ages 6-17). AX, MC, VI. Phone (912) 236-8097.

EVANGELICAL LUTHERAN CHURCH OF THE ASCENSION, on Wright Sq. at Bull and E. State sts., combines Norman and Gothic architectural features. The 1844 structure is noted for its stained-glass windows and exhibits about church history. The congregation was founded in 1741. Mon.-Fri. 9-1; closed holidays. Donations. Phone (912) 232-4151.

FACTOR'S WALK, a row of narrow buildings along the river bluff on the north side of Bay St., acquired its name in the 19th century when it was the meeting place for factors—sales agents and commission brokers such as cotton merchants—and was the center of commercial activities. Today is contains shops, restaurants and bars. A network of iron and concrete bridgeways connects the buildings to the bluff. The cobblestone streets were made from the ballast of ships from Europe.

FORSYTH PARK, on Gaston St. between Whitaker and Drayton sts., is particularly lovely in early spring during the azalea season. A fountain featuring a fanciful grouping of mermen, swans and a lone water nymph is the centerpiece of the original tract, laid out in 1851. The Confederate Monument is in the park extension. Daily 24 hours. Free.

FORT McALLISTER STATE HISTORIC PARK—*see attraction listing p. 90.*

GEM **FORT PULASKI NATIONAL MONUMENT**—*see place listing p. 74.*

GREEN-MELDRIM HOUSE, on Madison Sq. at 14 W. Macon St., was Gen. William Tecumseh Sherman's headquarters during his 1864 occupation of Savannah. The 1850 house is a fine example of Neo-Gothic Revival architecture. Today the house is used by the parish of St. John's Episcopal Church for church functions. Guided tours every half-hour Tues. and Thurs.-Fri. 10-4, Sat. 10-1 (unless a church function is scheduled). Last tour begins 30 minutes before closing. Closed holidays, the two weeks before Easter and Dec. 18 through mid-Jan. Admission $7; $3 (students with ID). Phone (912) 233-3845 to confirm availability.

JEPSON CENTER FOR THE ARTS is at jct. Barnard and W. York sts. on Telfair Square at 207 W. York St. The 64,000-square-foot building is one of three venues associated with the Telfair Academy of Arts and Sciences *(see attraction listing p. 98).* The center showcases terraces, gardens and galleries featuring permanent and temporary works of 20th- and

21st-century Southern art. ArtZeum, an area including interactive exhibits, allows visitors to use their creativity in the artistic process.

Allow 1 hour minimum. Mon. and Wed.-Sat. 10-5 (also Thurs. 5-8), Sun. noon-5; closed Jan. 1, Martin Luther King Jr. Day, Mar. 17, Easter, Labor Day, Thanksgiving and Dec. 25. Admission $10; $8 (senior citizens); $5 (students with ID); $4 (ages 5-12); $25 (family rate for two adults and two children). A combination ticket with Telfair's Owens-Thomas house and the Telfair Academy of Arts and Sciences $15; $30 (family rate). AX, DS, MC, VI. Phone (912) 790-8800.

MASSIE HERITAGE CENTER is at 207 E. Gordon St. Housed within a Greek Revival building, the center features three rooms of exhibits relating to Savannah's history. Highlights include a 3-D model of Savannah's Landmark Historic District and artifacts relating to the city's Victorian era. The Architecture Room showcases examples of the architectural styles found in Savannah. Street parking only is available. Allow 45 minutes minimum. Mon.-Fri. 9-4; guided tours are offered at 9 and 3. Closed school holidays. Admission for self-guiding tours $3. Guided tours $5. Phone (912) 201-5070.

MERCER WILLIAMS HOUSE is at 429 Bull St. Antiques dealer, preservation expert and socialite Jim Williams restored this 1860 mansion built for Gen. Hugh W. Mercer, great-grandfather of singer and songwriter Johnny Mercer. Events central to the book "Midnight in the Garden of Good and Evil," later a major film, took place in the house. Guides provide tours of the garden and first floor while offering history about the architecture, interior furnishings and Williams. Highlights include the spiral stairway below a stained-glass dome and the original English ceramic tile in the 60-foot entryway.

Allow 30 minutes minimum. Mon.-Sat. 10:30-4:10, Sun. 12:30-4; closed holidays. Phone ahead for tour schedule. Admission $12.50; $8 (military and students with ID). AX, DS, MC, VI. Phone (912) 236-6352 or (877) 430-6352.

MIGHTY EIGHTH AIR FORCE MUSEUM—*see Pooler p. 89.*

OLD FORT JACKSON, 3 mi. e. via President St., was built between 1808 and 1812. On the banks of the Savannah River and surrounded by a moat, the fort is one of the oldest remaining brickwork forts in Georgia. Exhibits depict the history of the fort's construction and its garrison during the War of 1812 and the Civil War. An orientation video provides an overview of the site's history.

There are frequent living-history presentations offered throughout the year, with cannon firings offered daily during summer. Allow 30 minutes minimum. Daily 9-5; closed Jan. 1, Thanksgiving and Dec. 25. Admission $4.25; $3.75 (ages 55+, military and students with ID); free (ages 0-5 with parent or guardian). AX, MC, VI. Phone (912) 232-3945.

Kudzu

Kudzu—that leafy green vine that entwines electric poles, decorates porch trellises and overtakes trees—has made the South its home.

The plant arrived in the United States innocently enough; the Japanese brought it to Philadelphia in the late 19th century to decorate their pavilion in the centennial celebration.

Kudzu grew in popularity as an ornamental shade plant until the 1930s, when experts at the U.S. Soil Conservation Service discovered how well it stopped soil erosion.

Soon Conservation Service workers had planted kudzu on farms all across the South. The plant not only stopped erosion; it sent tendrils in all directions in its quest for more space.

Southerners thought kudzu was pretty and planted it in their yards to hide tree stumps and compost piles. They soon learned kudzu's true nature, however.

Growing as much as a foot a day in hot weather, the vine spreads by sending roots into the earth where its leaves touch the ground. In a single season, one plant can creep 100 feet.

So far, kudzu has been successful in its search for space, spreading from Florida as far north as Maryland and as far west as Louisiana.

There is good news, though. In Japan, kudzu is ground into powder that is used for cooking and as a medicine. Kudzu adds its flavor to lemonade, sweet and sour sauce, apple pie and fried eggplant. Made into a cream, kudzu allegedly fights influenza, upset stomach, apoplexy and sexual apathy.

In the United States, meanwhile, cattle have found kudzu to be good eating. At the rate it is growing, our cattle will not go hungry.

RALPH MARK GILBERT CIVIL RIGHTS MUSEUM is at 460 Martin Luther King Jr. Blvd. The museum, named in honor of the late Dr. Ralph Mark Gilbert, NAACP leader and father of Georgia's civil rights movement, recounts the civil rights struggle of Georgia's oldest African-American community. Guided, narrated tours take visitors through three floors of interactive exhibits, videos and memorabilia. Allow 30 minutes minimum. Mon.-Sat. 9-5; closed Jan. 1, July 4, Labor Day, Thanksgiving and Dec. 25. Admission $4; $3 (ages 65+); $2 (students with ID). AX, MC, VI. Phone (912) 231-8900.

SAVE **RIVER STREET RIVERBOAT CO.,** departing from the dock at 9 E. River St., offers 1-hour narrated sightseeing harbor cruises, a 2-hour gospel music and Southern buffet dinner cruise, 90-minute Saturday lunch and Sunday brunch cruises, and 2-hour dinner/entertainment or 90-minute moonlight cruises aboard the 600-passenger vessels *Savannah River Queen* or *Georgia Queen,* both replicas of 19th-century stern-wheelers.

Sightseeing cruises depart Mon.-Fri. at 2 and 4, Sat.-Sun. at noon, 2 and 4, Apr.-Oct.; Sun.-Fri. at 2, Sat. at 2 and 4 in Nov.; Sat.-Sun. at 2, Dec.-Jan. (also Mon.-Fri. Dec. 26-31); Wed.-Fri. at 2, Sat. at 2 and 4, Sun. at 2 in Feb.; Mon.-Fri. at 2, Sat. at noon, 2 and 4, Sun. at noon and 2, in Mar. Phone for dinner and specialty cruise schedules.

Sightseeing fare $17.95; $9.95 (ages 0-12). Moonlight fare $16.95; $10.95 (ages 0-12). Murder mystery cruise $26.95; $18.95 (ages 0-12). Sat. luncheon cruise $32.95; $18.95 (ages 0-12). Gospel dinner cruise $35.95; $23.95 (ages 0-12). Sunday brunch cruise $35.95; $19.95 (ages 0-12). Dinner entertainment cruise $44.95; $27.95 (ages 0-12). Reservations are required for meal cruises. AX, DS, MC, VI. Phone (912) 232-6404 or (800) 786-6404.

SAVE **ROUNDHOUSE RAILROAD MUSEUM,** 601 W. Harris St., is said to be the nation's oldest and most complete railroad complex. More than a dozen buildings survive. Restored locomotives, railcars, machinery and a working model train also are displayed. Occasional steam demonstrations are offered and a children's area is available. Allow 30 minutes minimum. Daily 9-5; closed Jan. 1, Thanksgiving and Dec. 25. Admission $4.25; $3.75 (ages 55+, current and former railroad workers, military and students with ID); free (ages 0-6 with parent or guardian). AX, MC, VI. Phone (912) 651-6823.

GEM SAVE **SAVANNAH HISTORY MUSEUM** is in a restored mid-19th-century train passenger shed at 303 Martin Luther King Jr. Blvd. Artifacts and exhibits tell the story of the Savannah region from Native American settlement, to the city's founding in 1733, through the present.

Exhibits include the bench from the movie "Forrest Gump", one of the Oscars awarded to Savannah native and composer Johnny Mercer and displays of past fashions. A children's play area is available. Allow 1 hour, 30 minutes minimum. Mon.-Fri. 8:30-5, Sat.-Sun. 9-5; closed Jan. 1, Thanksgiving and Dec. 25. Admission $4.25; $3.75 (ages 55+, military and students with ID); free (ages 0-6 with parent or guardian). MC, VI. Phone (912) 651-6825.

SAVANNAH NATIONAL WILDLIFE REFUGE—*see Port Wentworth p. 90 and attraction listing in Hardeeville, S.C., p. 261.*

SAVE **SAVANNAH THEATRE** is at 222 Bull St. in the center of the historical district. Rotating 2-hour musical productions staged in this restored 1818 theater include a Christmas offering. Performances Wed.-Fri. at 8 p.m., Sat. at 3 and 8, Sun. at 3, Feb.-Dec. Tues. performances sometimes are scheduled; phone ahead. Admission $35; $16 (ages 0-17). DS, MC, VI. Phone (912) 233-7764.

SAVE **SHIPS OF THE SEA MARITIME MUSEUM,** 41 Martin Luther King Jr. Blvd., is in Scarbrough House, built in 1819 for William Scarbrough, a principal owner of the *Savannah,* the first steamship to cross the Atlantic. Exhibitions include ships models, maritime antiques and paintings from the 18th and 19th centuries. Four videotapes are shown. Of interest is the mid-1800s garden.

Allow 30 minutes minimum. Tues.-Sun. 10-5; closed Jan. 1, Mar. 17, Easter, Memorial Day, July 4, Labor Day, Thanksgiving, day after Thanksgiving, Dec. 24-25 and 31. Last admission is 45 minutes before closing. Admission $8; $6 (ages 65+ and students with ID); $20 (family rate for two adults and dependent children). Phone (912) 232-1511.

SORREL-WEED HOUSE is at 6 W. Harris St. A 6-minute video presentation introduces visitors to the house. A guided tour follows and shares the history, architecture and antiques of the former residence of Francis Sorrel and his family. Allow 45 minutes minimum. Daily 10-4:30; closed Thanksgiving and Dec. 25. Admission $10; free (ages 0-2). Phone (912) 236-8888.

TELFAIR ACADEMY OF ARTS AND SCIENCES is at 121 Barnard St. on Telfair Sq. Designed by William Jay in 1819, this Regency-style mansion includes two rooms furnished in period, including the impressive Octagon Room. The permanent collection features works by American Impressionists and European artists. On long-term loan is the "Bird Girl" statue popularized by the book "Midnight in the Garden of Good and Evil." Traveling exhibitions also are presented.

Mon. and Wed.-Sat. 10-5 (also Thurs. 5-8), Sun. noon-5; closed Jan. 1, Martin Luther King Day, Mar. 17, Easter, Labor Day, Thanksgiving and Dec. 25. Free guided tours are given Mon. and Wed.-Sat. at 11, 1 and 2, Sun. at 11 and 2. Admission $10; $8 (senior citizens); $5 (college students with ID); $4 (ages 5-12); $25 (family rate for two adults and two children). A combination ticket with Telfair's Owens-Thomas House and Jepson Center for the Arts $15; $30 (family rate). Admission may be more during special events. AX, MC, VI. Phone (912) 790-8880.

TELFAIR'S OWENS-THOMAS HOUSE, 124 Abercorn St. on Oglethorpe Sq., was designed by English architect William Jay. Influenced by classical antiquity, he built the elegant residence 1816-19 using domestic and imported materials and designed an innovative plumbing system. In 1825 the Marquis de Lafayette was a guest here.

The English Regency house is furnished with rare antiques and contains decorative arts that were owned by Savannah citizens in the 19th century. The carriage house contains an orientation gallery and the original slave quarters. An English inspired parterre garden connects the main buildings. Guided tours every half-hour Tues.-Sat. 10-5, Sun. 1-5, Mon. noon-5; closed major holidays and Mar. 17. Admission $10; $8 (military with ID and senior citizens); $5 (college students with ID); $4 (ages 5-12). A combination ticket with the Jepson Center for the Arts and the Telfair Academy of Arts and Sciences $15; $30 (family rate). AX, MC, VI. Phone (912) 233-9743.

TEMPLE MICKVE ISRAEL is in the historic district on Monterey Sq. on Bull St. at jct. Gordon and Wayne sts. This Gothic-style 1876 synagogue contains an archival museum displaying the Torah that the founders of the congregation brought to Savannah from England in 1733. Other items of interest are letters from George Washington, Thomas Jefferson, James Madison and several other presidents. Guided 45-minute tours Mon.-Fri. 10-1 and 2-4. Last tour begins 45 minutes before closing. Admission $3. MC, VI. Phone (912) 233-1547.

TOURS OF SAVANNAH, departing various locations, are conducted by several different companies and offer sightseeing tours of Savannah's historic district. Some feature nature tours, island tours, coastal low-country tours or specialty tours. Many include admission to one or two historic buildings.

Carriage Tours of Savannah depart from the City Market Visitor Center at Jefferson St. and W. Saint Julian St. Narrated 50-minute tours in horse-drawn carriages cover major points of interest in the historic district. Tours daily every half-hour 9-3 and ghost tours 6-9; closed Mar. 17, Easter, Thanksgiving and Dec. 25. Fare $20; $10 (ages 5-11). Garage or metered parking at some stops. Reservations are recommended. AX, DS, MC, VI. Phone (912) 236-6756.

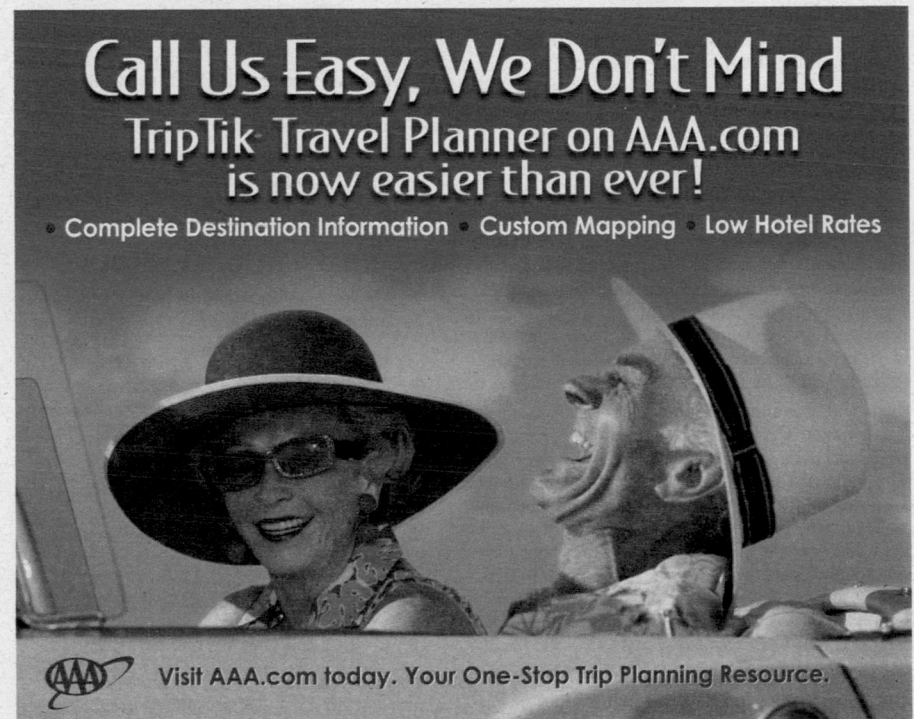

Cobblestone Tours Inc. departs from various city locations. The 90-minute Savannah Haunted History walking tour is given by guides in period costume. The tour begins at Colonial Park Cemetery and includes city history, local folklore and ghost stories. A 2-hour walking tour of local pubs, which is accompanied by local ghost stories, is available for those 21 and over. Allow 1 hour minimum. Haunted history tour departs daily at 7 p.m. and 9 p.m. Haunted history tour fee $10; $8 (ages 55+); $5 (ages 5-12). Reservations are required. Phone (912) 604-3007.

SAVE **The Freedom Trail Tour** departs the Savannah Visitor Information Center at 301 Martin Luther King Blvd. This 2-hour, narrated van tour passes and stops at historic sites important in the experiences and contributions of African Americans to the city and the region, from the founding of Savannah the present. Allow 2 hours minimum. Mon.-Sat. at 10, 1 and 3, Sun. at 1 and 3, spring and summer; daily at 1 and 3, rest of year. Fee $20; $17 (senior citizens); $15 (students with ID); $12 (ages 7-13). Phone (912) 398-2785.

The Ghosts & Legends of Savannah Tour offers tours departing from Johnson Sq. at the corner of E. Bryan and Bull sts. During these walking tours, knowledgeable guides lead visitors through Savannah, recounting the city's history as well as ghost stories and local legends along the way. Savannah has been described as one of the country's most haunted cities. Allow 1 hour, 30 minutes minimum. Daily at 6 p.m., 8 p.m. and 10 p.m., Memorial Day-Labor Day; at 6 and 8, rest of year. Closed Thanksgiving and Dec. 25. Fee $18; $10 (ages 8-14). Reservations are required. AX, DS, MC, VI. Phone (912) 236-4467 or (888) 419-4467.

SAVE **Gray Line Tours** depart the Gray Line office at 215 W. Boundary St., the visitor center at 301 Martin Luther King Jr. Blvd. and many downtown hotels. Guided tours include 90-minute trolley tours of the historic district and restored waterfront area, with departures every 20-30 minutes. Evening Haunted Trolley Tours are also available.

Daily 9-4:30; closed Mar. 17, Thanksgiving and Dec. 25. Fare for 90-minute historic district tour $10; haunted trolley tour $17; $10 (ages 5-11). AX, DS, MC, VI. Phone (912) 234-8687.

The Negro Heritage Trail Tour departs the Savannah Information Center at 301 Martin Luther King Jr. Blvd. This 90-minute, narrated van tour passes historic sites important in the experiences and contributions of African Americans to the city and the region, from the founding of Savannah to the present. Allow 2 hours minimum. Tours Tues.-Sat. at 10 and noon. Fare $20; $10 (ages 10-17). Phone (912) 234-8000 for reservations.

SAVE **Old Savannah Tours** depart the Savannah Visitor Center, 301 Martin Luther King Jr. Blvd. and from 250 Martin Luther King Jr. Blvd. The narrated historic tour with on/off privileges at 14 stops in the historic district is aboard open-air trolleys. Six specialty tours include a ghost tour, a land and sea tour and a Paula Deen food tour. On/off tours depart every 20 minutes daily 9-4:30. Phone for specialty tour schedules. Closed Mar. 17. On/off tour $24; $12 (ages 5-12). Specialty tours $21-$51; $10-$32 (ages 5-12). AX, MC, VI. Phone (912) 234-8128 or (800) 517-9007.

Old Town Trolley Tours depart from various downtown locations. The 90-minute narrated tours with on/off privileges feature more than 100 points of interest and pass through Savannah's city squares and Colonial, historic, Victorian and waterfront districts. Evening Ghosts & Gravestones tours are available by reservation. Allow 1 hour, 30 minutes minimum. On/off tours depart every 20 minutes daily 9-4:30. Ghosts & Gravestones tours available nightly; phone for schedule. Closed Mar. 17. Trolley on/off fare $23; $10 (ages 4-12). Ghosts & Gravestones fare $25; $10 (ages 4-12). AX, DS, MC, VI. Phone (912) 233-0083.

THE UNIVERSITY OF GEORGIA MARINE EDUCATION CENTER AQUARIUM, on Skidaway Island at 30 Ocean Science Cir., features saltwater aquariums displaying local marine life with additional exhibits focusing on the ecology, marine science, archeology and fossils of the coastal region. A self-guiding nature trail and boardwalk winds through maritime forest and salt marsh ecosystems. The 680-acre property, formerly portions of two plantations, is shared with the Skidaway Institute of Oceanography.

Picnicking is permitted. Mon.-Fri. 9-4, Sat. noon-5; closed major holidays. Admission $4; $2 (ages 3-12 and senior citizens). Phone (912) 598-3474 or (912) 598-2496.

WORMSLOE STATE HISTORIC SITE, 10 mi. s.e. at 7601 Skidaway Rd. on the Isle of Hope, was established in 1736 by Noble Jones, one of 114 colonists who came to Georgia with Gen. James E. Oglethorpe. The vestiges of his fortified tabby house, constructed 1739-45, are all that remain architecturally in Savannah of Georgia's first decade. A 1.5-mile oak-lined avenue leads to the plantation's ruins. A museum presents excavated artifacts and an audiovisual show about early settlement in Georgia.

Allow 1 hour minimum. Tues.-Sat. 9-5, Sun. 2-5:30; closed Jan. 1, Thanksgiving and Dec. 25. Admission $4; $3.50 (ages 62+); $2.50 (ages 6-18). AX, DC, DS, MC, VI. Phone (912) 353-3023.

SAVANNAH NATIONAL WILDLIFE REFUGE—*see Port Wentworth p. 90. and attraction listing in Hardeeville, S.C., p. 261.*

SEA ISLAND—*see Golden Isles p. 81.*

SOCIAL CIRCLE (C-3) pop. 3,379, elev. 861′

WINERIES

- **Fox Vineyards Winery**, I-20 exit 98, then 1 mi. s. to 225 SR 11S. Wed.-Sat. 10-6, Sun. 1-6; closed Jan. 1, Easter, Thanksgiving and Dec. 25. Phone (770) 787-5402.

STATESBORO (D-5) pop. 22,698, elev. 258′

Statesboro was established in 1803 and by 1902 it was shipping one-eighth of the world's supply of cotton. It remains a regional commercial and industrial center but it is also a center for higher education. Founded in 1906, the pine-studded, gently rolling 630-acre campus of Georgia Southern University is home to 15,000 students seeking traditional 4-year, graduate and doctoral degrees. Founded in 1991, Ogeechee Technical College's focused curriculum allows nearly 3,000 students the opportunity to pursue career-oriented studies.

Statesboro Convention & Visitors Bureau: 332 S. Main St., P.O. Box 1516, Statesboro, GA 30459; phone (912) 489-1869 or (800) 568-3301.

THE CENTER FOR WILDLIFE EDUCATION & THE LAMAR Q. BALL, JR. RAPTOR CENTER is on the campus of Georgia Southern University at Forest Dr. and Southern Dr. The center comprises almost 18 acres and features 11 species of eagles, falcons, hawks, owls and vultures in natural habitats. Indoor exhibits and weekend shows present a variety of birds and reptiles. A 12-acre wetland preserve focuses on ornithology and water resource conservation.

Picnicking is permitted. Mon.-Fri. 9-4:45, Sat. 1-5, Sept.-May; Mon.-Fri. 9-4:45, rest of year. Weekend reptile shows at 2 and raptor shows at 3. Closed holidays. Donations. Phone (912) 681-0831.

GEORGIA SOUTHERN BOTANICAL GARDEN, 1 mi. s. on SR 67 to 1505 Bland Ave., features 11 acres of nature trails and native flora. The focal point of the garden is the 1920s Bland Cottage, which houses a visitor center. Allow 30 minutes minimum. Garden open daily 9-dusk. Bland Cottage Visitor Center open Mon.-Fri. 10-4, Sun. 1-4. Closed holidays and academic breaks. Free. Phone (912) 871-1149.

GEORGIA SOUTHERN MUSEUM is in the Rosenwald Building on Southern Dr. on the grounds of Georgia Southern University, .5 mi. s. on US 301/25. This museum interprets the natural and cultural history of Georgia's coastal plain emphasizing the relationship between ancient and modern oceans. The main attraction is a 26-foot Mosasaur skeleton believed to be about 78 million years old. A replica of a 40 million-year-old whale skeleton is displayed. Two additional galleries present a variety of temporary exhibits.

Allow 1 hour minimum. Mon.-Fri. 9-5, Sat.-Sun. 2-5; closed holidays. Free. Phone (912) 478-5444.

STOCKBRIDGE (C-2) pop. 9,853, elev. 812′

PANOLA MOUNTAIN STATE CONSERVATION PARK, 9 mi. e. on SR 138, then 4 mi. n. on SR 155, encompasses a 100-acre granite mountain that shelters plants and animals indigenous to the Piedmont region. The 1,500-acre park offers a 30-acre play area, a 12-mile nature trail, a fishing lake and an interpretive center with displays about the natural history of the area. Nature programs and guided hikes for five or more persons are offered. Self-guiding hikes are permitted on three trails, but due to conservation concerns, hikes up the mountain are always guided.

Picnicking is permitted. Park open daily 7 a.m.-dusk. Nature center and park office open daily 8:30-5. Guided hikes (groups of five or more) Wed.-Fri. by reservation only. Admission $3 per private vehicle. Guided hikes $5. Phone (770) 389-7801.

STONE MOUNTAIN—*see Atlanta p. 62.*

TALLULAH FALLS (A-3)

pop. 164, elev. 1,629′

Near the turn of the 20th century, Tallulah Falls was a resort area with scenery and a mountain climate that brought visitors from other parts of Georgia and neighboring states.

TALLULAH GORGE STATE PARK, within the city limits at 11785 US 441N, offers 20 miles of trails including a 1.5-mile walking trail along the rim of Tallulah Gorge, a sheer-walled, 1,000-foot-deep crevice with waterfalls and lush vegetation. Overlooks at various points along the trail offer views of geologic formations as well as native flora and fauna. The Jane Hurt Yarn Interpretive Center offers presentations about history and safety. Entry to the gorge floor is by permit only, obtainable at the interpretive center.

Park open daily 8-dusk. Beach area daily 8-dusk, Memorial Day-Labor Day. Parking $4 per private vehicle; free (Wed.). Phone (706) 754-7970. *See Recreation Chart and the AAA Southeastern CampBook.*

THOMASVILLE (F-3) pop. 18,162, elev. 290′

Thomasville was spared most of the ravages of the Civil War. Afterward, railroad lines were repaired and Northerners soon were traveling south to enjoy the mild winter climate of the high pinelands; it was believed that the pine-scented air was of therapeutic value. By the 1880s Thomasville had become a popular winter resort with some of the country's finest hotels.

The winter residents brought money to this small town and left behind community improvements and a collection of shooting plantations, as they called their mansions. The Lapham-Patterson House Museum *(see attraction listing)* is an example of the fine Victorian "cottages" built during this period throughout the town.

One of the oldest residents of Thomasville is Big Oak, on the corner of E. Monroe and N. Crawford streets. Dating from the late 17th century, the tree is 68 feet high, with a trunk circumference of 24 feet and a limb spread of 162 feet.

Thomasville-Thomas Co. Visitor Center: Municipal Building at jct. Jackson and Crawford, Thomasville, GA 31792; phone (229) 228-7977 or (866) 577-3600.

Self-guiding tours: Visitor guides that include details about walking/driving tour of Thomasville's historic districts are available at the visitor center.

LAPHAM-PATTERSON HOUSE STATE HISTORIC SITE is at 626 N. Dawson St. Each room in this restored, asymmetrical, 1884 Victorian house is a different shape, and none is square. The house, built as a winter cottage for prosperous merchant C.W. Lapham, was late-19th-century state-of-the-art, with a gas lighting system, indoor plumbing with hot and cold running water, modern closets, a cantilevered balcony and an unusual double-flue chimney with a walk-through stairway.

Picnicking is permitted. Guided 45-minute tours begin on the hour Tues.-Sat. and Mon. holidays 9-5, Sun. 2-5:30; closed Jan. 1, Thanksgiving, Dec. 25 and the Tues. following Mon. holidays. Last tour begins at 4. Fee $5; $4.50 (ages 62+); $2.50 (ages 6-18). Phone (229) 225-4004.

PEBBLE HILL PLANTATION is 5 mi. s. on US 319. The former winter retreat of the Hanna family of Cleveland, Ohio, Pebble Hill has extensive grounds and a lavish main house typical of late 19th- and early 20th-century homes built in the area by wealthy Northerners. Extensive collections of sporting art, antiques, Audubon prints and American Indian relics are displayed in the main house. Grounds highlights include the stable complex, antique automobiles and carriages, and gardens.

Picnic facilities are available. Allow 2 hours minimum. Grounds open Tues.-Sat. 10-5, Sun. 1-5. Optional guided house tours Tues.-Sun. 10-3:45. Closed Jan. 1, Thanksgiving and Dec. 24-25. Last house tour begins at 3:45. Grounds $5; $2 (ages 0-11). Main house tour, not including grounds, $10; $4 (ages 6-12). Under grade 1 are not admitted to the main house. AX, MC, VI. Phone (229) 226-2344.

SAVE **THOMAS COUNTY MUSEUM OF HISTORY** is at 725 N. Dawson St. Museum exhibits depict the area's history and document the transformation of the county's antebellum cotton plantations into quail-hunting plantations. The museum consists of six historic buildings, including an 1860 log house, the 1893 Ewart bowling alley, the 1893 Metcalfe Courthouse and the 1910 Flowers Playhouse.

Allow 1 hour, 30 minutes minimum. Tours depart Mon.-Sat. 10-11:30 and 2-3:30; closed last two weeks of Aug. and major holidays. Admission $5; $1 (ages 0-17). Credit cards are not accepted. Phone (229) 226-7664.

THOMASVILLE CULTURAL CENTER, 600 E. Washington St., is housed in a restored 1915 Italianate elementary school. Highlights include 14-foot ceilings and hardwood floors. The center contains fine arts exhibitions and a 500-seat auditorium where concerts are held. Allow 30 minutes minimum. Mon.-Fri. 9-5, Sat. 1-5; closed holidays. Phone ahead for concert schedule. Cultural center free. Admission charged for concerts. Phone (229) 226-0588.

TIFTON (E-3) pop. 15,060, elev. 370′

Tifton was founded in 1890 and named for Nelson Tift, Georgia representative to the U.S. Congress 1868-69. Pecans, peanuts, tomatoes and honey are important to the region's agricultural base.

Tifton-Tift County Chamber of Commerce: 100 Central Ave., P.O. Box 165, Tifton, GA 31793; phone (229) 382-6200.

AGRIRAMA, GEORGIA'S MUSEUM OF AGRICULTURE & HISTORIC VILLAGE is off I-75 exit 63B at 1392 Whiddon Mill SAVE Rd. This agriculture museum and outdoor living-history village depicts life in the 1870-1910 era. Costumed interpreters operate the exhibits and discuss life in the region at that time. Visitors may ride a steam-powered logging train around the site.

The 35 structures on the 95-acre site includes the Tift House, a steam-powered sawmill, a cotton gin, farmhouses, blacksmith shop, 19th-century drugstore, Masonic hall, water-powered gristmill, newspaper office and turpentine still with cooper's shed. Events include the Folk Life Festival in April, the Old Fashioned Independence Day Celebration in July, and a Cane Grinding Party and Victorian Christmas Celebration in December.

Camping is available. Agrirama open Tues.-Sat. 9-5 (weather permitting); closed Thanksgiving, day after Thanksgiving and Dec. 24-Jan. 2. Admission $7; $6 (ages 55+); $4 (ages 4-16). AX, DS, MC, VI. Phone (229) 386-3344 or (800) 767-1875.

TOCCOA (A-3) pop. 9,323, elev. 1,045′

A mountain community bounded by the Chattahoochee National Forest *(see place listing p. 68)* and Lake Hartwell, Toccoa is significant in its military and American Indian history. During World War II, paratroopers trained at nearby Camp Toccoa and 1,740-foot-tall Currahee Mountain. In the 1700s, the area was the center of the Cherokee Nation.

Toccoa now is a popular vacation area and offers fishing, hunting, swimming, boating and water recreation. Toccoa Falls College, a four-year private institution with an enrollment of 925, offers guided campus tours; phone (888) 785-5624 to confirm tour schedule.

Toccoa-Stephens County Chamber of Commerce: 160 N Alexander St., P.O. Box 577, Toccoa, GA 30577; phone (706) 886-2132.

TOCCOA FALLS is 2 mi. n.e. on Alt. SR 17 on the campus of Toccoa Falls College, a short walk from the Gate Cottage. The 186-foot falls are one of the highest free-falling waterfalls east of the Mississippi River. Visitors have enjoyed this scenic spot since the early 1800s. Toccoa comes from a Cherokee word meaning "beautiful." Mon.-Sat. 8:30-6:30; Sun. noon-5. Admission $1; 50c (ages 60+); free (ages 0-12). Phone (706) 886-6831, ext. 5215.

TRAVELER'S REST HISTORIC SITE, 5 mi. e. off US 123 on Riverdale Rd., dates from 1815. Devereaux Jarrett, a Georgia planter and businessman, bought the dwelling in 1833 and expanded it not only to accommodate his family but also to serve as a stagecoach inn. The center of a thriving plantation, the structure became known as Traveler's Rest. At one time, it also was home to Mary Jarrett White; the first woman to vote in Georgia. The restored inn and plantation house are furnished in period. Special events are offered throughout the year.

Wed.-Sun. and Mon. holidays 9-5; closed Thanksgiving and Dec. 25. Admission $4; $3.50 (ages 62+); $2.50 (ages 6-18). Phone (706) 886-2256.

TUNNEL HILL (A-1) pop. 1,209, elev. 840′

TUNNEL HILL HERITAGE CENTER AND MUSEUM is at 215 Clisby Austin Rd. Displays relate the history of the town and historic 1850 railroad tunnel. The railroad tracks at the heritage center provide excellent opportunities for train viewing. A Civil War reenactment of the Battle of Tunnel Hill also is offered September 1 through first weekend after Labor Day. Allow 30 minutes minimum. Mon.-Sat. 9-5, Sun. 1-5; closed Jan. 1, Thanksgiving and Dec. 24-25. Admission $3; $2 (ages 0-12). Cash or check only is accepted. Phone (706) 876-1571.

TYBEE ISLAND (D-6) pop. 3,392

To visitors who flock to the island's 3 miles of sandy shoreline, Tybee means beach resort, but originally the name came from an American Indian word for salt. The island's strategic location at the mouth of the Savannah River resulted in the construction of a lighthouse in the 1770s and a defensive fortification in the 1880s.

Tybee Island Visitors Center: 802 First St., P.O. Box 491, Tybee Island, GA 31328; phone (912) 786-5444. *See color ad.*

TYBEE ISLAND MARINE SCIENCE CENTER is at the pier between 14th and 16th sts. Hands-on activities at the center provide visitors the opportunity to learn more about marine life in coastal Georgia. Aquariums contain fish and sea creatures indigenous to the south Georgia coast. Other displays include a touch tank and exhibits of shells, sea turtles, sharks, whales and various marine environments. Guided 90-minute beach discovery and marsh discovery walks are available.

Center open daily 10-5. Beach discovery walks depart daily at 10, June-Aug.; Mon., Wed. and Fri. at noon, Sat.-Sun. at 3, rest of year. Marsh discovery walks depart Fri. at 3. Schedule for discovery walks may vary; phone ahead to confirm. Closed Jan. 1, Mar. 17, Thanksgiving, day after Thanksgiving and Dec. 25-26. Admission $4; $3 (ages 3-16). Discovery walks $10; free (ages 0-2). Admission to center is included in walk fee. Reservations are suggested for discovery walks. MC, VI. Phone (912) 786-5917.

TYBEE MUSEUM is off US 80E at 30 Meddin Dr., adjacent to Fort Screven and on the n. end of Tybee Island. The museum is housed in one of the gun batteries of an 1898 fort and chronicles the history and multicultural influences of Tybee Island. Exhibits include paintings, dioramas, dolls, artifacts and historic weapons. A videotape relates the history of Fort Screven. The museum also features ocean views.

Allow 1 hour minimum. Wed.-Mon. 9-5:30; closed Jan. 1, St. Patrick's Day, Thanksgiving and Dec. 25. Last admission 1 hour before closing. Admission (includes Tybee Lighthouse) $6; $5 (ages 6-17, ages 62+ and military with ID). MC, VI. Phone (912) 786-5801.

Tybee Lighthouse, off US 80E at the n. end of Tybee Island at 30 Meddin Dr., is purported to be the tallest and oldest lighthouse in Georgia. This 1867 structure, built atop the lower 60 feet of the 1773 light, still has all support buildings intact on the 5-acre site. Among these are a fully restored keeper's house, which is open for tours, a summer kitchen and a fuel storage building. Ascending 178 stairs to the top of the lighthouse affords panoramic views of the ocean and Tybee Island.

Allow 1 hour minimum. Wed.-Mon. 9-5:30; closed Jan. 1, St. Patrick's Day, Thanksgiving and Dec. 25. Last admission 1 hour before closing. Admission (includes Tybee Museum) $6; $5 (ages 6-17, ages 62+ and military with ID). MC, VI. Phone (912) 786-5801.

VALDOSTA (F-3) pop. 43,724, elev. 215′

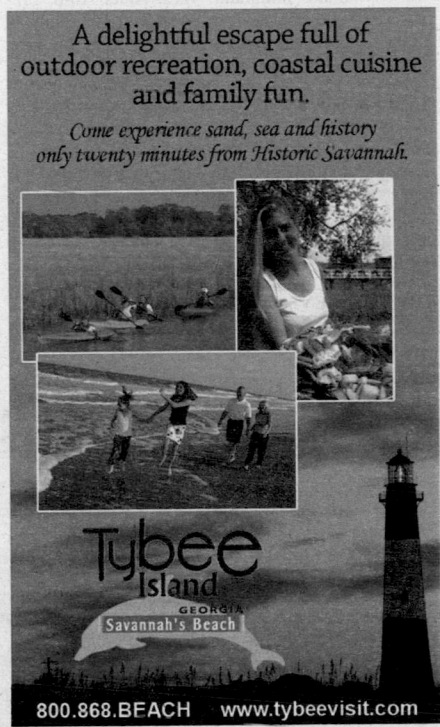

Valdosta's history is linked with transportation growth and a strategic location in the path of early westward expansion. Originally called Troupville, the settlement was designated a county seat in 1837. When it became evident that Troupville would not be on a proposed 1860 railroad route from Savannah to Mobile, Ala., the townsite was moved to take advantage of the potential prosperity. Troupville citizens renamed the town Valdosta for the governor's home Val de Aosta, or "Vale of Beauty."

The city has three historic districts featuring commercial and residential buildings of the Victorian era.

Valdosta-Lowndes County Conference Center and Tourism Authority: 1 Meeting Pl., Valdosta, GA 31601; phone (229) 245-0513 or (800) 569-8687.

Self-guiding tours: A brochure describing a driving tour of Valdosta's three historic districts can be obtained from the conference center and tourism authority.

Shopping areas: The Lake Park Outlets at I-75 exit 5 contains factory outlet shops. Anchor stores at the Valdosta Mall on SR 94W are Belk, JCPenney and Sears.

ANNETTE HOWELL TURNER CENTER FOR THE ARTS, 527 N. Patterson St., displays various types of art on a rotating monthly basis. The center's six galleries feature emerging and recognized local, national and international talent, with an emphasis on professional artists. Guided tours are available. Allow 30 minutes minimum. Tues.-Thurs. 10-6, Fri.-Sat. 10-4; closed Jan. 1-2, Memorial Day, July 4, Labor Day, Thanksgiving and last week in Dec. Free. Phone (229) 247-2787.

BARBER HOUSE, 416 N. Ashley St., was built by one of the early bottlers and promoters of Coca-Cola. The restored 1915 neoclassical mansion is decorated with late 19th-century furnishings. A home until 1977, the structure now houses the chamber of commerce. Allow 30 minutes minimum. Self-guiding tours Mon.-Fri. 8:30-5; closed major holidays. Free. Phone (229) 247-8100.

THE CRESCENT, 904 N. Patterson St., is a stately neoclassical mansion with a crescent-shaped tile and marble porch supported by 13 columns representing the 13 original Colonies. The 23-room 1898 house built by Sen. W.S. West is furnished in period. The house has a large ballroom and orchestra room, ornate woodwork, numerous fireplaces and a wide, curving stairway. An octagonal kindergarten schoolhouse, a chapel and five gardens complete the complex. Allow 30 minutes minimum. Mon.-Fri. 2-5; closed holidays. Donations. Phone (229) 244-6747.

LOWNDES COUNTY HISTORICAL SOCIETY AND MUSEUM, 305 W. Central Ave., has photographs, documents and memorabilia reflecting the development of Valdosta and the surrounding area. Among the displayed documents is an original Confederate secession decree. Period clothing, antique handworks, and city directories dating from 1904 are displayed along with an exhibit about John Henry "Doc" Holliday, who lived in the area in his youth. A genealogical library also is available. Allow 1 hour minimum. Mon.-Fri. 10-5, Sat. 10-2; closed holidays. Donations. Phone (229) 247-4780.

WILD ADVENTURES is off I-75 exit 13, then 4 mi. s. to 3766 Old Clyattville Rd. Offering more than 60 rides including nine roller coasters, Wild Adventures also features wild animals, shows, concerts by well-known entertainers, special events and a petting zoo. Splash Island Water Park, included in Wild Adventures admission, features water slides, a wave pool, a lazy river and a wet-play area. Go-carts and miniature golf are available for an additional fee.

Food is available. The park opens daily at 10, Memorial Day to mid-Aug.; open weekends and select days, rest of year. Closing time varies. Schedule may vary; phone ahead. Closed Thanksgiving and Dec. 25. Regular admission (includes second day free) $45; $40 (ages 3-9 and 55+). Parking $7-$9. AX, DS, MC, VI. Phone (229) 219-7080.

WARM SPRINGS (C-2) pop. 485, elev. 930'

The legendary curative powers of Warm Springs have lured the hopeful for centuries. Wounded American Indian warriors gathered at the springs before Europeans colonized the New World. In the late 1700s the springs were discovered by yellow fever victims, and by 1832 Warm Springs had become a popular summer health resort. The resort survived the torch of Gen. William Tecumseh Sherman only to be reduced to ashes by a runaway bonfire in 1865. Rebuilt, Warm Springs flourished in the 1880s and 1890s and was incorporated in 1893.

After contracting polio, Franklin Delano Roosevelt visited the springs in 1924 hoping to improve his health. A few years later he established the Warm Springs Foundation for the care and treatment of fellow polio victims who could not afford such medical help.

Although Warm Springs' popularity as a resort waned after Roosevelt's death, restoration efforts have attracted visitors who come to browse through the crafts shops housed in former grocery and dime stores. Artisans can be seen at work in more than 60 stores, and musicians and cloggers perform on the stage of the old Pavilion during events and on weekends.

FDR Warm Springs Welcome Center: 1 Broad St., Warm Springs, GA 31830; phone (706) 655-3322 or (800) 337-1927.

GEM **FDR'S LITTLE WHITE HOUSE STATE HISTORIC SITE** is .2 mi. s. on US 27A. Built by President Franklin Roosevelt in 1932, the Little White House was the site of his death on April 12, 1945, and is now a memorial shrine. Many of FDR's visionary programs were conceived within the walls of this house. A guest house, servant's quarters and garage also are on the grounds. One mile away is the Historic Pools Complex, where a small museum relates the story of the springs and of the town.

The self-guiding tour brochure also is available in French, Spanish, German and Japanese. Picnic facilities are available. Daily 9-4:45; closed Jan. 1, Thanksgiving and Dec. 25. Admission (includes site, memorial museum and pool museum) $7; $6 (ages 62+); $4 (ages 6-18). AX, DC, DS, MC, VI. Phone (706) 655-5870.

Franklin D. Roosevelt Memorial Museum is adjacent to Roosevelt's Little White House. The 11,000-square-foot museum features exhibits about Roosevelt's life and political career. Visitors can see his parade stagecoach, his hand-controlled 1938 Ford convertible and can listen to radio recordings of his "Fireside Chats." A film narrated by Walter Cronkite shows footage of FDR visiting his Warm Springs neighbors. Roosevelt died after suffering a stroke while posing for a portrait; the "Unfinished Portrait" is displayed.

Picnicking is permitted. Daily 9-4:45; closed Jan. 1, Thanksgiving and Dec. 25. Admission (includes site, memorial museum and pool museum) $7; $6 (ages 62+); $4 (ages 6-18). AX, DC, DS, MC, VI. Phone (706) 655-5870.

WARM SPRINGS NATIONAL FISH HATCHERY, s. on SR 41 to 5308 Spring St., also is a wildlife and wetlands habitat. The hatchery currently focuses its efforts on fish species in the southeastern United States. Although visitors see a variety of fish, research and management activities focus on striped bass, sturgeon, paddlefish and robust suckers. The hatchery features an aquarium and two outdoor display pools, a display of carnivorous plants, a nature trail and an enclosed wetland area containing two American alligators. Allow 30 minutes minimum. Daily 8-4; closed federal holidays. Free. Phone (706) 655-3382.

WARNER ROBINS (D-3)

pop. 48,804, elev. 381'

GEM SAVE **MUSEUM OF AVIATION,** 10 mi. e. of I-75 exit 144 to jct. SR 247 and Russell Pkwy., features more than 100 aircraft, missiles and cockpits and 200,000 square feet of indoor exhibits housed in four buildings. Aircraft displays include a B-1B bomber, F-4D MiG killer, U-2 spy plane, MiG-17, SR-71 Blackbird, F-15 Eagle, B-29 and a 60-foot cutaway replica of a B-17 bomber. Exhibits describe the World War II D-Day Invasion, CBI Hump pilots of World War II, Tuskegee Airmen, Gen. Robert L. Scott Jr. and the 14th Air Force Flying Tigers. A motion simulator allows visitors to experience 15 flying missions. The Georgia Aviation Hall of Fame recognizes commercial and military aviation greats from across the state.

Picnicking is permitted. Food is available. Comfortable walking shoes are advised. Allow 3 hours minimum. Daily 9-5; closed Jan. 1, Thanksgiving and Dec. 25. Museum free. Motion simulator $5. Phone (478) 926-6870. *See color ad.*

WASHINGTON (B-4) pop. 4,295, elev. 630′

Washington was established and designated temporary capital of Georgia in 1780. The town has antebellum Greek Revival mansions as well as Colonial-style houses dating from the days following the Revolution; some are occupied by descendants of the original owners. Tree-shaded streets bear such patriotic names as Jefferson and Liberty.

The Battle of Kettle Creek, the decisive battle of the Revolutionary War in Georgia, was fought west of town in 1779. A granite marker at the southwest corner of the courthouse indicates the location of the meeting that dissolved the government of the Confederacy on May 4, 1865.

Washington-Wilkes Chamber of Commerce: 29 W. Public Square, P.O. Box 661, Washington, GA 30673; phone (706) 678-2013.

CALLAWAY PLANTATION is 5 mi. w. on US 78 at 2160 Lexington Rd., across from the airport. This restored plantation includes an 1869 manor house, a smokehouse, a cemetery and a one-room schoolhouse. A 1785 hewn-log house, which was a settler's home, features domestic and agricultural implements. A 1790s two-story Federal Plainstyle house and an 1869 red brick Greek Revival house are furnished in period. These houses depict the increasing wealth and comfort of succeeding generations of a pioneer family.

Guided 45-minute tours leave on the hour Tues.-Sat. 10-5; closed Jan. 1, Thanksgiving and Dec. 25. Last tour leaves at closing. Admission $4; $2 (ages 5-12). MC, VI. Phone (706) 678-7060.

ROBERT TOOMBS HOUSE STATE HISTORIC SITE, 216 E. Robert Toombs Ave./Bus. Rte. 78, is the former home of the Confederate Secretary of State who was instrumental in leading Georgia to secession and war. The state has carefully restored the structure to its condition at the time of Toombs' death in 1885. The antebellum house displays furnishings once owned by the Toombs family. A 25-minute film relates Toombs' life.

Picnicking is permitted. Allow 1 hour minimum. Tues.-Sat. and Mon. holidays, 9-5; closed Jan. 1, Thanksgiving and Dec. 25. Admission $3; $2.50 (ages 62+); $1.50 (ages 6-18). Phone (706) 678-2226.

WASHINGTON HISTORICAL MUSEUM is at 308 E. Robert Toombs Ave./Bus. Rte. 78. Built about 1835, this museum houses antique furnishings and Confederate relics, including Jefferson Davis' camp chest. Tues.-Sat. 10-5, Sun. 12:30-3:30; closed major holidays. Admission $3; $2 (ages 6-12). Phone (706) 678-2105.

WAYCROSS (E-4) pop. 15,333, elev. 135′

Known as the "crossing of the ways" in the mid- to late 19th century because of the intersection of several railroad lines, Waycross has maintained its railroad heritage. At Rice Yard, the largest classification facility in the country, freight cars are organized into trains to move shipments across the nation. Other industries in the area include lumber and related concerns, manufactured housing, tobacco and pecan farming, bee culture and the production of honey. The town is at the northern entrance to the Okefenokee National Wildlife Refuge *(see attraction listing p. 73)*.

Waycross Tourism Bureau/Visitors Center: 315-A Plant Ave., Waycross, GA 31501; phone (912) 283-3744.

SAVE **OBEDIAH'S OKEFENOK,** US 82W to Gillmore St., then 8.5 mi. s. to 5115 Swamp Rd., offers a self-guiding tour, a 1,100-foot boardwalk through the Okefenokee Swamp, 75 wildlife exhibits and an 1870s homestead containing various exhibits and displays. Allow 1 hour, 30 minutes minimum. Daily 10-5; closed Easter and Dec. 25. Admission $4.50; $3.50 (ages 55+); $3 (ages 6-17). Phone (912) 287-0090.

OKEFENOKEE HERITAGE CENTER, 2 mi. n.w. via US 1/23, then 4 blks. w. to 1460 N. Augusta Ave., has an art gallery that features permanent and changing exhibits about history and the arts. The museum includes a late 19th-century printshop, a restored 1912 steam locomotive, train cars, a railroad depot and a restored 1840s farmhouse.

Allow 1 hour minimum. Tues.-Sat. 10-4:30; closed major holidays. Admission $3; free (ages 0-5). Phone (912) 285-4260.

SAVE **OKEFENOKEE SWAMP PARK** is 8 mi. s.e. on US 1/23, then 4.7 mi. s. on SR 177 to 5700 Okefenokee Swamp Park Rd. This 1,600-acre wildlife sanctuary on Cowhouse Island is the northern entrance to the Okefenokee Swamp *(see Folkston p. 73)*. The park features flower and seasonal butterfly gardens, a wilderness walkway and educational centers. Optional guided boat tours and rental canoes offer up-close looks at plants and wildlife. A 1.5-mile railroad provides transportation around the park. The Swamp Creation Center has dioramas, charts and animated exhibits explaining the swamp's evolution. The Living Swamp Ecological Center has a wildlife observation room and a carnivorous plant collection. The Nature Center includes a bear observatory and the animatronic "Okefenokee Bear Review." Outdoor museum displays at Pioneer Island pertain to the history of the swamp's early settlers.

Picnicking is permitted. Food is available. Park open daily, 9-5:30; closed Thanksgiving and Dec. 24-25. Optional guided boat tours ranging from 30 minutes to 1 hour depart daily (depending on water level and guide availability). Park $12; $11 (ages 3-11, ages 62+ and active military with ID). Combination park admission and boat tours $16-$30. Ask about boat tour refund policies. MC, VI. Phone (912) 283-0583.

SOUTHERN FOREST WORLD MUSEUM, 2 mi. n.w. via US 1/23, then 4 blks. w. to 1440 N. Augusta Ave., next to the Okefenokee Heritage Center, contains exhibits about the history of forestry in the

South. Visitors can walk up the inside of a 38-foot-tall model of a loblolly pine, step inside a giant cypress, listen to a talking tree or sit in the cab of a 1905 logging locomotive. Allow 30 minutes minimum. Wed.-Sat. 10-2; closed major holidays. Admission $3; free (ages 0-4). Phone (912) 285-4260.

WEST POINT (C-1) pop. 3,382, elev. 576′

Because of its strategic location on the Chattahoochee River at the Alabama state line, West Point was considered the key to the granary of the Tennessee Army during the Civil War. Word of Gen. Robert E. Lee's surrender was slow to reach the town, and the last battle east of the Mississippi River, the Battle of Fort Tyler, was fought a week after the war's official end.

Recovery after the war was ensured with the construction of two textile mills that eventually expanded into what is now WestPoint Home Inc., one of the world's largest textile manufacturing companies.

North of West Point is West Point Lake *(see Recreation Chart and the AAA Southeastern CampBook)*, a 25,900-acre man-made site offering a variety of recreational pursuits. A visitor center, 4 miles north off US 29, contains dioramas, photographs and a slide show describing the history of the region before, during and after construction of the dam that created the lake.

Greater Valley Area Chamber of Commerce: Write P.O. Box 205, Lanett, AL 36863; phone (334) 642-1411.

WHITE (B-1) pop. 693, elev. 856′

TELLUS: NORTHWEST GEORGIA SCIENCE MUSEUM is at 100 Tellus Dr. The museum has 125,000 square feet of exhibit space dedicated to minerals, fossils, transportation technology and interactive science displays. It also houses a 120-seat digital planetarium, a 200-seat theater, science trails and outdoor learning centers for hands-on exploration.

Note: The museum is currently closed; it is scheduled to re-open in late fall 2008. Phone ahead to confirm. Allow 30 minutes minimum. Mon.-Sat. 10-5; closed major holidays. Admission $4; $3.50 (ages 55+); $3 (ages 6-11). Hours and prices will increase for 2009; both were unable to be confirmed before going to press. Phone (770) 386-0576.

North Carolina

Blue Ridge & Smoky Mountains
Trails over rolling hills and through dense woods beckon nature lovers

Biltmore
Stroll through acres of vibrant gardens that surround Vanderbilt's stately 250-room château

Four National Forests
The Croatan, Nantahala, Pisgah and Uwharrie paint the state with green

Old Salem
An 18th-century atmosphere is preserved and celebrated

First in Flight
A memorial on the Outer Banks honors aviation pioneers Orville and Wilbur Wright

North Carolina Arboretum, Blue Ridge Parkway, south of Asheville

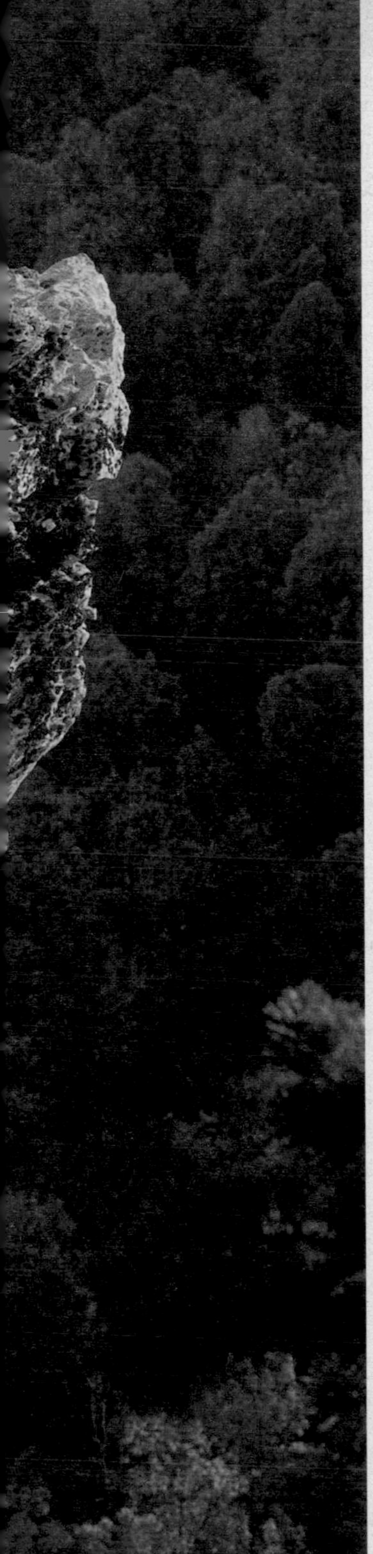

Hanging Rock State Park, Danbury
© Brian Sytnyk / Masterfile

When you set foot onto Tarheel soil, you will realize the meaning of the state motto, "esse quam videri"; to be rather than to seem. Culture, history and nature present themselves here in Kodachrome—genuine and vibrant.

Feel your heart beat in sync with the drums as you watch Cherokee Indian dancers, adorned in vivid native dress, perform the Eagle Dance. Attend an outdoor drama where the backdrop is a living canvas of mountains. At Seagrove, witness Carolina potters spin the wheel as they shape mounds of clay into whiskey jugs.

Trace the steps of residents of the first English settlement in America at Fort Raleigh. Imagine day-to-day life along the Pamlico River as you peek into Colonial homes and churches in pre-Revolutionary Bath.

Nature rules the roost in this state, where spring blossoms of white dogwoods fill nearly every nook. Gaze at mountains that embody such varied adjectives as craggy, rolling, smoky and bald. Marvel at waterfalls and rainbows of wildflowers.

Experience North Carolina. It not only *seems* sublime, it is.

Visit North Carolina for the simple, stunning beauty of it. The state is a carefully composed symphony of natural and man-made wonders. Mother Nature not only smiled on the northern of the two Carolina sisters; she spoiled her like an only child.

She played artiste in the northwest, mixing her color palette until the greens became blues and land became sky. So tall that they mingle with the clouds, the Smoky Mountains are blanketed with a bluish fog that protects still lakes, steep cliffs and carpets of fir trees. More colors dazzle us: Dotted with yellow and blue wildflowers, the mountains turn instantly cheerful in spring. Deep reds and golds flare in mid-October.

Falling water plummets, trickles, cascades and glides over cliffs and rocks throughout the central portion of the mountain region, creating a soothing melody. It's standing room only at Pisgah—one of four national forests—where the trees are so close they rub elbows. Lush valleys and gorges are so deep that the sun only permeates through to the cool clay at high noon.

Follow trails and winding roads to places devoid of footprints. Dig through nature's treasure box to find gold and precious gems. Dip your hand into waters where the fish jump to greet you. Smell the pungent pines. Listen to the rustle of deer's hooves and the echo of songbirds.

Miles of Sandy Shores

Mother Nature was a bit more tame with the coast, although no less spectacular. She shaped a coastal plain unfolding into smooth beaches and, as an afterthought, added a ribbon of barrier islands. The Outer Banks—including Cape Hatteras and Cape Lookout national seashores—form a broken strand of islands coddling the mainland.

Standing on the white sand, there is a distinct feeling that you can see as far south as Miami. Days begin with stretches of orange across the horizon and fade to puffs of clouds against a pink and purple sky. Windblown sand dunes, scattered grasslands, woods and marshlands display nature's different personalities. Wild ponies roam Ocracoke Island, nibbling on grass without a care; monarch butterflies flutter from flower to flower in late summer.

A sense of mystery pervades the coast through legends and stories. No one can be certain of the fate of the so-named "Lost Colony" that Sir Walter Raleigh established

North Carolina Historical Timeline

1585 Sir Walter Raleigh, under the sponsorship of Queen Elizabeth I, establishes a colony on Roanoke Island.

Library of Congress

1590 Gov. John White, in charge of a second colony, sails to England for supplies and upon his return finds no trace of the settlement.

1650s Virginia colonists make the first permanent settlement on Albemarle Sound.

1775 Mecklenburg County citizens meet in Charlotte and draw up a declaration of independence from England.

1789 North Carolina becomes the twelfth state.

on Roanoke Island; within 2 years it had disappeared with little clue save the word "Croatoan" carved into a tree.

Stories of Blackbeard and his visits to Ocracoke lie somewhere between myth and conjecture. It is said that the pirate blazed into battle with his beard bedecked with ribbons and left treasures along the coast.

Discover your own riches. Build a sandcastle. Snorkel in glistening blue waters. Wriggle your toes in the white sand. With a deep breath, take it all in.

Building on Her Blessings

When the setting was complete, North Carolina's people took over by accenting natural gifts with gems of their own.

They carved the Blue Ridge Parkway out of the mountains, creating overlooks that place panoramic vistas in the palm of your hand. Clad in dark green spruce, the scattered peaks of the Black Mountains—fog-topped in the distance—pose for the camera.

George Vanderbilt thought the scenery so inviting that he created a haven for himself. Nestled among acres of woodland, the Biltmore is an enormous replica of a 16th-century French château. Lavishly decorated and surrounded by immaculate gardens, the estate is a showplace that takes full advantage of its natural setting.

Residents also built for function. As much as Biltmore is opulent, Old Salem is modest. The restored 1766 village seems frozen in time; guides demonstrate trades of yesteryear and recall a simpler age.

Settlers shed light on the coastal region by building eight lighthouses that illuminate the barrier islands. These bright-eyed ladies serve as more than beacons to approaching vessels; their showy colors and upright stance contrast with the sandy dunes, tide and horizon. Cape Hatteras Lighthouse, arrayed in sashes of black and white, protects ships from destruction along the "Graveyard of the Atlantic." The tallest of its kind in the country, the brick tower is a regal sight to behold.

North Carolina has been a magnet for visionaries. When Orville and Wilbur Wright decided that the only way to go was up, they built the first powered airplane and flew it at Kitty Hawk. Looking up into the sky, these brothers had visions of grandeur.

What will the view from here do for you?

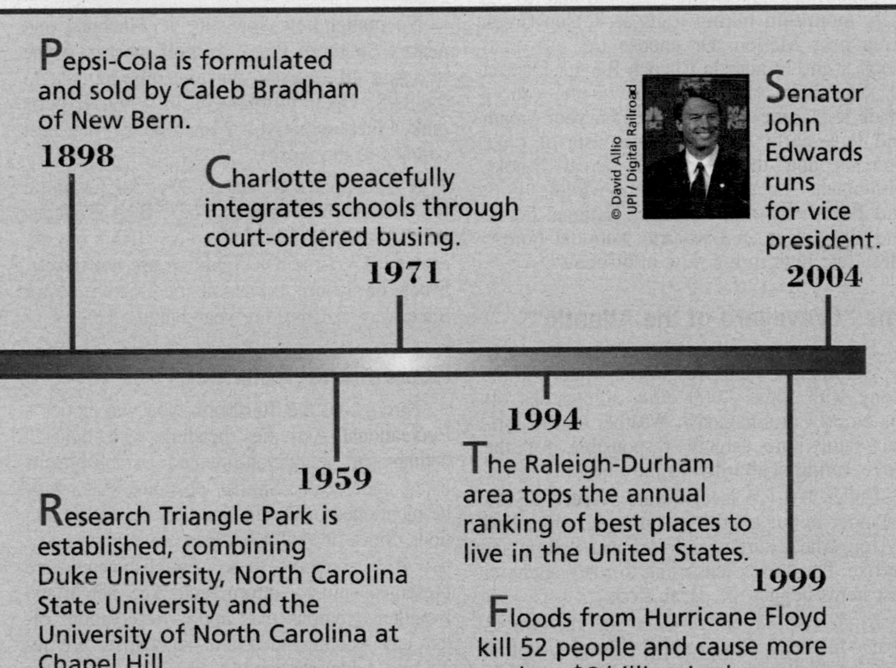

Pepsi-Cola is formulated and sold by Caleb Bradham of New Bern.
1898
Charlotte peacefully integrates schools through court-ordered busing.
1971
© David Allio UPI / Digital Railroad
Senator John Edwards runs for vice president.
2004
1959
Research Triangle Park is established, combining Duke University, North Carolina State University and the University of North Carolina at Chapel Hill.
1994
The Raleigh-Durham area tops the annual ranking of best places to live in the United States.
1999
Floods from Hurricane Floyd kill 52 people and cause more than $6 billion in damages.

Recreation

Ski, hike or bike in the mountains. Kayak, surf or scuba dive in the ocean. Fish, swim or boat in the lakes. With its diverse terrain, the best place to be in North Carolina is *outside.*

Cool lakes throughout the state refresh **swimmers** and **boaters. Campers** travel from across the country to pitch their tents in the unspoiled terrain of North Carolina's four national forests and state parks.

Anglers can cast their lines into lakes and mountain streams throughout the state for bass and rainbow and brook trout. Marlin swim in untamed surf at Oregon Inlet.

Hiking and Biking

Discover terrific trekking on hundreds of **hiking** trails that wind through the Blue Ridge Parkway and Nantahala and Pisgah national forests. The Appalachian Trail also passes through Great Smoky Mountains National Park. Grab a trail map at ranger stations within the parks and mosey to gaps, peaks, falls, balds and rushing streams. Mother Nature spoils spring and fall; reds and golds contrast with a clear blue sky in mid-October, while vivid wildflowers dot the hills in late April.

Don your helmets and pads and take to the hilly **mountain biking** trails at Wilson Creek Area near Marion. Or choose the left Tsali Loop in the Nantahala Cheoah Ranger District in Nantahala National Park. Once you've made it 11 miles to the top, catch your breath and look north for a stunning vista of Lake Fontana and the blue-green Great Smoky Mountains. Locals rave about Middle Fork and Twin Falls trails in Pisgah National Forest and Wood Run in Uwharrie National Forest; these rate high in fun, low in difficulty.

The "Graveyard of the Atlantic"

The *Queen Anne's Revenge,* presumed to be Blackbeard's ship, rests in its watery grave along with some 5,000 other shipwrecks off the North Carolina coast. Weather and historical battles are largely responsible for the trove, luring **scuba divers** into the salty sea.

Under 110-125 feet of water, **wreck divers** meander about encrusted hulls, accompanied by loggerhead turtles and blue and yellow angelfish. Purple sea fans cling to rusty anchors; lost items pepper the ocean floor.

Bottlenose dolphins frolic in the waves near Morehead City on the Crystal Coast, a popular diving departure point. Waters off Oregon Inlet and capes Fear, Hatteras and Lookout also guard waterlogged treasure. Olympus Dive Center arranges excursions; phone (252) 726-9432.

Each gust of wind changes the size and shape of sand dunes at Jockey's Ridge State Park in Nags Head. A hike up one of the tall, swooping dunes is rewarded with a jumping-off point for **hang gliders.** The waters off Nags Head are great for **sea kayaking** as well. Contact Kitty Hawk Kites, phone (877) 359-8447.

If **windsurfing** is more your style, check out the southwesterly winds at Canadian Hole on the Outer Banks, said to be the top choice of east coast windsurfers. Twilight at nearby Windmill Point brings flat water.

Rushing water attracts **rafters** and **kayakers** to Nantahala Falls, a class III rapid on the Nantahala River. Guide service can be secured in nearby Bryson City. Paddling trips on the Pigeon River depart from Marshall.

Skiers and **snowboarders** test the powder at ski slopes in the western part of the state. Runs at Ski Beech in Beech Mountain are open mid-November through March. Or share a bird's eye view with peregrine falcons while **rock climbing** at Whiteside Mountain in Highlands Ranger District.

No matter how you slice it, Pinehurst and nearby Southern Pines are **golf** meccas; home to some 40 courses, the area played host to the U.S. Open tournament in 1999. Experts rank Pinehurst's No. 2 as one of the best courses in the world.

If you prefer to watch, head to Charlotte for **professional sports.** The NBA's Bobcats, WNBA's Sting, NFL's Panthers, IHL's Checkers and AAA-rated Knights all are hot tickets. **Stock cars** burn rubber at the Lowe's Motor Speedway at Charlotte year-round.

Recreational Activities

Throughout the TourBook, you may notice a Recreational Activities heading with bulleted listings of recreation-oriented establishments listed underneath. Similar operations also may be mentioned in Destination City recreation sections. Since normal AAA inspection criteria cannot be applied, these establishments are presented only for information. Age, height and weight restrictions may apply. Reservations often are recommended and sometimes are required. Addresses and/or phone numbers are provided so visitors can contact the attraction for additional information.

Fast Facts

POPULATION: 8,049,313.

AREA: 52,586 square miles; ranks 27th.

CAPITAL: Raleigh.

HIGHEST POINT: 6,684 ft., Mount Mitchell.

LOWEST POINT: Sea level, Atlantic Ocean.

TIME ZONE(S): Eastern. DST.

TEEN DRIVING LAWS: No more than one passenger under age 21 is permitted; family members are exempt. If a family member younger than 21 is a passenger, then non-family passengers under age 21 are not permitted. Driving is not permitted 9 p.m.-5 a.m. The minimum age for an unrestricted driver's license is 16 years and 6 months.

SEAT BELT/CHILD RESTRAINT LAWS: Seat belts required for driver and front seat passengers 16 and older. Children 8 until 16 and over 80 pounds are required to be in a child restraint or seat belt; child restraints required for under age 8 and under 80 pounds.

HELMETS FOR MOTORCYCLISTS: Required.

RADAR DETECTORS: Permitted.

CELL PHONE RESTRICTIONS: Teen drivers are not permitted to use cell phones while driving.

MOVE OVER LAW: Driver is required to slow down and vacate the lane nearest stopped police, fire and rescue vehicles using audible or flashing signals. Law also requires driver to move over for tow truck drivers assisting motorists.

FIREARMS LAWS: Vary by state and/or county. Contact Law Enforcement Liaison Section, Attorney General's Office, P.O. Box 629, Raleigh, NC 27602-0629; phone (919) 716-6400.

HOLIDAYS: Jan. 1; Martin Luther King Jr. Day, Jan. (3rd Mon.); Good Friday (state and national banks only); Memorial Day, May (last Mon.); July 4; Labor Day, Sept. (1st Mon.); Veterans Day, Nov. 11; Thanksgiving; Christmas, Dec. 25.

TAXES: North Carolina's statewide sales tax is 4.5 percent, with local options for an additional 2.5 to 3 percent. Localities may impose a Room Occupancy Tax of varying percentages.

INFORMATION CENTERS: State welcome centers are found on I-85S near Kings Mountain; I-85N near Norlina; I-95N near Roanoke Rapids; I-95S near Rowland; I-77N near Dobson; I-77S near Charlotte; I-26 near Columbus; and I-40W near Waynesville. Information, free brochures and picnic and rest area facilities are available. Centers are open daily 8-5; closed federal holidays.

FURTHER INFORMATION FOR VISITORS:

Travel & Tourism Division
4301 Mail Service Center
Raleigh, NC 27699-4301
(919) 733-4151

RECREATION INFORMATION:

North Carolina Division of Parks and Recreation
1615 Mail Service Center
Raleigh, NC 27699-1615
(919) 733-4181

FISHING AND HUNTING REGULATIONS:

North Carolina Wildlife Resources Commission
1707 Mail Service Center
Raleigh, NC 27606
(919) 707-0007

NATIONAL FOREST INFORMATION:

U.S. Forest Service
160 Zillicoa St., Suite A
Asheville, NC 28801
(828) 257-4200
(877) 444-6777 (campground reservations only)

ROAD AND FERRY INFORMATION:

North Carolina Department of Transportation, Public Information Office, Customer Service Office
1503 Mail Service Center
Raleigh, NC 27699-1503
(919) 733-3109

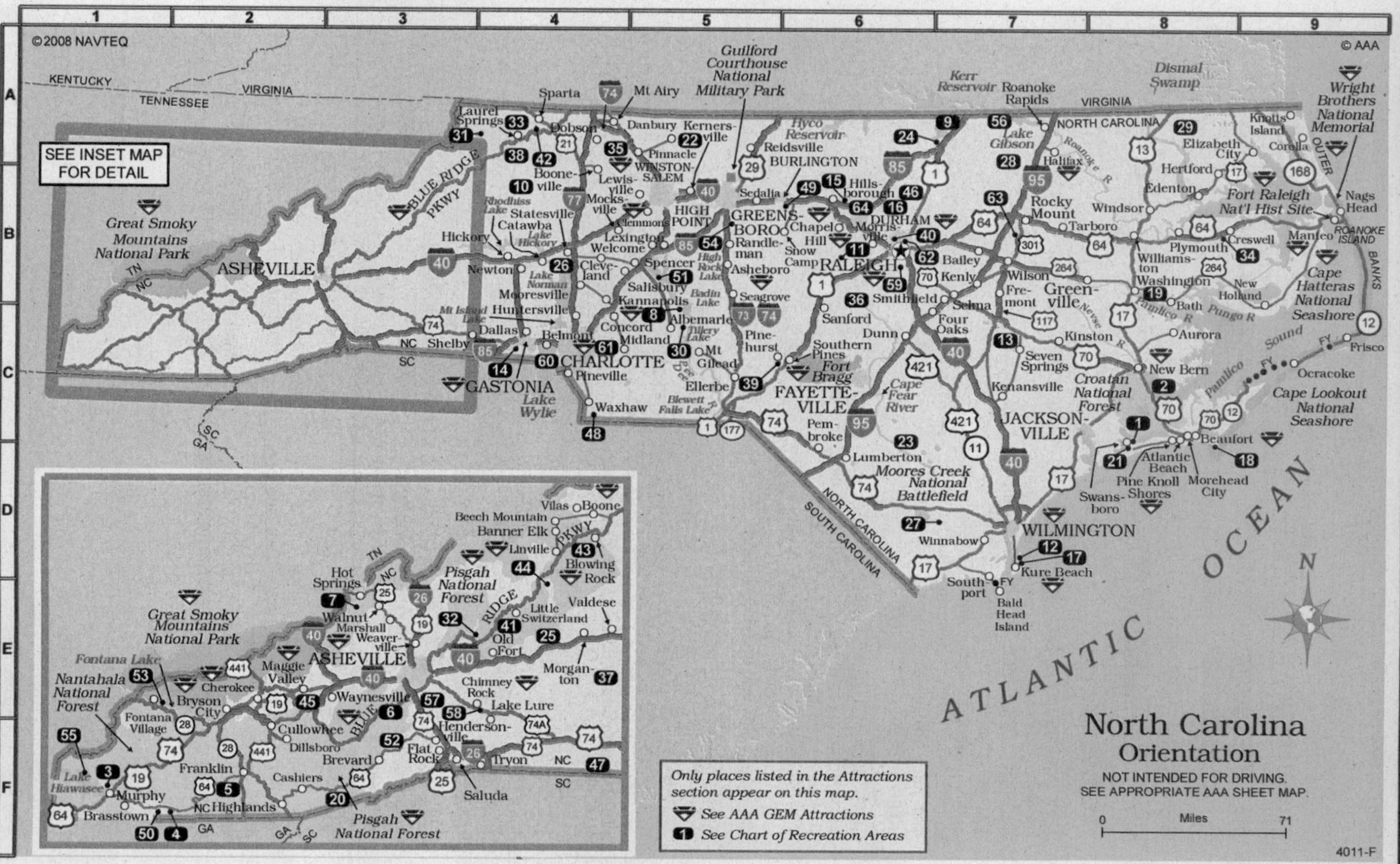

North Carolina
Orientation
NOT INTENDED FOR DRIVING.
SEE APPROPRIATE AAA SHEET MAP.
Miles
0
71
4011-F
© AAA
©2008 NAVTEQ
Only places listed in the Attractions section appear on this map.
See AAA GEM Attractions
See Chart of Recreation Areas
SEE INSET MAP FOR DETAIL
ATLANTIC
OCEAN
N
KENTUCKY
TENNESSEE
VIRGINIA
NORTH CAROLINA
SOUTH CAROLINA
Great Smoky Mountains National Park
ASHEVILLE
BLUE RIDGE PKWY
Laurel Springs
Sparta
Mt Airy
Dobson
Danbury
Kernersville
Pinnacle
WINSTON-SALEM
Booneville
Lewisville
Mocksville
Clemmons
Statesville
Catawba
Hickory
Newton
Mooresville
Huntersville
Dallas
Shelby
Belmont
GASTONIA
Lake Wylie
CHARLOTTE
Pineville
Waxhaw
Concord
Midland
Kannapolis
Salisbury
Spencer
Lexington
Welcome
Cleveland
HIGH POINT
GREENSBORO
Randleman
Asheboro
Seagrove
Albemarle
Mt Gilead
Ellerbe
Pinehurst
Southern Pines
Fort Bragg
FAYETTEVILLE
Pembroke
Lumberton
Moores Creek National Battlefield
Cape Fear River
Guilford Courthouse National Military Park
Hyco Reservoir
Reidsville
BURLINGTON
Sedalia
Hillsborough
Chapel Hill
Snow Camp
DURHAM
Morrisville
RALEIGH
Bailey
Kenly
Smithfield
Selma
Four Oaks
Dunn
Sanford
Kerr Reservoir
Roanoke Rapids
Lake Gibson
Halifax
Rocky Mount
Tarboro
Wilson
Fremont
Greenville
Kinston
Seven Springs
Kenansville
JACKSONVILLE
Croatan National Forest
New Bern
Windsor
Williamston
Washington
Bath
Aurora
Dismal Swamp
Elizabeth City
Hertford
Edenton
Plymouth
Creswell
New Holland
Knotts Island
Corolla
OUTER BANKS
Wright Brothers National Memorial
Nags Head
Fort Raleigh Nat'l Hist Site
Manteo
ROANOKE ISLAND
Cape Hatteras National Seashore
Frisco
Ocracoke
Pamlico Sound
Cape Lookout National Seashore
Beaufort
Morehead City
Atlantic Beach
Pine Knoll Shores
Swansboro
WILMINGTON
Kure Beach
Winnabow
Southport
Bald Head Island
Vilas
Boone
Beech Mountain
Banner Elk
Linville
Blowing Rock
Pisgah National Forest
Hot Springs
Walnut
Marshall
Weaverville
Little Switzerland
Valdese
Old Fort
Morganton
Fontana Lake
Nantahala National Forest
Maggie Valley
Cherokee
Bryson City
Fontana Village
Waynesville
Cullowhee
Dillsboro
Chimney Rock
Lake Lure
Hendersonville
Flat Rock
Brevard
Tryon
Saluda
Franklin
Cashiers
Highlands
Lake Hiwassee
Murphy
Brasstown
Pisgah National Forest

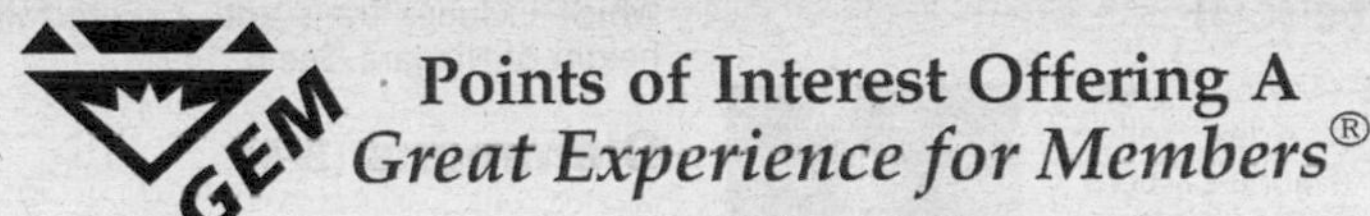

Points of Interest Offering A *Great Experience for Members®*

Asheboro (B-5)

NORTH CAROLINA ZOOLOGICAL PARK—More than 1,100 animals from two continents reside at the zoo in such habitats as a tropical forest, free-flight aviary, prairie, rocky coast and desert. See p. 124.

Asheville (E-3)

BILTMORE—Tours of George Washington Vanderbilt's spectacular 250-room French Renaissance-style château include the upstairs and downstairs, 75 acres of formal gardens, the conservatory and the winery. See p. 126.

Beaufort (C-8)

NORTH CAROLINA MARITIME MUSEUM—Exhibits at the museum are devoted to the state's coastal history and include ship models, birds and fish, fossils, decoys and saltwater aquariums. See p. 129.

Belmont (C-4)

DANIEL STOWE BOTANICAL GARDEN— Lush gardens, an 8,000-square-foot conservatory, a winding trail and 12 fountains create a polychromatic paradise. See p. 130.

Blowing Rock (D-4)

TWEETSIE RAILROAD—A ride on a restored narrow-gauge, coal-fired steam railroad takes visitors to the railroad town, which contains a jail, blacksmith shop and an 1880s general store. Watch out for train robbers along the way! See p. 130.

Blue Ridge Parkway

BLUE RIDGE PARKWAY—The scenic route offers stunning vistas of the Blue Ridge and surrounding mountain ranges. See p. 131.

MOUNT MITCHELL STATE PARK—The park is named for Dr. Elisha Mitchell, who fell to his death while attempting to ascend the 6,684-foot summit. See p. 133.

NORTH CAROLINA ARBORETUM—The 434-acre arboretum boasts 65 acres of gardens, 10 miles of forested recreational trails, a state-of-the-art greenhouse production facility and an impressive bonsai collection. See p. 134.

Boone (D-4)

"HORN IN THE WEST"—This musical drama takes the stage in an outside amphitheater. Costumed guides re-enact the lifestyle of early settlers in an 18th-century log village. See p. 134.

Bryson City (E-2)

GREAT SMOKY MOUNTAINS RAILROAD—Enjoy a spectacular train journey over bridges and through tunnels to view dramatic river gorges and lush valleys. See p. 135.

Cape Hatteras National Seashore (B-9)

CAPE HATTERAS NATIONAL SEASHORE—Two lighthouses and a wildlife refuge are highlights of this 45-mile stretch of sand. See p. 174.

Chapel Hill (B-6)

MOREHEAD PLANETARIUM AND SCIENCE CENTER—Having served as a NASA training center, the planetarium contains art and science exhibits. See p. 137.

Charlotte (C-4)

CAROWINDS—Various areas include water rides, roller coasters, Hanna-Barbera characters and a 16-story free-fall ride. See p. 143.

CHARLOTTE MUSEUM OF HISTORY AND HEZEKIAH ALEXANDER HOMESITE—Three hundred years of Carolina history are brought to life at this museum, which features a restored 1774 back-country house and the American Freedom Bell. See p. 144.

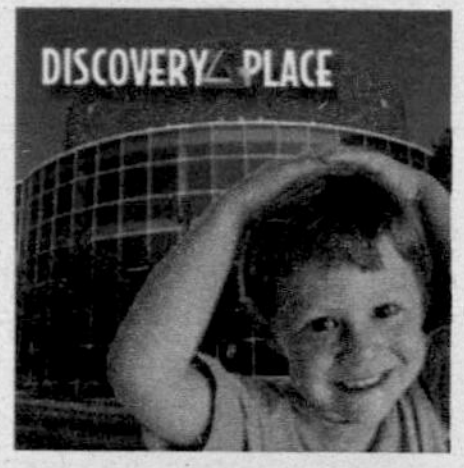

DISCOVERY PLACE—Hands-on exhibits focus on physiology, science, technology and nature. A rain forest, space station, planetarium, touch pools and an IMAX theater are included. See p. 144.

HENDRICK MOTORSPORTS MUSEUM—Two decades of HMS racing is represented within this 67-acre complex. Visitors may view exhibits including trophies and memorabilia as well as the construction of a race car from start to finish. See p. 144.

LEVINE MUSEUM OF THE NEW SOUTH—Interactive, multisensory exhibits interpret the history of the South since the Civil War in a way that is engaging to all who visit. See p. 144.

MINT MUSEUM OF ART—Housed in what served as the first branch of the U.S. Mint, the museum's collection includes American and European art, period costumes and pre-Columbian and African items. See p. 145.

Cherokee (E-2)

OCONALUFTEE INDIAN VILLAGE—Visitors are privy to American Indian craft demonstrations, a botanical garden, a council house, huts, cabins and nature trails. See p. 149.

"UNTO THESE HILLS"—A 2-hour outdoor historical drama depicts the tragic story of the Cherokees and their journey from Georgia to Oklahoma, known as The Trail of Tears. See p. 149.

Chimney Rock (E-4)

CHIMNEY ROCK PARK—A giant granite rock overlooking a lush gorge is the focus of the park, which includes trails and a waterfall twice the height of Niagara. See p. 149.

Clemmons (B-4)

TANGLEWOOD—This 1,400-acre park offers golf, tennis, nature trails, horseback riding and picnicking. See p. 149.

Durham (B-6)

DUKE UNIVERSITY CHAPEL—Housed in the chapel are the Flentrop Organ and a 50-bell carillon. See p. 152.

Fayetteville (C-6)

AIRBORNE AND SPECIAL OPERATIONS MUSEUM—Walk through time and experience the adventure, bravery and history of the U.S. Army's elite airborne and special operations forces. See p. 153.

Fort Raleigh National Historic Site (B-9)

ELIZABETHAN GARDENS—A memorial to the first English colonists in America, the gardens are modeled after a 16th-century formal English garden. See p. 177.

"THE LOST COLONY"—The outside drama portrays the disappearance of a short-lived colony on Roanoke Island established by Sir Walter Raleigh. See p. 178.

Gastonia (C-4)

THE SCHIELE MUSEUM OF NATURAL HISTORY—Found in the museum are a large collection of North American mammals, items relating to American Indian lifestyles, a back-country farm and a planetarium. See p. 155.

Great Smoky Mountains National Park

GREAT SMOKY MOUNTAINS NATIONAL PARK—The trademark blue haze that hangs over the park gives way to peaks, balds, gorges, varied plant life and streams. See p. 156.

Greensboro (B-5)

GREENSBORO HISTORICAL MUSEUM—The museum contains a reconstructed 19th-century village, two restored houses, a military history collection and an array of memorabilia. See p. 162.

Halifax (A-7)

HISTORIC HALIFAX STATE HISTORIC SITE—Guided tours take visitors through the center of the old town and include numerous significant town buildings. See p. 163.

Kannapolis (B-4)

CANNON VILLAGE VISITOR CENTER—The center features the Fieldcrest Cannon Textile Museum and Exhibition, which includes one of the world's largest towels, an antique hand loom and samples of textiles that are more than 1,200 years old. See p. 166.

Kure Beach (D-7)

NORTH CAROLINA AQUARIUM AT FORT FISHER—The aquarium features interactive exhibits and presentations that focus on aquatic life in the Cape Fear region and the ocean beyond. See p. 168.

Linville (D-4)

GRANDFATHER MOUNTAIN—When seen from the north, the peak resembles a bearded grandfather gazing toward the sky. See p. 169.

Maggie Valley (E-2)

WHEELS THROUGH TIME MUSEUM—The museum displays an impressive collection of vintage motorcycles and automobiles, dating 1903 to the present, along with thousands of artifacts that enhance each exhibit. See p. 169.

Manteo (B-9)

ROANOKE ISLAND FESTIVAL PARK, HOME OF *ELIZABETH II*—Living-history interpreters engage visitors with a compelling blend of facts, tales and legends while exhibits convey more than 400 years of Outer Banks history. See p. 179.

New Bern (C-8)

TRYON PALACE HISTORIC SITES & GARDENS—Home of Royalist governor William Tryon, the palace is furnished with period antiques, while the grounds display 18th-century English gardens. See p. 172.

Pine Knoll Shores (D-8)

NORTH CAROLINA AQUARIUM AT PINE KNOLL SHORES—Five of the state's aquatic zones are represented in the 93,000-square-foot aquarium, which is designed around the theme "From the Mountains to the Sea." See p. 181.

Pisgah National Forest

PISGAH NATIONAL FOREST—Roads and trails traverse the forest, which contains at least 20 massive peaks, a waterfall and an immense granite monolith. See p. 181.

Raleigh (B-6)

MARBLES KIDS MUSEUM—Through interactive exhibits and the Internet, this museum connects visitors to the world. See p. 182.

NORTH CAROLINA MUSEUM OF ART—Eight exhaustive collections span 5 centuries of Western art. See p. 184.

NORTH CAROLINA MUSEUM OF HISTORY—Exhibits depict state history from pre-Colonial through contemporary times. See p. 184.

NORTH CAROLINA MUSEUM OF NATURAL SCIENCES—From Venus flytraps to dinosaurs, the state's diverse geology, geography, plant life and wildlife are presented. See p. 184.

NORTH CAROLINA STATE CAPITOL—Completed in 1840, the restored Capitol is an example of the Greek Revival style of architecture and a fine symbol of the evolution of government in North Carolina history. See p. 184.

Wilmington (D-7)

BATTLESHIP *NORTH CAROLINA*—The ship earned 15 battle stars in World War II and now serves as a memorial to North Carolina service personnel who died in the war. See p. 191.

Winston-Salem (A-5)

OLD SALEM—The Moravian church town has been restored to its 18th-century appearance and functions as a living-history community complete with costumed interpreters who demonstrate crafts and trades. A self-guiding tour includes approximately 15 buildings. See p. 194.

REYNOLDA HOUSE MUSEUM OF AMERICAN ART—The beauty of the grounds, the museum and its collections is magical and founded upon smoke, not smoke and mirrors. See p. 195.

Wright Brothers National Memorial (A-9)

WRIGHT BROTHERS NATIONAL MEMORIAL—Dedicated "in commemoration of the conquest of the air," the visitor center displays replicas of the 1902 glider and 1903 flyer. See p. 180.

RECREATION AREAS

	MAP LOCATION	CAMPING	PICNICKING	HIKING TRAILS	BOATING	BOAT RAMP	BOAT RENTAL	FISHING	SWIMMING	PETS ON LEASH	BICYCLE TRAILS	NATURE PROGS.	VISITOR CENTER	LODGE/CABINS	FOOD SERVICE
NATIONAL PARKS *(See place listings)*															
Great Smoky Mountains (E-2) 520,000 acres. Horse rental.		•	•	•				•		•		•	•	•	
NATIONAL FORESTS *(See place listings)*															
Croatan 159,586 acres. Southeastern North Carolina.		•	•	•	•	•		•	•	•	•				
Cedar Point (C-8) 260 acres 1.25 mi. n. jct. SRs 24 and 58, 3 mi. s.e. of Swansboro.	1	•	•	•	•	•		•		•					
Neuse River (C-8) 240 acres 10 mi. s. of New Bern on US 70E.	2	•	•	•				•	•		•				
Nantahala 527,486 acres. Southwestern tip of North Carolina.		•	•	•	•	•		•	•	•	•				
Hanging Dog (F-1) 21 acres 5 mi. n.w. of Murphy on SR 1326.	3	•	•	•	•	•		•		•					
Jackrabbit Mountain (F-2) 28 acres 10 mi. n.e. of Hayesville via US 64, SR 175 and SR 1155.	4	•	•	•	•	•		•	•	•					
Standing Indian Mountain (F-2) 9 mi. w. of Franklin on US 64, 2 mi. e. on old US 64, then 2 mi. s. on FR 67.	5	•	•	•				•		•					
Pisgah 504,787 acres. Western North Carolina.		•	•	•	•			•	•	•	•	•	•		
Lake Powhatan (E-3) 30 acres 7 mi. s.w. of Asheville on SR 191 and FR 3484.	6	•	•	•				•	•	•	•	•			
Rocky Bluff (E-3) 10 acres 3 mi. s. of Hot Springs on SR 209.	7	•	•	•				•		•					
Uwharrie 50,189 acres. Central North Carolina.		•	•	•	•	•		•	•	•	•				
Badin Lake (C-5) 9,540 acres 10 mi. n. of Troy on SR 109.	8	•	•	•	•	•		•	•	•					
NATIONAL SEASHORES *(See place listings)*															
Cape Hatteras (C-9) 75 miles along the Outer Banks.		•	•	•	•	•		•	•	•		•	•	•	•
Cape Lookout (C-9) 55 miles along the Outer Banks.		•	•		•			•	•			•	•	•	
ARMY CORPS OF ENGINEERS															
John H. Kerr Reservoir (A-7) 106,860 acres n. of Henderson on the Virginia border off I-85. Water skiing.	9	•	•	•	•	•	•	•	•	•		•	•		
W. Kerr Scott Dam and Reservoir (B-4) 1,470 acres 4 mi. w. of Wilkesboro on SR 268W.	10	•	•	•	•	•		•	•	•		•	•		
STATE															
B. Everett Jordan (B-6) 47,000 acres 10 mi. w. of Apex off US 64.	11	•	•	•	•	•	•	•	•	•		•		•	•
Carolina Beach (D-7) 420 acres 1 mi. n.w. of Carolina Beach off US 421.	12	•	•	•	•	•		•		•		•	•		•
Cliffs of the Neuse (C-7) 751 acres 3 mi. w. on SR 55, then 2 mi. n. on SR 111. Scenic. Canoeing. *(See Seven Springs p. 187)*	13	•	•	•	•			•	•	•		•			•
Crowders Mountain (C-4) 2,587 acres 6 mi. w. of Gastonia off US 29/74 on SR 1125.	14	•	•	•	•		•	•		•		•			•
Eno River (B-6) 2,635 acres 3 mi. n.w. of Durham off CR 1569. Canoeing.	15	•	•	•				•		•		•			
Falls Lake (B-6) 38,000 acres 13 mi. n. of Raleigh off SR 50.	16	•	•	•	•	•	•	•	•	•	•	•			•
Fort Fisher (D-7) 287 acres 5 mi. s. of Carolina Beach off US 421.	17			•				•	•	•		•	•		•
Fort Macon (D-9) 389 acres 2 mi. e. on SR 1190. Historic. *(See Atlantic Beach p. 128)*	18		•	•				•	•	•		•	•		•
Goose Creek (B-8) 1,596 acres 8 mi. e. of Washington on US 264.	19	•	•	•	•	•		•	•	•		•	•		

RECREATION AREAS

RECREATION AREAS	MAP LOCATION	CAMPING	PICNICKING	HIKING TRAILS	BOATING	BOAT RAMP	BOAT RENTAL	FISHING	SWIMMING	PETS ON LEASH	BICYCLE TRAILS	NATURE PROGS.	VISITOR CENTER	LODGE/CABINS	FOOD SERVICE
Gorges (F-3) 7,200 acres in Sapphire at jct. SR 281S and US 64. Horseback riding; rare plant species, waterfall overlook.	20	•	•	•				•	•	•	•	•			
Hammocks Beach (D-8) 927 acres 4 mi. s. via SR 24 and ferry. Scenic. Shelling. *(See Swansboro p. 188)*	21	•	•	•				•	•	•		•	•		•
Hanging Rock (A-5) 6,457 acres 4 mi. n.w. off SR 89. Scenic. *(See Danbury p. 151)*	22	•	•	•	•		•	•	•	•		•	•	•	•
Jones Lake (C-6) 2,208 acres 4 mi. n. of Elizabethtown off SR 242.	23	•	•	•	•	•	•	•	•	•		•			•
Kerr Lake (A-6) 6,200 acres 11 mi. n. of Henderson on the Virginia border off I-85.	24	•	•	•	•	•	•	•	•	•		•	•	•	•
Lake James (E-4) 595 acres 5 mi. n.e. of Marion on SR 126. Canoeing.	25	•	•	•	•	•	•	•	•	•		•			•
Lake Norman (B-4) 32,510 acres n.w. of Huntersville off I-77.	26	•	•	•	•	•	•	•	•	•	•	•	•		•
Lake Waccamaw (D-6) 10,670 acres 6 mi. s. of Lake Waccamaw off US 74/76.	27	•	•	•				•		•		•	•		
Medoc Mountain (A-7) 2,287 acres 15 mi. s.w. of Roanoke Rapids via SR 40, then 2 mi. w. on SR 561.	28	•	•	•				•		•		•			
Merchants Millpond (A-8) 3,233 acres 6 mi. n.e. of Gatesville on SR 1403. Canoeing.	29	•	•	•			•	•		•		•			
Morrow Mountain (C-5) 4,742 acres 5 mi. e. via SR 24/27/73 and SR 1719 (near Badin). Scenic. *(See Albemarle p. 123)*	30	•	•	•	•	•	•	•	•	•		•	•	•	
Mount Jefferson (A-3) 489 acres 1.5 mi. s. of Jefferson off US 221.	31		•	•						•		•			
Mount Mitchell (E-3) 1,878 acres 35 mi. n.e. via the Blue Ridge Pkwy. and SR 128 at Milepost 355. Scenic. *(See Blue Ridge Parkway p. 133)*	32	•	•	•						•		•	•		•
New River (A-4) 1,488 acres 8 mi. s.e. of Jefferson via SR 88. Canoeing.	33	•	•	•		•		•		•		•			
Pettigrew (B-9) 17,743 acres 8 mi. s. via US 64. Scenic. *(See Creswell p. 150)*	34	•	•	•	•	•		•		•	•	•			
Pilot Mountain (A-4) 3,703 acres 24 mi. n. of Winston-Salem off US 52. Mountain climbing.	35	•	•	•				•		•		•			
Raven Rock (B-6) 3,549 acres 6 mi. n.w. of Lillington off US 421. Historic. Scenic. Horse trails.	36	•	•	•				•		•		•			
South Mountains (E-4) 11,660 acres 13 mi. s. of Morganton on CR 1904.	37	•	•	•				•		•	•	•			
Stone Mountain (A-4) 13,670 acres 7 mi. s.w. of Roaring Gap off US 21. Mountain climbing.	38	•	•	•				•		•		•	•		•
Weymouth Woods-Sandhills Nature Preserve (C-5) 755 acres 2 mi. s. of Southern Pines off US 1 on SR 2074.	39		•	•						•		•	•		
William B. Umstead (B-6) 5,337 acres 10 mi. n.w. of Raleigh off US 70 or 11 mi. w. on I-40. Canoe rental.	40	•	•	•			•	•	•	•	•	•	•		
BLUE RIDGE PARKWAY *(See place listing p. 131)*															
Crabtree Meadows (E-4) 253 acres at Milepost 340.	41	•	•	•						•		•			•
Doughton (A-4) 6,000 acres at Milepost 239.	42	•	•	•				•		•		•		•	•
Julian Price Memorial (D-4) 4,200 acres at Milepost 297. Horse trails.	43	•	•	•	•		•	•		•		•			
Linville Falls (D-4) 995 acres at Milepost 316.	44	•	•	•				•		•		•	•		
Mount Pisgah (E-2) 680 acres at Milepost 409.	45	•	•	•						•		•		•	•
OTHER															
Blue Jay Point (B-6) 234 acres in Raleigh 9 mi. n. on Six Forks Rd. from I-440, then following signs. Educational exhibits, garden area, playgrounds.	46		•	•				•		•		•	•		
Broad River Greenway (F-4) 436 acres 3 mi. s. of Boiling Springs on SR 150. Canoeing, tubing, flat-bottom boats only.	47			•	•	•	•	•	•	•	•	•			
Cane Creek (C-4) 1,050 acres 14 mi. s. of Monroe off SR 200.	48	•	•	•	•	•	•	•	•	•	•	•	•		•

RECREATION AREAS

RECREATION AREAS	MAP LOCATION	CAMPING	PICNICKING	HIKING TRAILS	BOATING	BOAT RAMP	BOAT RENTAL	FISHING	SWIMMING	PETS ON LEASH	BICYCLE TRAILS	NATURE PROGS.	VISITOR CENTER	LODGE/CABINS	FOOD SERVICE
Cedarock Park (B-6) 414 acres at 3916 R. Dean Coleman Rd. Historic. Canoeing, disc golf, hiking, kayaking, mountain biking, tent camping; horse trails. *(See Burlington p. 136)*	49	●	●	●				●			●				
Chatuge Lake (F-1) 7,050 acres 5 mi. e. of Hayesville via US 64.	50	●	●	●	●	●	●	●	●	●			●	●	●
Dan Nicholas (B-5) 350 acres 8 mi. s.e. of Salisbury on Bringle Ferry Rd. Tennis, paddleboats.	51	●	●	●	●		●	●		●		●	●		
DuPont State Forest (F-3) 10,400 acres 11 mi. w. of Hendersonville on US 64 to Crab Creek Rd., then 4.3 mi. s. to DuPont Rd., following signs. Boats with electric motors only. Bicycling, mountain biking; horse trails, waterfalls.	52		●	●	●			●		●					
Fontana Lake (E-1) 10,640 acres 2 mi. e. of Fontana Village. Horse rental, nature trails.	53	●	●	●	●	●	●	●	●	●	●	●	●	●	●
Hagan-Stone (B-5) 409 acres 6.5 mi. s. of Greensboro on US 421, then w. 2 mi. on park road.	54	●	●	●	●		●	●	●	●		●			●
Hiwassee Lake (F-1) 6,090 acres 15 mi. w. of Murphy via SR 294.	55	●	●		●	●	●	●	●	●			●	●	●
Lake Gaston (A-7) 20,300 acres on the Virginia border between I-95 and I-85. Jet skiing, tubing, wakeboarding, water skiing.	56	●	●		●	●		●	●						●
Lake Julian (E-3) 10 mi. s. of Asheville off I-26 on SR 280.	57	●	●		●	●	●	●		●					
Lake Lure (E-3) 1,500 acres 1 mi. e. on US 74. *(See place listing p. 168)*	58	●	●	●	●	●	●	●	●	●				●	●
Lake Wheeler (B-6) 700 acres 6 mi. s.w. of Raleigh via Lake Wheeler Rd.	59		●	●	●	●	●	●		●		●			●
McDowell Nature Preserve (C-4) 1,108 acres at 15222 York Rd. in Charlotte.	60	●	●	●	●	●		●		●		●	●		
Reedy Creek Park (C-4) 116 acres at 2900 Rocky River Rd. in Charlotte.	61		●	●				●		●		●	●		
Shelley Lake/Sertoma Park (B-6) 237 acres in n. Raleigh on W. Millbrook Rd. Boating allowed only on boats rented within park. Bicycle rental.	62		●	●	●		●	●		●	●	●			
Tar River Reservoir (B-7) 1,852 acres 5 mi. w. of Rocky Mount on SR 97, then 2 mi. n. on SR 1745.	63		●		●	●		●	●						●
West Point on the Eno (B-6) 40 acres, 5105 N. Roxboro St. Historic. *(See Durham p. 152)*	64		●	●				●		●	●	●			

North Carolina Temperature Averages Maximum/Minimum

From the records of The Weather Channel Interactive, Inc.

	JAN	FEB	MAR	APR	MAY	JUNE	JULY	AUG	SEPT	OCT	NOV	DEC
Asheville	46/27	50/29	58/36	67/44	74/52	81/60	84/64	83/62	77/56	68/45	58/37	50/30
Cape Hatteras	53/40	54/41	60/46	67/54	74/62	81/69	85/74	84/73	81/69	73/60	64/52	57/44
Charlotte	51/32	56/34	64/42	73/49	80/58	87/66	90/71	88/69	82/63	73/51	63/42	54/35
Raleigh	49/30	53/32	61/40	71/48	78/57	84/65	88/69	86/68	80/62	70/49	61/42	52/33
Winston-Salem	50/29	55/31	63/38	73/45	79/54	86/63	89/67	87/66	82/59	72/47	62/38	53/31

Points of Interest

ALBEMARLE (C-5) pop. 15,680, elev. 456′

Albemarle is on a crest of the Uwharrie Mountains, the worn slopes of which rise more than 1,800 feet and are older than the Appalachians. Founded in 1857 as the seat of Stanly County, Albemarle is an industrial center for textiles, lumber, bricks and aircraft tires.

North of the city in New London is the Cottonpatch Gold Mine, where rockhounds can pan for gold Wednesday through Sunday. Picnicking and camping facilities are available; phone (704) 463-5797.

Stanly County Visitor Center: 245 E. Main St., Albemarle, NC 28002; phone (704) 986-3777.

Self-guiding tours: A walking tour of downtown leads visitors to some 50 historic sites. A brochure featuring a map and description of the sites is available at the visitor center.

MORROW MOUNTAIN STATE PARK is 5 mi. e. via SR 24/27/73 and SR 1719 near Badin. In the Uwharrie Mountains on the Pee Dee River banks, this 4,742-acre park is one of the area's outstanding scenic spots. Information is available at the park office. Daily 8 a.m.-9 p.m., June-Aug.; 8-8, Mar.-May and Sept.-Oct.; 8-6, rest of year. Park office open Mon.-Fri. 8-5. Closed Dec. 25. Free. Phone (704) 982-4402. *See Recreation Chart and the AAA Southeastern CampBook.*

STANLY COUNTY MUSEUM, 245 E. Main St., traces civilization's development in the hills of North Carolina. Exhibits depict American Indian culture, pioneer life, slavery, the Civil War and modern events that shaped regional culture. Two restored 19th-century houses are located on museum grounds. Both feature period furniture and household implements. Allow 1 hour minimum. Tues.-Fri. 10-5, Sat. 10-4; closed holidays. Free. Phone (704) 986-3777.

ASHEBORO (B-5) pop. 21,672, elev. 855′

Once home of the Keyauwee, Saponi and other small American Indian tribes, the Asheboro area was settled about 1740 by German families fleeing European wars. English, Irish and Scottish pioneers soon followed. Asheboro was named for Samuel Ashe, governor of North Carolina 1795-98. The city and its early industries were nurtured by the waters of the Deep and Uwharrie rivers, along which several mills were built.

Situated near Asheboro is the Pisgah Covered Bridge, one of only two accessible covered bridges in the state. Also nearby is the Seagrove pottery region *(see place listing p. 186)*, on US 220, reputedly the nation's largest community of working potters.

The Heart of North Carolina: 222 Sunset Ave., Suite 107, Asheboro, NC 27203-2007; phone (336) 626-0364 or (800) 626-2672.

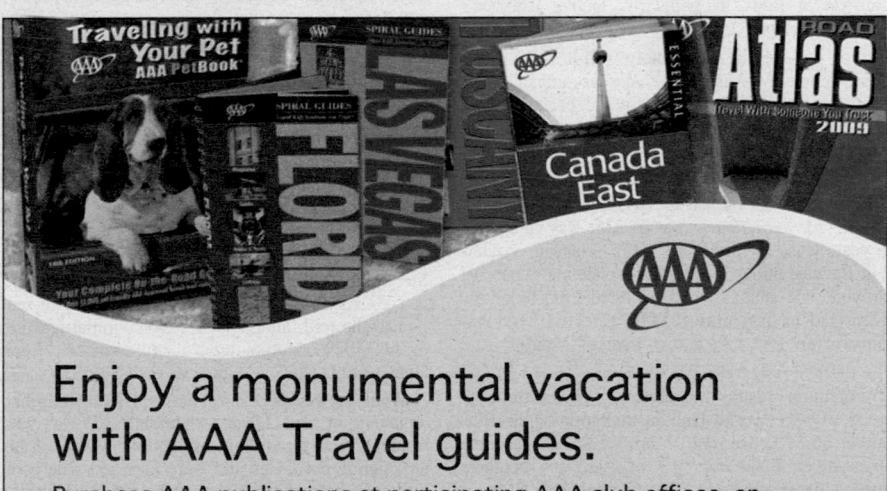

NORTH CAROLINA AVIATION MUSEUM is at the Asheboro Municipal Airport, 3 mi. s. on US 49, then e. on Tot Hill Farm Rd. to 2222-G Pilot View. Operated by the Peddycord Foundation for Aircraft Conservation, this museum focuses primarily on military aviation history. It houses more than a dozen planes from World War II and the Korean War, all of which still fly. The last plane ever flown by Orville Wright is displayed. Allow 1 hour minimum. Mon.-Sat. 10-5, Sun. 1-5; closed major holidays. Admission $5; $3 (students with ID); free (ages 0-6). Phone (336) 625-0170.

GEM SAVE **NORTH CAROLINA ZOOLOGICAL PARK,** 6 mi. s. on SR 159 following signs to 4401 Zoo Pkwy., contains more than 1,100 animals and 60,000 plants from two continents. The climate-controlled African Pavilion, a tropical forest setting, is home to 80 rare and unusual animals and 3,000 plants. A free-flight aviary contains 150 birds and tropical plants.

North American exhibits include a red wolf exhibit; The Prairie, featuring bison and elk in a 12-acre enclosure; Rocky Coast, home to polar bears, sea lions and Alaskan seabirds; and black and grizzly bears. North Carolina Streamside features the state's wildlife from the mountains to the coast and includes fish, snakes, frogs, otters and bobcats. At the Sonora Desert exhibit, visitors can view roadrunners, ocelots and other desert dwellers from the American Southwest.

Allow 3 hours minimum. Daily (weather permitting) 9-5, Apr.-Oct.; 9-4, rest of year. Closed Dec. 25. Admission $10; $8 (ages 62+); $6 (ages 2-12). MC, VI. Phone (336) 879-7200 or (800) 488-0444.

ASHEVILLE (E-3) pop. 68,889, elev. 2,250′

Asheville has been a tourist destination since the days when 19th-century doctors prescribed the city's fresh air, cool climate and abundant sulfur springs as treatments for tuberculosis and other illnesses. By the 1850s Asheville's renown as a health resort had already been established, and after the arrival of the railroad in 1880, its popularity among America's rich and famous soared.

One of Asheville's extremely well-heeled visitors was George W. Vanderbilt, who accompanied his mother here in 1888. Smitten by the beautiful Blue Ridge Mountains, he envisioned building a magnificent country estate in the area, and in 1889 construction of his dream house began.

The 250-room French Renaissance-style Biltmore house *(see attraction listing p. 126)* was completed 6 years later. To furnish his stately château, Vanderbilt traveled throughout Europe collecting expensive artwork and antiques, and he hired Frederick Law Olmstead to transform 125,000 acres of what was mostly farmland into a vast tract of carefully laid out gardens, parks and woods.

For those wealthy travelers who lacked the connections necessary to land an invitation to the Biltmore, the Grove Park Inn was a palatable alternative. Built in 1913 of hand-cut boulders hauled by wagon train from nearby Sunset Mountain, the inn was designed to resemble a rustic lodge, but one offering all the comforts and service of a top-notch hotel and resort. Although the inn has been restored and expanded, it still maintains the elegance it offered to such guests as Thomas Alva Edison, F. Scott Fitzgerald, Henry Ford, generations of Rockefellers and, so far, eight presidents.

Despite the massive scale of the Biltmore and Grove Park Inn, the city's biggest construction boom was still to come. By 1930 Asheville's skyline had been radically transformed by the addition of several impressive buildings, including the 1924 Gothic-style Jackson Building, which dominates Pack Square, the city's bustling center.

Also bordering Pack Square is Asheville's 1928 Art Deco city hall, designed by North Carolina native Douglas Ellington. With its distinctive octagonal, terra-cotta tile roof and chevron accents, city hall has become one of downtown's most recognized landmarks. Ellington also created two other city icons: The ornate 1929 S&W Cafeteria on Patton Avenue, which has been called his Art Deco masterpiece; and the 1927 First Baptist Church on Oak Street, which combines an Italian Renaissance-inspired design with Art Deco details.

Other notable buildings include the Grove Arcade, a 1929 Gothic-style indoor shopping mall at Battery Park and Page avenues that was completely renovated in 2002. The 1909 Basilica of St. Lawrence at 97 Haywood St. has a distinctive tile-and-mortar dome built without an underlying supporting structure. It was designed by Spanish-born builder and architect Rafael Guastavino, who came to Asheville to work on the Biltmore.

A wonderful way to view Asheville's architectural treasures and become acquainted with its history is by strolling along the Asheville Urban Trail. Pink granite markers embedded in sidewalks designate the 1.7-mile loop tour through downtown, and the city has installed 27 artworks along its length that interpret various aspects of Asheville's heritage. For instance, a giant, bronze flat iron stands at the intersection of Wall Street and Battery Park Avenue serving as a whimsical tribute to the adjacent wedge-shaped Flat Iron Building, completed in 1926.

CDs narrating the Urban Trail walking tour can be rented from the Asheville Art Museum *(see attraction listing p. 127)*. Urban Trail maps are available from the art museum, the chamber of commerce and many hotels and galleries throughout downtown; phone (828) 259-5800.

An Urban Trail focal point is the Thomas Wolfe Memorial at 52 N. Market St. *(see attraction listing p. 128)*. Asheville's favorite son merits his own section of the trail, although the town's initial reaction to his 1929 autobiographical masterpiece "Look Homeward, Angel" was far less enthusiastic.

Wolfe set his story in a fictional North Carolina mountain city he called "Altamont," but Asheville residents recognized their city and themselves in his unflattering portrayals and were outraged. The book was even banned for a time from the local library, and Wolfe felt so unwelcome that he stayed away from his hometown until 1937.

Asheville counts two other major 20th-century authors in a reckoning of its literary heritage: F. Scott Fitzgerald was a frequent visitor to the area while his wife, Zelda, was being treated at a local psychiatric hospital. O. Henry (William Porter) married an Asheville native and is buried in the city's Riverside Cemetery not far from Thomas Wolfe. Station four on the Urban Trail features a bronze comb and watch chain set into the pavement, symbols from O. Henry's Christmas story, "The Gift of the Magi."

One thing visitors may notice as they stroll through downtown is how cosmopolitan Asheville is for a city its size. Local bakeries, cafés and bistros offer all the variety one would expect to find in a major metropolis, and even the most jaded palates may encounter new flavors at the handful of trendy eateries serving fusion cuisine.

The area's rich craft tradition is represented by dozens of downtown galleries, and Pack Square is home to three museums. Concerts and cultural

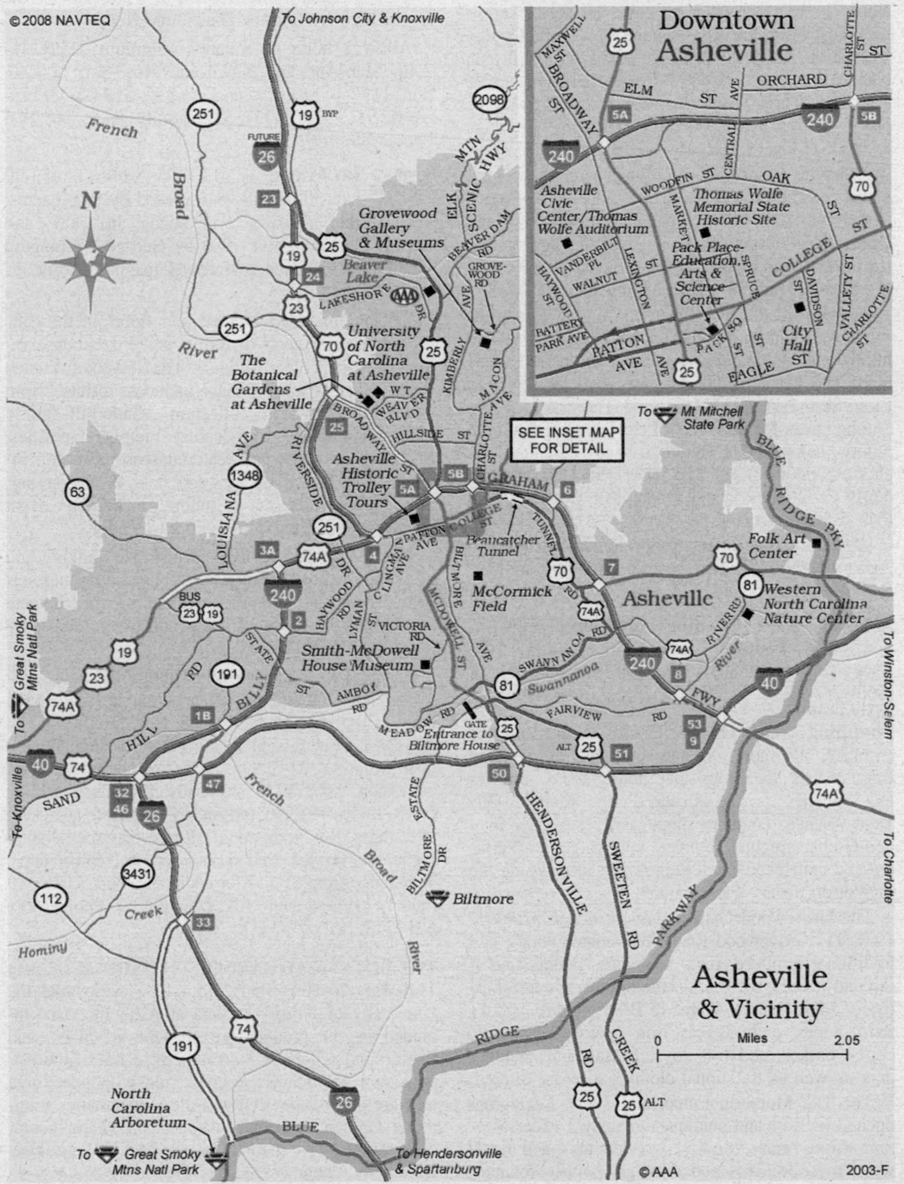

events are presented at several local venues, including the Asheville Civic Center/Thomas Wolfe Auditorium; phone (828) 259-5544. The Diana Wortham Theatre hosts more than 150 performances a year; phone (828) 257-4530. The Asheville Community Theatre has entertained since 1946; phone (828) 253-4931.

While Asheville offers many big-city diversions, its setting between the Blue Ridge and Smoky mountains is what stands out in the minds of most visitors. Many of the area's heavily forested slopes are threaded by winding roads and hiking trails designed to bring travelers to some of North Carolina's most beautiful vistas; phone Buncombe County Recreation Services at (828) 250-4260 or Pisgah National Forest, Pisgah Ranger District, (828) 877-3265. Three scenic highways pass through the city: The Blue Ridge Parkway *(see place listing p. 131)*, US 74 and I-40.

Asheville is divided by two rivers, the Swannanoa and the French Broad. Sections of the French Broad near Asheville are popular for kayaking and white-water rafting. Various adventure and family trips are offered by area outfitters; contact the chamber of commerce for a list of companies.

French Broad River Park, on Amboy Road just off I-240, includes a multi-use track for walking and biking, play and picnic areas and a dog park. Rollerblade and skateboard enthusiasts find fun at Food Lion SkatePark, at Cherry and Haywood streets. Skating areas for all levels of expertise are featured. Safety helmets are required and admission is charged; phone (828) 259-5800. The University of North Carolina at Asheville campus is home to more than 3,000 students.

SAVE Gray Line offers trolley tours of downtown Asheville, the River Arts District, Montford and surrounding areas; phone (828) 251-8687.

Asheville Area Chamber of Commerce/Convention & Visitors Bureau: 36 Montford Ave., Asheville, NC 28801; phone (828) 258-6101 or (800) 257-1300.

Shopping areas: On US 25 next to the Biltmore entrance, Biltmore Village consists of restored English-style dwellings that house shops, eateries and galleries. Grove Arcade Public Market, One Page Avenue, contains shops and restaurants in a neo-Gothic structure complete with gargoyles. Farmers and craftspeople sell their wares just outside the market on Battery Park Square.

The Grovewood Gallery *(see attraction listing p. 127)*, 111 Grovewood Rd., offers contemporary and traditional furniture, rugs, glassware, pottery, clothing and jewelry by some of the Southeast's finest artisans. Mast General Store, 15 Biltmore Ave., stocks retro goods such as cast-iron cookware, pottery, crafts, baskets and folk toys. Hiking and camping gear as well as traditional clothing also are offered.

The T.S. Morrison Emporium, 39 N. Lexington, opened in 1891 and continues to carry a wide selection, from penny candies, wooden toys and hardware, to collectibles and nostalgia items. Mountain crafts, produce and local specialties are offered daily at the 36-acre WNC Farmer's Market, 570 Brevard Rd.

SAVE **ASHEVILLE HISTORIC TROLLEY TOURS** stops at various locations. This sightseeing tour allows passengers to board and exit the trolley at various places that include the Grove Park Inn and Resort, Battery Park, Pack Square and Biltmore Village. Tickets may be purchased at the Chamber of Commerce Visitor Center, the Pack Place, the Renaissance Hotel, the Chelsea Tea Room, the New Morning Gallery, the Haywood Park Hotel, the Grove Park Inn and the Doubletree Hotel.

Allow 1 hour, 30 minutes minimum. Daily 11-2:40, Mar.-Apr. and Nov.-Dec.; Mon.-Sat. 11-4:40, Sun. 11-2:40, rest of year. Fare $19; $18 (senior citizens); $12 (ages 6-17); $45 (family). AX, MC, VI. Phone (888) 667-3600.

GEM **BILTMORE** is on US 25, 3 blks. n. of I-40 exit 50 or 50B. Surrounded by 8,000 acres, the mansion was begun in 1889 and opened Christmas Eve 1895 by George Washington Vanderbilt, grandson of railroad magnate Cornelius Vanderbilt.

Self-guiding tours include four floors of the Biltmore house, 75 acres of formal gardens, a conservatory and the Biltmore Winery. The 250-room French Renaissance-style château includes prints from Vanderbilt's vast art collection, Vanderbilt family china, crystal and 15th-century Flemish tapestries. Special events also are featured seasonally and include GEM Festival of Flowers, held in the spring; and GEM Christmas at Biltmore, a holiday event showcasing the house in yuletide splendor.

Note: All tours involve considerable walking and climbing. Access for physically impaired guests is provided to most parts of the estate, except for some sections of the Biltmore house and the gardens. Reduced admission is offered.

Photography is not permitted inside the house. Allow 4 hours minimum. Estate admission gate open daily 8:30-5, Apr.-Dec. (also 5-8, Nov.-Dec.); 9-4, rest of year. Last admission 1 hour before closing. Winery open Mon.-Sat. 11-7, Sun. noon-7. Estate all-inclusive admission $45; $27 (physically impaired); $22.50 (ages 10-16); $13.50 (physically impaired students); free (ages 0-9 with adult). Rates may be slightly higher on Fri.-Sat. and during seasonal celebrations. Fees range from $7-$17 for additional tours. Under 10 must be with an adult. AX, DS, MC, VI. Phone (800) 543-2961. *See color ad p. 108.*

THE BOTANICAL GARDENS AT ASHEVILLE is at 151 W.T. Weaver Blvd.; from US 19/23, take the University of North Carolina at Asheville exit. Included on the grounds are 10 acres of plants and flowers indigenous to the southern region of the Appalachian Mountains. A creek and a wooded area also are part of the scenery. Allow 30 minutes minimum. Garden open daily dawn-dusk. Visitor center open daily 10-4, second Sat. in Mar. to mid-Dec. Donations. Phone (828) 252-5190.

CHIMNEY ROCK PARK—
see Chimney Rock p. 149.

CRAGGY GARDENS—
see Blue Ridge Parkway p. 134.

FOLK ART CENTER—
see Blue Ridge Parkway p. 134.

GROVEWOOD GALLERY & MUSEUMS are at 111 Grovewood Rd., 1 mi. n. on Macon Ave. via Charlotte St. next to the Grove Park Inn. Established to preserve the Old World wool-manufacturing skills of mountain people, exhibits in the craft museum depict the history of Biltmore Industries and display examples of American crafts. The Estes-Winn Memorial Automobile Museum also is on the grounds and houses more than 20 vehicles, including a 1913 Model T, a 1959 Ford Edsel, a 1922 La France fire engine and horse-drawn carriages.

Allow 30 minutes minimum. Gallery open Mon.-Sat. 10-6, Sun. 11-5. Museums open Mon.-Sat. 10-5, Sun. 11-5, Apr.-Dec. Closed Jan. 1, Thanksgiving and Dec. 25. Free. Phone (828) 253-7651.

MOUNT MITCHELL STATE PARK—
see Blue Ridge Parkway p. 133.

NORTH CAROLINA ARBORETUM—
see Blue Ridge Parkway p. 134.

PACK PLACE—EDUCATION, ARTS & SCIENCE CENTER, 2 S. Pack Sq. in downtown, 3 blks. s. on US 25 from I-240 exit 5A, combines arts, science, culture and entertainment in one location. The complex contains museums, performance spaces, galleries and shops.

Allow 2 hours minimum. Tues.-Sat. 10-5, Sun. 1-5; closed Jan. 1, Thanksgiving and Dec. 25. Admission to each museum varies. Combination and multiday tickets are available. Ages 0-11 must be with an adult to visit museums. MC, VI. Phone (828) 257-4500.

Asheville Art Museum, 2 S. Pack Sq. in downtown, 3 blks. s. on US 25 from I-240 exit 5A, presents a permanent exhibit of 20th-century through contemporary American art. Changing exhibitions include displays of sculpture, paintings, and traditional and contemporary crafts. Admission $6; $5 (ages 4-12, ages 60+ and students with ID).

Colburn Gem & Mineral Museum, 2 S. Pack Sq. in downtown, 3 blks. s. on US 25 from I-240 exit 5A, displays North Carolina minerals as well as gemstones from around the world. Admission $4; $3 (ages 4-12, ages 60+ and students with ID).

SAVE **The Health Adventure,** 2 S. Pack Sq. in downtown, 3 blks. s. on US 25 from I-240 exit 5A, is a collection of hands-on health and science exhibits and programs including Nutri-Space, BodyWorks and BrainStorm. Galleries feature a scavenger hunt through the body and a talking transparent woman. Admission $7.50; $5 (ages 4-12, ages 60+ and students with ID). Phone (828) 254-6373.

YMI Cultural Center is at 2 S. Pack Sq. in downtown, 3 blks. s. on US 25 from I-240 exit 5A. Commissioned by George Vanderbilt in 1893, the center celebrates African-American life and history through exhibits and a permanent collection of African artifacts. Cultural insights also are revealed through music, drama and dance programs. Tues.-Fri. 10-5. Admission $5; $3 (ages 4-15, ages 60+ and students with ID).

SAVE **SMITH-McDOWELL HOUSE MUSEUM** is off I-40 exit 50B, .2 mi. n. on US 25 to Biltmore Ave., then 1.5 mi. n.e. to Victoria Rd. Built circa 1840 by an affluent businessman, the three-level house contains rooms furnished in various 19th-century styles including an 1850s bedroom, an 1860s sitting room and an 1880s parlor. Antique furniture, photographs, china and cookware are among the items displayed.

Allow 1 hour minimum. Thurs.-Sat. 10-4, Sun. noon-4. Admission $7; $3 (ages 5-18). Holiday admission mid-Nov. to mid-Jan. $10; $5 (ages 5-18). MC, VI. Phone (828) 253-9231.

THOMAS WOLFE MEMORIAL STATE HISTORIC SITE, 52 N. Market St., was the novelist's childhood home. Furnished with family possessions, the house retains the atmosphere of Dixieland, the boardinghouse in "Look Homeward, Angel." Personal items and a 20-minute film about Wolfe's life are presented in the visitor center.

Allow 30 minutes minimum. Tues.-Sat. 9-5, Sun. 1-5, Apr.-Oct.; Tues.-Sat. 10-4, Sun. 1-4, rest of year. Closed major holidays. Forty-five minute guided tours are offered at half-past the hour starting at 9:30. Last tour begins 30 minutes before closing. Admission $1; 50c (students with ID); free (ages 0-5). AX, MC, VI. Phone (828) 253-8304 to verify schedule.

WESTERN NORTH CAROLINA NATURE CENTER, 4 mi. e. on SR 81 at Gashes Creek Rd., contains indoor and outdoor exhibits of plant and animal life. Displays include nocturnal animals, freshwater life, snakes, cougars, deer, bears, raccoons, foxes, red and gray wolves, otters, waterfowl, turtles and farm stock. An aviary, petting zoo and self-guiding nature trail also are available.

Daily 10-5. Last admission 30 minutes before closing. Closed Jan. 1, Martin Luther King Jr. Day, Thanksgiving and Dec. 24-25. Admission $7; $6 (ages 65+); $3 (ages 3-15). MC, VI. Phone (828) 298-5600.

ATLANTIC BEACH (D-8) pop. 1,781

In the late 1800s, "surf bathing" was popular, and beachgoers were transported across the Intracoastal Waterway to Atlantic Beach by sailboat. A pavilion was built on the beach in 1887, which included refreshments and a place for changing clothes. Since then, Atlantic Beach has become a popular spot for summer tourists.

The 265-acre Theodore Roosevelt Natural Area is 7 miles northwest of Atlantic Beach; nature trails and observation decks afford views of the coastal woodlands. A Marine Resources Center is nearby off SR 24 on Bogue Sound.

FORT MACON STATE PARK, 389 acres, is 2 mi. e. on SR 58. Fort Macon was built 1826-34; young Lt. Robert E. Lee designed the garrison's jetties. The Confederacy captured the fort during the Civil War. Exhibits include re-creations of the mess hall, kitchen, living quarters and WWII barracks. Other features include a moat, powder magazines and several cannons. Food is available. Allow 30 minutes minimum. Daily 8-8, June-Aug; 8-7, Mar.-May and Sept.-Oct.; 9-5:30, rest of year. Closed Dec. 25. Guided tours are available Memorial Day-Labor Day. Free. Phone (252) 726-3775. *See Recreation Chart.*

AURORA (C-8) pop. 583

AURORA FOSSIL MUSEUM, 400 Main St., specializes in marine fossils, some of which include shells, skulls, sharks' teeth, coral and a walrus. An 18-minute videotape explains the local mining process. Visitors can search for fossils in a mound across the street and explore the learning center. Mon.-Sat. 9-4:30, Sun. 12:30-4:30; closed major holidays. Free. Phone (252) 322-4238.

BAILEY (B-7) pop. 670, elev. 1,728′

SAVE **THE COUNTRY DOCTOR MUSEUM,** s. from US 264 on SR 581 to 6629 Vance St., is dedicated to family physicians of the 19th century. Two restored doctors' buildings house an apothecary and a library, a doctor's office of the 1880s and an art of nursing building. Displayed are a tilting examination table from the Civil War era, medical equipment of a Confederate surgeon and a 1912 Model T used to make house calls.

Allow 1 hour minimum. Tues.-Sat. 10-4; closed major holidays. Admission $5; $4 (ages 55+); $3 (ages 3-17). Phone (252) 235-4165.

BALD HEAD ISLAND (E-7) pop. 173, elev. 5′

A barren, sandy mound on the island's shore inspired the unusual name and provided the perfect promontory for North Carolina's first lighthouse. Built in 1795, the tower guided sailors through churning waters at the confluence of the Atlantic Ocean and Cape Fear River. Shifting currents eventually threatened to topple the original lighthouse; it was replaced in 1818 with a brick and cement structure known today as "Old Baldy," said to be North Carolina's oldest lighthouse. Panoramas of this southernmost barrier island and its 14 miles of beaches await those who climb Old Baldy's steps.

Cape Fear, another aptly named landmark, lies on the island's Atlantic coast. In the early days, it served as a rescue outpost, manned by life-saving teams and lighthouse keepers who helped mariners navigate the treacherous Frying Pan Shoals.

Today's island visitors find smoother sailing via a 20-minute ferry ride from Southport *(see place listing p. 187)* down the Intracoastal waterway and across the Cape Fear River. For fares and schedules contact Bald Head Island Transportation; phone (910) 457-5003 or (800) 234-1666. Guided tours of historic landmarks are available. Because gasoline engines are prohibited on the island, electric carts and bicycles provide the primary means of transportation. These may be rented on a daily or weekly basis; for information phone (800) 432-7368.

BANNER ELK (D-4) pop. 811, elev. 3,739′

High peaks and rugged ridges surround the town of Banner Elk, which offers year-round beauty and plentiful recreational opportunities. Skiing, golf, horseback riding, rafting, hiking and fishing are some of the activities.

Avery/Banner Elk Chamber of Commerce—Banner Elk: Castle Shopping Center, jct. SRs 105 and 184, P.O. Box 335, Banner Elk, NC 28604; phone (828) 898-5605 or (800) 972-2183.

RECREATIONAL ACTIVITIES

Skiing

- **Sugar Mountain Resort**, off SR 184. Write P.O. Box 369, Banner Elk, NC 28604. Daily mid-Nov. to mid-Mar. Phone (828) 898-4521 or (800) 784-2768.

BATH (B-8) pop. 275

Originally called the Town of Pamticoe, Bath was founded along the Pamlico River in the late 17th century. Once a bustling trade center, Bath languished due to continual political friction, epidemics and American Indian warfare. The town boundaries remain about the same as when Bath was incorporated in 1705.

HISTORIC BATH STATE HISTORIC SITE is on SR 92. The oldest incorporated town in North Carolina, Bath was chartered in 1705. It was the colony's first official port of entry. When he was not plundering in the Caribbean, Blackbeard was a resident. Tours of the Bonner House and Palmer-Marsh House depart from the visitor center on Carteret Street. A 15-minute videotape presentation about the town precedes the tour.

Allow 1 hour, 30 minutes minimum. Mon.-Sat. 9-5, Sun. 1-5, Apr.-Oct.; Tues.-Sat. 10-4, Sun. 1-4, rest of year. Closed Thanksgiving, day after Thanksgiving and Dec. 24-26. Tours are given on the hour. Last tour departs 1 hour before closing. Admission $1 per house; 50c per house (students with ID); free (ages 0-4). Phone (252) 923-3971.

Bonner House, 200 Front St., has a collection of period furniture. Behind the 1830 house is the Ruth McCloud Smith Memorial Garden.

Palmer-Marsh House, 104 S. Main St., is a restored 1751 house. A Colonial kitchen, still in original condition, is in the cellar.

St. Thomas Episcopal Church is at the corner of Craven and Main sts. Built in 1734, it is said to be the oldest existing church in the state. The walls of the building are 2 feet thick and constructed of solid brick. Allow 30 minutes minimum. Daily 24 hours. Donations. Phone (252) 923-9141.

Van Der Veer House is at 103 S. Harding St. Built about 1790, the restored property contains exhibits depicting nearly 3 centuries of Bath's history.

BEAUFORT (C-8) pop. 3,771, elev. 12′

First known as Fish Town, Beaufort (BO-fort) was established in the early 1700s. A quaint seacoast town, its historic district is comprised of narrow streets and old houses.

In the Old Burying Ground, deeded to the town in 1731, the earliest legible date on a marker is 1756. The graveyard was declared full in 1825, yet townspeople continued to use it until the early 1900s. Graves face east in the oldest portion so that the occupants would face the sun on "Judgment Morn." Many interesting characters are buried here, including an English sailor buried upright so that he could salute the king.

Beaufort Historical Association Welcome Center: 130 Turner St., Beaufort, NC 28516; phone (252) 728-5225.

SAVE **BEAUFORT HISTORIC SITE,** 130 Turner Street, offers guided 1-hour tours led by docents in period dress. All tours depart from the Beaufort Historical Association Welcome Center. The site includes the 1796 Carteret County Courthouse, the 1829 county jail and an 1859 apothecary shop. The 1732 Rustell House serves as an art gallery. Historic district bus tours and Old Burying Ground cemetery walking tours also are offered.

Mon.-Sat. 9:30-5, Mar.-Nov.; 10-4, rest of year. Historic site tours are offered at 10, 11:30, 1 and 3. Last tour begins at 3. One-hour, double-decker bus tours to the historic district are given Mon., Wed. and Fri.-Sat. at 11 and 1:30, Apr.-Oct. Guided 45-minute tours of the Old Burying Ground are offered Tues.-Thurs. at 2:30, June-Sept. Admission $8; $4 (ages 7-12). Bus tour fare $8; $4 (ages 7-12). Old Burying Ground tour $8; $4 (ages 7-12). MC, VI. Phone (252) 728-5225 or (800) 575-7483.

GEM **NORTH CAROLINA MARITIME MUSEUM,** 315 Front St., depicts the state's maritime and coastal natural history. Exhibits include ship models, area small craft, birds and fish, fossils, decoys and saltwater aquariums. Field trips to coastal habitats are offered year-round for tidal flat and salt marsh exploration. Fossil, mushroom and wildflower hunts as well as bird-watching trips are available. A schedule of activities also is available.

Allow 1 hour minimum. Mon.-Fri. 9-5, Sat. 10-5, Sun. 1-5; closed Jan. 1, Thanksgiving and Dec.24-25. Free. Reservations for activities are required. Phone (252) 728-7317.

BEECH MOUNTAIN (D-3) pop. 310, elev. 4,000′

As one of the highest incorporated towns east of the Rockies, Beech Mountain is a resort community known for its natural beauty and year-round recreation. With summer temperatures rarely exceeding 72 degrees, it has long been a haven for vacationers seeking relief from the heat. Hiking trails traverse the mountain, which is home to deer, red foxes, wild turkeys and some 80 species of birds. In winter skiing, tubing, snowboarding and other cold-weather sports are popular. In summer activities such as golf and tennis can be enjoyed.

Beech Mountain Chamber of Commerce: 403-A Beech Mountain Pkwy., Beech Mountain, NC 28604; phone (828) 387-9283 or (800) 468-5506.

RECREATIONAL ACTIVITIES

Skiing

- **Ski Beech** is at 1007 Beech Mountain Pkwy. (SR 184), Beech Mountain, NC 28604. Daily mid-Nov. to mid-Mar. Phone (828) 387-2011 or (800) 438-2093.

BELMONT (C-4) pop. 8,705, elev. 685′

Belmont is home to Belmont Abbey, a Catholic college founded by Benedictine monks in 1876. The campus was built on the former grounds of the Caldwell Plantation.

SAVE **DANIEL STOWE BOTANICAL GARDEN,** 6500 S. New Hope Rd., features theme areas that include the Four Seasons Garden, the Cottage Garden, the Canal Garden, the Perennial Gardens and the .5-mile Woodland Trail. The Orchid Conservatory is an 8,000-square-foot home to a variety of orchids and tropical plants. Twelve fountains are scattered around the grounds, and a visitor pavilion sports a 1909 stained-glass dome. Picnicking is permitted. Allow 1 hour, 30 minutes minimum. Daily 9-5; closed Jan. 1, Thanksgiving and Dec. 25. Admission $10; $9 (ages 60+); $5 (ages 4-12). MC, VI. Phone (704) 825-4490.

BLACK MOUNTAIN (E-3)
pop. 7,511, elev. 2,405′

Black Mountain-Swannanoa Chamber of Commerce: 201 E. State St., Black Mountain, NC 28711; phone (828) 669-2300 or (800) 669-2301.

SWANNANOA VALLEY MUSEUM is at 223 W. State St. Allowing visitors a glimpse into Swannanoa Valley history, the museum features exhibits about early settlers, American Indians, valley watersheds, business expansion and the influence of the railroad. Allow 1 hour minimum. Tues.-Fri. 10-5, Sat. noon-4, Sun. 2-5, Apr.-Oct.; by appointment rest of year. Free. Phone (828) 669-9566.

BLOWING ROCK (D-4)
pop. 1,418, elev. 3,579′

Blowing Rock's cool summer temperatures are ideal for golf, fishing, riding and swimming. The region's four ski areas are popular in winter. Moses H. Cone and Julian Price memorial parks, comprising about 8,000 acres on the Blue Ridge Parkway *(see place listing p. 131)*, afford miles of horse and hiking trails. Bass Lake, .5 miles south on US 221, is a popular spot for walking, jogging and horseback riding. Climbers enjoy Grandfather Mountain in nearby Linville *(see place listing p. 169)* as well as Flat Top.

Blowing Rock Chamber of Commerce: 7738 Valley Blvd., Blowing Rock, NC 28605; phone (828) 295-7851.

Shopping areas: The SAVE Tanger Shoppes on the Parkway, on US 321, offers more than 45 stores and is open daily.

THE BLOWING ROCK, 2 mi. s. on US 321, is a large rock formation 4,000 ft. above sea level overhanging the John's River Gorge. The area is said to be the only place where snow falls upward. Lightweight objects cast over the cliff will return to the thrower when rising air currents are present. The observation tower affords a view of the gorge and surrounding mountain range.

Daily (weather permitting) 8:30-7, Memorial Day weekend-Labor Day; daily 9-5, Mar. 1-day before Memorial Day weekend and Nov.-Dec.; Sun.-Thurs. 9-6, Fri.-Sat. 9-7, day after Labor Day-Oct. 31; Sat.-Sun. 9-5, rest of year. Admission $6; $5 (ages 60+); $1 (ages 4-11). MC, VI. Phone (828) 295-7111.

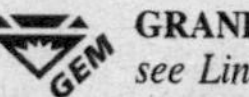

GRANDFATHER MOUNTAIN— *see Linville p. 169.*

MYSTERY HILL is 2 mi. n. on US 321/221. Because of a stronger than normal gravitational pull, visitors can watch a ball roll uphill and witness several optical illusions and natural enigmas. Exhibits and experiments at the Old Mystery House demonstrate these puzzling yet scientifically explainable phenomena. Allow 1 hour minimum. Daily 9-8, June 1-Labor Day; 9-5, rest of year. Closed Thanksgiving and Dec. 25. Admission $8; $7 (ages 60+); $6 (ages 5-12); free (ages 0-4 with adult). AX, DS, MC. Phone (828) 264-2792.

The Appalachian Heritage Museum, 2 mi. n. on US 221/321, is in a 19th-century house displaying 18th- and 19th-century furnishings. Area antiques and memorabilia are exhibited, and demonstrations related to mountain culture and crafts are occasionally presented. An exhibit featuring American Indian artifacts is situated on the lower level. Daily 9-8, June 1-Labor Day; 9-5, rest of year. Closed Thanksgiving and Dec. 25. Admission included with Mystery Hill. Phone (828) 264-2792 for demonstration schedule.

SAVE **TWEETSIE RAILROAD,** 4.2 mi. n. on US 321, is a Western theme park incorporating a restored narrow-gauge, coal-fired steam railroad that once ran from Boone *(see place listing p. 134)* to Johnson City, Tenn. Fond of the train's whistle, area residents coined the unusual name. Today's passengers experience mock robberies during the train ride. The railroad town has an 1880s general store, a blacksmith shop and jail.

Craft demonstrations and live musical shows are presented regularly. A chairlift runs to a re-created mining town, where children can pan for gold, visit the animal petting area or board a small train into Mouse Mine No. 9. The park affords scenic views of the surrounding area.

Food is available. Allow 2 hours minimum. Daily 9-6, Fri. before Memorial Day to mid-Aug. (also 6-9 p.m. July 4); Fri.-Sun. 9-6 in May and late Aug.-Oct. 31 (also Labor Day). Admission $30; $22 (ages 3-12). DS, MC, VI. Phone (828) 264-9061 or (800) 526-5740. *See color ad.*

GEM BLUE RIDGE PARKWAY

The Blue Ridge Parkway connects Shenandoah National Park in Virginia and Great Smoky Mountains National Park in North Carolina and Tennessee *(see place listing p. 156 and Recreation Chart and the AAA Southeastern CampBook)*. The 469-mile scenic road follows the crest of the Blue Ridge and other ranges at elevations from 649 to 6,047 feet.

The concept for the construction of the parkway began during Franklin D. Roosevelt's administration in the 1930s. The project, in addition to creating a scenic route linking the two new national parks and spurring tourism, was a way to provide jobs for many of those left unemployed during the peak of the Great Depression. Begun in 1935, the dedication of the complete parkway did not take place until 1987, although sections of the road have been enjoyed by travelers for many years.

The Blue Ridge Parkway, only 800 feet wide at certain points, is constructed free of billboards and with little residential encroachment, allowing leisurely drives and enjoyment of the surrounding area.

The parkway offers panoramas of the Southern Highlands. Among the areas of outstanding scenic interest are Humpback Rocks, Otter Creek, Peaks of Otter, Roanoke Mountain, Rocky Knob and Smart View in Virginia; and Crabtree Meadows, Craggy Gardens, Cumberland Knob, Doughton Park, E.B. Jeffress Park, Mount Pisgah, Waterrock Knob and Julian Price, Linville Falls and Moses H. Cone memorial parks in North Carolina.

Hiking trails, varying in length from short strolls to the lengthy and strenuous Appalachian Trail, can be reached from many overlooks and parking areas; information can be obtained at parkway visitor centers. During the summer season craft demonstrations and ranger programs at various points along the parkway provide insights into the everyday life and culture of mountain residents.

Wildflowers are in bloom mid-May through August; fall foliage is at its peak in October. Many visitor accommodations are open May through October only. Pets are permitted if confined or leashed; they are prohibited in overnight facilities. Picnic areas and drinking water are available at intervals along the parkway. Hunting is prohibited.

Food is available seasonally at Crabtree Meadows, Doughton Park, Mabry Mill, Mount Pisgah, Otter Creek and Peaks of Otter. There are overnight facilities at Peaks of Otter Lodge, housekeeping cabins at Rocky Knob and lodges at Doughton Park and Mount Pisgah. Other accommodations are nearby but off the parkway.

Concrete mileposts help keep track of mileage along the road, beginning at Milepost 0 at the northern portion and concluding at Milepost 469 at its southern terminus at Great Smoky Mountains National Park. The speed limit of 45 mph is enforced. To drive the entire length, plan on 2 to 4 days at an average speed of 35 mph. For additional information contact Blue Ridge Parkway, 199 Hemphill Knob Rd., Asheville, NC 28803.

The Travel Narrator Audio Driving Tour, covering Mileposts 390-469, is available at the Folk Art Center *(see attraction listing p. 134)*. These 90-minute narrated driving tour of the Blue Ridge Parkway from Asheville to Cherokee explores the region's history, people and lore; phone (828) 298-0495.

Go Blue Ridge Card is an all-access attraction pass offering admission to top attractions in Asheville and all along the Blue Ridge Parkway. The card is purchased by the day (2- ,3- or 5-day cards), and the visitor has up to 2 weeks to use the days purchased. The card includes a trolley pass, sightseeing tours, museums and historic sites. The card is priced as low as $31 per day (based on a 5-day card). Go Blue Ridge Card is available at the Asheville Area Chamber of Commerce at 36 Montford Ave. in Asheville and at the Smoky Mountain Host Visitor Center at 4437 Georgia Rd. in Franklin; phone (800) 887-9103.

The parkway is open all year, but sections of the road may be closed during icy or snowy weather. Most park facilities close November through April. Phone (828) 298-0398 for weather or other information.

North Carolina High Country Host: 1700 Blowing Rock Rd., Boone, NC 28607; phone (800) 438-7500.

Note: *The points of interest below are listed in order, from north to south, according to their nearness to the northern terminus of the road at Shenandoah National Park.*

HUMPBACK ROCKS VISITOR CENTER is at Milepost 5.8, 6 mi. s.e. of Afton, Va. The center features an outdoor museum of 1890s farm buildings. Picnicking is permitted. Allow 1 hour minimum. Daily 9-noon and 1-5, May-Oct. Schedule may vary; phone ahead. Free. Phone (540) 943-4716.

JAMES RIVER VISITOR CENTER, at Milepost 63.6, 3 mi. n. of Big Island, Va., chronicles the story of the James River and the Kanawha Canal. A pedestrian walkway crossing the river leads to a restored canal lock. Daily 9-5, June-Oct.; Sat.-Sun. 9-5, in May. Free. Phone (434) 299-5496.

PEAKS OF OTTER VISITOR CENTER, at Milepost 86, 10 mi. n.w. of Bedford, Va., houses exhibits about forest ecology and the history of the Peaks of Otter area. Nearby is an 1830s cabin that sheltered early travelers. A historic farm offers living-history demonstrations. Daily shuttle-bus trips to the summit of Sharp Top Mountain as well as a walking trail to the summit are available.

Allow 1 hour minimum. Visitor center open daily 9-5, Memorial Day-Oct. 31. Shuttle bus departs daily on the hour (weather permitting) 10-4 (also Sat.-Sun. 4-5), late May-Oct. 31. Farm and trail hours vary. Visitor center free. One-way bus fare $5; $4 (ages 0-11). Round-trip bus fare $8; $6 (ages 0-11). Phone (540) 586-4496 or (540) 586-4357.

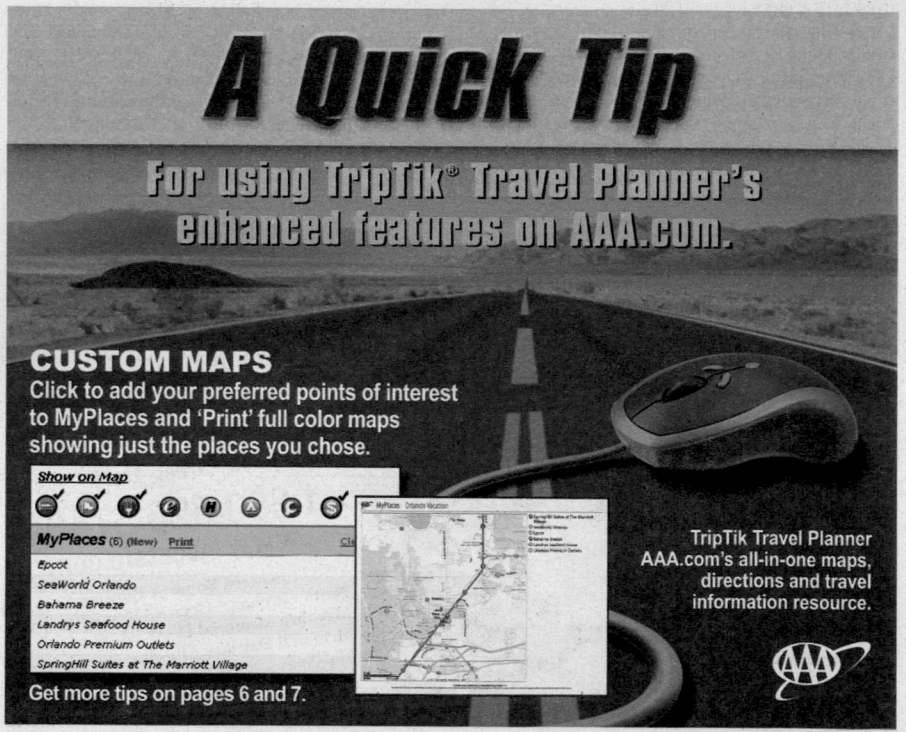

ROCKY KNOB VISITOR CENTER is at Milepost 169, 8 mi. n.e. of Meadows of Dan, Va. The center provides information about the Rocky Knob recreation area, which covers 4,000 acres. Daily 9-5, mid-May through Oct 31. Free. Phone (540) 745-9662.

MABRY MILL is at Milepost 176.1, just n. of the jct. US 58, 1 mi. n.w. of Meadows of Dan, Va. A display of pioneer items includes a blacksmith shop, a gristmill, a sawmill and a sorghum press. Allow 1 hour minimum. Daily 8-6, last weekend in Apr.-early Nov. Free. Phone (276) 952-2947.

BLUE RIDGE MUSIC CENTER is at Milepost 213, 1.2 mi. n.e. of Glendale Springs. Audiences can take in the natural scenic beauty of the Blue Ridge Parkway area while enjoying concerts and other special events here. Banjos and fiddles are regulars on both the center's main outdoor stage and its indoor theater. In the visitor center, an exhibit hall features displays relating the history of bluegrass music in Virginia as well as the genre's European and African roots.

Picnicking is permitted. Food is available. Allow 45 minutes minimum. Daily 9-5, Memorial Day-early Nov.; Wed.-Sat. 9-5, early May-day before Memorial Day. Concert schedule varies; phone ahead. Admission by donation. Fees for special events and concerts vary. Phone (276) 236-5309.

CUMBERLAND KNOB VISITORS CENTER, at Milepost 217.5, marks the site where the Civilian Conservation Corps began construction on the parkway in 1935. Picnic facilities and hiking trails are available. Daily 9-5, May-Oct. Free.

BLUE RIDGE MOUNTAIN FRESCOES are at Milepost 259 in Glendale Springs, 3 mi. n. of the parkway's jct. with SR 16, and in West Jefferson, following signs from jct. US 221 Bus. Rte. and SR 194. North Carolina artist Ben Long painted these religious artworks in two Episcopal churches, Holy Trinity in Glendale Springs and St. Mary's in West Jefferson. Taped narratives describe their history. Allow 1 hour minimum. Daily 24 hours. Donations. Phone (336) 982-3076.

PARKWAY CRAFT CENTER, at Milepost 294, 3 mi. w. of Blowing Rock, is in the former manor house at Moses H. Cone Memorial Park. It is operated by the Southern Highland Craft Guild. Cone, a wealthy textile manufacturer, built his country estate at the turn of the 20th century. Mountain crafts are demonstrated. Allow 30 minutes minimum. Daily 9-5, Mar. 15-Nov. 30. Free. Phone (828) 295-7938.

LINN COVE VIADUCT AND VISITORS CENTER is at Milepost 304.4, 5 mi. n.e. of Linville. Completed in 1983, the Linn Cove Viaduct is one of the most complicated concrete spans ever built. The quarter-mile bridge skirting the rugged perimeter of Grandfather Mountain was designed for minimal environmental impact. The visitor center has a scale model and a hiking trail leading under the viaduct for a closer look. Daily 9-5, May-Oct. Free. Phone (828) 733-1354.

LINVILLE FALLS RECREATION AREA, at Milepost 316.4, 2 mi. n.w. of Linville Falls, has trails to the pedestrian overlooks of Linville Falls and Linville Gorge. Picnicking and fishing are permitted in the campground only. Allow 3 hours minimum. Park open daily 24 hours. Visitor center open daily 9-5, May-Oct. Free. Phone (828) 765-1045. *See Recreation Chart and the AAA Southeastern CampBook.*

Linville Gorge is a scenic chasm within Linville Falls Recreation Area at Milepost 316.4. Linville Gorge Wilderness, below the falls, is part of Pisgah National Forest *(see place listing p. 181)* and has been set aside for scientific and recreational use. Wiseman's View observation point on the west overlooks the gorge. **Note:** The area is reached only by trail or cross-country travel. A few steep trails are moderately difficult and require some hiking skill. Free. Phone (828) 652-2144.

LINVILLE CAVERNS is at Milepost 317 at Linville Falls, then 4 mi. s. on US 221. In 1822 the spectacle of trout swimming in and out of the mountainside led settlers on a torch-lit expedition inside the caves. Ever since, their discovery has been a source of fascination, and sometimes shelter. During the Civil War, deserting soldiers from both armies sought refuge among the cathedral-like arches, columns and deep passageways.

The underground temperature is a constant 52 F; a jacket and comfortable walking shoes are recommended. Daily 9-6, June 1-Labor Day; daily 9-5, Apr.-May and day after Labor Day-Oct. 31; daily 9-4:30 in Nov. and Mar.; Sat.-Sun. 9-4:30, rest of year. Guided 30-minute tours depart every 15 minutes. Fee for tour $6; $4.50 (ages 62+); $4 (ages 5-12). DS, MC, VI. Phone (828) 756-4171 or (800) 419-0540.

MUSEUM OF NORTH CAROLINA MINERALS, at Milepost 331 on SR 226, 5 mi. s. of Spruce Pine, has samples of many rocks and minerals found within the area. Allow 30 minutes minimum. Daily 9-5, May-Oct.; 9-noon and 1-5, rest of year. Closed Jan. 1 and Dec. 25. Free. Phone (828) 765-2761.

GEM **MOUNT MITCHELL STATE PARK** is at Milepost 355, near Burnsville. The park encompasses the 6,684-foot summit of Mount Mitchell, highest peak east of the Mississippi River, and a portion of its slopes. The mountain was named for Dr. Elisha Mitchell, who fell to his death while attempting to prove the mountain's height.

Facilities at this 1,946-acre park include an interpretive center and observation platform. A naturalist is on duty in the summer. In spring and winter check road conditions before entering the park. **Note:** The summit and nearby trail sections are closed during construction of a new observation tower; reopening is scheduled for October 2008. Food is available May-Oct. Parking is available near the summit. Daily 8 a.m.-9 p.m., May-Aug.; 8-8, Mar.-Apr. and Sept.-Oct.; 8-6, rest of year. Closed

Dec. 25. Free. Phone (828) 675-4611. *See Recreation Chart.*

CRAGGY GARDENS is at Milepost 364.6, 18 mi. n.e. of Asheville. The Craggy Mountains, at an elevation of 5,500-6,000 feet, are a colorful sight when the rhododendrons bloom around mid-June. Trails and a visitor center are available. **CLOSURE INFORMATION:** The gardens are closed due to the collapse of a retaining wall; reopening is scheduled for May 2009. Phone for more information. Picnicking is permitted. Daily 9-5, May-Oct. Schedule may vary; phone ahead. Free. Phone (828) 298-0398 for the Blue Ridge Parkway information line, or (828) 271-4779, ext. 200.

FOLK ART CENTER is at Milepost 382, accessible from Asheville via I-40 to US 70W exit 55, following signs to the Blue Ridge Pkwy., then .5 mi. n. Operated by the Southern Highland Craft Guild, the center celebrates the tradition of craft work in the southern Appalachian region through demonstrations, special events and changing exhibits of past and present Southern Highlands crafts. A Blue Ridge Parkway information desk is in the center. Allow 30 minutes minimum. Daily 9-6, Apr.-Dec.; 9-5, rest of year. Closed Jan. 1, Thanksgiving and Dec. 25. Free. Phone (828) 298-7928.

GEM **NORTH CAROLINA ARBORETUM** is at Milepost 393, 9 mi. s. of Asheville. Fringed by the Southern Appalachian Mountains, the 434-acre arboretum offers 65 acres of cultivated gardens, 10 miles of forested hiking and biking trails, an education center, a state-of-the-art greenhouse production facility and what is reputed to be the finest bonsai collection in the southeastern United States. Garden demonstrations and educational programs also are featured.

Picnicking is permitted. Food is available. Allow 1 hour minimum. Arboretum daily 8 a.m.-9 p.m., Apr.-Oct; 8-7, rest of year. Closed Dec. 25. Education center Mon.-Sat. 9-5, Sun. noon-5; phone for holiday closures. Greenhouse production facility Mon.-Fri. 8-2; phone for holiday closures. Free. Parking $6; free (Tues.). Phone (828) 665-2492.

MOUNT PISGAH, at Milepost 408.6, has walking trails leading to the 5,721-foot summit. Educational programs are presented in an outdoor amphitheater most evenings June through October. Picnicking is permitted. Food is available. Free. Phone (828) 235-8228. *See Recreation Chart and the AAA Southeastern CampBook.*

RICHLAND BALSAM, near Milepost 431, 12 mi. n.e. of Balsam, is the highest point on the parkway, with a peak of 6,401 feet. A 1.5-mile walking trail winds to the summit of Richland Balsam Mountain, passing through a spruce and fir woodland that is native to climates usually found 1,000 miles north. Trail pamphlets describe this plant community, which is a living relic of the last ice age. Free. Phone (828) 456-9530, or (828) 298-0398 for the Blue Ridge Parkway information line.

WATERROCK KNOB, at Milepost 451.2, 8 mi. n.w. of Balsam, commands a 360-degree view of the main ranges of the southern Appalachian Mountains from a 6,000-foot elevation. A visitor information center in the parking area is open daily 10-5, May-Oct. Free. Phone (828) 298-0398 or (828) 456-9530.

WINERIES

- **Château Morrisette Winery**, exit Black Ridge Rd. (SR 726) between Mileposts 171 and 172, then s.w. on Winery Rd. (SR 777) to 287 Winery Rd. S.W. in Floyd. Wine tastings and tours are offered. Mon.-Sat. 10-5 (also Fri.-Sat. 5-6), Sun. 11-5; closed Jan. 1, Thanksgiving and Dec. 24-25. Tours are given Mon.-Sat. at 11, 1 and 3 (also Fri.-Sat. at 5), Sun. at noon, 2 and 4. Phone (540) 593-2865.

BOONE (D-4) pop. 13,472, elev. 3,333′

Named after Daniel Boone, who had a cabin in the area in the 1760s, the city is high atop the Blue Ridge Mountains, and is home to 12,000 students attending Appalachian State University. Boone is at the intersection of two scenic highways: A scenic portion of US 321 runs west across the Tennessee border, and a scenic portion of US 421 runs east to Winston-Salem.

Boone Convention & Visitors Bureau: 208 Howard St., Boone, NC 28607; phone (828) 262-3516 or (800) 852-9506.

Shopping areas: Mast General Store, 630 W. King St., operates out of a 1913 building, stocked with a variety of goods including cast-iron cookware, Amish rockers, boots and outdoor clothing.

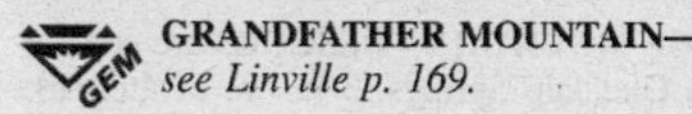

GRANDFATHER MOUNTAIN—*see Linville p. 169.*

GEM SAVE **"HORN IN THE WEST"**, .5 mi. s. of US 421 via Horn in the West Dr., is an outdoor musical drama portraying the struggle of Daniel Boone and his men to establish freedom in the Southern Appalachian Highlands. Hickory Ridge Homestead Museum contains a reconstructed log village typical of the 18th century. Costumed guides demonstrate the lifestyle of the early settlers.

Inquire about weather policies. Allow 2 hours minimum. Performances Tues.-Sun. at 8 p.m., mid-June to mid-Aug. Museum open Tues.-Sun. 1-8, mid-June to mid-Aug. Musical drama $18; $9 (senior citizens and ages 0-12). Museum $4.50; free with admission to "Horn in the West." AX, MC, VI. Phone (828) 264-2120.

RECREATIONAL ACTIVITIES

White-water Rafting

- **Wahoo's Adventures-Boone Outpost**, 1 mi. s. on US 321. Write P.O. Box 3094, Boone, NC 28607. Trips daily Apr.-Oct. Phone (828) 262-5774 or (800) 444-7238.

BOONVILLE (B-4) pop. 1,138, elev. 1,066′

WINERIES

- **RagApple Lassie Vineyards** is at 3820 Rockford Rd. Daily noon-6; closed Thanksgiving and Dec. 25. Phone (336) 367-6000 or (866) 724-2775.

BRASSTOWN (F-1)

JOHN C. CAMPBELL FOLK SCHOOL is in the center of town at 1 Folk School Rd. Visitors observe students at work in a variety of folk classes, including cooking, weaving, quilting, jewelry making and pottery. Self-guiding nature trails traverse the 300-acre campus; an on-site history center with photographs, crafts and exhibits preserves the school's heritage. Concerts and dance programs are held throughout the year. Mon.-Sat. 8-5, Sun. 1-5; closed Thanksgiving and Dec. 25. Free. Phone (828) 837-2775 or (800) 365-5724.

BREVARD (F-3) pop. 6,789, elev. 2,229′

Brevard is a Transylvania County treasure trove at the junction of Pisgah National Forest *(see place listing p. 181)*, Gorge State Park and DuPont State Forest. Aptly named "Land of Waterfalls," Transylvania County sports more than 250 named waterfalls such as Connestee Falls, Courthouse Falls and Laughing Falls.

A popular summer resort, Brevard allures visitors with its mountains, waterfalls, wilderness, arts and music. By day, be invigorated by the mountain air while fishing, hiking, biking, rock climbing or horseback riding; or head downtown and explore the rows of shops brimming with antiques and local arts and crafts. By night, soak in the sounds of summer at the Brevard Music Center, which features concerts each evening, late June to early August.

If you're lucky, you'll catch a glimpse of one of the most revered Brevard residents—the white squirrel. It is said that the creatures escaped during a carnival animal truck accident in Florida, were captured and presented as gifts to a Brevard resident, fled yet again, and began procreating. In 1986, a Brevard City Council ordinance declared white squirrels protected and designated the town a safe haven. It's no wonder the cherished inhabitants are honored annually at the White Squirrel Festival, held on Memorial Day weekend.

Brevard/Transylvania Chamber of Commerce and Visitor's Information Center: 35 W. Main St., P.O. Box 589, Brevard, NC 28712; phone (828) 883-3700 or (800) 648-4523.

BRYSON CITY (E-2) pop. 1,411, elev. 1,740′

Just south of Great Smoky Mountains National Park *(see place listing p. 156)* and east of Fontana Village *(see place listing p. 154)*, Bryson City is a center for recreational activities. The area offers boating, fishing, mountain biking, white-water rafting, hiking and camping opportunities.

Swain County Chamber of Commerce: 210 Main St., P.O. Box 509, Bryson City, NC 28713; phone (828) 488-3681 or (800) 867-9246.

SAVE **GREAT SMOKY MOUNTAINS RAILROAD,** departing the Bryson City and Dillsboro depots, operates various half-day and full-day round-trip excursions. Seating is offered in open cars, coaches, crown coaches and club cars. On weekends there are Gourmet Dinner Trains and Mystery Theatre Dinner Trains. The Polar Express runs November 7 through December 23.

"The Little Engine That Could," "Peanuts Pumpkin Patch Express" and "Thomas the Tank," rides with kid-oriented themes, are available in the spring and summer with limited dates. An animal petting area and musical entertainment also are offered.

Food is available. Allow 4 hours minimum. Trains run year-round; schedule varies. Sightseeing fares begin at $31; $16 (ages 3-12). Reservations are suggested. AX, DS, MC, VI. Phone (828) 586-8811 or (800) 872-4681 for reservations. *See color ad p. 156.*

Wildwater Ltd. Raft & Rail Excursion, departing the railroad depot in Bryson City, combines rail and white-water excursions in one outing. The adventure begins with a scenic 2-hour train trip across Fontana Lake to the top of Nantahala Gorge. Rafts are then boarded for a guided 3-hour trip down the Nantahala River. Lunch is included.

Children under 60 pounds are not permitted. Allow 7 hours minimum. Trips daily mid-Apr. to late Oct.; departure times vary. Fares begin at $74; $57 (ages 3-12). DS, MC, VI. Phone (828) 488-2384 or (800) 451-9972.

RECREATIONAL ACTIVITIES

White-water Rafting

- **Nantahala Outdoor Center**, 13 mi. s.w. on US 19/74W. Write 13077 Hwy. 19W, Bryson City, NC 28713. Trips daily Mar.-Oct. Phone (828) 488-2175 or (800) 232-7238.
- **USA Raft**, 12 mi. s. on US 19W. Write 11044 US 19W, Bryson City, NC 28713. Trips daily Mar.-Sept. Phone (828) 488-3316 or (800) 872-7238.
- **Wildwater Ltd.**, 12 mi. s.w. on US 19/74W. Write P.O. Box 309, Long Creek, SC 29658. Trips daily Apr.-Oct. Phone (828) 488-2384 or (800) 451-9972.

BURLINGTON (A-5) pop. 44,917, elev. 656′

Burlington is a textile industry center with numerous factory outlet shops that attract bargain hunters from nearby states. Clothing, leather goods, towels, blankets, sheets, carpets and furniture are popular products. The town began as a maintenance and repair community for the North Carolina Railroad; the 1880 engine house now serves as a train station and office complex.

The centerpiece of 76-acre City Park, at South Church Street and Overbrook Road, is a 1910 Dentzel Menagerie Carousel. Known for their detail and

THE UNIVERSITY OF NORTH CAROLINA AT CHAPEL HILL, off SR 15, was chartered in 1789. At the heart of the 700-acre campus is the historic Coker Arboretum, planted in 1903.

An audio walking tour of the campus is available; visitors may pick up a brochure and an audiotape player at the visitor center in the west lobby of the Morehead Planetarium and Science Center *(see attraction listing).*

Visitor parking is available in a number of municipal lots along Franklin and Rosemary streets. Visitor center open Mon.-Fri. 9-5. A guided tour is offered; reservations are required. Free. Phone (919) 962-1630 for tour information, or (800) 722-4335 for sports events tickets.

Ackland Art Museum is on campus near jct. S. Columbia and Franklin sts. Displays include paintings, drawings, sculpture, photographs, prints and artifacts of a wide range of cultures. Edgar Degas, Eugène Delacroix, Peter Paul Rubens, Max Weber and Emanuel de Witte are among the artists represented. Classical, Asian, 20th-century and contemporary and North Carolina folk art collections also are exhibited. Allow 1 hour minimum. Wed.-Sat. 10-5 (also second Fri. of every month 5-9 p.m.), Sun. 1-5; closed holidays. Free. Phone (919) 966-5736.

Carolina Athletic Memorabilia Room of the Dean E. Smith Center, on the second floor of the Smith Center on Skipper Bowles Dr., is dedicated to the UNC athletic tradition. Displayed are team artifacts, highlight tapes and NCAA championship trophies awarded to the Tar Heels in basketball and other varsity sports. The room also contains a communications studio where sports programs are taped. Allow 1 hour minimum. Mon.-Fri. 8-5; closed holidays and during events. Free. Phone (919) 962-6000.

Morehead-Patterson Bell Tower, on campus, e. off Columbia St. on South Rd., is a brick landmark that has 12 bells duplicating those at West Point. Chimes ring 15 minutes before the hour; songs are played at 8, noon, 6 and 9.

Morehead Planetarium and Science Center is on campus at 250 E. Franklin St. The planetarium served as a NASA training center for Mercury, Gemini, Apollo and Skylab astronauts; it contains arts and sciences exhibits, a 245-seat Star Theater, a rose garden and a large sundial. The west wing features an art gallery.

Allow 1 hour minimum. Sun.-Wed. 10:30-4 and 6:45-9:45 p.m., Thurs. Sat. 10-5 and 6:45-9:45 p.m., mid-June to mid-Aug.; Wed.-Sat. 10-5 and 7-9:45 p.m., Sun.-Tues. 12:30-5, rest of year. A variety of Star Theater shows is offered daily; phone for schedule. Exhibits free. Star Theater admission $6; $5 (ages 2-12, senior citizens and students with ID). MC, VI. Phone (919) 962-1236, or (919) 549-6863 for show information.

North Carolina Botanical Garden is on Old Mason Farm Rd. off US 15/501 bypass. This UNC facility consists of more than 600 acres and displays plants native to North Carolina and the Southeast. Aquatic, herb and family gardens, and a carnivorous plant collection also are presented. A fire ecology section explains the profuse return of vegetation following a burn. Nature trails also are on the grounds.

Allow 1 hour minimum. Gardens open Mon.-Fri. 8-5, Sat. 9-6, Sun. 1-6, during DST; Mon.-Fri. 8-5, Sat. 9-5, Sun. 1-5, rest of year. Nature trails open dawn-dusk. Free. Admission may be charged during special events and for programs. Phone (919) 962-0522.

The North Carolina Collection, on campus in the Wilson Library near Columbia St. and Cameron Ave., offers a gallery, reading room and photographic archive. The gallery contains exhibits pertaining to the history of North Carolina and the university. Historic rooms display Elizabethan and early Colonial furnishings, maps and statues; of note are the Sir Walter Raleigh rooms and the gold rush exhibit. The Hayes Library holds almost 2,000 volumes and imprints dating from the late 1500s to the mid-1900s.

Allow 1 hour, 30 minutes minimum. Gallery Mon.-Fri. 9-5, Sat. 9-1, Sun. 1-5. Reading room Mon.-Fri. 8-5, Sat. 9-1, Sun. 1-5. Photographic archives Mon.-Fri. 8-5. Closed holidays. Guided 30-minute tours by reservation. Free. Phone (919) 962-1172.

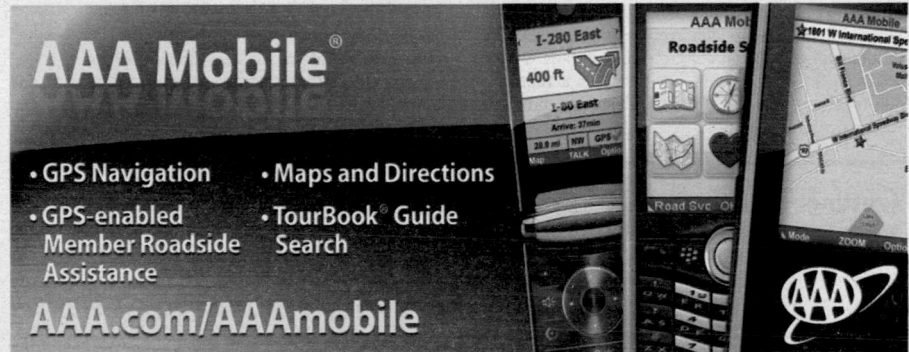

Charlotte

City Population: 540,828 **Elevation:** 734 ft.

Editor's Picks:

© James Schwabel / Panoramic Images

What started as a simple crossroads named for a young queen has grown into the second-largest financial center in the country. Still adhering to its nucleus, Charlotte has expanded upward and outward to become the largest metropolitan area in the Carolinas, draped with an attractive skyline.

The city came into being when a group of Scot-Irish immigrants en route from Philadelphia settled at the juncture of two American Indian trading posts. Since the nearby Catawba River posed certain navigational difficulties, colonists opted to establish roots east of the river. The intersection of Trade Street (named for the trading that took place there) and Tryon Street (named for Governor William Tryon, the Royal Governor of North Carolina at the time of the city's founding) remains the heart of Uptown.

German settlers, faithful to both England and Germany, named the town for German-born Queen Charlotte, wife to England's King George III. The county in which Charlotte resides adopted the name of the queen's birthplace and is known as Mecklenburg.

Charlotte's strong tie with England was severed when a convention of North Carolinians met to compose the Mecklenburg Resolves. Signed on May 31, 1775, the statement contained a number of resolutions that were intended to invalidate the authority of the king and parliament.

It is said that the proclamation contained phrases similar to those found in the Declaration of Independence a year later, yet no proof exists. Unfortunately, an original copy of the Resolves was not retained; the only tangible evidence is a reproduction from memory by one of the delegates, produced years later. Historians debate its authenticity.

Nevertheless, residents erected a monument to the signers at the County Courthouse, 600 E. Trade St. Thomas Polk, the founder of Charlotte, erected a log courthouse for the new county seat in 1768 at this site, the original crossroads.

The independent spirit that motivated the colonists to compose the Resolves continued, and British general Lord Cornwallis later would call Charlotte a "hornet's nest of rebellion" as a result of Patriot activity during his occupation of the city.

The intersection of Trade and Tryon streets, now known as The Square, historically has been the Uptown hub and serves as the center of commerce. Past, present and future are displayed in Raymond Kaskey's four bronze statues, found at each corner of the square. The statues tell Charlotte's story: A gold miner illustrates commerce; a female mill worker depicts a strong textile heritage; a railroad builder renders Charlotte's significance as a transportation mecca; and a mother lifting her child toward the sky represents hope for the city's future.

Charlotte's first burial ground, The Old Settlers' Cemetery, is 2 blocks northeast of The Square. Among those buried here are Thomas Polk, his wife Susannah Spratt Polk and Maj. Gen. George Graham, a Revolutionary War hero.

Concord Mills Outlet Mall / Visit Charlotte

Nicknamed the Queen City, Charlotte is the county seat of Mecklenburg County. Queen Charlotte's influence is omnipresent; street signs and the city flag are adorned with crowns shaped around the letter "M" for Mecklenburg. When lit up at night, the Bank of America Tower resembles a multi-tiered tiara. The building contains 60 floors, which matches the number of years of the queen's reign. Another of Kaskey's statues, a patinated bronze of the queen, is found at the north end of the airport. Finally, one of the nicer drives in town can be found along aptly-named Queens Road West, which boasts lavish Colonial-style houses.

Frescoes by artist Ben Long are found in the Bank of America Corporate Center lobby, 100 N. Tryon St. and the Trans-America Building at 401 N. Tryon St. The artist used Charlotte residents as models for the works and is known to have painted himself into the frescoes; look for a man with wavy hair and a grey beard.

Also called the City of Trees, Charlotte is known for its willow oaks, which line many residential and Uptown streets. The trees, which resemble black oaks but sport long, thin leaves similar to weeping willows, are native to Charlotte.

But Charlotte is mostly known for its wealth. The road to riches began in 1799 when a 17-pound nugget was found in nearby Concord *(see place listing p. 147)*, making Mecklenburg County a magnet for gold prospectors. A rather short boom ensued. This prosperity, coupled with the establishment of a Charlotte branch of the U.S. Mint in 1837, paved the way for Charlotte's financial notoriety.

The city now is a thriving financial center as well as a major service and distribution point for the Southeast. Next to New York City, more banking establishments are headquartered in Charlotte than any other U.S. city. Nine of the nation's top 200 banks operate out of Charlotte; Bank of America, the country's largest financial institution, and Wachovia, another financial giant, are headquartered here. It is no wonder that the city flag sports a green background—notably the color of money.

The University of North Carolina at Charlotte, the fourth largest of the institution's 16 campuses, has an enrollment of more than 17,000 students; phone (704) 687-2000. The 1,600-student Queens University was founded in 1857; phone (704) 332-7121. On the 100-acre campus of Johnson C. Smith University is a state historic landmark, Biddle Memorial Hall, built by students and volunteers in 1883; phone (704) 378-1000.

Mecklenburg Investment Company was a group of leading African-American citizens formed in 1921 with a mission to construct a facility that would provide office space to local professionals. The 1922 three-story brick building became a fixture in Charlotte's African-American community;

Destination Charlotte

Charlotte combines the hospitality of a traditional Southern Belle with the perspicacity of a contemporary Yankee Trader.

Her heritage is obvious in gracious Colonial and Victorian homes. Her savvy side is manifest in the skyscrapers that house the nation's second largest financial center, and in the amusements of the movers and shakers who inhabit them.

© Charlotte Museum of History and Hezekiah Alexander Homesite

Charlotte Museum of History and Hezekiah Alexander Homesite. Explore exhibit halls covering 300 years of Carolina heritage and experience late 18th-century life in the back country. (See listing page 144)

Lowe's Motor Speedway, Concord. Behind-the-scenes tours and three annual NASCAR Sprint Cup race weekends will surely satisfy your need for speed. (See listing page 147)

© Nigel Kinrade Transtock Jupiterimages

Historic Fourth Ward, Charlotte. Enjoy a stroll through this revitalized neighborhood, which features some 75 polychromatic Victorian homes. (See mention page 145)

© Vespasian / Alamy

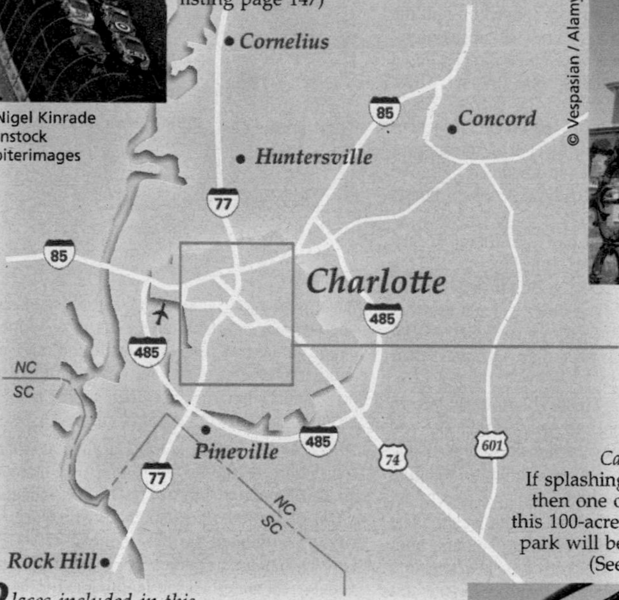

Cornelius
Concord
Huntersville
Charlotte
NC
SC
Pineville
Rock Hill

See Vicinity map page 143

Carowinds, Charlotte. If splashing isn't your thing, then one of the 50+ rides in this 100-acre theme and water park will be more your pace. (See listing page 143)

© Carowinds

Places included in this AAA Destination City:

The Informed Traveler

Sales Tax: North Carolina has a 4.5 percent sales tax. Charlotte has a tax of 11.25 percent for lodging and prepared food and an 11 percent tax for rental cars, with an additional $3.50 fee for vehicles rented at airport facilities.

WHOM TO CALL

Emergency: 911

Police (non-emergency): (704) 353-1000

Fire: (704) 336-2441

Time and Temperature: (704) 375-6711

Hospitals: Carolinas Medical Center, (704) 355-2000; Carolinas Med Center-Mercy, (704) 304-5000; Presbyterian Hospital, (704) 384-4000.

WHERE TO LOOK

Newspapers

The Charlotte Observer is the daily newspaper. *The Business Journal* is issued weekly.

Radio

WBT (1110 AM and 99.3 FM) is an all-news/weather station; WFAE (90.7 FM) is a member of National Public Radio.

Visitor Information

Visit Charlotte: 500 S. College St., Charlotte, NC 28202; phone (704) 331-2700 or (800) 231-4636.

The Visit Charlotte Visitor Center at 330 S. Tryon St. serves walk-in customers.

A visitor center at the Charlotte/Douglas Airport is staffed daily 7:45 a.m.-10:45 p.m.

TRANSPORTATION

Air Travel:

The Charlotte/Douglas International Airport is 7 miles west of the city on Josh Birmingham Parkway, and is accessible from Billy Graham Parkway or Wilkinson Boulevard. A hub for US Airways, the airport is served by other major airlines as well; phone (704) 359-4027. Service between the airport and Uptown is available Mon.-Fri. from Charlotte Transit. Concord Regional Airport, 9000 Aviation Blvd., is in nearby Concord; phone (704) 793-9000.

Rental Cars:

Hertz, 4102 Rental Car Rd., offers discounts to AAA members; phone (704) 359-0114 or (800) 654-3131. For listings of other agencies, check the telephone directory.

Rail Service:

Amtrak, (704) 376-4416, has a station at 1914 N. Tryon St.

Buses:

A Greyhound station serves Charlotte at 601 W. Trade St.; phone (704) 372-0456.

Taxis:

Cabs are metered and charge approximately $2 per mile. Crown Cab Co., (704) 334-6666, increases the base fare $2 for more than two passengers. Yellow Cab, (704) 332-6161, charges $2 per person for more than two passengers.

Public Transport:

Charlotte Transit, (704) 336-3366 or TTY (704) 336-5051, serves the city with local and express routes. Local fare is $1.30. Express fare (buses pick up in a limited area and travel directly to Uptown) is $1.75. Transfers from local to express are 45c; local to local transfers are free.

Most local buses operate Mon.-Sat. 5:30 a.m.-midnight, Sun. 7 a.m.-midnight. Express buses operate during rush hour, Mon.-Fri. 6-8 and 4-6. A free Center City Circuit electric shuttle bus has 45 stops and four routes throughout Uptown.

The LYNX Blue Line provides light-rail service between Uptown and I-485. One-way fare is $1.30; 65c (ages 62+ and grades K-12).

this National Historic Landmark is at 233 S. Brevard St.

Getting There

By Car

Interstates 77 and 277 provide access to Center City Charlotte. I-77 traverses north-south through the state, and I-277 circles the city. I-85 is an east-west route that bisects I-77 just north of the city.

From the north or south, I-77 connects directly with West Trade Street, which provides access through Uptown. From the east, US 74 connects with I-277 (John Belk Freeway) to the College Street exit; head northeast on SR 29/49 (Tryon Street) to reach Uptown. From the west, I-85 connects with SR 16 (Brookshire Expressway); head southwest on SR 29/49 to reach Uptown.

I-485 surrounds Charlotte, providing access to neighboring areas.

The Charlotte/Douglas International Airport is west of downtown and can be reached via I-85, I-77, the Billy Graham Parkway or Wilkinson Boulevard.

Getting Around

Street System

Center City Charlotte is encircled by I-277, which provides southern access. The uptown area is easily maneuverable; streets are laid out in a simple grid pattern. Numbered streets run southeast to northwest, and named streets are found perpendicular.

Charlotte's history is closely tied to its physical nucleus; the intersection of Trade and Tryon streets forms the main crossroads. Trade Street bisects the city east-west, and Tryon Street provides the north-south dividing line.

Parking

Charlotte has ample metered parking in Center City. Rates vary according to location; most metered spaces in popular areas charge 25c for 15 minutes, while those on the perimeter of the city charge 25c per hour.

Metered parking is available around the Charlotte-Mecklenburg Government Center on 1st, 2nd, 3rd, 4th, and Davidson streets. Near the City Center, metered spots are on College, Trade, Church and Tryon streets. Parking lots can be found on College Street between Stonewall and 2nd streets. Wachovia Plaza, Discovery Place and Founder's Hall have garages.

What To See

THE BILLY GRAHAM LIBRARY is at 4330 Westmont Dr. Perpetuating the mission of the Charlotte-born evangelist, the library allows visitors to delve into the story of Graham's life. Highlights include Graham's renovated childhood home, multimedia exhibits housed in a dairy barn, and a prayer garden in which Graham's mother was buried. Food is

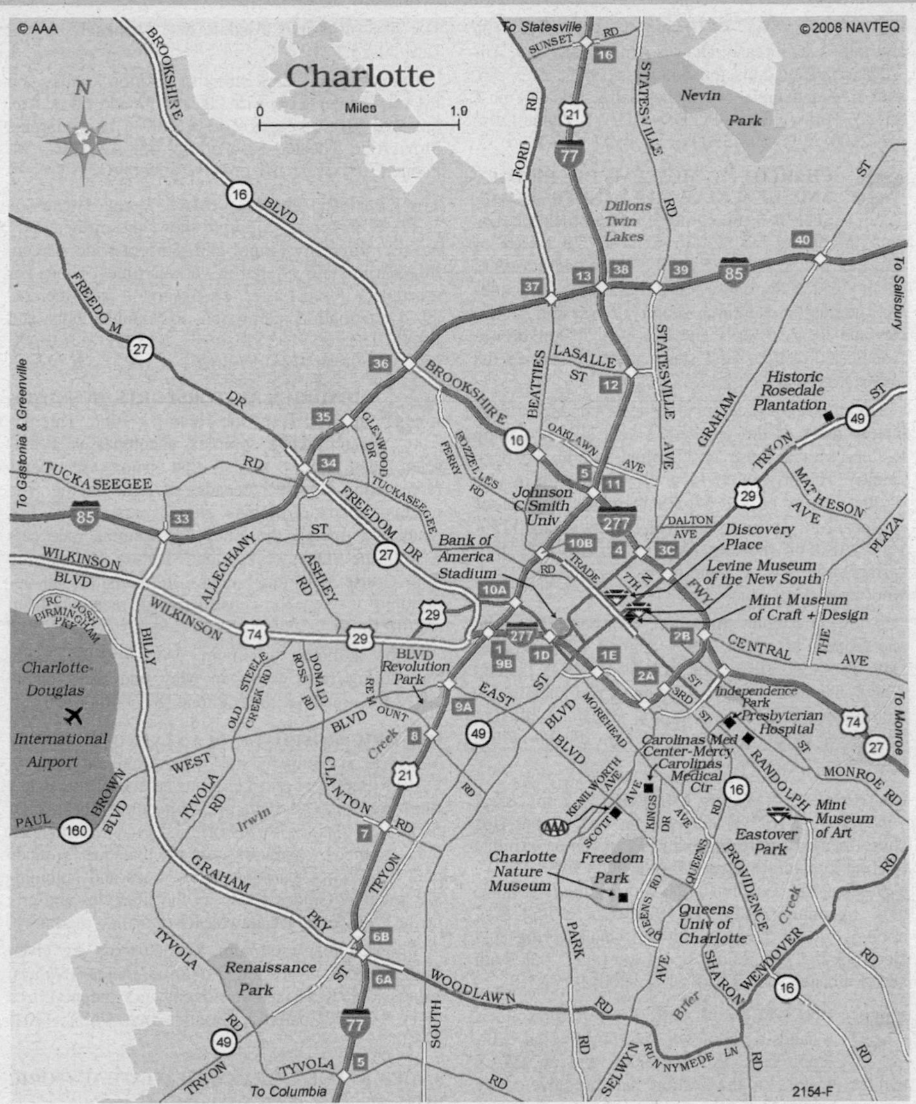

available. Allow 1 hour, 30 minutes minimum. Mon.-Sat. 9:30-5, Jan. 2-Dec. 23 and Dec. 26-30; 9:30-2:30, rest of year. Closed Jan. 1 and Dec. 25. Free. Phone (704) 401-2432.

GEM **CAROWINDS,** 10 mi. s. on I-77 to exit 90, is on the North Carolina/South Carolina border. The Nickelodeon Central section includes Phantom Flyers, interactive vehicles that glide through the air with a ghost-fighting superhero; The Flying Dutchman's Revenge; Little Bill's Cruisers; Rugrats Runaway Reptar; Wild Thornberrys River Adventure; and SpongeBob Square Pants.

Fred Flintstone, Scooby-Doo and other Hanna-Barbera characters are hosts at Animation Station, which has rides for children. Paramount Plaza re-creates the golden days of Hollywood.

The Thrill Zone is the place to go for daring rides, including the Southern Star, the Scream Weaver and the flying coaster Nighthawk. The Hurler treats riders to hills, dips and hairpin turns at 50 mph. Boomerang Bay, a 13-acre water park, has a giant wave pool and waterslides. Comedy and musical entertainment occur in the Paladium Amphitheatre.

Food is available. Kennel, stroller, wheelchair and locker rentals are available. Facilities include a first-aid station and campground. Pets are not permitted in the park. Park opens daily at 10, early June to mid-Aug.; Sat.-Sun. at 10, mid-Mar. to early June and mid-Aug. to early Oct. Closing times vary. All-inclusive park admission $45.99; $19.99 (ages 3-6, ages 62+ and under 48 inches tall). Two-day pass $51.99. Parking $10. AX, DS, MC, VI. Phone (704) 588-2600, (803) 548-5300 or (800) 888-4386.

CHARLOTTE MUSEUM OF HISTORY AND HEZEKIAH ALEXANDER HOMESITE is 3 mi. e. at 3500 Shamrock Dr. The museum allows visitors to explore 300 years of Carolina heritage. Three exhibit halls each cover a century of history, and a fourth holds rotating exhibits. The Lassiter Research Library focuses on American and local history. The 7-and-a-half-ton bronze American Freedom Bell stands in a garden on the museum grounds.

Docents in 18th-century costume conduct living-history tours of the wooded, 8-acre site, providing visitors with a sense of Carolina life in the back country. The original 1774 stone house, built by one of the signers of the Mecklenberg Declaration of Independence, is furnished with pieces dating 1750-1800. Also on the site are a re-created two-story springhouse and a hand-hewn log kitchen with working rock fireplace.

Allow one hour minimum. Museum, homesite and grounds Mon.-Sat. 10-5, Sun. 1-5, June 1-Labor Day; Tues.-Sat. 10-5, Sun. 1-5, rest of year. Guided 1-hour homesite tours are given at 1:15 and 3:15. Admission $6; $5 (ages 66+ and students with ID); $3 (ages 6-12); free (on Sun.). Phone (704) 568-1774.

CHARLOTTE NATURE MUSEUM, 2.5 mi. s. at 1658 Sterling Rd., is entered via East Blvd. This child-oriented nature museum has hands-on exhibits relating to natural history, a room with live animals, a pavilion and a nature trail. Allow 1 hour, 30 minutes minimum. Tues.-Fri. 9-5, Sat. 10-5, Sun. noon-5; closed Easter, July 4, Thanksgiving and Dec. 24-25. Admission $5; free (ages 0-2 with adult). Phone (704) 372-6261 or (800) 935-0553.

DISCOVERY PLACE, 301 N. Tryon St., is a hands-on complex incorporating an exhibition hall, a planetarium, and an IMAX theater. Visitors to the exhibit hall are greeted by roaring, animated dinosaurs. Exhibits are designed to enhance visitors' perceptions of science and technology. Traveling exhibits change three times a year. The Science Circus exposes visitors to basic scientific principles.

Other attractions include the Life Center, the Challenger Learning Center and the Aquarium Ocean Touch Pool. A chemistry hearth allows visitors to enjoy live shows. The Morphis MovieRide Theater launches visitors into the world of virtual reality. "Space Walk 2004" simulates a visit to the International Space Station and "Water Cycle" traces a raindrop's journey through the environment.

Food is available. Allow 1 hour, 30 minutes minimum. Exhibit halls open Mon.-Sat. 9-5, Sun. noon-6, June 1-Labor Day; Mon.-Sat. 10-6, Sun. 1-5, rest of year. Closed Easter, Thanksgiving and Dec. 24-25.

Combination admission to exhibit halls and IMAX Theater $16; $13 (ages 2-13 and 60+). Any one area $10; $8 (ages 2-13 and 60+). The Morphis MovieRide Theater $4. Parking $5. AX, MC, VI. Phone (704) 372-6261 or (800) 935-0553.

The Charlotte Observer IMAX Dome Theatre is at 301 N. Tryon St. Multiple shows are offered daily on the three-story-high and 80-foot-wide screen. IMAX films are offered at various times; phone for schedule. Closed Easter, Thanksgiving and Dec. 24-25. Combination admission to exhibit halls and IMAX Theater $16; $13 (ages 2-13 and 60+). AX, MC, VI. Phone (704) 372-6261 or (800) 935-0553.

HENDRICK MOTORSPORTS MUSEUM is at 4400 Papa Joe Hendrick Blvd. This 67-acre racing complex encompasses a museum and race shops that showcase items representing almost 2 decades of HMS racing. The museum displays include engine components, trophies and one of the Chevrolet Lumina race cars used in the "Days of Thunder" feature film starring Tom Cruise. The race shops afford visitors an opportunity to view the construction of race cars from start to finish.

Allow 2 hours minimum. Mon.-Fri. 9-5. Open Sat. during race weeks in May and Oct.; phone ahead for schedule. Free. Phone (877) 467-4890.

HISTORIC ROSEDALE PLANTATION is at 3427 N. Tryon St. Built by merchant Archibald Frew in 1815, Rosedale is considered to be one of the state's finest examples of Federal architecture. The plantation home is noted for its original French wallpaper, faux grained woodwork and picturesque grounds with a boxwood garden, mature trees and outbuilding remains. Guides focus on the lifestyles and arts of the 19th-century Catawba River Valley region.

Allow 1 hour minimum. Guided tours are given Thurs.-Sun. at 1:30 and 3; closed major holidays. Admission $5; $4 (senior citizens and students); free (ages 0-3 with parent). Grounds free. Phone (704) 335-0325.

JAMES K. POLK MEMORIAL STATE HISTORIC SITE—*see Pineville p. 148.*

LEVINE MUSEUM OF THE NEW SOUTH is at 200 E. Seventh St. Post Civil War history is interpreted through interactive, multisensory exhibits that chronicle the city's evolution from an industrial mill town to an international banking center. Exhibits include the early textile industry and a 1930s Main Street. The Banking Boomtown exhibit highlights the late 20th-century growth and progress that transformed Charlotte into one of the nation's leading cities. Changing exhibits also are available.

Free parking is available for 1 hour, 30 minutes in the Seventh St. Station deck adjacent to the museum. Allow 2 hours minimum. Mon.-Sat. 10-5, Sun. noon-5; closed major holidays. Admission $6;

$5 (ages 6-18, ages 62+ and students with ID); $17 (family); free (on Tues. 10-2). MC, VI. Phone (704) 333-1887.

GEM **MINT MUSEUM OF ART,** 2730 Randolph Rd., is housed in what served as the first branch of the U.S. Mint 1837-61. Before it was dismantled and moved to its present site in 1933, the Greek Revival building served as a Confederate hospital, an assay office and a federal courthouse.

The permanent collection, entitled Art in the Americas, features pre-Columbian, Spanish colonial and early North American works. Other highlights include European paintings and sculpture, period costumes, historic North Carolina pottery and gold coins minted in Charlotte. Changing exhibits and a student artists' gallery also are featured. The museum's pottery and porcelain collection is reputed to be one of the better in the country.

Of particular note is Alan Ramsey's coronation portraits of King George III and Queen Charlotte, the British monarchs who reigned during the American Revolutionary War. Included is the Delhom Collection, which ranges from ancient Chinese ceramics to late 18th-century Continental and English wares.

Allow 1 hour, 30 minutes minimum. Tues.-Sat. 10-5 (also Tues. 5-10), Sun. noon-5; closed Jan. 1, Easter, July 4, Thanksgiving and Dec. 24-25. Admission (including Mint Museum of Craft + Design) $6; $5 (ages 62+ and students with ID); $3 (ages 6-17); free (Tues. 5-10 and third Thurs. of the month 5-8). MC, VI. Phone (704) 337-2000.

MINT MUSEUM OF CRAFT + DESIGN, 220 N. Tryon St., features international objects in ceramics, glass, fiber, metal and wood. The collection traces the development of craft, from the utilitarian objects of 19th-century rural America to the contemporary art that studio craft is considered to be today. Also included are pottery, jewelry, tapestry and glass exhibits.

Allow 1 hour minimum. Tues.-Sat. 10-5, Sun noon-5; closed Jan. 1, Easter, July 4, Thanksgiving and Dec. 24-25. Admission (including Mint Museum of Art) $6; $5 (ages 62+ and students with ID); $3 (ages 6-17); free (Tues. 10-2 and third Thurs. of the month 5-8). MC, VI. Phone (704) 337-2000.

What To Do

Sightseeing

Walking Tours

Exploring on foot is a great way to get to know the Queen City. A walking tour of Uptown highlights 16 places of interest; maps are available at INFO! Charlotte, 330 S. Tryon St. Sites on the route include St. Peter's Catholic Church, which was established in 1851; Liberty Hall Monument, a stone obelisk that marks the location of a boys' academy that claimed Andrew Jackson as a former student; Kaskey's bronze statues at The Square; Thomas Polk Park; and Wachovia Plaza, which features a fountain complete with bronze figures of frolicking children.

Those interested in Victorian architecture will not want to miss Historic Fourth Ward. In 1869 residential Charlotte was divided into four voting districts called wards. Fourth Ward, the northwest quadrant, was occupied by merchants and ministers. The area, between 10th, Graham, 5th and Tryon streets, eventually fell into disrepair until restoration began in the late 1970s. Today the neighborhood contains approximately 75 colorfully painted Victorian residences; many are considered to be "Grand Old Ladies." A fountain marks the entrance to Fourth Ward Park, bordered by Pine, Poplar, 6th and 8th streets. Descriptive brochures with a detailed map are available at INFO! Charlotte as well as at various points in the neighborhood.

Visitors may opt to take a relaxing stroll through McGill Rose Garden at 940 N. Davidson St.; phone (704) 333-6497. This 1.3-acre urban sanctuary contains more than 200 varieties of roses along with annuals, perennials and herbs.

Sports and Recreation

Charlotte is a sports mecca, and residents love to root for the home teams. Spectators have their choice of numerous professional teams in the area. The Time Warner Cable Arena, uptown on East Trade Street, is where the National **Basketball** Association's Bobcats shoot hoops and the ECHL's Checkers play **hockey**; for tickets phone (704) 262-2287.

The Carolina Panthers1420, members of the National **Football** League, toss the pigskin at Bank of America Stadium, 800 S. Mint St.; phone the ticket office at (704) 358-7800 for schedule information.

Fans cheer on minor league **baseball** in nearby Fort Mill, S.C. The Charlotte Knights, a AAA affiliate for the Chicago White Sox, play in Knights Stadium, which is off I-77 at exit 88. The season runs April through September; phone (704) 357-8071, or (803) 548-8050 in S.C.

Golf opportunities can be found throughout Charlotte. Among the public courses are Charles T. Myers (18-hole), 7817 Harrisburg Rd., (704) 536-1692; Charlotte Golf Links (18-hole), 11500 Providence Rd., (704) 846-7990; Highland Creek Golf Course (18-hole), 7001 Highland Creek Pkwy., (704) 875-9000; Oak Hills Golf Course (18-hole), 4008 Oakdale Rd., (704) 394-2834; Olde Sycamore Golf Course (18-hole), 7504 Old Sycamore Dr., (704) 573-1000; Pawtuckett Golf Course (18-hole), 7942 Pawtuckett Rd., (704) 394-5890; Renaissance Park (18-hole), 1525 W. Tyvola Rd., (704) 357-3373; Revolution Park (nine-hole), 2661 Barringer Dr., (704) 342-1946; Sunset Hills Golf Club, 800 Radio Rd., (704) 399-0980; and The Tradition (18-hole), 3800 Prosperity Church Rd., (704) 549-9400. Most courses require tee time reservations.

More than 160 parks in Charlotte provide a multitude of recreational opportunities. Most parks have **picnic** areas and many have lakes; phone the Mecklenburg County Parks and Recreation Department for information, (704) 336-3854. Jetton Park, which consists of 106 acres on Lake Norman, offers **hiking** and **bicycling** trails as well as **tennis** courts and a playground. Nature enthusiasts will appreciate RibbonWalk at 4601 Nevin Rd., an urban botanical forest in the city that encompasses 155 acres of woodlands, natural wildlife and **hiking** trails; phone (704) 598-8857.

Northwest of Charlotte, Lake Norman *(see Recreation Chart)* is the state's largest man-made lake. Its 520 acres of shoreline make it a popular spot for **camping, swimming, sailing, windsurfing** and **water skiing**, (704) 528-6350. Lake Wylie, which runs along the Carolina border just south of Charlotte, also offers activities for water sports enthusiasts.

For those who prefer chlorinated water, swimming and **diving** are popular at the Mecklenburg County Aquatic Center, 800 Martin Luther King Jr. Blvd.; phone (704) 336-3483. Or try the Marion Diehl Pool Center, 2219 Tyvola Rd.; phone (704) 527-3175. One-hour **hot air balloon flights** are offered by Balloons Over Carolina; phone (704) 541-7058.

Stock car racing, courtesy of NASCAR, takes place at Lowe's Motor Speedway, 12 miles north on US 29. The season runs May and October. Phone (704) 455-3200 for information. *See attraction listing and Special Events.*

RECREATIONAL ACTIVITIES

White-water Rafting

- **U.S. National Whitewater Center** is at 820 Hawfield Rd. Write 820 Hawfield Rd., Charlotte, NC 28214. Other activities are offered. Trips depart daily year-round. Phone (704) 391-3900.

Shopping

From local pottery to antiques, Charlotte provides a diverse shopping experience. Those searching for nostalgia can find it at Old Firehouse Antiques and Gallery in Uptown at the corner of 5th and Graham streets. Antiquers are known to frequent various shops in Dilworth and Myers Park. The antique shops at 331 Main St. in nearby Pineville *(see place listing p. 148)* offer a bit of the past for purchase. JB's Hole in the Wall, 3813 South Blvd., offers a variety of items including everything from antiques to estate furniture, as well as gifts and collectibles. The market is open Tuesdays through Fridays 10:30-5, Saturdays 10:30-6 and Sundays 1-5. Sharon Corners, in SouthPark at the corner of Sharon and Fairview roads, features shops in a quaint setting.

Among Charlotte's many malls is SouthPark Mall, 4400 Sharon Rd., where the 130 stores include Belk, Coach Leather, Dillard's, Macy's, Nordstrom and Pottery Barn. Uptown shopping is found in the some 20 retail stores at Founder's Hall, 100 N. Tryon St. in the Bank of America Corporate Center.

Other malls in the area include Northlake Mall, 6801 Northlake Mall Dr., which is home to Belk, Dillard's and Macy's. Pineville's Carolina Place Mall, SR 51 and I-485, offers Belk, Dillard's, JCPenney, Macy's and Sears. While you are in the area, check out Peppermint Forest Christmas Shop behind the Carolina Place Mall on Carolina Place Parkway.

Home decor is all the rage at Interiors Marketplace, where booths displaying a variety of contemporary and antique collectibles share space in the restored Atherton Textile Mill. A trolley takes passengers from the marketplace, 2000 South Blvd. in Historic South End, to Uptown. Blacklion, at SR 51 and Park Road, offers more than 250 stores and boutiques.

Bargain hunters will find collections of outlet stores both north and south of the city. Crossroads Mall is south via I-77 at the Carowinds exit in Fort Mill, S.C.; phone (803) 548-5888. Among the standard outlet stores are Bass and Carolina Pottery. Discount stores and specialty shops are available for browsing at Cannon Village, Kannapolis, N.C., north on I-85 to exits 58 or 63. Concord Mills Outlet Mall, Concord, N.C., encompasses 125 shops and is north on I-85 to exit 49; phone (704) 979-3000.

Bass Pro Shops Outdoor World, north on I-85 to exit 49 in Concord, is a haven for sporting enthusiasts. This sprawling complex features a 30,000-gallon aquarium, archery and driving ranges, a putting green and NASCAR memorabilia; phone (704) 979-2200.

Performing Arts

Whatever your taste, Charlotte boasts several performing arts companies that provide entertainment. The Charlotte Philharmonic Orchestra, Charlotte Repertory Theatre, Charlotte Symphony Orchestra, North Carolina Dance Theatre and Opera Carolina all are resident companies at the North Carolina Blumenthal Performing Arts Center, 130 N. Tryon St. The center, which also plays host to Broadway musicals and performing artists, consists of Booth Playhouse, Belk Theater and Ovens Auditorium. Performances are held throughout the year. The box office is on the second floor of Founders Hall in Uptown; phone (704) 372-1000.

Spirit Square Center for Arts & Education, 345 N. College St., stages concerts and other performing arts programs. The center also sponsors art exhibits; phone (704) 372-1000.

The Children's Theatre of Charlotte, 300 E. 7th St., presents classic and new plays geared toward ages 3-18. The theater is open Mondays through Fridays 10-5. Performances are held throughout the year; phone the box office at (704) 973-2828.

Special Events

Queen City residents can always find something to do; an array of special events occur throughout the seasons. In late February the Southern Spring Show offers the first glimpse of the season with gardens, seminars, crafts and indoor and outdoor floral displays. The show takes place at the Merchandise Mart.

Charlotte's spring schedule is filled with ethnic festivals and community events. The third weekend in April finds residents engaged in a friendly competition of piping, drumming and dancing at the Loch Norman Highland Games. The Scottish festival features Celtic music and is held at Lake Norman *(see Recreation Chart and Sports and Recreation)*.

The NASCAR season kicks off in May with The Winston, which includes Goody's Pole Night, CarQuest 300 and the Coca-Cola 600.

Huntersville *(see place listing p. 147)* offers the Canoe Cornelius Paddlesports and Fishing Festival in April and the Lake Norman Balloon Regatta in September.

Also in September is the Charlotte Shout! festival, which draws crowds with its artwork, food and music.

More NASCAR events occur in October; the Bojangles' Pole Night, Little Trees 300 and the United Auto Workers General Motors Quality 500 are featured. Weekends from early October to mid-November find residents reliving the past at the Carolina Renaissance Festival. The "Christmas Made in the South" Craft Show takes place in late October.

Victorian homes are dressed up and put on display for the Fourth Ward Christmas Tour in early December.

Check the weekly *Creative Loafing* publication, found at newsstands, for additional entertainment and events information.

The Charlotte Vicinity

CONCORD (C-4) pop. 27,300, elev. 704′

In 1775 disagreeing German and Scot-Irish residents of Cabarrus County finally decided on the location of the county seat; they named the site Concord (meaning harmony) and the main thoroughfare Union Street to reflect the compromise that settled the issue.

A memorial garden on Spring Street between Cabarrus and Corban avenues contains the graves of many Concord founders.

The first gold nugget reputedly discovered in the nation was found nearby by a 12-year-old boy wading in Little Meadow Creek. Stories relate that the 17-pound chunk was used as a doorstop before the boy's father took it to Fayetteville in 1802 and sold it to a jeweler for the grand price of $3.50; it was worth approximately $3,600.

Cabarrus Regional Chamber of Commerce—Concord: 3003 Dale Earnhardt Blvd., Kannapolis, NC 28083; phone (704) 782-4000.

LOWE'S MOTOR SPEEDWAY is off I-85 exit 49, then 2 mi. e. on Speedway Blvd. Situated in the heart of stock-car racing country, the speedway annually hosts three NASCAR Sprint Cup race weekends, Food Lion AutoFairs and stock car racing schools. Guided tours include a van ride around the 1.5-mile super speedway and a photo opportunity in Victory Circle. Expanded, behind-the-scenes tours also are available by advance reservation.

Note: Previously scheduled time trials and racing events may affect tour availability; phone ahead. Food is available. Allow 1 hour, 30 minutes minimum. Tours Mon.-Sat. 9:30-3:30, Sun. 1:30-3:30; closed Jan. 1, Thanksgiving, Dec. 25 and race event days. Tours depart at 15 minutes before the hour. Admission $5; free (ages 0-2). MC, VI. Phone (704) 455-3204 for tour information, or (800) 455-3267 for ticket and event information.

CORNELIUS (B-4) pop. 11,969, elev. 804′

RACEWORLD USA is at 20310 Chartwell Center Dr. Home of the Michael Waltrip Racing team, the 140,000-square-foot facility offers a behind-the-scenes look at the process of preparing stock cars for NASCAR races. Visitors tour the Fabrication, Gears and Transmission, Shocks, Suspension and other shops in which crew members work on the cars that Michael Waltrip, Dale Jarrett and David Reutimann drive. Also featured are car-building videos and team memorabilia.

Guided tours are available. Allow 1 hour, 30 minutes minimum. Mon.-Sat. 9-6; closed Jan. 1, Thanksgiving and Dec. 25. Admission $15; $10 (senior citizens); $8 (ages 3-12). AX, DS, MC, VI. Phone (704) 897-5555.

HUNTERSVILLE (C-4) pop. 24,940, elev. 819′

DUKE POWER'S ENERGY EXPLORIUM, I-77 exit 25, then 5 mi. w. on SR 73, features hands-on displays explaining how electricity is produced. The grounds, along Lake Norman *(see Recreation Chart and Sports and Recreation section)*, also contain a nature trail. Picnicking is permitted. Allow 30 minutes minimum. Mon.-Fri. 9-5, Sat.-Sun. noon-5; closed Jan. 1, Easter, Thanksgiving and Dec. 24-25. Free. Phone (704) 875-5600.

LATTA PLANTATION NATURE PRESERVE is off I-77 exit 16B, .5 mi. w. on Sunset Rd., 4.8 mi. n. on Beatties Ford Rd., then w. on Sample Rd. following signs. A 1,290-acre nature preserve bordering Mountain Island Lake, the park has a nature center, an equestrian center, and hiking and horse trails. Boating and canoe access are available. Picnicking is permitted. Swimming is not allowed. Daily 7-dusk; closed Dec. 25. Free. Admission may be charged during special events. Phone (704) 875-1391.

SAVE **Carolina Raptor Center,** within Latta Plantation Nature Preserve at 5225 Sample Rd., provides care and rehabilitation for injured and orphaned birds of prey. Educational exhibits and weekend programs about raptors are presented. A nature trail is lined with aviaries containing many varieties of hawks, falcons and owls. Allow 2 hours minimum. Mon.-Sat. 10-5, Sun. noon-5; closed major holidays. Admission $7; $6 (ages 62+); $5 (ages 5-17). MC, VI. Phone (704) 875-6521.

SAVE **Historic Latta Place,** within Latta Plantation Nature Preserve at 5225 Sample Rd., is the restored 1800 river plantation house of James Latta, a successful merchant. The two-story Federal-style house is furnished in period; architectural highlights include a finely detailed staircase and elaborate mantels. Outbuildings include the kitchen, a smokehouse, provisions barn, pioneer cabin, wash house and well house.

Special programs for children are available. The house is open only by guided tour. Tues.-Sat. 10-5, Sun. 1-5, Sept.-May; Tues.-Sun. 10-5, rest of year. Closed major holidays. Tour $6; $5 (ages 6-12, ages 62+ and students with ID). Phone (704) 875-2312.

PINEVILLE (C-4) pop. 3,449, elev. 550′

JAMES K. POLK MEMORIAL STATE HISTORIC SITE, 1.6 mi. s. of I-485 exit 65 on Old US 521 (Lancaster Hwy.), preserves the birthplace of James K. Polk, 11th president of the United States. A 12-minute film in the museum and displays in the visitor center depict his life. Picnicking is permitted. Allow 1 hour minimum. Tues.-Sat. 9-5, Apr.-Oct.; 10-4, rest of year. Closed Thanksgiving and Dec. 25. Guided 30-minute tours of a restored 19th-century homestead are offered. Tours are given on the half-hour starting 30 minutes after opening. Last tour begins 30 minutes before closing. Free. Phone (704) 889-7145.

Nearby South Carolina

ROCK HILL (A-3) pop. 49,765, elev. 667′

The name Rock Hill is derived from the white flint rock encountered during the construction of the Charlotte, Columbia and Augusta Railroad. Not much more than a sprawling country crossroad for several decades following 1852, Rock Hill finally blossomed into an industrial town with the spread of cotton mills in the Upcountry and the development of hydroelectric power on the Catawba River.

In 1895 Rock Hill obtained Winthrop College from Columbia, where it had been founded in 1886. Today Winthrop University offers an art gallery, a golf course and a lake for public enjoyment.

Glencairn Garden, at Charlotte Avenue and Edgemont and Crest streets, is a manicured 6-acre city park with a fountain, lily pond and winding paths. In mid-April, the azaleas, dogwoods and wisteria reach their peak; tulips bloom in spring, annuals throughout the summer.

Rock Hill/York County Convention and Visitors Bureau—Rock Hill: 452 S. Anderson Rd., P.O. Box 11377, Rock Hill, SC 29731; phone (803) 329-5200 or (800) 866-5200.

Shopping areas: Crossroads Mall, I-77 exit 90, houses factory discount stores, including Adidas, Bass, Carolina Pottery and Van Heusen. Rock Hill Galleria, 2301 David Lyle Blvd., offers Belk and Sears.

HISTORIC BRATTONSVILLE—
see McConnells, S.C., p. 263.

MUSEUM OF YORK COUNTY, w. on SR 161 from I-77 exit 82A, then n. on Mount Gallant Rd., offers a planetarium, a large collection of mounted animals from Africa, history and natural history exhibits, and a nature trail. Also displayed are works by artist Vernon Grant. Picnicking is permitted. Museum open Mon.-Sat. 10-5, Sun. 1-5. Planetarium shows Sat.-Sun. at 2, 3 and 4 (also Sat. at 11 a.m.). Closed major holidays. Admission, including planetarium, $5; $4 (ages 60+); $3 (students with ID); free (ages 0-3). Phone (803) 329-2121.

This ends listings for the Charlotte Vicinity.
The following page resumes the alphabetical listings of cities in North Carolina.

CHEROKEE (E-2) elev. 1,991′

Near the southern entrance of Great Smoky Mountains National Park *(see place listing p. 156)* and the Blue Ridge Parkway *(see place listing p. 131)*, the 56,000-acre Qualla Boundary has been home to the Eastern Band of Cherokee Indians for thousands of years. Cherokee history and culture are presented at several museums, an outdoor drama and the Qualla Arts and Crafts Shop.

Cherokee Visitor Center: P.O. Box 460, Cherokee, NC 28719; phone (800) 438-1601 or (828) 497-9195. *See color ad p. 127 & p. 157.*

CHEROKEE MARKER, 2 mi. n. on US 441N, was erected by the United Daughters of the Confederacy in honor of all Cherokees who served with the Confederate Army. Free.

MUSEUM OF THE CHEROKEE INDIAN is at jct. US 441N and Drama Rd. The story of the Cherokee Nation from prehistory to modern times is depicted through audiovisual presentations and exhibits that include crafts, clothing and weapons. Interpretive displays describe the tribe's resettlement to western reservations and the hardships endured along the Trail of Tears.

Allow 1 hour minimum. Mon.-Sat. 9-7, Sun. 9-5, June-Aug.; daily 9-5, rest of year. Closed Jan. 1, Thanksgiving and Dec. 25. Admission $9; $6 (ages 6-13). AX, DS, MC, VI. Phone (828) 497-3481 or (888) 665-7249.

GEM SAVE **OCONALUFTEE INDIAN VILLAGE,** 2.5 mi. n. off US 441N, is a re-creation of a 1750s Cherokee community, where American Indians demonstrate the making of baskets, pottery, canoes, arrows and blowguns. Also of interest are a preserved seven-sided council house as well as huts and cabins containing articles used two centuries ago.

Nature trails and the Cherokee Botanical Gardens are on the grounds. Special programs are available. Guided tours are given daily every 15 minutes 9-5:30, May 15-Oct. 25. Last tour begins 15 minutes before closing. Admission $15; $6 (ages 6-13). MC, VI. Phone (828) 497-2315 or (828) 497-2111.

OCONALUFTEE VISITOR CENTER—
see Great Smoky Mountains National Park p. 160.

SAVE **SANTA'S LAND THEME PARK AND ZOO,** 3 mi. e. on US 19, is a Christmas theme park featuring amusement rides, a large exotic and domestic zoo, a mountain heritage section, and exhibits and entertainment. A Harvest Festival is held every weekend in October. Daily 9-6, day after Memorial Day to mid-Aug.; Mon.-Fri. 10-5, Sat.-Sun. 9-5, May 1-Memorial Day and mid-Aug. through Oct. 31. Admission $18.46; free (ages 0-1). Season pass $35. AX, DS, MC, VI. Phone (828) 497-9191 or (800) 648-7268.

GEM SAVE **"UNTO THESE HILLS",** .5 mi. n. on US 441N in the outdoor Mountainside Theater, is a 2-hour historical drama about the Cherokees. The play, first presented in 1950, covers the period from the arrival of Hernando de Soto in 1540 through the tragic Trail of Tears in 1839. Some descendants of Cherokees who lived the story appear in principal roles. Inquire about weather policies. Mon.-Sat. at 7:30 p.m., mid-June to late Aug. Reserved seating $22; $10 (ages 6-12). General admission $18; $8 (ages 6-12). MC, VI. Phone (828) 497-2111, or (866) 554-4557 for tickets.

GAMBLING ESTABLISHMENTS

- **Harrah's Cherokee Casino** is n. on US 19 at Bus. Rte. 441. Daily 24 hours. Phone (828) 497-7777 or (800) 427-7247.

CHIMNEY ROCK (E-4) pop. 175, elev. 1,040′

Chimney Rock lies in a gorge at the foot of its namesake, a giant granite monolith that rises sharply 315 feet. The town serves as an outfitting post for many recreational activities.

Hickory Nut Gorge Chamber of Commerce and Visitor Center: US 64/74A, P.O. Box 32, Chimney Rock, NC 28720; phone (828) 625-2725.

GEM SAVE **CHIMNEY ROCK PARK** on US 64/74A, is a 1,000-acre park encompassing the Chimney. For exceptional views, including Lake Lure *(see place listing p. 168, Recreation Chart and the AAA Southeastern CampBook)*, visitors can reach the summit by trail and stairs, or by an elevator built into the mountain. Three upper trails lead to 404-foot Hickory Nut Falls. A sheer drop twice the height of Niagara, the falls were featured as a backdrop in the 1992 movie "The Last of the Mohicans."

Two lower trails include the Great Woodland Trail, which has handcrafted sculptures depicting the park's creations; and the Four Seasons Trail, a more strenuous route winding from the meadow to the top of the mountain. Other points of interest include Devil's Head, Moonshiner's Cave and Needle's Eye.

Myriad wildflowers, birds and plants are indigenous to the park. One of the trails is steep in places and should be taken only by the surefooted. Guided hikes are led throughout the year by a park naturalist. Facilities include an observation lounge and a nature center.

Picnicking is permitted. Allow 2 hours minimum. Park open daily 8:30-7, during DST; 8:30-6, rest of year. Last admission 1 hour, 30 minutes before closing. Closed Jan. 1, Thanksgiving and Dec. 25. Admission (when majority of trails are open) $14; $6 (ages 6-15). Reduced admission for winter months $9; $5 (ages 6-15). AX, DS, MC, VI. Phone (828) 625-9611 or (800) 277-9611. *See color ad opposite title page.*

CLEMMONS (B-4) pop. 13,827

GEM **TANGLEWOOD,** 4060 Clemmons Rd., is a former horse farm and estate once owned by William Neal Reynolds, brother of tobacco entrepreneur R.J. Reynolds. The 1,400-acre park includes nature trails; rose, herb, friendship, fragrance and shade gardens; tennis courts; a 36-hole golf course designed by Robert Trent Jones, Sr.; a par-three course; stables; and paddleboat and canoe rentals. The Tanglewood Festival of Lights is held mid-November through January 1 and features more than 100 lighted displays. Picnicking is permitted. Daily dawn-dusk. Lake facilities open Memorial Day weekend-Labor Day. Admission $2 per private vehicle; use of facilities extra. Phone (336) 778-6300.

CLEVELAND (B-4) pop. 808, elev. 819′

PETER NEY'S GRAVE, in the graveyard at the Old Third Creek Presbyterian Church, is said to contain the body of Marshal Michel Ney, aide to Napoleon. According to legend, Ney escaped execution in France, came to America, died in 1846 and was buried under the name of Peter Stewart Ney.

CONCORD—*see Charlotte p. 147.*

CORNELIUS—*see Charlotte p. 147.*

COROLLA—*see Outer Banks p.175.*

CRESWELL (B-8) pop. 278, elev. 10′

PETTIGREW STATE PARK, 8 mi. s. via US 64, covers 17,743 acres and contains sections of an old plantation. Lake Phelps, a wildlife sanctuary, is lined with cypress trees; it also provides excellent fishing. Nature programs are held in the summer. Daily 8 a.m.-9 p.m., June-Aug.; 8-8, Mar.-May and in Oct.; 8-7, rest of year. Closed Dec. 25. Free. Fee for overnight camping. Phone (252) 797-4475. *See Recreation Chart and the AAA Southeastern CampBook.*

Somerset Place State Historic Site is on Lake Phelps. Built in the 1830s, the 14-room plantation house is an example of Greek Revival architecture. As one of North Carolina's most prosperous plantations, Somerset Place encompassed nearly 100,000 acres and produced rice, wheat and corn. Antebellum plantation life and early African-American customs and traditions are highlighted. Three buildings in the former slave community have been reconstructed.

Allow 30 minutes minimum. Mon.-Sat. 9-5, Sun. 1-5, Apr.-Oct.; Tues.-Sat. 10-4, Sun. 1-4, rest of year. Closed Jan. 1, Thanksgiving and Dec. 25. Guided 1.5-hour tours of the mansion, gardens, former slave community and restored outbuildings are conducted on request. Last tour begins 1 hour before closing. Free. Phone (252) 797-4560.

CROATAN NATIONAL FOREST

Elevations in the forest range from sea level to 46 ft. west of Great Lake. Refer to AAA maps for additional elevation information.

Covering 159,586 acres south of New Bern, Croatan National Forest consists mostly of pine and swamp hardwoods. As the most coastal of any national forest in the East, it contains many estuaries and waterfowl nesting areas, as well as public beaches. Three designated areas within the forest provide recreational facilities.

Some of the forest's most interesting wildlife is found in the pocosin ("swamp-on-a-hill"), a wet upland bog with a sponge-like top layer of soil. Among the plant life is the Venus flytrap, which cages insects in its leaves and digests them. The sundew and pitcher plants also supplement their soil diets with insects.

Black bears, alligators, woodpeckers, owls and a small number of bald eagles and falcons are part of the forest's ecosystem. Alligator and osprey habitats can be seen along the White Oak River and other coastal waterways. Canoes or small motorboats are best suited for navigation of the waterways. Both saltwater and freshwater fishing are possible, though fishing in the lakes is generally poor.

Cedar Point Tideland Trail, an elevated boardwalk originating at the mouth of the White Oak River across from Swansboro, winds through tidal marsh areas and hardwood and pine forests. Interpretive signs are found along both the 1- and 2-hour loops of the trail. Maps and camping information are available at the ranger office, 141 E. Fisher Ave., 9 mi. s. of New Bern via US 70E.

Open daily 24 hours. Ranger office open Mon.-Fri. 8-4:30; closed major holidays. Free. Camping $17, tent camping $12. For further information contact the U.S. Forest Service, 141 E. Fisher Ave., New Bern, NC 28560; phone (252) 638-5628. *See Recreation Chart and the AAA Southeastern CampBook.*

CULLOWHEE (F-2) pop. 3,579, elev. 2,400′

Primarily a college town, Cullowhee is the site of Western Carolina University, the University of North Carolina's mountain campus with an enrollment of 6,500. Students and visitors alike take advantage of the boating, fishing, canoeing, hiking and backpacking opportunities available in the nearby mountains and lakes.

Jackson County Travel & Tourism Authority—Cullowhee: 773 W. Main St., Sylva, NC 28779; phone (828) 586-2155 or (800) 962-1911. *See color ad p. 160.*

JUDACULLA ROCK, 3.5 mi. s. via SR 107, then 3 mi. e. on Caney Fork Rd., is a soapstone boulder covered with American Indian pictographs. According to Cherokee legend, these markings were made by a giant named Tsul'kula when he leaped from his mountaintop home to the Caney Fork Creek. Free. Phone (828) 586-2155.

MOUNTAIN HERITAGE CENTER, in the H.F. Robinson Administration Building on SR 107, chronicles the saga of the Scot-Irish, or Ulster-Scots, whose migration and settlement opened the country's frontier. Mon.-Fri. 8-5, Sun. 2-5, June-Oct.; Mon.-Fri. 8-5, rest of year. Free. Phone (828) 227-7129.

DALLAS (C-4) pop. 3,402, elev. 890′

Gaston County Travel & Tourism—Dallas: 620 N. Main St., Belmont, NC 28012; phone (704) 825-4044 or (800) 849-9994.

GASTON COUNTY MUSEUM OF ART AND HISTORY, 131 W. Main St., is in the former Hoffman Hotel on Dallas Square. The 1852 building has Victorian period rooms, a carriage and sleigh collection and changing exhibitions of art, local history and textile history. Brochures detailing Dallas' historic town square are available. Tues.-Fri. 10-5, Sat. noon-4, first Sun. of the month 2-5. Free. Phone (704) 852-6025 or (704) 922-7681.

DANBURY (A-5) pop. 108, elev. 825′

Danbury lies at the foot of the Sauratown Mountains near the Dan River. Union general George Stoneman made his headquarters in Danbury on Apr. 9, 1865, the day Gen. Robert E. Lee surrendered at Appomattox.

The *Danbury Reporter* is one of the oldest county weeklies in North Carolina. In the late 1800s the newspaper office was destroyed by fire, but the press was rescued and propped against a young tree. A new press was acquired and the old one forgotten. As the tree grew the original press became embedded in its trunk, and the two remained entwined until the tree died in the 1960s.

HANGING ROCK STATE PARK is 4 mi. n.w. off SR 8. The 6,921-acre park offers rugged mountain terrain, sparkling streams, waterfalls and a lake. More than 300 species of mountain flora are found within the park. Camping is permitted and cabins are available year-round; reservations are required. Swimming and bathhouse facilities are open June 1 through Labor Day.

Park open daily 8 a.m.-9 p.m., June-Aug.; 8-8, Apr.-May and in Sept.; 8-7 in Mar. and Oct.; 8-6, rest of year. Visitor center open daily 9-4:45. Closed Dec. 25. Free. Phone (336) 593-8480. *See Recreation Chart and the AAA Southeastern CampBook.*

DILLSBORO (F-2) pop. 205, elev. 1,983′

On the banks of the Tuckaseegee River, the four-block town of Dillsboro offers browsers more than 50 shops, galleries and studios specializing in traditional mountain crafts.

Jackson County Travel & Tourism Authority—Dillsboro: 773 W. Main St., Sylva, NC 28779; phone (828) 586-2155 or (800) 962-1911.

GREAT SMOKY MOUNTAINS RAILROAD—
see Bryson City p. 135.

DOBSON (A-4) pop. 1,457, elev. 1,259′

WINERIES

- **Shelton Vineyards** is at 286 Cabernet Ln. Guided tours Mon.-Sat. 10-6, Sun. 1-6; winter hours may vary. Closed Easter, Thanksgiving and Dec. 25. Tour and tasting $5 per person. Phone (336) 366-4724.

DUNN (C-6) pop. 9,196, elev. 214′

THE GENERAL WILLIAM C. LEE AIRBORNE MUSEUM, 209 W. Divine St., is in the former house of Gen. Lee. Known as the "Father of the Airborne," Lee was assigned by President Franklin D. Roosevelt to organize the development of Army airborne units. His efforts led to the establishment of the Airborne Command and earned him the Distinguished Service Medal. Exhibits include World War II memorabilia and historical documents.

Allow 1 hour minimum. Mon.-Fri. 10-4, Sat. 11-4; closed Thanksgiving and Dec. 25. Donations. Phone (910) 892-1947.

DURHAM (B-6) pop. 187,035, elev. 406′

Durham, home of Research Triangle Park, Duke University and North Carolina Central University, is known for excellence in medicine, education, research, technology and industry. With five major hospitals, including the Duke University Medical Center, and a physician-to-population ratio five times greater than the national average, the city has exchanged its old identity of "tobacco town" for that of "City of Medicine, USA."

The Research Triangle Region is an area twice the size of Rhode Island and half the size of the state of Connecticut. The term "Triangle" was first used to refer to an area anchored by the state's three major universities—University of North Carolina at Chapel Hill *(see listing p. 137)*, North Carolina State University in Raleigh and Duke. It now refers to a six-county metropolitan statistical area and a 13-county state planning region.

A 7,000-acre wooded tract of land, 4 miles south of downtown via SR 147, is known as Research Triangle Park. The park is a special Durham County tax district.

Durham Visitor Information Center: 101 East Morgan St., Durham, NC 27701; phone (919) 687-0288 or (800) 446-8604.

BENNETT PLACE STATE HISTORIC SITE is at 4409 Bennett Memorial Rd., 4 mi. n.w. off US 70/I-85 exit 173 southbound or 170 northbound. The site includes the restored Bennett House, where the largest Confederate troop surrender of the Civil War took place on April 26, 1865. It was here that Gen. Joseph E. Johnston surrendered some 89,000 soldiers to Gen. William T. Sherman. Additional exhibits pertaining to the Civil War also are displayed in the visitor center.

Picnicking is permitted. Allow 1 hour minimum. Visitor center Tues.-Sat. 10-5; closed major holidays. Hours may vary; phone ahead. Guided 30-minute tours are given daily on the half-hour, and an audiovisual show is presented every hour. Last tour begins 30 minutes before closing. Donations. Phone (919) 383-4345.

DUKE HOMESTEAD STATE HISTORIC SITE AND TOBACCO MUSEUM is off I-85 exit 175 to 2828 Duke Homestead Rd. The 1852 main house, two early tobacco factories, a packhouse and a curing barn reflect the historical impact of the tobacco industry on North Carolina. The museum includes a moving mannequin that plants tobacco and explains—with a North Carolina accent—the "13-month crop." The visitor center offers a museum and a movie about the history of tobacco.

Guided walking tours are available. Allow 1 hour, 30 minutes minimum. Tues.-Sat. 10-5; closed state holidays. Hours may vary; phone ahead. Free. Phone (919) 477-5498.

DUKE UNIVERSITY spans two campuses. The East Campus is s. off I-85 Guess Rd. exit, then w. on Broad St. For the West Campus take US 15/501 bypass to SR 751, then go e. to Duke University Rd. and follow signs. The West Campus features Gothic-style buildings while the architecture of the East Campus, formerly Trinity College, is predominantly Georgian. The combined enrollment is more than 12,000 students.

GEM **Duke University Chapel,** on the West Campus, is the central and dominant structure of the university buildings. The 50-bell carillon, with bells ranging in weight from 10 to 11,200 pounds, plays Mon.-Fri. at 5. The chapel houses the Flentrop Organ, which contains five keyboards and rises nearly 40 feet above the gallery floor. Allow 30 minutes minimum. Daily 8-5; closed Dec. 25 and for private occasions. Free. Phone (919) 684-2572.

SAVE **Nasher Museum of Art** is at 2001 Campus Dr. on the Duke University campus. The permanent collection focuses on medieval and Renaissance works, classical sculpture, and African and pre-Columbian art. Two additional galleries feature changing exhibits highlighting contemporary art. Allow 1 hour minimum. Tues.-Sat. 10-5 (also Thurs. 5-9), Sun. noon-5; closed major holidays. Guided tours are offered Sat.-Sun. at 2. Admission $5; $4 (ages 65+); $3 (students with ID); free (ages 0-16). Parking $2 per hour. MC, VI. Phone (919) 684-5135.

Sarah P. Duke Gardens, on the West Campus, encompasses 55 acres. This public garden space is a living museum dedicated to excellence in garden design, horticulture and plant collections. Seasonal colors can be enjoyed in the formal Terrace Garden. A 300-bush rose garden also is featured. Allow 1 hour minimum. Daily 8-dusk. Free. Phone (919) 684-3698.

HISTORIC STAGVILLE is off I-85S exit 177C, 1.4 mi. n. on Roxboro Rd., then 6.8 mi. e. to 5828 Old Oxford Hwy. This site represents the remnants of one of the South's largest antebellum plantations owned by the Bennehan-Cameron families. Stagville's furnished main house, slave quarters and large barn are all that remain of the former estate. Daily life, particularly that of the African-American community, is highlighted with exhibits and a 10-minute slide presentation.

Allow 1 hour, 30 minutes minimum. Tues.-Sat. 10-4; closed major holidays. Guided tours are available on the hour. Free. Phone (919) 620-0120.

MUSEUM OF LIFE AND SCIENCE is off I-85 Duke St. exit 176B, .7 mi. n. on US 501, then .2 mi. e. on Murray Ave. The museum explores the natural and physical sciences through interactive exhibits. Visitors can see native animals in the Nature Center, experience rare insects at the Bayer CropScience Insectarium, launch a Space Shuttle model and meet animals in the farmyard. Magic Wings Butterfly House is a three-story glass conservatory housing more than 500 tropical butterflies.

Food is available. Allow 2 hours minimum. Mon.-Sat. 10-5, Sun. noon-5, Jan. 1-Labor Day; Tues.-Sat. 10-5, Sun. noon-5, rest of year. Closed Jan. 1, Thanksgiving and Dec. 25. Admission $10.85; $8.85 (ages 65+ and military with ID); $7.85 (ages 3-12). Miniature train tour $2. MC, VI. Phone (919) 220-5429.

WEST POINT ON THE ENO, 5101 N. Roxboro Rd., is a 388-acre natural and historic city park on a 2-mile stretch of the Eno River. Hiking, canoeing, rafting and fishing are permitted. Environmental education programs and special events are offered throughout the year. Guided tours of the three historic buildings, West Point Mill, McCown-Mangum House and the Hugh Mangum Museum of Photography, are available on request.

Picnicking is permitted. Allow 1 hour minimum. Park open daily 8-dusk. Historic buildings open Sat.-Sun. 1-5, Mar.-Dec.; by appointment rest of year. Free. Phone (919) 471-1623. *See Recreation Chart.*

EDENTON (B-8) pop. 5,394, elev. 18'

One of the oldest communities in the state, Edenton served as a Colonial center of commerce, society and politics. Named for Lords Proprietary governor Charles Eden and incorporated in 1722, it was the first capital of the colony.

On the courthouse green is a marker commemorating the Edenton Tea Party, thought to be the first purely political action by women in the American Colonies–on Oct. 25, 1774, a group of 51 signed a resolution supporting the action of the North Carolina Provincial Assembly to boycott highly taxed British goods.

Historic Edenton State Historic Site Visitor Center: 108 N. Broad St., P.O. Box 474, Edenton, NC 27932; phone (252) 482-2637.

Self-guiding tours: The visitor center provides maps ($1 each) for several self-guiding walking tours originating there emphasizing the area's African-American history and architectural diversity; guided walking and trolley tours are available for a fee. Free maps and brochures outlining historic sites and attractions in the northeast region also are available at the center.

HISTORIC EDENTON STATE HISTORIC SITE includes several notable Colonial buildings of the old town. Guided walking and trolley tours begin at the Historic Edenton Visitor Center, a late 19th-century frame house at 108 N. Broad St. A 14-minute slide show and exhibits about the area are presented.

Wear comfortable shoes for the tours. Allow 2 hours minimum. The visitor center is open Mon.-Sat. 9-5, Sun. 1-4, Apr.-Oct.; Mon.-Sat. 10-4, Sun. 1-4, rest of year. Last tour departs 1 hour before closing. Forty-five minute trolley tours Tues.-Sat. at 10, 11, noon, 2, 3 and 4. Center closed Jan. 1, Martin Luther King Jr. Day, Good Friday, Veterans Day, Thanksgiving, day after Thanksgiving and Dec. 24-26.

Admission to visitor center free. Guided tour $10; $3.50 (grades K-12); $20 (family). Mini-tour (includes admission to two buildings) $4; $1.50 (grades K-12); $8 (family). Trolley tour $10; $2 (students). Phone (252) 482-2637.

Chowan County Courthouse, on E. King St., is an example of Georgian architecture. Built in 1767, it is said to be the most intact Colonial courthouse in America, and one of the oldest in the country.

Cupola House, 408 S. Broad St., was built in 1758. Its Georgian interior has elaborate woodwork and windows of wavy glass, with signatures more than 150 years old scratched into the panes.

James Iredell House State Historic Site, 105 E. Church St., was built in the early 1800s and was the homesite of Iredell, the first attorney general of North Carolina and a justice of the first U.S. Supreme Court.

St. Paul's Church (Episcopal), at Broad and Church sts., is a Colonial village church. The structure, built 1736-66, was partially burned in 1949 but was restored. Communion silver from 1725 is in use. The graves of three Colonial governors—Charles Eden, Henderson Walker and Thomas Pollack—are in the churchyard.

ELIZABETH CITY (A-8) pop. 17,188, elev. 6'

Elizabeth City is at the Narrows of the Pasquotank River, approximately 12 nautical miles from the Albemarle Sound. The Dismal Swamp Canal connects the Elizabeth River in Virginia and the Pasquotank River. After the canal was dug in 1790, Elizabeth City's development began.

By the early 1800s a vigorous trade with the West Indies was established. One hundred years later the freshwater, landlocked harbor on the Pasquotank River rivaled Baltimore as one of the East Coast's ports. It remains busy today. The city's revitalized waterfront and proximity to the Intracoastal Waterway draw pleasure boaters. Nearby are the large U.S. Coast Guard Air Station Elizabeth City and the Elizabeth City Shipyard.

Reminders of early days include the old Christ Episcopal Church and the Old Brick House.

Elizabeth City Area Convention & Visitors Bureau: 400 S. Water St., Suite 101, Elizabeth City, NC 27909; phone (866) 324-8948.

MUSEUM OF THE ALBEMARLE, 501 S. Water St., displays American Indian relics and other artifacts reflecting the history of the region. Visitors encounter hands-on exhibits in the Discovery Room. Allow 30 minutes minimum. Tues.-Sat. 9-5, Sun. 2-5; closed state holidays. Free. Phone (252) 335-1453.

ELLERBE (C-5) pop. 1,021, elev. 540'

Soothing mineral waters first lured people to the hamlet known in the early days as Ellerbe Springs. A rambling hotel built in 1906 with wide porches and Victorian appointments still stands. Today boating and fishing on the nearby Pee Dee River are popular summer pastimes.

RANKIN MUSEUM OF AMERICAN HERITAGE, 131 W. Church St., contains natural and cultural history exhibits. Included are a fossil collection spanning 500 million years; mounted animals from around the world; and 19th-century works by noted Piedmont potters. The Tribes of the Amazon exhibit contains art, ceremonial clothing and weapons from South America's indigenous peoples. Allow 1 hour minimum. Mon.-Fri. 10-4, Sat.-Sun. 2-5; closed major holidays. Admission $4; $1 (ages 5-18). Phone (910) 652-6378.

FAYETTEVILLE (C-6) pop. 121,015, elev. 135'

As North Carolina's most inland port, Fayetteville became an early trade center because of its position at the head of the Cape Fear River. When water transportation declined, Fayetteville responded by building a system of plank roads that revitalized commerce. Business generated by Fort Bragg *(see place listing p. 154)* and Pope Air Force Base military installations is Fayetteville's economic mainstay. At home in Fayetteville is the 4,000-student Fayetteville State University.

Fayetteville's historic sites include the Old Market House, which was built in 1832 in the center of downtown, and Heritage Square. Dick Street features three historic buildings. More contemporary buildings include the Cumberland County Coliseum Complex, which is home to The Fayetteville Force professional hockey team, as well as other sporting events, concerts and theater productions.

Fayetteville Area Convention and Visitors Bureau: 245 Person St., Fayetteville, NC 28301; phone (910) 483-5311 or (800) 255-8217.

Self-guiding tours: Brochures outlining Fayetteville's many historic houses and other points of interest are available from the convention and visitors bureau.

GEM SAVE **AIRBORNE AND SPECIAL OPERATIONS MUSEUM** is at 100 Bragg Blvd. This 59,000-square-foot museum features life-size dioramas, rare aircraft, artifacts and interactive displays commemorating this special sector of the armed forces from its inception in 1940 to the present. Highlights include a large-screen movie theater and a 24-seat motion simulator that places visitors in the midst of parachute jumps, helicopter gunship attacks and daring missions.

Allow 1 hour minimum. Tues.-Sat. and Mon. federal holidays 10-5, Sun. noon-5; closed Jan. 1, Easter, Thanksgiving and Dec. 25. Museum free. Motion simulator and theater each $4; free (ages 0-8 with adult). Combination ticket $7. Phone (910) 643-2766.

SAVE **CAPE FEAR BOTANICAL GARDEN** is 2 mi. n. of Market St. at 536 N. Eastern Blvd. Situated on 85 acres overlooking Cross Creek and the Cape Fear River, the garden includes an urban forest, formal gardens and more than 700 species of native plants and 2,500 varieties of ornamentals. A natural amphitheater, an 1886 farmhouse and a gazebo also are on the grounds. Seasonal events, garden tours and festivals are offered.

Picnicking is permitted. Allow 1 hour minimum. Mon.-Sat. 10-5, Sun. and holidays noon-5, Mar. 1 to mid-Dec.; Mon.-Sat. 10-5, rest of year. Closed Jan. 1-2, Good Friday, Thanksgiving and Dec. 24-31. Admission $5; $4 (military with ID); free (ages 0-12 and first Sat. of the month). MC, VI. Phone (910) 486-0221.

FASCINATE-U CHILDREN'S MUSEUM, 116 Green St., features hands-on exhibits encouraging children to explore their world through role-playing and interaction. Visitors can slide down the pole at a fire station, drive an ambulance, work at a bakery and shop in a grocery store. Allow 1 hour minimum. Tues.-Fri. 9-5 (also Wed. 5-7), Sat. 10-5, Sun. noon-5; closed holidays. Admission $3 (ages 1-12); $1 (adults); free (ages 1-7 on Wed.). AX, MC, VI. Phone (910) 829-9171.

FIRST PRESBYTERIAN CHURCH, Bow and Ann sts., was built in 1800, destroyed by fire in 1831 and rebuilt in 1832. It is an example of the classic Southern Colonial style of architecture. The communion silver, crystal chandeliers, hand-wrought-iron locks and hardware, and the carving on the galleries are noteworthy. Mon.-Fri. 8-5. Free. Phone (910) 483-0121.

MUSEUM OF THE CAPE FEAR, 801 Arsenal Ave., is a branch of the North Carolina Museum of History Division. The museum traces the events that shaped the development of southern North Carolina. Highlights include pottery and exhibits about the early settlements of American Indians, the antebellum period, the Civil War and the textile industry. Tours of the 1897 E. A. Poe House interpret late Victorian life 1897-1917.

Tues.-Sat. 10-5, Sun. 1-5; closed major holidays. Free. Phone (910) 486-1330.

FLAT ROCK (F-3) pop. 2,565, elev. 2,214′

Flat Rock is one of the oldest resort towns in western North Carolina. Flat Rock Playhouse, the state theater, presents performances from late April to mid-December. Matinees are given Wed.-Thurs. and Sat.-Sun. at 2:15; evening performances are Wed.-Sat. at 8:15 p.m. Phone (828) 693-0731 to confirm hours.

Henderson County Travel and Tourism/Visitor Information Center—Flat Rock: 201 South Main St., P.O. Box 721, Hendersonville, NC 28792; phone (828) 693-9708 or (800) 828-4244.

CARL SANDBURG HOME NATIONAL HISTORIC SITE (CONNEMARA), on Carl Sandburg Ln. off I-26 exit 53 following signs, was the house of the poet-historian from 1945 until his death in 1967. The house displays a collection of some 10,000 books as well as the poet's notes. While Sandburg wrote, his wife managed a 240-acre goat farm, still maintained on the grounds. Hiking trails are available; a bookstore contains exhibits and offers information on laser disk.

Guided house tours are offered. Picnicking is permitted. Grounds daily 9-5. Closed Dec. 25. First tour departs at 9:30. Last tour begins 30 minutes before closing. Tour $5; $3 (ages 62+); free (ages 0-15). Phone (828) 693-4178.

ST. JOHN'S IN THE WILDERNESS, on US 25 at 1905 Greenville Hwy., dates from 1832 and is one of the oldest churches in western North Carolina. Christopher G. Memminger, Secretary of the Treasury of the Confederacy, is buried at the church. Sunday services are held at 8:45 and 11. Daily 9-4. Free. Phone (828) 693-9783.

FONTANA VILLAGE (E-1) elev. 2,900′

Historic Fontana Village is a year-round resort at the southern edge of Great Smoky Mountains National Park *(see place listing p. 156)*. The village's location on the 10,600-acre Fontana Lake makes it a popular destination for camping, boating, fishing and swimming; lake tours and park shuttles are available. The resort also offers horseback riding, mountain biking, guided nature hikes and organized activities. Phone (800) 849-2258.

Fontana Dam, 3 miles northeast, is said to be the tallest dam in the eastern United States. The visitor building lobby is open daily 9-5, May-Oct. *(see Recreation Chart and the AAA Southeastern CampBook)*. SR 28 provides a scenic drive west along the Little Tennessee River to Tapoco.

FORT BRAGG (C-6)

FORT BRAGG, off I-95 exit 52 (SR 24) n.w. to Bragg Blvd., is one of America's largest and most important military installations. Valid ID is required and all vehicles will be subject to a search before proceeding on post.

82nd Airborne Division Museum, Ardennes St. at Gela St., is dedicated to the division's combat dead. The history of the division is told through pictures

intricate carvings, only 14 such carousels still exist worldwide. In addition to 26 horses, the hand-carved animals include a lion, tiger, giraffe and reindeer, four pigs, rabbits, ostriches and cats. The carousel operates seasonally and hours vary; phone (336) 222-5030.

Burlington/Alamance County Convention and Visitors Bureau: 610 S. Lexington Ave., P.O. Box 519, Burlington, NC 27216; phone (336) 570-1444 or (800) 637-3804.

Shopping areas: The Burlington Manufacturer's Outlet Center, at I-85/40, exit 145, houses more than 50 stores and is open daily.

ALAMANCE BATTLEGROUND STATE HISTORIC SITE, off I-40/85 exit 143, then 6 mi. s.w. on SR 62, commemorates the 1771 battle between Royalist governor William Tryon's militia and an inexperienced group of Colonial reformers known as the "Regulators," who protested taxes, corrupt officials and non-representation. The John Allen house, a log house typical of 1780s North Carolina, is on the battlefield near the visitor center. The visitor center offers a 20-minute audiovisual presentation about the battle.

Guided tours and special programs are available. Picnicking is permitted. Mon.-Sat. 9-5. Hours may vary; phone ahead. Free. Phone (336) 227-4785.

ALAMANCE COUNTY HISTORICAL MUSEUM is off I-40/85 exit 143 to 4777 SR 62S. The museum is inside the 19th-century home of Edwin Michael Holt, an early textile manufacturer. Guided tours take visitors through the two-story Italianate Revival plantation house, which contains furnishings and accessories from the mid-1800s as well as changing exhibits. The Holt family cemetery and several farm buildings constructed immediately after the Civil War also are on the premises.

Allow 1 hour minimum. Tues.-Fri. 9-5, Sat. 10:30-5, Sun. 1-5; closed major holidays. Free. Phone (336) 226-8254.

CEDAROCK PARK AND HISTORICAL FARM is at 3916 R. Dean Coleman Rd. Located on an 1830 farm that belonged to John and Polly Garrett, the 414-acre county park offers hiking, bicycling and horse trails; two 18-hole disc golf courses and a fishing pond (a state fishing license is required). The farm site features the original Garrett farmhouse and other buildings. Kids will enjoy the goats, sheep and other farm animals. Allow 1 hour minimum. Daily 8-6, with extended hours in summer. Park free. Rates for park activities vary. Phone (336) 229-2379. *See Recreation Chart.*

CAPE HATTERAS NATIONAL SEASHORE—*see Outer Banks p. 174.*

CAPE LOOKOUT NATIONAL SEASHORE—*see Outer Banks p. 174.*

CASHIERS (F-2) pop. 196

Cashiers is on a plateau surrounded by the Nantahala National Forest and the Appalachian Mountains in the southern crest of the Blue Ridge Mountains. The first European settlers, primarily from the British Isles, arrived in the early 1800s and by the end of the 19th century Cashiers was a summer home for many of the Southern elite. Still a resort town, summer activities include golfing, fishing, swimming, boating, horseback riding and tennis.

Cashiers Chamber of Commerce: P.O. Box 238, Cashiers, NC 28717; phone (828) 743-5191.

WHITEWATER FALLS SCENIC AREA is 10 mi. e. on US 64, then 10 mi. s. on US 281. The Whitewater River drops more than 400 feet in a series of falls and cascades. A point above the falls offers a view of the mountains and the South Carolina Piedmont. Picnicking is permitted. Phone (828) 743-5191.

CATAWBA (B-4) pop. 698

SAVE **HISTORIC MURRAY'S MILL COMPLEX,** 2.5 mi. w. on SR 10, then .5 mi. w. on Murray's Mill Rd., contains the homes of four generations of the Murray family. Included on the site are an operating turn-of-the-20th-century general store, a granary adapted as a folk art gallery, the restored 1913 miller's residence, and an operating gristmill with a 28-foot waterwheel.

Allow 1 hour minimum. Thurs.-Sat. 9-4, Sun. 1:30-4:30, Mar.-Dec.; closed major holidays. Guided 1-hour tours are available Fri.-Sat. 1-4, Sun. 1:30-4:30. Guided tours $3. Phone (828) 241-4299.

CHAPEL HILL (B-6) pop. 48,715, elev. 502′

Named for the New Hope Chapel that was erected on a hill at the crossing of two main roads, the community of Chapel Hill now centers on the campus of the University of North Carolina at Chapel Hill *(see attraction listing)*. The Research Triangle Park, a center for industrial and governmental research, is 12 miles east of Chapel Hill via SR 54 and I-40 *(see Durham p. 151)*.

Chapel Hill/Orange County Visitors Bureau: 501 W. Franklin St., Chapel Hill, NC 27516; phone (919) 968-2060 or (888) 968-2060.

PATTERSON'S MILL COUNTRY STORE is off I-40 exit 273B; take SR 54 s.w. to 5109 Farrington Rd. The store houses mercantile memorabilia, and many of the items displayed have been part of the store's inventory for more than a century. Exhibits include an extensive pharmaceutical collection and tobacco paraphernalia. A furnished, early 20th-century doctor's office and relics from the Patterson's Mill community also can be seen. Allow 1 hour minimum. Tues.-Sat. 10-5, Sun. 2-5; closed Easter and Dec. 25. Free. Phone (919) 493-8149.

and relics of its campaigns from 1917 to the present. Tues.-Sat. and Mon. holidays 10-4:30. Free. Phone (910) 432-3443.

John F. Kennedy Special Warfare Museum, at Ardennes and Marion sts. in Bldg. D 2502, serves as the branch museum for the U.S. Army Special Forces Training Group, the Green Berets. Exhibits illustrate the history of special operations units in the U.S. Army. Tues.-Sun. 11-4. Free. Phone (910) 432-1533.

FORT RALEIGH NATIONAL HISTORIC SITE—*see Outer Banks p. 177.*

FOUR OAKS (C-7) pop. 1,424, elev. 211′

BENTONVILLE BATTLEFIELD STATE HISTORIC SITE, 17 mi. s. off SR 1008 at 5466 Harper House Rd., saw the largest land engagement in North Carolina. One of the last conflicts of the Civil War was fought on this site March 19-21, 1865. The Harper House was used as a hospital by Union troops during the war and is furnished as a Civil War field hospital. The visitor center offers exhibits and an orientation presentation. Battle trenches, a cemetery and a history trail with exhibits also are on the grounds.

Allow 1 hour, 30 minutes minimum. Mon.-Sat. 9-5; closed major holidays. Guided tours are available on the hour. Free. Phone (910) 594-0789.

FRANKLIN (F-2) pop. 3,490, elev. 2,250′

Franklin, on a ridge overlooking the Little Tennessee River, was named for Jesse Franklin, governor of North Carolina 1820-21. The portion of SR 28 leading southeast to Highlands offers scenic views of the Nantahala National Forest *(see place listing p. 171, Recreation Chart and the AAA Southeastern CampBook).*

The city's major industries—sawmilling and talc—reflect the region's natural resources. Many precious and semiprecious stones are mined around Franklin.

Franklin Area Chamber of Commerce: 425 Porter St., Franklin, NC 28734; phone (828) 524-3161 or (800) 336-7829.

HORSESHOE BEND is about 20 mi. n. on SR 28, along the Little Tennessee River. The site offers a stunning panorama with abundant mountain flowers.

SAVE **ROSE CREEK MINE** is 5 mi. n. on SR 28 to Bennett Rd., n. on Rose Creek Rd., then w. on Lyle Downs Rd., following signs to 115 Terrace Ridge Dr. Gemstones that have been found at this site include amethysts, garnets, rose quartz, rubies, sapphires and topaz. Allow 1 hour minimum. Daily 9-5, Apr.-Oct. Admission (including one gravel-filled bucket) $6; $3 (ages 0-8). AX, DS, MC, VI. Phone (828) 349-3774.

SCOTTISH TARTANS MUSEUM, 86 E. Main St., depicts the history of the Scottish tartan from its earliest days in A.D. 325. Exhibits delineate the evolution of the kilt, from function to tradition. Displays include tartans and Highland dress from 1700 to the present and a complete registry of all publicly known tartans. Weaving demonstrations also are given, and visitors may view their family tartan by computer in the research library. Mon.-Sat. 10-5; closed major holidays. Admission $2; $1 (ages 0-9). AX, MC, VI. Phone (828) 524-7472.

STANDING INDIAN MOUNTAIN is 12 mi. w. on US 64, then 2 mi. e. on old US 64 and 2 mi. s. on FR 67. Noted for purple rhododendron and fine views, this 5,498-foot mountain is a part of the Nantahala National Forest *(see place listing p. 171, Recreation Chart and the AAA Southeastern CampBook).*

WAYAH BALD is 5 mi. s.w. on US 64, then 10 mi. w. on Wayah Bald Rd. and 6 mi. n. on FR 69. At 5,335 feet, Wayah Bald displays an array of mountain flowers in May and June and offers panoramic views of the mountains and four adjoining states from the John B. Byrne Memorial Tower. Daily 24 hours. Free.

FREMONT (B-7) pop. 1,463, elev. 153′

CHARLES B. AYCOCK BIRTHPLACE STATE HISTORIC SITE, approximately 1 mi. s. off US 117, is the birthplace of this former governor and founder of North Carolina's 20th-century public educational system. The restored farmhouse and one-room school date from 1870 and 1893, respectively. Farm animals are on the grounds. The visitor center offers a slide presentation and exhibits.

Picnicking is permitted. Mon.-Sat. 9-5, Apr.-Oct.; Tues.-Sat. 10-4, rest of year. Closed Jan. 1, Veterans Day, Thanksgiving, day after Thanksgiving and Dec. 24-27. Guided 1-hour tours are offered on request. Free. Phone (919) 242-5581.

FRISCO—*see Outer Banks p. 178.*

GASTONIA (C-4) pop. 66,277, elev. 825′

Gastonia is a textile-manufacturing city in the industrial Piedmont west of Charlotte. Nearby are Kings Mountain National Military Park, S.C., *(see place listing p. 262)* and Crowders Mountain State Park *(see Recreation Chart).*

A strike at Gastonia's Loray Mill in the 1920s became the subject of several novels: "A Stone Came Rolling" by Fielding Burke, "Strike" by Mary Heaton Vorse and "To Make My Bread" by Grace Lumpkin.

Gaston County Travel & Tourism-Gastonia: 620 N. Main St., Belmont, NC 28012; phone (704) 825-4044 or (800) 849-9994.

GEM SAVE **THE SCHIELE MUSEUM OF NATURAL HISTORY** is off I-85 exit 20 (New Hope Road), following signs to 1500 E. Garrison Blvd.. Regional dioramas are presented in the North Carolina Hall of Natural History. The Everglades, the Sonoran Desert and the Alaskan tundra are brought to life in the Hall of North American

Habitats. The Hall of North American Wildlife features an extensive collection including moose, elk, buffalo, birds, insects and live reptiles. The Robinson Hall of Earth and Man includes fossils, exhibits about prehistoric man, and one of the region's largest gem and mineral displays.

Tools, weapons, housing and adornments of 12 tribal groups are exhibited in the Henry Hall of the North American Indian. The James H. Lynn Planetarium offers astronomy and space science presentations. A half-mile nature trail features a Memorial Wildlife Garden, a Catawba Indian Village, a Stone Age Heritage Site and an 18th-century Backcountry Farm.

Allow 1 hour, 30 minutes minimum. Museum open Mon.-Sat. 9-5 (also second and fourth Tues. of the month 5-8), Sun. 1-5. Planetarium shows Mon.-Fri. at 3, Sat. at 1, 2 and 3, Sun. at 2 and 3, June 1 through mid-Aug.; Wed. at 3:30, Sat. at 1, 2 and 3, Sun. at 2 and 3, Sept.-May. Backcountry Farm and Catawba Indian Village open daily, June 1 through mid-Aug. Hours for farm and village may vary; phone ahead. Museum admission $4; $2 (ages 65+ and students with ID); free (ages 0-3 and on second and fourth Tues. of the month 4-8). Planetarium $3; $2 (ages 65+ and students with ID); free (ages 0-3). Phone (704) 866-6900 or (704) 866-6908.

GOLDSBORO (C-7) pop. 39,043, elev. 105′

WAYNE COUNTY MUSEUM is at 116 N. William St. Housed in a 1927 building once used by the Goldsboro Woman's Club and the United Service Organizations, the museum depicts the area's history through exhibits and artifacts. Highlights include a medical exhibit, a Civil War diorama and the Wayne County Wall of Fame. Allow 30 minutes minimum. Tues.-Sat. 11-4; closed major holidays. Free. Phone (919) 734-5023.

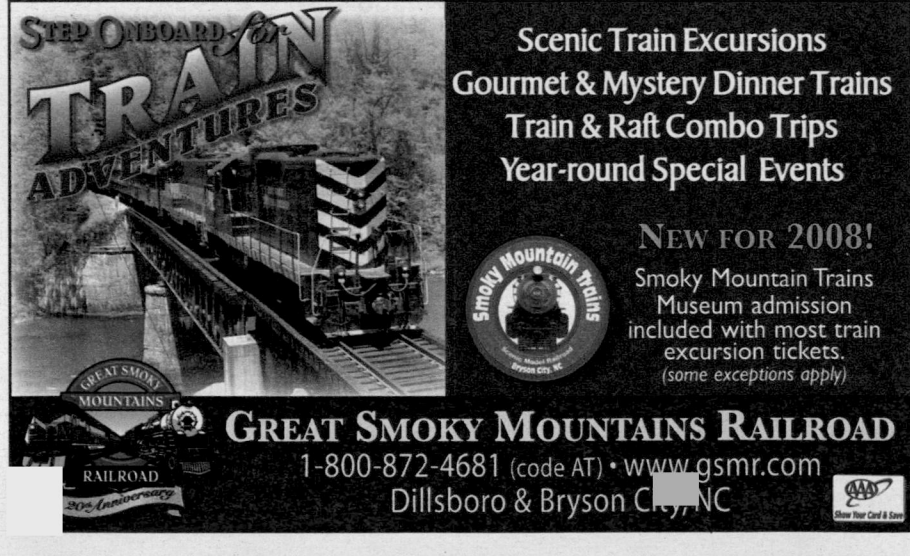

GREAT SMOKY MOUNTAINS NATIONAL PARK

Elevations in the park range from 840 ft. along Abrams Creek to 6,643 ft. at Clingmans Dome. Refer to AAA maps for additional elevation information.

Great Smoky Mountains National Park covers more than 520,000 acres divided between North Carolina and Tennessee. A blue, smokelike haze almost always hangs over the mountains—hence the name. Newfound Gap Road (US 441) bisects the park, which is 53 miles long and 18 miles wide.

With the exceptions of Mount Mitchell and Mount Craig, the highest mountain peaks in eastern North America are found in the Smokies—the most massive mountain uplift in the East and one of the oldest land areas on Earth. Sixteen mountain summits rise more than 6,000 feet, and the main ridge does not drop below 5,000 feet for a distance of 36 miles.

Few places in the United States have such varied vegetation. Because the mountains catch the region's copious rainfall, they support an exceptionally wide variety of plants. There are more than 100 native species of trees. A fine stand of Eastern deciduous trees and a large tract of red spruce constitute the park's 120,000 acres of old-growth forest. Much of the remainder is second growth.

Northern conifers, mainly spruce and fir, dominate the higher elevations; at intermediate heights grow hardwoods typical of the Northeast. Some mountaintops are covered only with grass or shrubs and thus are known as "balds."

Many streams are bordered with rhododendron, and in certain areas, such as on Gregory Bald, flame azalea grows in profusion. Rhododendron and sand myrtle are scattered throughout the mountain summits and knife-edged ridges. Dogwood and innumerable wildflowers usually bloom from mid-March to mid-May; other blossoms create spectacular displays into July.

Wildlife was scarce when the park was established in 1934, but hunting has since been outlawedand many species are recovering. Deer are often observed in Cades Cove *(see attraction listing)*, and ruffed grouse, wild turkeys and bears live in the park.

General Information and Activities

The park is open all year. Headquarters and the Sugarlands Visitor Center are 2 miles south of Gatlinburg, Tenn., on US 441. Information about naturalist-led hikes, campfire programs and other park activities can be obtained here and at the Oconaluftee Visitor Center, near the Cherokee *(see place listing p. 149)* entrance. Illustrated talks are given from mid-May through October in selected campgrounds and at the visitor centers.

There are 238 miles of paved and 146 miles of gravel park roads. Newfound Gap Road (US 441), a scenic 33-mile-long Cherokee-Gatlinburg route with an elevation of 5,048 feet at the state line, crosses the park. The 469-mile scenic Blue Ridge Parkway *(see place listing p. 131)* links the park with Virginia's Shenandoah National Park *(see Virginia)*. The Balsam Mountain Road, a 9-mile spur, branches off the parkway just north of the Cherokee Indian Reservation. Heintooga Ridge Road, a scenic loop drive, leads to an overlook.

CCinc. Auto Tape Tours, available at stores and motels in Gatlinburg, Tenn., and Cherokee, N.C., and by mail, allow driver and passengers to enjoy a guided tour of the park at their own pace; phone (201) 236-1666.

The park has more than 850 miles of horse and foot trails. Leaflets are provided at the start of short self-guiding nature trails. The most heavily used path is the section of the Appalachian Trail that runs the length of the park. Back-country shelters and campsites along the trail are spaced a day's hike apart and the camping limit is 1 day per site. Permits are required for all back-country camping.

Waterfalls are plentiful and welcome additions to the park's landscape. Although most require hikes of various lengths, one can be enjoyed from the road: Meigs Falls is 13 miles west of the Sugarlands Visitor Center.

Saddle horses and guides can be obtained in the park. Horseback trails lead from concessioner-operated stables at Smokemont and Deepcreek, as well as from Cades Cove and two stables near Gatlinburg, Tenn.

The ascent of Mount LeConte by foot or horseback from Gatlinburg offers awesome views. Lodging on the mountaintop is available by reservation. Also noted for spectacular views are Charlie's Bunion, reached by the Appalachian Trail 4 miles east from Newfound Gap, and the state's highest point, Clingmans Dome (see attraction listing).

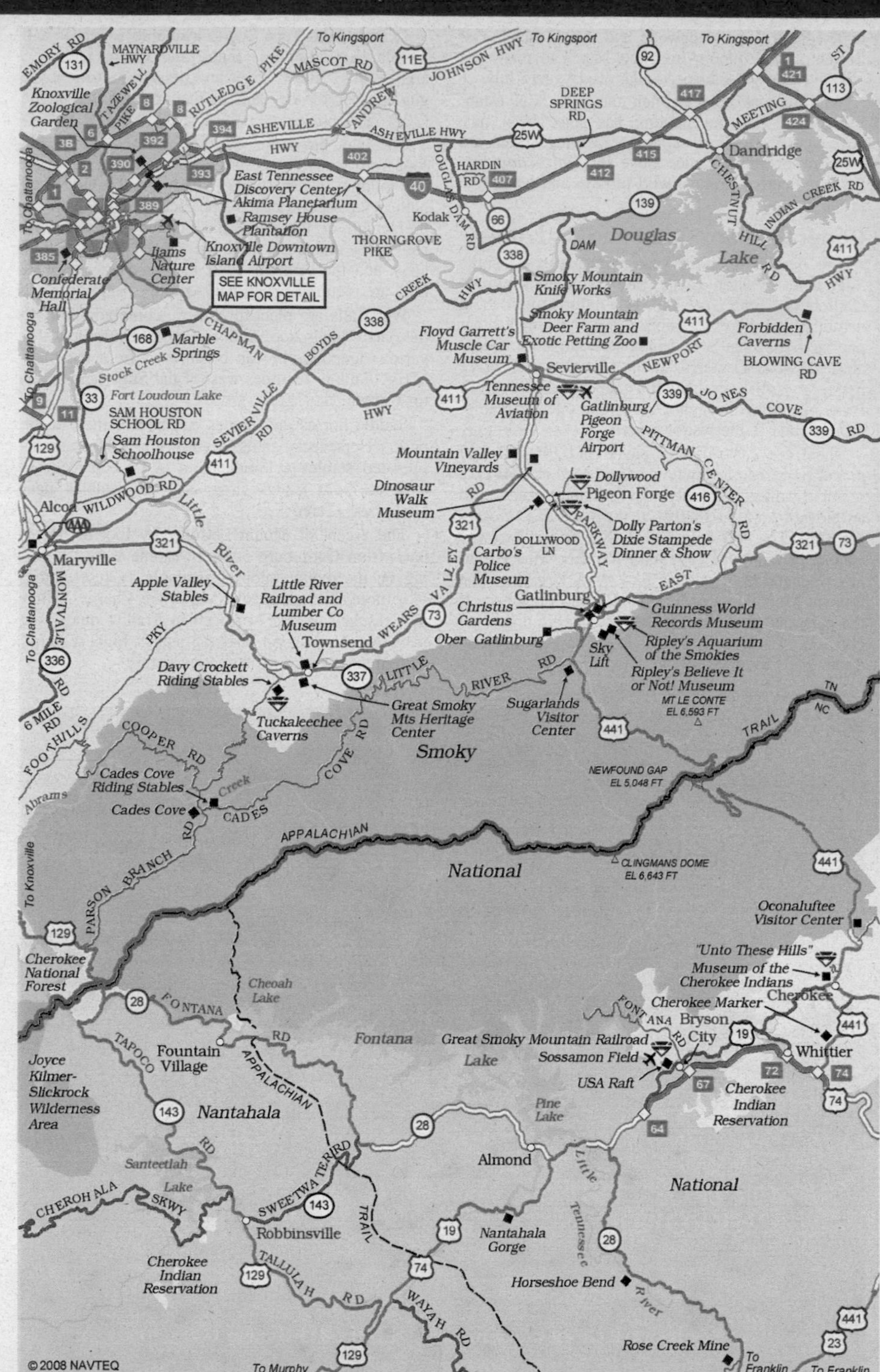

To Kingsport
To Kingsport
To Kingsport
Knoxville Zoological Garden
East Tennessee Discovery Center/ Akima Planetarium
Ramsey House Plantation
Knoxville Downtown Island Airport
Ijams Nature Center
Confederate Memorial Hall
SEE KNOXVILLE MAP FOR DETAIL
Dandridge
Douglas Lake
Smoky Mountain Knife Works
Smoky Mountain Deer Farm and Exotic Petting Zoo
Floyd Garrett's Muscle Car Museum
Forbidden Caverns
BLOWING CAVE RD
Marble Springs
Sevierville
Tennessee Museum of Aviation
Gatlinburg/ Pigeon Forge Airport
Fort Loudoun Lake
SAM HOUSTON SCHOOL RD
Sam Houston Schoolhouse
Mountain Valley Vineyards
Dinosaur Walk Museum
Dollywood
Pigeon Forge
Dolly Parton's Dixie Stampede Dinner & Show
Alcoa
Maryville
Carbo's Police Museum
Apple Valley Stables
Little River Railroad and Lumber Co Museum
Townsend
Gatlinburg
Christus Gardens
Guinness World Records Museum
Ober Gatlinburg
Ripley's Aquarium of the Smokies
Sky Lift
Ripley's Believe It or Not! Museum
Davy Crockett Riding Stables
Great Smoky Mts Heritage Center
Sugarlands Visitor Center
Tuckaleechee Caverns
MT LE CONTE EL 6,593 FT
Smoky
NEWFOUND GAP EL 5,048 FT
Cades Cove Riding Stables
Cades Cove
APPALACHIAN TRAIL
National
CLINGMANS DOME EL 6,643 FT
Oconaluftee Visitor Center
Cherokee National Forest
"Unto These Hills"
Museum of the Cherokee Indians
Cherokee
Cherokee Marker
Cheoah Lake
Bryson City
Fontana Lake
Great Smoky Mountain Railroad
Whittier
Sossamon Field
Fountain Village
Joyce Kilmer-Slickrock Wilderness Area
USA Raft
Cherokee Indian Reservation
Nantahala
Pine Lake
Almond
Santeetlah Lake
National
Robbinsville
Nantahala Gorge
Cherokee Indian Reservation
Horseshoe Bend
Rose Creek Mine
To Murphy
To Franklin
To Franklin
© 2008 NAVTEQ

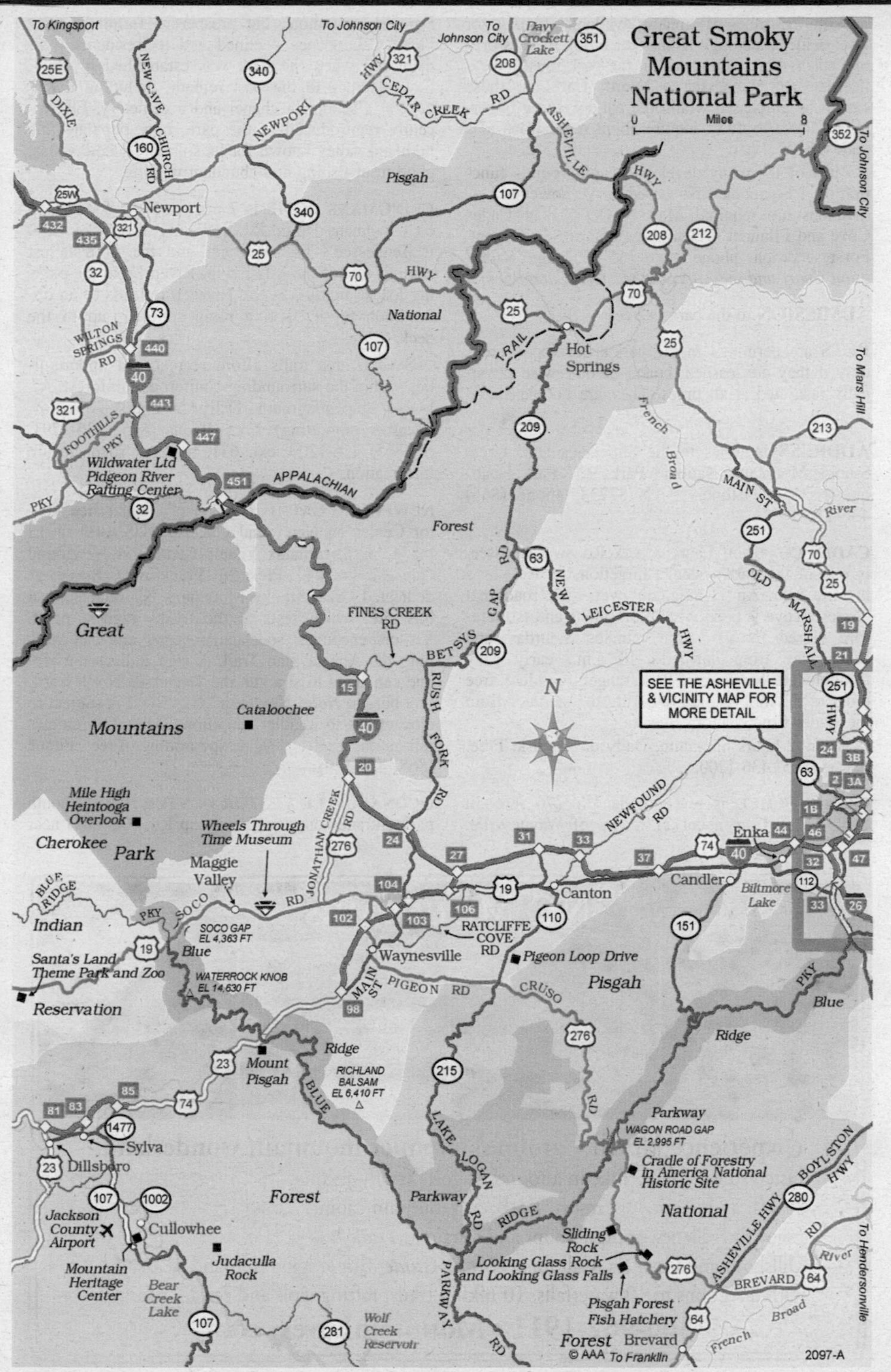
Great Smoky Mountains National Park
0 Miles 8
To Kingsport
To Johnson City
To Johnson City
Davy Crockett Lake
To Johnson City
To Mars Hill
To Hendersonville
To Franklin
Newport
Hot Springs
Wildwater Ltd Pidgeon River Rafting Center
APPALACHIAN TRAIL
Pisgah National Forest
FINES CREEK RD
Cataloochee
Great Smoky Mountains National Park
Mile High Heintooga Overlook
Cherokee Indian Reservation
Wheels Through Time Museum
Maggie Valley
SOCO GAP EL 4,363 FT
WATERROCK KNOB EL 14,630 FT
Santa's Land Theme Park and Zoo
SEE THE ASHEVILLE & VICINITY MAP FOR MORE DETAIL
Canton
Enka
Candler
Biltmore Lake
Waynesville
RATCLIFFE COVE RD
Pigeon Loop Drive
Mount Pisgah
RICHLAND BALSAM EL 6,410 FT
Blue Ridge Parkway
WAGON ROAD GAP EL 2,995 FT
Cradle of Forestry in America National Historic Site
Sylva
Dillsboro
Jackson County Airport
Cullowhee
Mountain Heritage Center
Judaculla Rock
Bear Creek Lake
Wolf Creek Reservoir
Sliding Rock
Looking Glass Rock and Looking Glass Falls
Pisgah Forest Fish Hatchery
Brevard
French Broad River
© AAA
2097-A

With 735 miles of streams available, fishing for trout is ideal, although fishing for brook trout is prohibited. Visitors fishing within the park must have a license from Tennessee or North Carolina; these cannot be purchased within the park. Fishing is permitted dawn to dusk; inquire about regulations at a park visitor center.

Most of the many developed campgrounds function on a first-come-first-served basis; however, reservations are required May 15-Oct. 31 at Cades Cove and Elkmont in Tennessee and at Smokemont. For reservations phone (800) 365-2267. *See Recreation Chart and the AAA Southeastern CampBook.*

ADMISSION to the park is free.

PETS are permitted in the park's developed areas only if they are leashed, crated or otherwise physically restricted at all times. They are not permitted on trails.

ADDRESS inquiries to the Superintendent, Great Smoky Mountains National Park, 107 Park Headquarters Rd., Gatlinburg, TN 37738; phone (865) 436-1200.

CADES COVE, off Laurel Creek Rd. in Tennessee, is one of the park's scenic attractions as well as a historic area. An 11-mile, one-way loop road that circles a cove is popular with bicyclists and is therefore closed to all motor vehicles Saturday and Wednesday from dawn to 10 a.m., early May through late September. Park rangers conduct free tours of the mill area daily during the summer from the Cades Cove visitor center.

Allow 2 hours minimum. Daily dawn-dusk. Free. Phone (865) 436-1200.

CATALOOCHEE is reached via US 276 through Cove Creek Gap, about 21 mi. n. of Waynesville. Formerly a remote, but prosperous farming settlement, Cataloochee declined and its residents were displaced when the park was established in 1934. Several clues to the past remain, including a few homes, a school, a chapel and a cemetery. Elk, recently reintroduced to the park, now populate this highland valley known for its solitude, scenic vistas, good trout fishing and abundant wildlife.

CLINGMANS DOME is 7 mi. s. of Newfound Gap on Clingmans Dome Rd. Towering at 6,643 feet, it is Tennessee's highest point and the third tallest summit east of the Mississippi River. From the parking lot, an uphill, .5-mile paved trail leads to an observation tower, with a ramp spiraling up to the deck.

Several area trails afford recreational opportunities within the surrounding coniferous rainforest. Allow 1 hour minimum. Daily 24 hours, Apr.-Nov. (weather permitting). Free. Phone (865) 436-1291, or (865) 436-1200, ext. 631, for park road closure information.

NEWFOUND GAP is 16 mi. n. of Oconaluftee Visitor Center on Newfound Gap Rd. (US 441) or 13 mi. s. of Sugarlands Visitor Center on Newfound Gap Rd. In 1940, President Franklin D. Roosevelt dedicated Great Smoky Mountains National Park at this site, which rests at the road's highest point. Visitors encounter spectacular views and can walk onto the Appalachian Trail. A sign indicates where one can stand to straddle the Tennessee-North Carolina border. **Note:** Newfound Gap Road is subject to closure due to weather conditions. Allow 30 minutes minimum. Daily, weather permitting. Free. Phone (865) 436-1291.

OCONALUFTEE VISITOR CENTER is at the south park entrance on Newfound Gap Rd. (US 441) near

The Smokies and AAA

Great Smoky Mountains National Park celebrates its 75th anniversary in 2009. The park became the 21st addition to the national park system and only the second in the eastern United States in 1934. Unlike the western parks carved from uninhabited, government-owned wilderness, the area proposed for Great Smoky Mountains National Park comprised more than 6,000 privately owned tracts held by farmers and lumber companies. From inception to congressional approval, the making of the park spanned 11 years.

After visiting Yellowstone National Park in 1923, Knoxville businessman Willis Davis, a director of the Knoxville Automobile Club, envisioned the Smoky Mountains as a national park. Davis' fellow board members believed that, in addition to protecting the area's natural resources, the establishment of a national park might also stimulate tourism and economic growth, particularly through the development of safe auto roads over the impassable mountain mass dividing North Carolina and Tennessee. On the club's behalf, Davis approached the Department of the Interior in Washington, D.C., and the seed of a movement was planted.

North Carolina Division of Tourism
Bill Russ

With bids for several eastern parks already being considered, the government needed convincing of the Smokies' worthiness. Through promotional campaigns, the automobile club raised support at local, state and national levels. When the movement gained momentum, supporters formed the Great Smoky Mountains Conservation Association, a separate committee devoted solely to the cause. In North Carolina, park advocates formed a counterpart organization to further the state's interests in a national park.

Congress approved the creation of the new national park in 1926, stipulating, however, that good-faith deeds for at least 150,000 acres be secured before the park could be placed under the protection of the National Park Service. Raising funds for land acquisitions proved to be the movement's greatest challenge. Seed money came from individual donors and through the sale of subscriptions. No amount was considered too small, not even $1,391.72 raised by more than 4,000 school children. Through legislation, Tennessee and North Carolina set aside $2 million each. But by the time the majority of money had been raised, appreciating land values threatened to deplete the acquisition fund. In 1928, the Rockefeller family saved the movement with a $5 million donation.

The first deeds were turned over to the government in 1930. Four years later, the movement realized its goal with the official establishment of Great Smoky Mountains National Park. Formal dedication of the park took place in 1940.

If Willis Davis is the father of the park movement, the creation of Great Smoky Mountains National Park was indeed a family affair. Members of the Knoxville Automobile Club, now AAA East Tennessee, played pivotal and ongoing roles in the park campaign, one that could not have succeeded without the support of countless volunteers, naturalists, civic leaders, state legislators and private benefactors. Mountains and other geographical features bear the names of those who made a difference.

Cherokee, N.C. Exhibits and information about the park are provided. Next to the center is the Mountain Farm Museum, which captures the feel of a typical 1880s Southern Appalachian farm. A small farmhouse displays the essentials of a late 19th-century pioneer home. Mingus Mill, an operating gristmill, is .5 miles north.

Visitor center open daily; hours vary seasonally. Closed Dec. 25. Free. Phone (828) 497-1900.

SUGARLANDS VISITOR CENTER is at jct. Newfound Gap Rd. (US 441) and Little River Rd. near park headquarters, 2 mi. s. of Gatlinburg. This center provides information, DVDs and exhibits about native plant and animal life. A nature trail and theater also are on site. Allow 30 minutes minimum. Visitor center open daily; hours vary seasonally. Closed Dec. 25. Free. Phone (865) 436-1291.

GREENSBORO (B-5) pop. 223,891, elev. 839′

Until the textile boom of the late 19th century, Greensboro was a quiet Piedmont town. The first steam-operated cotton mill began production in 1833, but real growth in textiles began after the Civil War. Textiles are still important to the economy but are supplemented by tobacco, electronics and insurance. Greensboro benefits from proximity to Winston-Salem and High Point, with the three forming an urban triangle.

Greensboro was home to several prominent Americans including William Sydney Porter (O. Henry), whose short stories are American classics. Porter's legacy was carried on by another Greensboro native, Wilbur Daniel Steele, winner of the O. Henry Prize for such works as "They Know Not What They Do" and "Can't Cross Jordan." Dolley Madison, wife of President James Madison, was a native of the area.

Greensboro Area Convention & Visitors Bureau: 2200 Pinecroft Rd., Greensboro, NC 27407; phone (336) 274-2282 or (800) 344-2282.

Shopping areas: Four Seasons Town Centre, off I-40 at jct. High Point Rd. and Koury Blvd., has more than 200 stores, including Belk, Dillard's and JCPenney. State Street Station features some 35 shops and restaurants housed in refurbished storefronts from the 1920s. Friendly Center, jct. Green Valley Rd. and West Friendly Ave., offers more than 100 restaurants and stores including Belk, Macy's and Sears. The Shops at Friendly Center, jct. Hobbs Rd. and West Friendly Ave., has several restaurants and counts Ann Taylor, Chico's, Coldwater Creek, J. Crew and Talbots among its stores.

BICENTENNIAL GARDEN is at 1105 Hobbs Rd. Trails meander through the gardens, leading visitors past flowering trees as well as mass plantings of bulbs, annuals and perennials. The park also includes a rose garden, a wedding garden with a brick gazebo, a small creek, and fragrance and herb gardens. Daily 7 a.m.-dusk. Free. Phone (336) 297-4162.

BLANDWOOD MANSION is near downtown at Edgeworth and Washington. The home of North Carolina Gov. John Motley Morehead, Blandwood was built as a farmhouse in the late 18th century. Redesigned in 1844 as an elegant Italian villa, the house contains many original furnishings. The mansion has been restored and the outbuildings, including the carriage house, have been reconstructed.

Guided tours are given Tues.-Sat. 11-2; Sun. 2-5, Feb.-Dec.; closed Jan. 1, Easter, Thanksgiving and Dec. 24-25. Last tour begins 30 minutes before closing. Admission $5; $4 (ages 66+); $2 (ages 0-12). Phone (336) 272-5003.

BOG GARDEN is at Hobbs Rd. and Starmount Farms Dr. across from the Bicentennial Garden. An elevated wooden walkway winds past surrounding wetlands and a small lake to provide easy viewing of plants that thrive in marshy areas and attract wildlife. Visitors also can hike Nell Lewis Trail, which scales a hillside. Daily 7 a.m.-dusk. Free. Phone (336) 373-2199.

GREENSBORO ARBORETUM, 401 Ashland Dr. in Lindley Park between West Market St. and Wendover Ave., features landscaped grounds and 12 labeled plant collections indigenous to the Piedmont region of North Carolina. Other features include an arbor, a lighted fountain and a gazebo. Daily dawn-dusk. Free. Phone (336) 292-2824.

SAVE **GREENSBORO CHILDREN'S MUSEUM** is at 220 N. Church St., across from the public library. "Our Town" is the theme of the museum's interactive games, exhibits and educational programs and includes a grocery store, post office and bank. A bubble gallery, music room and vegetable garden encourage hands-on learning. The Transportation Gallery includes a DC-9 jet with a flight simulator and a NASCAR Pontiac racing car. The Tot Spot offers activities for children under 6.

Food is available. Allow 2 hours minimum. Wed.-Thurs. and Sat. 9-5, Tues. 9-7, Fri. 9-8, Sun. 1-5; closed major holidays. Admission $6; $5 (ages 61+); $3 (on Fri. 5-8 and on Sun.); free (ages 0-1). MC, VI. Phone (336) 574-2898.

GEM **GREENSBORO HISTORICAL MUSEUM,** 130 Summit Ave., traces the development of Guilford County. Exhibits present an extensive military history collection, including more than 140 Confederate longarm rifles. Dolley Madison and O. Henry memorabilia, rare documents, decorative art works and a depiction of the 1960s civil rights movement lunch counter sit-ins also are featured. A reconstructed 19th-century Greensboro village displays a doctor's office, drugstore, schoolhouse and an antique fire engine.

Other highlights include the 18th-century Christian Isley House and the Francis McNairy House. Tues.-Sat. 10-5, Sun. 2-5; closed city holidays except July 4. Free. Phone (336) 373-2043.

GUILFORD COURTHOUSE NATIONAL MILITARY PARK—*see place listing p. 163.*

MATTYE REED AFRICAN HERITAGE CENTER is at 1601 E. Market St. on the campus of North Carolina A & T State University. The center houses what is reputedly one of the best collections of African cultural artifacts in the country. Approximately 3,500 art and craft items represent more than 30 African nations. Allow 1 hour minimum. Tues.-Fri. 10-5, Sat. 1-5; closed major holidays. Free. Phone (336) 334-3209.

NATURAL SCIENCE CENTER OF GREENSBORO, 4301 Lawndale Dr., displays a 36-foot Tyrannosaurus rex model and offers interactive exhibits pertaining to weather, geology, paleontology, energy, health and virtual reality. On the 30-acre grounds are the Omni-Sphere Theater; a reptile gallery; a marine gallery; small animal contact areas; a zoo containing lemurs, snakes and reptiles; and a children's petting zoo.

Center open Mon.-Sat. 9-5, Sun. 12:30-5; closed Jan. 1, Thanksgiving and Dec. 25. Theater shows daily on the hour 1-4. Admission $8; $7 (ages 3-13 and 65+). Theater admission $5 extra. MC, VI. Phone (336) 288-3769.

REPLACEMENTS, LTD. is off I-85/40 exit 132 (Mt. Hope Church Rd.) at 1089 Knox Rd. A museum holds more than 2,000 unusual and rare pieces of china, crystal, flatware and collectibles. Daily 9-7; closed Dec. 25. Holiday hours may vary; phone ahead. Tours are given every 30 minutes beginning at 9:30. Last tour begins 1 hour before closing. Free. Phone (336) 697-3000 or (800) 737-5223.

WEATHERSPOON ART MUSEUM, at Spring Garden and Tate sts. on the University of North Carolina at Greensboro campus, features six galleries devoted to modern and contemporary art by artists including Alexander Calder, Willem de Kooning and Henri Matisse. An outside exhibit displays sculpture. Displayed are works from the Weatherspoon's extensive collection as well as traveling exhibitions. Allow 1 hour minimum. Tues.-Fri. 10-5 (also Thurs. 5-9), Sat.-Sun. 1-5; closed university holidays. Free. Phone (336) 334-5770.

SAVE **WET 'N WILD EMERALD POINTE WATER PARK,** I-85 exit 121 to 3910 S. Holden Rd., contains numerous waterslides, a wave pool, a white-water adventure ride and a children's area. Food is available. Park is open Memorial Day weekend-Labor Day. Closing times and days of operation vary; phone ahead. All-day admission $29.99; $19.99 (under 48 inches tall); $19.99 (ages 55+); free (ages 0-2). After 4 p.m. $21.99; $14.99 (ages 55+); $16.99 (under 48 inches tall). Parking $5. AX, MC, VI. Phone (336) 852-9721 or (800) 555-5900.

GREENVILLE (B-7) pop. 60,476, elev. 75'

As one of the largest bright-leaf tobacco markets in the world, Greenville is an agricultural market and wholesale trading center. It also serves as a regional medical center for eastern North Carolina and is home to East Carolina University.

Greenville Pitt County Convention and Visitors Bureau: 303 S.W. Greenville Blvd., P.O. Box 8027, Greenville, NC 27835; phone (252) 329-4200 or (800) 537-5564.

GREENVILLE MUSEUM OF ART, 802 S. Evans St., displays 20th-century and contemporary American paintings, drawings, prints and sculpture. Allow 30 minutes minimum. Tues.-Fri. 10-4:30, Sat-Sun. 1-4; closed holidays. Guided tours are available on request Wed.-Fri. Free. Phone (252) 758-1946.

GUILFORD COURTHOUSE NATIONAL MILITARY PARK (A-5)

Guilford (GILL-ford) Courthouse National Military Park covers 226 acres in northwest Greensboro, off US 220. On March 15, 1781, the Battle of Guilford Courthouse pitted Gen. Nathanael Greene's mixed Continental and militia army against Lord Cornwallis' smaller, veteran forces.

Cornwallis, eager to avenge the British defeat at Cowpens, S.C., won the battle but took heavy losses and failed to destroy the American force. Although defeated in battle, Greene won his objective and Cornwallis soon moved to Virginia, where he finally surrendered his army at Yorktown on Oct. 19, 1781.

The site includes wayside exhibits throughout the battlefield and a visitor center with displays, films and brochures. A 2.5-mile auto tour leads to many of the monuments, including the graves of John Penn and William Hooper, signers of the Declaration of Independence.

Cavalry Monument honors all American cavalry, including Virginian Peter Francisco, known as "The Goliath of the Revolution." At the Battle of Guilford Courthouse, Francisco—who weighed 260 pounds and stood 6 feet 6 inches tall—supposedly fought with a 5-foot sword given to him by George Washington.

Tannenbaum Park, one-quarter mile west on US 220, contains picnic areas, two log cabins and a former British military hospital built in 1778. Explore History Days events are held throughout the year. The park is open Tues.-Sat. 10-4, March 1 through mid-December; otherwise varies. Phone (336) 545-5315.

The military park visitor center is open daily 8:30-5. For further information contact the Superintendent, Guilford Courthouse National Military Park, 2332 New Garden Rd., Greensboro, NC 27410-2355; phone (336) 288-1776.

HALIFAX (A-7) pop. 344, elev. 101'

GEM **HISTORIC HALIFAX STATE HISTORIC SITE** is on US 301 Bus. Rte. at St. David and Dobbs sts. Halifax was a commercial river port that became a political arena in 1776 when the "Halifax Resolves," recommending independence from England, were ratified by the colony of North Carolina. Founded in 1760, the town has many restored buildings that reflect its early history.

A free 60-minute guided tour includes the cemetery, Market Square, the 1808 Burgess Law Office, the 1838 jail, the 1832 Clerk of Courts Office, an archeological museum built over the remains of the 1762 Montfort house, the 1760 Owens House and the 1808 Sally-Billy Plantation House.

Maps of the village and brochures detailing a self-guiding tour are available at the visitor center, which displays artifacts and shows a 13-minute film Tues.-Sat. 10-4. Hours may vary; phone ahead. Free. Phone (252) 583-7191.

HATTERAS—*see Outer Banks p. 178.*

HENDERSONVILLE (F-3) pop. 10,420, elev. 2,200′

Once a hunting ground of the Cherokee, Hendersonville became a summer resort where many Low Country dwellers came to escape the season's intense heat. Nestled in the mountains of western North Carolina, Hendersonville continues to offer visitors year-round activities, including hiking, bicycling and antiquing.

Downtown on Main Street, the Mineral and Lapidary Museum of Henderson County displays gems, minerals, geodes and fossils from around the world; phone (828) 698-1977. Just a short distance from downtown on US 64W is Oakdale Cemetery, now home to the Italian marble angel statue that figures prominently in Thomas Wolfe's first novel, "Look Homeward, Angel." A historical marker explains its significance.

Henderson County Travel and Tourism/Visitor Information Center-Hendersonville: 201 South Main St., Hendersonville, NC 28793; phone (828) 693-9708 or (800) 828-4244.

Shopping areas: Historic Main Street, in downtown Hendersonville, is home to numerous antique shops and boutiques. Browse the retro offerings in the 1905 Mast General Store at 527 N. Main St. For a taste of local flavor, the Henderson County Curb Market, 2nd Ave. and Church St., offers a variety of handmade or locally grown items. The market is open select days; phone (828) 692-8012.

HISTORIC JOHNSON FARM is at 3346 Haywood Rd. In 1874 the Johnson Farm was purchased as a tobacco farm. It became a popular summer retreat for tourists during the Depression era. The site now operates as a farm museum and hands-on heritage learning center. Visitors may tour the 1880 farmhouse, the 1920 boarding house and the 1923 barnloft museum. Two nature trails and 15 acres of fields, forests and streams also are on site.

Picnicking is permitted. Allow 1 hour minimum. Tues.-Fri. 9-2:30, May-Oct. Guided tours of the farmhouse, boarding house and barn are given at 10:30 and 1:30. Closed major school holidays. Site free. Guided tours $3; $2 (ages 5-11). Phone (828) 891-6585.

JUMP-OFF ROCK is on the summit of Jump-off Mountain, 5 mi. w. via Fifth Ave. Legend holds that an American Indian chief and a Cherokee maiden often met on the rock. When she learned of her love's death in battle, the heartbroken maiden jumped off the ledge. Lore says that on some moonlit nights, the ghost of the maiden can be seen on the rock. Today, Jump-off Rock provides visitors with panoramic views of the Blue Ridge and Pisgah mountain ranges. Free.

HERTFORD (A-8) pop. 2,070, elev. 13′

Perquimans County Chamber of Commerce: 118 W. Market St., Hertford, NC 27944; phone (252) 426-5657.

SAVE **NEWBOLD-WHITE HOUSE,** 1.5 mi. off US 17 bypass on SR 1336 along the Perquimans River, is considered the oldest brick house in North Carolina. The 1730 house was painstakingly restored by hand, with original workmanship remaining in the two chimneys, 18-inch-thick brick walls and the second-floor woodwork.

Period furnishings are exhibited. Also on the grounds are a reconstructed 18th-century smokehouse and a 17th-century Quaker graveyard. Allow 30 minutes minimum. Tues.-Sat. 10-4, Mar.-Nov.; Sat. 10-4:30, in Dec.; by appointment rest of year. Admission $5; $3 (students with ID). Phone (252) 426-7567.

HICKORY (B-4) pop. 37,222, elev. 1,165′

Until 1900 Hickory was called Hickory Tavern Station, after the tavern and stagecoach stop that was the town's center of activity. Today Hickory supports a thriving furniture-manufacturing industry.

Just east of nearby Claremont on old US 70A is the 85-foot-long Bunker Hill Covered Bridge. Constructed in 1895, it is one of the few covered bridges remaining in the state. Though closed to automobiles, pedestrians may cross it during scheduled hours; phone (828) 465-0383.

Catawba County Chamber of Commerce: 1055 Southgate Corporate Park S.W., P.O. Box 1828, Hickory, NC 28602; phone (828) 328-6111.

Shopping areas: Catawba County is known for its many furniture manufacturers. More than 50 discount furniture stores are in the area. The 350,000-square-foot Catawba Furniture Mall, off I-40 exit 123B to US 70, features a variety of furniture and home decorating retailers. Hickory Furniture Mart, exit 126 on I-40, includes approximately 1,000 furniture lines in its 20 acres of showroom.

ARTS & SCIENCE CENTER OF CATAWBA VALLEY is off I-40 exit 125 to 243 Third Ave. N.E. The center houses the Hickory Museum of Art and the Catawba Science Center. Phone (828) 324-4906.

Catawba Science Center, 243 Third Ave. N.E., contains more than 12,000 square feet of interactive, hands-on science exhibits. Visitors can experience the trembling of an earthquake, see a living mountain stream, and more. Changing exhibits also are available. Allow 30 minutes minimum. Tues.-Fri.

10-5, Sat. 10-4, Sun. 1-4; closed major holidays. Admission $5; $3 (ages 3-18 and 62+). Phone (828) 322-8169.

Hickory Museum of Art, 243 Third Ave. N.E, presents changing exhibits and a permanent collection of 19th-century through contemporary American art. Works by Thomas Cole, Honoré Daumier, Robert Henri and Robert Reed are featured. Allow 30 minutes minimum. Tues.-Sat. 10-4, Sun. 1-4. Free. Phone (828) 327-8576.

HIGHLANDS (F-2) pop. 909, elev. 4,118′

Highlands is at the intersection of two scenic highways, US 64 running northeast to Brevard and SR 28 running northwest to Franklin. Near Highlands is Whiteside Mountain, accessible from US 64, which has some of the highest sheer cliffs in the eastern United States.

Within the Nantahala National Forest, the Highlands District Ranger Station is 5 miles east on US 64 and distributes trail maps of Van Hook Glade and Cliffside Lake; phone (828) 526-3765. Write Highlands District Ranger Station, 2010 Flat Mountain Rd., Highlands, NC 28741.

Highlands Chamber of Commerce: P.O. Box 404, Highlands, NC 28741; phone (828) 526-2112.

CULLASAJA RIVER GORGE, a deep canyon w. along US 64, has five waterfalls. The road passes under Bridal Veil Falls at the head of the gorge; farther along are Dry Falls and, almost halfway to Franklin *(see place listing p. 155)*, Cullasaja Falls.

Note: Because the road is narrow, travelers should pay strict attention to driving; designated overlooks provide opportunities for viewing the scenery.

HIGH POINT (B-5) pop. 85,839, elev. 939′

High Point earned its name by being the highest point on the original survey for the old North Carolina Railroad, but it is furniture design and production that drive the modern economy. With more than 125 manufacturers in the area, including 15 of the nation's largest, the city rightfully calls itself "The Home Furnishings Capital of the World." Twice a year furniture designers, buyers and sellers from around the world converge on High Point for The International Home Furnishings Market show.

The Bernice Bienenstock Furniture Library, 1009 N. Main St., contains a comprehensive collection of furniture books, including rare volumes dating to the 1600s. Tours are available; phone (336) 883-4011.

High Point Convention and Visitors Bureau: 300 S. Main St., P.O. Box 2273, High Point, NC 27261; phone (336) 884-5255 or (800) 720-5255.

ANGELA PETERSON DOLL AND MINIATURE MUSEUM, 101 W. Green Dr., presents more than 2,500 dolls and miniatures of various styles and from different periods. Featured are a dollhouse village, shadow boxes, displays of childhood toys and dolls, and collections of baby, foreign and religious dolls. Exhibitions rotate.

Mon.-Fri. 10-4, Sat. 9-4, Sun. 1-4, Apr.-Oct.; Tues.-Fri. 10-4, Sat. 9-4, rest of year. Admission $5; $4 (senior citizens); $2.50 (ages 6-15). MC, VI. Phone (336) 885-3655.

HIGH POINT MUSEUM & HISTORICAL PARK, 1859 E. Lexington Ave., portrays Southern history through museum exhibits and living-history demonstrations. The museum's Scrapbook of History gallery features artifacts, images and stories from Colonial through contemporary times. High Point's emergence as a furniture manufacturing center is depicted in the Hall of Commerce. Three 18th-century buildings are presented in the historical park.

Picnicking is permitted. Allow 1 hour minimum. Museum open Tues.-Sat. 10-4:30, Sun. 1-4:30. Historical park open Sat. 10-4, Sun. 1-4. Closed major holidays. Guided 45-minute tours of the historical park are available on weekends. Donations. Phone (336) 885-1859.

PIEDMONT ENVIRONMENTAL CENTER is 4 mi. e. on Lexington Ave., following signs to 1220 Penny Rd. This 376-acre nature preserve offers 11 miles of hiking trails and a topographical map that allows visitors to walk across a scale-size model of North Carolina. Environmental education and nature programs are offered in the 7,000-square-foot education building. Indigenous wildlife includes deer, fox, raccoons, owls, migratory songbirds and waterfowl. Picnicking is permitted. Allow 2 hours minimum. Mon.-Sat. 9-5, Sun. 1-5; closed major holidays. Free. Phone (336) 883-8531.

HILLSBOROUGH (B-6) pop. 5,446, elev. 538′

Hillsborough was founded on the site where the Great Indian Trading Path crossed the Eno River. The town was included in many historic events during the Colonial and Revolutionary periods, and its architecture reflects that of bygone days; the Alexander Dickson House, which now houses the Orange County Visitor Center, has sometimes been called the last headquarters of the Confederacy. Hillsborough was the site of the 1788 Constitutional Convention, at which delegates demanded a Bill of Rights before they would ratify the United States Constitution.

The city's historic district boasts more than 100 late 18th- and early 19th-century structures set along streets that retain pre-Revolutionary names, the most unmistakable being King and Queen streets. The Orange County Historical Museum has a gallery featuring the work of area artists and exhibits depicting the daily lives of early Orange County residents; phone (919) 732-2201.

The Ruffin-Roulhac House, Hillsborough's 1821 town hall, is open during business hours for self-guiding tours. Occaneechi Indian Village, along the banks of the Eno River, is a replica of a 17th-century settlement consisting of a stockade fence, huts, cooking area and sweat lodge. For information on either of these sites, phone (919) 732-7741.

Orange County Visitor Center: 150 E. King St., Hillsborough, NC 27278; phone (919) 732-7741.

Self-guiding tours: Walking-tour brochures and other visitor information are available at the visitor center.

AYR MOUNT HISTORIC SITE AND POET'S WALK is at 376 St. Mary's Rd. Scottish merchant William Kirkland built the brick 1815 plantation house which includes a Federal period collection of furniture, porcelain and crystal. Of interest is a set of North Carolina etchings by Louis Orr. The "Poet's Walk" is a trail that winds through landscaped grounds, woodlands and pastures.

Allow 1 hour minimum. Guided house tours Wed. at 11, Thurs.-Sat. at 11 and 2, Sun. at 2, late Mar.-late Dec. Poet's Walk daily 9-7, May-Aug.; 9-6, Mar.-Apr. and Sept.-Oct.; 9-5, rest of year. Closed major holidays. House tours $10. Poet's Walk free. Phone (919) 732-6886.

BURWELL SCHOOL HISTORIC SITE is at 319 N. Churton St. On the grounds is the 1821 frame house once inhabited by the Burwell family, who operated a school for young women 1837-57. Period and reproduction pieces reflect family and student life of the era in both the Burwell home and the 1840 brick school building. A self-guiding tour explores Civil War history.

Allow 30 minutes minimum. Guided tours Wed.-Sat. 11-4, Sun. 1-4, Feb. 1 to mid-Dec.; closed major holidays. Free. Phone (919) 732-7451.

HOT SPRINGS (D-3) pop. 645, elev. 1,329′

A popular resort since the early 1800s, Hot Springs is situated at the junction of the Appalachian Trail and the French Broad River. The town is named for the reputedly therapeutic hot mineral springs that continue to draw visitors today. Surrounded by the Pisgah National Forest, the area offers a variety of outdoor activities, including whitewater rafting, canoeing, fishing, mountain biking, hiking, horseback riding and camping. Scenic SR 209 runs through the heart of town, and nearby US 25/70 offers a picturesque drive through the river valley.

Madison County Visitors Center: 75 Anderson St., P.O. Box 1547, Mars Hill, NC 28754; phone (828) 680-9031 or (877) 262-3476.

HUNTERSVILLE—*see Charlotte p. 147.*

JACKSONVILLE (C-7) pop. 66,715, elev. 15′

Jacksonville, at the mouth of the New River and known for its outdoor water activities, is the commercial, banking, cultural and governmental center for the county. The 153,000-acre Marine Corps Base, Camp Lejeune, is central to the area's economy. The granite Beirut Memorial, built to honor marines and sailors killed in Beirut, Lebanon, and Grenada, stands just outside the gate of Camp Johnson on SR 17. Along Lejeune Boulevard, each Bradford pear tree stands for a life lost in Lebanon or Grenada.

Greater Jacksonville/Onslow Chamber of Commerce: 1099 Gum Branch Rd., P.O. Box 765, Jacksonville, NC 28541; phone (910) 347-3141.

CAMP LEJEUNE, e. on SR 24, is a 153,000-acre Marine Corps Base, home of Expeditionary Forces in Readiness, the 2nd Marine Division, 6th Marine Expeditionary Brigade, 2nd Force Service Support Group and 2nd Marine Expeditionary Force. Free. Phone (910) 451-2197.

KANNAPOLIS (B-4) pop. 36,910

Kannapolis (ka-NA-po-lis) was founded in 1887 as a company town around the Cannon Mills textile headquarters. Before the turn of the 20th century and the marketing of ready-made clothes, Cannon cloth was a staple in Southern homes. Kannapolis' central business district features Cannon Village, which depicts the architectural style of the early 20th century.

Cabarrus Regional Chamber of Commerce—Kannapolis: 3003 Dale Earnhardt Blvd., Kannapolis, NC 28083; phone (704) 782-4000.

Shopping areas: Tree-lined West Avenue offers bargain hunters a wide variety of factory outlet stores representing major manufacturers.

GEM **CANNON VILLAGE VISITOR CENTER,** off I-85 at 200 West Ave., is a welcome center featuring the Fieldcrest Cannon Textile Museum and Exhibition. Highlights of the exhibit include one of the world's largest towels, an antique hand loom and samples of textiles that are more than 1,200 years old.

Cannon Village Home Furnishings Market is a collection of Colonial-style buildings along tree-lined brick streets. A 9-foot bronze statue in tribute to native son Dale Earnhardt is in the village. A 12-minute audiovisual presentation shows the history of the village. Allow 1 hour minimum. Mon.-Sat. 9-5; closed Easter, Thanksgiving and Dec. 25. Free. Phone (704) 938-3200.

KENANSVILLE (C-7) pop. 1,149

Kenansville, in the fertile coastal plain of southeast North Carolina, was settled about 1735 by Swiss, German and Irish immigrants, who called their town Golden Grove. In 1818 Kenansville was renamed for Gen. James Kenan, a member of the House of Commons who fought in the Revolution and helped ratify the Constitution and formulate the Bill of Rights.

Many of Kenansville's old houses have been restored. There are three antebellum churches that have changed little since the 19th century; among them is 1736 Grove Church, the oldest Presbyterian congregation in the state. Brochures of Kenansville are available at the town hall on Rutledge Rd.; phone (910) 296-0369.

Duplin County Tourism Commission: 114 E. Hill St., P.O. Box 965, Kenansville, NC 28349-0929; phone (910) 296-2181.

COWAN MUSEUM is in the Kelly-Farrior House on SR 11/24/50/903 (S. Main St.). This two-story Greek Revival house contains more than 2,000 items dating mostly from the 18th, 19th and early 20th centuries. A few items, such as a 13th-century slave belt, come from ancient cultures. A blacksmith shop, one-room school, furnished log cabin and tobacco barn are on the grounds. Allow 30 minutes minimum. Tues.-Sat. 10-4, Sun. 2-4; closed major holidays. Donations. Phone (910) 296-2149.

LIBERTY HALL, on SR 11/24/50 (S. Main St.), is a Greek Revival house built in the early 1800s by Thomas Kenan II, son of Gen. James Kenan. The house has been restored as an ancestral memorial. Historical documents were used as references to create the wallpaper, upholstery and drapery fabric. Many of the furnishings are original. Historical exhibits and a 12-minute videotape are presented in the visitor center.

Other buildings on the estate include the necessary house (bathroom), smokehouse, chicken coop, carriage house and wash shed. Period music is played on a 1750 pianoforte.

Allow 1 hour minimum. Tues.-Sat. 10-4, Sun. 2-4; closed Jan. 1, Thanksgiving and Dec. 25. Admission $5; $2.50 (ages 6-11). Phone (910) 296-2175.

KENLY (B-7) pop. 1,569, elev. 204′

From May through September, Southern National Speedway is the scene of short-track stock car racing; for prices and schedules phone (919) 284-1114.

Johnston County Visitors Bureau—Kenly: 1535A Booker Dairy Rd., Smithfield, NC 27577; phone (919) 989-8687 or (800) 441-7829.

TOBACCO FARM LIFE MUSEUM, 1.5 mi. off I-95 exit 107 on US 301, offers a history of North Carolina tobacco farming and the economic changes brought about by the introduction of flue-cured tobacco. Displays include artifacts, tools and equipment used in the curing process.

Some exhibits illustrate social, educational and religious customs of early families of the area, and a restored farmstead re-creates rural life during the Great Depression. Videotapes show the history of tobacco and some of the phases involved in its production.

Allow 1 hour minimum. Mon.-Sat. 9:30-5, Sun. 2-5, early Jan.-Dec. 31; closed Easter, Thanksgiving and Dec. 25-26. Admission $6; $5 (ages 55+); $4 (students with ID). MC, VI. Phone (919) 284-3431.

KERNERSVILLE (A-5) pop. 17,126, elev. 1,023′

SAVE **KÖRNER'S FOLLY,** 413 S. Main St., is a 22-room mansion designed by 19th-century artist and interior decorator Jule Gilmer Körner, whose true genius emerged in the decades he spent designing and redesigning the home. Built on three floors and seven levels, the rooms feature a variety of ceiling heights and architectural curiosities such as hidden nooks, trap doors and pivoting windows.

Picnicking is permitted. Allow 1 hour minimum. Thurs.-Sat. 10-4, Sun. 1-4; closed Jan. 1, Easter, Thanksgiving and Dec. 24-25. Admission $8; $4 (ages 6-18). Phone (336) 996-7922.

KILL DEVIL HILLS—*see Outer Banks p. 178.*

KINSTON (C-7) pop. 23,688, elev. 43′

Kinston was founded in 1762 and originally named Kingston. After the Revolution, Patriots changed the spelling to avoid any reference to England. Today Kinston is one of the nation's leading bright-leaf tobacco markets. East of town on US 70, Lakeside Mills operates a 19th-century gristmill. Founded in Kinston in 1981, the Eastern North Carolina Bluegrass Association is dedicated to increasing public awareness of bluegrass music and its heritage.

Kinston/Lenoir County Chamber of Commerce: 301 N. Queen St., P.O. Box 157, Kinston, NC 28502-0157; phone (252) 527-1131.

CSS *NEUSE* STATE HISTORIC SITE AND THE GOVERNOR CASWELL MEMORIAL, 2612 W. Vernon Ave. (US 70), includes a museum; a memorial to Richard Caswell, first governor of the state of North Carolina; and the CSS *Neuse,* one of two remaining Confederate ironclads. A video also is presented.

Picnicking is permitted. Allow 1 hour minimum. Mon.-Sat. 9-5, Apr.-Oct.; Mon.-Fri. 10-4, rest of year. Closed major holidays. Hours may vary; phone ahead. Free. Phone (252) 522-2091.

KNOTTS ISLAND—*see Outer Banks p. 178.*

KURE BEACH (D-7) pop. 1,507

Cape Fear Coast Convention & Visitors Bureau—Kure Beach: 24 N. Third St., Wilmington, NC 28401; phone (910) 341-4030 or (877) 406-2356.

FORT FISHER STATE HISTORIC SITE, about 2 mi. s. at end of US 421, was one of the largest Confederate earthen seacoast fortifications. Reputedly scene to the largest naval bombardment and amphibious operation of the Civil War, the fort protected blockade runners en route to Wilmington with supplies before its fall in January 1865. The site has a monument commemorating the battle, a reconstructed gun emplacement and an interpretive history trail.

The visitor center features an audiovisual show and displays, models and dioramas that illustrate the history of the fort and the role played by the blockade runners. Guided tours are available. Allow 1 hour, 30 minutes minimum. Mon.-Sat. 9-5, Sun. 1-5,

Apr.-Sept.; Tues.-Sat. 10-4, rest of year. Closed Good Friday, Thanksgiving and Dec. 24-25. Free. Phone (910) 458-5538.

GEM **NORTH CAROLINA AQUARIUM AT FORT FISHER** is at 900 Loggerhead Rd. The aquarium features aquatic life found in and around the Cape Fear River and wetlands area as well as the ocean beyond. Exhibits include sea horses, alligators, sharks, jelly fish, stingrays and "Divers on the Cape Fear Shoals." At 3 p.m. each day, visitors also may watch some of the animals being fed by aquarium staff, while an educator is on hand to answer questions and offer insight.

Food is available. Allow 1 hour minimum. Daily 9-5; closed Jan. 1, Thanksgiving and Dec. 25. Admission $8; $7 (ages 62+); $6 (ages 6-17). MC, VI. Phone (910) 458-8257.

LAKE LURE (E-4) pop. 1,027, elev. 1,120′

Lake Lure takes its name from the 1,500-acre man-made lake east of town. It is surrounded by the Rumbling Bald mountain range; faults in the mountains have created landslides, exposing caves in the upper slopes. Scenic coves and inlets of the lake offer access for boating, swimming and fishing. Identified by deep violet blossoms, the paulownia—or empress tree—was brought to the vicinity by George Vanderbilt. *See Recreation Chart and the AAA Southeastern CampBook.*

Rutherford County Tourism: 1990 US 221S, Forest City, NC 28043; phone (828) 245-1492 or (800) 849-5998. *See color ad opposite title page.*

LAKE LURE TOURS, on US 64/74A at the town marina, features pontoon boat tours of the scenic lake. Narrated highlights include a stop at the film location used for the movie "Dirty Dancing." Local lore, such as the story of an entire town said to lie 100 feet beneath the surface, also is revealed. Dinner, champagne and twilight cruises are available.

Allow 1 hour minimum. Departures daily on the hour 10-6, Apr.-Oct.; Fri.-Sun. 10-4 in Mar. and Nov. Reservations are recommended for the twilight cruise and required for the dinner cruise. Fare $12; $10 (ages 62+); $6 (ages 4-12); free (ages 0-3 with adult). DS, MC, VI. Phone (828) 625-0077.

LAUREL SPRINGS (A-3) elev. 2,757′

WINERIES

- **Thistle Meadow Winery** is at 102 Thistle Meadow. Mon.-Sat. noon-5, Sun. 2-4; Apr.-Oct.; Mon.-Sat. noon-4, rest of year. Closed Dec. 25. Phone (800) 233-1505.

LENOIR (E-4) pop. 16,793, elev. 1,168′

Caldwell County Chamber of Commerce: 1909 Hickory Blvd. S.E., Lenoir, NC 28645; phone (828) 726-0323.

FORT DEFIANCE is off SR 268 at 1792 Fort Defiance Dr. Built by Revolutionary War general and politician William Lenoir, the 18th-century dwelling was occupied by the Lenoir family until 1961. Costumed guides offer tours of the restored house and the grounds; highlights include a cemetery, a garden, a smokehouse and more than 300 heirlooms. Historic reenactments also are featured.

Picnicking is permitted. Thurs.-Sat. 10-5, Sun. 1-5, Apr.-Oct. Schedule varies rest of year; phone ahead. Free. Phone (828) 758-1671.

LEWISVILLE (B-4) pop. 8,826, elev. 973′

WINERIES

- **Westbend Vineyards** is at 5394 Williams Rd. Tastings Tues.-Sat. 11-5, Sun. noon-5. Scheduled tours Sat. at noon, 1:30 and 3, Sun. at 1:30 and 3; Tues.-Fri. by appointment. Closed Easter, Thanksgiving and Dec. 25. Phone (336) 945-5032.

LEXINGTON (B-4) pop. 19,953, elev. 809′

Situated in the heart of the Piedmont region, the city is a furniture and textile center also known for its "Lexington style" barbecue. A walk through Historic Uptown Lexington reveals a revitalized area that offers a variety of shops and restaurants. The Bob Timberlake Gallery, 1714 E. Center St., features artwork by the local resident and nationally acclaimed painter; phone (800) 244-0095.

Lexington Tourism Authority: 16 E. Center St., Lexington, NC 27293; phone (336) 248-5929.

Self-guiding tours: A walking tour brochure highlighting historic homes and buildings is available from the convention and visitors bureau.

DAVIDSON COUNTY HISTORICAL MUSEUM is at 2 S. Main St. Housed in the 1858 county courthouse, the museum features permanent and changing

DID YOU KNOW

North Carolina has more than 200 waterfalls.

exhibits about life in the region from prehistory to the present. Among the historical artifacts displayed are Annie Oakley's saddle, recovered after a 1901 train wreck. A courtroom remains intact with its judge's bench, jury box and prisoners' holding cage.

Guided tours are available. Allow 30 minutes minimum. Tues.-Fri. 10-4 and first Sunday of each month 2-4; closed holidays. Free. Phone (336) 242-2035.

LINVILLE (D-4) elev. 3,800′

Three miles off the Blue Ridge Parkway *(see place listing p. 131)*, Linville is a resort community known for its excellent golf courses. The Linville River and nearby lakes provide good fishing opportunities, and hiking trails are plentiful on nearby Grandfather Mountain *(see attraction listing)*. In winter the region becomes a ski center.

Avery/Banner Elk Chamber of Commerce—Linville: Tyne Castle Shopping Center, jct. SRs 105 and 184, P.O. Box 335, Banner Elk, NC 28604; phone (828) 898-5605 or (800) 972-2183.

GEM SAVE **GRANDFATHER MOUNTAIN** is 2 mi. n. of Linville on US 221, or 1 mi. s. of jct. US 221 and Blue Ridge Pkwy. (Milepost 305). The rugged 5,964-foot peak was named by early pioneers for its profile: When viewed from the north, it resembles a bearded grandfather looking toward the sky.

A 2-mile road to the summit leads to a visitor center, a network of hiking and walking trails and the Mile High Swinging Bridge. Spectacular views and unusual rock formations are visible along the ascent. Halfway up the mountain is the Nature Center, which includes a museum and theater that shows nature movies filmed on location. Seven native wildlife habitats enable visitors to see black bears, golden and bald eagles, panthers, white-tailed deer and river otters.

Picnicking is permitted. Food is available. Allow 1 hour, 30 minutes minimum. Daily 8-7, Apr.-Oct.; 8-5, rest of year (weather permitting). Last admission 1 hour before closing. Closed Thanksgiving and Dec. 25. Admission $14; $12 (ages 60+); $6 (ages 4-12). AX, MC, VI. Phone (828) 733-4337 or (800) 468-7325.

LITTLE SWITZERLAND (E-4) elev. 3,479′

Captivated by natural beauty and abundant wildlife reminiscent of the Swiss Jura Mountains, early visitors named the town. Today, the nearby Blue Ridge Parkway provides easy access to many attractions, including the Orchard at Altapass, where guests may pick vintage apples, enjoy hayrides and listen to old-time music; phone (828) 765-9531.

EMERALD VILLAGE, 2.5 mi. w. on SR 1100, preserves the tradition of gem and mineral mining and features three historic mines. A self-guiding tour of the Bon Ami Mine, a source of feldspar, includes mining equipment. The Discovery Mill displays include railroad models, wildlife exhibits and a mineral gallery. Visitors may walk through a miniature town that re-creates mining life 1920-50. Gem mining is available.

Picnicking is permitted. Daily 9-6, late May-Sept. 1; 10-4 in Apr. and Nov. 1-15; 9 5, May 1-late May and Sept. 2-Oct. 31. Schedule may vary; phone ahead. Discovery Mill free. Mining tour $6; $5.50 (ages 55+); $5 (grades 1-12). AX, DS, MC, VI. Phone (828) 765-6463.

LUMBERTON (D-6) pop. 20,795, elev. 120′

Founded in 1787 by Revolutionary War officer Capt. John Willis, the city began as a shipping point for lumber and naval supplies transported down the Lumber River. Today the town's economy is centered around tobacco, farm produce and textile manufacturing. Situated directly off I-95, Lumberton serves as a halfway point between New York and Florida.

Lumberton Area Visitors Bureau: 3431 Lackey St., Lumberton, NC 28360; phone (910) 739-9999 or (800) 359-6971. *See color ad p. 751.*

ROBESON COUNTY SHOWCASE MUSEUM, 101 S. Elm St., displays local memorabilia along with mounted birds and small mammals native to the area. Items displayed include a 1909 record player, guns from the early 19th century and fossils found in the nearby Lumber River. Allow 30 minutes minimum. Tues.-Thurs. 1-5, Mon. and Fri. 9-1; closed holidays. Free. Phone (910) 738-7979.

MAGGIE VALLEY (E-2) pop. 607, elev. 3,020′

An all-year resort town, Maggie Valley is off the Blue Ridge Parkway near the east entrance to Great Smoky Mountains National Park *(see place listing p. 156)*. The community's name was selected in 1904 by the postmaster general, whose choice for the designation of the new postal district was limited to the name of one of a resident's three daughters.

Maggie Valley Area Chamber of Commerce: 2487 Soco Rd., P.O. Box 279, Maggie Valley, NC 28751; phone (828) 926-1686 or (800) 624-4431.

GHOST TOWN IN THE SKY is at 16 Fie Top Rd. Set within the replica of a western town, the park features a drop tower, a roller coaster, a 3,300-foot-high chairlift, shows and live music. Food is available. Stroller and wheelchair rentals are available. Allow 4 hours minimum. Daily 10-6, June-Aug.; Fri.-Sun. 10-6 in May and Sept.-Oct. Admission $30; $27 (ages 55+); $22 (ages 3-10). AX, DS, MC, VI. Phone (828) 926-1140.

GEM **WHEELS THROUGH TIME MUSEUM** is at 62 Vintage Ln. This 38,000-square-foot museum is said to feature the world's largest collection of rare American motorcycles, automobiles, related memorabilia and mementos dating 1903 to the present. More than 200 of these machines are operational and used regularly, and more than 100 are in their original condition.

The Decade Collection includes a 1914 Locomobile roadster/speedster and an original tomato red 1954 Cadillac Eldorado. Displays in the motorcycle collection include veteran (1903-26), military (WWI and WWII), Art Deco (1926-39), one-of-a-kind, post war (1946), speedway and special interest bikes. Changing exhibits also are featured regularly.

CLOSURE INFORMATION: The museum is scheduled to close permanently on Aug. 31, 2008. Guided tours are available. Picnicking is permitted. Allow 2 hours minimum. Daily 9-5, Apr.-Nov.; 10-4, rest of year. Closed Thanksgiving and Dec. 25. Admission $12; $10 (ages 65+); $6 (ages 5-12). AX, DS, MC, VI. Phone (828) 926-6266.

RECREATIONAL ACTIVITIES

White-water Rafting

- **Wildwater Ltd.** meets outside Bryson City on US 74W. Write P.O. Box 309, Long Creek, SC 29658. Daily Mar.-Oct. Reservations are required. Phone (800) 451-9972.

MANTEO—*see Outer Banks p. 179.*

MARSHALL (E-3) pop. 840, elev. 1,657′

RECREATIONAL ACTIVITIES

White-water Rafting

- **Nantahala Outdoor Center**, 9825 US 25/70. Write 13007 US 19W, Bryson City, NC 28713. Daily Mar.-Oct. Phone (828) 622-7260 or (800) 232-7238

MIDLAND (C-4) elev. 500′

REED GOLD MINE STATE HISTORIC SITE, 9621 Reed Mine Rd., was the first "placer" (creek) gold mine in the United States; a 17-pound gold nugget was discovered in 1799 on the farm of German immigrant John Reed. A visitor center has an orientation videotape, exhibits and mining equipment. Panning for gold is allowed April through October. A nature trail is on the grounds.

Picnicking is permitted. Allow 1 hour minimum. Tues.-Sat. 9-5; closed major holidays. Guided 30-minute tours of the mining area and underground tunnels begin 1 hour after opening. Last tour departs 45 minutes before closing. Museum and tour free; $2 charge to pan for gold. Phone (704) 721-4653.

MOCKSVILLE (B-4) pop. 4,178, elev. 850′

WINERIES

- **RayLen Vineyards & Winery** is at 3577 US 158. Mon.-Sat. 11-6; closed Jan. 1, Thanksgiving and Dec. 25. Phone (336) 998-3100.

MOORES CREEK NATIONAL BATTLEFIELD (D-6)

Moores Creek National Battlefield lies about 20 miles northwest of Wilmington and 4 miles west of US 421, on SR 210 near the town of Currie. This 87-acre site was the scene of a brief but decisive Revolutionary War battle on Feb. 27, 1776. Victory by the Colonists prevented the Loyalists from controlling North Carolina and helped block a British campaign to conquer the Southern colonies.

In the visitor center, displays and an audiovisual program depict the battle; two self-guiding trails with interpretive exhibits originate here. Picnicking is permitted. Daily 9-5; closed Jan. 1 and Dec. 25. Free. Phone (910) 283-5591.

MOORESVILLE (B-4) pop. 18,823, elev. 911′

Cotton drove the economy in Mooresville's quiet early years. Quite a different industry fuels today's growth. Due to its proximity to auto racing speedways at Wilmington and Charlotte and in Darlington, S.C., the community now calls itself Race City USA. Mooresville is home to more than 40 race teams representing some of the sport's biggest names.

Watercolorist Cotton Ketchie, known for his realistic depictions of North Carolina's mountain and coastal scenery, lives and paints in Mooresville. The Cotton Ketchie's Landmark Galleries and Pottery Museum, 212 N. Main St., features his work; phone (704) 664-4122 or (800) 842-8604.

Mooresville Convention and Visitors Bureau: 265 N. Main St., Mooresville, NC 28115; phone (704) 799-2400.

D.E. TURNER & COMPANY is 3 mi. e. of I-77 exit 36 on SR 150E to SR 152E, then 1 mi. to 111-115 Main St. Built in 1902, this old-fashioned hardware store has such period features as a hand-crank elevator and rolling ladders. The two-story building also contains examples of 19th- and 20th-century tools and materials. Allow 30 minutes minimum. Mon.-Sat. 8-6; closed Jan. 1, July 4, Thanksgiving and Dec. 25. Free. Phone (704) 664-5145.

LAZY 5 RANCH, 10 mi. e. on SR 150, contains more than 750 animals such as deer, elk, antelopes, giraffes, ostriches, emus, rhéas, white rhinos and zebras. Visitors may drive through the ranch via a 3.5-mile path or opt for a horse-drawn wagon ride; either affords the opportunity to pet and feed the animals. A petting zoo is on the grounds.

Picnicking is permitted. Allow 30 minutes minimum. Mon.-Sat. 9-5, Sun. 1-5. Admission $8.50; $5.50 (ages 2-11 and 61+). Wagon rides $13.50; $8.50 (ages 2-11 and 61+). Phone (704) 663-5100 or (704) 278-2618.

NORTH CAROLINA AUTO RACING HALL OF FAME, off I-77 exit 36, then .5 mi. w. on SR 150 to Lakeside Business Park, chronicles racing history with some 35 original race cars, memorabilia and personal items from the sport's best-known drivers. An art gallery features the works of motor sport artists and the Goodyear Mini-Theater presents 45-minute films highlighting racing achievements and winning drivers.

Allow 1 hour minimum. Mon.-Fri. 10-5, Sat.-Sun. 10-3; closed major holidays. Admission $5; $3 (ages

6-12 and 55+). AX, DS, MC, VI. Phone (704) 663-5331.

MOREHEAD CITY (D-8) pop. 7,691, elev. 16′

THE HISTORY PLACE is at 1008 Arendell St. The museum gallery includes local memorabilia in addition to exhibits about boat building, farming, hunting, fishing and the Civil War. A general store, school room, Victorian parlor and doctor's office depict early Carteret County life. Also onsite are a research library and historical society offices. Allow 1 hour minimum. Tues.-Sat. 10-4; closed major holidays. Free. Phone (252) 247-7533.

MORGANTON (E-4) pop. 17,310, elev. 1,191′

A series of dams on the Catawba River east and west of Morganton impounds a chain of lakes that provides many recreational opportunities. Optimist Park, 12 miles north on SR 181, offers swimming and picnicking. Nearby Lake James has areas for boating and is stocked with bass, walleye and bluegill. Both South Mountains State Park *(see Recreation Chart)* and Tuttle State Forest are nearby.

Burke County Travel & Tourism: 102 E. Union St., Morganton, NC 28655; phone (828) 433-6793 or (888) 462-2921.

OLD BURKE COUNTY COURTHOUSE, off I-40 exit 105, then 2 mi. n. on SR 18, was built in 1837. The Heritage Museum has changing exhibits and a replica of a turn-of-the-20th-century law office such as Sen. Sam Ervin might have used when he practiced law in Morganton. The Jailhouse Gallery offers art exhibits. Allow 30 minutes minimum. Tues.-Fri. 10-4; closed major holidays and Dec. 26-Jan. 2. Free. Phone (828) 437-4104.

MORRISVILLE (B-6) pop. 5,208, elev. 365′

WINERIES

- **Chatham Hill Winery** is at 3800 Gateway Centre Blvd., Suite 310. Mon.-Fri. 11-5, Sat. 11-6, Sun. 1-5; closed Jan. 1, Easter, Thanksgiving and Dec. 25. Phone (919) 380-7135 or (800) 808-6768.

MOUNT AIRY (A-5) pop. 8,484, elev. 1,014′

Although it was not incorporated until 1885, Mount Airy has had a long history. Originally a riverfront settlement dating from before 1750, its identity was that of a quiet small town until the late 19th century. When the railroad brought in manufacturing interests, Mount Airy began to grow. Now an industrialized city and trading center, it has endeavored to retain some of its old small-town atmosphere.

Despite its growth, Mount Airy still demonstrates that it served as the prototype for Mayberry of "The Andy Griffith Show." Griffith grew up in Mount Airy and later incorporated a number of its features into his fictional hometown. Griffith's former home is in the town's historic district, as is the Andy Griffith Playhouse, a former schoolhouse now used as a theater and arts center. The Mount Airy Visitor Center displays a collection of Andy Griffith memorabilia and other items of local historical significance.

Mount Airy Visitors Center/Greater Mount Airy Chamber of Commerce: 200 N. Main St., Mount Airy, NC 27030; phone (336) 786-6116 or (800) 948-0949.

Self-guiding tours: A brochure outlining a self-guiding driving tour of the city is available from the visitor center.

MOUNT GILEAD (C-5) pop. 1,389, elev. 433′

TOWN CREEK INDIAN MOUND STATE HISTORIC SITE is 5 mi. s.e. between SR 731 and SR 73. This 53-acre area was an important cultural, religious and political center, thought to have been developed during the 14th century by a Creek-related people. Several pre-Colonial buildings, including two temples and a mortuary, have been reconstructed. The visitor center offers interpretive exhibits and a DVD presentation.

Picnicking is permitted. Allow 1 hour minimum. Tues.-Sat. 9-5, Sun. 1-5; closed major winter holidays. Free. Phone (910) 439-6802.

MURPHY (F-1) pop. 1,568, elev. 1,578′

Murphy was the site of Fort Butler, built by Gen. Winfield Scott during the roundup of the Cherokees 1837-38. A marble shaft marks the fort's location. Hiwassee Dam and Lake *(see Recreation Chart and the AAA Southeastern CampBook)* are nearby.

Cherokee County Chamber of Commerce: 805 US 64W, Murphy, NC 28906; phone (828) 837-2242.

FIELDS OF THE WOOD, s. on US 64, then 10 mi. n.w. on SR 294, is a biblically inspired park. Highlights include a mountainside where the Ten Commandments are written in 6-foot-high letters made of huge white stones. Food is available. Allow 3 hours minimum. Daily dawn-dusk. Free. Phone (828) 494-7855.

NAGS HEAD—*see Outer Banks p. 179.*

NANTAHALA NATIONAL FOREST

Elevations in the forest range from 1,200 ft. on the Tusquetee River below the Appalachian Dam to 5,800 ft. at Lone Bald. Refer to AAA maps for additional elevation information.

The mountainous southwestern tip of North Carolina is overspread by the 527,486-acre Nantahala National Forest. The forest, which gives rise to 10 rivers, is named after the Cherokee word meaning "land of the noonday sun." The name refers to the deep gorges that are blessed with bright light only at noon, when the sun sits directly above.

Approximately 600 miles of roads and trails, including the Appalachian Trail and a 35-mile portion of the Bartram Trail, thread through the forest's interior. Scenic drives near Andrews pass Nantahala Lake and Wayah Bald; the "Trail of Tears" crosses the Snowbird Mountains from Andrews to Robbinsville. Joyce Kilmer Memorial Forest, named for the author of the poem "Trees," and Slickrock Wilderness also are in Nantahala. Several recreation areas in the vicinity are designated for public use.

Numerous waterfalls can be found in the forest. Whitewater Falls, 9 miles south of Sapphire on SR 281, plummets more than 400 feet in a number of smaller falls. At Glen Falls Scenic Area, 2 miles south of Highlands on SR 106, the river cascades over a 50-foot ledge for a spectacular show.

The Cherohala Skyway is a scenic 51-mile highway that begins in Robbinsville and traverses to Tellico Plains, Tenn. Known as the "mini Blue Ridge Parkway," it affords excellent views of the Nantahala National Forest. There are no facilities along the mountainous road.

Fishing and hunting are permitted; a license is required. Information is available from the district ranger stations at Robbinsville, Murphy, Highlands and Franklin or from the Visitor Information Center at the Forest Supervisor's Office, Federal Building, Post and Otis streets, P.O. Box 2750, Asheville, NC 28802. *For points of interest in the forest, see Cashiers p. 136, Franklin p. 155, Highlands p. 165 and Murphy p. 171; also see Recreation Chart and the AAA Southeastern CampBook.*

NANTAHALA GORGE is just n.e. of Topton on US 19. The gorge is 8 miles long and in places attains a depth of 2,000 feet.

NEW BERN (C-8) pop. 23,128, elev. 18'

Swiss and German colonists settled New Bern in 1710, naming it for Bern, Switzerland. By 1749 the thriving river port had the colony's first printing press; two years later printer James Davis founded the state's first newspaper, the *North Carolina Gazette.* As Colonial capital 1766-76 and state capital 1776-94, New Bern played an active part in the Revolution.

New Bern also is known as the birthplace of Pepsi-Cola, invented by Caleb Bradham in 1898. His pharmacy at the corner of Middle and Pollock streets now is a soda fountain and store dedicated to soft drink memorabilia.

The town streets are lined with historic sites and outstanding examples of American architecture, especially the early 19th-century Federal style. Bank of the Arts, housed in a 1912 bank building, features changing exhibits by regional and national artists. The Attmore-Oliver Civil War House Museum, 511 Broad St., contains 18th- and 19th-century furniture, New Bern historical objects and a doll collection; phone (252) 638-8558.

New Bern/Craven County Convention and Visitors Center: 203 S. Front St., P.O. Box 1713, New Bern, NC 28563; phone (252) 637-9400 or (800) 437-5767.

Self-guiding tours: Free tour maps are available from the convention and visitors center.

CHRIST EPISCOPAL CHURCH, Middle and Pollock sts., is the successor to the old "King's Chapel." The present Gothic Revival edifice dates from 1875 and has a silver communion service, Bible and prayer book presented by King George II in 1752. Mon.-Fri. 9-5. Free. Phone (252) 633-2109.

FIREMEN'S MUSEUM, 408 Hancock St., displays steam pumpers and firefighting equipment dating from the early 19th century. Exhibits include maps, old photographs, Civil War artifacts and items from Bern, Switzerland. Mon.-Sat. 10-4; closed Jan. 1, Thanksgiving, Dec. 24-26 and 31. Admission $5; $2.50 (students with ID and children). Phone (252) 636-4087.

FIRST PRESBYTERIAN CHURCH, 418 New St., was built in the Federal style 1819-22 and used as a hospital during the Civil War. Mon.-Fri. 9-5. Sunday services at 8:30 and 11. Closed major holidays. Free. Phone (252) 637-3270.

SAVE **NEW BERN TOURS & CONVENTION SERVICES** leaves from the corner of Pollock and George sts., and across from the Tryon Palace *(see attraction listing).* These narrated, 90-minute trolley tours explore the history and architecture of this former royal capital of North Carolina. Tours focusing on the Civil War and African-American history also are available. Trolley tours depart Mon.-Sat. at 11 and 2, Sun. at 2, Apr.-Oct.; by appointment rest of year. Phone ahead for Civil War and African-American history tours. Fare $15; $8 (ages 0-12). Phone (252) 637-7316 or (800) 849-7316.

GEM **TRYON PALACE HISTORIC SITES & GARDENS** is at the corner of George and Pollock sts. The imposing Georgian mansion, built by Royalist Governor William Tryon 1767-70, was designed to represent the British crown. Once built, it became North Carolina's first capitol and reputedly the finest government building in Colonial America. In 1798 a disastrous fire destroyed the palace; it was later reconstructed on the same site using the original architect's drawings.

The palace is furnished with rare 18th-century English and American antiques and decorative arts, and the 14 acres of grounds are landscaped in the manner of 18th-century English gardens. Visitors can see demonstrations of such Colonial crafts as weaving, blacksmithing, candle-dipping and cooking. The Reception Center shows a 20-minute orientation film.

Tours are conducted by costumed interpreters. Included in the tour is a stop by the New Bern Academy Museum, which contains exhibits on history, architecture, education and the Civil War in New Bern.

Guided tours every 30 minutes Mon.-Sat. 9-5, Sun. 1-5; closed Jan. 1, Thanksgiving and Dec. 24-26. Last tour begins at 4. Admission $15; $6 (grades

1-12). Rates may vary; phone ahead. MC, VI. Phone (252) 514-4900 or (800) 767-1560.

Gardens of Tryon Palace, 610 Pollock St., can be viewed on a self-guiding tour.

George W. Dixon House, 619 Pollock St., was built in the early 1830s. Antiques from the Federal and Empire periods decorate the interior.

John Wright Stanly House, 307 George St., was built around 1783. The town house's furnishings and garden are of period design.

Robert Hay House, Eden St., features costumed interpreters who portray historic New Bern characters from the 1850s.

NEW HOLLAND (B-9)

MATTAMUSKEET NATIONAL WILDLIFE REFUGE is entered on SR 94, 1 mi. n. of US 264. Covering approximately 50,000 acres and most of Lake Mattamuskeet, the refuge is a wintering area for migratory waterfowl. Within its boundaries is Salyer's Ridge Natural Area, where a mature loblolly pine forest is in the late stage of succession, transforming into a sweetgum and red maple forest.

The Mattamuskeet Lodge was built in 1915 as the world's largest water pumping station; it is now used as an environmental education and community center. Fishing, best in the spring and fall, is permitted early March through October. Daily dawn-dusk. Free. Phone (252) 926-4021.

NEWTON (B-4) pop. 12,560, elev. 969'

CATAWBA COUNTY MUSEUM OF HISTORY, 5 mi. s. on SR 16, is housed in a three-story former county courthouse built in 1924; the building is a neoclassic Revival structure in the center of a Southern courthouse square. Exhibits focus on the history of the Catawba River Valley and the western Piedmont area. Artifacts include military uniforms dating from the Revolution to the 20th century, items from the Civil War and an early 1930s race car.

Guided tours are available. Allow 1 hour minimum. Wed.-Sat. 9-4, Sun. 1:30-4:30; closed major holidays. Free. Phone (828) 465-0383.

OCRACOKE—*see Outer Banks p. 179.*

OLD FORT (E-4) pop. 963, elev. 1,438'

MOUNTAIN GATEWAY MUSEUM is at 24 Water St. Mountain lifestyle and history from pre-Colonial times to the 20th century are highlighted with displays, living-history exhibits and a videotape presentation. Collections include photographs, tools and household items. Two 1800s-era log cabins are on site. Picnicking is permitted. Allow 1 hour minimum. Tues.-Sat. 9-5, Sun. 2-5, Mon. noon-5; closed major holidays. Donations. Phone (828) 668-9259.

Outer Banks

The Outer Banks consist of a string of narrow islands and peninsulas that lie between the ocean and the sounds along 125 miles of North Carolina's coast. Through years of storms and shipwrecks, the islands have developed a distinctive culture. Certain areas are resorts, while others retain a relatively primitive charm. Residents closely identified with maritime activity have kept the speech patterns and customs handed down from the 17th century.

The area is rich in history. The first English colony attempted settlement on Roanoke Island in 1585. At Kill Devil Hills in 1903, Wilbur and Orville Wright successfully launched the first flight of a power-driven airplane.

The lands of the Outer Banks are constantly shifted by wind and wave action. Some believe the landmass is moving slowly toward the mainland; inlets connecting the ocean and sounds have a lifetime of less than 100 years. The result of storms, they regularly appear and disappear.

Outer Banks Visitors Bureau: One Visitor Center Circle, Manteo, NC 27954; phone (877) 629-4386. *See color ad p. 177.*

CAPE HATTERAS NATIONAL SEASHORE (B-9)

Covering approximately 45 square miles on North Carolina's Outer Banks, Cape Hatteras National Seashore is the most extensive stretch of undeveloped seashore on the Atlantic Coast. Except for a few villages on the islands, the national recreation area includes Ocracoke and Hatteras islands and part of Bodie (Body) Island. The islands are connected by a free bridge and a free ferry.

Vast expanses of sand and water are the main attractions in this area of wild beauty. Bottlenose dolphin sometimes are seen near the beach. The sand is treacherous for motorists; visitors should park in designated areas and only leave the road where indicated.

The lands are public property and residents and visitors have free access to the ocean. State and federal fishing regulations apply to waters inside and outside the boundaries. Regulated waterfowl hunting is permitted within the seashore, excluding Pea Island National Wildlife Refuge. Day-use facilities are at Coquina Beach, Cape Point and Ocracoke. *See Recreation Chart and the AAA Southeastern CampBook.*

BODIE ISLAND LIGHTHOUSE VISITOR CENTER is 8 mi. s. of jct. US 158 and US 64. The visitor center and lighthouse provide a glimpse of life as a lightkeeper in the late 1800s. **Note:** The lighthouse is not

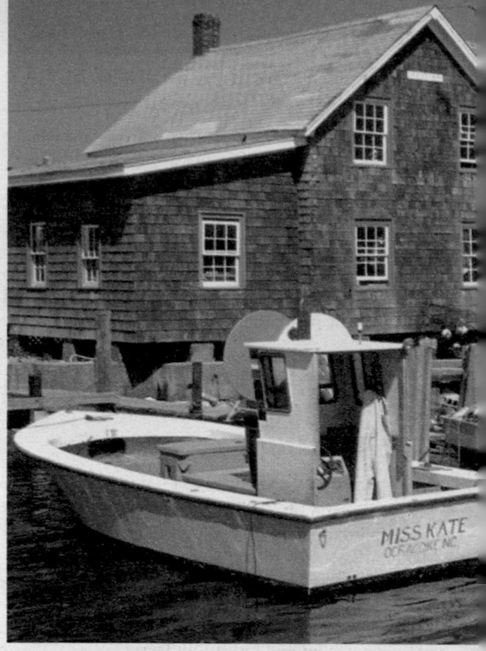

Ocracoke / © Gibson Stock Photography

open for climbing. Allow 30 minutes minimum. Daily 9-6, Memorial Day-Labor Day; 9-5, rest of year. Closed Dec. 25. Free. Phone (252) 441-5711.

CAPE HATTERAS LIGHTHOUSE, built in 1870, is about 1 mi. s.e. of Buxton. The tallest such brick structure in the United States, the 208-foot renovated lighthouse warns ships away from Diamond Shoals, the "Graveyard of the Atlantic." A balcony, perched at the top of a 268-step climb, offers an observation point. The keeper's quarters contains a visitor center and exhibits about area history. A self-guiding nature trail begins near the lighthouse.

Allow 30 minutes minimum. Lighthouse and visitor center open daily 9-6, Memorial Day-Labor Day; 9-5, rest of year. Closed Good Friday, Columbus Day and Dec. 25. Admission $7; $3.50 (ages 0-12 and 62+). Phone (252) 995-4474.

PEA ISLAND NATIONAL WILDLIFE REFUGE covers approximately 5,880 acres just s. of Oregon Inlet on Hatteras Island. Birds include more than 250 species of local and migratory fowl. Observation decks, about 5 miles south of the Oregon Inlet bridge, permit views of the ocean, wildlife and shipwrecks along the shore. Daily dawn-dusk; information office open daily 9-5, Apr.-Oct. Free. Phone (252) 987-2394 or (252) 473-1131.

CAPE LOOKOUT NATIONAL SEASHORE

Extending 55 miles along North Carolina's Outer Banks from Ocracoke Inlet in the north to Beaufort Inlet in the south, Cape Lookout National Seashore includes Portsmouth Island, Core Banks and Shackleford

Banks. Approximately 28,500 acres of undeveloped barrier islands lie within the national seashore.

Cape Lookout is reached only by boat, and on-island transportation is limited. Passenger and vehicle ferries leave regularly from Harkers Island, Atlantic and Davis; service is generally not available in winter. Charter service to Portsmouth can be arranged from Ocracoke. Rates for round-trip service to the park start at approximately $12 per person, $60-$80 per vehicle.

Popular recreational activities are seashell collecting, surf fishing, bird-watching, boating and camping. Shackleford Banks is home to a horse herd, maintained in its wild state with minimal human contact. While interesting to observe, they can be difficult to find. These horses, which graze in bachelor bands and harems across the island, reputedly have been residents of the Outer Banks since the early 1500s.

Portsmouth Village, once a prosperous pre-Civil War port, is on the northern end of Core Banks. The Portsmouth Village Historic District includes surviving buildings and structural remains dating from the 1850s. Cape Lookout Lighthouse, still operational, is in the Cape Village Historic District on Core Banks. The nearby Keepers' Quarters, which serves as a visitor center in summer, also is a meeting point for programs sponsored by park rangers. Rustic cabins are available for rent April through November; for reservations phone (877) 956-6568.

A visitor information station at the east end of Harkers Island Road is open daily 9-5; closed Jan. 1 and Dec. 25. For information contact the Superintendent, Cape Lookout National Seashore, 131 Charles St., Harkers Island, NC 28531; phone (252) 728-2250. *See Recreation Chart.*

Elizabethan Gardens, Fort Raleigh National Historic Site
Outer Banks Visitors Bureau

COROLLA (A-9) elev. 2′

CURRITUCK BEACH LIGHTHOUSE is at 1101 Corolla Village Rd. in Currituck Heritage Park. Visitors can climb to the top of the lighthouse, which has served as a navigational aid since 1875. A small exhibit inside explains the history of the various structures within the light station compound. The grounds are available for exploration. Allow 30 minutes minimum. Daily 10-6, Easter-Thanksgiving; closed major holidays. Lighthouse $7; free (ages 0-7). Grounds free. Phone (252) 453-4939.

WHALEHEAD CLUB is off SR12N at 1100 Club Way in Currituck Heritage Park. The Art Nouveau structure, built 1922-25, was the home of waterfowl hunting enthusiasts Mr. & Mrs. E.C. Knight, Jr. Said to be the first residence on the Outer Banks to contain a basement, elevator and swimming pool, the structure features original cork floors, "corduroy" walls and Tiffany light fixtures. A boathouse, boat basin and footbridge are on the grounds. Allow 1

Destination Outer Banks

Explore the nation's birth in the Outer Banks. Visit the *Elizabeth II*, a replica of the type of ship used to transport the first British Colonists. Then visit their settlement at Fort Raleigh.

But don't imagine you are seeing the land as the Colonists saw it. Not only have the storms and tides of the Atlantic changed it, but in the 1930s the WPA built more than 100 miles of duneline.

Outer Banks Visitors Bureau

Wright Brothers National Memorial, Kill Devil Hills.
Orville and Wilbur Wright's conquered dream of flight is celebrated on 431 acres. (See listing page 180)

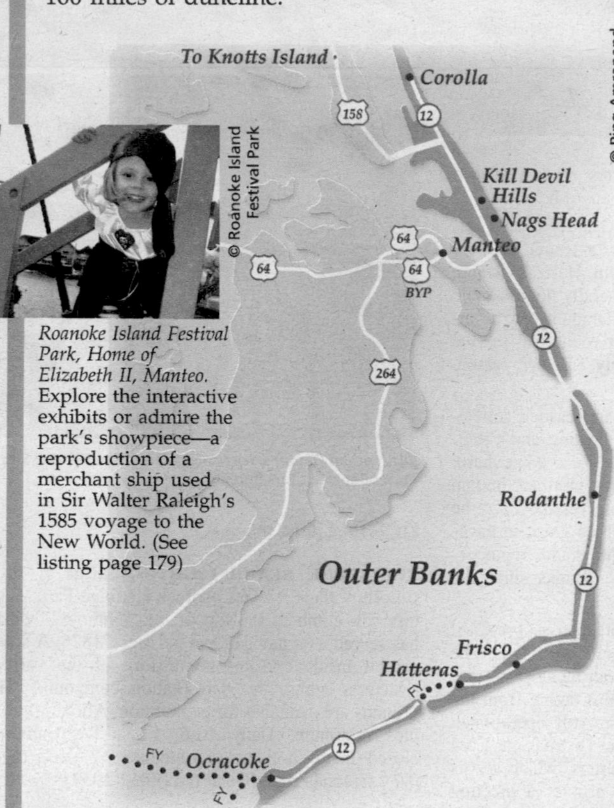

© Roanoke Island Festival Park

Roanoke Island Festival Park, Home of Elizabeth II, Manteo.
Explore the interactive exhibits or admire the park's showpiece—a reproduction of a merchant ship used in Sir Walter Raleigh's 1585 voyage to the New World. (See listing page 179)

© Ping Amranand SuperStock

Elizabethan Gardens, Fort Raleigh National Historic Site.
This replica of a 16th-century formal English garden pays tribute to the first English colonists in America. (See listing page 177)

© David R. Frazier Danita Delimont Stock Photography

Ocracoke Lighthouse.
The 75-foot structure is reputedly the oldest continually operating lighthouse on the North Carolina coast. (See mention page 179)

Places included in this AAA Destination Area:

hour minimum. Guided tours daily 9-5; closed major holidays. Admission $7; free (ages 0-8). MC, VI. Phone (252) 453-9040.

WILD HORSE SAFARI departs from Back Country Outfitters & Guides at 107-C Corolla Light Town Center. The 2.5-hour tour in an off-road vehicle allows visitors a glimpse of the Wild Spanish Mustangs that roam the Currituck beaches. A knowledgeable guide provides information about area history, including stories about Spanish conquistadores arriving with the mustangs. Birds, deer, goats, dolphins and other animals often are spotted.

Daily 9-5, Memorial Day-Labor Day. Schedule varies in the off-season; phone ahead. Fare $46; $23 (ages 4-11). Prices vary seasonally. Reservations must be made one week in advance. MC, VI. Phone (252) 453-0877.

FORT RALEIGH NATIONAL HISTORIC SITE (B-9)

Covering 143 acres, Fort Raleigh National Historic Site is on Roanoke Island, about 3 miles north of Manteo. In 1585 men sent to Roanoke Island by Sir Walter Raleigh attempted to establish the first English colony in what is now the eastern United States. Fort Raleigh was built, but the following year the survivors returned to England.

In 1587 Raleigh dispatched another expedition that included women and children to give permanence to the colony. Led by John White, these settlers rebuilt the fort. On Aug. 18, 1587, White's granddaughter, Virginia Dare, was born in the colony. She was the first English child born in the New World.

Several days later White sailed back to England for provisions, but Spanish hostilities delayed his return until 1590. He found no trace of the colonists. Many theories about the fate of the "Lost Colony" have been proposed, but the mystery remains unsolved.

Earthworks representing those that probably were part of the original fort have been reconstructed. A simple granite stone commemorates the birth of Virginia Dare. For visitor information relative to the site, phone (252) 473-5772.

GEM **ELIZABETHAN GARDENS,** reached by the park road into the fort, is a memorial to the first English colonists in America. This re-created, 16th-century formal English garden has antique statuary, period furniture, rose and herb beds, and indigenous shrubs, trees and flowers. Allow 1 hour minimum. Daily 9-8, June-Aug.; 9-5, rest of year. Closed Jan. 1, Thanksgiving and Dec. 24-25. Admission $8; $7 (ages 62+); $5 (ages 6-17). MC, VI. Phone (252) 473-3234.

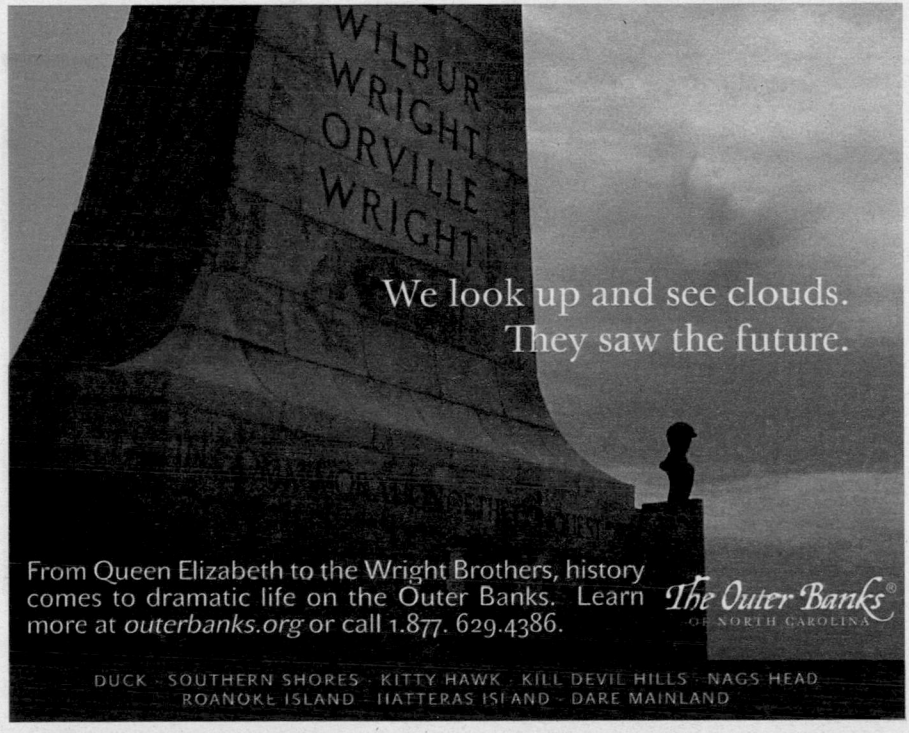

THE LINDSAY WARREN VISITOR CENTER, within Fort Raleigh, displays books, charts, pictures, American Indian artifacts and relics from the period of the first colony. A 17-minute laser disc presentation about the first English attempt to settle in the

New World is shown on the hour in the summer, on the half-hour off-season. Interpretive programs are held during summer. Allow 30 minutes minimum. Daily 9-6, Memorial Day-Labor Day; 9-5, rest of year. Closed Dec. 25. Free. Phone (252) 473-5772.

GEM SAVE **"THE LOST COLONY"** is presented in the Waterside Theater, 3 mi. n.w. of Manteo on Roanoke Island via US 64/264. This symphonic outdoor drama retells the story of the 1585 settlement on Roanoke Island. Inquire about weather policies. Performances Sun.-Fri. at 8:30 p.m., June-Aug. Admission $20 (preferred seating); $16 (adults); $15 (ages 62+); $8 (ages 0-11 Tues.-Thurs.); $4 (ages 0-11 Fri.-Sat.); free (ages 0-11 on Mon. with paying adult). DS, MC, VI. Phone (252) 473-3414 or (800) 488-5012.

FRISCO (C-9) elev. 10′

SAVE **FRISCO NATIVE AMERICAN MUSEUM & NATURAL HISTORY CENTER,** 53536 SR 12, includes a nationally recognized collection that showcases the history and culture of various tribes. Highlights include an exhibit detailing the tribes that inhabited Hatteras Island, a Hopi wishing drum and a dugout canoe. A self-guiding nature trail, designed to accommodate visually impaired visitors, points out many species of Outer Banks vegetation and wildlife.

Allow 30 minutes minimum. Tues.-Sun. 11-5, Mon. by appointment; closed Thanksgiving and Dec. 25. Admission $5; $3 (ages 65+); $15 (family). Phone (252) 995-4440.

HATTERAS (C-9) elev. 0′

GRAVEYARD OF THE ATLANTIC MUSEUM is at 59158 Coast Guard Rd. Featured are the original Cape Hatteras Lighthouse Fresnel lens, artifacts from the German submarine U-85, 2,000-year-old coins, and information about local Civil War activity. Allow 30 minutes minimum. Mon.-Sat. 10-4, mid-Sept. through Apr. 30; Tues.-Fri. 10-4, rest of year. Closed major holidays. Free. Phone (252) 986-2996.

KILL DEVIL HILLS (B-9) pop. 5,897, elev. 7′

NAGS HEAD WOODS PRESERVE is at 701 W. Ocean Acres Dr. The 1,092-acre preserve is home to more than 50 species of birds and more than 300 species of plants. Visitors can explore 5 miles of trails that reveal scenic views and an abundance of local flora and fauna. Allow 30 minutes minimum. Visitor center open Mon.-Sat. 10-3, in summer; Mon.-Fri. 10-3, rest of year. Trails open daily dawn-dusk. Free. Phone (252) 441-2525.

KNOTTS ISLAND (A-9) elev. 10′

WINERIES

- **Moonrise Bay Vineyard** is at 134 Moonrise Bay Landing. Daily noon-5, Apr.-Dec.; Thurs.-Sun. noon-5, rest of year. Closed Jan. 1, Thanksgiving and Dec. 25. Phone (252) 429-9463.

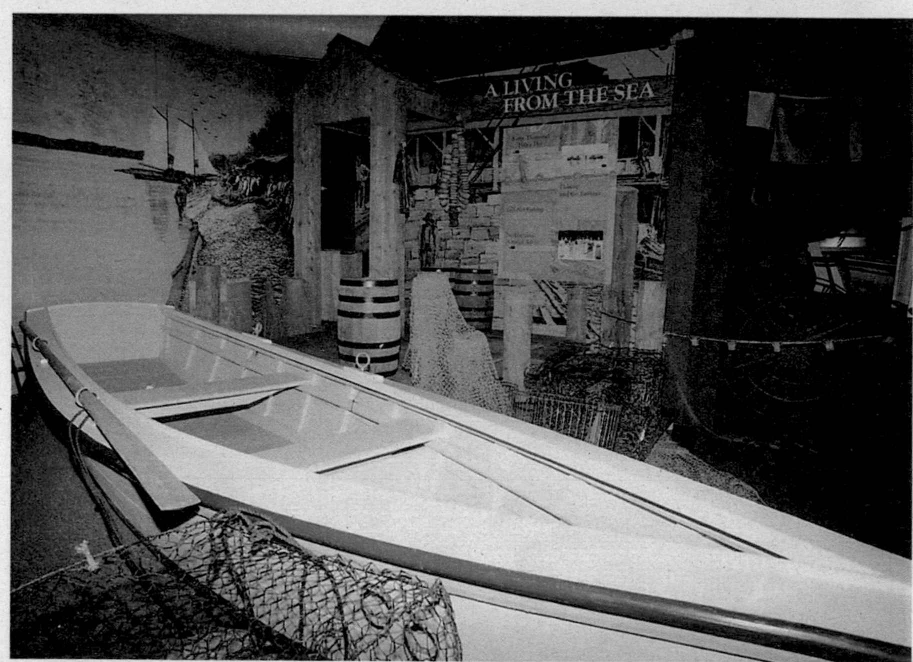

Roanoke Adventure Museum, Manteo / © Roanoke Island Festival Park

MANTEO (B-9) pop. 1,052, elev. 10′

On historic Roanoke Island, Manteo is reached by causeway from the east or west. In 1585 the English tried to establish their first New World colony at Roanoke Island *(see Fort Raleigh National Historic Site p. 177)*. Nearby, Gen. Ambrose E. Burnside's Union forces won the Battle of Roanoke Island in 1862. In 1902 the island and Hatteras were the scenes of Reginald A. Fessenden's experiments in wireless telegraphy.

"THE LOST COLONY"— *see Fort Raleigh National Historic Site p. 178.*

NORTH CAROLINA AQUARIUM ON ROANOKE ISLAND, 2 mi. n. on US 64, then 1 mi. s.w. on Airport Rd. (SR 1116), is a showcase for the state's diverse marine life. Exhibits include Waters of the Outer Banks, Close Encounters, Wetlands on the Edge and "Bite Shock Sting." In Graveyards of the Atlantic, sharks, sea turtles and reef fish inhabit a 285,000-gallon tank that also contains a replica of the USS *Monitor.* A nature trail with a shoreline boardwalk allows visitors to view nature and dig for fossilized shark teeth.

Allow 30 minutes minimum. Daily 9-5; closed Jan. 1, Thanksgiving and Dec. 25. Admission $8; $7 (ages 63+ and military with ID); $6 (ages 6-17). MC, VI. Phone (252) 473-3493 or (866) 332-3475.

GEM SAVE **ROANOKE ISLAND FESTIVAL PARK, HOME OF *ELIZABETH II*,** across from Manteo's waterfront, explores 400 years of the island's history. The park's centerpiece is a reproduction of a merchant ship used in Sir Walter Raleigh's 1585 voyage to the New World. Interpreters in Elizabethan costume re-create the lives of 16th-century mariners and soldiers.

The Roanoke Adventure Museum chronicles Outer Banks history through interactive exhibits, while the Settlement Site offers such demonstrations as woodworking, blacksmithing and leatherworking. An art gallery, history center and fossil pit also are on site. "The Legend of Two Path," a film about the colonists' impact on the American Indians of Roanoke Island, is shown several times daily. A summer performing arts series is presented late June-late July.

Picnicking is permitted. Food is available. Allow 2 hours minimum. Daily 9-6, Apr.-Nov.; 9-5, Feb.-Apr. and in Dec. Closed Thanksgiving and Dec. 24-25. Admission for 2 consecutive days $8; $5 (ages 6-17). MC, VI. Phone (252) 475-1500 or (252) 475-1506.

ROANOKE MARSHES LIGHT is at the end of the pier on the Manteo waterfront. A replica of an 1857 screwpile lighthouse, the structure features exhibits about Roanoke Island's nautical history, the lighthouse's construction and local boat builder Warren O'Neal. Allow 30 minutes minimum. Daily 9-5. Free. Phone (252) 475-1500.

NAGS HEAD (B-9) pop. 2,700

An oceanfront resort on the Outer Banks, Nags Head is a hotel and cottage colony. Facilities are excellent for swimming and fishing. According to local legend, the village of Nags Head acquired its name from the islanders' practice of tying lanterns to the necks of ponies and marching them along the dunes at night. The swinging lights simulated anchored boats, thus deceiving ship captains into running aground, where their cargo was seized. Wood from these shipwrecks was used to built homes, many of which are still standing today.

JOCKEY'S RIDGE STATE PARK, off US 158 bypass, contains two of the highest sand dunes on the East Coast. More than 100 feet high, Jockey's Ridge and Engagement Hill are popular takeoff points for hang gliders. Hang gliding permits can be obtained at the park office. Allow 1 hour minimum. Daily 8 a.m.-9 p.m., June-Aug.; 8-8, Mar.-May and Sept.-Oct.; 8-6, rest of year. Closed Dec. 25. Free. Phone (252) 441-7132.

Shopping areas: The SAVE Tanger Outlet Center, at Milepost 16 on US 158, offers more than 25 stores and is open daily.

OCRACOKE (C-9) pop. 769

On Ocracoke (OHK-ruh-coke) Island, the charming fishing village of Ocracoke is adjacent to Cape Hatteras National Seashore on the Outer Banks. Built mainly around Silver Lake, the houses were laid out with Old World irregularity along sandy streets overhung with moss-covered oaks and yaupon. Completed in 1823, the 75-foot Ocracoke Lighthouse is said to be the oldest continually operating lighthouse on the North Carolina coast.

Ocracoke also is known to have been a hangout of Edward Teach, alias Blackbeard; the notorious pirate and his crew were killed at Teach's Hole in 1718. Legend holds that Blackbeard still wanders the area in search of his severed head.

The British Cemetery is the resting place for four HMS Bedfordshire crew members who died in 1942 when their trawler was presumably torpedoed by German submarines. A public memorial service attended by members of the British Royal Navy and the U.S. Coast Guard honors these sailors—two of whom are unidentified—each May.

Bicycle rentals are available in town for those who seek a practical and enjoyable means of exploring Ocracoke Island. Several hundred bird species can be spotted, particularly during the spring and fall migratory seasons. At a 100-acre exhibit area 5 miles north of the village on scenic SR 12, visitors can observe the wild Banker horses that have roamed the island since the 1730s. According to one tale, the ponies were abandoned by 16th- and 17th-century European explorers who sought to minimize the cargo on recently wrecked ships.

For water and coastline aficionados, the island is a hot spot for clamming, crabbing, fishing, kayaking, scuba diving, surfing, swimming and whale watching. From sunset cruises to fishing expeditions to tours of nearby Portsmouth Island, boating activities abound. Those who, like a high tide, can't seem to pull themselves away from the shore might behold the marvelous sight of luminescent phosphorus in the nighttime surf.

The island is reached by a free ferry on SR 12 from Hatteras and by a toll ferry from Cedar Island and Swan Quarter. Note: Reservations are necessary for the Cedar Island and Swan Quarter toll ferries and can be made 30 days prior to departure date. Apply in person at the terminal or phone (252) 225-3551 or (800) 856-0343 for Cedar Island, (252) 928-3841 for Ocracoke, or (252) 926-1111 for Swan Quarter. The Hatteras ferry, however, does not accept reservations. For general information about ferry schedules, phone (800) 293-3779.

Ocracoke Island Visitor Center: Cape Hatteras National Seashore, 38 Irvin Garrish Hwy., Ocracoke, NC 27960; phone (252) 928-4531.

RODANTHE (B-9) elev. 3'

CHICAMACOMICO LIFE-SAVING STATION is at 23645 SR 12. A precursor of today's U.S. Coast Guard, the U.S. Life-Saving Service was established in 1871 with a mission to rescue shipwreck victims. Commissioned in 1874, Chicamacomico was the first operational station in the state.

A collection of photographs, documents and rescue gear allows visitors a glimpse into the lives of the dedicated service members. Also on the grounds are a 1911 station and a 1907 house. Allow 1 hour minimum. Mon.-Fri. noon-5; closed major holidays. Admission $6; $4 (ages 6-18 and 63+); $15 (family). DS, MC, VI. Phone (252) 987-1552.

GEM WRIGHT BROTHERS NATIONAL MEMORIAL (A-9)

This 431-acre area on the Outer Banks is on the US 158 bypass, at Milepost 8 in Kill Devil Hills. The Wright Memorial Shaft was dedicated in November 1932 to Orville and Wilbur Wright "in commemoration of the conquest of the air." The first sustained flights by a heavier-than-air powered machine were made nearby on Dec. 17, 1903.

The visitor center exhibit contains reproductions of the 1902 glider and 1903 flyer. The grounds have markers showing the distance traveled during the first four flights as well as replicas of the Wright brothers' workshop and living quarters.

Allow 1 hour minimum. Daily 9-6, Memorial Day-Labor Day; 9-5, rest of year. Closed Dec. 25. Admission $4, under 15 free. Phone (252) 441-7430.

Cape Hatteras Lighthouse, Cape Hatteras National Seashore / Outer Banks Visitors Bureau

This ends listings for the Outer Banks.
The following page resumes the alphabetical listings of cities in North Carolina.

PEMBROKE (C-6) pop. 2,399, elev. 169′

Pembroke is the center for the approximately 40,000 Lumbee Indians who live in Robeson County. It is theorized that some of these people are descendants of the "Lost Colony." The Lumbee Indians were initially denied full U.S. citizenship, but their protests during the Civil War and the persistence of their leader Henry Berry Lowrie eventually convinced the North Carolina Legislature to extend them voting rights.

Pembroke also is the home of the University of North Carolina at Pembroke. The Givens Performing Arts Center, on campus, features various performances September through May; phone (910) 521-6287.

Pembroke Area Chamber of Commerce: 205 Union Chapel Rd., P.O. Box 1978, Pembroke, NC 28372; phone (910) 521-0647.

PINEHURST (C-5) pop. 9,706, elev. 550′

A mild climate helped Pinehurst develop into a year-round resort community. The village's New England-style parks and roadways were laid out by Frederick Law Olmsted, designer of New York's Central Park and Asheville's Biltmore gardens. Handsome estates and other residences, many of Georgian Colonial design, are found throughout the village.

The Pinehurst area is noted for its more than 40 championship golf courses that often host PGA and LPGA tournaments. Tennis competitions are occasionally held in the town. Carriage rides throughout the village are available.

Pinehurst Area Convention and Visitors Bureau: 10677 Hwy. 15-501, P.O. Box 2270, Southern Pines, NC 28387; phone (800) 346-5362.

SANDHILLS HORTICULTURAL GARDENS is at 3395 Airport Rd. Sandhills Community College students maintain several gardens with a variety of landscape designs in this unique natural environment. Conifer, holly, woodland and annual gardens are among the collection. The "Circle of Peace" is a sculpture of seven children from diverse cultures. A visitor center is on the grounds. Daily dawn-dusk. Free. Phone (910) 695-3882.

PINE KNOLL SHORES (D-8) pop. 1,524, elev. 7′

GEM **NORTH CAROLINA AQUARIUM AT PINE KNOLL SHORES** is in the Theodore Roosevelt Natural Area, 5 mi. w. of Atlantic Beach on SR 58N at 1 Roosevelt Blvd. As visitors enter the building, they encounter a 32-foot waterfall. Five of the state's aquatic zones are represented in the aquarium, which is designed around the theme "From the Mountains to the Sea." The premier exhibit, "Living Shipwreck," presents a view of sharks, tarpons, groupers and other large fish swimming through the wreckage of a sunken German WWII submarine replica.

Additional exhibits include "Queen Anne's Revenge" that is a replica of a marine community and debris field of an 18th-century shipwreck as well as a river otter showcase, with feeding demonstrations. Allow 1 hour minimum. Daily 9-5; closed Jan. 1, Thanksgiving and Dec. 25. Admission $8; $7 (ages 62+ and military with ID); $6 (ages 6-17). MC, VI. Phone (252) 247-4003 or (866) 294-3477.

PINEVILLE—*see Charlotte p. 148.*

PINNACLE (A-5) elev. 1,079′

HORNE CREEK LIVING HISTORICAL FARM is off I-74/US 52 exit 129, 3.5 mi. s.w. on Perch Rd., then 3 mi. s. on Hauser Rd. This site, once farmed by generations of the Hauser and Sawyer families, gives a firsthand look at early farm life in North Carolina. Self-guiding tours of the homestead highlight agricultural practices and family life 1900-10. Livestock and heirloom crops typical of the period also are featured. Allow 1 hour minimum. Tues.-Sat. 10-4; closed major holidays. Donations. Phone (336) 325-2298.

GEM PISGAH NATIONAL FOREST

Elevations within the boundaries of the forest range from 1,200 ft. at Mulberry Creek to 6,285 ft. at Roan Mountain. Refer to AAA maps for additional elevation information.

The two segments of Pisgah National Forest cover 495,000 acres of the Appalachians in western North Carolina. Two main mountain chains and several lesser ranges encompassed by the forest have twenty 6,000-foot peaks, including 6,684-foot Mount Mitchell, highest summit east of the Mississippi River. Mount Mitchell is in a 1,677-acre state park *(see Recreation Chart)* surrounded by the forest and is next to the Blue Ridge Parkway.

A network of roads and miles of trails interlace the forest. Part of the Appalachian Trail winds along the northwestern boundary. US 276, which runs for 37 miles between Brevard and Waynesville, is part of the Forest Heritage National Scenic Byway and affords access to various points of interest.

District rangers are stationed at Marion, Burnsville, Pisgah Forest and Hot Springs. Pisgah headquarters is open Mon.-Fri. 8-4:30. Information can be obtained at these stations or from the Visitor Information Center at the Forest Supervisor's Office, Federal Building, 160A Zillicoa St., Asheville, NC 28804; phone (828) 257-4200.

Other points of interest within the forest are listed under Asheville, Brevard, Hot Springs, Linville and Waynesville. *See Recreation Chart and the AAA Southeastern CampBook.*

CRADLE OF FORESTRY IN AMERICA NATIONAL HISTORIC SITE is 14 mi. n. of Brevard via US 276. Two interpretive trails detail the history of forestry in the United States as well as the history of one of the first schools of forestry. In the Forest Discovery, visitors may explore an indoor forest. A ride in a helicopter simulator is available, and a logging locomotive is displayed on one of the trails. An old saw mill and historic cabins are on the grounds. An 18-minute film also is presented.

Visitor center daily 9-5, mid-Apr. to early Nov. Admission $5, free (ages 0-15 and on Tues.). DS, MC, VI. Phone (828) 877-3130.

LOOKING GLASS ROCK AND LOOKING GLASS FALLS are 8 mi. n.w. of Brevard via US 276, or 6 mi. from the south park entrance. The rock is believed to be the largest granite monolith in the southern Appalachians.

PISGAH FOREST FISH HATCHERY, on a forest service road 8 mi. n. of Brevard via US 276, is the state's largest hatchery. It produces brook, rainbow and brown trout for release throughout the state. Daily 8-5. Free. Phone (828) 877-4423.

SLIDING ROCK is 8 mi. n. of jct. US 276 and US 64. Sheets of very cool mountain water cascade down this 60-foot-long natural waterslide and drop gleeful riders into a 7-foot-deep natural pool from which they exit. While there are wading pools in the area, there are no pools for swimming.

Note: During thunder storms and times of high water run-off, Sliding Rock is closed; phone ahead to verify accessibility. Changing facilities are available in the summer. Picnicking and alcohol are prohibited. Open daily all year. Lifeguards are on duty daily 10-6, Memorial Day-Labor Day. Admission $1; free (ages 0-5). Phone (828) 877-3265.

WAGON ROAD GAP, atop the Pisgah ledge, is 20 mi. n.w. of Brevard via US 276, halfway between Waynesville and Brevard. The gap, intersecting US 276 at Milepost 412 on the Blue Ridge Parkway, affords a fine view of the surrounding area.

PLYMOUTH (B-8) pop. 4,107, elev. 6′

PORT O' PLYMOUTH ROANOKE RIVER MUSEUM is n. on Washington St. to 302 E. Water St. Once a railroad depot, the museum houses memorabilia relating to the Civil War Battle of Plymouth. Displays include a 1790 loom and an 1873 coffee grinder. Especially notable is a swivel cannon purchased in Austria by Benjamin Franklin.

Tues.-Sat. 9-4, Mon. 10-4; closed holidays. Admission $3; $2 (ages 14-18); $1 (ages 7-12). Phone (252) 793-1377.

ROANOKE RIVER LIGHTHOUSE & MARITIME MUSEUM is at 206 W. Water St. Guided tours of the lighthouse, which is a replica of one from 1866 to 1885, are offered. The museum depicts the area's history and includes such exhibits as a collection of antique outboard motors. Allow 30 minutes minimum. Tues.-Sat. 11-3; closed major holidays. Admission $3. Phone (252) 217-2204.

RALEIGH (B-6) pop. 276,093, elev. 352′

Founded in 1792 and named for Sir Walter Raleigh, the city was planned as the "unalterable seat of government" for North Carolina. Known as the "City of Oaks," Raleigh was established on land purchased specifically by the state to be used as the state's capital. Laid out in a square grid pattern, the capital city's expansion has slightly deviated from the original plans.

Preservation abounds in Raleigh as the citizens are dedicated to conserving the natural areas found throughout the community. In 1974 a system of public recreational trails was created, including 22 trails covering 46 miles. In 1975, Raleigh was named the first "Green Survival City" in the country.

Raleigh also is known as a cultural and educational center. It encompasses the southern portion of the Research Triangle region. *(see Durham p. 151).*

Pullen Park, next to the North Carolina State University campus via Western Boulevard, has attractions of interest to children, including a 1911 Dentzel carousel; phone (919) 831-6468.

Greater Raleigh Convention & Visitors Bureau: 421 Fayetteville Street Mall, Suite 1505, Raleigh, NC 27602; phone (919) 834-5900 or (800) 849-8499.

Self-guiding tours: Maps for self-guiding tours that include the Capitol, the legislative building and the Victorian-style neighborhood of Oakwood are available at Capital Area Visitor Services in the North Carolina Museum of History at 5 E. Edenton St., Raleigh, NC 27601. The center is open Mon.-Fri. 8-5; closed Jan. 1, Thanksgiving and Dec. 24-25. Phone (919) 807-7950.

Shopping areas: Cary Towne Center, I-40 exit 291, offers 130 stores as well as Dillard's, Hudson Belk, JCPenney, Macy's and Sears. Crabtree Valley Mall, SR 70, features more than 200 shops and eateries. Triangle Town Center, I-540 at US 1, offers more than 120 restaurants and stores such as Dillard's, Hudson Belk, Macy's, Saks Fifth Avenue and Sears.

GEM **MARBLES KIDS MUSEUM,** 201 E. Hargett St., connects people to the world through interactive computer activities, video conferences, the Internet, global art and artifacts. Hands-on galleries include Around Town!, Splash!, 2 B Me! and IdeaWorks. "The Exploris Journey" is shown daily in the museum theater. The giant five-story screen within the IMAX Theatre gives visitors a feeling of being in the midst of all the action.

Food is available. Allow 2 hours minimum. Tues.-Sat. 9-5, Sun. noon-5; closed Jan. 1, Easter, Thanksgiving and Dec. 24-25. Admission for museum $5; free (under 1). Admission for IMAX Theatre $8.95; $7.95 (ages 60+); $6.50 (ages 1-12). Combination ticket $12.95; $11.95 (ages 60+ and students with ID); $9.50 (ages 1-12). Fee for parking. AX, DS, MC, VI. Phone (919) 834-4040.

IMAX Theatre is at 201 E. Hargett St. Films presented in the 271-seat IMAX Theatre transport viewers to the center of the action as earth, sea and space are explored. Film titles and show times vary; phone ahead for schedule. Admission for museum $5; free (ages 0-3). Admission for IMAX Theatre $8.95; $7.95 (ages 60+); $6.50 (ages 1-12). Combination ticket $12.95; $11.95 (ages 60+ and students with ID); $9.50 (ages 1-12). Fee for parking. AX, DS, MC, VI. Phone (919) 834-4040.

HISTORIC OAK VIEW COUNTY PARK is at 4028 Carya Dr. The restored 17-acre site, originally founded in the 1830s, is comprised of the Cotton Museum, Farm History Center, carriage house, gardens, pecan grove, livestock barn, plank kitchen, cemetery and the Oak View Farmhouse, an 1855 Greek Revival structure. For almost 150 years, Oak View was a working farm, with cotton as the main cash crop until 1920. Brick walking paths allow easy access for touring the grounds. Allow 1 hour

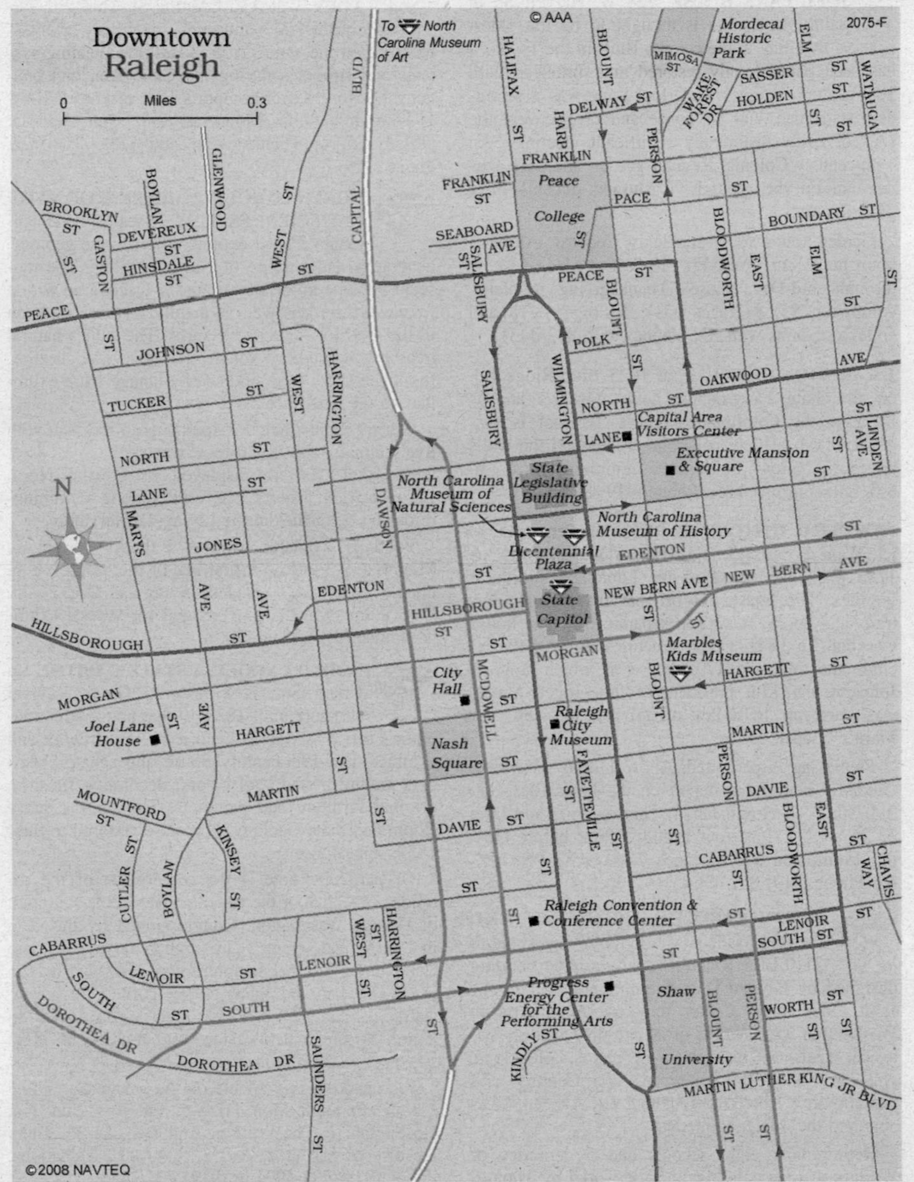

minimum. Daily 8:30-5; closed Jan. 1, Thanksgiving and Dec. 24-25. Free. Phone (919) 250-1013.

J.C. RAULSTON ARBORETUM is off the Hillsborough St. exit of the US 440 beltline at 4415 Beryl Rd. More than 5,000 kinds of plants are in this 8-acre horticultural park. Some highlights are the Japanese Garden, the Rose Garden, the White Garden and the Perennial Border. Allow 1 hour minimum. Daily 8-8, Apr.-Oct.; 8-5, rest of year. Free. Phone (919) 515-3132.

SAVE **JOEL LANE HOUSE,** 728 W. Hargett St. at Saint Mary's St., is thought to be the oldest existing dwelling in the county. Built in the 1770s, it has been painstakingly restored and furnished with 18th-century antiques. Col. Joel Lane was a prominent statesman, and his house and tavern were the sites of many historically significant meetings. An 18th-century Colonial Revival garden and herb garden are on the grounds. Costumed docents offer guided tours.

Garden tours are available by request. Allow 1 hour minimum. Wed.-Fri. 10-2, Sat. 1-4, Mar. 1 through mid-Dec.; closed Thanksgiving weekend. Admission $5; $4 (ages 62+); $3 (ages 7-18 and college students with ID). Phone (919) 833-3431.

J.S. DORTON ARENA, w. at 1025 Blue Ridge Rd. on the State Fairgrounds, holds concerts and is home to the Carolina Rollergirls. Its roof is suspended from 90-foot parabolic arches and the walls are glass. Allow 30 minutes minimum. Mon.-Fri. 8-5, unless in use. Free. Phone (919) 821-7400.

MORDECAI HISTORIC PARK, n. on Person St. to jct. Wake Forest Rd. and Mimosa St., contains the 1785 plantation house of the Lane and Mordecai families. The house has original furnishings, portraits and books. A kitchen separate from the house was built in 1842. Other structures in the park include the relocated 1795 house in which Andrew Johnson, the 17th president of the United States, was born; an 1810 law office; and the 1847 St. Mark's Chapel.

Picnicking is permitted. Allow 1 hour minimum. Guided 1-hour tours depart on the hour Tues.-Sat. 9-4, Sun. 1-4; closed Jan. 1, Thanksgiving and Dec. 24-25 and 31. Last tour begins 1 hour before closing. Admission $5; $3 (ages 7-17). AX, DS, MC, VI. Phone (919) 857-4364.

GEM **NORTH CAROLINA MUSEUM OF ART,** off I-40 Wade Ave. exit following signs to 2110 Blue Ridge Rd., is in a large building designed by Edward Durrell Stone, architect of the John F. Kennedy Center for Performing Arts in Washington, D.C. Works of art are displayed in historical sequence through eight major collections: Ancient, European, American, 20th-Century and contemporary, Jewish ceremonial art, African, Oceanic and the Ancient Americas.

Representing eight schools and 5 centuries of Western art, the paintings include works by Thomas Hart Benton, Sandro Botticelli, John Singleton Copley, Winslow Homer, Claude Monet, Georgia O'Keeffe, Raphael, Peter Paul Rubens, Anthony Van Dyck and Andrew Wyeth.

Changing exhibits are presented, as are films, concerts and lectures. Food is available. Allow 1 hour, 30 minutes minimum. Tues.-Sat. 9-5 (also Fri. 5-9), Sun. 10-5; closed major holidays. Tours are given at 1:30. Free. Admission may be charged for special exhibits. Phone (919) 839-6262.

GEM **NORTH CAROLINA MUSEUM OF HISTORY** is at 5 E. Edenton St. This 170,000-square-foot museum features exhibits focusing on the state's history, folklife, healing systems and struggles during the Civil War, and contains the North Carolina Sports Hall of Fame. Allow 1 hour minimum. Mon.-Sat. 9-5, Sun. noon-5; closed Jan. 1, Thanksgiving and Dec. 25. Free. Phone (919) 807-7900.

GEM **NORTH CAROLINA MUSEUM OF NATURAL SCIENCES,** 11 W. Jones St. on Bicentennial Plaza, explores the diverse geology, geography and wildlife of North Carolina. The museum is home to the first dinosaur discovered with a fossilized heart, as well as a fully restored skeleton of the predator Acrocanthosaurus. The state's natural treasures, including Venus flytraps, tiger beetles, fossilized shark teeth and scarlet tanagers are exhibited on the first floor.

Other exhibits include Mountains to the Sea, with live animals and a 20-foot waterfall. Five great whale skeletons are displayed in Coastal North Carolina, and visitors can walk among hummingbirds and butterflies in the Living Conservatory.

Food is available. Allow 2 hours minimum. Mon.-Sat. 9-5 (also 5-9 first Fri. of the month), Sun. noon-5; closed Jan. 1, Thanksgiving and Dec. 24-25. Free. Admission may be charged for special exhibits. Phone (919) 733-7450.

GEM **NORTH CAROLINA STATE CAPITOL,** on Union Sq., is a restored Greek Revival structure built 1833-40 that houses the governor's office as well as historic rooms, artwork and exhibits. The 19th-century house and senate chambers feature period wall colors, decorative finishes, original furniture and paintings. The State Library Room and State Geology Office are restored to their 1850s appearance.

Of particular note is the centerpiece of the rotunda—a replica of the neoclassical marble sculpture of George Washington. Commissioned by the state in 1815 and created by Italian artist Antonio Canova, the original sculpture was destroyed by fire in 1831 when the State House burned. A bronze statue of the first president also is displayed on Union Square, where statues and monuments total 14, most of them bronze on stone bases.

Free parking is available on the weekends. Allow 1 hour minimum. Mon.-Fri. 8-5, Sat. 10-4, Sun. 1-4; closed Jan. 1, Thanksgiving and Dec. 24-26. Tours are offered Sat. at 11 and 2, Sun. at 2. Donations. Phone (919) 733-4994 or (919) 733-3456.

RALEIGH CITY MUSEUM is at 220 Fayetteville Street Mall in the Briggs Bldg. The museum explores the city's history from its 1792 founding to the present through permanent and rotating exhibits. Local artifacts include sports memorabilia, vintage typewriters and a mock-up of a landmark downtown restaurant that closed in 2000.

Allow 1 hour minimum. Tues.-Fri. 10-4, Sat. 1-4; closed Jan. 1, Thanksgiving and Dec. 25. Donations. Phone (919) 832-3775.

STATE LEGISLATIVE BUILDING, 16 W. Jones St., is a colonnaded, marble-faced building rising from a 340-foot-wide podium of North Carolina granite. In front of the main entrance a 28-foot-diameter terrazzo mosaic of the Great Seal of the State of North Carolina is set into the podium. Interior garden courts and roof gardens complement the dramatic architecture. Allow 30 minutes minimum. Mon.-Sat. 9-5, Sun. 1-5; closed Jan. 1, Thanksgiving and Dec. 25. Free. Phone (919) 733-7928.

RANDLEMAN (B-5) pop. 3,557, elev. 680′

RICHARD PETTY MUSEUM, 142 W. Academy St., is a tribute to stock car racer Richard Petty. Race cars, trophies, photographs, racing signs, letters from government officials and other memorabilia fill the museum. A video details the racing legend's life. Allow 1 hour minimum. Mon.-Sat. 9-5; closed Thanksgiving and week of Dec. 25. Admission $5; $3 (ages 7-17). MC, VI. Phone (336) 495-1143.

REIDSVILLE (A-5) pop. 14,485, elev. 822′

Incorporated in 1873, Reidsville once conducted tobacco market operations. Penn House, 324 Maple Ave., is a Colonial Revival home built in 1932 by tobacco executive Charles Penn. Tours are available by reservation; phone (336) 349-1099.

Reidsville Chamber of Commerce: 513 S. Main St., Reidsville, NC 27323; phone (336) 349-8481.

Self-guiding tours: A brochure outlining a driving tour to several historic houses and buildings in Reidsville is available at the chamber of commerce.

ROANOKE ISLAND—*see Fort Raleigh National Historic Site in Outer Banks p. 177.*

ROANOKE RAPIDS (A-7) pop. 16,957, elev. 154′

Incorporated in 1897, the city sits along the banks of the mighty Roanoke River. The rapids are caused by the fall line; a granite shelf that runs the entire length of the East coast. In the early 1800s, the country's economy depended upon transportation of goods and produce for the west to seaports in the east. A canal was developed as a means to navigate the river to achieve this purpose.

Roanoke Rapids offers recreational activities that include canoeing, fishing, golfing and swimming. For entertainment, The Randy Parton Theater features musical performances by Grand Ole Opry legends; phone (877) 672-7866. Concerts, festivals and other events are held at the Carolina Crossroads Outdoor Amphitheater at 395 Wallace Fork Rd.; phone (888) 481-2726 for concert information or (252) 537-6252 for general information.

Halifax County Convention & Visitors Bureau: 260 Premier Blvd., Roanoke Rapids, NC 27870; phone (252) 535-1687 or (800) 522-4282.

ROANOKE CANAL MUSEUM AND TRAIL is at 15 Jackson St. Ext. Completed in 1823, the canal was constructed to facilitate transportation of goods on the Roanoke River; an aqueduct and locks regulated the water level. The museum features exhibits relating to the canal's development, 19th-century life along the canal and the area's wildlife. The 7.5-mile trail affords opportunities to observe a variety of plants and animals. Guided tours are available. Picnicking is permitted. Allow 30 minutes minimum. Museum open Tues.-Sat. 9-4. Trail open daily dawn-dusk. Closed major holidays. Admission by donations. Guided tours $2. Phone (252) 537-2769.

ROCKY MOUNT (B-7) pop. 55,893, elev. 120′

In the coastal plain of North Carolina, Rocky Mount was named for a large granite outcropping at the Falls of the Tar River. The surrounding area of the Falls, including the Cotton Mill building and Mill Village, dates back to the 1800s. The 3.5-mile Tar River Trail traces the banks of the Tar River and the Tar River Reservoir offers boating, water skiing, fishing, swimming and picnicking *(see Recreation Chart).*

Nash County Visitors Bureau: P.O. Box 7637, 107 Gateway Blvd., Rocky Mount, NC 27804; phone (252) 972-5080 or (800) 849-6825.

THE CHILDREN'S MUSEUM & SCIENCE CENTER AT THE IMPERIAL CENTRE is at 270 Gay St. A live animal gallery allows visitors an up-close encounter with animals and their habitats. Other highlights include a touch tank, a fitness course and an exhibit about mazes. The planetarium features full-dome video presentations and laser light shows. Food is available. Allow 1 hour, 30 minutes minimum. Tues.-Sat. 10-5, Sun. 1-5; closed Thanksgiving and Dec. 25. Planetarium hours vary; phone ahead. Admission $4; $3 (ages 3-16 and 60+). Planetarium $3.50. MC, VI. Phone (252) 972-1266.

RODANTHE—*see Outer Banks p. 180.*

SALISBURY (B-5) pop. 26,462, elev. 764′

Founded in 1753, Salisbury (SAULS-bur-y) was settled by Scot-Irish and German immigrants. It quickly became a trading, cultural and judicial center because of its location at the junction of two much-traveled routes. At different times during 1781 the city served as headquarters for the British general Lord Charles Cornwallis and Patriot general Nathanael Greene.

Salisbury had one of the largest prison camps maintained by Confederate forces. About 5,000

Union soldiers died there and are buried in a Salisbury National Cemetery nearby, at 202 Government Rd. A highlight of the historic district is the Dr. Josephus Hall House, the home of the prison surgeon.

The Civil War battles of 1865 destroyed much of the town, but the Rowan County Courthouse escaped damage. Styled after a Greek temple, it houses the Rowan Museum, which offers regional history exhibits; phone (704) 633-5946. Other historic structures are the Thyatira Church, Grimes Mill and the Old Stone House.

Rowan County Convention and Visitors Bureau: 204 E. Innes St., Suite 120, Salisbury, NC 28145; phone (704) 638-3100 or (800) 332-2343.

Self-guiding tours: A driving-tour audiotape of the Salisbury Confederate Prison Site and National Cemetery, as well as a walking-tour tape and brochure about the Salisbury historic district are offered at the visitor center. A driving-tour brochure about the African-American Heritage Trail also is available.

Shopping areas: The Salisbury Emporium, 230 E. Kerr St., is a collection of more than 85 shops and galleries. Housed in the 15,000-square-foot historic Frick Building, the emporium includes stores featuring art, antiques, books, furniture, garden accessories and militaria.

SALUDA (F-4) pop. 575, elev. 209′

PEARSON'S FALLS, 4 mi. n.w. via US 176, offers paths bordered by native plants. The focal point of this lush, natural area is a 90-foot waterfall that is reached via a quarter-mile trail. No pets are allowed. Picnicking is permitted. Pets are not permitted. Tues.-Sat. 10-6, Sun. noon-6, Mar.-Oct.; Wed.-Sat. 10-5, Sun. noon-5, rest of year. Closed major holidays. Admission $3; $1 (ages 6-12). Phone (828) 749-3031.

SANFORD (C-6) pop. 23,220, elev. 368′

HOUSE IN THE HORSESHOE STATE HISTORIC SITE is 12 mi. w. on SR 42, then 4 mi. s. on SR 2307 following signs. Built in 1772 on a horseshoe bend of the Deep River, this two-story frame plantation house still bears the scars and bullet holes from a Revolutionary War skirmish. Benjamin Williams, a four-term governor of North Carolina, acquired the house in 1798 and died on the plantation in 1814. The interior is furnished with period antiques and is distinguished by elaborate woodwork.

Allow 30 minutes minimum. Mon.-Sat. 9-5, Sun. 1-5; closed Jan. 1, Thanksgiving, day after Thanksgiving and Dec. 24-26. Hours may vary; phone ahead. Donations. Phone (910) 947-2051.

SCOTLAND NECK (B-7) pop. 2,362, elev. 98′

SAVE **SYLVAN HEIGHTS WATERFOWL PARK & ECO-CENTER,** at 4963 SR 258, is a breeding facility for more than 1,000 birds and 170 species of waterfowl. The eco-tourism center features a theater, exhibits and educational programs. Gardens, ponds and trails accent the 9-acre grounds. Picnicking is permitted. Allow 1 hour, 30 minutes minimum. Tues.-Sun. 9-5, Apr.-Sept.; 9-4, rest of year. Admission $7; $5 (ages 3-12 and 62+). AX, DS, MC, VI. Phone (252) 826-3186.

SEAGROVE (B-5) pop. 246, elev. 763′

The English settlers who moved to Seagrove in the mid-18th century were potters by trade and were attracted to the area by the abundance of surface clay, a resource that had been used by the area's native inhabitants for thousands of years. Throughout the 19th century, the large deposits of stoneware clay supported a thriving community of farmer-potters, who produced earthenware pieces used primarily for food preparation and preservation.

As mass-produced goods and technology such as refrigeration became more common in the late 19th and early 20th centuries, there was little need for these utilitarian wares and Prohibition eliminated the need for whiskey jugs. Pottery traditions throughout most of the United Stated died out.

North Carolina's pottery tradition survived uninterrupted because of its strong basis in family-owned and -operated potteries, and because of their ability to adapt to creating art pottery. Beginning in the 1920s, these primarily decorative items found new markets outside the local area and among tourists. Today, several potters in the area can claim seventh- and eighth-generation status.

The Seagrove area, with more than 100 shops, remains one of the nation's largest communities of working potters. Their work includes traditional and unusual shapes, forms and techniques. A map spotting Seagrove potteries is available in the lobby of the North Carolina Pottery Center.

NORTH CAROLINA POTTERY CENTER, 233 East Ave. at jct. US 220 and SR 705, preserves the history and tradition of regional pottery through exhibits, demonstrations and educational programs. Museum pieces range from prehistoric jars to the contemporary work of 100 area potteries. Picnicking is permitted. Tues.-Sat. 10-4; closed Jan. 1, July 4, Thanksgiving and Dec. 24-25. Admission $2; $1 (grades 9-12); free (grades K-8). MC, VI. Phone (336) 873-8430.

SEDALIA (B-5) pop. 618, elev. 704′

CHARLOTTE HAWKINS BROWN MUSEUM AT HISTORIC PALMER MEMORIAL INSTITUTE is 1 mi. off I-85 exit 135 following signs. This is the site of the former Palmer Memorial Institute, a boarding school for African-Americans, founded by Dr. Brown in 1902. Exhibits and audiovisual presentations document the school's history and Dr. Brown's contribution to African-American education. Guided tours are available. Allow 1 hour, 30 minutes minimum. Mon.-Sat. 9-5, Apr.-Oct.; Mon.-Fri. 10-4, rest of year. Closed holidays. Free. Phone (336) 449-4846.

SELMA (B-7) pop. 5,914, elev. 175′

ATKINSON'S MILL is at 95 Atkinson Mill Rd. This is the only operating mill in the area. Visitors can see how corn is ground and pushed by air through pipes to various stations, where it is further refined or mixed to make products that include hush puppy mix, corn meal and biscuit mix. Guided tours are offered. Allow 30 minutes minimum. Mon.-Fri. 8-5; closed Jan. 1, Thanksgiving and Dec. 25. Free. Phone (919) 965-3547 or (800) 948-5707.

SEVEN SPRINGS (C-7) pop. 86, elev. 20′

CLIFFS OF THE NEUSE STATE PARK is 3 mi. w. on SR 55, then 2 mi. n. on SR 111. Cliffs and vegetation line the Neuse River. A natural history museum, an 11-acre lake for fishing and boating, and interpretive nature trails are in the park. Camping sites are available from March 15 through November 30. Daily 8 a.m.-9 p.m., June-Aug.; 8-8, Mar.-May and Sept.-Oct.; 8-6, rest of year. Lake open Memorial Day-Labor Day. Park free; fees for camping and swimming. Phone (919) 778-6234. *See Recreation Chart and the AAA Southeastern CampBook.*

SHELBY (C-3) pop. 19,477, elev. 853′

Shelby may be best known as the home of a political dynasty that ruled North Carolina politics 1928-1954. The former homes of governors, senators and federal judges can be found in the central historic district, where architectural styles range from Colonial Revival to Art Deco. The 1919 Shelby City Park Carousel has been fully restored and operates year-round; phone (704) 484-6476.

Cleveland County Chamber of Commerce: 200 S. Lafayette St., Shelby, NC 28150; phone (704) 487-8521.

Self-guiding tours: A walking-tour map of the historic district is available from the chamber of commerce.

SMITHFIELD (B-6) pop. 11,510, elev. 153′

Chartered in 1777, Smithfield was named for John Smith, who owned much of the land on both sides of the nearby Neuse River. Downtown consists of several blocks of churches, restored buildings and shops. A walking tour takes visitors along the original Town Commons; check with the visitors bureau for more information.

Johnston County Visitors Bureau: 1115 Industrial Park Dr., Smithfield, NC 27577; phone (919) 989-8687 or (800) 441-7829. *See color ad p. 818.*

Shopping areas: More than 85 discount stores can be found at Carolina Outlet Center, exit 95 off I-95.

AVA GARDNER MUSEUM is off I-95 exit 95, then 1 mi. w. on US 70 Bus. Rte. to 325 E. Market St. This museum includes childhood memorabilia, film clips and costumes, posters, photographs, oil portraits, film scripts, magazine covers and other items related to Gardner, who was born and raised in the area.

Allow 1 hour minimum. Mon.-Sat. 9-5, Sun. 2-5; closed Jan. 1, Easter Monday, Thanksgiving and Dec. 24-25. Admission $6; $5 (ages 13-18 and 65+); $4 (ages 6-12). Phone (919) 934-5830.

SNOW CAMP (B-6)

SAVE **SNOW CAMP OUTDOOR THEATRE,** at the Snow Camp Historic Site on SR 1005, presents "Sword of Peace," a drama portraying the struggles of the Quakers during the Revolutionary War. Also presented is "Pathway to Freedom," a pre-Civil War drama recalling the events and people involved in the secret transfer of escaped slaves via the Underground Railroad. Children's theater is performed on Saturday. A musical is presented the last week of the season.

Presentations are shown Thurs.-Sat. at 8 p.m., late June-late Aug. Children's Theatre Sat. at 10, July-Aug. Admission $15; $13 (ages 60+); $7 (ages 1-11). Children's theater $5. AX, MC, VI. Phone (336) 376-6948 or (800) 726-5115.

SOUTHERN PINES (C-6) pop. 10,918, elev. 550′

An all-year resort area in the sandhills region, Southern Pines is known for its mild winters, outstanding golf courses, numerous equestrian activities and beautiful pine trees. Many professional and championship golf tournaments are played in the area. Other popular sports are bicycling, hunting and tennis.

Pinehurst Area Convention and Visitors Bureau-Southern Pines: 10677 US 15-501, Southern Pines, NC 28388; phone (800) 346-5362.

WEYMOUTH WOODS-SANDHILLS NATURE PRESERVE is at 1024 Ft. Bragg Rd. The 525-acre preserve contains 4 miles of hiking trails leading through pine forests and swamps. A nature exhibit hall contains displays and dioramas depicting regional flora and fauna. The Wall of Fire, a 10-foot-high illuminated mural, explains fire's role in forest ecology. A sound-activated "night sounds" display highlights various animals of the sandhills region. Interpretive programs are available. Allow 30 minutes minimum. Daily 8-8, Mar.-Oct.; 8-6, rest of year. Closed Dec. 25. Free. Phone (910) 692-2167. *See Recreation Chart.*

SOUTHPORT (D-7) pop. 2,351

Midway between New York and Miami on the Intracoastal Waterway, Southport's yacht harbor is a popular stopping point for boat traffic. The city also boasts both freshwater and saltwater fishing. Charter boats for deep-sea excursions are plentiful, and several piers accommodate the land-bound angler.

The city's position on a bluff at the mouth of the Cape Fear River made it a strategic location for the state's first fort, Fort Johnston, built in 1764. Today the fort, which was rebuilt after being destroyed by fire in 1775, is occupied by the Commanding Officer of the U.S. Army's Sunny Point Military Ocean Terminal.

Just across the Cape Fear River from Southport lies Bald Head Island *(see place listing p. 128)*, known for its pristine beaches, tidal creeks, salt marshes and the absence of automobiles. An island resort community offers daily bicycle and golf cart rentals, as well as restaurants and recreational activities. Ferry service from Southport is provided by Bald Head Island Transportation; phone (910) 457-5003 or (800) 234-1666.

Southport/Oak Island Chamber of Commerce: 4841 Longbeach Rd. S.E., Southport, NC 28461; phone (910) 457-6964.

NORTH CAROLINA MARITIME MUSEUM AT SOUTHPORT is at 116 N. Howe St. Exhibits relate the nautical history of the lower Cape Fear area. Early settlement, pirate activity, fishing and shipwrecks are among the subjects covered. A research library also is on site. Allow 45 minutes minimum. Tues.-Sat. 9-5; closed major holidays. Free. MC, VI. Phone (910) 457-0003.

PROGRESS ENERGY BRUNSWICK PLANT VISITOR CENTER, 2 mi. n. on SR 87, contains more than 30 displays about energy. Topics include electricity production, energy conservation, radiation and nuclear power. Films about energy-related subjects are shown. Picnicking is permitted. Allow 30 minutes minimum. Tues.-Thurs. 9-4; closed holidays. Hours may vary; phone ahead. Free. Phone (910) 457-6041.

SPARTA (A-4) pop. 1,817, elev. 2,939′

WINERIES

- **Chateau Laurinda Vineyard** is at 690 Reeves Ridge Rd. Tues.-Sat. 10-7, Sun. noon-5 in spring and summer; Tues.-Fri. 11-6, Sat. 10-6, Sun. noon-5, rest of year. Closed Dec. 25. Phone (336) 372-2562 or (800) 650-3236.

SPENCER (B-5) pop. 3,355, elev. 760′

SAVE **NORTH CAROLINA TRANSPORTATION MUSEUM,** off I-85 exit 79 at 411 S. Salisbury St., traces the history of transportation in North Carolina. The complex, once Southern Railway's primary staging and repair facility, includes the massive Back Shop, the 37-bay Roundhouse and nine other buildings. Among the displays are Conestoga wagons, antique automobiles, steam locomotives and a dugout canoe. Changing exhibits also are offered throughout the year.

Allow 1 hour, 30 minutes minimum. Museum and grounds Mon.-Sat. 9-5, Sun. 1-5, Apr.-Oct.; Tues.-Sat. 10-4, Sun. 1-4, rest of year. Closed major holidays. Train rides run Sat. at 11, 1, 2 and 3, Sun. at 1:30, 2:30 and 3:30, Mar.-Nov.; Sat. at 11 and 1 in Feb. Museum free. Train rides $6; $5 (ages 3-12 and 60+). MC, VI. Phone (704) 636-2889.

STATESVILLE (B-4) pop. 23,320, elev. 925′

Originally named Fourth Creek, Statesville was the site of Fort Dobbs, constructed to protect settlers during the French and Indian Wars. Today more than 100 historic buildings in downtown Statesville have been restored, including a 1911 train depot that houses the visitor information center and a gallery for local artists.

Statesville Convention & Visitors Bureau: 111 Depot Lane, Statesville, NC 28677; phone (704) 878-3480 or (877) 531-1819.

SWANSBORO (D-8) pop. 1,426

HAMMOCKS BEACH STATE PARK, 892 acres on Bear Island, is reached by a passenger ferry docked 4 miles s. of Swansboro via SR 24. Interpretive displays at the ferry dock describe plant and animal life native to the area. A bathhouse and primitive camping are available.

Park open daily 8-7, June-Aug.; 8-6, rest of year. Closed Dec. 25. Phone ahead for ferry departure times. Park admission free. Fare $5; $3 (ages 6-12 and senior citizens). Phone (910) 326-4881. *See Recreation Chart and the AAA Southeastern CampBook.*

TARBORO (B-7) pop. 11,138, elev. 71′

Founded in 1760 as a county government center, Tarboro became an important tobacco and cotton market. When North Carolina's itinerant legislature met in Tarboro, the assemblymen staying at Toole's Tavern were provided with gaming tables and theatrical entertainment. When the tavern ran out of heating fuel, guests warmed themselves with doses of spirits. Not surprisingly, George Washington later described the place as "lively and thriving."

Tarboro Edgecombe Chamber of Commerce: 325 N. Main St., Tarboro, NC 27886; phone (252) 823-7241.

Self-guiding tours: The Tarboro Historic District National Recreation Trail highlights Tarboro's many finely preserved Colonial, antebellum and Victorian houses. Brochures are available at the Blount-Bridgers House and at the chamber of commerce.

BLOUNT-BRIDGERS HOUSE, 130 Bridgers St., is a Federal-style structure built in 1808. Restored and furnished in period, the house contains the Hobson Pittman Memorial Gallery, which displays a collection of the artist's paintings and personal belongings. Mon.-Fri. 10-4, Sat.-Sun. 2-4; closed holidays. Free. Phone (252) 823-4159.

TRYON (F-4) pop. 1,760, elev. 1,090′

Tryon is a resort area noted for its horses. The Tryon Riding and Hunt Club maintains 500 miles of trails and sponsors equestrian events in the area. For information about the events contact the Tryon Riding Club, P.O. Box 1095, Tryon, NC 28782; phone (800) 438-3681.

Shunkawakan Falls, 5 mi. n. via SR 108 off a private road, near the top of White Oak Mountain, is one of the tallest waterfalls in the Southeast. From

Sunset Rock, also on White Oak Mountain, 16 counties in three states are visible.

Polk County Chamber of Commerce: 2753 Lynn Rd., Suite A, Tryon, NC 28782; phone (828) 859-6236.

UWHARRIE NATIONAL FOREST

Elevations in the forest range from 500 ft. to 1,000 ft. Refer to AAA maps for additional elevation information.

Covering more than 50,000 acres in the North Carolina Piedmont region, Uwharrie National Forest was established in 1961 and is one of the smaller national forests. Named for the Uwharrie Mountains, the forest is traversed by the Uwharrie, Yadkin and Pee Dee rivers.

Fishing and hunting are permitted in season. For information about regulations contact the North Carolina Wildlife Resources Commission; phone (919) 707-0010. The forest borders 8,000-acre Badin Lake, near Troy; campgrounds and boat ramps are available. For hikers, the 20-mile Uwharrie Trail runs north to south through the national forest. The ranger station is 2 miles east of Troy on SR 24/27. For further information contact the District Ranger, 789 SR 24/27E, Troy, NC 27371; phone (910) 576-6391. *See Recreation Chart and the AAA Southeastern CampBook.*

VALDESE (E-4) pop. 4,485, elev. 1,202′

Valdese traces its history to Waldensian settlers, who fled religious persecution in Italy and emigrated to the new country in the late 19th century. Their story is retold through The Trail of Faith and The Waldensian Museum as well as through the outdoor drama "From This Day Forward", presented at the Old Colony Players Amphitheater from mid-July to mid-August. For further information contact the Valdese Tourism Department; phone (828) 879-2126.

VALLE CRUCIS (D-4) elev. 2,671′

Shopping areas: Mast General Store, on SR 1112/194, operates as it did in 1883, complete with antique scales, counters and a potbellied stove. Country household items, food and clothing are offered. Just down the road, the Mast Store Annex offers an eclectic mix of dry goods and old-fashioned confections.

VILAS (D-4) elev. 2,746′

RECREATIONAL ACTIVITIES

Ziplines

- **Scream Time Ziplines** departs from 8483 US 421. Write 380 US 321, Boone, NC 28692. Daily 9-8, June-Aug; schedule varies rest of year. Reservations are required. Phone (828) 898-5404.

WASHINGTON (B-8) pop. 9,583

The first settlements in this region appeared in the 1690s and the present town began in the early 1770s as Forks of the Tar, named after the Tar River. Washington is the first community in the United States known to have been named for Gen. George Washington—the name appears on letterheads as early as 1775 and was officially adopted in 1776.

Washington/Beaufort County Chamber of Commerce: 102 Stewart Pkwy., Washington, NC 27889; Phone (252) 946-9168.

Self-guiding tours: A walking-tour brochure available from the chamber of commerce visitor center details a route past 30 noteworthy buildings, including the 1786 Beaufort County Courthouse and the 1795 Marsh House, which has a Civil War cannonball lodged in its facade.

THE NORTH CAROLINA ESTUARIUM, 223 E. Water St., uses some 200 exhibits, artwork, audiovisual presentations, a film and aquariums to explain the importance of estuaries, the places where freshwater meets saltwater. A pontoon boat tour of the Tar-Pamlico River waterways is given daily. Tues.-Sat. 10-4; closed Jan. 1, Thanksgiving and Dec. 24-25. Admission $3; $2 (students with ID). Boat tour free. Reservations are required for boat tour. MC, VI. Phone (252) 948-0000.

WAXHAW (C-4) pop. 1,625, elev. 645′

The Old Waxhaw Settlement, on the border of the Carolinas a few miles southwest of present-day Waxhaw, was President Andrew Jackson's 1767 birthplace. After the War of 1812, a dispute arose as to whether he was born in North or South Carolina. Jackson maintained he was a native of South Carolina. Attempts to resolve the mystery by finding the remains of the McKemey cabin site, where it is believed he was born, have been unsuccessful.

In June the drama "Listen and Remember" is presented in an outdoor amphitheater. It portrays the history of early settlers of the Old Waxhaw Settlement, including Jackson and his family. Shows are presented Friday and Saturday at 8:30 p.m.; phone (704) 843-2300 or (704) 764-7159.

A historic district offers quaint houses and commercial buildings.

Union County Chamber of Commerce: 903 Skyway Dr., P.O. Box 1789, Monroe, NC 28111; phone (704) 289-4567.

Shopping areas: Downtown's Antique Village contains about a dozen shops in turn-of-the-20th-century buildings.

MEXICO-CARDENAS MUSEUM is 5 mi. s. of SR 75, following signs to Davis Rd. The museum honors Mexican President Lázaro Cárdenas and contains artifacts depicting the customs and languages of Mexico's indigenous people. Pottery, costumes, folk art and photographs are displayed. A 1938 Chevrolet sedan, a gift from Cárdenas, also can be seen. Allow 1 hour minimum. Mon.-Sat. 9-noon and 1-4; closed holidays. Free. Phone (704) 843-6045.

MUSEUM OF THE ALPHABET is 5 mi. s. of SR 75, following signs to Davis Rd. The museum is dedicated to the study of written language from ancient times to the present. Included are 12 rooms of exhibits about languages from around the globe such as Armenian, Brahmi, Cyrillic and Visigoth. Notations of music, Braille and sign language also are included. Among other exhibits, visitors can view a replica of the Rosetta Stone and a working model of Gutenberg's press.

Allow 1 hour, 30 minutes minimum. Mon.-Sat. 9-noon and 1-4; closed holidays. Free. Phone (704) 843-6000.

MUSEUM OF THE WAXHAWS AND ANDREW JACKSON MEMORIAL is 5 mi. e. on SR 75. Named for its first inhabitants, the settlement was founded by the Scot-Irish about 1755. The museum's collection spans 1550-1900 and contains memorabilia and weapons from the Revolutionary and Civil wars, a working cotton gin, a display dedicated to Andrew Jackson, Scot-Irish settlement artifacts and an 1814 Conestoga wagon.

A short film detailing the history of the region is presented. Picnicking is permitted. Allow 1 hour minimum. Fri.-Sat. 10-5, Sun. 2-5; closed Jan. 1, Thanksgiving and Dec. 25. Admission $4; $2 (ages 6-12). Phone (704) 843-1832.

WAYNESVILLE (E-3) pop. 9,232, elev. 3,000′

English, Scot-Irish, German and Dutch immigrants who came from the coast to the mountains in search of better hunting and farming settled in Waynesville in the 18th century. Originally called Mount Prospect, Waynesville was renamed in honor of Revolutionary War general "Mad" Anthony Wayne. The World Methodist Council is headquartered 3 miles from Waynesville at Lake Junaluska.

Haywood County Chamber of Commerce: 591 N. Main St., P.O. Box 600, Waynesville, NC 28786-0600; phone (828) 456-3021.

Shopping Areas: Necessities such as stone-ground flour, boots and jawbreaker candies are stocked at the 1930s-era Mast General Store, 63 N. Main St.

MILE HIGH HEINTOOGA OVERLOOK, a spur of the Blue Ridge Parkway 8 mi. n.e. of Soco Gap, affords a view of Great Smoky Mountains National Park *(see place listing p. 156)*.

PIGEON LOOP DRIVE, US 276E to Woodrow, then SR 110N to Canton, then US 23/74W to US 276, traverses Pigeon Gap past many orchards that are colorful in the spring; the distance is 24 miles.

SOCO GAP, 13 mi. w. of Waynesville on the edge of Great Smoky Mountains National Park via US 276N and US 19W *(see place listing p. 156)*, affords excellent views.

WEAVERVILLE (E-3) pop. 2,416, elev. 2,176′

ZEBULON B. VANCE BIRTHPLACE STATE HISTORIC SITE, 911 Reems Creek Rd., contains the reconstructed two-story log house in which the state's Civil War-period governor was born on May 13, 1830. The site includes six farm buildings and a visitor center/museum.

Allow 1 hour minimum. Tues.-Sat. 9-5, Apr.-Oct.; Tues.-Sat. 10-4, rest of year. Closed major holidays. Hours may vary; phone ahead to verify schedule. Guided 1-hour tours are available on the hour. Last tour begins 1 hour before closing. Donations. Phone (828) 645-6706.

WELCOME (B-4) pop. 3,538, elev. 859′

RICHARD CHILDRESS RACING MUSEUM is off US 52 exit 97, then 2.5 mi. w. to 180 Industrial Dr. Dedicated to NASCAR racing, this 10-building complex houses 47 race vehicles and a collection of trophies, awards and driving memorabilia. Team cars of Robby Gordon, Jeff Green and Kevin Harvick are built on the site; tours of selected shop areas are offered. One exhibit area focuses on Richard Childress' passion for wildlife and natural resource conservation.

Allow 30 minutes minimum. Mon.-Fri. 9-5, Sat. 9-3; closed major holidays. Self-guiding shop tours Mon.-Fri. 8-5. Museum $12; $8 (ages 55+); $5 (ages 7-18). Phone (336) 731-3389 or (800) 476-3389.

WILLIAMSTON (B-8) pop. 5,843, elev. 75′

Williamston is known for being the birthplace of the first Confederate judge, Asa Biggs. The area's visitor center is located in Biggs' former residence—the family lived in the Federal-style home from 1835 until 1862, when they fled under the threat of approaching Union forces. A walking tour brochure available from the visitor center highlights a variety of architectural styles present in buildings throughout the town's two historic districts.

Horse shows and various sports events take place in the indoor coliseum at the Senator Bob Martin Eastern Agricultural Center on SR 125S; phone (252) 792-5111.

Martin County Visitor's Center: Asa Biggs House, 100 E. Church St., P.O. Box 382, Williamston, NC 27892; phone (252) 792-6605 or (800) 776-8566.

WILMINGTON (D-7) pop. 75,838, elev. 30′

Wilmington's maritime legacy is perpetuated by every blade of grass on the town's Civil War battlefields and every grain of sand on its 31 miles of beach. Anchored between the Cape Fear River and the Atlantic Ocean, Wilmington was the scene of Stamp Act resistance in 1765 and is North Carolina's principal deepwater port.

Best explored by riverboat, horse-drawn carriage, trolley or foot, the 230-block historic district boasts cobblestone walkways; fishing piers; museums; and centuries-old homes, churches, cemeteries and battlefields. Wilmington Adventure Tours provides guided 2-hour walking tours of the city April through October at 10 and 2; phone (910) 763-1785.

A shopping spree in downtown Wilmington might make you feel as if you've stepped back into the 1940s and '50s. Cotton Exchange and Chandler's Wharf, both of which have been renovated, house boutiques and restaurants amid a cluster of antique stores.

For those who can't get enough of the Great Outdoors, Wilmington is a hot spot for sailing, scuba diving, surfing and kiteboarding. If you'd prefer to stay dry, hike a nature trail, go horseback riding, or discover a new species of plant. The New Hanover County Arboretum, 6206 Oleander Dr., presents an array of exhibits designed to educate visitors about horticulture; phone (910) 798-7660.

Cape Fear Coast Convention & Visitors Bureau—Wilmington: 24 N. Third St., Wilmington, NC 28401; phone (910) 341-4030 or (877) 406-2356.

SAVE **AIRLIE GARDENS** is at 300 Airlie Rd. Three self-guiding tours of varying lengths wind throughout the 67-acre property, which includes 10 acres of freshwater lakes. Features include azaleas, camellias, statuary, various exhibits and the historic Airlie Oak, dating from the mid-1500s. Allow 30 minutes minimum. Daily 9-5, Apr.-Dec.; Mon.-Sat. 9-5, rest of year. Admission $5; $3 (ages 6-12). MC, VI. Phone (910) 798-7700.

GEM **BATTLESHIP *NORTH CAROLINA*** is at jct. US 17 and US 421N, on the Cape Fear River. Commissioned in 1941, the USS *North Carolina* served in every major naval offensive in the Pacific in World War II, earning 15 battle stars. A 2-hour self-guiding tour begins with an orientation exhibit and includes portions of nine decks, allowing visits to the crew's quarters, the bridge, gun turrets and plotting, radio and engine rooms. Many exhibits depict the World War II experiences of crew members and their loved ones.

Picnicking is permitted onshore. Daily 8-8, Memorial Day weekend Labor Day; 8-5, rest of year. Last admission 1 hour before closing. Admission $12; $10 (ages 65+ and military with ID); $6 (ages 6-11). MC, VI. Phone (910) 251-5797.

BELLAMY MANSION MUSEUM OF HISTORY AND DESIGN ARTS, 503 Market St., is a restored antebellum mansion that showcases several architectural styles including Italianate, neoclassic and Greek Revival. A slide show provides background information about the mansion and the Bellamy family. Changing exhibits also are featured. Allow 1 hour minimum. Tues.-Sat. 10-5, Sun. 1-5; closed major holidays. Tours are given on the hour. Last tour begins 1 hour before closing. Admission $10; $4 (ages 5-12). MC, VI. Phone (910) 251-3700.

BURGWIN-WRIGHT HOUSE AND GARDEN, at 3rd and Market sts., served as headquarters for Lord Cornwallis during the Revolutionary War. Occupied as a private residence until 1937, the 1770 Georgian house is restored to Colonial style and contains 18th-century furnishings. A separate, three-story cookhouse and seven gardens with original landscape designs also are featured. The massive stone walls of an old jail constitute the house's foundation.

Tues.-Sat. 10-4; closed July 4, Thanksgiving weekend and Dec. 25. Hours may vary; phone ahead. Guided 45-minute tours are given on the hour. Admission $8; $4 (students with ID); free (ages 0-4 with adult). Phone (910) 762-0570.

SAVE **CAPE FEAR MUSEUM,** 814 Market St., features a diorama of Fort Fisher; Waves and Currents, an exhibit about the history and culture of the lower Cape Fear area; a 17-foot-by-20-foot scale model of 1863 Wilmington; and an exhibit of the history of regional beaches. Daily 9-5, Sun. 1-5, Memorial Day-Labor Day; Tues.-Sat. 9-5, Sun. 1-5, rest of year. Closed major holidays. Admission $6; $5 (ages 66+ and students with ID); $3 (ages 3-17). MC, VI. Phone (910) 798-4350.

***CAPTAIN J.N. MAFFITT* RIVER CRUISES,** Riverfront Park at the corner of Market and Water sts., offers 45-minute narrated sightseeing cruises of the Cape Fear River. River taxi rides between Riverfront Park and the Battleship *North Carolina (see attraction listing)* also are offered.

Departures for sightseeing cruises Tues.-Sun. at 2:30, Apr.-Oct. River taxi rides depart daily every half-hour 10-5 (except 11:30 and 3:30), Memorial Day-Labor Day; Sat.-Sun. every half-hour 10-5, May 1-day before Memorial Day and day after Labor Day through mid-Dec. Sightseeing fare $15; $5 (ages 2-12). River taxi fare $4. Passengers must arrive 15 minutes before departure. Phone (910) 343-1611 or (800) 676-0162.

THE CHILDREN'S MUSEUM OF WILMINGTON is at 116 Orange St. Geared towards children ages 0-11, the museum features eight permanent exhibits that promote learning through role-playing. The following exhibits teach children about art, science and culture: International Diner, Imagination Circus, Ahoy Wilmington!, Toddler Room, Travelers' Stories, Animal Adventures, Star Maker Sound Stage and Grocery Store. Allow 1 hour, 30 minutes minimum. Mon.-Fri. 10-5, Sat. 10-6, Sun. 1-5. Admission: $8, free (0-11 months). MC, VI. Phone (910) 254-3534.

FORT FISHER STATE HISTORIC SITE—
see Kure Beach p. 167.

GREENFIELD PARK AND GARDENS, s. end of 3rd St. with entrance on 4th St., is a public park noted for its cypress trees, camellias, azaleas, roses and a 5-mile scenic drive around Greenfield Lake. The gardens are particularly colorful February through April. Recreational amenities include paddleboats, canoes, playgrounds, tennis courts, a skateboard park, and bicycle and nature trails.

Picnicking is permitted. Daily 6 a.m.-11 p.m. Skateboard park hours Tues.-Sat. noon-10, Sun. 1-8. Free. Rental fee for paddleboats and canoes $8 for first hour, $3 per each additional half-hour. Skateboard park $2. Phone (910) 341-7852, or (910) 362-8222 for information about the skateboard park.

HENRIETTA III**,** docked at 106 S. Water St. at the foot of Dock St., offers 90-minute narrated sightseeing cruises of the Cape Fear River, as well as 90-minute lunch cruises, 3-hour entertainment dinner cruises and 2-hour sunset dinner cruises. Special-events cruises also are offered.

Sightseeing cruises depart Tues.-Sun. at 2:30, Apr.-Oct. Boarding is 30 minutes before departure. Sightseeing cruise $15; $5 (ages 2-12). Because noon sightseeing cruises may be pre-empted by charters, phone for availability. DS, MC, VI. Phone (910) 343-1611 or (800) 676-0162 for other schedules and prices.

LOUISE WELLS CAMERON ART MUSEUM is at 3201 S. 17th St. This 42,000-square-foot facility houses an extensive collection of North Carolinian and American art from the 18th-century to the present. A set of prints by Mary Cassatt is featured. The grounds include a sculpture garden. Changing exhibits are presented. Guided tours are offered free to all at 1:30 the first Sunday and third Saturday of each month.

Food is available. Allow 1 hour minimum. Tues.-Sun. 11-5 (also Fri. 5-9); closed Jan. 1, Easter, July 4, Thanksgiving, Dec. 24-25 and 31. Admission $8; $3 (ages 2-12); $15 (family); free (on first Sun. of the month). Phone (910) 395-5999.

SAVE **POPLAR GROVE HISTORIC PLANTATION,** 9 mi. n. on US 17, consists of several historic buildings set on 16 acres of land that were once part of a vast, self-supporting agricultural community. Costumed guides conduct tours of the manor house and the outbuildings. Built by Joseph Mumford Foy in 1850, the manor house contains period furniture, clothing and memorabilia. Demonstrations by craftspeople are offered in the Cultural Arts Center.

Picnicking is permitted. Food is available. Allow 1 hour minimum. Mon.-Sat. 9-5, Sun. noon-5, first Mon. in Feb.-Fri. before Christmas; closed Easter and Thanksgiving. Guided 35- to 45-minute tours are offered at 9:30, 10:30, 11:30, 1, 2, 3 and 4. Admission $8; $7 (ages 63+); $5 (ages 6-15). MC, VI. Phone (910) 686-9518.

ST. JAMES EPISCOPAL CHURCH is at 3rd and Market sts. Built in 1751 it was used by the British as a riding school during the Revolutionary War. When rebuilt in 1839, the church structure was designed by T.U. Walter, architect of the U.S. Capitol dome and wings. The church house was designed in 1901 by Henry Bacon, architect of the Lincoln Memorial in Washington, D.C. "Ecce Homo," a Spanish painting taken from a captured ship in 1748, hangs in the church. Mon.-Fri. 9-4. Free. Phone (910) 763-1628.

THALIAN HALL, 310 Chestnut St., is the only surviving theater designed by 19th-century architect John Montague Trimble. In continuous use since 1858, the theater hosts more than 250 plays, films and musical performances a year. Self-guiding tours of the lobby are offered Mon.-Fri. noon-6, Sat. 2-6. Guided tours of the theater are available by appointment. Guided tours $10; $8 (senior citizens); $4 (children). Self-guiding tours $1. MC, VI. Phone (910) 343-3660 for tour reservations or the box office.

TREGEMBO ANIMAL PARK, 10 mi. s. on US 421, has more than 130 different birds, mammals and reptiles. Two small museums contain mounted animals and collections of fossils, currency, arrowheads, seashells and World War II memorabilia. Daily 10-5. Hours may vary; phone ahead. Admission $8; $7 (ages 62+); $6 (ages 2-11). MC, VI. Phone (910) 392-3604.

SAVE **WILMINGTON RAILROAD MUSEUM,** 505 Nutt St., commemorates the importance of railroads in local and national history. Exhibits include Wilmington and Weldon Railroad artifacts dating from 1840, as well as items from the Atlantic Coastline and other railroads. A steam locomotive, boxcar and caboose can be boarded. The Children's Corner offers toy trains and hands-on exhibits.

Mon.-Sat. 10-5, Sun. 1-5, Apr.-Sept.; Mon.-Sat. 10-4, rest of year. Closed Jan. 1, Easter, Thanksgiving and Dec. 25 and 31. Admission $6; $5 (ages 61+ and military with ID); $3 (ages 2-12). MC, VI. Phone (910) 763-2634.

SAVE **WILMINGTON TROLLEY** is at Dock and Water sts. Forty-five minute narrated tours allow visitors to receive an orientation of the city. The trolley passes by many of Wilmington's historic homes, attractions and other points of interest. Allow 1 hour minimum. Tours depart on the hour daily 10-5, Apr.-Oct.; Sat.-Sun. 10-5, in Mar. and Nov. Admission $11; $5 (ages 1-5). AX, MC, VI. Phone (910) 763-4483.

SAVE **ZEBULON LATIMER HOUSE,** 126 S. 3rd St., is a four-story Italianate Revival town residence built in 1852. Empire and Victorian furnishings grace the interior. Mon.-Fri. 10-4, Sat. noon-5; closed Jan. 1, Easter, Thanksgiving and Dec. 25. Guided 45-minute tours are available by request. Admission $8; $4 (students with ID and ages 6-18). Phone (910) 762-0492.

WILSON (B-7) pop. 44,405, elev. 145'

Primarily known as a bright-leaf tobacco market, Wilson also is an antique center. The city's central business district boasts many fine examples of late 19th- and early 20th-century architecture, while the older residential areas are noted for their restored bungalows.

The 1919 Edna Boykin Cultural Center is a lavishly decorated vaudeville house that offers live, professional performances; phone (252) 291-4329. Wilson Arts Center highlights the work of local and regional artists and is open Tues.-Fri. 10-5, Sat. 10-3; phone (252) 291-4329.

G.R. Hammond Gallery is open Saturdays and by appointment; phone (252) 234-6160 or (252)

291-4329. The Oliver Nestus Freeman Roundhouse Museum focuses on African-American history, art and culture and includes photographs chronicling the accomplishments of area citizens during the early 20th century; phone (252) 296-3056.

Auctioneers sell thousands of pounds of tobacco during the August through October market season. Free tours of tobacco auctions in area warehouses are offered Monday through Thursday at 9:30, July through October.

Wilson Visitors Bureau: 124 E. Nash St., Wilson, NC 27893; phone (252) 243-8440 or (800) 497-7398.

SAVE **IMAGINATION STATION,** 224 E. Nash St., is a hands-on science museum geared to children. Exhibits allow visitors to race against a cheetah, pilot a space shuttle, drive a fire engine and learn about electricity, optical illusions, exotic animals, music and magnets. Food is available. Allow 2 hours minimum. Mon.-Sat. 9-5; closed major holidays. Admission $5; $4 (ages 4-17 and 62+). MC, VI. Phone (252) 291-5113.

WINDSOR (B-8) pop. 2,283, elev. 277′

Windsor's beginnings date from 1717, when a plantation named Rosefield was established on 2,810 acres near the Cashie River. The possibilities of river transportation and the plantation's proximity to a road between Edenton and Halifax inspired landowner William Gray to give 100 acres for a new town. In 1773, a bill was passed moving the county seat from Wolfenden, or Hoggard's Mill, to Windsor. The town's streets still bear their old English names.

The Roanoke River National Wildlife Refuge, off US 17N, is home to more than 191 species of migrating birds and has informal trail systems available to the public; phone (252) 794-5326.

Windsor Area Chamber of Commerce: 102 N. York St., P.O. Box 572, Windsor, NC 27983; phone (252) 794-4277.

SAVE **HISTORIC HOPE PLANTATION,** 4.5 mi. w. on SR 308, is the restored early 19th-century mansion of David Stone, statesman and governor. It has Georgian and Federal elements and is furnished with period pieces. Also on the grounds are an 18th-century garden; an herb garden; a kitchen garden; and the King-Bazemore House, a mid-18th-century rural plantation house. Mon.-Sat. 10-5, Sun. 2-5, Apr.-Oct.; Mon.-Sat. 10-4, Sun. 2-5, rest of year. Admission $8; $7 (ages 65+); $3 (students with ID). MC, VI. Phone (252) 794-3140.

WINNABOW (D-6) elev. 50′

BRUNSWICK TOWN STATE HISTORIC SITE is on the Cape Fear River at 8884 St. Phillips Rd. S.E. One of Colonial North Carolina's leading seaports, residents fled at the outbreak of the Revolution and few returned when the war ended. Excavated foundations of Brunswick Town buildings are maintained as archeological exhibits. The ruins of St. Philip's Anglican Church are noteworthy and Fort Anderson was built on top of the old townsite by the Confederacy. A visitor center offers museum exhibits and a slide show.

Picnicking is permitted. Allow 1 hour minimum. Tues.-Sat. 10-4; closed major holidays. Free. Phone (910) 371-6613.

ORTON PLANTATION GARDENS are at 9149 Orton Rd., S.E. Azaleas, camellias, dogwoods, roses and flowering fruit trees are at their peak March through April. Day lilies, oleander, rhododendron, gardenia, magnolia and iris bloom May through June. Summer annuals and crape myrtle peak July through August.

The 1735 mansion, a fine example of antebellum architecture, is closed to the public. Picnicking is permitted. Daily 8-6, Mar.-Aug.; 10-5, Sept.-Nov. Closed Thanksgiving. Admission $9; $8 (ages 60+); $3 (ages 6-16). Phone (910) 371-6851.

WINSTON-SALEM (A-5)
pop. 185,776, elev. 912′

Winston-Salem dates from 1753, when a group of Pennsylvania Moravians purchased a large tract of land in the North Carolina Piedmont. Their settlement of Bethabara, meaning "House of Passage" or "Temporary Home," prospered and became a trading and crafts center. In 1766 Salem (from *Shalom*, Hebrew for "peace") was built nearby as the Moravians' permanent settlement.

Winston was founded in 1849. It grew rapidly because of the success of the tobacco and textile industries, and eventually surpassed Salem. The two towns consolidated in 1913.

Textiles and tobacco built the city, but the arts brought new life to downtown in the mid-20th century. The downtown was enhanced with a performing arts center, an arts and crafts school for children, and a park and amphitheater. The culmination of the program is the North Carolina School of the Arts, a branch of the University of North Carolina with about 1,200 students. The Stevens Center, a renovated 1929 movie palace in downtown Winston-Salem, is one of the school's performance centers.

In addition to being the home of Wake Forest University with its 4,000 undergrads and 2,300 graduate students, the city is home to Winston-Salem State University with an enrollment of 2,800. Founded in 1892 as Slater Industrial Academy, the university's name was changed to Winston-Salem Teacher's College in 1925—it was the first African-American institution in the country to award degrees in elementary education. Even older is Salem College. Founded in 1772 in the Moravian village of Salem, Salem College's 1,000 students attend classes on a 57-acre campus in Old Salem *(see attraction listing)*.

Recreational opportunities abound in Winston-Salem. The city operates and maintains 75 parks that include 16 miles of greenways for walking, jogging, skating and bicycling; phone (336) 727-2063.

Winston-Salem Visitor Center: 200 Brookstown Ave., Winston-Salem, NC 27101; phone (336) 728-4200 or (866) 728-4200.

Shopping areas: Old Salem provides numerous shopping opportunities. Several shops adjacent to Salem Square offer reproduction furniture and home furnishings reminiscent of 18th-century Moravian influences. T. Bagge-Merchant is in the 1775 building where Traugott Bagge once operated the town store. The Downtown Arts District, at Sixth and Trade streets, is the center of many cultural activities and features numerous working studios, galleries and shops.

Hanes Mall, off I-40, features over 200 stores including Belk, JCPenney, Macy's and Williams-Sonoma. For more than a century, the Historic West End has been the neighborhood place for shopping, dining and strolling, and offers a dozen or more antique and consignment shops. Reynolda Village, adjacent to Reynolda House Museum of American Art *(see attraction listing p. 195)*, is comprised of the barn and cottages of the Reynolds estate that have been converted to boutiques, shops and upscale restaurants.

GOD'S ACRE, the Moravian cemetery 1 blk. n. of Salem Sq. on Church St., contains more than 4,000 graves dating from 1771. The flat white marble markers symbolize the equality of the dead. Open daily 24 hours. Free.

HISTORIC BETHABARA PARK, on Bethabara Rd. 3 mi. n.w. off University Pkwy., is the 1753 site of the first Moravian settlement in the state. The grounds include the 1788 Gemeinhaus, or church; the 1782 Krause-Butner Potter's House; the 1803 Brewers House; excavations of 40 original foundations; a reconstructed 1756 fort in its original trench; the reconstructed 1759 community gardens; and a visitor center. The park has more than 20 miles of nature and history trails.

Picnicking is permitted. Park open daily dawn-dusk. Buildings open Tues.-Fri. 10:30-4:30, Sat.-Sun. 1:30-4:30, Apr.-Nov.; closed Thanksgiving. Costumed guides offer 1-hour tours on request. Grounds free. Buildings $2; $1 (students and children). Phone (336) 924-8191.

HOME MORAVIAN CHURCH, 529 S. Church St. on Salem Sq., is the center of Moravian church activities in the South. Services in the 1800 sanctuary are open to visitors. Volunteers are available to answer questions. Open daily 1:30-3:30, Easter-Nov. 30. Times may vary; phone ahead. Services Sun. at 8:45 and 11. Free. Phone (336) 722-6171.

GEM SAVE **OLD SALEM,** on Old Salem Rd. adjacent to downtown Winston-Salem, is a living-history re-creation of the Moravian church town of Salem founded in 1766. More than 100 buildings erected 1766-1850 have been restored or reconstructed on their original sites. Family gardens and orchards have been replanted, and streets and lighting have been adapted to re-create an 18th-century atmosphere.

Several of the buildings remain as private residences, including the half-timbered 1768 Fourth House, said to be the oldest house in Salem. Of the more than 90 restored buildings, 15 can be visited. Costumed interpreters throughout the town demonstrate historic trades and domestic activities.

Self-guiding tours begin with a brief orientation program at the Old Salem Visitor Center, 900 Old Salem Rd. Attraction tickets are purchased at the center, which contains exhibits detailing the history and lifestyles of the Moravian people. A noteworthy item to view is the restored Tannenberg Organ made in 1799-1800 by David Tannenberg, a Moravian immigrant and organ builder. Food is available. Historic area open Mon.-Sat. 9:30-4:30, Sun. 1-5, Mar.-Dec.; Tues.-Sat. 9:30-4:30, Sun. 1-5, rest of year. Closed Easter, Thanksgiving and Dec. 24-25. Visitor center and shops open at 9.

All-in-one combination ticket $21 or $24 (for 2 consecutive days); $10 (ages 6-16). AX, DC, DS, MC, VI. Phone (336) 721-7300 or (888) 348-4844.

Boys School (Wachovia Museum), facing Salem Sq., was built in 1794 and houses exhibits about various aspects of Moravian life, including examples of the early waterworks system and items relating to 17th- and 18th-century surveying. The second floor displays musical instruments, toys and an 18th-century schoolroom.

Market-Fire House, on Salem Sq., is divided into two sections. One holds two of the earliest fire engines used in North Carolina; the other is a former meat market. The original fire engines and firefighting equipment are displayed.

Miksch House and Garden, on S. Main St. just n. of Salem Sq., was built in 1771 by Matthew Miksch. An enterprising man, Miksch sold tobacco, candles and gingerbread. Behind the house is a log shed where seasonal activities often are demonstrated.

Museum of Early Southern Decorative Arts is at 924 S. Main St. Displayed in 24 rooms and seven galleries are furnishings and art produced 1690-1820. The objects are exhibited within homelike settings, and many of the rooms were actually moved from older buildings.

Guided 90-minute tours depart every half-hour Mon.-Sat. 9:30-4:30, Sun. 1-5, Mar.-Dec.; Tues.-Sat. 9:30-4:30, Sun. 1-5, rest of year. Closed Easter, Thanksgiving and Dec. 24-25. Tickets are issued for specific tour dates and times; reservations can be made at the visitor center upon arrival. AX, MC, VI. Phone (336) 721-7300, (336) 721-7350 for reservations, or (888) 348-4844.

The Old Salem Children's Museum, 924 S. Main St., is a hands-on history lesson for ages 4-9. Children can play in a miniature Moravian house, try on era costumes and learn about life in early Salem. Tues.-Sat. 9:30-4:30, Sun. 1-5, Mon. 1-4:30, Mar.-Dec.; Tues.-Sat. 9:30-4:30, Sun. 1-4:30, rest of year.

Closed Easter, Thanksgiving and Dec. 24-25. Admission $6. Admission included with All-in-One combination ticket. Tickets required for all children old enough to walk or play. AX, MC, VI. Phone (336) 721-7300 or (888) 348-4844.

The Old Salem Toy Museum is at 924 S. Main St. More than 1,200 antique toys dating from A.D. 225 to the 1920s are displayed. A large exhibit of miniature dollhouses is featured in addition to themed displays highlighting trains and circus items. An original set of Punch and Judy puppets also is part of the collection. Mon.-Sat. 9:30-4:30, Sun. 1-5; closed Easter, Thanksgiving and Dec. 24-25. Phone (888) 653-7253.

St. Philips Church, at 900 Church St., is thought to be the oldest standing African-American church in the state. The brick structure was built in 1861; an adjacent reconstruction of the 1823 log church interprets the African-American experience in Moravian Salem.

Salem Tavern, Annex and Barn are on 736 Main St. The tavern was built in 1784 and accommodated guests until 1850. The gentlemen's dining rooms, bedrooms and kitchen are furnished in period. George Washington was a guest for two nights in 1791. Behind the tavern is an 1840s heavy-timbered barn.

Shultz Shoe Shop, on 700 Main St., s. of Salem Sq., is a shoemaker's shop built in 1827. A costumed guide demonstrates 19th-century shoemaking and leatherworking.

Single Brothers House, facing Salem Sq. at 600 S. Main St., is a half-timbered, brick structure dating from 1769 with a 1786 addition. It served as the home and workplace for the community's single men and older boys. The building includes a dining room, kitchen, meeting hall and trade shops in which costumed artisans can be seen at work. Pewter casting, tailoring, blacksmithing and furniture making are among the demonstrations.

T. Vogler Gunsmith Shop is at 913 S. Main St., near the Horton Museum Center. Visitors can observe a blacksmith working at the forge and learn about the gun-making process as they view craftspeople creating rifles and pistols. Mon.-Sat. 9-5, Sun. 1-5; closed Easter, Thanksgiving and Dec. 24-25.

Vierling House is at 500 Church St., near God's Acre. Once the largest house in Salem, it was the residence of Dr. Benjamin Vierling, a prominent physician. Inside are an apothecary shop, dining room, kitchen and family quarters. A medical and health care exhibit is upstairs. At the rear of the 1802 building is a furnished wash-bake house, where household chores often are demonstrated.

Vogler House, at Main and West sts., was the 1819 house and shop of a silversmith. It contains many original 19th-century furnishings, including a Moravian tile stove, several clocks and a silhouette-making device. Silversmithing is demonstrated on select days.

Winkler Bakery, on S. Main St. n. of Salem Sq., was built in 1800. Inside the restored building, bakers demonstrate early baking methods using historic recipes and a wood-fired brick beehive oven.

REYNOLDA GARDENS OF WAKE FOREST UNIVERSITY is at 100 Reynolda Village. The 4-acre formal garden, 1912 greenhouses and natural areas were once part of Reynolda, the early 20th-century estate built by R.J. Reynolds. Antique and modern plants are cultivated, and the grounds have been restored to the historic design created by landscape architect Thomas Sears. Allow 30 minutes minimum. Gardens and grounds daily dawn-dusk. Greenhouses Mon.-Fri. 9-4, Sat. 10-4; closed Sat. in Jan. Free. Phone (336) 758-5593.

GEM SAVE **REYNOLDA HOUSE MUSEUM OF AMERICAN ART** is at 2250 Reynolda Rd. near Wake Forest University. Built by Katharine Smith and R.J. Reynolds 1912-17 on a 1,067-acre estate, this 64-room country house offers a fine collection of furnishings and American paintings, prints and sculpture from 1755 to the present. The works of Mary Cassatt, Frederic Church, John Singleton Copley, Thomas Eakins, Jacob Lawrence, Gilbert Stuart and Andrew Wyeth are represented.

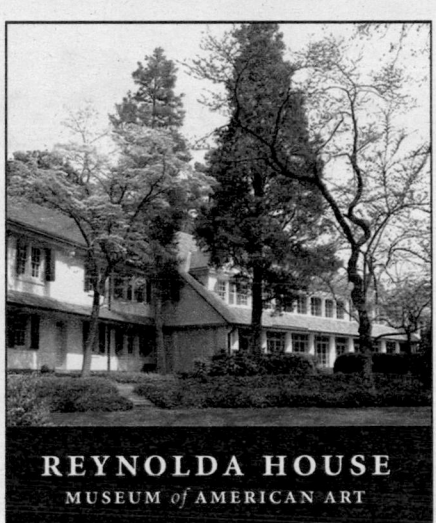

Also of interest are a ladies' costume collection 1905-50; an Aeolian residence organ; family clothing and memorabilia dating from 1905; and vintage children's toys. Outbuildings have been converted into a shopping village. Japanese cherry trees bloom in late March or early April, and the gardens offer lush seasonal vistas.

A 30,000-square-foot exhibition wing includes a visitor's center, museum shop, changing exhibits, oral history stations and a video. Reynolda House is restored to the 1917 period.

Allow 1 hour minimum. Self-guiding tours of the house Tues.-Sat. 9:30-4:30, Sun. 1:30-4:30; closed Jan. 1, Thanksgiving and Dec. 25. A staff-guided tour with admission is available Sun. at 2. House admission $10; $9 (ages 60+); free (students with ID). Gardens free. MC, VI. Phone (336) 758-5150 or (888) 663-1149. *See color ad p. 195.*

SAVE **SCIWORKS** is 7.5 mi. n. on US 52 to Hanes Mill Rd. exit, following signs. The center offers physical and natural science exhibits, nature trails, live animal exhibits, a discovery room and a planetarium. In addition, an outdoor animal habitat contains deer, river otters and wild birds. Allow 1 hour, 30 minutes minimum. Building open Mon.-Sat. 10-5, Memorial Day-Labor Day; Mon.-Fri. 10-4, Sat. 11-5, rest of year. Park closes 30 minutes before building. Closed Jan. 1, Thanksgiving and Dec. 25. Admission $10; $7 (ages 6-19 and 56+); $5 (ages 2-5). MC, VI. Phone (336) 767-6730.

SOUTHEASTERN CENTER FOR CONTEMPORARY ART, 750 Marguerite Dr. off Reynolda Rd., is in a Tudor-style mansion on 32 acres of landscaped grounds. The center houses works by contemporary American artists. Allow 1 hour minimum. Wed.-Sat. 10-5, Sun. 2-5; closed holidays. Guided tours are available Tues.-Fri. by reservation. Free. Phone (336) 725-1904.

WAKE FOREST UNIVERSITY is off Silas Creek Pkwy. at 1834 Wake Forest Rd. Campus highlights include the university's art collection in the Benson University Center, the Wait Chapel Carillon and the Scales Fine Arts Gallery. Student enrollment is 3,900 undergraduates and 2,000 graduate students. Campus tours can be arranged through the admissions office. Phone (336) 758-5201.

Wake Forest Museum of Anthropology, off University Pkwy., is North Carolina's only museum devoted to the study of various cultures. Relics from the Americas, Africa, Asia and Oceania are featured and include household and ceremonial items, textiles, hunting and fishing gear, and objects of personal adornment. Tues.-Sat. 10-4:30; closed major holidays. Free. Phone (336) 758-5282.

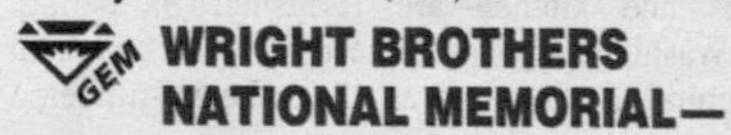

see Outer Banks p. 180.

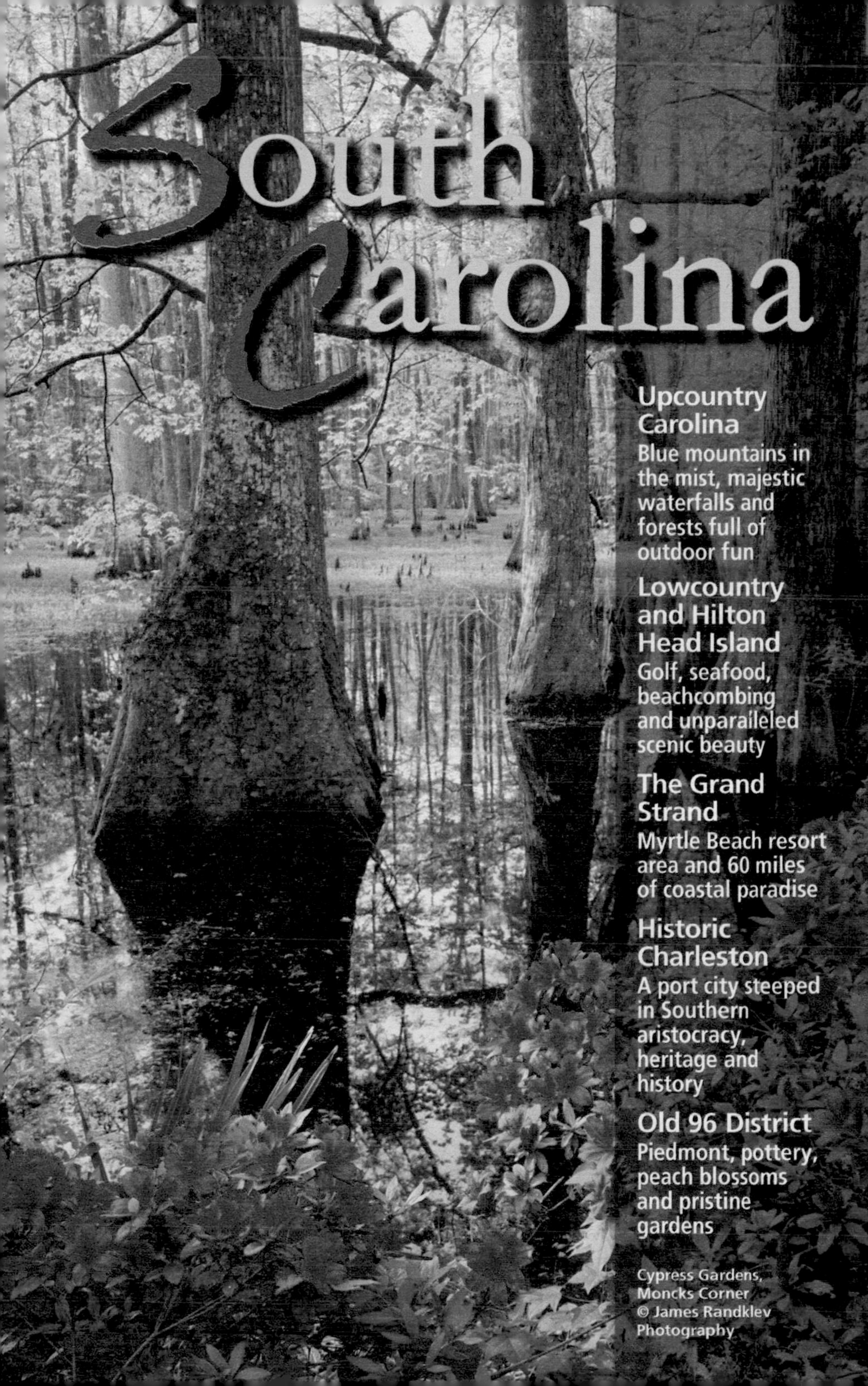

South Carolina
Upcountry Carolina
Blue mountains in the mist, majestic waterfalls and forests full of outdoor fun
Lowcountry and Hilton Head Island
Golf, seafood, beachcombing and unparalleled scenic beauty
The Grand Strand
Myrtle Beach resort area and 60 miles of coastal paradise
Historic Charleston
A port city steeped in Southern aristocracy, heritage and history
Old 96 District
Piedmont, pottery, peach blossoms and pristine gardens

Cypress Gardens, Moncks Corner © James Randklev Photography

Hilton Head Island / © Garry Black / Masterfile

"In my mind I'm going to Carolina." Once you've experienced South Carolina, no doubt you will venture back many times in your thoughts and dreams, just like the song says.

Why? Could it be the rolling blue mountains of the Upcountry, with their forests, waterfalls and scenic beauty?

Or perhaps it's the Lowcountry that lures you. Beachcombing on the barrier islands. Canoeing on the Edisto River. Golfing on Hilton Head Island.

The Grand Strand alone is enough to keep you coming back. Sun, sea and surf make Myrtle Beach a popular destination. The area's amusements and sumptuous seafood are an added bonus.

A city of culture and history, romantic Charleston will call you back again and again—that is, if you can leave it at all. Reflections of centuries past, the city's restored plantations, exotic gardens, galleries and museums offer a taste of the Old South that you won't forget.

Near quaint old harbor cities such as Beaufort and McClellanville, the barrier islands, with their lighthouses, shrimp trawlers and miles of Atlantic beaches, also tempt one.

Listen for a minute. Can't you hear the islands beckon in the ancient and lyrical dialect of Gullah? Can't you feel the sunshine and smell the salt air?

South Carolina will bring you back.

Pride and poise in present-day South Carolina show that you just can't keep a good state down. Despite the ravages of the Revolutionary and Civil wars, postwar economic chaos and one *really* big natural disaster, resilience has kept South Carolinians going.

One of the wealthiest colonies by the time of the American Revolution—courtesy of prolific rice and indigo plantations—South Carolina suffered more Revolutionary War battles than any other state, scarring both the land and its people.

Bouncing back with a prosperous trade in cotton, the people of South Carolina enjoyed a new period of plenty. Unfortunately, this boost died when trade restrictions and talk of abolishing slavery caused a rift between the state and the federal government. The first state to secede from the Union, it was soon thrust into war.

Again the ravages of combat—loss of men and property—were devastating. If that were not enough, Gen. William Tecumseh Sherman blazed through, torching towns and plantations; his fiery march nearly burned South Carolina off the map. Reconstruction followed with political strife and a sagging economy, but the state soon sprang back with the development of textile mills.

Indeed, South Carolina seems as resilient as Teflon—no matter what you throw at it, it just won't stick. In 1989 Hurricane Hugo assaulted the coast from Charleston to Myrtle Beach. But, resolute in rebuilding, the people recovered yet again and prospered once more.

Mountains, Piedmont and Sea

Adventure seekers and nature lovers enjoy exploring the mountainous Upcountry with its rivers, forests and waterfalls. And is any other state boundary as beautifully delineated as northwestern South Carolina's? The cascades of Whitewater Falls (actually two separate waterfalls) coolly divide the Carolinas. The falls are especially scenic when their curtains of water are enhanced by brilliant fall foliage.

Fresh produce and indigenous foods give you a true taste of the Carolinas. Spring in the Upcountry brings sweet-smelling peach and apple blossoms that yield the bountiful fruit harvested and sold at roadside stands in the fall. Try the homemade preserves and apple cider. And be sure to take home a bag of locally milled grits or cornmeal to savor the experience again and again.

As the foothills descend to the coastal plains of the Lowcountry, forests, marshes and moss-draped oaks give way to resort islands

South Carolina Historical Timeline

1521
Spaniard Francisco Cordilla becomes the first European to explore South Carolina.

1680
A decade after its founding, Charles Towne, the first permanent English settlement in Carolina, moves to the present site of Charleston.

1729
Carolina divides into southern and northern portions.

1788
South Carolina becomes the eighth state.

SC Department of Parks, Recreation & Tourism

1860-61
South Carolina secedes from the Union, and the Civil War begins when Confederate troops bombard Fort Sumter in Charleston Harbor.

Library of Congress

and white-sand beaches. Oysters, blue crabs and shrimp are gathered fresh daily on the Sea Islands, where some of the natives still speak Gullah, a lyrical mixture of English and African languages.

Preserving Their Heritage

Folk arts and crafts abound throughout the state; South Carolinians learned early on the value of resourcefulness. The handicrafts that survive have been passed down for generations. Essentially utilitarian although nonetheless beautiful, items are still made by hand the old-fashioned way—with pride.

Upcountry potters in Edgefield and Pickens have been making their wares by the traditional method—hand-thrown on a potter's wheel—since the 1800s. Shaping and trimming the clay by hand as it spins, they fashion pots, vases and bowls to be fired and glazed.

Craftspeople create a spirit of heritage in their handwoven baskets, always eager to share the history behind the art as they demonstrate their skills. Using products of the land, they fashion unique containers from pine needles, sweetgrass and rush strips. Quilters and rug makers likewise stitch and weave tradition into their patchwork quilts and rugs.

The Lowcountry coast is the place to go for Pawleys Island hammocks, those corded creations turned out by local artisans. Several shops in Charleston and along the Grand Strand feature them.

Quilts. Baskets. Rugs. Hammocks. It shouldn't be a surprise that South Carolina craftspeople excel in the fiber arts. After all, their ancestors—cotton growers and developers of some of our country's first textile mills—were the pioneers who weaved the future of this trade.

Indeed, the people of the Palmetto State take all preservation seriously, carefully refurbishing houses, churches, battlefields and cemeteries to their former dignity while retaining the historic integrity of the period. Old St. David's Episcopal Church in Cheraw withstood the Revolution, yet today its handsome steeple and white clapboard exterior make it look like a scene from a vintage postcard.

Some superb examples of historic preservation also are found in Camden. Here you can tour restored dwellings—from dovetailed log cabins to spacious mansions—and recall the craftsmanship of former times.

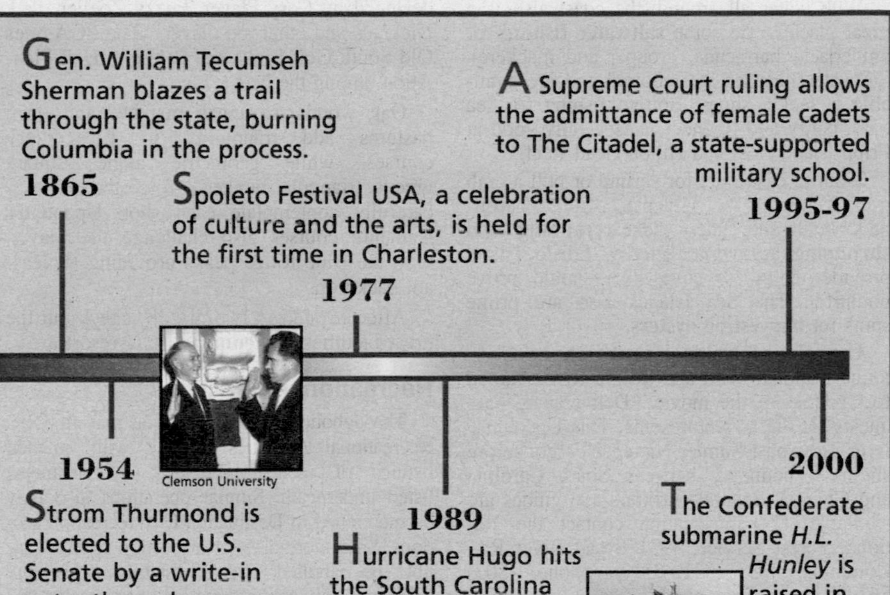

Gen. William Tecumseh Sherman blazes a trail through the state, burning Columbia in the process.
1865
Spoleto Festival USA, a celebration of culture and the arts, is held for the first time in Charleston.
1977
A Supreme Court ruling allows the admittance of female cadets to The Citadel, a state-supported military school.
1995-97
1954
Strom Thurmond is elected to the U.S. Senate by a write-in vote, the only person ever elected to the Senate in this manner.
1989
Hurricane Hugo hits the South Carolina coast, causing more than $3.7 billion in damages.
2000
The Confederate submarine *H.L. Hunley* is raised in Charleston Harbor.

Clemson University

Barbara Voulgaris / Naval Historical Center

Recreation

Outdoor activities are legion in South Carolina. You might tee off at Hilton Head or go rushing down a white-water river at Spartanburg. Whether you enjoy the scenic solitude of Cherokee Path, a woodsy trail that makes a northwest diagonal from Charleston to Keowee and was once used by American Indians, or the crowd-roaring excitement of the Carolina Cup horse race at Camden, adventure is here for the taking.

Water, Water Everywhere

A perfect blend of sun, sand and surf is waiting for you at the state's beaches and resorts. **Parasailing, surfing** and **swimming** lure ocean lovers to Hilton Head Island, Myrtle Beach and the Sea Islands along the Grand Strand.

Boating and **diving** enthusiasts should head for Beaufort or Port Royal. Both towns have plenty of marinas and boat ramps that make outings easy. And with Spanish explorers in the area as long ago as 1514, shipwrecks are hidden in the Intracoastal Waterway and the numerous saltwater creeks and rivers that wind between the islands. Who knows what treasures may yet lie undiscovered?

With water all around, the coast also is a great place to do some **saltwater fishing** for amberjack, barracuda, grouper and mackerel. Saltwater licenses are required and are available at tackle shops. Bottom fishing for sea bass, porgy and flounder is especially good at Fripp Island Reef and Hilton Head Reef.

Want to cast a net for shrimp or pull a crab trap? You're in the right place. South Carolina's tidal shorelines make **crabbing** and **shrimping** a favorite activity. Edisto Island provides countless coves that should prove bountiful. The Sea Islands also are prime spots for **harvesting oysters.**

Canoeing, kayaking or **rafting** the Chattooga National Wild and Scenic River, famed for its role in the movie "Deliverance," are quests for the adventuresome. This Upcountry river races past Sumter National Forest before slicing a boundary between South Carolina and Georgia. Several outfitters and guides are available. For information contact the National Forest Service, 4931 Broad River Rd., Columbia, SC 29212-3530; phone (803) 561-4000.

Playing in the Mountains

Upcountry mountains with their rolling, blue horizon embrace forests, rivers and waterfalls. One of the high spots, literally and figuratively, is Caesars Head State Park. At 3,208 feet, it crowns the Mountain Bridge Recreation and Wilderness Area, granting astounding views of the Blue Ridge Mountains. About a mile north is a trail to Raven Cliff Falls. If **hiking** doesn't take your breath away, the scenery will.

True hikers will want to check out Foothills Trail, winding for 85 miles over the ridges from Table Rock to Oconee State Park. Don't let the modest term "foothills" fool you, though. This is a real wilderness experience in rugged mountain country. Write to the Foothills Trail Conference, P.O. Box 3041, Greenville, SC 29602, for maps and information before you set out.

Croft State Park near Spartanburg is another good place for roughing it. You'll find nature trails for hiking and **horseback riding** as well as sites for **camping** and **fishing.**

Your Links to Fun

The word **"golf"** is practically synonymous with South Carolina, one of the most popular golf destinations in the country. Superb courses and a mild climate let you enjoy the links almost year-round. Hilton Head, home of the MCI Golf Classic, offers courses designed by Gary Player, Fuzzy Zoeller, Jack Nicklaus and other top players. The PGA rates Old South Golf Links and Palmetto Hall Plantation among the best.

Oak woods, savannah marshes and open pastures add tranquility to Lowcountry courses, while geometric angles—square greens, triangular bunkers—force the golfer to carefully contemplate each shot. Upcountry signature courses also challenge the player, with the Blue Ridge peaks providing a pleasant backdrop.

After a round or two of golf, check out the great facilities for **tennis** in these resort areas.

Recreational Activities

Throughout the TourBook, you may notice a Recreational Activities heading with bulleted listings of recreation-oriented establishments listed underneath. Similar operations also may be mentioned in Destination City recreation sections. Since normal AAA inspection criteria cannot be applied, these establishments are presented only for information. Age, height and weight restrictions may apply. Reservations often are recommended and sometimes are required. Addresses and/or phone numbers are provided so visitors can contact the attraction for additional information.

Fast Facts

POPULATION: 4,012,012.

AREA: 31,113 square miles; ranks 40th.

CAPITAL: Columbia.

HIGHEST POINT: 3,548 ft., Sassafras Mountain.

LOWEST POINT: Sea level, Atlantic Ocean.

TIME ZONE(S): Eastern. DST.

TEEN DRIVING LAWS: No more than 2 passengers are permitted unless supervised by driver at least 21 (family members and students to and from school exempt). Driving is not permitted 6 p.m.-6 a.m. (EST); 8 p.m.-6 a.m. (EDT). The minimum age for an unrestricted driver's license is 16 years, 6 months. For more information about South Carolina driver's license regulations phone (803) 896-5000.

SEAT BELT/CHILD RESTRAINT LAWS: Seat belts required for driver and all passengers 6 and older. Children 6 until 18 and over 80 pounds are required to be in a seat belt. Child restraints are required for under age 6 and under 80 pounds; children under age 6 must be in the rear seat if available.

HELMETS FOR MOTORCYCLISTS: Required for driver and passenger under 21.

RADAR DETECTORS: Permitted.

MOVE OVER LAW: Driver is required to slow down and vacate the lane nearest stopped police, fire and rescue vehicles using audible or flashing signals. Law also requires driver to move over for tow truck drivers assisting motorists on the side of the road.

FIREARMS LAWS: Vary by state or county. Contact South Carolina Law Enforcement, Regulatory Services Dept., P.O. Box 21398, Columbia, SC 29221; phone (803) 896-7014.

HOLIDAYS: Jan. 1; Washington's Birthday, Feb. (3rd Mon.); Memorial Day, May (last Mon.); July 4; Labor Day, Sept. (1st Mon.); Veterans Day, Nov. 11; Election Day, Nov. (2nd Tues. in even years); Thanksgiving (and day after); Christmas (Dec. 25) and Dec. 26.

TAXES: South Carolina sales tax is 6 percent. There is an admissions tax of 5 percent on most amusements and a 2 percent accommodations tax. The Charleston area has a lodging tax of 12 percent and a rental car tax of 10 percent.

INFORMATION CENTERS: State welcome centers can be found on US 17 near Little River, I-85S near Blacksburg, I-26E near Landrum, I-85N near Fair Play, I-20E near North Augusta, I-95S near Hamer, I-95S at Santee, I-95N near Hardeeville, I-77S near Fort Mill and US 301N near Allendale. Open daily 9-5:30 (also 5:30-6:30, Memorial Day-Labor Day); closed Jan. 1, Thanksgiving and Dec. 25.

FURTHER INFORMATION FOR VISITORS:
South Carolina Department of Parks, Recreation and Tourism
1205 Pendleton St.
Columbia, SC 29201
(866) 224-9339

FISHING AND HUNTING REGULATIONS:
South Carolina Department of Natural Resources
Division of Wildlife and Freshwater Fisheries
P.O. Box 167
Columbia, SC 29202
(803) 734-3886

NATIONAL FOREST INFORMATION:
U.S. Forest Service
4931 Broad River Rd.
Columbia, SC 29212-3530
(803) 561-4000
(877) 444-6777 (reservations)
TTY (803) 561-4023

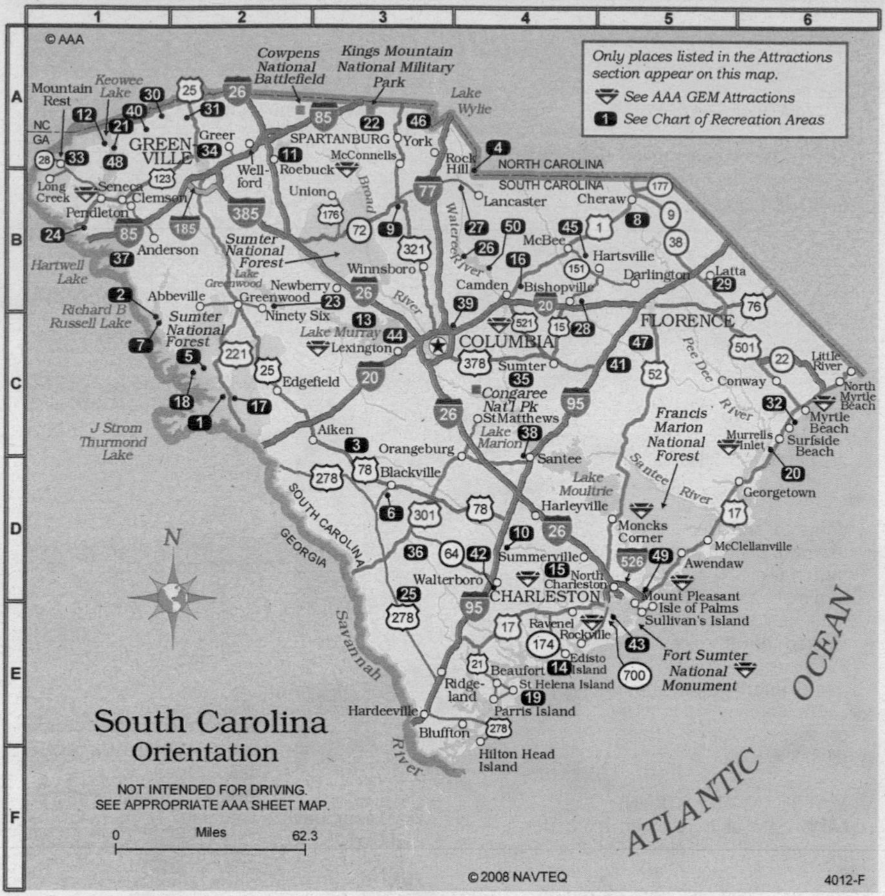

South Carolina Orientation

NOT INTENDED FOR DRIVING.
SEE APPROPRIATE AAA SHEET MAP.

Only places listed in the Attractions section appear on this map.

See AAA GEM Attractions

See Chart of Recreation Areas

© AAA © 2008 NAVTEQ 4012-F

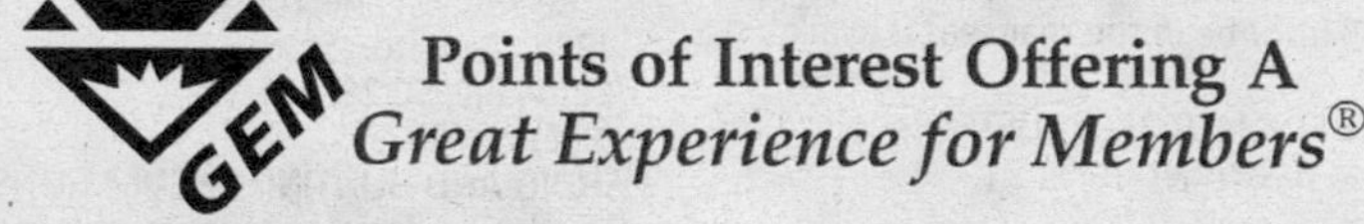

Points of Interest Offering A *Great Experience for Members®*

Charleston (E-5)

CALHOUN MANSION—This 35-room 1876 Italianate mansion is furnished with an impressive collection of antiques. See p. 218.

DOCK STREET THEATRE—The theater, opened in 1736, is believed to be America's first building designed solely for theatrical performances. See p. 218.

EDMONDSTON-ALSTON HOUSE—This 1825 house, built by a wealthy merchant, overlooks Charleston Harbor. See p. 219.

GIBBES MUSEUM OF ART—An outstanding collection of paintings, sculpture, engravings and other art objects is displayed. See p. 220.

HEYWARD-WASHINGTON HOUSE—This 1772 house was built by a prominent rice planter. Tours include the main house, kitchen building, a garden and servants' quarters. See p. 220.

HUGUENOT CHURCH—The last remaining independent Huguenot church in the nation is a fine example of Gothic Revival architecture. See p. 220.

JOSEPH MANIGAULT HOUSE—A hidden stairway connects the second and third floors of this notable 1803 house. See p. 220.

MAGNOLIA PLANTATION AND GARDENS—This Greek Revival plantation house depicts life since the Civil War, and the 60-acre garden dates from the 1680s. See p. 222.

MIDDLETON PLACE—Landscaped grounds feature azaleas, camellias, magnolias and roses, and demonstrations of period plantation chores are given. See p. 223.

NATHANIEL RUSSELL HOUSE—Set in a spacious garden, this Federal-style house features a freestanding spiral staircase and ornate interiors. See p. 221.

ST. MICHAEL'S EPISCOPAL CHURCH—This notable architectural achievement was begun in 1752 and modeled after the 1720s St. Martin-in-the-Fields Church in London. See p. 221.

SOUTH CAROLINA AQUARIUM—The area's diverse water habitats are showcased here with aquariums, an aviary and a touch tank. See p. 222.

Columbia (C-4)

HAMPTON-PRESTON MANSION AND GARDENS—This restored 1818 house, which was used for a variety of purposes through its history, reflects the life of antebellum Columbia. See p. 243.

RIVERBANKS ZOOLOGICAL PARK AND BOTANICAL GARDEN—The sanctuary is home to endangered species as well as domesticated farm friends—just a few of the more than 2,000 residents. See p. 244.

SOUTH CAROLINA STATE HOUSE—From its 18 landscaped acres with 25 monuments to its copper-sheathed dome, the state's seat of government is a historic treasure. See p. 245.

SOUTH CAROLINA STATE MUSEUM—Four floors of exhibits chronicle various aspects of state history, and a laser light show is presented regularly. See p. 245.

Fort Sumter National Monument (E-5)

FORT SUMTER NATIONAL MONUMENT—Learn about the role this brick fortification on a man-made island in Charleston Harbor played in the Civil War. See p. 236.

Lexington (C-3)

LEXINGTON COUNTY MUSEUM COMPLEX—Period buildings and demonstrations depict the lifestyle of the area during the 1830s. See p. 262.

Moncks Corner (D-5)

CYPRESS GARDENS—Flat-bottomed boat tours and walking trails show off this black-water swamp's flora and fauna. See p. 238.

OLD SANTEE CANAL PARK—The remnants of a vital 1800s commercial waterway are preserved within this park. See p. 238.

Mount Pleasant (D-5)

BOONE HALL PLANTATION & GARDENS—The evolution of a plantation is revealed through exhibits, history talks, performances by actors, original slave structures and tours of the house and grounds. See p. 238.

PATRIOTS POINT NAVAL AND MARITIME MUSEUM—The museum exhibits aircraft and maritime vessels and honors Congressional Medal of Honor recipients. See p. 239.

Murrells Inlet (C-6)

BROOKGREEN GARDENS—The garden museum, with its more than 725 sculptures, is on the site of four former rice plantations. See p. 252.

Myrtle Beach (C-6)

DOLLY PARTON'S DIXIE STAMPEDE DINNER & SHOW—Performances chronicle the North versus South rivalry and include feats of horsemanship and family entertainment combined with a four-course meal. See p. 256.

Rockville (E-4)

CHARLESTON TEA PLANTATION—Learn all about tea production with a factory tour and a tour of the extensive grounds. See p. 239.

Roebuck (A-2)

WALNUT GROVE PLANTATION—This 18th-century plantation is furnished with pre-1810 antiques and includes several outbuildings. See p. 265.

Seneca (B-1)

WORLD OF ENERGY—The center contains exhibits illustrating the use of water, coal and uranium in creating energy. See p. 266.

Spartanburg (A-3)

CHAPMAN CULTURAL CENTER—Art, history and science exhibits combine with performing arts to create an impressive cultural facility. See p. 266.

RECREATION AREAS

	MAP LOCATION	CAMPING	PICNICKING	HIKING TRAILS	BOATING	BOAT RAMP	BOAT RENTAL	FISHING	SWIMMING	PETS ON LEASH	BICYCLE TRAILS	NATURE PROGS.	VISITOR CENTER	LODGE/CABINS	FOOD SERVICE
NATIONAL PARKS *(See place listings)*															
Congaree C-4 22,200 acres in central South Carolina		●	●	●	●			●		●		●	●		
NATIONAL FORESTS *(See place listings)*															
Francis Marion 251,000 acres. Coastal Plain n. of Charleston.		●	●	●	●	●		●		●	●				
Sumter 360,000 acres. Western South Carolina.		●	●	●	●	●		●	●	●	●				
ARMY CORPS OF ENGINEERS															
J. Strom Thurmond Lake (C-2) 70,000 acres 30 mi. n.w. of Greenwood via US 221. Water skiing. Aquarium.	1	●	●	●	●	●		●	●	●		●	●		
Richard B. Russell Lake (B-1) 26,650 acres 1 mi. w. of Calhoun Falls on SR 72.	2	●	●	●	●	●		●	●	●			●		●
STATE															
Aiken (C-3) 1,067 acres 16 mi. e. of Aiken off US 78.	3	●	●	●	●	●	●	●	●	●					
Andrew Jackson (A-4) 360 acres 8 mi. n. of Lancaster on US 521. Historic. *(See Lancaster p. 262)*	4	●	●	●	●		●	●		●		●	●		
Baker Creek (C-2) 1,305 acres 4 mi. s.w. of McCormick on US 378.	5	●	●	●	●	●		●	●	●					
Barnwell (D-3) 307 acres 7 mi. n.e. of Barnwell on SR 3.	6	●	●	●	●		●	●	●	●				●	
Calhoun Falls (C-1) 438 acres 13 mi. w. of Abbeville on SR 81. Nature trail.	7	●	●		●	●		●	●	●					
Cheraw (B-5) 7,361 acres 4 mi. s.w. of Cheraw on US 1. *(See Cheraw p. 241)*	8	●	●	●	●		●	●	●	●				●	
Chester (B-3) 523 acres 3 mi. s.e. of Chester on SR 72.	9	●	●	●	●		●	●		●					
Colleton (D-4) 35 acres 11 mi. n. of Walterboro on US 15. Canoeing.	10	●	●	●	●	●		●		●					
Croft (A-2) 7,054 acres 3 mi. s.e. of Spartanburg off SR 56.	11	●	●	●	●		●	●	●	●					
Devils Fork (A-1) 644 acres 16 mi. n.w. of Pickens off SR 11.	12	●	●	●	●	●		●	●	●			●	●	
Dreher Island (C-3) 348 acres 6 mi. s.w. of Chapin off US 76.	13	●	●	●	●	●		●		●					
Edisto Beach (E-4) 1,255 acres 50 mi. s.w. of Charleston on SR 174. Shelling. *(See Edisto Island p. 236)*	14	●	●	●	●	●		●	●	●				●	
Givhans Ferry (D-4) 988 acres 16 mi. w. of Summerville on SR 61.	15	●	●	●				●		●				●	
Goodale (B-4) 763 acres 2 mi. n. of Camden off US 1. Golf.	16		●		●		●	●	●	●					
Hamilton Branch (C-2) 731 acres 12 mi. s.e. of McCormick off US 221.	17	●	●		●	●		●		●					
Hickory Knob (C-2) 1,091 acres 8 mi. s.w. of McCormick off US 378. Tennis, golf, archery.	18	●		●	●	●	●	●	●	●		●	●	●	●
Hunting Island (E-4) 5,000 acres 16 mi. s.e. of Beaufort on US 21. Lighthouse complex.	19	●	●	●	●			●	●	●		●	●	●	
Huntington Beach (D-6) 2,500 acres. Bird-watching. *(See Murrells Inlet p. 253)*	20	●	●	●				●	●	●		●			
Keowee-Toxaway (A-1) 1,000 acres on SR 11 at Lake Keowee, 12 mi. n.w. of Pickens.	21	●	●	●				●		●			●	●	
Kings Mountain (A-3) 6,471 acres 12 mi. n.w. of York on SR 161. Restored 1840s homestead. *(See York p. 268)*	22	●	●	●	●		●	●	●	●		●	●		
Lake Greenwood (B-3) 914 acres 17 mi. e. of Greenwood on SR 702.	23	●	●	●	●	●		●		●					
Lake Hartwell (B-1) 680 acres at Fair Play near jct. I-85 and SR 11.	24	●	●	●	●	●		●		●			●		
Lake Warren (D-3) 440 acres 5 mi. s.w. of Hampton off SR 363.	25	●	●	●	●	●		●		●			●		
Lake Wateree (B-4) 238 acres 30 mi. n. of Columbia off I-77.	26	●	●	●	●	●		●		●					
Landsford Canal (B-4) 244 acres 6 mi. n.w. of Lancaster off US 21.	27		●	●	●			●		●			●		
Lee (C-4) 2,839 acres 7 mi. e. of Bishopville off I-20.	28	●	●	●	●			●	●	●					
Little Pee Dee (B-5) 835 acres 11 mi. s.e. of Dillon off SR 57. Equestrian trails.	29	●	●	●	●	●	●			●					

RECREATION AREAS

	MAP LOCATION	CAMPING	PICNICKING	HIKING TRAILS	BOATING	BOAT RAMP	BOAT RENTAL	FISHING	SWIMMING	PETS ON LEASH	BICYCLE TRAILS	NATURE PROGS.	VISITOR CENTER	LODGE/CABINS	FOOD SERVICE
Mountain Bridge Wilderness Area															
Caesars Head (A-1) 7,467 acres 16 mi. n. of Greenville on US 276 at N.C. state line.	30	●	●	●				●		●		●	●		●
Jones Gap (A-2) 3,346 acres 3 mi. n.w. of Marietta off US 276.	31	●	●	●				●	●	●		●	●		
Myrtle Beach (C-6) 312 acres 3 mi. s. of Myrtle Beach on US 17.	32	●	●	●				●	●	●		●	●	●	
Oconee (A-1) 1,165 acres 12 mi. n.w. of Walhalla off SR 28. Self-guiding automobile tour.	33	●	●					●	●	●			●		●
Paris Mountain (A-2) 1,275 acres 6 mi. n. of Greenville off US 25.	34	●	●	●	●		●	●	●	●					
Poinsett (C-4) 1,000 acres 18 mi. s.w. of Sumter off SR 261.	35	●	●	●	●		●	●	●	●		●	●	●	
Rivers Bridge (D-3) 390 acres 7 mi. s.w. of Ehrhardt off SR 64.	36	●	●	●	●			●	●	●					
Sadlers Creek (B-1) 395 acres 13 mi. s.w. of Anderson off US 29. *(See Anderson p. 208)*	37	●	●	●	●	●		●		●					
Santee (C-4) 2,478 acres 3 mi. n.w. of Santee off US 301.	38	●	●	●	●	●	●	●	●	●		●	●	●	●
Sesquicentennial (B-4) 1,419 acres 13 mi. n.e. of Columbia on US 1.	39	●	●	●	●		●	●	●	●		●	●		
Table Rock (A-1) 3,083 acres 16 mi. n. of Pickens off SR 11.	40	●	●	●	●		●	●	●	●		●	●	●	●
Woods Bay (C-5) 1,541 acres 2.5 mi. s. of Olanta on US 301. Canoe rental.	41		●	●	●		●	●		●		●			
OTHER															
Great Swamp Sanctuary (D-4) 842 acres just e. of I-95 exit 53 in Walterboro. Canoeing, kayaking. *(See Walterboro p. 267)*	42		●	●	●					●	●				
James Island County Park (E-5) 640 acres 7 mi. s. of Charleston off SR 171. Pedal boat rental, playground.	43	●	●	●				●		●	●			●	●
Lake Murray (C-3) 50,000 acres 9 mi. w. of Columbia.	44	●	●		●	●	●		●	●	●				●
Lake Robinson (B-4) 2,250 acres 6 mi. w. of Hartsville off SR 151.	45		●		●	●		●	●				●		
Lake Wylie (A-3) 12,455 acres 17 mi. s. of Charlotte, N.C., off SR 49S. Water skiing.	46	●	●	●	●	●		●	●	●					●
Lynches River (C-5) 668 acres 13 mi. s.w. of Florence on US 52.	47		●	●	●			●	●	●					
Mile Creek Park (A-1) 155 acres 16 mi. n. of Clemson on SR 133.	48	●	●	●	●	●		●	●	●					
Palmetto Islands County Park (D-5) 943 acres 8 mi. n. of Charleston off US 17 bypass.	49		●	●	●		●	●	●	●	●		●		●
Wateree Lake (B-4) 13,710 acres 6 mi. n. of Camden on SR 97.	50	●	●	●	●	●		●	●	●					

South Carolina Temperature Averages Maximum/Minimum

From the records of The Weather Channel Interactive, Inc.

	JAN	FEB	MAR	APR	MAY	JUNE	JULY	AUG	SEPT	OCT	NOV	DEC
Charleston	57/42	60/45	66/52	73/59	80/67	85/74	89/77	87/76	83/72	75/62	68/53	60/45
Columbia	58/36	63/40	71/47	80/53	86/61	92/68	95/72	93/71	88/66	79/54	69/45	61/39
Florence	55/35	59/38	67/44	75/51	82/60	88/68	91/72	89/70	84/65	75/53	67/44	58/37
Myrtle Beach	57/34	61/37	68/44	75/50	82/59	88/67	91/71	89/70	85/65	76/53	69/44	60/37
Spartanburg	54/30	59/32	67/38	76/45	82/55	87/63	91/67	90/67	84/60	75/47	65/38	56/32

Points of Interest

ABBEVILLE (B-1) pop. 5,840, elev. 535′

The "Birthplace of the Confederacy" also was its deathbed; both the first organized secession meeting in 1860 and the last cabinet meeting of Confederate president Jefferson Davis in 1865 took place in Abbeville in what is known as Burt-Stark Mansion. John C. Calhoun, statesman and vice president of the United States 1825-32, was born in Abbeville, where he later practiced law.

The historic 1908 Abbeville Opera House on Town Square once presented well-known performers such as Fanny Brice, Jimmy Durante and Groucho Marx on its stage; today the restored theater offers a broad range of contemporary works.

Greater Abbeville Chamber of Commerce: 107 Court Sq., Abbeville, SC 29620; phone (864) 366-4600.

Self-guiding tours: A map detailing a walking tour is available at the chamber of commerce.

AIKEN (C-3) pop. 25,337, elev. 490′

Named for William Aiken, president of the South Carolina Canal and Railroad Co., Aiken grew from a mere crossroad in 1830 to a popular 1890s health resort thanks to the Best Friend, the first steam-powered passenger train to shuttle visitors inland from Charleston. Wealthy New York residents built estates for extended stays and introduced the game of polo; by the turn of the 20th century, Aiken was one of the country's foremost polo centers.

The terrain, sandy roads and mild climate of the sandhills region make Aiken an ideal equestrian sporting ground. Polo still is played, and Thoroughbreds and Standardbreds train on three racetracks. Carriage roads and bridle paths wind through Hitchcock Woods, a preserve off S. Boundary Avenue.

About 17 miles west of Aiken in North Augusta is Living History Park, which boasts a natural spring. Buildings representative of the 18th century are on the grounds, and living history demonstrations are held the last Saturday of each month between January and October. Annual events also take place in April, June, October and December. The park is open daily dawn to dusk and picnicking is permitted; phone (803) 279-7560 for event information.

Greater Aiken Chamber of Commerce: 121 Richland Ave. E., P.O. Box 892, Aiken, SC 29802; phone (803) 641-1111. *See color ad p. 861.*

Self-guiding tours: A map detailing a driving tour past historic landmarks is available from the chamber of commerce.

Shopping areas: Downtown Aiken offers a variety of art galleries, antique shops and boutiques.

AIKEN COUNTY HISTORICAL MUSEUM, 433 Newberry St. S.W., occupies Banksia, the 1930 estate of Richard Howe. Rooms depict late 18th- and early 19th-century life in Aiken County. Displays include military and American Indian artifacts, a drugstore from the former town of Dunbarton and a handmade miniature circus featuring 1,700 pieces. Tues.-Sat. 10-5, Sun. 2-5; closed holidays. Donations. Phone (803) 642-2015.

HOPELANDS GARDENS AND THOROUGHBRED RACING HALL OF FAME, .5 mi. s. off SR 19 at 149 Dupree Pl., is on the grounds of a former estate. A restored carriage house contains racing silks, trophies, photographs and other Thoroughbred racing memorabilia. There also is a changing equine art display. A touch and scent trail lined with identification plaques in Braille leads to the Performing Arts Stage. Open-air concerts are presented Monday evenings May through August.

Gardens daily 10-dusk. Hall of Fame Tues.-Sun. 2-5, Sept.-May; Sat.-Sun. 2-5, rest of year. Donations. Phone (803) 642-7630, or (803) 642-7631 for concert information.

ANDERSON (B-1) pop. 25,514, elev. 787′

Anderson was nicknamed "Electric City" because of its early innovation with electric power.

Anderson Convention and Visitors Bureau: 110 Federal St., Suite 8, Anderson, SC 29625; phone (864) 716-3660 or (877) 282-4650.

ANDERSON COUNTY MUSEUM, 202 E. Greenville St., has several local history displays, including quilts and cotton exhibits. Guided tours are available. Allow 15 minutes minimum. Tues.-Sat. 10-4 (also Tues. 4-7); closed major holidays. Donations. Phone (864) 260-4737.

SADLERS CREEK STATE RECREATION AREA is 7.2 mi. s. of jct. SRs 24 and 187 at 940 Sadlers Creek Rd. Primitive camping, hiking, boating and fishing are offered. Wildlife, including wild turkeys, can be seen. Picnicking is permitted. Allow 30 minutes minimum. Daily 6 a.m.-10 p.m. during DST; 7 a.m.-6 p.m. (also Fri. 6-8 p.m.), rest of year. Admission $2; $1.25 (ages 65+); free (ages 0-15). MC, VI. Phone (864) 226-8950. *See Recreation Chart.*

AWENDAW—*see Charleston p. 236.*

BEAUFORT (E-4) pop. 12,950, elev. 15′

A picturesque old port town, Beaufort (BEW-fort) retains the atmosphere of an earlier day. Its many pre-Revolutionary War and antebellum houses surrounded by quiet gardens stand along narrow oak-canopied streets. The oldest is the 1717 Thomas Hepworth House at Port Republic and New streets.

Established by charter from the Lords Proprietors in 1711, Beaufort is the second oldest town in the state. Its history dates back to Spanish exploration in 1520 and attempted settlements on nearby Parris Island by French Huguenots in 1562 and the Spanish in 1566 and 1577. Areas of early settlement have been the focus of several archeological digs.

In March 1863 the Beaufort National Cemetery was established. Today the remains of more than 7,500 Civil War soldiers as well as those of 6,500 other servicemen killed in action in subsequent wars are interred there. It is the final resting place of Marine Corps Pfc. Ralph H. Johnson, who posthumously received the Congressional Medal of Honor for service as a reconnaissance scout in Vietnam. The cemetery is surrounded by a brick wall, with the entrance at 1601 Boundary St.

Moviemakers have made their mark on Beaufort. "The Big Chill," "The Great Santini" and the blockbuster "Forrest Gump" are three of the movies that have been filmed in the city.

Facing the Intracoastal Waterway, Beaufort has one of the best natural harbors on the Atlantic coast. The Henry C. Chambers Waterfront Park, on the Beaufort River off Bay Street, includes a marina, pavilion and amphitheater. Also in the area is Lady's Island, across the Beaufort River.

Greater Beaufort Visitors Center: 2001 Boundary St., Suite 2, P.O. Box 910, Beaufort, SC 29902-0910; phone (843) 524-3163 or (800) 638-3525.

Self-guiding tours: Maps for walking tours of the historic district are available from the visitor center.

BEAUFORT ARSENAL MUSEUM, 713 Craven St., is housed in the 1798 Beaufort Arsenal, which features changing exhibits about the city's military and political history. **CLOSURE INFORMATION:** The museum is expected to be closed for renovations until spring 2009. Phone ahead to confirm reopening and to verify schedule and admission. Mon.-Sat. 10-4; closed holidays. Admission $4; free (ages 0-6). Phone (843) 379-3331.

ST. HELENA'S EPISCOPAL CHURCH is at 505 Church St. between King and North sts. and was founded in 1712. The wooden altar was carved by the crew of the USS *New Hampshire,* which was stationed nearby during Reconstruction. In the churchyard are tombstones used as operating tables during the Civil War and a brick sepulcher built for a doctor who feared being buried alive. His friends promised to place bread, water and an ax in his tomb to ensure his escape. The cemetery grounds are open to visitors. Tues.-Fri. 10-4, Sat. 10-noon. Donations. Phone (843) 522-1712.

SAVE **SPIRIT OF OLD BEAUFORT WALKING TOURS** depart from 103 West St. Extension. Guides in period attire comment on architecture, history, horticulture and other topics during a walking tour of historic Beaufort. Guides entertain guests with songs. An evening ghost tour, Whispers from the Grave, also is featured. An entertainment program showcasing historic Southern culture is available by reservation.

Allow 1 hour, 30 minutes minimum. Historical tour departs Mon.-Sat. at 10:30 and 2. Whispers From the Grave tour departs at 7. Fee $13; $8 (ages 6-12). Reservations are required. DS, MC, VI. Phone (843) 525-0459.

THE VERDIER HOUSE, 801 Bay St. across from Henry C. Chambers Waterfront Park, is a fine Federal-style residence built around 1802. Forty-minute guided tours point out highlights from when the home belonged to the prominent Verdier family, when the Marquis de Lafayette visited the house and spoke to Beaufort residents in 1825 and when the house served as headquarters for the Union Army during the Civil War. Nineteenth-century furnishings adorn the interior. Mon.-Sat. 10:30-3:30; closed major holidays. Admission $5; free (ages 0-6). Phone (843) 379-6335.

BISHOPVILLE (B-4) pop. 3,670, elev. 226′

Bishopville, seat of the state's largest cotton producing county, features a museum dedicated to the history of the cotton culture *(see attraction listing).* Visitors with a penchant for creative gardening can walk among 400 whimsical topiary plants on 3 acres in Fryar's Topiary Garden, created by an amateur gardener who gained national recognition as a plant artist. The garden is at 145 Broad Acres Rd.

SOUTH CAROLINA COTTON MUSEUM, 121 W. Cedar Ln., chronicles the history of cotton production in the South. Exhibits include scales, machines, cotton bales, photographs and a crop duster. A research library relates the history of cotton. Allow 30 minutes minimum. Mon.-Sat. 10-4; closed major holidays. Admission $5; $3 (ages 61+); $2 (students with ID); free (ages 0-5). MC, VI. Phone (803) 484-4497.

BLACKVILLE (D-3) pop. 2,973, elev. 292′

H. FLOWE TREXLER REGION 3 DISCOVERY CENTER is 3.5 mi. w. of jct. SR 3 on US 78 at 87 Heritage Rd. in the Clemson Agricultural Research Facility. Nearby rivers, railroads and crossroads are profiled at this interactive discovery center. Visitors can walk down a hallway designed to resemble a train car; television screens with outdoor images occupy the fictional window openings. Kiosks, videos, audio narratives and interpretive panels provide historical information.

Other exhibits feature early settlement and the Revolutionary and Civil wars. Guided tours are available. Allow 45 minutes minimum. Tues.-Sat. 10-5; closed major holidays. Donations. Phone (803) 284-3976.

BLUFFTON (E-3) pop. 1,275, elev. 25′

Bluffton was named for its location overlooking the May River. With giant, moss-draped oaks, small stores, antebellum houses and quaint country churches, the historic district has managed to retain its small-town charm despite the changing pace as nearby Hilton Head Island grew into a booming tourist destination. The highway that connects the island to the mainland runs through the outskirts of Bluffton.

The wooden, Gothic-style Church of the Cross, on Calhoun Street, was built in 1857 and has survived the onslaught of Union soldiers, hurricanes and modern development.

Bluffton Visitor Center: 70 Boundary St., P.O. Box 742, Bluffton, SC 29910; phone (843) 757-6293.

Shopping areas: More than 100 apparel, home and specialty stores, including Coach, Liz Claiborne, Nike, Polo Ralph Lauren and Seiko, comprise SAVE Tanger Factory Outlet Center, about 15 miles east of I-95 on US 278.

HEYWARD HOUSE HISTORIC CENTER, 70 Boundary St., was built in the 1840s as a summer retreat for plantation owner John James Cole. One of the area's few remaining antebellum residences, the simple, timber-frame house exemplifies Carolina farmhouse architecture and includes original furnishings. A summer kitchen and a slave cabin are on the grounds.

Guided tours are available. Allow 30 minutes minimum. Mon.-Fri. 10-3, Sat. 11-2; closed major holidays. Admission $5; $2 (students with ID); free (ages 0-9). DS, MC, VI. Phone (843) 757-6293.

CAMDEN (B-4) pop. 6,682, elev. 222'

Camden, the oldest inland town in the state, has roots dating back to the 1730s, and Irish Quakers arrived in the early 1750s. The town was called Fredericksburg and Pine Tree Hill before being changed in 1768 to honor Lord Camden, a friend of the Colonies.

More than a dozen Revolutionary War battles, including the Battle of Camden and the Battle of Hobkirk Hill, were fought within 30 miles of Camden. On May 8, 1781, the British evacuated Camden after burning most of it.

Bethesda Presbyterian Church, 502 DeKalb St., was designed in 1822 by Robert Mills, the architect of the Washington Monument. A granite monument in front of the church is dedicated to Baron DeKalb, a Revolutionary War soldier of Austrian descent killed in the Battle of Camden. The cornerstone was laid by the Marquis de Lafayette in 1825. Another memorial, Monument Square at Broad and Laurens streets, honors Camden's six Confederate generals.

Springdale Race Course hosts two steeplechases; the Carolina Cup is held in late March and the Colonial Cup in mid-November. Camden's polo field and 200 miles of bridle paths and country roads also lure equestrians.

Kershaw County Chamber of Commerce: 607 S. Broad St., P.O. Box 605, Camden, SC 29020; phone (803) 432-2525 or (800) 968-4037.

Self-guiding tours: A booklet detailing a driving tour past 63 historic sites, some of which are open to the public, is available from Historic Camden Revolutionary War Site, Camden Archives and Museum *(see attraction listings)* and the chamber of commerce for a cost of $5.

CAMDEN ARCHIVES AND MUSEUM, 1314 Broad St. in the 1915 Carnegie Library building, chronicles Camden's history and heritage. Displays include the original town clockworks dating from the 1820s and items from Confederate history, including an exhibit about Richard Kirkland, a local hero who fought at the Battle of Fredericksburg.

A library with genealogical and local history information also is available. Allow 30 minutes minimum. Mon.-Fri. 8-5, first and third Sun. of the month 1-5; closed holidays. Free. Phone (803) 425-6050.

FINE ARTS CENTER OF KERSHAW COUNTY, at 810 Lyttleton St., displays a variety of works of art and offers educational opportunities in the fine and performing arts. Allow 30 minutes minimum. Mon.-Fri. noon-6, Sat. by appointment only. Free. Phone (803) 425-7676.

SAVE **HISTORIC CAMDEN REVOLUTIONARY WAR SITE** is 1 mi. s. on US 521 at 222 S. Broad St. On the 107-acre site are restored buildings, including the Bradley, Craven, Cunningham and Drakeford houses. A nature trail leads to reconstructions of Revolutionary War fortifications, the powder magazine and the 1777 Kershaw-Cornwallis House, which British general Charles Cornwallis made his war headquarters. A Revolutionary War encampment is held the first full weekend in November.

Picnicking is permitted. Mon.-Sat. 10-5, Sun. 2-5; closed major holidays. Guided tours are given Fri. at 10:30, 1:30 and 3, Tues.-Thurs. at 10:30 and 3, Sat. 10:30-noon and 1:30-4, and Sun. 2:30-4. Phone ahead to verify schedule. Self-guiding tours are free. Guided tour $5; $4 (ages 65+ and military with ID); $3 (ages 6-18). Phone (803) 432-9841.

NATIONAL STEEPLECHASE MUSEUM is 1.7 mi. n. on US 521/601, then .9 mi. w. on Knights Hill Rd. to Springdale Race Course, which is a working steeplechase training facility. The museum presents the history of steeplechasing in the United States through interactive exhibits and memorabilia. Displays include photographs of competitions, silks of national champions, and trophies and awards. Equine history also is highlighted.

Allow 30 minutes minimum. Wed.-Sat. 10-4 and by appointment, Sept.-May; by appointment rest of year. Closed major holidays. Donations. Phone (803) 432-6513.

Charleston

City Population: 96,650 **Elevation:** 10 ft.

Editor's Picks:

Charleston Ghost Hunt ....*(see p. 227)*

Magnolia Plantation and Gardens............................*(see p. 222)*

South Carolina Aquarium ....*(see p. 222)*

Find more AAA top picks at AAA.com

© Jon Arnold Images / Danita Delimont Stock Photography

Preservation is a way of life in Charleston. From stately antebellum houses to the more utilitarian single houses that shoulder the narrow streets, this 300-year-old city is renowned for its splendid architecture. Embellished with fanciful wrought-iron details as intricate as window frost, and painted sparkling whites, pastels or whimsical rainbow hues, Charleston's houses delight the eye.

Once a cradle of Southern gentility, Charleston is now one of its last bastions. Ancestral pride runs deeper than the Ashley and Cooper rivers that shape the slender peninsula on which the city is built. A story that many locals tell illustrates the Charlestonian spirit. It concerns a wealthy matron who was asked repeatedly why she didn't spend some of her money on travel. "But my dear," she was said to reply, "why should I travel when I'm already here?" Charleston epitomizes the gracious air of the Old South, where life moves at the leisurely pace of a stroll along The Battery.

Though easygoing and elegant, Charleston gave America its first decisive victory in the Revolutionary War and the first defiant shots of the Civil War. A pioneer in civic affairs, the city established the country's first municipal chamber of commerce, municipal college and public museum. In 1931 it passed the first historic district zoning ordinance to preserve its architectural heritage.

Named for King Charles II, Charles Towne was founded in 1670 by English settlers along the marshy shores of nearby Albemarle Point. The settlement relocated to its present site 10 years later. Despite American Indian uprisings, a threat by the French, epidemics and privateers, Charles Towne had developed into a vigorous port and a prosperous and fashionable Colonial city by the mid-1700s.

Though drawn reluctantly into the Revolution, Charles Towne stubbornly repulsed a British attack by sea in 1776 and a second offensive by land 2 years later before it finally was captured in 1780. The British left in 1782, and the city was incorporated as Charleston the following year.

In 1860 South Carolina passed the first Ordinance of Secession at Charleston, and in April 1861 the Confederates occupied Fort Sumter. For 3 years Union ships blockaded the city, battering Fort Sumter with artillery fire, but the defenders refused to yield. Submarine warfare was introduced in Charleston when the Confederate vessel *H.L. Hunley* sank the USS *Housatonic*. The Confederate Army finally abandoned the city late in the war.

Charleston's historic district encompasses more than 2,000 buildings: 73 predate the Revolutionary War, 136 date from the late 1700s and more than 600 others were built in the early 1800s. So many church spires poke at the sky that Charleston once was nicknamed The Holy City. Many churches are

Getting There — *starting on p. 213*

Getting Around — *starting on p. 216*

What To See — *starting on p. 216*

What To Do — *starting on p. 224*

Where To Stay — *starting on p. 881*

Where To Dine — *starting on p. 895*

Essential Experiences — *visit AAA.com*

Editor's Event Picks — *visit AAA.com*

open for self-guiding and guided tours on a regular basis *(see attraction listings and AAA Walking Tours)*. The Unitarian Church, 4 Archdale St., offers tours on a limited schedule; phone (843) 723-4617 for details. Emanuel African Methodist Episcopal Church, 110 Calhoun St. between E. Bay and Meeting sts., is the oldest African Methodist Episcopal Church in the South. The 1891 structure reflects Gothic Revival architecture, and the exterior includes the dedication plaque; phone (843) 722-2561. The Jewish Heritage Collection, 205 Calhoun St., is in the Addlestone Library on the College of Charleston campus and is a research facility for Jewish history in South Carolina. The site is open Monday through Friday 9-5; phone (843) 953-8028.

Hurricane Hugo's assault in 1989 resulted in massive damages in Charleston as well as statewide, but 95 percent of the city's structures survived and the historic district remained intact.

The Battery, the waterfront along the edge of the historic district, offers fine views of the harbor. North of The Battery along E. Bay Street is a particularly colorful collection of houses known as Rainbow Row. A distinctive residential style is the single house, a narrow structure one room wide and two rooms deep with its gabled end, rather than its front, facing the street. Often a single house includes a piazza—the city's version of a veranda—and the pride of any Charleston home: a garden.

Nowhere does Charleston flaunt its beauty more than in its gardens. From the magnificent scale of the nearby plantation gardens to the more modest but equally enchanting walled gardens in the city, the area's lavish floral displays are known throughout the world. Charlestonians proudly show many of their private residences and gardens during the spring and fall tours of houses.

© David R. Frazier / Danita Delimont Stock Photography

Getting There

By Car

The major approach from the north and south is US 17, which angles into the city proper over the Ravenel Bridge on the east and the Ashley River bridges to the west. US 17 cuts directly across the heart of Charleston and provides easy access to all parts of the city. US 17 links with I-526 to bypass the city.

I-26 approaches from the west, terminating at US 17 near the center of Charleston. It provides a link with several important routes, including I-95, another major north-south highway.

SR 61 is a scenic approach paralleling the Ashley River on the west and giving access to several historic plantations. Other important approaches include US 52, which parallels I-26 immediately west of Charleston; SR 41, which traverses the Lowcountry to the north and terminates at US 17 northeast of the city; and US 701, also from the north, which merges with US 17 and terminates in Charleston.

Destination Charleston

Cultured and refined, Charleston is a beautifully preserved treasure. Steeped in history and quintessentially Southern, the city's past is evident in its genteel charm.

Architectural gems from the 18th- and 19th-centuries are easy to admire for their beauty, but they also help recall the city's Revolutionary War and Civil War heritage.

© Tumbleston Photography

Gibbes Museum of Art, Charleston. The extensive collection includes paintings and portraits that offer a peek into South Carolina's Colonial era as well as early 20th-century Charleston. (See listing page 220)

© Spoleto Festival U.S.A.

Spoleto Festival, U.S.A., Charleston. Memorial Day weekend ushers in this grand celebration of the arts, which lasts for more than 2 weeks. (See mention page 235)

© South Carolina Aquarium

South Carolina Aquarium, Charleston. Here you can get close-up views of amazing underwater inhabitants. (See listing page 222)

Moncks Corner
Harleyville
52
26
78
Summerville
McClellanville
Awendaw
North Charleston
Charleston
17
526
Mount Pleasant
Isle of Palms
Sullivan's Island
17
Rockville
Edisto Island

See Downtown map page 217

Middleton Place, Charleston. When you explore these grounds, you are walking in the country's oldest landscaped gardens, which date back to 1741. (See listing page 223)

© Middleton Place

Places included in this AAA Destination City:

The Informed Traveler

Sales Tax: South Carolina sales tax is 6 percent. There is an admissions tax of 5 percent on most amusements and a 2 percent accommodations tax. The Charleston area has a lodging tax of 12 percent and a rental car tax of 10 percent.

WHOM TO CALL

Emergency: 911

Police (non-emergency): (843) 577-7434

Hospitals: Bon Secours-St. Francis Hospital, (843) 402-1000; Medical University of South Carolina Medical Center, (843) 792-2300; Roper Hospital, (843) 724-2000; Trident Medical Center, (843) 797-7000.

WHERE TO LOOK

Newspapers

The major daily newspaper in Charleston is *The Post and Courier*. The area also is served by several local weekly newspapers.

Radio

Charleston radio station WTMZ (910 AM) is an all-news/weather station; WSCI (89.3 FM) is a member of National Public Radio.

Visitor Information

Charleston Area Convention and Visitors Bureau: 423 King St., Charleston, SC 29403; phone (843) 853-8000 or (800) 868-8118.

Operated by the Charleston Area Convention and Visitors Bureau, the Charleston Visitor Center is at 375 Meeting St. Self-guiding tour maps, brochures, information about events and performance schedules are available. The center is open daily 8:30-5 (also 5-5:30 during DST); phone (843) 853-8000 or (800) 868-8118.

TRANSPORTATION

Air Travel

Most major carriers serve Charleston International Airport, 12 miles west on I-26.

Rental Cars

Hertz, (843) 767-4550 or (800) 654-3080, is at the airport and offers discounts to AAA members. For listings of other agencies check the telephone directory.

Rail Service

The Amtrak train station, (800) 872-7245, is at 4565 Gaynor Ave. in North Charleston.

Buses

Service is provided by Greyhound Lines Inc., (843) 744-4247 or (800) 231-2222, at 3610 Dorchester Rd.

Taxis

Cab companies include Safety Cab, (843) 722-4066, and Yellow Cab, (843) 577-6565. Taxis are on the meter system; the fare is $2 upon entering the cab, and $1.75 per mile. Fares within the city limits average $3.50 for the first passenger, $1 for each additional passenger; outside the city limits $1 per mile is added to the base rate. Cabs must be ordered by phone.

Public Transport

Bus service is provided by Charleston Area Regional Transit Authority (CARTA); phone (843) 747-0922 for information about routes and schedules.

Getting Around

Street System

Crowded as they are onto a narrow peninsula, most Charleston streets are parallel or perpendicular, and many are narrow or one-way. While a rough grid is evident, the angle of the grid shifts along the dividing line of Beaufain and Hasell streets in the lower part of town.

Several major north-south streets traverse the city. King Street (US 78), one-way heading south below Calhoun St., and Meeting Street (US 52), a two-way street one block east, run through downtown and the historic districts. E. Bay Street (US 52A) branches off from Meeting Street in the north and winds down the east side, becoming E. Battery Street and then Murray Boulevard as it swings around The Battery. Ashley and Rutledge streets, a block apart and going one way north and south respectively, connect with the western end of Murray Boulevard.

Major east-west streets that cross all of the above thoroughfares south of the US 17 artery include Calhoun and Broad streets, both going two ways, and Tradd Street, one way eastbound. The speed limit is 30 mph unless otherwise posted.

Unless otherwise posted, a right turn on red and a left turn from a one-way street onto a one-way street are permitted after a complete stop.

Parking

Metered parking at 25c for 20 minutes can be found on downtown streets; metered spaces are free after 6 p.m. and on Sunday. Parking garages also are available throughout the area; fees are $1-$2 per hour. Some garages offer early-bird specials of $5-$10 for all-day parking.

What To See

AIKEN-RHETT HOUSE, 48 Elizabeth St., was built 1818 by merchant John Robinson and later remodeled by Gov. William Aiken Jr. The preserved mansion contains decorative items and furnishings purchased by the Aikens while touring Europe in the mid-19th century. An audio tour of the urban plantation guides visitors through the house and to several outbuildings, including the kitchen, stables and slave quarters.

Allow 1 hour minimum. Mon.-Sat. 10-5, Sun. 2-5; closed Thanksgiving and Dec. 24-25. Admission $10. Combination ticket with Nathaniel Russell House $16. DS, MC, VI. Phone (843) 723-1159.

AMERICAN MILITARY MUSEUM is at 360 Concord St. in Suite 9 at Aquarium Wharf. American military history since the Revolutionary War is presented through displays of artifacts, including badges, flags, medals, weapons and 400 uniforms. Several hundred miniature military figures are used throughout the exhibits. All branches of the military are represented.

Guided tours are available. Allow 30 minutes minimum. Mon.-Sat. 10-6, Sun. 1-5; closed Thanksgiving and Dec. 25. Admission $7; $5 (ages 55+ and military veterans with ID); $3 (ages 13-18); $2 (ages 6-12); free (active military duty). AX, DS, MC, VI. Phone (843) 577-7000.

Drayton Hall / © Gibson Stock Photography

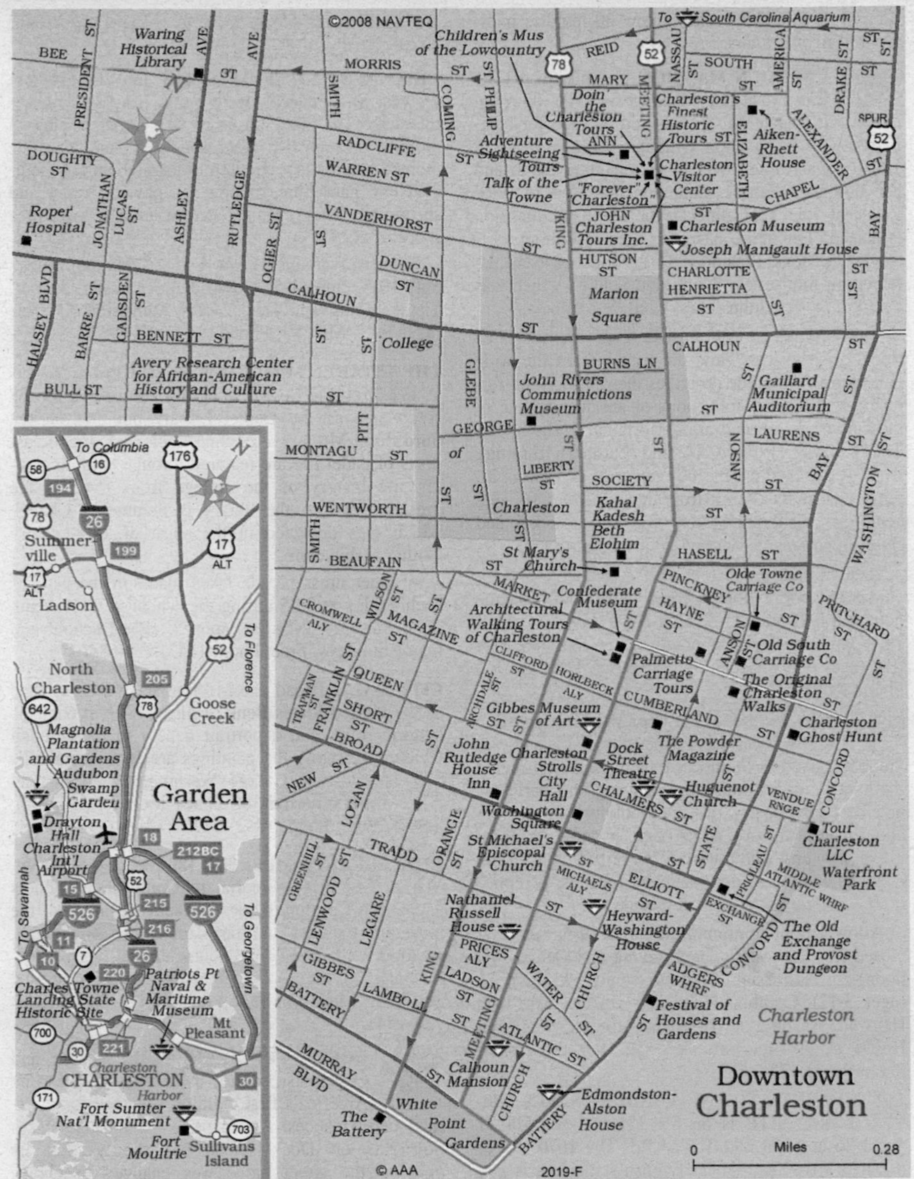

AVERY RESEARCH CENTER FOR AFRICAN-AMERICAN HISTORY AND CULTURE, 125 Bull St., offers regional art exhibits featuring sweetgrass baskets and handwoven fish nets as well as historical source materials documenting the relationship between the regions of West Africa and the Sea Islands of Georgia, Florida and the Carolinas. A video and linguistics display tracing African languages also can be viewed.

Guided tours are available. Allow 1 hour minimum. Mon.-Fri. 10-5, Sat. noon-5; closed holidays and Dec. 24-Jan. 4. Donations. Phone (843) 953-7609.

THE BATTERY is on Battery Point at the waterfront. The East, or High Battery, faces the Cooper River and Charleston Harbor, where some of the settlement's earliest fortifications were. White Point Gardens, planted with palmettos and live oaks, contains cannons, war relics and a monument to the defenders of Fort Moultrie and Fort Sumter. Many walking, motorized and carriage tours include The

Battery on their itineraries. Allow 30 minutes minimum. Daily 24 hours. Free.

GEM **CALHOUN MANSION** is 1 blk. n. of The Battery at 16 Meeting St. The 35-room Italianate house was built in 1876 for businessman George Walton Williams. After his death in 1903, it was turned over to his daughter Sarah and her husband, Patrick Calhoun (grandson of Vice President John C. Calhoun), for whom the mansion is named. The house has been used in filming various productions, including "The Notebook" and the television miniseries "North and South," which was based on author John Jakes' Civil War trilogy.

Thirty-minute tours include two of the three floors; visitors can view the rooms from the wide hallways as the guide describes their history and furnishings. The vast collections of antiques belong to the current owner and are not original to the house. There is American, Asian and European furniture from the 17th- through 19th centuries as well as international pieces of art from the 16th- through 19th centuries. Visitors can tour the Japanese koi and English gardens before and after the house tour.

A 90-minute grand tour also is available and includes the entire house. Tours depart daily on the hour and half-hour 11-5, Mar.-Nov.; 11-4:30, rest of year. Grand tour by appointment. Admission $15; free (ages 0-11). Grand tour $50. AX, DS, MC, VI. Phone (843) 722-8205.

SAVE **CHARLESTON MUSEUM,** 360 Meeting St. at John St., was established in 1773 and, although housed in a modern facility, is considered the nation's oldest museum. Focusing on Charleston and the Lowcountry, the museum houses displays about natural history, archeology, ornithology, decorative arts and cultural history. A children's room contains computers and hands-on exhibits. A replica of *H.L. Hunley* is displayed outside.

Allow 1 hour minimum. Mon.-Sat. 9-5, Sun. 1-5; closed Jan. 1, Easter, Thanksgiving and Dec. 24 (at noon)-25. Admission $10; $9 (senior citizens); $5 (ages 3-12). Combination tickets are available with Heyward-Washington House or Joseph Manigault House at $16 for two sites, $22 for three sites. Phone (843) 722-2996.

SAVE **CHARLES TOWNE LANDING STATE HISTORIC SITE** is on SR 171 between US 17 and I-26 at 1500 Old Towne Rd. The 1670 site of the state's first permanent English settlement is part of a 664-acre park in which early earthworks and a palisade have been reconstructed. Visitors can see a replica of a 17th-century trading vessel, a servants' living quarters, archeology digs and a 22-acre zoo featuring animal species known to the first settlers. A self-guiding audio tour explains the site's features. Exhibits in the visitor center showcase settlement life and the establishment of the new colony.

The site also includes 3 miles of interpretive trails, bicycle trails, history programs and a marsh boardwalk. Picnicking is permitted. Allow 3 hours minimum. Daily 9-5; closed Dec. 24-25. Admission $5; $3.25 (ages 65+); $3 (ages 6-15). Phone (843) 852-4200.

CHILDREN'S MUSEUM OF THE LOWCOUNTRY, 25 Ann St. between Meeting and King sts., houses interactive exhibits designed for children ages 3 months through 12 years and their families. The themed areas allow children to learn about the medieval era, gardening, motion and physics, water and shrimping. They can also create art and shop in a grocery store.

Food is available. Allow 1 hour minimum. Tues.-Sat. 10-5, Sun. 1-5; closed Jan. 1, Easter, July 4, Thanksgiving and Dec. 24-25. Admission $7; free (ages 0-1). MC, VI. Phone (843) 853-8962.

THE CITADEL MUSEUM is on the Citadel campus at 171 Moultrie St. The museum entrance is on the south side of the Daniel Library building on the third floor. Military, academic, social and athletic aspects of cadet life are featured through exhibits tracing the history of the college from 1842 to the present. Next to the library is Summerall Chapel, which was designed in the spirit of 14th-century Gothic architecture.

A cadet dress parade takes place on the campus each Friday at 3:45 during the school year. Museum open Sun.-Fri. 2-5, Sat. noon-5; closed school and major holidays. Free. Phone (843) 953-6846.

CITY HALL, Broad and Meeting sts., first was used as the United States Bank. Built in 1801, it contains historic relics and a portrait gallery in the Council Chamber. Among the paintings are John Trumbull's 1791 portrait of George Washington and Samuel F.B. Morse's portrait of James Monroe. Mon.-Fri. 8:30-5. Free. Phone (843) 577-6970.

CONFEDERATE MUSEUM, 188 Meeting St. at jct. Market St., is a memorial to Confederate soldiers and South Carolina heroes. Established in 1894, the museum displays military uniforms, equipment, weaponry, memorabilia, documents and flags. Allow 30 minutes minimum. Tues.-Sat. 11-3:30; closed holidays. Admission $5; $3 (ages 6-12). Phone (843) 723-1541.

GEM **DOCK STREET THEATRE,** Church and Queen sts., opened in 1736. It is said to be America's first building designed for theatrical performances. At that time the theater's location was on Dock Street, but shortly after its opening the street name was changed to Queen Street. The building is believed to have been destroyed by fire in 1740.

The Planter's Hotel was built on the site in 1809 and was a rendezvous for the gentry; the drink Planter's Punch is said to have originated there. In the mid-1930s the hotel was remodeled into the new Dock Street Theatre as a Works Progress Administration project.

Charleston Stage Company is the theater company in residence; frequent performances are staged in the theater and foyer. **CLOSURE INFORMATION:** The theater is closed for renovations and is scheduled to reopen spring 2010; phone ahead for updates. Phone (843) 577-5967 for Charleston Stage Company information.

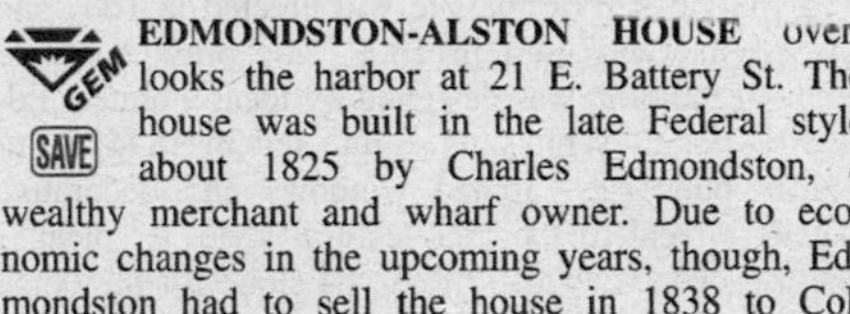

EDMONDSTON-ALSTON HOUSE overlooks the harbor at 21 E. Battery St. The house was built in the late Federal style about 1825 by Charles Edmondston, a wealthy merchant and wharf owner. Due to economic changes in the upcoming years, though, Edmondston had to sell the house in 1838 to Col. William Alston, who bought it for his son, Charles.

Charles Alston made additions, including a third-floor piazza and a rooftop parapet, to transform the house into the Greek Revival style. The house is furnished with Alston family possessions, including books, documents, portraits, engravings, furniture, silver and porcelain. It also contains elaborate and unconventional woodwork.

Two Confederate generals visited the house in 1861: Gen. P.T. Beauregard witnessed Fort Sumter's bombardment from here on April 12 and Gen. Robert E. Lee boarded on December 11 when a fire threatened his hotel.

Allow 30 minutes minimum. Guided 30-minute tours Tues.-Sat. 10-4:30, Sun.-Mon. 1:30-4:30 (also Mon. starting at 10, mid-Mar to mid-Apr.); closed Thanksgiving and Dec. 25. Last tour begins at closing. Admission $10; $8 (students with ID); free (ages 0-5). A combination ticket is available with Middleton Place. DS, MC, VI. Phone (843) 722-7171.

FALL TOUR OF HOMES & GARDENS locations vary, but all are downtown on the peninsula. To benefit The Preservation Society of Charleston, owners of private residences open up their homes in the autumn to allow visitors to take self-guiding tours. Gardens and public buildings also are included, but the majority of the sites are private houses. Each tour includes eight to ten locales representing a variety of architectural styles. A volunteer stays in each room and garden at each location on the tour.

Note: Tickets go on sale June 1 and often sell out in advance. They may be purchased at the Preservation Society's book shop and offices at 147 King St., and tickets that were pre-ordered must be picked up here as well. Backpacks and high-heeled shoes are not permitted on tours. Allow 2 hours minimum. Tours are offered Thurs.-Sat. 7-10 p.m., Sun. 2-5, Sept. 24-Oct. 25, 2009. Fee $45. Fee $120 (for a Thurs.-Sat. ticket for the same week). Under age 8 are not permitted. MC, VI. Phone (843) 722-4630.

FESTIVAL OF HOUSES AND GARDENS tickets may be purchased at 108 Meeting St. The festival features walking tours of private houses and gardens, most dating 1712-1850. Other events such as harbor cruises, luncheons and wine tastings also are offered. For dates of events write the Historic Charleston Foundation, P.O. Box 1120, Charleston, SC 29402. Afternoon tours 2-5, plantation oyster roasts 4:30-7 and candlelight tours 6-9 p.m., Mar.

Charleston Heritage Passport

Charleston Heritage Passport offers savings to those who plan to visit Charleston's historic and cultural attractions. Valid for 1 year from purchase, the passport covers the price of admission to nine sites: Aiken-Rhett House, Charleston Museum, Drayton Hall, Edmondston-Alston House, Gibbes Museum of Art, Heyward-Washington House, Joseph Manigault House, Middleton Place (gardens and stable yard only) and Nathaniel Russell House.

The passport may not be combined with any other discount and is not valid for admission during special events.

The passport can be purchased at the Charleston Visitor Center, 375 Meeting St., for $59.95. A 2-day pass is available for $39.95. For more information phone (843) 853-8000 or (800) 868-8118.

19-Apr. 18, 2009. Fee $45. Reservations are strongly recommended. AX, MC, VI. Phone (843) 722-3405 or (843) 723-1623.

"FOREVER CHARLESTON" is presented in the Charleston Visitor Center at 375 Meeting St. Using the voices of Charleston residents, the 24-minute film conveys the story of one of America's founding cities. The footage helps to orient visitors by cataloging the sights and sounds of Charleston and the Lowcountry, thereby revealing the beauty of the city and the heritage of its people.

Shows are given daily every 45 minutes 9-4:30, Apr.-Oct.; 9-3:45, rest of year. Closed Jan. 1, Thanksgiving and Dec. 25. Admission $2; $1.50 (ages 61+); $1 (ages 0-9). Phone (843) 723-5225.

FORT MOULTRIE—
see Fort Sumter National Monument p. 236.

GIBBES MUSEUM OF ART, 135 Meeting St., has an outstanding collection of American paintings, sculpture, engravings, photographs, miniature portraits and other art objects. Artists represented throughout the museum include Jonathan Green, Childe Hassam, Alfred Hutty, Henrietta Johnston, Alice Ravenel Huger Smith, Thomas Sully, Anna Heyward Taylor and Benjamin West.

A variety of portraits done by artists working with European techniques represents Colonial South Carolina. Early 20th-century Charleston is showcased in a collection of works featuring such themes as nature, architecture and everyday activities. Changing exhibits, concerts and lectures are presented throughout the year.

Allow 30 minutes minimum. Tues.-Sat. 10-5, Sun. 1-5; closed major holidays. Admission $9; $7 (ages 62+, military and students with ID); $5 (ages 6-12). AX, MC, VI. Phone (843) 722-2706.

HEYWARD-WASHINGTON HOUSE is at 87 Church St. The 1772 brick house was built by prominent rice planter Daniel Heyward for his son Thomas Heyward Jr., an artillery officer in South Carolina's militia during the American Revolution and a signer of the Declaration of Independence. The house was also named for George Washington, who was a guest during his visit to Charleston in May 1791.

Most of the furnishings are from Charleston. Guided house tours also include the servants' quarters, a 1740s kitchen building and a garden behind the main house. The formal garden showcases plants representative of those that would have been used in Charleston in the late 1700s.

Allow 30 minutes minimum. Mon.-Sat. 10-5, Sun. 1-5; closed Jan. 1, Easter, Thanksgiving and Dec. 24 (at noon)-25. Last tour begins 30 minutes before closing. Admission $10; $9 (senior citizens); $5 (ages 3-12). Combination tickets are available with Charleston Museum or Joseph Manigault House at $16 for two sites, $22 for three sites. Phone (843) 722-2996.

HUGUENOT CHURCH (French Protestant), 136 Church St., is the last remaining independent Huguenot church in the nation. The first church on the site was erected in 1687 and the second was built in 1800. The present Gothic Revival building was designed by local architect Edward Brickell White and completed in 1844; it includes buttresses, arched windows and decorative details typical of the architectural style. Atypical is the use of iron instead of carved stone for the detail work.

For 150 years services were conducted in French, but English is now used. A French liturgy service is held each year in the spring. Guided tours are available. Allow 30 minutes minimum. Mon.-Thurs. 10-4, Fri. 10-1, Mar.-June and Sept.-Nov.; closed holidays. Donations. Phone (843) 722-4385.

JOHN RIVERS COMMUNICATIONS MUSEUM is on the College of Charleston campus at 58 George St. The museum, housed in four rooms in the 1803 Bernard Elliot House, contains antiques representing the history of communications and broadcasting, including magic lanterns (antique oil-burning slide projectors), motion picture projectors, phonographs, radios and televisions. Visitors can learn about telegraphs, listen to old radio programs and watch early cartoons. The museum houses an impressive collection of music in all formats.

The museum is named after John Rivers Sr., president of Charleston's radio station WCSC, which later became a television station. Guided tours are available. Allow 45 minutes minimum. Mon.-Fri. noon-4, when college is in session; closed major holidays. Donations. Phone (843) 953-5810.

JOHN RUTLEDGE HOUSE INN, 116 Broad St., was the town house of John Rutledge, a leading South Carolina statesman and signer of the U.S. Constitution. Although it still operates as an inn, walk-in visitors can wander through the restored 1763 house and view public rooms. The house is furnished with antiques and period reproductions. Displayed in the upstairs parlor are relics from the restoration. Allow 30 minutes minimum. Open for walk-ins daily 10-4. Free. Phone (843) 723-7999.

JOSEPH MANIGAULT HOUSE, 350 Meeting St., was designed by Gabriel Manigault for his brother Joseph, a wealthy rice planter, and built in 1803. A notable house of the Adam style, it has fine examples of furniture made in Charleston, England and France. Some of the rooms have been restored and showcase original color schemes. A grand staircase leads to the second floor and a hidden stairway connects the second and third floors.

Visitors can tour the gardens on their own. Interpretive signs designate the location of such outbuildings as slave quarters and the stable that no longer exist. Each December, the Garden Club of Charleston decorates the house with plant varieties that would have been found in the area in the early 1800s.

Allow 30 minutes minimum. Guided tours Mon.-Sat. 10-5, Sun. 1-5; closed Jan. 1, Easter, Thanksgiving and Dec. 24 (at noon)-25. Last tour begins 30 minutes before closing. Admission $10; $9 (senior citizens); $5 (ages 3-12). Combination tickets are available with Charleston Museum or Heyward-Washington House at $16 for two sites, $22 for three sites. Phone (843) 722-2996.

KAHAL KADOSH BETH ELOHIM is at 90 Hasell St. Built by a congregation organized in 1749, the 1840 Greek Revival building is the nation's oldest synagogue in continuous use. The congregation's introduction in 1824 of instrumental music during a worship service made it a pioneer of Reform Judaism in the United States. A museum relates the history of the synagogue and Reform Judaism in the South. Guided temple tours are given Mon.-Fri. 10-noon and Sun. 12:30-3:45. Museum Mon.-Fri. and Sun. 10-noon. Free. Phone (843) 723-1090.

KARPELES MANUSCRIPT MUSEUM, 68 Spring St., is housed in a large 1847 Roman Revival temple that was used as a Confederate hospital and medical storehouse during the Civil War before the Union army attacked the city. It also served as the St. James Methodist Church. The building suffered much damage in 1989 from Hurricane Hugo and has since been renovated.

Displays of original historic documents representative of a variety of disciplines, including art, politics, religion and science, change quarterly. Translations are provided for non-English works. There also is a permanent photography exhibit about the construction of the new Cooper River Bridge. Allow 30 minutes minimum. Tues.-Sat. 11-4; closed major holidays. Free. Phone (843) 853-4651.

MAGNOLIA CEMETERY, about 1 mi. n. just off US 52 on the banks of the Cooper River, was established in 1849. Among its numerous ornate grave sites are those of South Carolina soldiers who died at Gettysburg as well as the crew from *H.L. Hunley.* Confederate Memorial Day services include a reading of Henry Timrod's ode, "Magnolia Cemetery," written for the first service in 1866. Allow 30 minutes minimum. Daily 8-5. Free.

MARION SQUARE is on Calhoun St. between King and Meeting sts. Also known as Citadel Green, the square has monuments to John C. Calhoun, vice president to John Quincy Adams, and to Wade Hampton, Confederate general and governor of South Carolina. The square also contains the Holocaust Memorial and the only remaining section of the bastion system of Colonial defense works. Fronting the square is the Old Citadel Building.

GEM **NATHANIEL RUSSELL HOUSE,** 51 Meeting St., was completed in 1808 for Nathaniel Russell, a wealthy merchant. Set in a spacious garden, the house is a fine example of Federal architecture. Notable features include a free-standing staircase that spirals up three floors as well as oval drawing rooms and ornate interior detailing. Period furnishings include works by Charleston craftsmen.

In 1857 Gov. Robert Francis Withers Allston bought the house, which his family owned until 1869. The following year the Sisters of Charity of Our Lady of Mercy purchased the house; these Catholic nuns ran a girls' school until 1901. The house belonged to the group until 1908, when a family moved into the home.

Allow 30 minutes minimum. Guided tours Mon.-Sat. 10-5, Sun. 2-5; closed Thanksgiving and Dec. 24-25. Last tour begins 30 minutes before closing. Admission $10; free (ages 0-5). Combination ticket with Aiken-Rhett House $16. AX, MC, VI. Phone (843) 724-8481.

THE OLD EXCHANGE AND PROVOST DUNGEON, 122 E. Bay St. at jct. Broad St., was built by the British in 1771 as the Exchange and Customs House for the prosperous city of Charles Towne. It was in the Great Hall that South Carolina ratified the Constitution in 1788. In the cellar where the British imprisoned prominent Patriots during the American Revolution, animatronics relate events important to early Charles Towne and the fledgling nation.

Allow 30 minutes minimum. Daily 9-5; closed Jan. 1, Thanksgiving and Dec. 25. Admission $7; $6 (ages 51+ and military with ID); $3.50 (ages 7-12). MC, VI. Phone (843) 727-2165 or (888) 763-0448.

THE POWDER MAGAZINE, 79 Cumberland St., was constructed 1712 during Charleston's proprietary period to store powder and weapons for the defense of the settlement. Reputed to be the oldest public building in the Carolinas, the restored magazine features artifacts and exhibits dealing with Colonial history. Allow 30 minutes minimum. Wed.-Sat. 10-4, late Mar.-early Nov. Hours may vary; phone ahead. Admission $2; $1 (ages 6-12). Phone (843) 722-9350.

ST. MARY'S CHURCH is between Meeting and King sts. at 89 Hasell St. Established in 1789, this is the Mother Church of the Catholic diocese of the Carolinas and Georgia. The church, dating from 1839, contains religious paintings. Mon.-Fri. 9:30-2. Donations. Phone (843) 722-7696.

GEM **ST. MICHAEL'S EPISCOPAL CHURCH** is at Broad and Meeting sts. Begun in 1752, St. Michael's was the second Episcopal church in Charleston. Designed after the 1720s St. Martin-in-the-Fields Church in London, it is considered a notable architectural achievement. Its Palladian Doric portico and steeple rise 186 feet above the street. The clock in the tower has marked the time since 1764, but the minute hand wasn't added until 1849. President George Washington attended the church on May 8, 1791, and Gen. Robert E. Lee visited during the early 1860s.

The richly ornamental interior includes box pews and the original pulpit. An old cemetery is on the grounds. Mon.-Wed. and Fri. 9-4:30, Thurs. 10-4:30. Donations. Phone (843) 723-0603.

SOUTH CAROLINA AQUARIUM, 100 Aquarium Wharf, showcases five regions of the Southeast Appalachian Watershed. Observation decks with viewing scopes overlook Charleston Harbor and the Cooper River. Free-flying birds inhabit the glass-enclosed aviary in the Mountain Forest Gallery, which includes indigenous plant life and stocked streams. The Piedmont Gallery explores the hill country's estuaries, reservoirs and aquatic insect species. The Saltmarsh Aviary features birds, marine life and plants found in salt marsh tidal creeks.

The Coast Gallery includes fish that can be found in the city's harbor. The Ocean Gallery's two-story, 385,000-gallon tank is filled with hundreds of sea animals. Snakes, turtles, frogs and fish live in the brackish waters of the Coastal Plain Gallery. The Touch Tank exhibit is filled with invertebrates. Behind-the-scenes tours are offered for an additional fee.

Food is available. Allow 1 hour, 30 minutes minimum. Mon.-Sat. 9-6, Sun. noon-6, Apr. 1-Aug. 15; Mon.-Sat. 9-5, Sun. noon-5, rest of year. Closed Thanksgiving and Dec. 25. Last admission 1 hour before closing. Phone for behind-the-scenes tour schedule. Admission $17; $16 (ages 62+); $10 (ages 2-11). Behind-the-scenes tour additional $10; $5 (ages 2-12). Parking under 1 hour, $1; 1-2 hours, $3; 3-4 hours, $5; 5-6 hours, $7. AX, DS, MC, VI. Phone (843) 720-1990.

WARING HISTORICAL LIBRARY, 175 Ashley Ave. on the Medical University of South Carolina campus, contains a large collection of medical books, some of which date back to the 1500s. There are prints, photographs, oral histories and more than 1,000 medical artifacts in this 1894 building. The MUSC archives also are housed here. Allow 20 minutes minimum. Mon.-Fri. 8:30-5; closed major state and federal holidays. Free. Phone (843) 792-2288.

Macaulay Museum of Dental History is on Ashley Ave. on the Medical University of South Carolina campus, adjacent to the Waring Historical Library at 175 Ashley Ave. Visitors must check in at the library before proceeding to the museum. South Carolina's history of dentistry is portrayed through artifacts, including dental chairs, manual drills, x-ray equipment and sets of teeth and dentures.

A highlight is an instrument that Revolutionary patriot Paul Revere made for Dr. Josiah Flagg, who was the first American born in this country to practice dentistry as his sole occupation. Allow 20 minutes minimum. Mon.-Fri. 8:30-5; closed major state and federal holidays. Free. Phone (843) 792-2288.

WASHINGTON SQUARE, or City Hall Park, at Broad and Meeting sts., includes several monuments honoring prominent South Carolinians. Among these are memorials to Henry Timrod, a noted South Carolina poet; Gen. P.G.T. Beauregard, leader of the city's defense during the Civil War; and the Washington Light Infantry. Also on the square is the Fireproof Building, the nation's first fireproof structure, designed by Robert Mills.

Gardens and Nearby Points of Interest

AUDUBON SWAMP GARDEN— *see Magnolia Plantation and Gardens p. 223.*

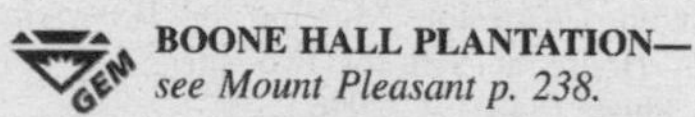
BOONE HALL PLANTATION— *see Mount Pleasant p. 238.*

DRAYTON HALL is 9 mi. n.w. on SR 61 at 3380 Ashley River Rd. Built about 1738 by John Drayton, a member of the Privy Council of the royal governor, the mansion remained in the family for seven generations. It is an outstanding example of Georgian Palladian architecture with hand-carved woodwork and plasterwork. Never modernized with electric lighting, plumbing or central heating, the house is virtually in its original condition. Drayton family history and information about the Bowens family, their slaves, is shared. Connections: From Africa to America is a 45-minute program showcasing slavery.

Visitors can rent portable DVD players for a self-guiding grounds tour. Picnicking is permitted. Grounds daily 8:30-5, Mar.-Oct.; 8:30-4, rest of year. Guided 50-minute house tours are given daily on the hour 9-4:30, Mar.-Oct.; 9-3:30, rest of year. The last tour of the day is the only tour departing on the half-hour. Connections programs daily at 11:15, 1:15 and 3:15. Closed Jan. 1, Thanksgiving and Dec. 24-25 and 31. House tour $14; $12 (military with ID); $8 (ages 12-18); $6 (ages 6-11). Grounds only $8. DVD rental additional $7. AX, MC, VI. Phone (843) 769-2600.

MAGNOLIA PLANTATION AND GARDENS is at 3550 Ashley River Rd. (SR 61), 10 mi. n.w. of jct. US 17. This 500-acre estate was acquired in 1676 by the Drayton family, whose heirs still own and manage it. The informal 60-acre garden, one of America's oldest, dates from around 1680 and contains 900 varieties of camellias, 250 types of azaleas and hundreds of other flowering species that provide year-round color while complementing the natural beauty of the surroundings.

Grounds include a petting zoo; antebellum cabins; a pasture with sheep and miniature horses; a horticultural maze; and biblical, herb and tropical gardens. Also offered are an orientation theater and bicycle and nature trails. House, boat and train tours as well as self-guiding tours of Audubon Swamp Garden are available for additional fees.

Restored slave cabins and an exhibit building featuring artifacts found on-site are scheduled to open February 2009; phone ahead for updates. Food is available. Picnicking and leashed pets are permitted. Allow 2 hours minimum.

Daily 8 a.m.-dusk. Last admission is at 5:30, mid-Feb. to mid-Nov.; at 4:30, rest of year. Admission to grounds and gardens $15; $10 (ages 6-12). AX, MC, VI. Phone (843) 571-1266 or (800) 367-3517. *See color ad p. 223.*

Audubon Swamp Garden, at Magnolia Plantation, 10 mi. n.w. of jct. US 17 on SR 61 (Ashley River Rd.), encompasses 60 acres of blackwater cypress and tupelo swamp accessible by boardwalks, bridges and dikes, with opportunities for viewing waterfowl, alligators and other wildlife as well as hundreds of species of blooming plants.

Note: The swamp garden has a separate entrance and may be visited without visiting the plantation grounds. Allow 1 hour minimum. Daily 8 a.m.-dusk. Last admission is at 5:30. Admission $7; free (ages 0-5). Visitors who choose to visit the plantation grounds beforehand will also be charged the Magnolia Plantation and Gardens general admission. AX, MC, VI. Phone (843) 571-1266 or (800) 367-3517.

Magnolia Plantation House, on Magnolia Plantation at 3550 Ashley River Rd. (SR 61), 10 mi. n.w. of jct. US 17, was built in the Greek Revival style and depicts life since the Civil War. Displays include Early American antiques and rare botanical and ornithological prints and books. The present house is a combination of the house burned during the Civil War and a pre-Revolutionary summer house that was disassembled and rebuilt on the charred brick remains of the burned house.

Guided 30-minute house tours are given daily 9-5, Apr.-Nov.; 9:30-4:30, rest of year. Admission $7 in addition to Magnolia Plantation and Gardens general admission; free (ages 0-5). AX, MC, VI. Phone (843) 571-1266 or (800) 367-3517. *See color ad.*

Nature Boat, on Magnolia Plantation at 3550 Ashley River Rd. (SR 61), 10 mi. n.w. of jct. US 17, offers a narrated 45-minute pontoon boat ride through a 125-acre pre-Civil War rice field, now a waterfowl refuge. The tour emphasizes Ashley River history and the rice culture and offers wildlife viewing. Daily 9:30-4, Mar.-Nov. (weather permitting); schedule varies. Fare $7 in addition to Magnolia Plantation and Gardens general admission; free (ages 0-5). AX, MC, VI. Phone (843) 571-1266 or (800) 367-3517.

Nature Train, on Magnolia Plantation at 3550 Ashley River Rd. (SR 61), 10 mi. n.w. of jct. US 17, offers a narrated 45-minute tour of the outskirts of the plantation and its wildlife refuges and focuses on plantation and natural history. Daily 9-4, Mar.-Nov.; 9:30-4, rest of year (weather permitting). Fare $7 in addition to Magnolia Plantation and Gardens general admission; free (ages 0-5). AX, MC, VI. Phone (843) 571-1266 or (800) 367-3517.

GEM SAVE **MIDDLETON PLACE** is on SR 61, 14 mi. n.w. of jct. US 17 at 4300 Ashley River Rd. The oldest landscaped gardens in America were begun in 1741 by Henry Middleton, later president of the First Continental Congress. It took 100 slaves 10 years to complete the landscaped terraces, camellia-lined walks and ornamental lakes. Azaleas bloom in the spring, magnolias and roses in the early summer, crape myrtles and perennials through the summer and fall, and camellias during the winter.

Demonstrations of spinning, weaving, blacksmithing, candle making, corn grinding and cow milking are given in the restored stable yard where skilled slaves would have performed similar tasks in the 18th and 19th centuries. African-American life is interpreted on a tour of a freedman's cabin, slave chapel and slave cemetery. A horse-drawn carriage tour and house tour are available for additional fees.

Food is available. Allow 2 hours minimum. Daily 9-5; closed Dec. 25. Gardens and stable yard $25; $5 (ages 7-15). Carriage tour $15. House tour $10. Combination ticket with carriage, house, gardens and stable yard $45; $30 (ages 7-15). A combination ticket is also available with Edmondston-Alston House. AX, MC, VI. Phone (843) 556-6020 or (800) 782-3608.

Middleton Place House, on Middleton Place Plantation at 4300 Ashley River Rd., was built in 1755. The house originally served as a guest wing, then became the Middleton family residence when the main portion of the house burned during the Civil War. It contains family furniture, paintings, books and silver. A silk copy of the Declaration of Independence was found among the personal mementos of Henry Middleton's son Arthur, a signer of the document.

Interior photography is not permitted. Allow 30 minutes minimum. Guided tours Tues.-Sun. 10-4:30, Mon. 1:30-4:30. Last tour begins at closing. Admission $10 (in addition to Middleton Place gardens and stable yard). Phone (843) 556-6020 or (800) 782-3608.

What To Do

Sightseeing

Before sightseeing in Charleston, park your car. Trying to negotiate the narrow streets while sightseeing is difficult, and your visit will be much more interesting if you move at a leisurely pace. So, follow one of the TourBook guide's walking tours or take one of the guided carriage, bus, van or trolley tours; boat tours are also offered. Tour operators are listed below.

A good place to begin your exploration is at the Charleston Visitor Center, 375 Meeting St. "Forever Charleston" *(see attraction listing p. 220)*, a multimedia presentation shown continuously at the center, provides an introduction to the city and its people. Self-guiding tour maps and brochures also are available.

Two of the most prominent features of the historic area are the two major architectural styles: the double house and the single house. The front doors of the double house face the street, with one room to each side. The typical single house is only one room wide with the narrow gable end turned toward the street. To one side is a door that opens onto a porch, and gardens or courtyards are beside or behind the house.

No one knows why there are so many single houses in Charleston, but past speculation, which is now often discounted, claimed that the design might have been prompted by taxes levied according to how many feet of a house faced the street. Similar houses were built during the 18th and early 19th centuries in New Orleans for this reason. The more likely explanation is that this design made the most of summer breezes and blocked the interior from the most intense sun during the day.

Many of Charleston's old houses have solid shutters on the first floor windows and louvered shutters on the windows of the floors above. The solid shutters helped keep the noise and dirt from entering the early houses, which had walls that rose from the edge of the street.

Perhaps the most common sight in Charleston is not a thing, but a color. Charleston green, such an extremely dark shade that it is almost black, is seen on everything from shutters to front doors to piazza trim. The color is said to have been devised during Reconstruction, when only black paint was available in quantity. Residents mixed in a small amount of yellow pigment and were able to use colored paint.

Boat Tours

SAVE Gray Line of Charleston offers a combination city tour of Charleston along with either a cruise to Fort Sumter or a cruise around the harbor; phone (843) 722-4444.

SAVE **CHARLESTON HARBOR TOURS** departs from the Charleston Maritime Center at 10 Wharfside St. The 1.5-hour narrated sightseeing cruise aboard the 1920s-style steamer *Carolina Belle* includes such sights as forts Sumter, Moultrie and Johnson; port facilities; the Battery; the Ravenel suspension bridge; and many of Charleston's fine waterfront houses and churches. A 2.5-hour tour combining the boat cruise and a 1-hour horse-drawn carriage tour also is available.

Food is available. Sightseeing cruises depart daily at 11:30, 1:30 and 3:30, mid-Feb. to late Nov. Sightseeing cruise fare $15.50; $14.50 (senior citizens); $11 (ages 4-11). Combination ticket $31; $17 (ages 4-11). Ages 0-11 must be with an adult. AX, MC, VI. Phone (843) 722-1112 or (800) 344-4483.

FORT SUMTER TOURS departs from Liberty Square, 340 Concord St. next to the South Carolina Aquarium, and from Patriots Point Naval and Maritime Museum *(see attraction listing p. 239)* in Mount Pleasant. The cruise consists of a 75-minute narrated tour of Charleston Harbor and a 1-hour tour of Fort Sumter *(see attraction listing p. 236)*. Interpretive exhibits are offered at the Liberty Square visitor center. National Park Service rangers are available at the fort to answer questions.

Tours depart from Liberty Square daily at 9:30, noon and 2:30 and from Patriots Point daily at 10:45, 1:30 and 4, Mar.-Aug.; otherwise varies. Visitors should arrive 25 minutes prior to departure. Visitor center daily 8:30-5; closed Jan. 1, Thanksgiving and Dec. 25. Fare $15; $13.50 (ages 62+); $9 (ages 6-11). AX, DS, MC, VI. Phone (843) 722-1691 or (800) 789-3678.

SAVE **SANDLAPPER WATER TOURS** departs from the Charleston Maritime Center at 10 Wharfside St. Visitors can view the local wildlife and spend some time on the beach at a barrier island while on the 2-hour Nature tour. A historian provides city history and tells maritime stories on the 90-minute History tour, which includes prominent landmarks. Stories about such past topics as wars, pirates, ships and seamen are shared on the 90-minute Haunted Harbor tour. Two-hour sunset tours also are available.

Food is available. Nature tour departs Tues.-Sat. (and Sun. of Memorial Day and Labor Day weekends) at 2, Apr.-Oct. History tour departs Wed. and Sat. (and Sun. of Memorial Day and Labor Day weekends) at 11 and 12:30, Apr.-Oct. Haunted Harbor and sunset tours are offered Apr.-Oct.; phone for schedules. Passengers should arrive 20 minutes prior to departure. Nature or sunset tour fare $25; $17 (ages 4-12). History tour fare $20; $15 (ages 4-12). Haunted Harbor tour fare $22; $16 (ages 4-12). Under age 3 are not permitted on the Haunted Harbor tour. Reservations are required. MC, VI. Phone (843) 849-8687.

THE SCHOONER *PRIDE*, at Aquarium Wharf, offers cruises aboard an 84-foot-tall ship around Charleston's historic harbor. The crew occasionally points out historic sites and wildlife on the trip. Guests are permitted to help with the sailing or just enjoy the ride. Sunset sails also are available.

Allow 2 hours minimum. Cruises offered daily Mar.-Oct. Schedule varies; phone for departure times. Daily sail fare $27; $21 (ages 0-11). Sunset sail fare $34; $25 (ages 0-11). Reservations are recommended. AX, DS, MC, VI. Phone (843) 559-9686 or (800) 344-4483.

SAVE **SPIRITLINE HARBOR TOUR** departs from the Fountain Walk dock at Aquarium Wharf, and from Patriots Point Naval and Maritime Museum in Mount Pleasant. The tour consists of a 1.5-hour narrated cruise around Charleston Harbor and features the history of the Old South. A dinner cruise also is available.

Harbor tours depart from Aquarium Wharf daily at 11 and 1, Mar.-Oct.; daily at 1, in Nov.; and from Patriots Point daily at 3, Mar.-Nov.; otherwise varies. Fare $15; $13.50 (ages 62+ and military with ID); $9 (ages 6-11). Phone for dinner cruise fare. Reservations are required for dinner cruises. AX, DS, MC, VI. Phone (843) 722-2628 or (800) 789-3678.

Bus and Carriage Tours

Motorized tours cater to weekend visitors seeking a quick overview of city architecture, culture and history or to those with plenty of time to explore Charleston's surroundings and historic plantations. SAVE Gray Line of Charleston offers several sightseeing options covering more than 100 points of interest including historic houses, Fort Sumter, the Battery and Charleston Harbor. For information phone (843) 722-4444. Routes for horse-drawn carriage tours are selected randomly.

ADVENTURE SIGHTSEEING TOURS departs from the Charleston Visitor Center at 375 Meeting St. Various van tours visit the city's major points of interest, including military sites, architectural landmarks, plantations, historic neighborhoods and gardens. Costumed guides narrate the tours.

Allow 1 hour, 30 minutes minimum. Daily 9-5; closed Jan. 1, Thanksgiving and Dec. 25. Tour times vary. Fare $17-$59; $16-$56 (ages 65+); $10-$25 (ages 1-11). Reservations are recommended. AX, DS, MC, VI. Phone (843) 762-0088 or (800) 722-5394.

SAVE **CHARLESTON'S FINEST HISTORIC TOURS** leaves from the visitor center at 375 Meeting St.; free pickup from downtown lodgings is available. Seasoned guides offer a narrated 90-minute city tour, 110-minute city tour, a nearly 4.5-hour Magnolia Plantation tour and a combination city and Magnolia Plantation tour. Highlights of the city tour include mansions, gardens, churches and The Battery.

The 90-minute city tour departs daily at 11:30 and 1:30. The 110-minute city tour and the combination tour depart daily at 10:30. Magnolia Plantation tour departs daily at 12:30. Closed Jan. 1, Thanksgiving and Dec. 25. Fare for 90-minute city tour $16; $9 (ages 4-12). Fare for 110-minute city tour $18; $17 (senior citizens); $9 (ages 4-12). Fare for Magnolia Plantation tour $48; $24 (ages 4-12). Combination tour fare $58; $29 (ages 4-12). Reservations are required. AX, MC, VI. Phone (843) 577-3311.

SAVE **CHARLESTON TOURS INC.** departs from the Charleston Visitor Center at 375 Meeting St.; transportation is available to and from area hotels. Several different tours are offered, each featuring the city's main points of interest. Highlights include plantations, waterfront houses, the French Quarter, the Slave Mart and Catfish Row. Tour guides narrate the trips. Full-day tours also are offered.

Allow 1 hour, 30 minutes minimum. Tours are offered Mon.-Sat. Departure times vary; phone ahead. Closed Jan. 1, Easter, Thanksgiving and Dec. 25. Fare $20-$65; $10-$30 (ages 3-12). Reservations are recommended. MC, VI. Phone (843) 571-0049.

SAVE **CLASSIC CARRIAGE TOURS INC.,** departing from 10 Guignard St. between E. Bay and Anson sts., provides 1-hour horse-driven carriage rides of Charleston with tour guides who share stories about the city's history and culture. Tours depart daily every half-hour 9-5, Mar.-Dec.; 10-5, rest of year. Evening tours are available by appointment. Closed Dec. 25. Fare $20; $12 (ages 5-12). Fare with reservation $18; $11 (ages 5-12). AX, MC, VI. Phone (843) 853-3747.

SAVE **DOIN' THE CHARLESTON TOURS** departs from the visitor center at 375 Meeting St. Free pickup at downtown lodgings and marinas is available 30 minutes before tour time. A bus tour of the historic district is offered. The guide brings history to life with 90 minutes of live narration, laser disc images and stories set to music. The 8-mile tour features a stop at The Battery.

Tours depart daily at 9:30, noon and 2:30 (also at 4:30, early Apr.-late Oct.). Fare $18; $13 (ages 0-11). Combination tickets are available. Not recommended for ages 0-5. MC, VI at the visitor center only. Phone (843) 763-1233 or (800) 647-4487. *See color ad.*

GULLAH TOURS departs from Gallery Chuma at 43 John St., across from Charleston Visitor Center. Tours aboard a 21-passenger bus take visitors by historic Charleston sites associated with African-American history, including Catfish Row, Old Slave Mart and places where the Underground Railroad was in operation. The tour guide shares lessons in the Gullah language.

Allow 1 hour, 30 minutes minimum. If traffic is heavy, tours can last 2 hours. Tours depart Sat. at 11, 1 and 3, Mon.-Fri. at 11 and 1; closed Thanksgiving and Dec. 25. Fare $18; $15 (ages 13-18); $12 (ages 8-12). Phone (843) 763-7551.

OLDE TOWNE CARRIAGE COMPANY, downtown between N. Market and Pinckney sts. at 20 Anson St., offers narrated, horse-drawn carriage rides through the city's oldest residential and business district. Allow 1 hour minimum. Daily 9-5 (weather permitting). Fare $20; $10 (ages 4-11). MC, VI. Phone (843) 722-1315 or (888) 800-5091.

SAVE **OLD SOUTH CARRIAGE CO.,** 14 Anson St., offers 1-hour tours of some 30 blocks in historic Charleston in surrey carriages. Guides in Confederate uniforms point out the sights. Daily 9-5, early Apr.-late Oct.; 9-4, rest of year. Fare $21; $13 (ages 3-11). MC, VI. Phone (843) 723-9712.

PALMETTO CARRIAGE TOURS, departing from the red barn at 40 N. Market St., offers 1-hour mule-drawn carriage excursions through historic Charleston. Three different tours rotate on a daily basis. Daily 9-5, during DST; 9-4, rest of year. Closed Dec. 25. Last tour begins at closing. Fare $20; $10 (ages 4-11). Parking free. AX, MC, VI. Phone (843) 723-8145.

TALK OF THE TOWNE tours depart from the Charleston Visitor Center at 375 Meeting St. These guided, motorized tours of the city's historic district include stops at Fort Sumter, The Battery, The Market and Rainbow Row. Two-hour trips include tours of the Nathaniel Russell House or the Edmondston-Alston House. Narrators provide background detail and point out areas of local interest.

Allow 1 hour, 30 minutes minimum. Mon.-Sat. 9:15-3:15, early Apr.-late Oct.; Mon.-Sat. 9:15-3, rest of year. Tour times vary. Fare $19-$28; $12-$16 (ages 0-12). MC, VI. Phone (843) 795-8199 or (888) 795-8199.

Guided Walking Tours

ARCHITECTURAL WALKING TOURS OF CHARLESTON, departing from the Meeting Street Inn at 173 Meeting St., provides 2-hour guided tours. The 18th-century tour of the original walled city emphasizes Georgian architecture. The 19th-century tour of Meeting Street and The Battery features Federal, Greek Revival and Victorian architecture. Tours include private houses and gardens as well as some public buildings and churches. A 3-day "Georgian Weekend" tour also is available.

Allow 2 hours minimum per tour. Both 2-hour tours depart Mon. and Wed.-Sat. at 10 and 2; closed Dec. 25. Fee $20; $15 (students with ID); free (ages 0-9). Reservations are recommended. Phone (843) 893-2327 or (800) 931-7761.

SAVE **BULLDOG TOURS** departs from several locations; ticket office is at 40 N. Market St. The 90-minute Charleston Ghost & Dungeon, the 90-minute Charleston Ghost & Graveyard and the 45-minute Haunted Jail walking tours explore the city's haunted history. The 90-minute Dark Side of Charleston walking tour includes historical narration of some of the city's dark and scandalous tales.

Due to the content in the Dark Side of Charleston Tour, under age 17 must be accompanied by a parent or adult guardian. Tours are offered daily 7-10 p.m.; phone for schedule. Fee $18; $12 (ages 7-12). Reservations are recommended. Phone (843) 722-8687.

CHARLESTON GHOST HUNT departs from the steps of the U.S. Custom House at jct. S. Market and E. Bay sts. Participants hear ghost stories on a 90-minute walking tour of downtown Charleston. Tours are given daily at 7 p.m. and 9 p.m. (also Fri.-Sat. at 10:45 p.m.). Fee $17. Not recommended for children ages 0-12. Reservations are required. MC, VI. Phone (843) 813-5055.

CHARLESTON PHOTO TOURS HISTORY WALK departs from Washington Square Park, by the statue of George Washington. This narrated walking tour, given by a professional photographer, combines sightseeing with helpful photography tips intended to guide visitors in taking better photographs and seeing the city's landmarks from a different perspective. The 1.5-mile route (with frequent rests) features historic cemeteries, churches, gardens, houses, public buildings and hidden walkways.

Allow 2 hours minimum. Tours depart daily at 10 and 4, during DST; at 10 and 3, rest of year. Closed holidays. Admission $18.50; 50c (ages 0-12). Reservations are required. Phone (843) 901-9283.

CHARLESTON STROLLS offers guided walking tours of the historic district. Tours leave from the Palmetto Cafe at Charleston Place Hotel, 130 Market St.; the Days Inn lobby at 155 Meeting St.; and the Mills House Hotel lobby at 115 Meeting St. Allow 2 hours minimum. Tours depart Mon.-Sat. from Charleston Place at 9:30, Days Inn at 9:40 and Mills House at 10. Fee $18; $10 (ages 7-12). Reservations are recommended. Phone (843) 766-2080.

CIVIL WAR WALKING TOUR departs from 115 Meeting St. A knowledgeable guide portrays a Confederate soldier on a walking tour highlighting the look and feel of 1860s Charleston, providing first-person accounts of daily life during the Civil War. Using a collection of historical photographs, the guide offers a then-and-now perspective of the city. Allow 2 hours minimum. Tour departs daily at 9, Mar.-Dec. Fee $17; $15 (ages 54+); free (ages 0-12). Phone (843) 722-7033.

ON THE MARKET TOUR departs from Market Hall, at the corner of Meeting and Market sts. The History Walk highlights architecture, gardens, graveyards and churches. Allow 1 hour, 45 minutes minimum. Tour departs daily at 11; closed holidays. Fee $20; $12 (ages 0-12). Reservations are required. MC, VI. Phone (843) 853-8687.

THE ORIGINAL CHARLESTON WALKS, departing from 45 S. Market St., offers various guided walking tours of the city. Tours include Ghosts & Legends, Historic Homes Walk, Civil War Walk, Slavery & Freedom Walk, Original Charleston Walk, Patriots of Charleston Walk, The Pub Walk, and Pirates & Buccaneers Walk.

It is recommended that visitors should be 21 for The Pub Walk. Daily 10:30-9:30; closed Dec. 25. Departure times vary with each tour. Visitors should arrive 15 minutes prior to departure. Fee $18.50-$29.50; $13-$16 (senior citizens); $10.50-$22.50 (ages 7-14). Reservations are required. AX, DS, MC, VI. Phone (843) 577-3800 or (800) 729-3420.

SAVE **TOUR CHARLESTON LLC,** departs from the circular fountain in Waterfront Park and from Marion Square and offers themed, guided walking tours. The Ghosts of Charleston I tour features entertaining stories of spirits. Charleston's sinister side is explored on the Ghosts of Charleston II tour. The Story of Charleston tour visits the Old Slave Market, mansions and historic sites. The Pirates of Charleston tour features pirate tales.

Allow 1 hour, 30 minutes minimum per tour. Tours are given daily; departure times vary. Closed Jan. 1, Easter, July 4, Thanksgiving and Dec. 25. Reservations are required. Fee $18; $12 (ages 5-11). Ghosts of Charleston II tour not recommended for ages 0-9. AX, MC, VI. Phone (843) 723-1670 or (800) 854-1670.

AAA Walking Tours

Exploring Charleston on foot allows you to peek into hidden gardens, walk through churchyards and parks and along cobblestone streets. A city ordinance stating that nothing older than 75 years may be torn down has preserved a city full of meticulously restored buildings, churches and houses, each with its own tale. Plaques from the Preservation Society of Charleston attest to the year in which the owner restored the building to its original state as well as interesting facts about the property and past residents.

Each walking tour will take 2-3 hours, allowing for a leisurely pace and stops for photography and plaque reading. The best way to see the city is to combine the walking tours with stops at the attractions along the way. *Names of sites listed in the What To See section are printed in bold type. Even if you don't tour a listed site, reading the listing when you reach that point will make the tour more interesting.*

The Battery

Park just north of Broad Street on Meeting Street, and walk a few steps south toward the intersection of Meeting and Broad. This intersection is known as The Four Corners of Law—buildings on each corner represent local, state, federal and religious law. **City Hall** 1, said to be the oldest in the country, is on your left on the northeast corner; the northwest corner is occupied by Charleston County Courthouse 2; the southwest corner houses the U.S. Post Office and Federal Court 3; and the large white church on the southeast corner is **St. Michael's Episcopal Church** 4. The church has an interesting history: During the Revolutionary War, its steeple was used as a target for British ship gunners, and the lead roof was melted to make bullets. Enter the church to see the cedar pews—used by George Washington and Gen. Robert E. Lee—and read the tombstones in its churchyard, where you'll find the graves of John Rutledge and Charles Cotesworth Pinckney, two signers of the Constitution.

In front of the post office and church you'll likely see ladies weaving and selling sweetgrass baskets. An African craft, basket making has been practiced throughout the Lowcountry since the 18th century; artisans use indigenous materials—sweetgrass, pine needles, bulrush and palmetto tree strips—to create the baskets.

Continue south on Meeting past St. Michael's Alley. On your left, the two-story building with the white columns is South Carolina Society Hall 5, which houses the charitable organization founded by French Huguenots in 1737. The Adamesque building was built in 1804; its portico, columns, dual staircase and iron filigreed railings were added in 1825. Glance up to see the Palladian window at the top of the portico.

To the right at 69 Meeting St. is the three-and-a-half story Adamesque Poyas-Mordecai House 6, built in 1788. This is a good (albeit large) example of a single house—meaning that the house is a single room wide. Many Charleston houses were built in this style to make the most of bay breezes in summer. By opening the front and back doors or windows, the breeze would pass through the house and cool it. Note the front door, called a privacy door. It grants access to the porch (called a piazza by Charlestonians), rather than the main house, allowing residents to relax on their porches without interruption from neighbors. The location of the piazza would also protect the interior of the house from the most intense sun during the day. In summers past, people often slept on them. The main entrance is off the piazza. If the gate is open, peek into the manicured garden fronting the piazzas.

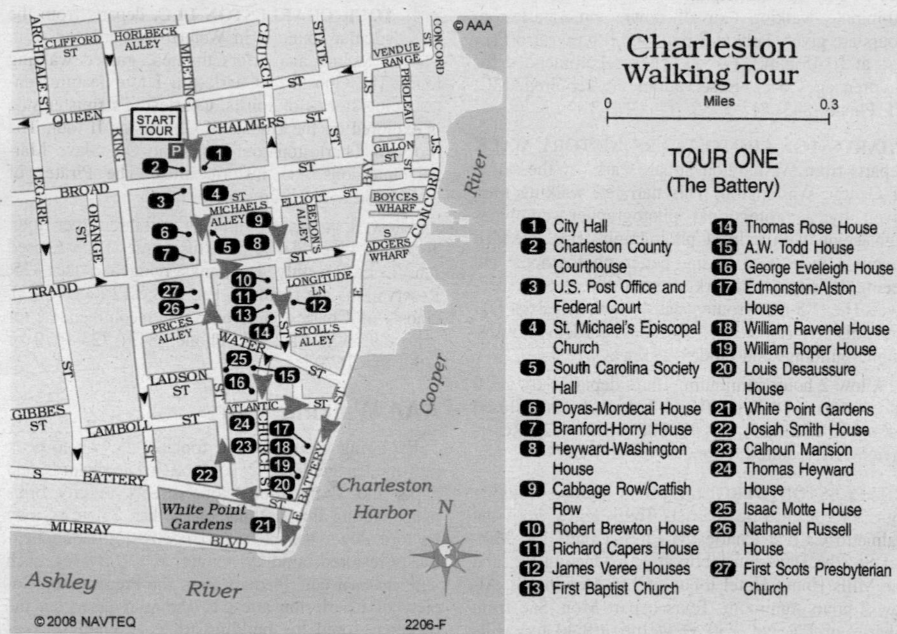

The large bolts on the side of the house are called earthquake bolts—you'll notice them on houses all over the historic district. Charleston sits on the Woodstock Fault, and on Aug. 31, 1886, the earth shook with an estimated magnitude of 7 (equivalent to 6 or 7 on today's Richter scale). Most brick homes crumbled. To save those with large cracks, these large screws were inserted through the floorboards of the houses and tightened, in effect cranking the brickwork back together. For visitors, they serve as historical markers: Whenever you see a building with an earthquake bolt, you know that the building was constructed before 1886.

Walk past Ropemaker's Lane to Tradd Street. On the northwest corner of Tradd and Meeting is the 1750 Branford-Horry House 7, a fine example of a double house (two rooms wide). The piazza, built over the sidewalk, was added in 1830. Iron railings on the second floor have the same pattern as those at the South Carolina Society Hall.

Turn left and walk down Tradd, chock full of historic properties, each marked with a plaque from the Preservation Society of Charleston. Now that you can recognize single and double houses, practice picking them out among the solid shuttered homes here; also note the earthquake bolts, as most buildings predate 1886. The narrow lane, gas lamps and hidden gardens make it one of Charleston's prettiest streets; it also runs the width of the city. By looking to the west, you can see the Ashley River, while the Cooper River is visible to the east. The distance from river to river is approximately 1 mile.

When offered for sale in 1770, the advertisement for 61 Tradd St. boasted that it was "new built." The single house at 60 Tradd St. was built in 1732 by shipbuilder George Ducat for his daughter and her new husband; he also built 56 Tradd St. (made of brick and Bermuda stone) and bequeathed it to his grandson in 1751. The three-and-a-half story brick house at 54 Tradd St. was built circa 1740; the balcony, rescued from a building on State Street, was added in the 1920s. Note the tenement at 51-53 Tradd St.

Take a quick detour onto Church Street by turning left. The three-story brick double house on your left at 87 Church St. is the **Heyward-Washington House** 8. Note the hitching posts and carriage step (which looks like a cement block) out front. A formal garden (behind the house) is impressive, and the interior features a mantel by Thomas Elfe, a Colonial cabinetmaker. Just a few steps farther, on your left at 89-91 Church St., is Cabbage Row 9—it's the three-story, gray stucco tenement with awnings. Residents gave the building its name by displaying vegetables for sale on the windowsills. You might wonder why a red "Catfish Row" sign dangles out front. In 1924, DuBose Heyward wrote the novel "Porgy," using the tenement as a model for the fictional Catfish Row. The book served as the basis for George Gershwin's opera "Porgy and Bess." If you can whistle, now might be a good time for a tune—"summertime, and the livin' is easy."

Built in 1805 by a merchant, 92 Church St. has served as the rectory of St. Philip's Church since 1908. The middle window on the first level was originally a door; this indicates that it was once a business. (If you look, you'll easily find other houses on this block that were once businesses.) Also notice the boot scrapers in front. Colorful Victorian houses at 93-99 Church St. were built around 1910.

Retrace your steps to Tradd Street and continue south on Church Street. On your right at 71 Church St. is the Robert Brewton House 10. Built in 1721, it is reputedly the oldest single house in the city. Note the quoins (square cornerstones) projecting from the building; the wrought-iron balcony; the key blocks over the windows; and the cornice, which is made from shaped bricks. An 18th-century-style garden is in the rear.

Next door at 69 Church St. is the Richard Capers House 11, a notable Georgian double house that differs from others in this period because the windows on the third floor are the same height as those on the lower two stories. The house has had various owners and occupants dating from the early 1700s, including Jacob Motte, who served for 27 years as the Public Treasurer (local banker). Since there were no banks at the time, the Public Treasurer personally held the government's funds. We assume he also kept busy with his 19 children. Peek into the garden to the left of the house.

A few steps ahead and across the street at 56, 58 and 60 Church St. are three wood frame houses known as the James Veree Houses 12, named after the local carpenter who built them. First Baptist Church 13, the large white building with wide columns and an iron fence, is on the right at 61 Church St. The church, dedicated in 1822, is said to be home to the oldest Baptist congregation in South Carolina and is decidedly Greek in style—note the Doric portico and pediment—yet the arches are Roman and the columns are Tuscan. During the Revolutionary War, the building was overtaken by British troops and used to store provisions.

Scared of ghosts? Then walk quickly past the early Georgian Thomas Rose House 14, 59 Church St.—the ghost of Dr. Joseph Brown Ladd, mortally wounded in a duel in 1786, is said to roam the halls. Continue to the Joseph Ball House, 53 Church St., where there is a great view of the two-story piazza.

Now walk a few steps to Water Street, named after Vanderhorst Creek, which once ran here. Thus far along your tour, you have been exploring the section of Charleston known as the walled city. From 1690-1720 Charleston was enclosed to protect from French, Spanish and American Indian invaders as well as pirates. The wall, which extended from Cumberland to Water streets (north-south) and from East Bay to Meeting streets (east-west), was destroyed in the mid-18th century, but an invisible boundary still exists: Most of the city's cobblestone streets and narrow alleys can be found within or very near the original walled city.

As you cross Water Street, look left (east) toward the Battery for a lovely view. Then continue south on Church Street. The second house on your right at 41 Church St. is the A.W. Todd House 15, built in 1909; notice the garage entrance through the base of the chimney. Next door is the George Eveleigh House 16, at 39 Church St., brick with white columns. When the home was built in the early 1700s, the creek was present—the mooring posts in front of the house date from this time. The house itself has an asymmetrical floor plan, which is unusual for this time period, and was rumored to have a secret staircase. Its original lot extended to Meeting Street, where the owner also built 34 Meeting St.

Continue walking south along Church Street for one block to Atlantic Street, then turn left. More single houses line Atlantic. Peek down Zig Zag Alley (on your left). When you reach East Battery Street, cross the street and climb the stairs to the elevated walkway running along the water. You are now in the area known as the High Battery. In 1755, the earth wall was held together with sticks and topped with grass, and wooden platforms along the top supported guns. In 1787 work began to extend East Bay Street south to create East Battery Street (the use of cannons here during the War of 1812 is purported to have given East Battery its name). After improvements were made to the wall—for example, using ships' ballast instead of mud—a granite wall was completed in 1820. Building along East Battery was possible after the wall's completion—the majority of the mansions were constructed 1820-50.

The elevated walkway overlooks Charleston Harbor, where the first shot of the Civil War was fired April 12, 1861, at Fort Sumter. During the bombardment that ensued, only one house along East Battery Street was destroyed; it sat at the corner of Atlantic and East Battery streets (a large pink Victorian house occupies the property now). Stroll along the walkway, enjoying the breeze and the antebellum mansions. Notice the **Edmondston-Alston House** 17, (the fourth house from Atlantic at 21 E. Battery St.), built in 1825 by merchant Charles Edmondston. Greek Revival elements were added by Charles Alston after his father William purchased the house in 1838; the roof parapet displays his family's coat of arms. General Beauregard watched the bombardment of Fort Sumter from the second-floor piazza.

When the Italian villa-style house at 19 E. Battery St. was built in 1920, it was one of the most expensive houses in Charleston. You can probably understand why. Look at the porte cochere (porch roof projecting over the driveway) at the William Ravenel House 18, 13 E. Battery St.; it runs underneath a gigantic drawing room rather than fronting it. This design enabled the huge house to be squeezed onto a relatively narrow lot.

Built in 1838, the brick Greek Revival William Roper House 19, at 9 E. Battery St., was the first on this section of the High Battery. Its huge white portico and Ionic columns can be seen from the harbor. Initials on the front door belong to Rudolph Siegling, publisher of the *News and Courier,* who purchased the house in 1877. Two details to look for are the earthquake bolts (covered by decorative plaques in the shape of lions' heads) and the rope-like trim around the front door. What you can't see is a 500-pound piece of cannon, said to be lodged in the attic since the Confederate evacuation in 1865, when a gun blew up at the corner of East Battery and South Battery streets.

The hot pink house at 5 E. Battery St. was built in 1847 by John Ravenel (if the name sounds familiar, it's because his brother built the house at 13 E. Battery St.). After being hit by the 1886 earthquake, it was rebuilt by a later owner, who added Victorian Italianate features popular at the time. The house remained in the hands of the Ravenel family until 1953. At the corner of East Battery and South Battery streets is the Louis Desaussure House 20, also damaged during the evacuation in February 1865; during repairs, a portion of the same gun was found in the upper section of this house.

To your right is White Point Gardens 21, named for the immense mound of oyster shells that covered the area in the city's early days. Continue along the elevated walkway to the bend, where a plaque set in the pavement points out the position of the harbor's forts: Sumter, Moultrie, Castle Pinckney and Johnson. Confederate forces first fired on Fort Sumter from Fort Johnson. Just past the bend on Murray Boulevard you will see stairs; descend the stairs here and cross Murray Boulevard, entering the park. Once a low, marshy area, the public garden was transformed and first enjoyed by residents in 1837. The live oaks that you see were planted in 1863; under their branches you'll find monuments, a gazebo and cannons that were part of Fort Sumter's "three-gun battery."

Cross the park to South Battery Street near Church Street and marvel at more antebellum castles, built mostly by bankers and merchants. Head west to Meeting Street. At the corner of Meeting and South Battery streets is a large Victorian house built around 1892 by George W. Williams, a wealthy banker, as a wedding present to his daughter. Not to be outdone, the groom's parents supposedly sent the couple on a 2-year tour of Europe, after which they returned to a house complete with stained-glass windows by Louis Comfort Tiffany. The house is now an inn called 2 Meeting Street. Turn right onto Meeting, heading north.

On your left at 7 Meeting St. is the Josiah Smith House 22, built of wood and brick, with a hipped roof and cupola. When the city fell into British hands in 1780, Smith, a rich merchant, was arrested and exiled to St. Augustine, Fla., returning to Charleston after the Revolution. A few houses farther at 11 Meeting St. is an 1850 pink Italianate house, which is covered with stucco scored to look like stone (this was a cheaper process than importing actual stone).

John Edwards, another exile, built 15 Meeting St. Aside from the brick basement, the rest of the house is cypress; the facade also is cut to resemble stone, and the portico is embellished with Corinthian columns and a double staircase. George W. Williams, Jr., later purchased this house, which is why it is often referred to as the Williams House. His father owned the 1876 **Calhoun Mansion** 23, which is the huge brick mansion across the street. (Recall, "Dad Williams" is the same banker who built 2 Meeting St. for his daughter). This 24,000-square-foot mansion, the city's largest building constructed as a single-family residence, contains 35 rooms (each with a fireplace), 14-foot-tall ceilings, a hand-carved, 75-foot-tall staircase and a ballroom with an elaborate skylight. The exterior also features cypress carved to look like stone.

Next door, at 18 Meeting St., is the Thomas Heyward House 24, a three-story Adamesque single house built around 1803 by Nathaniel Heyward for his brother Thomas Heyward, Jr., a signer of the Declaration of Independence. Cross Atlantic Street and note the three single houses on the left (23-27 Meeting St.), built 1750-88. Across the street at 26 Meeting St. is a formal, Regency-style house displaying three types of columns on its piazza: Doric columns are on the ground floor, the second story has Ionic columns and the top level is graced with Corinthian columns. The Isaac Motte House 25, another classic single house at 30 Meeting St., reputedly was occupied by German Hessian mercenaries during the British occupation; it is rumored that men hid in the fireplace to avoid capture following the Revolutionary War.

Continue past Water Street to the **Nathaniel Russell House** 26, at 51 Meeting St. Completed in 1808, the most impressive feature of this Federal structure is a free-flying mahogany staircase, which spirals up three floors. Notice the NR monogram on the front wrought-iron balcony. A few steps farther, at 53 Meeting St., is the First Scots Presbyterian Church 27. The present building, erected in 1814, employs twin towers topping the column-lined portico. Look at the stained-glass window over the main door—displayed is the Church of Scotland's seal.

You are now a few steps away from Tradd Street, where you turned off of Meeting Street. Continue north on Meeting for about two blocks to Broad Street, which is where you began your tour.

The Walled City

Park at the lot on Cumberland Street between Meeting and Church streets. A wall enclosed Charleston for protection against unwanted visitors during most of the time the settlement was owned by England. This was called the Lords Proprietors period, after the eight noblemen who governed what is now North and South Carolina. The barricade sheltered the area from Cumberland Street south to Water Street and from Meeting Street (near where you parked) east to East Bay Street (fronting the Cooper River). The riverside structure was a single wall, but the other three blockades consisted of double barriers separated by a moat; the city was accessed by two drawbridges at the intersection of Meeting and Broad streets, and wharves extended from East Bay Street. The following walking tour explores this area. To get your bearings, walk to the southeast corner of Meeting and Cumberland streets—the northwest corner of the walled city—where there is a plaque showing a map of the original city plan.

Now head east on Cumberland by turning right. It is believed that the stucco house on the right at 83 Cumberland St. 1 was the first brick house erected in the city and that Chief Justice Nicholas Trott lived here. Some surmise that 83 is the kitchen to the original building at 85 Cumberland St., based on the location of the chimney.

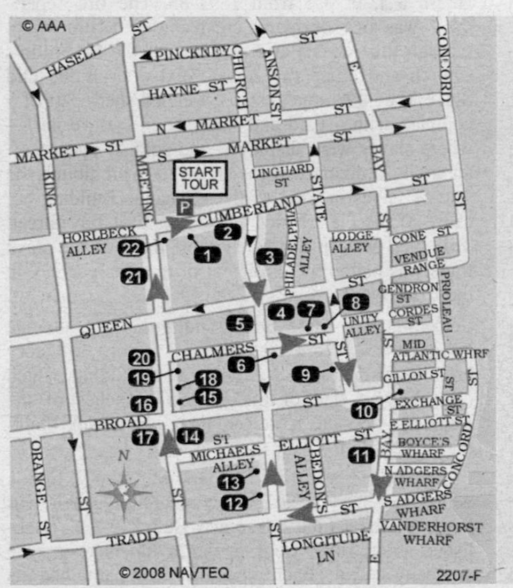

Charleston Walking Tour

0 Miles 0.22

TOUR TWO
(The Walled City)

1 Nicholas Trott House
2 Powder Magazine
3 St. Philip's Episcopal Church
4 French Huguenot Church
5 Dock Street Theatre
6 Pink House
7 German Fire Company Engine House
8 Old Slave Mart
9 Union Insurance Building
10 Old Exchange and Provost Dungeon
11 Rainbow Row
12 Heyward-Washington House
13 Cabbage Row/Catfish Row
14 St. Michael's Episcopal Church
15 City Hall
16 Charleston County Courthouse
17 U.S. Post Office and Federal Court
18 Washington Square
19 Fireproof Building
20 Hibernian Hall
21 Gibbes Museum of Art
22 Circular Congregational Church

Walk a few steps to the **Powder Magazine** 2 at 79 Cumberland St. This structure, said to be the only surviving building from the Lords Proprietors period, was Charleston's main storage facility for munitions and gunpowder. Note the steep hip roof, gables, brick vaulting and pan tiles on the roof. Although replaced by a new building in the mid-1700s, it was still used during the American Revolution, and it is rumored that paintings of George I were stored here for safekeeping during the war.

Continue just past the gate and turn right on Church Street. See the large iron crosses embedded into the side wall of the magazine? Those are earthquake bolts. After a damaging quake shook Charleston and neighboring Summerville in 1886, large screws were inserted through the buildings to hold brickwork together. These screws, which are much larger than the typical bolt, might have been used to penetrate the extremely thick walls, built to force potential explosions upward through the roof.

It's hard to miss the church with the giant steeple in the middle of Church Street. This is St. Philip's Episcopal Church 3. Three Tuscan porticoes grace the structure, built in 1835-38 to replace an earlier church building that burned. Following the blaze, the city wanted to widen Church Street at the expense of the steeple and porticoes. Members of the congregation argued that the steeple was surely more beautiful than a street. The compromise is what you see here: St. Philip's was moved a bit to the east, and the street curves around it.

The church took an active part in the Civil War. The English Renaissance-style steeple was used as a line-of-sight target during the Federal attack on Charleston—the church purportedly was hit 16 times. In addition, its bells were melted for cannons; the bells were not replaced until July 4, 1976.

The churchyard is divided in half by Church Street. Walk through the graveyards to see the burial plots (across the street from the church on the western side), which were reserved for strangers and other transient whites. However, some famous residents were later buried there, including John C. Calhoun, secretary of war and vice president of the United States; DuBose Heyward, author of the novel "Porgy"; Charles Pinckney, a signer of the Constitution; and Edward Rutledge, a signer of the Declaration of Independence. Ornate gates protecting this churchyard are said to be among the oldest wrought ironwork in the city.

Continue to 143 and 141 Church St. These two tenements were built about 1740 by a Huguenot merchant. The house at 143 is a double tenement (two rooms wide), while 141 is a single tenement (you guessed it—one room wide). A portion of 141 is built with Bermuda stone.

Across Queen Street on the left-hand side of Church Street is the white Gothic Revival **French Huguenot Church** 4, built in 1845. Details—such as the buttresses, pointed-arch windows and spires topped with finials—are typical of this style, but the cast iron accents are unusual and add interest. The windows are original. The house next to the church, 134 Church St., served as the church rectory until 1871. It has classic features of a single house—it is a single room wide, and the front door, called a privacy door, opens onto the veranda (called a piazza by Charlestonians) rather than into the main house. Another good example of a single house is the white clapboard dwelling at 132 Church St. Note the solid shutters, boot scraper and carriage step out front.

Now is a good time to notice the street signs, which point out that you are in Charleston's French Quarter, named for the French Huguenots who settled in this area.

A light blue filigreed balcony embellishes the **Dock Street Theatre** 5, said to be the country's first building designed specifically for dramatic performances. Since the settlement of Charles Towne was overseen by Charles II of England—a staunch supporter of the Globe Theater in London—he ordered the construction of the theater, which was completed in 1736. The balcony was added in the mid-1800s when the building operated as Planter's Hotel. Queen Street was once called Dock Street (due to the presence of a creek and a large dock)—hence the theater's name.

Stroll to Chalmers Street and turn left. This is the city's longest remaining cobblestone street, paved in 1760 with creek stones brought from Europe as ships' ballast. On the right at 17 Chalmers St. is the Pink House 6, which served as a tavern in Colonial days. Constructed of Bermuda stone (a coral limestone) about 1712, its most interesting feature is the gambrel roof, made of clay tiles, called thigh tiles because the clay was shaped over workers' thighs.

The stone Romanesque Revival building with three arches and octagon-shaped pillars at 8 Chalmers St. was the German Fire Company Engine House 7, in use from 1851-88. The fire department was one of many created after a fire swept through this area in 1838, damaging the St. Philip's Church and other structures. Next door is the Old Slave Mart 8—once an open-ended shed, part of a complex with a yard and "barracoon" (slave jail)—where slaves were displayed and sold. It opened after a city ordinance in the mid-1800s prohibited the sale of slaves in front of the Exchange Building because of the disturbance caused on East Bay Street. This mart was in use for a short time, as the slave trade was halted by the defeat of the Confederacy in the Civil War.

Continue to State Street and turn right. On the left (set back from the street) is a tiny two-story brick South Carolina National Bank building, which once housed one of the earliest branches of the Bank of America. A newer, three-story bank building is next door.

Across the street at 7 State St., you'll find a white, two-story Classic Revival building that was home to the Union Insurance Building 9, established about 1807. Look at the pediment to see the company's seal. Each insurance company had its own fire engine company, and residents would display a plaque on their house (similar to the seal) to show which company held their insurance. Although all fire companies would respond when a house caught fire, only the fire company whose plaque was displayed would be expected to fight the blaze.

Turn left onto Broad Street, logically named because it was once the broadest street in Charles Towne. It is still the city's main business street, and residents jokingly refer to locations as SOB (South of Broad) or SNOB (Slightly North of Broad). Head to the **Old Exchange and Provost Dungeon** **10**, the large Palladian-style building with the cupola at the end of the street. Since Charles Towne was a port and royal colony, this large exchange and customs house was completed in 1771 to manage trade activities. Once located adjacent to the Cooper River (the bay was later filled in, extending it east for two blocks), the exchange was where merchant ships docked and paid tariffs. Many historical events took place in the exchange's Great Hall. The yellow "don't tread on me" flag flying out front was designed in Charles Towne by Col. Christopher Gadsden. In the dungeon—created to store goods, but later used as a prison by the British during the occupation of 1780-82—you can see a portion of the original battery that surrounded the city.

On the north side of the Old Exchange, across Gillon Street, you can see another section of the original wall; it contains earthquake bolts and fronts a parking lot, facing East Bay Street.

Walk south along East Bay Street. The streets to your left are named for the warehouses and wharves that once stood there, before the bay was filled in. Catch a glimpse of the river by peering down one of these streets.

At Elliot Street, look back at the row of houses numbered 79-107. Known as Rainbow Row **11**, these colorful stucco houses are said to be the longest cluster of intact Georgian houses in the United States and are a favorite subject of artists. They were built 1723-40 by merchants who operated shops on the first floor and lived in the upper stories, reached by staircases from an inner courtyard. Once slums, they received the nickname in the 1930s when the facades were painted in pastel shades. Note the ropelike trim on one of the houses, which is the sign of a merchant—the thicker the rope, the richer the merchant.

Continue down East Bay Street to Tradd Street (opposite cobblestone Adgers Street) and turn right. Quaint Tradd Street runs the width of the city—looking ahead, you can see all the way to the Ashley River, Charleston's west boundary. In 1778 a fire destroyed the portion of Tradd Street from Church Street east toward the Cooper River; many homes here have been rebuilt. Plaques, bestowed by the Preservation Society of Charleston, detail their history. Stroll along Tradd, reading the plaques and peeking in the walled gardens as you pass.

The double tenements at 5 and 7 Tradd St. were built in the early 1700s. Destroyed by fire in 1740 and 1778, they were rebuilt both times according to the same plan. Notice the numerous earthquake bolts. At 14 Tradd St. you can see a fire plaque that shows the fire company to which the resident subscribed.

Continue to Church Street and turn right. On the left at 87 Church St. is the **Heyward-Washington House** **12**, built in 1772 by Daniel Heyward for his son, Thomas Heyward Jr., a signer of the Declaration of Independence. George Washington stayed here on his tour of the city in 1791.

Two doors down, at 89-91 Church St., awnings adorn Cabbage Row **13**, nicknamed because its residents once displayed vegetables for sale on the windowsills. The tenement provided inspiration for DuBose Heyward when he wrote the novel "Porgy"—characters in the book live at Catfish Row. The story, which later was the basis for George Gershwin's opera "Porgy and Bess," is set in a slum during the 1920s, and its main character, Porgy, was modeled after a Charleston resident named Samuel Smalls. The author lived at 76 Church St.

Built in 1805 by a merchant, 92 Church St. has served as the rectory of St. Philip's Church since 1908. The middle window on the first level was originally a door; this indicates that it was a business. Also notice the boot scrapers in front. Embellished single houses at 93-99 Church St. were built around 1910.

Continue on Church Street to St. Michael's Alley (opposite Elliott Street), turn left and walk down the alley to Meeting Street. As you walk, watch for cars; the last section of the alley is quite narrow. At 8 St. Michael's Alley is a Palladian-style building with brown shutters. Note the star-shaped earthquake bolts.

Once at Meeting Street, turn right, heading toward the large white church. Ahead you'll probably see women weaving baskets. An African craft, basket making has been practiced throughout the Lowcountry since the 18th century. Harvested from local marshes and swamps, sweetgrass is used as the basis for the baskets.

Stop at the corner of Broad and Meeting streets. You are now at the intersection known as the Four Corners of Law, because the buildings on each corner represent religious, local, state and federal law. The large white church to your right is **St. Michael's Episcopal Church** **14**. **City Hall** **15**, said to be the oldest in the country, is on the northeast corner. The northwest corner is occupied by Charleston County Courthouse **16**; and to your left, on the southwest corner, is the U.S. Post Office and Federal Court **17**. The church's most notable features are the giant portico and 186-foot-tall steeple, which was painted black during the American Revolution in an attempt to mask it from British ship gunners; instead, it became an easier target. City Hall, erected about 1800 in the Adamesque style, served as a branch of the first Bank of the United States. Inside, a gallery contains portraits of historical figures, including one of George Washington.

Since the Charleston County Courthouse was first built in 1753 to serve as the capitol for the colony of South Carolina, it has been modified several times. It is said that the Declaration of Independence was read from its second-story balcony overlooking Meeting Street. The U.S. Post Office and Federal Court building was constructed in 1896 in the Renaissance Revival style—featuring local gray granite, a rustic base and quoins, balconies with heavy balustrades and large double doors—in an effort to mimic an Italian palace.

Cross Broad Street and walk to the wrought-iron fence on the right that encloses **Washington Square** 18. The small, oak-draped plot features a monument to the Confederate military, among others. After exploring the park's brick paths, continue north on Meeting. Just past the park is the Fireproof Building 19—it's the large Palladian-style building with a Doric portico and double staircase at 100 Meeting St. Created to safely house public records, it is so solid that it suffered little damage in the 1886 earthquake. The South Carolina Historical Society occupies the building. Inside, an oval hall contains a stone staircase lit by an overhead cupola.

At Chalmers Street, look to the left to see Hibernian Hall 20, the white building with large Ionic columns. It was built in 1840 as a meeting place for the Hibernian Society, an Irish benevolent organization. Gilded harps are found in the panel over the front door and on the iron gates. A stone from Northern Ireland's Giant's Causeway, a world heritage site in County Antrim, also is in the portico. When the Mills House Hotel, 115 Meeting St., was originally constructed in 1853, it offered running water, among other amenities. Many famous people have stayed here, including Gen. Robert E. Lee in 1861, when a fire ravaged the street. It is rumored that hotel staff saved the building from destruction by hanging wet blankets from the windows.

Continue past Queen Street. **Gibbes Museum of Art** 21, in the stunning building at 135 Meeting St., houses an impressive collection of miniatures as well as other notable works. The Beaux Arts-style building is constructed of local granite and limestone and the red tile roof accents a large dome. A few steps farther, at 141 Meeting St., is a white Palladian-style building built about 1876 for the Charleston Gas Light Company.

Continue along Meeting, looking across the street to locate the Romanesque Circular Congregational Church 22 at 150 Meeting St. Settlers of Charles Towne dissenting from the Church of England—English Congregationalists, Scottish and Irish Presbyterians and French Huguenots—founded the independent church about 1681. The first church building, in the Pantheon style, was called the White Meeting House, which gave the street its name. Various changes were made to the structure until it burned in the fire of 1861, but the ruins stood until the 1886 earthquake, after which the Romanesque building you see was built, using the same bricks. Despite the name, the church is shaped more like a cloverleaf than a proper circle. The graveyard is said to be the oldest in the city; headstones date from 1690.

The next street is Cumberland. At this point, you can turn right to go to your car, or, if you'd like to shop, cross Meeting Street and walk down Horlbeck Alley to King Street for antique shops, boutiques and clothing stores. You also can cross Cumberland Street and walk up Meeting Street to Market Street, where restaurants surround the market.

Sports and Recreation

While recreational facilities within the historic district of Charleston are limited, the surrounding area offers ample choices for the outdoors enthusiast. Nearby state and county parks and the Francis Marion National Forest *(see place listing p. 236)* provide a variety of activities such as **picnicking, boating** and **hiking** and are only a few minutes' to an hour's drive away. **Camping** is permitted at Givhans Ferry and Edisto Beach state parks *(see Recreation Chart and the AAA Southeastern CampBook).*

The barrier islands that line the coast are the focus of much of Charleston's recreational activity. Once favored as a summer retreat from the threat of yellow fever, many of these islands now sport major resorts. Isle of Palms and Sullivan's Island, east of Charleston, and Edisto, Folly and Kiawah islands, south of the city, all have fine beaches for **swimming, sailing** and **surfing.**

The area is popular for both **freshwater** and **saltwater fishing.** Surf fishing is permitted on many beaches. Deep-sea fishing charters depart from Charleston City Marina. Some of the best fishing is in estuarine creeks. Bass, sheepshead, flounder and trout can be taken in fall and winter; crabbing is good in spring and summer. For information about fishing regulations write South Carolina Department of Natural Resources, Division of Wildlife and Freshwater Fisheries, P.O. Box 167, Columbia, SC 29202; phone (803) 734-3886.

Golf can be played at a number of 18-hole courses: Charleston Municipal Golf Course, (843) 795-6517, and Shadowmoss Golf Club, (843) 556-8251, in Charleston; Crooked Oaks and Ocean Winds, (843) 768-2529, on Seabrook Island; Turtle Point Golf Club, (843) 768-2121, on Kiawah Island; Patriots Point Golf Links, (843) 881-0042, in Mount Pleasant; and Wild Dunes, (843) 886-6000, on Isle of Palms.

Baseball fans can watch the Tampa Bay Devil Rays' minor league team, the Charleston RiverDogs, in action at Joseph P. Riley Jr. Park, 360 Fishburne St.; phone (843) 577-3647. Charleston also is home to the Charleston Battery **soccer** team, an A-League championship team that plays at Blackbaud Stadium, 1990 Daniel Island Dr.; phone (843) 971-4625.

For a quiet stroll in an urban setting, Charleston has several city parks, including White Point Gardens on The Battery, Waterfront Park along the

Cooper River, and Colonial Lake at Broad and Rutledge streets. Many of the parks have trails for **bicycling.** Rentals are available at The Bicycle Shop at 280 Meeting St.; phone (843) 722-8168.

Shopping

It is not surprising that antiques are one of the biggest shopping attractions in Charleston, a city more than 300 years old. An abundance of antique shops, art galleries, boutiques and specialty stores can be found along King Street, including Saks Fifth Avenue. Shops and stores also can be found along nearby Broad, Church, E. Bay and Meeting streets.

Specialty shops, boutiques and open-sided buildings with vendor and artisan booths can be found along N. and S. Market streets behind Market Hall, 188 Meeting St. This area, known as The Old City Market, was deeded to the city by the owners, who specified that it always must remain a public market.

Reproductions of 18th- and 19th-century Charleston antiques are available at the Historic Charleston Foundation's shop at 105 Broad St. Royalties generated from the sales are used to further the foundation's restoration work.

Such major department stores as Belk, Dillard's and JCPenney can be found in nearby shopping malls: Citadel Mall, US 17 and SR 7, and Northwoods Mall, I-26 at US 52.

Performing Arts

Charleston's cultural heritage goes back a long way. By the late 1730s the city had a music society and the Dock Street Theatre, said to be the first building in the Colonies designed solely for theatrical performances. Today the Charleston Stage Company performs in Dock Street Theatre *(see attraction listing p. 218)* at Church and Queen streets as well as at The Sottile Theatre, 44 George St., and at The American Theater, 446 King St.; phone (843) 577-5967 for information. Opera in Charleston also is a tradition: The first opera performance in America was presented here in 1735. Two centuries later George Gershwin wrote the opera "Porgy and Bess" in Cabbage Row, immortalized as Catfish Row in DuBose Heyward's novel "Porgy."

Gaillard Municipal Auditorium and Exhibition Hall, 77 Calhoun St., is home to the Charleston Ballet Theatre and the Charleston Symphony Orchestra. For information phone (843) 723-7334. The 2,300-seat Performing Arts Center in the North Charleston Area Convention Center Complex, 5001 Coliseum Dr., offers concerts and a variety of theatrical productions; phone (843) 529-5000.

Special Events

Oyster season runs September through April in Charleston, but the city celebrates this seafood tradition in January with the Lowcountry Oyster Festival. Oysters by the bucket are the main attraction of this winter event, but activities also include an oyster shucking contest, live music and children's events.

Wildlife connoisseurs of another sort have a month of their own: February in Charleston is Wildlife Month. The Southeastern Wildlife Exposition on the Friday, Saturday and Sunday preceding Presidents Day is one of the largest wildlife arts, crafts and collectibles shows in the South; phone (843) 723-1748.

Preeminent among Charleston's events is Spoleto Festival U.S.A., a celebration of the arts beginning Memorial Day weekend and continuing for 17 days. During the festival a full schedule of events encompassing music, dance, theater, opera, art, poetry and comedy takes place throughout the city; phone (843) 722-2764. The Piccolo Spoleto Festival serves as Charleston's companion festival and features local and regional performers and crafts; phone (843) 724-7305.

Every September a daylong international food festival, The Taste of Charleston, takes place. The cuisine of more than 50 of the city's finest restaurants can be sampled at one location.

Throughout December tours of traditionally decorated houses, churches and public buildings highlight the holiday season. Festivities also include the Parade of Boats in Charleston Harbor.

Many of Charleston's private houses are opened to the public two other times during the year. From mid-March to mid-April the Festival of Houses and Gardens *(see attraction listing p. 219)* offers afternoon and evening walking tours of private houses and gardens; phone (843) 722-3405 or (843) 723-1623. The Fall Tour of Homes & Gardens *(see attraction listing p. 219)*, held late September through late October, also offers an intimate glimpse of Charleston's architectural heritage; phone (843) 722-4630.

DID YOU KNOW

The first opera in America was performed in Charleston, Feb. 18, 1735.

The Charleston Vicinity

AWENDAW (D-5) pop. 1,195, elev. 20′

Cape Romain National Wildlife Refuge comprises undeveloped barrier islands and sea marshes that lie between the Atlantic Ocean and the Intracoastal Waterway; phone (843) 928-3368. All the islands—including primitive Bulls Island, which is popular with bird-watchers—can be reached only by ferry from Garris Landing; phone (843) 881-4582.

EDISTO ISLAND (E-4)

The Edistow Indians traded Edisto Island to the Lords Proprietors in 1674 for cloth, hatchets and goods. By the late 1700s, British settlers had developed a superior grade of cotton and prospered immensely from its export, giving them the means to establish large plantations. Union occupation during the Civil War forced planters to abandon their fine homes and cease tending the prized crop. The cotton industry recovered slowly after the war, then met its doom with the arrival of boll weevils in the 1920s.

Early plantation houses can be seen from the river, and some are open to the public during a home and church tour the second Saturday in October. Tour tickets and exhibits about area history are available at the Edisto Museum on Chisolm Plantation Road; phone (843) 869-1954.

Edisto's only inroad, SR 174, ends at the water's edge in Edisto Beach State Park. Swimming and shelling attract visitors to the pristine, secluded beach; phone (843) 869-2756. *See Recreation Chart.*

Edisto Chamber of Commerce: 430 SR 174, P.O. Box 206, Edisto Island, SC 29438; phone (843) 869-3867 or (888) 333-2781.

SAVE **EDISTO ISLAND SERPENTARIUM** is at 1374 SR 174. Snakes and reptiles from around the world are displayed in natural outdoor habitats and an indoor solarium. Handlers give demonstrations with live snakes at 11, 1, 3 and 5. Alligator feedings are offered twice daily at noon and 4. Allow 30 minutes minimum. Mon.-Sat. 10-6, May 23-Aug. 22; Thurs.-Sat. and Labor Day 10-6, Apr. 30-May 22 and Aug. 27-Aug. 30. Admission $12.95; $11.95 (ages 62+); $9.95 (ages 6-12); $5.95 (ages 4-5). MC, VI. Phone (843) 869-1171.

GEM FORT SUMTER NATIONAL MONUMENT (E-5)

Fort Sumter, a brick fortification built 1829-60 on a man-made island in Charleston Harbor, is accessible only by boat *(see What To Do, Boat Tours p. 224)*. On April 12, 1861, Confederate troops directed the opening shots of the Civil War against Fort Sumter, and after a 2-day bombardment, the small Union garrison surrendered.

Confederate forces occupied the fort until February 1865, successfully defying the blockade and foiling Federal attempts to capture Charleston, which remained a major port of the Confederacy. The fort contains some large cannons, and projectiles fired during the war still are embedded in the thick walls. A museum displays relics. National Park Service rangers present history talks.

Allow 2 hours, 30 minutes minimum. Tours depart daily from Liberty Square, 340 Concord St. next to the South Carolina Aquarium, at 9:30, noon and 2:30, and from Patriots Point Naval and Maritime Museum in Mount Pleasant at 10:45, 1:30 and 4, Mar.-Aug.; otherwise varies. Visitors should arrive 25 minutes prior to departure. Visitor center daily 8:30-5; closed Jan. 1, Thanksgiving and Dec. 25. Fort admission free. Fare $15; $13.50 (ages 62+ and military with ID); $9 (ages 6-11). AX, DS, MC, VI. Phone (843) 883-3123 for fort information, or (843) 722-1691 or (800) 789-3678 for boat schedule.

FORT MOULTRIE is on Sullivan's Island, reached via US 17 and SR 703. A military post for more than 170 years, the fort was the site of one of the first American victories of the Revolutionary War. The outnumbered Colonial garrison withstood bombardment by the British navy, whose shells were absorbed by the spongy palmetto log and sand defenses. Less than a century later the fort played a role during the Confederate attack on Fort Sumter.

A visitor center houses exhibits and shows a 20-minute film. Allow 1 hour, 30 minutes minimum. Daily 9-5; closed Jan. 1 and Dec. 25. Admission $3; $1 (senior citizens); free (ages 0-15); $5 (family). Phone (843) 883-3123.

FORT SUMTER TOURS—
see What To Do, Boat Tours p. 224.

FRANCIS MARION NATIONAL FOREST

Elevations in the forest range from sea level to 50 ft. Refer to AAA maps for additional elevation information.

North of Charleston, Francis Marion National Forest covers 251,000 acres of low flatlands, coastal sand areas, black swamp waters, moss-hung oaks, pines and little lakes, or Carolina Bays, thought to be water-filled meteorite impact depressions. The land had been heavily logged and was in poor condition when it was purchased from private owners in the 1930s. The newly created forest was named for the Revolutionary War general who engaged British troops in many skirmishes and battles in the area and then took refuge in the deep swamps, thus earning the nickname Swamp Fox. Much of the restoration performed over the succeeding 5 decades was undone by Hurricane Hugo in 1989, when more than 1 billion board feet of timber was destroyed.

Home to varied wildlife, the forest is a primary habitat of the red-cockaded woodpecker and of the swallow-tailed kite. At Rembert Dennis Wildlife Center in Bonneau off US 52, striped bass fingerlings are raised and studied; the center has free maps of the forest; phone (843) 825-3387.

For additional information contact the Forest Supervisor's Office, 4931 Broad River Rd., Columbia, SC 29212. Phone (803) 561-4000. *See Recreation Chart and the AAA Southeastern CampBook.*

HARLEYVILLE (D-4) pop. 594, elev. 92′

SAVE **AUDUBON CENTER AT FRANCIS BEIDLER FOREST** is off I-26W exit 187 or I-26E exit 177, following Beidler Forest signs. The 16,000-acre sanctuary contains the largest known stand of virgin cypress and tupelo trees in the world. A 1.75-mile boardwalk offers a close look at cypress trees that are more than 1,000 years old as well as abundant native wildlife and plant life. The visitor center has displays relating to the swamp. Guided 4-hour canoe trips are offered in spring.

Allow 1 hour minimum. Tues.-Sun. 9-5. Canoe trips Fri.-Sun. afternoons, Mar.-May. Closed Jan. 1, Thanksgiving and Dec. 24-25 and 31. Admission $7; $3.50 (ages 6-18). Canoe trip $25; $15 (ages 8-18). Reservations are required for canoe trips. Phone (843) 462-2150.

ISLE OF PALMS (D-5) pop. 4,583, elev. 3′

SAVE **BARRIER ISLAND ECOTOURS** departs from Isle of Palms Marina, jct. SRs 703 and 517. A narrated 3.5-hour excursion to Capers Island features wildlife sightings in salt-marsh tidal creeks and opportunities for shelling, bird-watching and island exploration. During the cruise, nets and habitat traps are pulled to give passengers a close look at marine creatures. Sunset cruises, crabbing clinics and kayak adventures also are available.

Allow 2 hours minimum. Capers Island excursions Tues., Thurs. and Sat. at 9, Fri. at 1:30, Memorial Day-Labor Day; Tues., Thurs. and Sat. at 9, rest of year. Phone for information about other tours. Fare $36; $32 (senior citizens); $26 (ages 0-11). Reservations are recommended. AX, MC, VI. Phone (843) 886-5000.

McCLELLANVILLE (D-5) pop. 459, elev. 9′

HAMPTON PLANTATION STATE HISTORIC SITE is at 1950 Rutledge Rd. The focus of this 322-acre park is the two-story Georgian grand mansion that grew from a six-room farmhouse built 1730-50 on this former rice plantation. The building is unfurnished in order to show its architectural detail, and walls have cutaway sections to reveal construction techniques. Fishing and nature trails are offered.

Picnicking is permitted. Allow 1 hour minimum. Park daily 9-6. Mansion Tues.-Sun. noon-4, Mar.-Oct.; Thurs.-Sun. noon-4, rest of year. Mansion tours are given on the hour. Last tour departs 1 hour before closing. Park free. Mansion $4; $3 (ages

6-15); $2.50 (senior citizens). Phone (843) 546-9361.

THE VILLAGE MUSEUM is at 401 Pinckney St. Guided tours through this museum provide insights into local history. Displays and exhibits showcase Seewee Indian villages and McClellanville's establishment as a coastal resort. Farming, timber harvesting and the seafood industry also are profiled. An archive provides extensive genealogical and area history resources. Thurs.-Sat. 10-noon and 1-5. Admission $3; free (children). Phone (843) 887-3030.

MONCKS CORNER (D-5)
pop. 5,952, elev. 50′

The Biggin Church Ruins can be found on SR 402. The St. John's Parish church dates to the early 18th century, and it suffered several fires in its history. Two were from forest fires, and one was set by the British, who were using it as an ammunition storage facility during the American Revolution. After the 1880s forest fire, it was not rebuilt. Two partial walls can be seen, and the cemetery is still in use. The site is open daily dawn to dusk.

GEM SAVE **CYPRESS GARDENS,** 5.2 mi. s.e. off US 52 at 3030 Cypress Gardens Rd., encompasses more than 170 acres of parkland in a setting of giant cypress trees growing out of a black-water swamp. Azaleas, camellias and daffodils seen from well-marked paths provide an unforgettable picture. Peak bloom occurs in March and April. The gardens and swamp once were part of Dean Hall, a prosperous early 18th-century rice plantation.

Animal sightings, like flora, vary by season, but wildlife viewing may include alligators, bald eagles, hawks, herons, otters and wood ducks. Bateaux—flat-bottomed boats—allow visitors to explore the swamp with a guide or on their own. A 24,000-gallon freshwater aquarium, a crocodile exhibit, a reptile center and an enclosed butterfly house also are on the grounds. About 4.5 miles of walking trails are available.

Food is available. Daily 9-5; closed Jan. 1, Thanksgiving and Dec. 24-25. Last admission is 1 hour before closing. Admission $10; $9 (ages 65+); $5 (ages 6-12). Guided boat ride $5 (per person). Boat rental for self-guiding tour $5 (per boatload). Phone ahead to verify prices. MC, VI. Phone (843) 553-0515.

MEPKIN ABBEY is 2 mi. s. on SR 402 from jct. US 52, 7.6 mi. s. on Mepkin Abbey Rd. then just w., following signs. This was once Mepkin Plantation, home to Revolutionary patriot and politician Henry Laurens, whose contributions include serving as president of the Continental Congress 1777-78. The serene terraced gardens and oak-strewn grounds overlooking the Cooper River are now home to Trappist monks. Visitors may walk the grounds on their own or take a tour given by one of the monks. Guided tours of the church and grounds include an explanation of monastic life and the history of the abbey.

Ring the bell at the reception center upon your arrival. Allow 1 hour, 30 minutes minimum. Grounds Tues.-Fri. 9-4:30, Sat. 9-4, Sun. 1-4:30. Guided tours are offered at 11:30 (includes the midday prayer service) and 3. Garden tours are available by appointment. Closed Easter, Thanksgiving and Dec. 25. Donations. Phone (843) 761-8509.

GEM SAVE **OLD SANTEE CANAL PARK** is 1 mi. e. off US 52 bypass at 900 Stony Landing Rd. The canal was constructed between the Santee and Cooper rivers in 1800 to flow goods from the Upcountry to Charleston Harbor. Within 50 years, the railroad had replaced the waterway for shipping, and most of the canal route is now covered by Lake Moultrie. The park preserves the canal's southern terminus.

An interpretive center highlights the history and workings of the canal through a scale model, an operating lock and archeological finds; wildlife displays focus on natural beauty. The Berkeley Museum traces regional history from early American Indian cultures to such 20th-century accomplishments as rural electrification. A special exhibit details the life of the elusive Revolutionary War hero Gen. Francis Marion (the Swamp Fox). Four miles of nature trails and boardwalks with observation decks allow visitors to view the bald cypress swamp, marl bluffs and resident wildlife including alligators, great blue herons and wood ducks.

Allow 3 hours minimum. Daily 9-5. Museum Tues.-Sat. 9-4:30, Sun. 1-4:30. Admission $3; free (ages 0-6). MC, VI. Phone (843) 899-5200, or (843) 899-5101 for the museum.

MOUNT PLEASANT (D-5)
pop. 47,609, elev. 24′

The making of baskets from native sweetgrass is a traditional art form begun in the Mount Pleasant community more than 300 years ago. Slaves brought to the area from West Africa have passed the skill from generation to generation. Originally used for the storage of staples, the baskets are prized today for their craftsmanship and artistry. Basket makers sell their wares from roadside stands along US 17 north of Mount Pleasant and near the Old City Market in downtown Charleston.

GEM SAVE **BOONE HALL PLANTATION & GARDENS,** 8 mi. n. on US 17 at 1235 Long Point Rd., traces its history to a 1681 land grant to Maj. John Boone. Primarily a cotton plantation, it also produced bricks and tiles. The current mansion, built in 1935 to resemble an antebellum house, contains plantation-made bricks as well as woodwork and flooring from an earlier house. Costumed docents lead tours of the first floor, which is furnished with antiques. Afterward, actors present a short skit portraying the antebellum South.

Nine brick slave cabins comprising a slave street contain furnishings and artifacts. Demonstrations of sweetgrass artistry and a presentation about Gullah culture are offered in separate slave buildings. The original circular smokehouse, a dock house built on the foundation of the original cotton dock, a stable built in the 1940s and a butterfly pavilion also can be seen.

Formal gardens with antique roses, camellias and azaleas grace the grounds. An in-depth coach tour of the former cotton fields, pecan groves, wetlands and working produce farm is available.

Food is available. Allow 3 hours minimum. Guided house tours are given Mon.-Sat. every 30 minutes 9-5, Sun. 1-4, day after Labor Day-March 31; Mon.-Sat. 8:30-6:30, Sun 1-5, rest of year. Last tour begins 30 minutes before closing. Coach tours, slave street history tours and Gullah talks are given throughout the day. Closed Thanksgiving and Dec. 25. Admission $17.50; $15 (ages 65+ and military with ID); $7.50 (ages 6-12). Ages 0-4 are not permitted on coach tour. Phone (843) 884-4371.

CHARLES PINCKNEY NATIONAL HISTORIC SITE is at 1254 Long Point Rd. This 28-acre site, once part of Charles Pinckney's 715-acre plantation known as Snee Farm, examines Pinckney's major role in the framing of the U.S. Constitution. The visitor center, in an 1828 farmhouse, has exhibits about Pinckney, the Constitution, Lowcountry plantation life and slavery. Daily 9-5; closed Jan. 1 and Dec. 25. Free. Phone (843) 881-5516.

GEM **PATRIOTS POINT NAVAL AND MARITIME MUSEUM,** 2 mi. e. on US 17 at 40 Patriots Point Rd., is dominated by the USS *Yorktown,* an aircraft carrier that served in World War II and Vietnam. On board is the Congressional Medal of Honor Museum, showcasing individuals who have received the highest military honor. The film "The Fighting Lady" is shown regularly; it depicts life aboard an aircraft carrier and was shot on the USS *Yorktown* during World War II; the ship carried the nickname Fighting Lady thereafter.

Twenty-six aircraft are displayed, and visitors can tour the ship's bridge, hangar bay, flight deck and other areas. The Carrier Hall of Fame also is included. Visitors can tour the submarine *Clamagore,* which patrolled Cuban waters during the 1962 Cuban missile crisis; the destroyer *Laffey,* which participated in the D-Day landings of Allied troops and was nicknamed the "Ship That Would Not Die"; and the Coast Guard cutter *Ingham,* which sank a U-boat in World War II. The complex includes the Cold War Submarine Memorial.

Guided tours are available. Food is available. Allow 3 hours minimum. Daily 9-6:30; closed Dec. 25. Admission $16; $13 (ages 62+ and military with ID); $8 (ages 6-11); free (military in uniform). MC, VI. Phone (866) 831-1720.

NORTH CHARLESTON (D-4)

pop. 79,641, elev. 20′

Shopping areas: Bargains can be found in dozens of stores at SAVE Tanger Outlet Center, 4840 Tanger Outlet Blvd.

***H.L. HUNLEY*/WARREN LASCH CONSERVATION CENTER** is off I-26 exit 216B, 1.1 mi. n. on SR 7 (Cosgrove Ave.), just n.w. on Spruill Ave. and e. on McMillan Ave. onto the former navy base to Building 255 at 1250 Supply St., following signs. Guided tours of this converted warehouse allow visitors to see the large tank that holds the Confederate submarine *H.L. Hunley* that sank during the Civil War and wasn't discovered until 1995. The vessel was recovered five years later. The facility also includes related exhibits.

Allow 30 minutes minimum. Sat. 10-5, Sun. noon-5. Admission $12; $10 (senior citizens and military with ID); free (ages 0-4). AX, CB, DC, DS, JC, MC, VI. Phone (843) 743-4865 for information or (877) 448-6539 for tickets.

SAVE **THE NORTH CHARLESTON AND AMERICAN LAFRANCE FIRE MUSEUM AND EDUCATION CENTER** is at 4975 Centre Pointe Dr. The facility features a collection of antique firefighting memorabilia, including 18 antique and new trucks. Interactive exhibits educate the public about fire safety and prevention as well as how to react in a fire. Charleston's fire history also is shared. Allow 45 minutes minimum. Mon.-Sat. 10-5; closed major holidays. Admission $6; free (ages 0-12). AX, DS, MC, VI. Phone (843) 740-5550.

ROCKVILLE (E-4) pop. 137, elev. 23′

GEM **CHARLESTON TEA PLANTATION** is nearby at 6617 Maybank Hwy. on Wadmalaw Island. A 15-minute factory tour introduces visitors to how tea is made from tea leaves. A window 125 feet in length allows visitors to look down and observe factory equipment, and footage of the manufacturing process is shown on large screens. A 20-minute trolley tour of the expansive grounds also is available. Visitors are driven through the tea fields and the guide reveals how the plants are grown and explains the history of tea. The harvest season is May through October.

Picnicking is permitted. Allow 45 minutes minimum. Wed.-Sat. 10-4, Sun. noon-4; closed major holidays. Factory tour free. Trolley tour $10; free (ages 0-6); $30 (family of 4; each additional child $3). AX, DS, MC, VI. Phone (843) 559-0383.

SULLIVAN'S ISLAND (E-5) pop. 1,911

Near Charleston Harbor, Sullivan's Island was named for Capt. Florence O'Sullivan of the *Carolina,* which, in 1670, was the first English ship to bring settlers. The island is the site of Fort Moultrie *(see Fort Sumter National Monument p. 236),* where American troops first triumphed over the British forces during the Revolution. It also was the setting for Edgar Allan Poe's "The Gold Bug." A lighthouse stands at the island's southern tip.

SUMMERVILLE (D-4) pop. 27,752, elev. 75′

Summerville was settled by coastal dwellers who moved inland in the summer to escape malaria. By the early 1890s the town became a popular health and winter resort. Much of its charm is derived from the natural beauty of its rambling streets, which wind around numerous pine trees protected by an ordinance prohibiting their removal. Azaleas, camellias and wisteria line the streets and provide seasonal blooms.

COLONIAL DORCHESTER STATE HISTORIC SITE, 6 mi. s. on SR 642, preserves the remnants of the former community of Dorchester, which was settled in 1697 by a small group of Congregationalists from Dorchester, Mass. Most moved to Midway, Ga., in the 1750s, and the village ultimately was destroyed by retreating British soldiers in 1781. Ruins of a fort and the bell tower of St. George's Church are all that remain.

A visitor center is on the grounds. Fishing and walking trails are offered. Archeological excavations are offered weekends. Picnicking is permitted. Allow 2 hours minimum. Daily 9-6. Admission $2; $1.25 (ages 65+); free (ages 0-15). Phone (843) 873-1740.

Nathaniel Russell House / © Rick Rhodes / Historic Charleston Foundation

This ends listings for the Charleston Vicinity.
The following page resumes the alphabetical listings of cities in South Carolina.

CHERAW (B-4) pop. 5,524, elev. 150′

Settled before 1750 and formally laid out in 1768, the town officially was named Cheraw in 1820 after a local American Indian tribe. Its position at the navigational head of the Pee Dee River made Cheraw an important trade center that grew proportionally with increased river traffic, particularly during the cotton era.

Gen. William T. Sherman's Union troops occupied Cheraw during the Civil War and were so taken by its charming atmosphere that they spared it from destruction. More than 50 antebellum houses and buildings and many late 19th- and early 20th-century structures can be found in the historic district, which encompasses 213 acres in the center of town. The original town green and parish church, Old St. David's, still grace Cheraw.

Local history exhibits and a tribute to native son Dizzy Gillespie are displayed at the Lyceum Museum on Market Street. A large bronze statue on the town green pays further homage to the late jazz musician. Keys to the museum and Old St. David's Church can be picked up at the chamber of commerce.

With more than 7,000 acres, Cheraw State Park on US 52 provides numerous opportunities for outdoor activity. Amenities include an 18-hole golf course and equestrian campsites. *See Recreation Chart and the AAA Southeastern CampBook.*

Cheraw Visitors Bureau: 221 Market St., Cheraw, SC 29520; phone (843) 537-7681.

Self-guiding tours: A brochure detailing a tour of the historic district is available at the Greater Cheraw Chamber of Commerce, located within the Cheraw Visitors Bureau.

CHERAW FISH HATCHERY, 6 mi. s. on US 1, raises large- and small-mouth bass; bluegill, red breast and red ear sunfish; channel catfish and striped bass for public lakes and rivers in South Carolina. The hatchery has 31 production ponds and two water-supply lakes. Picnicking is permitted. Allow 30 minutes minimum. Mon.-Fri. 7-3. Free. Phone (843) 537-7628.

CLEMSON (B-1) pop. 11,939, elev. 850′

Clemson was known as Calhoun when incorporated in 1892, then renamed in the 1940s. Land titles can be traced to relatives of John C. Calhoun, supporting one theory about the origin of the town name.

By the 1893 opening of the military-style Clemson Agricultural College, now Clemson University, Calhoun already had established itself as one of Pickens County's most important towns, boasting a railroad depot, cotton mill and general store as well as several boarding houses. Clemson's Old Calhoun District features historic buildings.

CLEMSON UNIVERSITY, 11 mi. w. of I-85 exit 19B on US 76, was established in 1889 as a scientific college on the former plantation of John C. Calhoun, a prominent statesman and U.S. vice president, senator and secretary of state. Maps and information for tours of the 1,400-acre campus can be obtained at the visitor center on Daniel Drive next to the Alumni Center.

Visitor center Mon.-Fri. 8-4:30, Sat. 9-4:30, Sun. 1-4:30. Guided 1.5-hour walking tours are given Mon.-Sat. at 9:45 and 1:45, some Sun at 1:45, during spring and fall semesters. Phone ahead to confirm tour schedule. Free. Phone (864) 656-4789.

Bob Campbell Geology Museum, 103 Garden Tr. at the South Carolina Botanical Garden, contains minerals, fossils and gemstones from around the world as well as American Indian artifacts. A replica of a saber-toothed cat skeleton is displayed. A darkened showroom features a collection of fluorescent rocks. Picnicking is permitted. Allow 1 hour minimum. Wed.-Sat. 10-5, Sun. 1-5; closed major holidays. Admission $3; $2 (ages 3-12). Phone (864) 656-4600.

Fort Hill, jct. Fort Hill St. and Calhoun Dr., was purchased by John C. Calhoun during his first term as U.S. vice president to John Quincy Adams. His son-in-law, Thomas G. Clemson, founded the university that now occupies the former plantation. Many original furnishings belonging to Calhoun and Clemson decorate the house. Guided tours are available. Mon.-Sat. 10-noon and 1-4:30, Sun. 2-4:30; closed university and major holidays. Admission $5; $4 (senior citizens); $2 (children). Phone (864) 656-2475.

Robert Muldrow Cooper Library is at the center of the Clemson University campus off S. Palmetto Blvd. The James F. Byrnes Room and Edgar A. Brown Room on the main floor exhibit collections of papers, furniture and other memorabilia pertaining to these two 20th-century statesmen. Changing exhibits are presented in the lobby. Daily 10 a.m.-midnight; closed holidays. Free. Phone (864) 656-3027.

Rudolph E. Lee Gallery, in Lee Hall on the w. side of the Clemson campus between Perimeter Rd. and S. Palmetto Blvd., displays works by leading architects, artists and craftspeople as well as works by art and architecture students. Mon.-Fri. 9-4:30, Sun. 2-5, during academic year; closed major holidays. Free. Phone (864) 656-3883.

South Carolina Botanical Garden, e. side of the campus off Perimeter Rd., is a 295-acre garden with an arboretum; gristmill; greenhouse; pagoda; and the Pioneer Complex, which has exhibits labeled in Braille. The garden contains 2,200 varieties of plants, including one of the largest shrub collections in the eastern United States. The wildflower, fern and bog gardens contain species native to the state. Hiking trails are available. Daily dawn-dusk. Free. Phone (864) 656-3405.

Strom Thurmond Institute, on Perimeter Rd. next to the parking lot s. of the Robert Muldrow Cooper Library, contains papers and memorabilia documenting the life and career of U.S. Sen. James Strom

Thurmond. Also featured are a rare book collection and documents from such important political leaders as John C. Calhoun; the university archives; and manuscript collections, the focus of which is primarily South Carolina. Changing exhibits are presented. Mon.-Fri. 8-4:30, during the academic year; closed major holidays. Free. Phone (864) 656-4700.

COLUMBIA (C-4) pop. 116,278, elev. 260′

Originally settled on the opposite bank of the Congaree River, Columbia was created and designated South Carolina's capital by a 1786 act of the legislature, which moved the seat of government from Charleston. On Dec. 17, 1860, a convention met to draw up the Ordinance of Secession, but because of a smallpox epidemic the convention moved to Charleston, where the ordinance was signed.

Gen. William Tecumseh Sherman entered Columbia on Feb. 17, 1865, and set a fire the same night that destroyed three-fourths of the city, including every house on Main Street except that of the French consul. The university, public buildings and statehouse also were spared. The South Carolina Governor's Mansion, the surviving structure of a destroyed military school, is open by appointment; phone (803) 737-1710.

Chartered in 1801, the University of South Carolina plays a prominent role in Columbia. The original campus of the university, known as the Horseshoe, contains 10 restored buildings dating to the early 19th century; the buildings are currently used for classrooms, offices and living quarters. The visitor center, on the corner of Assembly and Pendleton streets, has displays and interactive exhibits about the university's history and campus. Campus tours are conducted Monday through Friday at 10 and 2 during the academic year. Tour times vary during summer months; phone (803) 777-0169, (803) 777-2125 or (800) 922-9755 for information.

Finlay Park, set in the historic Congaree Vista, features lakes, waterfalls, walking trails, a Leland cypress tree, a playground and patios surrounding a plaza; phone (803) 545-3100.

Columbia Metropolitan Convention and Visitors Bureau and Visitors Center: 1101 Lincoln St., P.O. Box 15, Columbia, SC 29202; phone (803) 545-0000 or (800) 264-4884.

Shopping areas: Columbia Place, 7201 Two Notch Rd., features Dillard's, Macy's and Sears. Columbiana Centre, 100 Columbiana Cir., offers Ann Taylor Loft, Banana Republic and Dillard's. Old Mill Antique Mall, 310 State St., is home to some 75 antiques dealers. Produce, fresh flowers and specialty foods are sold Monday through Saturday at the State Farmers' Market, 1001 Bluff Rd.

THE COLUMBIA MUSEUM OF ART, Main and Hampton sts., features the Samuel H. Kress Collection of Italian Renaissance and Baroque paintings as

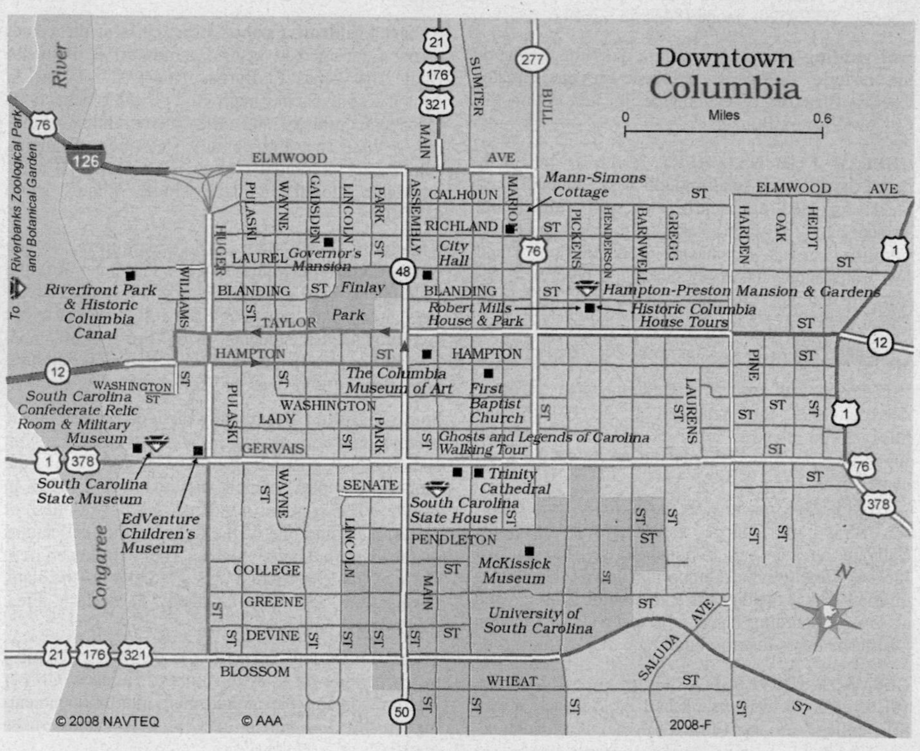

well as American and European art dating from the 18th century to the present day. An extensive collection of decorative arts includes bronze sculpture, textiles, furniture and glass pieces by Louis Comfort Tiffany. Allow 1 hour minimum. Wed.-Sat. 10-5 (also Fri. 5-9), Sun. 1-5. Admission $5; $4 (ages 60+); $2 (students with ID); free (Sat.). Phone (803) 799-2810.

EDVENTURE CHILDREN'S MUSEUM is .7 mi. s.w. at 211 Gervais St. This 67,000-square-foot museum features an array of interactive exhibits and activities designed for ages 1-12. Visitors can explore global cultures and climb a giant spider web. "Eddie," a 40-foot sculpture of a child, anchors the BodyWorks gallery. Other highlights include a talking skeleton, real fire trucks and tractors, a newsroom and a soft-sculpted pond where babies and toddlers can "swim" with tadpoles.

Allow 1 hour minimum. Mon.-Sat. 9-5, Sun. noon-5, Memorial Day-Labor Day; Tues.-Sat. 9-5, Sun. noon-5, rest of year. Closed Thanksgiving and Dec. 24-25. Admission $8.95; $6.95 (ages 1-12). MC, VI. Phone (803) 779-3100.

FIRST BAPTIST CHURCH is on Hampton St. near Marion St. Built in 1856, the church was the site of the first Secession Convention, which led to the Civil War. Mon.-Fri. 8:30-5. Free. Phone (803) 256-4251.

FORT JACKSON MUSEUM is at Fort Jackson; take Devine St. s.e. to Fort Jackson Blvd., then n. to the post. Fort Jackson is a U.S. Army Training Center established in 1917. The museum details the history of the post and the training of the soldiers. Large military equipment such as a helicopter, tanks and half-tracks is displayed outdoors. Mon.-Fri. 9-4, Sat. 9-6; closed federal holidays. Free. Phone (803) 751-7419.

SAVE **GHOSTS AND LEGENDS OF CAROLINA WALKING TOUR** departs from the State House at jct. Gervais and Main sts. A 90-minute tour introduces participants to Columbia's eerie side through stories of ghosts, legends, restless spirits and folk traditions. Daily at 8 p.m.; closed Thanksgiving and Dec. 25. Fee $18; $15 (ages 66+ and students with ID); $10 (ages 8-14). AX, MC, VI. Phone (803) 765-1837 or (866) 550-8939.

SAVE **HISTORIC COLUMBIA HOUSE TOURS,** departing from the Robert Mills Historic House, 1616 Blanding St., offers 45-minute guided tours of four 19th-century houses in downtown Columbia: Hampton-Preston Mansion and Gardens, Mann-Simons Cottage, Robert Mills House and Park, and Woodrow Wilson Family Home (closed throughout 2009). Tickets are issued at the Robert Mills House.

Guided tours are offered on the hour Tues.-Sat. 10-3, Sun. 1-4; closed major holidays. Admission (per house) $6; $5 (ages 66+, active military and students with ID); $3 (ages 6-17). Combination ticket for all three houses $15; $12 (ages 66+, active military and students with ID); $8 (ages 6-17). MC, VI. Phone (803) 252-1770.

GEM SAVE **Hampton-Preston Mansion and Gardens,** 1615 Blanding St., is a restored house reflecting life in antebellum Columbia. The 1818 house was purchased by Gen. Wade Hampton I in 1823 and at his death, his daughter and son in law, Caroline and John Preston, moved in. The couple built the north facade's addition 1845-50, which doubled the structure's size.

Over the years the house has served as Union Army Headquarters, the governor's mansion and two separate colleges. Many of the items and furnishings displayed throughout the house belonged to the family, including some Caroline and John brought home from their European travels.

Allow 45 minutes minimum. Guided tours are offered on the hour Tues.-Sat. 10-3, Sun. 1-4; closed major holidays. Admission $6; $5 (ages 66+, active military and students with ID); $3 (ages 6-17). Combination ticket with Mann-Simons Cottage and Robert Mills House and Park $15; $12 (ages 66+, active military and students with ID); $8 (ages 6-17). MC, VI. Phone (803) 252-1770.

SAVE **Mann-Simons Cottage,** 1403 Richland St., was the 1850 home of Celia Mann, a Charleston slave who purchased her freedom and walked to Columbia. The house features the original dining room table with hand-pressed nails, horsehair plaster walls and the original brick fireplace. The First Calvary Baptist Church was organized in the basement of the house.

Allow 45 minutes minimum. Guided tours are offered on the hour Tues.-Sat. 10-3, Sun. 1-4; closed major holidays. Admission $6; $5 (ages 66+, active military and students with ID); $3 (ages 6-17). Combination ticket with Hampton-Preston Mansion and Gardens and Robert Mills House and Park $15; $12 (ages 66+, active military and students with ID); $8 (ages 6-17). MC, VI. Phone (803) 252-1770.

SAVE **Robert Mills House and Park,** 1616 Blanding St., was designed by Robert Mills and houses a Regency decorative arts collection. The 1823 house features Venetian windows, formal English gardens and three floors of rooms furnished in the Regency style. Mills, the first federal architect of the United States, served seven presidents. His many notable designs include the Washington Monument and the U.S. Treasury Building in Washington, D.C.

Allow 45 minutes minimum. Guided tours are offered on the hour Tues.-Sat. 10-3, Sun. 1-4; closed major holidays. Admission $6; $5 (ages 66+, active military and students with ID); $3 (ages 6-17). Combination ticket with Hampton-Preston Mansion and Gardens and Mann-Simons Cottage $15; $12 (ages 66+, active military and students with ID); $8 (ages 6-17). MC, VI. Phone (803) 252-1770.

Woodrow Wilson Family Home, 1705 Hampton St., was built by Wilson's parents; young Wilson lived in the house 1872-75, from the age of 16 through 19. The house, a Victorian structure in the mode of a Tuscan villa, contains Wilson family memorabilia; original gas lighting fixtures; marble mantels; and period furnishings, including the bed in which Woodrow was born. **CLOSURE INFORMATION:** Due to renovations, the house is expected to be closed throughout 2009. Phone (803) 252-1770.

McKISSICK MUSEUM is at the head of the Historic Horseshoe area on the University of South Carolina campus, 2 blks. s. of the State House near Bull and Pendleton sts. Permanent collections, which focus on Southern folk art, culture and the natural environment, include the Howard Gemstone Collection and the Bernard Baruch Silver Collection as well as items pertaining to the history of the university and South Carolina. The museum also offers changing exhibits. Allow 1 hour minimum. Mon.-Fri. 8:30-5, Sat. 11-3; closed holidays. Free. Phone (803) 777-7251.

GEM **RIVERBANKS ZOOLOGICAL PARK AND BOTANICAL GARDEN,** at jct. Greystone Blvd. and I-126, is a sanctuary for more than 2,000 animals, including such endangered species as the Siberian tiger and black rhinoceros. Highlights include the African Plains, home to giraffes, zebras and ostriches; Ndoki Forest, a gorilla sanctuary; and a farm with domestic animals.

The Aquarium/Reptile Complex encompasses four display areas ranging from the South Carolina Gallery, with a spectrum of native amphibians and fish, to the exotic Tropic Gallery. Other park features include daily penguin and sea lion feedings, elephant shows and bird flight demonstrations.

The 70-acre botanical garden, across the Lower Saluda River and reached from within the park via tram or a woodlands walkway, is planted for year-round interest.

Food is available. Allow 2 hours minimum. Mon.-Fri. 9-5, Sat.-Sun. 9-6, late Mar. to mid-Oct.; daily 9-5, rest of year. Closed Thanksgiving and Dec. 25. Admission $9.75; $8.25 (ages 62+); $7.50 (students with ID); $7.25 (ages 3-12). MC, VI. Phone (803) 779-8717.

RIVERFRONT PARK AND HISTORIC COLUMBIA CANAL, Laurel and Gist sts., centers on the city's original waterworks and hydroelectric plant. A walkway leads to the Columbia Canal. The 1824 canal was an essential means of transportation prior to the railroad. It then became a major source of hydroelectric power. The park features several brick buildings, vintage-style lighting fixtures and wrought-iron fencing. Recreation includes biking, hiking and fishing. Picnicking is permitted. Allow 30 minutes minimum. Daily 7:30 a.m.-11 p.m. Free. Phone (803) 545-3100.

SOUTH CAROLINA ARCHIVES & HISTORY CENTER, 8301 Parklane Rd., houses governmental records of South Carolina dating back to 1671. Quarterly exhibits reflect the historic and cultural heritage of the state. Mon.-Fri. 8:30-5; closed major holidays. Free. Phone (803) 896-6100.

SOUTH CAROLINA CONFEDERATE RELIC ROOM & MILITARY MUSEUM, 301 Gervais St. in the former Columbia Mills building, contains a collection of military relics reflecting state military history, particularly the Civil War period. Flags, uniforms and weapons are among the displayed items. Guided tours are available. Allow 1 hour minimum. Tues.-Sat. 10-5, first Sun. of the month 1-5. Admission $4; $1 (first Sun. of the month); free (ages 0-20). Combination ticket with South Carolina State Museum (which is in the same building) $6. MC, VI. Phone (803) 737-8095.

SOUTH CAROLINA LAW ENFORCEMENT OFFICERS HALL OF FAME, 10 mi. n.w. at 5400 Broad River Rd., is a memorial to law enforcement officers who have died in the line of duty. Exhibits of photographs, artifacts, equipment, uniforms and insignia focus on historical and contemporary aspects of law enforcement in South Carolina. Also displayed are a 1955 Highway Patrol car, a 1930s prison cell and the Melvin Purvis firearms collection. Allow 30 minutes minimum. Mon.-Fri. 8:30-5; closed state holidays. Free. Phone (803) 896-8199.

GEM **SOUTH CAROLINA STATE HOUSE,** 1100 Gervais St., was constructed 1855-1907 and features a copper dome, original marble floors, cast-iron stairs and balcony supports, stained-glass windows and portraits of notable statesmen. Six bronze stars on the exterior walls mark the spots struck by Gen. William T. Sherman's Union Army cannonballs during the Civil War.

The 18-acre capitol complex encompasses landscaped grounds appointed with 25 monuments, including statues of George Washington, Civil War general Wade Hampton, and Sen. Strom Thurmond; a replica of the Liberty Bell; and a memorial to African-American history. A walking tour brochure is available.

Guided tours are available. Allow 1 hour minimum. Mon.-Fri. 9-5, Sat. 10-4, first Sun. of the month 1-4; closed holidays. Phone for tour schedule. Free. Phone (803) 734-2430.

GEM **SOUTH CAROLINA STATE MUSEUM,** 301 Gervais St., is in the former Columbia Mills building. Built in 1894, the structure was one of the first totally electric textile mills in the world. Today this facility has four floors of hands-on exhibits, displays and items chronicling state history, industry and transportation as well as science and technology and natural history. A laser light show is presented regularly. The Lipscomb Art Gallery offers changing exhibits.

The cultural history exhibits showcase some 14,000 years of area history. The natural history exhibits feature dinosaur fossils and dioramas depicting the state's major habitats. Highlights include a 43-foot-long model of a great white shark and a life-size mastodon reconstruction.

Allow 2 hours minimum. Tues.-Sat. 10-5, Sun. 1-5; closed Jan. 1, Easter, Thanksgiving and Dec. 24-25. Admission $5; $4 (ages 62+, military and students with ID); $3 (ages 3-12); $1 (first Sun. of the month). Ages 0-12 must be with an adult. Combination ticket with South Carolina Confederate Relic Room & Military Museum (which is in the same building) $6. Phone (803) 898-4921.

TRINITY CATHEDRAL (Episcopal), is at 1100 Sumter St. between Senate and Gervais sts. The mid-1800s structure is a beautiful example of English Gothic architecture. Modeled after Britain's York Cathedral, the cathedral has stained-glass windows from Munich, Germany, and a marble font and altar. Allow 30 minutes minimum. Tours are given Mon.-Fri. 10-2, mid-Mar. to mid-May and mid-Sept. to mid-Nov.; by appointment rest of year. Free. Phone (803) 771-7300.

CONGAREE NATIONAL PARK (C-4)

Elevations in the park range from 75 ft. to 136 ft.. Refer to AAA maps for additional elevation information.

Situated along the Congaree River, approximately 3 miles southeast of Hopkins off SR 48 (Bluff Rd.), following signs, the Congaree National Park encompasses 22,200 acres and is the largest intact tract of old-growth floodplain forest in North America. The park, a sanctuary for diverse flora and fauna, is characterized by giant hardwoods and towering pines and comprises one of the highest canopies in the world and some of the tallest trees in the eastern United States.

Over the centuries, the prehistoric forest has survived several significant challenges. From their arrival around 1700 and continuing through 1860, the European settlers attempted to make the land suitable for planting and grazing. Despite the settlers' best efforts, agricultural activity was prevented due to intermittent flooding, but the latter allowed for soil renewal and enabled the forest's trees to thrive. Bald Cypress, in particular, became a target for logging, and by 1905 much of the area had been acquired for logging purposes. Within 10 years, poor accessibility by land and the forest's perpetual dampness had suspended operations, leaving the forest predominantly untouched.

In 1969 private landowners considered resuming logging operations. The reaction was an effective campaign launched by a group of South Carolinian environmentalists and concerned individuals who banded together to protect the floodplain. In 1976 Congress established Congaree Swamp National Monument.

The force of Hurricane Hugo in September 1989 resulted in the park losing several national champion trees but the hurricane also proved to be a catalyst for new forest growth. Fallen trees have served as shelter for many species of organisms and standing dead trees provided new homes for a variety of plant and animal species. The Congaree Swamp National Monument was designated a national park in November 2003.

Recreational opportunities include picnicking, hiking, fishing, primitive camping, canoeing, kayaking, bird-watching, ranger-guided interpretive walks and canoe tours, nature study, and environmental education programs. More information about the park's activities is available at the visitor center.

Visitors may experience the park by way of six walking trails. The elevated 2.3-mile boardwalk loop moves from primeval swamp to massive pines and hardwood forests. The 1.7-mile Bluff Trail, near the visitor center, traverses a young loblolly pine forest. The 6.6-mile Oakridge Trail and the 4.4-mile Weston Trail pass through old-growth forests. At a length of 10 miles, the River Trail leads to the Congaree River. The 11-mile Kingsnake Trail to remote areas is likely to yield sightings of deer, opossums, raccoons and varied bird species, including barred owls. A marked canoe trail is on Cedar Creek, home to river otters.

Park open daily dawn-dusk. Visitor center daily 8:30-5; closed Dec. 25. Park gates close to vehicles at 5; parking is available outside the gates after 5.

For further information contact the Congaree National Park, 100 National Park Rd., Hopkins, SC 29061; phone (803) 776-4396. *See Recreation Chart.*

CONWAY—*see The Grand Strand p. 249.*

COWPENS NATIONAL BATTLEFIELD (A-2)

Encompassing 845 acres, Cowpens National Battlefield is 9 miles northwest of Gaffney and 18 miles northeast of Spartanburg, .2 miles east of the junction of SRs 11 and 110. At the battlefield Patriots commanded by Gen. Daniel Morgan outfought a more experienced British force under Lt. Col. Banastre Tarleton during the Revolutionary War.

After the Battle of Kings Mountain in 1780 British Gen. Charles Cornwallis chose to remain in South Carolina. Gen. Nathanael Greene, commissioned to reorganize the American forces, sent Morgan to divert Cornwallis' attention from the bulk of the American forces. Morgan threatened Ninety Six, where there was a British fort, so Cornwallis dispatched Tarleton to meet him.

When the two forces clashed at the cow pens on Jan. 17, 1781, the British infantry and dragoons outnumbered the Colonials, comprising Continental forces from Maryland and Delaware and militia units from the Carolinas, Georgia and Virginia.

Morgan, a brilliant strategist, divided his troops into three consecutive lines; the first two were meant to engage and slow the enemy, then fall back, leaving the brunt of the fighting to the more seasoned troops in the rear. The plan worked. Within an hour the Colonials sent the British regulars into a disorderly retreat. Morgan's losses were light; Tarleton's amounted to about 75 percent of his command.

Sites of major action are marked by exhibits along a 1.5-mile walking trail and a 3-mile automobile tour road. A restored 1830 log cabin also is beside the road.

The visitor center exhibits a lighted map tracing troop movements during the battle as well as oil paintings, woodcarvings and weapons. An audiovisual presentation, "Cowpens: A Battle Remembered," lasts about 20 minutes and is shown hourly. Picnicking is permitted until 4:30. Allow 1 hour minimum. Battlefield and visitor center open daily 9-5; closed Jan. 1, Thanksgiving and Dec. 25. Free. Phone (864) 461-2828.

DARLINGTON (B-5) pop. 6,720, elev. 155′

The rich farmland surrounding Darlington produces some of the largest tobacco crops in the state. The city was the site of the Darlington War of 1894, a brief citizens' revolt against harsh liquor regulations, which permitted private homes to be searched without a warrant. Gov. B.R. Tillman sent the state militia to restore peace.

Today, revving engines shatter the peace at Darlington Raceway *(see attraction listing)*, the home of major stock car races.

Greater Darlington Chamber of Commerce: 38 Public Sq., Darlington, SC 29532; phone (843) 393-2641.

DARLINGTON RACEWAY is .9 mi. w. of US 52 on SR 34/151 at 1301 Harry Byrd Hwy. The track dubbed "Too Tough to Tame" opened in 1950 with the Southern 500, which has since become its signature annual event. The culmination of local businessman Harold Brasington's dreams and labor, Darlington Raceway is a 1.366-mile egg-shaped oval whose lopsided west end was so configured to avoid destroying a neighboring landowner's fish pond.

Darlington's facilities include two towers, state-of-the-art grandstands and a pit road wide enough for the full lineup. Unless there is a special event, visitors can go to Gate 6 to have a look. The raceway gets a lot of attention in May when it hosts a NASCAR Nationwide series event as well as a NASCAR Sprint Cup event. Food is available. Phone (843) 395-8900 for information, or (843) 395-8806 or (866) 459-7223 for race ticket information.

Darlington Raceway Stock Car Museum & NMPA Hall of Fame is .9 mi. w. of US 52 on SR 34/151 at 1301 Harry Byrd Hwy. The facility displays stock cars, trophies and racing-related items. There are interactive exhibits, and a theater shows racing highlight clips. Food is available. Mon.-Sat. 9-5, Sun. 1-5; closed Thanksgiving and Dec. 25. Admission $5; free (ages 0-12). MC, VI. Phone (843) 395-8821.

EDGEFIELD (C-2) pop. 4,449, elev. 531′

REGION 2 DISCOVERY CENTER is at 405 Main St. Exhibits relating to the local history of Abbeville, Edgefield, Greenwood and McCormick counties are displayed in a restored 1840s farmhouse that has been relocated from Trenton. Topics showcased include natural history, early settlement, the Revolutionary and Civil wars, and the history of cotton in the state. An orientation theater and a virtual bike tour of the area also are offered. Guided tours are available. Tues.-Sat. 10-5; closed major holidays. Donations. Phone (803) 637-0877.

EDISTO ISLAND—*see Charleston p. 236.*

FLORENCE (C-5) pop. 30,248, elev. 137′

In 1853 Florence was an important junction of two newly completed railroads. During the Civil War the town developed into a shipping center and a point of embarkation for troops. A prison pen south of town held more than 8,000 captured Union soldiers. Most of them succumbed to typhoid fever and were buried in the Florence National Cemetery, 1 mile east of US 301S on National Cemetery Road. Florena Budwin, believed to be the first woman buried in a national cemetery, is interred here.

The railroads continue to play an important role in the town's economy: Florence is a major retail and wholesale distribution center for the various industrial plants in the town and the farms in the surrounding country. The Florence Railroad Museum on Irby Street consists of a box car and a caboose. The box car contains two model railroad layouts and local railroad artifacts. The caboose is set up to look as it did when it was built in 1967; guides explain the work that was done in this part of the train. Pictures from 1940s railroad yards also are featured. The cars can be toured by appointment; phone (843) 662-3351.

Numerous municipal parks present colorful floral displays in the spring. The 12-mile Beauty Trail is lined with marked gardens that begin to bloom in late March or early April. Timrod Park, at Timrod Park Drive and Coit Street, features test rose gardens and an azalea display in spring. Roses, camellias, azaleas and rhododendrons beautify Lucas Park, at Santee Drive, Azalea Lane and Park Avenue.

For outdoor activities, Freedom Florence Recreation Complex, 1515 Freedom Blvd., offers fishing, picnicking and a trail for jogging, walking or biking. Indoor ice-skating is available at the Florence Civic Center, 3300 W. Radio Dr.; phone (843) 679 9417.

Florence Convention and Visitors Center: 3290 W. Radio Rd., P.O. Box 3093, Florence, SC 29502; phone (843) 664-0330 or (800) 325-9005. *See color ad p. 959.*

Shopping areas: Magnolia Mall, 2701 David McLeod Blvd., offers Belk, JCPenney and Sears along with more than 60 stores. Pee Dee State Farmers Market, 2513 W. Lucas St., offers fresh produce, plants, garden accessories and specialty food items Monday through Saturday.

FLORENCE COUNTY LIBRARY, 509 S. Dargan St., contains more than 160,000 books. Its rare historical works include South Carolina genealogical material and family histories. It also houses an exhibit of fossils. Mon.-Thurs. 9-8:30, Fri.-Sat. 9-5:30, Sun. 2-6. Free. Phone (843) 662-8424.

FLORENCE MUSEUM OF ART, SCIENCE AND HISTORY, 558 Spruce St. at jct. Graham St., contains Asian and Western art as well as a collection of Southwestern American Indian pottery. The Hall of South Carolina History traces the development of the Palmetto State. Civil War artifacts, including uniforms, medical instruments and Confederate money, are displayed. Temporary exhibits also are included. Allow 15 minutes minimum. Tues.-Sat. 10-5, Sun. 2-5. Admission $1; free (ages 0-11 with an adult and students with ID). Phone (843) 662-3351.

FORT SUMTER NATIONAL MONUMENT—*see Charleston p. 236.*

FRANCIS MARION NATIONAL FOREST—*see Charleston p. 236.*

GEORGETOWN—*see The Grand Strand p. 251.*

The Grand Strand

Showers are welcome on The Grand Strand's award-winning golf courses only when accolades rain down. The sport's greatest players and architects have helped make Myrtle Beach and surrounds one of the nation's top golfing resorts. Esteemed course designer Robert Trent Jones Sr. created The Dunes and Waterway Hills. Arnold Palmer laid out King's North at Myrtle Beach National Golf Club, while Jack Nicklaus transformed the former rice fields of Pawleys Plantation in Pawleys Island into one of the Lowcountry's most beautiful upscale membership courses. And with a signature course at Barefoot Resort and a fine-dining restaurant at Barefoot Landing, Greg Norman may have scored a double eagle.

Promoters brag that The Grand Strand has more golf courses per-capita than any city in the world. Development as a golfing destination began as early as the 1920s with Pine Lakes Golf Club in Myrtle Beach, today a stronghold of traditional golf with its classic fairways, antebellum clubhouse and kilt-wearing attendants. Course designer Robert White hailed from St. Andrews, Scotland, and served as the first president of the Professional Golfer's Association of America (PGA).

Even miniature golf is big here. Would you believe there are at least 50 places to putt, each with an eye-catching theme? If you break for putting greens, look for life-size dinosaurs, towering volcanoes and pirate ship replicas conspicuously placed along the major thoroughfares. You can't miss them.

Music capital. Branson East. Grandiose nicknames capture the scope of The Strand's entertainment scene, and particularly its connections to the music industry. Alabama, one of country music's all-time-great bands, got its start playing in a Myrtle Beach shag dancing club in the 1970s. Shagging became an East Coast dance craze in the 1950s, while at the same time introducing a regional music genre later coined beach music. As superstars, Alabama wrote "Dancin', Shaggin'on the Boulevard," a tribute to their early years here. The group also established Alabama Theatre, one of The Strand's premiere performance venues, in North Myrtle Beach.

If longevity is a measure of success in the entertainment business, two of Myrtle Beach's most popular performance venues bear witness. The Carolina Opry, ongoing in the theater of the same name since 1986, is The Strand's granddaddy of variety shows. Conceived by Missouri-born singer, entrepreneur and Grand Ole Opry performer Calvin Gilmore, the revue combines dance and comedy with gamut-running music styles. After winning over folk in Pigeon Forge, Tenn., and Branson, Mo., with the Dixie Stampede Dinner & Show, country music icon Dolly Parton found another perfect fit for her blend of musical pageantry, wholesome comedy and endearing animal acts.

Georgetown
© J Sohm / VOA LLC / Panoramic Images

Dolly's double and Elvis, Rod, Garth, Elton, Brittney, Cher and other celebrity impersonators light up the Legends in Concert stage in Surfside Beach, while the House of Blues in North Myrtle Beach regularly brings in the real deal—headliners of rock, jazz and blues. Hard rock fans are still talking about the day Gene Simmons and fellow KISS band members opened the first KISS Coffeehouse at Broadway at the Beach in Myrtle Beach. With live entertainment as a menu staple, Jimmy Buffett's Margaritaville, also at Broadway, is right at home in this coastal resort.

The May 2008 debut of Hard Rock Park cranked up Myrtle Beach's entertainment profile a few bazillion decibels. Said to be the world's first theme park of its kind, Hard Rock Park delivers a musical journey for every member of the family. If grand-opening performances by The Moody Blues and The Eagles are any indication of what's to come, guests are in for the ride of their life.

Of course, the beach remains the superstar of The Grand Strand. With 60 miles of coastline for a theater, there isn't a bad seat in the house. Not on the wide, cottage-dappled shores of the northern strand; nor in the shadows of high-rise hotels and condos in Myrtle Beach proper; nor beside grassy inlets, fishing villages and cooling maritime forests on the less-populated southern strand. Visitors staying at

off-beach lodgings will really appreciate the plethora of public parking lots all along Ocean Boulevard.

A beach just isn't worth its salt air if it doesn't have a boardwalk, souvenir shops, swimwear boutiques, arcades, neon signs, open-air bars and at least one hot-dog dive. Suffice it to say that Myrtle Beach's worthiness is secure—for now—in the historic district of Ocean Boulevard between 9th and 21st avenues. Noticeably absent from the familiar beachscape is the old Pavilion Amusement Park, at one time the epicenter of summertime activity. To the dismay of many, it was dismantled after the 2006 season dubbed "The Last Ride." Nevertheless, those with fond memories of Myrtle Beach's most popular landmark can still pick up farewell-season T-shirts, postcards and other memorabilia, or better yet, visit a scaled-down version of the park in the southeast corner of Broadway at the Beach.

Wherever you stay or play on The Grand Strand will be within minutes of one of eight fishing piers. Some of the most popular are the Second Avenue Pier in Myrtle Beach's historic district; The Pier at Garden City, with rental fishing equipment and an arcade for kids; Springmaid Pier at Springmaid Resort, one of the widest; and Cherry Grove Pier in North Myrtle Beach, the only one with a raised observation deck.

CONWAY (C-5) pop. 11,788

Two constants have shaped the history of Conway—the Waccamaw River and the live oak trees that grace its streets. One of the oldest towns in South Carolina, Conway was created in 1734 and originally named Kingston, in honor of Great Britain's King George II. After the Revolutionary War its name was changed to Conwayborough after General Robert Conway. The name was shortened to Conway in 1883.

USS Kids-A-Float / © Children's Museum of South Carolina, Myrtle Beach

The town prospered in the 1820s as a busy port on the Waccamaw River. Its current city hall, formerly the Horry (pronounced O-ree) County courthouse, was built 1824-25. The structure, at the corner of Main Street and Third Avenue, was designed by Robert Mills, the architect of the Washington Monument.

The historic river town has preserved much of its past, including many centuries-old live oaks, some named after prominent citizens. The moss-draped trees, now protected by an ordinance, are so revered that traffic has been rerouted around them.

One such tree named for Confederate general and state governor Wade Hampton shades the Horry County Museum, 438 Main St., which chronicles area history and contains prehistoric artifacts, old farm tools, household implements and mercantile goods; phone (843) 915-5320.

Conway Area Chamber of Commerce: 203 Main St., P.O. Box 831, Conway, SC 29526; phone (843) 248-2273.

Destination The Grand Strand

The saying "something for everyone" certainly applies to The Grand Strand.

This vacation mecca includes both inland and beach destinations. There are cultural and historical options as well as more active choices like fishing, golfing, sailing and swimming.

The Carolina Opry, Myrtle Beach. Live entertainment at this elegant venue delights visitors. (See listing page 255)

Brookgreen Gardens, Murrells Inlet. Sculpture competes with gardens and wildlife for visitors' attention at this showcase of artistic and natural beauty. (See listing page 252)

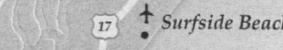

Myrtle Beach. Find that perfect shell to take home as a Myrtle Beach souvenir.

N.C.
S.C.
701
22
378
Conway
Little River
North Myrtle Beach
17
31
501
Myrtle Beach
Surfside Beach
17
701
Murrells Inlet
The Grand Strand
ALT. 17
521
Georgetown
17

Huntington Beach State Park, Murrells Inlet. In between recreational activities and wildlife viewing, take a tour of Atalaya, a 55-room 1930s mansion. (See listing page 253)

Places included in this AAA Destination Area:

Self-guiding tours: Copies of the Conway Historic Trail Map, which lists 39 of the city's historic sites, significant buildings and distinctive homes, and A Guide to Conway's Live Oaks, a walking tour describing many of the oaks the town has preserved since the 1780s, are available at the chamber of commerce.

GEORGETOWN (D-6) pop. 8,950, elev. 12'

In 1526 the Spanish attempted to settle at the head of Winyah Bay where Georgetown now stands, but were driven out by disease. The first permanent settlers arrived in the early 18th century; many of their buildings and houses still are in use. With a deepwater harbor that can accommodate oceangoing vessels, Georgetown has developed into an important shipping port.

Georgetown County Chamber of Commerce: 531 Front St., P.O. Box 1776, Georgetown, SC 29442; phone (843) 546-8436 or (800) 777-7705.

Self-guiding tours: Maps detailing walking and driving tours past historic sites are available from the chamber of commerce.

CAPTAIN SANDY'S TOURS departs several locations in Georgetown County for half-day Shell Island and half-day Plantation River tours. Other trips also are available. Island tours Wed. and Sat. at 10; River tours Tues. and Thurs.-Fri. at 1 (both weather permitting). Island tour $40; $30 (ages 0-12). River tour $35; $25 (ages 0-12). Reservations are recommended. Phone (843) 527-4106.

THE GEORGETOWN COUNTY MUSEUM is at 632 Prince St. at jct. Screven St. Photo and artifact displays in this historic Colonial bank building showcase more than 3 centuries of local history. Topics include American Indian as well as plantation life. The latter displays feature clothing, toys and slave bills of sale. Rice farming and the lumber and paper industries also are profiled. Allow 30 minutes minimum. Tues.-Sat. 10-5; closed major holidays. Admission $4; $3 (ages 65+); $2 (ages 6-18). Phone (843) 545-7020.

HOBCAW BARONY, 22 Hobcaw Rd., is a research facility and the former winter hunting retreat of native South Carolinian and Wall Street financier Bernard Baruch. The 17,500 acres encompass forests, salt marshes, swamps and former rice fields; the grounds are home to native wildlife. A tour in a 13-passenger van takes visitors to see the first floor of Hobcaw House (rebuilt in 1930), where many prominent guests once visited. Other sights include Bellefield Plantation, 19th-century slave cabins, the USC Marine Research Facility and Clemson Forestry Facility. The Hobcaw Barony Discovery Center houses history and animal exhibits as well as a theater that shows a short historical documentary.

Allow 3 hours minimum for the tour. Discovery center Mon.-Fri. 9-5. Tour departs Tues.-Fri. at 9:30; phone ahead to confirm. An afternoon tour sometimes is offered; phone for details. Closed major state and federal holidays. Visitor Center by donations. Tour $20. Reservations are required for tours. DS, MC, VI. Phone (843) 546-4623.

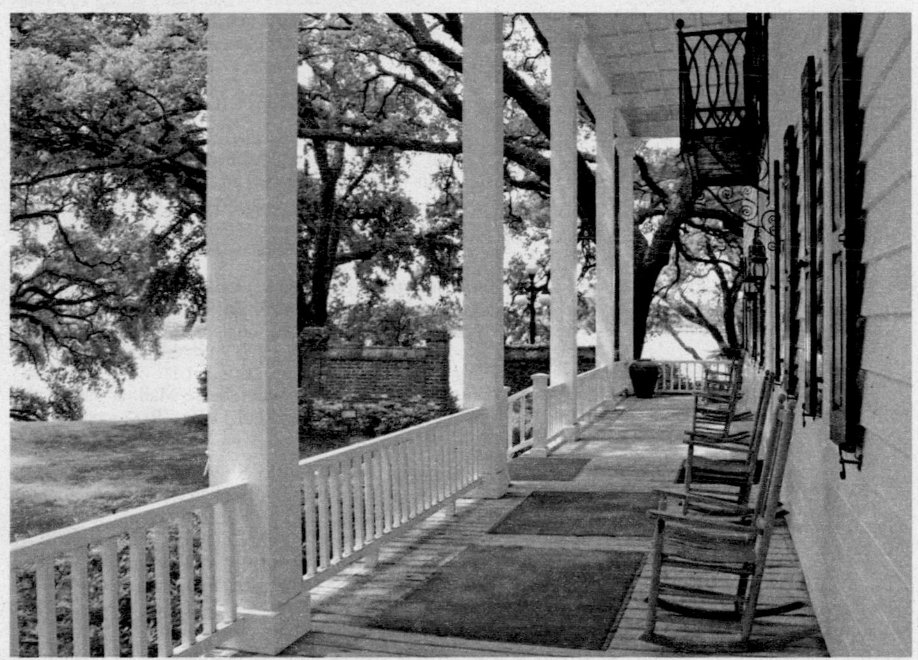

Kaminski House Museum, Georgetown / © Gibson Stock Photography

HOPSEWEE PLANTATION, 12 mi. s. on US 17 at 494 Hopsewee Rd., was the residence of Thomas Lynch, a South Carolina delegate to the Continental Congress, and the birthplace of his son Thomas Jr., who signed the Declaration of Independence. The 1740 plantation house has period furnishings. Mon.-Fri. 10-4, Feb.-Nov. Grounds $5 per private vehicle. House $15; $7.50 (ages 5-17). Phone (843) 546-7891.

SAVE **KAMINSKI HOUSE MUSEUM** is at 1003 Front St. Built in the 1760s, the house contains American and European furnishings from the 17th through the 20th century. Tours are given on the hour Mon.-Sat. 10-4, Sun. 1-4; closed Jan. 1, Easter, Thanksgiving and Dec. 25. Admission $7; $5 (ages 60+); $3 (ages 6-12). MC, VI. Phone (843) 546-7706 or (888) 233-0383.

LOWCOUNTRY PLANTATION TOURS departs jct. Front and Screven sts. behind the Town Clock. Three-hour Plantation River, 3-hour Lighthouse/Shell Island and 2-hour ghost tours are given aboard a pontoon boat. On the Lighthouse/Shell Island tour, visitors can disembark at a barrier island and spend an hour on the beach. Plantation tour Mon.-Sat. at 10. Lighthouse tour Mon.-Sat. at 2. Ghost tour Mon.-Fri. at 7, June-Aug. Fare $20-$25; $15-$20 (children). Reservations are recommended. Phone (843) 477-0287.

MISS NELL'S TOURS departs from 723 Front St. at Harborwalk Books. Guided walking tours given by a native of Georgetown feature information about the city's history, including ghost stories. Information about historic businesses, churches and houses is shared. The 30-minute tour covers eight blocks, the 1-hour tour covers 12 blocks and the 90-minute tour covers 24 blocks.

Tours depart by appointment only. Tour times are generally Tues.-Thurs. at 10:30 and 2:30 and other days and times by appointment; closed holidays. Fee $5-$9; free (ages 0-11). Reservations are required. Phone (843) 546-3975.

PRINCE GEORGE WINYAH CHURCH (Episcopal), 300 Broad St. at Highmarket St., dates from 1735. Colonists as well as Revolutionary and Confederate soldiers are buried at the site. Mon.-Fri. 11:30-4:30, Mar.-Oct. Donations. Phone (843) 546-4358.

RICE MUSEUM, Front and Screven sts., chronicles the history of the rice industry in the United States with maps, dioramas, photographs and artifacts. A maritime exhibit features the restored Browns Ferry vessel, a 50-foot river freighter that sunk in the Black River around 1730. The museum also has a cross-section scale model of a rice mill and an art gallery. Mon.-Sat. 10-4:30; closed major holidays. Admission $7; $5 (ages 60+); $3 (ages 6-21). Phone (843) 546-7423.

ROVER TOURS depart from the end of Broad St. at Harbor Walk. Narrated tours include the 3-hour Shelling and Lighthouse Cruise, which stops at a barrier island near the Georgetown Lighthouse; the 2-hour Pirate Adventure Sailing, which recounts Blackbeard's legend; and the 3-hour Alligator Alley Adventure Cruise. Mon.-Sat. 9-6. Departure times vary; phone ahead. Fares $24-$28; $12-$18 (ages 0-12). Phone (843) 546-8822 or (800) 705-9063.

SWAMP FOX TOURS departs from 624 Front St. at jct. Screven St. Bus and jeep-pulled tram tours provide historical information while showcasing the town's historic churches, graveyards, homes and the waterfront. Specialized tours, including plantation tours, also are available. Allow 1 hour minimum. Tours depart Mon.-Sat. on the hour 10-4 and other times by appointment; closed major holidays. Fare $10; $5 (ages 5-12). AX, MC, VI. Phone (843) 527-1112 or (843) 450-8433.

LITTLE RIVER (C-6) pop. 7,027, elev. 25'

SEA SCREAMER, 4495 Mineola Ave., offers two rides in one: a narrated leisurely cruise of the historical Intracoastal Waterway and then to the open water for a thrilling speedboat ride past the beaches and resorts of North Myrtle Beach. Dolphin sightings are guaranteed or the next ride is free. Casual clothing or a swimsuit is recommended.

Food is available. Allow 2 hours minimum. Tours are given Mon.-Sat. at 10, 1 and 4, June 15-Sept. 1. Schedule may vary; phone ahead. Fare $20; $15 (ages 3-12). MC, VI. Phone (843) 249-0870.

WINERIES

- **La Belle Amie Vineyard** is 4.4 mi. s.w. on US 17/SR 90 at 1120 St. Joseph Rd. Vineyard Mon.-Sat. 10-6. Tastings Mon.-Sat. 10-5. Tours are given Tues., Thurs. and Sat. at 11 (unless a festival is scheduled). Closed major holidays. Phone (843) 399-9463.

MURRELLS INLET (C-6) pop. 5,519

According to legend, the marshland community of Murrells Inlet was named for Capt. Murrell, a pirate who used the inlet as a base for his forays along the Atlantic coast. Today the area is known for seafood treasures, including oysters, crabs, clams and shrimp. Fishing boats leave the docks daily.

Myrtle Beach Area Chamber of Commerce-South Strand Visitor Information Center: 3401 S. U.S. 17, Murrells Inlet, SC 29576; phone (843) 651-1010.

Shopping areas: Inlet Square Mall, at the junction of US 17 bypass and US 17 Bus. Rte., includes Belk and JCPenney.

GEM SAVE **BROOKGREEN GARDENS,** 4 mi. s. on US 17 to 1931 Brookgreen Dr., encompasses more than 9,000 acres comprised of four former rice plantations. More than 725 sculptures by 19th-century and contemporary American artists are showcased in landscaped settings and garden rooms of the 35-acre Archer and Anna Hyatt Huntington Sculpture Garden.

Created by railroad heir Archer M. Huntington and his sculptor wife Anna Hyatt Huntington in the

1930s, the gardens are among the most beautiful in the South. More than 2,000 plant species are used in the landscape; many bloom from early April through September. Visitors can explore a wildlife preserve in a boat or an overland vehicle, or by walking a nature trail that contains history and animal exhibits. Programs are given daily.

Guided tours are available. Picnicking is permitted. Food is available. Allow 3 hours minimum. Daily 9:30-5. Open late during special events. Closed Dec. 25. Last admission is 30 minutes before closing. Admission $12; $10 (ages 13-18 and 65+); $5 (ages 6-12). AX, DS, MC, VI. (843) 235-6000 or (800) 849-1931.

Creek Excursions, at Brookgreen Gardens, 4 mi. s. on US 17 to 1931 Brookgreen Dr., offers narrated, 1-hour waterway tours in a 48-foot pontoon boat. Tickets must be purchased at least 10 minutes before the tour begins. Daily at 11, 1, 2 and 3, Mar.-Nov. (also 5:30 in Apr.). Schedule may vary; phone ahead. Fare $7; $4 (ages 0-11). AX, DS, MC, VI. Phone (843) 235-6000.

Trekker Excursions, at Brookgreen Gardens, takes visitors in a safari-type vehicle to seldom traveled areas of the plantation. A narrator highlights natural and historical points of interest. Tickets must be purchased at least 10 minutes before the tour begins. Allow 1 hour minimum. Daily at 11 and 2. Schedule may vary; phone ahead. Fare $7; $4 (ages 6-12). Not recommended for ages 0-5. AX, DS, MC, VI. Phone (843) 235-6000.

CAPT. DICK'S, 4123 US 17S Bus. Rte. on the waterfront, offers a variety of boat tours. The Saltwater Marsh Explorer Adventure is a 2.5-hour interactive ecology trip guided by a marine biologist. Cruisin' the Beach is a 2-hour ocean sightseeing cruise. Fishing trips and water sport rentals also are available.

Saltwater Marsh Explorer Adventure tour daily at 8, 11 and 2, Mar.-Nov. Cruisin' the Beach tour 6:30-8:30 p.m., mid-May to mid-Oct. (weather permitting). Reservations are recommended. Saltwater Marsh fare $21; $15 (ages 0-12). Cruisin' the Beach fare $19; $11 (ages 6-12). MC, VI. Phone (843) 651-3676 or (866) 557-3474.

HUNTINGTON BEACH STATE PARK, 3 mi. s. on US 17, offers nearly 2,500 acres of natural habitat and wildlife as well as camping and recreational facilities. The park features nature trails, beach areas, a saltwater marsh and a freshwater lagoon. Observation decks afford opportunities to view native wildlife, including shorebirds and alligators. Daily nature study programs are offered March through November.

Open daily 6 a.m.-10 p.m., Apr.-Nov.; Mon.-Sat. 6 a.m.-6 p.m. (also Fri. 6-8 p.m.), rest of year. Admission $5; $3.25 (senior citizens); $3 (ages 6-15). Phone (843) 237-4440. *See Recreation Chart and the AAA Southeastern CampBook.*

Atalaya, within Huntington Beach State Park, is a 55-room mansion. Atalaya is the Spanish term for "watchtower." Constructed in a square, the house built 1931-33 features a large open inner court; Anna Hyatt Huntington's sculpture studio; and a 40-foot-tall tower that once contained a 3,000-gallon water tank, the height of which created enough pressure to provide running water throughout the house. Guided tours are available daily February through October. Open daily 9-5. Free. Phone (843) 237-4440.

MYRTLE BEACH (C-6) pop. 22,759, elev. 30′

Envisioning a year-round golfing resort on 65,000 acres of undeveloped oceanfront property, John T. Woodside built a luxury hotel and had a Scottish golf course architect build the area's first course in 1927. The Depression waylaid Woodside's plans for further development, and he eventually sold out. The venerable golf club, later renamed Pine Lakes, is now the centerpiece of Myrtle Beach golfing.

More courses were added over the years, and by the late 1970s The Grand Strand had become a premiere golfing destination. Simultaneously, the beaches emerged as a favorite East Coast summertime getaway for middle-class Americans. Today, the area attracts vacationers from all over the country and annually courts thousands of returning Canadian visitors with its signature Canadian American Days Festival in March.

Resort hotels and high-rise condominiums, palatial theaters, and a smorgasbord of pay-one-price buffet restaurants have replaced most of the mom-and-pop hotels, dance pavilions and greasy spoons of old Myrtle Beach. But you can still stroll on the boardwalk, chow down on a foot-long chili dog, buy kitschy souvenirs, feed coins to arcade games or dangle a line from a fishing pier in the historic district of Ocean Boulevard, where the iconic—and recently demolished—Pavilion Amusement Park once lit up starry summer nights.

With the Gulf Stream pacing only 40 miles offshore, the temperate climate is perfect for water-oriented recreation. A day at the beach might include parasailing, swimming, snorkeling, shelling, riding on a banana boat or doing nothing at all. You can fish in the surf or from three piers without a license, or maybe charter a deep-sea fishing boat.

Musical variety shows figure prominently in Myrtle Beach's live entertainment offerings. Equally entertaining for all ages is Broadway at the Beach, a 350-acre village with shops, amusements, nightclubs, restaurants, attractions and an IMAX 3D Theatre *(see color ad)*. Also in the complex is The Pavilion Nostalgia Park. Nine rides from Myrtle Beach's former Pavilion Amusement Park have been relocated here, and there also is an arcade. A plaque at each ride details its history for nostalgic fans; phone (843) 913-9400.

Mealtime options are dizzying, with the highest concentration of establishments lining US 17 bypass, or Restaurant Row. While theater-size, pay-one-price seafood buffet restaurants are extremely popular, the discriminating diner can still find a cozy table for two, gourmet fare and a wine list behind less pretentious facades.

Myrtle Beach Area Chamber of Commerce: 1200 N. Oak St., P.O. Box 2115, Myrtle Beach, SC 29578; phone (843) 626-7444 for voice and TTY, or (800) 356-3016.

Shopping areas: One-stop shopping, dining and entertainment complexes such as Broadway at the Beach on US 17 bypass can turn an ordinary shopping excursion into a daylong event. And every imaginable amenity on 350 acres ensures that you do just that. You'll encounter an interesting mix of shops and experiences as you follow a boardwalk through a series of themed villages overlooking a lake. Surprise the kids with a teddy-making session at Build-A-Bear Workshop; sign up your little diva for a rock-star makeover at Club Libby Lu; and then treat yourself to a painting from the Thomas Kinkade Gallery or a future collectible from Department 56. You can even get motorcycling duds and accessories at a Harley Davidson shop. Broadway also features nearly 3 dozen restaurants and eateries as well as numerous attractions, amusements and nightspots. Oh, and lots of seagulls.

The Market Common on Farrow Parkway is a new urban village, the first of its kind in Myrtle Beach. Central to this luxury lifestyle community is a charming block of upscale shops including Tommy Bahama, White House/Black Market, Anthropologie, Chico's, and Coldwater Creek; there's also a Barnes & Noble bookstore and several fine-dining restaurants.

Finding two SAVE Tanger Outlets with nearly 200 stores combined within a few miles of each other is just too good to be true. Each mall has in common its share of the name brands Tanger bargain shoppers have come to expect—Brooks Brothers, Jones New York, OshKosh and Timberland, for example; however, many other sought-after brands are available only at one location. Before you begin a shopping spree, inquire about special offers and centerwide coupon books available at customer service stations at both the US 17 and US 501 Tanger Outlets.

More than 100 shops and three major department stores make Coastal Grand mall on US 17 bypass the largest conventional shopping mall on The Grand Strand—and in the state.

A big neon sign on Ocean Boulevard just north of 9th Avenue points across the street to The Gay Dolphin. This multilevel emporium has a staggering array of gifts, collectibles, beachwear, shells, postcards, kitschy gifts and stuff that has nothing to do with beaches. You have to go, if only to brag that you've been to Myrtle Beach's oldest souvenir shop. Be sure to exit through the back door to the boardwalk.

Nightlife: The partying begins long before sunset at beach hangouts such as Ocean Annie's Beach Bar, at the Sands Ocean Club Resort on Ocean Boulevard. Live beach music, killer margaritas and balmy breezes inspire camaraderie on the large oceanside deck. This is a fun place to chill out with locals and repeat resort guests.

With three clubs under one roof, 2001 Nightclub appeals to all ages. The cover charge gets you into Razzie's Beach Club—a Myrtle Beach institution—for live and DJ-spun R&B, oldies and beach music in a relaxed atmosphere, and into its brasher alter-ego, Funky Town, an updated disco with a lighted dance floor. Guests can segue from club to club through a bar serving as a sound barrier. Lounge seating, the hottest contemporary sounds and video-screen walls projecting what's happening on the dance floor take Club Touch, on the second floor, to the next level in clubbing.

Baby boomers are right at home among rock 'n' roll memorabilia, diner-style tile décor, neon signs, waitresses in cheerleader garb and dangling disco balls in Studebaker's. Music from the '50s, '60s, '70s and '80s gets everyone out of retro chrome chairs and onto the wooden dance floor to bop, shag, boogie or line dance.

Picture a discotheque in Superman's crystal fortress and you have an idea of what Club Kryptonite is like on a busy night. Go-go dancers on platforms, crisp shards of laser light bisecting the room and a master DJ perched high above the crowd of frenetic college students and young professionals fuel the rituals taking place on the dance floor.

By day, Celebrity Square at Broadway at the Beach is a quiet watering hole, a nice place to plop down for a beer or daiquiri, or maybe even a Rock-uccino from KISS Coffeehouse. After dark, neon lights and pulsing music from several trendy clubs battle for clubgoers' patronage while transforming the quadrangle into Myrtle Beach's go-to entertainment district. Pay the cover charge at one of three Celebrations clubs and get free admission to the other two. Dress up or go casual, but honor the liberal code if you want to get into this trio. Latin and hip-hop music infuses Club Boca with a South Beach vibe. A house band regularly belts the blues, oldies and pop music—in other words, something for everyone—at Froggy Bottomz, while Top 40 hits spun by dueling DJs enliven Malibu's Surf Bar.

There's more high energy and a lighted dance floor reminiscent of "Saturday Night Fever" in Revolutions, a retro dance club also on the square. If you'd rather sing than dance the night away at Broadway at the Beach, duck into Crocodile Rocks and watch dueling piano players work the crowd, or hang around for the late-night karaoke show in Broadway Louie's.

THE CAROLINA OPRY, jct. US 17 and US 17 bypass, presents family music and variety shows. Allow 2 hours minimum. Performances Mon.-Sat. at 8 p.m., Mar.-Oct.; Mon.-Sat. at 7 p.m., rest of year. Matinees also are offered on selected dates. Admission $34.95; $23 (students with ID); $17 (ages 3-16). Holiday specials $39.95 (Nov.-Dec.). Phone ahead to verify prices. Reservations are required. AX, DS, MC, VI. Phone (843) 913-4000 or (800) 843-6779.

SAVE **CHILDREN'S MUSEUM OF SOUTH CAROLINA,** 2501 N. Kings Hwy., inspires self-discovery in children through educational, interactive play stations. Among the exhibits are Bubble Mania, Kidz Medical Center, Discovery Lab and Magic School Bus. The USS Kids-A-Float exhibit simulates a high seas experience. Mon.-Sat. 10-4, Memorial Day-Labor Day; Tues.-Sat. 10-4, rest of year. Closed Jan. 1, Memorial Day, July 4,

Labor Day, Thanksgiving and Dec. 24-25. Admission $7; free (ages 0-1). Phone (843) 946-9469.

GEM SAVE **DOLLY PARTON'S DIXIE STAMPEDE DINNER & SHOW** is at the n. jct. of US 17 and US 17 bypass. The main show, presented in a 35,000-square-foot arena and accompanied by a four-course meal, chronicles the story of America and opens with a thunderous buffalo stampede. Entertainment includes feats of horsemanship, a North vs. South rivalry and a patriotic musical finale written by Dolly Parton.

Early arrivals can view the horses in their open-air stables prior to the evening's events. Breeds include Appaloosas, palominos, paint horses and quarter horses. A comedy performance in the Carriage Room precedes the arena event. Allow 3 hours minimum. Performances daily Mar.-Dec.; show times vary. Admission $43.79; $19.99 (ages 4-11). Reservations are recommended. AX, DS, MC, VI. Phone (843) 497-9700 or (800) 433-4401.

FAMILY KINGDOM AMUSEMENT PARK, 300 S. Ocean Blvd., is reminiscent of old-time amusement parks with its ornate carousel; wooden roller coaster; and Ferris wheel, which is said to be the largest in the state. Brave visitors can attempt the 110-foot drop on the Slingshot Drop Zone. A water park offers a lazy river, a children's area and a variety of waterslides.

Food is available. Allow 2 hours minimum. Amusement park late Mar.-late Sept. Water park late May-late Aug. Hours vary; phone ahead to verify schedule. Amusement park all-day unlimited ride wristband $22.75. Individual ride tickets $1.05 each (2-5 tickets per ride). Water park all-day unlimited ride wristband $17.95; $16.70 (under 48 inches tall). Combination ticket for an all-day unlimited ride wristband for each park $32.35; it can be used for both parks in one day or on separate days. Phone (843) 626-3447.

FRANKLIN G. BURROUGHS-SIMEON B. CHAPIN ART MUSEUM is at 3100 S. Ocean Blvd. Visitors can wander among works by renowned area artists housed in a restored 1920s beach villa. Tues.-Sat. 10-4, Sun. 1-4. Donations. Phone (843) 238-2510.

SAVE **GRAY LINE** tours depart from Hard Rock Cafe at 1322 Celebrity Cir. Pickup is available from select hotels for the Low Country tour. The 4.5-hour Low Country tour and 6.5-hour Gullah & Southern Heritage tour showcase the Grand Strand. Low Country tour departs Wed. and Fri. at 8:30, early Mar.-late Oct. Gullah & Southern Heritage tour departs Wed. and Fri. at 8:30, early Feb. to mid-Nov. Phone ahead to verify schedule. Fare $102. Reservations are required. Phone (800) 261-5991.

HARD ROCK PARK, 211 George Bishop Pkwy., celebrates rock 'n' roll with six themed areas: All Access Entry Plaza, Born in the USA, British Invasion, Cool Country, Lost in the 70s and Rock & Roll Heaven. Roller coasters, musical performances, stage shows, children's areas and shops inspired by these musical styles are featured. Origins Theater in the entry plaza shows short presentations about rock 'n' roll history and the creation of Hard Rock Park. Food is available. Admission $50; $40 (military); free (ages 0-3). Parking $10. Phone ahead to verify prices. AX, DS, MC, VI. Phone (843) 236-7625. *See color ad inside back cover.*

***JUNGLE PRINCESS* RIVERBOAT** departs from 8500 Enterprise Rd. Narrated sightseeing, sunset and pirate ghost story cruises on the Intracoastal Waterway and Waccamaw River are offered aboard a 150-passenger boat. Dinner cruises also are available. Allow 1 hour minimum. Tues.-Sat., mid-Apr. to early Oct.; phone for schedule rest of year. Schedule varies according to type of cruise; phone ahead. Sightseeing and pirate fare each $16; $8 (ages 3-12). Sunset cruise fare $17; $9 (ages 3-12). Phone (843) 650-6600 or (800) 685-6601.

SAVE **MEDIEVAL TIMES DINNER AND TOURNAMENT** is e. of US 17 bypass off US 501 at 2904 Fantasy Way. Guests dine in a European castle while watching an 11th-century royal tournament. The action includes jousting, horsemanship and hand-to-hand combat. In addition to the show, guests can visit the Hall of Arms with its medieval artifacts as well as a museum featuring medieval torture practices.

Allow 3 hours minimum. Performances daily at 6. Performance times may vary; phone ahead. Admission $46.95; $28.95 (ages 3-12). Reservations are required. AX, CB, MC, VI. Phone (843) 236-8080 or (800) 436-4386.

MYRTLE WAVES WATER PARK is at jct. US 17 bypass and 10th Ave. N. near Broadway at the Beach. The 20-acre water park features more than 30 rides and attractions, including a lazy river ride, wave pool, children's water park and a variety of waterslides.

Life vests, locker rooms, lounge chairs, showers and food are available. Allow 4 hours minimum. Open daily at 10, early June-late Aug.; Sat.-Sun. (also Memorial Day and Labor Day), early May-early June and late Aug.-early Sept. Closing times vary; phone ahead to verify schedule. Admission $28; $20 (ages 3-8 and 55+). Admission after 3 p.m. $18; $15 (ages 3-8 and 55+). Phone ahead to verify admission prices. MC, VI. Phone (843) 913-9260.

NASCAR SPEEDPARK, at US 17 bypass and 21st Ave. N. opposite Broadway at the Beach, is a 26-acre family theme park with seven speed tracks offering racing experiences for all ages. Speed bumper boats, two miniature golf courses and an arcade with simulator rides also are available. Allow 1 hour minimum. Open daily at 10 a.m.; closing times vary. Phone ahead to verify schedule. Admission $32; phone ahead to verify. AX, DS, MC, VI. Phone (843) 918-8725.

THE PALACE THEATRE, 1420 Celebrity Cir. at Broadway at the Beach, features live entertainment in an elegant 2,628-seat auditorium. Le Grande Cirque, the 2-hour resident show, is performed in the style of European circuses with vignettes featuring acrobat, dance and animal acts. Between acts, mimes entertain with skits that encourage some audience participation. During the 20-minute intermission, children can be photographed with the animals and animal trainer for an additional fee. Another show, The Magical Spirit of Ireland, is also offered and features Irish music and dance.

Le Grande Cirque Mon.-Sat. at 8; matinee and holiday hours vary. The Magical Spirit of Ireland Mon.-Sat. at 6. Phone to confirm schedule. Admission $34-$45; $10 (ages 3-12); free (ages 0-2 on lap). Reduced prices are offered for matinee shows. AX, DS, MC, VI. Phone (843) 448-0588 or (800) 905-4228.

RIPLEY'S AQUARIUM is at 1110 Celebrity Cir. in the Broadway at the Beach complex at jct. US 17 and 29th Ave. N. Visitors can walk through an underwater tunnel to view sharks, moray eels, great barracuda and a giant octopus. A touch tank displays horseshoe crabs, and a freshwater tank exhibits red-bellied piranhas. Hourly dive shows are presented. The aquarium also features interactive computer exhibits.

Food is available. Allow 1 hour, 30 minutes minimum. Daily 9 a.m.-10 p.m., Memorial Day-Labor Day; hours vary rest of year. Admission $18.99; $7.99 (ages 6-11); $3.99 (ages 2-5). Combination tickets with other Ripley's attractions are available. AX, DS, MC, VI. Phone (843) 916-0888 or (800) 734-8888.

RIPLEY'S BELIEVE IT OR NOT! ODDITORIUM, 901 N. Ocean Blvd. at 9th Ave. N., offers visitors more than 500 unusual and macabre exhibits, including shrunken heads, an elephant's foot humidor and a graveyard of strange epitaphs. Allow 30 minutes minimum. Daily 10 a.m.-1 a.m., Memorial Day-Labor Day; closing time varies rest of year. Admission $13.99; $7.99 (ages 6-11). Combination tickets with other Ripley's attractions are available. AX, DS, MC, VI. Phone (843) 448-2331.

RIPLEY'S HAUNTED ADVENTURE is at 915 N. Ocean Blvd. Costumed characters and special effects create a scary haunted-house experience. Allow 1 hour minimum. Daily noon-1 a.m., Memorial Day-Labor Day; schedule varies rest of year. Admission $13.99; $7.99 (ages 6-11). Ages 6-12 must be with an adult. Ages 0-5 are not permitted. Combination tickets with other Ripley's attractions are available. AX, DS, MC, VI. Phone (843) 916-8971.

RIPLEY'S MOVING THEATER, 917 N. Ocean Blvd., offers 15-minute rides created with huge movie screens, surround sound and seats that move in eight directions. Daily 10-7 (also Fri.-Sun. 7-9 p.m.). Hours may vary; phone ahead. Admission $13.99; $7.99 (children 43 inches tall-age 11). Under 43 inches are not permitted. Combination tickets with other Ripley's attractions are available. AX, DS, MC, VI. Phone (843) 626-0069.

SAVE **WACCATEE ZOO,** from US 17 bypass, 6 mi. s.w. via SR 707 to 8500 Enterprise Rd., is a haven for more than 100 animal species. The 500-acre farm provides a natural habitat for exotic and domestic animals, including miniature horses, leopards, buffaloes, llamas and alligators. The zoo also is a wildlife breeding ground for several species of migratory birds. A nature trail and petting zoo also are featured. Food is available. Allow 2 hours minimum. Daily 10-5 (weather permitting). Admission $7; $3.50 (ages 0-12). Phone (843) 650-8500.

NORTH MYRTLE BEACH (C-6)

pop. 10,974, elev. 8′

Dubbed the "quiet alternative" to the heavily developed beach community just to the south, North Myrtle Beach is not without its share of high-rise condominiums and resorts. Still, it is possible to drive along Ocean Boulevard and enjoy unencumbered views of the dunes, the wide beach and, ultimately, the sea. Ample public parking ensures easy access for visitors staying at off-beach lodgings.

The town is hailed as the cradle of shag dancing. Proclaimed the official state dance in 1984, the shag originated in beach pavilions and juke joints along the East Coast in the 1950s as teens adapted swing-style dances to emerging rhythm and blues music. Although shag dancing is not a freestyle response to the beat, its characteristic smooth moves and seemingly effortless fancy footwork have come to embody the carefree attitude of seaside living. Old and not-so-old dance clubs radiate from the intersection of Main Street and Ocean Boulevard.

North Myrtle Beach Chamber of Commerce: 270 US 17, North Myrtle Beach, SC 29582; phone (843) 281-2662 or (877) 332-2662.

Shopping areas: With its central lake, weathered boardwalks, floating pedestrian bridges and cottage-style clapboard structures, Barefoot Landing, on US 17, has the look and feel of coastal village. Popular retailers such as Chico's, Dress Barn, White House/Black Market and Ron Jon Surf Shop stand out among more than 80 boutique-style specialty shops. Expect the unexpected, like the Carolina Vineyards Winery store and tasting room. Kids will beg to ride the carousel, play in the mist at the Coca-Cola Cool Zone and toss purchased fish food to puckering carp. There are numerous restaurants and attractions on the boardwalk and in freestanding buildings surrounding this multifaceted entertainment complex. Barefoot Landing closes with a fireworks show on Monday nights during summer months.

Nightlife: Paneled walls with beach murals, contest memorabilia and photos of shag dance champions say it all: Fat Harold's on Main Street near Ocean Boulevard is shag-dance central, and has been for decades. The casual atmosphere recalls a time when the fast-dance craze evolved in East Coast beach pavilions. You can almost hear the shish of sand as you watch light-footed shaggers shuffle across Fat Harold's wooden dance floor. Like the music, the mostly middle-age crowd is laid-back. Other popular shag clubs within walking distance include Duck's, Duck's Too and OD Lounge.

Beach music and the state dance also get their due at the OD Beach Club, inside the Ocean Drive Beach & Golf Resort, which, by the way, houses the Shaggers Hall of Fame. But the resort's hottest dance floor is Spanish Galleon, where everything from hip-hop to Top 40 played by DJs and live bands whips dancers into a partying frenzy.

ALABAMA THEATRE, 4750 US 17S at Barefoot Landing, features "One-The Show," a Las Vegas-style revue with nonstop singing, dancing and comedy. A concert series by visiting performers also is offered. Show and concert schedule varies. Admission to "One" revue $34.70-$45.50; $17.95 (ages 3-16). Concert prices vary according to artist. There are no refunds or exchanges. Phone to verify prices. Reservations are required. AX, DS, MC, VI. Phone (843) 272-1111 or (800) 342-2262.

ALLIGATOR ADVENTURE, 4604 US 17 at Barefoot Landing, has more than 700 reptiles, including alligators, exotic snakes, lizards, tortoises, two albino alligators and a 20-foot crocodile. Visitors have the opportunity to watch two shows throughout the day. One is a reptile show, which usually features an alligator, snake and turtle. The other is an alligator show. In warm weather the show features alligator feedings, and during cool weather when alligators do not eat, the show becomes a handling and lecture show instead.

Allow 1 hour minimum. Daily 9 a.m.-11 p.m., mid-June through Aug. 31; daily 9-9, mid-May to mid-June; daily 9-6, late Apr. to mid-May; daily 10-6, mid-Mar. through late Apr. and in Sept.; daily 10-4, mid-Feb. to mid-Mar. and in Oct.; Fri.-Sun. 10-4, Nov.-Dec.; Fri.-Sat. 10-4, Jan. 1 to mid-Feb. Reptile shows presented on even hours, all year. Alligator feedings presented on odd hours, Apr.-Sept. Alligator handling/lectures presented on odd hours, Oct.-Mar. First show is 1 hour after opening; last show is 1 hour before closing. Admission $16.95; $14.95 (ages 62+); $10.95 (ages 4-12). DS, MC, VI. Phone (843) 361-0789.

GHOSTS AND LEGENDS THEATRE is at 4818 US 17S, at Barefoot Landing. Special effects combine with storytelling to create the Myrtle Beach Ghost Show, which presents local historic ghost stories told by the ghosts themselves from a southern parlor setting. The Blackbeard Encounter is another show that is offered.

Food is available. Allow 30 minutes minimum. Theater shows offered daily every 30 minutes. Theater opens at 10. Closing time varies; phone ahead. Last show begins 30 minutes before Barefoot Landing closes. Closed Dec. 25. Blackbeard Encounter conducted 1 hour after Barefoot Landing closes. Ghost Show admission $8.95; $5.95 (ages 4-12). Combination ticket with Ghost Walk $22.95; $14.95 (ages 4-12). Blackbeard Encounter $44.95. Children are not permitted for the Blackbeard Encounter; reservations are required. AX, DS, MC, VI. Phone (843) 361-2700.

Myrtle Beach Ghost Walk departs from 4818 US 17S, at Barefoot Landing. Guides dressed in period pirate attire lead visitors on nighttime tours through a 1-mile route within Gauses Swash while sharing 13 local tales.

Food is available. Allow 1 hour, 30 minutes minimum. Tours depart daily at 8 and 9:45, June 1-Sept.

1; at 8, early Sept.-late Sept.; at 7:30, early Mar.-May 31 and late Sept.-Oct. 31; at 6, Feb. 1-early Mar.; at 5:30, in Jan. and Nov.-Dec. Closed Dec. 24-25. Phone ahead to verify schedule. Fee $17.95; $12.95 (ages 4-12). Combination ticket with Ghosts and Legends Theatre $22.95; $14.95 (ages 4-12). Reservations are required. AX, DS, MC, VI. Phone (843) 361-2700.

SURFSIDE BEACH (C-6)

pop. 4,425, elev. 10′

Surfside Beach's 2 miles of pristine sand can be reached from most cross streets off Ocean Boulevard. A fishing pier extends into the ocean at Surfside Drive.

LEGENDS IN CONCERT, 301 US 17S Bus. Rte., presents tribute artists who re-create stage performances of such legendary stars as Elton John, Marilyn Monroe, Elvis Presley and Madonna. Each show features five impersonators. Performers change regularly. The impersonators use their own voices and are accompanied on stage by bands, dancers and special effects, and the performers interact with the audience.

Food is available. Allow 2 hours minimum. Performances Mon.-Thurs. at 6 and 9, Fri.-Sat. at 8, in July; Mon. and Thurs.-Sat. at 8, Tues.-Wed. at 6 and 9, in June and Aug.; Mon.-Sat. at 8 (also Tues. at 2), Feb.-May and Sept.-Dec. Closed Dec. 22-25. Additional performances are given Thanksgiving weekend and in Dec.; phone for schedule. Admission $34.95-$39.95; $14.95-$39.95 (ages 3-16). AX, DS, MC, VI. Phone (843) 238-7827 or (800) 960-7469.

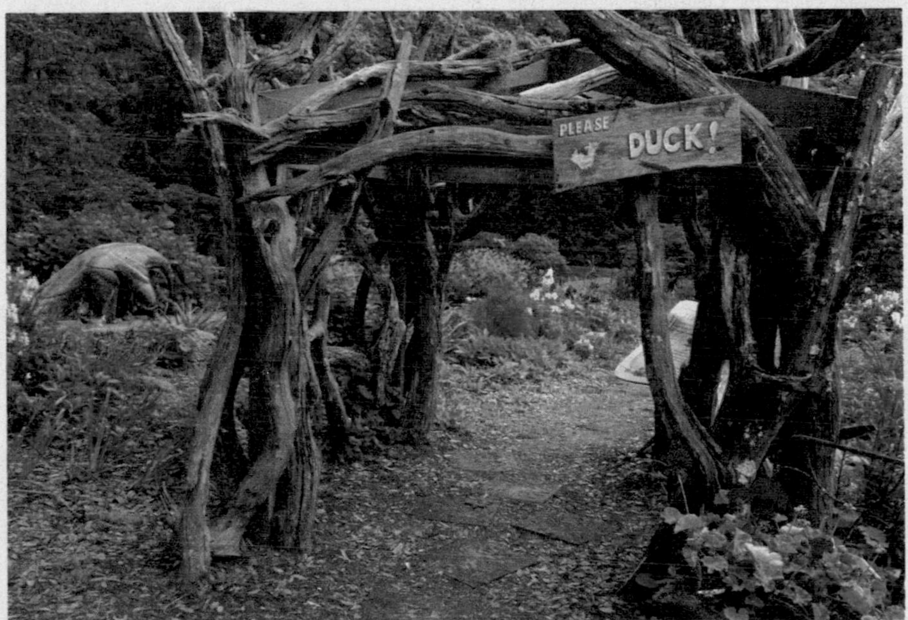

Brookgreen Gardens, Murrells Inlet / © Stephen Saks / Lonely Planet Images

This ends listings for The Grand Strand.
The following page resumes the alphabetical listings of cities in South Carolina.

GREENVILLE (A-1) pop. 56,002, elev. 1,040′

The Blue Ridge Mountains, visible from Greenville, present a compelling lure to many. By the early 19th century the region had become a summer resort for Lowcountry planters escaping the coastal heat and malaria. The town they built, Pleasantburg, soon was incorporated into Greenville as mills were erected to exploit the falls of the Reedy River in the heart of the community.

Despite the ravages of the Civil War, the city recovered. Greenville soon became known as the textile center of the world as many mills relocated from the Northeast. Falls Park on the Reedy preserves the site of the city's first settlement and the succession of mills that once stood there. The park offers gardens, waterfalls, picnic sites and several paths along the river.

During the Civil War Greenville was an important hospital center for Confederate soldiers. The city supports the Shriners Hospital for Children, which is one of the most modern hospitals of its kind; guided tours are available by phoning (864) 255-7848 between 10 and 3.

Performances by the Greenville Symphony Orchestra as well as ballet, chorale and theater groups are staged at the Peace Center for the Performing Arts, 300 S. Main St.; phone (864) 467-3000. The cultural and entertainment complex also includes an outdoor amphitheater and pavilion overlooking the Reedy River. The Greenville Little Theatre, established in 1926, presents six plays each year in the Charles E. Daniel Theatre, 444 College St.; phone (864) 233-6238.

Greenville has more than 60 city parks, including Cleveland Park, home to the Greenville Zoo *(see attraction listing)*. Cherokee Foothills Scenic Highway, northwest of Greenville, is lined with still lakes, greenery and historic sites.

Greenville Convention and Visitors Bureau: City Hall, 206 S. Main St., Greenville, SC 29601; phone (864) 233-0461 or (800) 717-0023.

Shopping areas: Belk, Dillard's, JCPenney, Macy's and Sears are among the 150 stores at Haywood Mall, 700 Haywood Rd. Tree-lined Main Street, in downtown, features antique shops and specialty stores.

BOB JONES UNIVERSITY MUSEUM & GALLERY is at 1700 Wade Hampton Blvd., 3 mi. n. on US 29 at jct. SR 291. The gallery contains more than 400 religious paintings by European artists from the 13th through 19th centuries. Allow 2 hours minimum. Tues.-Sun. 2-5; closed Jan. 1, Commencement Day (during the first week in May), July 4, Thanksgiving and Dec. 20-25. Admission $5; $4 (ages 60+); $3 (students with ID); free (ages 6-12). Ages 0-5 are not permitted. Phone (864) 770-1331.

GREENVILLE COUNTY MUSEUM OF ART, 420 College St., features a permanent collection that includes American art from the Colonial period to the present, with emphasis on Southern art. Temporary exhibits include contemporary art and explanations of aspects of American art history. Films, seminars and lectures are offered. Guided tours are given by appointment. Tues.-Sat. 11-5 (also Thurs. 5-8), Sun. 1-5; closed major holidays. Free. Phone (864) 271-7570.

GREENVILLE ZOO is w. off I-385 exit 42 to 150 Cleveland Park Dr. in Cleveland Park, following signs. Fourteen landscaped acres feature outdoor habitats with African elephants, primates, a red panda and exotic cats. The reptile exhibit houses a 75-pound python. Picnicking is permitted. Food is available. Allow 2 hours minimum. Daily 10-4:30; closed Jan. 1, Thanksgiving and Dec. 25. Admission $6; $3 (ages 3-15). Phone (864) 467-4300.

MUSEUM AND LIBRARY OF CONFEDERATE HISTORY is at 15 Boyce Ave. The museum features a research library as well as exhibits portraying the battles and the Southern home during the Civil War. Items include flags, photographs, uniforms and an extensive collection of weapons. Displayed is a derringer of the type John Wilkes Booth used to assassinate President Abraham Lincoln. Allow 30 minutes minimum. Mon. and Wed. 10-3, Fri. 1-9, Sat. 10-5, Sun. 1-5; closed Jan. 1 and Dec. 25. Donations. Phone (864) 421-9039.

GREENWOOD (B-2) pop. 22,071, elev. 665′

Named in 1824 for a local plantation, Greenwood became the seat of its namesake county in 1897. Cotton growing and textile manufacturing contributed to early growth; the latter industry is one of the city's leading employers.

The test gardens and display plots of George W. Park Seed Co., a seed mail-order house 6 miles north of Greenwood on SR 254, are open to the public. Tours of the company's experimental gardens are one of the attractions of the South Carolina Festival of Flowers, held the second through fourth weekends in June; phone (864) 223-8555 for tour information.

Greenwood Area Chamber of Commerce: 110 Phoenix St., P.O. Box 980, Greenwood, SC 29648; phone (864) 223-8431.

CALLIE SELF MEMORIAL CARILLON is next to the Callie Self Memorial Baptist Church at 509 W. Kirksey Dr. The 37 bells were cast in Holland and displayed as the Netherlands' exhibit at the New York World's Fair in 1939. Mon.-Fri. 9-2. Bells chime daily at 9, noon and 5. Phone (864) 227-2881.

THE MUSEUM, 106 Main St., houses items pertaining to the late 19th century, including such village reconstructions as an early drugstore, a Victorian parlor, a physician's office and a general store. Also featured are natural history displays and objects from Africa, Egypt, Japan and Latin America as well as changing art exhibits. Wed.-Sat. 10-5; closed major holidays. Admission $5; $2 (students with ID and senior citizens). Phone (864) 229-7093.

GREER (A-2) pop. 16,843, elev. 1,016′

BMW ZENTRUM is off I-85 exit 60, then w. to 1400 SR 101S, following signs. Displays highlight BMW achievements and products, including aircraft engines, motorcycles, formula racing cars, art cars and vehicles created for movies. A 15-minute video provides a factory tour as seen from the car's point of view and follows the creation of the models built at the adjacent BMW Manufacturing Co. Guided tours of the factory also are offered except during new model production.

Note: High- and open-heeled or open-toed shoes are not permitted on factory tours. Cameras are not allowed in the factory. Allow 1 hour minimum. Museum open Mon.-Fri. 9:30-5:30; closed holidays. Phone for factory tour schedule. Museum free. Plant tours $5; $3.50 (students with ID). Ages 0-11 are not permitted on factory tours. Reservations are required for tours. Phone (864) 989-5297, or (888) 868-7269 for tour reservations.

HARDEEVILLE (E-3) pop. 1,793, elev. 20′

SAVANNAH NATIONAL WILDLIFE REFUGE is off I-95 exit 5, 6.4 mi. s. on US 17, then 2.4 mi. s.w. on SR 170. Freshwater marshes, tidal rivers and forests provide sanctuary for waterfowl, deer, turkey and feral hogs. Many of the freshwater impoundments were originally created as plantation rice fields. The surrounding dikes and earthen berms create good trails for hiking and wildlife viewing. Birdwatching is best October through April. Vehicles are permitted on the Laurel Hill Wildlife Drive, a scenic 4-mile route off SR 170. Allow 30 minutes minimum. Daily dawn-dusk. Free. Phone (912) 652-4415.

HARLEYVILLE—*see Charleston p. 237.*

HARTSVILLE (B-5) pop. 7,556

Built on the plantation of Thomas Edward Hart, Hartsville grew into an active trading center largely through the efforts of the Coker family. Arriving in the mid-19th century, Maj. James Lide Coker established several businesses, constructed a railroad and founded Coker College, a 4-year liberal arts college with an enrollment of 950. David Coker, an agricultural expert who bred superior strains of cotton and other crops, also contributed to the town's prosperity.

Today only one-half of one percent of Hartsville's population is engaged in agriculture. The town accommodates several major manufacturers, including the international headquarters for a consumer and industrial packaging manufacturer. The town's development is documented at Hartsville Museum, 222 N. Fifth St.; phone (843) 383-3005.

Coker College's Kalmia Gardens, 2.6 miles west on W. Carolina Avenue (SR 151 Bus. Rte.), were developed in the 1930s on the site of the early 19th-century plantation of Thomas E. Hart. The gardens' natural setting can be explored by walking trails through a blackwater swamp forest; laurel thickets; a beech bluff; and pine, oak and holly uplands. Azaleas and camellias also bloom in the gardens' 30 acres. On the bluffs of Black Creek, the gardens are particularly lovely in May, when the mountain laurels are in bloom.

Greater Darlington County Tourism: 214 N. Fifth St., P.O. Box 578, Hartsville, SC 29551; phone (888) 427-8720.

HILTON HEAD ISLAND (F-4) pop. 33,862

Hilton Head Island, off the southern coast of South Carolina, is bordered by one of the last major unpolluted marine estuaries on the East Coast. The largest island between New Jersey and Florida, it is 12 miles long and up to 5 miles wide. Hilton Head was named for Capt. William Hilton, an Englishman who sailed into Port Royal Sound in 1663 and wrote about the green headlands of the island.

People lived on the island about 3,800 years ago. Beginning in 1526 Spanish, French and English colonists attempted to settle in the territory but were troubled by American Indian raids and pirates. By the mid-18th century English plantations were established. They prospered, growing indigo, rice and sea island cotton until the Civil War, when Union troops used the island as a base to block Confederate ports.

After the war the island was left to nature and the freed-slave, or Gullah, population, which developed a culture based on hunting, fishing and farming. Ruins of historic plantations and forts, including Baynard Ruins, a once prosperous sea island cotton plantation, still can be seen. The tomb of Thomas Heyward Jr., a signer of the Declaration of Independence, is visible from the intersection of US 278 and SC 462. The ruins of his Old House Plantation, burned by Union solders in 1864, also remain.

In 1956 the bridge to the mainland was completed, and the island developed into an all-year resort. Recreational facilities include about 25 golf courses, 300 tennis courts, riding stables, bicycle trails and marinas. Harbour Town Links is the site of the MCI Heritage Classic in April. The Hilton Head Island Celebrity Golf Tournament is played at Palmetto Dunes and Shipyard in September.

Wildlife and waterfowl habitats include the Sea Pines Forest Preserve, the Audubon Newhall Preserve and the Pinckney Island National Wildlife Refuge. Daily sightseeing cruises are available on Calibogue Sound, around the island and to Daufuskie Island, where many old Gullah traditions still are observed.

SAVE Gray Line offers motor coach sightseeing tours of the island's historical sites and resort communities. Extended tours to Beaufort also are available. For schedules and fares, or to make reservations, phone (843) 681-8212 or (800) 845-5582.

Hilton Head Island-Bluffton Chamber of Commerce and Visitor & Convention Bureau: P.O. Box 5647, Hilton Head Island, SC 29938-5647;

phone (843) 785-3673 or (800) 523-3373. Visitor information is available at 1 Chamber of Commerce Dr., Hilton Head Island, SC, 29928-3573. The walk-in welcome center is located at 100 William Hilton Pkwy., Hilton Head Island, SC 29926-1216.

Shopping areas: Coligny Plaza, N. Forest Beach Road, features some 60 specialty stores and restaurants. Upscale retailers Ann Taylor, Belk, Off 5th, Talbots and Williams-Sonoma are found at The Mall at Shelter Cove, on US 278 at mile marker 8.

COASTAL DISCOVERY MUSEUM, 100 William Pkwy., encourages hands-on discovery and features exhibits about animal and plant life, archeology, ecology and the region's cultural history. Guided off-site nature walks, history tours, cruises and kayak nature trips are available. Mon.-Sat. 9-4:30, Sun. 11-3. Donations. History and nature tours $12; $7 (ages 4-12). Cruises $19; $13 (ages 1-12). Kayak trip $27; $25 (ages 1-12). Reservations are required for tours. Phone (843) 689-6767.

ISLE OF PALMS—*see Charleston p. 237.*

KINGS MOUNTAIN NATIONAL MILITARY PARK (A-3)

South of the town of Kings Mountain, N.C., off I-85, is Kings Mountain National Military Park, one of the largest military parks in the United States. Spreading across York and Cherokee counties in South Carolina, this 3,950-acre area is a spur of the Kings Mountain Range. Battlefield Ridge, about 600 yards long, is a narrow hogback 60 feet above the surrounding valleys.

After several years of hostilities, only one Southern region remained undisturbed by the Revolutionary War—the southern Appalachians. That tenuous peace soon came to an end as British troops under Gen. Charles Cornwallis occupied vast areas of North and South Carolina.

In September 1780 Maj. Patrick Ferguson raided a mountain town. The threatened backwoodsmen joined forces with Whigs from Virginia, South Carolina and North Carolina and converged on Kings Mountain, where Ferguson was camped. Although outnumbered by the trained Loyalists, the mountain men advanced steadily against repeated bayonet charges and took the summit. Ferguson, who had threatened to lay their country waste with fire and sword, was killed.

The park is the southern terminus of the 220-mile Overmountain Victory National Historic Trail, which traces the Patriot army's assembly route from Abingdon, Va. Access to the trail primarily is by motor vehicles, but there are some hiking segments. In the park stand the United States Monument, Centennial Monument and other memorial markers. A self-guiding trail leads to significant battlefield sites. The visitor center offers exhibits, a film and a diorama of the battle as well as information about the national historic trail. Allow 1 hour minimum. Daily 9-5 (also Sat.-Sun. 5-6, in summer); closed Jan. 1, Thanksgiving and Dec. 25. Free. Phone (864) 936-7921.

LANCASTER (B-4) pop. 8,177

Settled in the early 1800s, Lancaster became the center of trade for the surrounding mill villages. Instrumental in the city's growth was a series of canals built on the Catawba-Wateree River during the 1820s. The locks made the waterway navigable despite its treacherous shoals and falls. A section of locks at Landsford Canal State Park *(see Recreation Chart),* northwest off US 21 and SR 330, has been restored.

Lancaster County Chamber of Commerce: 604 N. Main St., P.O. Box 430, Lancaster, SC 29721; phone (803) 283-4105.

ANDREW JACKSON STATE PARK is 8 mi. n. on US 521. Commemorating Andrew Jackson, who was born in the vicinity, the park contains an amphitheater and a museum with documents and relics of the frontier period as well as a one-room log schoolhouse with exhibits. Camping, fishing and picnicking are permitted, and trails are available.

Allow 2 hours minimum. Park open daily 9-9 during DST; 8-6, rest of year. Museum open Sat.-Sun. 1-5, Mon.-Fri. by appointment. Admission $2; $1.25 (ages 66+); free (ages 0-15). Phone (803) 285-3344. *See Recreation Chart and the AAA Southeastern CampBook.*

LATTA (B-5) pop. 1,410, elev. 105′

DILLON COUNTY MUSEUM, 101 S. Marion St., traces area history through documents, photographs and displays of agricultural artifacts. The museum is housed in a restored 1915 building and features a doctor's office furnished in period. Allow 1 hour minimum. Daily 1:30-4:30; closed Easter, Thanksgiving and Dec. 25. Donations. Phone (843) 752-9457.

LEXINGTON (C-3) pop. 9,793, elev. 360′

Formed in 1785, Lexington was named for the Massachusetts town where the first battle of the Revolutionary War was fought. However, this Lexington was not as quick to embrace the Patriot cause. The area's population, largely of German descent, was loyal to England's German king George III and his Lutheran queen Charlotte Sophia. The settlers finally did join their fellow colonists late in the war.

Lexington Chamber of Commerce: 321 S. Lake Dr., P.O. Box 44, Lexington, SC 29072; phone (803) 359-6113.

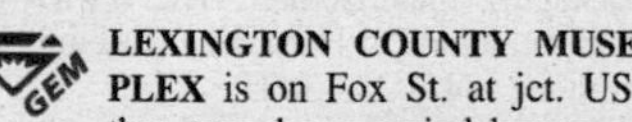

LEXINGTON COUNTY MUSEUM COMPLEX is on Fox St. at jct. US 378. More than two dozen period houses and outbuildings have been moved to this 7-acre site and depict the lifestyle of the area during the 1830s. Some buildings date to the late 1700s, including the county's oldest documented house. A hen house, cotton gin, carriage house, smokehouse, one-room schoolhouse, barns and corncribs are some of the structures included. A 19th-century garden also is on the grounds.

The buildings house collections of quilts, coverlets, American Indian artifacts and farm tools and equipment. Furnishings have been constructed by local craftspersons. Spinning and weaving demonstrations are offered. Guided tours are available; phone ahead to confirm availability. Allow 1 hour minimum. Tues.-Sat. 10-4, Sun. 1-4; closed major holidays and holiday weekends. Last tour begins 1 hour before closing. Admission $3; $2 (ages 0-11). Phone (803) 359-8369.

LITTLE RIVER—*see The Grand Strand p. 252.*

LONG CREEK (B-1) elev. 300′

Long Creek is surrounded by the Andrew Pickens District of Sumter National Forest *(see place listing p. 267)*. White-water enthusiasts frequent the nearby Chattooga Wild and Scenic River, where the motion picture "Deliverance" was filmed.

RECREATIONAL ACTIVITIES

White-water Rafting

- **Nantahala Outdoor Center** is at 851-A Chattooga Ridge Rd.; 10.1 mi. e. on US 76, then 2.5 mi. n. on Chattooga Ridge Rd. Write 13077 Hwy. 19W, Bryson City, NC 28713. Daily Mar.-Nov. Phone (800) 232-7238.
- **Wildwater Ltd. Rafting** is 1 mi. n. of US 76 in the Long Creek Academy Bldg., P.O. Box 309, Long Creek, SC 29658. Daily Mar.-Oct. Phone (864) 647-9587 or (800) 451-9972.

McBEE (B-4) pop. 714, elev. 490′

McBee traces its origin to 1900, when a barbecue was held and lots were sold at auction. Abandoning cotton and corn farming in favor of more marketable fruit cultivation, area farmers became renowned for their quality grapes, which are a favorite with winemakers.

CAROLINA SANDHILLS NATIONAL WILDLIFE REFUGE, 4 mi. n. on US 1, is 45,348 acres of forest, streamside, pond and open-field habitats supporting nearly 200 species of birds, deer and other wildlife. Sand dunes forming a line from Cheraw to North Augusta are the remains of an ancient coastline that once extended into the middle of the state. The refuge has 1- and 5-mile hiking trails, an automobile route, observation towers and approximately 310 acres of fishing waters. Mon.-Fri. 7-4:30. Free. Phone (843) 335-8401.

McCLELLANVILLE—*see Charleston p. 237.*

McCONNELLS (A-3) pop. 287

McConnells was established in the mid-1800s and named for one of the settling families. Local history is interpreted at nearby Historic Brattonsville *(see attraction listing)*.

HISTORIC BRATTONSVILLE, 2 mi. e. via SR 322 to 1444 Brattonsville Rd., following signs, comprises many restored structures, including an antebellum plantation house and supporting buildings. The buildings have been restored and furnished to reflect the 18th and 19th centuries. Interpretive programs are offered on the second and fourth Saturdays each month. Hiking trails are available. Phone ahead for information about mountain biking and horseback riding.

Mon.-Sat. 10-5, Sun. 1-5; closed Thanksgiving and Dec. 24-25. Last admission 30 minutes before closing. Admission $6; $5 (ages 60+); $3 (ages 4-17). MC, VI. Phone (803) 684-2327.

MONCKS CORNER—*see Charleston p. 238.*

MOUNTAIN REST (A-1)

WALHALLA STATE FISH HATCHERY is on SR 107 at the entrance to the Ellicott Rock Wilderness in the Sumter National Forest *(see place listing p. 267)*. The hatchery raises trout. Daily 8-4. Free. Phone (864) 638-2866.

MOUNT PLEASANT—*see Charleston p. 238.*

MURRELLS INLET—*see The Grand Strand p. 252.*

MYRTLE BEACH—*see The Grand Strand p. 254.*

NEWBERRY (B-2) pop. 10,580, elev. 495′

At Carter and Holmes Orchids, 629 Mendenhall Rd., visitors can peruse an abundance of orchids and houseplants in 18 greenhouses with the help of informational handouts. Guided tours are given by appointment and cost $5 per person (which buys visitors a coupon that can be used on plants); departures require a minimum of $50 in coupons. The site is open Monday through Saturday 9-5; phone (803) 276-0579 or (800) 873-7086.

NEWBERRY OPERA HOUSE is downtown at 1201 McKibben St. This structure, inspired by French Gothic architecture, was built in 1881 as a multipurpose facility. The upper floor was designated for performance space while the ground floor housed a fire station, police station, courthouse and other city offices. The building has since been restored and even enlarged. More than 250 dance, musical and theater performances are given throughout the year. Guided tours are offered, but access to the stage and backstage areas may not be available depending on the performance schedule.

Allow 45 minutes minimum. Mon.-Fri. 9-6, Sat. 11-4, Sun. 2-4; closed Jan. 1, Palm Sunday, Easter, July 4, Dec. 25. Tour by donations. Admission for shows varies. AX, DS, MC, VI. Phone (803) 276-5179.

NINETY SIX (C-2) pop. 1,936, elev. 571′

Settled along an American Indian trading route, Ninety Six was named for its distance in miles from the Cherokee village of Keowee in the Blue Ridge Mountains. Patriots and Tories fought the first land battle of the Revolutionary War in the South here in November 1775.

Ninety Six Chamber of Commerce: P.O. Box 8, 97 SR 34, Ninety Six, SC 29666. Until a phone number is established for this location, phone the city hall at (864) 543-2900.

NINETY SIX NATIONAL HISTORIC SITE is 2 mi. s. on SR 248. Two Revolutionary War battles occurred on this site, one in 1775 and the other in 1781, when Patriot general Nathanael Greene laid siege to a force of some 550 British Loyalists entrenched near the village of Ninety Six. Visitors can explore the earthworks, old roadbeds, traces of the village, a reconstructed stockade fort and an early log cabin along a mile-long trail. The visitor center houses a museum and auditorium.

Allow 1 hour, 30 minutes minimum. Park open daily dawn-dusk. Visitor center open daily 8-5; closed Jan. 1, Thanksgiving and Dec. 25. Free. Phone (864) 543-4068.

NORTH CHARLESTON—

see Charleston vicinity p. 239.

NORTH MYRTLE BEACH—

see The Grand Strand p. 258.

ORANGEBURG (C-3) pop. 12,765, elev. 252′

Since its settlement in the 1730s Orangeburg has been an important trade center for Orangeburg County's rich farmland. Such manufactured goods as wood products, textiles, chemicals and machinery sustain the town's economy.

Orangeburg County Chamber of Commerce: 155 Riverside Dr., P.O. Box 328, Orangeburg, SC 29116; phone (803) 534-6821 or (800) 545-6153.

EDISTO MEMORIAL GARDENS is a municipal park at 367 Green St. along the North Edisto River, one of the longest blackwater rivers in the world. Once a dismal riverbank swamp, the 110 acres of moss-draped oaks, cypresses, dogwoods, crab apples and azaleas are especially beautiful in late March and early April. A rose garden with about 200 varieties provides color from mid-April to mid-November. A boardwalk offers views of native plants and wildlife. Daily dawn-dusk. Free. Phone (803) 533-6020.

ORANGEBURG NATIONAL FISH HATCHERY, on US 21 bypass (Stonewall Jackson Blvd.), houses a display aquarium. On the premises blue gills, striped bass, catfish and shortnose sturgeon are raised. Guided tours are available. Picnicking is permitted. Mon.-Fri. 8-4; otherwise by appointment. Free. Phone (803) 534-4828.

PARRIS ISLAND (E-4) pop. 4,841

The U.S. Marine Corps Recruit Depot has occupied Parris Island since 1915. The Jean Ribault (or Huguenot) Monument marks the site of one of North America's first European settlements.

PARRIS ISLAND MUSEUM is on Panama St., Bldg. 111, at the Marine Corps Recruit Depot. The museum, located on an active military base, contains displays of uniforms, field equipment, official documents and photographs relating to the history of the Marine Corps and civilian life on Parris Island. Collections of weapons, ordnance and artillery, and scale models of aircraft, ships and amphibious landing craft also are displayed. Allow 1 hour minimum. Daily 10-4:30; closed Jan. 1, Easter, Thanksgiving and Dec. 25. Free. Phone (843) 228-2951.

PENDLETON (B-1) pop. 2,966, elev. 817′

The Pendleton district was formed soon after the Cherokees ceded their territory to South Carolina in 1777. Named for Judge Henry Pendleton of Culpeper, Va., whose Culpeper Minute Men were among the first Revolutionary militia in the South, the town became an important government, business and cultural center because of its location at the crossroads of two major American Indian trading paths.

Pendleton also became popular with wealthy Lowcountry families who built large plantations as summer retreats. Most notable are Ashtabula, on SR 88, and Woodburn, on US 76, both built in the 1820s; phone (864) 646-3782 for information.

The Pendleton Historic District, one of the largest national historic areas, is comprised of more than 6,000 acres with some 40 private residences and public and commercial buildings. Landmarks include the Farmer's Society Hall, an 1826 Greek Revival structure on the original village green; St. Paul's Episcopal Church, where the John C. Calhoun family worshipped; and Hunter's Store, an 1850s mercantile establishment.

Pendleton District Historical, Recreational and Tourism Commission: 125 E. Queen St., P.O. Box 565, Pendleton, SC 29670; phone (864) 646-3782.

Self-guiding tours: Guided walking tours and brochures are available from Pendleton District Historical, Recreational and Tourism Commission.

RAVENEL (E-4) pop. 2,214, elev. 38′

CAW CAW INTERPRETIVE CENTER is on US 17S, 2.6 mi. w. of SR 162. This 654-acre site within the Caw Caw Swamp contains remnants of 18th- and 19th-century rice plantations. Original earthen dikes and canals illustrate how the swampland was drained for cultivation. Now a wildlife sanctuary, the site provides a diverse habitat for more than 350 animal species. An 8-mile interpretive trail winds through forests, swamp and marshes. Birding specialists offer bird walks twice a week.

Allow 2 hours minimum. Wed.-Sun. 9-3 (also Sat.-Sun. 3-5). Bird walks Wed. and Sat. at 8:30. Closed major holidays. Admission $1; free (ages 0-3). Bird walk $5. AX, MC, VI. Phone (843) 889-8898.

RIDGELAND (E-3) pop. 2,518, elev. 62′

Ridgeland traces its origins to the railroad, which came through present-day Jasper County in the mid-1800s. The town, then known as Gopher Hill, had just begun to prosper when Union soldiers torched much of the region during the Civil War. By the early 1900s its location on US 17, the main route between New York City and Miami, put the town back on the map; but it was the arrival of I-95 that established it as a major travel service center. The Pauline Pratt Webel Museum, 451B E. Wilson St., documents town history through artifacts, documents and photographs; phone (843) 726-8126.

Jasper County Chamber of Commerce: 451B E. Wilson St., P.O. Box 1267, Ridgeland, SC 29936-0910; phone (843) 726-8126.

BLUE HERON NATURE TRAIL & LEARNING CENTER is off I-95 exit 21, n.w. to Wilson St., then just n. to 100 Bailey Ln. A 1-mile nature trail with raised boardwalks traverses a wetland habitat. Benches and swings encourage visitors to stop and enjoy Lowcountry flora and fauna. Alligators, herons, osprey and turtles are commonly seen. The learning center features wildlife exhibits. Picnicking is permitted. Allow 1 hour minimum. Trail daily dawn-dusk. Learning Center Mon.-Fri. 9-5; closed holidays. Free. Phone (843) 726-7611.

ROCK HILL—*see North Carolina p. 148.*

ROCKVILLE—*see Charleston vicinity p. 239.*

ROEBUCK (A-2) pop. 1,725, elev. 750′

GEM SAVE **WALNUT GROVE PLANTATION** is s. on US 221 to Still House Rd., following signs. The house on this 18th-century plantation was built in 1765 for Charles and Mary Moore. It is furnished with pre-1810 antiques. The kitchen building displays 18th-century utensils made from wood, wrought iron and tin as well as earthenware. Other outbuildings include a blacksmith shop, school, doctor's office, smokehouse and barns. An herb garden and nature trail also are on the grounds.

A family cemetery on the property includes at least 146 graves, including those of Charles and Mary, other relatives and friends, enslaved men and women, and Revolutionary War soldiers. Kate Moore Barry, the oldest Moore daughter, is interred here. She acted as a spy and scout during the war and is considered a heroine.

Tues.-Sat. 11-5, Apr.-Oct.; Sat. 11-5, Sun. 2-5, rest of year. Closed holidays. Tours are given on the hour. Admission $6; $5.50 (ages 65+); $3 (ages 6-18). Phone (864) 576-6546.

ST. HELENA ISLAND (E-4)

YORK W. BAILEY MUSEUM, off US 21 in the Penn Center Historic District, depicts the culture and history of the Sea Islands' African-American population since the Civil War. Penn Center was founded as Penn School in 1862 to provide formal

Spanish Moss

It's not Spanish and it's not moss; it is uniquely American and related to the pineapple. Spanish moss, the silver-green tresses that adorn trees from North Carolina to South America, is one of nature's most picturesque oddities.

Spanish moss is not a parasite but an epiphyte, a type of plant that has no roots but lives off moisture in the atmosphere. Tiny scales on the moss's tendrils trap rain for easier absorption and also keep internal moisture from evaporating. The plants are nourished by mineral-rich

cells that wash off the host tree; the greater the number of cells, the more prolific the moss, which is why masses of moss are often found on old or decaying trees.

Also called long moss or vegetable horsehair, it covers more trees than any other type of epiphyte. It does not bear fruit like its spiny distant cousin the pineapple, but it sometimes produces small yellow flowers.

Spanish moss stems can grow as long as 25 feet, with threadlike leaves 1 to 3 inches long sprouting from them. Primarily decorative, the moss sometimes is used as packing material and upholstery stuffing.

education and settlement assistance to former slaves. Mon.-Sat. 11-4; closed holidays. Admission $5; $4 (ages 55+); $2 (ages 6-11). Phone (843) 838-2474.

ST. MATTHEWS (C-4) pop. 2,107, elev. 257′

Originally the site of a trading post on the Cherokee Path, St. Matthews later was settled by Palatine Germans 1730-40. It was one of the first plantation domains in South Carolina beyond the Charleston tidewater region.

Calhoun County Chamber of Commerce: Courthouse Annex 114, St. Matthews, SC 29135; phone (803) 655-5650.

CALHOUN COUNTY MUSEUM AND CULTURAL CENTER, 313 Butler St., contains local historical memorabilia, period rooms, archeological artifacts, a library, archives and an art gallery. Tues.-Fri. 9-4; closed holidays. Archives open by appointment only. Free. Phone (803) 874-3964.

SANTEE (D-4) pop. 740

The Santee National Wildlife Refuge, I-95 exit 102, is a 15,095-acre sanctuary for migratory waterfowl; phone (803) 478-2217.

Shopping areas: Santee Factory Stores, I-95 exit 98, includes nearly a dozen factory outlet stores, including Bon Worth and IZOD.

SENECA (B-1) pop. 7,652, elev. 950′

Seneca was established 1873 at the junction of two railroad lines serving Atlanta and Charlotte. The town name is of Iroquois Indian origin. County history is chronicled at the Lunney Museum, a refurbished early 20th-century house at 211 W. South First St., in the historic district; phone (864) 882-4811.

Self-guiding tours: Tour maps of the Seneca Historic District are available at the Lunney Museum.

GEM **WORLD OF ENERGY,** jct. SRs 130 and 183, is Duke Power Co.'s information center. Next to Oconee Nuclear Station, the center contains exhibits that illustrate the use of water, coal and uranium in creating energy. Displays chart the story of power from lightning to light bulbs and describe energy conservation programs for the home.

The center also has specimens of local fish and a cold-water habitat, computer games concerning electricity and a Keowee Valley film. Visitors can enter a fission chamber that demonstrates atoms' role in energy creation. Views of Lake Keowee and the Keowee Valley are offered. A .25-mile nature trail is on the grounds. Picnicking is permitted. Allow 1 hour minimum. Mon.-Fri. 9-5, Sat.-Sun. noon-5; closed Jan. 1, Thanksgiving and Dec. 24-25. Free. Phone (864) 885-4600.

SPARTANBURG (A-3) pop. 39,673, elev. 875′

One of the South's leading textile-manufacturing cities, Spartanburg also is one of the world's largest peach shipping centers. Peach orchards and packing sheds can be visited June through August. The city was named for the Spartan Regiment, which represented it during the Revolutionary War. A statue honoring Gen. Daniel Morgan, the hero of the Battle of Cowpens, stands in Morgan Square.

Spartanburg Convention and Visitors Bureau: 298 Magnolia St., Spartanburg, SC 29306; phone (864) 594-5050 or (800) 374-8326.

GEM **CHAPMAN CULTURAL CENTER,** 200 E. St. John St., is home to the Spartanburg County Regional History Museum, Spartanburg Art Museum, and Spartanburg Science Center. A 500-seat theater, where visitors can watch performances by the Spartanburg Little Theatre and Spartanburg Repertory Company, also is located here. Concerts, dance and educational seminars are held throughout the year.

The history museum chronicles the area's history through archives, clothing, dolls, fine art, photographs, postcards and toys. The art museum features dozens of artworks, many of which were created by South Carolina artists. The science center explores an array of topics, including animals, astronomy, electricity, fossils, geology and the human body.

Allow 1 hour minimum. Tues.-Sat. 10-5 (also Thurs. 5-8); closed Thanksgiving and Dec. 25. Free through at least July 2009; phone to verify after that date. Phone (864) 583-2776.

HATCHER GARDEN AND WOODLAND PRESERVE is off I-26 exit 22, then 2 mi. e. This 10-acre site features forested areas, native plants, flower gardens, ponds and natural settings for wildlife viewing. Picnicking is permitted. Allow 30 minutes minimum. Daily dawn-dusk. Free. Phone (864) 574-7724.

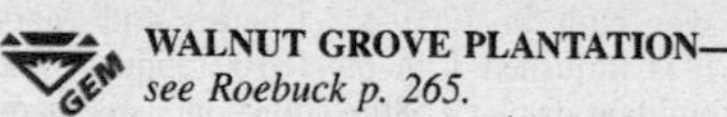
GEM **WALNUT GROVE PLANTATION—** *see Roebuck p. 265.*

SULLIVAN'S ISLAND—*see Charleston p. 239.*

SUMMERVILLE—*see Charleston p. 239.*

SUMTER (C-4) pop. 39,643, elev. 174′

Founded in 1785, Sumter was named for Gen. Thomas Sumter, a Revolutionary War hero and statesman. The British, impressed by Sumter's daring hit-and-run warfare, nicknamed him the Gamecock of the Revolution. Settled by a refined citizenry from surrounding plantations, the town developed a reputation as a cultural center. The arrival of road shows packed the old opera house, which now houses the city hall; for information about occasional productions phone (803) 436-2500.

One of the state's leading lumber and agricultural areas, Sumter is known for its furniture and woodworking industry. Further bolstering the city's economy are textile mills, chemical plants, foundries and the Palmetto Pigeon Plant, reputed to be the world's largest squab farm. Just west of Sumter is Shaw Air

Force Base, home to the F-16 Fighting Falcon and A-10 Thunderbolt II fighter crews.

Greater Sumter Chamber of Commerce: 32 E. Calhoun St., Sumter, SC 29150; phone (803) 775-1231.

SUMTER COUNTY MUSEUM, 122 N. Washington St., is in the restored 1916 Edwardian-style Williams-Brice residence. Period rooms contain textiles, decorative and fine arts, and articles that belonged to Gen. Thomas Sumter's family as well as displays about American military history.

On the grounds are formal gardens and a re-created pioneer settlement featuring an 1800s house and commissary along with several reproduction buildings. Allow 1 hour minimum. Tues.-Sat. 10-5; closed major holidays. Donations. Phone (803) 775-0908.

SUMTER GALLERY OF ART, 200 Hasel St., features changing exhibits of traditional and contemporary artwork in a variety of media and styles. The art gallery also showcases the work of Depression-era artist Elizabeth White. Born in Sumter in 1893, White is considered one of the state's leading artists. Tues.-Sat. 11-5, Sun. 1:30-5; closed holidays. Donations. Phone (803) 775-0543.

SWAN LAKE IRIS GARDENS is at 900 W. Liberty St. The eight species of swans from around the world are the dominant feature in the park. The 150 acres of lawns, landscaped gardens, lakes and pinewoods are known for a beautiful collection of Japanese irises, which bloom in mid-May. The Iris Festival, one of the state's oldest festivals, is held over Memorial Day weekend to celebrate the peak blooming season. Picnicking is permitted. Food is available. Daily 8-dusk. Free. Phone (800) 688-4748.

SUMTER NATIONAL FOREST

Elevations in the forest range from 150 ft. in the Enoree region to 3,500 ft. at Fork Mountain. Refer to AAA maps for additional elevation information.

Divided into three separate units in northwestern South Carolina, Sumter National Forest offers a variety of scenery within its 365,526 acres. The foothills of the southern Appalachians, the Piedmont's rolling terrain and the upper reaches of the Savannah River are enhanced by dogwoods, sourwoods and azaleas. A particularly scenic route is the 12-mile stretch of SR 107 that runs through the forest. The Chattooga Wild and Scenic River offers 31 miles of white-water rapids for canoeing or rafting.

Guided white-water rafting trips can be arranged with operators based in Long Creek *(see place listing p. 263)*. Forest facilities include campgrounds, picnic areas, rifle ranges and nature, hiking, canoeing and horse trails. Fishing is also permitted. For additional information contact the Forest Supervisor's Office, 4931 Broad River Rd., Columbia, SC 29212. Phone (803) 561-4000. *See Recreation Chart and the AAA Southeastern CampBook.*

SURFSIDE BEACH—

see The Grand Strand p. 259.

UNION (B-3) pop. 8,793, elev. 641′

ROSE HILL PLANTATION STATE HISTORIC SITE is on 44 acres off CR 2, 8 mi. s.w. via US 176 to 2677 Sardis Rd. The former site of secessionist Gov. William Henry Gist's cotton plantation, the park includes the governor's 1832 Federal mansion, which features the original wooden-peg staircase, large Renaissance Revival furnishings and some family clothing and belongings. The landscaped grounds offer gardens, nature trails and magnolia trees planted when the mansion was built.

Picnicking is permitted. Allow 30 minutes minimum. Park open Thurs.-Mon. 9-6. Guided mansion tours are given 1-4, holidays by appointment. Park free. Mansion $4; $2.50 (ages 65+); $3 (ages 6-16). Phone (864) 427-5966.

WALTERBORO (D-3) pop. 5,153, elev. 59′

Just east of I-95 exit 53 lies the Great Swamp Sanctuary, which encompasses 842 acres and offers visitors biking and hiking trails as well as canoeing and kayaking opportunities if the water level is sufficient. There are benches and boardwalks that enhance flora and wildlife viewing. Picnic tables also are provided. Insect repellent is recommended as is looking out for poison ivy. The site is open daily dawn to dusk; phone (843) 538-4353. *See Recreation Chart.*

Genealogy Research Center, 609 Black St., features research material for genealogical studies pertaining to Colleton and other nearby counties as well as legal records for several states in the Southeast. The facility is open Tuesday 9-5 and Saturday 9-1; phone (843) 538-4353.

Walterboro Welcome Center: 1273 Sniders Hwy., Walterboro, SC 29488; phone (843) 538-4353. *See color ad p. 1109.*

Self-guiding tours: Brochures for self-guiding walking tours of 55 historic sites are available at the Walterboro Welcome Center.

BEDON-LUCAS HOUSE MUSEUM is at 205 Church St. This 1820 Federal raised cottage was built high off the ground so its occupants could avoid mosquitoes but also benefit from summer breezes. The Clarence Lucas family bought the house from Richard Bedon, the first known occupant, late in the century and made renovations reflecting Victorian style. The separate kitchen house displays kitchen artifacts from other Colleton County homes.

Guided tours are available. Allow 20 minutes minimum. Thurs.-Sat. 1-4, Mar.-Nov. and other times by appointment; closed major holidays. Admission $3; $2 (ages 65+); free (ages 0-7). Phone (843) 549-9633.

COLLETON MUSEUM, 239 N. Jefferies Blvd., is housed in an 1850s neo-Gothic structure that once served as a jail. The building has undergone many changes, but it still resembles a castle. Exhibits showcase various aspects of local history, including a tribute to the Tuskegee Airmen who trained at the Walterboro base. Artifacts relating to domestic and military life are displayed and a natural history exhibit features animals found in the nearby ACE Basin. Space also is dedicated to rotating exhibits. Tues.-Fri. 10-5, Sat. noon-4; closed major holidays. Donations. Phone (843) 549-2303.

SAVE **SLAVE RELIC HISTORICAL MUSEUM** is at 208 Carn St. The African slave trade, the Underground Railroad and slavery in the South prior to the Civil War are chronicled through documents, photographs and both original and replica artifacts. Furniture, jewelry, quilts, a mock-up of slave quarters and an 1860 newspaper reprint advertising a slave auction are included. Guided tours are available. Allow 30 minutes minimum. Mon.-Thurs. 9:30-5, Sat. 10-3; closed major holidays. Admission $6; $5 (children and senior citizens). Phone (843) 549-9130.

WELLFORD (B-2) pop. 2,030, elev. 860′

HOLLYWILD ANIMAL PARK, 2325 Hampton Rd., is home to nearly 600 rare and exotic animals, many of which appeared in movies and television commercials. Numerous contact areas allow visitors to get close to the animals. Safaris and miniature steam train rides are available. During the holiday season the park is decorated with more than 3 million lights.

Picnicking is permitted. Allow 2 hours minimum. Mon.-Fri. 9-5, Sat. 9-7, Sun. 11-6, June-Aug.; Mon.-Fri. 9-4, Sat. 9-6, Sun. 11-6, in Apr.; Mon.-Fri. 9-4, Sat. 9-7, Sun. 11-6, in May; Sat. 9-6, Sun. 11-6 (also Labor Day), in Sept.; Sat. 9-5, Sun. 11-5 in Oct.; daily 6 p.m.-9 p.m. with extended hours Sat.-Sun. and Christmas week, late Nov.-Jan. 2. Phone to confirm schedule. Last admission 1 hour before closing. Admission $10; $8 (ages 2–12 and 65+). Train fare $1. Holiday drive-through $5 per person. MC, VI. Phone (864) 472-2038 or (877) 465-5994.

DID YOU KNOW

President Andrew Jackson was born in South Carolina.

WINNSBORO (B-3) pop. 3,599, elev. 539′

Winnsboro was named in honor of town founder and Revolutionary War colonel Richard Winn. In 1780 British troops under Gen. Charles Cornwallis occupied the town for 4 months before pressing onward to their eventual surrender at Yorktown, Va. In February 1865 Federal troops looted houses and stores and then burned part of Winnsboro.

Many of those buildings not destroyed by the fire are in the town's historic district. This area has several fine examples of early 19th-century architecture, including the Old Town Clock Building, Fairfield County Courthouse and Thespian Hall.

Fairfield County Chamber of Commerce: Town Clock Bldg., 100 Congress St., P.O. Box 297, Winnsboro, SC 29180; phone (803) 635-4242.

Self-guiding tours: Brochures detailing a walking or driving tour are available at the chamber of commerce and from local merchants.

FAIRFIELD COUNTY MUSEUM, 231 S. Congress St., was built in 1830 as a private residence. A noteworthy example of Federal architecture, the museum contains period furniture and clothing, local memorabilia, Victorian collectibles, farm and kitchen tools and American Indian artifacts. Allow 30 minutes minimum. Tues.-Fri. 10-5, Sat. 10-3; closed holidays. Donations. Phone (803) 635-9811.

YORK (A-3) pop. 6,985, elev. 756′

York was settled by Scot-Irish from Pennsylvania. The 340-acre historic district on US 321 and SR 5 contains more than 180 landmarks and structures.

Kings Mountain State Park has a re-creation of an 1850s farmstead with log and timber-frame structures. An interpreter is on the site June through August; phone (803) 222-3209. *See Recreation Chart and the AAA Southeastern CampBook.*

Greater York Chamber of Commerce: P.O. Box 97, 23 E. Liberty St., York, SC 29745; phone (803) 684-2590 or (877) 684-2590.

ENERGYQUEST AT CATAWBA NUCLEAR STATION is n. on SR 49 to SR 274, then 5 mi. n. to 4850 Concord Rd. The mirrored-glass building contains touch-activated computer terminals that display informative videos about nuclear energy. A film presentation and a nature trail are available. Picnicking is permitted. Allow 1 hour minimum. Mon.-Fri. 9-5; closed Jan. 1, Good Friday, Memorial Day, July 4, Labor Day, Thanksgiving and Dec. 24-25. Reservations are required. Free. Phone (800) 777-0006.

America on the Move is made possible by generous support from General Motors Corporation, AAA, State Farm Companies Foundation, The History Channel, United States Congress, U.S. Department of Transportation, Exxon Mobil, American Public Transportation Association, American Road & Transportation Builders Association, Association of American Railroads, National Asphalt Pavement Association, The UPS Foundation.

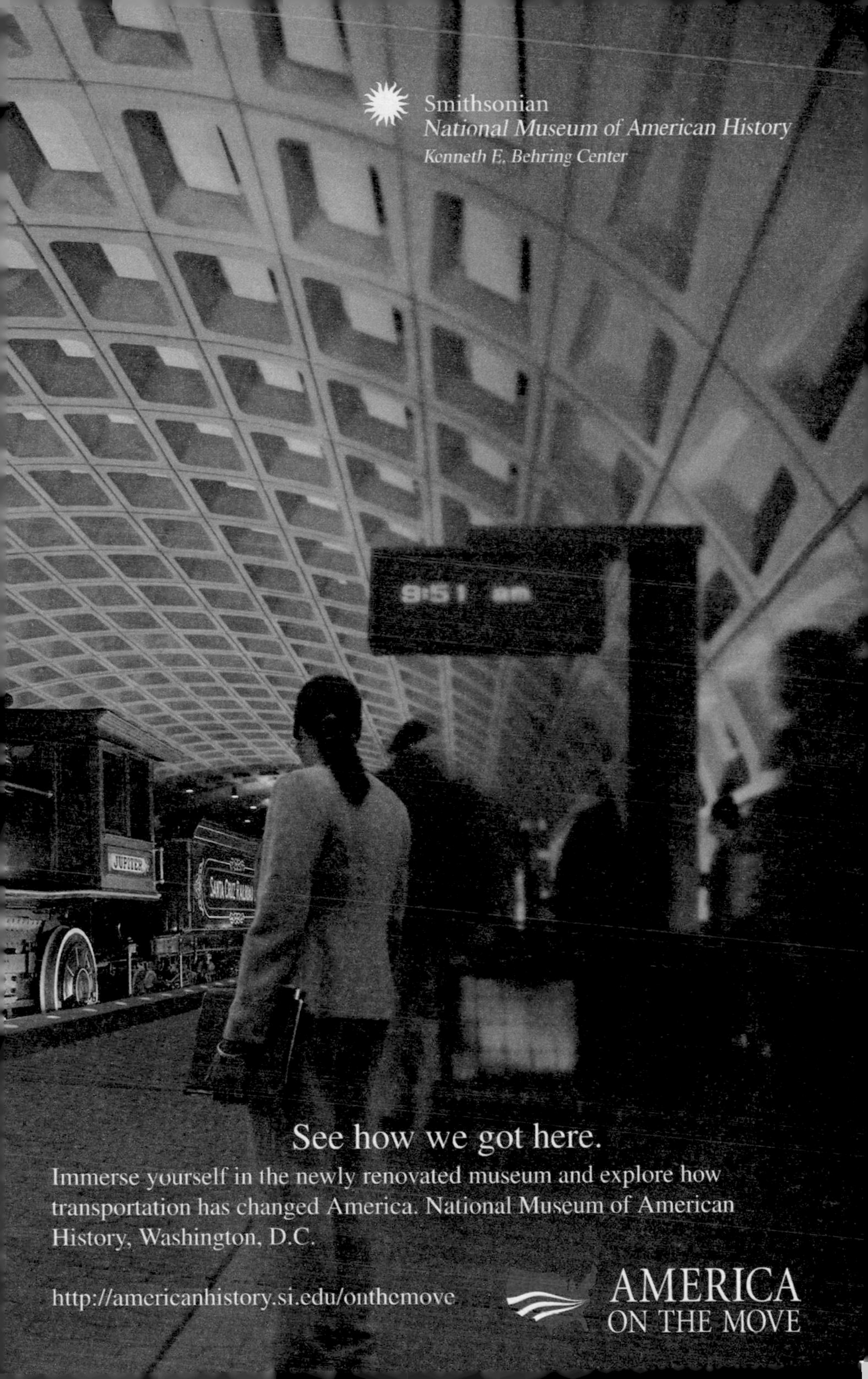
Smithsonian
National Museum of American History
Kenneth E. Behring Center
9:51 am
JUPITER
See how we got here.
Immerse yourself in the newly renovated museum and explore how transportation has changed America. National Museum of American History, Washington, D.C.
http://americanhistory.si.edu/onthemove
AMERICA
ON THE MOVE

Georgia

Forsyth Park, Savannah
© Bill Bachmann
Digital Railroad

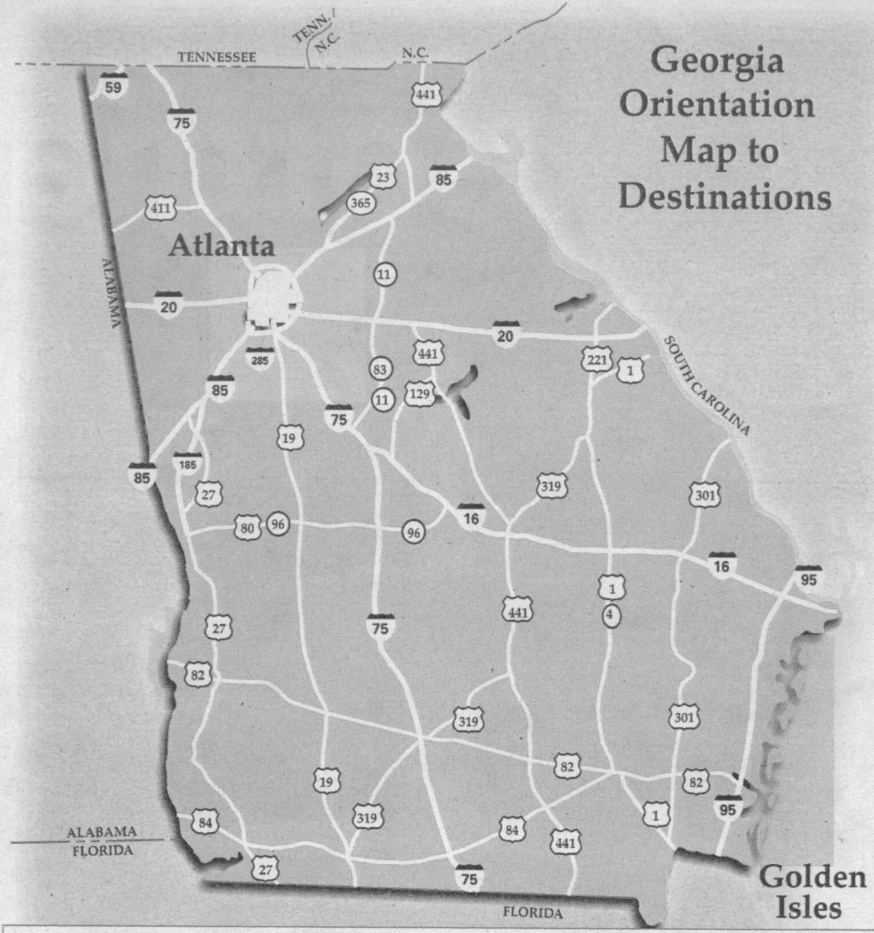

Major destinations are color-coded to index boxes, which display vicinity communities you will find listed within that destination's section of the book. Cities outside major destination vicinities are listed in alphabetical order throughout the book. Use the *Comprehensive City Index* at the back of the book to find every city's listing locations.

Atlanta (see p. 286)

The Atlanta Vicinity (see p. 368)

Golden Isles (see p. 474)

ACWORTH —*See Atlanta p. 368.*

ADAIRSVILLE pop. 2,542

WHERE TO STAY

BEST WESTERN COUNTRY SIDE INN *Book great rates at AAA.com* **Phone:** (770)773-3900

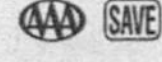

Hotel

$75-$110 All Year

Address: 100 Georgia North Cir **Location:** I-75, exit 306, just w. **Facility:** 51 one-bedroom standard units, some with whirlpools. 2 stories, interior corridors. **Parking:** on-site. **Amenities:** high-speed Internet, voice mail, irons, hair dryers. **Pool(s):** outdoor. **Guest Services:** valet laundry, wireless Internet. **Business Services:** fax. **Cards:** AX, CB, DC, DS, JC, MC, VI. **Free Special Amenities: expanded continental breakfast and high-speed Internet.**

CALL / SOME UNITS

AAA Benefit:

Members save up to 20%, plus 10% bonus points with rewards program.

COMFORT INN *Book great rates at AAA.com* **Phone:** (770)773-2886

Hotel

$60-$90 All Year

Address: 107 Princeton Blvd **Location:** I-75, exit 306, just w. **Facility:** 50 one-bedroom standard units, some with whirlpools. 2 stories (no elevator), exterior corridors. **Parking:** on-site. **Amenities:** video library (fee), high-speed Internet, irons, hair dryers. **Pool(s):** outdoor. **Guest Services:** wireless Internet. **Business Services:** fax. **Cards:** AX, CB, DC, DS, JC, MC, VI. **Free Special Amenities: expanded continental breakfast and high-speed Internet.**

CALL / SOME UNITS FEE

RAMADA LIMITED *Book at AAA.com* **Phone:** 770/769-9726

Hotel

Rates not provided

Address: 500 Georgia North Cir **Location:** I-75, exit 306, 0.3 mi w. **Facility:** 71 one-bedroom standard units. 2 stories, exterior corridors. **Parking:** on-site. **Amenities:** high-speed Internet, voice mail, irons, hair dryers. **Pool(s):** outdoor. **Guest Services:** coin laundry, wireless Internet. **Business Services:** meeting rooms, PC, fax (fee).

FEE CALL / SOME UNITS FEE

ADEL pop. 5,307

WHERE TO STAY

HAMPTON INN *Book great rates at AAA.com*

Hotel
$71-$99 All Year

Phone: (229)896-3099

Address: 1500 W 4th St **Location:** I-75, exit 39, just w. **Facility:** 74 one-bedroom standard units. 3 stories, interior corridors. *Bath:* combo or shower only. **Parking:** on-site. **Terms:** 1-30 night minimum stay, cancellation fee imposed. **Amenities:** voice mail, irons, hair dryers. **Pool(s):** outdoor. **Leisure Activities:** exercise room. **Guest Services:** coin laundry, wireless Internet. **Business Services:** meeting rooms, fax. **Cards:** AX, CB, DC, DS, MC, VI. **Free Special Amenities: expanded continental breakfast and high-speed Internet.** *(See color ad below)*

CALL / SOME UNITS FEE

AAA Benefit:
Members save up to 10% everyday!

SUPER 8 MOTEL I-75 *Book at AAA.com*

Motel
$45-$69 All Year

Phone: (229)896-2244

Address: 1103 W 4th St **Location:** I-75, exit 39, just e. **Facility:** 69 one-bedroom standard units. 2 stories, exterior corridors. **Parking:** on-site. **Amenities:** high-speed Internet. **Pool(s):** heated outdoor. **Guest Services:** wireless Internet. **Business Services:** fax (fee). **Cards:** AX, CB, DC, DS, MC, VI.

ASK / SOME UNITS FEE

ALBANY pop. 76,939

Airport Accommodations

SOUTHWEST GEORGIA REGIONAL	Diamond Rated	High Season	Page
Quality Inn-Merry Acres, 4.5 mi n of terminal	♦♦	$65-$85	279
Sleep Inn Albany, 4.6 mi n of terminal	♦♦	$65-$85	279

WHERE TO STAY

COMFORT SUITES *Book at AAA.com*

Hotel
$80-$95 All Year

Phone: (229)888-3939

Address: 1400 Dawson Rd **Location:** 3.3 mi w. **Facility:** Smoke free premises. 62 units. 60 one-bedroom standard units, some with whirlpools. 2 one-bedroom suites. 2 stories, interior corridors. *Bath:* combo or shower only. **Parking:** on-site. **Terms:** cancellation fee imposed. **Amenities:** voice mail, irons, hair dryers. **Guest Services:** complimentary laundry, wireless Internet. **Business Services:** meeting rooms, business center. **Cards:** AX, DS, MC, VI.

ASK

▼ See AAA listing above ▼

COUNTRY INN & SUITES BY CARLSON — **Phone:** 229/317-7100

fyi
Hotel
$89-$144 All Year

Too new to rate. **Address:** 2809 Nottingham Way **Location:** US 82/520, exit 7, just n. **Amenities:** 70 units, coffeemakers, microwaves, refrigerators. **Terms:** cancellation fee imposed. **Cards:** AX, CB, DC, DS, JC, MC, VI.

HAMPTON INN *Book great rates at AAA.com* — **Phone:** (229)883-3300

Hotel
$79-$99 All Year

Address: 806 N Westover Blvd **Location:** 7 mi w on Dawson Rd; 0.5 mi s of jct US 82 and SR 520. Located adjacent to Albany Mall. **Facility:** 82 one-bedroom standard units. 2 stories, exterior corridors. *Bath:* combo or shower only. **Parking:** on-site. **Terms:** 1-30 night minimum stay, cancellation fee imposed. **Amenities:** voice mail, irons, hair dryers. **Pool(s):** outdoor. **Leisure Activities:** exercise room. **Guest Services:** valet laundry, wireless Internet. **Business Services:** PC, fax. **Cards:** AX, DC, DS, MC, VI.

CALL / SOME UNITS

AAA Benefit:
Members save up to 10% everyday!

HILTON GARDEN INN ALBANY *Book great rates at AAA.com* — **Phone:** (229)888-1590

Hotel
$82-$135 All Year

Address: 101 S Front St **Location:** Between Oglethorpe Blvd and W Broad Ave. **Facility:** 122 one-bedroom standard units, some with whirlpools. 5 stories, interior corridors. *Bath:* combo or shower only. **Parking:** on-site. **Terms:** 1-30 night minimum stay, cancellation fee imposed. **Amenities:** video games, high-speed Internet, voice mail, irons, hair dryers. **Pool(s):** outdoor. **Leisure Activities:** whirlpool, exercise room. **Guest Services:** valet and coin laundry, wireless Internet. **Business Services:** meeting rooms, business center. **Cards:** AX, CB, DC, DS, JC, MC, VI.

/ SOME UNITS

Hilton Garden Inn

AAA Benefit:
Members save 5% or more everyday!

JAMESON INN *Book at AAA.com* — **Phone:** (229)435-3737

Hotel
$78-$85 All Year

Address: 2720 Dawson Rd **Location:** 0.5 mi s of jct US 82 and SR 520. **Facility:** 64 units. 62 one-bedroom standard units, some with whirlpools. 2 one-bedroom suites. 2 stories, exterior corridors. **Parking:** on-site. **Terms:** cancellation fee imposed. **Amenities:** irons, hair dryers. **Pool(s):** outdoor. **Leisure Activities:** exercise room. **Guest Services:** valet laundry, wireless Internet. **Business Services:** PC, fax. **Cards:** AX, DC, DS, MC, VI.

ASK / SOME UNITS FEE

QUALITY INN-MERRY ACRES *Book at AAA.com* — **Phone:** (229)435-7721

Motel
$65-$85 All Year

Address: 1500 Dawson Rd **Location:** 3.3 mi w. **Facility:** 110 units. 105 one-bedroom standard units. 5 two-bedroom suites with kitchens. 1 story, exterior corridors. **Parking:** on-site. **Amenities:** voice mail, irons, hair dryers. *Some:* high-speed Internet. **Pool(s):** outdoor. **Guest Services:** valet and coin laundry, wireless Internet. **Business Services:** conference facilities, PC, fax. **Cards:** AX, CB, DC, DS, MC, VI.

ASK / SOME UNITS FEE VCR

SLEEP INN ALBANY *Book at AAA.com* — **Phone:** (229)888-5595

Hotel
$65-$85 All Year

Address: 1525 Dawson Rd **Location:** 3.4 mi w. **Facility:** 81 one-bedroom standard units. 2 stories, interior corridors. *Bath:* combo or shower only. **Parking:** on-site. **Amenities:** voice mail, irons, hair dryers. **Pool(s):** outdoor. **Guest Services:** valet laundry, wireless Internet. **Business Services:** PC, fax. **Cards:** AX, CB, DC, DS, MC, VI.

ASK CALL / SOME UNITS

WINGATE INN *Book at AAA.com* — **Phone:** (229)883-9800

Hotel
$86 All Year

Address: 2735 Dawson Rd **Location:** Jct US 82 and SR 520, 0.4 mi s. **Facility:** 86 one-bedroom standard units. 3 stories, interior corridors. *Bath:* combo or shower only. **Parking:** on-site. **Terms:** check-in 4 pm. **Amenities:** video games, high-speed Internet, dual phone lines, voice mail, safes, irons, hair dryers. **Pool(s):** outdoor. **Leisure Activities:** whirlpool, exercise room. **Guest Services:** valet laundry, wireless Internet. **Business Services:** meeting rooms, business center. **Cards:** AX, CB, DC, DS, JC, MC, VI.

ASK CALL / SOME UNITS FEE

WHERE TO DINE

CASA TAPATIA — **Phone:** 229/903-8802

Mexican
$7-$13

Offering a large variety of Mexican favorites, like quesadillas and flautas with fresh pico de gallo, the small eatery is located on the west side of town. Casual dress. **Bar:** Full bar. **Hours:** 11 am-9:30 pm, Fri & Sat-10:30 pm. Closed: 4/12, 12/25. **Address:** 108 N Slappey Blvd **Location:** Just n of E Oglethorpe Blvd. **Parking:** on-site. **Cards:** AX, CB, DC, DS, JC, MC, VI.

MERRY ACRES RESTAURANT — **Phone:** 229/439-2261

Regional American
$4-$9

Known for its homemade cuisine, this eatery offers visitors a taste of elegance in a casual setting. Daily lunch specials complement specialties such as the savory stuffed grouper entree. An assortment of muffins is served with all meals. Casual dress. **Bar:** Full bar. **Hours:** 11 am-2 pm. **Address:** 1504 Dawson Rd **Location:** 3.3 mi w; adjacent to Quality Inn-Merry Acres. **Parking:** on-site. **Cards:** AX, MC, VI.

PLANTATION GRILLE BISTRO 717 WITHIN Phone: 229/439-1138

Seafood
$14-$25

This restaurant offers a serene, relaxing atmosphere achieved through subdued, earth-toned decor. Guests can start their meals with plantation dip and pita bread or crispy duck rolls before savoring distinctive preparations of beef, fish and pasta. The specialty among the all-homemade desserts is chocolate Kentucky Derby pie, luscious chocolate pecan pie served a la mode. Casual dress. **Bar:** Full bar. **Reservations:** accepted. **Hours:** 10 am-9:30 pm, Fri & Sat-10 pm. Closed: 1/1, 12/24, 12/25; also Sun. **Address:** 629 N Westover Blvd, Suite B **Location:** 0.5 mi s; in Westover Crossing Plaza. **Parking:** on-site. **Cards:** AX, DS, MC, VI.

SAN JOE'S MEXICAN GRILL Phone: 229/888-6056

Mexican
$4-$10

Offering traditional Mexican fare, the restaurant offers a relaxed dining experience. Casual dress. **Bar:** Beer & wine. **Hours:** 11 am-10 pm, Fri-10:30 pm, Sat & Sun-9 pm. Closed major holidays. **Address:** 232 W Broad St **Location:** Downtown. **Parking:** street. **Cards:** AX, DS, MC, VI.

SONNY'S REAL PIT BAR-B-Q Phone: 229/883-7427

Barbecue
$6-$15

House specialties include pork and chicken grilled over an open pit, barbecue ribs and fresh, homemade pie. The salad bar offers another popular option. Rustic and comfortable, the atmosphere is perfect for family meals. Casual dress. **Bar:** Beer only. **Hours:** 11 am-9:30 pm, Fri & Sat-10 pm. Closed: 11/26, 12/25. **Address:** 1900 N Slappey Blvd **Location:** 3.3 mi nw on US 19 business route and 82. **Parking:** on-site. **Cards:** AX, DS, MC, VI.

VILLA GARGANO ITALIAN RESTAURANT Phone: 229/436-7265

Italian
$7-$18

Established in 1968, this family-owned restaurant offers traditional favorites of Italian cuisine in an intimate setting. Italian murals and artifacts decorate the walls. Juicy chicken piccata, stuffed chicken parmigiana and spinach pizza are favorites. Casual dress. **Bar:** Beer & wine. **Reservations:** not accepted. **Hours:** 11 am-9:30 pm, Fri & Sat-10:30 pm. Closed major holidays; also 12/24 & Sun. **Address:** 1604 N Slappey Blvd **Location:** 3 mi nw on US 19 business route and 82. **Parking:** on-site. **Cards:** AX, DS, MC, VI.

ALMA pop. 3,236

WHERE TO STAY

DAYS INN *Book at AAA.com* Phone: (912)632-7000

Motel
$53-$63 All Year

Address: 930 S Pierce St **Location:** Jct SR 32/US 1, 0.4 mi s on US 1. **Facility:** 37 one-bedroom standard units, some with whirlpools. 2 stories (no elevator), exterior corridors. *Bath:* combo or shower only. **Parking:** on-site. **Terms:** 1-2 night minimum stay. **Amenities:** irons, hair dryers. **Pool(s):** outdoor. **Guest Services:** wireless Internet. **Business Services:** meeting rooms. **Cards:** AX, DS, MC, VI.

ASK / SOME UNITS FEE

ALPHARETTA —*See Atlanta p. 370.*

AMERICUS pop. 17,013

WHERE TO STAY

1906 PATHWAY INN BED & BREAKFAST Phone: 229/928-2078

AAA SAVE

Historic Bed & Breakfast
$99-$145 All Year

Address: 501 S Lee St **Location:** 0.5 mi s of US 280 on SR 377. Located in a historic neighborhood. **Facility:** This mansion is within walking distance to parks and a quaint downtown. Smoke free premises. 6 one-bedroom standard units, some with whirlpools. 2 stories (no elevator), interior corridors. *Bath:* combo or shower only. **Parking:** on-site. **Terms:** check-in 4 pm, 3 day cancellation notice-fee imposed. **Amenities:** video library, CD players, voice mail, hair dryers. **Guest Services:** valet laundry, wireless Internet. **Business Services:** meeting rooms, PC, fax. **Cards:** AX, DS, MC, VI. **Free Special Amenities: full breakfast and high-speed Internet.**

VCR / SOME UNITS FEE

HAMPTON INN *Book great rates at AAA.com* Phone: (229)924-3890

Hotel
$110 All Year

Address: 1609 E Lamar St **Location:** On US 280, just w of jct US 27. **Facility:** 55 one-bedroom standard units, some with whirlpools. 3 stories, interior corridors. *Bath:* combo or shower only. **Parking:** on-site. **Terms:** check-in 4 pm, 1-30 night minimum stay, cancellation fee imposed. **Amenities:** high-speed Internet, voice mail, irons, hair dryers. **Pool(s):** outdoor. **Leisure Activities:** exercise room. **Guest Services:** valet laundry, wireless Internet. **Business Services:** meeting rooms, business center. **Cards:** AX, CB, DC, DS, JC, MC, VI.

/ SOME UNITS

AAA Benefit:
Members save up to 10% everyday!

HOLIDAY INN EXPRESS *Book at AAA.com* Phone: (229)928-5400

Hotel
$80-$95 7/1-11/30
$70-$85 12/1-6/30

Address: 1611 E Lomar St **Location:** On US 280, just w of jct US 27. **Facility:** 62 one-bedroom standard units, some with whirlpools. 2 stories (no elevator), exterior corridors. *Bath:* combo or shower only. **Parking:** on-site. **Terms:** check-in 4 pm. **Amenities:** high-speed Internet, voice mail, irons, hair dryers. **Pool(s):** outdoor. **Guest Services:** valet laundry, wireless Internet. **Business Services:** meeting rooms, business center. **Cards:** AX, DC, DS, MC, VI.

ASK / SOME UNITS FEE

QUALITY INN *Book at AAA.com* **Phone:** (229)924-4431

Hotel
$84 All Year

Address: 1205 Martin Luther King Jr Blvd **Location:** On US 19 S, 1 mi w of downtown. **Facility:** 100 one-bedroom standard units. 2 stories (no elevator), exterior corridors. **Parking:** on-site. **Amenities:** voice mail, irons, hair dryers. *Some:* high-speed Internet. **Pool(s):** outdoor. **Guest Services:** coin laundry, wireless Internet. **Business Services:** meeting rooms. **Cards:** AX, DC, DS, MC, VI.

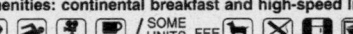

ASK / SOME UNITS FEE

WHERE TO DINE

THE GRAND DINING ROOM **Phone:** 229/924-1555

American
$8-$24

Dine on unusual specialties like pecan-crusted salmon or savory filet mignon in this elegant former ballroom with huge bay windows and upscale decor. The featured dishes change nightly at this lovely bistro which takes pride in its prompt service. Casual dress. **Bar:** Full bar. **Reservations:** suggested, for dinner. **Hours:** 11:30 am-2 & 6-9 pm, Sat from 6 pm, Sun 11 am-2 pm. Closed: 7/4, 9/7, 12/25, 12/26; also 1/2, 11/10 & 11/11. **Address:** 125 W Lamar St **Location:** On US 280; downtown; in The Windsor Hotel. **Parking:** on-site. **Cards:** AX, DC, DS, MC, VI. **Historic**

ASHBURN pop. 4,419

WHERE TO STAY

BEST WESTERN ASHBURN INN *Book great rates at AAA.com* **Phone:** (229)567-0080

Hotel
$59-$75 All Year

Address: 820 Shoney's Dr **Location:** I-75, exit 82, just w. **Facility:** 55 one-bedroom standard units. 2 stories, exterior corridors. **Parking:** on-site. **Amenities:** high-speed Internet, irons, hair dryers. *Some:* DVD players (fee). **Pool(s):** outdoor. **Guest Services:** valet laundry, wireless Internet. **Business Services:** PC, fax. **Cards:** AX, CB, DS, MC, VI. **Free Special Amenities: continental breakfast and high-speed Internet.**

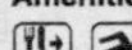  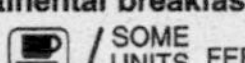  / SOME UNITS FEE 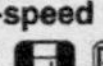 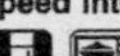

AAA Benefit:
Members save up to 20%, plus 10% bonus points with rewards program.

DAYS INN *Book great rates at AAA.com* **Phone:** (229)567-3346

Hotel
$55-$65 All Year

Address: 823 E Washington Ave **Location:** I-75, exit 82, just w on SR 112. **Facility:** 68 one-bedroom standard units. 2 stories, exterior corridors. **Parking:** on-site. **Amenities:** hair dryers. **Pool(s):** outdoor. **Leisure Activities:** playground. **Guest Services:** wireless Internet. **Business Services:** fax (fee). **Cards:** AX, DC, DS, MC, VI. **Free Special Amenities: continental breakfast and high-speed Internet.**

 / SOME UNITS FEE 

SUPER 8 MOTEL *Book at AAA.com* **Phone:** (229)567-4688

Hotel
$45-$65 All Year

Address: 749 E Washington Ave **Location:** I-75, exit 82, just w. **Facility:** 36 one-bedroom standard units. 2 stories, exterior corridors. *Bath:* combo or shower only. **Parking:** on-site. **Amenities:** hair dryers. **Guest Services:** wireless Internet. **Cards:** AX, DS, MC, VI.

ASK / SOME UNITS FEE

WHERE TO DINE

KEITH-A-QUE **Phone:** 229/567-0333

Barbecue
$4-$16

Smokin' for more than 10 years, the local favorite is near listed hotels and is definitely worth a visit — or several. The menu features buckets of fried chicken, smoked ribs, chicken, Boston butt, dogs, burgers, liver and gizzards and a few seafood plates. Portions are hearty, and there's a wide selection of sides to go with each selection. Everything, even Keith's own bottled barbecue sauce, can be packaged to go. Casual dress. **Hours:** 10 am-9 pm. Closed major holidays; also Sun. **Address:** 260 E Washington St **Location:** I-75, exit 82, 1.1 mi w. **Parking:** on-site. **Cards:** AX, DS, MC, VI.

ATHENS pop. 101,489

WHERE TO STAY

BEST WESTERN-COLONIAL INN *Book great rates at AAA.com* **Phone:** (706)546-7311

Motel
$70-$240 All Year

Address: 170 N Milledge Ave **Location:** Jct US 78 business route (Broad St), 0.5 mi w on SR 15. **Facility:** 70 one-bedroom standard units. 2 stories (no elevator), exterior corridors. **Parking:** on-site. **Terms:** 14 day cancellation notice-fee imposed. **Amenities:** high-speed Internet, voice mail, irons, hair dryers. **Pool(s):** heated outdoor. **Guest Services:** coin laundry, wireless Internet. **Cards:** AX, DC, DS, MC, VI. **Free Special Amenities: expanded continental breakfast and high-speed Internet.**

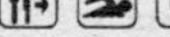   / SOME UNITS FEE 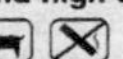

AAA Benefit:
Members save up to 20%, plus 10% bonus points with rewards program.

COMFORT INN Book great rates at AAA.com **Phone:** (706)227-9700

AAA SAVE

Hotel

$77-$120 All Year

Address: 3980 Atlanta Hwy **Location:** SR 10 Loop, exit 3, 0.7 mi w. **Facility:** 69 one-bedroom standard units, some with kitchens. 4 stories, interior corridors. **Parking:** on-site. **Terms:** 2 night minimum stay - seasonal, 3 day cancellation notice-fee imposed. **Amenities:** voice mail, irons, hair dryers. *Fee:* video games, safes. **Pool(s):** outdoor. **Leisure Activities:** exercise room. **Guest Services:** valet and coin laundry, wireless Internet. **Business Services:** meeting rooms, business center. **Cards:** AX, DC, DS, MC, VI. **Free Special Amenities: expanded continental breakfast and high-speed Internet.**

CALL / SOME UNITS

COMFORT SUITES ATHENS Book great rates at AAA.com **Phone:** (706)995-4000

AAA SAVE

Hotel

$89-$109 All Year

Address: 255 North Ave **Location:** SR 10 Loop, exit 11B (Dougherty St/North Ave); 1 mi n of downtown. **Facility:** Smoke free premises. 73 units. 67 one-bedroom standard units, some with whirlpools. 6 one-bedroom suites. 4 stories, interior corridors. *Bath:* combo or shower only. **Parking:** on-site. **Terms:** cancellation fee imposed. **Amenities:** voice mail, safes, irons, hair dryers. **Pool(s):** heated indoor. **Leisure Activities:** whirlpool, exercise room. **Guest Services:** valet and coin laundry, wireless Internet. **Business Services:** meeting rooms, PC. **Cards:** AX, DS, MC, VI. **Free Special Amenities: expanded continental breakfast and high-speed Internet.**

/ SOME UNITS FEE

COURTYARD BY MARRIOTT Book great rates at AAA.com **Phone:** (706)369-7000

Hotel

$119-$127 All Year

Address: 166 N Finley St **Location:** Corner of N Finley and W Broad sts. **Facility:** Smoke free premises. 105 units. 102 one-bedroom standard units. 3 one-bedroom suites. 3 stories, interior/exterior corridors. **Parking:** on-site. **Terms:** check-in 4 pm, cancellation fee imposed. **Amenities:** high-speed Internet, voice mail, irons, hair dryers. **Pool(s):** outdoor. **Leisure Activities:** whirlpool, exercise room. **Guest Services:** valet and coin laundry, wireless Internet. **Business Services:** meeting rooms, PC. **Cards:** AX, CB, DC, DS, JC, MC, VI.

/ SOME UNITS

COURTYARD Marriott

AAA Benefit:

Members save a minimum 5% off the best available rate.

DAYS INN Book at AAA.com **Phone:** (706)543-6511

Motel

$64-$145 All Year

Address: 230 N Finley St **Location:** 0.3 mi w on W Broad St, just n. **Facility:** 76 one-bedroom standard units. 2 stories (no elevator), exterior corridors. **Parking:** on-site. **Amenities:** irons, hair dryers. **Pool(s):** outdoor. **Guest Services:** wireless Internet. **Business Services:** PC. **Cards:** AX, CB, DC, DS, JC, MC, VI.

ASK / SOME UNITS

FOUNDARY PARK INN & SPA Book at AAA.com **Phone:** (706)549-7020

Hotel

$114-$145 All Year

Address: 295 E Dougherty St **Location:** Jct Thomas and Dougherty sts; downtown. **Facility:** 119 units. 112 one-bedroom standard units. 6 one- and 1 two-bedroom suites. 2 stories (no elevator), exterior corridors. **Parking:** on-site. **Terms:** 3 day cancellation notice-fee imposed. **Amenities:** dual phone lines, voice mail, irons, hair dryers. *Some:* DVD players (fee). **Pool(s):** outdoor. **Leisure Activities:** exercise room, spa. **Guest Services:** valet laundry, wireless Internet. **Business Services:** meeting rooms, PC. **Cards:** AX, CB, DC, DS, JC, MC, VI.

ASK / SOME UNITS FEE VCR

HILTON GARDEN INN Book great rates at AAA.com **Phone:** (706)353-6800

Hotel

$119-$199 All Year

Address: 390 E Washington St **Location:** Jct N Thomas St; downtown. **Facility:** Smoke free premises. 185 units. 182 one-bedroom standard units. 3 one-bedroom suites. 8 stories, interior corridors. *Bath:* combo or shower only. **Parking:** on-site (fee). **Terms:** 1-30 night minimum stay, cancellation fee imposed. **Amenities:** video games, high-speed Internet, dual phone lines, voice mail, irons, hair dryers. **Pool(s):** heated indoor. **Leisure Activities:** whirlpool, exercise room. **Guest Services:** valet and coin laundry, wireless Internet. **Business Services:** meeting rooms, business center. **Cards:** AX, CB, DC, DS, JC, MC, VI.

CALL

Hilton Garden Inn

AAA Benefit:

Members save 5% or more everyday!

HOLIDAY INN Book at AAA.com **Phone:** 706/549-4433

Hotel

Rates not provided

Address: 197 E Broad St **Location:** On US 78 business route (Broad St); jct N Hull St; center. **Facility:** 306 units. 297 one-bedroom standard units. 9 one-bedroom suites. 2-7 stories, interior/exterior corridors. *Bath:* combo or shower only. **Parking:** on-site. **Amenities:** high-speed Internet, voice mail, irons, hair dryers. *Some:* DVD players (fee). **Pool(s):** heated indoor. **Leisure Activities:** whirlpool, exercise room. **Guest Services:** valet and coin laundry, area transportation, wireless Internet. **Business Services:** conference facilities, PC.

/ SOME UNITS FEE FEE VCR

HOLIDAY INN EXPRESS Book at AAA.com **Phone:** 706/546-8122

Hotel

Rates not provided

Address: 513 W Broad St **Location:** On US 78 business route (Broad St); center. **Facility:** 160 one-bedroom standard units. 5 stories, interior corridors. **Parking:** on-site. **Amenities:** high-speed Internet, voice mail, irons, hair dryers. **Pool(s):** outdoor. **Leisure Activities:** exercise room. **Guest Services:** valet and coin laundry, area transportation, wireless Internet. **Business Services:** meeting rooms, PC.

CALL / SOME UNITS FEE FEE

MICROTEL INN *Book great rates at AAA.com* **Phone:** (706)548-5676

Hotel
$59-$130 3/1-11/30
$54-$85 12/1-2/28

Address: 1050 Ultimate Dr **Location:** Jct US 78 business route (Broad St) and SR 10 Loop, 1.4 mi e. **Facility:** 60 one-bedroom standard units. 2 stories (no elevator), interior corridors. *Bath:* combo or shower only. **Parking:** on-site. **Terms:** cancellation fee imposed. **Amenities:** hair dryers. **Guest Services:** coin laundry, wireless Internet. **Business Services:** PC. **Cards:** AX, DS, MC, VI.

CALL / SOME UNITS FEE

WHERE TO DINE

AQUA LINDA **Phone:** 706/543-1500

Mexican
$2-$14

The popular restaurant presents a menu of typical Mexican dishes, as well as fish and barbecue selections. Casual dress. **Bar:** Full bar. **Hours:** 11 am-10 pm, Fri & Sat-11 pm. Closed: 11/26, 12/25. **Address:** 1376 Prince Ave **Location:** SR 10 Loop, exit 7 (Prince Ave), 0.6 mi se. **Parking:** on-site. **Cards:** AX, MC, VI.

BARBERITOS **Phone:** 706/549-9008

Southwestern
$5-$8

The quick-serve restaurant offers a good selection of made-from-scratch burritos that come with meat or vegetarian ingredients. Also on the menu are tacos, nachos and salads. Casual dress. **Bar:** Beer only. **Hours:** 11 am-10 pm, Sun noon-9 pm. Closed: 11/26, 12/25. **Address:** 259 E Clayton St **Location:** Downtown. **Parking:** street. **Cards:** MC, VI.

BARBERITOS **Phone:** 706/549-9954

Southwestern
$2-$8

The quick-serve restaurant offers a good selection of made-from-scratch burritos that come with meat or vegetarian ingredients. Also on the menu are tacos, nachos and salads. Casual dress. **Bar:** Beer only. **Hours:** 11 am-10 pm, Sun-9 pm. Closed: 11/26, 12/25. **Address:** 1860 Barnett Shoals Rd **Location:** Corner of Barnett Shoals and Gaines School rds. **Parking:** on-site. **Cards:** MC, VI.

BAR-B-QUE SHACK **Phone:** 706/613-6752

Barbecue
$3-$8

Chicken, pork and stew are specialties of the well-known eatery. Those in a hurry can hit the drive-through window for ribs and banana pudding to go. Casual dress. **Hours:** 10 am-8 pm, Fri & Sat-9 pm. Closed major holidays; also Sun-Wed. **Address:** 4320 Lexington Rd **Location:** 4.2 mi e on US 78 business route (Broad St) and SR 10 Loop. **Parking:** on-site.

THE BASIL PRESS **Phone:** 706/227-8926

Mediterranean
$4-$24

On the menu at the cozy restaurant is a number of seafood and meat specials. Home-style desserts are worth saving some room. Outdoor seating is offered seasonally. Casual dress. **Bar:** Full bar. **Reservations:** suggested. **Hours:** 11:30 am-2 & 5-10 pm, Fri-11 pm, Sat 5 pm-11 pm. Closed: 11/26, 12/25. **Address:** 104 E Washington St **Location:** Downtown. **Parking:** street. **Cards:** AX, DS, MC, VI.

BIG CITY BREAD CAFE **Phone:** 706/353-0029

Deli
$4-$15

In a former Salvation Army building and fire station, the restaurant prepares breakfast plates; salads and sandwiches for lunch; and dinner fare at night. The pastries, cakes and breads are simply delicious. The patio opens seasonally. Casual dress. **Hours:** 7 am-9:30 pm, Sun-3 pm. Closed major holidays. **Address:** 393 N Finley St **Location:** Between Prince Ave and Broad St; downtown. **Parking:** on-site. **Cards:** AX, MC, VI.

CLOCKED **Phone:** 706/548-9175

American
$2-$10

The small, comfort-food eatery serves some of the best hamburgers and fries, fish and chips and vegetarian food in town. For dessert, try one of the fountain creations. Casual dress. **Bar:** Beer & wine. **Hours:** 11 am-10 pm, Fri & Sat-11 pm. Closed: 11/26, 12/25. **Address:** 259 W Washington St **Location:** Downtown. **Parking:** street. **Cards:** AX, DS, MC, VI.

COPPER CREEK BREWING COMPANY **Phone:** 706/546-1102

American
$2-$13

Many like this tavern as a place to meet over house-brewed beers, all of which go well with the menu items. Among choices are filet tips sauteed with brandy and served with rice pilaf and steamed vegetables. Casual dress. **Bar:** Full bar. **Hours:** 4 pm-2 am. Closed: 11/26, 12/25. **Address:** 140 E Washington St **Location:** Downtown. **Parking:** street. **Cards:** AX, DS, MC, VI.

DEPALMA'S ITALIAN CAFE **Phone:** 706/369-0085

Italian
$2-$21

Just like its downtown location, the restaurant has a number of delicious dishes on the menu, extensive wine and beer choices and the friendly service diners have come to expect. Casual dress. **Bar:** Full bar. **Hours:** 11 am-10 pm, Fri & Sat-11 pm. Closed: 11/26, 12/25. **Address:** 1965 Barnett Shoals Rd **Location:** 3.3 mi e; jct Gaines School Rd. **Parking:** on-site. **Cards:** AX, DC, DS, MC, VI.

DEPALMA'S ITALIAN CAFE **Phone:** 706/354-6966

Italian
$2-$20

The popular eatery is known for the number of delicious dishes on the menu, extensive wine and beer choices and the friendly service diners have come to expect. Casual dress. **Bar:** Full bar. **Hours:** 11 am-10 pm, Fri & Sat-midnight. Closed: 11/26, 12/25. **Address:** 401 E Broad St **Location:** Downtown. **Parking:** street. **Cards:** AX, DC, DS, MC, VI.

EAST WEST BISTRO

Phone: 706/546-4240

International

$4-$30

On the ground floor, the casual section of this restaurant serves fusion cuisine and tapas. Up the stairs on the second floor is a more upscale dining room in which Italian dishes tempt diners. The wine list is excellent. Casual dress. **Bar:** Full bar. **Reservations:** suggested, for upstairs dining. **Hours:** 11 am-10 pm, Fri-11 pm, Sat 11:30 am-11 pm, Sun 11:30 am-midnight. Closed: 7/4, 11/26, 12/25. **Address:** 251 E Broad St **Location:** Downtown. **Parking:** street. **Cards:** AX, MC, VI.

FIVE & TEN

Phone: 706/546-7300

New American

$16-$29

Earthy and unbridled decor matches the ambience of this spot as well as its chef's cuisine. A multifaceted menu offers ever-popular Low Country frogmore stew and other options to blend Old World style and refinement. Dishes feature fresh seasonal ingredients and local and organic items when possible. Also find excellent wine and cheese selections. Casual dress. **Bar:** Full bar. **Reservations:** suggested. **Hours:** 5:30 pm-10 pm, Fri & Sat-11 pm; Sunday brunch 10:30 am-2:30 pm. Closed major holidays. **Address:** 1653 S Lumpkin St **Location:** From US 78/10, 1 mi n on Milledgeville Rd, just e. **Parking:** on-site. **Cards:** AX, DS, MC, VI.

GAUTREAU'S CAJUN CAFE

Phone: 706/769-4177

Cajun

$4-$17

The restaurant and tavern presents a menu of delicious Cajun specialties, all served in a relaxed atmosphere. The boiled peanuts appetizer is a must-try for Northerners. Casual dress. **Bar:** Full bar. **Reservations:** accepted. **Hours:** 5 pm-9:30 pm, Fri & Sat-10:30 pm. Closed: 1/1, 11/26, 12/25; also Sun. **Address:** 1860 Barnett Shoals Rd **Location:** 3.2 mi e; jct Gaines School Rd. **Parking:** on-site. **Cards:** AX, DS, MC, VI.

GOLDEN DRAGON

Phone: 706/552-1688

Mandarin

$7-$17

The restaurant prepares an excellent selection of Mandarin cuisine, soups and vegetarian dishes. Many enjoy the lunch buffet due to the friendly service and relaxed atmosphere. Casual dress. **Bar:** Beer & wine. **Reservations:** accepted. **Hours:** 11 am-10 pm, Fri-11 pm, Sat noon-11 pm, Sun noon-10 pm. Closed: 7/4, 12/25. **Address:** 126 Alps Rd **Location:** Jct US 78 business route (Broad St), just s. **Parking:** on-site. **Cards:** AX, DS, MC, VI.

THE GRIT

Phone: 706/543-6592

Vegetarian

$2-$10

In an old brick building, the restaurant has become famous through word of mouth and the publication of The Grit Cookbook. The food is delicious, and those who have flipped through the book already know the menu is varied with ethnic choices. Casual dress. **Bar:** Beer & wine. **Hours:** 11 am-10 pm, Sat & Sun 10 am-3 & 5-10 pm. Closed: 1/1, 11/26, 12/25. **Address:** 199 Prince Ave **Location:** Downtown. **Parking:** on-site. **Cards:** MC, VI.

HARRY BISSETT'S NEW ORLEANS CAFE & OYSTER BAR

Phone: 706/353-7065

Cajun

$6-$24

This friendly, New Orleans-style restaurant overlooks the University of Georgia and attracts quite a crowd with its creative, Cajun fare. Use your imagination and have oysters any way your heart desires! Other dishes to try are the tender steak and veal. Casual dress. **Bar:** Full bar. **Reservations:** accepted. **Hours:** 11:30 am-3 & 5:30-10 pm, Fri & Sat-11 pm. Closed: 11/26, 12/24, 12/25; also for lunch Mon. **Address:** 279 E Broad St **Location:** On US 78 business route (Broad St); center; opposite main entrance to UGA. **Parking:** street. **Cards:** AX, DC, DS, MC, VI.

MARTI'S AT MIDDAY

Phone: 706/543-3541

Deli

$5-$12

The delightful eatery offers a number of soups, salads and gourmet sandwiches, all made from scratch. Desserts include cookies, brownies and cupcakes. Casual dress. **Hours:** 8 am-3:30 pm. Closed: 11/26, 12/25. **Address:** 1280 Prince Ave **Location:** SR 10 Loop, exit 7 (Prince Ave), 0.7 mi se. **Parking:** on-site.

PORTERHOUSE GRILL

Phone: 706/369-0990

Steak

$5-$34

Although this place is pegged as an American steakhouse—and the steaks are mouthwatering—its other choices are just as good. Among them are rabbit, pork chops, roast ducking, fresh seafood and a few vegetarian dishes. Casual dress. **Bar:** Full bar. **Reservations:** suggested. **Hours:** 5 pm-10 pm, Fri & Sat-11; Sunday brunch 11:30 am-2 pm. Closed: 11/26, 12/25. **Address:** 459 E Broad St **Location:** Downtown. **Parking:** street. **Cards:** AX, DS, MC, VI.

SONNY'S REAL PIT BAR-B-Q

Phone: 706/546-0385

Barbecue

$6-$15

House specialties include pork and chicken grilled over an open pit, barbecue ribs and fresh, homemade pie. The salad bar offers another popular option. Rustic and comfortable, the atmosphere is perfect for family meals. Casual dress. **Bar:** Beer only. **Hours:** 11 am-9:30 pm, Fri & Sat-10 pm. Closed: 11/26, 12/25. **Address:** 3755 Atlanta Hwy **Location:** Jct US 29/78, just w. **Parking:** on-site. **Cards:** AX, DS, MC, VI.

THE VARSITY

Phone: 706/548-6325

American

$2-$7

An Athens original, the fast-food restaurant has been in business more than 75 years. Hamburgers, fries, chili dogs, friendly counter service—you name it, it's worth a try if only for the memories. Casual dress. **Hours:** 10 am-10 pm, Fri & Sat-midnight. Closed: 11/26, 12/25. **Address:** 1000 W Broad St **Location:** Jct US 78 business route (Broad St) and SR 15A. **Parking:** on-site. **Cards:** MC, VI.

WILSON'S SOUL FOOD

Phone: 706/353-7289

Soul Food

$3-$6

Diners looking for an upscale restaurant won't find it here. Don't even think about ordering what's on the menu, as staffers have their own ideas about what to serve you—and it's polite to ask them. Casual dress. **Hours:** 8 am-4 pm, Fri-5 pm, Sat-3 pm. Closed: 4/12, 11/26, 12/25; also Sun. **Address:** 353 N Hull St **Location:** Downtown. **Parking:** street. **Cards:** MC, VI.

Destination Atlanta

pop. 416,474

Sugar and spice and everything nice. That's what Atlanta is made of. The city, as sweet as a slow, Southern accent and as spicy as an evening spent club-hopping in Buckhead, is a distinctive blend of old Southern charm and fast-paced sophistication.

Take yourself on a shopping spree at upscale Phipps Plaza, do lunch at one of many swank cafes or tour the bustling CNN studios. And when it's time to kick back, pack a picnic and head to Stone Mountain Park.

Georgia Department of Economic Development

Atlanta skyline.
Dramatic skyscrapers rose like a phoenix from the flames of Gen. William Tecumseh Sherman's 1864 raid on the city.

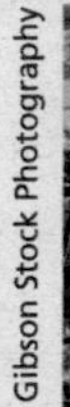

Farmers market, near Atlanta.
Shoppers have an array of goods to choose from at the local farmers market.

See Vicinity map page 296

See Buckhead map page 292

75
575
Acworth
Kennesaw
Marietta
Smyrna
6
285
Austell
278
Lithia Springs
20
Douglasville
Union City
Fairburn
85

See Vicinity map page 312

Places included in this AAA Destination City:

Georgia Department of Economic Development

Atlanta Braves.
A Braves team member prepares to swing into action. (See mention page 56)

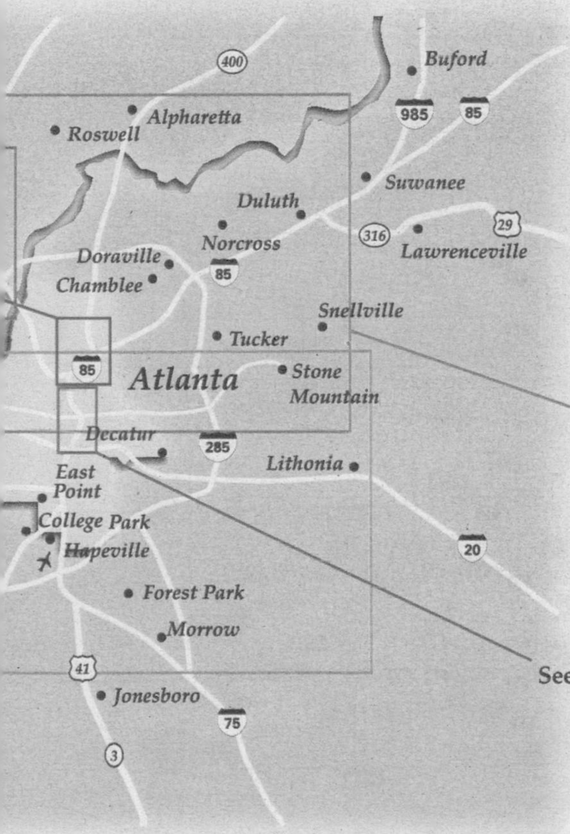

Georgia Department of Economic Development

Fishing in the Chattahoochee River.
Fishing is only one of many recreational activities available to visitors in, on or around the river. (See mention page 56)

400
Buford
985
85
Alpharetta
Roswell
Suwanee
Duluth
Norcross
316
29
Lawrenceville
Doraville
Chamblee
85
Snellville
Tucker
85
Atlanta
Stone Mountain
Decatur
285
Lithonia
East Point
College Park
Hapeville
20
Forest Park
Morrow
41
Jonesboro
75
3

See Vicinity map pages 302 & 303

See Downtown map page 288

Stone Mountain Park, Stone Mountain.
The paddlewheel riverboat, the *Scarlett O'Hara*, gracefully transports passengers for a cruise on Stone Mountain Lake. (See listing page 62)

Georgia Department of Economic Development

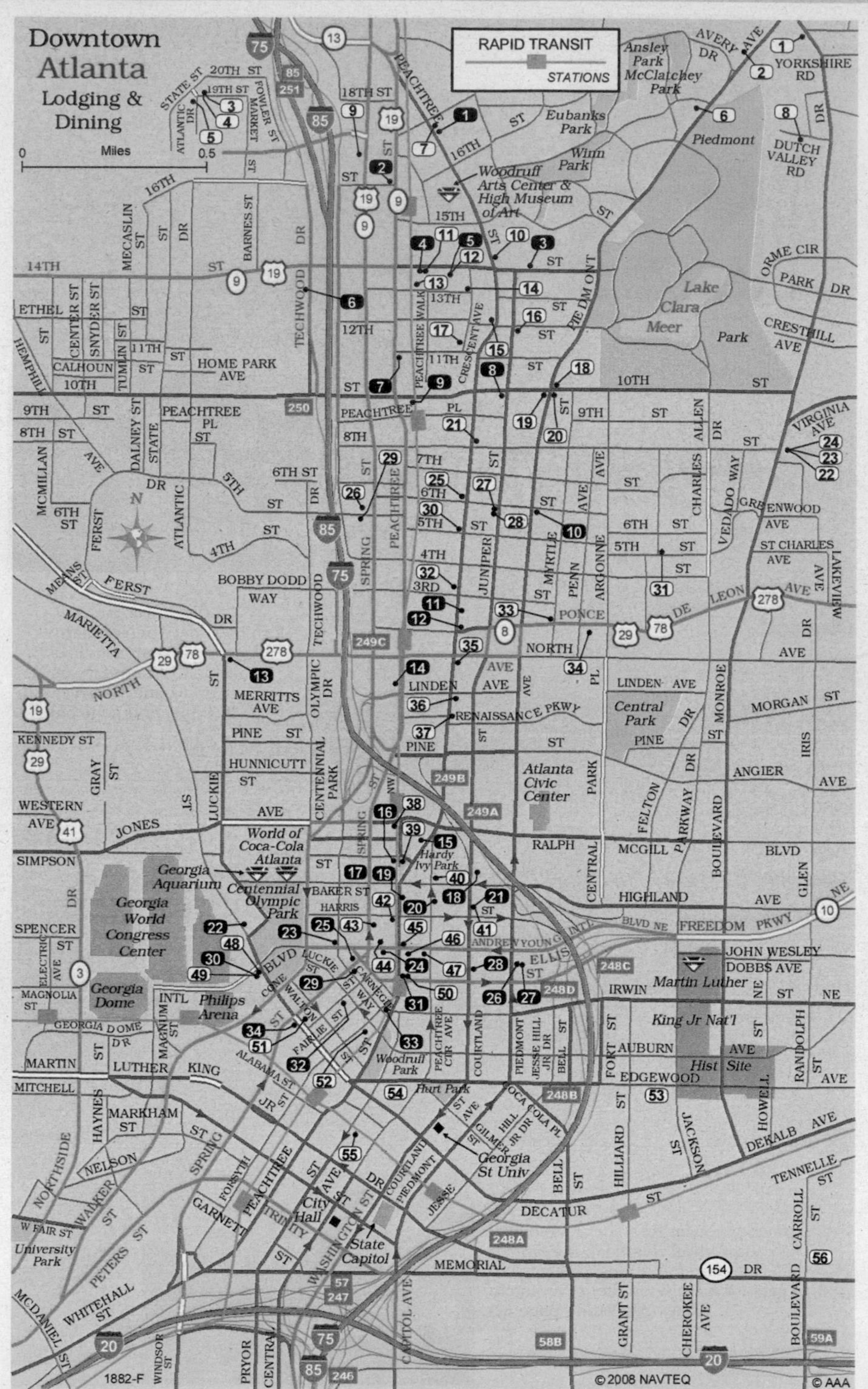

Downtown Atlanta
Lodging & Dining
0 Miles 0.5
RAPID TRANSIT
STATIONS
Woodruff Arts Center & High Museum of Art
Piedmont Park
Lake Clara Meer
Ansley Park McClatchey Park
Eubanks Park
Winn Park
Atlanta Civic Center
Central Park
World of Coca-Cola Atlanta
Georgia Aquarium
Centennial Olympic Park
Hardy Ivy Park
Georgia World Congress Center
Georgia Dome
Philips Arena
Martin Luther King Jr Nat'l Hist Site
Woodruff Park
Hurt Park
Georgia St Univ
City Hall
State Capitol
University Park
1882-F
©2008 NAVTEQ
© AAA

Downtown Atlanta

This index helps you "spot" where approved lodgings and restaurants are located on the corresponding detailed maps. Lodging daily rate range is for comparison only and show the property's high season. Restaurant rate range is a combination of lunch and/or dinner. Turn to the listing page for more detailed rate information and consult display ads for special promotions.

DOWNTOWN ATLANTA

Map Page	OA	Lodgings	Diamond Rated	High Season	Page
1 / p. 288		Residence Inn Atlanta Midtown at 17th Street	◆◆◆	$195-$215	329
2 / p. 288	AAA	**Best Western Granada Suite Hotel**	◆◆◆	$109-$209 SAVE	322
3 / p. 288	AAA	**W Atlanta Midtown**	◆◆◆◆	$199-$539 SAVE	331
4 / p. 288	AAA	**Atlanta Marriott Suites Midtown**	◆◆◆	$277-$298 SAVE	322
5 / p. 288	AAA	**Four Seasons Hotel Atlanta**	◆◆◆◆◆	$430-$4700 SAVE	324
6 / p. 288	AAA	**Courtyard by Marriott Atlanta Midtown**	◆◆◆	$205-$236 SAVE	323
7 / p. 288		Residence Inn by Marriott Midtown	◆◆◆	$220-$251	329
8 / p. 288		Wyndham Midtown Atlanta	◆◆◆	$129-$239	331
9 / p. 288	AAA	**Regency Suites Hotel**	◆◆◆	$119-$239 SAVE	327
10 / p. 288		Shellmont Inn	◆◆◆	$160-$350	330
11 / p. 288		Hotel Indigo	◆◆◆	Rates not provided	326
12 / p. 288		The Georgian Terrace Hotel	◆◆◆	$189-$349	324
13 / p. 288		Hampton Inn	◆◆◆	$124-$169	324
14 / p. 288	AAA	**Renaissance Atlanta Hotel Downtown - see color ad p 328**	◆◆◆	$256-$277 SAVE	328
15 / p. 288	AAA	**Hyatt Place Atlanta Downtown**	◆◆◆	$119-$299 SAVE	326
16 / p. 288		Inn at the Peachtrees	◆◆	$99-$119	327
17 / p. 288		Days Inn Downtown	◆◆	$99-$199	324
18 / p. 288		Red Roof Inn Atlanta Downtown	◆◆	Rates not provided	327
19 / p. 288	AAA	**Hyatt Regency Atlanta - see color ad p 326**	◆◆◆	$99-$399 SAVE	326
20 / p. 288	AAA	**Atlanta Marriott Marquis**	◆◆◆	$318-$339 SAVE	321
21 / p. 288		Hilton Atlanta	◆◆◆	$99-$299	325
22 / p. 288		Embassy Suites Centennial Olympic Park	◆◆◆	$135-$330	324
23 / p. 288		Holiday Inn Atlanta Downtown	◆◆◆	$89-$259	325
24 / p. 288	AAA	**The Westin Peachtree Plaza**	◆◆◆	$119-$405 SAVE	331
25 / p. 288		Atlanta Marriott Downtown	◆◆◆	$188-$202	320
26 / p. 288		Baymont Inn & Suites Atlanta Downtown	◆◆◆	$109-$219	322
27 / p. 288		Wyndham Garden Hotel Atlanta Downtown	◆◆◆	$119-$249	331
28 / p. 288	AAA	**Sheraton Atlanta Hotel**	◆◆◆	$119-$399 SAVE	330
29 / p. 288		Hampton Inn & Suites Atlanta Downtown	◆◆◆	$79-$250	325
30 / p. 288	AAA	**Omni Hotel at CNN Center**	◆◆◆◆	$159-$289 SAVE	327
31 / p. 288	AAA	**The Ritz-Carlton, Atlanta**	◆◆◆◆◆	Rates not provided SAVE	330
32 / p. 288	AAA	**Super 8 Downtown**	◆◆	$99-$129 SAVE	331
33 / p. 288	AAA	**Residence Inn by Marriott-Atlanta Downtown**	◆◆◆	$205-$236 SAVE	329
34 / p. 288		The Glenn Hotel	◆◆◆	$129-$389	324

Map Page	OA	Restaurants	Diamond Rated	Cuisine	Meal Range	Page
1 / p. 288		Agnes & Muriel's	◆◆	American	$2-$21	331

Map Page	OA	Restaurants (cont'd)	Diamond Rated	Cuisine	Meal Range	Page
2 / p. 288		Bangkok Thai Restaurant	◆◆	Thai	$3-$14	332
3 / p. 288		Ten Pin Alley	◆◆	American	$10-$15	336
4 / p. 288		Dolce Enoteca e Ristorante	◆◆◆	Italian	$9-$55	332
5 / p. 288		Geisha House	◆◆◆	Japanese	$3-$42	333
6 / p. 288		Tierra-Flavor of the Americas	◆◆	Latin American	$6-$24	336
7 / p. 288		Madison Grill	◆◆	American	$7-$22	334
8 / p. 288		One Midtown Kitchen	◆◆◆	American	$7-$21	335
9 / p. 288		Nan Thai Fine Dining	◆◆◆◆	Thai	$7-$32	334
10 / p. 288		Tamarind Seed	◆◆◆	Thai	$4-$29	336
11 / p. 288		Veni Vidi Vici	◆◆◆	Italian	$9-$29	337
12 / p. 288		Park 75	◆◆◆◆	New American	$10-$130	335
13 / p. 288		Vinocity Wine Bar & Restaurant	◆◆◆	American	$7-$27	337
14 / p. 288		South City Kitchen	◆◆◆	Regional American	$5-$36	336
15 / p. 288		Oceanaire	◆◆◆	Seafood	$8-$35	335
16 / p. 288		Einstein's	◆◆◆	American	$2-$21	332
17 / p. 288		Vickery's Bar & Grill	◆◆	American	$4-$20	337
18 / p. 288		Flying Biscuit Cafe	◆◆	American	$5-$14	332
19 / p. 288		Nickiemoto's	◆◆	Asian	$3-$23	335
20 / p. 288		Zocalo	◆◆	Mexican	$2-$16	337
21 / p. 288		Silk	◆◆◆	Asian	$4-$40	336
22 / p. 288		Nam	◆◆◆	New Vietnamese	$6-$24	334
23 / p. 288		F.R.O.G.S. Cantina & Tequileria	◆◆	Southwestern	$4-$15	333
24 / p. 288		Apres Diem	◆◆	Continental	$6-$20	332
25 / p. 288		Gordon Biersch Brewery & Restaurant	◆◆	American	$4-$23	333
26 / p. 288		The Globe	◆◆◆	American	$6-$26	333
27 / p. 288		Mu Lan	◆◆	Chinese	$6-$20	334
28 / p. 288		Mitra	◆◆◆	Southwestern	$5-$26	334
29 / p. 288		Tin Drum Asia Cafe	◆◆	Asian	$2-$7	336
30 / p. 288		Eno	◆◆◆	Mediterranean	$7-$27	332
31 / p. 288		Las Palmeras	◆◆	Cuban	$3-$14	334
32 / p. 288		Baraonda Caffe' Italiano	◆◆	Italian	$4-$22	332
33 / p. 288		Mary Mac's Tea Room	◆◆	Continental	$9-$18	334
34 / p. 288		M F Sushibar	◆◆◆	Sushi	$5-$30	334
35 / p. 288		The Varsity	◆	American	$3-$7	337
36 / p. 288		Pleasant Peasant	◆◆◆	American	$5-$29	335
37 / p. 288		Gladys & Ron's Chicken & Waffles	◆◆	American	$2-$15	333
38 / p. 288		French American Brasserie	◆◆◆	French	$7-$44	333
39 / p. 288	AAA	**Max Lager's American Grill & Brewery**	◆◆	American	$7-$25	334
40 / p. 288		Pacific Rim Bistro	◆◆◆	Pacific Rim	$4-$32	335

Map Page	OA	Restaurants (cont'd)	Diamond Rated	Cuisine	Meal Range	Page
41 / p. 288		Nikolai's Roof	◆◆◆◆	Continental	$9-$95	335
42 / p. 288		Ray's in the City	◆◆◆	Seafood	$4-$20	335
43 / p. 288		Haveli Indian Cuisine	◆◆	Indian	$8-$17	333
44 / p. 288		PittyPat's Porch	◆◆	Regional Southern	$14-$28	335
45 / p. 288		Hard Rock Cafe	◆◆	American	$12-$24 SAVE	333
46 / p. 288		Dailey's	◆◆	American	$8-$37	332
47 / p. 288		Hsu's Gourmet Chinese Restaurant	◆◆◆	Chinese	$7-$22	333
48 / p. 288		McCormick & Schmick's	◆◆◆	Seafood	$4-$38	334
49 / p. 288		Prime Meridian	◆◆◆	Steak & Seafood	$4-$29	335
50 / p. 288	AAA	**Atlanta Grill**	◆◆◆◆	American	$10-$30	332
51 / p. 288		Thrive	◆◆◆	American	$6-$32	336
52 / p. 288		Landmark Diner	◆◆	Continental	$4-$28	333
53 / p. 288		Rolling Bones	◆	Barbecue	$7-$37	336
54 / p. 288		City Grill	◆◆◆◆	Regional American	$7-$42	332
55 / p. 288		Tringali's	◆◆	Italian	$9-$22	337
56 / p. 288		Agave	◆◆◆	Southwestern	$14-$23	331

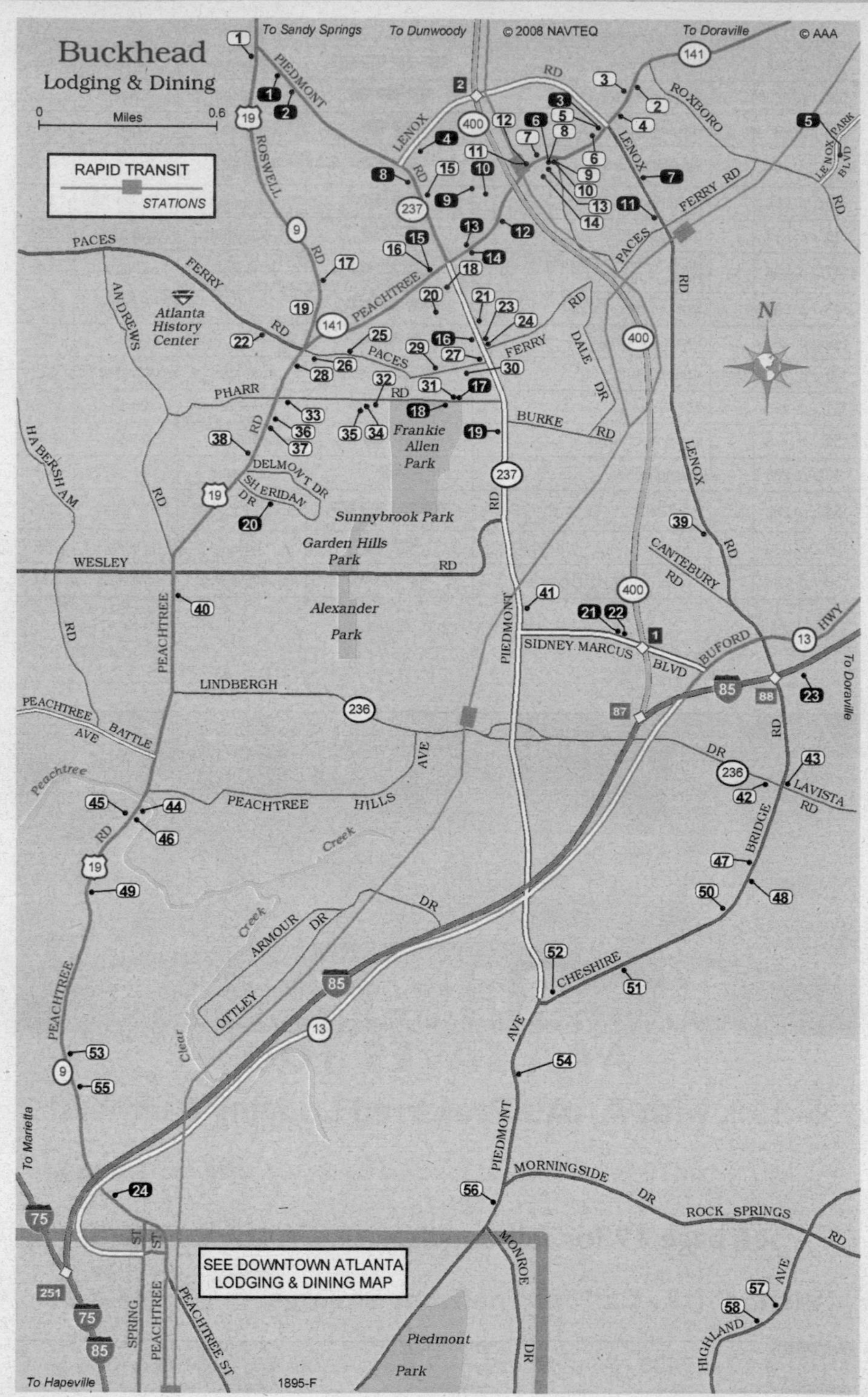
Buckhead
Lodging & Dining
0 Miles 0.6
RAPID TRANSIT
STATIONS
To Sandy Springs
To Dunwoody
© 2008 NAVTEQ
To Doraville
© AAA
Atlanta History Center
Frankie Allen Park
Sunnybrook Park
Garden Hills Park
Alexander Park
Piedmont Park
PACES FERRY RD
PEACHTREE
ROSWELL RD
PIEDMONT
LENOX RD
ROXBORO
PHARR RD
WESLEY RD
LINDBERGH
SIDNEY MARCUS BLVD
BUFORD HWY
CHESHIRE
MORNINGSIDE DR
ROCK SPRINGS RD
HIGHLAND AVE
MONROE DR
To Marietta
To Hapeville
To Doraville
SEE DOWNTOWN ATLANTA LODGING & DINING MAP
1895-F

Buckhead

This index helps you "spot" where approved lodgings and restaurants are located on the corresponding detailed maps. Lodging daily rate range is for comparison only and show the property's high season. Restaurant rate range is a combination of lunch and/or dinner. Turn to the listing page for more detailed rate information and consult display ads for special promotions.

BUCKHEAD

Map Page	OA	Lodgings	Diamond Rated	High Season	Page
1 / p. 292		Wingate Inn-Buckhead	◆◆◆	$119-$159	342
2 / p. 292		Homewood Suites-Atlanta Buckhead	◆◆◆	$189-$250	339
3 / p. 292	AAA	**The Ritz-Carlton, Buckhead**	◆◆◆◆◆	$369-$479 SAVE	341
4 / p. 292	AAA	**SpringHill Suites by Marriott-Atlanta Buckhead**	◆◆◆	$187-$201 SAVE	341
5 / p. 292	AAA	**Residence Inn-Buckhead/Lenox - see color ad p 341**	◆◆◆	$227-$243 SAVE	340
6 / p. 292	AAA	**The Westin Buckhead Atlanta**	◆◆◆◆	$169-$459 SAVE	342
7 / p. 292	AAA	**Atlanta Marriott Buckhead Hotel & Conference Center**	◆◆◆	Rates not provided SAVE	337
8 / p. 292		Hampton Inn Atlanta Buckhead	◆◆◆	$129-$169	339
9 / p. 292		DoubleTree Hotel Atlanta Buckhead	◆◆◆	$90-$198	338
10 / p. 292	AAA	**Courtyard by Marriott-Buckhead**	◆◆◆	$177-$190 SAVE	338
11 / p. 292	AAA	**JW Marriott Buckhead Atlanta**	◆◆◆◆	$365-$391 SAVE	340
12 / p. 292	AAA	**InterContinental Buckhead Atlanta**	◆◆◆◆◆	$219-$499 SAVE	340
13 / p. 292	AAA	**Grand Hyatt Atlanta - see color ad p 326**	◆◆◆◆	$139-$499 SAVE	338
14 / p. 292		Embassy Suites Hotel Atlanta Buckhead	◆◆◆	$134-$249	338
15 / p. 292	AAA	**Hyatt Place Atlanta/Buckhead**	◆◆◆	$89-$279 SAVE	340
16 / p. 292		Fairfield Inn-Atlanta/Buckhead	◆◆◆	$147-$158	338
17 / p. 292		Staybridge Suites	◆◆◆	$169-$269	342
18 / p. 292		Holiday Inn Express Hotel & Suites-Atlanta Buckhead	◆◆◆	$159-$259	339
19 / p. 292	AAA	**Residence Inn by Marriott-Atlanta/Buckhead**	◆◆◆	$227-$243 SAVE	341
20 / p. 292		Beverly Hills Inn	◆◆	$129-$249	337
21 / p. 292		Country Inn & Suites	◆◆	$119-$269	337
22 / p. 292		TownePlace Suites Atlanta Buckhead	◆◆◆	$197-$211	342
23 / p. 292		La Quinta Inn-Buckhead	◆◆◆	$64-$109	340
24 / p. 292		Super 8 Motel	◆◆	$79-$109	342

Map Page	OA	Restaurants	Diamond Rated	Cuisine	Meal Range	Page
1 / p. 292		Landmark Diner	◆◆	Continental	$7-$26	346
2 / p. 292		Ali-Oli	◆◆◆	Italian	$7-$24	342
3 / p. 292		Twist	◆◆◆	American	$5-$29	348
4 / p. 292		BluePointe	◆◆◆◆	Seafood	$4-$86	343
5 / p. 292	AAA	**The Dining Room**	◆◆◆◆◆	French	$92-$155	345
6 / p. 292		New York Prime	◆◆◆	Steak	$21-$45	346
7 / p. 292	AAA	**Dante's Down the Hatch**	◆◆	Specialty	$14-$28	345
8 / p. 292		The Atlanta Palm	◆◆◆	American	$10-$52	343
9 / p. 292		The Clubhouse	◆◆◆	American	$6-$46	344
10 / p. 292		Prime	◆◆◆	Specialty	$5-$39	347
11 / p. 292		Maggiano's Little Italy	◆◆◆	Italian	$11-$38	346

Map Page	OA	Restaurants (cont'd)	Diamond Rated	Cuisine	Meal Range	Page
12 / p. 292		Corner Bakery	◆	Deli	$5-$10	344
13 / p. 292		Hashiguchi Jr.	◆◆	Japanese	$2-$20	345
14 / p. 292		Dantanna's	◆◆	Steak & Seafood	$4-$39	344
15 / p. 292		Ru San's Sushi & Sake Bar-Buckhead Tower Place	◆◆	Japanese	$3-$26	347
16 / p. 292		Rock Bottom Brewery	◆◆	American	$8-$30	347
17 / p. 292		Annie's Thai Castle	◆◆	Thai	$6-$19	343
18 / p. 292		Bone's Restaurant	◆◆◆	Steak	$6-$45	343
19 / p. 292		One Star Ranch	◆	Barbecue	$5-$29	346
20 / p. 292		McKinnon's Louisiane Restaurant	◆◆	Cajun	$5-$26	346
21 / p. 292		Fogo De Chao	◆◆◆	Brazilian	$21-$50	345
22 / p. 292		Chops	◆◆◆	Steak	$7-$46	344
23 / p. 292		Kyma	◆◆◆	Greek	$9-$34	345
24 / p. 292		Buckhead Diner	◆◆◆	American	$11-$27	343
25 / p. 292		Rama 5 of Thailand	◆◆	Thai	$8-$15	347
26 / p. 292		The Capital Grille	◆◆◆	Steak	$6-$42	344
27 / p. 292		Buckhead Bread Company & Corner Cafe	◆◆	American	$9-$14	343
28 / p. 292		Nava	◆◆◆	Southwestern	$9-$32	346
29 / p. 292		Aria	◆◆◆◆	American	$21-$34	343
30 / p. 292		Antica Posta Tuscan Restaurant & Bar	◆◆◆	Italian	$18-$36	343
31 / p. 292		Pricci	◆◆◆	Italian	$9-$26	346
32 / p. 292		Taka	◆◆	Sushi	$4-$18	347
33 / p. 292		Atlanta Fish Market	◆◆◆	Seafood	$16-$38	343
34 / p. 292		Basil's	◆◆	Mediterranean	$4-$29	343
35 / p. 292		Anis Cafe & Bistro	◆◆	American	$6-$29	343
36 / p. 292		Grand China Restaurant	◆◆	Chinese	$7-$27	345
37 / p. 292		Raja Indian Restaurant	◆◆	Indian	$3-$20	347
38 / p. 292		Amaryn's Thai Bowl & Sushi Bar	◆	Asian	$5-$14	342
39 / p. 292		Cedar's	◆◆	Lebanese	$7-$18	344
40 / p. 292	AAA	**La Grotta Ristorante Italiano**	◆◆◆◆	Italian	$7-$39	346
41 / p. 292		Coco Loco Cafe	◆◆	Cuban	$2-$17	344
42 / p. 292		The Varsity Jr	◆	American	$3-$7	348
43 / p. 292		MesKerem	◆◆	Ethiopian	$7-$20	346
44 / p. 292	AAA	**The Imperial Fez**	◆◆	Moroccan	$45-$65	345
45 / p. 292		Georgia Grille	◆◆	Southwestern	$16-$25	345
46 / p. 292		Toulouse	◆◆◆	French	$11-$17	347
47 / p. 292		Taverna Plaka	◆◆	Greek	$4-$22	347
48 / p. 292		Taqueria del Sol	◆◆	Southwestern	$2-$11	347
49 / p. 292		Cafe Sunflower	◆◆	Vegetarian	$5-$16	344
50 / p. 292		Red Snapper	◆◆	Seafood	$5-$24	347
51 / p. 292		The Colonnade	◆◆	American	$3-$20	344

Map Page	OA	Restaurants (cont'd)	Diamond Rated	Cuisine	Meal Range	Page
52 / p. 292		Nakato	◆◆◆	Japanese	$4-$45	346
53 / p. 292		Cafe Intermezzo	◆◆	American	$7-$15	344
54 / p. 292		Fat Matt's Rib Shack	◆	Barbecue	$2-$19	345
55 / p. 292		R. Thomas Deluxe Grill	◆◆	Natural/Organic	$4-$15	347
56 / p. 292		Cowtippers	◆	American	$3-$19	344
57 / p. 292		Doc Chey's Noodle House	◆◆	Asian	$2-$11	345
58 / p. 292		Alon's Bakery & Market	◆	American	$4-$10	342

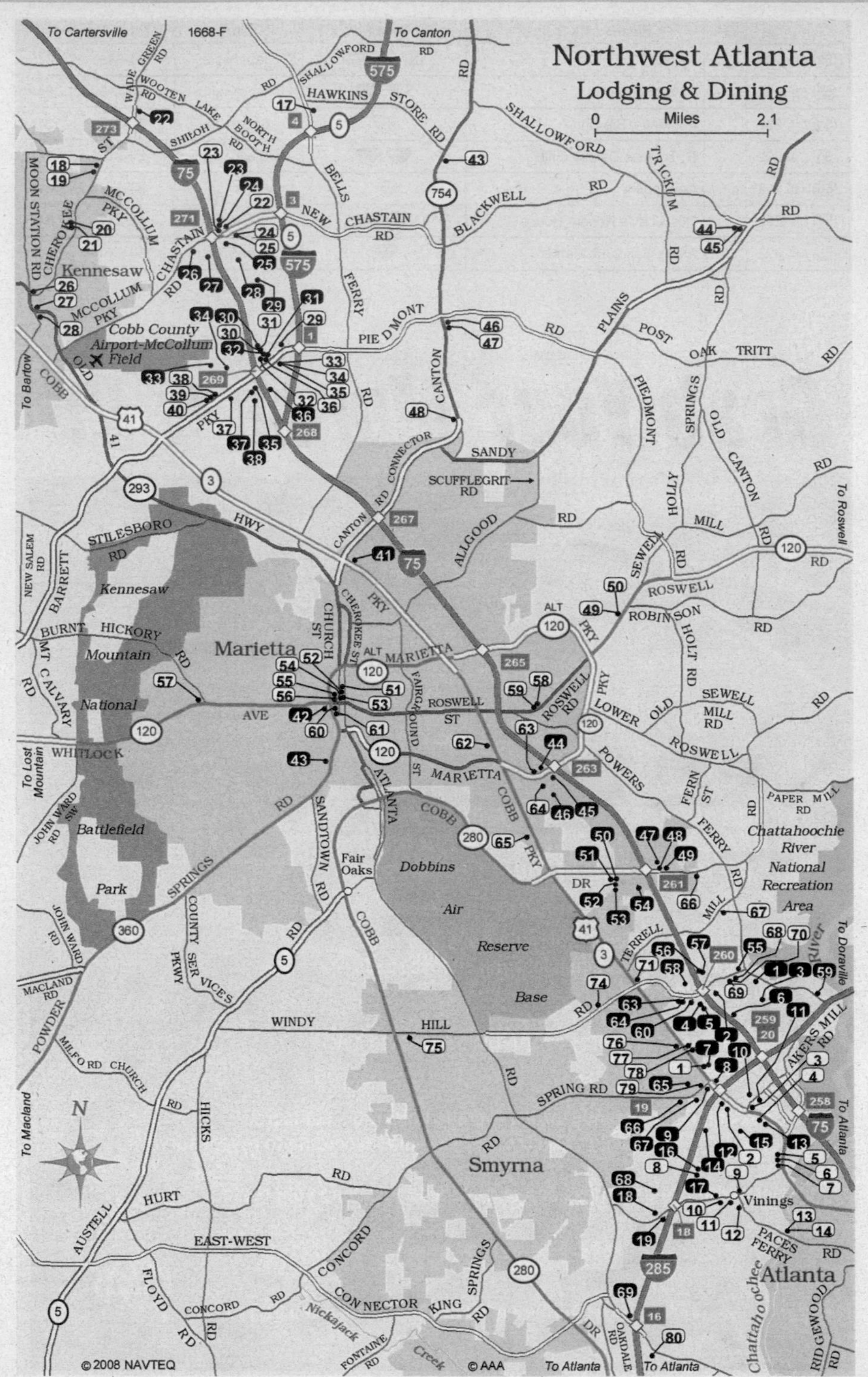
Northwest Atlanta
Lodging & Dining
0 Miles 2.1
To Cartersville
To Canton
Kennesaw
Cobb County Airport-McCollum Field
Marietta
Kennesaw Mountain National Battlefield Park
Dobbins Air Reserve Base
Chattahoochie River National Recreation Area
Smyrna
Vinings
Atlanta
To Roswell
To Doraville
To Atlanta
To Bartow
To Lost Mountain
To Macland
© 2008 NAVTEQ
© AAA

Northwest Atlanta

This index helps you "spot" where approved lodgings and restaurants are located on the corresponding detailed maps. Lodging daily rate range is for comparison only and show the property's high season. Restaurant rate range is a combination of lunch and/or dinner. Turn to the listing page for more detailed rate information and consult display ads for special promotions.

ATLANTA NORTHWEST

Map Page	OA	Lodgings	Diamond Rated	High Season	Page
1 / p. 296		Extended Stay Deluxe (Atlanta/Marietta/Powers Ferry Rd)	◆◆◆	$75-$85	350
2 / p. 296		Extended Stay Deluxe (Atlanta/Marietta/Windy Hill/Int. N Pkwy)	◆◆◆	$77-$87	350
3 / p. 296	AAA	**Hawthorn Suites-Atlanta NW**	◆◆◆	$129-$149 SAVE	350
4 / p. 296	AAA	**Country Inn & Suites by Carlson**	◆◆◆	$89-$159 SAVE	348
5 / p. 296		Days Inn-Atlanta/Marietta/Windy Hill Rd	◆◆	$49-$89	349
6 / p. 296		Atlanta Marriott Northwest	◆◆◆	$206-$221	348
7 / p. 296	AAA	**DoubleTree Guest Suites Atlanta-Galleria - see color ad p 349**	◆◆◆	$99-$209 SAVE	349
8 / p. 296		Hampton Inn & Suites Atlanta Galleria	◆◆◆	$89-$129	350
9 / p. 296		Wingate Inn Atlanta Galleria Center	◆◆◆	$89-$119	351
10 / p. 296	AAA	**Renaissance Waverly Hotel - see color ad p 328**	◆◆◆◆	$217-$233 SAVE	351
11 / p. 296		Embassy Suites Hotel-Galleria	◆◆◆	$119-$219	349
12 / p. 296	AAA	**Sheraton Suites Galleria**	◆◆◆	Rates not provided SAVE	351
13 / p. 296		Homewood Suites-Cumberland	◆◆◆	$89-$169	351
14 / p. 296		Hampton Inn Cumberland	◆◆◆	$109-$129	350
15 / p. 296	AAA	**Courtyard by Marriott-Cumberland Center**	◆◆◆	$177-$190 SAVE	348
16 / p. 296		Extended Stay Deluxe	◆◆◆	$70-$80	349
17 / p. 296		Courtyard by Marriott-Atlanta Vinings	◆◆◆	$169-$189	348
18 / p. 296		La Quinta Inn & Suites Atlanta (Paces Ferry/ Vinings)	◆◆◆	$69-$144	351
19 / p. 296		Fairfield Inn & Suites Atlanta/Vinings	◆◆◆	$128-$137	350

Map Page	OA	Restaurants	Diamond Rated	Cuisine	Meal Range	Page
1 / p. 296		Swapna Indian Cuisine	◆◆	Indian	$9-$15	352
2 / p. 296		Maggiano's	◆◆	Italian	$7-$30	352
3 / p. 296		Soup Garden	◆	American	$3-$8	352
4 / p. 296		Olde Mill Steakhouse	◆◆	American	$9-$23	352
5 / p. 296		Taverna Fiorentina	◆◆◆	Italian	$5-$27	353
6 / p. 296		C & S Seafood & Oyster Bar	◆◆◆	Seafood	$6-$47	352
7 / p. 296		Thai Dinner	◆◆	Thai	$8-$23	353
8 / p. 296		Willy's Mexicana Grill	◆	Mexican	$3-$6	353
9 / p. 296		Vinings Inn	◆◆◆	American	$9-$31	353
10 / p. 296		Meehan's Ale House	◆◆	Irish	$3-$16	352
11 / p. 296		La Paz Restaurante Cantina	◆◆	Mexican	$7-$15	352
12 / p. 296		Soho	◆◆◆	Specialty	$8-$25	352
13 / p. 296		Canoe	◆◆◆◆	American	$10-$33	352
14 / p. 296		The Orient at Vinings	◆◆	Chinese	$2-$20	352

KENNESAW

Map Page	OA	Lodgings	Diamond Rated	High Season	Page
22 / p. 296		Travelodge	◆◆	$49-$79	398
23 / p. 296	AAA	**Residence Inn by Marriott Town Center**	◆◆◆	$177-$190 SAVE	397
24 / p. 296		Fairfield Inn & Suites	◆◆◆	$123-$132	396
25 / p. 296	AAA	**Best Western Kennesaw Inn**	◆◆	$90-$100 SAVE	395
26 / p. 296		SpringHill Suites by Marriott	◆◆◆	$137-$147	397
27 / p. 296	AAA	**Country Inn & Suites by Carlson**	◆◆◆	$99-$155 SAVE	396
28 / p. 296		StudioPLUS	◆◆	$55-$75	397
29 / p. 296		Extended StayAmerica	◆◆	$55-$70	396
30 / p. 296		La Quinta Inn	◆◆◆	$69-$150	397
31 / p. 296		Holiday Inn Express-Town Center Mall	◆◆◆	$105-$179	397
32 / p. 296		Comfort Inn	◆◆◆	$89-$119	395
33 / p. 296		Hilton Garden Inn-Atlanta NW/Kennesaw Town Center	◆◆◆	$109-$179	396
34 / p. 296		Hampton Inn	◆◆◆	$120-$130	396
35 / p. 296		Quality Inn	◆◆	$55-$80	397
36 / p. 296	AAA	**Red Roof Inn-Town Center Mall**	◆◆	$50-$100 SAVE	397
37 / p. 296		Days Inn	◆◆	$55-$79	396
38 / p. 296	AAA	**Wingate By Wyndham**	◆◆◆	$119-$139 SAVE	398

Map Page	OA	Restaurants	Diamond Rated	Cuisine	Meal Range	Page
17 / p. 296		Bergamo	◆◆	Italian	$7-$15	398
18 / p. 296		Hamada Japanese Restaurant	◆◆	Japanese	$7-$34	399
19 / p. 296		Barbeque Street	◆	Barbecue	$6-$18	398
20 / p. 296		Bangkok Cabin	◆◆	Thai	$7-$13	398
21 / p. 296		Buckhead Burrito Grill	◆	Mexican	$3-$6	398
22 / p. 296		Los Reyes	◆◆	Tex-Mex	$5-$17	399
23 / p. 296		Sidelines Grille	◆◆	American	$5-$17	400
24 / p. 296		Froots	◆	Sandwiches	$2-$7	398
25 / p. 296		Marlow's Tavern	◆◆	American	$4-$17	399
26 / p. 296		Trackside Grill	◆◆◆	American	$7-$19	400
27 / p. 296		Caper's on Main Street	◆◆	American	$8-$20	398
28 / p. 296		My Country Kitchen	◆	Southern	$7-$13	399
29 / p. 296		The Varsity	◆	American	$3-$7	400
30 / p. 296		My Cousin Vinny's	◆◆	Italian	$2-$19	399
31 / p. 296		Happy China	◆◆	Chinese	$6-$16	399
32 / p. 296		Fuji Hana & Thai Peppers	◆◆	Asian	$7-$20	399
33 / p. 296		Ippolito's	◆◆	Italian	$7-$16	399
34 / p. 296	AAA	**New China Buffet**	◆◆	Chinese	$6-$12	399
35 / p. 296		Ru San's-Kennesaw	◆◆	Japanese	$5-$27	400
36 / p. 296		Penang Malaysian/Thai Cuisine	◆◆	Asian	$6-$18	400
37 / p. 296		Bahama Breeze	◆◆◆	Seafood	$11-$22	398

Map Page	OA	Restaurants (cont'd)	Diamond Rated	Cuisine	Meal Range	Page
38 / p. 296		Kuroshio Sushi Bar & Grille	◆◆	Japanese	$4-$23	399
39 / p. 296		El Nopalito	◆◆	Tex-Mex	$2-$12	398
40 / p. 296		Willy's Mexicana Grill	◆	Mexican	$3-$6	400

MARIETTA

Map Page	OA	Lodgings	Diamond Rated	High Season	Page
41 / p. 296		Hometown Inn	◆◆	Rates not provided	405
42 / p. 296		The Whitlock Inn Bed & Breakfast	◆◆◆	$125-$150	406
43 / p. 296		Hilton Atlanta/Marietta Hotel & Conference Center	◆◆◆	$89-$169	405
44 / p. 296		Hampton Inn Marietta	◆◆◆	$77-$97	405
45 / p. 296	AAA	**Crowne Plaza Atlanta-Marietta**	◆◆◆	$79-$189 SAVE	404
46 / p. 296	AAA	**Baymont Inn & Suites Marietta**	◆◆◆	$80-$110 SAVE	404
47 / p. 296	AAA	**Sleep Inn**	◆◆	$59-$89 SAVE	406
48 / p. 296		Drury Inn & Suites-Atlanta Northwest	◆◆◆	$70-$110	405
49 / p. 296	AAA	**Courtyard by Marriott-Marietta**	◆◆◆	$137-$147 SAVE	404
50 / p. 296		La Quinta Inn	◆◆◆	$39-$79	406
51 / p. 296		Wingate Inn	◆◆◆	$109-$149	406
52 / p. 296	AAA	**Quality Inn Atlanta/Marietta**	◆◆	$65-$100 SAVE	406
53 / p. 296		Comfort Inn-Marietta	◆◆◆	$79-$109	404
54 / p. 296		Days Inn	◆◆	Rates not provided	405
55 / p. 296	AAA	**Hyatt Regency Suites Perimeter Northwest**	◆◆◆	$79-$329 SAVE	406
56 / p. 296		Econo Lodge Northwest	◆◆	Rates not provided	405
57 / p. 296		Extended StayAmerica Atlanta-Marietta Windy Hill	◆◆	$55-$65	405
58 / p. 296	AAA	**Courtyard by Marriott-Windy Hill**	◆◆◆	$167-$179 SAVE	404
59 / p. 296		Homestead Studio Suites Hotel-Atlanta-Marietta-Powers Ferry Rd	◆◆◆	$70-$80	405
60 / p. 296	AAA	**Masters Inn Marietta**	◆	$45-$52 SAVE	406

Map Page	OA	Restaurants	Diamond Rated	Cuisine	Meal Range	Page
43 / p. 296		Tokyo Japanese Steak House	◆◆	Japanese	$11-$35	409
44 / p. 296		Aspens Signature Steaks	◆◆◆	Steak	$10-$33	407
45 / p. 296		New Lucky China	◆◆	Chinese	$6-$14	408
46 / p. 296		Basil Wraps	◆	Mediterranean	$2-$8	407
47 / p. 296		Cherokee Cattle Company	◆◆	Steak	$6-$20	407
48 / p. 296		The Rib Ranch	◆	Barbecue	$7-$23	409
49 / p. 296		Lemon Grass Thai Restaurant	◆◆	Thai	$7-$12	408
50 / p. 296		Wild Wing Cafe	◆	American	$4-$16	409
51 / p. 296		House of Lu	◆◆	Chinese	$6-$17	408
52 / p. 296		Efes	◆◆	Turkish	$7-$24	407
53 / p. 296		Willie Rae's	◆◆	Cajun	$7-$18	410

Map Page	OA	Restaurants (cont'd)	Diamond Rated	Cuisine	Meal Range	Page
54 / p. 296		Simpatico	◆◆◆	American	$14-$25	409
55 / p. 296		Blu Greek Taverna	◆◆	Greek	$5-$25	407
56 / p. 296		Thaicoon & Sushi Bar	◆◆◆	Asian	$8-$20	409
57 / p. 296		Chicago's Restaurant	◆◆	American	$8-$29	407
58 / p. 296	AAA	**Cafe Life**	◆	Natural/Organic	$4-$10	407
59 / p. 296		Williamson Bros Bar-B-Q	◆	Regional Barbecue	$7-$15	409
60 / p. 296		La Parrilla	◆◆	Tex-Mex	$6-$18	408
61 / p. 296		Kiosco	◆◆	Colombian	$1-$20	408
62 / p. 296		Marietta Diner	◆◆	Continental	$7-$24	408
63 / p. 296		Haveli Indian Cuisine	◆◆	Indian	$8-$15	408
64 / p. 296		Tasty China	◆◆	Chinese	$2-$14	409
65 / p. 296		Falafel Cafe	◆◆	Persian	$6-$15	407
66 / p. 296		Sabor do Brazil	◆	Brazilian	$7-$9	409
67 / p. 296		Vatica	◆◆	Indian	$9-$11	409
68 / p. 296		Barker's Red Hots	◆	American	$1-$5	407
69 / p. 296		My Friend's Place	◆	Deli	$5-$7	408
70 / p. 296		Hashiguchi	◆◆	Japanese	$8-$25	408
71 / p. 296		RuSan's Marietta	◆◆	Japanese	$5-$21	409

SMYRNA

Map Page	OA	Lodgings	Diamond Rated	High Season	Page
63 / p. 296	AAA	**Red Roof Inn-North**	◆◆	$50-$100 SAVE	420
64 / p. 296	AAA	**Best Western Atlanta Inn and Suites**	◆◆◆	$60-$80 SAVE	419
65 / p. 296	AAA	**Residence Inn-Atlanta Cumberland**	◆◆◆	$177-$190 SAVE	420
66 / p. 296		Homestead Studio Suites Hotel-Atlanta/Cumberland Mall	◆◆	$60-$70	420
67 / p. 296	AAA	**Holiday Inn Express Atlanta / Smyrna Cobb Galleria Center - see color ad p 325**	◆◆◆	$80-$100 SAVE	419
68 / p. 296	AAA	**Hyatt Place-Atlanta Galleria**	◆◆◆	$69-$209 SAVE	420
69 / p. 296		Holiday Inn Express, Vinings/Smyrna	◆◆◆	$70-$130	420

Map Page	OA	Restaurants	Diamond Rated	Cuisine	Meal Range	Page
74 / p. 296		Siam Square	◆◆	Thai	$7-$15	421
75 / p. 296		Old South Bar-B-Q	◆	Barbecue	$5-$12	421
76 / p. 296		Scalini's	◆◆	Italian	$5-$18	421
77 / p. 296		Yakitori Jinbei	◆◆	Japanese	$6-$14	421
78 / p. 296		House of Chan	◆◆	Chinese	$6-$30	421
79 / p. 296		Minato Japanese Restaurant	◆◆	Japanese	$1-$26	421
80 / p. 296		Blackstone	◆◆◆	Steak & Seafood	$11-$39	420

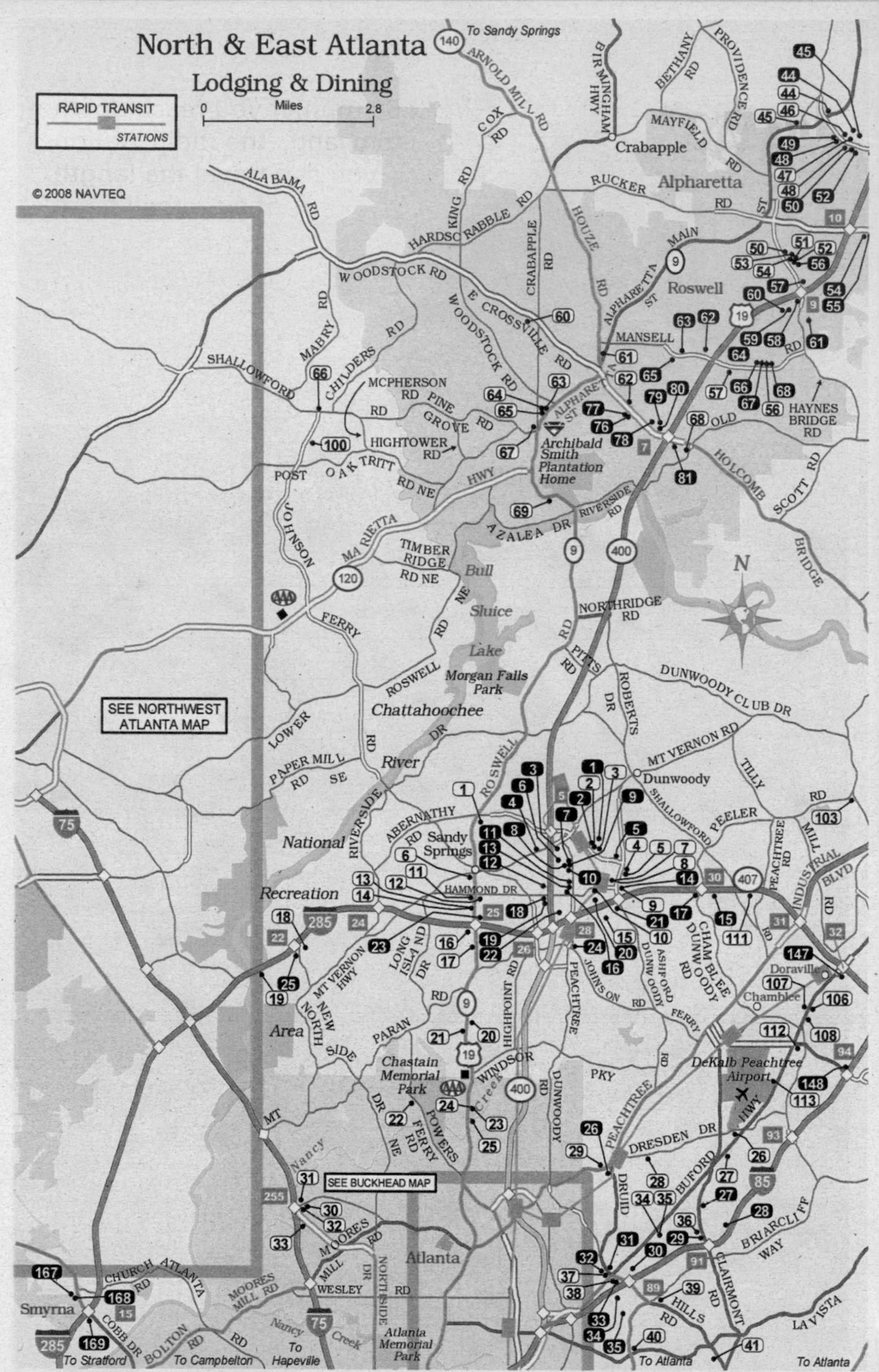
North & East Atlanta
Lodging & Dining
RAPID TRANSIT
STATIONS
Miles
© 2008 NAVTEQ
To Sandy Springs
Crabapple
Alpharetta
Roswell
Archibald Smith Plantation Home
Bull Sluice Lake
Morgan Falls Park
Chattahoochee River National Recreation Area
SEE NORTHWEST ATLANTA MAP
Dunwoody
Sandy Springs
Doraville
Chamblee
DeKalb Peachtree Airport
Chastain Memorial Park
SEE BUCKHEAD MAP
Atlanta
Smyrna
Atlanta Memorial Park
To Stratford
To Campbelton
To Hapeville
To Atlanta
To Atlanta

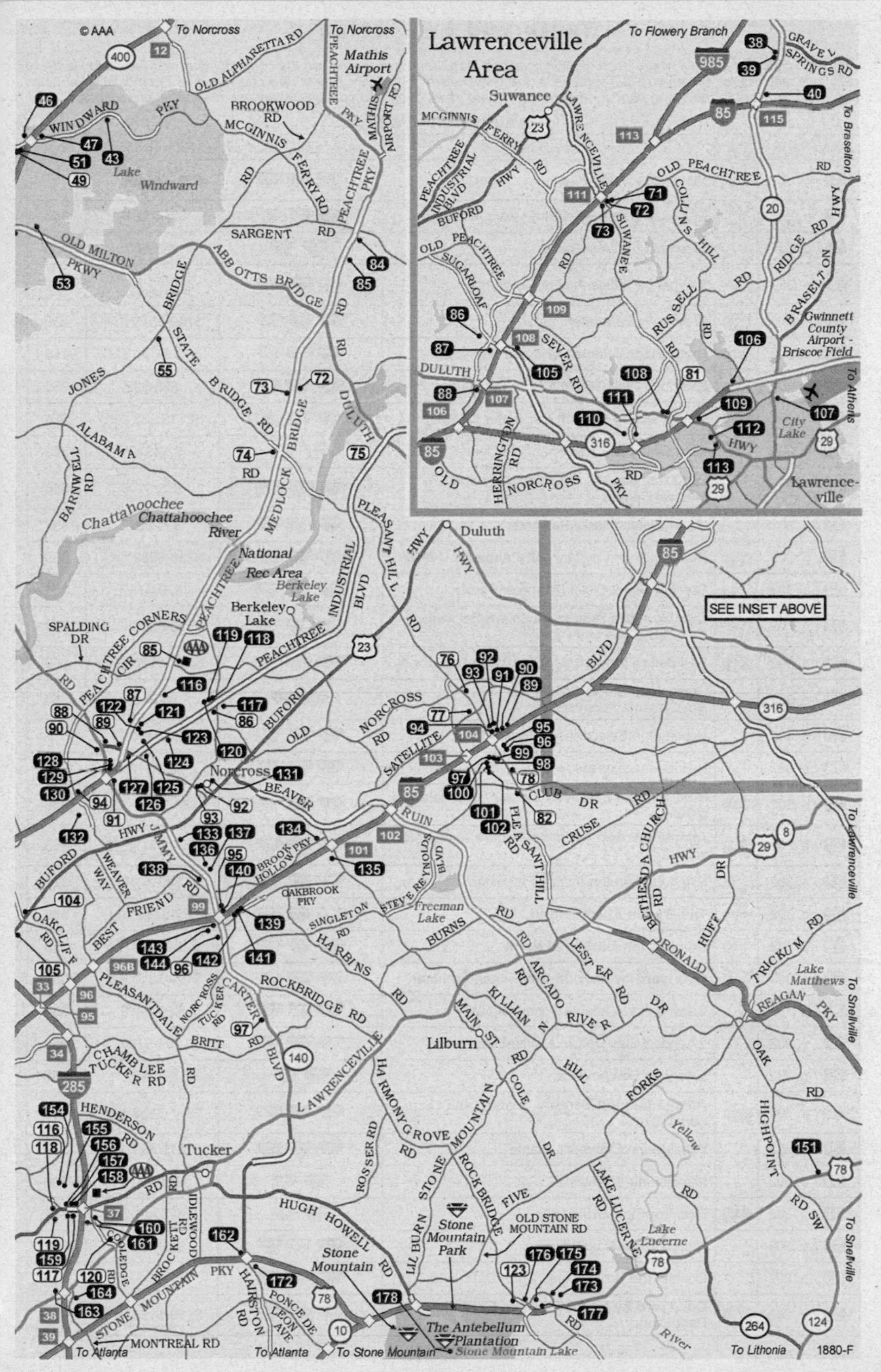

North and East Atlanta

This index helps you "spot" where approved lodgings and restaurants are located on the corresponding detailed maps. Lodging daily rate range is for comparison only and show the property's high season. Restaurant rate range is a combination of lunch and/or dinner. Turn to the listing page for more detailed rate information and consult display ads for special promotions.

ATLANTA NORTH & EAST

Map Page	OA	Lodgings	Diamond Rated	High Season	Page
1 / p. 302		Staybridge Suites Atlanta Perimeter	◆◆◆	Rates not provided	359
2 / p. 302		Embassy Suites Hotel Perimeter Center	◆◆◆	$114-$249	355
3 / p. 302		Extended StayAmerica	◆◆	$65-$90	355
4 / p. 302		Staybridge Suites-Atlanta-Mt. Vernon	◆◆◆	Rates not provided	359
5 / p. 302	AAA	**W Atlanta Perimeter**	◆◆◆	$109-$519 SAVE	360
6 / p. 302	AAA	**Hyatt Place Atlanta/Perimeter Center**	◆◆◆	$79-$239 SAVE	358
7 / p. 302		Extended Stay Deluxe Atlanta-Perimeter	◆◆◆	$78-$92	356
8 / p. 302	AAA	**Courtyard by Marriott Perimeter Center**	◆◆◆	$217-$233 SAVE	354
9 / p. 302		Microtel Inn & Suites-Perimeter Center	◆◆	$79-$129	359
10 / p. 302		La Quinta Inn & Suites Atlanta (Perimeter/ Medical Center)	◆◆◆	$55-$149	358
11 / p. 302		Hilton Suites Atlanta Perimeter	◆◆◆	$99-$279	357
12 / p. 302	AAA	**Residence Inn by Marriott-Perimeter Center**	◆◆◆	$236-$253 SAVE	359
13 / p. 302		Comfort Suites Hotel Perimeter Center	◆◆◆	$79-$159	354
14 / p. 302	AAA	**Crowne Plaza Atlanta-Ravinia Hotel** - see color ad p 355	◆◆◆	$125-$279 SAVE	354
15 / p. 302	AAA	**Residence Inn by Marriott Atlanta Dunwoody**	◆◆◆	$177-$190 SAVE	359
16 / p. 302		Homestead Studio Suites Hotel-Atlanta/Perimeter	◆◆	$60-$83	358
17 / p. 302		Holiday Inn Select Atlanta Perimeter	◆◆◆	$69-$139	357
18 / p. 302		Holiday Inn Express Hotel & Suites-Perimeter	◆◆◆	$77-$125	357
19 / p. 302	AAA	**Hampton Inn-Perimeter Center** - see color ad p 356	◆◆◆	$89-$149 SAVE	356
20 / p. 302	AAA	**Atlanta Marriott Perimeter Center** - see color ad p 321	◆◆◆	$296-$317 SAVE	353
21 / p. 302		Hilton Garden Inn-Atlanta Perimeter	◆◆◆	$89-$219	356
22 / p. 302	AAA	**The Westin Atlanta North**	◆◆◆	$99-$399 SAVE	360
23 / p. 302	AAA	**Comfort Inn-Buckhead North**	◆◆◆	$79-$169 SAVE	353
24 / p. 302	AAA	**Courtyard by Marriott-Glenridge/Perimeter**	◆◆◆	$197-$211 SAVE	354
25 / p. 302		Crowne Plaza Atlanta Perimeter NW	◆◆◆	$69-$219	354
26 / p. 302		Extended Stay Deluxe Atlanta-Lenox	◆◆◆	$80-$100	355
27 / p. 302		Extended StayAmerica	◆◆	$70-$87	355
28 / p. 302	AAA	**Atlanta Marriott Century Center** - see color ad p 320	◆◆◆	$217-$233 SAVE	353
29 / p. 302		Wingate Inn Clairmont-Atlanta	◆◆◆	$100-$119	360
30 / p. 302		Microtel Inn & Suites	◆◆	$59-$119	358
31 / p. 302	AAA	**Red Roof Inn-Druid Hills**	◆◆	$60-$100 SAVE	359
32 / p. 302		Hampton Inn-Druid Hills Road	◆◆◆	$124-$144	356
33 / p. 302		DoubleTree Hotel Atlanta North Druid Hills	◆◆◆	$94-$219	355
34 / p. 302	AAA	**Courtyard by Marriott Atlanta Executive Park/Emory**	◆◆◆	$169-$189 SAVE	354

ATLANTA NORTH & EAST (cont'd)

Map Page	OA	Lodgings (cont'd)	Diamond Rated	High Season	Page
35 / p. 302		Homestead Studio Suites Hotel-Atlanta/North Druid Hills	◆◆	$58-$70	357

Map Page	OA	Restaurants	Diamond Rated	Cuisine	Meal Range	Page
1 / p. 302		Mirage	◆◆	Persian	$6-$22	362
2 / p. 302		Joey D's Oak Room	◆◆	American	$5-$30	362
3 / p. 302		Tin Drum Asia Cafe	◆◆	Asian	$2-$7	364
4 / p. 302		Cafe Intermezzo	◆◆	American	$4-$15	360
5 / p. 302		McKendrick's Steak House	◆◆◆	Steak & Seafood	$15-$40	362
6 / p. 302		KC Pit BBQ	◆	Barbecue	$2-$19	362
7 / p. 302		Goldfish	◆◆◆	Seafood	$10-$40	361
8 / p. 302		Maggiano's Little Italy	◆◆◆	Italian	$11-$38	362
9 / p. 302	AAA	**La Grotta Ravinia Ristorante Italiano**	◆◆◆◆	Northern Italian	$7-$32	362
10 / p. 302		Chequers Seafood Grill	◆◆◆	Seafood	$6-$35	360
11 / p. 302		Canton Cooks	◆◆	Chinese	$4-$28	360
12 / p. 302		Cafe Sunflower	◆◆	Vegetarian	$4-$17	360
13 / p. 302		Sultan's	◆◆	Middle Eastern	$4-$20	363
14 / p. 302		Chicago's Restaurant	◆◆	American	$5-$30	361
15 / p. 302		Villa Christina	◆◆◆	Italian	$13-$38	364
16 / p. 302		China Cooks	◆◆	Chinese	$4-$28	361
17 / p. 302		Five Season's Brewing Company	◆◆	American	$3-$25	361
18 / p. 302		Sushi Huku	◆◆	Japanese	$4-$30	363
19 / p. 302		Ray's on the River	◆◆◆	Seafood	$5-$58	363
20 / p. 302		Food 101	◆◆◆	American	$9-$26	361
21 / p. 302		Pig-N-Chik	◆	Barbecue	$6-$20	363
22 / p. 302		Horseradish Grill	◆◆◆	Regional Southern	$6-$27	361
23 / p. 302		Chopstix Restaurant	◆◆◆	Chinese	$8-$26	361
24 / p. 302		Frontera Mex-Mex Grill	◆◆	Tex-Mex	$5-$13	361
25 / p. 302		10 Degrees South	◆◆◆	African	$16-$25	360
26 / p. 302		Pho Dai Loi	◆◆	Vietnamese	$3-$7	363
27 / p. 302		Pho #1	◆◆	Vietnamese	$2-$8	363
28 / p. 302		Haven	◆◆◆	New American	$17-$29	361
29 / p. 302		Terra Grille	◆◆	American	$3-$22	364
30 / p. 302		Pano's & Paul's	◆◆◆◆	Continental	$24-$46	363
31 / p. 302		Blue Ridge Grill	◆◆◆	Regional American	$15-$40	360
32 / p. 302		O K Cafe	◆	Southern	$6-$11	363
33 / p. 302		Joel	◆◆◆◆	French	$12-$36	362
34 / p. 302		Panahar Bangladeshi Cuisine	◆◆	Indian	$9-$15	363
35 / p. 302		Machu Picchu	◆◆	Peruvian	$7-$14	362
36 / p. 302		Violette	◆◆	French	$4-$22	364
37 / p. 302		Lawrence's Cafe	◆◆	Middle Eastern	$3-$20	362

Map Page	OA	Restaurants (cont'd)	Diamond Rated	Cuisine	Meal Range	Page
38 / p. 302		Havana Sandwich Shop	♦	Cuban	$4-$8	361
39 / p. 302		Queen of Sheba	♦♦	Ethiopian	$2-$16	363
40 / p. 302		Thai Chili	♦♦	Thai	$3-$23	364
41 / p. 302		Petite Auberge Restaurant	♦♦	Continental	$10-$27	363

BUFORD

Map Page	OA	Lodgings	Diamond Rated	High Season	Page
38 / p. 302		SpringHill Suites-Mall of Georgia	♦♦♦	$137-$147	377
39 / p. 302		Hampton Inn-Mall of Georgia	♦♦♦	$129-$149	377
40 / p. 302	AAA	**Country Inn & Suites By Carlson - see color ad p 377**	♦♦♦	$99-$139 SAVE	377

ALPHARETTA

Map Page	OA	Lodgings	Diamond Rated	High Season	Page
43 / p. 302	AAA	**Hilton Garden Inn Atlanta/North Alpharetta**	♦♦♦	$79-$189 SAVE	372
44 / p. 302		SpringHill Suites by Marriott	♦♦♦	$157-$169	374
45 / p. 302	AAA	**Courtyard by Marriott**	♦♦♦	$177-$190 SAVE	370
46 / p. 302		Hampton Inn & Suites	♦♦♦	$139-$179	371
47 / p. 302	AAA	**Atlanta Marriott Alpharetta**	♦♦♦	$217-$233 SAVE	370
48 / p. 302	AAA	**Hotel Sierra Alpharetta**	♦♦♦	$139-$199 SAVE	372
49 / p. 302		DoubleTree Hotel Atlanta/Alpharetta-Windward	♦♦♦	$69-$269	371
50 / p. 302		Holiday Inn Express	♦♦♦	Rates not provided	372
51 / p. 302	AAA	**Hyatt Place Atlanta/Alpharetta/Windward Parkway**	♦♦♦	$99-$299 SAVE	372
52 / p. 302	AAA	**Residence Inn by Marriott**	♦♦♦	$197-$211 SAVE	373
53 / p. 302		Staybridge Suites	♦♦♦	$135-$171	374
54 / p. 302		Extended Stay Deluxe Atlanta-Alpharetta-Northpoint	♦♦♦	$72-$87	371
55 / p. 302		StudioPLUS	♦♦	$62-$77	374
56 / p. 302		TownePlace Suites by Marriott	♦♦♦	$142-$152	374
57 / p. 302		Fairfield Inn & Suites	♦♦♦	$123-$132	371
58 / p. 302		Extended StayAmerica	♦♦	$57-$72	371
59 / p. 302		La Quinta Inn & Suites Atlanta (Alpharetta)	♦♦♦	$55-$139	373
60 / p. 302	AAA	**Residence Inn Atlanta Alpharetta North Point Mall**	♦♦♦	$179-$199 SAVE	373
61 / p. 302		Hilton Garden Inn-Atlanta North Point	♦♦♦	$59-$189	372
62 / p. 302		Homewood Suites	♦♦♦	$79-$149	372
63 / p. 302		Hampton Inn-Alpharetta/Roswell	♦♦♦	$79-$159	371
64 / p. 302	AAA	**Hyatt Place North Point**	♦♦♦	$99-$299 SAVE	373
65 / p. 302		Wingate Inn	♦♦♦	$114	374
66 / p. 302		Country Inn & Suites by Carlson	♦♦♦	$79-$119	370
67 / p. 302		Comfort Suites	♦♦♦	$90-$120	370
68 / p. 302		Ramada Limited	♦♦♦	$69-$75	373

Map Page	OA	Restaurants	Diamond Rated	Cuisine	Meal Range	Page
44 / p. 302		Ippolito's	♦♦	Italian	$7-$16	375
45 / p. 302		One Star Ranch	♦	Barbecue	$6-$25	375

Map Page	OA	Restaurants (cont'd)	Diamond Rated	Cuisine	Meal Range	Page
46 / p. 302		Xian China Bistro	◆◆	Chinese	$4-$30	376
47 / p. 302		Nahm Thai Cuisine	◆◆	Thai	$3-$22	375
48 / p. 302		Vinny's On Windward	◆◆◆	American	$6-$29	376
49 / p. 302		Cabernet	◆◆◆	Steak & Seafood	$6-$40	374
50 / p. 302		Rainwater Restaurant	◆◆◆	American	$10-$36	375
51 / p. 302		Village Tavern	◆◆◆	American	$5-$26	376
52 / p. 302		The Varsity	◆	American	$3-$7	375
53 / p. 302		Grouchy's-A New York Deli	◆	Deli	$2-$8	375
54 / p. 302		Thai Thai	◆◆	Thai	$4-$13	375
55 / p. 302		Sri Krishna Vilas	◆◆	Indian	$5-$12	375
56 / p. 302		Santoor	◆◆	Indian	$8-$17	375
57 / p. 302		Atlantic Seafood Company	◆◆◆	Seafood	$5-$47	374

SUWANEE

Map Page	OA	Lodgings	Diamond Rated	High Season	Page
71 / p. 302	AAA	**Comfort Suites**	◆◆◆	$89-$199 SAVE	423
72 / p. 302	AAA	**Comfort Inn**	◆◆	$75-$129 SAVE	423
73 / p. 302	AAA	**Best Western Gwinnett Inn**	◆◆	$80-$110 SAVE	423

ROSWELL

Map Page	OA	Lodgings	Diamond Rated	High Season	Page
76 / p. 302		Holiday Inn Hotel & Suites	◆◆◆	$99-$175	417
77 / p. 302	AAA	**Best Western Roswell Suites**	◆◆◆	$85-$109 SAVE	417
78 / p. 302		La Quinta Inn	◆◆◆	$44-$79	418
79 / p. 302		Brookwood Inn	◆◆	Rates not provided	417
80 / p. 302		Studio 6 #6025	◆◆	$64-$88	418
81 / p. 302		Courtyard by Marriott	◆◆◆	$153-$164	417

Map Page	OA	Restaurants	Diamond Rated	Cuisine	Meal Range	Page
60 / p. 302		Bistro VG	◆◆◆	American	$6-$34	418
61 / p. 302		Byblos	◆◆	Lebanese	$3-$20	418
62 / p. 302		Brookwood Grill	◆◆	American	$13-$23	418
63 / p. 302		Greenwood's on Green Street	◆◆	Southern	$8-$25	419
64 / p. 302		The Fickle Pickle	◆	Deli	$7-$10	419
65 / p. 302		The Swallow at the Hollow	◆◆	Barbecue	$7-$22	419
66 / p. 302		Chicago's Restaurant	◆◆	American	$10-$28	418
67 / p. 302		Pastis	◆◆◆	French	$5-$25	419
68 / p. 302		Angan	◆◆	Indian	$7-$15	418
69 / p. 302		Amalfi Ristorante	◆◆	Italian	$13-$20	418

DULUTH

Map Page	OA	Lodgings	Diamond Rated	High Season	Page
84 / p. 302		Hilton Garden Inn Atlanta-John's Creek	◆◆◆	$79-$154	388
85 / p. 302	AAA	**Hyatt Place Atlanta/Johns Creek**	◆◆◆	$99-$299 SAVE	388
86 / p. 302		Holiday Inn-Gwinnett Center	◆◆◆	$84-$169	388

DULUTH (cont'd)

Map Page	OA	Lodgings (cont'd)	Diamond Rated	High Season	Page
87 / p. 302		Hilton Garden Inn-Atlanta NE	♦♦♦	$99-$189	388
88 / p. 302	AAA	**La Quinta Inn Duluth**	♦♦♦	$59-$139 SAVE	389
89 / p. 302		Extended Stay Deluxe	♦♦♦	$75-$90	387
90 / p. 302		Wingate Inn	♦♦♦	Rates not provided	389
91 / p. 302		Quality Inn - Gwinnett Mall	♦♦	$60-$129	389
92 / p. 302	AAA	**Courtyard by Marriott-Gwinnett Mall**	♦♦♦	$153-$164 SAVE	387
93 / p. 302	AAA	**Hyatt Place Atlanta/Duluth/Gwinnett Mall**	♦♦♦	$69-$209 SAVE	388
94 / p. 302		Days Inn Gwinnett Place	♦♦	Rates not provided	387
95 / p. 302		Studio 6 #6023	♦♦	$59-$63	389
96 / p. 302		Country Inn & Suites by Carlson	♦♦♦	$119-$149	386
97 / p. 302		Holiday Inn Express	♦♦♦	$79-$119	388
98 / p. 302		Candlewood Suites-Atlanta	♦♦♦	Rates not provided	386
99 / p. 302		Atlanta Marriott Gwinnett Place	♦♦♦	$202-$216	386
100 / p. 302	AAA	**Comfort Suites-Atlanta Duluth**	♦♦♦	$80-$130 SAVE	386
101 / p. 302		Residence Inn-Atlanta Gwinnett	♦♦♦	$188-$202	389
102 / p. 302	AAA	**Hampton Inn & Suites-Gwinnett - see color ad p 387**	♦♦♦	$89-$179 SAVE	387

Map Page	OA	Restaurants	Diamond Rated	Cuisine	Meal Range	Page
72 / p. 302		Sia's	♦♦♦	New American	$6-$32	390
73 / p. 302		J.R.'s Log House	♦	American	$3-$13	390
74 / p. 302		Stoney River	♦♦♦	American	$7-$33	390
75 / p. 302		Kurt's and Vreny's Biergarten	♦♦♦	Continental	$4-$36	390
76 / p. 302		Athen's Pizza Kouzzina	♦♦	Mediterranean	$3-$24	389
77 / p. 302		HARU Ichiban Japanese Restaurant	♦♦	Japanese	$3-$33	389
78 / p. 302		Super Grand Buffet	♦♦	Asian	$6-$11	390

LAWRENCEVILLE

Map Page	OA	Lodgings	Diamond Rated	High Season	Page
105 / p. 302		Hampton Inn	♦♦♦	$90-$195	401
106 / p. 302		Microtel Inn & Suites-University Way/Lawrenceville	♦♦	$69-$79	402
107 / p. 302	AAA	**Best Western Lawrenceville Inn**	♦♦	$66-$86 SAVE	400
108 / p. 302	AAA	**Country Inn & Suites by Carlson**	♦♦♦	$119-$179 SAVE	401
109 / p. 302	AAA	**Days Inn**	♦♦	$70-$121 SAVE	401
110 / p. 302	AAA	**Comfort Suites**	♦♦♦	$119-$129 SAVE	401
111 / p. 302		Hampton Inn	♦♦♦	$79-$139	401
112 / p. 302		Holiday Inn Express Hotel & Suites	♦♦♦	Rates not provided	401
113 / p. 302		Extended StayAmerica Atlanta-Lawrenceville	♦♦	$55-$65	401

Map Page	OA	Restaurants	Diamond Rated	Cuisine	Meal Range	Page
81 / p. 302		Digger's Sports Grill	♦♦	American	$7-$18	402
82 / p. 302		Red Garlic Super Thai Cuisine	♦♦	Thai	$7-$16	402

NORCROSS

Map Page	OA	Lodgings	Diamond Rated	High Season	Page
116 / p. 302	AAA	**Hyatt Place Atlanta/Norcross/Peachtree**	◆◆◆	$69-$199 SAVE	415
117 / p. 302		Comfort Inn & Suites	◆◆◆	$79-$99	412
118 / p. 302		Baymont Inn & Suites	◆◆◆	Rates not provided	411
119 / p. 302		Days Inn & Suites	◆◆	$48-$99	413
120 / p. 302		Red Roof Inn & Suites	◆◆	$48-$52	415
121 / p. 302		Atlanta Marriott Norcross	◆◆◆	$187-$201	411
122 / p. 302		Homewood Suites by Hilton	◆◆◆	$69-$129	414
123 / p. 302		Hampton Inn	◆◆◆	$109-$139	414
124 / p. 302		Wingate Inn	◆◆◆	$65-$108	415
125 / p. 302		Hilton Atlanta Northeast	◆◆◆	$94-$199	414
126 / p. 302		Holiday Inn Select-Peachtree Corners	◆◆◆	Rates not provided	414
127 / p. 302	AAA	**Courtyard by Marriott-Peachtree Corners**	◆◆◆	$137-$147 SAVE	413
128 / p. 302		StudioPlus	◆◆	$60-$75	415
129 / p. 302		Homestead Studio Suites Hotel-Atlanta/Peachtree Corners	◆◆	$55-$65	414
130 / p. 302	AAA	**Best Western-Peachtree Corners**	◆◆◆	$79-$99 SAVE	412
131 / p. 302		Extended StayAmerica Atlanta-Norcross	◆◆	$58-$70	413
132 / p. 302		Super 8 Atlanta Northeast @ Technology Park	◆◆	$54-$69	415
133 / p. 302		Extended StayAmerica Atlanta-Jimmy Carter Blvd.	◆◆	$50-$65	413
134 / p. 302		Red Roof Inn-Indian Trail	◆◆	$50-$90	415
135 / p. 302	AAA	**GuestHouse Inn**	◆◆	$49-$89 SAVE	414
136 / p. 302		Microtel Inn & Suites	◆◆	Rates not provided	415
137 / p. 302	AAA	**Days Inn Atlanta NE**	◆◆	$56-$70 SAVE	413
138 / p. 302	AAA	**Country Inn & Suites by Carlson**	◆◆◆	$79-$109 SAVE	412
139 / p. 302	AAA	**La Quinta Inn**	◆◆◆	$59-$134 SAVE	415
140 / p. 302		Drury Inn & Suites-Atlanta Northeast	◆◆◆	$70-$125	413
141 / p. 302	AAA	**Comfort Inn & Suites Conference Centre - see color ad p 412**	◆◆◆	$74-$99 SAVE	412
142 / p. 302		America's Best Inn	◆◆	$59-$79	411
143 / p. 302	AAA	**Best Western North Atlanta-Norcross Inn**	◆◆◆	$55-$99 SAVE	411
144 / p. 302	AAA	**Courtyard by Marriott-Atlanta Norcross**	◆◆◆	$112-$123 SAVE	413

Map Page	OA	Restaurants	Diamond Rated	Cuisine	Meal Range	Page
85 / p. 302		Phoenix Noodle Cafe	◆◆	Asian	$5-$17	416
86 / p. 302		Thai Star	◆◆	Thai	$5-$18	417
87 / p. 302		Zapata	◆◆	Mexican	$5-$17	417
88 / p. 302		Hi Life	◆◆◆	American	$7-$26	416
89 / p. 302		The Palace	◆◆	Indian	$9-$20	416
90 / p. 302		Frontera Mex-Mex Grill	◆◆	Tex-Mex	$5-$13	416
91 / p. 302		Saigon Cafe	◆◆	Vietnamese	$7-$9	416
92 / p. 302		Norcross Station Cafe	◆◆◆	American	$6-$25	416

Map Page	OA	Restaurants (cont'd)	Diamond Rated	Cuisine	Meal Range	Page
93 / p. 302		Dominick's	◆◆	Italian	$7-$22	416
94 / p. 302		JR's Log House	◆	American	$5-$14	416
95 / p. 302		Ashiana	◆◆	Indian	$2-$15	416
96 / p. 302		The Varsity	◆	American	$2-$10	417
97 / p. 302		Pho Hien	◆	Vietnamese	$4-$9	416

DORAVILLE

Map Page	OA	Lodgings	Diamond Rated	High Season	Page
147 / p. 302	AAA	**Holiday Inn Northeast/Doraville**	◆◆◆	$104-$134 SAVE	384
148 / p. 302	AAA	**Super 8 Atlanta NE**	◆◆	$46-$65 SAVE	384

Map Page	OA	Restaurants	Diamond Rated	Cuisine	Meal Range	Page
103 / p. 302		Pho 79	◆◆	Vietnamese	$5-$10	384
104 / p. 302		Seoul Garden Restaurant	◆◆	Korean	$6-$21	385
105 / p. 302		Hae Woon Dae	◆◆	Korean	$6-$14	384
106 / p. 302		Pung Mie	◆◆	Chinese	$4-$30	385
107 / p. 302		Pho Hoa	◆◆	Vietnamese	$5-$7	385
108 / p. 302		Little Szechuan	◆◆	Chinese	$6-$18	384

SNELLVILLE

Map Page	OA	Lodging	Diamond Rated	High Season	Page
151 / p. 302	AAA	**Super 8 Motel**	◆◆◆	$74-$120 SAVE	421

TUCKER

Map Page	OA	Lodgings	Diamond Rated	High Season	Page
154 / p. 302	AAA	**Atlanta Northlake TownePlace Suites**	◆◆◆	$157-$169 SAVE	423
155 / p. 302		Hampton Inn Atlanta-Northlake	◆◆◆	$104-$129	424
156 / p. 302	AAA	**Holiday Inn Atlanta Northlake**	◆◆◆	$99-$129 SAVE	424
157 / p. 302	AAA	**Quality Inn Atlanta/Northlake**	◆◆	$75-$99 SAVE	425
158 / p. 302		DoubleTree Hotel NE/Northlake	◆◆◆	$89-$199	424
159 / p. 302	AAA	**Courtyard by Marriott-Northlake**	◆◆◆	$177-$190 SAVE	424
160 / p. 302	AAA	**Country Inn & Suites by Carlson**	◆◆◆	$96 SAVE	424
161 / p. 302	AAA	**Comfort Suites-Northlake**	◆◆◆	$90-$159 SAVE	423
162 / p. 302	AAA	**Econo Lodge**	◆◆	$50-$70 SAVE	424
163 / p. 302		Motel 6 #2007	◆◆	$35-$41	425
164 / p. 302	AAA	**Masters Inn Tucker**	◆	$42-$75 SAVE	424

Map Page	OA	Restaurants	Diamond Rated	Cuisine	Meal Range	Page
116 / p. 302		Dynasty Garden	◆◆	Chinese	$6-$9	425
117 / p. 302		Fuji Ya	◆◆	Japanese	$7-$30	425
118 / p. 302		Blue Ribbon Grill	◆◆	American	$7-$16	425
119 / p. 302		Northlake Thai Cuisine	◆◆◆	Thai	$9-$18	425
120 / p. 302		Lumiere Restaurant	◆◆	American	$4-$15	425

SMYRNA

Map Page	OA	Lodgings	Diamond Rated	High Season	Page
167 / p. 302	AAA	**Comfort Inn & Suites**	◆◆◆	$80-$121 SAVE	419
168 / p. 302		Baymont Inn & Suites	◆◆	Rates not provided	419

SMYRNA (cont'd)

Map Page	OA	Lodgings (cont'd)	Diamond Rated	High Season	Page
169 / p. 302	AAA	**Microtel Inn**	♦♦	$50-$70 SAVE	420

STONE MOUNTAIN

Map Page	OA	Lodgings	Diamond Rated	High Season	Page
172 / p. 302		Hampton Inn	♦♦♦	$99-$149	422
173 / p. 302		Days Inn	♦♦	$69-$129	422
174 / p. 302	AAA	**Best Western Stone Mountain**	♦♦	$80-$115 SAVE	421
175 / p. 302	AAA	**Holiday Inn Express**	♦♦♦	$99-$139 SAVE	422
176 / p. 302		Country Inn & Suites by Carlson	♦♦♦	$94-$179	422
177 / p. 302		Comfort Inn	♦♦♦	$99-$159	422
178 / p. 302		Stone Mountain Inn	♦♦♦	$167-$179	422

Map Page	OA	Restaurant	Diamond Rated	Cuisine	Meal Range	Page
123 / p. 302		MGR Palace	♦♦	Indian	$3-$8	423

MARIETTA

Map Page	OA	Restaurant	Diamond Rated	Cuisine	Meal Range	Page
100 / p. 302		Trattoria La Strada	♦♦	Italian	$12-$20	409

CHAMBLEE

Map Page	OA	Restaurants	Diamond Rated	Cuisine	Meal Range	Page
111 / p. 302		Bombay Grill	♦♦♦	Indian	$9-$19	378
112 / p. 302		Penang Malaysian Cuisine	♦♦	Asian	$5-$18	378
113 / p. 302		Pho Tan Tan	♦♦	Vietnamese	$5-$11	378

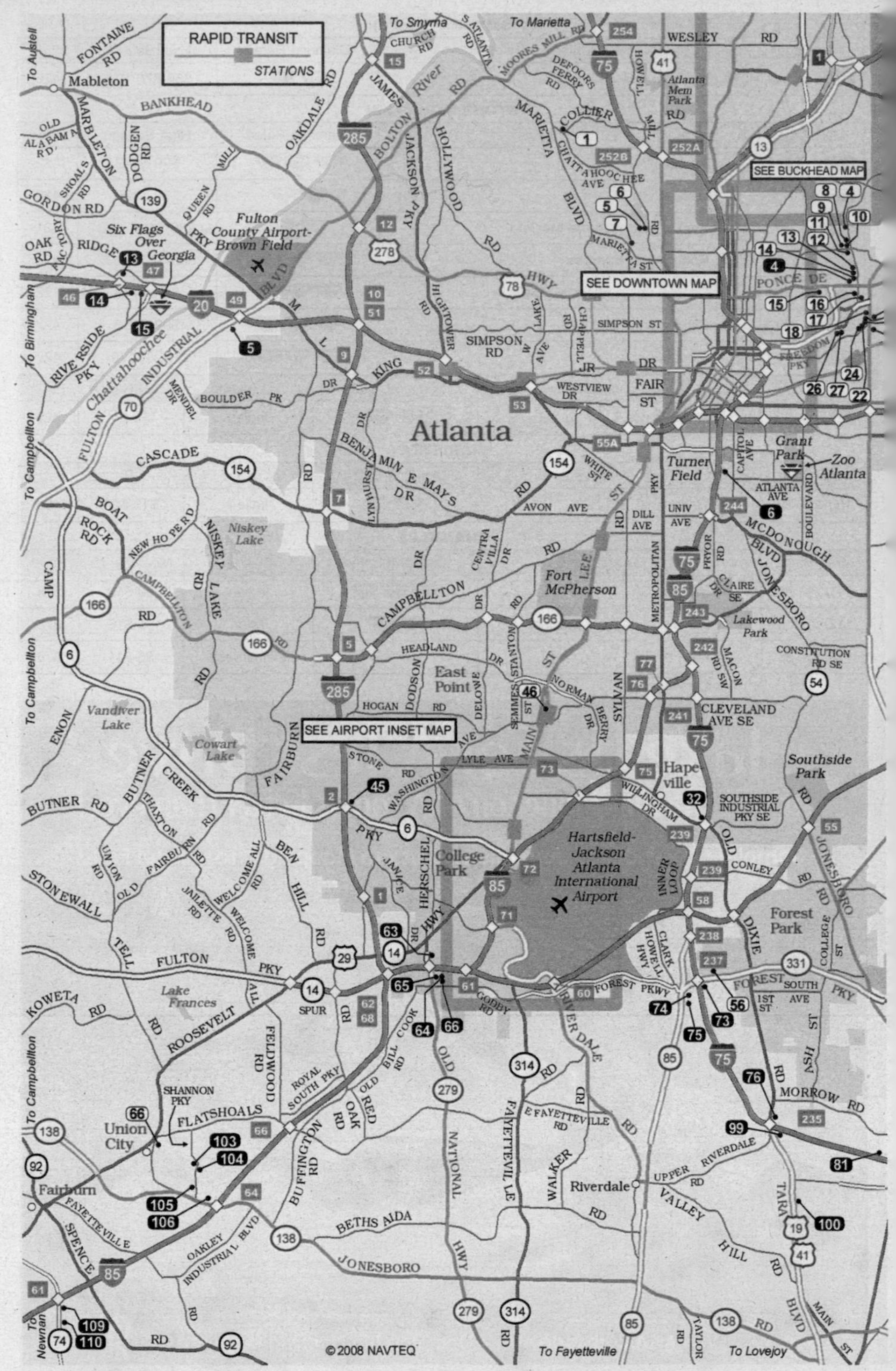
RAPID TRANSIT
STATIONS
SEE BUCKHEAD MAP
SEE DOWNTOWN MAP
SEE AIRPORT INSET MAP
Atlanta
Mableton
Six Flags Over Georgia
Fulton County Airport-Brown Field
Hartsfield-Jackson Atlanta International Airport
College Park
East Point
Hapeville
Forest Park
Union City
Fairburn
Riverdale
Fort McPherson
Turner Field
Grant Park
Zoo Atlanta
Lakewood Park
Southside Park
Niskey Lake
Vandiver Lake
Cowart Lake
Lake Frances
Atlanta Mem Park
To Smyrna
To Marietta
To Austell
To Birmingham
To Campbellton
To Newnan
To Fayetteville
To Lovejoy
© 2008 NAVTEQ

South Atlanta
Lodging & Dining
Miles
0
2.8
Atlanta
International
Airport Area
Hartsfield-Jackson
Atlanta
International
Airport
© AAA
To Greenville
To Doraville
To Snellville
To Conyers
To Jonesboro
To Macon
Decatur
Scottdale
Clarkston
Pine Lake
Avondale Estates
Stone Mountain
The Antebellum Plantation
Stone Mountain Park
Stone Mountain Lake
Venable Lake
Wade-Walker Park
East Lake
Panthersville
Lithonia
Conley
Fort Gillem
Ellenwood
Lake City
Morrow
Rex
CONVENTION CENTER CONCOURSE
1881-F

Airport Accommodations

Map Page	OA	THE WILLIAM B. HARTSFIELD ATLANTA INT'L	Diamond Rated	High Season	Page
7 / p. 312	AAA	**Renaissance Concourse Hotel, at the airport**	◆◆◆◆	$246-$264 SAVE	365
56 / p. 312	AAA	**Atlanta Airport Marriott, 2 mi sw of terminal**	◆◆◆	$236-$253 SAVE	378
48 / p. 312		Comfort Inn & Suites Atlanta Airport North, 1 mi n of terminal	◆◆◆	$99-$139	379
66 / p. 312		Comfort Inn & Suites-Atlanta Airport/South, 1.5 mi s of terminal	◆◆◆	$89-$199	379
67 / p. 312		Country Inn & Suites by Carlson, 1.3 mi s of terminal	◆◆◆	$90-$119	379
60 / p. 312	AAA	**Courtyard by Marriott Airport South, 1 mi s of terminal**	◆◆◆	$197-$211 SAVE	379
69 / p. 312		Days Inn Airport South, 1.3 mi s of terminal	◆◆	Rates not provided	379
63 / p. 312		Econo Lodge, 1.3 mi sw of terminal	◆◆	$50-$55	380
50 / p. 312		Embassy Suites Hotel at Atlanta Airport, opposite terminal	◆◆◆	$99-$209	380
59 / p. 312		Fairfield Inn & Suites Atlanta Airport South, 1 mi s of terminal	◆◆◆	$147-$158	380
55 / p. 312		Hampton Inn-Atlanta Airport, 1 mi s of terminal	◆◆◆	$94-$159	380
49 / p. 312		Holiday Inn Express-Atlanta Airport, 2 mi sw of terminal	◆◆◆	$79-$159	380
54 / p. 312	AAA	**Hyatt Place Atlanta Airport-South, 1 mi s of terminal**	◆◆◆	$79-$209 SAVE	381
61 / p. 312	AAA	**La Quinta Inn & Suites Atlanta Airport, 1 mi s of terminal**	◆◆◆	$80-$190 SAVE	381
62 / p. 312	AAA	**Microtel Inn-Atlanta Airport, 1 mi s of terminal**	◆◆	$69-$89 SAVE	381
68 / p. 312		Quality Hotel & Conference Center-Atlanta Airport, 1.3 mi s of terminal	◆◆◆	$80	381
64 / p. 312	AAA	**Quality Inn & Suites, 1.5 mi s of terminal**	◆◆	$74-$79 SAVE	381
58 / p. 312	AAA	**Sheraton Gateway Hotel, Atlanta Airport, 1 mi s of terminal**	◆◆◆	$89-$269 SAVE	382
52 / p. 312	AAA	**The Westin Hotel-Atlanta Airport, 1 mi s of terminal**	◆◆◆	$99-$529 SAVE	382
38 / p. 312	AAA	**Country Inn & Suites By Carlson, 1 mi n of terminal**	◆◆◆	$97-$105 SAVE	390
41 / p. 312		Crowne Plaza Hotel and Resort Atlanta Airport, 1 mi n of terminal	◆◆◆	$89-$209	391
35 / p. 312		DoubleTree Club Hotel Atlanta Airport, 1 mi n of terminal	◆◆◆	$79-$179	391
42 / p. 312		Drury Inn & Suites-Atlanta Airport, 1 mi n of terminal	◆◆◆	$90-$170	391
36 / p. 312		Fairfield Inn & Suites, 1 mi n of terminal	◆◆◆	$128-$137	391
44 / p. 312	AAA	**Ramada Atlanta Airport Conference Center, 1 mi n of terminal**	◆◆◆	$109-$159 SAVE	391
39 / p. 312	AAA	**Hyatt Place Atlanta Airport - North, 1 mi n of terminal**	◆◆◆	$99-$299 SAVE	392
43 / p. 312		Red Roof Inn-Atlanta Airport North, 1 mi n of terminal	◆◆	$71-$81	392
40 / p. 312	AAA	**Wellesley Inn (Atlanta/Hartsfield Int'l Airport), 1 mi n of terminal**	◆◆	$79-$119 SAVE	392
32 / p. 312	AAA	**Best Western Atlanta Airport East, 1 mi ne of terminal**	◆◆◆	$90-$150 SAVE	394
29 / p. 312	AAA	**Courtyard by Marriott Atlanta Airport North, 1 mi n of terminal**	◆◆◆	$197-$211 SAVE	394
31 / p. 312		Hilton Atlanta Airport, 0.8 mi n of terminal	◆◆◆◆	$99-$229	395
30 / p. 312	AAA	**Residence Inn Atlanta Airport, 1 mi n of terminal**	◆◆◆	$246-$264 SAVE	395

South Atlanta

This index helps you "spot" where approved lodgings and restaurants are located on the corresponding detailed maps. Lodging daily rate range is for comparison only and show the property's high season. Restaurant rate range is a combination of lunch and/or dinner. Turn to the listing page for more detailed rate information and consult display ads for special promotions.

ATLANTA SOUTH

Map Page	OA	Lodgings	Diamond Rated	High Season	Page
1 / p. 312		Emory Inn	◆◆◆	Rates not provided	364
2 / p. 312		Emory Conference Center Hotel	◆◆◆	$195-$229	364
3 / p. 312	AAA	**University Inn at Emory**	◆◆	$135-$250 SAVE	365
4 / p. 312		The Gaslight Inn B&B	◆◆◆	$115-$215	365
5 / p. 312		Days Inn Atlanta West/Six Flags	◆◆	$60-$100	364
6 / p. 312	AAA	**Comfort Inn @ Turner Field**	◆◆	$89-$149 SAVE	364
7 / p. 312	AAA	**Renaissance Concourse Hotel - see color ad p 328**	◆◆◆◆	$246-$264 SAVE	365

Map Page	OA	Restaurants	Diamond Rated	Cuisine	Meal Range	Page
1 / p. 312		Nuevo Laredo Cantina	◆◆	Mexican	$3-$18	366
2 / p. 312		Floataway Cafe	◆◆◆	New American	$15-$36	366
3 / p. 312		Dusty's Barbeque	◆	Barbecue	$5-$15	365
4 / p. 312		Sala-Sabor de Mexico	◆◆◆	Regional Mexican	$5-$20	367
5 / p. 312		Bacchanalia	◆◆◆◆	Northern American	$72-$125	365
6 / p. 312		JCT Kitchen & Bar	◆◆	American	$4-$29	366
7 / p. 312	AAA	**The Food Studio**	◆◆◆◆	New American	$6-$32	366
8 / p. 312		Highland Tap	◆◆	American	$4-$40	366
9 / p. 312		La Tavola Trattoria	◆◆◆	Italian	$4-$26	366
10 / p. 312		Noche	◆◆	Spanish	$4-$15	366
11 / p. 312		Murphy's	◆◆	American	$5-$24	366
12 / p. 312		Osteria 832	◆◆	Italian	$3-$13	367
13 / p. 312		Surin of Thailand	◆◆	Thai	$6-$17	367
14 / p. 312		Belly General Store	◆	Deli	$2-$7	365
15 / p. 312		Cameli's Gourmet Pizza Joint	◆	Pizza	$3-$30	365
16 / p. 312		Soul Vegetarian II	◆◆	Vegetarian	$6-$14	367
17 / p. 312		Babette's Cafe	◆◆◆	French	$3-$25	365
18 / p. 312		Savage Pizza	◆	Pizza	$2-$20	367
19 / p. 312		Planet Bombay	◆◆	Indian	$6-$25	367
20 / p. 312		The Vortex Bar & Grill	◆	American	$4-$9	367
21 / p. 312		Little 5 Corner Tavern	◆◆	American	$5-$15	366
22 / p. 312		Calcutta	◆◆	Indian	$4-$15	365
23 / p. 312		Flying Biscuit Cafe	◆◆	American	$5-$15	366
24 / p. 312		Sweet Lime	◆◆	Asian	$4-$18	367
25 / p. 312		Sabroso	◆◆	Spanish	$4-$10	367
26 / p. 312		Sotto Sotto	◆◆◆	Italian	$7-$34	367
27 / p. 312		Fritti	◆◆	Regional Italian	$4-$14	366

STONE MOUNTAIN

Map Page	OA	Lodging	Diamond Rated	High Season	Page
10 / p. 312	AAA	**Marriott Evergreen Conference Resort**	◆◆◆◆	$195-$215 SAVE	422

Map Page	OA	Restaurant	Diamond Rated	Cuisine	Meal Range	Page
30 / p. 312		Continental Park Cafe	◆◆	American	$7-$9	423

AUSTELL

Map Page	OA	Lodgings	Diamond Rated	High Season	Page
13 / p. 312		Baymont Inn-Six Flags	◆◆◆	$60-$76	376
14 / p. 312	AAA	**Sleep Inn**	◆◆	$55-$120 SAVE	376
15 / p. 312		Wingate By Wyndham at Six Flags	◆◆◆	$89-$210	376

DECATUR

Map Page	OA	Lodgings	Diamond Rated	High Season	Page
18 / p. 312	AAA	**Holiday Inn Express, Atlanta-Emory**	◆◆◆	$100-$169 SAVE	383
19 / p. 312	AAA	**Super 8 Motel**	◆◆	$60-$150 SAVE	383
20 / p. 312		Holiday Inn Select	◆◆◆	Rates not provided	383
21 / p. 312		America's Best Inn & Suites	◆◆	$65	382
22 / p. 312		Econo Lodge	◆◆	$45-$150	382

Map Page	OA	Restaurants	Diamond Rated	Cuisine	Meal Range	Page
33 / p. 312		Madras Saravana Bhavan	◆◆	Indian	$3-$12	383
34 / p. 312		Udipi Cafe	◆◆	Indian	$5-$15	384
35 / p. 312		Cafe Istanbul	◆◆	Turkish	$7-$17	383
36 / p. 312		Athens Pizza House	◆◆	Greek	$5-$11	383
37 / p. 312		Watershed	◆◆	Southern American	$8-$34	384
38 / p. 312		Cafe' Alsace	◆◆	French	$3-$21	383
39 / p. 312		Crescent Moon	◆◆	American	$1-$14	383
40 / p. 312		Brick Store Pub	◆◆	American	$4-$9	383
41 / p. 312		SAGE	◆◆◆	American	$6-$22	384
42 / p. 312		Feast Restaurant	◆◆◆	Continental	$2-$24	383
43 / p. 312		Universal Joint	◆◆	American	$5-$9	384

LITHONIA

Map Page	OA	Lodgings	Diamond Rated	High Season	Page
25 / p. 312		Super 8 Motel	◆◆	Rates not provided	404
26 / p. 312	AAA	**Red Roof Inn**	◆◆	$80-$90 SAVE	403

HAPEVILLE

Map Page	OA	Lodgings	Diamond Rated	High Season	Page
29 / p. 312	AAA	**Courtyard by Marriott Atlanta Airport North**	◆◆◆	$197-$211 SAVE	394
30 / p. 312	AAA	**Residence Inn Atlanta Airport**	◆◆◆	$246-$264 SAVE	395
31 / p. 312		Hilton Atlanta Airport	◆◆◆◆	$99-$229	395
32 / p. 312	AAA	**Best Western Atlanta Airport East - see color ad p 322**	◆◆◆	$90-$150 SAVE	394

EAST POINT

Map Page	OA	Lodgings	Diamond Rated	High Season	Page
35 / p. 312		DoubleTree Club Hotel Atlanta Airport	◆◆◆	$79-$179	391
36 / p. 312		Fairfield Inn & Suites	◆◆◆	$128-$137	391

EAST POINT (cont'd)

Map Page	OA	Lodgings (cont'd)	Diamond Rated	High Season	Page
37 / p. 312		Hampton Inn & Suites-Atlanta Airport North	3 Diamonds	$109-$199	391
38 / p. 312	AAA	**Country Inn & Suites By Carlson**	3 Diamonds	$97-$105 SAVE	390
39 / p. 312	AAA	**Hyatt Place Atlanta Airport - North**	3 Diamonds	$99-$299 SAVE	391
40 / p. 312	AAA	**Wellesley Inn (Atlanta/Hartsfield Int'l Airport)**	2 Diamonds	$79-$119 SAVE	392
41 / p. 312		Crowne Plaza Hotel and Resort Atlanta Airport	3 Diamonds	$89-$209	391
42 / p. 312		Drury Inn & Suites-Atlanta Airport	3 Diamonds	$90-$170	391
43 / p. 312		Red Roof Inn-Atlanta Airport North	2 Diamonds	$71-$81	392
44 / p. 312	AAA	**Ramada Atlanta Airport Conference Center**	3 Diamonds	$109-$159 SAVE	392
45 / p. 312		Comfort Inn & Suites Atlanta Airport Camp Creek	2 Diamonds	$79-$119	390

Map Page	OA	Restaurants	Diamond Rated	Cuisine	Meal Range	Page
46 / p. 312		Lov'n It Live	2 Diamonds	Natural/Organic	$9-$18	392
47 / p. 312		Giovanna's Italian Kitchen	2 Diamonds	Italian	$5-$24	392
48 / p. 312		Malone's Steak & Seafood	2 Diamonds	American	$8-$22	392

COLLEGE PARK

Map Page	OA	Lodgings	Diamond Rated	High Season	Page
48 / p. 312		Comfort Inn & Suites Atlanta Airport North	3 Diamonds	$99-$139	379
49 / p. 312		Holiday Inn Express-Atlanta Airport	3 Diamonds	$79-$159	380
50 / p. 312		Embassy Suites Hotel at Atlanta Airport	3 Diamonds	$99-$209	380
51 / p. 312	AAA	**Holiday Inn Select-Atlanta Airport South**	3 Diamonds	$99-$194 SAVE	381
52 / p. 312	AAA	**The Westin Hotel-Atlanta Airport**	3 Diamonds	$99-$529 SAVE	382
53 / p. 312		Sleep Inn/Atlanta Airport	2 Diamonds	$65-$150	382
54 / p. 312	AAA	**Hyatt Place Atlanta Airport-South**	3 Diamonds	$79-$209 SAVE	381
55 / p. 312		Hampton Inn-Atlanta Airport	3 Diamonds	$94-$159	380
56 / p. 312	AAA	**Atlanta Airport Marriott**	3 Diamonds	$236-$253 SAVE	378
57 / p. 312	AAA	**Hilton Garden Inn-Atlanta Airport/Millenium Center**	3 Diamonds	$89-$199 SAVE	380
58 / p. 312	AAA	**Sheraton Gateway Hotel, Atlanta Airport**	3 Diamonds	$89-$269 SAVE	382
59 / p. 312		Fairfield Inn & Suites Atlanta Airport South	3 Diamonds	$147-$158	380
60 / p. 312	AAA	**Courtyard by Marriott Airport South**	3 Diamonds	$197-$211 SAVE	379
61 / p. 312	AAA	**La Quinta Inn & Suites Atlanta Airport**	3 Diamonds	$80-$190 SAVE	381
62 / p. 312	AAA	**Microtel Inn-Atlanta Airport**	2 Diamonds	$69-$89 SAVE	381
63 / p. 312		Econo Lodge	2 Diamonds	$50-$55	380
64 / p. 312	AAA	**Quality Inn & Suites**	2 Diamonds	$74-$79 SAVE	381
65 / p. 312		Clarion Hotel-Atlanta Airport	3 Diamonds	$89	379
66 / p. 312		Comfort Inn & Suites-Atlanta Airport/South	3 Diamonds	$89-$199	379
67 / p. 312		Country Inn & Suites by Carlson	3 Diamonds	$90-$119	379
68 / p. 312		Quality Hotel & Conference Center-Atlanta Airport	3 Diamonds	$80	381
69 / p. 312		Days Inn Airport South	2 Diamonds	Rates not provided	379
70 / p. 312	AAA	**Best Western Hotel & Suites**	3 Diamonds	$89-$99 SAVE	379

Map Page	OA	Restaurants	Diamond Rated	Cuisine	Meal Range	Page
51 / p. 312		Brake Pad	1 Diamond	American	$6-$11	382

Map Page	OA	Restaurants (cont'd)	Diamond Rated	Cuisine	Meal Range	Page
52 / p. 312		Simon's	◆◆	American	$3-$33	382
53 / p. 312		The Feed Store	◆◆	American	$8-$35	382

FOREST PARK

Map Page	OA	Lodgings	Diamond Rated	High Season	Page
73 / p. 312		Econo Lodge	◆◆	$40-$53	394
74 / p. 312		Days Inn-Airport East	◆◆	$53-$95	393
75 / p. 312		Ramada Limited Suites	◆◆◆	$65-$125	394
76 / p. 312		Super 8 Motel	◆◆	$50-$100	394

Map Page	OA	Restaurant	Diamond Rated	Cuisine	Meal Range	Page
56 / p. 312		Oakwood Cafe	◆◆	Southern	$3-$16	394

MORROW

Map Page	OA	Lodgings	Diamond Rated	High Season	Page
79 / p. 312	AAA	**Best Western Southlake Inn**	◆◆	$59-$99 SAVE	410
80 / p. 312	AAA	**Comfort Suites Morrow**	◆◆◆	$79-$199 SAVE	410
81 / p. 312	AAA	**Red Roof Inn-South**	◆◆	$50-$90 SAVE	411
82 / p. 312		Drury Inn & Suites-Atlanta South	◆◆◆	$85-$140	410
83 / p. 312		Hampton Inn Southlake	◆◆◆	$85-$129	410
84 / p. 312	AAA	**Country Inn & Suites by Carlson-Atlanta I-75 South**	◆◆◆	$89-$99 SAVE	410
85 / p. 312		Sleep Inn	◆◆	$55-$90	411
86 / p. 312		Extended StayAmerica-Atlanta-Morrow	◆◆	$60-$75	410

Map Page	OA	Restaurant	Diamond Rated	Cuisine	Meal Range	Page
59 / p. 312		China Cafe	◆◆	Chinese	$6-$20	411

STOCKBRIDGE

Map Page	OA	Lodgings	Diamond Rated	High Season	Page
89 / p. 312	AAA	**Quality Inn & Suites**	◆◆	$54-$77 SAVE	548
90 / p. 312	AAA	**Hampton Inn-Atlanta-Stockbridge**	◆◆◆	$109-$165 SAVE	547
91 / p. 312	AAA	**La Quinta Inn & Suites**	◆◆◆	$74-$134 SAVE	548
92 / p. 312	AAA	**Country Hearth Inn & Suites**	◆◆	Rates not provided SAVE	547
93 / p. 312	AAA	**Comfort Suites Stockbridge**	◆◆◆	$99-$159 SAVE	547
94 / p. 312		Sleep Inn & Suites	◆◆◆	$60-$149	548
95 / p. 312		Holiday Inn Hotel & Suites	◆◆◆	$117-$275	547
96 / p. 312	AAA	**Howard Johnson Stockbridge**	◆◆	$60-$140 SAVE	547

Map Page	OA	Restaurants	Diamond Rated	Cuisine	Meal Range	Page
62 / p. 312		Frontera Mex-Mex Grill	◆◆	Mexican	$5-$14	548
63 / p. 312		Chin Chin Osaki	◆◆	Asian	$6-$20	548

JONESBORO

Map Page	OA	Lodgings	Diamond Rated	High Season	Page
99 / p. 312	AAA	**Holiday Inn Atlanta South Jonesboro**	◆◆◆	$75-$175 SAVE	395
100 / p. 312		Tara Inn & Suites	◆◆	$70-$130	395

UNION CITY

Map Page	OA	Lodgings	Diamond Rated	High Season	Page
103 / p. 312	AAA	**Microtel Inn & Suites**	◆◆	$50-$70 SAVE	426
104 / p. 312		Days Inn Shannon Mall	◆◆	$60-$85	426

UNION CITY (cont'd)

Map Page	OA	Lodgings (cont'd)	Diamond Rated	High Season	Page
105 / p. 312	AAA	**Best Western Union City Inn & Suites**	◆◆◆	$60-$99 SAVE	425
106 / p. 312	AAA	**Comfort Inn Atlanta Airport Union City**	◆◆◆	$79-$99 SAVE	425

Map Page	OA	Restaurant	Diamond Rated	Cuisine	Meal Range	Page
66 / p. 312		The Historic Green Manor Restaurant	◆◆	Southern	$11-$15	426

FAIRBURN

Map Page	OA	Lodgings	Diamond Rated	High Season	Page
109 / p. 312		Hampton Inn Atlanta/Fairburn	◆◆◆	$99-$129	393
110 / p. 312		Wingate Inn	◆◆◆	$99	393

DOWNTOWN ATLANTA

(See map and index starting on p. 288)

WHERE TO STAY

ATLANTA MARRIOTT DOWNTOWN Book great rates at AAA.com Phone: (404)688-8600 

Hotel
$189-$202 All Year

Address: 160 Spring St NW **Location:** I-75/85, exit 248C (International Blvd) northbound; exit 249C (Williams St) southbound. **Facility:** Smoke free premises. 312 units. 286 one-bedroom standard units. 24 one- and 2 two-bedroom suites, some with whirlpools. 9 stories, interior corridors. *Bath:* combo or shower only. **Parking:** valet. **Terms:** cancellation fee imposed. **Amenities:** high-speed Internet (fee), dual phone lines, voice mail, irons, hair dryers. *Some:* CD players. **Pool(s):** heated outdoor. **Leisure Activities:** exercise room. **Guest Services:** valet laundry, wireless Internet. **Business Services:** conference facilities, business center. **Cards:** AX, CB, DC, DS, JC, MC, VI.

FEE 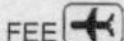    

Marriott HOTELS & RESORTS

AAA Benefit:
Members save a minimum 5% off the best available rate.

▼ See AAA listing p 353 ▼

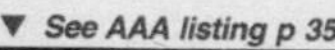

(See map and index starting on p. 288)

ATLANTA MARRIOTT MARQUIS *Book great rates at AAA.com* **Phone:** (404)521-0000 20

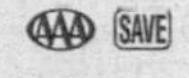

Hotel
$318-$339 All Year

Address: 265 Peachtree Center Ave **Location:** I-75/85, exit 249A, 0.3 mi s to International Blvd, just w to Peachtree Center Ave, then just n. **Facility:** Smoke free premises. 1675 units. 1607 one-bedroom standard units. 68 one-bedroom suites. 47 stories, interior corridors. **Parking:** valet. **Terms:** cancellation fee imposed. **Amenities:** high-speed Internet (fee), dual phone lines, voice mail, safes, irons, hair dryers. *Some:* video games (fee). **Dining:** 4 restaurants. **Pool(s):** heated indoor/outdoor. **Leisure Activities:** saunas, whirlpool, steamroom, spa. **Guest Services:** valet laundry, wireless Internet. **Business Services:** conference facilities, business center. **Cards:** AX, CB, DC, DS, JC, MC, VI. **Free Special Amenities:** newspaper.

 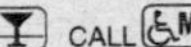 CALL  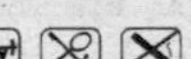 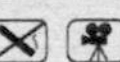 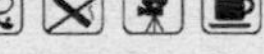

Marriott HOTELS & RESORTS

AAA Benefit:
Members save a minimum 5% off the best available rate.

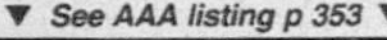
▼ See AAA listing p 353 ▼

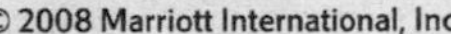

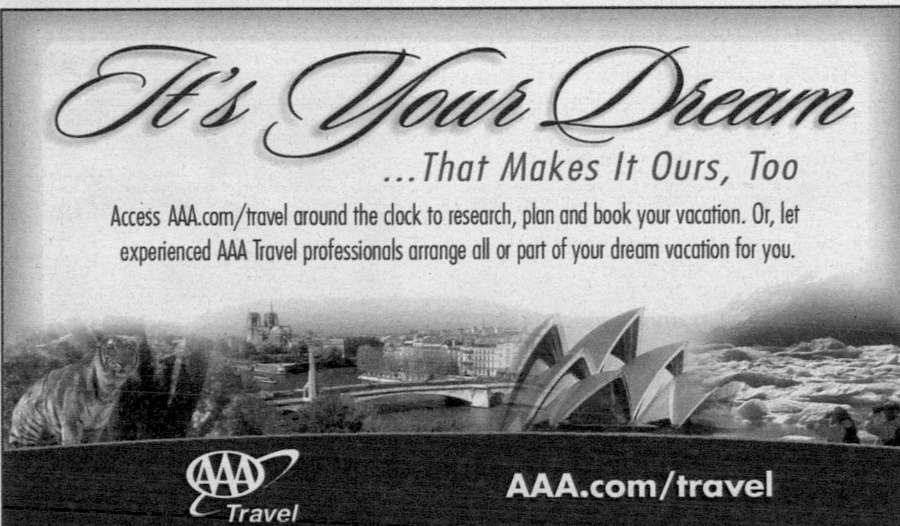

(See map and index starting on p. 288)

ATLANTA MARRIOTT SUITES MIDTOWN Book great rates at AAA.com Phone: (404)876-8888 

Hotel
$277-$298 All Year

Address: 35 14th St **Location:** I-75/85, exit 250 (14th St), 0.3 mi e. **Facility:** Smoke free premises. 254 one-bedroom suites. 19 stories, interior corridors. **Parking:** on-site (fee) and valet. **Terms:** check-in 4 pm, cancellation fee imposed. **Amenities:** voice mail, irons, hair dryers. *Fee:* video games, high-speed Internet. **Pool(s):** heated indoor/outdoor. **Leisure Activities:** whirlpool, exercise room. **Guest Services:** valet and coin laundry, wireless Internet. **Business Services:** meeting rooms, business center. **Cards:** AX, CB, DC, DS, JC, MC, VI. **Free Special Amenities:** newspaper.

FEE

Marriott HOTELS & RESORTS
AAA Benefit:
Members save a minimum 5% off the best available rate.

BAYMONT INN & SUITES ATLANTA DOWNTOWN Book at AAA.com Phone: (404)659-7777 26

Hotel
$109-$219 All Year

Address: 175 Piedmont Ave NE **Location:** I-75/85, exit 248C northbound; exit 249A southbound, 0.3 mi s on Courtland St to Ellis, then just e. **Facility:** 242 units. 231 one-bedroom standard units. 11 one-bedroom suites. 6 stories, exterior corridors. **Parking:** on-site (fee). **Terms:** cancellation fee imposed. **Amenities:** video games (fee), high-speed Internet, voice mail, irons, hair dryers. **Pool(s):** outdoor. **Leisure Activities:** whirlpool, exercise room. **Guest Services:** valet and coin laundry, wireless Internet. **Business Services:** meeting rooms, PC, fax (fee). **Cards:** AX, CB, DC, DS, JC, MC, VI.

ASK FEE CALL / SOME UNITS

BEST WESTERN GRANADA SUITE HOTEL Book great rates at AAA.com Phone: (404)876-6100 2

Hotel
$109-$209 All Year

Address: 1302 W Peachtree St **Location:** I-75/85, exit 250 (14th St), just e, then just n on W Peachtree St to 16th St. **Facility:** 104 units. 77 two-bedroom standard units, some with efficiencies, kitchens and/or whirlpools. 20 one- and 7 two-bedroom suites, some with kitchens. 3 stories, interior corridors. *Bath:* combo or shower only. **Parking:** on-site. **Amenities:** video games (fee), high-speed Internet, voice mail, irons, hair dryers. **Leisure Activities:** pool privileges, exercise room. **Guest Services:** valet and coin laundry, area transportation-within 3 mi, wireless Internet. **Business Services:** meeting rooms, PC. **Cards:** AX, DS, MC, VI.

FEE / SOME UNITS FEE

AAA Benefit:
Members save up to 20%, plus 10% bonus points with rewards program.

▼ See AAA listing p 394 ▼

(See map and index starting on p. 288)

COURTYARD BY MARRIOTT ATLANTA MIDTOWN Book great rates at AAA.com **Phone:** (404)607-1112 

Hotel

$205-$236 All Year

Address: 1132 Techwood Dr **Location:** I-75/85, exit 250, just s. **Facility:** Smoke free premises. 164 units. 150 one-bedroom standard units. 14 one-bedroom suites. 7 stories, interior corridors. **Parking:** on-site. **Terms:** cancellation fee imposed. **Amenities:** high-speed Internet (fee), voice mail, irons, hair dryers. **Pool(s):** outdoor. **Leisure Activities:** whirlpool, exercise room. **Guest Services:** valet and coin laundry, wireless Internet. **Business Services:** meeting rooms, business center. **Cards:** AX, CB, DC, DS, JC, MC, VI. **Free Special Amenities: newspaper and high-speed Internet.**

FEE   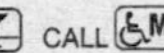 CALL     / SOME UNITS

AAA Benefit:

Members save a minimum 5% off the best available rate.

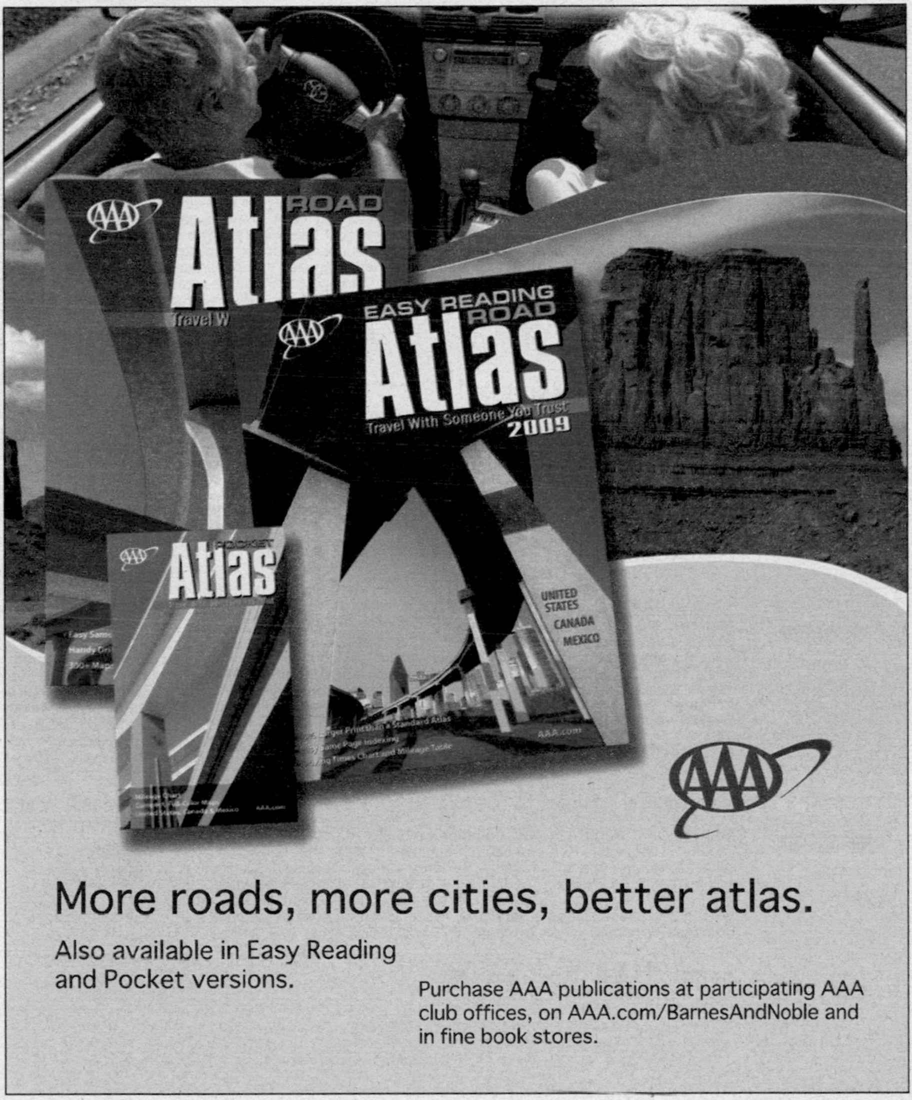

(See map and index starting on p. 288)

DAYS INN DOWNTOWN Book great rates at AAA.com Phone: (404)523-1144 17

Hotel
$99-$199 All Year

Address: 300 Spring St **Location:** I-75/85, exit 248C northbound; exit 249C southbound, 0.4 mi s. Located across from Apparel Mart. **Facility:** 263 one-bedroom standard units. 10 stories, interior corridors. **Parking:** on-site (fee). **Terms:** 3 day cancellation notice. **Amenities:** high-speed Internet, voice mail, irons, hair dryers. *Fee:* video games, safes. *Some:* dual phone lines. **Pool(s):** outdoor. **Leisure Activities:** exercise room. **Guest Services:** valet and coin laundry, wireless Internet. **Business Services:** meeting rooms, fax. **Cards:** AX, CB, DC, DS, MC, VI.

ASK FEE CALL / SOME UNITS

EMBASSY SUITES CENTENNIAL OLYMPIC PARK Book great rates at AAA.com Phone: (404)223-2300 22

Hotel
$135-$330 All Year

Address: 267 Marietta St **Location:** Just w of International Blvd and Marietta St. **Facility:** 321 one-bedroom standard units. 8 stories, interior corridors. **Parking:** valet. **Terms:** 1-30 night minimum stay, cancellation fee imposed. **Amenities:** dual phone lines, voice mail, safes, irons, hair dryers. *Fee:* video games, high-speed Internet. **Pool(s):** heated outdoor. **Leisure Activities:** sauna, whirlpool, exercise room. **Guest Services:** valet and coin laundry, wireless Internet. **Business Services:** conference facilities, business center. **Cards:** AX, CB, DC, DS, MC, VI.

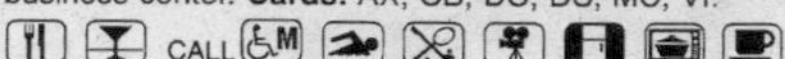

AAA Benefit:
Members save 5% or more everyday!

FOUR SEASONS HOTEL ATLANTA Book great rates at AAA.com Phone: (404)881-9898 5

Hotel
$430-$4700 All Year

Address: 75 14th St **Location:** I-75/85, exit 250 (14th St), 0.3 mi e. Located in art and business district. **Facility:** An imported crystal chandelier lights the grand staircase's red Spanish marble at this service-oriented hotel. 244 units. 226 one-bedroom standard units. 14 one- and 4 two-bedroom suites. 19 stories, interior corridors. **Parking:** on-site (fee) and valet. **Terms:** cancellation fee imposed. **Amenities:** video library, DVD players, CD players, dual phone lines, voice mail, safes, honor bars, irons, hair dryers. *Fee:* video games, high-speed Internet. *Some:* fax. **Dining:** Park 75, see separate listing. **Pool(s):** heated indoor. **Leisure Activities:** saunas, whirlpool, steamrooms, spa. **Guest Services:** valet laundry, area transportation-within 7 mi, personal trainer, wireless Internet. **Business Services:** meeting rooms, business center. **Cards:** AX, DC, DS, MC, VI. **Free Special Amenities: local telephone calls and newspaper.**

FEE 24 CALL / SOME UNITS

THE GEORGIAN TERRACE HOTEL Book at AAA.com Phone: (404)897-1991 12

Classic Hotel
$189-$349 All Year

Address: 659 Peachtree St **Location:** I-75/85, exit 249D, 0.5 mi e to Peachtree St, then just n. **Facility:** The 1911 Atlanta landmark, which hosted the 1939 "Gone With The Wind" premiere in its grand ballroom, has been renovated to maintain its elegance. 307 units. 80 one-bedroom standard units, some with kitchens. 196 one-, 23 two- and 8 three-bedroom suites with kitchens. 19 stories, interior corridors. **Parking:** on-site (fee) and valet. **Amenities:** high-speed Internet, dual phone lines, voice mail, irons, hair dryers. **Pool(s):** heated outdoor. **Leisure Activities:** exercise room. **Guest Services:** valet and coin laundry, wireless Internet. **Business Services:** conference facilities, business center. **Cards:** AX, DC, DS, MC, VI.

ASK FEE / SOME UNITS

THE GLENN HOTEL Book at AAA.com Phone: (404)521-2250 34

Hotel
$129-$389 All Year

Address: 110 Marietta St NW **Location:** I-75/85, exit 248C northbound, 0.8 mi w, then just n; exit 249A southbound, just s to Baker St, just w, then just n. **Facility:** 110 units. 95 one-bedroom standard units. 15 one-bedroom suites. 10 stories, interior corridors. *Bath:* combo or shower only. **Parking:** valet. **Terms:** 3 day cancellation notice-fee imposed. **Amenities:** video games (fee), high-speed Internet, dual phone lines, voice mail, safes, honor bars, irons, hair dryers. *Some:* CD players. **Leisure Activities:** exercise room. **Guest Services:** valet laundry, wireless Internet. **Business Services:** meeting rooms, business center. **Cards:** AX, DS, MC, VI.

ASK FEE CALL / SOME UNITS FEE

HAMPTON INN Book great rates at AAA.com Phone: (404)881-0881 13

Hotel
$124-$169 All Year

Address: 244 North Ave NW **Location:** I-75/85, exit 249D, 0.4 mi w. **Facility:** 108 units. 106 one-bedroom standard units. 2 one-bedroom suites. 6 stories, interior corridors. **Parking:** on-site. **Terms:** 1-30 night minimum stay, cancellation fee imposed. **Amenities:** high-speed Internet, voice mail, irons, hair dryers. **Leisure Activities:** exercise room. *Fee:* game room. **Guest Services:** valet laundry, wireless Internet. **Business Services:** meeting rooms, PC, fax (fee). **Cards:** AX, CB, DC, DS, JC, MC, VI.

AAA Benefit:
Members save up to 10% everyday!

(See map and index starting on p. 288)

HAMPTON INN & SUITES ATLANTA DOWNTOWN *Book great rates at AAA.com* **Phone:** (404)589-1111 29

Hotel

$79-$250 All Year

Address: 161 Spring St NW **Location:** I-75/85, exit 248C northbound, 0.5 mi w, then just s; exit 249C southbound, 0.5 mi s. **Facility:** 119 units. 77 one-bedroom standard units, some with efficiencies. 42 one-bedroom suites with efficiencies. 8 stories, interior corridors. **Parking:** on-site (fee). **Terms:** 1-30 night minimum stay, cancellation fee imposed. **Amenities:** high-speed Internet, dual phone lines, voice mail, irons, hair dryers. **Leisure Activities:** exercise room. **Guest Services:** valet and coin laundry, wireless Internet. **Business Services:** meeting rooms, business center. **Cards:** AX, CB, DC, DS, MC, VI.

FEE  / SOME UNITS

AAA Benefit:
Members save up to 10% everyday!

HILTON ATLANTA *Book great rates at AAA.com* **Phone:** (404)659-2000 21

Hotel

$99-$299 All Year

Address: 255 Courtland St NE **Location:** I-75/85, exit 249A southbound; exit 248C northbound, just w to Piedmont Ave, just n to Baker St, then just w. **Facility:** 1226 units. 1184 one-bedroom standard units. 40 one- and 2 two-bedroom suites. 28 stories, interior corridors. **Parking:** on-site (fee) and valet. **Terms:** 1-30 night minimum stay, cancellation fee imposed. **Amenities:** high-speed Internet (fee), dual phone lines, voice mail, safes, honor bars, irons, hair dryers. **Dining:** Nikolai's Roof, Trader Vic's, see separate listings. **Pool(s):** outdoor. **Leisure Activities:** saunas, steamroom, jogging, basketball. *Fee:* 3 lighted tennis courts, massage. **Guest Services:** valet laundry, wireless Internet. **Business Services:** conference facilities, business center. **Cards:** AX, CB, DC, DS, JC, MC, VI.

    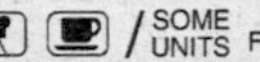 / SOME UNITS FEE 

AAA Benefit:
Members save 5% or more everyday!

HOLIDAY INN ATLANTA DOWNTOWN *Book at AAA.com* **Phone:** (404)524-5555 23

Hotel

$89-$259 All Year

Address: 101 Andrew Young International Blvd **Location:** I-75/85, exit 248C northbound, 0.6 mi w; exit 249C southbound, 0.5 mi s. **Facility:** 260 units. 257 one-bedroom standard units. 3 one-bedroom suites. 11 stories, interior corridors. **Parking:** valet. **Amenities:** video games (fee), high-speed Internet, dual phone lines, voice mail, irons, hair dryers. **Pool(s):** outdoor. **Leisure Activities:** whirlpool, exercise room. **Guest Services:** valet and coin laundry, wireless Internet. **Business Services:** meeting rooms, business center. **Cards:** AX, DC, DS, MC, VI.

ASK FEE 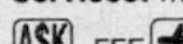  CALL  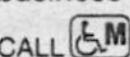  / SOME UNITS 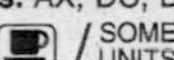   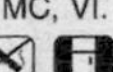 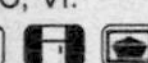

▼ *See AAA listing p 419* ▼

(See map and index starting on p. 288)

HOTEL INDIGO Book at AAA.com Phone: 404/874-9200 11

Hotel
Rates not provided

Address: 683 Peachtree St NE **Location:** I-75/85, exit 249D, 0.5 mi e to Peachtree St, then just n. **Facility:** 140 one-bedroom standard units. 12 stories, interior corridors. *Bath:* shower only. **Parking:** on-site. **Amenities:** CD players, high-speed Internet, voice mail, irons, hair dryers. *Some:* DVD players. **Leisure Activities:** exercise room. **Guest Services:** valet laundry, area transportation, wireless Internet. **Business Services:** meeting rooms, PC, fax (fee).

FEE CALL / SOME UNITS VCR

HYATT PLACE ATLANTA DOWNTOWN Book great rates at AAA.com Phone: (404)577-1980 15

SAVE

Hotel
$119-$299 All Year

Address: 330 Peachtree St NE **Location:** I-75/85, exit 249A to Baker St, 0.3 mi w to Peachtree St, then just n. **Facility:** 94 one-bedroom standard units. 10 stories, interior corridors. **Parking:** on-site (fee). **Terms:** cancellation fee imposed. **Amenities:** high-speed Internet, dual phone lines, voice mail, irons, hair dryers. **Leisure Activities:** limited exercise equipment. **Guest Services:** valet laundry, area transportation-within 3 mi, wireless Internet. **Business Services:** meeting rooms, business center. **Cards:** AX, CB, DC, DS, JC, MC, VI. **Free Special Amenities: continental breakfast and high-speed Internet.**

FEE VCR / SOME UNITS

HYATT PLACE
AAA Benefit:
Ask for the AAA rate and save 10%.

HYATT REGENCY ATLANTA Book great rates at AAA.com Phone: (404)577-1234 19

SAVE

Hotel
$99-$399 All Year

Address: 265 Peachtree St NE **Location:** I-75/85, exit 248C northbound, 0.4 mi w, then just n; exit 249A southbound, just s to Baker St, then just w; in Peachtree Center Shopping and Office Complex. **Facility:** 1260 units. 1208 one-bedroom standard units. 41 one- and 11 two-bedroom suites. 22-24 stories, interior corridors. *Bath:* combo or shower only. **Parking:** valet. **Terms:** cancellation fee imposed. **Amenities:** high-speed Internet (fee), dual phone lines, voice mail, safes, irons, hair dryers. **Dining:** 3 restaurants. **Pool(s):** outdoor. **Leisure Activities:** *Fee:* massage. **Guest Services:** valet laundry, wireless Internet. **Business Services:** conference facilities, business center. **Cards:** AX, CB, DC, DS, JC, MC, VI. **Free Special Amenities: newspaper and early check-in/late check-out.** ***(See color ad below)***

FEE FEE / SOME UNITS

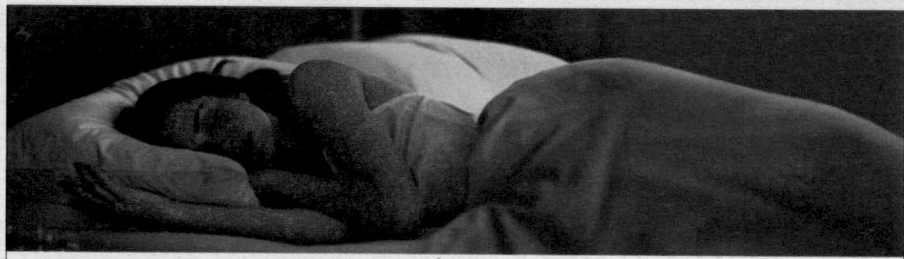

HYATT HOTELS & RESORTS
AAA Benefit:
Ask for the AAA rate and save 10%.

(See map and index starting on p. 288)

INN AT THE PEACHTREES Book great rates at AAA.com Phone: (404)577-6970 16

Hotel
$90-$110 All Year

Address: 330 W Peachtree St **Location:** I-75/85, exit 248C northbound, 0.4 mi w to Peachtree St, then 0.3 mi n; exit 249C southbound, just s to Peachtree Pl, then just e. **Facility:** 112 one-bedroom standard units, some with kitchens. 4 stories, interior/exterior corridors. *Bath:* combo or shower only. **Parking:** on-site (fee). **Terms:** 7 day cancellation notice-fee imposed. **Amenities:** video games (fee), high-speed Internet, voice mail, irons, hair dryers. **Leisure Activities:** exercise room. **Guest Services:** valet and coin laundry, wireless Internet. **Business Services:** meeting rooms, business center. **Cards:** AX, CB, DC, DS, JC, MC, VI.

FEE / SOME UNITS FEE

OMNI HOTEL AT CNN CENTER Book great rates at AAA.com Phone: (404)659-0000 30

AAA SAVE

Hotel
$159-$289 All Year

Address: 100 CNN Center **Location:** I-75/85, exit 248C northbound, 0.8 mi w; exit 249C southbound to International Blvd, then 0.5 mi w. **Facility:** Centrally located, the hotel offers proximity to CNN and the World Congress Center. 1067 units. 1034 one-bedroom standard units. 33 one-bedroom suites. 15 stories, interior corridors. **Parking:** valet. **Terms:** cancellation fee imposed. **Amenities:** dual phone lines, voice mail, honor bars, irons, hair dryers. *Fee:* video games, high-speed Internet. *Some:* safes. **Dining:** 3 restaurants, also, Prime Meridian, see separate listing. **Pool(s):** heated outdoor. **Leisure Activities:** saunas, whirlpool, spa. **Guest Services:** valet laundry, wireless Internet. **Business Services:** conference facilities, business center. **Cards:** AX, CB, DC, DS, JC, MC, VI.

FEE 24 / SOME UNITS FEE FEE

RED ROOF INN ATLANTA DOWNTOWN Book at AAA.com Phone: 404/659-4545 18

Hotel
Rates not provided

Address: 311 Courtland St NE **Location:** I-75/85, exit 249A southbound; exit 249B northbound. **Facility:** 69 one-bedroom standard units. 3 stories, interior/exterior corridors. *Bath:* shower only. **Parking:** on-site. **Amenities:** high-speed Internet, voice mail, irons. **Pool(s):** outdoor. **Guest Services:** valet laundry, wireless Internet. **Business Services:** fax (fee).

FEE CALL M / SOME UNITS

REGENCY SUITES HOTEL Book great rates at AAA.com Phone: (404)876-5003 9

AAA SAVE

Hotel
$119-$239 All Year

Address: 975 W Peachtree St **Location:** I-75/85, exit 250 (10th St), just e; corner of 10th St. Located adjacent to rapid transit station. **Facility:** 96 one-bedroom standard units. 9 stories, interior corridors. **Parking:** on-site (fee). **Amenities:** high-speed Internet, dual phone lines, voice mail, safes, irons, hair dryers. **Leisure Activities:** exercise room. **Guest Services:** valet and coin laundry, area transportation-within 3 mi, wireless Internet. **Business Services:** meeting rooms, PC, fax. **Cards:** AX, CB, DC, DS, MC, VI. **Free Special Amenities: expanded continental breakfast and high-speed Internet.**

FEE / SOME UNITS

(See map and index starting on p. 288)

RENAISSANCE ATLANTA HOTEL DOWNTOWN *Book great rates at AAA.com* **Phone:** (404)881-6000 

Hotel
$256-$277 All Year

Address: 590 W Peachtree St NW **Location:** I-75/85, exit 249D, just e; between North and Linden aves. **Facility:** Smoke free premises. 502 one-bedroom standard units. 25 stories, interior corridors. *Bath:* combo or shower only. **Parking:** valet. **Terms:** cancellation fee imposed. **Amenities:** dual phone lines, voice mail, irons, hair dryers. *Fee:* video games, high-speed Internet. *Some:* CD players. **Dining:** 2 restaurants. **Pool(s):** outdoor. **Leisure Activities:** exercise room. **Guest Services:** valet laundry, wireless Internet. **Business Services:** conference facilities, business center. **Cards:** AX, CB, DC, DS, JC, MC, VI. **Free Special Amenities: newspaper.** ***(See color ad below)***

CALL / SOME UNITS

AAA Benefit:
Members save a minimum 5% off the best available rate.

(See map and index starting on p. 288)

RESIDENCE INN ATLANTA MIDTOWN AT 17TH STREET Book great rates at AAA.com

Phone: (404)745-1000 1

Hotel
$195-$215 All Year

Address: 1365 Peachtree St **Location:** I-75/85, exit 250 (14th St), 0.5 mi e to Peachtree St, then 0.3 mi n. **Facility:** Smoke free premises. 160 units. 148 one- and 12 two-bedroom standard units, some with efficiencies or kitchens. 7 stories, interior corridors. **Parking:** on-site. **Terms:** check-in 4 pm, cancellation fee imposed. **Amenities:** video games (fee), high-speed Internet, dual phone lines, voice mail, irons, hair dryers. *Some:* CD players. **Leisure Activities:** exercise room. **Guest Services:** valet and coin laundry, wireless Internet. **Business Services:** meeting rooms, PC, fax (fee). **Cards:** AX, CB, DC, DS, JC, MC, VI.

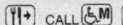

FEE CALL  / SOME UNITS FEE

AAA Benefit:
Members save a minimum 5% off the best available rate.

RESIDENCE INN BY MARRIOTT-ATLANTA DOWNTOWN Book great rates at AAA.com

Phone: (404)522-0950 33

AAA SAVE

Hotel
$205-$236 All Year

Address: 134 Peachtree St NW **Location:** I-75/85, exit 248C northbound, 0.4 mi w, then just s; exit 249A southbound to International Blvd, just w, then just s. **Facility:** Smoke free premises. 160 units. 70 one-bedroom standard units, some with efficiencies. 88 one- and 2 two-bedroom suites with efficiencies. 20 stories, interior corridors. **Parking:** valet. **Terms:** cancellation fee imposed. **Amenities:** high-speed Internet, voice mail, irons, hair dryers. *Some:* CD players. **Leisure Activities:** exercise room. **Guest Services:** valet and coin laundry, wireless Internet. **Business Services:** meeting rooms, PC, fax (fee). **Cards:** AX, DS, JC, MC, VI. **Free Special Amenities: full breakfast and high-speed Internet.**

FEE    / SOME UNITS FEE

AAA Benefit:
Members save a minimum 5% off the best available rate.

RESIDENCE INN BY MARRIOTT MIDTOWN Book great rates at AAA.com

Phone: (404)872-8885 7

Hotel
$220-$251 All Year

Address: 1041 W Peachtree St **Location:** I-75/85, exit 250 (10th St), just e to W Peachtree St, then just n; corner of 11th St. **Facility:** Smoke free premises. 78 units. 72 one- and 6 two-bedroom standard units with kitchens. 7 stories, interior corridors. **Parking:** on-site (fee). **Terms:** cancellation fee imposed. **Amenities:** high-speed Internet, voice mail, irons, hair dryers. **Leisure Activities:** exercise room. **Guest Services:** valet and coin laundry, wireless Internet. **Business Services:** fax. **Cards:** AX, CB, DC, DS, JC, MC, VI.

FEE CALL 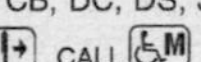    / SOME UNITS FEE

AAA Benefit:
Members save a minimum 5% off the best available rate.

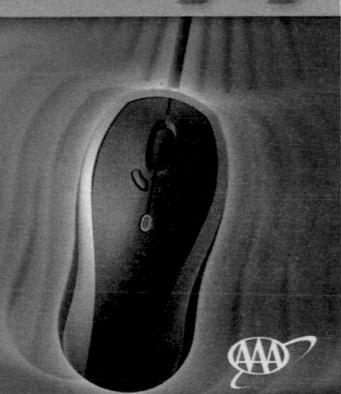

(See map and index starting on p. 288)

THE RITZ-CARLTON, ATLANTA *Book great rates at AAA.com* **Phone:** 404/659-0400 **31**

AAA SAVE

Hotel
Rates not provided

Address: 181 Peachtree St NE **Location:** I-75/85, exit 248C northbound, 0.4 mi w, then just s; exit 249A southbound, just s to International Blvd, just w, then just s. **Facility:** Polished woods, crystal chandeliers and plush carpets are standard at this service-oriented property. Smoke free premises. 444 units. 416 one-bedroom standard units. 28 one-bedroom suites. 25 stories, interior corridors. *Bath:* combo or shower only. **Parking:** on-site (fee) and valet. **Amenities:** DVD players, CD players, dual phone lines, voice mail, safes, honor bars, irons, hair dryers. *Fee:* video games, high-speed Internet. **Dining:** Atlanta Grill, see separate listing, entertainment. **Leisure Activities:** saunas, steamrooms, recreation programs, exercise room. *Fee:* massage. **Guest Services:** valet laundry, airport transportation (fee)-The William B. Hartsfield Atlanta Int'l Airport, area transportation-within 5 mi, wireless Internet. **Business Services:** conference facilities, business center. **Free Special Amenities: newspaper and preferred room (subject to availability with advance reservations).**

FEE CALL VCR / SOME UNITS FEE

SHELLMONT INN **Phone:** (404)872-9290 **10**

Historic Bed & Breakfast
$160-$350 All Year

Address: 821 Piedmont Ave NE **Location:** I-75/85, exit 249D, just e, then just n. **Facility:** This historic Victorian home features secluded verandas and Tiffany windows, as well as original garland moldings inside and out. Fruit basket and soft drinks upon arrival. Designated smoking area. 5 units. 3 one- and 2 two-bedroom standard units, some with whirlpools. 2 stories (no elevator), interior corridors. *Bath:* combo or shower only. **Parking:** on-site. **Terms:** 2 night minimum stay - weekends, age restrictions may apply, 7 day cancellation notice-fee imposed. **Amenities:** video library, DVD players, CD players, high-speed Internet, irons, hair dryers. **Guest Services:** valet laundry. **Business Services:** fax (fee). **Cards:** AX, CB, DC, DS, JC, MC, VI.

/ SOME UNITS 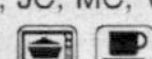

SHERATON ATLANTA HOTEL *Book great rates at AAA.com* **Phone:** (404)659-6500 **28**

AAA SAVE

Hotel
$119-$399 All Year

Address: 165 Courtland St **Location:** I-75/85, exit 249A southbound; exit 248C northbound, just w. **Facility:** 760 units. 735 one-bedroom standard units. 5 one- and 20 two-bedroom suites, some with whirlpools. 4-12 stories, interior corridors. *Bath:* combo or shower only. **Parking:** on-site (fee) and valet. **Amenities:** dual phone lines, voice mail, irons, hair dryers. *Fee:* video games, high-speed Internet. *Some:* CD players, safes, honor bars. **Dining:** 3 restaurants. **Pool(s):** heated indoor/outdoor. **Leisure Activities:** whirlpool, exercise room. **Guest Services:** valet laundry, wireless Internet. **Business Services:** conference facilities, business center. **Cards:** AX, CB, DC, DS, JC, MC, VI. **Free Special Amenities: newspaper and preferred room (subject to availability with advance reservations).**

Sheraton HOTELS & RESORTS
AAA Benefit:
Members get up to 15% off, plus Starwood Preferred Guest® bonuses.

/ SOME UNITS

(See map and index starting on p. 288)

SUPER 8 DOWNTOWN Book great rates at AAA.com **Phone:** (404)524-7000 32

AAA SAVE

Hotel
$99-$129 All Year

Address: 111 Cone St NW **Location:** Jct Cone and Luckie sts. **Facility:** 190 units. 168 one-bedroom standard units. 22 one-bedroom suites. 10 stories, interior corridors. *Bath:* combo or shower only. **Parking:** on-site (fee). **Terms:** 3 day cancellation notice. **Amenities:** high-speed Internet, voice mail, irons, hair dryers. **Leisure Activities:** exercise room. **Guest Services:** valet laundry, wireless Internet. **Business Services:** meeting rooms, fax (fee). **Cards:** AX, DC, DS, MC, VI. **Free Special Amenities: continental breakfast and high-speed Internet.**

/ SOME UNITS

W ATLANTA MIDTOWN Book great rates at AAA.com **Phone:** (404)892-6000 

AAA SAVE

Hotel
$199-$539 All Year

Address: 188 14th St NE **Location:** I-75/85, exit 250, 0.5 mi. Adjoins a shopping mall in the Art-Center District. **Facility:** The new hotel is equipped with the latest technology and features a swank, hip decor throughout; the nightclub is popular with high-profile celebs. 466 units. 434 one-bedroom standard units. 32 one-bedroom suites. 27 stories, interior corridors. *Bath:* combo or shower only. **Parking:** valet. **Amenities:** DVD players, dual phone lines, voice mail, irons, hair dryers. *Fee:* video library, video games, high-speed Internet. *Some:* fax. **Dining:** 2 restaurants, nightclub. **Pool(s):** outdoor. **Leisure Activities:** sauna, whirlpool, exercise room, spa. **Guest Services:** valet laundry, area transportation-within 4 mi, wireless Internet. **Business Services:** conference facilities, business center. **Cards:** AX, CB, DC, DS, JC, MC, VI.

AAA Benefit:
Special member room rates, plus Starwood Preferred Guest® bonuses.

THE WESTIN PEACHTREE PLAZA Book great rates at AAA.com **Phone:** (404)659-1400 24

AAA SAVE

Hotel
$119-$405 All Year

Address: 210 Peachtree St **Location:** I-75/85, exit 248C northbound, 0.4 mi w; exit 249C southbound, 0.5 mi s. **Facility:** Smoke free premises. 1068 units. 1029 one-bedroom standard units. 39 one-bedroom suites, some with whirlpools. 73 stories, interior corridors. **Parking:** on-site (fee) and valet. **Amenities:** dual phone lines, voice mail, safes, honor bars, irons, hair dryers. *Fee:* video games, high-speed Internet. *Some:* CD players. **Dining:** 2 restaurants. **Pool(s):** heated indoor/outdoor. **Leisure Activities:** *Fee:* massage. **Guest Services:** valet laundry, wireless Internet. **Business Services:** conference facilities, business center. **Cards:** AX, CB, DC, DS, JC, MC, VI.

24 / SOME UNITS

AAA Benefit:
Enjoy up to 15% off your next stay, plus Starwood Preferred Guest® bonuses.

WYNDHAM GARDEN HOTEL ATLANTA DOWNTOWN Book at AAA.com **Phone:** (404)659-2727 27

Hotel
$119-$249 All Year

Address: 175 Piedmont Ave N **Location:** I-75/85, exit 248C northbound; exit 249A southbound, 0.3 mi s on Courtland St to Ellis, then just e. **Facility:** 211 units. 205 one-bedroom standard units. 6 one-bedroom suites. 8 stories, interior corridors. **Parking:** on-site (fee). **Terms:** cancellation fee imposed. **Amenities:** video games (fee), high-speed Internet, voice mail, safes, irons, hair dryers. **Pool(s):** outdoor. **Leisure Activities:** whirlpool, exercise room. **Guest Services:** valet and coin laundry, wireless Internet. **Business Services:** meeting rooms, business center. **Cards:** AX, DC, DS, JC, MC, VI.

ASK FEE CALL / SOME UNITS

WYNDHAM MIDTOWN ATLANTA Book at AAA.com **Phone:** (404)873-4800 8

Hotel
$129-$239 All Year

Address: 125 10th St NE **Location:** I-75/85, exit 250 (14th St), 0.5 mi e. Located in an office/commercial complex. **Facility:** 191 one-bedroom standard units. 11 stories, interior corridors. **Parking:** on-site (fee) and valet. **Terms:** cancellation fee imposed. **Amenities:** dual phone lines, voice mail, irons, hair dryers. *Fee:* video games, high-speed Internet. *Some:* CD players. **Pool(s):** heated indoor. **Leisure Activities:** whirlpool, exercise room. **Guest Services:** valet laundry, area transportation, wireless Internet. **Business Services:** meeting rooms, fax (fee). **Cards:** AX, CB, DC, DS, MC, VI.

ASK / SOME UNITS

WHERE TO DINE

AGAVE **Phone:** 404/588-0006 56

Southwestern
$14-$23

Known for its "eclectic Southwestern cuisine," the restaurant nurtures a cozy Southwestern atmosphere. Guests dine in front of a roaring fireplace during the winter or outdoors on the patio, which overlooks the city, in the summer. An outstanding choices is red wine-, herb- and honey-marinated free-range venison served over a spicy tomato puree. It's quite a delicious dish. Dressy casual. **Bar:** Full bar. **Hours:** 5 pm-10 pm, Fri & Sat-11 pm. **Address:** 242 Boulevard SE **Location:** 0.9 mi s of jct Freedom Pkwy. **Parking:** on-site. **Cards:** AX, DS, MC, VI.

AGNES & MURIEL'S **Phone:** 404/885-1000 1

American
$2-$21

The walls of this bustling, '50s-style diner in a refurbished brick home are dotted with whimsical kitsch. Modern-day adaptations of down-home cooking give a nod to the era of green goddess dressing and congealed cherry salad. Sides include an impressive list of vegetables. Dressy casual. **Bar:** Beer & wine. **Reservations:** suggested. **Hours:** 11 am-10 pm, Fri-11 pm, Sat 10 am-11 pm, Sun 10 am-10 pm. Closed: 12/25. **Address:** 1514 Monroe Dr NE **Location:** Jct Monroe Dr and Piedmont Ave, just s. **Parking:** on-site and valet. **Cards:** AX, CB, DC, DS, MC, VI.

(See map and index starting on p. 288)

APRES DIEM

Phone: 404/872-3333 (24)

Continental
$6-$20

Mediterranean dishes like hummus and fatoosh are served in a bustling, hip, bohemian setting. A Continental menu—with eclectic entrees, fresh salads and amazing desserts—offers an excellent value. Expect good service. Casual dress. **Bar:** Full bar. **Hours:** 11:30 am-midnight, Fri-2 am, Sat 11 am-2 am, Sun 11 am-midnight. **Address:** 931 Monroe Dr **Location:** Jct 10th St, just s; in Midtown Promenade Shopping Center. **Parking:** on-site. **Cards:** AX, CB, DC, DS, JC, MC, VI.

ATLANTA GRILL

Phone: 404/659-0400 (50)

AAA

American
$10-$30

Prime rib and seafood are at the heart of the menu in the bustling dining room, which also has a popular bar. Linen tablecloths and napkins hide the casual atmosphere. Well-trained servers are quick to give guests attention. The signature dessert, pecan torte with homemade ice cream, is a must. Dressy casual. Entertainment. **Bar:** Full bar. **Reservations:** suggested. **Hours:** 6:30 am-midnight. **Address:** 181 Peachtree St NE **Location:** I-75/85, exit 248C northbound, 0.4 mi w, then just s; exit 249A southbound, just s to International Blvd, just w, then just s; in The Ritz-Carlton, Atlanta. **Parking:** valet and street. **Cards:** AX, DS, MC, VI.

CALL

BANGKOK THAI RESTAURANT

Phone: 404/874-2514 (2)

Thai
$3-$14

The establishment holds the distinction of being the first Thai restaurant to open its doors in Georgia. Expect friendly, dependable service and tried-and-true traditional fare. The delicious food also is a good value. Casual dress. **Bar:** Beer & wine. **Reservations:** accepted. **Hours:** 11:30 am-2:30 & 5:30-10 pm, Fri-10:30 pm, Sat 5:30 pm-10:30 pm. Closed major holidays; also Sun. **Address:** 1492A Piedmont Ave NE **Location:** Jct Piedmont and Monroe aves, just s; in Ansley Square. **Parking:** on-site. **Cards:** AX, DC, DS, MC, VI.

BARAONDA CAFFE' ITALIANO

Phone: 404/879-9962 (32)

Italian
$4-$22

Everyone should be so lucky as to have such a warm, intimate space in their neighborhood. On the menu are more than 20 types of pizza and calzones, as well as varied pasta dishes and other Italian standards. Casual dress. **Bar:** Full bar. **Reservations:** suggested. **Hours:** 11 am-10:30 pm, Fri-midnight, Sat noon-midnight, Sun noon-10 pm. Closed: major holidays; also 12/26, 12/26. **Address:** 710 Peachtree St NE **Location:** I-75/85, exit 249D, 0.5 mi e to Peachtree St NE, then just n. **Parking:** valet and street. **Cards:** AX, DC, DS, MC, VI.

CITY GRILL

Phone: 404/524-2489 (54)

Regional American
$7-$42

In an elegant, Federalist-style building with a dramatic marble rotunda, modern American cuisine is served with regional flavor. The daily menu may include the signature crab cakes on corn chowder or Southern-fried quail with raspberry pepper biscuit. Dressy casual. **Bar:** Full bar. **Reservations:** suggested. **Hours:** 11:30 am-2 & 5-10 pm, Sat from 5 pm. Closed major holidays; also Sun. **Address:** 50 Hurt Plaza, Suite 200 **Location:** I-75/85, exit 248B northbound, 0.5 mi w; exit 249A southbound to Edgewood, 0.3 mi w. **Parking:** on-site and valet. **Cards:** AX, DS, MC, VI.

DAILEY'S

Phone: 404/681-3303 (46)

American
$8-$37

A majestic staircase and old merry-go-round horses lend to the decor at the restaurant. Downstairs has a jazz club feel, with a casual menu of sandwiches and hamburgers, and upstairs has white-tablecloth dining and a fabulous dessert bar. Casual dress. Entertainment. **Bar:** Full bar. **Reservations:** suggested. **Hours:** 11:30 am-2:30 & 5:30-11 pm, Fri-midnight, Sat 5:30 pm-midnight, Sun 5:30 pm-11 pm. Closed major holidays. **Address:** 17 International Blvd **Location:** I-75/85, exit 248C northbound, 0.3 mi w; exit 249A southbound, just s, then just w. **Parking:** on-site (fee). **Cards:** AX, CB, DC, DS, MC, VI.

DOLCE ENOTECA E RISTORANTE

Phone: 404/872-3902 (4)

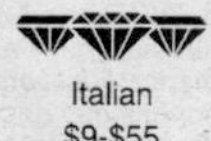

Italian
$9-$55

Contemporary surroundings and dim lighting characterize the loud and hip restaurant, where patrons savor choices such as forest risotti, pumpkin ravioli and Tuscan rib-eye pizzaiola. Dressy casual. **Bar:** Full bar. **Reservations:** accepted. **Hours:** 5 pm-midnight, Fri & Sat-1 am. Closed major holidays. **Address:** 261 19th St NW **Location:** I-75, exit 251, just w; in Atlantic Station. **Parking:** on-site. **Cards:** AX, DC, MC, VI.

CALL

EINSTEIN'S

Phone: 404/876-7925 (16)

American
$2-$21

The waterfall wall at the entrance prepares guests for the tranquil setting that awaits. The centerpiece of the restaurant is a free-standing fireplace surrounded by leather benches. The reactor dessert will end the evening with a bang. Dressy casual. **Bar:** Full bar. **Reservations:** accepted. **Hours:** 11 am-11 pm, Fri-midnight, Sat 10 am-midnight, Sun 10 am-11 pm. Closed: 11/26, 12/25. **Address:** 1077 Juniper St **Location:** Jct 12th St. **Parking:** street. **Cards:** AX, DC, DS, MC, VI.

ENO

Phone: 404/685-3191 (30)

Mediterranean
$7-$27

An extremely well-stocked wine cellar, which offers excellent choices by the taste or by the glass, and cutting-edge Mediterranean cuisine reflecting Southern European influences, are the hallmarks of the trendy Midtown eatery. Dressy casual. **Bar:** Full bar. **Reservations:** suggested. **Hours:** 11:30 am-11 pm, Fri-midnight, Sat 5 pm-midnight, Sun 5:30 pm-10 pm. Closed major holidays; also Mon. **Address:** 800 Peachtree St NE, Suite A **Location:** Jct Peachtree and 5th sts; in Midtown. **Parking:** valet. **Cards:** AX, CB, DC, DS, JC, MC, VI.

FLYING BISCUIT CAFE

Phone: 404/874-8887 (18)

American
$5-$14

Near historic Piedmont Park, the friendly neighborhood restaurant in Midtown prepares eccentric vegetarian and Southern fare. Although this place is known for its namesake biscuits, the menu also lists such choices as scrambled tofu, chipotle barbecue salmon and stoup, a combination between soup and stew. Casual dress. **Bar:** Beer & wine. **Hours:** 7 am-10 pm, Fri & Sat-10:30 pm. Closed: 11/26, 12/25. **Address:** 1001 Piedmont Ave **Location:** Jct 10th St. **Parking:** on-site. **Cards:** AX, MC, VI.

(See map and index starting on p. 288)

FRENCH AMERICAN BRASSERIE — **Phone:** 404/266-1440 (38)

French
$7-$44

The multi-level dining room is a canvas of influential Art Nouveau. The grand brasserie features succulent French cuisine served in a delightful setting. You'll literally be taken back in time. A local, all-time favorite is the skate wings as is the white bean soup with truffle oil. The desserts are wonderfully prepared and end the dining experience in an explosive manner. Casual dress. **Bar:** Full bar. **Reservations:** suggested. **Hours:** 11:30 am-10 pm, Fri & Sat-11 pm. Closed major holidays. **Address:** 30 Ivan Allen Jr Blvd **Location:** I-75/85, exit 248C northbound, 0.4 mi w to Peachtree St, then 0.4 mi n; exit 249C southbound, just s to Peachtree Pl, then just e. **Parking:** on-site (fee). **Cards:** AX, MC, VI.

F.R.O.G.S. CANTINA & TEQUILERIA — **Phone:** 404/607-9967 (23)

Southwestern
$4-$15

The atmosphere is casual inside and out, but the food and more than 50 tequilas are serious. The menu comprises traditional Mexican and Southwestern favorites. Fresh is another key word here, as preservatives find no place in this food. Casual dress. **Bar:** Full bar. **Hours:** 11 am-11 pm, Sun-10 pm. Closed: 1/1, 11/26, 12/25. **Address:** 931 Monroe Dr NE **Location:** Jct 10th St, just s; in Midtown Promenade Shopping Center. **Parking:** on-site. **Cards:** AX, MC, VI.

GEISHA HOUSE — **Phone:** 404/872-3903 (5)

Japanese
$3-$42

Menu offerings include sushi and sashimi, miso soups, tempura, Robata-Yaki and udon noodles as well as a variety of hot (grilled Alaskan salmon teriyaki) and cold (albacore carpaccio) entrees. Both the dining room's decor and waitstaff's efficient conduct define the hip, chic atmosphere. Dressy casual. **Bar:** Full bar. **Reservations:** accepted. **Hours:** 5 pm-midnight, Fri & Sat-1 am. Closed major holidays. **Address:** 1380 Atlantic Dr **Location:** I-75, exit 251, just w; in Atlantic Station. **Parking:** on-site. **Cards:** AX, DC, MC, VI.

CALL

GLADYS & RON'S CHICKEN & WAFFLES — **Phone:** 404/874-9393 (37)

American
$2-$15

Home cooking and the breakfast namesakes can all be enjoyed at the entertainer's dining spot. Casual dress. **Reservations:** not accepted. **Hours:** 11 am-11 pm, Fri & Sat-4 am, Sun-8 pm. Closed major holidays; also 12/24. **Address:** 529 Peachtree St NE **Location:** I-75/85, exit 249A to Barker St, 0.3 mi w to Peachtree St, then 0.5 mi n; across from Crawford-Long Hospital. **Parking:** on-site. **Cards:** AX, CB, DC, DS, MC, VI.

CALL

THE GLOBE — **Phone:** 404/541-1487 (26)

American
$6-$26

In a relaxed yet hip and trendy setting, the urban bistro prepares dishes with ingredients and cooking techniques from around the world. The wine menu includes a range of classic styles and varietals. Casual dress. **Bar:** Full bar. **Reservations:** accepted. **Hours:** 11 am-11 pm, Thurs-Sat to 2 am. Closed: 11/26; also Sun. **Address:** 75 5th St NW **Location:** I-75/85, exit 250 (10th/14th sts), just e to 10th St; northwest corner of Spring and 5th sts. **Parking:** street. **Cards:** AX, DC, DS, MC, VI.

GORDON BIERSCH BREWERY & RESTAURANT — **Phone:** 404/870-0805 (25)

American
$4-$23

Asian-influenced American cuisine and hand-crafted beers are the draw at the contemporarily outfitted pub. Casual dress. **Bar:** Full bar. **Reservations:** accepted. **Hours:** 11:30 am-12:30 am, Fri & Sat-2 am. Closed: 11/26, 12/25. **Address:** 848 Peachtree St **Location:** Jct Peachtree and 5th sts, just n. **Parking:** valet and street. **Cards:** AX, CB, DC, DS, JC, MC, VI.

HARD ROCK CAFE — **Phone:** 404/688-7625 (45)

American
$12-$24

Rock 'n' roll memorabilia decorates the walls of the popular theme restaurant. Live music on the weekends contributes to the bustling atmosphere. On the menu is a wide variety of American cuisine—from burgers and sandwiches to seafood, steaks and pasta. Casual dress. **Bar:** Full bar. **Hours:** 11 am-11 pm. **Address:** 215 Peachtree St NE **Location:** I-75/85, exit 248C northbound, 0.4 mi w; exit 249A southbound, just s; jct International Blvd. **Parking:** on-site (fee). **Cards:** AX, DS, JC, MC, VI.

CALL

HAVELI INDIAN CUISINE — **Phone:** 404/522-4545 (43)

Indian
$8-$17

Tasty lamb dishes are highlights at this downtown favorite. Featured are baingan bharta, fish tikka and a lunchtime buffet. Traditional Indian decor enhances the relaxed setting of this place, which occupies an apparel mart and shopping center. Service enhances the exotic experience here. Casual dress. **Bar:** Full bar. **Reservations:** accepted. **Hours:** 11:30 am-2:30 & 5:30-9:45 pm, Sat from noon, Sun from 5:30 pm. Closed major holidays. **Address:** 225 Spring St **Location:** In Gift Mart Shopping Center. **Parking:** street. **Cards:** AX, DC, DS, MC, VI.

HSU'S GOURMET CHINESE RESTAURANT — **Phone:** 404/659-2788 (47)

Chinese
$7-$22

The longtime downtown fixture pleases guests with an array of Hong Kong- and Cantonese-style gourmet cuisine served in an intimate, casual atmosphere. Peking duck is a popular house specialty, as is the succulent fresh fish. Casual dress. **Bar:** Full bar. **Reservations:** accepted. **Hours:** 11:30 am-2:30 & 5-10 pm, Fri-10:30 pm, Sat 5 pm-10:30 pm, Sun 5 pm-10 pm. Closed major holidays. **Address:** 192 Peachtree Center Ave **Location:** I-75/85, exit 248C northbound, just w; exit 249A southbound, just s to International Blvd, then just w. **Parking:** on-site (fee). **Cards:** AX, DC, DS, MC, VI.

LANDMARK DINER — **Phone:** 404/659-1756 (52)

Continental
$4-$28

Fresh daily specials and large portions. Desserts are very good and nicely presented. Casual dress. **Hours:** 24 hours. Closed major holidays. **Address:** 60 Luckie St **Location:** I-75/85, exit 249A southbound; exit 248C northbound, 0.5 mi s on Courtland Ave to Auburn Ave, then 0.3 mi s. **Parking:** street. **Cards:** AX, DC, DS, MC, VI.

CALL

(See map and index starting on p. 288)

LAS PALMERAS

Phone: 404/872-0846 (31)

Cuban
$3-$14

Plenty of food is heaped on each plate at the quaint, no-frills restaurant, a best-kept secret in the middle of a residential neighborhood. Casual dress. **Bar:** Beer & wine. **Hours:** 11:30 am-3 & 5:30-9:45 pm, Sat from noon. Closed major holidays; also Sun-Tues. **Address:** 366 5th St NE **Location:** Just e of Durant St; Midtown. **Parking:** street. **Cards:** AX, MC, VI.

MADISON GRILL

Phone: 404/475-1188 (7)

American
$7-$22

The chic and contemporary new addition to the Atlanta scene turns out upscale comfort food, including preparations of seafood, pasta and beef. Georgia mountain trout is a real keeper. Casual dress. **Bar:** Full bar. **Reservations:** accepted. **Hours:** 11 am-midnight, Fri & Sat-2 am. Closed: 11/26, 12/25. **Address:** 1375 Peachtree St **Location:** I-75/85, exit 250 (14th St), 0.5 mi e, then 0.3 mi n. **Parking:** on-site and street. **Cards:** AX, CB, DC, DS, JC, MC, VI.

CALL

MARY MAC'S TEA ROOM

Phone: 404/876-1800 (33)

Continental
$9-$18

The restaurant blends traditional Southern cuisine and warm service in an atmosphere reminiscent of an old boarding house. Casual dress. **Bar:** Full bar. **Hours:** 11 am-9 pm. Closed major holidays; also 12/22-12/26. **Address:** 224 Ponce de Leon Ave **Location:** Jct Ponce de Leon Ave and Myrtle St. **Parking:** on-site. **Cards:** AX, CB, DC, DS, JC, MC, VI.

MAX LAGER'S AMERICAN GRILL & BREWERY

Phone: 404/525-4400 (39)

AAA

American
$7-$25

The restaurant lets diners sample wood-fired cuisine and a variety of hand-crafted beverages. The brew pub occupies a converted warehouse with exposed brick walls and slate floors. Servers are knowledgeable and attentive. Casual dress. **Bar:** Full bar. **Reservations:** accepted. **Hours:** 11:30 am-10 pm, Sun from 4 pm. Closed: 11/26, 12/25. **Address:** 320 Peachtree St NW **Location:** I-75/85, exit 249A to Baker St, 0.3 mi w to Peachtree St, then just n. **Parking:** street. **Cards:** AX, DC, DS, MC, VI.

MCCORMICK & SCHMICK'S

Phone: 404/521-1236 (48)

Seafood
$4-$38

This place is all about seafood, which is imported from all over the world. Among good choices are Washington state oysters, Maine clams, delicate Hawaiian escolar and tuna from Ecuador. The clublike decor is cozy, and expert staff provide able assistance. Casual dress. **Bar:** Full bar. **Reservations:** accepted. **Hours:** 11 am-11 pm, Sat from 4 pm, Sun 4 pm-10 pm. Closed: 11/26, 12/25. **Address:** One CNN Center, Suite 200 **Location:** I-75/85, exit 248C northbound; exit 249C southbound to International Blvd, then 0.5 mi w. **Parking:** on-site. **Cards:** AX, DC, DS, MC, VI.

M F SUSHIBAR

Phone: 404/815-8844 (34)

Sushi
$5-$30

First-timers shouldn't let the heavy sounds of techno music dissuade them from waiting in line with other impatient diners at the elegantly sleek space. Lending his name to the restaurant, Chef "Magic Fingers" creates an exciting seasonal menu of incredibly fresh, perfectly prepared, jewel-like morsels of sushi and sashimi only. The graceful wait staff can guide guests through an incredible selection of sakes. Dressy casual. **Bar:** Wine only. **Reservations:** suggested. **Hours:** 11:30 am-2:30 & 5:30-10:30 pm, Fri-11:30 pm, Sat 5:30 pm-11:30 pm, Sun 6 pm-10 pm. Closed major holidays. **Address:** 265 Ponce de Leon Ave NE, Unit B **Location:** 0.4 mi e of jct Peachtree St NE and Ponce de Leon Ave NE, at 4th St. **Parking:** valet and street. **Cards:** AX, DS, MC, VI.

CALL

MITRA

Phone: 404/875-5515 (28)

Southwestern
$5-$26

The interesting spot has a fine-dining feel, with a bit of an art deco flair courtesy of hand-crafted wrought-iron artwork and abstract architecture. An eye-catching waterfall is at the entrance. Chef Ramos creates myriad items, including jalapeno-lime caramelized sea scallops with manchego cheese grits; banana leaf roasted gulf snapper with chile escabeche; crispy lobster tail; and filet of beef with chayote squash salad. Dressy casual. **Bar:** Full bar. **Hours:** 5 pm-10 pm, Fri & Sat-11 pm. Closed major holidays; also Sun. **Address:** 818 Juniper St NE **Location:** Just n of jct 14th St NE. **Parking:** on-site (fee) and valet. **Cards:** AX, DS, MC, VI.

MU LAN

Phone: 404/877-5797 (27)

Chinese
$6-$20

In a lovely converted Victorian, this place offers some upscale twists on tried-and-true Chinese cuisine. Porch seating is an option here. Casual dress. **Bar:** Full bar. **Reservations:** accepted. **Hours:** 11:30 am-10:30 pm, Fri & Sat noon-11 pm, Sun noon-10:30 pm. Closed major holidays. **Address:** 824 Juniper St **Location:** Jct Juniper and 5th sts; Midtown. **Parking:** on-site. **Cards:** AX, DS, MC, VI.

NAM

Phone: 404/541-9997 (22)

New Vietnamese
$6-$24

A far cry from the typical noodle house, the elegant space, which features modernist light sculptures and the owner's flowing artwork, epitomizes white tablecloth dining. Nouveau Vietnamese cuisine replicates the sort of subtle yet clean flavors one would could only hope to find in a major West Coast city. Dressy casual. **Bar:** Wine only. **Reservations:** suggested. **Hours:** 11:30 am-2 & 5:30-9:30 pm, Fri & Sat-10:30 pm. Closed major holidays; also Sun. **Address:** 931 Monroe Dr, Suite 101A **Location:** Jct 10th St, just s; in Midtown Promenade Shopping Center. **Parking:** on-site. **Cards:** AX, DC, DS, MC, VI.

CALL

NAN THAI FINE DINING

Phone: 404/870-9933 (9)

Thai
$7-$32

The refined establishment includes a stunning contemporary dining room and an upscale lounge. Beautiful presentations characterize the cutting-edge Thai cuisine. Dressy casual. **Bar:** Full bar. **Reservations:** suggested. **Hours:** 11 am-2:30 & 5:30-10 pm, Fri-11 pm, Sat 5 pm-11 pm, Sun 5 pm-10 pm. Closed major holidays. **Address:** 1350 Spring St, Suite 1 **Location:** I-79/85, exit 250 (14th St), just w to W Peachtree St, 0.5 mi n, just w on 19th St, then just s. **Parking:** on-site. **Cards:** AX, MC, VI.

CALL

(See map and index starting on p. 288)

NICKIEMOTO'S — **Phone:** 404/253-2010 (19)

Asian
$3-$23

Locals gather at the trendy sushi bar for cocktails and tapas with an Asian flair. Dumplings, stir-fried noodle and rice dishes and such house specialties as beef tenderloin medallions with butter ponzu, bok choy and mashed potato roll round out the menu. Patio seating is available. Casual dress. **Bar:** Full bar. **Reservations:** accepted. **Hours:** 11:30 am-11 pm, Fri-midnight, Sat 1 pm-midnight, Sun 1 pm-10 pm. Closed: major holidays; also 12/26. **Address:** 990 Piedmont Ave NE **Location:** Jct 10th St NE **Parking:** valet. **Cards:** AX, DC, DS, MC, VI.

NIKOLAI'S ROOF — **Phone:** 404/221-6362 (41)

Continental
$9-$95

A wait staff in Cossack attire, an expansive view of the city from the 28th floor and expertly prepared and presented three-, four and six-course French-Continental menus with Russian specialties all add up to an impressive evening out. A fine starter is flavored house-marinated Russian vodka, such as orange or peach, and peroshkis. Formal attire. **Bar:** Full bar. **Reservations:** suggested. **Hours:** 5:30 pm-10:30 pm. Closed: Sun & Mon. **Address:** 255 Courtland St NE **Location:** I-75/85, exit 249 southbound; exit 248C northbound, just w to Piedmont Ave, just n to Baker St, then just w; in Hilton Atlanta. **Parking:** valet. **Cards:** AX, CB, DC, DS, MC, VI.

OCEANAIRE — **Phone:** 404/475-2277 (15)

Seafood
$8-$35

Fresh fish and shellfish are flown in daily from around the globe. The sleek, handsomely designed dining room has a raw bar and is tastefully appointed in an art deco/nautical theme. The menu notes the seafood available daily and the varied preparation styles, such as broiled, grilled and blackened. Casual dress. **Bar:** Full bar. **Reservations:** suggested. **Hours:** 11 am-10 pm, Fri-11 pm, Sat 5 pm-11 pm, Sun 5 pm-10 pm. Closed major holidays. **Address:** 1100 Peachtree St NW **Location:** I-75, exit 249D, just e to Linden Ave NW, then just n. **Parking:** valet and street. **Cards:** AX, DC, DS, MC, VI.

ONE MIDTOWN KITCHEN — **Phone:** 404/892-4111 (8)

American
$7-$21

The popular and extremely hip bistro offers trendy small plates and entrees along with a "bottomless-glass" wine concept. The contemporary atmosphere has a funky feel. Casual dress. **Bar:** Full bar. **Reservations:** suggested. **Hours:** 5:30 pm-10 pm, Tues-Thurs to 11 pm, Fri & Sat-midnight. Closed major holidays. **Address:** 559 Dutch Valley Rd NE **Location:** Jct Monroe Dr, 0.3 mi w. **Parking:** on-site. **Cards:** AX, CB, DC, DS, JC, MC, VI.

CALL &M

PACIFIC RIM BISTRO — **Phone:** 404/893-0018 (40)

Pacific Rim
$4-$32

A melange of Chinese, Korean and Thai flavors melds nicely in dishes at the chic, downtown restaurant. Dressy casual. **Bar:** Full bar. **Reservations:** suggested. **Hours:** 11:30 am-2:30 & 5-10:30 pm, Sat from 5 pm. Closed: 11/26, 12/25. **Address:** 303 Peachtree Center Ave NE **Location:** I-75/85, exit 249A southbound, just s to International Blvd, just w, then 0.3 mi n; exit 248C northbound, just w, then 0.3 mi w. **Parking:** street. **Cards:** AX, DC, DS, MC, VI.

PARK 75 — **Phone:** 404/881-9898 (12)

New American
$10-$130

Sleek, ultra-contemporary decor elements create a striking, casually elegant look. Park 75 offers cutting-edge cuisine, such as variations on Arctic char, bison and foie gras. Dressy casual. **Bar:** Full bar. **Reservations:** suggested. **Hours:** 6:30-11 am, 11:30-2 & 5:30-10:30 pm, Sun 7 am-2 pm. **Address:** 75 14th St **Location:** I-75/85, exit 250 (14th St), 0.3 mi e; in Four Seasons Hotel Atlanta. **Parking:** valet. **Cards:** AX, CB, DC, DS, MC, VI.

CALL &M

PITTYPAT'S PORCH — **Phone:** 404/525-8228 (44)

Regional Southern
$14-$28

A country theme weaves through this quaint bistro, which offers its guests a touch of the South right out of "Gone with the Wind." For dinner, guests savor the freshness of scrumptious pork tenderloin with curried peanut sauce or Aunt PittyPat's fried chicken. A favorite dessert is Georgia peach cobbler with cinnamon ice cream. Mint juleps are a specialty of the house. Casual dress. Entertainment. **Bar:** Full bar. **Reservations:** suggested. **Hours:** 5 pm-9 pm, Fri & Sat-10 pm. Closed major holidays. **Address:** 25 International Blvd NW **Location:** I-75/85, exit 249A southbound; exit 248C northbound, 0.5 mi w. **Parking:** on-site (fee). **Cards:** AX, DC, DS, MC, VI.

PLEASANT PEASANT — **Phone:** 404/874-3223 (36)

American
$5-$29

A great spot to take a date, the charming, casual bistro serves an eclectic menu of American cuisine, including preparations of fresh seafood, steak and pasta. A romantic ambience is evident in everything from the tile floors to the original pressed tin ceiling. Casual dress. **Bar:** Full bar. **Reservations:** accepted. **Hours:** 11 am-2:30 & 5-10 pm, Fri & Sat-11 pm; Saturday & Sunday brunch 11 am-3 pm. Closed major holidays. **Address:** 555 Peachtree St NE **Location:** I-75/85, exit 248, 0.3 mi e on North Ave to Peachtree St, then just s. **Parking:** valet. **Cards:** AX, DC, DS, MC, VI.

PRIME MERIDIAN — **Phone:** 404/818-4450 (49)

Steak & Seafood
$4-$29

The menu lists steak, seafood and regional dishes prepared with a Continental flair. The view from the dining room overlooks Centennial Park and the Atlanta skyline. Dressy casual. **Bar:** Full bar. **Reservations:** suggested. **Hours:** 6:30 am-2:30 & 5-10:30 pm. **Address:** 100 CNN Center **Location:** I-75/85, exit 248C northbound, 0.8 mi w; exit 249C southbound to International Blvd, 0.5 mi w; in Omni Hotel at CNN Center. **Parking:** on-site. **Cards:** AX, CB, DC, DS, JC, MC, VI.

RAY'S IN THE CITY — **Phone:** 404/524-9224 (42)

Seafood
$4-$20

Fresh seafood arrives up to five times daily at the downtown hot spot. In addition to sushi and oyster bar offerings, the menu includes a lengthy list of fresh fish, steak and lobster. Among house specialties are shrimp and crawfish etouffee, grilled salmon Oscar and Maryland-style lump crab cakes. Dressy casual. **Bar:** Full bar. **Reservations:** accepted. **Hours:** 11 am-10 pm, Sat & Sun from 4 pm. Closed major holidays. **Address:** 240 Peachtree St **Location:** Jct Harris St, just n; across from Peachtree Center MARTA Station. **Parking:** street. **Cards:** AX, DC, DS, MC, VI.

(See map and index starting on p. 288)

RISING ROLL

Phone: 404/815-6787

Deli
$3-$8

As upscale as a self-serve delicatessen can be, the office complex location can be busy during the lunch rush. Featuring a variety of in-house-made breads, the standards of sandwiches, soups and salads are given a few distinctive and creative twists. Casual dress. **Hours:** 10:30 am-3 pm. Closed major holidays; also Sat & Sun. **Address:** 1180 W Peachtree St, Suite 190 **Location:** I-75/85, exit 250 (14th St), just e; in Atlantic Center Plaza Building. **Parking:** on-site (fee). **Cards:** AX, MC, VI.

CALL

ROLLING BONES

Phone: 404/222-2324 (53)

Barbecue
$7-$37

It may not be in the best part of town, but this downtown favorite turns out some tasty mesquite-smoked Texas barbecue, including the killer hand-sliced-to-order brisket. Minimalist '40s art deco appointments lend to the style of the eatery, which occupies what once was a gas station. Outside seating is all about casual comfort. Casual dress. **Bar:** Beer only. **Hours:** 11 am-9 pm, Fri & Sat-10 pm, Sun 12:30 pm-8 pm. Closed major holidays. **Address:** 377 Edgewood Ave **Location:** I-75/85, exit 248B, 0.3 mi e. **Parking:** on-site. **Cards:** AX, MC, VI.

SILK

Phone: 678/705-8888 (21)

Asian
$4-$40

The Midtown location, with its sleek and contemporary decor, is popular with locals who seek certified Angus steak, lobster and sushi prepared with Asian flair. Also offered is a lengthy list of Asian-style tapas and entrees, including Chilean sea bass in sake-miso marinade. Dressy casual. **Bar:** Full bar. **Reservations:** accepted. **Hours:** 11:30 am-2 & 5-10 pm, Fri-11 pm, Sat 5 pm-11 pm, Sun 5 pm-9:30 pm. Closed major holidays. **Address:** 919 Peachtree St **Location:** Jct 8th St NE; in Metropolis Building. **Parking:** on-site and valet. **Cards:** AX, MC, VI.

SOUTH CITY KITCHEN

Phone: 404/873-7358 (14)

Regional American
$5-$36

Contemporary Southern cuisine is served in a cool converted home with wide windows and high ochre-tinted walls. Food offerings are creative and complex in composition, and the servers are sharply knowledgeable of the menu and preparation styles. The BLT is an incredible choice for Sunday brunch. Casual dress. **Bar:** Full bar. **Reservations:** accepted. **Hours:** 11 am-3:30 & 5-11 pm, Fri & Sat-midnight, Sun-10 pm. Closed major holidays. **Address:** 1144 Crescent Ave **Location:** I-75/85, exit 250 (14th St), 0.3 mi e to Crescent Ave, then just s. **Parking:** street. **Cards:** AX, DC, MC, VI.

TAMARIND SEED

Phone: 404/873-4888 (10)

Thai
$4-$29

A contemporary ambiance, genteel service and excellent Thai dishes combine for an exceptional experience. Favored by locals and celebrities alike, choice selections include spicy lamb with basil, roast duck panang curry and barbecue lemongrass chicken. Casual dress. **Bar:** Full bar. **Reservations:** accepted. **Hours:** 11 am-2:30 & 5-10 pm, Fri-11 pm, Sat 4 pm-11 pm, Sun 11 am-9 pm. **Address:** 1197 Peachtree St NW, Suite 110 **Location:** I-75/85, exit 250, 0.5 mi e; in Colony Square. **Parking:** on-site. **Cards:** AX, MC, VI.

CALL

TEN PIN ALLEY

Phone: 404/872-3364 (3)

American
$10-$15

In an actual bowling alley, the hip, chic eatery prepares bar food with a funky twist. Kobe beef burgers, lobster, skewers, Brie pizza and yummy desserts are among offerings. Casual dress. **Bar:** Full bar. **Hours:** 7 pm-1 am, Fri & Sat 6 pm-2 am, Sun 6 pm-midnight. Closed major holidays. **Address:** 261 19th St NW **Location:** I-75, exit 251, just w; in Atlantic Station. **Parking:** on-site. **Cards:** AX, DC, MC, VI.

THRIVE

Phone: 404/389-1000 (51)

American
$6-$32

Named one of the city's top 50 in the Atlanta Journal Constitution, the hot, trendy downtown restaurant exudes chic contemporary style. A heavy Asian influence peppers American fare, such as grilled grouper over a sushi rice cake with coconut curry. The sushi bar is popular late at night. Hip staffers provide service. Casual dress. **Bar:** Full bar. **Reservations:** suggested. **Hours:** 11:30 am-2:30 & 5:30-10 pm, Thurs-Sat to 2 am. Closed major holidays. **Address:** 101 Marietta St **Location:** I-75/85, exit 248C northbound, 0.8 mi w, then just n; exit 249A southbound, just s to Baker St, just w, then just n; in Centennial Tower. **Parking:** street. **Cards:** AX, CB, DC, DS, JC, MC, VI.

CALL

TIERRA-FLAVOR OF THE AMERICAS

Phone: 404/874-5951 (6)

Latin American
$6-$24

The bistro-style eatery prepares innovative combinations of flavors and foods that exhibit influences from most of the Pan American countries. Casual dress. **Bar:** Full bar. **Reservations:** suggested. **Hours:** 6 pm-10 pm, Fri & Sat-10:30 pm. Closed major holidays; also Sun & Mon. **Address:** 1425-B Piedmont Ave **Location:** Jct 14th St and Piedmont Ave, 0.5 mi n. **Parking:** on-site. **Cards:** AX, DC, MC, VI.

TIN DRUM ASIA CAFE

Phone: 404/881-1368 (29)

Asian
$2-$7

The quick-serve restaurant dishes up large portions of fresh and value-priced Asian cuisine. Contemporary minimalist style marks the dining room. Casual dress. **Bar:** Beer & wine. **Hours:** 11 am-9 pm, Sat & Sun noon-3 & 5-9 pm. **Address:** 88 5th St **Location:** I-75/85, exit 250 southbound, just e to Spring St, 0.9 mi s to 5th St, then just w; exit 249D northbound, just e to W Peachtree St, just n to 5th St, then just w. **Parking:** street. **Cards:** AX, DS, MC, VI.

CALL

TRADER VIC'S

Phone: 404/221-6339

Polynesian
$20-$45

Chinese wood-fired ovens serve to prepare exotic Polynesian dishes, including white meat fish and fowl roasted in roti. Casual dress. **Bar:** Full bar. **Reservations:** suggested. **Hours:** 6 pm-10:30 pm. Closed major holidays. **Address:** 255 Courtland St NE **Location:** I-75/85, exit 249A southbound; exit 248C northbound, just w to Piedmont Ave, just n to Baker St, then just w; in Hilton Atlanta. **Parking:** on-site. **Cards:** AX, CB, DC, DS, MC, VI.

(See map and index starting on p. 288)

TRINGALI'S **Phone:** 404/522-6568 (55)

Italian
$0-$22

At Underground Atlanta, this casual and fun eatery serves pasta, Northern Italian veal entrees and fresh brick-oven pizza. Some of the sweet desserts are made on the premises. The tummy-pleasing fare is reason enough for this place's popularity. Casual dress. **Bar:** Full bar. **Reservations:** suggested. **Hours:** 11 am-9 pm, Sat from 2 pm, Sun from 5 pm. Closed major holidays. **Address:** 94 Upper Pryor St **Location:** Pryor and Alabama sts. **Parking:** on-site (fee). **Cards:** AX, DC, DS, JC, MC, VI.

THE VARSITY **Phone:** 404/881-1706 (35)

American
$3-$7

This Atlanta landmark has been serving chili dogs and onion rings, among many other fast food favorites, since the 1920s. Casual dress. **Hours:** 10 am-11:30 pm, Fri & Sat-12:30 am. **Address:** 61 North Ave NE **Location:** I-75/85, exit 249; exit 249D, just e. **Parking:** on-site. **Cards:** MC, VI.

VENI VIDI VICI **Phone:** 404/875-8424 (11)

Italian
$9-$29

A classic, open design lends New York chic to this experience. Authentic Italian cuisine is the focus, with well-prepared dishes such as the recommended crispy half duck, which is grilled over a fire rotisserie. Pre- and post-theater specialties are offered, as is an excellent Italian wine list. The wait staff is well versed in the menu and efficient. Dressy casual. **Bar:** Full bar. **Reservations:** suggested. **Hours:** 11:30 am-10 pm, Fri-11 pm, Sat 5 pm-11 pm, Sun 5 pm-10 pm. Closed major holidays. **Address:** 41 14th St NW **Location:** I-75/85, exit 250 (14th St); corner of 14th and W Peachtree sts; midtown. **Parking:** valet. **Cards:** AX, CB, DC, DS, JC, MC, VI.

VICKERY'S BAR & GRILL **Phone:** 404/881-1106 (17)

American
$4-$20

The nifty spot serves great sandwiches, soups, salads and burgers and even better full meals, such as pecan-crusted salmon, grilled jerk chicken and low-country grits with crawfish tails, shrimp, lump crabmeat and andouille sausage. There is something for everyone, and the atmosphere is relaxing. Casual dress. **Bar:** Full bar. **Hours:** 11 am-11 pm, Fri & Sat-1 am; Sunday brunch. Closed: 12/25. **Address:** 1106 Crescent Ave **Location:** Just n of jct 12th St NE. **Parking:** on-site (fee). **Cards:** AX, DC, DS, MC, VI.

VINOCITY WINE BAR & RESTAURANT **Phone:** 404/870-8886 (13)

American
$7-$27

The new Midtown hot spot is housed in a newly renovated 1890's house, where an abundant array of wines, cheeses and exciting new dishes can be sampled. Dressy casual. **Bar:** Full bar. **Reservations:** accepted. **Hours:** 11:30 am-11 pm, Sunday brunch 8 am-3 pm. Closed major holidays. **Address:** 36 13th St **Location:** I-75/85, exit 250 (14th St), just e to W Peachtree St, then just e. **Parking:** street. **Cards:** AX, DC, DS, MC, VI.

ZOCALO **Phone:** 404/249-7576 (20)

Mexican
$2-$16

The restaurant and bar specializes in Mexican food, including some of the best margaritas around. Casual dress. **Bar:** Full bar. **Hours:** 11 am-11 pm, Sun 10 am-10 pm. Closed major holidays. **Address:** 187 10th St **Location:** I-75/85, exit 250 (14th St), 1 mi e. **Parking:** on-site. **Cards:** AX, DC, DS, MC, VI.

BUCKHEAD (See map and index starting on p. 292)

WHERE TO STAY

ATLANTA MARRIOTT BUCKHEAD HOTEL & CONFERENCE CENTER **Phone:** 404/261-9250 (7)

AAA SAVE

Hotel
Rates not provided

Address: 3405 Lenox Rd NE **Location:** I-85, exit 88 southbound; exit 86 northbound, 1.8 mi n. Located in a commercial area opposite Lenox Square. **Facility:** 369 units. 362 one-bedroom standard units. 7 one-bedroom suites. 10 stories, interior corridors. **Parking:** on-site (fee) and valet. **Amenities:** high-speed Internet (fee), dual phone lines, voice mail, irons, hair dryers. *Some:* fax. **Pool(s):** outdoor. **Leisure Activities:** exercise room. **Guest Services:** valet laundry, airport transportation (fee)-The William B. Hartfield Atlanta Int'l Airport, area transportation-within 3 mi, wireless Internet. **Business Services:** conference facilities, business center. **Free Special Amenities: newspaper.**

FEE / SOME UNITS FEE FEE

Marriott HOTELS & RESORTS
AAA Benefit:
Members save a minimum 5% off the best available rate.

BEVERLY HILLS INN *Book at AAA.com* **Phone:** (404)233-8520 (20)

Historic Bed & Breakfast
$129-$249 All Year

Address: 65 Sheridan Dr NE **Location:** Jct Piedmont and Peachtree rds, 1.1 mi s on Peachtree Rd to Sheridan Dr, then just e. **Facility:** This European-style inn close to shopping and restaurants is furnished with antiques. 18 units. 14 one- and 4 two-bedroom standard units, some with kitchens and/or whirlpools. 3 stories (no elevator), interior corridors. **Parking:** on-site. **Terms:** 3 day cancellation notice-fee imposed. **Amenities:** high-speed Internet, irons, hair dryers. **Guest Services:** wireless Internet. **Business Services:** PC, fax. **Cards:** AX, DS, JC, MC, VI.

ASK / SOME UNITS FEE

COUNTRY INN & SUITES *Book at AAA.com* **Phone:** (404)949-4000 (21)

Hotel
$119-$269 All Year

Address: 800 Sidney Marcus Blvd **Location:** I-85, exit 86 northbound, 1.9 mi n to Sidney Marcus Blvd, then just w; exit 88 southbound, just w to Sidney Marcus Blvd, then just w. **Facility:** 142 units. 136 one-bedroom standard units. 6 one-bedroom suites. 6 stories, interior corridors. *Bath:* shower only. **Parking:** on-site. **Amenities:** high-speed Internet, voice mail, irons, hair dryers. **Pool(s):** outdoor. **Leisure Activities:** exercise room. **Guest Services:** complimentary and valet laundry, area transportation, wireless Internet. **Business Services:** meeting rooms, business center. **Cards:** AX, CB, DC, DS, JC, MC, VI.

ASK FEE CALL &M / SOME UNITS

(See map and index starting on p. 292)

COURTYARD BY MARRIOTT-BUCKHEAD

Book great rates at AAA.com

Phone: (404)869-0818 10

Hotel

$177-$190 All Year

Address: 3332 Peachtree Rd NE **Location:** I-85, exit 88 southbound; exit 86 northbound, 3 mi n on Lenox Rd, then 0.8 mi sw. **Facility:** Smoke free premises. 181 units. 172 one-bedroom standard units, some with whirlpools. 9 one-bedroom suites. 10 stories, interior corridors. **Parking:** on-site (fee) and valet. **Terms:** cancellation fee imposed. **Amenities:** high-speed Internet, voice mail, irons, hair dryers. **Pool(s):** heated indoor. **Leisure Activities:** whirlpool, exercise room. **Guest Services:** valet and coin laundry, area transportation-within 3 mi, wireless Internet. **Business Services:** meeting rooms, business center. **Cards:** AX, CB, DC, DS, JC, MC, VI.

FEE CALL

AAA Benefit:

Members save a minimum 5% off the best available rate.

DOUBLETREE HOTEL ATLANTA BUCKHEAD

Book great rates at AAA.com

Phone: (404)231-1234 

Hotel

$90-$198 All Year

Address: 3342 Peachtree Rd NE **Location:** Jct Piedmont and Peachtree rds NE, just e. **Facility:** 230 units. 229 one-bedroom standard units. 1 one-bedroom suite. 6 stories, interior corridors. **Parking:** on-site (fee) and valet. **Amenities:** dual phone lines, voice mail, irons, hair dryers. *Fee:* video games, high-speed Internet. **Guest Services:** valet laundry, area transportation, wireless Internet. **Business Services:** meeting rooms, business center. **Cards:** AX, DC, DS, MC, VI.

FEE CALL 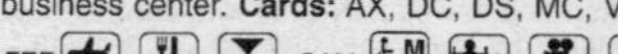 / SOME UNITS

AAA Benefit:

Members save 5% or more everyday!

EMBASSY SUITES HOTEL ATLANTA BUCKHEAD

Book great rates at AAA.com

Phone: (404)261-7733 14

Hotel

$134-$249 All Year

Address: 3285 Peachtree Rd NE **Location:** Jct Piedmont and Peachtree rds NE, 0.3 mi e. **Facility:** 317 units. 304 one- and 13 two-bedroom suites, some with whirlpools. 16 stories, interior corridors. *Bath:* combo or shower only. **Parking:** on-site (fee) and valet. **Terms:** 1-30 night minimum stay, cancellation fee imposed. **Amenities:** dual phone lines, voice mail, safes, irons, hair dryers. *Fee:* video games, high-speed Internet. **Pool(s):** outdoor, heated indoor. **Leisure Activities:** whirlpool, exercise room. **Guest Services:** valet and coin laundry, area transportation, wireless Internet. **Business Services:** conference facilities, business center. **Cards:** AX, CB, DC, DS, JC, MC, VI.

FEE 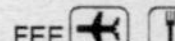  CALL    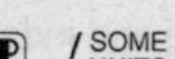 / SOME UNITS

AAA Benefit:

Members save 5% or more everyday!

FAIRFIELD INN-ATLANTA/BUCKHEAD

Book great rates at AAA.com

Phone: (404)846-0900 

Hotel

$147-$158 All Year

Address: 3092 Piedmont Rd NE **Location:** Jct Piedmont and Peachtree rds NE, just s. **Facility:** Smoke free premises. 115 one-bedroom standard units. 5 stories, interior corridors. **Parking:** on-site. **Terms:** cancellation fee imposed. **Amenities:** high-speed Internet, dual phone lines, voice mail, irons, hair dryers. *Some:* DVD players, CD players. **Pool(s):** heated indoor. **Leisure Activities:** whirlpool, exercise room. **Guest Services:** valet and coin laundry, area transportation, wireless Internet. **Business Services:** meeting rooms, business center. **Cards:** AX, CB, DC, DS, JC, MC, VI.

FEE  CALL 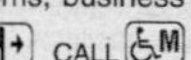 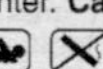 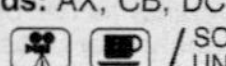 / SOME UNITS 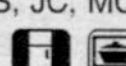

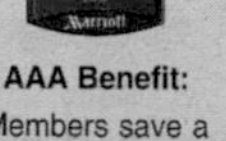

AAA Benefit:

Members save a minimum 5% off the best available rate.

GRAND HYATT ATLANTA

Book great rates at AAA.com

Phone: (404)237-1234 

Hotel

$139-$499 All Year

Address: 3300 Peachtree Rd NE **Location:** Corner of Peachtree and Piedmont rds. **Facility:** A Georgian-style high-rise hotel offering very large guest rooms with comfortable pillow-top mattresses and marble baths. 438 units. 413 one-bedroom standard units. 25 one-bedroom suites, some with whirlpools. 25 stories, interior corridors. **Parking:** on-site (fee) and valet. **Terms:** cancellation fee imposed. **Amenities:** dual phone lines, voice mail, fax, safes, honor bars, irons, hair dryers. *Fee:* video games, high-speed Internet. **Pool(s):** heated outdoor. **Leisure Activities:** saunas, steamrooms. *Fee:* massage. **Guest Services:** valet laundry, airport transportation (fee)-The William B. Hartsfield Atlanta Int'l Airport, area transportation-within 2 mi, wireless Internet. **Business Services:** conference facilities, business center. **Cards:** AX, CB, DC, DS, JC, MC, VI. **Free Special Amenities: newspaper and early check-in/late check-out.** ***(See color ad p 326)***

HYATT
HOTELS & RESORTS

AAA Benefit:

Ask for the AAA rate and save 10%.

FEE  CALL 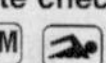    / SOME UNITS FEE  

(See map and index starting on p. 292)

HAMPTON INN ATLANTA BUCKHEAD *Book great rates at AAA.com* **Phone:** (404)233-5656 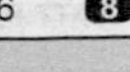

Hotel
$129-$169 All Year

Address: 3398 Piedmont Rd NE **Location:** Jct Piedmont and Peachtree rds NE, just w. **Facility:** 152 one-bedroom standard units. 6 stories, interior corridors. **Parking:** on-site. **Terms:** 1-30 night minimum stay, cancellation fee imposed. **Amenities:** video games (fee), high-speed Internet, voice mail, irons, hair dryers. **Pool(s):** outdoor. **Leisure Activities:** exercise room. **Guest Services:** valet laundry, area transportation, wireless Internet. **Business Services:** meeting rooms, business center. **Cards:** AX, CB, DC, DS, MC, VI.

FEE CALL / SOME UNITS

AAA Benefit:
Members save up to 10% everyday!

HOLIDAY INN EXPRESS HOTEL & SUITES-ATLANTA BUCKHEAD *Book at AAA.com* **Phone:** (404)262-7880 18

Hotel
$159-$259 All Year

Address: 505 Pharr Rd **Location:** Jct Pharr Rd and Maple Dr; just w of Piedmont Rd. **Facility:** 87 units. 49 one- and 38 two-bedroom standard units with kitchens. 3 stories (no elevator), interior/exterior corridors. **Parking:** on-site. **Amenities:** video library (fee), CD players, high-speed Internet, dual phone lines, voice mail, safes, irons, hair dryers. **Pool(s):** heated outdoor. **Leisure Activities:** whirlpool, exercise room. **Guest Services:** valet and coin laundry, area transportation, wireless Internet. **Business Services:** meeting rooms, business center. **Cards:** AX, CB, DC, DS, JC, MC, VI.

ASK FEE VCR / SOME UNITS FEE

HOMEWOOD SUITES-ATLANTA BUCKHEAD *Book great rates at AAA.com* **Phone:** (404)365-0001 2

Hotel
$189-$250 All Year

Address: 3566 Piedmont Rd **Location:** SR 400, exit 2, just s to Piedmont Rd, then 1 mi w. **Facility:** 92 units. 86 one- and 6 two-bedroom standard units with efficiencies. 4 stories, interior corridors. **Parking:** on-site. **Terms:** cancellation fee imposed. **Amenities:** video games (fee), high-speed Internet, dual phone lines, voice mail, safes, irons, hair dryers. **Pool(s):** outdoor. **Leisure Activities:** exercise room. **Guest Services:** valet and coin laundry, area transportation, wireless Internet. **Business Services:** meeting rooms, business center. **Cards:** AX, DC, DS, MC, VI.

FEE CALL / SOME UNITS FEE

AAA Benefit:
Members save 5% or more everyday!

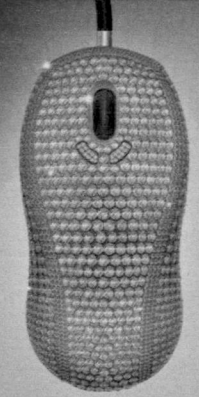

(See map and index starting on p. 292)

HYATT PLACE ATLANTA/BUCKHEAD Book great rates at AAA.com Phone: (404)869-6161 15

AAA SAVE

Hotel

$89-$279 All Year

Address: 3242 Peachtree Rd NE **Location:** Jct Peachtree and Piedmont rds NE, just s. **Facility:** 170 one-bedroom standard units. 8 stories, interior corridors. **Parking:** on-site. **Terms:** cancellation fee imposed. **Amenities:** high-speed Internet, dual phone lines, voice mail, safes, irons, hair dryers. **Pool(s):** outdoor. **Leisure Activities:** exercise room. **Guest Services:** valet laundry, area transportation-within 2 mi, wireless Internet. **Business Services:** meeting rooms, business center. **Cards:** AX, CB, DC, DS, JC, MC, VI. **Free Special Amenities: continental breakfast and high-speed Internet.**

FEE CALL

HYATT PLACE

AAA Benefit:

Ask for the AAA rate and save 10%.

INTERCONTINENTAL BUCKHEAD ATLANTA Book great rates at AAA.com Phone: (404)946-9000 12

AAA SAVE

Hotel

$219-$499 All Year

Address: 3315 Peachtree Rd NE **Location:** Jct Piedmont and Peachtree rds NE, just e. **Facility:** An impressive high-rise hotel in the heart of Buckhead; elegant guest rooms feature floor-to-ceiling windows, pillow-top bedding and marble baths. 422 units. 401 one-bedroom standard units. 21 one-bedroom suites. 22 stories, interior corridors. **Parking:** on-site and valet. **Amenities:** video library, CD players, dual phone lines, voice mail, safes, honor bars, irons, hair dryers. *Fee:* video games, high-speed Internet. *Some:* DVD players. **Pool(s):** heated outdoor. **Leisure Activities:** whirlpool, spa. **Guest Services:** valet laundry, area transportation-within 2 mi, wireless Internet. **Business Services:** conference facilities, business center. **Cards:** AX, DC, DS, MC, VI.

24 CALL / SOME UNITS FEE

JW MARRIOTT BUCKHEAD ATLANTA Book great rates at AAA.com Phone: (404)262-3344 11

AAA SAVE

Hotel

$365-$392 All Year

Address: 3300 Lenox Rd NE **Location:** I-85, exit 88 southbound; exit 86 northbound, 1.8 mi n. Adjoins a shopping mall. **Facility:** This angular glass-and-marble high-rise features richly appointed public areas as well as compact but lush grounds. Smoke free premises. 371 units. 367 one-bedroom standard units. 4 one-bedroom suites. 25 stories, interior corridors. **Parking:** on-site (fee). **Terms:** check-in 4 pm, cancellation fee imposed. **Amenities:** CD players, dual phone lines, voice mail, safes, honor bars, irons, hair dryers. *Fee:* video games, high-speed Internet. **Pool(s):** heated indoor. **Leisure Activities:** saunas, whirlpool, steamroom, spa. **Guest Services:** valet laundry, airport transportation (fee)-The William B. Hartfield Atlanta Int'l Airport, area transportation-within 3 mi, wireless Internet. **Business Services:** conference facilities, business center. **Cards:** AX, CB, DC, DS, JC, MC, VI.

FEE 24 CALL

JW MARRIOTT. HOTELS & RESORTS

AAA Benefit:

A deluxe level of comfort and a Member rate.

LA QUINTA INN-BUCKHEAD Book great rates at AAA.com Phone: (404)321-0999 23

Hotel

$64-$109 All Year

Address: 2535 Chantilly Dr NE **Location:** I-85, exit 88 southbound; exit 86 northbound, 2 mi on Buford Hwy to Lenox Rd, then just e under highway. **Facility:** 96 units. 94 one-bedroom standard units. 2 one-bedroom suites. 3 stories, interior corridors. **Parking:** on-site. **Amenities:** video games (fee), high-speed Internet, voice mail, irons, hair dryers. **Leisure Activities:** exercise room. **Guest Services:** valet and coin laundry, area transportation, wireless Internet. **Business Services:** meeting rooms, fax (fee). **Cards:** AX, DC, DS, MC, VI.

ASK FEE / SOME UNITS

RESIDENCE INN-BUCKHEAD/LENOX Book great rates at AAA.com Phone: (404)467-1660 5

AAA SAVE

Hotel

$227-$244 All Year

Address: 2220 Lake Blvd **Location:** I-85, exit 89, 1.6 mi w on N Druid Hills (becomes E Roxboro), then just n on Lenox Park Blvd. **Facility:** Smoke free premises. 150 units. 126 one- and 24 two-bedroom standard units, some with efficiencies or kitchens. 4 stories, interior corridors. *Bath:* combo or shower only. **Parking:** on-site. **Terms:** check-in 4 pm, cancellation fee imposed. **Amenities:** high-speed Internet, dual phone lines, voice mail, irons, hair dryers. **Pool(s):** heated outdoor. **Leisure Activities:** whirlpool, jogging, exercise room, sports court. **Guest Services:** valet and coin laundry, area transportation-within 3 mi, wireless Internet. **Business Services:** meeting rooms, PC, fax (fee). **Cards:** AX, CB, DC, DS, JC, MC, VI. **Free Special Amenities: full breakfast and high-speed Internet.** *(See color ad p 341)*

Residence Inn Marriott

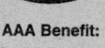

AAA Benefit:

Members save a minimum 5% off the best available rate.

CALL / SOME UNITS FEE

(See map and index starting on p. 292)

RESIDENCE INN BY MARRIOTT-ATLANTA/BUCKHEAD Book great rates at AAA.com Phone: (404)239-0677 19

Hotel

$227-$244 All Year

Address: 2960 Piedmont Rd NE **Location:** Jct Piedmont and Pharr rds, just s. **Facility:** Smoke free premises. 136 units. 102 one- and 34 two-bedroom standard units with kitchens. 2 stories, exterior corridors. **Parking:** on-site. **Terms:** cancellation fee imposed. **Amenities:** high-speed Internet, voice mail, irons, hair dryers. **Pool(s):** outdoor. **Leisure Activities:** whirlpool, gas grills, exercise room, sports court. **Guest Services:** valet and coin laundry, area transportation-within 3 mi, wireless Internet. **Business Services:** meeting rooms, business center. **Cards:** AX, CB, DC, DS, JC, MC, VI. **Free Special Amenities: full breakfast and high-speed Internet.**

FEE / SOME UNITS FEE

AAA Benefit:

Members save a minimum 5% off the best available rate.

THE RITZ-CARLTON, BUCKHEAD Book great rates at AAA.com Phone: (404)237-2700 3

Hotel

$369-$479 All Year

Address: 3434 Peachtree Rd NE **Location:** I-85, exit 86, 1.8 mi n on Cheshire Bridge-Lenox Rd. Located opposite Phipps Plaza Mall. **Facility:** The hotel's mahogany paneling, crystal chandeliers, marble floors and old-world oil paintings in gilded frames exude elegance. Smoke free premises. 517 units. 459 one-bedroom standard units. 58 one-bedroom suites, some with whirlpools. 22 stories, interior corridors. *Bath:* combo or shower only. **Parking:** on-site (fee) and valet. **Terms:** cancellation fee imposed. **Amenities:** DVD players, CD players, high-speed Internet (fee), dual phone lines, voice mail, safes, honor bars, irons, hair dryers. **Dining:** 2 restaurants, also, The Dining Room, see separate listing, entertainment. **Pool(s):** heated indoor. **Leisure Activities:** saunas, whirlpool, steamroom, CD library. *Fee:* massage. **Guest Services:** valet laundry, area transportation-within 3 mi, wireless Internet. **Business Services:** conference facilities, business center. **Cards:** AX, DC, DS, JC, MC, VI.

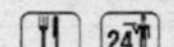 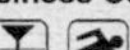    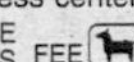 / SOME UNITS FEE 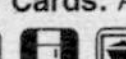 

SPRINGHILL SUITES BY MARRIOTT-ATLANTA BUCKHEAD Book great rates at AAA.com Phone: (404)844-4800 4

Hotel

$188-$201 All Year

Address: 3459 Buckhead Loop NE **Location:** SR 400, exit 2, just w on Lenox Rd. **Facility:** Smoke free premises. 220 one-bedroom standard units, some with whirlpools. 11 stories, interior corridors. **Parking:** on-site (fee). **Terms:** cancellation fee imposed. **Amenities:** video games (fee), high-speed Internet, voice mail, irons, hair dryers. **Pool(s):** heated indoor. **Leisure Activities:** whirlpool, exercise room. **Guest Services:** valet and coin laundry, area transportation-within 2 mi, wireless Internet. **Business Services:** meeting rooms, business center. **Cards:** AX, DS, MC, VI. **Free Special Amenities: high-speed Internet.**

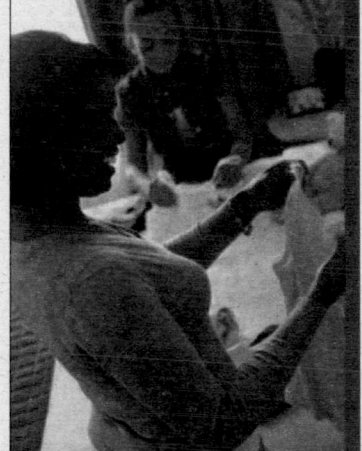

FEE 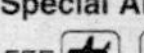 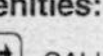 CALL 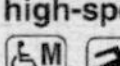 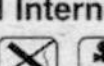  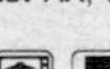

AAA Benefit:

Members save a minimum 5% off the best available rate.

▼ See AAA listing p 340 ▼

(See map and index starting on p. 292)

STAYBRIDGE SUITES   Book at AAA.com   **Phone:** (404)842-0800   17

Hotel
$169-$269 All Year

Address: 540 Pharr Rd **Location:** Jct Pharr and Piedmont rds, just w. **Facility:** 83 units. 74 one- and 9 two-bedroom standard units with efficiencies. 6 stories, interior corridors. **Parking:** on-site. **Amenities:** high-speed Internet, dual phone lines, voice mail, irons, hair dryers. **Pool(s):** heated indoor. **Leisure Activities:** whirlpool, exercise room. **Guest Services:** complimentary laundry, area transportation, wireless Internet. **Business Services:** meeting rooms, business center. **Cards:** AX, CB, DC, DS, JC, MC, VI.

ASK FEE / SOME UNITS FEE

SUPER 8 MOTEL   Book at AAA.com   **Phone:** (404)873-5731   24

Motel
$79-$109 All Year

Address: 1641 Peachtree St NE **Location:** I-75/85, exit 250, 0.3 mi e to W Peachtree St, then 1 mi n. **Facility:** 56 one-bedroom standard units. 3 stories, interior/exterior corridors. **Parking:** on-site. **Amenities:** high-speed Internet, hair dryers. **Guest Services:** coin laundry, wireless Internet. **Business Services:** fax (fee). **Cards:** AX, DS, MC, VI.

ASK / SOME UNITS FEE

TOWNEPLACE SUITES ATLANTA BUCKHEAD   Book great rates at AAA.com   **Phone:** (404)949-4820   22

Hotel
$197-$212 All Year

Address: 820 Sidney Marcus Blvd **Location:** I-85, exit 86 northbound, 1.9 mi n to Sidney Marcus Blvd, then just w; exit 88 southbound, just w to Sidney Marcus Blvd, then just w. **Facility:** Smoke free premises. 75 units. 67 one- and 8 two-bedroom standard units with efficiencies. 4 stories, interior corridors. **Parking:** on-site. **Terms:** office hours 7 am-11 pm, cancellation fee imposed. **Amenities:** high-speed Internet, dual phone lines, voice mail, irons, hair dryers. **Leisure Activities:** limited exercise equipment. **Guest Services:** valet and coin laundry, area transportation, wireless Internet. **Business Services:** PC, fax. **Cards:** AX, DS, MC, VI.

FEE CALL / SOME UNITS FEE

AAA Benefit:
Members save a minimum 5% off the best available rate.

THE WESTIN BUCKHEAD ATLANTA   Book great rates at AAA.com   **Phone:** (404)365-0065   6

Hotel
$169-$459 All Year

Address: 3391 Peachtree Rd NE **Location:** Adjacent to Lenox Square Mall. **Facility:** This high-rise hotel's post-modern and contemporary artwork and Biedermeier-style furnishings complement its white-metal-and-glass exterior. Smoke free premises. 365 units. 354 one-bedroom standard units. 11 one-bedroom suites, some with whirlpools. 22 stories, interior corridors. **Parking:** on-site (fee) and valet. **Amenities:** dual phone lines, voice mail, fax, safes, honor bars, irons, hair dryers. *Fee:* video games, high-speed Internet. *Some:* CD players. **Dining:** The Atlanta Palm, see separate listing. **Pool(s):** heated indoor. **Leisure Activities:** sauna, steamroom, sun deck, spa. *Fee:* golf & tennis privileges. **Guest Services:** valet laundry, area transportation-within 2 mi, wireless Internet. **Business Services:** conference facilities, business center. **Cards:** AX, CB, DC, DS, JC, MC, VI.

FEE / SOME UNITS

WESTIN
HOTELS & RESORTS

AAA Benefit:
Enjoy up to 15% off your next stay, plus Starwood Preferred Guest® bonuses.

WINGATE INN-BUCKHEAD   Book at AAA.com   **Phone:** (404)869-1100   1

Hotel
$119-$159 All Year

Address: 3600 Piedmont Rd NE **Location:** SR 400, exit 2, just s to Piedmont Rd, then 1.1 mi w. **Facility:** 101 units. 83 one-bedroom standard units. 18 one-bedroom suites with whirlpools. 5 stories, interior corridors. **Parking:** on-site. **Amenities:** video games (fee), high-speed Internet, dual phone lines, voice mail, safes, irons, hair dryers. **Pool(s):** outdoor. **Leisure Activities:** whirlpool, exercise room. **Guest Services:** valet laundry, area transportation, wireless Internet. **Business Services:** meeting rooms, business center. **Cards:** AX, CB, DC, DS, JC, MC, VI.

ASK FEE CALL / SOME UNITS

WHERE TO DINE

ALI-OLI   **Phone:** 404/266-0414   2

Italian
$7-$24

High ceilings and a beautiful bar mark the intimate, sophisticated dining area, where patrons sit down to delicious Italian-Mediterranean cuisine. Casual dress. **Bar:** Full bar. **Reservations:** accepted. **Hours:** 11:30 am-3 & 5:30-10 pm, Fri & Sat-11 pm. Closed major holidays; also Sun. **Address:** 3535 Peachtree Rd **Location:** In Lenox Marketplace. **Parking:** on-site. **Cards:** AX, DC, MC, VI.

CALL

ALON'S BAKERY & MARKET   **Phone:** 404/872-6000   58

American
$4-$10

The bakery tempts patrons with European desserts, pastries, artisan breads, salads and sandwiches. In the market are specialty wines and cheeses and prepared to-go foods. Casual dress. **Hours:** 7 am-8 pm, Sat from 8 am, Sun 9 am-4 pm. Closed major holidays. **Address:** 1394 N Highland Ave **Location:** Jct Virginia and N Highland aves, 1.5 mi n. **Parking:** on-site. **Cards:** MC, VI.

AMARYN'S THAI BOWL & SUSHI BAR   **Phone:** 404/841-2990   38

Asian
$5-$14

A bit different from its two sister restaurants, the quick-serve eatery prepares both Japanese and Thai food from a great location. Casual dress. **Bar:** Beer & wine. **Hours:** 11:30 am-3 & 5-10 pm. Closed: 11/26, 12/25. **Address:** 2900 Peachtree Rd **Location:** Jct Peachtree and W Paces Ferry rds, 0.4 mi s. **Parking:** on-site. **Cards:** AX, DS, MC, VI.

(See map and index starting on p. 292)

ANIS CAFE & BISTRO — **Phone:** 404/233-9889 (35)

American
$6-$29

On a side street, the converted residence is decorated with a mixture of media, giving the feel of a casual, relaxed bistro. Enclosed patio seating also is available. Creative, well-prepared appetizers and entrees include a pate of the day, mussels, escargots, lamb shank, fresh seafood and a daily flatbroad pizza. Casual dress. **Bar:** Full bar. **Reservations:** accepted. **Hours:** 11:30 am-2:30 & 6-10 pm, Fri & Sat-10:30 pm, Sun 6 pm-9 pm. Closed: 11/26, 12/25. **Address:** 2974 Grandview Ave **Location:** Jct Peachtree Rd, 0.3 mi s. **Parking:** on-site. **Cards:** AX, MC, VI.

ANNIE'S THAI CASTLE — **Phone:** 404/264-9546 (17)

Thai
$6-$19

Variations on traditional Thai themes are done nicely at the tastefully appointed Buckhead spot. Basil rolls and masaman curry highlight the list of favorites. The patio is a nice seating option in good weather. Casual dress. **Bar:** Full bar. **Reservations:** accepted. **Hours:** 11 am-2:30 & 5:30-10 pm, Fri-Sun from 4 pm. Closed major holidays; also Mon. **Address:** 3195 Roswell Rd **Location:** Jct Peachtree and W Paces Ferry rds, just n. **Parking:** on-site. **Cards:** AX, MC, VI.

ANTICA POSTA TUSCAN RESTAURANT & BAR — **Phone:** 404/262-7112 (30)

Italian
$18-$36

In a quiet area, the quaint converted house is popular for its fresh and authentic Tuscan dishes, such as white zolfini beans in olive oil and char-grilled rib-eye steak over arugula with a squeeze of lemon. Dressy casual. **Bar:** Full bar. **Reservations:** suggested. **Hours:** 4 pm-10 pm, Fri-11 pm, Sat noon-11 pm. Closed major holidays. **Address:** 519 E Paces Ferry Rd NE **Location:** Jct E Paces Ferry and Piedmont rds, just w. **Parking:** valet. **Cards:** AX, DC, DS, MC, VI.

ARIA — **Phone:** 404/233-7673 (29)

American
$21-$34

Contemporary preparations—such as farfalle pasta, Dungeness crab and veal medallions—reflect French and Mediterranean influences. Dressy casual. **Bar:** Full bar. **Reservations:** suggested. **Hours:** 6 pm-10 pm. Closed major holidays; also Sun. **Address:** 490 E Paces Ferry Rd **Location:** Jct E Paces Ferry and Peachtree rds, 0.3 mi e. **Parking:** valet. **Cards:** AX, DS, MC, VI.

ATLANTA FISH MARKET — **Phone:** 404/262-3165 (33)

Seafood
$16-$38

A gigantic fish statue marks the entrance to this popular Buckhead eatery, which has the bustling ambience of a warm and casual Savannah-style fish market. A wide variety of fresh fish entrees are offered, in addition to pasta, chicken and duck. Mouthwatering desserts include white chocolate chunk banana creme brulee. The wait staff is prompt, efficient and knowledgeable. Dressy casual. **Bar:** Full bar. **Reservations:** suggested. **Hours:** 11:30 am-11 pm, Fri & Sat 11 am-midnight, Sun 4 pm-10 pm. Closed: 11/26, 12/25. **Address:** 265 Pharr Rd **Location:** Jct Peachtree and Pharr rds, 2 blks e. **Parking:** valet. **Cards:** AX, DC, DS, MC, VI.

THE ATLANTA PALM — **Phone:** 404/814-1955 (8)

American
$10-$52

USDA Prime steak and seafood specialties are presented in a classic New York steakhouse setting. Steaks are cooked to order, and portions are monstrous. Particularly good is the filet, thinly sliced and served over garlic mashed potatoes, with a colossal salad. The staff is friendly, casual and knowledgeable. Dressy casual. **Bar:** Full bar. **Reservations:** suggested. **Hours:** 6:30 am-10:30 & 11:30-11 pm, Sun 7 am-11 & noon-10 pm. **Address:** 3391 Peachtree Rd NE **Location:** Adjacent to Lenox Square Mall; in The Westin Buckhead Atlanta. **Parking:** valet. **Cards:** AX, CB, DC, DS, JC, MC, VI.

BASIL'S — **Phone:** 404/233-9755 (34)

Mediterranean
$4-$29

This cozy little cafe serves Mediterranean dishes, many of which are not only inventive, but healthy as well. Well-prepared and nicely presented, a recommended selection is shrimp with vegetables served over rice, topped with an oil-based dressing. Casual dress. **Bar:** Full bar. **Reservations:** suggested. **Hours:** 11:30 am-2:30 & 5:30-10:30 pm, Fri & Sat 5:30 pm-10 pm. Closed major holidays; also for lunch Mon. **Address:** 2985 Grandview Ave **Location:** Off Pharr Rd, just s on Grandview Ave; in the heart of Buckhead. **Parking:** on-site. **Cards:** AX, CB, DC, DS, MC, VI.

BLUEPOINTE — **Phone:** 404/237-9070 (4)

Seafood
$4-$86

Excellent fusion cuisine with heavy Asian and Southwestern influences are featured. Located in a stunning, chic and very contemporary dining room. Dressy casual. **Bar:** Full bar. **Reservations:** suggested. **Hours:** 11:30 am-2:30 & 5:30-11 pm, Fri & Sat-midnight, Sun 5:30 pm-10 pm. Closed: 11/26, 12/25. **Address:** 3455 Peachtree Rd **Location:** Jct Peachtree and Lenox rds; in Pinnacle Building. **Parking:** valet. **Cards:** AX, CB, DC, DS, JC, MC, VI.

BONE'S RESTAURANT — **Phone:** 404/237-2663 (18)

Steak
$6-$45

This restaurant has the feel of a New York club with a comfortable ambience and available private rooms. The menu features aged prime beef and fresh seafood. Try an excellent petite New York strip, cooked to perfection and served with sauteed mushrooms. Dressy casual. **Bar:** Full bar. **Reservations:** suggested. **Hours:** 11:30 am-2:30 & 5:30-10 pm, Sat 5:30 pm-11 pm, Sun 5:30 pm-10 pm. Closed major holidays. **Address:** 3130 Piedmont Rd NE **Location:** Jct Piedmont and Peachtree rds NE, just s. **Parking:** valet. **Cards:** AX, CB, DC, DS, MC, VI.

BUCKHEAD BREAD COMPANY & CORNER CAFE — **Phone:** 404/240-1978 (27)

American
$9-$14

Creative sandwiches and salad fill the new American menu. The upbeat bistro-style atmosphere is light and airy, featuring culinary murals, slate floors and wooden tables. Also in the facility is a bakery that offers a wide selection of fresh bread. Casual dress. **Bar:** Beer & wine. **Hours:** 6:30 am-5:30 pm, Sat & Sun from 8 am. Closed: 11/26, 12/25. **Address:** 3070 Piedmont Rd NE **Location:** Corner of Piedmont NE and E Paces Ferry rds. **Parking:** on-site. **Cards:** AX, DC, DS, MC, VI.

CALL &M

BUCKHEAD DINER — **Phone:** 404/262-3336 (24)

American
$11-$27

Patrons can hop on board a reproduction of a luxury railroad dining car for a fine meal. This eclectic dining spot serves unusual cutting-edge cuisine, such as the distinctively seasoned blackened mahi mahi. The experience here is unforgettable. Casual dress. **Bar:** Full bar. **Hours:** 11 am-midnight, Sat & Sun 10 am-10 pm. Closed: 11/26, 12/25. **Address:** 3073 Piedmont Rd NE **Location:** Corner of Piedmont NE and E Paces Ferry rds. **Parking:** valet. **Cards:** AX, DC, DS, MC, VI.

(See map and index starting on p. 292)

CAFE INTERMEZZO **Phone:** 404/355-0411 (53)

American
$7-$15

The stylish European coffee bar and restaurant serves tasty, attractively presented dishes and delicious dessert specialties. A nice brunch is featured on Saturdays and Sundays. Prompt yet casual service rounds out an overall pleasant experience. Casual dress. **Bar:** Full bar. **Hours:** 10 am-2 am, Fri & Sat-3 am. **Address:** 1845 Peachtree Rd NE **Location:** Jct Collier Rd, 0.4 mi s. **Parking:** on-site. **Cards:** AX, CB, DC, DS, JC, MC, VI.

CAFE SUNFLOWER **Phone:** 404/352-8859 (49)

Vegetarian
$5-$16

Playful yet sophisticated, the vegetarian restaurant's atmosphere combines sunflowers and other colorful accessories. The elaborate menu caters primarily to the New Age crowd and features many tasty entrees and luscious desserts. Casual dress. **Bar:** Beer & wine. **Reservations:** accepted. **Hours:** 11:30 am-2:30 & 5-9:30 pm, Fri-10 pm, Sat noon-2:30 & 5-10 pm. Closed major holidays; also Sun. **Address:** 2140 Peachtree Rd **Location:** Jct Colonial Homes Dr; in Brookwood Square Center. **Parking:** on-site. **Cards:** AX, CB, DC, DS, JC, MC, VI.

CALL &M

THE CAPITAL GRILLE **Phone:** 404/262-1162 (26)

Steak
$6-$42

Cherry wood and red leather assist in making this "clubby" dining room a beautiful spot to dine on excellent cuts of dry-aged beef. The staff is highly attentive and knowledgeable. Dressy casual. **Bar:** Full bar. **Reservations:** suggested. **Hours:** 11:30 am-3 & 5-10 pm, Fri & Sat-11 pm, Sun 5 pm-9 pm. Closed major holidays. **Address:** 255 E Paces Ferry Rd **Location:** Jct Peachtree and E Paces Ferry rds; in Capital Building. **Parking:** valet. **Cards:** AX, CB, DC, DS, JC, MC, VI.

CEDAR'S **Phone:** 404/261-1826 (39)

Lebanese
$7-$18

The lunch buffet is popular in this neighborhood storefront, but evenings also are busy with folks enjoying the various salad, kebobs, chops and casseroles, each accompanied by fragrant rice and a salad. Casual dress. **Bar:** Full bar. **Reservations:** suggested. **Hours:** 11:30 am-2:30 & 6-9:30 pm, Fri & Sat-10:30 pm, Sun noon-3 & 6-9 pm. Closed: 1/1, 11/26, 12/25. **Address:** 2770 Lenox Rd **Location:** I-85, exit 88 southbound; exit Cheshire Bridge and Lenox Rd northbound, 0.5 mi w. **Parking:** on-site. **Cards:** AX, DC, DS, MC, VI.

CHOPS **Phone:** 404/262-2675 (22)

Steak
$7-$46

The cosmopolitan New York-style steakhouse, with an exhibition kitchen, is a step above the everyday steakhouse. Prime beef cuts are delicious and well-prepared, as is the lobster bisque appetizer. A selection from the extensive wine list makes the meal complete. Dressy casual. **Bar:** Full bar. **Reservations:** suggested. **Hours:** 11:30 am-2:30 & 5:30-11 pm, Fri-midnight, Sat 5:30 pm-midnight, Sun 5:30 pm-10 pm. Closed major holidays. **Address:** 70 W Paces Ferry Rd **Location:** Just w of Peachtree Rd; in Buckhead Plaza. **Parking:** valet. **Cards:** AX, CB, DC, DS, MC, VI.

THE CLUBHOUSE **Phone:** 404/442-8891 (9)

American
$6-$46

This cavernous and upscale establishment features the latest take on steak, seafood, pasta and burgers and the like on the Buckhead "see and be seen" circuit. Its list of celebrity co-owners include Jack Nicklaus and Kevin Costner. Dressy casual. **Bar:** Full bar. **Reservations:** accepted. **Hours:** 11:30 am-10:30 pm, Fri & Sat-11:30 pm, Sun-9:30 pm. Closed: 12/25. **Address:** 3393 Peachtree Rd NE **Location:** In Lenox Square Mall. **Parking:** on-site and valet. **Cards:** AX, CB, DC, DS, MC, VI.

COCO LOCO CAFE **Phone:** 404/364-0212 (41)

Cuban
$2-$17

Served in a fun and festive atmosphere, Caribbean and Cuban cuisine makes up the menu. Casual dress. **Bar:** Full bar. **Reservations:** accepted. **Hours:** 11 am-2:30 & 6-10 pm, Fri & Sat 11:30 am-10:30 pm, Sun 1 pm-9 pm. Closed major holidays. **Address:** 2625 Piedmont Rd, Suite 40 **Location:** Jct Piedmont Rd and Sidney Marcus Blvd; in Buckhead Crossing Mall. **Parking:** on-site. **Cards:** AX, CB, DC, DS, JC, MC, VI.

THE COLONNADE **Phone:** 404/874-5642 (51)

American
$3-$20

This family owned favorite has been a standby for years for such staples as homestyle fried chicken, seafood and southern style vegetables and dessert. Casual dress. **Bar:** Full bar. **Hours:** 5 pm-9 pm, Sat noon-10 pm, Sun 11:30 am-9 pm. Closed: 7/4, 12/25. **Address:** 1879 Cheshire Bridge Rd **Location:** I-85, exit 86 northbound, 1.9 mi n to Cheshire Bridge Rd, then 1.1 mi e; exit 88 southbound, 1.1 mi e. **Parking:** on-site.

CORNER BAKERY **Phone:** 404/816-5100 (12)

Deli
$5-$10

This cafeteria-style restaurant specializes in sandwiches, soup, salad, fresh-baked bread and desserts. All dishes are served in tasty, large portions by efficient servers. For a yummy twist on the traditional tuna sandwich, try it with potato dill bread. Casual dress. **Hours:** 7 am-9 pm, Sat & Sun from 7:30 am. Closed: 11/26, 12/25. **Address:** 3368 Peachtree Rd NE **Location:** I-85, exit 88, n on Lenox Rd to Peachtree Rd NE, then 0.3 mi sw. **Parking:** street. **Cards:** AX, DC, DS, MC, VI.

CALL &M

COWTIPPERS **Phone:** 404/874-3751 (56)

American
$3-$19

Featuring all things meat ranging from steaks to hamburgers, the boisterous Texas roadhouse is as comfortable as a pair of broken-in jeans. This place is popular with the neighborhood crowd. Casual dress. **Bar:** Full bar. **Hours:** 11:30 am-11 pm, Fri & Sat-midnight. Closed major holidays. **Address:** 1600 Piedmont Ave NE **Location:** Jct Monroe Dr NE, just s. **Parking:** on-site. **Cards:** AX, DC, DS, MC, VI.

DANTANNA'S **Phone:** 404/760-8873 (14)

Steak & Seafood
$4-$39

Convenient for shoppers, the upscale sports bar adjacent to Lenox Square offers fresh seafood and strong service. Casual dress. **Bar:** Full bar. **Hours:** 11 am-2:30 am, Sun noon-midnight. Closed: 11/26, 12/25. **Address:** 3400 Around Lenox Dr, Suite 304 **Location:** Adjacent to Lenox Square Mall. **Parking:** on-site. **Cards:** AX, DS, MC, VI.

CALL &M

(See map and index starting on p. 292)

DANTE'S DOWN THE HATCH Phone: 404/266-1600 (7)

Specialty
$14-$28

Guests can watch crocodiles swim in a moat around an 18th-century sailing vessel and listen to music from a jazz trio at the comfortable restaurant. Fondues combine beef, pork, chicken, shrimp, Chinese dumplings and vegetables with assorted dips, including broths and cheese. Dressy casual. Entertainment **Bar:** Full bar. **Reservations:** suggested. **Hours:** 4 pm-11 pm, Fri & Sat-midnight, Sun 5 pm-11 pm. Closed major holidays; also Super Bowl Sun. **Address:** 3380 Peachtree Rd **Location:** Just e of Piedmont Rd. **Parking:** on-site. **Cards:** AX, DC, DS, MC, VI.

THE DINING ROOM Phone: 404/237-2700 (5)

French
$92-$155

Silk upholstery, classically rendered paintings, intimate lighting, exotic flowers and soft orchestral music provide the ultimate in luxurious dining. Modern French cuisine with Asian overtones features selections that are imaginatively adventurous. Polished service with gracious civility extended to all guests. Formal attire. Entertainment. **Bar:** Full bar. **Reservations:** suggested. **Hours:** 6 pm-9 pm, Fri & Sat-9:30 pm. Closed: 12/25; also Sun & Mon. **Address:** 3434 Peachtree Rd NE **Location:** I-85, exit 86, 1.8 mi n on Cheshire Bridge-Lenox Rd; in The Ritz-Carlton, Buckhead. **Parking:** on-site. **Cards:** AX, DC, DS, JC, MC, VI.

CALL (♿M)

DOC CHEY'S NOODLE HOUSE Phone: 404/888-0777 (57)

Asian
$2-$11

This funky, crowded restaurant offers a fun mix of dishes from Asian cultures, including sushi handroos and udon noodles from Japan, vermicilli bowls and basil rolls from Vietnam, curries from Thailand and vegetable stir-fry from the Szechuan region of China. The large patio is an ideal spot for people watching. The food is a super value. Casual dress. **Bar:** Beer & wine. **Hours:** 11:30 am-10 pm. Closed major holidays; also Super Bowl Sun. **Address:** 1424 N Highland Ave **Location:** In Virginia-Highlands at University Dr; in Highland Walk. **Parking:** on-site. **Cards:** AX, DS, MC, VI.

FAT MATT'S RIB SHACK Phone: 404/607-1622 (54)

Barbecue
$2-$19

"Messy" ribs and down-home barbecue are a great fix at this "dive" which also serves up some dynamite "blues" each evening. Casual dress. **Bar:** Beer only. **Hours:** 11:30 am-11:30 pm, Fri & Sat-12:30 am, Sun 1 pm-11:30 pm. Closed major holidays. **Address:** 1181 Piedmont Rd NE **Location:** I-85, exit 86 northbound, just n to Monroe Dr, just e to Piedmont Rd NE, then just s; exit 88 southbound, just e to Lenot Rd, just e to Cheshire Bridge Rd, 1.5 mi e s to Piedmont Rd, then just e. **Parking:** on-site. **Cards:** MC, VI.

FOGO DE CHAO Phone: 404/266-9988 (21)

Brazilian
$21-$50

This Southern Brazilian styled churrascaria features fifteen select cuts of meat served tableside by "Gauchos". An extremely well-stocked salad bar is available also. The service staff is most attentive. Casual dress. **Bar:** Full bar. **Reservations:** suggested. **Hours:** 11 am-2 & 5-10 pm, Fri-10:30 pm, Sat 4:30 pm-10:30 pm, Sun 4:30 pm-9:30 pm. Closed: 11/26, 12/25. **Address:** 3101 Piedmont Rd NE **Location:** Jct Piedmont and Peachtree rds NE, just s. **Parking:** on-site and valet. **Cards:** AX, CB, DC, DS, JC, MC, VI.

GEORGIA GRILLE Phone: 404/352-3517 (45)

Southwestern
$16-$25

This pleasant, sunny bistro features excellent, creative Southwestern cuisine. One of the most renowned dishes is the lobster enchilada, a must on a first visit, which, when followed by an exquisite chocolate mousse, makes an extraordinary meal. Highly attentive servers ably assist guests in making good choice to suit their tastes. Casual dress. **Bar:** Full bar. **Reservations:** suggested, weekends. **Hours:** 6 pm-10 pm, Fri & Sat-11 pm, Sun 5:30 pm-9 pm. Closed major holidays; also Mon. **Address:** 2290 Peachtree Rd **Location:** Just s of Peachtree Rd and Peachtree Battle Ave; in Peachtree Square. **Parking:** on-site. **Cards:** AX, MC, VI.

GRAND CHINA RESTAURANT Phone: 404/231-8690 (36)

Chinese
$7-$27

This lovely restaurant has pleased local residents for many years with its exotic menu of Hunan, Cantonese, Szechuan and Mandarin entrees and gracious service. Dim lighting, fresh flowers and soft orchestral music help achieve a comfortable, casual ambience. Casual dress. **Bar:** Full bar. **Reservations:** accepted. **Hours:** 11:30 am-10:45 pm, Fri-11 pm, Sat noon-11 pm, Sun noon-10 pm. Closed: 11/26. **Address:** 2975 Peachtree Rd **Location:** Jct Peachtree and W Paces Ferry rds, 3 blks s. **Parking:** on-site. **Cards:** AX, CB, DC, DS, MC, VI.

HASHIGUCHI JR. Phone: 404/841-9229 (13)

Japanese
$2-$20

Affordable sushi is the star at the often-crowded restaurant, but plenty of other fresh fish choices appeal to those who prefer cooked food. Casual dress. **Bar:** Beer & wine. **Reservations:** accepted. **Hours:** 11:30 am-2 & 5:30-11:30 pm. **Address:** 3400 Around Lenox Rd, Suite C520 **Location:** Adjacent to Lenox Square Mall. **Parking:** on-site. **Cards:** AX, DS, MC, VI.

THE IMPERIAL FEZ ***Menu on AAA.com*** Phone: 404/351-0870 (44)

Moroccan
$45-$65

Surrender your shoes and dine in an opulent nest of pillows, rugs and brilliantly patterned drapery. Five-courses of Moroccan Mediterranean cuisine are staged in an exotic setting while belly dancers fascinate with graceful movement and colorful costumes. Dressy casual. **Bar:** Full bar. **Reservations:** suggested. **Hours:** 6 pm-11:30 pm; to 11 pm in winter. **Address:** 2285 Peachtree Rd NE, Suite 102 **Location:** Between Collier and 26th. **Parking:** on site and valet. **Cards:** AX, DC, DS, MC, VI.

KYMA Phone: 404/262-0702 (23)

Greek
$9-$34

The contemporary Greek restaurant features excellent preparations of fish. The decor is chic and the servers well-versed. Dressy casual. **Bar:** Full bar. **Reservations:** suggested. **Hours:** 5 pm-11 pm. Closed major holidays; also Sun. **Address:** 3085 Piedmont Rd NE **Location:** Jct Piedmont NE and E Paces Ferry rds. **Parking:** valet. **Cards:** AX, CB, DC, DS, JC, MC, VI.

(See map and index starting on p. 292)

LA GROTTA RISTORANTE ITALIANO **Phone:** 404/231-1368 (40)

AAA

Italian
$7-$39

With a relaxed formal atmosphere, this local favorite always delights with Northern Italian seafood, veal, chicken and beef entrees, as well as homemade pasta specialties like Ravioloni con Caprino. Delectable desserts and an excellent wine list complete a great meal. Semi-formal attire. **Bar:** Full bar. **Reservations:** suggested. **Hours:** 6 pm-10:30 pm. Closed major holidays; also Sun & 6/22-7/6. **Address:** 2637 Peachtree Rd NE **Location:** Jct Peachtree and Wesley Chapel rds, just s. **Parking:** valet. **Cards:** AX, DC, DS, MC, VI.

LANDMARK DINER **Phone:** 404/816-9090 (1)

Continental
$7-$26

Fresh daily specials, large portions and mountainous desserts are just a few of the reasons Atlantans have been frequenting the eatery for years. Adjoining is a lounge that has become a popular night spot. Casual dress. **Bar:** Full bar. **Hours:** 24 hours. **Address:** 3652 Roswell Rd NE **Location:** SR 400, exit 2, 1 mi n to Roswell Rd. **Parking:** on-site. **Cards:** AX, CB, DC, DS, JC, MC, VI.

MAGGIANO'S LITTLE ITALY **Phone:** 404/816-9650 (11)

Italian
$11-$38

Diners savor scrumptious, traditional favorites served in a bustling atmosphere reminiscent of Little Italy. The dining area projects an early-20th-century feel; loud conversations bouncing off high ceilings evoke a sense of the Roaring 20s. Casual dress. **Bar:** Full bar. **Reservations:** accepted. **Hours:** 11 am-10 pm, Fri & Sat-11 pm, Sun-9 pm. Closed: 12/25. **Address:** 3368 Peachtree Rd NE **Location:** I-85, exit 88, n on Lenox Rd to Peachtree Rd NE, then 0.3 mi sw. **Parking:** valet. **Cards:** AX, CB, DC, DS, JC, MC, VI.

CALL &M

MAMA FU'S **Phone:** 404/367-5443

Asian
$6-$9

The funky, crowded restaurant offers a fun mix of dishes from Asian cultures, including ahi tuna from Japan, noodle bowls and basil rolls from Vietnam, curries from Thailand and lo mein pot stickers from China. The food is a super value. Casual dress. **Bar:** Beer & wine. **Hours:** 11 am-9 pm, Fri & Sat-10 pm. Closed major holidays. **Address:** 1935 Peachtree Rd **Location:** Between Collier and Brighton rds. **Parking:** no self-parking. **Cards:** AX, DS, MC, VI.

CALL &M

MCKINNON'S LOUISIANE RESTAURANT **Phone:** 404/237-1313 (20)

Cajun
$5-$26

Seafood items have a spicy touch, as does the homemade seasoned jambalaya. A small cocktail bar separates the elegant, candlelit dining room from the casual bistro. Service shows a touch of sophistication. Casual dress. **Bar:** Full bar. **Reservations:** suggested. **Hours:** 5:30 pm-10 pm. Closed major holidays. **Address:** 3209 Maple Dr **Location:** Jct Piemont and Peachtree rds, just s on Peachtree to Maple Dr. **Parking:** on-site. **Cards:** AX, DC, DS, MC, VI.

MESKEREM **Phone:** 404/417-0991 (43)

Ethiopian
$7-$20

Gracious, slow-paced service and some of the tastiest Ethopian food in Atlanta are featured at this eatery. Casual dress. **Bar:** Full bar. **Reservations:** accepted. **Hours:** 11:30 am-11 pm. Closed major holidays. **Address:** 2781 Clairmont Rd **Location:** I-85, exit 91, just w. **Parking:** on-site. **Cards:** AX, DC, DS, MC, VI.

NAKATO **Phone:** 404/873-6582 (52)

Japanese
$4-$45

A bit on the outskirts, the fine-dining establishment is worth the drive. The rich, elegant dining room features staff in traditional Japanese attire. Diners can choose from teppenyaki tables, a sushi bar or dining room service. Teppenyaki tables provide good theatrics as the chef displays his cooking talents. Select ingredients flavor such dishes as yakitori, tempura, sushi, sashimi and varied noodles. Dressy casual. **Bar:** Full bar. **Reservations:** accepted. **Hours:** 5:30 pm-10 pm, Fri & Sat-11 pm, Sun 5 pm-10 pm. **Address:** 1776 Cheshire Bridge Rd **Location:** Between La Vista and Piedmont rds; just e of jct Cheshire Bridge and Monroe rds. **Parking:** on-site and valet. **Cards:** AX, CB, DC, DS, JC, MC, VI.

NAVA **Phone:** 404/240-1984 (28)

Southwestern
$9-$32

Such superbly crafted dishes as chili-cured lamb rack and fire-roasted quail are examples of the highly creative Southwestern cuisine offered here. The sophisticated and upscale ambience has been exactingly executed to offer diners an experience that rivals anything in Santa Fe. Dressy casual. **Bar:** Full bar. **Reservations:** suggested. **Hours:** 11:30 am-2:30 & 5:30-11 pm, Sat from 5 pm, Sun 5:30 pm-10 pm. Closed major holidays. **Address:** 3060 Peachtree Rd **Location:** Jct Peachtree and W Paces Ferry rds. **Parking:** on-site and valet. **Cards:** AX, CB, DC, DS, JC, MC, VI.

NEW YORK PRIME **Phone:** 404/846-0644 (6)

Steak
$21-$45

Customers are invited to relax, take their time and enjoy dinner at the popular steakhouse. Only USDA prime beef is used. Courses are prepared when ordered, using fresh products of the highest quality. The service staff is attentive to guests' comfort and needs, as well as helpful and knowledgeable regarding the menu. When the meal is finished, venture to the martini and cigar bar. Dressy casual. **Bar:** Full bar. **Reservations:** accepted. **Hours:** 5 pm-11 pm, Sun-10 pm. Closed: 7/4, 11/26. **Address:** 3424 Peachtree Rd NE **Location:** Jct Lenox Ave, just sw; in Monarch Tower. **Parking:** valet. **Cards:** AX, DC, DS, MC, VI.

CALL &M

ONE STAR RANCH **Phone:** 404/233-7644 (19)

Barbecue
$5-$29

Simple, straightforward Texas-style barbecue makes up a menu that lists enormous ribs, brisket and tasty vegetable sides, which go well with cold beer. Patio seating lets guests sit back and relax. Casual dress. **Bar:** Full bar. **Hours:** 11 am-10 pm, Fri & Sat-11 pm, Sun 11:30-10 pm. Closed major holidays. **Address:** 25 Irby Ave **Location:** Jct Roswell Rd and Irby Ave, just w. **Parking:** on-site. **Cards:** AX, MC, VI.

PRICCI **Phone:** 404/237-2941 (31)

Italian
$9-$26

Taste buds wake up to creative Italian meals served in an upscale atmosphere. Patrons can follow up savory vitello alla parmigiana for dinner with a luscious dessert afterward. Dressy casual. **Bar:** Full bar. **Reservations:** suggested. **Hours:** 11:30 am-2:30 & 5-10 pm, Fri-11 pm, Sat from 5 pm-11 pm, Sun 5 pm-10 pm. Closed major holidays. **Address:** 500 Pharr Rd **Location:** Jct Pharr Rd and Maple Dr, just w of Piedmont Rd. **Parking:** valet. **Cards:** AX, DC, DS, MC, VI.

(See map and index starting on p. 292)

PRIME **Phone:** 404/812-0555 (10)

Specialty
$5-$39

The hip, distinctive concept combines Japanese and American cuisine with similarly themed decor. On the menu are USDA prime cuts of beef as well as the freshest in seafood and sushi. Fried lobster tail is a favorite. Dressy casual. **Bar:** Full bar. **Reservations:** suggested. **Hours:** 11:30 am-10 pm, Fri & Sat-11 pm, Sun 4 pm-9 pm. Closed: 11/26, 12/25. **Address:** 3393 Peachtree Rd **Location:** In Lenox Square Mall. **Parking:** on-site and valet. **Cards:** AX, CB, DC, DS, MC, VI.

RAJA INDIAN RESTAURANT **Phone:** 404/237-2661 (37)

Indian
$3-$20

The restaurant features traditional Indian favorites such as tandoori and vindaloo. Amiable servers are familiar with the menu and can help diners to make satisfying choices. Dressy casual. **Bar:** Beer & wine. **Reservations:** accepted. **Hours:** 11:30 am-2:30 & 5:30-10 pm, Fri-10:30 pm, Sat 12:30 pm-3 & 5:30-10:30 pm, Sun 5:30 pm-10 pm. Closed: 11/26, 12/25. **Address:** 2955A-2 Peachtree Rd NE **Location:** Jct Peachtree and W Paces Ferry rds, 3 blks s. **Parking:** on-site. **Cards:** AX, CB, DS, MC, VI.

RAMA 5 OF THAILAND **Phone:** 404/442-7522 (25)

Thai
$8-$15

The authentic Thai dishes, which can be ordered mild, hot or "thai hot," are draws here. Enjoy this fare either inside or on the patio. Casual dress. **Bar:** Full bar. **Hours:** 11:30 am-2:30 & 5:30-10 pm, Sat noon-2:30 & 5:30-11 pm, Sun noon-2:30 & 5:30-10 pm. Closed: 11/26. **Address:** 318 E Paces Ferry Rd **Location:** Jct Peachtree and E Paces Ferry rds, just e. **Parking:** on-site. **Cards:** AX, DS, MC, VI.

RED SNAPPER **Phone:** 404/634-8947 (50)

Seafood
$5-$24

Several preparations of snapper and many other succulent seafood specials are on the traditional restaurant's menu. A romantic ambience is part of the dining experience. Casual dress. **Bar:** Full bar. **Hours:** 11:30 am-2 & 5:30-10 pm, Fri & Sat-10:30 pm, Sun 5:30 pm-9:30 pm. Closed: 9/7, 11/26; also Mon. **Address:** 2100 Cheshire Bridge Rd **Location:** I-85, exit 86 northbound, 2.4 mi n, then 0.5 mi e; exit 88 southbound, 0.5 mi e. **Parking:** on-site. **Cards:** AX, CB, DC, DS, JC, MC, VI.

ROCK BOTTOM BREWERY **Phone:** 404/264-0253 (16)

American
$8-$30

Hand-crafted beers, grilled entrees, pasta dishes, salads, ribs and wings are among offerings at the brewery, an always-popular spot with the after-work crowd. Casual dress. **Bar:** Full bar. **Hours:** 11 am-midnight, Fri & Sat-2 am. Closed: 11/26, 12/25. **Address:** 3242 Peachtree Rd NE **Location:** Jct Peachtree and Piedmont rds, just w. **Parking:** on-site. **Cards:** AX, CB, DC, DS, JC, MC, VI.

R. THOMAS DELUXE GRILL **Phone:** 404/872-2942 (55)

Natural/Organic
$4-$15

In a garden atmosphere replete with exotic birds, the funky and distinctive eatery serves healthy fare and is remarkably veggie-friendly. Casual dress. **Bar:** Beer & wine. **Reservations:** accepted. **Hours:** 24 hours. Closed: 11/26, 12/25. **Address:** 1812 Peachtree Rd NW **Location:** Between Collier Rd and 26th St. **Parking:** on-site. **Cards:** AX, CB, DC, DS, JC, MC, VI.

RU SAN'S SUSHI & SAKE BAR BUCKHEAD TOWER PLACE **Phone:** 404/239-9557 (15)

Japanese
$3-$26

The bustling, trendy establishment presents an extensive menu of sushi, creative appetizers, salads, fried and grilled fish and Pacific Rim seafood dinners. The lunch buffet is popular. Casual dress. **Bar:** Beer & wine. **Hours:** 11:30 am-11 pm, Fri & Sat-midnight. **Address:** 3365 Piedmont Rd **Location:** Jct Piedmont and Peachtree rds, just n. **Parking:** on-site. **Cards:** AX, DC, DS, MC, VI.

TAKA **Phone:** 404/869-2802 (32)

Sushi
$4-$18

Lots of fresh fish choices make up the menu at the contemporary restaurant, but sushi is the star. It's sometimes crowded in the soothingly decorated spot. Critics and customers alike shower rave reviews on this place. Casual dress. **Bar:** Beer & wine. **Reservations:** accepted. **Hours:** 5:30 pm-10:30 pm, Fri & Sat-11:30 pm. Closed major holidays; also Sun. **Address:** 375 Pharr Rd, Suite 600 **Location:** Jct Peachtree and Pharr rds, 0.3 mi e. **Parking:** on-site. **Cards:** AX, CB, DC, DS, JC, MC, VI.

TAQUERIA DEL SOL **Phone:** 404/321-1118 (48)

Southwestern
$2-$11

At lunch, lines form at the counter to order various pork, chicken, beef or fish tacos and cups of poblano corn chowder, and guests seat themselves. The method changes to table service at dinner, when diners can order innovative Southwestern dishes, such as pork medallions with roasted jalapeno gravy, smoked beef brisket, shellfish burritos, the enchilada sampler or the like. Casual dress. **Bar:** Full bar. **Hours:** 11 am-2 & 5:30-9 pm, Sat 5:30 pm-10 pm. Closed major holidays; also Sun. **Address:** 2165 Cheshire Bridge Rd **Location:** I-85, exit 86 northbound, 2.4 mi n, then 0.5 mi e; exit 88 southbound, 0.5 mi e. **Parking:** on-site. **Cards:** AX, MC, VI.

TAVERNA PLAKA **Phone:** 404/636-2284 (47)

Greek
$4-$22

Guests can experience a Greek celebration with food, drink and dancing that takes place both indoors and out; call for times. On the menu are varied meats, seafood and desserts with Greek flavors. Casual dress. Entertainment. **Bar:** Full bar. **Hours:** 4 pm-11 pm, Fri-2:30 am, Sat 5 pm-2:30 am. **Address:** 2196 Cheshire Bridge Rd **Location:** I-85, exit 88, just e. **Parking:** valet. **Cards:** MC, VI.

CALL

TOULOUSE **Phone:** 404/351-9533 (46)

French
$11-$17

Featuring Southern French cuisine, the menu here includes braised lamb shank with sweet pepper sauce and sauteed sea bass with tarragon. The work of local artists decorates the walls. An open, loft-style dining room sets a relaxed tone for guests in this French bistro style setting. Dressy casual. **Bar:** Full bar. **Reservations:** suggested. **Hours:** 5:30 pm-10 pm, Fri & Sat-11 pm. Closed: 1/1, 12/25. **Address:** 2293-B Peachtree Rd NE **Location:** Just s of Peachtree Battle; between Peachtree Memorial and Peachtree Hills. **Parking:** on-site. **Cards:** AX, DC, MC, VI.

(See map and index starting on p. 292)

TWIST

Phone: 404/869-1191 (3)

American
$5-$29

Upscale, contemporary decor meets an energetic atmosphere at the popular restaurant. Whether dining inside or outside on the front patio, guests receive friendly, attentive service. Varied ethnic influences enhance sushi, sashimi, satays, wraps and meat and seafood entrees. A wide variety of tapas selections can be shared. Save room for a delicious dessert in a regular or small portion. Plaza valet parking is available adjacent to the restaurant. Dressy casual. **Bar:** Full bar. **Reservations:** accepted. **Hours:** 11:30 am-11 pm, Fri & Sat-midnight, Sun 3 pm-10 pm. Closed: 11/26, 12/25. **Address:** 3500 Peachtree Rd NE **Location:** Jct Lenox Rd; in Phipps Plaza. **Parking:** on-site. **Cards:** AX, DC, DS, MC, VI.

CALL

THE VARSITY JR

Phone: 404/261-5200 (42)

American
$3-$7

A smaller branch of the famous downtown Varsity, this eatery serves the same fast food and frozen orange drinks. Dieters should waive their best intentions for a meal, as the only options here are greasy (but good). Casual dress. **Hours:** 10:30 am-10 pm, Fri & Sat-11 pm, Sun 11 am-10 pm. Closed: 4/12. **Address:** 1085 Lindbergh Dr **Location:** I-85, exit 86 northbound, 2.4 mi n, then 1 mi e; exit 88 southbound, 1 mi e. **Parking:** on-site. **Cards:** MC, VI.

CALL

ATLANTA NORTHWEST (See map and index starting on p. 296)

— WHERE TO STAY —

ATLANTA MARRIOTT NORTHWEST Book great rates at AAA.com

Phone: (770)952-7900 (6)

Hotel
$207-$222 All Year

Address: 200 Interstate North Pkwy **Location:** I-75, exit 260 (Windy Hill Rd), 0.5 mi se. Located in a corporate business park area. **Facility:** Smoke free premises. 401 units. 400 one-bedroom standard units. 1 one-bedroom suite. 5-16 stories, interior corridors. **Parking:** on-site. **Terms:** check-in 4 pm, cancellation fee imposed. **Amenities:** dual phone lines, voice mail, irons, hair dryers. *Fee:* video games, high-speed Internet. **Pool(s):** heated indoor/outdoor. **Leisure Activities:** whirlpool. **Guest Services:** valet and coin laundry, area transportation, wireless Internet. **Business Services:** conference facilities, business center. **Cards:** AX, CB, DC, DS, JC, MC, VI.

FEE CALL

Marriott
HOTELS & RESORTS

AAA Benefit:
Members save a minimum 5% off the best available rate.

COUNTRY INN & SUITES BY CARLSON Book great rates at AAA.com

Phone: (770)956-9919 (4)

Hotel
$89-$159 All Year

Address: 4500 Circle 75 Pkwy **Location:** I-75, exit 260 (Windy Hill Rd), just w to Circle 75 Pkwy, then just s. **Facility:** 149 units. 134 one-bedroom standard units. 15 one-bedroom suites. 3-5 stories, interior corridors. **Parking:** on-site. **Amenities:** high-speed Internet, voice mail, irons, hair dryers. **Pool(s):** heated indoor. **Leisure Activities:** whirlpool, exercise room. **Guest Services:** valet and coin laundry, area transportation-within 5 mi, wireless Internet. **Business Services:** meeting rooms, business center. **Cards:** AX, DC, DS, JC, MC, VI. **Free Special Amenities: expanded continental breakfast and high-speed Internet.**

FEE CALL / SOME UNITS

COURTYARD BY MARRIOTT-ATLANTA VININGS Book great rates at AAA.com

Phone: (770)432-5555 (17)

Hotel
$169-$189 All Year

Address: 2857 Paces Ferry Rd **Location:** I-285, exit 18, 0.6 mi e. **Facility:** Smoke free premises. 159 units. 154 one-bedroom standard units. 5 one-bedroom suites. 4 stories, interior corridors. **Parking:** on-site. **Terms:** cancellation fee imposed. **Amenities:** high-speed Internet (fee), dual phone lines, voice mail, irons, hair dryers. *Some:* CD players. **Pool(s):** outdoor. **Leisure Activities:** whirlpool, exercise room. **Guest Services:** valet laundry, area transportation, wireless Internet. **Business Services:** meeting rooms, fax. **Cards:** AX, DS, MC, VI.

CALL / SOME UNITS

AAA Benefit:
Members save a minimum 5% off the best available rate.

COURTYARD BY MARRIOTT-CUMBERLAND CENTER Book great rates at AAA.com

Phone: (770)952-2555 (15)

Hotel
$177-$190 All Year

Address: 3000 Cumberland Blvd **Location:** I-285, exit 19 northbound; exit 20 southbound, 0.5 mi s to Akers Mill Rd, then just w. **Facility:** Smoke free premises. 182 one-bedroom standard units. 8 stories, interior corridors. **Parking:** on-site. **Terms:** cancellation fee imposed. **Amenities:** high-speed Internet, dual phone lines, voice mail, irons, hair dryers. **Pool(s):** heated indoor. **Leisure Activities:** sauna, whirlpool, exercise room. **Guest Services:** valet laundry, area transportation-within 3 mi, wireless Internet. **Business Services:** meeting rooms, business center. **Cards:** AX, CB, DC, DS, JC, MC, VI. **Free Special Amenities: newspaper and high-speed Internet.**

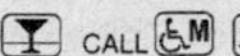

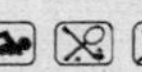

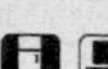

/ SOME UNITS

COURTYARD
Marriott

AAA Benefit:
Members save a minimum 5% off the best available rate.

(See map and index starting on p. 296)

DAYS INN-ATLANTA/MARIETTA/WINDY HILL RD Book at AAA.com Phone: (770)541-9399 5

Hotel
$49-$89 All Year

Address: 4502 Circle 75 Pkwy **Location:** I-75, exit 260 (Windy Hill Rd), just w to Circle 75 Pkwy, then just s. **Facility:** 82 one-bedroom standard units. 3 stories, interior corridors. **Parking:** on-site. **Amenities:** high-speed Internet, voice mail, hair dryers. **Pool(s):** heated indoor. **Leisure Activities:** limited exercise equipment. **Guest Services:** coin laundry, wireless Internet. **Business Services:** meeting rooms, fax (fee). **Cards:** AX, DC, DS, MC, VI.

ASK FEE / SOME UNITS

DOUBLETREE GUEST SUITES ATLANTA-GALLERIA Book great rates at AAA.com Phone: (770)980-1900 7

Hotel
$99-$209 All Year

Address: 2780 Windy Ridge Pkwy **Location:** I-285, exit 20 westbound; exit 19 eastbound, just n on US 41 (Cobb Pkwy). **Facility:** 154 units. 140 one- and 14 two-bedroom standard units with whirlpools. 8 stories, interior corridors. **Parking:** on-site. **Terms:** 1-30 night minimum stay, cancellation fee imposed. **Amenities:** dual phone lines, voice mail, irons, hair dryers. *Fee:* video games, high-speed Internet. **Pool(s):** outdoor. **Leisure Activities:** exercise room. **Guest Services:** valet laundry, area transportation-within 3 mi, wireless Internet. **Business Services:** conference facilities, business center. **Cards:** AX, CB, DC, DS, JC, MC, VI. **Free Special Amenities: local telephone calls and newspaper.** ***(See color ad below)***

DoubleTree
Hotels·Suites·Resorts·Clubs
AAA Benefit:
Members save 5% or more everyday!

FEE CALL / SOME UNITS

EMBASSY SUITES HOTEL-GALLERIA Book great rates at AAA.com Phone: (770)984-9300 11

Hotel
$119-$219 All Year

Address: 2815 Akers Mill Rd **Location:** I-75, exit 258, just w. **Facility:** 261 units. 243 one- and 18 two-bedroom standard units. 9 stories, interior corridors. **Parking:** on-site. **Terms:** 1-30 night minimum stay, cancellation fee imposed. **Amenities:** dual phone lines, voice mail, irons, hair dryers. *Fee:* video games, high-speed Internet. **Pool(s):** heated indoor. **Leisure Activities:** sauna, whirlpool, exercise room. **Guest Services:** valet laundry, area transportation, wireless Internet. **Business Services:** meeting rooms, business center. **Cards:** AX, CB, DC, DS, JC, MC, VI.

FEE / SOME UNITS

AAA Benefit:
Members save 5% or more everyday!

EXTENDED STAY DELUXE Book at AAA.com Phone: (770)436-1511 16

Hotel
$70-$80 All Year

Address: 2474 Cumberland Pkwy SE **Location:** I-285, exit 18, just e. **Facility:** 98 one-bedroom standard units with kitchens. 4 stories, interior corridors. **Parking:** on-site. **Terms:** office hours 7 am-11 pm. **Amenities:** DVD players, CD players, high-speed Internet (fee), voice mail, irons, hair dryers. **Pool(s):** outdoor. **Leisure Activities:** limited exercise equipment. **Guest Services:** coin laundry, wireless Internet. **Business Services:** fax (fee). **Cards:** AX, CB, DC, DS, JC, MC, VI.

ASK FEE CALL / SOME UNITS FEE

▼ *See AAA listing above* ▼

(See map and index starting on p. 296)

EXTENDED STAY DELUXE (ATLANTA/MARIETTA/ POWERS FERRY RD) *Book at AAA.com* **Phone:** (770)933-8010 **1**

Hotel
$75-$85 All Year

Address: 2010 Powers Ferry Rd **Location:** I-75, exit 260 (Windy Hill Rd), 0.5 mi e, then just s. **Facility:** 88 one-bedroom standard units with efficiencies. 3 stories, interior corridors. **Parking:** on-site. **Amenities:** DVD players, CD players, high-speed Internet (fee), dual phone lines, voice mail, irons, hair dryers. **Pool(s):** heated outdoor. **Leisure Activities:** limited exercise equipment. **Guest Services:** valet and coin laundry, wireless Internet. **Business Services:** fax (fee). **Cards:** AX, CB, DC, DS, JC, MC, VI.

ASK FEE CALL / SOME UNITS FEE

EXTENDED STAY DELUXE (ATLANTA/MARIETTA/ WINDY HILL/INT. N PKWY) *Book at AAA.com* **Phone:** (770)226-0242 **2**

Hotel
$77-$87 All Year

Address: 2225 Interstate North Pkwy **Location:** I-75, exit 260 (Windy Hill Rd), just e to Interstate North Pkwy, then just s. **Facility:** 100 units. 30 one-bedroom standard units with efficiencies. 70 one-bedroom suites with efficiencies. 3 stories, interior corridors. **Parking:** on-site. **Amenities:** DVD players, CD players, high-speed Internet (fee), dual phone lines, voice mail, irons, hair dryers. **Pool(s):** outdoor. **Leisure Activities:** exercise room. **Guest Services:** coin laundry, wireless Internet. **Business Services:** meeting rooms, fax. **Cards:** AX, CB, DC, DS, JC, MC, VI.

ASK FEE CALL / SOME UNITS FEE

FAIRFIELD INN & SUITES ATLANTA/VININGS *Book great rates at AAA.com* **Phone:** (770)435-4500 **19**

Hotel
$128-$137 All Year

Address: 2450 Paces Ferry Rd **Location:** I-285, exit 18, just w. **Facility:** Smoke free premises. 145 units. 142 one-bedroom standard units. 3 one-bedroom suites. 7 stories, interior corridors. **Parking:** on-site. **Terms:** cancellation fee imposed. **Amenities:** high-speed Internet, voice mail, irons, hair dryers. *Some:* CD players, dual phone lines. **Pool(s):** outdoor. **Leisure Activities:** whirlpool, limited exercise equipment. **Guest Services:** complimentary and valet laundry, wireless Internet. **Business Services:** meeting rooms, business center. **Cards:** AX, CB, DC, DS, JC, MC, VI.

AAA Benefit:
Members save a minimum 5% off the best available rate.

HAMPTON INN & SUITES ATLANTA GALLERIA *Book great rates at AAA.com* **Phone:** (770)955-1110 **8**

Hotel
$89-$129 All Year

Address: 2733 Circle 75 Pkwy **Location:** I-285, exit 19 eastbound; exit 20 westbound, just n. **Facility:** 106 units. 78 one-bedroom standard units, some with efficiencies and/or whirlpools. 28 one-bedroom suites, some with efficiencies. 8 stories, interior corridors. **Parking:** on-site. **Terms:** 1-30 night minimum stay, cancellation fee imposed. **Amenities:** high-speed Internet, dual phone lines, voice mail, irons, hair dryers. **Pool(s):** heated indoor. **Guest Services:** valet and coin laundry, area transportation, wireless Internet. **Business Services:** meeting rooms, business center. **Cards:** AX, CB, DC, DS, JC, MC, VI.

FEE CALL FEE / SOME UNITS

Hampton Inn & Suites

AAA Benefit:
Members save up to 10% everyday!

HAMPTON INN CUMBERLAND *Book great rates at AAA.com* **Phone:** (770)333-6006 **14**

Hotel
$109-$129 All Year

Address: 2775 Cumberland Pkwy **Location:** I-285, exit 20 westbound; exit 19 eastbound, 0.5 mi sw. Located behind the Cumberland Mall. **Facility:** 128 one-bedroom standard units. 4 stories, interior corridors. *Bath:* combo or shower only. **Parking:** on-site. **Terms:** 1-30 night minimum stay, cancellation fee imposed. **Amenities:** video games (fee), high-speed Internet, voice mail, irons, hair dryers. **Pool(s):** outdoor. **Leisure Activities:** exercise room. **Guest Services:** valet and coin laundry, area transportation, wireless Internet. **Business Services:** meeting rooms, business center. **Cards:** AX, CB, DC, DS, MC, VI.

FEE CALL / SOME UNITS

Hampton Inn

AAA Benefit:
Members save up to 10% everyday!

HAWTHORN SUITES-ATLANTA NW *Book great rates at AAA.com* **Phone:** (770)952-9595 **3**

AAA SAVE

Hotel
$129-$149 All Year

Address: 1500 Parkwood Cir **Location:** I-75, exit 260 (Windy Hill Rd), 0.5 mi e, then 0.3 mi s on Powers Ferry Rd. Located in an office park area. **Facility:** 280 units. 158 one- and 122 two-bedroom standard units, some with kitchens. 3 stories, exterior corridors. **Parking:** on-site. **Terms:** cancellation fee imposed. **Amenities:** high-speed Internet, dual phone lines, voice mail, irons, hair dryers. **Pool(s):** heated outdoor. **Leisure Activities:** whirlpool, 2 lighted tennis courts, gas grills, exercise room, basketball. **Guest Services:** valet and coin laundry, area transportation-within 3 mi, wireless Internet. **Business Services:** meeting rooms, business center. **Cards:** AX, DC, DS, JC, MC, VI. **Free Special Amenities: full breakfast and high-speed Internet.**

FEE / SOME UNITS FEE

(See map and index starting on p. 296)

HOMEWOOD SUITES-CUMBERLAND *Book great rates at AAA.com* **Phone:** (770)988-9449 **13**

Hotel

$89-$169 All Year

Address: 3200 Cobb Pkwy SW **Location:** I-285, exit 19 eastbound; exit 20 westbound, 0.7 mi se on US 41 (Cobb Pkwy). **Facility:** 124 units. 120 one- and 4 two-bedroom standard units with efficiencies. 3 stories, interior/exterior corridors. *Bath:* combo or shower only. **Parking:** on-site. **Terms:** 1-30 night minimum stay, cancellation fee imposed. **Amenities:** video games (fee), high-speed Internet, voice mail, irons, hair dryers. *Some:* DVD players. **Pool(s):** outdoor. **Leisure Activities:** whirlpool, limited exercise equipment, sports court. **Guest Services:** valet and coin laundry, area transportation, wireless Internet. **Business Services:** meeting rooms, business center. **Cards:** AX, CB, DC, DS, MC, VI.

FEE CALL

/ SOME UNITS FEE VCR

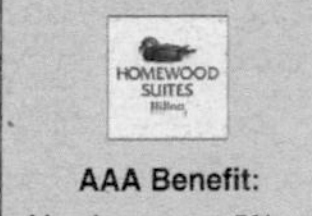

AAA Benefit:

Members save 5% or more everyday!

LA QUINTA INN & SUITES ATLANTA (PACES FERRY/VININGS) *Book great rates at AAA.com* **Phone:** (770)801-9002 **18**

Hotel

$69-$144 All Year

Address: 2415 Paces Ferry Rd SE **Location:** I-285, exit 18, just w. **Facility:** 140 units. 133 one-bedroom standard units. 7 one-bedroom suites. 6 stories, interior corridors. **Parking:** on-site. **Amenities:** video games (fee), high-speed Internet, voice mail, irons, hair dryers. *Some:* dual phone lines. **Pool(s):** heated outdoor. **Leisure Activities:** whirlpool, exercise room. **Guest Services:** valet and coin laundry, area transportation, wireless Internet. **Business Services:** meeting rooms, business center. **Cards:** AX, DC, DS, MC, VI.

ASK FEE CALL / SOME UNITS

RENAISSANCE WAVERLY HOTEL *Book great rates at AAA.com* **Phone:** (770)953-4500 **10**

Hotel

$217-$233 All Year

Address: 2450 Galleria Pkwy **Location:** I-285, exit 20 westbound to Cobb Pkwy, just s on US 41 (Cobb Pkwy); exit 19 eastbound, just s on US 41 (Cobb Pkwy). Adjoins shopping mall and convention center. **Facility:** Sophisticated accommodations, especially the 14-story atrium with hand-carved teak bells from Thailand. Smoke free premises. 521 units. 497 one-bedroom standard units. 24 one-bedroom suites. 14 stories, interior corridors. **Parking:** on-site and valet. **Terms:** cancellation fee imposed. **Amenities:** dual phone lines, voice mail, irons, hair dryers. *Fee:* video games, high-speed Internet. *Some:* DVD players (fee). **Dining:** 3 restaurants. **Pool(s):** heated outdoor, heated indoor. **Leisure Activities:** sauna, whirlpool, steamroom, spa. *Fee:* racquetball courts. **Guest Services:** valet laundry, area transportation-within 3 mi, wireless Internet. **Business Services:** conference facilities, business center. **Cards:** AX, CB, DC, DS, JC, MC, VI. ***(See color ad p 328)***

FEE / SOME UNITS FEE VCR

RENAISSANCE. HOTELS & RESORTS

AAA Benefit:

Members save a minimum 5% off the best available rate.

SHERATON SUITES GALLERIA *Book great rates at AAA.com* **Phone:** 770/955-3900 **12**

Hotel

Rates not provided

Address: 2844 Cobb Pkwy SE **Location:** I-285, exit 20 westbound; exit 19 eastbound, just s on US 41 (Cobb Pkwy). Located adjacent to the Cumberland Mall. **Facility:** 278 units. 277 one- and 1 two-bedroom standard units. 17 stories, interior corridors. **Parking:** on-site. **Amenities:** dual phone lines, voice mail, irons, hair dryers. *Fee:* video games, high-speed Internet. **Pool(s):** heated indoor/outdoor. **Leisure Activities:** whirlpool, exercise room. **Guest Services:** valet and coin laundry, area transportation-within 3 mi, wireless Internet. **Business Services:** meeting rooms, business center.

FEE CALL

/ SOME UNITS FEE

AAA Benefit:

Members get up to 15% off, plus Starwood Preferred Guest® bonuses.

WINGATE INN ATLANTA GALLERIA CENTER *Book at AAA.com* **Phone:** (678)214-6000 **9**

Hotel

$89-$119 All Year

Address: 2762 Cobb Pkwy SE **Location:** I-285, exit 20 westbound, just n to Spring Rd, then just s; exit 19 eastbound. **Facility:** 103 units. 91 one-bedroom standard units. 12 one-bedroom suites. 4 stories, interior corridors. **Parking:** on-site. **Terms:** 30 day cancellation notice-fee imposed. **Amenities:** video games (fee), high-speed Internet, dual phone lines, voice mail, safes, irons, hair dryers. **Pool(s):** heated indoor. **Leisure Activities:** whirlpool, exercise room. **Guest Services:** valet and coin laundry, area transportation, wireless Internet. **Business Services:** meeting rooms, business center. **Cards:** AX, CB, DC, DS, MC, VI.

ASK FEE CALL / SOME UNITS

(See map and index starting on p. 296)

WHERE TO DINE

C & S SEAFOOD & OYSTER BAR **Phone:** 770/272-0999 (6)

Seafood
$6-$47

Designed to resemble an upscale saloon—complete with large brass doors, mosaic tile floors, tin ceiling tiles and a 35-foot mahogany bar—you can expect to find the freshest seafood and an excellent raw bar. Market-fresh fish selections include Alaskan halibut, black grouper, organic Scottish salmon and Chilean sea bass. Landlubbers can select from several steak entrees. Waitstaff are well-equipped and knowledgeable. Dressy casual. **Bar:** Full bar. **Reservations:** accepted. **Hours:** 11:30 am-2:30 & 5-11 pm, Sat 4 pm-midnight, Sun 4 pm-10 pm. **Address:** 3240 Cobb Pkwy **Location:** I-285, exit 20 westbound; exit 19 eastbound, 1.3 mi s; in Riverview Village. **Parking:** on-site. **Cards:** AX, MC, VI.

CALL

CANOE **Phone:** 770/432-2808 (13)

American
$10-$33

Succulent seafood and other cutting-edge cuisine is served at the canoe-shaped restaurant on the banks of the Chattahoochee River. Eclectic surroundings add a sense of mystery to the splendid fare. Dressy casual. **Bar:** Full bar. **Reservations:** suggested. **Hours:** 11:30 am-2:30 & 5:30-10 pm, Fri-11 pm, Sat 5:30 pm-11 pm, Sun 10:30 am-2:30 & 5:30-9:30 pm; Sunday brunch. Closed major holidays; also Super Bowl Sun. **Address:** 4199 Paces Ferry Rd NW **Location:** I-285, exit 18, 0.6 mi e, then 1 mi s. **Parking:** on-site and valet. **Cards:** AX, CB, DC, DS, MC, VI.

LA PAZ RESTAURANTE CANTINA **Phone:** 770/801-0020 (11)

Mexican
$7-$15

Located in a converted church building, this festive, atmospheric restaurant has expanded original Tex-Mex themes in fresh, creative ways. The signature dish is the La Paz Platter, which includes a gulf shrimp enchilada, chili relleno and a beef taco. Casual dress. **Bar:** Full bar. **Hours:** 11:30 am-10 pm, Fri-11 pm, Sat noon-11 pm, Sun noon-10 pm. Closed major holidays. **Address:** 2950 New Paces Ferry Rd **Location:** I-285, exit 18, 0.8 mi e to New Paces Ferry Rd, then just s. **Parking:** on-site. **Cards:** AX, DC, DS, MC, VI.

MAGGIANO'S **Phone:** 770/799-1580 (2)

Italian
$7-$30

Friendly, observant staff members provide service at the busy restaurant, which evokes Little Italy in an early-20th-century dining room reminiscent of the Roaring '20s. Patrons sit down to traditional Italian favorites and carry on noisy, lively conversations that bounce off the high ceilings. Cobb Galleria serves as the convenient home of the handsome architectural building. Casual dress. **Bar:** Full bar. **Reservations:** accepted. **Hours:** 11 am-10 pm, Fri & Sat-11 pm. Closed: 12/25. **Address:** 1601 Cumberland Mall SE, Suite 200 **Location:** I-285, exit 20 westbound; exit 19 eastbound, just s; in Cumberland Mall. **Parking:** on-site. **Cards:** AX, CB, DC, DS, JC, MC, VI.

CALL

MEEHAN'S ALE HOUSE **Phone:** 770/433-1920 (10)

Irish
$3-$16

Finger foods, Irish favorites and a very good selection of beers and ales await you at Meehan's. Casual dress. **Bar:** Full bar. **Hours:** 11:30 am-2 am, Sat-3 am, Sun noon-midnight. Closed major holidays. **Address:** 2810 Paces Ferry Rd, Suite 302 **Location:** I-285, exit 18, 0.5 mi e; in Station at Vinings. **Parking:** on-site. **Cards:** AX, CB, DC, DS, JC, MC, VI.

CALL

OLDE MILL STEAKHOUSE **Phone:** 770/952-6042 (4)

American
$9-$23

Good old, straightforward preparations of beef are the specialty at this popular lunch spot. Casual dress. **Bar:** Full bar. **Reservations:** accepted. **Hours:** 11 am-11 pm. Closed: 11/26, 12/25. **Address:** 2960 Cobb Pkwy **Location:** I-285, exit 19 eastbound; exit 20 westbound, 0.4 mi se. **Parking:** on-site. **Cards:** AX, DC, DS, MC, VI.

THE ORIENT AT VININGS **Phone:** 770/438-8866 (14)

Chinese
$2-$20

Chinese-American cuisine emphasizes fresh ingredients and eschews preservatives at this eatery near the Chattahoochee River. In addition to delicious blackened pepper chicken, the menu lists preparations of scallops, shrimp and duck. Casual dress. **Bar:** Full bar. **Reservations:** suggested. **Hours:** 11 am-3 & 4:30-10 pm, Fri & Sat-11 pm. Closed major holidays. **Address:** 4199 Paces Ferry Rd SE **Location:** I-285, exit 18, 1.5 mi se. **Parking:** on-site. **Cards:** AX, DS, MC, VI.

SOHO **Phone:** 770/801-0069 (12)

Specialty
$8-$25

The hot spot is known for excellent preparations of eclectic cuisine, including Southwestern and Asian dishes. Patio dining is a nice relaxing option, and service is friendly and attentive. Chocolate bread pudding is a decadent pleasure. An excellent selection of wines by the glass is available. Casual dress. **Bar:** Full bar. **Reservations:** accepted. **Hours:** 11:30 am-2:30 & 5:30-10 pm, Fri-11 pm, Sat 5:30 pm-11 pm, Sun 11 am-3 & 5-9 pm; Sunday brunch. Closed major holidays. **Address:** 4300 Paces Ferry Rd, Suite 107 **Location:** I-285, exit 18, 0.7 mi e; in Vinings Jubilee Plaza. **Parking:** on-site. **Cards:** AX, CB, DC, DS, JC, MC, VI.

SOUP GARDEN **Phone:** 770/955-5726 (3)

American
$3-$8

An enormous salad bar is the focal point of the long-time favorite near the Cobb Galleria. Sandwiches, soups and desserts also are popular. Casual dress. **Hours:** 11 am-9 pm, Sat-8 pm. Closed major holidays; also Sun. **Address:** 2945 Cobb Pkwy **Location:** I-285, exit 19 eastbound; exit 20 westbound, 0.4 mi s; in Akers Mill Plaza. **Parking:** on-site. **Cards:** MC, VI.

SWAPNA INDIAN CUISINE **Phone:** 770/956-7589 (1)

Indian
$9-$15

The well-stocked buffet satisfies lunch guests, while the varied menu of Indian dishes offers plenty of dinner choices. Casual dress. **Bar:** Beer only. **Reservations:** accepted. **Hours:** 11:30 am-2:30 & 5:30-10 pm, Sat & Sun 11:30 am-3 & 5:30-10 pm. Closed: 11/26. **Address:** 2655 S Cobb Pkwy **Location:** I-285, exit 19 eastbound; exit 20 westbound, just n. **Parking:** on-site. **Cards:** AX, CB, DS, MC, VI.

(See map and index starting on p. 296)

TAVERNA FIORENTINA — Phone: 770/272-9825 (5)

Italian
$5-$27

Fresh ingredients are predominantly used in preparation of the traditional Italian dishes, like pasta, wild boar and the fish of the day. The dining room offers an intimate setting with a few hints of upscale touches. You'll find the service to be smooth. Casual dress. **Bar:** Full bar. **Reservations:** suggested. **Hours:** 11:30 am-2:30 & 5:30-10:30 pm, Fri-Sun to 11:30 pm. Closed major holidays. **Address:** 3324 Cobb Pkwy **Location:** I-75, exit 258, 0.5 mi w to Cobb Pkwy, then 0.3 mi s; in Riverview Village. **Parking:** on-site. **Cards:** AX.

THAI DINNER — Phone: 770/859-9898 (7)

Thai
$8-$23

Solid standards and creative specials are among the flavorful choices. A large and tastefully done dining room helps make the dining experience all the more enjoyable. Casual dress. **Hours:** 11 am-2:30 & 5-10 pm, Fri-10:30 pm, Sat 5 pm-10:30 pm, Sun 5 pm-10 pm. Closed major holidays. **Address:** 3280 Cobb Pkwy **Location:** I-285, exit 20 westbound; exit 19 eastbound, 1.3 mi s; in Riverview Village. **Parking:** on-site. **Cards:** AX, DC, DS, MC, VI.

CALL

VININGS INN — Phone: 770/438-2282 (9)

American
$9-$31

The cozy, established restaurant prepares some new takes on traditional Southern-style cuisine, such as the can't-miss shrimp and grits. Dressy casual. **Bar:** Full bar. **Reservations:** suggested. **Hours:** 11:30 am-2:30 & 5:30-10 pm, Fri & Sat-10:30 pm. Closed: 1/1, 12/25; also Sun. **Address:** 3011 Paces Mill Rd **Location:** I-285, exit 18, 0.8 mi e. **Parking:** valet. **Cards:** AX, CB, DC, DS, JC, MC, VI.

WILLY'S MEXICANA GRILL — Phone: 770/801-8633 (8)

Mexican
$3-$6

Massive, made-to-order burritos are the real draw, but tacos, chips and salsa also are "can't miss" items on the short but sweet menu. Casual dress. **Bar:** Beer only. **Hours:** 11 am-10 pm. **Address:** 2460 Cumberland Pkwy **Location:** I-285, exit 18, just e. **Parking:** on-site. **Cards:** AX, MC, VI.

ATLANTA NORTH & EAST (See map and index starting on p. 302)

WHERE TO STAY

ATLANTA MARRIOTT CENTURY CENTER — *Book great rates at AAA.com* — Phone: (404)325-0000 (28)

AAA SAVE

Hotel
$217-$233 All Year

Address: 2000 Century Blvd NE **Location:** I-85, exit 91, 0.3 mi w to Century Blvd, then 0.5 mi n. **Facility:** Smoke free premises. 287 one-bedroom standard units. 15 stories, interior corridors. **Parking:** on-site. **Terms:** cancellation fee imposed. **Amenities:** high-speed Internet (fee), voice mail, irons, hair dryers. *Some:* CD players. **Pool(s):** heated outdoor. **Leisure Activities:** exercise room. **Guest Services:** valet laundry, area transportation-within 3 mi, wireless Internet. **Business Services:** conference facilities, business center. **Cards:** AX, CB, DC, DS, JC, MC, VI. ***(See color ad p 320)***

FEE

ATLANTA MARRIOTT PERIMETER CENTER — *Book great rates at AAA.com* — Phone: (770)394-6500 (20)

AAA SAVE

Hotel
$296-$318 All Year

Address: 246 Perimeter Center Pkwy **Location:** I-285, exit 29 (Ashford-Dunwoody Rd), just n, 0.3 mi w on Hammond Dr, then just s. **Facility:** Smoke free premises. 400 units. 396 one-bedroom standard units. 4 one-bedroom suites. 16 stories, interior corridors. **Parking:** on-site. **Terms:** check-in 4 pm, cancellation fee imposed. **Amenities:** dual phone lines, voice mail, irons, hair dryers. *Fee:* video games, high-speed Internet. **Pool(s):** heated indoor/outdoor. **Leisure Activities:** saunas, whirlpool, exercise room. **Guest Services:** valet and coin laundry, area transportation-within 2 mi, wireless Internet. **Business Services:** conference facilities, business center. **Cards:** AX, CB, DC, DS, JC, MC, VI. **Free Special Amenities: newspaper.** ***(See color ad p 321)***

FEE CALL / SOME UNITS

COMFORT INN-BUCKHEAD NORTH — *Book great rates at AAA.com* — Phone: (404)252-6400 (23)

AAA SAVE

Hotel
$79-$169 All Year

Address: 5793 Roswell Rd NE **Location:** I-285, exit 25, just n. **Facility:** 80 one-bedroom standard units. 4 stories, interior corridors. **Parking:** on-site. **Terms:** cancellation fee imposed. **Amenities:** high-speed Internet, voice mail, safes (fee), irons, hair dryers. **Pool(s):** outdoor. **Leisure Activities:** sauna, exercise room. **Guest Services:** valet laundry, wireless Internet. **Business Services:** meeting rooms, business center. **Cards:** AX, CB, DC, DS, JC, MC, VI. **Free Special Amenities: continental breakfast and high-speed Internet.**

FEE / SOME UNITS

(See map and index starting on p. 302)

COMFORT SUITES HOTEL PERIMETER CENTER *Book at AAA.com* **Phone:** (770)828-0330 **13**

Hotel
$79-$159 All Year

Address: 6110 Peachtree-Dunwoody Rd **Location:** I-285, exit 28 westbound, 1 mi n; exit 26 eastbound, 0.5 mi n to Hammond Dr, 0.7 mi e to Peachtree-Dunwoody Rd, then just n. **Facility:** Smoke free premises. 121 units. 103 one-bedroom standard units. 18 one-bedroom suites, some with whirlpools. 7 stories, interior corridors. **Parking:** on-site. **Terms:** cancellation fee imposed. **Amenities:** CD players, high-speed Internet, dual phone lines, voice mail, irons, hair dryers. **Pool(s):** outdoor. **Leisure Activities:** sauna, exercise room. **Guest Services:** valet and coin laundry, wireless Internet. **Business Services:** meeting rooms, business center. **Cards:** AX, CB, DC, DS, JC, MC, VI.

ASK FEE CALL

COURTYARD BY MARRIOTT ATLANTA EXECUTIVE PARK/EMORY *Book great rates at AAA.com* **Phone:** (404)728-0708 **34**

AAA SAVE

Hotel
$169-$189 All Year

Address: 1236 Executive Park Dr **Location:** I-85, exit 89, just e to Exective Park Dr, then just s. **Facility:** Smoke free premises. 145 units. 133 one-bedroom standard units. 12 one-bedroom suites. 4 stories, interior corridors. **Parking:** on-site. **Terms:** cancellation fee imposed. **Amenities:** high-speed Internet, voice mail, irons, hair dryers. **Pool(s):** outdoor. **Leisure Activities:** whirlpool, limited exercise equipment. **Guest Services:** valet and coin laundry, wireless Internet. **Business Services:** meeting rooms, business center. **Cards:** AX, CB, DC, DS, JC, MC, VI. **Free Special Amenities: newspaper and high-speed Internet.**

CALL / SOME UNITS

AAA Benefit:
Members save a minimum 5% off the best available rate.

COURTYARD BY MARRIOTT-GLENRIDGE/PERIMETER *Book great rates at AAA.com* **Phone:** (404)843-2300 **24**

AAA SAVE

Hotel
$197-$212 All Year

Address: 5601 Peachtree-Dunwoody Rd **Location:** I-285, exit 28 westbound, 0.8 mi s; exit 26 eastbound, 0.5 mi e on Johnson Ferry Rd. **Facility:** Smoke free premises. 128 units. 108 one-bedroom standard units. 20 one-bedroom suites. 2 stories, interior corridors. **Parking:** on-site. **Terms:** cancellation fee imposed. **Amenities:** high-speed Internet, dual phone lines, voice mail, irons, hair dryers. **Pool(s):** outdoor. **Leisure Activities:** whirlpool, exercise room. **Guest Services:** valet and coin laundry, area transportation-within 3 mi, wireless Internet. **Business Services:** meeting rooms. *Fee:* PC, fax. **Cards:** AX, CB, DC, DS, JC, MC, VI. **Free Special Amenities: newspaper and high-speed Internet.**

AAA Benefit:
Members save a minimum 5% off the best available rate.

COURTYARD BY MARRIOTT PERIMETER CENTER *Book great rates at AAA.com* **Phone:** (770)393-1000 **8**

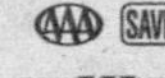

Hotel
$217-$233 All Year

Address: 6250 Peachtree-Dunwoody Rd **Location:** I-285, exit 26 eastbound, 0.5 mi n, 0.7 mi e on Hammond Dr to Peachtree-Dunwoody Rd, then 0.5 mi n; exit 28 westbound, 0.8 mi n. **Facility:** Smoke free premises. 145 units. 133 one-bedroom standard units. 12 one-bedroom suites. 4 stories, interior corridors. **Parking:** on-site. **Terms:** cancellation fee imposed. **Amenities:** video games (fee), high-speed Internet, dual phone lines, voice mail, irons, hair dryers. **Pool(s):** outdoor. **Leisure Activities:** whirlpool, exercise room. **Guest Services:** valet and coin laundry, area transportation-within 3 mi, wireless Internet. **Business Services:** meeting rooms, business center. **Cards:** AX, CB, DC, DS, MC, VI. **Free Special Amenities: newspaper and high-speed Internet.**

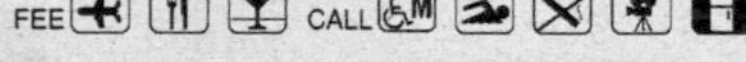

AAA Benefit:
Members save a minimum 5% off the best available rate.

CROWNE PLAZA ATLANTA PERIMETER NW *Book at AAA.com* **Phone:** (770)955-1700 **25**

Hotel
$69-$219 All Year

Address: 6345 Powers Ferry Rd NW **Location:** I-285, exit 22, southeast corner. **Facility:** 296 one-bedroom standard units. 9 stories, interior corridors. **Parking:** on-site. **Terms:** cancellation fee imposed. **Amenities:** CD players, dual phone lines, voice mail, irons, hair dryers. *Fee:* video games, high-speed Internet. **Pool(s):** heated indoor/outdoor. **Leisure Activities:** exercise room. **Guest Services:** valet and coin laundry, area transportation, wireless Internet. **Business Services:** conference facilities, business center. **Cards:** AX, CB, DC, DS, JC, MC, VI.

CROWNE PLAZA ATLANTA-RAVINIA HOTEL *Book great rates at AAA.com* **Phone:** (770)395-7700 **14**

AAA SAVE

Hotel
$125-$279 All Year

Address: 4355 Ashford-Dunwoody Rd **Location:** I-285, exit 29 (Ashford-Dunwoody Rd), northeast corner. **Facility:** 495 units. 462 one-bedroom standard units. 33 one-bedroom suites, some with whirlpools. 15 stories, interior corridors. **Parking:** on-site and valet. **Amenities:** CD players, high-speed Internet (fee), dual phone lines, voice mail, safes, irons, hair dryers. *Some:* honor bars. **Dining:** 2 restaurants, also, La Grotta Ravinia Ristorante Italiano, see separate listing, entertainment. **Pool(s):** heated indoor. **Leisure Activities:** saunas, whirlpool, lighted tennis court, jogging, basketball. *Fee:* massage. **Guest Services:** valet laundry, area transportation-within 2 mi, wireless Internet. **Business Services:** conference facilities, business center. **Cards:** AX, DC, DS, MC, VI.
(See color ad p 355)

/ SOME UNITS

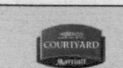

(See map and index starting on p. 302)

DOUBLETREE HOTEL ATLANTA NORTH DRUID HILLS *Book great rates at AAA.com* **Phone:** (404)321-4174 33

Hotel
$94-$219 All Year

Address: 2061 N Druid Hills Rd NE **Location:** I-85, exit 89, just w. **Facility:** 208 one-bedroom standard units. 9 stories, interior corridors. **Parking:** on-site. **Terms:** 1-30 night minimum stay, cancellation fee imposed. **Amenities:** high-speed Internet, dual phone lines, voice mail, irons, hair dryers. *Some:* CD players. **Pool(s):** outdoor. **Leisure Activities:** exercise room. **Guest Services:** valet laundry, area transportation, wireless Internet. **Business Services:** meeting rooms, business center. **Cards:** AX, DC, DS, MC, VI.

FEE CALL / SOME UNITS

AAA Benefit:
Members save 5% or more everyday!

EMBASSY SUITES HOTEL PERIMETER CENTER *Book great rates at AAA.com* **Phone:** (770)394-5454 2

Hotel
$114-$249 All Year

Address: 1030 Crown Pointe Pkwy **Location:** I-285, exit 29 (Ashford-Dunwoody Rd), 0.5 mi n to Perimeter Center W Rd, then 0.5 mi w. Located opposite the Perimeter Mall. **Facility:** 241 units. 240 one- and 1 two-bedroom standard units. 10 stories, interior corridors. **Parking:** on-site. **Terms:** 1-30 night minimum stay, cancellation fee imposed. **Amenities:** dual phone lines, voice mail, irons, hair dryers. *Fee:* video games, high-speed Internet. **Pool(s):** heated indoor. **Leisure Activities:** whirlpool, exercise room. **Guest Services:** valet and coin laundry, area transportation, wireless Internet. **Business Services:** meeting rooms, business center. **Cards:** AX, CB, DC, DS, JC, MC, VI.

FEE CALL / SOME UNITS

EMBASSY SUITES HOTELS

AAA Benefit:
Members save 5% or more everyday!

EXTENDED STAYAMERICA *Book at AAA.com* **Phone:** (404)679-4333 27

Hotel
$70-$87 All Year

Address: 3115 Clairmont Rd **Location:** I-85, exit 91, 0.6 mi w. **Facility:** 104 one-bedroom standard units with efficiencies. 3 stories, interior corridors. **Parking:** on-site. **Terms:** office hours 7 am-11 pm. **Amenities:** high-speed Internet (fee), voice mail, irons. **Guest Services:** coin laundry, wireless Internet. **Business Services:** fax (fee). **Cards:** AX, CB, DC, DS, JC, MC, VI.

ASK CALL / SOME UNITS FEE

EXTENDED STAYAMERICA *Book at AAA.com* **Phone:** (770)396-5600 3

Hotel
$65-$90 All Year

Address: 905 S Crestline Pkwy **Location:** I-285, exit 28 westbound, 0.7 mi n; exit 26 eastbound, 0.5 mi n to Hammond Dr, 0.5 mi e, then 0.3 mi n. **Facility:** 97 one-bedroom standard units with efficiencies. 4 stories, interior corridors. **Parking:** on-site. **Terms:** office hours 7 am-11 pm. **Amenities:** high-speed Internet (fee), dual phone lines, voice mail, irons. *Some:* hair dryers. **Guest Services:** coin laundry, wireless Internet. **Business Services:** fax (fee). **Cards:** AX, CB, DC, DS, JC, MC, VI.

ASK CALL / SOME UNITS FEE

EXTENDED STAY DELUXE ATLANTA-LENOX *Book at AAA.com* **Phone:** (404)237-9100 26

Hotel
$80-$100 All Year

Address: 3967 Peachtree Rd **Location:** I-85, exit 89, 2.8 mi w. **Facility:** 91 one-bedroom standard units with efficiencies. 4 stories, interior corridors. **Parking:** on-site. **Amenities:** DVD players, CD players, high-speed Internet (fee), dual phone lines, voice mail, irons, hair dryers. **Pool(s):** outdoor. **Leisure Activities:** limited exercise equipment, picnic tables & grills. **Guest Services:** valet and coin laundry, wireless Internet. **Business Services:** fax (fee). **Cards:** AX, CB, DC, DS, JC, MC, VI.

ASK CALL / SOME UNITS FEE

▼ *See AAA listing p 354* ▼

(See map and index starting on p. 302)

EXTENDED STAY DELUXE ATLANTA-PERIMETER *Book at AAA.com* **Phone:** (770)379-0111 7

Hotel
$78-$92 All Year

Address: 6330 Peachtree-Dunwoody Rd NE **Location:** I-285, exit 28 westbound, 0.7 mi n; exit 26 eastbound, 0.5 mi n to Hammond Dr, 0.5 mi e, then 0.3 mi n. **Facility:** 99 one-bedroom standard units with efficiencies. 3 stories, interior corridors. **Parking:** on-site. **Amenities:** high-speed Internet (fee), dual phone lines, voice mail, irons, hair dryers. *Some:* DVD players. **Pool(s):** outdoor. **Leisure Activities:** exercise room. **Guest Services:** coin laundry, wireless Internet. **Business Services:** fax. **Cards:** AX, CB, DC, DS, JC, MC, VI.

ASK CALL / SOME UNITS FEE

HAMPTON INN-DRUID HILLS ROAD *Book great rates at AAA.com* **Phone:** (404)320-6600  32

Hotel
$124-$144 All Year

Address: 1975 N Druid Hills Rd **Location:** I-85, exit 89, just w. **Facility:** 111 one-bedroom standard units, some with whirlpools. 5 stories, interior corridors. **Parking:** on-site. **Terms:** 1-30 night minimum stay, cancellation fee imposed. **Amenities:** high-speed Internet, voice mail, irons, hair dryers. **Pool(s):** outdoor. **Leisure Activities:** exercise room. **Guest Services:** valet laundry, wireless Internet. **Business Services:** meeting rooms, business center. **Cards:** AX, CB, DC, DS, JC, MC, VI.

FEE CALL / SOME UNITS

AAA Benefit:
Members save up to 10% everyday!

HAMPTON INN-PERIMETER CENTER *Book great rates at AAA.com* **Phone:** (404)303-0014  19

Hotel
$89-$149 All Year

Address: 769 Hammond Dr **Location:** I-285, exit 26 eastbound, 0.5 mi n to Hammond Dr, then 0.5 mi e; exit 28 westbound, 0.5 mi n to Hammond Dr, then 0.5 mi w. **Facility:** 131 one-bedroom standard units. 8 stories, interior corridors. **Parking:** on-site. **Amenities:** video games (fee), high-speed Internet, voice mail, irons, hair dryers. **Pool(s):** outdoor. **Leisure Activities:** exercise room. **Guest Services:** valet and coin laundry, wireless Internet. **Business Services:** meeting rooms, fax (fee). **Cards:** AX, CB, DC, DS, JC, MC, VI. **Free Special Amenities: expanded continental breakfast and high-speed Internet.** *(See color ad below)*

FEE CALL / SOME UNITS FEE

AAA Benefit:
Members save up to 10% everyday!

HILTON GARDEN INN-ATLANTA PERIMETER *Book great rates at AAA.com* **Phone:** (404)459-0500  21

Hotel
$89-$219 All Year

Address: 1501 Lake Hearn Dr **Location:** I-285, exit 29 (Ashford-Dunwoody Rd), just s to Lake Hearn Dr, then just w. **Facility:** 193 units. 188 one-bedroom standard units. 5 one-bedroom suites. 7 stories, interior corridors. **Parking:** on-site. **Terms:** 1-30 night minimum stay, cancellation fee imposed. **Amenities:** video games (fee), high-speed Internet, dual phone lines, voice mail, irons, hair dryers. **Pool(s):** heated indoor. **Leisure Activities:** whirlpool, exercise room. **Guest Services:** valet and coin laundry, area transportation, wireless Internet. **Business Services:** meeting rooms, business center. **Cards:** AX, CB, DC, DS, JC, MC, VI.

    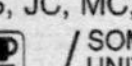

FEE CALL / SOME UNITS

AAA Benefit:
Members save 5% or more everyday!

(See map and index starting on p. 302)

HILTON SUITES ATLANTA PERIMETER Book great rates at AAA.com Phone: (770)668-0808 11

Hotel
$99-$279 All Year

Address: 6120 Peachtree-Dunwoody Rd **Location:** I-285, exit 28 westbound, 0.4 mi n; exit 26 eastbound, 0.5 mi n to Hammond Dr, 0.5 mi e to Peachtree-Dunwoody Rd, then just n. **Facility:** 224 one-bedroom standard units, some with whirlpools. 6 stories, interior corridors. **Parking:** on-site. **Terms:** 1-30 night minimum stay, cancellation fee imposed. **Amenities:** dual phone lines, voice mail, irons, hair dryers. *Fee:* video games, high-speed Internet. **Pool(s):** heated indoor/outdoor. **Leisure Activities:** whirlpool, exercise room. **Guest Services:** valet laundry, area transportation, wireless Internet. **Business Services:** meeting rooms, business center. **Cards:** AX, CB, DC, DS, JC, MC, VI.

CALL

Hilton
AAA Benefit:
Members save 5% or more everyday!

HOLIDAY INN EXPRESS HOTEL & SUITES-PERIMETER Book at AAA.com Phone: (404)250-4450 18

Hotel
$77-$125 All Year

Address: 765 Hammond Dr **Location:** I-285, exit 26 eastbound, 0.5 mi n, then 0.3 mi e; exit 28 westbound, 0.5 mi n to Hammond Dr, then 0.5 mi w. **Facility:** 107 one-bedroom standard units, some with efficiencies and/or whirlpools. 8 stories, interior corridors. **Parking:** on-site. **Terms:** cancellation fee imposed. **Amenities:** high-speed Internet, dual phone lines, voice mail, irons, hair dryers. **Pool(s):** outdoor. **Leisure Activities:** exercise room. **Guest Services:** valet and coin laundry, area transportation, wireless Internet. **Business Services:** meeting rooms, business center. **Cards:** AX, DC, DS, MC, VI.

ASK FEE CALL / SOME UNITS

HOLIDAY INN SELECT ATLANTA PERIMETER Book at AAA.com Phone: (770)457-6363 17

Hotel
$69-$139 All Year

Address: 4386 Chamblee-Dunwoody Rd **Location:** I-285, exit 30 eastbound, just s; exit westbound, follow access road 1.3 mi to Chamblee-Dunwoody Rd, then just s. **Facility:** 250 one-bedroom standard units. 5 stories, interior corridors. **Parking:** on-site. **Terms:** cancellation fee imposed. **Amenities:** video games (fee), high-speed Internet, voice mail, irons, hair dryers. **Pool(s):** heated outdoor. **Leisure Activities:** exercise room. **Guest Services:** valet and coin laundry, area transportation, wireless Internet. **Business Services:** conference facilities, business center. **Cards:** AX, CB, DC, DS, JC, MC, VI.

ASK FEE CALL / SOME UNITS FEE FEE FEE

HOMESTEAD STUDIO SUITES HOTEL-ATLANTA/ NORTH DRUID HILLS Book at AAA.com Phone: (404)325-1223 35

Hotel
$58-$70 All Year

Address: 1339 Executive Park Dr NE **Location:** I-85, exit 89, just e to Executive Park Dr, then just s. **Facility:** 138 one-bedroom standard units with efficiencies. 2 stories, exterior corridors. **Parking:** on-site. **Terms:** office hours 7 am-11 pm. **Amenities:** high-speed Internet (fee), voice mail, irons, hair dryers. *Some:* safes. **Guest Services:** coin laundry, wireless Internet. **Business Services:** fax (fee). **Cards:** AX, CB, DC, DS, JC, MC, VI.

ASK FEE CALL FEE / SOME UNITS FEE

(See map and index starting on p. 302)

HOMESTEAD STUDIO SUITES HOTEL-ATLANTA/PERIMETER *Book at AAA.com* **Phone:** (770)522-0025 16

Hotel
$60-$83 All Year

Address: 1050 Hammond Dr **Location:** I-285, exit 26 eastbound, 0.5 mi n to Hammond Dr, then 0.5 mi e; exit 28 westbound, just n to Hammond Dr, then just w. **Facility:** 127 units. 122 one-bedroom standard units with efficiencies. 5 one-bedroom suites with efficiencies. 2 stories, exterior corridors. **Parking:** on-site. **Amenities:** high-speed Internet (fee), dual phone lines, voice mail, irons. **Guest Services:** coin laundry, wireless Internet. **Business Services:** fax (fee). **Cards:** AX, CB, DC, DS, JC, MC, VI.

ASK CALL / SOME UNITS FEE

HYATT PLACE ATLANTA/PERIMETER CENTER *Book great rates at AAA.com* **Phone:** (770)730-9300 

Hotel
$79-$239 All Year

Address: 1005 Crestline Pkwy **Location:** SR 400, exit 5A (Dunwoody Rd), 0.3 mi e. **Facility:** 150 one-bedroom standard units. 6 stories, interior corridors. **Parking:** on-site. **Terms:** cancellation fee imposed. **Amenities:** high-speed Internet, dual phone lines, voice mail, safes (fee), irons, hair dryers. **Pool(s):** heated outdoor. **Leisure Activities:** exercise room. **Guest Services:** valet and coin laundry, area transportation-within 3 mi, wireless Internet. **Business Services:** meeting rooms, business center. **Cards:** AX, CB, DC, DS, JC, MC, VI. **Free Special Amenities: continental breakfast and high-speed Internet.**

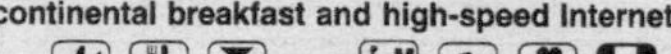

HYATT PLACE
AAA Benefit:
Ask for the AAA rate and save 10%.

LA QUINTA INN & SUITES ATLANTA (PERIMETER/ MEDICAL CENTER) *Book great rates at AAA.com* **Phone:** (770)350-6177 10

Hotel
$55-$149 All Year

Address: 6260 Peachtree-Dunwoody **Location:** I-285, exit 28 westbound, 0.7 mi n; exit 26 eastbound, 0.5 mi n to Hammond Dr, 0.7 mi e, then 0.5 mi n. **Facility:** 143 units. 128 one-bedroom standard units. 15 one-bedroom suites. 7 stories, interior corridors. **Parking:** on-site. **Amenities:** video games (fee), high-speed Internet, voice mail, irons, hair dryers. *Some:* dual phone lines. **Pool(s):** heated outdoor. **Leisure Activities:** whirlpool, exercise room. **Guest Services:** valet and coin laundry, area transportation, wireless Internet. **Business Services:** meeting rooms, fax (fee). **Cards:** AX, DS, MC, VI.

ASK FEE CALL / SOME UNITS

MICROTEL INN & SUITES *Book at AAA.com* **Phone:** (404)325-4446 30

Hotel
$59-$119 All Year

Address: 1840 Corporate Blvd **Location:** I-85, exit 89, just w to Buford Hwy, 0.3 mi n to Corporate Blvd, then just e. **Facility:** 97 one-bedroom standard units. 3 stories, interior corridors. **Parking:** on-site. **Amenities:** high-speed Internet, voice mail. *Some:* dual phone lines, irons, hair dryers. **Guest Services:** wireless Internet. **Business Services:** meeting rooms, fax (fee). **Cards:** AX, DC, DS, MC, VI.

ASK FEE CALL / SOME UNITS

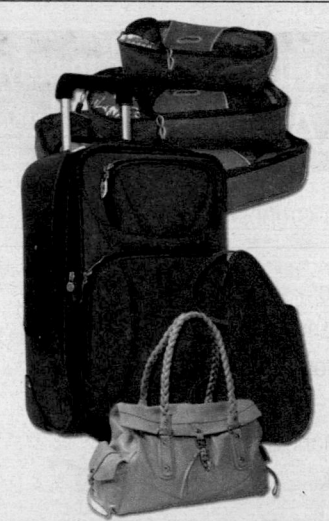

(See map and index starting on p. 302)

MICROTEL INN & SUITES PERIMETER CENTER *Book at AAA.com* **Phone:** (678)781-4000 9

Hotel
$79-$129 All Year

Address: 6280 Peachtree-Dunwoody Rd **Location:** SR 400, exit 5A (Dunwoody Rd), just e to Peachtree Dunwoody Rd, then 0.5 mi s. **Facility:** 80 one-bedroom standard units. 4 stories, interior corridors. **Parking:** on-site. **Amenities:** video games (fee), high-speed Internet, voice mail, irons, hair dryers. *Some:* dual phone lines. **Pool(s):** outdoor. **Leisure Activities:** exercise room. **Guest Services:** complimentary laundry, area transportation, wireless Internet. **Business Services:** meeting rooms, fax (fee). **Cards:** AX, CB, DC, DS, MC, VI.

ASK FEE CALL / SOME UNITS

RED ROOF INN-DRUID HILLS *Book great rates at AAA.com* **Phone:** (404)321-1653 31

AAA SAVE

Motel
$60-$100 All Year

Address: 1960 N Druid Hills Rd **Location:** I-85, exit 89, just w. **Facility:** 115 one-bedroom standard units. 3 stories, exterior corridors. **Parking:** on-site. **Terms:** 14 day cancellation notice. **Amenities:** voice mail. *Fee:* video games, high-speed Internet. **Guest Services:** wireless Internet. **Business Services:** fax (fee). **Cards:** AX, CB, DC, DS, MC, VI. **Free Special Amenities: local telephone calls.**

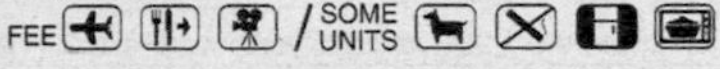

RESIDENCE INN BY MARRIOTT ATLANTA DUNWOODY *Book great rates at AAA.com* **Phone:** (770)455-4446 15

AAA SAVE

Hotel
$177-$190 All Year

Address: 1901 Savoy Dr **Location:** I-285, exit 30, just e. **Facility:** Smoke free premises. 144 units. 108 one- and 36 two-bedroom standard units with kitchens. 2 stories (no elevator), exterior corridors. **Parking:** on-site. **Terms:** cancellation fee imposed. **Amenities:** video library, high-speed Internet, voice mail, irons, hair dryers. **Pool(s):** outdoor. **Leisure Activities:** whirlpool, exercise room, sports court. **Guest Services:** valet and coin laundry, area transportation-within 5 mi, wireless Internet. **Business Services:** meeting rooms, business center. **Cards:** AX, CB, DC, DS, JC, MC, VI. **Free Special Amenities: full breakfast and high-speed Internet.**

FEE / SOME UNITS FEE

AAA Benefit:
Members save a minimum 5% off the best available rate.

RESIDENCE INN BY MARRIOTT-PERIMETER CENTER *Book great rates at AAA.com* **Phone:** (404)252-5066 12

AAA SAVE

Hotel
$237-$254 All Year

Address: 6096 Barfield Rd **Location:** I-285, exit 26 eastbound, 0.5 mi n on Glenridge to Hammond Dr, then 0.3 mi e to Barfield Rd; exit 28 westbound (Peachtree-Dunwoody Rd), 0.5 mi n to Hammond Dr, then just w. **Facility:** Smoke free premises. 128 units. 96 one- and 32 two-bedroom standard units with kitchens. 2 stories, exterior corridors. **Parking:** on-site. **Terms:** cancellation fee imposed. **Amenities:** video games (fee), high-speed Internet, voice mail, irons, hair dryers. **Pool(s):** outdoor. **Leisure Activities:** whirlpool, exercise room, sports court. **Guest Services:** valet and coin laundry, area transportation-within 3 mi, wireless Internet. **Business Services:** meeting rooms, business center. **Cards:** AX, CB, DC, DS, JC, MC, VI. **Free Special Amenities: full breakfast and high-speed Internet.**

FEE / SOME UNITS FEE

AAA Benefit:
Members save a minimum 5% off the best available rate.

STAYBRIDGE SUITES-ATLANTA-MT. VERNON *Book at AAA.com* **Phone:** 404/250-0110 4

Hotel
Rates not provided

Address: 760 Mt Vernon Hwy NE **Location:** I-285, exit 25, 0.8 mi n on Roswell Rd, then 1 mi e. **Facility:** 122 units. 63 one- and 59 two-bedroom standard units with kitchens. 2-3 stories (no elevator), interior/exterior corridors. **Parking:** on-site. **Amenities:** video library (fee), DVD players, CD players, high-speed Internet, voice mail, safes, irons, hair dryers. *Some:* dual phone lines. **Pool(s):** heated outdoor. **Leisure Activities:** whirlpool, limited exercise equipment. **Guest Services:** complimentary laundry, area transportation, wireless Internet. **Business Services:** meeting rooms, business center.

FEE VCR / SOME UNITS FEE

STAYBRIDGE SUITES ATLANTA PERIMETER *Book at AAA.com* **Phone:** 678/320-0111 1

Hotel
Rates not provided

Address: 4601 Ridgeview Rd **Location:** I-285, exit 29 (Ashford-Dunwoody Rd), 0.5 mi n, 0.5 mi w on Perimeter Center W to Crowne Pointe Dr, then just n. **Facility:** 143 units. 114 one- and 29 two-bedroom standard units with efficiencies. 5 stories, interior corridors. **Parking:** on-site. **Amenities:** DVD players, high-speed Internet, dual phone lines, voice mail, irons, hair dryers. *Fee:* video library, video games. **Pool(s):** heated outdoor. **Leisure Activities:** whirlpool, exercise room. **Guest Services:** valet and coin laundry, area transportation, wireless Internet. **Business Services:** meeting rooms, business center.

FEE CALL VCR / SOME UNITS FEE

(See map and index starting on p. 302)

W ATLANTA PERIMETER Book great rates at AAA.com **Phone:** (770)396-6800 5

AAA SAVE

Hotel
$109-$519 All Year

Address: 111 Perimeter Center W **Location:** I-285 E, exit 29 (Ashford-Dunwoody Rd), 0.5 mi n. **Facility:** 275 units. 121 one-bedroom standard units. 154 one-bedroom suites with kitchens. 11 stories, interior corridors. *Bath:* combo or shower only. **Parking:** on-site (fee) and valet. **Amenities:** DVD players, CD players, high-speed Internet (fee), dual phone lines, voice mail, safes, honor bars, irons, hair dryers. **Pool(s):** outdoor. **Leisure Activities:** whirlpool, exercise room. **Guest Services:** valet laundry, area transportation-within 3 mi, wireless Internet. **Business Services:** meeting rooms, business center. **Cards:** AX, CB, DC, DS, JC, MC, VI.

/ SOME UNITS FEE

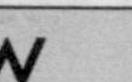

HOTELS

AAA Benefit:
Special member room rates, plus Starwood Preferred Guest® bonuses.

THE WESTIN ATLANTA NORTH Book great rates at AAA.com **Phone:** (770)395-3900 22

AAA SAVE

Hotel
$99-$399 All Year

Address: 7 Concourse Pkwy **Location:** I-285, exit 28 westbound; exit 26 eastbound, 0.5 mi n to Hammond Dr, then 0.4 mi e. **Facility:** Smoke free premises. 369 units. 349 one-bedroom standard units. 20 one-bedroom suites, some with whirlpools. 20 stories, interior corridors. *Bath:* combo or shower only. **Parking:** on-site and valet. **Amenities:** dual phone lines, voice mail, safes, honor bars, irons, hair dryers. *Fee:* video games, high-speed Internet. *Some:* CD players, fax. **Pool(s):** heated outdoor. **Leisure Activities:** sauna, whirlpool, steamroom, basketball. *Fee:* 7 lighted tennis courts, racquetball courts, 3 squash courts. **Guest Services:** valet laundry, area transportation-within 2 mi, wireless Internet. **Business Services:** conference facilities, business center. **Cards:** AX, CB, DC, DS, JC, MC, VI. **Free Special Amenities: room upgrade and preferred room (each subject to availability with advance reservations).**

FEE / SOME UNITS FEE

WESTIN HOTELS & RESORTS

AAA Benefit:
Enjoy up to 15% off your next stay, plus Starwood Preferred Guest® bonuses.

WINGATE INN CLAIRMONT-ATLANTA Book at AAA.com **Phone:** (404)248-1550 29

Hotel
$100-$119 All Year

Address: 2920 Clairmont Rd **Location:** I-85, exit 91, just w. **Facility:** 80 one-bedroom standard units. 4 stories, interior corridors. **Parking:** on-site. **Amenities:** video games (fee), high-speed Internet, dual phone lines, voice mail, safes, irons, hair dryers. **Leisure Activities:** whirlpool, exercise room. **Guest Services:** valet laundry, wireless Internet. **Business Services:** meeting rooms, business center. **Cards:** AX, DC, DS, MC, VI.

ASK FEE CALL / SOME UNITS

WHERE TO DINE

10 DEGREES SOUTH **Phone:** 404/705-8870 25

African
$16-$25

A nice surprise, the restaurant serves authentic South African cuisine and distinctive wine selections in a handsome dining room or outside in the back. Dressy casual. **Bar:** Full bar. **Reservations:** accepted. **Hours:** 5:30 pm-10:30 pm, Fri & Sat-11 pm. Closed major holidays; also Sun. **Address:** 4183 Roswell Rd NE **Location:** Between Piedmont and Wieuca rds. **Parking:** on-site. **Cards:** AX, CB, DC, DS, JC, MC, VI.

BLUE RIDGE GRILL **Phone:** 404/233-5030 31

Regional American
$15-$40

This rustic Adirondack-style restaurant features creative American cuisine. Favorites of horseradish-crusted grouper and blackened mahi mahi pair well with fresh organic vegetables. Wood beams and antiques surround the dining room. Casual dress. **Bar:** Full bar. **Reservations:** suggested. **Hours:** 11:30 am-2:30 & 5:30-10 pm, Sat from 5:30 pm. Closed major holidays. **Address:** 1261 W Paces Ferry Rd **Location:** I-75, exit 255, northeast corner. **Parking:** on-site and valet. **Cards:** AX, CB, DC, DS, MC, VI.

CAFE INTERMEZZO **Phone:** 770/396-1344 4

American
$4-$15

The stylish European coffee bar and restaurant serves tasty, attractively presented dishes and delicious dessert specialties. Saturdays and Sundays usher in a nice brunch. Friendly service rounds out an overall pleasant experience. Casual dress. **Bar:** Full bar. **Reservations:** not accepted. **Hours:** 10 am-1 am, Fri & Sat-2 am. **Address:** 4505 Ashford-Dunwoody Rd **Location:** I-285, exit 29 (Ashford-Dunwoody Rd), 0.5 mi n; in Park Plaza Shopping Center. **Parking:** on-site. **Cards:** AX, CB, DC, DS, JC, MC, VI.

CAFE SUNFLOWER **Phone:** 404/256-1675 12

Vegetarian
$4-$17

Enjoy the playful and sophisticated atmosphere of sunflowers and other colorful accessories at this vegetarian restaurant. The elaborate menu caters primarily to the New-Age crowd and features many tasty main dishes as well as luscious desserts. Casual dress. **Reservations:** accepted. **Hours:** 11:30 am-2:30 & 5-9 pm, Fri-9:30 pm, Sat noon-2:30 & 5-9:30 pm. Closed: 11/26, 12/25; also Sun. **Address:** 5975 Roswell Rd **Location:** I-285, exit 25, 0.5 mi n; in Hammonds Springs Shopping Center. **Parking:** on-site. **Cards:** AX, DC, DS, MC, VI.

CANTON COOKS **Phone:** 404/252-0322 11

Chinese
$4-$28

The sleek, contemporary dining room at Canton Cooks is the setting for some exciting variations on basic Chinese cuisine themes. Casual dress. **Bar:** Beer & wine. **Hours:** 11:30 am-2:30 & 4:30-2:30 am, Sat & Sun noon-2:30 am. **Address:** 5984 Roswell Rd **Location:** I-285, exit 25, 0.5 mi n; in The Exchange at Hammond. **Parking:** on-site. **Cards:** AX, CB, DC, DS, JC, MC, VI.

CHEQUERS SEAFOOD GRILL **Phone:** 770/391-9383 10

Seafood
$6-$35

Relax and enjoy creative renditions of fresh seafood at this upscale, yet casual, restaurant. Dressy casual. **Bar:** Full bar. **Reservations:** accepted. **Hours:** 11 am-10 pm, Sat from 4 pm, Sun 10:30 am-2:30 & 4-9:30 pm. Closed major holidays. **Address:** 236 Perimeter Center Pkwy **Location:** I-285, exit 26 eastbound, 0.5 mi to Hammond Dr, then 0.6 mi e; exit 28 westbound, just n to Hammond Dr, then just e. **Parking:** on-site and valet. **Cards:** AX, CB, DC, DS, MC, VI.

CALL

(See map and index starting on p. 302)

CHICAGO'S RESTAURANT **Phone:** 404/257-8883 (14)

American
$5-$30

Seafood mixed grill, sauteed shrimp and scallops, stockyard steak and varied other quality menu items are popular at the casual, neighborhood-style restaurant. The tasty filet is cooked to order. Freshly ground espresso and cappuccino are served in the on-site pastry shop. Casual dress. **Bar:** Full bar. **Hours:** 11 am-10 pm, Fri & Sat-11 pm, Sun-9 pm. Closed major holidays; also Super Bowl Sun. **Address:** 5920 Roswell Rd NE **Location:** I-285, exit 25, 0.4 mi n; in Parkside Shopping Center. **Parking:** on-site. **Cards:** AX, CB, DC, DS, JC, MC, VI.

CHINA COOKS **Phone:** 404/252-6611 (16)

Chinese
$4-$28

Patrons frequent the longtime standby for traditional Chinese food that is both tasty and satisfying. Casual dress. **Bar:** Beer & wine. **Reservations:** accepted. **Hours:** 11 am-2 am, Sat & Sun from noon. Closed major holidays. **Address:** 215 Northwood Dr **Location:** I-285, exit 25, just s; in Copeland Village Shopping Center. **Parking:** on-site. **Cards:** AX, DS, MC, VI.

CHOPSTIX RESTAURANT **Phone:** 404/255-4868 (23)

Chinese
$8-$26

Fresh, quality ingredients go into the distinctive blends of old and new cuisine that make up the menu at this spot near busy Buckhead and the perimeter north areas. Among more creative offerings are stir-fried lobster, venison with garlic brown sauce and crawfish spring rolls. Gracious service enhances the experience here. Guests can expect fine dining, with double-clothed tables, fresh flowers, oil lamps and a pianist. Dressy casual. Entertainment. **Bar:** Full bar. **Reservations:** suggested. **Hours:** 11:30 am-2 & 6-10 pm, Fri & Sat-10:30 pm. Closed major holidays. **Address:** 4279 Roswell Rd **Location:** I-285, exit 17, 2.6 mi s; in Chastain Square. **Parking:** on-site. **Cards:** AX, DC, DS, MC, VI.

FIVE SEASON'S BREWING COMPANY **Phone:** 404/255-5911 (17)

American
$3-$25

The brew pub serves some creative entrees, such as crispy buffalo quail, grilled pizzas and tasty handcrafted beers. Service is friendly and helpful. Casual dress. **Bar:** Full bar. **Reservations:** accepted. **Hours:** 11 am-10 pm, Thurs-10:30 pm, Fri & Sat-11 pm, Sun noon-10 pm. Closed major holidays. **Address:** 5600 Roswell Rd, Suite 21 **Location:** I-285, exit 27, just s; in The Prado. **Parking:** on-site. **Cards:** AX, CB, DC, DS, JC, MC, VI.

FOOD 101 **Phone:** 404/497-9700 (20)

American
$9-$26

In an easily accessible corner of a new shopping center, the restaurant creates new takes on such old favorites as braised lamb shank. The decor is both chic and upscale. Servers are knowledgeable and helpful. Casual dress. **Bar:** Full bar. **Reservations:** suggested. **Hours:** 11:30 am-2:30 & 5:30-10 pm, Fri-11 pm, Sat 5:30 pm-11:30 pm; Sunday brunch 11 am-3 pm. Closed major holidays. **Address:** 4969 Roswell Rd, Suite 200 **Location:** I-285, exit 25, 1.5 mi s; in Belle Isle Shopping Center. **Parking:** on-site. **Cards:** AX, CB, DC, DS, MC, VI.

CALL &M

FRONTERA MEX-MEX GRILL **Phone:** 404/236-0777 (24)

Tex-Mex
$5-$13

Diners get what they'd expect from this place: chips and salsa, yummy Tex-Mex, margaritas and varied lunch specials. Casual dress. **Bar:** Full bar. **Hours:** 11 am-10:30 pm, Sat from noon, Sun noon-10 pm. Closed major holidays. **Address:** 4279 Roswell Rd NE **Location:** I-285, exit 25, 2.6 mi s; in Chastain Square. **Parking:** on-site. **Cards:** AX, CB, DC, DS, JC, MC, VI.

CALL &M

GOLDFISH **Phone:** 770/671-0100 (7)

Seafood
$10-$40

Colorful murals on high ceilings offer visual appeal at the large, comfortable palace of salt water and freshwater delights. Excellent sushi—along with the freshest sea bass, grouper and tuna—highlights the seafood choices. Prime steaks are available for landlubbers. Dressy casual. **Bar:** Full bar. **Reservations:** suggested. **Hours:** 11:30 am-10 pm, Fri-11 pm, Sat noon-11 pm, Sun noon-10 pm. Closed: 11/26, 12/25. **Address:** 4400 Ashford-Dunwoody Rd **Location:** I-285, exit 29 (Ashford-Dunwoody Rd), 0.3 mi n; in Perimeter Mall. **Parking:** on-site and valet. **Cards:** AX, CB, DC, DS, JC, MC, VI.

CALL &M

HAVANA SANDWICH SHOP **Phone:** 404/636-4094 (38)

Cuban
$4-$8

Although not much on decor, the basic sandwich shop makes some of the best Cubans around. Friendly, welcoming servers make sure the food is just right. Casual dress. **Hours:** 10:30 am-9:30 pm, Sun 11 am-8 pm. Closed major holidays. **Address:** 2905 Buford Hwy NE **Location:** Jct N Druid Hills Rd. **Parking:** on-site. **Cards:** MC, VI.

HAVEN **Phone:** 404/969-0700 (28)

New American
$17-$29

The chic, upscale restaurant pairs creative American cuisine with fine wines. Guests enjoy the sizzle and flame emanating from the exhibition kitchen while enjoying a cocktail or a glass of one of the many wine varieties. On the menu are small plates, entrees and sumptuous desserts. Among notable specialties are wild mushroom carpaccio, smoked salmon tostada, wood-grilled filet mignon and Dreamsicle-infused creme brulee. Dressy casual. **Bar:** Full bar. **Hours:** 5 pm-10 pm, Fri & Sat-11 pm. Closed: 11/26, 12/25; also Mon. **Address:** 1441 Dresden Dr NE, Suite 160 **Location:** Jct SR 141, 0.5 mi w; in Village Plaza Place. **Parking:** on-site and valet. **Cards:** AX, DS, MC, VI.

CALL &M

HORSERADISH GRILL **Phone:** 404/255-7277 (22)

Regional Southern
$6-$27

The restaurant serves a taste of the new South in distinctive and imaginative regional cuisine that includes homegrown vegetables from a garden right on the premises. Beautifully decorated in wood and natural stone, the restored barn is accented with modern paintings. Dressy casual. **Bar:** Full bar. **Reservations:** suggested. **Hours:** 11:30 am-2:30 & 5-9 pm, Fri-10 pm, Sat 5 pm-10 pm, Sun 11 am-2:30 & 5-9 pm; Sunday brunch. Closed major holidays. **Address:** 4320 Powers Ferry Rd **Location:** Corner of W Wieuca and Powers Ferry rds; at Chastain Park. **Parking:** valet. **Cards:** AX, CB, DC, DS, MC, VI.

(See map and index starting on p. 302)

JOEL

Phone: 404/233-3500 (33)

French
$12-$36

Featuring French cuisine with Mediterranean and Asian influences, the restaurant features minimalist decor and informed waitstaff that enhance the dining experience. Dressy casual. **Bar:** Full bar. **Reservations:** suggested. **Hours:** 11:30 am-2 & 5:30-10 pm Sat from 5:30 pm. Closed major holidays; also Sun. **Address:** 3290 Northside Pkwy, Suite 120 **Location:** I-75, exit 255, just e to Northside Pkwy, then just s; in Piazza at Paces. **Parking:** valet. **Cards:** AX, CB, DC, DS, JC, MC, VI.

CALL

JOEY D'S OAK ROOM

Phone: 770/512-7063 (2)

American
$5-$30

An informal dining room decked out with acres of oak parquet flooring is the setting for delicious steaks and sandwiches. Try the corned beef sandwich with its massive amount of lean corned beef said to be specially flown in from the Carnegie Deli. Casual dress. **Bar:** Full bar. **Hours:** 11 am-10 pm, Fri-11 pm, Sat 4:30 pm-11 pm, Sun 4:30 pm-10 pm. Closed: 7/4, 11/26, 12/25. **Address:** 1015 Crown Pointe Pkwy **Location:** I-285, exit 29 (Ashford-Dunwoody Rd), 0.5 mi n, then 0.5 mi w on Perimeter Center W. **Parking:** on-site. **Cards:** AX, DC, DS, MC, VI.

CALL

KC PIT BBQ

Phone: 404/459-6497 (6)

Barbecue
$2-$19

Guests should get ready to chow down on huge portions of ribs, pork, chicken and an array of side items. The eatery is modeled after its namesake. Casual dress. **Bar:** Full bar. **Reservations:** accepted. **Hours:** 11 am-9 pm, Fri & Sat-10 pm, Sun noon-9 pm. Closed major holidays; also 1/1-1/4. **Address:** 234 Hilderbrand Rd **Location:** I-285, exit 25, 0.8 mi n. **Parking:** on-site. **Cards:** AX, DS, MC, VI.

LA GROTTA RAVINIA RISTORANTE ITALIANO

Phone: 770/395-9925 (9)

Northern Italian
$7-$32

Expect elegant dining in candlelit ambience. Attractively presented dishes include veal chops, seafood such as tuna, lamb chops and a wide variety of pasta selections. An excellent choice of Italian wines are sure to complement any meal. Dressy casual. **Bar:** Full bar. **Reservations:** suggested. **Hours:** 11:30 am-2 & 5:45-10 pm, Sat from 5:45 pm. Closed major holidays; also Sun. **Address:** 4355 Ashford-Dunwoody Rd **Location:** I-285, exit 29 (Ashford-Dunwoody Rd), northeast corner; in Crowne Plaza Atlanta-Ravinia Hotel. **Parking:** on-site and valet. **Cards:** AX, DC, DS, JC, MC, VI.

LAWRENCE'S CAFE

Phone: 404/320-7756 (37)

Middle Eastern
$3-$20

Middle Eastern Lebanese cuisine is the focus of the menu at this little "find" near several local lodgings. The combination platter is a good way to sample many of the favorites. Casual dress. **Bar:** Beer & wine. **Hours:** 11 am-2:45 & 5-9 pm, Fri-10 pm, Sat noon-10 pm. Closed: 7/4, 11/26, 12/24, 12/25; also Sun. **Address:** 2888 Buford Hwy **Location:** I-85, exit 94, just w to Buford Hwy, then just s. **Parking:** on-site. **Cards:** AX, CB, DC, DS, MC, VI.

MACHU PICCHU

Phone: 404/320-3226 (35)

Peruvian
$7-$14

A Peruvian dining experience awaits at the simple, warm and inviting restaurant, which offers several seviche appetizers as well as authentic specials such as tripe and beef hearts. Earnest and helpful servers circulate through this place, which occupies a shopping center with many other eateries and retail outlets. Casual dress. **Bar:** Beer & wine. **Reservations:** accepted. **Hours:** 11 am-10 pm, Fri & Sat-11 pm. Closed: 11/26; also Tues. **Address:** 3375 Buford Hwy NE, Bldg 1130 **Location:** I-85, exit 89, just w to Buford Hwy, then 0.8 mi n; in Northeast Plaza. **Parking:** on-site. **Cards:** AX, DS, MC, VI.

MAGGIANO'S LITTLE ITALY

Phone: 770/804-3313 (8)

Italian
$11-$38

Diners savor scrumptious, traditional favorites served in a bustling atmosphere reminiscent of Little Italy. The dining area projects an early-20th-century feel; loud conversations bouncing off high ceilings evoke a sense of the Roaring 20s. Casual dress. **Bar:** Full bar. **Reservations:** accepted. **Hours:** 11 am-10 pm, Fri & Sat-11 pm. Closed: 12/25. **Address:** 4400 Ashford-Dunwoody Rd **Location:** I-285, exit 29 (Ashford-Dunwoody Rd), 0.3 mi n; in Perimeter Mall. **Parking:** on-site. **Cards:** AX, CB, DC, DS, JC, MC, VI.

MAMA FU'S

Phone: 404/844-6262

Asian
$6-$9

The funky, crowded restaurant offers a fun mix of dishes from Asian cultures, including ahi tuna from Japan, noodle bowls and basil rolls from Vietnam, curries from Thailand and lo mein pot stickers from China. The food is a super value. Casual dress. **Bar:** Beer & wine. **Hours:** 11 am-10 pm. **Address:** 3027 N Druid Hills Rd **Location:** I-85, exit 89, 1.7 mi e; in Toco Hills Plaza. **Parking:** on-site. **Cards:** AX, DS, MC, VI.

CALL

MCKENDRICK'S STEAK HOUSE

Phone: 770/512-8888 (5)

Steak & Seafood
$15-$40

In an upscale shopping plaza, the posh steakhouse presents an extensive wine list to complement its prime beef and varied seafood dishes. A good meal might include stuffed scallops, New York strip and the beefsteak tomato salad. Dressy casual is the mode of attire. Servers are highly attentive, knowledgeable and responsive. Dressy casual. **Bar:** Full bar. **Reservations:** suggested. **Hours:** 11:30 am-2:30 & 5:30-10 pm, Fri-11 pm, Sat 5:30 pm-11 pm, Sun 5:30 pm-10 pm. Closed major holidays. **Address:** 4505 Ashford-Dunwoody Rd **Location:** I-285, exit 29 (Ashford-Dunwoody Rd), 0.5 mi n. **Parking:** on-site and valet. **Cards:** AX, CB, DC, DS, MC, VI.

MIRAGE

Phone: 404/843-8300 (1)

Persian
$6-$22

Among cuisine highlights are a variety of kebabs and other fresh foods and breads. Service is friendly and the atmosphere honest. The food and culture are accurately represented. Casual dress. **Bar:** Beer & wine. **Reservations:** accepted. **Hours:** 11 am-10 pm, Fri & Sat-11 pm. **Address:** 6631 Roswell Rd, Suite B/C **Location:** I-285, exit 25, 1.6 mi n; in Abernathy Square. **Parking:** on-site. **Cards:** AX, CB, DC, DS, JC, MC, VI.

(See map and index starting on p. 302)

O K CAFE **Phone:** 404/233-2888 (32)

Southern
$6-$11

The well-lighted cafe takes guests back in time with its plaid motif and diner-style menu. Monstrous portions of fresh comfort foods—such as country-fried steak and homemade desserts—are served by the fast, friendly staff. Casual dress. **Bar:** Beer & wine. **Hours:** 7 am-11 pm, Fri & Sat-midnight. Closed major holidays. **Address:** 1284 W Paces Ferry Rd **Location:** I-75, exit 255, just e. **Parking:** on-site. **Cards:** AX, DS, MC, VI.

PANAHAR BANGLADESHI CUISINE **Phone:** 404/633-6655 (34)

Indian
$9-$15

A weekday lunch buffet provides a nice alternative to the eatery's menu of exotic dinner items, including chicken and lamb karai, shrimp sagwala and many vegetarian dishes. Casual dress. **Reservations:** accepted. **Hours:** 11:30 am-2:30 & 5:30-10:30 pm. Closed: Mon. **Address:** 3375 Buford Hwy, Suite 1060 **Location:** I-85, exit 89, just w to N Druid Hills Rd, then 0.8 mi n; in North East Plaza. **Parking:** on-site. **Cards:** AX, CB, DC, DS, JC, MC, VI.

PANO'S & PAUL'S **Phone:** 404/261-3662 (30)

Continental
$24-$46

The restaurant's extraordinary chef creates such culinary masterpieces as sauteed veal sweetbreads, Chilean sea bass and the signature fried lobster tail. The lavish decor evokes the retro feel of the 1940s. Dressy casual. **Bar:** Full bar. **Reservations:** suggested. **Hours:** 6 pm-11 pm, Sat from 5:30 pm. Closed major holidays; also Sun. **Address:** 1232 W Paces Ferry Rd NW **Location:** I-75, exit 255, just e; jct Northside Dr and W Paces Ferry Rd. **Parking:** on-site and valet. **Cards:** AX, CB, DC, DS, JC, MC, VI.

PETITE AUBERGE RESTAURANT **Phone:** 404/634-6268 (41)

Continental
$10-$27

Diners can experience a friendly Old World atmosphere at the quaint bistro, where each dish flaunts creativity and good taste. Authentic German fare is available to those seeking something other than traditional beef, chicken, veal and seafood meals. Dressy casual. **Bar:** Full bar. **Reservations:** suggested. **Hours:** 11:30 am-10 pm, Sat from 4 pm. Closed major holidays; also Sun. **Address:** 2935 N Druid Hills Rd **Location:** I-85, exit 89, 1.7 mi se; in Toco Hills Center. **Parking:** on-site. **Cards:** AX, DC, DS, MC, VI.

CALL M

PHO #1 **Phone:** 404/633-0776 (27)

Vietnamese
$2-$8

The restaurant is known for its hot, tasty, comforting and filling pho (Vietnamese soup) and also serves other traditional Vietnamese fare, including spring rolls and rice dishes. Patrons sip interesting beverages, such as soy bean milk and the salty plum drink, in the simple surroundings. Casual dress. **Hours:** 10 am-10 pm. **Address:** 4051 Buford Hwy, Suite A **Location:** I-85, exit 91, 1 mi w to Buford Hwy, then 0.3 mi n. **Parking:** on-site. **Cards:** MC, VI.

PHO DAI LOI **Phone:** 404/633-2111 (26)

Vietnamese
$3-$7

Piping-hot bowls of pho and other Vietnamese favorites, such as fresh basil rolls, satisfy patrons of the eatery, where earnest servers circulate through a dining room appointed in pleasing traditional Vietnamese decor. Casual dress. **Hours:** 9:30 am-9 pm. Closed: 11/26, 12/25. **Address:** 4186 Buford Hwy, Suite G **Location:** I-285, exit 32, 2.8 mi s. **Parking:** on-site. **Cards:** AX, DS, MC, VI.

CALL M

PIG-N-CHIK **Phone:** 404/255-6368 (21)

Barbecue
$6-$20

Although pulled pork is the staple here, patrons averse to it can try salmon instead. Lines are a given at this popular spot. Music lends to the atmosphere on alternating Fridays. Outside seating offers no frills. Casual dress. **Bar:** Beer only. **Hours:** 10:30 am-10 pm. Closed major holidays. **Address:** 4920 Roswell Rd NE **Location:** I-285, exit 25, 1.5 mi s; in Fountain Oaks Shopping Center. **Parking:** on-site. **Cards:** AX, MC, VI.

QUEEN OF SHEBA **Phone:** 404/321-1493 (39)

Ethiopian
$2-$16

Dishes are served in the authentic style at the classic Ethiopian restaurant. Casual dress. **Bar:** Full bar. **Reservations:** accepted. **Hours:** 11 am-11:30 pm, Fri-Sun to 2 am. Closed: 12/25. **Address:** 1594 Woodcliff Dr NE **Location:** Jct Briarcliff Rd and N Druid Hills Rd, just s; in Briarcliff Station Shopping Center. **Parking:** on-site. **Cards:** AX, DS, MC, VI.

RAY'S ON THE RIVER **Phone:** 770/955-1187 (19)

Seafood
$5-$58

Savor a delicious meal of horseradish-crusted grouper at this bustling seafood spot on the banks of the Chattahoochie River. Catch an early evening sunset from the huge picture windows off of the dining room. Casual dress. Entertainment. **Bar:** Full bar. **Hours:** 11 am-10 pm, Fri & Sat 5 pm-11 pm, Sun 9:30 am-3 & 5-9 pm. Closed: 7/4, 9/7, 12/25; also Super Bowl Sun. **Address:** 6700 Powers Ferry Rd **Location:** I-285, exit 22, 0.8 mi sw; at Powers Ferry Landing. **Parking:** on-site. **Cards:** AX, CB, DC, DS, MC, VI.

SULTAN'S **Phone:** 404/257-2220 (13)

Middle Eastern
$4-$20

The menu of Turkish and Lebanese food lines up choices such as traditional kibbeh, grape leaves and kebabs, in addition to pita platters. Diners relax in the pleasant setting. Casual dress. **Bar:** Beer & wine. **Reservations:** accepted. **Hours:** 11:30 am-2:30 & 5:30-10:30 pm, Fri & Sat-11:30 pm. Closed: 11/26, 12/25. **Address:** 5920 Roswell Rd **Location:** I-285, exit 25, 0.4 mi n; in Parkside Shopping Center. **Parking:** on-site. **Cards:** AX, CB, DC, DS, JC, MC, VI.

SUSHI HUKU **Phone:** 770/956-9559 (18)

Japanese
$4-$30

Delectable sushi/tempura dishes are nicely presented and made with very fresh ingredients. Well-prepared dishes include pork in ginger sauce and shrimp Sushi Huku, both delicious and highly recommended. Sample the Sake and Asahitkirin beers with your meal. Casual dress. **Bar:** Beer & wine. **Reservations:** accepted. **Hours:** 5:30 pm-10:30 pm. Closed major holidays; also Mon. **Address:** 6300 Powers Ferry Rd **Location:** I-285, exit 22; in shopping center; opposite Crowne Plaza-Atlanta Powers Ferry. **Parking:** on-site. **Cards:** AX, DC, DS, MC, VI.

(See map and index starting on p. 302)

TERRA GRILLE

Phone: 404/841-1032 (29)

American
$3-$22

The menu focuses on healthy, lean cuisine. In addition to a broad selection of choices geared to Atkins dieters, diners can choose from among farm-raised buffalo burgers and meatloaf, chicken, trout, turkey and vegetarian dishes. Casual dress. **Bar:** Beer & wine. **Hours:** 11 am-4 & 5:30-10 pm, Fri & Sat-11:30 pm. Closed: 11/26; also Sun. **Address:** 3974-C Peachtree Rd **Location:** SR 400, exit 2, just w to Peachtree Rd NE, then 1.5 mi ne; in Brookhaven Plaza. **Parking:** on-site. **Cards:** AX, DC, MC, VI.

CALL

THAI CHILI

Phone: 404/315-6750 (40)

Thai
$3-$23

Expertly prepared authentic Thai cuisine features noteworthy culinary creations daily. Start with fried tofu with a sweet peanut sauce for dipping, then indulge in an entree of fried soft shell crab. For the adventurous palate, try the coconut milk soup. Casual dress. **Bar:** Beer & wine. **Reservations:** accepted. **Hours:** 11 am-10 pm, Fri & Sat-11 pm. Closed major holidays. **Address:** 2169 Briarcliff Rd **Location:** I-85, exit 89, 0.3 mi e to Briarcliff Rd, then 0.9 mi s; in Briar Vista Shopping Center. **Parking:** on-site. **Cards:** AX, DC, DS, MC, VI.

TIN DRUM ASIA CAFE

Phone: 770/393-3006 (3)

Asian
$2-$7

Examples of the contemporary-styled cafe's quick-serve Japanese, Chinese and Thai cuisine include spring rolls, noodle bowls, fried tempura dishes, hot soups and fried rice. The Asian wraps, known as drumrolls, deserve special consideration. Casual dress. **Bar:** Beer & wine. **Hours:** 11 am-4 & 5-9:30 pm, Sat & Sun noon-4 & 5-9 pm. Closed major holidays. **Address:** 4530 Olde Perimeter Way, Suite 200 **Location:** I-285, exit 29, 0.5 mi n, then 0.4 mi w on Perimeter Center West; in Perimeter Place. **Parking:** on-site. **Cards:** AX, DS, MC, VI.

VILLA CHRISTINA

Phone: 404/303-0133 (15)

Italian
$13-$38

Nestled in a convenient yet secluded locale within a three-story Italian villa, the restaurant is surrounded by more than eight acres of landscaped gardens. The contemporary Italian menu lists highly unusual and creative variations on fish, lamb, steak, pork and chicken. Dressy casual. **Bar:** Full bar. **Reservations:** suggested. **Hours:** 11:30 am-2:30 & 6-10 pm, Sat from 6 pm. Closed major holidays; also Sun. **Address:** 4000 Summit Blvd **Location:** I-285, exit 29 (Ashford-Dunwoody Rd), just s to Lake Hearn Dr, follow signs to Perimeter Summit Complex, then just n. **Parking:** on-site and valet. **Cards:** AX, DC, DS, MC, VI.

VIOLETTE

Phone: 404/633-3363 (36)

French
$4-$22

The charming French bistro has a nice selection of wines and offers diners a good value. Casual dress. **Bar:** Full bar. **Reservations:** accepted. **Hours:** 11:30 am-2:30 & 5:30-10 pm, Sat from 5:30 pm. Closed: Sun. **Address:** 2948 Clairmont Rd **Location:** I-85, exit 91, just w. **Parking:** on-site. **Cards:** AX, CB, DC, DS, JC, MC, VI.

ATLANTA SOUTH

(See map and index starting on p. 312)

WHERE TO STAY

COMFORT INN @ TURNER FIELD *Book great rates at AAA.com*

Phone: (404)658-1610 (6)

AAA SAVE

Hotel
$89-$149 3/26-11/30
$84-$124 12/1-3/25

Address: 795 Pollard Blvd **Location:** I-75/85, exit 245 northbound; exit 246 southbound, just e. Adjacent to Turner Field. **Facility:** 89 one-bedroom standard units. 6 stories, interior corridors. **Parking:** on-site. **Terms:** check-in 4 pm, 3 day cancellation notice-fee imposed. **Amenities:** high-speed Internet, voice mail, irons, hair dryers. **Pool(s):** outdoor. **Leisure Activities:** exercise room privileges. **Guest Services:** coin laundry, wireless Internet. **Business Services:** business center. **Cards:** AX, DS, MC, VI. **Free Special Amenities: continental breakfast and high-speed Internet.**

FEE / SOME UNITS

DAYS INN ATLANTA WEST/SIX FLAGS *Book at AAA.com*

Phone: (404)505-8880 (5)

Hotel
$60-$100 All Year

Address: 4330 Fulton Industrial Blvd **Location:** I-20, exit 49, just s. **Facility:** 155 one-bedroom standard units. 7 stories, interior corridors. **Parking:** on-site. **Terms:** cancellation fee imposed. **Amenities:** high-speed Internet, irons, hair dryers. **Pool(s):** outdoor. **Guest Services:** coin laundry, wireless Internet. **Business Services:** meeting rooms, fax (fee). **Cards:** AX, CB, DC, DS, JC, MC, VI.

ASK / SOME UNITS

EMORY CONFERENCE CENTER HOTEL *Book at AAA.com*

Phone: (404)712-6000 (2)

Hotel
$195-$229 All Year

Address: 1615 Clifton Rd **Location:** I-85, exit 91, 3.8 mi s on Clairmont Rd to N Decatur Rd, 0.9 mi e to Clifton Rd, then 1 mi n. Located opposite Emory University & Center for Disease Control. **Facility:** 198 units. 195 one-bedroom standard units. 3 one-bedroom suites, some with whirlpools. 5 stories, interior corridors. **Parking:** on-site. **Terms:** check-in 4 pm, cancellation fee imposed. **Amenities:** dual phone lines, voice mail, irons, hair dryers. *Fee:* video games, high-speed Internet. **Pool(s):** heated indoor. **Leisure Activities:** saunas, whirlpool, exercise room, spa. **Guest Services:** valet and coin laundry, area transportation, wireless Internet. **Business Services:** conference facilities, business center. **Cards:** AX, DC, DS, MC, VI.

ASK FEE CALL / SOME UNITS FEE FEE

EMORY INN *Book at AAA.com*

Phone: 404/712-6700 (1)

Hotel
Rates not provided

Address: 1641 Clifton Rd **Location:** I-85, exit 91, 3.8 mi s to N Decatur Rd, 0.9 mi w to Clifton Rd, then 1 mi n. Located next to Emory University. **Facility:** 107 one-bedroom standard units. 2-3 stories (no elevator), exterior corridors. **Parking:** on-site. **Terms:** check-in 4 pm. **Amenities:** high-speed Internet (fee), voice mail, irons, hair dryers. **Pool(s):** outdoor. **Leisure Activities:** whirlpool, exercise room privileges. **Guest Services:** valet and coin laundry, area transportation. **Business Services:** conference facilities, fax (fee).

FEE CALL / SOME UNITS

(See map and index starting on p. 312)

THE GASLIGHT INN B&B — Phone: 404/875-1001 (4)

Bed & Breakfast
$115-$215 All Year

Address: 1001 St Charles Ave NE **Location:** I-75/85, exit 248C to Ponce de Leon Ave, just e, n on Frederica, then just e. **Facility:** Hand-painted 18th-century furniture is displayed in some rooms of this Craftsman-style home built in 1913. Smoke free premises. 8 units. 5 one- and 3 two-bedroom standard units, some with whirlpools. 2 stories (no elevator), interior corridors. *Bath:* combo or shower only. **Parking:** on-site. **Terms:** 2 night minimum stay - weekends, 14 day cancellation notice-fee imposed. **Amenities:** video library, CD players, irons, hair dryers. *Some:* DVD players, high-speed Internet, voice mail. **Guest Services:** wireless Internet. **Business Services:** PC, fax. **Cards:** AX, DS, MC, VI.

ASK

RENAISSANCE CONCOURSE HOTEL *Book great rates at AAA.com* — Phone: (404)209-9999 (7)

AAA SAVE

Hotel
$246-$264 All Year

Address: One Hartsfield Centre Pkwy **Location:** I-85, exit 73A northbound; exit 73 southbound, just e to Toffie Terrace, then just se. **Facility:** Located next to airport with some units overlooking the adjacent runways; spacious guest units are decorated with a contemporary flair. Smoke free premises. 387 units. 383 one-bedroom standard units. 4 one-bedroom suites with whirlpools. 11 stories, interior corridors. **Parking:** on-site (fee) and valet. **Terms:** check-in 4 pm, cancellation fee imposed. **Amenities:** voice mail, irons, hair dryers. *Fee:* video games, high-speed Internet. *Some:* CD players, dual phone lines. **Pool(s):** outdoor, heated indoor. **Leisure Activities:** saunas, whirlpool. **Guest Services:** valet and coin laundry, airport transportation-The William B. Hartsfield Atlanta Int'l Airport, area transportation-within 2 mi, wireless Internet. **Business Services:** conference facilities, business center. **Cards:** AX, CB, DC, DS, JC, MC, VI. **Free Special Amenities: newspaper and early check-in/late check-out.** ***(See color ad p 328)***

AAA Benefit:
Members save a minimum 5% off the best available rate.

CALL

UNIVERSITY INN AT EMORY *Book great rates at AAA.com* — Phone: (404)634-7327 (8)

AAA SAVE

Hotel
$135-$250 All Year

Address: 1767 N Decatur Rd **Location:** I-85, exit 91, 3.8 mi s on Clairmont Rd to N Decatur Rd, then 0.8 mi w. Located opposite Emory Medical Complex. **Facility:** Smoke free premises. 34 one-bedroom standard units, some with kitchens. 2-3 stories (no elevator), exterior corridors. **Parking:** on-site. **Terms:** office hours 6:30 am-11 pm, cancellation fee imposed. **Amenities:** high-speed Internet, voice mail, irons, hair dryers. **Pool(s):** outdoor. **Guest Services:** coin laundry, wireless Internet. **Business Services:** fax. **Cards:** AX, CB, DC, DS, MC, VI. **Free Special Amenities: expanded continental breakfast and high-speed Internet.**

FEE / SOME UNITS FEE

WHERE TO DINE

BABETTE'S CAFE — Phone: 404/523-9121 (17)

French
$3-$25

This critically acclaimed bistro serves European provincial cuisine in a casual atmosphere. The mouthwatering cassoulet is popular. Top off your savory meal with a dessert like the yummy homemade chocolate bread pudding with banana ice cream. Casual dress. **Bar:** Full bar. **Reservations:** accepted. **Hours:** 5:30 pm-10 pm, Sun 10:30 am-2 & 5-9 pm; Sunday brunch. Closed: 7/4, 11/26, 12/25; also Mon. **Address:** 573 N Highland Ave **Location:** Jct Ponce de Leon and Highland aves, 0.5 mi s. **Parking:** on-site. **Cards:** AX, DC, DS, MC, VI.

BACCHANALIA — Phone: 404/365-0410 (5)

Northern American
$72-$125

New American cuisine with a Northern California influence is offered in their new location in a transitioning warehouse district. The industrial space is softened with velvet and soft-lighting. A wall of windows view the chrome kitchen which prodcues a weekly changing menu of creative fresh fare. A new addition is their gourmet market up front. Dressy casual. **Bar:** Full bar. **Reservations:** suggested. **Hours:** 6 pm-10 pm. Closed major holidays; also Sun. **Address:** 1198 Howell Mill Rd **Location:** I-75/85, exit 252, 1.4 mi w. **Parking:** on-site. **Cards:** AX, DC, MC, VI.

BELLY GENERAL STORE — Phone: 404/872-1003 (14)

Deli
$2-$7

The general store is a gathering place for those interested in homemade cookies, cupcakes, breads, sandwiches with artisan flair and organic coffee drinks. Casual dress. **Hours:** 7 am-7 pm, Sun 8 am-5 pm. Closed major holidays. **Address:** 772 N Highland Ave **Location:** Ponce de Leon Ave, e to N Highland Ave, then n. **Parking:** street. **Cards:** AX, MC, VI.

CALCUTTA — Phone: 404/681-1838 (22)

Indian
$4-$15

Classic Indian cuisine is served from this spot in the funky Little Five Points neighborhood. Although a bit tired, the decor is fitting. Excellent breads complement such choices as vindaloo and tandoori items. Casual dress. **Bar:** Beer & wine. **Reservations:** accepted. **Hours:** 11:30 am-2:30 & 5-10 pm, Fri & Sat-11 pm, Sun 5 pm-10:30 pm. Closed major holidays. **Address:** 1138 Euclid Ave **Location:** Jct Euclid and Moreland aves, just w. **Parking:** street. **Cards:** AX, CB, DC, DS, JC, MC, VI.

CAMELI'S GOURMET PIZZA JOINT — Phone: 404/249-9020 (15)

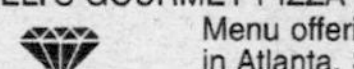

Pizza
$3-$30

Menu offerings at the "joint" include traditional Italian dishes and, what some consider to be, the best pizza in Atlanta. Service is solid and consistent. Casual dress. **Bar:** Beer & wine. **Hours:** 11:30 am-10 pm, Fri & Sat-11 pm, Sat noon-11 pm, Sun 5 pm-10 pm. **Address:** 699 Ponce de Leon Ave **Location:** I-75/85, exit 249D, 0.5 mi e to Piedmont Rd, just n to Ponce de Leon Ave, then 1.5 mi e. **Parking:** on-site.

DUSTY'S BARBEQUE — Phone: 404/320-6264 (3)

Barbecue
$5-$15

Around since the '70s, the rustic restaurant specializes in simple fare, particularly great North Carolina vinegar-based barbecue. Alcohol no longer is served here. Casual dress. **Hours:** 11 am-9 pm, Fri & Sat-10 pm. Closed major holidays. **Address:** 1815 Briarcliff Rd **Location:** I-85, exit 89 (S Druid Hills Rd), 0.3 mi e to Briarcliff Rd, then 1.6 mi s. **Parking:** on-site.

(See map and index starting on p. 312)

FLOATAWAY CAFE — Phone: 404/892-1414 (2)

New American
$15-$36

In a warehouse district, the chic, contemporary digs are cutting-edge in style. An excellent wine list and superb cuisine make the restaurant a top choice. Desserts are exquisite. Dressy casual. **Bar:** Full bar. **Reservations:** suggested. **Hours:** 6 pm-10 pm. Closed major holidays; also Sun & Mon. **Address:** 1123 Zonolite Rd NE **Location:** I-85, exit 89, just e on S Druid Hills Rd, 1.8 mi s on Briarcliff Rd, then 0.5 mi sw. **Parking:** on-site. **Cards:** AX, DC, MC, VI.

FLYING BISCUIT CAFE — Phone: 404/687-8888 (23)

American
$5-$15

Hailed by many as having the best breakfast and biscuits in town, the non-breakfast selections here are excellent also. Funky, off-beat decor and atmosphere lend charm. Casual dress. **Bar:** Beer & wine. **Hours:** 7 am-10 pm, Fri & Sat-10:30 pm. **Address:** 1655 McLendon Ave **Location:** In Candler Park. **Parking:** on-site. **Cards:** AX, MC, VI.

THE FOOD STUDIO *Menu on AAA.com* — Phone: 404/815-6677 (7)

New American
$6-$32

Contemporary, bold American cuisine lines the menu of the restaurant, which occupies a converted farm equipment factory. The interior is strikingly redone in an upscale, "artsy" fashion. Servers are highly knowledgeable and personable. Dressy casual. **Bar:** Full bar. **Reservations:** suggested. **Hours:** 11:30 am-2 & 5:30-10 pm, Fri & Sat-11 pm. Closed major holidays; also Sun. **Address:** 887 W Marietta St SW Studio K-102 **Location:** I-75, exit 250, follow 10th St w to Brady S; in King Plow Arts Center. **Parking:** on-site and valet. **Cards:** AX, CB, DC, DS, MC, VI.

FRITTI — Phone: 404/880-9559 (27)

Regional Italian
$4-$14

In a former garage, the casual Italian eatery has an operating garage door for al fresco dining when the weather is appropriate. Notable preparations include the wood-fired pizzas for which this place has won awards, but guests also appreciate the full selection of eclectic appetizers. Casual dress. **Bar:** Full bar. **Hours:** 11:30 am-3 & 5:30-11 pm, Fri & Sat-midnight, Sun 1 pm-10 pm. Closed: 11/26, 12/25. **Address:** 309 N Highland Ave **Location:** Jct US 23/SR 42 and US 29/78/278, just w to N Highland Ave NE, then 0.9 mi s. **Parking:** valet and street. **Cards:** AX, MC, VI.

HIGHLAND TAP — Phone: 404/875-3673 (8)

American
$4-$40

Super steaks and martinis are hallmarks of the restaurant, which enjoys a buzzing bar scene. Casual dress. **Bar:** Full bar. **Hours:** 11 am-3 am, Mon from 5 pm. Closed major holidays. **Address:** 1026 N Highland Ave NE **Location:** Jct Virginia and Highland aves. **Parking:** on-site. **Cards:** AX, CB, DC, DS, JC, MC, VI.

JCT KITCHEN & BAR — Phone: 404/355-2252 (6)

American
$4-$29

Contemporary style merges with comfortable warmth in the open dining room, while live music in the upstairs bar enhances the atmosphere. Fried chicken is the signature dish on a menu of New American food. Casual dress. **Bar:** Full bar. **Reservations:** accepted. **Hours:** 11 am-2:30 & 5-10 pm, Fri & Sat-11 pm. Closed major holidays; also Sun. **Address:** 1198 Howell Mill Rd, Suite 18 **Location:** I-75/85, exit 252, 1.4 mi w; in Westside Urban Market. **Parking:** on-site. **Cards:** AX, CB, DC, DS, JC, MC, VI.

CALL M

LA TAVOLA TRATTORIA — Phone: 404/873-5430 (9)

Italian
$4-$26

In the trendy Virginia-Highlands area, the sleek, contemporary restaurant has a rich interior with granite tabletops, wood accents and modern artwork. Menu favorites include seared scallops with polenta and sauteed spinach and tomato-onion compote and ricotta and sage ravioli. To complete the experience, the chef's sampling of signature desserts cannot be missed. Casual dress. **Bar:** Full bar. **Reservations:** accepted. **Hours:** 5:30 pm-11 pm, Fri & Sat-midnight, Sun 11 am-3 & 5:30-10 pm. Closed: 11/26, 12/24, 12/25. **Address:** 992 Virginia Ave NE **Location:** Jct N Highland and Virginia aves. **Parking:** valet. **Cards:** AX, DC, MC, VI.

LITTLE 5 CORNER TAVERN — Phone: 404/521-0667 (21)

American
$5-$15

At one of the city's hippest intersections, the modish nightspot has the feel of a British pub. Guests can play a game of pool while waiting for salads, appetizers, sandwiches and entrees. Casual dress. **Bar:** Full bar. **Hours:** 11 am-2:30 am, Sun-midnight. Closed major holidays. **Address:** 1174 E Euclid Ave **Location:** Jct Euclid and Moreland aves. **Parking:** street. **Cards:** AX, MC, VI.

MURPHY'S — Phone: 404/872-0904 (11)

American
$5-$24

Renovations—which include a wine shop and sharp, contemporary decor—go well with the neighborhood favorite's tried, true and trusted cuisine. Casual dress. **Bar:** Full bar. **Hours:** 11 am-10 pm, Fri-midnight, Sat 8 am-11 pm, Sun 8 am-10 pm. Closed: 11/26, 12/25. **Address:** 997 Virginia Ave NE **Location:** Jct Virginia and Highland aves, just w. **Parking:** on-site. **Cards:** AX, DS, MC, VI.

NOCHE — Phone: 404/815-9155 (10)

Spanish
$4-$15

Award winning margaritas, a happening bar scene and Spanish influenced tapas including blue cornmeal fried green tomatoes, veggie empanadas and lobster tacos draw people to this restaurant. Casual dress. **Bar:** Full bar. **Reservations:** accepted. **Hours:** 5:30 pm-11 pm, Fri-midnight, Sat 1 pm-midnight, Sun 1 pm-10 pm. Closed: 11/26, 12/25. **Address:** 1000 Virginia Ave **Location:** Ponce de Leon Ave, e to N Highland Ave, n to Virginia Ave; jct Virginia and Highland aves. **Parking:** street. **Cards:** AX, DC, DS, MC, VI.

CALL M

NUEVO LAREDO CANTINA — Phone: 404/352-9009 (1)

Mexican
$3-$18

In business since 1992, the award-winning restaurant centers its menu on home-style Mexican cooking. Specialties include brisket Barbacoa, chicken mole, over-stuffed poblano chiles rellenos and lobster or fish (grilled salmon) tacos. The owner refers to his cuisine as "cult Mexican for die-hard fans.". Casual dress. **Bar:** Beer & wine. **Hours:** 11 am-10 pm, Fri & Sat-11 pm. Closed: 11/26, 12/25; also Sun. **Address:** 1495 Chattahoochee Ave **Location:** I-75, exit 252, 0.4 mi s on Howell Mill Rd, nw to Chattahoochee Ave NW, then 1.5 mi nw. **Parking:** on-site. **Cards:** AX, MC, VI.

(See map and index starting on p. 312)

OSTERIA 832 **Phone:** 404/897-1414 (12)

Italian
$3-$13

In the historic Virginia-Highlands neighborhood, the casual Italian eatery presents a menu of pizza and pasta dishes to satisfy any appetite. Casual dress. **Bar:** Beer & wine. **Hours:** 5 pm-10 pm, Fri-11 pm, Sat 9 am-11 pm, Sun 9 am-10 pm. Closed major holidays. **Address:** 832 N Highland Ave **Location:** Ponce de Leon Ave, e to N Highland Ave, then n. **Parking:** on-site. **Cards:** AX, DC, DS, MC, VI.

PLANET BOMBAY **Phone:** 404/688-0005 (19)

Indian
$6-$25

The menu comprises traditional dishes, such as tandoori items, as well as some good curry preparations. Many options of naan complement a filling lunch or dinner. Casual dress. **Bar:** Beer & wine. **Reservations:** accepted. **Hours:** 11:30 am-3 & 5:30-10:30 pm, Fri-11 pm, Sat noon-3 & 5:30-11 pm, Sun 5:30 pm-10:30 pm. Closed major holidays. **Address:** 451 Moreland Ave NE **Location:** Jct Moreland and Colquit aves, just n. **Parking:** street. **Cards:** AX, DS, MC, VI.

SABROSO **Phone:** 404/475-8888 (25)

Spanish
$4-$10

Tapas dishes that pick up on Spanish and American influences line the menu at the funky Little Five Points eatery. Hip, chic decor characterizes the spot. Casual dress. **Bar:** Full bar. **Reservations:** accepted. **Hours:** 11 am-11 pm, Fri-1 am, Sat-2 am. Closed major holidays. **Address:** 351 Moreland Ave **Location:** Jct Euclid and Moreland aves, just s. **Parking:** on-site. **Cards:** AX, DS, MC, VI.

CALL

SALA-SABOR DE MEXICO **Phone:** 404/872-7203 (4)

Regional Mexican
$5-$20

In a trendy neighborhood, the restaurant with chic decor takes Mexican cuisine to a new level. Diners might begin with one of several seviche appetizers before trying the house favorite pork asado and fish tacos. Refreshing designer margaritas are a must. Save room for one of the homemade desserts. Dressy casual. **Bar:** Full bar. **Reservations:** accepted. **Hours:** 5:30 pm-10 pm, Fri-11 pm, Sat & Sun noon-11 pm. Closed: 11/26, 12/24, 12/25. **Address:** 1186 N Highland Ave NE **Location:** Jct N Highland Ave NE and Amsterdam Ave; in Virginia-Highland neighborhood. **Parking:** on-site. **Cards:** AX, DC, MC, VI.

SAVAGE PIZZA **Phone:** 404/523-0500 (18)

Pizza
$2-$20

The busy, charming pizza joint serves great New York-style, thin-crust pizza—available by the slice or as a whole pie—as well as calzones and subs. Adorning the walls and ceilings are images of super heroes. Casual dress. **Bar:** Beer & wine. **Hours:** 11:30 am-10:30 pm, Fri & Sat-11:30 pm, Sun noon-10:30 pm. Closed major holidays. **Address:** 484 Moreland Ave **Location:** Jct Euchid and Moreland aves, just n. **Parking:** on-site. **Cards:** AX, MC, VI.

SOTTO SOTTO **Phone:** 404/523-6678 (26)

Italian
$7-$34

There is something sassy about this with-it trattoria, from the "peer in" kitchen to the rough, sanded walls. Wood-roasted dishes, a few meats and homemade pasta in minimalist herb-enhanced sauce can be enjoyed amid bustle and a constant din. Wood-roasted whole fish, including the favorite pompano, is the signature dish. Panna cotta is another "can't miss" item, as is the Belgian chocolate soup ordered at almost every table. Dressy casual. **Bar:** Full bar. **Reservations:** suggested. **Hours:** 5:30 pm-11 pm, Fri & Sat-midnight, Sun-10 pm. Closed major holidays. **Address:** 313 N Highland Ave NE **Location:** Jct Ponce de Leon and N Highland aves, 0.8 mi s. **Parking:** valet. **Cards:** AX, DC, MC, VI.

SOUL VEGETARIAN II **Phone:** 404/875-0145 (16)

Vegetarian
$6-$14

The vegan eatery prepares dishes with a decidedly Southern twist. Great vegetables include collards, corn and potatoes, while salads, soups, tempeh and tofu are among other choices. Everything is organic, and even the "ice cream" is free of dairy products. Casual dress. **Hours:** 11 am-10 pm, Sat from 10 am, Sun 10 am-2 & 5-10 pm. Closed major holidays; also Mon. **Address:** 652 N Highland Ave **Location:** Jct North and Highland aves, just s. **Parking:** on-site. **Cards:** AX, DC, DS, MC, VI.

CALL

SURIN OF THAILAND **Phone:** 404/892-7789 (13)

Thai
$6-$17

In the fashionable Virginia Highlands district, the restaurant prepares authentic Thai dishes with varied sauces, spices and marinades. The large, energetic dining room has an original tin ceiling. Full bar service is available. Casual dress. **Bar:** Full bar. **Hours:** 11:30 am-2:30 & 5:30-10:30 pm, Fri-11:30 pm, Sat noon-2:30 & 5:30-11:30 pm, Sun noon-2:30 & 5:30-10:30 pm. Closed: 11/26, 12/25. **Address:** 810 N Highland Ave **Location:** Jct Ponce de Leon and N Highland aves, just n. **Parking:** street. **Cards:** AX, DS, MC, VI.

SWEET LIME **Phone:** 404/589-9696 (24)

Asian
$4-$18

Primarily Japanese cuisine, including sushi and other traditional dishes, makes up the menu at the hip neighborhood spot. The food here is a good value. Casual dress. **Bar:** Full bar. **Reservations:** accepted. **Hours:** noon-10:30 pm, Fri & Sat-11:30 pm. Closed major holidays. **Address:** 1128 Euclid Ave **Location:** Jct Euclid and Moreland aves, just w. **Parking:** street. **Cards:** AX, CB, DC, DS, JC, MC, VI.

THE VORTEX BAR & GRILL **Phone:** 404/688-1828 (20)

American
$4-$9

A huge selection of burgers and other pub fare is offered at this eatery. The walls are covered in photographs, memorabilia and nostalgic items; servers are upbeat and efficient. Casual dress. **Bar:** Full bar. **Reservations:** not accepted. **Hours:** 11 am-midnight, Fri & Sat-3 am. Closed: 11/26. **Address:** 438 Moreland Ave **Location:** Just n of jct Euclid and Moreland aves. **Parking:** on-site. **Cards:** AX, DC, DS, MC, VI.

The Atlanta Vicinity

ACWORTH pop. 13,422

WHERE TO STAY

AMERICA'S BEST INN *Book great rates at AAA.com* **Phone:** (770)974-5400

AAA SAVE

Motel
$45-$50 All Year

Address: 5320 Cherokee St **Location:** I-75, exit 278, just w. **Facility:** 48 one-bedroom standard units. 2 stories, exterior corridors. **Parking:** on-site. **Terms:** 7 day cancellation notice. **Amenities:** high-speed Internet, hair dryers. **Pool(s):** outdoor. **Guest Services:** wireless Internet. **Business Services:** fax. **Cards:** AX, DS, MC, VI. **Free Special Amenities: continental breakfast and high-speed Internet.**

/ SOME UNITS FEE

BEST WESTERN ACWORTH INN *Book great rates at AAA.com* **Phone:** (770)974-0116

AAA SAVE

Motel
$55-$80 All Year

Address: 5155 Cowan Rd **Location:** I-75, exit 277, just w. **Facility:** 84 one-bedroom standard units. 2 stories, exterior corridors. **Parking:** on-site. **Amenities:** high-speed Internet, irons, hair dryers. **Pool(s):** outdoor. **Guest Services:** coin laundry, wireless Internet. **Business Services:** fax (fee). **Cards:** AX, DS, MC, VI. **Free Special Amenities: expanded continental breakfast and high-speed Internet.**

/ SOME UNITS FEE

AAA Benefit:
Members save up to 20%, plus 10% bonus points with rewards program.

ECONO LODGE *Book great rates at AAA.com* **Phone:** (770)974-1922

AAA SAVE

Motel
$55-$65 All Year

Address: 4980 Cowan Rd **Location:** I-75, exit 277, just w. **Facility:** 58 one-bedroom standard units. 2-3 stories (no elevator), exterior corridors. **Parking:** on-site. **Amenities:** high-speed Internet. **Pool(s):** outdoor. **Guest Services:** wireless Internet. **Business Services:** fax (fee). **Cards:** AX, DC, DS, MC, VI.

/ SOME UNITS FEE

HOLIDAY INN EXPRESS *Book at AAA.com* **Phone:** (770)975-9920

Hotel
$89-$119 All Year

Address: 184 N Point Way **Location:** I-75, exit 277, just e. **Facility:** 44 one-bedroom standard units, some with whirlpools. 3 stories, interior/exterior corridors. **Parking:** on-site. **Amenities:** high-speed Internet, dual phone lines, voice mail, irons, hair dryers. **Pool(s):** outdoor. **Leisure Activities:** exercise room. **Guest Services:** valet laundry, wireless Internet. **Business Services:** business center. **Cards:** AX, DC, DS, MC, VI.

ASK FEE CALL / SOME UNITS

MOTEL 6 **Phone:** (770)974-1700

Motel
$45-$65 All Year

Address: 5035 Cowan Rd **Location:** I-75, exit 277, just w. **Facility:** 60 one-bedroom standard units. 2 stories, exterior corridors. **Parking:** on-site. **Terms:** cancellation fee imposed. **Amenities:** high-speed Internet, hair dryers. **Pool(s):** outdoor. **Guest Services:** wireless Internet. **Business Services:** fax (fee). **Cards:** AX, DC, DS, MC, VI.

ASK / SOME UNITS FEE

RAMADA LIMITED *Book at AAA.com* **Phone:** (770)975-9000

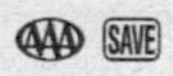

Hotel
$66-$80 All Year

Address: 164 N Point Way **Location:** I-75, exit 277, just e. **Facility:** 40 one-bedroom standard units. 2 stories, exterior corridors. **Parking:** on-site. **Amenities:** high-speed Internet, voice mail, irons, hair dryers. **Guest Services:** wireless Internet. **Business Services:** PC, fax (fee). **Cards:** AX, CB, DC, DS, MC, VI.

ASK / SOME UNITS

SUPER 8 MOTEL *Book great rates at AAA.com* **Phone:** (770)966-9700

AAA SAVE

Motel
$60-$80 All Year

Address: 4970 Cowan Rd **Location:** I-75, exit 277, just w. **Facility:** 49 one-bedroom standard units, some with whirlpools. 2-3 stories (no elevator), exterior corridors. **Parking:** on-site. **Terms:** cancellation fee imposed. **Amenities:** high-speed Internet, hair dryers. **Pool(s):** outdoor. **Guest Services:** wireless Internet. **Business Services:** fax (fee). **Cards:** AX, DC, DS, MC, VI. **Free Special Amenities: continental breakfast and high-speed Internet.**

/ SOME UNITS FEE

WHERE TO DINE

FUSCO'S VIA ROMA **Phone:** 770/974-1110

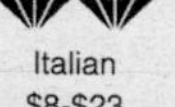

Italian
$8-$23

A downtown jewel, the restaurant serves well-prepared Italian favorites with choices from a good wine list. Servers are informed. Casual dress. **Bar:** Full bar. **Reservations:** accepted. **Hours:** 11 am-10 pm, Thurs-Sat to 11 pm; Sun 4 pm-9 pm in summer & fall. Closed major holidays; also Mon. **Address:** 4815A S Main St NW **Location:** I-75, exit 278, 1 mi w; downtown. **Parking:** street. **Cards:** AX, DS, MC, VI.

GRAND ASIAN BUFFET **Phone:** 770/975-5898

Asian
$2-$11

Offering an excellent value, the restaurant's enormous buffet includes more than 300 items with a huge variety of Chinese, Korean and Japanese cuisine. The contemporary dining room is bright and fresh. Casual dress. **Hours:** 11 am-10 pm, Fri & Sat-11 pm. Closed: 12/25. **Address:** 3335 Cobb Pkwy, Suite 830 **Location:** Jct US 41/SR 92, 1 mi s; in Best Buy Shopping Plaza. **Parking:** on-site. **Cards:** AX, DS, MC, VI.

CALL

GREEN TOMATO HOME COOKING **Phone:** 770/928-2303

Southern
$6

Home-style cooking is served on a buffet. In addition to salad fixings, the tables line up meats, vegetables and fruit. Casual dress. **Hours:** 11 am-8:30 pm. Closed major holidays; also Sun. **Address:** 6199 Hwy 92 **Location:** Jct SR 92 and Wade Green Rd, just e. **Parking:** on-site. **Cards:** MC, VI.

CALL

HENRY'S LOUISIANA GRILL **Phone:** 770/966-1515

Cajun
$7-$19

It wouldn't be surprising for diners to say "Louisiana ooh la la" after diving into the dish of the same name. Other authentic preparations include jambalaya du jour, po'boys and succulent bread pudding. Casual dress. **Bar:** Full bar. **Hours:** 11 am-10 pm, Fri & Sat-11 pm. Closed major holidays; also Sun. **Address:** 4849 N Main St **Location:** I-75, exit 278, 1 mi w; downtown. **Parking:** street. **Cards:** AX, DS, MC, VI.

HONG KONG STAR **Phone:** 770/917-0688

Chinese
$6-$24

The eatery is a true up-and-coming spot on the North Side dining scene. Lovely decor and delicious food are big reasons why. Casual dress. **Bar:** Beer & wine. **Hours:** 11:30 am-10 pm, Fri & Sat-10:30 pm. Closed major holidays. **Address:** 3451 Cobb Pkwy, Suite 9 **Location:** Jct US 41 (Cobb Pkwy) and Due West Rd. **Parking:** on-site. **Cards:** AX, DS, MC, VI.

MEXICO TIPICO **Phone:** 770/975-7708

Tex-Mex
$2-$15

Noch on traditional, quick-serve Tex-Mex dishes like tacos, burritos, enchiladas and fajitas. Chips and fresh salsa are served before the meal. Casual dress. **Bar:** Full bar. **Hours:** 11 am-2 & 5-10 pm, Fri & Sat 11 am-10 pm. Closed: 11/26, 12/25; also Sun. **Address:** 4417 S Main St **Location:** I-75, exit 277, 1.5 mi w to Main St, then just s. **Parking:** on-site. **Cards:** AX, DS, MC, VI.

THE OLD MILL **Phone:** 678/388-1630

American
$8-$21

As the name implies, the restaurant is nestled downtown in a former abandoned mill. High ceilings, exposed brick walls, hardwood floors and live music dancing through the air define the relaxed atmosphere. Uniquely prepared, old favorites—such as fried green tomatoes, catfish, steak and seafood—take on a new taste. Casual dress. **Bar:** Full bar. **Reservations:** suggested. **Hours:** 11 am-10 pm, Fri & Sat-11 pm, Sun 11 am-3 & 5-10 pm. Closed major holidays; also Mon. **Address:** 4271 Southside Dr **Location:** I-75, exit 278, 1 mi w; downtown. **Parking:** valet. **Cards:** AX, CB, DC, DS, JC, MC, VI.

CALL

PACHAMAMA **Phone:** 770/928-7977

Peruvian
$4-$15

Located in a converted Pizza Hut building, the eatery offers fresh Peruvian-style dishes, like the rotisserie chicken special. Casual dress. **Bar:** Beer & wine. **Hours:** 11 am-9 pm, Sat noon-10 pm, Sun noon-8 pm. Closed major holidays; also Mon. **Address:** 6822 Hwy 92 **Location:** Jct Bells Ferry Rd and SR 92. **Parking:** on-site. **Cards:** MC, VI.

PACIFIC SPICE **Phone:** 770/529-8300

Asian
$6-$26

A newcomer to the area dining scene, the contemporary restaurant focuses on a wide variety of Chinese and Japanese fare, including sushi. Casual dress. **Bar:** Beer & wine. **Reservations:** accepted. **Hours:** 11 am-10 pm, Fri & Sat-10:30 pm. Closed major holidays. **Address:** 6110 Cedar Crest Rd, Suite 310 **Location:** Jct US 41 (Cobb Pkwy) and Cedar Crest Rd; in Governor's Towne Square. **Parking:** on-site. **Cards:** AX, DS, MC, VI.

CALL

PAISANO'S PIZZERIA & ITALIAN RESTAURANT **Phone:** 678/213-5500

Italian
$3-$20

New York-style pizza merits pride of place among the restaurant's many Italian choices. The recently opened spot offers some outside seating. Casual dress. **Bar:** Beer & wine. **Hours:** 11 am-9 pm, Fri & Sat-10 pm. Closed major holidays. **Address:** 3979 S Main St, Suite 250 **Location:** 1 mi s; in Main Street Exchange. **Parking:** on-site. **Cards:** AX, MC, VI.

CALL

RED PEPPER'S **Phone:** 770/529-3636

International
$6-$18

The restaurant prepares what it bills as international cuisine: many Latin favorites, including Mexican and Cuban fare, in addition to other choices. The atmosphere and decor are simple. Many diners choose the delicious Cuban sandwich, and even Atlantans make the drive to this place. Casual dress. **Bar:** Full bar. **Reservations:** accepted. **Hours:** 11 am-2:30 & 5-10 pm, Sun 11 am-3 & 5-8 pm. Closed major holidays. **Address:** 4439 S Main St **Location:** I-75, exit 277, 1.5 mi w to Main St, then just s. **Parking:** on-site. **Cards:** AX, DC, DS, MC, VI.

CALL

STROMBOLI'S **Phone:** 770/424-0000

Italian
$8-$13

Simple and satisfying food in large portions is what diners find at the new restaurant. On the menu is anything from pasta to pizza to a little bit more. Casual dress. **Bar:** Beer & wine. **Hours:** 11 am-10 pm. Closed: 4/12, 11/26, 12/25. **Address:** 3365 Acworth Oaks Dr **Location:** I-75, exit 277, just w to Baker Rd, then just s; behind car wash. **Parking:** on-site. **Cards:** AX, DS, MC, VI.

THAI BASIL & SUSHI ZEN
Phone: 770/975-8909

Asian
$6-$15

Both Thai and Japanese dishes are served at the traditional restaurant, which employs friendly servers and has a sushi bar. Casual dress. **Reservations:** accepted. **Hours:** 11 am-2:30 & 4:30-10 pm, Sat 11:30 am-3 & 4:30-10:30 pm, Sun 4 pm-10 pm. Closed major holidays. **Address:** 3330 Cobb Pkwy, #15 **Location:** Jct Cobb Pkwy (US 41) and Acworth Due West Rd. **Parking:** on-site. **Cards:** AX, DS, MC, VI.

CALL

THAI GINGER
Phone: 678/494-0880

Thai
$6-$15

The menu blends traditional curry and noodle dishes with more adventurous fare, such as the house specialty shellfish hoe ra par. Casual dress. **Bar:** Beer & wine. **Reservations:** accepted. **Hours:** 11:30 am-2:30 & 5-9:30 pm, Fri-10 pm, Sat & Sun 5 pm-10 pm. Closed major holidays; also Mon. **Address:** 5399 Bells Ferry Rd **Location:** Jct Bells Ferry Rd and SR 92, just s; in Market Center Shopping Center. **Parking:** on-site. **Cards:** AX, CB, DC, DS, JC, MC, VI.

WATERSTONE GRILL
Phone: 770/974-4899

American
$3-$29

Offering the feel of a neighborhood restaurant, staff at the downtown eatery use fresh ingredients during preparation of the global cuisine. Casual dress. **Bar:** Full bar. **Reservations:** accepted. **Hours:** 11:30 am-2 & 5-9:30 pm. Closed major holidays; also Sun & Mon. **Address:** 4849 N Main St **Location:** I-75, exit 278, 1 mi w; downtown. **Parking:** street. **Cards:** AX, CB, DC, DS, JC, MC, VI.

ALPHARETTA pop. 34,854 (See map and index starting on p. 302)

WHERE TO STAY

ATLANTA MARRIOTT ALPHARETTA *Book great rates at AAA.com* **Phone:** (770)754-9600 47

Hotel
$217-$233 All Year

Address: 5750 Windward Pkwy **Location:** SR 400, exit 11, just e. **Facility:** Smoke free premises. 318 units. 316 one-bedroom standard units. 2 one-bedroom suites. 8 stories, interior corridors. **Parking:** on-site. **Terms:** cancellation fee imposed. **Amenities:** dual phone lines, voice mail, irons, hair dryers. *Fee:* video games, high-speed Internet. **Pool(s):** heated outdoor, heated indoor. **Leisure Activities:** whirlpool, accessibility lift in pool, exercise room. **Guest Services:** valet and coin laundry, area transportation-within 5 mi, wireless Internet. **Business Services:** conference facilities, business center. **Cards:** AX, CB, DC, DS, JC, MC, VI. **Free Special Amenities: newspaper.**

FEE CALL / SOME UNITS

Marriott HOTELS & RESORTS
AAA Benefit:
Members save a minimum 5% off the best available rate.

COMFORT SUITES *Book at AAA.com* **Phone:** (770)645-6060 67

Hotel
$90-$120 All Year

Address: 3000 Mansell Rd **Location:** SR 400, exit 8, 0.7 mi e. **Facility:** Smoke free premises. 75 one-bedroom standard units, some with efficiencies and/or whirlpools. 3 stories, interior corridors. **Parking:** on-site. **Amenities:** high-speed Internet, voice mail, irons, hair dryers. **Pool(s):** outdoor. **Leisure Activities:** exercise room. **Guest Services:** valet laundry, wireless Internet. **Business Services:** meeting rooms, business center. **Cards:** AX, DC, DS, MC, VI.

ASK FEE CALL

COUNTRY INN & SUITES BY CARLSON *Book at AAA.com* **Phone:** (770)552-0006 66

Hotel
$79-$119 All Year

Address: 2950 Mansell Rd **Location:** SR 400, exit 8, 0.7 mi e. **Facility:** 66 units. 57 one-bedroom standard units. 9 one-bedroom suites. 3 stories, interior corridors. **Parking:** on-site. **Terms:** cancellation fee imposed. **Amenities:** high-speed Internet, dual phone lines, voice mail, irons, hair dryers. **Pool(s):** heated indoor. **Leisure Activities:** whirlpool, limited exercise equipment. **Guest Services:** valet and coin laundry, wireless Internet. **Business Services:** meeting rooms, business center. **Cards:** AX, CB, DC, DS, MC, VI.

ASK FEE / SOME UNITS

COURTYARD BY MARRIOTT *Book great rates at AAA.com* **Phone:** (678)366-3360 45

Hotel
$177-$190 All Year

Address: 12655 Deerfield Pkwy **Location:** SR 400, exit 11, 0.5 mi w to Deerfield Pkwy, then just n. **Facility:** Smoke free premises. 154 units. 149 one-bedroom standard units, some with whirlpools. 5 one-bedroom suites. 3 stories, interior corridors. **Parking:** on-site. **Terms:** cancellation fee imposed. **Amenities:** high-speed Internet, dual phone lines, voice mail, irons, hair dryers. **Pool(s):** outdoor. **Leisure Activities:** whirlpool, exercise room. **Guest Services:** valet and coin laundry, wireless Internet. **Business Services:** meeting rooms, business center. **Cards:** AX, CB, DC, DS, MC, VI. **Free Special Amenities: newspaper and high-speed Internet.**

FEE CALL / SOME UNITS

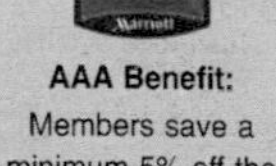

AAA Benefit:
Members save a minimum 5% off the best available rate.

(See map and index starting on p. 302)

DOUBLETREE HOTEL ATLANTA/ALPHARETTA-WINDWARD *Book great rates at AAA.com* **Phone:** (678)347-0022 49

Hotel
$69-$269 All Year

Address: 2925 Jordan Ct **Location:** SR 400, exit 11, 0.7 mi w. **Facility:** 79 one-bedroom standard units. 4 stories, interior corridors. *Bath:* shower only. **Parking:** on-site. **Terms:** 1-30 night minimum stay, cancellation fee imposed. **Amenities:** video games (fee), voice mail, irons, hair dryers. **Pool(s):** outdoor. **Leisure Activities:** exercise room. **Guest Services:** valet laundry, area transportation, wireless Internet. **Business Services:** meeting rooms, business center. **Cards:** AX, CB, DC, DS, MC, VI.

FEE CALL / SOME UNITS

AAA Benefit: Members save 5% or more everyday!

EXTENDED STAYAMERICA *Book at AAA.com* **Phone:** (770)475-2676 58

Hotel
$57-$72 All Year

Address: 1950 Rock Mill Rd **Location:** SR 400, exit 9, just e. **Facility:** 101 one-bedroom standard units with efficiencies. 3 stories, interior corridors. **Parking:** on-site. **Terms:** office hours 7 am-11 pm. **Amenities:** high-speed Internet (fee), voice mail, irons. **Guest Services:** coin laundry, wireless Internet. **Business Services:** fax (fee). **Cards:** AX, CB, DC, DS, JC, MC, VI.

ASK CALL / SOME UNITS FEE

EXTENDED STAY DELUXE ATLANTA-ALPHARETTA-NORTHPOINT *Book at AAA.com* **Phone:** (770)569-1730 54

Hotel
$72-$87 All Year

Address: 3329 Old Milton Pkwy **Location:** SR 400, exit 10, just e. **Facility:** 91 one-bedroom standard units with efficiencies. 3 stories, interior corridors. *Bath:* combo or shower only. **Parking:** on-site. **Amenities:** high-speed Internet (fee), dual phone lines, voice mail, irons, hair dryers. *Some:* DVD players. **Pool(s):** outdoor. **Leisure Activities:** exercise room. **Guest Services:** coin laundry, wireless Internet. **Business Services:** fax (fee). **Cards:** AX, CB, DC, DS, JC, MC, VI.

ASK FEE CALL / SOME UNITS FEE

FAIRFIELD INN & SUITES *Book great rates at AAA.com* **Phone:** (770)663-4000 57

Hotel
$123-$132 All Year

Address: 11385 Haynes Bridge Rd **Location:** SR 400, exit 9, just w. **Facility:** Smoke free premises. 87 one-bedroom standard units. 3 stories, interior corridors. **Parking:** on-site. **Terms:** cancellation fee imposed. **Amenities:** high-speed Internet, dual phone lines, voice mail, irons, hair dryers. *Some:* DVD players, CD players. **Pool(s):** heated outdoor. **Leisure Activities:** limited exercise equipment. **Guest Services:** valet and coin laundry, wireless Internet. **Business Services:** meeting rooms, business center. **Cards:** AX, CB, DC, DS, JC, MC, VI.

FEE CALL / SOME UNITS VCR

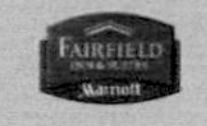

AAA Benefit: Members save a minimum 5% off the best available rate.

HAMPTON INN-ALPHARETTA/ROSWELL *Book great rates at AAA.com* **Phone:** (770)640-5511 63

Hotel
$79-$159 All Year

Address: 10740 Westside Pkwy **Location:** SR 400, exit 8, 0.6 mi w. **Facility:** 106 units. 103 one-bedroom standard units, some with whirlpools. 3 one-bedroom suites with whirlpools. 5 stories, interior corridors. **Parking:** on-site. **Terms:** 1-30 night minimum stay, cancellation fee imposed. **Amenities:** high-speed Internet, dual phone lines, voice mail, irons, hair dryers. **Pool(s):** outdoor. **Leisure Activities:** exercise room. **Guest Services:** valet laundry, area transportation, wireless Internet. **Business Services:** meeting rooms, business center. **Cards:** AX, CB, DC, DS, JC, MC, VI.

FEE CALL / SOME UNITS

AAA Benefit: Members save up to 10% everyday!

HAMPTON INN & SUITES *Book great rates at AAA.com* **Phone:** (678)393-0990 

Hotel
$139-$179 All Year

Address: 16785 Old Morris Rd **Location:** SR 400, exit 11, 1.2 mi nw, follow Deerfield Pkwy and Old Morris Rd. **Facility:** 103 units. 78 one-bedroom standard units. 25 one-bedroom suites with efficiencies. 6 stories, interior corridors. **Parking:** on-site. **Terms:** 1-30 night minimum stay, cancellation fee imposed. **Amenities:** video games (fee), high-speed Internet, dual phone lines, voice mail, irons, hair dryers. **Pool(s):** outdoor. **Leisure Activities:** exercise room. **Guest Services:** valet and coin laundry, area transportation, wireless Internet. **Business Services:** meeting rooms, business center. **Cards:** AX, DC, DS, MC, VI.

AAA Benefit: Members save up to 10% everyday!

(See map and index starting on p. 302)

HILTON GARDEN INN ATLANTA/NORTH ALPHARETTA *Book great rates at AAA.com* **Phone:** (770)360-7766 43

Hotel
$79-$189 All Year

Address: 4025 Windward Plaza Dr **Location:** SR 400, exit 11, 1.1 mi e to Windward Plaza Dr, then just se. **Facility:** 164 one-bedroom standard units. 6 stories, interior corridors. **Parking:** on-site. **Amenities:** video games (fee), high-speed Internet, dual phone lines, voice mail, irons, hair dryers. **Pool(s):** heated indoor. **Leisure Activities:** whirlpool, exercise room. **Guest Services:** valet and coin laundry, area transportation-within 5 mi, wireless Internet. **Business Services:** meeting rooms, business center. **Cards:** AX, CB, DC, DS, JC, MC, VI. **Free Special Amenities: newspaper and high-speed Internet.**

CALL / SOME UNITS

Hilton Garden Inn
AAA Benefit:
Members save 5% or more everyday!

HILTON GARDEN INN-ATLANTA NORTH POINT *Book great rates at AAA.com* **Phone:** (678)566-3900 61

Hotel
$59-$189 All Year

Address: 10975 Georgia Ln **Location:** SR 400, exit 9, 0.5 mi to Georgia Ln, then just n. **Facility:** 125 units. 105 one-bedroom standard units, some with whirlpools. 20 one-bedroom suites with whirlpools. 5 stories, interior corridors. **Parking:** on-site. **Terms:** 1-30 night minimum stay, cancellation fee imposed. **Amenities:** video games (fee), high-speed Internet, dual phone lines, voice mail, irons, hair dryers. **Pool(s):** heated outdoor. **Leisure Activities:** whirlpool, exercise room. **Guest Services:** valet and coin laundry, area transportation, wireless Internet. **Business Services:** meeting rooms, business center. **Cards:** AX, CB, DC, DS, JC, MC, VI.

FEE CALL / SOME UNITS

Hilton Garden Inn
AAA Benefit:
Members save 5% or more everyday!

HOLIDAY INN EXPRESS *Book at AAA.com* **Phone:** 770/664-6661 50

Hotel
Rates not provided

Address: 5455 Windward Pkwy **Location:** SR 400, exit 11, 0.4 mi w. **Facility:** 65 one-bedroom standard units. 4 stories, interior corridors. **Parking:** on-site. **Amenities:** high-speed Internet, voice mail, irons, hair dryers. **Leisure Activities:** exercise room. **Guest Services:** valet laundry, wireless Internet. **Business Services:** PC, fax (fee).

FEE CALL / SOME UNITS

HOMEWOOD SUITES *Book great rates at AAA.com* **Phone:** (770)998-1622 62

Hotel
$79-$149 All Year

Address: 10775 Davis Dr **Location:** SR 400, exit 8, northwest corner. **Facility:** 112 units. 107 one- and 5 two-bedroom standard units with efficiencies. 6 stories, interior corridors. **Parking:** on-site. **Terms:** 1-30 night minimum stay, cancellation fee imposed. **Amenities:** video games (fee), high-speed Internet, voice mail, irons, hair dryers. **Pool(s):** outdoor. **Leisure Activities:** exercise room. **Guest Services:** valet and coin laundry, area transportation, wireless Internet. **Business Services:** meeting rooms, business center. **Cards:** AX, CB, DC, DS, JC, MC, VI.

FEE CALL
/ SOME UNITS FEE

HOMEWOOD SUITES
AAA Benefit:
Members save 5% or more everyday!

HOTEL SIERRA ALPHARETTA *Book great rates at AAA.com* **Phone:** (678)339-0505 48

Hotel
$139-$199 All Year

Address: 12505 Cingular Way **Location:** SR 400, exit 11, 0.5 mi w. **Facility:** 124 one-bedroom standard units, some with efficiencies. 6 stories, interior corridors. **Parking:** on-site. **Amenities:** high-speed Internet, dual phone lines, voice mail, irons, hair dryers. **Pool(s):** heated outdoor. **Leisure Activities:** exercise room. **Guest Services:** valet and coin laundry, area transportation-within 5 mi, wireless Internet. **Business Services:** meeting rooms, business center. **Cards:** AX, CB, DC, DS, JC, MC, VI. **Free Special Amenities: full breakfast and high-speed Internet.**

FEE CALL / SOME UNITS FEE

HYATT PLACE ATLANTA/ALPHARETTA/WINDWARD PARKWAY *Book great rates at AAA.com* **Phone:** (770)343-9566 51

Hotel
$99-$299 All Year

Address: 5595 Windward Pkwy **Location:** SR 400, exit 11, just w. **Facility:** 127 one-bedroom standard units. 6 stories, interior corridors. **Parking:** on-site. **Terms:** cancellation fee imposed. **Amenities:** high-speed Internet, dual phone lines, voice mail, irons, hair dryers. **Pool(s):** outdoor. **Leisure Activities:** exercise room. **Guest Services:** valet laundry, area transportation-within 5 mi, wireless Internet. **Business Services:** meeting rooms, business center. **Cards:** AX, CB, DC, DS, JC, MC, VI. **Free Special Amenities: continental breakfast and high-speed Internet.**

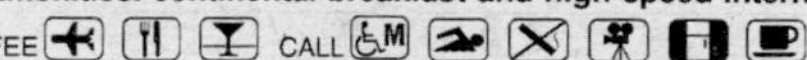

AAA Benefit:
Ask for the AAA rate and save 10%.

(See map and index starting on p. 302)

HYATT PLACE NORTH POINT *Book great rates at AAA.com* **Phone:** (770)594-8788 **64**

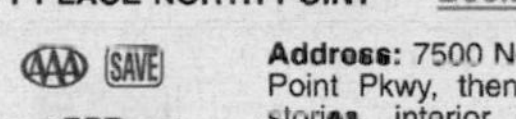

Hotel
$99-$299 All Year

Address: 7500 North Point Pkwy **Location:** SR 400, exit 8, just e to North Point Pkwy, then just n. **Facility:** 124 one-bedroom standard units. 6 stories, interior corridors. **Parking:** on-site. **Terms:** cancellation fee imposed. **Amenities:** high-speed Internet, voice mail, irons, hair dryers. **Pool(s):** heated outdoor. **Leisure Activities:** exercise room. **Guest Services:** valet laundry, area transportation-within 5 mi, wireless Internet. **Business Services:** meeting rooms, business center. **Cards:** AX, CB, DC, DS, JC, MC, VI. **Free Special Amenities: continental breakfast and high-speed Internet.**

CALL

HYATT PLACE
AAA Benefit:
Ask for the AAA rate and save 10%.

LA QUINTA INN & SUITES ATLANTA (ALPHARETTA) *Book great rates at AAA.com* **Phone:** (770)754-7800 **59**

Hotel
$55-$139 All Year

Address: 1350 North Point Dr **Location:** SR 400, exit 9, 0.5 mi e. **Facility:** 131 units. 125 one-bedroom standard units. 6 one-bedroom suites. 6 stories, interior corridors. **Parking:** on-site. **Amenities:** video games (fee), high-speed Internet, voice mail, irons, hair dryers. *Some:* dual phone lines. **Pool(s):** heated outdoor. **Leisure Activities:** whirlpool, exercise room. **Guest Services:** valet and coin laundry, area transportation, wireless Internet. **Business Services:** meeting rooms, business center. **Cards:** AX, DS, MC, VI.

ASK FEE CALL / SOME UNITS

RAMADA LIMITED *Book at AAA.com* **Phone:** (678)461-7300 **68**

Hotel
$69-$75 All Year

Address: 3020 Mansell Rd **Location:** SR 400, exit 8, 0.7 mi e. **Facility:** 62 one-bedroom standard units, some with efficiencies and/or whirlpools. 3 stories, interior corridors. **Parking:** on-site. **Amenities:** high-speed Internet, voice mail, irons, hair dryers. **Pool(s):** heated indoor. **Leisure Activities:** limited exercise equipment. **Guest Services:** valet and coin laundry, wireless Internet. **Business Services:** meeting rooms, PC, fax (fee). **Cards:** AX, CB, DC, DS, MC, VI.

ASK FEE / SOME UNITS

RESIDENCE INN ATLANTA ALPHARETTA NORTH POINT MALL *Book great rates at AAA.com* **Phone:** (770)587-1151 **60**

Hotel
$179-$199 All Year

Address: 1325 North Point Dr **Location:** SR 400, exit 9, just e to North Point Dr, then just s. **Facility:** Smoke free premises. 120 units. 100 one- and 20 two-bedroom standard units, some with efficiencies or kitchens. 3 stories, interior corridors. **Parking:** on-site, winter plug-ins (fee). **Terms:** cancellation fee imposed. **Amenities:** high-speed Internet, voice mail, irons, hair dryers. **Pool(s):** outdoor. **Leisure Activities:** whirlpool, exercise room, sports court. **Guest Services:** valet and coin laundry, wireless Internet. **Business Services:** meeting rooms, PC, fax (fee). **Cards:** AX, CB, DC, DS, JC, MC, VI. **Free Special Amenities: full breakfast and high-speed Internet.**

CALL    

AAA Benefit:
Members save a minimum 5% off the best available rate.

RESIDENCE INN BY MARRIOTT *Book great rates at AAA.com* **Phone:** (770)664-0664 **52**

Hotel
$197-$212 All Year

Address: 5465 Windward Pkwy W **Location:** SR 400, exit 11, 0.4 mi w. Located in a business park area. **Facility:** Smoke free premises. 103 units. 83 one- and 20 two-bedroom standard units with efficiencies. 2-3 stories, interior/exterior corridors. *Bath:* combo or shower only. **Parking:** on-site. **Terms:** cancellation fee imposed. **Amenities:** high-speed Internet, dual phone lines, voice mail, irons, hair dryers. **Pool(s):** outdoor. **Leisure Activities:** whirlpool, exercise room, sports court. **Guest Services:** valet and coin laundry, wireless Internet. **Business Services:** meeting rooms, business center. **Cards:** AX, CB, DC, DS, JC, MC, VI. **Free Special Amenities: full breakfast and high-speed Internet.**

FEE CALL / SOME UNITS FEE

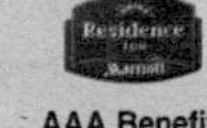

AAA Benefit:
Members save a minimum 5% off the best available rate.

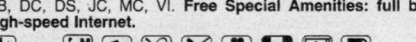

(See map and index starting on p. 302)

SPRINGHILL SUITES BY MARRIOTT *Book great rates at AAA.com* **Phone:** (770)751-6900 44

Hotel
$158-$169 All Year

Address: 12730 Deerfield Pkwy **Location:** SR 400, exit 11, 0.5 mi w to Deerfield Pkwy, then just n. **Facility:** Smoke free premises. 82 one-bedroom standard units. 3 stories, interior corridors. **Parking:** on-site. **Terms:** cancellation fee imposed. **Amenities:** high-speed Internet, dual phone lines, voice mail, irons, hair dryers. **Pool(s):** outdoor. **Leisure Activities:** whirlpool, exercise room. **Guest Services:** valet and coin laundry, area transportation, wireless Internet. **Business Services:** meeting rooms, business center. **Cards:** AX, CB, DC, DS, JC, MC, VI.

FEE CALL

AAA Benefit:
Members save a minimum 5% off the best available rate.

STAYBRIDGE SUITES *Book at AAA.com* **Phone:** (770)569-7200 53

Hotel
$135-$171 All Year

Address: 3980 North Point Pkwy **Location:** SR 400, exit 10, 0.5 mi e. **Facility:** 118 units. 98 one- and 20 two-bedroom standard units with efficiencies. 3 stories, interior corridors. **Parking:** on-site. **Terms:** cancellation fee imposed. **Amenities:** DVD players, CD players, high-speed Internet, dual phone lines, voice mail, irons, hair dryers. **Pool(s):** heated outdoor. **Leisure Activities:** exercise room, sports court. **Guest Services:** valet and coin laundry, area transportation, wireless Internet. **Business Services:** meeting rooms, business center. **Cards:** AX, CB, DC, DS, MC, VI.

ASK FEE CALL VCR / SOME UNITS FEE

STUDIOPLUS *Book at AAA.com* **Phone:** (770)475-7871 55

Hotel
$62-$77 All Year

Address: 3331 Old Milton Pkwy **Location:** SR 400, exit 10, just e. **Facility:** 92 units. 90 one- and 2 two-bedroom standard units with kitchens. 3 stories, interior corridors. **Parking:** on-site. **Terms:** office hours 7 am-11 pm. **Amenities:** high-speed Internet (fee), dual phone lines, voice mail, irons. **Pool(s):** outdoor. **Leisure Activities:** exercise room. **Guest Services:** coin laundry, wireless Internet. **Business Services:** meeting rooms, fax (fee). **Cards:** AX, CB, DC, DS, JC, MC, VI.

ASK FEE CALL / SOME UNITS FEE

TOWNEPLACE SUITES BY MARRIOTT *Book great rates at AAA.com* **Phone:** (770)664-1300 56

Hotel
$143-$153 All Year

Address: 7925 S Westside Pkwy **Location:** SR 400, exit 9, 0.3 mi w. **Facility:** Smoke free premises. 89 units. 66 one- and 23 two-bedroom standard units with kitchens. 3 stories, interior corridors. **Parking:** on-site. **Terms:** check-in 4 pm, cancellation fee imposed. **Amenities:** high-speed Internet, dual phone lines, voice mail, irons, hair dryers. **Pool(s):** outdoor. **Leisure Activities:** exercise room. **Guest Services:** valet and coin laundry, area transportation, wireless Internet. **Business Services:** business center. **Cards:** AX, CB, DC, DS, JC, MC, VI.

FEE CALL
/ SOME UNITS FEE

AAA Benefit:
Members save a minimum 5% off the best available rate.

WINGATE INN *Book at AAA.com* **Phone:** (770)649-0955 65

Hotel
$114 All Year

Address: 1005 Kingswood Pl **Location:** SR 400, exit 8, 0.7 mi w. **Facility:** 84 one-bedroom standard units. 4 stories, interior corridors. **Parking:** on-site. **Amenities:** video games (fee), high-speed Internet, dual phone lines, voice mail, safes, irons, hair dryers. **Leisure Activities:** whirlpool, limited exercise equipment. **Guest Services:** valet and coin laundry, area transportation, wireless Internet. **Business Services:** meeting rooms, business center. **Cards:** AX, CB, DC, DS, JC, MC, VI.

ASK FEE CALL / SOME UNITS

WHERE TO DINE

ALE HOUSE (MILLERS) **Phone:** 678/277-2581

American
$6-$13

Diners savor selections of clams on the half shell, oysters and peel-and-eat shrimp from the raw bar, in addition to such appetizing menu choices as the 8-ounce filet, baby back ribs and chicken parmigiana. Casual dress. **Bar:** Full bar. **Hours:** 11 am-2 am. Closed: 11/26. **Address:** 10750 Davis Dr **Location:** Just n of jct Mansell Dr. **Parking:** on-site. **Cards:** AX, DC, DS, MC, VI.

CALL

ATLANTIC SEAFOOD COMPANY **Phone:** 770/640-0488 57

Seafood
$5-$47

The popular up-and-comer builds its menu on saltwater dishes, including ahi tuna, salmon and sea bass. Also offered is a fresh selection of daily specials, including raw oysters from many areas. Dressy casual. **Bar:** Full bar. **Reservations:** accepted. **Hours:** 11:30 am-2:30 & 5-10 pm, Fri-11 pm, Sat noon-11 pm. Closed: 11/26, 12/25; also Sun. **Address:** 2345 Mansell Rd **Location:** SR 400, exit 8, just e. **Parking:** on-site and valet. **Cards:** AX, CB, DC, DS, JC, MC, VI.

CALL

CABERNET **Phone:** 770/777-5955 49

Steak & Seafood
$6-$40

The rock-salt-crusted rib-eye for two is renowned at the upscale steakhouse on the northern fringes of the metropolitan area. Dressy casual. **Bar:** Full bar. **Reservations:** suggested. **Hours:** 11:30 am-2 & 5-10 pm, Fri-11 pm, Sat 5 pm-11 pm. Closed major holidays; also Sun. **Address:** 5575 Windward Pkwy **Location:** SR 400, exit 11, just w. **Parking:** valet. **Cards:** AX, CB, DC, DS, JC, MC, VI.

(See map and index starting on p. 302)

GROUCHY'S-A NEW YORK DELI **Phone:** 770/667-6933 (53)

Deli
$2-$8

Enjoy the house special succulent and lean pastrami sandwich or choose from other New York style specialties at Grouchy's. Casual dress. **Hours:** 6:30 am-2:30 pm, Sat from 8 am. Closed major holidays; also Sun. **Address:** 11525 Haynes Bridge Rd **Location:** SR 400, exit 9, 0.3 mi w. **Parking:** on-site. **Cards:** AX, DS, MC, VI.

IPPOLITO'S **Phone:** 678/624-1900 (44)

Italian
$7-$16

Skillfully served pasta dishes bathed in excellent homemade sauces are highlights at the warm, family-oriented eatery. Worth a splurge are the delicious homemade desserts, including spumoni served with a coconut macaroon. Casual dress. **Bar:** Beer & wine. **Hours:** 11 am-10 pm, Fri & Sat-11 pm, Sun noon-10 pm. **Address:** 12850 State Hwy 9 **Location:** SR 400, exit 11, 1.2 mi w; in Windward Commons. **Parking:** on-site. **Cards:** AX, DS, MC, VI.

NAHM THAI CUISINE **Phone:** 678/762-1818 (47)

Thai
$3-$22

The casual eatery presents a menu of freshly prepared Thai cuisine, including some dishes that reflect a French influence. Luncheon specials offer exceptional value and include a piece of the decadent specialty cakes. Varied level of such spices as curry, ginger and chili please all taste buds. Warm, personable service complements the pleasant, cozy dining room. Casual dress. **Bar:** Full bar. **Reservations:** suggested. **Hours:** 11 am-3 & 5-10 pm, Fri & Sat-10:30 pm, Sun 5 pm-10 pm. **Address:** 5310 Windward Pkwy, Suite C **Location:** SR 400, exit 11, 0.5 mi w on the north side. **Parking:** on-site. **Cards:** AX, CB, DC, DS, MC.

ONE STAR RANCH **Phone:** 770/475-6695 (45)

Barbecue
$6-$25

Texas-style barbecue, including beef ribs, plies patrons of the classic roadhouse. Patio seating is an option during nice weather. Music pumps up the atmosphere on the weekend. Casual dress. **Bar:** Full bar. **Hours:** 11 am-10 pm, Tues & Thurs-11 pm, Fri & Sat-1 am, Sun noon-9 pm. Closed major holidays. **Address:** 732 N Main St **Location:** 1.8 mi n on SR 9. **Parking:** on-site. **Cards:** AX, MC, VI.

PAPPADEAUX SEAFOOD **Phone:** 770/992-5566

Regional Seafood
$11-$22

A seafood lover's delight, the restaurant taps into a little bit of New Orleans with its Cajun dishes and elaborate menu selections. Patrons might start off with a creative choice of blackened oyster and shrimp fondeaux with crayfish and let the feast begin. While music plays in the background, patrons can dig into dirty rice or spicy gumbo loaded with seafood. Well-seasoned shrimp and fish are prepared in varied ways. Casual dress. **Bar:** Full bar. **Hours:** 11 am-9 pm. Closed: 11/26, 12/25. **Address:** 10795 Davis Dr **Location:** US 19, exit 8 (Mansell Rd), just w to Davis Rd, then just n. **Parking:** on-site. **Cards:** AX, DC, DS, MC, VI.

RAINWATER RESTAURANT **Phone:** 770/777-0033 (50)

American
$10-$36

Artful presentations and imaginative creations characterize standard meat, fish and chicken dishes. The chic, vineyard-themed dining room also adds to the delightful ambience. Dressy casual. **Bar:** Full bar. **Reservations:** suggested. **Hours:** 11:30 am-2:30 & 5:30-9 pm, Fri-10 pm, Sat 5:30 pm-10 pm. Closed major holidays; also Sun. **Address:** 11655 Haynes Bridge Rd **Location:** SR 400, exit 9. 0.5 mi w. **Parking:** on-site and valet. **Cards:** AX, CB, DC, DS, MC, VI.

CALL

RISING ROLL **Phone:** 770/752-8082

Deli
$7-$9

As upscale as a self-serve delicatessen can be,this location can be busy during the lunch rush. Featuring a variety of in-house-made breads, the standards of sandwiches, soups and salads are given a few distinctive and creative twists. Casual dress. **Hours:** 10:30 am-4 pm. Closed: 12/25; also Sun. **Address:** 11417 Haynes Bridge Rd **Location:** SR 400, exit 9, just w. **Parking:** on-site. **Cards:** AX, MC, VI.

CALL

SANTOOR **Phone:** 770/650-8802 (56)

Indian
$8-$17

From the traditional, authentic style of decor to the delectable, well-prepared dishes, the restaurant enables diners to experience a true dining treat. Shrimp vindaloo and chicken massala are spicy favorites. Casual dress. **Bar:** Beer & wine. **Reservations:** accepted. **Hours:** 11:30 am-2:30 & 5-10 pm, Fri-10:30 pm, Sat noon-3 & 5-10:30 pm, Sun noon-3 & 5-10 pm. **Address:** 3050 Mansell Rd, Suite A **Location:** SR 400, exit 8, 0.7 mi e. **Parking:** on-site. **Cards:** AX, CB, DS, MC, VI.

SRI KRISHNA VILAS **Phone:** 770/475-9195 (55)

Indian
$5-$12

Tucked in a quiet strip mall, the eatery is a perfect spot to sample a wide selection of freshly prepared and well-spiced cuisine. The menu includes a good choice of vegetarian dishes, as well as such traditional favorites as tandoori, dosai and uthappam, an Indian-style pancake. The setting is relaxed and comfortable and the service warm and personable. Casual dress. **Bar:** Full bar. **Hours:** 11:30 am-2:30 & 6-10 pm, Fri-11 pm, Sat & Sun 11:30-3 & 6-10 pm. Closed major holidays; also Mon. **Address:** 10875 Jones Bridge Rd, Suite 7 **Location:** SR 400, exit 10, 3.5 mi e, then s. **Parking:** on-site. **Cards:** AX, MC, VI.

THAI THAI **Phone:** 770/777-1306 (54)

Thai
$4-$13

The restaurant is noted for quick, efficient service and tasty Thai food that is easy on the purse. Casual dress. **Bar:** Beer & wine. **Hours:** 11 am-3 & 5-10 pm, Sat from 5 pm, Sun 4:30 pm-9:30 pm. Closed major holidays. **Address:** 11525 Haynes Bridge Rd, Suite 150 **Location:** SR 400, exit 9, 0.3 mi w. **Parking:** on-site. **Cards:** AX, DS, MC, VI.

THE VARSITY **Phone:** 770/777-4004 (52)

American
$3-$7

You can indulge in chili dogs, onion rings, hamburgers and frosted oranges at this outpost of the long-time Atlanta favorite. **Hours:** 10:30 am-9 pm, Fri & Sat-10 pm, Sun 11 am-9 pm. Closed: 4/12, 11/26, 12/25. **Address:** 11556 Rainwater Dr **Location:** SR 400, exit 9, 0.3 mi w to Westside Pkwy, then just n. **Parking:** on-site. **Cards:** MC, VI.

CALL

(See map and index starting on p. 302)

VILLAGE TAVERN — Phone: 770/777-6490 (51)

American
$5-$26

The warm, inviting dining room is enhanced by beautiful rafters and a two-sided fireplace. New American cuisine is good at this tavern, which also is popular for a drink in the evenings. Dressy casual. **Bar:** Full bar. **Hours:** 11 am-10 pm, Fri-11 pm, Sat 4 pm-11 pm, Sun 10 am-10 pm; Sunday brunch. Closed major holidays. **Address:** 11555 Rainwater Dr **Location:** SR 400, exit 9, 0.3 mi w to Westside Pkwy, then just n. **Parking:** on-site. **Cards:** AX, DC, MC, VI.

VINNY'S ON WINDWARD — Phone: 770/772-4644 (48)

American
$6-$29

Contemporary, creative American cuisine flavored with Italian influences is served in an upscale, stylish atmosphere. Try the fettuccine and seafood entree, filled with mussels, sea bass, scallops, shrimp, onion and tomato. Don't forget the tiramisu! Casual dress. **Bar:** Full bar. **Reservations:** suggested. **Hours:** 11 am-midnight, Sun from 5 pm. Closed major holidays. **Address:** 5355 Windward Pkwy W **Location:** SR 400, exit 11, 0.5 mi w. **Parking:** valet. **Cards:** AX, CB, DC, DS, MC, VI.

CALL

XIAN CHINA BISTRO — Phone: 770/442-9996 (46)

Chinese
$4-$30

A sleek, contemporary dining room at Xian is the setting for some exciting variations on basic Chinese cuisine themes. Casual dress. **Bar:** Full bar. **Reservations:** accepted. **Hours:** 11 am-10 pm, Fri-11 pm, Sat & Sun 11 am-midnight. **Address:** 5316-A Windward Pkwy **Location:** SR 400, exit 11, 0.5 mi w; in Deerfield Village. **Parking:** on-site. **Cards:** AX, CB, DC, DS, JC, MC, VI.

CALL

AUSTELL pop. 5,359 (See maps and indexes starting on p. 312)

WHERE TO STAY

BAYMONT INN-SIX FLAGS *Book at AAA.com* — Phone: (770)944-2110 (13)

Hotel
$60-$76 All Year

Address: 7377 Six Flags Dr **Location:** I-20, exit 46 eastbound; exit 46B westbound, just n. **Facility:** 106 units. 104 one-bedroom standard units. 2 one-bedroom suites. 3 stories, interior/exterior corridors. **Parking:** on-site. **Amenities:** video games (fee), high-speed Internet, voice mail, irons, hair dryers. **Pool(s):** outdoor. **Guest Services:** coin laundry, wireless Internet. **Business Services:** meeting rooms, fax (fee). **Cards:** AX, DS, MC, VI.

ASK FEE / SOME UNITS FEE

SLEEP INN *Book great rates at AAA.com* — Phone: (770)819-2805 (14)

AAA SAVE

Hotel
$55-$120 All Year

Address: 125 S Service Rd **Location:** I-20, exit 47 westbound; exit 46 eastbound. Located adjacent to an amusement park. **Facility:** 49 one-bedroom standard units. 2 stories, interior corridors. *Bath:* shower only. **Parking:** on-site. **Amenities:** video library (fee), high-speed Internet, irons, hair dryers. **Pool(s):** heated indoor. **Guest Services:** wireless Internet. **Business Services:** fax (fee). **Cards:** AX, DC, DS, MC, VI.

CALL / SOME UNITS FEE VCR

WINGATE BY WYNDHAM AT SIX FLAGS *Book great rates at AAA.com* — Phone: (770)948-7877 (15)

Hotel
$89-$210 All Year

Address: 65 S Service Rd **Location:** I-20, exit 47 westbound; exit 46 eastbound. **Facility:** 101 units. 95 one-bedroom standard units. 6 one-bedroom suites with whirlpools. 4 stories, interior corridors. **Parking:** on-site. **Terms:** cancellation fee imposed. **Amenities:** video games (fee), high-speed Internet, dual phone lines, voice mail, safes, irons, hair dryers. **Pool(s):** outdoor. **Leisure Activities:** whirlpool, exercise room. **Guest Services:** valet and coin laundry, wireless Internet. **Business Services:** meeting rooms, business center. **Cards:** AX, CB, DC, DS, JC, MC, VI.

ASK FEE CALL / SOME UNITS

WHERE TO DINE

WALLACE BARBECUE — Phone: 770/739-1686

Barbecue
$3-$11

Using family recipes dating back to 1947, the staff serves traditional Georgia hickory-pit barbecue, including delicious smoked pork and beef dishes. A nice combination is ribs with onion rings and a cold glass of sweet tea. Casual dress. **Hours:** 10:30 am-9 pm, Fri & Sat-10 pm. Closed major holidays; also Sun & Mon. **Address:** 3035 Veterans Memorial Hwy **Location:** I-20, exit 44, 2.8 mi n on Thornton Rd, then 0.5 mi e on US 78/278. **Parking:** on-site. **Cards:** AX, MC, VI.

BUFORD pop. 10,668 (See map and index starting on p. 302)

WHERE TO STAY

AMERICAS BEST VALUE INN *Book at AAA.com* — Phone: (770)932-0111

Motel
$70-$100 All Year

Address: 4267 Buford Dr **Location:** I-985, exit 4, 1 mi w. **Facility:** 39 one-bedroom standard units. 2 stories (no elevator), exterior corridors. **Parking:** on-site. **Amenities:** high-speed Internet, hair dryers. **Guest Services:** wireless Internet. **Business Services:** fax (fee). **Cards:** AX, DS, MC, VI.

ASK / SOME UNITS FEE FEE

(See map and index starting on p. 302)

COUNTRY INN & SUITES BY CARLSON *Book great rates at AAA.com* **Phone:** (770)271-1441 

Hotel

$99-$139 All Year

Address: 1395 Mall of Georgia Blvd **Location:** I-85, exit 115, 1.2 mi w to Mall of Georgia Blvd, then 0.3 mi s. **Facility:** 77 units. 61 one-bedroom standard units. 16 one-bedroom suites. 4 stories, interior corridors. **Parking:** on-site. **Amenities:** high-speed Internet, voice mail, irons, hair dryers. *Some:* DVD players (fee). **Pool(s):** heated indoor. **Leisure Activities:** whirlpool, limited exercise equipment. **Guest Services:** valet and coin laundry, airport transportation (fee)-The William B. Hartsfield Atlanta Int'l Airport, wireless Internet. **Business Services:** meeting rooms, fax. **Cards:** AX, DC, DS, MC, VI. **Free Special Amenities: expanded continental breakfast and high-speed Internet.**

(See color ad below)

FEE CALL / SOME UNITS

HAMPTON INN-MALL OF GEORGIA *Book great rates at AAA.com* **Phone:** (678)546-1200 

Hotel

$129-$149 All Year

Address: 3240 Buford Dr **Location:** I-85, exit 115, 1.5 mi w. **Facility:** 92 one-bedroom standard units. 5 stories, interior corridors. **Parking:** on-site. **Amenities:** high-speed Internet, dual phone lines, voice mail, irons, hair dryers. **Pool(s):** outdoor. **Leisure Activities:** limited exercise equipment. **Guest Services:** valet and coin laundry, wireless Internet. **Business Services:** meeting rooms, PC, fax. **Cards:** AX, DC, DS, MC, VI.

FEE / SOME UNITS

AAA Benefit:

Members save up to 10% everyday!

HOLIDAY INN EXPRESS HOTEL & SUITES *Book at AAA.com* **Phone:** (678)318-1080

Hotel

$115-$169 All Year

Address: 2499 Satellite Blvd **Location:** I-985, exit 4, just w. **Facility:** 79 units. 77 one-bedroom standard units. 2 one-bedroom suites with whirlpools. 3 stories, interior corridors. **Parking:** on-site. **Amenities:** high-speed Internet, dual phone lines, voice mail, irons, hair dryers. **Pool(s):** outdoor. **Leisure Activities:** whirlpool, limited exercise equipment. **Guest Services:** valet and coin laundry, wireless Internet. **Business Services:** meeting rooms, business center. **Cards:** AX, DC, DS, MC, VI.

ASK FEE CALL / SOME UNITS

SPRINGHILL SUITES-MALL OF GEORGIA *Book great rates at AAA.com* **Phone:** (678)714-2150 

Hotel

$138-$148 All Year

Address: 3250 Buford Dr **Location:** I-85, exit 115, 1.5 mi w. **Facility:** Smoke free premises. 97 one-bedroom standard units. 5 stories, interior corridors. **Parking:** on-site. **Terms:** cancellation fee imposed. **Amenities:** high-speed Internet, dual phone lines, voice mail, irons, hair dryers. **Pool(s):** outdoor. **Leisure Activities:** whirlpool, exercise room. **Guest Services:** valet and coin laundry, wireless Internet. **Business Services:** meeting rooms, business center. **Cards:** AX, CB, DC, DS, JC, MC, VI.

FEE CALL

AAA Benefit:

Members save a minimum 5% off the best available rate.

(See map and index starting on p. 302)

WHERE TO DINE

37-MAIN — Phone: 770/614-7197

Spanish
$3-$21

So many tapas, so little time. The speakeasy offers a good variety of delicious tapas, a nightly entree special and entertainment off and on during the week. Casual dress. **Bar:** Full bar. **Hours:** 5 pm-11 pm, Fri & Sat-12:30 am. Closed: 11/26, 12/25; also Sun & Mon. **Address:** 37 E Main St **Location:** Downtown; in historic district. **Parking:** street. **Cards:** AX, DC, DS, MC, VI.

AQUA TERRA BISTRO — Phone: 770/271-3000

International
$6-$27

An example of the cozy restaurant's tempting entrees is grilled red grouper over basil, goat cheese and crab risotto with English peas and white asparagus. Other selections include chargrilled steaks, blackened chicken and rack of lamb. Dressy casual. **Bar:** Full bar. **Reservations:** not accepted. **Hours:** 11 am-2:30 & 5-10 pm. Closed: 11/26, 12/25. **Address:** 55 E Main St **Location:** Downtown; in historic district. **Parking:** street. **Cards:** AX, DC, DS, MC, VI.

SAIGON BANGKOK — Phone: 678/546-0406

Asian
$5-$11

Guests exploring the Mall of Georgia can recharge their shopping batteries at the nearby restaurant, which presents a menu of Vietnamese and Thai fare, including tasty and filling bowls of pho. Casual dress. **Hours:** 11 am-9:30 pm, Sun noon-8 pm. Closed: 11/26, 12/25. **Address:** 4060 Buford Dr, Suite A **Location:** I-985, exit 4, just w. **Parking:** on-site. **Cards:** AX, MC, VI.

CALL

SONNY'S REAL PIT BAR-B-Q — Phone: 770/831-5002

Barbecue
$6-$15

House specialties include pork and chicken grilled over an open pit, barbecue ribs and fresh, homemade pie. The salad bar offers another popular option. Rustic and comfortable, the atmosphere is perfect for family meals. Casual dress. **Bar:** Beer only. **Hours:** 11 am-9:30 pm, Fri & Sat-10 pm. Closed: 11/26, 12/25. **Address:** 1905 Buford Mill Dr **Location:** I-985, exit 4 (SR 20), just se. **Parking:** on-site. **Cards:** AX, DS, MC, VI.

THIRD COAST GRILLE — Phone: 770/614-9508

American
$7-$27

The restaurant and tavern lets guests choose from a good selection of finger foods, steaks and such seafood dishes as seared Cajun catfish and almond-crusted rainbow trout. Casual dress. **Bar:** Full bar. **Reservations:** not accepted. **Hours:** 11:30 am-10 pm, Fri & Sat-11 pm, Sun 11 am-10 pm. Closed: 11/26, 12/25. **Address:** 5713 Holiday Rd **Location:** I-985, exit 8 (Friendship Rd), 1.5 mi nw, 0.3 mi sw on Peachtree Industrial Blvd/McEver Rd, then 0.3 mi nw. **Parking:** on-site. **Cards:** AX, CB, DC, DS, MC, VI.

CHAMBLEE pop. 9,552 (See map and index starting on p. 302)

WHERE TO DINE

BOMBAY GRILL — Phone: 678/530-9555 (111)

Indian
$9-$19

The fine dining establishment offers a very good ambiance. The menu lists a wide selection of Indian cuisine including tandoori specialties, seafood, chicken, lamb, rice and vegetarian dishes. There is a daily lunch buffet as well as a Sunday dinner buffet. Casual dress. **Bar:** Beer & wine. **Reservations:** accepted. **Hours:** 11:30 am-2:30 & 5:30-10 pm, Fri-11 pm, Sat noon-3 & 5:30-11 pm, Sun noon-3 & 6-10:30 pm. **Address:** 2165 Savoy Dr **Location:** I-285, exit 30, 0.5 mi w. **Parking:** on-site. **Cards:** AX, CB, DC, DS, JC, MC, VI.

PENANG MALAYSIAN CUISINE — Phone: 770/220-0308 (112)

Asian
$5-$18

Menu favorites include whole fish with Thai sauce and pancakes with chicken curry. The atmosphere duplicates a Malaysian village right down to the bamboo. Casual dress. **Bar:** Beer & wine. **Reservations:** accepted. **Hours:** 11 am-11 pm. **Address:** 4897 Buford Hwy, Suite 113 **Location:** I-285, exit 32, 1.5 mi s; in Orient Center. **Parking:** on-site. **Cards:** MC, VI.

PHO TAN TAN — Phone: 770/455-9474 (113)

Vietnamese
$5-$11

Enjoy an evening of heaping bowls of pho, rice paper rolls and "rex" dancing. An array of fresh and tasty side condiments enhance each meal. Casual dress. **Bar:** Full bar. **Reservations:** accepted. **Hours:** 10 am-10 pm. **Address:** 4646 Buford Hwy, #R **Location:** I-285, exit 32, 2.1 mi s. **Parking:** on-site. **Cards:** MC, VI.

COLLEGE PARK pop. 20,382 (See map and index starting on p. 312)

WHERE TO STAY

ATLANTA AIRPORT MARRIOTT *Book great rates at AAA.com* — Phone: (404)766-7900 (56)

AAA SAVE

Hotel
$237-$254 All Year

Address: 4711 Best Rd **Location:** I-85, exit 71, just w, se on access road to Best Rd, then just s. Located in office park area. **Facility:** Smoke free premises. 638 units. 635 one-bedroom standard units. 3 one-bedroom suites. 16 stories, interior corridors. *Bath:* combo or shower only. **Parking:** on-site (fee) and valet. **Terms:** cancellation fee imposed. **Amenities:** dual phone lines, voice mail, irons, hair dryers. *Fee:* video games, high-speed Internet. **Dining:** 3 restaurants. **Pool(s):** heated indoor/outdoor. **Leisure Activities:** saunas, whirlpool, 2 lighted tennis courts. **Guest Services:** valet laundry, airport transportation-The William B. Hartsfield Atlanta Int'l Airport, wireless Internet. **Business Services:** conference facilities, business center. **Cards:** AX, CB, DC, DS, JC, MC, VI. **Free Special Amenities: newspaper.**

CALL

(See map and index starting on p. 312)

BEST WESTERN HOTEL & SUITES *Book great rates at AAA.com* **Phone:** (770)996-5800 70

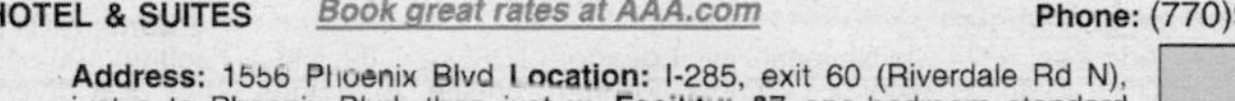

Hotel
$89-$99 All Year

Address: 1556 Phoenix Blvd **Location:** I-285, exit 60 (Riverdale Rd N), just s to Phoenix Blvd, then just w. **Facility:** 87 one-bedroom standard units, some with whirlpools. 5 stories, interior corridors. *Bath:* combo or shower only. **Parking:** on-site. **Amenities:** high-speed Internet, irons, hair dryers. **Pool(s):** outdoor. **Leisure Activities:** whirlpool, exercise room. **Guest Services:** valet laundry, airport transportation-The William B. Hartsfield Atlanta Int'l Airport. **Business Services:** meeting rooms, PC. **Cards:** AX, CB, DC, DS, MC, VI.

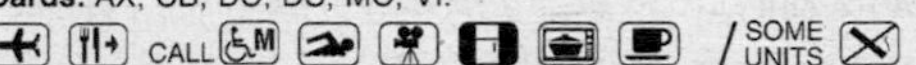

AAA Benefit:
Members save up to 20%, plus 10% bonus points with rewards program.

CLARION HOTEL-ATLANTA AIRPORT *Book at AAA.com* **Phone:** (404)768-9199 65

Hotel
$89 All Year

Address: 5010 Old National Hwy **Location:** I-285, exit 62, just s. **Facility:** 232 units. 230 one-bedroom standard units. 2 one-bedroom suites. 7 stories, interior corridors. **Parking:** on-site. **Terms:** cancellation fee imposed. **Amenities:** video games (fee), high-speed Internet, voice mail, irons, hair dryers. *Some:* CD players. **Pool(s):** heated indoor/outdoor. **Leisure Activities:** whirlpool, exercise room. **Guest Services:** valet and coin laundry, wireless Internet. **Business Services:** meeting rooms, business center. **Cards:** AX, CB, DC, DS, JC, MC, VI.

ASK CALL / SOME UNITS

COMFORT INN & SUITES ATLANTA AIRPORT NORTH *Book great rates at AAA.com* **Phone:** (404)768-7800 48

Hotel
$99-$139 All Year

Address: 1419 Virginia Ave **Location:** I-85, exit 73 southbound; exit 73B northbound, just w. **Facility:** 247 one-bedroom standard units, some with whirlpools. 6 stories, interior corridors. **Parking:** on-site. **Amenities:** high-speed Internet, voice mail, irons, hair dryers. **Pool(s):** outdoor. **Leisure Activities:** exercise room. **Guest Services:** valet and coin laundry, area transportation, wireless Internet. **Business Services:** meeting rooms, business center. **Cards:** AX, DS, MC, VI.

ASK / SOME UNITS

COMFORT INN & SUITES-ATLANTA AIRPORT/SOUTH *Book at AAA.com* **Phone:** (404)684-9898 66

Hotel
$89-$199 All Year

Address: 2450 Old National Pkwy **Location:** I-85, exit 69; exit 69B northbound; I-285, exit 62, just s. **Facility:** 75 units. 41 one-bedroom standard units, some with whirlpools. 34 one-bedroom suites, some with whirlpools. 3 stories, interior corridors. **Parking:** on-site. **Terms:** 3 day cancellation notice-fee imposed. **Amenities:** high-speed Internet, dual phone lines, voice mail, safes (fee), irons, hair dryers. **Pool(s):** heated indoor. **Leisure Activities:** whirlpool, exercise room. **Guest Services:** valet and coin laundry, wireless Internet. **Business Services:** meeting rooms, business center. **Cards:** AX, DC, DS, MC, VI.

ASK CALL / SOME UNITS

COUNTRY INN & SUITES BY CARLSON *Book great rates at AAA.com* **Phone:** (770)991-1099 67

Hotel
$90-$119 All Year

Address: 1808 Phoenix Blvd **Location:** I-285, exit 60 (Riverdale Rd N), just s, then 0.5 mi w. **Facility:** 186 units. 182 one-bedroom standard units. 4 one-bedroom suites. 4 stories, interior corridors. **Parking:** on-site. **Amenities:** video games (fee), high-speed Internet, voice mail, irons, hair dryers. **Pool(s):** outdoor. **Leisure Activities:** exercise room. **Guest Services:** valet and coin laundry, area transportation, wireless Internet. **Business Services:** meeting rooms, PC, fax. **Cards:** AX, DS, MC, VI.

ASK CALL / SOME UNITS

COURTYARD BY MARRIOTT AIRPORT SOUTH *Book great rates at AAA.com* **Phone:** (770)997-2220 60

Hotel
$197-$212 All Year

Address: 2050 Sullivan Rd **Location:** I-85, exit 71, 0.4 mi e to Airport Rd, just s, then just w. **Facility:** Smoke free premises. 144 units. 129 one-bedroom standard units. 15 one-bedroom suites. 3 stories, interior corridors. **Parking:** on-site. **Terms:** cancellation fee imposed. **Amenities:** high-speed Internet (fee), voice mail, irons, hair dryers. **Pool(s):** heated indoor. **Leisure Activities:** whirlpool, limited exercise equipment. **Guest Services:** valet and coin laundry, wireless Internet. **Business Services:** meeting rooms, business center. **Cards:** AX, CB, DC, DS, JC, MC, VI. **Free Special Amenities: newspaper and high-speed Internet.**

CALL / SOME UNITS

AAA Benefit:
Members save a minimum 5% off the best available rate.

DAYS INN AIRPORT SOUTH *Book at AAA.com* **Phone:** 770/996-7300 69

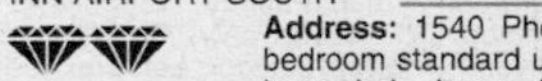

Hotel
Rates not provided

Address: 1540 Phoenix Blvd **Location:** I-285, exit 60 (Riverdale Rd N), just s. **Facility:** 49 one-bedroom standard units. 2 stories (no elevator), interior corridors. **Parking:** on-site. **Amenities:** safes, irons, hair dryers. **Pool(s):** outdoor. **Leisure Activities:** exercise room. **Guest Services:** wireless Internet. **Business Services:** meeting rooms, business center.

/ SOME UNITS

(See map and index starting on p. 312)

ECONO LODGE Book at AAA.com Phone: (404)768-1241 63

Motel
$50-$55 All Year

Address: 4874 Old National Hwy **Location:** I-285, exit 62, just n. **Facility:** 120 one-bedroom standard units. 2 stories, exterior corridors. **Parking:** on-site. **Amenities:** irons, hair dryers. **Pool(s):** outdoor. **Guest Services:** wireless Internet. **Business Services:** PC, fax. **Cards:** AX, DS, MC, VI.

ASK / SOME UNITS FEE

EMBASSY SUITES HOTEL AT ATLANTA AIRPORT Book great rates at AAA.com Phone: (404)767-1988 50

Hotel
$99-$209 All Year

Address: 4700 Southport Rd **Location:** I-85, exit 71, 0.3 mi w on Riverdale Rd. **Facility:** 233 one-bedroom suites. 5 stories, interior corridors. **Parking:** on-site. **Terms:** 1-30 night minimum stay, cancellation fee imposed. **Amenities:** video games (fee), dual phone lines, voice mail, irons, hair dryers. **Pool(s):** outdoor, heated indoor. **Leisure Activities:** sauna, whirlpool, exercise room. **Guest Services:** valet and coin laundry, wireless Internet. **Business Services:** meeting rooms, business center. **Cards:** AX, CB, DC, DS, JC, MC, VI.

CALL / SOME UNITS

EMBASSY SUITES HOTELS
AAA Benefit:
Members save 5% or more everyday!

FAIRFIELD INN & SUITES ATLANTA AIRPORT SOUTH Book great rates at AAA.com Phone: (770)994-3666 59

Hotel
$147-$158 All Year

Address: 2020 Sullivan Rd **Location:** I-85, exit 71, just e to Airport Rd, just s, then just w. **Facility:** Smoke free premises. 127 one-bedroom standard units, some with whirlpools. 4 stories, interior corridors. **Parking:** on-site. **Terms:** cancellation fee imposed. **Amenities:** video games (fee), dual phone lines, voice mail, safes, irons, hair dryers. *Some:* CD players. **Leisure Activities:** whirlpool, exercise room. **Guest Services:** valet and coin laundry, wireless Internet. **Business Services:** meeting rooms, business center. **Cards:** AX, CB, DC, DS, JC, MC, VI.

CALL

AAA Benefit:
Members save a minimum 5% off the best available rate.

HAMPTON INN-ATLANTA AIRPORT Book great rates at AAA.com Phone: (770)996-2220 55

Hotel
$94-$159 All Year

Address: 1888 Sullivan Rd **Location:** I-85, exit 71, 0.4 mi e to Airport Rd, then just s. **Facility:** 127 one-bedroom standard units. 4 stories, interior corridors. **Parking:** on-site. **Terms:** 1-30 night minimum stay, cancellation fee imposed. **Amenities:** video games (fee), high-speed Internet, voice mail, irons, hair dryers. **Pool(s):** outdoor. **Leisure Activities:** limited exercise equipment. **Guest Services:** valet laundry, wireless Internet. **Business Services:** meeting rooms, business center. **Cards:** AX, CB, DC, DS, MC, VI.

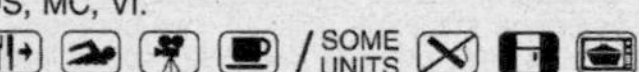

/ SOME UNITS

AAA Benefit:
Members save up to 10% everyday!

HILTON GARDEN INN-ATLANTA AIRPORT/MILLENIUM CENTER Book great rates at AAA.com Phone: (404)766-0303 57

Hotel
$89-$199 All Year

Address: 2301 Sullivan Rd **Location:** I-85, exit 71, just e, just s, then 0.7 mi w. **Facility:** 200 one-bedroom standard units, some with whirlpools. 6 stories, interior corridors. *Bath:* combo or shower only. **Parking:** on-site. **Terms:** 1-30 night minimum stay, cancellation fee imposed. **Amenities:** video games (fee), high-speed Internet, voice mail, safes, irons, hair dryers. **Pool(s):** heated indoor. **Leisure Activities:** whirlpool, exercise room. **Guest Services:** valet and coin laundry, area transportation-within 5 mi, wireless Internet. **Business Services:** conference facilities, business center. **Cards:** AX, CB, DC, DS, JC, MC, VI.

/ SOME UNITS

AAA Benefit:
Members save 5% or more everyday!

HOLIDAY INN EXPRESS-ATLANTA AIRPORT Book great rates at AAA.com Phone: (404)761-6500 49

Hotel
$79-$159 All Year

Address: 4601 Best Rd **Location:** I-85, exit 71, northwest corner. **Facility:** 160 one-bedroom standard units. 6 stories, interior corridors. *Bath:* combo or shower only. **Parking:** on-site. **Amenities:** high-speed Internet, voice mail, irons, hair dryers. **Pool(s):** outdoor. **Leisure Activities:** exercise room. **Guest Services:** valet laundry, area transportation, wireless Internet. **Business Services:** meeting rooms, business center. **Cards:** AX, CB, DC, DS, MC, VI.

ASK CALL / SOME UNITS FEE

(See map and index starting on p. 312)

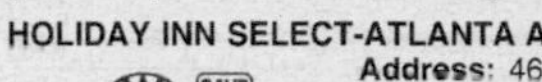

HOLIDAY INN SELECT-ATLANTA AIRPORT SOUTH *Book great rates at AAA.com* **Phone:** (404)763-8800 51

Hotel
\$99-\$194 All Year

Address: 4669 Airport Blvd **Location:** I-85, exit 71, just e to Airport Blvd, then just s; I-285, exit 60 (Riverdale Rd N), 1 mi n to Airport Blvd, then just s. **Facility:** 190 one-bedroom standard units. 6 stories, interior corridors. *Bath:* combo or shower only. **Parking:** on site. **Terms:** check-in 4 pm. **Amenities:** video games (fee), high-speed Internet, dual phone lines, voice mail, safes, irons, hair dryers. **Pool(s):** heated indoor. **Leisure Activities:** whirlpool, exercise room. **Guest Services:** complimentary and valet laundry, wireless Internet. **Business Services:** meeting rooms, business center. **Cards:** AX, CB, DC, DS, MC, VI. **Free Special Amenities: newspaper and high-speed Internet.**

HYATT PLACE ATLANTA AIRPORT-SOUTH *Book great rates at AAA.com* **Phone:** (770)994-2997 54

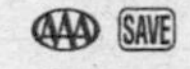

Hotel
\$79-\$209 All Year

Address: 1899 Sullivan Rd **Location:** I-85, exit 71, just e to Sullivan Rd, then just s; I-285, exit 60 (Riverdale Rd N), 1 mi to Sullivan Rd, then just s. **Facility:** 123 one-bedroom standard units. 6 stories, interior corridors. **Parking:** on-site. **Terms:** cancellation fee imposed. **Amenities:** video games (fee), high-speed Internet, dual phone lines, voice mail, irons, hair dryers. **Pool(s):** outdoor. **Leisure Activities:** exercise room. **Guest Services:** valet laundry, airport transportation-The William B. Hartsfield Atlanta Int'l Airport, wireless Internet. **Business Services:** meeting rooms, business center. **Cards:** AX, CB, DC, DS, JC, MC, VI. **Free Special Amenities: continental breakfast and high-speed Internet.**

HYATT
PLACE
AAA Benefit:
Ask for the AAA rate
and save 10%.

LA QUINTA INN & SUITES ATLANTA AIRPORT *Book great rates at AAA.com* **Phone:** (770)996-0000 61

Hotel
\$80-\$190 All Year

Address: 4820 Massachusetts Blvd **Location:** I-85, exit 71, just e to Airport Rd, then just s. **Facility:** 70 units. 63 one-bedroom standard units, some with whirlpools. 7 one-bedroom suites. 4 stories, interior corridors. **Parking:** on-site. **Amenities:** high-speed Internet, voice mail, irons, hair dryers. **Pool(s):** outdoor. **Leisure Activities:** exercise room. **Guest Services:** valet laundry, airport transportation-The William B. Hartsfield Atlanta Int'l Airport, area transportation-within 2 mi, wireless Internet. **Business Services:** meeting rooms, business center. **Cards:** AX, DC, DS, MC, VI. **Free Special Amenities: expanded continental breakfast and high-speed Internet.**

MICROTEL INN-ATLANTA AIRPORT *Book great rates at AAA.com* **Phone:** (770)994-3003 62

Hotel
\$69-\$89 All Year

Address: 4839 Massachusetts Blvd **Location:** I-85, exit 71, just e to Airport Rd, then just s; I-285, exit 60 (Riverdale Rd N), 1 mi to Sullivan Rd, then just s. **Facility:** 83 one-bedroom standard units. 3 stories, interior corridors. **Parking:** on-site. **Amenities:** high-speed Internet, dual phone lines, irons, hair dryers. **Guest Services:** coin laundry, wireless Internet. **Business Services:** meeting rooms, fax (fee). **Cards:** AX, CB, DC, DS, JC, MC, VI.

CALL / SOME UNITS FEE

QUALITY HOTEL & CONFERENCE CENTER-ATLANTA AIRPORT *Book at AAA.com* **Phone:** (770)996-4321 63

Hotel
\$80 All Year

Address: 1551 Phoenix Blvd **Location:** I-285, exit 60 (Riverdale Rd N), just sw. **Facility:** 142 units. 134 one-bedroom standard units. 8 one-bedroom suites. 6 stories, interior/exterior corridors. **Parking:** on-site. **Terms:** 7 day cancellation notice. **Amenities:** voice mail, irons, hair dryers. **Pool(s):** outdoor. **Leisure Activities:** exercise room. **Guest Services:** valet and coin laundry, wireless Internet. **Business Services:** meeting rooms, PC, fax. **Cards:** AX, DC, DS, MC, VI.

ASK / SOME UNITS

QUALITY INN & SUITES *Book great rates at AAA.com* **Phone:** (404)761-8371 64

Hotel
\$74-\$79 All Year

Address: 2451 Old National Pkwy **Location:** I-85, exit 69; I-285, exit 62, just s. **Facility:** 115 units. 107 one-bedroom standard units. 8 one-bedroom suites. 3 stories, interior/exterior corridors. **Parking:** on-site. **Amenities:** high-speed Internet, voice mail, irons, hair dryers. **Pool(s):** outdoor. **Leisure Activities:** exercise room. **Guest Services:** coin laundry, airport transportation-The William B. Hartsfield Atlanta Int'l Airport, wireless Internet. **Business Services:** meeting rooms, PC. **Cards:** AX, CB, DC, DS, JC, MC, VI.

(See map and index starting on p. 312)

SHERATON GATEWAY HOTEL, ATLANTA AIRPORT *Book great rates at AAA.com* **Phone:** (770)997-1100 58

Hotel
$89-$269 All Year

Address: 1900 Sullivan Rd **Location:** I-85, exit 71, just e to Airport Rd, then just s. Located adjacent to the convention center. **Facility:** 395 units. 382 one-bedroom standard units. 13 one-bedroom suites. 12 stories, interior corridors. **Parking:** on-site (fee) and valet. **Amenities:** video games (fee), voice mail, irons, hair dryers. *Some:* high-speed Internet (fee), dual phone lines. **Pool(s):** heated indoor/outdoor. **Leisure Activities:** whirlpool, exercise room. **Guest Services:** valet laundry, airport transportation-The William B. Hartsfield Atlanta Int'l Airport, wireless Internet. **Business Services:** conference facilities, business center. **Cards:** AX, CB, DC, DS, JC, MC, VI. **Free Special Amenities: newspaper and early check-in/late check-out.**

/ SOME UNITS

AAA Benefit:
Members get up to 15% off, plus Starwood Preferred Guest® bonuses.

SLEEP INN/ATLANTA AIRPORT *Book at AAA.com* **Phone:** (770)996-6100 53

Hotel
$65-$150 All Year

Address: 1911 Sullivan Rd **Location:** I-85, exit 71, just e to Airport Blvd, just s to Sullivan Rd, then just w; I-285, exit 60 (Riverdale Rd N), 1 mi to Airport Blvd, just s to Sullivan Rd, then just w. **Facility:** 63 one-bedroom standard units. 4 stories, interior corridors. *Bath:* shower only. **Parking:** on-site. **Terms:** cancellation fee imposed. **Amenities:** irons, hair dryers. **Leisure Activities:** exercise room. **Guest Services:** valet and coin laundry, wireless Internet. **Business Services:** meeting rooms, PC, fax (fee). **Cards:** AX, DS, MC, VI.

ASK / SOME UNITS

THE WESTIN HOTEL-ATLANTA AIRPORT *Book great rates at AAA.com* **Phone:** (404)762-7676 52

Hotel
$99-$529 All Year

Address: 4736 Best Rd **Location:** I-85, exit 71, just w, se on access road to Best Rd, then just s. **Facility:** Smoke free premises. 495 units. 491 one-bedroom standard units. 4 one-bedroom suites. 10 stories, interior corridors. **Parking:** on-site (fee) and valet. **Amenities:** video games (fee), voice mail, honor bars, irons, hair dryers. **Pool(s):** heated indoor/outdoor. **Leisure Activities:** whirlpool, exercise room. **Guest Services:** valet laundry, airport transportation-The William B. Hartsfield Atlanta Int'l Airport, wireless Internet. **Business Services:** conference facilities, business center. **Cards:** AX, CB, DC, DS, JC, MC, VI. **Free Special Amenities: newspaper and preferred room (subject to availability with advance reservations).**

CALL / SOME UNITS

AAA Benefit:
Enjoy up to 15% off your next stay, plus Starwood Preferred Guest® bonuses.

WHERE TO DINE

BRAKE PAD **Phone:** 404/766-1515 51

American
$6-$11

The former gas station now is a haven for burgers, wings and healthy bar food as well. Smoking permitted after 9 pm. Casual dress. **Bar:** Full bar. **Hours:** 11 am-1 am. Closed major holidays. **Address:** 3403 Main St **Location:** Downtown. **Parking:** on-site. **Cards:** AX, MC, VI.

THE FEED STORE **Phone:** 404/209-7979 53

American
$8-$35

Recycled farm tools and colorful farm art adorn the walls of this eclectic restaurant, which is housed in an original 1920s feed store. Fresh ingredients go into tasty American foods. Casual dress. **Bar:** Full bar. **Reservations:** accepted. **Hours:** 11 am-2 & 5-10 pm, Fri-11 pm, Sat 5 pm-11 pm. Closed major holidays; also Sun. **Address:** 3841 Main St **Location:** Jct Roosevelt Hwy and Main St, just n. **Parking:** on-site. **Cards:** AX, MC, VI.

SIMON'S **Phone:** 404/768-0143 52

American
$3-$33

The American-style grill with upscale touches and earnest servers offers steaks, seafood, pastas, burgers, salads and sandwiches. Casual dress. **Bar:** Full bar. **Reservations:** accepted. **Hours:** 11 am-10 pm, Fri & Sat-11 pm. Closed major holidays. **Address:** 3529 Main St **Location:** I-85, exit 73 (southbound), 1 mi w to Howell Slade Cir, just e to Main St, then just s; exit 73B northbound. **Parking:** on-site. **Cards:** AX, CB, DC, DS, JC, MC, VI.

CALL

DECATUR pop. 18,147 (See maps and indexes starting on p. 302, 312)

WHERE TO STAY

AMERICA'S BEST INN & SUITES *Book at AAA.com* **Phone:** (404)286-2500 21

Motel
$65 All Year

Address: 4095 Covington Hwy **Location:** I-285, exit 43, just w. **Facility:** 47 units. 44 one-bedroom standard units, some with whirlpools. 3 one-bedroom suites. 2 stories (no elevator), exterior corridors. **Parking:** on-site. **Amenities:** high-speed Internet, voice mail, irons. *Some:* hair dryers. **Pool(s):** outdoor. **Guest Services:** wireless Internet. **Business Services:** fax. **Cards:** AX, DS, MC, VI.

ASK FEE CALL / SOME UNITS FEE

ECONO LODGE *Book at AAA.com* **Phone:** (404)243-4422 22

Motel
$45-$150 All Year

Address: 2574 Candler Rd **Location:** I-20, exit 65, just n. **Facility:** 59 one-bedroom standard units, some with whirlpools. 2 stories, exterior corridors. **Parking:** on-site. **Terms:** cancellation fee imposed. **Amenities:** high-speed Internet, irons. **Guest Services:** wireless Internet. **Business Services:** fax. **Cards:** AX, DS, MC, VI.

ASK / SOME UNITS

(See maps and indexes starting on p. 302, 312)

HOLIDAY INN EXPRESS, ATLANTA EMORY Book great rates at AAA.com Phone: (404)320-0888 18

Hotel
$100-$169 All Year

Address: 2183 N Decatur Rd **Location:** I-85, exit 91, 0.8 mi e to N Decatur Rd, then just n. **Facility:** 62 one-bedroom standard units with efficiencies, some with whirlpools. 4 stories, interior corridors. **Parking:** on-site. **Terms:** 7 day cancellation notice fee imposed. **Amenities:** high-speed Internet, dual phone lines, voice mail, irons, hair dryers. **Pool(s):** indoor. **Leisure Activities:** sauna, exercise room. **Guest Services:** valet and coin laundry, wireless Internet. **Business Services:** meeting rooms, business center. **Cards:** AX, CB, DC, DS, MC, VI. **Free Special Amenities: full breakfast and high-speed Internet.**

FEE CALL

HOLIDAY INN SELECT Book at AAA.com Phone: 404/371-0204 20

Hotel
Rates not provided

Address: 130 Clairmont Ave **Location:** Downtown. **Facility:** 184 units. 180 one-bedroom standard units. 4 one-bedroom suites. 5 stories, interior corridors. **Parking:** on-site (fee). **Amenities:** video games (fee), high-speed Internet, voice mail, irons, hair dryers. **Pool(s):** heated indoor. **Leisure Activities:** exercise room. **Guest Services:** valet and coin laundry, area transportation, wireless Internet. **Business Services:** conference facilities, business center.

FEE / SOME UNITS FEE

SUPER 8 MOTEL Book great rates at AAA.com Phone: (404)378-3765 19

Motel
$60-$150 All Year

Address: 917 Church St **Location:** I 285, exit 39A, 2.5 mi w to Church St, then 1.5 mi sw. **Facility:** 33 one-bedroom standard units, some with whirlpools. 3 stories (no elevator), exterior corridors. **Parking:** on-site. **Terms:** cancellation fee imposed. **Amenities:** high-speed Internet, irons, hair dryers. *Some:* DVD players. **Guest Services:** wireless Internet. **Business Services:** fax (fee). **Cards:** AX, DC, DS, MC, VI. **Free Special Amenities: continental breakfast and high-speed Internet.**

CALL / SOME UNITS VCR

WHERE TO DINE

ATHENS PIZZA HOUSE Phone: 404/636-1100 36

Greek
$5-$11

The casual spot is a favorite of families and nearby Emory students alike. Good choices include Mediterranean pizza with gyro meat and feta, famous Greek salad, pita wraps and hot subs. Other home-style specialties, created from family recipes that haven't changed in generations, include moussaka and pastitsio. The large patio is breezy and welcoming. Casual dress. **Bar:** Beer & wine. **Hours:** 11 am-11 pm, Fri & Sat-midnight. Closed major holidays. **Address:** 1341 Clairmont Rd, Suite A **Location:** Jct N Decatur Rd. **Parking:** on-site. **Cards:** AX, DC, DS, MC, VI.

BRICK STORE PUB Phone: 404/687-0990 40

American
$4-$9

A delightful hideaway, the local pub is atypical in that it lacks televisions and loud music. Comfort foods are served in ample portions. On hand is an excellent selection of draft beers, 65 bottled varieties and fine single malts. Casual dress. **Bar:** Full bar. **Hours:** 11 am-2 am, Mon-1 am, Sun noon-1 am. Closed: 1/1, 12/24, 12/25. **Address:** 125 E Court Square **Location:** Just s of Ponce de Leon Ave; in historic square. **Parking:** street. **Cards:** AX, MC, VI.

CAFE' ALSACE Phone: 404/373-5622 38

French
$3-$21

The chef prepares food in the Alsatian style, which blends elements of French and German cuisine. The quaint dining room is appointed in a rustic French country kitchen style. This place is popular, so typically it can be busy as food is prepared to order. Casual dress. **Bar:** Beer & wine. **Hours:** 11:30 am-2:15 & 6-10 pm, Sat from 6 pm; Sunday brunch 10 am-2 pm. Closed: 11/26, 12/25; also Mon. **Address:** 121 E Ponce de Leon Ave **Location:** Just w of Church St. **Parking:** street. **Cards:** AX, DS, MC, VI.

CAFE ISTANBUL Phone: 404/320-0054 35

Turkish
$7-$17

Guests can taste succulent and satisfying Turkish cuisine at a table or in a relaxing loungelike setting. The experience is like entering a Middle Eastern habitat. **Bar:** Beer & wine. **Reservations:** accepted, Fri & Sat. **Hours:** noon-10 pm, Fri & Sat-midnight, Sun 1 pm-10 pm. Closed major holidays. **Address:** 1850 Lawrenceville Hwy **Location:** I-285, exit 39A, 2.3 mi w. **Parking:** on-site. **Cards:** AX, MC, VI.

CRESCENT MOON Phone: 404/377-5623 39

American
$1-$14

In the heart of town, the wonderful family restaurant serves breakfast, lunch and dinner. Portions are ample, and the food is well-prepared. Casual dress. **Bar:** Beer & wine. **Reservations:** not accepted. **Hours:** 7:30 am-9:30 pm, Sat 7:30 am-3 & 5:30-9:30 pm, Sun & Mon-3 pm. Closed: 11/26, 12/25. **Address:** 174 W Ponce de Leon Ave **Location:** At Commerce Dr; center. **Parking:** street. **Cards:** AX, DC, MC, VI.

FEAST RESTAURANT Phone: 404/377-2000 42

Continental
$2-$24

A hip renovation enhances the style of this former feed store, which has exposed brick walls and a relaxed patio. Fresh ingredients go into small and large plates of Continental fare, including tuna tartare, whole roasted trout, vegetable ravioli and delicious pizza. Burgers, soups and salads are among lighter offerings. The educated staff carries out prompt service. Casual dress. **Bar:** Full bar. **Reservations:** accepted. **Hours:** 11 am-10 pm, Fri & Sat-11 pm. Closed: 11/26, 12/25. **Address:** 314 E Howard Ave **Location:** Jct Barry St, just e. **Parking:** valet. **Cards:** AX, DS, MC, VI.

MADRAS SARAVANA BHAVAN Phone: 404/636-4400 33

Indian
$3-$12

The enormous variety of menu options is all vegetarian, and the buffet always is a popular choice. The South Indian eatery is widely praised. Casual dress. **Bar:** Beer & wine. **Reservations:** accepted. **Hours:** 11:30 am-2:30 & 5:30-10 pm, Fri & Sat 11:30 am-10 pm. **Address:** 2179 Lawrenceville Hwy **Location:** I-285, exit 38, 1.5 mi w. **Parking:** on-site. **Cards:** AX, DC, DS, MC, VI.

(See maps and indexes starting on p. 302, 312)

SAGE **Phone:** 404/373-5574 (41)

American
$6-$22

The spacious restaurant is a local favorite and can be lively. The extensive menu lines up a selection of meat and seafood items, including rainbow trout, crab cakes, filet mignon and pepper steak. A few vegetarian choices also are available. Casual dress. **Bar:** Full bar. **Reservations:** accepted. **Hours:** 5:30-9:30 pm, Fri & Sat-10:30 pm, Sun 5 pm-9 pm. Closed major holidays; also Mon. **Address:** 121 Sycamore St **Location:** Downtown; in historic square. **Parking:** street. **Cards:** AX, DC, DS, MC, VI.

UDIPI CAFE **Phone:** 404/325-1933 (34)

Indian
$5-$15

The Indian-vegetarian menu teems with bold, spicy, inexpensive items, such as the special vegetable curry, Indian-style pancakes and sambar. Not far from downtown, the cafe occupies a small plaza and has sparse but comfortable decor. Servers are earnest and congenial. Casual dress. **Hours:** 11:30 am-9:30 pm, Fri-Sun to 10 pm. **Address:** 1850 Lawrenceville Hwy, Suite 700 **Location:** I-285, exit 38, 2.3 mi w. **Parking:** on-site. **Cards:** AX, MC, VI.

UNIVERSAL JOINT **Phone:** 404/373-6260 (43)

American
$5-$9

In a converted garage, the funky joint has a large patio for outdoor dining. The atmosphere is extremely relaxed, and good, simple foods and beverages are the focus. Patrons can save a few calories because no desserts are available. Casual dress. **Bar:** Full bar. **Reservations:** not accepted. **Hours:** 11:30 am-midnight. **Address:** 906 Oakview Rd **Location:** Corner of East Lake Dr; adjacent to Oakhurst Park. **Parking:** on-site and street. **Cards:** AX, MC, VI.

WATERSHED **Phone:** 404/378-4900 (37)

Southern American
$8-$34

In a converted old gas station downtown, the restaurant is redone in a funky style. Featured on the menu are dishes that reflect innovative twists on soup, salad, sandwiches, homemade pasta and seafood. Emily Saliers of the Indigo Girls is one of the owners of this spot. Casual dress. **Bar:** Full bar. **Reservations:** suggested. **Hours:** 11 am-10 pm; Sunday brunch 10 am-3 pm. Closed major holidays. **Address:** 406 W Ponce de Leon Ave **Location:** Just w of center of town. **Parking:** on-site. **Cards:** AX, MC, VI.

CALL

DORAVILLE pop. 9,862 (See map and index starting on p. 302)

— WHERE TO STAY —

HOLIDAY INN NORTHEAST/DORAVILLE *Book great rates at AAA.com* **Phone:** (770)455-3700 (147)

Hotel
$104-$134 3/2-11/30
$99-$129 12/1-3/1

Address: 2001 Clearview Ave **Location:** I-285, exit 32, southeast corner. **Facility:** 230 units. 228 one-bedroom standard units, some with whirlpools. 2 one-bedroom suites. 4 stories, interior corridors. **Parking:** on-site. **Amenities:** video games (fee), high-speed Internet, voice mail, irons, hair dryers. **Pool(s):** outdoor. **Leisure Activities:** exercise room. **Guest Services:** valet and coin laundry, area transportation, wireless Internet. **Business Services:** meeting rooms, business center. **Cards:** AX, DC, DS, MC, VI. **Free Special Amenities: newspaper and high-speed Internet.**

FEE / SOME UNITS FEE

SUPER 8 ATLANTA NE *Book great rates at AAA.com* **Phone:** (770)458-2671 (148)

Motel
$46-$65 All Year

Address: 2822 Chamblee Tucker Rd **Location:** I-85, exit 94, just w. **Facility:** 52 one-bedroom standard units. 2-3 stories (no elevator), exterior corridors. **Parking:** on-site. **Terms:** cancellation fee imposed. **Amenities:** video games (fee), high-speed Internet, hair dryers. **Guest Services:** coin laundry, wireless Internet. **Business Services:** fax. **Cards:** AX, DC, DS, MC, VI. **Free Special Amenities: continental breakfast and high-speed Internet.**

/ SOME UNITS FEE

— WHERE TO DINE —

HAE WOON DAE **Phone:** 770/458-6999 (105)

Korean
$6-$14

Korean barbecue is at its tastiest in the comfortable and unpretentious little restaurant. Casual dress. **Bar:** Full bar. **Reservations:** accepted. **Hours:** 11 am-6 am, Wed-midnight. **Address:** 5805 Buford Hwy, Suite 5 **Location:** I-285, exit 32, 0.5 mi n; in Treasure Village. **Parking:** on-site. **Cards:** AX, CB, DC, DS, JC, MC, VI.

LITTLE SZECHUAN **Phone:** 770/451-0192 (108)

Chinese
$6-$18

Often crowded with loyal lunch goers, the family-size restaurant offers a large menu of both familiar and slightly exotic dishes. Among tasty choices are sesame chicken, crispy tea duck, shrimp with cashews, squid with yellow chives, Mongolian beef and brisket in Szechuan sauce. Casual dress. **Bar:** Beer & wine. **Hours:** 11:30 am-3 & 5-9:30 pm. Closed: 9/7. **Address:** 5091-C Buford Hwy **Location:** I-285, exit 32, 0.4 mi n of Chamblee Tucker Rd; jct US 285; in Northwoods Plaza. **Parking:** on-site. **Cards:** MC, VI.

CALL

PHO 79 **Phone:** 404/477-3317 (103)

Vietnamese
$6-$10

Noodle bowls are inexpensive and filling at the Vietnamese outlet. Videos enhance the color of the dining experience. Casual dress. **Bar:** Beer & wine. **Reservations:** accepted. **Hours:** 11 am-10 pm. **Address:** 5000 Winters Chapel Rd **Location:** I-285, exit 31B, 1.5 mi n, 0.4 mi n, then 0.8 mi w. **Parking:** on-site. **Cards:** AX, DS, MC, VI.

CALL

(See map and index starting on p. 302)

PHO HOA — **Phone:** 770/455-8729 (107)

Vietnamese
$5-$7

Patrons enjoy heaping bowls of pho and spring rolls, along with other Vietnamese dishes. An array of fresh and tasty condiments on the side enhances each meal. Casual dress. **Reservations:** accepted. **Hours:** 10 am-10 pm. **Address:** 5150 Buford Hwy, Suite C120 **Location:** I-285, exit 32, 0.8 mi s; in Asian Square. **Parking:** on-site. **Cards:** AX, MC, VI.

PUNG MIE — **Phone:** 770/455-0435 (106)

Chinese
$4-$30

Fountains, art and large ornamental vases contribute to the lovely setting. Among the authentic dishes are dumplings and the house special: pan-fried rolls and shark-fin soup. Casual dress. **Bar:** Full bar. **Hours:** 11:30 am-10:30 pm, Sun-10 pm. **Address:** 5145 Buford Hwy **Location:** I-285, exit 32, 0.8 mi s. **Parking:** on-site. **Cards:** AX, DC, DS, MC, VI.

SEOUL GARDEN RESTAURANT — **Phone:** 770/452-0123 (104)

Korean
$6-$21

The restaurant features authentic Korean and Japanese dishes, as well as a sushi bar. Fragrant seasonings and vegetables flavor a large variety of hearty soups filled with crab, lamb, beef, dumplings or fish. A favorite is steamed chicken soup with a choice of side dishes. Barbecue entrees also are top choices. Casual dress. **Bar:** Beer & wine. **Reservations:** accepted. **Hours:** 10:30 am-midnight, Sat & Sun from 3:30 pm. **Address:** 5938 Buford Hwy **Location:** I-85, exit 103. **Parking:** on-site. **Cards:** AX, MC, VI.

SONNY'S REAL PIT BAR-B-Q — **Phone:** 770/447-6616

Barbecue
$6-$15

House specialties include pork and chicken grilled over an open pit, barbecue ribs and fresh, homemade pie. The salad bar offers another popular option. Rustic and comfortable, the atmosphere is perfect for family meals. Casual dress. **Bar:** Beer only. **Hours:** 11 am-9:30 pm, Fri & Sat-10 pm. Closed: 11/26, 12/25. **Address:** 6869 Peachtree Industrial Blvd **Location:** I-285, exit 31 (SR 141 N), 1.7 mi ne, on S Access Rd; 0.3 mi sw of Winters Chapel Rd/Amwiler Rd exit. **Parking:** on-site. **Cards:** AX, DS, MC, VI.

DOUGLASVILLE pop. 20,065

WHERE TO STAY

BEST WESTERN GARDEN INN & SUITES *Book great rates at AAA.com* — **Phone:** (770)489-4863

AAA SAVE

Hotel
$85-$95 All Year

Address: 8304 Cherokee Blvd **Location:** I-20, exit 37, just n to Cherokee Blvd, then just e. **Facility:** 56 units. 55 one-bedroom standard units, some with whirlpools. 1 one-bedroom suite. 3 stories, interior corridors. **Parking:** on-site. **Terms:** 3 day cancellation notice. **Amenities:** high-speed Internet, voice mail, irons, hair dryers. **Pool(s):** outdoor. **Leisure Activities:** exercise room. **Guest Services:** coin laundry, wireless Internet. **Business Services:** meeting rooms, PC, fax. **Cards:** AX, DS, MC, VI. **Free Special Amenities: continental breakfast and high-speed Internet.**

AAA Benefit:
Members save up to 20%, plus 10% bonus points with rewards program.

COMFORT INN *Book great rates at AAA.com* — **Phone:** (678)504-2000

AAA SAVE

Hotel
$85-$95 All Year

Address: 5487 Westmoreland Plaza **Location:** I-20, exit 37, northeast corner. **Facility:** 69 one-bedroom standard units, some with kitchens and/or whirlpools. 3 stories, interior corridors. **Parking:** on-site. **Terms:** cancellation fee imposed. **Amenities:** high-speed Internet, dual phone lines, voice mail, irons, hair dryers. **Pool(s):** outdoor. **Leisure Activities:** exercise room. **Guest Services:** complimentary laundry, wireless Internet. **Business Services:** meeting rooms, PC. **Cards:** AX, CB, DC, DS, JC, MC, VI. **Free Special Amenities: continental breakfast and high-speed Internet.**

FEE / SOME UNITS

DAYS INN *Book at AAA.com* — **Phone:** (770)949-1499

Motel
$50-$95 All Year

Address: 5489 Westmoreland Plaza **Location:** I-20, exit 37, just n. **Facility:** 57 one-bedroom standard units. 2 stories (no elevator), exterior corridors. **Parking:** on-site. **Amenities:** high-speed Internet, hair dryers. *Some:* irons. **Pool(s):** outdoor. **Guest Services:** coin laundry, wireless Internet. **Business Services:** PC, fax (fee). **Cards:** AX, DS, MC, VI.

ASK / SOME UNITS FEE

HOLIDAY INN EXPRESS *Book at AAA.com* — **Phone:** (770)920-9228

Hotel
$99-$125 All Year

Address: 7101 Concourse Pkwy **Location:** I-20, exit 34. **Facility:** 102 one-bedroom standard units. 5 stories, interior corridors. **Parking:** on-site. **Terms:** 7 day cancellation notice-fee imposed. **Amenities:** high-speed Internet, voice mail, irons, hair dryers. **Pool(s):** outdoor. **Leisure Activities:** limited exercise equipment. **Guest Services:** coin laundry, wireless Internet. **Business Services:** meeting rooms, PC, fax (fee). **Cards:** AX, DC, DS, JC, MC, VI.

ASK CALL / SOME UNITS

HOLIDAY INN EXPRESS-SIX FLAGS AREA/ATLANTA — **Phone:** 770/949-5730

Hotel
Rates not provided

Address: 5479 Westmoreland Plaza **Location:** I-20, exit 37, northeast corner. **Facility:** 50 units. 49 one-bedroom standard units, some with kitchens (no utensils) and/or whirlpools. 1 one-bedroom suite. 2 stories (no elevator), exterior corridors. **Parking:** on-site. **Amenities:** high-speed Internet, voice mail, irons, hair dryers. **Pool(s):** outdoor. **Guest Services:** wireless Internet. **Business Services:** fax (fee).

FEE CALL / SOME UNITS

LA QUINTA INN & SUITES *Book great rates at AAA.com* **Phone:** (770)577-3838

Hotel
$69-$135 All Year

Address: 1000 Linnenkohl Dr **Location:** I-20, exit 34, just n. **Facility:** 90 one-bedroom standard units. 5 stories, interior corridors. **Parking:** on-site. **Amenities:** high-speed Internet, dual phone lines, voice mail, irons, hair dryers. **Pool(s):** outdoor. **Leisure Activities:** exercise room. **Guest Services:** coin laundry, wireless Internet. **Business Services:** meeting rooms, PC, fax. **Cards:** AX, CB, DC, DS, MC, VI.

CALL / SOME UNITS

SLEEP INN *Book at AAA.com* **Phone:** (770)920-8887

Hotel
$71-$89 4/1-11/30
$62-$71 12/1-3/31

Address: 7055 Concourse Pkwy **Location:** I-20, exit 34, just n. **Facility:** 60 one-bedroom standard units. 3 stories, interior corridors. *Bath:* shower only. **Parking:** on-site. **Amenities:** high-speed Internet, irons, hair dryers. **Guest Services:** wireless Internet. **Business Services:** PC, fax (fee). **Cards:** AX, DC, DS, JC, MC, VI.

ASK CALL / SOME UNITS

WHERE TO DINE

GUMBEAUX'S, A CAJUN CAFE **Phone:** 770/947-8288

Cajun
$5-$19

The spicy Cajun and New Orleans-style food is as close to authentic as diners can fine without actually making the trip to Louisiana. A bayou-style atmosphere adds to the delicious food. Casual dress. **Bar:** Full bar. **Hours:** 11 am-2 & 5-10 pm. Closed major holidays; also Sun & Mon. **Address:** 6712 Broad St **Location:** I-20, exit 36, 2 mi n on Campbellton Rd, then just w. **Parking:** on-site. **Cards:** AX, CB, DC, DS, MC, VI.

DULUTH pop. 22,122 (See map and index starting on p. 302)

WHERE TO STAY

ATLANTA MARRIOTT GWINNETT PLACE *Book great rates at AAA.com* **Phone:** (770)923-1775 99

Hotel
$202-$217 All Year

Address: 1775 Pleasant Hill Rd **Location:** I-85, exit 104, just e. **Facility:** Smoke free premises. 426 units. 421 one-bedroom standard units. 5 one-bedroom suites, some with whirlpools. 9-17 stories, interior corridors. **Parking:** on-site. **Terms:** check-in 4 pm, cancellation fee imposed. **Amenities:** dual phone lines, voice mail, irons, hair dryers. *Fee:* video games, high-speed Internet. **Pool(s):** heated indoor/outdoor. **Leisure Activities:** whirlpool. **Guest Services:** valet and coin laundry, area transportation, wireless Internet. **Business Services:** conference facilities, business center. **Cards:** AX, CB, DC, DS, JC, MC, VI.

CALL

CANDLEWOOD SUITES-ATLANTA *Book at AAA.com* **Phone:** 678/380-0414 98

Hotel
Rates not provided

Address: 3665 Shackleford Rd **Location:** I-85, exit 104, just e, then just s. **Facility:** 122 units. 98 one-bedroom standard units with efficiencies. 24 one-bedroom suites with efficiencies. 3 stories, interior corridors. **Parking:** on-site. **Terms:** office hours 7 am-11 pm. **Amenities:** video library, DVD players, CD players, high-speed Internet, dual phone lines, voice mail, irons, hair dryers. **Leisure Activities:** exercise room. **Guest Services:** valet laundry. **Business Services:** fax (fee).

FEE CALL VCR / SOME UNITS FEE

COMFORT SUITES-ATLANTA DULUTH *Book great rates at AAA.com* **Phone:** (770)931-9299 100

AAA SAVE

Hotel
$80-$130 All Year

Address: 3700 Shackleford Rd **Location:** I-85, exit 104, just e to Shackleford Rd, then just s. **Facility:** Smoke free premises. 85 one-bedroom standard units. 2 stories, interior corridors. **Parking:** on-site. **Amenities:** video games (fee), high-speed Internet, dual phone lines, voice mail, irons, hair dryers. **Pool(s):** heated indoor. **Leisure Activities:** limited exercise equipment. **Guest Services:** valet laundry, wireless Internet. **Business Services:** meeting rooms, business center. **Cards:** AX, CB, DC, DS, MC, VI.

FEE CALL

COUNTRY INN & SUITES BY CARLSON *Book at AAA.com* **Phone:** (678)405-2900 96

Hotel
$119-$149 All Year

Address: 3530 Breckinridge Blvd **Location:** I-85, exit 104, just e. **Facility:** 104 units. 81 one-bedroom standard units, some with whirlpools. 23 one-bedroom suites. 5 stories, interior corridors. **Parking:** on-site. **Terms:** cancellation fee imposed. **Amenities:** high-speed Internet, voice mail, irons, hair dryers. **Pool(s):** heated indoor. **Leisure Activities:** whirlpool, exercise room. **Guest Services:** valet and coin laundry, area transportation, wireless Internet. **Business Services:** meeting rooms, PC, fax. **Cards:** AX, DC, DS, MC, VI.

ASK FEE / SOME UNITS

(See map and index starting on p. 302)

COURTYARD BY MARRIOTT-GWINNETT MALL *Book great rates at AAA.com* **Phone:** (770)476-4666 

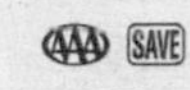

Hotel
$153-$164 All Year

Address: 3550 Venture Pkwy **Location:** I-85, exit 104, just w to Venture Pkwy, then just n. **Facility:** Smoke free premises. 146 units. 135 one-bedroom standard units. 11 one-bedroom suites. 3 stories, interior corridors. **Parking:** on-site. **Terms:** cancellation fee imposed. **Amenities:** high-speed Internet, voice mail, irons, hair dryers. **Pool(s):** outdoor. **Leisure Activities:** whirlpool, exercise room. **Guest Services:** valet and coin laundry, airport transportation (fee)-The William B. Hartsfield Atlanta Int'l Airport, area transportation-within 3 mi, wireless Internet. **Business Services:** meeting rooms, business center. **Cards:** AX, CB, DC, DS, JC, MC, VI. **Free Special Amenities: newspaper and high-speed Internet.**

FEE CALL / SOME UNITS

AAA Benefit:
Members save a minimum 5% off the best available rate.

DAYS INN GWINNETT PLACE *Book at AAA.com* **Phone:** 770/476-8700 94

Hotel
Rates not provided

Address: 1920 Pleasant Hill Rd **Location:** I-85, exit 104; northwest corner. **Facility:** 38 one-bedroom standard units. 3 stories, interior corridors. **Parking:** on-site. **Amenities:** high-speed Internet, hair dryers. **Guest Services:** wireless Internet. **Business Services:** meeting rooms, fax (fee).

FEE / SOME UNITS FEE

EXTENDED STAY DELUXE *Book at AAA.com* **Phone:** (770)623-6800 89

Hotel
$75-$90 All Year

Address: 3390 Venture Pkwy NW **Location:** I-85, exit 104, just w to Venture Pkwy, then just n. **Facility:** 114 one-bedroom standard units with efficiencies. 6 stories, interior corridors. **Parking:** on-site. **Amenities:** DVD players, high-speed Internet (fee), dual phone lines, voice mail, irons, hair dryers. **Pool(s):** heated outdoor. **Leisure Activities:** exercise room. **Guest Services:** coin laundry, wireless Internet. **Business Services:** meeting rooms, fax (fee). **Cards:** AX, CB, DC, DS, JC, MC, VI.

ASK FEE CALL / SOME UNITS FEE

HAMPTON INN & SUITES-GWINNETT *Book great rates at AAA.com* **Phone:** (770)931-9800 102

AAA SAVE

Hotel
$89-$179 All Year

Address: 1725 Pineland Rd **Location:** I-85, exit 104, 0.3 mi e to Crestwood, then just s. **Facility:** 136 units. 104 one-bedroom standard units. 32 one-bedroom suites with kitchens. 8 stories, interior corridors. **Parking:** on-site. **Amenities:** video games (fee), high-speed Internet, voice mail, irons, hair dryers. **Pool(s):** outdoor. **Leisure Activities:** exercise room. **Guest Services:** valet and coin laundry, wireless Internet. **Business Services:** meeting rooms, business center. **Cards:** AX, CB, DC, DS, JC, MC, VI. **Free Special Amenities: expanded continental breakfast and high-speed Internet.** *(See color ad below)*

FEE CALL / SOME UNITS VCR

AAA Benefit:
Members save up to 10% everyday!

(See map and index starting on p. 302)

HILTON GARDEN INN ATLANTA-JOHN'S CREEK *Book great rates at AAA.com* **Phone:** (770)476-1966 84

Hotel
$79-$154 All Year

Address: 11695 Medlock Bridge Rd **Location:** Jct SR 141 and 120, 1 mi n. **Facility:** 124 units. 111 one-bedroom standard units, some with whirlpools. 13 one-bedroom suites with whirlpools. 5 stories, interior corridors. **Parking:** on-site. **Terms:** 1-30 night minimum stay, cancellation fee imposed. **Amenities:** high-speed Internet, dual phone lines, voice mail, irons, hair dryers. **Pool(s):** outdoor. **Leisure Activities:** whirlpool, exercise room. **Guest Services:** valet and coin laundry, area transportation, wireless Internet. **Business Services:** meeting rooms, business center. **Cards:** AX, CB, DC, DS, JC, MC, VI.

FEE 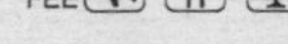  CALL   / SOME UNITS

Hilton Garden Inn
AAA Benefit:
Members save 5% or more everyday!

HILTON GARDEN INN-ATLANTA NE *Book great rates at AAA.com* **Phone:** (770)495-7600  

Hotel
$99-$189 All Year

Address: 2040 Sugarloaf Cir **Location:** I-85, exit 108, just w. **Facility:** 122 units. 116 one-bedroom standard units. 6 one-bedroom suites with whirlpools. 5 stories, interior corridors. **Parking:** on-site. **Terms:** 1-30 night minimum stay, cancellation fee imposed. **Amenities:** video games (fee), high-speed Internet, dual phone lines, voice mail, irons, hair dryers. **Pool(s):** heated indoor. **Leisure Activities:** whirlpool, exercise room. **Guest Services:** valet and coin laundry, area transportation, wireless Internet. **Business Services:** meeting rooms, business center. **Cards:** AX, CB, DC, DS, JC, MC, VI.

FEE CALL / SOME UNITS

AAA Benefit:
Members save 5% or more everyday!

HOLIDAY INN EXPRESS *Book at AAA.com* **Phone:** (770)935-7171 97

Hotel
$79-$119 All Year

Address: 3670 Shackleford Rd **Location:** I-85, exit 104, just e to Shackleford Rd, then just s. **Facility:** 68 one-bedroom standard units, some with whirlpools. 3 stories, interior corridors. **Parking:** on-site. **Amenities:** video games (fee), high-speed Internet, dual phone lines, voice mail, irons, hair dryers. **Pool(s):** outdoor. **Leisure Activities:** exercise room. **Guest Services:** valet laundry, wireless Internet. **Business Services:** meeting rooms, fax (fee). **Cards:** AX, DC, DS, JC, MC, VI.

ASK FEE / SOME UNITS FEE

HOLIDAY INN-GWINNETT CENTER *Book at AAA.com* **Phone:** (770)476-2022 86

Hotel
$84-$169 All Year

Address: 6310 Sugarloaf Pkwy **Location:** I-85, exit 108, just w. **Facility:** 143 one-bedroom standard units. 6 stories, interior corridors. *Bath:* combo or shower only. **Parking:** on-site. **Amenities:** video games (fee), high-speed Internet, dual phone lines, voice mail, safes, irons, hair dryers. **Pool(s):** indoor. **Leisure Activities:** exercise room. **Guest Services:** valet and coin laundry, area transportation, wireless Internet. **Business Services:** meeting rooms, PC, fax (fee). **Cards:** AX, DC, DS, MC, VI.

ASK FEE CALL / SOME UNITS FEE

HYATT PLACE ATLANTA/DULUTH/GWINNETT MALL *Book great rates at AAA.com* **Phone:** (770)623-9699 93

AAA SAVE

Hotel
$69-$209 All Year

Address: 3530 Venture Pkwy **Location:** I-85, exit 104, just w to Venture Pkwy, then just n. **Facility:** 123 one-bedroom standard units. 6 stories, interior corridors. **Parking:** on-site. **Terms:** cancellation fee imposed. **Amenities:** video games (fee), high-speed Internet, voice mail, irons, hair dryers. **Pool(s):** outdoor. **Leisure Activities:** exercise room. **Guest Services:** valet laundry, area transportation-within 5 mi, wireless Internet. **Business Services:** meeting rooms, business center. **Cards:** AX, CB, DC, DS, JC, MC, VI. **Free Special Amenities: continental breakfast and high-speed Internet.**

FEE CALL

HYATT PLACE
AAA Benefit:
Ask for the AAA rate and save 10%.

HYATT PLACE ATLANTA/JOHNS CREEK *Book great rates at AAA.com* **Phone:** (770)622-5858 85

AAA SAVE

Hotel
$99-$299 All Year

Address: 11505 Medlock Bridge Rd **Location:** Jct SR 141 and 120, 0.7 mi n. **Facility:** 122 one-bedroom standard units. 5 stories, interior corridors. **Parking:** on-site. **Terms:** cancellation fee imposed. **Amenities:** video games (fee), high-speed Internet, dual phone lines, voice mail, irons, hair dryers. **Pool(s):** heated outdoor. **Leisure Activities:** exercise room. **Guest Services:** valet laundry, airport transportation (fee)-The William B. Hartsfield Atlanta Int'l Airport, area transportation-within 5 mi, wireless Internet. **Business Services:** meeting rooms, business center. **Cards:** AX, CB, DC, DS, JC, MC, VI. **Free Special Amenities: continental breakfast and high-speed Internet.**

FEE CALL

HYATT PLACE
AAA Benefit:
Ask for the AAA rate and save 10%.

(See map and index starting on p. 302)

LA QUINTA INN DULUTH Book great rates at AAA.com Phone: (678)957-0500 88

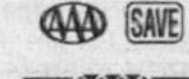

Hotel
$59-$139 All Year

Address: 2370 Stephen Center Dr **Location:** I-85, exit 107, just w. **Facility:** 83 one-bedroom standard units. 3 stories, interior corridors. **Parking:** on-site. **Amenities:** high-speed Internet, dual phone lines, voice mail, irons, hair dryers. **Pool(s):** heated outdoor. **Leisure Activities:** exercise room. **Guest Services:** valet and coin laundry, wireless Internet. **Business Services:** meeting rooms, PC, fax. **Cards:** AX, DS, MC, VI. **Free Special Amenities: expanded continental breakfast and high-speed Internet.**

CALL / SOME UNITS

QUALITY INN - GWINNETT MALL Book at AAA.com Phone: (770)623-9300 91

Hotel
$60-$129 All Year

Address: 3500 Venture Pkwy **Location:** I-85, exit 104, just w to Venture Pkwy, then just n. **Facility:** 111 one-bedroom standard units. 3 stories, interior/exterior corridors. **Parking:** on-site. **Terms:** cancellation fee imposed. **Amenities:** high-speed Internet, voice mail, irons, hair dryers. **Pool(s):** outdoor. **Leisure Activities:** exercise room. **Guest Services:** valet laundry, wireless Internet. **Business Services:** meeting rooms, business center. **Cards:** AX, CB, DC, DS, JC, MC, VI.

ASK FEE CALL / SOME UNITS FEE

RESIDENCE INN-ATLANTA GWINNETT Book great rates at AAA.com Phone: (770)921-2202 101

Hotel
$189-$202 All Year

Address: 1760 Pineland Rd **Location:** I-85, exit 104, just e to Shackleford Rd, just s to Pineland Rd, then just e. **Facility:** Smoke free premises. 132 units. 108 one- and 24 two-bedroom standard units, some with efficiencies or kitchens. 3 stories, interior corridors. **Parking:** on-site. **Terms:** cancellation fee imposed. **Amenities:** video games (fee), high-speed Internet, voice mail, irons, hair dryers. **Pool(s):** outdoor. **Leisure Activities:** whirlpool, exercise room, sports court. **Guest Services:** valet and coin laundry, area transportation, wireless Internet. **Business Services:** meeting rooms, business center. **Cards:** AX, CB, DC, DS, JC, MC, VI.

Residence Inn Marriott

AAA Benefit:
Members save a minimum 5% off the best available rate.

FEE CALL / SOME UNITS FEE

STUDIO 6 #6023 Book at AAA.com Phone: (770)931-3113 95

Hotel
$59-$63 5/23-11/30
$57-$61 12/1-5/22

Address: 3525 Breckinridge Blvd **Location:** I-85, exit 104, just e to Breckinridge Blvd, then just n. **Facility:** 130 one-bedroom standard units with efficiencies. 2 stories (no elevator), exterior corridors. **Parking:** on-site. **Terms:** office hours 7 am-2 pm. **Amenities:** high-speed Internet (fee), voice mail, irons. **Guest Services:** coin laundry, wireless Internet. **Business Services:** fax (fee). **Cards:** AX, CB, DC, DS, JC, MC, VI.

FEE CALL / SOME UNITS FEE

WINGATE INN Book at AAA.com Phone: 770/622-7277 90

Hotel
Rates not provided

Address: 3450 Venture Pkwy **Location:** I-85, exit 104, just w to Venture Pkwy, then just n. **Facility:** 90 units. 86 one-bedroom standard units. 4 one-bedroom suites. 5 stories, interior corridors. **Parking:** on-site. **Amenities:** video games (fee), high-speed Internet, dual phone lines, voice mail, safes, irons, hair dryers. **Pool(s):** outdoor. **Leisure Activities:** whirlpool, exercise room. **Guest Services:** valet and coin laundry, area transportation, wireless Internet. **Business Services:** meeting rooms, business center.

FEE CALL / SOME UNITS

WHERE TO DINE

ATHEN'S PIZZA KOUZZINA Phone: 770/813-1369 76

Mediterranean
$3-$24

Kouzzina—from the Greek word meaning "kitchen"—serves a nice selection of Greek specialties, including moussaka, souvlaki and gyros. Pizza and Italian favorites round out the menu. Casual dress. **Bar:** Full bar. **Hours:** 11 am-9 pm, Fri & Sat-10 pm. Closed: 4/12, 11/26, 12/25. **Address:** 2205 Pleasant Hill Rd **Location:** I-85, exit 104, 0.8 mi w; opposite Gwinnett Mall; in Pleasant Hill Square. **Parking:** on-site. **Cards:** AX, DS, MC, VI.

CALIFORNIA DREAMING Phone: 770/813-9240

American
$8-$23

The full-service, fine-dining restaurant appeals to adults, particularly those with an appetite for innovative concepts in food. Revised weekly, the menu consistently incorporates sophisticated, cutting-edge California dishes with Pacific Rim influences throughout. Among house specialties are flatbread appetizers baked in a brick oven, sushi, sashimi and some vegetarian dishes. The wine list focuses primarily on California vintages. Casual dress. **Bar:** Full bar. **Hours:** 11 am-10 pm, Fri & Sat-11 pm. **Address:** 1630 Distribution Dr **Location:** I-85, exit 108, just w, then just s. **Parking:** on-site. **Cards:** AX, DC, DS, MC, VI.

HARU ICHIBAN JAPANESE RESTAURANT Phone: 770/622-4060 77

Japanese
$3-$33

Both traditional and contemporary Japanese cuisines are featured on the restaurant's menu. Casual dress. **Bar:** Beer & wine. **Reservations:** accepted, weekdays. **Hours:** 11:30 am-2:30 & 6-10:30 pm, Sat from 6 pm. Closed: 12/25; also Sun. **Address:** 3646 Satellite Blvd **Location:** I-85, exit 104, 0.3 mi w; in Mall Corners Shopping Center. **Parking:** on-site. **Cards:** AX, MC, VI.

CALL

(See map and index starting on p. 302)

J.R.'S LOG HOUSE **Phone:** 770/476-1766 (73)

American
$3-$13

The family restaurant prides itself on pit-cooked barbecue and Brunswick stew. Homemade desserts, including peach cobbler, round out the menu. Casual dress. **Bar:** Beer & wine. **Hours:** 7 am-8:30 pm, Fri & Sat-9 pm, Sun 8 am-8:30 pm. Closed: 11/26, 12/25. **Address:** 10270 Medlock Bridge Rd **Location:** Jct Wilson Rd, just s. **Parking:** on-site. **Cards:** AX, DC, DS, MC, VI.

KURT'S AND VRENY'S BIERGARTEN **Phone:** 770/623-4128 (75)

Continental
$4-$36

Enjoy fine dining in a quiet, rural setting. Gracious servers attend to your needs as you sample traditional German dishes like Wiener schnitzel. A flambe dessert or a Bavarian-style chocolate cake would be the perfect ending to a very nice meal. Dressy casual. **Bar:** Full bar. **Reservations:** suggested. **Hours:** 5:30 pm-11 pm. Closed: 1/1, 12/25; also Sun. **Address:** 4225 River Green Pkwy **Location:** Jct Peachtree Industrial Blvd and Pleasant Hill Rd, 1 mi n. **Parking:** on-site. **Cards:** AX, CB, DC, DS, MC, VI.

LA MADELEINE FRENCH BAKERY & CAFE **Phone:** 770/814-0355

French
$7-$15

The aroma of fresh breads and pastries fills the dining room, which nurtures a cafe atmosphere. Topped with sun-dried tomatoes and mozzarella, pizza Rivera is a mouthwatering treat rivaled only by the pastries on display at the entrance. Infusions of flowers always delight, and breakfast is served all day. Casual dress. **Bar:** Beer & wine. **Hours:** 7 am-10 pm. Closed: 12/25. **Address:** 2255 Pleasant Hill Rd, Suite 480 **Location:** I-85, exit 104, just n. **Parking:** on-site. **Cards:** AX, DS, MC, VI.

MAMA FU'S **Phone:** 678/213-0521

Asian
$7-$15

The funky, crowded restaurant offers a fun mix of dishes from Asian cultures, including ahi tuna from Japan, noodle bowls and basil rolls from Vietnam, curries from Thailand and lo mein pot stickers from China. The food is a super value. Casual dress. **Bar:** Beer & wine. **Hours:** 11 am-9 pm, Fri & Sat-10 pm. **Address:** 6590 Sugarloaf Pkwy, Suite 201 **Location:** I-85, exit 108, 0.8 mi w. **Parking:** on-site. **Cards:** AX, DS, MC, VI.

CALL

SIA'S **Phone:** 770/497-9727 (72)

New American
$6-$32

The excellent cuisine here is creative, innovative and imaginative with strong Southwestern slant and a touch of Asian influence. The sleek, chic contemporary dining room enhances the dining experience. Dressy casual. **Bar:** Full bar. **Reservations:** suggested. **Hours:** 11:30 am-2 & 5:30-10 pm, Fri & Sat 5 pm-10:30 pm. Closed major holidays; also Sun, except Mother's Day. **Address:** 10305 Medlock Bridge Rd **Location:** In Shoppes at St. Ives. **Parking:** on-site. **Cards:** AX, CB, DC, DS, JC, MC, VI.

CALL

STONEY RIVER **Phone:** 770/497-6676 (74)

American
$7-$33

Flagstone, leather and polished wood contribute to the ambience of an upscale lodge. In addition to well-prepared cuts of steak, patrons can choose from such tempting side dishes as sauteed spinach and onion mashed potatoes. Dressy casual. **Bar:** Full bar. **Reservations:** suggested. **Hours:** 5 pm-10:30 pm, Fri-11 pm, Sat 4 pm-11 pm, Sun noon-10 pm. Closed major holidays. **Address:** 5800 State Bridge Rd **Location:** Corner of State Bridge and Medlock Bridge rds. **Parking:** on-site. **Cards:** AX, DC, DS, MC, VI.

SUPER GRAND BUFFET **Phone:** 770/923-6660 (78)

Asian
$6-$11

The enormous buffet lines up Chinese, Japanese, Korean, Italian and American dishes, in addition to sushi preparations and Mongolian barbecue. The quality is a cut above the typical buffet standards. Casual dress. **Hours:** 10:30 am-10:30 pm, Fri-Sun to 11 pm. Closed: 12/25. **Address:** 1630 Pleasant Hill Rd **Location:** I-85, exit 104, 0.5 mi e; in Wal-Mart Shopping Center. **Parking:** on-site. **Cards:** AX, CB, DC, DS, JC, MC, VI.

CALL

EAST POINT pop. 39,595 (See map and index starting on p. 312)

WHERE TO STAY

COMFORT INN & SUITES ATLANTA AIRPORT CAMP CREEK *Book at AAA.com* **Phone:** (404)762-5566 (45)

Hotel
$79-$119 All Year

Address: 3601 N Desert Dr **Location:** I-285, exit 2, just e. **Facility:** 188 one-bedroom standard units, some with efficiencies. 5 stories, interior corridors. **Parking:** on-site. **Terms:** 30 day cancellation notice-fee imposed. **Amenities:** high-speed Internet, voice mail, irons, hair dryers. **Pool(s):** heated indoor. **Leisure Activities:** whirlpool, exercise room. **Guest Services:** valet and coin laundry, wireless Internet. **Business Services:** meeting rooms, business center. **Cards:** AX, CB, DC, DS, JC, MC, VI.

ASK CALL / SOME UNITS FEE

COUNTRY INN & SUITES BY CARLSON *Book great rates at AAA.com* **Phone:** (404)767-9787 (38)

AAA SAVE

Hotel
$97-$105 All Year

Address: 1365 Hardin Ave **Location:** I-85, exit 73 southbound; exit 73B northbound, just w. **Facility:** 71 units. 43 one-bedroom standard units. 28 one-bedroom suites. 3 stories, interior corridors. **Parking:** on-site. **Terms:** cancellation fee imposed. **Amenities:** high-speed Internet, dual phone lines, voice mail, safes, irons, hair dryers. **Pool(s):** heated indoor. **Leisure Activities:** whirlpool, exercise room. **Guest Services:** valet and coin laundry, airport transportation-The William B. Hartsfield Atlanta Int'l Airport, area transportation-MARTA, wireless Internet. **Business Services:** meeting rooms, business center. **Cards:** AX, DS, MC, VI. **Free Special Amenities: expanded continental breakfast and high-speed Internet.**

(See map and index starting on p. 312)

CROWNE PLAZA HOTEL AND RESORT ATLANTA AIRPORT *Book at AAA.com* **Phone:** (404)768-6660 41

Hotel
$89-$209 All Year

Address: 1325 Virginia Ave **Location:** I-85, exit 73 southbound; exit 73B northbound, just w. **Facility:** 378 units. 376 one-bedroom standard units. 2 one-bedroom suites. 12 stories, interior corridors. *Bath:* combo or shower only. **Parking:** on-site. **Amenities:** video games (fee), CD players, voice mail, irons, hair dryers. **Pool(s):** outdoor. **Leisure Activities:** exercise room. **Guest Services:** valet and coin laundry, wireless Internet. **Business Services:** conference facilities, business center. **Cards:** AX, CB, DC, DS, JC, MC, VI.

ASK CALL / SOME UNITS FEE

DOUBLETREE CLUB HOTEL ATLANTA AIRPORT *Book great rates at AAA.com* **Phone:** (404)763-1600 35

Hotel
$79-$179 All Year

Address: 3400 Norman Berry Dr **Location:** I-85, exit 73 southbound, just e to Bobby Brown Pkwy, 0.4 mi n to Norman Berry Dr, then just s; exit 73B northbound. **Facility:** 220 one-bedroom standard units. 6 stories, interior corridors. *Bath:* combo or shower only. **Parking:** on-site. **Terms:** 1-30 night minimum stay, cancellation fee imposed. **Amenities:** dual phone lines, voice mail, irons, hair dryers. **Pool(s):** heated outdoor. **Leisure Activities:** whirlpool, exercise room. **Guest Services:** valet laundry, area transportation, wireless Internet. **Business Services:** meeting rooms, business center. **Cards:** AX, CB, DC, DS, JC, MC, VI.

CALL / SOME UNITS

DOUBLETREE
HOTELS·SUITES·RESORTS·CLUBS
AAA Benefit:
Members save 5% or more everyday!

DRURY INN & SUITES-ATLANTA AIRPORT *Book at AAA.com* **Phone:** (404)761-4900 42

Hotel
$90-$170 All Year

Address: 1270 Virginia Ave **Location:** I-85, exit 73 southbound; exit 73A northbound, just e. **Facility:** 152 units. 133 one-bedroom standard units. 19 one-bedroom suites. 6 stories, interior corridors. **Parking:** on-site. **Amenities:** high-speed Internet, voice mail, irons, hair dryers. **Pool(s):** heated indoor/outdoor. **Leisure Activities:** whirlpool, exercise room. **Guest Services:** valet and coin laundry, wireless Internet. **Business Services:** meeting rooms, business center. **Cards:** AX, DC, DS, MC, VI.

ASK CALL / SOME UNITS

FAIRFIELD INN & SUITES *Book great rates at AAA.com* **Phone:** (404)767-5374 36

Hotel
$128-$137 All Year

Address: 1255 Walker Ave **Location:** I-85, exit 73 southbound; exit 73B northbound, just e to Bobby Brown Pkwy, then just n. **Facility:** Smoke free premises. 85 units. 55 one-bedroom standard units, some with whirlpools. 30 one-bedroom suites, some with whirlpools. 6 stories, interior corridors. *Bath:* combo or shower only. **Parking:** on-site. **Terms:** cancellation fee imposed. **Amenities:** high-speed Internet, dual phone lines, voice mail, irons, hair dryers. *Some:* CD players. **Pool(s):** outdoor. **Leisure Activities:** limited exercise equipment. **Guest Services:** valet and coin laundry, area transportation, wireless Internet. **Business Services:** meeting rooms, business center. **Cards:** AX, DS, MC, VI.

CALL

AAA Benefit:
Members save a minimum 5% off the best available rate.

HAMPTON INN & SUITES-ATLANTA AIRPORT NORTH *Book great rates at AAA.com* **Phone:** (404)767-9300 37

Hotel
$109-$199 All Year

Address: 3450 Bobby Brown Pkwy **Location:** I-85, exit 73 southbound; exit 73B northbound, just e to Bobby Brown Pkwy, then just n. **Facility:** 105 units. 85 one-bedroom standard units, some with whirlpools. 20 one-bedroom suites. 8 stories, interior corridors. **Parking:** on-site. **Terms:** 3 day cancellation notice. **Amenities:** video games (fee), dual phone lines, voice mail, irons, hair dryers. **Pool(s):** outdoor. **Leisure Activities:** exercise room. **Guest Services:** valet and coin laundry, area transportation, wireless Internet. **Business Services:** meeting rooms, business center. **Cards:** AX, CB, DC, DS, JC, MC, VI.

/ SOME UNITS

AAA Benefit:
Members save up to 10% everyday!

HYATT PLACE ATLANTA AIRPORT - NORTH *Book great rates at AAA.com* **Phone:** (404)768-8484

AAA SAVE

Hotel
$99-$299 All Year

Address: 3415 Norman Berry Dr **Location:** I-85, exit 73 southbound, just e to Bobby Brown Pkwy, then just n; exit 73B northbound. **Facility:** 150 one-bedroom standard units. 6 stories, interior corridors. **Parking:** on-site. **Terms:** cancellation fee imposed. **Amenities:** video games (fee), high-speed Internet, voice mail, safes, irons, hair dryers. **Pool(s):** outdoor. **Leisure Activities:** exercise room. **Guest Services:** valet laundry, airport transportation-The William B. Hartsfield Atlanta Int'l Airport, area transportation-MARTA, wireless Internet. **Business Services:** meeting rooms, business center. **Cards:** AX, CB, DS, MC, VI. **Free Special Amenities: continental breakfast and high-speed Internet.**

CALL / SOME UNITS

HYATT
PLACE
AAA Benefit:
Ask for the AAA rate and save 10%.

(See map and index starting on p. 312)

RAMADA ATLANTA AIRPORT CONFERENCE CENTER — **Phone:** (404)762-8411 44

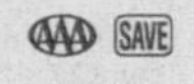

Hotel
$109-$159 All Year

Address: 1380 Virginia Ave **Location:** I-85, exit 73 southbound; exit 73B northbound, just w. **Facility:** 493 units. 492 one-bedroom standard units. 1 one-bedroom suite. 4-5 stories, interior/exterior corridors. **Parking:** on-site. **Terms:** cancellation fee imposed. **Amenities:** video games (fee), voice mail, irons, hair dryers. **Pool(s):** outdoor. **Leisure Activities:** limited exercise equipment. **Guest Services:** valet and coin laundry, airport transportation-The William B. Hartsfield Atlanta Int'l Airport, area transportation-MARTA, wireless Internet. **Business Services:** conference facilities, business center. **Cards:** AX, CB, DC, DS, MC, VI. **Free Special Amenities: preferred room (subject to availability with advance reservations) and high-speed Internet.**

CALL / SOME UNITS FEE

RED ROOF INN-ATLANTA AIRPORT NORTH — *Book great rates at AAA.com* — **Phone:** (404)209-1800 43

Hotel
$71-$81 All Year

Address: 1200 Virginia Ave **Location:** I-85, exit 73 southbound; exit 73A northbound, just e. **Facility:** 193 one-bedroom standard units. 6 stories, interior corridors. **Parking:** on-site. **Terms:** cancellation fee imposed. **Amenities:** high-speed Internet, voice mail, irons, hair dryers. **Pool(s):** outdoor. **Leisure Activities:** exercise room. **Guest Services:** valet and coin laundry, wireless Internet. **Business Services:** business center. **Cards:** AX, DS, MC, VI.

ASK CALL / SOME UNITS FEE

WELLESLEY INN (ATLANTA/HARTSFIELD INT'L AIRPORT) — *Book great rates at AAA.com* — **Phone:** (404)762-5111 40

Hotel
$79-$119 All Year

Address: 1377 Virginia Ave **Location:** I-85, exit 73 southbound; exit 73B northbound, just w. **Facility:** 191 one-bedroom standard units. 6 stories, interior corridors. **Parking:** on-site. **Amenities:** video games (fee), high-speed Internet, voice mail, irons, hair dryers. **Pool(s):** outdoor. **Leisure Activities:** exercise room. **Guest Services:** valet and coin laundry, airport transportation-The William B. Hartsfield Atlanta Int'l Airport, wireless Internet. **Business Services:** meeting rooms, PC, fax (fee). **Cards:** AX, DC, DS, MC, VI. **Free Special Amenities: local telephone calls and high-speed Internet.**

/ SOME UNITS FEE

WHERE TO DINE

GIOVANNA'S ITALIAN KITCHEN — **Phone:** 404/762-6755 47

Italian
$5-$24

Menu offerings include a great variety of classic, Italian pasta dishes, steaks, seafood and other traditional American favorites. The decor is handsome and the service very competent. Casual dress. **Bar:** Full bar. **Reservations:** accepted. **Hours:** 6:30 am-10 & 11-11 pm. Closed major holidays. **Address:** 1375 Virginia Ave **Location:** I-85, exit 73, just w. **Parking:** on-site. **Cards:** AX, CB, DC, DS, JC, MC, VI.

LOV'N IT LIVE — **Phone:** 404/765-9220 46

Natural/Organic
$9-$18

The eatery specializes in "slow" and "live" food that's organic, natural, whole, vegetarian and prepared to retain enzymes to optimize health benefits and nutrition. Daily specials are worth consideration, as is the sage "burger". Casual dress. **Reservations:** accepted. **Hours:** 11 am-8 pm, Thurs-7 pm, Fri-9 pm, Sat 2 pm-9 pm, Sun 2 pm-7 pm. Closed: Mon. **Address:** 2796 E Point St **Location:** Just w of Main St; downtown. **Parking:** street. **Cards:** MC, VI.

MALONE'S STEAK & SEAFOOD — **Phone:** 404/762-5577 48

American
$8-$22

Near the airport, this casual restaurant presents a traditional menu of certified Angus beef steaks, ribs, seafood, sandwiches and salads. Casual dress. **Bar:** Full bar. **Reservations:** accepted. **Hours:** 11 am-midnight, Fri & Sat-1 am, Sun-11:30 pm. Closed: 11/26, 12/25. **Address:** 1258 Virginia Ave **Location:** I-85, exit 73 southbound; exit 73A northbound, just e. **Parking:** on-site. **Cards:** AX, DC, DS, MC, VI.

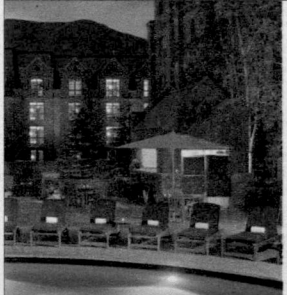

FAIRBURN pop. 5,464 (See map and index starting on p. 312)

WHERE TO STAY

HAMPTON INN ATLANTA/FAIRBURN *Book great rates at AAA.com* Phone: (678)782-4600 109

Hotel
$99-$129 All Year

Address: 7790 Ella Ln **Location:** I-85, exit 61, just e. Located behind McDonald's. **Facility:** 99 one-bedroom standard units. 4 stories, interior corridors. *Bath:* combo or shower only. **Parking:** on-site. **Terms:** 5 day cancellation notice. **Amenities:** video games, high-speed Internet, voice mail, irons, hair dryers. **Pool(s):** outdoor. **Leisure Activities:** exercise room. **Guest Services:** valet and coin laundry, area transportation, wireless Internet. **Business Services:** meeting rooms, business center. **Cards:** AX, DC, DS, JC, MC, VI.

CALL / SOME UNITS

AAA Benefit:
Members save up to 10% everyday!

HOLIDAY INN EXPRESS HOTEL & SUITES FAIRBURN

fyi
Hotel
$89-$129 All Year

Too new to rate, opening scheduled for October 2008. **Address:** 7905 Peachtree Landing Cir **Location:** I-85, exit 61. **Amenities:** 82 units, coffeemakers, microwaves, refrigerators, pool. **Terms:** 10 day cancellation notice-fee imposed. **Cards:** AX, DC, DS, MC, VI. ***(See color ad below)***

WINGATE INN *Book at AAA.com* Phone: (770)892-3006 110

Hotel
$99 All Year

Address: 7882 Senoia Rd **Location:** I-85, exit 61, 0.3 mi se on SR 74. **Facility:** 66 units. 58 one-bedroom standard units, some with whirlpools. 8 one-bedroom suites. 4 stories, interior corridors. *Bath:* combo or shower only. **Parking:** on-site. **Terms:** cancellation fee imposed. **Amenities:** video games (fee), high-speed Internet, dual phone lines, voice mail, safes, irons, hair dryers. **Pool(s):** indoor. **Leisure Activities:** sauna, whirlpool, exercise room. **Guest Services:** valet laundry, wireless Internet. **Business Services:** meeting rooms, business center. **Cards:** AX, CB, DC, DS, JC, MC, VI.

ASK / SOME UNITS

FOREST PARK pop. 21,447 (See map and index starting on p. 312)

WHERE TO STAY

DAYS INN-AIRPORT EAST *Book at AAA.com* Phone: (404)768-6400 74

Motel
$53-$95 All Year

Address: 5116 Hwy 85 **Location:** I-75, exit 237A southbound; exit 237 northbound, 0.5 mi w. **Facility:** 199 one-bedroom standard units. 4 stories, exterior corridors. **Parking:** on-site. **Amenities:** voice mail, safes, hair dryers. *Some:* high-speed Internet. **Pool(s):** outdoor. **Leisure Activities:** exercise room privileges. **Guest Services:** valet and coin laundry, wireless Internet. **Business Services:** meeting rooms, fax (fee). **Cards:** AX, CB, DC, DS, MC, VI.

ASK / SOME UNITS FEE

▼ *See AAA listing above* ▼

(See map and index starting on p. 312)

ECONO LODGE Book at AAA.com Phone: (404)363-6429 73

Motel
$40-$53 All Year

Address: 5060 Frontage Rd **Location:** I-75, exit 237, just e to Frontage Rd, then just s. **Facility:** 58 one-bedroom standard units. 2 stories, exterior corridors. **Parking:** on-site. **Terms:** cancellation fee imposed. **Amenities:** high-speed Internet, irons, hair dryers. **Guest Services:** coin laundry, wireless Internet. **Business Services:** fax. **Cards:** AX, DC, DS, MC, VI.

ASK / SOME UNITS FEE

RAMADA LIMITED SUITES Book at AAA.com Phone: (404)768-7799 75

Hotel
$65-$125 All Year

Address: 357 Lee St **Location:** I-75, exit 237A southbound; exit 237 northbound, 0.5 mi w. **Facility:** 79 one-bedroom standard units. 4 stories, interior corridors. **Parking:** on-site **Amenities:** high-speed Internet, voice mail, safes (fee), irons, hair dryers. **Pool(s):** outdoor. **Leisure Activities:** exercise room. **Guest Services:** valet and coin laundry, wireless Internet. **Business Services:** meeting rooms, PC, fax (fee). **Cards:** AX, CB, DC, DS, JC, MC, VI.

ASK CALL / SOME UNITS

SUPER 8 MOTEL Book at AAA.com Phone: (404)363-8811 76

Motel
$50-$100 All Year

Address: 410 Old Dixie Way **Location:** I-75, exit 235, just e. **Facility:** 53 one-bedroom standard units, some with whirlpools. 2 stories (no elevator), exterior corridors. **Parking:** on-site. **Amenities:** high-speed Internet, hair dryers. **Pool(s):** outdoor. **Guest Services:** coin laundry, wireless Internet. **Business Services:** PC, fax. **Cards:** AX, CB, DC, DS, MC, VI.

ASK / SOME UNITS FEE

WHERE TO DINE

OAKWOOD CAFE Phone: 404/214-5663 56

Southern
$3-$16

"Good ole country cookin" is the staple at this hugely popular restaurant, which is set at the Farmer's Market on the south side of Atlanta. There's no denying the vegetables are fresh and tasty; they're hand-selected from the market next door. Casual dress. **Hours:** 6 am-9 pm, Sat from 7 am. Closed major holidays; also Sun. **Address:** 16 Forest Pkwy **Location:** I-75, exit 237, just e; in State Farmers. **Parking:** on-site. **Cards:** AX, DS, MC, VI.

HAPEVILLE pop. 6,180 (See map and index starting on p. 312)

WHERE TO STAY

BEST WESTERN ATLANTA AIRPORT EAST Book great rates at AAA.com Phone: (404)479-1100 32

AAA SAVE

Hotel
$90-$150 All Year

Address: 301 N Central Ave **Location:** I-75, exit 239, just w; I-85, exit 75, 1.5 mi e. **Facility:** 188 one-bedroom standard units, some with efficiencies and/or whirlpools. 2-10 stories, interior corridors. **Parking:** on-site. **Amenities:** video games (fee), high-speed Internet, voice mail, irons, hair dryers. **Pool(s):** outdoor. **Leisure Activities:** exercise room. **Guest Services:** valet and coin laundry, airport transportation-The William B. Hartsfield Atlanta Int'l Airport, wireless Internet. **Business Services:** meeting rooms, business center. **Cards:** AX, DC, DS, MC, VI. **Free Special Amenities: continental breakfast and high-speed Internet.** *(See color ad p 322)*

AAA Benefit:
Members save up to 20%, plus 10% bonus points with rewards program.

/ SOME UNITS

COURTYARD BY MARRIOTT ATLANTA AIRPORT NORTH Book great rates at AAA.com Phone: (404)559-1043 29

AAA SAVE

Hotel
$197-$212 All Year

Address: 3399 International Blvd **Location:** I-85, exit 73 southbound; exit 73A northbound, 0.5 mi e to International Blvd, then just n. **Facility:** Smoke free premises. 151 units. 139 one-bedroom standard units. 12 one-bedroom suites. 4 stories, interior corridors. **Parking:** on-site. **Terms:** cancellation fee imposed. **Amenities:** video games (fee), dual phone lines, voice mail, irons, hair dryers. **Pool(s):** outdoor. **Leisure Activities:** whirlpool, exercise room. **Guest Services:** valet and coin laundry, airport transportation-The William B. Hartsfield Atlanta Int'l Airport, wireless Internet. **Business Services:** meeting rooms, business center. **Cards:** AX, CB, DC, DS, JC, MC, VI. **Free Special Amenities: newspaper and high-speed Internet.**

AAA Benefit:
Members save a minimum 5% off the best available rate.

(See map and index starting on p. 312)

HILTON ATLANTA AIRPORT *Book great rates at AAA.com* **Phone:** (404)767-9000 31

Hotel
$99-$229 All Year

Address: 1031 Virginia Ave **Location:** I-85, exit 73 southbound; exit 73A northbound, just e. **Facility:** The atrium and common area decor provide a feeling of elegance. 504 units. 499 one-bedroom standard units. 5 one-bedroom suites. 17 stories, interior corridors. **Parking:** on-site (fee) and valet. **Terms:** 1-30 night minimum stay, cancellation fee imposed. **Amenities:** dual phone lines, voice mail, irons, hair dryers. *Fee:* video games, high-speed Internet. **Pool(s):** outdoor, heated indoor. **Leisure Activities:** whirlpool. *Fee:* lighted tennis court. **Guest Services:** valet laundry, area transportation, beauty salon, wireless Internet. **Business Services:** conference facilities, business center. **Cards:** AX, CB, DC, DS, JC, MC, VI.

CALL / SOME UNITS

AAA Benefit:
Members save 5% or more everyday!

RESIDENCE INN ATLANTA AIRPORT *Book great rates at AAA.com* **Phone:** (404)761-0511 30

AAA SAVE

Hotel
$246-$264 All Year

Address: 3401 International Blvd **Location:** I-85, exit 73 southbound; exit 73A northbound, 0.5 mi e to International Blvd, then just n. **Facility:** Smoke free premises. 126 units. 94 one- and 32 two-bedroom standard units with kitchens. 2 stories (no elevator), interior/exterior corridors. **Parking:** on-site. **Terms:** cancellation fee imposed. **Amenities:** video games (fee), high-speed Internet, voice mail, irons, hair dryers. **Pool(s):** outdoor. **Leisure Activities:** whirlpool, exercise room, sports court. **Guest Services:** valet and coin laundry, airport transportation-The William B. Hartsfield Atlanta Int'l Airport, area transportation, wireless Internet. **Business Services:** meeting rooms, business center. **Cards:** AX, CB, DC, DS, JC, MC, VI. **Free Special Amenities: full breakfast and high-speed Internet.**

/ SOME UNITS FEE

AAA Benefit:
Members save a minimum 5% off the best available rate.

JONESBORO pop. 3,829 (See map and index starting on p. 312)

WHERE TO STAY

HOLIDAY INN ATLANTA SOUTH JONESBORO *Book great rates at AAA.com* **Phone:** (770)968-4300 99

AAA SAVE

Hotel
$75-$175 All Year

Address: 6288 Old Dixie Hwy **Location:** I-75, exit 235, just w. **Facility:** 180 one-bedroom standard units. 6 stories, interior corridors. *Bath:* combo or shower only. **Parking:** on-site. **Amenities:** video games (fee), high-speed Internet, voice mail, irons, hair dryers. **Pool(s):** outdoor. **Leisure Activities:** playground, exercise room. **Guest Services:** valet and coin laundry, wireless Internet. **Business Services:** meeting rooms, PC. **Cards:** AX, CB, DC, DS, MC, VI.

CALL / SOME UNITS FEE

TARA INN & SUITES *Book at AAA.com* **Phone:** (678)674-1360 100

Hotel
$70-$130 All Year

Address: 628 Southside Commercial Pkwy **Location:** I-75, exit 235, 1.1 mi sw on US 19/41; in Southside Commercial Park. **Facility:** 127 units. 125 one-bedroom standard units, some with efficiencies and/or whirlpools. 2 one-bedroom suites with kitchens. 3 stories, interior corridors. **Parking:** on-site. **Amenities:** high-speed Internet, voice mail. *Some:* DVD players (fee), hair dryers. **Pool(s):** outdoor. **Leisure Activities:** whirlpool, exercise room. **Guest Services:** coin laundry, wireless Internet. **Business Services:** meeting rooms. **Cards:** AX, CB, DC, DS, JC, MC, VI.

ASK / SOME UNITS FEE VCR

WHERE TO DINE

SONNY'S REAL PIT BAR-B-Q **Phone:** 770/968-0052

Barbecue
$6-$15

House specialties include pork and chicken grilled over an open pit, barbecue ribs and fresh, homemade pie. The salad bar offers another popular option. Rustic and comfortable, the atmosphere is perfect for family meals. Casual dress. **Bar:** Beer only. **Hours:** 11 am-9:30 pm, Fri & Sat-10 pm. Closed: 11/26, 12/25. **Address:** 641 Mount Zion Rd **Location:** Jct US 19/41, just e on Morrow Industrial Blvd. **Parking:** on-site. **Cards:** AX, DS, MC, VI.

KENNESAW pop. 21,675 (See map and index starting on p. 296)

WHERE TO STAY

BEST WESTERN KENNESAW INN *Book great rates at AAA.com* **Phone:** (770)424-7666 25

AAA SAVE

Hotel
$90-$100 All Year

Address: 3375 Busbee Dr **Location:** I-75, exit 271, just e. **Facility:** 106 one-bedroom standard units. 2 stories, exterior corridors. **Parking:** on-site. **Amenities:** irons, hair dryers. *Some:* high-speed Internet. **Pool(s):** outdoor. **Guest Services:** coin laundry, wireless Internet. **Business Services:** fax (fee). **Cards:** AX, CB, DC, DS, JC, MC, VI. **Free Special Amenities: continental breakfast and high-speed Internet.**

FEE / SOME UNITS FEE

Best Western

AAA Benefit:
Members save up to 20%, plus 10% bonus points with rewards program.

COMFORT INN *Book at AAA.com* **Phone:** (770)499-9200 32

Hotel
$89-$119 All Year

Address: 2489 George Busbee Pkwy **Location:** I-75, exit 269. Located adjacent to Holiday Inn Express and Town Center Mall. **Facility:** 61 one-bedroom standard units. 5 stories, interior corridors. **Parking:** on-site. **Amenities:** high-speed Internet, irons, hair dryers. **Guest Services:** valet laundry, wireless Internet. **Business Services:** meeting rooms, fax. **Cards:** AX, DS, MC, VI.

ASK FEE CALL / SOME UNITS

(See map and index starting on p. 296)

COUNTRY INN & SUITES BY CARLSON *Book great rates at AAA.com* **Phone:** (770)423-7105 27

AAA SAVE

Hotel
$99-$155 All Year

Address: 3192 Barrett Lakes Blvd **Location:** I-75, exit 271, just w to Barrett Lakes Blvd, then just s. **Facility:** 46 units. 33 one-bedroom standard units. 13 one-bedroom suites, some with whirlpools. 2 stories, interior corridors. **Parking:** on-site. **Terms:** 2 night minimum stay - seasonal and/or weekends. **Amenities:** high-speed Internet, voice mail, safes, irons, hair dryers. **Pool(s):** outdoor. **Leisure Activities:** exercise room. **Guest Services:** valet and coin laundry, wireless Internet. **Business Services:** meeting rooms, business center. **Cards:** AX, CB, DC, DS, JC, MC, VI. **Free Special Amenities: expanded continental breakfast and high-speed Internet.**

/ SOME UNITS

DAYS INN *Book at AAA.com* **Phone:** (770)419-1576 37

Hotel
$55-$79 All Year

Address: 760 Cobb Place Blvd **Location:** I-75, exit 269, just w. **Facility:** 80 one-bedroom standard units. 2 stories (no elevator), exterior corridors. **Parking:** on-site. **Terms:** 7 day cancellation notice. **Amenities:** high-speed Internet, voice mail, irons, hair dryers. **Pool(s):** outdoor. **Guest Services:** valet and coin laundry, wireless Internet. **Business Services:** conference facilities, PC, fax (fee). **Cards:** AX, DC, DS, MC, VI.

ASK FEE CALL / SOME UNITS FEE

EXTENDED STAYAMERICA *Book at AAA.com* **Phone:** (770)422-1403 29

Hotel
$55-$70 All Year

Address: 3000 George Busbee Pkwy **Location:** I-75, exit 269, just e to George Busbee Pkwy, then 0.8 mi n. **Facility:** 104 one-bedroom standard units with efficiencies. 3 stories, interior corridors. **Parking:** on-site. **Terms:** office hours 7 am-11 pm. **Amenities:** high-speed Internet (fee), voice mail, irons. **Guest Services:** coin laundry, wireless Internet. **Business Services:** fax (fee). **Cards:** AX, CB, DC, DS, JC, MC, VI.

ASK CALL / SOME UNITS FEE

FAIRFIELD INN & SUITES *Book great rates at AAA.com* **Phone:** (770)427-9700 24

Hotel
$123-$132 All Year

Address: 3425 Busbee Dr **Location:** I-75, exit 271, just e. **Facility:** Smoke free premises. 87 one-bedroom standard units. 3 stories, interior corridors. **Parking:** on-site. **Terms:** cancellation fee imposed. **Amenities:** high-speed Internet, dual phone lines, voice mail, irons, hair dryers. *Some:* DVD players, CD players. **Pool(s):** outdoor. **Leisure Activities:** whirlpool, limited exercise equipment. **Guest Services:** valet and coin laundry, wireless Internet. **Business Services:** meeting rooms, business center. **Cards:** AX, CB, DC, DS, JC, MC, VI. .

FEE CALL / SOME UNITS VCR

Fairfield Inn & Suites Marriott

AAA Benefit:
Members save a minimum 5% off the best available rate.

GREEN ROOF INN & SUITES *Book great rates at AAA.com* **Phone:** (770)529-3370

AAA SAVE

Motel
$45-$120 All Year

Address: 3027 Cobb Pkwy NW **Location:** I-75, exit 271, 2.5 mi w, then 2.2 mi n on US 41. **Facility:** 40 one-bedroom standard units, some with whirlpools. 2 stories, exterior corridors. **Parking:** on-site. **Amenities:** high-speed Internet, irons, hair dryers. *Some:* DVD players (fee). **Guest Services:** coin laundry, wireless Internet. **Business Services:** fax. **Cards:** AX, DC, DS, MC, VI. **Free Special Amenities: local telephone calls and high-speed Internet.**

CALL / SOME UNITS FEE FEE VCR

HAMPTON INN *Book great rates at AAA.com* **Phone:** (770)426-0017 34

Hotel
$120-$130 All Year

Address: 871 Cobb Place Blvd **Location:** I-75, exit 269, just w to Cobb Place Blvd, then just n. **Facility:** 59 one-bedroom standard units. 3 stories, interior corridors. *Bath:* combo or shower only. **Parking:** on-site. **Terms:** 1-30 night minimum stay, cancellation fee imposed. **Amenities:** video games (fee), high-speed Internet, dual phone lines, voice mail, irons, hair dryers. **Pool(s):** outdoor. **Leisure Activities:** exercise room. **Guest Services:** valet laundry, wireless Internet. **Business Services:** meeting rooms, fax (fee). **Cards:** AX, DC, DS, MC, VI.

FEE CALL / SOME UNITS

Hampton Inn

AAA Benefit:
Members save up to 10% everyday!

HILTON GARDEN INN-ATLANTA NW/KENNESAW TOWN CENTER *Book great rates at AAA.com* **Phone:** (678)322-1140 33

Hotel
$109-$179 All Year

Address: 895 Cobb Place Blvd **Location:** I-75, exit 269, just w to Cobb Place Blvd, then just n. **Facility:** 114 units. 107 one-bedroom standard units, some with whirlpools. 7 one-bedroom suites with whirlpools. 5 stories, interior corridors. **Parking:** on-site. **Amenities:** video games (fee), high-speed Internet, dual phone lines, voice mail, irons, hair dryers. **Pool(s):** heated indoor/outdoor. **Leisure Activities:** whirlpool, exercise room. **Guest Services:** valet and coin laundry, wireless Internet. **Business Services:** meeting rooms, business center. **Cards:** AX, CB, DC, DS, MC, VI.

AAA Benefit:
Members save 5% or more everyday!

(See map and index starting on p. 296)

HOLIDAY INN EXPRESS-TOWN CENTER MALL Book at AAA.com Phone: (770)427-5210 31

Hotel
$105-$179 All Year

Address: 2485 George Busbee Pkwy NW **Location:** I-75, exit 269, northeast corner. Located adjacent to Town Center Mall. **Facility:** 147 units. 146 one-bedroom standard units. 1 one-bedroom suite. 6 stories, interior corridors. **Parking:** on-site. **Terms:** cancellation fee imposed. **Amenities:** high-speed Internet, dual phone lines, voice mail, irons, hair dryers. **Pool(s):** outdoor. **Guest Services:** valet and coin laundry, wireless Internet. **Business Services:** meeting rooms, business center. **Cards:** AX, CB, DC, DS, MC, VI.

ASK FEE CALL / SOME UNITS

LA QUINTA INN Book great rates at AAA.com Phone: (770)426-0045 30

Hotel
$69-$150 All Year

Address: 2625 George Busbee Pkwy **Location:** I-75, exit 269, just e to George Busbee Pkwy, then just n. Located adjacent to Town Center Mall. **Facility:** 59 units. 56 one-bedroom standard units, some with whirlpools. 3 one-bedroom suites with whirlpools. 4 stories, interior corridors. **Parking:** on-site. **Amenities:** high-speed Internet, voice mail, irons, hair dryers. **Pool(s):** outdoor. **Leisure Activities:** limited exercise equipment. **Guest Services:** wireless Internet. **Business Services:** fax (fee). **Cards:** AX, DC, DS, MC, VI.

ASK FEE CALL / SOME UNITS

QUALITY INN Book at AAA.com Phone: (770)419-1530 35

Hotel
$55-$80 All Year

Address: 750 Cobb Place Blvd **Location:** I-75, exit 269, just w. **Facility:** 80 one-bedroom standard units. 2 stories (no elevator), exterior corridors. **Parking:** on-site. **Terms:** 7 day cancellation notice-fee imposed. **Amenities:** high-speed Internet, voice mail, irons, hair dryers. **Pool(s):** outdoor. **Guest Services:** valet and coin laundry, wireless Internet. **Business Services:** conference facilities, PC, fax. **Cards:** AX, CB, DC, DS, MC, VI.

ASK FEE CALL / SOME UNITS FEE

RED ROOF INN-TOWN CENTER MALL Book great rates at AAA.com Phone: (770)429-0323 36

AAA SAVE

Motel
$50-$100 All Year

Address: 520 Roberts Ct NW **Location:** I-75, exit 269, just e. Located opposite Town Center Mall. **Facility:** 135 one-bedroom standard units. 3 stories, exterior corridors. **Parking:** on-site. **Terms:** 14 day cancellation notice. **Amenities:** video games (fee), high-speed Internet, voice mail. **Guest Services:** wireless Internet. **Business Services:** meeting rooms, fax (fee). **Cards:** AX, CB, DC, DS, MC, VI. **Free Special Amenities: local telephone calls.**

FEE CALL / SOME UNITS

RESIDENCE INN BY MARRIOTT TOWN CENTER Book great rates at AAA.com Phone: (770)218-1018 23

AAA SAVE

Hotel
$177-$190 All Year

Address: 3443 Busbee Dr **Location:** I-75, exit 271, just e. **Facility:** Smoke free premises. 120 units. 96 one- and 24 two-bedroom standard units, some with efficiencies or kitchens. 3 stories, interior corridors. **Parking:** on-site. **Terms:** cancellation fee imposed. **Amenities:** video games (fee), high-speed Internet, dual phone lines, voice mail, irons, hair dryers. **Pool(s):** outdoor. **Leisure Activities:** whirlpool, exercise room, sports court. **Guest Services:** valet and coin laundry, area transportation-within 5 mi, wireless Internet. **Business Services:** meeting rooms, PC, fax (fee). **Cards:** AX, CB, DC, DS, MC, VI. **Free Special Amenities: full breakfast and high-speed Internet.**

FEE CALL / SOME UNITS FEE

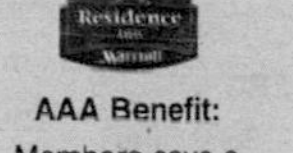

AAA Benefit:
Members save a minimum 5% off the best available rate.

SPRINGHILL SUITES BY MARRIOTT Book great rates at AAA.com Phone: (770)218-5550 26

Hotel
$138-$148 All Year

Address: 3399 Town Point Dr **Location:** I-75, exit 271, just w. **Facility:** Smoke free premises. 90 one-bedroom standard units. 3 stories, interior corridors. **Parking:** on-site. **Terms:** cancellation fee imposed. **Amenities:** high-speed Internet, dual phone lines, voice mail, irons, hair dryers. **Pool(s):** outdoor. **Leisure Activities:** whirlpool, exercise room. **Guest Services:** valet and coin laundry, wireless Internet. **Business Services:** meeting rooms, business center. **Cards:** AX, CB, DC, DS, MC, VI.

FEE CALL

AAA Benefit:
Members save a minimum 5% off the best available rate.

STUDIOPLUS Book at AAA.com Phone: (770)425-6101 28

Hotel
$55-$75 All Year

Address: 3316 Busbee Dr **Location:** I-75, exit 271, just e to Busbee Dr, then just s. **Facility:** 85 one-bedroom standard units with kitchens. 3 stories, interior corridors. **Parking:** on-site. **Terms:** office hours 7 am-11 pm. **Amenities:** high-speed Internet (fee), dual phone lines, voice mail, irons. **Pool(s):** outdoor. **Leisure Activities:** limited exercise equipment. **Guest Services:** coin laundry, wireless Internet. **Business Services:** fax (fee). **Cards:** AX, CB, DC, DS, JC, MC, VI.

ASK FEE CALL / SOME UNITS FEE

(See map and index starting on p. 296)

TRAVELODGE Book at AAA.com Phone: (770)590-0519 22

Motel
$49-$79 All Year

Address: 1460 George Busbee Pkwy **Location:** I-75, exit 273, just e. **Facility:** 54 one-bedroom standard units, some with whirlpools. 2 stories, exterior corridors. **Parking:** on-site. **Amenities:** high-speed Internet, safes, irons, hair dryers. **Pool(s):** outdoor. **Guest Services:** wireless Internet. **Business Services:** meeting rooms, fax (fee). **Cards:** AX, DS, MC, VI.

ASK FEE / SOME UNITS FEE

WINGATE BY WYNDHAM Book great rates at AAA.com Phone: (770)514-7344 38

AAA SAVE

Hotel
$119-$139 All Year

Address: 560 Greers Chapel Dr NW **Location:** I-75, exit 269, just w. **Facility:** 84 units. 82 one-bedroom standard units, some with whirlpools. 2 one-bedroom suites with whirlpools. 3 stories, interior corridors. **Parking:** on-site. **Amenities:** video games (fee), high-speed Internet, dual phone lines, voice mail, safes, irons, hair dryers. **Pool(s):** outdoor. **Leisure Activities:** whirlpool, exercise room. **Guest Services:** valet laundry, area transportation-within 5 mi, wireless Internet. **Business Services:** meeting rooms, business center. **Cards:** AX, DS, MC, VI. **Free Special Amenities: full breakfast and high-speed Internet.**

FEE CALL / SOME UNITS

WHERE TO DINE

BAHAMA BREEZE Phone: 678/354-7777 37

Seafood
$11-$22

Capturing the sights, sounds and sensations of the Caribbean, the restaurant caters to those seeking an exciting evening out. In addition to delicious food, such as fresh mahi mahi and Key lime pie, patrons will find a full bar and scheduled live entertainment. Casual dress. **Bar:** Full bar. **Hours:** 11 am-11 pm, Fri & Sat-midnight. Closed: 11/26, 12/25. **Address:** 755 Ernest Barrett Pkwy NW **Location:** I-75, exit 269, just w. **Parking:** on-site. **Cards:** AX, CB, DC, DS, JC, MC, VI.

BAILEY'S PUB & GRILLE Phone: 770/794-4444

American
$8-$18

Not your typical stuffy Old English Pub, sister restaurants, Bailey's and Fox. Casual dress. **Bar:** Full bar. **Hours:** 11 am-2 am. Closed: 12/25. **Address:** 2500 Cobb Place Ln, Suite 900 **Location:** I-75, exit 269, just w to Cobb Place Ln, then just n. **Parking:** on-site. **Cards:** AX, MC, VI.

BANGKOK CABIN Phone: 770/427-5287 20

Thai
$7-$13

Nestled in a nicely refurbished cottage with a tasteful Asian decor, the restaurant prepares some of the best Thai food outside the Atlanta perimeter. Casual dress. **Bar:** Beer & wine. **Reservations:** accepted. **Hours:** 11 am-2:30 & 5-9 pm, Fri-10 pm, Sat noon-10 pm. Closed major holidays; also Sun. **Address:** 3413 Cherokee St **Location:** I-75, exit 273, 1.3 mi w. **Parking:** on-site. **Cards:** AX, DS, MC, VI.

BARBEQUE STREET Phone: 770/419-2626 19

Barbecue
$6-$18

The family restaurant prides itself on pit-cooked barbecue and Brunswick stew. Other offerings include beef, pork and chicken entrees. Homemade desserts round out the menu. Casual dress. **Hours:** 10:30 am-9 pm, Fri & Sat-10 pm. Closed major holidays; also Sun. **Address:** 3815 Cherokee St **Location:** I-75, exit 273, 0.5 mi w. **Parking:** on-site. **Cards:** AX, MC, VI.

BERGAMO Phone: 678/445-8585 17

Italian
$7-$15

This bustling cafe presents a good variety of pizza, pasta, chicken and veal dishes in an authentic Italian family-style atmosphere. Casual dress. **Bar:** Beer & wine. **Hours:** 11:30 am-9 pm, Fri & Sat-10 pm, Sun noon-9 pm. Closed major holidays; also Mon. **Address:** 4290 Bells Ferry Rd NW, Suite 114 **Location:** I-575, exit 4, just n. **Parking:** on-site. **Cards:** AX, DS, MC, VI.

BUCKHEAD BURRITO GRILL Phone: 770/420-7118 21

Mexican
$3-$6

Made-to-order burritos and tacos are loaded with your favorite ingredients. Casual dress. **Bar:** Beer only. **Hours:** 11 am-9 pm. Closed major holidays; also Sun. **Address:** 3393 Cherokee St **Location:** I-75, exit 273, 1.5 mi w. **Parking:** on-site. **Cards:** AX, DS, MC, VI.

CAPER'S ON MAIN STREET Phone: 678/594-7735 27

American
$8-$20

The American-style grill serves fish, chicken, pork and beef favorites in a casual and contemporary atmosphere. Dining on the porch is a popular option. Casual dress. **Bar:** Full bar. **Reservations:** accepted, Sun-Thurs. **Hours:** 11 am-2:30 & 5-10 pm, Fri-11 pm, Sat 11 am-11 pm, Sun 11 am-10 pm; Sunday brunch. Closed major holidays; also Mon & Tues. **Address:** 2756 S Main St **Location:** Downtown. **Parking:** on-site. **Cards:** AX, DS, MC, VI.

CALL

EL NOPALITO Phone: 770/590-9253 39

Tex-Mex
$2-$12

Classic Tex-Mex fare includes burritos, tacos, enchiladas and fajitas. Service is consistent. Chips and salsa are served while you peruse the menu. Casual dress. **Bar:** Full bar. **Hours:** 11 am-10:30 pm, Fri & Sat-11 pm. Closed major holidays. **Address:** 840 Barrett Pkwy, Suite 600 **Location:** I-75, exit 269, 0.3 mi w. **Parking:** on-site. **Cards:** AX, CB, DC, DS, JC, MC, VI.

CALL

FROOTS Phone: 770/499-8200 24

Sandwiches
$2-$7

If you're looking for health-conscience fare, you're search is over. You'll find wraps, salads and fruit smoothies on the menu at this quick-serve eatery. Casual dress. **Hours:** 10 am-8 pm, Sat & Sun 11 am-5 pm. Closed major holidays. **Address:** 745 Chastain Rd, Suite 1020 **Location:** I-75, exit 271, 0.4 mi e; in Madison Place Village. **Parking:** on-site. **Cards:** AX, DS, MC, VI.

CALL

(See map and index starting on p. 296)

FUJI HANA & THAI PEPPERS **Phone:** 770/419-9500 (32)

Asian
$7-$20

Tasteful Oriental decor and a casual ambience set the stage for excellent sushi, traditional Japanese favorites and tried-and-true Thai preparations. Casual dress. **Bar:** Beer & wine. **Hours:** 11:30 am-2:30 & 5-10:30 pm, Fri-11 pm, Sat noon-3:30 & 5-11 pm, Sun noon-3:30 & 5-10 pm. **Address:** 2700 Town Center Dr, Suite E **Location:** I-75, exit 269; opposite Town Center Mall; in the Esplanade. **Parking:** on-site. **Cards:** AX, DC, DS, MC, VI.

HAMADA JAPANESE RESTAURANT **Phone:** 678/797-5978 (18)

Japanese
$7-$34

Both traditional and contemporary Japanese dishes are featured on the restaurant's menu. Patrons can take advantage of the sushi bar or hibachi tables. Casual dress. **Bar:** Beer & wine. **Reservations:** accepted. **Hours:** 11:30 am-2 & 5-10 pm, Sat 5 pm-11 pm, Sun 5 pm-10 pm. Closed major holidays. **Address:** 3895 Cherokee St **Location:** I-75, exit 273, 0.5 mi w; in Shiloh Square. **Parking:** on-site. **Cards:** AX, DC, DS, MC, VI.

HAPPY CHINA **Phone:** 770/428-8818 (31)

Chinese
$6-$16

Patrons can expect traditional Chinese cuisine and decor, in addition to prompt service, at this eatery, which also has other locations. Lunch specials entice midday visitors. Casual dress. **Bar:** Beer & wine. **Hours:** 11 am-10 pm, Fri-11 pm, Sat 11:30 am-11 pm, Sun 11:30 am-10 pm. Closed major holidays. **Address:** 2615 George Busbee Pkwy, Suite 1 **Location:** I-75, exit 69, just e to George Busbee Pkwy, then just n. **Parking:** on-site. **Cards:** AX, MC, VI.

CALL

IPPOLITO'S **Phone:** 770/514-8500 (33)

Italian
$7-$16

This bustling cafe presents a good variety of pizza, pasta, chicken and veal dishes. The chicken tetrazzini is outstanding especially when accompanied by hot garlic rolls. Very good desserts, like chocolate banana cream pie, bring the meal to a sweet end. Casual dress. **Bar:** Beer & wine. **Hours:** 11 am-10 pm, Fri-11 pm, Sat noon-11 pm, Sun noon-10 pm. Closed major holidays; also 12/24. **Address:** 425 Ernest Barret Pkwy **Location:** I-75, exit 269, 0.3 mi e. **Parking:** on-site. **Cards:** AX, DS, MC, VI.

KUROSHIO SUSHI BAR & GRILLE **Phone:** 770/499-7160 (38)

Japanese
$4-$23

In addition to sushi, the specialty here, there are a variety of traditional Japanese dishes available, all served by congenial staff in a hip, contemporary atmosphere. Diners can watch sporting events on the televisions located throughout the dining room. Casual dress. **Bar:** Full bar. **Reservations:** accepted. **Hours:** 11:30 am-10 pm, Fri & Sat-11 pm, Sun 2 pm-10-pm. **Address:** 840 Earnest Barrett Pkwy, Suite 500 **Location:** I-75, exit 69, 0.3 mi w. **Parking:** on-site. **Cards:** AX, CB, DC, DS, JC, MC, VI.

CALL

LOS REYES **Phone:** 770/420-9181 (22)

Tex-Mex
$5-$17

Tex-Mex fare is served in a relaxed atmosphere that simulates a starry night in Mexico. Casual dress. **Bar:** Full bar. **Hours:** 11 am-10:30 pm, Fri & Sat-11 pm. Closed major holidays. **Address:** 777 Town Park Dr **Location:** I-75, exit 271, just e. **Parking:** on-site. **Cards:** AX, DC, DS, MC, VI.

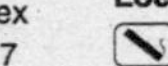

MARLOW'S TAVERN **Phone:** 770/425-8777 (25)

American
$4-$17

A great neighborhood tavern serving good appetizers, sides and salads as well as well-prepared entrees like grouper. A popular entree is the fish taco but don't miss out on the okra, possibly the best in the area. The dining room is casual but does offer some upscale touches. Casual dress. **Bar:** Full bar. **Hours:** 11:30 am-midnight, Thurs-Sat to 2 am. Closed major holidays. **Address:** 745 Chastain Rd NW, Suite 1160 **Location:** I-75, exit 271, 0.4 mi e; in Chastain Creek Village. **Parking:** on-site. **Cards:** AX, CB, DC, DS, JC, MC, VI.

CALL

MY COUNTRY KITCHEN **Phone:** 770/423-9448 (28)

Southern
$7-$13

An array of freshly-prepared Southern favorites—such as fried chicken, mashed potatoes and greens—are served buffet-style. Casual dress. **Hours:** 6 am-9 pm, Sat-2 pm, Sun 8 am-4 pm. Closed: 11/26, 12/25. **Address:** 2740 Summers St **Location:** Downtown. **Parking:** on-site. **Cards:** AX, DS, MC, VI.

MY COUSIN VINNY'S **Phone:** 770/423-0391 (30)

Italian
$2-$19

Select from gourmet, brick-oven pizzas or other Italian favorites like salads, veal, chicken, seafood and pasta dishes. You might find what you crave in the featured daily special. Seating is available in the no-frills dining room or at the outdoor patio. Casual dress. **Bar:** Beer & wine. **Reservations:** accepted. **Hours:** 11 am-10 pm, Fri & Sat-11 pm, Sun noon-9 pm. Closed major holidays. **Address:** 2615 George Busbee Pkwy, Suite 26 **Location:** I-75, exit 269, just e to George Busbee Pkwy, then just n. **Parking:** on-site. **Cards:** AX, DS, MC, VI.

NEW CHINA BUFFET **Phone:** 770/792-2262 (34)

Chinese
$6-$12

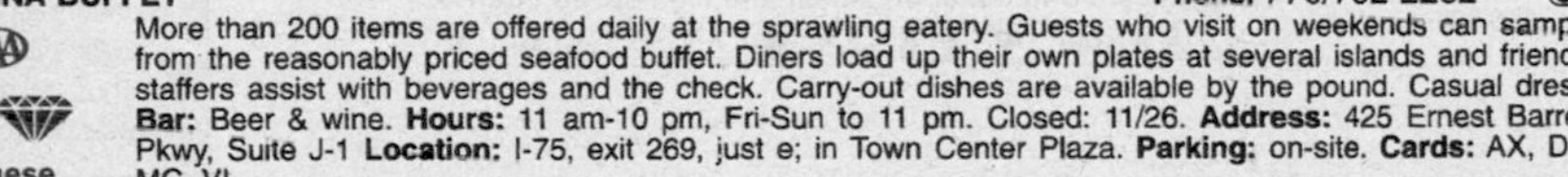

More than 200 items are offered daily at the sprawling eatery. Guests who visit on weekends can sample from the reasonably priced seafood buffet. Diners load up their own plates at several islands and friendly staffers assist with beverages and the check. Carry-out dishes are available by the pound. Casual dress. **Bar:** Beer & wine. **Hours:** 11 am-10 pm, Fri-Sun to 11 pm. Closed: 11/26. **Address:** 425 Ernest Barrett Pkwy, Suite J-1 **Location:** I-75, exit 269, just e; in Town Center Plaza. **Parking:** on-site. **Cards:** AX, DS, MC, VI.

(See map and index starting on p. 296)

PENANG MALAYSIAN/THAI CUISINE
Phone: 678/213-4848 (36)

Asian
$6-$18

The enormous menu lists interesting and delicious dishes. Diners unwind in a dining room evocative of a banana palm and a house made of bamboo. Casual dress. **Bar:** Beer & wine. **Reservations:** accepted. **Hours:** 11 am-11 pm, Fri-Sun to 11:30 pm. **Address:** 2491 George Busbee Pkwy **Location:** I-75, exit 269, just e to George Busbee Pkwy, then just n. **Parking:** on-site. **Cards:** MC, VI.

CALL

PROVINO'S
Phone: 678/594-5055

Italian
$10-$17

Traditional Italian favorites are served in a neighborhood-style atmosphere. Of particular interest are the distinctive house salad and delicious cheesecake. Casual dress. **Bar:** Beer & wine. **Hours:** 11:30 am-10 pm, Fri & Sat-11 pm. Closed: 7/4, 11/26, 12/24, 12/25. **Address:** 440-A Ernest Barrett Pkwy, Suite 1 **Location:** I-75, exit 269, just w. **Parking:** on-site. **Cards:** AX, CB, DC, DS, JC, MC, VI.

CALL

RAFFERTY'S RESTAURANT & BAR
Phone: 770/792-8001

American
$7-$19

American grilled food include preparations of fish, beef, chicken and pasta. Also on the menu are good entree salads. This place is convenient to the mall and movie theaters. Casual dress. **Bar:** Full bar. **Hours:** 11 am-10 pm, Fri & Sat-11 pm. Closed: 11/26, 12/25. **Address:** 2501 Cobb Place Ln NW **Location:** I-75, exit 269, just w to Cobb Place Ln, then just n. **Parking:** on-site. **Cards:** AX, CB, DC, DS, JC, MC, VI.

CALL

RU SAN'S-KENNESAW
Phone: 678/766-0598 (35)

Japanese
$5-$27

The menu lists a wide array of creations, with an emphasis on sushi. Tempura and ahi tuna are of particular interest. Casual dress. **Bar:** Full bar. **Reservations:** accepted. **Hours:** 11:30 am-11 pm, Fri & Sat-midnight, Sun 11 am-11 pm. **Address:** 425 Ernest Barrett Pkwy, Suite H-10 **Location:** I-75, exit 269, 0.3 mi e; in Town Center Plaza. **Parking:** on-site. **Cards:** AX, CB, DC, DS, JC, MC, VI.

SIDELINES GRILLE
Phone: 678/797-0006 (23)

American
$5-$17

Enjoy your favorite sporting event while savoring such "bar food" favorites as wings, nachos, burgers and steaks. Casual dress. **Bar:** Full bar. **Hours:** 11 am-2 am. Closed: 11/26, 12/25. **Address:** 3405 Busbee Dr **Location:** I-75, exit 271, just e. **Parking:** on-site. **Cards:** AX, CB, DC, DS, JC, MC, VI.

CALL

TRACKSIDE GRILL
Phone: 770/499-0874 (26)

American
$7-$19

Receiving good marks for its innovative interpretations of American cuisine, the grill offers noteworthy seafood dishes. Casual dress. **Bar:** Full bar. **Reservations:** accepted. **Hours:** 11 am-3 & 5-9 pm, Fri & Sat-10 pm; Saturday & Sunday brunch. Closed: 7/4, 11/26, 12/24, 12/25. **Address:** 2840 S Main St **Location:** Downtown. **Parking:** on-site. **Cards:** AX, MC, VI.

THE VARSITY
Phone: 770/795-0802 (29)

American
$3-$7

A branch of a longtime Atlanta landmark, the restaurant offers fast food favorites. Casual dress. **Hours:** 10:30 am-9:30 pm, Fri & Sat-10:30 pm, Sun 11 am-9:30 pm. Closed: 4/12, 11/26, 12/25. **Address:** 2790 Town Center Dr **Location:** I-75, exit 269, just e; behind Town Center Mall. **Parking:** on-site. **Cards:** MC, VI.

WILLY'S MEXICANA GRILL
Phone: 770/429-9515 (40)

Mexican
$3-$6

Fast, fresh Tex Mex includes burritos and tacos made to order in a cafeteria-style line. Beer is among beverage choices. Varied salsas complement the chips. Casual dress. **Bar:** Beer only. **Hours:** 11 am-10 pm. Closed major holidays. **Address:** 840 Ernest Barrett Pkwy **Location:** I-75, exit 269, 0.3 mi w. **Parking:** on-site. **Cards:** AX, MC, VI.

CALL

LAWRENCEVILLE pop. 22,397 (See map and index starting on p. 302)

WHERE TO STAY

BEST WESTERN LAWRENCEVILLE INN *Book great rates at AAA.com*
Phone: (770)513-0028 (107)

AAA SAVE

Hotel
$66-$86 All Year

Address: 571 Budford Dr **Location:** Jct SR 316 and 20/124, 0.5 mi s. **Facility:** 54 one-bedroom standard units. 2 stories, interior corridors. **Parking:** on-site. **Amenities:** high-speed Internet, irons, hair dryers. **Pool(s):** outdoor. **Guest Services:** coin laundry, wireless Internet. **Business Services:** PC. **Cards:** AX, DS, MC, VI. **Free Special Amenities: continental breakfast and high-speed Internet.**

CALL / SOME UNITS FEE

Best Western

AAA Benefit:
Members save up to 20%, plus 10% bonus points with rewards program.

(See map and index starting on p. 302)

COMFORT SUITES Book great rates at AAA.com Phone: (678)377-0003 110

AAA SAVE

Hotel

$119-$129 3/31-11/30
$99-$109 12/1-3/30

Address: 2225 Riverside Pkwy **Location:** I-85, exit 106, just n. **Facility:** Smoke free premises. 52 one-bedroom standard units, some with whirlpools. 3 stories, interior corridors. **Parking:** on-site. **Terms:** cancellation fee imposed. **Amenities:** high-speed Internet, irons, hair dryers. **Leisure Activities:** limited exercise equipment. **Guest Services:** valet and coin laundry, wireless Internet. **Business Services:** meeting rooms, business center. **Cards:** AX, DC, DS, MC, VI. **Free Special Amenities: expanded continental breakfast and high-speed Internet.**

FEE CALL

COUNTRY INN & SUITES BY CARLSON Book great rates at AAA.com Phone: (770)339-1991 108

AAA SAVE

Hotel

$119-$179 All Year

Address: 989 Duluth Hwy (SR 120) **Location:** I-85, exit 106 northbound, 5 mi e; exit 115 southbound, 4.4 mi e. **Facility:** 49 units. 39 one-bedroom standard units. 10 one-bedroom suites, some with whirlpools. 3 stories, interior corridors. **Parking:** on-site. **Terms:** cancellation fee imposed. **Amenities:** high-speed Internet, dual phone lines, voice mail, irons, hair dryers. **Pool(s):** outdoor. **Leisure Activities:** exercise room. **Guest Services:** valet and coin laundry, wireless Internet. **Business Services:** meeting rooms, business center. **Cards:** AX, CB, DC, DS, MC, VI. **Free Special Amenities: expanded continental breakfast and high-speed Internet.**

FEE CALL / SOME UNITS

DAYS INN Book great rates at AAA.com Phone: (770)995-7782 109

AAA SAVE

Motel

$70-$121 All Year

Address: 731 Duluth Hwy **Location:** Jct SR 316, just e on SR 120. Located across from Gwinnett Medical Center. **Facility:** 53 one-bedroom standard units. 1 story, exterior corridors. **Parking:** on-site. **Terms:** cancellation fee imposed. **Amenities:** high-speed Internet, irons, hair dryers. **Leisure Activities:** limited exercise equipment. **Guest Services:** wireless Internet. **Business Services:** PC, fax. **Cards:** AX, DC, DS, MC, VI.

/ SOME UNITS FEE

EXTENDED STAYAMERICA ATLANTA-LAWRENCEVILLE Book at AAA.com Phone: (770)962-5660 113

Hotel

$55-$65 All Year

Address: 474 W Pike St **Location:** SR 316, exit SR 120, 0.8 mi s. **Facility:** 121 units. 115 one-bedroom standard units with efficiencies. 6 one-bedroom suites with efficiencies. 2 stories (no elevator), exterior corridors. **Parking:** on-site. **Terms:** office hours 7 am-11 pm. **Amenities:** high-speed Internet (fee), voice mail, irons. **Guest Services:** coin laundry, wireless Internet. **Business Services:** fax (fee). **Cards:** AX, CB, DC, DS, JC, MC, VI.

ASK CALL / SOME UNITS FEE

HAMPTON INN Phone: (678)407-0018 105

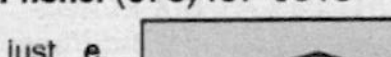

Hotel

$90-$195 All Year

Address: 6010 Sugarloaf Pkwy **Location:** I-85, exit 108, just e. **Facility:** 127 units. 119 one-bedroom standard units. 8 one-bedroom suites with whirlpools. 5 stories, interior corridors. **Parking:** on-site. **Terms:** 14 day cancellation notice-fee imposed. **Amenities:** video games (fee), high-speed Internet, dual phone lines, voice mail, irons, hair dryers. *Some:* DVD players. **Pool(s):** outdoor. **Leisure Activities:** exercise room. **Guest Services:** valet and coin laundry, area transportation, wireless Internet. **Business Services:** meeting rooms, business center. **Cards:** AX, CB, DC, DS, JC, MC, VI.

FEE / SOME UNITS

Hampton Inn

AAA Benefit:

Members save up to 10% everyday!

HAMPTON INN Book great rates at AAA.com Phone: (770)338-9600 111

Hotel

$79-$139 All Year

Address: 1135 Lakes Pkwy **Location:** SR 316, exit Riverside Pkwy, just n. **Facility:** 85 one-bedroom standard units. 3 stories, interior corridors. *Bath:* combo or shower only. **Parking:** on-site. **Terms:** 1-30 night minimum stay, cancellation fee imposed. **Amenities:** video games (fee), high-speed Internet, dual phone lines, voice mail, irons, hair dryers. **Pool(s):** outdoor. **Leisure Activities:** limited exercise equipment. **Guest Services:** valet laundry, wireless Internet. **Business Services:** meeting rooms, fax (fee). **Cards:** AX, CB, DC, DS, MC, VI.

FEE CALL

/ SOME UNITS FEE

AAA Benefit:

Members save up to 10% everyday!

HOLIDAY INN EXPRESS HOTEL & SUITES Book at AAA.com Phone: 770/277-8009 112

Hotel

Rates not provided

Address: 520 John B Wilson Ct **Location:** I-85, exit 106 northbound, jct SR 316, 0.7 mi e on SR 120. **Facility:** 62 one-bedroom standard units, some with whirlpools. 4 stories, interior corridors. **Parking:** on-site. **Amenities:** high-speed Internet, dual phone lines, voice mail, irons, hair dryers. **Pool(s):** outdoor. **Leisure Activities:** exercise room. **Guest Services:** valet laundry, wireless Internet. **Business Services:** meeting rooms, business center.

(See map and index starting on p. 302)

MICROTEL INN & SUITES-UNIVERSITY WAY/LAWRENCEVILLE Book at AAA.com

Phone: (770)237-5992 106

Hotel

$69-$79 4/1-11/30

$66-$73 12/1-3/31

Address: 215 Collins Industrial Way **Location:** I-85, exit 106 northbound, 4.5 mi e to Collins Hill Rd, just n to Collins Industrial Way, then just w; exit 115 southbound, 4.4 mi s on SR 20 to SR 316, then 0.5 mi w. **Facility:** 92 one-bedroom standard units. 3 stories, interior corridors. **Parking:** on-site. **Amenities:** video games (fee), high-speed Internet. *Some:* irons, hair dryers. **Guest Services:** coin laundry, wireless Internet. **Business Services:** meeting rooms, fax (fee). **Cards:** AX, DC, DS, MC, VI.

ASK FEE CALL / SOME UNITS

WHERE TO DINE

DIGGER'S SPORTS GRILL

Phone: 678/377-8660 81

American

$7-$18

Visitors can fill up on huge portions of Southern comfort food, such as chicken-fried steak, wings, burgers and large sandwiches. All meals are freshly prepared. Television screens surround the room so that patrons can enjoy their favorite sporting events. Servers are fast, friendly and attentive. Casual dress. **Bar:** Full bar. **Hours:** 11:30 am-1:30 am, Sun noon-midnight. Closed: 11/26, 12/25. **Address:** 909 Parkside Walk Ln **Location:** I-85, exit 106 northbound, 5 mi e; exit 115 southbound, 4.4 mi e. **Parking:** on-site. **Cards:** AX, DC, DS, MC, VI.

CALL

RED GARLIC SUPER THAI CUISINE

Phone: 770/923-3010 82

Thai

$7-$16

Thai preparations, tantalizing seafood choices and Chinese cuisine can be seasoned to taste, from mild to sweat-on-the-brow spicy. The intimate restaurant is a popular lunch spot. Casual dress. **Bar:** Beer & wine. **Hours:** 11 am-3 & 5-9:30 pm, Fri & Sat-10:30 pm, Sun 5 pm-9:30 pm. Closed: 7/4, 11/26, 12/25. **Address:** 1455 Pleasant Hill Rd, #603 **Location:** I-85, exit 104, 0.8 mi e; in Pleasant Hill Pointe Shopping Center. **Parking:** on-site. **Cards:** AX, DS, MC, VI.

SONNY'S REAL PIT BAR-B-Q

Phone: 770/822-3330

Barbecue

$6-$15

House specialties include pork and chicken grilled over an open pit, barbecue ribs and fresh, homemade pie. The salad bar offers another popular option. Rustic and comfortable, the atmosphere is perfect for family meals. Casual dress. **Bar:** Beer only. **Hours:** 11 am-9:30 pm, Fri & Sat-10 pm. Closed: 11/26, 12/25. **Address:** 660 W Pike St **Location:** I-85, exit 106 northbound, 5 mi e; exit 107 southbound, 4.5 mi e to Duluth exit, then 0.9 mi e on SR 120. **Parking:** on-site. **Cards:** AX, DS, MC, VI.

LITHIA SPRINGS pop. 2,072

WHERE TO STAY

COMFORT INN AT SIX FLAGS Book great rates at AAA.com

Phone: (770)941-5384

AAA SAVE

Hotel

$85-$115 3/1-11/30

$79-$99 12/1-2/28

Address: 850 Crestmark Dr **Location:** I-20, exit 44, just n. **Facility:** 92 one-bedroom standard units. 4 stories, interior corridors. **Parking:** on-site. **Terms:** cancellation fee imposed. **Amenities:** high-speed Internet, voice mail, irons, hair dryers. **Pool(s):** outdoor. **Leisure Activities:** exercise room. **Guest Services:** valet laundry, wireless Internet. **Business Services:** meeting rooms, fax (fee). **Cards:** AX, DC, DS, JC, MC, VI.

CALL / SOME UNITS

COUNTRY INN & SUITES-ATLANTA SIX FLAGS Book at AAA.com

Phone: 678/945-0945

Hotel

Rates not provided

Address: 960 West Point Ct **Location:** I-20, exit 44, just s. **Facility:** 91 units. 53 one-bedroom standard units. 38 one-bedroom suites, some with whirlpools. 5 stories, interior corridors. **Parking:** on-site. **Amenities:** high-speed Internet, dual phone lines, voice mail, irons, hair dryers. **Pool(s):** heated indoor. **Leisure Activities:** whirlpool, exercise room. *Fee:* game room. **Guest Services:** valet and coin laundry, wireless Internet. **Business Services:** meeting rooms, business center.

FEE CALL / SOME UNITS

COURTYARD BY MARRIOTT Book great rates at AAA.com

Phone: (678)945-4444

Hotel

$138-$148 All Year

Address: 950 Bob Arnold Blvd **Location:** I-20, exit 44, 0.5 mi s. **Facility:** Smoke free premises. 78 units. 75 one-bedroom standard units. 3 one-bedroom suites with whirlpools. 3 stories, interior corridors. **Parking:** on-site. **Terms:** cancellation fee imposed. **Amenities:** high-speed Internet, dual phone lines, voice mail, irons, hair dryers. **Pool(s):** heated indoor. **Leisure Activities:** whirlpool, exercise room. **Guest Services:** valet and coin laundry, wireless Internet. **Business Services:** meeting rooms, business center. **Cards:** AX, CB, DC, DS, JC, MC, VI.

AAA Benefit:

Members save a minimum 5% off the best available rate.

FAIRFIELD INN BY MARRIOTT *Book great rates at AAA.com* **Phone:** (770)739-2800

Hotel
$112-$139 All Year

Address: 976 West Point Ct **Location:** I-20, exit 44, just s. **Facility:** Smoke free premises. 81 one-bedroom standard units. 3 stories, interior corridors. **Parking:** on-site. **Terms:** cancellation fee imposed. **Amenities:** high-speed Internet, irons, hair dryers. **Pool(s):** heated indoor. **Leisure Activities:** whirlpool. **Guest Services:** valet laundry, wireless Internet. **Business Services:** fax (fee). **Cards:** AX, CB, DC, DS, JC, MC, VI.

FEE CALL / SOME UNITS

AAA Benefit: Members save a minimum 5% off the best available rate.

SPRINGHILL SUITES BY MARRIOTT ATLANTA-THORNTON ROAD/SIX FLAGS *Book great rates at AAA.com* **Phone:** (770)819-9906

Hotel
$123-$133 All Year

Address: 960 Bob Arnold Blvd **Location:** I-20, exit 44, 0.5 mi s. **Facility:** Smoke free premises. 78 one-bedroom standard units. 3 stories, interior corridors. **Parking:** on-site. **Terms:** cancellation fee imposed. **Amenities:** high-speed Internet, dual phone lines, voice mail, irons, hair dryers. **Pool(s):** heated indoor. **Leisure Activities:** whirlpool, exercise room. **Guest Services:** valet and coin laundry, wireless Internet. **Business Services:** meeting rooms, business center. **Cards:** AX, CB, DC, DS, JC, MC, VI.

FEE CALL

AAA Benefit: Members save a minimum 5% off the best available rate.

WHERE TO DINE

BEAVER CREEK BISCUITS & BBQ **Phone:** 770/739-0200

Barbecue
$5-$9

The breakfast entrees and barbecue dishes are popular selections. Casual dress. **Reservations:** not accepted. **Hours:** 5:30 am-5 pm, Sat 7 am-3 pm. Closed major holidays; also Sun. **Address:** 1451 Six Flags Rd **Location:** I-20, exit 44, 1 mi w, then just e. **Parking:** on-site. **Cards:** AX, MC, VI.

LITHONIA pop. 2,187 (See map and index starting on p. 312)

WHERE TO STAY

FAIRFIELD INN & SUITES *Book great rates at AAA.com* **Phone:** (770)484-9993

Hotel
$108-$116 All Year

Address: 7850 Stonecrest Sq **Location:** I-20, exit 75, just s on Turner Hill Rd, then 0.8 mi w; rear of Stonecrest Mall. **Facility:** Smoke free premises. 85 units. 56 one-bedroom standard units. 29 one-bedroom suites. 4 stories, interior corridors. **Parking:** on-site. **Terms:** cancellation fee imposed. **Amenities:** high-speed Internet, voice mail, irons, hair dryers. *Some:* CD players. **Pool(s):** heated indoor. **Leisure Activities:** whirlpool, exercise room. **Guest Services:** valet and coin laundry, wireless Internet. **Business Services:** meeting rooms, business center. **Cards:** AX, CB, DC, DS, JC, MC, VI.

FEE 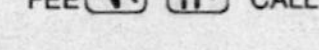 CALL   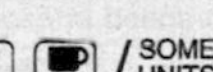 / SOME UNITS 

AAA Benefit: Members save a minimum 5% off the best available rate.

HYATT PLACE ATLANTA-EAST/LITHONIA *Book great rates at AAA.com* **Phone:** (770)484-4384

Hotel
$99-$299 All Year

Address: 7900 Mall Ring Rd **Location:** I-20, exit 75, just s on Turner Hill Rd, then 0.7 mi w; at rear of Stonecrest Mall. **Facility:** 83 one-bedroom standard units. 5 stories, interior corridors. *Bath:* combo or shower only. **Parking:** on-site. **Terms:** cancellation fee imposed. **Pool(s):** outdoor. **Leisure Activities:** exercise room. **Guest Services:** valet laundry, wireless Internet. **Business Services:** meeting rooms, business center. **Cards:** AX, CB, DC, DS, MC, VI. **Free Special Amenities: continental breakfast and high-speed Internet.**

 / SOME UNITS

AAA Benefit: Ask for the AAA rate and save 10%.

RED ROOF INN *Book great rates at AAA.com* **Phone:** (770)332-1400 26

Hotel
$80-$90 5/1-11/30
$70-$80 12/1-4/30

Address: 5400 Fairington Rd **Location:** I-20, exit 71, just s to Fairington Rd, then just ne. **Facility:** 63 one-bedroom standard units. 3 stories, interior corridors. *Bath:* shower only. **Parking:** on-site. **Terms:** cancellation fee imposed. **Amenities:** high-speed Internet. **Guest Services:** wireless Internet. **Business Services:** fax. **Cards:** AX, DS, MC, VI. **Free Special Amenities: local telephone calls and high-speed Internet.**

CALL  / SOME UNITS

(See map and index starting on p. 312)

SUPER 8 MOTEL Book at AAA.com Phone: 770/987-5128 25

Motel
Rates not provided

Address: 5354 Snapfinger Park Dr **Location:** I-20, exit 71, just n. **Facility:** 50 one-bedroom standard units, some with whirlpools. 2 stories (no elevator), exterior corridors. **Parking:** on-site. **Amenities:** high-speed Internet, hair dryers. **Guest Services:** wireless Internet. **Business Services:** fax.

/ SOME UNITS

WHERE TO DINE

ARIZONA'S Phone: 678/526-7775

American
$5-$32

Offering classic American favorites like steaks, chops and seafood, the dining room is large with upscale touches though casual. A popular spot for lunch, so expect heavy traffic. The bar area is great for meeting friends and relaxing. Casual dress. **Bar:** Full bar. **Reservations:** accepted. **Hours:** 11:30 am-10 pm, Tues & Sat-11 pm, Fri-1 am, Sun-9 pm. Closed major holidays. **Address:** 2940 Stonecrest Cir **Location:** I-20, exit 75, just s. **Parking:** on-site. **Cards:** AX, CB, DC, DS, JC, MC, VI.

CALL

MARIETTA pop. 58,748 (See maps and indexes starting on p. 296, 302)

WHERE TO STAY

BAYMONT INN & SUITES MARIETTA Book great rates at AAA.com **Phone:** (678)355-5050 46

AAA SAVE

Hotel
$80-$110 All Year

Address: 639 Franklin Rd SE **Location:** I-75, exit 263, 0.3 mi w to Franklin Rd, then 0.3 mi s. **Facility:** 44 units. 39 one-bedroom standard units, some with whirlpools. 5 one-bedroom suites. 2-3 stories, interior corridors. *Bath:* combo or shower only. **Parking:** on-site. **Terms:** cancellation fee imposed. **Amenities:** high-speed Internet, irons, hair dryers. *Some:* dual phone lines. **Pool(s):** indoor. **Leisure Activities:** whirlpool, exercise room. **Guest Services:** wireless Internet. **Business Services:** meeting rooms, fax (fee). **Cards:** AX, DC, DS, MC, VI. **Free Special Amenities: continental breakfast and high-speed Internet.**

FEE CALL / SOME UNITS

COMFORT INN-MARIETTA Book at AAA.com **Phone:** (770)952-3000 53

Hotel
$79-$109 5/1-11/30
$69-$99 12/1-4/30

Address: 2100 Northwest Pkwy **Location:** I-75, exit 261, 0.3 mi w to Franklin Rd, then just s. **Facility:** 184 one-bedroom standard units with efficiencies. 5 stories, exterior corridors. **Parking:** on-site. **Amenities:** video games (fee), high-speed Internet, voice mail, irons, hair dryers. **Pool(s):** outdoor. **Leisure Activities:** exercise room. **Guest Services:** valet and coin laundry, area transportation, wireless Internet. **Business Services:** meeting rooms, PC, fax (fee). **Cards:** AX, CB, DC, DS, JC, MC, VI.

ASK FEE / SOME UNITS FEE

COURTYARD BY MARRIOTT-MARIETTA Book great rates at AAA.com **Phone:** (770)956-1188 49

AAA SAVE

Hotel
$138-$148 All Year

Address: 2455 Delk Rd **Location:** I-75, exit 261, 0.3 mi e. **Facility:** Smoke free premises. 146 units. 134 one-bedroom standard units. 12 one-bedroom suites. 3 stories, interior corridors. **Parking:** on-site. **Terms:** cancellation fee imposed. **Amenities:** high-speed Internet, dual phone lines, voice mail, irons, hair dryers. **Pool(s):** outdoor. **Leisure Activities:** whirlpool, exercise room. **Guest Services:** valet and coin laundry, wireless Internet. **Business Services:** meeting rooms, business center. **Cards:** AX, CB, DC, DS, MC, VI. **Free Special Amenities: newspaper and high-speed Internet.**

FEE CALL / SOME UNITS

AAA Benefit:
Members save a minimum 5% off the best available rate.

COURTYARD BY MARRIOTT-WINDY HILL Book great rates at AAA.com **Phone:** (770)955-3838 58

AAA SAVE

Hotel
$168-$180 All Year

Address: 2045 S Park Pl **Location:** I-75, exit 260, 0.3 mi w to S Park Pl, then just n. **Facility:** Smoke free premises. 127 units. 107 one-bedroom standard units. 20 one-bedroom suites. 2 stories, interior corridors. **Parking:** on-site. **Terms:** cancellation fee imposed. **Amenities:** high-speed Internet, dual phone lines, voice mail, irons, hair dryers. **Pool(s):** outdoor. **Leisure Activities:** whirlpool, exercise room. **Guest Services:** valet and coin laundry, wireless Internet. **Business Services:** meeting rooms, business center. **Cards:** AX, CB, DC, DS, MC, VI. **Free Special Amenities: newspaper and high-speed Internet.**

FEE CALL / SOME UNITS

AAA Benefit:
Members save a minimum 5% off the best available rate.

CROWNE PLAZA ATLANTA-MARIETTA Book great rates at AAA.com **Phone:** (770)428-4400 45

AAA SAVE

Hotel
$79-$189 All Year

Address: 1775 Parkway Pl NW **Location:** I-75, exit 263, just w. **Facility:** 218 one-bedroom standard units. 10 stories, interior corridors. **Parking:** on-site. **Terms:** cancellation fee imposed. **Amenities:** video games (fee), CD players, high-speed Internet, voice mail, irons, hair dryers. **Pool(s):** outdoor. **Leisure Activities:** exercise room. **Guest Services:** valet laundry, area transportation-within 5 mi, wireless Internet. **Business Services:** meeting rooms, business center. **Cards:** AX, CB, DC, DS, JC, MC, VI. **Free Special Amenities: local telephone calls and high-speed Internet.**

FEE CALL / SOME UNITS FEE

(See maps and indexes starting on p. 296, 302)

DAYS INN Book at AAA.com Phone: 770/952-9863 54

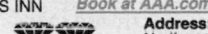

Hotel
Rates not provided

Address: 2191 Northwest Pkwy **Location:** I-75, exit 261, just w on Delk Rd to Franklin Rd, just s to Northwest Pkwy, then just e. Located in an office park/light-commercial area. **Facility:** 131 one-bedroom standard units. 3 stories, interior/exterior corridors. **Parking:** on-site. **Amenities:** high-speed Internet, irons, hair dryers. **Pool(s):** outdoor. **Guest Services:** valet and coin laundry, wireless Internet. **Business Services:** meeting rooms, PC, fax (fee).

CALL / SOME UNITS

DRURY INN & SUITES-ATLANTA NORTHWEST Book at AAA.com Phone: (770)612-0900 48

Hotel
$70-$110 All Year

Address: 1170 Powers Ferry Pl **Location:** I-75, exit 261, just e. **Facility:** 143 units. 119 one-bedroom standard units. 24 one-bedroom suites. 7 stories, interior corridors. **Parking:** on-site. **Amenities:** high-speed Internet, voice mail, irons, hair dryers. **Pool(s):** heated indoor/outdoor. **Leisure Activities:** whirlpool, exercise room. **Guest Services:** valet and coin laundry, wireless Internet. **Business Services:** meeting rooms, business center. **Cards:** AX, DC, DS, MC, VI.

ASK FEE CALL / SOME UNITS

ECONO LODGE NORTHWEST Book at AAA.com Phone: 770/952-0052 56

Hotel
Rates not provided

Address: 1940 Leland Dr **Location:** I-75, exit 260, just e, then 0.3 mi n. Located in a quiet area. **Facility:** 100 one-bedroom standard units. 3 stories, interior/exterior corridors. **Parking:** on-site. **Amenities:** high-speed Internet. **Guest Services:** coin laundry, wireless Internet. **Business Services:** meeting rooms, fax (fee).

/ SOME UNITS FEE

EXTENDED STAYAMERICA ATLANTA-MARIETTA WINDY HILL Book at AAA.com Phone: (770)690-9477 57

Hotel
$55-$65 All Year

Address: 1967 Leland Dr **Location:** I-75, exit 260, just e to Leland Dr, then just n. **Facility:** 113 one-bedroom standard units with efficiencies. 3 stories, interior corridors. **Parking:** on-site. **Terms:** office hours 7 am-11 pm. **Amenities:** high-speed Internet (fee), voice mail, irons. **Guest Services:** coin laundry, wireless Internet. **Business Services:** fax (fee). **Cards:** AX, CB, DC, DS, JC, MC, VI.

ASK FEE CALL / SOME UNITS FEE

HAMPTON INN MARIETTA Book great rates at AAA.com Phone: (770)425-9977 44

Hotel
$77-$97 All Year

Address: 455 Franklin Rd **Location:** I-75, exit 263, just w. **Facility:** 139 one-bedroom standard units. 2-4 stories, interior/exterior corridors. **Parking:** on-site. **Terms:** 1-30 night minimum stay, cancellation fee imposed. **Amenities:** video games (fee), high-speed Internet, voice mail, irons, hair dryers. **Pool(s):** outdoor. **Leisure Activities:** exercise room. **Guest Services:** valet laundry, wireless Internet. **Business Services:** meeting rooms, business center. **Cards:** AX, CB, DC, DS, MC, VI.

FEE CALL / SOME UNITS

AAA Benefit:
Members save up to 10% everyday!

HILTON ATLANTA/MARIETTA HOTEL & CONFERENCE CENTER Book great rates at AAA.com Phone: (770)427-2500 43

Hotel
$89-$169 All Year

Address: 500 Powder Springs St **Location:** I-75, exit 263, 3.5 mi w to Powder Springs St, then just w. **Facility:** 199 units. 193 one-bedroom standard units. 6 one-bedroom suites, some with whirlpools. 6 stories, interior corridors. **Parking:** on-site and valet. **Terms:** 1-30 night minimum stay, cancellation fee imposed. **Amenities:** high-speed Internet (fee), dual phone lines, voice mail, irons, hair dryers. *Some:* CD players, safes. **Pool(s):** heated outdoor. **Leisure Activities:** saunas, whirlpool, 2 lighted tennis courts, exercise room. *Fee:* golf-18 holes, massage. **Guest Services:** valet laundry, area transportation, personal trainer, wireless Internet. **Business Services:** conference facilities, business center.

24 CALL / SOME UNITS VCR

AAA Benefit:
Members save 5% or more everyday!

HOMESTEAD STUDIO SUITES HOTEL-ATLANTA-MARIETTA-POWERS FERRY RD Book at AAA.com Phone: (770)303-0043 59

Hotel
$70-$80 All Year

Address: 2239 Powers Ferry Rd **Location:** I-285, exit 22, just n. **Facility:** 123 units. 113 one-bedroom standard units with efficiencies. 10 one-bedroom suites with efficiencies. 3 stories, interior corridors. **Parking:** on-site. **Amenities:** high-speed Internet (fee), dual phone lines, voice mail, irons, hair dryers. **Guest Services:** valet and coin laundry, wireless Internet. **Business Services:** fax (fee). **Cards:** AX, CB, DC, DS, JC, MC, VI.

ASK FEE CALL / SOME UNITS FEE

HOMETOWN INN Book at AAA.com Phone: 770/499-9550 41

Hotel
Rates not provided

Address: 1051 Canton Rd **Location:** I-75, exit 267A northbound, 1.8 mi w. **Facility:** 120 one-bedroom standard units with efficiencies. 3 stories, exterior corridors. **Parking:** on-site. **Terms:** office hours 8 am-11 pm. **Amenities:** high-speed Internet (fee), voice mail. **Guest Services:** coin laundry, wireless Internet. **Business Services:** fax (fee).

/ SOME UNITS FEE

(See maps and indexes starting on p. 296, 302)

HYATT REGENCY SUITES PERIMETER NORTHWEST *Book great rates at AAA.com*

Phone: (770)956-1234 55

Hotel
$79-$329 All Year

Address: 2999 Windy Hill Rd **Location:** I-75, exit 260, 0.5 mi e at Powers Ferry Rd. **Facility:** 202 one-bedroom standard units. 7 stories, interior corridors. **Parking:** on-site. **Terms:** 3 day cancellation notice-fee imposed. **Amenities:** dual phone lines, voice mail, irons, hair dryers. *Fee:* video games, high-speed Internet. *Some:* DVD players, CD players. **Pool(s):** outdoor. **Leisure Activities:** exercise room. **Guest Services:** valet laundry, area transportation-within 5 mi, wireless Internet. **Business Services:** conference facilities, business center. **Cards:** AX, CB, DC, DS, JC, MC, VI.

FEE CALL / SOME UNITS FEE VCR

HYATT HOTELS & RESORTS

AAA Benefit:
Ask for the AAA rate and save 10%.

LA QUINTA INN *Book great rates at AAA.com*

Phone: (770)951-0026 50

Hotel
$39-$79 All Year

Address: 2170 Delk Rd **Location:** I-75, exit 261, 0.3 mi w. **Facility:** 130 one-bedroom standard units. 3 stories, interior/exterior corridors. **Parking:** on-site. **Amenities:** video games (fee), high-speed Internet, voice mail, irons, hair dryers. *Some:* dual phone lines. **Pool(s):** outdoor. **Guest Services:** wireless Internet. **Business Services:** meeting rooms, fax (fee). **Cards:** AX, DS, MC, VI.

ASK FEE / SOME UNITS

MASTERS INN MARIETTA *Book great rates at AAA.com*

Phone: (770)951-2005 60

Motel
$45-$52 All Year

Address: 2682 Windy Hill Rd **Location:** I-75, exit 260, just w to Circle 75 Pkwy, then just s. **Facility:** 87 one-bedroom standard units. 2 stories, exterior corridors. **Parking:** on-site. **Terms:** 5 day cancellation notice. **Amenities:** high-speed Internet. **Guest Services:** coin laundry, wireless Internet. **Business Services:** fax. **Cards:** AX, DC, DS, MC, VI. **Free Special Amenities: local telephone calls.**

/ SOME UNITS FEE

QUALITY INN ATLANTA/MARIETTA *Book great rates at AAA.com*

Phone: (770)955-0004 52

Hotel
$65-$100 All Year

Address: 1255 Franklin Rd **Location:** I-75, exit 261, 0.3 mi w to Franklin Rd, then just s. **Facility:** 96 units. 93 one-bedroom standard units, some with whirlpools. 3 one-bedroom suites. 3 stories, interior corridors. **Parking:** on-site. **Terms:** cancellation fee imposed. **Amenities:** high-speed Internet, irons, hair dryers. *Some:* DVD players. **Pool(s):** outdoor. **Leisure Activities:** exercise room. **Guest Services:** coin laundry, wireless Internet. **Business Services:** fax (fee). **Cards:** AX, DC, DS, MC, VI. **Free Special Amenities: continental breakfast and high-speed Internet.**

FEE / SOME UNITS VCR

SLEEP INN *Book great rates at AAA.com*

Phone: (770)952-9005 47

Hotel
$59-$89 All Year

Address: 1175 Powers Ferry Pl **Location:** I-75, exit 261, just e. **Facility:** 90 one-bedroom standard units. 3 stories, interior corridors. *Bath:* shower only. **Parking:** on-site. **Amenities:** high-speed Internet, irons, hair dryers. **Pool(s):** heated indoor. **Leisure Activities:** whirlpool, exercise room. **Guest Services:** coin laundry, wireless Internet. **Business Services:** business center. **Cards:** AX, DC, DS, MC, VI. **Free Special Amenities: expanded continental breakfast and high-speed Internet.**

CALL / SOME UNITS

THE WHITLOCK INN BED & BREAKFAST

Phone: 770/428-1495 42

Historic Bed & Breakfast
$125-$150 All Year

Address: 57 Whitlock Ave **Location:** I-75, exit 263, 2.7 mi w to Powder Springs Rd, 0.3 mi n to Whitlock Ave, then just w. **Facility:** This B&B, in a restored Victorian mansion surrounded by gardens, includes a large ballroom. Smoke free premises. 5 one-bedroom standard units. 2 stories (no elevator), interior corridors. **Parking:** on-site. **Terms:** age restrictions may apply. **Amenities:** high-speed Internet, irons, hair dryers. **Guest Services:** wireless Internet. **Business Services:** meeting rooms, fax. **Cards:** AX, DS, MC, VI.

ASK

WINGATE INN *Book at AAA.com*

Phone: (770)989-0071 51

Hotel
$109-$149 All Year

Address: 1250 Franklin Rd **Location:** I-75, exit 261, 0.3 mi w to Franklin Rd, then just s. **Facility:** 80 one-bedroom standard units, some with whirlpools. 5 stories, interior corridors. **Parking:** on-site. **Amenities:** video games (fee), high-speed Internet, dual phone lines, voice mail, safes, irons, hair dryers. **Leisure Activities:** whirlpool, exercise room. **Guest Services:** valet and coin laundry, wireless Internet. **Business Services:** meeting rooms, business center. **Cards:** AX, CB, DC, DS, JC, MC, VI.

ASK FEE CALL / SOME UNITS

(See maps and indexes starting on p. 296, 302)

WHERE TO DINE

ASPENS SIGNATURE STEAKS **Phone:** 770/419-1744

American
$15-$35

The monu comprises both great steaks and seafood, which are served with good side dishes and great wines, at this spot appointed in upscale Adirondack-style decor. Early-bird specials offer good savings. Dressy casual. **Reservations:** accepted. **Hours:** 5 pm-10 pm, Fri & Sat-11 pm, Sun 11 am-3 & 5-9 pm. Closed major holidays. **Address:** 3625 Dallas Hwy **Location:** Just w of jct Due West Rd and Dallas Hwy; in Avenue of West Cobb. **Parking:** on-site. **Cards:** AX, CB, DC, DS, MC, VI.

CALL

ASPENS SIGNATURE STEAKS **Phone:** 678/236-1400 (44)

Steak
$10-$33

Certified Angus steaks, palate-pleasing and imaginative appetizers and salads, and mouthwatering desserts all are on the restaurant's menu. The dining room re-creates an upscale ski lodge, and the service staff is adept at pointing patrons in the right direction. Dressy casual. **Bar:** Full bar. **Reservations:** suggested. **Hours:** 5 pm-10 pm, Fri & Sat-11 pm, Sun-9 pm. Closed major holidays. **Address:** 2942 Shallowford Rd **Location:** Jct Shallowford and Sandy Plains rds. **Parking:** on-site. **Cards:** AX, CB, DC, DS, JC, MC, VI.

BARKER'S RED HOTS **Phone:** 770/272-0407 (68)

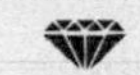

American
$1-$5

Modeled after an old-style Coney stand, the quick-serve eatery has a small dining room in which patrons nosh on charcoal-broiled hot dogs, red hots, Italian sausage and even veggie dogs with all the fixings. This place originated as a street vendor in 1984. Casual dress. **Hours:** 11 am-8 pm, Sat-4 pm. Closed major holidays. **Address:** 3000 Windy Hill Rd, Suite B-6 **Location:** I-75, exit 260, 0.5 mi e; in Terrace at Windy Hill Plaza. **Parking:** on-site. **Cards:** AX, DS, MC, VI.

CALL

BASIL WRAPS **Phone:** 770/514-9990 (46)

Mediterranean
$2-$8

Everything is made from scratch at this small, family-owned and -operated, Middle Eastern eatery. Expect to find quick service and warm, sincere owners. You can't go wrong with the hummus, falafel, wraps or salads. Casual dress. **Hours:** 10 am-8 pm. Closed: 1/1, 12/25; also Sun. **Address:** 2800 Canton Rd, Suite 1220 J **Location:** I-75, exit 267A, 2.6 mi ne; in Piedmont Village. **Parking:** on-site. **Cards:** MC, VI.

BLU GREEK TAVERNA **Phone:** 770/429-4096 (55)

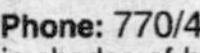

Greek
$5-$25

In the historic downtown square, the authentic Greek taverna is drenched in shades of blue and nurtures a soothing and casual Mediterranean feel. Dolmades (stuffed grape leaves), hummus and pita bread share menu space with great fish dishes, such as whole red snapper. Casual dress. **Bar:** Full bar. **Reservations:** accepted. **Hours:** 11:30 am-2:30 & 5:30-10 pm. Closed major holidays. **Address:** 26 Mill St **Location:** Just w of Historic Marietta Square; downtown. **Parking:** street. **Cards:** AX, CB, DC, DS, JC, MC, VI.

CALL

CAFE LIFE **Phone:** 770/977-9583 (58)

Natural/Organic
$4-$10

Food is organic, natural and whole at the vegetarian spot, which has an adjoining food store where some foods can be bought by the pound. The decor is nondescript. Juices and teas are among beverages choices. Fresh baked goods, grab-and-go items and gluten-free and raw foods are available. Casual dress. **Hours:** 11 am-7 pm, Sun noon-5 pm. Closed major holidays. **Address:** 1453 Roswell Rd **Location:** In London Square Plaza. **Parking:** on-site. **Cards:** AX, DS, MC, VI.

CHEROKEE CATTLE COMPANY **Phone:** 770/427-0490 (47)

Steak
$7-$20

Old license plates, animal trophies, barbed wire and neon signs are among rustic appointments decorating this Texas-style roadhouse. Patrons can kick back with a cold one while they wait for mesquite grilled steak, prime rib, fish or chicken. Casual dress. **Bar:** Full bar. **Hours:** 11 am-10 pm, Fri & Sat-11 pm. **Address:** 2710 Canton Rd **Location:** I-75, exit 267A, 2.5 mi ne. **Parking:** on-site. **Cards:** AX, MC, VI.

CHICAGO'S RESTAURANT **Phone:** 770/590-1500 (57)

American
$8-$29

Steak and seafood are the specialties here, along with some nice Italian selections. A casual neighborhood atmosphere is enhanced by a very British decor. Vintage photographs, black marbleized tile floors and brass fixtures add an air of nostalgia. The friendly and professional service staff seeks to assist in making guests' experiences good ones. Casual dress. **Bar:** Full bar. **Hours:** 5 pm-10 pm, Fri & Sat-11 pm, Sun 11 am-9 pm, Mon 5 pm-9 pm; Sunday brunch. Closed major holidays. **Address:** 990 Whitlock Ave **Location:** 2 mi w on SR 120. **Parking:** on-site. **Cards:** AX, DC, DS, MC, VI.

CALL

EFES **Phone:** 770/419-0159 (52)

Turkish
$7-$24

Belly dancers, an attentive and smartly attired wait staff and delicious food all combine to make dining here a fun and fulfilling experience. Casual dress. **Bar:** Beer & wine. **Reservations:** accepted, weekends. **Hours:** 11 am-3 & 4:30-10 pm, Sat noon-3 & 5-11 pm, Sun noon-9 pm. Closed: 11/26, 12/25. **Address:** 113 N Park Square **Location:** On square; downtown. **Parking:** street. **Cards:** AX, DS, MC, VI.

FALAFEL CAFE **Phone:** 770/429-8999 (65)

Persian
$6-$15

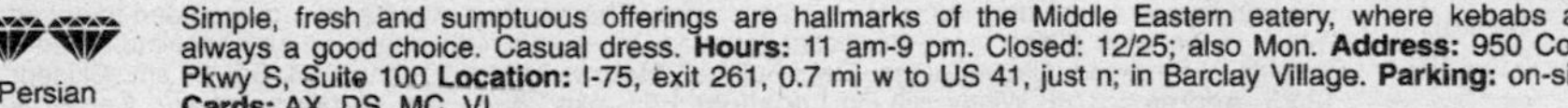

Simple, fresh and sumptuous offerings are hallmarks of the Middle Eastern eatery, where kebabs are always a good choice. Casual dress. **Hours:** 11 am-9 pm. Closed: 12/25; also Mon. **Address:** 950 Cobb Pkwy S, Suite 100 **Location:** I-75, exit 261, 0.7 mi w to US 41, just n; in Barclay Village. **Parking:** on-site. **Cards:** AX, DS, MC, VI.

(See maps and indexes starting on p. 296, 302)

HASHIGUCHI — **Phone:** 770/955-2337 (70)

Japanese
$8-$25

Both traditional and contemporary Japanese dishes make appearances on the restaurant's menu. Casual dress. **Bar:** Beer & wine. **Hours:** 11:30 am-2 & 5:30-10 pm, Sat from 5:30 pm. Closed major holidays; also Sun. **Address:** 3000 Windy Hill Rd **Location:** I-75, exit 260, 0.5 mi e; in Terrace at Windy Hill Plaza. **Parking:** on-site. **Cards:** AX, CB, DC, DS, JC, MC, VI.

HAVELI INDIAN CUISINE — **Phone:** 770/422-8000 (63)

Indian
$8-$15

The lunch buffet is a popular offering at this establishment, which also prepares Indian dishes from a large evening menu. Casual dress. **Bar:** Full bar. **Hours:** 11:30 am-2:30 & 5:30-10 pm, Sat & Sun from noon. Closed major holidays. **Address:** 490 Franklin Rd **Location:** I-75, exit 263, just w. **Parking:** on-site. **Cards:** AX, DC, DS, MC, VI.

HOUSE OF LU — **Phone:** 770/794-8831 (51)

Chinese
$6-$17

Traditional Chinese decor and cuisine are hallmarks of the long-established downtown staple, which also counts some other locations. Service is prompt. Casual dress. **Bar:** Beer & wine. **Reservations:** accepted. **Hours:** 11 am-10 pm, Fri & Sat-10:30 pm. Closed: 12/25. **Address:** 89 Cherokee St, Marietta Square **Location:** Downtown; on Historic Marietta Square. **Parking:** street. **Cards:** AX, CB, DC, DS, JC, MC, VI.

KIOSCO — **Phone:** 678/337-7999 (61)

Colombian
$1-$20

Owned and operated by natives, menu selections include traditional Colombian fare, such as carnes, pescado and pollo as well as yuccas and empanadas. For a perfect ending, order the figs in syrup with cheese. Casual dress. **Bar:** Beer & wine. **Reservations:** accepted. **Hours:** 11 am-3 & 5:45-9:30 pm, Sat from noon. Closed major holidays. **Address:** 48 Powder Springs St **Location:** Just s of Historic Marietta Square. **Parking:** on-site. **Cards:** AX, CB, DC, DS, JC, MC, VI.

CALL

LA PARRILLA — **Phone:** 770/427-0055 (60)

Tex-Mex
$6-$18

The Tex-Mex establishment is a cut above many in terms of food, service and decor. Patrons can sip a margarita while nibbling on chips and salsa and soak up the festive atmosphere while waiting on their entrees. Casual dress. **Bar:** Full bar. **Hours:** 11 am-10 pm, Thurs-Sat to 10:30 pm. Closed: 1/1, 7/4, 12/25. **Address:** 29 S Marietta Pkwy **Location:** Just w of Historic Marietta Square; downtown. **Parking:** on-site. **Cards:** AX, CB, DC, DS, JC, MC, VI.

LEMON GRASS THAI RESTAURANT — **Phone:** 770/973-7478 (49)

Thai
$7-$12

Varied Thai dishes are served in a relaxing, classy atmosphere. Gracious servers bring well-prepared, spicy selections, such as rama chicken sauteed with vegetables and basil in hot curry sauce. Hot tea rounds out a tasty meal. Casual dress. **Bar:** Beer & wine. **Reservations:** accepted. **Hours:** 11:30 am-2:30 & 5-10 pm, Fri-10:30 pm, Sat 5 pm-10:30 pm. Closed major holidays; also Sun. **Address:** 2145 Roswell Rd, Suite 190 **Location:** I-75, exit 265, 1.6 mi se on SR 120 Loop to SR 120, then 0.6 mi e; in East Lake Shopping Center. **Parking:** on-site. **Cards:** AX, DC, DS, MC, VI.

MARIETTA DINER — **Phone:** 770/423-9390 (62)

Continental
$7-$24

A seemingly endless array of choices—all served in heaping portions—awaits patrons. Desserts must be seen to be believed. Casual dress. **Bar:** Beer & wine. **Hours:** 24 hours. **Address:** 306 Cobb Pkwy **Location:** I-75, exit 263, 0.4 mi w to Cobb Pkwy, then just n. **Parking:** on-site. **Cards:** AX, DC, MC, VI.

MY FRIEND'S PLACE — **Phone:** 770/956-7545 (69)

Deli
$5-$7

The quick-serve deli does a brisk lunchtime business, offering soups, salads and sandwiches. Casual dress. **Hours:** 10 am-4 pm, Sat-3 pm. Closed major holidays; also Sun. **Address:** 3000 Windy Hill Rd **Location:** I-75, exit 260, 0.5 mi e; in Terrace at Windy Hill Plaza. **Parking:** on-site. **Cards:** AX, CB, DC, DS, JC, MC, VI.

NEW LUCKY CHINA — **Phone:** 770/565-9666 (45)

Chinese
$6-$14

The menu blends well-prepared Chinese dishes and a handful of Thai offerings. Twice-cooked pork is a can't miss for those who favor hot and spicy selections. Fish, fowl, beef and pork all are represented. Casual dress. **Bar:** Beer & wine. **Hours:** 11:30 am-3 & 4-9:30 pm, Fri & Sat 11:30 am-11 pm. Closed major holidays. **Address:** 2960 Shallowford Rd, Suite 201 **Location:** Jct Shallowford and Sandy Plains rds; in Sandy Plains Shopping Center. **Parking:** on-site. **Cards:** AX, DC, DS, MC, VI.

PAPPADEAUX SEAFOOD — **Phone:** 770/984-8899

Regional Seafood
$11-$22

A seafood lover's delight, the restaurant taps into a little bit of New Orleans with its Cajun dishes and elaborate menu selections. Patrons might start off with a creative choice of blackened oyster and shrimp fondeaux with crayfish and let the feast begin. While music plays in the background, patrons can dig into dirty rice or spicy gumbo loaded with seafood. Well-seasoned shrimp and fish are prepared in varied ways. Casual dress. **Bar:** Full bar. **Reservations:** accepted, for lunch Sat & Sun. **Hours:** 11 am-9 pm. Closed: 11/26, 12/25. **Address:** 2830 Windy Hill Rd **Location:** I-75, exit 260, just e. **Parking:** on-site. **Cards:** AX, DC, DS, MC, VI.

CALL

PAPPASITO'S CANTINA — **Phone:** 770/541-6100

Tex-Mex
$11-$40

Fine traditional offerings are served in an upscale cantina atmosphere. Often crowded during peak hours, the immensely popular stop dishes up generous portions of sizzling fajitas, enchiladas and other traditional Mexican favorites, including some shrimp specialties. The terrific margaritas are guaranteed to get attention. Tables in the large dining room are closely spaced. Ice cream with cinnamon on chocolate bread pudding shouldn't be missed. Casual dress. **Bar:** Full bar. **Hours:** 11 am-10 pm, Fri & Sat-11 pm. Closed: 11/26, 12/25. **Address:** 2788 Windy Hill Rd **Location:** I-75, exit 260, just e. **Parking:** on-site. **Cards:** AX, DC, MC, VI.

(See maps and indexes starting on p. 296, 302)

THE RIB RANCH **Phone:** 770/422-5755 (48)

Barbecue
$7-$23

House specialties include barbecue ribs, pork and chicken grilled over an open pit and fresh homemade pie. Rustic and comfortable, the atmosphere is perfect for family meals. Casual dress. **Bar:** Beer & wine. **Hours:** 11 am-9:30 pm, Fri & Sat-10:30 pm, Sun noon-9:30 pm. Closed: 4/12, 11/26, 12/25. **Address:** 2063 Canton Rd **Location:** I-75, exit 267A, 1 mi ne. **Parking:** on-site. **Cards:** AX, DS, MC, VI.

RUSAN'S MARIETTA **Phone:** 770/933-8315 (71)

Japanese
$5-$21

The extensive menu features sushi, tempura, yakatori, nouveau Pacific Rim and other Japanese fusion items. The atmosphere is chic, trendy and bustling, with the owner's stark black-and-white artwork. The sushi lunch buffet lines up a generous sampling. Casual dress. **Bar:** Full bar. **Reservations:** accepted. **Hours:** 11:30 am-2:30 & 4:30-10:30 pm, Fri & Sat-11:30 pm, Sun 4:30 pm-10 pm. Closed: 11/26, 12/25. **Address:** 2313 Windy Hill Rd **Location:** I-75, exit 260, 0.5 mi w; in Windy Hill Crossing. **Parking:** on-site. **Cards:** AX, MC, VI.

SABOR DO BRAZIL **Phone:** 770/541-2625 (66)

Brazilian
$7-$9

The little eatery stays busy due in large part to a well-stocked buffet with some enticing South American food preparations. Casual dress. **Hours:** 11 am-10 pm, Sat-9 pm, Sun 11:30 am-5 pm. **Address:** 2800 Delk Rd, Suite E **Location:** I-75, exit 261, 0.5 mi e. **Parking:** on-site. **Cards:** AX, DC, DS, MC, VI.

SIMPATICO **Phone:** 770/792-9086 (54)

American
$14-$25

The Marietta Square newcomer receives good marks for its innovative interpretations of American cuisine. The seafood dishes are particularly noteworthy. Casual dress. **Bar:** Full bar. **Reservations:** accepted. **Hours:** 5:30 pm-10 pm, Fri & Sat-11 pm. Closed major holidays; also Sun & Mon. **Address:** 23 N Park Square **Location:** Downtown; on Historic Marietta Square. **Parking:** street. **Cards:** AX, MC, VI.

TASTY CHINA **Phone:** 770/419-9849 (64)

Chinese
$2-$14

Named among Atlanta's top 50 restaurants by the Atlanta Journal-Constitution, this place prepares authentic Szechuan cuisine, including spicy originals as well as more Americanized dishes. Bold choices include fried dry eggplant and sharp pepper fish. The owner can steer diners to some real treats. Casual dress. **Hours:** 11 am-10 pm, Fri & Sat-11 pm, Sun noon-10 pm. **Address:** 585 Franklin Rd, Suite B-3 **Location:** I-75, exit 263, 0.3 mi w to Franklin Rd; in shopping plaza. **Parking:** on-site. **Cards:** MC, VI.

THAICOON & SUSHI BAR **Phone:** 678/766-0641 (56)

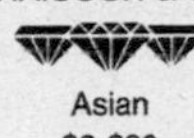

Asian
$8-$20

Visually appealing Japanese and Thai dishes coexist harmoniously on the modestly upscale restaurant's menu. The charming and tasteful decor incorporates elegant artwork and fresh flowers. Casual dress. **Bar:** Beer & wine. **Reservations:** accepted. **Hours:** 11:30 am-2:30 & 5-10 pm, Fri-11 pm, Sat 5 pm-11 pm, Sun 11:30 am-10 pm. Closed: 11/26, 12/25. **Address:** 34 Mill St **Location:** 1 blk w of Historic Marietta Square; downtown. **Parking:** street. **Cards:** AX, MC, VI.

CALL M

TOKYO JAPANESE STEAK HOUSE **Phone:** 770/928-9386 (43)

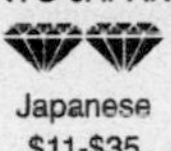

Japanese
$11-$35

Entertaining expert chefs prepare hibachi-style food tableside. The experience at the longtime local haunt is satisfying and fun. Casual dress. **Bar:** Full bar. **Reservations:** accepted. **Hours:** 4:30 pm-10 pm, Fri & Sat-11 pm. Closed: 11/26. **Address:** 3920 Canton Rd **Location:** I-75, exit 267A, 3.6 mi ne. **Parking:** on-site. **Cards:** AX, CB, DC, DS, JC, MC, VI.

TRATTORIA LA STRADA **Phone:** 770/640-7008 (100)

Italian
$12-$20

Traditional cuisine is served in a friendly, neighborhood eatery atmosphere. Local residents rave about the food, which is very good and a truly good value. Menu choices include fried calamari, veal Marsala, linguine with marinara sauce and tiramisu. The well-trained staff is eager to please. Casual dress. **Bar:** Full bar. **Hours:** 5 pm-10 pm, Fri & Sat-11 pm. Closed: 11/26, 12/25. **Address:** 2930 Johnson Ferry Rd NE **Location:** Jct Shallowford and Johnson Ferry rds, 0.5 mi s. **Parking:** on-site. **Cards:** AX, CB, DC, DS, MC, VI.

VATICA **Phone:** 770/955-3740 (67)

Indian
$9-$11

The Indian-vegetarian menu teems with bold, spicy and inexpensive items, such as the special vegetable curry, Indian-style pancakes and sambar. Casual dress. **Hours:** 11 am-3 & 5-9:30 pm. Closed major holidays. **Address:** 1475 Terrell Mill Rd, Suite 105 **Location:** I-75, exit 261, 1 mi e to Powers Ferry Rd, 0.4 mi s, then just w. **Parking:** on-site. **Cards:** AX, MC, VI.

WILD WING CAFE **Phone:** 770/509-9464 (50)

American
$4-$16

This fun and boisterous sports bar boasts a huge selection of draft and imported beer. Specialties include the 25-wing sampler platter, with a dozen or so sauce flavors ranging from honey mustard and ranchilada to Chernobyl and China Syndrome. Casual dress. **Bar:** Full bar. **Reservations:** not accepted. **Hours:** 11 am-2 am, Sun noon-midnight. Closed: 12/25. **Address:** 2145 Roswell Rd NE **Location:** I-75, exit 265, 1.6 mi e on SR 120 Loop to SR 120, 0.6 mi e; in East Lake Shopping Center. **Parking:** on-site. **Cards:** AX, DC, DS, MC, VI.

WILLIAMSON BROS BAR-B-Q **Phone:** 770/971-3201 (59)

Regional Barbecue
$7-$15

House specialties include barbecue ribs, pork and chicken grilled over an open pit and fresh homemade pie. Rustic and comfortable, the atmosphere is perfect for family meals. Fried dill pickles and fried red tomatoes in a thick batter are worth a try. Casual dress. **Bar:** Beer & wine. **Hours:** 10:30 am-9:30 pm, Fri & Sat-10:30 pm. Closed major holidays. **Address:** 1425 Roswell Rd **Location:** I-75, exit 263 northbound, 0.5 mi w to US 41, 0.5 mi n to Roswell Rd, then 0.5 mi e; exit 265 southbound, 0.3 mi e to US 41, then 0.5 mi s. **Parking:** on-site. **Cards:** AX, DC, DS, MC, VI.

(See maps and indexes starting on p. 296, 302)

WILLIE RAE'S

Phone: 770/792-9995 (53)

Cajun
$7-$18

Both traditional and creative Cajun dishes satisfy diners at the popular establishment on historic Marietta Square. Casual dress. **Bar:** Full bar. **Reservations:** accepted. **Hours:** 11:30 am-9:30 pm, Fri-10:30 pm, Sat noon-10:30 pm. Closed major holidays; also Sun. **Address:** 25 N Park Square **Location:** Downtown; on Historic Marietta Square. **Parking:** street. **Cards:** AX, MC, VI.

MORROW pop. 4,882 (See map and index starting on p. 312)

WHERE TO STAY

BEST WESTERN SOUTHLAKE INN *Book great rates at AAA.com*

Phone: (770)961-6300 (79)

AAA SAVE

Hotel
$59-$99 All Year

Address: 6437 Jonesboro Rd **Location:** I-75, exit 233, just e. **Facility:** 113 one-bedroom standard units, some with whirlpools. 2 stories, exterior corridors. **Parking:** on-site. **Amenities:** high-speed Internet, irons, hair dryers. **Pool(s):** outdoor. **Guest Services:** coin laundry, wireless Internet. **Business Services:** PC, fax (fee). **Cards:** AX, DC, DS, MC, VI. **Free Special Amenities: expanded continental breakfast and high-speed Internet.**

/ SOME UNITS FEE

Best Western

AAA Benefit:
Members save up to 20%, plus 10% bonus points with rewards program.

COMFORT SUITES MORROW *Book great rates at AAA.com*

Phone: (678)674-1300 (80)

AAA SAVE

Hotel
$79-$199 All Year

Address: 1444 Southlake Plaza Dr **Location:** I-75, exit 233, just n, then just w. **Facility:** Smoke free premises. 74 one-bedroom standard units, some with whirlpools. 3 stories, interior corridors. **Parking:** on-site. **Amenities:** high-speed Internet, voice mail, irons, hair dryers. **Pool(s):** heated indoor. **Leisure Activities:** whirlpool, exercise room. **Guest Services:** coin laundry, wireless Internet. **Business Services:** meeting rooms, business center. **Cards:** AX, DC, DS, MC, VI. **Free Special Amenities: expanded continental breakfast and high-speed Internet.**

COUNTRY INN & SUITES BY CARLSON-ATLANTA I-75 SOUTH *Book great rates at AAA.com*

Phone: (770)603-3232 (84)

AAA SAVE

Hotel
$89-$99 All Year

Address: 2192 Mt. Zion Pkwy **Location:** I-75, exit 231, just w to Mt. Zion Pkwy, then just s. **Facility:** 62 units. 52 one-bedroom standard units. 10 one-bedroom suites, some with whirlpools. 3 stories, interior corridors. **Parking:** on-site. **Amenities:** voice mail, irons, hair dryers. **Pool(s):** outdoor. **Leisure Activities:** exercise room. **Guest Services:** coin laundry, wireless Internet. **Business Services:** meeting rooms, PC, fax. **Cards:** AX, CB, DC, DS, JC, MC, VI. **Free Special Amenities: full breakfast and high-speed Internet.**

CALL / SOME UNITS

DRURY INN & SUITES-ATLANTA SOUTH *Book at AAA.com*

Phone: (770)960-0500 (82)

Hotel
$85-$140 All Year

Address: 6520 S Lee St **Location:** I-75, exit 233, just e. **Facility:** 134 units. 110 one-bedroom standard units. 24 one-bedroom suites. 7 stories, interior corridors. *Bath:* combo or shower only. **Parking:** on-site. **Terms:** 3 day cancellation notice-fee imposed. **Amenities:** high-speed Internet, voice mail, irons, hair dryers. **Pool(s):** heated indoor/outdoor. **Leisure Activities:** whirlpool, exercise room. **Guest Services:** valet and coin laundry, wireless Internet. **Business Services:** meeting rooms, business center. **Cards:** AX, DC, DS, MC, VI.

ASK CALL / SOME UNITS

EXTENDED STAYAMERICA-ATLANTA-MORROW *Book at AAA.com*

Phone: (770)472-0727 (86)

Hotel
$60-$75 All Year

Address: 2265 Mt. Zion Pkwy **Location:** I-75, exit 231, just w, then 1.3 mi s. **Facility:** 104 one-bedroom standard units with efficiencies. 3 stories, interior corridors. **Parking:** on-site. **Terms:** office hours 7 am-11 pm. **Amenities:** high-speed Internet (fee), voice mail, irons. **Guest Services:** coin laundry, wireless Internet. **Business Services:** fax (fee). **Cards:** AX, CB, DC, DS, JC, MC, VI.

ASK / SOME UNITS FEE

HAMPTON INN SOUTHLAKE *Book great rates at AAA.com*

Phone: (770)968-8990 (83)

Hotel
$85-$129 All Year

Address: 1533 Southlake Pkwy **Location:** I-75, exit 233, just w, then just s. **Facility:** 125 one-bedroom standard units. 5 stories, interior corridors. *Bath:* combo or shower only. **Parking:** on-site. **Terms:** 1-30 night minimum stay, cancellation fee imposed. **Amenities:** video games (fee), voice mail, irons, hair dryers. **Pool(s):** outdoor. **Leisure Activities:** exercise room. **Guest Services:** valet and coin laundry, wireless Internet. **Business Services:** meeting rooms, PC. **Cards:** AX, CB, DC, DS, MC, VI.

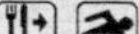  / SOME UNITS  

Hampton Inn

AAA Benefit:
Members save up to 10% everyday!

(See map and index starting on p. 312)

RED ROOF INN-SOUTH *Book great rates at AAA.com* **Phone:** (770)968-1483 81

AAA SAVE

Motel
$50-$90 All Year

Address: 1348 Southlake Plaza Dr **Location:** I-75, exit 233, just e to Southlake Plaza Dr, then just n. **Facility:** 108 one-bedroom standard units. 2 stories (no elevator), exterior corridors. **Parking:** on-site. **Terms:** 14 day cancellation notice. **Amenities:** video games (fee), voice mail. **Guest Services:** wireless Internet. **Business Services:** fax (fee). **Cards:** AX, CB, DC, DS, MC, VI. **Free Special Amenities: local telephone calls.**

/ SOME UNITS

SLEEP INN *Book at AAA.com* **Phone:** (770)472-9800 85

Hotel
$55-$90 All Year

Address: 2185 Mt. Zion Pkwy **Location:** I-75, exit 231, just w to Mt. Zion Pkwy, then just s. **Facility:** 90 one-bedroom standard units, some with whirlpools. 3 stories, interior corridors. *Bath:* shower only. **Parking:** on-site. **Amenities:** irons, hair dryers. **Pool(s):** outdoor. **Leisure Activities:** whirlpool, limited exercise equipment. **Guest Services:** valet and coin laundry, wireless Internet. **Business Services:** meeting rooms, PC, fax (fee). **Cards:** AX, CB, DC, DS, JC, MC, VI.

ASK CALL / SOME UNITS FEE VCR

WHERE TO DINE

CHINA CAFE **Phone:** 770/968-1100 59

Chinese
$6-$20

Traditional Chinese cuisine, such as flaming steak cooked tableside, is the focus of the family-owned restaurant's menu. Combinations of chicken, shrimp, pork and vegetables mingle with Asian sauces. The decor lights up the dining room. Casual dress. **Bar:** Beer & wine. **Hours:** 11 am-10 pm, Fri & Sat-11 pm. Closed: 11/26. **Address:** 1500 Mt. Zion Rd, Suite 201 **Location:** I-75, exit 233, 0.3 mi w to Mt. Zion Rd, then just s. **Parking:** on-site. **Cards:** AX, DS, MC, VI.

NORCROSS pop. 8,410 (See map and index starting on p. 302)

WHERE TO STAY

AMERICA'S BEST INN *Book at AAA.com* **Phone:** (770)449-7322 142

Hotel
$59-$79 All Year

Address: 6045 Oakbrook Pkwy **Location:** I-85, exit 99, just e to Live Oak Pkwy, 1 mi n, then w. **Facility:** 50 one-bedroom standard units. 2 stories (no elevator), interior/exterior corridors. **Parking:** on-site. **Amenities:** high-speed Internet, voice mail, irons, hair dryers. **Leisure Activities:** exercise room. **Guest Services:** coin laundry, wireless Internet. **Business Services:** meeting rooms, fax (fee). **Cards:** AX, CB, DC, DS, JC, MC, VI.

ASK FEE / SOME UNITS FEE

ATLANTA MARRIOTT NORCROSS *Book great rates at AAA.com* **Phone:** (770)263-8558 121

Hotel
$188-$201 All Year

Address: 475 Technology Pkwy **Location:** I-85, exit 99, 4 mi w to Peachtree Industrial Blvd, w on Holcomb Bridge Rd, then 0.8 mi n on Peachtree Pkwy (SR 141); I-285, exit 31B, 5 mi n on SR 141. **Facility:** Smoke free premises. 222 units. 218 one-bedroom standard units. 4 one-bedroom suites. 6 stories, interior corridors. **Parking:** on-site. **Terms:** cancellation fee imposed. **Amenities:** voice mail, irons, hair dryers. *Fee:* video games, high-speed Internet. **Pool(s):** heated indoor. **Leisure Activities:** whirlpool, exercise room. **Guest Services:** valet laundry, area transportation, wireless Internet. **Business Services:** meeting rooms, business center. **Cards:** AX, CB, DC, DS, JC, MC, VI.

FEE CALL / SOME UNITS FEE

Marriott
HOTELS & RESORTS
AAA Benefit:
Members save a minimum 5% off the best available rate.

BAYMONT INN & SUITES *Book at AAA.com* **Phone:** 770/449-5144 118

Hotel
Rates not provided

Address: 5375 Peachtree Industrial Blvd **Location:** I-285, exit 31B, 5.5 mi n; I-85, exit 99, 4 mi w to Peachtree Industrial Blvd, then 1.5 mi n. **Facility:** 130 units. 129 one-bedroom standard units. 1 one-bedroom suite. 3 stories, interior/exterior corridors. **Parking:** on-site. **Amenities:** high-speed Internet, voice mail, irons, hair dryers. *Some:* dual phone lines. **Pool(s):** outdoor. **Guest Services:** coin laundry, wireless Internet. **Business Services:** meeting rooms, PC, fax (fee).

FEE / SOME UNITS FEE

BEST WESTERN NORTH ATLANTA-NORCROSS INN *Book great rates at AAA.com* **Phone:** (770)448-8686 143

AAA SAVE

Hotel
$55-$99 All Year

Address: 6187 Dawson Blvd **Location:** I-85, exit 99, just e to McDonough Dr, then just s. Located in an office park/commercial area. **Facility:** 130 one-bedroom standard units. 3 stories, exterior corridors. **Parking:** on-site. **Terms:** 7 day cancellation notice. **Amenities:** high-speed Internet, voice mail, irons, hair dryers. **Pool(s):** outdoor. **Guest Services:** wireless Internet. **Business Services:** meeting rooms, PC, fax (fee). **Cards:** AX, DS, MC, VI. **Free Special Amenities: continental breakfast and high-speed Internet.**

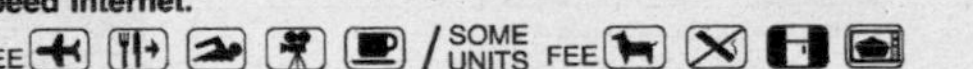

AAA Benefit:
Members save up to 20%, plus 10% bonus points with rewards program.

(See map and index starting on p. 302)

BEST WESTERN-PEACHTREE CORNERS Phone: (770)409-0004 130

AAA SAVE

Hotel
$79-$99 All Year

Address: 7035 Jimmy Carter Blvd **Location:** I-85, exit 99, 4 mi w; I-285, exit 31B, 4 mi n. **Facility:** 81 one-bedroom standard units, some with whirlpools. 3 stories, interior corridors. **Parking:** on-site. **Terms:** 3 day cancellation notice-fee imposed. **Amenities:** high-speed Internet, voice mail, irons, hair dryers. **Pool(s):** outdoor. **Leisure Activities:** limited exercise equipment. **Guest Services:** valet and coin laundry, wireless Internet. **Business Services:** meeting rooms, fax (fee). **Cards:** AX, DC, DS, MC, VI. **Free Special Amenities: continental breakfast and high-speed Internet.**

FEE CALL / SOME UNITS

AAA Benefit:
Members save up to 20%, plus 10% bonus points with rewards program.

COMFORT INN & SUITES *Book at AAA.com* Phone: (770)263-8883 117

Hotel
$79-$99 All Year

Address: 5200 Peachtree Industrial Blvd **Location:** I-285, exit 31B, 5.5 mi n; I-85, exit 99, 4 mi w to Peachtree Industrial Blvd, then 1.5 mi n. **Facility:** 62 units. 40 one-bedroom standard units, some with whirlpools. 22 one-bedroom suites. 3 stories, interior corridors. **Parking:** on-site. **Amenities:** high-speed Internet, dual phone lines, voice mail, irons, hair dryers. **Pool(s):** outdoor. **Leisure Activities:** limited exercise equipment. **Guest Services:** valet and coin laundry, wireless Internet. **Business Services:** meeting rooms, business center. **Cards:** AX, DC, DS, MC, VI.

ASK FEE CALL / SOME UNITS FEE

COMFORT INN & SUITES CONFERENCE CENTRE *Book great rates at AAA.com* Phone: (770)662-8175 141

AAA SAVE

Hotel
$74-$99 All Year

Address: 5985 Oakbrook Pkwy **Location:** I-85, exit 99, 0.5 mi e to Live Oak Pkwy, 0.8 mi n, then w. Located in an office park area. **Facility:** 115 units. 95 one-bedroom standard units. 20 one-bedroom suites, some with whirlpools. 3 stories, interior corridors. **Parking:** on-site. **Terms:** cancellation fee imposed. **Amenities:** high-speed Internet, voice mail, irons, hair dryers. **Pool(s):** outdoor. **Leisure Activities:** exercise room. **Guest Services:** valet and coin laundry, wireless Internet. **Business Services:** meeting rooms, PC, fax (fee). **Cards:** AX, CB, DC, DS, JC, MC, VI. **Free Special Amenities: continental breakfast and high-speed Internet.** *(See color ad below)*

FEE / SOME UNITS FEE

COUNTRY INN & SUITES BY CARLSON *Book great rates at AAA.com* Phone: (770)449-5051 138

AAA SAVE

Hotel
$79-$109 All Year

Address: 5970 Jimmy Carter Blvd **Location:** I-85, exit 99, 0.8 mi w. **Facility:** 51 units. 29 one-bedroom standard units. 22 one-bedroom suites. 3 stories, interior corridors. **Parking:** on-site. **Terms:** cancellation fee imposed. **Amenities:** high-speed Internet, dual phone lines, voice mail, irons, hair dryers. *Some:* DVD players (fee). **Pool(s):** outdoor. **Leisure Activities:** limited exercise equipment. **Guest Services:** valet and coin laundry, wireless Internet. **Business Services:** business center. **Cards:** AX, DS, MC, VI. **Free Special Amenities: expanded continental breakfast and high-speed Internet.**

FEE CALL / SOME UNITS

▼ *See AAA listing above* ▼

(See map and index starting on p. 302)

COURTYARD BY MARRIOTT-ATLANTA NORCROSS 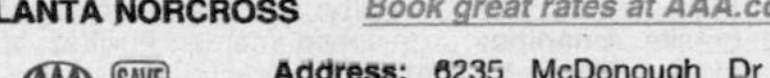 Book great rates at AAA.com

Phone: (770)242-7172 144

Hotel
$112-$123 All Year

Address: 6235 McDonough Dr **Location:** I-85, exit 99, just e to McDonough Dr, then just s. **Facility:** Smoke free premises. 122 units. 111 one-bedroom standard units. 11 one-bedroom suites. 2 stories (no elevator), interior corridors. **Parking:** on-site. **Terms:** cancellation fee imposed. **Amenities:** video games (fee), high-speed Internet, voice mail, irons, hair dryers. **Pool(s):** outdoor. **Leisure Activities:** whirlpool, exercise room. **Guest Services:** valet and coin laundry, wireless Internet. **Business Services:** meeting rooms, business center. **Cards:** AX, CB, DC, DS, JC, MC, VI. **Free Special Amenities: newspaper and high-speed Internet.**

FEE CALL / SOME UNITS

AAA Benefit:
Members save a minimum 5% off the best available rate.

COURTYARD BY MARRIOTT-PEACHTREE CORNERS Book great rates at AAA.com

Phone: (770)446-3777 127

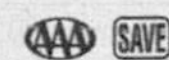

Hotel
$138-$148 All Year

Address: 3209 Holcomb Bridge Rd **Location:** I-85, exit 99, 4 mi w, then 0.5 mi n; I-285, exit 31B, 4 mi n to Holcomb Bridge Rd, then just w. **Facility:** Smoke free premises. 131 units. 109 one-bedroom standard units. 22 one-bedroom suites. 2-3 stories (no elevator), interior corridors. **Parking:** on-site. **Terms:** cancellation fee imposed. **Amenities:** high-speed Internet, voice mail, irons, hair dryers. **Pool(s):** outdoor. **Leisure Activities:** whirlpool, exercise room. **Guest Services:** valet and coin laundry, wireless Internet. **Business Services:** meeting rooms, business center. **Cards:** AX, CB, DC, DS, JC, MC, VI. **Free Special Amenities: newspaper and high-speed Internet.**

FEE CALL / SOME UNITS

AAA Benefit:
Members save a minimum 5% off the best available rate.

DAYS INN & SUITES Book at AAA.com

Phone: (770)416-9021 119

Hotel
$48-$99 All Year

Address: 5385 Peachtree Industrial Blvd **Location:** I-285, exit 31B, 5.5 mi n; I-85, exit 99, 4 mi w to Peachtree Industrial Blvd, then 1.5 mi n. **Facility:** 57 one-bedroom standard units, some with whirlpools. 2 stories, interior corridors. **Parking:** on-site. **Amenities:** high-speed Internet, safes (fee), irons, hair dryers. **Pool(s):** indoor. **Leisure Activities:** whirlpool, limited exercise equipment. **Guest Services:** wireless Internet. **Business Services:** meeting rooms, PC, fax (fee). **Cards:** AX, DC, DS, MC, VI.

ASK FEE CALL / SOME UNITS FEE

DAYS INN ATLANTA NE Book great rates at AAA.com

Phone: (770)368-0218 137

Motel
$56-$70 All Year

Address: 5990 Western Hills Dr **Location:** I-85, exit 99, 0.8 mi w to Norcross Tucker Rd to Western Hills Dr, then just n. Located in a light industrial/residential area. **Facility:** 90 one-bedroom standard units, some with whirlpools. 2 stories, exterior corridors. **Parking:** on-site. **Amenities:** high-speed Internet, hair dryers. **Pool(s):** outdoor. **Guest Services:** coin laundry, wireless Internet. **Business Services:** meeting rooms, PC, fax (fee). **Cards:** AX, DC, DS, JC, MC, VI. **Free Special Amenities: continental breakfast and high-speed Internet.**

/ SOME UNITS FEE

DRURY INN & SUITES-ATLANTA NORTHEAST Book at AAA.com

Phone: (770)729-0060 140

Hotel
$70-$125 All Year

Address: 5655 Jimmy Carter Blvd **Location:** I-85, exit 99, just w. **Facility:** 136 units. 128 one-bedroom standard units. 8 one-bedroom suites. 5 stories, interior corridors. **Parking:** on-site. **Amenities:** high-speed Internet, dual phone lines, voice mail, irons, hair dryers. **Pool(s):** heated indoor/outdoor. **Leisure Activities:** whirlpool, exercise room. **Guest Services:** valet and coin laundry, wireless Internet. **Business Services:** meeting rooms, business center. **Cards:** AX, DC, DS, MC, VI.

ASK FEE CALL / SOME UNITS

EXTENDED STAYAMERICA ATLANTA-JIMMY CARTER BLVD. Book at AAA.com

Phone: (770)446-9245 133

Hotel
$50-$65 All Year

Address: 6295 Jimmy Carter Blvd **Location:** I-85, exit 99, 2.5 mi w. **Facility:** 195 one-bedroom standard units with efficiencies. 2 stories (no elevator), exterior corridors. *Bath:* combo or shower only. **Parking:** on-site. **Terms:** office hours 7 am-11 pm. **Amenities:** high-speed Internet (fee), voice mail, irons. **Guest Services:** coin laundry, wireless Internet. **Business Services:** fax (fee). **Cards:** AX, CB, DC, DS, JC, MC, VI.

ASK CALL / SOME UNITS FEE

EXTENDED STAYAMERICA ATLANTA-NORCROSS Book at AAA.com

Phone: (770)729-8100 131

Hotel
$58-$70 All Year

Address: 200 Lawrenceville St **Location:** Downtown; behind post office. **Facility:** 132 one-bedroom standard units with efficiencies. 2-3 stories (no elevator), exterior corridors. **Parking:** on-site. **Terms:** office hours 7 am-11 pm. **Amenities:** high-speed Internet (fee), voice mail, irons. **Guest Services:** coin laundry, wireless Internet. **Business Services:** fax (fee). **Cards:** AX, CB, DC, DS, JC, MC, VI.

ASK CALL / SOME UNITS FEE

(See map and index starting on p. 302)

GUESTHOUSE INN Book great rates at AAA.com **Phone:** (770)564-0492 135

SAVE

Hotel
$49-$89 All Year

Address: 2050 Willowtrail Pkwy **Location:** I-85, exit 101, just e. **Facility:** 144 one-bedroom standard units. 3 stories, exterior corridors. **Parking:** on-site. **Amenities:** high-speed Internet. **Pool(s):** outdoor. **Guest Services:** valet laundry, wireless Internet. **Business Services:** meeting rooms, fax (fee). **Cards:** AX, DS, MC, VI. **Free Special Amenities: continental breakfast and high-speed Internet.**

FEE / SOME UNITS FEE

HAMPTON INN Book great rates at AAA.com **Phone:** (770)729-0015 123

Hotel
$109-$139 All Year

Address: 440 Technology Pkwy **Location:** I-85, exit 99, 4 mi w to Peachtree Industrial Blvd, then 0.8 mi n on Peachtree Pkwy (SR 141); I-285, exit 31B, 5 mi n on SR 141. **Facility:** 149 one-bedroom standard units. 5 stories, interior corridors. **Parking:** on-site. **Terms:** 1-30 night minimum stay, cancellation fee imposed. **Amenities:** video games (fee), high-speed Internet, voice mail, irons, hair dryers. **Pool(s):** heated indoor. **Leisure Activities:** whirlpool, exercise room. **Guest Services:** valet laundry, area transportation, wireless Internet. **Business Services:** meeting rooms, PC, fax (fee). **Cards:** AX, CB, DC, DS, MC, VI.

FEE CALL / SOME UNITS

AAA Benefit:
Members save up to 10% everyday!

HILTON ATLANTA NORTHEAST Book great rates at AAA.com **Phone:** (770)447-4747 125

Hotel
$94-$199 All Year

Address: 5993 Peachtree Industrial Blvd **Location:** I-285, exit 31B, 4.5 mi ne. **Facility:** 272 units. 269 one-bedroom standard units. 3 one-bedroom suites. 10 stories, interior corridors. **Parking:** on-site. **Terms:** 1-30 night minimum stay, cancellation fee imposed. **Amenities:** high-speed Internet (fee), dual phone lines, voice mail, safes, irons, hair dryers. **Pool(s):** heated indoor/outdoor. **Leisure Activities:** saunas, whirlpool, exercise room. **Guest Services:** valet and coin laundry, area transportation, wireless Internet. **Business Services:** conference facilities, business center. **Cards:** AX, CB, DC, DS, JC, MC, VI.

FEE CALL
/ SOME UNITS FEE

AAA Benefit:
Members save 5% or more everyday!

HOLIDAY INN SELECT-PEACHTREE CORNERS Book at AAA.com **Phone:** 770/448-4400 126

Hotel
Rates not provided

Address: 6050 Peachtree Industrial Blvd NW **Location:** I-285, exit 31B, 4.5 mi ne; I-85, exit 99, 4 mi w to Peachtree Industrial Blvd, 0.4 mi n, then just w on Holcomb Bridge Rd. Located in business park. **Facility:** 243 one-bedroom standard units. 9 stories, interior corridors. **Parking:** on-site. **Amenities:** high-speed Internet, voice mail, irons, hair dryers. **Pool(s):** heated indoor/outdoor. **Leisure Activities:** whirlpool, exercise room. **Guest Services:** valet and coin laundry, area transportation, wireless Internet. **Business Services:** conference facilities, business center.

FEE CALL / SOME UNITS

HOMESTEAD STUDIO SUITES HOTEL-ATLANTA/ PEACHTREE CORNERS Book at AAA.com **Phone:** (770)449-9966 129

Hotel
$55-$65 All Year

Address: 7049 Jimmy Carter Blvd **Location:** I-85, exit 99, 4 mi n; I-285, exit 31B, 4 mi n. **Facility:** 137 one-bedroom standard units with efficiencies. 2 stories, exterior corridors. **Parking:** on-site. **Amenities:** high-speed Internet (fee), voice mail, irons, hair dryers. **Guest Services:** valet and coin laundry, wireless Internet. **Business Services:** fax (fee). **Cards:** AX, CB, DC, DS, JC, MC, VI.

ASK CALL / SOME UNITS FEE

HOMEWOOD SUITES BY HILTON Book great rates at AAA.com **Phone:** (770)448-4663 122

Hotel
$69-$129 All Year

Address: 450 Technology Pkwy **Location:** I-85, exit 99, 4 mi w to Peachtree Industrial Blvd, 0.4 mi n, w on Holcomb Bridge Rd, then 2 blks n on Peachtree Pkwy; I-285, exit 31B, 5 mi n on SR 141. Located in a business park area. **Facility:** 92 units. 88 one- and 4 two-bedroom standard units with efficiencies. 3 stories, interior/exterior corridors. **Parking:** on-site. **Terms:** 1-30 night minimum stay, cancellation fee imposed. **Amenities:** video games (fee), high-speed Internet, voice mail, irons, hair dryers. *Some:* DVD players. **Pool(s):** outdoor. **Leisure Activities:** whirlpool, exercise room, sports court. **Guest Services:** valet and coin laundry, area transportation, wireless Internet. **Business Services:** meeting rooms, business center. **Cards:** AX, DC, DS, MC, VI.

FEE CALL
/ SOME UNITS FEE VCR

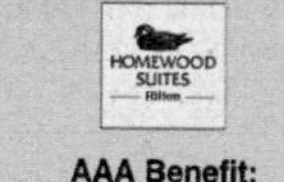

AAA Benefit:
Members save 5% or more everyday!

(See map and index starting on p. 302)

HYATT PLACE ATLANTA/NORCROSS/PEACHTREE Book great rates at AAA.com **Phone:** (770)416-7655 116

Hotel
$69-$199 All Year

Address: 5600 Peachtree Pkwy **Location:** I-285, exit 31B, 4 mi n on SR 141, then 1 mi n. **Facility:** 126 one-bedroom standard units. 6 stories, interior corridors. **Parking:** on-site. **Terms:** cancellation fee imposed. **Amenities:** high-speed Internet, voice mail, irons, hair dryers. **Pool(s):** heated outdoor. **Leisure Activities:** exercise room. **Guest Services:** valet laundry, area transportation-within 3 mi, wireless Internet. **Business Services:** meeting rooms, business center. **Cards:** AX, CB, DC, DS, JC, MC, VI. **Free Special Amenities: continental breakfast and high-speed Internet.**

CALL / SOME UNITS

AAA Benefit: Ask for the AAA rate and save 10%.

LA QUINTA INN Book great rates at AAA.com **Phone:** (770)368-9400 139

Hotel
$59-$134 All Year

Address: 5945 Oakbrook Pkwy **Location:** I-85, exit 99, 0.5 mi e to Live Oak Pkwy, then 0.8 mi w. Located in an office park area. **Facility:** 121 units. 102 one-bedroom standard units, some with whirlpools. 19 one-bedroom suites. 3 stories, interior corridors. **Parking:** on-site. **Amenities:** high-speed Internet, dual phone lines, voice mail, irons, hair dryers. **Pool(s):** heated outdoor. **Leisure Activities:** exercise room. **Guest Services:** coin laundry, wireless Internet. **Business Services:** meeting rooms, PC, fax (fee). **Cards:** AX, DC, DS, MC, VI. **Free Special Amenities: full breakfast and high-speed Internet.**

FEE / SOME UNITS

MICROTEL INN & SUITES Book at AAA.com **Phone:** 678/291-9888 136

Hotel
Rates not provided

Address: 2150 N Norcross Tucker Rd **Location:** I-85, exit 99, 0.8 mi w to Norcross Tucker Rd, then just n. **Facility:** 46 one-bedroom standard units. 3 stories, interior corridors. **Parking:** on-site. **Amenities:** high-speed Internet, hair dryers. **Guest Services:** coin laundry, wireless Internet. **Business Services:** fax (fee).

CALL / SOME UNITS

RED ROOF INN & SUITES Book at AAA.com **Phone:** (770)446-2882 120

Hotel
$48-$52 All Year

Address: 5395 Peachtree Industrial Blvd **Location:** I-285, exit 31B, 5.5 mi n; I-85, exit 99, 4 mi w to Peachtree Industrial Blvd, then 1.5 mi n. **Facility:** 132 units. 121 one-bedroom standard units. 11 one-bedroom suites with efficiencies (no utensils). 3 stories, interior corridors. **Parking:** on-site. **Amenities:** high-speed Internet, voice mail, irons, hair dryers. **Pool(s):** outdoor. **Guest Services:** coin laundry, wireless Internet. **Business Services:** meeting rooms, fax (fee). **Cards:** AX, CB, DC, DS, MC, VI.

ASK FEE / SOME UNITS

RED ROOF INN-INDIAN TRAIL Book at AAA.com **Phone:** (770)448-8944 134

Motel
$50-$90 1/1-11/30
$45-$70 12/1-12/31

Address: 5171 Brook Hollow Pkwy **Location:** I-85, exit 101, just w to Brook Hollow Pkwy, then just s. **Facility:** 115 one-bedroom standard units. 3 stories, exterior corridors. **Parking:** on-site. **Terms:** 14 day cancellation notice. **Amenities:** voice mail. *Fee:* video games, high-speed Internet. **Guest Services:** wireless Internet. **Business Services:** fax (fee). **Cards:** AX, CB, DC, DS, MC, VI.

/ SOME UNITS

STUDIOPLUS Book at AAA.com **Phone:** (770)582-9984 128

Hotel
$60-$75 All Year

Address: 7065 Jimmy Carter Blvd **Location:** I-85, exit 99, 4 mi n; I-285, exit 31B, 4 mi n. **Facility:** 72 one-bedroom standard units with kitchens. 3 stories, interior corridors. **Parking:** on-site. **Terms:** office hours 7 am-11 pm. **Amenities:** high-speed Internet (fee), voice mail, irons. **Pool(s):** outdoor. **Leisure Activities:** exercise room. **Guest Services:** coin laundry, wireless Internet. **Business Services:** fax (fee). **Cards:** AX, CB, DC, DS, JC, MC, VI.

ASK FEE CALL / SOME UNITS FEE

SUPER 8 ATLANTA NORTHEAST @ TECHNOLOGY PARK Book at AAA.com **Phone:** (770)441-1999 132

Hotel
$54-$69 All Year

Address: 6650 Bay Circle Dr **Location:** I-285, exit 31B, 3 mi n on Peachtree Industrial Blvd to Jones Mill Rd. Located in an industrial business park area. **Facility:** 130 one-bedroom standard units. 3 stories, interior/exterior corridors. **Parking:** on-site. **Terms:** cancellation fee imposed. **Amenities:** high-speed Internet, irons, hair dryers. **Pool(s):** outdoor. **Guest Services:** coin laundry, wireless Internet. **Business Services:** business center. **Cards:** AX, DC, DS, MC, VI.

ASK FEE CALL / SOME UNITS

WINGATE INN Book at AAA.com **Phone:** (770)263-2020 124

Hotel
$65-$108 All Year

Address: 5800 Peachtree Industrial Blvd **Location:** I-285, exit 31B, 5 mi n; I-85, exit 99, 4 mi w to Peachtree Industrial Blvd, then 1 mi n. **Facility:** 118 units. 114 one-bedroom standard units. 4 one-bedroom suites with whirlpools. 4 stories, interior corridors. **Parking:** on-site. **Terms:** cancellation fee imposed. **Amenities:** video games (fee), high-speed Internet, dual phone lines, voice mail, safes, irons, hair dryers. **Pool(s):** outdoor. **Leisure Activities:** whirlpool, exercise room. **Guest Services:** valet and coin laundry, area transportation, wireless Internet. **Business Services:** meeting rooms, business center. **Cards:** AX, DC, DS, MC, VI.

ASK FEE CALL / SOME UNITS

(See map and index starting on p. 302)

WHERE TO DINE

ASHIANA

Indian
$2-$15

Phone: 770/446-8081 (95)

Offerings of traditional Indian food are served in a contemporary setting. Pickled relish, naan, curries and many vegetable options often find their way onto the popular lunch buffet. Casual dress. **Bar:** Full bar. **Reservations:** accepted. **Hours:** 11:30 am-3 & 5:30-10 pm, Sat & Sun from noon. Closed: Mon. **Address:** 5675 Jimmy Carter Blvd **Location:** I-85, exit 99, just w. **Parking:** on-site. **Cards:** AX, CB, DC, DS, JC, MC, VI.

DOMINICK'S

Italian
$7-$22

Phone: 770/449-1611 (93)

In old town Norcross, this fun, friendly restaurant nurtures a bustling ambience that comes straight from the heart of Little Italy. A shining example of the sumptuously prepared traditional favorites is the highly recommended veal Dominick with provolone cheese. The staff facilitates guests' relaxed experiences. Casual dress. **Bar:** Full bar. **Hours:** 11 am-2 & 5-10 pm, Sat from 5 pm, Sun 5 pm-9 pm. Closed major holidays; also 12/24 & Super Bowl Sun. **Address:** 95 S Peachtree St **Location:** Corner of Peachtree St and Holcomb Bridge Rd; downtown. **Parking:** street. **Cards:** AX, CB, DC, DS, MC, VI.

FRONTERA MEX-MEX GRILL

Tex-Mex
$5-$13

Phone: 770/441-3488 (90)

Diners get what they'd expect from this place: chips and salsa, yummy Tex-Mex, margaritas and varied lunch specials. Casual dress. **Bar:** Full bar. **Hours:** 11 am-10:30 pm, Sun-10 pm. Closed major holidays. **Address:** 7190 Jimmy Carter Blvd **Location:** I-85, exit 99, 4 mi n; I-285, exit 31B, 4 mi n, then just w. **Parking:** on-site. **Cards:** AX, DS, MC, VI.

CALL

HI LIFE

American
$7-$26

Phone: 770/409-0101 (88)

The atmosphere is ritzy in the upscale New American eatery, which appeals to both locals and out-of-towners. Casual dress. **Bar:** Full bar. **Reservations:** accepted. **Hours:** 11 am-10 pm, Fri-11 pm, Sat 5 pm-11 pm. Closed major holidays; also Sun. **Address:** 3380 Holcomb Bridge Rd **Location:** Jct Jimmy Carter Blvd. **Parking:** on-site. **Cards:** AX, MC, VI.

JR'S LOG HOUSE

American
$5-$14

Phone: 770/449-6426 (94)

The popular local spot has been cooking and catering barbecue for more than 30 years. Daily specials are served in generous portions. Casual dress. **Bar:** Beer & wine. **Hours:** 7 am-8:30 pm, Fri & Sat-9 pm, Sun 8 am-8:30 pm. Closed: 11/26, 12/25. **Address:** 6601 Peachtree Industrial Blvd **Location:** Jct Jones Mill Rd and Peachtree Industrial Blvd. **Parking:** on-site. **Cards:** AX, DC, DS, MC, VI.

NORCROSS STATION CAFE

American
$6-$25

Phone: 770/409-9889 (92)

Trains still pass the interesting railroad train station that houses the welcoming restaurant. Ribs and Calabash shrimp are two favorites from the menu of creative cuisine. Casual dress. **Bar:** Full bar. **Hours:** 11 am-9:30 pm, Fri & Sat-10 pm. Closed major holidays; also Sun. **Address:** 40 S Peachtree St **Location:** I-85, exit 99, 1.6 mi w to S Peachtree St, just past SR 23, then 0.6 mi n. **Parking:** on-site. **Cards:** AX, CB, DC, DS, MC, VI.

THE PALACE

Indian
$9-$20

Phone: 770/840-7770 (89)

A well-stocked lunch buffet and traditional dinner favorites make their mark at the spacious suburban stop. Casual dress. **Bar:** Full bar. **Reservations:** accepted. **Hours:** 11:30 am-2:30 & 5:30-10 pm, Fri-11 pm, Sat & Sun noon-3 & 5:30-10 pm. **Address:** 6131 Peachtree Pkwy **Location:** I-85, exit 99, 4 mi w to Peachtree Industrial Blvd, 0.4 mi n, w on Holcomb Bridge Rd, then just n; I-285, exit 31B, 5 mi n on SR 141. **Parking:** on-site. **Cards:** AX, CB, DC, DS, JC, MC, VI.

PAPPADEAUX SEAFOOD

Regional Seafood
$11-$22

Phone: 770/849-0600

A seafood lover's delight, the restaurant taps into a little bit of New Orleans with its Cajun dishes and elaborate menu selections. Patrons might start off with a creative choice of blackened oyster and shrimp fondeaux with crayfish and let the feast begin. While music plays in the background, patrons can dig into dirty rice or spicy gumbo loaded with seafood. Well-seasoned shrimp and fish are prepared in varied ways. Casual dress. **Bar:** Full bar. **Reservations:** accepted, for lunch Mon-Sat. **Hours:** 11 am-9 pm. Closed: 11/26, 12/25. **Address:** 5635 Jimmy Carter Blvd **Location:** I-85, exit 99, just w. **Parking:** on-site. **Cards:** AX, DC, DS, MC, VI.

CALL

PHOENIX NOODLE CAFE

Asian
$5-$17

Phone: 770/449-8585 (85)

Diners who visit the sophisticated restaurant can expect a refined and intimate experience. Global flavors go into seafood and steak preparations, while the chicken salad platter offers a fresh and nicely presented version of a lighter favorite. The experienced and accommodating staff provides service. Casual dress. **Bar:** Beer & wine. **Hours:** 10:30 am-10 pm, Fri & Sat-11 pm. Closed: 11/26; also Mon. **Address:** 5450 Peachtree Pkwy NW **Location:** I-85, exit 99, 4 mi w to Peachtree Industrial Blvd, 0.4 mi n, just w on Holcomb Bridge Rd, then 1.2 mi n. **Parking:** on-site. **Cards:** AX, DS, MC, VI.

PHO HIEN

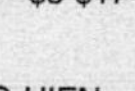

Vietnamese
$4-$9

Phone: 678/924-3610 (97)

The restaurant's Vietnamese cuisine can be carried out or savored in the cozy dining room. Casual dress. **Hours:** 10 am-9 pm. **Address:** 4782 Jimmy Carter Blvd **Location:** I-85, exit 99, 1 mi e. **Parking:** on-site. **Cards:** MC, VI.

SAIGON CAFE

Vietnamese
$7-$9

Phone: 770/368-8968 (91)

The pleasant Asian decor includes full-size palm, bamboo and mango trees. Guests can savor large portions of beef rice noodle soup, rice vermicelli and other rice plates. Casual dress. **Bar:** Beer & wine. **Hours:** 10:30 am-10 pm, Sun-9 pm. **Address:** 7040 Jimmy Carter Blvd **Location:** I-85, exit 99, 4 mi n; I-285, exit 31B, 4 mi n. **Parking:** on-site. **Cards:** AX, CB, DS, MC, VI.

(See map and index starting on p. 302)

THAI STAR — Phone: 770/326-9991 (86)

Thai
$5-$18

Solid standards and creative specials all are part of the tasty treats here. A large and tastefully done dining room helps to make the dining experience all the more enjoyable. Casual dress. **Bar:** Full bar. **Reservations:** accepted. **Hours:** 11 am-2:30 & 5-9:30 pm, Fri-10 pm, Sat noon-10 pm, Sun noon-9:30 pm. Closed: 1/1, 12/25. **Address:** 5370 Peachtree Industrial Blvd **Location:** I-285, exit 31B, 5.5 mi n; I-85, exit 99, 4 mi w to Peachtree Industrial Blvd, then 1.5 mi n. **Parking:** on-site. **Cards:** AX, CB, DC, DS, MC, VI.

THE VARSITY — Phone: 770/840-8519 (96)

American
$2-$10

A branch of a longtime Atlanta landmark, the restaurant offers fast food favorites. Casual dress. **Hours:** 10:30 am-9 pm. Closed: 4/12, 11/26, 12/25; also Sun. **Address:** 6045 Dawson Blvd **Location:** I-85, exit 99, 0.3 mi e to Dawson Blvd, then just s. **Parking:** on-site. **Cards:** AX, MC, VI.

ZAPATA — Phone: 770/248-0052 (87)

Mexican
$5-$17

The eclectic menu lines up a wide selection of Mexican dishes prepared from traditional recipes. Seafood and vegetarian preparations are among offerings. Casual dress. **Bar:** Full bar. **Hours:** 11 am-2:30 & 5-10 pm, Sat 12:30 pm-10 pm, Sun 11:30 am-9 pm. Closed: 11/26, 12/25. **Address:** 5975 Peachtree Pkwy NW **Location:** I-285, exit 31B, 4 mi n on SR 141, then 1.4 mi n. **Parking:** on-site. **Cards:** AX, DC, DS, MC, VI.

ROSWELL pop. 79,334 (See map and index starting on p. 302)

— WHERE TO STAY —

BEST WESTERN ROSWELL SUITES — Book great rates at AAA.com — Phone: (770)552-5599 (77)

AAA SAVE

Hotel
$85-$109 All Year

Address: 907 Holcomb Bridge Rd **Location:** SR 400, exit 7B, 0.7 mi w. **Facility:** 93 one-bedroom standard units, some with whirlpools. 3 stories, interior corridors. **Parking:** on-site. **Amenities:** video games (fee), high-speed Internet, voice mail, irons, hair dryers. **Pool(s):** outdoor. **Leisure Activities:** whirlpool, exercise room. **Guest Services:** valet and coin laundry, area transportation-within 5 mi, wireless Internet. **Business Services:** meeting rooms, business center. **Cards:** AX, CB, DC, DS, JC, MC, VI. **Free Special Amenities: continental breakfast and high-speed Internet.**

FEE CALL / SOME UNITS 

AAA Benefit: Members save up to 20%, plus 10% bonus points with rewards program.

BROOKWOOD INN — Book at AAA.com — Phone: 770/587-5161 (79)

Hotel
Rates not provided

Address: 9995 Old Dogwood Rd **Location:** SR 400, exit 7B, just w to Old Dogwood Rd, then just n. Located in a light commercial area. **Facility:** 90 one-bedroom standard units. 3 stories, exterior corridors. **Parking:** on-site. **Amenities:** high-speed Internet, dual phone lines, voice mail, irons, hair dryers. **Pool(s):** outdoor. **Leisure Activities:** limited exercise equipment. **Guest Services:** valet and coin laundry, wireless Internet. **Business Services:** meeting rooms, PC, fax (fee).

FEE / SOME UNITS FEE

COURTYARD BY MARRIOTT — Book great rates at AAA.com — Phone: (770)992-7200 (81)

Hotel
$153-$164 All Year

Address: 1500 Market Blvd **Location:** SR 400, exit 7A northbound, exit 7; southbound, just e. Located in a commercial/business area. **Facility:** Smoke free premises. 154 units. 140 one-bedroom standard units. 14 one-bedroom suites. 2-4 stories, interior corridors. **Parking:** on-site. **Terms:** cancellation fee imposed. **Amenities:** video games (fee), high-speed Internet, voice mail, irons, hair dryers. **Pool(s):** outdoor. **Leisure Activities:** whirlpool, exercise room. **Guest Services:** valet and coin laundry, wireless Internet. **Business Services:** meeting rooms, business center. **Cards:** AX, CB, DC, DS, MC, VI.

FEE CALL / SOME UNITS

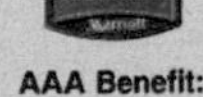

AAA Benefit: Members save a minimum 5% off the best available rate.

HOLIDAY INN HOTEL & SUITES — Book at AAA.com — Phone: (770)817-1414 (76)

Hotel
$99-$175 All Year

Address: 909 Holcomb Bridge Rd **Location:** SR 400, exit 7B, 0.7 mi w. **Facility:** 102 one-bedroom standard units. 3 stories, interior corridors. *Bath:* combo or shower only. **Parking:** on-site. **Amenities:** high-speed Internet, voice mail, irons, hair dryers. **Pool(s):** heated outdoor. **Leisure Activities:** exercise room. **Guest Services:** coin laundry, wireless Internet. **Business Services:** meeting rooms, business center. **Cards:** AX, DS, MC, VI.

(See map and index starting on p. 302)

LA QUINTA INN — Book great rates at AAA.com — Phone: (770)552-0200 78

Hotel
$44-$79 All Year

Address: 575 Old Holcomb Bridge Rd **Location:** SR 400, exit 7B, just w. **Facility:** 83 units. 79 one-bedroom standard units. 3 one- and 1 two-bedroom suites. 4 stories, interior corridors. **Parking:** on-site. **Amenities:** video games (fee), high-speed Internet, voice mail, irons, hair dryers. **Pool(s):** outdoor. **Leisure Activities:** exercise room. **Guest Services:** coin laundry, wireless Internet. **Business Services:** meeting rooms, fax (fee). **Cards:** AX, DC, DS, MC, VI.

ASK FEE CALL / SOME UNITS

STUDIO 6 #6025 — Book at AAA.com — Phone: (770)992-9449 80

Hotel
$64-$68 5/22-11/30
$61-$65 12/1-5/21

Address: 9955 Old Dogwood Rd **Location:** SR 400, exit 7B, just w. **Facility:** 141 one-bedroom standard units with efficiencies. 2 stories, exterior corridors. **Parking:** on-site. **Terms:** office hours 7 am-8 pm. **Amenities:** voice mail, irons. **Guest Services:** coin laundry, wireless Internet. **Business Services:** fax (fee). **Cards:** AX, CB, DC, DS, MC, VI.

CALL / SOME UNITS FEE

WHERE TO DINE

AMALFI RISTORANTE — Phone: 770/645-9983 69

Italian
$13-$20

The lively restaurant recalls Little Italy. Guests might start with complimentary olives, then dive into antipasto or calamari. Rigatoni with meatballs is representative of the nightly specials. Delectable desserts aim to please. Casual dress. **Bar:** Full bar. **Hours:** 5:30 pm-10 pm, Fri & Sat-11 pm. Closed major holidays; also Sun. **Address:** 292 S Atlanta St **Location:** 1 mi s of town square. **Parking:** on-site. **Cards:** AX, DC, DS, MC, VI.

ANGAN — Phone: 770/993-0010 68

Indian
$7-$15

A sumptuous buffet that lays out a lineup of varied options is a big draw at the Indian eatery. Casual dress. **Bar:** Beer & wine. **Reservations:** accepted. **Hours:** 5 pm-9:30 pm, Sat & Sun 11 am-3 & 5-10 pm; Saturday & Sunday brunch. Closed: 11/26, 12/25; also Mon. **Address:** 1475 Holcomb Bridge Rd, Suite 155 **Location:** SR 400, exit 7A, 0.3 mi e; in King's Market. **Parking:** on-site. **Cards:** AX, CB, DC, DS, JC, MC, VI.

BISTRO VG — Phone: 770/993-1156 60

American
$6-$34

This eatery never seems to disappoint with its consistently good food and top-notch service. "Can't miss" dishes include rack of lamb and the excellent strawberry creme brulee. Artwork enhances the intimate atmosphere. Dressy casual. **Bar:** Full bar. **Reservations:** suggested. **Hours:** 11:30 am-11 pm, Sun from 5 pm. Closed major holidays; also Sun. **Address:** 70 W Crossville Rd **Location:** SR 400, exit 7B, 2.7 mi w, follow via Holcomb Bridge Rd (SR 92); jct Crabapple Rd. **Parking:** valet. **Cards:** AX, DS, MC, VI.

CALL

BROOKWOOD GRILL — Phone: 770/587-0102 62

American
$13-$23

Favorites at the small, cozy restaurant are hickory-grilled chicken and steak. The salads are large and the pasta fresh. All desserts are noticeably made from scratch. Dressy casual. **Bar:** Full bar. **Reservations:** accepted. **Hours:** 11 am-10:30 pm, Fri-11:30 pm, Sat 10 am-11:30 pm, Sun 10 am-10 pm; Saturday & Sunday brunch. Closed: 11/26, 12/25. **Address:** 880A Holcomb Bridge Rd **Location:** SR 400, exit 7B, 0.8 mi w. **Parking:** on-site. **Cards:** AX, DC, DS, MC, VI.

BYBLOS — Phone: 678/352-0321 61

Lebanese
$3-$20

Kebabs, hummus, tabbouleh and kibbeh are some of the assorted Lebanese favorites. Guests also can savor more unusual items, such as aged yogurt cheese with spices and minced raw beef with bulgur. Casual dress. **Bar:** Beer & wine. **Reservations:** accepted. **Hours:** 11 am-2:30 & 5:30-9:30 pm, Fri & Sat-11 pm, Sun 11 am-3 & 5:30-9:30 pm. Closed: Mon. **Address:** 10684 Alpharetta Hwy, Commerce Row #500 **Location:** SR 400, exit 7B, 1.5 mi w to Alpharetta Hwy, then just n. **Parking:** on-site. **Cards:** AX, DS, MC, VI.

CHICAGO'S RESTAURANT — Phone: 770/993-7464 66

American
$10-$28

The seafood mixed grill, sauteed shrimp and scallops, stockyard steak and other quality dishes make up the menu at the casual neighborhood-style restaurant. The cooked-to-order filet is a tasty choice. Freshly ground espresso and cappuccino are favorite beverage options. Casual dress. Entertainment. **Bar:** Full bar. **Hours:** 5 pm-10 pm, Fri & Sat-11 pm, Sun 11:30 am-9 pm; Sunday brunch. Closed major holidays. **Address:** 4401 Shallowford Rd, Suite 106 **Location:** Jct Shallowford and Johnson's Ferry rds; in Shallowford Corners Shopping Center. **Parking:** on-site. **Cards:** AX, DC, DS, MC, VI.

CALL

DREAMLAND BAR-B-QUE — Phone: 678/352-7999

Barbecue
$7-$18

Like its sister restaurant in Alabama, the establishment focuses on ribs and other barbecue dishes. Casual dress. **Bar:** Beer only. **Hours:** 10 am-10 pm, Sun 11 am-9 pm. Closed: 11/26, 12/25. **Address:** 10730 Alpharetta Hwy **Location:** SR 400, exit 7B, 1.5 mi w to Alpharetta Hwy, then just n. **Parking:** on-site. **Cards:** AX, DC, DS, MC, VI.

(See map and index starting on p. 302)

THE FICKLE PICKLE — Phone: 770/650-9838 (64)

Deli
$7-$10

In a restored old house, the self-service bakery/sandwich shop is a delightful find. The menu is limited to soups, salads and sandwiches, as well as a wonderful array of homemade desserts and goodies, including pies, cookies and scrumptious brownies. All orders are made to order. Casual dress. **Bar:** Beer & wine. **Reservations:** not accepted. **Hours:** 11 am-9 pm, Mon-3 pm. Closed major holidays; also Sun. **Address:** 1085 Canton St **Location:** Downtown. **Parking:** on-site. **Cards:** AX, DS, MC, VI.

GREENWOOD'S ON GREEN STREET — Phone: 770/992-5383 (63)

Southern
$8-$25

The charming restaurant occupies a 150-plus-year-old clapboard house that's protected by the historical society. After a meal of dreamily good crispy fried chicken, guests often indulge in a huge slice of sinful coconut cream pie. Casual dress. **Bar:** Beer & wine. **Hours:** 5 pm-9 pm, Fri & Sat 11:30 am-10 pm, Sun 11:30 am-9 pm. Closed major holidays; also Mon & Tues. **Address:** 1087 Green St **Location:** SR 400, exit 4, 1.5 mi w to Alpharetta St, 1 mi s to Woodstock St, 1.3 mi w to Green St, then just s. **Parking:** on-site.

PASTIS — Phone: 770/640-3870 (67)

French
$5-$25

The appealing French bistro sustains a Mediterranean feel and prepares delicious authentic cuisine, including fresh salads, cheese plates and dishes such as salmon en croute, tuna nicoise and filet mignon. Patrons relax on the upstairs balcony and in the downstairs lounge. Friendly staff members provide casual service. Casual dress. **Bar:** Full bar. **Reservations:** accepted. **Hours:** 11:30 am-2:30 & 5:30-9:30 pm, Fri & Sat-10:30 pm. Closed: 1/1, 12/25. **Address:** 936 Canton St **Location:** Downtown. **Parking:** street. **Cards:** AX, CB, DC, DS, JC, MC, VI.

THE SWALLOW AT THE HOLLOW — Phone: 678/352-1975 (65)

Barbecue
$7-$22

This rustic and woodsy eatery serves savory barbecue, such as baby back ribs and pork, in addition to grilled portobello mushroom sandwiches and mouthwatering banana chocolate chip pudding. Nashville's best songwriters perform on Friday and Saturday evenings, and fast, friendly servers make the down-home dining experience even more enjoyable. Casual dress. **Bar:** Beer & wine. **Hours:** 11 am-2:30 & 5-9 pm, Sat 11 am-10 pm, Sun 11 am-9 pm. Closed major holidays; also Mon & Tues. **Address:** 1072 Green St **Location:** SR 400, exit 4, 1.5 mi w to Alpharetta St, 1.2 mi s to Green St, then 0.3 mi w. **Parking:** on-site. **Cards:** AX, MC, VI.

SMYRNA pop. 40,999 (See maps and indexes starting on p. 296, 302)

WHERE TO STAY

BAYMONT INN & SUITES — *Book at AAA.com* — Phone: 404/794-1600 (168)

Hotel
Rates not provided

Address: 5130 S Cobb Dr **Location:** I-285, exit 15, 0.3 mi w. **Facility:** 56 one-bedroom standard units, some with whirlpools. 2 stories (no elevator), interior corridors. **Parking:** on-site. **Amenities:** high-speed Internet, voice mail, irons, hair dryers. **Pool(s):** heated indoor. **Leisure Activities:** whirlpool, limited exercise equipment. **Guest Services:** wireless Internet. **Business Services:** meeting rooms, fax (fee).

CALL / SOME UNITS FEE

BEST WESTERN ATLANTA INN AND SUITES — *Book great rates at AAA.com* — Phone: (770)541-1499 (64)

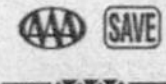

Hotel
$60-$80 All Year

Address: 2221 Corporate Plaza **Location:** I-75, exit 260, just w. **Facility:** 75 units. 43 one-bedroom standard units. 32 one-bedroom suites. 2-3 stories, interior corridors. **Parking:** on-site. **Amenities:** high-speed Internet, voice mail, irons, hair dryers. **Pool(s):** heated indoor. **Leisure Activities:** sauna, exercise room. **Guest Services:** valet and coin laundry, wireless Internet. **Business Services:** meeting rooms, business center. **Cards:** AX, DS, MC, VI. **Free Special Amenities: continental breakfast and local telephone calls.**

FEE CALL / SOME UNITS

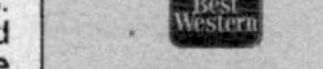

AAA Benefit:
Members save up to 20%, plus 10% bonus points with rewards program.

COMFORT INN & SUITES — *Book great rates at AAA.com* — Phone: (678)309-1200 (167)

Hotel
$80-$121 All Year

Address: 2800 Highlands Pkwy **Location:** I-285, exit 15, just w to Highlands Pkwy, then just s. **Facility:** 72 units. 70 one-bedroom standard units, some with whirlpools. 2 one-bedroom suites, some with whirlpools. 3 stories, interior corridors. **Parking:** on-site. **Amenities:** high-speed Internet, dual phone lines, voice mail, safes (fee), irons, hair dryers. **Pool(s):** heated indoor. **Leisure Activities:** limited exercise equipment. **Guest Services:** valet and coin laundry, wireless Internet. **Business Services:** meeting rooms, business center. **Cards:** AX, CB, DC, DS, JC, MC, VI. **Free Special Amenities: continental breakfast and high-speed Internet.**

FEE CALL / SOME UNITS FEE

HOLIDAY INN EXPRESS ATLANTA / SMYRNA COBB GALLERIA CENTER — *Book great rates at AAA.com* — Phone: (770)435-4990 (67)

Hotel
$80-$100 All Year

Address: 2855 Springhill Pkwy **Location:** I-285, exit 20 westbound; exit 19 eastbound, just n on US 41 (Cobb Pkwy), then just w on Spring Rd. **Facility:** 143 one-bedroom standard units. 6 stories, interior corridors. **Parking:** on-site. **Terms:** cancellation fee imposed. **Amenities:** high-speed Internet, voice mail, irons, hair dryers. **Pool(s):** outdoor. **Leisure Activities:** exercise room. *Fee:* game room. **Guest Services:** valet and coin laundry, area transportation-within 3 mi, wireless Internet. **Business Services:** meeting rooms, business center. **Cards:** AX, DC, DS, JC, MC, VI. ***(See color ad p 325)***

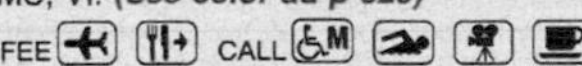

FEE CALL / SOME UNITS FEE

(See maps and indexes starting on p. 296, 302)

HOLIDAY INN EXPRESS, VININGS/SMYRNA Book at AAA.com Phone: (770)333-9910 69

Hotel
$70-$130 All Year

Address: 1200 Winchester Pkwy **Location:** I-285, exit 16, just w. **Facility:** 117 one-bedroom standard units. 5 stories, interior corridors. **Parking:** on-site. **Terms:** 14 day cancellation notice-fee imposed. **Amenities:** high-speed Internet, voice mail, irons, hair dryers. **Pool(s):** outdoor. **Leisure Activities:** exercise room. **Guest Services:** valet and coin laundry, wireless Internet. **Business Services:** meeting rooms, business center. **Cards:** AX, CB, DC, DS, MC, VI.

ASK FEE / SOME UNITS

HOMESTEAD STUDIO SUITES HOTEL-ATLANTA/CUMBERLAND MALL Book at AAA.com Phone: (770)432-4000 66

Hotel
$60-$70 All Year

Address: 3103 Sports Ave **Location:** I-285, exit 20 westbound; exit 19 eastbound, just n to Spring Rd, then 0.3 mi w. **Facility:** 125 units. 115 one-bedroom standard units with efficiencies. 10 one-bedroom suites with efficiencies. 2 stories (no elevator), exterior corridors. **Parking:** on-site. **Terms:** office hours 7 am-10 pm. **Amenities:** high-speed Internet (fee), voice mail, irons. *Some:* hair dryers. **Guest Services:** coin laundry, wireless Internet. **Business Services:** fax. **Cards:** AX, CB, DC, DS, JC, MC, VI.

ASK FEE CALL / SOME UNITS FEE

HYATT PLACE-ATLANTA GALLERIA Book great rates at AAA.com Phone: (770)384-0060 68

Hotel
$69-$209 All Year

Address: 2876 Springhill Pkwy **Location:** I-285, exit 20 westbound; exit 19 eastbound, just n to Spring Rd, then just w. **Facility:** 123 one-bedroom standard units. 6 stories, interior corridors. **Parking:** on-site. **Terms:** cancellation fee imposed. **Amenities:** high-speed Internet, voice mail, irons, hair dryers. **Pool(s):** outdoor. **Leisure Activities:** exercise room. **Guest Services:** valet laundry, area transportation-within 5 mi, wireless Internet. **Business Services:** meeting rooms, business center. **Cards:** AX, CB, DC, DS, JC, MC, VI. **Free Special Amenities: continental breakfast and high-speed Internet.**

FEE CALL

HYATT PLACE
AAA Benefit:
Ask for the AAA rate and save 10%.

MICROTEL INN Book great rates at AAA.com Phone: (404)799-7000 169

Hotel
$50-$70 All Year

Address: 5300 S Cobb Dr SE **Location:** I-285, exit 15, just e. **Facility:** 87 one-bedroom standard units. 3 stories, interior corridors. **Parking:** on-site. **Amenities:** high-speed Internet, safes (fee), irons, hair dryers. **Guest Services:** wireless Internet. **Business Services:** fax (fee). **Cards:** AX, CB, DC, DS, MC, VI. **Free Special Amenities: continental breakfast and local telephone calls.**

CALL / SOME UNITS

RED ROOF INN-NORTH Book great rates at AAA.com Phone: (770)952-6966 63

Motel
$50-$100 All Year

Address: 2200 Corporate Plaza **Location:** I-75, exit 260, just w to Corporate Plaza, then just s. **Facility:** 136 one-bedroom standard units. 2 stories, exterior corridors. **Parking:** on-site. **Terms:** 14 day cancellation notice. **Amenities:** voice mail. *Fee:* video games, high-speed Internet. **Guest Services:** wireless Internet. **Business Services:** fax. **Cards:** AX, CB, DC, DS, MC, VI. **Free Special Amenities: local telephone calls.**

CALL / SOME UNITS

RESIDENCE INN-ATLANTA CUMBERLAND Book great rates at AAA.com Phone: (770)433-8877 65

Hotel
$177-$190 All Year

Address: 2771 Cumberland Blvd **Location:** I-285, exit 20 westbound; exit 19 eastbound, just n to Spring Rd, 0.3 mi w to Cumberland Blvd, then just n. **Facility:** Smoke free premises. 130 one-bedroom standard units with kitchens. 3 stories, exterior corridors. **Parking:** on-site. **Terms:** cancellation fee imposed. **Amenities:** video games (fee), high-speed Internet, voice mail, irons, hair dryers. **Pool(s):** heated outdoor. **Leisure Activities:** whirlpool, exercise room, sports court. **Guest Services:** valet and coin laundry, wireless Internet. **Business Services:** meeting rooms, PC, fax (fee). **Cards:** AX, CB, DC, DS, JC, MC, VI. **Free Special Amenities: full breakfast and high-speed Internet.**

FEE CALL / SOME UNITS FEE

AAA Benefit:
Members save a minimum 5% off the best available rate.

WHERE TO DINE

BLACKSTONE Phone: 404/794-6100 80

Steak & Seafood
$11-$39

The upscale establishment serves USDA prime, grain-fed Midwestern beef, which is aged a minimum of 21 days. Seafood entrees include Alaskan halibut, grilled Atlantic salmon and cold-water lobster tail. The wine list offers a good selection and value. Dressy casual. **Bar:** Full bar. **Reservations:** accepted. **Hours:** 5:30 pm-10 pm, Fri & Sat-11 pm. Closed major holidays. **Address:** 4686 S Atlanta Rd **Location:** I-285, exit 16, 0.3 mi e. **Parking:** on-site. **Cards:** AX, CB, DC, DS, MC, VI.

CALL

(See maps and indexes starting on p. 296, 302)

HOUSE OF CHAN — Phone: 770/955-9444 (78)

Chinese $6-$30

Diners can feast on ample portions of well-prepared family recipes, including the popular bass and duck entrees. Casual dress. **Bar:** Beer & wine. **Reservations:** accepted. **Hours:** 11:30 am-2:30 & 5-10 pm, Sun noon-3 & 5-10 pm. Closed: 11/26, also Sat **Address:** 2469 Cobb Pkwy **Location:** I-285, exit 20 westbound; exit 19 eastbound, 1 mi n on US 41 (Cobb Pkwy). **Parking:** on-site. **Cards:** AX, DC, MC, VI.

MINATO JAPANESE RESTAURANT — Phone: 770/432-6012 (79)

Japanese $1-$26

Enjoy sushi or tempura, or relax and let a tableside chef cook you shrimp, chicken or beef, hibachi style. Casual dress. **Bar:** Beer & wine. **Hours:** 11:30 am-2:30 & 5:30-10 pm, Fri-11 pm, Sat 5:30 pm-11 pm. Closed major holidays; also Sun. **Address:** 2697 Spring Rd **Location:** I-285, exit 20 westbound; exit 19 eastbound, just n to Spring Rd, then just w. **Parking:** on-site. **Cards:** AX, CB, DC, DS, JC, MC, VI.

OLD SOUTH BAR-B-Q — Phone: 770/435-4215 (75)

Barbecue $5-$12

Serving some of the most delicious ribs in the area, the eatery also serves mouthwatering barbecue pork and Brunswick stew. Top off your meal with a slice of homemade pie. Casual dress. **Hours:** 11 am-8 pm, Fri & Sat-9 pm. Closed major holidays; also Mon. **Address:** 601 Burbank Cir **Location:** I-75, exit 260, 3 mi w; corner of Windy Hill Rd and Burbank Cir. **Parking:** on-site. **Cards:** MC, VI.

SCALINI'S — Phone: 770/952-7222 (76)

Italian $5-$18

Skillfully served pasta dishes bathed in excellent homemade sauces are highlights at the warm, family-oriented eatory. Worth a splurge are the delicious homemade desserts, including spumoni served with a coconut macaroon. Casual dress. **Bar:** Full bar. **Hours:** 4:30 pm-10 pm, Fri & Sat-11 pm, Sun 4 pm-10 pm. Closed: 11/26, 12/24, 12/25. **Address:** 2390 Cobb Pkwy SE **Location:** I-285, exit 20 westbound; exit 19 eastbound, 1 mi n on US 41 (Cobb Pkwy); in The Promenade. **Parking:** on-site. **Cards:** AX, CB, DC, DS, MC, VI.

SIAM SQUARE — Phone: 770/333-1700 (74)

Thai $7-$15

Gracious servers deliver well-prepared Thai selections, such as pad thai and panang curry. The atmosphere is relaxed yet classy. Casual dress. **Bar:** Beer & wine. **Reservations:** accepted. **Hours:** 11:30 am-2:30 & 5:30-10 pm, Sat from 5 pm. Closed major holidays; also Sun. **Address:** 1995 Windy Hill Rd **Location:** I-75, exit 260, 1 mi w; in Windy Hill West Shopping Center. **Parking:** on-site. **Cards:** AX, DS, MC, VI.

YAKITORI JINBEI — Phone: 770/818-9215 (77)

Japanese $6-$14

Visit the restaurant for an authentic Japanese dining experience and the house specialty yakitori. Casual dress. **Bar:** Beer & wine. **Reservations:** accepted. **Hours:** 11:30 am-2 & 5:30-10 pm, Fri & Sat-11 pm. Closed major holidays; also Sun & Mon. **Address:** 2421 Cobb Pkwy **Location:** I-285, exit 20 westbound; exit 19 eastbound, 1 mi n. **Parking:** on-site. **Cards:** AX, CB, DC, DS, JC, MC, VI.

SNELLVILLE pop. 15,351 (See map and index starting on p. 302)

WHERE TO STAY

CRESTWOOD SUITES — *Book at AAA.com* — Phone: (770)982-5250

Hotel $50-$70 All Year

Address: 1784 Presidential Cir **Location:** Jct Ronald Reagan Pkwy and SR 124, just w. **Facility:** 130 units. 127 one-bedroom standard units with efficiencies. 3 one-bedroom suites, some with kitchens. 3 stories, interior corridors. **Parking:** on-site. **Terms:** cancellation fee imposed. **Amenities:** high-speed Internet, voice mail, irons, hair dryers. **Guest Services:** coin laundry, wireless Internet. **Business Services:** meeting rooms, fax (fee). **Cards:** AX, DS, MC, VI.

ASK / SOME UNITS FEE

SUPER 8 MOTEL — *Book great rates at AAA.com* — Phone: (770)736-4723 (151)

AAA SAVE

Hotel **$74-$120 All Year**

Address: 2971 W Main St **Location:** Jct US 78 and SR 124, 0.6 mi w. **Facility:** 57 one-bedroom standard units, some with whirlpools. 2-3 stories, interior corridors. **Parking:** on-site. **Amenities:** high-speed Internet, irons, hair dryers. **Pool(s):** indoor. **Leisure Activities:** exercise room. **Guest Services:** coin laundry, wireless Internet. **Business Services:** meeting rooms, business center. **Cards:** AX, DC, DS, MC, VI. **Free Special Amenities: expanded continental breakfast and high-speed Internet.**

CALL / SOME UNITS FEE

STONE MOUNTAIN pop. 7,145 (See maps and indexes starting on p. 302, 312)

WHERE TO STAY

BEST WESTERN STONE MOUNTAIN — *Book great rates at AAA.com* — Phone: (770)465-1022 (174)

AAA SAVE

Hotel **$80-$115 All Year**

Address: 1595 E Park Place Blvd **Location:** US 78, exit E Park Place Blvd, just n. **Facility:** 60 one-bedroom standard units, some with whirlpools. 2 stories (no elevator), exterior corridors. **Parking:** on-site. **Terms:** 3 day cancellation notice-fee imposed. **Amenities:** high-speed Internet, voice mail, safes (fee), irons, hair dryers. **Pool(s):** outdoor. **Guest Services:** coin laundry, wireless Internet. **Business Services:** meeting rooms, PC, fax (fee). **Cards:** AX, CB, DC, DS, JC, MC, VI. **Free Special Amenities: expanded continental breakfast and high-speed Internet.**

AAA Benefit: Members save up to 20%, plus 10% bonus points with rewards program.

(See maps and indexes starting on p. 302, 312)

COMFORT INN *Book at AAA.com*

Hotel
$99-$159 All Year

Phone: (770)465-1888 177

Address: 5355 Stone Mountain Hwy **Location:** US 78, exit 9. **Facility:** 57 one-bedroom standard units, some with whirlpools. 3 stories, interior corridors. **Parking:** on-site. **Terms:** check-in 4 pm. **Amenities:** high-speed Internet, voice mail, irons, hair dryers. **Pool(s):** heated indoor. **Leisure Activities:** exercise room. **Guest Services:** coin laundry, wireless Internet. **Business Services:** meeting rooms, business center. **Cards:** AX, CB, DC, DS, MC, VI.

ASK FEE CALL / SOME UNITS

COUNTRY INN & SUITES BY CARLSON *Book at AAA.com*

Hotel
$94-$179 All Year

Phone: (770)465-6515 176

Address: 1852 Rockbridge Rd **Location:** US 78, exit 9. **Facility:** 72 units. 57 one-bedroom standard units, some with whirlpools. 15 one-bedroom suites. 3 stories, interior corridors. **Parking:** on-site. **Terms:** cancellation fee imposed. **Amenities:** high-speed Internet, dual phone lines, voice mail, irons, hair dryers. **Pool(s):** indoor. **Leisure Activities:** whirlpool, limited exercise equipment. **Guest Services:** coin laundry, wireless Internet. **Business Services:** meeting rooms, business center. **Cards:** AX, DS, MC, VI.

ASK FEE / SOME UNITS

DAYS INN *Book at AAA.com*

Motel
$69-$129 All Year

Phone: (770)879-0800 173

Address: 2006 Glen Club Dr & Hwy 78 E **Location:** US 78, 1.3 mi e of entrance to Stone Mountain Park; behind Krystal Restaurant. **Facility:** 81 one-bedroom standard units. 2 stories, exterior corridors. **Parking:** on-site. **Terms:** cancellation fee imposed. **Amenities:** high-speed Internet, irons, hair dryers. **Pool(s):** outdoor. **Guest Services:** coin laundry, wireless Internet. **Business Services:** fax (fee). **Cards:** AX, CB, DC, DS, MC, VI.

ASK FEE / SOME UNITS

HAMPTON INN *Book great rates at AAA.com*

Hotel
$99-$149 All Year

Phone: (770)934-0004 172

Address: 1737 Mountain Industrial Blvd **Location:** US 78, exit 4 (Mountain Industrial Blvd), just s. **Facility:** 112 units. 95 one-bedroom standard units. 17 one-bedroom suites. 4 stories, interior corridors. *Bath:* combo or shower only. **Parking:** on-site. **Terms:** 1-30 night minimum stay, cancellation fee imposed. **Amenities:** high-speed Internet, voice mail, irons, hair dryers. *Some:* DVD players, CD players. **Pool(s):** outdoor. **Leisure Activities:** exercise room. **Guest Services:** valet and coin laundry, wireless Internet. **Business Services:** meeting rooms, business center. **Cards:** AX, CB, DC, DS, MC, VI.

FEE CALL / SOME UNITS VCR

AAA Benefit:
Members save up to 10% everyday!

HOLIDAY INN EXPRESS *Book great rates at AAA.com*

AAA SAVE

Hotel
$99-$139 All Year

Phone: (770)465-8847 175

Address: 1790 E Park Place Blvd **Location:** US 78, exit 9, 0.3 mi n. **Facility:** 63 one-bedroom standard units, some with whirlpools. 3 stories, interior corridors. **Parking:** on-site. **Amenities:** high-speed Internet, dual phone lines, voice mail, irons, hair dryers. **Pool(s):** outdoor. **Leisure Activities:** limited exercise equipment. **Guest Services:** valet and coin laundry, wireless Internet. **Business Services:** meeting rooms, business center. **Cards:** AX, CB, DS, MC, VI. **Free Special Amenities: expanded continental breakfast and high-speed Internet.**

FEE CALL / SOME UNITS

MARRIOTT EVERGREEN CONFERENCE RESORT *Book great rates at AAA.com*

AAA SAVE

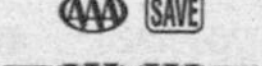

Resort Hotel
$195-$215 All Year

Phone: (770)879-9900 10

Address: 4021 Lakeview Dr **Location:** US 78, exit 8; I-285, exit 39B; in Stone Mountain Park. **Facility:** Rooms feature either a balcony or patio with views of the lake; located in Stone Mountain Park with a natural setting. Smoke free premises. 336 units. 327 one-bedroom standard units. 8 one- and 1 two-bedroom suites, some with whirlpools. 5 stories, interior corridors. **Parking:** on-site and valet. **Terms:** check-in 4 pm, cancellation fee imposed. **Amenities:** dual phone lines, voice mail, irons, hair dryers. *Fee:* video games, high-speed Internet. **Dining:** 2 restaurants. **Pool(s):** heated outdoor, heated indoor. **Leisure Activities:** whirlpools, hiking trails, jogging, exercise room, spa. *Fee:* golf-36 holes, tennis club privileges, game room. **Guest Services:** valet laundry, area transportation-within the park, wireless Internet. **Business Services:** conference facilities, business center. **Cards:** AX, CB, DC, DS, JC, MC, VI. **Free Special Amenities: newspaper.**

FEE

Marriott HOTELS & RESORTS

AAA Benefit:
Members save a minimum 5% off the best available rate.

STONE MOUNTAIN INN *Book great rates at AAA.com*

Hotel
$168-$180 All Year

Phone: (770)469-3311 178

Address: 1058 Robert E Lee Blvd **Location:** US 78, exit 8. **Facility:** Smoke free premises. 92 one-bedroom standard units. 2 stories, interior/exterior corridors. **Parking:** on-site. **Terms:** check-in 4 pm, 3 day cancellation notice-fee imposed. **Amenities:** voice mail, irons, hair dryers. *Fee:* video games, high-speed Internet. **Pool(s):** outdoor. **Leisure Activities:** *Fee:* golf-36 holes. **Guest Services:** valet and coin laundry, area transportation, wireless Internet. **Business Services:** meeting rooms, business center. **Cards:** AX, CB, DC, DS, JC, MC, VI.

Marriott HOTELS & RESORTS

AAA Benefit:
Members save a minimum 5% off the best available rate.

(See maps and indexes starting on p. 302, 312)

WHERE TO DINE

CONTINENTAL PARK CAFE — Phone: 770/413-6448 (30)

American
$7-$9

Distinctive food, flavorful appetizers, salads and entrees are served at reasonable prices. Delicious homemade cakes and pies satisfy a sweet tooth, as do the many milkshake varieties. A hearty cup of fine coffee, espresso or cappuccino is a great way to end the meal. Casual dress. **Reservations:** accepted. **Hours:** 11 am-3 pm, Thurs-Sat also 5 pm-10 pm. Closed: 11/26, 12/25. **Address:** 941-A Main St **Location:** Center; in Stone Mountain Village. **Parking:** street. **Cards:** AX, DS, MC, VI.

MGR PALACE — Phone: 770/413-1415 (123)

Indian
$3-$8

Serving superb Southern Indian entrees including curries, uthappam, dosa, rice and bread. You'll find earnest service and a proud chef/owner. Casual dress. **Bar:** Beer & wine. **Hours:** 11 am-10 pm. **Address:** 1825 Rockbridge Rd, Suite 14A **Location:** US 78, exit 9, just e; in Stone Mountain Festival Plaza. **Parking:** on-site. **Cards:** AX, DS, MC, VI.

SUWANEE pop. 8,725 (See map and index starting on p. 302)

WHERE TO STAY

BEST WESTERN GWINNETT INN — *Book great rates at AAA.com* — Phone: (770)271-5559 (73)

AAA SAVE
Hotel
$80-$110 All Year

Address: 77 Gwinco Blvd **Location:** I-85, exit 111, just e to Gwinco Blvd, then just s. **Facility:** 49 one-bedroom standard units. 2 stories (no elevator), interior corridors. **Parking:** on-site. **Amenities:** high-speed Internet, voice mail, irons, hair dryers. *Some:* DVD players. **Pool(s):** outdoor. **Guest Services:** coin laundry, wireless Internet. **Business Services:** meeting rooms, fax (fee). **Cards:** AX, DS, MC, VI. **Free Special Amenities: continental breakfast and high-speed Internet.**

FEE CALL / SOME UNITS FEE

Best Western
AAA Benefit:
Members save up to 20%, plus 10% bonus points with rewards program.

COMFORT INN — *Book great rates at AAA.com* — Phone: (770)945-1608 (72)

AAA SAVE
Hotel
$75-$129 All Year

Address: 2945 Hwy 317 **Location:** I-85, exit 111, just e. **Facility:** 80 one-bedroom standard units. 2 stories (no elevator), exterior corridors. **Parking:** on-site. **Amenities:** high-speed Internet, voice mail, safes (fee), irons, hair dryers. **Pool(s):** outdoor. **Leisure Activities:** exercise room privileges. **Guest Services:** valet and coin laundry, airport transportation (fee)-The William B. Hartsfield Atlanta Int'l Airport, wireless Internet. **Business Services:** business center. **Cards:** AX, CB, DC, DS, MC, VI.

FEE / SOME UNITS FEE

COMFORT SUITES — *Book great rates at AAA.com* — Phone: (678)714-7707 (71)

AAA SAVE
Hotel
$89-$199 All Year

Address: 2945-A Hwy 317 **Location:** I-85, exit 111, just e. **Facility:** Smoke free premises. 65 units. 64 one-bedroom standard units, some with whirlpools. 1 one-bedroom suite. 4 stories, interior corridors. **Parking:** on-site. **Amenities:** high-speed Internet, dual phone lines, voice mail, irons, hair dryers. **Pool(s):** heated indoor. **Leisure Activities:** whirlpool, limited exercise equipment. **Guest Services:** valet and coin laundry, airport transportation (fee)-The William B. Hartsfield Atlanta Int'l Airport, wireless Internet. **Business Services:** meeting rooms, business center. **Cards:** AX, CB, DC, DS, MC, VI. **Free Special Amenities: expanded continental breakfast and high-speed Internet.**

FEE CALL

TUCKER pop. 26,532 (See map and index starting on p. 302)

WHERE TO STAY

ATLANTA NORTHLAKE TOWNEPLACE SUITES — *Book great rates at AAA.com* — Phone: (770)938-0408 (154)

AAA SAVE
Hotel
$158-$169 All Year

Address: 3300 Northlake Pkwy **Location:** I-285, exit 36 southbound, just w; exit 37 northbound, just w to Parklake Dr, 0.5 mi n, then just w. **Facility:** Smoke free premises. 98 units. 79 one- and 19 two-bedroom standard units with kitchens. 5 stories, interior corridors. **Parking:** on-site. **Terms:** cancellation fee imposed. **Amenities:** high-speed Internet, voice mail, irons, hair dryers. **Pool(s):** outdoor. **Leisure Activities:** limited exercise equipment. **Guest Services:** valet and coin laundry, wireless Internet. **Business Services:** PC, fax. **Cards:** AX, CB, DC, DS, JC, MC, VI. **Free Special Amenities: expanded continental breakfast and high-speed Internet.**

FEE CALL / SOME UNITS FEE

AAA Benefit:
Members save a minimum 5% off the best available rate.

COMFORT SUITES-NORTHLAKE — *Book great rates at AAA.com* — Phone: (770)496-1070 (161)

AAA SAVE
Hotel
$90-$159 All Year

Address: 2060 Crescent Centre Blvd **Location:** I-285, exit 37, 0.5 mi se. **Facility:** Smoke free premises. 110 one-bedroom standard units, some with whirlpools. 6 stories, interior corridors. **Parking:** on-site. **Terms:** cancellation fee imposed. **Amenities:** DVD players, CD players, high-speed Internet, dual phone lines, voice mail, safes (fee), irons, hair dryers. **Pool(s):** outdoor. **Leisure Activities:** exercise room. **Guest Services:** valet and coin laundry, wireless Internet. **Business Services:** meeting rooms, business center. **Cards:** AX, CB, DC, DS, JC, MC, VI. **Free Special Amenities: expanded continental breakfast and high-speed Internet.**

CALL VCR

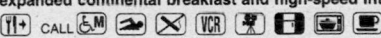

(See map and index starting on p. 302)

COUNTRY INN & SUITES BY CARLSON Book great rates at AAA.com **Phone:** (770)270-9009 160

AAA SAVE

Hotel
$96 All Year

Address: 2081 Northlake Pkwy **Location:** I-285, exit 37, 0.4 mi se. **Facility:** 49 units. 26 one-bedroom standard units, some with whirlpools. 23 one-bedroom suites. 5 stories, interior corridors. **Parking:** on-site. **Amenities:** high-speed Internet, voice mail, irons, hair dryers. **Leisure Activities:** exercise room. **Guest Services:** valet and coin laundry, wireless Internet. **Business Services:** meeting rooms, fax (fee). **Cards:** AX, CB, DC, DS, MC, VI.

FEE CALL / SOME UNITS

COURTYARD BY MARRIOTT-NORTHLAKE Book great rates at AAA.com **Phone:** (770)938-1200 159

AAA SAVE

Hotel
$177-$190 All Year

Address: 4083 La Vista Rd **Location:** I-285, exit 37, just w. **Facility:** Smoke free premises. 128 units. 108 one-bedroom standard units. 20 one-bedroom suites. 2 stories, interior corridors. **Parking:** on-site. **Terms:** cancellation fee imposed. **Amenities:** high-speed Internet, dual phone lines, voice mail, irons, hair dryers. **Pool(s):** outdoor. **Leisure Activities:** whirlpool, exercise room. **Guest Services:** valet and coin laundry, wireless Internet. **Business Services:** meeting rooms, business center. **Cards:** AX, CB, DC, DS, JC, MC, VI. **Free Special Amenities: newspaper and high-speed Internet.**

FEE / SOME UNITS

AAA Benefit:
Members save a minimum 5% off the best available rate.

DOUBLETREE HOTEL NE/NORTHLAKE Book great rates at AAA.com **Phone:** (770)938-1026 158

Hotel
$89-$199 All Year

Address: 4156 La Vista Rd **Location:** I-285, exit 37, just w. **Facility:** 183 one-bedroom standard units. 5 stories, interior corridors. **Parking:** on-site. **Terms:** 1-30 night minimum stay, cancellation fee imposed. **Amenities:** voice mail, irons, hair dryers. *Fee:* video games, high-speed Internet. **Pool(s):** outdoor. **Leisure Activities:** exercise room. **Guest Services:** valet and coin laundry, wireless Internet. **Business Services:** meeting rooms, PC. **Cards:** AX, CB, DC, DS, MC, VI.

CALL / SOME UNITS FEE

DOUBLETREE
HOTELS·SUITES·RESORTS·CLUBS

AAA Benefit:
Members save 5% or more everyday!

ECONO LODGE Book great rates at AAA.com **Phone:** (770)939-8440 162

AAA SAVE

Motel
$50-$70 All Year

Address: 1820 Mountain Industrial Blvd **Location:** US 78, exit 4, just n. **Facility:** 48 one-bedroom standard units. 2 stories (no elevator), interior corridors. **Parking:** on-site. **Guest Services:** coin laundry, wireless Internet. **Business Services:** meeting rooms, fax. **Cards:** AX, CB, DC, DS, JC, MC, VI. **Free Special Amenities: continental breakfast and high-speed Internet.**

/ SOME UNITS FEE

HAMPTON INN ATLANTA-NORTHLAKE Book great rates at AAA.com **Phone:** (770)493-1966 155

Hotel
$104-$129 All Year

Address: 3400 Northlake Pkwy **Location:** I-285, exit 37, just w to Parklake Dr, then 0.5 mi n. Located in an office park area. **Facility:** 122 one-bedroom standard units. 5 stories, interior corridors. **Parking:** on-site. **Terms:** 1-30 night minimum stay, cancellation fee imposed. **Amenities:** video games (fee), high-speed Internet, voice mail, irons, hair dryers. **Pool(s):** outdoor. **Leisure Activities:** exercise room. **Guest Services:** valet and coin laundry, wireless Internet. **Business Services:** meeting rooms, business center. **Cards:** AX, CB, DC, DS, MC, VI.

FEE / SOME UNITS

AAA Benefit:
Members save up to 10% everyday!

HOLIDAY INN ATLANTA NORTHLAKE Book great rates at AAA.com **Phone:** (770)934-6000 156

AAA SAVE

Hotel
$99-$129 All Year

Address: 2158 Ranchwood Dr NE **Location:** I-285, exit 37, 0.4 mi w to Ranchwood Dr, then just n. **Facility:** 129 one-bedroom standard units. 5 stories, interior corridors. **Parking:** on-site. **Amenities:** high-speed Internet, dual phone lines, voice mail, irons, hair dryers. **Pool(s):** outdoor. **Leisure Activities:** sauna, exercise room. **Guest Services:** coin laundry, wireless Internet. **Business Services:** meeting rooms, business center. **Cards:** AX, DC, DS, MC, VI. **Free Special Amenities: full breakfast and high-speed Internet.**

FEE CALL FEE FEE / SOME UNITS

MASTERS INN TUCKER **Phone:** (770)938-3552 164

AAA SAVE

Motel
$42-$75 All Year

Address: 1435 Montreal Rd **Location:** I-285, exit 38, just w. **Facility:** 104 one-bedroom standard units. 3 stories, exterior corridors. **Parking:** on-site. **Amenities:** high-speed Internet. **Pool(s):** outdoor. **Guest Services:** coin laundry. **Business Services:** meeting rooms, fax (fee). **Cards:** AX, DC, DS, MC, VI. **Free Special Amenities: local telephone calls.**

/ SOME UNITS FEE FEE FEE

(See map and index starting on p. 302)

MOTEL 6 #2007 Book at AAA.com **Phone:** (770)496-1311 163

Motel
$35-$41 All Year

Address: 2810 Lawrenceville Hwy **Location:** I-285, exit 38, just w. Located in a light-commercial area. **Facility:** 116 one-bedroom standard units. 3 stories, exterior corridors. **Parking:** on-site. **Amenities:** voice mail. **Guest Services:** coin laundry. **Business Services:** fax (fee). **Cards:** AX, DC, DS, MC, VI.

/ SOME UNITS

QUALITY INN ATLANTA/NORTHLAKE Book great rates at AAA.com **Phone:** (770)491-7444 157

AAA SAVE

Hotel
$75-$99 All Year

Address: 2155 Ranchwood Dr **Location:** I-285, exit 37, 0.4 mi w, then just n. **Facility:** 133 one-bedroom standard units. 3 stories, interior/exterior corridors. **Parking:** on-site. **Amenities:** high-speed Internet, irons, hair dryers. **Pool(s):** outdoor. **Guest Services:** valet and coin laundry, wireless Internet. **Business Services:** fax (fee). **Cards:** AX, DC, DS, MC, VI. **Free Special Amenities: expanded continental breakfast and high-speed Internet.**

FEE CALL / SOME UNITS FEE

WHERE TO DINE

BLUE RIBBON GRILL **Phone:** 770/491-1570 118

American
$7-$16

Praised for its comfort foods, menu favorites include catfish and meatloaf. Families enjoy the restaurant's simple decor and setting. Casual dress. **Bar:** Full bar. **Hours:** 11:15 am-9 pm, Fri & Sat-10 pm, Sun-8:30 pm; Saturday & Sunday brunch. Closed major holidays. **Address:** 4006 La Vista Rd **Location:** I-285, exit 37, 0.3 mi w. **Parking:** on-site. **Cards:** AX, DS, MC, VI.

DYNASTY GARDEN **Phone:** 770/492-8683 116

Chinese
$6-$9

Offering over 200 buffet selections, choose from a variety of traditional Chinese fare, seafood, salads and desserts. Casual dress. **Hours:** 11 am-10 pm, Fri & Sat-11 pm. Closed: 11/26. **Address:** 3274 Northlake Pkwy **Location:** I-285, exit 36, 0.4 mi w. **Parking:** on-site. **Cards:** AX, DC, MC, VI.

FUJI YA **Phone:** 770/270-9962 117

Japanese
$7-$30

Patrons can order from the sushi bar or the menu. Options vary from traditional chicken and pork offerings to things for the more adventurous, such as baby octopus salad. Casual dress. **Bar:** Full bar. **Reservations:** accepted. **Hours:** 11:30 am-10 pm, Fri-11 pm, Sat noon-11 pm, Sun noon-10 pm. Closed major holidays. **Address:** 4139 Lavista Rd **Location:** I-285, exit 37, just w; in Northlake Square Shopping Center. **Parking:** on-site. **Cards:** AX, CB, DC, DS, MC, VI.

LUMIERE RESTAURANT **Phone:** 770/723-3507 120

American
$4-$15

Situated in a culinary arts institute, the exceptional entrees are prepared by student chefs using fresh ingredients. The changing menu features regional, American food with a French twist. Conscientious servers swiftly move about the dining room, which boasts a few upscale elements. Casual dress. **Bar:** Beer & wine. **Hours:** 11 am-1 & 7-11 pm. Closed major holidays; also Sat-Mon. **Address:** 1927 Lakeside Pkwy **Location:** I-285, exit 37, just e to Northlake Pkwy, 0.5 mi s to Robin Hill Ln, then just e; in LeCordon Blue College of Culinary Arts. **Parking:** on-site. **Cards:** AX, DS, MC, VI.

CALL

NORTHLAKE THAI CUISINE **Phone:** 770/938-2223 119

Thai
$9-$18

Offering creative "Eurasian Thai" dishes—such as lamb chops with basil sauce, Thai eggplant and green curry with chicken—Northlake's specialties are free of salt and monosodium glutamate (MSG).Dishes are presented in an upscale manner. Casual dress. **Bar:** Beer & wine. **Reservations:** accepted. **Hours:** 11 am-3 & 5-10 pm, Fri & Sat 5 pm-11 pm. Closed major holidays; also Sun. **Address:** 3939 Lavista Rd **Location:** I-285, exit 37, 0.5 mi w to Montreal Rd, then just s. **Parking:** on-site. **Cards:** AX, MC, VI.

UNION CITY pop. 11,621 (See map and index starting on p. 312)

WHERE TO STAY

BEST WESTERN UNION CITY INN & SUITES Book great rates at AAA.com **Phone:** (770)969-4567 105

AAA SAVE

Hotel
$60-$99 All Year

Address: 6743 Shannon Pkwy **Location:** I-85, exit 64, 0.3 mi w, then just n. **Facility:** 60 one-bedroom standard units. 3 stories, interior corridors. **Parking:** on-site. **Terms:** 3 day cancellation notice. **Amenities:** high-speed Internet, dual phone lines, voice mail, irons, hair dryers. **Pool(s):** outdoor. **Guest Services:** wireless Internet. **Business Services:** business center. **Cards:** AX, DS, MC, VI. **Free Special Amenities: expanded continental breakfast and high-speed Internet.**

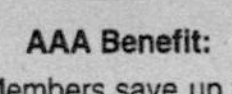

AAA Benefit:
Members save up to 20%, plus 10% bonus points with rewards program.

COMFORT INN ATLANTA AIRPORT UNION CITY Book great rates at AAA.com **Phone:** (770)306-2677 106

AAA SAVE

Hotel
$79-$99 All Year

Address: 6800 Shannon Way **Location:** I-85, exit 64, just w to Shannon Pkwy, then just n. **Facility:** 59 one-bedroom standard units. 4 stories, interior corridors. **Parking:** on-site. **Amenities:** video library (fee), high-speed Internet, voice mail, irons, hair dryers. **Pool(s):** heated indoor. **Leisure Activities:** whirlpool, exercise room. **Guest Services:** coin laundry, wireless Internet. **Business Services:** meeting rooms, business center. **Cards:** AX, CB, DC, DS, JC, MC, VI. **Free Special Amenities: expanded continental breakfast and high-speed Internet.**

(See map and index starting on p. 312)

DAYS INN SHANNON MALL Book at AAA.com Phone: (770)306-6067 104

Hotel

$60-$85 5/1-11/30
$55-$85 12/1-4/30

Address: 6840 Shannon Pkwy S **Location:** I-85, exit 64, 0.3 mi w to Shannon Pkwy, then just s. Located opposite Shannon Southpark Mall. **Facility:** 73 one-bedroom standard units, some with whirlpools. 2 stories, exterior corridors. **Parking:** on-site. **Amenities:** voice mail, irons, hair dryers. *Some:* DVD players. **Pool(s):** outdoor. **Leisure Activities:** exercise room. **Guest Services:** coin laundry, wireless Internet. **Business Services:** meeting rooms, PC, fax. **Cards:** AX, CB, DC, DS, MC, VI.

ASK / SOME UNITS FEE

MICROTEL INN & SUITES Book great rates at AAA.com Phone: (770)306-3800 103

AAA SAVE

Hotel

$50-$70 All Year

Address: 6690 Shannon Pkwy **Location:** I-85, exit 64, 0.3 mi w to Shannon Pkwy, then just n. **Facility:** 65 one-bedroom standard units. 3 stories, interior corridors. **Parking:** on-site. **Amenities:** dual phone lines, voice mail, irons, hair dryers. **Guest Services:** coin laundry, wireless Internet. **Business Services:** PC, fax (fee). **Cards:** AX, DC, DS, JC, MC, VI. **Free Special Amenities: continental breakfast and high-speed Internet.**

CALL / SOME UNITS FEE

WHERE TO DINE

THE HISTORIC GREEN MANOR RESTAURANT Phone: 770/964-4343 66

Southern

$11-$15

Feast on sumptuous Southern-style buffet at the stately, turn-of-the-20th-century mansion. Fried chicken, smothered steak, banana pudding and many tasty vegetables are staples. Casual dress. **Bar:** Full bar. **Reservations:** accepted. **Hours:** 11:30 am-2:30 pm, Fri also 6 pm-8:30 pm, Sun 11:30 am-5 pm. Closed: 1/1, 7/4, 12/25; also Sat. **Address:** 6400 Westbrook St **Location:** I-85, exit 66, 3 mi w to Westbrook St, then just s. **Parking:** on-site. **Cards:** AX, DS, MC, VI.

Stone Mountain Park, Stone Mountain / Georgia Department of Economic Development

This ends listings for the Atlanta Vicinity.
The following page resumes the alphabetical listings of cities in Georgia.

AUGUSTA pop. 199,775

WHERE TO STAY

BAYMONT INN & SUITES
Book great rates at AAA.com

Phone: (706)733-5900

Hotel

$88-$165 All Year

Address: 2905 Riverwest Dr **Location:** I-20, exit 200, just w. **Facility:** 65 units. 63 one-bedroom standard units, some with whirlpools. 2 one-bedroom suites. 3 stories, interior corridors. *Bath:* combo or shower only. **Parking:** on-site. **Terms:** 3 day cancellation notice-fee imposed. **Amenities:** high-speed Internet, voice mail, irons, hair dryers. **Pool(s):** outdoor. **Leisure Activities:** exercise room, gas grills. **Guest Services:** valet and coin laundry, wireless Internet. **Business Services:** business center. **Cards:** AX, CB, DC, DS, MC, VI. **Free Special Amenities: full breakfast and high-speed Internet.**

/ SOME UNITS

BEST WESTERN GARDEN CITY INN
Book great rates at AAA.com

Phone: (706)736-9292

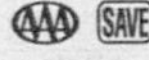

Hotel

$75-$85 All Year

Address: 2562 Center West Pkwy **Location:** I-20, exit 199, just se. **Facility:** 60 one-bedroom standard units, some with whirlpools. 3 stories, interior corridors. *Bath:* combo or shower only. **Parking:** on-site. **Amenities:** voice mail, irons, hair dryers. **Pool(s):** heated outdoor. **Leisure Activities:** whirlpool, exercise room. **Guest Services:** coin laundry, wireless Internet. **Business Services:** meeting rooms, PC. **Cards:** AX, DC, DS, MC, VI. **Free Special Amenities: continental breakfast and high-speed Internet.**

CALL / SOME UNITS

AAA Benefit:
Members save up to 20%, plus 10% bonus points with rewards program.

CLARION SUITES
Book great rates at AAA.com

Phone: (706)868-1800

Hotel

$79-$89 All Year

Address: 3038 Washington Rd **Location:** I-20, exit 199, just w. **Facility:** 176 units. 24 one-bedroom standard units. 152 one-bedroom suites, some with whirlpools. 4 stories, exterior corridors. **Parking:** on-site. **Terms:** 3 day cancellation notice-fee imposed. **Amenities:** voice mail, irons, hair dryers. **Pool(s):** outdoor. **Guest Services:** valet and coin laundry, wireless Internet. **Business Services:** meeting rooms, business center. **Cards:** AX, DC, DS, MC, VI. **Free Special Amenities: full breakfast and high-speed Internet.**

/ SOME UNITS

COMFORT INN MEDICAL CENTER
Book great rates at AAA.com

Phone: (706)722-2224

Hotel

$75 12/1-4/5 & 4/14-11/30

Address: 1455 Walton Way **Location:** I-20, exit 199 (Washington Rd), 4.5 mi e on SR 28, then just sw on 15th St. **Facility:** 100 one-bedroom standard units. 2 stories (no elevator), exterior corridors. *Bath:* combo or shower only. **Parking:** on-site. **Terms:** open 12/1-4/5 & 4/14-11/30, cancellation fee imposed. **Amenities:** voice mail, irons, hair dryers. *Some:* high-speed Internet. **Pool(s):** outdoor. **Guest Services:** valet and coin laundry, wireless Internet. **Business Services:** PC. **Cards:** AX, CB, DC, DS, MC, VI.

/ SOME UNITS FEE

COURTYARD BY MARRIOTT-AUGUSTA
Book great rates at AAA.com

Phone: (706)737-3737

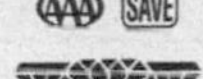

Hotel

$159-$164 All Year

Address: 1045 Stevens Creek Rd **Location:** I-20, exit 199 (Washington Rd), just w, then just ne. **Facility:** Smoke free premises. 130 units. 118 one-bedroom standard units. 12 one-bedroom suites. 2 stories (no elevator), interior corridors. *Bath:* combo or shower only. **Parking:** on-site. **Terms:** cancellation fee imposed. **Amenities:** video games (fee), high-speed Internet, dual phone lines, voice mail, irons, hair dryers. **Pool(s):** outdoor. **Leisure Activities:** whirlpool, exercise room. **Guest Services:** valet and coin laundry, wireless Internet. **Business Services:** meeting rooms, business center. **Cards:** AX, CB, DC, DS, MC, VI. **Free Special Amenities: newspaper and high-speed Internet.**

CALL

AAA Benefit:
Members save a minimum 5% off the best available rate.

DAYS INN WHEELER RD
Book great rates at AAA.com

Phone: (706)868-8610

Motel

$55-$265 All Year

Address: 3654 Wheeler Rd **Location:** I-520, exit 1C (Wheeler Rd), 0.5 mi w. **Facility:** 55 one-bedroom standard units. 2 stories (no elevator), exterior corridors. **Parking:** on-site. **Amenities:** safes (fee), hair dryers. **Pool(s):** outdoor. **Guest Services:** coin laundry, wireless Internet. **Cards:** AX, DS, MC, VI.

/ SOME UNITS

DOUBLETREE HOTEL AUGUSTA Book great rates at AAA.com Phone: (706)855-8100

Hotel
$110-$199 All Year

Address: 2651 Perimeter Pkwy **Location:** I-520, exit 1C (Wheeler Rd), just w to Perimeter Pkwy, then just n. **Facility:** 179 units. 150 one-bedroom standard units. 29 one-bedroom suites with whirlpools. 6 stories, interior corridors. *Bath:* combo or shower only. **Parking:** on-site. **Terms:** cancellation fee imposed. **Amenities:** dual phone lines, voice mail, safes (fee), irons, hair dryers. **Pool(s):** outdoor, heated indoor. **Leisure Activities:** whirlpool, exercise room, volleyball. **Guest Services:** valet and coin laundry, area transportation, wireless Internet. **Business Services:** conference facilities, business center. **Cards:** AX, DC, DS, MC, VI.

CALL / SOME UNITS FEE

AAA Benefit:
Members save 5% or more everyday!

HAMPTON INN Book great rates at AAA.com Phone: (706)737-1122

Hotel
$102-$117 All Year

Address: 3030 Washington Rd **Location:** I-20, exit 199 (Washington Rd), just nw. Located in a commercial area. **Facility:** 145 one-bedroom standard units. 2 stories (no elevator), exterior corridors. **Parking:** on-site. **Terms:** 1-30 night minimum stay, cancellation fee imposed. **Amenities:** video games (fee), high-speed Internet, voice mail, irons, hair dryers. **Pool(s):** outdoor. **Leisure Activities:** sauna, exercise room. **Guest Services:** valet laundry, wireless Internet. **Business Services:** PC. **Cards:** AX, CB, DC, DS, MC, VI.

/ SOME UNITS

AAA Benefit:
Members save up to 10% everyday!

HOLIDAY INN GORDON HIGHWAY AT BOBBY JONES Book at AAA.com Phone: (706)737-2300

Hotel
$111 All Year

Address: 2155 Gordon Hwy **Location:** I-520, exit 3A (US 78), just w. **Facility:** Smoke free premises. 150 one-bedroom standard units. 2 stories (no elevator), exterior corridors. *Bath:* combo or shower only. **Parking:** on-site, winter plug-ins. **Terms:** check-in 4 pm. **Amenities:** video games (fee), high-speed Internet, voice mail, irons, hair dryers. **Pool(s):** outdoor. **Leisure Activities:** exercise room. **Guest Services:** valet and coin laundry, area transportation, wireless Internet. **Business Services:** meeting rooms, PC. **Cards:** AX, CB, DC, DS, JC, MC, VI.

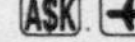      / SOME UNITS FEE

HOMEWOOD SUITES BY HILTON Book great rates at AAA.com Phone: (706)738-3131

Hotel
$98-$475 All Year

Address: 1049 Stevens Creek Rd **Location:** I-20, exit 199 (Washington Rd), just w, then n. **Facility:** 65 units. 61 one- and 4 two-bedroom suites with efficiencies. 5 stories, interior corridors. *Bath:* combo or shower only. **Parking:** on-site. **Terms:** 1-30 night minimum stay, cancellation fee imposed. **Amenities:** high-speed Internet, voice mail, irons, hair dryers. **Pool(s):** outdoor. **Leisure Activities:** limited exercise equipment. **Guest Services:** valet and coin laundry, wireless Internet. **Business Services:** meeting rooms, business center. **Cards:** AX, CB, DC, DS, MC, VI.

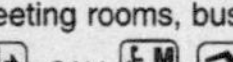 CALL  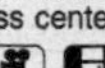  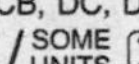 / SOME UNITS

AAA Benefit:
Members save 5% or more everyday!

LA QUINTA INN AUGUSTA Book great rates at AAA.com Phone: (706)733-2660

Hotel
$49-$99 All Year

Address: 3020 Washington Rd **Location:** I-20, exit 199 (Washington Rd), just w. **Facility:** 129 units. 127 one-bedroom standard units. 2 one-bedroom suites. 3 stories, interior/exterior corridors. **Parking:** on-site. **Amenities:** video games (fee), voice mail, irons, hair dryers. **Pool(s):** outdoor. **Guest Services:** valet laundry, wireless Internet. **Cards:** AX, DC, DS, MC, VI.

ASK CALL / SOME UNITS

MARRIOTT AUGUSTA HOTEL & SUITES Book great rates at AAA.com Phone: (706)722-8900

AAA SAVE

Hotel
$188-$201 All Year

Address: 2 10th St **Location:** I-20, exit 200 (River Watch Pkwy), 5.4 mi se, then just n; downtown. **Facility:** Smoke free premises. 372 units. 228 one-bedroom standard units. 144 one-bedroom suites, some with whirlpools. 11 stories, interior corridors. *Bath:* combo or shower only. **Parking:** on-site (fee) and valet. **Terms:** check-in 4 pm, cancellation fee imposed. **Amenities:** video games (fee), dual phone lines, voice mail, irons, hair dryers. *Some:* high-speed Internet, safes. **Pool(s):** heated outdoor, heated indoor. **Leisure Activities:** saunas, whirlpool, exercise room. **Guest Services:** valet and coin laundry, airport transportation-Bush Field Airport, wireless Internet. **Business Services:** conference facilities, business center. **Cards:** AX, DS, JC, MC, VI. **Free Special Amenities: local telephone calls and high-speed Internet.**

Marriott HOTELS & RESORTS
AAA Benefit:
Members save a minimum 5% off the best available rate.

CALL / SOME UNITS FEE

THE PARTRIDGE INN Book great rates at AAA.com Phone: (706)737-8888

AAA SAVE

Historic Hotel
$99-$249 All Year

Address: 2110 Walton Way **Location:** 1.3 mi w off 15th St. **Facility:** Dating from 1890, this historic hotel offers Old World charm with a variety of room types, some with balconies, and lots of modern amenities. Smoke free premises. 145 units. 120 one-bedroom standard units. 24 one- and 1 three-bedroom suites, some with kitchens. 6 stories, interior corridors. *Bath:* combo or shower only. **Parking:** valet and street. **Amenities:** high-speed Internet, dual phone lines, voice mail, irons, hair dryers. **Pool(s):** outdoor. **Leisure Activities:** exercise room. **Guest Services:** valet and coin laundry, airport transportation-Bush Field Airport, area transportation-local, wireless Internet. **Business Services:** meeting rooms, business center. **Cards:** AX, CB, DC, DS, MC, VI.

/ SOME UNITS FEE

WEST BANK INN Book great rates at AAA.com Phone: (706)733-1724

AAA SAVE

Motel
$54-$69 All Year

Address: 2904 Washington Rd **Location:** I-20, exit 199 (Washington Rd), just e. Located in a commercial area. **Facility:** Smoke free premises. 47 one-bedroom standard units. 2 stories (no elevator), exterior corridors. **Parking:** on-site. **Amenities:** voice mail, irons, hair dryers. *Some:* DVD players (fee). **Guest Services:** coin laundry, wireless Internet. **Business Services:** PC. **Cards:** AX, CB, DC, DS, JC, MC, VI. **Free Special Amenities: continental breakfast and high-speed Internet.**

WINGATE INN Book at AAA.com Phone: 706/729-1616

Hotel
Rates not provided

Address: 2123 Noland Connector **Location:** I-520, exit 3A (Gordon Hwy), just w. **Facility:** 64 one-bedroom standard units. 3 stories, interior corridors. *Bath:* combo or shower only. **Parking:** on-site. **Amenities:** video games (fee), high-speed Internet, dual phone lines, voice mail, safes, irons, hair dryers. **Leisure Activities:** whirlpool, exercise room. **Guest Services:** valet laundry, wireless Internet. **Business Services:** meeting rooms, business center.

CALL / SOME UNITS

WHERE TO DINE

THE BOLL WEEVIL - A CAFE & SWEETERY Phone: 706/722-7772

American
$6-$18

Soups, salads and sandwiches on homemade bread all are part of an extensive, trendy menu. An on-site bakery turns out a wide selection of tantalizing desserts. Casual dress. **Bar:** Beer & wine. **Reservations:** not accepted. **Hours:** 11 am-10 pm, Fri & Sat-11 pm. Closed major holidays; also 12/24 & 12/31. **Address:** 10 9th St **Location:** End of 9th St; next to Riverwalk. **Parking:** on-site. **Cards:** AX, DS, MC, VI.

CALIFORNIA DREAMING Phone: 706/860-6206

American
$8-$23

The full-service, fine-dining restaurant appeals to adults, particularly those with an appetite for innovative concepts in food. Revised weekly, the menu consistently incorporates sophisticated, cutting-edge California dishes with Pacific Rim influences throughout. Among house specialties are flatbread appetizers baked in a brick oven, sushi, sashimi and some vegetarian dishes. The wine list focuses primarily on California vintages. Casual dress. **Bar:** Full bar. **Hours:** 11 am-10 pm, Fri & Sat-11 pm. **Address:** 3241 Washington Rd **Location:** I-20, exit 199 (Washington Rd), 1.2 mi nw. **Parking:** valet. **Cards:** AX, DC, DS, MC, VI.

CALVERT'S Phone: 706/738-4514

Continental
$19-$35

The dining area blends sophistication and coziness. Guests can choose from attractively garnished dishes that take into account texture and presentation. Desserts and full cocktail service also are available. Dressy casual. **Bar:** Full bar. **Reservations:** suggested. **Hours:** 5 pm-9 pm, Fri & Sat-10 pm. Closed major holidays; also Sun. **Address:** 475 Highland Ave **Location:** I-20, exit 199 (Washington Rd), 1.2 mi e to Berckmans Rd, then 1.8 mi s; in Surrey Center. **Parking:** on-site. **Cards:** AX, DC, DS, MC, VI.

FRENCH MARKET GRILLE — **Phone:** 706/737-4865

Regional American
$8-$26

The festive eatery nurtures a Mardi Gras theme and an energetic attitude. Spicy cuisine, such as seafood crepes drizzled with cheese sauce, is sure to please. The award-winning peanut butter pie is the perfect way to end a meal. Casual dress. **Bar:** Full bar. **Hours:** 11 am-10 pm, Fri & Sat-11 pm. Closed major holidays; also Sun. **Address:** 425 Highland Ave **Location:** Jct SR 28, 1.8 mi s on Berckmans Rd; in Surrey Center. **Parking:** on-site. **Cards:** AX, DC, DS, MC, VI.

LA MAISON ON TELFAIR — **Phone:** 706/722-4805

Continental
$16-$38

Quartered in a beautifully restored 1855 Victorian home, the restaurant projects Southern charm and elegance. The owner, a certified executive chef, prepares Continental and international dishes, such as rack of lamb, crab cakes, pecan-smoked salmon, creme brulee and walnut tarts. The extensive wine cellar will suit the most discriminating tastes. Dressy casual. **Bar:** Full bar. **Reservations:** suggested. **Hours:** 6 pm-10 pm. Closed major holidays; also Sun. **Address:** 404 Telfair St **Location:** 0.5 mi s, just e of US 1 (Gordon Hwy); in Olde Town. **Parking:** on-site. **Cards:** AX, DC, DS, MC, VI.

MIKOTO JAPANESE RESTAURANT — **Phone:** 706/855-0009

Japanese
$5-$18

The tempura is flavorful and teriyaki dishes are well-prepared, but sushi is the obvious star. Guests sit at either of two long sushi bars to watch the sushi chefs cut, prepare and garnish selections. Standard choices, such as salmon and rainbow rolls, join interesting in-house specialties. A large selection of Japanese beers and sakes accompanies the wine list. Casual dress. **Bar:** Beer & wine. **Reservations:** suggested. **Hours:** 11:30 am-2 & 5-9:30 pm, Fri-10:30 pm, Sat 5 pm-10:30 pm, Mon 5 pm-9:30 pm. Closed: 11/26, 12/25; also Sun. **Address:** 3102 Washington Rd **Location:** I-20, exit 199 (Washington Rd), 0.6 mi n. **Parking:** on-site. **Cards:** AX, DS, MC, VI.

MIMMO'S TASTE OF ITALY — **Phone:** 706/860-0888

Italian
$6-$19

The restaurant's reputation is well-deserved for its excellent food and broad menu, which lists standard favorites and a host of specialties. Entrees incorporate many varieties of pasta, as well as meat, veal, shellfish and vegetable accompaniments and perfect sauces. Zuppa pavese and wedding soup each are excellent starters. Casual dress. **Bar:** Beer & wine. **Reservations:** accepted. **Hours:** 11:30 am-9 pm, Fri & Sat-10 pm, Sun & Mon 5 pm-9 pm. Closed major holidays. **Address:** 362 Furys Ferry Rd **Location:** I-20, exit 199 (Washington Rd), 2 mi w; in Winn Dixie Plaza. **Parking:** on-site. **Cards:** AX, MC, VI.

RAES COASTAL CAFE — **Phone:** 706/738-1313

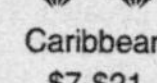

Caribbean
$7-$21

The cafe is a good place in which to escape to a Caribbean hideaway. Light reggae background music and a fun staff add to the comfortable atmosphere indoors and on the garden patio. On the menu are excellently prepared Cuban, Southern, Caribbean and American favorites. This is a great place to unwind. Casual dress. **Bar:** Full bar. **Hours:** 11:30 am-2 & 5:30-10 pm, Fri-11 pm, Sat 5:30 pm-11 pm, Sun 5:30 pm-10 pm. Closed major holidays; also Mon. **Address:** 3208 W Wimbledon Dr **Location:** I-520, exit 1C (Wheeler Rd), 0.7 mi ne to Walton Way, 0.4 mi s to W Lake Forest Dr, just s to Kerry Pl, then just sw to Forest Hills residential area, follow signs. **Parking:** on-site. **Cards:** AX, DS, MC, VI.

S & S CAFETERIA — **Phone:** 706/736-2972

American
$4-$8

A longtime favorite for comfort food, the family-owned cafeteria invites diners to load a plate with traditionally prepared chicken, beef, vegetables, salad and dessert. Casual dress. **Hours:** 11 am-2:15 & 5-8 pm. Closed: 12/25. **Address:** 1616 Walton Way **Location:** Jct Bobler Ave and Walton Way. **Parking:** on-site. **Cards:** AX, DS, MC, VI.

THE SNUG STEAK & GRILL — **Phone:** 706/863-1118

Steak & Seafood
$9-$33

Serving certified Angus beef and seafood, the romantic cabin-style restaurant is just northwest of the city. On the menu are such offerings as rib-eye steaks up to 24 ounces, Alaskan king crab and Canadian lobster tails, all served with a house salad and sides. The "toss me silly" salad, which the diner gets to toss, is a fun way to kick off a great meal. Casual dress. **Bar:** Full bar. **Reservations:** suggested. **Hours:** 11:30 am-2 & 4:30-9 pm, Fri & Sat-9:30 pm, Mon from 4:30 pm. Closed major holidays; also Sun. **Address:** 240 Davis Rd **Location:** I-20, exit 196B (Bobby Jones Expwy), just n to Scott Nixon Memorial Dr, just e to Davis Rd, then just n. **Parking:** on-site. **Cards:** AX, DS, MC, VI.

STICKY FINGERS RIB HOUSE — **Phone:** 706/733-7427

Barbecue
$7-$26

Diners can put down their silverware and get their fingers ready for classic Carolina sweet ribs, as well as ribs cooked in the Texas and Tennessee styles. Hearty sides of baked beans and coleslaw complement entrees at the friendly cafe. Casual dress. **Bar:** Full bar. **Hours:** 11 am-close. Closed: 11/26, 12/25. **Address:** 277 Robert C. Daniel Pkwy **Location:** I-20, exit 196B (Bobby Jones Expwy), just ne. **Parking:** on-site. **Cards:** AX, DC, DS, MC, VI.

T-BONZ STEAKHOUSE — **Phone:** 706/796-1875

Steak & Seafood
$6-$18

The restaurant offers casual dining in a Southwestern steakhouse atmosphere. Friendly, efficient service from a knowledgeable staff makes for a comfortable meal. The flowering fried onion and beer-boiled shrimp are popular starters. The house special drunken rib-eye steak, marinated in Kentucky bourbon sauce, and the "gill and grill" specials are favorite entrees. Casual dress. **Bar:** Full bar. **Hours:** 11 am-10 pm. Closed: 11/26, 12/25. **Address:** 1654 Gordon Hwy **Location:** Jct US 1/78; on southwest side of city. **Parking:** on-site. **Cards:** AX, DS, MC, VI.

T-BONZ STEAKHOUSE-WASHINGTON ROAD — **Phone:** 706/737-8325

Steak
$8-$20

Families gather for casual dining and attentive service in a lively atmosphere. Recipes are simple but offer variety. Check out the many scrumptious desserts and full cocktail bar. Casual dress. **Bar:** Full bar. **Reservations:** accepted. **Hours:** 11 am-10:30 pm, Fri & Sat-11 pm, Sun-10 pm. Closed: 11/26, 12/25. **Address:** 2856 Washington Rd **Location:** I-20, exit 199 (Washington Rd), just e. **Parking:** on-site. **Cards:** AX, DS, MC, VI.

VILLA EUROPA

German
$5-$20

Phone: 706/798-6211
In business since 1974, the modest family-owned restaurant is popular with families and friends for lunch and dinner. Favorites on a menu of mostly American and Italian food are German salad, fried mushrooms with horseradish sauce and herring in creamer. Service is warm and friendly. Casual dress. **Bar:** Full bar. **Reservations:** accepted. **Hours:** 11 am-3 & 5-10 pm, Sat & Sun from 5 pm. Closed: 1/1, 11/26, 12/25. **Address:** 3044 Deans Bridge Rd **Location:** I-520, exit 5B (US 1), 0.9 mi ne. **Parking:** on-site. **Cards:** AX, CB, DC, DS, MC, VI.

AUSTELL —*See Atlanta p. 376.*

BAINBRIDGE pop. 11,722

WHERE TO STAY

JAMESON INN *Book at AAA.com*

Hotel
$88-$93 All Year

Phone: (229)243-7000
Address: 1403 Tallahassee Hwy **Location:** Just s of US 84 Bypass on US 27. **Facility:** 61 one-bedroom standard units. 2 stories, exterior corridors. *Bath:* combo or shower only. **Parking:** on-site. **Terms:** cancellation fee imposed. **Amenities:** irons, hair dryers. **Pool(s):** outdoor. **Leisure Activities:** exercise room. **Guest Services:** valet laundry, wireless Internet. **Business Services:** PC. **Cards:** AX, DC, DS, MC, VI.

ASK / SOME UNITS FEE

BARNESVILLE pop. 5,972

WHERE TO STAY

COUNTRY HEARTH INN *Book at AAA.com*

Hotel
Rates not provided

Phone: 770/358-0967
Address: 648 Hwy 341 S **Location:** Jct US 341 and 41, 2.3 mi s. **Facility:** 40 one-bedroom standard units, some with whirlpools. 2 stories (no elevator), interior corridors. *Bath:* combo or shower only. **Parking:** on-site. **Amenities:** hair dryers. **Guest Services:** wireless Internet.

/ SOME UNITS FEE

WHERE TO DINE

HIGH FALLS BAR-B-QUE AND BEVERAGE

Barbecue
$5-$10

Phone: 478/992-6616
After a meal of traditional barbecue, including beef or pulled pork, diners can taste delicious homemade desserts, including peach ice cream. Casual dress. **Hours:** 11 am-9 pm, Fri & Sat-10 pm. Closed major holidays. **Address:** 5047 Highfalls Rd **Location:** I-75, exit 198, just e. **Parking:** on-site. **Cards:** MC, VI.

BAXLEY pop. 4,150

WHERE TO STAY

KEY WEST INN *Book at AAA.com*

Hotel
Rates not provided

Phone: 912/367-6653
Address: 53 Heritage St **Location:** 0.8 mi e on US 341. **Facility:** 51 one-bedroom standard units, some with whirlpools. 2 stories (no elevator), interior corridors. *Bath:* combo or shower only. **Parking:** on-site. **Amenities:** irons, hair dryers. **Pool(s):** outdoor. **Guest Services:** valet laundry, wireless Internet. **Business Services:** PC.

/ SOME UNITS

WHERE TO DINE

CAPTAIN JOE'S SEAFOOD

Seafood
$7-$19

Phone: 912/367-7795
Friendly, nautical ambience combined with generous portions and attentive service make this a pleasant experience. Do not miss the heavenly onion rings made with homegrown Vidalia onions and served with bleu cheese dressing. Casual dress. **Reservations:** accepted. **Hours:** 11 am-9 pm, Fri & Sat-10 pm. Closed: 11/26, 12/24, 12/25. **Address:** 2115 Golden Isles E **Location:** 2 mi e on US 341 and SR 27. **Parking:** on-site. **Cards:** AX, DS, MC, VI.

BLAIRSVILLE pop. 659

WHERE TO STAY

BEST WESTERN MILTON INN *Book great rates at AAA.com*

Hotel
$69-$109 All Year

Phone: (706)745-6995
Address: 222 Hwy 515 **Location:** Jct SR 19/US 129 and SR 515/US 76, just e. **Facility:** 60 one-bedroom standard units. 2 stories (no elevator), interior/exterior corridors. **Parking:** on-site. **Terms:** 3 day cancellation notice-fee imposed. **Amenities:** high-speed Internet, irons, hair dryers. **Pool(s):** outdoor. **Guest Services:** wireless Internet. **Business Services:** fax. **Cards:** AX, DS, MC, VI. **Free Special Amenities: expanded continental breakfast and high-speed Internet.**

AAA Benefit:
Members save up to 20%, plus 10% bonus points with rewards program.

HOLIDAY INN EXPRESS Book at AAA.com

Hotel
Rates not provided

Phone: 706/745-6844

Address: 333 Fisher St **Location:** Jct SR 19/US 129 and SR 515/US 76, just e. **Facility:** 65 one-bedroom standard units, some with whirlpools. 2 stories (no elevator), interior corridors. **Parking:** on-site. **Amenities:** high-speed Internet, dual phone lines, voice mail, irons, hair dryers. **Pool(s):** heated indoor. **Leisure Activities:** limited exercise equipment. **Guest Services:** valet laundry, wireless Internet. **Business Services:** PC, fax (fee).

CALL / SOME UNITS

WHERE TO DINE

COOKIE JAR RESTAURANT

Southern
$2-$17

Phone: 706/745-3600

Find down-home, Southern cooking served buffet-style with such favorites as fried chicken, collard greens, mashed potatoes and cornbread. And, don't forget to order some sweet tea to wash everything down. Casual dress. **Hours:** 11 am-8 pm, Fri & Sat-9 pm. Closed: 1/1, 12/25. **Address:** 199 Wellborn St **Location:** Just off SR 515 and US 76. **Parking:** on-site. **Cards:** AX, CB, DC, DS, JC, MC, VI.

CALL

WORLD FAMOUS BLAIRSVILLE RESTAURANT

American
$3-$16

Phone: 706/745-6921

Both buffet and full service highlight country cooking. Friendly servers circulate through the down-home setting. Casual dress. **Hours:** 5:30 am-2:30 pm, Wed-Fri also 5:30 pm-8 pm. Closed major holidays. **Address:** 229 Earnest St **Location:** Downtown. **Parking:** on-site. **Cards:** AX, DS, MC, VI.

BLAKELY pop. 5,696

WHERE TO STAY

DAYS INN OF BLAKELY Book at AAA.com

Hotel
Rates not provided

Phone: 229/723-5858

Address: 1097 Arlington Ave **Location:** On US 27. **Facility:** 30 one-bedroom standard units, some with whirlpools. 2 stories, exterior corridors. **Parking:** on-site. **Amenities:** high-speed Internet, irons, hair dryers. **Pool(s):** outdoor. **Guest Services:** coin laundry, wireless Internet. **Business Services:** fax (fee).

CALL / SOME UNITS

BLUE RIDGE pop. 1,210

WHERE TO STAY

DAYS INN Book at AAA.com

Motel
Rates not provided

Phone: 706/632-2100

Address: 4970 Appalachian Hwy **Location:** On SR 515 and US 76. **Facility:** 60 one-bedroom standard units. 2 stories (no elevator), exterior corridors. **Parking:** on-site. **Amenities:** high-speed Internet, irons, hair dryers. **Pool(s):** outdoor. **Guest Services:** wireless Internet. **Business Services:** fax.

/ SOME UNITS

DOUGLAS INN & SUITES

AAA SAVE

Motel
$45-$69 All Year

Phone: (706)258-3600

Address: 1192 Windy Ridge Rd **Location:** Just off SR 515 and US 76. **Facility:** 26 units. 18 one-bedroom standard units. 8 one-bedroom suites with kitchens. 1 story, exterior corridors. **Parking:** on-site. **Amenities:** high-speed Internet. *Some:* irons, hair dryers. **Pool(s):** outdoor. **Guest Services:** coin laundry, wireless Internet. **Business Services:** fax (fee). **Cards:** AX, CB, DC, DS, JC, MC, VI. **Free Special Amenities: local telephone calls and high-speed Internet.**

/ SOME UNITS FEE

RAMADA LIMITED Book at AAA.com

Hotel
$59-$99 All Year

Phone: (706)632-4444

Address: 30 Overview Dr **Location:** Just off SR 515 and US 76; behind Taco Bell. **Facility:** 42 one-bedroom standard units, some with whirlpools. 2 stories (no elevator), interior corridors. **Parking:** on-site. **Amenities:** video library, high-speed Internet, voice mail, irons, hair dryers. *Some:* DVD players (fee). **Pool(s):** heated indoor. **Guest Services:** wireless Internet. **Business Services:** fax (fee). **Cards:** AX, DC, DS, MC, VI.

ASK CALL / SOME UNITS

WHERE TO DINE

TOCCOA RIVERSIDE RESTAURANT & GENERAL STORE

AAA

American
$4-$16

Phone: 706/632-7891

Overlook the Toccoa River as you savor home-style favorites like chicken-fried steak, homemade mashed potatoes and fried okra. Juicy steak; seafood and an extensive salad bar top off the menu at this relaxed, country-themed restaurant. Casual dress. **Hours:** 11:30-3 & 4:30-9 pm, Fri & Sat-9:30 pm. Closed major holidays. **Address:** 8055 Aska Rd **Location:** 8 mi s. **Parking:** on-site. **Cards:** AX, MC, VI.

BRASELTON pop. 1,206

WHERE TO STAY

BEST WESTERN BRASELTON INN *Book great rates at AAA.com* **Phone:** (706)654-3081

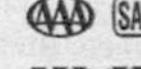

Hotel
$89-$165 All Year

Address: 303 Zion Church Rd **Location:** I-85, exit 129, 0.3 mi n. **Facility:** 55 one-bedroom standard units. 2 stories, exterior corridors. **Parking:** on-site. **Amenities:** DVD players, high-speed Internet, irons, hair dryers. **Pool(s):** outdoor. **Guest Services:** wireless Internet. **Business Services:** PC, fax (fee). **Cards:** AX, DC, DS, MC, VI. **Free Special Amenities: expanded continental breakfast and high-speed Internet.**

/ SOME UNITS FEE

AAA Benefit:
Members save up to 20%, plus 10% bonus points with rewards program.

CHATEAU ELAN LODGE BY HOLIDAY INN EXPRESS *Book great rates at AAA.com* **Phone:** (770)867-8100

Hotel
$90-$130 All Year

Address: 2069 Hwy 211 NW **Location:** I-85, exit 126, just w. **Facility:** 80 one-bedroom standard units. 2 stories, interior corridors. **Parking:** on-site. **Amenities:** high-speed Internet, voice mail, irons, hair dryers. **Pool(s):** outdoor. **Guest Services:** valet laundry, area transportation-Chateau Elan, wireless Internet. **Business Services:** PC, fax (fee). **Cards:** AX, DC, DS, MC, VI. **Free Special Amenities: expanded continental breakfast and high-speed Internet.**

FEE / SOME UNITS FEE

CHATEAU ELAN WINERY AND RESORT *Book at AAA.com* **Phone:** (678)425-0900

Resort Hotel
$164-$259 All Year

Address: 100 rue Charlemagne **Location:** I-85, exit 126, just w. **Facility:** This beautiful and sprawling resort, designed like a French chateau, has been a repeat destination for luminaries and locals alike since its inception. 306 units. 296 one-bedroom standard units. 1 one-bedroom suite with whirlpool. 9 cottages. 5 stories, interior corridors. **Parking:** on-site and valet. **Terms:** 3 day cancellation notice-fee imposed. **Amenities:** high-speed Internet (fee), voice mail, safes, irons, hair dryers. *Some:* CD players, dual phone lines. **Pool(s):** 2 outdoor, 2 heated indoor. **Leisure Activities:** saunas, whirlpools, steamrooms, 7 lighted tennis courts, recreation programs, rental bicycles, hiking trails, playground, spa, basketball, volleyball. *Fee:* golf-63 holes. **Guest Services:** valet laundry, area transportation, wireless Internet. **Business Services:** conference facilities, business center. **Cards:** AX, DC, DS, MC, VI. Affiliated with A Preferred Hotel.

ASK CALL / SOME UNITS

WHERE TO DINE

HOUNDSTOOTH GRILL & TAVERN **Phone:** 770/967-2225

American
$4-$27

An American version of an English restaurant and tavern, the decor is reminiscent of a hunting lodge. Surprisingly, the food doesn't reflect this as menu selections include traditional American grilled foods and some Italian favorites as well as salads, sandwiches, seafood, steaks and pork chops. Casual dress. **Bar:** Full bar. **Hours:** 11 am-9 pm, Fri & Sat-10 pm, Sun-8:30 pm. Closed major holidays. **Address:** 6323 Grand Hickory Dr **Location:** I-85, exit 126, 1.6 mi w; in Mulberry Walk. **Parking:** on-site. **Cards:** AX, CB, DC, DS, JC, MC, VI.

CALL 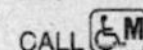

BREMEN pop. 4,579

WHERE TO STAY

DAYS INN Book great rates at AAA.com

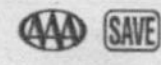

Hotel
$65 All Year

Phone: (770)537-4646

Address: 35 Price Creek Rd **Location:** I-75, exit 11, just n. **Facility:** 62 one-bedroom standard units. 2 stories (no elevator), exterior corridors. **Parking:** on-site. **Amenities:** high-speed Internet, safes (fee), hair dryers. **Pool(s):** outdoor. **Guest Services:** coin laundry, wireless Internet. **Business Services:** PC, fax. **Cards:** AX, DS, MC, VI. **Free Special Amenities: expanded continental breakfast and high-speed Internet.**

/ SOME UNITS FEE

HAMPTON INN Book great rates at AAA.com

Hotel
$94-$104 All Year

Phone: (770)537-9001

Address: 28 Price Creek Rd **Location:** I-20, exit 11, just n. **Facility:** 56 units. 55 one-bedroom standard units. 1 one-bedroom suite with whirlpool. 3 stories, interior corridors. **Parking:** on-site. **Terms:** cancellation fee imposed. **Amenities:** high-speed Internet, voice mail, irons, hair dryers. **Pool(s):** outdoor. **Leisure Activities:** exercise room. **Guest Services:** valet laundry, wireless Internet. **Business Services:** meeting rooms, PC, fax (fee). **Cards:** AX, DC, DS, MC, VI.

CALL / SOME UNITS

AAA Benefit:
Members save up to 10% everyday!

HOLIDAY INN EXPRESS HOTEL & SUITES Book great rates at AAA.com

Hotel
$90-$100 All Year

Phone: (770)537-3770

Address: 125 US Hwy 27 Bypass **Location:** I-20, exit 11, just n. **Facility:** 60 units. 58 one- and 2 two-bedroom standard units, some with whirlpools. 3 stories, interior corridors. **Parking:** on-site. **Amenities:** high-speed Internet, dual phone lines, voice mail, irons, hair dryers. **Pool(s):** heated indoor. **Leisure Activities:** whirlpool, exercise room. **Guest Services:** valet and coin laundry, wireless Internet. **Business Services:** meeting rooms, business center. **Cards:** AX, CB, DC, DS, JC, MC, VI. **Free Special Amenities: expanded continental breakfast and high-speed Internet.** *(See color ad below)*

CALL / SOME UNITS FEE

MICROTEL INN & SUITES Book great rates at AAA.com

Hotel
Rates not provided

Phone: 770/537-8000

Address: 104 Price Creek Rd **Location:** I-20, exit 11, just n. **Facility:** 62 one-bedroom standard units. 4 stories, interior corridors. **Parking:** on-site. **Amenities:** high-speed Internet, voice mail, irons, hair dryers. **Pool(s):** outdoor. **Leisure Activities:** exercise room. **Guest Services:** wireless Internet. **Business Services:** meeting rooms, PC, fax. **Free Special Amenities: expanded continental breakfast and high-speed Internet.**

CALL / SOME UNITS FEE

▼ See AAA listing above ▼

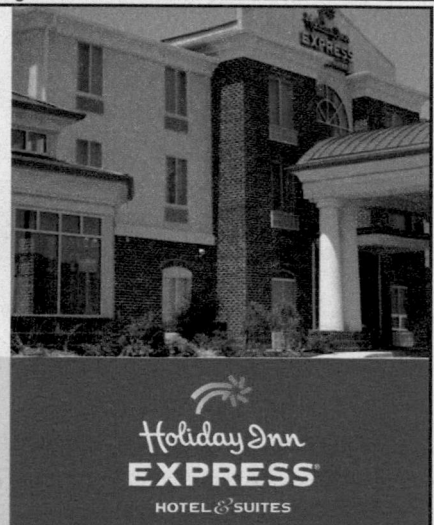

WHERE TO DINE

BILBO'S BARBEQUE

Phone: 770/537-4180

Barbecue
$1-$19

Barbecue pork, ribs and Brunswick stew are traditional favorites at the unpretentious spot. Casual dress. **Hours:** 11 am-8 pm, Fri & Sat-9 pm. Closed major holidays; also Sun & Mon. **Address:** 769 Atlantic Ave **Location:** I-20, exit 11, 1.5 mi n to US 78/SR 8, just e. **Parking:** on-site. **Cards:** AX, DS, MC, VI.

BRUNSWICK pop. 15,600

WHERE TO STAY

BEST WESTERN BRUNSWICK INN *Book great rates at AAA.com*

Phone: (912)264-0144

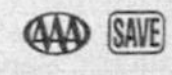

Hotel
$75-$135 All Year

Address: 5323 New Jesup Hwy **Location:** I-95, exit 36B (New Jesup Hwy/US 25), just nw. **Facility:** 144 one-bedroom standard units, some with efficiencies. 2 stories (no elevator), exterior corridors. *Bath:* combo or shower only. **Parking:** on-site. **Amenities:** voice mail, irons, hair dryers. *Some:* high-speed Internet. **Dining:** Matteo's Italian Restaurant, see separate listing. **Pool(s):** outdoor. **Leisure Activities:** whirlpool, covered picnic area with grill. **Guest Services:** coin laundry, wireless Internet. **Business Services:** meeting rooms. **Cards:** AX, CB, DC, DS, MC, VI. **Free Special Amenities: expanded continental breakfast and high-speed Internet.** ***(See color ad below)***

AAA Benefit:
Members save up to 20%, plus 10% bonus points with rewards program.

COMFORT INN *Book great rates at AAA.com*

Phone: (912)264-6540

Hotel
$79-$109 All Year

Address: 5308 New Jesup Hwy **Location:** I-95, exit 36B (New Jesup Hwy/US 25), just nw. **Facility:** Smoke free premises. 118 one-bedroom standard units, some with whirlpools. 5 stories, interior corridors. *Bath:* combo or shower only. **Parking:** on-site. **Terms:** 3 day cancellation notice. **Amenities:** voice mail, safes (fee), irons, hair dryers. **Pool(s):** outdoor. **Guest Services:** valet laundry, wireless Internet. **Business Services:** meeting rooms. **Cards:** AX, CB, DC, DS, MC, VI. **Free Special Amenities: expanded continental breakfast and high-speed Internet.**

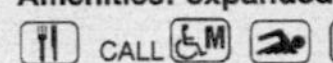

COMFORT SUITES

Phone: 912/267-4440

fyi

Hotel
$99-$209 All Year

Too new to rate. **Address:** 25 Ashton Dr **Location:** I-95, exit 29. **Amenities:** 72 units, coffeemakers, microwaves, refrigerators, pool. **Cards:** AX, CB, DC, DS, JC, MC, VI.

COUNTRY INN & SUITES BY CARLSON *Book great rates at AAA.com*

Phone: (912)264-2888

Hotel
$99-$169 All Year

Address: 211 Gateway Center Blvd **Location:** I-95, exit 38 (Golden Isles Pkwy), just se, then ne. **Facility:** 65 units. 56 one-bedroom standard units, some with whirlpools. 9 one-bedroom suites. 3 stories, interior corridors. *Bath:* combo or shower only. **Parking:** on-site. **Amenities:** high-speed Internet, voice mail, irons, hair dryers. **Pool(s):** heated indoor. **Leisure Activities:** sauna, whirlpool, exercise room. **Guest Services:** valet and coin laundry, wireless Internet. **Business Services:** meeting rooms, business center. **Cards:** AX, DC, DS, MC, VI. **Free Special Amenities: expanded continental breakfast and high-speed Internet.**

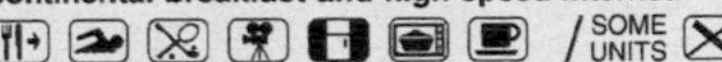

▼ *See AAA listing above* ▼

COURTYARD BY MARRIOTT BRUNSWICK *Book great rates at AAA.com*

Phone: (912)265-2644

Hotel
$128-$137 All Year

Address: 580 Millennium Dr **Location:** I-95, exit 38 (Golden Isles Pkwy), just w, then just n. **Facility:** Smoke free premises. 93 units. 90 one-bedroom standard units, some with whirlpools. 3 one-bedroom suites. 3 stories, interior corridors. *Bath:* combo or shower only. **Parking:** on-site. **Terms:** cancellation fee imposed. **Amenities:** high-speed Internet, dual phone lines, voice mail, irons, hair dryers. **Leisure Activities:** whirlpool, exercise room. **Guest Services:** valet and coin laundry, wireless Internet. **Business Services:** meeting rooms, business center. **Cards:** AX, CB, DC, DS, MC, VI.

AAA Benefit:
Members save a minimum 5% off the best available rate.

ECONO LODGE *Book great rates at AAA.com*

Phone: (912)264-8666

AAA SAVE

Hotel
$65-$85 All Year

Address: 2300 Perry Lane Rd **Location:** I-95, exit 38 (Golden Isles Pkwy), just n, then just w. **Facility:** 69 one-bedroom standard units. 2 stories (no elevator), interior/exterior corridors. **Parking:** on-site. **Pool(s):** outdoor. **Guest Services:** coin laundry, wireless Internet. **Business Services:** meeting rooms. **Cards:** AX, CB, DC, DS, JC, MC, VI. **Free Special Amenities: continental breakfast and high-speed Internet.**

CALL / SOME UNITS

EMBASSY SUITES HOTEL *Book great rates at AAA.com*

Phone: (912)264-6100

Hotel
$109-$189 All Year

Address: 500 Mall Blvd **Location:** I-95, exit 38 (Golden Isles Pkwy), 2 mi se, then just e. Adjoins Colonial Mall. **Facility:** 130 units. 127 one- and 3 two-bedroom suites. 5 stories, interior corridors. **Parking:** on-site. **Terms:** 1-30 night minimum stay, cancellation fee imposed. **Amenities:** video games (fee), voice mail, irons, hair dryers. **Pool(s):** outdoor. **Leisure Activities:** exercise room. **Guest Services:** valet laundry, area transportation, wireless Internet. **Business Services:** meeting rooms, PC. **Cards:** AX, CB, DC, DS, JC, MC, VI.

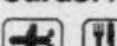    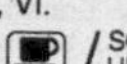 

/ SOME UNITS FEE VCR

AAA Benefit:
Members save 5% or more everyday!

FAIRFIELD INN AND SUITES BY MARRIOTT *Book great rates at AAA.com* **Phone:** (912)264-2060

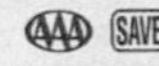

Hotel
$92-$102 All Year

Address: 107 Gateway Center Cir **Location:** I-95, exit 38 (Golden Isles Pkwy), just se. Located in a quiet area. **Facility:** Smoke free premises. 81 one-bedroom standard units. 3 stories, interior corridors. *Bath:* combo or shower only. **Parking:** on-site. **Terms:** cancellation fee imposed. **Amenities:** high-speed Internet, voice mail, irons, hair dryers. **Pool(s):** outdoor. **Leisure Activities:** whirlpool, limited exercise equipment. **Guest Services:** valet and coin laundry, wireless Internet. **Business Services:** meeting rooms, business center. **Cards:** AX, CB, DC, DS, MC, VI. **Free Special Amenities: expanded continental breakfast and high-speed Internet.**

 CALL  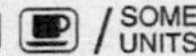  / SOME UNITS

AAA Benefit:
Members save a minimum 5% off the best available rate.

HAMPTON INN *Book great rates at AAA.com* **Phone:** (912)261-0002

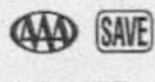

Hotel
$89-$109 All Year

Address: 230 Warren Mason Blvd **Location:** I-95, exit 36A (New Jesup Hwy/US 25), just se, then just sw on Tourist Dr. **Facility:** 129 one-bedroom standard units. 3 stories, interior/exterior corridors. **Parking:** on-site. **Terms:** 1-30 night minimum stay, cancellation fee imposed. **Amenities:** video games (fee), voice mail, irons, hair dryers. **Pool(s):** outdoor. **Guest Services:** valet laundry, wireless Internet. **Business Services:** PC. **Cards:** AX, CB, DC, DS, MC, VI. **Free Special Amenities: full breakfast and high-speed Internet.**
(See color ad below)

 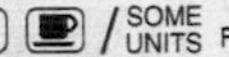  / SOME UNITS FEE  

AAA Benefit:
Members save up to 10% everyday!

HOLIDAY INN HOTEL & SUITES *Book at AAA.com* **Phone:** 912/264-3300

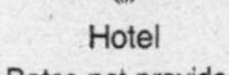

Hotel
Rates not provided

Address: 138 Glynco Pkwy **Location:** I-95, exit 38 (Golden Isles Pkwy), just se. **Facility:** 103 units. 81 one-bedroom standard units. 22 one-bedroom suites. 5 stories, interior corridors. *Bath:* combo or shower only. **Parking:** on-site. **Amenities:** high-speed Internet, voice mail, irons, hair dryers. **Dining:** Millhouse Steakhouse, see separate listing. **Pool(s):** heated indoor. **Leisure Activities:** exercise room. **Guest Services:** valet and coin laundry, wireless Internet. **Business Services:** meeting rooms, business center.

 CALL / SOME UNITS

JAMESON INN BRUNSWICK *Book at AAA.com* **Phone:** (912)267-0800

Hotel
$78-$85 All Year

Address: 661 Scranton Rd **Location:** I-95, exit 38 (Golden Isles Pkwy), 1.6 mi se, then just sw. **Facility:** Smoke free premises. 62 one-bedroom standard units, some with whirlpools. 2 stories, exterior corridors. *Bath:* combo or shower only. **Parking:** on-site. **Terms:** cancellation fee imposed. **Amenities:** hair dryers. **Pool(s):** outdoor. **Leisure Activities:** exercise room. **Guest Services:** wireless Internet. **Business Services:** PC. **Cards:** AX, DC, DS, MC, VI.

  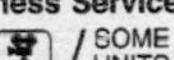 / SOME UNITS FEE   

▼ See AAA listing above ▼

LA QUINTA INN & SUITES BRUNSWICK *Book great rates at AAA.com*

Hotel
$39-$79 All Year

Phone: (912)265-7725

Address: 165 Warren Mason Blvd **Location:** I-95, exit 36A (New Jesup Hwy/US 25), just se, then sw on Tourist Dr. **Facility:** 102 one-bedroom standard units. 3 stories, interior corridors. **Parking:** on-site. **Amenities:** video games (fee), dual phone lines, voice mail, irons, hair dryers. **Pool(s):** outdoor. **Guest Services:** coin laundry, wireless Internet. **Business Services:** PC. **Cards:** AX, DC, DS, MC, VI.

ASK / SOME UNITS

MICROTEL INN & SUITES *Book at AAA.com*

Hotel
$50-$82 All Year

Phone: (912)261-0118

Address: 325 Palisades Dr **Location:** I-95, exit 29, just w. **Facility:** 61 one-bedroom standard units, some with whirlpools. 3 stories, interior corridors. *Bath:* combo or shower only. **Parking:** on-site. **Amenities:** hair dryers. **Pool(s):** outdoor. **Guest Services:** coin laundry, wireless Internet. **Business Services:** PC. **Cards:** AX, DS, MC, VI.

ASK CALL / SOME UNITS

MICROTEL INN & SUITES *Book great rates at AAA.com*

Hotel
$69-$139 All Year

Phone: (912)554-1430

Address: 146 Gateway Center Blvd **Location:** I-95, exit 38 (Golden Isles Pkwy), just se to Glynco Tpke, then just ne. **Facility:** Smoke free premises. 62 one-bedroom standard units, some with whirlpools. 3 stories, interior corridors. *Bath:* combo or shower only. **Parking:** on-site. **Amenities:** dual phone lines, voice mail, hair dryers. **Pool(s):** outdoor. **Guest Services:** wireless Internet. **Business Services:** PC. **Cards:** AX, DC, DS, MC, VI. **Free Special Amenities: continental breakfast and high-speed Internet.** *(See color ad below)*

CALL / SOME UNITS

QUALITY INN *Book at AAA.com*

Hotel
$79-$109 All Year

Phone: (912)265-4600

Address: 125 Venture Dr **Location:** I-95, exit 38 (Golden Isles Pkwy), just nw. **Facility:** 83 one-bedroom standard units, some with whirlpools. 2 stories (no elevator), interior/exterior corridors. **Parking:** on-site. **Amenities:** high-speed Internet, irons, hair dryers. **Pool(s):** outdoor. **Guest Services:** coin laundry, wireless Internet. **Business Services:** meeting rooms. **Cards:** AX, CB, DC, DS, JC, MC, VI.

RODEWAY INN *Book at AAA.com*

Hotel
$50-$55 All Year

Phone: (912)261-0670

Address: 5272 New Jesup Hwy **Location:** I-95, exit 36B (New Jesup Hwy/US 25), just nw. **Facility:** Smoke free premises. 93 one-bedroom standard units, some with whirlpools. 2 stories (no elevator), interior corridors. *Bath:* combo or shower only. **Parking:** on-site. **Amenities:** irons, hair dryers. **Pool(s):** outdoor. **Guest Services:** wireless Internet. **Business Services:** PC. **Cards:** AX, DS, MC, VI.

/ SOME UNITS

▼ *See AAA listing above* ▼

SUPER 8 MOTEL **Phone:** (912)264-8800

Hotel
$45-$125 All Year

Address: 5280 New Jesup Hwy **Location:** I-95, exit 36B (New Jesup Hwy/US 25), just nw. **Facility:** 59 one-bedroom standard units. 3 stories, interior corridors. **Parking:** on-site. **Terms:** cancellation fee imposed. **Amenities:** irons, hair dryers. **Guest Services:** coin laundry, wireless Internet. **Business Services:** PC. **Cards:** AX, DC, DS, MC, VI. **Free Special Amenities: continental breakfast and high-speed Internet.**

/ SOME UNITS FEE

WHERE TO DINE

BARBERITOS **Phone:** 912/264-8804

Mexican
$3-$6

Diners order at the counter and pay, then watch as their orders are prepared. The quick-serve eatery is a favorite for tacos, burritos, quesadillas and salads, as well as some vegetarian and vegan dishes. Casual dress. **Bar:** Beer only. **Hours:** 11 am-9 pm, Fri & Sat-10 pm. Closed major holidays. **Address:** 250 Golden Isles Plaza Dr, Suite 100 **Location:** I-95, exit 38 (Golden Isles Pkwy), 1.4 mi se, then just s on Scranton Rd: **Parking:** on-site. **Cards:** AX, MC, VI.

CALL

CARGO PORTSIDE GRILL **Phone:** 912/267-7330

Northern American
$19-$27

In the heart of historic downtown, minutes from the barrier islands, the restaurant boasts a contemporary nautical decor in an airy dining room. Expect to find skillfully prepared fresh seafood with international touches. Save room for dessert and enjoy delicious peach poundcake. Dressy casual. **Bar:** Full bar. **Reservations:** suggested. **Hours:** 5:30 pm-9:30 pm, Fri & Sat-10 pm. Closed major holidays; also Sun & Mon. **Address:** 1423 Newcastle St **Location:** I-95, exit 36A (New Jesup Hwy/US 25), 5.4 mi s on US 25; between Gloucester and Monck sts; downtown. **Parking:** street. **Cards:** AX, MC, VI.

CALL

CHRISTIE'S **Phone:** 912/262-0699

American
$8-$29

In the downtown historic area, this intimate eatery presents guests with some sophisticated entree options: lobster macaroni and cheese, roast duck breast and fennel- and coriander-crusted ahi tuna. As much as possible, ingredients are purchased from local producers. While the dining room has a distinctive look, the atmosphere remains casual. Casual dress. **Bar:** Full bar. **Hours:** 11 am-3 & 6-10 pm, Sat from 6 pm, Mon-3 pm. Closed major holidays; also Sun. **Address:** 1618 Newcastle St **Location:** I-95, exit 36A (New Jesep Hwy/US 25), 5.4 mi s on US 25; downtown. **Parking:** street. **Cards:** AX, MC, VI.

JINRIGHT'S SEAFOOD HOUSE **Phone:** 912/267-1590

Seafood
$5-$25

The family-owned restaurant is just minutes from the ocean. Reasonably priced fried seafood platters are served in portions ample enough to satisfy any appetite. The nautical decor adds to the ambience. Casual dress. **Bar:** Beer & wine. **Hours:** 11 am-9 pm, Fri & Sat-10 pm. Closed: 1/1, 11/26, 12/24, 12/25. **Address:** 2815 Glynn Ave **Location:** Jct US 25 Spur/Golden Isles Pkwy and US 17, 0.9 mi s on US 17; jct US 17/25, 2.6 mi n on US 17. **Parking:** on-site. **Cards:** DS, MC, VI.

JOE'S JAPANESE STEAKHOUSE

Phone: 912/554-0073

Steak & Seafood

$8-$29

Hibachi-style dining means guests, particularly groups seeking a fun dinner experience, are treated to an entertaining show from the table chef. Predominant entrees of steak and seafood come with soup and salad. Casual dress. **Bar:** Full bar. **Reservations:** suggested. **Hours:** 11 am-2 & 5-10 pm, Sat & Sun from 5 pm. Closed: 11/26, 12/25. **Address:** 704 Mall Blvd **Location:** I-95, exit 38 (Golden Isles Pkwy), 1.6 mi se on US 25 Spur; adjacent to Colonial Mall; next to Spankeys Mallside. **Parking:** on-site. **Cards:** AX, DS, MC, VI.

LA FUENTE DE PABLO MEXICAN RESTAURANT

Phone: 912/279-0606

Mexican

$6-$14

In addition to the traditional tacos, burritos and enchiladas typical of many Mexican restaurants, the casual restaurant prepares varied chicken, beef and seafood entrees. Much of the food is made in house. Service is informal. Casual dress. **Bar:** Full bar. **Hours:** 11 am-10 pm, Sun-9 pm. Closed: 1/1, 11/26, 12/25. **Address:** 2450 Perry Lane Rd **Location:** I-95, exit 38 (Golden Isles Pkwy), just nw. **Parking:** on-site. **Cards:** AX, DS, MC, VI.

CALL

MATTEO'S ITALIAN RESTAURANT

Phone: 912/267-0248

Italian

$5-$16

Right off the interstate, the restaurant invites guests to sit at wrought-iron tables and dine on fine Italian-American favorites and tasty garlic rolls. Tasty pasta dishes and eggplant parmigiana all are served in good-size portions. Dress is casual, and the decor resembles an Italian garden. Casual dress. **Bar:** Beer & wine. **Reservations:** accepted. **Hours:** 11 am-2:30 & 5-9:30 pm, Sat from 4 pm. Closed: 7/4, 11/26, 12/25; also Sun. **Address:** 5323 New Jesup Hwy **Location:** I-95, exit 36B (New Jesup Hwy/US 25), just nw; in Best Western Brunswick Inn. **Parking:** on-site. **Cards:** AX, MC, VI.

CALL

MILLHOUSE STEAKHOUSE

Phone: 912/264-3424

Steak

$9-$28

Wood and muted colors in a rustic theme give this restaurant a country impression. The menu offers a variety of meat and seafood, including steaks, duck, lamb, salmon, mussels and shrimp. Special ingredients, such as Brie, Gorgonzola and portobello mushrooms, take dining to a higher level of enjoyment. Casual dress. **Bar:** Full bar. **Reservations:** accepted. **Hours:** 4 pm-10:30 pm, Fri & Sat-11 pm. **Address:** 124 Glynco Pkwy **Location:** I-95, exit 38 (Golden Isles Pkwy), just se; in Holiday Inn Hotel & Suites. **Parking:** on-site. **Cards:** AX, DS, MC, VI.

ORLANDO'S

Phone: 912/264-5200

Mexican

$5-$13

Friendly staff members serve large portions of well-prepared traditional Tex-Mex food. Flavorful dishes are thoroughly enjoyable. The atmosphere is casual and informal. Fried ice cream is a real treat for dessert. Casual dress. **Bar:** Full bar. **Hours:** 11 am-10 pm, Fri & Sat-11 pm. Closed major holidays. **Address:** 3384 Cypress Mill Rd **Location:** Jct SR 25, just s. **Parking:** on-site. **Cards:** AX, DS, MC, VI.

SONNY'S REAL PIT BAR-B-Q

Phone: 912/264-9184

Barbecue

$6-$15

House specialties include pork and chicken grilled over an open pit, barbecue ribs and fresh, homemade pie. The salad bar offers another popular option. Rustic and comfortable, the atmosphere is perfect for family meals. Casual dress. **Bar:** Beer only. **Hours:** 11 am-9:30 pm, Fri & Sat-10 pm. Closed: 11/26, 12/25. **Address:** 5328 New Jesup Hwy **Location:** I-95, exit 36B (New JesupHwy/US 25), just nw. **Parking:** on-site. **Cards:** AX, DS, MC, VI.

SPANKY'S MALLSIDE

Phone: 912/554-0222

Seafood

$7-$20

Patrons can dine on healthy portions of steak, seafood and burgers at the lively gathering spot near the mall. Casual dress. **Bar:** Full bar. **Hours:** 11 am-10 pm, Fri & Sat-11 pm. Closed: 11/26, 12/25. **Address:** 704 Mall Blvd **Location:** I-95, exit 38 (Golden Isles Pkwy), 1.5 mi s on US 25 Spur; adjacent to Colonial Mall. **Parking:** on-site. **Cards:** AX, DS, MC, VI.

BUFORD

—*See Atlanta p. 376.*

BYRON pop. 2,887

WHERE TO STAY

BEST WESTERN INN & SUITES *Book great rates at AAA.com* **Phone:** (478)956-3056

AAA Benefit: Members save up to 20%, plus 10% bonus points with rewards program.

AAA SAVE

Hotel
$63-$69 All Year

Address: 101 Dunbar Rd **Location:** I-75, exit 149 (SR 49), just ne. **Facility:** 70 one-bedroom standard units, some with whirlpools. 2 stories (no elevator), exterior corridors. *Bath:* combo or shower only. **Parking:** on-site, winter plug-ins. **Amenities:** irons, hair dryers. *Some:* DVD players, high-speed Internet. **Pool(s):** heated indoor. **Leisure Activities:** whirlpool, exercise room. **Guest Services:** coin laundry, wireless Internet. **Business Services:** PC. **Cards:** AX, CB, DC, DS, MC, VI. **Free Special Amenities: continental breakfast and high-speed Internet.** *(See color ad below)*

   / SOME UNITS FEE  VCR

COMFORT SUITES **Phone:** 478/956-1222

fyi

Hotel

Under construction, scheduled to open January 2009. **Address:** 103 Dunbar Rd **Location:** I-75, exit 149. **Amenities:** 71 units, coffeemakers, microwaves, refrigerators, pool. ***(See color ad below)***

▼ *See AAA listing above* ▼

▼ *See AAA listing above* ▼

HOLIDAY INN EXPRESS HOTEL & SUITES Book great rates at AAA.com **Phone:** (478)956-7829

Hotel
$95-$120 All Year

Address: 102 Holiday Ct **Location:** I-75, exit 149 (SR 49), just ne. **Facility:** 61 one-bedroom standard units. 4 stories, interior corridors. *Bath:* combo or shower only. **Parking:** on-site. **Terms:** 14 day cancellation notice. **Amenities:** high-speed Internet, dual phone lines, voice mail, irons, hair dryers. **Pool(s):** outdoor. **Leisure Activities:** limited exercise equipment. **Guest Services:** valet and coin laundry. **Business Services:** meeting rooms, fax (fee). **Cards:** AX, CB, DC, DS, MC, VI.

CALL / SOME UNITS

QUALITY INN **Phone:** (478)956-1600

Hotel
$70-$115 All Year

Address: 115 Chapman Rd **Location:** I-75, exit 149 (SR 49), just sw, then n. **Facility:** 60 one-bedroom standard units, some with whirlpools. 2 stories (no elevator), exterior corridors. *Bath:* combo or shower only. **Parking:** on-site. **Amenities:** high-speed Internet, irons, hair dryers. **Pool(s):** heated indoor. **Guest Services:** coin laundry, wireless Internet. **Business Services:** fax (fee). **Cards:** AX, DS, MC, VI.

ASK / SOME UNITS FEE

SUPER 8 MOTEL Book great rates at AAA.com **Phone:** (478)956-3311

Hotel
$65-$70 All Year

Address: 305 Hwy 49 N **Location:** I-75, exit 149 (SR 49), just ne. **Facility:** 57 one-bedroom standard units, some with whirlpools. 2 stories (no elevator), exterior corridors. *Bath:* combo or shower only. **Parking:** on-site. **Amenities:** irons, hair dryers. **Pool(s):** outdoor. **Guest Services:** coin laundry, wireless Internet. **Business Services:** fax (fee). **Cards:** AX, CB, DC, DS, MC, VI. **Free Special Amenities: continental breakfast and high-speed Internet.**

/ SOME UNITS

WHERE TO DINE

COUNTRY CUPBOARD RESTAURANT **Phone:** 478/956-4771

American
$4-$12

Guests seeking freshly prepared comfort food can get it from the buffet or the menu. Just off the interstate, the restaurant is a great stop for a quick, filling and inexpensive meal. Casual dress. **Hours:** 6:30 am-9:30 pm. Closed: 11/26, 12/25. **Address:** 107 Chapman Rd **Location:** I-75, exit 149 (SR 49), just sw, then n. **Parking:** on-site. **Cards:** AX, DS, MC, VI.

CAIRO pop. 9,239

WHERE TO STAY

BEST WESTERN EXECUTIVE INN Book great rates at AAA.com **Phone:** (229)377-8000

Hotel
$60-$100 All Year

Address: 2800 Hwy 84 E **Location:** 2 mi e. **Facility:** 50 one-bedroom standard units, some with whirlpools. 2 stories (no elevator), exterior corridors. **Parking:** on-site. **Amenities:** voice mail, irons, hair dryers. **Pool(s):** outdoor. **Leisure Activities:** sauna, limited exercise equipment. **Guest Services:** valet laundry, wireless Internet. **Cards:** AX, CB, DC, DS, MC, VI. **Free Special Amenities: expanded continental breakfast and high-speed Internet.**

/ SOME UNITS FEE

AAA Benefit:
Members save up to 20%, plus 10% bonus points with rewards program.

CALHOUN pop. 10,667

WHERE TO STAY

COMFORT INN Book at AAA.com **Phone:** (706)629-8271

Hotel
$60-$70 All Year

Address: 742 Hwy 53 SE **Location:** I-75, exit 312, just w. **Facility:** 90 one-bedroom standard units, some with whirlpools. 2 stories (no elevator), exterior corridors. **Parking:** on-site. **Amenities:** high-speed Internet, voice mail, irons, hair dryers. *Some:* dual phone lines. **Pool(s):** outdoor. **Guest Services:** coin laundry, wireless Internet. **Business Services:** meeting rooms, fax (fee). **Cards:** AX, CB, DC, DS, MC, VI.

ASK FEE / SOME UNITS FEE

COUNTRY INN & SUITES Book at AAA.com **Phone:** (706)625-6500

Hotel
$76-$149 All Year

Address: 1033 Fairmount Hwy **Location:** I-75, exit 312, just e. **Facility:** 64 units. 54 one-bedroom standard units. 10 one-bedroom suites. 4 stories, interior corridors. **Parking:** on-site. **Amenities:** high-speed Internet, voice mail, irons, hair dryers. **Pool(s):** heated indoor. **Leisure Activities:** whirlpool, limited exercise equipment. **Guest Services:** coin laundry, wireless Internet. **Business Services:** meeting rooms, business center. **Cards:** AX, DC, DS, MC, VI.

HAMPTON INN *Book great rates at AAA.com* **Phone:** (706)629-0999

Hotel

$72-$88 All Year

Address: 115 Hampton Dr SE **Location:** I-75, exit 312, just w. **Facility:** 59 one-bedroom standard units, some with whirlpools. 2 stories, exterior corridors. **Parking:** on-site. **Amenities:** high-speed Internet, voice mail, irons, hair dryers. **Pool(s):** outdoor. **Leisure Activities:** exercise room. **Guest Services:** wireless Internet. **Business Services:** business center. **Cards:** AX, DC, DS, MC, VI.

CALL / SOME UNITS

AAA Benefit: Members save up to 10% everyday!

HOLIDAY INN EXPRESS *Book at AAA.com* **Phone:** (706)629-8566

Hotel

$89-$149 All Year

Address: 125 Hampton Dr **Location:** I-75, exit 312, just w. **Facility:** 62 one-bedroom standard units. 2 stories, interior corridors. **Parking:** on-site. **Amenities:** high-speed Internet, dual phone lines, voice mail, irons, hair dryers. **Pool(s):** outdoor. **Leisure Activities:** exercise room. **Guest Services:** valet and coin laundry, wireless Internet. **Business Services:** meeting rooms, business center. **Cards:** AX, CB, DC, DS, JC, MC, VI.

ASK CALL / SOME UNITS

JAMESON INN *Book at AAA.com* **Phone:** (706)629-8133

Hotel

$83-$90 All Year

Address: 189 Jameson St **Location:** I-75, exit 312, just w. **Facility:** 59 one-bedroom standard units, some with whirlpools. 2 stories, exterior corridors. **Parking:** on-site. **Terms:** cancellation fee imposed. **Amenities:** high-speed Internet, irons, hair dryers. **Pool(s):** outdoor. **Leisure Activities:** exercise room. **Guest Services:** wireless Internet. **Business Services:** PC, fax. **Cards:** AX, DC, DS, MC, VI.

ASK / SOME UNITS FEE

QUALITY INN CALHOUN **Phone:** (706)629-9501

Hotel

$55-$75 All Year

Address: 915 Hwy 53 E SE **Location:** I-75, exit 312, just e. **Facility:** 90 one-bedroom standard units. 2 stories, exterior corridors. **Parking:** on-site. **Amenities:** high-speed Internet, irons, hair dryers. **Pool(s):** outdoor. **Guest Services:** coin laundry, wireless Internet. **Business Services:** meeting rooms, business center. **Cards:** AX, CB, DC, DS, JC, MC, VI.

ASK / SOME UNITS FEE

RAMADA LIMITED *Book at AAA.com* **Phone:** (706)629-9207

Motel

$55-$100 All Year

Address: 1204 Red Bud Rd NE **Location:** I-75, exit 315, just w. **Facility:** 47 one-bedroom standard units. 2 stories (no elevator), exterior corridors. **Parking:** on-site. **Amenities:** high-speed Internet, voice mail, irons, hair dryers. **Pool(s):** outdoor. **Guest Services:** coin laundry, wireless Internet. **Business Services:** fax (fee). **Cards:** AX, DC, DS, MC, VI.

ASK / SOME UNITS FEE

SMITH MOTEL **Phone:** (706)629-8427

AAA SAVE

Motel

$33 6/1-11/30

$30 12/1-5/31

Address: 1437 US Hwy 41 N **Location:** I-75, exit 318, just w. **Facility:** 40 one-bedroom standard units. 2 stories (no elevator), exterior corridors. **Parking:** on-site. **Amenities:** high-speed Internet. **Guest Services:** wireless Internet. **Business Services:** fax. **Cards:** AX, DS, MC, VI.

/ SOME UNITS FEE

WHERE TO DINE

BJ'S RESTAURANT **Phone:** 706/629-3461

AAA

Southern

$5-$15

The local gathering spot delivers a touch of Southern hospitality. Fried green tomatoes, fried chicken and peanut butter pie are a few of the more down-home offerings served alongside such creative dishes as orange-glazed pecan chicken. Casual dress. **Hours:** 11 am-8:30 pm, Thurs-Sat to 9 pm, Sun-2:30 pm. Closed major holidays. **Address:** 273 Hwy 53 E **Location:** I-75, exit 312, 0.8 mi w; in Midtown Square. **Parking:** on-site. **Cards:** AX, DS, MC, VI.

GONDOLIER ITALIAN RESTAURANT AND PIZZA **Phone:** 706/625-2322

Pizza

$3-$13

In addition to daily specials, diners can select from a tempting variety of calzones and such standards as spaghetti, manicotti and ravioli. Servers are fast and friendly. Casual dress. **Bar:** Beer & wine. **Hours:** 11 am-10 pm, Fri & Sat-11 pm. Closed: 11/26, 12/25. **Address:** 427 Hwy 53 **Location:** I-75, exit 312, 0.7 mi w. **Parking:** on-site. **Cards:** AX, DS, MC, VI.

GOURMET DAY CAFE

Deli
$2-$8

Phone: 706/624-9001

Fresh, tasty and satisfying sandwiches, soups and salads are featured at Gourmet Day Cafe. Lucious desserts should not be missed if you are so inclined. Casual dress. **Hours:** 10:30 am-2 pm. Closed major holidays; also Sun. **Address:** 100 Peters St, Suite 15 **Location:** I-75, exit 312, 1 mi w to US 41, then 1 mi n; in Gordon Hills Shopping Center. **Parking:** on-site. **Cards:** AX, DS, MC, VI.

CANTON pop. 7,709

— WHERE TO STAY —

COMFORT INN Book at AAA.com

Hotel
$65-$100 All Year

Phone: (770)345-1994

Address: 138 Keith Dr **Location:** I-575, exit 20, just e. **Facility:** 51 one-bedroom standard units, some with whirlpools. 2 stories (no elevator), interior corridors. **Parking:** on-site. **Terms:** cancellation fee imposed. **Amenities:** high-speed Internet, voice mail, irons, hair dryers. **Pool(s):** outdoor. **Leisure Activities:** exercise room. **Guest Services:** valet and coin laundry, wireless Internet. **Business Services:** meeting rooms, PC, fax (fee). **Cards:** AX, CB, DC, DS, JC, MC, VI.

ASK CALL / SOME UNITS

DAYS INN Book at AAA.com

Hotel
$63-$70 4/1-11/30
$58-$70 12/1-3/31

Phone: (770)479-0301

Address: 101 Juniper St **Location:** I-575, exit 20, 1.4 mi w. **Facility:** 39 one-bedroom standard units. 2 stories, exterior corridors. **Parking:** on-site. **Terms:** cancellation fee imposed. **Amenities:** high-speed Internet, irons, hair dryers. **Pool(s):** outdoor. **Guest Services:** wireless Internet. **Business Services:** fax (fee). **Cards:** AX, DS, MC, VI.

ASK / SOME UNITS

HOLIDAY INN EXPRESS HOTEL & SUITES Book at AAA.com

Hotel
$80-$90 All Year

Phone: (770)479-7300

Address: 713 Transit Ave **Location:** I-575, exit 20, just w. **Facility:** 61 one-bedroom standard units, some with whirlpools. 3 stories, interior corridors. **Parking:** on-site. **Terms:** cancellation fee imposed. **Amenities:** high-speed Internet, dual phone lines, voice mail, irons, hair dryers. **Pool(s):** heated indoor. **Leisure Activities:** limited exercise equipment. **Guest Services:** valet and coin laundry, wireless Internet. **Business Services:** meeting rooms, PC, fax (fee). **Cards:** AX, CB, DC, DS, MC, VI.

ASK CALL / SOME UNITS

MICROTEL INN & SUITES

Hotel
Rates not provided

Phone: 770/345-8700

Too new to rate. **Address:** 114 River Pointe Pkwy **Location:** I-575, exit 20, 0.3 mi e to River Ponte Pkwy. **Amenities:** 71 units, refrigerators, pool.

— WHERE TO DINE —

DOWNTOWN KITCHEN

American
$4-$28

Phone: 770/479-1616

A downtown jewel well outside the Atlanta perimeter, the restaurant pairs well-prepared comfort foods with selections from a good wine list. Funky art of music icons and exposed brick walls add to the trendy feel. Servers are informed. Casual dress. **Bar:** Full bar. **Reservations:** accepted. **Hours:** 11 am-2 & 5-close, Sat from 5 pm. Closed: 11/26, 12/25; also Sun. **Address:** 140 E Marietta St **Location:** Downtown. **Parking:** on-site. **Cards:** AX, DS, MC, VI.

LITTLE RIVER GRILLE

American
$6-$16

Phone: 770/345-4444

The restaurant serves standard American grill fare in a beautiful lakeside setting. Diners can pull right up in their boat. Casual dress. **Bar:** Beer & wine. **Hours:** 11 am-11 pm, Fri & Sat-midnight, Sun 11 am-10 pm; hours vary in winter. Closed: 11/26, 12/25. **Address:** 6979 Bells Ferry Rd **Location:** I-575, exit 11, 3 mi w, then 3 mi s. **Parking:** on-site. **Cards:** AX, DS, MC, VI.

PROVINO'S

Italian
$5-$18

Phone: 770/720-9676

Traditional Italian favorites——are served in a warm and pleasant setting. Buttery garlic rolls taste delicious. Casual dress. **Bar:** Beer & wine. **Hours:** 4:30 pm-10 pm, Sat-11 pm, Sun 11:30 am-9 pm. Closed: 11/26, 12/25. **Address:** 1365 Riverstone Pkwy **Location:** I-575, exit 20, 1 mi w. **Parking:** on-site. **Cards:** AX, CB, DC, DS, JC, MC, VI.

CALL

WILLIAMSON BROS BAR-B-Q

Barbecue
$7-$17

Phone: 770/345-9067

House specialties include barbecue ribs, pork and chicken grilled over an open pit and fresh homemade pie. Rustic and comfortable, the atmosphere is perfect for family meals. Fried dill pickles and fried red tomatoes in a thick batter are worth a try. Casual dress. **Bar:** Full bar. **Hours:** 10 am-9 pm, Fri & Sat-10 pm. Closed major holidays. **Address:** 1600 Marietta Hwy **Location:** I-575, exit 16, 0.8 mi w. **Parking:** on-site. **Cards:** AX, CB, DC, DS, JC, MC, VI.

CARROLLTON pop. 19,843

WHERE TO STAY

BEST WESTERN CARROLLTON INN & SUITES *Book great rates at AAA.com* **Phone:** (770)830-1000

Hotel
$70-$149 All Year

Address: 1111 Bankhead Hwy **Location:** Jct SR 166 and S Bypass 166, just w. Adjacent to Lake Carroll Mall. **Facility:** 50 one-bedroom standard units. 2 stories (no elevator), interior corridors. **Parking:** on-site. **Terms:** 2 night minimum stay. **Amenities:** high-speed Internet, voice mail, irons, hair dryers. **Pool(s):** heated indoor. **Leisure Activities:** exercise room. **Guest Services:** coin laundry, wireless Internet. **Business Services:** meeting rooms, PC, fax. **Cards:** AX, CB, DC, DS, MC, VI. **Free Special Amenities: continental breakfast and high-speed Internet.**

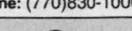

CALL / SOME UNITS

AAA Benefit: Members save up to 20%, plus 10% bonus points with rewards program.

HAMPTON INN *Book great rates at AAA.com* **Phone:** (770)838-7722

Hotel
$79-$115 All Year

Address: 102 S Cottage Hill Rd **Location:** Jct US 27 and SR 166, just s. **Facility:** 77 one-bedroom standard units, some with whirlpools. 4 stories, interior corridors. **Parking:** on-site. **Terms:** 1-30 night minimum stay, cancellation fee imposed. **Amenities:** video games (fee), high-speed Internet, voice mail, irons, hair dryers. **Pool(s):** outdoor. **Leisure Activities:** exercise room. **Guest Services:** valet laundry, wireless Internet. **Business Services:** meeting rooms, PC, fax. **Cards:** AX, CB, DC, DS, MC, VI.

/ SOME UNITS

AAA Benefit: Members save up to 10% everyday!

HOLIDAY INN EXPRESS *Book great rates at AAA.com* **Phone:** (770)838-0508

Hotel
$95-$99 All Year

Address: 104 S Cottage Hill Rd **Location:** Jct US 27 and SR 166, just s. **Facility:** 83 one-bedroom standard units. 4 stories, interior corridors. **Parking:** on-site. **Amenities:** voice mail, irons, hair dryers. **Pool(s):** outdoor. **Leisure Activities:** exercise room. **Guest Services:** valet laundry, wireless Internet. **Business Services:** meeting rooms, PC, fax. **Cards:** AX, CB, DC, DS, JC, MC, VI.

/ SOME UNITS

JAMESON INN *Book at AAA.com* **Phone:** (770)834-2600

Hotel
$78-$85 All Year

Address: 700 S Park St **Location:** On US 27, just s of downtown. **Facility:** 59 one-bedroom standard units. 2 stories (no elevator), exterior corridors. **Parking:** on-site. **Terms:** cancellation fee imposed. **Amenities:** irons, hair dryers. **Pool(s):** outdoor. **Leisure Activities:** exercise room. **Guest Services:** valet and coin laundry, wireless Internet. **Business Services:** PC. **Cards:** AX, DC, DS, MC, VI.

ASK CALL / SOME UNITS FEE

WHERE TO DINE

MAPLE STREET MANSION **Phone:** 770/834-2657

American
$7-$20

Located in a restored home built circa 1894, the establishment features both dining and sports bar areas. Prime rib is the specialty of the house and many Southern-style favorites are also offered. Delectable desserts round off the menu. Casual dress. **Bar:** Full bar. **Reservations:** accepted. **Hours:** 11 am-2 & 4-10 pm, Sat 4 pm-11 pm. Closed major holidays; also Sun & Mon. **Address:** 401 Maple St **Location:** Just w of US 27; downtown. **Parking:** on-site. **Cards:** AX, DC, DS, MC, VI.

CARTERSVILLE pop. 15,925

WHERE TO STAY

BEST WESTERN GARDEN INN & SUITES *Book great rates at AAA.com* **Phone:** (770)386-1569

Hotel
$60-$85 All Year

Address: 5663 Hwy 20 NE **Location:** I-75, exit 290, 0.3 mi e. **Facility:** 46 one-bedroom standard units, some with whirlpools. 3 stories, exterior corridors. **Parking:** on-site. **Amenities:** high-speed Internet, voice mail, irons, hair dryers. **Pool(s):** outdoor. **Guest Services:** coin laundry, wireless Internet. **Business Services:** meeting rooms, fax. **Cards:** AX, CB, DC, DS, JC, MC, VI. **Free Special Amenities: expanded continental breakfast and high-speed Internet.**

FEE CALL / SOME UNITS FEE

AAA Benefit: Members save up to 20%, plus 10% bonus points with rewards program.

BUDGET HOST INN *Book at AAA.com* **Phone:** (770)386-0350

Motel
$44 All Year

Address: 851 Cass-White Rd **Location:** I-75, exit 296, just w. Located in a quiet rural area. **Facility:** 87 one-bedroom standard units. 2 stories, exterior corridors. **Parking:** on-site. **Terms:** cancellation fee imposed. **Amenities:** voice mail. **Pool(s):** outdoor. **Guest Services:** coin laundry. **Business Services:** fax (fee). **Cards:** AX, DS, MC, VI.

ASK / SOME UNITS FEE

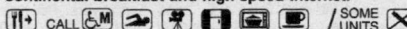

COMFORT INN *Book great rates at AAA.com* **Phone:** (770)387-1800

AAA SAVE

Motel
$60-$70 All Year

Address: 28 SR 20 Spur **Location:** I-75, exit 290, 0.3 mi se. **Facility:** 56 one-bedroom standard units, some with whirlpools. 2 stories, exterior corridors. **Parking:** on-site. **Amenities:** high-speed Internet, irons, hair dryers. **Pool(s):** outdoor. **Guest Services:** wireless Internet. **Business Services:** fax (fee). **Cards:** AX, CB, DC, DS, JC, MC, VI. **Free Special Amenities: expanded continental breakfast and high-speed Internet.**

COUNTRY INN & SUITES BY CARLSON *Book at AAA.com* **Phone:** (770)386-5888

Hotel
$81-$149 All Year

Address: 43 SR 20 Spur **Location:** I-75, exit 290, 0.3 mi se. **Facility:** 62 units. 35 one-bedroom standard units. 27 one-bedroom suites, some with whirlpools. 3 stories, interior corridors. **Parking:** on-site. **Amenities:** high-speed Internet, voice mail, irons, hair dryers. **Pool(s):** heated indoor. **Leisure Activities:** whirlpool, exercise room. **Guest Services:** valet and coin laundry. **Business Services:** meeting rooms, business center. **Cards:** AX, DC, DS, MC, VI.

DAYS INN *Book great rates at AAA.com* **Phone:** (770)382-1824

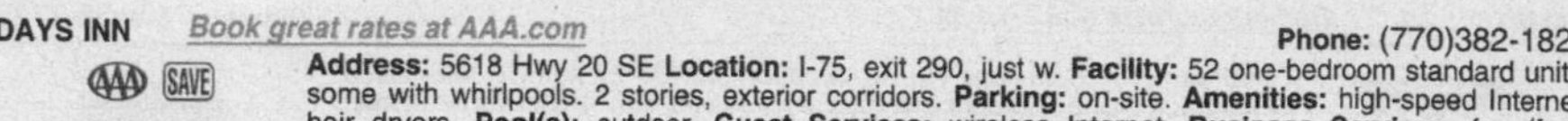

AAA SAVE

Hotel
$55-$60 All Year

Address: 5618 Hwy 20 SE **Location:** I-75, exit 290, just w. **Facility:** 52 one-bedroom standard units, some with whirlpools. 2 stories, exterior corridors. **Parking:** on-site. **Amenities:** high-speed Internet, hair dryers. **Pool(s):** outdoor. **Guest Services:** wireless Internet. **Business Services:** fax (fee). **Cards:** AX, DC, DS, MC, VI. **Free Special Amenities: continental breakfast and high-speed Internet.**

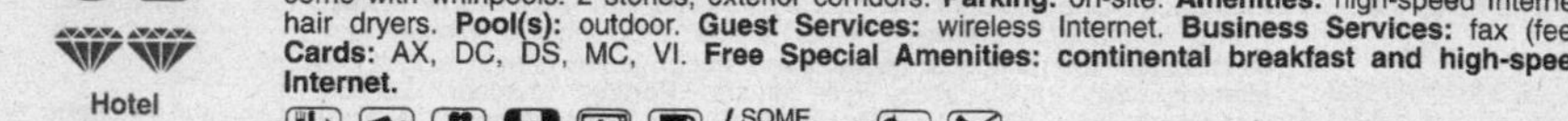

HAMPTON INN *Book great rates at AAA.com* **Phone:** (770)382-8999

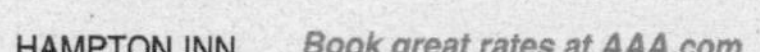

Hotel
$86-$92 All Year

Address: 5600 Hwy 20 SE **Location:** I-75, exit 290, just w. **Facility:** 66 one-bedroom standard units. 3 stories, interior corridors. **Parking:** on-site. **Terms:** 1-30 night minimum stay, cancellation fee imposed. **Amenities:** high-speed Internet, voice mail, irons, hair dryers. **Pool(s):** outdoor. **Leisure Activities:** exercise room. **Guest Services:** wireless Internet. **Business Services:** meeting rooms, business center. **Cards:** AX, CB, DC, DS, MC, VI.

HOLIDAY INN *Book at AAA.com* **Phone:** 770/386-0830

Hotel
Rates not provided

Address: 2336 Hwy 411 **Location:** I-75, exit 293, southwest corner. Located in a quiet rural area. **Facility:** 144 units. 138 one-bedroom standard units. 6 one-bedroom suites with whirlpools. 2 stories, interior corridors. **Parking:** on-site. **Amenities:** high-speed Internet, voice mail, irons, hair dryers. **Pool(s):** outdoor. **Leisure Activities:** exercise room. **Guest Services:** valet and coin laundry, wireless Internet. **Business Services:** meeting rooms, business center.

HOWARD JOHNSON EXPRESS *Book at AAA.com* **Phone:** 770/386-0700

Motel
Rates not provided

Address: 25 Carson Loop NW **Location:** I-75, exit 296, just w. **Facility:** 57 one-bedroom standard units. 2 stories, exterior corridors. **Parking:** on-site. **Amenities:** high-speed Internet, safes, irons, hair dryers. *Some:* DVD players (fee). **Pool(s):** outdoor. **Leisure Activities:** playground. **Guest Services:** wireless Internet. **Business Services:** fax (fee).

KNIGHTS INN *Book great rates at AAA.com* **Phone:** (770)386-7263

AAA SAVE

Motel
$55-$75 All Year

Address: 420 E Church St **Location:** I-75, exit 288, 1.5 mi w. **Facility:** 65 one-bedroom standard units. 1 story, exterior corridors. **Parking:** on-site. **Amenities:** high-speed Internet. **Pool(s):** outdoor. **Guest Services:** wireless Internet. **Business Services:** fax. **Cards:** AX, DC, DS, MC, VI. **Free Special Amenities: continental breakfast and high-speed Internet.**

MOTEL 6 - 4046 *Book at AAA.com* **Phone:** (770)386-1449

Motel
$43-$47 All Year

Address: 5657 Hwy 20 NE **Location:** I-75, exit 290, 0.3 mi e. **Facility:** 48 one-bedroom standard units. 2 stories (no elevator), exterior corridors. **Parking:** on-site. **Terms:** 3 day cancellation notice. **Amenities:** high-speed Internet. **Pool(s):** outdoor. **Guest Services:** wireless Internet. **Business Services:** fax (fee). **Cards:** AX, CB, DC, DS, JC, MC, VI.

QUALITY INN *Book at AAA.com* **Phone:** 770/386-0510

Hotel
Rates not provided

Address: 235 Dixie Ave **Location:** I-75, exit 288, 2.5 mi w. **Facility:** 85 one-bedroom standard units. 2 stories, exterior corridors. **Parking:** on-site. **Amenities:** high-speed Internet, voice mail, irons, hair dryers. **Pool(s):** outdoor. **Guest Services:** coin laundry, wireless Internet. **Business Services:** meeting rooms, PC, fax (fee).

RED TOP MOUNTAIN LODGE **Phone:** 770/975-0055

Resort Hotel

$70-$130 All Year

Address: 50 Lodge Rd **Location:** I-75, exit 285, 3 mi ne, follow signs; in state park. **Facility:** The lodge offers a tranquil mountain-forest setting. 51 units. 32 one-bedroom standard units. 1 one-bedroom suite. 18 cottages. 2 stories, exterior corridors. **Parking:** on-site. **Terms:** check-in 4 pm, 2 night minimum stay - seasonal and/or weekends, 3 day cancellation notice-fee imposed. **Amenities:** high-speed Internet, voice mail, irons, hair dryers. **Pool(s):** outdoor. **Leisure Activities:** rental boats, marina, fishing, 2 lighted tennis courts, recreation programs, hiking trails, playground. *Fee:* miniature golf. **Guest Services:** wireless Internet. **Business Services:** meeting rooms, fax (fee). **Cards:** AX, DS, MC, VI.

FEE CALL / SOME UNITS

SLEEP INN *Book great rates at AAA.com* **Phone:** (770)386-9259

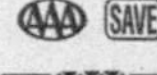

Hotel

$90 All Year

Address: 11 Kent Dr **Location:** I-75, exit 296, just e. **Facility:** 54 one-bedroom standard units. 3 stories, interior corridors. *Bath:* combo or shower only. **Parking:** on-site. **Terms:** cancellation fee imposed. **Amenities:** high-speed Internet, voice mail, irons, hair dryers. **Pool(s):** outdoor. **Leisure Activities:** exercise room. **Guest Services:** coin laundry, wireless Internet. **Business Services:** meeting rooms, PC, fax. **Cards:** AX, DS, MC, VI. **Free Special Amenities: continental breakfast and high-speed Internet.**

CALL / SOME UNITS FEE

SUPER 8 MOTEL *Book great rates at AAA.com* **Phone:** (770)382-8881

Motel

$48-$65 All Year

Address: 41 SR 20 Spur SE **Location:** I-75, exit 290, 0.3 mi e. **Facility:** 61 one-bedroom standard units. 3 stories (no elevator), interior corridors. **Parking:** on-site. **Amenities:** high-speed Internet, hair dryers. **Pool(s):** outdoor. **Guest Services:** wireless Internet. **Business Services:** fax (fee). **Cards:** AX, DS, MC, VI. **Free Special Amenities: continental breakfast and high-speed Internet.**

/ SOME UNITS FEE

WHERE TO DINE

ANTONINOS ITALIAN GROTTO **Phone:** 770/387-9664

Italian

$5-$18

The family eatery prepares some nice takes on traditional dishes, including the particularly good veal entrees. Also available are fine wines and delicious desserts. Casual dress. **Bar:** Full bar. **Hours:** 11 am-2 & 5-9:30 pm, Fri & Sat-10 pm. Closed major holidays; also Sun & Mon. **Address:** 28 Wall St **Location:** I-75, exit 288, 2.1 mi w. **Parking:** on-site. **Cards:** AX, CB, DC, DS, JC, MC, VI.

APPALACHIAN GRILL **Phone:** 770/607-5357

American

$9-$23

Steaks and seafood are some staples that have made the grill a downtown favorite. Casual dress. **Bar:** Full bar. **Hours:** 11 am-9 pm, Fri & Sat-10 pm, Sun noon-10 pm. Closed major holidays. **Address:** 14 E Church St **Location:** I-75, exit 288, 2.1 mi w to Wall St, just n; under the bridge. **Parking:** street. **Cards:** AX, CB, DC, DS, MC, VI.

D MORGAN'S **Phone:** 770/383-3535

New American

$8-$27

Excellent New American cuisine includes baked goat cheese salad, Australian rack of lamb and seared duck breast, all prepared with chef Morgan's freshest ingredients and magic touch. Situated in an 125-year-old building, the original hardwood floors and exposed brick walls define the upscale ambiance. The wine cellar lounge offers an extensive list of wines. Service is flawless. Dressy casual. **Bar:** Full bar. **Reservations:** suggested. **Hours:** 5 pm-10 pm. Closed: 4/12, 11/26, 12/25; also Sun & Mon. **Address:** 28 W Main St **Location:** I-75, exit 288, 2.2 mi w; downtown. **Parking:** street. **Cards:** AX, DS, MC, VI.

GOLDEN CITY **Phone:** 770/386-6877

Chinese

$2-$20

Chinese and American favorites, including preparations of steak and seafood, are served in a contemporary dining room. Among top choices are hot and sour soup, egg rolls and classic chicken and pork dishes. Casual dress. **Bar:** Beer & wine. **Reservations:** accepted. **Hours:** 11 am-10 pm, Fri & Sat-11 pm, Sun noon-9:30 pm. **Address:** 460 Cherokee Pl **Location:** I-75, exit 288, 1.3 mi w; in Main Street Shopping Center. **Parking:** on-site. **Cards:** AX, CB, DC, DS, JC, MC, VI.

THE MEATING PLACE DELI & CAFE **Phone:** 770/386-4563

American

$6-$12

The hidden location offers many rewards for its small size. Cheery servers bring fresh sandwiches, soups, salads and grilled meats. Homemade chicken salad and white chocolate hazelnut cheesecake are two of the specialties. Casual dress. **Hours:** 11 am-2:30 & 5-9 pm, Tues & Wed-2:30 pm. Closed major holidays; also Sun & Mon. **Address:** 485 E Main St **Location:** I-75, exit 288, 1.5 mi w; in Main Street East Shopping Center. **Parking:** on-site. **Cards:** AX, MC, VI.

VILLAGE GRILL **Phone:** 770/276-2002

Pakistani

$5-$16

Enthusiastic staff serve made-from-scratch Pakistani dishes, such as hummus and samosas, at the family-owned grill. The Hookah lounge is the ideal spot to meet friends for a drink and conversation. Casual dress. **Reservations:** accepted. **Hours:** 11 am-10 pm. Closed: Mon. **Address:** 5698 Hwy 20, Suite J **Location:** I-75, exit 290, 0.5 mi e. **Parking:** on-site. **Cards:** AX, CB, DC, DS, JC, MC, VI.

CEDARTOWN pop. 9,470

WHERE TO STAY

COUNTRY HEARTH INN *Book at AAA.com* **Phone:** 770/749-9951

Hotel

Rates not provided

Address: 925 N Main St **Location:** 1.5 mi n on US 27. **Facility:** 40 one-bedroom standard units, some with whirlpools. 2 stories (no elevator), interior corridors. *Bath:* combo or shower only. **Parking:** on-site. **Amenities:** high-speed Internet, safes. *Some:* hair dryers. **Guest Services:** wireless Internet. **Business Services:** fax (fee).

CALL / SOME UNITS FEE

CHAMBLEE —*See Atlanta p. 378.*

CHATSWORTH pop. 3,531

WHERE TO STAY

BEST WESTERN FAIRWINDS INN & SUITES *Book great rates at AAA.com* **Phone:** (706)695-1411

Motel
$79-$89 All Year

Address: 613 S 3rd Ave **Location:** On US 411/SR 76, 0.3 mi s. **Facility:** 32 one-bedroom standard units, some with whirlpools. 1 story, exterior corridors. **Parking:** on-site. **Terms:** 3 night minimum stay - seasonal and/or weekends, cancellation fee imposed. **Amenities:** high-speed Internet, irons, hair dryers. **Pool(s):** outdoor. **Guest Services:** coin laundry, wireless Internet. **Business Services:** fax. **Cards:** AX, DS, MC, VI. **Free Special Amenities: continental breakfast and high-speed Internet.**

CALL / SOME UNITS FEE

AAA Benefit: Members save up to 20%, plus 10% bonus points with rewards program.

KEY WEST INN *Book at AAA.com* **Phone:** 706/517-1155

Motel
Rates not provided

Address: 501 Gl Maddox Pkwy **Location:** Jct SR 76 and US 411. **Facility:** 41 one-bedroom standard units. 2 stories (no elevator), exterior corridors. **Parking:** on-site. **Amenities:** high-speed Internet, hair dryers. **Guest Services:** coin laundry, wireless Internet. **Business Services:** fax (fee).

/ SOME UNITS FEE

WHERE TO DINE

EDNA'S RESTAURANT *Menu on AAA.com* **Phone:** 706/695-4960

Regional Southern
$4-$10

Edna's Restaurant is a long-established, straightforward eatery serving home-style, Southern comfort foods like fried chicken and ham shanks. A popular dessert selection is their heirloom recipe peanut butter, coconut or chocolate pies. Casual dress. **Hours:** 11 am-7:45 pm. Closed major holidays; also Sun, Mon, last week in June, first week in July, week of Thanksgiving, 2 weeks at Christmas. **Address:** 1300 Hwy 411 S **Location:** 1 mi s. **Parking:** on-site. **Cards:** MC, VI.

CLAYTON pop. 2,019

WHERE TO STAY

AMERICAS BEST VALUE INN *Book at AAA.com* **Phone:** (706)782-4702

Hotel
$55-$95 6/1-11/30
$45-$55 12/1-5/31

Address: 698 Hwy 441 S **Location:** 0.8 mi s. **Facility:** 30 one-bedroom standard units. 2 stories (no elevator), interior corridors. **Parking:** on-site. **Terms:** 21 day cancellation notice-fee imposed. **Amenities:** high-speed Internet, voice mail, hair dryers. *Some:* irons. **Guest Services:** wireless Internet. **Business Services:** fax (fee). **Cards:** AX, DS, MC, VI.

ASK / SOME UNITS FEE

BEECHWOOD INN **Phone:** 706/782-5485

Country Inn
$199-$229 All Year

Address: 220 Beechwood Dr **Location:** Jct US 76 and 441, just e on US 76 to Beechwood Dr, then just n. **Facility:** Heartwood pine floors throughout the mountain cottage add a warm, inviting ambiance; many of the cozy guest rooms overlook the 100-year-old gardens. Smoke free premises. 8 one-bedroom standard units. 2 stories, interior corridors. **Parking:** on-site. **Terms:** office hours 6 am-10 pm, 14 day cancellation notice-fee imposed. **Amenities:** video library, CD players, irons, hair dryers. **Guest Services:** wireless Internet. **Business Services:** fax. **Cards:** MC, VI.

/ SOME UNITS FEE

DAYS INN *Book at AAA.com* **Phone:** (706)782-4258

Hotel
$56-$100 6/1-11/30
$56-$66 12/1-5/31

Address: 54 Hwy 441 **Location:** Center. **Facility:** 60 one-bedroom standard units. 2 stories (no elevator), exterior corridors. **Parking:** on-site. **Amenities:** high-speed Internet, hair dryers. *Some:* irons. **Pool(s):** outdoor. **Guest Services:** wireless Internet. **Business Services:** fax. **Cards:** AX, DC, DS, MC, VI.

ASK / SOME UNITS FEE

OLD CLAYTON INN **Phone:** 706/782-7722

Hotel
Rates not provided

Address: 60 S Main St **Location:** 1 blk s of US 76; 2 blks w of US 441; downtown. **Facility:** 30 units. 28 one-bedroom standard units, some with whirlpools. 1 one- and 1 two-bedroom suites. 2 stories (no elevator), interior corridors. *Bath:* combo or shower only. **Parking:** on-site. **Dining:** restaurant, see separate listing. **Guest Services:** wireless Internet. **Business Services:** meeting rooms, fax (fee).

QUALITY INN & SUITES *Book great rates at AAA.com* **Phone:** (706)782-2214

Hotel
$90-$109 5/1-11/30
$70-$90 12/1-4/30

Address: 834 Hwy 441 S **Location:** 0.8 mi s. **Facility:** 57 units. 47 one-bedroom standard units. 10 one-bedroom suites, some with whirlpools. 2 stories (no elevator), exterior corridors. **Parking:** on-site. **Terms:** cancellation fee imposed. **Amenities:** high-speed Internet, voice mail, irons, hair dryers. **Pool(s):** outdoor. **Guest Services:** wireless Internet. **Business Services:** fax (fee). **Cards:** AX, DS, MC, VI.

/ SOME UNITS

REGAL INN **Phone:** 706/782-4269

Motel
$42-$95 5/1-11/30
$37-$45 12/1-4/30

Address: 707 Hwy 441 S **Location:** 0.8 mi s. **Facility:** 19 one-bedroom standard units. 1 story, exterior corridors. **Parking:** on-site. **Amenities:** high-speed Internet. **Guest Services:** wireless Internet. **Business Services:** fax (fee). **Cards:** AX, DS, MC, VI.

/ SOME UNITS FEE

WHERE TO DINE

OLD CLAYTON INN **Phone:** 706/782-7722

American
$5-$17

In addition to home-cooked items on the buffet, diners can opt for simple steaks and seafood off the menu. Nothing is fancy about this spot in the historic Old Clayton Inn. Casual dress. **Bar:** Beer & wine. **Hours:** 7 am-9:30 & 11-2 pm, Fri & Sat also 5 pm-9 pm; Sunday buffet. **Address:** 60 S Main St **Location:** 1 blk s of US 76; 2 blks w of US 441; downtown; in Old Clayton Inn. **Parking:** on-site and street. **Cards:** MC, VI.

CLEVELAND pop. 1,907

WHERE TO DINE

WEST FAMILY RESTAURANT **Phone:** 706/865-0525

Southern
$2-$19

The buffet, which is spread out for all meals, is the draw here. A wide selection of down-home Southern favorites is lined up. Casual dress. **Hours:** 7 am-9 pm. Closed: 12/23-12/26. **Address:** 1963 Tom Bell Rd **Location:** 4.5 mi n on SR 75. **Parking:** on-site. **Cards:** AX, DS, MC, VI.

COLLEGE PARK —*See Atlanta p. 378.*

COLQUITT pop. 1,939

WHERE TO STAY

TARRER INN **Phone:** 229/758-2888

Country Inn
Rates not provided

Address: 155 S Cuthbert St **Location:** Corner of SR 91 and 27; center of town square. **Facility:** Located near a city park; a service-oriented property with a dining facility on the first floor and guest rooms situated on the second floor. Smoke free premises. 17 one-bedroom standard units. 2 stories, interior corridors. **Parking:** on-site. **Guest Services:** wireless Internet. **Business Services:** meeting rooms, fax.

CALL

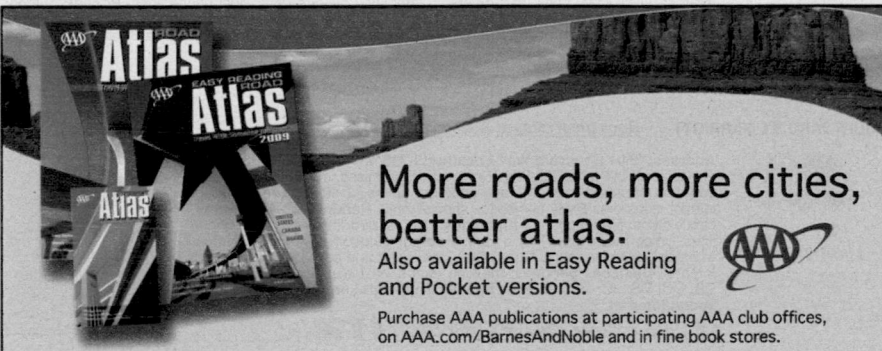

COLUMBUS pop. 186,291

Airport Accommodations

OA	COLUMBUS METROPOLITAN	Diamond Rated	High Season	Page
AAA	**Courtyard by Marriott, 2.3 mi se of terminal**	3 diamonds	$143-$153 SAVE	450
	Fairfield Inn & Suites, 1.2 mi sw of terminal	3 diamonds	$98-$105	451
AAA	**Hampton Inn Airport, 1 mi nw of terminal**	2 diamonds	$104-$124 SAVE	451
	La Quinta Inn Columbus State University, 2 mi sw of terminal	2 diamonds	$79-$129	452
	Wingate by Wyndham, 1.5 mi nw of terminal	3 diamonds	Rates not provided	453

WHERE TO STAY

BEST WESTERN COLUMBUS *Book great rates at AAA.com* **Phone:** (706)568-3300

Motel

$70-$110 All Year

Address: 3443B Macon Rd **Location:** I-185, exit 6, just e. **Facility:** 82 one-bedroom standard units. 3-4 stories, exterior corridors. *Bath:* combo or shower only. **Parking:** on-site. **Amenities:** irons, hair dryers. *Some:* high-speed Internet. **Pool(s):** outdoor. **Leisure Activities:** exercise room. **Guest Services:** valet laundry, wireless Internet. **Business Services:** PC. **Cards:** AX, CB, DC, DS, JC, MC, VI. **Free Special Amenities: continental breakfast and high-speed Internet.**

AAA Benefit: Members save up to 20%, plus 10% bonus points with rewards program.

COMFORT INN COLUMBUS *Book great rates at AAA.com* **Phone:** (706)256-3093

Hotel

$99-$149 2/15-11/30
$94-$139 12/1-2/14

Address: 3460 Macon Rd **Location:** I-185, exit 6, just e. **Facility:** 73 one-bedroom standard units, some with kitchens and/or whirlpools. 3 stories, interior corridors. *Bath:* combo or shower only. **Parking:** on-site. **Amenities:** high-speed Internet, voice mail, irons, hair dryers. *Some:* dual phone lines. **Pool(s):** heated indoor. **Leisure Activities:** exercise room. **Guest Services:** valet and coin laundry, wireless Internet. **Business Services:** business center. **Cards:** AX, CB, DC, DS, MC, VI. **Free Special Amenities: expanded continental breakfast and high-speed Internet.**

/ SOME UNITS

COUNTRY INN & SUITES **Phone:** 706/256-6390

fyi

Hotel

$110-$189 5/16-11/30
$99-$149 12/1-5/15

Too new to rate. **Address:** 1664 Rollins Way **Location:** I-185, exit 10 to I-80 W, exit 3A. **Amenities:** 64 units, coffeemakers, microwaves, refrigerators, pool. **Terms:** cancellation fee imposed. **Cards:** AX, CB, DC, DS, JC, MC, VI.

COUNTRY INN & SUITES BY CARLSON *Book great rates at AAA.com* **Phone:** (706)660-1880

AAA SAVE

Hotel

$119-$169 All Year

Address: 1720 Fountain Ct **Location:** I-185, exit 12, just w, then just s on Williams Way. Located in a quiet area across from the Visitor Center. **Facility:** 62 units. 50 one-bedroom standard units, some with whirlpools. 12 one-bedroom suites, some with whirlpools. 3 stories, interior corridors. *Bath:* combo or shower only. **Parking:** on-site. **Terms:** 2-3 night minimum stay - seasonal. **Amenities:** high-speed Internet, voice mail, irons, hair dryers. *Some:* DVD players (fee), dual phone lines. **Pool(s):** outdoor. **Leisure Activities:** exercise room. **Guest Services:** valet and coin laundry, wireless Internet. **Business Services:** meeting rooms, PC. **Cards:** AX, CB, DC, DS, MC, VI. **Free Special Amenities: full breakfast and high-speed Internet.**

/ SOME UNITS

COURTYARD BY MARRIOTT *Book great rates at AAA.com* **Phone:** (706)323-2323

AAA SAVE

Hotel

$143-$153 All Year

Address: 3501 Courtyard Way **Location:** I-185, exit 7 southbound; exit 7A northbound, 0.7 mi e. **Facility:** Smoke free premises. 139 units. 127 one-bedroom standard units. 12 one-bedroom suites. 2 stories (no elevator), interior corridors. *Bath:* combo or shower only. **Parking:** on-site. **Terms:** cancellation fee imposed. **Amenities:** high-speed Internet, dual phone lines, voice mail, irons, hair dryers. **Pool(s):** outdoor. **Leisure Activities:** whirlpool, exercise room. **Guest Services:** valet and coin laundry, wireless Internet. **Business Services:** meeting rooms, business center. **Cards:** AX, CB, DC, DS, JC, MC, VI. **Free Special Amenities: newspaper and high-speed Internet.**

CALL / SOME UNITS

AAA Benefit: Members save a minimum 5% off the best available rate.

ECONO LODGE INN & SUITES FORT BENNING *Book at AAA.com* **Phone:** 706/682-3803

Hotel

Rates not provided

Address: 4483 Victory Dr **Location:** I-185, exit 1B, just w. **Facility:** 80 one-bedroom standard units. 2 stories (no elevator), exterior corridors. *Bath:* combo or shower only. **Parking:** on-site. **Amenities:** irons. *Some:* hair dryers. **Pool(s):** outdoor. **Guest Services:** valet and coin laundry, wireless Internet. **Business Services:** meeting rooms.

/ SOME UNITS

EXTENDED STAYAMERICA-COLUMBUS-AIRPORT *Book at AAA.com* **Phone:** (706)653-0131

Hotel

$70-$85 All Year

Address: 5020 Armour Rd **Location:** I-185, exit 8, 1.5 mi e, then 0.5 mi n. **Facility:** 108 one-bedroom standard units with efficiencies. 3 stories, exterior corridors. *Bath:* combo or shower only. **Parking:** on-site. **Terms:** office hours 7 am-11 pm. **Amenities:** voice mail, irons. *Some:* hair dryers. **Guest Services:** coin laundry, wireless Internet. **Cards:** AX, CB, DC, DS, JC, MC, VI.

ASK / SOME UNITS FEE

EXTENDED STAYAMERICA-COLUMBUS-BRADLEY PARK *Book at AAA.com* **Phone:** (706)653-9938

Hotel

$65-$85 All Year

Address: 1721 Rollins Way **Location:** I-185, exit 10 (US 80 and SR 22), 1.5 mi w on US 80, exit 3A, just s to Whittlesey Rd, 0.3 mi e to Rollins Way, then just n. Located behine Bradley Park Crossing Shopping Center. **Facility:** 92 one-bedroom standard units with efficiencies. 3 stories, interior corridors. *Bath:* combo or shower only. **Parking:** on-site. **Amenities:** voice mail, irons, hair dryers. **Guest Services:** coin laundry, wireless Internet. **Cards:** AX, CB, DC, DS, JC, MC, VI.

FAIRFIELD INN & SUITES *Book great rates at AAA.com* **Phone:** (706)317-3600

Hotel

$98-$106 All Year

Address: 4510 E Armour Rd **Location:** I-185, exit 7B southbound; exit 7A northbound, just w to Armour Rd, then just n. **Facility:** Smoke free premises. 79 one-bedroom standard units. 3 stories, interior corridors. *Bath:* combo or shower only. **Parking:** on-site. **Terms:** cancellation fee imposed. **Amenities:** high-speed Internet, voice mail, irons, hair dryers. *Some:* CD players, dual phone lines. **Pool(s):** heated indoor. **Leisure Activities:** whirlpool, exercise room. **Guest Services:** valet and coin laundry, wireless Internet. **Business Services:** PC. **Cards:** AX, CB, DC, DS, MC, VI.

CALL / SOME UNITS

AAA Benefit:

Members save a minimum 5% off the best available rate.

HAMPTON INN AIRPORT *Book great rates at AAA.com* **Phone:** (706)576-5303

AAA SAVE

Hotel

$104-$124 All Year

Address: 5585 Whitesville Rd **Location:** I-185, exit 8, 0.5 mi w, then just n; behind Harmony Place Shops. **Facility:** 118 one-bedroom standard units. 2 stories (no elevator), exterior corridors. **Parking:** on-site. **Terms:** 1-30 night minimum stay, cancellation fee imposed. **Amenities:** video games (fee), voice mail, irons, hair dryers. **Pool(s):** outdoor. **Guest Services:** valet laundry, wireless Internet. **Business Services:** meeting rooms, PC. **Cards:** AX, CB, DC, DS, JC, MC, VI. **Free Special Amenities: expanded continental breakfast and high-speed Internet.** *(See color ad below)*

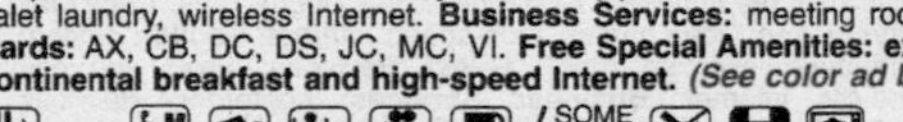

AAA Benefit:

Members save up to 10% everyday!

▼ See AAA listing above ▼

HILTON GARDEN INN COLUMBUS *Book great rates at AAA.com* **Phone:** (706)660-1000

Hotel
$99-$179 All Year

Address: 1500 Bradley Lakes Blvd **Location:** I-185, exit 10 (US 80 and SR 22), 1.4 mi w on US 80, exit 3B, then just nw. **Facility:** 120 units. 117 one-bedroom standard units, some with whirlpools. 3 one-bedroom suites. 5 stories, interior corridors. *Bath:* combo or shower only. **Parking:** on-site. **Terms:** 1-30 night minimum stay, cancellation fee imposed. **Amenities:** high-speed Internet, dual phone lines, voice mail, irons, hair dryers. **Pool(s):** heated indoor. **Leisure Activities:** whirlpool, exercise room. **Guest Services:** valet and coin laundry, wireless Internet. **Business Services:** conference facilities, business center. **Cards:** AX, CB, DC, DS, JC, MC, VI.

/ SOME UNITS

AAA Benefit:
Members save 5% or more everyday!

HOWARD JOHNSON EXPRESS INN & SUITES *Book great rates at AAA.com* **Phone:** (706)322-6641

Hotel
$65-$99 All Year

Address: 1011 Veterans Pkwy **Location:** I-185, exit 7 southbound; exit 7A northbound, 1.2 mi w to Veterans Pkwy, then 3.2 mi s. **Facility:** 110 units. 90 one-bedroom standard units. 20 one-bedroom suites. 2 stories (no elevator), exterior corridors. *Bath:* combo or shower only. **Parking:** on-site. **Amenities:** high-speed Internet, voice mail, safes (fee), irons, hair dryers. *Some:* DVD players. **Pool(s):** outdoor. **Guest Services:** valet and coin laundry, wireless Internet. **Business Services:** meeting rooms, PC. **Cards:** AX, DS, MC, VI. ***(See color ad below)***

ASK / SOME UNITS FEE

LA QUINTA INN COLUMBUS MIDTOWN *Book great rates at AAA.com* **Phone:** (706)568-1740

Hotel
$59-$99 All Year

Address: 3201 Macon Rd **Location:** I-185, exit 6, just w. **Facility:** 122 units. 120 one-bedroom standard units. 2 one-bedroom suites. 2 stories (no elevator), interior/exterior corridors. *Bath:* combo or shower only. **Parking:** on-site. **Amenities:** video games (fee), voice mail, irons, hair dryers. *Some:* high-speed Internet, dual phone lines. **Pool(s):** outdoor. **Guest Services:** coin laundry, wireless Internet. **Cards:** AX, DC, DS, MC, VI.

ASK / SOME UNITS

LA QUINTA INN COLUMBUS STATE UNIVERSITY *Book great rates at AAA.com* **Phone:** (706)323-4344

Hotel
$79-$129 All Year

Address: 2919 Warm Springs Rd **Location:** I-185, exit 7 southbound; exit 7A northbound, just e. **Facility:** 98 units. 96 one-bedroom standard units. 2 one-bedroom suites. 3 stories, interior corridors. **Parking:** on-site. **Amenities:** video games (fee), voice mail, irons, hair dryers. **Pool(s):** outdoor. **Guest Services:** valet laundry, wireless Internet. **Cards:** AX, DC, DS, MC, VI.

ASK / SOME UNITS

MARRIOTT HOTEL-COLUMBUS *Book great rates at AAA.com* **Phone:** (706)324-1800

Hotel
$174-$184 All Year

Address: 800 Front Ave **Location:** Jct 9th St and Broadway; edge of historic district; downtown. **Facility:** Smoke free premises. 177 units. 175 one-bedroom standard units. 2 one-bedroom suites with whirlpools. 3-6 stories, interior corridors. *Bath:* combo or shower only. **Parking:** on-site. **Terms:** cancellation fee imposed. **Amenities:** dual phone lines, voice mail, irons, hair dryers. *Fee:* video games, high-speed Internet. **Pool(s):** outdoor. **Leisure Activities:** exercise room. **Guest Services:** valet and coin laundry, wireless Internet. **Business Services:** conference facilities, business center. **Cards:** AX, CB, DC, DS, JC, MC, VI.

Marriott HOTELS & RESORTS

AAA Benefit:
Members save a minimum 5% off the best available rate.

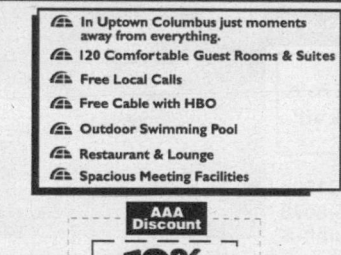

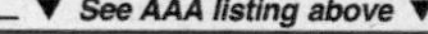

MOTEL 6 #58 Book at AAA.com **Phone:** (706)687-7214

Motel
$49-$59 All Year

Address: 3050 Victory Dr **Location:** I-185, exit 1B, 3 mi w. **Facility:** 111 one-bedroom standard units. 2 stories (no elevator), exterior corridors. *Bath:* shower only. **Parking:** on-site. **Pool(s):** outdoor. **Guest Services:** coin laundry. **Cards:** AX, CB, DC, DS, JC, MC, VI.

/ SOME UNITS

ROTHSCHILD-POUND HOUSE INN Book at AAA.com **Phone:** (706)322-4075

Historic Country Inn
$175-$365 All Year

Address: 201 7th St **Location:** Jct US 27 (Veterans Pkwy/7th St), just w; downtown. **Facility:** Convenient to the riverfront, the 1870 Victorian home occupies much of one block; select from units in the main home or several adjacent cottages. Smoke free premises. 18 units. 10 one-bedroom standard units, some with whirlpools. 2 one-bedroom suites, some with kitchens and/or whirlpools. 6 cottages. 1-2 stories (no elevator), interior/exterior corridors. *Bath:* combo or shower only. **Parking:** street. **Terms:** age restrictions may apply, 14 day cancellation notice-fee imposed. **Amenities:** video library, irons, hair dryers. *Some:* DVD players. **Dining:** Cafe 222, see separate listing. **Leisure Activities:** *Fee:* massage. **Guest Services:** valet laundry, wireless Internet. **Cards:** AX, DS, MC, VI.

ASK / SOME UNITS FEE

WINGATE BY WYNDHAM Book at AAA.com **Phone:** 706/225-1000

Hotel
Rates not provided

Address: 1711 Rollins Way **Location:** I-185, exit 10 (US 80 and SR 22), 1.5 mi w on US 80, exit 3A, just s to Whittlesey Rd, 0.3 mi e to Rollins Way, then just n. Located behind Bradley Park Crossing Shopping Center. **Facility:** 84 units. 82 one-bedroom standard units. 2 one-bedroom suites with whirlpools. 3 stories, interior corridors. *Bath:* combo or shower only. **Parking:** on-site. **Amenities:** video games (fee), high-speed Internet, dual phone lines, voice mail, safes, irons, hair dryers. **Pool(s):** heated outdoor. **Leisure Activities:** whirlpool, exercise room. **Guest Services:** valet and coin laundry, area transportation, wireless Internet. **Business Services:** meeting rooms, business center.

CALL / SOME UNITS

WHERE TO DINE

BUCKHEAD GRILL AND BAR **Phone:** 706/571-9995

AAA

Steak
$10-$26

This restaurant is a longtime local favorite on the Columbus dining scene. It features steaks, crab cakes, pasta, chicken and other American standards. Set in a lovely wooded area, it offers a welcome respite for a weary traveler. Casual dress. **Bar:** Full bar. **Hours:** 5 pm-10 pm, Fri & Sat-11 pm. Closed: 11/26, 12/25. **Address:** 5010 Armour Rd **Location:** I-185, exit 8, just w to Sidney Simons Blvd, 0.3 mi s to Armour Rd, then just w. **Parking:** on-site. **Cards:** AX, CB, DC, DS, JC, MC, VI.

CAFE 222 **Phone:** 706/576-2231

American
$9

Located in the historic district, the building was originally a butcher shop in the 1880s. The original pressed tin ceiling tiles, decorative plaster and wood trim accent the dining room, lending to the casual, comfortable atmosphere. Breakfast is ordered from a menu while lunch is either from a self-serve buffet or ordered from the selections written on a chalkboard located at the entrance. Casual dress. **Bar:** Beer & wine. **Hours:** 7 am-2 pm, Sat & Sun from 8 am. Closed major holidays. **Address:** 222 7th St **Location:** Jct US 27 (Veterans Pkwy/7th St), just w; downtown; in Rothschild-Pound House Inn. **Parking:** street. **Cards:** AX, DC, DS, MC, VI. **Historic**

CANNON BREWPUB **Phone:** 706/653-2337

American
$7-$17

Hand-crafted beers, wood-fired pizza, steak, pasta and homemade burgers are highlights at the eatery in the riverfront entertainment district. Casual dress. **Bar:** Full bar. **Hours:** 11 am-11 pm, Sun noon-10 pm. Closed major holidays. **Address:** 1041 Broadway **Location:** In historic uptown district. **Parking:** street. **Cards:** AX, DS, MC, VI.

CHEF LEE'S PEKING II **Phone:** 706/653-8888

Chinese
$6-$26

Ornate, palatial surroundings and traditional Chinese food, including selections on a well-stocked lunch buffet, are hallmarks of the comfortable restaurant. Casual dress. **Bar:** Beer & wine. **Hours:** 11 am-10 pm, Fri & Sat-11 pm, Sun 10 am-10 pm. Closed: 11/26, 12/24, 12/25; also Mon. **Address:** 6100 Bradley Park Dr **Location:** US 80 and SR 22, exit 3A, 0.5 mi s. **Parking:** on-site. **Cards:** AX, DS, MC, VI.

COUNTRY'S BARBECUE **Phone:** 706/563-7604

Barbecue
$5-$15

Pulled pork, ribs and more are all favorites at this popular barbecue house. Friendly servers and a laid-back atmosphere help make you feel at home. Casual dress. **Bar:** Beer & wine. **Hours:** 11 am-10 pm, Fri & Sat-11 pm. Closed major holidays. **Address:** 3137 Mercury Dr **Location:** I-185, exit 6, 0.3 mi w. **Parking:** on-site. **Cards:** AX, DS, MC, VI.

COUNTRY'S BBQ NORTH **Phone:** 706/660-1415

Barbecue
$5-$15

In a more modern building, the chain eatery prepares basic country barbecue meals with slaw and Brunswick stew. Casual dress. **Hours:** 11 am-10 pm, Fri & Sat-11 pm. Closed major holidays. **Address:** 6298 Veterans Pkwy **Location:** Jct Weems Rd. **Parking:** on-site. **Cards:** MC, VI.

COUNTRY'S ON BROAD — **Phone:** 706/596-8910

Barbecue
$5-$15

In a historic bus depot, the chain eatery prepares basic country barbecue meals with slaw and Brunswick stew. Crowds are common at lunchtime. Casual dress. **Hours:** 11 am-10 pm, Fri & Sat-11 pm. Closed major holidays. **Address:** 1329 Broadway **Location:** Center. **Parking:** on-site. **Cards:** AX, DS, MC, VI.

DEORIO'S PIZZA INN — **Phone:** 706/563-5887

Italian
$2-$17

This Columbus staple has been dishing up great pizza and pasta for more than 40 years. Casual dress. **Bar:** Beer & wine. **Hours:** 11 am-2:30 & 4:30-9:30 pm, Fri & Sat-10:30 pm. Closed major holidays; also Sun. **Address:** Cross Country Plaza **Location:** I-185, exit 6, 0.3 mi w; in Cross Country Plaza Shopping Center. **Parking:** on-site. **Cards:** AX, MC, VI.

MAYURI INDIAN CUISINE — **Phone:** 706/568-9992

Indian
$6-$14

Select from an extensive menu of prepared-to-order authentic dishes, including chicken, lamb and seafood specialties as well as vegetarian and rice dishes. During preparation, entrees are spiced to the requested level. Staff are knowledgeable about menu preparations and very attentive. Casual dress. **Bar:** Beer & wine. **Hours:** 11:30 am-2:30 & 5-9:30 pm. **Address:** 2009 Auburn Ave **Location:** I-185, exit 6, 0.5 mi w, then just n. **Parking:** on-site. **Cards:** AX, MC, VI.

MINNIE'S UPTOWN RESTAURANT — **Phone:** 706/322-2766

Southern
$5-$7

Along the edge of Columbus' historic district you will find traditional Southern cooking just like mom's. Extremely friendly, helpful servers added to the exceptionally good home cooking will leave you smiling on your way out and coming back for more. Casual dress. **Hours:** 10:45 am-2:30 pm. Closed major holidays; also Sat, Sun & week following 12/25. **Address:** 104 8th St **Location:** Corner of 8th St and 1st Ave; in historic district. **Parking:** street.

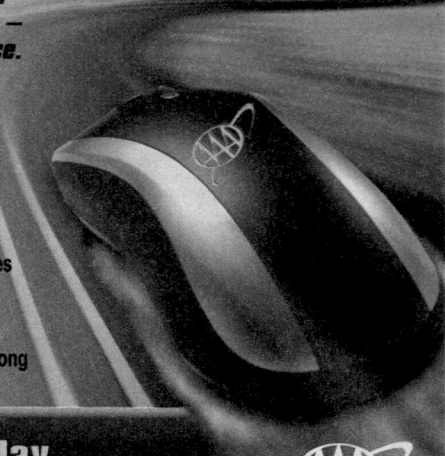

COMMERCE pop. 5,292

WHERE TO STAY

BEST WESTERN COMMERCE INN *Book great rates at AAA.com* **Phone:** (706)335-3640

Hotel
$55-$160 All Year

Address: 157 Eisenhower Dr **Location:** I-85, exit 149, just ne. **Facility:** 51 one-bedroom standard units, some with whirlpools. 3 stories, interior corridors. **Parking:** on-site. **Terms:** check-in 4 pm, cancellation fee imposed. **Amenities:** irons, hair dryers. *Some:* DVD players. **Pool(s):** outdoor. **Leisure Activities:** exercise room. **Guest Services:** valet and coin laundry, wireless Internet. **Business Services:** PC. **Cards:** AX, DC, DS, MC, VI. **Free Special Amenities: expanded continental breakfast and high-speed Internet.**

CALL / SOME UNITS

AAA Benefit:
Members save up to 20%, plus 10% bonus points with rewards program.

COMFORT INN *Book at AAA.com* **Phone:** (706)335-9001

Motel
$70-$150 All Year

Address: 165 Eisenhower Dr **Location:** I-85, exit 149, just ne. **Facility:** 61 one-bedroom standard units, some with whirlpools. 2 stories (no elevator), exterior corridors. **Parking:** on-site. **Terms:** 2-3 night minimum stay - seasonal and/or weekends, cancellation fee imposed. **Amenities:** safes (fee), irons, hair dryers. **Pool(s):** outdoor. **Guest Services:** wireless Internet. **Business Services:** PC, fax. **Cards:** AX, DS, MC, VI.

ASK / SOME UNITS FEE

COMFORT SUITES **Phone:** 706/336-0000

fyi

Hotel
$79-$139 All Year

Too new to rate, opening scheduled for January 2009. **Address:** 30484 Hwy 441 S **Location:** I-85, exit 149. **Amenities:** 74 units, coffeemakers, microwaves, refrigerators, pool. **Cards:** AX, CB, DC, DS, JC, MC, VI. ***(See color ad below)***

HAMPTON INN *Book great rates at AAA.com* **Phone:** (706)335-6161

Hotel
$89-$100 All Year

Address: 153 Hampton Ct **Location:** I-85, exit 149, just e. **Facility:** 61 one-bedroom standard units. 3 stories, interior corridors. **Parking:** on-site. **Terms:** 1-30 night minimum stay, cancellation fee imposed. **Amenities:** voice mail, irons, hair dryers. **Pool(s):** outdoor. **Leisure Activities:** limited exercise equipment. **Guest Services:** valet laundry, wireless Internet. **Business Services:** meeting rooms, PC. **Cards:** AX, CB, DC, DS, MC, VI.

CALL
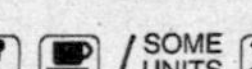

/ SOME UNITS

AAA Benefit:
Members save up to 10% everyday!

▼ *See AAA listing above* ▼

HOWARD JOHNSON INN & SUITES *Book at AAA.com* **Phone:** (706)335-5581

Motel

$53-$140 4/1-11/30
$53-$69 12/1-3/31

Address: 148 Eisenhower Dr **Location:** I-85, exit 149, just ne. **Facility:** 69 one-bedroom standard units. 2 stories (no elevator), exterior corridors. **Parking:** on-site. **Amenities:** voice mail, safes, irons, hair dryers. **Pool(s):** outdoor. **Guest Services:** wireless Internet. **Cards:** AX, DS, MC, VI.

ASK / SOME UNITS FEE

SUPER 8 MOTEL *Book at AAA.com* **Phone:** (706)336-8008

Motel

$49-$140 4/1-11/30
$49-$69 12/1-3/31

Address: 152 Eisenhower Dr **Location:** I-85, exit 149, just ne. **Facility:** 44 one-bedroom standard units. 2 stories, exterior corridors. **Parking:** on-site. **Terms:** office hours 6 am-2 am. **Amenities:** hair dryers. **Guest Services:** wireless Internet. **Cards:** AX, DS, MC, VI.

ASK / SOME UNITS FEE

WHERE TO DINE

GRAND BUFFET **Phone:** 706/335-0877

Chinese

$1-$11

As the restaurant's name makes clear, this place lays out an all-you-can-eat lunch and dinner buffet that includes a salad bar, a good selection of Chinese, Japanese and American entrees and an ice cream bar. Casual dress. **Hours:** 11 am-10 pm, Fri & Sat-11 pm. Closed: 11/26. **Address:** 108 Pottery Factory Dr **Location:** I-85, exit 149, just se. **Parking:** on-site. **Cards:** MC, VI.

SONNY'S REAL PIT BAR-B-Q **Phone:** 706/335-4741

Barbecue

$6-$15

House specialties include pork and chicken grilled over an open pit, barbecue ribs and fresh, homemade pie. The salad bar offers another popular option. Rustic and comfortable, the atmosphere is perfect for family meals. Casual dress. **Bar:** Beer only. **Hours:** 11 am-9:30 pm, Fri & Sat-10 pm. Closed: 11/26, 12/25. **Address:** 30975 Hwy 441 S **Location:** I-85, exit 149, 0.5 mi se. **Parking:** on-site. **Cards:** AX, DS, MC, VI.

CONYERS pop. 10,689

WHERE TO STAY

COMFORT INN *Book at AAA.com* **Phone:** (770)760-0300

Hotel

$79-$129 All Year

Address: 1363 Klondike Rd **Location:** I-20, exit 80, just s. **Facility:** 83 one-bedroom standard units, some with whirlpools. 4-5 stories, interior corridors. **Parking:** on-site. **Terms:** 7 day cancellation notice. **Amenities:** high-speed Internet, irons, hair dryers. **Pool(s):** outdoor. **Leisure Activities:** exercise room. **Guest Services:** valet and coin laundry, wireless Internet. **Business Services:** meeting rooms, fax (fee). **Cards:** AX, DC, DS, MC, VI.

ASK CALL M / SOME UNITS FEE 

▼ See AAA listing p 457 ▼

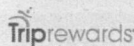

DAYS INN *Book at AAA.com* **Phone:** (770)922-3314

Motel

$80-$145 All Year

Address: 1350 Dogwood Dr **Location:** I-20, exit 82, just n, then just e. **Facility:** 59 one-bedroom standard units. 2 stories (no elevator), exterior corridors. **Parking:** on-site. **Amenities:** high-speed Internet, hair dryers. **Pool(s):** outdoor. **Guest Services:** coin laundry, wireless Internet. **Business Services:** fax. **Cards:** AX, CB, DC, DS, MC, VI.

ASK / SOME UNITS

HAMPTON INN *Book great rates at AAA.com* **Phone:** (770)483-8838

Hotel

$104-$145 All Year

Address: 1340 Dogwood Dr **Location:** I-20, exit 82, just n, then just e. **Facility:** 104 one-bedroom standard units. 4 stories, interior corridors. **Parking:** on-site. **Terms:** 1-30 night minimum stay, cancellation fee imposed. **Amenities:** high-speed Internet, voice mail, irons, hair dryers. **Pool(s):** outdoor. **Leisure Activities:** limited exercise equipment. **Guest Services:** valet laundry, wireless Internet. **Business Services:** business center. **Cards:** AX, CB, DC, DS, JC, MC, VI.

CALL / SOME UNITS FEE

AAA Benefit:

Members save up to 10% everyday!

JAMESON INN *Book at AAA.com* **Phone:** (770)760-1230

Hotel

$88-$95 All Year

Address: 1161 Dogwood Dr **Location:** I-20, exit 82, just n, then just w. **Facility:** 59 one-bedroom standard units. 2 stories (no elevator), exterior corridors. **Parking:** on-site. **Terms:** cancellation fee imposed. **Amenities:** high-speed Internet, dual phone lines, hair dryers. *Some:* irons. **Pool(s):** outdoor. **Leisure Activities:** exercise room. **Guest Services:** valet laundry, wireless Internet. **Business Services:** meeting rooms, PC, fax. **Cards:** AX, DC, DS, MC, VI.

ASK / SOME UNITS FEE

LA QUINTA INN & SUITES ATLANTA (CONYERS) *Book great rates at AAA.com* **Phone:** (770)918-0092

Hotel

$74-$139 All Year

Address: 1184 Dogwood Dr **Location:** I-20, exit 82, just n, then just w. **Facility:** 119 units. 113 one-bedroom standard units. 6 one-bedroom suites. 6 stories, interior corridors. **Parking:** on-site. **Amenities:** video games (fee), high-speed Internet, voice mail, irons, hair dryers. **Pool(s):** outdoor. **Leisure Activities:** whirlpool, exercise room. **Guest Services:** valet and coin laundry, wireless Internet. **Business Services:** meeting rooms, fax (fee). **Cards:** AX, DS, MC, VI.

ASK CALL / SOME UNITS

RAMADA INN & CONFERENCE CENTER *Book great rates at AAA.com* **Phone:** (770)483-3220

Hotel

$49-$109 All Year

Address: 1351 Dogwood Dr **Location:** I-20, exit 80, just n, then 0.4 mi w. **Facility:** 122 units. 114 one-bedroom standard units. 8 two-bedroom suites. 2 stories, exterior corridors. **Parking:** on-site. **Terms:** cancellation fee imposed. **Amenities:** high-speed Internet, voice mail, irons, hair dryers. **Pool(s):** outdoor. **Leisure Activities:** exercise room. **Guest Services:** valet and coin laundry, wireless Internet. **Business Services:** meeting rooms, business center. **Cards:** AX, DS, MC, VI. **Free Special Amenities: full breakfast and high-speed Internet.** ***(See color ad p 456)***

WHERE TO DINE

BAAN THAI **Phone:** 770/761-6161

Thai

$4-$16

Seafood and curried preparations are specialties at this traditional Thai eatery. Casual dress. **Bar:** Beer & wine. **Hours:** 11:30 am-3 & 4:30-9:30 pm, Fri & Sat-10 pm. Closed major holidays; also Mon. **Address:** 1745 Hwy 138 **Location:** I-20, exit 82, 0.9 mi s; in Kroger Plaza. **Parking:** on-site. **Cards:** AX, CB, DC, DS, JC, MC, VI.

SEVEN GABLES RESTAURANT **Phone:** 770/922-8824

Continental

$5-$21

Presented in a lovely Swiss chalet setting, the European cuisine features traditional French bouillabaisse, roasted rack of lamb, and grilled seafood. A well-known eatery in its 12th year of operation, it is located in the "bedroom community" of Atlanta. Casual dress. **Bar:** Full bar. **Reservations:** accepted. **Hours:** 5:30 pm-10 pm. Closed: 12/25; also Sun. **Address:** 1897 SR 20 S **Location:** I-20, exit 82, 1.5 mi s. **Parking:** on-site. **Cards:** AX, DS, MC, VI.

SONNY'S REAL PIT BAR-B-Q **Phone:** 770/860-0099

Barbecue

$6-$15

House specialties include pork and chicken grilled over an open pit, barbecue ribs and fresh, homemade pie. The salad bar offers another popular option. Rustic and comfortable, the atmosphere is perfect for family meals. Casual dress. **Bar:** Beer only. **Hours:** 11 am-9:30 pm, Fri & Sat-10 pm. Closed: 11/26, 12/25. **Address:** 1870 Hwy 20 S **Location:** I-20, exit 82, 1.5 mi s. **Parking:** on-site. **Cards:** AX, DS, MC, VI.

CORDELE pop. 11,608

WHERE TO STAY

BEST WESTERN COLONIAL INN

Book great rates at AAA.com

Phone: (229)273-5420

AAA SAVE

Hotel

$62-$69 All Year

Address: 1706 E 16th Ave (US 280) **Location:** I-75, exit 101 (US 280), just w. **Facility:** 93 one-bedroom standard units. 2 stories (no elevator), interior/exterior corridors. **Parking:** on-site. **Terms:** 10 day cancellation notice. **Amenities:** irons, hair dryers. *Some:* high-speed Internet. **Pool(s):** outdoor. **Leisure Activities:** playground. **Guest Services:** wireless Internet. **Business Services:** PC, fax (fee). **Cards:** AX, CB, DC, DS, JC, MC, VI. **Free Special Amenities: expanded continental breakfast and high-speed Internet.**

/ SOME UNITS FEE

AAA Benefit:

Members save up to 20%, plus 10% bonus points with rewards program.

COMFORT INN

Book great rates at AAA.com

Phone: (229)273-2371

AAA SAVE

Hotel

$70-$130 All Year

Address: 1601 E 16th Ave (US 280) **Location:** I-75, exit 101 (US 280), just w. Located adjacent to railroad. **Facility:** 59 one-bedroom standard units, some with whirlpools. 2 stories (no elevator), exterior corridors. **Parking:** on-site. **Amenities:** irons, hair dryers. **Pool(s):** outdoor. **Guest Services:** wireless Internet. **Business Services:** meeting rooms, fax (fee). **Cards:** AX, CB, DC, DS, MC, VI.

/ SOME UNITS

COUNTRY INN & SUITES

Book great rates at AAA.com

Phone: (229)273-7117

AAA SAVE

Hotel

$79-$209 6/1-11/30

$59-$189 12/1-5/31

Address: 2803 Frontage Rd **Location:** I-75, exit 99 (SR 300), just w, then n. **Facility:** Smoke free premises. 107 units. 72 one-bedroom standard units. 35 one-bedroom suites, some with efficiencies (no utensils). 5 stories, interior corridors. *Bath:* combo or shower only. **Parking:** on-site. **Terms:** cancellation fee imposed. **Amenities:** high-speed Internet, voice mail, irons, hair dryers. **Pool(s):** outdoor. **Leisure Activities:** whirlpool, exercise room. **Guest Services:** coin laundry, wireless Internet. **Business Services:** meeting rooms, business center. **Cards:** AX, CB, DC, DS, MC, VI.

CALL / SOME UNITS

FAIRFIELD INN & SUITES

Book great rates at AAA.com

Phone: (229)273-0042

Hotel

$103-$111 All Year

Address: 2001 E 16th Ave **Location:** I-75, exit 101 (US 280), just e. **Facility:** Smoke free premises. 69 units. 65 one-bedroom standard units. 4 one-bedroom suites. 3 stories, interior corridors. *Bath:* combo or shower only. **Parking:** on-site. **Terms:** cancellation fee imposed. **Amenities:** high-speed Internet, voice mail, safes, irons, hair dryers. **Pool(s):** heated indoor. **Leisure Activities:** whirlpool, exercise room. **Guest Services:** valet and coin laundry, wireless Internet. **Business Services:** meeting rooms, business center. **Cards:** AX, CB, DC, DS, JC, MC, VI.

AAA Benefit:

Members save a minimum 5% off the best available rate.

HAMPTON INN

Book great rates at AAA.com

Phone: (229)273-0737

Hotel

$95-$140 All Year

Address: 1603 16th Ave E (US 280) **Location:** I-75, exit 101 (US 280), just w. Located adjacent to railroad. **Facility:** 80 one-bedroom standard units, some with whirlpools. 2 stories (no elevator), exterior corridors. *Bath:* combo or shower only. **Parking:** on-site. **Amenities:** high-speed Internet, voice mail, irons, hair dryers. **Pool(s):** outdoor. **Leisure Activities:** whirlpool, limited exercise equipment. **Guest Services:** valet laundry. **Business Services:** meeting rooms, business center. **Cards:** AX, CB, DC, DS, MC, VI.

/ SOME UNITS

AAA Benefit:

Members save up to 10% everyday!

HOLIDAY INN EXPRESS

Book at AAA.com

Phone: (229)273-9477

Hotel

$84-$89 All Year

Address: 416 S Greer St **Location:** I-75, exit 101 (US 280), just w, then just n. Located adjacent to railroad. **Facility:** 51 units. 50 one-bedroom standard units, some with whirlpools. 1 one-bedroom suite. 2 stories (no elevator), interior corridors. *Bath:* combo or shower only. **Parking:** on-site. **Amenities:** high-speed Internet, dual phone lines, voice mail, irons, hair dryers. **Pool(s):** heated indoor. **Leisure Activities:** exercise room. **Guest Services:** valet laundry, wireless Internet. **Business Services:** PC, fax (fee). **Cards:** AX, DC, DS, MC, VI.

ASK / SOME UNITS

LAKE BLACKSHEAR RESORT & GOLF CLUB **Phone:** 229/276-1004

Resort Hotel
$99-$199 All Year

Address: 2459-H US 280 W **Location:** I-75, exit 101 (US 280), 10 mi w. Located in Georgia Veterans Memorial State Park. **Facility:** Some units have balconies at this resort in a state park; outdoor enthusiasts will appreciate the picnic areas, trails and boating facilities. 78 one-bedroom standard units. 2 stories, interior/exterior corridors. *Bath:* combo or shower only. **Parking:** on-site. **Terms:** check-in 4 pm, 7 day cancellation notice-fee imposed. **Amenities:** high-speed Internet, dual phone lines, voice mail, irons, hair dryers. **Dining:** 2 restaurants. **Pool(s):** heated outdoor, heated indoor. **Leisure Activities:** whirlpool, limited beach access, rental boats, marina, fishing, rental bicycles, hiking trails, jogging, playground, limited exercise equipment, volleyball. *Fee:* golf-18 holes. **Guest Services:** wireless Internet. **Business Services:** conference facilities, fax (fee). **Cards:** AX, DS, MC, VI. **Free Special Amenities: local telephone calls and high-speed Internet.**

CALL / SOME UNITS FEE

RAMADA INN *Book great rates at AAA.com* **Phone:** (229)273-5000

Hotel
$69-$79 All Year

Address: 2016 E 16th Ave (US 280) **Location:** I-75, exit 101 (US 280), just e. **Facility:** 103 one-bedroom standard units, some with whirlpools. 2 stories (no elevator), exterior corridors. **Parking:** on-site. **Amenities:** voice mail, irons, hair dryers. **Pool(s):** outdoor. **Guest Services:** valet laundry, wireless Internet. **Business Services:** meeting rooms, PC, fax (fee). **Cards:** AX, CB, DC, DS, MC, VI. **Free Special Amenities: expanded continental breakfast and high-speed Internet.**

/ SOME UNITS

TRAVELODGE *Book great rates at AAA.com* **Phone:** (229)273-2456

Motel
$45-$60 All Year

Address: 1618 16th Ave E (US 280) **Location:** I-75, exit 101 (US 280), just w. **Facility:** 44 one-bedroom standard units. 2 stories (no elevator), exterior corridors. **Parking:** on-site. **Amenities:** hair dryers. **Guest Services:** wireless Internet. **Business Services:** fax (fee). **Cards:** AX, CB, DC, DS, MC, VI. **Free Special Amenities: continental breakfast and high-speed Internet.**

/ SOME UNITS

WHERE TO DINE

CUTTERS STEAKS & BUFFET **Phone:** 229/273-8204

American
$5-$13

A good selection of cuts of beef can be cooked to order, or the diner can feast on salads, soup and meat entrees, including fried chicken, riblets and barbecue pork, from the large buffet. This is a great place for a quick, inexpensive and filling meal. Casual dress. **Hours:** 11 am-9 pm, Fri & Sat-10 pm. Closed: 11/26, 12/25. **Address:** 1309 16th Ave E (US 280) **Location:** I-75, exit 101 (US 280), 0.6 mi w. **Parking:** on-site. **Cards:** MC, VI.

CALL

DAPHNE LODGE RESTAURANT **Phone:** 229/273-2596

Steak & Seafood
$9-$25

In a cozy red cabin nestled among pine trees, the family-owned restaurant serves award-winning regional dishes. Among favorites are baked Parmesan grouper and fried catfish. All desserts are homemade. Casual dress. **Bar:** Beer & wine. **Reservations:** suggested, weekends. **Hours:** 4:30 pm-9 pm. Closed major holidays; also Sun & Mon. **Address:** US Hwy 280 W **Location:** I-75, exit 101 (US 280), 10.2 mi w. **Parking:** on-site. **Cards:** AX, DS, MC, VI.

LOS COMPADRES **Phone:** 229/273-1350

Mexican
$6-$11

Located just off the highway, expect to find traditional quick Mexican meals including quesadillas, chimichangas or carne asada. Casual dress. **Bar:** Beer only. **Hours:** 11 am-10:30 pm. **Address:** 111 16th Ave **Location:** I-75, exit 101 (US 280), 1.3 mi w. **Parking:** on-site. **Cards:** AX, MC, VI.

THE OLDE INN RESTAURANT **Phone:** 229/273-1229

Steak & Seafood
$10-$25

In the pines, the converted late-1800s cabin offers excellent service and food. Steak and seafood dominate the menu, but there also are unusual specialty items that shouldn't be overlooked. An appetizer such as spicy sausage and cheese dip is a wonderful prelude to a hearty portion of spicy Mexican snapper or Portuguese pasta: a medley of ham, shrimp and Parmesan over fettuccine. Casual dress. **Bar:** Beer & wine. **Reservations:** suggested, weekends. **Hours:** 5:30 pm-10 pm. Closed major holidays; also Sun & Thurs. **Address:** 2536 US Hwy 280 W **Location:** I-75, exit 101 (US 280), 10.3 mi w. **Parking:** on-site. **Cards:** AX, MC, VI.

CORNELIA pop. 3,674

WHERE TO STAY

COMFORT INN *Book at AAA.com* **Phone:** (706)778-9573

Hotel
$79-$109 All Year

Address: 2965 J Warren Rd **Location:** Jct SR 365 and US 441 business route, just w. **Facility:** 60 units. 58 one-bedroom standard units. 2 one-bedroom suites with whirlpools. 2 stories (no elevator), interior corridors. **Parking:** on-site. **Terms:** 2 night minimum stay - seasonal and/or weekends, cancellation fee imposed. **Amenities:** high-speed Internet, irons, hair dryers. **Pool(s):** outdoor. **Guest Services:** valet laundry, wireless Internet. **Business Services:** meeting rooms, PC, fax (fee). **Cards:** AX, CB, DC, DS, JC, MC, VI.

ASK CALL / SOME UNITS FEE VCR

HAMPTON INN *Book great rates at AAA.com* **Phone:** (706)778-0040

Hotel
$72-$87 All Year

Address: 161 Market Corners Dr **Location:** Jct SR 365 and US 441 business route, just e. **Facility:** 81 units. 80 one-bedroom standard units. 1 one-bedroom suite. 3 stories, interior corridors. **Parking:** on-site. **Terms:** 1-30 night minimum stay, cancellation fee imposed. **Amenities:** video games (fee), high-speed Internet, voice mail, irons, hair dryers. **Pool(s):** outdoor. **Leisure Activities:** exercise room. **Guest Services:** valet laundry, wireless Internet. **Business Services:** meeting rooms, PC, fax (fee). **Cards:** AX, CB, DC, DS, MC, VI.

AAA Benefit:
Members save up to 10% everyday!

HOLIDAY INN EXPRESS *Book at AAA.com* **Phone:** 706/778-3600

Hotel
Rates not provided

Address: 1105 Business 441 **Location:** Jct SR 365 and US 441 business route, just e. **Facility:** 60 one-bedroom standard units, some with whirlpools. 2 stories, interior corridors. **Parking:** on-site. **Amenities:** high-speed Internet, irons, hair dryers. **Pool(s):** heated indoor. **Leisure Activities:** whirlpool, exercise room. **Guest Services:** valet laundry, wireless Internet. **Business Services:** business center.

CALL / SOME UNITS

COVINGTON pop. 11,547

— WHERE TO STAY —

AMERICAS BEST VALUE INN *Book great rates at AAA.com* **Phone:** (770)786-4133

AAA SAVE

Motel
$40-$100 All Year

Address: 10101 Alcovy Rd **Location:** I-20, exit 92, just n. **Facility:** 50 one-bedroom standard units. 2 stories (no elevator), exterior corridors. **Parking:** on-site. **Terms:** cancellation fee imposed. **Amenities:** hair dryers. **Guest Services:** coin laundry. **Business Services:** fax (fee). **Cards:** AX, DS, MC, VI. **Free Special Amenities: continental breakfast and preferred room (subject to availability with advance reservations).**

/ SOME UNITS

BAYMONT INN & SUITES *Book great rates at AAA.com* **Phone:** (770)787-4900

AAA SAVE

Motel
$70-$150 All Year

Address: 10111 Alcovy Rd **Location:** I-20, exit 92, just n. **Facility:** 50 one-bedroom standard units, some with whirlpools. 2 stories (no elevator), exterior corridors. *Bath:* combo or shower only. **Parking:** on-site. **Amenities:** irons, hair dryers. *Some:* safes. **Pool(s):** outdoor. **Leisure Activities:** exercise room. **Guest Services:** coin laundry, wireless Internet. **Business Services:** meeting rooms, PC, fax. **Cards:** AX, DC, DS, MC, VI. **Free Special Amenities: expanded continental breakfast and high-speed Internet.**

CALL / SOME UNITS FEE

QUALITY INN *Book at AAA.com* **Phone:** (770)784-1849

Motel
$53-$160 All Year

Address: 10225 Hwy 142 N **Location:** I-20, exit 93, just s. **Facility:** 42 one-bedroom standard units, some with whirlpools. 2 stories (no elevator), exterior corridors. **Parking:** on-site. **Terms:** cancellation fee imposed. **Amenities:** high-speed Internet, safes (fee), irons, hair dryers. **Pool(s):** outdoor. **Leisure Activities:** exercise room. **Guest Services:** coin laundry, wireless Internet. **Business Services:** PC. **Cards:** AX, DS, MC, VI.

ASK CALL / SOME UNITS

SUPER 8 MOTEL-COVINGTON *Book at AAA.com* **Phone:** (770)786-5800

Motel
$55-$150 All Year

Address: 10130 Alcovy Rd **Location:** I-20, exit 92, just n. **Facility:** 77 one-bedroom standard units. 2 stories (no elevator), exterior corridors. **Parking:** on-site. **Terms:** 3 day cancellation notice. **Amenities:** high-speed Internet, irons, hair dryers. **Guest Services:** coin laundry, wireless Internet. **Business Services:** meeting rooms, PC. **Cards:** AX, CB, DC, DS, JC, MC, VI.

ASK / SOME UNITS FEE

CUMMING pop. 4,220

— WHERE TO STAY —

COMFORT SUITES *Book great rates at AAA.com* **Phone:** (770)889-4141

AAA SAVE

Hotel
$99-$119 3/2-11/30
$99-$109 12/1-3/1

Address: 905 Buford Rd **Location:** SR 400, exit 14, 0.3 mi e. **Facility:** Smoke free premises. 71 one-bedroom standard units, some with whirlpools. 3 stories, interior corridors. **Parking:** on-site. **Terms:** 7 day cancellation notice. **Amenities:** high-speed Internet, irons, hair dryers. **Pool(s):** outdoor. **Leisure Activities:** exercise room. **Guest Services:** coin laundry, wireless Internet. **Business Services:** meeting rooms, PC, fax (fee). **Cards:** AX, CB, DC, DS, JC, MC, VI. **Free Special Amenities: full breakfast and high-speed Internet.**

FEE CALL

HAMPTON INN Book great rates at AAA.com Phone: (770)889-0877

Hotel
$109 All Year

Address: 915 Ronald Reagan Blvd **Location:** SR 400, exit 14, just e. **Facility:** 71 one-bedroom standard units, some with whirlpools. 4 stories, interior corridors. **Parking:** on-site. **Terms:** 1-30 night minimum stay, cancellation fee imposed. **Amenities:** video games (fee), high-speed Internet, dual phone lines, voice mail, irons, hair dryers. **Pool(s):** outdoor. **Leisure Activities:** exercise room. **Guest Services:** valet and coin laundry, wireless Internet. **Business Services:** meeting rooms, business center. **Cards:** AX, DC, DS, MC, VI.

FEE CALL / SOME UNITS

AAA Benefit: Members save up to 10% everyday!

DAHLONEGA pop. 3,638

WHERE TO STAY

DAYS INN Book at AAA.com Phone: (706)864-2338

Motel
$51-$150 All Year

Address: 833 S Chestatee St **Location:** 0.5 mi s on US 19 and SR 60. **Facility:** 41 one-bedroom standard units, some with whirlpools. 2 stories (no elevator), exterior corridors. **Parking:** on-site. **Amenities:** high-speed Internet, irons, hair dryers. **Pool(s):** outdoor. **Guest Services:** wireless Internet. **Business Services:** fax (fee). **Cards:** AX, DC, DS, MC, VI.

ASK / SOME UNITS

ECONO LODGE Book great rates at AAA.com Phone: (706)864-6191

AAA SAVE

Motel
$55-$130 All Year

Address: 619 N Grove St **Location:** 0.5 mi n on US 19 business route. **Facility:** 42 one-bedroom standard units, some with whirlpools. 2-4 stories, exterior corridors. **Parking:** on-site. **Amenities:** high-speed Internet, hair dryers. *Some:* irons. **Pool(s):** outdoor. **Guest Services:** wireless Internet. **Business Services:** PC, fax (fee). **Cards:** AX, DC, DS, MC, VI. **Free Special Amenities: continental breakfast and high-speed Internet.**

/ SOME UNITS FEE

HOLIDAY INN EXPRESS Book at AAA.com Phone: (706)867-7777

Hotel
$79-$169 All Year

Address: 835 S Chestatee St **Location:** 0.5 mi s on US 19 and SR 60. **Facility:** 81 one-bedroom standard units, some with whirlpools. 3 stories, interior corridors. **Parking:** on-site. **Amenities:** high-speed Internet, irons, hair dryers. **Pool(s):** outdoor. **Guest Services:** valet laundry, wireless Internet. **Business Services:** meeting rooms, fax (fee). **Cards:** AX, CB, DC, DS, MC, VI.

ASK CALL / SOME UNITS

LILY CREEK LODGE Phone: (706)864-6848

Bed & Breakfast
$115-$145 All Year

Address: 2608 Auraria Rd **Location:** Northbound, jct SR 400 and Burnt Stand Rd, 2.5 mi w to Auraria Rd, then 2 mi n; southbound, jct US 60 and SR 52 and 9, 1.8 mi w on SR 52 and 9 to Auraria Rd, then 2.5 mi s. **Facility:** This European-style chalet is nestled in a quiet, wooded valley and features feather comforters, art, collectibles and an art nouveau-style parlor. Smoke free premises. 13 units. 8 one-bedroom standard units, some with efficiencies or kitchens. 5 one-bedroom suites, some with kitchens and/or whirlpools. 3 stories (no elevator), interior corridors. *Bath:* combo or shower only. **Parking:** on-site. **Terms:** 3 day cancellation notice-fee imposed. **Amenities:** high-speed Internet. *Some:* DVD players, hair dryers. **Pool(s):** outdoor. **Leisure Activities:** whirlpool. *Fee:* massage. **Guest Services:** wireless Internet. **Business Services:** fax. **Cards:** AX, MC, VI.

ASK / SOME UNITS VCR

SUPER 8 MOTEL Book at AAA.com Phone: 706/864-4343

Motel
Rates not provided

Address: 20 Mountain Dr **Location:** 0.5 mi s on US 19 and SR 60. **Facility:** 60 one-bedroom standard units, some with whirlpools. 2 stories (no elevator), exterior corridors. **Parking:** on-site. **Amenities:** high-speed Internet, hair dryers. *Some:* irons. **Pool(s):** outdoor. **Guest Services:** wireless Internet. **Business Services:** PC, fax (fee).

/ SOME UNITS FEE

WHERE TO DINE

CARUSO'S ITALIAN GRILL & DAHLONEGA BREWING COMPANY Phone: 706/864-4664

Italian
$6-$15

Set in an older building in historic Dahlonega, this casual, Italian-style cafe serves meats, pasta, pizza and sandwiches. Veal Marsala is favored by guests. Local artists' work cover the walls adding personality and familiarity to the room. Casual dress. **Bar:** Beer & wine. **Hours:** 11 am-1 am, Fri-Sun to midnight. Closed: 11/26, 12/25. **Address:** 19B E Main St **Location:** Downtown; by the square. **Parking:** street. **Cards:** AX, DS, MC, VI.

DALLAS pop. 5,056

WHERE TO STAY

DAYS INN Book at AAA.com

Phone: (770)505-4567

Motel

$60-$70 3/1-11/30
$59-$65 12/1-2/28

Address: 1007 Old Harris Rd **Location:** Jct Business Rt SR 6 (Atlanta Hwy). **Facility:** 44 one-bedroom standard units. 2 stories, exterior corridors. **Parking:** on-site. **Amenities:** high-speed Internet, voice mail, hair dryers. **Guest Services:** coin laundry, wireless Internet. **Business Services:** fax (fee). **Cards:** AX, DS, MC, VI.

ASK CALL / SOME UNITS FEE

DALTON pop. 27,912

WHERE TO STAY

AMERICA'S BEST INN Book great rates at AAA.com

Phone: (706)226-1100

AAA SAVE

Motel

$44-$69 All Year

Address: 1529 W Walnut Ave **Location:** I-75, exit 333, just e. **Facility:** 92 one-bedroom standard units. 2 stories, exterior corridors. **Parking:** on-site. **Amenities:** high-speed Internet, irons, hair dryers. **Pool(s):** outdoor. **Guest Services:** coin laundry, wireless Internet. **Business Services:** fax. **Cards:** AX, CB, DC, DS, MC, VI. **Free Special Amenities: expanded continental breakfast and high-speed Internet.**

/ SOME UNITS FEE

BEST WESTERN INN OF DALTON Book great rates at AAA.com

Phone: (706)226-5022

AAA SAVE

Hotel

$59-$74 All Year

Address: 2106 Chattanooga Rd **Location:** I-75, exit 336, just w. **Facility:** 96 one-bedroom standard units. 2 stories, exterior corridors. **Parking:** on-site. **Amenities:** high-speed Internet, irons, hair dryers. **Pool(s):** outdoor. **Guest Services:** coin laundry, wireless Internet. **Business Services:** fax (fee). **Cards:** AX, CB, DC, DS, MC, VI.

CALL / SOME UNITS FEE 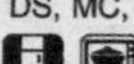

Best Western

AAA Benefit:

Members save up to 20%, plus 10% bonus points with rewards program.

COMFORT INN & SUITES Book at AAA.com

Phone: (706)259-2583

Hotel

$89-$219 All Year

Address: 905 Westbridge Rd **Location:** I-75, exit 333, just w to Westbridge Rd, then just s. **Facility:** 75 units. 64 one-bedroom standard units, some with whirlpools. 11 one-bedroom suites. 4 stories, interior corridors. **Parking:** on-site. **Amenities:** high-speed Internet, dual phone lines, voice mail, irons, hair dryers. **Pool(s):** heated indoor. **Leisure Activities:** whirlpool, limited exercise equipment. **Guest Services:** valet and coin laundry, wireless Internet. **Business Services:** meeting rooms, business center. **Cards:** AX, CB, DC, DS, JC, MC, VI.

ASK CALL / SOME UNITS FEE

COUNTRY INN & SUITES BY CARLSON Book great rates at AAA.com

Phone: (706)278-9700

AAA SAVE

Hotel

$115-$175 All Year

Address: 903 Westbridge Rd **Location:** I-75, exit 333, just w to Westbridge Rd, then just s. **Facility:** 68 units. 48 one-bedroom standard units, some with whirlpools. 20 one-bedroom suites. 3 stories, interior corridors. **Parking:** on-site. **Amenities:** video library (fee), DVD players, high-speed Internet, voice mail, irons, hair dryers. *Some:* dual phone lines. **Pool(s):** heated indoor. **Leisure Activities:** exercise room. **Guest Services:** valet and coin laundry, wireless Internet. **Business Services:** meeting rooms, business center. **Cards:** AX, DS, MC, VI.

CALL / SOME UNITS

COURTYARD BY MARRIOTT Book great rates at AAA.com

Phone: (706)275-7215

Hotel

$119-$127 All Year

Address: 785 College Dr **Location:** I-75, exit 333, just w, then 0.3 mi n. **Facility:** Smoke free premises. 93 units. 90 one-bedroom standard units, some with whirlpools. 3 one-bedroom suites. 3 stories, interior corridors. **Parking:** on-site. **Terms:** cancellation fee imposed. **Amenities:** high-speed Internet, dual phone lines, voice mail, irons, hair dryers. **Pool(s):** heated indoor. **Leisure Activities:** whirlpool, exercise room. **Guest Services:** valet and coin laundry, wireless Internet. **Business Services:** meeting rooms, business center. **Cards:** AX, DS, MC, VI.

CALL / SOME UNITS

AAA Benefit:

Members save a minimum 5% off the best available rate.

ECONO LODGE Book great rates at AAA.com

Phone: (706)278-4300

AAA SAVE

Motel

$43-$100 12/1-10/31
$43-$70 11/1-11/30

Address: 2007 Tampico Way **Location:** I-75, exit 336, just e. **Facility:** 96 one-bedroom standard units. 2 stories (no elevator), interior corridors. **Parking:** on-site. **Amenities:** high-speed Internet. **Pool(s):** outdoor. **Guest Services:** coin laundry, wireless Internet. **Business Services:** fax (fee). **Cards:** AX, DS, MC, VI. **Free Special Amenities: continental breakfast and high-speed Internet.**

/ SOME UNITS FEE   

HAMPTON INN *Book great rates at AAA.com* **Phone:** (706)226-4333

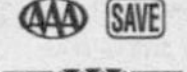

Hotel
$98-$100 All Year

Address: 1000 Market St **Location:** I-75, exit 333, just e to Market St, then just s. Located opposite Dalton Factory Stores Mall. **Facility:** 125 one-bedroom standard units. 3 stories, exterior corridors. **Parking:** on-site. **Terms:** 1-30 night minimum stay, cancellation fee imposed. **Amenities:** high-speed Internet, dual phone lines, voice mail, irons, hair dryers. **Pool(s):** outdoor. **Leisure Activities:** whirlpool, limited exercise equipment, sports court. **Guest Services:** valet and coin laundry, wireless Internet. **Business Services:** meeting rooms, business center. **Cards:** AX, CB, DC, DS, MC, VI. **Free Special Amenities: expanded continental breakfast and high-speed Internet.**

CALL / SOME UNITS

AAA Benefit:
Members save up to 10% everyday!

JAMESON INN *Book at AAA.com* **Phone:** (706)281-1880

Hotel
$73-$78 All Year

Address: 790 College Dr **Location:** I-75, exit 333, just w, then 0.3 mi n. **Facility:** 59 one-bedroom standard units. 2 stories (no elevator), exterior corridors. **Parking:** on-site. **Terms:** cancellation fee imposed. **Amenities:** high-speed Internet, irons, hair dryers. **Pool(s):** outdoor. **Leisure Activities:** exercise room. **Guest Services:** coin laundry, wireless Internet. **Business Services:** PC, fax (fee). **Cards:** AX, DC, DS, MC, VI.

ASK FEE / SOME UNITS FEE

LA QUINTA INN & SUITES *Book at AAA.com* **Phone:** (706)272-9099

Hotel
$89-$169 All Year

Address: 715 College Dr **Location:** I-75, exit 333, just w to Holiday Dr, then 0.5 mi n. **Facility:** 86 units. 82 one-bedroom standard units. 4 one-bedroom suites, some with whirlpools. 4 stories, interior corridors. **Parking:** on-site. **Terms:** cancellation fee imposed. **Amenities:** video games (fee), high-speed Internet, dual phone lines, voice mail, safes, irons, hair dryers. **Pool(s):** outdoor. **Leisure Activities:** whirlpool, exercise room. **Guest Services:** valet and coin laundry, wireless Internet. **Business Services:** meeting rooms, business center. **Cards:** AX, CB, DC, DS, MC, VI.

ASK FEE CALL / SOME UNITS FEE

RAMADA INN & SUITES *Book at AAA.com* **Phone:** (706)217-6200

Hotel
$70-$90 All Year

Address: 795 College Dr **Location:** I-75, exit 333, just w to Holiday Dr, then just n. **Facility:** 71 one-bedroom standard units, some with whirlpools. 2 stories (no elevator), interior corridors. **Parking:** on-site. **Terms:** check-in 4 pm. **Amenities:** high-speed Internet, voice mail, irons, hair dryers. **Pool(s):** heated indoor. **Leisure Activities:** exercise room. **Guest Services:** valet and coin laundry, wireless Internet. **Business Services:** meeting rooms, business center. **Cards:** AX, DS, MC, VI.

ASK FEE CALL / SOME UNITS

WHERE TO DINE

THE CELLAR RESTAURANT **Phone:** 706/226-6029

Continental
$5-$32

The gently elegant atmosphere makes dining on fresh seafood, rack of lamb, and certified Black Angus beef all the more enjoyable. An extensive dessert menu includes table side preparation of bananas foster and cherries jubilee. Special dietary requests are honored. Dressy casual. **Bar:** Full bar. **Reservations:** accepted. **Hours:** 11 am-2 & 5-10 pm, Sat from 5 pm. Closed major holidays; also Sun. **Address:** 1331 W Walnut Ave **Location:** I-75, exit 333, 0.5 mi e; in Dalton Shopping Center. **Parking:** on-site. **Cards:** AX, DS, MC, VI.

DARIEN pop. 1,719

WHERE TO STAY

COMFORT INN *Book great rates at AAA.com* **Phone:** (912)437-4200

Hotel
$85-$250 All Year

Address: 703 Frontage Rd **Location:** I-95, exit 49 (SR 251), just nw. Located adjacent to the Prime Outlet Mall. **Facility:** 66 one-bedroom standard units, some with whirlpools. 2 stories (no elevator), interior corridors. *Bath:* combo or shower only. **Parking:** on-site. **Amenities:** irons, hair dryers. **Pool(s):** outdoor. **Guest Services:** coin laundry, wireless Internet. **Business Services:** PC. **Cards:** AX, DC, DS, MC, VI.

/ SOME UNITS FEE

HAMPTON INN *Book great rates at AAA.com* **Phone:** (912)437-5558

Hotel
$89 All Year

Address: 610 Hwy 251 **Location:** I-95, exit 49 (SR 251), just nw. Located across from the Prime Outlet Mall. **Facility:** 63 one-bedroom standard units. 3 stories, interior corridors. *Bath:* combo or shower only. **Parking:** on-site. **Terms:** 1-30 night minimum stay, cancellation fee imposed. **Amenities:** dual phone lines, voice mail, irons, hair dryers. *Some:* DVD players. **Pool(s):** outdoor. **Leisure Activities:** limited exercise equipment. **Guest Services:** coin laundry, wireless Internet. **Business Services:** meeting rooms. **Cards:** AX, CB, DC, DS, MC, VI.

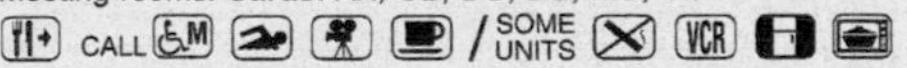

AAA Benefit:
Members save up to 10% everyday!

QUALITY INN *Book at AAA.com* **Phone:** 912/437-5373

Hotel
Rates not provided

Address: GA Hwy 251 & I-95 exit 49 **Location:** I-95, exit 49 (SR 251), just w. **Facility:** 60 one-bedroom standard units, some with whirlpools. 2 stories (no elevator), interior corridors. *Bath:* combo or shower only. **Parking:** on-site. **Terms:** check-in 4 pm. **Amenities:** irons, hair dryers. **Pool(s):** outdoor. **Guest Services:** coin laundry, wireless Internet. **Business Services:** business center.

/ SOME UNITS FEE

WHERE TO DINE

SKIPPER'S FISH CAMP **Phone:** 912/437-3474

Seafood
$11-$25

The riverfront restaurant affords views of the boats and marshlands from the large wooden deck, which is great for kicking back and relaxing. Nautical appointments decorate the dining room, which incorporates extensive use of brick and wood trim and accents. A fresh look and nice landscaping mark the inviting exterior. Comfort foods and Southern dishes, including barbecue, share the menu with specialties of fresh seafood. Service is casual yet attentive. Casual dress. **Bar:** Full bar. **Hours:** 11 am-10 pm. Closed: 11/26, 12/25. **Address:** 85 Screven St **Location:** I-95, exit 49, 1.1 mi se to US 17, 1.2 mi s to Broad St (before bridge), then just w. **Parking:** on-site. **Cards:** AX, DC, DS, MC, VI.

DAWSONVILLE pop. 619

WHERE TO STAY

AMICALOLA FALLS LODGE **Phone:** 706/265-8888

Hotel
Rates not provided

Address: 418 Amicalola Falls Lodge Dr **Location:** Jct SR 53 and 183, 13 mi n on SR 183, just e on SR 52. **Facility:** 56 one-bedroom standard units, some with efficiencies and/or whirlpools. 4 stories, interior corridors. **Parking:** on-site. **Terms:** check-in 4 pm. **Amenities:** high-speed Internet, voice mail, irons, hair dryers. **Leisure Activities:** fishing, recreation programs, hiking trails, jogging. **Guest Services:** wireless Internet. **Business Services:** conference facilities, fax.

CALL / SOME UNITS

BEST WESTERN DAWSON VILLAGE INN *Book great rates at AAA.com* **Phone:** (706)216-4410

AAA SAVE

Hotel
$70-$90 All Year

Address: 76 N Georgia Ave **Location:** Jct SR 400/53, 0.5 mi s. **Facility:** 64 one-bedroom standard units, some with whirlpools. 2 stories (no elevator), interior corridors. **Parking:** on-site. **Terms:** 7 day cancellation notice. **Amenities:** high-speed Internet, voice mail, safes, irons, hair dryers. **Pool(s):** heated indoor. **Leisure Activities:** whirlpool, exercise room. **Guest Services:** coin laundry, wireless Internet. **Business Services:** meeting rooms, PC, fax (fee). **Cards:** AX, DS, MC, VI. **Free Special Amenities: continental breakfast and high-speed Internet.**

CALL / SOME UNITS FEE

AAA Benefit:
Members save up to 20%, plus 10% bonus points with rewards program.

COMFORT INN *Book at AAA.com* **Phone:** (706)216-1900

Hotel
$114-$134 10/1-11/30
$71-$114 12/1-9/30

Address: 127 Beartooth Pkwy **Location:** Jct SR 400/53, 0.5 mi s. **Facility:** 50 one-bedroom standard units, some with whirlpools. 2 stories (no elevator), interior corridors. **Parking:** on-site. **Terms:** 15 day cancellation notice. **Amenities:** high-speed Internet, voice mail, safes (fee), irons, hair dryers. **Pool(s):** outdoor. **Leisure Activities:** exercise room. **Guest Services:** coin laundry, wireless Internet. **Business Services:** meeting rooms, business center. **Cards:** AX, CB, DC, DS, MC, VI.

ASK CALL / SOME UNITS FEE

SUPER 8 MOTEL *Book at AAA.com* **Phone:** (706)216-6801

Hotel
$49-$99 All Year

Address: 205 N 400 Center Ln **Location:** Jct SR 400/53, just n. **Facility:** 53 one-bedroom standard units, some with whirlpools. 2 stories (no elevator), interior corridors. **Parking:** on-site. **Amenities:** high-speed Internet, voice mail, hair dryers. **Pool(s):** heated indoor. **Leisure Activities:** whirlpool. **Guest Services:** wireless Internet. **Business Services:** meeting rooms, PC, fax (fee). **Cards:** AX, DS, MC, VI.

ASK CALL / SOME UNITS FEE

WHERE TO DINE

CHIN CHIN **Phone:** 706/216-2017

Chinese
$6-$20

One of a few locations, this restaurant offers traditional Chinese decor and cuisine, as well as prompt service and lunch specials. Casual dress. **Bar:** Full bar. **Reservations:** accepted. **Hours:** 11:30 am-10 pm, Fri & Sat-10:30 pm, Sun noon-10 pm. **Address:** 837 Hwy 400 S, Suite 115 **Location:** Jct SR 400/53, 0.8 mi s; in Dawson Promenade. **Parking:** on-site. **Cards:** AX, DS, MC, VI.

CALL

DECATUR —*See Atlanta p. 382.*

DILLARD pop. 198

WHERE TO STAY

DILLARD HOUSE Phone: (706)746-5348

AAA SAVE

Hotel
$59-$149 All Year

Address: 768 Franklin St **Location:** US 441, just e via Old Dillard Rd. Located in a quiet area. **Facility:** 84 units. 78 one-bedroom standard units. 6 one-bedroom suites, some with whirlpools. 1-2 stories (no elevator), exterior corridors. **Parking:** on-site. **Terms:** 3 day cancellation notice-fee imposed. **Amenities:** high-speed Internet, voice mail, irons, hair dryers. *Some:* DVD players. **Pool(s):** outdoor. **Leisure Activities:** whirlpool, fishing, 2 tennis courts, petting zoo, horseshoes. *Fee:* horseback riding. **Guest Services:** wireless Internet. **Business Services:** meeting rooms, business center. **Cards:** AX, DC, DS, MC, VI. **Free Special Amenities: room upgrade (subject to availability with advance reservations) and high-speed Internet.**
(See color ad below)

/ SOME UNITS FEE

KNIGHTS INN Book at AAA.com Phone: (706)746-5321

Motel
$60-$140 All Year

Address: 3 Best Inn Way **Location:** Center. **Facility:** 65 one-bedroom standard units. 1-2 stories (no elevator), exterior corridors. **Parking:** on-site. **Amenities:** high-speed Internet, voice mail, irons, hair dryers. **Pool(s):** outdoor. **Leisure Activities:** fishing. **Guest Services:** coin laundry, wireless Internet. **Business Services:** meeting rooms, PC, fax (fee). **Cards:** AX, CB, DC, DS, MC, VI.

ASK / SOME UNITS FEE

MOUNTAIN VALLEY INN Book great rates at AAA.com Phone: (706)746-5373

AAA SAVE

Motel
$45-$98 4/2-11/30
$35-$45 12/1-4/1

Address: 13 Royalty Ln **Location:** Just n of town center. **Facility:** 40 one-bedroom standard units. 2 stories (no elevator), exterior corridors. **Parking:** on-site. **Amenities:** high-speed Internet, hair dryers. **Pool(s):** outdoor. **Leisure Activities:** grills, picnic tables, playground. **Guest Services:** wireless Internet. **Business Services:** meeting rooms, fax. **Cards:** AX, DS, MC, VI. **Free Special Amenities: continental breakfast and high-speed Internet.**

/ SOME UNITS FEE

DORAVILLE —*See Atlanta p. 384.*

DOUGLAS pop. 10,639

WHERE TO STAY

HAMPTON INN Book great rates at AAA.com Phone: (912)383-7550

AAA SAVE

Hotel
$88 All Year

Address: 1604 S Peterson Ave **Location:** Jct US 221/441/SR 31 and SR 206/353, just s. **Facility:** 61 one-bedroom standard units. 3 stories, interior corridors. *Bath:* combo or shower only. **Parking:** on-site. **Terms:** 1-30 night minimum stay, cancellation fee imposed. **Amenities:** video games (fee), dual phone lines, voice mail, irons, hair dryers. **Pool(s):** outdoor. **Leisure Activities:** limited exercise equipment. **Guest Services:** valet laundry, wireless Internet. **Business Services:** meeting rooms. **Cards:** AX, CB, DC, DS, MC, VI. **Free Special Amenities: expanded continental breakfast and high-speed Internet.**

CALL / SOME UNITS

AAA Benefit:
Members save up to 10% everyday!

▼ *See AAA listing above* ▼

JAMESON INN

Motel

Rates not provided

Book at AAA.com

Phone: 912/384-9432

Address: 1628 S Peterson Ave **Location:** Jct US 221/441/SR 31 and SR 206/353, just s. **Facility:** 39 one-bedroom standard units, some with whirlpools. 2 stories (no elevator), exterior corridors. *Bath:* combo or shower only. **Parking:** on-site. **Amenities:** irons, hair dryers. **Pool(s):** outdoor. **Leisure Activities:** exercise room. **Guest Services:** wireless Internet. **Business Services:** PC.

/ SOME UNITS

DOUGLASVILLE —*See Atlanta p. 385.*

DUBLIN pop. 15,857

WHERE TO STAY

COMFORT INN

Hotel

$55-$90 All Year

Book at AAA.com

Phone: (478)274-8000

Address: 2110 Hwy 441 S **Location:** I-16, exit 51 (US 441), 0.6 mi n. **Facility:** 52 one-bedroom standard units, some with whirlpools. 2 stories (no elevator), exterior corridors. **Parking:** on-site, winter plug-ins. **Terms:** cancellation fee imposed. **Amenities:** high-speed Internet, irons, hair dryers. **Pool(s):** outdoor. **Leisure Activities:** exercise room. **Guest Services:** valet and coin laundry, wireless Internet. **Business Services:** business center. **Cards:** AX, DC, DS, MC, VI.

ASK CALL / SOME UNITS FEE

HAMPTON INN DUBLIN

Hotel

$79-$91 All Year

Book great rates at AAA.com

Phone: (478)275-1600

Address: 2108 Hwy 441 S **Location:** I-16, exit 51 (US 441), 0.6 mi n. **Facility:** 71 one-bedroom standard units. 2 stories (no elevator), exterior corridors. *Bath:* combo or shower only. **Parking:** on-site. **Terms:** 1-30 night minimum stay, cancellation fee imposed. **Amenities:** voice mail, irons, hair dryers. **Pool(s):** outdoor. **Guest Services:** valet laundry, wireless Internet. **Business Services:** meeting rooms, PC, fax (fee). **Cards:** AX, CB, DC, DS, MC, VI.

/ SOME UNITS

AAA Benefit:

Members save up to 10% everyday!

HOLIDAY INN EXPRESS HOTEL & SUITES

Hotel

Rates not provided

Book great rates at AAA.com

Phone: 478/272-7862

Address: 2192 Hwy 441 S **Location:** I-16, exit 51 (US 441), just n. **Facility:** 92 one-bedroom standard units, some with whirlpools. 3 stories, interior corridors. *Bath:* combo or shower only. **Parking:** on-site. **Amenities:** high-speed Internet, dual phone lines, voice mail, irons, hair dryers. **Pool(s):** outdoor. **Leisure Activities:** exercise room. **Guest Services:** coin laundry, wireless Internet. **Business Services:** meeting rooms, business center. ***(See color ad below)***

CALL / SOME UNITS

JAMESON INN

Motel

$78-$85 All Year

Book at AAA.com

Phone: (478)275-3008

Address: 100 PM Watson Dr **Location:** I-16, exit 51 (US 441), just n. **Facility:** 40 units. 38 one-bedroom standard units. 2 one-bedroom suites with whirlpools. 2 stories (no elevator), exterior corridors. **Parking:** on-site. **Terms:** cancellation fee imposed. **Amenities:** hair dryers. **Pool(s):** outdoor. **Leisure Activities:** exercise room. **Guest Services:** wireless Internet. **Business Services:** PC, fax (fee). **Cards:** AX, DC, DS, MC, VI.

ASK / SOME UNITS FEE

▼ *See AAA listing above* ▼

LA QUINTA INN & SUITES *Book at AAA.com* **Phone:** (478)272-3110

Hotel

$59-$129 All Year

Address: 101 Travel Center Blvd **Location:** I-16, exit 51 (US 441), just s. Located behind the Cracker Barrel. **Facility:** Smoke free premises. 69 units. 67 one-bedroom standard units, some with whirlpools. 2 one-bedroom suites. 3 stories, interior corridors. *Bath:* combo or shower only. **Parking:** on-site. **Amenities:** high-speed Internet, voice mail, safes, irons, hair dryers. *Some:* DVD players. **Pool(s):** heated indoor. **Leisure Activities:** whirlpool, exercise room. **Guest Services:** coin laundry, wireless Internet. **Business Services:** meeting rooms, business center. **Cards:** AX, DS, MC, VI.

ASK / SOME UNITS

SUPER 8 MOTEL *Book great rates at AAA.com* **Phone:** (478)272-5141

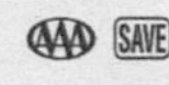

Hotel

$50-$80 All Year

Address: 2150 Hwy 441 S **Location:** I-16, exit 51 (US 441), just n. **Facility:** 52 one-bedroom standard units, some with whirlpools. 2 stories (no elevator), exterior corridors. **Parking:** on-site. **Terms:** 3 day cancellation notice-fee imposed. **Amenities:** high-speed Internet, irons, hair dryers. **Pool(s):** outdoor. **Guest Services:** coin laundry, wireless Internet. **Cards:** AX, CB, DC, DS, JC, MC, VI. **Free Special Amenities: expanded continental breakfast and high-speed Internet.**

/ SOME UNITS

TRAVELODGE SUITES AND CONFERENCE CENTER *Book great rates at AAA.com* **Phone:** (478)275-2650

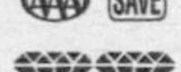

Hotel

$50-$60 All Year

Address: 2121 Hwy 441 S **Location:** I-16, exit 51 (US 441), 0.5 mi n. **Facility:** 88 units. 64 one-bedroom standard units. 24 one-bedroom suites. 2 stories (no elevator), exterior corridors. **Parking:** on-site. **Terms:** 3 day cancellation notice-fee imposed. **Amenities:** voice mail, irons, hair dryers. *Some:* high-speed Internet. **Pool(s):** outdoor. **Leisure Activities:** exercise room. **Guest Services:** valet and coin laundry, wireless Internet. **Business Services:** meeting rooms, PC, fax (fee). **Cards:** AX, DC, DS, MC, VI. **Free Special Amenities: expanded continental breakfast and high-speed Internet.**

— WHERE TO DINE —

SONNY'S REAL PIT BAR-B-Q **Phone:** 478/275-7180

Barbecue

$6-$15

House specialties include pork and chicken grilled over an open pit, barbecue ribs and fresh, homemade pie. The salad bar offers another popular option. Rustic and comfortable, the atmosphere is perfect for family meals. Casual dress. **Bar:** Beer only. **Hours:** 11 am-9:30 pm, Fri & Sat-10 pm. Closed: 11/26, 12/25. **Address:** 2201 Veterans Blvd **Location:** 3 mi w on US 80/SR 26. **Parking:** on-site. **Cards:** AX, DS, MC, VI.

DULUTH *—See Atlanta p. 386.*

EAST ELLIJAY pop. 707

— WHERE TO STAY —

BEST WESTERN MOUNTAIN VIEW INN *Book great rates at AAA.com* **Phone:** (706)515-1500

Hotel

$79-$150 All Year

Address: 43 Coosawattee Dr **Location:** 0.8 mi s on SR 515. **Facility:** 49 one-bedroom standard units, some with whirlpools. 2 stories (no elevator), interior corridors. **Parking:** on-site. **Terms:** cancellation fee imposed. **Amenities:** high-speed Internet, voice mail, irons, hair dryers. **Pool(s):** heated indoor. **Leisure Activities:** whirlpool. **Guest Services:** wireless Internet. **Business Services:** fax (fee). **Cards:** AX, DC, DS, MC, VI. **Free Special Amenities: continental breakfast and high-speed Internet.**

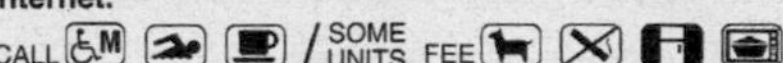

AAA Benefit:

Members save up to 20%, plus 10% bonus points with rewards program.

STRATFORD MOTOR INN **Phone:** (706)276-1080

Hotel

$80-$100 5/1-11/30

$60-$70 12/1-4/30

Address: 79 Maddox Cir **Location:** Jct Maddox Cir and SR 515; behind KFC. **Facility:** 60 one-bedroom standard units. 2 stories, exterior corridors. **Parking:** on-site. **Amenities:** high-speed Internet, irons, hair dryers. **Pool(s):** outdoor. **Guest Services:** wireless Internet. **Business Services:** meeting rooms, fax (fee). **Cards:** AX, DS, MC, VI.

/ SOME UNITS FEE

EAST POINT *—See Atlanta p. 390.*

EATONTON pop. 6,764

WHERE TO STAY

THE LODGE ON LAKE OONEE **Phone:** (706)485-7785

Hotel

$109-$169 All Year

Address: 930 Lake Oconee Pkwy **Location:** I-20, exit 130, 12.3 mi s. **Facility:** Smoke free premises. 81 one-bedroom standard units, some with whirlpools. 3 stories, interior corridors. *Bath:* combo or shower only. **Parking:** on-site. **Terms:** cancellation fee imposed. **Amenities:** high-speed Internet, voice mail, irons, hair dryers. **Pool(s):** outdoor. **Leisure Activities:** sauna, whirlpool, exercise room. *Fee:* boat dock. **Guest Services:** valet and coin laundry, wireless Internet. **Business Services:** meeting rooms, business center. **Cards:** AX, CB, DC, DS, JC, MC, VI.

ASK

ELBERTON pop. 4,743

WHERE TO STAY

DAYS INN *Book great rates at AAA.com* **Phone:** (706)283-2300

AAA SAVE

Motel

$70-$84 All Year

Address: 302 Elbert St **Location:** Jct SR 77/17, 0.4 mi se on SR 17. **Facility:** 34 one-bedroom standard units, some with whirlpools. 2 stories (no elevator), exterior corridors. **Parking:** on-site. **Amenities:** irons, hair dryers. **Pool(s):** outdoor. **Guest Services:** wireless Internet. **Business Services:** PC. **Cards:** AX, DS, MC, VI.

/ SOME UNITS

ELLIJAY pop. 1,584

WHERE TO STAY

The following lodging was either not evaluated or did not meet AAA rating requirements but is listed for your information only.

BEAVER FOREST CHALET VILLAS **Phone:** 706/276-1075

fyi

Not evaluated. **Address:** 147 Beaver Lake Dr. Facilities, services, and decor characterize a mid-scale property.

FAIRBURN —*See Atlanta p. 393.*

FITZGERALD pop. 8,758

WHERE TO STAY

COUNTRY HEARTH INN *Book at AAA.com* **Phone:** (229)409-9911

Hotel

$50-$90 All Year

Address: 125 Stuart Way **Location:** Just n of US 319/107, just e. **Facility:** 40 one-bedroom standard units, some with whirlpools. 2 stories, interior corridors. *Bath:* combo or shower only. **Parking:** on-site. **Amenities:** hair dryers. **Guest Services:** wireless Internet. **Business Services:** fax. **Cards:** AX, DC, DS, MC, VI.

ASK / SOME UNITS

WESTERN MOTEL **Phone:** 229/424-9500

Hotel

Rates not provided

Address: 111 Bull Run Rd **Location:** Just n of US 319/107, on US 129. **Facility:** 39 one-bedroom standard units, some with whirlpools. 2 stories, exterior corridors. **Parking:** on-site. **Amenities:** hair dryers. **Pool(s):** outdoor. **Leisure Activities:** exercise room. **Guest Services:** wireless Internet. **Business Services:** fax.

/ SOME UNITS FEE

FLOWERY BRANCH pop. 1,806

WHERE TO STAY

WHITWORTH INN **Phone:** (770)967-2386

Bed & Breakfast

$75-$89 All Year

Address: 6593 McEver Rd **Location:** I-985, exit 8, 1.4 mi w to McEver Rd, then 1.2 mi n. **Facility:** Minutes from Lake Sidney Lanier, this inn set well back from the road features a pleasant gazebo under tall trees. Smoke free premises. 9 one-bedroom standard units. 2 stories (no elevator), interior corridors. *Bath:* combo or shower only. **Parking:** on-site. **Terms:** 3 day cancellation notice. **Amenities:** high-speed Internet, hair dryers. *Some:* DVD players. **Guest Services:** wireless Internet. **Business Services:** meeting rooms, PC, fax. **Cards:** AX, MC, VI.

WHERE TO DINE

SONNY'S REAL PIT BAR-B-Q **Phone:** 770/287-1622

Barbecue

$6-$15

House specialties include pork and chicken grilled over an open pit, barbecue ribs and fresh, homemade pie. The salad bar offers another popular option. Rustic and comfortable, the atmosphere is perfect for family meals. Casual dress. **Bar:** Beer only. **Hours:** 11 am-9:30 pm, Fri & Sat-10 pm. Closed: 11/26, 12/25. **Address:** 3445 Mundy Mill Rd **Location:** I-985, exit Mundy Mill Rd, 0.4 mi sw. **Parking:** on-site. **Cards:** AX, DS, MC, VI.

FOLKSTON pop. 2,178

— WHERE TO STAY —

THE INN AT FOLKSTON — **Phone:** 912/496-6256

Bed & Breakfast
$105-$160 All Year

Address: 509 W Main St **Location:** Jct US 1/301 and SR 23, 0.4 mi w of downtown. **Facility:** Front-porch rocking chairs add charm to this cottage home with a certified backyard wildlife habitat; guest rooms feature feather beds and bathrobes. Smoke free premises. 4 one-bedroom standard units, some with whirlpools. 1 story, interior corridors. *Bath:* combo or shower only. **Parking:** on-site. **Terms:** 5 day cancellation notice-fee imposed. **Amenities:** irons, hair dryers. **Leisure Activities:** whirlpool. **Guest Services:** TV in common area, wireless Internet. **Cards:** AX, DS, MC, VI.

ASK

WESTERN MOTEL — **Phone:** (912)496-4711

AAA SAVE

Motel
$80-$145 All Year

Address: 1207 S 2nd St **Location:** 0.9 mi s of jct SR 23/121 and US 1/301, on US 1/301. **Facility:** 30 one-bedroom standard units, some with whirlpools. 2 stories (no elevator), exterior corridors. **Parking:** on-site. **Terms:** 2 night minimum stay - seasonal, cancellation fee imposed. **Amenities:** hair dryers. **Pool(s):** outdoor. **Guest Services:** wireless Internet. **Cards:** AX, DC, DS, MC, VI. **Free Special Amenities: continental breakfast and high-speed Internet.**

/ SOME UNITS

FOREST PARK —*See Atlanta p. 393.*

FORSYTH pop. 3,776

— WHERE TO STAY —

BEST WESTERN HILLTOP INN *Book great rates at AAA.com* — **Phone:** (478)994-9260

AAA SAVE

Motel
$60-$116 All Year

Address: 951 Hwy 42 N **Location:** I-75, exit 188 (SR 42), just ne via Frontage Rd. **Facility:** 90 one-bedroom standard units. 2 stories, exterior corridors. **Parking:** on-site. **Terms:** cancellation fee imposed. **Amenities:** irons, hair dryers. **Pool(s):** outdoor. **Guest Services:** wireless Internet. **Business Services:** meeting rooms, PC, fax (fee). **Cards:** AX, CB, DC, DS, MC, VI. **Free Special Amenities: continental breakfast and room upgrade (subject to availability with advance reservations).** *(See color ad p 497)*

AAA Benefit:
Members save up to 20%, plus 10% bonus points with rewards program.

/ SOME UNITS FEE

COMFORT INN *Book great rates at AAA.com* — **Phone:** (478)994-3400

Hotel
$69-$99 All Year

Address: 333 Harold G Clark Pkwy **Location:** I-75, exit 185 (SR 18), just w. **Facility:** 59 one-bedroom standard units. 2 stories (no elevator), exterior corridors. *Bath:* combo or shower only. **Parking:** on-site. **Amenities:** voice mail, irons, hair dryers. **Pool(s):** outdoor. **Leisure Activities:** exercise room. **Guest Services:** wireless Internet. **Business Services:** PC, fax (fee). **Cards:** AX, DC, DS, MC, VI. **Free Special Amenities: expanded continental breakfast and high-speed Internet.**

/ SOME UNITS FEE

COMFORT SUITES — **Phone:** 478/994-9494

fyi

Hotel
$90-$130 All Year

Too new to rate. **Address:** 343 Harold G Clark Pkwy **Location:** I-75, exit 185. **Amenities:** 53 units. **Cards:** AX, DC, DS, MC, VI.

ECONO LODGE *Book great rates at AAA.com* — **Phone:** (478)994-5603

AAA SAVE

Motel
$50-$80 All Year

Address: 320 Cabiness Rd **Location:** I-75, exit 187 (SR 83), just ne. **Facility:** 72 one-bedroom standard units. 2 stories (no elevator), interior corridors. **Parking:** on-site. **Pool(s):** outdoor. **Guest Services:** coin laundry, wireless Internet. **Business Services:** PC, fax (fee). **Cards:** AX, DC, DS, MC, VI. **Free Special Amenities: continental breakfast and high-speed Internet.**

/ SOME UNITS FEE

HOLIDAY INN EXPRESS *Book at AAA.com* — **Phone:** (478)994-9697

Hotel
$109-$169 All Year

Address: 520 Holiday Cir **Location:** I-75, exit 186 (Juliette Rd), just w, then just s on Aaron St. **Facility:** 121 units. 120 one-bedroom standard units. 1 one-bedroom suite. 4 stories, interior corridors. **Parking:** on-site. **Amenities:** high-speed Internet, voice mail, irons, hair dryers. **Leisure Activities:** exercise room. **Guest Services:** wireless Internet. **Business Services:** meeting rooms, PC, fax. **Cards:** AX, DS, MC, VI.

ASK CALL / SOME UNITS FEE

HOLIDAY INN FORSYTH *Book at AAA.com* **Phone:** (478)994-5691

Hotel
$96 All Year

Address: 480 Holiday Cir **Location:** I-75, exit 186 (Juliette Rd), just w, then just s on Aaron St. **Facility:** 120 one-bedroom standard units. 2 stories (no elevator), exterior corridors. *Bath:* combo or shower only. **Parking:** on-site. **Amenities:** voice mail, irons, hair dryers. **Pool(s):** outdoor. **Leisure Activities:** exercise room. **Guest Services:** coin laundry, wireless Internet. **Business Services:** conference facilities, PC, fax. **Cards:** AX, DS, MC, VI.

ASK / SOME UNITS FEE

SUPER 8 MOTEL *Book great rates at AAA.com* **Phone:** (478)994-5101

AAA SAVE

Hotel
$58-$100 All Year

Address: 436 Tift College Dr **Location:** I-75, exit 186 (Juliette Rd), just w. **Facility:** 66 one-bedroom standard units. 2 stories, interior/exterior corridors. **Parking:** on-site. **Amenities:** hair dryers. **Pool(s):** outdoor. **Guest Services:** wireless Internet. **Business Services:** PC, fax (fee). **Cards:** AX, CB, DC, DS, MC, VI.

/ SOME UNITS FEE

WHERE TO DINE

GRITS CAFE **Phone:** 478/994-8325

Regional American
$7-$22

The quality of meals surprises at the homespun-sounding cafe, where the chef takes Southern style to new heights. Hearty soups, such as cream of mushroom with roasted red peppers, warm the heart. The signature shrimp and grits combines spicy, sauced shrimp with smoked gouda cheese-blended grit cakes. Although desserts such as homemade turtle sundae or cappuccino creme brulee are big enough to share, diners won't want to. Dressy casual. **Bar:** Full bar. **Reservations:** accepted. **Hours:** 11 am-2 & 5:30-9 pm, Fri & Sat-10 pm. Closed major holidays; also Sun & Mon. **Address:** 17 W Johnston St **Location:** I-75, exit 186 (Juliette Rd), 1 mi w. **Parking:** street. **Cards:** AX, DS, MC, VI.

FORT GAINES pop. 1,110

WHERE TO STAY

GEORGE T. BAGBY STATE PARK & LODGE **Phone:** 229/768-2571

Motel
$70-$75 4/1-11/30
$65-$70 12/1-3/31

Address: 330 Bagby Park Way **Location:** On SR 39, 4 mi n of jct SR 37, 1.8 mi w, then s on park road; in George T Bagby State Park. **Facility:** Smoke free premises. 66 units. 58 one-bedroom standard units. 2 one-bedroom suites. 6 cabins. 1 story, exterior corridors. *Bath:* combo or shower only. **Parking:** on-site. **Terms:** check-in 4 pm, 2 night minimum stay - weekends, 3 day cancellation notice-fee imposed. **Amenities:** voice mail, irons, hair dryers. **Pool(s):** outdoor. **Leisure Activities:** rental boats, rental canoes, waterskiing, fishing, 2 lighted tennis courts, recreation programs, rental bicycles, hiking trails, playground. *Fee:* marina, golf-18 holes. **Guest Services:** wireless Internet. **Business Services:** meeting rooms. **Cards:** AX, DS, MC, VI.

/ SOME UNITS

FORT OGLETHORPE pop. 6,940

WHERE TO STAY

BEST WESTERN BATTLEFIELD INN *Book great rates at AAA.com* **Phone:** (706)866-0222

AAA SAVE

Hotel
$49-$99 All Year

Address: 2120 Lafayette Rd **Location:** Jct US 27 and SR 2, just n. **Facility:** 38 one-bedroom standard units, some with whirlpools. 1-2 stories (no elevator), exterior corridors. **Parking:** on-site. **Terms:** 3 day cancellation notice. **Amenities:** high-speed Internet, irons, hair dryers. **Pool(s):** heated indoor. **Guest Services:** wireless Internet. **Business Services:** PC, fax (fee). **Cards:** AX, DS, MC, VI. **Free Special Amenities: continental breakfast and high-speed Internet.**

VCR / SOME UNITS FEE

AAA Benefit:
Members save up to 20%, plus 10% bonus points with rewards program.

CAPTAINS QUARTERS B & B INN **Phone:** (706)858-0624

Bed & Breakfast
$135-$185 All Year

Address: 13 Barnhardt Cir **Location:** 0.8 mi s of jct US 27 and SR 2, just w on Harker, then just s. **Facility:** Walking distance to Chickamauga and Chattanooga National Military Park, this B&B features fireplaces in four guest rooms. Smoke free premises. 9 units. 7 one- and 2 two-bedroom standard units. 2 stories (no elevator), interior corridors. *Bath:* some shared or private, combo or shower only. **Parking:** street. **Terms:** age restrictions may apply, 7 day cancellation notice. **Amenities:** high-speed Internet, irons, hair dryers. **Guest Services:** wireless Internet. **Business Services:** fax. **Cards:** AX, DS, MC, VI.

ASK

SUPER 8 MOTEL *Book great rates at AAA.com* **Phone:** (706)861-1744

AAA SAVE

Hotel
$50-$75 All Year

Address: 2044 Lafayette Rd **Location:** Jct US 27 and SR 2, just n. **Facility:** 45 one-bedroom standard units, some with whirlpools. 2 stories (no elevator), exterior corridors. **Parking:** on-site. **Amenities:** high-speed Internet, voice mail, irons, hair dryers. **Pool(s):** outdoor. **Guest Services:** wireless Internet. **Business Services:** meeting rooms, fax. **Cards:** AX, DC, DS, MC, VI. **Free Special Amenities: expanded continental breakfast and high-speed Internet.**

WHERE TO DINE

THAI GARDEN

Thai
$2-$21

Phone: 706/866-7025

Featuring authentic Thai cuisine with very good curries and the traditional favorites served with beef, chicken, pork or tofu. The owner delivers charming service. Casual dress. **Reservations:** accepted. **Hours:** 11 am-9 pm, Sun-8:30 pm. Closed: 11/26, 12/25. **Address:** 685 Battlefield Pkwy **Location:** Jct US 27/SR 2 and Battlefield Pkwy, 0.3 mi e; in Battlefield Shopping Center. **Parking:** on-site. **Cards:** AX, DS, MC, VI.

FORT VALLEY pop. 8,005

WHERE TO STAY

DAYS INN & SUITES

Motel
$69-$129 All Year

Book at AAA.com

Phone: (478)825-3600

Address: 300 Commercial Heights **Location:** Jct SR 49, just se on US 341/SR 96. **Facility:** 40 one-bedroom standard units, some with whirlpools. 2 stories (no elevator), exterior corridors. **Parking:** on-site. **Amenities:** irons, hair dryers. **Pool(s):** outdoor. **Guest Services:** coin laundry, wireless Internet. **Cards:** AX, DC, DS, MC, VI.

ASK / SOME UNITS

WHERE TO DINE

PEACHTREE CAFE'

American
$5-$8

Phone: 478/825-3592

After a tasty sandwich with all the fixings, guests can partake of the peach cobbler and homemade ice cream for which this place is known. Guided and self-guided tours wend through the packing facilities. The staff takes orders at the counter and then brings meals out to the table. Casual dress. **Hours:** 9 am-5 pm. Closed major holidays. **Address:** 50 Lane Rd **Location:** I-75, exit 142 (SR 96), 4.9 mi w; in Lane Southern Orchard. **Parking:** on-site. **Cards:** AX, DS, MC, VI.

TAPATIO

Mexican
$5-$12

Phone: 478/827-0250

On the menu are choices such as fajitas, soft tacos with grilled steak or marinated pork, shrimp with rice and a variety of burritos and enchiladas. Casual dress. **Bar:** Beer only. **Hours:** 11 am-9 pm, Fri & Sat-10 pm, Sun-8 pm. Closed major holidays. **Address:** 600 Vineville St **Location:** Jct US 341/SR 96 (Vineville St), 0.6 mi w. **Parking:** on-site. **Cards:** AX, DS, MC, VI.

GAINESVILLE pop. 25,578

WHERE TO STAY

AMERICAS BEST VALUE INN

Motel
$50-$75 All Year

Book at AAA.com

Phone: (770)534-0303

Address: 809 Jesse Jewell Pkwy **Location:** I-985, exit 20, 2 mi w on SR 60/Queen City Pkwy, then just s. **Facility:** 39 one-bedroom standard units, some with whirlpools. 2 stories (no elevator), exterior corridors. **Parking:** on-site. **Amenities:** high-speed Internet, voice mail, irons, hair dryers. **Pool(s):** outdoor. **Leisure Activities:** whirlpool. **Guest Services:** wireless Internet. **Business Services:** fax (fee). **Cards:** AX, CB, DC, DS, JC, MC, VI.

ASK / SOME UNITS

▼ See AAA listing p 472 ▼

DAYS INN Book great rates at AAA.com **Phone:** (770)535-8100

Hotel
$55-$80 All Year

Address: 520 Queen City Pkwy SW **Location:** I-985, exit 20, 1.8 mi nw on SR 60/Queen City Pkwy. **Facility:** 98 one-bedroom standard units. 2 stories (no elevator), exterior corridors. **Parking:** on-site. **Terms:** cancellation fee imposed. **Amenities:** high-speed Internet, irons, hair dryers. **Pool(s):** outdoor. **Guest Services:** valet and coin laundry, wireless Internet. **Business Services:** meeting rooms, PC, fax (fee). **Cards:** AX, CB, DC, DS, MC, VI. **Free Special Amenities: full breakfast and high-speed Internet.** *(See color ad p 471)*

/ SOME UNITS FEE

HAMPTON INN Book great rates at AAA.com **Phone:** (770)503-0300

Hotel
$98 All Year

Address: 450 Jesse Jewell Pkwy **Location:** I-985, exit 20, 2 mi on SR 60/Queen City Pkwy, then just n. **Facility:** 74 one-bedroom standard units. 4 stories, interior corridors. **Parking:** on-site. **Terms:** 1-30 night minimum stay, cancellation fee imposed. **Amenities:** high-speed Internet, voice mail, irons, hair dryers. **Pool(s):** outdoor. **Guest Services:** valet laundry, wireless Internet. **Business Services:** PC, fax (fee). **Cards:** AX, CB, DC, DS, JC, MC, VI.

FEE CALL / SOME UNITS

AAA Benefit:
Members save up to 10% everyday!

HOLIDAY INN LANIER CENTRE Book great rates at AAA.com **Phone:** (770)531-0907

Hotel
$140-$170 3/31-11/30
$130-$160 12/1-3/30

Address: 400 E E Butler Pkwy **Location:** I-985, exit 22, 1 mi w on US 129 business route. **Facility:** 122 one-bedroom standard units, some with efficiencies and/or whirlpools. 4 stories, interior corridors. **Parking:** on-site. **Terms:** 3 day cancellation notice-fee imposed. **Amenities:** high-speed Internet, dual phone lines, voice mail, irons, hair dryers. **Pool(s):** outdoor. **Leisure Activities:** exercise room. **Guest Services:** valet and coin laundry, wireless Internet. **Business Services:** meeting rooms, PC, fax (fee). **Cards:** AX, CB, DC, DS, MC, VI. **Free Special Amenities: full breakfast and high-speed Internet.**

FEE / SOME UNITS

▼ *See AAA listing p 473* ▼

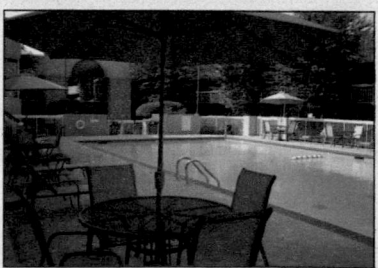

QUALITY INN & SUITES *Book great rates at AAA.com* **Phone:** 770/536-4451

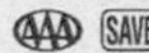

Hotel
Rates not provided

Address: 726 Jessie Jewell Pkwy **Location:** I-985, exit 20, 1.9 mi w to Jesse Jewell Pkwy, then just s. **Facility:** 96 units. 94 one-bedroom standard units. 2 one-bedroom suites. 3 stories, exterior corridors. **Parking:** on-site. **Amenities:** high-speed Internet, irons, hair dryers. **Pool(s):** outdoor. **Leisure Activities:** exercise room. **Guest Services:** valet and coin laundry, airport transportation (fee)-Gainesville Regional Airport, wireless Internet. **Business Services:** meeting rooms, fax. **Free Special Amenities: full breakfast and high-speed Internet.** *(See color ad p 472)*

FEE CALL / SOME UNITS FEE

RAMADA LIMITED *Book at AAA.com* **Phone:** (770)287-3205

Motel
$56-$60 All Year

Address: 766 Jesse Jewell Pkwy **Location:** I-985, exit 20, 1.9 mi w to Jesse Jewell Pkwy, then just s. **Facility:** 47 one-bedroom standard units. 3 stories, exterior corridors. **Parking:** on-site. **Amenities:** high-speed Internet, voice mail, irons, hair dryers. **Guest Services:** coin laundry, wireless Internet. **Business Services:** PC, fax (fee). **Cards:** AX, CB, DC, DS, MC, VI.

ASK / SOME UNITS FEE

WHERE TO DINE

RUDOLPH'S ON GREEN STREET **Phone:** 770/534-2226

American
$11-$42

In a turn-of-the-20th-century mansion, this restaurant serves traditional cuisine. Scones served with peanut butter honey spread are a delicious alternative to typical bread and butter. Prix fixe chef's dinners are available on Friday and Saturday. Casual dress. **Bar:** Full bar. **Reservations:** suggested, weekends. **Hours:** 11:30 am-2 & 5:30-9 pm, Fri-10 pm, Sat 5:30 pm-10 pm, Sun 11:30 am-2 pm; Sunday brunch. Closed major holidays; also Mon. **Address:** 700 Green St **Location:** I-985, exit 22, 2 mi nw on US 129 and SR 60. **Parking:** on-site. **Cards:** AX, DC, DS, MC, VI. **Historic**

GARDEN CITY pop. 11,289 (See map and index starting on p. 520)

WHERE TO STAY

BAYMONT INN & SUITES *Book great rates at AAA.com* **Phone:** 912/964-8669 58

Hotel
Rates not provided

Address: 357 Main St **Location:** I-95, exit 109 (SR 21), 6.5 mi se to Spur SR 21 (Brampton Rd), 0.3 mi n to Coastal Hwy/Main St, then just se. **Facility:** 57 units. 39 one-bedroom standard units. 18 one-bedroom suites. 2 stories, interior corridors. *Bath:* combo or shower only. **Parking:** on-site. **Amenities:** high-speed Internet, voice mail, irons, hair dryers. *Some:* DVD players. **Pool(s):** outdoor. **Leisure Activities:** whirlpool. **Guest Services:** valet and coin laundry, area transportation, wireless Internet. **Business Services:** business center. ***(See color ad p 524)***

/ SOME UNITS FEE

GLENNVILLE pop. 3,641

WHERE TO STAY

CHEERI-O INN **Phone:** (912)654-2176

Motel
$45-$50 All Year

Address: 820 S Downing Musgrove St **Location:** 0.8 mi s on US 25 and 301. **Facility:** 25 one-bedroom standard units. 1 story, exterior corridors. *Bath:* combo or shower only. **Parking:** on-site. **Terms:** cancellation fee imposed. **Leisure Activities:** picnic tables. **Cards:** AX, DS, MC, VI. **Free Special Amenities: local telephone calls and early check-in/late check-out.**

/ SOME UNITS FEE

Destination Golden Isles

The Golden Isles contain all the ingredients for a perfect beach getaway. Don your bathing suit and flip-flops and head to one of many sandy shores for a stroll. Or spread out a towel, slather on some SPF and take advantage of the sunshine.

And when the orange glow of the sun has dropped below the horizon, enjoy seafood under the protective eye of an ancient lighthouse.

Georgia Department of Economic Development

Sand castles, Jekyll Island. A young beachgoer enjoys the sand and ocean breeze on Jekyll Island.

Georgia Department of Economic Development

Bird-watching on St. Simons Island. Eager bird-watching enthusiasts spend time trying to spot some fine-feathered friends.

Georgia Department of Economic Development

Golfing, Jekyll Island. Jekyll Island offers golfers a number of greens on which to play.

Shopping. Finding that perfect item can be very rewarding.

Georgia Department of Economic Development

Places included in this AAA Destination Area:

Golden Isles

JEKYLL ISLAND

There is a $3.00 fee every time you enter Jekyll Island.

WHERE TO STAY

THE BEACHVIEW CLUB

Hotel

$169-$279 6/1-11/30
$119-$259 12/1-5/31

Phone: 912/635-2256

Address: 721 N Beachview Dr **Location:** Jct Ben Fortson Pkwy (SR 520)/Beachview Dr, 1.7 mi n. **Facility:** Smoke free premises. 38 units. 37 one-bedroom standard units, some with efficiencies and/or whirlpools. 1 one-bedroom suite with efficiency. 2 stories (no elevator), exterior corridors. *Bath:* combo or shower only. **Parking:** on-site. **Terms:** check-in 4 pm, 2 night minimum stay - weekends, 3 day cancellation notice. **Amenities:** dual phone lines, voice mail, irons, hair dryers. *Some:* DVD players. **Pool(s):** heated outdoor. **Leisure Activities:** whirlpool. *Fee:* bicycles. **Guest Services:** coin laundry, area transportation, wireless Internet. **Business Services:** meeting rooms. **Cards:** AX, CB, DC, DS, MC, VI.

A$K / SOME UNITS VCR

DAYS INN & SUITES

AAA SAVE

Hotel

$140-$280 5/23-11/30
$75-$205 12/1-5/22

Book great rates at AAA.com

Phone: (912)635-9800

Address: 60 S Beachview Dr **Location:** Oceanfront. Jct Ben Fortson Pkwy (SR 520)/Beachview Dr, just s. **Facility:** 124 units. 84 one-bedroom standard units. 40 one-bedroom suites with efficiencies. 2 stories, exterior corridors. *Bath:* combo or shower only. **Parking:** on-site. **Terms:** check-in 4 pm, 2 night minimum stay - seasonal and/or weekends, 3 day cancellation notice. **Amenities:** voice mail, irons, hair dryers. *Some:* high-speed Internet, dual phone lines. **Pool(s):** 2 outdoor. **Leisure Activities:** *Fee:* bicycles. **Guest Services:** coin laundry, airport transportation-Jekyll Island Airport, wireless Internet. **Business Services:** meeting rooms. **Cards:** AX, DC, DS, MC, VI. **Free Special Amenities: expanded continental breakfast and newspaper.**

/ SOME UNITS

JEKYLL ISLAND CLUB HOTEL

AAA SAVE

Classic Historic Hotel

$149-$439 All Year

Book great rates at AAA.com

Phone: (912)635-2600

Address: 371 Riverview Dr **Location:** 0.5 mi n of Ben Fortson Pkwy (SR 520)/Beachview Dr, follow signs; in historic district. **Facility:** Offering a rare glimpse at the Gilded Age, the hotel includes well-appointed rooms and cottages, fine dining and an array of recreation options. 157 units. 141 one-bedroom standard units, some with whirlpools. 16 one-bedroom suites, some with whirlpools. 2-4 stories, interior corridors. **Parking:** on-site and valet. **Terms:** check-in 4 pm, 2 night minimum stay - weekends, cancellation fee imposed. **Amenities:** video library (fee), DVD players, voice mail, safes, honor bars, irons, hair dryers. *Some:* high-speed Internet. **Dining:** 2 restaurants, also, The Grand Dining Room, see separate listing. **Pool(s):** heated outdoor. **Leisure Activities:** beach access, putting green, recreation programs, croquet court, lending library, jogging. *Fee:* fishing, charter fishing, bicycles, massage. **Guest Services:** valet laundry, airport transportation (fee)-Jacksonville, Brunswick & Savannah/Hilton Head International airports, area transportation-on island, wireless Internet. **Business Services:** conference facilities, PC. **Cards:** AX, CB, DC, DS, JC, MC, VI. **Free Special Amenities: newspaper and high-speed Internet.** *(See color ad below)*

FEE / SOME UNITS FEE

▼ *See AAA listing above* ▼

QUALITY INN & SUITES *Book great rates at AAA.com* **Phone:** (912)635-2202

Hotel

$99-$169 All Year

Address: 700 N Beachview Dr **Location:** Jct Ben Fortson Pkwy (SR 520)/Beachview Dr, 1.5 mi n. Located next to a public park. **Facility:** 72 units. 23 one-bedroom standard units, some with efficiencies. 16 one- and 33 two-bedroom suites with kitchens. 2 stories (no elevator), exterior corridors. *Bath:* combo or shower only. **Parking:** on-site. **Terms:** 2 night minimum stay - seasonal and/or weekends, cancellation fee imposed. **Amenities:** voice mail, irons, hair dryers. **Pool(s):** outdoor. **Leisure Activities:** beach access, shuffleboard. *Fee:* bicycles. **Guest Services:** coin laundry, wireless Internet. **Business Services:** meeting rooms, PC. **Cards:** AX, DC, DS, MC, VI. **Free Special Amenities: expanded continental breakfast and high-speed Internet.**

/ SOME UNITS FEE

VILLAS BY THE SEA *Book great rates at AAA.com* **Phone:** (912)635-2521

Vacation Rental Condominium

$129-$349 5/23-11/30

$129-$289 12/1-5/22

Address: 1175 N Beachview Dr **Location:** Jct Ben Fortson Pkwy (SR 520)/Beachview Dr, 4 mi n. **Facility:** The oceanside resort is set amid lush natural landscaping and towering oaks; boardwalks lead through greenery to the uncrowded beach. 167 units. 7 one-bedroom standard units, some with efficiencies. 160 condominiums. 1-3 stories (no elevator), exterior corridors. *Bath:* combo or shower only. **Parking:** on-site. **Terms:** check-in 4 pm, 2-3 night minimum stay - seasonal and/or weekends, 7 day cancellation notice-fee imposed. **Amenities:** video library, dual phone lines, voice mail, irons, hair dryers. *Some:* DVD players, high-speed Internet. **Pool(s):** outdoor. **Leisure Activities:** fishing, barbecue grill, bike trail, picnic tables, croquet, jogging, playground, exercise room, basketball, horseshoes, volleyball. *Fee:* bicycles. **Guest Services:** coin laundry, wireless Internet. **Business Services:** meeting rooms, PC. **Cards:** AX, DC, DS, MC, VI. **Free Special Amenities: high-speed Internet.** *(See color ad below)*

CALL / SOME UNITS VCR

▼ See AAA listing above ▼

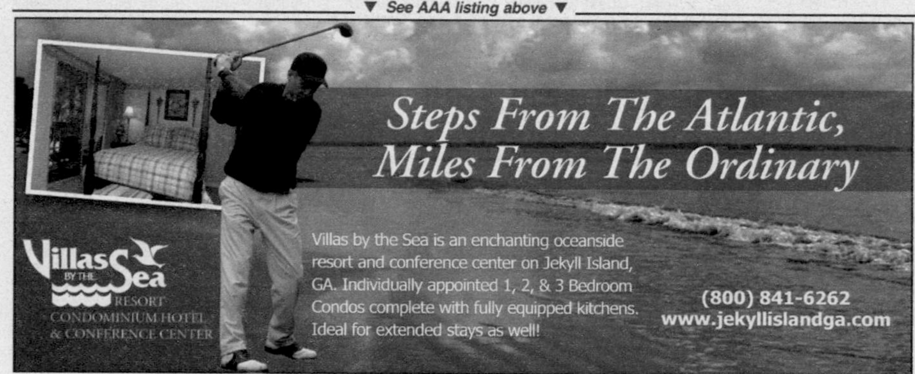

WHERE TO DINE

BLACKBEARDS RESTAURANT — **Phone:** 912/635-3522

Steak & Seafood
$6-$22

Settle down to good ol' Georgia cookin' in an unpretentious setting with wonderful ocean views. The menu features a variety of seafood, steak and chicken dishes with an emphasis on sandwiches at lunch. Try the crab bisque with yesterday's hush puppies. Casual dress. **Bar:** Full bar. **Reservations:** accepted. **Hours:** 11 am-3:30 & 5-9 pm, Fri & Sat-10 pm. Closed: 12/25. **Address:** 200 N Beachview Dr **Location:** Jct Ben Fortson Pkwy (SR 520)/Beachview Dr, 0.5 mi n. **Parking:** on-site. **Cards:** AX, DS, MC, VI.

CALL

THE GRAND DINING ROOM *Menu on AAA.com* — **Phone:** 912/635-2400

Continental
$9-$32

Stop and experience a taste of creative, gourmet food, in an elegant, sophisticated dining room. Brunswick stew is a great way to spice up your meal, literally! This eatery is casual for breakfast and lunch, while jackets are required at dinner. Dressy casual. Entertainment. **Bar:** Full bar. **Reservations:** suggested. **Hours:** 7-11 am, 11:30-2 & 6-10 pm; Sunday brunch. **Address:** 371 Riverview Dr **Location:** 0.5 mi n of Ben Fortson Pkwy (SR 520)/Beachview Dr, follow signs; in historic district; in Jekyll Island Club Hotel. **Parking:** on-site and valet. **Cards:** AX, CB, DC, DS, MC, VI. **Historic**

LATITUDE 31 — **Phone:** 912/635-3800

American
$18-$32

Juicy chicken and marinara sauce pair with some of the delicious seafood and pasta entrees at the comfortable restaurant. Guests can dine indoors or unwind outside on the pier with summer evening entertainment. Casual dress. **Bar:** Full bar. **Hours:** 5:30 pm-close. Closed major holidays; also Mon. **Address:** 1 Pier Rd **Location:** 1 mi n from Jekyll Island Bridge. **Parking:** on-site. **Cards:** DS, MC, VI.

SAYDEE'S RESTAURANT & MARTINI BAR — **Phone:** 912/635-3588

Steak & Seafood
$6-$18

Specializing in steaks and fresh local seafood, the popular restaurant features daily early-bird specials and provides cool jazz background music. After dinner, guests can enjoy live entertainment in the Riptides lounge. Casual dress. **Bar:** Full bar. **Reservations:** accepted. **Hours:** 11 am-2 & 5-9 pm, Fri & Sat-10 pm. Closed: 1/1, 12/24, 12/25; also Sun. **Address:** 1175 N Beachview Dr **Location:** Jct Ben Fortson Pkwy (SR 520)/Beachview Dr, 4 mi n; in Villas by the Sea. **Parking:** on-site. **Cards:** AX, MC, VI.

CALL

ZACHRY'S SEAFOOD RESTAURANT — **Phone:** 912/635-3128

Seafood
$6-$18

At the end of a small strip mall, the casual restaurant presents a menu of mostly fresh local seafood but with a few selections of steak and chicken. Desserts are homemade. The staff provides informal service. Casual dress. **Bar:** Beer & wine. **Hours:** 11 am-9 pm, Fri & Sat-10 pm; to 8 pm, Fri & Sat-9 pm in winter. Closed major holidays; also 2 weeks before Christmas. **Address:** 44 Beachview Dr **Location:** Just n of jct Ben Fortson Pkwy (SR 520)/Beachview Dr. **Parking:** on-site. **Cards:** DS, MC, VI.

ST. SIMONS ISLAND

WHERE TO STAY

BEST WESTERN ISLAND INN *Book great rates at AAA.com* — **Phone:** (912)638-7805

SAVE

Hotel
$89-$159 All Year

Address: 301 Main St **Location:** Jct Demere Rd and Main St, just n; in Plantation Village. **Facility:** 61 units. 50 one-bedroom standard units. 11 one-bedroom suites. 2 stories (no elevator), exterior corridors. **Parking:** on-site. **Terms:** 3 night minimum stay - seasonal and/or weekends, cancellation fee imposed. **Amenities:** high-speed Internet, voice mail, irons, hair dryers. **Pool(s):** heated outdoor. **Leisure Activities:** whirlpool. **Guest Services:** wireless Internet. **Business Services:** meeting rooms. **Cards:** AX, DS, MC, VI.

  / SOME UNITS  

AAA Benefit: Members save up to 20%, plus 10% bonus points with rewards program.

HAMPTON INN *Book great rates at AAA.com* — **Phone:** (912)634-2204

Hotel
$129-$159 2/2-11/30
$119-$149 12/1-2/1

Address: 2204 Demere Rd **Location:** Jct Frederica and Demere rds, just w. **Facility:** 79 one-bedroom standard units, some with whirlpools. 3 stories, interior corridors. *Bath:* combo or shower only. **Parking:** on-site. **Amenities:** dual phone lines, voice mail, irons, hair dryers. **Pool(s):** outdoor. **Leisure Activities:** whirlpool. **Guest Services:** valet and coin laundry, wireless Internet. **Business Services:** meeting rooms, PC. **Cards:** AX, DC, DS, MC, VI.

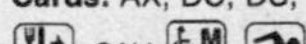
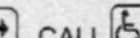 CALL  FEE   / SOME UNITS

AAA Benefit: Members save up to 10% everyday!

HOLIDAY INN EXPRESS *Book at AAA.com* — **Phone:** 912/634-2175

Hotel
Rates not provided

Address: 299 Main St **Location:** Jct Demere Rd and Main St, just n; in Plantation Village. **Facility:** Smoke free premises. 60 one-bedroom standard units. 2 stories (no elevator), interior corridors. **Parking:** on-site. **Amenities:** voice mail, irons, hair dryers. **Pool(s):** outdoor. **Guest Services:** valet laundry, wireless Internet. **Business Services:** meeting rooms.

     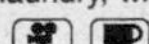

THE LODGE AT SEA ISLAND *Book great rates at AAA.com* **Phone:** (912)634-3992

Resort Hotel

$650-$850 3/1-11/30
$450-$550 12/1-2/28

Address: 100 Retreat Ave **Location:** FJ Torras Cswy, 1.6 mi se on Kings Way, just s. **Facility:** A long, tree-lined drive leads to this property; impressive interior touches include imported slate floors and mahogany accents throughout. Designated smoking area. 40 units. 38 one-bedroom standard units. 2 one-bedroom suites. 3 stories, interior corridors. **Parking:** valet. **Terms:** check-in 4 pm, 2-3 night minimum stay - seasonal and/or weekends, 30 day cancellation notice. **Amenities:** video library, DVD players, CD players, high-speed Internet, dual phone lines, voice mail, safes, honor bars, irons, hair dryers. **Dining:** 3 restaurants, entertainment. **Leisure Activities:** recreation programs, bicycles, exercise room, spa and resort privileges. *Fee:* golf-54 holes, massage. **Guest Services:** valet laundry, airport transportation (fee)-Jacksonville & Savannah/Hilton Head International airports, area transportation-within 15 mi, wireless Internet. **Business Services:** meeting rooms, business center. **Cards:** AX, DC, DS, MC, VI. **Free Special Amenities: newspaper and high-speed Internet.** Affiliated with A Preferred Hotel.

FEE

QUEEN'S COURT **Phone:** 912/638-8459

Motel
Rates not provided

Address: 437 Kings Way **Location:** Just w; corner of Frederica Rd and Kings Way; center. **Facility:** Smoke free premises. 23 units. 14 one- and 9 two-bedroom standard units, some with efficiencies. 2 stories (no elevator), exterior corridors. *Bath:* shower only. **Parking:** on-site. **Amenities:** irons. **Pool(s):** outdoor.

/ SOME UNITS

VILLAGE INN & PUB *Book at AAA.com* **Phone:** 912/634-6056

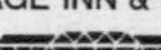

Bed & Breakfast
Rates not provided

Address: 500 Mallory St **Location:** Jct Frederica Rd and Kings Way, 0.7 mi s on Kings Way, then just n. **Facility:** Nestled among live oaks, this property was designed to complement the natural environment; all rooms feature upscale appointments. Smoke free premises. 28 one-bedroom standard units. 2 stories (no elevator), exterior corridors. *Bath:* combo or shower only. **Parking:** on-site. **Terms:** office hours 7 am-8 pm. **Amenities:** voice mail, irons, hair dryers. **Pool(s):** outdoor. **Guest Services:** valet laundry, wireless Internet. **Business Services:** meeting rooms.

WHERE TO DINE

BARBARA JEAN'S RESTAURANTS **Phone:** 912/634-6500

Regional American
$7-$20

Take a break from shopping to enjoy down-home, country cooking at this small, downtown eatery, which boasts friendly service and menu favorites like salmon, crab cakes, fried catfish, meatloaf and fruit cobbler. Casual dress. **Bar:** Full bar. **Reservations:** not accepted. **Hours:** 11 am-10 pm; Sun-Thurs to 9 pm off season. Closed: 12/25. **Address:** 214 Mallery St **Location:** Between Beachview Dr and Lord Ave; on south side of island. **Parking:** street. **Cards:** AX, DS, MC, VI.

BENNIE'S RED BARN **Phone:** 912/638-2844

American
$13-$25

A Golden Isles tradition since 1954, the restaurant builds its menu around fresh local seafood and steaks cooked over a wood fire. Servers deliver a pleasant recitation of the menu and don't mind a request to repeat it. Casual dress. **Bar:** Full bar. **Reservations:** accepted. **Hours:** 6 pm-10 pm, Fri & Sat-11 pm. Closed major holidays. **Address:** 5514 Frederica Rd **Location:** Jct Demere and Frederica rds, 3.5 mi n. **Parking:** on-site. **Cards:** AX, DS, MC, VI.

BLACKWATER GRILL **Phone:** 912/634-6333

American
$14-$24

A nautical theme weaves through the relaxed dining room, where guests sit down to low-country and Cajun dishes. Servers are friendly and casual. Casual dress. **Bar:** Full bar. **Reservations:** accepted. **Hours:** 5:30 pm-9 pm, Fri & Sat-10 pm. Closed: 1/1, 11/26, 12/24, 12/25. **Address:** 260 Redfern Village **Location:** Jct Demere and Fredrica rds, just n. **Parking:** on-site. **Cards:** AX, DS, MC, VI.

BONEFISH GRILL **Phone:** 912/634-0246

Seafood
$13-$20

Fish is the house specialty, and the menu and nightly specials offer a variety of choices. Well-prepared food is cooked to perfection. Service is casual in nature, and the staff is skilled and attentive. Dressy casual. **Bar:** Full bar. **Reservations:** accepted. **Hours:** 4 pm-close. Closed: 11/26, 12/25. **Address:** 202 Retreat Village, #3 **Location:** Jct Demere and Fredrica rds, just s. **Parking:** on-site. **Cards:** AX, DC, DS, MC, VI.

CALL

CRABDADDY'S RESTAURANT **Phone:** 912/634-1120

Seafood
$18-$26

Come enjoy dining in a restaurant with a nautical theme. Seafood and fish are available grilled, blackened, steamed or sauteed. There are a variety of pasta-inspired dishes available as well. Casual dress. **Bar:** Full bar. **Reservations:** accepted. **Hours:** 5 pm-10 pm, Fri & Sat-10:30 pm. Closed: 11/26, 12/25. **Address:** 1217 Ocean Blvd **Location:** Just s of jct CR 226 and Ocean Blvd. **Parking:** on-site. **Cards:** AX, DS, MC, VI.

DELANEY'S BISTRO **Phone:** 912/638-1330

American
$8-$27

Service is casual and informal at this pleasant, contemporary bistro located in a small business center. Seafood, duck, chicken, veal, beef and lamb selections are carefully prepared to ensure a flavorful, palate-pleasing experience. Casual dress. **Bar:** Full bar. **Reservations:** suggested. **Hours:** 11 am-2 & 6-10 pm. Closed major holidays; also Sun & Mon. **Address:** 3415 Frederica Rd **Location:** Jct Frederica and Demere rds, 3 mi n. **Parking:** on-site. **Cards:** AX, DC, DS, MC, VI.

THE FREDERICA HOUSE
Steak & Seafood
$10-$30

Phone: 912/638-6789
Guests find a bustling atmosphere at the cozy, family dining establishment. Taking pride in its fresh seafood selections, the restaurant has crab soup with a thick, white cream broth. The rustic setting attracts locals and tourists alike. Casual dress. **Bar:** Full bar. **Reservations:** suggested. **Hours:** 5:30 pm-9:30 pm, Fri & Sat-10 pm. Closed major holidays; also 12/24 & Super Bowl Sun. **Address:** 3611 Frederica Rd **Location:** Jct Demere and Frederica rds, 2.3 mi n. **Parking:** on-site. **Cards:** AX, DS, MC, VI.

SEA ISLAND

WHERE TO STAY

The following lodging was either not evaluated or did not meet AAA rating requirements but is listed for your information only.

THE CLOISTER
fyi

Phone: 912/638-3611
Not evaluated. **Address:** 100 Cloister Dr **Location:** Just over Sea Island Bridge Cswy. Facilities, services, and decor characterize an upscale property.

Jekyll Island / Georgia Department of Economic Development

This ends listings for the Golden Isles.
The following page resumes the alphabetical listings of cities in Georgia.

GREENSBORO pop. 3,238

WHERE TO STAY

THE RITZ-CARLTON LODGE, REYNOLDS PLANTATION Book at AAA.com

Phone: (706)467-0600

Resort Hotel

$219-$559 All Year

Address: One Lk Oconee Tr **Location:** I-20, exit 130, 7.2 mi sw on SR 44 (Old Eatonton Rd), 1.5 mi e on Linger Longer Rd, then 2 mi ne. **Facility:** Charming guest rooms are elegant and comfortable; set on 35 acres overlooking Lake Oconee. Smoke free premises. 251 units. 217 one-bedroom standard units. 22 one-bedroom suites. 12 cottages. 5 stories, interior/exterior corridors. *Bath:* combo or shower only. **Parking:** on-site (fee) and valet. **Terms:** cancellation fee imposed. **Amenities:** video library, CD players, dual phone lines, voice mail, safes, honor bars, irons, hair dryers. *Fee:* video games, high-speed Internet. *Some:* DVD players (fee). **Dining:** Georgia's, Linger Longer Bar & Grill, see separate listings. **Pool(s):** heated outdoor, heated indoor. **Leisure Activities:** saunas, whirlpools, steamrooms, limited beach access, rental canoes, boat dock, fishing, recreation programs, rental bicycles, hiking trails, jogging, playground, spa, horseshoes. *Fee:* paddleboats, charter fishing, golf-99 holes, 9 tennis courts (2 lighted), horseback riding. **Guest Services:** valet laundry, area transportation, beauty salon, wireless Internet. **Business Services:** conference facilities, business center. **Cards:** AX, DC, DS, MC, VI.

ASK FEE CALL

/ SOME UNITS FEE

WHERE TO DINE

GEORGIA'S

Phone: 706/467-0600

Regional American

$12-$40

A taste of the New South. This casually elegant dining room specializes in Southern cuisine with a gourmet flair, incorporating such regional ingredients as pecans, peaches and Vidalia onions. Dressy casual. **Bar:** Full bar. **Reservations:** suggested. **Hours:** 6:30 am-11 & 5:30-10 pm. **Address:** One Lake Oconee Tr **Location:** I-20, exit 130, 7.2 mi sw on SR 44 (Old Eatonton Rd), 1.5 mi e on Linger Longer Rd, then 2 mi ne; in The Ritz-Carlton Lodge, Reynolds Plantation. **Parking:** valet. **Cards:** AX, CB, DC, DS, JC, MC, VI.

CALL

LINGER LONGER BAR & GRILL

Phone: 706/467-0600

Steak & Seafood

$10-$45

The tavern-style moniker belies the casually elegant atmosphere at this clubhouse restaurant overlooking Lake Oconee. Diverse palates appreciate the many burgers, sandwiches and lighter "post-golf" entrees for lunch and the comprehensive dinner selection of steaks, chops and seafood, which can be prepared with signature sauces or in classic dishes such as steak Rossini, steak Oscar or rue Orleans. Professional servers deliver each fresh dish and eagerly ensure each guest's needs are met. Dressy casual. **Bar:** Full bar. **Reservations:** suggested. **Hours:** 11 am-3:30 & 6-10 pm. Closed: Wed. **Address:** One Lake Oconee Tr **Location:** I-20, exit 130, 7.2 mi sw on SR 44 (Old Eatonton Rd), 1.5 mi e on Linger Longer Rd, then 2 mi ne; in The Ritz-Carlton Lodge, Reynolds Plantation. **Parking:** valet. **Cards:** AX, CB, DC, DS, JC, MC, VI.

GRIFFIN pop. 23,451

WHERE TO STAY

BEST WESTERN GRIFFIN Book great rates at AAA.com

Phone: (770)227-8400

Hotel

$70-$200 All Year

Address: 1616 N Expressway **Location:** 1 mi n on US 41 and 19. **Facility:** 48 units. 46 one-bedroom standard units. 2 one-bedroom suites with whirlpools. 2 stories (no elevator), exterior corridors. **Parking:** on-site. **Terms:** 2-3 night minimum stay - weekends, 3 day cancellation notice. **Amenities:** high-speed Internet, irons, hair dryers. **Pool(s):** outdoor. **Leisure Activities:** exercise room. **Guest Services:** valet and coin laundry, wireless Internet. **Business Services:** PC, fax (fee). **Cards:** AX, CB, DC, DS, MC, VI. **Free Special Amenities: continental breakfast and high-speed Internet.**

/ SOME UNITS

AAA Benefit:

Members save up to 20%, plus 10% bonus points with rewards program.

COMFORT INN & SUITES Book at AAA.com

Phone: (770)229-6001

Hotel

$59-$199 All Year

Address: 2014 N Expressway **Location:** 2.1 mi n on US 41 and 19. **Facility:** 48 one-bedroom standard units. 2 stories, exterior corridors. **Parking:** on-site. **Terms:** 7 day cancellation notice. **Amenities:** dual phone lines, irons, hair dryers. **Pool(s):** outdoor. **Leisure Activities:** exercise room. **Guest Services:** coin laundry, wireless Internet. **Business Services:** meeting rooms, PC, fax (fee). **Cards:** AX, CB, DC, DS, MC, VI.

HAMPTON INN GRIFFIN *Book great rates at AAA.com* **Phone:** (770)229-9900

Hotel
$65-$71 All Year

Address: 2007 N Expressway **Location:** 2 mi n on US 41 and 19. **Facility:** 53 one-bedroom standard units. 2 stories, exterior corridors. *Bath:* combo or shower only. **Parking:** on-site. **Terms:** 1-30 night minimum stay, cancellation fee imposed. **Amenities:** video games, high-speed Internet, voice mail, irons, hair dryers. **Pool(s):** outdoor. **Leisure Activities:** exercise room. **Guest Services:** valet and coin laundry. **Business Services:** PC. **Cards:** AX, CB, DC, DS, MC, VI.

/ SOME UNITS

AAA Benefit:
Members save up to 10% everyday!

HOLIDAY INN EXPRESS HOTEL & SUITES *Book at AAA.com* **Phone:** (770)228-9799

Hotel
$100-$330 All Year

Address: 1900 N Expressway **Location:** 2 mi n on US 41 and 19. **Facility:** Smoke free premises. 82 units. 79 one-bedroom standard units, some with whirlpools. 3 one-bedroom suites. 2 stories, interior corridors. **Parking:** on-site. **Terms:** cancellation fee imposed. **Amenities:** high-speed Internet, dual phone lines, voice mail, safes, irons, hair dryers. **Pool(s):** heated indoor. **Leisure Activities:** sauna, whirlpool, exercise room. **Guest Services:** valet and coin laundry, wireless Internet. **Business Services:** meeting rooms, business center. **Cards:** AX, CB, DC, DS, JC, MC, VI.

ASK

IRIS INN & SUITES *Book great rates at AAA.com* **Phone:** (770)233-4747

AAA SAVE

Hotel
$70-$249 All Year

Address: 1906 N Expressway **Location:** 2 mi n on US 41 and 19. **Facility:** 43 one-bedroom standard units. 2 stories, interior corridors. **Parking:** on-site. **Amenities:** voice mail, irons, hair dryers. **Leisure Activities:** limited exercise equipment. **Guest Services:** valet and coin laundry, wireless Internet. **Business Services:** meeting rooms, business center. **Cards:** AX, DS, MC, VI.

CALL

GROVETOWN pop. 6,089

WHERE TO STAY

AMERICA'S BEST INN & SUITES *Book great rates at AAA.com* **Phone:** (706)855-9111

AAA SAVE

Hotel
$59-$399 All Year

Address: 461 Park West Dr **Location:** I-20, exit 194 (SR 383), just s. **Facility:** 64 one-bedroom standard units, some with whirlpools. 3 stories, interior corridors. *Bath:* combo or shower only. **Parking:** on-site. **Amenities:** DVD players, high-speed Internet, voice mail, irons, hair dryers. **Pool(s):** outdoor. **Leisure Activities:** limited exercise equipment. **Guest Services:** coin laundry, wireless Internet. **Business Services:** PC. **Cards:** AX, CB, DC, DS, MC, VI. **Free Special Amenities: expanded continental breakfast and high-speed Internet.**

/ SOME UNITS

BEST WESTERN EVANS HOTEL *Book great rates at AAA.com* **Phone:** (706)651-9100

AAA SAVE

Hotel
$95-$500 All Year

Address: 452 Park West Dr **Location:** I-20, exit 194 (SR 383), just s. **Facility:** 58 one-bedroom standard units, some with whirlpools. 3 stories, interior corridors. *Bath:* combo or shower only. **Parking:** on-site. **Terms:** cancellation fee imposed. **Amenities:** high-speed Internet, voice mail, irons, hair dryers. *Some:* DVD players. **Pool(s):** outdoor. **Leisure Activities:** exercise room. **Guest Services:** coin laundry, wireless Internet. **Business Services:** PC. **Cards:** AX, CB, DC, DS, MC, VI. **Free Special Amenities: full breakfast and high-speed Internet.**

/ SOME UNITS VCR

AAA Benefit:
Members save up to 20%, plus 10% bonus points with rewards program.

HAMPTON INN & SUITES AUGUSTA WEST *Book great rates at AAA.com* **Phone:** (706)860-1610

Hotel
$350 All Year

Address: 4081 Jimmie Dyess Pkwy **Location:** I-20, exit 194 (SR 383), just s. **Facility:** 83 one-bedroom standard units, some with whirlpools. 5 stories, interior corridors. *Bath:* combo or shower only. **Parking:** on-site. **Terms:** 1-30 night minimum stay, cancellation fee imposed. **Amenities:** video games (fee), high-speed Internet, dual phone lines, voice mail, safes, irons, hair dryers. **Pool(s):** heated indoor. **Leisure Activities:** whirlpool, exercise room. **Guest Services:** valet laundry, wireless Internet. **Business Services:** meeting rooms, business center. **Cards:** AX, CB, DC, DS, MC, VI.

CALL / SOME UNITS

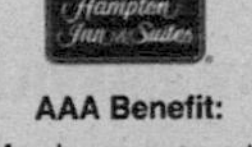

AAA Benefit:
Members save up to 10% everyday!

HOLIDAY INN AUGUSTA WEST *Book at AAA.com* **Phone:** (706)396-4600

Hotel
$130-$175 All Year

Address: 441 Park West Dr **Location:** I-20, exit 194 (SR 383), just s, then w. **Facility:** 130 units. 126 one-bedroom standard units, some with whirlpools. 4 one-bedroom suites. 5 stories, interior corridors. *Bath:* combo or shower only. **Parking:** on-site. **Amenities:** high-speed Internet, dual phone lines, voice mail, safes, irons, hair dryers. **Pool(s):** heated indoor. **Leisure Activities:** whirlpool, exercise room. **Guest Services:** valet and coin laundry, wireless Internet. **Business Services:** meeting rooms, business center. **Cards:** AX, CB, DC, DS, JC, MC, VI.

SUPER 8 MOTEL-AUGUSTA *Book at AAA.com* **Phone:** (706)396-1600

Hotel
$80-$425 All Year

Address: 456 Park West Dr **Location:** I-20, exit 194 (SR 383), just s, then w. **Facility:** 65 units. 64 one-bedroom standard units, some with whirlpools. 1 one-bedroom suite. 3 stories, interior corridors. *Bath:* combo or shower only. **Parking:** on-site. **Amenities:** high-speed Internet, voice mail, irons, hair dryers. **Pool(s):** outdoor. **Leisure Activities:** exercise room. **Guest Services:** coin laundry, area transportation, wireless Internet. **Business Services:** business center. **Cards:** AX, CB, DC, DS, JC, MC, VI.

A$K / SOME UNITS FEE

HAMILTON pop. 307

WHERE TO STAY

MAGNOLIA HALL BED & BREAKFAST **Phone:** 706/628-4566

Historic Bed & Breakfast
$115-$135 All Year

Address: 127 Barnes Mill Rd **Location:** Jct US 27/SR 1/116, just e; behind courthouse; center. **Facility:** Well-appointed rooms with upgraded amenities are featured at this service-oriented B&B; convenient to Callaway Gardens. Smoke free premises. 5 units. 3 one-bedroom standard units. 2 one-bedroom suites. 2 stories (no elevator), interior corridors. *Bath:* shower only. **Parking:** on-site. **Terms:** check-in 4 pm, 4 day cancellation notice. **Amenities:** video library, irons, hair dryers. **Leisure Activities:** hiking trails. **Guest Services:** wireless Internet. **Cards:** AX, DS, MC, VI.

A$K VCR

HAMPTON pop. 3,857

WHERE TO STAY

COUNTRY HEARTH INN *Book at AAA.com* **Phone:** (770)707-1477

Hotel
$62-$65 All Year

Address: 1078 Bear Creek Blvd **Location:** 1 mi w of center of town; at US 41 and 19. Located opposite the Atlanta Motor Speedway. **Facility:** 40 one-bedroom standard units, some with whirlpools. 2 stories (no elevator), interior corridors. *Bath:* combo or shower only. **Parking:** on-site. **Amenities:** hair dryers. **Guest Services:** wireless Internet. **Cards:** AX, DS, MC, VI.

A$K CALL / SOME UNITS

HAPEVILLE —*See Atlanta p. 394.*

HARTWELL pop. 4,188

WHERE TO STAY

BEST WESTERN LAKE HARTWELL INN & SUITES *Book great rates at AAA.com* **Phone:** (706)376-4700

AAA SAVE

Hotel
$80 All Year

Address: 1357 E Franklin St **Location:** I-85, exit 177, 2 mi on US 29 E. **Facility:** 40 one-bedroom standard units, some with whirlpools. 2 stories (no elevator), interior corridors. **Parking:** on-site. **Amenities:** video library, high-speed Internet, irons, hair dryers. *Some:* DVD players. **Pool(s):** outdoor. **Guest Services:** wireless Internet. **Business Services:** PC, fax. **Cards:** AX, DS, MC, VI.

/ SOME UNITS FEE

Best Western
AAA Benefit:
Members save up to 20%, plus 10% bonus points with rewards program.

THE SKELTON HOUSE **Phone:** 706/376-7969

Historic Bed & Breakfast
$100-$135 All Year

Address: 97 Benson St **Location:** Just se of jct US 29/8 and SR 77 (Benson St). **Facility:** Dating from 1896, this Victorian home offers appealing individually decorated guest rooms as well as pleasant porches overlooking the grounds. Smoke free premises. 7 one-bedroom standard units, some with whirlpools. 2 stories (no elevator), interior/exterior corridors. *Bath:* combo or shower only. **Parking:** on-site. **Terms:** 3 day cancellation notice-fee imposed. **Amenities:** hair dryers. *Some:* DVD players, irons. **Guest Services:** wireless Internet. **Cards:** AX, DC, DS, MC, VI.

A$K / SOME UNITS

HAWKINSVILLE pop. 3,280

WHERE TO STAY

BEST WESTERN HAWKINSVILLE INN & SUITES *Book great rates at AAA.com* **Phone:** (478)783-1300

AAA SAVE

Hotel
$70-$75 All Year

Address: 100 Buchan Dr (Hwy 341 Bypass) **Location:** 0.5 mi w on Commerce St, then just n on US 129/341. **Facility:** 26 one-bedroom standard units. 2 stories (no elevator), exterior corridors. *Bath:* combo or shower only. **Parking:** on-site. **Amenities:** high-speed Internet, irons, hair dryers. **Pool(s):** outdoor. **Guest Services:** coin laundry. **Cards:** AX, DC, DS, MC, VI. **Free Special Amenities: continental breakfast and high-speed Internet.**

/ SOME UNITS

AAA Benefit:
Members save up to 20%, plus 10% bonus points with rewards program.

BUDGET INN Book great rates at AAA.com **Phone:** (478)783-2002

Motel
$55-$65 3/1-11/30
$53-$60 12/1-2/28

Address: 509 Broad St **Location:** Downtown. **Facility:** 20 one-bedroom standard units, some with whirlpools. 1 story, exterior corridors. **Parking:** on-site. **Terms:** 3 night minimum stay, 3 day cancellation notice-fee imposed. **Amenities:** hair dryers. **Pool(s):** outdoor. **Guest Services:** coin laundry, wireless Internet. **Business Services:** fax (fee). **Cards:** AX, DS, MC, VI. **Free Special Amenities: local telephone calls and high-speed Internet.**

/ SOME UNITS

WHERE TO DINE

THE STEAK HOUSE **Phone:** 478/892-3383

Steak & Seafood
$5-$16

Specialties at the family-run, family-friendly restaurant include charbroiled flavored steaks, a weekend seafood buffet and fresh homemade desserts. Casual dress. **Reservations:** accepted. **Hours:** 11 am-9 pm, Fri & Sat-10 pm, Sun-2:30 pm. Closed major holidays. **Address:** 101 Buchan Dr (Hwy 341 Bypass) **Location:** 0.5 mi w of downtown on Commerce St, just n on US 129/341. **Parking:** on-site. **Cards:** AX, DS, MC, VI.

CALL

HAZLEHURST pop. 3,787

WHERE TO STAY

BEST WESTERN HAZLEHURST Book great rates at AAA.com **Phone:** (912)375-3400

Motel
$59 All Year

Address: 143 Martin Luther King Dr **Location:** Just n of center on US 23/341. **Facility:** 44 one-bedroom standard units, some with whirlpools. 1 story, exterior corridors. **Parking:** on-site. **Amenities:** irons, hair dryers. *Some:* high-speed Internet. **Pool(s):** outdoor. **Leisure Activities:** exercise room. **Guest Services:** coin laundry, wireless Internet. **Business Services:** PC. **Cards:** AX, CB, DC, DS, MC, VI. **Free Special Amenities: continental breakfast and high-speed Internet.**

/ SOME UNITS

AAA Benefit:
Members save up to 20%, plus 10% bonus points with rewards program.

MCDONALD'S LODGE Book at AAA.com **Phone:** (912)379-1770

Hotel
$52 All Year

Address: 160 W Coffee St **Location:** Just n of center on US 23/341. **Facility:** 41 one-bedroom standard units, some with whirlpools. 2 stories (no elevator), interior corridors. *Bath:* combo or shower only. **Parking:** on-site, winter plug-ins. **Terms:** 3 day cancellation notice. **Amenities:** high-speed Internet, hair dryers. **Pool(s):** outdoor. **Guest Services:** wireless Internet. **Business Services:** meeting rooms, PC. **Cards:** AX, DS, MC, VI.

ASK / SOME UNITS

HELEN pop. 430

WHERE TO STAY

BEST WESTERN RIVERPARK INN & CONFERENCE CENTER ALPINE HELEN Book great rates at AAA.com **Phone:** (706)878-2111

Hotel
$45-$259 All Year

Address: 8220 S Main St **Location:** 0.5 mi s on SR 17 and 75. **Facility:** 65 one-bedroom standard units, some with whirlpools. 2 stories (no elevator), interior/exterior corridors. **Parking:** on-site. **Amenities:** high-speed Internet, irons, hair dryers. **Pool(s):** outdoor. **Guest Services:** wireless Internet. **Business Services:** meeting rooms, PC, fax. **Cards:** AX, DC, DS, MC, VI. **Free Special Amenities: expanded continental breakfast and high-speed Internet.** *(See color ad p 484)*

/ SOME UNITS

AAA Benefit:
Members save up to 20%, plus 10% bonus points with rewards program.

CHALET KRISTY MOTEL & CABINS **Phone:** 706/878-2155

Motel
$55-$139 5/21-11/30
$45-$69 12/1-5/20

Address: 134 River St **Location:** Just w off Main St. **Facility:** 34 one-bedroom standard units, some with kitchens and/or whirlpools. 2 stories (no elevator), exterior corridors. **Parking:** on-site. **Terms:** 3 day cancellation notice-fee imposed. **Amenities:** high-speed Internet, irons, hair dryers. **Leisure Activities:** fishing. **Guest Services:** wireless Internet. **Business Services:** fax (fee). **Cards:** AX, DS, MC, VI.

COMFORT INN Book great rates at AAA.com

Phone: (706)878-8000

Hotel

$60-$180 4/2-11/30
$50-$70 12/1-4/1

Address: 101 Edelweiss Strasse **Location:** 1 mi s on SR 75. Located in a semi-rural area. **Facility:** 57 one-bedroom standard units, some with whirlpools. 2 stories (no elevator), exterior corridors. **Parking:** on-site. **Amenities:** high-speed Internet, irons, hair dryers. **Pool(s):** outdoor. **Guest Services:** wireless Internet. **Business Services:** meeting rooms, fax (fee). **Cards:** AX, DS, MC, VI.

/ SOME UNITS

COUNTRY INN & SUITES BY CARLSON Book great rates at AAA.com

Phone: (706)878-9000

Hotel

$59-$179 All Year

Address: 877 Edelweiss Strasse **Location:** 0.4 mi s on SR 75 and 17. **Facility:** 63 units. 47 one-bedroom standard units, some with whirlpools. 16 one-bedroom suites. 3 stories, interior corridors. **Parking:** on-site. **Terms:** 2-3 night minimum stay - seasonal and/or weekends. **Amenities:** high-speed Internet, voice mail, irons, hair dryers. **Pool(s):** heated indoor. **Leisure Activities:** whirlpool, limited exercise equipment. **Guest Services:** coin laundry, wireless Internet. **Business Services:** meeting rooms, fax (fee). **Cards:** AX, CB, DC, DS, JC, MC, VI. **Free Special Amenities: expanded continental breakfast and high-speed Internet.**

CALL

HAMPTON INN Book great rates at AAA.com

Phone: (706)878-3310

Hotel

$69-$119 All Year

Address: 147 Unicoi St **Location:** Jct Spring St, just e of N Main St. **Facility:** 67 units. 55 one-bedroom standard units, some with whirlpools. 12 one-bedroom suites with whirlpools. 3 stories, interior corridors. **Parking:** on-site, winter plug-ins. **Terms:** check-in 4 pm, 1-30 night minimum stay, cancellation fee imposed. **Amenities:** video games (fee), high-speed Internet, dual phone lines, voice mail, irons, hair dryers. **Pool(s):** outdoor. **Leisure Activities:** limited exercise equipment. **Guest Services:** coin laundry, wireless Internet. **Business Services:** meeting rooms, fax (fee). **Cards:** AX, CB, DC, DS, MC, VI.

/ SOME UNITS

AAA Benefit:
Members save up to 10% everyday!

THE HELENDORF RIVER INN & CONFERENCE CENTER

Phone: (706)878-2271

Hotel

$64-$159 5/22-11/30
$34-$109 12/1-5/21

Address: 33 Munichstrasse **Location:** SR 17 and 75; center. **Facility:** 98 units. 95 one-bedroom standard units, some with kitchens (no utensils) and/or whirlpools. 3 one-bedroom suites with whirlpools. 2-3 stories, exterior corridors. **Parking:** on-site. **Terms:** 2 night minimum stay - seasonal and/or weekends, 10 day cancellation notice. **Amenities:** irons, hair dryers. *Some:* high-speed Internet. **Pool(s):** heated indoor. **Leisure Activities:** fishing. **Guest Services:** coin laundry, wireless Internet. **Business Services:** meeting rooms, fax (fee). **Cards:** MC, VI.

/ SOME UNITS FEE

▼ *See AAA listing p 483* ▼

KOUNTRY PEDDLER TANGLEWOOD RESORT CABINS — Phone: 706/878-3286

Vacation Rental Cabin
$99-$169 5/21-11/30
$89-$149 12/1-5/20

Address: 3387 Hwy 356 **Location:** 1 mi n on SR 75, then 3 mi ne. Located in a rural area. **Facility:** The property offers individual cabins secluded in a wooded, mountainous area. 38 cabins. 1-2 stories, exterior corridors. **Parking:** on-site. **Terms:** check-in 4 pm, 2 night minimum stay - seasonal and/or weekends, 14 day cancellation notice-fee imposed. **Amenities:** video library (fee), DVD players, irons. *Some:* CD players, hair dryers. **Leisure Activities:** playground, horseshoes, volleyball. *Fee:* game room. **Guest Services:** wireless Internet. **Business Services:** meeting rooms, fax. **Cards:** MC, VI.

ASK VCR / SOME UNITS FEE

PREMIER VACATION RENTALS — Phone: 706/348-8323

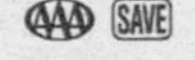

Vacation Rental Cabin
$99-$495 All Year

Address: 5156 Helen Hwy **Location:** 3.5 mi s on SR 75. **Facility:** You can rent your choice of a large and luxurious home or a smaller abode, and all are situated in the mountains of north Georgia. 65 units. 21 houses and 44 cabins. 1-4 stories (no elevator), exterior corridors. **Parking:** on-site. **Terms:** 2-4 night minimum stay, 14 day cancellation notice-fee imposed. **Amenities:** DVD players, CD players, high-speed Internet, irons. *Some:* video games (fee). **Leisure Activities:** pool access, golf & tennis privileges in some units. **Business Services:** meeting rooms. **Cards:** DS, MC, VI. **Free Special Amenities: local telephone calls and early check-in/late check-out.**

/ SOME UNITS FEE VCR

QUALITY INN & SUITES *Book at AAA.com* — Phone: (706)878-2268

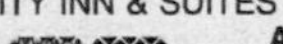

Motel
$59-$209 5/24-11/30
$49-$109 12/1-5/23

Address: 15 Yonah St **Location:** Just w of Mack St. **Facility:** 46 units. 38 one-bedroom standard units. 8 cabins. 1-2 stories (no elevator), exterior corridors. **Parking:** on-site. **Terms:** 3 day cancellation notice. **Amenities:** high-speed Internet, irons, hair dryers. **Pool(s):** outdoor. **Guest Services:** wireless Internet. **Business Services:** meeting rooms, PC, fax (fee). **Cards:** AX, DS, MC, VI.

/ SOME UNITS FEE

RAMADA LIMITED *Book great rates at AAA.com* — Phone: (706)878-1451

Hotel
$50-$130 All Year

Address: 11 Edelweiss St **Location:** 1 mi s on SR 75. **Facility:** 54 one-bedroom standard units, some with whirlpools. 2 stories (no elevator), exterior corridors. **Parking:** on-site. **Amenities:** high-speed Internet, voice mail, irons, hair dryers. **Pool(s):** heated indoor. **Leisure Activities:** whirlpool. **Guest Services:** wireless Internet. **Business Services:** meeting rooms, fax (fee). **Cards:** AX, DS, MC, VI.

/ SOME UNITS

SUPER 8 MOTEL *Book great rates at AAA.com* — Phone: (706)878-2191

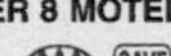

Hotel
$35-$245 All Year

Address: 8396 S Main St **Location:** 0.3 mi s on SR 17 and 75. **Facility:** 61 one-bedroom standard units, some with whirlpools. 2 stories (no elevator), exterior corridors. **Parking:** on-site. **Amenities:** high-speed Internet, hair dryers. **Pool(s):** heated indoor/outdoor. **Guest Services:** wireless Internet. **Business Services:** fax (fee). **Cards:** AX, DS, MC, VI. **Free Special Amenities: continental breakfast and high-speed Internet.** *(See color ad below)*

/ SOME UNITS

▼ See AAA listing above ▼

The following lodgings were either not evaluated or did not meet AAA rating requirements but are listed for your information only.

INNSBRUCK IGLS GOLF VILLAS **Phone:** 706/878-2400

fyi

Not evaluated. **Address:** 98 Schwarzwald Strasse. Facilities, services, and decor characterize a mid-scale property.

LORELY **Phone:** 706/878-2238

fyi

Not evaluated. **Address:** 387 Brucken St. Facilities, services, and decor characterize a mid-scale property.

WHERE TO DINE

CAFE INTERNATIONAL **Phone:** 706/878-3102

Continental
$4-$15

A nice selection of schnitzels, cheeses and side dishes, as well as sumptuous desserts, await you at this cafe on the river. Outdoor dining is popular at this scenic spot. Casual dress. **Bar:** Beer & wine. **Hours:** 11 am-8:45 pm; hours vary in winter. Closed: 1/1, 11/26, 12/25; also for dinner 11/10-4/15. **Address:** 8546 Main St **Location:** Downtown. **Parking:** on-site. **Cards:** AX, CB, DC, DS, JC, MC, VI.

HANS RESTAURANT AND LOUNGE **Phone:** 706/878-2312

German
$2-$20

Among offerings at the downtown eatery are prime rib, chicken, seafood and German specialties. Patrons can dine both inside and out. Casual dress. **Bar:** Full bar. **Hours:** 11 am-9 pm, Fri & Sat-10 pm. Closed major holidays. **Address:** 8735 N Main St **Location:** Downtown. **Parking:** on-site. **Cards:** MC, VI.

HOFBRAU RIVERFRONT RESTAURANT **Phone:** 706/878-2248

Continental
$4-$32

In the picturesque Bavarian-style village of Helen, this eclectic restaurant combines French, Italian, German and American cuisines. Modeled after an elegant German guest house, it has a river garden and large windows that afford a lovely mountain view. Casual dress. **Bar:** Full bar. **Reservations:** suggested. **Hours:** 5 pm-10 pm. Closed: 12/25. **Address:** 9001 Main St **Location:** 0.3 mi n on SR 75. **Parking:** on-site. **Cards:** AX, CB, DC, DS, JC, MC, VI.

LA CABANA **Phone:** 706/878-3456

Tex-Mex
$4-$15

Guests can wash down chips and salsa and traditional Tex-Mex with tasty margaritas. Lunch specials appeal to the midday crowd. Casual dress. **Bar:** Full bar. **Hours:** 11 am-10 pm. Closed major holidays. **Address:** 8160 S Main St, Bldg A-5 & A-5B **Location:** 0.6 mi s on SR 17 and 75. **Parking:** on-site. **Cards:** AX, DS, MC, VI.

CALL M

LYNN & JULIE'S COUNTRY DINER **Phone:** 706/878-7738

American
$5-$7

Home-cooked food exemplifies what guests find at this "meat-and-three" type eatery. Huge hamburgers are a specialty. Casual dress. **Hours:** 8 am-2 pm, Sun-noon. Closed major holidays. **Address:** 8988 N Main St **Location:** 0.3 mi n on SR 75. **Parking:** on-site. **Cards:** MC, VI.

NACOOCHEE GRILL **Phone:** 706/878-8020

American
$5-$29

Fresh ingredients and well-prepared regional favorites are strong points at the restaurant, which features such dishes as trout. Guests can bring their own bottle. Casual dress. **Bar:** Wine only. **Reservations:** accepted. **Hours:** 11:30 am-9 pm, Fri & Sat-10 pm, Sun 11 am-9 pm. Closed: 1/1, 11/26, 12/25. **Address:** 7277 S Main St **Location:** 1.3 mi s on SR 75 and 17. **Parking:** on-site. **Cards:** AX, CB, DS, MC, VI.

PAUL'S STEAKHOUSE & LOUNGE **Phone:** 706/878-2468

Steak
$14-$24

Paul's Steakhouse pays tribute to country music with photos of its stars—and of Elvis—and those kinds of songs playing in the dining rooms and lounge. Guests can look out over the Chattahoochee River and the downtown area while feasting on seafood platters and prime rib. Casual dress. **Bar:** Full bar. **Hours:** 4 pm-10 pm, Fri & Sat-11 pm. Closed: 11/26, 12/25. **Address:** 8537 S Main St **Location:** Downtown; by river. **Parking:** on-site. **Cards:** AX, DS, MC, VI.

TANGLEWOOD RESTAURANT **Phone:** 706/878-1044

American
$5-$17

Absorb the peaceful and scenic mountain view while dining on fine, country cooking. The lovely ponderosa pine interior with comfortable seating for the entire family makes the meal just like home. For dessert, try the fresh homemade cobbler. Casual dress. **Hours:** 4:30 pm-8:30 pm, Sat 8 am-8 pm, Sun 8 am-3 pm; hours vary in winter. Closed major holidays; also Mon. **Address:** Hwy 356 **Location:** 1 mi n on SR 75, 3 mi ne. **Parking:** on-site. **Cards:** MC, VI.

HIAWASSEE pop. 808

WHERE TO STAY

ENOTA B & B, CABINS & CONFERENCE LODGE **Phone:** 706/896-9966

Cabin
$80-$165 All Year

Address: 1000 Hwy 180 **Location:** E on US 76 to SR 75/17, 6 mi s to SR 180, then 3 mi w. **Facility:** 52 units. 37 one-bedroom standard units. 15 cabins. 1 story, exterior corridors. *Bath:* some shared or private, combo or shower only. **Parking:** on-site. **Terms:** check-in 4 pm, 2-4 night minimum stay. **Amenities:** video library (fee), high-speed Internet. *Some:* DVD players. **Leisure Activities:** whirlpool, limited beach access, recreation programs in summer, hiking trails, playground, horseshoes, volleyball, game room. *Fee:* fishing, massage. **Guest Services:** coin laundry, wireless Internet. **Business Services:** meeting rooms, PC, fax. **Cards:** AX, MC, VI.

HOLIDAY INN EXPRESS HOTEL & SUITES *Book at AAA.com* **Phone:** (706)896-8884

Hotel
$79-$170 All Year

Address: 300 Big Sky Dr **Location:** On US 76; center. **Facility:** 74 one-bedroom standard units, some with whirlpools. 3 stories, interior corridors. **Parking:** on-site. **Terms:** cancellation fee imposed. **Amenities:** high-speed Internet, dual phone lines, voice mail, irons, hair dryers. **Pool(s):** heated indoor. **Leisure Activities:** whirlpool, bicycles, limited exercise equipment. **Guest Services:** valet and coin laundry, wireless Internet. **Business Services:** meeting rooms, PC, fax (fee). **Cards:** AX, DC, DS, MC, VI.

ASK CALL / SOME UNITS

RAMADA AT LAKE CHATUGE LODGE *Book at AAA.com* **Phone:** (706)896-5253

Hotel
$89-$139 5/1-11/30
$69-$109 12/1-4/30

Address: 653 US Hwy 76 **Location:** 1 mi w. Located adjacent to the fairgrounds. **Facility:** 103 units. 99 one-bedroom standard units, some with whirlpools. 4 two-bedroom suites. 3 stories, interior corridors. **Parking:** on-site. **Amenities:** high-speed Internet, voice mail, irons, hair dryers. **Leisure Activities:** exercise room. **Guest Services:** coin laundry, wireless Internet. **Business Services:** meeting rooms, PC, fax (fee). **Cards:** AX, DS, MC, VI.

ASK CALL / SOME UNITS FEE FEE

THE RIDGES RESORT & CLUB ON LAKE CHATUGE *Book great rates at AAA.com* **Phone:** 706/896-2262

AAA SAVE

Resort Hotel
Rates not provided

Address: 3499 US Hwy 76 W **Location:** US 76, 3 mi w. **Facility:** Balconies, many with lake views, are included in all of the upscale, country units. Smoke free premises. 66 one-bedroom standard units, some with whirlpools. 2 stories, interior corridors. **Parking:** on-site. **Terms:** check-in 4 pm. **Amenities:** high-speed Internet, dual phone lines, voice mail, irons, hair dryers. *Some:* honor bars. **Dining:** Hiawassee Grill, see separate listing. **Pool(s):** outdoor. **Leisure Activities:** whirlpools, rental boats, rental canoes, rental paddleboats, rental sailboats, marina, fishing, golf privileges, 2 lighted tennis courts, recreation programs, amusement park, cinema, rental bicycles, hiking trails, jogging, playground, exercise room, spa, horseshoes, shuffleboard, volleyball. *Fee:* charter fishing, personal watercraft, houseboats, pontoons, game room. **Guest Services:** valet laundry, wireless Internet. **Business Services:** conference facilities, business center.

/ SOME UNITS

WHERE TO DINE

HIAWASSEE GRILL **Phone:** 706/896-4141

Continental
$13-$25

In a resort area on a marina, the upbeat, family-oriented restaurant treats guests to striking lake and mountain views, in addition to sports and entertainment. The nautically themed menu lines up some fun and interesting choices. Casual dress. **Bar:** Full bar. **Reservations:** suggested, weekends. **Hours:** 7-10 am, 11-2 & 5-9 pm, Fri & Sat-10 pm; Sunday brunch 11 am-2:30 pm. **Address:** Hwy 76 W **Location:** US 76, 3 mi w; in The Ridges Resort & Club on Lake Chatuge. **Parking:** on-site. **Cards:** AX, DS, MC, VI.

HINESVILLE pop. 30,392

WHERE TO STAY

BEST WESTERN FT. STEWART INN & SUITES *Book great rates at AAA.com* **Phone:** (912)408-4444

AAA SAVE

Hotel
$70-$110 All Year

Address: 773 Frank Cochran Dr **Location:** Jct SR 119/196, 1 mi sw on SR 196, then just nw. **Facility:** 52 one-bedroom standard units, some with whirlpools. 2 stories, interior corridors. *Bath:* combo or shower only. **Parking:** on-site. **Amenities:** irons, hair dryers. *Some:* high-speed Internet. **Pool(s):** outdoor. **Guest Services:** coin laundry, wireless Internet. **Business Services:** PC. **Cards:** AX, CB, DC, DS, JC, MC, VI. **Free Special Amenities: expanded continental breakfast and high-speed Internet.**

CALL / SOME UNITS FEE

AAA Benefit:
Members save up to 20%, plus 10% bonus points with rewards program.

COUNTRY INN & SUITES BY CARLSON *Book at AAA.com* **Phone:** 912/877-7777

Hotel
Rates not provided

Address: 742 General Stewart Way **Location:** Jct US 84 and SR 38C. **Facility:** 65 units. 63 one-bedroom standard units, some with efficiencies (no utensils) and/or whirlpools. 2 one-bedroom suites with whirlpools. 3 stories, interior corridors. *Bath:* combo or shower only. **Parking:** on-site. **Amenities:** high-speed Internet, dual phone lines, voice mail, safes, irons, hair dryers. **Pool(s):** outdoor. **Leisure Activities:** sauna, whirlpool, exercise room. **Guest Services:** coin laundry, wireless Internet. **Business Services:** meeting rooms, business center.

CALL / SOME UNITS

HAMPTON INN *Book great rates at AAA.com* **Phone:** (912)877-4090

Hotel
$75-$85 All Year

Address: 1148 E Oglethorpe Hwy **Location:** Jct US 84 and SR 38C, just ne. **Facility:** 60 one-bedroom standard units. 3 stories, interior corridors. *Bath:* combo or shower only. **Parking:** on-site. **Terms:** 1-30 night minimum stay, cancellation fee imposed. **Amenities:** high-speed Internet, dual phone lines, voice mail, irons, hair dryers. **Pool(s):** outdoor. **Leisure Activities:** exercise room. **Guest Services:** complimentary laundry, wireless Internet. **Business Services:** meeting rooms, business center. **Cards:** AX, CB, DC, DS, MC, VI.

AAA Benefit:
Members save up to 10% everyday!

HOLIDAY INN EXPRESS HOTEL & SUITES Book at AAA.com Phone: (912)877-5611

Hotel
$90-$125 All Year

Address: 1388 E Oglethorpe Hwy **Location:** Jct US 84 and SR 38C, 0.3 mi ne. **Facility:** 86 one-bedroom standard units, some with efficiencies (no utensils) and/or whirlpools. 3 stories, interior corridors. *Bath:* combo or shower only. **Parking:** on-site. **Amenities:** high-speed Internet, voice mail, irons, hair dryers. **Pool(s):** heated indoor. **Leisure Activities:** sauna, whirlpool, exercise room. **Guest Services:** coin laundry, wireless Internet. **Business Services:** meeting rooms, business center. **Cards:** AX, CB, DC, DS, MC, VI.

ASK CALL / SOME UNITS

WHERE TO DINE

ZUM ROSENHOF Phone: 912/876-2191

German
$6-$19

It's easy to fall in love with the quaint cafe. Guests can sit at the bar with an authentic German beer or take a seat at one of the tables to nosh on a full-course meal of bratwurst, rippchen, schnitzel or other favorites prepared by the German chef/owner. Reservations are recommended. Casual dress. **Bar:** Beer & wine. **Reservations:** suggested, weekends. **Hours:** 11 am-10 pm. Closed: 12/25; also Sun. **Address:** 103 Midway Ct **Location:** Downtown; adjacent to courthouse. **Parking:** street. **Cards:** DS, MC, VI.

HIRAM pop. 1,361

WHERE TO STAY

COUNTRY INN & SUITES BY CARLSON Book at AAA.com Phone: (770)222-0456

Hotel
$75-$120 All Year

Address: 70 Enterprise Path **Location:** Jct SR 92/6 and US 278, 0.3 mi w. **Facility:** 62 units. 48 one-bedroom standard units, some with whirlpools. 14 one-bedroom suites. 3 stories, interior corridors. **Parking:** on-site. **Terms:** cancellation fee imposed. **Amenities:** high-speed Internet, voice mail, irons, hair dryers. **Pool(s):** heated indoor. **Leisure Activities:** whirlpool. **Guest Services:** valet and coin laundry, wireless Internet. **Business Services:** meeting rooms, fax (fee). **Cards:** AX, DC, DS, MC, VI.

ASK / SOME UNITS FEE

HOLIDAY INN EXPRESS HOTEL & SUITES Book at AAA.com Phone: 770/222-9494

Hotel
Rates not provided

Address: 1340 Pace Rd **Location:** Jct SR 92/6 and US 278, just w. **Facility:** 51 units. 50 one-bedroom standard units, some with kitchens and/or whirlpools. 1 one-bedroom suite. 2 stories, interior corridors. **Parking:** on-site. **Amenities:** high-speed Internet, voice mail, irons, hair dryers. **Pool(s):** outdoor. **Leisure Activities:** limited exercise equipment. **Guest Services:** valet and coin laundry, wireless Internet. **Business Services:** meeting rooms, business center.

CALL / SOME UNITS

WHERE TO DINE

FIESTA BRAVA Phone: 770/222-4410

Tex-Mex
$2-$12

Standard Tex Mex offerings include tasty quesadillas, tacos, burritos and fajitas, as well as combination dinners and vegetarian plates. Top-shelf tequila enhances the drink selection. Casual dress. **Bar:** Full bar. **Hours:** 11 am-10 pm, Fri-11 pm, Sat-11:30 am-11 pm, Sun 11:30 am-10 pm. Closed major holidays. **Address:** 45 Enterprise Path **Location:** Jct SR 92/6 and US 278, 0.3 mi w. **Parking:** on-site. **Cards:** AX, DS, MC, VI.

CALL

HOGANSVILLE pop. 2,774

WHERE TO STAY

KEY WEST INN & SUITES Phone: (706)637-9395

Motel
$60-$120 All Year

Address: 1888 E Main St **Location:** I-85, exit 28, just w. **Facility:** 44 one-bedroom standard units. 2 stories (no elevator), exterior corridors. **Parking:** on-site. **Terms:** cancellation fee imposed. **Amenities:** *Some:* irons, hair dryers. **Pool(s):** outdoor. **Guest Services:** coin laundry, wireless Internet. **Cards:** AX, DS, MC, VI.

ASK / SOME UNITS FEE

WHERE TO DINE

ROGER'S BAR-B-QUE — **Phone:** 706/637-4100

American
$3-$18

At lunch you will find good old "meat and throes," and at dinner you can feast on barbecue chicken, ribs or pork, which are all quite savory. Casual dress. **Hours:** 11 am-9 pm, Fri & Sat-10 pm. Closed: 11/26, 12/25; also Sun. **Address:** 1863 E Main St **Location:** I-85, exit 28, just w. **Parking:** on-site. **Cards:** AX, DS, MC, VI.

JACKSON pop. 3,934

WHERE TO STAY

BEST WESTERN PLANTATION INN & SUITES — **Phone:** (770)504-8811

Hotel
$79-$175 All Year

Address: 385 Macon Ave **Location:** 1 mi s on SR 23/42; center. **Facility:** 37 units. 28 one-bedroom standard units, some with whirlpools. 9 one-bedroom suites. 2 stories, interior/exterior corridors. *Bath:* combo or shower only. **Parking:** on-site. **Amenities:** high-speed Internet, irons, hair dryers. **Pool(s):** outdoor. **Guest Services:** coin laundry, wireless Internet. **Business Services:** meeting rooms, PC, fax (fee). **Cards:** AX, DS, MC, VI.

AAA Benefit:
Members save up to 20%, plus 10% bonus points with rewards program.

JASPER pop. 2,167

WHERE TO STAY

MICROTEL INN & SUITES — *Book at AAA.com* — **Phone:** (706)299-5500

Hotel
$59-$129 All Year

Address: 171 H Mullins Ct **Location:** Jct SR 515/53; 0.9 mi n. **Facility:** 70 one-bedroom standard units. 3 stories, interior corridors. **Parking:** on-site **Terms:** cancellation fee imposed. **Amenities:** high-speed Internet, voice mail. **Guest Services:** wireless Internet. **Business Services:** PC. **Cards:** AX, DC, DS, MC, VI.

ASK / SOME UNITS

SUPER 8 MOTEL — *Book at AAA.com* — **Phone:** 706/253-3297

Motel
Rates not provided

Address: 100 Whitfield Dr **Location:** Jct SR 515/53; in Lawsons Crossing. **Facility:** 44 one-bedroom standard units, some with whirlpools. 2 stories (no elevator), exterior corridors. **Parking:** on-site. **Amenities:** high-speed Internet, irons, hair dryers. **Pool(s):** outdoor. **Guest Services:** coin laundry, wireless Internet. **Business Services:** fax (fee).

CALL / SOME UNITS FEE

JEFFERSON pop. 3,825

WHERE TO STAY

COMFORT INN — *Book great rates at AAA.com* — **Phone:** (706)693-4582

Hotel
$75-$130 3/16-11/30
$65-$90 12/1-3/15

Address: 4880 US Hwy 129 N **Location:** I-85, exit 137, just e. **Facility:** 50 one-bedroom standard units, some with whirlpools. 2 stories (no elevator), interior corridors. **Parking:** on-site. **Terms:** check-in 4 pm. **Amenities:** irons, hair dryers. **Pool(s):** heated indoor. **Leisure Activities:** whirlpool, exercise room. **Guest Services:** coin laundry, wireless Internet. **Business Services:** meeting rooms. **Cards:** AX, DC, DS, JC, MC, VI. **Free Special Amenities: expanded continental breakfast and high-speed Internet.**

/ SOME UNITS

JEKYLL ISLAND —*See Golden Isles p. 475.*

JESUP pop. 9,279

WHERE TO STAY

JAMESON INN OF JESUP — *Book at AAA.com* — **Phone:** (912)427-6800

Motel
$73-$78 All Year

Address: 205 N Hwy 301 **Location:** Jct US 341, just n. **Facility:** 61 one-bedroom standard units, some with whirlpools. 2 stories (no elevator), exterior corridors. **Parking:** on-site. **Terms:** cancellation fee imposed. **Amenities:** hair dryers. *Some:* DVD players (fee), irons. **Pool(s):** outdoor. **Leisure Activities:** exercise room. **Guest Services:** wireless Internet. **Business Services:** PC. **Cards:** AX, DC, DS, MC, VI.

ASK / SOME UNITS FEE FEE VCR

WHERE TO DINE

CAPTAIN JOE'S SEAFOOD — **Phone:** 912/427-7729

Seafood
$5-$17

You'll find a friendly, nautical ambience with generous portions of fried, local seafood at this family-operated restaurant. Dip into the seafood sampler and treat yourself to a taste of everything. Don't miss the hearty corn chowder with fresh corn. Casual dress. **Reservations:** accepted. **Hours:** 11 am-9 pm, Fri & Sat-10 pm. Closed: 11/26, 12/24, 12/25. **Address:** 2686 Savannah Hwy 301 **Location:** On US 84/301, 3.3 mi n of jct US 341. **Parking:** on-site. **Cards:** AX, DS, MC, VI.

OVERPASS STEAKHOUSE — **Phone:** 912/530-6900

American
$5-$25

The family-owned and -operated steakhouse serves up a variety of cuts of beef: On the menu are rib-eyes, New York strips and filet mignon as well as chicken and ribs. All main courses come with a baked potato, french fries, coleslaw or beans. Casual dress. **Hours:** 11 am-7:45 pm, Thurs-Sat to 9:15 pm. Closed: Sun. **Address:** 123 E Pine St **Location:** 1 mi nw of jct US 301 and 341; north side of overpass. **Parking:** on-site. **Cards:** AX, DS, MC, VI.

JONESBORO —*See Atlanta p. 395.*

KENNESAW —*See Atlanta p. 395.*

KINGSLAND pop. 10,506

— WHERE TO STAY —

COUNTRY INN & SUITES BY CARLSON *Book great rates at AAA.com* — **Phone:** (912)576-1616

AAA SAVE

Hotel
$90-$100 All Year

Address: 135 The Lakes Blvd **Location:** I-95, exit 3 (SR 40), just se. **Facility:** 64 units. 54 one-bedroom standard units, some with whirlpools. 10 one-bedroom suites. 3 stories, interior corridors. *Bath:* combo or shower only. **Parking:** on-site. **Terms:** cancellation fee imposed. **Amenities:** high-speed Internet, voice mail, irons, hair dryers. **Pool(s):** heated indoor. **Leisure Activities:** whirlpool, exercise room. **Guest Services:** coin laundry, wireless Internet. **Business Services:** meeting rooms. **Cards:** AX, DC, DS, MC, VI. **Free Special Amenities: expanded continental breakfast and high-speed Internet.**

CALL / SOME UNITS

ECONO LODGE *Book at AAA.com* — **Phone:** (912)673-7336

Motel
$62 All Year

Address: 1135 E King Ave **Location:** I-95, exit 3 (SR 40), just nw. **Facility:** 52 one-bedroom standard units, some with whirlpools. 2 stories (no elevator), exterior corridors. *Bath:* combo or shower only. **Parking:** on-site. **Amenities:** hair dryers. **Pool(s):** outdoor. **Guest Services:** wireless Internet. **Cards:** AX, DS, MC, VI.

ASK CALL / SOME UNITS FEE

HAMPTON INN *Book great rates at AAA.com* — **Phone:** (912)729-1900

AAA SAVE

Hotel
$85-$90 All Year

Address: 1363 Hwy 40 E **Location:** I-95, exit 3 (SR 40), just se. **Facility:** 57 one-bedroom standard units, some with whirlpools. 2 stories, exterior corridors. *Bath:* combo or shower only. **Parking:** on-site. **Terms:** 1-30 night minimum stay, cancellation fee imposed. **Amenities:** high-speed Internet, voice mail, irons, hair dryers. **Pool(s):** outdoor. **Leisure Activities:** whirlpool. **Guest Services:** valet laundry, wireless Internet. **Cards:** AX, CB, DC, DS, MC, VI. **Free Special Amenities: high-speed Internet.**

CALL  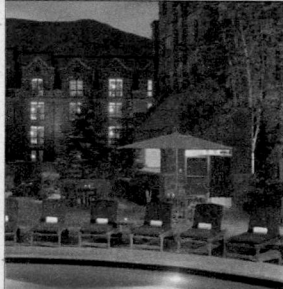   / SOME UNITS

AAA Benefit:
Members save up to 10% everyday!

HAWTHORN SUITES *Book great rates at AAA.com* — **Phone:** (912)882-4170

AAA SAVE

Extended Stay Hotel
$99-$119 All Year

Address: 1323 E King Ave **Location:** I-95, exit 3 (SR 40), just w. **Facility:** The property's contemporary, upscale decor and furnishings provide a high level of comfort and amenities for both business and leisure travelers. Smoke free premises. 66 one-bedroom suites with efficiencies, some with whirlpools. 3 stories, interior corridors. *Bath:* combo or shower only. **Parking:** on-site. **Amenities:** DVD players, CD players, high-speed Internet, voice mail, safes, irons, hair dryers. **Pool(s):** outdoor. **Leisure Activities:** whirlpool, exercise room. **Guest Services:** coin laundry, wireless Internet. **Business Services:** meeting rooms, business center. **Cards:** AX, DS, MC, VI. **Free Special Amenities: full breakfast and high-speed Internet.**

   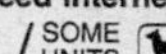 / SOME UNITS

HOLIDAY INN EXPRESS Book at AAA.com **Phone:** (912)882-8200

Hotel

$99-$119 All Year

Address: 1375 Hospitality Ave **Location:** I-95, exit 3 (SR 40), just se. **Facility:** Smoke free premises. 54 one-bedroom standard units. 2 stories, interior corridors. *Bath:* shower only. **Parking:** on-site. **Amenities:** high-speed Internet, voice mail, irons, hair dryers. **Pool(s):** heated outdoor. **Leisure Activities:** exercise room. **Guest Services:** valet and coin laundry, wireless Internet. **Business Services:** meeting rooms, business center. **Cards:** AX, CB, DC, DS, JC, MC, VI.

ASK

JAMESON INN Book at AAA.com **Phone:** (912)729-9600

Motel

$78-$85 All Year

Address: 105 May Creek Blvd **Location:** I-95, exit 3 (SR 40), just w, then s at Boone Ave. **Facility:** 41 one-bedroom standard units, some with whirlpools. 2 stories (no elevator), exterior corridors. **Parking:** on-site. **Terms:** cancellation fee imposed. **Amenities:** irons, hair dryers. **Pool(s):** outdoor. **Leisure Activities:** exercise room. **Guest Services:** wireless Internet. **Business Services:** PC. **Cards:** AX, DC, DS, MC, VI.

ASK CALL / SOME UNITS FEE

MAGNOLIA INN Book great rates at AAA.com **Phone:** (912)576-4777

AAA SAVE

Motel

$60-$100 All Year

Address: 1325 Hospitality Ave **Location:** I-95, exit 3 (SR 40), 0.5 mi e, then just n on JSJ Ave. **Facility:** 44 one-bedroom standard units, some with whirlpools. 2 stories (no elevator), exterior corridors. **Parking:** on-site. **Terms:** 3 day cancellation notice. **Amenities:** voice mail, hair dryers. *Some:* DVD players. **Leisure Activities:** pool privileges. **Guest Services:** wireless Internet. **Cards:** AX, CB, DS, MC, VI. **Free Special Amenities: expanded continental breakfast and high-speed Internet.**

/ SOME UNITS FEE VCR

MICROTEL INN & SUITES Book great rates at AAA.com **Phone:** (912)729-1555

AAA SAVE

Hotel

$49-$79 All Year

Address: 1325 E King Ave **Location:** I-95, exit 3 (SR 40), just ne. **Facility:** 59 one-bedroom standard units. 3 stories, interior corridors. *Bath:* combo or shower only. **Parking:** on-site. **Amenities:** high-speed Internet, irons, hair dryers. **Guest Services:** coin laundry, wireless Internet. **Business Services:** PC. **Cards:** AX, DC, DS, MC, VI. **Free Special Amenities: expanded continental breakfast and high-speed Internet.**

/ SOME UNITS FEE

SLEEP INN & SUITES Book at AAA.com **Phone:** (912)673-7116

Hotel

$63-$72 All Year

Address: 1321 Hospitality Ave **Location:** I-95, exit 3 (SR 40), just e. **Facility:** 73 one-bedroom standard units. 3 stories, interior corridors. *Bath:* combo or shower only. **Parking:** on-site. **Amenities:** high-speed Internet, voice mail, safes (fee), irons, hair dryers. **Pool(s):** outdoor. **Leisure Activities:** exercise room. **Guest Services:** coin laundry, wireless Internet. **Business Services:** PC. **Cards:** AX, DS, MC, VI.

ASK / SOME UNITS

SUPER 8 MOTEL Book great rates at AAA.com **Phone:** (912)729-6888

AAA SAVE

Motel

$50-$100 All Year

Address: 120 Robert L Edenfield Dr **Location:** I-95, exit 3 (SR 40), just se. Located in a quiet area. **Facility:** 59 one-bedroom standard units. 3 stories (no elevator), interior corridors. **Parking:** on-site. **Amenities:** hair dryers. **Guest Services:** wireless Internet. **Cards:** AX, DC, DS, MC, VI. **Free Special Amenities: continental breakfast and high-speed Internet.**

/ SOME UNITS FEE

WHERE TO DINE

ANGELO'S RESTAURANT OF KINGSLAND **Phone:** 912/882-1212

Italian

$7-$15

Word to the wise: Come hungry and order light. The diversity and length of the menu is surpassed only by the size of the portions. Casual dress. **Hours:** 10 am-10 pm. Closed major holidays; also Sat & Sun. **Address:** 1371A Hwy 40 E **Location:** I-95, exit 3 (SR 40), 0.5 mi se. **Parking:** on-site. **Cards:** AX, DS, MC, VI.

BONZAI JAPANESE STEAK HOUSE **Phone:** 912/882-8600

Japanese

$10-$20

Tableside preparation, family-style table seating around a hibachi grill and a staff of skilled, entertaining chefs make for an enjoyable night out. Portions are huge so come hungry. Small parties will be seated with others to ensure the grill-seating is full. Casual dress. **Bar:** Full bar. **Hours:** 4 pm-10 pm, Sun-9 pm. Closed: 11/26. **Address:** 1202 Hospitality Ave **Location:** I-95, exit 3 (SR 40), 0.6 mi se on SR 40. **Parking:** on-site. **Cards:** AX, DC, DS, MC, VI.

SONNY'S REAL PIT BAR-B-Q **Phone:** 912/673-7262

Barbecue

$6-$15

House specialties include pork and chicken grilled over an open pit, barbecue ribs and fresh, homemade pie. The salad bar offers another popular option. Rustic and comfortable, the atmosphere is perfect for family meals. Casual dress. **Bar:** Beer only. **Hours:** 11 am-9:30 pm, Fri & Sat-10 pm. Closed: 11/26, 12/25. **Address:** 1380 E Boone Ave **Location:** I-95, exit 3 (SR 40), 0.4 mi e. **Parking:** on-site. **Cards:** AX, DS, MC, VI.

LA FAYETTE pop. 6,702

WHERE TO STAY

DAYS INN *Book great rates at AAA.com* **Phone:** (706)639-9362

AAA SAVE

Motel
$50-$65 All Year

Address: 2209 N Main St **Location:** 2.5 mi n on US 27. **Facility:** 35 one-bedroom standard units, some with whirlpools. 2 stories (no elevator), exterior corridors. **Parking:** on-site. **Amenities:** high-speed Internet, hair dryers. **Pool(s):** outdoor. **Guest Services:** wireless Internet. **Business Services:** fax. **Cards:** AX, DS, MC, VI. **Free Special Amenities: continental breakfast and high-speed Internet.**

/ SOME UNITS FEE

KEY WEST INN *Book at AAA.com* **Phone:** (706)638-8200

Motel
$47-$60 All Year

Address: 2221 N Main St **Location:** 2.5 mi n on US 27. **Facility:** 38 one-bedroom standard units, some with whirlpools. 2 stories (no elevator), exterior corridors. **Parking:** on-site. **Terms:** 3 day cancellation notice. **Amenities:** high-speed Internet, irons, hair dryers. **Pool(s):** outdoor. **Guest Services:** coin laundry, wireless Internet. **Business Services:** PC, fax (fee). **Cards:** AX, DC, DS, MC, VI.

ASK CALL / SOME UNITS FEE

LAGRANGE pop. 25,998

WHERE TO STAY

BEST WESTERN LAFAYETTE GARDEN INN & CONFERENCE CENTER *Book great rates at AAA.com* **Phone:** (706)884-6175

AAA SAVE

Hotel
$65-$85 All Year

Address: 1513 Lafayette Pkwy **Location:** I-85, exit 18 (Lafayette Pkwy), just w. **Facility:** 109 units. 105 one-bedroom standard units. 4 one-bedroom suites. 2 stories (no elevator), exterior corridors. **Parking:** on-site. **Amenities:** voice mail, safes, irons, hair dryers. *Some:* dual phone lines. **Pool(s):** outdoor. **Leisure Activities:** exercise room. **Guest Services:** valet and coin laundry, wireless Internet. **Business Services:** conference facilities, PC. **Cards:** AX, DC, DS, MC, VI. **Free Special Amenities: full breakfast and high-speed Internet.**

AAA Benefit:
Members save up to 20%, plus 10% bonus points with rewards program.

DAYS INN-LAGRANGE/CALLAWAY GARDENS *Book great rates at AAA.com* **Phone:** (706)882-8881

AAA SAVE

Hotel
$60 All Year

Address: 2606 Whitesville Rd **Location:** I-85, exit 13, just e. **Facility:** 107 one-bedroom standard units. 2 stories (no elevator), exterior corridors. *Bath:* combo or shower only. **Parking:** on-site. **Amenities:** voice mail, irons, hair dryers. *Some:* dual phone lines. **Pool(s):** outdoor. **Guest Services:** coin laundry, wireless Internet. **Business Services:** meeting rooms, PC. **Cards:** AX, DS, MC, VI. **Free Special Amenities: continental breakfast and high-speed Internet.**

/ SOME UNITS FEE

HAMPTON INN *Book great rates at AAA.com* **Phone:** (706)845-1115

Hotel
$95-$120 All Year

Address: 100 Willis Cir **Location:** I-85, exit 14, just w. **Facility:** 81 one-bedroom standard units. 3 stories, interior corridors. **Parking:** on-site. **Terms:** 1-30 night minimum stay, cancellation fee imposed. **Amenities:** video games (fee), high-speed Internet, dual phone lines, voice mail, irons, hair dryers. **Pool(s):** outdoor. **Leisure Activities:** exercise room. **Guest Services:** valet and coin laundry, wireless Internet. **Business Services:** meeting rooms, PC, fax. **Cards:** AX, CB, DC, DS, MC, VI.

/ SOME UNITS

AAA Benefit:
Members save up to 10% everyday!

JAMESON INN *Book at AAA.com* **Phone:** (706)882-8700

Hotel
$78-$85 All Year

Address: 110 Jameson Dr **Location:** I-85, exit 18 (Lafayette Pkwy), 0.3 mi w. **Facility:** 57 one-bedroom standard units. 2 stories (no elevator), exterior corridors. *Bath:* combo or shower only. **Parking:** on-site. **Terms:** office hours 5:30 am-11 pm, cancellation fee imposed. **Amenities:** irons, hair dryers. **Pool(s):** outdoor. **Leisure Activities:** exercise room. **Guest Services:** wireless Internet. **Business Services:** PC. **Cards:** AX, DC, DS, MC, VI.

ASK CALL / SOME UNITS FEE

QUALITY INN & SUITES *Book at AAA.com* **Phone:** (706)882-9540

Hotel
$69-$139 All Year

Address: 1601 Lafayette Pkwy **Location:** I-85, exit 18 (Lafayette Pkwy), just e. **Facility:** 82 units. 72 one-bedroom standard units. 10 one-bedroom suites. 2 stories (no elevator), exterior corridors. **Parking:** on-site. **Terms:** cancellation fee imposed. **Amenities:** voice mail, irons, hair dryers. **Pool(s):** outdoor. **Guest Services:** valet laundry, wireless Internet. **Business Services:** meeting rooms, PC. **Cards:** AX, CB, DC, DS, MC, VI.

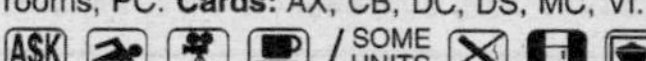

LAKE PARK pop. 549

WHERE TO STAY

DAYS INN Book great rates at AAA.com **Phone:** (229)559-0229

Hotel
$59-$89 All Year

Address: 4913 Timber Dr **Location:** I-75, exit 5, just nw. **Facility:** Smoke free premises. 94 one-bedroom standard units. 2 stories (no elevator), exterior corridors. **Parking:** on-site. **Amenities:** hair dryers. **Pool(s):** outdoor. **Guest Services:** wireless Internet. **Cards:** AX, DC, DS, MC, VI. **Free Special Amenities: expanded continental breakfast and high-speed Internet.**

/ SOME UNITS FEE

QUALITY INN Book great rates at AAA.com **Phone:** (229)559-5181

Hotel
$59-$115 All Year

Address: 1198 Lakes Blvd **Location:** I-75, exit 5, just e. **Facility:** 66 one-bedroom standard units. 2 stories, exterior corridors. **Parking:** on-site. **Terms:** cancellation fee imposed. **Amenities:** dual phone lines, voice mail, irons, hair dryers. **Pool(s):** outdoor. **Guest Services:** coin laundry, wireless Internet. **Business Services:** PC. **Cards:** AX, DC, DS, MC, VI. **Free Special Amenities: continental breakfast and high-speed Internet.**

/ SOME UNITS FEE

SUPER 8 MOTEL Book great rates at AAA.com **Phone:** (229)559-8111

Hotel
$55-$75 All Year

Address: 4907 Timber Dr **Location:** I-75, exit 5, just w, then n. **Facility:** 44 one-bedroom standard units, some with whirlpools. 2 stories, exterior corridors. **Parking:** on-site. **Amenities:** *Some:* hair dryers. **Guest Services:** wireless Internet. **Business Services:** fax (fee). **Cards:** AX, DC, DS, MC, VI. **Free Special Amenities: continental breakfast and local telephone calls.**

/ SOME UNITS FEE

VALDOSTA-LAKE PARK HAMPTON INN Book great rates at AAA.com **Phone:** (229)559-5565

Hotel
$94-$99 All Year

Address: 4906 Timber Dr **Location:** I-75, exit 5, just w, then n. **Facility:** 70 units. 68 one-bedroom standard units, some with whirlpools. 2 one-bedroom suites with whirlpools. 3 stories, interior corridors. *Bath:* combo or shower only. **Parking:** on-site. **Amenities:** video games, voice mail, irons, hair dryers. **Pool(s):** outdoor. **Leisure Activities:** exercise room. *Fee:* game room. **Guest Services:** coin laundry, wireless Internet. **Business Services:** meeting rooms, business center. **Cards:** AX, DC, DS, MC, VI.

CALL / SOME UNITS

AAA Benefit:
Members save up to 10% everyday!

WHERE TO DINE

RODEO MEXICAN RESTAURANT **Phone:** 229/559-3320

Mexican
$6-$14

Just off the interstate, the festive restaurant features a wide selection of Mexican standards served by a friendly wait staff. Well-portioned selections are inexpensive and tasty. The lunch menu features a wide variety of combination selections, and fajitas are great anytime. Casual dress. **Bar:** Full bar. **Hours:** 11 am-10 pm. Closed: 4/12, 12/25. **Address:** 1219 Lakes Blvd **Location:** I-75, exit 5, just e. **Parking:** on-site. **Cards:** AX, CB, DC, DS, JC, MC, VI.

SONNY'S REAL PIT BAR-B-Q **Phone:** 229/559-0052

Barbecue
$6-$15

House specialties include pork and chicken grilled over an open pit, barbecue ribs and fresh, homemade pie. The salad bar offers another popular option. Rustic and comfortable, the atmosphere is perfect for family meals. Casual dress. **Bar:** Beer only. **Hours:** 11 am-9:30 pm, Fri & Sat-10 pm. Closed: 11/26, 12/25. **Address:** 1088 Lakes Blvd **Location:** I-75, exit 5, 0.3 mi e. **Parking:** on-site. **Cards:** AX, DS, MC, VI.

LAVONIA pop. 1,827

WHERE TO STAY

BEST WESTERN REGENCY INN & SUITES Book great rates at AAA.com **Phone:** (706)356-4000

Motel
$63-$120 All Year

Address: 13705 Jones St **Location:** I-85, exit 173, just e. **Facility:** 92 one-bedroom standard units. 2 stories (no elevator), exterior corridors. **Parking:** on-site. **Amenities:** irons, hair dryers. **Pool(s):** outdoor. **Guest Services:** wireless Internet. **Business Services:** PC, fax. **Cards:** AX, CB, DC, DS, JC, MC, VI. **Free Special Amenities: continental breakfast and high-speed Internet.**

  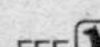  / SOME UNITS FEE 

AAA Benefit:
Members save up to 20%, plus 10% bonus points with rewards program.

SLEEP INN *Book great rates at AAA.com*

Hotel
$80-$100 3/1-11/30
$65-$80 12/1-2/28

Phone: (706)356-2268
Address: 890 Ross Pl **Location:** I-85, exit 173, just e. **Facility:** 74 one-bedroom standard units, some with whirlpools. 2 stories (no elevator), interior corridors. *Bath:* combo or shower only. **Parking:** on-site. **Amenities:** irons, hair dryers. **Pool(s):** outdoor. **Guest Services:** wireless Internet. **Cards:** AX, CB, DC, DS, MC, VI. **Free Special Amenities: continental breakfast and high-speed Internet.**

CALL / SOME UNITS

SUPER 8 MOTEL-LAVONIA *Book at AAA.com*

Hotel
$48-$90 All Year

Phone: (706)356-8848
Address: 14227 Jones St **Location:** I-85, exit 173, just w. **Facility:** 60 one-bedroom standard units. 2 stories (no elevator), exterior corridors. *Bath:* combo or shower only. **Parking:** on-site. **Amenities:** high-speed Internet, irons, hair dryers. **Pool(s):** outdoor. **Guest Services:** wireless Internet. **Business Services:** meeting rooms. **Cards:** AX, CB, DC, DS, JC, MC, VI.

ASK CALL / SOME UNITS FEE

LAWRENCEVILLE —*See Atlanta p. 400.*

LITHIA SPRINGS —*See Atlanta p. 402.*

LITHONIA —*See Atlanta p. 403.*

LOCUST GROVE pop. 2,322

WHERE TO STAY

ECONO LODGE *Book at AAA.com*

Motel
Rates not provided

Phone: 770/957-2601
Address: 4829 Bill Gardner Pkwy **Location:** I-75, exit 212, just e. **Facility:** 94 one-bedroom standard units. 2 stories (no elevator), exterior corridors. **Parking:** on-site. **Amenities:** *Some:* hair dryers. **Guest Services:** coin laundry, wireless Internet. **Business Services:** fax (fee).

/ SOME UNITS FEE

LA QUINTA INN & SUITES *Book great rates at AAA.com*

Hotel
$80-$110 4/1-11/30
$69-$95 12/1-3/31

Phone: (678)583-0004
Address: 4832 Bill Gardner Pkwy **Location:** I-75, exit 212, just e. **Facility:** 65 units. 57 one-bedroom standard units, some with whirlpools. 8 one-bedroom suites. 3-4 stories, interior corridors. *Bath:* combo or shower only. **Parking:** on-site. **Amenities:** high-speed Internet, voice mail, irons, hair dryers. *Some:* dual phone lines. **Pool(s):** heated indoor. **Leisure Activities:** exercise room. **Guest Services:** coin laundry, wireless Internet. **Business Services:** meeting rooms, business center. **Cards:** AX, CB, DC, DS, JC, MC, VI. **Free Special Amenities: expanded continental breakfast and high-speed Internet.** *(See color ad below)*

CALL / SOME UNITS

RAMADA LIMITED *Book at AAA.com*

Hotel
$60-$150 All Year

Phone: (770)898-1216
Address: 197 Stanley Tanger Blvd **Location:** I-75, exit 212, just e. **Facility:** 44 one-bedroom standard units, some with whirlpools. 2 stories, interior corridors. **Parking:** on-site. **Amenities:** high-speed Internet, voice mail, irons, hair dryers. **Pool(s):** heated indoor. **Guest Services:** coin laundry, wireless Internet. **Business Services:** PC. **Cards:** AX, DC, DS, MC, VI.

ASK / SOME UNITS

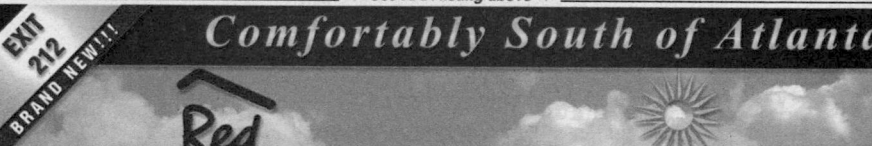

▼ *See AAA listing above* ▼

RED ROOF — Phone: 678/583-0004

fyi — Hotel — Rates not provided

Too new to rate, opening scheduled for December 2008. **Address:** 4840 Bill Gardner Pkwy **Location:** I-75, exit 212, just e. **Amenities:** 64 units, pets, microwaves, refrigerators, pool. ***(See color ad p 494)***

SUPER 8 MOTEL — *Book great rates at AAA.com* — Phone: (770)957-2936

AAA SAVE — Motel — $55-$135 All Year

Address: 4605 Bill Gardner Pkwy **Location:** I-75, exit 212, just w. **Facility:** 56 one-bedroom standard units. 2 stories, exterior corridors. **Parking:** on-site. **Terms:** cancellation fee imposed. **Amenities:** hair dryers. **Guest Services:** coin laundry, wireless Internet. **Business Services:** fax (fee). **Cards:** AX, DC, DS, MC, VI. **Free Special Amenities: continental breakfast and high-speed Internet.**

/ SOME UNITS

LOOKOUT MOUNTAIN pop. 1,617

— WHERE TO STAY —

CHANTICLEER INN — Phone: (706)820-2002

Bed & Breakfast — $120-$220 All Year

Address: 1300 Mockingbird Ln **Location:** I-24, exit 178 westbound; exit 174 eastbound, follow signs to Lookout Mountain, Rock City. Located adjacent to Rock City. **Facility:** Built in 1930. Individually decorated rooms with some antique furnishings. Smoke free premises. 17 units. 16 one-bedroom standard units, some with whirlpools. 1 one-bedroom suite. 1 story, interior/exterior corridors. *Bath:* combo or shower only. **Parking:** on-site. **Terms:** age restrictions may apply, 7 day cancellation notice. **Amenities:** high-speed Internet, voice mail, irons, hair dryers. *Some:* CD players. **Pool(s):** outdoor. **Guest Services:** wireless Internet. **Business Services:** meeting rooms, fax (fee). **Cards:** AX, DS, MC, VI.

/ SOME UNITS

MACON pop. 97,255

— WHERE TO STAY —

1842 INN — *Book great rates at AAA.com* — Phone: (478)741-1842

AAA SAVE — Historic Bed & Breakfast — $189-$255 All Year

Address: 353 College St **Location:** I-75, exit 164 (US 41), 0.5 mi e, then just n. **Facility:** This Greek Revival-style inn offers inviting garden seating on its manicured grounds; rooms are well-appointed and public areas are spacious. Smoke free premises. 19 one-bedroom standard units, some with whirlpools. 2 stories (no elevator), interior/exterior corridors. **Parking:** on-site. **Terms:** 7 day cancellation notice-fee imposed. **Amenities:** voice mail, irons, hair dryers. **Leisure Activities:** golf & tennis privileges. **Guest Services:** valet laundry, wireless Internet. **Business Services:** PC. **Cards:** AX, DC, MC, VI. **Free Special Amenities: full breakfast and high-speed Internet.**

THE BAYMONT INN AND SUITES OF MACON — *Book at AAA.com* — Phone: (478)474-8004

Motel — $70-$140 All Year

Address: 150 Plantation Inn Dr **Location:** I-475, exit 9 (Zebulon Rd), just e to Peake Rd, then just s. **Facility:** 59 units. 57 one-bedroom standard units, some with whirlpools. 2 one-bedroom suites. 2 stories, exterior corridors. **Parking:** on-site, winter plug-ins. **Amenities:** safes, irons, hair dryers. **Pool(s):** outdoor. **Leisure Activities:** exercise room. **Guest Services:** wireless Internet. **Business Services:** PC, fax (fee). **Cards:** AX, CB, DC, DS, MC, VI.

ASK / SOME UNITS FEE

▼ *See AAA listing p 496* ▼

BEST WESTERN INN & SUITES OF MACON *Book great rates at AAA.com* **Phone:** (478)781-5300

Motel
$71-$83 All Year

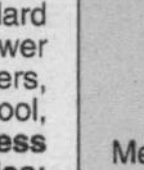

Address: 4681 Chambers Rd **Location:** I-475, exit 3 (Eisenhower Pkwy/US 80), just ne, then just se. **Facility:** 56 one-bedroom standard units. 2 stories (no elevator), exterior corridors. *Bath:* combo or shower only. **Parking:** on-site. **Amenities:** irons, hair dryers. *Some:* DVD players, high-speed Internet. **Pool(s):** heated indoor. **Leisure Activities:** whirlpool, exercise room. **Guest Services:** coin laundry, wireless Internet. **Business Services:** fax (fee). **Cards:** AX, DS, MC, VI. **Free Special Amenities: expanded continental breakfast and high-speed Internet.**
(See color ad p 495)

/ SOME UNITS FEE

AAA Benefit:
Members save up to 20%, plus 10% bonus points with rewards program.

BEST WESTERN RIVERSIDE INN *Book great rates at AAA.com* **Phone:** (478)743-6311

Hotel
$60-$75 All Year

Address: 2400 Riverside Dr **Location:** I-75, exit 167 (Riverside Dr), just w, then 0.4 mi se. **Facility:** 115 one-bedroom standard units. 2 stories (no elevator), interior corridors. **Parking:** on-site. **Amenities:** irons, hair dryers. **Pool(s):** outdoor. **Leisure Activities:** gazebo, exercise room. **Guest Services:** coin laundry, wireless Internet. **Business Services:** meeting rooms, PC. **Cards:** AX, CB, DC, DS, JC, MC, VI. **Free Special Amenities: expanded continental breakfast and high-speed Internet.**
(See color ad below)

   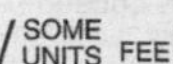  / SOME UNITS FEE

AAA Benefit:
Members save up to 20%, plus 10% bonus points with rewards program.

COURTYARD BY MARRIOTT *Book great rates at AAA.com* **Phone:** (478)477-8899

Hotel
$153-$164 All Year

Address: 3990 Sheraton Dr **Location:** I-75, exit 169 (Arkwright Rd), just n, then just nw. **Facility:** Smoke free premises. 108 units. 102 one-bedroom standard units. 6 one-bedroom suites. 3 stories, interior corridors. *Bath:* combo or shower only. **Parking:** on-site. **Terms:** cancellation fee imposed. **Amenities:** high-speed Internet, voice mail, irons, hair dryers. **Pool(s):** heated outdoor. **Leisure Activities:** whirlpool, exercise room. **Guest Services:** valet and coin laundry, wireless Internet. **Business Services:** meeting rooms, business center. **Cards:** AX, CB, DC, DS, JC, MC, VI. **Free Special Amenities: newspaper and high-speed Internet.**

CALL     / SOME UNITS

AAA Benefit:
Members save a minimum 5% off the best available rate.

FAIRFIELD INN & SUITES MACON *Book great rates at AAA.com* **Phone:** (478)738-9007

Hotel
$128-$137 All Year

Address: 4035 Sheraton Dr **Location:** I-75, exit 169 (Arkwright Rd), just n, then just nw. **Facility:** Smoke free premises. 78 one-bedroom standard units. 3 stories, interior corridors. *Bath:* combo or shower only. **Parking:** on-site. **Terms:** cancellation fee imposed. **Amenities:** high-speed Internet, dual phone lines, voice mail, irons, hair dryers. *Some:* DVD players. **Pool(s):** outdoor. **Leisure Activities:** whirlpool, exercise room. **Guest Services:** valet and coin laundry, wireless Internet. **Business Services:** meeting rooms, business center. **Cards:** AX, CB, DC, DS, MC, VI.

CALL / SOME UNITS

AAA Benefit:
Members save a minimum 5% off the best available rate.

▼ *See AAA listing above* ▼

FAIRFIELD INN-MACON/WEST *Book great rates at AAA.com*

Phone: (478)474-9922

Hotel
$94-$100 All Year

Address: 110 Plantation Inn Dr **Location:** I-475, exit 9 (Zebulon Rd), just e to Peake Rd, then just s. Located in a quiet area. **Facility:** Smoke free premises. 65 one-bedroom standard units, some with whirlpools. 3 stories, interior corridors. *Bath:* combo or shower only. **Parking:** on-site. **Terms:** cancellation fee imposed. **Amenities:** voice mail, irons, hair dryers. **Pool(s):** outdoor. **Leisure Activities:** whirlpool. **Guest Services:** valet laundry, wireless Internet. **Business Services:** PC, fax (fee). **Cards:** AX, CB, DC, DS, JC, MC, VI.

CALL / SOME UNITS

AAA Benefit:
Members save a minimum 5% off the best available rate.

HAMPTON INN I-475 *Book great rates at AAA.com*

Phone: (478)757-9711

Hotel
$68-$97 All Year

Address: 5010 Eisenhower Pkwy (US 80) **Location:** I-475, exit 3 (Eisenhower Pkwy/US 80), just ne. **Facility:** 62 one-bedroom standard units, some with whirlpools. 2 stories, exterior corridors. *Bath:* combo or shower only. **Parking:** on-site. **Terms:** 1-30 night minimum stay, cancellation fee imposed. **Amenities:** video games (fee), high-speed Internet, voice mail, irons, hair dryers. **Pool(s):** outdoor. **Guest Services:** valet and coin laundry, wireless Internet. **Business Services:** PC. **Cards:** AX, CB, DC, DS, MC, VI.

/ SOME UNITS

AAA Benefit:
Members save up to 10% everyday!

HILTON GARDEN INN MACON/MERCER UNIVERSITY *Book great rates at AAA.com*

Phone: (478)741-5527

Hotel
$89-$179 All Year

Address: 1220 Stadium Dr **Location:** I-75, exit 163, just s. **Facility:** 101 one-bedroom standard units. 4 stories, interior corridors. *Bath:* combo or shower only. **Parking:** on-site. **Terms:** 1-30 night minimum stay, cancellation fee imposed. **Amenities:** high-speed Internet, voice mail, irons, hair dryers. **Pool(s):** outdoor. **Leisure Activities:** whirlpool, exercise room. **Guest Services:** complimentary laundry, wireless Internet. **Business Services:** meeting rooms, business center. **Cards:** AX, CB, DC, DS, MC, VI.

/ SOME UNITS

Hilton Garden Inn

AAA Benefit:
Members save 5% or more everyday!

▼ *See AAA listing p 469* ▼

LA QUINTA INN & SUITES MACON *Book great rates at AAA.com*

Phone: (478)475-0206

Hotel

$79-$139 All Year

Address: 3944 River Place Dr **Location:** I-75, exit 169 (Arkwright Rd), just n, then e. **Facility:** 141 units. 134 one-bedroom standard units. 7 one-bedroom suites. 3 stories, interior corridors. *Bath:* combo or shower only. **Parking:** on-site. **Amenities:** video games (fee), high-speed Internet, voice mail, irons, hair dryers. *Some:* dual phone lines. **Pool(s):** outdoor. **Leisure Activities:** whirlpool, exercise room. **Guest Services:** valet and coin laundry, wireless Internet. **Business Services:** meeting rooms, PC, fax (fee). **Cards:** AX, DC, DS, MC, VI.

ASK CALL / SOME UNITS

MACON I-75 HAMPTON INN & SUITES *Book great rates at AAA.com*

Phone: (478)803-5000

Hotel

$109-$129 All Year

Address: 3954 River Place Dr **Location:** I-75, exit 169 (Arkwright Rd), just e, then just s. **Facility:** 83 one-bedroom standard units. 4 stories, interior corridors. *Bath:* combo or shower only. **Parking:** on-site. **Terms:** 1-30 night minimum stay, cancellation fee imposed. **Amenities:** high-speed Internet, voice mail, irons, hair dryers. **Pool(s):** heated indoor. **Leisure Activities:** exercise room. **Guest Services:** coin laundry, wireless Internet. **Business Services:** meeting rooms, business center. **Cards:** AX, CB, DC, DS, MC, VI.

/ SOME UNITS

Hampton Inn & Suites

AAA Benefit:

Members save up to 10% everyday!

QUALITY INN & SUITES *Book great rates at AAA.com*

Phone: (478)474-4000

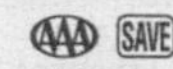

AAA SAVE

Hotel

$55-$70 All Year

Address: 115 Riverside Pkwy **Location:** I-75, exit 169 (Arkwright Rd), just sw, then just nw. Located in a commercial area. **Facility:** 86 one-bedroom standard units. 2 stories (no elevator), exterior corridors. *Bath:* combo or shower only. **Parking:** on-site. **Amenities:** irons, hair dryers. **Pool(s):** outdoor. **Leisure Activities:** whirlpool. **Guest Services:** coin laundry, wireless Internet. **Business Services:** PC, fax (fee). **Cards:** AX, DC, DS, MC, VI. **Free Special Amenities: full breakfast and high-speed Internet.**

/ SOME UNITS

RODEWAY INN *Book great rates at AAA.com*

Phone: (478)781-4343

AAA SAVE

Motel

$49-$59 All Year

Address: 4999 Eisenhower Pkwy **Location:** I-475, exit 3 (Eisenhower Pkwy/US 80), just ne. **Facility:** 58 one-bedroom standard units. 2 stories (no elevator), exterior corridors. **Parking:** on-site. **Amenities:** video library (fee). *Some:* hair dryers. **Pool(s):** outdoor. **Guest Services:** coin laundry, wireless Internet. **Business Services:** fax (fee). **Cards:** AX, CB, DC, DS, MC, VI. **Free Special Amenities: continental breakfast and high-speed Internet.** *(See color ad below)*

/ SOME UNITS FEE VCR

SLEEP INN *Book great rates at AAA.com*

Phone: (478)757-8300

AAA SAVE

Hotel

$60-$100 All Year

Address: 3928 River Place Dr **Location:** I-75, exit 169 (Arkwright Rd), just n, then e. **Facility:** 59 one-bedroom standard units. 2 stories (no elevator), interior corridors. *Bath:* combo or shower only. **Parking:** on-site. **Amenities:** irons, hair dryers. **Pool(s):** indoor/outdoor. **Leisure Activities:** whirlpool. **Guest Services:** wireless Internet. **Business Services:** PC. **Cards:** AX, DC, DS, MC, VI. **Free Special Amenities: continental breakfast and high-speed Internet.**

/ SOME UNITS

▼ *See AAA listing above* ▼

SLEEP INN I-475 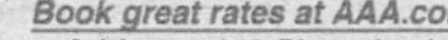 **Phone:** (478)476-8111

Hotel
$59-$99 All Year

Address: 140 Plantation Inn Dr **Location:** I-475, exit 9 (Zebulon Rd), just e to Peake Rd, then just s. **Facility:** 52 one-bedroom standard units, some with whirlpools. 3 stories, interior corridors. *Bath:* combo or shower only. **Parking:** on-site. **Terms:** cancellation fee imposed. **Amenities:** high-speed Internet, irons, hair dryers. **Pool(s):** heated indoor. **Guest Services:** wireless Internet. **Business Services:** PC, fax (fee). **Cards:** AX, DS, JC, MC, VI.

CALL / SOME UNITS FEE

WINGATE INN *Book at AAA.com* **Phone:** (478)476-8100

Hotel
$89 All Year

Address: 100 Northcrest Blvd **Location:** I-75, exit 169 (Arkwright Rd), just sw to Riverside Dr, then 0.4 mi nw. **Facility:** 80 one-bedroom standard units, some with whirlpools. 3 stories, interior corridors. *Bath:* combo or shower only. **Parking:** on-site. **Terms:** cancellation fee imposed. **Amenities:** high-speed Internet, dual phone lines, voice mail, safes, irons, hair dryers. *Some:* DVD players. **Pool(s):** heated outdoor. **Leisure Activities:** whirlpool, exercise room. **Guest Services:** valet laundry, wireless Internet. **Business Services:** meeting rooms, business center. **Cards:** AX, DC, DS, MC, VI.

ASK / SOME UNITS VCR

WHERE TO DINE

THE BACK BURNER RESTAURANT **Phone:** 478/746-3336

French
$13-$25

The quaint cottage's dining room has a homey feel with its several small dining rooms, wood floors, artwork and comfortable furnishings. Continental dishes, which change often, reflect a heavy French influence. Delicate, perfectly prepared sauces complement favorites such as crab cakes laden with lump crab, chicken breast in Burgundy sauce, salmon in basil cream and halibut in tomato caper sauce. The wait staff is well versed in the many wine offerings and competently make pairing suggestions. Casual dress. **Bar:** Full bar. **Reservations:** accepted. **Hours:** 11:30 am-2 & 5:30-9:30 pm. Closed major holidays; also Sun. **Address:** 2242 Ingleside Ave **Location:** Jct Riverside and Ingleside, 0.5 mi w. **Parking:** on-site. **Cards:** AX, CB, DC, DS, JC, MC, VI.

DOWNTOWN GRILL **Phone:** 478/742-5999

Steak
$15-$35

Downtown in the alley is an unimposing building that houses great food served in a relaxed Southern style. The competent servers' verbal review of the evening menu whets appetites for morsels such as crab cakes or cheese grits for starters and a variety of steaks, chops and fish prepared in varying styles. The signature pork loin with Vidalia onion barbecue sauce shouldn't be missed. Dessert specialties are a fitting end to any meal. Dressy casual. **Bar:** Full bar. **Reservations:** suggested. **Hours:** 5 pm-10 pm, Fri & Sat-10:30 pm. Closed major holidays; also Sun. **Address:** 562 Mulberry Street Ln **Location:** Center of town. **Parking:** valet and street. **Cards:** AX, DS, MC, VI.

EL AZTECA **Phone:** 478/475-9199

Tex-Mex
$5-$15

A large colorful dining room adds to this festive experience. Diners can choose from a wide selection of Tex/Mex favorites delivered by a friendly and attentive wait staff. Known locally for great margaritas. Casual dress. **Bar:** Full bar. **Hours:** 11 am-10 pm, Fri & Sat-11 pm. Closed major holidays. **Address:** 169 Tom Hill Sr Blvd **Location:** I-75, exit 169 (Arkwright Rd), just sw. **Parking:** on-site. **Cards:** AX, DC, DS, MC, VI.

H & H RESTAURANT **Phone:** 478/742-9810

Regional American
$6-$8

Down-home vittles come from Mama Louise's kitchen. Operating since 1968, the soul-food establishment was routinely visited by members of the Allman Brothers band. The walls are a memorial to them. Casual dress. **Hours:** 6 am-4 pm. Closed major holidays; also Sun & Martin Luther King Day. **Address:** 807 Forsyth St **Location:** I-75, exit 164 (US 41), 0.8 mi se. **Parking:** street. **Cards:** MC, VI.

J.L.'S OPEN PIT BAR-B-Q **Phone:** 478/788-1989

Barbecue
$3-$18

Jumbo pork, beef or smoked turkey sandwiches served sliced or chopped and a large salad bar are crowd pleasers in the popular restaurant. Half and full racks of ribs, as well as choice cut steaks and prime rib, also are available. Good portions add up to good value. Service is friendly. Casual dress. **Bar:** Beer only. **Reservations:** accepted. **Hours:** 11 am-9 pm, Fri & Sat-9:30 pm. Closed: 11/26, 12/25. **Address:** 5001 Brookhaven Rd **Location:** I-475, exit 3 (Eisenhower Pkwy/US 80), just ne. **Parking:** on-site. **Cards:** AX, DC, DS, MC, VI.

MARGARITAS MEXICAN GRILL **Phone:** 478/477-2410

Mexican
$4-$18

The grill is another outstanding member of a small central Georgia chain. Guests can expect Mexican fare in a colorful and friendly atmosphere. Fajitas Texanas is a tasty medley of grilled shrimp, chicken and beef served with refried beans, rice and all the standard toppings. Casual dress. **Bar:** Full bar. **Hours:** 11 am-10 pm, Fri & Sat-11 pm. Closed: 1/1, 5/25, 12/24, 12/25. **Address:** 6012 Zebulon Rd **Location:** I-475, exit 9 (Zebulon Rd), just e. **Parking:** on-site. **Cards:** AX, DS, MC, VI.

CALL

MIDTOWN GRILL **Phone:** 478/745-8595

American
$11-$22

Established in 1996, the successful eatery has spawned several other similarly popular restaurants in the Perry/Macon area. The menu is filled with simple favorites prepared from the freshest cuts of meat and seafood. The friendly staff serves "mother's cooking" in a casually upscale dining room. Those who arrive between 5 and 6 pm can order inexpensive early-bird specials. Casual dress. **Bar:** Full bar. **Hours:** 5 pm-10 pm, Fri & Sat-10:30 pm. Closed: 11/26, 12/25; also Sun. **Address:** 3065 Vineville Ave **Location:** I-75, exit 164 (US 41), 1.7 mi w on Hardeman/Vineville Ave. **Parking:** on-site. **Cards:** AX, DS, MC, VI.

NATALIA'S RESTAURANT **Phone:** 478/741-1380

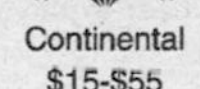

Continental
$15-$55

Subdued lighting creates an intimate, yet a bit whimsical, atmosphere that's perfect for a romantic dinner for two. The menu features fish in parchment, ricotta salata with bowtie pasta, and triple-cut lamb chops. Servers will recommend the specials, which change often. Beverage choices include espresso and selections from an extensive wine list. Dressy casual. **Bar:** Full bar. **Reservations:** suggested. **Hours:** 5:30 pm-9:30 pm, Fri & Sat-10:30 pm. Closed major holidays; also Sun & week of 7/4. **Address:** 2720 Riverside Dr **Location:** I-75, exit 167 (Riverside Dr), just nw, then just w; in Riverstreet Corners. **Parking:** on-site. **Cards:** AX, MC, VI.

S & S CAFETERIA

Phone: 478/788-5913

American
$4-$8

A longtime favorite for comfort food, the family-owned cafeteria invites diners to load a plate with traditionally prepared chicken, beef, vegetables, salad and dessert. Casual dress. **Hours:** 11 am-2:15 & 5-8 pm. Closed: 12/25. **Address:** 3724 Bloomfield Village Dr **Location:** Jct SR 408, 2 mi e. **Parking:** on-site. **Cards:** AX, DS, MC, VI.

S & S CAFETERIA

Phone: 478/746-9406

American
$4-$8

A longtime favorite for comfort food, the family-owned cafeteria invites diners to load a plate with traditionally prepared chicken, beef, vegetables, salad and dessert. Casual dress. **Reservations:** not accepted. **Hours:** 11 am-2:15 & 5-8 pm. Closed: 12/25. **Address:** 2626 Riverside Dr **Location:** I-75, exit 167 (Riverside Dr), just w. **Parking:** on-site. **Cards:** AX, DS, MC, VI.

SONNY'S REAL PIT BAR-B-Q

Phone: 478/477-7787

Barbecue
$6-$15

House specialties include pork and chicken grilled over an open pit, barbecue ribs and fresh, homemade pie. The salad bar offers another popular option. Rustic and comfortable, the atmosphere is perfect for family meals. Casual dress. **Bar:** Beer only. **Hours:** 11 am-9:30 pm, Fri & Sat-10 pm. Closed: 11/26, 12/25. **Address:** 4684 Presidential Pkwy **Location:** I-475, exit 3 (US 80), 0.3 mi e, then 0.4 mi n. **Parking:** on-site. **Cards:** AX, DS, MC, VI.

TAYLORMADE GRILL

Phone: 478/405-6678

American
$10-$25

In a shopping center, the family-owned-and-operated restaurant offers comfortable, well-spaced seating arrangements. Guests can enjoy handsomely presented and tasty dishes, such as bourbon-marinated grilled salmon over a bed of wilted garlic spinach. Casual dress. **Bar:** Full bar. **Hours:** 5 pm-9 pm. Closed: 11/26, 12/25, 12/26; also Sun. **Address:** 157 Tom Hill Sr Blvd **Location:** I-75, exit 169 (Arkwright Rd), just sw; in Rivergate Shopping Center. **Parking:** on-site. **Cards:** AX, DS, MC, VI.

MADISON pop. 3,636

WHERE TO DINE

MADISON CHOPHOUSE GRILLE

Phone: 706/342-0910

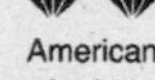

American
$7-$19

The large, bistro-style dining room bustles with an upbeat atmosphere. The menu features many entrees—from burgers and sandwiches to pasta, steak, ribs and salmon. All are well prepared and served in ample portions. Homemade desserts are mouthwatering, but cappuccino or espresso are fitting alternatives for those who prefer a lighter meal ending. Casual dress. **Bar:** Full bar. **Hours:** 11 am-9 pm, Fri & Sat-10 pm. Closed: 11/26, 12/25. **Address:** 202 S Main St **Location:** I-20, exit 114, 3 mi n on US 441; on Historic Town Square. **Parking:** on-site. **Cards:** AX, DC, DS, MC, VI.

YE OLDE COLONIAL RESTAURANT

Phone: 706/342-2211

Southern
$5-$8

An 1800s bank building located in the charming Historic Town Square is home to Southern cooking served cafeteria-style. Simple food like Southern fried chicken and black-eye peas go well with fresh iced tea. You'll enjoy a classic meal in a classic setting. Casual dress. **Hours:** 5:30 am-8:30 pm. Closed major holidays; also Sun. **Address:** 108 E Washington St **Location:** I-20, exit 114, 3 mi n on US 441; on Historic Town Square. **Parking:** street. **Cards:** AX, DS, MC, VI.

MARIETTA —*See Atlanta p. 404.*

MCDONOUGH pop. 8,493

WHERE TO STAY

BEST WESTERN MCDONOUGH INN & SUITES *Book great rates at AAA.com*

Phone: (770)898-1006

Hotel
$100-$110 All Year

Address: 805 Industrial Blvd **Location:** I-75, exit 218, just e to Industrial Blvd, then just s. **Facility:** 64 units. 62 one-bedroom standard units, some with kitchens and/or whirlpools. 2 one-bedroom suites. 3 stories, interior corridors. *Bath:* combo or shower only. **Parking:** on-site. **Terms:** cancellation fee imposed. **Amenities:** high-speed Internet, voice mail, irons, hair dryers. **Pool(s):** heated indoor. **Leisure Activities:** whirlpool, exercise room. **Guest Services:** coin laundry, wireless Internet. **Business Services:** meeting rooms, PC. **Cards:** AX, DC, DS, MC, VI. **Free Special Amenities: continental breakfast and local telephone calls.**

CALL / SOME UNITS

AAA Benefit:
Members save up to 20%, plus 10% bonus points with rewards program.

COMFORT INN *Book great rates at AAA.com*

Phone: (770)954-9110

Hotel
$85-$175 All Year

Address: 80 Hwy 81 W **Location:** I-75, exit 218, just nw. **Facility:** 59 one-bedroom standard units. 2 stories (no elevator), exterior corridors. **Parking:** on-site. **Amenities:** high-speed Internet, voice mail, irons, hair dryers. **Pool(s):** outdoor. **Guest Services:** valet and coin laundry, wireless Internet. **Business Services:** PC, fax. **Cards:** AX, CB, DC, DS, MC, VI. **Free Special Amenities: expanded continental breakfast and high-speed Internet.**

COUNTRY INN & SUITES BY CARLSON-MCDONOUGH Book great rates at AAA.com Phone: (770)957-0082

Hotel
$89-$190 All Year

Address: 115 E Greenwood Rd **Location:** I-75, exit 216, just w. **Facility:** 57 units. 47 one- and 2 two-bedroom standard units, some with whirlpools. 8 one-bedroom suites. 3 stories, interior corridors. *Bath:* combo or shower only. **Parking:** on-site. **Amenities:** high-speed Internet, voice mail, irons, hair dryers. **Pool(s):** heated indoor. **Leisure Activities:** whirlpool, exercise room. **Guest Services:** coin laundry, wireless Internet. **Business Services:** fax. **Cards:** AX, DS, MC, VI.

CALL / SOME UNITS

DAYS INN Book at AAA.com Phone: (770)957-5261

Hotel
$59-$120 All Year

Address: 744 Hwy 155 S **Location:** I-75, exit 216, just e. **Facility:** 57 one-bedroom standard units. 2 stories, exterior corridors. **Parking:** on-site. **Amenities:** high-speed Internet, irons, hair dryers. **Pool(s):** outdoor. **Guest Services:** valet and coin laundry, wireless Internet. **Business Services:** business center. **Cards:** AX, CB, DC, DS, JC, MC, VI.

ASK / SOME UNITS FEE

ECONO LODGE Book at AAA.com Phone: 770/957-2651

Motel
Rates not provided

Address: 1279 Hwy 20 W **Location:** I-75, exit 218, just w. **Facility:** 40 one-bedroom standard units. 2 stories (no elevator), exterior corridors. **Parking:** on-site. **Guest Services:** coin laundry, wireless Internet. **Business Services:** fax.

/ SOME UNITS FEE

HAMPTON INN Book great rates at AAA.com Phone: (770)914-0077

Motel
$69-$200 All Year

Address: 855 Industrial Blvd **Location:** I-75, exit 218, just e to Industrial Blvd, then just s. **Facility:** 74 one-bedroom standard units. 2 stories, exterior corridors. *Bath:* combo or shower only. **Parking:** on-site. **Terms:** 1-30 night minimum stay, cancellation fee imposed. **Amenities:** voice mail, irons, hair dryers. **Pool(s):** outdoor. **Leisure Activities:** exercise room. **Guest Services:** wireless Internet. **Business Services:** meeting rooms, PC. **Cards:** AX, CB, DC, DS, MC, VI.

CALL / SOME UNITS

AAA Benefit:
Members save up to 10% everyday!

HOLIDAY INN EXPRESS HOTEL & SUITES Book at AAA.com Phone: (678)782-1100

Hotel
$129-$295 All Year

Address: 1315 Hwy 20 W **Location:** I-75, exit 218, just w. **Facility:** 84 one-bedroom standard units. 4 stories, interior corridors. *Bath:* combo or shower only. **Parking:** on-site. **Terms:** cancellation fee imposed. **Amenities:** high-speed Internet, dual phone lines, voice mail, irons, hair dryers. **Pool(s):** heated indoor. **Leisure Activities:** whirlpool, exercise room. **Guest Services:** valet and coin laundry, wireless Internet. **Business Services:** meeting rooms, business center. **Cards:** AX, CB, DC, DS, JC, MC, VI.

ASK / SOME UNITS

QUALITY INN & SUITES CONFERENCE CENTER Book great rates at AAA.com Phone: (770)957-5291

Motel
$79-$199 All Year

Address: 930 Hwy 155 S **Location:** I-75, exit 216, just w. **Facility:** 90 units. 81 one-bedroom standard units. 9 one-bedroom suites. 2 stories (no elevator), exterior corridors. **Parking:** on-site. **Amenities:** voice mail, irons, hair dryers. **Pool(s):** outdoor. **Leisure Activities:** limited exercise equipment. **Guest Services:** valet and coin laundry, wireless Internet. **Business Services:** meeting rooms. **Cards:** AX, CB, DC, DS, JC, MC, VI. **Free Special Amenities: full breakfast and newspaper.**

CALL / SOME UNITS FEE

SLEEP INN Book at AAA.com Phone: (770)898-0804

Hotel
$72-$80 All Year

Address: 945 Hwy 155 S **Location:** I-75, exit 216, just w. **Facility:** 51 one-bedroom standard units. 3 stories, interior corridors. *Bath:* shower only. **Parking:** on-site. **Terms:** cancellation fee imposed. **Amenities:** voice mail, irons, hair dryers. **Pool(s):** heated indoor. **Guest Services:** coin laundry, wireless Internet. **Business Services:** meeting rooms, fax. **Cards:** AX, DS, MC, VI.

ASK CALL / SOME UNITS

WHERE TO DINE

O. B.'S B-B-Q Phone: 678/432-6002

Barbecue
$6-$20

Ribs and pork stand out among the restaurant's offerings of slow-cooked hickory-pit barbecue, but fried catfish also merits some thought. Down-home flavors satisfy the usually lively clientele. A large stone fireplace serves as the focal point of the rustic log cabin, a welcoming woodsy spot. Casual dress. **Reservations:** accepted. **Hours:** 11 am-9 pm, Sun-8 pm. Closed major holidays. **Address:** 725 Industrial Blvd **Location:** I-75, exit 218, just e to Industrial Blvd, then 0.3 mi s. **Parking:** on-site. **Cards:** AX, MC, VI.

UP THE CREEK FISH CAMP & GRILL Phone: 770/914-5644

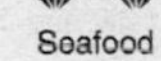

Seafood
$6-$20

Among the broad array of seafood prepared fried, grilled or broiled are tuna, catfish and shrimp. Desserts such as key lime pie are hard to pass up. Casual dress. **Bar:** Full bar. **Hours:** 11 am-11 pm, Fri & Sat-midnight. Closed: 11/26, 12/25. **Address:** 1120 Hwy 20/81 W **Location:** I-75, exit 218, just e. **Parking:** on-site. **Cards:** AX, DS, MC, VI.

MCRAE pop. 2,682

— WHERE TO STAY —

PETE PHILLIPS LODGE

Phone: 229/868-7474

Motel

Rates not provided

Address: US Hwy 441 **Location:** On US 441, 3 mi n. Located in Little Ocmulgee State Park. **Facility:** 60 units. 58 one-bedroom standard units. 2 one-bedroom suites. 1 story, exterior corridors. *Bath:* combo or shower only. **Parking:** on-site. **Terms:** check-in 4 pm. **Amenities:** voice mail, irons, hair dryers. **Dining:** The Fairways Grill, see separate listing. **Pool(s):** outdoor. **Leisure Activities:** rental canoes, rental paddleboats, fishing, 2 lighted tennis courts, rental bicycles, hiking trails, jogging, playground, volleyball. *Fee:* golf-18 holes, miniature golf. **Guest Services:** coin laundry, wireless Internet. **Business Services:** meeting rooms, fax (fee).

/ SOME UNITS

— WHERE TO DINE —

THE FAIRWAYS GRILL

Phone: 229/868-7474

American

$4-$12

In picturesque Little Ocmulgee State Park, the restaurant lets diners watch golfers and wildlife. The menu centers on regional offerings. Also available are a salad bar and several soups. Friendly servers dish out Southern hospitality. Casual dress. **Bar:** Beer & wine. **Hours:** 7-10 am, 11:30-2 & 5-9 pm, Sun-2 pm. **Address:** US Hwy 441 **Location:** On US 441, 3 mi n; in Pete Phillips Lodge. **Parking:** on-site. **Cards:** AX, DC, DS, MC, VI.

METTER pop. 3,879

— WHERE TO STAY —

HOLIDAY INN EXPRESS *Book at AAA.com*

Phone: 912/685-3000

Hotel

Rates not provided

Address: 1225 S Lewis **Location:** I-16, exit 104 (SR 121), just n. **Facility:** 61 one-bedroom standard units. 2 stories (no elevator), exterior corridors. *Bath:* combo or shower only. **Parking:** on-site. **Amenities:** irons, hair dryers. **Pool(s):** outdoor. **Guest Services:** wireless Internet. **Business Services:** meeting rooms.

/ SOME UNITS

MILLEDGEVILLE pop. 18,757

— WHERE TO STAY —

ANTEBELLUM INN

Phone: 478/453-3993

Historic Bed & Breakfast

$109-$189 All Year

Address: 200 N Columbia St **Location:** Just s of Business Rt US 441 (Columbia St); between SR 22 and 49; downtown. **Facility:** Dating from 1890, this Greek Revival-style inn is among Milledgeville's many historic antebellum buildings. Smoke free premises. 5 units. 4 one-bedroom standard units. 1 cottage. 2 stories (no elevator), interior corridors. **Parking:** on-site. **Terms:** check-in 4 pm, 3 day cancellation notice-fee imposed. **Amenities:** video library, hair dryers. **Pool(s):** outdoor. **Guest Services:** wireless Internet. **Business Services:** meeting rooms. **Cards:** AX, DS, MC, VI.

ASK VCR

COMFORT SUITES *Book at AAA.com*

Phone: 478/453-2212

Hotel

Rates not provided

Address: 2621 N Columbia St **Location:** US 441, 3.7 mi n of downtown. **Facility:** Smoke free premises. 47 one-bedroom standard units, some with whirlpools. 2 stories (no elevator), interior corridors. *Bath:* combo or shower only. **Parking:** on-site. **Amenities:** high-speed Internet, voice mail, irons, hair dryers. **Pool(s):** heated indoor. **Leisure Activities:** exercise room. **Guest Services:** valet laundry, wireless Internet. **Business Services:** meeting rooms, business center.

HAMPTON INN *Book great rates at AAA.com*

Phone: (478)451-0050

Hotel

$74-$82 All Year

Address: 2461 N Columbia St **Location:** US 441, 2.6 mi n of downtown. Located on north side of the city. **Facility:** 75 one-bedroom standard units. 3 stories, interior corridors. *Bath:* combo or shower only. **Parking:** on-site, winter plug-ins. **Terms:** 1-30 night minimum stay, cancellation fee imposed. **Amenities:** video games (fee), high-speed Internet, dual phone lines, voice mail, irons, hair dryers. **Pool(s):** outdoor. **Leisure Activities:** exercise room. **Guest Services:** valet laundry, wireless Internet. **Business Services:** meeting rooms, PC. **Cards:** AX, CB, DC, DS, MC, VI.

/ SOME UNITS

Hampton Inn

AAA Benefit:

Members save up to 10% everyday!

HOLIDAY INN EXPRESS HOTEL & SUITES *Book at AAA.com*

Phone: 478/454-9000

Hotel

Rates not provided

Address: 1839 N Columbia St **Location:** US 441, 2 mi n of downtown. **Facility:** 68 one-bedroom standard units, some with whirlpools. 3 stories, interior corridors. *Bath:* combo or shower only. **Parking:** on-site. **Amenities:** high-speed Internet, dual phone lines, voice mail, irons, hair dryers. **Pool(s):** heated indoor. **Leisure Activities:** whirlpool, exercise room. **Guest Services:** valet and coin laundry, wireless Internet. **Business Services:** meeting rooms, PC.

CALL / SOME UNITS FEE

WHERE TO DINE

BO JO'S BOARDWALK CAFE — **Phone:** 478/453-3234

American
$6-$24

The popular family-run steak and seafood house serves regional American dishes in good portion sizes. The friendly staff and pleasant setting make for a nice dining experience. Casual dress. **Bar:** Full bar. **Hours:** 4 pm-10 pm. Closed major holidays; also Sun. **Address:** 3021 N Columbia St **Location:** Jct SR 24 E, 8.3 mi n on US 441. **Parking:** on-site. **Cards:** MC, VI.

MARGARITAS MEXICAN GRILL — **Phone:** 478/453-9547

Mexican
$6-$16

Near area hotels, the colorful restaurant prepares Mexican food in a bright, lively atmosphere. Casual dress. **Bar:** Full bar. **Hours:** 11 am-10 pm, Fri & Sat-11 pm. Closed: 1/1, 5/25, 12/24, 12/25. **Address:** 2400 N Columbia St **Location:** Jct US Business Rt 441/US 441 Bypass, just n. **Parking:** on-site. **Cards:** AX, DS, MC, VI.

CALL

MONTEZUMA pop. 3,999

WHERE TO STAY

DAYS INN MONTEZUMA *Book great rates at AAA.com* — **Phone:** 478/472-4565

Motel
Rates not provided

Address: 520 Spaulding Rd **Location:** Jct SR 26/90, just n. **Facility:** 30 one-bedroom standard units. 2 stories (no elevator), exterior corridors. *Bath:* combo or shower only. **Parking:** on-site. **Amenities:** irons, hair dryers. **Pool(s):** outdoor. **Guest Services:** coin laundry, wireless Internet. **Business Services:** fax (fee).

/ SOME UNITS

WHERE TO DINE

YODERS DEITSCH HAUS — **Phone:** 478/472-2024

American
$5-$10

The restaurant is well-known locally for a generous buffet of homemade braised roast, fried chicken, sausages and kraut, fish and a host of savory vegetables and rolls served by young Mennonite girls. Cream and fruit pies make tasty dessert choices. Diners seat themselves and pay at the counter. An on-premises bakery tempts with mouthwatering aromas. Casual dress. **Hours:** 11:30 am-2 & 5-8:30 pm, Wed-2 pm. Closed major holidays; also Sun & Mon. **Address:** 5252 SR 26 E **Location:** I-75, exit 127 (SR 26), 13.2 mi w. **Parking:** on-site.

MORROW —*See Atlanta p. 410.*

MOULTRIE pop. 14,387

WHERE TO STAY

BARBER-TUCKER HOUSE — **Phone:** 229/890-0714

Bed & Breakfast
$125-$190 All Year

Address: 704 3rd St SW **Location:** Jct US 319 business route and 7th Ave SW, just w, then s; downtown. **Facility:** Large guest rooms are decorated with antiques; property located among shade trees in a quiet, tranquil location. Smoke free premises. 6 one-bedroom standard units. 2 stories (no elevator), interior/exterior corridors. *Bath:* combo or shower only. **Parking:** on-site. **Terms:** 2 night minimum stay - weekends, 3 day cancellation notice-fee imposed. **Amenities:** video library, CD players, high-speed Internet, irons, hair dryers. *Some:* DVD players. **Pool(s):** outdoor. **Guest Services:** wireless Internet. **Business Services:** business center. **Cards:** AX, DS, MC, VI.

ASK / SOME UNITS VCR

BEST WESTERN EXPO INN — **Phone:** 229/890-8652

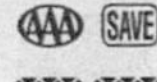

Hotel
$66-$160 All Year

Address: 1300 Veterans Pkwy **Location:** Northern jct US 319 and 319 business route, just e. **Facility:** 60 one-bedroom standard units. 2 stories (no elevator), interior corridors. *Bath:* combo or shower only. **Parking:** on-site. **Amenities:** irons, hair dryers. **Pool(s):** heated indoor. **Guest Services:** wireless Internet. **Business Services:** PC. **Cards:** AX, DS, MC, VI. **Free Special Amenities: continental breakfast and high-speed Internet.**

AAA Benefit:
Members save up to 20%, plus 10% bonus points with rewards program.

WHERE TO DINE

THE BAR-B-QUE PIT — **Phone:** 229/985-5314

Barbecue
$4-$17

If you have an appetite for barbecue, get ready for this town's best. The friendly server will walk you through the selections and then tell you about the sauces to choose from. And, yes, the sauce is made in the back. Casual dress. **Hours:** 11 am-9 pm, Fri & Sat-10 pm. Closed major holidays; also Sun. **Address:** 311 1st Ave SE **Location:** 1.3 mi w of US 319. **Parking:** on-site.

NEWNAN pop. 16,242

WHERE TO STAY

BEST WESTERN-SHENANDOAH INN Book great rates at AAA.com **Phone:** (770)304-9700

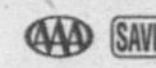

Hotel
$59-$109 All Year

Address: 620 Hwy 34 E **Location:** I-85, exit 47, just w. **Facility:** 42 one-bedroom standard units, some with whirlpools. 2 stories (no elevator), exterior corridors. *Bath:* combo or shower only. **Parking:** on-site. **Terms:** 7 day cancellation notice. **Amenities:** high-speed Internet, voice mail, irons, hair dryers. *Some:* dual phone lines. **Pool(s):** outdoor. **Leisure Activities:** exercise room. **Guest Services:** valet laundry, wireless Internet. **Business Services:** PC. **Cards:** AX, CB, DC, DS, JC, MC, VI. **Free Special Amenities: expanded continental breakfast and high-speed Internet.**

CALL / SOME UNITS FEE

AAA Benefit: Members save up to 20%, plus 10% bonus points with rewards program.

COMFORT INN-ATLANTA/NEWNAN Book great rates at AAA.com **Phone:** (770)502-8688

Hotel
$79-$109 All Year

Address: 590 Bullsboro Dr **Location:** I-85, exit 47, 0.3 mi w. **Facility:** 58 units. 56 one-bedroom standard units, some with whirlpools. 2 one-bedroom suites. 3-4 stories, interior corridors. *Bath:* combo or shower only. **Parking:** on-site. **Terms:** 7 day cancellation notice. **Amenities:** high-speed Internet, voice mail, irons, hair dryers. *Some:* dual phone lines. **Pool(s):** outdoor. **Leisure Activities:** exercise room. **Guest Services:** valet and coin laundry, wireless Internet. **Business Services:** meeting rooms, PC. **Cards:** AX, CB, DC, DS, JC, MC, VI. **Free Special Amenities: expanded continental breakfast and high-speed Internet.**

CALL / SOME UNITS

COUNTRY INN & SUITES BY CARLSON Book great rates at AAA.com **Phone:** (770)304-8500

Hotel
$90-$215 All Year

Address: 1125 Newnan Crossing Blvd **Location:** I-85, exit 47, 0.3 mi e. **Facility:** 64 units. 49 one-bedroom standard units, some with whirlpools. 15 one-bedroom suites, some with whirlpools. 3-4 stories, interior corridors. **Parking:** on-site. **Terms:** 7 day cancellation notice-fee imposed. **Amenities:** voice mail, irons, hair dryers. **Pool(s):** heated indoor. **Leisure Activities:** whirlpool, exercise room. **Guest Services:** valet and coin laundry, wireless Internet. **Business Services:** meeting rooms, business center. **Cards:** AX, DC, DS, MC, VI. **Free Special Amenities: expanded continental breakfast and local telephone calls.**

CALL / SOME UNITS

HAMPTON INN Book great rates at AAA.com **Phone:** (770)253-9922

Hotel
$110-$130 All Year

Address: 50 Hampton Way **Location:** I-85, exit 47, just e. **Facility:** 91 one-bedroom standard units. 3 stories, interior corridors. *Bath:* combo or shower only. **Parking:** on-site. **Terms:** 1-30 night minimum stay, cancellation fee imposed. **Amenities:** high-speed Internet, voice mail, irons, hair dryers. *Some:* dual phone lines. **Pool(s):** outdoor. **Leisure Activities:** exercise room. **Guest Services:** valet laundry, wireless Internet. **Business Services:** meeting rooms, PC, fax. **Cards:** AX, CB, DC, DS, MC, VI.

CALL / SOME UNITS

AAA Benefit: Members save up to 10% everyday!

HOWARD JOHNSON INN Book at AAA.com **Phone:** (770)683-1499

Motel
$50-$75 All Year

Address: 1310 Hwy 29 S **Location:** I-85, exit 41, just w. **Facility:** 58 one-bedroom standard units, some with whirlpools. 2 stories (no elevator), exterior corridors. **Parking:** on-site. **Amenities:** voice mail, safes (fee), irons, hair dryers. **Pool(s):** outdoor. **Guest Services:** coin laundry, wireless Internet. **Cards:** AX, DS, MC, VI.

ASK / SOME UNITS FEE

SPRINGHILL SUITES BY MARRIOTT Book great rates at AAA.com **Phone:** (770)254-8900

Hotel
$124-$133 All Year

Address: 1119 Bullsboro Dr **Location:** I-85, exit 47, 0.3 mi e. **Facility:** Smoke free premises. 82 one-bedroom standard units. 3 stories, interior corridors. *Bath:* combo or shower only. **Parking:** on-site. **Terms:** cancellation fee imposed. **Amenities:** video games (fee), high-speed Internet, dual phone lines, voice mail, irons, hair dryers. **Pool(s):** outdoor. **Leisure Activities:** whirlpool, exercise room. **Guest Services:** valet and coin laundry, wireless Internet. **Business Services:** meeting rooms, PC. **Cards:** AX, CB, DC, DS, JC, MC, VI.

CALL

AAA Benefit: Members save a minimum 5% off the best available rate.

WHERE TO DINE

EL CAZADOR MEXICAN RESTAURANT **Phone:** 770/251-0104

Mexican
$5-$15

Combination plates, house specialties and old standbys like tacos, enchiladas and burritos are the staples at El Cazador. Casual dress. **Bar:** Beer & wine. **Hours:** 10 am-10 pm, Fri & Sat-11 pm. Closed major holidays. **Address:** 1108 Bullsboro Dr **Location:** I-85, exit 47, just w. **Parking:** on-site. **Cards:** AX, DS, MC, VI.

GINGER GRILL & NOODLE HOUSE Phone: 770/502-8883

Asian
$6-$27

Just east of downtown, the storefront restaurant features a wide selection of Asian fare, with tastes that are a cut above. The casual and well-coordinated dining room widely incorporates bamboo accents and greenery into its contemporary look. Casual dress. **Bar:** Full bar. **Reservations:** accepted. **Hours:** 11:30 am-2:30 & 5-10 pm, Fri & Sat-10:30 pm. Closed: 11/26, 12/25. **Address:** 1435 E Hwy 34 **Location:** I-85, exit 47, 0.7 mi e. **Parking:** on-site. **Cards:** AX, CB, DC, DS, JC, MC, VI.

CALL

GOLDENS ON THE SQUARE **Phone:** 770/251-4300

Southern
$5-$7

Freshly prepared Southern favorites, such as fried chicken, mashed potatoes and greens, line cafeteria-style tables at the casual restaurant. Casual dress. **Hours:** 11 am-9 pm. Closed: 1/1, 12/25; also Mon. **Address:** 9 E Court Square **Location:** Downtown. **Parking:** street. **Cards:** MC, VI.

SPRAYBERRY'S BAR-B-QUE **Phone:** 770/253-4421

Regional American
$5-$15

Serving up delicious barbecue since 1926, this family-owned establishment provides three modestly furnished, clean and comfortable dining areas. A tasty lunch might comprise the sliced pork sandwich with hearty onion rings and a slice of scrumptious fried pie. Casual dress. **Hours:** 10:30 am-9 pm. Closed: 1/1, 11/26, 12/25; also Sun. **Address:** 229 Jackson St **Location:** On SR 14, 1 mi n of SR 34. **Parking:** on-site. **Cards:** MC, VI.

SPRAYBERRY'S BAR-B-QUE/I-85 **Phone:** 770/253-5080

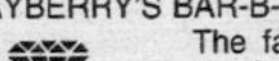

Barbecue
$3-$17

The family-owned establishment provides tasty barbecue lunches and dinners, such as the sliced pork sandwich with hearty onion rings. Fried pie is scrumptious. Casual dress. **Hours:** 10:30 am-9 pm. Closed major holidays; also Sun. **Address:** 1060 Hwy 34 E **Location:** I-85, exit 47, just e. **Parking:** on-site. **Cards:** MC, VI.

NORCROSS —*See Atlanta p. 411.*

OAKWOOD pop. 2,689

WHERE TO STAY

COMFORT INN *Book at AAA.com* **Phone:** (770)287-1000

Hotel
$85-$125 3/2-11/30
$70-$125 12/1-3/1

Address: 3469 Branch Rd **Location:** I-985, exit 16, just e. **Facility:** 72 one-bedroom standard units, some with whirlpools. 2 stories (no elevator), exterior corridors. **Parking:** on-site. **Terms:** 2-3 night minimum stay - seasonal, 3 day cancellation notice. **Amenities:** high-speed Internet, voice mail, irons, hair dryers. **Pool(s):** outdoor. **Guest Services:** valet and coin laundry, wireless Internet. **Business Services:** meeting rooms, PC, fax (fee). **Cards:** AX, CB, DC, DS, JC, MC, VI.

ASK / SOME UNITS

COUNTRY INN & SUITES BY CARLSON *Book at AAA.com* **Phone:** 770/535-8080

Hotel
Rates not provided

Address: 4535 Oakwood Rd **Location:** I-985, exit 16, just sw. **Facility:** 61 units. 46 one-bedroom standard units, some with whirlpools. 15 one-bedroom suites. 3 stories, interior corridors. **Parking:** on-site. **Amenities:** high-speed Internet, dual phone lines, voice mail, irons, hair dryers. **Pool(s):** outdoor. **Guest Services:** valet and coin laundry, wireless Internet. **Business Services:** fax (fee).

FEE / SOME UNITS FEE

JAMESON INN *Book at AAA.com* **Phone:** 770/533-9400

Hotel
Rates not provided

Address: 3780 Merchants Way **Location:** I-985, exit 16, 0.4 mi w. **Facility:** 42 one-bedroom standard units, some with whirlpools. 2 stories (no elevator), exterior corridors. **Parking:** on-site. **Amenities:** high-speed Internet, irons, hair dryers. **Pool(s):** outdoor. **Leisure Activities:** exercise room. **Guest Services:** wireless Internet. **Business Services:** PC, fax (fee).

CALL / SOME UNITS

PEACHTREE CITY pop. 31,580

WHERE TO STAY

BEST WESTERN INN & SUITES *Book great rates at AAA.com* **Phone:** (770)632-9700

AAA SAVE

Motel
$90-$130 All Year

Address: 976 Crosstown Dr **Location:** Jct SR 74 and 54, 2.1 mi s on SR 74. **Facility:** 50 one-bedroom standard units. 2 stories, exterior corridors. *Bath:* combo or shower only. **Parking:** on-site. **Amenities:** high-speed Internet, irons, hair dryers. *Some:* dual phone lines. **Pool(s):** outdoor. **Leisure Activities:** exercise room. **Guest Services:** valet laundry. **Business Services:** PC. **Cards:** AX, CB, DC, DS, MC, VI. **Free Special Amenities: continental breakfast and high-speed Internet.**

CALL    / SOME UNITS FEE

AAA Benefit:
Members save up to 20%, plus 10% bonus points with rewards program.

HAMPTON INN *Book great rates at AAA.com* **Phone:** (770)486-8800

Hotel

$84-$109 All Year

Address: 300 Westpark Dr **Location:** Jct SR 74 and 54, 0.3 mi n on SR 74. **Facility:** 61 one-bedroom standard units. 2 stories (no elevator), interior corridors. *Bath:* combo or shower only. **Parking:** on-site. **Terms:** 1-30 night minimum stay, cancellation fee imposed. **Amenities:** high-speed Internet, voice mail, irons, hair dryers. **Pool(s):** outdoor. **Leisure Activities:** exercise room. **Guest Services:** valet and coin laundry, wireless Internet. **Business Services:** meeting rooms, PC. **Cards:** AX, CB, DC, DS, JC, MC, VI.

CALL / SOME UNITS

AAA Benefit:

Members save up to 10% everyday!

SLEEP INN *Book at AAA.com* **Phone:** (770)486-0044

Hotel

$95-$109 All Year

Address: 109 City Cir **Location:** Jct SR 74 and 54; in The Avenue Shopping Center. **Facility:** 61 one-bedroom standard units, some with whirlpools. 2 stories, interior corridors. *Bath:* shower only. **Parking:** on-site. **Amenities:** high-speed Internet, voice mail, irons, hair dryers. **Leisure Activities:** exercise room. **Guest Services:** valet and coin laundry, wireless Internet. **Business Services:** meeting rooms, PC. **Cards:** AX, DC, DS, JC, MC, VI.

ASK CALL / SOME UNITS

WYNDHAM PEACHTREE HOTEL & CONFERENCE CENTER *Book at AAA.com* **Phone:** (770)487-2000

Resort Hotel

$179 All Year

Address: 2443 Hwy 54 W **Location:** Jct SR 74 and 54, 1 mi e. **Facility:** On extensive grounds, the property features large rooms and spacious public areas. 250 units. 245 one-bedroom standard units. 5 one-bedroom suites. 4 stories, interior corridors. *Bath:* combo or shower only. **Parking:** on-site. **Terms:** cancellation fee imposed. **Amenities:** dual phone lines, voice mail, irons, hair dryers. *Fee:* video games, high-speed Internet. *Some:* CD players. **Pool(s):** outdoor, heated indoor. **Leisure Activities:** saunas, whirlpool, steamrooms, 3 lighted tennis courts, racquetball courts, hiking trails, jogging, sports court. *Fee:* bicycles, massage. **Guest Services:** complimentary laundry, area transportation, wireless Internet. **Business Services:** conference facilities, business center. **Cards:** AX, DC, DS, JC, MC, VI.

ASK CALL / SOME UNITS

WHERE TO DINE

PASCAL'S BISTRO **Phone:** 770/632-0112

Italian

$12-$25

The owner/chef has been known to greet each guest at this Continental eatery. At lunch, the pasta buffet lines up 14 meats and vegetables, four types of pasta and four complementary sauces, Caesar salad and garlic bread. In the evening, white tablecloth service kicks in. Among flavorful dishes are grouper imperial, steak au poivre and mustard-crusted pork tenderloin, and diners also can opt for the reasonably priced three-course prix fixe meal. The long wine list includes a Champagne selection. Casual dress. **Bar:** Full bar. **Hours:** 11 am-2 & 5-9 pm, Fri-10 pm, Sat 5 pm-10 pm. **Address:** 217 Commerce Dr **Location:** At jct SR 54 & 74; in West Park Shopping Center. **Parking:** on-site. **Cards:** AX, CB, DC, DS, JC, MC, VI.

PERRY pop. 9,602

WHERE TO STAY

BEST WESTERN BRADBURY INN & SUITES *Book great rates at AAA.com* **Phone:** (478)218-5200

Hotel

$60-$95 All Year

Address: 205 Lect Dr **Location:** I-75, exit 135 (US 41), just e, then just n. **Facility:** 75 units. 59 one-bedroom standard units, some with whirlpools. 16 one-bedroom suites. 3 stories, interior corridors. *Bath:* combo or shower only. **Parking:** on-site. **Terms:** cancellation fee imposed. **Amenities:** high-speed Internet, dual phone lines, voice mail, irons, hair dryers. **Pool(s):** indoor/outdoor. **Leisure Activities:** whirlpool. **Guest Services:** valet and coin laundry, wireless Internet. **Business Services:** fax (fee). **Cards:** AX, DC, DS, MC, VI.

/ SOME UNITS

AAA Benefit:

Members save up to 20%, plus 10% bonus points with rewards program.

HAMPTON INN *Book great rates at AAA.com* **Phone:** (478)987-7681

Hotel

$107 All Year

Address: 102 Hampton Ct **Location:** I-75, exit 136 (Sam Nunn Blvd), just se. **Facility:** 98 one-bedroom standard units. 2 stories, interior corridors. *Bath:* combo or shower only. **Parking:** on-site. **Terms:** 1-30 night minimum stay, cancellation fee imposed. **Amenities:** high-speed Internet, voice mail, irons, hair dryers. **Pool(s):** outdoor. **Guest Services:** valet laundry, wireless Internet. **Business Services:** PC, fax (fee). **Cards:** AX, CB, DC, DS, MC, VI.

AAA Benefit:

Members save up to 10% everyday!

HENDERSON VILLAGE **Phone:** 478/988-8696

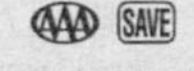

Resort Country Inn
$159-$297 All Year

Address: 125 S Langston Cir **Location:** I-75, exit 127 (SR 26), 1.3 mi w. Located in a quiet rural area. **Facility:** This expansive 18-acre property situated on well-tended grounds includes buildings dating back to the early 1800's. Smoke free premises. 24 units. 19 one-bedroom standard units, some with whirlpools. 5 one-bedroom suites, some with whirlpools. 1-2 stories (no elevator), interior/exterior corridors. **Parking:** on-site. **Terms:** 3 day cancellation notice-fee imposed. **Amenities:** video library, CD players, irons, hair dryers. **Dining:** Langston House, see separate listing. **Pool(s):** outdoor. **Leisure Activities:** fishing, bicycles, hiking trails, horseshoes, game room. *Fee:* clay shooting, table tennis, darts, checkers, horseback riding, massage. **Guest Services:** wireless Internet. **Business Services:** meeting rooms. **Cards:** AX, DS, MC, VI. **Free Special Amenities: full breakfast.**

/ SOME UNITS FEE

HOLIDAY INN *Book at AAA.com* **Phone:** (478)987-3313

Hotel
$95-$120 10/1-11/30
$80-$95 12/1-9/30

Address: 200 Valley Dr **Location:** I-75, exit 136 (Sam Nunn Blvd), just w, then s. **Facility:** 203 one-bedroom standard units. 2 stories (no elevator), exterior corridors. **Parking:** on-site. **Amenities:** high-speed Internet, voice mail, irons, hair dryers. *Some:* safes. **Dining:** Green Derby Restaurant & Bar, see separate listing. **Pool(s):** outdoor. **Leisure Activities:** putting green, limited exercise equipment. **Guest Services:** valet and coin laundry, wireless Internet. **Business Services:** meeting rooms, PC, fax (fee). **Cards:** AX, CB, DC, DS, JC, MC, VI.

ASK / SOME UNITS

JAMESON INN-PERRY *Book at AAA.com* **Phone:** 478/987-5060

Motel
Rates not provided

Address: 200 Market Place Dr **Location:** I-75, exit 136 (Sam Nunn Blvd), just e, then s. **Facility:** 42 one-bedroom standard units, some with whirlpools. 2 stories (no elevator), exterior corridors. **Parking:** on-site. **Amenities:** high-speed Internet, hair dryers. **Pool(s):** outdoor. **Leisure Activities:** limited exercise equipment. **Guest Services:** valet laundry, wireless Internet. **Business Services:** PC, fax (fee).

/ SOME UNITS

NEW PERRY HOTEL *Book at AAA.com* **Phone:** (478)987-1000

Historic Hotel
$59-$125 All Year

Address: 800 Main St **Location:** I-75, exit 136 (Sam Nunn Blvd) southbound, 1.2 mi se on US 341, then just w; exit 135 (US 41) northbound, 1.5 mi ne, then just s. **Facility:** This 1925 hotel is within walking distance of the downtown district that is filled with antique stores and specialty shops. 42 units. 40 one-bedroom standard units. 2 one-bedroom suites. 1-3 stories (no elevator), interior/exterior corridors. *Bath:* combo or shower only. **Parking:** on-site. **Amenities:** high-speed Internet. **Dining:** The Restaurant, see separate listing. **Pool(s):** outdoor. **Guest Services:** valet laundry, wireless Internet. **Business Services:** meeting rooms, business center. **Cards:** AX, DS, MC, VI.

ASK / SOME UNITS FEE

QUALITY INN *Book great rates at AAA.com* **Phone:** (478)987-1345

Motel
$65-$95 All Year

Address: 1504 Sam Nunn Blvd **Location:** I-75, exit 136 (Sam Nunn Blvd), just w. **Facility:** 56 units. 54 one-bedroom standard units. 2 one-bedroom suites. 1 story, exterior corridors. **Parking:** on-site. **Terms:** 30 day cancellation notice. **Amenities:** voice mail, irons, hair dryers. **Dining:** Angelina's Italian Garden Cafe, see separate listing. **Pool(s):** outdoor. **Guest Services:** wireless Internet. **Business Services:** business center. **Cards:** AX, CB, DC, DS, JC, MC, VI. **Free Special Amenities: continental breakfast and high-speed Internet.**

/ SOME UNITS FEE

SUPER 8 MOTEL *Book great rates at AAA.com* **Phone:** 478/987-0999

Hotel
Rates not provided

Address: 102 Plaza Dr **Location:** I-75, exit 136 (Sam Nunn Blvd), just e. **Facility:** 56 one-bedroom standard units, some with whirlpools. 2 stories (no elevator), exterior corridors. *Bath:* combo or shower only. **Parking:** on-site. **Amenities:** high-speed Internet. **Pool(s):** outdoor. **Guest Services:** coin laundry, wireless Internet. **Business Services:** fax (fee). **Free Special Amenities: expanded continental breakfast and high-speed Internet.**

/ SOME UNITS FEE

WHERE TO DINE

ANGELINA'S ITALIAN GARDEN CAFE **Phone:** 478/987-9494

Italian
$6-$17

The Old World eatery brings the outside in with umbrellas, flower beds and a fountain. Freshly cut veal and prime rib, homemade garlic rolls and the well-known family salad bowl are a few of the features on a traditional menu. Casual dress. **Reservations:** accepted. **Hours:** noon-2 & 5-9:30 pm, Fri-10 pm, Sat 5 pm-10 pm. Closed: major holidays; also 12/24, Sun. **Address:** 1500 Sam Nunn Blvd **Location:** I-75, exit 136 (Sam Nunn Blvd), just w; in Quality Inn. **Parking:** on-site. **Cards:** AX, DC, DS, MC, VI.

GREEN DERBY RESTAURANT & BAR **Phone:** 478/987-8877

Regional American
$5-$15

This restaurant and lounge features a full-service entree menu accompanied by a soup and salad bar. Local and regional favorites are prepared to order. Service is casual and friendly. Casual dress. **Bar:** Full bar. **Reservations:** accepted. **Hours:** 6:30 am-10 pm. Closed: for lunch & dinner 12/25. **Address:** 200 Valley Dr **Location:** I-75, exit 136 (Sam Nunn Blvd), just w, then s; in Holiday Inn. **Parking:** on-site. **Cards:** AX, DC, DS, MC, VI.

CALL

LANGSTON HOUSE **Phone:** 478/988-8696

Continental
$8-$29

Patrons experience the civility of yesterday in the historic 1838 Langston House. The restaurant serves preparations of veal, fresh fish, pork tenderloin and filet of beef. The menu changes every Tuesday, and daily chef's specials won't disappoint. In-house desserts are sweet temptations. Hearty Southern breakfasts are cooked to order each morning. Casual dress. **Bar:** Full bar. **Reservations:** suggested. **Hours:** 7-10 am, 11:30-2 & 6-9 pm, Fri & Sat 6 pm-10 pm. Closed: for dinner Sun & Mon. **Address:** 125 S Langston Cir **Location:** I-75, exit 127 (SR 26), 1.3 mi w; in Henderson Village. **Parking:** on-site. **Cards:** AX, CB, DC, DS, JC, MC, VI. **Historic**

MY SISTER'S CAFE **Phone:** 478/987-3131

American
$5-$15

The cafe's friendly staff serves satisfying comfort foods and tends tables of guests who opt instead for the lunch buffet. Casual dress. **Hours:** 8 am-9 pm. **Address:** 107 Perimeter Rd **Location:** I-75, exit 136 (Sam Nunn Blvd), just e. **Parking:** on-site. **Cards:** MC, VI.

THE RESTAURANT **Phone:** 478/987-1000

American
$7-$19

Find a home away from home in the bright dining rooms of this restaurant serving regional, down-home cooking. Homemade pastry and dessert are a perfect way to have a happy ending in finishing off your meal. Enjoy the gracious, efficient servers. Casual dress. **Bar:** Full bar. **Hours:** 11 am-2 & 5-9 pm, Sun-3 pm. Closed: 12/25. **Address:** 800 Main St **Location:** I-75, exit 136 (Sam Nunn Blvd) southbound, 1.2 mi se on US 341, then just w; exit 135 (US 41) northbound, 1.5 mi ne, then just s; in New Perry Hotel. **Parking:** on-site. **Cards:** AX, DS, MC, VI.

SONNY'S REAL PIT BAR-B-Q **Phone:** 478/218-2100

Barbecue
$6-$15

House specialties include pork and chicken grilled over an open pit, barbecue ribs and fresh, homemade pie. The salad bar offers another popular option. Rustic and comfortable, the atmosphere is perfect for family meals. Casual dress. **Bar:** Beer only. **Hours:** 11 am-9:30 pm, Fri & Sat-10 pm. Closed: 11/26, 12/25. **Address:** 1001 St. Patricks Dr **Location:** I-75, exit 136 (Sam Nunn Blvd), just e, then 0.4 mi n. **Parking:** on-site. **Cards:** AX, DS, MC, VI.

THE SWANSON **Phone:** 478/987-1938

AAA

American
$5-$22

Housed in a historic building in the heart of downtown, the Southern-style establishment doesn't skimp on hospitality and offers some delectable selections. Dressy casual. **Hours:** 11 am-2 & 5-9 pm, Sun-2 pm. Closed: 1/1, 12/25. **Address:** 933 Carroll St **Location:** I-75, exit 136 (Sam Nunn Blvd); corner of Washington and Carroll St; downtown. **Parking:** on-site. **Cards:** AX, DS, MC, VI.

PINE MOUNTAIN pop. 1,141

WHERE TO STAY

THE COTTAGES AT CALLAWAY GARDENS **Phone:** 706/663-2281

AAA SAVE

Resort Cottage
$194-$377 All Year

Address: 3168 Calloway Southern Pine Dr **Location:** Jct US 27/SR 1, 2 mi w on SR 354; in Callaway Gardens. **Facility:** Surrounded by a beautiful garden, these spacious and handsome dwellings are a favorite of leisure travelers, especially golfers. Smoke free premises. 310 units. 155 one-bedroom standard units. 155 one-bedroom suites with efficiencies. 1 story, exterior corridors. **Parking:** on-site. **Terms:** check-in 4 pm, 2-4 night minimum stay, 7 day cancellation notice-fee imposed. **Amenities:** voice mail, irons, hair dryers. *Fee:* video games, high-speed Internet. **Pool(s):** heated indoor. **Leisure Activities:** whirlpool. *Fee:* golf-36 holes. **Guest Services:** valet and coin laundry, airport transportation-Harris County Municipal Airport, area transportation-resort. **Cards:** AX, DS, MC, VI. **Free Special Amenities: local telephone calls.**

/ SOME UNITS

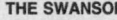

DAVIS INN **Phone:** 706/663-2522

Motel
Rates not provided

Address: 5585 Hwy 354 **Location:** Jct US 27/SR 1, just e. Located in a quiet area adjacent to Callaway Gardens. **Facility:** Smoke free premises. 10 one-bedroom standard units, some with kitchens. 1 story, exterior corridors. **Parking:** on-site. **Terms:** office hours 8 am-5 pm. **Amenities:** voice mail, irons, hair dryers. **Guest Services:** wireless Internet.

THE LODGE AND SPA AT CALLAWAY GARDENS **Phone:** 706/663-2281

AAA SAVE

Resort Hotel
$227-$317 All Year

Address: 3168 Callaway Southern Pine Dr **Location:** Jct US 27 and SR 1, 2 mi w on SR 354. **Facility:** A luxury lodge located on the grounds of Callaway Gardens, a AAA GEM attraction, sharing all of the resort facilities. Smoke free premises. 150 units. 143 one-bedroom standard units. 7 one-bedroom suites, some with whirlpools. 4 stories, interior corridors. *Bath:* combo or shower only. **Parking:** on-site and valet. **Terms:** check-in 4 pm, 7 day cancellation notice-fee imposed. **Amenities:** video games (fee), high-speed Internet, voice mail, safes, irons, hair dryers. **Dining:** Piedmont Dining Room at Callaway, see separate listing. **Pool(s):** heated outdoor. **Leisure Activities:** whirlpools, beach access, rental canoes, rental paddleboats, fishing, recreation programs in summer, rental bicycles, hiking trails, playground, spa, shuffleboard. *Fee:* golf-36 holes. **Guest Services:** valet and coin laundry, airport transportation-Harris County Municipal Airport, area transportation-resort, wireless Internet. **Business Services:** conference facilities, business center. **Cards:** AX, DS, MC, VI. **Free Special Amenities: local telephone calls.**

CALL / SOME UNITS

MOUNTAIN CREEK INN AT CALLAWAY GARDENS *Book great rates at AAA.com* **Phone:** 706/663-2281

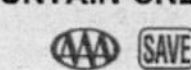

Resort Motel
$129-$171 All Year

Address: 17800 Hwy 27 **Location:** Jct SR 354, 1.5 mi s on US 27/SR 1; in Callaway Gardens. **Facility:** A popular resort centrally located, offering access to many local facilities. Smoke free premises. 323 one-bedroom standard units. 1-4 stories, exterior corridors. **Parking:** on-site. **Terms:** check-in 4 pm, 2-4 night minimum stay, 7 day cancellation notice. **Amenities:** voice mail, irons, hair dryers. *Fee:* video games, high-speed Internet. **Pool(s):** outdoor. **Leisure Activities:** exercise room. *Fee:* golf-36 holes. **Guest Services:** valet and coin laundry, airport transportation (fee)-Harris County Municipal Airport, area transportation-resort. **Cards:** AX, DS, MC, VI. **Free Special Amenities: local telephone calls.**

FEE CALL / SOME UNITS FEE

THE VILLAS AT CALLAWAY GARDENS **Phone:** 706/663-2281

Resort Condominium
$148-$728 All Year

Address: 17800 Hwy 27 **Location:** Jct SR 354, 1.5 mi s on US 27/SR 1; in Callaway Gardens. **Facility:** Well-equipped villas are situated on the grounds of Callaway Gardens, offering easy access to the resort's amenities. Smoke free premises. 147 units. 97 one-bedroom standard units. 50 condominiums. 1-2 stories (no elevator), exterior corridors. **Parking:** on-site. **Terms:** check-in 4 pm, 2-4 night minimum stay, 7 day cancellation notice-fee imposed. **Amenities:** high-speed Internet (fee), voice mail, irons, hair dryers. **Pool(s):** outdoor. **Leisure Activities:** whirlpool. *Fee:* golf-36 holes. **Guest Services:** valet and coin laundry, airport transportation-Harris County Municipal Airport, area transportation-resort. **Cards:** AX, DS, MC, VI. **Free Special Amenities: local telephone calls.**

WHITE COLUMNS MOTEL **Phone:** (706)663-2312

Motel
$59-$80 All Year

Address: 524 S Main Ave **Location:** Jct SR 354, just n on US 27/SR 1. **Facility:** 14 units. 13 one-bedroom standard units, some with kitchens. 1 one-bedroom suite. 1-2 stories, exterior corridors. **Parking:** on-site. **Terms:** 2-3 night minimum stay - seasonal and/or weekends, 3 day cancellation notice-fee imposed. **Amenities:** voice mail, hair dryers. *Some:* irons. **Guest Services:** wireless Internet. **Cards:** AX, DS, MC, VI.

ASK / SOME UNITS FEE

WHERE TO DINE

CRICKET'S RESTAURANT **Phone:** 706/663-8136

American
$9-$29

Leave the normal hustle and bustle of the city behind and slip into nature at this New Orleans-style restaurant located in the cozy comfort of the woods. Take in a great view of nature while dining on catfish, spicy jambalaya and other Creole specialties. Casual dress. **Bar:** Beer & wine. **Hours:** 5 pm-9 pm. Closed: 12/25. **Address:** Hwy 18 **Location:** Jct US 27/SR 1, 4 mi w on SR 18. **Parking:** on-site. **Cards:** AX, DC, DS, MC, VI.

PIEDMONT DINING ROOM AT CALLAWAY **Phone:** 706/663-2281

American
$8-$37

Prime steak, seafood, chicken and pasta are on the menu at this casual, upscale restaurant, which is located at Callaway Gardens. The breakfast menu features made-to-order omelets and other tasty fare. Dressy casual. **Bar:** Full bar. **Reservations:** suggested. **Hours:** 7-10:30 am, 11:30-2 & 5-9 pm. **Address:** 3168 Calloway Southern Pine Dr **Location:** US 27/SR 1, 2 mi w on SR 354; in The Lodge & Spa at Calloway. **Parking:** on-site. **Cards:** AX, DC, DS, MC, VI.

CALL

PLAINS pop. 637

WHERE TO STAY

PLAINS HISTORIC INN **Phone:** 229/824-4517

Bed & Breakfast
$75-$110 All Year

Address: 106 Main St **Location:** Center. **Facility:** A historic building restored and owned by former President Jimmy Carter; guest rooms are individually decorated from various decades. Smoke free premises. 7 one-bedroom standard units, some with whirlpools. 2 stories, interior corridors. **Parking:** street. **Terms:** office hours 10 am-6 pm, cancellation fee imposed. **Amenities:** video library, hair dryers. **Guest Services:** wireless Internet. **Business Services:** fax. **Cards:** AX, DS, MC, VI.

ASK / SOME UNITS VCR

POOLER pop. 6,239 (See map and index starting on p. 520)

WHERE TO STAY

BEST WESTERN BRADBURY SUITES *Book great rates at AAA.com* **Phone:** (912)330-0330 51

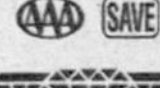

Hotel
$79-$189 All Year

Address: 155 Bourne Ave **Location:** I-95, exit 102 (US 80), just e. Located adjacent to the Mighty 8th Air Force Museum. **Facility:** 92 units. 87 one-bedroom standard units. 5 one-bedroom suites with whirlpools. 3 stories, interior corridors. *Bath:* combo or shower only. **Parking:** on-site. **Amenities:** dual phone lines, voice mail, irons, hair dryers. **Pool(s):** heated indoor. **Leisure Activities:** sauna, whirlpool, exercise room. **Guest Services:** valet and coin laundry, wireless Internet. **Business Services:** meeting rooms, business center. **Cards:** AX, CB, DC, DS, JC, MC, VI. **Free Special Amenities: expanded continental breakfast.**

CALL / SOME UNITS

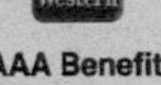

AAA Benefit:
Members save up to 20%, plus 10% bonus points with rewards program.

HOLIDAY INN SAVANNAH WEST *Book at AAA.com* **Phone:** (912)330-5100 53

Hotel
$125-$165 All Year

Address: 103 San Dr **Location:** I-95, exit 102 (US 80), just w. **Facility:** 102 one-bedroom standard units, some with whirlpools. 4 stories, interior corridors. *Bath:* combo or shower only. **Parking:** on-site. **Terms:** cancellation fee imposed. **Amenities:** high-speed Internet, dual phone lines, voice mail, irons, hair dryers. **Pool(s):** heated indoor. **Leisure Activities:** whirlpool, exercise room. **Guest Services:** valet laundry, area transportation, wireless Internet. **Business Services:** meeting rooms, business center. **Cards:** AX, CB, DC, DS, MC, VI.

ASK / SOME UNITS FEE

JAMESON INN *Book at AAA.com* **Phone:** (912)748-0017 52

Hotel
$93-$100 All Year

Address: 125 Bourne Ave **Location:** I-95, exit 102 (US 80), just e. **Facility:** 55 units. 53 one-bedroom standard units. 2 one-bedroom suites. 3 stories, interior corridors. *Bath:* combo or shower only. **Parking:** on-site. **Terms:** cancellation fee imposed. **Amenities:** voice mail, irons, hair dryers. **Pool(s):** outdoor. **Leisure Activities:** exercise room. **Guest Services:** valet laundry, wireless Internet. **Business Services:** meeting rooms, PC. **Cards:** AX, DC, DS, MC, VI.

ASK / SOME UNITS FEE

LA QUINTA INN & SUITES *Book at AAA.com* **Phone:** (912)748-3771 50

Hotel
$69-$139 All Year

Address: 414 Gray St **Location:** I-95, exit 102 (US 80), just w. **Facility:** Smoke free premises. 63 units. 61 one-bedroom standard units. 2 one-bedroom suites. 3 stories, interior corridors. **Parking:** on-site. **Amenities:** high-speed Internet, voice mail, irons, hair dryers. **Pool(s):** heated outdoor. **Leisure Activities:** whirlpool, exercise room. **Guest Services:** coin laundry, area transportation (fee), wireless Internet. **Business Services:** meeting rooms, business center. **Cards:** AX, DC, DS, MC, VI.

/ SOME UNITS

MICROTEL INN & SUITES *Book great rates at AAA.com* **Phone:** (912)748-1112 55

AAA SAVE

Hotel
$60-$160 All Year

Address: 125 Continental Blvd **Location:** I-95, exit 102 (US 80), just e. **Facility:** 71 one-bedroom standard units. 2 stories (no elevator), interior corridors. *Bath:* combo or shower only. **Parking:** on-site. **Amenities:** voice mail, hair dryers. *Some:* irons. **Pool(s):** outdoor. **Guest Services:** wireless Internet. **Cards:** AX, CB, DC, DS, MC, VI.

/ SOME UNITS

TRAVELODGE SUITES *Book great rates at AAA.com* **Phone:** (912)748-6363 54

AAA SAVE

Hotel
$59-$149 All Year

Address: 130 Continental Blvd **Location:** I-95, exit 102 (US 80), just e. **Facility:** 72 units. 70 one-bedroom standard units, some with whirlpools. 2 one-bedroom suites. 3 stories, interior corridors. *Bath:* combo or shower only. **Parking:** on-site. **Amenities:** voice mail, hair dryers. **Pool(s):** heated indoor. **Guest Services:** coin laundry, wireless Internet. **Business Services:** PC. **Cards:** AX, DS, MC, VI. **Free Special Amenities: expanded continental breakfast and high-speed Internet.**

/ SOME UNITS FEE

WHERE TO DINE

FETTUCCINI & CO **Phone:** 912/450-3463 25

Italian
$9-$15

Some of the well-prepared traditional Italian entrees can take on an interesting and flavorful slant. The dining room decor has a casual, Mediterranean theme; a ceiling mural and hanging arbor add to the ambience. Casual dress. **Bar:** Full bar. **Hours:** 11 am-9 pm, Fri-10 pm, Sat 4 pm-10 pm, Sun 4 pm-9 pm. Closed major holidays; also Mon. **Address:** 125 Foxfield Way, Suite F **Location:** I-95, exit 104 (Pooler Pkwy), 0.3 mi w to Benton Blvd, then just n; at west end of strip plaza. **Parking:** on-site. **Cards:** AX, MC, VI.

CALL &M

LOVEZZOLA'S PIZZA RESTAURANT **Phone:** 912/748-6414 26

Italian
$5-$19

Sheltered by large old oaks, this wonderful little eatery with colorful awnings and red-and-white-checkered tablecloths serves excellent homemade pizza, a seemingly endless variety of hot and cold sandwiches and popular dishes such as lasagna, ravioli and spaghetti. A buffet is set up at lunch and on Sunday night. Casual dress. **Bar:** Beer & wine. **Hours:** 10 am-10 pm, Fri & Sat-11 pm. Closed major holidays. **Address:** 320 E Hwy 80 **Location:** I-95, exit 102 (US 80), just nw. **Parking:** on-site. **Cards:** AX, MC, VI.

MIWA JAPANESE RESTAURANT **Phone:** 912/748-8228 24

Japanese
$6-$19

The menu features teriyaki, grilled, yakiniku and katsu preparations of chicken, steak and a few seafood items as well as made-to-order sushi. Expect a relaxed dining experience. Casual dress. **Bar:** Beer & wine. **Hours:** 11 am-2 & 5-9 pm, Sat from noon. Closed major holidays; also Sun. **Address:** 125 Foxfield Way **Location:** I-95, exit 104, 0.3 mi w on Benton Blvd, then just n; in Towne Plaza. **Parking:** on-site. **Cards:** AX, MC, VI.

PORT WENTWORTH pop. 3,276 (See map and index starting on p. 520)

WHERE TO STAY

COMFORT SUITES SAVANNAH NORTH Book at AAA.com Phone: 912/965-1445 42

Hotel
Rates not provided

Address: 115 Travelers Way **Location:** I-95, exit 109 (SR 21), just nw. **Facility:** Smoke free premises. 83 one-bedroom standard units, some with whirlpools. 3 stories, interior corridors. *Bath:* combo or shower only. **Parking:** on-site. **Amenities:** high-speed Internet, voice mail, irons, hair dryers. **Pool(s):** heated indoor. **Leisure Activities:** whirlpool, exercise room. **Guest Services:** coin laundry, wireless Internet. **Business Services:** meeting rooms, business center.

COUNTRY INN & SUITES SAVANNAH NORTH Book great rates at AAA.com Phone: (912)964-2300 44

AAA SAVE
Hotel
$80-$134 All Year

Address: 200 Raley Rd **Location:** I-95, exit 109 (SR 21), just s. **Facility:** 61 units. 50 one-bedroom standard units, some with whirlpools. 11 one-bedroom suites. 3 stories, interior corridors. *Bath:* combo or shower only. **Parking:** on-site. **Amenities:** high-speed Internet, voice mail, irons, hair dryers. **Pool(s):** heated indoor. **Leisure Activities:** whirlpool. **Guest Services:** valet and coin laundry, wireless Internet. **Business Services:** meeting rooms. **Cards:** AX, DC, DS, MC, VI. **Free Special Amenities: full breakfast and high-speed Internet.**

/ SOME UNITS

DAYS INN & SUITES Book at AAA.com Phone: (912)629-1900 43

Hotel
$60-$199 All Year

Address: 105 Travelers Way **Location:** I-95, exit 109 (SR 21), just nw. **Facility:** Smoke free premises. 63 one-bedroom standard units. 3 stories, interior corridors. *Bath:* combo or shower only. **Parking:** on-site. **Terms:** 2 night minimum stay. **Amenities:** high-speed Internet, voice mail, irons, hair dryers. **Pool(s):** outdoor. **Leisure Activities:** limited exercise equipment. **Guest Services:** coin laundry, wireless Internet. **Business Services:** business center. **Cards:** AX, DC, DS, MC, VI.

ASK

HOLIDAY INN EXPRESS SAVANNAH NORTH Book at AAA.com Phone: (912)964-8900 41

Hotel
$89-$149 All Year

Address: 7210 Hwy 21 **Location:** I-95, exit 109 (SR 21), just n. **Facility:** 82 one-bedroom standard units. 2 stories, interior corridors. *Bath:* combo or shower only. **Parking:** on-site. **Terms:** cancellation fee imposed. **Amenities:** high-speed Internet, dual phone lines, voice mail, irons, hair dryers. **Pool(s):** outdoor. **Leisure Activities:** exercise room. **Guest Services:** valet and coin laundry, wireless Internet. **Business Services:** meeting rooms, business center. **Cards:** AX, CB, DC, DS, JC, MC, VI.

ASK / SOME UNITS VCR

INN AT MULBERRY GROVE Book at AAA.com Phone: (912)965-9666 46

Hotel
$90-$200 All Year

Address: 101 O'Leary Rd **Location:** I-95, exit 109 (SR 21), just e. **Facility:** Smoke free premises. 47 one-bedroom standard units, some with whirlpools. 2 stories (no elevator), exterior corridors. *Bath:* combo or shower only. **Parking:** on-site. **Terms:** cancellation fee imposed. **Amenities:** high-speed Internet, irons, hair dryers. **Guest Services:** coin laundry, wireless Internet. **Business Services:** business center. **Cards:** AX, DS, MC, VI.

ASK

QUALITY INN & SUITES Book at AAA.com Phone: (912)965-1313 40

Hotel
$75-$175 All Year

Address: 7220 Hwy 21 **Location:** I-95, exit 109 (SR 21), just n. **Facility:** 60 units. 54 one-bedroom standard units, some with whirlpools. 6 one-bedroom suites. 2 stories, interior corridors. *Bath:* combo or shower only. **Parking:** on-site. **Amenities:** high-speed Internet, dual phone lines, irons, hair dryers. **Pool(s):** outdoor. **Guest Services:** valet and coin laundry, wireless Internet. **Business Services:** meeting rooms, PC. **Cards:** AX, CB, DC, DS, JC, MC, VI.

ASK / SOME UNITS

SLEEP INN-SAVANNAH NORTH Book great rates at AAA.com Phone: (912)966-9800 47

AAA SAVE
Hotel
$69-$145 All Year

Address: 7206 Hwy 21 **Location:** I-95, exit 109 (SR 21), just n. **Facility:** 85 one-bedroom standard units. 2 stories (no elevator), interior corridors. *Bath:* combo or shower only. **Parking:** on-site. **Amenities:** safes, irons, hair dryers. **Pool(s):** outdoor. **Guest Services:** wireless Internet. **Business Services:** PC. **Cards:** AX, CB, DC, DS, JC, MC, VI. **Free Special Amenities: continental breakfast and high-speed Internet.**

/ SOME UNITS

WINGATE INN Book great rates at AAA.com Phone: (912)964-0840 45

AAA SAVE
Hotel
$69-$129 All Year

Address: 115 O' Leary Rd **Location:** I-95, exit 109 (SR 21), just e, then just n. **Facility:** 83 one-bedroom standard units. 4 stories, interior corridors. *Bath:* combo or shower only. **Parking:** on-site. **Amenities:** high-speed Internet, dual phone lines, voice mail, safes, irons, hair dryers. **Leisure Activities:** whirlpool, exercise room. **Guest Services:** valet and coin laundry, wireless Internet. **Business Services:** meeting rooms, business center. **Cards:** AX, DC, DS, MC, VI. **Free Special Amenities: expanded continental breakfast and high-speed Internet.**

CALL M / SOME UNITS FEE

WHERE TO DINE

ISLAND GRILL — Phone: 912/966-0969 (21)

Seafood
$8-$20

The atmosphere bustles at the popular sports bar, which has a basically constructed dining room. Examples of nicely prepared food include varied sandwiches and some standard-type entrees. Casual dress. **Bar:** Full bar. **Hours:** 11 am-10 pm, Sun from 11:30 am. Closed: 12/25. **Address:** 7222 Hwy 21 **Location:** I-95, exit 109 (SR 21), 0.5 mi n. **Parking:** on-site. **Cards:** AX, DS, MC, VI.

CALL

RICHMOND HILL pop. 6,959

WHERE TO STAY

BEST WESTERN RICHMOND HILL INN — Book great rates at AAA.com — **Phone:** (912)756-7070

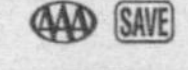

Hotel
$79-$129 All Year

Address: 4564 Hwy 17 **Location:** I-95, exit 87 (Ocean Hwy/US 17), just w. **Facility:** 59 one-bedroom standard units. 3 stories, interior corridors. *Bath:* combo or shower only. **Parking:** on-site. **Amenities:** high-speed Internet, voice mail, irons, hair dryers. **Pool(s):** heated indoor. **Leisure Activities:** whirlpool, exercise room. **Guest Services:** coin laundry, wireless Internet. **Business Services:** business center. **Cards:** AX, CB, DC, DS, JC, MC, VI. **Free Special Amenities: expanded continental breakfast and high-speed Internet.** *(See color ad p 537)*

/ SOME UNITS FEE

AAA Benefit:
Members save up to 20%, plus 10% bonus points with rewards program.

COMFORT SUITES — Book great rates at AAA.com — **Phone:** (912)756-6668

Hotel
$89-$109 All Year

Address: 4601 Hwy 17 **Location:** I-95, exit 87 (Ocean Hwy/US 17), 0.4 mi sw. **Facility:** Smoke free premises. 65 one-bedroom standard units, some with whirlpools. 3 stories, interior corridors. *Bath:* combo or shower only. **Parking:** on-site. **Terms:** 14 day cancellation notice. **Amenities:** high-speed Internet, voice mail, irons, hair dryers. **Pool(s):** outdoor. **Leisure Activities:** sauna, whirlpools, limited exercise equipment. **Guest Services:** coin laundry, wireless Internet. **Business Services:** meeting rooms, business center. **Cards:** AX, CB, DC, DS, JC, MC, VI. **Free Special Amenities: local telephone calls and high-speed Internet.**

/ SOME UNITS FEE

ECONO LODGE-RICHMOND HILL — Book great rates at AAA.com — **Phone:** (912)756-3312

Motel
$50-$75 All Year

Address: 4701 US 17 **Location:** I-95, exit 87 (Ocean Hwy/US 17), 0.4 mi sw. **Facility:** 47 one-bedroom standard units. 2 stories, exterior corridors. **Parking:** on-site. **Amenities:** high-speed Internet, irons, hair dryers. **Guest Services:** coin laundry, wireless Internet. **Cards:** AX, DS, MC, VI. **Free Special Amenities: full breakfast and high-speed Internet.**

/ SOME UNITS

HAMPTON INN — Book great rates at AAA.com — **Phone:** (912)756-2272

Hotel
$72-$200 All Year

Address: 4679 Hwy 17 **Location:** I-95, exit 87 (Ocean Hwy/US 17), 0.4 mi sw. **Facility:** 64 one-bedroom standard units. 3 stories, interior corridors. *Bath:* combo or shower only. **Parking:** on-site. **Terms:** cancellation fee imposed. **Amenities:** high-speed Internet, voice mail, irons, hair dryers. **Pool(s):** outdoor. **Leisure Activities:** limited exercise equipment. **Guest Services:** coin laundry, wireless Internet. **Business Services:** PC. **Cards:** AX, DC, DS, MC, VI. **Free Special Amenities: full breakfast and high-speed Internet.**

/ SOME UNITS

AAA Benefit:
Members save up to 10% everyday!

HOLIDAY INN — Book great rates at AAA.com — **Phone:** (912)756-3351

Hotel
$72-$81 All Year

Address: 4300 Coastal Hwy 17 S **Location:** I-95, exit 87 (Ocean Hwy/US 17), just sw. **Facility:** 136 one-bedroom standard units. 2 stories (no elevator), exterior corridors. **Parking:** on-site. **Amenities:** dual phone lines, voice mail, irons, hair dryers. **Dining:** The Dining Room and Lounge, see separate listing. **Pool(s):** outdoor. **Leisure Activities:** exercise room. **Guest Services:** valet and coin laundry, wireless Internet. **Business Services:** meeting rooms, PC. **Cards:** AX, DS, MC, VI. **Free Special Amenities: local telephone calls and high-speed Internet.**

/ SOME UNITS

WHERE TO DINE

THE DINING ROOM AND LOUNGE — **Phone:** 912/756-3351

American
$7-$18

The original chicken pot pie recipe (without vegetables) has been a cornerstone of the menu for more than three decades. But the crowd that gathers here also enjoys steak and local, fresh seafood where the atmosphere is relaxed and the service attentive. Buffet is served at lunch. Casual dress. **Bar:** Full bar. **Hours:** 6:30-10 am, 11:30-2 & 6-9 pm, Sat 6:30 am-10 & 6-9 pm, Sun-10 am. Closed major holidays. **Address:** 4300 Coastal Hwy 17 S **Location:** I-95, exit 87 (Ocean Hwy/US 17), just sw; in Holiday Inn. **Parking:** on-site. **Cards:** AX, DC, DS, MC, VI.

MOLLY MACPHERSON'S SCOTTISH PUB & GRILL **Phone:** 912/459-9600

Scottish
$9-$18

The pub decor and atmosphere add to the enjoyment of a casual, carefree dining experience. A large and varied selection of single malt scotches complements the Scottish pub fare, such as bangers and mash and shepherd's pie, as well as more traditional American entrees. Service, while informal, is attentive. Casual dress. **Bar:** Full bar. **Hours:** 11 am-10 pm. Closed major holidays; also Sun. **Address:** 3742 Hwy 17 S **Location:** I-95, exit 87, 0.4 mi e; in Park South Plaza. **Parking:** on-site. **Cards:** AX, DS, MC, VI.

SOUTHERN IMAGE RESTAURANT **Phone:** 912/756-3535

American
$5-$16

The accent is on Southern preparations of chicken, fried seafood, steaks and sandwiches. Daily multicourse lunch and dinner specials are popular and reasonably priced. The atmosphere is casual and relaxed. Casual dress. **Hours:** 11 am-2 pm, Thurs-Sun to 9 pm. Closed: 1/1, 12/25. **Address:** 3881 Coastal Hwy **Location:** I-95, exit 87 (Ocean Hwy/US 17), just e. **Parking:** on-site. **Cards:** AX, DC, DS, MC, VI.

CALL

THE UPPER CRUST **Phone:** 912/756-6990

Italian
$6-$12

This place is not just about the pizza. Tasty, well-prepared Italian dishes abound, and all are prepared freshly in house. Cold drinks are served in mason jars with pasta straws. Great food is served in a family atmosphere. Casual dress. **Bar:** Beer & wine. **Hours:** 11 am-10 pm, Sun 4 pm-9:30 pm. Closed major holidays. **Address:** 1702 US 17 **Location:** Jct US 17/SR 144 (Ford Ave), just ne. **Parking:** on-site. **Cards:** AX, DS, MC, VI.

RINCON pop. 4,376

WHERE TO STAY

MICROTEL INN & SUITES *Book at AAA.com* **Phone:** (912)826-5055

Hotel
$62-$99 All Year

Address: 6132 Hwy 21 S **Location:** I-95, exit 109, 4.5 mi nw. **Facility:** 59 one-bedroom standard units. 3 stories, interior corridors. *Bath:* combo or shower only. **Parking:** on-site. **Terms:** 3 day cancellation notice. **Amenities:** voice mail, hair dryers. **Guest Services:** valet laundry, wireless Internet. **Cards:** AX, DC, DS, MC, VI.

ASK / SOME UNITS

RINGGOLD pop. 2,422

WHERE TO STAY

COMFORT INN *Book great rates at AAA.com* **Phone:** (706)935-4000

SAVE

Hotel
$79-$119 All Year

Address: 177 Industrial Blvd **Location:** I-75, exit 348, just w. **Facility:** 63 one-bedroom standard units, some with whirlpools. 3 stories, interior corridors. **Parking:** on-site. **Amenities:** high-speed Internet, irons, hair dryers. **Pool(s):** outdoor. **Guest Services:** coin laundry, wireless Internet. **Business Services:** fax (fee). **Cards:** AX, DC, DS, MC, VI. **Free Special Amenities: expanded continental breakfast and high-speed Internet.**

/ SOME UNITS FEE

HOMETOWN INN **Phone:** (706)937-7070

SAVE

Hotel
$60-$75 All Year

Address: 22 Gateway Business Park Dr **Location:** I-75, exit 350, just e. **Facility:** 40 one-bedroom standard units, some with efficiencies (no utensils). 2 stories, interior corridors. **Parking:** on-site. **Terms:** cancellation fee imposed. **Amenities:** high-speed Internet, voice mail, irons, hair dryers. *Some:* DVD players. **Pool(s):** outdoor. **Guest Services:** valet and coin laundry, wireless Internet. **Business Services:** PC, fax. **Cards:** AX, DC, DS, MC, VI. **Free Special Amenities: continental breakfast and high-speed Internet.**

CALL / SOME UNITS FEE VCR

SUPER 8 MOTEL *Book at AAA.com* **Phone:** 706/965-7080

Motel
Rates not provided

Address: 5400 Alabama Hwy **Location:** I-75, exit 348, just e. **Facility:** 40 one-bedroom standard units. 2 stories (no elevator), exterior corridors. **Parking:** on-site, winter plug-ins. **Amenities:** high-speed Internet, hair dryers. **Pool(s):** outdoor. **Guest Services:** wireless Internet. **Business Services:** fax.

CALL / SOME UNITS FEE

WHERE TO DINE

AUNT EFFIE'S **Phone:** 706/935-6525

American
$5-$10

Straightforward, down-home country cooking is the draw at the unpretentious North Georgia eatery. Casual dress. **Hours:** 11 am-8 pm. Closed major holidays; also Sat & Sun. **Address:** 5287 Alabama Hwy **Location:** I-75, exit 348, just e. **Parking:** on-site. **Cards:** MC, VI.

ROCKMART pop. 3,870

WHERE TO STAY

DAYS INN *Book at AAA.com* **Phone:** 770/684-9955

Motel
Rates not provided

Address: 105 GTM Pkwy **Location:** Jct US 278 and SR 101, just n. **Facility:** 38 one-bedroom standard units, some with whirlpools. 2 stories, exterior corridors. **Parking:** on-site. **Amenities:** high-speed Internet, safes (fee), hair dryers. **Leisure Activities:** exercise room. **Guest Services:** wireless Internet. **Business Services:** fax (fee).

CALL / SOME UNITS FEE

ROME pop. 34,980

WHERE TO STAY

BEST WESTERN EXECUTIVE INN

Book great rates at AAA.com

Phone: (706)234-3161

Hotel
$82-$84 All Year

Address: 217 Hwy 411 E **Location:** 2.3 mi e. **Facility:** 45 one-bedroom standard units, some with whirlpools. 2 stories (no elevator), exterior corridors. **Parking:** on-site. **Amenities:** high-speed Internet, irons, hair dryers. **Pool(s):** outdoor. **Guest Services:** valet laundry, wireless Internet. **Business Services:** fax (fee). **Cards:** AX, CB, DC, DS, JC, MC, VI. **Free Special Amenities: continental breakfast and high-speed Internet.**

/ SOME UNITS

AAA Benefit:
Members save up to 20%, plus 10% bonus points with rewards program.

COMFORT INN

Book at AAA.com

Phone: (706)802-1223

Hotel
$70-$130 All Year

Address: 2209 Shorter Ave **Location:** 3.5 mi w on SR 20. **Facility:** 50 one-bedroom standard units, some with whirlpools. 3 stories, interior corridors. **Parking:** on-site. **Amenities:** high-speed Internet, irons, hair dryers. **Pool(s):** outdoor. **Guest Services:** valet and coin laundry, wireless Internet. **Business Services:** fax (fee). **Cards:** AX, DS, JC, MC, VI.

ASK / SOME UNITS

COUNTRY INN & SUITES BY CARLSON

Book at AAA.com

Phone: (706)232-3380

Hotel
$85-$94 All Year

Address: 231 Hwy 411 SE **Location:** 2.3 mi e. **Facility:** 60 units. 30 one-bedroom standard units. 30 one-bedroom suites. 3 stories, interior corridors. **Parking:** on-site. **Amenities:** high-speed Internet, dual phone lines, voice mail, irons, hair dryers. **Pool(s):** outdoor. **Leisure Activities:** exercise room. **Guest Services:** valet and coin laundry, wireless Internet. **Business Services:** business center. **Cards:** AX, CB, DC, DS, JC, MC, VI.

ASK CALL

DAYS INN ROME

Book at AAA.com

Phone: (706)295-0400

Hotel
$59-$95 3/1-11/30
$59-$75 12/1-2/28

Address: 840 Turner McCall Blvd **Location:** On SR 20 and US 27; downtown. **Facility:** 105 one-bedroom standard units. 5 stories, interior corridors. **Parking:** on-site. **Amenities:** high-speed Internet, voice mail, hair dryers. *Some:* dual phone lines. **Pool(s):** outdoor. **Leisure Activities:** exercise room. **Guest Services:** coin laundry, wireless Internet. **Business Services:** meeting rooms, business center. **Cards:** AX, CB, DC, DS, JC, MC, VI.

ASK / SOME UNITS

HAMPTON INN

Book great rates at AAA.com

Phone: (706)232-9551

Hotel
$80-$97 All Year

Address: 21 Chateau Dr **Location:** 2 mi e on US 411. **Facility:** 64 units. 60 one-bedroom standard units. 4 one-bedroom suites. 2 stories, interior corridors. **Parking:** on-site. **Terms:** 1-30 night minimum stay, cancellation fee imposed. **Amenities:** high-speed Internet, voice mail, irons, hair dryers. **Pool(s):** outdoor. **Leisure Activities:** exercise room. **Guest Services:** valet and coin laundry, wireless Internet. **Business Services:** meeting rooms, business center. **Cards:** AX, CB, DC, DS, MC, VI.

CALL / SOME UNITS

AAA Benefit:
Members save up to 10% everyday!

HOLIDAY INN-SKY TOP CENTER *Book at AAA.com* **Phone:** (706)295-1100

Hotel
$94 All Year

Address: 20 US 411 E **Location:** 2 mi e. **Facility:** 150 units. 141 one-bedroom standard units. 9 one-bedroom suites. 2 stories, exterior corridors. **Parking:** on-site. **Amenities:** high-speed Internet, dual phone lines, voice mail, irons, hair dryers. **Pool(s):** heated indoor/outdoor. **Leisure Activities:** whirlpool, exercise room. **Guest Services:** valet and coin laundry, wireless Internet. **Business Services:** meeting rooms, PC, fax (fee). **Cards:** AX, DS, MC, VI.

ASK CALL / SOME UNITS

JAMESON INN *Book at AAA.com* **Phone:** (706)291-7797

Hotel
$93-$100 All Year

Address: 40 Grace Dr **Location:** On US 411, 2.2 mi e. **Facility:** 67 one-bedroom standard units. 3 stories, interior corridors. **Parking:** on-site. **Terms:** cancellation fee imposed. **Amenities:** high-speed Internet, voice mail, irons, hair dryers. **Pool(s):** heated indoor/outdoor. **Leisure Activities:** exercise room. **Guest Services:** wireless Internet. **Business Services:** meeting rooms, PC, fax (fee). **Cards:** AX, DC, DS, MC, VI.

ASK CALL / SOME UNITS FEE

WHERE TO DINE

GONDOLIER ITALIAN RESTAURANT AND PIZZA **Phone:** 706/291-8080

Pizza
$3-$13

In addition to daily specials, diners can select from a tempting variety of calzones and such standards as spaghetti, manicotti and ravioli. Servers are fast and friendly. Casual dress. **Bar:** Beer & wine. **Hours:** 11 am-10 pm, Fri & Sat-11 pm. Closed: 11/26, 12/25. **Address:** 152 Shorter Ave **Location:** Jct US 27, 0.4 mi w on SR 20. **Parking:** on-site. **Cards:** AX, DS, MC, VI.

SONNY'S REAL PIT BAR-B-Q **Phone:** 706/234-1441

Barbecue
$6-$15

House specialties include pork and chicken grilled over an open pit, barbecue ribs and fresh, homemade pie. The salad bar offers another popular option. Rustic and comfortable, the atmosphere is perfect for family meals. Casual dress. **Bar:** Beer only. **Hours:** 11 am-9:30 pm, Fri & Sat-10 pm. Closed: 11/26, 12/25. **Address:** 2103 Shorter Ave **Location:** 3.3 mi w on SR 20. **Parking:** on-site. **Cards:** AX, DS, MC, VI.

ROSWELL —*See Atlanta p. 417.*

ST. MARYS pop. 13,761

WHERE TO STAY

CUMBERLAND INN & SUITES KINGS BAY *Book great rates at AAA.com* **Phone:** (912)882-6250

AAA SAVE

Hotel
$79-$129 All Year

Address: 2710 Osborne Rd **Location:** I-95, exit 3 (SR 40), 5.5 mi e. **Facility:** 79 units. 41 one-bedroom standard units. 38 one-bedroom suites, some with kitchens and/or whirlpools. 2 stories (no elevator), exterior corridors. **Parking:** on-site. **Amenities:** high-speed Internet, voice mail, irons, hair dryers. **Pool(s):** outdoor. **Leisure Activities:** picnic tables, charcoal grills, limited exercise equipment. **Guest Services:** coin laundry, wireless Internet. **Business Services:** meeting rooms, business center. **Cards:** AX, DS, MC, VI. **Free Special Amenities: expanded continental breakfast and high-speed Internet.** ***(See color ad below)***

/ SOME UNITS

▼ *See AAA listing above* ▼

SPENCER HOUSE INN BED & BREAKFAST Phone: (912)882-1872

Historic Bed & Breakfast
$125-$235 All Year

Address: 200 Osborne St **Location:** I-95, exit 3 (SR 40), 9 mi se. Located within easy access to the Cumberland Island Ferry. **Facility:** Showcasing Victorian-era architecture, this 1872 home close to Cumberland Island Ferry features individually decorated rooms and a guest elevator. Smoke free premises. 14 units. 13 one-bedroom standard units. 1 one-bedroom suite. 3 stories, interior corridors. *Bath:* combo or shower only. **Parking:** on-site. **Terms:** 7 day cancellation notice. **Amenities:** hair dryers. *Some:* DVD players. **Guest Services:** area transportation, wireless Internet. **Business Services:** meeting rooms, fax (fee). **Cards:** AX, DS, MC, VI.

ASK

The following lodging was either not evaluated or did not meet AAA rating requirements but is listed for your information only.

GREYFIELD INN Phone: 904/261-6408

Not evaluated. **Address:** Cumberland Island **Location:** Park at Amelia Island Deck D, board ferry to Cumberland Island. Facilities, services, and decor characterize an upscale property.

WHERE TO DINE

BORRELL CREEK LANDING RESTAURANT Phone: 912/673-6300

American
$6-$35

The upscale, waterfront restaurant sustains a cozy feel that lends to its popularity as an exceptional dining spot. Good preparations of beef, poultry and seafood are complemented by a broad wine list of potential pairings by the glass or bottle. Their motto is, "The view, the food, the service.". Casual dress. **Bar:** Full bar. **Reservations:** suggested, weekends. **Hours:** 11 am-2:30 & 5-10 pm, Sat & Sun from 5 pm. Closed: 11/26, 12/25; also Father's Day. **Address:** 1101 Hwy 40 E **Location:** I-95, exit 3 (SR 40), 6 mi se, then just sw to Borrell Creek Landing. **Parking:** on-site. **Cards:** AX, DS, MC, VI.

ST. SIMONS ISLAND —*See Golden Isles p. 477.*

SANDERSVILLE pop. 6,144

WHERE TO STAY

DAYS INN SANDERSVILLE *Book at AAA.com* Phone: 478/553-0393

Motel
Rates not provided

Address: 128 Commerce St **Location:** On SR 15 at jct SR 77, just s. **Facility:** 45 units. 44 one-bedroom standard units, some with whirlpools. 1 one-bedroom suite with kitchen. 2 stories (no elevator), exterior corridors. *Bath:* combo or shower only. **Parking:** on-site. **Amenities:** voice mail, irons, hair dryers. **Pool(s):** outdoor. **Guest Services:** coin laundry, wireless Internet. **Business Services:** meeting rooms.

CALL   / SOME UNITS FEE 

HOLIDAY INN EXPRESS *Book at AAA.com* Phone: 478/553-1414

Hotel
Rates not provided

Address: 508 S Harris St **Location:** Jct SR 242 E, just n on SR 15. **Facility:** 53 one-bedroom standard units, some with whirlpools. 2 stories (no elevator), interior corridors. *Bath:* combo or shower only. **Parking:** on-site. **Amenities:** high-speed Internet, voice mail, irons, hair dryers. **Pool(s):** outdoor. **Leisure Activities:** exercise room. **Guest Services:** wireless Internet. **Business Services:** meeting rooms, PC.

/ SOME UNITS VCR

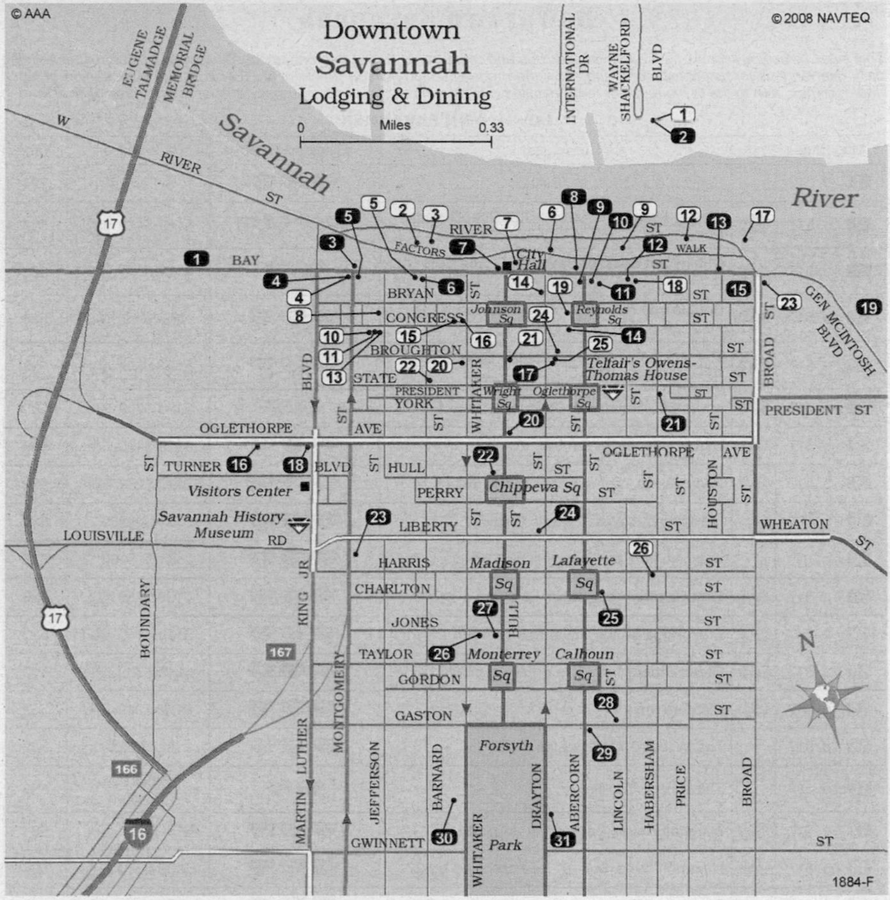

© AAA

Downtown Savannah Lodging & Dining

0 Miles 0.33

© 2008 NAVTEQ

Savannah River

W RIVER ST, BAY ST, RIVER ST, FACTORS WALK, BRYAN ST, CONGRESS ST, BROUGHTON ST, STATE ST, PRESIDENT ST, YORK ST, OGLETHORPE AVE, HULL ST, PERRY ST, LIBERTY ST, HARRIS ST, CHARLTON ST, JONES ST, TAYLOR ST, GORDON ST, GASTON ST, GWINNETT ST, TURNER BLVD, LOUISVILLE RD, WHEATON ST, GEN MCINTOSH BLVD, EUGENE TALMADGE MEMORIAL BRIDGE, INTERNATIONAL DR, WAYNE SHACKELFORD BLVD, BOUNDARY ST, MARTIN LUTHER KING JR BLVD, MONTGOMERY ST, JEFFERSON ST, BARNARD ST, WHITAKER ST, BULL ST, DRAYTON ST, ABERCORN ST, LINCOLN ST, HABERSHAM ST, PRICE ST, HOUSTON ST, BROAD ST

City Hall, Johnson Sq, Reynolds Sq, Telfair's Owens-Thomas House, Wright Sq, Oglethorpe Sq, Chippewa Sq, Visitors Center, Savannah History Museum, Madison Sq, Lafayette Sq, Monterrey Sq, Calhoun Sq, Forsyth Park

17, 16, 166, 167

N

1884-F

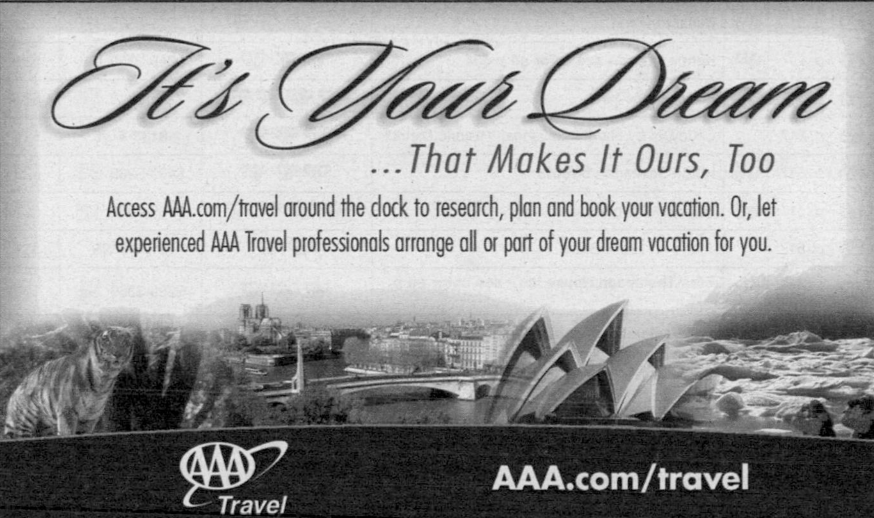

Downtown Savannah

This index helps you "spot" where approved lodgings and restaurants are located on the corresponding detailed maps. Lodging daily rate range is for comparison only and show the property's high season. Restaurant rate range is a combination of lunch and/or dinner. Turn to the listing page for more detailed rate information and consult display ads for special promotions.

DOWNTOWN SAVANNAH

Map Page	OA	Lodgings	Diamond Rated	High Season	Page
1 / p. 517		Comfort Suites Historic District	◆◆◆	$129-$289	524
2 / p. 517	AAA	**Westin Savannah Harbor Golf Resort and Spa**	◆◆◆◆	$169-$439 SAVE	533
3 / p. 517	AAA	**Quality Inn Heart of Savannah - see color ad p 532**	◆◆	$119-$179 SAVE	532
4 / p. 517	AAA	**DoubleTree Hotel Historic Savannah - see color ad p 529**	◆◆◆	$99-$249 SAVE	526
5 / p. 517	AAA	**The Hilton Garden Inn Historic Savannah - see color ad p 529**	◆◆◆	$104-$499 SAVE	528
6 / p. 517	AAA	**Inn at Ellis Square, A Days Hotel**	◆◆	$139-$209 SAVE	530
7 / p. 517	AAA	**Hyatt Regency Savannah**	◆◆◆	$129-$400 SAVE	530
8 / p. 517	AAA	**River Street Inn - see color ad p 533**	◆◆◆	$119-$289 SAVE	532
9 / p. 517		Holiday Inn Express Historic District	◆◆◆	$109-$239	530
10 / p. 517		Hampton Inn-Savannah Historic District	◆◆◆	$152-$186	528
11 / p. 517	AAA	**East Bay Inn - see color ad p 531**	◆◆◆	$189-$269 SAVE	526
12 / p. 517	AAA	**Staybridge Suites Savannah Historic District**	◆◆◆	$120-$140 SAVE	533
13 / p. 517	AAA	**Olde Harbour Inn - see color ad p 531**	◆◆◆	$219-$309 SAVE	532
14 / p. 517	AAA	**Planters Inn**	◆◆◆	$149-$249 SAVE	532
15 / p. 517		The Mulberry-A Holiday Inn Hotel	◆◆◆	$209-$259	532
16 / p. 517		The Thunderbird Inn	◆◆	Rates not provided	533
17 / p. 517	AAA	**Marshall House - see color ad p 531**	◆◆◆	$159-$269 SAVE	531
18 / p. 517	AAA	**Hampton Inn & Suites - see color ad p 527**	◆◆◆	$139-$389 SAVE	527
19 / p. 517		Savannah Marriott Riverfront	◆◆◆	$196-$227	533
20 / p. 517	AAA	**Ballastone Inn**	◆◆◆◆	$215-$395 SAVE	524
21 / p. 517	AAA	**Kehoe House - see color ad p 531**	◆◆◆	$249-$359 SAVE	531
22 / p. 517	AAA	**Foley House Inn**	◆◆◆◆	$225-$410 SAVE	527
23 / p. 517		Courtyard by Marriott-Savannah Historic District	◆◆◆	$133-$195	524
24 / p. 517	AAA	**Hilton Savannah DeSoto**	◆◆◆	$109-$269 SAVE	529
25 / p. 517	AAA	**Hamilton-Turner Inn**	◆◆◆◆	$189-$369 SAVE	527
26 / p. 517		Joan's on Jones B & B	◆◆	$175-$195	531
27 / p. 517	AAA	**Eliza Thompson House Inn - see color ad p 531**	◆◆◆	$209-$369 SAVE	526
28 / p. 517	AAA	**The Gastonian - see color ad p 531**	◆◆◆◆	$235-$435 SAVE	527
29 / p. 517		Dresser Palmer House	◆◆◆	$149-$429	526
30 / p. 517		The Forsyth Park Inn	◆◆◆	$175-$275	527
31 / p. 517	AAA	**The Mansion on Forsyth Park**	◆◆◆◆	$229-$509 SAVE	531

Map Page	OA	Restaurants	Diamond Rated	Cuisine	Meal Range	Page
1 / p. 517		Aqua Star Restaurant	◆◆◆	Regional American	$9-$35	534

Map Page	OA	Restaurants (cont'd)	Diamond Rated	Cuisine	Meal Range	Page
2 / p. 517		Cobblestone Conch House	♦♦	Seafood	$12-$24	535
3 / p. 517		River House Seafood & Bakery	♦♦	Seafood	$9-$35	536
4 / p. 517		John Ryan's Bistro & Pub	♦♦	Regional American	$7-$28	535
5 / p. 517		Chart House	♦♦♦	Steak & Seafood	$18-$26 SAVE	535
6 / p. 517		Huey's New Orleans Cafe	♦♦	Regional American	$6-$27	535
7 / p. 517		Vic's On The River Restaurant & Bar	♦♦	American	$7-$29	536
8 / p. 517		Belford's	♦♦	Steak & Seafood	$8-$35	534
9 / p. 517		Boar's Head Grill & Tavern	♦♦	Steak & Seafood	$9-$30	534
10 / p. 517		Garibaldi's Cafe	♦♦	Seafood	$13-$32	535
11 / p. 517		Molly MacPherson's Scottish Pub & Grill	♦♦	Scottish	$9-$18	535
12 / p. 517	AAA	**Shrimp Factory**	♦♦	Seafood	$12-$32	536
13 / p. 517		Bistro Savannah	♦♦♦	Continental	$15-$24	534
14 / p. 517		Isaac's on Drayton	♦♦	American	$7-$30	535
15 / p. 517		The Lady & Sons	♦♦	Southern	$9-$25	535
16 / p. 517		Sapphire Grill	♦♦♦	American	$26-$40	536
17 / p. 517		The Oyster Bar	♦♦	Seafood	$9-$23	536
18 / p. 517		B. Matthew's Eatery	♦♦	American	$5-$20	534
19 / p. 517		The Olde Pink House	♦♦♦	Regional American	$15-$29	536
20 / p. 517	AAA	**A Vida Restaurant & Wine Bar**	♦♦♦	New American	$24-$38	534
21 / p. 517		Il Pasticcio	♦♦♦	Italian	$23-$45	535
22 / p. 517		Alligator Soul	♦♦♦	American	$28-$36	534
23 / p. 517		The Pirates' House	♦♦	Southern Seafood	$7-$26	536
24 / p. 517	AAA	**Casbah Moroccan Restaurant**	♦♦	Moroccan	$16-$26	534
25 / p. 517		45 Bistro at the Marshall House	♦♦♦	Continental	$18-$34	534
26 / p. 517		Firefly Cafe	♦♦	American	$9-$22	535

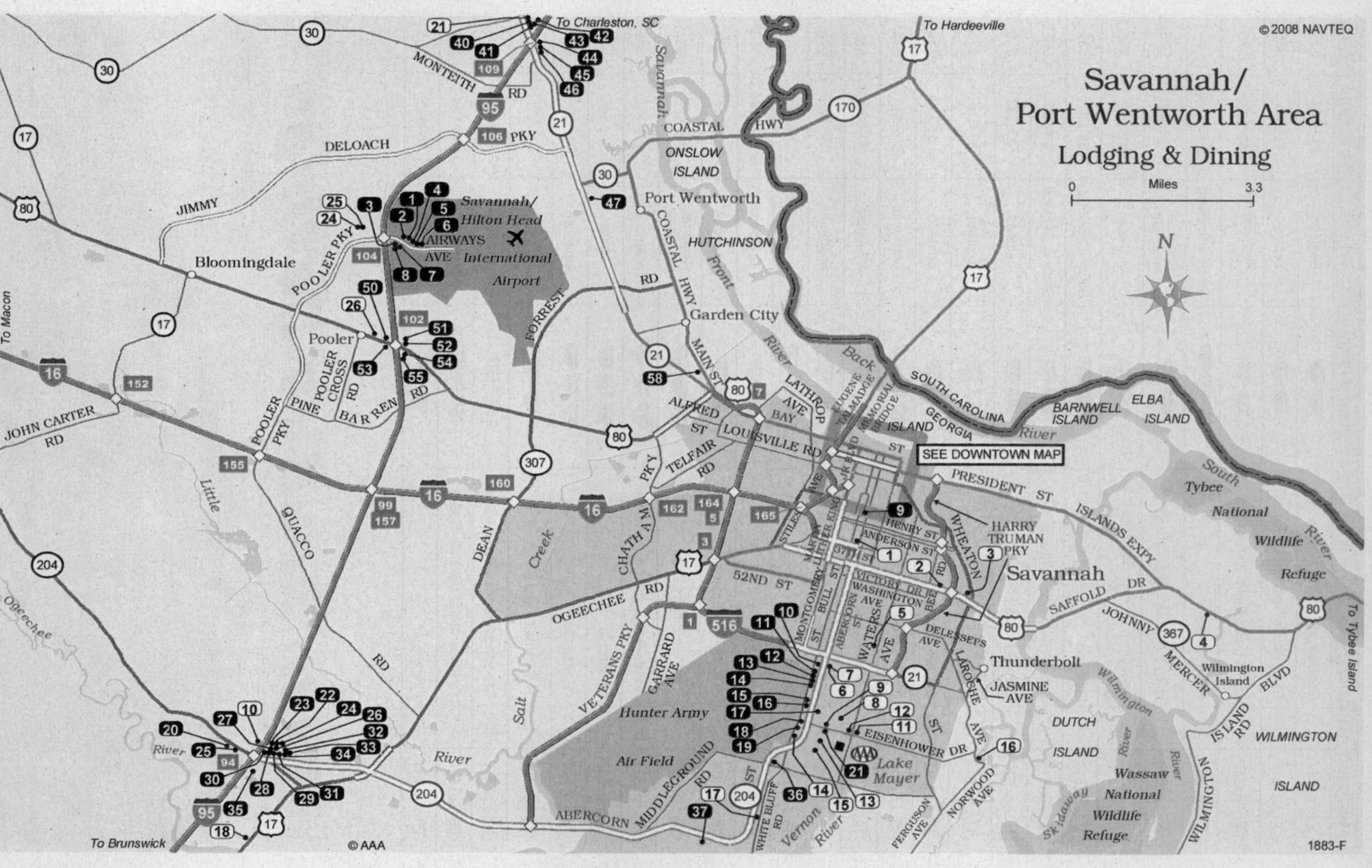
Savannah/
Port Wentworth Area
Lodging & Dining
Miles
0
3.3
N
© 2008 NAVTEQ
© AAA
1883-F
SEE DOWNTOWN MAP
To Hardeeville
To Charleston, SC
To Tybee Island
To Brunswick
To Macon
Savannah
Port Wentworth
Garden City
Pooler
Bloomingdale
Thunderbolt
Wilmington Island
Savannah/Hilton Head International Airport
Hunter Army Air Field
Lake Mayer
South Tybee National Wildlife Refuge
Wassaw National Wildlife Refuge
ELBA ISLAND
BARNWELL ISLAND
HUTCHINSON
ONSLOW ISLAND
DUTCH ISLAND
WILMINGTON ISLAND
SOUTH CAROLINA
GEORGIA
Savannah River
Back River
Front River
Wilmington River
Skidaway River
Vernon River
Little Ogeechee River
Ogeechee
Salt Creek
ISLANDS EXPY
PRESIDENT ST
HARRY TRUMAN PKY
VETERANS PKY
ABERCORN
MIDDLEGROUND RD
WHITE BLUFF RD
OGEECHEE RD
DEAN FOREST RD
POOLER PKY
QUACCO RD
JOHN CARTER RD
DELOACH
JIMMY
MONTEITH RD
COASTAL HWY
LOUISVILLE RD
CHATHAM PKY
EUGENE TALMADGE MEMORIAL BRIDGE

Airport Accommodations

Map Page	OA	SAVANNAH/HILTON HEAD INTERNATIONAL AIRPORT	Diamond Rated	High Season	Page
6 / p. 520		Cambria Suites Savannah Airport, 1 mi w of terminal	◆◆◆	Rates not provided	537
5 / p. 520		Comfort Suites Savannah Airport, 1 mi w of terminal	◆◆◆	$109-$129	538
N/A		Country Inn & Suites Savannah Airport, 1 mi w of terminal		$95-$115	538
3 / p. 520		Fairfield Inn Savannah Airport, 1.1 mi w of terminal	◆◆	$137-$147	539
1 / p. 520	AAA	**Four Points by Sheraton, 1 mi w of terminal**	◆◆◆	Rates not provided SAVE	539
7 / p. 520	AAA	**Hawthorn Suites, 1 mi w of terminal**	◆◆◆	$109-$159 SAVE	539
8 / p. 520		Hilton Garden Inn, 1 mi w of terminal	◆◆◆	$79-$179	540
2 / p. 520		SpringHill Suites by Marriott Savannah Airport, 1 mi w of terminal	◆◆◆	$137-$147	542
4 / p. 520		TownePlace Suites Savannah Airport, 1 mi w of terminal	◆◆	$123-$132	542

Savannah/Port Wentworth

This index helps you "spot" where approved lodgings and restaurants are located on the corresponding detailed maps. Lodging daily rate range is for comparison only and show the property's high season. Restaurant rate range is a combination of lunch and/or dinner. Turn to the listing page for more detailed rate information and consult display ads for special promotions.

SAVANNAH

Map Page	OA	Lodgings	Diamond Rated	High Season	Page
1 / p. 520	AAA	**Four Points by Sheraton**	◆◆◆	Rates not provided SAVE	539
2 / p. 520		SpringHill Suites by Marriott Savannah Airport	◆◆◆	$137-$147	542
3 / p. 520		Fairfield Inn Savannah Airport	◆◆	$137-$147	539
4 / p. 520		TownePlace Suites Savannah Airport	◆◆	$123-$132	542
5 / p. 520		Comfort Suites Savannah Airport	◆◆◆	$109-$129	538
6 / p. 520		Cambria Suites Savannah Airport	◆◆◆	Rates not provided	537
7 / p. 520	AAA	**Hawthorn Suites**	◆◆◆	$109-$159 SAVE	539
8 / p. 520		Hilton Garden Inn	◆◆◆	$79-$179	540
9 / p. 520		Catherine Ward House Inn	◆◆◆	$369	537
10 / p. 520		Extended StayAmerica-Midtown	◆◆	$70-$185	538
11 / p. 520	AAA	**Hilton Garden Inn Savannah Midtown** - see color ad p 529	◆◆◆	$79-$399 SAVE	540
12 / p. 520		Residence Inn by Marriott Savannah	◆◆◆	$159-$169	541
13 / p. 520		Homewood Suites by Hilton	◆◆◆	$149-$229	540
14 / p. 520		Fairfield Inn	◆◆	$81-$102	538
15 / p. 520	AAA	**Savannah Midtown Courtyard by Marriott**	◆◆◆	$147-$158 SAVE	542
16 / p. 520		La Quinta Inn Savannah (Midtown)	◆◆	$59-$129	541
17 / p. 520		Red Roof Inn Savannah Midtown	◆◆	$70-$110	539
18 / p. 520	AAA	**Best Western Central**	◆◆	$69-$109 SAVE	536
19 / p. 520	AAA	**Country Inn & Suites by Carlson**	◆◆◆	$108-$119 SAVE	538

SAVANNAH (cont'd)

Map Page	OA	Lodgings (cont'd)	Diamond Rated	High Season	Page
20 / p. 520		Microtel Inn & Suites	◆◆	$40-$90	541
21 / p. 520	AAA	**Oglethorpe Inn & Suites**	◆◆	$89-$195 SAVE	541
22 / p. 520		Comfort Suites Gateway	◆◆◆	$80-$300	537
23 / p. 520		Holiday Inn Express	◆◆◆	$100-$109	540
24 / p. 520		Hampton Inn & Suites I-95 Gateway	◆◆◆	$129-$169	539
25 / p. 520	AAA	**Travelodge**	◆◆	$40-$299 SAVE	543
26 / p. 520	AAA	**Clarion Inn & Suites**	◆◆◆	$89-$169 SAVE	537
27 / p. 520	AAA	**Fairfield Inn & Suites I-95 South**	◆◆	$88-$118 SAVE	538
28 / p. 520	AAA	**Wingate by Wyndham-Savannah - see color ad p 525**	◆◆◆	$99-$119 SAVE	543
29 / p. 520		SpringHill Suites by Marriott I-95 South	◆◆◆	$137-$147	542
30 / p. 520	AAA	**Best Western Savannah Gateway - see color ad p 525**	◆◆	$59-$139 SAVE	537
31 / p. 520		Ramada I-95 Gateway	◆◆	$66-$125	541
32 / p. 520	AAA	**Country Inn & Suites by Carlson-Savannah Gateway**	◆◆◆	$89-$170 SAVE	538
33 / p. 520		Red Roof Inn	◆◆	$45-$107	541
34 / p. 520		Howard Johnson Express Inn	◆◆	$79-$99	540
35 / p. 520		La Quinta Inn Savannah (I-95)	◆◆	$55-$109	541
36 / p. 520		La Quinta Inn & Suites	◆◆	$59-$149	540
37 / p. 520		SpringHill Suites by Marriott	◆◆◆	$101-$108	542

Map Page	OA	Restaurants	Diamond Rated	Cuisine	Meal Range	Page
1 / p. 520		Elizabeth on 37th	◆◆◆	Regional American	$25-$33	543
2 / p. 520	AAA	**Johnny Harris Restaurant**	◆◆	American	$6-$24	543
3 / p. 520	AAA	**The New South Cafe**	◆◆◆	American	$8-$34	544
4 / p. 520		Uncle Bubba's Seafood & Oyster House	◆◆	Seafood	$6-$25	545
5 / p. 520		Kasey's Grille	◆◆	American	$7-$24	543
6 / p. 520		The Italian Garden	◆◆	Italian	$7-$15	543
7 / p. 520		Bonefish Grill	◆◆◆	Seafood	$13-$20	543
8 / p. 520	AAA	**Toucan Cafe**	◆◆◆	International	$6-$25	545
9 / p. 520		King and I	◆◆	Thai	$10-$21	543
10 / p. 520		The Shell House Restaurant	◆	Seafood	$8-$22	544
11 / p. 520		Old Savannah Diner	◆◆	American	$7-$15	544
12 / p. 520	AAA	**Sweet Potatoes Kitchen**	◆◆	American	$6-$10	544
13 / p. 520		Fiddler's Crab House & Oyster Barn	◆◆	Seafood	$12-$25	543
14 / p. 520		Chiriya's Thai Cuisine	◆◆	Thai	$11-$25	543
15 / p. 520		Taste of India	◆◆	Indian	$7-$15	544
16 / p. 520		Pearl's Saltwater Grille	◆◆	Steak & Seafood	$15-$30	544
17 / p. 520		Troy Mediterranean Cuisine	◆◆	Mediterranean	$12-$24	545

Map Page	OA	Restaurants (cont'd)	Diamond Rated	Cuisine	Meal Range	Page
18 / p. 520		Love's Seafood Restaurant	♦♦	Steak & Seafood	$9-$22	544

PORT WENTWORTH

Map Page	OA	Lodgings	Diamond Rated	High Season	Page
40 / p. 520		Quality Inn & Suites	♦♦♦	$75-$175	511
41 / p. 520		Holiday Inn Express Savannah North	♦♦♦	$89-$149	511
42 / p. 520		Comfort Suites Savannah North	♦♦♦	Rates not provided	511
43 / p. 520		Days Inn & Suites	♦♦	$60-$199	511
44 / p. 520	AAA	**Country Inn & Suites Savannah North**	♦♦♦	$80-$134 SAVE	511
45 / p. 520	AAA	**Wingate Inn**	♦♦♦	$69-$129 SAVE	511
46 / p. 520		Inn at Mulberry Grove	♦♦	$90-$200	511
47 / p. 520	AAA	**Sleep Inn-Savannah North**	♦♦	$69-$145 SAVE	511

Map Page	OA	Restaurant	Diamond Rated	Cuisine	Meal Range	Page
21 / p. 520		Island Grill	♦	Seafood	$8-$20	512

POOLER

Map Page	OA	Lodgings	Diamond Rated	High Season	Page
50 / p. 520		La Quinta Inn & Suites	♦♦♦	$69-$139	510
51 / p. 520	AAA	**Best Western Bradbury Suites**	♦♦♦	$79-$189 SAVE	509
52 / p. 520		Jameson Inn	♦♦	$93-$100	510
53 / p. 520		Holiday Inn Savannah West	♦♦♦	$125-$165	510
54 / p. 520	AAA	**Travelodge Suites**	♦♦	$59-$149 SAVE	510
55 / p. 520	AAA	**Microtel Inn & Suites**	♦♦	$60-$160 SAVE	510

Map Page	OA	Restaurants	Diamond Rated	Cuisine	Meal Range	Page
24 / p. 520		MIWA Japanese Restaurant	♦♦	Japanese	$6-$19	510
25 / p. 520		Fettuccini & Co	♦♦	Italian	$9-$15	510
26 / p. 520		Lovezzola's Pizza Restaurant	♦	Italian	$5-$19	510

GARDEN CITY

Map Page	OA	Lodging	Diamond Rated	High Season	Page
58 / p. 520		Baymont Inn & Suites - see color ad p 524	♦♦	Rates not provided	473

DOWNTOWN SAVANNAH

(See map and index starting on p. 517)

WHERE TO STAY

BALLASTONE INN

Phone: (912)236-1484 20

Historic Bed & Breakfast
$215-$395 All Year

Address: 14 E Oglethorpe Ave **Location:** Between Bull and Drayton sts. **Facility:** This restored antebellum inn, built in 1838, was Savannah's first B&B; it is tastefully furnished with Victorian antiques and reproductions. Smoke free premises. 16 one-bedroom standard units, some with whirlpools. 4 stories, interior corridors. **Parking:** on-site. **Terms:** 2 night minimum stay - weekends, 21 day cancellation notice-fee imposed. **Amenities:** video library, CD players, hair dryers. **Leisure Activities:** courtyard patio. **Guest Services:** wireless Internet. **Business Services:** PC. **Cards:** AX, MC, VI. **Free Special Amenities: full breakfast and high-speed Internet.**

COMFORT SUITES HISTORIC DISTRICT

Book at AAA.com

Phone: (912)629-2001 1

Hotel
$129-$289 3/1-11/30
$99-$179 12/1-2/28

Address: 630 W Bay St **Location:** I-16, exit 167 (Montgomery St), 0.9 mi n to Bay St, then just w. **Facility:** Smoke free premises. 76 units. 74 one-bedroom standard units. 2 one-bedroom suites. 3 stories, interior corridors. *Bath:* combo or shower only. **Parking:** on-site. **Amenities:** high-speed Internet, dual phone lines, voice mail, irons, hair dryers. **Pool(s):** heated indoor. **Leisure Activities:** whirlpool, limited exercise equipment. **Guest Services:** valet and coin laundry, wireless Internet. **Business Services:** meeting rooms, business center. **Cards:** AX, DC, DS, JC, MC, VI.

ASK CALL

COUNTRY INN & SUITES SAVANNAH HISTORIC DISTRICT

Phone: 912/912-5300

fyi
Hotel
Rates not provided

Too new to rate. **Address:** 320 Montgomery St **Location:** Just s of W Liberty St. **Amenities:** 101 units, restaurant, coffeemakers, microwaves, refrigerators, pool. ***(See color ad p 526)***

COURTYARD BY MARRIOTT-SAVANNAH HISTORIC DISTRICT

Book great rates at AAA.com

Phone: (912)790-8287 23

Hotel
$133-$195 All Year

Address: 415 W Liberty St **Location:** I-16, exit 167 (Montgomery St), 0.4 mi n. **Facility:** Smoke free premises. 156 units. 147 one-bedroom standard units, some with whirlpools. 9 one-bedroom suites. 5 stories, interior corridors. *Bath:* combo or shower only. **Parking:** valet. **Terms:** cancellation fee imposed. **Amenities:** high-speed Internet, dual phone lines, voice mail, irons, hair dryers. **Pool(s):** heated outdoor. **Leisure Activities:** whirlpool, exercise room. **Guest Services:** valet and coin laundry, wireless Internet. **Business Services:** meeting rooms, business center. **Cards:** AX, CB, DC, DS, MC, VI.

 CALL    / SOME UNITS

AAA Benefit:
Members save a minimum 5% off the best available rate.

▼ *See AAA listing p 473* ▼

(See map and index starting on p. 517)

DOUBLETREE HOTEL HISTORIC SAVANNAH Book great rates at AAA.com **Phone:** (912)790-7000 4

Hotel
$99-$249 All Year

Address: 411 W Bay St **Location:** I-16, exit 167 (Montgomery St), 0.8 mi ne. Located in the historic district. **Facility:** 150 units. 148 one-bedroom standard units, some with whirlpools. 2 one-bedroom suites with whirlpools. 6 stories, interior corridors. *Bath:* combo or shower only. **Parking:** valet. **Terms:** check-in 4 pm, 1-30 night minimum stay, cancellation fee imposed. **Amenities:** video games (fee), dual phone lines, voice mail, irons, hair dryers. **Dining:** John Ryan's Bistro & Pub, see separate listing. **Pool(s):** heated outdoor. **Leisure Activities:** whirlpool, exercise room. **Guest Services:** valet and coin laundry, wireless Internet. **Business Services:** meeting rooms, business center. **Cards:** AX, CB, DC, DS, MC, VI. **Free Special Amenities: local telephone calls and high-speed Internet.** *(See color ad p 529)*

AAA Benefit:
Members save 5% or more everyday!

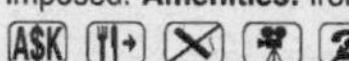 / SOME UNITS FEE VCR

DRESSER PALMER HOUSE Book at AAA.com **Phone:** (912)238-3294 29

Historic Bed & Breakfast
$149-$429 All Year

Address: 211 E Gaston St **Location:** Between Abercorn and Lincoln sts. **Facility:** This 1876 Italianate-style townhouse offers spacious rooms and a large front porch furnished with comfortable wicker chairs. Smoke free premises. 15 one-bedroom standard units, some with whirlpools. 3 stories (no elevator), interior/exterior corridors. *Bath:* combo or shower only. **Parking:** on-site. **Terms:** 2 night minimum stay - seasonal and/or weekends, age restrictions may apply, 7 day cancellation notice-fee imposed. **Amenities:** irons, hair dryers. **Guest Services:** wireless Internet. **Cards:** AX, DS, MC, VI.

ASK

EAST BAY INN Book great rates at AAA.com **Phone:** (912)238-1225 11

Historic Country Inn
$189-$269 All Year

Address: 225 E Bay St **Location:** I-16, exit 167 (Montgomery St), 0.8 mi ne, then 0.4 mi se; in historic district. **Facility:** Four-poster rice beds and 18-foot ceilings are among the elegant features found in this restored 1853 cotton warehouse's individually decorated rooms. Smoke free premises. 28 one-bedroom standard units. 3 stories, interior corridors. **Parking:** on-site. **Terms:** 2-3 night minimum stay - weekends, 7 day cancellation notice. **Amenities:** CD players, safes, irons, hair dryers. **Guest Services:** valet laundry, wireless Internet. **Business Services:** meeting rooms. **Cards:** AX, CB, DC, DS, MC, VI. **Free Special Amenities: expanded continental breakfast and high-speed Internet.** *(See color ad p 531)*

/ SOME UNITS FEE

ELIZA THOMPSON HOUSE INN Book great rates at AAA.com **Phone:** (912)236-3620 27

Historic Bed & Breakfast
$209-$369 All Year

Address: 5 W Jones **Location:** Between Whitaker and Bull sts. **Facility:** The inn, housed in a restored 1847 home, features an attractive courtyard area complete with a fountain. Smoke free premises. 25 one-bedroom standard units. 3 stories (no elevator), interior/exterior corridors. *Bath:* combo or shower only. **Parking:** street. **Terms:** 2 night minimum stay - weekends, age restrictions may apply, 7 day cancellation notice. **Amenities:** CD players, irons, hair dryers. *Some:* DVD players. **Guest Services:** wireless Internet. **Cards:** AX, DC, DS, MC, VI. **Free Special Amenities: expanded continental breakfast and high-speed Internet.** *(See color ad p 531)*

(See map and index starting on p. 517)

FOLEY HOUSE INN — Phone: 912/232-6622 **22**

Historic Bed & Breakfast

$225-$410 All Year

Address: 14 W Hull St on Chippewa Square **Location:** Between Bull and Whitaker sts; in historic district. **Facility:** This inn offers upscale accommodations furnished with period antiques and luxurious amenities; two private garden courtyards are also on premises. Smoke free premises. 19 one-bedroom standard units, some with whirlpools. 2-4 stories (no elevator), interior/exterior corridors. **Parking:** on-site (fee) and street. **Terms:** age restrictions may apply, 10 day cancellation notice-fee imposed. **Amenities:** voice mail, safes, irons, hair dryers. **Guest Services:** valet laundry, wireless Internet. **Cards:** AX, DS, MC, VI. **Free Special Amenities: full breakfast and high-speed Internet.**

/ SOME UNITS FEE

THE FORSYTH PARK INN — Phone: 912/233-6800 **30**

Historic Bed & Breakfast

$175-$275 All Year

Address: 102 W Hall St **Location:** Between Whitaker and Howard sts; on Forsyth Park. **Facility:** An original oak staircase and 12-foot solid-oak doors distinguish this restored Victorian mansion, which overlooks Savannah's largest park. Smoke free premises. 12 units. 11 one-bedroom standard units, some with whirlpools. 1 cottage. 3 stories (no elevator), interior corridors. *Bath:* combo or tub only. **Parking:** street. **Terms:** 2 night minimum stay - weekends, 14 day cancellation notice-fee imposed. **Amenities:** hair dryers. **Guest Services:** wireless Internet. **Cards:** AX, DS, MC, VI.

ASK / SOME UNITS FEE

THE GASTONIAN *Book great rates at AAA.com* — Phone: (912)232-2869 **28**

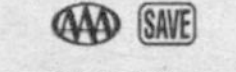

Classic Historic Bed & Breakfast

$235-$435 All Year

Address: 220 E Gaston St **Location:** Between Abercorn and Lincoln sts; in historic district. **Facility:** All accommodations in this inn's conjoined 1868 houses are furnished with English antiques and include a fireplace. Smoke free premises. 17 units. 16 one-bedroom standard units, some with whirlpools. 1 one-bedroom suite. 4 stories (no elevator), interior/exterior corridors. *Bath:* combo or shower only. **Parking:** on-site and street. **Terms:** 2 night minimum stay - weekends, age restrictions may apply, 10 day cancellation notice. **Amenities:** DVD players, CD players, irons, hair dryers. **Guest Services:** valet laundry, wireless Internet. **Cards:** AX, DC, DS, MC, VI. **Free Special Amenities: full breakfast and high-speed Internet.** *(See color ad p 531)*

HAMILTON-TURNER INN — Phone: 912/233-1833 **25**

Historic Bed & Breakfast

$189-$369 All Year

Address: 330 Abercorn St **Location:** Between E Charlton and E Harris sts; overlooking Lafayette Square; in historic district. **Facility:** Southern ambience is evident in this converted Second French Empire-style mansion furnished with period antiques from area estates. Smoke free premises. 17 one-bedroom standard units, some with whirlpools. 4 stories (no elevator), interior/exterior corridors. **Parking:** street. **Terms:** 2 night minimum stay - weekends, age restrictions may apply, 10 day cancellation notice-fee imposed. **Amenities:** video library, DVD players, CD players, voice mail, irons, hair dryers. **Guest Services:** wireless Internet. **Business Services:** PC. **Cards:** AX, DC, DS, MC, VI. **Free Special Amenities: full breakfast and high-speed Internet.**

/ SOME UNITS FEE

HAMPTON INN & SUITES *Book great rates at AAA.com* — Phone: (912)721-1600 **18**

Hotel

$139-$389 All Year

Address: 201 Martin Luther King Jr Blvd **Location:** Jct Oglethorpe Ave. **Facility:** 154 one-bedroom standard units. 6 stories, interior corridors. *Bath:* combo or shower only. **Parking:** on-site. **Terms:** check-in 4 pm, cancellation fee imposed. **Amenities:** video games (fee), high-speed Internet, voice mail, irons, hair dryers. **Pool(s):** heated outdoor. **Leisure Activities:** exercise room. **Guest Services:** valet and coin laundry, wireless Internet. **Business Services:** meeting rooms, PC. **Cards:** AX, CB, DC, DS, JC, MC, VI. **Free Special Amenities: expanded continental breakfast and high-speed Internet.** *(See color ad below)*

/ SOME UNITS

AAA Benefit:
Members save up to 10% everyday!

▼ *See AAA listing above* ▼

(See map and index starting on p. 517)

HAMPTON INN-SAVANNAH HISTORIC DISTRICT *Book great rates at AAA.com* **Phone:** (912)231-9700 **10**

Hotel

$152-$186 All Year

Address: 201 E Bay St **Location:** Corner of Abercorn St; in historic district. **Facility:** 144 one-bedroom standard units. 7 stories, interior corridors. *Bath:* combo or shower only. **Terms:** check-in 4 pm, 1-30 night minimum stay, cancellation fee imposed. **Amenities:** high-speed Internet, voice mail, irons, hair dryers. **Pool(s):** outdoor. **Leisure Activities:** exercise room. **Guest Services:** valet laundry, wireless Internet. **Business Services:** meeting rooms, PC. **Cards:** AX, CB, DC, DS, MC, VI.

CALL / SOME UNITS

AAA Benefit:

Members save up to 10% everyday!

THE HILTON GARDEN INN HISTORIC SAVANNAH *Book great rates at AAA.com* **Phone:** (912)721-5000 **5**

Hotel

$104-$499 All Year

Address: 321 W Bay St **Location:** I-16, exit 167 (Montgomery St), 0.8 mi ne; in historic district. **Facility:** 133 units. 103 one-bedroom standard units, some with whirlpools. 30 one-bedroom suites. 6 stories, interior corridors. *Bath:* combo or shower only. **Parking:** valet. **Terms:** check-in 4 pm, 1-30 night minimum stay, cancellation fee imposed. **Amenities:** video games (fee), high-speed Internet, voice mail, irons, hair dryers. *Some:* DVD players. **Pool(s):** heated outdoor. **Leisure Activities:** whirlpool, exercise room. **Guest Services:** valet and coin laundry, wireless Internet. **Business Services:** meeting rooms, business center. **Cards:** AX, DC, DS, MC, VI. **Free Special Amenities: local telephone calls and high-speed Internet.** *(See color ad p 529)*

Hilton Garden Inn

AAA Benefit:

Members save 5% or more everyday!

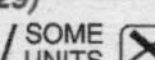

/ SOME UNITS

(See map and index starting on p. 517)

HILTON SAVANNAH DESOTO Book great rates at AAA.com **Phone:** (912)232-9000 24

Hotel
$109-$269 All Year

Address: 15 E Liberty St **Location:** Between Bull and Drayton sts; in historic district. **Facility:** 246 units. 243 one-bedroom standard units. 3 one-bedroom suites. 15 stories, interior corridors. **Parking:** on-site (fee) and valet. **Terms:** check-in 4 pm, cancellation fee imposed. **Amenities:** video games (fee), dual phone lines, voice mail, irons, hair dryers. **Pool(s):** heated outdoor. **Leisure Activities:** limited exercise equipment. **Guest Services:** valet laundry, wireless Internet. **Business Services:** conference facilities, business center. **Cards:** AX, DS, MC, VI.

SOME UNITS / VCR FEE

Hilton
AAA Benefit:
Members save 5% or more everyday!

(See map and index starting on p. 517)

HOLIDAY INN EXPRESS HISTORIC DISTRICT *Book at AAA.com* **Phone:** (912)231-9000 9

Hotel
$109-$239 All Year

Address: 199 E Bay St **Location:** Corner of Abercorn St. **Facility:** Smoke free premises. 143 one-bedroom standard units. 8 stories, interior corridors. *Bath:* combo or shower only. **Parking:** valet. **Terms:** check-in 4 pm, cancellation fee imposed. **Amenities:** high-speed Internet, voice mail, irons, hair dryers. **Pool(s):** heated outdoor. **Leisure Activities:** whirlpool, exercise room. **Guest Services:** valet laundry, wireless Internet. **Business Services:** meeting rooms, PC. **Cards:** AX, DS, MC, VI.

ASK

HYATT REGENCY SAVANNAH *Book great rates at AAA.com* **Phone:** (912)238-1234 

Hotel
$129-$400 All Year

Address: 2 W Bay St **Location:** I-16, exit 167 (Montgomery St), 0.8 mi ne, then just se. Located next to City Hall. **Facility:** Smoke free premises. 351 units. 346 one-bedroom standard units. 5 one-bedroom suites. 7 stories, interior corridors. *Bath:* combo or shower only. **Parking:** valet. **Terms:** 3 day cancellation notice-fee imposed. **Amenities:** voice mail, safes, irons, hair dryers. *Some:* dual phone lines. **Pool(s):** heated indoor. **Leisure Activities:** exercise room. *Fee:* boat dock. **Guest Services:** valet laundry, wireless Internet. **Business Services:** conference facilities, business center. **Cards:** AX, CB, DC, DS, JC, MC, VI. **Free Special Amenities: full breakfast and newspaper.**

HYATT HOTELS & RESORTS

AAA Benefit:
Ask for the AAA rate and save 10%.

INN AT ELLIS SQUARE, A DAYS HOTEL *Book great rates at AAA.com* **Phone:** (912)236-4440 6

Hotel
$139-$209 All Year

Address: 201 W Bay St **Location:** I-16, exit 167 (Montgomery St), 0.8 mi ne, then just se; between Whitaker and Jefferson sts; in historic district. **Facility:** Smoke free premises. 252 units. 195 one-bedroom standard units. 50 one- and 7 two-bedroom suites. 3-7 stories, interior corridors. *Bath:* combo or shower only. **Parking:** on-site (fee). **Terms:** check-in 4 pm, cancellation fee imposed. **Amenities:** CD players, voice mail, safes, irons, hair dryers. *Some:* high-speed Internet. **Pool(s):** outdoor. **Leisure Activities:** exercise room. **Guest Services:** wireless Internet. **Business Services:** meeting rooms, business center. **Cards:** AX, DS, MC, VI. **Free Special Amenities: expanded continental breakfast and room upgrade (subject to availability with advance reservations).**

SOME UNITS

(See map and index starting on p. 517)

JOAN'S ON JONES B & B | **Phone:** 912/234-3863 | 26

Historic Bed & Breakfast
$175-$195 All Year

Address: 17 W Jones St **Location:** Between Whitaker and Bull sts. **Facility:** Suites at this B&B have private ground-level entrances, and all rooms access a stocked refrigerator. Smoke free premises. 2 one-bedroom suites, some with efficiencies or kitchens. 1 story, exterior corridors. **Parking:** on-site. **Terms:** 2 night minimum stay - weekends, 7 day cancellation notice. **Amenities:** irons, hair dryers. **Guest Services:** wireless Internet.

/ SOME UNITS FEE

KEHOE HOUSE | *Book great rates at AAA.com* | **Phone:** (912)232-1020 | 21

AAA SAVE

Historic Bed & Breakfast
$249-$359 All Year

Address: 123 Habersham St **Location:** Between E President and E State sts; on Columbia Square; in historic district. **Facility:** An 1892 Victorian mansion with a dark brick exterior is elegantly furnished. Smoke free premises. 13 one-bedroom standard units. 2-4 stories, interior corridors. *Bath:* combo or shower only. **Parking:** on-site. **Terms:** 2 night minimum stay - seasonal and/or weekends, age restrictions may apply, 7 day cancellation notice. **Amenities:** DVD players, CD players, voice mail, hair dryers. **Guest Services:** valet laundry, wireless Internet. **Business Services:** meeting rooms, business center. **Cards:** AX, CB, DC, DS, MC, VI. **Free Special Amenities: full breakfast and high-speed Internet.** *(See color ad below)*

/ SOME UNITS VCR

THE MANSION ON FORSYTH PARK | *Book great rates at AAA.com* | **Phone:** (912)238-5158 | 31

AAA SAVE

Hotel
$229-$509 All Year

Address: 700 Drayton St **Location:** Between E Hall and E Gwinnett sts; on Forsyth Park. **Facility:** The hotel features a culinary school, restaurants, art gallery, spa, fitness center and nightclub; a modern-retro decor adorns the guest rooms. Smoke free premises. 120 one-bedroom standard units, some with whirlpools. 1 one-bedroom suite with kitchen. 2 stories (no elevator), exterior corridors. *Bath:* combo or shower only. **Parking:** valet. **Terms:** check-in 4 pm, 3 day cancellation notice-fee imposed. **Amenities:** voice mail, irons, hair dryers. **Dining:** entertainment. **Pool(s):** outdoor, heated outdoor. **Leisure Activities:** exercise room, spa. **Guest Services:** coin laundry, area transportation-within historic district, wireless Internet. **Business Services:** conference facilities, business center. **Cards:** AX, CB, DC, DS, MC, VI. **Free Special Amenities: newspaper and high-speed Internet.** Affiliated with A Preferred Hotel.

24 / SOME UNITS FEE FEE VCR

MARSHALL HOUSE | *Book great rates at AAA.com* | **Phone:** (912)644-7896 | 17

AAA SAVE

Classic Country Inn
$159-$269 All Year

Address: 123 E Broughton St **Location:** Between Drayton and Abercorn sts; in historic district. **Facility:** A restored 1851 property offering the charm and friendly warmth of a B&B with all the amenities expected of a modern hotel. 68 units. 65 one-bedroom standard units. 3 one-bedroom suites. 4 stories, interior corridors. *Bath:* combo or shower only. **Parking:** valet and street. **Terms:** 2 night minimum stay - seasonal and/or weekends, 7 day cancellation notice. **Amenities:** CD players, high-speed Internet, dual phone lines, voice mail, safes, irons, hair dryers. **Dining:** 45 Bistro at the Marshall House, see separate listing. **Guest Services:** valet laundry, wireless Internet. **Business Services:** meeting rooms, business center. **Cards:** AX, CB, DC, DS, MC, VI. **Free Special Amenities: expanded continental breakfast and high-speed Internet.** *(See color ad below)*

(See map and index starting on p. 517)

THE MULBERRY-A HOLIDAY INN HOTEL *Book great rates at AAA.com* **Phone:** (912)238-1200 15

Hotel
$209-$259 All Year

Address: 601 E Bay St **Location:** Between Broad and Houston sts; east side of historic district. **Facility:** 145 units. 120 one-bedroom standard units. 25 one-bedroom suites. 3 stories, interior/exterior corridors. *Bath:* combo or shower only. **Parking:** on-site (fee). **Terms:** check-in 4 pm. **Amenities:** high-speed Internet, dual phone lines, voice mail, irons, hair dryers. *Some:* DVD players, safes. **Pool(s):** outdoor. **Leisure Activities:** whirlpool, exercise room. **Guest Services:** valet laundry, wireless Internet. **Business Services:** meeting rooms, PC. **Cards:** AX, CB, DC, DS, JC, MC, VI.

ASK / SOME UNITS VCR

OLDE HARBOUR INN *Book great rates at AAA.com* **Phone:** (912)234-4100 13

AAA SAVE

Historic Bed & Breakfast
$219-$309 3/1-11/30
$199-$279 12/1-2/28

Address: 508 E Factors Walk **Location:** Lincoln St ramp off E Bay St; in historic riverfront district. **Facility:** The inn offers one- and two-bedroom accommodations that include a living room and kitchen; some rooms have river views. 24 units. 4 one-bedroom standard units. 14 one- and 6 two-bedroom suites. 3 stories (no elevator), exterior corridors. **Parking:** on-site (fee). **Terms:** 2 night minimum stay - weekends, 7 day cancellation notice. **Amenities:** CD players, safes, irons, hair dryers. *Some:* DVD players. **Guest Services:** valet laundry, wireless Internet. **Cards:** AX, CB, DC, DS, MC, VI. **Free Special Amenities: expanded continental breakfast and high-speed Internet.** *(See color ad p 531)*

/ SOME UNITS FEE

PLANTERS INN *Book great rates at AAA.com* **Phone:** (912)232-5678 14

AAA SAVE

Historic Boutique Hotel
$149-$249 2/14-11/30
$129-$199 12/1-2/13

Address: 29 Abercorn St **Location:** Corner of E Congress; on Reynolds Square; in historic district. **Facility:** Individually decorated rooms and 18-foot ceilings add charm to this inn. Smoke free premises. 60 one-bedroom standard units. 7 stories, interior corridors. *Bath:* combo or shower only. **Parking:** valet and street. **Terms:** check-in 4 pm, 2 night minimum stay - seasonal and/or weekends. **Amenities:** safes, irons, hair dryers. **Guest Services:** valet laundry, wireless Internet. **Business Services:** meeting rooms. **Cards:** AX, MC, VI. **Free Special Amenities: expanded continental breakfast and high-speed Internet.**

/ SOME UNITS

QUALITY INN HEART OF SAVANNAH *Book great rates at AAA.com* **Phone:** (912)236-6321 3

AAA SAVE

Motel
$119-$179 All Year

Address: 300 W Bay St **Location:** Between N Montgomery and N Jefferson sts; in historic district. **Facility:** 52 one-bedroom standard units. 2 stories (no elevator), exterior corridors. **Parking:** on-site. **Amenities:** irons, hair dryers. **Guest Services:** wireless Internet. **Cards:** AX, CB, DC, DS, JC, MC, VI. **Free Special Amenities: expanded continental breakfast and high-speed Internet.** *(See color ad below)*

/ SOME UNITS

RIVER STREET INN *Book great rates at AAA.com* **Phone:** (912)234-6400 8

AAA SAVE

Historic Country Inn
$119-$289 All Year

Address: 124 E Bay St **Location:** I-16, exit 167 (Montgomery St), 0.8 mi ne, then 0.4 mi se; in historic district. **Facility:** In a former cotton warehouse, the inn offers rooms with waterfront views and simple elegance. Smoke free premises. 86 units. 85 one-bedroom standard units, some with whirlpools. 1 one-bedroom suite. 5 stories, interior corridors. *Bath:* combo or shower only. **Parking:** on-site (fee) and street. **Terms:** check-in 4 pm. **Amenities:** CD players, dual phone lines, voice mail, safes, hair dryers. **Dining:** 2 restaurants. **Leisure Activities:** rooftop sun deck, billiards, exercise room. **Guest Services:** wireless Internet. **Business Services:** meeting rooms, PC. **Cards:** AX, CB, DC, DS, MC, VI. **Free Special Amenities: local telephone calls and newspaper.** *(See color ad p 533)*

▼ *See AAA listing above* ▼

(See map and index starting on p. 517)

SAVANNAH MARRIOTT RIVERFRONT Book great rates at AAA.com **Phone:** (912)233-7722 

Hotel
$196-$227 All Year

Address: 100 General McIntosh Blvd **Location:** East end of E Bay St. **Facility:** Smoke free premises. 391 units. 385 one-bedroom standard units. 6 one-bedroom suites. 8 stories, interior corridors. *Bath:* combo or shower only. **Parking:** on-site (fee) and valet. **Terms:** check-in 4 pm, cancellation fee imposed. **Amenities:** high-speed Internet (fee), dual phone lines, voice mail, irons, hair dryers. **Pool(s):** outdoor, heated indoor. **Leisure Activities:** whirlpool, exercise room, spa. **Guest Services:** valet and coin laundry, wireless Internet. **Business Services:** conference facilities, business center. **Cards:** AX, CB, DC, DS, JC, MC, VI.

/ SOME UNITS

Marriott HOTELS & RESORTS
AAA Benefit:
Members save a minimum 5% off the best available rate.

STAYBRIDGE SUITES SAVANNAH HISTORIC DISTRICT Book great rates at AAA.com **Phone:** (912)721-9000 12

AAA SAVE

Extended Stay Hotel
$120-$140 All Year

Address: 301 E Bay St **Location:** Corner of Lincoln St; in historic district. **Facility:** Located within walking distance of River Street and many restaurants, the extended-stay hotel offers features and amenities for comfort. 104 units. 102 one-bedroom standard units with efficiencies. 2 one-bedroom suites with efficiencies. 2-4 stories, interior corridors. *Bath:* combo or shower only. **Parking:** valet. **Terms:** 2 night minimum stay - weekends, 90 day cancellation notice-fee imposed. **Amenities:** high-speed Internet, voice mail, irons, hair dryers. **Leisure Activities:** exercise room. **Guest Services:** valet and coin laundry, wireless Internet. **Business Services:** meeting rooms, business center. **Cards:** AX, DS, MC. **Free Special Amenities: full breakfast and high-speed Internet.**

THE THUNDERBIRD INN Book great rates at AAA.com **Phone:** 912/232-2661 16

Motel
Rates not provided

Address: 611 W Oglethorpe Ave **Location:** Just w of Martin Luther King Jr Blvd. **Facility:** Smoke free premises. 42 one-bedroom standard units. 2 stories (no elevator), exterior corridors. **Parking:** on-site. **Amenities:** high-speed Internet, irons, hair dryers. **Guest Services:** wireless Internet.

/ SOME UNITS FEE

WESTIN SAVANNAH HARBOR GOLF RESORT AND SPA Book great rates at AAA.com **Phone:** (912)201-2000 

Resort Hotel
$169-$439 All Year

Address: 1 Resort Dr **Location:** On Hutchinson Island; 1 mi se of first exit after Eugene Talmadge Memorial Bridge and US 17. **Facility:** The resort offers well-appointed rooms overlooking river and harbor activities; a water-taxi service to historic River Street is available. Smoke free premises. 403 units. 390 one-bedroom standard units. 13 one-bedroom suites. 16 stories, interior corridors. *Bath:* combo or shower only. **Parking:** on-site and valet. **Amenities:** dual phone lines, voice mail, safes, honor bars, irons, hair dryers. *Fee:* video games, high-speed Internet. *Some:* CD players. **Dining:** 2 restaurants, also, Aqua Star Restaurant, see separate listing. **Pool(s):** heated outdoor. **Leisure Activities:** saunas, whirlpools, steamrooms, boat dock, 4 lighted tennis courts, jogging, spa. *Fee:* golf-18 holes. **Guest Services:** valet laundry, wireless Internet. **Business Services:** conference facilities, business center. **Cards:** AX, CB, DC, DS, JC, MC, VI. **Free Special Amenities: newspaper.**

/ SOME UNITS

WESTIN HOTELS & RESORTS
AAA Benefit:
Enjoy up to 15% off your next stay, plus Starwood Preferred Guest® bonuses.

▼ See AAA listing p 532 ▼

(See map and index starting on p. 517)

WHERE TO DINE

45 BISTRO AT THE MARSHALL HOUSE — **Phone:** 912/234-3111 (25)

Continental
$18-$34

This sister to the famous 45 South is a strong contender for downtown's top dining spot. The atrium garden setting, professional wait staff and gourmet menu combine to create a relaxing dining experience and a great meal. Highlights include crisp lasagna of jumbo sea scallops, osso buco, fillet of salmon gratinee and grilled black Angus fillet. All dishes are prepared to perfection and presented with an imaginative array of accompaniments. Dressy casual. **Bar:** Full bar. **Reservations:** suggested. **Hours:** 6 pm-10 pm. Closed: 11/26, 12/25; also Sun. **Address:** 123 E Broughton St **Location:** Between Drayton and Abercorn sts; in historic district; in Marshall House. **Parking:** valet and street. **Cards:** AX, DS, MC, VI.

ALLIGATOR SOUL — **Phone:** 912/232-7899 (22)

American
$28-$36

The chef prepares creative cuisine on the premises. There is always something new, with the entree menu changing seasonally and the appetizer and dessert menus changing weekly to biweekly. Dining is relaxed and comfortable and the staff attentive and congenial. The dining room is downstairs below ground level, with an elevator available for diners with special needs. Dressy casual. **Bar:** Full bar. **Reservations:** accepted. **Hours:** 5:30 pm-10 pm. Closed: 7/4, 12/25; also Sun. **Address:** 114 Barnard St **Location:** Between Congress and Broughton sts; in historic district. **Parking:** street. **Cards:** AX, DS, MC, VI.

CALL &M

AQUA STAR RESTAURANT — **Phone:** 912/201-2000 (1)

Regional American
$9-$35

Enjoy fine dining at The Westin's casually elegant signature restaurant. Diners can choose from a selection of fresh local seafood while watching the ships sail by against the backdrop of Savannah's historical skyline. The 2nd story location and large picture windows overlooking the river give the effect of dining on a ship. The chef's specialties include cedar plank salmon and Aqua Star lump crab cakes, both enormously popular and for good reason. Casual dress. **Bar:** Full bar. **Reservations:** suggested, for major events. **Hours:** 6:30 am-3 & 5:30-10 pm. **Address:** 1 Resort Dr **Location:** On Hutchinson Island; 1 mi se of first exit after Eugene Talmadge Memorial Bridge and US 17; in Westin Savannah Harbor Golf Resort and Spa. **Parking:** on-site and valet. **Cards:** AX, CB, DC, DS, JC, MC, VI.

CALL &M

A VIDA RESTAURANT & WINE BAR — **Phone:** 912/232-8432 (20)

AAA

New American
$24-$38

Casual eclectic atmosphere and chic decor make this award-winning restaurant an excellent dining choice. The menu offers a diverse selection of exotic creations combining traditional meats and seafoods with unusual sauces and vegetables. Vegan and vegetarian dishes are also available. Casual dress. **Bar:** Full bar. **Reservations:** suggested. **Hours:** 5 pm-10 pm, Fri & Sat-11 pm. Closed major holidays; also Sun. **Address:** 113 W Broughton **Location:** Between Whitaker and Barnard sts. **Parking:** street. **Cards:** AX, DS, MC, VI.

BELFORD'S — **Phone:** 912/233-2626 (8)

Steak & Seafood
$8-$35

Boasting brick walls, large arched windows and wood floors, the restaurant resides in a historic building constructed circa 1902. A popular menu selection is the fine Angus beef, cut in house, with buttermilk mashed potatoes and sauteed asparagus. You'll also find several well-prepared seafood entrees and such distinctive appetizers as the Parmesan tomato stack. Casual dress. **Bar:** Full bar. **Reservations:** suggested. **Hours:** 8-11 am, 11:30-3 & 5:30-10 pm, Sun from 11:30 am. Closed: 11/26, 12/25. **Address:** 315 W St. Julian St **Location:** Between Montgomery and Jefferson sts; in historic district at city market. **Parking:** street. **Cards:** AX, DC, DS, MC, VI.

BISTRO SAVANNAH — **Phone:** 912/233-6266 (13)

Continental
$15-$24

Set in an eclectic surrounding, menu offering include an array of excellent entrees prepared with a Southern flair. The artfully presented dishes won't disappoint. Desserts, such as flambeed berries, are luscious and delicious. Casual dress. **Bar:** Full bar. **Reservations:** suggested. **Hours:** 5 pm-10 pm, Fri & Sat-10:30 pm. Closed: 11/26, 12/25. **Address:** 309 W Congress St **Location:** Between Montgomery and Jefferson sts; in historic district at city market. **Parking:** street. **Cards:** AX, MC, VI.

B. MATTHEW'S EATERY — **Phone:** 912/233-1319 (18)

American
$5-$20

Somewhat reminiscent of a roadside inn from bygone days, the shop is in a historic building with brick walls and dark woods. The quality of the products, as well as the chef's skill, combine to create flavorful, upscale cuisine. Casual dress. **Bar:** Wine only. **Reservations:** accepted, for dinner. **Hours:** 7:30 am-3:30 & 5:30-10 pm, Sun & Mon-3:30 pm. Closed: 1/1, 12/25. **Address:** 325 E Bay St **Location:** Between Habersham and Price sts; on east side of historic district. **Parking:** street. **Cards:** AX, DS, MC, VI.

BOAR'S HEAD GRILL & TAVERN — **Phone:** 912/651-9660 (9)

Steak & Seafood
$9-$30

The restored cotton warehouse affords nice views of the river. A Southern flair infuses the award-winning, chef-owner's New American cuisine, which is beautifully presented. The menu is diverse, service is good, and the distinctive dessert creations are worth saving room for. Casual dress. **Bar:** Full bar. **Reservations:** accepted. **Hours:** 11 am-10 pm, Fri & Sat-11 pm, Sun noon-10 pm. Closed: 11/26, 12/25. **Address:** 1 N Lincoln St **Location:** Corner of Lincoln and River sts. **Parking:** street. **Cards:** AX, DC, DS, MC, VI. **Historic**

CASBAH MOROCCAN RESTAURANT *Menu on AAA.com* — **Phone:** 912/234-6168 (24)

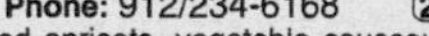

AAA

Moroccan
$16-$26

Dine opulently on traditional Moroccan fare such as lamb with caramelized apricots, vegetable couscous, fish tangine or harina. Various marinated and grilled kabobs are served with honey-nutmeg sauce. Belly dancers captivate the audience in the ceremonial Moroccan tent-like decor. Casual dress. Entertainment. **Bar:** Full bar. **Reservations:** suggested. **Hours:** 5:30 pm-10:30 pm. Closed: 12/25. **Address:** 118 E Broughton St **Location:** Between Drayton and Abercorn sts. **Parking:** street. **Cards:** AX, DC, DS, MC, VI.

(See map and index starting on p. 517)

CHART HOUSE — **Phone:** 912/234-6686 (5)

Steak & Seafood
$18-$26

Directly on the water, the restaurant offers a great view of the waterway and its many yachts. Examples of the fabulous food include prime rib, filet mignon, tomato-basil chicken and varied fresh fish and seafood dishes. Casual dress. **Bar:** Full bar. **Reservations:** suggested. **Hours:** 5 pm-10 pm, Sat-10:30 pm, Sun-9 pm. **Address:** 202 W Bay St **Location:** Between Montgomery and Whitaker sts. **Parking:** street. **Cards:** AX, DC, DS, MC, VI. **Historic**

COBBLESTONE CONCH HOUSE — **Phone:** 912/232-5551 (2)

Seafood
$12-$24

Overlooking the Savannah River, the restaurant has two spacious floors decorated in a Caribbean theme. Such Caribbean-influenced dishes as conch fritters, jerk chicken and coconut shrimp show evidence of a Southern twist. Casual dress. **Bar:** Full bar. **Reservations:** accepted. **Hours:** 11 am-10 pm, Fri & Sat-11 pm. Closed: 11/26, 12/25. **Address:** 225 W River St **Location:** On historic riverfront. **Parking:** street. **Cards:** AX, MC, VI.

FIREFLY CAFE — **Phone:** 912/234-1971 (26)

American
$9-$22

Located in a building originally constructed in 1869, the casual, neighborhood cafe serves comfort foods, seafood and other favorites prepared with creative touches. The menu also denotes items that can be prepared vegan. There are a few tables on the sidewalk for al fresco dining, where dogs are also welcome. Casual dress. **Bar:** Wine only. **Reservations:** accepted. **Hours:** 7:30 am-8:30 pm, Fri-9:30 pm, Sat 9 am-9 pm, Sun 9 am-3 pm. Closed major holidays; also Mon. **Address:** 321 Habersham St **Location:** S of E Liberty St, at Harris St; on Troup Square. **Parking:** street. **Cards:** MC, VI.

GARIBALDI'S CAFE — **Phone:** 912/232-7118 (10)

Seafood
$13-$32

Set in a restored 1871 German firehouse, diners can select from a bar-like, bustling eatery or a more traditional dining room on the second floor, which was the former firemen's ballroom. Highlights include eclectic recipes and daily specials. Casual dress. **Bar:** Full bar. **Reservations:** required. **Hours:** 5 pm-10:30 pm, Fri & Sat-11 pm, Sun-10 pm. Closed: 12/25. **Address:** 315 W Congress St **Location:** Between Montgomery and Jefferson sts; on southeast side of Franklin Square; in historic district at city market. **Parking:** street. **Cards:** AX, MC, VI.

HUEY'S NEW ORLEANS CAFE — **Phone:** 912/234-7385 (6)

Regional American
$6-$27

The popular restaurant serves N'awlins-style fare, such as gumbo, red beans and rice and shrimp Creole. Views of the river are wonderful. Casual dress. **Bar:** Full bar. **Reservations:** accepted. **Hours:** 7 am-10 pm, Fri-11 pm, Sat 8 am-11 pm, Sun 8 am-10 pm. Closed: 11/26, 12/25. **Address:** 115 E River St **Location:** On historic riverfront. **Parking:** street. **Cards:** AX, DS, MC, VI.

IL PASTICCIO — **Phone:** 912/231-8888 (21)

Italian
$23-$45

Traditional Italian cuisine share space on the menu with several veal dishes. The bistro is lively and offers an eclectic interior and friendly service. Casual dress. **Bar:** Full bar. **Reservations:** required. **Hours:** 5:30 pm-10 pm, Fri & Sat-11:30 pm, Sun-9:30 pm. Closed: 1/1, 11/26, 12/25; also Super Bowl Sun. **Address:** 2 E Broughton St **Location:** Corner of Broughton and Bull sts; between Bull and Drayton sts. **Parking:** street. **Cards:** AX, DC, DS, MC, VI.

ISAAC'S ON DRAYTON — **Phone:** 912/231-0100 (14)

American
$7-$30

Said to be haunted by a bare knuckles fighter hanged after killing a local fighter, the restaurant's focal point has to be the large bar that was built in England in the 1700s. The chef prepares excellent fare, accentuated by flavorful seasonings and sauces: Specifically, the orange marmalade butter adds a delightful treat to the bread. Dine on the open, outside deck located upstairs, if you choose. Casual dress. **Bar:** Full bar. **Reservations:** accepted. **Hours:** 11 am-10 pm. Closed: 12/25. **Address:** 9 Drayton St **Location:** Between Bay and Bryan sts; opposite Bryan St parking garage. **Parking:** street. **Cards:** AX, DC, MC, VI.

JOHN RYAN'S BISTRO & PUB — **Phone:** 912/790-7000 (4)

Regional American
$7-$28

The hotel restaurant prepares a great selection of local favorites for dinner and a wide variety of sandwiches and lighter meals for lunch. Also, a lunch buffet is set up on weekdays. Happy hour light bites also are served on weekdays. Casual dress. **Bar:** Full bar. **Reservations:** accepted. **Hours:** 6-10:30 am, 11:30-1:30 & 5-10 pm. **Address:** 411 W Bay St **Location:** I-16, exit 167 (Montgomery St), 0.8 mi ne; in DoubleTree Hotel Historic Savannah. **Parking:** valet. **Cards:** AX, CB, DS, MC, VI.

CALL

THE LADY & SONS — **Phone:** 912/233-2600 (15)

Southern
$9-$25

The energetic atmosphere and bustling activity make for an exciting dining experience, where the wait staff may surprise you by simply bursting into song. Appetizers include crispy fried green tomatoes and crab-stuffed portobello mushrooms. Barbecue shrimp over grits and chicken pot pie are two house specialties that give you a sample of Southern cookery at its best. Cheese biscuits melt in your mouth, and the pear cobbler and sock-it-to-me cake are fitting finales. Sunday is buffet only. Casual dress. **Bar:** Full bar. **Hours:** 11 am-3 & 5-9 pm, Sun-5 pm. Closed: 1/1, 12/25, 12/26. **Address:** 102 W Congress St **Location:** Between Jefferson and Montgomery sts; in historic district at city market. **Parking:** street. **Cards:** AX, DC, DS, MC, VI.

MOLLY MACPHERSON'S SCOTTISH PUB & GRILL — **Phone:** 912/239-9600 (11)

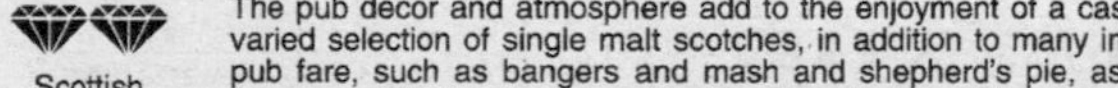

Scottish
$9-$18

The pub decor and atmosphere add to the enjoyment of a casual, carefree dining experience. A large and varied selection of single malt scotches, in addition to many international beers, complements the Scottish pub fare, such as bangers and mash and shepherd's pie, as well as more traditional American entrees. Service, while informal, is attentive. Casual dress. **Bar:** Full bar. **Hours:** 11 am-10 pm, Sun from noon. Closed major holidays. **Address:** 311 W Congress St **Location:** Just e of Montgomery St, across from city market. **Parking:** street. **Cards:** AX, DS, MC, VI.

(See map and index starting on p. 517)

THE OLDE PINK HOUSE Phone: 912/232-4286 (19)

Regional American
$15-$29

Housed in a converted 18th-century mansion, the restaurant prides itself on hearty, classic Southern cuisine and tip-top service. Menu favorites are grilled salmon with capers and new potatoes, crispy scored flounder and Colonial apple pie. Casual dress. **Bar:** Full bar. **Reservations:** suggested, weekends. **Hours:** 5:30 pm-10:30 pm, Fri & Sat-11 pm. **Address:** 23 Abercorn St **Location:** Between E Bryan and E Saint Julian sts; facing Reynold Square. **Parking:** street. **Cards:** AX, MC, VI. **Historic**

THE OYSTER BAR Phone: 912/232-1565 (17)

Seafood
$9-$23

The converted warehouse along the Savannah River features local seafood, fresh oysters and a raw bar. Try crab-stuffed mushrooms in butter sauce for starters and seafood Diane with fresh shrimp, scallops and artichokes for the main course. Casual dress. **Bar:** Full bar. **Reservations:** accepted. **Hours:** 4 pm-10 pm, Fri & Sat-10:30 pm. Closed: 11/26, 12/25. **Address:** 411 E River St **Location:** 0.4 mi e on historic riverfront. **Parking:** street. **Cards:** AX, DC, DS, MC, VI.

THE PIRATES' HOUSE Phone: 912/233-5757 (23)

Southern Seafood
$7-$26

Dating back to the early 1700s, The Pirates' House began as a tavern and now that same yesteryear charm greets diners in historic Savannah. Steak, seafood, chicken and Southern-style side dishes are served in 16 dining rooms decorated with period pieces. Casual dress. **Bar:** Full bar. **Reservations:** suggested. **Hours:** 11 am-10 pm. Closed: 12/25. **Address:** 20 E Broad & Bay St **Location:** Between E Bay and E Broughton sts; on east side of historic district at Trustees' Garden. **Parking:** on-site. **Cards:** AX, DC, DS, MC, VI. **Historic**

RIVER HOUSE SEAFOOD & BAKERY Phone: 912/234-1900 (3)

Seafood
$9-$35

Although off the beaten path, this riverfront eatery, offering fresh and flavorful entrees in a nautical atmosphere, does a brisk business. There's seafood, pasta and chops, and warm pecan pie with vanilla ice cream and other homemade treats on the menu. Casual dress. **Bar:** Full bar. **Reservations:** suggested. **Hours:** 11 am-10 pm, Fri & Sat-11 pm, Sun 11:30 am-10 pm. Closed: 11/26, 12/25. **Address:** 125 W River St **Location:** On historic riverfront. **Parking:** on-site and street. **Cards:** AX, DC, DS, MC, VI.

SAPPHIRE GRILL Phone: 912/443-9962 (16)

American
$26-$40

In a historic building, the dining rooms combine the charm of brick walls and wood-plank floors with distinctive, upscale decor. The chef uses fresh ingredients to create innovative cuisine. Artistic presentations are a feast for the eyes, as well as a treat for the palate. Dressy casual. **Bar:** Full bar. **Reservations:** suggested. **Hours:** 6 pm-10:30 pm, Fri & Sat 5:30 pm-11:30 pm. Closed: 1/1, 11/26, 12/25. **Address:** 110 W Congress St **Location:** Jct Whitaker St; 2 blks s of Bay St. **Parking:** street. **Cards:** AX, DC, MC, VI.

SHRIMP FACTORY Phone: 912/236-4229 (12)

Seafood
$12-$32

This active dining spot in a 1820s cotton warehouse with a river view and nautical theme serves up a variety of seafood like shrimp strudel full of spinach and cheese. Try the historic pine bark stew, the recipe for which dates back hundreds of years. Casual dress. **Bar:** Full bar. **Reservations:** accepted. **Hours:** 11 am-10 pm, Fri & Sat-11 pm, Sun noon-10 pm. Closed: 11/26, 12/25. **Address:** 313 E River St **Location:** On historic riverfront. **Parking:** on-site (fee). **Cards:** AX, DC, DS, MC, VI.

VIC'S ON THE RIVER RESTAURANT & BAR Phone: 912/721-1000 (7)

American
$7-$29

Entry to the restaurant is via Bay Street or an elevator from River Street. The historic building once served as a warehouse and a gathering place for Union officers during the Civil War. During a renovation, a portion of a wall-drawn map chronicling General Sherman's march through the South was uncovered; patrons are invited to take a peek. Waits aren't unusual at the popular spot, which earns praise for its casual service, laid-back atmosphere and hearty comfort foods, Southern favorites and traditional fare. Casual dress. **Bar:** Full bar. **Reservations:** accepted. **Hours:** 11 am-10 pm, Fri & Sat-11 pm. Closed: 11/26, 12/25. **Address:** 26 E Bay St **Location:** On River; in historic district; entrance also at 15 E River St. **Parking:** street. **Cards:** AX, DS, MC, VI.

CALL

SAVANNAH pop. 131,510 (See map and index starting on p. 520)

WHERE TO STAY

BEST WESTERN CENTRAL *Book great rates at AAA.com* **Phone:** (912)355-1000 (18)

Hotel
$69-$109 All Year

Address: 45 Eisenhower Dr **Location:** 1.3 mi s of jct SR 21/204 (Abercorn St), then just w. Located adjacent to Hunter Army Air Field. **Facility:** 129 one-bedroom standard units. 2 stories (no elevator), exterior corridors. **Parking:** on-site. **Terms:** 3 day cancellation notice-fee imposed. **Amenities:** irons, hair dryers. **Pool(s):** outdoor. **Guest Services:** wireless Internet. **Business Services:** meeting rooms. **Cards:** AX, DC, DS, JC, MC, VI. **Free Special Amenities: expanded continental breakfast and high-speed Internet.**

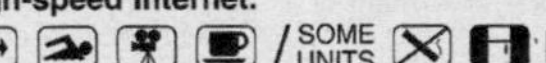

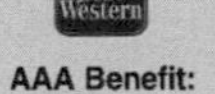

AAA Benefit:

Members save up to 20%, plus 10% bonus points with rewards program.

(See map and index starting on p. 520)

BEST WESTERN SAVANNAH GATEWAY *Book great rates at AAA.com* **Phone:** (912)925-2420 30

Hotel

$59-$139 All Year

Address: 1 Gateway Blvd **Location:** I-95, exit 94 (SR 204/Abercorn St), just e. **Facility:** 122 one-bedroom standard units. 2 stories (no elevator), exterior corridors. **Parking:** on-site. **Terms:** 7 day cancellation notice-fee imposed. **Amenities:** voice mail, irons, hair dryers. **Pool(s):** outdoor. **Leisure Activities:** whirlpool. **Guest Services:** valet laundry, wireless Internet. **Business Services:** meeting rooms. **Cards:** AX, CB, DC, DS, JC, MC, VI. **Free Special Amenities: continental breakfast and high-speed Internet.** *(See color ad p 525)*

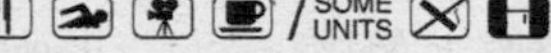

AAA Benefit:

Members save up to 20%, plus 10% bonus points with rewards program.

CAMBRIA SUITES SAVANNAH AIRPORT *Book at AAA.com* **Phone:** 912/965-9595 6

Hotel

Rates not provided

Address: 50 Yvette Johnson Hagins Dr **Location:** I-95, exit 104, just e. **Facility:** Smoke free premises. 97 units. 87 one- and 2 two-bedroom standard units. 8 one-bedroom suites. 4 stories, interior corridors. *Bath:* combo or shower only. **Parking:** on-site. **Amenities:** DVD players, CD players, high-speed Internet, voice mail, irons, hair dryers. **Pool(s):** heated outdoor. **Leisure Activities:** whirlpool, exercise room. **Guest Services:** valet and coin laundry, area transportation, wireless Internet. **Business Services:** meeting rooms, business center.

CALL

CATHERINE WARD HOUSE INN **Phone:** (912)234-8564 9

Historic Bed & Breakfast

$369 All Year

Address: 118 E Waldburg St **Location:** Between Drayton and Abercorn sts. **Facility:** Gingerbread embellishments, a parlor filled with fine antiques, and beautifully decorated rooms make this an ideal choice for a romantic getaway. Smoke free premises. 9 one-bedroom standard units, some with whirlpools. 3 stories (no elevator), interior/exterior corridors. *Bath:* combo or shower only. **Parking:** street. **Terms:** 2 night minimum stay - weekends, 3 day cancellation notice-fee imposed. **Amenities:** CD players, hair dryers. *Some:* DVD players. **Guest Services:** wireless Internet. **Cards:** AX, DS, MC, VI.

ASK / SOME UNITS FEE

CLARION INN & SUITES *Book great rates at AAA.com* **Phone:** (912)920-3200 26

AAA SAVE

Hotel

$89-$169 12/1-8/10

$79-$119 8/11-11/30

Address: 16 Gateway Blvd E **Location:** I-95, exit 94 (SR 204/Abercorn St), just e. **Facility:** 72 one-bedroom standard units. 3 stories, interior corridors. *Bath:* combo or shower only. **Parking:** on-site. **Amenities:** dual phone lines, voice mail, irons, hair dryers. **Pool(s):** heated indoor. **Leisure Activities:** whirlpool, limited exercise equipment. **Guest Services:** coin laundry, wireless Internet. **Business Services:** meeting rooms, business center. **Cards:** AX, CB, DC, DS, JC, MC, VI. **Free Special Amenities: expanded continental breakfast and high-speed Internet.**

CALL / SOME UNITS FEE

COMFORT SUITES GATEWAY *Book at AAA.com* **Phone:** (912)920-9499 22

Hotel

$80-$300 All Year

Address: 596 Al Henderson Blvd **Location:** I-95, exit 94 (SR 204/Abercorn St), just e to Gateway Blvd, then 0.3 mi n. **Facility:** Smoke free premises. 90 units. 86 one-bedroom standard units, some with whirlpools. 4 one-bedroom suites, some with whirlpools. 4 stories, interior corridors. *Bath:* combo or shower only. **Parking:** on-site. **Amenities:** high-speed Internet, voice mail, safes, irons, hair dryers. **Pool(s):** heated indoor. **Leisure Activities:** whirlpool, exercise room. **Guest Services:** valet and coin laundry, wireless Internet. **Business Services:** meeting rooms, business center. **Cards:** AX, CB, DC, DS, MC, VI.

ASK

▼ *See AAA listing p 512* ▼

(See map and index starting on p. 520)

COMFORT SUITES SAVANNAH AIRPORT *Book at AAA.com* **Phone:** (912)721-9100 5

Hotel

$109-$129 All Year

Address: 1 Yvette Johnson Hagins Dr **Location:** I-95, exit 104, 0.4 mi e. **Facility:** Smoke free premises. 80 one-bedroom standard units. 3 stories, interior corridors. *Bath:* combo or shower only. **Parking:** on-site. **Amenities:** high-speed Internet, voice mail, irons, hair dryers. **Pool(s):** heated indoor. **Leisure Activities:** whirlpool, limited exercise equipment. **Guest Services:** valet and coin laundry, area transportation, wireless Internet. **Business Services:** business center. **Cards:** AX, DC, DS, MC, VI.

ASK / SOME UNITS FEE

COUNTRY INN & SUITES BY CARLSON *Book great rates at AAA.com* **Phone:** (912)692-0404 19

AAA SAVE

Hotel

$108-$119 All Year

Address: 7576 White Bluff Rd **Location:** Jct SR 21, 1.5 mi s. Located adjacent to Hunter Army Air Field. **Facility:** Smoke free premises. 62 units. 31 one-bedroom standard units, some with whirlpools. 29 one- and 2 two-bedroom suites. 3 stories, interior corridors. *Bath:* combo or shower only. **Parking:** on-site. **Amenities:** high-speed Internet, dual phone lines, voice mail, irons, hair dryers. **Pool(s):** heated indoor. **Leisure Activities:** whirlpool, exercise room. **Guest Services:** coin laundry, wireless Internet. **Cards:** AX, CB, DC, DS, MC, VI.

CALL / SOME UNITS

COUNTRY INN & SUITES BY CARLSON-SAVANNAH GATEWAY *Book great rates at AAA.com* **Phone:** (912)921-1940 32

AAA SAVE

Hotel

$89-$170 All Year

Address: 17009 Abercorn St **Location:** I-95, exit 94 (SR 204/Abercorn St), just e. **Facility:** Smoke free premises. 54 units. 39 one-bedroom standard units. 15 one-bedroom suites. 4 stories, interior corridors. *Bath:* combo or shower only. **Parking:** on-site. **Terms:** cancellation fee imposed. **Amenities:** high-speed Internet, dual phone lines, voice mail, irons, hair dryers. **Pool(s):** heated indoor. **Leisure Activities:** whirlpool, limited exercise equipment. **Guest Services:** coin laundry, wireless Internet. **Cards:** AX, DS, MC, VI.

COUNTRY INN & SUITES SAVANNAH AIRPORT **Phone:** 912/966-1717

fyi

Hotel

$95-$115 All Year

Too new to rate. **Address:** 21 Yvette Johnson Hagins Dr **Location:** I-95, exit 104, just e. **Amenities:** 82 units, coffeemakers, microwaves, refrigerators, pool. **Terms:** cancellation fee imposed. **Cards:** AX, DS, MC, VI.

EXTENDED STAYAMERICA-MIDTOWN *Book at AAA.com* **Phone:** (912)692-0076 10

Hotel

$70-$185 All Year

Address: 5511 Abercorn St **Location:** Jct SR 21 and 204 (Abercorn St), just s. **Facility:** 104 one-bedroom standard units with efficiencies. 3 stories, interior corridors. *Bath:* combo or shower only. **Parking:** on-site. **Terms:** office hours 7 am-11 pm. **Amenities:** dual phone lines, voice mail, irons, hair dryers. **Guest Services:** coin laundry, wireless Internet. **Cards:** AX, CB, DC, DS, JC, MC, VI.

ASK / SOME UNITS FEE

FAIRFIELD INN *Book great rates at AAA.com* **Phone:** (912)353-7100 14

Hotel

$81-$102 All Year

Address: 2 Lee Blvd **Location:** Jct SR 21 and 204 (Abercorn St), 0.6 mi s on Abercorn St, then just w. **Facility:** Smoke free premises. 131 one-bedroom standard units. 3 stories, interior/exterior corridors. *Bath:* combo or shower only. **Parking:** on-site. **Terms:** cancellation fee imposed. **Amenities:** voice mail, irons, hair dryers. **Pool(s):** outdoor. **Leisure Activities:** exercise room. **Guest Services:** valet and coin laundry, wireless Internet. **Business Services:** PC. **Cards:** AX, CB, DC, DS, JC, MC, VI.

/ SOME UNITS

AAA Benefit:

Members save a minimum 5% off the best available rate.

FAIRFIELD INN & SUITES I-95 SOUTH *Book great rates at AAA.com* **Phone:** (912)925-5050 27

Hotel

$88-$118 All Year

Address: 17027 Abercorn St **Location:** I-95, exit 94 (SR 204/Abercorn St), just e. **Facility:** Smoke free premises. 80 one-bedroom standard units. 3 stories, interior corridors. *Bath:* combo or shower only. **Parking:** on-site. **Terms:** cancellation fee imposed. **Amenities:** high-speed Internet, voice mail, irons, hair dryers. *Some:* CD players. **Pool(s):** heated indoor. **Leisure Activities:** whirlpool, exercise room. **Guest Services:** valet and coin laundry, wireless Internet. **Business Services:** PC. **Cards:** AX, CB, DC, DS, JC, MC, VI. **Free Special Amenities: expanded continental breakfast and high-speed Internet.**

/ SOME UNITS

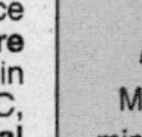

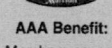

AAA Benefit:

Members save a minimum 5% off the best available rate.

(See map and index starting on p. 520)

FAIRFIELD INN SAVANNAH AIRPORT Book great rates at AAA.com **Phone:** (912)965-9777 3

Hotel
$138-$148 All Year

Address: 10 Stephen S Green Dr **Location:** I-95, exit 104, just e. **Facility:** Smoke free premises. 80 one-bedroom standard units, some with whirlpools. 3 stories, interior corridors. *Bath:* combo or shower only. **Parking:** on-site. **Terms:** cancellation fee imposed. **Amenities:** voice mail, irons, hair dryers. **Pool(s):** heated indoor. **Leisure Activities:** whirlpool, exercise room. **Guest Services:** valet laundry, area transportation, wireless Internet. **Business Services:** meeting rooms, PC. **Cards:** AX, CB, DC, DS, JC, MC, VI.

CALL / SOME UNITS FEE

AAA Benefit:
Members save a minimum 5% off the best available rate.

FOUR POINTS BY SHERATON Book great rates at AAA.com **Phone:** 912/629-1500 

Hotel
Rates not provided

Address: 15 Jay R Turner Dr **Location:** I-95, exit 104, 0.4 mi e. **Facility:** Smoke free premises. 79 units. 73 one-bedroom standard units. 6 one-bedroom suites. 3 stories, interior corridors. *Bath:* combo or shower only. **Parking:** on-site. **Amenities:** high-speed Internet, voice mail, irons, hair dryers. **Pool(s):** heated outdoor. **Leisure Activities:** exercise room. **Guest Services:** valet laundry, area transportation-within 5 mi, wireless Internet. **Business Services:** business center. **Free Special Amenities: local telephone calls and newspaper.**

/ SOME UNITS FEE

FOUR POINTS BY SHERATON

AAA Benefit:
Members get up to 15% off, plus Starwood Preferred Guest® bonuses.

HAMPTON INN & SUITES I-95 GATEWAY Book great rates at AAA.com **Phone:** (912)921-1515 

Hotel
$129-$169 All Year

Address: 591 Al Henderson Blvd **Location:** I-95, exit 94 (SR 204/Abercorn St), just ne. **Facility:** 92 one-bedroom standard units, some with whirlpools. 6 stories, interior corridors. *Bath:* combo or shower only. **Parking:** on-site. **Amenities:** voice mail, safes, irons, hair dryers. **Pool(s):** heated indoor. **Leisure Activities:** whirlpool, exercise room. **Guest Services:** valet and coin laundry, wireless Internet. **Business Services:** meeting rooms, business center. **Cards:** AX, CB, DC, DS, MC, VI.

CALL    / SOME UNITS

AAA Benefit:
Members save up to 10% everyday!

HAWTHORN SUITES Book great rates at AAA.com **Phone:** (912)966-0020 7

Hotel
$109-$159 All Year

Address: 4 Stephen S Green Ave **Location:** I-95, exit 104, 0.4 mi e. **Facility:** 85 one-bedroom suites, some with efficiencies, kitchens and/or whirlpools. 3 stories, interior corridors. *Bath:* combo or shower only. **Parking:** on-site. **Terms:** cancellation fee imposed. **Amenities:** video library (fee), DVD players, high-speed Internet, dual phone lines, voice mail, safes, irons, hair dryers. **Pool(s):** outdoor. **Leisure Activities:** exercise room. **Guest Services:** valet and coin laundry, airport transportation-Savannah/Hilton Head International Airport, area transportation-within 5 mi, wireless Internet. **Business Services:** meeting rooms, business center. **Cards:** AX, DC, DS, MC, VI. **Free Special Amenities: continental breakfast and early check-in/late check-out.**

CALL / SOME UNITS

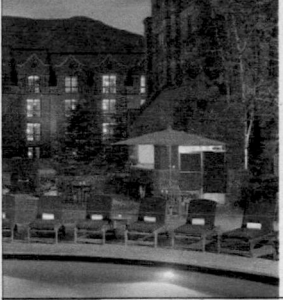

(See map and index starting on p. 520)

HILTON GARDEN INN *Book great rates at AAA.com* **Phone:** (912)964-5550 8

Hotel
$79-$179 All Year

Address: 80 Clyde E Martin Dr **Location:** I-95, exit 104, just se. **Facility:** 105 units. 103 one-bedroom standard units. 2 one-bedroom suites with whirlpools. 3 stories, interior corridors. *Bath:* combo or shower only. **Parking:** on-site. **Terms:** 1-30 night minimum stay, cancellation fee imposed. **Amenities:** video games (fee), high-speed Internet, dual phone lines, voice mail, irons, hair dryers. **Pool(s):** outdoor. **Leisure Activities:** whirlpool, exercise room. **Guest Services:** valet and coin laundry, area transportation, wireless Internet. **Business Services:** meeting rooms, business center. **Cards:** AX, CB, DC, DS, JC, MC, VI.

CALL / SOME UNITS

HILTON GARDEN INN SAVANNAH MIDTOWN *Book great rates at AAA.com* **Phone:** (912)652-9300 11

Hotel
$79-$399 All Year

Address: 5711 Abercorn St **Location:** Jct SR 204/21, just s. **Facility:** 131 units. 116 one-bedroom standard units, some with whirlpools. 15 one-bedroom suites. 6 stories, interior corridors. *Bath:* combo or shower only. **Parking:** on-site. **Terms:** check-in 4 pm, 1-30 night minimum stay, cancellation fee imposed. **Amenities:** video games (fee), high-speed Internet, dual phone lines, voice mail, irons, hair dryers. **Pool(s):** heated outdoor. **Leisure Activities:** whirlpool, exercise room. **Guest Services:** valet and coin laundry, area transportation-historic district. **Business Services:** meeting rooms, business center. **Cards:** AX, DC, DS, MC, VI. **Free Special Amenities: local telephone calls and high-speed Internet.** ***(See color ad p 529)***

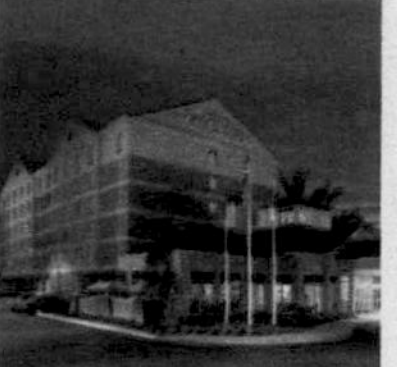

CALL / SOME UNITS

HOLIDAY INN EXPRESS *Book great rates at AAA.com* **Phone:** (912)925-2700 23

Hotel
$100-$109 All Year

Address: 17 Gateway Blvd E **Location:** I-95, exit 94 (SR 204/Abercorn St), just e. **Facility:** 96 one-bedroom suites, some with whirlpools. 3 stories, interior corridors. *Bath:* combo or shower only. **Parking:** on-site. **Terms:** check-in 4 pm. **Amenities:** high-speed Internet, dual phone lines, voice mail, safes, irons, hair dryers. **Pool(s):** outdoor. **Guest Services:** coin laundry, wireless Internet. **Business Services:** meeting rooms, business center. **Cards:** AX, DC, DS, MC, VI.

ASK / SOME UNITS

HOMEWOOD SUITES BY HILTON *Book great rates at AAA.com* **Phone:** (912)353-8500 13

Hotel
$149-$229 3/1-11/30
$139-$229 12/1-2/28

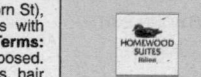

Address: 5820 White Bluff Rd **Location:** Jct SR 21 and 204 (Abercorn St), 0.5 mi s. **Facility:** 106 units. 97 one- and 9 two-bedroom suites with efficiencies. 2-3 stories, interior/exterior corridors. **Parking:** on-site. **Terms:** 3 night minimum stay - seasonal, cancellation fee imposed. **Amenities:** video games (fee), high-speed Internet, voice mail, irons, hair dryers. **Pool(s):** heated outdoor. **Leisure Activities:** whirlpool, exercise room, sports court. **Guest Services:** valet and coin laundry, wireless Internet. **Business Services:** meeting rooms, business center. **Cards:** AX, DC, DS, MC, VI.

/ SOME UNITS FEE

HOWARD JOHNSON EXPRESS INN *Book at AAA.com* **Phone:** (912)925-7050 34

Motel
$79-$99 All Year

Address: 17003 Abercorn St **Location:** I-95, exit 94 (SR 204), just e. **Facility:** 66 one-bedroom standard units. 2 stories (no elevator), exterior corridors. *Bath:* combo or shower only. **Parking:** on-site. **Amenities:** voice mail, safes, irons, hair dryers. **Pool(s):** outdoor. **Guest Services:** wireless Internet. **Business Services:** PC. **Cards:** AX, DC, DS, MC, VI.

ASK / SOME UNITS

LA QUINTA INN & SUITES *Book at AAA.com* **Phone:** (912)927-7660 35

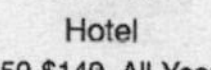

Hotel
$59-$149 All Year

Address: 8484 Abercorn St **Location:** 2.4 mi s of jct SR 21 and 204 (Abercorn St). **Facility:** 100 units. 99 one-bedroom standard units. 1 one-bedroom suite. 3 stories, interior corridors. **Parking:** on-site. **Amenities:** video games (fee), voice mail, irons, hair dryers. *Some:* high-speed Internet. **Pool(s):** outdoor. **Leisure Activities:** limited exercise equipment. **Guest Services:** coin laundry, wireless Internet. **Business Services:** PC. **Cards:** AX, DC, DS, MC, VI.

 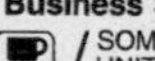  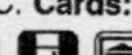

ASK / SOME UNITS

(See map and index starting on p. 520)

LA QUINTA INN SAVANNAH (I-95) Book great rates at AAA.com **Phone:** (912)925-9505 35

Hotel
$55-$109 All Year

Address: 6 Gateway Blvd S **Location:** I-95, exit 94 (SR 204/Abercorn St), just e, then s. **Facility:** 120 one-bedroom standard units. 2 stories (no elevator), exterior corridors. *Bath:* combo or shower only. **Parking:** on-site. **Amenities:** video games (fee), voice mail, irons, hair dryers. *Some:* high-speed Internet. **Pool(s):** outdoor. **Guest Services:** coin laundry, wireless Internet. **Cards:** AX, DS, MC, VI.

ASK CALL / SOME UNITS

LA QUINTA INN SAVANNAH (MIDTOWN) Book great rates at AAA.com **Phone:** (912)355-3004 16

Hotel
$59-$129 All Year

Address: 6805 Abercorn St **Location:** 1 mi s of jct SR 21 and 204 (Abercorn St). **Facility:** 154 units. 152 one-bedroom standard units. 2 one-bedroom suites. 2 stories (no elevator), interior/exterior corridors. **Parking:** on-site. **Amenities:** video games (fee), voice mail, irons, hair dryers. *Some:* high-speed Internet. **Pool(s):** outdoor. **Guest Services:** coin laundry, wireless Internet. **Cards:** AX, DS, MC, VI.

ASK / SOME UNITS

MICROTEL INN & SUITES Book at AAA.com **Phone:** (912)920-1920 20

Hotel
$40-$90 All Year

Address: 45 Ft Argyle Rd **Location:** I-95, exit 94 (SR 204/Abercorn St), just w. **Facility:** 67 one-bedroom standard units. 3 stories, interior corridors. *Bath:* combo or shower only. **Parking:** on-site. **Amenities:** voice mail, irons, hair dryers. **Pool(s):** heated indoor. **Leisure Activities:** whirlpool, limited exercise equipment. **Guest Services:** coin laundry, wireless Internet. **Cards:** AX, DC, DS, MC, VI.

ASK CALL / SOME UNITS

OGLETHORPE INN & SUITES Book great rates at AAA.com **Phone:** (912)354-8560 21

AAA SAVE

Hotel
$89-$195 All Year

Address: 7110 Hodgson Memorial Dr **Location:** Jct SR 21 and 204 (Abercorn St), 1.3 mi s, just e on Eisenhower Dr, then just s. **Facility:** Smoke free premises. 52 units. 47 one-bedroom standard units. 5 one-bedroom suites with whirlpools. 3 stories, interior corridors. *Bath:* combo or shower only. **Parking:** on-site. **Amenities:** voice mail, irons, hair dryers. **Pool(s):** outdoor. **Leisure Activities:** exercise room. **Guest Services:** coin laundry, wireless Internet. **Business Services:** meeting rooms, PC. **Cards:** AX, DC, DS, MC, VI. **Free Special Amenities: continental breakfast and high-speed Internet.**

RAMADA I-95 GATEWAY Book at AAA.com **Phone:** (912)925-1212 31

Motel
$66-$125 All Year

Address: 17007 Abercorn St **Location:** I-95, exit 94 (SR 204/Abercorn St), just e. **Facility:** 60 one-bedroom standard units, some with whirlpools. 2 stories (no elevator), exterior corridors. **Parking:** on-site. **Amenities:** voice mail, safes, irons, hair dryers. **Pool(s):** outdoor. **Cards:** AX, DS, MC, VI.

ASK / SOME UNITS

RED ROOF INN Book at AAA.com **Phone:** (912)920-3535 33

Hotel
$45-$107 All Year

Address: 405 Al Henderson Blvd **Location:** I-95, exit 94 (SR 204/Abercorn St), just e. **Facility:** 75 one-bedroom standard units, some with efficiencies and/or whirlpools. 3 stories, interior corridors. *Bath:* combo or shower only. **Parking:** on-site. **Amenities:** voice mail, irons, hair dryers. **Pool(s):** outdoor. **Guest Services:** coin laundry. **Business Services:** PC. **Cards:** AX, DC, DS, MC, VI.

ASK CALL / SOME UNITS

RED ROOF INN SAVANNAH MIDTOWN Book at AAA.com **Phone:** (912)355-4100 17

Hotel
$70-$110 All Year

Address: 201 Stephenson Ave **Location:** 1.1 mi s of jct SR 21 and 204 (Abercorn St), just e. **Facility:** 127 one-bedroom standard units. 2 stories (no elevator), exterior corridors. **Parking:** on-site. **Terms:** 1-30 night minimum stay, cancellation fee imposed. **Amenities:** voice mail, irons, hair dryers. **Pool(s):** outdoor. **Guest Services:** valet laundry, area transportation, wireless Internet. **Business Services:** meeting rooms. **Cards:** AX, CB, DC, DS, MC, VI.

/ SOME UNITS

RESIDENCE INN BY MARRIOTT SAVANNAH Book great rates at AAA.com **Phone:** (912)356-3266 12

Hotel
$159-$169 All Year

Address: 5710 White Bluff Rd **Location:** Jct SR 21, 0.5 mi s. **Facility:** Smoke free premises. 66 units. 18 one-bedroom standard units with efficiencies. 36 one- and 12 two-bedroom suites, some with efficiencies or kitchens. 3 stories, interior corridors. **Parking:** on-site. **Terms:** check-in 4 pm, cancellation fee imposed. **Amenities:** high-speed Internet, voice mail, irons, hair dryers. *Some:* DVD players. **Pool(s):** heated indoor. **Leisure Activities:** whirlpool, limited exercise equipment, sports court. **Guest Services:** valet and coin laundry, wireless Internet. **Business Services:** meeting rooms, PC. **Cards:** AX, CB, DC, DS, JC, MC, VI.

/ SOME UNITS FEE VCR

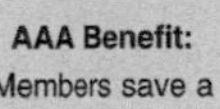

AAA Benefit:
Members save a minimum 5% off the best available rate.

(See map and index starting on p. 520)

SAVANNAH MIDTOWN COURTYARD BY MARRIOTT Book great rates at AAA.com **Phone:** (912)354-7878 15

Hotel
$147-$158 All Year

Address: 6703 Abercorn St **Location:** Jct SR 21 and 204 (Abercorn St), 0.8 mi s. **Facility:** Smoke free premises. 144 units. 132 one-bedroom standard units. 12 one-bedroom suites. 3 stories, interior corridors. *Bath:* combo or shower only. **Parking:** on-site. **Terms:** cancellation fee imposed. **Amenities:** high-speed Internet, voice mail, irons, hair dryers. **Pool(s):** outdoor. **Leisure Activities:** whirlpool, exercise room. **Guest Services:** valet and coin laundry, wireless Internet. **Business Services:** meeting rooms, business center. **Cards:** AX, CB, DC, DS, JC, MC, VI. **Free Special Amenities: newspaper and high-speed Internet.**

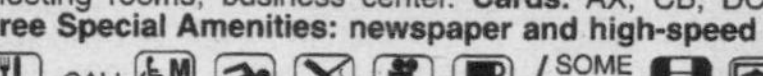

AAA Benefit:
Members save a minimum 5% off the best available rate.

SPRINGHILL SUITES BY MARRIOTT Book great rates at AAA.com **Phone:** (912)920-3787 37

Hotel
$101-$109 All Year

Address: 11317 Abercorn St **Location:** Jct SR 21 and 204 (Abercorn St), 4.6 mi s. **Facility:** Smoke free premises. 79 one-bedroom standard units. 3 stories, interior corridors. *Bath:* combo or shower only. **Parking:** on-site. **Terms:** cancellation fee imposed. **Amenities:** voice mail, irons, hair dryers. **Pool(s):** heated indoor. **Leisure Activities:** whirlpool, exercise room. **Guest Services:** valet and coin laundry, wireless Internet. **Business Services:** meeting rooms, business center. **Cards:** AX, CB, DC, DS, MC, VI.

AAA Benefit:
Members save a minimum 5% off the best available rate.

SPRINGHILL SUITES BY MARRIOTT I-95 SOUTH Book great rates at AAA.com **Phone:** (912)629-7777 29

Hotel
$138-$148 All Year

Address: 4 Gateway Blvd E **Location:** I-95, exit 94 (SR 204/Abercorn St), just ne. Located next to Cracker Barrel & Houlihan's Restaurant. **Facility:** Smoke free premises. 86 one-bedroom standard units. 3 stories, interior corridors. *Bath:* combo or shower only. **Parking:** on-site. **Terms:** cancellation fee imposed. **Amenities:** high-speed Internet, voice mail, irons, hair dryers. **Pool(s):** heated indoor. **Leisure Activities:** whirlpool, exercise room. **Guest Services:** valet and coin laundry, wireless Internet. **Business Services:** meeting rooms, business center. **Cards:** AX, CB, DC, DS, MC, VI.

AAA Benefit:
Members save a minimum 5% off the best available rate.

SPRINGHILL SUITES BY MARRIOTT SAVANNAH AIRPORT Book great rates at AAA.com **Phone:** (912)330-5555 2

Hotel
$138-$148 All Year

Address: One Jay R Turner Dr **Location:** I-95, exit 104, just e. **Facility:** Smoke free premises. 92 one-bedroom standard units. 3 stories, interior corridors. *Bath:* combo or shower only. **Parking:** on-site. **Terms:** cancellation fee imposed. **Amenities:** high-speed Internet, voice mail, irons, hair dryers. **Pool(s):** heated indoor. **Leisure Activities:** whirlpool, exercise room. **Guest Services:** valet and coin laundry, area transportation, wireless Internet. **Business Services:** meeting rooms, business center. **Cards:** AX, DS, MC, VI.

AAA Benefit:
Members save a minimum 5% off the best available rate.

TOWNEPLACE SUITES SAVANNAH AIRPORT Book great rates at AAA.com **Phone:** (912)629-7775 4

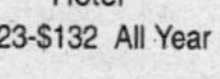

Hotel
$123-$132 All Year

Address: 4 Jay R Turner Dr **Location:** I-95, exit 104, just e. **Facility:** Smoke free premises. 63 units. 57 one-bedroom standard units with efficiencies. 6 one-bedroom suites with efficiencies. 4 stories, interior corridors. *Bath:* combo or shower only. **Parking:** on-site. **Terms:** cancellation fee imposed. **Amenities:** high-speed Internet, voice mail, irons, hair dryers. **Leisure Activities:** whirlpool, exercise room. **Guest Services:** valet and coin laundry, area transportation, wireless Internet. **Business Services:** business center. **Cards:** AX, DS, MC, VI.

AAA Benefit:
Members save a minimum 5% off the best available rate.

(See map and index starting on p. 520)

TRAVELODGE *Book great rates at AAA.com* **Phone:** (912)925-2640 25

Motel
$40-$299 All Year

Address: 1 Fort Argyle Rd **Location:** I-95, exit 94 (SR 204/Abercorn St), just w. **Facility:** 88 one-bedroom standard units, some with whirlpools. 2 stories (no elevator), exterior corridors. *Bath:* combo or shower only. **Parking:** on-site. **Amenities:** hair dryers. *Some:* irons. **Pool(s):** outdoor. **Guest Services:** coin laundry, wireless Internet. **Cards:** AX, DC, DS, MC, VI. **Free Special Amenities: continental breakfast and high-speed Internet.**

/ SOME UNITS FEE

WINGATE BY WYNDHAM-SAVANNAH *Book great rates at AAA.com* **Phone:** (912)925-2525 28

Hotel
$99-$119 All Year

Address: 11 Gateway Blvd E **Location:** I-95, exit 94 (SR 204/Abercorn St), just e. **Facility:** 101 one-bedroom standard units, some with whirlpools. 4 stories, interior corridors. *Bath:* combo or shower only. **Parking:** on-site. **Amenities:** high-speed Internet, dual phone lines, voice mail, safes, irons, hair dryers. **Pool(s):** outdoor. **Leisure Activities:** whirlpool, limited exercise equipment. *Fee:* golf privileges. **Guest Services:** valet laundry, wireless Internet. **Business Services:** meeting rooms, business center. **Cards:** AX, CB, DC, DS, MC, VI. **Free Special Amenities: expanded continental breakfast and high-speed Internet.** *(See color ad p 525)*

CALL / SOME UNITS

WHERE TO DINE

BONEFISH GRILL **Phone:** 912/691-2575 7

Seafood
$13-$20

Fish is the house specialty, and the menu and nightly specials offer a variety of choices. Well-prepared food is cooked to perfection. Service is casual in nature, and the staff is skilled and attentive. Casual dress. **Bar:** Full bar. **Hours:** 4 pm-close. Closed: 11/26, 12/25. **Address:** 5500 Abercorn St, Suite 44 **Location:** Jct SR 21 and 204, 0.4 mi s. **Parking:** on-site. **Cards:** AX, DC, DS, MC, VI.

CHIRIYA'S THAI CUISINE **Phone:** 912/303-0555 14

Thai
$11-$25

The menu offers well-prepared Thai and Hawaiian cuisine that are full of flavor and attractively presented. Many items are made-to-order and can be spiced to the guest's preference. Some menu selections can be prepared vegetarian-style. Casual dress. **Bar:** Beer & wine. **Reservations:** accepted. **Hours:** 11 am-2:30 & 5-10 pm, Sat from noon, Sun from 5 pm. Closed: 11/26, 12/25. **Address:** 7805 Abercorn St **Location:** 2 mi s of jct SR 21 and 204. **Parking:** on-site. **Cards:** AX, DS, MC, VI.

ELIZABETH ON 37TH **Phone:** 912/236-5547 1

Regional American
$25-$33

Southern charm combines with a sophisticated menu of imaginative dishes including seafood, poultry, beef, lamb and pork. House desserts satisfy sweet-tooth cravings. Dressy casual. **Bar:** Full bar. **Reservations:** required. **Hours:** 6 pm-9:30 pm. Closed major holidays; also 12/24 & 2 weeks in Aug. **Address:** 105 E 37th St **Location:** Corner of Drayton and 37th St. **Parking:** street. **Cards:** AX, DC, DS, MC, VI. **Historic**

FIDDLER'S CRAB HOUSE & OYSTER BARN **Phone:** 912/351-2274 13

Seafood
$12-$25

The restaurant's exterior resembles an old fish camp, with an inviting waterfall that flows from the roof and into a small man-made pond. That atmosphere continues inside, with rustic woods and a nautical theme punctuated with maritime decor and local photographs. The menu emphasizes fresh local seafood, as well as varied American items. A signature dish is oysters on the half-shell. Casual dress. **Bar:** Full bar. **Reservations:** accepted. **Hours:** 11 am-midnight. Closed: 11/26, 12/25. **Address:** 7201 Hodgson Memorial Drive **Location:** Jct SR 21 and 204 (Abercorn St), 1.4 mi s, just e on Mall Blvd. **Parking:** on-site. **Cards:** AX, DS, MC, VI.

CALL

THE ITALIAN GARDEN **Phone:** 912/355-2101 6

Italian
$7-$15

Serving traditional Italian favorites as well as a variety of seafood and meat items with pasta, the restaurant's atmosphere and service are casual. Casual dress. **Bar:** Beer & wine. **Reservations:** accepted. **Hours:** 11 am-10 pm. Closed major holidays. **Address:** 5500 Abercorn St **Location:** Jct SR 21 and 204 (Abercorn St/Derenne Rd), just s. **Parking:** on-site. **Cards:** AX, DS, MC, VI.

JOHNNY HARRIS RESTAURANT *Menu on AAA.com* **Phone:** 912/354-7810 2

American
$6-$24

A popular area landmark since 1924, this restaurant features a round dining room with a domed blue ceiling lit by artificial stars. Many of the freshly made entrees go well with the hickory-smoked barbecue sauce at each table. Casual dress. **Bar:** Full bar. **Reservations:** suggested, weekends. **Hours:** 11:30 am-9:30 pm, Fri & Sat-10:30 pm. Closed: 1/1, 12/25; also Sun. **Address:** 1651 E Victory Dr **Location:** Jct Truman Pkwy/US 80 (E Victory Dr), just w. **Parking:** on-site. **Cards:** AX, DS, MC, VI.

CALL

KASEY'S GRILLE **Phone:** 912/355-9250 5

American
$7-$24

The interior combines various media for visual impact, and all contribute to an overall casual and comfortable atmosphere. The knowledgeable and professional wait staff provides attentive service. On the menu is a varied selection of innovative entrees. In addition to the standard menu, lighter entrees are available at dinner. Dressy casual. **Bar:** Full bar. **Reservations:** accepted. **Hours:** 11 am-2:30 & 5-10 pm, Sat from 5 pm. Closed major holidays. **Address:** 4829 Waters Ave **Location:** Jct SR 21 and 204 (Abercorn St/Derenne Rd), 0.8 mi e, then 0.4 mi n. **Parking:** on-site. **Cards:** AX, DS, MC, VI.

KING AND I **Phone:** 912/355-2100 9

Thai
$10-$21

Traditional cuisine is made-to-order and spiced to preference. Casual dress. **Bar:** Beer & wine. **Hours:** 11 am-3 & 5-9 pm, Fri-9:30 pm, Sat noon-9:30 pm, Sun noon-9 pm. Closed major holidays. **Address:** 7098 Hodgson Memorial Dr **Location:** Jct SR 24 and 204 (Abercorn St), 1.3 mi s to Eisenhower Dr, just e; in Eisenhower Shopping Plaza. **Parking:** on-site. **Cards:** AX, DS, MC, VI.

CALL

(See map and index starting on p. 520)

LOVE'S SEAFOOD RESTAURANT **Phone:** 912/925-3616 (18)

Steak & Seafood
$9-$22

Select your dining preference from four indoor dining rooms and a cozy patio, most overlooking the Ogeechee River. Family-operated since 1949, the restaurant specializes in golden-fried river catfish. Casual dress. **Bar:** Full bar. **Hours:** 5 pm-10 pm, Sun noon-9 pm. Closed: 11/26, 12/25; also Mon. **Address:** 6817 Chief O F Love Rd **Location:** I-95, exit 94 (SR 204), 1.9 mi e to US 17 S, 2.8 mi sw to Basin Rd, then just ne of Ogeechee River at Kings Ferry Bridge. **Parking:** on-site. **Cards:** AX, DC, DS, MC, VI.

CALL

THE NEW SOUTH CAFE **Phone:** 912/233-7568 (3)

American
$8-$34

This restaurant offers a fine-dining experience in a casual and relaxed atmosphere. Graduates of the Culinary Institute of America, the chef-owners take Southern food upscale with inventive spins on comfort food, in addition to Latin and Asian selections. Local and regional ingredients factor heavily in new interpretations of traditional favorites, and artful plate presentations heighten the overall appeal. While the service style is casual and informal, the staff is attentive. Casual dress. **Bar:** Beer & wine. **Hours:** 11 am-3 & 5-10 pm. Closed major holidays; also Sun, Mon & week of Thanksgiving. **Address:** 2601 Skidaway Rd **Location:** Just n of US 80 (Victory Dr). **Parking:** on-site. **Cards:** AX, DS, MC, VI.

OLD SAVANNAH DINER **Phone:** 912/355-3404 (11)

American
$7-$15

Vinyl booths and chairs, a counter with stools and walls heavily decorated with pictures and caricatures help give the dining room the feel of an old-time diner. The menu sticks to the same theme, with burgers, sandwiches, salads and the expected comfort foods. Among surprises on the vast menu are some ethnic choices, including preparations of Greek, Italian, Asian, Mexican and Continental fare. Breakfast is always available. Casual dress. **Bar:** Beer & wine. **Hours:** 6 am-midnight. **Address:** 6730 Waters Ave **Location:** Just n of Eisenhower Dr; in Midtown area. **Parking:** on-site. **Cards:** AX, DC, DS, MC, VI.

PEARL'S SALTWATER GRILLE **Phone:** 912/352-8221 (16)

Steak & Seafood
$15-$30

The riverside location complements the subtle nautical appointments and freshly caught seafood. Landlubbers have plenty of menu options, too. A good variety of desserts made in house top off the meal nicely. Casual dress. **Bar:** Full bar. **Reservations:** suggested. **Hours:** 5 pm-10 pm, Fri & Sat-10:30 pm. Closed: 1/1, 11/26, 12/25; also Super Bowl Sun. **Address:** 7000 LaRoche Ave **Location:** 5.8 mi sw via SR 204 (Abercorn St) to Eisenhower Dr, 2.5 mi e to LaRoche Ave, then just s (Eisenhower Dr becomes Nottingham Rd). **Parking:** on-site. **Cards:** AX, DC, DS, MC, VI.

CALL

SAM SNEAD'S BAR & GRILL **Phone:** 912/963-0797

American
$9-$28

Menu offerings consist of beef, seafood and chicken entrees. Served in a relaxed, casual setting, the dining room is decorated with golf memorabilia, photos and artwork, giving the room a country club ambiance. Staff provide attentive, knowledgeable service. Casual dress. **Bar:** Full bar. **Reservations:** accepted. **Hours:** 11 am-11 pm, Sat from 5 pm, Sun 5 pm-10 pm. Closed: 11/26, 12/25. **Address:** 7 Sylvester C. Formey Dr **Location:** I-95, exit 104, 0.4 mi e. **Parking:** on-site. **Cards:** AX, DC, DS, MC, VI.

CALL

THE SHELL HOUSE RESTAURANT **Phone:** 912/927-3280 (10)

Seafood
$8-$22

Finger-licking menu offering include peel-and-eat shrimp, lobster and crab. Large wood tables and a picnic-like atmosphere is ideal for families. Casual dress. **Bar:** Full bar. **Hours:** 4 pm-10 pm, Fri & Sat-11 pm. Closed major holidays. **Address:** 8 Gateway Blvd **Location:** I-95, exit 94 (SR 204), just w, then just n. **Parking:** on-site. **Cards:** DS, MC, VI.

STICKY FINGERS RIB HOUSE **Phone:** 912/925-7427

Barbecue
$7-$26

Diners can put down their silverware and get their fingers ready for classic Carolina sweet ribs, as well as ribs cooked in the Texas and Tennessee styles. Hearty sides of baked beans and coleslaw complement entrees at the friendly cafe. Casual dress. **Bar:** Full bar. **Hours:** 11 am-close. Closed: 11/26, 12/25. **Address:** 7921 Abercorn St **Location:** Jct SR 204 (Abercorn St) and White Bluff Rd, just sw. **Parking:** on-site. **Cards:** AX, DC, DS, MC, VI.

CALL

SWEET POTATOES KITCHEN **Phone:** 912/352-3434 (12)

American
$6-$10

The menu lists comfort foods and seafood marked by home-style and Southern influences. The namesake sweet potato is highlighted in such items as the sweet potato of the day and sweet potato cake. The eatery has a laid-back, easygoing style. The primary decor feature is the field of flowers painted along the walls. Casual dress. **Bar:** Beer & wine. **Hours:** 11 am-9 pm. Closed: 11/26, 12/24, 12/25; also Sun. **Address:** 6825 Waters Ave **Location:** SR 21 and 204 (Abercorn St), 1.2 mi s, then 0.9 mi e on Eisenhower Dr. **Parking:** on-site. **Cards:** AX, MC, VI.

CALL

TASTE OF INDIA **Phone:** 912/356-1020 (15)

Indian
$7-$15

Guests peruse an extensive menu of well-prepared dishes, including lamb, chicken, goat, seafood and vegetarian specialties—all spiced to the requested level. Servers are knowledgeable about menu preparations and attentive. Casual and relaxed dining combines with prepared-to-order cuisine for a pleasurable experience. A lunch buffet is offered daily. Casual dress. **Bar:** Full bar. **Reservations:** required. **Hours:** 11 am-3 & 5-10 pm, Sat & Sun from 5 pm. **Address:** 401 Mall Blvd **Location:** Just e of SR 204 (Abercorn St); jct Hodgson Memorial Dr. **Parking:** on-site. **Cards:** AX, DC, DS, MC, VI.

CALL

(See map and index starting on p. 520)

TOUCAN CAFE **Phone:** 912/352-2233 (8)

International
$6-$25

Although the restaurant's name suggests it's for the birds, nothing could be further from the truth. The bright atmosphere, attentive wait staff and quiet music combine to create a wonderful ambience, and the food is outstanding. The chef, Jim Le Clair, prepares International-inspired dishes around seafood, pork, beef and vegetarian bases and garnishes each entree with fresh herbs, tasty vegetables and crisp salad. In-house desserts are a treat, especially the Cappuccino pie. Casual dress. **Bar:** Beer & wine. **Hours:** 11:30 am-2:30 & 5-9 pm, Fri & Sat-10 pm. Closed major holidays; also Sun. **Address:** 531 Stephenson Ave **Location:** SR 21/204 (Abercorn St), 1.1 mi s, 0.6 mi e. **Parking:** on-site. **Cards:** AX, DS, MC, VI.

TROY MEDITERRANEAN CUISINE **Phone:** 912/921-5117 (17)

Mediterranean
$12-$24

Made-to-order and favored with Mediterranean seasonings, a variety of pasta, seafood, chicken, beef, lamb and pork share space on the menu. Soft colors and a subtle Mediterranean decor provide a welcoming and peaceful surrounding. Casual dress. **Bar:** Beer & wine. **Reservations:** accepted. **Hours:** 11 am-10 pm. Closed: 12/25. **Address:** 10510 Abercorn St **Location:** Jct SR 21 and 204, 3.6 mi s. **Parking:** on-site. **Cards:** AX, DS, MC, VI.

UNCLE BUBBA'S SEAFOOD & OYSTER HOUSE **Phone:** 912/897-6101 (4)

Seafood
$6-$25

Dine in the traditional dining room or al fresco on the large outdoor deck. Whatever you choose, you'll enjoy views of Turner Creek and the surrounding marsh. Come hungry: Well-prepared local seafood is served in enormous portions. Casual dress. **Bar:** Full bar. **Reservations:** accepted. **Hours:** 11 am-3 & 5-9 pm, Thurs-Sat to 10 pm. Closed: 1/1, 12/25, 12/26. **Address:** 104 Bryan Woods Rd **Location:** Jct Harry S Truman Pkwy/US 80, 5.1 mi e on US 80, then just s; just w of Turner Creek Bridge. **Parking:** on-site. **Cards:** AX, DC, DS, MC, VI.

SEA ISLAND —*See Golden Isles p. 479.*

SMYRNA —*See Atlanta p. 419.*

SNELLVILLE —*See Atlanta p. 421.*

SOCIAL CIRCLE pop. 3,379

WHERE TO DINE

BLUE WILLOW INN RESTAURANT *Menu on AAA.com* **Phone:** 770/464-2131

Southern
$13-$24

The cordial wait staff at this Greek-Revival mansion with a beautiful fountain serves a traditional, home-cooked Southern buffet. Wash down your meal with a specialty lemonade or tea made on the premises. Casual dress. **Reservations:** suggested. **Hours:** 11 am-2:30 & 5-8 pm, Fri-9 pm, Sat 11 am-2:30 & 4:30-9 pm, Sun 11 am-8 pm; hours may vary in winter. Closed: 12/24, 12/25; also Mon. **Address:** 294 N Cherokee Rd **Location:** I-20, exit 98, 4 mi n on SR 11. **Parking:** on-site. **Cards:** DS, MC, VI.

STATESBORO pop. 22,698

WHERE TO STAY

BEST WESTERN UNIVERSITY INN *Book great rates at AAA.com* **Phone:** (912)681-7900

Motel
$62-$69 All Year

Address: 1 Jameson Ave **Location:** Jct US 25/301 and SR 67, 0.9 mi s on US 25/301. Located opposite Georgia Southern University. **Facility:** 39 one-bedroom standard units. 2 stories (no elevator), exterior corridors. **Parking:** on-site. **Amenities:** irons, hair dryers. **Pool(s):** outdoor. **Guest Services:** wireless Internet. **Cards:** AX, DC, DS, JC, MC, VI. **Free Special Amenities: continental breakfast and high-speed Internet.**

 / SOME UNITS FEE 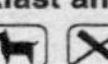

AAA Benefit:
Members save up to 20%, plus 10% bonus points with rewards program.

COMFORT INN & SUITES *Book at AAA.com* **Phone:** 912/681-2400

Hotel
Rates not provided

Address: 17870 Hwy 67 **Location:** Jct US 301 Bypass and SR 67, just s. **Facility:** Smoke free premises. 78 units. 70 one-bedroom standard units, some with whirlpools. 8 one-bedroom suites. 3 stories, interior corridors. *Bath:* combo or shower only. **Parking:** on-site. **Amenities:** high-speed Internet, voice mail, irons, hair dryers. *Some:* dual phone lines. **Pool(s):** outdoor. **Leisure Activities:** exercise room. **Guest Services:** coin laundry, wireless Internet. **Business Services:** meeting rooms, business center.

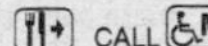 CALL    

LA QUINTA INN STATESBORO *Book great rates at AAA.com* **Phone:** (912)871-2525

Hotel

$63-$119 All Year

Address: 225 Lanier Dr **Location:** Jct US 301 Bypass and SR 67, 1.2 mi w on US 301, just n of Georgia Southern University. **Facility:** 63 one-bedroom standard units. 3 stories, interior corridors. *Bath:* combo or shower only. **Parking:** on-site. **Amenities:** voice mail, irons, hair dryers. **Pool(s):** heated indoor. **Leisure Activities:** whirlpool, limited exercise equipment. **Guest Services:** wireless Internet. **Business Services:** business center. **Cards:** AX, DC, DS, MC, VI.

ASK CALL / SOME UNITS

QUALITY INN & SUITES *Book great rates at AAA.com* **Phone:** 912/489-3995

AAA SAVE

Hotel

Rates not provided

Address: 230 S Main St **Location:** On US 301/25, 0.8 mi s of center; near downtown. **Facility:** 97 one-bedroom standard units, some with whirlpools. 2 stories (no elevator), exterior corridors. *Bath:* combo or shower only. **Parking:** on-site. **Amenities:** high-speed Internet, voice mail, irons, hair dryers. **Pool(s):** outdoor. **Leisure Activities:** exercise room. **Guest Services:** valet and coin laundry, wireless Internet. **Business Services:** meeting rooms, business center. **Free Special Amenities: expanded continental breakfast and high-speed Internet.**

/ SOME UNITS FEE

STATESBORO INN & RESTAURANT **Phone:** 912/489-8628

Historic Country Inn

Rates not provided

Address: 106 S Main St **Location:** US 301/25, just s of town center; downtown. **Facility:** This 1904 late-Victorian, neoclassic home features a wrap-around porch; some guest rooms have fireplaces and private screened porches. Smoke free premises. 17 units. 16 one-bedroom standard units, some with whirlpools. 1 one-bedroom suite. 2 stories (no elevator), interior corridors. **Parking:** on-site. **Amenities:** CD players, voice mail, irons, hair dryers. **Dining:** restaurant, see separate listing. **Guest Services:** valet laundry, wireless Internet. **Business Services:** meeting rooms, administrative services, fax (fee).

/ SOME UNITS FEE VCR

TRELLIS GARDEN INN **Phone:** (912)489-8781

Hotel

$75-$105 All Year

Address: 107 S Main St (US 301/25) **Location:** On US 301/25, just s of center; downtown. **Facility:** 39 one-bedroom standard units. 2 stories (no elevator), exterior corridors. **Parking:** on-site. **Amenities:** irons, hair dryers. *Some:* high-speed Internet. **Pool(s):** outdoor. **Guest Services:** valet laundry, wireless Internet. **Cards:** AX, DC, DS, MC, VI.

ASK / SOME UNITS

WHERE TO DINE

THE BEAVER HOUSE **Phone:** 912/764-2821

Regional American

$7-$15

The well-kept decor and glass-top tables help define the restaurant's impressive Southern-style. Menu selections include cornbread, biscuits, salad dressings and desserts, all made in-house. Casual dress. **Bar:** Full bar. **Reservations:** accepted. **Hours:** 11 am-2:30 & 5:30-8:30 pm, Fri & Sat-9 pm, Sun-2:30 pm. Closed: 1/1, 12/25. **Address:** 121 S Main St, Box 189 **Location:** On US 301/25, just s of center; downtown. **Parking:** on-site. **Cards:** AX, DS, MC, VI. **Historic**

CHRISTOPHER'S **Phone:** 912/681-6188

American

$15-$29

Decorated in a minimalist contemporary style, this upscale restaurant prepares distinctive American fare from fresh regional ingredients. In addition to daily specials, the menu lists some seasonally changing choices. A knowledgeable and attentive staff supports the chef/owner's culinary accomplishments in the kitchen. Dressy casual. **Bar:** Full bar. **Reservations:** accepted. **Hours:** 5 pm-10 pm. Closed: 12/24, 12/25; also Sun & Mon. **Address:** 441 S Main St **Location:** Jct US 301/25 and SR 67, just s. **Parking:** on-site. **Cards:** AX, MC, VI.

CALL

HEIWA'S TEPPAN YAKI **Phone:** 912/681-3881

Japanese

$7-$15

At the small art deco restaurant, contemporary Japanese cuisine is grilled to perfection in front of patrons. The short menu lists a variety of teriyaki dishes, marinated steak and fish rolls. This is a great stop for a light, well-prepared meal. Casual dress. **Bar:** Beer & wine. **Hours:** 11:30 am-2:30 & 5-9 pm, Sat from noon. Closed: Sun. **Address:** 100 Brampton Ave **Location:** Jct US 301 Bypass and SR 67, 0.8 nw on SR 67. **Parking:** on-site. **Cards:** AX, MC, VI.

R J 'S SEAFOOD & STEAKS **Phone:** 912/489-8658

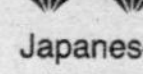

Steak & Seafood

$6-$16

This casual, small-town diner consistently serves up good food, cafeteria-style. The selections are broad — steak and plenty of seafood and an extensive, inviting salad bar. Want a great end to a good meal? Select a slice of rich German chocolate cake. Casual dress. **Reservations:** accepted. **Hours:** 11 am-9:30 pm, Fri-Sun to 10 pm. Closed: 1/1, 7/4, 12/25. **Address:** 434 S Main St (US 301/25) **Location:** Jct US 301/25 and SR 67, just s. **Parking:** on-site. **Cards:** AX, MC, VI.

SONNY'S REAL PIT BAR-B-Q **Phone:** 912/871-6146

Barbecue

$6-$15

House specialties include pork and chicken grilled over an open pit, barbecue ribs and fresh, homemade pie. The salad bar offers another popular option. Rustic and comfortable, the atmosphere is perfect for family meals. Casual dress. **Reservations:** required. **Hours:** 11 am-9:30 pm, Fri & Sat-10 pm. Closed: 11/26, 12/25. **Address:** 1602 Statesboro Place Cir **Location:** From US 301 Bypass (Veterans Memorial), 0.3 mi n on Lanier Rd, just e on Robin Hood Tr, then just s. **Parking:** on-site. **Cards:** AX, DS, MC, VI.

THE STATESBORO INN RESTAURANT **Phone:** 912/489-8628

American
$7-$9

An historic inn houses this class act in fine dining. Beef, seafood, poultry and lamb, complemented by a small but thoughtful wine list, makes the Statesboro a popular stop. Try the homemade soup, daily "catch", and freshly prepard dessert. Casual dress. **Reservations:** suggested. **Hours:** 11 am-2 pm. Closed: 12/25; also Sat. **Address:** 106 S Main St **Location:** US 301/25, just s of center; downtown; in Statesboro Inn & Restaurant. **Parking:** on-site. **Cards:** DS, MC, VI. **Historic**

STOCKBRIDGE pop. 9,853 (See map and index starting on p. 312)

WHERE TO STAY

BAYMONT INN & SUITES *Book great rates at AAA.com* **Phone:** (770)507-6500

Motel
$59-$99 All Year

Address: 100 N Park Ct **Location:** I-75, exit 224, just e, then just n on Rock Quarry Rd. **Facility:** 56 one-bedroom standard units, some with whirlpools. 2 stories (no elevator), interior corridors. *Bath:* combo or shower only. **Parking:** on-site. **Amenities:** voice mail, safes (fee), irons, hair dryers. **Pool(s):** heated indoor. **Leisure Activities:** whirlpool, limited exercise equipment. **Guest Services:** wireless Internet. **Business Services:** meeting rooms, PC. **Cards:** AX, CB, DC, DS, MC, VI. **Free Special Amenities: expanded continental breakfast and high-speed Internet.**

SOME UNITS FEE

COMFORT SUITES STOCKBRIDGE *Book great rates at AAA.com* **Phone:** (770)507-0444 93

Hotel
$99-$159 All Year

Address: 3540 Cameron Pkwy **Location:** I-75, exit 228, just w on SR 138, then just n; I-675, exit 1, just e on SR 138, then just n. **Facility:** Smoke free premises. 80 units. 68 one-bedroom standard units, some with whirlpools. 12 one-bedroom suites. 4 stories, interior corridors. *Bath:* combo or shower only. **Parking:** on-site. **Terms:** 4 day cancellation notice. **Amenities:** high-speed Internet, voice mail, safes, irons, hair dryers. **Pool(s):** heated indoor. **Leisure Activities:** sauna, whirlpool, exercise room. **Guest Services:** valet and coin laundry, wireless Internet. **Business Services:** meeting rooms, business center. **Cards:** AX, DC, DS, JC, MC, VI. **Free Special Amenities: full breakfast and high-speed Internet.**

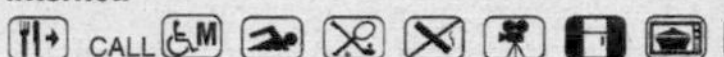

CALL

COUNTRY HEARTH INN & SUITES *Book great rates at AAA.com* **Phone:** 770/474-0555 92

Motel
Rates not provided

Address: 7395 Davidson Cir E **Location:** I-675, exit 1, just e; I-75, exit 228, 1 mi e. **Facility:** 58 one-bedroom standard units, some with whirlpools. 2 stories (no elevator), exterior corridors. **Parking:** on-site. **Amenities:** voice mail, irons, hair dryers. **Pool(s):** outdoor. **Guest Services:** valet laundry, wireless Internet. **Business Services:** meeting rooms, PC. **Free Special Amenities: expanded continental breakfast and high-speed Internet.**

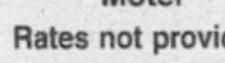

SOME UNITS

HAMPTON INN-ATLANTA-STOCKBRIDGE  *Book great rates at AAA.com* **Phone:** (770)389-0065 90

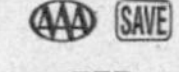

Hotel
$109-$165 All Year

Address: 7342 Hanover Pkwy N **Location:** I-75, exit 228, just e on SR 138, then just n; I-675, exit 1, just w on SR 138, then just n. **Facility:** 72 units. 70 one-bedroom standard units. 2 one-bedroom suites with whirlpools. 3 stories, interior corridors. *Bath:* combo or shower only. **Parking:** on-site. **Amenities:** video games (fee), high-speed Internet, voice mail, irons, hair dryers. **Pool(s):** heated indoor. **Leisure Activities:** sauna, whirlpool, exercise room. **Guest Services:** valet and coin laundry, wireless Internet. **Business Services:** meeting rooms, business center. **Cards:** AX, CB, DC, DS, JC, MC, VI.

CALL 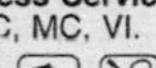   SOME UNITS

HOLIDAY INN HOTEL & SUITES *Book at AAA.com* **Phone:** (678)782-4000 95

Hotel
$117-$275 All Year

Address: 638 Hwy 138 W **Location:** I-75, exit 228, just e; I-675, exit 1, just w. **Facility:** Smoke free premises. 112 units. 80 one-bedroom standard units. 32 one-bedroom suites. 5 stories, interior corridors. *Bath:* combo or shower only. **Parking:** on-site. **Terms:** cancellation fee imposed. **Amenities:** CD players, high-speed Internet, voice mail, safes, irons, hair dryers. **Pool(s):** heated indoor/outdoor. **Leisure Activities:** exercise room. **Guest Services:** valet and coin laundry, wireless Internet. **Business Services:** conference facilities, business center. **Cards:** AX, DC, DS, MC, VI.

ASK CALL

HOWARD JOHNSON STOCKBRIDGE **Phone:** (770)474-8771 96

Address: 619 Hwy 138 **Location:** I-75, exit 228, just e; I-675, exit 1, 0.5 mi w. **Facility:** 116 one-bedroom standard units. 2 stories (no elevator), exterior corridors. **Parking:** on-site. **Terms:** 3 day cancellation notice. **Amenities:** irons, hair dryers. **Pool(s):** outdoor. **Guest Services:** coin laundry, wireless Internet. **Business Services:** meeting rooms. **Cards:** AX, DC, DS, MC, VI. **Free Special Amenities: local telephone calls and high-speed Internet.**

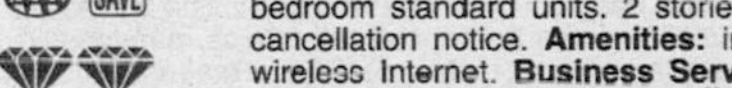

Motel

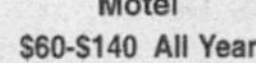

$60-$140 All Year

SOME UNITS

(See map and index starting on p. 312)

LA QUINTA INN & SUITES *Book great rates at AAA.com* **Phone:** (770)506-9991 91

AAA SAVE

Hotel

$74-$134 All Year

Address: 3581 Cameron Pkwy **Location:** I-75, exit 228, just e on SR 138, then just n; I-675, exit 1, just w on SR 138, then just n. **Facility:** 71 units. 68 one-bedroom standard units, some with whirlpools. 3 one-bedroom suites. 4 stories, interior corridors. *Bath:* combo or shower only. **Parking:** on-site. **Amenities:** dual phone lines, voice mail, irons, hair dryers. *Some:* high-speed Internet. **Pool(s):** heated indoor. **Leisure Activities:** sauna, whirlpool, exercise room. **Guest Services:** valet and coin laundry, wireless Internet. **Business Services:** meeting rooms, business center. **Cards:** AX, DC, DS, MC, VI. **Free Special Amenities: expanded continental breakfast and high-speed Internet.**

CALL / SOME UNITS FEE

MICROTEL INN & SUITES *Book at AAA.com* **Phone:** (678)782-6100

Hotel

$65-$150 All Year

Address: 195 Country Club Dr **Location:** I-75, exit 224, just e, then just se. **Facility:** 62 one-bedroom standard units. 3 stories, interior corridors. *Bath:* combo or shower only. **Parking:** on-site. **Amenities:** *Some:* irons, hair dryers. **Pool(s):** outdoor. **Leisure Activities:** exercise room. **Guest Services:** coin laundry, wireless Internet. **Business Services:** meeting rooms. **Cards:** AX, DS, MC, VI.

ASK CALL / SOME UNITS

QUALITY INN & SUITES *Book great rates at AAA.com* **Phone:** (770)507-7911 89

AAA SAVE

Motel

$54-$77 All Year

Address: 7325 Davidson Pkwy N **Location:** I-675, exit 1, just e, then just n; I-75, exit 228, 1 mi e on SR 138, then just n. **Facility:** 51 one-bedroom standard units, some with whirlpools. 2 stories (no elevator), exterior corridors. *Bath:* combo or shower only. **Parking:** on-site. **Amenities:** irons, hair dryers. **Pool(s):** outdoor. **Guest Services:** coin laundry, wireless Internet. **Business Services:** PC. **Cards:** AX, CB, DC, DS, MC, VI. **Free Special Amenities: expanded continental breakfast and high-speed Internet.**

/ SOME UNITS

SLEEP INN & SUITES *Book at AAA.com* **Phone:** (770)474-3870 94

Hotel

$60-$149 All Year

Address: 7423 Davidson Cir W **Location:** I-675, exit 1, just e, then just s; I-75, exit 228, 1 mi e on SR 138, then just s. **Facility:** Smoke free premises. 73 one-bedroom standard units, some with whirlpools. 3 stories, interior corridors. *Bath:* combo or shower only. **Parking:** on-site. **Terms:** cancellation fee imposed. **Amenities:** high-speed Internet, voice mail, irons, hair dryers. **Pool(s):** outdoor. **Leisure Activities:** exercise room. **Guest Services:** valet and coin laundry, wireless Internet. **Business Services:** business center. **Cards:** AX, DS, MC, VI.

ASK CALL / SOME UNITS FEE

SUPER 8 MOTEL ATLANTA SOUTH *Book great rates at AAA.com* **Phone:** (770)474-5758

AAA SAVE

Motel

$54-$60 All Year

Address: 1451 Hudson Bridge Rd **Location:** I-75, exit 224, just w. **Facility:** 56 one-bedroom standard units. 2 stories (no elevator), exterior corridors. **Parking:** on-site. **Amenities:** hair dryers. **Pool(s):** heated outdoor. **Guest Services:** coin laundry, wireless Internet. **Cards:** AX, DC, DS, MC, VI.

/ SOME UNITS FEE

WHERE TO DINE

CHIN CHIN OSAKI **Phone:** 770/507-0288 63

Asian

$6-$20

The casual bistro offers both Chinese and Japanese fare, including a lengthy sushi menu. Dining is a la carte, and lunch specials are featured daily. Specialties include tangerine beef in a sweet and spicy brown sauce, Kung Pao chicken and sashimi platters, plus more. Casual dress. **Bar:** Full bar. **Hours:** 11:30 am-10 pm, Fri & Sat-11 pm, Sun noon-10 pm. **Address:** 3570 Hwy 138 **Location:** I-75, exit 228, just e; I-675, exit 1, just w. **Parking:** on-site. **Cards:** AX, DS, MC, VI.

FRONTERA MEX-MEX GRILL **Phone:** 770/474-1540 62

Mexican

$5-$14

Traditional Tex-Mex food served quickly and in cheery surroundings is Frontera's claim to fame. Chips and two salsas (one smoked chipotle) precede the entree. Margaritas are made from scratch and live music is complimentary Wednesday through Sunday. Casual dress. **Bar:** Full bar. **Hours:** 11 am-10:30 pm, Sun-10 pm. Closed: 12/25. **Address:** 3607 SE Hwy 138 **Location:** I-75, exit 228, just e; I-675, exit 1, just w. **Parking:** on-site. **Cards:** AX, CB, DC, DS, MC, VI.

NONNA MARIA'S ITALIAN EATERY **Phone:** 678/565-9500

Italian

$8-$19

Menu offerings at this casual-romantic eatery include veal, chicken, seafood and pasta dishes, as well as pizza. Specials not to be missed are the veal piccata, grilled center-cut pork chops, pan-roasted salmon, lasagna, penne carbonara and margherita pizza. Casual dress. **Bar:** Full bar. **Reservations:** accepted. **Hours:** 5 pm-9 pm, Fri & Sat-11 pm, Sun also 11 am-3 pm. Closed: 1/1, 11/26, 12/25. **Address:** 1445 Rock Quarry Rd **Location:** I-75, exit 224, just e, then just n. **Parking:** on-site. **Cards:** AX, DS, MC, VI.

STONE MOUNTAIN *—See Atlanta p. 421.*

SUWANEE *—See Atlanta p. 423.*

SWAINSBORO pop. 6,943

WHERE TO STAY

BEST WESTERN BRADFORD INN *Book great rates at AAA.com* **Phone:** (478)237-2400

Motel
$65 12/1-9/1
$60 9/2-11/30

Address: 688 S Main St **Location:** I-16, exit 90 (US 1), 12.4 mi n. **Facility:** 50 one-bedroom standard units, some with whirlpools. 2 stories (no elevator), exterior corridors. **Parking:** on-site, winter plug-ins. **Amenities:** irons, hair dryers. *Some:* high-speed Internet. **Pool(s):** outdoor. **Leisure Activities:** golf club privileges. **Guest Services:** wireless Internet. **Cards:** AX, DC, DS, MC, VI. **Free Special Amenities: continental breakfast and high-speed Internet.**

/ SOME UNITS FEE

AAA Benefit: Members save up to 20%, plus 10% bonus points with rewards program.

SYLVANIA pop. 2,675

WHERE TO DINE

POP'S KITCHEN **Phone:** 912/564-2988

American
$5-$10

You can saddle up to the buffet or opt for table service at this down-home restaurant staffed with eager to please servers. Breakfast, lunch and dinner consist of a good selection of favorites, from barbecue to meatloaf and everything in between. Casual dress. **Hours:** 6 am-4 pm, Wed-Sat to 9 pm, Sun-3 pm. Closed major holidays. **Address:** 109 Mims Rd **Location:** Jct US 301 business route and SR 21, 0.9 mi e; in Harvey's Shopping Center. **Parking:** on-site. **Cards:** MC, VI.

TALLAPOOSA pop. 2,789

WHERE TO STAY

COMFORT INN *Book at AAA.com* **Phone:** (770)574-5575

Hotel
$70-$500 All Year

Address: 788 Hwy 100 **Location:** I-20, exit 5, just s. **Facility:** 51 one-bedroom standard units, some with whirlpools. 2 stories (no elevator), interior corridors. **Parking:** on-site. **Terms:** 2 night minimum stay - seasonal, cancellation fee imposed. **Amenities:** high-speed Internet, voice mail, irons, hair dryers. **Pool(s):** outdoor. **Guest Services:** coin laundry, wireless Internet. **Business Services:** PC, fax (fee). **Cards:** AX, CB, DC, DS, JC, MC, VI.

ASK CALL / SOME UNITS

THOMASTON pop. 9,411

WHERE TO STAY

JAMESON INN *Book at AAA.com* **Phone:** (706)648-2232

Hotel
$73-$80 All Year

Address: 1010 Hwy 19 N **Location:** Jct SR 74, 2.3 mi n. **Facility:** 57 one-bedroom standard units, some with whirlpools. 2 stories, exterior corridors. **Parking:** on-site. **Terms:** cancellation fee imposed. **Amenities:** hair dryers. *Some:* irons. **Pool(s):** outdoor. **Leisure Activities:** exercise room. **Guest Services:** coin laundry, wireless Internet. **Business Services:** meeting rooms, PC, fax (fee). **Cards:** AX, DC, DS, MC, VI.

ASK / SOME UNITS FEE

WHERE TO DINE

NORRIS' FINE FOOD **Phone:** 706/647-8216

Southern
$5-$12

Friendly service and Southern-style food is a menu mainstay. Of course, there's fried chicken and roast beef and more, but add to that a cool dish of chocolate mousse in a graham cracker crust with whipped cream and you have a scrumptious, hearty meal. Casual dress. **Hours:** 6:30 am-2:30 & 5-8 pm, Sat 6 am-2 pm, Sun 11 am-2:30 pm. Closed: 11/26, 12/25. **Address:** 695 Short E St **Location:** Just off SR 19; downtown. **Parking:** street. **Cards:** MC, VI.

THOMASVILLE pop. 18,162

WHERE TO STAY

1884 PAXTON HOUSE INN **Phone:** 229/226-5197

Historic Bed & Breakfast
$165-$295 All Year

Address: 445 Remington Ave **Location:** Corner of Hansell; just e of downtown. Located in a historical residential area. **Facility:** Bathrobes and fresh fruit are provided at this Victorian mansion furnished with antiques and collectibles; cottage rooms are available. Smoke free premises. 9 units. 4 one-bedroom standard units. 2 one- and 1 two-bedroom suites. 2 cottages. 2 stories (no elevator), interior/exterior corridors. **Parking:** on-site. **Terms:** age restrictions may apply, 7 day cancellation notice-fee imposed. **Amenities:** video library, DVD players, high-speed Internet, irons, hair dryers. **Pool(s):** heated indoor. **Leisure Activities:** whirlpool. **Guest Services:** wireless Internet. **Business Services:** business center. **Cards:** AX, MC, VI. **Free Special Amenities: full breakfast and preferred room (subject to availability with advance reservations).**

COMFORT INN Book at AAA.com

Motel
$65-$83 All Year

Phone: (229)228-5555

Address: 14866 US 19 S **Location:** Jct SR 300/US 19 and 84/SR 122. **Facility:** 94 one-bedroom standard units. 2 stories, exterior corridors. **Parking:** on-site. **Terms:** cancellation fee imposed. **Amenities:** voice mail, irons, hair dryers. **Pool(s):** outdoor. **Leisure Activities:** exercise room. **Guest Services:** wireless Internet. **Business Services:** PC, fax (fee). **Cards:** AX, DS, MC, VI.

ASK / SOME UNITS FEE FEE FEE

DAWSON STREET INN

Bed & Breakfast
$120-$155 All Year

Phone: (229)226-7515

Address: 324 N Dawson St **Location:** 0.4 mi n of US 319. **Facility:** This circa 1856 property is nestled in the heart of the historic district; decorated in the antebellum period. Designated smoking area. 6 one-bedroom standard units. 2 stories (no elevator), interior corridors. *Bath:* combo, shower or tub only. **Parking:** on-site. **Terms:** check-in 4 pm, age restrictions may apply, 7 day cancellation notice. **Amenities:** hair dryers. **Pool(s):** outdoor. **Leisure Activities:** bicycles. **Guest Services:** wireless Internet. **Cards:** AX, MC, VI.

ASK

HAMPTON INN THOMASVILLE Book great rates at AAA.com

Hotel
$88-$108 All Year

Phone: (229)227-0040

Address: 1950 GA Hwy 122 (Pavo Rd) **Location:** Jct US 19/84 and SR 122/300. **Facility:** 67 one-bedroom standard units. 3 stories, interior corridors. *Bath:* combo or shower only. **Parking:** on-site. **Terms:** 1-30 night minimum stay, cancellation fee imposed. **Amenities:** voice mail, irons, hair dryers. **Pool(s):** outdoor. **Leisure Activities:** sauna, whirlpool, exercise room. **Guest Services:** wireless Internet. **Business Services:** PC, fax (fee). **Cards:** AX, CB, DC, DS, MC, VI.

CALL / SOME UNITS

AAA Benefit:
Members save up to 10% everyday!

HOLIDAY INN EXPRESS HOTEL & SUITES Book at AAA.com

Hotel
$99-$180 All Year

Phone: (229)226-4666

Address: 452 Liberty St **Location:** Jct US 19 S and 84 E. **Facility:** 81 one-bedroom standard units, some with whirlpools. 3 stories, interior corridors. *Bath:* combo or shower only. **Parking:** on-site. **Amenities:** high-speed Internet, dual phone lines, voice mail, irons, hair dryers. **Pool(s):** heated indoor. **Leisure Activities:** whirlpool, exercise room. **Guest Services:** coin laundry, wireless Internet. **Business Services:** meeting rooms, business center. **Cards:** AX, CB, DC, DS, JC, MC, VI.

ASK / SOME UNITS

JAMESON INN Book at AAA.com

Motel
$78-$81 All Year

Phone: (229)227-9500

Address: 1470 Remington Ave **Location:** US 19, just w on CR 122. **Facility:** 40 one-bedroom standard units, some with whirlpools. 2 stories, exterior corridors. *Bath:* combo or shower only. **Parking:** on-site. **Terms:** cancellation fee imposed. **Amenities:** hair dryers. **Pool(s):** outdoor. **Leisure Activities:** exercise room. **Guest Services:** wireless Internet. **Business Services:** PC, fax (fee). **Cards:** AX, DC, DS, MC, VI.

ASK CALL / SOME UNITS FEE

QUALITY INN & SUITES Book great rates at AAA.com

AAA SAVE

Motel
$55-$69 All Year

Phone: (229)225-2134

Address: 15138 Hwy 19 S **Location:** 0.3 mi s of US 319. **Facility:** 75 units. 66 one-bedroom standard units. 9 one-bedroom suites. 2 stories, exterior corridors. **Parking:** on-site. **Terms:** cancellation fee imposed. **Amenities:** voice mail, irons, hair dryers. *Some:* dual phone lines. **Pool(s):** outdoor. **Leisure Activities:** exercise room. **Guest Services:** coin laundry, wireless Internet. **Business Services:** meeting rooms, PC, fax. **Cards:** AX, DS, MC, VI. **Free Special Amenities: full breakfast and early check-in/late check-out.**

CALL / SOME UNITS FEE

WHERE TO DINE

CHANDLER'S HAMBURGERS

American
$3-$7

Phone: 229/226-0222

The restaurant's no-frills decor includes a large-screen TV. Hamburgers are made fresh to order, and thick milk shakes have real ice cream. Casual dress. **Hours:** 6:30 am-10 pm. Closed major holidays. **Address:** 1010 E Jackson St **Location:** Just w of jct SR 19. **Parking:** on-site. **Cards:** MC, VI.

GEORGE & LOUIE'S FRESH SEAFOOD RESTAURANT

Seafood
$5-$14

Phone: 229/226-1218

Dine on fresh seafood in a pristine dining area with stainless steel tables and chairs. The family-style seafood platter is the house specialty, and the country Greek salad is worth a try as well. Sandwiches come with great sauces, and desserts tempt from a display case at the counter. Casual dress. **Bar:** Beer & wine. **Hours:** 11 am-9 pm. Closed major holidays; also Sun. **Address:** 217 Remington Ave **Location:** Downtown. **Parking:** on-site.

GRANDDADDY'S BARBEQUE

Barbecue
$5-$16

Phone: 229/225-9500

A variety of barbecue dishes are served in a simple, casual setting at this family-style, self-service restaurant. Casual dress. **Hours:** 11 am-9 pm. **Address:** 2128 Smith Ave **Location:** Jct SR 19 and 84. **Parking:** on-site. **Cards:** AX, DS, MC, VI.

LA FOGATA **Phone:** 229/228-9787

Mexican
$5-$14

Authentic recipes, a friendly staff and good-size portions are trademarks of this spot, which is adorned in colorful walls with framed posters and prints. Casual dress. **Bar:** Beer & wine. **Hours:** 11 am-10 pm, Fri & Sat-11 pm. Closed: 1/1, 12/25; also Sun. **Address:** 14418 Hwy 19 S **Location:** Jct US 284 and 19, just n. **Parking:** on-site. **Cards:** MC, VI.

MOM & DAD'S ITALIAN RESTAURANT **Phone:** 229/226-6265

Italian
$8-$20

Family owned for 27 years, this Italian, family-style restaurant is known for its delicious pasta dishes with various sauces. The Italian salad dressing is made fresh, in-house. Two specials you will want to try are sauteed grouper and chicken Florentine. Casual dress. **Bar:** Full bar. **Hours:** 5 pm-10 pm. Closed major holidays; also Sun, Mon & week of 7/4. **Address:** 1800 Smith Ave **Location:** 2.5 mi e on US 84 E. **Parking:** on-site. **Cards:** AX, DS, MC, VI. **Classic**

SONNY'S REAL PIT BAR-B-Q **Phone:** 229/558-9000

Barbecue
$6-$15

House specialties include pork and chicken grilled over an open pit, barbecue ribs and fresh, homemade pie. The salad bar offers another popular option. Rustic and comfortable, the atmosphere is perfect for family meals. Casual dress. **Hours:** 11 am-9:30 pm, Fri & Sat-10 pm. Closed: 11/26, 12/25. **Address:** 14293 US Hwy 19 S **Location:** 0.4 mi n of jct US 84 S. **Parking:** on-site. **Cards:** AX, DS, MC, VI.

THOMSON pop. 6,828

WHERE TO STAY

BEST WESTERN WHITE COLUMNS INN *Book great rates at AAA.com* **Phone:** (706)595-8000

AAA SAVE

Hotel
$82 All Year

Address: 1890 Washington Rd **Location:** I-20, exit 172 (US 78), just s. **Facility:** 133 units. 126 one-bedroom standard units, some with whirlpools. 7 one-bedroom suites, some with efficiencies (no utensils) and/or whirlpools. 2 stories (no elevator), exterior corridors. **Parking:** on-site, winter plug-ins. **Terms:** 3 day cancellation notice. **Amenities:** video games (fee), voice mail, irons, hair dryers. *Some:* high-speed Internet. **Dining:** Stirrup Cup Restaurant & Lounge, see separate listing. **Pool(s):** outdoor. **Leisure Activities:** barbecue grills, gazebo, picnic tables, walk/jog path & deck, hiking trails, jogging, exercise room. **Guest Services:** coin laundry, airport transportation-The Thomson McDuffie-Regional Airport, wireless Internet. **Business Services:** meeting rooms, PC. **Cards:** AX, DC, DS, MC, VI. **Free Special Amenities: expanded continental breakfast and high-speed Internet.**

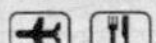

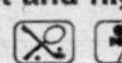

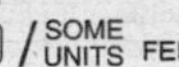
/ SOME UNITS FEE

AAA Benefit:
Members save up to 20%, plus 10% bonus points with rewards program.

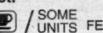

WHERE TO DINE

STIRRUP CUP RESTAURANT & LOUNGE **Phone:** 706/595-8000

American
$4-$30

Touted by the owner as the best food in the South, the restaurant's menu includes such basic fare as steak, prime rib and shrimp. Historical artwork relating to the family and property hangs on the walls of the plantation replica, which was created on an upscale horse theme. Casual dress. **Bar:** Full bar. **Reservations:** suggested. **Hours:** 6:30-10 am, 11-2 & 6-10 pm, Sat from 6 pm. Closed: major holidays; also 12/24, Sun. **Address:** 1890 Washington Rd **Location:** I-20, exit 172 (US 78), just s; in Best Western White Columns Inn. **Parking:** on-site. **Cards:** AX, DC, MC, VI.

TIFTON pop. 15,060

WHERE TO STAY

COMFORT INN & SUITES Book at AAA.com Phone: (229)382-8250

Hotel
$79-$139 All Year

Address: 905 W 7th St **Location:** I-75, exit 62, adjacent to interchange. **Facility:** Smoke free premises. 93 units. 90 one-bedroom standard units, some with whirlpools. 3 one-bedroom suites. 4 stories, interior corridors. **Parking:** on-site. **Amenities:** high-speed Internet, voice mail, irons, hair dryers. **Pool(s):** outdoor. **Leisure Activities:** exercise room. **Guest Services:** coin laundry, wireless Internet. **Business Services:** meeting rooms, PC. **Cards:** AX, CB, DC, DS, MC, VI.

ASK

COURTYARD BY MARRIOTT Book great rates at AAA.com Phone: (229)388-0803

Hotel
$128-$137 All Year

Address: 814 W 7th St **Location:** I-75, exit 62, just e on US 319. **Facility:** Smoke free premises. 90 units. 87 one-bedroom standard units, some with whirlpools. 3 one-bedroom suites. 3 stories, interior corridors. *Bath:* combo or shower only. **Parking:** on-site. **Terms:** cancellation fee imposed. **Amenities:** video games, voice mail, irons, hair dryers. **Pool(s):** heated indoor. **Leisure Activities:** whirlpool, exercise room. **Guest Services:** valet and coin laundry, wireless Internet. **Business Services:** meeting rooms, PC, fax (fee). **Cards:** AX, CB, DC, DS, MC, VI.

CALL / SOME UNITS

AAA Benefit:
Members save a minimum 5% off the best available rate.

DAYS INN & SUITES Book at AAA.com Phone: (229)382-8505

Hotel
$59-$89 All Year

Address: 1199 Hwy 82 W **Location:** I-75, exit 62, just w. **Facility:** 80 one-bedroom standard units. 3 stories, interior corridors. *Bath:* combo or shower only. **Parking:** on-site. **Amenities:** high-speed Internet, irons, hair dryers. **Pool(s):** outdoor. **Leisure Activities:** exercise room. **Guest Services:** wireless Internet. **Business Services:** PC, fax (fee). **Cards:** AX, CB, DC, DS, MC, VI.

ASK / SOME UNITS FEE

FAIRFIELD INN & SUITES Book great rates at AAA.com Phone: (229)387-8288

Hotel
$119-$127 All Year

Address: 806 W 7th St **Location:** I-75, exit 62, just e. **Facility:** Smoke free premises. 81 one-bedroom standard units. 3 stories, interior corridors. *Bath:* combo or shower only. **Parking:** on-site. **Terms:** cancellation fee imposed. **Amenities:** high-speed Internet, voice mail, irons, hair dryers. *Some:* CD players. **Pool(s):** outdoor. **Leisure Activities:** whirlpool, exercise room. **Guest Services:** valet and coin laundry, wireless Internet. **Business Services:** meeting rooms, business center. **Cards:** AX, DS, MC, VI.

/ SOME UNITS

AAA Benefit:
Members save a minimum 5% off the best available rate.

HAMPTON INN Book great rates at AAA.com Phone: (229)382-8800

Hotel
$95-$175 All Year

Address: 720 Hwy 319 S **Location:** I-75, exit 62, just e. **Facility:** 82 one-bedroom standard units. 2 stories, exterior corridors. **Parking:** on-site. **Terms:** 1-30 night minimum stay, cancellation fee imposed. **Amenities:** high-speed Internet, dual phone lines, voice mail, irons, hair dryers. **Pool(s):** outdoor. **Guest Services:** valet laundry, wireless Internet. **Business Services:** PC, fax (fee). **Cards:** AX, CB, DC, DS, MC, VI.

/ SOME UNITS

AAA Benefit:
Members save up to 10% everyday!

HILTON GARDEN INN Phone: 229/382-8484

Hotel

Under construction, scheduled to open April 2009. **Address:** 201 Boo Dr **Location:** I-75, exit 62, left on US 82W, left at light for McCormick, then left. **Amenities:** 105 units, coffeemakers, microwaves, refrigerators, pool. ***(See color ad p 553)***

Hilton Garden Inn

AAA Benefit:
Members save 5% or more everyday!

HOLIDAY INN *Book great rates at AAA.com* **Phone:** (229)382-6687

Hotel
$80-$109 All Year

Address: 1208 Hwy 82 W **Location:** I-75, exit 62, at jct US 82 and 319. **Facility:** 188 one-bedroom standard units. 2 stories, exterior corridors. **Parking:** on-site. **Terms:** cancellation fee imposed. **Amenities:** high-speed Internet, voice mail, irons, hair dryers. **Pool(s):** outdoor. **Leisure Activities:** exercise room. **Guest Services:** valet and coin laundry, wireless Internet. **Business Services:** meeting rooms, fax (fee). **Cards:** AX, DC, DS, MC, VI. **Free Special Amenities: full breakfast and local telephone calls.** *(See color ad below)*

MICROTEL INNS & SUITES *Book at AAA.com* **Phone:** (229)387-0112

Hotel
$45-$199 All Year

Address: 196 S Virginia Ave **Location:** I-75, exit 62, just n. **Facility:** 82 one-bedroom standard units. 3 stories, interior corridors. *Bath:* combo or shower only. **Parking:** on-site. **Terms:** cancellation fee imposed. **Pool(s):** outdoor. **Leisure Activities:** limited exercise equipment. **Guest Services:** wireless Internet. **Business Services:** PC, fax. **Cards:** AX, DC, DS, MC, VI.

ASK CALL / SOME UNITS

RAMADA LIMITED AND CONFERENCE CENTER *Book at AAA.com* **Phone:** (229)382-8500

Hotel
$59-$109 All Year

Address: 1211 Hwy 82 W **Location:** I-75, exit 62, just w. **Facility:** 94 one-bedroom standard units. 2 stories, exterior corridors. *Bath:* combo or shower only. **Parking:** on-site. **Amenities:** voice mail, irons, hair dryers. **Pool(s):** outdoor. **Leisure Activities:** exercise room. **Guest Services:** coin laundry, wireless Internet. **Business Services:** meeting rooms, PC. **Cards:** AX, CB, DC, DS, MC, VI.

ASK / SOME UNITS FEE

▼ *See AAA listing p 552* ▼

▼ *See AAA listing above* ▼

WHERE TO DINE

EL CAZADOR MEXICAN RESTAURANT — **Phone:** 229/386-2126

Mexican
$5-$19

The colorful, casual eatery offers friendly service and basic Mexican fare. Casual dress. **Bar:** Full bar. **Hours:** 11 am-10 pm. Closed: 11/26, 12/25. **Address:** 1021 W 2nd St **Location:** I-75, exit 64, just e. **Parking:** on-site. **Cards:** AX, DS, MC, VI.

PIT STOP BAR-B-QUE & GRILL *Menu on AAA.com* — **Phone:** 229/387-0888

Barbecue
$5-$14

Select from flavorful pork, beef and turkey barbecue sandwiches as well as grilled grouper and hearty Brunswick stew. Dining options include the comfortable interior or picnic tables on the back porch. A nice selection of pies and cakes are available. Don't be surprised if you have to wait for a table at this popular eatery. **Bar:** Beer & wine. **Hours:** 11 am-9 pm, Fri & Sat-10 pm. Closed: 12/25. **Address:** 1112 W 8th St **Location:** I-75, exit 63B, just w. **Parking:** on-site. **Cards:** AX, MC, VI.

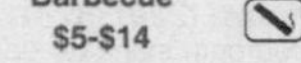

SONNY'S REAL PIT BAR-B-Q — **Phone:** 229/386-0606

Barbecue
$6-$15

House specialties include pork and chicken grilled over an open pit, barbecue ribs and fresh, homemade pie. The salad bar offers another popular option. Rustic and comfortable, the atmosphere is perfect for family meals. Casual dress. **Hours:** 11 am-9:30 pm, Fri & Sat-10 pm. Closed: 11/26, 12/25. **Address:** 1616 Hwy 82 W **Location:** I-75, exit 62, 0.5 mi w. **Parking:** on-site. **Cards:** AX, DS, MC, VI.

TRENTON pop. 1,942

WHERE TO STAY

DAYS INN *Book at AAA.com* — **Phone:** (706)657-2550

Hotel
$60-$70 5/1-11/30
$57-$60 12/1-4/30

Address: 95 Killian Ave **Location:** I-59, exit 11, just e. **Facility:** 45 one-bedroom standard units, some with whirlpools. 2 stories (no elevator), exterior corridors. **Parking:** on-site. **Terms:** cancellation fee imposed. **Amenities:** high-speed Internet, irons, hair dryers. **Pool(s):** outdoor. **Guest Services:** coin laundry, wireless Internet. **Business Services:** meeting rooms, fax (fee). **Cards:** AX, DC, DS, MC, VI.

ASK CALL / SOME UNITS FEE

TUCKER —*See Atlanta p. 423.*

TYBEE ISLAND pop. 3,392

WHERE TO STAY

DUNES INN & SUITES — **Phone:** (912)786-4591

SAVE

Motel
$109-$249 3/1-11/30
$59-$149 12/1-2/28

Address: 1409 Butler Ave **Location:** On US 80; center. **Facility:** 32 one-bedroom standard units, some with efficiencies and/or whirlpools. 2 stories (no elevator), exterior corridors. **Parking:** on-site. **Terms:** 3 day cancellation notice-fee imposed. **Amenities:** irons, hair dryers. **Pool(s):** outdoor. **Cards:** AX, DS, MC, VI. **Free Special Amenities: continental breakfast and early check-in/late check-out.**

/ SOME UNITS

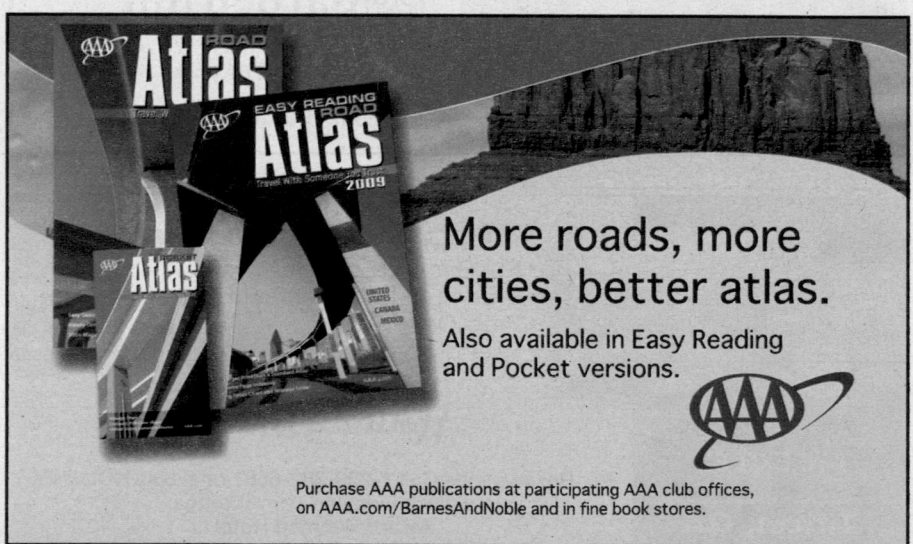

HOWARD JOHNSON-ADMIRAL'S INN Book at AAA.com Phone: (912)786-0700

Hotel
$80-$175 3/1-11/30
$50-$70 12/1-2/28

Address: 1501 Butler Ave **Location:** On US 80 E; near south end of Island. **Facility:** 41 one-bedroom standard units, some with whirlpools. 2 stories (no elevator), interior corridors. **Parking:** on-site. **Terms:** 2 night minimum stay - seasonal and/or weekends, cancellation fee imposed. **Amenities:** voice mail, irons, hair dryers. **Pool(s):** outdoor. **Guest Services:** wireless Internet. **Cards:** AX, CB, DC, DS, JC, MC, VI.

ASK CALL / SOME UNITS

OCEAN PLAZA BEACH RESORT Book great rates at AAA.com **Phone:** 912/786-7777

AAA SAVE
Hotel
Rates not provided

Address: 1401 Strand Ave **Location:** Just e on US 80 E; near south end of island; downtown. **Facility:** Smoke free premises. 204 units. 200 one-bedroom standard units. 4 one-bedroom suites. 4 stories, interior corridors. *Bath:* combo or shower only. **Parking:** on-site. **Terms:** check-in 4 pm. **Amenities:** video games (fee), voice mail, irons, hair dryers. **Pool(s):** 2 outdoor. **Guest Services:** wireless Internet. **Business Services:** conference facilities, PC. **Free Special Amenities: high-speed Internet.**

/ SOME UNITS FEE FEE

WHERE TO DINE

THE HUNTER HOUSE **Phone:** 912/786-7515

Regional American
$15-$30

Cozy dining is the hallmark of the renovated beach house, which dates back to 1910. Beautifully presented, Southern regional selections include preparations of fresh, local seafood, chicken, pork and beef. Casual dress. **Bar:** Full bar. **Reservations:** suggested, weekends. **Hours:** Open 12/1-12/31 & 1/16-11/30; 6 pm-9 pm. Closed: Sun 9/1-5/31. **Address:** 1701 Butler Ave **Location:** Corner of 17th St and Butler Ave, just s of jct US 80, just sw of Atlantic Ocean. **Parking:** on-site. **Cards:** AX, DS, MC, VI.

UNADILLA pop. 2,772

WHERE TO STAY

SUGAR HILL BED & BREAKFAST **Phone:** 478/627-3557

Historic Bed & Breakfast
$60-$80 All Year

Address: 2540 Sugar Hill Rd **Location:** I-75, exit 122 (SR 230), 2.1 mi e, then 2.3 mi n on Ransom Rd. **Facility:** The B&B, build in 1850, offers a quiet, pastoral farm setting that is convenient to the interstate. Smoke free premises. 4 one-bedroom standard units, some with whirlpools. 2 stories (no elevator), interior corridors. **Parking:** on-site. **Terms:** age restrictions may apply, 7 day cancellation notice-fee imposed. **Amenities:** video library. *Some:* CD players. **Pool(s):** outdoor. **Cards:** MC, VI.

/ SOME UNITS VCR

UNION CITY —*See Atlanta p. 425.*

VALDOSTA pop. 43,724

WHERE TO STAY

BEST WESTERN KING OF THE ROAD

Book great rates at AAA.com

Phone: (229)244-7600

AAA Benefit: Members save up to 20%, plus 10% bonus points with rewards program.

Hotel
$69-$89 All Year

Address: 1403 N St Augustine Rd **Location:** I-75, exit 18, just w off of SR 94. **Facility:** 137 units. 131 one-bedroom standard units. 5 one- and 1 two-bedroom suites, some with kitchens. 3 stories, exterior corridors. **Parking:** on-site. **Terms:** 7 day cancellation notice. **Amenities:** irons, hair dryers. **Pool(s):** outdoor. **Guest Services:** valet laundry, wireless Internet. **Business Services:** meeting rooms, PC, fax. **Cards:** AX, DC, DS, MC, VI. **Free Special Amenities: expanded continental breakfast and high-speed Internet.**

/ SOME UNITS FEE

COMFORT INN CONFERENCE CENTER

Book great rates at AAA.com

Phone: (229)242-1212

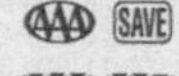

Hotel
$95-$100 All Year

Address: 2101 W Hill Ave **Location:** I-75, exit 16, just w. **Facility:** 138 units. 136 one-bedroom standard units. 2 one-bedroom suites. 2 stories (no elevator), interior/exterior corridors. *Bath:* combo or shower only. **Parking:** on-site. **Amenities:** voice mail, irons, hair dryers. *Some:* dual phone lines. **Pool(s):** outdoor. **Leisure Activities:** picnic pavilion, shuffleboard, volleyball. **Guest Services:** valet and coin laundry, wireless Internet. **Business Services:** meeting rooms, PC, fax (fee). **Cards:** AX, DC, DS, MC, VI. **Free Special Amenities: expanded continental breakfast and high-speed Internet.**

/ SOME UNITS

COMFORT SUITES

Book at AAA.com

Phone: (229)249-8880

Hotel
$89-$149 All Year

Address: 1332 N St Augustine Rd **Location:** I-75, exit 18, adjacent to interchange. **Facility:** Smoke free premises. 88 units. 85 one-bedroom standard units. 3 one-bedroom suites. 3 stories, interior corridors. *Bath:* combo or shower only. **Parking:** on-site. **Amenities:** high-speed Internet, voice mail, irons, hair dryers. **Pool(s):** outdoor. **Leisure Activities:** exercise room. **Guest Services:** valet and coin laundry, wireless Internet. **Business Services:** meeting rooms, PC. **Cards:** AX, CB, DC, DS, MC, VI.

ASK / SOME UNITS

COUNTRY INN & SUITES BY CARLSON

Book at AAA.com

Phone: (229)245-1700

Hotel
$139-$159 All Year

Address: 1308 N St Augustine Rd **Location:** I-75, exit 18, just e. **Facility:** Designated smoking area. 71 units. 45 one-bedroom standard units, some with whirlpools. 26 one-bedroom suites, some with whirlpools. 5 stories, interior corridors. *Bath:* combo or shower only. **Parking:** on-site. **Amenities:** high-speed Internet, dual phone lines, voice mail, safes, irons, hair dryers. **Pool(s):** heated indoor. **Leisure Activities:** whirlpool, exercise room. **Guest Services:** valet and coin laundry, wireless Internet. **Business Services:** meeting rooms, business center. **Cards:** AX, MC, VI.

ASK

DAYS INN I-75 NORTH

Book at AAA.com

Phone: (229)244-4460

Hotel
$54-$79 All Year

Address: 4598 N Valdosta Rd **Location:** I-75, exit 22, just w. **Facility:** 100 one-bedroom standard units. 2 stories, exterior corridors. **Parking:** on-site. **Amenities:** irons, hair dryers. **Pool(s):** outdoor. **Leisure Activities:** *Fee:* game room. **Guest Services:** wireless Internet. **Business Services:** meeting rooms, fax. **Cards:** AX, CB, DC, DS, MC, VI.

ASK / SOME UNITS FEE

ECONO LODGE

Book at AAA.com

Phone: 229/671-1511

Hotel
Rates not provided

Address: 3022 James Rd **Location:** I-75, exit 18, just w. **Facility:** 65 one-bedroom standard units, some with efficiencies. 3 stories, interior corridors. *Bath:* combo or shower only. **Parking:** on-site. **Amenities:** high-speed Internet, voice mail, irons, hair dryers. **Pool(s):** heated outdoor. **Guest Services:** wireless Internet. **Business Services:** fax.

/ SOME UNITS FEE

HAMPTON INN & SUITES

Book great rates at AAA.com

Phone: (229)241-1234

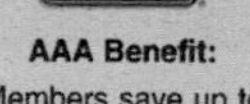

AAA Benefit: Members save up to 10% everyday!

Hotel
$104 All Year

Address: 2 Meeting Place Dr **Location:** I-75, exit 16, just e, then 0.3 mi n. Located next to the convention center. **Facility:** 184 one-bedroom standard units. 4 stories, interior corridors. *Bath:* combo or shower only. **Parking:** on-site. **Terms:** 1-30 night minimum stay, cancellation fee imposed. **Amenities:** video games (fee), high-speed Internet, dual phone lines, voice mail, irons, hair dryers. **Pool(s):** outdoor. **Leisure Activities:** whirlpool, exercise room. **Guest Services:** coin laundry, wireless Internet. **Business Services:** business center. **Cards:** AX, CB, DC, DS, MC, VI.

/ SOME UNITS

HILTON GARDEN INN

Phone: 229/219-1011

fyi

Hotel

$109-$229 All Year

Too new to rate, opening scheduled for September 2008. **Address:** 1702 Gornto Rd **Location:** I-75, exit 18 (SR 133), 0.3 mi e. **Amenities:** 163 units, restaurant, coffeemakers, microwaves, refrigerators, pool. **Terms:** 1-30 night minimum stay, cancellation fee imposed. **Cards:** DC, DS, MC, VI.

Hilton Garden Inn

AAA Benefit:

Members save 5% or more everyday!

HOLIDAY INN HOTEL AND CONFERENCE CENTER

Book at AAA.com

Phone: (229)244-1111

Hotel

$99-$189 All Year

Address: 1805 W Hill Ave **Location:** I-75, exit 16, 0.4 mi e. **Facility:** 158 units. 152 one-bedroom standard units, some with whirlpools. 6 one-bedroom suites. 6 stories, interior corridors. *Bath:* combo or shower only. **Parking:** on-site. **Amenities:** high-speed Internet, dual phone lines, voice mail, safes, irons, hair dryers. **Pool(s):** outdoor. **Leisure Activities:** whirlpool, exercise room. **Guest Services:** valet and coin laundry, wireless Internet. **Business Services:** conference facilities, business center. **Cards:** AX, CB, DC, DS, MC, VI.

ASK   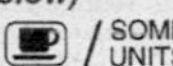    / SOME UNITS

LA QUINTA INN & SUITES VALDOSTA

Book great rates at AAA.com

Phone: (229)247-7755

SAVE

Hotel

$89-$149 All Year

Address: 1800 Clubhouse Dr **Location:** I-75, exit 18, 0.3 mi e, then just s off SR 94. **Facility:** 121 units. 104 one-bedroom standard units. 17 one-bedroom suites, some with whirlpools. 2 stories, interior corridors. *Bath:* combo or shower only. **Parking:** on-site. **Terms:** cancellation fee imposed. **Amenities:** high-speed Internet, voice mail, irons, hair dryers. **Pool(s):** outdoor. **Leisure Activities:** hot tub, exercise room. **Guest Services:** complimentary laundry, wireless Internet. **Business Services:** meeting rooms, business center. **Cards:** AX, CB, DC, DS, MC, VI. **Free Special Amenities: full breakfast and high-speed Internet.**

(See color ad below)

/ SOME UNITS

▼ See AAA listing above ▼

QUALITY INN NORTH — Book great rates at AAA.com

Hotel
$55-$75 All Year

Phone: (229)244-8510

Address: 1209 St Augustine Rd **Location:** I-75, exit 18, 0.3 mi e on SR 94. **Facility:** 84 one-bedroom standard units. 2 stories, exterior corridors. **Parking:** on-site. **Amenities:** voice mail, irons, hair dryers. **Pool(s):** outdoor. **Leisure Activities:** lighted tennis court, picnic tables & grills. **Guest Services:** valet and coin laundry, wireless Internet. **Business Services:** meeting rooms, PC, fax (fee). **Cards:** AX, CB, DC, DS, MC, VI. **Free Special Amenities: expanded continental breakfast and high-speed Internet.**

/ SOME UNITS FEE

QUALITY INN SOUTH — Book at AAA.com

Hotel
$50-$90 All Year

Phone: (229)244-4520

Address: 1902 W Hill Ave **Location:** I-75, exit 16, just e on US 84. **Facility:** 48 one-bedroom standard units. 2 stories, exterior corridors. **Parking:** on-site. **Amenities:** high-speed Internet, irons, hair dryers. **Pool(s):** outdoor. **Leisure Activities:** putting green, playground. **Guest Services:** coin laundry, wireless Internet. **Business Services:** PC, fax (fee). **Cards:** AX, CB, DC, DS, MC, VI.

ASK / SOME UNITS FEE

RAMADA LIMITED — Book at AAA.com

Motel
Rates not provided

Phone: 229/242-1225

Address: 2008 W Hill Ave **Location:** I-75, exit 16, just e on US 84. **Facility:** 82 one-bedroom standard units. 2 stories, exterior corridors. *Bath:* combo or shower only. **Parking:** on-site. **Amenities:** high-speed Internet, voice mail, irons, hair dryers. **Pool(s):** outdoor. **Guest Services:** valet laundry, wireless Internet. **Business Services:** meeting rooms, fax.

/ SOME UNITS FEE

SLEEP INN & SUITES — Book great rates at AAA.com

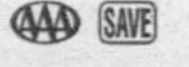

Hotel
Rates not provided

Phone: 229/671-1111

Address: 3026 James Rd **Location:** I-75, exit 18, just w. **Facility:** 73 units. 70 one-bedroom standard units. 3 one-bedroom suites with whirlpools. 3 stories, interior corridors. *Bath:* combo or shower only. **Parking:** on-site. **Amenities:** high-speed Internet, dual phone lines, voice mail, irons, hair dryers. **Pool(s):** heated outdoor. **Leisure Activities:** exercise room. **Guest Services:** coin laundry. **Business Services:** meeting rooms, PC, fax. **Free Special Amenities: continental breakfast and high-speed Internet.**

/ SOME UNITS

WINGATE BY WYNDHAM VALDOSTA

fyi
Hotel
$122-$170 All Year

Phone: 229/242-1225

Too new to rate, opening scheduled for July 2008. **Address:** 2008 W Hill Ave **Location:** I-75, exit 16. **Amenities:** 132 units, pets, coffeemakers, microwaves, refrigerators, pool. **Terms:** 3 day cancellation notice-fee imposed. **Cards:** AX, CB, DC, DS, MC, VI. ***(See color ad below)***

▼ *See AAA listing above* ▼

AAA CAA TourBookMark

Lodging Listing Symbols

Member Values (see pgs. 12-13)

- Official Appointment
- Offers lowest public rate or minimum 10% discount
- May offer discount
- Informational listing only

Member Services

- Airport transportation
- Pets allowed (call property for restrictions and fees)
- Restaurant on premises
- Restaurant off premises (walking distance)
- 24-hour room service
- Full bar
- Child care
- Accessible features (call property for available services and amenities)

Leisure Activities

- Full-service casino
- Pool
- Health club on premises
- Health club off premises (walking distance)
- Recreational activities

In-Room Amenities

- Designated non-smoking rooms
- VCR
- Movies
- Refrigerator
- Microwave
- Coffee maker
- No air conditioning
- No TV
- No cable TV
- No telephones

Safety Features (see page 24)

(Mexico and Caribbean only)

- S Sprinklers
- D Smoke detectors

Call property for detailed information about fees and restrictions relating to the lodging listing symbols.

CHOICE HOTELS INTERNATIONAL®

Book today at choicehotels.com or 800.228.1222

We'll see you there.

CHOICE HOTELS INTERNATIONAL®

WHERE TO DINE

306 NORTH — **Phone:** 229/249-5333

American
$6-$25

Well-trained, attentive servers circulate through the open dining room, which has an upscale feel with open beam ceilings and large watercolor art pieces. Pan-seared duck with sweet corn whippers, tuna with sesame spinach, grilled filet and shrimp with fettuccine represent the menu choices. Dressy casual. **Bar:** Full bar. **Reservations:** accepted. **Hours:** 11 am-2 & 5-9 pm, Fri & Sat-10 pm. Closed: 11/26, 12/24, 12/25; also Sun. **Address:** 306 N Patterson St **Location:** Downtown. **Parking:** on-site. **Cards:** AX, CB, DC, DS, JC, MC, VI.

ALIGATOU JAPANESE STEAKHOUSE & SEAFOOD — **Phone:** 229/244-4784

Japanese
$5-$20

Energetic chefs prepare your Japanese/Chinese meal tableside with skill, humor and flair. If sushi's your choice, you'll enjoy the fresh selection and reasonable prices at the sushi bar, along with a serving of soup and salad with ginger dressing. Casual dress. **Bar:** Full bar. **Hours:** 5 pm-10 pm. Closed: 11/26, 12/25. **Address:** 1922 W Hill Ave **Location:** I-75, exit 16, just e. **Parking:** on-site. **Cards:** AX, DS, MC, VI.

CHARLIE TRIPPER'S — **Phone:** 229/247-0366

American
$14-$25

Vaulted ceilings lend a roomy feel to the rustic, country dining area. On the menu are delicious salad, steak and seafood prepared with an American flair. For dessert, try the creme brulee. A pianist entertains during dinner hours. Dressy casual. **Bar:** Full bar. **Reservations:** suggested, weekends. **Hours:** 6 pm-10 pm. Closed: 12/24, 12/25; also Sun & Mon. **Address:** 4479 N Valdosta Rd **Location:** I-75, exit 22, 0.3 mi e. **Parking:** on-site. **Cards:** AX, DC, DS, MC, VI.

CRYSTAL RIVER SEAFOOD — **Phone:** 229/249-9515

Seafood
$6-$25

Seafood choices are plentiful on the menu, and guests can pick a favorite or try something new. Flavors are good and portions ample. Casual dress. **Bar:** Beer & wine. **Hours:** 11 am-9 pm, Fri & Sat-10 pm. Closed: 11/26, 12/25. **Address:** 985 N St Augustine Rd **Location:** I-75, exit 18, 0.6 mi w on SR 94. **Parking:** on-site. **Cards:** AX, DS, MC, VI.

HEIDI'S BROOKLYN DELI — **Phone:** 229/241-9944

Deli
$5-$10

The nationally popular franchise prepares a wide selection of delicatessen fare, including cold and hot sandwiches, wraps, salads, soups and a variety of freshly baked breads. Casual dress. **Hours:** 7 am-8 pm. Closed major holidays. **Address:** 1407 W Hill Ave **Location:** I-75, exit 16, 1.8 mi e. **Parking:** on-site. **Cards:** AX, DS, MC, VI.

LAS BANDERAS MEXICAN FOOD — **Phone:** 229/245-9797

Mexican
$5-$12

Fine artwork adorns the walls of this restaurant, which plays host to fiesta and salsa nights. Selections include La Panchanga sampler platter, alambre veracruzano and marinated chicken, steak, shrimp and vegetable shish kebab. Casual dress. **Bar:** Full bar. **Hours:** 11 am-10:30 pm, Thurs-Sat to 11 pm, Sun noon-9 pm. Closed: 1/1, 12/25. **Address:** 904 Baytree Rd **Location:** Just e of jct Norman Dr. **Parking:** on-site. **Cards:** AX, CB, DC, DS, JC, MC, VI.

LOCOS GRILL & PUB — **Phone:** 229/245-1994

Deli
$7-$17

Dining options include a lively pub with televisions for watching your favorite sports or a traditional deli where the atmosphere is calmer and menu selections include finger foods such as sandwiches, burgers and steak. Casual dress. **Bar:** Full bar. **Hours:** 11 am-midnight, Sun-10 pm. Closed: 1/1, 11/26, 12/25. **Address:** 1703 Gornto Rd **Location:** I-75, exit 18, just e. **Parking:** on-site. **Cards:** AX, DS, MC, VI.

MICHAEL'S DELI & SEAFOOD — **Phone:** 229/293-9905

Deli
$5-$11

The quick-serve deli offers a large seating area and serves subs on hoagie rolls, large salads and fried mushrooms. Seafood offerings include tilapia, flounder and Alaskan pollock. Casual dress. **Hours:** 10 am-9 pm. Closed major holidays. **Address:** 1307 N Ashley St **Location:** Downtown. **Parking:** on-site. **Cards:** MC, VI.

MOM & DAD'S ITALIAN RESTAURANT — **Phone:** 229/333-0848

Italian
$8-$16

Savor the delicious pasta dishes and various sauces served at this family-owned Italian restaurant decorated with attractively framed Italian landscapes and cityscapes. The homemade Italian dressing bursts with flavor, as does the stuffed tortellini. Casual dress. **Bar:** Full bar. **Hours:** 5 pm-10 pm. Closed major holidays; also Sun & Mon. **Address:** 4143 N Valdosta Rd **Location:** I-75, exit 22, 1.5 mi e. **Parking:** on-site. **Cards:** AX, CB, DC, DS, MC, VI.

SISTERS PIZZA & MUSSELS — **Phone:** 229/241-9004

Pizza
$6-$18

Between downtown and many listed hotels, the small storefront restaurant serves pizza prepared in varied styles, in addition to salads, sandwiches, pasta and, like the name says, steamed mussels in spicy sauce. Casual dress. **Hours:** 11 am-10 pm, Fri & Sat-midnight. Closed major holidays. **Address:** 1407 W Hill Ave **Location:** I-75, exit 16, 0.8 mi e. **Parking:** on-site. **Cards:** MC, VI.

SONNY'S REAL PIT BAR-B-Q — **Phone:** 229/241-8090

Barbecue
$6-$15

House specialties include pork and chicken grilled over an open pit, barbecue ribs and fresh, homemade pie. The salad bar offers another popular option. Rustic and comfortable, the atmosphere is perfect for family meals. Casual dress. **Bar:** Beer only. **Hours:** 11 am-9:30 pm, Fri & Sat-10 pm. Closed: 11/26, 12/25. **Address:** 1701 Norman Dr **Location:** I-75, exit 18, 0.6 mi e on St Augustine Rd, then just n. **Parking:** on-site. **Cards:** AX, DS, MC, VI.

STEAMHOUSE SEAFOOD

Phone: 229/245-9008

Seafood
$8-$15

Next to the interstate and near listed hotels, the unpretentious, family-friendly restaurant counts foil-steamed fish and Chesapeake crab dip among its popular choices. The menu also lists delicious steamed shrimp, oysters and corn on the cob. Service is relaxed and casual, and prices are reasonable. Casual dress. **Bar:** Full bar. **Hours:** 4 pm-10 pm, Fri & Sat-11 pm. Closed: 12/24; also Sun. **Address:** 3008 James Rd **Location:** I-75, exit 18, just w. **Parking:** on-site. **Cards:** AX, CB, DC, DS, JC, MC, VI.

VIDALIA pop. 10,491

WHERE TO STAY

COMFORT INN *Book great rates at AAA.com*

Phone: (912)538-8100

AAA SAVE

Hotel
$75-$99 All Year

Address: 1509 E First St **Location:** 1.3 mi e on US 280. Located in a quiet area. **Facility:** 67 one-bedroom standard units, some with whirlpools. 2 stories (no elevator), interior corridors. *Bath:* combo or shower only. **Parking:** on-site. **Amenities:** voice mail, irons, hair dryers. *Some:* high-speed Internet. **Pool(s):** indoor. **Leisure Activities:** whirlpool, limited exercise equipment. **Guest Services:** valet laundry, wireless Internet. **Business Services:** meeting rooms, business center. **Cards:** AX, CB, DC, DS, JC, MC, VI. **Free Special Amenities: expanded continental breakfast and high-speed Internet.**

/ SOME UNITS

DAYS INN *Book great rates at AAA.com*

Phone: (912)537-9251

AAA SAVE

Hotel
$69-$79 All Year

Address: 1503 Lyons Hwy E **Location:** 1 mi e on US 280. **Facility:** 64 one-bedroom standard units. 1-2 stories (no elevator), exterior corridors. **Parking:** on-site, winter plug-ins. **Terms:** check-in 4 pm, 7 day cancellation notice. **Amenities:** voice mail, irons, hair dryers. **Pool(s):** outdoor. **Guest Services:** valet laundry, wireless Internet. **Cards:** AX, CB, DC, DS, MC, VI. **Free Special Amenities: expanded continental breakfast and high-speed Internet.**

/ SOME UNITS FEE

HOLIDAY INN EXPRESS *Book at AAA.com*

Phone: (912)537-9000

Hotel
$79-$102 All Year

Address: 2619 E First St **Location:** 2.5 mi e on US 280. **Facility:** 65 units. 59 one-bedroom standard units, some with whirlpools. 6 one-bedroom suites with whirlpools. 2 stories (no elevator), exterior corridors. *Bath:* combo or shower only. **Parking:** on-site, winter plug-ins. **Amenities:** voice mail, irons, hair dryers. **Pool(s):** outdoor. **Leisure Activities:** jogging. **Guest Services:** valet laundry, wireless Internet. **Business Services:** business center. **Cards:** AX, DC, DS, MC, VI.

ASK / SOME UNITS FEE

WHERE TO DINE

STEEPLECHASE GRILLE AND TAVERN

Phone: 912/537-7900

American
$5-$20

Appetizers, such as spinach con queso or fried mushrooms, are a great starter. A smorgasbord of selections, the menu includes items such as freshly baked quiche, filet mignon, salmon and pasta. A salad bar is include with all meals. To wrap up your meal, any of the sweet temptations from the dessert tray will do the trick. Casual dress. **Bar:** Full bar. **Reservations:** accepted. **Hours:** 11 am-2:30 & 4:30-10 pm, Fri-11 pm, Sat 5 pm-10 pm. Closed major holidays; also Sun. **Address:** 306 E 2nd St **Location:** Just off US 280; southwest of center. **Parking:** on-site. **Cards:** AX, MC, VI.

VILLA RICA pop. 4,134

WHERE TO STAY

BEST WESTERN VILLA RICA INN *Book great rates at AAA.com*

Phone: (770)459-6669

AAA SAVE

Hotel
$69-$84 All Year

Address: 124 Hwy 61 Connector **Location:** I-20, exit 24, just n. **Facility:** 39 one-bedroom standard units, some with whirlpools. 2 stories (no elevator), exterior corridors. **Parking:** on-site. **Amenities:** high-speed Internet, irons, hair dryers. *Some:* DVD players, CD players. **Pool(s):** outdoor. **Guest Services:** coin laundry, wireless Internet. **Cards:** AX, CB, DC, DS, MC, VI. **Free Special Amenities: continental breakfast and high-speed Internet.**

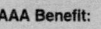

CALL / SOME UNITS VCR

AAA Benefit:
Members save up to 20%, plus 10% bonus points with rewards program.

COMFORT INN & SUITES *Book at AAA.com*

Phone: (678)941-3401

Hotel
$80-$140 All Year

Address: 132 Hwy 61 Connector **Location:** I-20, exit 24, just n. **Facility:** 59 units. 56 one-bedroom standard units, some with whirlpools. 3 one-bedroom suites. 4 stories, interior corridors. **Parking:** on-site. **Amenities:** high-speed Internet, voice mail, irons, hair dryers. **Pool(s):** heated indoor. **Leisure Activities:** exercise room. **Guest Services:** coin laundry, wireless Internet. **Business Services:** meeting rooms, PC, fax. **Cards:** AX, DC, DS, MC, VI.

DAYS INN *Book at AAA.com* **Phone:** (770)459-8888

Hotel

$55-$115 1/1-11/30
$55-$79 12/1-12/31

Address: 195 Hwy 61 Connector **Location:** I-20, exit 24, just n. **Facility:** 61 one-bedroom standard units, some with whirlpools. 2 stories, interior corridors. **Parking:** on-site. **Amenities:** high-speed Internet, hair dryers. **Pool(s):** outdoor. **Guest Services:** coin laundry, wireless Internet. **Business Services:** fax (fee). **Cards:** AX, DS, MC, VI.

ASK CALL / SOME UNITS FEE

SUPER 8 MOTEL *Book great rates at AAA.com* **Phone:** 770/459-8000

AAA SAVE

Hotel

Rates not provided

Address: 128 Hwy 61 Connector **Location:** I-20, exit 24, just n. **Facility:** 61 one-bedroom standard units, some with whirlpools. 2 stories, exterior corridors. **Parking:** on-site. **Amenities:** high-speed Internet, voice mail, irons, hair dryers. **Pool(s):** outdoor. **Leisure Activities:** limited exercise equipment. **Guest Services:** wireless Internet. **Business Services:** meeting rooms, PC, fax (fee). **Free Special Amenities: continental breakfast and high-speed Internet.**

/ SOME UNITS FEE

The following lodging was either not evaluated or did not meet AAA rating requirements but is listed for your information only.

FAIRFIELD PLANTATION **Phone:** 770/834-7781

fyi

Not evaluated. **Address:** 1602 Lakeview Pkwy **Location:** I-20, exit 24, 6.5 mi s to SR 61, then 2.1 mi e, follow signs. Facilities, services, and decor characterize a mid-scale property.

WARNER ROBINS pop. 48,804

WHERE TO STAY

BEST WESTERN PEACH INN **Phone:** (478)953-3800

Hotel

$49-$69 All Year

Address: 2739 Watson Blvd **Location:** I-75, exit 146 (SR 247C), 4.1 mi e. **Facility:** 50 one-bedroom standard units, some with whirlpools. 2 stories (no elevator), exterior corridors. *Bath:* combo or shower only. **Parking:** on-site. **Terms:** 7 day cancellation notice. **Amenities:** video library (fee), high-speed Internet, irons, hair dryers. *Some:* DVD players (fee). **Pool(s):** outdoor. **Leisure Activities:** exercise room. **Guest Services:** coin laundry, wireless Internet. **Business Services:** fax (fee). **Cards:** AX, CB, DS, JC, MC, VI. **Free Special Amenities: continental breakfast and high-speed Internet.**

/ SOME UNITS FEE FEE VCR

AAA Benefit:

Members save up to 20%, plus 10% bonus points with rewards program.

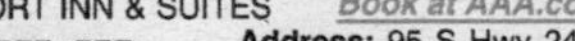

COMFORT INN & SUITES *Book at AAA.com* **Phone:** (478)922-7555

Hotel

$82-$150 All Year

Address: 95 S Hwy 247 **Location:** Jct SR 247C and US 129/SR 247, 1.6 mi s on US 129/SR 247. **Facility:** 77 units. 45 one-bedroom standard units, some with whirlpools. 32 one-bedroom suites. 1-2 stories (no elevator), interior/exterior corridors. **Parking:** on-site. **Terms:** cancellation fee imposed. **Amenities:** irons, hair dryers. **Pool(s):** outdoor. **Leisure Activities:** limited exercise equipment. **Guest Services:** valet and coin laundry, wireless Internet. **Business Services:** meeting rooms, business center. **Cards:** AX, CB, DC, DS, JC, MC, VI.

ASK / SOME UNITS FEE FEE VCR

COUNTRY INN & SUITES *Book at AAA.com* **Phone:** (478)971-1660

Hotel

$92-$96 All Year

Address: 220 Margie Dr **Location:** I-75, exit 146 (SR 247C), 3.2 mi e, then just s. **Facility:** Smoke free premises. 61 units. 32 one-bedroom standard units. 29 one-bedroom suites. 3 stories, interior corridors. *Bath:* combo or shower only. **Parking:** on-site. **Amenities:** dual phone lines, voice mail, irons, hair dryers. *Some:* high-speed Internet. **Pool(s):** indoor. **Leisure Activities:** whirlpool, limited exercise equipment. **Guest Services:** valet and coin laundry, wireless Internet. **Business Services:** PC, fax (fee). **Cards:** AX, CB, DC, DS, JC, MC, VI.

ASK

DAYS INN-WARNER ROBINS *Book at AAA.com* **Phone:** (478)953-6866

Motel

$65-$80 All Year

Address: 215 Margie Dr **Location:** I-75, exit 146 (SR 247C), 3.2 mi e, then just s. **Facility:** 61 one-bedroom standard units. 2 stories (no elevator), exterior corridors. *Bath:* combo or shower only. **Parking:** on-site. **Amenities:** high-speed Internet, irons, hair dryers. **Pool(s):** outdoor. **Guest Services:** coin laundry, wireless Internet. **Business Services:** meeting rooms, PC. **Cards:** AX, CB, DC, DS, JC, MC, VI.

ASK / SOME UNITS VCR

HAMPTON INN-WARNER ROBINS *Book great rates at AAA.com* **Phone:** (478)953-9443

Hotel
$90-$109 All Year

Address: 4000 Watson Blvd **Location:** I-75, exit 146 (SR 247C), 2.8 mi e. **Facility:** 87 units. 78 one-bedroom standard units. 9 one-bedroom suites, some with whirlpools. 3 stories, interior corridors. *Bath:* combo or shower only. **Parking:** on-site. **Terms:** 1-30 night minimum stay, cancellation fee imposed. **Amenities:** high-speed Internet, dual phone lines, voice mail, irons, hair dryers. **Pool(s):** heated indoor. **Leisure Activities:** sauna, whirlpool, exercise room. **Guest Services:** valet and coin laundry, wireless Internet. **Business Services:** meeting rooms, business center. **Cards:** AX, CB, DC, DS, MC, VI.

AAA Benefit:
Members save up to 10% everyday!

HOLIDAY INN OF WARNER ROBINS *Book at AAA.com* **Phone:** 478/923-8871

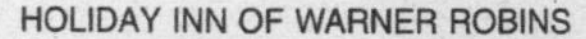

Motel
Rates not provided

Address: 2024 Watson Blvd **Location:** I-75, exit 146 (SR 247C), 5.6 mi e. **Facility:** 152 one-bedroom standard units. 2 stories (no elevator), exterior corridors. *Bath:* combo or shower only. **Parking:** on-site. **Amenities:** voice mail, irons, hair dryers. **Pool(s):** outdoor. **Leisure Activities:** exercise room. **Guest Services:** valet and coin laundry, wireless Internet. **Business Services:** meeting rooms, PC.

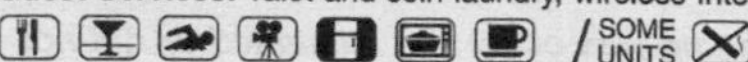

JAMESON INN-WARNER ROBINS *Book at AAA.com* **Phone:** (478)953-5522

Hotel
$78-$85 All Year

Address: 2731 Watson Blvd **Location:** I-75, exit 146 (SR 247C), 4.1 mi e. **Facility:** 61 one-bedroom standard units, some with whirlpools. 2 stories (no elevator), exterior corridors. *Bath:* combo or shower only. **Parking:** on-site. **Terms:** cancellation fee imposed. **Amenities:** irons, hair dryers. **Pool(s):** outdoor. **Leisure Activities:** exercise room. **Guest Services:** valet laundry, wireless Internet. **Business Services:** PC, fax (fee). **Cards:** AX, DC, DS, MC, VI.

WHERE TO DINE

CHEF AUDREY'S BISTRO & BAKERY **Phone:** 478/953-7480

European
$7-$25

The storefront European-style bistro and bakery presents a menu of eclectic lighter fare, such as salads, vegetable plates and fruit and cheese platters, alongside traditional Continental entrees, including beef Wellington. Delicate sauces accompany rack of lamb and roasted pork loin. This place's secret is its owner, Chef Audrey, a professionally trained pastry chef who prepares the always fresh bread and deadly good desserts, which pair well with fresh espresso beverages. Casual dress. **Hours:** 11 am-3 pm & 5:30 pm-close. Closed: Sun. **Address:** 2728 Ste D Watson Blvd **Location:** I-75, exit 146 (SR 247C), 4.5 mi e, then just n; in Wal-mart Center. **Parking:** on-site. **Cards:** DS, MC, VI.

EL BRONCO MEXICAN RESTAURANT **Phone:** 478/328-0344

Mexican
$5-$11

A colorful decor sets the stage for the authentic Mexican dishes of chicken enchiladas, chile rellenos, carne asada, fajita burritos, vegetarian dishes and combination platters. Casual dress. **Bar:** Full bar. **Hours:** 11 am-10 pm, Fri-11 pm, Sat-10:30 pm, Sun-8:30 pm. Closed: 4/12, 11/26, 12/25. **Address:** 2067 Watson Blvd **Location:** I-75, exit 146 (SR 247C), 5.3 mi e. **Parking:** on-site. **Cards:** AX, DS, MC, VI.

PIER 97 **Phone:** 478/328-6111

Seafood
$5-$20

Recommended by locals, this restaurant offers fresh seafood in a casual, comfortable setting. Casual dress. **Bar:** Beer & wine. **Hours:** 11:30 am-9:30 pm, Fri & Sat-10 pm. Closed: 11/26, 12/25; also Sun. **Address:** 2056 Watson Blvd **Location:** I-75, exit 146 (SR 247C), 5.2 mi e. **Parking:** on-site. **Cards:** AX, CB, DC, DS, JC, MC, VI.

THE SHIPWRECK RESTAURANT **Phone:** 478/923-6565

Seafood
$4-$18

The restaurant offers a salad bar and a variety of seafood items, such as shrimp and trout. Service is friendly and efficient, and the atmosphere is casual. Casual dress. **Hours:** 11 am-8:30 pm, Mon-2 pm, Fri-9 pm, Sat 4 pm-9 pm. Closed major holidays; also Sun. **Address:** 100 S Hwy 247 **Location:** Jct SR 247C/US 129, 2.2 mi s on US 129. **Parking:** on-site. **Cards:** MC, VI.

SONNY'S REAL PIT BAR-B-Q **Phone:** 478/929-3333

Barbecue
$6-$15

House specialties include pork and chicken grilled over an open pit, barbecue ribs and fresh, homemade pie. The salad bar offers another popular option. Rustic and comfortable, the atmosphere is perfect for family meals. Casual dress. **Bar:** Beer only. **Hours:** 11 am-9:30 pm, Fri & Sat-10 pm. Closed: 11/26, 12/25. **Address:** 811 Russell Pkwy **Location:** Jct US 129/SR 247, 2 mi w. **Parking:** on-site. **Cards:** AX, DS, MC, VI.

SUSHI THAI RESTAURANT **Phone:** 478/923-0898

Thai
$8-$16

Select items from a traditional Thai menu or from a Japanese sushi menu. Chef specialties include curry duck, spicy catfish and Thai royal duck (roasted, then fried and topped with a secret sauce). Casual dress. **Bar:** Beer & wine. **Hours:** 11 am-2:30 & 4:30-9:30 pm, Sat noon-10 pm, Sun 4:30 pm-9:30 pm. **Address:** 2624 Watson Blvd **Location:** Just e of Carl Vinson Pkwy. **Parking:** on-site. **Cards:** AX, DS, MC, VI.

WASHINGTON pop. 4,295

WHERE TO STAY

LAFAYETTE MANOR INN — **Phone:** 706/678-5922

Historic Country Inn
$125-$175 All Year

Address: 219 E Robert Toombs Ave (SR 17) **Location:** Downtown; just e of town square. **Facility:** Guest can expect a delightful experience at the non-traditional country inn. 7 units. 5 one-bedroom standard units. 1 two-bedroom suite. 1 cottage. 2 stories, interior corridors. *Bath:* combo or shower only. **Parking:** on-site. **Terms:** check-in 4 pm, age restrictions may apply, 14 day cancellation notice-fee imposed. **Amenities:** *Some:* DVD players, CD players. **Dining:** restaurant, see separate listing. **Leisure Activities:** gazebo, garden. **Guest Services:** wireless Internet. **Business Services:** meeting rooms. **Cards:** AX, DS, MC, VI. **Free Special Amenities: full breakfast and high-speed Internet.**

/ SOME UNITS

WHERE TO DINE

LAFAYETTE MANOR INN DINING ROOM — **Phone:** 706/678-5922

French
$9-$45

Experience a truly gourmet dinner in the dining room of a historic bed and breakfast. Five courses are typical with this prix fixe menu featuring French cuisine with an Asian influence. Advanced reservations are required, as the chef commutes to Atlanta in order to personally select premium seasonal and regional offerings from her choice of purveyors. The atmosphere is a comfortable middle ground between casual and formal, and the result is a genuine, pleasing experience. If you choose to relax in the parlor after dinner, your host will entertain you with his talents on the grand piano. Dressy casual. Entertainment. **Bar:** Beer & wine. **Reservations:** required. **Hours:** 11:30 am-2 pm; 7:30 pm seating. Closed: Mon. **Address:** 219 E Robert Toombs Ave (SR 17) **Location:** Downtown; just e of town square; in Lafayette Manor Inn. **Parking:** on-site. **Cards:** AX, DS, MC, VI.

WAYCROSS pop. 15,333

WHERE TO STAY

BEST WESTERN BRADBURY INN & SUITES — Book great rates at AAA.com — **Phone:** (912)284-0095

Hotel
$85-$100 All Year

Address: 2750 Memorial Dr **Location:** Jct US 1 and 82, 1.5 mi s on US 1. **Facility:** 38 one-bedroom standard units, some with whirlpools. 2 stories, interior corridors. *Bath:* combo or shower only. **Parking:** on-site. **Amenities:** high-speed Internet, voice mail, safes, irons, hair dryers. **Pool(s):** outdoor. **Guest Services:** coin laundry, wireless Internet. **Business Services:** business center. **Cards:** AX, DC, DS, MC, VI. **Free Special Amenities: continental breakfast and high-speed Internet.**

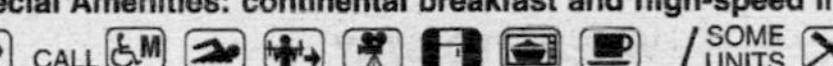

AAA Benefit: Members save up to 20%, plus 10% bonus points with rewards program.

COMFORT INN WAYCROSS — Book at AAA.com — **Phone:** 912/283-3300

Motel
Rates not provided

Address: 1903 Memorial Dr **Location:** Between US 1 and 82, at S City Blvd. **Facility:** 70 one-bedroom standard units, some with whirlpools. 2 stories (no elevator), exterior corridors. *Bath:* combo or shower only. **Parking:** on-site. **Amenities:** irons, hair dryers. **Pool(s):** outdoor. **Leisure Activities:** limited exercise equipment. **Guest Services:** valet and coin laundry, wireless Internet. **Business Services:** meeting rooms.

/ SOME UNITS

HAMPTON INN — Book great rates at AAA.com — **Phone:** (912)285-5515

Hotel
$89-$105 All Year

Address: 1720 Brunswick Hwy (US 82) **Location:** Jct US 1 and 82, just e. **Facility:** 69 one-bedroom standard units. 3 stories, interior corridors. *Bath:* combo or shower only. **Parking:** on-site. **Amenities:** dual phone lines, voice mail, irons, hair dryers. **Pool(s):** outdoor. **Leisure Activities:** limited exercise equipment. **Guest Services:** valet and coin laundry, wireless Internet. **Business Services:** meeting rooms. **Cards:** AX, CB, DC, DS, MC, VI.

AAA Benefit: Members save up to 10% everyday!

JAMESON INN — Book at AAA.com — **Phone:** (912)283-3800

Motel
$73-$78 All Year

Address: 950 City Blvd **Location:** Between US 1 and 82, east of city. **Facility:** 62 one-bedroom standard units, some with whirlpools. 2 stories (no elevator), exterior corridors. **Parking:** on-site. **Terms:** cancellation fee imposed. **Amenities:** irons, hair dryers. **Pool(s):** outdoor. **Leisure Activities:** exercise room. **Guest Services:** valet laundry, wireless Internet. **Business Services:** PC. **Cards:** AX, DC, DS, MC, VI.

ASK CALL / SOME UNITS FEE

WHERE TO DINE

ANDREW'S CAFE & GRILL — **Phone:** 912/285-1545

American
$9-$21

Craft collections adorn the walls of the storefront restaurant. Well-prepared selections line the diverse menu, including salmon in dill sauce. Casual dress. **Bar:** Full bar. **Reservations:** accepted. **Hours:** 5:30 pm-10 pm. Closed major holidays; also Sun-Tues. **Address:** 412 Elizabeth St **Location:** Downtown; across from Confederate Memorial Park; in historic shopping district. **Parking:** street. **Cards:** AX, MC, VI.

POND VIEW DOWNTOWN INN & RESTAURANT **Phone:** 912/283-9300

Continental
$11-$25

In a historic storefront, the charming restaurant serves a wide selection of entrees, from spaghetti to duck, with choices from a well-selected wine list. Professional service and a warm greeting from the host enhance the experience. Casual dress. **Bar:** Beer & wine. **Reservations:** suggested. **Hours:** 5:30 pm-9:30 pm. Closed major holidays; also Sun & Mon. **Address:** 311 Pendleton St **Location:** Just e of US 84; between Mary and Elizabeth sts. **Parking:** street. **Cards:** AX, DS, MC, VI.

WAYNESBORO pop. 5,813

WHERE TO STAY

BEST WESTERN EXECUTIVE INN *Book great rates at AAA.com* **Phone:** (706)554-0806

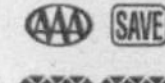

Hotel
$75-$209 All Year

Address: 1224 N Liberty St **Location:** 0.8 mi n of downtown center on US 25. **Facility:** 38 one-bedroom standard units, some with whirlpools. 2 stories (no elevator), interior corridors. *Bath:* combo or shower only. **Parking:** on-site. **Terms:** 3 day cancellation notice. **Amenities:** safes (fee), irons, hair dryers. **Pool(s):** outdoor. **Guest Services:** wireless Internet. **Business Services:** PC. **Cards:** AX, DS, MC, VI. **Free Special Amenities: full breakfast and high-speed Internet.**

/ SOME UNITS

AAA Benefit:
Members save up to 20%, plus 10% bonus points with rewards program.

JAMESON INN *Book at AAA.com* **Phone:** (706)437-0500

Motel
$78-$85 All Year

Address: 1436 N Liberty St **Location:** 0.9 mi n of downtown center on US 25. **Facility:** 42 one-bedroom standard units, some with whirlpools. 2 stories (no elevator), exterior corridors. **Parking:** on-site. **Terms:** cancellation fee imposed. **Amenities:** irons, hair dryers. **Pool(s):** outdoor. **Leisure Activities:** exercise room. **Guest Services:** wireless Internet. **Business Services:** PC. **Cards:** AX, DC, DS, MC, VI.

ASK / SOME UNITS FEE

WINDER pop. 10,201

WHERE TO STAY

BEST WESTERN WINDER HOTEL **Phone:** (770)868-5303

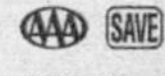

Hotel
$67-$121 All Year

Address: 177 W Athens St **Location:** Jct Broad St, 0.8 mi n; downtown. **Facility:** 42 one-bedroom standard units. 2 stories (no elevator), interior corridors. **Parking:** on-site. **Terms:** check-in 4 pm, 15 day cancellation notice. **Amenities:** voice mail, irons, hair dryers. **Pool(s):** outdoor. **Leisure Activities:** limited exercise equipment. **Guest Services:** wireless Internet. **Business Services:** PC. **Cards:** AX, DC, DS, MC, VI. **Free Special Amenities: continental breakfast and high-speed Internet.**

CALL / SOME UNITS FEE

AAA Benefit:
Members save up to 20%, plus 10% bonus points with rewards program.

JAMESON INN *Book at AAA.com* **Phone:** (770)867-1880

Motel
$83-$90 All Year

Address: 9 Stafford St **Location:** Jct SR 81, 11, 53 and 8; center. **Facility:** 40 one-bedroom standard units, some with whirlpools. 2 stories (no elevator), exterior corridors. **Parking:** on-site. **Terms:** cancellation fee imposed. **Amenities:** hair dryers. **Pool(s):** outdoor. **Leisure Activities:** exercise room. **Guest Services:** wireless Internet. **Business Services:** meeting rooms, PC. **Cards:** AX, DC, DS, MC, VI.

ASK / SOME UNITS FEE

WOODSTOCK pop. 10,050

WHERE TO STAY

COMFORT SUITES *Book great rates at AAA.com* **Phone:** (770)517-9650

Hotel
$80-$99 All Year

Address: 340 Parkway 575 **Location:** I-575, exit 7, just e to Parkway 575, then just n. **Facility:** Smoke free premises. 59 units. 47 one-bedroom standard units, some with whirlpools. 12 one-bedroom suites, some with whirlpools. 3 stories, interior corridors. **Parking:** on-site. **Amenities:** high-speed Internet, voice mail, irons, hair dryers. **Pool(s):** outdoor. **Leisure Activities:** exercise room. **Guest Services:** valet and coin laundry, wireless Internet. **Business Services:** meeting rooms, business center. **Cards:** AX, CB, DC, DS, JC, MC, VI.

FEE CALL

HAMPTON INN *Book great rates at AAA.com* **Phone:** (770)592-2323

Hotel
$86-$106 All Year

Address: 450 Parkway 575 **Location:** I-575, exit 7, just e to Parkway 575, then just n. **Facility:** 60 one-bedroom standard units. 3 stories, interior corridors. **Parking:** on-site. **Terms:** 1-30 night minimum stay, cancellation fee imposed. **Amenities:** high-speed Internet, dual phone lines, voice mail, irons, hair dryers. **Pool(s):** outdoor. **Leisure Activities:** limited exercise equipment. **Guest Services:** valet and coin laundry, wireless Internet. **Business Services:** meeting rooms, business center. **Cards:** AX, CB, DC, DS, MC, VI.

FEE  CALL 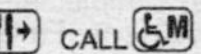   / SOME UNITS 

AAA Benefit:
Members save up to 10% everyday!

WHERE TO DINE

B. L. D.'S RESTAURANT **Phone:** 678/213-3393

American
$2-$16

The property's name stands for breakfast, lunch and dinner. A wide variety of American favorites are served in a diner-style setting. Casual dress. **Hours:** 7 am-9 pm, Fri & Sat-10 pm, Sun 7 am-8 pm. **Address:** 295 Molly Ln, Suite 100 **Location:** I-575, exit 7, just w. **Parking:** on-site. **Cards:** AX, DS, MC, VI.

CALL

CHILITOS **Phone:** 770/926-7200

Mexican
$2-$7

Fast, fresh Tex-Mex includes burritos and tacos made-to-order in a cafeteria-style line. Beer is among beverage choices. Varied salsas complement the chips. Casual dress. **Hours:** 11 am-9 pm. Closed major holidays; also Sun. **Address:** 6424 Bells Ferry Rd, Suite 116 **Location:** Jct Bells Ferry Rd and Eagle Dr. **Parking:** on-site. **Cards:** AX, MC, VI.

CALL

CHINA BAY **Phone:** 770/928-1668

Chinese
$6-$22

A good variation of basic Chinese cuisines are served in a sleek, contemporary dining room. Casual dress. **Bar:** Beer & wine. **Reservations:** accepted. **Hours:** 11 am-10 pm, Fri & Sat-11 pm, Sat 3:30 pm-11 pm. Closed major holidays. **Address:** 2035 Towne Lake Pkwy, Suite 150 **Location:** I-575, exit 8, 1 mi w. **Parking:** on-site. **Cards:** AX, CB, DC, DS, JC, MC, VI.

CALL

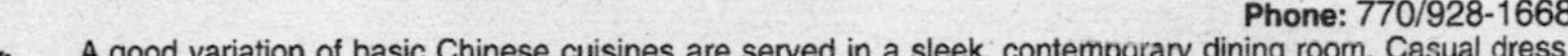

EL RANCHERO **Phone:** 770/516-6616

Tex-Mex
$2-$18

The neighborhood eatery is known for friendly service and a menu of standard Tex Mex, including fajitas, tacos, burritos and enchiladas, which taste great with fresh salsas. Casual dress. **Bar:** Full bar. **Hours:** 11 am-10:30 pm, Sun 11:30 am-9 pm. Closed: 11/26, 12/25. **Address:** 1025 Rose Creek Dr, Suite 180 **Location:** I-575, exit 8, 1.3 mi w to Towne Lake Pkwy, then 2.3 mi n. **Parking:** on-site. **Cards:** AX, CB, DC, DS, JC, MC, VI.

CALL

J. D.'S BAR-B-QUE **Phone:** 678/445-7730

Barbecue
$5-$11

The family restaurant prides itself on pit-cooked barbecue and Brunswick stew. Homemade desserts round out the menu. Casual dress. **Hours:** 10:30 am-9 pm, Sun noon-7 pm. Closed: 4/12, 11/26, 12/25; also Mon. **Address:** 6557 Bells Ferry Rd **Location:** Jct SR 92 and Bells Ferry Rd, 2.5 mi n. **Parking:** on-site. **Cards:** MC, VI.

KANI HOUSE **Phone:** 770/592-5264

Japanese
$8-$29

A no-frills Asian decor defines the relaxed atmosphere. Hibachi dinners, tempura, teriyaki, noodles, sushi and combination platters make up the extensive menu. Lunchbox specials are big favorites. Casual dress. **Bar:** Beer & wine. **Reservations:** accepted. **Hours:** 11:30 am-2 & 5-10 pm, Fri-11 pm, Sat 5 pm-11 pm, Sun 5 pm-10 pm. Closed major holidays. **Address:** 2455 Towne Lake Pkwy, Suite 110 **Location:** I-575, exit 8. **Parking:** on-site. **Cards:** AX, DC, DS, MC, VI.

CALL

PACIFIC SPICE **Phone:** 770/928-1899

Asian
$6-$18

The contemporary restaurant focuses on a wide variety of Chinese and Thai fare. Casual dress. **Bar:** Beer & wine. **Reservations:** accepted. **Hours:** 11 am-10 pm, Fri & Sat-10:30 pm, Sun noon-10 pm. **Address:** 6234 Old Hwy 5, Suite D15 **Location:** Jct Canton Hwy (Old Hwy 5) and E Cherokee; in Village Shoppes of East Cherokee. **Parking:** on-site. **Cards:** AX, MC, VI.

CALL

PEKING & TOKYO **Phone:** 770/591-8895

Asian
$6-$22

Set in a pleasant atmosphere, you will find standard Chinese and Japanese favorites including a sushi bar. Lunch specials are a great bargain. Casual dress. **Bar:** Beer & wine. **Reservations:** accepted. **Hours:** 11:30 am-2:30 & 4:30-9:30 pm, Fri-10:30 pm, Sat noon-10:30 pm, Sun noon-9:30 pm. Closed: 7/4, 11/26. **Address:** 200 Park Brooke Dr, Suite 160 **Location:** I-575, exit 8, 1.5 mi w; in Shops at Towne Lake. **Parking:** on-site. **Cards:** AX, CB, DC, DS, JC, MC, VI.

CALL

SAIGON CAFE

Asian
$6-$10

Phone: 770/384-8599

Cafe patrons can choose from steaming-hot noodle bowls and Thai favorites. Casual dress. **Bar:** Beer & wine. **Reservations:** accepted. **Hours:** 10:30 am-10 pm, Fri & Sat-11 pm, Sun-9 pm. Closed: 11/26, 12/25. **Address:** 12195 Hwy 92, Suite 132 **Location:** I-575, exit 7, 3 mi e; in Centre at Woodstock. **Parking:** on-site. **Cards:** AX, DS, MC, VI.

CALL

TECALI GRILLE

Tex-Mex
$6-$11

Phone: 770/926-1031

Three types of salsa, including habanero and tomatillo, complement the grill's Tex-Mex and vegetarian options. Casual dress. **Bar:** Full bar. **Hours:** 11 am-9:30 pm, Fri & Sat-10 pm. Closed: 11/26, 12/25. **Address:** 1105 Parkside Ln, Suite 1330 **Location:** I-575, exit 8, 1 mi w; in Southpointe at Towne Lake. **Parking:** on-site. **Cards:** AX, CB, DC, DS, JC, MC, VI.

TUSCANY ITALIAN GRILL

Italian
$8-$17

Phone: 678/453-0888

This bustling cafe serves a good variety of pizza, pasta, veal and chicken dishes in a family-friendly atmosphere. Casual dress. **Bar:** Beer & wine. **Hours:** 11:30 am-2:30 & 5-9 pm, Fri & Sat-10 pm. Closed major holidays; also Sun. **Address:** 1428 Towne Lake Pkwy, Suite 105 **Location:** I-575, exit 8, 0.7 mi w. **Parking:** on-site. **Cards:** AX, DS, MC, VI.

CALL

VILLA ROMA

Italian
$4-$17

Phone: 770/591-1966

Find authentic, Little Italy, family-style dining at this spot, which serves heaping bowls of salad, great pizza and a very good selection of pastas and sauces. Casual dress. **Bar:** Full bar. **Reservations:** accepted. **Hours:** 11 am-10 pm, Fri & Sat-11 pm. Closed major holidays. **Address:** 1025 Rose Creek Dr **Location:** In Towne Lake Village Shopping Center. **Parking:** on-site. **Cards:** AX, CB, DC, DS, JC, MC, VI.

CALL

WOODSTOCK COFFEEHOUSE

Deli
$6-$8

Phone: 770/928-2901

Choose from a multitude of organic coffees, lattes, espressos, juices and smoothies at this environment-conscious coffeehouse. If you're hungry, select from a variety of sandwiches, salads, soups and homemade desserts. Casual dress. **Hours:** 7 am-9 pm, Fri & Sat-10 pm. Closed major holidays. **Address:** 1428 Towne Lake Pkwy **Location:** I-575, exit 8, 0.7 mi w. **Parking:** on-site. **Cards:** AX, DS, MC, VI.

CALL

YOUNG HARRIS pop. 604

WHERE TO STAY

BRASSTOWN VALLEY RESORT *Book at AAA.com*

Resort Hotel
Rates not provided

Phone: 706/379-9900

Address: 6321 US Hwy 76 **Location:** US 76 and US 76/SR 515. Located in a quiet area. **Facility:** Nestled in the quiet mountains, this resort offers twig furniture, panoramic mountain views and outdoor activities such as fly fishing. 134 units. 102 one-bedroom standard units. 32 cottages. 5 stories, interior corridors. **Parking:** on-site. **Terms:** check-in 4 pm. **Amenities:** video games (fee), high-speed Internet, dual phone lines, voice mail, safes, irons, hair dryers. **Pool(s):** heated indoor/outdoor. **Leisure Activities:** saunas, whirlpools, steamrooms, fishing, recreation programs, hiking trails, jogging, playground, spa, horseshoes, volleyball. *Fee:* golf-18 holes, 4 lighted tennis courts, horseback riding, game room. **Guest Services:** valet and coin laundry, wireless Internet. **Business Services:** conference facilities, business center.

   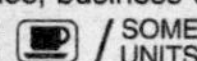 / SOME UNITS FEE  

North Carolina

North Carolina Arboretum, Blue Ridge Parkway, south of Asheville
© Pat & Chuck Blackley

North Carolina Orientation Map to Destinations

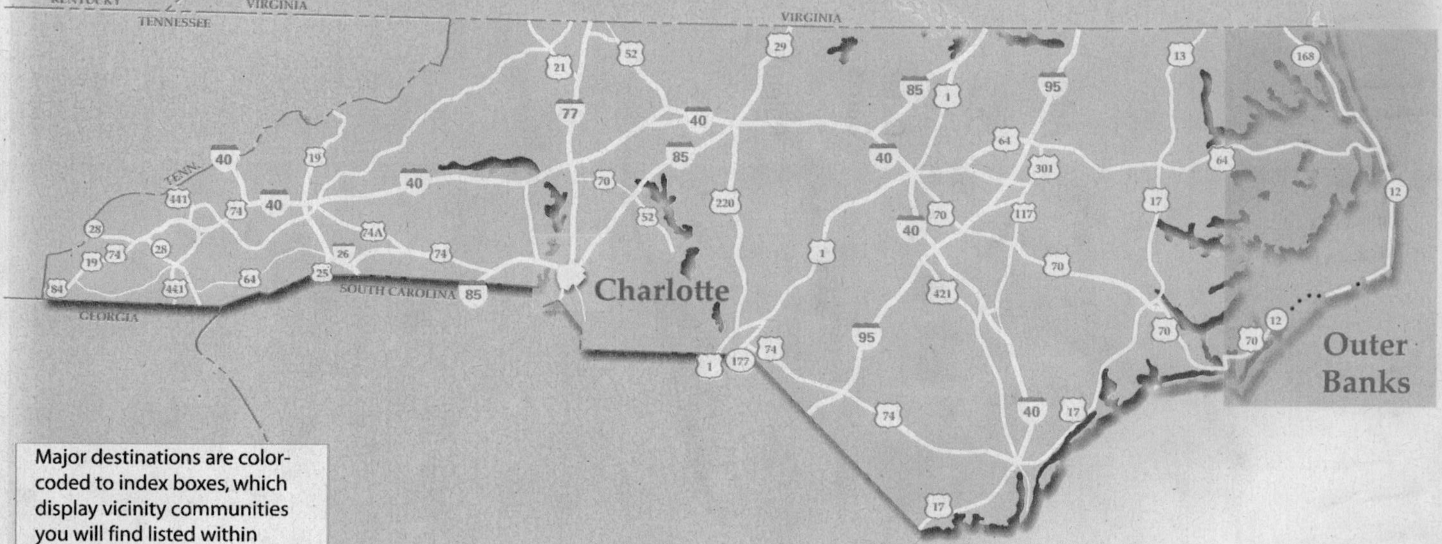

Charlotte

Outer Banks

Major destinations are color-coded to index boxes, which display vicinity communities you will find listed within that destination's section of the book.
Cities outside major destination vicinities are listed in alphabetical order throughout the book.
Use the Comprehensive City Index at the back of this book to find every city's listing locations.

The Charlotte Vicinity (see p. 660)

Outer Banks (see p. 769)

ABERDEEN pop. 3,400

WHERE TO STAY

HAMPTON INN & SUITES *Book great rates at AAA.com* **Phone:** (910)693-4330

AAA SAVE

Hotel
$159 All Year

Address: 200 Columbus Dr **Location:** Jct US 1, just n on US 15/501, then just s. **Facility:** Smoke free premises. 103 one-bedroom standard units, some with whirlpools. 4 stories, interior corridors. *Bath:* combo or shower only. **Parking:** on-site. **Terms:** 1-30 night minimum stay, cancellation fee imposed. **Amenities:** video games (fee), high-speed Internet, voice mail, irons, hair dryers. **Pool(s):** heated indoor. **Leisure Activities:** exercise room. **Guest Services:** valet and coin laundry, wireless Internet. **Business Services:** meeting rooms, business center. **Cards:** AX, CB, DC, DS, MC, VI. **Free Special Amenities: expanded continental breakfast and high-speed Internet.**

/ SOME UNITS

AAA Benefit:
Members save up to 10% everyday!

MOTEL 6-1234 *Book at AAA.com* **Phone:** (910)944-5633

Motel
$45-$51 4/4-11/30
$43-$49 12/1-4/3

Address: 1408 Sandhills Blvd **Location:** Jct US 15/501 N, just s on US 1. **Facility:** 80 one-bedroom standard units. 1 story, exterior corridors. *Bath:* combo or shower only. **Parking:** on-site. **Pool(s):** outdoor. **Cards:** AX, DC, DS, MC, VI.

/ SOME UNITS

SANDHILLS VALUE INN *Book at AAA.com* **Phone:** (910)944-2369

Motel
$49-$129 All Year

Address: 1500 Sandhills Blvd **Location:** Jct US 15/501 N, just s on US 1. **Facility:** 50 one-bedroom standard units. 1-2 stories (no elevator), exterior corridors. *Bath:* combo or shower only. **Parking:** on-site. **Amenities:** irons, hair dryers. *Some:* high-speed Internet. **Pool(s):** outdoor. **Guest Services:** valet and coin laundry, wireless Internet. **Business Services:** meeting rooms. **Cards:** AX, CB, DC, DS, MC, VI.

ASK / SOME UNITS FEE FEE VCR

WHERE TO DINE

THAI ORCHID **Phone:** 910/944-9299

Thai
$6-$17

Patrons savor traditional Thai cuisine in a casually intimate setting. The menu lists fried rice and noodle dishes, as well as vegetarian, chicken, beef, pork and seafood ingredients prepared in curries, basil, ginger and chili sauces. Chef's specialties include Bangkok duck and Thai grilled steak. Casual dress. **Bar:** Beer & wine. **Hours:** 11:30 am-2 & 5-9:30 pm, Mon & Sat from 5 pm. Closed: 11/26, 12/25. **Address:** 1404 Sandhills Blvd **Location:** Jct US 15/501 N, just s on US 1. **Parking:** on-site. **Cards:** AX, MC, VI.

ALBEMARLE pop. 15,680

WHERE TO STAY

EXECUTIVE INN *Book at AAA.com* **Phone:** 704/983-6990

Hotel
$65-$89 All Year

Address: 735 Hwy 24/27 Bypass **Location:** Jct US 52 S, 1.4 mi e. **Facility:** 80 one-bedroom standard units, some with efficiencies (no utensils). 2 stories (no elevator), exterior corridors. **Parking:** on-site. **Terms:** cancellation fee imposed. **Amenities:** voice mail, irons, hair dryers. *Some:* high-speed Internet. **Pool(s):** outdoor. **Guest Services:** valet laundry, wireless Internet. **Business Services:** meeting rooms, PC. **Cards:** AX, DC, DS, MC, VI.

ASK / SOME UNITS FEE

HAMPTON INN *Book great rates at AAA.com* **Phone:** (704)985-1111

Hotel
$85-$129 All Year

Address: 2300 US 52 N **Location:** Jct SR 73 W, 3.5 mi n on US 52 Bypass. **Facility:** 50 one-bedroom standard units, some with whirlpools. 2 stories (no elevator), interior corridors. *Bath:* combo or shower only. **Parking:** on-site. **Terms:** 1-30 night minimum stay, cancellation fee imposed. **Amenities:** voice mail, irons, hair dryers. **Pool(s):** outdoor. **Leisure Activities:** limited exercise equipment. **Guest Services:** valet and coin laundry, wireless Internet. **Business Services:** meeting rooms. **Cards:** AX, CB, DC, DS, MC, VI.

AAA Benefit:
Members save up to 10% everyday!

SLEEP INN & SUITES *Book at AAA.com* **Phone:** (704)983-2770

Hotel
$65-$130 All Year

Address: 621 Hwy 24/27 Bypass **Location:** Jct US 52 S, 1.1 mi e. **Facility:** 62 one-bedroom standard units, some with whirlpools. 3 stories, interior corridors. *Bath:* combo or shower only. **Parking:** on-site. **Terms:** cancellation fee imposed. **Amenities:** voice mail, irons, hair dryers. *Some:* high-speed Internet, dual phone lines. **Pool(s):** heated indoor. **Leisure Activities:** limited exercise equipment. **Guest Services:** valet and coin laundry, wireless Internet. **Business Services:** meeting rooms, PC. **Cards:** AX, DS, MC, VI.

ASK CALL / SOME UNITS

WHERE TO DINE

THE BOARDROOM BAR & BISTRO **Phone:** 704/982-1908

Northern Italian
$8-$35

In a restored 1908 building, this casual eatery presents a seasonally changing menu of dishes prepared from fresh ingredients. In addition to classic pasta dishes such as shrimp fra diavolo and linguine carbonara, entrees of veal, chicken and fresh fish appeal to diners. At lunch, offerings center on grilled pizza, salads and paninis. Casual dress. **Bar:** Full bar. **Hours:** 11:30 am-2 & 5:30-10 pm, Sat from 5:30 pm. Closed: 7/4, 11/26, 12/25, 12/26; also Sun & Mon. **Address:** 135 W Main St **Location:** Center. **Parking:** street. **Cards:** MC, VI.

HARMANCO'S **Phone:** 704/982-5414

Cajun
$5-$20

Cajun favorites are served in a casual atmosphere. Among choices are jambalaya, red beans and rice and gumbo, as well as steaks, chicken, seafood and sandwiches. Casual dress. **Bar:** Full bar. **Reservations:** accepted. **Hours:** 11 am-10 pm, Mon, Fri & Sat-11 pm. Closed: 11/26, 12/25. **Address:** 1407 E Main St **Location:** Jct US 52 S, 1.8 mi e on SR 24/27, 0.7 mi n. **Parking:** on-site. **Cards:** MC, VI.

ANDREWS pop. 1,602

WHERE TO STAY

HAWKESDENE HOUSE MOUNTAIN RETREAT **Phone:** (828)321-6027

Bed & Breakfast
$179-$209 All Year

Address: 381 Phillips Creek Rd **Location:** US 19 business route, 3.2 mi s on Cherry St, then 0.5 mi s. Located in a quiet area. **Facility:** English-country styling brings charm to the architecture of this property's guest rooms and cottages; the manicured grounds border a stream. Smoke free premises. 8 units. 5 one-bedroom standard units, some with whirlpools. 3 cottages. 1-2 stories (no elevator), interior/exterior corridors. *Bath:* combo or shower only. **Parking:** on-site. **Terms:** age restrictions may apply, 7 day cancellation notice, 14 day for cottages-fee imposed. **Amenities:** video library, hair dryers. *Some:* irons. **Leisure Activities:** hiking trails. **Guest Services:** complimentary laundry, wireless Internet. **Business Services:** fax. **Cards:** AX, DS, MC, VI.

ASK / SOME UNITS VCR

APEX pop. 20,212 (See map and index starting on p. 790)

WHERE TO STAY

COMFORT INN Book at AAA.com **Phone:** (919)387-4600

Hotel
$59-$129 All Year

Address: 1411 E Williams St **Location:** US 1, exit 95, just e on SR 55. **Facility:** 68 one-bedroom standard units, some with whirlpools. 2 stories (no elevator), interior corridors. *Bath:* combo or shower only. **Parking:** on-site. **Amenities:** irons, hair dryers. **Pool(s):** outdoor. **Guest Services:** valet and coin laundry, wireless Internet. **Business Services:** meeting rooms, PC. **Cards:** AX, CB, DC, DS, JC, MC, VI.

ASK CALL &M / SOME UNITS

HOLIDAY INN EXPRESS Book at AAA.com **Phone:** (919)387-3636 75

Hotel
$91 All Year

Address: 1006 Marco Dr **Location:** US 1, exit 95, just w on SR 55. **Facility:** 64 one-bedroom standard units, some with whirlpools. 4 stories, interior corridors. *Bath:* combo or shower only. **Parking:** on-site. **Amenities:** high-speed Internet, dual phone lines, voice mail, irons, hair dryers. **Pool(s):** outdoor. **Leisure Activities:** limited exercise equipment. **Guest Services:** valet laundry, wireless Internet. **Business Services:** meeting rooms, business center. **Cards:** AX, CB, DC, DS, JC, MC, VI.

ASK CALL &M / SOME UNITS

WHERE TO DINE

DANIEL'S RESTAURANT & CATERING **Phone:** 919/303-1006

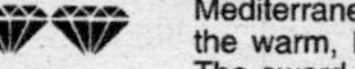

Italian
$7-$18

Mediterranean influences are detected in the homemade sauces, fresh bread and desserts. Contributing to the warm, European atmosphere are dining room walls adorned with murals, photographs and paintings. The award-winning wine list features more than 450 labels. Casual dress. **Bar:** Beer & wine. **Hours:** 11:30 am-10 pm, Sat from 5 pm, Sun & Mon 11:30 am-9 pm. Closed major holidays. **Address:** 1430 Hwy 55 **Location:** Jct US 64, just n. **Parking:** on-site. **Cards:** AX, DS, MC, VI.

THE PEAK CITY GRILL & BAR **Phone:** 919/303-8001 52

American
$8-$25

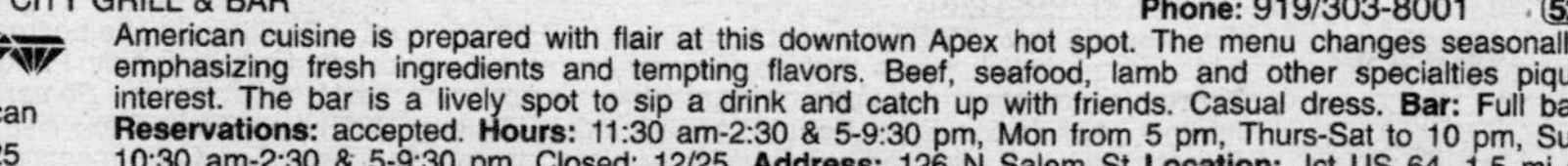

American cuisine is prepared with flair at this downtown Apex hot spot. The menu changes seasonally, emphasizing fresh ingredients and tempting flavors. Beef, seafood, lamb and other specialties pique interest. The bar is a lively spot to sip a drink and catch up with friends. Casual dress. **Bar:** Full bar. **Reservations:** accepted. **Hours:** 11:30 am-2:30 & 5-9:30 pm, Mon from 5 pm, Thurs-Sat to 10 pm, Sun 10:30 am-2:30 & 5-9:30 pm. Closed: 12/25. **Address:** 126 N Salem St **Location:** Jct US 64, 1.5 mi s. **Parking:** on-site. **Cards:** AX, DS, MC, VI.

ARCHDALE pop. 9,014

WHERE TO STAY

BEST WESTERN-HIGH POINT *Book great rates at AAA.com* **Phone:** (336)861-3000

SAVE

Hotel
$85-$199 All Year

Address: 1202 Liberty Rd **Location:** I-85, exit 113, just s on SR 62. **Facility:** 45 one-bedroom standard units, some with whirlpools. 3 stories, interior corridors. **Parking:** on-site. **Amenities:** voice mail, irons, hair dryers. **Pool(s):** outdoor. **Guest Services:** wireless Internet. **Business Services:** PC. **Cards:** AX, CB, DC, DS, MC, VI. **Free Special Amenities: expanded continental breakfast and high-speed Internet.**

/ SOME UNITS FEE

AAA Benefit:
Members save up to 20%, plus 10% bonus points with rewards program.

THE BOULDIN HOUSE B & B-HIGH POINT **Phone:** 336/431-4909

Historic Bed & Breakfast
Rates not provided

Address: 4332 Archdale Rd **Location:** I-85, exit 111, just n on US 311, 0.8 mi sw on Balfour Dr, then just w. **Facility:** Comfortable rooms in this four-square home feature fireplaces and some antiques, and common areas are attractive. Smoke free premises. 5 one-bedroom standard units. 2 stories (no elevator), interior corridors. *Bath:* combo or shower only. **Parking:** on-site. **Terms:** check-in 5 pm, age restrictions may apply. **Amenities:** video library, irons, hair dryers. **Guest Services:** wireless Internet.

/ SOME UNITS VCR

COMFORT INN *Book great rates at AAA.com* **Phone:** (336)434-4797

SAVE

Hotel
$175 All Year

Address: 10123 N Main St **Location:** I-85, exit 111, just n on US 311, then just sw on Balfour Dr. **Facility:** 74 one-bedroom standard units, some with whirlpools. 2 stories (no elevator), interior corridors. *Bath:* combo or shower only. **Parking:** on-site. **Amenities:** irons, hair dryers. **Pool(s):** outdoor. **Leisure Activities:** exercise room. **Guest Services:** valet and coin laundry, wireless Internet. **Business Services:** meeting rooms, PC. **Cards:** AX, CB, DC, DS, JC, MC, VI. **Free Special Amenities: expanded continental breakfast and high-speed Internet.**

CALL / SOME UNITS FEE

COUNTRY INN & SUITES **Phone:** 336/861-2233

fyi

Hotel
$90-$160 All Year

Too new to rate, opening scheduled for October 2008. **Address:** 10151 N Main St **Location:** I-85, exit 111. **Amenities:** 68 units, coffeemakers, microwaves, refrigerators, pool. **Cards:** DS, MC, VI.
(See color ad p 737)

FAIRFIELD INN & SUITES BY MARRIOTT *Book great rates at AAA.com* **Phone:** (336)434-0055

SAVE

Hotel
$98-$106 All Year

Address: 10141 N Main St **Location:** I-85, exit 111, just n on US 311. **Facility:** Smoke free premises. 74 one-bedroom standard units. 3 stories, interior corridors. *Bath:* combo or shower only. **Parking:** on-site. **Terms:** cancellation fee imposed. **Amenities:** high-speed Internet, dual phone lines, voice mail, irons, hair dryers. *Some:* CD players. **Pool(s):** heated indoor. **Leisure Activities:** whirlpool, exercise room. **Guest Services:** valet and coin laundry, wireless Internet. **Business Services:** meeting rooms, PC. **Cards:** AX, CB, DC, DS, JC, MC, VI.

AAA Benefit:
Members save a minimum 5% off the best available rate.

HAMPTON INN-HIGH POINT *Book great rates at AAA.com* **Phone:** (336)434-5200

Hotel
$79-$109 All Year

Address: 10066 N Main St **Location:** I-85, exit 111, just n on US 311. **Facility:** 104 one-bedroom standard units. 4 stories, interior corridors. *Bath:* combo or shower only. **Parking:** on-site. **Amenities:** video games (fee), dual phone lines, voice mail, irons, hair dryers. **Pool(s):** outdoor. **Guest Services:** valet laundry, wireless Internet. **Business Services:** meeting rooms, PC. **Cards:** AX, CB, DC, DS, JC, MC, VI.

/ SOME UNITS FEE

AAA Benefit:
Members save up to 10% everyday!

HOLIDAY INN EXPRESS HOTEL & SUITES *Book at AAA.com* **Phone:** (336)861-3310

Hotel
$93-$97 All Year

Address: 10050 N Main St **Location:** I-85, exit 111, just n on US 311. **Facility:** 71 one-bedroom standard units. 3 stories, interior corridors. *Bath:* combo or shower only. **Parking:** on-site. **Terms:** 3 day cancellation notice. **Amenities:** high-speed Internet, dual phone lines, voice mail, irons, hair dryers. **Pool(s):** outdoor. **Guest Services:** valet laundry, wireless Internet. **Business Services:** PC. **Cards:** AX, CB, DC, DS, JC, MC, VI.

ASK / SOME UNITS FEE

INNKEEPER HIGH POINT *Book at AAA.com* **Phone:** (336)434-5151

Motel
$55 All Year

Address: 10002 S Main St **Location:** I-85, exit 111, just s on US 311. **Facility:** 117 one-bedroom standard units, some with whirlpools. 2-3 stories, interior/exterior corridors. **Parking:** on-site. **Terms:** 3 day cancellation notice. **Amenities:** *Some:* hair dryers. **Pool(s):** outdoor. **Guest Services:** wireless Internet. **Business Services:** PC. **Cards:** AX, CB, DC, DS, JC, MC, VI.

ASK / SOME UNITS FEE

WHERE TO DINE

PIONEER FAMILY RESTAURANT **Phone:** 336/861-6247

American
$5-$14

Classic home-cooking is served daily on the lunch and dinner buffets. Featured are items like char-grilled steaks, chicken, fried seafood and burgers. Casual dress. **Hours:** 11 am-9 pm. Closed: 7/4, 12/24, 12/25. **Address:** 10914 N Main St **Location:** I-85, exit 111, 1 mi n on US 311. **Parking:** on-site. **Cards:** AX, DS, MC, VI.

ARDEN (See map and index starting on p. 576)

WHERE TO STAY

QUALITY INN & SUITES BILTMORE SOUTH *Book at AAA.com* **Phone:** (828)684-6688 57

Hotel
$85-$179 4/1-11/30
$70-$109 12/1-3/31

Address: 1 Skyline Inn Dr **Location:** I-26, exit 37. **Facility:** 107 units. 97 one-bedroom standard units. 10 one-bedroom suites. 4 stories, interior corridors. *Bath:* combo or shower only. **Parking:** on-site. **Amenities:** voice mail, irons, hair dryers. **Pool(s):** heated indoor. **Leisure Activities:** whirlpool, limited exercise equipment. **Guest Services:** valet laundry, wireless Internet. **Business Services:** meeting rooms, PC, fax (fee). **Cards:** CB, DC, JC, MC, VI.

ASK / SOME UNITS FEE

WHERE TO DINE

ASIAN GRILL **Phone:** 828/277-1558 43

Chinese
$6-$22

Sushi lovers should be on alert. Here, they can sample fresh, masterfully carved fish steaks beautifully adorned with garnishes and served in special bowls or on special plates, one for each fish type. Pacific Rim cuisine is done well, with a large selection of Chinese, Thai, Polynesian and Vietnamese dishes. There is plenty of seating in comfy booths. Casual dress. **Bar:** Full bar. **Reservations:** not accepted. **Hours:** 11 am-10 pm, Fri & Sat-10:30 pm. Closed: 11/26. **Address:** 2635 Hendersonville Rd **Location:** I-40, exit 50 (US 25), 4.5 mi s. **Parking:** on-site. **Cards:** AX, DS, MC, VI.

THE BLACK FOREST RESTAURANT **Phone:** 828/687-7980 41

German
$13-$24

The menu features a good variety of steaks, Northern Italian and German seafood dishes and beef, pork and poultry entrees. Preparation is simple but thoughtful, and the ambience is relaxed and casual. The friendly staff provides attentive service. Casual dress. **Bar:** Full bar. **Reservations:** suggested. **Hours:** 4 pm-10 pm; to 9 pm in winter. Closed major holidays. **Address:** 2155 Hendersonville Rd **Location:** I-26, exit 40, 1.8 mi e on SR 146, then 0.3 mi s on US 25. **Parking:** on-site. **Cards:** AX, MC, VI.

POMODOROS GREEK & ITALIAN CAFE **Phone:** 828/687-3828 40

Greek
$7-$24

Served in a warm, contemporary dining room, Greek and Italian dishes are prepared in-house with fresh ingredients. Some innovative touches punctuate traditional preparations of pasta and other entrees. Dressy casual. **Bar:** Full bar. **Reservations:** suggested. **Hours:** 11 am-10 pm, Sun 10 am-9:30 pm. Closed: 11/26, 12/25. **Address:** 75 Long Shoals Rd **Location:** I-26, exit 37, 2 mi e. **Parking:** on-site. **Cards:** AX, MC, VI.

CALL

SAGEBRUSH STEAKHOUSE **Phone:** 828/684-5049

American
$5-$19

Born from the spirit of Texas cattle drives, the restaurant presents a menu of hearty steaks, prime rib, chicken, seafood and baby back ribs. Yummy desserts merit a splurge. Guests can call ahead to facilitate seating. Casual dress. **Bar:** Full bar. **Hours:** 11 am-10 pm, Fri & Sat-11 pm. Closed: 12/25. **Address:** 2250 Hendersonville Rd **Location:** Jct US 25/25A, 1.1 mi n on US 25. **Parking:** on-site. **Cards:** AX, DC, DS, MC, VI.

CALL

TIJUANA JUNCTION MEXICAN RESTAURANT **Phone:** 828/684-6013 42

Mexican
$5-$9

Traditional Mexican favorites make up the menu. Informal dining rooms are suited for a casual experience. Casual dress. **Bar:** Full bar. **Hours:** 11 am-10 pm, Fri & Sat-11 pm, Sun noon-9 pm. Closed: 11/26, 12/25. **Address:** 2424 Hendersonville Rd **Location:** I-26, exit 40, 1.8 mi e. **Parking:** on-site. **Cards:** AX, DS, MC, VI.

ASHEBORO pop. 21,672

WHERE TO STAY

HAMPTON INN Book great rates at AAA.com **Phone:** (336)625-9000

Hotel
$71-$105 All Year

Address: 1137 E Dixie Dr **Location:** Jct SR 42, 0.4 mi w on US 64. **Facility:** 109 units. 102 one-bedroom standard units, some with whirlpools. 7 one-bedroom suites, some with whirlpools. 3 stories, interior corridors. *Bath:* combo or shower only. **Parking:** on-site. **Terms:** 1-30 night minimum stay, cancellation fee imposed. **Amenities:** dual phone lines, voice mail, irons, hair dryers. **Pool(s):** outdoor, heated indoor. **Leisure Activities:** sauna, whirlpool, exercise room. *Fee:* golf and tennis privileges. **Guest Services:** valet and coin laundry, wireless Internet. **Business Services:** meeting rooms, business center. **Cards:** AX, DC, DS, MC, VI.

CALL / SOME UNITS

AAA Benefit: Members save up to 10% everyday!

HOLIDAY INN EXPRESS HOTEL & SUITES Book at AAA.com **Phone:** 336/636-5222

Hotel
Rates not provided

Address: 1113 E Dixie Dr **Location:** Jct SR 42, 0.5 mi w on US 64. **Facility:** 64 one-bedroom standard units, some with whirlpools. 3 stories, interior corridors. *Bath:* combo or shower only. **Parking:** on-site. **Amenities:** dual phone lines, voice mail, safes, irons, hair dryers. **Pool(s):** outdoor. **Leisure Activities:** exercise room. **Guest Services:** valet and coin laundry, wireless Internet. **Business Services:** meeting rooms, PC.

CALL / SOME UNITS

QUALITY INN **Phone:** (336)626-3680

Hotel
$75-$130 All Year

Address: 242 Lakecrest Rd **Location:** US 64, just nw on SR 42. Located behind Randolph Mall. **Facility:** 42 one-bedroom standard units, some with whirlpools. 2 stories (no elevator), exterior corridors. **Parking:** on-site. **Amenities:** irons, hair dryers. **Pool(s):** outdoor. **Leisure Activities:** exercise room. **Guest Services:** valet laundry, wireless Internet. **Business Services:** PC. **Cards:** AX, CB, DC, DS, MC, VI. **Free Special Amenities: continental breakfast and high-speed Internet.**

/ SOME UNITS FEE

WHERE TO DINE

BAMBOO GARDEN **Phone:** 336/629-0203

Chinese
$5-$16

Daily lunch and dinner buffets and reasonable prices attract diners seeking traditional Chinese fare, such as sweet and sour chicken and vegetable lo mein. Casual dress. **Hours:** 11 am-9:30 pm. Closed: 11/26, 12/25. **Address:** 801 W Dixie Dr **Location:** Jct US 220, just e on US 64. **Parking:** on-site. **Cards:** MC, VI.

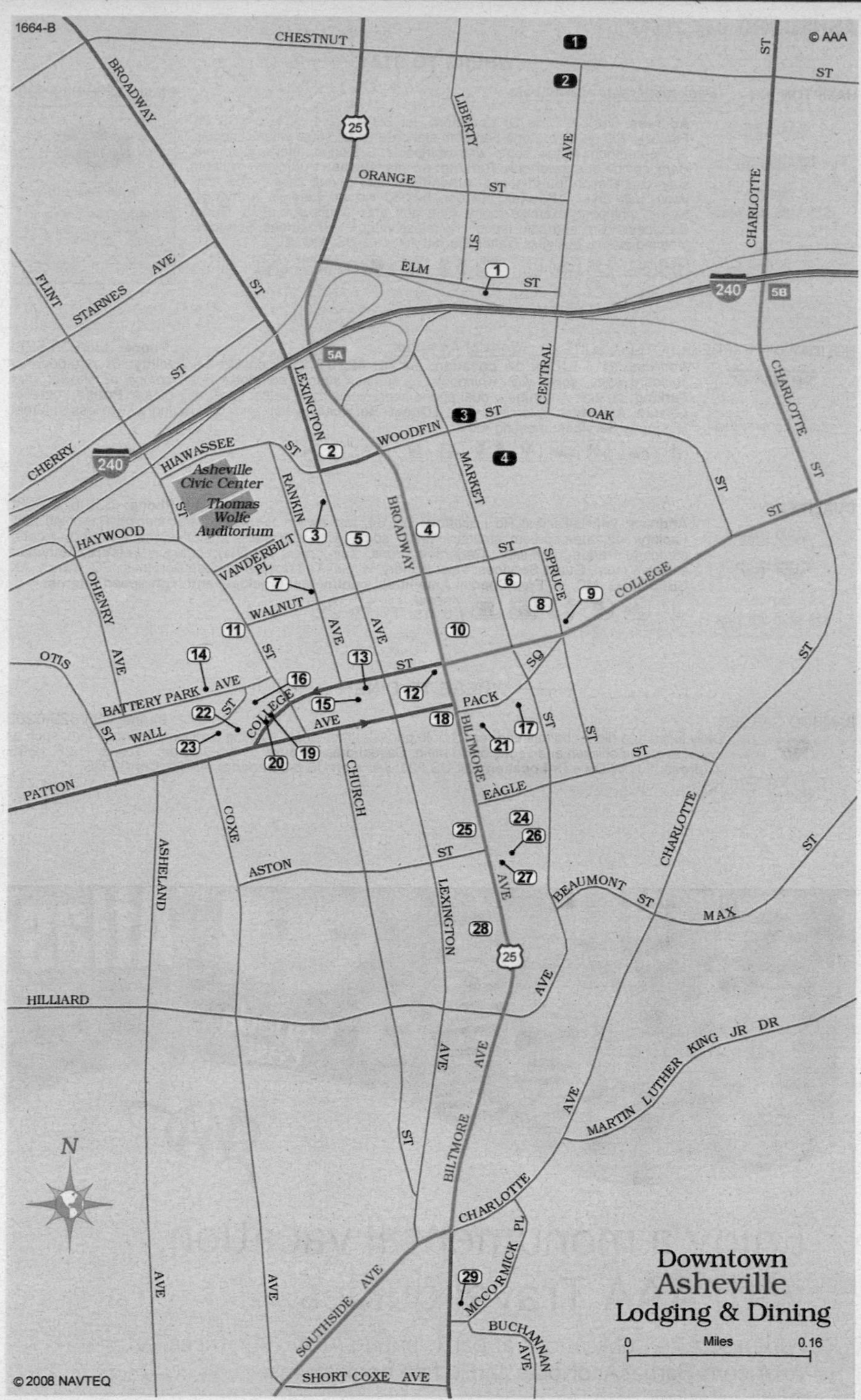
1664-B
© AAA
CHESTNUT
BROADWAY
LIBERTY
ORANGE
ST
ELM
CHARLOTTE
FLINT
STARNES
AVE
CHERRY
HIAWASSEE
Asheville Civic Center
Thomas Wolfe Auditorium
LEXINGTON
WOODFIN
CENTRAL
OAK
MARKET
RANKIN
HAYWOOD
VANDERBILT PL
OHENRY
WALNUT
SPRUCE
COLLEGE
OTIS
BATTERY PARK
WALL
PATTON
PACK SQ
BILTMORE
CHURCH
EAGLE
COXE
ASTON
ASHELAND
BEAUMONT
MAX
HILLIARD
MARTIN LUTHER KING JR DR
CHARLOTTE
MCCORMICK PL
SOUTHSIDE AVE
BUCHANNAN AVE
SHORT COXE AVE
© 2008 NAVTEQ
Downtown Asheville Lodging & Dining
0 Miles 0.16

Downtown Asheville

This index helps you "spot" where approved lodgings and restaurants are located on the corresponding detailed maps. Lodging daily rate range is for comparison only and show the property's high season. Restaurant rate range is a combination of lunch and/or dinner. Turn to the listing page for more detailed rate information and consult display ads for special promotions.

DOWNTOWN ASHEVILLE

Map Page	OA	Lodgings	Diamond Rated	High Season	Page
1 / p. 574	AAA	**Chestnut Street Inn**	◆◆◆	$129-$249 SAVE	580
2 / p. 574		1889 WhiteGate Inn & Cottage	◆◆◆	$169-$369	580
3 / p. 574	AAA	**Four Points by Sheraton Asheville Downtown**	◆◆◆	Rates not provided SAVE	580
4 / p. 574		Renaissance Asheville Hotel	◆◆◆	$153-$195	580

Map Page	OA	Restaurants	Diamond Rated	Cuisine	Meal Range	Page
1 / p. 574		La Caterina Trattoria	◆◆◆	Italian	$11-$24	581
2 / p. 574		Rosetta's Kitchen	◆	Natural/Organic	$4-$9	582
3 / p. 574		Heiwa Shokudo	◆◆	Japanese	$5-$16	581
4 / p. 574		Mellow Mushroom	◆◆	Pizza	$5-$12	582
5 / p. 574		Mela	◆◆	Indian	$2-$15	582
6 / p. 574		Magnolia's Raw Bar & Grille	◆◆	American	$10-$25	581
7 / p. 574		Zambra	◆◆◆	Spanish	$7-$14	583
8 / p. 574		Vicenzo's	◆◆◆	Northern Italian	$10-$32	583
9 / p. 574		Fiore's Cottonwood Ristorante Toscana	◆◆	Italian	$7-$20	581
10 / p. 574		Sushi-Thai	◆◆	American	$8-$22	582
11 / p. 574		Bier Garden	◆◆	American	$6-$15	580
12 / p. 574		Wasabi Japanese Restaurant	◆◆	Japanese	$7-$25	583
13 / p. 574		Table	◆◆◆	American	$8-$34	582
14 / p. 574		True Confections	◆	Breads/Pastries	$3-$8	582
15 / p. 574		The Lobster Trap	◆◆	Seafood	$10-$47	581
16 / p. 574		Early Girl Eatery	◆◆	American	$5-$14	581
17 / p. 574		Bistro 1896	◆◆◆	American	$7-$28	581
18 / p. 574		Salsa's	◆◆	Caribbean	$6-$17	582
19 / p. 574		Tupelo Honey Cafe	◆◆	New Southern	$5-$17	582
20 / p. 574		The Market Place	◆◆◆	New American	$19-$31	582
21 / p. 574		The New French Bar Courtyard Cafe	◆◆	French	$6-$10	582
22 / p. 574		Asheville Barbecue Company	◆	Barbecue	$6-$15	580
23 / p. 574		Laughing Seed Cafe	◆◆	Vegetarian	$7-$16	581
24 / p. 574		Limones	◆◆	Mexican	$15-$28	581
25 / p. 574		Doc Chey's Noodle House	◆◆	Asian	$5-$8	581
26 / p. 574		Ed Boudreaux's Bayou Bar-B-Que	◆◆	Barbecue	$4-$17	581
27 / p. 574		Barley's Taproom & Pizzaria	◆	American	$5-$10	580
28 / p. 574		Mamacitas Mexican Grill	◆	Mexican	$3-$8	582
29 / p. 574		Athenian Bistro	◆	Mediterranean	$4-$6	580

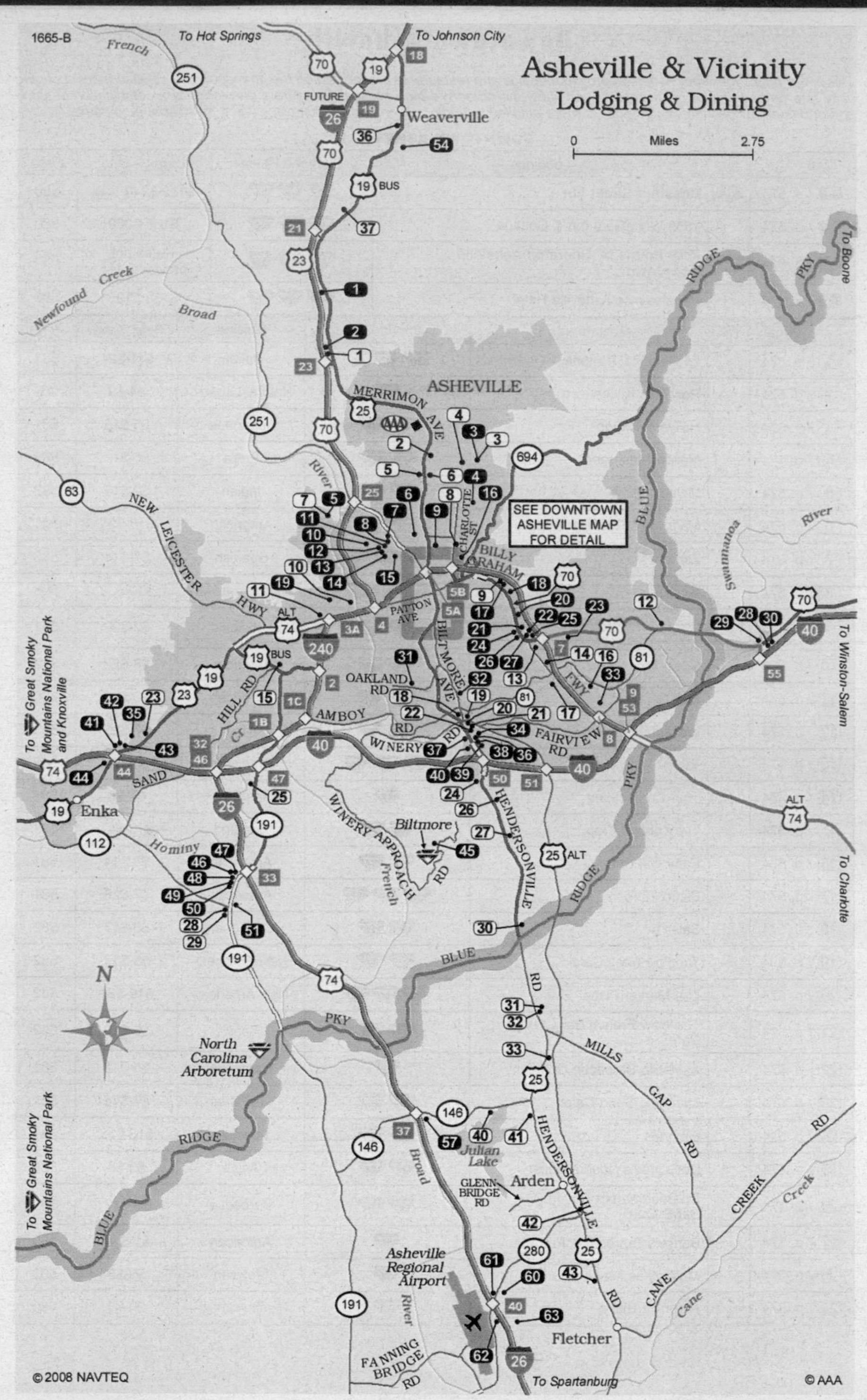
1665-B
Asheville & Vicinity
Lodging & Dining
0 Miles 2.75
To Hot Springs
To Johnson City
Weaverville
ASHEVILLE
SEE DOWNTOWN ASHEVILLE MAP FOR DETAIL
To Boone
To Winston-Salem
To Charlotte
To Great Smoky Mountains National Park and Knoxville
To Great Smoky Mountains National Park
Enka
Biltmore
North Carolina Arboretum
Julian Lake
Arden
Asheville Regional Airport
Fletcher
To Spartanburg
MERRIMON AVE
PATTON AVE
BILTMORE AVE
CHARLOTTE ST
BILLY GRAHAM
NEW LEICESTER HWY
HILL RD
SAND
AMBOY RD
OAKLAND RD
WINERY RD
WINERY APPROACH RD
FAIRVIEW RD
HENDERSONVILLE RD
BLUE RIDGE PKY
MILLS GAP RD
CANE CREEK RD
GLENN BRIDGE RD
FANNING BRIDGE RD
French Broad River
Newfound Creek
Swannanoa River
Hominy
Cane Creek
© 2008 NAVTEQ
© AAA

Airport Accommodations

Map Page	OA	ASHEVILLE REGIONAL	Diamond Rated	High Season	Page
57 / p. 576		Quality Inn & Suites Biltmore South, 1 mi from terminal	◆◆	$85-$179	672
62 / p. 576		Fairfield Inn by Marriott, across the road	◆◆	$87-$128	705
60 / p. 576	AAA	**Hampton Inn & Suites Asheville, 0.3 mi e on Airport Rd**	◆◆◆	$99-$189 SAVE	706
61 / p. 576		Holiday Inn Asheville-Airport, 0.3 mi e	◆◆◆	$89-$169	706

Asheville and Vicinity

This index helps you "spot" where approved lodgings and restaurants are located on the corresponding detailed maps. Lodging daily rate range is for comparison only and show the property's high season. Restaurant rate range is a combination of lunch and/or dinner. Turn to the listing page for more detailed rate information and consult display ads for special promotions.

ASHEVILLE

Map Page	OA	Lodgings	Diamond Rated	High Season	Page
1 / p. 576	AAA	**The Log Cabin Motor Court**	◆	$55-$110 SAVE	593
2 / p. 576		Days Inn North	◆◆	$59-$159	588
3 / p. 576	AAA	**The Grove Park Inn Resort & Spa - see color ad p 589**	◆◆◆◆	$300-$415 SAVE	589
4 / p. 576	AAA	**Albemarle Inn**	◆◆◆◆	$125-$380 SAVE	583
5 / p. 576	AAA	**Richmond Hill Inn**	◆◆◆◆	$205-$615 SAVE	595
6 / p. 576		Hill House Bed & Breakfast Inn	◆◆◆	$125-$270	590
7 / p. 576	AAA	**Applewood Manor Inn Bed & Breakfast**	◆◆◆	$160-$225 SAVE	584
8 / p. 576	AAA	**Abbington Green Bed & Breakfast Inn**	◆◆◆	$150-$450 SAVE	583
9 / p. 576	AAA	**Beaufort House Inn**	◆◆◆	Rates not provided SAVE	584
10 / p. 576	AAA	**The Wright Inn & Carriage House**	◆◆◆	$105-$360 SAVE	596
11 / p. 576		At Cumberland Falls Bed & Breakfast Inn	◆◆◆	$125-$259	584
12 / p. 576		1900 Inn on Montford	◆◆◆	$145-$625	583
13 / p. 576	AAA	**Black Walnut B&B Inn**	◆◆◆	$145-$295 SAVE	586
14 / p. 576	AAA	**The Lion & the Rose Bed & Breakfast**	◆◆◆	$165-$225 SAVE	593
15 / p. 576		Carolina Bed & Breakfast	◆◆	$135-$225	586
16 / p. 576		Princess Anne Hotel	◆◆◆	$119-$299	594
17 / p. 576	AAA	**Holiday Inn Hotel & Suites - see color ad p 585**	◆◆◆	$100-$400 SAVE	592
18 / p. 576	AAA	**Homewood Suites by Hilton - see color ad p 593**	◆◆◆	$119-$249 SAVE	592
19 / p. 576		Crowne Plaza Resort	◆◆◆	$119-$179	587
20 / p. 576		Extended StayAmerica	◆◆	$90-$120	589
21 / p. 576	AAA	**Econo Lodge Biltmore**	◆◆	$44-$126 SAVE	588
22 / p. 576		SpringHill Suites by Marriott	◆◆◆	$107-$153	596
23 / p. 576	AAA	**Best Western of Asheville Biltmore East - see color ad p 584**	◆◆	$49-$199 SAVE	585
24 / p. 576	AAA	**Days Inn-Asheville Mall - see color ad p 587**	◆◆	$49-$249 SAVE	587
25 / p. 576		Courtyard by Marriott	◆◆◆	$112-$153	587
26 / p. 576	AAA	**Country Inn & Suites**	◆◆◆	$109-$250 SAVE	586
27 / p. 576	AAA	**Hampton Inn Tunnel Road - see color ad p 591**	◆◆◆	$99-$189 SAVE	590

ASHEVILLE (cont'd)

Map Page	OA	Lodgings (cont'd)	Diamond Rated	High Season	Page
28 / p. 576		Holiday Inn-Biltmore East at the Blue Ridge Parkway	◆◆◆	$89-$169	590
29 / p. 576		Quality Inn & Suites	◆◆	$55-$199	594
30 / p. 576	AAA	**Days Inn-Biltmore East** - see color ad p 588	◆◆	$55-$199 SAVE	588
31 / p. 576	AAA	**North Lodge on Oakland**	◆◆◆	$120-$180 SAVE	593
32 / p. 576	AAA	**1891 Cedar Crest Inn**	◆◆◆	$145-$300 SAVE	583
33 / p. 576	AAA	**Ramada** - see color ad p 594	◆◆	$84-$129 SAVE	594
34 / p. 576	AAA	**Biltmore Village Inn**	◆◆◆	$220-$325 SAVE	586
35 / p. 576	AAA	**Sleep Inn Biltmore West** - see color ad p 595	◆◆	$49-$189 SAVE	595
36 / p. 576	AAA	**Howard Johnson Inn Biltmore**	◆	$90-$170 SAVE	592
37 / p. 576		Doubletree Biltmore Hotel	◆◆◆	$89-$229	588
38 / p. 576	AAA	**Baymont Inn-Biltmore** - see color ad p 585	◆◆	$79-$189 SAVE	584
39 / p. 576	AAA	**Holiday Inn Express-Biltmore** - see color ad p 585	◆◆	$99-$169 SAVE	590
40 / p. 576		Sleep Inn Biltmore	◆◆	$89-$180	595
41 / p. 576		Comfort Inn-West	◆◆	$59-$169	586
42 / p. 576	AAA	**Red Roof Inn-West**	◆	$50-$90 SAVE	594
43 / p. 576		Super 8 Motel Central	◆	Rates not provided	596
44 / p. 576		Holiday Inn Biltmore West	◆◆◆	$89-$199	590
45 / p. 576	AAA	**Inn on Biltmore Estate** - see color ad p 108	◆◆◆◆	$299-$549 SAVE	592
46 / p. 576	AAA	**Hampton Inn - Biltmore Square** - see color ad p 591	◆◆◆	$99-$189 SAVE	590
47 / p. 576	AAA	**Fairfield Inn & Suites by Marriott Biltmore Square Mall**	◆◆◆	$118-$127 SAVE	589
48 / p. 576	AAA	**Holiday Inn Express Hotel & Suites**	◆◆◆	$115-$189 SAVE	592
49 / p. 576		Super 8 Motel at Biltmore Square	◆◆	$59-$159	596
50 / p. 576	AAA	**Country Inn & Suites by Carlson**	◆◆◆	$104-$175 SAVE	587
51 / p. 576		Comfort Suites-Biltmore Square Mall	◆◆◆	$69-$189	586

Map Page	OA	Restaurants	Diamond Rated	Cuisine	Meal Range	Page
1 / p. 576		Bellagio Bistro	◆◆	Mediterranean	$5-$8	597
2 / p. 576		Usual Suspects	◆◆	International	$7-$18	600
3 / p. 576		Horizons	◆◆◆◆	American	$75-$125	598
4 / p. 576		Grovewood Cafe	◆◆◆	Continental	$7-$35	598
5 / p. 576		Urban Burrito	◆	Mexican	$5-$7	599
6 / p. 576		Savoy Restaurant & Martini Bar	◆◆◆	Continental	$8-$43	599
7 / p. 576	AAA	**Gabrielle's at Richmond Hill**	◆◆◆◆	Regional American	$60-$80	598
8 / p. 576		Charlotte Street Grill & Pub	◆◆	Steak	$6-$25	597
9 / p. 576		Fiddlin' Pig Blue Grass & Barbecue	◆◆	Southern American	$6-$20	597
10 / p. 576		Red Orchid Thai Restaurant	◆◆◆	Thai	$6-$18	599
11 / p. 576		Green Tea Japanese Kitchen & Sushi Bar	◆◆	Japanese	$4-$18	598
12 / p. 576		Pomodoros Greek & Italian Cafe	◆◆	Greek	$7-$24	599
13 / p. 576		China Palace	◆◆	Chinese	$6-$14	597

Map Page	OA	Restaurants (cont'd)	Diamond Rated	Cuisine	Meal Range	Page
14 / p. 576		India Garden Authentic Indian Cuisine	♦♦	Indian	$6-$17	598
15 / p. 576		Westville Pub	♦	American	$5-$10	600
16 / p. 576		Spirits on the River Native American Restaurant	♦♦	Specialty	$7-$18	599
17 / p. 576		Bonefish Grill	♦♦♦	Seafood	$13-$20	597
18 / p. 576		Asaka Japanese Restaurant	♦	Japanese	$5-$11	596
19 / p. 576		Fig	♦♦♦	American	$8-$30	597
20 / p. 576		Rezaz Mediterranean Cuisine	♦♦♦	Mediterranean	$4-$22	599
21 / p. 576		La Paz Restaurant	♦♦	Mexican	$5-$15	598
22 / p. 576		Chelsea's Cafe & Tea Room	♦♦	English	$10-$12	597
23 / p. 576		Asiana Grand Buffet	♦	Chinese	$6-$12	596
24 / p. 576		Apollo Flame Bistro	♦♦	Greek	$5-$12	596
25 / p. 576		The Moose Cafe	♦	Southern	$5-$10	599
26 / p. 576		Province 620	♦♦	American	$7-$22	599
27 / p. 576		Amici Trattoria	♦♦♦	Italian	$7-$23	596
28 / p. 576		Stone Ridge Tavern	♦♦	American	$6-$24	599
29 / p. 576		Apollo Flame Bistro	♦♦	Greek	$6-$15	596
30 / p. 576		Flat Rock Grille	♦♦	Seafood	$9-$25	597
31 / p. 576		El Charro	♦♦	Mexican	$5-$15	597
32 / p. 576		Frankie Bones Restaurant & Lounge	♦♦♦	Italian	$6-$25	598
33 / p. 576		LaCarreta	♦♦	Mexican	$5-$15	598

WEAVERVILLE

Map Page	OA	Lodging	Diamond Rated	High Season	Page
54 / p. 576		Inn on Main Street	♦♦♦	$125-$165	831

Map Page	OA	Restaurants	Diamond Rated	Cuisine	Meal Range	Page
36 / p. 576		Sunnyside Cafe	♦♦	American	$6-$10	831
37 / p. 576		Stoney Knob Cafe	♦♦	American	$7-$28	831

ARDEN

Map Page	OA	Lodging	Diamond Rated	High Season	Page
57 / p. 576		Quality Inn & Suites Biltmore South	♦♦	$85-$179	572

Map Page	OA	Restaurants	Diamond Rated	Cuisine	Meal Range	Page
40 / p. 576		Pomodoros Greek & Italian Cafe	♦♦	Greek	$7-$24	572
41 / p. 576		The Black Forest Restaurant	♦♦♦	German	$13-$24	572
42 / p. 576		Tijuana Junction Mexican Restaurant	♦	Mexican	$5-$9	572
43 / p. 576		Asian Grill	♦♦	Chinese	$6-$22	572

FLETCHER

Map Page	OA	Lodgings	Diamond Rated	High Season	Page
60 / p. 576	AAA	**Hampton Inn & Suites Asheville - see color ad p 591**	♦♦♦	$99-$189 SAVE	706
61 / p. 576		Holiday Inn Asheville-Airport	♦♦♦	$89-$169	706
62 / p. 576		Fairfield Inn by Marriott	♦♦	$87-$128	705
63 / p. 576	AAA	**Econo Lodge Airport**	♦♦	Rates not provided SAVE	705

DOWNTOWN ASHEVILLE (See map and index starting on p. 574)

WHERE TO STAY

1889 WHITEGATE INN & COTTAGE — Phone: 828/253-2553 — 2

Bed & Breakfast
$169-$369 All Year

Address: 173 E Chestnut St **Location:** I-240, exit 5B (Charlotte St), just n, then just w; in historic district. Located in a residential area. **Facility:** A picturesque glass conservatory centers the impressive gardens at this 1899 home; accommodations include a cottage and new suite. Designated smoking area. 9 units. 7 one-bedroom standard units, some with whirlpools. 2 one-bedroom suites with whirlpools, some with kitchens. 3 stories (no elevator), interior/exterior corridors. *Bath:* combo or shower only. **Parking:** on-site. **Terms:** 2-3 night minimum stay - seasonal and/or weekends, 14 day cancellation notice-fee imposed. **Amenities:** video library, DVD players, CD players, irons, hair dryers. **Leisure Activities:** spa. **Guest Services:** wireless Internet. **Cards:** AX, MC, VI.

VCR / SOME UNITS FEE

CHESTNUT STREET INN — Phone: 828/285-0705 — 1

AAA SAVE

Bed & Breakfast
$129-$249 All Year

Address: 176 E Chestnut St **Location:** I-240, exit 5B (Charlotte St), just n, then just w. Located in historic district/residential area. **Facility:** Rooms are attractively decorated with period pieces and reproductions at this B&B dating from 1905; a cottage suite is available. Smoke free premises. 8 units. 7 one-bedroom standard units, some with whirlpools. 1 one-bedroom suite with whirlpool. 1-3 stories (no elevator), interior/exterior corridors. *Bath:* combo or shower only. **Parking:** on-site. **Terms:** office hours 10 am-10 pm, 2 night minimum stay - weekends, age restrictions may apply, 14 day cancellation notice-fee imposed. **Amenities:** hair dryers. *Some:* DVD players, irons. **Guest Services:** wireless Internet. **Cards:** AX, DS, MC, VI. **Free Special Amenities: full breakfast and early check-in/late check-out.**

/ SOME UNITS VCR

FOUR POINTS BY SHERATON ASHEVILLE DOWNTOWN — *Book great rates at AAA.com* — Phone: 828/253-1851 — 3

AAA SAVE

Hotel
Rates not provided

Address: 22 Woodfin St **Location:** I-240, exit 5A (Merrimon Ave). **Facility:** Smoke free premises. 150 one-bedroom standard units. 5 stories, interior corridors. *Bath:* combo or shower only. **Parking:** on-site. **Amenities:** voice mail, irons, hair dryers. **Pool(s):** heated outdoor. **Leisure Activities:** exercise room. **Guest Services:** valet laundry, wireless Internet. **Business Services:** meeting rooms, business center. **Free Special Amenities: newspaper.**

/ SOME UNITS

FOUR POINTS BY SHERATON
AAA Benefit:
Members get up to 15% off, plus Starwood Preferred Guest® bonuses.

RENAISSANCE ASHEVILLE HOTEL — *Book great rates at AAA.com* — Phone: (828)252-8211 — 4

Hotel
$153-$195 All Year

Address: 31 Woodfin St **Location:** I-240, exit 5A (Merrimon Ave). Located adjacent to Thomas Wolfe Memorial Home. **Facility:** Smoke free premises. 280 units. 276 one-bedroom standard units. 4 one-bedroom suites. 12 stories, interior corridors. *Bath:* combo or shower only. **Parking:** on-site. **Terms:** check-in 4 pm, cancellation fee imposed. **Amenities:** high-speed Internet (fee), dual phone lines, voice mail, honor bars, irons, hair dryers. **Pool(s):** heated indoor. **Leisure Activities:** whirlpool, exercise room. **Guest Services:** valet and coin laundry, wireless Internet. **Business Services:** conference facilities, business center. **Cards:** AX, CB, DC, DS, JC, MC, VI.

RENAISSANCE. HOTELS & RESORTS
AAA Benefit:
Members save a minimum 5% off the best available rate.

WHERE TO DINE

ASHEVILLE BARBECUE COMPANY — Phone: 828/232-0809 — 22

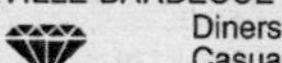

Barbecue
$6-$15

Diners make their way to the center of town to get to the casual spot, which serves no-frills barbecue. Casual dress. Entertainment. **Bar:** Full bar. **Hours:** 4 pm-2 am, Sat from noon. Closed: 11/26, 12/25. **Address:** 4 College St **Location:** East of federal building. **Parking:** street. **Cards:** MC, VI.

ATHENIAN BISTRO — Phone: 828/254-0477 — 29

Mediterranean
$4-$6

The eatery serves all of the typical Greek fare including gyros, Greek salads, hummus, tabbouleh and more in a friendly and casual setting. Casual dress. **Bar:** Beer & wine. **Hours:** 6 am-8 pm. Closed major holidays. **Address:** 224 Biltmore Ave **Location:** 0.5 mi s on US 25 from center. **Parking:** on-site. **Cards:** MC, VI.

BARLEY'S TAPROOM & PIZZARIA — Phone: 828/255-0504 — 27

American
$5-$10

The casual pizzeria also serves salads, sandwiches and wraps. This place prides itself on an extensive beer menu that appeals to connoisseurs. Casual dress. **Bar:** Beer & wine. **Hours:** 11:30 am-midnight, Fri & Sat-1 am, Sun noon-11 pm. Closed: 11/26, 12/25; also for dinner 12/24. **Address:** 42 Biltmore Ave **Location:** Between Eagle and Astor sts; just s of College St. **Parking:** street. **Cards:** AX, DS, MC, VI. **Historic**

BIER GARDEN — Phone: 828/285-0002 — 11

American
$6-$15

The eatery's name says it all. Pub standards, and the requisite beers to go with them, make up the offerings. Patrons nosh on nachos, wings, sandwiches, burgers and salads as they gaze at passers-by through open picture windows. Casual dress. **Bar:** Full bar. **Hours:** 11 am-midnight, Fri & Sat-1 am, Sun noon-midnight. Closed: 12/25. **Address:** 46 Haywood St **Location:** Just n of College and Haywood sts. **Parking:** street. **Cards:** AX, DC, DS, MC, VI.

(See map and index starting on p. 574)

BISTRO 1896 — **Phone:** 828/251-1300 (17)

American
$7-$28

Enjoy an array of pasta dishes, fresh seafood and innovatively prepared meats at this charming Bistro located near shopping and the theatre. This is a perfect place for al fresco dining during the warmer months. Dressy casual. **Bar:** Full bar. **Reservations:** suggested. **Hours:** 11:30 am-4 & 5-10 pm, Fri & Sat-10:30 pm, Sun 10:30 am-4 pm; Sunday brunch; seasonal hours vary. Closed: 11/26, 12/25. **Address:** 7 Pack Square **Location:** Center; in Pack Square. **Parking:** street. **Cards:** AX, DS, MC, VI.

DOC CHEY'S NOODLE HOUSE — **Phone:** 828/252-8220 (25)

Asian
$5-$8

The affordable noodle house dishes up large portions of fresh Pan-Asian cuisine. Guests might start with a dim sum selection then choose from an assortment of noodle bowls and rice plates. Most every dish is made with the choice of chicken, salmon, shrimp or vegetables. Casual dress. **Bar:** Beer & wine. **Hours:** 11:30 am-10 pm, Fri & Sat-11 pm. Closed major holidays. **Address:** 37 Biltmore Ave **Location:** I-40, exit 50, just s from Pack Square; center. **Parking:** street. **Cards:** AX, DS, MC, VI.

EARLY GIRL EATERY — **Phone:** 828/259-9292 (16)

American
$5-$14

This restaurant prides itself on its made-from-scratch food, using quality fresh produce and ingredients. Casual dress. **Bar:** Beer & wine. **Reservations:** not accepted. **Hours:** 7:30 am-3 pm, Tues-Thurs also 5 pm-9 pm, Fri & Sat 9 am-3 & 5-10 pm, Sun 9 am-3 pm; hours vary in winter. Closed: 7/4, 11/26, 12/25. **Address:** 8 Wall St **Location:** Just e of federal building. **Parking:** street. **Cards:** MC, VI.

ED BOUDREAUX'S BAYOU BAR-B-QUE — **Phone:** 828/296-0100 (26)

Barbecue
$4-$17

Cajun-style barbecue flavors kick up the taste in pork, beef and chicken dishes. A sauce bar with 14 in-house sauces lets diners find the heat that suits them best. The downtown spot also satisfies with an array of sandwiches, local brews and down-home entertainment. Casual dress. **Bar:** Full bar. **Hours:** 11:30 am-11 pm. Closed: 11/26, 12/25. **Address:** 48 Biltmore Ave **Location:** Just s of Pack Square. **Parking:** street. **Cards:** MC, VI.

FIORE'S COTTONWOOD RISTORANTE TOSCANA — **Phone:** 828/281-0710 (9)

Italian
$7-$20

In an unobtrusive storefront, the area favorite offers an intimate dining experience. Roomy private booths line an entire wall, and attractively presented plates offer great Italian food in portions large enough to share. The decor is old-timey, with lots of posters of the city's good old days. The atmosphere is charming, and service is friendly. Dressy casual. **Bar:** Full bar. **Reservations:** accepted. **Hours:** 11:30 am-3:30 & 4:30-9:30 pm, Fri & Sat-10 pm. Closed: 9/7, 12/25; also Sun. **Address:** 122 College St **Location:** I-240, exit 5B (Charlotte St), just s, then just w. **Parking:** street. **Cards:** AX, MC, VI.

HEIWA SHOKUDO — **Phone:** 828/254-7761 (3)

Japanese
$5-$16

Sushi with a vegetarian twist has been hard to find until now. The restaurant offers lots of tofu and vegetables with Japanese flair. Soba noodles, fresh fish and tempura round out the menu. Large bowls of soup, meals in themselves, complement plates of steaming vegetables, served with or without meat. Popular with the young college crowd, this place is just off the main square downtown. Casual dress. **Bar:** Beer & wine. **Hours:** 11:30 am-2:30 & 5:30-9:30 pm, Sat noon-3 & 5:30-9:30 pm. Closed major holidays; also Sun & Mon. **Address:** 87 N Lexington Ave **Location:** East of civic center; 0.5 mi n of intersection of Patton Ave; at intersection of Hiawasse St; center. **Parking:** on-site and street. **Cards:** AX, DS, MC, VI.

LA CATERINA TRATTORIA — **Phone:** 828/254-1148 (1)

Italian
$11-$24

Homemade mozzarella cheese is just one of the items that will never leave the seasonal menu, and for good reason. A family operation, the popular trattoria maintains a high standard of freshness and quality. Dining alfresco, which gives patrons the feel they are in Italy watching people in the square, is a highlight. Casual dress. **Bar:** Full bar. **Reservations:** suggested. **Hours:** 5 pm-10 pm. Closed major holidays. **Address:** 39 Elm St **Location:** I-240, exit 5A (Merrimon Ave); northeast corner of jct I-240 and US 25. **Parking:** on-site. **Cards:** AX, MC, VI.

LAUGHING SEED CAFE — **Phone:** 828/252-3445 (23)

Vegetarian
$7-$16

The cafe serves creative, vegetarian cuisine in a funky atmosphere. Quality is mixed into each dish. Casual dress. **Bar:** Full bar. **Hours:** 11:30 am-9 pm, Fri & Sat-10 pm, Sun 10 am-9 pm; Sunday brunch. Closed: 4/12, 11/26, 12/25; also Tues. **Address:** 40 Wall St **Location:** Just e of federal building. **Parking:** street. **Cards:** AX, DS, MC, VI.

LIMONES — **Phone:** 828/252-2327 (24)

Mexican
$15-$28

A cozy setting with an inspirational mix of Mexican and Californian cuisine, the restaurant has a frequently changing menu featuring seasonal, local and fresh ingredients; start with the fresh tuna ceviche and save plenty of room for the homemade flan. Casual dress. **Bar:** Full bar. **Reservations:** suggested. **Hours:** 5 pm-10 pm, Fri & Sat-11 pm, Sun 11 am-3 pm; call for holiday hours. **Address:** 13 Eagle St **Location:** Just s of Pack Square. **Parking:** street. **Cards:** MC, VI.

THE LOBSTER TRAP — **Phone:** 828/350-0505 (15)

Seafood
$10-$47

The casual eatery prepares not only fresh local mountain trout but also the fresh Maine lobster that reminds the owner of her roots. A native of Portland, Maine, she grew up working on the docks and now flies fresh lobster in every day. Casual dress. Entertainment. **Bar:** Full bar. **Hours:** 5 pm-11 pm. **Address:** 35 Patton Ave **Location:** Just w of Pack Square. **Parking:** street. **Cards:** AX, MC, VI.

MAGNOLIA'S RAW BAR & GRILLE — **Phone:** 828/251-5211 (6)

American
$10-$25

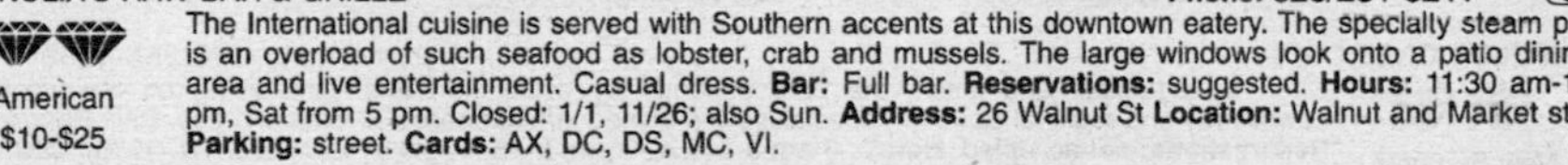

The International cuisine is served with Southern accents at this downtown eatery. The specialty steam pot is an overload of such seafood as lobster, crab and mussels. The large windows look onto a patio dining area and live entertainment. Casual dress. **Bar:** Full bar. **Reservations:** suggested. **Hours:** 11:30 am-10 pm, Sat from 5 pm. Closed: 1/1, 11/26; also Sun. **Address:** 26 Walnut St **Location:** Walnut and Market sts. **Parking:** street. **Cards:** AX, DC, DS, MC, VI.

(See map and index starting on p. 574)

MAMACITAS MEXICAN GRILL **Phone:** 828/255-8080 (28)

Mexican
$3-$8

The contemporary downtown Mexican taqueria specializes in hand-crafted tacos, burritos, salads and daily specials. Casual dress. **Bar:** Beer & wine. **Hours:** 11 am-10 pm. Closed major holidays. **Address:** 77A Biltmore Ave **Location:** Between Aston and Hilliard sts; just s of center. **Parking:** street. **Cards:** AX, MC, VI.

THE MARKET PLACE **Phone:** 828/252-4162 (20)

New American
$19-$31

Serving creative cuisine for more than 29 years, the stylish, high-ceiling restaurant and wine bar has an informal, comfortable atmosphere. Local ingredients—which include fresh fish, seafood, beef and seasonal produce—all excellently prepared and presented. Among favorites are Clemson blue cheese salad, local red trout and Atlantic grouper. Service is refined yet friendly. Bar 100 offers a lighter menu and premium cocktails. Dressy casual. **Bar:** Full bar. **Reservations:** suggested. **Hours:** 5:30 pm-9 pm. Closed major holidays; also Mon 1/1-3/31 & Sun 11/1-9/30. **Address:** 20 Wall St **Location:** Just e of federal building. **Parking:** street. **Cards:** AX, CB, DC, DS, JC, MC, VI.

MELA **Phone:** 828/225-8880 (5)

Indian
$2-$15

A good stop for tasty Indian cuisine, the restaurant sets up a lunch buffet with a nice selection of dishes. In keeping with the cuisine, the decor enhances overall dining experience. Casual dress. **Bar:** Beer & wine. **Reservations:** accepted. **Hours:** 11:30 am-2:30 & 5:30-9:30 pm. Closed: 12/25. **Address:** 70 N Lexington Ave **Location:** Jct Walnut St, just n. **Parking:** street. **Cards:** AX, DS, MC, VI.

CALL M

MELLOW MUSHROOM **Phone:** 828/236-9800 (4)

Pizza
$5-$12

Such products as hearth-baked pizza and calzones are made fresh-to-order with natural spring-water dough. Also on the menu are sandwiches and salads. Casual dress. **Bar:** Full bar. **Hours:** 11 am-10 pm, Fri & Sat-11 pm, Sun noon-10 pm. Closed major holidays. **Address:** 50 Broadway **Location:** Corner of Walnut St and Broadway. **Parking:** street. **Cards:** AX, DS, MC, VI.

THE NEW FRENCH BAR COURTYARD CAFE **Phone:** 828/225-6445 (21)

French
$6-$10

The downtown restaurant showcases local artwork and live entertainment. Patrons can choose a table in the courtyard, restaurant or bar area and enjoy traditional French fare served in a non-traditional tapas style. Hand-crafted desserts are a delicious cap to any meal. Casual dress. **Bar:** Full bar. **Hours:** 3 pm-2 am, Sat from 11 am, Sun 10:30 am-10 pm. Closed major holidays; also Mon. **Address:** 12 Biltmore Ave **Location:** Next to Pack Square. **Parking:** street. **Cards:** MC, VI.

ROSETTA'S KITCHEN **Phone:** 828/232-0738 (2)

Natural/Organic
$4-$9

Bustling and informal, Rosetta's is a vegetarian restaurant conveniently located in the center of downtown Asheville. Entrees for every taste are offered, homemade in their own kitchen each day. Try the yummy vegan chocolate cake, or browse along the display counter and choose from assorted salads and entrees. Every employee counts here; lots of the recipes are created by the staff. Always something new, different, and oh-so-good! Casual dress. **Bar:** Beer & wine. **Reservations:** not accepted. **Hours:** 10 am-11 am, Fri & Sat-3 am, Sun-3 pm. Closed major holidays; also 11/1. **Address:** 116 N Lexington Ave **Location:** Jct College and Broadway sts, just w on College St, then just s. **Parking:** street. **Cards:** AX, MC, VI.

SALSA'S **Phone:** 828/252-9805 (18)

Caribbean
$6-$17

The funky, eclectic, colorful and popular restaurant lets patrons sample menu offerings influenced by Spanish, Caribbean and Mexican cuisine. Casual dress. **Bar:** Full bar. **Hours:** 11:30 am-2:30 & 5:30-9 pm, Sat & Sun noon-3 & 5:30-9:30 pm. Closed: 1/1, 11/26, 12/24, 12/25. **Address:** 6 Patton Ave **Location:** Center; in Pack Square. **Parking:** street. **Cards:** DS, MC, VI.

SUSHI-THAI **Phone:** 828/225-8885 (10)

American
$8-$22

This fusion restaurant lets patrons choose from a full sushi bar and a classic menu of Thai dishes. The flavorful dishes don't disappoint. Casual dress. **Hours:** 11:30 am-3 & 5:30-10 pm, Fri-Sun 11:30 am-10:30 pm. Closed: 11/26, 12/25. **Address:** 3 Biltmore Ave **Location:** Just s of Pack Square. **Parking:** street. **Cards:** AX, DS, MC, VI.

TABLE **Phone:** 828/254-8980 (13)

American
$8-$34

The decor may be minimalist, but the menu is complex with fresh flavors. Daily changing menu items might include seared foie gras, curried scallops, porterhouse steak or fresh seafood. Dressy casual. **Bar:** Full bar. **Reservations:** suggested. **Hours:** 11:30 am-2:30 & 5:30-11 pm, Sat & Sun from 10:30 am. Closed: 11/26, 12/25; also Tues. **Address:** 48 College St **Location:** Jct College and Lexington sts. **Parking:** street. **Cards:** AX, MC, VI.

TRUE CONFECTIONS **Phone:** 828/350-9480 (14)

Breads/Pastries
$3-$8

The new bake shop's owner is a culinary school graduate who spent many years perfecting the tastes of scrumptious sweets. The specialty here is the confections, loaded with real butter, eggs, imported chocolate and other goodies. The downtown shop is in the newly remodeled Grove Arcade. Fresh ground coffee, herbal teas and some savories also are served. Casual dress. **Reservations:** not accepted. **Hours:** 7:30 am-9 pm, Fri-11 pm, Sat 9 am-11 pm, Sun 10 am-5 pm. Closed: 11/26, 12/25. **Address:** One Page Ave, Suite 147 **Location:** Center; in Grove Arcade. **Parking:** street.

TUPELO HONEY CAFE **Phone:** 828/255-4863 (19)

New Southern
$5-$17

Open for breakfast and lunch, the cafe expands its hours with late-night dining on the weekends. Lowcountry and regional Southern specialties are dished in huge portions. Casual dress. **Bar:** Beer & wine. **Reservations:** not accepted. **Hours:** 9 am-3 & 5:30-9 pm, Fri & Sat-11 pm. Closed: 1/1, 11/26, 12/25; also Mon. **Address:** 12 College St **Location:** East of federal building. **Parking:** street. **Cards:** AX, MC, VI.

(See map and index starting on p. 574)

VICENZO'S **Phone:** 828/254-4698 (8)

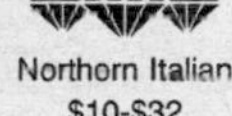

Northern Italian
$10-$32

Pasta is the popular dish at the elegant restaurant. Uncomplicated preparation emphasizes taste in menu offerings of veal, fish, chicken and homemade desserts. The second-floor dining room, set with a formal serving presentation, allows for a traditional and comforting special-occasion experience. The downstairs bistro encompasses a cigar bar and live music. Dressy casual. Entertainment. **Bar:** Full bar. **Reservations:** suggested. **Hours:** 5:30 pm-10 pm, Fri & Sat-11 pm, Sun-9 pm. Closed major holidays. **Address:** 10 N Market St **Location:** Walnut St at Market St; center. **Parking:** on-site. **Cards:** AX, DC, DS, MC, VI.

WASABI JAPANESE RESTAURANT **Phone:** 828/225-2551 (12)

Japanese
$7-$25

Serving some of the freshest sushi in town, the Japanese restaurant has a cozy atmosphere, friendly staff and, for those who enjoy watching it all come together, an attractive sushi bar to view the creations in progress. Casual dress. **Bar:** Full bar. **Reservations:** suggested. **Hours:** noon-3 & 5-10 pm, Fri & Sat-10:30 pm, Sun 5 pm-10 pm. Closed: 11/26. **Address:** 19 Broadway **Location:** Between College and Walnut sts; just n from Pack Square. **Parking:** street. **Cards:** AX, DS, MC, VI.

ZAMBRA **Phone:** 828/232-1060 (7)

Spanish
$7-$14

The romantic atmosphere is reminiscent of a Spanish bodega, where diners feast on tapas. The chef's innovation shines through in Portuguese, Spanish and Moroccan preparations. An extensive Spanish wine list is presented. Casual dress. **Bar:** Full bar. **Hours:** 5:30 pm-9:30 pm, Fri & Sat-10 pm, Sun-9 pm. Closed major holidays; also call for days in Jan. **Address:** 85 W Walnut St **Location:** Jct Lexington and Walnut sts. **Parking:** street. **Cards:** AX, DS, MC, VI.

CALL

The following restaurant has not been evaluated by AAA but is listed for your information only.

FLYING FROG CAFE **Phone:** 828/254-9411

fyi

Not evaluated. The casually elegant restaurant's menu lines up a delicious combination of French and Indian dishes, which are served by friendly, knowledgeable staffers. **Address:** 1 Battery Park **Location:** Corner of Haywood St; downstairs of Haywood Park Hotel Complex.

ASHEVILLE pop. 68,889 (See map and index starting on p. 576)

WHERE TO STAY

1891 CEDAR CREST INN **Phone:** (828)252-1389 (32)

SAVE

Historic Bed & Breakfast
$145-$300 All Year

Address: 674 Biltmore Ave **Location:** I-40, exit 50, 1.1 mi n. **Facility:** This 1891 Victorian mansion has original interior woodwork; upscale accommodations of varied sizes include two cottages and a new suite. Smoke free premises. 12 units. 8 one-bedroom standard units. 2 one- and 1 two-bedroom suites, some with whirlpools. 1 cottage. 3 stories (no elevator), interior/exterior corridors. *Bath:* combo, shower or tub only. **Parking:** on-site. **Terms:** 2-3 night minimum stay - seasonal, age restrictions may apply, 14 day cancellation notice-fee imposed. **Amenities:** irons, hair dryers. *Some:* CD players. **Guest Services:** wireless Internet. **Business Services:** meeting rooms. **Cards:** AX, MC, VI. **Free Special Amenities: full breakfast and high-speed Internet.**

/ SOME UNITS VCR

1900 INN ON MONTFORD **Phone:** (828)254-9569 (12)

Historic Bed & Breakfast
$145-$625 All Year

Address: 296 Montford Ave **Location:** I-240, exit 4C (Montford Ave/Haywood St), 0.7 mi n; in historic district. Located in a residential area. **Facility:** Dating from 1900, this home features gas fireplaces, antique furnishings and heated towel bars in all accommodations. Designated smoking area. 8 units. 5 one-bedroom standard units, some with whirlpools. 3 one-bedroom suites with whirlpools. 3 stories (no elevator), interior/exterior corridors. **Parking:** on-site. **Terms:** office hours 7 am-9 pm, 2-3 night minimum stay - seasonal and/or weekends, age restrictions may apply, 14 day cancellation notice-fee imposed. **Amenities:** video library, DVD players, CD players, high-speed Internet, dual phone lines, irons, hair dryers. **Guest Services:** wireless Internet. **Business Services:** meeting rooms, PC, fax. **Cards:** AX, DC, DS, MC, VI.

/ SOME UNITS

ABBINGTON GREEN BED & BREAKFAST INN **Phone:** (828)251-2454 (8)

SAVE

Historic Bed & Breakfast
$150-$450 All Year

Address: 46 Cumberland Cir **Location:** I-240, exit 4C (Montford Ave/Haywood St), n to W Chestnut St, just e to Cumberland Ave, then 0.3 mi n; in historic district. Located in residential area. **Facility:** Guest rooms feature English-style furnishings, antiques and canopy or four-poster beds at this 1908 Colonial Revival home with gardens. Smoke free premises. 8 units. 6 one-bedroom standard units. 1 one- and 1 two-bedroom suites, some with kitchens and/or whirlpools. 2 stories (no elevator), interior/exterior corridors. **Parking:** on-site. **Terms:** 2-3 night minimum stay, 30 day cancellation notice-fee imposed. **Amenities:** video library, irons, hair dryers. *Some:* CD players. **Guest Services:** wireless Internet. **Cards:** AX, DS, MC, VI. **Free Special Amenities: full breakfast and high-speed Internet.**

/ SOME UNITS FEE VCR

ALBEMARLE INN **Phone:** (828)255-0027 (4)

SAVE

Historic Bed & Breakfast
$125-$380 All Year

Address: 86 Edgemont Rd **Location:** I-240, exit 5B (Charlotte St), 0.9 mi nw, then 0.3 mi e. Located in a quiet residential area. **Facility:** This 1909 Greek Revival mansion has many spacious accommodations; breakfast is served on the enclosed patio overlooking extensive manicured gardens. Smoke free premises. 11 one-bedroom standard units, some with whirlpools. 3 stories (no elevator), interior corridors. **Parking:** on-site. **Terms:** 2 night minimum stay - seasonal and/or weekends, age restrictions may apply, 14 day cancellation notice-fee imposed. **Amenities:** high-speed Internet, hair dryers. **Leisure Activities:** veranda. *Fee:* massage. **Guest Services:** wireless Internet. **Business Services:** meeting rooms. **Cards:** AX, DS, MC, VI. **Free Special Amenities: full breakfast and high-speed Internet.**

CALL / SOME UNITS

(See map and index starting on p. 576)

APPLEWOOD MANOR INN BED & BREAKFAST **Phone:** 828/254-2244 7

AAA SAVE

Historic Bed & Breakfast

$160-$225 All Year

Address: 62 Cumberland Cir **Location:** I-240, exit 4C (Montford Ave/Haywood St), n on Montford Ave, e on W Chestnut St, n on Cumberland Ave, then ne; in historic district. Located in residential area. **Facility:** On a two-acre garden lot, this 1910 Colonial Revival inn is partly furnished with antiques; most rooms have a fireplace and balcony. Smoke free premises. 6 units. 5 one-bedroom standard units. 1 cottage. 2 stories (no elevator), interior/exterior corridors. *Bath:* combo or shower only. **Parking:** on-site. **Terms:** 2 night minimum stay, 7 day cancellation notice-fee imposed. **Amenities:** hair dryers. *Some:* DVD players. **Guest Services:** wireless Internet. **Cards:** AX, DS, MC, VI. **Free Special Amenities: full breakfast and high-speed Internet.**

/ SOME UNITS FEE

AT CUMBERLAND FALLS BED & BREAKFAST INN **Phone:** 828/253-4085 11

Bed & Breakfast

$125-$259 All Year

Address: 254 Cumberland Ave **Location:** I-240, exit 4C (Montford Ave/Haywood St), 0.5 mi nw on Montford Ave to Soco St, just n, then just nw. **Facility:** Converted 1930 home, tastefully decorated guest rooms. Attractive landscaped grounds. Smoke free premises. 6 one-bedroom standard units, some with whirlpools. 3 stories (no elevator), interior corridors. *Bath:* combo or tub only. **Parking:** on-site. **Terms:** office hours 6 am-6 pm, 2-3 night minimum stay - seasonal and/or weekends, 30 day cancellation notice-fee imposed. **Amenities:** video library, DVD players, CD players, irons, hair dryers. **Leisure Activities:** *Fee:* massage. **Guest Services:** valet laundry, wireless Internet. **Business Services:** fax (fee). **Cards:** DS, MC, VI.

VCR / SOME UNITS

BAYMONT INN-BILTMORE *Book great rates at AAA.com* **Phone:** (828)274-2022 38

AAA SAVE

Hotel

$79-$189 3/30-11/30

$69-$139 12/1-3/29

Address: 204 Hendersonville Rd **Location:** I-40, exit 50 eastbound; exit 50B westbound, just n on US 25. Located near Biltmore Estate. **Facility:** 71 one-bedroom standard units. 5 stories, interior corridors. *Bath:* combo or shower only. **Parking:** on-site. **Amenities:** high-speed Internet, voice mail, irons, hair dryers. **Pool(s):** heated indoor. **Leisure Activities:** whirlpool, exercise room. **Guest Services:** valet and coin laundry, wireless Internet. **Cards:** AX, CB, DC, DS, MC, VI. **Free Special Amenities: expanded continental breakfast and high-speed Internet.** *(See color ad p 585)*

CALL / SOME UNITS

BEAUFORT HOUSE INN **Phone:** 828/254-8334 9

AAA SAVE

Historic Bed & Breakfast

Rates not provided

Address: 61 N Liberty St **Location:** I-240, exit 5A (Merrimon Ave), just n to 2nd light, e on Chestnut St to N Liberty St, then just n. Located in a quiet residential area. **Facility:** This handsome 1894 Victorian home features graciously furnished guest rooms and a wraparound porch. Smoke free premises. 10 one-bedroom standard units, some with whirlpools. 3 stories (no elevator), interior/exterior corridors. *Bath:* combo, shower or tub only. **Parking:** on-site. **Terms:** age restrictions may apply. **Amenities:** video library, CD players, hair dryers. *Some:* DVD players. **Leisure Activities:** badminton, swings, volleyball. **Guest Services:** wireless Internet. **Free Special Amenities: full breakfast and high-speed Internet.**

VCR / SOME UNITS

▼ See AAA listing p 585 ▼

(See map and index starting on p. 576)

BEST WESTERN OF ASHEVILLE BILTMORE EAST Book great rates at AAA.com **Phone:** (828)298-5562 

Motel
$49-$199 All Year

Address: 501 Tunnel Rd **Location:** I-240, exit 7, 0.5 mi e on US 70 (Tunnel Rd). **Facility:** 89 one-bedroom standard units. 2 stories (no elevator), exterior corridors. **Parking:** on-site. **Terms:** 3 day cancellation notice-fee imposed. **Amenities:** safes, irons, hair dryers. *Some:* high-speed Internet. **Pool(s):** heated outdoor. **Guest Services:** wireless Internet. **Business Services:** PC. **Cards:** AX, CB, DC, DS, JC, MC, VI. **Free Special Amenities: expanded continental breakfast and high-speed Internet.** *(See color ad p 584)*

AAA Benefit:
Members save up to 20%, plus 10% bonus points with rewards program.

    / SOME UNITS FEE 

(See map and index starting on p. 576)

BILTMORE VILLAGE INN *Book great rates at AAA.com* **Phone:** (828)274-8707 34

AAA SAVE

Historic Bed & Breakfast

$220-$325 All Year

Address: 119 Dodge St **Location:** I-40, exit 50/50B (US 25 N), 0.5 mi n, just e on Lula St, just n on Reed St, just e on Warren Ave, then just s. Located in a residential area. **Facility:** Natural woodwork throughout the house has been carefully preserved by the owners of this B&B, which is perched on a rise overlooking Biltmore Village. Smoke free premises. 7 units. 4 one-bedroom standard units with whirlpools. 2 one-bedroom suites with whirlpools. 1 house. 2 stories (no elevator), interior/exterior corridors. **Parking:** on-site. **Terms:** 2 night minimum stay - weekends, age restrictions may apply, 14 day cancellation notice-fee imposed. **Amenities:** video library, irons, hair dryers. **Guest Services:** wireless Internet. **Cards:** AX, DS, MC, VI. **Free Special Amenities: full breakfast and high-speed Internet.**

VCR / SOME UNITS FEE

BLACK WALNUT B&B INN **Phone:** 828/254-3878 13

AAA SAVE

Historic Bed & Breakfast

$145-$295 All Year

Address: 288 Montford Ave **Location:** I-240, exit 4C (Montford Ave/Haywood St), 0.5 mi n; in historic district. Located in a residential area. **Facility:** A garden with a fountain adds appeal to the grounds of this inn housed in an 1899 Tudor/Arts and Crafts manor. Smoke free premises. 6 one-bedroom standard units, some with whirlpools. 2 stories (no elevator), interior/exterior corridors. *Bath:* combo or shower only. **Parking:** on-site. **Terms:** 2 night minimum stay, age restrictions may apply, 15 day cancellation notice-fee imposed. **Amenities:** video library, irons, hair dryers. *Some:* DVD players. **Guest Services:** wireless Internet. **Cards:** AX, MC, VI. **Free Special Amenities: full breakfast and high-speed Internet.**

/ SOME UNITS VCR

CAROLINA BED & BREAKFAST **Phone:** (828)254-3608 15

Bed & Breakfast

$135-$225 3/23-11/30

$120-$200 12/1-3/22

Address: 177 Cumberland Ave **Location:** I-240, exit 4C (Montford Ave/Haywood St), 0.5 mi n on Montford Ave, just e on Chestnut St, then just n. **Facility:** 7 units. 6 one-bedroom standard units, some with whirlpools. 1 cottage. 2 stories (no elevator), interior/exterior corridors. *Bath:* combo or shower only. **Parking:** on-site. **Terms:** check-in 4 pm, 2 night minimum stay - seasonal and/or weekends, age restrictions may apply, cancellation fee imposed. **Amenities:** DVD players, hair dryers. *Some:* irons. **Guest Services:** wireless Internet. **Cards:** AX, DS, MC, VI.

/ SOME UNITS FEE

COMFORT INN-WEST *Book at AAA.com* **Phone:** (828)665-6500 41

Hotel

$59-$169 4/1-11/30

$49-$119 12/1-3/31

Address: 15 Crowell Rd **Location:** I-40, exit 44, just n on US 19 and 23, just w on Old Haywood Rd, then just s. **Facility:** 63 one-bedroom standard units, some with whirlpools. 3 stories, interior corridors. *Bath:* combo or shower only. **Parking:** on-site. **Terms:** cancellation fee imposed. **Amenities:** high-speed Internet, safes, irons, hair dryers. **Pool(s):** outdoor. **Leisure Activities:** exercise room. **Guest Services:** valet and coin laundry, wireless Internet. **Business Services:** meeting rooms, PC. **Cards:** AX, DS, MC, VI.

ASK CALL / SOME UNITS

COMFORT SUITES-BILTMORE SQUARE MALL *Book at AAA.com* **Phone:** (828)665-4000 51

Hotel

$69-$189 4/1-11/30

$69-$129 12/1-3/31

Address: 890 Brevard Rd **Location:** I-26, exit 33, 0.3 mi w. **Facility:** Smoke free premises. 125 one-bedroom standard units, some with whirlpools. 5 stories, interior corridors. *Bath:* combo or shower only. **Parking:** on-site. **Terms:** cancellation fee imposed. **Amenities:** voice mail, irons, hair dryers. **Pool(s):** heated outdoor. **Leisure Activities:** exercise room. **Guest Services:** valet and coin laundry, wireless Internet. **Business Services:** meeting rooms, business center. **Cards:** AX, CB, DC, DS, JC, MC, VI.

ASK CALL / SOME UNITS FEE

COUNTRY INN & SUITES *Book great rates at AAA.com* **Phone:** (828)254-4311 26

AAA SAVE

Hotel

$109-$250 7/1-11/30

$99-$160 12/1-6/30

Address: 199 Tunnel Rd **Location:** I-240, exit 6, 0.5 mi e on US 70 (Tunnel Rd). **Facility:** Smoke free premises. 74 units. 63 one-bedroom standard units, some with whirlpools. 11 one-bedroom suites. 5 stories, interior corridors. *Bath:* combo or shower only. **Parking:** on-site. **Terms:** cancellation fee imposed. **Amenities:** high-speed Internet, voice mail, irons, hair dryers. **Pool(s):** heated indoor. **Leisure Activities:** whirlpool, exercise room. **Guest Services:** valet and coin laundry, wireless Internet. **Business Services:** meeting rooms, PC, fax (fee). **Cards:** AX, DC, DS, MC, VI. **Free Special Amenities: expanded continental breakfast and high-speed Internet.**

CALL / SOME UNITS

COUNTRY INN & SUITES BY CARLSON *Book great rates at AAA.com* **Phone:** (828)670-9000 50

AAA SAVE

Hotel

$104-$175 5/1-11/30

$89-$105 12/1-4/30

Address: 845 Brevard Rd **Location:** I-26, exit 33, just w. **Facility:** Smoke free premises. 57 units. 45 one-bedroom standard units. 12 one-bedroom suites, some with whirlpools. 3 stories, interior corridors. *Bath:* combo or shower only. **Parking:** on-site. **Terms:** cancellation fee imposed. **Amenities:** voice mail, irons, hair dryers. *Some:* high-speed Internet. **Pool(s):** heated outdoor. **Leisure Activities:** exercise room. **Guest Services:** valet and coin laundry, wireless Internet. **Business Services:** PC, fax (fee). **Cards:** AX, DC, DS, JC, MC, VI. **Free Special Amenities: expanded continental breakfast and high-speed Internet.**

(See map and index starting on p. 576)

COURTYARD BY MARRIOTT *Book great rates at AAA.com* **Phone:** (828)281-0041 

Hotel
$112-$153 All Year

Address: 1 Buckstone Pl **Location:** I-240, exit 6, 0.5 mi e on US 70 (Tunnel Rd). **Facility:** Smoke free premises. 78 units. 75 one-bedroom standard units, some with whirlpools. 3 one-bedroom suites with efficiencies. 3 stories, interior corridors. *Bath:* combo or shower only. **Parking:** on-site. **Terms:** check-in 4 pm, cancellation fee imposed. **Amenities:** voice mail, irons, hair dryers. **Pool(s):** heated indoor. **Leisure Activities:** whirlpool, exercise room. **Guest Services:** valet and coin laundry, wireless Internet. **Business Services:** meeting rooms, PC, fax (fee). **Cards:** AX, CB, DC, DS, JC, MC, VI.

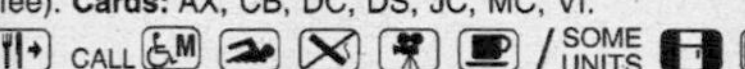

AAA Benefit:
Members save a minimum 5% off the best available rate.

CROWNE PLAZA RESORT *Book great rates at AAA.com* **Phone:** (828)254-3211 19

Resort Hotel
$119-$179 4/1-11/30
$89-$139 12/1-3/31

Address: 1 Resort Dr **Location:** I-240, exit 3B (Resort Dr), just w. **Facility:** A manicured, 87-acre golf course forms the backdrop for this property featuring attractive public areas. 279 units. 275 one-bedroom standard units. 2 one- and 2 two-bedroom suites, some with kitchens and/or whirlpools. 2-5 stories, interior corridors. *Bath:* combo or shower only. **Parking:** on-site. **Terms:** check-in 4 pm, cancellation fee imposed. **Amenities:** CD players, voice mail, irons, hair dryers. **Pool(s):** heated outdoor. **Leisure Activities:** 4 tennis courts, playground, exercise room. *Fee:* golf-9 holes. **Guest Services:** valet laundry, wireless Internet. **Business Services:** conference facilities, business center. **Cards:** AX, MC, VI.

ASK / SOME UNITS FEE 

DAYS INN-ASHEVILLE MALL *Book great rates at AAA.com* **Phone:** (828)252-4000 24

AAA SAVE

Motel
$49-$249 All Year

Address: 201 Tunnel Rd **Location:** I-240, exit 6, 0.5 mi e, on south side of road. **Facility:** 129 units. 128 one-bedroom standard units, some with whirlpools. 1 one-bedroom suite with whirlpool. 2 stories (no elevator), exterior corridors. **Parking:** on-site. **Amenities:** voice mail, safes, irons, hair dryers. *Some:* DVD players, CD players, high-speed Internet. **Pool(s):** outdoor. **Guest Services:** coin laundry, wireless Internet. **Business Services:** meeting rooms, PC. **Cards:** AX, CB, DC, DS, MC, VI. **Free Special Amenities: full breakfast and high-speed Internet.** *(See color ad below)*

/ SOME UNITS FEE

▼ *See AAA listing above* ▼

(See map and index starting on p. 576)

DAYS INN-BILTMORE EAST *Book great rates at AAA.com* **Phone:** (828)298-4000 

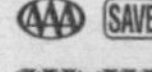

Hotel
$55-$199 4/1-11/30
$42-$119 12/1-3/31

Address: 1435 Tunnel Rd **Location:** I-40, exit 55, just n. **Facility:** 84 one-bedroom standard units. 3 stories, interior corridors. **Parking:** on-site. **Terms:** cancellation fee imposed. **Amenities:** safes, hair dryers. *Some:* irons. **Pool(s):** heated outdoor. **Guest Services:** wireless Internet. **Business Services:** PC. **Cards:** AX, CB, DC, DS, JC, MC, VI. ***(See color ad below)***

 / SOME UNITS FEE 

DAYS INN NORTH *Book at AAA.com* **Phone:** (828)645-9191 **2**

Motel
$59-$159 All Year

Address: 3 Reynolds Mountain Blvd **Location:** US 19/23, exit 23, just n. **Facility:** 49 one-bedroom standard units, some with whirlpools. 2 stories (no elevator), exterior corridors. *Bath:* combo or shower only. **Parking:** on-site. **Amenities:** hair dryers. *Some:* irons. **Pool(s):** outdoor. **Guest Services:** wireless Internet. **Cards:** AX, DC, DS, MC, VI.

ASK / SOME UNITS

DOUBLETREE BILTMORE HOTEL *Book great rates at AAA.com* **Phone:** (828)274-1800 **37**

Hotel
$89-$229 All Year

Address: 115 Hendersonville Rd **Location:** I-40, exit 50 eastbound; exit 50B westbound, just n on US 25. Located near the Biltmore Estate. **Facility:** 160 units. 145 one-bedroom standard units. 15 one-bedroom suites. 5 stories, interior corridors. *Bath:* combo or shower only. **Parking:** on-site. **Terms:** 1-30 night minimum stay, cancellation fee imposed. **Amenities:** video games (fee), high-speed Internet, dual phone lines, voice mail, safes, irons, hair dryers. *Some:* DVD players (fee). **Pool(s):** outdoor. **Leisure Activities:** whirlpool, exercise room. **Guest Services:** valet laundry, wireless Internet. **Business Services:** meeting rooms, PC. **Cards:** AX, CB, DC, DS, MC, VI.

/ SOME UNITS FEE VCR

DOUBLETREE
HOTELS·SUITES·RESORTS·CLUBS
AAA Benefit:
Members save 5% or more everyday!

ECONO LODGE BILTMORE *Book great rates at AAA.com* **Phone:** (828)254-9521 **21**

Motel
$44-$126 3/21-11/30
$42-$89 12/1-3/20

Address: 190 Tunnel Rd **Location:** I-240, exit 6, 0.5 mi e on US 70 (Tunnel Rd). **Facility:** 53 one-bedroom standard units. 2 stories (no elevator), exterior corridors. **Parking:** on-site. **Guest Services:** wireless Internet. **Cards:** AX, CB, DC, DS, MC, VI. **Free Special Amenities: expanded continental breakfast and high-speed Internet.**

 / SOME UNITS

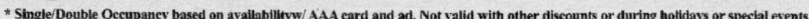

(See map and index starting on p. 576)

EXTENDED STAYAMERICA Book at AAA.com **Phone:** (828)253-3483 20

Hotel
$90-$120 All Year

Address: 6 Kenilworth Knoll **Location:** I-240, exit 6, 0.7 mi e on US 70 (Tunnel Rd), then just n. **Facility:** 101 one-bedroom standard units with kitchens. 3 stories, interior corridors. *Bath:* combo or shower only. **Parking:** on-site. **Terms:** office hours 7 am-11 pm. **Amenities:** voice mail, irons. **Guest Services:** coin laundry, wireless Internet. **Business Services:** fax (fee). **Cards:** AX, CB, DC, DS, JC, MC, VI.

ASK CALL / SOME UNITS FEE

FAIRFIELD INN & SUITES BY MARRIOTT BILTMORE SQUARE MALL Book great rates at AAA.com **Phone:** (828)665-4242 47

AAA SAVE

Hotel
$119-$127 All Year

Address: 11 Rocky Ridge Rd **Location:** I-26, exit 33. **Facility:** Smoke free premises. 92 one-bedroom standard units, some with whirlpools. 6 stories, interior corridors. *Bath:* combo or shower only. **Parking:** on-site. **Terms:** cancellation fee imposed. **Amenities:** high-speed Internet, dual phone lines, voice mail, safes, irons, hair dryers. *Some:* CD players. **Pool(s):** heated indoor. **Leisure Activities:** whirlpool, board games, exercise room. **Guest Services:** valet and coin laundry, wireless Internet. **Business Services:** meeting rooms, business center. **Cards:** AX, CB, DC, DS, MC, VI. **Free Special Amenities: expanded continental breakfast and high-speed Internet.**

CALL

Fairfield Inn & Suites Marriott

AAA Benefit:
Members save a minimum 5% off the best available rate.

THE GROVE PARK INN RESORT & SPA Book great rates at AAA.com **Phone:** (828)252-2711 3

AAA SAVE

Resort Hotel
$300-$415 4/1-11/30
$205-$405 12/1-3/31

Address: 290 Macon Ave **Location:** I-240, exit 5B (Charlotte St), 2 mi n on Macon Ave via Charlotte St, follow signs. **Facility:** A golf course, manicured grounds, spa and on-site restaurants are featured at this 1913 hotel constructed using granite. 512 units. 498 one-bedroom standard units, some with whirlpools. 14 one-bedroom suites. 6-11 stories, interior corridors. *Bath:* combo or shower only. **Parking:** on-site and valet. **Terms:** check-in 4 pm, 2-7 night minimum stay - seasonal and/or weekends, 7 day cancellation notice-fee imposed. **Amenities:** video games (fee), CD players, voice mail, safes, irons, hair dryers. *Some:* high-speed Internet. **Dining:** 4 restaurants, also, Horizons, see separate listing, entertainment. **Pool(s):** 2 heated outdoor, 5 heated indoor, heated indoor/outdoor. **Leisure Activities:** miniature golf, recreation programs, jogging, playground, spa, basketball. *Fee:* saunas, whirlpools, steamrooms, golf-18 holes, 6 tennis courts (3 indoor), racquetball court, aerobics & tennis instruction. **Guest Services:** valet laundry, airport transportation (fee)-Asheville Regional Airport, personal fitness trainer, wireless Internet. **Business Services:** conference facilities, business center. **Cards:** AX, DC, DS, MC, VI. *(See color ad below)*

FEE

▼ See AAA listing above ▼

(See map and index starting on p. 576)

HAMPTON INN - BILTMORE SQUARE *Book great rates at AAA.com* **Phone:** (828)667-2022 46

Hotel
$99-$189 4/1-11/30
$99-$129 12/1-3/31

Address: 1 Rocky Ridge Rd **Location:** I-26, exit 33. **Facility:** 121 one-bedroom standard units, some with whirlpools. 5 stories, interior corridors. **Parking:** on-site. **Terms:** 2-3 night minimum stay - seasonal and/or weekends, 3 day cancellation notice-fee imposed. **Amenities:** voice mail, irons, hair dryers. **Pool(s):** heated indoor. **Leisure Activities:** sauna, whirlpool, exercise room. **Guest Services:** valet laundry, airport transportation-Asheville Regional Airport, wireless Internet. **Business Services:** meeting rooms, PC. **Cards:** AX, DC, DS, MC, VI. **Free Special Amenities: expanded continental breakfast and high-speed Internet.** *(See color ad p 591)*

AAA Benefit:
Members save up to 10% everyday!

CALL / SOME UNITS

HAMPTON INN TUNNEL ROAD *Book great rates at AAA.com* **Phone:** (828)255-9220 

Hotel
$99-$189 4/1-11/30
$99-$129 12/1-3/31

Address: 204 Tunnel Rd **Location:** I-240, exit 6, 0.5 mi e, then n. Located across from mall. **Facility:** 120 one-bedroom standard units, some with whirlpools. 5 stories, interior corridors. *Bath:* combo or shower only. **Parking:** on-site. **Terms:** 2-3 night minimum stay - seasonal and/or weekends, 3 day cancellation notice-fee imposed. **Amenities:** voice mail, irons, hair dryers. *Some:* high-speed Internet. **Pool(s):** heated indoor. **Leisure Activities:** sauna, whirlpool, exercise room. **Guest Services:** valet laundry, wireless Internet. **Business Services:** meeting rooms, PC, fax (fee). **Cards:** AX, DS, MC, VI. **Free Special Amenities: expanded continental breakfast and high-speed Internet.** *(See color ad p 591)*

AAA Benefit:
Members save up to 10% everyday!

CALL / SOME UNITS

HILL HOUSE BED & BREAKFAST INN **Phone:** 828/232-0345 6

Bed & Breakfast
$125-$270 All Year

Address: 120 Hillside St **Location:** I-240, exit 5A (Merrimon Ave/US 25), just n, then w. **Facility:** With its original tin roof, this grand Victorian painted lady is shaded by century-old oaks and a beautiful garden setting. Located in a quiet residential area; enjoy the privacy of nicely appointed guestrooms or the fresh air on the large wraparound porch. 9 units. 7 one-bedroom standard units, some with whirlpools. 1 one-bedroom suite. 1 cottage. 2 stories (no elevator), interior/exterior corridors. *Bath:* combo or shower only. **Parking:** on-site. **Terms:** check-in 4 pm, 2 night minimum stay - weekends, age restrictions may apply, 14 day cancellation notice-fee imposed. **Amenities:** CD players, irons, hair dryers. *Some:* DVD players. **Leisure Activities:** limited exercise equipment. **Guest Services:** wireless Internet. **Cards:** DS, MC, VI.

/ SOME UNITS VCR

HOLIDAY INN-BILTMORE EAST AT THE BLUE RIDGE PARKWAY *Book at AAA.com* **Phone:** (828)298-5611 28

Hotel
$89-$169 5/1-11/30
$69-$99 12/1-4/30

Address: 1450 Tunnel Rd **Location:** I-40, exit 55, just n. **Facility:** 111 one-bedroom standard units. 4 stories, interior corridors. *Bath:* combo or shower only. **Parking:** on-site. **Amenities:** dual phone lines, voice mail, irons, hair dryers. **Pool(s):** heated outdoor. **Leisure Activities:** exercise room. **Guest Services:** valet and coin laundry, wireless Internet. **Business Services:** meeting rooms, PC, fax. **Cards:** AX, CB, DC, DS, JC, MC, VI.

ASK / SOME UNITS FEE

HOLIDAY INN BILTMORE WEST *Book great rates at AAA.com* **Phone:** (828)665-2161 44

Hotel
$89-$199 4/1-11/30
$79-$169 12/1-3/31

Address: 435 Smokey Park Hwy **Location:** I-40, exit 44 on US 19 and 23. **Facility:** 156 one-bedroom standard units, some with whirlpools. 6 stories, interior corridors. *Bath:* combo or shower only. **Parking:** on-site. **Amenities:** high-speed Internet, voice mail, irons, hair dryers. **Pool(s):** heated outdoor, heated indoor/outdoor. **Leisure Activities:** whirlpool, exercise room. *Fee:* game room. **Guest Services:** valet and coin laundry, wireless Internet. **Business Services:** conference facilities, business center. **Cards:** AX, CB, DC, DS, JC, MC, VI.

CALL / SOME UNITS

HOLIDAY INN EXPRESS-BILTMORE *Book great rates at AAA.com* **Phone:** (828)274-0101 39

Hotel
$99-$169 All Year

Address: 234 Hendersonville Rd **Location:** I-40, exit 50, exit 50 eastbound; exit 50B westbound, just n on US 25. Located near entrance to Biltmore Estate. **Facility:** 71 one-bedroom standard units. 3 stories (no elevator), exterior corridors. *Bath:* combo or shower only. **Parking:** on-site. **Terms:** 3 day cancellation notice-fee imposed. **Amenities:** high-speed Internet, voice mail, irons, hair dryers. **Pool(s):** outdoor. **Guest Services:** valet laundry, wireless Internet. **Cards:** AX, CB, DC, DS, JC, MC, VI. **Free Special Amenities: expanded continental breakfast and high-speed Internet.** *(See color ad p 585)*

(See map and index starting on p. 576)

HOLIDAY INN EXPRESS HOTEL & SUITES Book great rates at AAA.com **Phone:** (828)665-6519 48

AAA SAVE

Hotel

$115-$189 6/1-11/30
$89-$189 12/1-5/31

Address: 1 Wedgefield Dr **Location:** I-26, exit 33. **Facility:** 108 one-bedroom standard units, some with whirlpools. 5 stories, interior corridors. *Bath:* combo or shower only. **Parking:** on-site. **Terms:** 7 day cancellation notice. **Amenities:** voice mail, irons, hair dryers. **Pool(s):** outdoor. **Leisure Activities:** whirlpool, exercise room. **Guest Services:** valet and coin laundry, wireless Internet. **Business Services:** meeting rooms, business center. **Cards:** AX, DS, MC, VI. **Free Special Amenities: expanded continental breakfast and high-speed Internet.**

CALL / SOME UNITS

HOLIDAY INN HOTEL & SUITES Book great rates at AAA.com **Phone:** (828)225-5550 17

AAA SAVE

Hotel

$100-$400 All Year

Address: 42 Tunnel Rd **Location:** I-240, exit 6, 0.4 mi e on US 70 (Tunnel Rd). **Facility:** Smoke free premises. 111 units. 87 one-bedroom standard units. 22 one- and 2 two-bedroom suites, some with whirlpools. 6 stories, interior corridors. *Bath:* some combo or shower only. **Parking:** on-site. **Terms:** cancellation fee imposed. **Amenities:** voice mail, safes, irons, hair dryers. *Some:* dual phone lines. **Pool(s):** heated indoor/outdoor. **Leisure Activities:** whirlpool, exercise room. **Guest Services:** wireless Internet. **Business Services:** meeting rooms, business center. **Cards:** AX, DS, MC, VI. **Free Special Amenities: newspaper and high-speed Internet.** *(See color ad p 585)*

CALL

HOMEWOOD SUITES BY HILTON Book great rates at AAA.com **Phone:** (828)252-5400 18

AAA SAVE

Hotel

$119-$249 4/1-11/30
$109-$199 12/1-3/31

Address: 88 Tunnel Rd **Location:** I-240, exit 6, just n. **Facility:** 94 one-bedroom suites with kitchens, some with whirlpools. 6 stories, interior corridors. *Bath:* combo or shower only. **Parking:** on-site. **Terms:** 2-3 night minimum stay - seasonal and/or weekends, 3 day cancellation notice-fee imposed. **Amenities:** video library, DVD players, high-speed Internet, voice mail, irons, hair dryers. **Pool(s):** heated indoor. **Leisure Activities:** whirlpool. **Guest Services:** valet and coin laundry, area transportation-within 5 mi, wireless Internet. **Business Services:** meeting rooms, PC. **Cards:** AX, DS, MC, VI. **Free Special Amenities: expanded continental breakfast and high-speed Internet.** *(See color ad p 593)*

HOMEWOOD SUITES Hilton

AAA Benefit:
Members save 5% or more everyday!

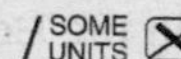
/ SOME UNITS

HOWARD JOHNSON INN BILTMORE Book great rates at AAA.com **Phone:** (828)274-2300 36

AAA SAVE

Motel

$90-$170 7/1-11/30
$70-$140 12/1-6/30

Address: 190 Hendersonville Rd **Location:** I-40, exit 50 eastbound; exit 50B westbound, just n on US 25. Located near Biltmore Estate. **Facility:** 68 one-bedroom standard units. 2 stories (no elevator), interior corridors. **Parking:** on-site. **Terms:** 5 day cancellation notice. **Amenities:** irons, hair dryers. **Pool(s):** outdoor. **Guest Services:** valet laundry. **Business Services:** meeting rooms. **Cards:** AX, DC, DS, MC, VI. **Free Special Amenities: continental breakfast and high-speed Internet.**

/ SOME UNITS

INN ON BILTMORE ESTATE **Phone:** (828)225-1660 45

AAA SAVE

Hotel

$299-$549 All Year

Address: 1 Antler Hill Rd **Location:** I-40, exit 50/50B, 0.8 mi n on US 25, follow signs to Biltmore Estate. **Facility:** The hotel is on the 8,000-acre grounds of the Biltmore Estate and offers luxuriously appointed accommodations. Smoke free premises. 213 units. 206 one-bedroom standard units, some with whirlpools. 7 one-bedroom suites with whirlpools. 7 stories, interior corridors. *Bath:* combo or shower only. **Parking:** on-site and valet. **Terms:** check-in 4 pm, 14 day cancellation notice-fee imposed. **Amenities:** video games (fee), CD players, high-speed Internet, dual phone lines, voice mail, safes, irons, hair dryers. *Some:* DVD players (fee). **Dining:** entertainment. **Pool(s):** heated outdoor. **Leisure Activities:** whirlpool, fishing, hiking trails, exercise room. *Fee:* river rafting, segway, Land Rover experience, bicycles, horseback riding. **Guest Services:** valet laundry, area transportation-estate grounds, wireless Internet. **Business Services:** conference facilities, business center. **Cards:** AX, DC, DS, MC, VI. *(See color ad p 108)*

24 CALL / SOME UNITS FEE VCR

(See map and index starting on p. 576)

THE LION & THE ROSE BED & BREAKFAST — **Phone:** 828/255-7673 14

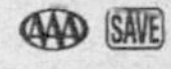

Historic Bed & Breakfast

$165-$225 All Year

Address: 276 Montford Ave **Location:** I-240, exit 4C (Montford Ave/Haywood St), just w, then 0.7 mi n; In historic district. Located in a residential area. **Facility:** This 1895 Queen Anne/Georgian-style home has upscale, individually decorated guest rooms and lush grounds with appealing gardens. Smoke free premises. 5 units. 4 one-bedroom standard units. 1 one-bedroom suite with whirlpool. 3 stories (no elevator), interior corridors. *Bath:* combo or shower only. **Parking:** on-site. **Terms:** 2 night minimum stay - seasonal and/or weekends, age restrictions may apply, 14 day cancellation notice-fee imposed. **Amenities:** video library, DVD players, CD players, hair dryers. *Some:* irons. **Guest Services:** wireless Internet. **Cards:** AX, DS, MC, VI. **Free Special Amenities: full breakfast and high-speed Internet.**

/ SOME UNITS

THE LOG CABIN MOTOR COURT — **Phone:** (828)645-6546 1

Vacation Rental Cabin

$55-$110 All Year

Address: 330 Weaverville Hwy **Location:** US 19/23, exit 21 (New Stock Rd), 1 mi s on Weaverville Hwy. **Facility:** The property features rustic log cabins built in the 1920s and '30s; some have full kitchens. 19 units. 1 house and 18 cabins. 1-2 stories, exterior corridors. *Bath:* combo or shower only. **Parking:** on-site. **Terms:** 2 night minimum stay, 14 day cancellation notice-fee imposed. **Leisure Activities:** picnic tables & grills. **Guest Services:** coin laundry, wireless Internet. **Cards:** AX, DS, MC, VI. **Free Special Amenities: high-speed Internet.**

/ SOME UNITS FEE AC VCR

NORTH LODGE ON OAKLAND — **Phone:** 828/252-6433 31

Bed & Breakfast

$120-$180 All Year

Address: 84 Oakland Rd **Location:** I-40, exit 50, 0.4 mi n to Biltmore Rd, 1 mi n to Victoria Rd, 0.7 mi sw, then just w. **Facility:** This traditional B&B, recently renovated, offers modern guest-room decor and is surrounded by extensive gardens. Smoke free premises. 6 one-bedroom standard units. 3 stories (no elevator), interior corridors. **Parking:** on-site. **Terms:** office hours 10 am-9 pm, check-in 4 pm, 2-3 night minimum stay - weekends, age restrictions may apply, 7 day cancellation notice-fee imposed. **Amenities:** video library, DVD players, CD players, irons, hair dryers. **Leisure Activities:** gazebo, English gardens. *Fee:* massage. **Guest Services:** wireless Internet. **Cards:** MC, VI. **Free Special Amenities: full breakfast and high-speed Internet.**

/ SOME UNITS

▼ See AAA listing p 592 ▼

(See map and index starting on p. 576)

PRINCESS ANNE HOTEL

Boutique Hotel

$119-$299 All Year

Phone: 828/258-0986 16

Address: 301 Chestnut St **Location:** I-240, exit 5B (Charlotte St), just e. Located in a residential area, near town center. **Facility:** Located in a quiet residential setting, the elegant, lovingly restored inn offers the charm of a bygone era with the casual comforts of today. Smoke free premises. 16 units. 6 one-bedroom standard units. 10 one-bedroom suites, some with kitchens. 3 stories, interior corridors. *Bath:* combo or shower only. **Parking:** on-site. **Terms:** office hours 7:30 am-9:30 pm, 3 day cancellation notice-fee imposed. **Amenities:** high-speed Internet, voice mail, safes. *Some:* DVD players. **Guest Services:** coin laundry, wireless Internet. **Business Services:** PC. **Cards:** AX, MC, VI.

CALL / SOME UNITS

QUALITY INN & SUITES *Book great rates at AAA.com*

Motel

$55-$199 All Year

Phone: (828)298-5519 29

Address: 1430 Tunnel Rd **Location:** I-40, exit 55, just n. **Facility:** 132 one-bedroom standard units, some with whirlpools. 2 stories (no elevator), exterior corridors. *Bath:* combo or shower only. **Parking:** on-site. **Terms:** cancellation fee imposed. **Amenities:** high-speed Internet, voice mail, irons, hair dryers. **Pool(s):** outdoor. **Leisure Activities:** exercise room. **Guest Services:** coin laundry, wireless Internet. **Business Services:** PC, fax. **Cards:** AX, CB, DC, DS, JC, MC, VI.

ASK / SOME UNITS FEE

RAMADA *Book great rates at AAA.com*

AAA SAVE

Hotel

$84-$129 5/1-11/30
$74-$109 12/1-4/30

Phone: (828)298-9141 33

Address: 800 Fairview Rd **Location:** I-240, exit 8; jct I-40 and US 74. Located above River Ridge Market Place. **Facility:** 177 units. 153 one-bedroom standard units. 24 one-bedroom suites with whirlpools. 3 stories (no elevator), interior corridors. **Parking:** on-site. **Terms:** check-in 4 pm, 7 day cancellation notice. **Amenities:** high-speed Internet, voice mail, irons, hair dryers. **Pool(s):** outdoor. **Leisure Activities:** whirlpool, picnic area with grills, playground, exercise room, basketball, volleyball. **Guest Services:** valet and coin laundry, wireless Internet. **Business Services:** meeting rooms, PC. **Cards:** AX, CB, DC, DS, MC, VI. **Free Special Amenities: full breakfast and high-speed Internet.**
(See color ad below)

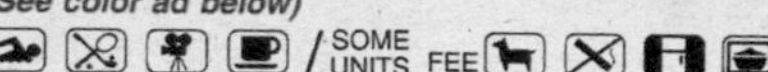

RED ROOF INN-WEST *Book great rates at AAA.com*

AAA SAVE

Motel

$50-$90 All Year

Phone: (828)667-9803 42

Address: 16 Crowell Rd **Location:** I-40, exit 44, just n on US 19 and 23, just w on Old Haywood Rd, then just s. **Facility:** 109 one-bedroom standard units. 3 stories, exterior corridors. *Bath:* combo or shower only. **Parking:** on-site. **Terms:** 14 day cancellation notice. **Amenities:** video games (fee), voice mail. **Cards:** AX, CB, DC, DS, MC, VI. **Free Special Amenities: local telephone calls.**

/ SOME UNITS

(See map and index starting on p. 576)

THE RESIDENCES AT BILTMORE — Phone: 828/350-8000

fyi
Hotel
$139-$519 All Year

Too new to rate, opening scheduled for August 2008. **Address:** 700 Biltmore Ave **Location:** I-40, exit 50, on US 25 (Hendersonville Rd). **Amenities:** 114 units, pets, coffeemakers, microwaves, refrigerators, pool. **Cards:** AX, DC, DS, MC, VI.

RICHMOND HILL INN — **Phone:** (828)252-7313 5

AAA SAVE
Country Inn
$205-$615 All Year

Address: 87 Richmond Hill Dr **Location:** I-240, exit 4A (Weaverville Hwy); US 19/23, exit SR 251, just w on Broadway, under overpass, 1st light s (Riverside Dr), 0.5 mi to Pearson Bridge Rd, then just w (across bridge). **Facility:** This Victorian mansion on six acres of manicured grounds offers rooms in the main inn, a newer wing and private cottages. Smoke free premises. 37 units. 25 one-bedroom standard units, some with whirlpools. 3 one-bedroom suites with whirlpools, some with kitchens. 9 cottages. 3 stories (no elevator), interior/exterior corridors. *Bath:* combo or shower only. **Parking:** on-site and valet. **Terms:** 2 night minimum stay - seasonal and/or weekends, 7 day cancellation notice. **Amenities:** video library, DVD players, CD players, hair dryers. *Some:* irons. **Dining:** Gabrielle's at Richmond Hill, see separate listing. **Leisure Activities:** sauna, croquet, hiking trails, limited exercise equipment, spa. **Guest Services:** valet laundry, wireless Internet. **Business Services:** meeting rooms, business center. **Cards:** AX, MC, VI. **Free Special Amenities: full breakfast and local telephone calls.**

/ SOME UNITS

SLEEP INN BILTMORE — *Book at AAA.com* — **Phone:** (828)277-1800 40

Hotel
$89-$180 4/1-11/30
$69-$139 12/1-3/31

Address: 117 Hendersonville Rd **Location:** I-40, exit 50 eastbound; exit 50B westbound, just n on US 25. Located near Biltmore Estate. **Facility:** 64 one-bedroom standard units. 3 stories, interior corridors. *Bath:* combo or shower only. **Parking:** on-site. **Amenities:** irons. *Some:* hair dryers. **Guest Services:** wireless Internet. **Cards:** AX, CB, DC, DS, MC, VI.

ASK CALL / SOME UNITS FEE

SLEEP INN BILTMORE WEST — *Book great rates at AAA.com* — **Phone:** (828)670-7600 35

AAA SAVE
Hotel
$49-$189 All Year

Address: 1918 Old Haywood Rd **Location:** I-40, exit 44, just n on US 19 and 23, then just w. **Facility:** 74 one-bedroom standard units. 3 stories, interior corridors. *Bath:* combo or shower only. **Parking:** on-site. **Amenities:** irons, hair dryers. **Leisure Activities:** exercise room. **Guest Services:** valet and coin laundry, wireless Internet. **Business Services:** meeting rooms, PC. **Cards:** AX, DS, MC, VI. **Free Special Amenities: expanded continental breakfast and high-speed Internet.**
(See color ad below)

/ SOME UNITS

(See map and index starting on p. 576)

SPRINGHILL SUITES BY MARRIOTT Book great rates at AAA.com Phone: (828)253-4666 22

Hotel
$107-$153 All Year

Address: 2 Buckstone Pl **Location:** I-240, exit 6, 0.5 mi e on US 70 (Tunnel Rd), follow signs. **Facility:** Smoke free premises. 88 one-bedroom standard units. 3 stories, interior corridors. *Bath:* combo or shower only. **Parking:** on-site. **Terms:** check-in 4 pm, cancellation fee imposed. **Amenities:** high-speed Internet, voice mail, irons, hair dryers. **Pool(s):** heated indoor. **Leisure Activities:** whirlpool, exercise room. **Guest Services:** valet and coin laundry, wireless Internet. **Business Services:** meeting rooms, business center. **Cards:** AX, CB, DC, DS, JC, MC, VI.

AAA Benefit: Members save a minimum 5% off the best available rate.

SUPER 8 MOTEL AT BILTMORE SQUARE Book at AAA.com Phone: (828)670-8800 49

Hotel
$59-$159 All Year

Address: 9 Wedgefield Dr **Location:** I-26, exit 33, just nw. Located behind the Holiday Inn Express Hotel & Suites. **Facility:** 65 one-bedroom standard units. 5 stories, interior corridors. *Bath:* combo or shower only. **Parking:** on-site. **Amenities:** video library, hair dryers. *Some:* DVD players (fee). **Guest Services:** coin laundry, wireless Internet. **Business Services:** PC, fax (fee). **Cards:** AX, CB, DC, DS, MC, VI.

ASK CALL / SOME UNITS FEE

SUPER 8 MOTEL CENTRAL Book at AAA.com Phone: 828/667-8706 43

Motel
Rates not provided

Address: 8 Crowell Rd **Location:** I-40, exit 44, just n on US 19 and 23. **Facility:** 62 one-bedroom standard units. 3 stories (no elevator), interior corridors. **Parking:** on-site. **Amenities:** hair dryers. **Guest Services:** coin laundry, wireless Internet. **Business Services:** *Fee:* PC, fax.

CALL / SOME UNITS FEE

THE WRIGHT INN & CARRIAGE HOUSE Phone: (828)251-0789 10

AAA SAVE

Historic Bed & Breakfast
$105-$360 All Year

Address: 235 Pearson Dr **Location:** I-240, exit 4C (Montford Ave/Haywood St), 0.8 mi n to Wautauga, then just w; in historic district. Located in a residential area. **Facility:** Antiques are among the furnishings of the tastefully appointed guest rooms at this restored 1899 Victorian mansion with gardens. Smoke free premises. 11 one-bedroom standard units, some with whirlpools. 4 stories (no elevator), interior/exterior corridors. *Bath:* combo or shower only. **Parking:** on-site. **Terms:** age restrictions may apply, 14 day cancellation notice-fee imposed. **Amenities:** hair dryers. *Some:* DVD players, CD players. **Leisure Activities:** bicycles, horseshoes. **Guest Services:** wireless Internet. **Cards:** AX, DS, MC, VI. **Free Special Amenities: full breakfast and high-speed Internet.**

/ SOME UNITS VCR

WHERE TO DINE

AMICI TRATTORIA Phone: 828/277-1010 27

Italian
$7-$23

Patrons can sample traditional Italian fare in a contemporary setting. Among choices are varied antipasti, primi and secondi dishes, as well as beef carpaccio, calamari, risotto, rigatoni and flat-iron steak with Gorgonzola mashed potatoes and ratatouille. Casual dress. **Bar:** Full bar. **Reservations:** suggested. **Hours:** 11 am-2 & 5-9 pm, Fri-10 pm, Sat 5 pm-10 pm. Closed: 11/26, 12/25; also Sun. **Address:** 900 Hendersonville Rd, Suite 201 **Location:** I-40, exit 50 (US 25), 1 mi s. **Parking:** on-site. **Cards:** AX, DS, MC, VI.

APOLLO FLAME BISTRO Phone: 828/665-0080 29

Greek
$6-$15

The casual eatery is popular with the locals for its varied Greek and Italian selections, friendly service and relaxed atmosphere. Casual dress. **Bar:** Beer & wine. **Hours:** 11 am-10 pm. Closed major holidays; also Sun. **Address:** 1025 Brevard Rd **Location:** I-26, exit 33, 0.3 mi w; in The Center at Biltmore Square. **Parking:** on-site. **Cards:** AX, MC, VI.

APOLLO FLAME BISTRO Phone: 828/274-3582 24

Greek
$5-$12

In a small shopping center, the casual eatery is popular with the locals. The restaurant is known for huge portions and Greek salads served with every entree. Casual dress. **Bar:** Beer & wine. **Reservations:** not accepted. **Hours:** 11 am-10 pm. Closed major holidays; also Sun. **Address:** 485 Hendersonville Rd **Location:** I-40, exit 50 (US 25), 0.5 mi s; in Forest Edge Shopping Center. **Parking:** on-site. **Cards:** AX, DS, MC, VI.

CALL

ASAKA JAPANESE RESTAURANT Phone: 828/250-9301 18

Japanese
$5-$11

The casual restaurant has a limited menu of nicely prepared Japanese entrees of steak, chicken, shrimp and scallops. Table service is offered in the evenings. At lunch, customers order and pay at the counter, and the food is brought to their table. Casual dress. **Reservations:** not accepted. **Hours:** 11 am-10 pm. Closed major holidays. **Address:** 801 Biltmore Ave **Location:** I-40, exit 50 (US 25), 0.9 mi n via Hendersonville Rd. **Parking:** on-site. **Cards:** AX, DS, MC, VI.

ASIANA GRAND BUFFET Phone: 828/667-0410 23

Chinese
$6-$12

In a shopping center, the restaurant specializes in all-you-can-eat buffets for lunch and dinner. Buffet offerings include cooked-to-order and Thai barbecue stations. In addition to traditional dishes, diners can try more unusual Chinese and Vietnamese choices, as well as sushi. Casual dress. **Bar:** Beer & wine. **Hours:** 11 am-3:30 & 4-10 pm. Closed: 7/4, 11/26, 12/25. **Address:** 153 Smokey Park Hwy **Location:** I-40, exit 44, 0.3 mi n. **Parking:** on-site. **Cards:** AX, DS, MC, VI.

CALL

(See map and index starting on p. 576)

BELLAGIO BISTRO — **Phone:** 828/658-9700 (1)

Mediterranean
$6-$8

Between Asheville and Weaverville, the bistro presents a menu of Greek salads, pasta, pizza, gyros and sandwiches. Casual dress. **Bar:** Beer & wine. **Reservations:** not accepted. **Hours:** 11 am-10 pm. Closed major holidays; also Sun. **Address:** 133 Weaverville Hwy **Location:** US 19/23, exit New Bridge northbound; exit N Asheville/Merrimon Ave southbound, just n on US 25. **Parking:** on-site. **Cards:** AX, DS, MC, VI.

CALL

BONEFISH GRILL — **Phone:** 828/298-6530 (17)

Seafood
$13-$20

Fish is the house specialty, and the menu and nightly specials offer a variety of choices. Well-prepared food is cooked to perfection. Service is casual in nature, and the staff is skilled and attentive. Dressy casual. **Bar:** Full bar. **Reservations:** accepted. **Hours:** 4 pm-close. Closed: 11/26, 12/25. **Address:** 105 River Hills Rd **Location:** I-240, exit 7, 1.1 mi e on Tunnel Rd. **Parking:** on-site. **Cards:** AX, DC, DS, MC, VI.

CHARLOTTE STREET GRILL & PUB — **Phone:** 828/253-5348 (8)

Steak
$6-$25

You can find just about anything you are craving on the large menu at this grill and pub. Burgers, pasta, steak are just a few of the satisfying meals served here. A pleasant wait staff adds to the enjoyment of your meal. Casual dress. **Bar:** Full bar. **Reservations:** suggested. **Hours:** 11:30 am-2 & 5-9 pm, Fri & Sat-10 pm. Closed major holidays; also Sun. **Address:** 157 Charlotte St **Location:** I-240, exit 5B (Charlotte St), 0.5 mi n. **Parking:** on-site. **Cards:** AX, DC, DS, MC, VI.

CHELSEA'S CAFE & TEA ROOM — **Phone:** 828/274-4400 (22)

English
$10-$12

Guests enjoy a delightful lunch setting amidst English and Country French antiques, crockery, linens and decor. Browse through their specialty store and relax during English afternoon tea, which is served at 3:30 pm. Casual dress. **Bar:** Beer & wine. **Hours:** 10 am-5 pm, Sun 10:30 am-3 pm. Closed: Sun & 1/1-2/1. **Address:** 6 Boston Way **Location:** I-40, exit 50 (US 25), just n; in Historic Biltmore Village. **Parking:** street. **Cards:** AX, DS, MC, VI.

CHINA PALACE — **Phone:** 828/298-7098 (13)

Chinese
$6-$14

Taste the all-natural ingredients of classic Chinese fare at this pleasant restaurant with an extensive menu of options. Try the precious duck cooked in a five-spice sauce over rice and Oriental vegetables. The authentic decor adds a touch of class. Casual dress. **Bar:** Beer & wine. **Reservations:** accepted. **Hours:** 11 am-10 pm, Sun from noon. Closed: 11/26. **Address:** 4 S Tunnel Rd **Location:** On US 74A; opposite Asheville Mall, just 200 yards south of jct US 70 (Tunnel Rd) and 74A. **Parking:** on-site. **Cards:** AX, MC, VI.

EL CHARRO — **Phone:** 828/277-2248 (31)

Mexican
$5-$15

Situated in a small shopping strip, El Charro presents a menu of traditional Mexican favorites set in an informal, casual dining room. Casual dress. **Bar:** Full bar. **Hours:** 11 am-10 pm. Closed: 7/4, 11/26, 12/25. **Address:** 1788 Hendersonville Rd **Location:** I-40, exit 50 (US 25), 4.5 mi s; beside K-Mart Shopping Plaza. **Parking:** on-site. **Cards:** AX, DS, MC, VI.

FATZ CAFE — **Phone:** 828/665-9950

American
$7-$18

Friendly staff and appealing country decor help set the tone for a relaxed and enjoyable dining experience. It's not unusual for guests to wait to be seated at the popular spot, which earns raves for its well-prepared variations on chicken, steak, ribs and pasta, as well as salads and sandwiches. The signature Southern-style peach cobbler served with vanilla ice cream and walnuts is scrumptious. Casual dress. **Bar:** Full bar. **Reservations:** not accepted. **Hours:** 11 am-10 pm, Fri & Sat-11 pm, Sun-9 pm. Closed: 11/26, 12/25. **Address:** 5 Spartan Ave **Location:** I-40, exit 44, just n. **Parking:** on-site. **Cards:** AX, DC, DS, MC, VI.

CALL

FIDDLIN' PIG BLUE GRASS & BARBECUE — **Phone:** 828/251-1979 (9)

Southern American
$6-$20

Southern hospitality and mouthwatering barbecue satisfy patrons of this family restaurant, a favorite for good ol' down-home cooking with a little foot-stomping bluegrass on the side. Delicious Southern sides—such as fried okra, collard greens and macaroni and cheese—complement beef brisket, pork and St. Louis-style ribs, which are slow-smoked over hickory wood. Casual dress. Entertainment. **Bar:** Full bar. **Reservations:** not accepted. **Hours:** 11:30 am-10 pm, Fri & Sat-11 pm. Closed: 1/1, 11/26, 12/24, 12/25. **Address:** 28 Tunnel Rd **Location:** I-240, exit 6, just e on US 70 (Tunnel Rd). **Parking:** on-site. **Cards:** AX, DS, MC, VI.

FIG — **Phone:** 828/277-0889 (19)

American
$8-$30

The casual restaurant nurtures an upscale feel. Glass walls overlook the street activity. Dressy casual. **Bar:** Full bar. **Reservations:** suggested. **Hours:** 11:30 am-3 & 5:30-9 pm, Fri & Sat-10 pm. Closed major holidays; also Sun. **Address:** 18 Brook St, Suite 101 **Location:** I-40, exit 50 (US 25), 0.3 mi n to US 25A, just s; in Biltmore Village. **Parking:** on-site. **Cards:** AX, DS, MC, VI.

FLAT ROCK GRILLE — **Phone:** 828/277-1212 (30)

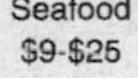

Seafood
$9-$25

The family restaurant lets diners create their own dish by choosing their fish and its accompanying sauce. Salads and steaks are other options. It's worth planning ahead for one of the well-portioned desserts. Casual dress. **Bar:** Full bar. **Hours:** 11 am-9:30 pm, Fri & Sat-10:30 pm, Sun-9 pm. Closed: 11/26, 12/25. **Address:** 1302 Hendersonville Rd **Location:** I-40, exit 50A; US 25 S (Hendersonville Rd), 3 mi. **Parking:** on-site. **Cards:** AX, DS, MC, VI.

(See map and index starting on p. 576)

FRANKIE BONES RESTAURANT & LOUNGE **Phone:** 828/274-7111 (32)

Italian
$6-$25

While the name may sound like that of a rib house, this classic American-Italian restaurant offers an array of choices. Steaks, pasta, chicken and fish are served in a clublike setting reminiscent of the late '60s. Patrons relax in a softly light room accented with dark wood and high-back booths (or on the patio, weather permitting) while crooners of that era sing softly in the background. Grandma Jean's homemade carrot cake makes a meal complete. Casual dress. **Bar:** Full bar. **Reservations:** accepted. **Hours:** 11:30 am-10 pm, Fri & Sat-11 pm, Sun 10 am-10 pm. Closed major holidays. **Address:** 2 Gerber Rd, Suite 101 **Location:** I-40, exit Hendersonville Rd S. **Parking:** on-site. **Cards:** AX, CB, DC, DS, JC, MC, VI.

GABRIELLE'S AT RICHMOND HILL **Phone:** 828/252-7313 (7)

AAA

Regional American
$60-$80

You will be treated to gracious service either in the Victorian dining room or on the glass-enclosed veranda. Featured are some unique Southern variations on many dishes, a high degree of preparation and presentation, and fresh, quality ingredients. Dining room will accommodate large parties. Dressy casual. **Bar:** Full bar. **Reservations:** suggested. **Hours:** 6 pm-10 pm. **Address:** 87 Richmond Hill Dr **Location:** I-240, exit 4A (Weaverville Hwy); US 19/23, exit SR 251, just w on Broadway, under overpass, 1st light s (Riverside Dr), 0.5 mi to Pearson Bridge Rd, then just w (across bridge); in Richmond Hill Inn. **Parking:** on-site. **Cards:** AX, MC, VI.

GREEN TEA JAPANESE KITCHEN & SUSHI BAR **Phone:** 828/252-8300 (11)

Japanese
$4-$18

In a strip mall across the French Broad River, the casual restaurant entices guests with fresh sushi and friendly service. Casual dress. **Bar:** Beer & wine. **Reservations:** accepted. **Hours:** 11:30 am-3 & 4:30-10 pm, Fri & Sat-10:30 pm, Sun 1 pm-10 pm. Closed: 11/26. **Address:** 2 Regent Park Blvd **Location:** Jct SR 74A (Patton Ave) and US 240, just w on Patton Ave; in Regent Park Shopping Center. **Parking:** on-site. **Cards:** AX, MC, VI.

GROVEWOOD CAFE **Phone:** 828/258-8956 (4)

Continental
$7-$35

Gracious and homey, this upscale cafe with a splendid view serves delicious Southern recipes that are said to be the best kept secrets in the mountains. Feast on fresh salad and flavorful, seasonally changing dishes. There is something for just about everyone. A few vegetarian offerings. Smoking allowed on patio in season. Dressy casual. **Bar:** Full bar. **Reservations:** suggested. **Hours:** 11 am-2:30 & 5-9 pm; hours may vary in winter. **Address:** 111 Grovewood Rd **Location:** I-240, exit 5B (Charlotte St), 2 mi n via Charlotte St and Macon Ave; adjacent to Grove Park Inn Resort & Spa. **Parking:** on-site. **Cards:** AX, DC, DS, MC, VI.

HARBOR INN SEAFOOD **Phone:** 828/665-9940

Seafood
$4-$14

The laid-back restaurant is known for its broiled and fried seafood. Informal servers pay attention to customer needs. There can be a wait for seating in the nautical dining room, especially on weekends. Casual dress. **Hours:** 11 am-9 pm, Fri & Sat-10 pm. Closed: 4/12, 11/26, 12/25; also Mon. **Address:** 880 Brevard Rd **Location:** I-26, exit 33, just w. **Parking:** on-site. **Cards:** AX, DS, MC, VI.

CALL

HORIZONS **Phone:** 828/252-2711 (3)

American
$75-$125

The spacious, attractive dining area is nicely decorated with elegant, arts-and-crafts-style furnishings and affords a nice view of a nearby golf course and hillside. Superior, innovative cuisine is served under silver cover by a cordial, competent staff. Semi-formal attire. Entertainment. **Bar:** Full bar. **Reservations:** required. **Hours:** 6 pm-9:30 pm. Closed: Sun & Mon. **Address:** 290 Macon Ave **Location:** I-240, exit 5B (Charlotte St), 2 mi n on Macon Ave via Charlotte St, follow signs; in The Grove Park Inn Resort & Spa. **Parking:** on-site and valet. **Cards:** AX, CB, DC, DS, JC, MC, VI.

CALL

INDIA GARDEN AUTHENTIC INDIAN CUISINE **Phone:** 828/298-5001 (14)

Indian
$6-$17

Guests savor well-prepared chicken, lamb, seafood and vegetarian dishes that are spiced to the requested level. Staff are knowledgeable about menu preparations and attentive to the guest. The relaxed setting combines with prepared-to-order cuisine for a pleasurable experience. Dressy casual. **Bar:** Beer & wine. **Reservations:** suggested. **Hours:** 11 am-3 & 5-9:30 pm, Fri & Sat-11 pm. Closed: 12/25. **Address:** 156 S Tunnel Rd **Location:** I-240, exit 7, just w, then 0.3 mi s; in Overlook Village Shopping Center, opposite Asheville Mall. **Parking:** on-site. **Cards:** AX, DC, MC, VI.

CALL

J & S CAFETERIA **Phone:** 828/298-0507

American
$3-$10

Guests are served steaming entrees, homemade bread and cold items from the comfortable cafeteria's buffet. The dessert area overflows with homemade, tasty treats. Casual dress. **Hours:** 6:15-10 am, 10:45-2:15 & 3:45-8 pm, Fri & Sat 6:15 am-10:30 & 10:45-8:30 pm, Sun 10:45 am-8 pm. Closed: 12/25. **Address:** 800 Fairview Rd **Location:** I-240, exit 8, just n to River Ridge Market Place. **Parking:** on-site. **Cards:** MC, VI.

LACARRETA **Phone:** 828/651-4462 (33)

Mexican
$5-$15

Friendly, helpful staff members serve ample portions of traditional Mexican cuisine. The newly constructed restaurant lets diners unwind in an adobe setting. Casual dress. **Bar:** Full bar. **Hours:** 11 am-10 pm, Fri & Sat-11 pm. Closed major holidays. **Address:** 1916 Hendersonville Rd **Location:** I-40, exit 50 (US 25), 5 mi s. **Parking:** on-site. **Cards:** AX, DS, MC, VI.

LA PAZ RESTAURANT **Phone:** 828/277-8779 (21)

Mexican
$5-$15

A traditional Mexican and Southwestern menu features seafood dishes, stuffed peppers, great margaritas and fresh salsa made on the premises daily. The ambience is lively, upscale gourmet in a casual setting, decorated with traditional Mexican handicrafts. Casual dress. **Bar:** Full bar. **Hours:** 11 am-10 pm, Fri & Sat-11 pm. Closed: 11/26, 12/24, 12/25. **Address:** 10 Biltmore Plaza **Location:** I-40, exit 50 (US 25), 0.3 mi n to SR 81, just e to US 25A, then just s; in Biltmore Village. **Parking:** street. **Cards:** MC, VI.

(See map and index starting on p. 576)

THE MOOSE CAFE **Phone:** 828/255-0920 (25)

Southern
$5-$10

All plates come with two fresh vegetables and a main dish of ham, fried chicken, roast turkey with cornbread dressing or roast beef. Be sure to sample Southern-only specialties like sweet potato souffle. Sip some sweet tea or lomonade and take in the million dollar view high up in the Blue Ridge Mountains. **Hours:** 7 am-8:30 pm, Fri & Sat-9 pm; hours may vary in winter. Closed: 12/25; also for dinner 11/24. **Address:** 570 Brevard Rd **Location:** I-40, exit 47; adjacent to the Farmer's Market. **Parking:** on-site. **Cards:** MC, VI.

CALL

POMODOROS GREEK & ITALIAN CAFE **Phone:** 828/299-3032 (12)

Greek
$7-$24

Greek and Italian dishes are made in house using fresh ingredients. Some innovative touches punctuate traditional preparations of pasta and other entrees. The dining room has a contemporary look. Outdoor dining is a seasonal option. Dressy casual. **Bar:** Full bar. **Reservations:** suggested. **Hours:** 11:30 am-9:30 pm, Fri & Sat-10 pm, Sun 10:30 am-9 pm; Sunday brunch. Closed: 11/26, 12/25. **Address:** 1070 Tunnel Rd **Location:** I-240, exit 7, 1.8 mi e; I-40, exit 55, just n, then 1.5 mi w. **Parking:** on-site. **Cards:** AX, MC, VI.

CALL

PROVINCE 620 **Phone:** 828/277-0355 (26)

American
$7-$22

Dark woods give a rich, distinctive look to the casual dining room. Service is accommodating and informal. In addition to chicken, steak and seafood options, the menu includes Italian and Greek items. The signature appetizer is breaded and fried Parmesan-stuffed green olives. Dressy casual. **Bar:** Full bar. **Reservations:** not accepted. **Hours:** 11 am-10 pm, Sat from 4 pm. Closed: 1/1, 12/25; also Super Bowl Sun. **Address:** 620 Hendersonville Rd **Location:** I-40, exit 50 (US 25), 0.6 mi s. **Parking:** on-site. **Cards:** AX, DS, MC, VI.

CALL

RED ORCHID THAI RESTAURANT **Phone:** 828/281-4155 (10)

Thai
$6-$18

Top-flight traditional Thai specialties make up the menu. Each aromatic dish is prepared to order using fresh ingredients. Exotic spices and fruits, along with the judicious use of chili, enable tastes to meld and blend lusciously on the palate. Fantastic edible garnishes lend to the stunning, innovative presentations. The intimate dining room has real wood and authentic artwork. Dressy casual. **Bar:** Full bar. **Reservations:** accepted. **Hours:** 11:30 am-2:30 & 5-9 pm, Fri & Sat-9:30 pm, Sun noon-2:30 & 5-9 pm. Closed: 11/26, 12/25. **Address:** 70 Westgate Hwy **Location:** I-240, exit 3B (Holiday Inn Dr), just w; in Westgate Shopping Center. **Parking:** on-site. **Cards:** AX, DC, MC, VI.

CALL

REZAZ MEDITERRANEAN CUISINE **Phone:** 828/277-1510 (20)

Mediterranean
$4-$22

The owner/chef creatively prepares nouveau Mediterranean and Middle Eastern food. The upscale, elegant dining room sits in historic Biltmore Square. Dressy casual. **Bar:** Full bar. **Reservations:** suggested. **Hours:** 11:30 am-2 & 5:30-9:30 pm, Fri & Sat-10:30 pm. Closed major holidays; also Sun. **Address:** 28 Hendersonville Rd **Location:** I-40, exit 50 (US 25), 1 mi n; in Historic Biltmore Village. **Parking:** on-site. **Cards:** AX, MC, VI.

SAVOY RESTAURANT & MARTINI BAR **Phone:** 828/253-1077 (6)

Continental
$8-$43

Enjoy a different creative dish each visit as the menu changes nightly. Excellent desserts are made to on the premises. Casual dress. **Bar:** Full bar. **Reservations:** suggested. **Hours:** 11:30 am-2 & 5:30-9 pm, Sat & Sun 5:30 pm-10 pm. Closed: 7/4, 11/26, 12/25. **Address:** 641 Merrimon Ave **Location:** I-240, exit 5A (Merrimon Ave), 1.8 mi n. **Parking:** on-site. **Cards:** AX, DS, MC, VI.

CALL

SPIRITS ON THE RIVER NATIVE AMERICAN RESTAURANT **Phone:** 828/299-1404 (16)

Specialty
$7-$18

Vegetables and grains enhance the unique but well-prepared, tasty entrees. Using traditional Native American techniques, rattlesnake, alligator and buffalo are prepared to perfection. Guests can dine indoors in an adobe-like setting or with nature, overlooking the river. Casual dress. **Bar:** Beer & wine. **Hours:** noon-9 pm, Wed from 5 pm, Sun noon-8 pm; hours may vary in winter. Closed major holidays; also Mon & Tues. **Address:** 571 Swannanoa River Rd (SR 81) **Location:** I-240, exit 8, 0.5 mi ne on US 74A, then just w. **Parking:** on-site. **Cards:** MC, VI.

STONE RIDGE TAVERN **Phone:** 828/665-3333 (28)

American
$6-$24

Lending to the large tavern's mountain retreat atmosphere are stone accents and a waterfall. Menu items include soups, salads, sandwiches, burgers and grilled entrees. Casual dress. **Bar:** Full bar. **Reservations:** not accepted. **Hours:** 11 am-10 pm, Fri-11 pm, Sat 4 pm-11 pm. Closed: 11/26, 12/25. **Address:** 1003 Brevard Rd **Location:** I-26, exit 33, 0.3 mi w. **Parking:** on-site. **Cards:** AX, DS, MC, VI.

URBAN BURRITO **Phone:** 828/251-1921 (5)

Mexican
$5-$7

Quick serve that is fresh, fast and affordable. This California-style Mexican grill is a friendly alternative to fast food. Order from a list of burritos, tacos, salads or soups, and watch as it's prepared with your choice of ingredients. Casual dress. **Bar:** Beer only. **Hours:** 11 am-9 pm, Fri & Sat-10 pm. Closed: 7/4, 11/26, 12/25. **Address:** 640 Merrimon Ave, Suite 203 **Location:** I-240, exit 5A (Merrimon Ave), 1.8 mi n. **Parking:** on-site. **Cards:** AX, DS, MC, VI.

(See map and index starting on p. 576)

USUAL SUSPECTS
Phone: 828/350-8181 (2)

International
$7-$18

The northside neighborhood bar and restaurant has a relaxed atmosphere and friendly staff. Guests unwind in a converted building turned contemporary, casual dining space and peruse a menu of global selections. Casual dress. **Bar:** Full bar. **Hours:** noon-1:30 am, Tues-Sat from 5:30 pm. Closed: Sun. **Address:** 791 Merrimon Ave **Location:** I-240, exit 5A (Merrimon Ave), 1.8 mi n. **Parking:** on-site. **Cards:** AX, MC, VI.

WESTVILLE PUB
Phone: 828/225-9782 (15)

American
$5-$10

Westside residents favor the eatery for typical pub fare, including nachos, wraps and sandwiches. The food is fresh and the staff friendly. Casual dress. **Bar:** Full bar. **Hours:** noon-2 am. Closed: 1/1, 11/26, 12/25. **Address:** 777 Haywood Rd **Location:** Jct US 26 and 240, 0.7 mi e on Haywood Rd (West Asheville). **Parking:** street. **Cards:** AX, CB, DC, DS, JC, MC, VI.

ATLANTIC BEACH pop. 1,781

WHERE TO DINE

AMOS MOSQUITO'S RESTAURANT AND BAR
Phone: 252/247-6222

American
$12-$28

Seafood, steak and pasta are featured at the casual, family-friendly restaurant. Patio seating is an option. Casual dress. **Bar:** Full bar. **Reservations:** not accepted. **Hours:** Open 12/1-1/1 & 2/15-11/30; 5 pm-9 pm, Fri & Sat-10 pm; hours may vary off season. Closed: 11/26, 12/24, 12/25. **Address:** 703 E Fort Macon Rd **Location:** 0.5 mi e on SR 58. **Parking:** on-site. **Cards:** AX, DS, MC, VI.

CHANNEL MARKER RESTAURANT
Phone: 252/247-2344

Steak & Seafood
$15-$32

On the waterfront of Bogue Sound, the casual restaurant is popular with locals and vacationers. Steamed, broiled and fried seafood grounds the menu. Casual dress. **Bar:** Full bar. **Hours:** 5 pm-9 pm; to 10 pm, also Sat & Sun 7 am-2 pm in season. **Address:** 718 Atlantic Beach Cswy **Location:** Just over bridge from Morehead City. **Parking:** on-site. **Cards:** AX, MC, VI.

AVON —*See Outer Banks p. 775.*

BALD HEAD ISLAND pop. 173

WHERE TO STAY

THEODOSIA'S BED & BREAKFAST
Phone: 910/457-6563

Bed & Breakfast
Rates not provided

Address: 2 Keelson Row **Location:** Jct SR 87, 0.9 mi s on SR 211, then w on W 9th St to ferry terminal; catch ferry at Indigo Plantation in Southport. Located off the marina in the Harbor Row area. **Facility:** Balconies at this inn offer scenic views of a peaceful, quiet island where no motor vehicles are permitted; spacious rooms are tastefully decorated. Smoke free premises. 10 one-bedroom standard units, some with whirlpools. 3 stories (no elevator), interior/exterior corridors. *Bath:* combo or shower only. **Parking:** on-site (fee). **Terms:** age restrictions may apply. **Amenities:** video library, voice mail, irons, hair dryers. *Some:* CD players. **Leisure Activities:** bicycles. **Guest Services:** area transportation, wireless Internet. **Business Services:** meeting rooms.

BANNER ELK pop. 811

WHERE TO STAY

1902 TURNPIKE HOUSE *Book at AAA.com*
Phone: (828)898-5611

Historic Bed & Breakfast
$89-$159 All Year

Address: 317 Old Turnpike Rd **Location:** From center, just w on SR 184 (toward Beech Mountain), then just w. **Facility:** Tucked on a residential street at the base of Beech Mountain, this renovated home features modestly furnished rooms in a tranquil setting. Smoke free premises. 7 one-bedroom standard units, some with whirlpools. 2 stories (no elevator), interior/exterior corridors. *Bath:* combo or shower only. **Parking:** on-site. **Terms:** 2 night minimum stay - seasonal and/or weekends, 10 day cancellation notice-fee imposed. **Amenities:** video library. *Some:* DVD players, irons, hair dryers. **Leisure Activities:** whirlpool. **Guest Services:** wireless Internet. **Cards:** AX, DS, MC, VI.

SOME UNITS

AZALEA INN
Phone: (828)898-8195

Bed & Breakfast
$99-$209 All Year

Address: 149 Azalea Cir **Location:** Jct SR 184 and 194, just e to Azalea Cir, then just s. **Facility:** The flower gardens at this renovated 1934 home have won awards; shops and restaurants are within walking distance. Designated smoking area. 11 units. 6 one-bedroom standard units, some with whirlpools. 2 one-bedroom suites with whirlpools. 3 cottages. 2 stories (no elevator), interior/exterior corridors. *Bath:* combo or shower only. **Parking:** on-site. **Terms:** age restrictions may apply, 14 day cancellation notice. **Amenities:** video library. *Some:* DVD players, irons, hair dryers. **Guest Services:** wireless Internet. **Cards:** AX, CB, DC, DS, JC, MC, VI.

THE BANNER ELK INN B&B AND COTTAGES

Phone: (828)898-6223

Bed & Breakfast

$90-$250 All Year

Address: 407 Main St E **Location:** Jct SR 184 and 194, 0.3 mi n on SR 194. **Facility:** This B&B in a restored 1912 home provides a cozy environment enhanced by antique furnishings from around the world. Designated smoking area. 8 units. 5 one-bedroom standard units, some with whirlpools. 1 cabin and 2 cottages. 2 stories (no elevator), interior corridors. **Parking:** on-site. **Terms:** 2-3 night minimum stay - seasonal and/or weekends, age restrictions may apply, 30 day cancellation notice-fee imposed. **Amenities:** high-speed Internet. *Some:* DVD players. **Guest Services:** wireless Internet. **Cards:** AX, DS, MC, VI.

/ SOME UNITS

BEST WESTERN MOUNTAIN LODGE AT BANNER ELK *Book great rates at AAA.com*

Phone: (828)898-4571

Hotel

$80-$210 12/1-3/1

$80-$190 3/2-11/30

Address: 1615 Tynecastle Hwy **Location:** 1 mi se on SR 184. **Facility:** Smoke free premises. 100 units. 99 one-bedroom standard units. 1 one-bedroom suite with whirlpool. 2 stories (no elevator), exterior corridors. *Bath:* combo or shower only. **Parking:** on-site, winter plug-ins. **Terms:** 2-4 night minimum stay - seasonal and/or weekends, 3 day cancellation notice-fee imposed. **Amenities:** video library, DVD players, high-speed Internet, voice mail, irons, hair dryers. **Pool(s):** heated outdoor. **Leisure Activities:** grills & picnic tables, gazebo, tiki bar, game room. **Guest Services:** coin laundry, wireless Internet. **Business Services:** conference facilities, PC, fax (fee). **Cards:** AX, CB, DC, DS, JC, MC, VI. **Free Special Amenities: newspaper and high-speed Internet.**

(See color ad below)

AAA Benefit:

Members save up to 20%, plus 10% bonus points with rewards program.

HIGHLANDS AT SUGAR

Phone: 828/898-9601

Vacation Rental Condominium

Rates not provided

Address: 2173 Sugar Mountain Dr **Location:** Jct SR 184 and Sugar Mountain Dr, 4 mi w. Located in a quiet rural area. **Facility:** Atop one of the highest mountains in the area, this property offers outstanding views. 57 units. 30 one- and 27 two-bedroom suites with kitchens and whirlpools. 1-2 stories (no elevator), exterior corridors. **Parking:** on-site. **Terms:** check-in 4 pm. **Amenities:** video library (fee), DVD players, CD players, voice mail, irons, hair dryers. **Pool(s):** heated indoor. **Leisure Activities:** sauna, whirlpool, hiking trails, playground, exercise room. *Fee:* game room. **Guest Services:** wireless Internet.

THE PERRY HOUSE BED & BREAKFAST

Phone: (828)898-3535

Bed & Breakfast

$69-$139 All Year

Address: 153 Klonteska Dr **Location:** Just n of town center. **Facility:** A front porch furnished with rockers overlooks both Main Street as well as the distant mountains. Smoke free premises. 5 one-bedroom standard units. 2 stories, interior corridors. *Bath:* shower only. **Parking:** on-site. **Terms:** check-in 4 pm, 14 day cancellation notice-fee imposed. **Amenities:** video library. **Business Services:** PC, fax. **Cards:** AX, DS, MC, VI.

ASK

VALLE CRUCIS BED & BREAKFAST

Phone: 828/963-2525

Bed & Breakfast

$139-$225 All Year

Address: 2171 Broadstone Rd **Location:** Jct SR 321, 4.7 mi w on SR 105, then 2 mi n. **Facility:** The sumptuous decor at the rustic, mountain property is sure to offer guests a comfortable, relaxed visit. Smoke free premises. 5 one-bedroom standard units, some with whirlpools. 1-2 stories (no elevator), interior/exterior corridors. **Parking:** on-site. **Terms:** 2 night minimum stay - weekends, 7 day cancellation notice-fee imposed. **Amenities:** irons, hair dryers. *Some:* DVD players. **Leisure Activities:** whirlpool. **Guest Services:** wireless Internet. **Cards:** MC, VI.

/ SOME UNITS

▼ *See AAA listing above* ▼

WHERE TO DINE

THE CORNER PALATE

Phone: 828/898-8668

American
$5-$22

The saloon-turned-restaurant has the feel of a spot blissfully stuck in another era. Fresh ingredients and a friendly staff help make this a locals' favorite. Casual dress. **Bar:** Full bar. **Reservations:** accepted. **Hours:** 4 pm-9 pm, Fri & Sat-10 pm; hours may vary. **Address:** 115 Shawneehaw Ave S **Location:** Corner of Tyne Castle and SR 194 S; center. **Parking:** street. **Cards:** AX, DS, MC, VI.

LOUISIANA PURCHASE

Phone: 828/898-5656

Creole
$16-$34

The intimate restaurant's chef creatively prepares traditional Creole and Cajun dishes. The wait staff is knowledgeable and attentive. Dressy casual. **Bar:** Full bar. **Reservations:** suggested. **Hours:** 6 pm-10 pm; seasonal hours vary. Closed major holidays; also Sun & Mon. **Address:** 397 Shawneehaw Ave **Location:** SR 184 S; center. **Parking:** on-site. **Cards:** AX, CB, DC, DS, JC, MC, VI.

THE MOUNTAIN TAVERN & GRILLE

Phone: 828/898-8887

American
$17-$32

As you sip a fine glass of wine, savor such menu offerings as Kobe beef, carpaccio and ahi tuna. To wrap up the meal, you can't go wrong with the chocolate tart. Casual dress. **Bar:** Full bar. **Reservations:** accepted. **Hours:** 5 pm-10 pm, Fri & Sat-11 pm; hours vary seasonally. Closed major holidays; also 12/24, Sun & Mon 11/1-4/30. **Address:** 3990 Hwy 105, Suite 6 **Location:** Jct SR 105 and 184 N; in Grandfather Shopping Center. **Parking:** on-site. **Cards:** AX, DC, DS, MC, VI.

SORRENTO'S BISTRO

Phone: 828/898-5214

Italian
$5-$30

Traditional cuisine is consistently well-prepared at the family-owned eatery. Casual dress. **Bar:** Full bar. **Hours:** noon-10 pm, Fri & Sat-11 pm; hours may vary in winter. Closed major holidays; also Tues. **Address:** 140 Azalea Cir **Location:** Center; in Village Shops. **Parking:** on-site. **Cards:** AX, DC, DS, MC, VI.

STONE WALLS

Phone: 828/898-5550

American
$12-$30

This popular eatery serves traditional American food with a regional flare. Casual dress. **Bar:** Full bar. **Reservations:** accepted. **Hours:** 5 pm-10 pm, Fri & Sat-11 pm. Closed: 4/12, 11/26, 12/25. **Address:** SR 184 S **Location:** Just s of town center. **Parking:** on-site. **Cards:** AX, MC, VI.

CALL

BEAUFORT pop. 3,771

WHERE TO STAY

BEAUFORT INN

Phone: (252)728-2600

Hotel
$79-$169 All Year

Address: 101 Ann St **Location:** Jct US 70, just s on Moore St, then just w. Located in the historic district. **Facility:** Smoke free premises. 40 units. 36 one-bedroom standard units. 4 one-bedroom suites. 3 stories, exterior corridors. **Parking:** on-site. **Terms:** 2-3 night minimum stay - weekends, 4 day cancellation notice. **Amenities:** irons, hair dryers. **Leisure Activities:** whirlpool, fishing, rental bicycles, exercise room. *Fee:* marina. **Guest Services:** wireless Internet. **Business Services:** meeting rooms. **Cards:** AX, CB, DC, DS, MC, VI. **Free Special Amenities: full breakfast and high-speed Internet.**

/ SOME UNITS

OLD SEAPORT INN

Phone: (252)728-4300

Historic Bed & Breakfast
$99-$150 All Year

Address: 217 Turner St **Location:** Jct US 70, just s; corner of Broad St. Located in the historic district. **Facility:** A manicured garden and patio area add charm to the restored 1866 home; guests are welcome to stroll through the owner's onsite gallery. Smoke free premises. 3 one-bedroom standard units. 2 stories (no elevator), interior corridors. *Bath:* shower only. **Parking:** on-site. **Terms:** 2 night minimum stay - seasonal and/or weekends, 5 day cancellation notice-fee imposed. **Guest Services:** TV in common area, wireless Internet. **Cards:** MC, VI.

ASK

PECAN TREE INN

Phone: (252)728-6733

Historic Bed & Breakfast
$140-$190 4/1-11/30
$110-$150 12/1-3/31

Address: 116 Queen St **Location:** Jct US 70, just s. Located in the historic district. **Facility:** A half-block from the waterfront, this 1866 Victorian inn features handsomely appointed rooms and public areas and an English flower and herb garden. Smoke free premises. 7 one-bedroom standard units, some with whirlpools. 2 stories (no elevator), interior/exterior corridors. *Bath:* combo or shower only. **Parking:** on-site. **Terms:** 2 night minimum stay - seasonal and/or weekends, age restrictions may apply, 7 day cancellation notice-fee imposed. **Amenities:** hair dryers. **Leisure Activities:** bicycles. **Guest Services:** wireless Internet. **Cards:** AX, DS, MC, VI.

ASK

WHERE TO DINE

BEAUFORT GROCERY CO.

Phone: 252/728-3899

American
$8-$35

The eatery welcomes a stop for a gourmet or delicatessen sandwich at lunchtime or a return at dinner for innovative cuisine and nightly specials such as yellowfin grilled tuna or veal scaloppine. Homemade desserts, including an array of delectable cheesecakes, demand attention. Casual dress. **Bar:** Full bar. **Reservations:** suggested. **Hours:** Open 12/1-12/31 & 2/1-11/30; 11:30 am-2:30 & 5:30-9 pm. Closed: 11/26, 12/25; also Tues off season. **Address:** 117 Queen St **Location:** Jct US 70, just s; in historic district. **Parking:** on-site. **Cards:** AX, DS, MC, VI.

CLAWSON'S 1905 RESTAURANT & PUB **Phone:** 252/728-2133

American
$6-$20

Located in a vintage building across from the waterfront, the casual, family-friendly restaurant features seafood, steaks and pasta as well as burgers and sandwiches. The award-winning mud pie dessert is centered around rocky road ice cream and will satisfy any sweet tooth. The pub is a favorite hang-out for tourists and locals alike. Casual dress. **Bar:** Full bar. **Reservations:** accepted. **Hours:** 11:30 am-9 pm, Fri & Sat-9:30 pm; 11:30 am-9:30 pm, Fri & Sat-10 pm, Sun 4:30 pm-9:30 pm in summer. Closed: 1/1, 11/26, 12/24, 12/25; also Sun. **Address:** 425 Front St **Location:** On waterfront; downtown. **Parking:** on-site. **Cards:** DS, MC, VI.

FINZ GRILL & BAR **Phone:** 252/728-7459

Seafood
$5-$20

Fried seafood and burgers, along with hot wings, quesadillas and steak, are on the menu at the waterfront eatery. During warmer weather, guests can enjoy their meal outside on the covered deck. Casual dress. **Bar:** Full bar. **Hours:** 11 am-9 pm; to 10 pm in summer. Closed: 1/1, 12/25. **Address:** 330 Front St **Location:** On waterfront. **Parking:** on-site. **Cards:** DS, MC, VI.

BELMONT pop. 8,705

WHERE TO STAY

HAMPTON INN - BELMONT AT MONTCROSS *Book great rates at AAA.com* **Phone:** (704)825-6100

Hotel
$99-$149 All Year

Address: 820 Cecilia Alexander Dr **Location:** I-85, exit 26 northbound, just e; exit southbound, just e, then just s. **Facility:** Smoke free premises. 85 one-bedroom standard units. 4 stories, interior corridors. *Bath:* combo or shower only. **Parking:** on-site. **Terms:** 1-30 night minimum stay, cancellation fee imposed. **Amenities:** high-speed Internet, voice mail, irons, hair dryers. **Pool(s):** outdoor. **Leisure Activities:** exercise room. **Guest Services:** valet and coin laundry, wireless Internet. **Business Services:** meeting rooms, business center. **Cards:** AX, CB, DC, DS, MC, VI.

AAA Benefit:
Members save up to 10% everyday!

BLACK MOUNTAIN pop. 7,511

WHERE TO STAY

COMFORT INN *Book great rates at AAA.com* **Phone:** (828)669-9950

AAA SAVE

Motel
$49-$129 All Year

Address: 585 Hwy 9 **Location:** I-40, exit 64, just s. **Facility:** 57 one-bedroom standard units, some with whirlpools. 2 stories (no elevator), exterior corridors. *Bath:* combo or shower only. **Parking:** on-site. **Amenities:** voice mail, safes, irons, hair dryers. *Some:* DVD players. **Pool(s):** outdoor. **Guest Services:** coin laundry, wireless Internet. **Business Services:** PC. **Cards:** AX, CB, DC, DS, MC, VI. **Free Special Amenities: expanded continental breakfast and high-speed Internet.**

CALL / SOME UNITS VCR

INN ON MILL CREEK **Phone:** 828/668-1115

Bed & Breakfast
$145-$200 All Year

Address: 3895 Mill Creek Rd **Location:** I-40, exit 66, just n, 0.9 mi e on Ridgecrest Rd, 0.9 mi n on Yates Ave to white gate, then 1.5 mi n. Located in a remote location. **Facility:** This modern property, set beside a brook with a small waterfall and swimming hole, has large guest rooms and a community kitchen. Designated smoking area. 7 one-bedroom standard units, some with whirlpools. 2 stories, interior/exterior corridors. *Bath:* combo or shower only. **Parking:** on-site. **Terms:** 2 night minimum stay - weekends, 30 day cancellation notice-fee imposed. **Amenities:** video library, hair dryers. *Some:* DVD players, irons. **Leisure Activities:** canoeing, paddleboats, fishing, hiking trails. *Fee:* massage. **Guest Services:** wireless Internet. **Business Services:** meeting rooms, PC, fax. **Cards:** DS, MC, VI.

VCR / SOME UNITS

WHERE TO DINE

VERNADA CAFE & GIFTS **Phone:** 828/669-8864

American
$3-$8

A historic building houses this quaint storefront lunch room, where patrons find six daily homemade soups, creative sandwiches, wraps and vegetarian options. Casual dress. **Bar:** Beer & wine. **Reservations:** not accepted. **Hours:** 11 am-3 pm. Closed major holidays; also Sun. **Address:** 119 Cherry St **Location:** Center. **Parking:** street. **Cards:** AX, MC, VI.

BLOWING ROCK pop. 1,418

WHERE TO STAY

ALPEN ACRES MOTEL **Phone:** (828)295-7981

AAA SAVE

Motel
$59-$134 5/22-11/30
$54-$119 12/1-5/21

Address: 318 Old US Hwy 321 **Location:** 1.3 mi n on US 221 and 321; 0.3 mi n of Blue Ridge Pkwy at MM 292. **Facility:** 19 units. 18 one-bedroom standard units, some with kitchens. 1 cottage. 1 story, exterior corridors. *Bath:* combo or shower only. **Parking:** on-site. **Terms:** 3 day cancellation notice. **Amenities:** *Some:* DVD players, irons. **Pool(s):** heated outdoor. **Leisure Activities:** grills & picnic area, playground, horseshoes, shuffleboard, volleyball. **Guest Services:** wireless Internet. **Cards:** AX, DS, MC, VI.

ALPINE VILLAGE INN

Motel

$59-$119 5/1-11/30
$49-$89 12/1-4/30

Phone: 828/295-7206

Address: 297 Sunset Dr **Location:** Just e of Main St. **Facility:** Smoke free premises. 17 one-bedroom standard units, some with whirlpools. 1-2 stories (no elevator), exterior corridors. *Bath:* combo or shower only. **Parking:** on-site, winter plug-ins. **Terms:** 2-3 night minimum stay - seasonal and/or weekends, 7 day cancellation notice-fee imposed. **Amenities:** *Some:* DVD players, irons, hair dryers. **Cards:** DS, MC, VI.

CALL / SOME UNITS VCR

BLOWING ROCK INN

Motel

$69-$159 4/1-11/30

Phone: 828/295-7921

Address: 788 N Main St **Location:** Just n on US 221 and 321 business route. **Facility:** 24 units. 20 one-bedroom standard units. 4 one-bedroom suites with efficiencies. 1 story, exterior corridors. **Parking:** on-site. **Terms:** open 4/1-11/30, 2 night minimum stay - seasonal and/or weekends, 7 day cancellation notice-fee imposed. **Amenities:** *Some:* irons. **Cards:** AX, MC, VI.

/ SOME UNITS

BOB TIMBERLAKE INN AT CHETOLA RESORT

Country Inn

$241-$370 4/24-11/30
$204-$370 12/1-4/23

Phone: (828)295-5500

Address: 538 N Main St **Location:** 1 mi e on US 321 business route, follow signs off US 321 Bypass; 0.5 mi n of Blue Ridge Pkwy via US 321. **Facility:** The small inn's unique furnishings, artwork and accessories were created and hand-selected by the property's renowned namesake artist. Smoke free premises. 8 one-bedroom standard units with whirlpools. 3 stories, interior corridors. **Parking:** on-site. **Terms:** 2 night minimum stay - weekends, 3 day cancellation notice. **Amenities:** DVD players, CD players, voice mail, safes, irons, hair dryers. **Dining:** The Manor House at Chetola Resort, see separate listing. **Pool(s):** heated indoor. **Leisure Activities:** sauna, whirlpool, rental boats, rental canoes, rental paddleboats, fishing, 3 tennis courts, recreation programs, hiking trails, playground, exercise room, horseshoes, volleyball. *Fee:* massage, facials, yoga & pilates instruction. **Guest Services:** valet and coin laundry, wireless Internet. **Business Services:** conference facilities, PC. **Cards:** AX, DS, MC, VI.

ASK CALL

BOXWOOD LODGE

Motel

$75-$179 12/1-1/1 & 4/1-11/30

Phone: 828/295-9984

Address: 671 N Main St **Location:** US 221 and 321 business route. **Facility:** Smoke free premises. 23 units. 21 one-bedroom standard units, some with efficiencies, kitchens and/or whirlpools. 1 one-bedroom suite. 1 cabin. 1-2 stories (no elevator), interior/exterior corridors. *Bath:* combo or shower only. **Parking:** on-site. **Terms:** open 12/1-1/1 & 4/1-11/30, 7 day cancellation notice-fee imposed. **Amenities:** irons, hair dryers. **Guest Services:** wireless Internet. **Cards:** AX, MC, VI.

CALL / SOME UNITS VCR

CHETOLA RESORT AT BLOWING ROCK

Resort Hotel

$185-$355 4/24-11/30
$142-$319 12/1-4/23

Phone: (828)295-5500

Address: 538 N Main St St **Location:** Jct US 321, just e on US 321 business route. **Facility:** Overlooking a small lake adjoining Moses H. Cone Memorial Park and the Blue Ridge Parkway, the lodge offers some units with lake-view balconies. Smoke free premises. 42 units. 37 one-bedroom standard units. 5 one-bedroom suites, some with whirlpools. 3 stories, interior corridors. **Parking:** on-site, winter plug-ins. **Terms:** 2 night minimum stay - seasonal and/or weekends, 3 day cancellation notice. **Amenities:** video library (fee), DVD players, CD players, voice mail, irons, hair dryers. **Pool(s):** heated indoor. **Leisure Activities:** sauna, whirlpool, rental boats, rental canoes, rental paddleboats, fishing, 3 tennis courts, recreation programs, hiking trails, playground, exercise room, horseshoes, volleyball. *Fee:* massage. **Guest Services:** valet and coin laundry, wireless Internet. **Business Services:** conference facilities, PC. **Cards:** AX, DS, MC, VI.

ASK VCR

CLIFF DWELLERS INN *Book at AAA.com*

Motel

Rates not provided

Phone: 828/295-3121

Address: 116 Lakeview Terr **Location:** Just off US 321 Bypass at jct US 221; 0.8 mi s from Blue Ridge Pkwy at MM 292. **Facility:** Smoke free premises. 22 units. 19 one-bedroom standard units. 2 one- and 1 two-bedroom suites, some with kitchens and/or whirlpools. 1-3 stories (no elevator), exterior corridors. **Parking:** on-site. **Amenities:** video games (fee), voice mail, hair dryers. *Some:* irons. **Guest Services:** wireless Internet. **Business Services:** fax.

/ SOME UNITS

HILLWINDS INN *Book great rates at AAA.com* **Phone:** (828)295-7660

Motel
$89-$359 5/1-11/30
$69-$249 12/1-4/30

Address: 315 Sunset Dr **Location:** Just e of Main St. **Facility:** 20 units. 16 one-bedroom standard units. 2 one-bedroom suites, some with kitchens and/or whirlpools. 2 cottages. 1-2 stories (no elevator), interior/exterior corridors. **Parking:** on-site. **Terms:** office hours 7 am-8 pm, 3 day cancellation notice-fee imposed. **Amenities:** voice mail, irons, hair dryers. **Guest Services:** wireless Internet. **Business Services:** meeting rooms, PC. **Cards:** MC, VI. ***(See color ad p 604)***

HOMESTEAD INN **Phone:** 828/295-9559

Motel
$49-$99 5/1-11/30
$45-$79 12/1-4/30

Address: 153 Morris St **Location:** Just s of US 321 business route; just e of town park. **Facility:** 14 one-bedroom standard units, some with whirlpools. 1 story, exterior corridors. *Bath:* combo or shower only. **Parking:** on-site. **Terms:** 2-3 night minimum stay - seasonal and/or weekends, 7 day cancellation notice-fee imposed. **Amenities:** video library, DVD players, hair dryers. *Some:* CD players. **Guest Services:** wireless Internet. **Cards:** AX, DS, MC, VI.

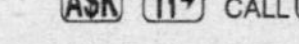
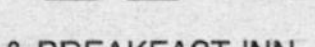

MAPLE LODGE BED & BREAKFAST INN **Phone:** 828/295-3331

Bed & Breakfast
Rates not provided

Address: 152 Sunset Dr **Location:** Just s on Sunset Dr from town park; center. **Facility:** Handsomely decorated rooms, some with four-poster or canopy beds, are featured here; one room houses a library. Smoke free premises. 11 units. 10 one-bedroom standard units. 1 one-bedroom suite. 2 stories (no elevator), interior/exterior corridors. *Bath:* combo or shower only. **Parking:** on-site. **Terms:** open 4/1-11/30, office hours 8 am-6 pm, age restrictions may apply. **Amenities:** CD players, hair dryers. *Some:* irons. **Guest Services:** wireless Internet.

MEADOWBROOK INN **Phone:** (828)295-4300

Hotel
$129-$299 5/1-11/30
$79-$269 12/1-4/30

Address: 711 Main St **Location:** Just n on US 221 and 321 business route. **Facility:** Smoke free premises. 63 units. 51 one-bedroom standard units, some with whirlpools. 9 one- and 2 two-bedroom suites, some with whirlpools. 1 house. 4 stories, interior corridors. *Bath:* combo or shower only. **Parking:** on-site. **Terms:** cancellation fee imposed. **Amenities:** voice mail, irons, hair dryers. *Some:* DVD players. **Pool(s):** heated indoor. **Leisure Activities:** whirlpool, exercise room. **Guest Services:** coin laundry, wireless Internet. **Business Services:** meeting rooms. **Cards:** DS, MC, VI.

RIDGEWAY INN *Book great rates at AAA.com* **Phone:** (828)295-7321

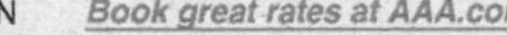

Motel
$89-$359 5/1-11/30
$69-$249 12/1-4/30

Address: 131 Yonahlossee **Location:** Just n of jct US 221 and 321 business route, on US 221 business route. **Facility:** Smoke free premises. 22 units. 18 one-bedroom standard units. 4 cottages. 1-2 stories (no elevator), interior/exterior corridors. *Bath:* combo or shower only. **Parking:** on-site. **Terms:** office hours 7 am-8 pm, 3 day cancellation notice-fee imposed. **Amenities:** voice mail, irons, hair dryers. **Guest Services:** wireless Internet. **Business Services:** PC. **Cards:** MC, VI. ***(See color ad p 604)***

THE VILLAGE INN *Book great rates at AAA.com* **Phone:** (828)295-3380

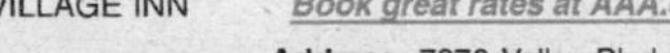

Motel
$89-$359 5/1-11/30
$75-$249 12/1-4/30

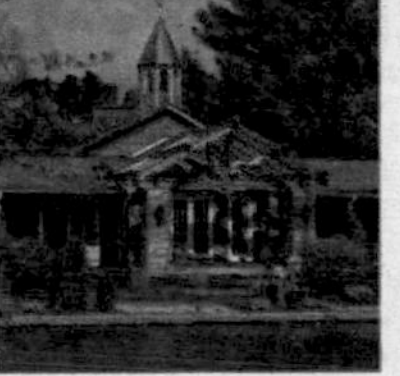

Address: 7876 Valley Blvd **Location:** On US 321 Bypass, just e of city park. **Facility:** Smoke free premises. 22 units. 19 one-bedroom standard units with kitchens, some with whirlpools. 3 cottages. 1 story, exterior corridors. *Bath:* combo or shower only. **Parking:** on-site, winter plug-ins. **Terms:** office hours 7:30 am-10 pm, 3 day cancellation notice-fee imposed. **Amenities:** irons, hair dryers. **Guest Services:** wireless Internet. **Business Services:** PC. **Cards:** MC, VI. ***(See color ad p 604)***

WHERE TO DINE

THE BEST CELLAR **Phone:** 828/295-3466

American
$24-$38

Visitors to the authentic log cabin will receive a friendly greeting and prompt, professional service. Featuring seafood, prime rib, roast duck, veal and a raw bar option, the restaurant strives for good taste and well-presented meals. Casual dress. **Bar:** Full bar. **Reservations:** suggested. **Hours:** 5:30 pm-9 pm, Fri & Sat-9:30 pm. Closed: 11/26, 12/25; also Sun 5/1-11/30; also Tues & Wed 12/1-4/30. **Address:** 203 Sunset Dr **Location:** center, just e; in The Inn @ Raggedy Gardens. **Parking:** on-site. **Cards:** AX, MC, VI.

BLOWING ROCK GRILLE AND BERT'S BAR

Phone: 828/295-9474

American
$7-$20

Pleasant servers make you feel welcome in this cozy and comfortable eatery. Homemade soup, fresh mountain trout and a "monster" vegetarian burrito are hallmarks of a varied and unique menu, as are the famous strawberry bran muffins. Casual dress. **Bar:** Full bar. **Hours:** 11 am-10 pm, Sun-8 pm. Closed: 12/25. **Address:** 349 Sunset Dr **Location:** Just e of Main St; just w of US 321. **Parking:** on-site. **Cards:** AX, MC, VI.

CANYONS OF THE BLUE RIDGE

Phone: 828/295-7661

Southwestern
$6-$18

Menu offerings range from finger foods to fresh Southwestern fare to traditional entrees of sirloin, salmon and chicken. Popular for its awesome sunset and mountain views, patrons also enjoy a Sunday jazz brunch. Monday evening karaoke and live music four days a week. Casual dress. Entertainment. **Bar:** Full bar. **Hours:** 11 am-9:30 pm, Fri & Sat-10 pm; hours vary in winter. Closed: 11/26, 12/24, 12/25. **Address:** 8960 Valley Blvd (US 321) **Location:** US 321 N; n of jct US 231. **Parking:** on-site. **Cards:** AX, DS, MC, VI.

CALL

CRIPPEN'S COUNTRY INN & RESTAURANT

Phone: 828/295-3487

American
$16-$40

The chef prepares delicious gourmet nouvelle American dishes. Inventive presentations are served in an intimate bed-and-breakfast setting. Casual dress. **Bar:** Full bar. **Reservations:** suggested. **Hours:** call for hours. **Address:** 239 Sunset Dr **Location:** Just e; center. **Parking:** street. **Cards:** AX, DS, MC, VI.

CALL

STORIE STREET GRILLE

Phone: 828/295-7075

American
$10-$23

A downtown favorite of both locals and tourists, the grille offers casual dining in sophisticated surroundings. Indulge in a culinary experience, whether by choosing the eggplant Napoleon lunch plate or one of the dinner special entrees—try Gorgonzola beef tenderloin or linguine with asparagus and walnuts. Whatever your fancy, dining here is sure to be distinctive. Casual dress. **Bar:** Full bar. **Hours:** 11 am-3 & 5-9 pm; seasonal hours may vary. Closed: Sun. **Address:** 1167 Main St **Location:** Center of downtown. **Parking:** street. **Cards:** AX, DS, MC, VI.

TWIGS RESTAURANT & BAR

Phone: 828/295-5050

Continental
$15-$34

The intimate, quiet hideaway is known for its offerings of inventive seasonal cuisine. Servers are knowledgeable and prompt. Dressy casual. **Bar:** Full bar. **Reservations:** suggested. **Hours:** 5:30 pm-9:30 pm, Fri & Sat-10 pm. Closed: 11/26, 12/24, 12/25; also Mon. **Address:** 7956 Valley Blvd **Location:** US 321 at Sunset Dr. **Parking:** on-site. **Cards:** AX, DS, MC, VI.

WOODLANDS BBQ

Phone: 828/295-3651

Barbecue
$5-$18

Get your fingers ready for the luscious barbecue baby-back ribs at this personable eatery located near the Blue Ridge Parkway. Guests gather at this rustic establishment to get a taste of the delicious chopped chicken and original barbecue sauce. Casual dress. Entertainment. **Bar:** Full bar. **Hours:** 11 am-9 pm, Fri & Sat-10 pm. Closed major holidays; also Mon 11/1-5/25 & Christmas week. **Address:** 8304 Valley Blvd (321 Bypass) **Location:** 0.5 mi s on US 321 Bypass from Sunset Dr. **Parking:** on-site. **Cards:** DS, MC, VI.

The following restaurant has not been evaluated by AAA but is listed for your information only.

THE MANOR HOUSE AT CHETOLA RESORT

Phone: 828/295-5505

fyi

Not evaluated. Situated in what was the home of one of the Lodge's former owners and local socialites of the early 1930s, the restaurant is open for breakfast and lunch and offers the chef's expertly-prepared Continental dinner menu. **Address:** 185 Chetola Lake Dr **Location:** 1 mi e on US 321 business route, follow signs off US 321 Bypass; 0.5 mi n of Blue Ridge Pkwy via US 321; in Bob Timberlake Inn at Chetola Resort.

BOILING SPRINGS pop. 3,866

WHERE TO STAY

AMERICINN LODGE & SUITES Book at AAA.com

Phone: (704)434-9996

Hotel
$85 All Year

Address: 428 E College Ave **Location:** On SR 150; 0.7 mi e of town center. **Facility:** 53 units. 52 one-bedroom standard units, some with whirlpools. 1 one-bedroom suite with whirlpool. 2 stories (no elevator), interior corridors. *Bath:* combo or shower only. **Parking:** on-site. **Terms:** cancellation fee imposed. **Amenities:** high-speed Internet, voice mail, irons, hair dryers. **Pool(s):** heated indoor. **Leisure Activities:** whirlpool. **Guest Services:** coin laundry. **Business Services:** PC. **Cards:** AX, DS, MC, VI.

ASK CALL / SOME UNITS

WHERE TO DINE

ITALIAN GARDEN RESTAURANT

Phone: 704/434-9290

Italian
$7-$11

The casual, family-friendly eatery features Italian dishes such as pizza, hot subs, spaghetti, lasagna, chicken parmigiana as well as a few Greek specialties like souvlaki. Casual dress. **Hours:** 11 am-10 pm. Closed: 7/4, 11/26, 12/25. **Address:** 105 N Main St **Location:** Jct SR 150, just n. **Parking:** on-site. **Cards:** AX, DS, MC, VI.

BOONE pop. 13,472

WHERE TO STAY

BEST WESTERN BLUE RIDGE PLAZA Book great rates at AAA.com **Phone:** (828)266-1100

Hotel
$70-$170 All Year

Address: 840 E King St **Location:** Jct US 321, 0.7 mi e on US 421. **Facility:** 73 one-bedroom standard units, some with whirlpools. 3 stories, interior corridors. *Bath:* combo or shower only. **Parking:** on-site. **Terms:** 3 day cancellation notice-fee imposed. **Amenities:** high-speed Internet, voice mail, irons, hair dryers. *Some:* DVD players. **Pool(s):** heated indoor. **Leisure Activities:** exercise room. *Fee:* game room. **Guest Services:** valet laundry, wireless Internet. **Business Services:** meeting rooms. **Cards:** AX, CB, DC, DS, JC, MC, VI. **Free Special Amenities: expanded continental breakfast and high-speed Internet.**

CALL / SOME UNITS VCR

AAA Benefit:
Members save up to 20%, plus 10% bonus points with rewards program.

COMFORT SUITES Book at AAA.com **Phone:** (828)268-0099

Hotel
$59-$299 All Year

Address: 1184 Hwy 105 **Location:** Jct US 321, 0.4 mi sw. **Facility:** Smoke free premises. 96 one-bedroom standard units, some with whirlpools. 3 stories, interior corridors. **Parking:** on-site. **Terms:** cancellation fee imposed. **Amenities:** video library (fee), high-speed Internet, voice mail, irons, hair dryers. *Some:* video games. **Pool(s):** heated indoor. **Leisure Activities:** limited exercise equipment, game room. **Guest Services:** valet and coin laundry, wireless Internet. **Business Services:** PC, fax (fee). **Cards:** AX, DC, DS, MC, VI.

ASK VCR

COUNTRY INN & SUITES **Phone:** (828)264-4234

Hotel
$80-$210 6/1-11/30
$70-$200 12/1-5/31

Address: 818 King St (Hwy 421) **Location:** Jct US 321, 0.7 mi e on US 421. **Facility:** 68 one-bedroom standard units. 3 stories, interior corridors. *Bath:* combo or shower only. **Parking:** on-site. **Amenities:** high-speed Internet, irons, hair dryers. **Pool(s):** heated indoor. **Leisure Activities:** whirlpool, exercise room. **Guest Services:** coin laundry, wireless Internet. **Cards:** AX, DS, MC, VI.

ASK / SOME UNITS

FAIRFIELD INN & SUITES-BOONE Book great rates at AAA.com **Phone:** (828)268-0677

Hotel
$74-$89 All Year

Address: 2060 Blowing Rock Rd **Location:** On US 321, 0.8 mi s of jct SR 105 and US 321. **Facility:** Smoke free premises. 100 units. 96 one-bedroom standard units, some with whirlpools. 4 one-bedroom suites. 3 stories, interior corridors. *Bath:* combo or shower only. **Parking:** on-site. **Terms:** cancellation fee imposed. **Amenities:** dual phone lines, voice mail, irons, hair dryers. *Some:* CD players. **Pool(s):** heated indoor. **Leisure Activities:** limited exercise equipment. **Guest Services:** valet and coin laundry, wireless Internet. **Business Services:** meeting rooms, business center. **Cards:** AX, CB, DC, DS, MC, VI.

CALL / SOME UNITS

AAA Benefit:
Members save a minimum 5% off the best available rate.

HAMPTON INN Book great rates at AAA.com

Phone: (828)264-0077

Hotel
$109-$199 All Year

Address: 1075 Hwy 105 **Location:** Jct US 321, just sw. **Facility:** 96 one-bedroom standard units. 5 stories, interior corridors. *Bath:* combo or shower only. **Parking:** on-site. **Amenities:** voice mail, irons, hair dryers. **Pool(s):** heated indoor. **Leisure Activities:** whirlpool, exercise room. **Guest Services:** valet laundry, wireless Internet. **Business Services:** PC, fax. **Cards:** AX, DS, MC, VI.

SOME UNITS

AAA Benefit:
Members save up to 10% everyday!

HOLIDAY INN EXPRESS Book great rates at AAA.com

Phone: (828)264-2451

Hotel
$99-$259 All Year

Address: 1943 Blowing Rock Rd **Location:** Jct SR 105, 0.8 mi s on US 321. **Facility:** 129 units. 124 one-bedroom standard units, some with whirlpools. 5 one-bedroom suites with whirlpools. 5 stories, interior corridors. *Bath:* combo or shower only. **Parking:** on-site. **Amenities:** high-speed Internet, dual phone lines, voice mail, irons, hair dryers. **Pool(s):** heated outdoor. **Leisure Activities:** exercise room. **Guest Services:** valet and coin laundry, wireless Internet. **Business Services;** meeting rooms, PC, fax. **Cards:** AX, DC, DS, MC, VI.

ASK / SOME UNITS

LA QUINTA INN & SUITES Book at AAA.com

Phone: (828)262-1234

Hotel
$69-$219 All Year

Address: 165 Hwy 105 Ext **Location:** US 321 NW, 1 mi n of jct US 321. **Facility:** Smoke free premises. 77 units. 63 one-bedroom standard units, some with whirlpools. 14 one-bedroom suites. 3 stories, interior corridors. *Bath:* combo or shower only. **Parking:** on-site. **Amenities:** high-speed Internet, voice mail, irons, hair dryers. *Some:* dual phone lines. **Pool(s):** heated indoor. **Leisure Activities:** whirlpool, exercise room. **Guest Services:** valet and coin laundry, wireless Internet. **Business Services:** meeting rooms. **Cards:** AX, DC, DS, MC, VI.

CALL / SOME UNITS

LOVILL HOUSE INN

Phone: 828/264-4204

AAA SAVE

Historic Bed & Breakfast
$159-$219 12/1-4/30
$179-$209 5/1-11/30

Address: 404 Old Bristol Rd **Location:** 1 mi n on US 421/321, 0.5 mi e. Located in a quiet area. **Facility:** A wraparound porch adds charm to this restored farmhouse inn; set on 11 acres, the building dates from 1875. Smoke free premises. 6 units. 5 one-bedroom standard units. 1 cottage. 2 stories (no elevator), interior/exterior corridors. **Parking:** on-site. **Terms:** 14 day cancellation notice-fee imposed. **Amenities:** video library, hair dryers. **Leisure Activities:** gazebo, walking paths, waterfall, hiking trails, spa. **Guest Services:** wireless Internet. **Cards:** MC, VI. **Free Special Amenities: full breakfast and high-speed Internet.**

VCR / SOME UNITS

SLEEP INN Book at AAA.com

Phone: (828)262-0020

Hotel
$59-$149 All Year

Address: Hwy 105 Extension **Location:** Just n; center. **Facility:** 82 one-bedroom standard units. 3 stories, interior corridors. *Bath:* combo or shower only. **Parking:** on-site. **Amenities:** high-speed Internet, voice mail, irons, hair dryers. **Pool(s):** heated outdoor. **Guest Services:** coin laundry, wireless Internet. **Business Services:** fax (fee). **Cards:** AX, DC, DS, MC, VI.

ASK CALL / SOME UNITS

WHERE TO DINE

THE BISTRO

Phone: 828/265-0500

Continental
$11-$23

French and Italian entrees are presented with a cosmopolitan flair. Sauces made in-house enhance the flavor of each meal. Small and upscale, the dining room features live plants and continually updated original artwork. Dressy casual. **Bar:** Beer & wine. **Reservations:** suggested. **Hours:** 5:30 pm-close. Closed: 12/24, 12/25; also Sun. **Address:** 115 New Market Center **Location:** 1.2 mi s on US 421. **Parking:** on-site. **Cards:** AX, DS, MC, VI.

CASA RUSTICA

Phone: 828/262-5128

Italian
$10-$25

Located in the mountains off the Blue Ridge Pkwy, this cozy eatery with its stone fireplace and log cabin ambience has been the site of many marriage proposals! Try the delicious manicotti, a signature dish made lighter with crepes instead of pasta. Casual dress. **Bar:** Beer & wine. **Reservations:** suggested. **Hours:** 5 pm-10 pm; seasonal hours may vary. Closed: 11/26, 12/25; also Super Bowl Sun. **Address:** 1348 Hwy 105 S **Location:** 0.5 mi w on SR 105 S; jct US 321, 0.3 mi s. **Parking:** on-site. **Cards:** AX, DS, MC, VI.

DAN'L BOONE INN

Phone: 828/264-8657

American
$9-$15

Informal, country decor. Located in one of the oldest buildings in town. Served family style, with one price for the meal. Inexpensive; within walking distance of ASU and downtown area; very popular. Wait staff in period country attire. Casual dress. **Reservations:** accepted. **Hours:** 11:30 am-9 pm, Sat & Sun from 8 am; call for off season hours. Closed: 12/24, 12/25. **Address:** 130 Hardin St **Location:** Jct US 321 and 421, on southwest corner. **Parking:** on-site.

GAMEKEEPER RESTAURANT & BAR Phone: 828/963-7400

Regional American

$24-$31

Located along a winding mountain road this historic, 50's style stone cottage is a delightful destination filled with charm and a romantic flair. The chef/owner's passion is to create a Southern style "mountain" cuisine, and is accomplished by preparing a seasonal menu which includes fresh local produce, fish, beef and some surprises - think pheasant, ostrich and venison. Dressy casual. **Bar:** Full bar. **Reservations:** required. **Hours:** 6 pm-9 pm; Sat 5:30 pm-9:30 pm 5/1 10/31; Thurs-Sat 5 pm-9 pm in winter. Closed: 1/1, 4/12, 12/25. **Address:** 3005 Shulls Mill Rd **Location:** Ne on SR 1557, 4.5 mi from center. **Parking:** on-site. **Cards:** AX, DC, MC, VI.

THE PEDDLER STEAK HOUSE **Phone:** 828/264-4433

Steak

$17-$30

Diners select their own rib-eye and create their own salad at the gourmet salad bar. Among other choices are filet mignon, New York strip and king crab legs. Casual dress. **Bar:** Beer & wine. **Reservations:** accepted. **Hours:** 5 pm-9:30 pm, Fri-10 pm, Sat 4:30 pm-10 pm. Closed: 11/26, 12/25. **Address:** 1972 Blowing Rock Rd **Location:** Jct SR 105, 0.8 mi on US 321. **Parking:** on-site. **Cards:** AX, DC, DS, MC, VI.

SAGEBRUSH STEAKHOUSE **Phone:** 828/265-4448

American

$5-$19

Born from the spirit of Texas cattle drives, the restaurant presents a menu of hearty steaks, prime rib, chicken, seafood and baby back ribs. Yummy desserts merit a splurge. Guests can call ahead to facilitate seating. Casual dress. **Bar:** Beer & wine. **Hours:** 11 am-10 pm, Fri & Sat-11 pm. Closed: 12/25. **Address:** 1111 Hwy 105 **Location:** Jct US 221/SR 105, just sw. **Parking:** on-site. **Cards:** AX, DC, DS, MC, VI.

CALL

BREVARD pop. 6,789

WHERE TO STAY

HAMPTON INN-BREVARD *Book great rates at AAA.com* **Phone:** (828)883-4800

Hotel

$79-$189 All Year

Address: 800 Forest Gate Center **Location:** 3.3 mi e on US 64, just e on SR 280, then just n. Adjoins Forest Gate Shopping Center. **Facility:** 80 one-bedroom standard units. 3 stories, interior corridors. *Bath:* combo or shower only. **Parking:** on-site. **Terms:** 1-30 night minimum stay, cancellation fee imposed. **Amenities:** video games (fee), voice mail, irons, hair dryers. **Pool(s):** outdoor. **Guest Services:** wireless Internet. **Business Services:** meeting rooms, PC. **Cards:** AX, CB, DC, DS, JC, MC, VI.

  / SOME UNITS  

AAA Benefit:

Members save up to 10% everyday!

HOLIDAY INN EXPRESS *Book great rates at AAA.com* **Phone:** (828)862-8900

SAVE

Hotel

$89-$179 5/1-11/30

$89-$149 12/1-4/30

Address: 1570 Asheville Hwy **Location:** 3 mi e on US 64. **Facility:** 63 one-bedroom standard units, some with whirlpools. 3 stories, interior corridors. *Bath:* combo or shower only. **Parking:** on-site. **Terms:** 2-3 night minimum stay - seasonal and/or weekends. **Amenities:** dual phone lines, voice mail, irons, hair dryers. **Pool(s):** heated outdoor. **Leisure Activities:** exercise room. **Guest Services:** coin laundry, wireless Internet. **Business Services:** meeting rooms, PC, fax (fee). **Cards:** AX, CB, DC, DS, JC, MC, VI. *(See color ad below)*

CALL / SOME UNITS FEE

▼ See AAA listing above ▼

THE INN AT BREVARD

Phone: 828/884-2105

Historic Bed & Breakfast

$110-$235 All Year

Address: 315 E Main St **Location:** I-26, exit Asheville Airport, just w on Broad St, then just e; center. **Facility:** This property offers a choice of rooms in an 1885 main inn or in a pine-walled annex. Smoke free premises. 14 one-bedroom standard units, some with whirlpools. 2 stories (no elevator), interior/exterior corridors. *Bath:* combo or shower only. **Parking:** on-site. **Terms:** 2 night minimum stay - seasonal and/or weekends, 14 day cancellation notice-fee imposed. **Amenities:** irons, hair dryers. **Guest Services:** wireless Internet. **Business Services:** meeting rooms, fax (fee). **Cards:** MC, VI.

/ SOME UNITS

WHERE TO DINE

THE FALLS LANDING

Phone: 828/884-2835

American

$5-$22

People of all ages will enjoy the seafood served with a Caribbean flair at this eatery. The custom made mahogany table and chairs accent the Mexican tile floor in the dining area. Choose from an array of seafood like mussels and clams in white sauce. Casual dress. **Bar:** Full bar. **Reservations:** suggested. **Hours:** 11:30-3 & 5-9 pm. Closed: 11/26, 12/25; also Sun. **Address:** 18 E Main St **Location:** Center. **Parking:** street. **Cards:** AX, DS, MC, VI.

HOBNOB

Phone: 828/966-4662

American

$5-$28

Creative variety of dishes served in a casually elegant atmosphere at the restored Victorian house. Dressy casual. **Bar:** Full bar. **Reservations:** suggested. **Hours:** 11:30 am-2:30 & 5-9 pm, Sun from 11 am. Closed: 11/26, 12/25. **Address:** 226 W Main St **Location:** Center. **Parking:** street. **Cards:** AX, MC, VI.

SAGEBRUSH STEAKHOUSE

Phone: 828/966-4767

American

$5-$19

Born from the spirit of Texas cattle drives, the restaurant presents a menu of hearty steaks, prime rib, chicken, seafood and baby back ribs. Yummy desserts merit a splurge. Guests can call ahead to facilitate seating. Casual dress. **Bar:** Full bar. **Hours:** 11 am-10 pm, Fri & Sat-11 pm. Closed: 12/25. **Address:** 391 Asheville Hwy **Location:** 1 mi n on US 64/276. **Parking:** on-site. **Cards:** AX, DC, DS, MC, VI.

BRYSON CITY pop. 1,411

WHERE TO STAY

THE HISTORIC CALHOUN HOUSE HOTEL

Phone: (828)488-1234

Bed & Breakfast

$104-$148 All Year

Address: 135 Everett St **Location:** Just n of US 19; downtown. **Facility:** Smoke free premises. 20 one-bedroom standard units. 3 stories (no elevator), interior corridors. *Bath:* some shared or private, combo, shower or tub only. **Parking:** on-site. **Terms:** office hours 7 am-11 pm, cancellation fee imposed. **Amenities:** *Some:* DVD players. **Guest Services:** wireless Internet. **Cards:** AX, DS, MC, VI.

ASK / SOME UNITS VCR

▼ See AAA listing p 611 ▼

SLEEP INN BRYSON CITY  Book great rates at AAA.com **Phone:** (828)488-0326

Hotel
$59-$159 All Year

Address: 500 Veterans Blvd **Location:** US 74, exit 67, just w. **Facility:** 50 one-bedroom standard units. 2 stories (no elevator), interior corridors. *Bath:* combo or shower only. **Parking:** on-site. **Amenities:** irons, hair dryers. **Pool(s):** outdoor. **Guest Services:** coin laundry, wireless Internet. **Business Services:** fax (fee). **Cards:** AX, CB, DC, DS, MC, VI. **Free Special Amenities: expanded continental breakfast and high-speed Internet.** *(See color ad p 610)*

CALL / SOME UNITS

WHERE TO DINE

EVERETT STREET DINER **Phone:** 828/488-0123

Regional American
$5-$8

Open only for breakfast and lunch, the restaurant draws a loyal local clientele. The menu lists innovative twists on traditional dishes, which are served in ample portions. Homemade flavors lend to the delicious taste. Casual dress. **Reservations:** not accepted. **Hours:** 7 am-2 pm, Sat from 8 am. Closed major holidays; also Sun. **Address:** 126 Everett St **Location:** Center. **Parking:** street. **Cards:** AX, CB, DC, DS, JC, MC, VI.

FRYEMONT INN **Phone:** 828/488-2159

Regional Southern
$14-$27

Tasty food, particularly the trout preparations, is served in a rustic atmosphere. The inn, of which the restaurant is a part, is on the historic registry. Meals are included in the room price for guests, so reservations are necessary. Guests can take advantage of the breathtaking mountain views while relaxing in rocking chairs on the porch. A huge hearth adds warmth to the restaurant and lobby. Casual dress. **Bar:** Full bar. **Reservations:** suggested. **Hours:** Open 4/18-11/30; 8 am-10 & 6-8 pm, Fri & Sat-9 pm. **Address:** 245 Fryemont St **Location:** US 74, exit 67, just w. **Parking:** on-site. **Cards:** DS, MC, VI. **Historic**

PASQUALINO'S ITALIAN RESTAURANT **Phone:** 828/488-9555

Italian
$5-$23

In the heart of the city is a touch of Italy. A fresh Caesar salad, pasta carbonara and tiramisu is a meal fit to end a day of outdoor activities. Lunch patrons might try pizza or a fresh pasta dish. Casual dress. **Bar:** Full bar. **Reservations:** accepted. **Hours:** 11:30 am-10 pm. Closed: 11/26, 12/25; also 1/1-1/20 & Wed 12/1-3/1. **Address:** 25 Everett St **Location:** Center. **Parking:** on-site. **Cards:** AX, MC, VI.

RELIA'S GARDEN **Phone:** 828/488-2175

American
$12-$22

On the Nantahala River just west of downtown, the restaurant is worth the drive. While dining on delicious fresh local trout, patrons can unwind in the wooded mountain setting. Most dishes are prepared using herbs from the surrounding garden. Casual dress. **Bar:** Beer & wine. **Hours:** Open 4/11-10/31; 5 pm-9 pm, Fri & Sat-10 pm. **Address:** 13077 US Hwy 19 W **Location:** 13 mi w on US 19/74, just n over bridge; in Nantahala Outdoor Center. **Parking:** on-site. **Cards:** DS, MC, VI.

BURLINGTON pop. 44,917

WHERE TO STAY

BEST WESTERN BURLINGTON INN Book great rates at AAA.com **Phone:** (336)584-0151

Hotel
$91-$120 All Year

Address: 770 Huffman Mill Rd **Location:** I-40/85, exit 141, just n. **Facility:** 144 units. 143 one-bedroom standard units. 1 one-bedroom suite. 2 stories (no elevator), interior corridors. *Bath:* combo or shower only. **Parking:** on-site. **Amenities:** voice mail, irons, hair dryers. *Some:* DVD players, high-speed Internet. **Dining:** Chop House Grille, see separate listing. **Pool(s):** outdoor. **Leisure Activities:** exercise room. **Guest Services:** valet and coin laundry, wireless Internet. **Business Services:** conference facilities, business center. **Cards:** AX, CB, DC, DS, MC, VI. **Free Special Amenities: full breakfast and high-speed Internet.** *(See color ad p 612)*

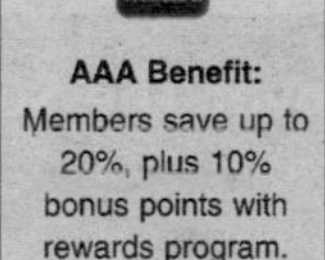

Best Western
AAA Benefit:
Members save up to 20%, plus 10% bonus points with rewards program.

/ SOME UNITS VCR

COMFORT INN Book at AAA.com **Phone:** (336)584-4447

Hotel
$79-$179 All Year

Address: 2701 Kirkpatrick Rd **Location:** I-40/85, exit 141, just s, then e. **Facility:** 113 units. 110 one-bedroom standard units. 3 one-bedroom suites. 4 stories, interior corridors. **Parking:** on-site. **Amenities:** voice mail, irons, hair dryers. **Pool(s):** outdoor. **Leisure Activities:** limited exercise equipment. **Guest Services:** valet laundry, wireless Internet. **Business Services:** meeting rooms, business center. **Cards:** AX, DC, DS, MC, VI.

ASK / SOME UNITS

COUNTRY SUITES BY CARLSON Book at AAA.com **Phone:** (336)584-1115

Hotel
$125-$135 All Year

Address: 3211 Wilson Dr **Location:** I-40/85, exit 141, just n, 0.3 mi w on Garden Rd, then just s. **Facility:** Smoke free premises. 75 units. 4 one-bedroom standard units, some with whirlpools. 71 one-bedroom suites. 3 stories, interior corridors. *Bath:* combo or shower only. **Parking:** on-site. **Amenities:** high-speed Internet, voice mail, irons, hair dryers. **Pool(s):** outdoor. **Leisure Activities:** exercise room. **Guest Services:** valet and coin laundry. **Business Services:** meeting rooms, PC. **Cards:** AX, CB, DC, DS, JC, MC, VI.

ASK CALL

COURTYARD BY MARRIOTT *Book great rates at AAA.com* **Phone:** (336)585-1888

Hotel
$128-$137 All Year

Address: 3141 Wilson Dr **Location:** I-40/85, exit 141, just n, just w on Garden Rd, then just s. **Facility:** Smoke free premises. 122 units. 118 one-bedroom standard units. 4 one-bedroom suites. 4 stories, interior corridors. *Bath:* combo or shower only. **Parking:** on-site. **Terms:** cancellation fee imposed. **Amenities:** voice mail, irons, hair dryers. **Pool(s):** outdoor. **Leisure Activities:** whirlpool, exercise room. **Guest Services:** valet and coin laundry, wireless Internet. **Business Services:** meeting rooms, PC. **Cards:** AX, CB, DC, DS, JC, MC, VI.

CALL / SOME UNITS

AAA Benefit:
Members save a minimum 5% off the best available rate.

ECONO LODGE *Book great rates at AAA.com* **Phone:** (336)227-1270

Hotel
$46-$60 All Year

Address: 2133 W Hanford Rd **Location:** I-40/85, exit 145, just s on SR 49, then just w. **Facility:** 124 one-bedroom standard units. 2 stories (no elevator), interior corridors. **Parking:** on-site. **Terms:** 10 day cancellation notice-fee imposed. **Amenities:** *Some:* irons, hair dryers. **Pool(s):** outdoor. **Guest Services:** wireless Internet. **Business Services:** PC. **Cards:** AX, DS, MC, VI. **Free Special Amenities: continental breakfast and high-speed Internet.**

  / SOME UNITS FEE

HAMPTON INN & SUITES *Book great rates at AAA.com* **Phone:** (336)584-8585

Hotel
$129 All Year

Address: 2935 Saconn Dr **Location:** I-40/85, exit 141, just s on Huffman Mill Rd, just e on Kirkpatrick Rd, then just n. **Facility:** 92 one-bedroom standard units, some with whirlpools. 5 stories, interior corridors. *Bath:* combo or shower only. **Parking:** on-site. **Terms:** 1-30 night minimum stay, cancellation fee imposed. **Amenities:** high-speed Internet, voice mail, irons, hair dryers. **Pool(s):** heated outdoor. **Leisure Activities:** exercise room. **Guest Services:** coin laundry, wireless Internet. **Business Services:** meeting rooms, business center. **Cards:** AX, CB, DC, DS, MC, VI.

  CALL 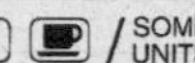  / SOME UNITS 

AAA Benefit:
Members save up to 10% everyday!

MICROTEL INN & SUITES *Book great rates at AAA.com* **Phone:** (336)227-1515

Hotel
$70-$110 All Year

Address: 2185 W Hanford Rd **Location:** I-40/85, exit 145, just s on SR 49, then just w. **Facility:** 60 one-bedroom standard units. 2 stories, interior corridors. *Bath:* combo or shower only. **Parking:** on-site. **Terms:** cancellation fee imposed. **Amenities:** irons, hair dryers. **Guest Services:** valet and coin laundry, wireless Internet. **Business Services:** PC. **Cards:** AX, CB, DC, DS, MC, VI. **Free Special Amenities: continental breakfast and high-speed Internet.**

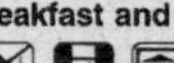 / SOME UNITS

▼ *See AAA listing p 611* ▼

MOTEL 6 - 1257 *Book at AAA.com* **Phone:** (336)226-1325

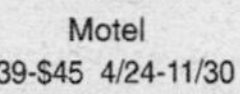

Motel
$39-$45 4/24-11/30
$37-$43 12/1-4/23

Address: 2155 Hanford Rd **Location:** I-40/85, exit 145, just s on SR 49, then just w. **Facility:** 111 one-bedroom standard units. 1 story, exterior corridors. *Bath:* combo or shower only. **Parking:** on-site. **Pool(s):** outdoor. **Guest Services:** coin laundry. **Cards:** AX, DC, DS, MC, VI.

/ SOME UNITS

QUALITY INN BURLINGTON *Book great rates at AAA.com* **Phone:** (336)229-5203

SAVE

Hotel
$50-$80 All Year

Address: 2444 Maple Ave **Location:** I-40/85, exit 145, just n. **Facility:** 131 units. 127 one-bedroom standard units. 4 one-bedroom suites with whirlpools. 2 stories (no elevator), interior corridors. **Parking:** on-site. **Amenities:** video games (fee), dual phone lines, voice mail, irons, hair dryers. **Pool(s):** outdoor. **Leisure Activities:** exercise room. **Guest Services:** valet laundry, wireless Internet. **Business Services:** meeting rooms, business center. **Cards:** AX, DS, MC, VI. **Free Special Amenities: expanded continental breakfast and high-speed Internet.**

CALL / SOME UNITS FEE

SUPER 8 **Phone:** (336)584-8787

SAVE

Motel
$55-$89 All Year

Address: 802 Huffman Mill Rd **Location:** I-40/85, exit 141, just n. **Facility:** 26 one-bedroom standard units. 2 stories (no elevator), exterior corridors. **Parking:** on-site. **Amenities:** irons, hair dryers. **Guest Services:** wireless Internet. **Business Services:** PC. **Cards:** AX, CB, DC, DS, MC, VI. **Free Special Amenities: continental breakfast and high-speed Internet.**

/ SOME UNITS

WHERE TO DINE

B. CHRISTOPHER'S RESTAURANT **Phone:** 336/222-1177

Steak & Seafood
$15-$35

The menu at this casually upscale bistro features steak, seafood and pasta dishes. Dressy casual. **Bar:** Full bar. **Reservations:** accepted. **Hours:** 5 pm-10 pm. Closed major holidays; also Sun. **Address:** 2461 S Church St **Location:** I-40/85, exit 141, 1.2 mi n on Huffman Mill Rd, then just e on US 70. **Parking:** on-site. **Cards:** AX, MC, VI.

CHOP HOUSE GRILLE **Phone:** 336/524-9941

Steak & Seafood
$8-$30

Both families and professionals feel at home at the casually upscale grill—and they leave well fed. Quality, center-cut Angus beef steaks and choice seafood share the menu with pasta and chicken dishes. Side dishes are sized for sharing, as are the desserts. Dressy casual. **Bar:** Full bar. **Reservations:** accepted. **Hours:** 11:30 am-10 pm, Sat from 4:30 pm. Closed: 11/26, 12/25; also Sun. **Address:** 710 Huffman Mill Rd **Location:** I-40/85, exit 141, just n. **Parking:** on-site. **Cards:** AX, DS, MC, VI.

THE CUTTING BOARD **Phone:** 336/229-2770

American
$7-$25

The newest incarnation of this longtime favorite still features Choice steaks grilled over hickory charcoal as the focal point of the menu. Burgers, sandwiches, chicken, pasta and fish, along with a salad bar, round out the offerings. Casual dress. **Bar:** Full bar. **Hours:** 11 am-10 pm, Fri & Sat-11 pm, Sun-9:30 pm. Closed: 11/26, 12/25. **Address:** 2699 Ramada Rd **Location:** I-40/85, exit 143, just n, then just w. **Parking:** on-site. **Cards:** AX, DS, MC, VI.

BURNSVILLE pop. 1,623

WHERE TO STAY

CLEAR CREEK GUEST RANCH **Phone:** (828)675-4510

Ranch
$120-$230 4/1-11/30

Address: 100 Clearcreek Dr **Location:** Blue Ridge Pkwy, 5 mi n on SR 80; from jct SR 19 E, 10 mi s on SR 80. Located near the Pisgah National Forest. **Facility:** Nestled near Mt. Mitchell, the authentic dude ranch offers horseback rides and the dining room has gourmet fare and a panoramic view of the mountains. Smoke free premises. 18 units. 12 one- and 4 two-bedroom standard units. 2 three-bedroom suites. 1 story, exterior corridors. *Bath:* combo or shower only. **Parking:** on-site. **Terms:** open 4/1-11/30, 2-4 night minimum stay - seasonal, 30 day cancellation notice. **Pool(s):** heated outdoor. **Leisure Activities:** whirlpool, fishing, recreation programs, hiking trails, horseback riding, basketball, horseshoes, volleyball. *Fee:* game room. **Guest Services:** TV in common area, coin laundry. **Business Services:** meeting rooms. **Cards:** MC, VI.

BUXTON —*See Outer Banks p. 775.*

CALABASH pop. 711

WHERE TO STAY

BRUNSWICK PLANTATION RESORT VILLAS *Book great rates at AAA.com* **Phone:** (910)845-7000

AAA SAVE

Condominium
$59-$149 1/22-11/30
$45-$89 12/1-1/21

Address: 330 S Middleton Dr **Location:** US 17, 3 mi n of NC/SC state line. **Facility:** This property offers condominium-style guest accommodations as well as studio suites and 27 holes of golf. 400 condominiums. 3 stories (no elevator), exterior corridors. *Bath:* combo or shower only. **Parking:** on-site. **Terms:** office hours 7 am-11 pm, 3 night minimum stay, age restrictions may apply, 14 day cancellation notice-fee imposed. **Amenities:** high-speed Internet (fee), voice mail, irons. **Pool(s):** 2 outdoor, heated indoor. **Leisure Activities:** whirlpools, picnic area, grilling stations, exercise room, volleyball. *Fee:* golf-27 holes. **Business Services:** PC (fee). **Cards:** AX, MC, VI. **Free Special Amenities: local telephone calls and preferred room (subject to availability with advance reservations).**

WHERE TO DINE

THE BOUNDARY HOUSE RESTAURANT **Phone:** 910/579-8888

Seafood
$7-$27

Menu selections at this casual eatery include steaks, seafood, pasta, chicken, sandwiches and salads. Casual dress. **Bar:** Full bar. **Hours:** 11 am-10 pm. Closed: 12/25. **Address:** 1045 River Rd **Location:** US 17, 1.7 mi e on SR 179, just s at stoplight. **Parking:** on-site. **Cards:** AX, DS, MC, VI.

ELLA'S OF CALABASH **Phone:** 910/579-6728

Seafood
$5-$16

Since 1950, the reliable eatery has served Carolina-style seafood, such as shrimp, deviled crab and hushpuppies. Service in the quaint, simple, nautical dining room reflects a genuine Southern attitude. Casual dress. **Bar:** Full bar. **Hours:** 11 am-9 pm. Closed: 12/25. **Address:** 1148 River Rd **Location:** US 17, 1.7 mi e on SR 179, just s at stoplight. **Parking:** on-site. **Cards:** MC, VI.

CANDLER

WHERE TO STAY

DAYS INN WEST #6116 *Book great rates at AAA.com* **Phone:** (828)667-9321

AAA SAVE

Motel
$50-$140 All Year

Address: 2551 Smoky Park Hwy **Location:** I-40, exit 37, just w, then n. **Facility:** 112 one-bedroom standard units. 3 stories (no elevator), exterior corridors. **Parking:** on-site. **Terms:** office hours 8 am-5 pm. **Amenities:** voice mail, hair dryers. **Pool(s):** outdoor. **Guest Services:** wireless Internet. **Cards:** AX, CB, DC, DS, MC, VI. **Free Special Amenities: full breakfast and early check-in/late check-out.**

/ SOME UNITS FEE

OWL'S NEST INN AND ENGADINE CABINS **Phone:** 828/665-8325

AAA SAVE

Bed & Breakfast
$145-$250 All Year

Address: 2630 Smoky Park Hwy **Location:** I-40, exit 37, 0.5 mi w on SR 19/23. **Facility:** Set upon a hill in a country setting, this B&B and cabins afford guests fantastic views in a quiet setting. Smoke free premises. 11 units. 5 one-bedroom standard units with kitchens, some with whirlpools. 6 cabins. 1-2 stories (no elevator), interior/exterior corridors. *Bath:* combo or shower only. **Parking:** on-site. **Terms:** 14 day cancellation notice-fee imposed. **Amenities:** video library, DVD players, CD players, high-speed Internet, voice mail, irons, hair dryers. **Leisure Activities:** hiking trails. **Guest Services:** wireless Internet. **Cards:** AX, DS, MC, VI.

/ SOME UNITS FEE VCR

CANTON pop. 4,029

WHERE TO STAY

COMFORT INN *Book at AAA.com* **Phone:** (828)648-4881

Hotel
$60-$140 All Year

Address: 737 Champion Dr **Location:** I-40, exit 31, just s. **Facility:** 76 units. 72 one-bedroom standard units. 4 one-bedroom suites with efficiencies and whirlpools. 2 stories (no elevator), interior corridors. **Parking:** on-site. **Amenities:** irons, hair dryers. **Pool(s):** outdoor. **Leisure Activities:** limited exercise equipment. **Guest Services:** coin laundry, wireless Internet. **Business Services:** meeting rooms, PC. **Cards:** AX, CB, DC, DS, JC, MC, VI.

ASK / SOME UNITS

DAYS INN *Book at AAA.com* **Phone:** 828/648-0300

Motel
Rates not provided

Address: 1963 Champion Dr **Location:** I-40, exit 31. **Facility:** 39 one-bedroom standard units. 2 stories (no elevator), exterior corridors. **Parking:** on-site. **Amenities:** hair dryers. **Pool(s):** outdoor. **Guest Services:** coin laundry, wireless Internet.

/ SOME UNITS FEE

WHERE TO DINE

SAGEBRUSH STEAKHOUSE **Phone:** 828/646-3750

American
$5-$19

Born from the spirit of Texas cattle drives, the restaurant presents a menu of hearty steaks, prime rib, chicken, seafood and baby back ribs. Yummy desserts merit a splurge. Guests can call ahead to facilitate seating. Casual dress. **Bar:** Full bar. **Hours:** 11 am-10 pm, Fri & Sat-11 pm. Closed: 12/25. **Address:** 1941 Champion Dr **Location:** I-40, exit 31, just s. **Parking:** on-site. **Cards:** AX, DC, DS, MC, VI.

CALL

CAPE CARTERET pop. 1,214

WHERE TO DINE

THE FISHTRAP — Phone: 252/393-1433

Seafood
$5-$22

Seafood figures prominently on the casual eatery's menu, it also lists such landlubber fare as pasta, steaks and sandwiches. Casual dress. **Bar:** Full bar. **Reservations:** accepted. **Hours:** 11 am-2:30 & 5-9 pm, Fri-10 pm, Sat 11 am-10 pm, Sun 11 am-9 pm. Closed: 11/26, 12/25; also 2 weeks in winter. **Address:** 1000 WB McLean Dr **Location:** Jct SR 58, 1.4 mi e on SR 24. **Parking:** on-site. **Cards:** MC, VI.

CAROLINA BEACH pop. 4,701

WHERE TO STAY

COURTYARD BY MARRIOTT — *Book great rates at AAA.com* — Phone: (910)458-2030

Hotel
$92-$205 All Year

Address: 100 Charlotte Ave **Location:** Oceanfront. From Snow's Cut Bridge, 1.8 mi s on Lake Park Blvd, then just e. **Facility:** Smoke free premises. 144 units. 126 one-bedroom standard units, some with whirlpools. 18 one-bedroom suites. 10 stories, interior corridors. *Bath:* combo or shower only. **Parking:** on-site. **Terms:** cancellation fee imposed. **Amenities:** high-speed Internet, dual phone lines, voice mail, irons, hair dryers. **Pool(s):** outdoor, heated indoor. **Leisure Activities:** whirlpool, exercise room. **Guest Services:** valet and coin laundry, wireless Internet. **Business Services:** conference facilities, PC. **Cards:** AX, CB, DC, DS, MC, VI.

  CALL  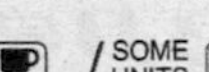 / SOME UNITS

AAA Benefit:
Members save a minimum 5% off the best available rate.

MICROTEL INN & SUITES — *Book at AAA.com* — Phone: (910)458-1300

Hotel
$59-$179 All Year

Address: 907 N Lake Park Blvd **Location:** From Snow's Cut Bridge, 1.2 mi se. **Facility:** 59 units. 58 one-bedroom standard units. 1 two-bedroom suite with kitchen (no utensils). 3 stories, interior corridors. *Bath:* combo or shower only. **Parking:** on-site. **Terms:** 2 night minimum stay - seasonal and/or weekends, 3 day cancellation notice-fee imposed. **Amenities:** high-speed Internet, voice mail, safes (fee). *Some:* irons, hair dryers. **Pool(s):** outdoor. **Guest Services:** wireless Internet. **Cards:** AX, DS, MC, VI.

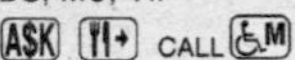 CALL  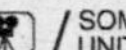  / SOME UNITS  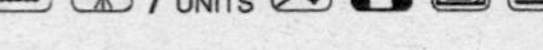

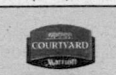

WHERE TO DINE

MICHAEL'S SEAFOOD RESTAURANT & CATERING — Phone: 910/458-7761

Seafood
$7-$32

Patrons savor fresh seafood, chops, steaks and pasta under the eyes of the mermaids who adorn the walls of the casual and beautifully decorated bistro. The award-winning seafood chowder is a must. Casual dress. **Bar:** Full bar. **Hours:** 11 am-10 pm, Fri & Sat-11 pm; to 9 pm, Fri & Sat-10 pm in winter. Closed: 11/26, 12/25. **Address:** 1206 N Lake Park Blvd **Location:** From Snow's Cut Bridge, just e; in Cross Bridge Shopping Center. **Parking:** on-site. **Cards:** AX, DS, MC, VI.

CARRBORO pop. 16,782 (See map and index starting on p. 681)

WHERE TO STAY

THE INN AT BINGHAM SCHOOL — Phone: 919/563-5583

Historic Bed & Breakfast
$150-$195 All Year

Address: 6720 Mebane Oaks Rd **Location:** I-40/85, exit 154 (Mebane Oaks Rd), 8.3 mi s; jct SR 54. Located in a secluded rural area. **Facility:** The rustic inn features a log home that was built in stages beginning more than 200 years ago; guest rooms are spacious and well-appointed. Smoke free premises. 4 units. 3 one-bedroom standard units, some with whirlpools. 1 one-bedroom suite with whirlpool. 2 stories (no elevator), exterior corridors. **Parking:** on-site. **Terms:** 7 day cancellation notice-fee imposed. **Amenities:** video library, CD players, irons, hair dryers. *Some:* DVD players. **Leisure Activities:** hiking trails. **Guest Services:** wireless Internet. **Business Services:** meeting rooms. **Cards:** AX, DS, MC, VI.

/ SOME UNITS VCR

WHERE TO DINE

SPOTTED DOG RESTAURANT & BAR — Phone: 919/933-1117 (46)

American
$7-$13

Original artwork lines the walls of the tiny cafe, where the menu lists an eclectic mix of pasta, sandwiches, salads and other fare, including many vegetarian offerings of Greek pasta and marinated or grilled tofu over vegetables and rice. Also sharing menu space are such favorites as chargrilled tuna steak sandwich and crab cakes. Casual dress. **Bar:** Full bar. **Hours:** 11:30 am-midnight. Closed: 4/12, 11/26, 12/25; also Mon. **Address:** 111 E Main St **Location:** Just e; center. **Parking:** on-site. **Cards:** AX, DS, MC, VI.

CARY pop. 94,536 (See map and index starting on p. 790)

WHERE TO STAY

BEST WESTERN CARY INN & EXTENDED STAY SUITES
Book great rates at AAA.com

Phone: (919)481-1200 48

AAA SAVE

Hotel
$60-$130 All Year

Address: 1722 Walnut St **Location:** I-40, exit 293A, just s on US 1, exit 101A, then just e. **Facility:** 140 units. 100 one-bedroom standard units, some with whirlpools. 40 one-bedroom suites. 2-4 stories, interior/exterior corridors. **Parking:** on-site. **Amenities:** high-speed Internet, irons, hair dryers. **Pool(s):** outdoor. **Leisure Activities:** whirlpool, limited exercise equipment. **Guest Services:** valet and coin laundry, wireless Internet. **Business Services:** meeting rooms, PC. **Cards:** AX, CB, DC, DS, MC, VI. **Free Special Amenities: expanded continental breakfast and high-speed Internet.**

/ SOME UNITS FEE

AAA Benefit:
Members save up to 20%, plus 10% bonus points with rewards program.

CANDLEWOOD SUITES-RALEIGH/CARY
Book at AAA.com

Phone: (919)468-4222 46

Hotel
$95-$100 12/1-10/9
$93-$96 10/10-11/30

Address: 1020 Buck Jones Rd **Location:** I-40, exit 293A, just s on US 1, exit 101B, 0.5 mi nw; in Buck Jones Village. **Facility:** 81 units. 69 one-bedroom standard units with kitchens. 12 one-bedroom suites with kitchens. 3 stories, interior corridors. *Bath:* combo or shower only. **Parking:** on-site. **Terms:** cancellation fee imposed. **Amenities:** video library, DVD players, CD players, high-speed Internet, voice mail, irons, hair dryers. **Leisure Activities:** exercise room. **Guest Services:** complimentary and valet laundry. **Cards:** AX, CB, DC, DS, JC, MC, VI.

ASK VCR / SOME UNITS FEE

COMFORT SUITES HOTEL
Book at AAA.com

Phone: (919)852-4318 51

Hotel
$79-$129 All Year

Address: 350 Ashville Ave **Location:** US 1, exit 98A, 0.8 mi e on Tryon Rd, then just n. Located adjacent to Western Wake Medical Center. **Facility:** Smoke free premises. 121 one-bedroom standard units. 6 stories, interior corridors. *Bath:* combo or shower only. **Parking:** on-site. **Terms:** cancellation fee imposed. **Amenities:** dual phone lines, voice mail, irons, hair dryers. *Some:* high-speed Internet. **Pool(s):** heated indoor. **Leisure Activities:** whirlpool, exercise room. **Guest Services:** valet laundry, wireless Internet. **Business Services:** meeting rooms, PC. **Cards:** AX, DC, DS, MC, VI.

ASK CALL M / SOME UNITS FEE

DAYS INN
Book at AAA.com

Phone: 919/481-4011 47

Motel
Rates not provided

Address: 1716 Walnut St **Location:** I-40, exit 293A, just s on US 1, exit 101A, then just e. **Facility:** 120 one-bedroom standard units. 2 stories (no elevator), exterior corridors. **Parking:** on-site. **Amenities:** dual phone lines, voice mail, irons, hair dryers. **Pool(s):** outdoor. **Guest Services:** wireless Internet. **Business Services:** meeting rooms.

CALL M / SOME UNITS FEE FEE

EMBASSY SUITES-RALEIGH-DURHAM/RESEARCH TRIANGLE
Book great rates at AAA.com

Phone: (919)677-1840 41

AAA SAVE

Hotel
$119-$259 All Year

Address: 201 Harrison Oaks Blvd **Location:** I-40, exit 287, just s, then just w. **Facility:** 273 one-bedroom suites. 9 stories, interior corridors. *Bath:* combo or shower only. **Parking:** on-site. **Terms:** 1-30 night minimum stay, cancellation fee imposed. **Amenities:** dual phone lines, voice mail, irons, hair dryers. *Fee:* video games, high-speed Internet. **Pool(s):** heated indoor. **Leisure Activities:** sauna, whirlpool, 2 lighted tennis courts, exercise room. **Guest Services:** complimentary and valet laundry, airport transportation-Raleigh-Durham International Airport, area transportation-Weston Pkwy, Harrison Square & Arboretum Shopping Center, wireless Internet. **Business Services:** conference facilities, business center. **Cards:** AX, CB, DC, DS, MC, VI. **Free Special Amenities: full breakfast and newspaper.**

/ SOME UNITS

AAA Benefit:
Members save 5% or more everyday!

EXTENDED STAYAMERICA-RALEIGH/CARY

Phone: (919)468-5828 53

Hotel
$77-$87 All Year

Address: 1500 Regency Pkwy **Location:** US 1, exit 98A, 0.5 mi e on Tryon Rd, then just s. **Facility:** 122 one-bedroom standard units with efficiencies. 3 stories, interior corridors. *Bath:* combo or shower only. **Parking:** on-site. **Terms:** office hours 7 am-11 pm. **Amenities:** voice mail, irons. **Guest Services:** coin laundry, wireless Internet. **Cards:** AX, CB, DC, DS, JC, MC, VI.

ASK / SOME UNITS FEE

EXTENDED STAY DELUXE RALEIGH-CARY-REGENCY PARKWAY
Book at AAA.com

Phone: (919)460-1161 56

Hotel
$92-$102 All Year

Address: 3100 Regency Pkwy **Location:** US 1, exit 98A, 0.5 mi e on Tryon Rd, then just s. **Facility:** 83 one-bedroom standard units with efficiencies. 3 stories, interior corridors. *Bath:* combo or shower only. **Parking:** on-site. **Terms:** office hours 7 am-11 pm. **Amenities:** DVD players, voice mail, irons, hair dryers. **Pool(s):** outdoor. **Leisure Activities:** exercise room. **Guest Services:** coin laundry, wireless Internet. **Cards:** AX, CB, DC, DS, JC, MC, VI.

ASK / SOME UNITS FEE

(See map and index starting on p. 790)

HAMPTON INN Book great rates at AAA.com **Phone:** (919)859-5559 50

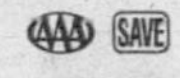

Hotel
$79-$149 All Year

Address: 201 Ashville Ave **Location:** US 1, exit 98A, 0.8 mi e on Tryon Rd, then just n. Located across from Western Wake Medical Center. **Facility:** 129 one-bedroom standard units. 5 stories, interior corridors. *Bath:* combo or shower only. **Parking:** on-site. **Terms:** 1-7 night minimum stay. **Amenities:** video games (fee), voice mail, irons, hair dryers. **Pool(s):** outdoor. **Leisure Activities:** exercise room. **Guest Services:** valet laundry, wireless Internet. **Business Services:** meeting rooms, PC. **Cards:** AX, DC, DS, JC, MC, VI. **Free Special Amenities: expanded continental breakfast and high-speed Internet.** *(See color ad p 797)*

CALL / SOME UNITS

AAA Benefit:
Members save up to 10% everyday!

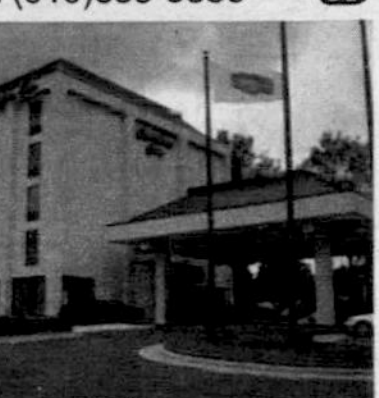

HAMPTON INN & SUITES Book great rates at AAA.com **Phone:** (919)233-1798 45

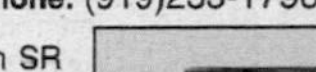

Hotel
$119-$139 All Year

Address: 111 Hampton Woods Ln **Location:** I-40, exit 290, just w on SR 54, then just s. **Facility:** 124 units. 93 one-bedroom standard units. 31 one-bedroom suites with efficiencies, some with whirlpools. 6 stories, interior corridors. *Bath:* combo or shower only. **Parking:** on-site. **Terms:** 1-30 night minimum stay, cancellation fee imposed. **Amenities:** dual phone lines, voice mail, irons, hair dryers. *Some:* DVD players, CD players. **Pool(s):** outdoor. **Leisure Activities:** exercise room. **Guest Services:** valet and coin laundry, area transportation, wireless Internet. **Business Services:** meeting rooms, PC. **Cards:** AX, CB, DC, DS, MC, VI.

CALL / SOME UNITS

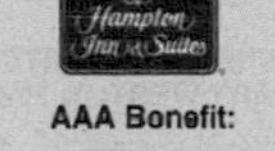

AAA Benefit:
Members save up to 10% everyday!

HOLIDAY INN HOTEL & SUITES Book great rates at AAA.com **Phone:** (919)851-1220 49

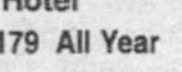

Hotel
$89-$179 All Year

Address: 5630 Dillard Dr **Location:** I-40, exit 293A, just s on US 1, exit 101A, 0.5 mi e on Walnut St, then just n. **Facility:** 120 units. 75 one-bedroom standard units, some with whirlpools. 45 one-bedroom suites. 6 stories, interior corridors. *Bath:* combo or shower only. **Parking:** on-site. **Terms:** 14 day cancellation notice-fee imposed. **Amenities:** high-speed Internet, dual phone lines, voice mail, irons, hair dryers. **Pool(s):** heated indoor. **Leisure Activities:** whirlpool, exercise room. **Guest Services:** valet and coin laundry, wireless Internet. **Business Services:** meeting rooms, PC. **Cards:** AX, DC, DS, MC, VI. **Free Special Amenities: room upgrade (subject to availability with advance reservations) and high-speed Internet.**

CALL / SOME UNITS

HOMEWOOD SUITES Book great rates at AAA.com **Phone:** (919)467-4444 

Hotel
$89-$179 All Year

Address: 100 MacAlyson Ct **Location:** US 1, exit 98B, just w on US 64, then just s on Edinburgh Dr; in MacGregor Park. **Facility:** 150 units. 30 one-bedroom standard units. 110 one- and 10 two-bedroom suites with efficiencies. 4 stories, interior corridors. *Bath:* combo or shower only. **Parking:** on-site. **Terms:** cancellation fee imposed. **Amenities:** video games (fee), voice mail, irons, hair dryers. **Pool(s):** outdoor. **Leisure Activities:** whirlpool, jogging, exercise room, basketball, horseshoes. **Guest Services:** valet and coin laundry, wireless Internet. **Business Services:** meeting rooms, business center. **Cards:** AX, CB, DC, DS, JC, MC, VI. **Free Special Amenities: full breakfast and high-speed Internet.** *(See color ad p 797)*

CALL / SOME UNITS FEE

AAA Benefit:
Members save 5% or more everyday!

LA QUINTA INN & SUITES RALEIGH (CARY) Book great rates at AAA.com **Phone:** (919)851-2850 52

Hotel
$79-$129 All Year

Address: 191 Crescent Commons Dr **Location:** US 1, exit 98A, 0.5 mi e on Tryon Rd, then just n. **Facility:** 128 units. 123 one-bedroom standard units. 5 one-bedroom suites. 5 stories, interior corridors. *Bath:* combo or shower only. **Parking:** on-site. **Amenities:** video games (fee), high-speed Internet, voice mail, irons, hair dryers. **Pool(s):** heated outdoor. **Leisure Activities:** whirlpool, exercise room. **Guest Services:** valet and coin laundry, wireless Internet. **Business Services:** meeting rooms, PC. **Cards:** AX, DC, DS, MC, VI.

(See map and index starting on p. 790)

RESIDENCE INN  **Phone:** (919)467-4080 55

Hotel
$172-$185 All Year

Address: 2900 Regency Pkwy **Location:** US 1, exit 98A, 0.5 mi e on Tryon Rd, then just s. **Facility:** Smoke free premises. 108 units. 37 one-bedroom standard units with efficiencies. 47 one- and 24 two-bedroom suites with efficiencies. 3 stories, interior corridors. *Bath:* combo or shower only. **Parking:** on-site. **Terms:** check-in 4 pm, cancellation fee imposed. **Amenities:** high-speed Internet, dual phone lines, voice mail, irons, hair dryers. **Pool(s):** outdoor. **Leisure Activities:** whirlpool, exercise room, sports court. **Guest Services:** valet and coin laundry, wireless Internet. **Business Services:** meeting rooms, PC. **Cards:** AX, CB, DC, DS, JC, MC, VI.

CALL / SOME UNITS FEE

AAA Benefit:
Members save a minimum 5% off the best available rate.

STUDIOPLUS-HARRISON AVE *Book at AAA.com* **Phone:** (919)677-9910 43

Hotel
$90-$100 All Year

Address: 600 Weston Pkwy **Location:** I-40, exit 287, 0.5 mi s on Harrison Ave, then just w. **Facility:** 71 one-bedroom standard units with kitchens. 3 stories (no elevator), interior corridors. *Bath:* combo or shower only. **Parking:** on-site. **Terms:** office hours 7 am-11 pm. **Amenities:** voice mail, irons. **Pool(s):** outdoor. **Leisure Activities:** exercise room. **Guest Services:** coin laundry, wireless Internet. **Cards:** AX, CB, DC, DS, JC, MC, VI.

ASK / SOME UNITS FEE

TOWNEPLACE SUITES BY MARRIOTT - RALEIGH/ CARY/WESTON PARKWAY *Book great rates at AAA.com* **Phone:** (919)678-0005 44

AAA SAVE

Hotel
$183-$196 All Year

Address: 120 Sage Commons Way **Location:** I-40, exit 287, 0.5 mi s on Harrison Ave, 2.3 w on Weston Pkwy, then just n. **Facility:** Smoke free premises. 97 units. 77 one-bedroom standard units with kitchens. 6 one- and 14 two-bedroom suites with kitchens. 4 stories, interior corridors. *Bath:* combo or shower only. **Parking:** on-site. **Terms:** cancellation fee imposed. **Amenities:** high-speed Internet, dual phone lines, voice mail, irons, hair dryers. **Pool(s):** outdoor. **Leisure Activities:** exercise room. **Guest Services:** valet and coin laundry, wireless Internet. **Business Services:** PC. **Cards:** AX, CB, DC, DS, MC, VI. **Free Special Amenities: continental breakfast and high-speed Internet.**

CALL / SOME UNITS FEE

AAA Benefit:
Members save a minimum 5% off the best available rate.

THE UMSTEAD HOTEL & SPA *Book great rates at AAA.com* **Phone:** (919)447-4000 42

AAA SAVE

Hotel
$199-$425 All Year

Address: 100 Woodland Pond Dr **Location:** I-40, exit 287, just s on Harrison Ave, just e on SAS Campus Dr, then just n. **Facility:** Located amid a bevy of gardens on the banks of a small lake, the luxury hotel features spacious rooms with 42 inch plasma TVs and posh marble baths. Designated smoking area. 150 units. 136 one-bedroom standard units. 14 one-bedroom suites. 7 stories, interior corridors. *Bath:* combo or shower only. **Parking:** on-site and valet. **Terms:** cancellation fee imposed. **Amenities:** video library, DVD players, CD players, high-speed Internet, dual phone lines, voice mail, safes, honor bars, irons, hair dryers. **Dining:** Herons Restaurant, see separate listing. **Pool(s):** heated outdoor. **Leisure Activities:** saunas, whirlpools, steamrooms, jogging, spa. *Fee:* golf & tennis privileges. **Guest Services:** valet laundry, airport transportation (fee)-Raleigh-Durham International Airport, area transportation-SAS Campus & The Arboretum Complex, wireless Internet. **Business Services:** conference facilities, business center. **Cards:** AX, CB, DC, DS, JC, MC, VI. **Free Special Amenities: newspaper and high-speed Internet.**

FEE / SOME UNITS FEE

WHERE TO DINE

AN, NEW WORLD CUISINE **Phone:** 919/677-9229 32

Asian
$13-$50

A world-class chef prepares delectable specialties, such as braised catfish, taro crab cake, curry lamb chops, stone crab claws and several types of spring and fresh rolls. The cutting-edge design makes way for a sushi bar, a raw bar and a Viet bar where patrons can select from a list of appetizer and sampling choices. A multi-course tasting menu offers diners the opportunity to sample a variety of offerings. Casual dress. **Bar:** Full bar. **Reservations:** required. **Hours:** 11 am-2:30 & 5-10 pm, Fri & Sat-11 pm. Closed: 11/26, 12/25; also Sun. **Address:** 2800 Renaissance Park Pl **Location:** I-40, exit 287, 0.7 mi s on Harrison Pkwy, then just w. **Parking:** on-site. **Cards:** MC, VI.

CALL

BENTLEY'S AT CROSSROADS **Phone:** 919/854-0644 40

American
$6-$29

The casually upscale eatery features steaks, fresh seafood, lamb chops, sauteed chicken and pasta dishes, cajun tuna and more. Casual dress. **Bar:** Full bar. **Reservations:** accepted. **Hours:** 11 am-11 pm, Sat & Sun from 4 pm. Closed: 1/1, 11/26, 12/25. **Address:** 2007 Walnut St **Location:** I-40, exit 293A, just s on US 1, exit 101A, then 0.4 mi e. **Parking:** on-site. **Cards:** AX, MC, VI.

BIAGGI'S RISTORANTE ITALIANO **Phone:** 919/468-7229 34

Italian
$6-$21

Cool, upscale decor surrounds diners who savor freshly prepared creations. Delicious combinations of quality, unusual ingredients make for an adventurous dining experience. Casual dress. **Bar:** Full bar. **Reservations:** accepted. **Hours:** 11 am-10 pm, Fri & Sat-11 pm, Sun-9 pm. Closed: 11/26, 12/25. **Address:** 1060 Darrington Dr **Location:** I-40, exit 287, 1.1 mi s on Harrison Ave, 3.4 mi sw on Cary Pkwy, then just e. **Parking:** on-site. **Cards:** AX, DS, MC, VI.

(See map and index starting on p. 790)

GYPSY'S SHINY DINER — **Phone:** 919/469-3663 39

American
$4-$8

Oldies pipe from the tabletop jukebox as patrons enjoy burgers, shakes and other diner classics, including grilled chicken and hamburger steak. Casual dress. **Hours:** 7 am-midnight, Fri & Sat 24 hours, Sun 7 am-9 pm. Closed: 11/26, 12/24, 12/25. **Address:** 1550 Buck Jones Rd **Location:** I-40, exit 293A, just s on US 1, exit 101B, just nw. **Parking:** on-site. **Cards:** MC, VI.

HERONS RESTAURANT — **Phone:** 919/447-4200 31

American
$11-$39

Modern American cuisine with regional influences is the focus of the menu, and products from area farms and herbs from the hotel's garden are blended into the chef's creations. Signature dishes include salt-brined pork loin with black-eyed pea and corn succotash, and roast chicken with house-made duck sausage and caramelized sweet potatoes. A comfortably elegant dining room provides a sophisticated setting, in which guests will feel at home in business casual attire. An extensive wine list is offered, and brunch is featured on Sundays. Dressy casual. **Bar:** Full bar. **Reservations:** suggested. **Hours:** 6:30-10 am, 11:30-2 & 5:30-10 pm, Sun 6:30-10:30 am, 11-2:30 & 5-9 pm. **Address:** 100 Woodland Pond Dr **Location:** I-40, exit 287, just s on Harrison Ave, just e on SAS Campus Dr, then just n; in The Umstead Hotel & Spa. **Parking:** on-site and valet. **Cards:** AX, DC, DS, MC, VI.

CALL

HIBERNIAN RESTAURANT & IRISH PUB — **Phone:** 919/467-9000 38

American
$5-$20

Traditional Irish pub fare joins American food prepared with flair. The menu includes such favorites as bangers and mash and shepherd's pie, as well as steaks, pasta, sandwiches and salads. Casual dress. **Bar:** Full bar. **Reservations:** accepted. **Hours:** 11 am-2 am. Closed: 12/25. **Address:** 1144 Kildaire Farm Rd **Location:** Jct Cary Pkwy, 0.6 mi n. **Parking:** on-site. **Cards:** AX, DS, MC, VI.

INDIA GARDEN — **Phone:** 919/319-3722 36

Indian
$6-$15

At the mall, the cozy restaurant's large lunch and dinner buffet lines up traditional dishes, including seafood, chicken and lamb entrees and vegetarian fare. A la carte choices are another option. Casual dress. **Bar:** Full bar. **Reservations:** accepted. **Hours:** 11:30 am-2:30 & 5-10 pm, Sat noon-3 & 5-10:30 pm, Sun noon-3 pm. Closed: 12/25; also for Easter dinner. **Address:** 1105 Walnut St, Suite E101A **Location:** I-40, exit 291, 0.5 mi sw on Cary Towne Blvd, then just s; at Cary Towne Center Mall; northwest entrance. **Parking:** on-site. **Cards:** AX, DC, DS, MC, VI.

JIMMY V'S STEAKHOUSE & TAVERN — **Phone:** 919/380-8210 41

Steak
$20-$45

Diners savor Certified Angus beef steaks and New Zealand cold water lobster tails, in addition to a few Italian entrees, in a casually upscale atmosphere. The wine list is extensive. Casual dress. **Bar:** Full bar. **Reservations:** accepted. **Hours:** 5 pm-10 pm, Fri & Sat-11 pm. Closed major holidays; also Sun. **Address:** 107 Edinburgh Dr S, Suite 131 **Location:** US 1, exit 98A, just w on US 64, then just s; in MacGregor Village Shopping Center. **Parking:** on-site. **Cards:** AX, DC, DS, MC, VI.

KABUKI JAPANESE STEAKHOUSE & SUSHI — **Phone:** 919/380-8081 37

Japanese
$6-$30

Japanese steak, seafood and sushi, as well as other traditional delicacies, are prepared tableside with theatrical showmanship. Dishes are served with flair. Casual dress. **Bar:** Full bar. **Reservations:** accepted. **Hours:** 11:30 am-2 & 5-9:15 pm, Fri-10:15 pm, Sat 5 pm-10:15 pm. Closed major holidays. **Address:** 220 Nottingham Dr **Location:** I-40, exit 293A, just s on US 1, exit 101B, 0.5 mi nw on Buck Jones Rd, then just w. **Parking:** on-site. **Cards:** AX, DC, DS, MC, VI.

THE KING AND I — **Phone:** 919/460-9265 33

Thai
$7-$16

The popular restaurant's lengthy menu all but guarantees patrons will find their favorite Thai dish or discover a new one. Pork, chicken and seafood dishes abound, as do curries and fried rice and noodle entrees. Casual dress. **Bar:** Full bar. **Reservations:** accepted. **Hours:** 11 am-2:30 & 5-9:30 pm, Fri & Sat-10:30 pm, Sun 5 pm-9:30 pm. Closed: 12/25. **Address:** 926 NE Maynard Rd **Location:** I-40, exit 290, 1 mi w on SR 54, then just n; in Reedy Creek Plaza. **Parking:** on-site. **Cards:** AX, MC, VI.

LUCKY 32 — **Phone:** 919/233-1632 44

Regional American
$7-$25

The menu changes monthly at the comfortably upscale eatery. Regional American fare incorporates fresh, locally grown ingredients. Casual dress. **Bar:** Full bar. **Reservations:** accepted. **Hours:** 11:15 am-10:30 pm, Fri & Sat-11 pm, Sun 10 am-9 pm. Closed: 11/26, 12/25. **Address:** 7307 Tryon Rd **Location:** US 1, exit 98A, 0.5 mi e. **Parking:** on-site. **Cards:** AX, DC, MC, VI.

MACGREGOR DRAFT HOUSE — **Phone:** 919/461-1633 42

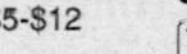

American
$5-$12

Burgers, beer and sports best describes MacGregor's. Casual dress. **Bar:** Full bar. **Hours:** 11 am-2 pm, Sun noon-midnight. Closed: 7/4, 11/26, 12/24, 12/25. **Address:** 107 Edinburgh S, Suite 120 **Location:** US 1, exit 98B, just w on US 64, then just s; in MacGregor Village Shopping Center. **Parking:** on-site. **Cards:** AX, DC, DS, MC, VI.

(See map and index starting on p. 790)

SAN REMO ITALIAN GRILL

Phone: 919/363-9009

Italian
$5-$20

The popular, neighborhood bistro features friendly service and tasty dishes, such as Mediterranean chicken with a light and tangy lemon sauce as well as many traditional pasta favorites. A nice lunch buffet is offered on weekdays and Sundays. Casual dress. **Bar:** Full bar. **Reservations:** accepted. **Hours:** 11 am-3 & 4:30-10 pm, Sun 11:30 am-9 pm. Closed major holidays. **Address:** 3450-150 Kildaire Farm Rd **Location:** Jct CR 1010 and Kildaire Farm Rd; in Mill Pond Shopping Center. **Parking:** on-site. **Cards:** AX, MC, VI.

TONY'S BOURBON STREET OYSTER BAR

Phone: 919/462-6226 (43)

Seafood
$7-$30

For more than 10 years, the Mardi Gras-themed restaurant has served Creole favorites, such as jambalaya and red beans and rice, in a laid-back environment. Fresh seafood is at the menu's core, and oysters are shucked in front of guests perched at the bar. Live entertainment is scheduled late nights from Thursday through Saturday. Casual dress. **Bar:** Full bar. **Reservations:** accepted. **Hours:** 5 pm-10 pm, Tues-11 pm, Wed & Thurs-midnight, Fri & Sat-2 am. Closed: 1/1, 11/26, 12/25. **Address:** 107 Edinburgh Dr, Suite 129 **Location:** US 1, exit 98B, just w on US 64, then just s; in MacGregor Village Shopping Center. **Parking:** on-site. **Cards:** AX, DC, DS, MC, VI.

VESPA

Phone: 919/319-5656 (35)

Italian
$9-$20

A light, contemporary decor and a spacious patio provide a comfortable atmosphere in which patrons can appreciate the fine service and traditional Italian dishes. Casual dress. **Bar:** Full bar. **Reservations:** accepted. **Hours:** 11:30 am-2 & 5:30-9 pm, Fri & Sat-10 pm, Sun noon-2 & 5:30-9 pm. Closed major holidays. **Address:** 200 S Academy St **Location:** 2 blks s; center. **Parking:** on-site. **Cards:** AX, DS, MC, VI.

CASHIERS pop. 196

WHERE TO STAY

HIGH HAMPTON INN & COUNTRY CLUB

Phone: (828)743-2411

AAA SAVE

Resort Hotel
$264-$369 All Year

Address: 1525 Hwy 107 S **Location:** Jct US 64, 1.5 mi s. **Facility:** Heirloom trees shade the manicured grounds of this family-owned lakeside inn offering rustic rooms and cottages; recreational facilities are on site. 135 units. 120 one-bedroom standard units. 15 cottages. 3 stories (no elevator), interior/exterior corridors. **Parking:** on-site. **Terms:** 3 night minimum stay - seasonal and/or weekends, cancellation fee imposed. **Amenities:** irons, hair dryers. **Dining:** entertainment. **Leisure Activities:** rental boats, rental canoes, rental paddleboats, fishing, table tennis, recreation programs, exercise trail, croquet, bocci, badminton, hiking trails, jogging, playground, spa, horseshoes, shuffleboard, volleyball. *Fee:* sailboats, golf-18 holes, covered driving range, 6 tennis courts, tennis & golf clinics. **Guest Services:** coin laundry, airport transportation (fee)-Asheville Regional & Greenville-Spartanburg airports, wireless Internet. **Business Services:** conference facilities, PC. **Cards:** AX, DC, DS, MC, VI. **Free Special Amenities: full breakfast and high-speed Internet.** ***(See color ad below)***

FEE / SOME UNITS FEE

INNISFREE VICTORIAN INN & GARDEN HOUSE

Phone: (828)743-2946

AAA SAVE

Bed & Breakfast
$150-$330 All Year

Address: 108 Innisfree Dr **Location:** Jct US 64, 5 mi n on SR 107, just w on Glenville School Rd, then just s. Located in a quiet area. **Facility:** Most rooms have a private balcony, garden tub and gas fireplace at this mountain inn overlooking surrounding hills and gardens. Smoke free premises. 9 units. 3 one-bedroom standard units, some with whirlpools. 6 one-bedroom suites. 2 stories (no elevator), interior/exterior corridors. *Bath:* combo or shower only. **Parking:** on-site. **Terms:** 2 night minimum stay - weekends, 21 day cancellation notice-fee imposed. **Amenities:** video library, irons, hair dryers. *Some:* CD players. **Leisure Activities:** boat dock, fishing, sunset cruise, nature trail, hiking trails. *Fee:* ballroom dance class & studio. **Guest Services:** valet laundry, wireless Internet. **Cards:** MC, VI. **Free Special Amenities: full breakfast and room upgrade (subject to availability with advance reservations).**

/ SOME UNITS VCR

▼ See AAA listing above ▼

LAURELWOOD MOUNTAIN INN **Phone:** 828/743-9939

Motel

$79-$99 5/1-11/30

$69-$89 12/1-4/30

Address: 58 Hwy 107 **Location:** Jct US 64, just n. **Facility:** 22 units. 18 one-bedroom standard units, some with efficiencies. 3 two-bedroom suites with kitchens and whirlpools. 1 cabin. 1-2 stories (no elevator), exterior corridors. *Bath:* combo or shower only. **Parking:** on-site. **Terms:** 2 night minimum stay - seasonal and/or weekends, 3 day cancellation notice-fee imposed. **Amenities:** voice mail, irons, hair dryers. **Leisure Activities:** playground. **Guest Services:** wireless Internet. **Cards:** AX, DS, MC, VI.

A$K CALL / SOME UNITS FEE

WHERE TO DINE

CORNUCOPIA GOURMET **Phone:** 828/743-3750

American

$8-$14

Frequented by locals and travelers alike, this is touted as the friendliest patio in town. The chef-owner uses his culinary talents to add new twists to gourmet sandwiches, soups and desserts as well as inventive dinner specials. Casual dress. **Bar:** Beer & wine. **Hours:** Open 3/15-11/2; 11 am-3 pm; 6 pm-9 pm 5/1-11/1. **Address:** 107 Schoolhouse Rd **Location:** Jct SR 64, 0.5 mi s on SR 107. **Parking:** on-site. **Cards:** MC, VI.

CALL

CHAPEL HILL pop. 48,715 (See map and index starting on p. 681)

WHERE TO STAY

CAROLINA INN *Book great rates at AAA.com* **Phone:** (919)933-2001 45

AAA SAVE

Historic Hotel

$109-$234 All Year

Address: 211 Pittsboro St **Location:** Jct Franklin St, just s on Columbia St (SR 86). **Facility:** Opened in 1924, the hotel is centrally located on the UNC campus and offers handsomely-appointed accommodations in a variety of room sizes. Smoke free premises. 184 units. 177 one-bedroom standard units. 7 one-bedroom suites. 3 stories, interior corridors. *Bath:* combo or shower only. **Parking:** on-site (fee) and valet. **Terms:** 1-30 night minimum stay, cancellation fee imposed. **Amenities:** video games (fee), high-speed Internet, dual phone lines, voice mail, irons, hair dryers. *Some:* CD players. **Dining:** Carolina Crossroads, see separate listing. **Leisure Activities:** exercise room. **Guest Services:** valet and coin laundry, airport transportation (fee)-Raleigh-Durham International Airport, wireless Internet. **Business Services:** conference facilities, business center. **Cards:** AX, CB, DC, DS, JC, MC, VI. **Free Special Amenities: local telephone calls and high-speed Internet.**

FEE CALL / SOME UNITS FEE VCR

▼ See AAA listing p 622 ▼

(See map and index starting on p. 681)

COURTYARD BY MARRIOTT-CHAPEL HILL *Book great rates at AAA.com* **Phone:** (919)883-0700 48

Hotel
$174-$184 All Year

Address: 100 Marriott Way **Location:** I-40, exit 273 & 273A, 1.8 mi w on SR 54, just s on Friday Center Dr, then just e. **Facility:** Smoke free premises. 169 units. 153 one-bedroom standard units. 16 one-bedroom suites. 5 stories, interior corridors. *Bath:* combo or shower only. **Parking:** on-site. **Terms:** cancellation fee imposed. **Amenities:** dual phone lines, voice mail, irons, hair dryers. *Some:* high-speed Internet. **Pool(s):** heated indoor. **Leisure Activities:** whirlpool, exercise room. **Guest Services:** valet and coin laundry, wireless Internet. **Business Services:** meeting rooms, business center. **Cards:** AX, DS, MC, VI. **Free Special Amenities: newspaper and high-speed Internet.** *(See color ad p 621)*

CALL / SOME UNITS

AAA Benefit:
Members save a minimum 5% off the best available rate.

HAMPTON INN *Book great rates at AAA.com* **Phone:** (919)968-3000 43

Hotel
$95-$115 All Year

Address: 1740 Fordham Blvd **Location:** I-40, exit 270, 1 mi s on US 15/501, just e on Europa Dr, then just s on service road. **Facility:** 120 one-bedroom standard units. 2 stories (no elevator), exterior corridors. **Parking:** on-site. **Terms:** 1-30 night minimum stay, cancellation fee imposed. **Amenities:** video games (fee), voice mail, irons, hair dryers. **Pool(s):** outdoor. **Leisure Activities:** exercise room. **Guest Services:** valet laundry, wireless Internet. **Business Services:** meeting rooms, PC. **Cards:** AX, CB, DC, DS, JC, MC, VI.

CALL / SOME UNITS

AAA Benefit:
Members save up to 10% everyday!

HAMPTON INN & SUITES *Book great rates at AAA.com* **Phone:** (919)403-8700 46

Hotel
$99-$279 All Year

Address: 6121 Farrington Rd **Location:** I-40, exit 273 and 273A, just w on SR 54, then just se. **Facility:** 92 units. 63 one-bedroom standard units. 29 one-bedroom suites with efficiencies, some with whirlpools. 4 stories, interior corridors. *Bath:* combo or shower only. **Parking:** on-site. **Amenities:** dual phone lines, voice mail, irons, hair dryers. *Some:* high-speed Internet. **Pool(s):** outdoor. **Leisure Activities:** gas grills, exercise room. **Guest Services:** valet and coin laundry, area transportation-UNC hospitals, universities & Streets of Southpoint Mall, wireless Internet. **Business Services:** meeting rooms, business center. **Cards:** AX, DC, DS, MC, VI. **Free Special Amenities: expanded continental breakfast and high-speed Internet.**

CALL / SOME UNITS VCR

AAA Benefit:
Members save up to 10% everyday!

HOLIDAY INN *Book at AAA.com* **Phone:** (919)929-2171 40

Hotel
$99-$129 All Year

Address: 1301 N Fordham Blvd **Location:** I-40, exit 270, 2 mi s on US 15/501. **Facility:** 134 one-bedroom standard units. 2 stories (no elevator), exterior corridors. **Parking:** on-site. **Amenities:** video games (fee), dual phone lines, voice mail, irons, hair dryers. **Pool(s):** outdoor. **Leisure Activities:** exercise room. **Guest Services:** valet and coin laundry, wireless Internet. **Business Services:** meeting rooms, PC. **Cards:** AX, CB, DC, DS, JC, MC, VI.

/ SOME UNITS FEE FEE FEE

HOLIDAY INN EXPRESS *Book great rates at AAA.com* **Phone:** (919)489-7555 47

Hotel
$89-$269 All Year

Address: 6119 Farrington Rd **Location:** I-40, exit 273 and 273A, just w on SR 54, then just se. **Facility:** 64 one-bedroom standard units. 4 stories, interior corridors. *Bath:* combo or shower only. **Parking:** on-site. **Terms:** cancellation fee imposed. **Amenities:** high-speed Internet, dual phone lines, voice mail, irons, hair dryers. **Leisure Activities:** pool privileges, limited exercise equipment. **Guest Services:** valet laundry, area transportation-UNC hospitals, universities & Streets of Southpoint Mall, wireless Internet. **Business Services:** PC. **Cards:** AX, DC, DS, MC, VI. **Free Special Amenities: expanded continental breakfast and high-speed Internet.**

CALL / SOME UNITS

RESIDENCE INN BY MARRIOTT-CHAPEL HILL *Book great rates at AAA.com* **Phone:** (919)933-4848 41

Hotel
$197-$212 All Year

Address: 101 Erwin Rd **Location:** I-40, exit 270, 1.2 mi s on US 15/501, then just w. **Facility:** Smoke free premises. 108 units. 66 one-bedroom standard units with efficiencies. 36 one- and 6 two-bedroom suites with efficiencies. 3 stories, interior corridors. *Bath:* combo or shower only. **Parking:** on-site. **Terms:** cancellation fee imposed. **Amenities:** high-speed Internet, voice mail, irons, hair dryers. **Pool(s):** heated outdoor. **Leisure Activities:** whirlpool, putting green, billiards, grills, exercise room. **Guest Services:** valet and coin laundry, area transportation-within Chapel Hill, wireless Internet. **Business Services:** meeting rooms, PC. **Cards:** AX, DS, MC, VI. **Free Special Amenities: full breakfast and high-speed Internet.**

CALL / SOME UNITS FEE

AAA Benefit:
Members save a minimum 5% off the best available rate.

(See map and index starting on p. 681)

SHERATON CHAPEL HILL *Book great rates at AAA.com* **Phone:** (919)968-4900 42

Hotel
$99-$410 All Year

Address: 1 Europa Dr **Location:** I-40, exit 270, 1 mi s, then just e. **Facility:** 168 units. 164 one-bedroom standard units. 4 one-bedroom suites. 4 stories, interior corridors. *Bath:* combo or shower only. **Parking:** on-site. **Amenities:** high-speed Internet, dual phone lines, voice mail, irons, hair dryers. **Pool(s):** outdoor. **Leisure Activities:** exercise room. **Guest Services:** valet laundry, area transportation-within 5 mi, wireless Internet. **Business Services:** conference facilities, business center. **Cards:** AX, CB, DC, DS, JC, MC, VI. **Free Special Amenities: local telephone calls and high-speed Internet.**

FEE / SOME UNITS FEE

AAA Benefit:
Members get up to 15% off, plus Starwood Preferred Guest® bonuses.

THE SIENA HOTEL *Book great rates at AAA.com* **Phone:** (919)929-4000 44

Boutique Hotel
$119-$300 All Year

Address: 1505 E Franklin St **Location:** I-40, exit 270, 2 mi s on US 15/501, then 0.5 mi w. **Facility:** Modeled on a beautiful Tuscan villa, the property offers a warm and inviting ambiance with luxury appointments. 79 one-bedroom standard units. 4 stories, interior corridors. *Bath:* combo or shower only. **Parking:** on-site. **Terms:** check-in 4 pm, cancellation fee imposed. **Amenities:** high-speed Internet, dual phone lines, voice mail, irons, hair dryers. **Dining:** Il Palio Ristorante, see separate listing. **Guest Services:** valet laundry, area transportation-within Chapel Hill, wireless Internet. **Business Services:** meeting rooms, PC. **Cards:** AX, DC, MC, VI. **Free Special Amenities: full breakfast and high-speed Internet.**

WHERE TO DINE

411 WEST ITALIAN CAFE **Phone:** 919/967-2782 37

Italian
$6-$24

The aromas of American and Italian cuisine seep from the wood-burning ovens at the Mediterranean bistro. Lively surroundings add flavor to the freshly made pasta, grilled seafood and pizza. Patio seating lends to the relaxed ambience. Casual dress. **Bar:** Full bar. **Hours:** 11:30 am-2:30 & 5-10 pm, Fri-10:30 pm, Sat noon-3 & 5-10:30 pm, Sun 10:30 am-2 & 5-9:30 pm; Sunday brunch. Closed: 7/4, 11/26, 12/24, 12/25. **Address:** 411 W Franklin St **Location:** Jct Columbia St, 0.5 mi w **Parking:** street. **Cards:** AX, DC, DS, MC, VI.

BIN 54 **Phone:** 919/969-1155 43

Steak & Seafood
$25-$50

Sophistication punctuates the contemporary restaurant, where the breads, sauces and desserts are made on site. The menu lists superior cuts of beef and fish, in addition to some wild game and organic vegetable dishes. Presentations are simple and sauces come on the side so that the dishes' savory flavors stand out. Dressy casual. **Bar:** Full bar. **Reservations:** suggested. **Hours:** 5:30 pm-10 pm, Fri & Sat-11 pm. Closed: 11/26, 12/25; also Sun. **Address:** 1201-M Raleigh Rd **Location:** I-40, exit 273, 2.7 mi w on SR 54; in Glen Lennox Shopping Center. **Parking:** on-site. **Cards:** AX, DS, MC, VI.

CALL

CAROLINA BREWERY **Phone:** 919/942-1800 38

American
$6-$20

Brewed under the strict guidelines of the Bavarian Purity Act of 1516, hand-crafted beers complement contemporary American menu offerings. The signature North Carolina catfish with chips and homemade focaccia pizza are popular choices. Some desserts are made with beer. On game days, the brewery provides complimentary shuttle service to and from Dean Smith Center and Kenan Stadium. Brunch is offered on weekends. Casual dress. **Bar:** Full bar. **Hours:** 11:30 am-midnight, Fri-Sat to 1 am, Sun 11 am-11 pm. Closed: 1/1, 11/26, 12/25. **Address:** 460 W Franklin St **Location:** Jct Columbia St, 0.6 mi w. **Parking:** on-site. **Cards:** AX, DS, MC, VI.

CAROLINA CROSSROADS **Phone:** 919/918-2777 40

Regional American
$9-$24

An excellent choice for intimate, upscale dining, the restaurant serves Southern cuisine in superior presentations. Exquisite artwork and exotic orchids add style and flair. The wine list showcases fine American labels. Dressy casual. **Bar:** Full bar. **Reservations:** suggested. **Hours:** 6:30 am-2 & 5:30-10 pm. **Address:** 211 Pittsboro St **Location:** Jct Franklin St, just s on Columbia St (SR 86); in Carolina Inn. **Parking:** on-site. **Cards:** AX, CB, DC, DS, JC, MC, VI. **Historic**

CROOK'S CORNER **Phone:** 919/929-7643 41

Southern
$11-$22

The restaurant's upscale, ever-evolving decor rotates new works from a local artist every month. The accomplished chef's imaginative Southern cuisine includes many noteworthy items, particularly shrimp and grits and green Tabasco chicken. Weather permitting, seating is available on the patio. Casual dress. **Bar:** Full bar. **Reservations:** accepted. **Hours:** 5:30 pm-9:30 pm, Fri & Sat-10 pm, Sun-9 pm; 5:30 pm-10 pm, Fri & Sat-10:30 pm, Sun-9:30 pm 4/15-10/31. Closed major holidays; also Mon. **Address:** 610 W Franklin St **Location:** Jct Franklin St and Merritt Mill Rd. **Parking:** on-site. **Cards:** AX, DS, MC, VI.

ELAINE'S ON FRANKLIN *Menu on AAA.com* **Phone:** 919/960-2770 36

New World
$22-$35

The focus at the tiny bistro is on the best fresh and local bounty for all items that appear on the ever-changing menu. The wine list has earned prestigious awards. Dressy casual. **Bar:** Full bar. **Reservations:** suggested. **Hours:** 5:30 pm-9:30 pm, Fri & Sat-10 pm. Closed: 1/1, 11/26, 12/25; also Sun & Mon. **Address:** 454 W Franklin St **Location:** Jct Franklin St, 1.2 mi w. **Parking:** street. **Cards:** AX, DC, DS, MC, VI.

(See map and index starting on p. 681)

IL PALIO RISTORANTE — **Phone:** 919/918-2545 (31)

New Italian
$9-$30

The elegantly appointed dining room projects a casually upscale feel. Varied selections of meat, seafood and poultry are featured beside a wide selection of pasta, gnocchi, risotto and polenta dishes. All of the delicious, well-presented meals are cooked to order. Dressy casual. Entertainment. **Bar:** Full bar. **Reservations:** suggested. **Hours:** 6-10 am, 11:30-2 & 5:30-10 pm, Sat & Sun 7-11 am, 11:30-2 & 5:30-10 pm. Closed: 1/1. **Address:** 1505 E Franklin St **Location:** I-40, exit 270, 2 mi s on US 15/501, then 0.5 mi w; in The Siena Hotel. **Parking:** on-site. **Cards:** AX, DC, MC, VI.

CALL

JUJUBE — **Phone:** 919/960-0555 (42)

Asian
$6-$20

Guests can visit the bar for a drink and quick bite, take a seat in the dining room or dine al fresco if the weather is nice. Dishes merge fresh ingredients and Asian flavors. Casual dress. **Bar:** Full bar. **Reservations:** accepted. **Hours:** 11:30 am-2:30 & 5:30-10 pm, Sat from 5:30 pm. Closed major holidays; also Sun. **Address:** 1201-L Raleigh Rd **Location:** I-40, exit 273, 2.7 mi w on SR 54; in Glen Lennox Shopping Center. **Parking:** on-site. **Cards:** AX, DS, MC, VI.

LANTERN — **Phone:** 919/969-8846 (39)

Asian
$19-$29

The bistro earns raves for innovative Asian dishes made from the freshest ingredients. Chic but unpretentious style marks the tiny dining room, while coziness is the mode in the lounge, where diners often enjoy a late-night snack. Casual dress. **Bar:** Full bar. **Reservations:** accepted. **Hours:** 5:30 pm-10 pm. Closed major holidays; also Sun. **Address:** 423 W Franklin St **Location:** Jct Columbia St, 0.5 mi w. **Parking:** on-site. **Cards:** AX, MC, VI.

LA RESIDENCE — **Phone:** 919/967-2506 (32)

Continental
$7-$27

An intimate, candlelit atmosphere sets the stage for a romantic dining experience. Friendly service and eclectic European cuisine, including delicious preparations of lamb and salmon, are restaurant hallmarks. The enclosed, heated patio allows for year-round seating. Dressy casual. **Bar:** Full bar. **Reservations:** suggested. **Hours:** 6 pm-10:30 pm. Closed: 12/24-12/26. **Address:** 202 W Rosemary St **Location:** Jct Franklin St, just n on Columbia St, then just w. **Parking:** on-site (fee) and street. **Cards:** AX, DC, DS, MC, VI.

MAMA DIP'S KITCHEN — **Phone:** 919/942-5837 (34)

American
$6-$15

Home-style favorites at the family-owned cafe include fried chicken and cobblers. For more than 25 years, Mama has made fresh bread, country vegetables and irresistible pies. Friendly service is standard at the homey eatery. Casual dress. **Bar:** Beer & wine. **Reservations:** not accepted. **Hours:** 8 am-9:30 pm, Sun-9 pm. Closed: major holidays; also 12/26. **Address:** 408 W Rosemary St **Location:** Jct Columbia St, just w. **Parking:** on-site. **Cards:** DS, MC, VI.

ORIENTAL GARDEN CHINESE & THAI RESTAURANT — **Phone:** 919/967-8818 (35)

Chinese
$4-$11

Diners can relax in a lovely indoor garden while sampling Chinese and Thai cuisine. A friendly greeting awaits those entering the atrium, then cordial servers offer a tempting array of dishes featuring fresh vegetables in well-prepared compositions. Casual dress. **Bar:** Beer & wine. **Reservations:** accepted. **Hours:** 11:30 am-2 & 5-9:30 pm, Fri & Sat-10:30 pm. Closed: Mon. **Address:** 503 W Rosemary St **Location:** Jct Columbia St, just w. **Parking:** on-site. **Cards:** AX, DC, DS, MC, VI.

SQUID'S RESTAURANT & OYSTER BAR — **Phone:** 919/942-8757 (30)

Seafood
$10-$20

Guests can enjoy savory mesquite-grilled or broiled seafood in the spacious, nautical-themed dining room. The menu also lists some steak and pasta entrees. Casual dress. **Bar:** Full bar. **Hours:** 5 pm-9:30 pm, Fri & Sat-10 pm, Sun & Mon-9 pm; oyster bar opens 4 pm. Closed: major holidays; also 12/24, Super Bowl Sun. **Address:** 1201 N Fordham Blvd **Location:** Jct US 54, 1.5 mi n; on US 15/501 Bypass. **Parking:** on-site. **Cards:** AX, DC, DS, MC, VI.

TOP OF THE HILL RESTAURANT & BREWERY — **Phone:** 919/929-8676 (33)

American
$8-$20

The downtown hot spot is at the top of many local "best of" lists for both the contemporary American menu and the great views of Franklin Street offered from the third-floor covered deck. The dining room is casually upscale, and servers are friendly. The on-site microbrewery is considered one of the top in the nation. Guests can smoke on the terrace. Casual dress. **Bar:** Full bar. **Reservations:** accepted. **Hours:** 11 am-2 am, Sun from noon. Closed: 11/26, 12/25. **Address:** 100 E Franklin St, 3rd Floor **Location:** Jct Columbia and Franklin sts. **Parking:** on-site. **Cards:** AX, DC, MC, VI.

WEATHERVANE — **Phone:** 919/929-9466 (29)

American
$6-$25

Diners can relax on the cafe's huge patio to savor such dishes as salmon over orzo with hot homemade bread. The adjacent gourmet store features an extensive collection of beers and wines, along with delicatessen and bakery items. A brunch is offered all day on Sunday. Casual dress. **Bar:** Full bar. **Reservations:** suggested. **Hours:** 7 am-9 pm, Fri & Sat-10 pm, Sun 10 am-6 pm. Closed major holidays. **Address:** 201 S Estes Dr **Location:** I-40, exit 270, 2.7 mi s on US 15/501 Bypass; at University Mall in "A Southern Season". **Parking:** on-site. **Cards:** AX, DS, MC, VI.

Destination Charlotte

pop. 540,828

Charlotte's movers and shakers work hard and smart, so they relax with verve and style.

Sports range from the WNBA's Sting to NASCAR's mean machines. Thrills range from stomach-churning roller coasters to goose-bump-raising symphonies. And restaurant fare runs the gamut from down-home to haute cuisine.

© SuperStock
age fotostock

Bank of America Stadium, Charlotte. A pair of 8-foot panther sculptures safeguards each of the stadium's three entrances. (See mention page 145)

Mike Hewitt
Getty Images

Rowing Competition, Charlotte. Whether they're racing or rowing for the sheer pleasure of it, water sports enthusiasts head to Charlotte's lakes for exercise and entertainment.

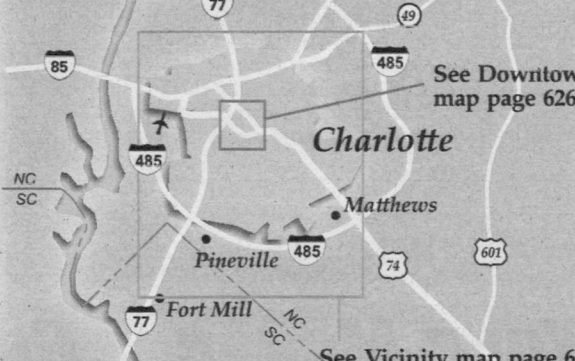

Davidson
Cornelius
Concord
Huntersville
85
77
49
485
See Downtown map page 626
Charlotte
NC
SC
Matthews
Pineville
601
74
Fort Mill
Rock Hill
See Vicinity map page 628

© Gibson Stock Photography

Charlotte Skyline. Skyscrapers cast shadows where the subjects of George III and Queen Charlotte once walked.

Dining in the Charlotte area. From home cooking to nouvelle cuisine, Charlotte's restaurants please with flavorful culinary creations.

Visit Charlotte

Places included in this AAA Destination City:

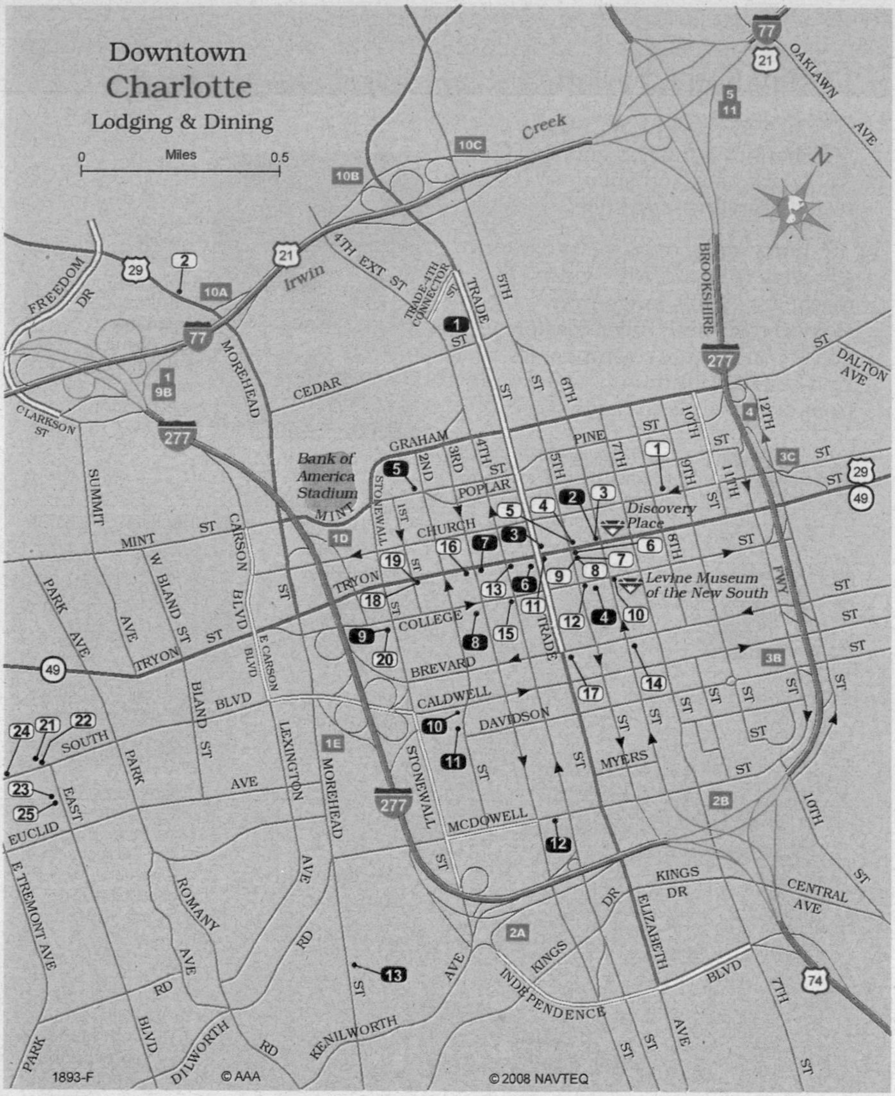

Downtown Charlotte Lodging & Dining

0 Miles 0.5

1893-F © AAA © 2008 NAVTEQ

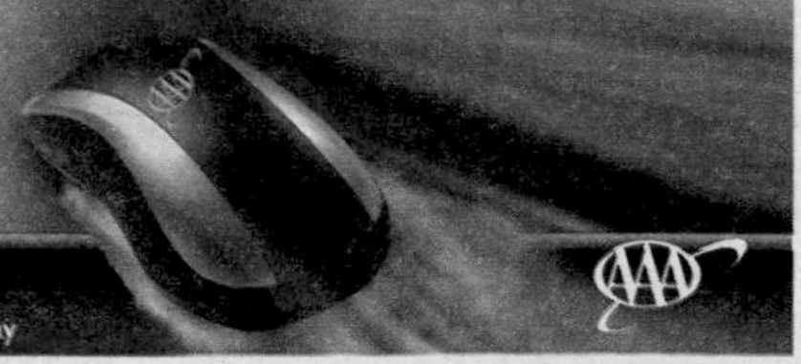

Downtown Charlotte

This index helps you "spot" where approved lodgings and restaurants are located on the corresponding detailed maps. Lodging daily rate range is for comparison only and show the property's high season. Restaurant rate range is a combination of lunch and/or dinner. Turn to the listing page for more detailed rate information and consult display ads for special promotions.

DOWNTOWN CHARLOTTE

Map Page	OA	Lodgings	Diamond Rated	High Season	Page
1 / p. 626	AAA	**DoubleTree Hotel Charlotte-Gateway Village**	♦♦♦	$89-$229 SAVE	635
2 / p. 626	AAA	**The Dunhill Hotel**	♦♦♦	$179-$269 SAVE	635
3 / p. 626		Marriott Charlotte City Center	♦♦♦	$226-$246	636
4 / p. 626		Holiday Inn Center City	♦♦♦	$109-$289	636
5 / p. 626	AAA	**Residence Inn by Marriott-Charlotte Uptown**	♦♦♦	$267-$277 SAVE	637
6 / p. 626	AAA	**Omni Charlotte Hotel**	♦♦♦♦	$237-$267 SAVE	636
7 / p. 626		Courtyard by Marriott-Charlotte City Center	♦♦♦	$206-$221	635
8 / p. 626	AAA	**Hilton Charlotte Center City**	♦♦♦♦	$109-$349 SAVE	636
9 / p. 626	AAA	**The Westin Charlotte**	♦♦♦♦	$119-$379 SAVE	637
10 / p. 626		Hilton Garden Inn-Charlotte Uptown	♦♦♦	$99-$199	636
11 / p. 626		Hampton Inn-Charlotte Uptown	♦♦♦	$129-$194	635
12 / p. 626	AAA	**Crowne Plaza - Charlotte**	♦♦♦	$119-$289 SAVE	635
13 / p. 626		Morehead Inn	♦♦♦	Rates not provided	636

Map Page	OA	Restaurants	Diamond Rated	Cuisine	Meal Range	Page
1 / p. 626	AAA	**McNinch House**	♦♦♦♦	Continental	$89	639
2 / p. 626		Open Kitchen	♦	Italian	$7-$16	639
3 / p. 626		Monticello Restaurant	♦♦♦	American	$8-$34	639
4 / p. 626		The Capital Grille	♦♦♦	Steak & Seafood	$11-$37	638
5 / p. 626		Zink American Kitchen	♦♦♦	American	$5-$25	640
6 / p. 626		Ri-Ra Irish Pub	♦♦	Irish	$10-$21	639
7 / p. 626		Luce Ristorante	♦♦♦	Italian	$9-$30	638
8 / p. 626		Blue Restaurant & Bar	♦♦♦	Mediterranean	$20-$45	637
9 / p. 626		Coco Osteria	♦♦	Italian	$10-$22	638
10 / p. 626		Cosmos Cafe	♦♦	International	$7-$26	638
11 / p. 626		Sonoma Modern American Cuisine	♦♦♦	American	$7-$34	640
12 / p. 626		Mert's Heart & Soul	♦♦	Southern	$5-$14	639
13 / p. 626		Harry & Jean's	♦♦♦	American	$6-$35	638
14 / p. 626		La Vecchia's Seafood Grille	♦♦♦	Seafood	$17-$36	638
15 / p. 626		Bentley's on 27	♦♦♦	French	$9-$54	637
16 / p. 626		Mimosa Grill	♦♦♦	American	$8-$36	639
17 / p. 626		Carpe Diem Restaurant	♦♦♦	American	$14-$28	638
18 / p. 626		Aquavina	♦♦♦	Seafood	$7-$38	637
19 / p. 626	AAA	**Ratcliffe on the Green**	♦♦♦	Southern	$11-$40	639
20 / p. 626		Ember Grille	♦♦♦	American	$6-$32	638
21 / p. 626		McIntosh's Steak & Seafood	♦♦♦	Steak & Seafood	$25-$55	639
22 / p. 626		Pewter Rose Bistro	♦♦♦	American	$6-$22	639
23 / p. 626	AAA	**Bonterra Dining & Wine Room**	♦♦♦♦	American	$17-$52	638
24 / p. 626		Sullivan's Steakhouse	♦♦♦	Steak	$20-$40	640
25 / p. 626		300 East	♦♦	American	$8-$21	637

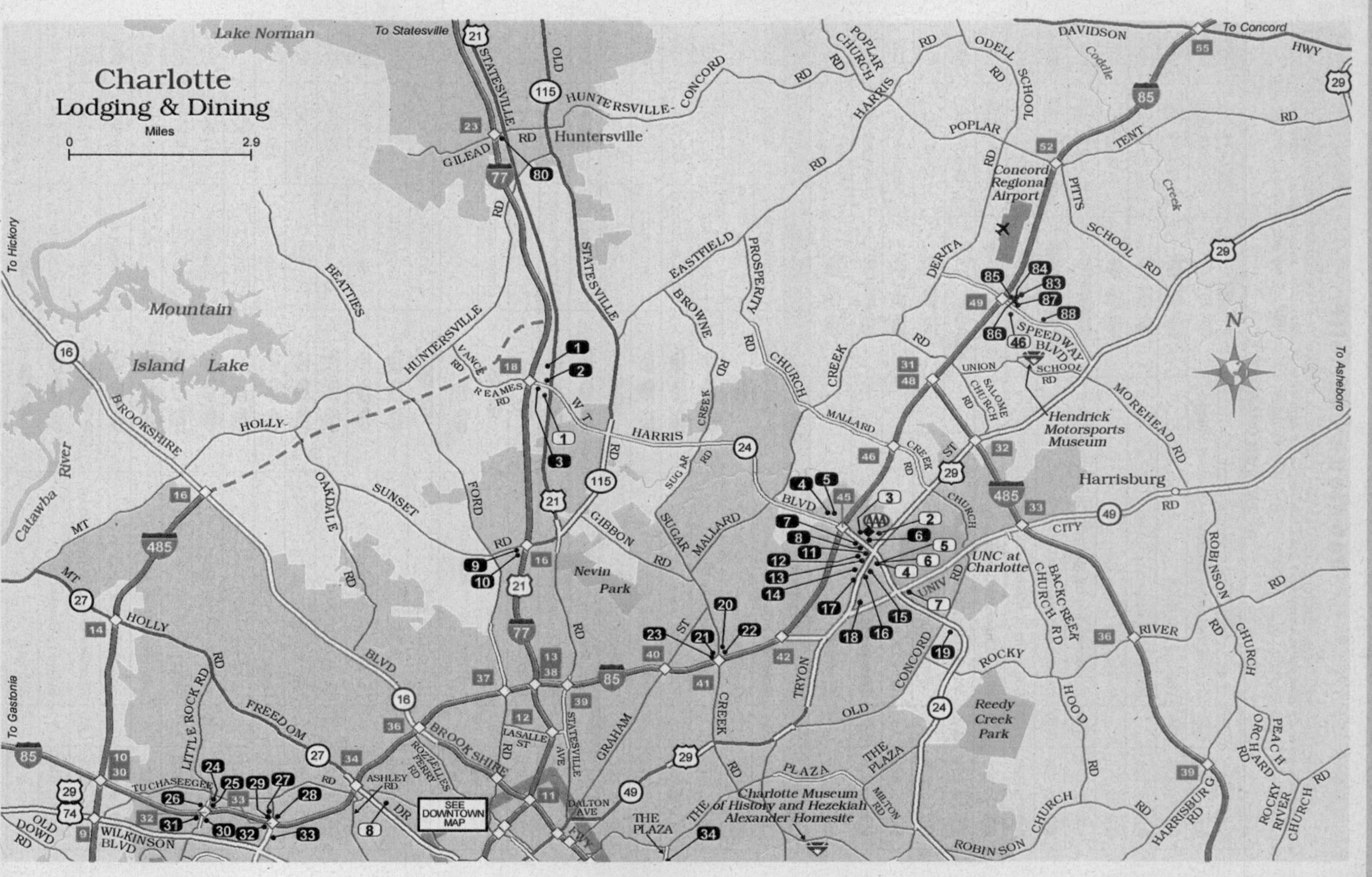
Charlotte
Lodging & Dining
Miles
0
2.9
To Statesville
To Concord
To Hickory
To Gastonia
To Asheboro
Lake Norman
Mountain Island Lake
Catawba River
Huntersville
Harrisburg
Concord Regional Airport
Hendrick Motorsports Museum
UNC at Charlotte
Nevin Park
Reedy Creek Park
Charlotte Museum of History and Hezekiah Alexander Homesite
SEE DOWNTOWN MAP

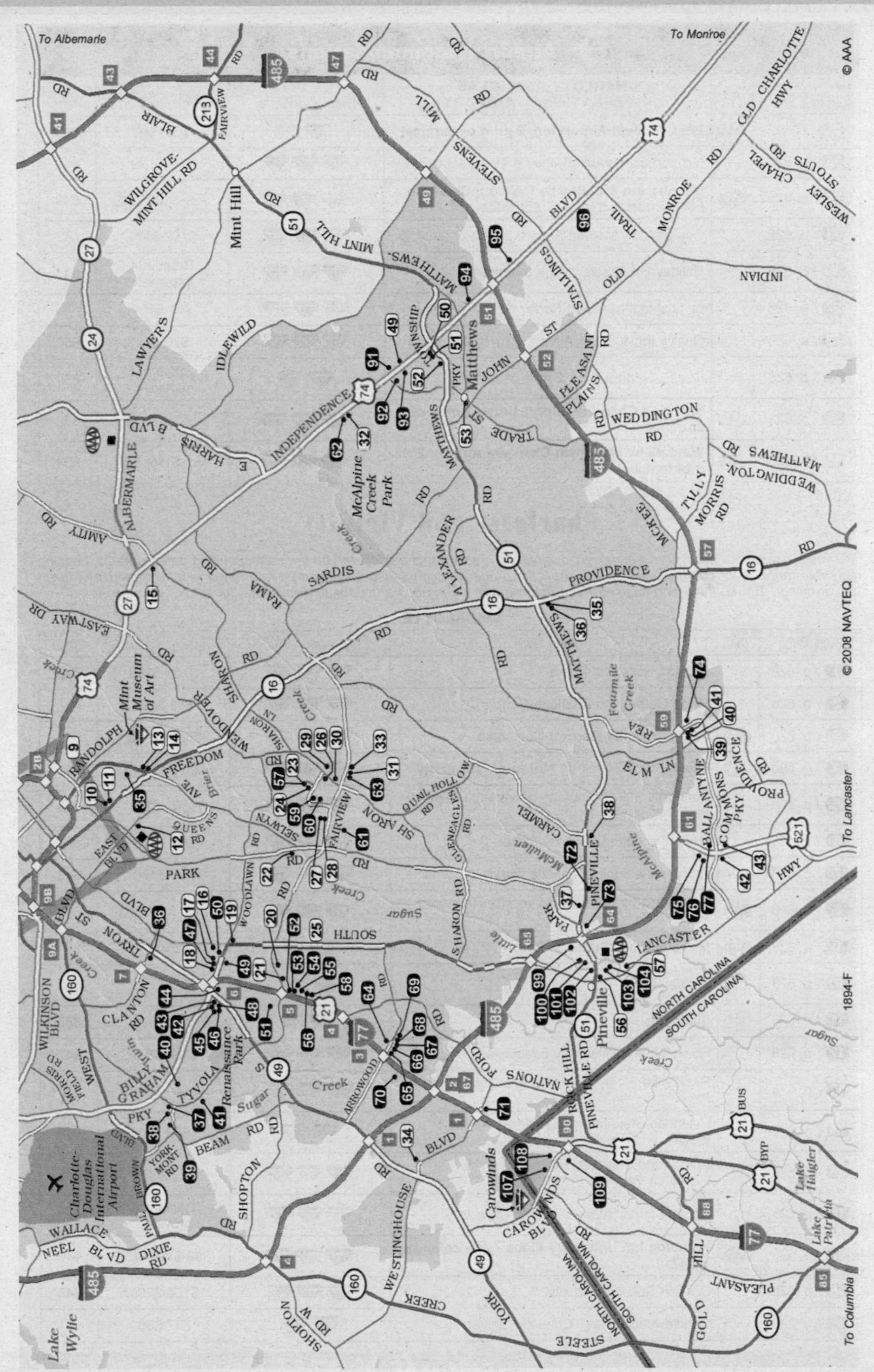
To Albemarle
To Monroe
To Lancaster
To Columbia
Mint Hill
Matthews
Pineville
Carowinds
McAlpine Creek Park
Mint Museum of Art
Renaissance Park
Charlotte-Douglas International Airport
Lake Wylie
Lake Hagler
Lake Patricia
NORTH CAROLINA
SOUTH CAROLINA
INDEPENDENCE
ALBEMARLE
PROVIDENCE
SARDIS
WEDDINGTON
TYVOLA
BILLY GRAHAM PKY
WILKINSON BLVD
WESTINGHOUSE BLVD
NATIONS FORD
ARROWOOD
STEELE CREEK
WILGROVE-MINT HILL RD
LAWYERS
IDLEWILD
BALLANTYNE COMMONS PKY
PINEVILLE
RANDOLPH
FREEDOM
WENDOVER
SHARON
FAIRVIEW
SELWYN
WOODLAWN
QUAIL HOLLOW
CARMEL
PARK
SOUTH
TRYON
CLANTON
TRADE ST
JOHN ST
STEVENS MILL
STALLINGS
OLD MONROE
WESLEY CHAPEL STOUTS RD
INDIAN TRAIL
OLD CHARLOTTE HWY
© AAA
© 2038 NAVTEQ
1894-F

Airport Accommodations

Map Page	OA	CHARLOTTE-DOUGLAS INTERNATIONAL AIRPORT	Diamond Rated	High Season	Page
25 / p. 628	AAA	**Best Western-Airport Inn, 2 mi n of terminal**	◆◆	$69 SAVE	640
33 / p. 628		Comfort Suites/Airport, 2 mi e of entrance	◆◆◆	$89-$199	642
24 / p. 628	AAA	**Country Inn & Suites by Carlson, Charlotte, I-85 Airport, 1.5 mi n of entrance**	◆◆◆	$99-$109 SAVE	643
31 / p. 628		Courtyard by Marriott-Airport, 2 mi n of terminal	◆◆◆	$162-$174	643
30 / p. 628		Holiday Inn Airport, 1 mi n of entrance	◆◆◆	Rates not provided	647
27 / p. 628		La Quinta Inn- Airport North, 2 mi n of terminal	◆◆◆	$59-$109	649
28 / p. 628		Quality Inn & Suites Airport, 2 mi n of terminal	◆◆◆	$70-$80	650
29 / p. 628		Red Roof Inn-Airport, 2 mi e of airport	◆◆	Rates not provided	650
32 / p. 628	AAA	**Sheraton Charlotte Airport Hotel, 2 mi e of entrance**	◆◆◆	$99-$279 SAVE	652
26 / p. 628	AAA	**Wingate by Wyndham-Charlotte Airport, 2 mi n of terminal**	◆◆◆	$69-$199 SAVE	654

Charlotte and Vicinity

This index helps you "spot" where approved lodgings and restaurants are located on the corresponding detailed maps. Lodging daily rate range is for comparison only and show the property's high season. Restaurant rate range is a combination of lunch and/or dinner. Turn to the listing page for more detailed rate information and consult display ads for special promotions.

CHARLOTTE

Map Page	OA	Lodgings	Diamond Rated	High Season	Page
1 / p. 628		Comfort Suites-Northlake	◆◆◆	$109-$189	642
2 / p. 628		Hilton Garden Inn-Charlotte North	◆◆◆	$89-$199	647
3 / p. 628	AAA	**Fairfield Inn by Marriott-Northlake**	◆◆◆	$98-$105 SAVE	646
4 / p. 628	AAA	**TownePlace Suites by Marriott - University**	◆◆◆	$195-$205 SAVE	653
5 / p. 628		SpringHill Suites Charlotte University Research Park	◆◆◆	$147-$158	652
6 / p. 628		Hilton Charlotte University Place	◆◆◆	$99-$349	647
7 / p. 628		Drury Inn & Suites-Charlotte North	◆◆◆	$90-$170	645
8 / p. 628	AAA	**Courtyard by Marriott-University Research Park**	◆◆◆	$147-$158 SAVE	644
9 / p. 628	AAA	**Microtel Inn & Suites**	◆◆	$49-$140 SAVE	650
10 / p. 628		Sunset Inn	◆◆	Rates not provided	653
11 / p. 628	AAA	**Sleep Inn**	◆◆	$70-$170 SAVE	652
12 / p. 628		Holiday Inn at University Executive Park	◆◆◆	$99-$289	647
13 / p. 628		Residence Inn by Marriott-University Research Park	◆◆◆	$159-$299	651
14 / p. 628		Extended StayAmerica-Charlotte-University Place	◆◆	$80-$90	645
15 / p. 628		Homewood Suites by Hilton-University Research Park	◆◆◆	$79-$239	648
16 / p. 628		Country Inn & Suites-Charlotte University	◆◆◆	Rates not provided	643
17 / p. 628	AAA	**Hampton Inn University Place - see color ad p 647**	◆◆◆	$99-$169 SAVE	646
18 / p. 628		Comfort Suites-University	◆◆◆	$100-$200	643
19 / p. 628		Candlewood Suites - Charlotte University	◆◆	$77-$80	641

CHARLOTTE (cont'd)

Map Page	OA	Lodgings (cont'd)	Diamond Rated	High Season	Page
20 / p. 628		Rodeway Inn	◆◆	$40-$125	652
21 / p. 628		Super 8 Motel	◆◆	Rates not provided	653
22 / p. 628	AAA	**Ramada Northeast**	◆◆	$49-$54 SAVE	650
23 / p. 628	AAA	**Comfort Inn-UNCC - see color ad p 642**	◆◆	$70-$159 SAVE	642
24 / p. 628	AAA	**Country Inn & Suites by Carlson, Charlotte, I-85 Airport**	◆◆◆	$99-$109 SAVE	643
25 / p. 628	AAA	**Best Western-Airport Inn**	◆◆	$69 SAVE	640
26 / p. 628	AAA	**Wingate by Wyndham-Charlotte Airport**	◆◆◆	$69-$199 SAVE	654
27 / p. 628		La Quinta Inn- Airport North	◆◆◆	$59-$109	649
28 / p. 628		Quality Inn & Suites Airport	◆◆◆	$70-$80	650
29 / p. 628		Red Roof Inn-Airport	◆◆	Rates not provided	650
30 / p. 628		Holiday Inn Airport	◆◆◆	Rates not provided	647
31 / p. 628		Courtyard by Marriott-Airport	◆◆◆	$162-$174	643
32 / p. 628	AAA	**Sheraton Charlotte Airport Hotel**	◆◆◆	$99-$279 SAVE	652
33 / p. 628		Comfort Suites/Airport	◆◆◆	$89-$199	642
34 / p. 628		The Vanlandingham Estate	◆◆◆	$149-$239	653
35 / p. 628	AAA	**The Duke Mansion Historic Inn & Meeting Place**	◆◆◆◆	$179-$299 SAVE	645
36 / p. 628		Super 8 Motel	◆◆	$40-$125	653
37 / p. 628	AAA	**Hyatt Place Charlotte Airport/Tyvola Road**	◆◆◆	$69-$209 SAVE	648
38 / p. 628	AAA	**DoubleTree Hotel-Charlotte Airport - see color ad p 644**	◆◆◆	$89-$209 SAVE	644
39 / p. 628		Homewood Suites by Hilton Airport	◆◆◆	$69-$189	648
40 / p. 628	AAA	**Renaissance Charlotte Suites Hotel**	◆◆◆	$187-$201 SAVE	651
41 / p. 628	AAA	**Hyatt Place Charlotte/City Park**	◆◆◆	$69-$209 SAVE	649
42 / p. 628		Homestead Studio Suites Hotel-Charlotte/Airport	◆◆	$95-$105	648
43 / p. 628		Embassy Suites	◆◆◆	$119-$239	645
44 / p. 628		Holiday Inn-Billy Graham Parkway	◆◆◆	Rates not provided	648
45 / p. 628		Sleep Inn-Yorkmont	◆◆	$80-$130	652
46 / p. 628	AAA	**Hyatt Summerfield Suites**	◆◆◆	$99-$299 SAVE	649
47 / p. 628		Ramada Conference Center "Airport South"	◆◆	Rates not provided	650
48 / p. 628		La Quinta Inn & Suites Charlotte Airport South	◆◆◆	$69-$129	649
49 / p. 628	AAA	**Best Western Sterling Hotel**	◆◆◆	$69-$99 SAVE	641
50 / p. 628	AAA	**Four Points by Sheraton-Charlotte**	◆◆◆	Rates not provided SAVE	646
51 / p. 628		Wingate by Wyndham	◆◆◆	$99-$149	654
52 / p. 628	AAA	**Comfort Inn-Executive Park**	◆◆◆	$54-$84 SAVE	642
53 / p. 628	AAA	**Charlotte Marriott Executive Park**	◆◆◆	$206-$221 SAVE	642
54 / p. 628	AAA	**Quality Inn-Executive Park**	◆◆◆	$75-$195 SAVE	650
55 / p. 628		Residence Inn by Marriott-Charlotte South	◆◆◆	$172-$184	651
56 / p. 628		Candlewood Suites-Executive Park	◆◆	Rates not provided	641

CHARLOTTE (cont'd)

Map Page	OA	Lodgings (cont'd)	Diamond Rated	High Season	Page
57 / p. 628	AAA	**Marriott-Charlotte SouthPark**	◆◆◆◆	$217-$233 SAVE	650
58 / p. 628		StudioPLUS-Tyvola	◆◆	$83-$93	653
59 / p. 628	AAA	**DoubleTree Guest Suites-South Park**	◆◆◆	$99-$289 SAVE	644
60 / p. 628		Renaissance Charlotte SouthPark	fyi	$205-$226	651
61 / p. 628		Courtyard by Marriott-South Park	◆◆◆	$147-$158	643
62 / p. 628	AAA	**Best Western Independence Hotel**	◆◆◆	$89-$129 SAVE	640
63 / p. 628		Hampton Inn & Suites South Park	◆◆◆	$110-$245	646
64 / p. 628		TownePlace Suites by Marriott-Arrowood	◆◆◆	$133-$143	653
65 / p. 628		Fairfield Inn by Marriott-Arrowood	◆◆◆	$108-$115	645
66 / p. 628	AAA	**Hyatt Place Charlotte/Arrowood**	◆◆◆	$99-$299 SAVE	649
67 / p. 628		MainStay Suites	◆◆	Rates not provided	650
68 / p. 628		Staybridge Suites-Arrowood	◆◆◆	Rates not provided	652
69 / p. 628		Holiday Inn Express Hotel & Suites	◆◆◆	$100-$300	648
70 / p. 628		Hampton Inn & Suites-Arrowood	◆◆◆	$130-$157	646
71 / p. 628		Super 8 Charlotte/Carowinds/Airport	◆◆	$55-$120	653
72 / p. 628		Extended Stay Deluxe-Charlotte/Pineville	◆◆◆	$99-$109	645
73 / p. 628		Extended StayAmerica-Charlotte-Pineville	◆◆	$85-$95	645
74 / p. 628		Residence Inn by Marriott-Piper Glen	◆◆◆	$217-$233	651
75 / p. 628		Courtyard by Marriott-Ballantyne Resort	◆◆◆	$157-$169	643
76 / p. 628		Staybridge Suites Charlotte-Ballantyne	◆◆◆	$169-$349	652
77 / p. 628	AAA	**Ballantyne Resort, A Luxury Collection Resort - see color ad p 641**	◆◆◆◆	$209-$429 SAVE	640

Map Page	OA	Restaurants	Diamond Rated	Cuisine	Meal Range	Page
1 / p. 628		Hickory Tavern	◆◆	American	$8-$33	656
2 / p. 628		Ciro's Italian Restaurant	◆◆	Italian	$7-$25	655
3 / p. 628	AAA	**Lava Bistro & Bar**	◆◆◆	American	$7-$29	656
4 / p. 628		Chen's Bistro	◆◆	Chinese	$6-$16	655
5 / p. 628		Bombay Cuisine	◆◆	Indian	$5-$19	654
6 / p. 628		Thai House	◆◆	Thai	$6-$17	659
7 / p. 628		Amalfi Pasta & Pizza	◆◆	Italian	$5-$15	654
8 / p. 628		Beauregards Restaurant	◆◆	American	$5-$14	654
9 / p. 628		Cajun Queen Restaurant	◆◆	Cajun	$14-$25	655
10 / p. 628		Mama Ricotta's	◆◆	Italian	$6-$18	657
11 / p. 628		Maharani	◆◆	Indian	$7-$16	656
12 / p. 628		Sole' Spanish Grille	◆◆◆	Spanish	$8-$24	658
13 / p. 628		Primo Tuscan Grille	◆◆◆	Italian	$18-$35	658
14 / p. 628		Providence Cafe	◆◆◆	American	$7-$23	658
15 / p. 628		The Middle East Deli	◆	Middle Eastern	$4-$10	657
16 / p. 628		Beef & Bottle	◆◆	Steak	$16-$39	654
17 / p. 628		Tryon House	◆◆	American	$5-$14	659

Map Page	OA	Restaurants (cont'd)	Diamond Rated	Cuisine	Meal Range	Page
18 / p. 628		Murphy's Food & Spirits	◆◆	American	$7-$20	657
19 / p. 628		Villa Antonio Fine Italian Ristorante	◆◆	Italian	$6-$35	659
20 / p. 628		Carolina Country Barbecue	◆◆	Regional Southern	$5-$12	655
21 / p. 628		Derby Diner	◆◆	American	$6-$15	655
22 / p. 628		Portofino Italian Restaurant	◆◆	Italian	$6-$20	658
23 / p. 628		The Grill	◆◆◆	American	$8-$29	656
24 / p. 628		Frank Manzetti's Tavern at Southpark	◆◆	American	$5-$25	656
25 / p. 628		Pho 98 Authentic Vietnamese Restaurant	◆◆	Vietnamese	$6-$13	657
26 / p. 628		M5 Modern Mediterranean	◆◆◆	Mediterranean	$9-$35	656
27 / p. 628		Oceanaire	◆◆◆	Seafood	$10-$38	657
28 / p. 628		Brio Tuscan Grille	◆◆◆	Italian	$12-$30	655
29 / p. 628		Restaurant J Basul Noble	◆◆◆	New Italian	$8-$38	658
30 / p. 628	AAA	**Zebra Restaurant and Fine Catering**	◆◆◆◆	French	$8-$39	659
31 / p. 628		P.F. Chang's China Bistro	◆◆◆	New Asian	$10-$21	657
32 / p. 628		Crown Point Family Restaurant	◆◆	American	$5-$12	655
33 / p. 628		Upstream	◆◆◆	Seafood	$7-$37	659
34 / p. 628		John's Family Restaurant	◆◆	American	$5-$9	656
35 / p. 628		Mickey & Mooch, The Other Joint	◆◆◆	Continental	$11-$37	657
36 / p. 628		New South Kitchen & Bar	◆◆◆	American	$10-$19	657
37 / p. 628		Bombay Grille	◆◆	Indian	$7-$18	654
38 / p. 628		Bangkok Ocha	◆◆	Thai	$6-$16	654
39 / p. 628		Miro Spanish Grille	◆◆◆	Spanish	$7-$20	657
40 / p. 628		JoJo China Bistro	◆◆	Chinese	$7-$18	656
41 / p. 628		Firebirds Wood Fired Grill	◆◆◆	American	$8-$36	655
42 / p. 628		Table Restaurant & Bar	◆◆◆	American	$20-$40	659
43 / p. 628		Zapata's Mexican Restaurant	◆◆	Mexican	$6-$13	659

HUNTERSVILLE

Map Page	OA	Lodging	Diamond Rated	High Season	Page
80 / p. 628		Holiday Inn Express	◆◆	$88-$180	664

CONCORD

Map Page	OA	Lodgings	Diamond Rated	High Season	Page
83 / p. 628		Wingate by Wyndham	◆◆◆	$116-$129	662
84 / p. 628		Comfort Suites-Concord Mills	◆◆◆	$110-$345	660
85 / p. 628		SpringHill Suites-Charlotte Concord Mills	◆◆◆	$137-$147	661
86 / p. 628		Holiday Inn Express Hotel & Suites-Charlotte/ Concord	◆◆◆	$109-$316	661
87 / p. 628		Hampton Inn & Suites-Speedway Blvd/Concord Mills	◆◆◆	$115-$290	661
88 / p. 628	AAA	**Embassy Suites Charlotte-Concord Golf Resort & Spa**	◆◆◆	$129-$189 SAVE	660

Map Page	OA	Restaurant	Diamond Rated	Cuisine	Meal Range	Page
46 / p. 628		Tsunami Japanese Steakhouse & Sushi Bar	◆◆	Japanese	$7-$32	662

MATTHEWS

Map Page	OA	Lodgings	Diamond Rated	High Season	Page
91 / p. 628	AAA	**Comfort Inn**	◆◆◆	$84-$195 SAVE	665
92 / p. 628		Hampton Inn-Matthews	◆◆◆	$104-$124	665
93 / p. 628		Sleep Inn	◆◆	$69-$119	666
94 / p. 628		Courtyard by Marriott	◆◆◆	$137-$147	665
95 / p. 628	AAA	**Country Inn & Suites-Matthews**	◆◆◆	$99-$119 SAVE	665
96 / p. 628		Holiday Inn Express Hotel & Suites	◆◆◆	$90-$150	665

Map Page	OA	Restaurants	Diamond Rated	Cuisine	Meal Range	Page
49 / p. 628		Elliot's BBQ	◆	Barbecue	$6-$9	666
50 / p. 628		Township Grille	◆◆	American	$5-$13	666
51 / p. 628		Fontanella Italiano Ristorante	◆◆	Italian	$5-$20	666
52 / p. 628		Buffet Dynasty	◆◆	Chinese	$7-$15	666
53 / p. 628		Sante	◆◆◆	American	$8-$28	666

PINEVILLE

Map Page	OA	Lodgings	Diamond Rated	High Season	Page
99 / p. 628		Comfort Suites	◆◆◆	$109-$165	667
100 / p. 628	AAA	**Best Western Crown Suites**	◆◆◆	$120-$140 SAVE	666
101 / p. 628		Holiday Inn Express	◆◆◆	$99-$175	667
102 / p. 628	AAA	**Quality Suites**	◆◆◆	$99-$159 SAVE	667
103 / p. 628		Hampton Inn & Suites-Charlotte/Pineville	◆◆◆	$116-$199	667
104 / p. 628		Hilton Garden Inn-Charlotte/Pineville	◆◆◆	$95-$179	667

Map Page	OA	Restaurants	Diamond Rated	Cuisine	Meal Range	Page
56 / p. 628		China Buffet	◆	Chinese	$4-$12	667
57 / p. 628		Waldhorn Restaurant	◆◆	German	$7-$22	667

FORT MILL

Map Page	OA	Lodgings	Diamond Rated	High Season	Page
107 / p. 628		Sleep Inn Carowinds	◆◆	$69-$119	668
108 / p. 628		Comfort Inn Carowinds	◆◆	Rates not provided	668
109 / p. 628	AAA	**Best Western Carowinds**	◆◆◆	$75-$89 SAVE	668

DOWNTOWN CHARLOTTE (See map and index starting on p. 626)

— WHERE TO STAY —

COURTYARD BY MARRIOTT-CHARLOTTE CITY CENTER Book great rates at AAA.com Phone: (704)926-5800 **7**

Hotel
$207-$222 All Year

Address: 237 S Tryon St **Location:** I-77, exit 10 or 10B, 0.6 mi e on Trade St, just s on Church St, then just e on 3rd St. **Facility:** Smoke free premises. 181 units. 177 one-bedroom standard units, some with whirlpools. 4 one-bedroom suites. 11 stories, interior corridors. *Bath:* combo or shower only. **Parking:** on-site (fee). **Terms:** cancellation fee imposed. **Amenities:** high-speed Internet, dual phone lines, voice mail, irons, hair dryers. **Pool(s):** heated outdoor. **Leisure Activities:** whirlpool, exercise room. **Guest Services:** valet and coin laundry, wireless Internet. **Business Services:** meeting rooms, business center. **Cards:** AX, CB, DC, DS, JC, MC, VI.

AAA Benefit:
Members save a minimum 5% off the best available rate.

CROWNE PLAZA - CHARLOTTE Book great rates at AAA.com Phone: (704)372-7550 **12**

AAA SAVE

Hotel
$119-$289 All Year

Address: 201 S McDowell St **Location:** I-277, exit 2A, just w on 4th St, then just s. **Facility:** 193 units. 191 one-bedroom standard units. 2 one-bedroom suites. 11 stories, interior corridors. *Bath:* combo or shower only. **Parking:** on-site (fee). **Terms:** cancellation fee imposed. **Amenities:** video games (fee), CD players, high-speed Internet, voice mail, irons, hair dryers. **Pool(s):** outdoor. **Leisure Activities:** exercise room. **Guest Services:** valet laundry, area transportation-within 3 mi, wireless Internet. **Business Services:** meeting rooms, business center. **Cards:** AX, DC, DS, JC, MC, VI. **Free Special Amenities: newspaper and high-speed Internet.**

/ SOME UNITS FEE

DOUBLETREE HOTEL CHARLOTTE-GATEWAY VILLAGE Book great rates at AAA.com Phone: (704)347-0070 **1**

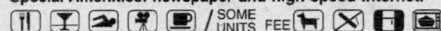

Hotel
$89-$229 All Year

Address: 895 W Trade St **Location:** I-77, exit 10 or 10B, just e. **Facility:** 187 one-bedroom standard units. 8 stories, interior corridors. *Bath:* combo or shower only. **Parking:** on-site (fee). **Terms:** 1-30 night minimum stay, cancellation fee imposed. **Amenities:** dual phone lines, voice mail, safes, irons, hair dryers. *Fee:* video games, high-speed Internet. **Pool(s):** outdoor. **Leisure Activities:** exercise room. **Guest Services:** valet laundry, wireless Internet. **Business Services:** meeting rooms, business center. **Cards:** AX, CB, DC, DS, JC, MC, VI. **Free Special Amenities: newspaper and early check-in/late check-out.**

CALL / SOME UNITS

AAA Benefit:
Members save 5% or more everyday!

THE DUNHILL HOTEL Book great rates at AAA.com Phone: (704)332-4141 **2**

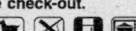

AAA SAVE

Historic Hotel
$179-$269 All Year

Address: 237 N Tryon St **Location:** I-77, exit 10 or 10B, 1 mi e on Trade St, just n on College St, then just w on 6th St. **Facility:** Originally opened in 1929, the downtown hotel retains its historic charm with elegant guestroom furnishings and attractive public areas. 60 units. 59 one-bedroom standard units, some with whirlpools. 1 one-bedroom suite. 10 stories, interior corridors. **Parking:** on-site (fee) and valet. **Terms:** 2-3 night minimum stay - seasonal. **Amenities:** CD players, dual phone lines, voice mail, irons, hair dryers. **Dining:** Monticello Restaurant, see separate listing. **Guest Services:** valet laundry, area transportation-within 5 mi, wireless Internet. **Business Services:** meeting rooms, PC. **Cards:** AX, DS, MC, VI. **Free Special Amenities: newspaper and high-speed Internet.**

24 FEE / SOME UNITS FEE VCR

HAMPTON INN-CHARLOTTE UPTOWN Book great rates at AAA.com Phone: (704)373-0917 **11**

Hotel
$129-$194 All Year

Address: 530 Dr Martin Luther King Jr Blvd **Location:** Jct Caldwell St, just e. **Facility:** 149 units. 129 one-bedroom standard units, some with whirlpools. 20 one-bedroom suites, some with whirlpools. 11 stories, interior corridors. *Bath:* combo or shower only. **Parking:** on-site (fee). **Terms:** 1-30 night minimum stay, cancellation fee imposed. **Amenities:** high-speed Internet, dual phone lines, voice mail, irons, hair dryers. **Pool(s):** heated indoor. **Leisure Activities:** whirlpool, exercise room. **Guest Services:** complimentary and valet laundry, area transportation, wireless Internet. **Business Services:** meeting rooms, business center. **Cards:** AX, CB, DC, DS, JC, MC, VI.

CALL / SOME UNITS VCR

AAA Benefit:
Members save up to 10% everyday!

(See map and index starting on p. 626)

HILTON CHARLOTTE CENTER CITY Book great rates at AAA.com Phone: (704)377-1500 8

Hotel
$109-$349 All Year

Address: 222 E 3rd St **Location:** I-77, exit 10 or 10B, 0.8 mi e on Trade St, just s on Church St, then just e; jct S College St. **Facility:** The high-rise property offers tastefully furnished rooms in the Hilton tradition. Designated smoking area. 400 units. 396 one-bedroom standard units. 4 one-bedroom suites, some with whirlpools. 22 stories, interior corridors. *Bath:* combo or shower only. **Parking:** on-site and valet. **Terms:** 1-30 night minimum stay, cancellation fee imposed. **Amenities:** dual phone lines, voice mail, irons, hair dryers. *Fee:* video games, high-speed Internet. *Some:* CD players. **Guest Services:** valet laundry, wireless Internet. **Business Services:** conference facilities, business center. **Cards:** AX, CB, DC, DS, JC, MC, VI.

CALL FEE

Hilton
AAA Benefit:
Members save 5% or more everyday!

HILTON GARDEN INN-CHARLOTTE UPTOWN Book great rates at AAA.com Phone: (704)347-5972 10

Hotel
$99-$199 All Year

Address: 508 E Martin Luther King Jr Blvd **Location:** Jct Caldwell St, just e. **Facility:** 181 units. 142 one-bedroom standard units, some with whirlpools. 39 one-bedroom suites, some with whirlpools. 15 stories, interior corridors. *Bath:* combo or shower only. **Parking:** on-site (fee). **Terms:** 1-30 night minimum stay, cancellation fee imposed. **Amenities:** video games (fee), high-speed Internet, dual phone lines, voice mail, irons, hair dryers. **Pool(s):** heated indoor. **Leisure Activities:** whirlpool, exercise room. **Guest Services:** complimentary and valet laundry, area transportation, wireless Internet. **Business Services:** meeting rooms, business center. **Cards:** AX, CB, DC, DS, JC, MC, VI.

/ SOME UNITS

Hilton Garden Inn
AAA Benefit:
Members save 5% or more everyday!

HOLIDAY INN CENTER CITY Book at AAA.com Phone: (704)335-5400 4

Hotel
$109-$289 All Year

Address: 230 N College St **Location:** I-77, exit 10 or 10B, 1 mi e on Trade St, then just n; jct 6th St. **Facility:** 296 units. 282 one-bedroom standard units. 14 one-bedroom suites. 14 stories, interior corridors. **Parking:** on-site (fee) and valet. **Terms:** 3 day cancellation notice-fee imposed. **Amenities:** high-speed Internet, dual phone lines, voice mail, irons, hair dryers. **Pool(s):** outdoor. **Leisure Activities:** whirlpool, exercise room. **Guest Services:** valet laundry, wireless Internet. **Business Services:** conference facilities, business center. **Cards:** AX, CB, DC, DS, JC, MC, VI.

ASK CALL / SOME UNITS

MARRIOTT CHARLOTTE CITY CENTER Book great rates at AAA.com Phone: (704)333-9000 3

Hotel
$226-$246 All Year

Address: 100 W Trade St **Location:** I-77, exit 10 or 10B, 0.7 mi e; jct Tryon St. **Facility:** Smoke free premises. 438 units. 434 one-bedroom standard units. 4 one-bedroom suites. 19 stories, interior corridors. *Bath:* combo or shower only. **Parking:** on-site (fee) and valet. **Terms:** cancellation fee imposed. **Amenities:** high-speed Internet (fee), dual phone lines, voice mail, irons, hair dryers. *Some:* DVD players (fee), safes. **Pool(s):** heated indoor. **Leisure Activities:** whirlpool, exercise room. **Guest Services:** complimentary and valet laundry, tanning facilities, wireless Internet. **Business Services:** conference facilities, business center. **Cards:** AX, CB, DC, DS, JC, MC, VI.

/ SOME UNITS FEE VCR

Marriott HOTELS & RESORTS
AAA Benefit:
Members save a minimum 5% off the best available rate.

MOREHEAD INN Book at AAA.com Phone: 704/376-3357 13

Bed & Breakfast
Rates not provided

Address: 1122 E Morehead St **Location:** I-277, exit Kenilworth Ave, 0.9 mi s, then just w; corner of Berkeley Ave. **Facility:** Dating from 1917, the in-town mansion offers spacious, attractive guest rooms and a few suites. Smoke free premises. 13 units. 9 one-bedroom standard units, some with whirlpools. 4 one-bedroom suites, some with whirlpools. 2 stories (no elevator), interior/exterior corridors. *Bath:* combo or shower only. **Parking:** on-site. **Amenities:** video library, DVD players, high-speed Internet, dual phone lines, voice mail, irons, hair dryers. **Guest Services:** valet laundry, wireless Internet. **Business Services:** meeting rooms.

/ SOME UNITS

OMNI CHARLOTTE HOTEL Book great rates at AAA.com Phone: (704)377-0400 6

Hotel
$237-$267 All Year

Address: 132 E Trade St **Location:** I-77, exit 10 or 10B, 0.8 mi e; jct Tryon St. **Facility:** This upscale, contemporary hotel is in a complex containing a shopping mall, a civic center and business offices. 374 one-bedroom standard units. 15 stories, interior corridors. *Bath:* combo or shower only. **Parking:** on-site (fee) and valet. **Amenities:** CD players, dual phone lines, voice mail, honor bars, irons, hair dryers. **Pool(s):** outdoor. **Leisure Activities:** *Fee:* massage. **Guest Services:** valet laundry, wireless Internet. **Business Services:** conference facilities, business center. **Cards:** AX, CB, DC, DS, MC, VI. **Free Special Amenities: local telephone calls and newspaper.**

(See map and index starting on p. 626)

RESIDENCE INN BY MARRIOTT-CHARLOTTE UPTOWN Book great rates at AAA.com **Phone:** (704)340-4000 **5**

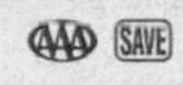

Extended Stay Hotel
$267-$277 All Year

Address: 404 S Mint St **Location:** I-77, exit 10 or 10B, 0.6 mi e on Trade St, then just s. Across from Bank of America Stadium. **Facility:** Just across from the stadium, this extended-stay hotel is centrally located near the downtown core. Smoke free premises. 150 units. 80 one-bedroom standard units with efficiencies. 51 one- and 19 two-bedroom suites, some with efficiencies, kitchens and/or whirlpools. 11 stories, interior corridors. *Bath:* combo or shower only. **Parking:** on-site (fee). **Terms:** cancellation fee imposed. **Amenities:** high-speed Internet, dual phone lines, voice mail, irons, hair dryers. **Leisure Activities:** pool privileges, exercise room. **Guest Services:** valet and coin laundry, area transportation-within 3 mi, wireless Internet. **Business Services:** meeting rooms, business center. **Cards:** AX, CB, DC, DS, JC, MC, VI. **Free Special Amenities: full breakfast and high-speed Internet.**

AAA Benefit:
Members save a minimum 5% off the best available rate.

  CALL  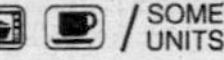  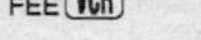 / SOME UNITS FEE  FEE VCR

THE WESTIN CHARLOTTE Book great rates at AAA.com **Phone:** (704)375-2600 **9**

Hotel
$119-$379 All Year

Address: 601 S College St **Location:** I-277, exit College St, just n; jct E Stonewall St. **Facility:** The hotel has become popular for both business and leisure travelers; its upscale decor combines contemporary features with trendy stylings. Smoke free premises. 700 units. 678 one-bedroom standard units. 22 one-bedroom suites, some with whirlpools. 25 stories, interior corridors. *Bath:* combo or shower only. **Parking:** on-site (fee) and valet. **Amenities:** dual phone lines, voice mail, safes, honor bars, irons, hair dryers. *Fee:* video games, high-speed Internet. *Some:* DVD players, CD players. **Dining:** Ember Grille, see separate listing. **Pool(s):** heated indoor. **Leisure Activities:** saunas, exercise room. *Fee:* massage. **Guest Services:** valet laundry, wireless Internet. **Business Services:** conference facilities, business center. **Cards:** AX, CB, DC, DS, JC, MC, VI. **Free Special Amenities: newspaper.**

AAA Benefit:
Enjoy up to 15% off your next stay, plus Starwood Preferred Guest® bonuses.

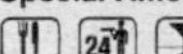  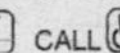 CALL 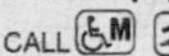  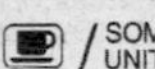  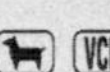 / SOME UNITS 

WHERE TO DINE

300 EAST **Phone:** 704/332-6507 **25**

American
$8-$21

Ensconced in the historic Dilworth area, in a converted vintage home, the restaurant offers innovative American cuisine in a casual, friendly setting. Other than the popular Sunday brunch, menu favorites include ancho lime pork tenderloin and Gorgonzola-stuffed filet mignon. When weather permits, request a seat at the outdoor patio. Casual dress. **Bar:** Full bar. **Reservations:** accepted. **Hours:** 11 am-10 pm, Fri & Sat-11 pm, Sun 10 am-10 pm. Closed: 1/1, 11/26, 12/25. **Address:** 300 East Blvd **Location:** I-77, exit 7 (Clanton Rd), 0.5 mi e on Clanton Rd, 1.5 mi n on South Blvd, then just e. **Parking:** on-site. **Cards:** AX, DC, DS, MC, VI.

CALL

AQUAVINA **Phone:** 704/377-9911 **18**

Seafood
$7-$38

The innovative decor includes replica native canoes hanging from the ceiling, as well as a variety of mediums to elicit a relaxed, upscale feel. The menu includes high quality steaks and seafood. The cuisine is creative in the combinations of sauces and ingredients and is presented in an enhanced style. The overall effect of all elements of the dining experience is one of fine dining in a comfortable atmosphere. Wine is offered by the taste as well as by the glass or bottle. Dressy casual. **Bar:** Full bar. **Reservations:** accepted. **Hours:** 11 am-3 & 5-10 pm, Sat from 5 pm. Closed: 11/26, 12/25; also Sun. **Address:** 435 S Tryon St **Location:** Between 1st and 2nd sts; in Radcliffe Building on the Green. **Parking:** on-site. **Cards:** AX, DC, DS, MC, VI.

CALL

BENTLEY'S ON 27 **Phone:** 704/343-9201 **15**

French
$9-$54

Enjoy classic French and American cuisine along with views of downtown from the 27th floor of the Charlotte Plaza building. Tableside preparations add drama to the polished service, and an extensive wine list, elegant atmosphere and refined cuisine make this a popular spot for both business gatherings and romantic interludes. Dressy casual. **Bar:** Full bar. **Reservations:** suggested. **Hours:** 11:30 am-2 & 5:30-9:30 pm, Fri-10:30 pm, Sat 5:30 pm-10:30 pm. Closed major holidays; also Sun. **Address:** 201 S College St **Location:** I-77, exit 10 or 10B, 0.8 mi e on Trade St, just s on Tryon St, just e on 3rd St, then just n; on 27th floor of the Charlotte Plaza building. **Parking:** on-site (fee) and valet. **Cards:** AX, DS, MC, VI.

CALL

BLUE RESTAURANT & BAR **Phone:** 704/927-2583 **8**

Mediterranean
$20-$45

The chef presents flavors of the Mediterranean region in the cuisine and cheese selections. On the menu are creative interpretations of the culinary tastes of various countries. The cordial staff attends to customers in a relaxed yet skilled and efficient manner. The dining room's blend of modern and contemporary decor, accented by jazz background music, combines with the other elements to offer patrons a casual, enjoyable dining experience. Live jazz enhances the Sunday brunch. Dressy casual. **Bar:** Full bar. **Reservations:** suggested. **Hours:** 5 pm-10 pm, Fri & Sat-11 pm. Closed: 1/1, 11/26, 12/25; also Sun. **Address:** 214 N Tryon St **Location:** Corner of 5th and College sts. **Parking:** valet and street. **Cards:** AX, DC, DS, MC, VI.

CALL 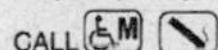

(See map and index starting on p. 626)

BONTERRA DINING & WINE ROOM **Phone:** 704/333-9463 (23)

AAA

American
$17-$52

In a former 1914 church, the restaurant sustains an upscale air in part due to distinctive, yet subtle and subdued, decor elements in its dining room. The chef transforms high-quality ingredients into flavorful culinary creations. The staff is intent on each guest enjoying the dining experience. More than 200 wines are offered by the glass. Dressy casual. **Bar:** Full bar. **Reservations:** accepted. **Hours:** 5:30 pm-11 pm. Closed major holidays; also Sun. **Address:** 1829 Cleveland Ave **Location:** I-77, exit 7 (Clanton Rd), 0.5 mi e, 1.4 mi n on South Blvd, just e on East Blvd, then just s. **Parking:** valet and street. **Cards:** AX, DC, DS, MC, VI.

CALL

THE CAPITAL GRILLE **Phone:** 704/348-1400 (4)

Steak & Seafood
$11-$37

Cherry wood and red leather assist in making this "clubby" dining room a beautiful spot to dine on excellent cuts of dry-aged beef. The staff is highly attentive and knowledgeable. Dressy casual. **Bar:** Full bar. **Reservations:** accepted. **Hours:** 11:30 am-3 & 5-10 pm, Fri-11 pm, Sat 5 pm-11 pm, Sun 5 pm-9 pm. Closed major holidays. **Address:** 201 N Tryon St **Location:** Jct W 5th and N Tryon sts. **Parking:** valet and street. **Cards:** AX, CB, DC, DS, MC, VI.

CARPE DIEM RESTAURANT **Phone:** 704/377-7976 (17)

American
$14-$28

New American cuisine favorites at Carpe Diem, a casual bistro eatery, include a warm goat cheese salad in an apricot jalapeno vinaigrette, the pistachio-crusted trout and their vegetable lasagna. Dressy casual. **Bar:** Full bar. **Reservations:** suggested. **Hours:** 5 pm-10 pm, Fri & Sat-11 pm. Closed major holidays; also Sun. **Address:** 1535 Elizabeth Ave **Location:** I-77, exit 10 or 10B, 2.2 mi w on Trade St (which becomes Elizabeth Ave). **Parking:** on-site. **Cards:** AX, DC, MC, VI.

COCO OSTERIA **Phone:** 704/344-8878 (9)

Italian
$10-$22

Offering a cozy, uptown ambiance, perfect for enjoying Tuscan fare from the seasonally changing menu, items such as lasagna with meat sauce and braised lamb shank. Dressy casual. **Bar:** Full bar. **Reservations:** suggested. **Hours:** 11:30 am-2 & 5-10 pm, Fri-11 pm, Sat 5 pm-11 pm. Closed major holidays; also Sun. **Address:** 214 N Tryon St, Plaza Suite 3 **Location:** I-77, exit 10 or 10B, 0.8 mi e on Trade St, then just n. **Parking:** street. **Cards:** AX, MC, VI.

COSMOS CAFE **Phone:** 704/372-3553 (10)

International
$7-$26

Amid a funky and eclectic decor, diners will find a little something from most corners of the cuisine world: tapas, sushi, pizza, pasta and home-style favorites such as meatloaf. The cafe is open for lunch, dinner and late-night dining. Casual dress. **Bar:** Full bar. **Reservations:** accepted. **Hours:** 11 am-2 am, Sat from 5 pm. Closed: 11/26, 12/25; also Sun. **Address:** 300 N College St **Location:** I-77, exit 10 or 10B, 1 mi e on Trade St, then just n; jct 6th St. **Parking:** street. **Cards:** AX, MC, VI.

EMBER GRILLE **Phone:** 704/335-2064 (20)

American
$6-$32

The dining room presents a two-course prix fixe menu, with variety in each course to appeal to all tastes. Custom-made warmers on each table help keep bread and portions of the meal from cooling. The staff is personable and accommodating, while providing skilled, knowledgeable assistance. Upscale contemporary decor is subdued and the atmosphere relaxed and casual. Patio seating is a seasonal option. Dressy casual. **Bar:** Full bar. **Reservations:** accepted. **Hours:** 6:30 am-3 & 5-10 pm. **Address:** 601 S College St **Location:** I-277, exit College St, just n; jct E Stonewall St; in The Westin Charlotte. **Parking:** on-site (fee) and valet. **Cards:** AX, CB, DC, DS, JC, MC, VI.

CALL

HARRY & JEAN'S **Phone:** 704/333-4300 (13)

American
$6-$35

Passionately prepared American food is on the menu at this popular downtown eatery. Flair distinguishes such home-style meals as pecan-crusted catfish, coconut chicken and cranberry and apple pork loin. Guests can enjoy a cocktail in the casually upscale bar, where live music is featured Wednesday through Sunday. Casual dress. **Bar:** Full bar. **Hours:** 11 am-2:30 & 5-10 pm, Sat from 5 pm. Closed: 11/26, 12/25; also Sun. **Address:** 201 S Tryon St, Suite 101 **Location:** I-77, exit 10 or 10B, 0.8 mi e, then just s; in Tryon Square Building. **Parking:** street. **Cards:** AX, DC, DS, MC, VI.

LA VECCHIA'S SEAFOOD GRILLE **Phone:** 704/370-6776 (14)

Seafood
$17-$36

This downtown hot spot boasts whimsical, energetic decor with colorful oversize sculptures. The menu features a nice blend of classic and non-traditional seafood. Live Maine lobster is a specialty; other tasty selections include almond-crusted tilapia and stuffed jumbo shrimp. Dressy casual. **Bar:** Full bar. **Reservations:** accepted. **Hours:** 5:30 pm-10 pm, Fri & Sat-11 pm. Closed major holidays; also Sun. **Address:** 225 E 6th St **Location:** Corner of 6th and Brevard sts. **Parking:** valet. **Cards:** AX, DC, DS, MC, VI.

CALL

LUCE RISTORANTE **Phone:** 704/344-9222 (7)

Italian
$9-$30

Distinctive upscale decor—including marble floors, wainscoting and a hand-painted fresco—surrounds patrons of the pleasurable restaurant. A Tuscan influence is evident in the cuisine, which exudes freshness and highlights the chef's innovative flair. Skilled servers are attentive. Outside seating is a seasonal option. Dressy casual. **Bar:** Full bar. **Reservations:** suggested. **Hours:** 11:30 am-2:30 & 5:30-10 pm, Fri-11 pm, Sat 5:30 pm-11 pm. Closed: 11/26, 12/25; also Sun. **Address:** 214 N Tryon St **Location:** Between 5th and 6th sts; in The Hearst Tower Courtyard. **Parking:** on-site. **Cards:** AX, MC, VI.

CALL

(See map and index starting on p. 626)

MCINTOSH'S STEAK & SEAFOOD — **Phone:** 704/342-1088 (21)

Steak & Seafood
$25-$55

The relaxed, intimate dining rooms at the upscale steakhouse are decorated with wood panels and large framed artwork. Prime beef and fresh seafood dominate the menu. Diners can listen to live piano music in the bar nightly. Outdoor dining is offered in warmer weather. Dressy casual. Entertainment. **Bar:** Full bar. **Reservations:** suggested. **Hours:** 5 pm-10 pm, Fri & Sat-11 pm. Closed major holidays; also Sun. **Address:** 1812 South Blvd **Location:** I-77, exit 7 (Clanton Rd), 0.5 mi e on Clanton Rd, then 1.5 mi n; jct East Blvd. **Parking:** on-site. **Cards:** AX, DC, DS, MC, VI.

MCNINCH HOUSE — **Phone:** 704/332-6159 (1)

Continental
$89

In a restored house, built circa 1892, elegance abounds with candlelit tables, beautiful flowers and antique china and crystal. The owner/chef provides personalized service, including inquiries about food preferences and possible food allergies. French Continental with Southern twist; their signature entree is roasted rack of lamb with crusted rosemary and mustard. 20% service charge. Semi-formal attire. **Bar:** Full bar. **Reservations:** required. **Hours:** 6:30 pm-10 pm. Closed: 7/4, 12/25; also Sun & Mon. **Address:** 511 N Church St **Location:** I-277, exit Church St, just sw. **Parking:** valet and street. **Cards:** AX, MC, VI. **Historic**

MERT'S HEART & SOUL — **Phone:** 704/342-4222 (12)

Southern
$5-$14

Southern hospitality is served in liberal helpings along with down-home Southern cooking, such as fried chicken, pork chops, salmon cakes, warm cornbread, greens, steamed squash, okra and fresh vegetables. Crowds can be expected at lunchtime. Parking is available on the nearby Holiday Inn deck. Casual dress. **Bar:** Beer & wine. **Hours:** 11 am-9 pm, Fri-11 pm, Sat 9 am-11 pm, Sun 9 am-9 pm, Mon 11 am-3 pm. Closed major holidays. **Address:** 214 N College St **Location:** I-77, exit 10 or 10B, 1 mi e on Trade St, then just n. **Parking:** no self-parking. **Cards:** AX, DS, MC, VI.

MIMOSA GRILL — **Phone:** 704/343-0700 (16)

American
$8-$36

Complimentary valet parking is available on 2nd Street after 5:30 pm. The chef turns out well-prepared cuisine with creative flavor combinations. The food reflects regional and Low Country influences. The upscale yet comfortable and casual dining room has a subdued decor, with wood and stone treatments and distinctive quality accents. Dressy casual. **Bar:** Full bar. **Reservations:** suggested. **Hours:** 11 am-10 pm, Fri-11 pm, Sat 5 pm-11 pm, Sun 5 pm-10 pm. Closed: 7/4, 12/25. **Address:** Two Wachovia Center, 327 S Tryon St **Location:** Between 2nd and 3rd sts. **Parking:** valet and street. **Cards:** AX, DC, DS, MC, VI.

CALL

MONTICELLO RESTAURANT — **Phone:** 704/342-1193 (3)

American
$8-$34

This intimate restaurant presents a menu of well-prepared of well-prepared beef, chicken, pork and lamb In a array of preparations. Window seats are the perfect place to while away the time people-watching. Casual dress. **Bar:** Full bar. **Reservations:** accepted. **Hours:** 6:30-11 am, 11:30-3 & 5:30-11 pm. **Address:** 235 N Tryon St **Location:** I-77, exit 10 or 10B, 1 mi e on Trade St, just n on College St, then just w on 6th St; in The Dunhill Hotel. **Parking:** on-site. **Cards:** AX, DC, MC, VI.

OPEN KITCHEN — **Phone:** 704/375-7449 (2)

Italian
$7-$16

Since 1952, the family-owned eatery has served pizza, spaghetti, chicken and veal dishes in a classic, home-like setting with red-and-white checkered tablecloths and family photos displayed throughout. Casual dress. **Bar:** Full bar. **Hours:** 11 am-9:30 pm, Fri-10 pm, Sat 4 pm-10 pm, Sun 4 pm-9:30 pm. Closed: 1/1, 11/26, 12/24, 12/25. **Address:** 1318 W Morehead St **Location:** I-77, exit 10A southbound, just w; exit 9C northbound, just w; exit 1A (Wilkinson Blvd), just n on Freedom Dr, then just e. **Parking:** on-site. **Cards:** AX, MC, VI.

PEWTER ROSE BISTRO — **Phone:** 704/332-8149 (22)

American
$6-$22

On the second floor of a turn-of-the-20th-century textile warehouse, the popular restaurant displays classic, upscale decor with live plants and eclectic, bright and bold color accents. The chef combines fresh ingredients, including organic selections, into flavorful and visually appealing creations for a menu of diverse ethnic cuisine. In addition to seafood, beef, chicken and pasta dishes, the menu also lists vegetarian and vegan selections. Dressy casual. **Bar:** Full bar. **Reservations:** accepted. **Hours:** 11 am-2:30 & 5-10 pm, Fri-11 pm, Sat 10 am-2:30 & 5-11 pm, Sun 10 am-2:30 pm. Closed: 1/1, 11/26, 12/24, 12/25. **Address:** 1820 South Blvd **Location:** I-77, exit 7 (Clanton Rd), 0.5 mi e on Clanton Rd, then 1.5 mi n; jct East Blvd. **Parking:** valet. **Cards:** AX, DC, DS, MC, VI.

RATCLIFFE ON THE GREEN — **Phone:** 704/358-9898 (19)

Southern
$11-$40

Fresh ingredients, many of which come from local or regional farms, are used in the restaurant's flavorful contemporary Carolina cuisine. The menu changes frequently but may include dishes such as shrimp and grits, pan-seared duck breast, grilled pork chop with Southern succotash or flounder meuniere. The atmosphere in the intimate dining room is quietly upscale, and service is attentive. Dressy casual. **Bar:** Full bar. **Reservations:** accepted. **Hours:** 11:30 am-2 & 5-10 pm, Sat from 5 pm. Closed major holidays; also Sun. **Address:** 435 S Tryon St, Suite 100 **Location:** I-77, exit 10 or 10B, 0.7 mi e on Trade St, 0.4 mi s on Church St, then just e on 1st St. **Parking:** on-site. **Cards:** AX, DS, MC, VI.

RI-RA IRISH PUB — **Phone:** 704/333-5554 (6)

Irish
$10-$21

The restaurant specializes in traditional Irish cuisine with a contemporary twist. Some examples include beef and Guinness pie and classic fish and chips. The noise level can be loud at times due to the pub's popularity and folk bands that regularly play. Casual dress. **Bar:** Full bar. **Hours:** 11:30 am-10 pm. Closed: 12/25. **Address:** 208 N Tryon St **Location:** Between 5th and 6th sts. **Parking:** street. **Cards:** AX, MC, VI.

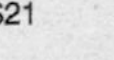

(See map and index starting on p. 626)

SONOMA MODERN AMERICAN CUISINE — **Phone:** 704/332-1132 (11)

American
$7-$34

The atmosphere at this uptown hot spot is as sleek and tony as its menu. Examples of the fabulous fare may include shiitake coconut poached barramundi or kurobuto center-cut pork chop with goat cheese mac 'n' cheese. The hip bar, with its expansive wine list and trendy martini offerings, is the place to see and be seen. Dressy casual. **Bar:** Full bar. **Reservations:** suggested. **Hours:** 11:30 am-2 & 5:30-10 pm, Fri-11 pm, Sat 5:30 pm-11 pm. Closed: 11/26, 12/25; also Sun. **Address:** 100 N Tryon St **Location:** Jct Trade St. **Parking:** valet. **Cards:** AX, DS, MC, VI.

SULLIVAN'S STEAKHOUSE — **Phone:** 704/335-8228 (24)

Steak
$20-$40

Named for John L. Sullivan, heavyweight champion of the world in the 1880s, the upscale steak house prepares a wide selection of steaks, chops and seafood. Decorated with black-and-white photographs of Sullivan, Jack Dempsey and other boxing legends. Dressy casual. **Bar:** Full bar. **Reservations:** accepted. **Hours:** 11 am-1 am. Closed: 12/25. **Address:** 1928 South Blvd, Suite 200 **Location:** I-77, exit 7 (Clanton Rd), 0.5 mi e, then 1.8 mi n; in Southend Steelyard. **Parking:** on-site. **Cards:** AX, DC, MC, VI.

ZINK AMERICAN KITCHEN — **Phone:** 704/444-9001 (5)

American
$5-$25

The zinc bar at the casually upscale spot is a hot spot for the uptown, after-work crowd to enjoy martinis and mixing. The dining room features dramatic black and red decor, as well as an eclectic menu with small plates and sushi, seafood, steak, chicken and sandwiches. Dressy casual. **Bar:** Full bar. **Reservations:** accepted. **Hours:** 11:30 am-11 pm, Wed & Thurs-midnight, Fri-1 am, Sat 5 pm-1 am, Sun 11:30 am-2 & 5-10 pm; Sunday brunch. **Address:** 201 N Tryon St **Location:** Just n; center; in IJL Building. **Parking:** street. **Cards:** AX, MC, VI.

CHARLOTTE pop. 540,828 (See map and index starting on p. 628)

WHERE TO STAY

BALLANTYNE RESORT, A LUXURY COLLECTION RESORT *Book great rates at AAA.com* — **Phone:** (704)248-4000 (77)

Hotel
$209-$429 All Year

Address: 10000 Ballantyne Commons Pkwy **Location:** I-485, exit 61 or 61B, just s on US 521. **Facility:** An award-winning golf course is on the grounds of this luxurious hotel, which is distinguished by an Old World ambience and modern amenities. Smoke free premises. 214 units. 200 one-bedroom standard units. 14 one-bedroom suites. 7 stories, interior corridors. *Bath:* combo or shower only. **Parking:** on-site and valet. **Terms:** check-in 4 pm. **Amenities:** high-speed Internet (fee), dual phone lines, voice mail, safes, honor bars, irons, hair dryers. *Some:* DVD players, CD players. **Pool(s):** heated indoor. **Leisure Activities:** saunas, whirlpool, 2 continuous wave lap pools, spa. *Fee:* golf-18 holes, golf/tennis instruction. **Guest Services:** valet laundry, wireless Internet. **Business Services:** conference facilities, business center. **Cards:** AX, CB, DC, DS, JC, MC, VI. ***(See color ad p 641)***

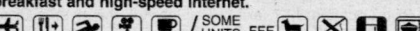

THE LUXURY COLLECTION
AAA Benefit:
Inspiring travels with your AAA Preferred rates.

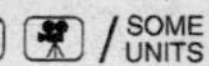

CALL / SOME UNITS

BEST WESTERN-AIRPORT INN *Book great rates at AAA.com* — **Phone:** (704)394-4111 (25)

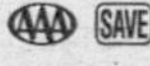

Motel
$69 All Year

Address: 2625 Little Rock Rd **Location:** I-85, exit 32, just w. **Facility:** 120 one-bedroom standard units. 2 stories (no elevator), exterior corridors. **Parking:** on-site. **Terms:** 30 day cancellation notice. **Amenities:** irons, hair dryers. **Pool(s):** outdoor. **Leisure Activities:** exercise room. **Guest Services:** airport transportation-Charlotte/Douglas International Airport, wireless Internet. **Business Services:** meeting rooms, PC. **Cards:** AX, CB, DC, DS, JC, MC, VI. **Free Special Amenities: expanded continental breakfast and high-speed Internet.**

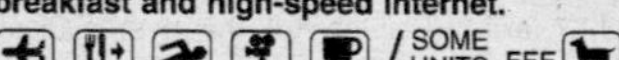

/ SOME UNITS FEE

AAA Benefit:
Members save up to 20%, plus 10% bonus points with rewards program.

BEST WESTERN INDEPENDENCE HOTEL *Book great rates at AAA.com* — **Phone:** (704)845-2810 (62)

Hotel
$89-$129 All Year

Address: 2501 Sardis Rd N **Location:** I-485, exit 51A, 3.3 mi w on US 74, then just s. **Facility:** 93 one-bedroom standard units. 3 stories, interior corridors. **Parking:** on-site. **Terms:** 3 day cancellation notice. **Amenities:** voice mail, irons, hair dryers. **Leisure Activities:** exercise room. **Guest Services:** coin laundry, wireless Internet. **Business Services:** meeting rooms, PC. **Cards:** AX, DC, DS, MC, VI. **Free Special Amenities: expanded continental breakfast and high-speed Internet.**

/ SOME UNITS

AAA Benefit:
Members save up to 20%, plus 10% bonus points with rewards program.

(See map and index starting on p. 628)

BEST WESTERN STERLING HOTEL Book great rates at AAA.com **Phone:** (704)525-5454 49

Hotel
$69-$99 All Year

Address: 242 E Woodlawn Rd **Location:** I-77, exit 6A, 0.4 mi e. **Facility:** 98 one-bedroom standard units. 3 stories, interior corridors. **Parking:** on-site. **Terms:** 3 day cancellation notice. **Amenities:** voice mail, irons, hair dryers. **Leisure Activities:** limited exercise equipment. **Guest Services:** valet and coin laundry, airport transportation-Charlotte-Douglas International Airport, wireless Internet. **Business Services:** meeting rooms, business center. **Cards:** AX, DS, MC, VI.

/ SOME UNITS

AAA Benefit:
Members save up to 20%, plus 10% bonus points with rewards program.

CANDLEWOOD SUITES - CHARLOTTE UNIVERSITY Book at AAA.com **Phone:** (704)598-9863 19

Hotel
$77-$80 All Year

Address: 8812 University East Dr **Location:** I-85, exit 45A (W.T. Harris Blvd), 2.5 mi e on SR 24, then just s; in University East Business Park. **Facility:** 122 units. 98 one-bedroom standard units with efficiencies. 24 one-bedroom suites with efficiencies. 3 stories, interior corridors. *Bath:* combo or shower only. **Parking:** on-site. **Terms:** office hours 7 am-11 pm, cancellation fee imposed. **Amenities:** video library, DVD players, high-speed Internet, voice mail, irons, hair dryers. **Leisure Activities:** exercise room. **Guest Services:** complimentary and valet laundry. **Cards:** AX, DC, DS, MC, VI.

ASK / SOME UNITS FEE

CANDLEWOOD SUITES-EXECUTIVE PARK Book at AAA.com **Phone:** 704/529-7500 56

Hotel
Rates not provided

Address: 5840 Westpark Dr **Location:** I-77, exit 5 (Tyvola Rd), just e, then 0.5 mi s. **Facility:** 81 units. 69 one-bedroom standard units with efficiencies. 12 one-bedroom suites with efficiencies. 3 stories, interior corridors. *Bath:* combo or shower only. **Parking:** on-site. **Terms:** office hours 7 am-11 pm. **Amenities:** video library, DVD players, high-speed Internet, dual phone lines, voice mail, irons, hair dryers. **Leisure Activities:** exercise room. **Guest Services:** complimentary and valet laundry.

CALL VCR / SOME UNITS FEE

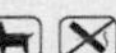

▼ See AAA listing p 640 ▼

(See map and index starting on p. 628)

CHARLOTTE MARRIOTT EXECUTIVE PARK *Book great rates at AAA.com* **Phone:** (704)527-9650 53

Hotel
$207-$222 All Year

Address: 5700 Westpark Dr **Location:** I-77, exit 5 (Tyvola Rd), just e, then just s. **Facility:** Smoke free premises. 297 units. 296 one-bedroom standard units. 1 one-bedroom suite. 19 stories, interior corridors. *Bath:* combo or shower only. **Parking:** on-site. **Terms:** cancellation fee imposed. **Amenities:** dual phone lines, voice mail, irons, hair dryers. **Pool(s):** heated indoor/outdoor. **Leisure Activities:** sauna, whirlpool, exercise room, volleyball. **Guest Services:** valet laundry, airport transportation-Charlotte-Douglas International Airport, area transportation-within 3 mi, wireless Internet. **Business Services:** conference facilities, business center. **Cards:** AX, CB, DC, DS, JC, MC, VI. **Free Special Amenities: newspaper.**

CALL / SOME UNITS

Marriott
HOTELS & RESORTS

AAA Benefit:
Members save a minimum 5% off the best available rate.

COMFORT INN-EXECUTIVE PARK *Book great rates at AAA.com* **Phone:** (704)525-2626 52

Hotel
$54-$84 3/1-11/30
$54 12/1-2/28

Address: 5822 Westpark Dr **Location:** I-77, exit 5 (Tyvola Rd), just e, then 0.5 mi s. **Facility:** 144 units. 140 one-bedroom standard units, some with whirlpools. 4 one-bedroom suites, some with kitchens and/or whirlpools. 6 stories, interior corridors. *Bath:* combo or shower only. **Parking:** on-site. **Amenities:** video games (fee), voice mail, irons, hair dryers. **Pool(s):** outdoor. **Leisure Activities:** exercise room. **Guest Services:** valet laundry, wireless Internet. **Business Services:** meeting rooms, PC. **Cards:** AX, DC, DS, MC, VI.

/ SOME UNITS FEE

COMFORT INN-UNCC *Book great rates at AAA.com* **Phone:** (704)598-0007 23

Hotel
$70-$159 All Year

Address: 5111 Equipment Dr **Location:** I-85, exit 41, just w, then just s. **Facility:** 87 one-bedroom standard units. 2 stories (no elevator), interior corridors. **Parking:** on-site. **Terms:** 3 night minimum stay. **Amenities:** irons, hair dryers. **Pool(s):** outdoor. **Leisure Activities:** limited exercise equipment. **Guest Services:** wireless Internet. **Business Services:** meeting rooms. **Cards:** AX, CB, DC, DS, JC, MC, VI. **Free Special Amenities: expanded continental breakfast and high-speed Internet.** *(See color ad below)*

/ SOME UNITS FEE

COMFORT SUITES/AIRPORT *Book great rates at AAA.com* **Phone:** (704)971-4400 33

Hotel
$89-$199 All Year

Address: 3425 Mulberry Church Rd **Location:** I-85, exit 33, just e, then just n. **Facility:** Smoke free premises. 84 units. 40 one-bedroom standard units. 44 one-bedroom suites with efficiencies (no utensils). 5 stories, interior corridors. *Bath:* combo or shower only. **Parking:** on-site. **Amenities:** high-speed Internet, dual phone lines, voice mail, irons, hair dryers. **Pool(s):** heated indoor. **Leisure Activities:** exercise room. **Guest Services:** valet and coin laundry, wireless Internet. **Business Services:** meeting rooms, business center. **Cards:** AX, CB, DC, DS, JC, MC, VI.

ASK CALL

COMFORT SUITES-NORTHLAKE *Book at AAA.com* **Phone:** (704)598-0478 1

Hotel
$109-$189 All Year

Address: 7315 Smith Corners Blvd **Location:** I-77, exit 18 (W. T. Harris Blvd), just e on SR 24, 0.4 mi n on US 21, then just w. **Facility:** Smoke free premises. 104 one-bedroom standard units, some with whirlpools. 5 stories, interior corridors. *Bath:* combo or shower only. **Parking:** on-site. **Terms:** cancellation fee imposed. **Amenities:** high-speed Internet, dual phone lines, voice mail, irons, hair dryers. **Pool(s):** outdoor. **Leisure Activities:** limited exercise equipment. **Guest Services:** complimentary and valet laundry, wireless Internet. **Business Services:** meeting rooms, business center. **Cards:** AX, CB, DC, DS, JC, MC, VI.

ASK

▼ *See AAA listing above* ▼

(See map and index starting on p. 628)

COMFORT SUITES-UNIVERSITY Book at AAA.com Phone: (704)547-0049 18

Hotel
$100-$200 All Year

Address: 7735 University City Blvd **Location:** I-85, exit 45A (W. T. Harris Blvd), 1 mi e on SR 24, then 0.5 mi s on SR 49. **Facility:** Smoke free premises. 120 one-bedroom standard units, some with whirlpools. 7 stories, interior corridors. *Bath:* combo or shower only. **Parking:** on-site. **Amenities:** voice mail, irons, hair dryers. **Pool(s):** outdoor. **Leisure Activities:** limited exercise equipment. **Guest Services:** valet and coin laundry, wireless Internet. **Business Services:** meeting rooms, PC. **Cards:** AX, CB, DC, DS, JC, MC, VI.

ASK CALL / SOME UNITS FEE

COUNTRY INN & SUITES BY CARLSON, CHARLOTTE, I-85 AIRPORT Book great rates at AAA.com Phone: (704)394-2000 24

AAA SAVE

Hotel
$99-$109 All Year

Address: 2541 Little Rock Rd **Location:** I-85, exit 32, just w. **Facility:** 119 units. 108 one-bedroom standard units. 11 one-bedroom suites. 2 stories (no elevator), interior corridors. **Parking:** on-site. **Terms:** cancellation fee imposed. **Amenities:** voice mail, irons, hair dryers. **Pool(s):** outdoor. **Leisure Activities:** exercise room. **Guest Services:** coin laundry, airport transportation-Charlotte-Douglas International Airport, wireless Internet. **Business Services:** meeting rooms, PC. **Cards:** AX, DC, DS, MC, VI. **Free Special Amenities: expanded continental breakfast and high-speed Internet.**

/ SOME UNITS

COUNTRY INN & SUITES-CHARLOTTE UNIVERSITY Book at AAA.com Phone: 704/549-8770 16

Hotel
Rates not provided

Address: 131 E McCullough Dr **Location:** I-85, exit 45A (W. T. Harris Blvd), 0.5 mi e on SR 24, 0.4 mi s on US 29 (N Tryon St), then just e. **Facility:** Smoke free premises. 100 units. 63 one-bedroom standard units, some with whirlpools. 37 one-bedroom suites. 3 stories, interior corridors. *Bath:* combo or shower only. **Parking:** on-site. **Amenities:** high-speed Internet, dual phone lines, voice mail, irons, hair dryers. **Pool(s):** heated indoor/outdoor. **Leisure Activities:** whirlpool, exercise room. **Guest Services:** valet and coin laundry, wireless Internet. **Business Services:** meeting rooms, business center.

CALL / SOME UNITS FEE

COURTYARD BY MARRIOTT-AIRPORT Book great rates at AAA.com Phone: (704)319-9900 31

Hotel
$163-$175 All Year

Address: 2700 Little Rock Rd **Location:** I-85, exit 32, just e. **Facility:** Smoke free premises. 90 units. 87 one-bedroom standard units, some with whirlpools. 3 one-bedroom suites. 3 stories, interior corridors. *Bath:* combo or shower only. **Parking:** on-site. **Terms:** cancellation fee imposed. **Amenities:** high-speed Internet, dual phone lines, voice mail, irons, hair dryers. **Pool(s):** heated indoor. **Leisure Activities:** whirlpool, exercise room. **Guest Services:** valet and coin laundry, area transportation, wireless Internet. **Business Services:** meeting rooms, PC. **Cards:** AX, CB, DC, DS, JC, MC, VI.

CALL / SOME UNITS

AAA Benefit: Members save a minimum 5% off the best available rate.

COURTYARD BY MARRIOTT-BALLANTYNE RESORT Book great rates at AAA.com Phone: (704)341-0041 75

Hotel
$158-$169 All Year

Address: 15660 John J Delaney Dr **Location:** I-485, exit 61 or 61B, just s, then just w. Located in Ballantyne Corporate Park West. **Facility:** Smoke free premises. 90 units. 87 one-bedroom standard units, some with whirlpools. 3 one-bedroom suites. 3 stories, interior corridors. *Bath:* combo or shower only. **Parking:** on-site. **Terms:** cancellation fee imposed. **Amenities:** high-speed Internet, dual phone lines, voice mail, irons, hair dryers. **Pool(s):** heated indoor. **Leisure Activities:** whirlpool, limited exercise equipment. **Guest Services:** complimentary and valet laundry, area transportation, wireless Internet. **Business Services:** meeting rooms, business center. **Cards:** AX, CB, DC, DS, JC, MC, VI.

/ SOME UNITS

AAA Benefit: Members save a minimum 5% off the best available rate.

COURTYARD BY MARRIOTT-SOUTH PARK Book great rates at AAA.com Phone: (704)552-7333 61

Hotel
$147-$158 All Year

Address: 6023 Park South Dr **Location:** I-77, exit 5 (Tyvola Rd), 3 mi e on Tyvola/Fairview rds, then just s. **Facility:** Smoke free premises. 149 units. 137 one-bedroom standard units. 12 one-bedroom suites. 3 stories, interior corridors. *Bath:* combo or shower only. **Parking:** on-site. **Terms:** cancellation fee imposed. **Amenities:** high-speed Internet, voice mail, irons, hair dryers. **Pool(s):** outdoor. **Leisure Activities:** whirlpool, exercise room. **Guest Services:** valet and coin laundry, wireless Internet. **Business Services:** meeting rooms, business center. **Cards:** AX, CB, DC, DS, JC, MC, VI.

AAA Benefit: Members save a minimum 5% off the best available rate.

(See map and index starting on p. 628)

COURTYARD BY MARRIOTT-UNIVERSITY RESEARCH PARK

Phone: (704)549-4888 8

Hotel

$147-$158 All Year

Address: 333 W W. T. Harris Blvd **Location:** I-85, exit 45A (W. T. Harris Blvd), just e on SR 24. **Facility:** Smoke free premises. 152 units. 140 one-bedroom standard units. 12 one-bedroom suites. 4 stories, interior corridors. *Bath:* combo or shower only. **Parking:** on-site. **Terms:** cancellation fee imposed. **Amenities:** high-speed Internet, dual phone lines, voice mail, irons, hair dryers. **Pool(s):** outdoor. **Leisure Activities:** whirlpool, exercise room. **Guest Services:** valet and coin laundry, wireless Internet. **Business Services:** meeting rooms, business center. **Cards:** AX, CB, DC, DS, MC, VI. **Free Special Amenities: high-speed Internet.**

CALL / SOME UNITS

AAA Benefit:

Members save a minimum 5% off the best available rate.

DOUBLETREE GUEST SUITES-SOUTH PARK *Book great rates at AAA.com*

Phone: (704)364-2400 59

Hotel

$99-$289 All Year

Address: 6300 Morrison Blvd **Location:** I-77, exit 5 (Tyvola Rd), 3.3 mi e on Tyvola/Fairview rds, just n on Barclay Downs, then just e. Adjacent to South Park Mall. **Facility:** 208 units. 187 one- and 21 two-bedroom suites, some with kitchens. 3-6 stories, interior corridors. *Bath:* combo or shower only. **Parking:** on-site. **Terms:** cancellation fee imposed. **Amenities:** video games (fee), dual phone lines, voice mail, irons, hair dryers. *Some:* high-speed Internet (fee). **Pool(s):** outdoor. **Leisure Activities:** exercise room. **Guest Services:** valet and coin laundry, wireless Internet. **Business Services:** conference facilities, business center. **Cards:** AX, CB, DC, DS, MC, VI.

/ SOME UNITS

AAA Benefit:

Members save 5% or more everyday!

DOUBLETREE HOTEL-CHARLOTTE AIRPORT *Book great rates at AAA.com*

Phone: (704)357-9100 38

Hotel

$89-$209 All Year

Address: 2600 Yorkmont Rd **Location:** I-77, exit 6B, 2 mi nw on Billy Graham Pkwy, exit Coliseum/Tyvola Rd, just se on Tyvola Rd, then just w; in Lake Pointe Business Park. **Facility:** 173 units. 167 one-bedroom standard units. 6 one-bedroom suites. 3 stories, interior corridors. *Bath:* combo or shower only. **Parking:** on-site. **Terms:** 1-30 night minimum stay, cancellation fee imposed. **Amenities:** high-speed Internet (fee), dual phone lines, voice mail, irons, hair dryers. **Pool(s):** heated outdoor. **Leisure Activities:** exercise room. **Guest Services:** valet laundry, airport transportation-Charlotte-Douglas International Airport, wireless Internet. **Business Services:** meeting rooms, business center. **Cards:** AX, DC, DS, MC, VI. *(See color ad below)*

CALL / SOME UNITS

AAA Benefit:

Members save 5% or more everyday!

▼ See AAA listing above ▼

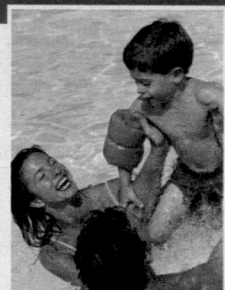

(See map and index starting on p. 628)

DRURY INN & SUITES-CHARLOTTE NORTH *Book at AAA.com* **Phone:** (704)593-0700 7

Hotel

$90-$170 All Year

Address: 415 W WT Harris Blvd **Location:** I-85, exit 45A (W. T. Harris Blvd), just e on SR 24. **Facility:** 142 units. 127 one-bedroom standard units. 15 one-bedroom suites. 5 stories, interior corridors. *Bath:* combo or shower only. **Parking:** on-site. **Amenities:** high-speed Internet, voice mail, irons, hair dryers. **Pool(s):** heated indoor/outdoor. **Leisure Activities:** whirlpool, exercise room. **Guest Services:** valet and coin laundry, wireless Internet. **Business Services:** meeting rooms, business center. **Cards:** AX, DC, DS, MC, VI.

A$K CALL / SOME UNITS

DRURY INN & SUITES-CHARLOTTE NORTHLAKE **Phone:** 704/599-8882

fyi

Hotel

$70-$145 All Year

Too new to rate, opening scheduled for October 2008. **Address:** 6920 Northlake Mall Dr **Location:** I-77, exit 18 (W.T. Harris Blvd), just e on SR 24. **Amenities:** 180 units, pets, coffeemakers, microwaves, refrigerators, pool. **Cards:** AX, DC, DS, MC, VI.

THE DUKE MANSION HISTORIC INN & MEETING PLACE *Book great rates at AAA.com* **Phone:** (704)714-4400 35

AAA SAVE

Bed & Breakfast

$179-$299 All Year

Address: 400 Hermitage Rd **Location:** I-277, exit 2A, 1.5 mi e on 3rd St/Providence Rd, just s on Ardsley Rd, then just w. **Facility:** The 1915 historic home, replete with Southern charm and elegance, is nestled in a quiet neighborhood close to downtown; guest rooms are spacious. Smoke free premises. 20 one-bedroom standard units, some with whirlpools. 3 stories, interior corridors. *Bath:* combo or shower only. **Parking:** on-site. **Terms:** cancellation fee imposed. **Amenities:** video library, CD players, high-speed Internet, voice mail, irons, hair dryers. *Some:* DVD players. **Leisure Activities:** croquet, limited exercise equipment. **Guest Services:** valet laundry, wireless Internet. **Business Services:** conference facilities. **Cards:** AX, DS, MC, VI. **Free Special Amenities: full breakfast and high-speed Internet.**

/ SOME UNITS VCR

EMBASSY SUITES *Book great rates at AAA.com* **Phone:** (704)527-8400 43

Hotel

$119-$239 All Year

Address: 4800 S Tryon St **Location:** I-77, exit 6B northbound, just w, then just s; exit southbound, just s. **Facility:** 274 units. 272 one- and 2 two-bedroom suites, some with whirlpools. 8 stories, interior corridors. *Bath:* combo or shower only. **Parking:** on-site. **Terms:** 1-30 night minimum stay, cancellation fee imposed. **Amenities:** video games (fee), dual phone lines, voice mail, irons, hair dryers. **Pool(s):** heated indoor. **Leisure Activities:** whirlpool, exercise room. **Guest Services:** valet and coin laundry, area transportation, wireless Internet. **Business Services:** meeting rooms, business center. **Cards:** AX, CB, DC, DS, JC, MC, VI.

CALL / SOME UNITS

EMBASSY SUITES HOTELS

AAA Benefit:

Members save 5% or more everyday!

EXTENDED STAYAMERICA-CHARLOTTE-PINEVILLE *Book at AAA.com* **Phone:** (704)341-0929 73

Hotel

$85-$95 All Year

Address: 10930 Park Rd **Location:** I-485, exit 64A, just n on SR 51, then just e; behind Terraces at Park Place Shopping Center. **Facility:** 107 one-bedroom standard units with efficiencies. 3 stories, interior corridors. *Bath:* combo or shower only. **Parking:** on-site. **Amenities:** voice mail, irons. **Guest Services:** coin laundry, wireless Internet. **Cards:** AX, CB, DC, DS, JC, MC, VI.

A$K CALL / SOME UNITS FEE

EXTENDED STAYAMERICA-CHARLOTTE-UNIVERSITY PLACE *Book at AAA.com* **Phone:** (704)510-1636 14

Hotel

$80-$90 All Year

Address: 8211 University Executive Park Dr **Location:** I-85, exit 45A (W. T. Harris Blvd), 0.5 mi e on SR 24, then 0.5 mi s on US 29 (N Tryon St). **Facility:** 113 one-bedroom standard units with efficiencies. 3 stories, interior corridors. *Bath:* combo or shower only. **Parking:** on-site. **Terms:** office hours 7 am-11 pm. **Amenities:** voice mail, irons. **Guest Services:** coin laundry, wireless Internet. **Cards:** AX, CB, DC, DS, JC, MC, VI.

A$K / SOME UNITS FEE

EXTENDED STAY DELUXE-CHARLOTTE/PINEVILLE *Book at AAA.com* **Phone:** (704)542-9521 72

Hotel

$99-$109 All Year

Address: 8405 Pineville-Matthews Rd **Location:** I-485, exit 64A, 0.7 mi n on SR 51. **Facility:** 76 one-bedroom suites with kitchens. 3 stories, interior corridors. *Bath:* combo or shower only. **Parking:** on-site. **Amenities:** DVD players, voice mail, irons, hair dryers. **Pool(s):** outdoor. **Leisure Activities:** exercise room. **Guest Services:** coin laundry, wireless Internet. **Cards:** AX, CB, DC, DS, JC, MC, VI.

A$K / SOME UNITS FEE

FAIRFIELD INN BY MARRIOTT-ARROWOOD *Book great rates at AAA.com* **Phone:** (704)319-5100 65

Hotel

$108-$116 All Year

Address: 7920 Arrowridge Blvd **Location:** I-77, exit 3 southbound; exit 2 northbound, just e on Arrowood Rd, then just s. **Facility:** Smoke free premises. 82 one-bedroom standard units. 3 stories, interior corridors. *Bath:* combo or shower only. **Parking:** on-site. **Terms:** cancellation fee imposed. **Amenities:** high-speed Internet, irons, hair dryers. **Pool(s):** outdoor. **Leisure Activities:** exercise room. **Guest Services:** valet and coin laundry, wireless Internet. **Business Services:** meeting rooms, PC. **Cards:** AX, CB, DC, DS, MC, VI.

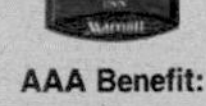

AAA Benefit:

Members save a minimum 5% off the best available rate.

(See map and index starting on p. 628)

FAIRFIELD INN BY MARRIOTT-NORTHLAKE *Book great rates at AAA.com* **Phone:** (704)509-0123 

Hotel

$98-$106 All Year

Address: 9230 Harris Corners Pkwy **Location:** I-77, exit 18 (W. T. Harris Blvd), just e on SR 24, just s on Maple View Ln, then just w. **Facility:** Smoke free premises. 93 one-bedroom standard units. 3 stories, interior corridors. *Bath:* combo or shower only. **Parking:** on-site. **Terms:** cancellation fee imposed. **Amenities:** high-speed Internet, dual phone lines, voice mail, irons, hair dryers. **Pool(s):** outdoor. **Leisure Activities:** whirlpool. **Guest Services:** valet and coin laundry, wireless Internet. **Business Services:** meeting rooms, PC. **Cards:** AX, CB, DC, DS, MC, VI. **Free Special Amenities: expanded continental breakfast and high-speed Internet.**

AAA Benefit:

Members save a minimum 5% off the best available rate.

FOUR POINTS BY SHERATON-CHARLOTTE *Book great rates at AAA.com* **Phone:** 704/522-0852 

Hotel

Rates not provided

Address: 315 E Woodlawn Rd **Location:** I-77, exit 6A, 0.5 mi e. **Facility:** Smoke free premises. 132 units. 76 one-bedroom standard units. 56 one-bedroom suites. 6 stories, interior corridors. **Parking:** on-site. **Amenities:** dual phone lines, voice mail, safes, irons, hair dryers. **Pool(s):** outdoor. **Leisure Activities:** exercise room. **Guest Services:** valet and coin laundry, airport transportation-Charlotte/Douglas International Airport, wireless Internet. **Business Services:** meeting rooms, business center. **Free Special Amenities: newspaper and high-speed Internet.**

/ SOME UNITS

AAA Benefit:

Members get up to 15% off, plus Starwood Preferred Guest® bonuses.

HAMPTON INN & SUITES-ARROWOOD *Book great rates at AAA.com* **Phone:** (704)525-3333 70

Hotel

$130-$157 All Year

Address: 9110 Southern Pines Blvd **Location:** I-77, exit 3 southbound; exit 2 northbound, just w. **Facility:** 100 units. 66 one-bedroom standard units, some with whirlpools. 34 one-bedroom suites with efficiencies and whirlpools. 7 stories, interior corridors. *Bath:* combo or shower only. **Parking:** on-site. **Terms:** cancellation fee imposed. **Amenities:** dual phone lines, voice mail, safes, irons, hair dryers. **Pool(s):** outdoor. **Leisure Activities:** exercise room. **Guest Services:** valet and coin laundry, area transportation, wireless Internet. **Business Services:** meeting rooms, business center. **Cards:** AX, DC, DS, MC, VI.

CALL / SOME UNITS VCR

AAA Benefit:

Members save up to 10% everyday!

HAMPTON INN & SUITES SOUTH PARK *Book great rates at AAA.com* **Phone:** (704)319-5700 

Hotel

$110-$245 All Year

Address: 6700 Phillips Place Ct **Location:** I-77, exit 5 (Tyvola Rd), 3.7 mi e on Tyvola/Fairview rds, then just e; in Phillips Plaza. **Facility:** 124 units. 88 one-bedroom standard units, some with whirlpools. 36 one-bedroom suites, some with whirlpools. 6 stories, interior corridors. *Bath:* combo or shower only. **Parking:** on-site. **Terms:** 1-30 night minimum stay, cancellation fee imposed. **Amenities:** dual phone lines, voice mail, irons, hair dryers. **Pool(s):** outdoor. **Leisure Activities:** exercise room. **Guest Services:** valet and coin laundry, area transportation, wireless Internet. **Business Services:** meeting rooms, business center. **Cards:** AX, CB, DC, DS, MC, VI.

   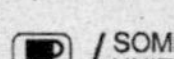 / SOME UNITS VCR

AAA Benefit:

Members save up to 10% everyday!

HAMPTON INN UNIVERSITY PLACE *Book great rates at AAA.com* **Phone:** (704)548-0905 17

Hotel

$99-$169 All Year

Address: 8419 N Tryon St **Location:** I-85, exit 45A (W. T. Harris Blvd), 0.5 mi e on SR 24, then just s on US 29 (N Tryon St). **Facility:** 126 one-bedroom standard units. 6 stories, interior corridors. *Bath:* combo or shower only. **Parking:** on-site. **Amenities:** voice mail, irons, hair dryers. **Pool(s):** outdoor. **Guest Services:** valet laundry, wireless Internet. **Business Services:** meeting rooms, business center. **Cards:** AX, CB, DC, DS, JC, MC, VI. **Free Special Amenities: expanded continental breakfast and high-speed Internet.** *(See color ad p 647)*

AAA Benefit:

Members save up to 10% everyday!

(See map and index starting on p. 628)

HILTON CHARLOTTE UNIVERSITY PLACE *Book great rates at AAA.com* **Phone:** (704)547-7444 

Hotel

$99-$349 All Year

Address: 8629 J M Keynes Dr **Location:** I-85, exit 45A (W. T. Harris Blvd), just e on SR 24, then just n. **Facility:** Designated smoking area. 393 units. 388 one-bedroom standard units. 5 one-bedroom suites. 12 stories, interior corridors. *Bath:* combo or shower only. **Parking:** on-site. **Terms:** check-in 4 pm, 1-30 night minimum stay, cancellation fee imposed. **Amenities:** high-speed Internet (fee), dual phone lines, voice mail, safes, irons, hair dryers. **Pool(s):** outdoor. **Leisure Activities:** exercise room. **Guest Services:** valet laundry, area transportation, wireless Internet. **Business Services:** conference facilities, business center. **Cards:** AX, CB, DC, DS, MC, VI.

CALL / SOME UNITS

AAA Benefit:

Members save 5% or more everyday!

HILTON GARDEN INN CHARLOTTE AIRPORT **Phone:** 843/669-0855

fyi

Hotel

Under construction, scheduled to open August 2009. **Address:** 2300 Cascade Pointe Blvd **Location:** I-77, exit 6A. **Amenities:** 137 units, restaurant, coffeemakers, microwaves, refrigerators, pool.

AAA Benefit:

Members save 5% or more everyday!

HILTON GARDEN INN-CHARLOTTE NORTH *Book great rates at AAA.com* **Phone:** (704)597-7655 

Hotel

$89-$199 All Year

Address: 9315 Statesville Rd **Location:** I-77, exit 18 (W. T. Harris Blvd), just e on SR 24, then just n on US 21. **Facility:** 112 units. 108 one-bedroom standard units, some with whirlpools. 4 one-bedroom suites, some with whirlpools. 5 stories, interior corridors. *Bath:* combo or shower only. **Parking:** on-site. **Terms:** 1-30 night minimum stay, cancellation fee imposed. **Amenities:** high-speed Internet, dual phone lines, voice mail, irons, hair dryers. **Pool(s):** heated indoor/outdoor. **Leisure Activities:** whirlpool, exercise room. **Guest Services:** complimentary and valet laundry, area transportation, wireless Internet. **Business Services:** meeting rooms, business center. **Cards:** AX, CB, DC, DS, MC, VI.

CALL / SOME UNITS

AAA Benefit:

Members save 5% or more everyday!

HOLIDAY INN AIRPORT *Book at AAA.com* **Phone:** 704/394-4301 30

Hotel

Rates not provided

Address: 2707 Little Rock Rd **Location:** I-85, exit 32, just e. **Facility:** 212 units. 210 one-bedroom standard units. 2 one-bedroom suites. 4 stories, interior corridors. *Bath:* combo or shower only. **Parking:** on-site. **Amenities:** video games (fee), high-speed Internet, dual phone lines, voice mail, irons, hair dryers. **Pool(s):** outdoor. **Leisure Activities:** exercise room. **Guest Services:** valet and coin laundry, wireless Internet. **Business Services:** conference facilities, business center.

  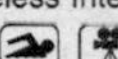 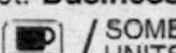   

/ SOME UNITS FEE

HOLIDAY INN AT UNIVERSITY EXECUTIVE PARK *Book at AAA.com* **Phone:** (704)547-0999 12

Hotel

$99-$289 All Year

Address: 8520 University Executive Park Dr **Location:** I-85, exit 45A (W. T. Harris Blvd), just e on SR 24, then just s. **Facility:** 174 units. 173 one-bedroom standard units. 1 one-bedroom suite. 7 stories, interior corridors. *Bath:* combo or shower only. **Parking:** on-site. **Terms:** cancellation fee imposed. **Amenities:** dual phone lines, voice mail, irons, hair dryers. **Pool(s):** heated outdoor. **Leisure Activities:** exercise room. **Guest Services:** valet laundry, wireless Internet. **Business Services:** meeting rooms, business center. **Cards:** AX, DC, DS, MC, VI.

ASK  CALL 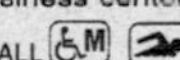  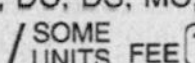 / SOME UNITS FEE 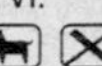 

▼ *See AAA listing p 646* ▼

(See map and index starting on p. 628)

HOLIDAY INN-BILLY GRAHAM PARKWAY Book at AAA.com Phone: 704/523-1400 44

Hotel
Rates not provided

Address: 321 W Woodlawn Rd **Location:** I-77, exit 6B northbound, just w; exit southbound, just s on S Tryon St. **Facility:** 177 units. 173 one-bedroom standard units. 4 one-bedroom suites. 6 stories, interior corridors. *Bath:* combo or shower only. **Parking:** on-site. **Amenities:** voice mail, safes, irons, hair dryers. *Some:* DVD players, CD players. **Pool(s):** outdoor. **Leisure Activities:** whirlpool, exercise room. **Guest Services:** valet and coin laundry, wireless Internet. **Business Services:** conference facilities, business center.

CALL / SOME UNITS FEE VCR

HOLIDAY INN EXPRESS HOTEL & SUITES Book at AAA.com Phone: (704)971-8720 69

Hotel
$100-$300 All Year

Address: 805 W Arrowood Rd **Location:** I-77, exit 3 southbound; exit 2 northbound, just e. **Facility:** Smoke free premises. 98 one-bedroom standard units. 4 stories, interior corridors. *Bath:* combo or shower only. **Parking:** on-site. **Amenities:** high-speed Internet, dual phone lines, voice mail, irons, hair dryers. **Pool(s):** heated indoor/outdoor. **Leisure Activities:** exercise room. **Guest Services:** valet and coin laundry, wireless Internet. **Business Services:** meeting rooms, business center. **Cards:** AX, CB, DC, DS, JC, MC, VI.

CALL

HOMESTEAD STUDIO SUITES HOTEL-CHARLOTTE/AIRPORT Book at AAA.com Phone: (704)676-0083 42

Extended Stay Motel
$95-$105 All Year

Address: 710 Yorkmont Rd **Location:** I-77, exit 6B northbound, just w, just s on S Tryon St, then just w; exit southbound, just s on S Tryon St, then just w. **Facility:** Compact, economy-style accommodations are designed for long-term visits; all units include an efficiency kitchenette. 137 one-bedroom standard units with efficiencies. 2 stories (no elevator), exterior corridors. *Bath:* combo or shower only. **Parking:** on-site. **Amenities:** voice mail, irons. **Guest Services:** coin laundry, wireless Internet. **Cards:** AX, CB, DC, DS, JC, MC, VI.

ASK / SOME UNITS FEE

HOMEWOOD SUITES BY HILTON AIRPORT Book great rates at AAA.com Phone: (704)357-0500 39

Hotel
$69-$189 All Year

Address: 2770 Yorkmont Rd **Location:** I-77, exit 6B, 2 mi nw on Billy Graham Pkwy, exit Coliseum/Tyvola Rd, just se on Tyvola Rd, then just w. Located in Lake Pointe Business Park. **Facility:** 102 units. 98 one- and 4 two-bedroom suites with efficiencies. 3 stories, interior corridors. *Bath:* combo or shower only. **Parking:** on-site. **Terms:** 1-30 night minimum stay, cancellation fee imposed. **Amenities:** video library (fee), high-speed Internet, dual phone lines, voice mail, irons, hair dryers. **Pool(s):** outdoor. **Leisure Activities:** putting green, exercise room. **Guest Services:** valet and coin laundry, wireless Internet. **Business Services:** meeting rooms, business center. **Cards:** AX, CB, DC, DS, JC, MC, VI.

CALL VCR / SOME UNITS FEE

AAA Benefit:
Members save 5% or more everyday!

HOMEWOOD SUITES BY HILTON-UNIVERSITY RESEARCH PARK Book great rates at AAA.com Phone: (704)549-8800 15

Hotel
$79-$239 All Year

Address: 8340 N Tryon St **Location:** I-85, exit 45A (W. T. Harris Blvd), 0.5 mi e on SR 24, then just s on US 29. **Facility:** 112 units. 100 one- and 12 two-bedroom suites with efficiencies. 2-3 stories, interior/exterior corridors. **Parking:** on-site. **Terms:** 1-30 night minimum stay, cancellation fee imposed. **Amenities:** video library (fee), DVD players, dual phone lines, voice mail, irons, hair dryers. **Pool(s):** outdoor. **Leisure Activities:** fishing, exercise room, sports court. **Guest Services:** valet and coin laundry, wireless Internet. **Business Services:** meeting rooms, business center. **Cards:** AX, CB, DC, DS, JC, MC, VI.

CALL / SOME UNITS

AAA Benefit:
Members save 5% or more everyday!

HYATT PLACE CHARLOTTE AIRPORT/TYVOLA ROAD Book great rates at AAA.com Phone: (704)423-9931 37

Hotel
$69-$209 All Year

Address: 2950 Oak Lake Blvd **Location:** I-77, exit 6B, 2 mi nw on Billy Graham Pkwy, exit Coliseum/Tyvola Rd, just se on Tyvola Rd, just w on Yorkmont Rd, then just n. Located in Lake Pointe Business Park. **Facility:** 128 one-bedroom standard units. 6 stories, interior corridors. *Bath:* combo or shower only. **Parking:** on-site. **Terms:** cancellation fee imposed. **Amenities:** video games (fee), voice mail, irons, hair dryers. **Pool(s):** outdoor. **Leisure Activities:** exercise room. **Guest Services:** valet and coin laundry, airport transportation-Charlotte-Douglas International Airport, wireless Internet. **Business Services:** meeting rooms, PC. **Cards:** AX, CB, DC, DS, JC, MC, VI. **Free Special Amenities: continental breakfast and high-speed Internet.**

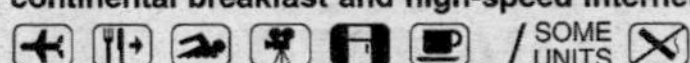

AAA Benefit:
Ask for the AAA rate and save 10%.

(See map and index starting on p. 628)

HYATT PLACE CHARLOTTE/ARROWOOD Book great rates at AAA.com **Phone:** (704)522-8400 66

Hotel
$99-$299 All Year

Address: 7900 Forest Point Blvd **Location:** I-77, exit 3 southbound; exit 2 northbound, just e. **Facility:** 128 one-bedroom standard units. 6 stories, interior corridors. *Bath:* combo or shower only. **Parking:** on-site. **Terms:** cancellation fee imposed. **Amenities:** voice mail, safes (fee), irons, hair dryers. *Some:* high-speed Internet, dual phone lines. **Pool(s):** heated outdoor. **Leisure Activities:** exercise room. **Guest Services:** valet and coin laundry, airport transportation-Charlotte-Douglas International Airport, wireless Internet. **Business Services:** meeting rooms. **Cards:** AX, CB, DC, DS, JC, MC, VI. **Free Special Amenities: continental breakfast and high-speed Internet.**

CALL / SOME UNITS FEE

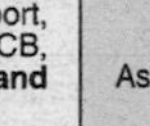

AAA Benefit:
Ask for the AAA rate and save 10%.

HYATT PLACE CHARLOTTE/CITY PARK Book great rates at AAA.com **Phone:** (704)357-8555 

Hotel
$69-$209 All Year

Address: 4119 S Stream Blvd **Location:** I-77, exit 6B, 2 mi nw on Billy Graham Pkwy, exit Coliseum/Tyvola Rd, then 0.8 mi se on Tyvola Rd. **Facility:** 122 one-bedroom standard units. 6 stories, interior corridors. **Parking:** on-site. **Terms:** cancellation fee imposed. **Amenities:** voice mail, irons, hair dryers. **Pool(s):** heated outdoor. **Leisure Activities:** exercise room. **Guest Services:** valet laundry, airport transportation-Charlotte-Douglas International Airport, wireless Internet. **Business Services:** meeting rooms, PC. **Cards:** AX, CB, DC, DS, JC, MC, VI. **Free Special Amenities: continental breakfast and high-speed Internet.**

/ SOME UNITS

AAA Benefit:
Ask for the AAA rate and save 10%.

HYATT SUMMERFIELD SUITES Book great rates at AAA.com **Phone:** (704)525-2600 46

Hotel
$99-$299 All Year

Address: 4920 S Tryon St **Location:** I-77, exit 6B northbound, just w, then just s; exit southbound, just s. **Facility:** 135 units. 126 one- and 9 two-bedroom suites, some with efficiencies. 5 stories, interior corridors. **Parking:** on-site. **Terms:** cancellation fee imposed. **Amenities:** DVD players, high-speed Internet, dual phone lines, voice mail, irons, hair dryers. **Pool(s):** outdoor. **Leisure Activities:** whirlpool, barbecue grills, exercise room, sports court. **Guest Services:** valet and coin laundry, wireless Internet. **Business Services:** meeting rooms, business center. **Cards:** AX, CB, DC, DS, JC, MC, VI. **Free Special Amenities: full breakfast and high-speed Internet.**

CALL / SOME UNITS FEE

AAA Benefit:
Ask for the AAA rate and save 10%.

LA QUINTA INN- AIRPORT NORTH Book great rates at AAA.com **Phone:** (704)392-1600 27

Hotel
$59-$109 All Year

Address: 3127 Sloan Dr **Location:** I-85, exit 33, just w, then just s. **Facility:** 119 units. 117 one-bedroom standard units. 2 one-bedroom suites. 4 stories, interior corridors. **Parking:** on-site. **Amenities:** voice mail, irons, hair dryers. *Some:* high-speed Internet. **Leisure Activities:** exercise room. **Guest Services:** valet and coin laundry, wireless Internet. **Business Services:** meeting rooms. **Cards:** AX, DC, DS, MC, VI.

ASK / SOME UNITS

LA QUINTA INN & SUITES CHARLOTTE AIRPORT SOUTH Book great rates at AAA.com **Phone:** (704)523-5599 48

Hotel
$69-$129 All Year

Address: 4900 S Tryon St **Location:** I-77, exit 6B northbound, just w, then just s; exit southbound, just s. **Facility:** 131 units. 125 one-bedroom standard units. 6 one-bedroom suites. 6 stories, interior corridors. *Bath:* combo or shower only. **Parking:** on-site. **Amenities:** video games (fee), high-speed Internet, voice mail, irons, hair dryers. *Some:* dual phone lines. **Pool(s):** outdoor. **Leisure Activities:** whirlpool, exercise room. **Guest Services:** valet and coin laundry, wireless Internet. **Business Services:** meeting rooms, PC. **Cards:** AX, DC, DS, MC, VI.

ASK CALL / SOME UNITS

MAINSTAY SUITES Book at AAA.com **Phone:** 704/521-3232 67

Hotel
Rates not provided

Address: 7926 Forest Pine Dr **Location:** I-77, exit 3 southbound; exit 2 northbound, just e, then just s. **Facility:** 76 units. 51 one-bedroom standard units with efficiencies. 25 one-bedroom suites with efficiencies. 3 stories, interior corridors. *Bath:* combo or shower only. **Parking:** on-site. **Amenities:** high-speed Internet, dual phone lines, voice mail, irons, hair dryers. **Pool(s):** outdoor. **Leisure Activities:** limited exercise equipment. **Guest Services:** coin laundry, wireless Internet. **Business Services:** meeting rooms, business center.

CALL VCR / SOME UNITS FEE

(See map and index starting on p. 628)

MARRIOTT-CHARLOTTE SOUTHPARK *Book great rates at AAA.com* **Phone:** (704)364-8220 57

AAA SAVE
Hotel
$217-$233 All Year

Address: 2200 Rexford Rd **Location:** I-77, exit 5 (Tyvola Rd), 3.6 mi e on Tyvola/Fairview rds, just n on Sharon Rd, just w on Morrison Blvd, just n on Roxborough Rd, then just w. **Facility:** Fine English furniture and original artwork add a warm ambience to this hotel's appealing public areas. Smoke free premises. 195 units. 187 one-bedroom standard units. 8 one-bedroom suites. 6 stories, interior corridors. *Bath:* combo or shower only. **Parking:** on-site and valet. **Terms:** check-in 4 pm, cancellation fee imposed. **Amenities:** dual phone lines, voice mail, safes, irons, hair dryers. *Fee:* video games, high-speed Internet. *Some:* DVD players, CD players. **Dining:** The Grill, see separate listing. **Pool(s):** outdoor. **Leisure Activities:** whirlpool, exercise room. *Fee:* golf privileges, massage. **Guest Services:** valet laundry, wireless Internet. **Business Services:** conference facilities, business center. **Cards:** AX, CB, DC, DS, JC, MC, VI. **Free Special Amenities: room upgrade (subject to availability with advance reservations) and high-speed Internet.**

CALL / SOME UNITS FEE

Marriott HOTELS & RESORTS
AAA Benefit:
Members save a minimum 5% off the best available rate.

MICROTEL INN & SUITES *Book great rates at AAA.com* **Phone:** (704)227-3377 9

AAA SAVE
Hotel
$49-$140 All Year

Address: 6309 Banner Elk Dr **Location:** I-77, exit 16B, just w on Sunset Rd, then just s. **Facility:** 64 one-bedroom standard units, some with whirlpools. 3 stories, interior corridors. *Bath:* combo or shower only. **Parking:** on-site. **Amenities:** high-speed Internet, voice mail, irons, hair dryers. *Some:* dual phone lines. **Pool(s):** outdoor. **Leisure Activities:** exercise room. **Guest Services:** coin laundry, wireless Internet. **Business Services:** PC. **Cards:** AX, CB, DC, DS, MC, VI. **Free Special Amenities: expanded continental breakfast and high-speed Internet.**

CALL / SOME UNITS

QUALITY INN & SUITES AIRPORT *Book at AAA.com* **Phone:** (704)393-5306 28

Hotel
$70-$80 All Year

Address: 3100 Queen City Dr **Location:** I-85, exit 33, just w, then just n. **Facility:** 130 one-bedroom standard units. 3 stories, interior/exterior corridors. **Parking:** on-site. **Terms:** 14 day cancellation notice. **Amenities:** video games (fee), voice mail, irons, hair dryers. **Pool(s):** outdoor. **Guest Services:** valet laundry, wireless Internet. **Business Services:** meeting rooms. **Cards:** AX, DC, DS, MC, VI.

ASK CALL / SOME UNITS FEE

QUALITY INN-EXECUTIVE PARK *Book great rates at AAA.com* **Phone:** (704)525-0747 54

AAA SAVE
Hotel
$75-$195 All Year

Address: 440 Griffith Rd **Location:** I-77, exit 5 (Tyvola Rd), just e, just s on Westpark Dr, then just e. Located in an office park area. **Facility:** 151 units. 142 one-bedroom standard units. 9 one-bedroom suites, some with efficiencies and/or whirlpools. 4 stories, interior corridors. **Parking:** on-site. **Amenities:** voice mail, irons, hair dryers. **Pool(s):** outdoor. **Leisure Activities:** exercise room. **Guest Services:** valet laundry, airport transportation-Charlotte/Douglas International Airport, wireless Internet. **Business Services:** meeting rooms, PC. **Cards:** AX, DC, DS, MC, VI. **Free Special Amenities: full breakfast and high-speed Internet.**

/ SOME UNITS FEE

RAMADA CONFERENCE CENTER "AIRPORT SOUTH" *Book at AAA.com* **Phone:** 704/525-8350 47

Hotel
Rates not provided

Address: 212 W Woodlawn Rd **Location:** I-77, exit 6A, just e. **Facility:** 425 one-bedroom standard units. 4 stories, interior corridors. *Bath:* combo or shower only. **Parking:** on-site. **Amenities:** voice mail, irons, hair dryers. **Pool(s):** outdoor. **Leisure Activities:** exercise room. **Guest Services:** complimentary and valet laundry, wireless Internet. **Business Services:** conference facilities, PC.

/ SOME UNITS FEE

RAMADA NORTHEAST *Book great rates at AAA.com* **Phone:** (704)596-2999 22

AAA SAVE
Motel
$49-$54 All Year

Address: 5415 Equipment Dr **Location:** I-85, exit 41, just w, then 0.4 mi n. **Facility:** 125 one-bedroom standard units. 3 stories, interior/exterior corridors. *Bath:* combo or shower only. **Parking:** on-site. **Terms:** cancellation fee imposed. **Amenities:** voice mail, irons, hair dryers. **Pool(s):** outdoor. **Guest Services:** valet laundry, wireless Internet. **Business Services:** meeting rooms, PC. **Cards:** AX, DS, JC, MC, VI. **Free Special Amenities: continental breakfast and high-speed Internet.**

CALL / SOME UNITS FEE

RED ROOF INN-AIRPORT *Book at AAA.com* **Phone:** 704/392-2316 29

Motel
Rates not provided

Address: 3300 Queen City Dr **Location:** I-85, exit 33, just w, then just s. **Facility:** 84 one-bedroom standard units. 2 stories (no elevator), exterior corridors. *Bath:* combo or shower only. **Parking:** on-site. **Amenities:** video games (fee), voice mail.

CALL / SOME UNITS FEE FEE

(See map and index starting on p. 628)

RENAISSANCE CHARLOTTE SOUTHPARK | **Phone:** (704)501-2510 60

fyi
Hotel
$205-$226 All Year

Under major renovation, scheduled to be completed September 2008. **Last rated:** ♦♦♦ **Address:** 5501 Carnegie Blvd **Location:** I-77, exit 5 (Tyvola Rd), 3.3 mi e on Tyvola/Fairview rds, then just n on Barclay Downs. **Facility:** Smoke free premises. 264 one-bedroom standard units. 7 stories, interior corridors. **Parking:** on-site. **Terms:** cancellation fee imposed. **Amenities:** irons, hair dryers. **Guest Services:** wireless Internet. **Business Services:** conference facilities. **Cards:** AX, DS, MC, VI.

RENAISSANCE. HOTELS & RESORTS
AAA Benefit:
Members save a minimum 5% off the best available rate.

RENAISSANCE CHARLOTTE SUITES HOTEL *Book great rates at AAA.com* | **Phone:** (704)357-1414 40

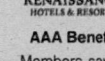

Hotel
$188-$201 All Year

Address: 2800 Coliseum Centre Dr **Location:** I-77, exit 6B, 2 mi nw on Billy Graham Pkwy, exit Coliseum/Tyvola Rd, just se on Tyvola Rd, just e on Yorkmont Rd, then just s. **Facility:** Smoke free premises. 275 one-bedroom suites. 9 stories, interior corridors. *Bath:* combo or shower only. **Parking:** on-site. **Terms:** check-in 4 pm, cancellation fee imposed. **Amenities:** dual phone lines, voice mail, irons, hair dryers. *Fee:* video games, high-speed Internet. **Pool(s):** heated indoor. **Leisure Activities:** sauna, whirlpool, exercise room. **Guest Services:** valet and coin laundry, airport transportation-Charlotte-Douglas International Airport, wireless Internet. **Business Services:** conference facilities, business center. **Cards:** AX, CB, DC, DS, JC, MC, VI. **Free Special Amenities: newspaper.**

RENAISSANCE. HOTELS & RESORTS
AAA Benefit:
Members save a minimum 5% off the best available rate.

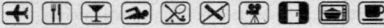

RESIDENCE INN BY MARRIOTT-CHARLOTTE SOUTH *Book great rates at AAA.com* | **Phone:** (704)527-8110 55

Extended Stay Hotel
$172-$185 All Year

Address: 5816 Westpark Dr **Location:** I-77, exit 5 (Tyvola Rd), just e, then 0.4 mi s. **Facility:** Fireplaces are featured in some guest rooms of the hotel, which offers an optional grocery delivery service; the three-story building has an elevator. Smoke free premises. 116 units. 60 one-bedroom standard units with kitchens. 33 one- and 23 two-bedroom suites with kitchens. 2-3 stories (no elevator), interior/exterior corridors. **Parking:** on-site. **Terms:** cancellation fee imposed. **Amenities:** dual phone lines, voice mail, irons, hair dryers. *Some:* high-speed Internet. **Pool(s):** outdoor. **Leisure Activities:** whirlpool, exercise room, sports court. **Guest Services:** valet and coin laundry, wireless Internet. **Business Services:** meeting rooms, business center. **Cards:** AX, CB, DC, DS, JC, MC, VI.

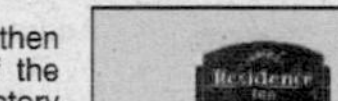

CALL / SOME UNITS FEE

AAA Benefit:
Members save a minimum 5% off the best available rate.

RESIDENCE INN BY MARRIOTT-PIPER GLEN *Book great rates at AAA.com* | **Phone:** (704)319-3900 74

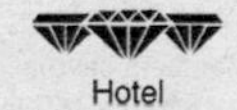

Hotel
$217-$233 All Year

Address: 5115 Piper Station Dr **Location:** I-485, exit 59, just s on Rea Rd, then just e. **Facility:** Smoke free premises. 114 units. 45 one-bedroom standard units with efficiencies. 44 one- and 25 two-bedroom suites, some with efficiencies or kitchens. 5 stories, interior corridors. *Bath:* combo or shower only. **Parking:** on-site. **Terms:** cancellation fee imposed. **Amenities:** high-speed Internet, dual phone lines, voice mail, irons, hair dryers. **Pool(s):** outdoor. **Leisure Activities:** whirlpool, exercise room, sports court. **Guest Services:** valet and coin laundry, wireless Internet. **Business Services:** meeting rooms, business center. **Cards:** AX, CB, DC, DS, JC, MC, VI.

CALL / SOME UNITS FEE

AAA Benefit:
Members save a minimum 5% off the best available rate.

RESIDENCE INN BY MARRIOTT-UNIVERSITY RESEARCH PARK *Book great rates at AAA.com* | **Phone:** (704)547-1122 13

Hotel
$159-$299 All Year

Address: 8503 N Tryon St **Location:** I-85, exit 45A (W. T. Harris Blvd), 0.5 mi e on SR 24, then just s on US 29 (N Tryon St). **Facility:** Smoke free premises. 91 units. 67 one- and 24 two-bedroom standard units with kitchens. 2 stories (no elevator), exterior corridors. *Bath:* combo or shower only. **Parking:** on-site. **Terms:** cancellation fee imposed. **Amenities:** high-speed Internet, voice mail, irons, hair dryers. **Pool(s):** outdoor. **Leisure Activities:** exercise room, sports court, basketball. **Guest Services:** valet and coin laundry, area transportation, wireless Internet. **Business Services:** meeting rooms, business center. **Cards:** AX, CB, DC, DS, JC, MC, VI.

AAA Benefit:
Members save a minimum 5% off the best available rate.

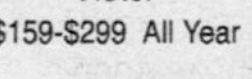

CALL / SOME UNITS FEE

(See map and index starting on p. 628)

RODEWAY INN Book at AAA.com Phone: (704)597-5074 20

Hotel
$40-$125 All Year

Address: 1416 W Sugar Creek Rd **Location:** I-85, exit 41, just w. **Facility:** 55 one-bedroom standard units. 2 stories (no elevator), exterior corridors. **Parking:** on-site. **Terms:** cancellation fee imposed. **Pool(s):** outdoor. **Guest Services:** wireless Internet. **Cards:** AX, DC, DS, MC, VI.

ASK CALL / SOME UNITS

SHERATON CHARLOTTE AIRPORT HOTEL Book great rates at AAA.com Phone: (704)392-1200 32

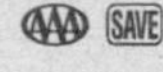

Hotel
$99-$279 All Year

Address: 3315 Scott Futrell Dr **Location:** I-85, exit 33, just e, then just s. **Facility:** 222 units. 219 one-bedroom standard units. 3 one-bedroom suites. 8 stories, interior corridors. *Bath:* combo or shower only. **Parking:** on-site. **Amenities:** video games (fee), voice mail, irons, hair dryers. **Pool(s):** heated indoor/outdoor. **Leisure Activities:** whirlpool, exercise room. **Guest Services:** valet and coin laundry, airport transportation-Charlotte-Douglas International Airport, wireless Internet. **Business Services:** conference facilities, business center. **Cards:** AX, CB, DC, DS, JC, MC, VI.

Sheraton HOTELS & RESORTS
AAA Benefit:
Members get up to 15% off, plus Starwood Preferred Guest® bonuses.

SLEEP INN Book great rates at AAA.com Phone: (704)549-4544 11

Hotel
$70-$170 All Year

Address: 8525 N Tryon St **Location:** I-85, exit 45A (W. T. Harris Blvd), 0.5 mi e on SR 24, just s on US 29 (N Tryon St). **Facility:** 121 one-bedroom standard units. 5 stories, interior corridors. *Bath:* combo or shower only. **Parking:** on-site. **Terms:** cancellation fee imposed. **Amenities:** video games (fee), dual phone lines, voice mail, irons, hair dryers. **Pool(s):** heated outdoor. **Guest Services:** valet laundry, wireless Internet. **Business Services:** PC. **Cards:** AX, CB, DC, DS, JC, MC, VI. **Free Special Amenities: expanded continental breakfast and high-speed Internet.**

CALL / SOME UNITS FEE

SLEEP INN-YORKMONT Book at AAA.com Phone: (704)525-5005 45

Hotel
$80-$130 All Year

Address: 701 Yorkmont Rd **Location:** I-77, exit 6B northbound, just w, just s on S Tryon St, then just w; exit southbound, just s on Tryon St, then just w. **Facility:** 79 one-bedroom standard units, some with whirlpools. 3 stories, interior corridors. *Bath:* combo or shower only. **Parking:** on-site. **Terms:** 14 day cancellation notice. **Amenities:** dual phone lines, voice mail, irons, hair dryers. **Pool(s):** outdoor. **Leisure Activities:** exercise room. **Guest Services:** wireless Internet. **Business Services:** meeting rooms, business center. **Cards:** AX, CB, DC, DS, JC, MC, VI.

ASK CALL / SOME UNITS FEE

SPRINGHILL SUITES CHARLOTTE UNIVERSITY RESEARCH PARK Book great rates at AAA.com Phone: (704)503-4800 5

Hotel
$147-$158 All Year

Address: 8700 Research Dr **Location:** I-85, exit 45B, just w on SR 24, then just n. **Facility:** Smoke free premises. 136 one-bedroom standard units. 4 stories, interior corridors. *Bath:* combo or shower only. **Parking:** on-site. **Terms:** cancellation fee imposed. **Amenities:** video games (fee), high-speed Internet, dual phone lines, voice mail, irons, hair dryers. **Pool(s):** heated indoor. **Leisure Activities:** whirlpool, exercise room. **Guest Services:** valet and coin laundry. **Business Services:** meeting rooms, business center. **Cards:** AX, CB, DC, DS, JC, MC, VI.

CALL

AAA Benefit:
Members save a minimum 5% off the best available rate.

STAYBRIDGE SUITES-ARROWOOD Book at AAA.com Phone: 704/527-6767 68

Hotel
Rates not provided

Address: 7924 Forest Pine Dr **Location:** I-77, exit 3 southbound; exit 2 northbound, just e, then just s. **Facility:** 117 units. 54 one-bedroom standard units with efficiencies. 40 one- and 23 two-bedroom suites with efficiencies. 3 stories, interior corridors. *Bath:* some combo or shower only. **Parking:** on-site. **Amenities:** DVD players, dual phone lines, voice mail, irons, hair dryers. **Pool(s):** outdoor. **Leisure Activities:** exercise room, sports court. **Guest Services:** complimentary and valet laundry, wireless Internet. **Business Services:** meeting rooms, PC.

CALL VCR / SOME UNITS FEE

STAYBRIDGE SUITES CHARLOTTE-BALLANTYNE Book at AAA.com Phone: (704)248-5000 76

Hotel
$169-$349 3/1-11/30
$149-$229 12/1-2/28

Address: 15735 John J Delaney Dr **Location:** I-485, exit 61 or 61B, just s. **Facility:** Smoke free premises. 118 units. 43 one-bedroom standard units with efficiencies. 52 one- and 23 two-bedroom suites with efficiencies. 3 stories, interior corridors. *Bath:* combo or shower only. **Parking:** on-site. **Terms:** cancellation fee imposed. **Amenities:** high-speed Internet, dual phone lines, voice mail, irons, hair dryers. **Pool(s):** heated indoor. **Leisure Activities:** whirlpool, putting green, exercise room. **Guest Services:** complimentary and valet laundry, area transportation, wireless Internet. **Business Services:** meeting rooms, business center. **Cards:** AX, CB, DC, DS, JC, MC, VI.

ASK CALL

(See map and index starting on p. 628)

STUDIOPLUS-TYVOLA *Book at AAA.com* **Phone:** (704)527-1960 58

Hotel
$83-$93 All Year

Address: 5830 Westpark Dr **Location:** I-77, exit 5 (Tyvola Rd), just e, then 0.4 mi s. **Facility:** 72 one-bedroom standard units with efficiencies. 3 stories (no elevator), interior corridors. **Parking:** on-site. **Amenities:** voice mail, irons. **Pool(s):** outdoor. **Leisure Activities:** exercise room. **Guest Services:** coin laundry, wireless Internet. **Cards:** AX, CB, DC, DS, JC, MC, VI.

ASK / SOME UNITS FEE

SUNSET INN **Phone:** 704/399-7778 10

Hotel
Rates not provided

Address: 6300 Banner Elk Dr **Location:** I-77, exit 16B, just w on Sunset Rd, then just s. **Facility:** 71 one-bedroom standard units. 5 stories, interior corridors. *Bath:* combo or shower only. **Parking:** on-site. **Amenities:** irons, hair dryers. **Pool(s):** heated indoor. **Leisure Activities:** limited exercise equipment. **Guest Services:** coin laundry, wireless Internet.

/ SOME UNITS

SUPER 8 CHARLOTTE/CAROWINDS/AIRPORT *Book at AAA.com* **Phone:** (704)588-8488 71

Hotel
$55-$120 All Year

Address: 11300 Texland Blvd **Location:** I-77, exit 1, just e, then just s. Located in an industrial area. **Facility:** 60 one-bedroom standard units. 3 stories (no elevator), interior corridors. **Parking:** on-site. **Guest Services:** wireless Internet. **Cards:** AX, DC, DS, MC, VI.

ASK / SOME UNITS

SUPER 8 MOTEL *Book at AAA.com* **Phone:** 704/598-8820 21

Hotel
Rates not provided

Address: 5125 Equipment Dr **Location:** I-85, exit 41, just w, then just s. **Facility:** 80 one-bedroom standard units. 2 stories (no elevator), interior corridors. **Parking:** on-site. **Amenities:** hair dryers. *Some:* irons. **Pool(s):** outdoor. **Guest Services:** coin laundry. **Business Services:** PC.

/ SOME UNITS

SUPER 8 MOTEL *Book at AAA.com* **Phone:** (704)523-1404 36

Motel
$40-$125 All Year

Address: 505 Clanton Rd **Location:** I-77, exit 7, just e. **Facility:** 54 one-bedroom standard units. 2 stories (no elevator), exterior corridors. **Parking:** on-site. **Amenities:** high-speed Internet, irons, hair dryers. **Pool(s):** outdoor. **Cards:** AX, DC, DS, MC, VI.

ASK / SOME UNITS

TOWNEPLACE SUITES BY MARRIOTT-ARROWOOD *Book great rates at AAA.com* **Phone:** (704)227-2000 64

Hotel
$133-$143 All Year

Address: 7805 Forest Point Blvd **Location:** I-77, exit 3 southbound; exit 2 northbound, just e. **Facility:** Smoke free premises. 96 units. 74 one-bedroom standard units, some with kitchens. 22 two-bedroom suites with kitchens. 3 stories, interior corridors. *Bath:* combo or shower only. **Parking:** on-site. **Terms:** cancellation fee imposed. **Amenities:** high-speed Internet, dual phone lines, voice mail, irons, hair dryers. **Pool(s):** outdoor. **Leisure Activities:** limited exercise equipment. **Guest Services:** valet and coin laundry, wireless Internet. **Business Services:** meeting rooms, PC. **Cards:** AX, CB, DC, DS, MC, VI.

CALL / SOME UNITS FEE

AAA Benefit:
Members save a minimum 5% off the best available rate.

TOWNEPLACE SUITES BY MARRIOTT - UNIVERSITY *Book great rates at AAA.com* **Phone:** (704)548-0388 4

AAA SAVE

Hotel
$195-$205 All Year

Address: 8710 Research Dr **Location:** I-85, exit 45B, just w on SR 24, then just n. **Facility:** Smoke free premises. 96 units. 70 one-bedroom standard units with kitchens. 4 one- and 22 two-bedroom suites with kitchens. 3 stories, interior corridors. *Bath:* combo or shower only. **Parking:** on-site. **Terms:** cancellation fee imposed. **Amenities:** dual phone lines, voice mail, irons, hair dryers. **Pool(s):** outdoor. **Leisure Activities:** limited exercise equipment. **Guest Services:** valet and coin laundry, wireless Internet. **Business Services:** meeting rooms, business center. **Cards:** AX, CB, DC, DS, JC, MC, VI. **Free Special Amenities: continental breakfast and high-speed Internet.**

CALL / SOME UNITS FEE VCR

TownePlace SUITES Marriott

AAA Benefit:
Members save a minimum 5% off the best available rate.

THE VANLANDINGHAM ESTATE *Book at AAA.com* **Phone:** (704)334-8909 34

Historic Bed & Breakfast
$149-$239 All Year

Address: 2010 The Plaza **Location:** Independence Blvd (US 74), exit Briar Creek Rd, just n, 1.2 mi w on Commonwealth Ave, then 0.7 mi n. **Facility:** Garden paths add charm to this home, which is set back from the road in a quiet residential neighborhood. Smoke free premises. 9 units. 8 one-bedroom standard units, some with whirlpools. 1 one-bedroom suite with whirlpool. 2 stories (no elevator), interior corridors. *Bath:* combo or shower only. **Parking:** on-site. **Amenities:** dual phone lines, voice mail, irons, hair dryers. **Leisure Activities:** bicycles. **Guest Services:** valet laundry, wireless Internet. **Business Services:** meeting rooms. **Cards:** AX, DS, MC, VI.

ASK / SOME UNITS

(See map and index starting on p. 628)

WINGATE BY WYNDHAM Book at AAA.com Phone: (704)523-3366 51

Hotel
$99-$149 All Year

Address: 6057 Nations Ford Rd **Location:** I-77, exit 5 (Tyvola Rd), just w. **Facility:** 122 one-bedroom standard units, some with whirlpools. 4 stories, interior corridors. *Bath:* combo or shower only. **Parking:** on-site. **Amenities:** video games (fee), high-speed Internet, dual phone lines, voice mail, safes, irons, hair dryers. **Pool(s):** outdoor. **Leisure Activities:** whirlpool, exercise room. **Guest Services:** valet and coin laundry, wireless Internet. **Business Services:** meeting rooms, business center. **Cards:** AX, DC, DS, MC, VI.

ASK / SOME UNITS

WINGATE BY WYNDHAM-CHARLOTTE AIRPORT Book great rates at AAA.com Phone: (704)395-3600 26

SAVE

Hotel
$69-$199 All Year

Address: 4238 Business Center Dr **Location:** I-85, exit 32 (Little Rock Rd), just w, then s. **Facility:** 80 one-bedroom standard units. 5 stories, interior corridors. *Bath:* combo or shower only. **Parking:** on-site. **Terms:** check-in 4 pm, cancellation fee imposed. **Amenities:** video games (fee), high-speed Internet, dual phone lines, voice mail, safes, irons, hair dryers. **Leisure Activities:** whirlpool, exercise room. **Guest Services:** valet and coin laundry, airport transportation-Charlotte-Douglas International Airport, wireless Internet. **Business Services:** meeting rooms, business center. **Cards:** AX, DS, MC, VI. **Free Special Amenities: full breakfast and high-speed Internet.**

CALL / SOME UNITS

WHERE TO DINE

AMALFI PASTA & PIZZA Phone: 704/547-8651 7

Italian
$5-$15

Located in a strip mall, the family-friendly, active pizzeria serves other favorites such as pasta dishes and chicken, veal and seafood entrees. Casual dress. **Bar:** Beer & wine. **Hours:** 11 am-2:30 & 4-10 pm, Fri & Sat 11 am-11 pm, Sun noon-9:30 pm. Closed: 4/12, 11/26, 12/25; also Mon. **Address:** 8542 University City Blvd **Location:** I-85, exit 45A (W.T. Harris Blvd), 1 mi e on SR 24, exit SR 49, then just n; in Town Center Plaza. **Parking:** on-site. **Cards:** AX, DC, DS, MC, VI.

BAILEY'S PUB & GRILLE Phone: 704/541-0794

American
$8-$18

Not your typical stuffy Old English Pub, sister restaurants, Bailey's and Fox. Casual dress. **Bar:** Full bar. **Hours:** 11 am-2 am. Closed: 12/25. **Address:** 8500 Pineville-Matthews Rd **Location:** I-485, exit 64, just s on SR 51. **Parking:** on-site. **Cards:** AX, MC, VI.

BANGKOK OCHA Phone: 704/544-7770 38

Thai
$6-$16

Various traditional dishes, as well as chef's specialties, are made as spicy as diners can handle. Lunch specials are reasonably priced and include soup and a spring roll. Casual dress. **Bar:** Beer & wine. **Hours:** 11 am-2:15 & 5-9 pm. Closed major holidays; also Sun. **Address:** 7629-B Pineville-Mathews Rd **Location:** I-485, exit 64A, 1.5 mi n on SR 51; in Carmel Commons Shopping Center. **Parking:** on-site. **Cards:** AX, DC, DS, MC, VI.

BEAUREGARDS RESTAURANT Phone: 704/399-5155 8

American
$5-$14

Since 1974, the family-friendly restaurant has presented a menu of pasta, chicken, steaks and sandwiches. Entrees include baby back ribs, lasagna, prime rib and catfish fillets. Casual dress. **Bar:** Full bar. **Reservations:** accepted. **Hours:** 11 am-10 pm, Sat 4 pm-11 pm, Sun 11 am-9 pm. Closed: 7/4, 11/26, 12/25. **Address:** 3030 Freedom Dr **Location:** I-85, exit 34, 0.5 mi e on US 27. **Parking:** on-site. **Cards:** AX, CB, DC, DS, MC, VI.

BEEF & BOTTLE Phone: 704/523-9977 16

Steak
$16-$39

The restaurant specializes in steak and seafood. From the complimentary cheddar cheese spread and crackers to guests creating their own salads from fixings brought to the table, to a relaxed and casual atmosphere, the emphasis is on a pleasant experience. Casual dress. **Bar:** Full bar. **Reservations:** suggested. **Hours:** 5:30 pm-10 pm, Fri & Sat-10:30 pm. Closed: 1/1, 11/26, 12/24, 12/25; also Sun, 4/13 & 7/1-7/7. **Address:** 4538 South Blvd **Location:** I-77, exit 6A, 0.7 mi e on Woodlawn Rd, then just n. **Parking:** on-site. **Cards:** AX, MC, VI.

BOMBAY CUISINE Phone: 704/503-5558 5

Indian
$5-$19

Charming hosts serve traditional cuisine, including some vegetarian dishes, in a cozy, intimate setting. Food is spiced to the patron's liking, but mostly it's intense, well-balanced and expertly cooked. Dishes are made to order, so diners should plan to take their time. An extensive lunch buffet is also offered. Dressy casual. **Bar:** Beer & wine. **Reservations:** suggested. **Hours:** 11 am-10 pm, Fri & Sat-11 pm. Closed: 11/26. **Address:** 230 E W.T. Harris Blvd **Location:** I-85, exit 45A (W. T. Harris Blvd), 0.7 mi e on SR 24; in The Promenade Place Shopping Center, upstairs. **Parking:** on-site. **Cards:** AX, DS, MC, VI.

CALL

BOMBAY GRILLE Phone: 704/542-3933 37

Indian
$7-$18

The menu features well-prepared East Indian cuisine as well as several vegetarian selections. A lunch buffet is offered weekdays. Casual dress. **Bar:** Beer & wine. **Hours:** 11 am-2:30 & 5-9:30 pm, Fri-10:30 pm, Sat noon-3 & 5-10:30 pm, Sun noon-3 & 5-9:30 pm. Closed: 7/4, 11/26, 12/25. **Address:** 8706-170 Pineville-Mathews Rd **Location:** I-485, exit 64A, just n; in Tower Place Shopping Center. **Parking:** on-site. **Cards:** AX, DC, DS, MC, VI.

(See map and index starting on p. 628)

BRIO TUSCAN GRILLE **Phone:** 704/571-4214 (28)

Italian
$12-$30

While the atmosphere is casual, upscale Tuscan villa-style decor lends a sophisticated touch to the dining experience. Both lunch and dinner offer all the attentiveness a diner expects. From the garlic, spinach and artichoke dip starter to beef, chicken, veal, seafood and homemade pasta entrees, there is a selection to satisfy all tastes. Among specialties are home-made mozzarella, crisp flat breads and wood-fired oven-baked pizza, in addition to a selection of steak. Dressy casual. **Bar:** Full bar. **Reservations:** suggested. **Hours:** 11 am-10 pm, Fri & Sat-11 pm. Closed: 11/26, 12/25. **Address:** 4720 Piedmont Row Dr, Suite 150 **Location:** I-77, exit 5, 3.3 mi e on Tyvola/Fairview rds, then just n; in Piedmont Town Center. **Parking:** on-site. **Cards:** AX, DS, MC, VI.

CALL

CAJUN QUEEN RESTAURANT **Phone:** 704/377-9017 (9)

Cajun
$14-$25

This energetic eatery serves New Orleans-style cuisine ranging from barbecue shrimp to fresh, blackened fish with a seafood topping and a traditional gumbo. Located in a historic house, this eatery has cordial service and live Dixieland jazz every night. Casual dress. Entertainment. **Bar:** Full bar. **Hours:** 5 pm-9:30 pm, Fri & Sat-10:30 pm. Closed: 11/26, 12/25. **Address:** 1800 E 7th St **Location:** Jct Central Ave, 0.5 mi e. **Parking:** on-site. **Cards:** AX, DC, DS, MC, VI.

CAROLINA COUNTRY BARBECUE **Phone:** 704/525-0337 (20)

Regional Southern
$5-$12

Guests chow down on western North Carolina-style chopped pork barbecue smothered in a spicy tomato-based sauce at the family-friendly eatery. Also on the menu are ribs, chicken and all the traditional fixings, including coleslaw and hushpuppies. Casual dress. **Hours:** 11 am-8 pm, Fri & Sat-8:30 pm, Sun-3 pm. Closed: 11/26, 12/25. **Address:** 838 Tyvola Rd **Location:** I-77, exit 5 (Tyvola Rd), 0.5 mi e. **Parking:** on-site. **Cards:** AX, DS, MC, VI.

CHEN'S BISTRO **Phone:** 704/510-9889 (4)

Chinese
$6-$16

In a shopping and dining complex, the restaurant sets out all-you-can-eat buffets for lunch and dinner. Included are preparations cooked to order at the hibachi station. The extensive Oriental offerings range from the traditional to the more unusual. Among them are sushi bar preparations, crab legs and various preparations of oysters. Guests also can order from the menu. Casual dress. **Bar:** Full bar. **Hours:** 11 am-10 pm, Fri-11 pm, Sat 11:30 am-11 pm, Sun 11:30 am-10 pm. **Address:** 230 W.T. Harris Blvd, #C4 **Location:** I-85, exit 45A (W. T. Harris Blvd), 0.7 mi e; in The Promonade Place Shopping Center, upstairs. **Parking:** on-site. **Cards:** AX, DS, MC, VI.

CALL

CIRO'S ITALIAN RESTAURANT **Phone:** 704/510-0012 (2)

Italian
$7-$25

In a busy shopping plaza, the casual restaurant employs a friendly staff. Pizza, pasta, veal, chicken and seafood choices line the menu, which entices with classic dishes such as linguine in clam sauce and spaghetti alla puttanesca, in addition to whiskey shrimp and chicken, veal saltimbocca and chicken piccata. Casual dress. **Bar:** Full bar. **Hours:** 11 am-10 pm, Fri & Sat-11 pm, Sun noon-9 pm. Closed major holidays. **Address:** 8927 JM Keynes Dr, Suite 100 **Location:** I-85, exit 45A (W. T. Harris Blvd), 0.5 mi e on SR 24, just n on US 29 (N Tryon St), then just w; in Boardwalk Plaza at The Shoppes at University Place. **Parking:** on-site. **Cards:** AX, DC, DS, MC, VI.

CROWN POINT FAMILY RESTAURANT **Phone:** 704/847-1212 (32)

American
$5-$12

Representative of the casual eatery's home-style cooking are chopped steak, meatloaf, beef tips over rice and liver and onions. Also on the lengthy menu are chicken dishes, steaks, seafood and Italian favorites. Casual dress. **Bar:** Full bar. **Hours:** 6 am-9 pm, Fri & Sat-10 pm. Closed: 11/26, 12/25; also Sun. **Address:** 2518 Sardis Rd N **Location:** I-485, exit 51A, 3.3 mi w on US 74, then just s; in Crown Point Shopping Center. **Parking:** on-site. **Cards:** AX, MC, VI.

DERBY DINER **Phone:** 704/522-9977 (21)

American
$6-$15

The dining room has a rustic and appealing country decor with shelves full of old-time collectibles. While the menu is not large, it does list a good selection of homemade comfort foods including steaks, ribs, chicken, seafood and a few Italian entrees. Attentive, helpful staff set the tone for a casual and relaxed dining experience. Casual dress. **Bar:** Beer & wine. **Hours:** 11 am-9 pm, Sat from 4 pm. Closed major holidays; also Sun, Memorial Day & Labor Day weekends. **Address:** 516 Tyvola Rd **Location:** I-77, exit 5 (Tyvola Rd), just e. **Parking:** on-site. **Cards:** AX, DC, DS, MC, VI.

CALL

FIREBIRDS WOOD FIRED GRILL **Phone:** 704/752-7979 (41)

American
$8-$36

The restaurant re-creates the atmosphere of a mountain lodge. Hand-cut steaks and seafood dominate the menu, which also lists a few pork and chicken entrees, as well as elk tenderloin medallions and buffalo meatloaf. The kitchen uses wood grilling, and pizzas bake in a wood-burning oven. Flavorful food, enhanced presentations and a skilled, knowledgeable and attentive staff, together with distinctive physical elements, make this place appealing. Dressy casual. **Bar:** Full bar. **Hours:** 11 am-10 pm, Fri & Sat-11 pm. Closed: 1/1, 11/26, 12/25. **Address:** 7716 Rea Rd **Location:** I-485, exit 59, just s; in Stonecrest Shopping Center. **Parking:** on-site. **Cards:** AX, DC, DS, MC, VI.

(See map and index starting on p. 628)

FOX & HOUND SMOKEHOUSE & TAVERN — **Phone:** 704/544-8902

American
$6-$18

The casual theme restaurant presents a lengthy menu of pub fare, including burgers, sandwiches and pizza, as well as steaks and ribs. Diners can catch their favorite sport on one of the TVs lining the walls or hang out with friends in the boisterous gathering spot. Casual dress. **Bar:** Full bar. **Hours:** 11 am-2 am. **Address:** 15235 John J Delaney Dr **Location:** I-485, exit 61, 1 mi s on US 521; in Ballantyne Commons East. **Parking:** on-site. **Cards:** AX, DS, MC, VI.

CALL

FRANK MANZETTI'S TAVERN AT SOUTHPARK — **Phone:** 704/364-9334 (24)

American
$5-$25

Short of making the trip to Pennsylvania, this is a good way to try a Pittsburgh steak. Steaks are prepared charred on the outside with a tender and juicy interior. Also offered are ribs, fresh fish, chicken and pastas. Casual dress. **Bar:** Full bar. **Reservations:** accepted. **Hours:** 11 am-10 pm, Fri & Sat-11 pm. Closed: 11/26, 12/25. **Address:** 6401 Morrison Blvd **Location:** I-77, exit 5 (Tyvola Rd), 3.6 mi e on Tyvola/Fairview rds, just n on Sharon Rd, then just w; in The Specialty Shops on the Park; opposite South Park Mall. **Parking:** on-site. **Cards:** AX, DC, DS, MC, VI.

THE GRILL — **Phone:** 704/364-8220 (23)

American
$8-$29

Guests indulge in well-prepared entrees of beef, seafood and other fine fare while cordial, professional servers tend to their every need in the casually upscale dining room. Fresh desserts often bring smiles. A lunch buffet is set up weekdays. Dressy casual. **Bar:** Full bar. **Reservations:** suggested. **Hours:** 6:30 am-10:30 pm. **Address:** 2200 Rexford Rd **Location:** I-77, exit 5 (Tyvola Rd), 3.6 mi e on Tyvola/Fairview rds, just n on Sharon Rd, just w on Morrison Blvd, just n on Roxborough Rd, then just w; in Marriott-Charlotte Southpark. **Parking:** on-site. **Cards:** AX, DC, DS, MC, VI.

HICKORY TAVERN — **Phone:** 704/921-4466 (1)

American
$8-$33

With its lengthy menu of steaks, seafood, burgers and other munchie delights, the tavern is a great place to hang out with friends and catch the big game or race on one of the dozens of televisions sprinkled around the dining room. Live music is featured on a regular basis; call for details. Casual dress. **Bar:** Full bar. **Hours:** 11 am-midnight, Fri-2 am, Sat 11:30 am-2 am, Sun 11:30 am-midnight. Closed: 11/26, 12/24, 12/25. **Address:** 9010 Harris Corners Pkwy **Location:** I-77, exit 18, just e on Harris Blvd, then just s on US 29. **Parking:** on-site. **Cards:** AX, MC, VI.

JOHN'S FAMILY RESTAURANT — **Phone:** 704/588-6613 (34)

American
$5-$9

Home-style cooking makes up the menu at the bustling restaurant. Patrons savor such entrees as beef tips over rice, meatloaf and chopped steak, as well as Italian favorites, including spaghetti, lasagna and chicken piccata. Homemade pies and cakes lend the meal a sweet finish. Casual dress. **Bar:** Beer & wine. **Hours:** 11 am-9 pm. Closed major holidays; also Sun. **Address:** 2002 Westinghouse Blvd **Location:** I-77, exit 1, 1.4 mi w. **Parking:** on-site. **Cards:** AX, DS, MC, VI.

CALL

JOJO CHINA BISTRO — **Phone:** 704/541-6488 (40)

Chinese
$7-$18

The colorful, sophisticated bistro blends traditional Chinese cuisine and some innovative dishes on its menu. In addition to chicken, beef, seafood and vegetarian entrees, specialties include steamed sea bass Hong Kong-style, scallops in black bean sauce and spicy tangerine chicken. The dining patio overlooks several fountains. Casual dress. **Bar:** Full bar. **Hours:** 11:30 am-2:30 & 5-10 pm, Fri-11 pm, Sat noon-3 & 5-11 pm, Sun 5 pm-10 pm. Closed: 11/26, 12/25. **Address:** 7800-A Rea Rd **Location:** I-485, exit 59, just s; in Stonecrest at Piper Glen Shopping Center. **Parking:** on-site. **Cards:** AX, DS, MC, VI.

LAVA BISTRO & BAR — **Phone:** 704/549-0050 (3)

American
$7-$29

Lava Bistro & Bar, a trendy and pleasant eatery, is situated in the vicinity of Carolinas Medical Center-University and University of North Carolina-Charlotte. The trendy, stylish bistro and bar offers fantastic views of the boardwalk and lake. Menu offerings include such favorites as peppered ahi tuna, fettuccine primavera and espresso-rubbed filet mignon. A Sunday brunch buffet is available. Casual dress. **Bar:** Full bar. **Reservations:** accepted. **Hours:** 11:30 am-10 pm, Fri & Sat-11 pm, Sun 10:30 am-3 pm. Closed: 11/26, 12/24, 12/25. **Address:** 8708 JW Clay Blvd, Suite 1 **Location:** I-85, exit 45A (W. T. Harris Blvd), just e, then just n on JW Clay Blvd; in Shoppes at University Place, next to the AAA office. **Parking:** on-site. **Cards:** AX, DS, MC, VI.

M5 MODERN MEDITERRANEAN — **Phone:** 704/909-5500 (26)

Mediterranean
$9-$35

Enjoy Mediterranean dishes such as pan-roasted salmon with roasted beets and couscous salad, lamb shank with risotto milanese or porcini-crusted mahi with caramelized onions served in a relaxed, modern setting. More than 30 wines are offered by-the-glass. Al fresco dining is available. Dressy casual. **Bar:** Full bar. **Reservations:** accepted. **Hours:** 11 am-10 pm, Fri & Sat-11 pm. Closed: 12/25. **Address:** 4310 Sharon Rd, Suite W01 **Location:** I-77, exit 5 (Tyvola Rd), 3.6 mi e on Tyvola/Fairview rds, then 0.4 mi n; in The Village; adjacent to South Park Mall. **Parking:** on-site. **Cards:** AX, DC, DS, MC, VI.

MAHARANI — **Phone:** 704/370-2455 (11)

Indian
$7-$16

Guests are invited to enjoy well-prepared, authentic dishes spiced to the requested level, including chicken, lamb and seafood specialties, as well as vegetarian selections. Staff are knowledgeable about menu preparations and attentive to the guest. Casual and relaxed dining combines with prepared-to-order cuisine for a pleasurable experience. A lunch buffet is offered daily. Casual dress. **Bar:** Beer & wine. **Hours:** 11:30 am-2:30 & 5-10 pm, Fri-11 pm, Sat noon-3 & 5-11 pm, Sun noon-3 & 5-10 pm. **Address:** 901 S Kings Dr, Suite 115 **Location:** I-277, exit 2A, just s on Kenilworth Ave, just e on Baxter St, then 0.9 mi s; in King's Court Plaza. **Parking:** on-site. **Cards:** AX, DS, MC, VI.

(See map and index starting on p. 628)

MAMA RICOTTA'S — **Phone:** 704/343-0148 (10)

Italian
$6-$18

The restaurant offers the same gourmet-style, progressive regional Italian fare and professional, efficient service in its newly renovated and decoratively lit dining room. The atmosphere is upbeat and bustling. Complimentary garlic rolls with red pepper and garlic-spiked olive oil are great, and the mozzarella is fresh and homemade. Try one of the favorites: penne ala vodka or Tuscan-style grilled Angus ribeye. Casual dress. **Bar:** Full bar. **Reservations:** accepted. **Hours:** 11 am-10 pm, Sat-11 pm, Sun 10 am-9 pm. Closed: 1/1, 11/26, 12/24, 12/25. **Address:** 601 S Kings Dr **Location:** Jct Morehead St, just n; in King's Pointe Shopping Center. **Parking:** on-site. **Cards:** AX, DC, DS, MC, VI.

MICKEY & MOOCH, THE OTHER JOINT — **Phone:** 704/752-8080 (35)

Continental
$11-$37

The dining rooms have a contemporary styling, accented by lighted interior stained-glass window effects, painted and finished woods and high painted murals around the bar. Playing in the background is the music of Frank Sinatra or other tunes of the era. Fresh, high-quality ingredients abound in preparations of steak, chops, seafood, pasta, chicken and ribs. Sushi also appears on the menu. Dressy casual. **Bar:** Full bar. **Reservations:** accepted. **Hours:** 5 pm-10 pm, Fri-11 pm, Sat 4:30 pm-11 pm. Closed: 11/26, 12/24, 12/25; also Super Bowl Sun. **Address:** 8128 Providence Rd, Suite 1200 **Location:** I-485, exit 57, 2.6 mi n; in Arboretum Shopping Center, on southwest side. **Parking:** on-site. **Cards:** AX, MC, VI.

CALL

THE MIDDLE EAST DELI — **Phone:** 704/536-9847 (15)

Middle Eastern
$4-$10

The quick-serve delicatessen offers a wide array of selections including gyro sandwich platters and falafel platters, which are served with traditional Middle Eastern sides of tabbouleh or chickpea dip. An a la carte menu is also available. The pistachio dessert is a must-have. Casual dress. **Hours:** 10 am-8 pm, Sun-6 pm. Closed: 12/25. **Address:** 4508 Independence Blvd **Location:** 4 mi e on US 74, jct Sharon Amity Rd; in Bascom's Corner Shopping Center. **Parking:** on-site. **Cards:** DS, MC, VI.

MIRO SPANISH GRILLE — **Phone:** 704/540-7374 (39)

Spanish
$7-$20

Flavorful Spanish cuisine makes up the menu at the popular bistro. Tapas, chicken, steaks and seafood dishes share menu space with vegetarian and traditional paella, carne asada, salmon a la plancha and grilled seasoned pork tenderloin. The patio allows for al fresco dining. Casual dress. **Bar:** Full bar. **Reservations:** accepted. **Hours:** 11:30 am-2 & 5-10 pm, Fri-11 pm, Sat 5 pm-11 pm, Sun 5 pm-10 pm. Closed: 11/26, 12/25. **Address:** 7804-A Rea Rd **Location:** I-485, exit 59, just s; in Stonecrest at Piper Glen Shopping Center. **Parking:** on-site. **Cards:** AX, DS, MC, VI.

MURPHY'S FOOD & SPIRITS — **Phone:** 704/527-8002 (18)

American
$7-$20

A great place to catch live music, enjoy karaoke performances or watch the big game. Murphy's serves typical pub fare like burgers, sandwiches and hearty fare like babyback ribs, fish and chips, and corned beef and cabbage. Casual dress. **Bar:** Full bar. **Hours:** 11 am-2 am, Sat from noon, Sun noon-midnight. Closed: 12/25. **Address:** 131 E Woodlawn Rd **Location:** I-77, exit 6A, just e. **Parking:** on-site. **Cards:** AX, DS, MC, VI.

NEW SOUTH KITCHEN & BAR — **Phone:** 704/541-9990 (36)

American
$10-$19

The chef/owner excels in preparing innovative upscale Southern cuisine. His imaginative flavor and ingredient combinations fascinate the taste buds. The expansive menu lists both large and small plates and places an emphasis on fresh Carolina seafood. Selections might include shrimp and grits, slow-roasted pork shoulder in bacon-mustard sauce and the signature meatloaf. Casual dress. **Bar:** Full bar. **Hours:** 5 pm-10 pm, Sun-9 pm. Closed major holidays. **Address:** 8140 Providence Rd, Suite 300 **Location:** I-485, exit 57, 3 mi n on SR 16; in Arboretum Shopping Center. **Parking:** on-site. **Cards:** AX, DS, MC, VI.

CALL

OCEANAIRE — **Phone:** 704/554-8811 (27)

Seafood
$10-$38

Fresh fish and shellfish are flown in daily from around the globe. The sleek, handsomely designed dining room has a raw bar and is tastefully appointed in an art deco/nautical theme. The menu notes the seafood available daily and the varied preparation styles, such as broiled, grilled and blackened. Dressy casual. **Bar:** Full bar. **Reservations:** suggested. **Hours:** 11:30 am-10 pm, Fri-11 pm, Sat 5 pm-11 pm. Closed: 11/26, 12/25; also Sun. **Address:** 4620 Piedmont Row Dr, Suite 110 **Location:** I-77, exit 5 (Tyvola Rd), 3.2 mi e on Tyvola/Fairview rds, then just n; in Piedmont Town Center. **Parking:** on-site and valet. **Cards:** AX, DS, MC, VI.

CALL

P.F. CHANG'S CHINA BISTRO — **Phone:** 704/552-6644 (31)

New Asian
$10-$21

Trendy, upscale decor provides a pleasant backdrop for New Age Chinese dining. Appetizers, soups and salads are a meal by themselves. Vegetarian plates and sides, noodles, meins, chicken and meat dishes are created from exotic, fresh ingredients. Casual dress. **Bar:** Full bar. **Reservations:** accepted. **Hours:** 11 am-11 pm, Fri & Sat-midnight. Closed: 11/26, 12/25. **Address:** 6809 Phillips Place Ct, Suite F **Location:** I-77, exit 5 (Tyvola Rd), 3.7 mi e on Tyvola/Fairview rds, then just s; in Phillips Plaza. **Parking:** on-site. **Cards:** AX, DC, DS, MC, VI.

CALL

PHO 98 AUTHENTIC VIETNAMESE RESTAURANT — **Phone:** 704/643-1243 (25)

Vietnamese
$6-$13

Tucked in a strip shopping center, the restaurant presents a menu of tasty food, including huge bowls of pho and other equally as good traditional dishes. Many vegetarian and other healthily prepared offerings are available. Casual dress. **Bar:** Beer & wine. **Hours:** 11 am-9 pm, Fri & Sat-10 pm. Closed major holidays. **Address:** 5937 South Blvd **Location:** I-77, exit 5 (Tyvola Rd), 1 mi e, then 0.6 mi s; in Food Lion Shopping Center. **Parking:** on-site. **Cards:** AX, DS, MC, VI.

(See map and index starting on p. 628)

PORTOFINO ITALIAN RESTAURANT **Phone:** 704/527-0702 (22)

Italian
$6-$20

The casual neighborhood restaurant's menu features a lengthy list of pasta dishes, as well as chicken, veal, seafood, pizza and submarine sandwiches. Guests select their pasta choice and pair it with one of more than a dozen sauces, including bolognese, clam sauce and Mediteraneo. Other classic dishes include veal Marsala, chicken parmigiana and shrimp scampi. Casual dress. **Bar:** Full bar. **Hours:** 11 am-10 pm, Fri & Sat-11 pm, Sun noon-10 pm. Closed: 4/12, 12/25. **Address:** 5126 Park Rd **Location:** I-77, exit 5 (Tyvola Rd), 2.7 mi e, then 0.5 mi n; in Park Selwyn Terrace Shopping Center. **Parking:** on-site. **Cards:** AX, MC, VI.

PRIMO TUSCAN GRILLE **Phone:** 704/334-3346 (13)

Italian
$18-$35

Classic Italian cuisine is created from fresh ingredients at this casual and cozy neighborhood bistro. Traditional penne primavera, linguine with clams and other pasta dishes share menu space with entrees such as stuffed chicken breast in Marsala cream sauce, veal francese, lobster ravioli and lamb osso buco. Casual dress. **Bar:** Full bar. **Reservations:** accepted. **Hours:** 5:30 pm-10 pm, Sat-11 pm. Closed: 4/12, 11/26, 12/25; also Sun & Mon. **Address:** 116 Middleton Dr **Location:** Jct Queens Rd, just n on Providence Rd (SR 16), then just e. **Parking:** on-site. **Cards:** AX, DS, MC, VI.

PROVIDENCE CAFE **Phone:** 704/376-2008 (14)

American
$7-$23

The dining room's distinctive contemporary-classic look mixes light colors with dark woods and upscale appointments. In addition to the regular menu of well-prepared and inventive meat and seafood selections, the chef creates an evening special menu. Staff competently perform their duties while accommodating the guest's pace and preferences in a casual and relaxed atmosphere. The chef skillfully blends common and not-so-common ingredients into tempting and appealing creations. Dressy casual. **Bar:** Full bar. **Hours:** 11 am-10 pm, Fri & Sat-11 pm, Sun 10 am-10 pm. Closed major holidays. **Address:** 110 Perrin Pl **Location:** Jct Queens and Providence rds, just n, then just e. **Parking:** on-site. **Cards:** AX, DC, MC, VI.

CALL

RAFFERTY'S RESTAURANT & BAR **Phone:** 704/643-0050

American
$6-$18

Hearty portions and friendly service are the hallmarks of this bustling, casual eatery. The menu includes steak, seafood, burgers, pasta and ribs. Casual dress. **Bar:** Full bar. **Reservations:** accepted. **Hours:** 11 am-10 pm, Fri & Sat-11 pm. Closed: 11/26, 12/25. **Address:** 9501 South Blvd **Location:** I-485, exit 65A, just n. **Parking:** on-site. **Cards:** AX, DC, DS, MC, VI.

RESTAURANT J BASUL NOBLE **Phone:** 704/367-9463 (29)

New Italian
$8-$38

French-Mediterranean seafood and meat favorites are grilled California-style in an open, oak-hickory wood-fired oven, adding just the right flavoring. Dressy casual. **Bar:** Full bar. **Reservations:** suggested. **Hours:** 11:30 am-2:30 & 6-10 pm, Fri-11 pm, Sat 6 pm-11 pm. Closed major holidays; also Sun. **Address:** 6801 Morrison Blvd **Location:** I-77, exit 5 (Tyvola Rd), 3.6 mi e on Tyvola/Fairview rds, just n on Sharon Rd, then just e. **Parking:** on-site and valet. **Cards:** AX, DC, DS, MC, VI.

SOLE' SPANISH GRILLE **Phone:** 704/343-9890 (12)

Spanish
$8-$24

Pleasant and accommodating staff serve a variety of vibrantly flavored Spanish and Mediterranean beef, pork and seafood entrees in an intimate, subdued setting. Dressy casual. **Bar:** Full bar. **Reservations:** accepted. **Hours:** 5 pm-10 pm, Fri-11 pm. Closed: 1/1, 12/25; also Super Bowl Sun. **Address:** 1608 East Blvd **Location:** I-77, exit 7 (Clanton Rd), 0.5 mi e on Clanton Rd, 1.5 mi n on South Blvd, then 2 mi e. **Parking:** on-site. **Cards:** AX, DS, MC, VI.

CALL

SONNY'S REAL PIT BAR-B-Q **Phone:** 704/554-7550

Barbecue
$6-$15

House specialties include pork and chicken grilled over an open pit, barbecue ribs and fresh, homemade pie. The salad bar offers another popular option. Rustic and comfortable, the atmosphere is perfect for family meals. Casual dress. **Bar:** Beer only. **Hours:** 11 am-9:30 pm, Fri & Sat-10 pm. Closed: 11/26, 12/25. **Address:** 9500 South Blvd **Location:** I-485, exit 65A, n on US 521 (South Blvd). **Parking:** on-site. **Cards:** AX, DS, MC, VI.

SONNY'S REAL PIT BAR-B-Q **Phone:** 704/333-3792

Barbecue
$6-$15

House specialties include pork and chicken grilled over an open pit, barbecue ribs and fresh, homemade pie. The salad bar offers another popular option. Rustic and comfortable, the atmosphere is perfect for family meals. Casual dress. **Bar:** Beer only. **Hours:** 11 am-9:30 pm, Fri & Sat-10 pm. Closed: 11/26, 12/25. **Address:** 4301 Monroe Rd **Location:** From N Wendover Rd, just e. **Parking:** on-site. **Cards:** AX, DS, MC, VI.

SONNY'S REAL PIT BAR-B-Q **Phone:** 704/523-1053

Barbecue
$6-$15

House specialties include pork and chicken grilled over an open pit, barbecue ribs and fresh, homemade pie. The salad bar offers another popular option. Rustic and comfortable, the atmosphere is perfect for family meals. Casual dress. **Bar:** Beer only. **Hours:** 11 am-9:30 pm, Fri & Sat-10 pm. Closed: 11/26, 12/25. **Address:** 440 Tyvola Rd **Location:** I-77, exit 5 (Tyvola Rd), just e. **Parking:** on-site. **Cards:** AX, DS, MC, VI.

(See map and index starting on p. 628)

TABLE RESTAURANT & BAR **Phone:** 704/369-5170 (42)

American
$20-$40

You will be in awe as you enter the glamorous, dramatic dining room where one of the main focal points is the enormous marble-topped table where the chef uses fresh ingredients to uniquely prepare small tasting courses from the seasonal menu. Menu selections might include grilled venison, spice-braised lamb shank and seared yellowfin tuna. Extensive cheese and wine menus also are available. Dressy casual. **Bar:** Full bar. **Reservations:** suggested. **Hours:** 5 pm-10 pm, Fri & Sat-11 pm. Closed: 1/1, 11/26, 12/24, 12/25; also Sun. **Address:** 14835 John J Delaney Dr, Suite 150 **Location:** I-485, exit 61 or 61B, just s on US 521; in Ballantyne Village. **Parking:** on-site. **Cards:** AX, DC, DS, MC, VI.

THAI HOUSE **Phone:** 704/717-8006 (6)

Thai
$6-$17

In the University area, the restaurant prepares traditional cuisine to guests' specified level of spiciness. Knowledgeable servers enhance the cozy atmosphere. Casual dress. **Bar:** Beer & wine. **Hours:** 11 am-2:45 & 5-10 pm, Fri-11 pm, Sat noon-11 pm, Sun noon-10 pm. Closed: 12/25. **Address:** 230 E W.T. Harris Blvd, B-9 **Location:** I-85, exit 45A (W. T. Harris Blvd), 0.7 mi e; in Promenade Place Shopping Center, downstairs. **Parking:** on-site. **Cards:** AX, DC, DS, MC, VI.

TRYON HOUSE **Phone:** 704/527-6545 (17)

American
$5-$14

A pleasant decor and rock 'n' roll oldies background music set the stage for relaxed, comfortable family dining. The menu lists seafood dishes, steaks and several Italian specialties as well as a large selection of sandwiches. Breakfast features all the usual favorites, like blueberry pancakes, bacon, eggs and waffles. Casual dress. **Bar:** Beer & wine. **Hours:** 6 am-10 pm. Closed: 7/4, 11/26, 12/25; also Sun. **Address:** 215 E Exmore St **Location:** I-77, exit 6A, 0.4 mi e on Woodlawn Rd, then just n on Old Pineville Rd; in Woodlawn Station Shopping Center. **Parking:** on-site. **Cards:** AX, DC, DS, MC, VI.

CALL

UPSTREAM **Phone:** 704/556-7730 (33)

Seafood
$7-$37

Patrons may have a hard time choosing from creatively prepared seafood dishes imported from around the world. Floating sculptures help create a peaceful atmosphere. Those who visit the upscale restaurant's champagne bar often favor the oysters. Dressy casual. **Bar:** Full bar. **Reservations:** suggested. **Hours:** 11:30 am-3 & 5:30-10 pm, Fri & Sat-11 pm, Sun 10:30 am-2 & 5:30-10 pm. Closed: 12/25. **Address:** 6902 Phillips Place Ct **Location:** I-77, exit 5 (Tyvola Rd), 3.7 mi e on Tyvola/Fairview rds, then just s; in Phillips Plaza. **Parking:** on-site and valet. **Cards:** AX, DC, DS, MC, VI.

CALL

VILLA ANTONIO FINE ITALIAN RISTORANTE **Phone:** 704/523-1594 (19)

Italian
$6-$35

Diners can savor the freshness of delicious osso buco or veal chops at an upscale Italian bistro characterized by a quiet, intimate atmosphere. This is a lovely place to enjoy a wide variety of food freshly prepared by a professional staff. A guitarist performs on Friday and Saturday evenings. Dressy casual. **Bar:** Full bar. **Reservations:** suggested. **Hours:** 11 am-11 pm, Fri-2 am, Sat 5 pm-2 am, Sun 5 pm-11 pm. **Address:** 4707 South Blvd **Location:** I-77, exit 6A, 0.8 mi e on Woodlawn Rd, then just s. **Parking:** on-site. **Cards:** AX, DC, DS, MC, VI.

ZAPATA'S MEXICAN RESTAURANT **Phone:** 704/752-6869 (43)

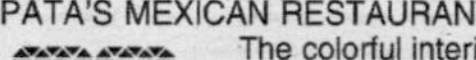

Mexican
$6-$13

The colorful interior of the popular, festive eatery replicates an outdoor dining area. Fresh ingredients go into the traditional Mexican fare and plates come from the kitchen piping hot and heaping full. Enjoy such favorites as tortilla soup, enchiladas and carne asada. Casual dress. **Bar:** Full bar. **Hours:** 11 am-10:30 pm. Closed: 11/26, 12/25. **Address:** 15105 John J Delaney Dr **Location:** I-485, exit 61 or 61B, 1 mi s on US 521; in Ballantyne Commons East Shopping Center. **Parking:** on-site. **Cards:** AX, DS, MC, VI.

ZEBRA RESTAURANT AND FINE CATERING *Menu on AAA.com* **Phone:** 704/442-9525 (30)

French
$8-$39

Patrons should allow the chef/owner to wow them with his creations at the popular Southpark restaurant. Worldly influences, techniques and ingredients lend flavor to dishes of contemporary French cuisine. The dining room incorporates stylish black and white decor. The wine list is extensive. Grand tastings are offered nightly. Dressy casual. **Bar:** Full bar. **Reservations:** suggested. **Hours:** 7:30-10 am, 11:30-2 & 6-10 pm, Sat from 6 pm. Closed major holidays; also Sun. **Address:** 4521 Sharon Rd **Location:** I-77, exit 5 (Tyvola Rd), 3.6 mi e on Tyvola/Fairview rds, just n; in Wall Street Capitol Building, first floor. **Parking:** on-site. **Cards:** AX, CB, DS, MC, VI.

The Charlotte Vicinity

CONCORD pop. 27,300 (See map and index starting on p. 628)

WHERE TO STAY

AMERICAS BEST VALUE INN Book great rates at AAA.com **Phone:** (704)788-8550

AAA SAVE

Motel
$135 All Year

Address: 2451 Kannapolis Hwy **Location:** I-85, exit 58, just s on US 29, then just w. **Facility:** 32 one-bedroom standard units. 2 stories (no elevator), exterior corridors. **Parking:** on-site. **Terms:** 3 day cancellation notice-fee imposed. **Guest Services:** wireless Internet. **Cards:** AX, DC, DS, JC, MC, VI.

/ SOME UNITS FEE

COMFORT SUITES-CONCORD MILLS Book at AAA.com **Phone:** (704)979-3800 84

Hotel
$110-$345 All Year

Address: 7800 Gateway Ln NW **Location:** I-85, exit 49, just e, just n on Weddington Rd, then just w. Located across from Concord Mills Mall. **Facility:** Smoke free premises. 84 units. 45 one-bedroom standard units. 39 one-bedroom suites with efficiencies (no utensils). 5 stories, interior corridors. *Bath:* combo or shower only. **Parking:** on-site. **Amenities:** dual phone lines, voice mail, irons, hair dryers. **Pool(s):** heated indoor. **Leisure Activities:** exercise room. **Guest Services:** valet and coin laundry, wireless Internet. **Business Services:** meeting rooms, business center. **Cards:** AX, CB, DC, DS, JC, MC, VI.

ASK

EMBASSY SUITES CHARLOTTE-CONCORD GOLF RESORT & SPA Book great rates at AAA.com **Phone:** (704)455-8200 88

AAA SAVE

Hotel
$129-$189 All Year

Address: 5400 John Q Hammons Dr **Location:** I-85, exit 49 (Speedway Blvd), 1 mi e, then just n. **Facility:** 308 units. 288 one- and 20 two-bedroom suites, some with whirlpools. 11 stories, interior corridors. *Bath:* combo or shower only. **Parking:** on-site. **Terms:** 2-3 night minimum stay - weekends, 3 day cancellation notice-fee imposed. **Amenities:** voice mail, safes, irons, hair dryers. *Fee:* video games, high-speed Internet. **Pool(s):** heated indoor. **Leisure Activities:** whirlpool, exercise room, spa. *Fee:* golf-18 holes. **Guest Services:** valet and coin laundry, airport transportation-Concord Regional Airport, area transportation-Concord Mills Outlet Mall, wireless Internet. **Business Services:** conference facilities, business center. **Cards:** AX, DC, DS, MC, VI. **Free Special Amenities: full breakfast and newspaper.**

CALL / SOME UNITS

EMBASSY SUITES HOTELS
AAA Benefit:
Members save 5% or more everyday!

▼ See AAA listing p 661 ▼

(See map and index starting on p. 620)

GREAT WOLF LODGE CONCORDE

Phone: 704/549-8206

fyi

Hotel

Under construction, scheduled to open March 2009. **Address:** 10175 Weddington Rd **Location:** I-85, to Speedway Blvd. **Amenities:** 402 units, restaurant, coffeemakers, microwaves, refrigerators, pool. ***(See color ad p 660)***

HAMPTON INN Book great rates at AAA.com

Phone: (704)793-9700

Hotel

$99-$175 All Year

Address: 612 Dickens Pl NE **Location:** I-85, exit 60, just e, then just s. **Facility:** 101 one-bedroom standard units, some with whirlpools. 5 stories, interior corridors. *Bath:* combo or shower only. **Parking:** on-site. **Terms:** cancellation fee imposed. **Amenities:** video games (fee), voice mail, irons, hair dryers. **Pool(s):** outdoor. **Leisure Activities:** exercise room. **Guest Services:** complimentary and valet laundry, wireless Internet. **Business Services:** meeting rooms, business center. **Cards:** AX, DS, MC, VI.

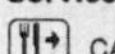 CALL   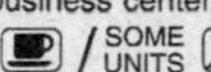 / SOME UNITS  

AAA Benefit:

Members save up to 10% everyday!

HAMPTON INN & SUITES-SPEEDWAY BLVD/ CONCORD MILLS Book great rates at AAA.com

Phone: (704)979-5600 87

Hotel

$115-$290 All Year

Address: 9850 Weddington Rd **Location:** I-85, exit 49, just e, then just n. **Facility:** 125 units. 90 one-bedroom standard units, some with whirlpools. 35 one-bedroom suites with efficiencies, some with whirlpools. 6 stories, interior corridors. *Bath:* combo or shower only. **Parking:** on-site. **Terms:** 1-30 night minimum stay, cancellation fee imposed. **Amenities:** high-speed Internet, dual phone lines, voice mail, irons, hair dryers. *Some:* CD players. **Pool(s):** outdoor. **Leisure Activities:** whirlpool, exercise room. **Guest Services:** complimentary and valet laundry, area transportation, wireless Internet. **Business Services:** meeting rooms, business center. **Cards:** AX, CB, DC, DS, JC, MC, VI.

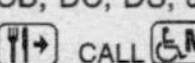   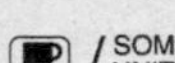 / SOME UNITS  

AAA Benefit:

Members save up to 10% everyday!

HOLIDAY INN EXPRESS HOTEL & SUITES-CHARLOTTE/CONCORD Book at AAA.com

Phone: (704)979-7900 86

Hotel

$109-$316 All Year

Address: 7772 Gateway Ln NW **Location:** I-85, exit 49, just e, just n on Weddington Rd, then just w. **Facility:** 79 one-bedroom standard units, some with efficiencies and/or whirlpools. 4 stories, interior corridors. *Bath:* combo or shower only. **Parking:** on-site. **Amenities:** high-speed Internet, dual phone lines, voice mail, irons, hair dryers. **Pool(s):** outdoor. **Leisure Activities:** sauna, whirlpool, exercise room. **Guest Services:** valet and coin laundry, wireless Internet. **Business Services:** meeting rooms, business center. **Cards:** AX, CB, DC, DS, JC, MC, VI.

ASK CALL  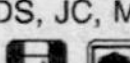 / SOME UNITS

SLEEP INN Book at AAA.com

Phone: (704)788-2150

Hotel

$70-$230 All Year

Address: 1120 Copperfield Blvd **Location:** I-85, exit 60, just e. **Facility:** 82 one-bedroom standard units. 3 stories, interior corridors. *Bath:* combo or shower only. **Parking:** on-site. **Terms:** cancellation fee imposed. **Amenities:** voice mail, irons, hair dryers. **Pool(s):** heated indoor. **Leisure Activities:** limited exercise equipment. **Guest Services:** wireless Internet. **Business Services:** PC. **Cards:** AX, DS, MC, VI.

ASK CALL / SOME UNITS FEE

SPRINGHILL SUITES-CHARLOTTE CONCORD MILLS Book great rates at AAA.com

Phone: (704)979-2500 85

Hotel

$138-$148 All Year

Address: 7811 Gateway Ln NW **Location:** I-85, exit 49, just e, just n on Weddington Rd, then just w. **Facility:** Smoke free premises. 95 one-bedroom standard units. 5 stories, interior corridors. *Bath:* combo or shower only. **Parking:** on-site. **Terms:** cancellation fee imposed. **Amenities:** high-speed Internet, dual phone lines, voice mail, irons, hair dryers. **Pool(s):** heated indoor. **Leisure Activities:** whirlpool, limited exercise equipment. **Guest Services:** valet and coin laundry, wireless Internet. **Business Services:** meeting rooms, business center. **Cards:** AX, CB, DC, DS, MC, VI.

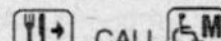     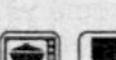

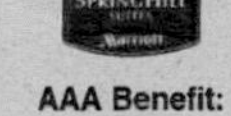

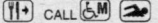

AAA Benefit:

Members save a minimum 5% off the best available rate.

(See map and index starting on p. 628)

WINGATE BY WYNDHAM *Book at AAA.com* **Phone:** (704)979-1300 83

Hotel
$117-$129 All Year

Address: 7841 Gateway Ln NW **Location:** I-85, exit 49, just e, just n on Weddington Rd, then just w. **Facility:** 93 one-bedroom standard units, some with whirlpools. 4 stories, interior corridors. *Bath:* combo or shower only. **Parking:** on-site. **Terms:** 7 day cancellation notice. **Amenities:** video games (fee), high-speed Internet, dual phone lines, voice mail, safes, irons, hair dryers. **Pool(s):** outdoor. **Leisure Activities:** whirlpool, exercise room. **Guest Services:** complimentary and valet laundry, wireless Internet. **Business Services:** meeting rooms, business center. **Cards:** AX, DC, DS, MC, VI.

ASK CALL / SOME UNITS

WHERE TO DINE

COSTELLO'S PIZZA & PASTA **Phone:** 704/784-2328

Italian
$5-$15

The colorful cafe's menu lists Chicago-style stuffed pizza and such Italian entrees as shrimp scampi, scallops Romano, chicken parmigiana and sausage and peppers, as well as a fish of the day. Casual dress. **Bar:** Full bar. **Reservations:** accepted. **Hours:** 11 am-10 pm, Fri & Sat-11 pm. Closed: 11/26, 12/25. **Address:** 970-180 Branchview Dr NE **Location:** I-85, exit 60, 1.5 mi e on Copperfield Blvd, then just s on SR 3; in North Branch Center. **Parking:** on-site. **Cards:** AX, MC, VI.

SONNY'S REAL PIT BAR-B-Q **Phone:** 704/979-0073

Barbecue
$6-$15

House specialties include pork and chicken grilled over an open pit, barbecue ribs and fresh, homemade pie. The salad bar offers another popular option. Rustic and comfortable, the atmosphere is perfect for family meals. Casual dress. **Bar:** Beer only. **Hours:** 11 am-9:30 pm, Fri & Sat-10 pm. Closed: 11/26, 12/25. **Address:** 7820 Lyles Ln **Location:** I-85, exit 49, just e on Speedway Blvd, just s to Fireball Roberts Rd, then just n. **Parking:** on-site. **Cards:** AX, DS, MC, VI.

TSUNAMI JAPANESE STEAKHOUSE & SUSHI BAR **Phone:** 704/979-3400 46

Japanese
$7-$32

In a shopping center, the restaurant serves Japanese cuisine in a cozy setting. A sushi bar occupies one room, while in another the chef entertains patrons while he prepares and cooks meals tableside. Casual dress. **Bar:** Full bar. **Hours:** 11:30 am-2 & 4:30-10 pm, Fri & Sat-10:30 pm, Sun-9:30 pm. Closed: 11/26, 12/25. **Address:** 10025 Weddington Rd **Location:** I-85, exit 49, just e; in Shoppes at King's Grant. **Parking:** on-site. **Cards:** AX, DS, MC, VI.

CALL

CORNELIUS pop. 11,969

WHERE TO STAY

CLARION INN - LAKE NORMAN *Book great rates at AAA.com* **Phone:** (704)896-0660

AAA SAVE

Hotel
$95-$150 4/1-11/30
$80-$130 12/1-3/31

Address: 19608 Liverpool Pkwy **Location:** I-77, exit 28, just w, then s. **Facility:** 80 units. 70 one- and 1 two-bedroom standard units, some with whirlpools. 9 one-bedroom suites, some with whirlpools. 4 stories, interior corridors. **Parking:** on-site. **Terms:** check-in 4 pm. **Amenities:** high-speed Internet, voice mail, irons, hair dryers. **Pool(s):** outdoor. **Leisure Activities:** whirlpool, exercise room. **Guest Services:** valet laundry, wireless Internet. **Business Services:** meeting rooms, PC. **Cards:** AX, DC, DS, JC, MC, VI. **Free Special Amenities: expanded continental breakfast and high-speed Internet.**

/ SOME UNITS FEE

COMFORT INN & SUITES *Book great rates at AAA.com* **Phone:** (704)896-7622

AAA SAVE

Hotel
$95-$259 3/1-11/30
$90-$130 12/1-2/28

Address: 19521 Liverpool Pkwy **Location:** I-77, exit 28, just w, then s. **Facility:** 65 one-bedroom standard units, some with whirlpools. 4 stories, interior corridors. *Bath:* combo or shower only. **Parking:** on-site. **Terms:** cancellation fee imposed. **Amenities:** voice mail, irons, hair dryers. **Pool(s):** outdoor. **Leisure Activities:** whirlpool, limited exercise equipment. **Guest Services:** valet and coin laundry, wireless Internet. **Business Services:** meeting rooms, business center. **Cards:** AX, DC, DS, MC, VI. **Free Special Amenities: continental breakfast and high-speed Internet.**

/ SOME UNITS FEE VCR

DAYS INN-LAKE NORMAN *Book at AAA.com* **Phone:** (704)892-9120

Hotel
$65-$139 All Year

Address: 19901 Holiday Ln **Location:** I-77, exit 28, just e, then just n. **Facility:** 116 one-bedroom standard units. 2 stories (no elevator), exterior corridors. **Parking:** on-site. **Amenities:** voice mail, irons, hair dryers. **Pool(s):** outdoor. **Leisure Activities:** limited exercise equipment. **Guest Services:** valet and coin laundry, wireless Internet. **Business Services:** meeting rooms, business center. **Cards:** AX, CB, DC, DS, MC, VI.

ASK CALL / SOME UNITS FEE

ECONO LODGE LAKE NORMAN *Book at AAA.com* **Phone:** (704)892-3500

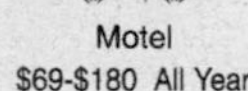

Motel
$69-$180 All Year

Address: 20740 Torrence Chapel Rd **Location:** I-77, exit 28, just w, then just n. **Facility:** 90 units. 84 one-bedroom standard units, some with whirlpools. 6 one-bedroom suites with whirlpools. 2-3 stories, exterior corridors. **Parking:** on-site. **Terms:** cancellation fee imposed. **Amenities:** hair dryers. **Pool(s):** outdoor. **Guest Services:** coin laundry, wireless Internet. **Business Services:** meeting rooms. **Cards:** AX, DC, DS, MC, VI.

ASK / SOME UNITS FEE

HAMPTON INN LAKE NORMAN *Book great rates at AAA.com* **Phone:** (704)892-9900

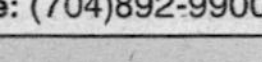

Hotel
$114-$124 All Year

Address: 19501 Statesville Rd **Location:** I-77, exit 28, just e, then just s. **Facility:** 116 one-bedroom standard units. 5 stories, interior corridors. **Parking:** on-site. **Amenities:** high-speed Internet, voice mail, irons, hair dryers. **Pool(s):** outdoor. **Leisure Activities:** exercise room. **Guest Services:** valet laundry, wireless Internet. **Business Services:** meeting rooms, business center. **Cards:** AX, CB, DC, DS, JC, MC, VI.

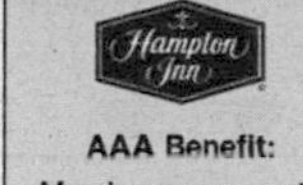

AAA Benefit:
Members save up to 10% everyday!

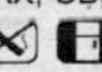

/ SOME UNITS

WHERE TO DINE

131 MAIN RESTAURANT **Phone:** 704/896-0131

American
$7-$28

This casually upscale eatery prides itself on its service and the fresh ingredients that go into every made-from-scratch dish. On the menu are salads, sandwiches, steak and seafood, as well as tasty fare such as baby back ribs and herb-roasted chicken. Casual dress. **Bar:** Full bar. **Reservations:** accepted. **Hours:** 11 am-9:30 pm, Fri & Sat-10:30 pm. Closed: 11/26, 12/25. **Address:** 17830 Statesville Rd **Location:** I-77, exit 28, just e, then 1.7 mi s on US 21; in Village at Oakhurst. **Parking:** on-site. **Cards:** AX, MC, VI.

CALL

ACROPOLIS CAFE & GRILL **Phone:** 704/894-0191

Greek
$6-$15

In addition to daily specials, the menu at this casual eatery features steak, lamb, pizza and pasta dishes, as well as Greek specialties like pastitsio, a Greek-style lasagna, or moussaka. Casual dress. **Bar:** Full bar. **Hours:** 7 am-10 pm, Fri-11 pm, Sat 8 am-11 pm, Sun 8 am-10 pm. Closed: 11/26, 12/25. **Address:** 20659 Catawba Ave **Location:** I-77, exit 28, just e, then just n. **Parking:** on-site. **Cards:** AX, DC, DS, MC, VI.

DAVIDSON pop. 7,139

WHERE TO STAY

DAVIDSON VILLAGE INN **Phone:** 704/892-8044

Bed & Breakfast
$125-$195 All Year

Address: 117 Depot St **Location:** I-77, exit 30, 1 mi e, just s on Main St (SR 115), then just w. **Facility:** Common areas at this homey inn set in a historic district include a large private library; most guest rooms feature four-poster beds. Smoke free premises. 18 one-bedroom standard units. 3 stories, interior corridors. **Parking:** on-site. **Terms:** office hours 7 am-11 pm, 3 day cancellation notice-fee imposed. **Amenities:** high-speed Internet, dual phone lines, irons, hair dryers. *Some:* DVD players. **Guest Services:** valet laundry, wireless Internet. **Business Services:** meeting rooms, PC. **Cards:** AX, DC, DS, MC, VI.

ASK CALL FEE / SOME UNITS

WHERE TO DINE

THE SODA SHOP **Phone:** 704/896-7743

American
$3-$7

The sidewalk soda fountain opened its doors in 1951 and a "yesteryear" feeling permeates the tiny cafe. It's often packed at lunchtime as locals flock in for soups, sandwiches, wraps, quesadillas and, of course, the ice cream! A thick, old-fashioned milk shake is a treat. Casual dress. **Bar:** Beer & wine. **Hours:** 8 am-8 pm, Fri-9 pm. Closed major holidays. **Address:** 104 S Main St **Location:** I-77, exit 30, 1 mi e, then s on Main St (SR 115) to town center shops. **Parking:** street.

HUNTERSVILLE pop. 24,940 (See map and index starting on p. 628)

WHERE TO STAY

CANDLEWOOD SUITES *Book at AAA.com* **Phone:** (704)895-3434

Hotel
$110-$170 All Year

Address: 16530 Northcross Dr **Location:** I-77, exit 25, just w on SR 73, then just s. **Facility:** 75 units. 60 one-bedroom standard units with efficiencies. 15 one-bedroom suites with efficiencies. 3 stories, interior corridors. *Bath:* combo or shower only. **Parking:** on-site. **Amenities:** video library, DVD players, CD players, high-speed Internet, dual phone lines, voice mail, irons, hair dryers. **Leisure Activities:** exercise room. **Guest Services:** complimentary and valet laundry, wireless Internet. **Cards:** AX, CB, DC, MC, VI.

ASK / SOME UNITS FEE

COUNTRY SUITES BY CARLSON-LAKE NORMAN *Book at AAA.com* **Phone:** (704)895-6565

Hotel
$119-$209 All Year

Address: 16617 Statesville Rd **Location:** I-77, exit 25, just e on SR 73, then just s on US 21. **Facility:** Smoke free premises. 87 units. 14 one-bedroom standard units, some with whirlpools. 73 one-bedroom suites. 5 stories, interior corridors. *Bath:* combo or shower only. **Parking:** on-site. **Amenities:** high-speed Internet, dual phone lines, voice mail, safes, irons, hair dryers. **Pool(s):** heated indoor. **Leisure Activities:** whirlpool, exercise room. **Guest Services:** valet and coin laundry, wireless Internet. **Business Services:** meeting rooms, business center. **Cards:** AX, CB, DC, DS, JC, MC, VI.

(See map and index starting on p. 628)

COURTYARD BY MARRIOTT-CHARLOTTE/LAKE NORMAN *Book great rates at AAA.com* **Phone:** (704)949-4900

Hotel
$168-$180 All Year

Address: 16700 Northcross Dr **Location:** I-77, exit 25, just w on SR 73, then just s. **Facility:** Smoke free premises. 90 units. 87 one-bedroom standard units, some with whirlpools. 3 one-bedroom suites. 3 stories, interior corridors. *Bath:* combo or shower only. **Parking:** on-site. **Terms:** cancellation fee imposed. **Amenities:** high-speed Internet, dual phone lines, voice mail, irons, hair dryers. **Pool(s):** heated indoor. **Leisure Activities:** whirlpool, exercise room. **Guest Services:** valet and coin laundry, wireless Internet. **Business Services:** meeting rooms, business center. **Cards:** AX, CB, DC, DS, JC, MC, VI.

CALL / SOME UNITS

AAA Benefit:
Members save a minimum 5% off the best available rate.

HAWTHORN SUITES LTD *Book at AAA.com* **Phone:** (704)892-9487

Hotel
$109-$159 All Year

Address: 16905 Caldwell Creek Dr **Location:** I-77, exit 25, just e on SR 73, just n on US 21, then just w. **Facility:** 91 one-bedroom standard units, some with efficiencies. 5 stories, interior corridors. *Bath:* combo or shower only. **Parking:** on-site. **Terms:** cancellation fee imposed. **Amenities:** dual phone lines, voice mail, irons, hair dryers. **Pool(s):** outdoor. **Leisure Activities:** limited exercise equipment. **Guest Services:** valet and coin laundry, wireless Internet. **Business Services:** meeting rooms. **Cards:** AX, DC, DS, MC, VI.

ASK VCR / SOME UNITS

HOLIDAY INN EXPRESS *Book at AAA.com* **Phone:** (704)875-1165 (80)

Hotel
$88-$180 All Year

Address: 14135 Statesville Rd **Location:** I-77, exit 23, just e, then just s. **Facility:** 60 one-bedroom standard units, some with whirlpools. 2 stories (no elevator), exterior corridors. *Bath:* combo or shower only. **Parking:** on-site. **Amenities:** high-speed Internet, dual phone lines, voice mail, irons, hair dryers. **Pool(s):** outdoor. **Leisure Activities:** limited exercise equipment. **Guest Services:** valet laundry, wireless Internet. **Cards:** AX, CB, DC, DS, JC, MC, VI.

CALL / SOME UNITS

QUALITY INN *Book at AAA.com* **Phone:** (704)892-6597

Hotel
$60-$169 All Year

Address: 16825 Caldwell Creek Dr **Location:** I-77, exit 25, just e on SR 73, just n on US 21, then just w. **Facility:** 66 one-bedroom standard units. 3 stories, interior/exterior corridors. *Bath:* combo or shower only. **Parking:** on-site. **Terms:** 14 day cancellation notice-fee imposed. **Amenities:** voice mail, irons, hair dryers. **Guest Services:** coin laundry, wireless Internet. **Cards:** AX, DC, DS, MC, VI.

ASK / SOME UNITS FEE

RESIDENCE INN BY MARRIOTT-LAKE NORMAN *Book great rates at AAA.com* **Phone:** (704)584-0000

Hotel
$217-$233 All Year

Address: 16830 Kenton Dr **Location:** I-77, exit 25, 1 mi w on SR 73, then just n. **Facility:** Smoke free premises. 78 units. 33 one-bedroom standard units with kitchens. 27 one- and 18 two-bedroom suites with kitchens. 3 stories, interior corridors. *Bath:* combo or shower only. **Parking:** on-site. **Terms:** cancellation fee imposed. **Amenities:** video games (fee), high-speed Internet, dual phone lines, voice mail, irons, hair dryers. **Pool(s):** outdoor. **Leisure Activities:** whirlpool, limited exercise equipment, sports court. **Guest Services:** valet and coin laundry, wireless Internet. **Business Services:** meeting rooms, PC. **Cards:** AX, DS, MC, VI.

CALL / SOME UNITS FEE

AAA Benefit:
Members save a minimum 5% off the best available rate.

SLEEP INN *Book at AAA.com* **Phone:** (704)766-2500

Hotel
$101-$111 All Year

Address: 16508 Northcross Dr **Location:** I-77, exit 25, just w on SR 73, then just s. **Facility:** 108 units. 100 one-bedroom standard units. 8 one-bedroom suites. 4 stories, interior corridors. *Bath:* combo or shower only. **Parking:** on-site. **Amenities:** high-speed Internet, voice mail, safes (fee), irons, hair dryers. **Leisure Activities:** exercise room. **Guest Services:** coin laundry, wireless Internet. **Business Services:** meeting rooms, PC. **Cards:** AX, CB, DC, DS, JC, MC, VI.

ASK / SOME UNITS

WHERE TO DINE

DRESSLER'S RESTAURANT **Phone:** 704/987-1779

American
$15-$29

Located in Birkdale Village, an upscale shopping complex, the bistro features well-prepared seafood, beef and chicken. House-made desserts, like the chocolate volcano cake or carrot cake with cream cheese frosting, wrap up the meal nicely. Dressy casual. **Bar:** Full bar. **Reservations:** accepted. **Hours:** 5 pm-10 pm, Sun-9 pm. Closed major holidays; also Super Bowl Sun. **Address:** 8630-1A Lindholm Dr **Location:** 0.6 mi w on Sam Furr Rd (SR 73), then just n on Birkdale Commons Dr; in Birkdale Village. **Parking:** on-site and valet. **Cards:** AX, DS, MC, VI.

HOUSE OF TAIPEI *Menu on AAA.com* **Phone:** 704/987-7997

Chinese
$5-$16

The a la carte menu includes traditional Chinese dishes and some chef's specialties, including honey-walnut shrimp or chicken, pepper steak and sweet-and-sour chicken. Vegetarians also have several options. Casual dress. **Bar:** Full bar. **Hours:** 11:30 am-3 & 5-10 pm, Sat noon-3 & 5:30-10 pm, Sun noon-3 & 5-9:30 pm. Closed: 7/4, 11/26, 12/25. **Address:** 16500 Northcross Dr **Location:** I-77, exit 25, just w on SR 73, then just s. **Parking:** on-site. **Cards:** AX, DS, MC, VI.

(See map and index starting on p. 628)

MICKEY & MOOCH

Phone: 704/895-6654

American
$12-$26

An old-fashioned revolving door and Sinatra crooning in the background will have you taking a trip down memory lane..right back to the '40s and '50s. Menu selections include homemade sauces, aged center-cut steaks, chops, fresh salads and delicious desserts. Casual dress. **Bar:** Full bar. **Reservations:** accepted. **Hours:** 5 pm-10 pm, Fri-11 pm, Sat 4:30 pm-11 pm, Sun 4:30 pm-9 pm. Closed: 11/26, 12/24, 12/25; also Super Bowl Sun. **Address:** 9723 Sam Furr Rd **Location:** I-77, exit 25, just e; in Northcross Shopping Center. **Parking:** on-site. **Cards:** AX, MC, VI.

RED ROCKS CAFE

Phone: 704/892-9999

American
$9-$25

Jazzy background music sets the scene for casually elegant dining with contemporary American cuisine. Steak, poultry, seafood and pasta populate the menu, and dishes are named for both the famous and not-so-famous. Dressy casual. **Bar:** Full bar. **Reservations:** accepted. **Hours:** 11 am-1 am, Thurs-Sat to 2 am, Sun-midnight. Closed: 12/25. **Address:** 8712 Lindholm Dr **Location:** I-77, exit 25, 0.4 mi w on SR 73, then just n; in Birkdale Village. **Parking:** on-site. **Cards:** AX, DC, MC, VI.

MATTHEWS pop. 22,127 (See map and index starting on p. 628)

WHERE TO STAY

COMFORT INN *Book great rates at AAA.com*

Phone: (704)845-5911 91

AAA SAVE

Hotel
$84-$195 All Year

Address: 9701 E Independence Blvd **Location:** I-485, exit 51A, 1.8 mi w on US 74, just n on Windsor Square Dr, then just w. **Facility:** 93 one-bedroom standard units, some with whirlpools. 3 stories, interior corridors. **Parking:** on-site. **Amenities:** irons, hair dryers. **Pool(s):** outdoor. **Leisure Activities:** exercise room. **Guest Services:** coin laundry, wireless Internet. **Business Services:** meeting rooms, business center. **Cards:** AX, DS, MC, VI. **Free Special Amenities: full breakfast and high-speed Internet.**

/ SOME UNITS

COUNTRY INN & SUITES-MATTHEWS *Book great rates at AAA.com*

Phone: (704)846-8000 95

AAA SAVE

Hotel
$99-$119 All Year

Address: 2001 Mount Harmony Church Rd **Location:** I-485, exit 51B, 0.5 mi e on US 74, just n on Independence Commerce Dr, then just w. **Facility:** 72 units. 54 one-bedroom standard units, some with whirlpools. 18 one-bedroom suites. 3 stories, interior corridors. *Bath:* combo or shower only. **Parking:** on-site. **Terms:** cancellation fee imposed. **Amenities:** high-speed Internet, dual phone lines, voice mail, safes, irons, hair dryers. **Pool(s):** heated indoor. **Leisure Activities:** limited exercise equipment. **Guest Services:** valet and coin laundry, wireless Internet. **Business Services:** meeting rooms, business center. **Cards:** AX, CB, DC, DS, JC, MC, VI. **Free Special Amenities: expanded continental breakfast and high-speed Internet.**

CALL / SOME UNITS FEE

COURTYARD BY MARRIOTT *Book great rates at AAA.com*

Phone: (704)846-4466 94

Hotel
$138-$148 All Year

Address: 11425 E Independence Blvd **Location:** I-485, exit 51A, just w on US 74. **Facility:** Smoke free premises. 121 units. 116 one-bedroom standard units, some with whirlpools. 5 one-bedroom suites. 3 stories, interior corridors. *Bath:* combo or shower only. **Parking:** on-site. **Terms:** cancellation fee imposed. **Amenities:** dual phone lines, voice mail, irons, hair dryers. **Pool(s):** outdoor. **Leisure Activities:** whirlpool, exercise room. **Guest Services:** valet and coin laundry, wireless Internet. **Business Services:** meeting rooms. **Cards:** AX, CB, DC, DS, JC, MC, VI.

CALL / SOME UNITS

COURTYARD Marriott

AAA Benefit:
Members save a minimum 5% off the best available rate.

HAMPTON INN-MATTHEWS *Book great rates at AAA.com*

Phone: (704)841-1155 92

Hotel
$104-$124 All Year

Address: 9615 Independence Point Pkwy **Location:** I-485, exit 51A, 2 mi w on US 74, then just s. **Facility:** 91 one-bedroom standard units, some with whirlpools. 5 stories, interior corridors. *Bath:* combo or shower only. **Parking:** on-site. **Terms:** 1-30 night minimum stay, cancellation fee imposed. **Amenities:** video games (fee), voice mail, irons, hair dryers. **Pool(s):** outdoor. **Leisure Activities:** exercise room. **Guest Services:** complimentary and valet laundry, wireless Internet. **Business Services:** meeting rooms, PC. **Cards:** AX, CB, DC, DS, MC, VI.

CALL / SOME UNITS

AAA Benefit:
Members save up to 10% everyday!

HOLIDAY INN EXPRESS HOTEL & SUITES *Book at AAA.com*

Phone: (704)821-9800 96

Hotel
$90-$150 All Year

Address: 13470 E Independence Blvd **Location:** I-485, exit 51B, 1 mi e on US 74. **Facility:** 118 one-bedroom standard units, some with whirlpools. 2-3 stories, interior/exterior corridors. *Bath:* combo or shower only. **Parking:** on-site. **Terms:** 5 day cancellation notice-fee imposed. **Amenities:** high-speed Internet, dual phone lines, voice mail, irons, hair dryers. **Pool(s):** outdoor. **Leisure Activities:** exercise room. **Guest Services:** valet and coin laundry, wireless Internet. **Business Services:** meeting rooms, business center. **Cards:** AX, DC, DS, MC, VI.

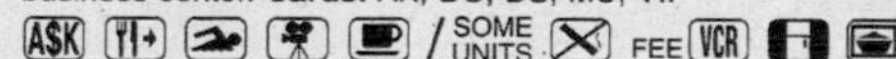

(See map and index starting on p. 628)

SLEEP INN Book at AAA.com Phone: (704)841-1660 93

Hotel
$69-$119 All Year

Address: 9900 Matthews Park Dr **Location:** I-485, exit 51A, 1.8 mi w on US 74, then just s. **Facility:** 79 one-bedroom standard units, some with whirlpools. 4 stories, interior corridors. *Bath:* combo or shower only. **Parking:** on-site. **Terms:** 3 day cancellation notice-fee imposed. **Amenities:** voice mail, safes (fee), irons, hair dryers. **Pool(s):** outdoor. **Guest Services:** coin laundry, wireless Internet. **Business Services:** meeting rooms, PC. **Cards:** AX, DC, DS, JC, MC, VI.

ASK CALL / SOME UNITS

WHERE TO DINE

BUFFET DYNASTY Phone: 704/844-8150 52

Chinese
$7-$15

Select from a variety of fresh, tasty Oriental selections served buffet-style at the popular restaurant. Casual dress. **Bar:** Beer & wine. **Hours:** 11:30 am-4 & 5-9 pm, Fri & Sat-10 pm. Closed: 11/26, 12/25. **Address:** 1709 Matthews Township Pkwy **Location:** Jct US 74, just s on SR 51. **Parking:** on-site. **Cards:** AX, MC, VI.

CALL

ELLIOT'S BBQ Phone: 704/847-6000 49

Barbecue
$6-$9

Service is straightforward at Elliot's: Place your order at the counter, and it's delivered with a smile. Smoked pork, beef brisket, chicken and baby back ribs come with your choice of baked beans, coleslaw or onion rings, to name a few options. Portions are huge and tasty—all the better to sample the variety of barbecue sauces clustered on each table. Casual dress. **Bar:** Beer only. **Hours:** 11 am-8 pm, Fri & Sat-9 pm, Sun-3 pm. Closed: 11/26, 12/25; also Mon. **Address:** 9949 E Independence Blvd **Location:** I-485, exit 51B, 1.6 mi w on US 74; in Windsor Square Shopping Center. **Parking:** on-site. **Cards:** AX, DS, MC, VI.

FONTANELLA ITALIANO RISTORANTE Phone: 704/844-0103 51

Italian
$5-$20

Traditional Italian favorites can be savored in a casually romantic setting. Pizza and pasta are the backbone of the menu, but other tasty dishes with chicken, veal and seafood also are available. Casual dress. **Bar:** Full bar. **Hours:** 11:30 am-10 pm, Fri & Sat-11:30 pm. Closed major holidays. **Address:** 10412 E Independence Blvd **Location:** I-485, exit 51A, 1.4 mi w on US 74. **Parking:** on-site. **Cards:** AX, DS, MC, VI.

HOPS RESTAURANT Phone: 704/844-8300

American
$6-$20

Specially brewed beers, brewmaster steaks and hot honey muffin croissants are a few of the mouthwatering choices at the casual restaurant. Casual dress. **Bar:** Full bar. **Hours:** 11 am-10:30 pm, Fri & Sat-11 pm. Closed: 11/26, 12/25. **Address:** 9950 E Independence Blvd **Location:** I-485, exit 51A, 1.6 mi w on US 74. **Parking:** on-site. **Cards:** AX, DC, DS, MC, VI.

SANTE Phone: 704/845-1899 53

American
$8-$28

Taking the spot light at this cozy downtown bistro are French-influenced American cuisines including osso bucco, slow-roasted duck breast and pan-seared veal. An extensive wine list is available. Dressy casual. **Bar:** Full bar. **Reservations:** accepted. **Hours:** 11 am-2 & 5-9 pm. Closed: 1/1, 11/26, 12/25; also Sun & Mon. **Address:** 165 N Trade St **Location:** I-485, exit 52, 1.2 mi w on John St, then just e. **Parking:** street. **Cards:** AX, MC, VI.

TOWNSHIP GRILLE Phone: 704/847-2480 50

American
$5-$13

Menu offerings at the casual eatery feature comfort foods like pot roast and a meatloaf sandwich as well as steak, chicken and pasta dishes and sandwiches and burgers. On cooler days, locals flock to Township Grille to gorge on their large selection of chili. Casual dress. **Bar:** Beer & wine. **Hours:** 11 am-10 pm, Fri & Sat-11 pm, Sun-9 pm. Closed: 4/12, 11/26, 12/25. **Address:** 10400 E Independence Blvd **Location:** I-485, exit 51A, 1.6 mi w on US 74; in Matthews Festival Shopping Center. **Parking:** on-site. **Cards:** AX, DS, MC, VI.

PINEVILLE pop. 3,449 (See map and index starting on p. 628)

WHERE TO STAY

BEST WESTERN CROWN SUITES Book great rates at AAA.com **Phone:** (704)540-8500 100

AAA SAVE

Hotel
$120-$140 All Year

Address: 9705 Leitner Dr **Location:** I-485, exit 64B, just s on SR 51, then w. **Facility:** 85 one-bedroom standard units. 5 stories, interior corridors. *Bath:* combo or shower only. **Parking:** on-site. **Terms:** 2 night minimum stay - seasonal and/or weekends. **Amenities:** high-speed Internet, dual phone lines, voice mail, irons, hair dryers. **Pool(s):** outdoor. **Leisure Activities:** exercise room. **Guest Services:** valet and coin laundry, wireless Internet. **Business Services:** meeting rooms, business center. **Cards:** AX, CB, DC, DS, MC, VI. **Free Special Amenities: expanded continental breakfast and high-speed Internet.**

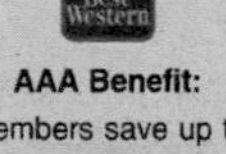

AAA Benefit:
Members save up to 20%, plus 10% bonus points with rewards program.

(See map and index starting on p. 628)

COMFORT SUITES — Book at AAA.com — **Phone:** (704)540-0069 (99)

Hotel
$109-$165 All Year

Address: 10415 Centrum Pkwy **Location:** I-485, exit 64B, just s on SR 51, then w. **Facility:** Smoke free premises. 116 units. 113 one-bedroom standard units. 3 one-bedroom suites with efficiencies and whirlpools. 5 stories, interior corridors. *Bath:* combo or shower only. **Parking:** on-site. **Terms:** cancellation fee imposed. **Amenities:** dual phone lines, voice mail, irons, hair dryers. **Pool(s):** outdoor. **Leisure Activities:** exercise room. **Guest Services:** valet and coin laundry, wireless Internet. **Business Services:** meeting rooms. **Cards:** AX, CB, DC, DS, JC, MC, VI.

ASK / SOME UNITS VCR

HAMPTON INN & SUITES-CHARLOTTE/PINEVILLE — Book great rates at AAA.com — **Phone:** (704)889-2700 (103)

Hotel
$116-$199 All Year

Address: 401 Towne Centre Blvd **Location:** I-485, exit 64B, 0.5 mi s on SR 51, then just e. **Facility:** 111 units. 79 one-bedroom standard units, some with whirlpools. 32 one-bedroom suites with efficiencies, some with whirlpools. 5 stories, interior corridors. *Bath:* combo or shower only. **Parking:** on-site. **Amenities:** video games (fee), voice mail, irons, hair dryers. *Some:* dual phone lines. **Pool(s):** outdoor. **Leisure Activities:** exercise room. **Guest Services:** complimentary and valet laundry, wireless Internet. **Business Services:** meeting rooms, business center. **Cards:** AX, CB, DC, DS, JC, MC, VI.

CALL / SOME UNITS

Hampton Inn & Suites
AAA Benefit:
Members save up to 10% everyday!

HILTON GARDEN INN-CHARLOTTE/PINEVILLE — Book great rates at AAA.com — **Phone:** (704)889-3279 (104)

Hotel
$95-$179 All Year

Address: 425 Towne Centre Blvd **Location:** I-485, exit 64B, 0.5 mi s on SR 51, then just e. **Facility:** 112 units. 108 one-bedroom standard units, some with whirlpools. 4 one-bedroom suites, some with whirlpools. 5 stories, interior corridors. *Bath:* combo or shower only. **Parking:** on-site. **Terms:** 1-30 night minimum stay, cancellation fee imposed. **Amenities:** video games (fee), high-speed Internet, dual phone lines, voice mail, irons, hair dryers. **Pool(s):** heated indoor/outdoor. **Leisure Activities:** whirlpool, exercise room. **Guest Services:** complimentary and valet laundry, wireless Internet. **Business Services:** meeting rooms, business center. **Cards:** AX, CB, DC, DS, JC, MC, VI.

CALL / SOME UNITS

Hilton Garden Inn
AAA Benefit:
Members save 5% or more everyday!

HOLIDAY INN EXPRESS — Book at AAA.com — **Phone:** (704)341-1190 (101)

Hotel
$99-$175 All Year

Address: 9825 Leitner Dr **Location:** I-485, exit 64B, just s on SR 51, then w. **Facility:** 95 one-bedroom standard units, some with whirlpools. 4 stories, interior corridors. *Bath:* combo or shower only. **Parking:** on-site. **Terms:** cancellation fee imposed. **Amenities:** voice mail, irons, hair dryers. **Pool(s):** outdoor. **Guest Services:** valet and coin laundry, wireless Internet. **Business Services:** meeting rooms, PC. **Cards:** AX, CB, DC, DS, JC, MC, VI.

ASK / SOME UNITS

QUALITY SUITES — Book great rates at AAA.com — **Phone:** (704)889-7095 (102)

AAA SAVE

Hotel
$99-$159 All Year

Address: 9840 Pineville Matthews Rd **Location:** I-485, exit 64B, 0.4 mi s on SR 51. **Facility:** 75 one-bedroom standard units, some with whirlpools. 3 stories, interior corridors. *Bath:* combo or shower only. **Parking:** on-site. **Amenities:** voice mail, irons, hair dryers. **Pool(s):** heated indoor. **Leisure Activities:** exercise room. **Guest Services:** valet and coin laundry, wireless Internet. **Business Services:** meeting rooms, business center. **Cards:** AX, CB, DC, DS, JC, MC, VI. **Free Special Amenities: full breakfast and local telephone calls.**

CALL / SOME UNITS

WHERE TO DINE

CHINA BUFFET — **Phone:** 704/889-2828 (56)

Chinese
$4-$12

Beef with broccoli, spring rolls, sesame chicken, dumplings and many other offerings line the expansive buffet. Sushi and some American favorites complement the predominant traditional Chinese fare. Casual dress. **Bar:** Beer & wine. **Hours:** 11 am-10 pm, Fri & Sat-11 pm. **Address:** 9931 Lee St **Location:** I-485, exit 64B, 0.5 mi s on SR 51. **Parking:** on-site. **Cards:** AX, MC, VI.

HARPER'S RESTAURANT — **Phone:** 704/541-5255

American
$8-$24

All menu items are made from scratch daily on the premises. Offerings include well-prepared salmon, chicken, ribs and prime rib dishes as well as salads, sandwiches and wood-fired pizzas. Casual dress. **Bar:** Full bar. **Reservations:** accepted. **Hours:** 11 am-10 pm, Fri & Sat-11 pm, Sun-9 pm. Closed: 11/26, 12/25. **Address:** 11059 Carolina Place Pkwy **Location:** I-485, exit 64B, just s on SR 51, then just e; at Carolina Place Mall; south entrance. **Parking:** on-site. **Cards:** AX, DC, DS, MC, VI.

WALDHORN RESTAURANT — **Phone:** 704/540-7047 (57)

German
$7-$22

You don't have to wait for Oktoberfest to enjoy authentic German dishes like sauerbraten and wienerschnitzel. To wash it down, a large selection of German beers are available. The Sunday brunch is popular and festival. American cuisines are also available. Casual dress. **Bar:** Full bar. **Hours:** 11:30 am-3 & 5-10 pm, Sat 11:30 am-10 pm, Sun 11:30 am-9 pm. Closed: 7/4, 11/26, 12/25; also Mon. **Address:** 12101 Lancaster Hwy **Location:** I-485, exit 64B, 0.6 mi s on SR 51, then 0.5 mi s on Polk St. **Parking:** on-site. **Cards:** AX, DC, MC, VI.

Nearby South Carolina

FORT MILL pop. 7,587 (See map and index starting on p. 628)

WHERE TO STAY

BEST WESTERN CAROWINDS *Book great rates at AAA.com* **Phone:** (704)542-8488 109

AAA SAVE

Hotel
$75-$89 All Year

Address: 3675 Foothills Way **Location:** I-77, exit 90, just nw, then just s. **Facility:** 52 one-bedroom standard units, some with whirlpools. 3 stories, interior corridors. *Bath:* combo or shower only. **Parking:** on-site. **Terms:** 3 day cancellation notice. **Amenities:** high-speed Internet, voice mail, irons, hair dryers. **Pool(s):** outdoor. **Leisure Activities:** exercise room. **Guest Services:** coin laundry. **Business Services:** meeting rooms, business center. **Cards:** AX, CB, DC, DS, JC, MC, VI. **Free Special Amenities: expanded continental breakfast and high-speed Internet.**

/ SOME UNITS

AAA Benefit:
Members save up to 20%, plus 10% bonus points with rewards program.

COMFORT INN CAROWINDS *Book at AAA.com* **Phone:** 803/548-5200 108

Hotel
Rates not provided

Address: 3725 Avenue of the Carolinas **Location:** I-77, exit 90, just nw. **Facility:** 153 units. 143 one-bedroom standard units. 10 one-bedroom suites with whirlpools, some with kitchens. 4 stories, interior corridors. **Parking:** on-site. **Amenities:** video games (fee), voice mail, irons, hair dryers. *Some:* safes. **Pool(s):** outdoor. **Leisure Activities:** exercise room. **Guest Services:** valet laundry, wireless Internet. **Business Services:** meeting rooms, PC, fax (fee).

/ SOME UNITS

SLEEP INN CAROWINDS *Book at AAA.com* **Phone:** (803)547-2300 107

Hotel
$69-$119 All Year

Address: 3540 Lakemont Blvd **Location:** I-77, exit 90, just nw. **Facility:** 80 one-bedroom standard units, some with whirlpools. 4 stories, interior corridors. *Bath:* combo or shower only. **Parking:** on-site. **Amenities:** voice mail, irons, hair dryers. **Pool(s):** outdoor. **Guest Services:** valet laundry, wireless Internet. **Business Services:** meeting rooms, business center. **Cards:** AX, DS, MC, VI.

ASK CALL / SOME UNITS

ROCK HILL pop. 49,765

WHERE TO STAY

BAYMONT INN & SUITES *Book great rates at AAA.com* **Phone:** (803)329-1330

AAA SAVE

Hotel
$75-$115 3/1-11/30
$74-$80 12/1-2/28

Address: 1106 N Anderson Rd **Location:** I-77, exit 82B (US 21), 0.4 mi sw to US 21 Bypass, then just s. **Facility:** 60 one-bedroom standard units. 2 stories (no elevator), interior corridors. **Parking:** on-site. **Terms:** cancellation fee imposed. **Amenities:** irons, hair dryers. *Some:* safes. **Pool(s):** outdoor. **Leisure Activities:** whirlpool. **Guest Services:** coin laundry, wireless Internet. **Business Services:** meeting rooms, fax (fee). **Cards:** AX, DC, DS, MC, VI. **Free Special Amenities: full breakfast and high-speed Internet.** *(See color ad p 669)*

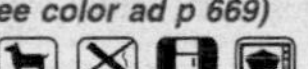

/ SOME UNITS FEE

THE BOOK & THE SPINDLE **Phone:** (803)328-1913

Bed & Breakfast
$90-$105 All Year

Address: 626 Oakland Ave **Location:** I-77, exit 82B (US 21), 3.1 mi s; before Aiken. Located opposite Winthrop University. **Facility:** Constructed in the 1930s, this property features South Carolina-themed guest rooms; phone for seasonal closures. 4 units. 3 one-bedroom standard units, some with kitchens. 1 one-bedroom suite with kitchen. 2 stories (no elevator), interior corridors. *Bath:* combo or shower only. **Parking:** on-site. **Terms:** age restrictions may apply, 10 day cancellation notice-fee imposed. **Guest Services:** wireless Internet. **Business Services:** fax (fee). **Cards:** AX, MC, VI.

ASK / SOME UNITS FEE

COURTYARD BY MARRIOTT-ROCK HILL *Book great rates at AAA.com* **Phone:** (803)324-1400

Hotel
$138-$148 All Year

Address: 1300 River Run Ct **Location:** I-77, exit 82A southbound, just w, then just n; exit 82A northbound, just ne to Celanese Rd (SR 161), 0.5 mi w to River Chase, then just n. Located beside Outback Steakhouse. **Facility:** Smoke free premises. 90 units. 87 one-bedroom standard units, some with whirlpools. 3 one-bedroom suites. 3 stories, interior corridors. *Bath:* combo or shower only. **Parking:** on-site. **Terms:** cancellation fee imposed. **Amenities:** dual phone lines, voice mail, irons, hair dryers. **Pool(s):** heated indoor. **Leisure Activities:** whirlpool, exercise room. **Guest Services:** valet and coin laundry, wireless Internet. **Business Services:** meeting rooms, PC, fax (fee). **Cards:** AX, CB, DC, DS, JC, MC, VI.

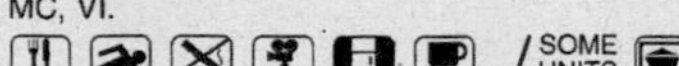

/ SOME UNITS

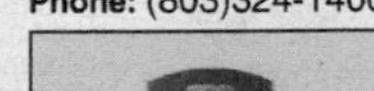

AAA Benefit:
Members save a minimum 5% off the best available rate.

DAYS INN Book great rates at AAA.com **Phone:** (803)329-2171

Motel
$55-$95 All Year

Address: 875 Riverview Rd **Location:** I-77, exit 82B (US 21), just sw, then s. **Facility:** 99 one-bedroom standard units. 2 stories (no elevator), exterior corridors. **Parking:** on-site. **Amenities:** irons, hair dryers. **Pool(s):** outdoor. **Guest Services:** coin laundry, wireless Internet. **Business Services:** PC, fax (fee). **Cards:** AX, DC, DS, MC, VI. **Free Special Amenities: continental breakfast and high-speed Internet.**

/ SOME UNITS

EAST MAIN GUEST HOUSE **Phone:** 803/366-1161

Historic Bed & Breakfast
$79-$99 All Year

Address: 600 E Main St **Location:** I-77, exit 77 (SR 5), 2.2 mi w. **Facility:** This 1919 Craftsman house features guest rooms furnished in traditional 18th-century style, some with fireplaces. Smoke free premises. 3 one-bedroom standard units, some with whirlpools. 2 stories (no elevator), interior corridors. **Parking:** on-site. **Terms:** age restrictions may apply, 7 day cancellation notice. **Amenities:** hair dryers. **Cards:** AX, MC, VI.

ASK

HAMPTON INN ROCK HILL Book great rates at AAA.com **Phone:** (803)325-1100

Hotel
$114-$124 All Year

Address: 2111 Tabor Dr **Location:** I-77, exit 79, just n on frontage road. Adjacent to Galleria Mall. **Facility:** 162 one-bedroom standard units, some with whirlpools. 5 stories, interior corridors. **Parking:** on-site. **Terms:** 1-30 night minimum stay, cancellation fee imposed. **Amenities:** video games (fee), dual phone lines, voice mail, irons, hair dryers. *Some:* DVD players. **Pool(s):** outdoor. **Leisure Activities:** sauna, exercise room. **Guest Services:** valet and coin laundry, wireless Internet. **Business Services:** meeting rooms, business center. **Cards:** AX, CB, DC, DS, MC, VI.

/ SOME UNITS VCR

AAA Benefit: Members save up to 10% everyday!

HILTON GARDEN INN Book great rates at AAA.com **Phone:** (803)325-2800

Hotel
$89-$189 All Year

Address: 650 Tinsley Way **Location:** I-77, exit 79, just w. Located in Manchester Village Shopping area. **Facility:** 127 units. 116 one-bedroom standard units, some with whirlpools. 11 one-bedroom suites. 6 stories, interior corridors. *Bath:* combo or shower only. **Parking:** on-site. **Terms:** 1-30 night minimum stay, cancellation fee imposed. **Amenities:** video games (fee), high-speed Internet, dual phone lines, voice mail, irons, hair dryers. **Pool(s):** outdoor. **Leisure Activities:** whirlpool, exercise room. **Guest Services:** valet and coin laundry, area transportation, wireless Internet. **Business Services:** conference facilities, business center. **Cards:** AX, CB, DC, DS, JC, MC, VI.

CALL / SOME UNITS

Hilton Garden Inn

AAA Benefit: Members save 5% or more everyday!

▼ *See AAA listing p 668* ▼

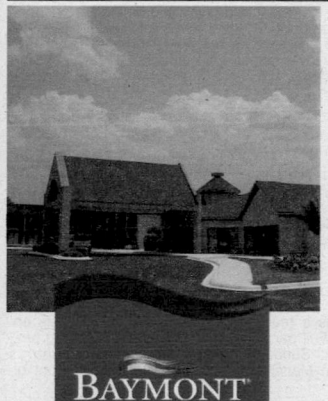

HOWARD JOHNSON INN *Book at AAA.com* **Phone:** 803/329-7900

Motel
Rates not provided

Address: 911 Riverview Rd **Location:** I-77, exit 82B (US 21), just sw, then just s. **Facility:** 54 one-bedroom standard units, some with whirlpools. 2 stories (no elevator), exterior corridors. **Parking:** on-site. **Amenities:** irons, hair dryers. **Leisure Activities:** exercise room. **Guest Services:** wireless Internet. **Business Services:** meeting rooms, fax (fee).

/ SOME UNITS FEE

MICROTEL INN & SUITES *Book great rates at AAA.com* **Phone:** (803)817-7700

AAA SAVE
Hotel
$51-$91 All Year

Address: 1047 Riverview Rd **Location:** I-77, exit 82B (US 21), just sw, then just nw. **Facility:** 77 one-bedroom standard units. 4 stories, interior corridors. *Bath:* combo or shower only. **Parking:** on-site. **Amenities:** voice mail, hair dryers. **Guest Services:** coin laundry, wireless Internet. **Business Services:** business center. **Cards:** AX, CB, DC, DS, MC, VI. **Free Special Amenities: expanded continental breakfast and high-speed Internet.**

/ SOME UNITS

SUPER 8 MOTEL *Book at AAA.com* **Phone:** (803)980-0400

Hotel
$50-$60 All Year

Address: 888 Riverview Rd **Location:** I-77, exit 82B (US 21), just sw, then just s. **Facility:** 62 one-bedroom standard units, some with whirlpools. 3 stories, interior corridors. *Bath:* combo or shower only. **Parking:** on-site. **Terms:** cancellation fee imposed. **Amenities:** irons, hair dryers. **Guest Services:** valet and coin laundry, wireless Internet. **Business Services:** fax (fee). **Cards:** AX, DS, MC, VI.

ASK CALL / SOME UNITS FEE

WINGATE INN-ROCK HILL *Book at AAA.com* **Phone:** 803/324-9000

Hotel
Rates not provided

Address: 760 Galleria Blvd **Location:** I-77, exit 79, just se. Located across from Galleria Mall. **Facility:** 92 units. 90 one-bedroom standard units. 1 one-bedroom suite. 5 stories, interior corridors. *Bath:* combo or shower only. **Parking:** on-site. **Amenities:** *Some:* video games (fee), high-speed Internet, dual phone lines, voice mail, safes, irons, hair dryers. **Pool(s):** outdoor. **Leisure Activities:** whirlpool, limited exercise equipment. **Guest Services:** valet laundry, area transportation, wireless Internet. **Business Services:** meeting rooms, business center.

FEE CALL / SOME UNITS

WHERE TO DINE

CAPTAIN'S GALLEY SEAFOOD RESTAURANT **Phone:** 803/366-0300

American
$7-$20

The restaurant is decorated in a colorful, nautical theme. The menu offers an extensive selection of seafood, with a few chicken and steak items as well. Casual dress. **Hours:** 3 pm-9 pm, Fri & Sat-10 pm, Sun noon-9 pm. Closed major holidays; also Mon. **Address:** 2349 Cherry Rd, Suite 49 **Location:** I-77, exit 82B (US 21), 0.7 mi sw; in The Market on Cherry Road Shopping Center. **Parking:** on-site. **Cards:** MC, VI.

CALL

CHARANDA MEXICAN GRILL & CANTINA **Phone:** 803/985-0809

Mexican
$5-$13

Located at the end of a shopping center, the restaurant offers well-prepared traditional Mexican selections. The use of quality ingredients is evident by the very good flavors of the food. The fresh, upbeat dining room and use of bold color accents set the mood for dining that is relaxed and informal. Casual dress. **Bar:** Full bar. **Hours:** 11 am-10 pm, Fri & Sat-11 pm. Closed: 11/26, 12/25. **Address:** 2260 Cross Pointe Dr **Location:** I-77, exit 79, just e; in Food Lion Shopping Center. **Parking:** on-site. **Cards:** AX, DS, MC, VI.

CALL

FATZ CAFE **Phone:** 803/980-6500

American
$7-$18

Friendly staff and appealing country decor help set the tone for a relaxed and enjoyable dining experience. It's not unusual for guests to wait to be seated at the popular spot, which earns raves for its well-prepared variations on chicken, steak, ribs and pasta, as well as salads and sandwiches. The signature Southern-style peach cobbler served with vanilla ice cream and walnuts is scrumptious. Casual dress. **Hours:** 11 am-10 pm, Fri & Sat-11 pm, Sun-9 pm. Closed: 11/26, 12/25. **Address:** 478 S Herlong Ave **Location:** Jct SR 274 (Ebeneezer Rd), 0.8 mi w. **Parking:** on-site. **Cards:** AX, DS, MC, VI.

CALL

FIREBONZ ALL AMERICAN BAR-B-QUE & GRILL **Phone:** 803/366-1555

Barbecue
$6-$17

Menu offerings include a wide variety of barbecue creations but also sharing menu space are steaks, ribs, chicken and seafood entrees. Little tykes can select a favorite dish from the children's menu. A View-Master slide viewer offers a 3D look at available desserts, making the ordering process fun and inventive. Casual dress. **Bar:** Full bar. **Hours:** 11 am-10 pm. Closed: 12/25. **Address:** 2445 Cherry Rd **Location:** I-77, exit 82A northbound; exit 82B southbound, 0.4 mi sw on US 21 (Cherry Rd). **Parking:** on-site. **Cards:** MC, VI.

CALL

HARRY & JEAN'S **Phone:** 803/366-7878

American
$7-$30

Located in a shopping area, the friendly, meet-and-eat spot is a real find. Creative and tasty twists on traditional American cuisine are delightful. Casual dress. **Bar:** Full bar. **Hours:** 11:30 am-2:30 & 5-10 pm, Fri-10:30 pm, Sat 5 pm-10:30 pm, Sun 11 am-3 & 4-9 pm; Sunday brunch. Closed major holidays. **Address:** 1940 Cinema Dr **Location:** I-77, exit 79, just w; in Manchester Shopping Village; in front of cinema. **Parking:** on-site. **Cards:** AX, CB, DC, DS, JC, MC, VI.

CALL

JING JING CHINESE CUISINE **Phone:** 803/366-1211

Chinese
$5-$12

Open since 2001, the simple eat-in/take-out restaurant is near hotels on the east side of the city. The menu lists the standard wide selection of soups, appetizers and entrees, which can be spiced to the your liking. The house specialty is Thai noodles with chicken and shrimp. Casual dress. **Hours:** 11:30 am-10 pm, Fri & Sat-10:30 pm, Sun noon-10 pm. Closed: 11/26. **Address:** 2260 Crosspointe Dr, #99 **Location:** I-77, exit 79, just e. **Parking:** on-site. **Cards:** AX, DS, MC, VI.

SAGEBRUSH STEAKHOUSE **Phone:** 803/366-8331

American

$5-$19

Born from the spirit of Texas cattle drives, the restaurant presents a menu of hearty steaks, prime rib, chicken, seafood and baby back ribs. Yummy desserts merit a splurge. Guests can call ahead to facilitate seating. Casual dress. **Bar:** Full bar. **Hours:** 11 am-10 pm, Fri & Sat-11 pm. Closed: 12/25. **Address:** 680 Tinsley Way **Location:** I-77, exit 79, just w, then just n; behind Hilton Garden Inn. **Parking:** on-site. **Cards:** AX, DC, DS, MC, VI.

CALL

SONNY'S REAL PIT BAR-B-Q **Phone:** 803/324-7984

Barbecue

$6-$15

House specialties include pork and chicken grilled over an open pit, barbecue ribs and fresh, homemade pie. The salad bar offers another popular option. Rustic and comfortable, the atmosphere is perfect for family meals. Casual dress. **Bar:** Beer only. **Hours:** 11 am-9:30 pm, Fri & Sat-10 pm. Closed: 11/26, 12/25. **Address:** 2781 Cherry Rd **Location:** I-77, exit 82A, just ne; in Home Depot Shopping Center. **Parking:** on-site. **Cards:** AX, DS, MC, VI.

THE STATION BAR & GRILL **Phone:** 803/980-4853

American

$8-$20

Even though the old building's exterior has been updated, it still is recognizable as originally having been a gas station. The renovated interior belies its origins, providing a comfortable, yet distinctive, contemporary look. Menu selections, which appeal to all tastes, include salads, wraps, sandwiches, specialty pizzas, noodle and rice bowls and a variety of pork, beef, chicken and seafood specialty entrees. Finish off the meal with a tempting dessert. Casual dress. **Bar:** Full bar. **Reservations:** accepted. **Hours:** 11 am-9 pm, Fri & Sat-10 pm. Closed major holidays; also Sun. **Address:** 122 S Oakland Ave **Location:** 0.3 mi n of Main St; downtown. **Parking:** on-site. **Cards:** AX, DS, MC, VI.

CALL

TROPICAL ESCAPE CAFE & BAR **Phone:** 803/366-3888

Pacific Rim

$5-$19

Much of the Pacific Rim cuisine is prepared in house, using fresh ingredients. Entrees reflect influences from China and the Philippines, with lots of flavors and spices that are sure to arouse the palate. The service is informal yet very attentive. Casual dress. **Bar:** Full bar. **Reservations:** accepted. **Hours:** 11:30 am-2:30 & 5-10 pm, Sat from 5 pm. Closed major holidays; also Sun. **Address:** 564 N Anderson Rd **Location:** I-77, exit 82B (US 21) southbound, 0.6 mi sw, then 1.4 mi s on Bypass US 21; exit 79 northbound, 1.6 mi w on Dave Lyle Blvd, then 0.9 mi n on Bypass US 21; in Twenty One Plaza. **Parking:** on-site. **Cards:** AX, DS, MC, VI.

SpongeBob SquarePants / © Carowinds

This ends listings for the Charlotte Vicinity.
The following page resumes the alphabetical listings of cities in North Carolina.

CHEROKEE

WHERE TO STAY

BAYMONT INN-CHEROKEE/SMOKY MOUNTAINS

Book great rates at AAA.com

Phone: (828)497-2102

AAA SAVE

Hotel

$69-$149 All Year

Address: 1455 Acquoni Rd **Location:** 2.5 mi n, just w off US 441 N. **Facility:** 67 one-bedroom standard units. 3 stories, interior corridors. *Bath:* combo or shower only. **Parking:** on-site. **Terms:** 2 night minimum stay - seasonal and/or weekends. **Amenities:** voice mail, irons, hair dryers. **Pool(s):** outdoor. **Guest Services:** coin laundry, area transportation-casino, wireless Internet. **Business Services:** fax (fee). **Cards:** AX, CB, DC, DS, MC, VI. **Free Special Amenities: expanded continental breakfast and high-speed Internet.**

CALL FEE / SOME UNITS

BEST WESTERN GREAT SMOKIES INN

Book great rates at AAA.com

Phone: (828)497-2020

AAA SAVE

Motel

$59-$149 12/1-10/31
$49-$99 11/1-11/30

Address: 1636 Acquoni Rd **Location:** US 441 N, 2.5 mi n; downtown. **Facility:** 152 one-bedroom standard units. 2 stories (no elevator), exterior corridors. **Parking:** on-site. **Amenities:** voice mail, irons, hair dryers. *Some:* high-speed Internet. **Pool(s):** outdoor. **Guest Services:** coin laundry, area transportation-casino, wireless Internet. **Business Services:** meeting rooms, fax (fee). **Cards:** AX, CB, DC, DS, JC, MC, VI.

/ SOME UNITS FEE FEE FEE

AAA Benefit:
Members save up to 20%, plus 10% bonus points with rewards program.

CHEROKEE SLEEP INN

Phone: 828/497-4730

AAA SAVE

Hotel

Rates not provided

Address: 344 Seven Clans Ln (US 441) **Location:** US 74/441, exit 74, 4.6 mi n. **Facility:** 84 one-bedroom standard units, some with whirlpools. 3 stories, interior corridors. *Bath:* some combo or shower only. **Parking:** on-site. **Amenities:** voice mail, irons, hair dryers. **Pool(s):** heated indoor. **Leisure Activities:** whirlpool. **Guest Services:** coin laundry, area transportation-casino, wireless Internet. **Business Services:** meeting rooms, PC, fax (fee). **Free Special Amenities: continental breakfast and high-speed Internet.**

/ SOME UNITS

COMFORT INN

Book at AAA.com

Phone: (828)497-2411

Motel

$59-$159 5/16-11/30
$49-$159 12/1-5/15

Address: 44 Tsalagi Rd **Location:** Jct US 19 and 441, just w on US 19 S. **Facility:** 88 one-bedroom standard units, some with whirlpools. 2 stories (no elevator), exterior corridors. *Bath:* combo or shower only. **Parking:** on-site. **Amenities:** high-speed Internet, irons, hair dryers. **Pool(s):** outdoor. **Leisure Activities:** whirlpool, fishing. **Guest Services:** area transportation, wireless Internet. **Business Services:** meeting rooms. **Cards:** AX, CB, DC, DS, JC, MC, VI.

A$K CALL / SOME UNITS

COMFORT SUITES

Book at AAA.com

Phone: (828)497-3500

Motel

$69-$159 4/1-11/30
$49-$159 12/1-3/31

Address: 1223 Tsalagi Rd **Location:** US 441, 1 mi n. **Facility:** Smoke free premises. 91 one-bedroom standard units, some with whirlpools. 3 stories, interior corridors. *Bath:* combo or shower only. **Parking:** on-site. **Amenities:** high-speed Internet, voice mail, safes, irons, hair dryers. **Pool(s):** outdoor. **Leisure Activities:** whirlpool. **Guest Services:** coin laundry, area transportation, wireless Internet. **Business Services:** meeting rooms, fax. **Cards:** AX, CB, DC, DS, JC, MC, VI.

A$K

DAYS INN

Book at AAA.com

Phone: 828/497-2300

Motel

Rates not provided

Address: 660 Painttown Rd **Location:** On US 19 N. Located across from Harrah's Cherokee Casino & Hotel. **Facility:** 52 one-bedroom standard units. 2 stories (no elevator), exterior corridors. *Bath:* combo or shower only. **Parking:** on-site. **Amenities:** hair dryers. **Pool(s):** outdoor. **Guest Services:** wireless Internet.

CALL / SOME UNITS

EL CAMINO MOTEL

Phone: 828/497-3600

Motel

$58-$140 All Year

Address: 15 Painttown Rd **Location:** Jct US 441, 0.3 mi n. Located adjacent to casino. **Facility:** 30 one-bedroom standard units. 1 story, exterior corridors. **Parking:** on-site. **Pool(s):** outdoor. **Cards:** AX, DS, MC, VI.

/ SOME UNITS

FAIRFIELD INN & SUITES

Book great rates at AAA.com

Phone: (828)497-0400

Hotel

$129-$139 All Year

Address: 568 Painttown Rd **Location:** US 19 N. Located across from Harrah's Cherokee Casino & Hotel. **Facility:** Smoke free premises. 100 units. 96 one-bedroom standard units, some with whirlpools. 4 one-bedroom suites. 3 stories, interior corridors. *Bath:* combo or shower only. **Parking:** on-site. **Terms:** cancellation fee imposed. **Amenities:** video games (fee), dual phone lines, voice mail, irons, hair dryers. *Some:* CD players. **Pool(s):** heated indoor. **Leisure Activities:** exercise room. **Guest Services:** coin laundry, wireless Internet. **Business Services:** meeting rooms, PC, fax. **Cards:** AX, CB, DC, DS, JC, MC, VI.

/ SOME UNITS

AAA Benefit:
Members save a minimum 5% off the best available rate.

HAMPTON INN *Book great rates at AAA.com* **Phone:** (828)497-3115

Hotel
$55-$165 All Year

Address: 185 Tsalagi Rd **Location:** Jct US 441 S and 19 S. **Facility:** 67 one-bedroom standard units. 2 stories (no elevator), interior corridors. *Bath:* combo or shower only. **Parking:** on-site. **Terms:** cancellation fee imposed. **Amenities:** voice mail, irons, hair dryers. **Pool(s):** outdoor. **Leisure Activities:** exercise room privileges. **Guest Services:** coin laundry, area transportation-casino, wireless Internet. **Business Services:** fax (fee). **Cards:** AX, CB, DC, DS, MC, VI.

CALL / SOME UNITS FEE

AAA Benefit:
Members save up to 10% everyday!

HOLIDAY INN *Book great rates at AAA.com* **Phone:** (828)497-9181

Motel
$49-$169 All Year

Address: 37 Tsalagi Rd **Location:** 0.8 mi w on US 19 S. **Facility:** 154 one-bedroom standard units. 2 stories (no elevator), exterior corridors. *Bath:* combo or shower only. **Parking:** on-site. **Terms:** check-in 4 pm, cancellation fee imposed. **Amenities:** voice mail, irons, hair dryers. **Pool(s):** outdoor, heated indoor. **Leisure Activities:** whirlpool, indoor recreation area, playground, limited exercise equipment. *Fee:* massage. **Guest Services:** coin laundry, area transportation-casino, wireless Internet. **Business Services:** meeting rooms, fax (fee). **Cards:** AX, CB, DC, DS, MC, VI.

/ SOME UNITS FEE

HOLIDAY INN EXPRESS HOTEL & SUITES CASINO *Book at AAA.com* **Phone:** (828)497-3113

Hotel
$69-$189 All Year

Address: 376 Painttown Rd **Location:** On US 19 N; across from Harrah's Cherokee Casino & Hotel. **Facility:** 93 one-bedroom standard units. 3 stories, interior corridors. *Bath:* combo or shower only. **Parking:** on-site. **Amenities:** high-speed Internet, dual phone lines, voice mail, irons, hair dryers. **Pool(s):** outdoor. **Leisure Activities:** exercise room. **Business Services:** meeting rooms. **Cards:** AX, DC, DS, JC, MC, VI.

A$K CALL / SOME UNITS

MICROTEL INN & SUITES *Book great rates at AAA.com* **Phone:** 828/497-7800

Hotel
Rates not provided

Address: 674 Casino Tr **Location:** Jct US 441 and Business Rt US 441 S. **Facility:** 63 one-bedroom standard units, some with whirlpools. 3 stories, interior corridors. *Bath:* combo or shower only. **Parking:** on-site. **Amenities:** dual phone lines, safes, hair dryers. *Some:* irons. **Pool(s):** outdoor. **Guest Services:** coin laundry, area transportation-casino, wireless Internet. **Free Special Amenities: expanded continental breakfast and high-speed Internet.**

CALL / SOME UNITS FEE

PIONEER MOTEL **Phone:** (828)497-2435

Motel
$48-$80 All Year

Address: 122 Tsalagi Rd **Location:** 0.8 mi w on US 19 S. **Facility:** 27 units. 21 one-bedroom standard units. 6 cottages. 1 story, exterior corridors. **Parking:** on-site. **Terms:** 3 day cancellation notice, 30 day for cottages-fee imposed. **Pool(s):** outdoor. **Leisure Activities:** fishing, picnic area with barbecue grill, playground, basketball, horseshoes. **Cards:** AX, DS, MC, VI. **Free Special Amenities: local telephone calls.**

CALL / SOME UNITS FEE

RAMADA LIMITED *Book great rates at AAA.com* **Phone:** 828/497-4231

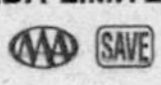

Hotel
Rates not provided

Address: 196 Painttown Rd **Location:** Jct US 19 N and 441 business route. Located across from Harrah's Cherokee Casino. **Facility:** 90 one-bedroom standard units, some with whirlpools. 1-4 stories, interior/exterior corridors. *Bath:* combo or shower only. **Parking:** on-site. **Amenities:** voice mail, irons, hair dryers. **Pool(s):** heated outdoor. **Guest Services:** area transportation-casino, wireless Internet. **Business Services:** meeting rooms, fax (fee). **Free Special Amenities: continental breakfast and local telephone calls.**

/ SOME UNITS

TWO RIVERS LODGE **Phone:** 828/488-2284

Motel
$49-$120 5/1-11/30
$35-$95 12/1-4/30

Address: 5280 Ela Rd **Location:** 5 mi e on US 19 S. Located in a rural area. **Facility:** 21 one-bedroom standard units. 1 story, exterior corridors. **Parking:** on-site. **Terms:** 4 day cancellation notice-fee imposed. **Pool(s):** outdoor. **Leisure Activities:** fishing. **Guest Services:** wireless Internet. **Cards:** AX, DS, MC, VI.

A$K / SOME UNITS FEE

WHERE TO DINE

LEE GARDEN CHINESE RESTAURANT **Phone:** 828/497-4388

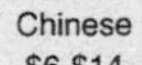

Chinese
$6-$14

Situated in a shopping plaza, the modern restaurant specializes in all-you-can-eat lunch and dinner buffets. Also offered is a full menu of well-prepared traditional entrees. The dining room is adorned with Oriental art and offers both table and booth seating. Service is casual yet very courteous. Casual dress. **Reservations:** not accepted. **Hours:** 11 am-9 pm, Fri & Sat-10 pm, Sun noon-9 pm. Closed: 11/26, 12/25. **Address:** 16 Cherokee Crossing **Location:** US 441; in Food Lion Center. **Parking:** on-site. **Cards:** MC, VI.

NEW HAPPY GARDEN CHINESE RESTAURANT — Phone: 828/497-4310

Chinese
$6-$12

Many Oriental selections are served in a traditional, relaxed setting. Both buffet and menu options are available. Casual dress. **Reservations:** not accepted. **Hours:** 11 am-8 pm; hours vary in winter. Closed: 1/1, 11/26, 12/25; also Mon. **Address:** Great Smoky Center, Acquoni Rd **Location:** 2.5 mi n on US 441, then just e. **Parking:** on-site. **Cards:** AX, DS, MC, VI.

CALL

PETER'S PANCAKES AND WAFFLES — **Phone:** 828/497-5116

American
$4-$8

What a treat to eat a mile-high stack of your favorite pancakes while looking out the window at the picturesque river. The local folks flock here for the morning ritual of breakfast and the newspaper. Casual dress. **Hours:** 7 am-2 pm. Closed: 12/25. **Address:** 1384 US 441 N **Location:** US 441, 1.5 mi n. **Parking:** on-site. **Cards:** DS, MC, VI.

SYCAMORES ON THE CREEK — **Phone:** 828/497-8706

New American
$10-$30

A large selection of steaks, chops and seafood is served in hefty portions. The walls are covered with river rock and wavy Plexiglas dividers section off the cozy dining room, which offers the best dining experience in the casino. No alcohol is served on the reservation. Dressy casual. **Reservations:** suggested. **Hours:** 5 pm-10 pm, Fri & Sat-11 pm. Closed: Mon & Tues. **Address:** 777 Casino Dr **Location:** In Harrah's Cherokee Casino & Hotel. **Parking:** on-site and valet. **Cards:** AX, CB, DC, DS, JC, MC, VI.

CALL

CHIMNEY ROCK pop. 175

WHERE TO STAY

THE ESMERALDA — **Phone:** (828)625-2999

Country Inn
$139-$245 All Year

Address: 910 Main St **Location:** 1 mi w on US 74. **Facility:** Rebuilt in 1999 after fire destroyed the original 1890 structure, the inn offers varied-size guest rooms with a country decor. Smoke free premises. 14 one-bedroom standard units. 3 stories, interior corridors. **Parking:** on-site. **Terms:** 2 night minimum stay - seasonal and/or weekends, age restrictions may apply, 21 day cancellation notice-fee imposed. **Amenities:** DVD players, CD players, voice mail. **Guest Services:** wireless Internet. **Business Services:** meeting rooms. **Cards:** AX, DS, MC, VI.

ASK CALL

MOUNTAIN VILLAGE CHALETS — **Phone:** 828/625-9783

SAVE

Vacation Rental Cottage
$89-$336 5/1-11/30
$67-$252 12/1-4/30

Address: 950 Main St **Location:** 1 mi w on US 74A. **Facility:** A mountain setting is the scenic backdrop of this property's varied-size chalet and motel units. 18 units. 3 two-bedroom standard units, some with whirlpools. 3 one-, 2 two- and 3 three-bedroom suites, some with efficiencies, kitchens and/or whirlpools. 7 cottages. 2 stories (no elevator), exterior corridors. **Parking:** on-site. **Terms:** 14 day cancellation notice-fee imposed. **Amenities:** *Some:* DVD players. **Leisure Activities:** croquet, pavilion, hiking trails. **Guest Services:** wireless Internet. **Cards:** AX, DS, MC, VI. **Free Special Amenities: local telephone calls and high-speed Internet.**

/ SOME UNITS FEE VCR

CLAREMONT pop. 1,038

WHERE TO STAY

SUPER 8 MOTEL — *Book great rates at AAA.com* — **Phone:** (828)459-7777

SAVE

Motel
$66-$85 All Year

Address: 3054 N Oxford St **Location:** I-40, exit 135, just s. **Facility:** 60 one-bedroom standard units, some with whirlpools. 2 stories (no elevator), interior/exterior corridors. *Bath:* combo or shower only. **Parking:** on-site. **Terms:** cancellation fee imposed. **Amenities:** safes, irons, hair dryers. **Pool(s):** outdoor. **Leisure Activities:** exercise room. **Guest Services:** coin laundry, wireless Internet. **Business Services:** meeting rooms. **Cards:** AX, DS, MC, VI. **Free Special Amenities: continental breakfast and high-speed Internet.**

/ SOME UNITS FEE

WHERE TO DINE

BOXCAR GRILLE — **Phone:** 828/459-9287

American
$7-$15

A large menu offers a range of options from to choose from; entrees such as fried catfish, sirloins and chicken tenders come with a choice of side items, add the garden station for an extra fee. Top it all off with the house favorite blackberry cobbler. Casual dress. **Bar:** Full bar. **Hours:** 11 am-10 pm. Closed: 11/26, 12/24, 12/25. **Address:** 3140 N Oxford St **Location:** I-40, exit 135, just s. **Parking:** on-site. **Cards:** AX, DS, MC, VI.

CLAYTON pop. 6,973

WHERE TO STAY

COMFORT SUITES Book at AAA.com **Phone:** (919)553-1234

Hotel

$100-$150 All Year

Address: 761 Enterprise Dr **Location:** I-40, exit 306B, 6 mi e on US 70, then just n. **Facility:** Smoke free premises. 60 units. 54 one-bedroom standard units. 6 one-bedroom suites with whirlpools. 3 stories, interior corridors. *Bath:* combo or shower only. **Parking:** on-site. **Amenities:** voice mail, irons, hair dryers. **Pool(s):** outdoor. **Leisure Activities:** exercise room. **Guest Services:** valet laundry, wireless Internet. **Business Services:** meeting rooms, business center. **Cards:** AX, DC, DS, MC, VI.

ASK CALL

HAMPTON INN RALEIGH/CLAYTON I-40 Book great rates at AAA.com **Phone:** (919)773-1977

Hotel

$79-$99 All Year

Address: 100 Hampton Dr **Location:** I-40, exit 312, just w on SR 42, then just n. **Facility:** 72 one-bedroom standard units, some with whirlpools. 3 stories, interior corridors. *Bath:* combo or shower only. **Parking:** on-site. **Terms:** 1-30 night minimum stay, cancellation fee imposed. **Amenities:** dual phone lines, voice mail, irons, hair dryers. *Some:* high-speed Internet. **Pool(s):** outdoor. **Leisure Activities:** exercise room. **Guest Services:** valet and coin laundry, wireless Internet. **Business Services:** meeting rooms, business center. **Cards:** AX, CB, DC, DS, MC, VI.

/ SOME UNITS

AAA Benefit:

Members save up to 10% everyday!

HOLIDAY INN EXPRESS Book at AAA.com **Phone:** 919/719-3415

Hotel

Rates not provided

Address: 105 Leone Ct **Location:** I-40, exit 312, just e on SR 42, then just s. **Facility:** 67 one-bedroom standard units, some with whirlpools. 3 stories, interior corridors. *Bath:* combo or shower only. **Parking:** on-site. **Amenities:** dual phone lines, voice mail, irons, hair dryers. *Some:* high-speed Internet. **Pool(s):** outdoor. **Leisure Activities:** exercise room. **Guest Services:** valet laundry, wireless Internet. **Business Services:** meeting rooms.

CALL / SOME UNITS

MORNING GLORY INN **Phone:** 919/550-8547

Historic Bed & Breakfast

$99-$119 All Year

Address: 507 E 2nd St **Location:** Jct US 70, just n on Main St, then just nw. **Facility:** This 1907 Victorian inn features spacious rooms painted in inviting colors and offers guests access to a small, fully stocked kitchen. Smoke free premises. 5 one-bedroom standard units. 2 stories (no elevator), interior corridors. *Bath:* combo or shower only. **Parking:** on-site and street. **Amenities:** hair dryers. **Leisure Activities:** croquet. **Guest Services:** TV in common area, complimentary laundry, wireless Internet. **Business Services:** meeting rooms. **Cards:** AX, DS, MC, VI.

ASK

SLEEP INN Book at AAA.com **Phone:** 919/772-7771

Hotel

Rates not provided

Address: 105 Commerce Pkwy **Location:** I-40, exit 312, just w on SR 42, then just s. **Facility:** 88 one-bedroom standard units. 3 stories, interior corridors. *Bath:* combo or shower only. **Parking:** on-site. **Amenities:** dual phone lines, voice mail, irons, hair dryers. *Some:* high-speed Internet. **Pool(s):** outdoor. **Leisure Activities:** exercise room. **Guest Services:** wireless Internet. **Business Services:** meeting rooms.

CALL / SOME UNITS FEE

SUPER 8 MOTEL Book at AAA.com **Phone:** (919)661-1991

Hotel

$60-$70 All Year

Address: 101 Leone Ct **Location:** I-40, exit 312, just e on SR 42, then just s. **Facility:** 38 one-bedroom standard units. 2 stories (no elevator), exterior corridors. **Parking:** on-site. **Amenities:** hair dryers. **Pool(s):** outdoor. **Guest Services:** wireless Internet. **Cards:** AX, DC, DS, MC, VI.

ASK / SOME UNITS FEE

CLEMMONS pop. 13,827

WHERE TO STAY

HOLIDAY INN EXPRESS Book at AAA.com **Phone:** (336)778-1500

Hotel

$90-$130 All Year

Address: 6320 Amp Dr **Location:** I-40, exit 184, just n, then just e. **Facility:** 60 one-bedroom standard units, some with whirlpools. 2 stories, interior corridors. *Bath:* combo or shower only. **Parking:** on-site. **Amenities:** voice mail, irons, hair dryers. **Leisure Activities:** limited exercise equipment. **Guest Services:** valet laundry, wireless Internet. **Business Services:** meeting rooms, PC. **Cards:** AX, CB, DC, DS, MC, VI.

ASK / SOME UNITS

SUPER 8 MOTEL Book at AAA.com **Phone:** (336)778-0931

Hotel

$66-$116 All Year

Address: 6204 Ramada Dr **Location:** I-40, exit 184, just s, then just e. **Facility:** 56 one-bedroom standard units, some with whirlpools. 2 stories (no elevator), interior corridors. *Bath:* combo or shower only. **Parking:** on-site. **Terms:** cancellation fee imposed. **Amenities:** voice mail, irons, hair dryers. **Guest Services:** wireless Internet. **Cards:** AX, DC, DS, MC, VI.

ASK CALL / SOME UNITS

THE VILLAGE INN GOLF & CONFERENCE CENTER Book at AAA.com Phone: (336)766-9121

Hotel
$68-$79 All Year

Address: 6205 Ramada Dr **Location:** I-40, exit 184, just s, then just e. **Facility:** 145 units. 142 one-bedroom standard units. 3 one-bedroom suites, some with whirlpools. 2 stories (no elevator), interior corridors. *Bath:* combo or shower only. **Parking:** on-site. **Terms:** 3 day cancellation notice. **Amenities:** voice mail, hair dryers. *Some:* irons. **Pool(s):** outdoor. **Leisure Activities:** limited exercise equipment. **Guest Services:** valet and coin laundry, area transportation (fee), wireless Internet. **Business Services:** conference facilities. **Cards:** AX, DC, DS, MC, VI.

ASK FEE / SOME UNITS FEE

WHERE TO DINE

COZUMEL MEXICAN RESTAURANT Phone: 336/778-0300

Mexican
$4-$10

The casual cantina's menu lists traditional Mexican favorites, as well as several flavorful specialties of the house. The informal dining room is suited for a casual dining experience. Casual dress. **Bar:** Full bar. **Reservations:** accepted. **Hours:** 11 am-10 pm, Fri & Sat-11 pm, Sun-9 pm. Closed major holidays. **Address:** 2630 Lewisville-Clemmons Rd **Location:** I-40, exit 184, 0.7 mi s. **Parking:** on-site. **Cards:** AX, DC, DS, MC, VI.

CALL

I BAMBINI Phone: 336/778-1838

Italian
$5-$16

The popular restaurant presents an extensive menu of well-prepared classic pasta dishes, steaks, chicken, veal, seafood, pizzas and sandwiches. The small, comfortable dining room is casual but features some upscale treatments. A buffet is offered at lunch Monday through Friday. Casual dress. **Bar:** Beer & wine. **Hours:** 11 am-10 pm, Fri-10:30 pm, Sat 11:30 am-10:30 pm, Sun 11:30 am-10 pm. Closed: 11/26, 12/25. **Address:** 2385 Lewisville Clemmons Rd **Location:** I-40, exit 184, just n. **Parking:** on-site. **Cards:** AX, DC, DS, MC, VI.

SAGEBRUSH STEAKHOUSE Phone: 336/712-0901

American
$5-$19

Born from the spirit of Texas cattle drives, the restaurant presents a menu of hearty steaks, prime rib, chicken, seafood and baby back ribs. Yummy desserts merit a splurge. Guests can call ahead to facilitate seating. Casual dress. **Bar:** Full bar. **Hours:** 11 am-10 pm, Fri & Sat-11 pm. Closed: 12/25. **Address:** 2560 Lewisville-Clemmons Rd **Location:** I-40, exit 184, 0.4 mi s. **Parking:** on-site. **Cards:** AX, DC, DS, MC, VI.

CALL

CLINTON pop. 8,600

WHERE TO STAY

COMFORT INN Book at AAA.com Phone: (910)592-8220

Hotel
$75-$126 All Year

Address: 1412 Sunset Ave **Location:** Jct US 701, 1 mi w on SR 24. **Facility:** 50 one-bedroom standard units, some with whirlpools. 2 stories (no elevator), interior corridors. *Bath:* combo or shower only. **Parking:** on-site. **Amenities:** high-speed Internet, dual phone lines, voice mail, irons, hair dryers. **Pool(s):** outdoor. **Leisure Activities:** exercise room. **Guest Services:** wireless Internet. **Business Services:** meeting rooms, business center. **Cards:** AX, DC, DS, MC, VI.

ASK / SOME UNITS

DAYS INN Book great rates at AAA.com Phone: (910)590-0660

AAA SAVE

Motel
$60-$80 All Year

Address: 508 Southeast Blvd **Location:** Jct US 701 business route and SR 24 E. **Facility:** 50 one-bedroom standard units, some with whirlpools. 2 stories (no elevator), exterior corridors. **Parking:** on-site. **Amenities:** safes, hair dryers. **Pool(s):** outdoor. **Guest Services:** wireless Internet. **Cards:** AX, DS, MC, VI. **Free Special Amenities: continental breakfast and high-speed Internet.**

/ SOME UNITS

INN AT CLINTON Book at AAA.com Phone: (910)592-1990

Hotel
$65-$120 All Year

Address: 1406 Sunset Ave **Location:** Jct US 701, 1 mi w on SR 24. **Facility:** 49 one-bedroom standard units. 2 stories (no elevator), interior corridors. **Parking:** on-site. **Amenities:** high-speed Internet, dual phone lines, voice mail, irons, hair dryers. **Guest Services:** wireless Internet. **Cards:** AX, DC, DS, MC, VI.

ASK CALL / SOME UNITS

COLUMBUS pop. 992

WHERE TO STAY

DAYS INN Book great rates at AAA.com Phone: 828/894-3303

AAA SAVE

Motel
Rates not provided

Address: 626 W Mills St **Location:** I-26, exit 67, just w on SR 108. **Facility:** 59 one-bedroom standard units, some with whirlpools. 2 stories (no elevator), exterior corridors. **Parking:** on-site. **Amenities:** hair dryers. **Pool(s):** outdoor. **Guest Services:** wireless Internet. **Business Services:** fax (fee). **Free Special Amenities: continental breakfast and high-speed Internet.**

FEE / SOME UNITS FEE

CONCORD —*See Charlotte p. 660.*

CONOVER pop. 6,604

WHERE TO STAY

DAYS INN *Book great rates at AAA.com* **Phone:** (828)465-2378

AAA SAVE

Motel
$62-$140 All Year

Address: 1710 Fairgrove Church Rd SE **Location:** I-40, exit 128, just s. **Facility:** 60 one-bedroom standard units, some with whirlpools. 2 stories (no elevator), exterior corridors. **Parking:** on-site. **Terms:** 5 day cancellation notice. **Amenities:** safes, hair dryers. *Some:* irons. **Pool(s):** outdoor. **Guest Services:** valet and coin laundry. **Business Services:** meeting rooms, fax (fee). **Cards:** AX, CB, DC, DS, JC, MC, VI. **Free Special Amenities: continental breakfast and high-speed Internet.**

CALL / SOME UNITS FEE VCR

HOLIDAY INN EXPRESS HOTEL & SUITES *Book at AAA.com* **Phone:** (828)465-7070

Hotel
$92-$100 All Year

Address: 104 10th St NW **Location:** I-40, exit 132, just n on SR 16. **Facility:** 92 units. 66 one-bedroom standard units. 26 one-bedroom suites with efficiencies. 4 stories, interior corridors. *Bath:* combo or shower only. **Parking:** on-site, winter plug-ins. **Amenities:** video games (fee), voice mail, irons, hair dryers. **Pool(s):** outdoor. **Leisure Activities:** exercise room. **Guest Services:** valet and coin laundry, wireless Internet. **Business Services:** meeting rooms, PC, fax. **Cards:** AX, CB, DC, DS, JC, MC, VI.

ASK CALL / SOME UNITS

WHERE TO DINE

CAFE' RENDEZVOUS **Phone:** 828/466-3122

Continental
$5-$19

Don't let the unassuming exterior fool you, as the dining experience is far from ordinary. The bright bistro is filled with amazing artwork, and the cuisine is the work of three chef-owners who create their own artwork in the kitchen. Fresh, local and organic ingredients set the canvas for a range of such tasty delights as homemade soups, five-cheese pizza, pecan-encrusted, honey-Dijon salmon or beef tenderloin with bearnaise, not to mention the homemade desserts. Casual dress. **Bar:** Full bar. **Reservations:** accepted. **Hours:** 11 am-10 pm, Fri-11 pm, Sat 5 pm-11 pm, Sun 11 am-2 pm. Closed: 11/26, 12/25. **Address:** 102 10th St NW **Location:** I-40, exit 132, just n on SR 16. **Parking:** on-site. **Cards:** VI.

CORNELIUS —*See Charlotte p. 662.*

COROLLA —*See Outer Banks p. 775.*

CREEDMOOR pop. 2,232

WHERE TO STAY

COMFORT INN *Book great rates at AAA.com* **Phone:** (919)528-9296

AAA SAVE

Hotel
$85-$105 All Year

Address: 1585 SR 56 **Location:** I-85, exit 191, 0.3 mi e. **Facility:** 51 one-bedroom standard units, some with whirlpools. 2 stories (no elevator), interior corridors. *Bath:* combo or shower only. **Parking:** on-site. **Terms:** 2 night minimum stay - seasonal and/or weekends. **Amenities:** irons, hair dryers. **Pool(s):** outdoor. **Leisure Activities:** exercise room. **Guest Services:** coin laundry, wireless Internet. **Cards:** AX, CB, DC, DS, JC, MC, VI. **Free Special Amenities: expanded continental breakfast and high-speed Internet.**

/ SOME UNITS

RAMADA LIMITED *Book great rates at AAA.com* **Phone:** (919)575-6565

AAA SAVE

Motel
$60-$79 All Year

Address: 2575 W Lyon Station Rd **Location:** I-85, exit 191, just w. **Facility:** 65 one-bedroom standard units. 2 stories (no elevator), exterior corridors. **Parking:** on-site. **Amenities:** voice mail, irons, hair dryers. **Leisure Activities:** limited exercise equipment. **Guest Services:** wireless Internet. **Business Services:** meeting rooms. **Cards:** AX, DC, DS, MC, VI. **Free Special Amenities: continental breakfast and high-speed Internet.**

/ SOME UNITS

WHERE TO DINE

BOB'S BARBECUE **Phone:** 919/528-2081

Regional Southern
$3-$10

A quick lunch might consist of sweet and tangy pulled pork barbecue or fried chicken. Casual dress. **Hours:** 10 am-8 pm. Closed major holidays; also Sun. **Address:** 1589 Hwy 56 **Location:** I-85, exit 191, 0.3 mi e. **Parking:** on-site. **Cards:** AX, DC, MC, VI.

JON'S MAIN STREET BAR & GRILL **Phone:** 919/528-7777

American
$6-$19

The downtown eatery's menu features pasta, ribs, steaks and sandwiches. On weekends, patrons often relax on the outdoor patio and enjoy the entertainment. Casual dress. **Bar:** Beer & wine. **Hours:** 11 am-9 pm, Fri & Sat-10 pm, Sun-8 pm. Closed major holidays. **Address:** 406 N Main St **Location:** I-85, exit 191, 2.8 mi e on SR 56, then just s on SR 50. **Parking:** on-site. **Cards:** MC, VI.

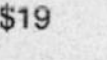

CULLOWHEE pop. 3,579

WHERE TO STAY

UNIVERSITY INN

Motel
$59-$120 All Year

Phone: 828/293-5442

Address: 563 N Country Club Dr **Location:** 0.5 mi sw of SR 107. **Facility:** 32 one-bedroom standard units, some with kitchens (no utensils). 1-3 stories (no elevator), exterior corridors. **Parking:** on-site. **Terms:** 2 night minimum stay - seasonal. **Amenities:** *Some:* irons, hair dryers. **Guest Services:** wireless Internet. **Cards:** AX, DS, MC, VI.

ASK / SOME UNITS

DAVIDSON —*See Charlotte p. 663.*

DENVER

WHERE TO DINE

SAGEBRUSH STEAKHOUSE

American
$5-$19

Phone: 704/483-8550

Born from the spirit of Texas cattle drives, the restaurant presents a menu of hearty steaks, prime rib, chicken, seafood and baby back ribs. Yummy desserts merit a splurge. Guests can call ahead to facilitate seating. Casual dress. **Bar:** Beer & wine. **Hours:** 11 am-10 pm, Fri & Sat-11 pm. Closed: 12/25. **Address:** 6170 Hwy 16 S **Location:** Jct SR 73/16, just sw. **Parking:** on-site. **Cards:** AX, DC, DS, MC, VI.

CALL

DILLSBORO pop. 205

WHERE TO STAY

BEST WESTERN RIVER ESCAPE INN & SUITES

Phone: (828)586-6060

Hotel
$100-$230 All Year

Address: 248 WBI Dr **Location:** SR 23/74, exit 81, 0.5 mi s, then just w on Haywood Rd, follow signs. Located on the Tuckaseegee River. **Facility:** 65 one-bedroom standard units, some with whirlpools. 3 stories, interior corridors. *Bath:* combo or shower only. **Parking:** on-site. **Terms:** 3 day cancellation notice-fee imposed. **Amenities:** high-speed Internet, dual phone lines, voice mail, safes, irons, hair dryers. **Pool(s):** heated indoor. **Leisure Activities:** whirlpool, charcoal grill, picnic tables, outdoor deck, exercise room. **Guest Services:** coin laundry, wireless Internet. **Business Services:** meeting rooms, business center. **Cards:** AX, DC, DS, MC, VI. **Free Special Amenities: expanded continental breakfast and high-speed Internet.**

/ SOME UNITS

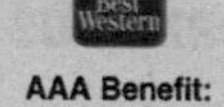

AAA Benefit:
Members save up to 20%, plus 10% bonus points with rewards program.

THE CHALET INN

Bed & Breakfast
$96-$190 3/20-11/30
$96-$180 12/1-1/2

Phone: (828)586-0251

Address: 285 Lone Oak Dr **Location:** 3 mi w on US 74/441, just s on Barkers Creek Rd (at the Old Steel Girder Bridge), 1.1 mi e on Thomas Valley Rd, then 0.3 mi sw on Nations Creek Rd. Located in a quiet area. **Facility:** This handsome chalet-type home reminiscent of a European Alpine dwelling is nestled in a mountain cove; suites feature gas fireplaces. Smoke free premises. 6 units. 4 one-bedroom standard units. 2 one-bedroom suites, some with whirlpools. 3 stories (no elevator), interior/exterior corridors. *Bath:* combo or shower only. **Parking:** on-site. **Terms:** open 12/1-1/2 & 3/20-11/30, 2 night minimum stay - seasonal and/or weekends, 30 day cancellation notice-fee imposed. **Amenities:** CD players. **Leisure Activities:** fishing, badminton, bocci, croquet, picnic area with barbecue grill, country club, pool & golf privileges, hiking trails, massage, horseshoes, game room. **Guest Services:** wireless Internet. **Cards:** AX, DS, MC, VI. **Free Special Amenities: full breakfast and high-speed Internet.**

/ SOME UNITS

HOLIDAY INN EXPRESS

Hotel
$120-$140 All Year

Phone: (828)631-1111

Address: 26 Robinson Rd **Location:** I-40, exit 27 to US 23/74 to exit 81. **Facility:** 67 one-bedroom standard units, some with whirlpools. 3 stories, interior corridors. *Bath:* combo or shower only. **Parking:** on-site. **Terms:** check-in 4 pm, cancellation fee imposed. **Amenities:** dual phone lines, voice mail, irons, hair dryers. **Pool(s):** heated indoor. **Leisure Activities:** whirlpool, exercise room. **Guest Services:** coin laundry, wireless Internet. **Business Services:** meeting rooms, business center. **Cards:** AX, DC, DS, MC, VI.

ASK CALL / SOME UNITS

MOUNTAIN BROOK COTTAGES

Vacation Rental Cottage
$90-$140 All Year

Phone: (828)586-4329

Address: 208 Mountain Brook Rd **Location:** 9 mi s of Dillsboro on US 23 and 441; Franklin-Atlanta, exit 81 off US 19 and 23. **Facility:** These rustic housekeeping cottages near a mountain stream each have a fireplace. 12 cottages. 1 story, exterior corridors. *Bath:* combo or shower only. **Parking:** on-site. **Terms:** 2 night minimum stay - weekends, 30 day cancellation notice-fee imposed. **Amenities:** *Some:* CD players. **Leisure Activities:** sauna, whirlpool, picnic area, hiking trails, playground. *Fee:* fishing, game room.

/ SOME UNITS

WHERE TO DINE

DILLSBORO SMOKEHOUSE **Phone:** 828/586-9556

Barbecue
$5-$15

Smokin' for more than a decade, this establishment lives up to its name. The menu lists fall-off-the-bone barbecue and smoked items, including pork, beef, chicken, turkey, ham and baby back ribs with all the fixings. Locals flock here for the lively atmosphere and friendly service. Casual dress. **Bar:** Beer & wine. **Reservations:** not accepted. **Hours:** 11 am-9 pm; hours may vary in winter. Closed major holidays. **Address:** 403 Haywood Rd **Location:** Center. **Parking:** on-site. **Cards:** AX, MC, VI.

DOBSON pop. 1,457

WHERE TO STAY

HAMPTON INN & SUITES-SHELTON VINEYARDS *Book great rates at AAA.com* **Phone:** (336)353-9400

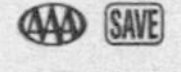

Hotel
$104-$299 All Year

Address: 150 Charlestowne Dr **Location:** I-77, exit 93, just e on Zephyr Rd, then just s on Twin Oaks Rd. **Facility:** 102 one-bedroom standard units, some with whirlpools. 5 stories, interior corridors. *Bath:* combo or shower only. **Parking:** on-site. **Amenities:** video games (fee), high-speed Internet, voice mail, irons, hair dryers. **Pool(s):** heated indoor. **Leisure Activities:** whirlpool, bicycles, exercise room. **Guest Services:** valet and coin laundry, wireless Internet. **Business Services:** meeting rooms, business center. **Cards:** AX, CB, DC, DS, MC, VI. **Free Special Amenities: full breakfast and high-speed Internet.**

CALL / SOME UNITS

AAA Benefit:
Members save up to 10% everyday!

WHERE TO DINE

HARVEST GRILL AT SHELTON VINEYARDS **Phone:** 336/366-3590

Continental
$17-$30

The dining room overlooks the acres of grapevines that comprise the vineyards, and the menu features delicious fare to sample with the wines they generate. Seasonally changing selections include dishes along the lines of smoked turkey panini at lunch or grilled pork chops with apple cider, pecan and bacon demi-glace at dinner. From 3 to 5 pm, patrons can request the tasting menu. Casual dress. **Bar:** Wine only. **Reservations:** accepted. **Hours:** 10 am-10 pm, Sun 11 am-6 pm. Closed: 11/26, 12/25. **Address:** 230 Cabernet Ln **Location:** I-77, exit 93, just e on Zephyr Rd, then 2.5 mi s on Twin Oaks Rd. **Parking:** on-site. **Cards:** AX, MC, VI.

THE WOLF'S LAIR RESTAURANT

Phone: 336/374-2532

American
$5-$26

The road to the restaurant runs through the vineyards with which this place is associated. The decor in the dining rooms has the look and feel of a hunting lodge. The chef creates interesting combinations of ingredients that excite the imagination and please the taste buds. Touches of refinement and accommodating service enhance the informal dining experience. Dressy casual. **Bar:** Beer & wine. **Reservations:** suggested. **Hours:** 11 am-2:30 pm, Thurs-Sat also 5 pm-10 pm, Sun noon-8 pm. Closed: 7/4, 12/25. **Address:** 283 Vineyard Ln **Location:** I-77, exit 93, 6 mi e to Main St, just s to Atkins St, 1 mi e to US 601, then 0.3 mi n. **Parking:** on-site. **Cards:** AX, MC, VI.

CALL

DUCK —*See Outer Banks p. 776.*

DUNN pop. 9,196

WHERE TO STAY

COMFORT INN *Book at AAA.com*

Phone: 910/891-2511

Hotel
Rates not provided

Address: 131 Bud Hawkins Rd **Location:** I-95, exit 72 (Pope Rd), just e, then just s. **Facility:** 57 one-bedroom standard units, some with whirlpools. 3 stories, interior corridors. *Bath:* combo or shower only. **Parking:** on-site. **Amenities:** irons, hair dryers. **Pool(s):** outdoor. **Guest Services:** wireless Internet.

CALL / SOME UNITS

HAMPTON INN *Book great rates at AAA.com*

Phone: (910)892-4333

Hotel
$94-$119 All Year

Address: 100 Jesse Tart Cir **Location:** I-95, exit 73, just w, then just s. **Facility:** 120 units. 115 one-bedroom standard units. 5 one-bedroom suites. 5 stories, interior corridors. *Bath:* combo or shower only. **Parking:** on-site. **Terms:** 1-30 night minimum stay, cancellation fee imposed. **Amenities:** voice mail, irons, hair dryers. *Some:* DVD players (fee). **Pool(s):** outdoor. **Leisure Activities:** exercise room. **Guest Services:** valet laundry, wireless Internet. **Business Services:** meeting rooms, business center. **Cards:** AX, CB, DC, DS, MC, VI.

CALL / SOME UNITS FEE VCR

Hampton Inn
AAA Benefit:
Members save up to 10% everyday!

HOLIDAY INN EXPRESS *Book great rates at AAA.com*

Phone: (910)892-4400

AAA SAVE

Hotel
$81-$96 All Year

Address: 900 E Pearsall St **Location:** I-95, exit 73, just w, then just s. **Facility:** 69 one-bedroom standard units, some with whirlpools. 2 stories (no elevator), interior corridors. *Bath:* combo or shower only. **Parking:** on-site. **Amenities:** high-speed Internet, voice mail, irons, hair dryers. **Leisure Activities:** limited exercise equipment. **Guest Services:** valet laundry, wireless Internet. **Business Services:** meeting rooms, business center. **Cards:** AX, DC, DS, MC, VI. **Free Special Amenities: continental breakfast and high-speed Internet.**

/ SOME UNITS

JAMESON INN *Book at AAA.com*

Phone: (910)891-5758

Motel
$83-$90 All Year

Address: 901 Jackson Rd **Location:** I-95, exit 73, just w, then just s. **Facility:** 42 one-bedroom standard units, some with whirlpools. 2 stories (no elevator), exterior corridors. **Parking:** on-site. **Terms:** cancellation fee imposed. **Amenities:** irons, hair dryers. **Pool(s):** outdoor. **Leisure Activities:** exercise room. **Guest Services:** wireless Internet. **Business Services:** PC. **Cards:** AX, DC, DS, MC, VI.

ASK CALL / SOME UNITS FEE

WHERE TO DINE

BRASS LANTERN

Phone: 910/892-6309

Steak
$8-$35

Combining attentive and accommodating service, a well-maintained and clean facility and good food quality makes this a popular choice for locals and tourists. Menu favorites include the fresh salad bar and generous portions of prime rib and seafood entrees. Casual dress. **Bar:** Beer & wine. **Hours:** 5 pm-9 pm, Fri & Sat-9:30 pm. Closed: 11/26, 12/25; also Sun. **Address:** 515 Spring Branch Rd **Location:** I-95, exit 72 (Pope Rd), just w. **Parking:** on-site. **Cards:** AX, DS, MC, VI.

KIM'S BARBECUE & SEAFOOD

Phone: 910/892-7750

Regional Southern
$4-$10

Don't let the no-frills decor fool you, Kim's is a local favorite for delicious North Carolina-style pulled pork barbecue, fried chicken and seafood. Complementing the entrees is slaw, Brunswick stew and hush puppies. Expect friendly, efficient service. Casual dress. **Hours:** 11 am-8 pm. Closed major holidays; also Sat & Sun. **Address:** 900 W Broad St **Location:** I-95, exit 73, 0.7 mi n on US 421, just se on US 301, then just nw. **Parking:** on-site. **Cards:** MC, VI.

SAGEBRUSH STEAKHOUSE

Phone: 910/892-7744

American
$5-$19

Born from the spirit of Texas cattle drives, the restaurant presents a menu of hearty steaks, prime rib, chicken, seafood and baby back ribs. Yummy desserts merit a splurge. Guests can call ahead to facilitate seating. Casual dress. **Bar:** Full bar. **Hours:** 11 am-10 pm, Fri & Sat-11 pm. Closed: 12/25. **Address:** 1006 E Cumberland St **Location:** I-95, exit 73, just w. **Parking:** on-site. **Cards:** AX, DC, DS, MC, VI.

CALL

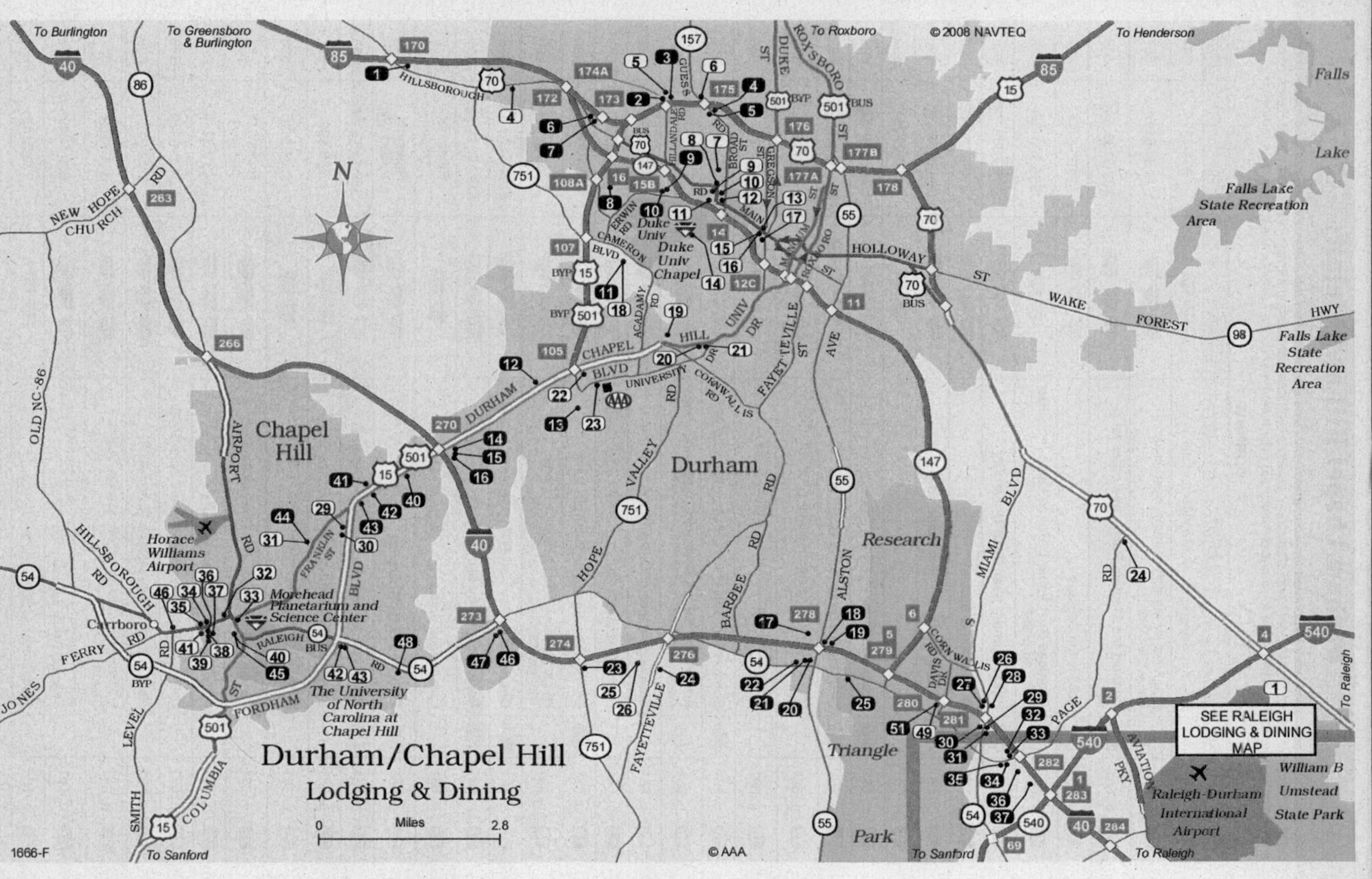
Durham/Chapel Hill
Lodging & Dining
© 2008 NAVTEQ
© AAA
SEE RALEIGH LODGING & DINING MAP
Miles
0
2.8
To Burlington
To Greensboro & Burlington
To Henderson
To Roxboro
To Raleigh
To Sanford
Falls Lake
Falls Lake State Recreation Area
Falls Lake State Recreation Area
Duke Univ
Duke Univ Chapel
Durham
Research
Triangle
Park
Chapel Hill
Horace Williams Airport
Carrboro
Morehead Planetarium and Science Center
The University of North Carolina at Chapel Hill
Raleigh-Durham International Airport
William B Umstead State Park
1666-F

Durham/Chapel Hill and Vicinity

This index helps you "spot" where approved lodgings and restaurants are located on the corresponding detailed maps. Lodging daily rate range is for comparison only and show the property's high season. Restaurant rate range is a combination of lunch and/or dinner. Turn to the listing page for more detailed rate information and consult display ads for special promotions.

DURHAM

Map Page	OA	Lodgings	Diamond Rated	High Season	Page
1 / p. 681		Durham Skyland Inn, A Magnuson Hotel	◆◆	$59-$99	687
2 / p. 681		Courtyard by Marriott Durham near Duke University/Downtown	◆◆◆	$137-$147	687
3 / p. 681	AAA	**Comfort Inn Medical Park - see color ad p 686**	◆◆◆	$99-$139 SAVE	686
4 / p. 681		Holiday Inn Express	◆◆◆	$105-$114	689
5 / p. 681	AAA	**Americas Best Value Carolina Duke Inn - see color ad p 685**	◆◆	$55-$60 SAVE	685
6 / p. 681	AAA	**Hilton Durham near Duke University**	◆◆◆	$119-$309 SAVE	688
7 / p. 681	AAA	**Quality Inn & Suites**	◆◆◆	$72-$77 SAVE	690
8 / p. 681	AAA	**Millennium Hotel - see color ad p 691**	◆◆◆	$89-$169 SAVE	690
9 / p. 681		University Inn	◆◆	$73-$125	692
10 / p. 681	AAA	**Brookwood Inn**	◆◆	$89-$169 SAVE	685
11 / p. 681	AAA	**Washington Duke Inn & Golf Club**	◆◆◆◆	$339-$369 SAVE	692
12 / p. 681		La Quinta Inn & Suites Raleigh (Durham-Chapel Hill)	◆◆◆	$65-$129	690
13 / p. 681		Homestead Studio Suites Hotel-Durham/ University	◆◆	$77-$87	689
14 / p. 681	AAA	**Comfort Inn University - see color ad p 687**	◆◆◆	$79-$119 SAVE	686
15 / p. 681	AAA	**Homewood Suites Durham/Chapel Hill - see color ad p 689**	◆◆◆	$109-$164 SAVE	689
16 / p. 681		Staybridge Suites of Durham	◆◆◆	$149-$299	692
17 / p. 681		DoubleTree Guest Suites	◆◆◆	$99-$229	687
18 / p. 681	AAA	**Comfort Inn-Research Triangle Park**	◆◆◆	$69-$169 SAVE	686
19 / p. 681		La Quinta Inn & Suites Raleigh (Research Triangle Park)	◆◆◆	$59-$139	690
20 / p. 681	AAA	**Courtyard by Marriott-RTP/Durham**	◆◆◆	$167-$179 SAVE	687
21 / p. 681	AAA	**Residence Inn by Marriott**	◆◆◆	$197-$211 SAVE	690
22 / p. 681		Candlewood Suites	◆◆	Rates not provided	685
23 / p. 681	AAA	**Four Points by Sheraton**	◆◆◆	Rates not provided SAVE	688
24 / p. 681	AAA	**Hilton Garden Inn - Durham/Southpoint**	◆◆◆	$89-$269 SAVE	688
25 / p. 681		StudioPLUS-Research Triangle Park	◆◆	$86-$96	692
26 / p. 681		Extended Stay Deluxe-Durham-RTP-Miami Blvd North	◆◆	$105-$115	688
27 / p. 681		Wyndham Hotel-Research Triangle Park	◆◆◆	Rates not provided	693
28 / p. 681		Marriott at Research Triangle Park	◆◆◆	$219-$249	690
29 / p. 681		Extended Stay Deluxe-RTP-Miami Blvd-South	◆◆◆	$110-$120	688
30 / p. 681		Holiday Inn Express Hotel & Suites-RTP	◆◆◆	$144-$154	689
31 / p. 681		Homewood Suites by Hilton-Raleigh Durham Airport	◆◆◆	$94-$159	689
32 / p. 681		Hilton-Raleigh-Durham Airport at Research Triangle Park - see color ad p 692	◆◆◆	$99-$249	688
33 / p. 681		Sleep Inn-RDU/RTP	◆◆	$79-$149	691

DURHAM (cont'd)

Map Page	OA	Lodgings (cont'd)	Diamond Rated	High Season	Page
34 / p. 681		Comfort Suites Hotel RTP/RDU	◆◆◆	$72-$180	686
35 / p. 681		Wingate Inn by Wyndham - RTP/RDU Airport	◆◆◆	Rates not provided	692
36 / p. 681	AAA	**Sheraton Imperial Hotel & Convention Center**	◆◆◆	$79-$350 SAVE	691
37 / p. 681	AAA	**SpringHill Suites by Marriott-RTP/Airport**	◆◆◆	$153-$164 SAVE	691

Map Page	OA	Restaurants	Diamond Rated	Cuisine	Meal Range	Page
4 / p. 681		Bennett Pointe Grill	◆◆	American	$6-$19	693
5 / p. 681		Papa's Grille	◆◆◆	Regional Mediterranean	$7-$30	695
6 / p. 681		Honey's Restaurant	◆◆	American	$5-$12	694
7 / p. 681		Magnolia Grill	◆◆◆	American	$22-$28	694
8 / p. 681		Vin Rouge	◆◆◆	French	$10-$22	695
9 / p. 681		George's Garage	◆◆◆	Seafood	$12-$30	694
10 / p. 681		Blue Corn Cafe	◆◆	Latin American	$8-$15	693
11 / p. 681		Parizade	◆◆◆	Mediterranean	$6-$35	695
12 / p. 681		The Mad Hatter's Cafe & Bake Shop	◆	Deli	$5-$10	694
13 / p. 681		Anotherthyme	◆◆◆	Continental	$12-$30	693
14 / p. 681		Nasher Museum Cafe	◆◆	American	$4-$16	694
15 / p. 681		Satisfaction Restaurant & Bar	◆	American	$5-$12	695
16 / p. 681		Taverna Nikos	◆◆◆	Greek	$6-$19	695
17 / p. 681		Pop's-A Durham Trattoria	◆◆	Italian	$9-$18	695
18 / p. 681	AAA	**The Fairview Dining Room**	◆◆◆◆	American	$10-$40	693
19 / p. 681		Four Square Restaurant	◆◆◆◆	American	$19-$30	694
20 / p. 681	AAA	**Pao Lim Asian Bistro & Bar**	◆◆	Chinese	$5-$16	695
21 / p. 681		Nana's	◆◆◆	New American	$17-$28	694
22 / p. 681		Spartacus Restaurant	◆◆	Mediterranean	$7-$23	695
23 / p. 681		Rick's Diner	◆◆	American	$6-$18	695
24 / p. 681		Kemp's Seafood House	◆◆	Seafood	$8-$20	694
25 / p. 681		Firebirds Wood Fired Grill	◆◆◆	American	$8-$36	693
26 / p. 681		Maggiano's Little Italy	◆◆◆	Southern Italian	$11-$38	694

CHAPEL HILL

Map Page	OA	Lodgings	Diamond Rated	High Season	Page
40 / p. 681		Holiday Inn	◆◆	$99-$129	622
41 / p. 681	AAA	**Residence Inn by Marriott-Chapel Hill**	◆◆◆	$197-$211 SAVE	622
42 / p. 681	AAA	**Sheraton Chapel Hill**	◆◆◆	$99-$410 SAVE	623
43 / p. 681		Hampton Inn	◆◆◆	$95-$115	622
44 / p. 681	AAA	**The Siena Hotel**	◆◆◆◆	$119-$300 SAVE	623
45 / p. 681	AAA	**Carolina Inn**	◆◆◆◆	$109-$234 SAVE	621
46 / p. 681	AAA	**Hampton Inn & Suites**	◆◆◆	$99-$279 SAVE	622
47 / p. 681	AAA	**Holiday Inn Express**	◆◆◆	$89-$269 SAVE	622
48 / p. 681	AAA	**Courtyard by Marriott-Chapel Hill - see color ad p 621**	◆◆◆	$174-$184 SAVE	622

Map Page	OA	Restaurants	Diamond Rated	Cuisine	Meal Range	Page
29 / p. 681	AAA	**Weathervane**	◆◆	American	$6-$25	624
30 / p. 681		Squid's Restaurant & Oyster Bar	◆◆	Seafood	$10-$20	624
31 / p. 681	AAA	**Il Palio Ristorante**	◆◆◆◆	New Italian	$9-$30	624
32 / p. 681		La Residence	◆◆◆	Continental	$7-$27	624
33 / p. 681		Top of the Hill Restaurant & Brewery	◆◆	American	$8-$20	624
34 / p. 681		Mama Dip's Kitchen	◆◆	American	$6-$15	624
35 / p. 681		Oriental Garden Chinese & Thai Restaurant	◆◆	Chinese	$4-$11	624
36 / p. 681	AAA	**Elaine's on Franklin**	◆◆◆	New World	$22-$35	623
37 / p. 681		411 West Italian Cafe	◆◆	Italian	$6-$24	623
38 / p. 681		Carolina Brewery	◆◆	American	$6-$20	623
39 / p. 681		Lantern	◆◆◆	Asian	$19-$29	624
40 / p. 681	AAA	**Carolina Crossroads**	◆◆◆◆	Regional American	$9-$24	623
41 / p. 681		Crook's Corner	◆◆	Southern	$11-$22	623
42 / p. 681		Jujube	◆◆	Asian	$6-$20	624
43 / p. 681		Bin 54	◆◆◆	Steak & Seafood	$25-$50	623

RESEARCH TRIANGLE PARK

Map Page	OA	Lodging	Diamond Rated	High Season	Page
51 / p. 681		Radisson Hotel in Research Triangle Park	◆◆◆	$199-$239	806

Map Page	OA	Restaurant	Diamond Rated	Cuisine	Meal Range	Page
49 / p. 681		The Galeria	◆◆◆	American	$8-$21	806

RALEIGH

Map Page	OA	Restaurant	Diamond Rated	Cuisine	Meal Range	Page
1 / p. 681		The Angus Barn	◆◆◆	Steak	$30-$60	802

CARRBORO

Map Page	OA	Restaurant	Diamond Rated	Cuisine	Meal Range	Page
46 / p. 681		Spotted Dog Restaurant & Bar	◆◆	American	$7-$13	615

DURHAM pop. 187,035 (See map and index starting on p. 681)

WHERE TO STAY

AMERICAS BEST VALUE CAROLINA DUKE INN *Book great rates at AAA.com* **Phone:** (919)286-0771 5

AAA SAVE

Motel
$55-$60 All Year

Address: 2517 Guess Rd **Location:** I-85, exit 175, just e. **Facility:** 100 one-bedroom standard units. 2 stories (no elevator), exterior corridors. **Parking:** on-site. **Amenities:** voice mail, irons. **Pool(s):** outdoor. **Leisure Activities:** picnic area with grills. **Guest Services:** coin laundry, area transportation-Duke & VA hospitals, within 3 mi, wireless Internet. **Business Services:** meeting rooms. **Cards:** AX, DS, MC, VI. **Free Special Amenities: continental breakfast and high-speed Internet.** *(See color ad below)*

/ SOME UNITS FEE

ARROWHEAD INN BED AND BREAKFAST **Phone:** 919/477-8430

AAA SAVE

Bed & Breakfast
$140-$350 All Year

Address: 106 Mason Rd **Location:** 7 mi n of I-85 on US 501 (Roxboro Rd). **Facility:** The restored 1775 manor house on 6 acres is furnished with antiques and reproductions, and all rooms have a gas or wood-burning fireplace. Smoke free premises. 9 units. 4 one-bedroom standard units, some with whirlpools. 3 one-bedroom suites, some with whirlpools. 1 cabin and 1 cottage. 2 stories (no elevator), interior/exterior corridors. *Bath:* combo or shower only. **Parking:** on-site. **Terms:** 3 day cancellation notice-fee imposed. **Amenities:** video library, DVD players, CD players, voice mail, irons, hair dryers. **Leisure Activities:** croquet, horseshoes, volleyball. **Guest Services:** wireless Internet. **Cards:** AX, DS, MC, VI. **Free Special Amenities: full breakfast and high-speed Internet.**

VCR / SOME UNITS

BROOKWOOD INN *Book great rates at AAA.com* **Phone:** (919)286-3111 10

AAA SAVE

Hotel
$89-$169 All Year

Address: 2306 Elba St **Location:** SR 147, exit 15B (Hillandale Rd/Fulton St), just w. Located across from Duke & VA hospitals. **Facility:** 148 units. 146 one-bedroom standard units. 2 one-bedroom suites. 5-8 stories, interior corridors. **Parking:** on-site. **Terms:** cancellation fee imposed. **Amenities:** voice mail, irons, hair dryers. *Fee:* video games, safes. **Leisure Activities:** exercise room. **Guest Services:** valet and coin laundry, area transportation-within 3 mi, wireless Internet. **Business Services:** business center. **Cards:** AX, CB, DC, DS, MC, VI. **Free Special Amenities: local telephone calls and high-speed Internet.**

/ SOME UNITS

CANDLEWOOD SUITES *Book at AAA.com* **Phone:** 919/484-9922 22

Hotel
Rates not provided

Address: 1818 E NC Hwy 54 **Location:** I-40, exit 278, just s, then just w. **Facility:** 122 units. 98 one-bedroom standard units with efficiencies. 24 one-bedroom suites with efficiencies. 3 stories, interior corridors. *Bath:* combo or shower only. **Parking:** on-site. **Amenities:** video library, DVD players, CD players, high-speed Internet, dual phone lines, voice mail, irons, hair dryers. **Leisure Activities:** exercise room, basketball. **Guest Services:** complimentary and valet laundry. **Business Services:** business center.

CALL VCR / SOME UNITS FEE

▼ *See AAA listing above* ▼

(See map and index starting on p. 681)

COMFORT INN MEDICAL PARK *Book great rates at AAA.com* **Phone:** (919)471-6100 **3**

AAA SAVE

Hotel
$99-$139 All Year

Address: 1816 Hillandale Rd **Location:** I-85, exit 174, just w. **Facility:** 136 one-bedroom standard units. 5 stories, interior corridors. *Bath:* combo or shower only. **Parking:** on-site. **Amenities:** video games (fee), high-speed Internet, voice mail, irons, hair dryers. **Pool(s):** outdoor. **Leisure Activities:** sauna, exercise room. **Guest Services:** valet and coin laundry, area transportation-within 5 mi, wireless Internet. **Business Services:** meeting rooms, PC. **Cards:** AX, DS, MC, VI. **Free Special Amenities: expanded continental breakfast and high-speed Internet.** *(See color ad below)*

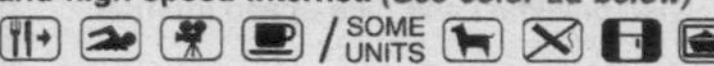

COMFORT INN-RESEARCH TRIANGLE PARK *Book great rates at AAA.com* **Phone:** (919)361-2656 **18**

AAA SAVE

Hotel
$69-$169 All Year

Address: 4507 NC Hwy 55 **Location:** I-40, exit 278, just n. **Facility:** 94 one-bedroom standard units, some with whirlpools. 3 stories, interior/exterior corridors. **Parking:** on-site. **Amenities:** high-speed Internet, dual phone lines, voice mail, irons, hair dryers. **Leisure Activities:** exercise room. **Guest Services:** valet and coin laundry, wireless Internet. **Business Services:** meeting rooms. **Cards:** AX, CB, DC, DS, JC, MC, VI. **Free Special Amenities: expanded continental breakfast and early check-in/late check-out.**

CALL / SOME UNITS

COMFORT INN UNIVERSITY *Book great rates at AAA.com* **Phone:** (919)490-4949 **14**

AAA SAVE

Hotel
$79-$119 All Year

Address: 3508 Mt Moriah Rd **Location:** I-40, exit 270, just n on US 15/501, then just e. **Facility:** 135 units. 117 one-bedroom standard units. 18 one-bedroom suites with whirlpools. 4 stories, interior corridors. *Bath:* combo or shower only. **Parking:** on-site. **Amenities:** voice mail, irons, hair dryers. **Pool(s):** outdoor. **Leisure Activities:** exercise room. **Guest Services:** valet and coin laundry, wireless Internet. **Business Services:** meeting rooms. **Cards:** AX, CB, DC, DS, JC, MC, VI. **Free Special Amenities: expanded continental breakfast and high-speed Internet.** *(See color ad p 687)*

 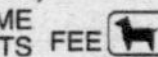  

/ SOME UNITS FEE

COMFORT SUITES HOTEL RTP/RDU *Book at AAA.com* **Phone:** (919)314-1200 **34**

Hotel
$72-$180 All Year

Address: 5219 Page Rd **Location:** I-40, exit 282, just s. **Facility:** Smoke free premises. 125 one-bedroom standard units, some with whirlpools. 5 stories, interior corridors. **Parking:** on-site. **Amenities:** high-speed Internet, dual phone lines, voice mail, irons, hair dryers. **Pool(s):** outdoor. **Leisure Activities:** whirlpool, exercise room. **Guest Services:** valet and coin laundry, area transportation, wireless Internet. **Business Services:** meeting rooms, business center. **Cards:** AX, DC, DS, MC, VI.

ASK CALL 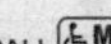    

▼ *See AAA listing above* ▼

(See map and index starting on p. 681)

COURTYARD BY MARRIOTT DURHAM NEAR DUKE UNIVERSITY/DOWNTOWN *Book great rates at AAA.com* **Phone:** (919)309-1500 **2**

Hotel
$138-$148 All Year

Address: 1815 Front St **Location:** I-85, exit 174, just w on Hillandale Rd, then just s. **Facility:** Smoke free premises. 151 units. 146 one-bedroom standard units. 5 one-bedroom suites. 4 stories, interior corridors. *Bath:* combo or shower only. **Parking:** on-site. **Terms:** cancellation fee imposed. **Amenities:** video games (fee), voice mail, irons, hair dryers. **Pool(s):** outdoor. **Leisure Activities:** whirlpool, exercise room. **Guest Services:** valet and coin laundry, wireless Internet. **Business Services:** meeting rooms, PC. **Cards:** AX, DS, MC, VI.

/ SOME UNITS

AAA Benefit:
Members save a minimum 5% off the best available rate.

COURTYARD BY MARRIOTT-RTP/DURHAM *Book great rates at AAA.com* **Phone:** (919)484-2900 

Hotel
$168-$180 All Year

Address: 301 Residence Inn Blvd **Location:** I-40, exit 278, just s on SR 55, then just w. **Facility:** Smoke free premises. 123 units. 117 one-bedroom standard units, some with whirlpools. 6 one-bedroom suites. 3 stories, interior corridors. *Bath:* combo or shower only. **Parking:** on-site. **Terms:** cancellation fee imposed. **Amenities:** high-speed Internet, dual phone lines, voice mail, irons, hair dryers. **Pool(s):** outdoor. **Leisure Activities:** whirlpool, exercise room. **Guest Services:** valet and coin laundry, wireless Internet. **Business Services:** meeting rooms, PC. **Cards:** AX, CB, DC, DS, MC, VI. **Free Special Amenities: newspaper and high-speed Internet.**

CALL / SOME UNITS

AAA Benefit:
Members save a minimum 5% off the best available rate.

DOUBLETREE GUEST SUITES *Book great rates at AAA.com* **Phone:** (919)361-4660 **17**

Hotel
$99-$229 All Year

Address: 2515 Meridian Pkwy **Location:** I-40, exit 278, just n on SR 55, then just w. **Facility:** 203 units. 201 one- and 2 two-bedroom suites, some with whirlpools. 7 stories, interior corridors. **Parking:** on-site. **Terms:** 1-30 night minimum stay, cancellation fee imposed. **Amenities:** voice mail, irons, hair dryers. **Pool(s):** heated indoor/outdoor. **Leisure Activities:** sauna, whirlpool, rental paddleboats, lighted tennis court, rental bicycles, jogging, exercise room, basketball, volleyball. **Guest Services:** valet and coin laundry, area transportation. **Business Services:** meeting rooms, business center. **Cards:** AX, DC, DS, MC, VI.

CALL / SOME UNITS

DOUBLETREE
HOTELS·SUITES·RESORTS·CLUBS

AAA Benefit:
Members save 5% or more everyday!

DURHAM SKYLAND INN, A MAGNUSON HOTEL *Book at AAA.com* **Phone:** (919)383-2508 **1**

Motel
$59-$99 All Year

Address: 5400 US 70 W **Location:** I-85, exit 170, 0.3 mi e on US 70, then just n. Located in a quiet wooded area. **Facility:** 31 one-bedroom standard units. 1 story, exterior corridors. **Parking:** on-site. **Amenities:** high-speed Internet, voice mail, irons, hair dryers. **Pool(s):** outdoor. **Leisure Activities:** playground. **Guest Services:** wireless Internet. **Business Services:** business center. **Cards:** AX, DC, DS, MC, VI.

ASK / SOME UNITS FEE

▼ *See AAA listing p 686* ▼

(See map and index starting on p. 681)

EXTENDED STAY DELUXE-DURHAM-RTP-MIAMI BLVD NORTH *Book at AAA.com* **Phone:** (919)941-2878 26

Hotel
$105-$115 All Year

Address: 4610 S Miami Blvd **Location:** I-40, exit 281, just n. **Facility:** 84 one-bedroom standard units with kitchens. 3 stories, interior corridors. *Bath:* combo or shower only. **Parking:** on-site. **Amenities:** DVD players, voice mail, irons, hair dryers. **Pool(s):** outdoor. **Leisure Activities:** exercise room. **Guest Services:** coin laundry, wireless Internet. **Cards:** AX, CB, DC, DS, JC, MC, VI.

ASK / SOME UNITS FEE

EXTENDED STAY DELUXE-RTP-MIAMI BLVD-SOUTH *Book at AAA.com* **Phone:** (919)998-0400 29

Hotel
$110-$120 All Year

Address: 4919 S Miami Blvd **Location:** I-40, exit 281, just s. **Facility:** 138 units. 129 one-bedroom standard units with efficiencies. 9 one-bedroom suites with efficiencies. 3 stories, interior corridors. *Bath:* some combo or shower only. **Parking:** on-site. **Amenities:** DVD players, dual phone lines, voice mail, irons, hair dryers. **Pool(s):** outdoor. **Leisure Activities:** exercise room. **Guest Services:** coin laundry, area transportation, wireless Internet. **Business Services:** PC. **Cards:** AX, CB, DC, DS, JC, MC, VI.

ASK CALL / SOME UNITS FEE

FOUR POINTS BY SHERATON *Book great rates at AAA.com* **Phone:** 919/806-8200 23

AAA SAVE
Hotel
Rates not provided

Address: 7807 Leonardo Dr **Location:** I-40, exit 274, just s on SR 751. **Facility:** Smoke free premises. 98 units. 93 one-bedroom standard units. 5 one-bedroom suites. 6 stories, interior corridors. *Bath:* combo or shower only. **Parking:** on-site. **Amenities:** high-speed Internet, voice mail, irons, hair dryers. **Pool(s):** heated indoor. **Leisure Activities:** exercise room. **Guest Services:** valet laundry, airport transportation-Raleigh-Durham International Airport, area transportation-Southpoint Mall, wireless Internet. **Business Services:** meeting rooms, business center.

/ SOME UNITS FEE

FOUR POINTS BY SHERATON
AAA Benefit:
Members get up to 15% off, plus Starwood Preferred Guest® bonuses.

HILTON DURHAM NEAR DUKE UNIVERSITY *Book great rates at AAA.com* **Phone:** (919)383-8033 6

AAA SAVE
Hotel
$119-$309 All Year

Address: 3800 Hillsborough Rd **Location:** I-85, exit 173, just e on Cole Mill Rd, then 0.5 mi w on US 70 business route. **Facility:** Smoke free premises. 195 one-bedroom standard units. 6 stories, interior corridors. *Bath:* combo or shower only. **Parking:** on-site. **Terms:** 1-30 night minimum stay, cancellation fee imposed. **Amenities:** video games (fee), high-speed Internet, dual phone lines, voice mail, irons, hair dryers. **Dining:** 2 restaurants. **Pool(s):** outdoor. **Leisure Activities:** whirlpool, exercise room. **Guest Services:** valet and coin laundry, area transportation-within 5 mi, wireless Internet. **Business Services:** conference facilities, business center. **Cards:** AX, CB, DC, DS, JC, MC, VI. **Free Special Amenities: newspaper and high-speed Internet.**

/ SOME UNITS

Hilton
AAA Benefit:
Members save 5% or more everyday!

HILTON GARDEN INN - DURHAM/SOUTHPOINT *Book great rates at AAA.com* **Phone:** (919)544-6000 24

Hotel
$89-$269 All Year

Address: 7007 Fayetteville Rd **Location:** I-40, exit 276, just s. Located across from Streets of Southpoint Mall. **Facility:** Smoke free premises. 150 units. 145 one-bedroom standard units. 5 one-bedroom suites with whirlpools. 6 stories, interior corridors. *Bath:* combo or shower only. **Parking:** on-site. **Terms:** 1-30 night minimum stay, cancellation fee imposed. **Amenities:** high-speed Internet, voice mail, irons, hair dryers. **Pool(s):** heated indoor. **Leisure Activities:** whirlpool, exercise room. **Guest Services:** valet and coin laundry, wireless Internet. **Business Services:** meeting rooms, business center. **Cards:** AX, DC, DS, MC, VI. **Free Special Amenities: newspaper and high-speed Internet.**

CALL

Hilton Garden Inn
AAA Benefit:
Members save 5% or more everyday!

HILTON-RALEIGH-DURHAM AIRPORT AT RESEARCH TRIANGLE PARK *Book great rates at AAA.com* **Phone:** (919)941-6000 

Hotel
$99-$249 All Year

Address: 4810 Page Creek Ln **Location:** I-40, exit 282, just s on Page Rd, then just w. **Facility:** Smoke free premises. 249 units. 240 one-bedroom standard units. 9 one-bedroom suites. 4-5 stories, interior corridors. *Bath:* combo or shower only. **Parking:** on-site. **Terms:** 1-30 night minimum stay, cancellation fee imposed. **Amenities:** dual phone lines, voice mail, irons, hair dryers. **Pool(s):** outdoor. **Leisure Activities:** exercise room. **Guest Services:** complimentary and valet laundry, area transportation, wireless Internet. **Business Services:** conference facilities, business center. **Cards:** AX, CB, DC, DS, JC, MC, VI. ***(See color ad p 692)***

   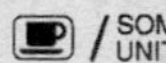  / SOME UNITS

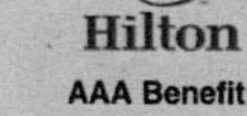

AAA Benefit:
Members save 5% or more everyday!

(See map and index starting on p. 681)

HOLIDAY INN EXPRESS *Book at AAA.com* **Phone:** (919)313-3244 4

Hotel
$105-$114 All Year

Address: 2516 Guess Rd **Location:** I-85, exit 175, just e. **Facility:** 79 one-bedroom standard units. 4 stories, interior corridors. *Bath:* combo or shower only. **Parking:** on-site. **Terms:** 3 day cancellation notice. **Amenities:** high-speed Internet, dual phone lines, voice mail, irons, hair dryers. **Pool(s):** outdoor. **Guest Services:** valet laundry, wireless Internet. **Business Services:** meeting rooms, PC. **Cards:** AX, CB, DC, DS, JC, MC, VI.

ASK / SOME UNITS FEE

HOLIDAY INN EXPRESS HOTEL & SUITES-RTP *Book at AAA.com* **Phone:** (919)474-9800 30

Hotel
$144-$154 All Year

Address: 4912 S Miami Blvd **Location:** I-40, exit 281, just s. **Facility:** 81 one-bedroom standard units. 4 stories, interior corridors. *Bath:* combo or shower only. **Parking:** on-site. **Terms:** 3 day cancellation notice. **Amenities:** high-speed Internet, dual phone lines, voice mail, irons, hair dryers. **Leisure Activities:** exercise room. **Guest Services:** valet and coin laundry, area transportation, wireless Internet. **Business Services:** meeting rooms, PC. **Cards:** AX, CB, DC, DS, JC, MC, VI.

ASK CALL M / SOME UNITS FEE

HOMESTEAD STUDIO SUITES HOTEL-DURHAM/UNIVERSITY *Book at AAA.com* **Phone:** (919)402-1700 13

Hotel
$77-$87 All Year

Address: 1920 Ivy Creek Blvd **Location:** I-40, exit 270, 2 mi n on US 15/501, exit 105B, then just e on Martin Luther King Jr Pkwy; in University Place. **Facility:** 127 units. 117 one-bedroom standard units with efficiencies. 10 one-bedroom suites with efficiencies. 2 stories (no elevator), exterior corridors. *Bath:* combo or shower only. **Parking:** on-site. **Terms:** office hours 7 am-11 pm. **Amenities:** voice mail, irons. **Guest Services:** valet and coin laundry, wireless Internet. **Cards:** AX, CB, DC, DS, JC, MC, VI.

ASK / SOME UNITS FEE

HOMEWOOD SUITES BY HILTON-RALEIGH DURHAM AIRPORT *Book great rates at AAA.com* **Phone:** (919)474-9900 31

Hotel
$94-$159 All Year

Address: 4603 Central Park Dr **Location:** I-40, exit 281, just s. **Facility:** 122 units. 115 one- and 7 two-bedroom suites with efficiencies. 7 stories, interior corridors. *Bath:* combo or shower only. **Parking:** on-site. **Terms:** 1-30 night minimum stay, cancellation fee imposed. **Amenities:** high-speed Internet, dual phone lines, voice mail, irons, hair dryers. **Pool(s):** outdoor. **Leisure Activities:** sauna, whirlpool, exercise room. **Guest Services:** valet and coin laundry, area transportation, wireless Internet. **Business Services:** meeting rooms, business center. **Cards:** AX, CB, DC, DS, MC, VI.

/ SOME UNITS

HOMEWOOD SUITES Hilton
AAA Benefit:
Members save 5% or more everyday!

HOMEWOOD SUITES DURHAM/CHAPEL HILL *Book great rates at AAA.com* **Phone:** (919)401-0610 15

AAA SAVE

Hotel
$109-$164 All Year

Address: 3600 Mt Moriah Rd **Location:** I-40, exit 270, just n on US 15/501, then just e. **Facility:** 96 units. 93 one- and 3 two-bedroom suites. 4 stories, interior corridors. *Bath:* combo or shower only. **Parking:** on-site. **Amenities:** video games (fee), dual phone lines, voice mail, irons, hair dryers. **Pool(s):** outdoor. **Leisure Activities:** exercise room. **Guest Services:** valet and coin laundry, area transportation-within 5 mi, wireless Internet. **Business Services:** meeting rooms. **Cards:** AX, CB, DC, DS, JC, MC, VI. **Free Special Amenities: full breakfast and high-speed Internet.** *(See color ad below)*

CALL M / SOME UNITS FEE

AAA Benefit:
Members save 5% or more everyday!

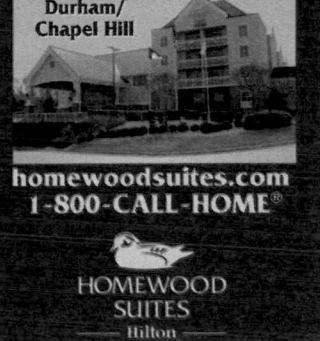

▼ See AAA listing above ▼

(See map and index starting on p. 681)

LA QUINTA INN & SUITES RALEIGH (DURHAM-CHAPEL HILL) *Book great rates at AAA.com* **Phone:** (919)401-9660 12

Hotel
$65-$129 All Year

Address: 4414 Durham Chapel Hill Blvd **Location:** I-40, exit 270, 1.7 mi n on US 15/501. **Facility:** 130 units. 118 one-bedroom standard units. 12 one-bedroom suites. 4 stories, interior corridors. *Bath:* combo or shower only. **Parking:** on-site. **Amenities:** video games (fee), high-speed Internet, voice mail, irons, hair dryers. *Some:* dual phone lines. **Pool(s):** heated indoor. **Leisure Activities:** whirlpool, exercise room. **Guest Services:** valet and coin laundry, wireless Internet. **Business Services:** meeting rooms. **Cards:** AX, DC, DS, MC, VI.

ASK CALL / SOME UNITS

LA QUINTA INN & SUITES RALEIGH (RESEARCH TRIANGLE PARK) *Book great rates at AAA.com* **Phone:** (919)484-1422 19

Hotel
$59-$139 All Year

Address: 1910 W Park Dr **Location:** I-40, exit 278, just n on SR 55, then just e. **Facility:** 141 units. 135 one-bedroom standard units. 6 one-bedroom suites. 6 stories, interior corridors. *Bath:* combo or shower only. **Parking:** on-site. **Amenities:** video games (fee), high-speed Internet, voice mail, irons, hair dryers. *Some:* dual phone lines. **Pool(s):** heated outdoor. **Leisure Activities:** whirlpool, exercise room. **Guest Services:** valet and coin laundry, wireless Internet. **Business Services:** meeting rooms. **Cards:** AX, DC, DS, MC, VI.

ASK CALL / SOME UNITS

MARRIOTT AT RESEARCH TRIANGLE PARK *Book great rates at AAA.com* **Phone:** (919)941-6200 28

Hotel
$219-$249 All Year

Address: 4700 Guardian Dr **Location:** I-40, exit 281, just n on Miami Blvd, then just e. **Facility:** Smoke free premises. 224 units. 222 one-bedroom standard units. 2 one-bedroom suites. 6 stories, interior corridors. *Bath:* combo or shower only. **Parking:** on-site. **Terms:** check-in 4 pm, cancellation fee imposed. **Amenities:** high-speed Internet (fee), dual phone lines, voice mail, irons, hair dryers. *Some:* CD players. **Pool(s):** heated indoor. **Leisure Activities:** whirlpool, exercise room. **Guest Services:** valet laundry, area transportation, wireless Internet. **Business Services:** conference facilities, business center. **Cards:** AX, CB, DC, DS, JC, MC, VI.

CALL / SOME UNITS FEE VCR

Marriott HOTELS & RESORTS
AAA Benefit:
Members save a minimum 5% off the best available rate.

MILLENNIUM HOTEL *Book great rates at AAA.com* **Phone:** (919)383-8575 8

AAA SAVE
Hotel
$89-$169 All Year

Address: 2800 Campus Walk Ave **Location:** US 15/501 Bypass, exit 108A(Morreene Rd), just e, then just n. **Facility:** 313 units. 307 one-bedroom standard units. 6 one-bedroom suites. 4 stories, interior corridors. *Bath:* combo or shower only. **Parking:** on-site. **Terms:** 7 day cancellation notice. **Amenities:** voice mail, irons, hair dryers. *Some:* high-speed Internet (fee). **Pool(s):** heated indoor. **Leisure Activities:** whirlpool, exercise room. **Guest Services:** valet and coin laundry, airport transportation (fee)-Raleigh-Durham International Airport, area transportation-Duke Hospital & area shopping, wireless Internet. **Business Services:** conference facilities, business center. **Cards:** AX, CB, DC, DS, JC, MC, VI. ***(See color ad p 691)***

FEE / SOME UNITS

QUALITY INN & SUITES *Book great rates at AAA.com* **Phone:** (919)382-3388 7

AAA SAVE
Hotel
$72-$77 All Year

Address: 3710 Hillsborough Rd **Location:** I-85, exit 173, just e on Cole Mill Rd, then just w on US 70 business route. **Facility:** 114 units. 105 one-bedroom standard units. 9 one-bedroom suites, some with efficiencies (no utensils). 3 stories, interior/exterior corridors. *Bath:* combo or shower only. **Parking:** on-site. **Amenities:** irons, hair dryers. **Pool(s):** outdoor. **Leisure Activities:** exercise room. **Guest Services:** coin laundry, area transportation-Duke & VA hospitals, wireless Internet. **Business Services:** meeting rooms, PC. **Cards:** AX, CB, DC, DS, JC, MC, VI. **Free Special Amenities: expanded continental breakfast and high-speed Internet.**

/ SOME UNITS FEE

RESIDENCE INN BY MARRIOTT *Book great rates at AAA.com* **Phone:** (919)361-1266 21

AAA SAVE
Hotel
$197-$212 All Year

Address: 201 Residence Inn Blvd **Location:** I-40, exit 278, just s, then just w. **Facility:** Smoke free premises. 122 units. 78 one-bedroom standard units with kitchens. 8 one- and 36 two-bedroom suites with efficiencies. 2 stories (no elevator), interior/exterior corridors. **Parking:** on-site. **Terms:** cancellation fee imposed. **Amenities:** high-speed Internet, voice mail, irons, hair dryers. **Pool(s):** outdoor. **Leisure Activities:** whirlpool, grills, exercise room, sports court. **Guest Services:** valet and coin laundry, wireless Internet. **Business Services:** meeting rooms, PC. **Cards:** AX, CB, DC, DS, JC, MC, VI. **Free Special Amenities: full breakfast and high-speed Internet.**

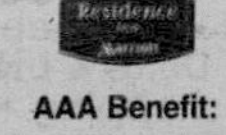

AAA Benefit:
Members save a minimum 5% off the best available rate.

(See map and index starting on p. 681)

SHERATON IMPERIAL HOTEL & CONVENTION CENTER *Book great rates at AAA.com* **Phone:** (919)941-5050 36

AAA SAVE

Hotel
$79-$350 All Year

Address: 4700 Emperor Blvd **Location:** I-40, exit 282, just s, then just e. **Facility:** Smoke free premises. 331 one-bedroom standard units. 10 stories, interior corridors. **Parking:** on-site. **Amenities:** video games (fee), high-speed Internet, dual phone lines, voice mail, irons, hair dryers. *Some:* fax. **Dining:** 2 restaurants. **Pool(s):** outdoor. **Leisure Activities:** 2 lighted tennis courts, jogging. **Guest Services:** valet laundry, airport transportation-Raleigh-Durham International Airport, area transportation-Research Triangle Park, wireless Internet. **Business Services:** conference facilities, business center. **Cards:** AX, CB, DC, DS, JC, MC, VI. **Free Special Amenities: local telephone calls and high-speed Internet.**

FEE / SOME UNITS FEE VCR

AAA Benefit:
Members get up to 15% off, plus Starwood Preferred Guest® bonuses.

SLEEP INN-RDU/RTP *Book at AAA.com* **Phone:** (919)993-3393 33

Hotel
$79-$149 All Year

Address: 5208 Page Rd **Location:** I-40, exit 282, just s. **Facility:** 73 one-bedroom standard units. 4 stories, interior corridors. *Bath:* combo or shower only. **Parking:** on-site. **Amenities:** high-speed Internet, dual phone lines, voice mail, safes (fee), irons, hair dryers. **Leisure Activities:** exercise room. **Guest Services:** valet and coin laundry, area transportation, wireless Internet. **Business Services:** meeting rooms, PC. **Cards:** AX, CB, DC, DS, MC, VI.

SPRINGHILL SUITES BY MARRIOTT-RTP/AIRPORT *Book great rates at AAA.com* **Phone:** (919)998-9500 37

AAA SAVE

Hotel
$153-$164 All Year

Address: 920 Slater Rd **Location:** I-40, exit 282, just s, 0.5 mi e on Emperor Rd, then just n. **Facility:** Smoke free premises. 120 one-bedroom standard units. 4 stories, interior corridors. *Bath:* combo or shower only. **Parking:** on-site. **Terms:** cancellation fee imposed. **Amenities:** high-speed Internet, dual phone lines, voice mail, irons, hair dryers. **Pool(s):** heated indoor. **Leisure Activities:** whirlpool, jogging, exercise room. **Guest Services:** valet and coin laundry, wireless Internet. **Business Services:** meeting rooms, PC. **Cards:** AX, CB, DC, DS, JC, MC, VI. **Free Special Amenities: expanded continental breakfast and high-speed Internet.**

CALL

AAA Benefit:
Members save a minimum 5% off the best available rate.

▼ *See AAA listing p 690* ▼

(See map and index starting on p. 681)

STAYBRIDGE SUITES OF DURHAM Book at AAA.com **Phone:** (919)401-9800 16

Extended Stay Hotel
$149-$299 All Year

Address: 3704 Mt. Moriah Rd **Location:** I-40, exit 270, just n on US 15/501, then just e. **Facility:** Opened in 2008, the casually upscale hotel offers studio suites and one- to two-bedroom floorplans, each with an efficiency kitchenette. 99 units. 58 one-bedroom standard units with efficiencies. 30 one- and 11 two-bedroom suites with efficiencies. 4 stories, interior corridors. *Bath:* combo or shower only. **Parking:** on-site. **Terms:** 3 night minimum stay - seasonal and/or weekends, cancellation fee imposed. **Amenities:** high-speed Internet, voice mail, irons, hair dryers. **Pool(s):** outdoor. **Leisure Activities:** exercise room. **Guest Services:** complimentary and valet laundry, area transportation, wireless Internet. **Business Services:** meeting rooms, business center. **Cards:** AX, CB, DC, DS, JC, MC, VI.

ASK CALL / SOME UNITS FEE

STUDIOPLUS-RESEARCH TRIANGLE PARK Book at AAA.com **Phone:** (919)361-1853 25

Hotel
$86-$96 All Year

Address: 2504 NC Hwy 54 **Location:** I-40, exit 278, just s on SR 55, then just e. **Facility:** 72 one-bedroom standard units with kitchens. 3 stories, interior corridors. *Bath:* combo or shower only. **Parking:** on-site. **Terms:** office hours 7 am-11 pm. **Amenities:** voice mail, irons. **Pool(s):** outdoor. **Leisure Activities:** limited exercise equipment. **Guest Services:** coin laundry, wireless Internet. **Cards:** AX, CB, DC, DS, JC, MC, VI.

ASK / SOME UNITS FEE

UNIVERSITY INN Book at AAA.com **Phone:** (919)286-4421 9

Hotel
$73-$125 All Year

Address: 502 Elf St **Location:** SR 147 (Durham Frwy), exit 15B (Hillandale/Fulton St), just w on Fulton St, then just e on Elba St. Located at Duke and VA Hospitals. **Facility:** 48 one-bedroom standard units. 4 stories, interior corridors. **Parking:** on-site. **Amenities:** high-speed Internet, irons, hair dryers. **Guest Services:** coin laundry, area transportation. **Cards:** AX, DS, MC, VI.

/ SOME UNITS

WASHINGTON DUKE INN & GOLF CLUB Book great rates at AAA.com **Phone:** (919)490-0999 11

AAA SAVE

Hotel
$339-$369 All Year

Address: 3001 Cameron Blvd **Location:** US 15/501 Bypass, exit 107, 0.8 mi s on SR 751. **Facility:** Located in a quiet, wooded area. Displays throughout the hotel honor the Washington Duke family; some rooms offer views of the golf course. Smoke free premises. 271 units. 229 one-bedroom standard units. 38 one- and 4 two-bedroom suites, some with whirlpools. 5 stories, interior corridors. *Bath:* combo or shower only. **Parking:** on-site and valet. **Terms:** cancellation fee imposed. **Amenities:** video games (fee), high-speed Internet, voice mail, safes, honor bars, irons, hair dryers. *Some:* CD players. **Dining:** 3 restaurants, also, The Fairview Dining Room, see separate listing. **Pool(s):** heated indoor. **Leisure Activities:** whirlpool, golf driving range, jogging, exercise room. *Fee:* golf-18 holes, 6 lighted tennis courts. **Guest Services:** valet laundry, area transportation-Duke campus & medical center, wireless Internet. **Business Services:** conference facilities, business center. **Cards:** AX, DC, DS, JC, MC, VI. **Free Special Amenities: newspaper and high-speed Internet.**

24 / SOME UNITS

WINGATE INN BY WYNDHAM - RTP/RDU AIRPORT Book at AAA.com **Phone:** 919/941-2854 35

Hotel
Rates not provided

Address: 5223 Page Rd **Location:** I-40, exit 282, just s. **Facility:** 84 one-bedroom standard units, some with whirlpools. 4 stories, interior corridors. *Bath:* combo or shower only. **Parking:** on-site. **Amenities:** video games (fee), high-speed Internet, dual phone lines, voice mail, safes, irons, hair dryers. **Leisure Activities:** whirlpool, jogging, exercise room. **Guest Services:** valet laundry, area transportation, wireless Internet. **Business Services:** meeting rooms, business center.

/ SOME UNITS

▼ *See AAA listing p 688* ▼

(See map and index starting on p. 681)

WYNDHAM HOTEL-RESEARCH TRIANGLE PARK Book at AAA.com Phone: 919/941-6066 (27)

Hotel
Rates not provided

Address: 4620 S Miami Blvd **Location:** I-40, exit 281, just n. **Facility:** 175 one-bedroom standard units. 7 stories, interior corridors. *Bath:* combo or shower only. **Parking:** on-site. **Amenities:** high-speed Internet (fee), dual phone lines, voice mail, irons, hair dryers. *Some:* CD players. **Pool(s):** outdoor. **Leisure Activities:** exercise room. **Guest Services:** valet laundry, area transportation, wireless Internet. **Business Services:** meeting rooms, business center.

/ SOME UNITS FEE FEE VCR

WHERE TO DINE

ANOTHERTHYME Phone: 919/682-5225 (13)

Continental
$12-$30

The neighborhood bistro has been a popular dining spot for more than 30 years. The eclectic, seasonal changing menu has its roots in vegetarian and other healthy fare. Entrees may include pan-seared herb-rubbed pork chops or almond-coated free-range fried chicken. Casual dress. **Bar:** Full bar. **Reservations:** accepted. **Hours:** 5:30 pm-9:30 pm, Fri & Sat-10 pm. Closed: 1/1, 11/26, 12/24, 12/25. **Address:** 109 N Gregson St **Location:** SR 147 (Durham Frwy), exit 12C (Duke St), 0.5 mi n, just w on Morgan St, then just s. **Parking:** on-site. **Cards:** AX, DS, MC, VI.

BENNETT POINTE GRILL Phone: 919/382-9431 (4)

American
$6-$19

Daily specials and pasta and seafood entrees are prepared in a comfortable neighborhood atmosphere. The menu lists such specialties as shrimp and grits and slow-roasted pork tenderloin, as well as pasta entrees, steaks, sandwiches and salads. Casual dress. **Bar:** Full bar. **Hours:** 11:30 am-2:30 & 5-9:30 pm, Sat from 5 pm. Closed: 4/12, 11/26, 12/25; also Sun. **Address:** 4625 Hillsborough Rd **Location:** I-85, exit 173, just e, then 1.9 mi s; in Bennett Pointe Shopping Center. **Parking:** on-site. **Cards:** AX, DS, MC, VI.

BLUE CORN CAFE Phone: 919/286-9600 (10)

Latin American
$8-$15

Local artists provide a changing display on the walls of the casual eatery's dining room, where Cuban, Puerto Rican and Mexican dishes are the focus. Favorites include ropa vieja, picadillo and grilled chicken in mole sauce. Several vegetarian selections are offered as well. Casual dress. **Bar:** Full bar. **Hours:** 11:30 am-9 pm, Fri & Sat-9:30 pm. Closed: 1/1, 11/26, 12/24-12/26; also Sun. **Address:** 716 Ninth St **Location:** SR 147 (Durham Frwy), exit 14 (Swift Ave), just n, just w on Main St, then just n. **Parking:** on-site. **Cards:** AX, DS, MC, VI.

THE FAIRVIEW DINING ROOM Phone: 919/493-6699 (18)

AAA

American
$10-$40

Tranquil elegance combines with a casual resort ambience in this dining room overlooking the golf course. The atmosphere becomes more lively before Duke University events. Well-prepared and nicely presented regional American cuisine utilizes fresh ingredients and incorporates French and Italian influences. A pianist entertains nightly. Dressy casual. Entertainment. **Bar:** Full bar. **Reservations:** suggested. **Hours:** 7-10:30 am, 11:30-2:30 & 5:30-10 pm. **Address:** 3001 Cameron Blvd **Location:** US 15/501 Bypass, exit 107, 0.8 mi s on SR 751; in Washington Duke Inn & Golf Club. **Parking:** on-site and valet. **Cards:** AX, CB, DC, DS, MC, VI.

CALL M

FIREBIRDS WOOD FIRED GRILL Phone: 919/544-6332 (25)

American
$8-$36

The restaurant re-creates the atmosphere of a mountain lodge. Hand-cut steaks and seafood dominate the menu, which also lists a few pork and chicken entrees, as well as elk tenderloin medallions and buffalo meatloaf. The kitchen uses wood grilling, and pizzas bake in a wood-burning oven. Flavorful food, enhanced presentations and a skilled, knowledgeable and attentive staff, together with distinctive physical elements, make this place appealing. Casual dress. **Bar:** Full bar. **Hours:** 11 am-10 pm, Fri & Sat-11 pm. Closed: 1/1, 11/26, 12/25. **Address:** 8030 Renaissance Pkwy **Location:** I-40, exit 276, 0.3 mi s; in Southpoint Mall on Main Street. **Parking:** on-site. **Cards:** AX, DC, DS, MC, VI.

(See map and index starting on p. 681)

FOUR SQUARE RESTAURANT **Phone:** 919/401-9877 (19)

American
$19-$30

Built in 1908, the neo-Classical, revival-style Victorian home is listed on the National Register of Historic Places. The talented owner/chefs are known for their excellent presentations. With the exception of the seasonally changing desserts, every course changes monthly. The screened porch offers cozy seating during nice weather. Dressy casual. **Bar:** Full bar. **Reservations:** suggested. **Hours:** 5:30 pm-9:30 pm. Closed: 1/1, 7/4, 12/25, 12/26; also Sun, week after 1/1 & week of 7/4. **Address:** 2701 Chapel Hill Rd **Location:** US 15/501 Bypass, exit 106 (Cornwallis St), 1.2 mi e, then just n on Pickett; immediately across road at dead end. **Parking:** on-site. **Cards:** AX, DC, MC, VI. **Historic**

GEORGE'S GARAGE **Phone:** 919/286-4131 (9)

Seafood
$12-$30

The smartly casual eatery presents a menu of fresh seafood and sushi, along with freshly baked breads and desserts. The gourmet food market adjacent to the dining room is a local favorite for lunch, offering a hot and cold buffet for eat-in or carry-out. Dressy casual. **Bar:** Full bar. **Reservations:** accepted. **Hours:** 5 pm-10 pm, Fri & Sat-11 pm. Closed: 12/25. **Address:** 737 Ninth St **Location:** SR 147 (Durham Frwy), exit 14 (Swift Ave), just n, just w on Main St, then just n. **Parking:** on-site. **Cards:** AX, DC, DS, MC, VI.

HONEY'S RESTAURANT **Phone:** 919/477-2181 (6)

American
$5-$12

Breakfast is served around the clock at this family-friendly diner where home-cooking is "queen bee." Favorites like meat loaf, pot roast and fried chicken are dished up with an assortment of vegetables. Casual dress. **Hours:** 24 hours. Closed: 12/25. **Address:** 2700 Guess Rd **Location:** I-85, exit 175, just w. **Parking:** on-site. **Cards:** AX, DS, MC, VI.

KEMP'S SEAFOOD HOUSE **Phone:** 919/957-7155 (24)

Seafood
$8-$20

Calabash-style battered and fried seafood is the specialty of the house although broiled, Cajun-broiled and steamed items also are offered. Portions are huge, and the hush puppies are plump, flavorful and served piping hot. The dining room is spacious and casual, and the service is efficient. Casual dress. **Bar:** Full bar. **Hours:** 5 pm-9 pm, Fri-Sun from 4 pm. Closed: 11/26, 12/25. **Address:** 115 Page Point Cir **Location:** I-540, exit 4, 3.4 mi w on US 70, just s on Page Rd, then just e. **Parking:** on-site. **Cards:** AX, DS, MC, VI.

THE MAD HATTER'S CAFE & BAKE SHOP **Phone:** 919/286-1987 (12)

Deli
$5-$10

The casual cafe and bakery occupies a vintage corner across from the Duke University campus and is popular with students and locals for its gourmet soups, salads, sandwiches, wraps and Pacific Rim noodle bowls. Breakfast is served all day. Displays of cookies, cakes and other confections in the bakery cases delight both the eye and, later, the sweet tooth. Casual dress. **Hours:** 7 am-9 pm, Sun 8 am-4 pm. Closed: 1/1, 11/26, 12/25. **Address:** 1802 W Main St **Location:** SR 147 (Durham Frwy), exit 14 (Swife Ave), 0.4 mi n on Broad St. **Parking:** on-site. **Cards:** AX, MC, VI.

MAGGIANO'S LITTLE ITALY **Phone:** 919/572-0070 (26)

Southern Italian
$11-$38

Diners savor scrumptious, traditional favorites served in a bustling atmosphere reminiscent of Little Italy. The dining area projects an early-20th-century feel; loud conversations bouncing off high ceilings evoke a sense of the Roaring 20s. **Bar:** Full bar. **Reservations:** suggested. **Hours:** 11 am-10 pm, Fri & Sat-11 pm. Closed: 12/25. **Address:** 8030 Renaissance Pkwy, Suite 890 **Location:** I-40, exit 276, just s; in Southpoint Mall on Main Street. **Parking:** on-site. **Cards:** AX, CB, DC, DS, JC, MC, VI.

MAGNOLIA GRILL **Phone:** 919/286-3609 (7)

American
$22-$28

Considered one of the Triangle's top dining destinations, the Magnolia Grill features seasonal American cuisine by a James Beard Award-winning chef on a menu that changes almost daily, as well as an extensive, well-priced wine list. Dressy casual. **Bar:** Full bar. **Reservations:** suggested. **Hours:** 6 pm-8:30 pm, Fri & Sat 5:30 pm-9:30 pm. Closed major holidays; also Sun & Mon. **Address:** 1002 Ninth St **Location:** SR 147 (Durham Frwy), exit 14 (Swift Ave), just n, just w on Main St, then 0.5 mi n. **Parking:** on-site. **Cards:** AX, MC, VI.

NANA'S **Phone:** 919/493-8545 (21)

New American
$17-$28

For more than 10 years, the restaurant has been considered one of the top dining destinations in the Triangle. Patrons discover why when they settle into the cozy dining room and sample courses from a seasonally changing menu that features fresh ingredients prepared with flair. Fresh fish is always on the menu, along with a risotto appetizer, although the preparation style varies to showcase the chef's talents and innovations. Dressy casual. **Bar:** Full bar. **Reservations:** suggested. **Hours:** 5:30 pm-10 pm. Closed major holidays; also Sun. **Address:** 2514 University Dr **Location:** SR 147 (Durham Frwy), exit 12B, 1.9 mi s on US 15/501 business route to University Dr, then 1 mi. **Parking:** on-site. **Cards:** AX, DC, DS, MC, VI.

NASHER MUSEUM CAFE **Phone:** 919/684-6032 (14)

American
$4-$16

After exploring the exhibits inside Nasher Museum on the west campus of Duke University, art lovers can savor a tasty repast in the casual cafe. Seasonally changing dishes, which draw on a Southern influence, rely on fresh local produce, meats and cheeses. Soups, salads, sandwiches and varied desserts are favorite choices. Casual dress. **Bar:** Wine only. **Hours:** 10 am-4:30 pm, Thurs-8:30 pm, Sun noon-4:30 pm. Closed major holidays; also Mon. **Address:** 2001 Campus Dr **Location:** SR 147 (Durham Frwy), exit 14 (Swift Ave), just s, then just w on Duke University Rd; in Nasher Museum of Art. **Parking:** on-site (fee). **Cards:** AX, DS, MC, VI.

CALL

(See map and index starting on p. 681)

PAO LIM ASIAN BISTRO & BAR — **Phone:** 919/419-1771 (20)

Chinese
$5-$16

The busy eatery's menu is a showcase for the chef-owner's flair for Indian-Chinese fusion cuisine. Also offered are traditional Chinese favorites and some Thai fare. Dressy casual. **Bar:** Full bar. **Reservations:** accepted. **Hours:** 11:30 am-9:30 pm, Fri-10 pm, Sat noon-10 pm, Sun noon-9:30 pm. Closed: 11/26, 12/25. **Address:** 2505 Durham-Chapel Hill Blvd **Location:** I-40, exit 270, 2.3 mi n on US 15/501, exit 105A, 2.2 mi n on US 15/501 business route. **Parking:** on-site. **Cards:** AX, DS, MC, VI.

PAPA'S GRILLE — **Phone:** 919/383-8502 (5)

Regional Mediterranean
$7-$30

For more than 10 years, this family-owned-and-operated bistro has offered well-prepared, contemporary Mediterranean Rim cuisine in comfortably elegant surroundings. The focus of the frequently changing menu is on fresh ingredients, including seasonal vegetables and homemade pastas. Casual dress. **Bar:** Full bar. **Reservations:** suggested, weekends. **Hours:** 11:30 am-2:30 & 5-10 pm, Fri & Sat-10:30 pm. Closed: 1/1, 11/26, 12/25; also Sun. **Address:** 1821 Hillandale Rd **Location:** I-85, exit 174A, just w; in Loehmann's Plaza. **Parking:** on-site. **Cards:** AX, DC, DS, MC, VI.

PARIZADE — **Phone:** 919/286-9712 (11)

Mediterranean
$6-$35

Contemporary Mediterranean fare shares the menu with vegetarian selections at the casually upscale cafe, a favorite for the local business crowd. The lively dining room sports hammered-copper accents and colorful paintings, and diners are afforded a view of the kitchen. Dressy casual. **Bar:** Full bar. **Reservations:** suggested. **Hours:** 11:30 am-2:30 & 5:30-10 pm, Fri-11 pm, Sat 5:30 pm-11 pm, Sun 5:30 pm-9 pm. Closed: 1/1, 9/7, 12/25. **Address:** 2200 W Main St **Location:** SR 147 (Durham Frwy), exit 14 (Swift Ave), just n, then 0.4 mi w; in Erwin Square. **Parking:** on-site. **Cards:** AX, DC, DS, MC, VI.

POP'S-A DURHAM TRATTORIA — **Phone:** 919/956-7677 (17)

Italian
$9-$18

In the Brightleaf district downtown, the former warehouse has an open kitchen with a wood-fired oven. Fresh, local ingredients are incorporated into pizzas, pastas and other Northern Italian dishes. Casual dress. **Bar:** Full bar. **Reservations:** accepted. **Hours:** 5:30 pm-9 pm. Closed major holidays. **Address:** 810 W Peabody St **Location:** SR 147 (Durham Frwy), exit 12C (Duke St) northbound, just n, then just w; exit 13 (Chapel Hill St) southbound, just w, then just n. **Parking:** on-site. **Cards:** AX, DS, MC, VI.

RICK'S DINER — **Phone:** 919/419-0907 (23)

American
$6-$18

Hearty, daily specials share space on a menu offering such classics as meatloaf, hamburger steak, burgers and vegetable plates. Casual dress. **Bar:** Beer & wine. **Hours:** 7 am-3 pm, Wed-Sat to 8:30 pm. Closed: 11/26, 12/25. **Address:** 4015 Univeristy Dr **Location:** I-40, exit 270, 2 mi n on US 15/501, exit 105B, just e on Martin Luther King Jr Pkwy, then 0.4 mi n; in BB&T Plaza. **Parking:** on-site. **Cards:** AX, DS, MC, VI.

SATISFACTION RESTAURANT & BAR — **Phone:** 919/682-7397 (15)

American
$5-$12

The restaurant builds its menu on hand-spun pizzas, vegetarian entrees and gourmet burgers. Wash down a meal with your choice of one of 13 beers on tap, 80 beers in bottles or a choice from an expanded wine list. Patrons can catch the game of the day on one of many TVs scattered around the bar. Casual dress. **Bar:** Full bar. **Hours:** 11 am-1 am, Sun noon-10 pm. Closed: 7/4, 11/26, 12/24, 12/25. **Address:** 905 W Main St **Location:** SR 147 (Durham Frwy), exit 12C (Duke St), just n, then just w; in Brightleaf Square. **Parking:** on-site. **Cards:** AX, DS, MC, VI.

SPARTACUS RESTAURANT — **Phone:** 919/489-2848 (22)

Mediterranean
$7-$23

Tasty, traditional Greek dishes—such as roasted lamb and beef, pasta and spanakopita—are on the menu at the popular eatery. Guests can check out daily lunch buffets, in addition to dinner buffets on Wednesday and Sunday. Casual dress. **Bar:** Full bar. **Reservations:** accepted. **Hours:** 11 am-10 pm, Fri & Sat-11 pm, Sun noon-9 pm. Closed: 11/26, 12/25. **Address:** 4139 Chapel Hill Blvd **Location:** I-40, exit 270, 2 mi n on US 15/501, exit 105 A, just n on US 15/501 business route; access via Service Rd. **Parking:** on-site. **Cards:** AX, DC, DS, MC, VI.

TAVERNA NIKOS — **Phone:** 919/682-0043 (16)

Greek
$6-$19

Salads, hearty entrees, sandwiches and appetizers are prepared with a Mediterranean flair. The large, bustling warehouse also houses shops for after-dinner browsing. Casual dress. **Bar:** Full bar. **Reservations:** suggested. **Hours:** 11 am-3 & 5-10 pm. Closed major holidays; also Sun. **Address:** 905 W Main St **Location:** SR 147 (Durham Frwy), exit 12C (Duke St), just n then just w; in Brightleaf Square. **Parking:** on-site. **Cards:** AX, DC, DS, MC, VI.

VIN ROUGE — **Phone:** 919/416-0406 (8)

French
$10-$22

Provencal cooking is on the menu at the cozy French cafe and wine bar. Outdoor seating is available in the garden. Casual dress. **Bar:** Full bar. **Reservations:** suggested. **Hours:** 5:30 pm-10 pm, Fri & Sat-11 pm; Sun 10:30 am-2 & 5:30-9 pm. Closed: 11/26, 12/25; also Mon. **Address:** 2010 Hillsborough Rd **Location:** SR 147 (Durham Frwy), exit 14 (Swift Ave), just n, just w on Main St, then 0.4 mi n on Ninth St. **Parking:** on-site. **Cards:** AX, DC, DS, MC, VI.

EDEN pop. 15,908

WHERE TO STAY

HAMPTON INN *Book great rates at AAA.com* **Phone:** (336)627-1111

Hotel
$99-$111 All Year

Address: 724 S Van Buren Rd **Location:** Jct SR 700/770, 1.4 mi s on SR 87/14. **Facility:** 72 one-bedroom standard units, some with whirlpools. 3 stories, interior corridors. *Bath:* combo or shower only. **Parking:** on-site. **Amenities:** high-speed Internet, voice mail, irons, hair dryers. **Pool(s):** outdoor. **Leisure Activities:** exercise room. **Guest Services:** valet and coin laundry, wireless Internet. **Business Services:** meeting rooms, PC. **Cards:** AX, CB, DC, DS, JC, MC, VI.

/ SOME UNITS FEE

AAA Benefit: Members save up to 10% everyday!

JAMESON INN *Book at AAA.com* **Phone:** (336)627-0472

Motel
$73-$78 All Year

Address: 716 Linden Dr **Location:** Jct SR 700/770, 1.4 mi s on SR 87/14, then just e. **Facility:** 41 one-bedroom standard units, some with whirlpools. 2 stories (no elevator), exterior corridors. **Parking:** on-site. **Terms:** cancellation fee imposed. **Amenities:** irons, hair dryers. **Pool(s):** outdoor. **Leisure Activities:** exercise room. **Guest Services:** valet laundry, wireless Internet. **Business Services:** PC. **Cards:** AX, DC, DS, MC, VI.

ASK CALL / SOME UNITS FEE

EDENTON pop. 5,394

WHERE TO STAY

HAMPTON INN *Book great rates at AAA.com* **Phone:** (252)482-3500

Hotel
$87-$99 All Year

Address: 115 Hampton Dr **Location:** US 17 Bypass, exit 227, just n on SR 32. **Facility:** 61 units. 58 one-bedroom standard units, some with whirlpools. 3 one-bedroom suites. 3 stories, interior corridors. *Bath:* combo or shower only. **Parking:** on-site. **Terms:** 1-30 night minimum stay, cancellation fee imposed. **Amenities:** dual phone lines, voice mail, irons, hair dryers. **Pool(s):** outdoor. **Leisure Activities:** exercise room. **Guest Services:** valet and coin laundry, wireless Internet. **Business Services:** meeting rooms, business center. **Cards:** AX, CB, DC, DS, MC, VI.

CALL / SOME UNITS

AAA Benefit: Members save up to 10% everyday!

SUPER 8 MOTEL *Book at AAA.com* **Phone:** 252/482-2017

Motel
Rates not provided

Address: 501 Virginia Rd **Location:** US 17 Bypass, exit 227, just n on SR 32. **Facility:** 66 one-bedroom standard units. 2 stories (no elevator), exterior corridors. **Parking:** on-site. **Amenities:** irons, hair dryers. **Pool(s):** outdoor. **Guest Services:** wireless Internet.

CALL / SOME UNITS

THE TRESTLE HOUSE INN **Phone:** 252/482-2282

Bed & Breakfast
Rates not provided

Address: 632 Soundside Rd **Location:** Jct US 17 business route (Broad St), 2 mi s on SR 32 S (E Church St), then 2.8 mi w on SR 94 S. **Facility:** Smoke free premises. 5 one-bedroom standard units. 3 stories (no elevator), interior corridors. *Bath:* combo or shower only. **Parking:** on-site. **Terms:** age restrictions may apply. **Leisure Activities:** rental canoes, fishing, recreation programs, rental bicycles. *Fee:* horseback riding. **Guest Services:** TV in common area, wireless Internet. **Business Services:** meeting rooms.

WHERE TO DINE

CHERO'S MARKET CAFE & CATERING **Phone:** 252/482-5525

American
$6-$20

Nestled across from the waterfront, the casual, colorful cafe serves sandwiches, wraps and quesadillas for lunch and more innovative chicken, seafood, pasta and beef dishes at dinner. During warm weather, outdoor seating is an appealing option. Casual dress. **Bar:** Full bar. **Hours:** 11:30 am-2 & 5:30-9 pm, Sun & Tues-2 pm; Sunday brunch. Closed: 11/26; also Mon. **Address:** 112 W Water St **Location:** Jct Broad St, just w; downtown. **Parking:** on-site. **Cards:** MC, VI.

KRISTY'S PLACE **Phone:** 252/482-7655

Pizza
$7-$16

The family-friendly restaurant presents a menu of tasty pizza, pasta and sandwiches. Casual dress. **Bar:** Beer & wine. **Hours:** 11 am-9 pm, Fri & Sat-10 pm. Closed: 11/26, 12/25; also Sun. **Address:** 321 S Broad St **Location:** Just n from waterfront; downtown. **Parking:** street. **Cards:** MC, VI.

WATERMAN'S GRILL **Phone:** 252/482-7733

Seafood
$11-$21

The raw bar, numerous daily specials and a host of steak and seafood favorites draw crowds to the casual grill, which has a two-story dining room. Save room for a slice of one of the homemade pies. Casual dress. **Bar:** Full bar. **Hours:** 4:30 pm-9 pm, Fri & Sat-9:30 pm. Closed: 11/26, 12/24, 12/25; also Sun & 1/1-1/4. **Address:** 427 S Broad St **Location:** Just n from waterfront; town center. **Parking:** street. **Cards:** AX, DC, DS, MC, VI.

ELIZABETH CITY pop. 17,188

WHERE TO STAY

THE CULPEPPER INN **Phone:** (252)335-9235

Bed & Breakfast
$105-$175 All Year

Address: 609 W Main St **Location:** Jct US 158, just s on US 17, 0.4 mi s; in historic district. **Facility:** Comprised of a 1936 Colonial Revival home and contemporary guest house; some units feature a working fireplace and two-person soaking tub. Smoke free premises. 11 one-bedroom standard units. 2 stories (no elevator), interior/exterior corridors. *Bath:* combo or shower only. **Parking:** on-site. **Terms:** check-in 4 pm, age restrictions may apply. **Amenities:** DVD players, CD players, hair dryers. **Guest Services:** wireless Internet. **Business Services:** meeting rooms. **Cards:** AX, DS, MC, VI. **Free Special Amenities: full breakfast and high-speed Internet.**

  / SOME UNITS   

FAIRFIELD INN & SUITES *Book great rates at AAA.com* **Phone:** (252)333-1003

Hotel
$136 All Year

Address: 1640 City Center Blvd **Location:** US 17 Bypass, exit 258, 2.5 mi se on Halstead Blvd Ext (SR 344), just s on Ridgefield Dr, then just se. **Facility:** Smoke free premises. 97 units. 95 one-bedroom standard units, some with whirlpools. 2 one-bedroom suites. 4 stories, interior corridors. *Bath:* combo or shower only. **Parking:** on-site. **Amenities:** high-speed Internet, dual phone lines, voice mail, irons, hair dryers. **Pool(s):** heated indoor. **Leisure Activities:** whirlpool, exercise room. **Guest Services:** valet and coin laundry, wireless Internet. **Business Services:** meeting rooms, business center. **Cards:** AX, DS, MC, VI.

AAA Benefit:
Members save a minimum 5% off the best available rate.

HAMPTON INN *Book great rates at AAA.com* **Phone:** (252)333-1800

Hotel
$93-$190 All Year

Address: 402 Halstead Blvd **Location:** US 17 Bypass, exit 258, 3 mi s on SR 344. **Facility:** 101 one-bedroom standard units, some with whirlpools. 5 stories, interior corridors. *Bath:* combo or shower only. **Parking:** on-site. **Terms:** 1-30 night minimum stay, cancellation fee imposed. **Amenities:** voice mail, irons, hair dryers. **Pool(s):** outdoor. **Leisure Activities:** whirlpool, exercise room. **Guest Services:** valet laundry, wireless Internet. **Business Services:** meeting rooms, PC. **Cards:** AX, CB, DC, DS, MC, VI.

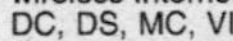 CALL  / SOME UNITS

AAA Benefit:
Members save up to 10% everyday!

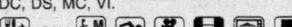

HOLIDAY INN EXPRESS *Book at AAA.com* **Phone:** 252/338-8900

Hotel
Rates not provided

Address: 306 S Hughes Blvd **Location:** US 17 Bypass, exit 258, 3 mi se on Halstead Blvd Ext (SR 344), then 0.4 mi n. **Facility:** 79 one-bedroom standard units. 5 stories, interior corridors. **Parking:** on-site. **Amenities:** dual phone lines, voice mail, irons, hair dryers. **Pool(s):** outdoor. **Guest Services:** valet and coin laundry, wireless Internet.

/ SOME UNITS

MICROTEL INN & SUITES *Book at AAA.com* **Phone:** 252/331-7751

Hotel
Rates not provided

Address: 848 Halstead Blvd **Location:** US 17 Bypass, exit 258, 3.5 mi s on SR 344. **Facility:** 80 units. 78 one-bedroom standard units. 2 one-bedroom suites. 3 stories, interior corridors. *Bath:* combo or shower only. **Parking:** on-site. **Amenities:** voice mail. **Guest Services:** wireless Internet.

/ SOME UNITS

THE POND HOUSE INN **Phone:** (252)335-9834

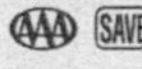

Bed & Breakfast
$108-$160 All Year

Address: 915 Rivershore Rd **Location:** Jct US 17 business route, 2.1 mi se on Halstead Blvd, 1.2 mi n on Edgewood Dr, keep straight on Park Dr and Rivershore Rd. **Facility:** On the Pasquotank River, the classic Colonial Revival house offers views of the water from every room; the property is close to downtown attractions. Smoke free premises. 4 one-bedroom standard units. 2 stories (no elevator), interior/exterior corridors. *Bath:* combo or shower only. **Parking:** on-site. **Terms:** 2 night minimum stay - seasonal and/or weekends, 7 day cancellation notice. **Amenities:** video library, DVD players, irons, hair dryers. **Leisure Activities:** canoeing, boat dock, bicycles. **Guest Services:** wireless Internet. **Business Services:** meeting rooms. **Cards:** AX, MC, VI. **Free Special Amenities: full breakfast and high-speed Internet.**

FEE / SOME UNITS

WHERE TO DINE

THE CIRCLE II RESTAURANT **Phone:** 252/338-3060

American
$4-$14

The locally popular diner features a lengthy menu ranging from salads and sandwiches to such comfort foods as hamburger, steak and fried chicken. A few Italian and Greek favorites round out the list. Casual dress. **Bar:** Beer & wine. **Hours:** 6 am-9 pm, Fri & Sat-10 pm; to 10 pm, Fri & Sat-11 pm 5/31-9/1. Closed: 11/26, 12/25. **Address:** 205 S Hughes Blvd **Location:** Jct US 158, 0.7 mi s on US 17. **Parking:** on-site. **Cards:** DS, MC, VI.

THE CITY WINE SELLAR BAKERY, DELI & WINE BAR

Phone: 252/335-1163

Deli
$4-$8

Huge sandwiches in a dozen varieties are on the menu at the tiny delicatessen, which is near the waterfront. Casual dress. **Bar:** Beer & wine. **Reservations:** not accepted. **Hours:** 7 am-6 pm, Fri-9 pm, Sat 10 am-3 pm. Closed: 1/1, 11/26, 12/24-12/26; also Sun. **Address:** 102 Water St **Location:** Corner of Main and Water sts; downtown. **Parking:** on-site. **Cards:** AX, DS, MC, VI.

CYPRESS CREEK GRILL

Phone: 252/334-9915

American
$6-$20

The menu at the casual downtown eatery lists seafood, steaks, sandwiches and homemade soups, as well as items from its Texas grill, including fajitas and Monterey chicken. Casual dress. **Bar:** Full bar. **Hours:** 11 am-9 pm, Fri-10 pm, Sat 5 pm-10 pm. Closed major holidays; also Sun. **Address:** 113 S Water St **Location:** Center. **Parking:** street. **Cards:** AX, MC, VI.

GROUPER'S WATERFRONT GRILLE

Phone: 252/331-2431

American
$5-$20

Guests can settle into a warm, tavern-like atmosphere and enjoy a panoramic view of the Pasquotank River. Fresh ingredients and appealing presentations are elements of the owner/chef's tasty cuisine. When the weather permits, unwind on the patio. Casual dress. **Bar:** Full bar. **Hours:** 11:30 am-10 pm, Sun noon-9 pm. Closed: 12/25. **Address:** 400 S Water St **Location:** Downtown; in Water Works Building. **Parking:** on-site. **Cards:** AX, DS, MC, VI.

MARINA RESTAURANT & BAR

Phone: 252/335-7307

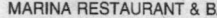

Seafood
$4-$19

A good variety of broiled and fried seafood, sandwiches and appetizers is served in small, wood-paneled dining rooms overlooking the Pasquotank River. Seasonal deck dining is an option, and the oyster and raw bars are open year-round. Casual dress. **Bar:** Full bar. **Hours:** 11 am-2 & 5-9 pm, Sat from 5 pm, Sun 11 am-9 pm. Closed: 12/24, 12/25; also Mon. **Address:** 35 Camden Cswy **Location:** On US 158, just e of Camden Bridge. **Parking:** on-site. **Cards:** AX, MC, VI.

ROMA'S ITALIAN RESTAURANT

Phone: 252/333-1700

Italian
$5-$16

Just north of town, Roma's welcomes your family for pizza, pasta and submarine sandwiches. If it's your birthday, let the chef/own regale you with an operatic rendition of "Happy Birthday" and bring you a sweet something from the kitchen. Casual dress. **Bar:** Beer & wine. **Hours:** 11 am-10 pm, Fri & Sat-11 pm. Closed major holidays; also Mon. **Address:** 2012-D N Road St **Location:** Jct US 158, 5 mi n on US 17; in Mildred's Plaza. **Parking:** on-site. **Cards:** AX, DS, MC, VI.

ELIZABETHTOWN pop. 3,698

WHERE TO DINE

THE FRONT PORCH

Phone: 910/862-3330

American
$6-$12

The popular eating place serves steaks, chicken and other dishes with a Southern flavor. A large buffet is laid out at lunch and dinner. Casual dress. **Bar:** Beer & wine. **Reservations:** accepted. **Hours:** 11 am-9 pm. Closed: 12/24, 12/25. **Address:** 1100 W Broad St **Location:** Just n on SR 87 business route; center. **Parking:** on-site. **Cards:** AX, DC, DS, MC, VI.

ELKIN pop. 4,109

WHERE TO STAY

FAIRFIELD INN & SUITES ELKIN JONESVILLE

Phone: 336/353-2008

fyi

Hotel
$89-$119 All Year

Too new to rate, opening scheduled for July 2008. **Address:** 628 CC Camp Rd **Location:** I-77, exit 85. **Amenities:** 65 units, pool. **Terms:** cancellation fee imposed. **Cards:** AX, DS, MC, VI.

AAA Benefit:
Members save a minimum 5% off the best available rate.

WHERE TO DINE

PIRATES LANDING

Phone: 336/366-4150

Seafood
$5-$18

In essence, guests dine in a pirate ship. The building resembles a ship, and dining rooms are decorated nautically with riggings and cargo nets. On the menu are pasta and baked, grilled and blackened seafood dishes, as well as limited beef and chicken items. Staff are accommodating and informal. The setting is relaxed and casual. Casual dress. **Bar:** Beer & wine. **Reservations:** accepted. **Hours:** 2 pm-10 pm, Sun noon-9 pm. Closed: 11/26, 12/25; also Mon. **Address:** 161 Interstate Way **Location:** I-77, exit 85, just e, 0.5 mi s, then just sw, follow signs. **Parking:** on-site. **Cards:** AX, MC, VI.

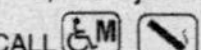

EMERALD ISLE pop. 3,488

WHERE TO STAY

EMERALD ISLE INN & BED & BREAKFAST

Phone: (252)354-3222

Bed & Breakfast
$99-$169 All Year

Address: 502 Ocean Dr **Location:** On SR 58 and 5th St at MM 12.5. **Facility:** Smoke free premises. 4 units. 2 one-bedroom standard units. 2 two bedroom suites with kitchens. 2 stories (no elevator), interior/exterior corridors. **Parking:** on-site. **Terms:** office hours 8 am-7 pm, 2 night minimum stay, age restrictions may apply, 7 day cancellation notice-fee imposed. **Amenities:** video library, CD players, irons, hair dryers. **Leisure Activities:** fishing. **Business Services:** meeting rooms. **Cards:** MC, VI.

ASK VCR

THE ISLANDER SUITES

Phone: 252/354-3464

Motel
$75-$260 All Year

Address: 102 Islander Dr **Location:** Oceanfront. From Intracoastal Waterway bridge, 0.6 mi n on SR 58. **Facility:** 81 one-bedroom standard units. 2 stories (no elevator), exterior corridors. **Parking:** on-site. **Terms:** cancellation fee imposed. **Amenities:** hair dryers. *Some:* DVD players, safes. **Pool(s):** outdoor. **Leisure Activities:** limited beach access, exercise room. **Guest Services:** wireless Internet. **Business Services:** meeting rooms. **Cards:** AX, MC, VI.

ASK / SOME UNITS

ENKA

WHERE TO DINE

J & S CAFETERIA

Phone: 828/665-1911

American
$5-$10

Guests are served steaming entrees, homemade bread and cold items from the comfortable cafeteria's buffet. The dessert area overflows with homemade, tasty treats. Casual dress. **Hours:** 10:45 am-2:15 & 3:45-8 pm, Fri 10:45 am-8:30 pm, Sat 7 am-8:30 pm, Sun 7 am-8 pm. Closed: 12/25. **Address:** 900 Smokey Park Hwy **Location:** I-40, exit 44, 1.3 mi s on US 19 and 23; in Westridge Mall. **Parking:** on-site. **Cards:** MC, VI.

CALL

FAYETTEVILLE pop. 121,015

WHERE TO STAY

COMFORT INN CROSS CREEK *Book great rates at AAA.com*

Phone: (910)867-1777

AAA SAVE
Hotel
$99-$119 All Year

Address: 1922 Skibo Rd **Location:** All American Frwy, exit US 401 Bypass, 0.8 mi s. **Facility:** 123 units. 115 one-bedroom standard units. 8 one-bedroom suites with whirlpools. 4 stories, interior corridors. **Parking:** on-site. **Amenities:** irons, hair dryers. **Pool(s):** outdoor. **Guest Services:** valet and coin laundry, wireless Internet. **Cards:** AX, DC, DS, MC, VI. **Free Special Amenities: expanded continental breakfast and high-speed Internet.**

FEE / SOME UNITS FEE

COMFORT INN-FAYETTEVILLE *Book great rates at AAA.com*

Phone: (910)323-8333

Motel
$72-$99 All Year

Address: 1957 Cedar Creek Rd **Location:** I-95, exit 49, just w. **Facility:** 120 one-bedroom standard units, some with whirlpools. 2 stories (no elevator), exterior corridors. **Parking:** on-site. **Amenities:** safes (fee), irons, hair dryers. **Pool(s):** outdoor. **Leisure Activities:** exercise room. **Guest Services:** valet laundry, wireless Internet. **Business Services:** meeting rooms. **Cards:** AX, CB, DC, DS, JC, MC, VI.

ASK / SOME UNITS FEE

COUNTRY HEARTH INN & SUITES *Book great rates at AAA.com*

Phone: (910)438-0748

AAA SAVE
Motel
$60-$90 All Year

Address: 1902 Cedar Creek Rd **Location:** I-95, exit 49, just w. **Facility:** 55 one-bedroom standard units, some with whirlpools. 2 stories (no elevator), exterior corridors. *Bath:* combo or shower only. **Parking:** on-site. **Amenities:** irons, hair dryers. **Pool(s):** outdoor. **Leisure Activities:** exercise room. **Guest Services:** coin laundry, wireless Internet. **Business Services:** PC. **Cards:** AX, CB, DC, DS, MC, VI.

CALL / SOME UNITS FEE

COURTYARD BY MARRIOTT *Book great rates at AAA.com*

Phone: (910)487-5557

AAA SAVE

Hotel
$138-$148 All Year

Address: 4192 Sycamore Dairy Rd **Location:** All American Frwy, exit Morganton Rd, just e, then just n. **Facility:** Smoke free premises. 108 units. 102 one-bedroom standard units. 6 one-bedroom suites. 3 stories, interior corridors. *Bath:* combo or shower only. **Parking:** on-site. **Terms:** cancellation fee imposed. **Amenities:** high-speed Internet, voice mail, irons, hair dryers. **Pool(s):** outdoor. **Leisure Activities:** whirlpool, exercise room. **Guest Services:** valet and coin laundry, wireless Internet. **Business Services:** meeting rooms, PC. **Cards:** AX, CB, DC, DS, MC, VI. **Free Special Amenities: newspaper and high-speed Internet.**

CALL / SOME UNITS

AAA Benefit:
Members save a minimum 5% off the best available rate.

ECONO LODGE I-95 Book great rates at AAA.com

Motel

$60-$90 All Year

Phone: (910)433-2100

Address: 1952 Cedar Creek Rd **Location:** I-95, exit 49, just w. **Facility:** 150 one-bedroom standard units, some with whirlpools. 2 stories (no elevator), exterior corridors. **Parking:** on-site. **Amenities:** irons, hair dryers. **Pool(s):** outdoor. **Guest Services:** valet and coin laundry, airport transportation-Fayetteville Regional Airport, area transportation-bus & train stations, wireless Internet. **Cards:** AX, CB, DC, DS, JC, MC, VI. **Free Special Amenities: expanded continental breakfast and high-speed Internet.** *(See color ad below)*

/ SOME UNITS FEE

EXTENDED STAYAMERICA Book at AAA.com

Motel

$99-$109 All Year

Phone: (910)485-2747

Address: 408 Owen Dr **Location:** Jct All American Frwy. **Facility:** 120 one-bedroom standard units with efficiencies. 3 stories, exterior corridors. *Bath:* combo or shower only. **Parking:** on-site. **Terms:** office hours 7 am-11 pm. **Amenities:** voice mail, irons. **Guest Services:** coin laundry, wireless Internet. **Cards:** AX, CB, DC, DS, JC, MC, VI.

ASK / SOME UNITS FEE

EXTENDED STAY DELUXE FAYETTEVILLE-CROSS CREEK MALL Book at AAA.com

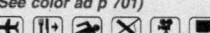

Hotel

$109-$119 All Year

Phone: (910)868-5662

Address: 4105 Sycamore Dairy Rd **Location:** All American Frwy, exit Morganton Rd, just e, then just n. **Facility:** 76 units. 7 one-bedroom standard units with kitchens. 69 one-bedroom suites with kitchens. 3 stories, interior corridors. *Bath:* combo or shower only. **Parking:** on-site. **Terms:** office hours 7 am-11 pm. **Amenities:** DVD players, voice mail, irons, hair dryers. **Pool(s):** outdoor. **Leisure Activities:** exercise room. **Guest Services:** coin laundry, wireless Internet. **Business Services:** meeting rooms. **Cards:** AX, CB, DC, DS, JC, MC, VI.

ASK / SOME UNITS FEE

FAIRFIELD INN-I-95 Book great rates at AAA.com

Hotel

$94-$100 All Year

Phone: (910)433-2666

Address: 1925 Cedar Creek Rd **Location:** I-95, exit 49, just w. **Facility:** Smoke free premises. 64 one-bedroom standard units. 3 stories, interior corridors. *Bath:* combo or shower only. **Parking:** on-site. **Terms:** cancellation fee imposed. **Amenities:** safes, irons, hair dryers. **Pool(s):** outdoor. **Leisure Activities:** whirlpool, exercise room. **Guest Services:** valet laundry, airport transportation-Fayetteville Regional Airport, area transportation-within 8 mi, wireless Internet. **Business Services:** meeting rooms. **Cards:** AX, CB, DC, DS, JC, MC, VI. **Free Special Amenities: continental breakfast and high-speed Internet.** *(See color ad p 701)*

AAA Benefit: Members save a minimum 5% off the best available rate.

HAMPTON INN Book great rates at AAA.com

Hotel

$79-$104 All Year

Phone: (910)323-0011

Address: 1922 Cedar Creek Rd **Location:** I-95, exit 49, just w. **Facility:** 121 one-bedroom standard units. 2 stories (no elevator), exterior corridors. **Parking:** on-site. **Terms:** 1-30 night minimum stay, cancellation fee imposed. **Amenities:** video games (fee), voice mail, irons, hair dryers. **Pool(s):** outdoor. **Guest Services:** valet laundry, wireless Internet. **Business Services:** meeting rooms, PC. **Cards:** AX, CB, DC, DS, JC, MC, VI. **Free Special Amenities: expanded continental breakfast and high-speed Internet.** *(See color ad p 702)*

/ SOME UNITS

Hampton Inn

AAA Benefit: Members save up to 10% everyday!

▼ See AAA listing above ▼

Fayetteville, I-95

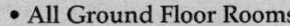

BY CHOICE HOTELS

800-828-2346
Call Direct

$64.95 plus 13% tax

1-2 Persons w/ Ad & AAA card. Subject to Availability. Not Available for special events or groups.

Fayetteville, NC
6 miles from I-95
Northbound
(Exit 40)
Southbound
(Exit 56)

- All Ground Floor Rooms
- Cable TV w/ HBO
- Non-Smoking Rooms
- Pancake House • Golf Packages
- Free High Speed Internet Access

800-235-5363
Call Direct

Spacious rooms with comfortable sitting area. Free HSIA and local calls.

$84.95 plus 13% tax

1-4 Persons w/ Ad & AAA card. Subject to Availability. Not Available for special events or groups.

- Complimentary Continental Breakfast
- Pool, Exercise Room
- Free High Speed Internet Access
- Earn Marriott Points or Miles
- All Non-Smoking Rooms & Public Areas
- Golf Package

800-538-0015
Call Direct

$69.95 plus 13% tax

1-4 Persons w/ Ad & AAA card. Subject to Availability. Not Available for special events or groups.

- Free Deluxe Continental Breakfast
- King Size Beds • Cable TV w/ HBO
- Non-Smoking Rooms
- Restaurant Adjacent • Golf Packages
- Fresh Baked Cookies & Milk
- Free High Speed Internet Access

Visit Us Online at www.ammonshotels.com

HAMPTON INN-CROSS CREEK *Book great rates at AAA.com* **Phone:** (910)487-4006

Hotel
$109 All Year

Address: 1700 Skibo Rd **Location:** All American Frwy, exit US 401 Bypass, just s; enter thru Cross Creek Plaza entrance. **Facility:** 131 one-bedroom standard units. 4 stories, interior corridors. *Bath:* combo or shower only. **Parking:** on-site. **Amenities:** video games (fee), voice mail, irons, hair dryers. **Pool(s):** outdoor. **Guest Services:** valet and coin laundry, wireless Internet. **Business Services:** meeting rooms, PC. **Cards:** AX, CB, DC, DS, JC, MC, VI.

CALL / SOME UNITS

AAA Benefit:
Members save up to 10% everyday!

HILTON GARDEN INN-FAYETTEVILLE/FORT BRAGG *Book great rates at AAA.com* **Phone:** (910)860-3600

Hotel
$79-$279 All Year

Address: 4025 Sycamore Dairy Rd **Location:** US 401 Bypass, just e on MacPhearson Church Rd, then just s. **Facility:** 104 units. 99 one-bedroom standard units. 5 one-bedroom suites with whirlpools. 4 stories, interior corridors. *Bath:* combo or shower only. **Parking:** on-site. **Terms:** 1-30 night minimum stay, cancellation fee imposed. **Amenities:** video games (fee), high-speed Internet, dual phone lines, voice mail, irons, hair dryers. **Pool(s):** heated indoor. **Leisure Activities:** whirlpool, exercise room. **Guest Services:** valet and coin laundry, wireless Internet. **Business Services:** meeting rooms, business center. **Cards:** AX, CB, DC, DS, JC, MC, VI.

CALL / SOME UNITS

AAA Benefit:
Members save 5% or more everyday!

HOLIDAY INN BORDEAUX *Book at AAA.com* **Phone:** (910)323-0111

Hotel
$99-$375 All Year

Address: 1707 Owen Dr **Location:** Jct I-95 business route/US 301 S, 2.3 mi w. **Facility:** 289 one-bedroom standard units. 3-6 stories, interior/exterior corridors. **Parking:** on-site. **Terms:** cancellation fee imposed. **Amenities:** video games (fee), high-speed Internet, voice mail, irons, hair dryers. *Some:* dual phone lines. **Pool(s):** outdoor. **Leisure Activities:** exercise room. **Guest Services:** valet and coin laundry, area transportation, wireless Internet. **Business Services:** conference facilities, PC. **Cards:** AX, CB, DC, DS, JC, MC, VI.

/ SOME UNITS FEE

HOLIDAY INN EXPRESS HOTEL & SUITES-FAYETTEVILLE/FORT BRAGG *Book at AAA.com* **Phone:** (910)867-6777

Hotel
$104-$259 All Year

Address: 1706 Skibo Rd **Location:** All American Frwy, exit US 401 Bypass, just s; enter thru Cross Creek Plaza entrance. **Facility:** 89 one-bedroom standard units, some with whirlpools. 3-4 stories, interior corridors. *Bath:* combo or shower only. **Parking:** on-site. **Amenities:** CD players, high-speed Internet, dual phone lines, voice mail, irons, hair dryers. **Pool(s):** outdoor. **Leisure Activities:** exercise room. **Guest Services:** valet and coin laundry, wireless Internet. **Business Services:** meeting rooms, business center. **Cards:** AX, DC, DS, MC, VI.

ASK CALL / SOME UNITS

HOLIDAY INN I-95 *Book great rates at AAA.com* **Phone:** (910)323-1600

AAA SAVE

Hotel
$108-$120 1/1-11/30
$103 12/1-12/31

Address: 1944 Cedar Creek Rd **Location:** I-95, exit 49, just w. **Facility:** 198 units. 171 one-bedroom standard units. 27 one-bedroom suites. 2 stories (no elevator), interior/exterior corridors. *Bath:* combo or shower only. **Parking:** on-site. **Terms:** 3 day cancellation notice. **Amenities:** video games (fee), voice mail, irons, hair dryers. *Some:* DVD players (fee). **Pool(s):** heated indoor. **Leisure Activities:** exercise room. **Guest Services:** valet and coin laundry, airport transportation-Fayetteville Regional Airport, area transportation-within 5 mi, wireless Internet. **Business Services:** conference facilities. **Cards:** AX, CB, DC, DS, JC, MC, VI. **Free Special Amenities: newspaper and high-speed Internet.**

/ SOME UNITS FEE FEE VCR

▼ *See AAA listing p 700* ▼

INNKEEPER-CROSS CREEK Book at AAA.com Phone: (910)867-7659

Motel

$71 All Year

Address: 1720 Skibo Rd **Location:** All American Frwy, exit US 401 Bypass, just s; enter thru Cross Creek Plaza entrance. **Facility:** 124 one-bedroom standard units, some with whirlpools. 2-3 stories (no elevator), interior/exterior corridors. **Parking:** on-site. **Terms:** 3 day cancellation notice. **Amenities:** *Some:* irons, hair dryers. **Pool(s):** outdoor. **Guest Services:** coin laundry, wireless Internet. **Business Services:** PC. **Cards:** AX, CB, DC, DS, JC, MC, VI.

ASK / SOME UNITS FEE

QUALITY INN AMBASSADOR Book great rates at AAA.com Phone: (910)485-8135

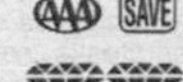

Motel

$65-$139 All Year

Address: 2035 Eastern Blvd **Location:** Jct SR 87, 1.2 mi s on I-95 business route/US 301; jct Owen Dr. **Facility:** 62 units. 61 one-bedroom standard units. 1 one-bedroom suite. 1 story, exterior corridors. **Parking:** on-site. **Amenities:** irons, hair dryers. **Pool(s):** outdoor. **Guest Services:** valet laundry, wireless Internet. **Business Services:** meeting rooms. **Cards:** AX, CB, DC, DS, MC, VI. **Free Special Amenities: local telephone calls and high-speed Internet.** ***(See color ad p 701)***

/ SOME UNITS

QUALITY MOTEL Phone: (910)323-9850

Motel

$69-$99 All Year

Address: 2111 Cedar Creek Rd **Location:** I-95, exit 49, just e. **Facility:** 100 one-bedroom standard units. 2 stories (no elevator), interior corridors. **Parking:** on-site. **Amenities:** high-speed Internet, irons, hair dryers. **Pool(s):** outdoor. **Guest Services:** wireless Internet. **Cards:** AX, DS, MC, VI.

ASK / SOME UNITS

RED ROOF INN Book great rates at AAA.com Phone: (910)321-1460

Hotel

$56-$85 All Year

Address: 1569 Jim Johnson Rd **Location:** I-95, exit 49, just w on SR 53, then just n. Located behind the Cracker Barrel Restaurant. **Facility:** 61 units. 57 one-bedroom standard units. 4 one-bedroom suites with whirlpools. 3 stories, interior corridors. *Bath:* combo or shower only. **Parking:** on-site. **Amenities:** high-speed Internet, irons, hair dryers. **Pool(s):** outdoor. **Guest Services:** coin laundry, wireless Internet. **Cards:** AX, DS, MC, VI.

CALL / SOME UNITS VCR

RESIDENCE INN BY MARRIOTT-FAYETTEVILLE-CROSS CREEK-FT. BRAGG Book great rates at AAA.com Phone: (910)868-9005

Extended Stay Hotel

$147-$158 All Year

Address: 1468 Skibo Rd **Location:** Jct SR 24/87, just s on US 401 Bypass. **Facility:** Enjoy clean, comfortable accommodations designed for the extended-stay guest, whether traveling for business or leisure. Smoke free premises. 92 units. 58 one-bedroom standard units with efficiencies. 18 one- and 16 two-bedroom suites, some with efficiencies or kitchens. 4 stories, interior corridors. *Bath:* combo or shower only. **Parking:** on-site. **Terms:** cancellation fee imposed. **Amenities:** high-speed Internet, dual phone lines, voice mail, irons, hair dryers. **Pool(s):** heated indoor. **Leisure Activities:** whirlpool, exercise room, sports court. **Guest Services:** valet and coin laundry, wireless Internet. **Business Services:** meeting rooms, business center. **Cards:** AX, DS, MC, VI.

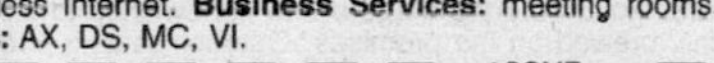

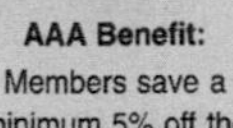

AAA Benefit:

Members save a minimum 5% off the best available rate.

SLEEP INN Book great rates at AAA.com Phone: (910)433-9090

Hotel

$79-$99 All Year

Address: 1915 Cedar Creek Rd **Location:** I-95, exit 49, just w. **Facility:** Smoke free premises. 63 one-bedroom standard units. 2 stories (no elevator), interior corridors. *Bath:* combo or shower only. **Parking:** on-site. **Amenities:** safes, irons, hair dryers. **Leisure Activities:** pool & exercise room privileges. **Guest Services:** valet laundry, airport transportation-Fayetteville Regional Airport, area transportation-within 8 mi, wireless Internet. **Cards:** AX, CB, DC, DS, JC, MC, VI. ***(See color ad p 701)***

CALL / SOME UNITS

WINGATE BY WYNDHAM Book at AAA.com Phone: (910)826-9200

Hotel

$111-$350 All Year

Address: 4182 Sycamore Dairy Rd **Location:** All American Frwy, exit Morganton Rd, just e, then just n. **Facility:** 85 one-bedroom standard units, some with whirlpools. 4 stories, interior corridors. *Bath:* combo or shower only. **Parking:** on-site. **Terms:** cancellation fee imposed. **Amenities:** video games (fee), high-speed Internet, dual phone lines, voice mail, safes, irons, hair dryers. **Leisure Activities:** whirlpool, exercise room. **Guest Services:** valet laundry, wireless Internet. **Business Services:** meeting rooms, business center. **Cards:** AX, CB, DC, DS, MC, VI.

ASK CALL / SOME UNITS

WHERE TO DINE

CHRIS'S OPEN HEARTH STEAK HOUSE Phone: 910/485-2948

Steak & Seafood

$14-$22

A favorite spot for the locals since 1963, the casually upscale steakhouse offers seafood, a small salad bar and steaks grilled to perfection. Casual dress. **Bar:** Full bar. **Hours:** 5 pm-10 pm, Fri & Sat-11 pm. Closed: 1/1, 11/26, 12/25. **Address:** 2620 Raeford Rd **Location:** Jct All American Frwy, exit US 401 business route, 1 mi n. **Parking:** on-site. **Cards:** AX, DS, MC, VI.

HAYMONT GRILL & STEAK HOUSE **Phone:** 910/484-0261

American
$5-$15

The family-owned eatery has been a landmark in the historic Haymount neighborhood for more than 50 years. Lunchtime attracts many locals for daily specials of down-home favorites, sandwiches and burgers. Also on the menu are hearty portions of Greek and Italian fare, fresh seafood, hand-cut steaks and daily specials. Desserts are homemade, and pineapple cake is a perennial favorite. Casual dress. **Bar:** Beer & wine. **Hours:** 6 am-10 pm, Sun 7 am-3 pm. Closed major holidays. **Address:** 1304 Morganton Rd **Location:** SR 87, exit 104B, 0.5 mi w on Hay St; 1.5 mi nw of center. **Parking:** on-site. **Cards:** MC, VI.

HILLTOP HOUSE RESTAURANT & CATERING **Phone:** 910/484-6699

Continental
$9-$26

In the historic Haymount neighborhood, the early-20th-century home features individually decorated dining rooms with elegant touches for a casually upscale dining experience. The menu features steaks, seafood and nightly specials. Crab cakes are a house specialty. Casual dress. **Bar:** Full bar. **Reservations:** accepted. **Hours:** 11 am-2 & 5-9 pm, Fri & Sat-10 pm; Sunday brunch 10:30 am-2:30 pm. Closed: 11/26, 12/25. **Address:** 1240 Ft Bragg Rd **Location:** SR 87, exit 104B, 0.5 mi w on Hay St to Ft Bragg Rd; 1.5 mi nw of center. **Parking:** on-site. **Cards:** AX, DS, MC, VI.

HUSKE HARDWARE HOUSE BREWING COMPANY **Phone:** 910/437-9905

American
$6-$17

The open and airy downtown pub features seafood, steak and pasta entrees, along with homebrewed draft beer and live music every night. Casual dress. **Bar:** Full bar. **Reservations:** accepted. **Hours:** 11 am-10 pm. Closed: 1/1, 11/26, 12/25; also Sun. **Address:** 405 Hay St **Location:** 4 blks w of traffic circle; downtown. **Parking:** on-site. **Cards:** AX, DS, MC, VI.

LUIGI'S ITALIAN RESTAURANT & BAR **Phone:** 910/864-1810

Italian
$9-$30

Pleasant, attentive servers tend to their duties in the family-owned-and-operated restaurant's casually upscale dining room. Homemade sauces, hand-cut steaks and chops and an award-winning wine list draw a loyal following. A few examples of the tasty offerings include pasta classics of fettuccine Alfredo and baked manicotti, along with rib-eye Marsala, grilled veal chop, blackened salmon and chicken with artichokes. Casual dress. **Bar:** Full bar. **Reservations:** accepted. **Hours:** 11:30 am-2:30 & 5-10 pm, Sat noon-10 pm, Sun noon-9 pm. Closed major holidays. **Address:** 528 N McPherson Church Rd **Location:** US 401 Bypass, just e. **Parking:** on-site. **Cards:** AX, DS, MC, VI.

MAIN GARDEN SUPER BUFFET **Phone:** 910/829-9080

Chinese
$5-$14

Southern Chinese dishes and Mongolian barbecue are at the core of the popular restaurant's offerings. Crab legs are among selections on the dinner buffet. Casual dress. **Bar:** Beer only. **Hours:** 11 am-10 pm, Fri & Sat-11 pm, Sun 11:30 am-10 pm. Closed: 11/26. **Address:** 2807 Raeford Rd **Location:** Jct All American Frwy, 0.7 mi n on US 401 business route. **Parking:** on-site. **Cards:** MC, VI.

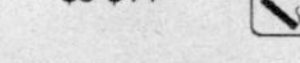

THE MASH HOUSE RESTAURANT & BREWERY **Phone:** 910/867-9223

American
$8-$27

The eclectic menu at this casually upscale eatery includes a wide variety of dishes ranging from wood-fired pizzas and mouthwatering burgers and sandwiches to steak, seafood and pasta entrees. Signature beers are freshly brewed on the premises. Outdoor seating is offered on the patio. Casual dress. **Bar:** Full bar. **Reservations:** accepted. **Hours:** 5 pm-10 pm, Sat noon-11 pm, Sun noon-9 pm. Closed: 7/4, 11/26, 12/25. **Address:** 4150 Sycamore Dairy Rd **Location:** All American Frwy, exit Morganton Rd, just e, then just n. **Parking:** on-site. **Cards:** AX, DS, MC, VI.

RAINBOW RESTAURANT **Phone:** 910/822-0431

American
$5-$14

A quick scan of the menu—which includes burgers, sandwiches and a range of classic dishes, such as hamburger steak, fried chicken, grilled steaks and fried or broiled seafood—shows the restaurant aims to please all members of the family. The casual dining room is spacious and relaxed. Service is attentive. Casual dress. **Hours:** 5:30 am-9 pm, Sun 7 am-3 pm. Closed major holidays. **Address:** 3708 Ramsey St **Location:** Jct SR 24, 3.5 mi n on US 401. **Parking:** on-site. **Cards:** AX, MC, VI.

FEARRINGTON VILLAGE

WHERE TO STAY

THE FEARRINGTON HOUSE INN *Book great rates at AAA.com* **Phone:** (919)542-2121

Country Inn
$250-$575 All Year

Address: 2000 Fearrington Village Center **Location:** US 64, exit 383, 6 mi n on US 15/501. **Facility:** In a rural village complex of shops and above-the-store lodgings. The inn offers rooms overlooking a garden courtyard. Smoke free premises. 35 units. 15 one-bedroom standard units, some with whirlpools. 20 one-bedroom suites, some with whirlpools. 2 stories (no elevator), interior/exterior corridors. *Bath:* combo or shower only. **Parking:** on-site and valet. **Terms:** age restrictions may apply, cancellation fee imposed. **Amenities:** video library, DVD players, CD players, high-speed Internet, voice mail, honor bars, irons, hair dryers. *Some:* safes. **Dining:** restaurant, see separate listing. **Pool(s):** outdoor. **Leisure Activities:** whirlpool, croquet, 2 tennis courts, bicycles, jogging, playground. *Fee:* massage. **Guest Services:** valet laundry, beauty salon, wireless Internet. **Business Services:** meeting rooms, PC. **Cards:** AX, MC, VI. **Free Special Amenities: full breakfast and high-speed Internet.**

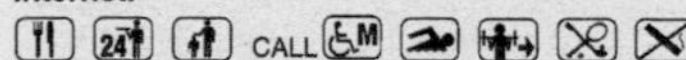

WHERE TO DINE

THE FEARRINGTON HOUSE RESTAURANT

Regional American
$69-$110

Phone: 919/542-2121

Candlelit dining rooms overlook beautiful gardens and arbors where you will enjoy fine, intimate dining in a restored farmhouse setting. Southern cuisine interpreted with artistic touches includes sophisticated dessert presentations like the Mango Fool. Semi-formal attire. **Bar:** Full bar. **Reservations:** required. **Hours:** 6 pm-9 pm, Sun-8 pm. Closed: Mon. **Address:** 2000 Fearrington Village Center **Location:** US 64, exit 383, 6 mi n on US 15/501; in The Fearrington House Inn. **Parking:** on-site and valet. **Cards:** AX, MC, VI.

FLAT ROCK pop. 2,565

WHERE TO STAY

HIGHLAND LAKE INN

Resort Hotel
$89-$259 4/1-11/30
$79-$199 12/1-3/31

Phone: 828/693-6812

Address: 86 Lily Pad Ln **Location:** I-26, exit 53, 2.1 mi w. **Facility:** The inn offers a variety of lodgings from basic cabins and cottages to upscale lodge and inn rooms. Smoke free premises. 66 units. 36 one-bedroom standard units, some with whirlpools. 1 one-bedroom suite with whirlpool. 10 cabins and 19 cottages. 1-2 stories (no elevator), interior/exterior corridors. **Parking:** on-site. **Terms:** check-in 4 pm, 2 night minimum stay - seasonal and/or weekends, 7 day cancellation notice. **Amenities:** voice mail, irons, hair dryers. *Some:* DVD players. **Dining:** Season's at Highland Lake Inn, see separate listing. **Pool(s):** outdoor. **Leisure Activities:** canoeing, paddleboats, fishing, 2 tennis courts, bicycles, basketball, horseshoes, volleyball, game room. *Fee:* massage. **Guest Services:** wireless Internet. **Business Services:** meeting rooms, business center. **Cards:** AX, DS, MC, VI.

ASK / SOME UNITS VCR

WHERE TO DINE

FLAT ROCK VILLAGE BAKERY

American
$6-$12

Phone: 828/693-1313

It's worth the drive to this tiny pocket of a bakery/cafe tucked into a corner shop in historic, downtown Flat Rock. Dine on fresh-baked breads, cookies, desserts and pizzas with big flavors. Homemade soups, sandwiches and daily specials are served inside at four neighborly-near tables, or outside in a court area if the weather permits. **Reservations:** not accepted. **Hours:** 7 am-3 pm, Fri & Sat-5:30 pm. Closed major holidays; also Sun & Mon. **Address:** 2710 Greenville Hwy **Location:** I-26, exit 53 (E Upward Rd), follow signs to historic Flat Rock. **Parking:** on-site.

SEASON'S AT HIGHLAND LAKE INN

American
$7-$28

Phone: 828/696-9094

The restaurant is located on the resort grounds, affording pleasant views of the landscaping and buildings. The dining room decor hints of French country and uses a variety of mediums to enhance the overall appeal. The cuisine enters the realm of fine dining, offering a diversity in selection and preparation. Entrees include innovative preparations of chicken, fish, lamb, duck, pork and steak. Dressy casual. **Bar:** Full bar. **Reservations:** suggested. **Hours:** 7:30-9:30 am, 11:30-2:30 & 5-8 pm, Sun 10:30 am-2 pm; Sunday brunch; hours vary in winter. **Address:** 180 Highland Lake Rd **Location:** I-26, exit 53, 2.1 mi w; in Highland Lake Inn. **Parking:** on-site. **Cards:** AX, DS, MC, VI.

FLETCHER pop. 4,185 (See map and index starting on p. 576)

WHERE TO STAY

ECONO LODGE AIRPORT *Book great rates at AAA.com*

Motel
Rates not provided

Phone: 828/684-1200 63

Address: 196 Underwood Rd **Location:** I-26, exit 40, just e, then s on service road, follow signs. **Facility:** 60 one-bedroom standard units. 2 stories (no elevator), exterior corridors. **Parking:** on-site. **Amenities:** high-speed Internet, irons, hair dryers. **Pool(s):** outdoor. **Free Special Amenities: continental breakfast and high-speed Internet.**

/ SOME UNITS

FAIRFIELD INN BY MARRIOTT *Book great rates at AAA.com*

Hotel
$87-$128 All Year

Phone: (828)684-1144 62

Address: 31 Airport Park Rd **Location:** I-26, exit 40, 0.3 mi w on Airport Rd. Located next to J&S Cafeteria. **Facility:** Smoke free premises. 107 one-bedroom standard units. 3 stories, interior corridors. *Bath:* combo or shower only. **Parking:** on-site. **Terms:** cancellation fee imposed. **Amenities:** video games (fee), irons, hair dryers. **Pool(s):** heated indoor. **Leisure Activities:** whirlpool, limited exercise equipment. **Guest Services:** valet and coin laundry, wireless Internet. **Business Services:** meeting rooms, business center. **Cards:** AX, CB, DC, DS, JC, MC, VI.

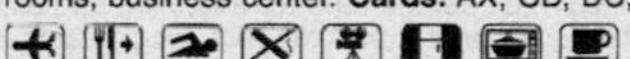

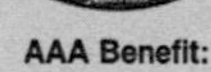

AAA Benefit:
Members save a minimum 5% off the best available rate.

(See map and index starting on p. 576)

HAMPTON INN & SUITES ASHEVILLE *Book great rates at AAA.com* **Phone:** (828)687-0806 60

Hotel
$99-$189 4/1-11/30
$99-$129 12/1-3/31

Address: 18 Rockwood Rd **Location:** I-26, exit 40, just se. **Facility:** 96 units. 73 one-bedroom standard units. 23 one-bedroom suites with kitchens and whirlpools. 5 stories, interior corridors. *Bath:* combo or shower only. **Parking:** on-site. **Terms:** 2-3 night minimum stay - seasonal and/or weekends, 3 day cancellation notice-fee imposed. **Amenities:** voice mail, irons, hair dryers. *Some:* dual phone lines. **Pool(s):** heated outdoor. **Leisure Activities:** sauna, whirlpools, gas barbecues, exercise room. **Guest Services:** valet and coin laundry, wireless Internet. **Business Services:** meeting rooms, PC, fax (fee). **Cards:** AX, CB, DS, MC, VI. **Free Special Amenities: expanded continental breakfast and high-speed Internet.** *(See color ad p 591)*

CALL / SOME UNITS

HOLIDAY INN ASHEVILLE-AIRPORT *Book great rates at AAA.com* **Phone:** (828)684-1213 61

Hotel
$89-$169 3/15-11/30
$79-$109 12/1-3/14

Address: 550 Airport Rd **Location:** I-26, exit 40, just e. **Facility:** 152 one-bedroom standard units. 2 stories (no elevator), interior corridors. *Bath:* combo or shower only. **Parking:** on-site. **Terms:** check-in 4 pm. **Amenities:** voice mail, irons, hair dryers. **Pool(s):** heated indoor/outdoor. **Leisure Activities:** exercise room. **Guest Services:** valet and coin laundry. **Business Services:** meeting rooms, business center. **Cards:** AX, DC, DS, MC, VI.

ASK / SOME UNITS FEE FEE FEE

WHERE TO DINE

BLUE SKY CAFE **Phone:** 828/684-1247

American
$5-$10

The casual little cafe packs dishes with a lot of fresh flavor. Guests can sit indoors or on the patio to savor wraps, sandwiches, orzo pasta salad and burgers. Casual dress. **Bar:** Beer & wine. **Reservations:** not accepted. **Hours:** 11 am-8:30 pm. Closed major holidays; also Sun. **Address:** 3987 Hendersonville Rd **Location:** I-26, exit 40, 2 mi e on New Airport Rd, then 2.3 mi s. **Parking:** on-site. **Cards:** AX, DS, MC, VI.

J & S CAFETERIA **Phone:** 828/684-3418

American
$4-$10

Guests are served steaming entrees, homemade bread and cold items from the comfortable cafeteria's buffet. The dessert area overflows with homemade, tasty treats. Casual dress. **Hours:** 10:45 am-2:15 & 3:45-8 pm, Fri-Sun 10:45 am-8 pm. Closed: 12/25. **Address:** 645 New Airport Rd **Location:** I-26, exit 40, just s. **Parking:** on-site. **Cards:** MC, VI.

FOREST CITY pop. 7,549

WHERE TO STAY

HOLIDAY INN EXPRESS *Book at AAA.com* **Phone:** (828)755-2000

Hotel
$85-$95 All Year

Address: 200 Holiday Inn Dr **Location:** US 74 Bypass, exit 181, 2 mi nw on US 74A, then just s. **Facility:** 63 one-bedroom standard units, some with efficiencies and/or whirlpools. 3 stories, interior corridors. *Bath:* combo or shower only. **Parking:** on-site. **Amenities:** voice mail, irons, hair dryers. **Leisure Activities:** exercise room. **Guest Services:** coin laundry, wireless Internet. **Business Services:** meeting rooms, business center. **Cards:** AX, DC, DS, MC, VI.

ASK CALL / SOME UNITS

JAMESON INN *Book at AAA.com* **Phone:** (828)287-8788

Motel
$78-$85 All Year

Address: 164 Jameson Inn Dr **Location:** US 74 Bypass, exit 181, 1.8 mi nw on US 74A. **Facility:** 61 one-bedroom standard units, some with whirlpools. 2 stories (no elevator), exterior corridors. *Bath:* combo or shower only. **Parking:** on-site. **Terms:** cancellation fee imposed. **Amenities:** hair dryers. **Pool(s):** outdoor. **Leisure Activities:** exercise room. **Guest Services:** wireless Internet. **Business Services:** PC. **Cards:** AX, DC, DS, MC, VI.

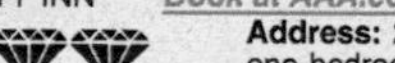

ASK CALL / SOME UNITS FEE

QUALITY INN *Book at AAA.com* **Phone:** (828)248-3400

Motel
$80-$90 All Year

Address: 205 Commercial Dr **Location:** US 74 Bypass, exit 181, 1.8 mi nw on US 74A. **Facility:** 49 one-bedroom standard units, some with whirlpools. 2 stories (no elevator), exterior corridors. **Parking:** on-site. **Amenities:** irons, hair dryers. **Pool(s):** outdoor. **Guest Services:** coin laundry, wireless Internet. **Business Services:** meeting rooms, PC. **Cards:** AX, DC, DS, MC, VI.

ASK / SOME UNITS

WHERE TO DINE

FATZ CAFE **Phone:** 828/286-8996

American
$7-$15

Friendly staff and appealing country decor help set the tone for a relaxed and enjoyable dining experience. It's not unusual for guests to wait to be seated at the popular spot, which earns raves for its well-prepared variations on chicken, steak, ribs and pasta, as well as salads and sandwiches. The signature Southern-style peach cobbler served with vanilla ice cream and walnuts is scrumptious. Casual dress. **Bar:** Full bar. **Hours:** 11 am-10 pm, Fri & Sat-11 pm, Sun-9 pm. Closed: 11/26, 12/25. **Address:** 118 Hill Top Way **Location:** US 74 Bypass, exit 181, 1.8 mi nw on US 74 A. **Parking:** on-site. **Cards:** AX, DC, DS, MC, VI.

CALL

HICKORY LOG BARBEQUE **Phone:** 828/245-6241

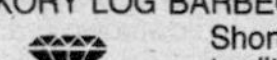

Regional Southern
$3-$9

Short and simple best describes the menu of pork or beef barbecue, prepared in the western-North Carolina tradition. A side of coleslaw and hushpuppies is a must, as is a slice of pie to wrap up the meal. Casual dress. **Hours:** 11 am-8 pm, Fri & Sat-9 pm. Closed: Sun & Mon. **Address:** 1163 W Main St **Location:** 2 mi on US 74 business route. **Parking:** on-site. **Cards:** AX, DS, MC, VI.

MI PUEBLITO MEXICAN RESTAURANT **Phone:** 828/288-3600

Mexican
$4-$11

Enjoy traditional favorites at the family-friendly eatery. The menu includes popular combination platters that mix and match burritos, tacos and enchiladas as well as house specialties like carne asada, pollo ranchero and shrimp fajitas. Casual dress. **Bar:** Full bar. **Hours:** 11 am-2 & 5-10 pm. Closed: 11/26, 12/25. **Address:** 220 Oak St Ext **Location:** US 74 Bypass, exit 181, 1.8 mi nw on US 74A, then just w. **Parking:** on-site. **Cards:** AX, DS, MC, VI.

FRANKLIN pop. 3,490

WHERE TO STAY

COMFORT INN *Book at AAA.com* **Phone:** (828)369-9200

Hotel
$80-$300 5/1-11/30
$70-$300 12/1-4/30

Address: 313 Cunningham Rd **Location:** Jct US 441 Bypass, 0.5 mi nw. **Facility:** 61 units. 55 one-bedroom standard units. 6 one-bedroom suites with whirlpools. 3 stories, interior corridors. *Bath:* combo or tub only. **Parking:** on-site. **Amenities:** high-speed Internet, irons, hair dryers. **Pool(s):** heated indoor. **Leisure Activities:** whirlpool, exercise room. **Guest Services:** wireless Internet. **Business Services:** PC, fax (fee). **Cards:** AX, CB, DC, DS, JC, MC, VI.

ASK CALL / SOME UNITS

THE FRANKLIN MOTEL **Phone:** 828/524-4431

Motel
$60-$70 4/1-11/30
$50-$60 12/1-3/31

Address: 17 W Palmer St **Location:** Jct US 441 Bypass, 1 mi n on US 441 business route; downtown. **Facility:** 51 one-bedroom standard units. 1-2 stories (no elevator), exterior corridors. *Bath:* combo or shower only. **Parking:** on-site. **Pool(s):** outdoor. **Cards:** AX, CB, DC, DS, JC, MC, VI.

ASK / SOME UNITS FEE

HAMPTON INN *Book great rates at AAA.com* **Phone:** (828)369-0600

Hotel
$99-$149 All Year

Address: 244 Cunningham Rd **Location:** Jct US 441 Bypass, 0.5 mi nw. **Facility:** Smoke free premises. 80 one-bedroom standard units. 3 stories, interior corridors. *Bath:* combo or shower only. **Parking:** on-site. **Terms:** check-in 4 pm, 2-3 night minimum stay - seasonal and/or weekends, cancellation fee imposed. **Amenities:** high-speed Internet, voice mail, irons, hair dryers. **Pool(s):** outdoor. **Guest Services:** wireless Internet. **Business Services:** meeting rooms, business center. **Cards:** AX, CB, DC, DS, JC, MC, VI.

/ SOME UNITS

MICROTEL INN & SUITES *Book at AAA.com* **Phone:** (828)349-9000

Hotel
$70-$130 5/1-11/30
$60-$100 12/1-4/30

Address: 81 Allman Dr **Location:** Jct US 441 Bypass, 0.4 mi s on US 441 and 23. **Facility:** 61 one-bedroom standard units. 2 stories (no elevator), interior corridors. *Bath:* combo or shower only. **Parking:** on-site. **Terms:** cancellation fee imposed. **Guest Services:** coin laundry, wireless Internet. **Business Services:** PC. **Cards:** AX, DS, MC, VI.

ASK FEE / SOME UNITS FEE

WHERE TO DINE

THE CHEF & HIS WIFE..AN AMERICAN GRILLE *Menu on AAA.com* **Phone:** 828/369-0575

AAA

American
$5-$31

The chef serves only the freshest fish in the elegant restaurant. Attention to quality is evident in all the gourmet menu offerings. The wait staff is attentive. Casual dress. **Bar:** Beer & wine. **Reservations:** accepted. **Hours:** 11 am-2:30 & 5-9 pm, Mon-2:30 pm. Closed major holidays; also Sun. **Address:** 15 Courthouse Plaza **Location:** Center; behind Courthouse. **Parking:** street. **Cards:** MC, VI.

THE FROG & OWL MOUNTAIN BISTRO & WINE BAR **Phone:** 828/349-4112

AAA

American
$7-$30

In the center of town, the friendly bistro presents a menu with an array of intercontinental items. Casual dress. **Bar:** Wine only. **Reservations:** suggested. **Hours:** 11 am-3 & 5:30-9 pm, Sun 10:30 am-3 pm. Closed: 11/26, 12/25. **Address:** 46 E Main St **Location:** Center of downtown. **Parking:** street. **Cards:** AX, MC, VI.

GAZEBO CREEKSIDE CAFE **Phone:** 828/524-8783

American
$4-$7

A simple and satisfying meal is what you get at this small, creek-side eatery located in downtown Franklin. Enjoy the stunning surroundings on the three-leveled open-air gazebo (heated on chilly days) while you devour sandwiches, soup or salad. Casual dress. **Hours:** 10:30 am-3 pm. Closed major holidays; also Sun 10/1-2/28. **Address:** 44 Heritage Hollow **Location:** Off US 441 business route; in Heritage Shopping Village. **Parking:** on-site. **Cards:** MC, VI.

MOTOR CO. GRILL **Phone:** 828/524-0099

American
$3-$10

This is not just another hamburger joint. Burgers are made from hand-ground beef, sandwiches feature fresh chicken breast fillets, and other menu standouts include hand-cut fries and onion rings, homemade chili and old-fashioned shakes and sodas. Nostalgia flows forth from the retro-designed dining room and soda fountain. Casual dress. **Reservations:** not accepted. **Hours:** 11 am-8 pm. Closed major holidays; also Mon. **Address:** 86 W Main St **Location:** US 441 business route; center of downtown. **Parking:** on-site. **Cards:** DS, MC, VI.

FUQUAY-VARINA pop. 7,898

WHERE TO STAY

COMFORT INN Book at AAA.com **Phone:** (919)557-9000

Hotel
$79-$179 All Year

Address: 7616 Purfoy Rd **Location:** Jct SR 55, 1 mi n on US 401/SR 55, then just e. **Facility:** 60 units. 56 one-bedroom standard units. 4 one-bedroom suites, some with whirlpools. 3 stories, interior corridors. *Bath:* combo or shower only. **Parking:** on-site. **Amenities:** voice mail, irons, hair dryers. **Pool(s):** outdoor. **Leisure Activities:** exercise room. **Guest Services:** valet and coin laundry, wireless Internet. **Business Services:** meeting rooms, PC. **Cards:** AX, DS, MC, VI.

ASK / SOME UNITS

WHERE TO DINE

COOLEYS RESTAURANT & PUB **Phone:** 919/552-0543

American
$6-$20

The longtime downtown fixture prepares sandwiches and burgers at lunch and steaks, seafood and pasta at dinner. Casual dress. **Bar:** Full bar. **Hours:** 11 am-9 pm. Closed major holidays; also Sun. **Address:** 305 S Main St **Location:** Jct US 401 and E Vance St; downtown. **Parking:** on-site. **Cards:** AX, DS, MC, VI.

GARNER pop. 17,757 (See map and index starting on p. 790)

WHERE TO STAY

ECONO LODGE SOUTH Book at AAA.com **Phone:** 919/779-7888 78

Motel
Rates not provided

Address: 1602 Mechanical Blvd **Location:** I-40, exit 298A, 1.9 mi e on US 70, then just n. **Facility:** 60 one-bedroom standard units, some with whirlpools. 2 stories (no elevator), exterior corridors. **Parking:** on-site. **Amenities:** video library (fee), high-speed Internet, irons, hair dryers. **Pool(s):** outdoor. **Leisure Activities:** exercise room. **Guest Services:** valet and coin laundry, wireless Internet. **Business Services:** meeting rooms.

/ SOME UNITS FEE VCR

HAMPTON INN Book great rates at AAA.com **Phone:** (919)772-6500 81

Hotel
$95 All Year

Address: 110 Drexmere St **Location:** I-40, exit 298A, 2.3 mi e on US 70, just n on McCormick, then just e. Located behind IHOP restaurant. **Facility:** 68 one-bedroom standard units, some with whirlpools. 3 stories, interior corridors. *Bath:* combo or shower only. **Parking:** on-site. **Terms:** 1-30 night minimum stay, cancellation fee imposed. **Amenities:** high-speed Internet, dual phone lines, voice mail, irons, hair dryers. **Pool(s):** outdoor. **Leisure Activities:** exercise room. **Guest Services:** wireless Internet. **Business Services:** meeting rooms, PC. **Cards:** AX, CB, DC, DS, MC, VI.

CALL / SOME UNITS

Hampton Inn

AAA Benefit:
Members save up to 10% everyday!

HOLIDAY INN EXPRESS **Phone:** 919/662-4890 80

Hotel
Rates not provided

Address: 1595 Mechanical Blvd **Location:** I-40, exit 298A, 1.9 mi e on US 70, then just n. **Facility:** 52 one-bedroom standard units. 2 stories (no elevator), interior corridors. *Bath:* combo or shower only. **Parking:** on-site. **Amenities:** high-speed Internet, dual phone lines, voice mail, irons, hair dryers. **Guest Services:** complimentary and valet laundry, wireless Internet. **Business Services:** business center.

VCR / SOME UNITS

WINGATE BY WYNDHAM-RALEIGH SOUTH Book at AAA.com **Phone:** 919/779-7441 79

Hotel
Rates not provided

Address: 1542 Mechanical Blvd **Location:** I-40, exit 298A, 1.9 mi e on US 70, then just n. **Facility:** 85 one-bedroom standard units, some with whirlpools. 4 stories, interior corridors. *Bath:* combo or shower only. **Parking:** on-site. **Amenities:** video games (fee), high-speed Internet, dual phone lines, voice mail, safes, irons, hair dryers. **Pool(s):** outdoor. **Leisure Activities:** exercise room. **Guest Services:** complimentary and valet laundry, wireless Internet. **Business Services:** meeting rooms, business center.

CALL / SOME UNITS

(See map and index starting on p. 790)

WHERE TO DINE

CAROLINA BARBECUE — Phone: 919/773-0222

Regional Southern
$5-$10

The backbone of the menu is eastern North Carolina-style pulled-pork barbecue with a vinegar and spice sauce that pops in the mouth. Fried chicken, shrimp, scallops and fish round out the offerings, and a side of hushpuppies and Brunswick stew is a must. Casual dress. **Hours:** 11 am-9 pm. Closed: 11/26, 12/25. **Address:** 733 Hwy 70 W **Location:** I-40, exit 298A, 3.5 mi e. **Parking:** on-site. **Cards:** MC, VI.

RAGAZZI'S — Phone: 919/772-9772 (55)

Italian
$5-$13

Italian favorites—including lasagna, manicotti, fettuccine Alfredo and pizza—are the focus at the casual eatery. Homemade salad dressing is delicious, and the breadsticks are plentiful. Casual dress. **Bar:** Full bar. **Hours:** 11 am-10 pm, Sun-9 pm. Closed: 11/26, 12/25. **Address:** 1514 W US 70 **Location:** I-40, exit 298A, 2 mi e. **Parking:** on-site. **Cards:** AX, MC, VI.

GASTONIA pop. 66,277

WHERE TO STAY

BEST WESTERN EXECUTIVE INN GASTONIA — *Book great rates at AAA.com* — Phone: (704)868-2000

Motel
$70-$199 All Year

Address: 360 Best Western Ct **Location:** I-85, exit 20, just n on SR 279, then just e. **Facility:** 63 one-bedroom standard units, some with whirlpools. 3 stories (no elevator), interior/exterior corridors. **Parking:** on-site. **Terms:** 3 day cancellation notice. **Amenities:** high-speed Internet, voice mail, irons, hair dryers. **Pool(s):** outdoor. **Guest Services:** wireless Internet. **Business Services:** PC. **Cards:** AX, DC, DS, MC, VI. **Free Special Amenities: expanded continental breakfast and high-speed Internet.**

/ SOME UNITS

AAA Benefit:
Members save up to 20%, plus 10% bonus points with rewards program.

COMFORT SUITES — *Book at AAA.com* — Phone: (704)865-6688

Hotel
$90-$105 All Year

Address: 1874 Remount Rd **Location:** I-85, exit 20, just n on SR 279, then just e. **Facility:** Smoke free premises. 109 one-bedroom standard units, some with whirlpools. 5 stories, interior corridors. *Bath:* combo or shower only. **Parking:** on-site. **Terms:** cancellation fee imposed. **Amenities:** video games (fee), voice mail, irons, hair dryers. **Pool(s):** outdoor. **Leisure Activities:** exercise room. **Guest Services:** complimentary and valet laundry, wireless Internet. **Business Services:** meeting rooms, PC. **Cards:** AX, CB, DC, DS, MC, VI.

ASK CALL / SOME UNITS VCR

▼ See AAA listing p 710 ▼

COURTYARD BY MARRIOTT *Book great rates at AAA.com* **Phone:** (704)852-4411

Hotel
$123-$132 All Year

Address: 1856 Remount Rd **Location:** I-85, exit 20, just n on SR 279, then just e. **Facility:** Smoke free premises. 130 units. 124 one-bedroom standard units, some with whirlpools. 6 one-bedroom suites, some with whirlpools. 4 stories, interior corridors. *Bath:* combo or shower only. **Parking:** on-site. **Terms:** cancellation fee imposed. **Amenities:** video games (fee), high-speed Internet, dual phone lines, voice mail, irons, hair dryers. **Pool(s):** heated indoor. **Leisure Activities:** whirlpool, exercise room. **Guest Services:** valet and coin laundry, wireless Internet. **Business Services:** meeting rooms, business center. **Cards:** AX, CB, DC, DS, JC, MC, VI.

CALL

AAA Benefit:
Members save a minimum 5% off the best available rate.

FAIRFIELD INN BY MARRIOTT *Book great rates at AAA.com* **Phone:** (704)867-5073

Hotel
$89-$95 All Year

Address: 1860 Remount Rd **Location:** I-85, exit 20, just n on SR 279, then just e. **Facility:** Smoke free premises. 89 one-bedroom standard units, some with whirlpools. 4 stories, interior corridors. *Bath:* combo or shower only. **Parking:** on-site. **Terms:** cancellation fee imposed. **Amenities:** irons, hair dryers. **Pool(s):** heated indoor. **Leisure Activities:** whirlpool, exercise room. **Guest Services:** valet and coin laundry, wireless Internet. **Business Services:** meeting rooms, PC. **Cards:** AX, CB, DC, DS, MC, VI.

CALL

AAA Benefit:
Members save a minimum 5% off the best available rate.

HAMPTON INN *Book great rates at AAA.com* **Phone:** (704)866-9090

Hotel
$99-$159 All Year

Address: 1859 Remount Rd **Location:** I-85, exit 20, just n on SR 279, then just e. **Facility:** 108 one-bedroom standard units. 5 stories, interior corridors. **Parking:** on-site. **Terms:** 1-30 night minimum stay, cancellation fee imposed. **Amenities:** voice mail, irons, hair dryers. **Pool(s):** outdoor. **Guest Services:** valet laundry, wireless Internet. **Business Services:** meeting rooms. **Cards:** AX, CB, DC, DS, MC, VI. **Free Special Amenities: expanded continental breakfast and high-speed Internet.**
(See color ad p 709)

CALL / SOME UNITS

Hampton Inn

AAA Benefit:
Members save up to 10% everyday!

KNIGHTS INN *Book at AAA.com* **Phone:** (704)864-8744

Motel
$49-$59 All Year

Address: 1400 E Franklin Blvd **Location:** I-85, exit 20, 0.5 mi s on SR 279, then just w on US 29/74. Located in a busy commercial area. **Facility:** 58 one-bedroom standard units. 2 stories (no elevator), exterior corridors. **Parking:** on-site. **Amenities:** irons, hair dryers. *Some:* high-speed Internet. **Leisure Activities:** exercise room. **Cards:** AX, DS, MC, VI.

ASK / SOME UNITS FEE

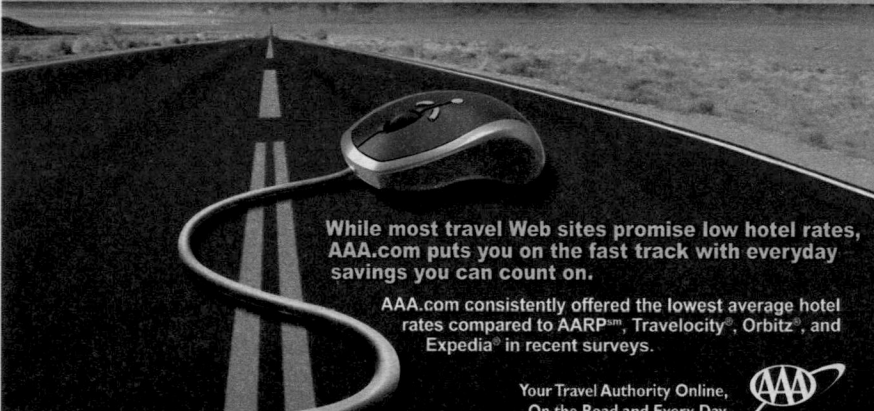

WHERE TO DINE

BILLIE JEAN'S GRASSHOPPER FARM AMERICAN GRILL — **Phone:** 704/853-8661

American
$5-$15

The popular local eatery presents a lengthy menu of chicken, steaks, pork chops, ribs, sandwiches, burgers and salads. Young ones can order from the kids' menu. Casual dress. **Bar:** Full bar. **Hours:** 11 am-midnight, Sun-11 pm. Closed: 11/26, 12/25. **Address:** 911 Union Rd **Location:** I-85, exit 20 (New Hope Rd), 1.2 mi se on SR 279, 1.0 mi w on E Garrison Blvd, then just e. **Parking:** on-site. **Cards:** AX, MC, VI.

CALL

FIESTA MARGARITA MEXICAN RESTAURANT — **Phone:** 704/854-4848

Mexican
$6-$14

The colorful, casual eatery serves traditional Mexican favorites like fajitas, burritos, quesadillas and other specialties of the house. Casual dress. **Bar:** Full bar. **Hours:** 11 am-10 pm. Closed: 11/26, 12/25. **Address:** 1414 E Franklin Blvd. **Parking:** on-site. **Cards:** AX, MC, VI.

HILLBILLY'S BBQ & STEAKS — **Phone:** 704/861-8787

Barbecue
$4-$15

Steaks, chicken, ribs, beef and pork are grilled over hickory wood at the quick, casual eatery. Seniors' and children's menus are offered. Casual dress. **Hours:** 11 am-9 pm, Fri & Sat-9:30 pm, Sun-3 pm. Closed: 11/26, 12/25. **Address:** 930 E Garrison Blvd **Location:** I-85, exit 20 (New Hope Rd), 1.2 mi se on SR 279, then 1.2 mi w. **Parking:** on-site. **Cards:** AX, DS, MC, VI.

MILANO'S ITALIAN RESTAURANT — **Phone:** 704/854-3946

Italian
$6-$17

Homemade sauce, dressing and soup enhance a menu that features many chicken entrees and an excellent Greek salad. Veal scaloppini, a house specialty, is a delicious blend of veal, onions, peppers and mushrooms sauteed in olive oil, butter and lemon. Casual dress. **Bar:** Full bar. **Hours:** 11 am-10 pm, Sat from noon. Closed: 1/1, 11/26, 12/25; also Mon. **Address:** 904-C S New Hope Rd **Location:** I-85, exit 20, 1.2 mi s on SR 279. **Parking:** on-site. **Cards:** AX, DS, MC, VI.

GERTON

WHERE TO STAY

MOUNTAIN MEADOWS MOTEL — **Phone:** (828)625-1025

AAA SAVE

Motel
$64-$95 4/1-11/30
$59-$74 12/1-3/31

Address: 5793 Gerton Hwy **Location:** On US 74A, 12.5 mi se of Asheville. **Facility:** 10 units. 4 one-bedroom standard units. 4 one-bedroom suites. 2 cottages. 1 story, exterior corridors. *Bath:* combo or shower only. **Parking:** on-site. **Terms:** office hours 8:30 am-9:30 pm, 2 night minimum stay - seasonal and/or weekends, 7 day cancellation notice. **Amenities:** *Some:* DVD players, video games. **Leisure Activities:** boating, paddleboats, fishing, lake, hot tub, barbecue grills, picnic tables, tetherball, swings, hiking trails, basketball, horseshoes, volleyball. **Guest Services:** wireless Internet. **Cards:** DS, MC, VI. **Free Special Amenities: high-speed Internet.**

/ SOME UNITS VCR

GIBSONVILLE pop. 4,372

WHERE TO STAY

The following lodging was either not evaluated or did not meet AAA rating requirements but is listed for your information only.

THE BURKE MANOR INN — **Phone:** 336/449-6266

fyi

Not evaluated. **Address:** 303 Burke St **Location:** Just w of downtown center. Facilities, services, and decor characterize a mid-scale property.

GOLDSBORO pop. 39,043

WHERE TO STAY

BEST WESTERN GOLDSBORO INN *Book great rates at AAA.com* — **Phone:** (919)735-7911

Motel
$62-$180 All Year

Address: 801 US 70 E Bypass **Location:** US 70 E Bypass, exit Wayne Memorial Dr eastbound, just n, just w on Eleventh St, then 0.4 mi sw on service road; exit westbound, straight on Eleventh St, then 0.4 mi sw on service road. **Facility:** 112 units. 109 one-bedroom standard units. 3 one-bedroom suites. 2 stories (no elevator), exterior corridors. *Bath:* combo or shower only. **Parking:** on-site. **Terms:** cancellation fee imposed. **Amenities:** irons, hair dryers. **Pool(s):** outdoor. **Leisure Activities:** exercise room. **Guest Services:** coin laundry, wireless Internet. **Business Services:** meeting rooms. **Cards:** AX, DC, DS, MC, VI. **Free Special Amenities: continental breakfast and high-speed Internet.**

     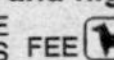  

AAA Benefit:
Members save up to 20%, plus 10% bonus points with rewards program.

COMFORT SUITES Book at AAA.com

Hotel

Rates not provided

Phone: 919/759-0098

Address: 2613 N Park Dr **Location:** US 70 E Bypass, exit Spence Ave, just n, then just e. **Facility:** Smoke free premises. 83 one-bedroom standard units, some with whirlpools. 3 stories, interior corridors. *Bath:* combo or shower only. **Parking:** on-site. **Amenities:** dual phone lines, voice mail, irons, hair dryers. **Pool(s):** heated indoor. **Leisure Activities:** sauna, exercise room. **Guest Services:** coin laundry, wireless Internet. **Business Services:** meeting rooms, PC.

CALL / SOME UNITS FEE VCR

COUNTRY INN & SUITES BY CARLSON Book at AAA.com

Hotel

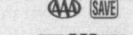

Rates not provided

Phone: 919/581-0503

Address: 2302 Norwood Ave **Location:** US 70 Bypass, exit Wayne Memorial Dr, just n, just w on Eleventh St, then just sw on Lincoln Mercury Dr. **Facility:** 66 units. 50 one-bedroom standard units, some with whirlpools. 16 one-bedroom suites. 4 stories, interior corridors. *Bath:* combo or shower only. **Parking:** on-site. **Amenities:** high-speed Internet, dual phone lines, voice mail, irons, hair dryers. *Some:* DVD players. **Pool(s):** outdoor. **Leisure Activities:** whirlpool, exercise room. **Guest Services:** valet and coin laundry, wireless Internet. **Business Services:** meeting rooms.

CALL / SOME UNITS FEE VCR

HAMPTON INN Book great rates at AAA.com

AAA SAVE

Hotel

$91-$111 All Year

Phone: (919)778-1800

Address: 905 N Spence Ave **Location:** US 70 E Bypass, exit Spence Ave, just s. **Facility:** 111 units. 101 one-bedroom standard units. 10 one-bedroom suites with whirlpools. 4 stories, interior corridors. *Bath:* combo or shower only. **Parking:** on-site. **Terms:** 1-30 night minimum stay, cancellation fee imposed. **Amenities:** video games (fee), high-speed Internet, voice mail, irons, hair dryers. **Pool(s):** outdoor. **Leisure Activities:** exercise room. **Guest Services:** valet and coin laundry, wireless Internet. **Business Services:** meeting rooms, PC. **Cards:** AX, CB, DC, DS, MC, VI. **Free Special Amenities: expanded continental breakfast and high-speed Internet.**

/ SOME UNITS

AAA Benefit:

Members save up to 10% everyday!

HOLIDAY INN EXPRESS GOLDSBORO Book great rates at AAA.com

AAA SAVE

Hotel

$105-$195 All Year

Phone: (919)751-1999

Address: 909 N Spence Ave **Location:** US 70 E Bypass, exit Spence Ave, just s. **Facility:** 120 units. 116 one-bedroom standard units, some with whirlpools. 4 one-bedroom suites with whirlpools. 5 stories, interior corridors. *Bath:* combo or shower only. **Parking:** on-site. **Terms:** cancellation fee imposed. **Amenities:** high-speed Internet, voice mail, irons, hair dryers. **Pool(s):** outdoor. **Leisure Activities:** exercise room. **Guest Services:** valet and coin laundry, wireless Internet. **Business Services:** meeting rooms, business center. **Cards:** AX, CB, DC, DS, JC, MC, VI. **Free Special Amenities: expanded continental breakfast and high-speed Internet.**

/ SOME UNITS FEE

JAMESON INN Book at AAA.com

Hotel

$83-$90 All Year

Phone: (919)778-9759

Address: 1408 Harding Dr **Location:** US 70 E Bypass, exit Spence Ave, just n, then just e on North Park Dr. **Facility:** 67 one-bedroom standard units. 3 stories, interior corridors. *Bath:* combo or shower only. **Parking:** on-site. **Terms:** cancellation fee imposed. **Amenities:** high-speed Internet, voice mail, irons, hair dryers. **Pool(s):** outdoor. **Leisure Activities:** exercise room. **Business Services:** meeting rooms, PC. **Cards:** AX, DC, DS, MC, VI.

ASK CALL / SOME UNITS FEE FEE VCR

WHERE TO DINE

CENTRAL LUNCH RESTAURANT

American

$6-$8

Phone: 919/735-7979

The Southern cafe has been in continual operation since 1905. Classic entrees, such as roast beef with gravy and hamburger steak, join a list of sandwiches and cold plates on the menu. Daily changing sides range from applesauce to yams. Breakfast also is served. Casual dress. **Hours:** 7:30 am-2:30 pm. Closed major holidays; also Sat & Sun. **Address:** 103 N Center St **Location:** US 70/117 business route, just s; downtown. **Parking:** street. **Cards:** AX, DS, MC, VI.

MCCALL'S BAR-B-QUE & SEAFOOD

Regional Southern

$6-$15

Phone: 919/751-0072

Down-home country cooking lines the popular spot's lunch and dinner buffets. Among offerings are fried and barbecued chicken, fried fish, pulled-pork and chopped barbecue in a spicy vinegar sauce and plenty of sides and vegetables. Casual dress. **Hours:** 11 am-9 pm. Closed: 12/25. **Address:** 139 Miller's Chapel Rd **Location:** Jct US 70 and SR 111 S. **Parking:** on-site. **Cards:** AX, DS, MC, VI.

STEAK BARN

Steak & Seafood

$10-$30

Phone: 919/734-3544

Since 1968, the large, family-run restaurant has been a local favorite for steak. The salad bar is another popular offering. Casual dress. **Bar:** Full bar. **Reservations:** accepted. **Hours:** 5 pm-9:30 pm, Fri & Sat-10 pm. Closed: 11/26, 12/25; also Mon. **Address:** 1324 W Grantham St **Location:** Jct US 13, 0.8 mi w on US 70. **Parking:** on-site. **Cards:** AX, DS, MC, VI.

TEXAS STEAKHOUSE & SALOON

Steak

$6-$25

Phone: 919/778-7998

The typical Texas-style roadhouse focuses on freshly cut steaks, including the popular Duke entree with fries. Southwestern decor and arrows stuck in the walls get diners' minds wandering back to the old days. The popular draft beer is the microbrewed Red Oak lager. Casual dress. **Bar:** Full bar. **Hours:** 11 am-10 pm, Fri & Sat-11 pm. Closed: 11/26, 12/24, 12/25. **Address:** 330 Spence Ave **Location:** US 70 Bypass, exit Spence Ave, just s. **Parking:** on-site. **Cards:** AX, DS, MC, VI.

WILBER'S BBQ & RESTAURANT — Phone: 919/778-5218

Regional American
$2-$13

Join the crowd at the popular family eatery, which serves good ol' North Carolina barbecue. Sauces for the beef, pork and chicken are pepper- and vinegar-based for a little extra flavor. Try the fresh coleslaw and hush puppies. Casual dress. **Reservations:** accepted. **Hours:** 6 am-9 pm, Sun from 7 am. Closed: 11/26, 12/25; also for dinner 12/24. **Address:** 4172 US 70 E **Location:** Jct SR 111 S, just w. **Parking:** on-site. **Cards:** MC, VI.

GRAHAM pop. 12,833

WHERE TO STAY

COMFORT SUITES — *Book great rates at AAA.com* — **Phone:** (336)221-9199

AAA SAVE

Hotel
$79-$99 All Year

Address: 769 Woody Dr **Location:** I-40/85, exit 148, just s, then just w. **Facility:** Smoke free premises. 81 one-bedroom standard units, some with whirlpools. 3 stories, interior corridors. *Bath:* combo or shower only. **Parking:** on-site. **Amenities:** high-speed Internet, voice mail, irons, hair dryers. **Pool(s):** heated indoor. **Leisure Activities:** whirlpool, exercise room. **Guest Services:** valet and coin laundry, wireless Internet. **Business Services:** meeting rooms, PC. **Cards:** AX, CB, DC, DS, JC, MC, VI. **Free Special Amenities: full breakfast and high-speed Internet.**

CALL

WHERE TO DINE

SAGEBRUSH STEAKHOUSE — **Phone:** 336/227-8369

American
$5-$19

Born from the spirit of Texas cattle drives, the restaurant presents a menu of hearty steaks, prime rib, chicken, seafood and baby back ribs. Yummy desserts merit a splurge. Guests can call ahead to facilitate seating. Casual dress. **Bar:** Beer & wine. **Hours:** 11 am-10 pm, Fri & Sat-11 pm. Closed: 12/25. **Address:** 800 S Main St **Location:** I-40, exit 147, just s. **Parking:** on-site. **Cards:** AX, DC, DS, MC, VI.

CALL

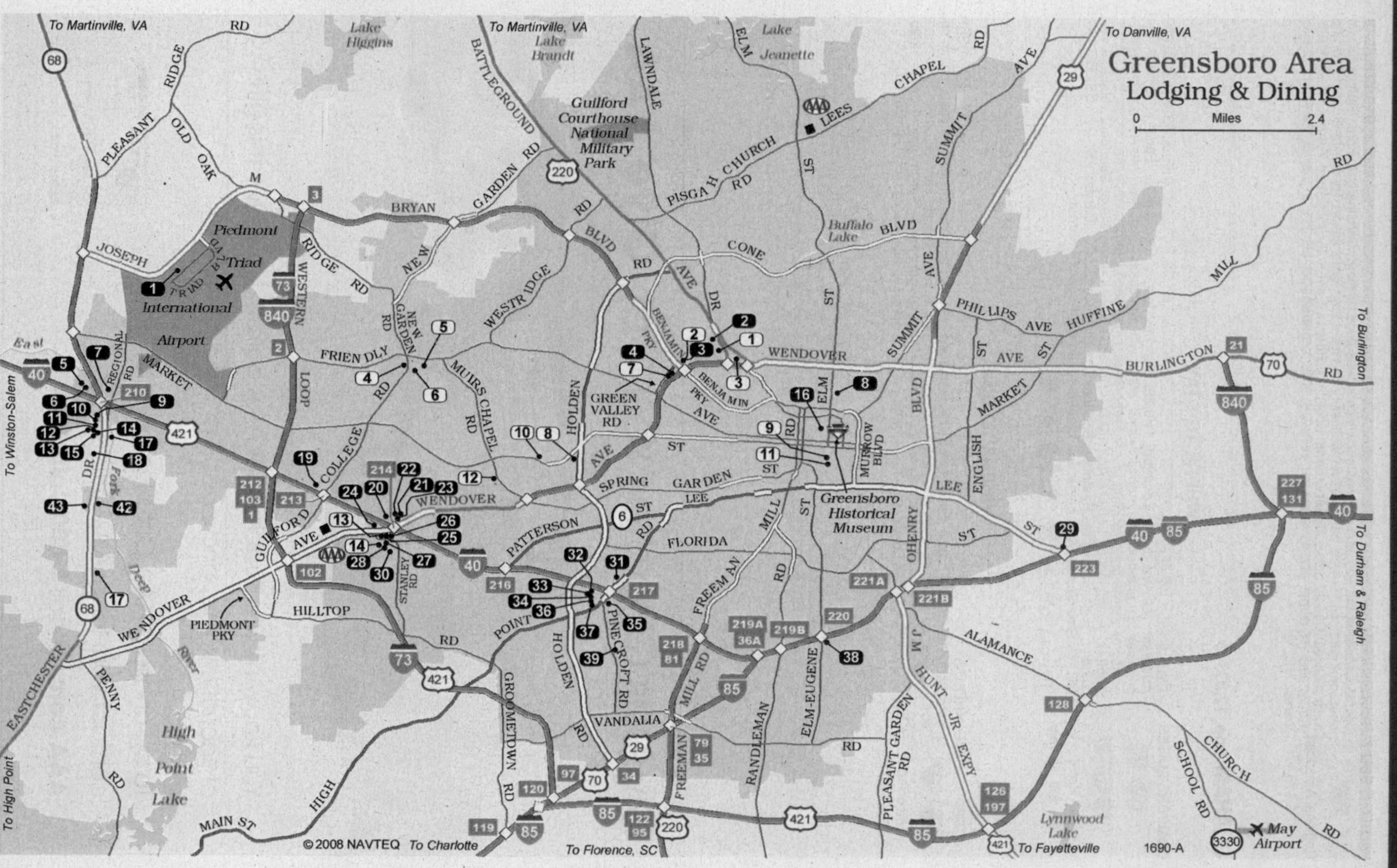
Greensboro Area
Lodging & Dining
0
Miles
2.4
To Martinville, VA
To Martinville, VA
To Danville, VA
To Burlington
To Durham & Raleigh
To Winston-Salem
To High Point
To Charlotte
To Florence, SC
To Fayetteville
Lake Higgins
Lake Brandt
Lake Jeanette
Buffalo Lake
Guilford Courthouse National Military Park
Piedmont Triad International Airport
Greensboro Historical Museum
High Point Lake
Lynnwood Lake
May Airport
BATTLEGROUND
LAWNDALE
PISGAH CHURCH RD
BRYAN
GARDEN RD
CONE
WENDOVER
BURLINGTON RD
SUMMIT AVE
PHILLIPS AVE
HUFFINE MILL RD
MARKET
WESTERN LOOP
NEW GARDEN RD
FRIENDLY
WESTRIDGE
MUIRS CHAPEL RD
HOLDEN
COLLEGE
GREEN VALLEY RD
SPRING GARDEN ST
PATTERSON
FLORIDA
FREEMAN MILL RD
ELM-EUGENE
RANDLEMAN
PLEASANT GARDEN RD
J M HUNT JR EXPY
ALAMANCE
SCHOOL RD
CHURCH
GROOMETOWN RD
VANDALIA
PINECROFT RD
HILLTOP
PIEDMONT PKY
EASTCHESTER
PENNY RD
HIGH
MAIN ST
© 2008 NAVTEQ
1690-A

Airport Accommodations

Map Page	OA	PIEDMONT TRIAD INTERNATIONAL	Diamond Rated	High Season	Page
11 / p. 714	AAA	**Best Western Deep River, 3 mi sw of airport**	◆◆◆	$84-$189 SAVE	717
13 / p. 714		Candlewood Suites, 3 mi sw of airport	◆◆◆	$90-$120	717
12 / p. 714		Comfort Suites Airport, 3 mi sw of airport	◆◆◆	$99-$229	718
18 / p. 714		Crestwood Suites, 3.2 mi sw of airport	◆◆	Rates not provided	718
6 / p. 714	AAA	**Embassy Suites Hotel, 2.5 mi sw of airport**	◆◆◆	$139-$199 SAVE	718
15 / p. 714		Extended Stay Deluxe, 3 mi sw of airport	◆◆	$100-$110	719
14 / p. 714		Fairfield Inn by Marriott Piedmont-Triad International Airport, 3 mi sw of airport	◆◆◆	$118-$127	719
9 / p. 714	AAA	**Hampton Inn-Greensboro Airport, 3 mi sw of airport**	◆◆◆	$139 SAVE	720
5 / p. 714	AAA	**Homewood Suites by Hilton-Greensboro Airport, 2.5 mi sw of airport**	◆◆◆	$99-$269 SAVE	720
1 / p. 714		Marriott Greensboro Airport, 0.5 mi w of airport	◆◆◆	$177-$190	721
17 / p. 714	AAA	**Red Roof Inn Airport, 3 mi sw of airport**	◆◆	$50-$106 SAVE	722
10 / p. 714		Residence Inn by Marriott-Greensboro Airport, 3 mi sw of airport	◆◆◆	$147-$158	723
7 / p. 714		Sleep Inn-Airport, 2.8 mi sw of airport	◆◆	$100-$170	723
43 / p. 714		Ashford Suites Hotel, 4 mi s of airport	◆◆◆	$106-$116	736
42 / p. 714		Biltmore Suites Hotel, 4 mi s of airport	◆◆◆	Rates not provided	736

Greensboro Area

This index helps you "spot" where approved lodgings and restaurants are located on the corresponding detailed maps. Lodging daily rate range is for comparison only and show the property's high season. Restaurant rate range is a combination of lunch and/or dinner. Turn to the listing page for more detailed rate information and consult display ads for special promotions.

GREENSBORO

Map Page	OA	Lodgings	Diamond Rated	High Season	Page
1 / p. 714		Marriott Greensboro Airport	◆◆◆	$177-$190	721
2 / p. 714	AAA	**Battleground Inn**	◆◆	$68-$99 SAVE	717
3 / p. 714	AAA	**Proximity Hotel - see color ad p 722**	◆◆◆◆	$229-$239 SAVE	722
4 / p. 714	AAA	**O. HENRY HOTEL - see color ad p 722**	◆◆◆◆	$249-$259 SAVE	721
5 / p. 714	AAA	**Homewood Suites by Hilton-Greensboro Airport**	◆◆◆	$99-$269 SAVE	720
6 / p. 714	AAA	**Embassy Suites Hotel**	◆◆◆	$139-$199 SAVE	718
7 / p. 714		Sleep Inn-Airport	◆◆	$100-$170	723
8 / p. 714		Greenwood Bed & Breakfast LLC	◆◆◆	Rates not provided	719
9 / p. 714	AAA	**Hampton Inn-Greensboro Airport**	◆◆◆	$139 SAVE	720
10 / p. 714		Residence Inn by Marriott-Greensboro Airport	◆◆◆	$147-$158	723
11 / p. 714	AAA	**Best Western Deep River**	◆◆◆	$84-$189 SAVE	717
12 / p. 714		Comfort Suites Airport	◆◆◆	$99-$229	718
13 / p. 714		Candlewood Suites	◆◆◆	$90-$120	717
14 / p. 714		Fairfield Inn by Marriott Piedmont-Triad International Airport	◆◆◆	$118-$127	719
15 / p. 714		Extended Stay Deluxe	◆◆	$100-$110	719
16 / p. 714		Marriott Greensboro Downtown	◆◆◆	$168-$180	721
17 / p. 714	AAA	**Red Roof Inn Airport**	◆◆	$50-$106 SAVE	722
18 / p. 714		Crestwood Suites	◆◆	Rates not provided	718
19 / p. 714		Clarion Hotel-Airport	◆◆◆	$86-$115	717

GREENSBORO (cont'd)

Map Page	OA	Lodgings (cont'd)	Diamond Rated	High Season	Page
20 / p. 714		Extended StayAmerica-Greensboro-Wendover Ave	◆◆	$72-$82	719
21 / p. 714	AAA	**Fairfield Inn & Suites by Marriott-Wendover**	◆◆◆	$118-$127 SAVE	719
22 / p. 714		Hilton Garden Inn	◆◆◆	$134-$164	720
23 / p. 714		Holiday Inn Express	◆◆◆	$99	720
24 / p. 714	AAA	**Courtyard by Marriott-Greensboro**	◆◆◆	$137-$147 SAVE	718
25 / p. 714	AAA	**Best Western Wendover Plaza**	◆◆◆	$70-$170 SAVE	717
26 / p. 714	AAA	**Hyatt Place Greensboro/Wendover**	◆◆◆	$79-$199 SAVE	721
27 / p. 714		La Quinta Inn & Suites Greensboro	◆◆◆	$69-$129	721
28 / p. 714		Wingate by Wyndham	◆◆◆	Rates not provided	723
29 / p. 714		Quality Inn & Suites	◆◆	$69-$199	722
30 / p. 714		SpringHill Suites by Marriott	◆◆◆	$132-$142	723
31 / p. 714		DoubleTree Hotel	◆◆◆	$109-$269	718
32 / p. 714	AAA	**Comfort Inn**	◆◆	$68-$84 SAVE	717
33 / p. 714		Residence Inn by Marriott	◆◆◆	$123-$132	722
34 / p. 714	AAA	**Hampton Inn-Four Seasons**	◆◆◆	$79-$119 SAVE	720
35 / p. 714	AAA	**Sheraton Greensboro at Four Seasons**	◆◆◆	Rates not provided SAVE	723
36 / p. 714	AAA	**Best Western Windsor Suites**	◆◆◆	$94-$150 SAVE	717
37 / p. 714		Drury Inn & Suites-Greensboro	◆◆◆	$80-$145	718
38 / p. 714		Econo Lodge Inn & Suites	◆◆	$49-$159	718
39 / p. 714		The Twin Lakes Lodge	◆◆◆	$150-$250	723

Map Page	OA	Restaurants	Diamond Rated	Cuisine	Meal Range	Page
1 / p. 714		Lucky 32	◆◆◆	Regional American	$7-$25	725
2 / p. 714		Print Works Bistro	◆◆◆	French	$9-$31	725
3 / p. 714		Taste of Thai-Oriental Grill	◆◆	Thai	$5-$16	725
4 / p. 714		Red Oak Brew Pub	◆◆	American	$6-$20	725
5 / p. 714		Bistro Sofia	◆◆◆	New American	$16-$35	724
6 / p. 714		Revival Grill	◆◆◆	American	$12-$28	725
7 / p. 714		Green Valley Grill	◆◆◆	Continental	$9-$27	724
8 / p. 714		Gate City Chop House	◆◆◆	Steak	$8-$36	724
9 / p. 714		Liberty Oak	◆◆◆	American	$8-$26	724
10 / p. 714		Leblon Churrascaria	◆◆◆	Brazilian	$27	724
11 / p. 714		Natty Greene's Pub & Brewing Company	◆◆	American	$6-$18	725
12 / p. 714		Pho Hien Vuong	◆	Vietnamese	$5-$12	725
13 / p. 714		Imperial Gourmet	◆	Chinese	$6-$13	724
14 / p. 714		Villa Rosa Italian Restaurant and Grill	◆◆	Italian	$8-$16	725

HIGH POINT

Map Page	OA	Lodgings	Diamond Rated	High Season	Page
42 / p. 714		Biltmore Suites Hotel	◆◆◆	Rates not provided	736
43 / p. 714		Ashford Suites Hotel	◆◆◆	$106-$116	736

Map Page	OA	Restaurant	Diamond Rated	Cuisine	Meal Range	Page
17 / p. 714		Chop House Grille	◆◆◆	Steak & Seafood	$8-$35	738

GREENSBORO pop. 223,891 (See map and index starting on p. 714)

WHERE TO STAY

BATTLEGROUND INN — **Phone:** (336)272-4737 — 2

AAA SAVE — Hotel — $68-$99 All Year

Address: 1517 Westover Terr **Location:** Wendover Ave, exit US 220 N/Westview Terr/Battleground Ave N, 0.5 mi n. **Facility:** 48 one-bedroom standard units, some with whirlpools. 4 stories, interior corridors. **Parking:** on-site. **Amenities:** hair dryers. **Guest Services:** wireless Internet. **Business Services:** PC. **Cards:** AX, DS, MC, VI. **Free Special Amenities: continental breakfast and high-speed Internet.**

CALL / SOME UNITS

BEST WESTERN DEEP RIVER — *Book great rates at AAA.com* — **Phone:** (336)454-0333 — 11

AAA SAVE — Hotel — $84-$189 All Year

Address: 7800 National Service Rd **Location:** I-40, exit 210 (SR 68), just s, just w on Thorndike Rd, then just n. **Facility:** 61 one-bedroom standard units. 4 stories, interior corridors. *Bath:* combo or shower only. **Parking:** on-site. **Terms:** 7 day cancellation notice. **Amenities:** high-speed Internet, dual phone lines, voice mail, irons, hair dryers. **Pool(s):** outdoor. **Leisure Activities:** exercise room. **Guest Services:** valet and coin laundry, airport transportation-Piedmont Triad International Airport, wireless Internet. **Business Services:** meeting rooms, PC. **Cards:** AX, DS, MC, VI. **Free Special Amenities: expanded continental breakfast and high-speed Internet.**

/ SOME UNITS FEE

AAA Benefit: Members save up to 20%, plus 10% bonus points with rewards program.

BEST WESTERN WENDOVER PLAZA — *Book great rates at AAA.com* — **Phone:** (336)297-1055 — 25

AAA SAVE — Hotel — $70-$170 All Year

Address: 1103 Lanada Rd **Location:** I-40 business route, exit 26 or 26A, just sw on Wendover Ave, then just e on Stanley Rd. **Facility:** 111 one-bedroom standard units. 5 stories, interior corridors. *Bath:* combo or shower only. **Parking:** on-site. **Amenities:** high-speed Internet, voice mail, irons, hair dryers. **Pool(s):** outdoor. **Leisure Activities:** exercise room. **Guest Services:** valet and coin laundry, wireless Internet. **Business Services:** meeting rooms, business center. **Cards:** AX, DC, DS, MC, VI. **Free Special Amenities: expanded continental breakfast and high-speed Internet.**

/ SOME UNITS

AAA Benefit: Members save up to 20%, plus 10% bonus points with rewards program.

BEST WESTERN WINDSOR SUITES — *Book great rates at AAA.com* — **Phone:** (336)294-9100 — 36

AAA SAVE — Hotel — $94-$150 All Year

Address: 2006 Veasley St **Location:** I-40 business route, exit 29, just s on High Point Rd, then just w. **Facility:** 76 one-bedroom standard units, some with whirlpools. 3 stories, interior corridors. *Bath:* combo or shower only. **Parking:** on-site. **Terms:** 3 night minimum stay - seasonal, 3 day cancellation notice. **Amenities:** voice mail, irons, hair dryers. **Pool(s):** outdoor. **Leisure Activities:** exercise room. **Guest Services:** valet and coin laundry, wireless Internet. **Business Services:** meeting rooms, PC. **Cards:** AX, DC, DS, MC, VI. **Free Special Amenities: expanded continental breakfast and high-speed Internet.**

/ SOME UNITS

AAA Benefit: Members save up to 20%, plus 10% bonus points with rewards program.

CANDLEWOOD SUITES — *Book at AAA.com* — **Phone:** (336)454-0078 — 13

Hotel — $90-$120 All Year

Address: 7623 Thorndike Rd **Location:** I-40, exit 210 (SR 68), just s, then just w. **Facility:** 122 units. 98 one-bedroom standard units with efficiencies. 24 one-bedroom suites with efficiencies. 3 stories, interior corridors. *Bath:* combo or shower only. **Parking:** on-site. **Terms:** cancellation fee imposed. **Amenities:** video library, DVD players, CD players, high-speed Internet, dual phone lines, voice mail, irons, hair dryers. **Leisure Activities:** exercise room. **Guest Services:** complimentary and valet laundry. **Cards:** AX, DC, DS, MC, VI.

ASK CALL VCR / SOME UNITS FEE

CLARION HOTEL-AIRPORT — *Book at AAA.com* — **Phone:** (336)299-7650 — 19

Hotel — $86-$115 All Year

Address: 415 Swing Rd **Location:** I-40 business route, exit 25, just n, then just w. **Facility:** 192 one-bedroom standard units. 4 stories, interior corridors. **Parking:** on-site. **Terms:** cancellation fee imposed. **Amenities:** dual phone lines, voice mail, irons, hair dryers. **Pool(s):** outdoor. **Leisure Activities:** exercise room. **Guest Services:** valet laundry, wireless Internet. **Business Services:** conference facilities, business center. **Cards:** AX, DC, DS, MC, VI.

COMFORT INN — *Book great rates at AAA.com* — **Phone:** (336)294-6220 — 32

AAA SAVE — Hotel — $68-$84 All Year

Address: 2001 Veasley St **Location:** I-40 business route, exit 29, just s on High Point Rd, then just w. **Facility:** 123 one-bedroom standard units. 2 stories (no elevator), interior corridors. **Parking:** on-site. **Terms:** 7 day cancellation notice-fee imposed. **Amenities:** voice mail, irons, hair dryers. **Pool(s):** outdoor. **Guest Services:** wireless Internet. **Business Services:** PC. **Cards:** AX, DS, MC, VI. **Free Special Amenities: expanded continental breakfast and high-speed Internet.**

/ SOME UNITS FEE

(See map and index starting on p. 714)

COMFORT SUITES AIRPORT *Book at AAA.com* **Phone:** (336)882-6666 12

Hotel

$99-$229 All Year

Address: 7619 Thorndike Rd **Location:** I-40, exit 210 (SR 68), just s, then just w. **Facility:** Smoke free premises. 113 one-bedroom standard units, some with whirlpools. 5 stories, interior corridors. *Bath:* combo or shower only. **Parking:** on-site. **Terms:** cancellation fee imposed. **Amenities:** high-speed Internet, dual phone lines, voice mail, safes (fee), irons, hair dryers. *Some:* DVD players (fee). **Pool(s):** outdoor. **Leisure Activities:** exercise room. **Guest Services:** valet and coin laundry, wireless Internet. **Business Services:** meeting rooms, PC. **Cards:** AX, DC, DS, JC, MC, VI.

CALL / SOME UNITS FEE FEE VCR

COURTYARD BY MARRIOTT-GREENSBORO *Book great rates at AAA.com* **Phone:** (336)294-3800 

Hotel

$138-$148 All Year

Address: 4400 W Wendover Ave **Location:** I-40 business route, exit 26 or 26A, just sw. **Facility:** Smoke free premises. 149 units. 138 one-bedroom standard units. 11 one-bedroom suites. 3 stories, interior corridors. *Bath:* combo or shower only. **Parking:** on-site. **Terms:** cancellation fee imposed. **Amenities:** high-speed Internet, voice mail, irons, hair dryers. **Pool(s):** outdoor. **Leisure Activities:** whirlpool, exercise room. **Guest Services:** valet and coin laundry, wireless Internet. **Business Services:** meeting rooms, business center. **Cards:** AX, CB, DC, DS, JC, MC, VI. **Free Special Amenities: preferred room (subject to availability with advance reservations) and high-speed Internet.**

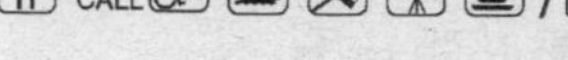

AAA Benefit:
Members save a minimum 5% off the best available rate.

CRESTWOOD SUITES *Book at AAA.com* **Phone:** 336/886-1250 18

Hotel

Rates not provided

Address: 501 Americhase Dr **Location:** I-40, exit 210 (SR 68), 0.5 mi s. **Facility:** 137 units. 121 one-bedroom standard units with efficiencies. 16 one-bedroom suites with efficiencies. 3 stories, interior corridors. *Bath:* combo or shower only. **Parking:** on-site. **Terms:** office hours 7 am-9 pm. **Amenities:** voice mail, irons, hair dryers. **Guest Services:** coin laundry, wireless Internet.

DOUBLETREE HOTEL *Book great rates at AAA.com* **Phone:** (336)292-4004 31

Hotel

$109-$269 All Year

Address: 3030 High Point Rd **Location:** I-40 business route, exit 29, just n. **Facility:** 175 one-bedroom standard units. 12 stories, interior corridors. *Bath:* combo or shower only. **Parking:** on-site. **Terms:** 1-30 night minimum stay, cancellation fee imposed. **Amenities:** high-speed Internet, voice mail, irons, hair dryers. **Pool(s):** heated indoor. **Leisure Activities:** exercise room. **Guest Services:** valet and coin laundry, wireless Internet. **Business Services:** conference facilities, business center. **Cards:** AX, CB, DC, DS, MC, VI.

CALL / SOME UNITS FEE FEE

AAA Benefit:
Members save 5% or more everyday!

DRURY INN & SUITES-GREENSBORO *Book at AAA.com* **Phone:** (336)856-9696 37

Hotel

$80-$145 All Year

Address: 3220 High Point Rd **Location:** I-40 business route, exit 29, just s. **Facility:** 143 units. 127 one-bedroom standard units. 16 one-bedroom suites. 5 stories, interior corridors. *Bath:* combo or shower only. **Parking:** on-site. **Amenities:** high-speed Internet, dual phone lines, voice mail, irons, hair dryers. **Pool(s):** heated indoor/outdoor. **Leisure Activities:** whirlpool, limited exercise equipment. **Guest Services:** valet and coin laundry, wireless Internet. **Business Services:** meeting rooms, PC. **Cards:** AX, DC, DS, MC, VI.

ASK / SOME UNITS

ECONO LODGE INN & SUITES *Book at AAA.com* **Phone:** (336)275-9575 38

Motel

$49-$159 All Year

Address: 120 Seneca Rd **Location:** I-40/Business 85, exit 37, just s, then e. **Facility:** 115 units. 105 one-bedroom standard units. 10 one-bedroom suites. 2 stories (no elevator), interior/exterior corridors. **Parking:** on-site. **Terms:** 14 day cancellation notice. **Amenities:** voice mail, irons, hair dryers. **Pool(s):** outdoor. **Leisure Activities:** playground. **Guest Services:** wireless Internet. **Business Services:** meeting rooms, PC. **Cards:** AX, DS, MC, VI.

ASK / SOME UNITS FEE

EMBASSY SUITES HOTEL *Book great rates at AAA.com* **Phone:** (336)668-4535 6

Hotel

$139-$199 All Year

Address: 204 Centreport Dr **Location:** I-40, exit 210 (SR 68), just n, just w on Triad Center Dr, then just s. **Facility:** 219 one-bedroom suites. 7 stories, interior corridors. *Bath:* combo or shower only. **Parking:** on-site. **Terms:** cancellation fee imposed. **Amenities:** video games (fee), voice mail, irons, hair dryers. **Pool(s):** heated indoor. **Leisure Activities:** sauna, whirlpool, sun deck, exercise room. **Guest Services:** valet and coin laundry, airport transportation-Piedmont Triad International Airport, wireless Internet. **Business Services:** conference facilities, business center. **Cards:** AX, CB, DC, DS, JC, MC, VI. **Free Special Amenities: full breakfast and newspaper.**

AAA Benefit:
Members save 5% or more everyday!

(See map and index starting on p. 714)

EXTENDED STAYAMERICA-GREENSBORO-WENDOVER AVE *Book at AAA.com* **Phone:** (336)299-0200 20

Motel
$72-$82 All Year

Address: 4317 Big Tree Way **Location:** I-40 business route, exit 26 or 26B, just ne on Wendover Ave, then just w. **Facility:** 129 one-bedroom standard units with efficiencies. 3 stories (no elevator), exterior corridors. *Bath:* combo or shower only. **Parking:** on-site. **Terms:** office hours 7 am-11 pm. **Amenities:** voice mail, irons. **Guest Services:** coin laundry, wireless Internet. **Cards:** AX, CB, DC, DS, JC, MC, VI.

ASK / SOME UNITS FEE

EXTENDED STAY DELUXE *Book at AAA.com* **Phone:** (336)454-0080 15

Hotel
$100-$110 All Year

Address: 7617 Thorndike Rd **Location:** I-40, exit 210 (SR 68), just s, then just w. **Facility:** 84 units. 83 one-bedroom standard units with kitchens. 1 two-bedroom suite with kitchen. 4 stories, interior corridors. *Bath:* combo or shower only. **Parking:** on-site. **Amenities:** DVD players, voice mail, irons, hair dryers. **Pool(s):** outdoor. **Leisure Activities:** exercise room. **Guest Services:** coin laundry, wireless Internet. **Cards:** AX, CB, DC, DS, JC, MC, VI.

ASK / SOME UNITS FEE

FAIRFIELD INN & SUITES BY MARRIOTT-WENDOVER *Book great rates at AAA.com* **Phone:** (336)369-1300 21

AAA SAVE

Hotel
$119-$127 All Year

Address: 4308 Big Tree Way **Location:** I-40 business route, exit 26 or 26B, just ne on Wendover Ave, then just w. **Facility:** Smoke free premises. 98 one-bedroom standard units. 4 stories, interior corridors. *Bath:* combo or shower only. **Parking:** on-site. **Terms:** cancellation fee imposed. **Amenities:** CD players, high-speed Internet, voice mail, irons, hair dryers. **Pool(s):** heated indoor. **Leisure Activities:** whirlpool, exercise room. **Guest Services:** valet and coin laundry, wireless Internet. **Business Services:** meeting rooms, business center. **Cards:** AX, DS, MC, VI. **Free Special Amenities: expanded continental breakfast and high-speed Internet.**

/ SOME UNITS

AAA Benefit:
Members save a minimum 5% off the best available rate.

FAIRFIELD INN BY MARRIOTT PIEDMONT-TRIAD INTERNATIONAL AIRPORT *Book great rates at AAA.com* **Phone:** (336)841-0140 14

Hotel
$119-$127 All Year

Address: 7615 Thorndike Rd **Location:** I-40, exit 210 (SR 68), just s, then just w. **Facility:** Smoke free premises. 81 one-bedroom standard units. 5 stories, interior corridors. *Bath:* combo or shower only. **Parking:** on-site. **Terms:** cancellation fee imposed. **Amenities:** high-speed Internet, voice mail, irons, hair dryers. **Pool(s):** outdoor. **Leisure Activities:** whirlpool. **Guest Services:** valet and coin laundry, wireless Internet. **Business Services:** PC. **Cards:** AX, CB, DC, DS, MC, VI.

CALL / SOME UNITS

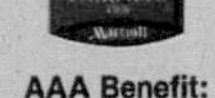

AAA Benefit:
Members save a minimum 5% off the best available rate.

GRANDOVER RESORT & CONFERENCE CENTER GOLF & SPA *Book at AAA.com* **Phone:** (336)294-1800

Resort Hotel
$189-$295 All Year

Address: 1000 Club Rd **Location:** I-85, exit 118, 0.7 mi s on I-85 business route, exit Guilford College Rd, 0.4 mi w, then 1.3 mi n on Grandover Pkwy. **Facility:** The grand resort features an imposing lobby replete with old world charm, and elegant guest rooms sport views of a world-class golf course. 247 units. 242 one-bedroom standard units, some with whirlpools. 3 one- and 2 two-bedroom suites with whirlpools. 12 stories, interior corridors. *Bath:* combo or shower only. **Parking:** on-site and valet. **Terms:** check-in 4 pm. **Amenities:** high-speed Internet, voice mail, irons, hair dryers. **Dining:** Di Valletta, see separate listing. **Pool(s):** heated indoor/outdoor. **Leisure Activities:** sauna, whirlpool, jogging, spa, volleyball. *Fee:* golf-36 holes, 4 lighted tennis courts, racquetball courts. **Guest Services:** valet laundry, wireless Internet. **Business Services:** conference facilities, business center. **Cards:** AX, DC, DS, MC, VI.

ASK FEE 24 CALL / SOME UNITS

GREENWOOD BED & BREAKFAST LLC **Phone:** 336/274-6350 8

Historic Bed & Breakfast
Rates not provided

Address: 205 N Park Dr **Location:** 0.8 mi n on N Elm St, just e; downtown. **Facility:** The property, furnished with antiques and centered in a well-tended garden, is located on a quiet residential street, across from a park. Smoke free premises. 4 one-bedroom standard units. 2 stories (no elevator), interior corridors. *Bath:* combo or shower only. **Parking:** street. **Terms:** age restrictions may apply. **Amenities:** hair dryers. **Guest Services:** TV in common area, wireless Internet. **Business Services:** PC.

(See map and index starting on p. 714)

HAMPTON INN-FOUR SEASONS Book great rates at AAA.com **Phone:** (336)854-8600 

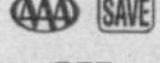

Hotel
$79-$119 All Year

Address: 2004 Veasley St **Location:** I-40 business route, exit 29, just s on High Point Rd, then just w. **Facility:** 120 one-bedroom standard units. 2 stories (no elevator), exterior corridors. **Parking:** on-site. **Terms:** 1-30 night minimum stay, cancellation fee imposed. **Amenities:** video games (fee), voice mail, irons, hair dryers. **Pool(s):** outdoor. **Guest Services:** wireless Internet. **Business Services:** meeting rooms, PC. **Cards:** AX, DC, DS, MC, VI. **Free Special Amenities: expanded continental breakfast and high-speed Internet.**

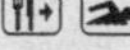 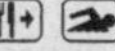   / SOME UNITS

AAA Benefit:
Members save up to 10% everyday!

HAMPTON INN-GREENSBORO AIRPORT Book great rates at AAA.com **Phone:** (336)605-5500 

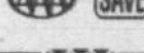

Hotel
$139 All Year

Address: 7803 National Service Rd **Location:** I-40, exit 210 (SR 68), just s, just w on Thorndike Rd, then just n. **Facility:** 125 one-bedroom standard units, some with whirlpools. 5 stories, interior corridors. *Bath:* combo or shower only. **Parking:** on-site. **Terms:** cancellation fee imposed. **Amenities:** video games (fee), high-speed Internet, voice mail, irons, hair dryers. **Pool(s):** outdoor. **Leisure Activities:** exercise room. **Guest Services:** valet laundry, airport transportation-Piedmont Triad International Airport, area transportation-within 10 mi, wireless Internet. **Business Services:** meeting rooms, PC. **Cards:** AX, DC, DS, MC, VI.

CALL   / SOME UNITS

AAA Benefit:
Members save up to 10% everyday!

HILTON GARDEN INN Book great rates at AAA.com **Phone:** (336)852-1491 

Hotel
$134-$164 All Year

Address: 4307 Big Tree Way **Location:** I-40 business route, exit 26 or 26B, just ne on Wendover Ave, then just w. **Facility:** 134 units. 132 one-bedroom standard units. 2 one-bedroom suites. 5 stories, interior corridors. *Bath:* combo or shower only. **Parking:** on-site. **Amenities:** video games (fee), high-speed Internet, voice mail, irons, hair dryers. **Pool(s):** heated indoor. **Leisure Activities:** whirlpool, exercise room. **Guest Services:** valet and coin laundry, wireless Internet. **Business Services:** meeting rooms, business center. **Cards:** AX, CB, DC, DS, JC, MC, VI.

CALL / SOME UNITS

AAA Benefit:
Members save 5% or more everyday!

HOLIDAY INN EXPRESS Book at AAA.com **Phone:** (336)854-0090 

Hotel
$99 All Year

Address: 4305 Big Tree Way **Location:** I-40 business route, exit 26 or 26B, just ne on Wendover Ave, then just w. **Facility:** 121 one-bedroom standard units, some with whirlpools. 4 stories, interior corridors. *Bath:* combo or shower only. **Parking:** on-site. **Terms:** 3 day cancellation notice. **Amenities:** high-speed Internet, dual phone lines, voice mail, irons, hair dryers. **Pool(s):** outdoor. **Guest Services:** valet laundry, wireless Internet. **Business Services:** meeting rooms, PC. **Cards:** AX, CB, DC, DS, JC, MC, VI.

     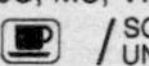

ASK CALL / SOME UNITS FEE

HOMEWOOD SUITES BY HILTON-GREENSBORO AIRPORT Book great rates at AAA.com **Phone:** (336)393-0088 

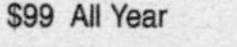

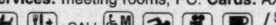

Hotel
$99-$269 All Year

Address: 201 Centreport Dr **Location:** I-40, exit 210 (SR 68), just n, just w on Triad Center Dr, then just s. **Facility:** 104 units. 90 one- and 14 two-bedroom suites with kitchens. 3 stories, interior corridors. *Bath:* combo or shower only. **Parking:** on-site. **Terms:** 1-30 night minimum stay, cancellation fee imposed. **Amenities:** video library, video games (fee), voice mail, irons, hair dryers. *Some:* high-speed Internet. **Pool(s):** outdoor. **Leisure Activities:** whirlpool, exercise room, basketball. **Guest Services:** valet and coin laundry, airport transportation-Piedmont Triad International Airport, wireless Internet. **Business Services:** meeting rooms, business center. **Cards:** AX, CB, DC, DS, JC, MC, VI. **Free Special Amenities: expanded continental breakfast and newspaper.**

/ SOME UNITS

AAA Benefit:
Members save 5% or more everyday!

(See map and index starting on p. 714)

HYATT PLACE GREENSBORO/WENDOVER Book great rates at AAA.com **Phone:** (336)852-1443 26

Hotel
$79-$199 All Year

Address: 1619 Stanley Rd **Location:** I-40 business route, exit 26 or 26A, just sw on Wendover Ave, then just e. **Facility:** 124 one-bedroom standard units. 6 stories, interior corridors. *Bath:* combo or shower only. **Parking:** on-site. **Terms:** cancellation fee imposed. **Amenities:** video games (fee), voice mail, irons, hair dryers. *Some:* high-speed Internet. **Pool(s):** outdoor. **Leisure Activities:** exercise room. **Guest Services:** valet laundry, airport transportation-Piedmont Triad International Airport, area transportation-within 5 mi, wireless Internet. **Business Services:** meeting rooms, business center. **Cards:** AX, CB, DC, DS, JC, MC, VI. **Free Special Amenities: continental breakfast and high-speed Internet.**

/ SOME UNITS

HYATT PLACE
AAA Benefit:
Ask for the AAA rate and save 10%.

LA QUINTA INN & SUITES GREENSBORO Book great rates at AAA.com **Phone:** (336)316-0100 27

Hotel
$69-$129 All Year

Address: 1201 Lanada Rd **Location:** I-40 business route, exit 26 or 26A, just sw on Wendover Ave, then just e on Stanley Rd. **Facility:** 131 units. 125 one-bedroom standard units. 6 one-bedroom suites. 6 stories, interior corridors. *Bath:* combo or shower only. **Parking:** on-site. **Amenities:** high-speed Internet, dual phone lines, voice mail, irons, hair dryers. **Pool(s):** heated outdoor. **Leisure Activities:** whirlpool, exercise room. **Guest Services:** valet and coin laundry, wireless Internet. **Business Services:** meeting rooms, PC. **Cards:** AX, DC, DS, MC, VI.

ASK CALL / SOME UNITS

MARRIOTT GREENSBORO AIRPORT Book great rates at AAA.com **Phone:** (336)852-6450 1

Hotel
$177-$190 All Year

Address: 1 Marriott Dr **Location:** I-40, exit 210 (SR 68), 2 mi n, 1.5 mi e on Bryan Blvd, 0.7 mi sw on Airport Pkwy. **Facility:** Smoke free premises. 299 one-bedroom standard units. 6 stories, interior corridors. *Bath:* combo or shower only. **Parking:** on-site. **Terms:** cancellation fee imposed. **Amenities:** high-speed Internet (fee), voice mail, irons, hair dryers. *Some:* DVD players (fee). **Pool(s):** heated indoor/outdoor. **Leisure Activities:** whirlpool, exercise room, horseshoes, volleyball. **Guest Services:** complimentary and valet laundry. **Business Services:** conference facilities, business center. **Cards:** AX, CB, DC, DS, JC, MC, VI.

CALL / SOME UNITS FEE VCR

Marriott HOTELS & RESORTS
AAA Benefit:
Members save a minimum 5% off the best available rate.

MARRIOTT GREENSBORO DOWNTOWN Book great rates at AAA.com **Phone:** (336)379-8000 16

Hotel
$168-$181 All Year

Address: 304 N Greene St **Location:** Just n on Elm St, just w on Lindsay St, then just s. **Facility:** Smoke free premises. 280 one-bedroom standard units, some with whirlpools. 11 stories, interior corridors. *Bath:* combo or shower only. **Parking:** on-site (fee). **Terms:** cancellation fee imposed. **Amenities:** high-speed Internet (fee), dual phone lines, voice mail, irons, hair dryers. **Pool(s):** heated indoor. **Leisure Activities:** sauna, whirlpool, exercise room. **Guest Services:** valet laundry, wireless Internet. **Business Services:** conference facilities, business center. **Cards:** AX, DS, MC, VI.

   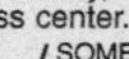 / SOME UNITS

Marriott HOTELS & RESORTS
AAA Benefit:
Members save a minimum 5% off the best available rate.

O. HENRY HOTEL Book great rates at AAA.com **Phone:** (336)854-2000 4

Hotel
$249-$259 All Year

Address: 624 Green Valley Rd **Location:** Wendover Ave, exit Benjamin Pkwy, just n, then just w. **Facility:** This European-style hotel features well-appointed common areas and guest rooms with a vintage ambience; afternoon tea is served in the social lobby. 131 units. 124 one-bedroom standard units. 7 one-bedroom suites with whirlpools. 8 stories, interior corridors. *Bath:* combo or shower only. **Parking:** on-site and valet. **Terms:** cancellation fee imposed. **Amenities:** video games (fee), CD players, high-speed Internet, dual phone lines, voice mail, safes, irons, hair dryers. **Dining:** Green Valley Grill, see separate listing. **Pool(s):** outdoor. **Leisure Activities:** jogging, exercise room. **Guest Services:** valet laundry, airport transportation-Piedmont Triad International Airport, area transportation-within 5 mi, wireless Internet. **Business Services:** conference facilities, business center. **Cards:** AX, DC, DS, MC, VI. **Free Special Amenities: full breakfast and high-speed Internet.** *(See color ad p 722)*

CALL / SOME UNITS VCR

(See map and index starting on p. 714)

PROXIMITY HOTEL Book great rates at AAA.com **Phone:** (336)379-8200 3

Hotel
$229-$239 All Year

Address: 704 Green Valley Rd **Location:** Wendover Ave, exit Benjamin Pkwy, just n, then just e. **Facility:** An eco-friendly property, the stylish hotel features a loft-like atmosphere with custom furnishings, rich textiles and local artwork. Smoke free premises. 147 one-bedroom standard units. 8 stories, interior corridors. *Bath:* combo or shower only. **Parking:** on-site and valet. **Terms:** cancellation fee imposed. **Amenities:** CD players, high-speed Internet, dual phone lines, voice mail, safes, irons, hair dryers. *Some:* DVD players (fee). **Dining:** Print Works Bistro, see separate listing. **Pool(s):** outdoor. **Leisure Activities:** bicycles, hiking trails. **Guest Services:** valet laundry, airport transportation-Piedmont Triad International Airport, area transportation-within 1 mi, wireless Internet. **Business Services:** conference facilities, business center. **Cards:** AX, DC, DS, MC, VI. **Free Special Amenities: local telephone calls and high-speed Internet.** *(See color ad below)*

QUALITY INN & SUITES Book at AAA.com **Phone:** (336)697-4000 29

Hotel
$69-$199 All Year

Address: 3114 Cedar Park Rd **Location:** I-85 business route, exit 41, just w on SR 6, then just n. **Facility:** 140 one-bedroom standard units. 2 stories (no elevator), exterior corridors. *Bath:* combo or shower only. **Parking:** on-site. **Terms:** 3 day cancellation notice. **Amenities:** voice mail, irons, hair dryers. **Pool(s):** outdoor. **Leisure Activities:** exercise room. **Guest Services:** valet laundry, wireless Internet. **Business Services:** conference facilities, PC. **Cards:** AX, DC, DS, MC, VI.

ASK CALL / SOME UNITS

RED ROOF INN AIRPORT Book great rates at AAA.com **Phone:** (336)271-2636 17

Motel
$50-$106 All Year

Address: 615 Regional Rd S **Location:** I-40, exit 210 (SR 68), just s, then just e. **Facility:** 112 one-bedroom standard units. 2 stories (no elevator), exterior corridors. *Bath:* combo or shower only. **Parking:** on-site. **Amenities:** video games (fee), voice mail. **Cards:** AX, CB, DC, DS, MC, VI. **Free Special Amenities: local telephone calls.**

CALL / SOME UNITS

RESIDENCE INN BY MARRIOTT Book great rates at AAA.com **Phone:** (336)294-8600 33

Hotel
$123-$132 All Year

Address: 2000 Veasley St **Location:** I-40 business route, exit 29, just s on High Point Rd, then 0.4 mi w. **Facility:** Smoke free premises. 128 units. 96 one- and 32 two-bedroom standard units with kitchens. 2 stories (no elevator), exterior corridors. **Parking:** on-site. **Terms:** cancellation fee imposed. **Amenities:** high-speed Internet, voice mail, irons, hair dryers. **Pool(s):** outdoor. **Leisure Activities:** whirlpool, sports court. **Guest Services:** coin laundry, wireless Internet. **Business Services:** PC. **Cards:** AX, CB, DC, DS, JC, MC, VI.

/ SOME UNITS FEE

Residence Inn Marriott
AAA Benefit:
Members save a minimum 5% off the best available rate.

(See map and index starting on p. 714)

RESIDENCE INN BY MARRIOTT-GREENSBORO AIRPORT Book great rates at AAA.com Phone: (336)632-4666 10

Hotel
$147-$158 All Year

Address: 7616 Thorndike Rd **Location:** I-40, exit 210, just s on SR 68, then just w. **Facility:** Smoke free premises. 116 units. 79 one-bedroom standard units with efficiencies. 22 one- and 15 two-bedroom suites, some with efficiencies or kitchens. 4 stories, interior corridors. *Bath:* combo or shower only. **Parking:** on-site. **Terms:** cancellation fee imposed. **Amenities:** high-speed Internet, voice mail, irons, hair dryers. **Pool(s):** heated indoor. **Leisure Activities:** whirlpool, putting green, exercise room. **Guest Services:** valet and coin laundry, area transportation, wireless Internet. **Business Services:** meeting rooms, business center. **Cards:** AX, CB, DC, DS, MC, VI.

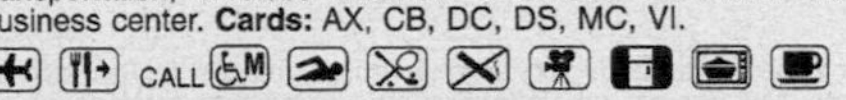

/ SOME UNITS FEE

AAA Benefit:
Members save a minimum 5% off the best available rate.

SHERATON GREENSBORO AT FOUR SEASONS Book great rates at AAA.com Phone: 336/292-9161 35

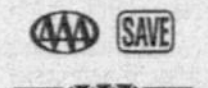

Hotel
Rates not provided

Address: 3121 High Point Rd **Location:** I-40 business route, exit 29, just s. Attached to Joseph S Koury Convention Center. **Facility:** 990 units. 914 one-bedroom standard units, some with whirlpools. 76 one-bedroom suites, some with whirlpools. 5-28 stories, interior corridors. *Bath:* combo or shower only. **Parking:** on-site. **Amenities:** high-speed Internet, dual phone lines, voice mail, irons, hair dryers. **Dining:** 4 restaurants, nightclub, entertainment. **Pool(s):** heated indoor/outdoor. **Leisure Activities:** sauna, whirlpool, racquetball court. **Guest Services:** valet and coin laundry, wireless Internet. **Business Services:** conference facilities, business center. **Free Special Amenities: newspaper and high-speed Internet.**

FEE CALL

/ SOME UNITS FEE FEE

AAA Benefit:
Members get up to 15% off, plus Starwood Preferred Guest® bonuses.

SLEEP INN-AIRPORT Book at AAA.com Phone: (336)931-1272 7

Hotel
$100-$170 All Year

Address: 7 Sharps Airpark Ct **Location:** I-40, exit 210 (SR 68) westbound, follow Regional Rd sign, just n; exit 210 eastbound, just e on Albert Pick Rd, then just n on Regional Rd. **Facility:** 116 one-bedroom standard units. 7 stories, interior corridors. *Bath:* combo or shower only. **Parking:** on-site. **Amenities:** dual phone lines, voice mail, irons, hair dryers. **Pool(s):** outdoor. **Guest Services:** valet and coin laundry, wireless Internet. **Cards:** AX, CB, DC, DS, MC, VI.

ASK CALL / SOME UNITS

SPRINGHILL SUITES BY MARRIOTT Book great rates at AAA.com Phone: (336)809-0909 30

Hotel
$133-$143 All Year

Address: 6006 Landmark Center Blvd **Location:** I-40 business route, exit 26 or 26A, just sw on Wendover Ave, 0.4 mi e on Stanley Rd, then just s. **Facility:** Smoke free premises. 82 one-bedroom standard units. 4 stories, interior corridors. *Bath:* combo or shower only. **Parking:** on-site. **Terms:** cancellation fee imposed. **Amenities:** high-speed Internet, dual phone lines, voice mail, irons, hair dryers. **Pool(s):** heated indoor. **Leisure Activities:** whirlpool, exercise room. **Guest Services:** valet and coin laundry, wireless Internet. **Business Services:** meeting rooms, business center. **Cards:** AX, DS, JC, MC, VI.

CALL

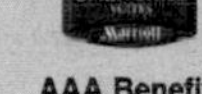

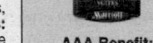

AAA Benefit:
Members save a minimum 5% off the best available rate.

THE TWIN LAKES LODGE Phone: 336/852-6968 39

Bed & Breakfast
$150-$250 All Year

Address: 2700 Twin Lakes Dr **Location:** I-40 business route, exit 29 eastbound, 0.7 mi se on Pinecroft Rd, over bridge, then just nw on 2nd Twin Lakes Dr entrance; exit westbound, just s on High Point Rd, then 0.7 mi se on Pinecroft Rd over bridge, then just nw on 2nd Twin Lakes Dr entrance. **Facility:** Set in a wooded area overlooking a small lake, the inn's spacious guest rooms feature a fireplace and a two-person whirlpool tub. Smoke free premises. 4 one-bedroom standard units with whirlpools. 2 stories (no elevator), exterior corridors. **Parking:** on-site. **Terms:** 3 day cancellation notice-fee imposed. **Amenities:** video library, CD players, hair dryers. **Leisure Activities:** fishing. **Guest Services:** wireless Internet. **Business Services:** meeting rooms, PC. **Cards:** AX, MC, VI.

WINGATE BY WYNDHAM Book at AAA.com Phone: 336/854-8610 28

Hotel
Rates not provided

Address: 6007 Landmark Center Blvd **Location:** I-40 business route, exit 26 or 26A, just sw on Wendover Ave, just e on Stanley Rd, then just se on Lanada Rd. **Facility:** 105 one-bedroom standard units. 5 stories, interior corridors. *Bath:* combo or shower only. **Parking:** on-site. **Amenities:** video games (fee), high-speed Internet, dual phone lines, voice mail, safes, irons, hair dryers. **Pool(s):** outdoor. **Leisure Activities:** whirlpool, exercise room. **Guest Services:** valet and coin laundry, wireless Internet. **Business Services:** meeting rooms, business center.

(See map and index starting on p. 714)

WHERE TO DINE

ARIGATO JAPANESE STEAK HOUSE — **Phone:** 336/299-1003

Japanese
$18-$30

Seated around the grill, diners watch as their meal is prepared with flair by Japanese chefs. Selections include hibachi steak, chicken, shrimp and sauteed vegetables, all served in large portions so come hungry. Casual dress. **Bar:** Full bar. **Reservations:** suggested, weekends. **Hours:** 5 pm-10 pm, Fri-10:30 pm, Sat 4 pm-10:30 pm, Sun 4 pm-9:30 pm. Closed: 11/26, 12/24, 12/25. **Address:** 1200 S Holden Rd **Location:** I-40, exit 217, just n, 0.4 mi w on Meadowview Rd, then 0.4 mi n. **Parking:** on-site. **Cards:** AX, MC, VI.

BISTRO SOFIA — **Phone:** 336/855-1313 (5)

New American
$16-$35

Elegant but not stuffy, the warm and cozy dining room provides for an intimate dining experience. The helpful, knowledgeable staff serves exquisite French cuisine that satisfies all epicurean desires. Outdoor dining is an option. Dressy casual. **Bar:** Full bar. **Reservations:** suggested. **Hours:** 5 pm-10 pm. Closed major holidays; also Mon. **Address:** 616 Dolley Madison Rd **Location:** I-40, exit 213, 2 mi n on Guilford College Rd, just e on Friendly Ave, then just s. **Parking:** on-site. **Cards:** AX, DC, MC, VI.

DI VALLETTA — **Phone:** 336/294-1800

Continental
$9-$29

The serene setting, which reflects the ambience of a European castle, affords excellent views of manicured gardens and the 18th hole of the east course. The menu features fresh seafood, Angus beef and other quality ingredients. Dressy casual. **Bar:** Full bar. **Reservations:** suggested. **Hours:** 6 am-2:30 & 5:30-10:30 pm. **Address:** 1000 Club Rd **Location:** I-85, exit 118, 0.7 mi s on I-85 business route, exit Guilford College Rd, 0.4 mi w, then 1.3 mi n on Grandover Pkwy; in Grandover Resort & Conference Center Golf & Spa. **Parking:** on-site and valet. **Cards:** AX, CB, DC, DS, MC, VI.

GATE CITY CHOP HOUSE — **Phone:** 336/294-9977 (8)

Steak
$8-$36

Menu offerings include quality steaks, seafood, chicken, lamb, pork and pasta. Specialties at the upscale eatery are grilled sea bass with warm pineapple-ponzu sauce, seared jumbo scallops, center-cut Angus beef in a variety of cuts and rack of lamb with mint demi-glace. Dressy casual. **Bar:** Full bar. **Reservations:** accepted. **Hours:** 11:30 am-10 pm, Sat from 4:30 pm. Closed major holidays; also 12/24 & Sun. **Address:** 106 S Holden Rd **Location:** I-40, exit 214 or 214B, 1.8 mi e on Wendover Ave, then 0.3 mi n. **Parking:** on-site. **Cards:** AX, DS, MC, VI.

GREEN VALLEY GRILL — **Phone:** 336/854-2015 (7)

Continental
$9-$27

With arched windows, tile mosaics and brick walls, the decor has a distinct turn-of-the-century feel. Every four weeks the menu changes, offering many European influenced entrees prepared on a wood fired rotisserie or in a wood burning oven, appealingly presented. Dressy casual. **Bar:** Full bar. **Reservations:** suggested. **Hours:** 11:15 am-10:30 pm, Fri & Sat-11 pm, Sun 9 am-10 pm. **Address:** 622 Green Valley Rd **Location:** Wendover Ave, exit Benjamin Pkwy, just n, then just w; in O. Henry Hotel. **Parking:** on-site. **Cards:** AX, CB, DC, DS, MC, VI.

CALL

HARPER'S RESTAURANT — **Phone:** 336/299-8850

American
$8-$26

Convenient to shops and the highway, the casual eatery prepares tasty steak, seafood, chicken and salads. Casual dress. **Bar:** Full bar. **Reservations:** accepted. **Hours:** 11:15 am-10 pm, Fri & Sat-11 pm, Sun 10:30 am-10 pm. Closed: 12/25. **Address:** 601 Friendly Center Rd **Location:** Jct Wendover Ave, just w; in Friendly Center Shopping Center. **Parking:** on-site. **Cards:** AX, DC, DS, MC, VI.

IMPERIAL GOURMET — **Phone:** 336/547-8868 (13)

Chinese
$6-$13

The restaurant specializes in all-you-can-eat buffets for lunch and dinner. Included in the buffet are a barbecue bar, carved roast beef and a sushi and dim sum selection. Buffet items include a variety of traditional and unusual Oriental items, as well as crab legs. Menu service is also available. Casual dress. **Bar:** Full bar. **Hours:** 11 am-10 pm, Fri & Sat-11 pm, Sun noon-10 pm. **Address:** 4408 Landover Rd **Location:** I-40 business route, exit 26 or 26A, just sw on Wendover Ave. **Parking:** on-site. **Cards:** AX, MC, VI.

CALL

LEBLON CHURRASCARIA — **Phone:** 336/294-2605 (10)

Brazilian
$27

Features of the hot-and-cold buffet include whipped sweet potatoes, fried bananas, salad fixings, brie in honey with pistachios and smoked salmon, leg of lamb, flank steak, bacon-wrapped filet mignon, parmesan-crusted pork loin and many other items. Meats are carved and served tableside at this upscale Brazilian steakhouse. Dressy casual. **Bar:** Full bar. **Reservations:** suggested. **Hours:** 5 pm-9:30 pm. Closed: 12/25; also Sun. **Address:** 4512 W Market St **Location:** I-40, exit 214 or 214B, 1.8 mi e on Wendover Ave, exit Holden Rd, just n, then 0.8 mi w. **Parking:** on-site. **Cards:** AX, DS, MC, VI.

LIBERTY OAK — **Phone:** 336/273-7057 (9)

American
$8-$26

The vintage downtown building nurtures a casually upscale dining atmosphere. The menu features dishes that combine fresh ingredients in inventive ways, such as in stuffed rainbow trout and lamb with honey-mint pesto. Also offered are down-home favorites prepared with flair, including roasted pulled pork, fried chicken and shrimp and grits. Casual dress. **Bar:** Full bar. **Reservations:** accepted. **Hours:** 11:30 am-9:30 pm, Fri-10 pm, Sat noon-10 pm. Closed major holidays; also Sun. **Address:** 100-D W Washington St **Location:** Jct S Elm St, just w; downtown. **Parking:** street. **Cards:** AX, DS, MC, VI.

(See map and index starting on p. 714)

LUCKY 32 **Phone:** 336/370-0707 (1)

Regional American
$7-$25

The menu changes monthly at the comfortably upscale eatery, with the focus of the cuisine on incorporating fresh, locally grown ingredients into regional American fare. Casual dress. **Bar:** Full bar. **Reservations:** accepted. **Hours:** 11:15 am-10:30, Fri & Sat-11 pm, Sun 10 am-10 pm. Closed: 11/26, 12/25. **Address:** 1421 Westover Terrace **Location:** Wendover Ave, exit US 220 N/Westover Terrace/Battleground Ave N, just n. **Parking:** on-site. **Cards:** AX, DS, MC, VI.

NATTY GREENE'S PUB & BREWING COMPANY **Phone:** 336/274-1373 (11)

American
$6-$18

The downtown brewery is as popular for its lengthy menu of burgers, wraps, sandwiches and hearty pub fare as it is for its house-brewed ales and stout. Outdoor seating is offered during warm weather. Casual dress. **Bar:** Full bar. **Hours:** 11 am-2 am, Sun-midnight. Closed: 11/26, 12/24, 12/25. **Address:** 345 S Elm St **Location:** Jct McGee St; downtown. **Parking:** street. **Cards:** AX, DS, MC, VI.

PHO HIEN VUONG **Phone:** 336/294-5551 (12)

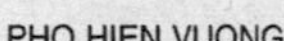

Vietnamese
$5-$12

Traditional pho (soup) or bun (vermicelli) is at its tastiest and is served with a smile in the comfortable, unpretentious restaurant. Casual dress. **Bar:** Beer & wine. **Hours:** 11 am-3:30 & 5-9:30 pm, Fri-Sun 11 am-9:30 pm. **Address:** 4109-A Spring Garden Rd **Location:** I-40, exit 214 or 214 B, 1.8 mi ne on Wendover Ave, exit Spring Garden Rd, then 0.5 mi w. **Parking:** on-site. **Cards:** AX, DS, MC, VI.

PRINT WORKS BISTRO **Phone:** 336/379-0699 (2)

French
$9-$31

Adjacent to the chic, eco-friendly Proximity Hotel, the bistro offers the tastes and ambience of France. Windows surround the elegant dining room, which affords beautiful views of the gardens, while tables on the large patio sit next to a small stream. Offerings of traditional French bistro cuisine include bouillabaisse, salmon and lentils, gougeres (warm house-baked cheese puffs), steak and frites, mussels and a daily fresh fruit tart. A sophisticated wine and cocktail list is presented. Casual dress. **Bar:** Full bar. **Reservations:** accepted. **Hours:** 11:15 am-10:30 pm, Fri-11 pm, Sat 7:30 am-11 pm, Sun 7:30 am-10:30 pm. Closed: 11/26, 12/25. **Address:** 702 Green Valley Rd **Location:** Wendover Ave, exit Benjamin Pkwy, just n, then just e; in Proximity Hotel. **Parking:** on-site. **Cards:** MC, VI.

CALL

RED OAK BREW PUB **Phone:** 336/299-3649 (4)

American
$6-$20

Red Oak lager is a cool complement to such favorites as gourmet sandwiches, fish and chips, the signature drunken chicken entree and preparations of Black Angus beef. Sauces, dressings and soups are homemade. An appointment is needed to tour the on-site brewery. Casual dress. **Bar:** Full bar. **Hours:** 11 am-11 pm, Sat 4 pm-midnight, Sun 4 pm-9 pm. Closed: 11/26, 12/25. **Address:** 714 Francis King St **Location:** I-40, exit 213, 2 mi n on Guilford College Rd, just w on Hunt Club Rd, then just n. **Parking:** on-site. **Cards:** DS, MC, VI.

REVIVAL GRILL **Phone:** 336/297-0950 (6)

American
$12-$28

This extremely popular restaurant recently expanded to this newly constructed building, located behind a shopping center, and well worth finding. The atmosphere is informal, yet the menu offerings are cutting edge. All service is personable, yet professional. Dressy casual. **Bar:** Full bar. **Reservations:** accepted. **Hours:** 5:30 pm-9:30 pm. Closed: 12/25; also Sun & Mon. **Address:** 604 Milner Dr **Location:** I-40, exit 213, 2 mi n, then just e on Hunt Club Rd; behind Quaker Village Shopping Center. **Parking:** on-site. **Cards:** AX, DC, DS, MC, VI.

CALL

TASTE OF THAI-ORIENTAL GRILL **Phone:** 336/273-1318 (3)

Thai
$5-$16

The pleasant, attentive staff enhance the dining experience at the cafe, a favorite for traditional Thai cuisine. Casual dress. **Bar:** Full bar. **Hours:** 11:30 am-3 & 5-10 pm, Fri & Sat-10:30 pm. Closed: 11/26. **Address:** 1500 Mill St, Suite 101 **Location:** Jct Wendover Ave, exit US 220/Westover Terrace/Battleground Ave N, just n, then just e. **Parking:** on-site. **Cards:** AX, DC, DS, MC, VI.

VILLA ROSA ITALIAN RESTAURANT AND GRILL **Phone:** 336/294-8688 (14)

Italian
$8-$16

Classic selections of pasta, steak and seafood are prepared to order. Together with an upscale look to the dining room, these two features combine to create an enjoyable experience. Dining is comfortable and relaxed. The dining room, which takes on an Old World Mediterranean decor, re-creates a sense of dining al fresco. Knowledgeable staff are attentive to guests' needs. Dressy casual. **Bar:** Full bar. **Reservations:** suggested. **Hours:** 11 am-10 pm, Fri & Sat-11 pm. Closed: 11/26, 12/25. **Address:** 6010 Landmark Center Blvd **Location:** I-40 business route, exit 26 or 26A, just sw on Wendover Ave, then just e. **Parking:** on-site. **Cards:** AX, DS, MC, VI.

CALL 

GREENVILLE pop. 60,476

WHERE TO STAY

BAYMONT INN & SUITES Book at AAA.com **Phone:** (252)355-2521

Hotel
$69-$109 All Year

Address: 3439 S Memorial Dr **Location:** Jct US 264 alternate route, just s on SR 11/903. **Facility:** 116 one-bedroom standard units. 2 stories (no elevator), exterior corridors. **Parking:** on-site. **Terms:** check-in 4 pm. **Amenities:** voice mail, irons, hair dryers. **Pool(s):** outdoor. **Leisure Activities:** exercise room. **Guest Services:** valet laundry, wireless Internet. **Business Services:** meeting rooms, PC. **Cards:** AX, DC, DS, MC, VI.

ASK / SOME UNITS FEE

BEST WESTERN SUITES-GREENVILLE Book great rates at AAA.com **Phone:** (252)752-2378

AAA SAVE
Hotel
$89-$91 All Year

Address: 2310 NE Greenville Blvd **Location:** Jct US 264 alternate route and SR 33, just e. **Facility:** Smoke free premises. 70 one-bedroom standard units, some with whirlpools. 2 stories, interior corridors. *Bath:* combo or shower only. **Parking:** on-site. **Terms:** check-in 4 pm, 2 night minimum stay, 3 day cancellation notice-fee imposed. **Amenities:** high-speed Internet, dual phone lines, voice mail, irons, hair dryers. **Pool(s):** outdoor. **Leisure Activities:** exercise room. **Guest Services:** valet and coin laundry, airport transportation-Pitt-Greenville Airport, area transportation-industrial park & university, wireless Internet. **Business Services:** meeting rooms, business center. **Cards:** AX, DC, DS, MC, VI. **Free Special Amenities: expanded continental breakfast and high-speed Internet.**

AAA Benefit:
Members save up to 20%, plus 10% bonus points with rewards program.

CITY HOTEL AND BISTRO Book at AAA.com **Phone:** 252/355-8300

Hotel
Rates not provided

Address: 203 W Greenville Blvd **Location:** Jct SR 11/903, 1 mi e on US 264 alternate route. **Facility:** 192 one-bedroom standard units, some with whirlpools. 4 stories, interior corridors. **Parking:** on-site. **Amenities:** dual phone lines, voice mail, irons, hair dryers. **Pool(s):** outdoor. **Leisure Activities:** exercise room. **Guest Services:** valet laundry, wireless Internet. **Business Services:** conference facilities, business center.

/ SOME UNITS

COMFORT INN Book great rates at AAA.com **Phone:** (252)355-0070

AAA SAVE
Hotel
$68-$99 All Year

Address: 3900 S Memorial Dr **Location:** Jct US 264 alternate route, 1 mi s on SR 11/903. **Facility:** 60 one-bedroom standard units, some with whirlpools. 2 stories (no elevator), interior corridors. *Bath:* combo or shower only. **Parking:** on-site. **Terms:** 2 night minimum stay - seasonal, cancellation fee imposed. **Amenities:** irons, hair dryers. **Pool(s):** outdoor. **Leisure Activities:** limited exercise equipment. **Guest Services:** valet laundry, wireless Internet. **Business Services:** PC. **Cards:** AX, DC, DS, MC, VI. **Free Special Amenities: expanded continental breakfast and high-speed Internet.**

/ SOME UNITS

COURTYARD BY MARRIOTT Book great rates at AAA.com **Phone:** (252)329-2900

Hotel
$128-$137 All Year

Address: 2225 Stantonsburg Rd **Location:** Jct US 13/SR 11, 0.5 mi w. Located across from Pitt County Memorial Hospital. **Facility:** Smoke free premises. 84 one-bedroom standard units. 3 stories, interior corridors. *Bath:* combo or shower only. **Parking:** on-site. **Terms:** cancellation fee imposed. **Amenities:** high-speed Internet, dual phone lines, voice mail, irons, hair dryers. **Pool(s):** heated indoor. **Leisure Activities:** whirlpool, exercise room. **Guest Services:** valet and coin laundry, wireless Internet. **Business Services:** meeting rooms, business center. **Cards:** AX, CB, DC, DS, MC, VI.

/ SOME UNITS

AAA Benefit:
Members save a minimum 5% off the best available rate.

DAYS INN Book at AAA.com **Phone:** (252)752-0214

Motel
$86-$95 All Year

Address: 810 S Memorial Dr **Location:** Jct US 264 alternate route, just s on US 13/SR 11. **Facility:** 47 one-bedroom standard units. 2 stories (no elevator), exterior corridors. **Parking:** on-site. **Amenities:** high-speed Internet, irons, hair dryers. **Pool(s):** outdoor. **Guest Services:** coin laundry, wireless Internet. **Business Services:** PC. **Cards:** AX, DC, DS, MC, VI.

ASK / SOME UNITS

EAST CAROLINA INN **Phone:** (252)752-2122

AAA SAVE
Motel
$55-$95 All Year

Address: 2095 Stantonsburg Rd (US 264 Alternate) **Location:** Jct US 13/SR 11, just w. Located opposite Pitt County Memorial Hospital. **Facility:** 53 units. 52 one-bedroom standard units. 1 one-bedroom suite with whirlpool. 2 stories (no elevator), exterior corridors. **Parking:** on-site. **Amenities:** irons, hair dryers. **Guest Services:** wireless Internet. **Business Services:** meeting rooms. **Cards:** AX, DS, MC, VI. **Free Special Amenities: continental breakfast and high-speed Internet.**

FEE / SOME UNITS VCR

HILTON GREENVILLE *Book great rates at AAA.com* **Phone:** (252)355-5000

Hotel
$119-$199 All Year

Address: 207 SW Greenville Blvd **Location:** Jct SR 11/903, 1 mi e on US 264 alternate route. **Facility:** Designated smoking area. 141 units. 135 one-bedroom standard units. 4 one- and 2 two-bedroom suites. 6 stories, interior corridors. **Parking:** on-site. **Terms:** cancellation fee imposed. **Amenities:** dual phone lines, voice mail, irons, hair dryers. *Some:* high-speed Internet. **Pool(s):** outdoor. **Leisure Activities:** whirlpool, exercise room. **Guest Services:** valet laundry, wireless Internet. **Business Services:** conference facilities, business center. **Cards:** AX, DC, DS, MC, VI.

/ SOME UNITS FEE VCR

HOLIDAY INN EXPRESS *Book at AAA.com* **Phone:** (252)754-8300

Hotel
$106-$154 All Year

Address: 909 Moye Blvd **Location:** Jct US 264 alternate route, just s on US 13/SR 11, then just w on Crosswinds St. **Facility:** 124 one-bedroom standard units, some with whirlpools. 4 stories, interior corridors. *Bath:* combo or shower only. **Parking:** on-site. **Terms:** check-in 4 pm. **Amenities:** voice mail, irons, hair dryers. **Pool(s):** outdoor. **Leisure Activities:** whirlpool. **Guest Services:** valet laundry, wireless Internet. **Business Services:** meeting rooms, business center. **Cards:** AX, DS, MC, VI.

ASK CALL / SOME UNITS

HOME-TOWNE SUITES *Book at AAA.com* **Phone:** (252)752-3411

Hotel
$79-$130 3/1-11/30
$59-$110 12/1-2/28

Address: 2111 W Arlington Blvd **Location:** Jct US 13/SR 11, 0.4 mi w on Stantonsburg Rd, then just s. **Facility:** 69 units. 61 one- and 8 two-bedroom standard units with efficiencies. 2 stories (no elevator), interior corridors. *Bath:* combo or shower only. **Parking:** on-site. **Terms:** office hours 8 am-10 pm, cancellation fee imposed. **Amenities:** dual phone lines, voice mail, irons. **Leisure Activities:** horseshoes. **Guest Services:** coin laundry, wireless Internet. **Cards:** AX, DC, DS, MC, VI.

ASK FEE / SOME UNITS FEE

JAMESON INN *Book at AAA.com* **Phone:** (252)752-7382

Motel
$73-$78 All Year

Address: 920 Crosswinds St **Location:** Jct US 264 alternate route, just s on US 13/SR 11, then just w. Located behind Waffle House. **Facility:** 40 one-bedroom standard units, some with whirlpools. 2 stories (no elevator), exterior corridors. **Parking:** on-site. **Terms:** cancellation fee imposed. **Amenities:** hair dryers. **Pool(s):** outdoor. **Leisure Activities:** exercise room. **Business Services:** PC. **Cards:** AX, DC, DS, MC, VI.

ASK CALL / SOME UNITS FEE

MICROTEL INN & SUITES **Phone:** 252/758-7282

fyi
Hotel
$69-$149 All Year

Too new to rate, opening scheduled for October 2008. **Address:** 450 Moye Blvd **Location:** US 264. **Amenities:** 90 units, coffeemakers, microwaves, refrigerators. **Terms:** 3 day cancellation notice. **Cards:** AX, MC, VI.

QUALITY INN *Book at AAA.com* **Phone:** (252)758-5544

Motel
$59-$140 All Year

Address: 821 S Memorial Dr **Location:** Jct US 264 alternate route, just s on US 13/SR 11. **Facility:** 110 one-bedroom standard units. 2 stories (no elevator), exterior corridors. **Parking:** on-site. **Terms:** 2 night minimum stay - seasonal and/or weekends. **Amenities:** irons, hair dryers. **Pool(s):** outdoor. **Leisure Activities:** limited exercise equipment. **Guest Services:** wireless Internet. **Cards:** AX, CB, DC, DS, JC, MC, VI.

ASK CALL / SOME UNITS

TRAVELODGE *Book at AAA.com* **Phone:** (252)355-5699

Motel
$45-$55 All Year

Address: 3435 S Memorial Dr **Location:** Jct US 264 alternate route, just s on SR 11/903. **Facility:** 58 one-bedroom standard units, some with whirlpools. 1 story, exterior corridors. **Parking:** on-site. **Amenities:** safes, hair dryers. **Pool(s):** outdoor. **Cards:** AX, CB, DS, MC, VI.

ASK / SOME UNITS

WINGATE BY WYNDHAM *Book at AAA.com* **Phone:** 252/355-4283

Hotel
Rates not provided

Address: 3212 S Memorial Dr **Location:** Jct US 264 alternate route, just n on SR 11/903. **Facility:** 87 units. 85 one-bedroom standard units, some with whirlpools. 2 one-bedroom suites. 4 stories, interior corridors. *Bath:* combo or shower only. **Parking:** on-site. **Amenities:** video games (fee), high-speed Internet, dual phone lines, voice mail, safes, irons, hair dryers. **Pool(s):** heated indoor. **Leisure Activities:** whirlpool, exercise room. **Guest Services:** valet laundry, area transportation, wireless Internet. **Business Services:** meeting rooms, business center.

/ SOME UNITS FEE VCR

WHERE TO DINE

BEEF BARN **Phone:** 252/756-1161

Steak
$6-$25

An award-winning wine list, from which mini-tastings are offered, and choice cuts of beef are the steakhouse's pride. Fresh fixings line the salad bar. Casual dress. **Bar:** Full bar. **Reservations:** accepted. **Hours:** 11:30 am-2 & 5-10 pm, Sat from 5 pm. Closed major holidays. **Address:** 400 St Andrews Dr **Location:** Jct SR 11, 0.5 mi e on US 264 alternate route, then just n. **Parking:** on-site. **Cards:** AX, DC, DS, MC, VI.

CHEFS 505 **Phone:** 252/355-7505

American
$6-$30

The menu at the intimate bistro changes nightly, but crab cakes are always available. Fresh seafood, steaks and decadent desserts will please the palate. Casual dress. **Bar:** Full bar. **Reservations:** suggested. **Hours:** 11:30 am-2:30 & 5:30-9:30 pm; Sunday brunch. Closed: 11/26, 12/25. **Address:** 505 Red Banks Rd **Location:** Jct SR 11, 2 mi e on US 264 alternate route, just s; in Lynndale Shoppes. **Parking:** on-site. **Cards:** AX, MC, VI.

CHICO'S MEXICAN RESTAURANT **Phone:** 252/757-1666

Mexican
$5-$14

The eatery is popular with East Carolina University students and faculty. Colorfully decorated dining rooms are the backdrop for a good variety of well-prepared dishes, such as tasty burritos and delicious chicken soup. In pleasant weather, outdoor seating is offered on the patio. Casual dress. **Bar:** Full bar. **Reservations:** accepted. **Hours:** 11 am-10 pm, Fri & Sat-11 pm. Closed: 4/12, 11/26, 12/25. **Address:** 521 Cotanche St **Location:** Jct Reade Cir and Cotanche St; across from ECU; downtown. **Parking:** on-site. **Cards:** AX, DS, MC, VI.

COURTYARD TAVERN **Phone:** 252/321-0202

American
$6-$15

Referred to as "Greenville's gathering place," the casual eatery presents a lengthy menu of sandwiches, burgers, entree-sized salads and chicken, salmon and steak dishes. Patio seating is available. Musicians perform on Sunday nights. Casual dress. **Bar:** Full bar. **Hours:** 11:30-midnight, Fri & Sat-1 am. Closed: 12/25. **Address:** 703 SE Greenville Blvd **Location:** Jct SR 11/903, 2 mi e on US 264 alternate route; in Greenville Square Shopping Center. **Parking:** on-site. **Cards:** AX, MC, VI.

CPW'S FINE FOOD & SPIRITS **Phone:** 252/757-7756

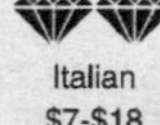

Italian
$7-$18

Diners can dig into a gourmet pizza or heaping bowl of pasta at the open, airy restaurant. Also popular are selections from the chef's ever-changing monthly themed menu. Casual dress. **Bar:** Full bar. **Reservations:** accepted. **Hours:** 11 am-10 pm, Fri & Sat-11 pm. Closed: 11/26, 12/25. **Address:** 2422 Stantonsburg Rd **Location:** Jct Stantonsbury Rd and Arlington Blvd; in Stanton Square Shopping Center. **Parking:** on-site. **Cards:** AX, MC, VI.

PARKER'S BARBECUE **Phone:** 252/756-2388

Regional Southern
$5-$8

Served with a spicy vinegar sauce, the restaurant's eastern North-Carolina-style pulled-pork barbecue is served with all the trimmings like Brunswick stew and hushpuppies. Other menu offerings include fried chicken and seafood. Casual dress. **Hours:** 9 am-9 pm. Closed: 12/25. **Address:** 3109 S Memorial Dr **Location:** Jct US 264 alternate route, 0.5 mi n on SR 11/903. **Parking:** on-site.

THE STARLIGHT CAFE **Phone:** 252/707-9033

Continental
$6-$30

The cozy neighborhood atmosphere invites guests to relax over quick-serve lunches, including gourmet sandwiches and salads as well as quiche and daily specials. Culinary horizons broaden at dinner, with such fare as handmade papardelle pasta, jambalaya, Eastern Carolina farm-raised striped bass and shrimp in coconut-lime sauce. Casual dress. **Bar:** Full bar. **Reservations:** accepted. **Hours:** 11:30 am-2 & 5:30-9 pm, Fri-10 pm, Sat 5:30 pm-10 pm, Mon 11:30 am-2 pm. Closed major holidays; also Sun. **Address:** 104 Martin Luther King Jr Dr **Location:** Jct Evans and Fifth sts. **Parking:** on-site. **Cards:** AX, MC, VI.

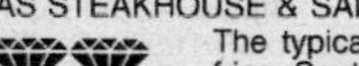

TEXAS STEAKHOUSE & SALOON **Phone:** 252/321-2905

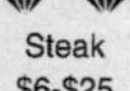

Steak
$6-$25

The typical Texas-style roadhouse focuses on freshly cut steaks, including the popular Duke entree with fries. Southwestern decor and arrows stuck in the walls get diners' minds wandering back to the old days. The popular draft beer is the microbrewed Red Oak lager. Casual dress. **Bar:** Full bar. **Hours:** 11 am-10 pm, Fri & Sat-11 pm. Closed: 11/26, 12/24, 12/25. **Address:** 400 SW Greenville Blvd **Location:** Jct SR 11/903, 1 mi e on US 264 alternate route. **Parking:** on-site. **Cards:** AX, DS, MC, VI.

HAVELOCK pop. 22,442

—— WHERE TO STAY ——

HAMPTON INN *Book great rates at AAA.com* **Phone:** (252)447-9400

Hotel
$83-$104 All Year

Address: 105 Tourist Center Dr **Location:** Jct SR 101, 1 mi w on US 70. **Facility:** 60 one-bedroom standard units, some with whirlpools. 3 stories, interior corridors. *Bath:* combo or shower only. **Parking:** on-site. **Terms:** 1-30 night minimum stay, cancellation fee imposed. **Amenities:** video games (fee), dual phone lines, voice mail, irons, hair dryers. **Pool(s):** outdoor. **Leisure Activities:** exercise room. **Guest Services:** valet laundry, wireless Internet. **Business Services:** meeting rooms, PC. **Cards:** AX, CB, DC, DS, JC, MC, VI.

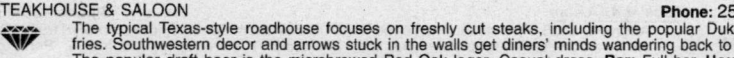

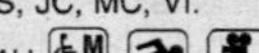

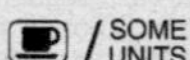

CALL / SOME UNITS

AAA Benefit:
Members save up to 10% everyday!

QUALITY INN *Book at AAA.com* **Phone:** (252)444-1111

Hotel
$83 All Year

Address: 400 Hwy 70 W **Location:** Jct SR 101, 1.9 mi w. **Facility:** 102 one-bedroom standard units. 2 stories (no elevator), interior corridors. **Parking:** on-site. **Amenities:** voice mail, irons, hair dryers. *Some:* high-speed Internet. **Pool(s):** outdoor. **Leisure Activities:** exercise room. **Guest Services:** valet and coin laundry, wireless Internet. **Business Services:** meeting rooms. **Cards:** AX, CB, DC, DS, MC, VI.

ASK CALL / SOME UNITS

HAW RIVER pop. 1,908

WHERE TO STAY

DAYS INN *Book at AAA.com* **Phone:** (336)578-2666

Hotel
$70-$80 All Year

Address: 1370 Truby Dr **Location:** I-85/40, exit 150, just n. **Facility:** 54 one-bedroom standard units, some with whirlpools. 2 stories (no elevator), interior corridors. *Bath:* combo or shower only. **Parking:** on-site. **Terms:** 3 day cancellation notice-fee imposed. **Amenities:** voice mail, irons, hair dryers. *Some:* dual phone lines. **Pool(s):** outdoor. **Leisure Activities:** exercise room. **Guest Services:** coin laundry, wireless Internet. **Cards:** AX, CB, DC, DS, MC, VI.

ASK CALL / SOME UNITS

HAYESVILLE pop. 297

WHERE TO STAY

CHATUGE MOUNTAIN INN **Phone:** 828/389-9340

Motel
$60-$80 All Year

Address: 4238 Hwy 64 E **Location:** Jct SR 69, 4.2 mi e. Located in a country setting. **Facility:** 14 one-bedroom standard units, some with efficiencies or kitchens. 1 story, exterior corridors. **Parking:** on-site. **Amenities:** *Some:* irons, hair dryers. **Guest Services:** wireless Internet. **Cards:** AX, DS, MC, VI.

ASK / SOME UNITS

DEERFIELD INN **Phone:** 828/389-8272

AAA SAVE

Motel
$60-$100 All Year

Address: 40 Chatuge Ln **Location:** 3 mi e on US 64. Facing the Blue Ridge Mountains and Chatuge Lake; in the country. **Facility:** 20 one-bedroom standard units. 1 story, exterior corridors. **Parking:** on-site. **Terms:** cancellation fee imposed. **Amenities:** voice mail, hair dryers. *Some:* irons. **Guest Services:** wireless Internet. **Cards:** AX, DS, MC, VI. **Free Special Amenities: continental breakfast and high-speed Internet.**

CALL / SOME UNITS FEE

HENDERSON pop. 16,095

WHERE TO STAY

BUDGET HOST INN *Book great rates at AAA.com* **Phone:** (252)492-2013

AAA SAVE

Motel
$49-$69 All Year

Address: 1727 N Garnett St **Location:** I-85, exit 215, just e, then just w on US 158. **Facility:** 25 one-bedroom standard units. 2 stories (no elevator), exterior corridors. **Parking:** on-site. **Terms:** cancellation fee imposed. **Amenities:** irons. **Guest Services:** wireless Internet. **Cards:** AX, CB, DC, DS, MC, VI. **Free Special Amenities: continental breakfast and high-speed Internet.**

CALL / SOME UNITS

ECONO LODGE **Phone:** (252)438-8511

Motel
$45-$75 All Year

Address: 112 Parham Rd **Location:** I-85, exit 215, just e on US 158. Located behind Burger King. **Facility:** 51 one-bedroom standard units. 2 stories (no elevator), exterior corridors. *Bath:* combo or shower only. **Parking:** on-site. **Amenities:** irons, hair dryers. **Pool(s):** outdoor. **Guest Services:** wireless Internet. **Cards:** AX, DS, MC, VI.

ASK / SOME UNITS FEE

HAMPTON INN *Book great rates at AAA.com* **Phone:** (252)492-3007

Hotel
$84-$89 All Year

Address: 385 Ruin Creek Rd **Location:** I-85, exit 212, just w, then just n. **Facility:** 75 units. 70 one-bedroom standard units. 5 one-bedroom suites. 5 stories, interior corridors. *Bath:* combo or shower only. **Parking:** on-site. **Terms:** 1-30 night minimum stay. **Amenities:** voice mail, irons, hair dryers. **Pool(s):** outdoor. **Leisure Activities:** exercise room. **Guest Services:** wireless Internet. **Business Services:** meeting rooms. **Cards:** AX, CB, DC, DS, MC, VI.

/ SOME UNITS

AAA Benefit:
Members save up to 10% everyday!

HOLIDAY INN EXPRESS *Book at AAA.com* **Phone:** (252)438-6300

Hotel
$79-$125 All Year

Address: 200 Simmons St **Location:** I-85, exit 212, just w on Ruin Creek Rd, 0.5 mi n on N Cooper Dr, then just e. **Facility:** 69 one-bedroom standard units, some with whirlpools. 2 stories, interior corridors. *Bath:* combo or shower only. **Parking:** on-site. **Amenities:** high-speed Internet, dual phone lines, voice mail, irons, hair dryers. **Leisure Activities:** exercise room. **Guest Services:** valet laundry, wireless Internet. **Business Services:** meeting rooms, PC. **Cards:** AX, DC, DS, MC, VI.

ASK / SOME UNITS

JAMESON INN Book at AAA.com

Hotel
$78-$85 All Year

Phone: (252)430-0247

Address: 400 N Cooper Dr **Location:** I-85, exit 212, just w on Ruin Creek Rd, then just n. **Facility:** 67 units. 65 one-bedroom standard units. 2 one-bedroom suites. 3 stories, interior corridors. *Bath:* combo or shower only. **Parking:** on-site. **Terms:** cancellation fee imposed. **Amenities:** dual phone lines, voice mail, irons, hair dryers. **Pool(s):** outdoor. **Leisure Activities:** exercise room. **Guest Services:** wireless Internet. **Business Services:** meeting rooms, PC. **Cards:** AX, DC, DS, MC, VI.

A$K CALL / SOME UNITS FEE

LAMPLIGHT INN B&B

Bed & Breakfast
$90-$120 12/1-12/31 & 3/1-11/30

Phone: (252)438-6311

Address: 1680 Flemingtown Rd **Location:** I-85, exit 220, 1.5 mi nw. **Facility:** Smoke free premises. 4 one-bedroom standard units, some with whirlpools. 2 stories, interior corridors. *Bath:* combo or shower only. **Parking:** on-site. **Terms:** open 12/1-12/31 & 3/1-11/30, 7 day cancellation notice-fee imposed. **Amenities:** video library. *Some:* CD players. **Leisure Activities:** horseshoes. **Cards:** AX, DS, MC, VI.

/ SOME UNITS VCR

SLEEP INN Book great rates at AAA.com

AAA SAVE

Hotel
$59-$85 All Year

Phone: (252)433-9449

Address: 18 Market St **Location:** I-85, exit 212, just w on Ruin Creek Rd, then just se on Zeb Robinson Rd. **Facility:** 54 one-bedroom standard units. 3 stories, interior corridors. *Bath:* combo or shower only. **Parking:** on-site. **Terms:** cancellation fee imposed. **Amenities:** high-speed Internet, dual phone lines, voice mail, irons, hair dryers. **Leisure Activities:** exercise room. **Guest Services:** coin laundry, wireless Internet. **Business Services:** meeting rooms. **Cards:** AX, CB, DC, DS, MC, VI. **Free Special Amenities: expanded continental breakfast and high-speed Internet.**

/ SOME UNITS FEE

WHERE TO DINE

BAMBOO GARDEN

Chinese
$5-$12

Phone: 252/438-8080

Sit back and relax in an inviting dining room as you savor such delights as sweet and sour chicken and house specialties like crispy duck. Casual dress. **Bar:** Full bar. **Reservations:** accepted. **Hours:** 9:30 am-9:30 pm, Sun from 10 am. Closed: 11/26, 12/25. **Address:** 1520 Dabney Dr **Location:** I-85, exit 213, just e; in Dabney West Shopping Center. **Parking:** on-site. **Cards:** AX, DC, DS, MC, VI.

PINO'S ITALIAN RESTAURANT & PIZZERIA

AAA

Italian
$4-$18

Phone: 252/438-1341

Patrons of the family-friendly eatery enjoy pizza and all the traditional Italian favorites, including spaghetti, lasagna and stuffed shells. Casual dress. **Bar:** Beer & wine. **Hours:** 11 am-10 pm, Fri & Sat-11 pm. Closed major holidays; also Sun. **Address:** 901-D Beckford Dr **Location:** I-85, exit 213, 0.5 mi e on Dabney Dr, then just n; in Marketplace Shopping Center. **Parking:** on-site. **Cards:** AX, DS, MC, VI.

SILO STEAK HOUSE & BAR

AAA

Steak & Seafood
$10-$25

Phone: 252/492-6772

Diners can dig into a choice cut of beef and the expansive salad bar at the quaint, barn-themed restaurant. Casual dress. **Bar:** Full bar. **Reservations:** suggested. **Hours:** 4 pm-10 pm, Sun 11:30 am-9 pm; Sunday brunch. **Address:** 2002 Graham Ave **Location:** I-85, exit 212, just e, then just n. **Parking:** on-site. **Cards:** AX, DC, DS, MC, VI.

UPTOWN ROSE RESTAURANT & PUB

American
$4-$22

Phone: 252/433-4846

Well-prepared beef, chicken and seafood entrees make up the menu at the quiet, downtown bistro. The pub opens at 5:30 pm and serves appetizer specials on Mondays and Wednesdays from 6 to 7 pm. Casual dress. **Bar:** Full bar. **Reservations:** suggested. **Hours:** 11:45 am-2 & 6-9 pm. Closed major holidays; also Sun, except Mother's Day & Father's Day. **Address:** 130 W Montgomery St **Location:** Just s on Garnett St (US 1 business route), just w; downtown. **Parking:** on-site. **Cards:** AX, DC, MC, VI.

THE WILDFLOWER CAFE

American
$5-$24

Phone: 252/430-1775

Local artwork is on display at the downtown eatery, where patrons sample delicious sandwiches and entrees such as lemon chicken linguine. Casual dress. **Bar:** Beer & wine. **Reservations:** suggested, for dinner. **Hours:** 7 am-2:30 pm, Thurs & Fri also 5:30 pm-9 pm. Closed: 7/4, 12/25; also Sat & Sun. **Address:** 200 S Garnett St **Location:** US 1 business route; downtown. **Parking:** on-site. **Cards:** AX, DS, MC, VI.

HENDERSONVILLE pop. 10,420

WHERE TO STAY

BEST WESTERN HENDERSONVILLE INN Book great rates at AAA.com **Phone:** (828)692-0521

Motel
$45-$160 All Year

Address: 105 Sugarloaf Rd **Location:** I-26, exit 49A, just e. **Facility:** 100 one-bedroom standard units. 2 stories (no elevator), exterior corridors. *Bath:* combo or shower only. **Parking:** on-site. **Amenities:** voice mail, irons, hair dryers. *Some:* DVD players, video games, high-speed Internet. **Dining:** El Paso, see separate listing. **Pool(s):** outdoor. **Guest Services:** wireless Internet. **Business Services:** meeting rooms, fax (fee). **Cards:** AX, DC, DS, MC, VI. **Free Special Amenities: expanded continental breakfast and high-speed Internet.**

/ SOME UNITS FEE

AAA Benefit:
Members save up to 20%, plus 10% bonus points with rewards program.

CLADDAGH INN **Phone:** 828/693-6737

Historic Bed & Breakfast
$105-$175 5/1-11/30
$95-$155 12/1-4/30

Address: 755 N Main St **Location:** I-26, exit 49B, 2 mi w on US 64 W, then just n. Located on a busy street. **Facility:** Dating from 1888, this Victorian inn houses a library, a large parlor and lodgings of varied size and decor. Smoke free premises. 16 units. 15 one-bedroom standard units. 1 one-bedroom suite. 3 stories (no elevator), interior corridors. *Bath:* combo or shower only. **Parking:** on-site. **Terms:** 7 day cancellation notice. **Amenities:** voice mail. **Guest Services:** wireless Internet. **Cards:** AX, MC, VI.

ASK / SOME UNITS

COMFORT INN Book great rates at AAA.com **Phone:** (828)693-8800

Hotel
$55-$149 All Year

Address: 206 Mitchell Dr **Location:** I-26, exit 49B, just w. **Facility:** 85 one-bedroom standard units, some with whirlpools. 2 stories (no elevator), exterior corridors. **Parking:** on-site. **Amenities:** irons, hair dryers. **Pool(s):** outdoor. **Guest Services:** valet laundry, wireless Internet. **Business Services:** PC. **Cards:** AX, CB, DC, DS, JC, MC, VI.

/ SOME UNITS FEE

DAYS INN **Phone:** 828/697-5999

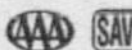

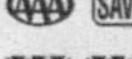

Motel
$70-$120 5/1-11/30
$60-$70 12/1-4/30

Address: 102 Mitchell Dr **Location:** I-26, exit 49B, just sw. **Facility:** 46 one-bedroom standard units. 2 stories (no elevator), exterior corridors. **Parking:** on-site. **Amenities:** high-speed Internet, irons, hair dryers. **Guest Services:** wireless Internet. **Cards:** AX, DC, DS, MC, VI.

/ SOME UNITS

ECHO MOUNTAIN INN **Phone:** 828/693-9626

Historic Bed & Breakfast
$85-$195 All Year

Address: 2849 Laurel Park Hwy **Location:** I-26, exit 49B, just s to 5th Ave W, then 3 mi w on 5th Ave (Laurel Park Hwy). **Facility:** This 1896 stone manor offers outstanding mountain views and quiet country charm. Smoke free premises. 33 units. 29 one-bedroom standard units, some with efficiencies. 4 one-bedroom suites. 2 stories (no elevator), interior/exterior corridors. *Bath:* combo or shower only. **Parking:** on-site. **Terms:** office hours 9 am-5 pm, 2 night minimum stay - seasonal, cancellation fee imposed. **Amenities:** voice mail, hair dryers. *Some:* DVD players, irons. **Pool(s):** outdoor. **Leisure Activities:** hiking trails, shuffleboard, game room. **Guest Services:** wireless Internet. **Business Services:** meeting rooms, business center. **Cards:** AX, MC, VI.

ASK / SOME UNITS VCR

HAMPTON INN Book great rates at AAA.com **Phone:** (828)697-2333

Hotel
$89-$225 All Year

Address: 155 Sugarloaf Rd **Location:** I-26, exit 49A, just e. **Facility:** 109 units. 103 one-bedroom standard units. 6 one-bedroom suites. 4 stories, interior corridors. *Bath:* combo or shower only. **Parking:** on-site. **Amenities:** video games (fee), voice mail, irons, hair dryers. *Some:* high-speed Internet. **Pool(s):** outdoor. **Guest Services:** valet laundry, wireless Internet. **Business Services:** meeting rooms, business center. **Cards:** AX, CB, DC, DS, MC, VI. **Free Special Amenities: expanded continental breakfast and high-speed Internet.**

AAA Benefit:
Members save up to 10% everyday!

HOLIDAY INN EXPRESS-HENDERSONVILLE/FLATROCK Book great rates at AAA.com **Phone:** (828)698-8899

Hotel
$100-$150 5/15-11/30
$75-$120 12/1-5/14

Address: 111 Commercial Blvd **Location:** I-26, exit 53, just sw on Upward Rd. **Facility:** 66 one-bedroom standard units, some with whirlpools. 2 stories, interior corridors. *Bath:* combo or shower only. **Parking:** on-site. **Terms:** cancellation fee imposed. **Amenities:** dual phone lines, voice mail, irons, hair dryers. **Pool(s):** heated indoor. **Guest Services:** valet laundry, wireless Internet. **Business Services:** PC, fax (fee). **Cards:** AX, CB, DC, DS, JC, MC, VI. **Free Special Amenities: expanded continental breakfast and high-speed Internet.**

RAMADA LIMITED *Book great rates at AAA.com* **Phone:** (828)697-0006

Hotel

$50-$130 All Year

Address: 150 Sugarloaf Rd **Location:** I-26, exit 49A, just e on US 64 (Bat Cave Rd), then just s. **Facility:** 53 units. 52 one-bedroom standard units. 1 one-bedroom suite with whirlpool. 2 stories, interior corridors. *Bath:* combo or shower only. **Parking:** on-site. **Amenities:** voice mail, irons, hair dryers. **Guest Services:** wireless Internet. **Business Services:** PC. **Cards:** AX, DC, DS, MC, VI. **Free Special Amenities: full breakfast and high-speed Internet.**

CALL / SOME UNITS FEE

THE WAVERLY INN *Book at AAA.com* **Phone:** (828)693-9193

Historic Bed & Breakfast

$199-$305 4/2-11/30

$189-$285 12/1-4/1

Address: 783 N Main St **Location:** I-26, exit 49B, 2 mi w on US 64, then just n. Located on a busy street. **Facility:** In a building established in 1898, this B&B offers well-appointed rooms, some with canopy beds and period furniture or reproductions. Smoke free premises. 14 units. 13 one-bedroom standard units. 1 one-bedroom suite. 3 stories (no elevator), interior corridors. *Bath:* combo or shower only. **Parking:** on-site. **Terms:** 2 night minimum stay - weekends, 7 day cancellation notice-fee imposed. **Amenities:** video library, DVD players, hair dryers. **Guest Services:** wireless Internet. **Business Services:** PC, fax. **Cards:** AX, CB, DC, JC, MC, VI.

/ SOME UNITS VCR

WHERE TO DINE

A DAY IN THE COUNTRY **Phone:** 828/692-7914

American

$5-$8

Guests can dine outdoors under bowers of roses, wisteria and grapes or have lunch inside the greenhouse surrounded by flowers, scented candles and soaps. Flowers are the theme here. Sandwich platters are offered along with creamy made-from-scratch soup. Desserts and breads also are prepared in house. Casual dress. **Reservations:** not accepted. **Hours:** 10:30 am-3:30 pm. Closed: 4/12, 12/25; also Sun & Mon. **Address:** 130 Sugarloaf Rd **Location:** I-26, exit 49A, just e, then just s. **Parking:** on-site. **Cards:** AX, DS, MC, VI.

BLACK ROSE PUBLIC HOUSE **Phone:** 828/698-2622

American

$6-$15

Although the eatery's pub fare is expected, the twists used to create it are not. In addition to quiches and soups of the day, the menu lists fresh salads, nachos, wraps and sandwiches. Guests can expect pleasant service. Casual dress. **Bar:** Full bar. **Hours:** 11 am-2 am. Closed: 12/25. **Address:** 222 N Main St **Location:** Center of historic downtown. **Parking:** street. **Cards:** AX, MC, VI.

CYPRESS CELLAR **Phone:** 828/698-1005

Cajun

$7-$18

Guests who take the few steps downstairs are transported to a lively French Quarter-style eatery. Well-prepared entrees are served in ample portions. Patio seating is popular when the weather cooperates. Casual dress. **Bar:** Full bar. **Reservations:** not accepted. **Hours:** 11 am-9 pm, Fri & Sat-10 pm. Closed major holidays; also Sun. **Address:** 321-C N Main St **Location:** Center of historic downtown. **Parking:** street. **Cards:** AX, MC, VI.

EL PASO **Phone:** 828/694-0201

Mexican

$5-$15

Traditional, well-prepared Mexican cuisine makes up the menu at the popular eatery. Casual dress. **Bar:** Full bar. **Hours:** 11 am-10 pm, Fri & Sat-10:30 pm. **Address:** 105 Sugarloaf Rd **Location:** I-26, exit 49A, just e; in Best Western Hendersonville Inn. **Parking:** on-site. **Cards:** AX, MC, VI.

FLIGHT WOOD GRILL & WINE BAR *Menu on AAA.com* **Phone:** 828/694-1030

Continental

$18-$34

Specialties of the house at the casually upscale bistro are prepared over an apple-wood fire. Pizza and baked Italian entrees share menu space with fresh homemade pastas, as well as seafood, beef and other delicious fare. Dressy casual. **Bar:** Full bar. **Reservations:** suggested. **Hours:** 5 pm-10 pm, Fri & Sat-10:30 pm. Closed: 1/1, 12/25; also Sun. **Address:** 401 N Main St **Location:** Center; just s. **Parking:** on-site. **Cards:** AX, DS, MC, VI.

HANNAH FLANAGAN'S IRISH PUB & RESTAURANT **Phone:** 828/696-1665

Irish

$5-$10

A favorite with the locals, the Irish pub has something on the menu for everyone. Bangers and mash, fish and chips and Irish and Guinness stews are just a few of the traditional choices available. Casual dress. **Bar:** Full bar. **Reservations:** not accepted. **Hours:** 11 am-2 am, Sun from 11:30 am. Closed: 11/26, 12/25. **Address:** 300 N Main St **Location:** I-26, exit 49B, 2 mi w on US 64, then just s on US 25. **Parking:** street. **Cards:** AX, DS, MC, VI.

SINBAD RESTAURANT **Phone:** 828/696-2039

Mediterranean

$6-$28

Mediterranean cuisine—including Greek, Lebanese, Indian and seafood dishes—is served in a casual atmosphere. Dressy casual. **Bar:** Full bar. **Reservations:** suggested. **Hours:** Open 12/1-12/31 & 1/31-11/30; 11:30 am-2 & 5:30-close. Closed: Sun & Mon. **Address:** 202 S Washington St **Location:** Downtown. **Parking:** on-site and street. **Cards:** AX, DS, MC, VI.

HERTFORD pop. 2,070

WHERE TO DINE

CAPTAIN BOB'S

American
$4-$16

Phone: 252/333-0553

Conveniently located between Edenton and Elizabeth City. Fried, grilled or broiled, the restaurant is popular for its North Carolina-style, pulled-pork barbecue, fried chicken and fresh seafood. Casual dress. **Hours:** 5:30 am-9 pm, Sun from 6:30 am. Closed: 7/4, 11/26, 12/25. **Address:** 2337 Harvey Point Rd **Location:** On US 17. **Parking:** on-site. **Cards:** MC, VI.

HICKORY pop. 37,222

WHERE TO STAY

COMFORT SUITES *Book at AAA.com*

Motel
$85-$119 All Year

Phone: (828)323-1211

Address: 1125 13th Ave Dr SE **Location:** I-40, exit 125, just s, then just w. Located in a commercial area. **Facility:** Smoke free premises. 116 one-bedroom standard units, some with whirlpools. 2 stories (no elevator), interior/exterior corridors. **Parking:** on-site. **Terms:** cancellation fee imposed. **Amenities:** dual phone lines, voice mail, irons, hair dryers. **Pool(s):** outdoor. **Leisure Activities:** exercise room. **Guest Services:** valet and coin laundry, wireless Internet. **Business Services:** meeting rooms. **Cards:** AX, CB, DC, DS, JC, MC, VI.

ASK

COURTYARD BY MARRIOTT *Book great rates at AAA.com*

Hotel
$144-$154 All Year

Phone: (828)267-2100

Address: 1946 13th Ave Dr SE **Location:** I-40, exit 125, just s, then 0.5 mi e. Located in a commercial area. **Facility:** Smoke free premises. 140 one-bedroom standard units, some with whirlpools. 4 stories, interior corridors. *Bath:* combo or shower only. **Parking:** on-site. **Terms:** cancellation fee imposed. **Amenities:** high-speed Internet, dual phone lines, voice mail, irons, hair dryers. **Pool(s):** heated indoor. **Leisure Activities:** whirlpool, exercise room. **Guest Services:** valet and coin laundry, wireless Internet. **Business Services:** meeting rooms, business center. **Cards:** AX, CB, DC, DS, JC, MC, VI.

CALL / SOME UNITS

AAA Benefit:
Members save a minimum 5% off the best available rate.

FAIRFIELD INN & SUITES BY MARRIOTT *Book great rates at AAA.com*

Hotel
$103-$111 All Year

Phone: (828)431-3000

Address: 1950 13th Ave Dr SE **Location:** I-40, exit 125, just s, then 0.5 mi e. **Facility:** Smoke free premises. 108 one-bedroom standard units. 4 stories, interior corridors. *Bath:* combo or shower only. **Parking:** on-site. **Terms:** cancellation fee imposed. **Amenities:** voice mail, irons, hair dryers. **Pool(s):** heated indoor. **Leisure Activities:** limited exercise equipment. **Guest Services:** valet and coin laundry, wireless Internet. **Business Services:** meeting rooms, business center. **Cards:** AX, CB, DC, DS, JC, MC, VI.

/ SOME UNITS

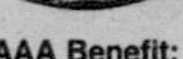

AAA Benefit:
Members save a minimum 5% off the best available rate.

HAMPTON INN *Book great rates at AAA.com*

Hotel
$84-$119 All Year

Phone: (828)323-1150

Address: 1520 13th Ave Dr SE **Location:** I-40, exit 125, 2 blks s on Lenoir Rhyne Blvd, then 2 blks e. Located below Hickory Metro Convention Center. **Facility:** 118 one-bedroom standard units. 2 stories (no elevator), interior/exterior corridors. **Parking:** on-site. **Amenities:** voice mail, irons, hair dryers. **Pool(s):** outdoor. **Leisure Activities:** exercise room. **Guest Services:** valet laundry, wireless Internet. **Business Services:** PC, fax (fee). **Cards:** AX, CB, DC, DS, JC, MC, VI.

/ SOME UNITS

AAA Benefit:
Members save up to 10% everyday!

HOLIDAY INN SELECT *Book at AAA.com*

Hotel
$115-$165 All Year

Phone: (828)323-1000

Address: 1385 Lenoir Rhyne Blvd SE **Location:** I-40, exit 125, just s. **Facility:** 198 units. 196 one-bedroom standard units. 2 one-bedroom suites. 2 stories, interior/exterior corridors. **Parking:** on-site. **Amenities:** voice mail, irons, hair dryers. **Pool(s):** heated indoor. **Leisure Activities:** sauna, exercise room. **Guest Services:** valet and coin laundry, area transportation, wireless Internet. **Business Services:** conference facilities, business center. **Cards:** AX, DC, DS, MC, VI.

ASK / SOME UNITS

JAMESON INN *Book at AAA.com*

Motel
$78-$85 All Year

Phone: (828)304-0410

Address: 1120 13th Ave Dr SE **Location:** I-40, exit 125, just s, then 0.4 mi w. **Facility:** 60 one-bedroom standard units, some with whirlpools. 2 stories (no elevator), exterior corridors. *Bath:* combo or shower only. **Parking:** on-site. **Terms:** cancellation fee imposed. **Amenities:** irons, hair dryers. **Pool(s):** outdoor. **Leisure Activities:** exercise room. **Guest Services:** wireless Internet. **Business Services:** PC, fax (fee). **Cards:** AX, DC, DS, MC, VI.

ASK CALL / SOME UNITS FEE

PARK INN GATEWAY CONFERENCE CENTER *Book at AAA.com* **Phone:** (828)328-5101

Hotel

$88-$150 1/1-11/30

$86-$145 12/1-12/31

Address: 909 US 70 SW **Location:** I-40, exit 123, just n on US 321, then just e at jct US 70 E. **Facility:** 109 units. 100 one-bedroom standard units. 9 one-bedroom suites. 2 stories, interior/exterior corridors. *Bath:* combo or shower only. **Parking:** on-site. **Amenities:** dual phone lines, voice mail, irons, hair dryers. **Pool(s):** outdoor. **Leisure Activities:** exercise room. **Guest Services:** valet and coin laundry, area transportation, wireless Internet. **Business Services:** conference facilities, PC, fax (fee). **Cards:** AX, CB, DC, DS, MC, VI.

ASK / SOME UNITS

RED ROOF INN HICKORY *Book great rates at AAA.com* **Phone:** (828)323-1500

Motel

$50-$80 All Year

Address: 1184 Lenoir Rhyne Blvd **Location:** I-40, exit 125, just n. **Facility:** 108 one-bedroom standard units. 2 stories (no elevator), exterior corridors. *Bath:* combo or shower only. **Parking:** on-site. **Terms:** 14 day cancellation notice. **Amenities:** video games (fee), voice mail. **Cards:** AX, CB, DC, DS, MC, VI. **Free Special Amenities: local telephone calls.**

/ SOME UNITS

WHERE TO DINE

1859 CAFE **Phone:** 828/322-1859

Continental

$16-$25

Intimate dining rooms in a restored 1859 home evoke a casually elegant ambience. A piano bar, a patio with a garden view and an extensive collection of antiques are a few of the amenities offered. Try the tasty Asian crab cakes with a mango-ginger salsa. Casual dress. **Bar:** Full bar. **Reservations:** suggested. **Hours:** 5:30 pm-10 pm. Closed: 11/26, 12/25; also Sun. **Address:** 443 2nd Ave SW **Location:** I-40, exit 123, 0.5 mi e on US 70 E, 0.5 mi n on 4th St SW, 0.3 mi w on 1st Ave SW, just s on 6th St SW, then just e. **Parking:** on-site. **Cards:** AX, CB, DC, DS, MC, VI. **Historic**

FIREBONZ **Phone:** 828/327-2232

Barbecue

$6-$17

Flavorful smoked meats come in sandwiches and on platters, with a selection of six barbecue sauces in serve-yourself containers. The congenial staff takes interest in ensuring customers enjoy their meals. Save room for the rich and delicious signature bread pudding. Casual dress. **Bar:** Beer only. **Reservations:** not accepted. **Hours:** 11 am-9 pm, Fri & Sat-10 pm. Closed: 12/25. **Address:** 1520 Hwy 70 SE **Location:** I-40, exit 125, just s. **Parking:** on-site. **Cards:** AX, DS, MC, VI.

CALL

GONDOLIER ITALIAN RESTAURANT AND PIZZA **Phone:** 828/322-2025

Pizza

$9-$14

In addition to daily specials, diners can select from a tempting variety of calzones and such standards as spaghetti, manicotti and ravioli. Servers are fast and friendly. Casual dress. **Bar:** Beer & wine. **Hours:** 11 am-10 pm, Fri & Sat-11 pm. Closed: 11/26, 12/25. **Address:** 1991 15th Ave Pl SE **Location:** I-40, exit 125, just s, 0.5 mi w on US 321 business route, then just n. **Parking:** on-site. **Cards:** AX, DS, MC, VI.

J & S CAFETERIA **Phone:** 828/326-8926

American

$4-$10

Guests are served steaming entrees, homemade bread and cold items from the comfortable cafeteria's buffet. The dessert area overflows with homemade, tasty treats. Casual dress. **Hours:** 10:45 am-2:15 & 3:45-8 pm, Fri-Sun 7 am-10 & 10:30-8 pm. Closed: 12/25. **Address:** 1940 13th Ave Dr SE **Location:** I-40, exit 125, just s, then 0.5 mi e; next to Hampton Inn. **Parking:** on-site. **Cards:** MC, VI.

SAGEBRUSH STEAKHOUSE **Phone:** 828/267-7243

American

$5-$19

Born from the spirit of Texas cattle drives, the restaurant presents a menu of hearty steaks, prime rib, chicken, seafood and baby back ribs. Yummy desserts merit a splurge. Guests can call ahead to facilitate seating. Casual dress. **Bar:** Full bar. **Hours:** 11 am-10 pm, Fri & Sat-11 pm. Closed: 12/25. **Address:** 2410 Hwy 70 SE **Location:** I-40, exit 126, just s. **Parking:** on-site. **Cards:** AX, DC, DS, MC, VI.

CALL

SHELL'S BAR-B-Q **Phone:** 828/256-2275

American

$3-$10

Reminiscent of a 1950s diner, the restaurant turns out more than just hamburgers and milk shakes. In addition to sandwiches, the menu includes chicken and beef dishes. Rock 'n' roll music plays in the background of a dining area decorated with much memorabilia. Breakfast is served all day. Casual dress. **Bar:** Beer only. **Reservations:** accepted. **Hours:** 6 am-9 pm. Closed: 11/26, 12/25; also Sun, July 4th & Labor day week. **Address:** 2609 Springs Rd **Location:** I-40, exit 125, 2 mi n on Lenoir Rhyme Blvd, 0.8 mi e on Highlands, then 1.9 mi ne on 16th St. **Parking:** on-site. **Cards:** AX, DS, MC, VI.

YOUSSEF 242 **Phone:** 828/324-2005

American

$8-$30

With made-to-order pizza, creatively prepared fish and chicken and large portions of delicious steak, this place is a welcome addition to the city's restaurant scene. Off the busy highway and in a quiet residential area, the eatery provides a change of pace and a quiet place for drinks and dinner. Booths allow for comfortable group dining, and the artwork and lighting contribute to the easy atmosphere. Dressy casual. **Bar:** Full bar. **Reservations:** suggested. **Hours:** 11:30 am-2 & 5:30-10 pm, Fri-10:30 pm, Sat 5:30 pm-10:30 pm. Closed major holidays; also Sun. **Address:** 242 11th Ave NE **Location:** I-40, exit 123, 2 mi n on SR 127. **Parking:** on-site. **Cards:** AX, MC, VI.

HIGHLANDS pop. 909

WHERE TO STAY

HIGHLANDS SUITE HOTEL

Phone: (828)526-4502

Hotel

$149-$209 4/1-11/30

$69-$149 12/1-3/31

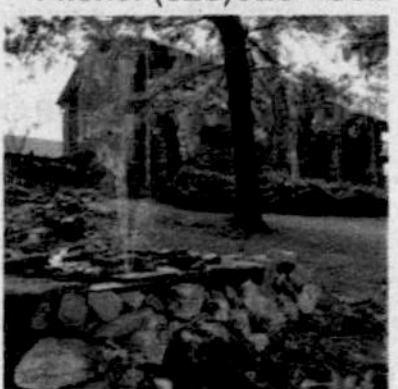

Address: 205 Main St **Location:** Just w on US 64; downtown. **Facility:** 28 one-bedroom suites with whirlpools. 2 stories, exterior corridors. **Parking:** on-site. **Terms:** check-in 4 pm, 2 night minimum stay - seasonal and/or weekends, 7 day cancellation notice-fee imposed. **Amenities:** irons, hair dryers. **Guest Services:** wireless Internet. **Cards:** AX, DS, MC, VI. **Free Special Amenities: continental breakfast and local telephone calls.** *(See color ad below)*

MITCHELL'S LODGE & COTTAGES

Phone: 828/526-2267

Motel

$64-$275 All Year

Address: 264 Dillard Rd **Location:** Jct US 64, just s on SR 106 (Dillard Rd). **Facility:** 27 units. 21 one-bedroom standard units, some with kitchens and/or whirlpools. 2 one-bedroom suites with kitchens. 4 cottages. 2 stories (no elevator), exterior corridors. *Bath:* combo or shower only. **Parking:** on-site. **Terms:** office hours 8 am-11 pm, check-in 4 pm, 2 night minimum stay - seasonal and/or weekends, 60 day cancellation notice fee imposed. **Amenities:** voice mail. *Some:* irons, hair dryers. **Leisure Activities:** whirlpool. **Guest Services:** complimentary laundry, wireless Internet. **Cards:** AX, DS, MC, VI.

CALL / SOME UNITS

MOUNTAIN HIGH LODGE

Phone: (828)526-2790

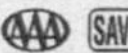

Motel

$49-$189 All Year

Address: 200 Main St **Location:** Just w on US 64; downtown. **Facility:** 49 units. 48 one-bedroom standard units, some with whirlpools. 1 one-bedroom suite with whirlpool. 2 stories (no elevator), exterior corridors. **Parking:** on-site. **Terms:** check-in 4 pm, 2 night minimum stay - seasonal and/or weekends, 7 day cancellation notice-fee imposed. **Amenities:** hair dryers. **Guest Services:** wireless Internet. **Business Services:** meeting rooms. **Cards:** AX, DS, MC, VI. **Free Special Amenities: continental breakfast and local telephone calls.** *(See color ad below)*

CALL / SOME UNITS

OLD EDWARDS INN AND SPA

Book great rates at AAA.com

Phone: (828)526-8008

Country Inn

$360-$2100 5/22-11/30

$320-$2000 12/1-5/21

Address: 445 Main St **Location:** At Main and 4th sts; downtown. **Facility:** Having welcomed guests for more than a century, the inn was recently renovated, fusing modern technology and amenities with old-world charm. Smoke free premises. 57 units. 42 one-bedroom standard units, some with whirlpools. 8 one- and 2 two-bedroom suites with whirlpools. 5 condominiums. 1-3 stories (no elevator), interior/exterior corridors. **Parking:** valet. **Terms:** check-in 4 pm, 2 night minimum stay - weekends, 30 day cancellation notice-fee imposed. **Amenities:** DVD players, voice mail, irons, hair dryers. *Some:* fax, safes. **Dining:** 2 restaurants, also, Madison's Restaurant and Wine Garden, see separate listing. **Pool(s):** heated outdoor. **Leisure Activities:** steamroom, putting green, golf privileges, 2 lighted tennis courts, recreation programs, exercise room, spa. **Guest Services:** valet laundry, airport transportation (fee)-Asheville Regional & Greenville-Spartanburg airports, wireless Internet. **Business Services:** conference facilities, PC. **Cards:** AX, DS, MC, VI. **Free Special Amenities: expanded continental breakfast and high-speed Internet.**

FEE / SOME UNITS

WHERE TO DINE

LAKESIDE RESTAURANT

Phone: 828/526-9419

Continental

$20-$32

Innovative preparations of traditional entrees delight diners' taste buds. The lake views are beautiful from the intimate and popular dining spot. Casual dress. **Bar:** Wine only. **Reservations:** suggested. **Hours:** Open 4/15-11/5; 5:30 pm-9 pm. Closed major holidays; also Sun & Mon. **Address:** 531 Smallwood Ave **Location:** Center; on Harris Lake. **Parking:** on-site. **Cards:** MC, VI.

THE LOG CABIN STEAK HOUSE **Phone:** 828/526-3380

American
$23-$40

Built in 1924, the true log cabin is a charming place in which to relax and enjoy steak, chops, seafood and wild game. Locally made furniture decorates the inviting dining room. Homemade dessert and specialty coffees are special surprises. Casual dress. **Bar:** Full bar. **Reservations:** suggested. **Hours:** 5:30 pm-9 pm; hours vary in summer. Closed: 4/12, 12/25; also Tues & Wed 11/1-5/1. **Address:** 130 Log Cabin Ln **Location:** Jct US 64, just s on SR 106 (Dillard Rd), then just w; behind Hampton Inn. **Parking:** on-site. **Cards:** AX, MC, VI.

MADISON'S RESTAURANT AND WINE GARDEN **Phone:** 828/787-2525

American
$8-$39

Enjoy an elegant setting overlooking the inn's intimate gardens through large picture windows; the menu changes regularly and features their signature Carolina High Country cuisine. Dressy casual. **Bar:** Full bar. **Reservations:** required. **Hours:** 11:30 am-2 & 5:30-9 pm. **Address:** 445 Main St **Location:** At Main and 4th sts; downtown; in Old Edwards Inn and Spa. **Parking:** valet and street. **Cards:** AX, DC, DS, MC, VI.

..ON THE VERANDAH **Phone:** 828/526-2338

American
$22-$36

Guests, indeed, may sit on the verandah, overlooking the water, or may request seating in the intimate dining room. Either way, expect friendly, knowledgeable service. The menu changes seasonally, and the chef's creative, well-prepared offerings are delightful. Casual dress. **Bar:** Wine only. **Reservations:** suggested. **Hours:** Open 12/1-1/1 & 3/16-11/30; 6 pm-9 pm; Sunday brunch 11 am-2 pm. Closed: 12/25. **Address:** 1536 Franklin Rd **Location:** Jct SR 106 (Dillard Rd) and 64, 2 mi w on US 64. **Parking:** on-site. **Cards:** AX, DS, MC, VI.

PAOLETTI'S **Phone:** 828/526-4906

Northern Italian
$18-$34

Creative dishes are served in an Old World atmosphere. The outstanding wine list has received the Wine Spectator Award of Excellence for 12 years. Dressy casual. **Bar:** Full bar. **Reservations:** required, in season. **Hours:** 5:30 pm-close. Closed: 11/26, 12/24, 12/25; also Wed. **Address:** 440 Main St **Location:** Center. **Parking:** on-site. **Cards:** AX, MC, VI.

WILD THYME GOURMET **Phone:** 828/526-4035

New Continental
$8-$29

The menu blends fresh local fish and regional seafood with creatively prepared traditional offerings. The upbeat atmosphere and patio dining make the gourmet restaurant a fun place to eat. Dressy casual. **Bar:** Wine only. **Reservations:** suggested. **Hours:** 11:30 am-4 & 5:30-close; seasonal hours vary. Closed: 7/4, 11/26, 12/25; also Sun & Tues. **Address:** 490 Carolina Way **Location:** Center. **Parking:** on-site. **Cards:** MC, VI.

HIGH POINT pop. 85,839 (See map and index starting on p. 714)

WHERE TO STAY

ASHFORD SUITES HOTEL Book at AAA.com **Phone:** (336)812-8787 43

Hotel
$106-$116 All Year

Address: 3901 Sedgebrook Rd **Location:** I-40, exit 210, 1.3 mi s on SR 68, then just w on Regency Dr. **Facility:** 81 one-bedroom standard units, some with whirlpools. 3 stories, interior corridors. *Bath:* combo or shower only. **Parking:** on-site. **Terms:** cancellation fee imposed. **Amenities:** CD players, high-speed Internet, dual phone lines, voice mail, safes (fee), honor bars, irons, hair dryers. **Pool(s):** heated indoor. **Leisure Activities:** exercise room. **Guest Services:** valet laundry, area transportation, wireless Internet. **Business Services:** meeting rooms, business center. **Cards:** AX, DC, DS, MC, VI.

ASK CALL / SOME UNITS FEE VCR

ATRIUM INN **Phone:** 336/884-8838

Motel
$69-$79 All Year

Address: 425 S Main St **Location:** Just s on US 311 business route; center. **Facility:** 38 one-bedroom standard units. 2 stories (no elevator), exterior corridors. *Bath:* combo or shower only. **Parking:** on-site. **Amenities:** irons, hair dryers. **Guest Services:** wireless Internet. **Cards:** AX, DS, MC, VI.

ASK / SOME UNITS

BILTMORE SUITES HOTEL Book at AAA.com **Phone:** 336/812-8188 42

Hotel
Rates not provided

Address: 4400 Regency Dr **Location:** I-40, exit 210, 1.3 mi s on SR 68. **Facility:** 62 one-bedroom standard units, some with whirlpools. 3 stories, interior corridors. *Bath:* combo or shower only. **Parking:** on-site. **Amenities:** voice mail, irons, hair dryers. **Leisure Activities:** limited exercise equipment. **Guest Services:** valet laundry, area transportation, wireless Internet. **Business Services:** meeting rooms, PC.

CALL / SOME UNITS

COURTYARD BY MARRIOTT - HIGH POINT Book great rates at AAA.com **Phone:** (336)882-3600

Hotel
$138-$148 All Year

Address: 1000 Mall Loop Rd **Location:** Jct US 311 Bypass, 1.5 mi s on SR 68, just nw. Located adjacent to Oak Hollow Mall. **Facility:** Smoke free premises. 107 units. 99 one-bedroom standard units. 8 one-bedroom suites, some with whirlpools. 4 stories, interior corridors. *Bath:* combo or shower only. **Parking:** on-site. **Terms:** cancellation fee imposed. **Amenities:** high-speed Internet, dual phone lines, voice mail, irons, hair dryers. **Pool(s):** heated indoor. **Leisure Activities:** whirlpool, exercise room. **Guest Services:** valet and coin laundry, wireless Internet. **Business Services:** meeting rooms, business center. **Cards:** AX, CB, DC, DS, JC, MC, VI. **Free Special Amenities: newspaper and high-speed Internet.**

CALL / SOME UNITS

AAA Benefit:
Members save a minimum 5% off the best available rate.

(See map and index starting on p. 714)

DAYS INN & SUITES Book great rates at AAA.com **Phone:** (336)885-6000

AAA SAVE

Motel

$57-$74 All Year

Address: 120 SW Cloverleaf Pl **Location:** I-85 business route, exit US 311 S northbound, on exit ramp; exit southbound, just s, then just w. **Facility:** 93 one-bedroom standard units, some with whirlpools. 2 stories (no elevator), interior/exterior corridors. **Parking:** on-site. **Terms:** check-in 4 pm. **Amenities:** voice mail, irons, hair dryers. *Some:* dual phone lines, safes. **Pool(s):** outdoor. **Leisure Activities:** exercise room. **Guest Services:** coin laundry, wireless Internet. **Business Services:** meeting rooms, PC. **Cards:** AX, CB, DC, DS, MC, VI. **Free Special Amenities: expanded continental breakfast and high-speed Internet.**

/ SOME UNITS

ECONO LODGE-HIGH POINT Book great rates at AAA.com **Phone:** (336)882-4103

AAA SAVE

Motel

$49-$69 All Year

Address: 400 S Main St **Location:** Just s on US 311 business route; center. **Facility:** 40 one-bedroom standard units. 2 stories (no elevator), exterior corridors. **Parking:** on-site. **Terms:** 3 day cancellation notice. **Amenities:** irons, hair dryers. **Guest Services:** valet laundry, wireless Internet. **Business Services:** PC. **Cards:** AX, DS, MC, VI. **Free Special Amenities: expanded continental breakfast and newspaper.** *(See color ad below)*

/ SOME UNITS

J. H. ADAMS INN **Phone:** (336)882-3267

Hotel

$139-$269 All Year

Address: 1108 N Main St **Location:** 1 mi n; center. **Facility:** Smoke free premises. 31 units. 29 one-bedroom standard units, some with whirlpools. 1 one- and 1 two-bedroom suites, some with kitchens. 2-3 stories, interior corridors. **Parking:** on-site. **Terms:** 3 day cancellation notice-fee imposed. **Amenities:** high-speed Internet, voice mail, safes, irons, hair dryers. **Leisure Activities:** exercise room. **Guest Services:** valet laundry. **Business Services:** meeting rooms, PC. **Cards:** AX, MC, VI.

ASK CALL / SOME UNITS

(See map and index starting on p. 714)

RADISSON HOTEL HIGH POINT *Book at AAA.com* **Phone:** (336)889-8888

Hotel
$89 All Year

Address: 135 S Main St **Location:** On US 311 business route; center. **Facility:** 252 one-bedroom standard units. 8 stories, interior corridors. **Parking:** on-site (fee). **Terms:** 3 day cancellation notice. **Amenities:** high-speed Internet, voice mail, irons, hair dryers. **Pool(s):** heated indoor. **Leisure Activities:** exercise room. **Guest Services:** valet laundry, wireless Internet. **Business Services:** conference facilities, business center. **Cards:** AX, DC, DS, MC, VI.

ASK / SOME UNITS

WHERE TO DINE

CHOP HOUSE GRILLE **Phone:** 336/841-7156 (17)

Steak & Seafood
$8-$35

Both families and business associates will feel at home, and will leave well-fed, at the casually upscale grill. Quality, center-cut Angus beef steaks and choice seafood share the menu with pasta and chicken dishes. Side dishes are portioned for sharing, as are the desserts. Dressy casual. **Bar:** Full bar. **Reservations:** accepted. **Hours:** 11:30 am-10 pm, Sat from 4:30 pm. Closed major holidays; also Sun. **Address:** 4001 Meeting Way **Location:** I-40, exit 210, 2.2 mi s on SR 68. **Parking:** on-site. **Cards:** AX, MC, VI.

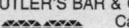

GIANNOS **Phone:** 336/885-0762

Italian
$5-$22

Chicken, veal, seafood, chops, steaks, pizza and pasta are on the menu at the popular eatery. Many entrees are prepared on the grill or in the stone oven. Guests can create their own pasta dish with a variety of sauces and toppings. Also, a pizza buffet is set up for weekday lunches. Casual dress. **Bar:** Full bar. **Hours:** 11 am-10 pm. Closed: 11/26, 12/25; also Sun. **Address:** 1124 Eastchester Dr **Location:** Jct US 311 Bypass, 1 mi s on SR 68. **Parking:** on-site. **Cards:** AX, DS, MC, VI.

CALL

J BUTLER'S BAR & GRILLE **Phone:** 336/861-5758

American
$6-$18

Catch up on the latest sporting events—televisions are scattered throughout the dining room—as you chow on burgers, sandwiches, salads and house specialties like babyback ribs, grilled steaks and fajitas. Casual dress. **Bar:** Full bar. **Hours:** 11 am-1 am, Sun-midnight. Closed: 11/26, 12/25. **Address:** 3030 S Main St **Location:** I-85, exit 111, 1.5 mi n on US 311; in Achdale Commons Shopping Center. **Parking:** on-site. **Cards:** AX, DS, MC, VI.

LIBERTY STEAKHOUSE BREWERY **Phone:** 336/882-4677

Steak
$5-$22

As the name hints, the decor at this popular steakhouse and microbrewery plays homage to American liberty with pictures and icons, such as a bald eagle, adorning the dining room. The menu focuses on steaks and seafood but brick-oven pizzas, burgers and sandwiches also are available. Select from eight beers, including a seasonal selection, masterfully created by the brewmaster. Casual dress. **Bar:** Full bar. **Reservations:** accepted. **Hours:** 11 am-10 pm, Fri & Sat-11 pm. Closed: 11/26, 12/25. **Address:** 914 Mall Loop Rd **Location:** Jct US 311, 1.3 mi s on SR 68, then just sw; adjacent to Oak Hollow Mall. **Parking:** on-site. **Cards:** AX, DS, MC, VI.

CALL

RESTAURANT J BASUL NOBLE **Phone:** 336/889-3354

Continental
$16-$33

An upscale bistro, the restaurant offers a lengthy menu of pasta, fowl, seafood, lamb, beef and veal selections, all prepared with fresh ingredients. An extensive wine list is also available. They did a good job of making the expansive interior feel like an intimate indoor courtyard. The plaza level dining room can be accessed by elevator. Dressy casual. **Bar:** Full bar. **Reservations:** suggested. **Hours:** 5:30 pm-10 pm, Fri & Sat-11 pm, Sun 11 am-2:30 pm; Sunday brunch. Closed major holidays. **Address:** 101 S Main St **Location:** On US 311 business route; center; In GE Capital Building, lower level. **Parking:** on-site (fee). **Cards:** AX, DS, MC, VI.

THAI CHIANG MAI **Phone:** 336/869-0908

Thai
$5-$15

The family-operated restaurant, with a lovely Thai-themed decor, offers an extensive menu of authentic Thai dishes. On some evenings, the owner is known to perform traditional music. Casual dress. **Bar:** Beer & wine. **Hours:** 11 am-2:30 & 5-9:30 pm, Fri-10 pm, Sat noon-10 pm. Closed major holidays; also Sun. **Address:** 2209 N Main St **Location:** Jct SR 68, just n on US 311 business route. **Parking:** on-site. **Cards:** AX, DS, MC, VI.

HILLSBOROUGH pop. 5,446

WHERE TO STAY

HOLIDAY INN EXPRESS *Book great rates at AAA.com* **Phone:** (919)644-7997

AAA SAVE

Hotel
$95-$230 All Year

Address: 202 Cardinal Dr **Location:** I-85, exit 164, just e, then just s. **Facility:** 83 one-bedroom standard units, some with whirlpools. 3 stories, interior corridors. *Bath:* combo or shower only. **Parking:** on-site. **Amenities:** voice mail, irons, hair dryers. *Some:* high-speed Internet. **Pool(s):** outdoor. **Leisure Activities:** exercise room. **Guest Services:** coin laundry, wireless Internet. **Business Services:** meeting rooms. **Cards:** AX, DC, DS, MC, VI.

WHERE TO DINE

TUPELO'S — **Phone:** 919/643-7722

Creole
$5-$22

In the heart of downtown, the family-run bistro prepares regional Southern cuisine with a Creole flair. Specialties of the house include jambalaya and gumbo, as well as fillet of beef bordelaise and catfish Louisianne. At lunch, the menu centers on varied sandwiches and salads. Casual dress. **Bar:** Full bar. **Hours:** 11:30 am-3 & 5-9 pm, Fri & Sat-10 pm. Closed: 11/26, 12/25; also Sun. **Address:** 101 N Churton St **Location:** Center. **Parking:** street. **Cards:** DS, MC, VI.

HOT SPRINGS pop. 645

WHERE TO DINE

PADDLER'S PUB — **Phone:** 828/622-0001

American
$8-$22

After a long day of hiking or rafting, guests can kick back with a cold beer and a plate of home-cooked food at the casual spot. The surprisingly eclectic menu comprises buffalo burgers, crab cakes, hand-cut steaks, organic salads, pizza and pasta dishes. Casual dress. **Bar:** Beer & wine. **Reservations:** not accepted. **Hours:** 11:30 am-midnight; seasonal hours may vary. Closed: 1/1, 11/26, 12/25. **Address:** 159 Bridge St **Location:** US 25/70; center. **Parking:** street. **Cards:** AX, CB, DC, DS, JC, MC, VI.

HUNTERSVILLE —*See Charlotte p. 663.*

JACKSONVILLE pop. 66,715

WHERE TO STAY

AMERICAS BEST VALUE INN *Book great rates at AAA.com* — **Phone:** (910)455-6888

Hotel
$70-$90 All Year

Address: 2149 N Marine Blvd **Location:** Jct Western Blvd, just n on US 17. **Facility:** 60 one-bedroom standard units. 2 stories (no elevator), interior corridors. **Parking:** on-site. **Amenities:** high-speed Internet, safes (fee). **Pool(s):** outdoor. **Guest Services:** coin laundry, wireless Internet. **Cards:** AX, DC, DS, MC, VI. **Free Special Amenities: continental breakfast and local telephone calls.**

/ SOME UNITS FEE

COMFORT SUITES *Book at AAA.com* — **Phone:** 910/346-8900

Hotel
Rates not provided

Address: 130 Workshop Ln **Location:** Jct Western Blvd, just n on US 17. **Facility:** Smoke free premises. 72 one-bedroom standard units, some with whirlpools. 3 stories, interior corridors. *Bath:* combo or shower only. **Parking:** on-site. **Amenities:** voice mail, safes (fee), irons, hair dryers. **Pool(s):** outdoor. **Leisure Activities:** sauna, limited exercise equipment. **Guest Services:** valet and coin laundry, wireless Internet. **Business Services:** meeting rooms, PC.

CALL

DAYS INN *Book at AAA.com* — **Phone:** 910/347-5131

Motel
Rates not provided

Address: 505 N Marine Blvd **Location:** Jct Western Blvd, 2 mi w on US 17 business route. **Facility:** 73 one-bedroom standard units, some with whirlpools. 2 stories (no elevator), exterior corridors. **Parking:** on-site. **Amenities:** irons, hair dryers. **Pool(s):** outdoor. **Guest Services:** wireless Internet.

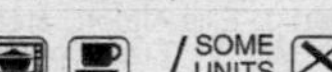

/ SOME UNITS

EXTENDED STAYAMERICA *Book at AAA.com* — **Phone:** (910)347-7684

Hotel
$99-$169 All Year

Address: 20 McDaniel Dr **Location:** Jct Western Blvd, just n on US 17, then just w. **Facility:** 98 one-bedroom standard units with efficiencies. 3 stories, interior corridors. *Bath:* combo or shower only. **Parking:** on-site. **Amenities:** voice mail, irons. **Guest Services:** coin laundry, wireless Internet. **Cards:** AX, CB, DC, DS, JC, MC, VI.

ASK CALL FEE / SOME UNITS FEE

FAIRFIELD INN & SUITES BY MARRIOTT *Book great rates at AAA.com* — **Phone:** (910)938-4499

Hotel
$98-$106 All Year

Address: 121 Circuit Ln **Location:** Jct US 17, 0.4 mi w on Western Blvd, then just s. **Facility:** Smoke free premises. 79 one-bedroom standard units, some with whirlpools. 3 stories, interior corridors. *Bath:* combo or shower only. **Parking:** on-site. **Terms:** cancellation fee imposed. **Amenities:** voice mail, irons, hair dryers. **Pool(s):** outdoor. **Leisure Activities:** whirlpool, exercise room. **Guest Services:** valet and coin laundry, wireless Internet. **Business Services:** meeting rooms, PC. **Cards:** AX, DS, MC, VI.

CALL

AAA Benefit:
Members save a minimum 5% off the best available rate.

HAMPTON INN Book great rates at AAA.com **Phone:** (910)347-6500

Hotel
$79-$129 All Year

Address: 474 Western Blvd **Location:** Jct US 17, just n. **Facility:** 122 one-bedroom standard units. 2 stories (no elevator), exterior corridors. **Parking:** on-site. **Terms:** cancellation fee imposed. **Amenities:** video games (fee), voice mail, irons, hair dryers. **Pool(s):** outdoor. **Guest Services:** valet and coin laundry, wireless Internet. **Cards:** AX, CB, DC, DS, JC, MC, VI. **Free Special Amenities: expanded continental breakfast and high-speed Internet.**

/ SOME UNITS FEE

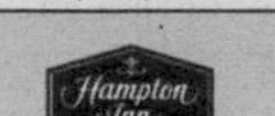

AAA Benefit: Members save up to 10% everyday!

HOLIDAY INN EXPRESS Book at AAA.com **Phone:** (910)347-1900

Hotel
$104-$114 All Year

Address: 2115 Hwy 17 N **Location:** Jct Western Blvd, just n on US 17, then just w. **Facility:** 118 one-bedroom standard units. 4 stories, interior corridors. *Bath:* combo or shower only. **Parking:** on-site. **Terms:** check-in 4 pm, cancellation fee imposed. **Amenities:** voice mail, irons, hair dryers. **Pool(s):** outdoor. **Guest Services:** valet and coin laundry, wireless Internet. **Business Services:** PC. **Cards:** AX, CB, DC, DS, MC, VI.

ASK / SOME UNITS

INNKEEPER Book at AAA.com **Phone:** (910)938-0800

Hotel
$80 All Year

Address: 2139 N Marine Blvd **Location:** Jct Western Blvd, just n on US 17. **Facility:** 82 one-bedroom standard units. 3 stories, interior corridors. *Bath:* combo or shower only. **Parking:** on-site. **Terms:** 3 day cancellation notice. **Amenities:** hair dryers. **Pool(s):** outdoor. **Guest Services:** coin laundry, wireless Internet. **Business Services:** meeting rooms, PC. **Cards:** AX, CB, DC, DS, JC, MC, VI.

ASK / SOME UNITS FEE

LIBERTY INN **Phone:** 910/353-3336

Hotel
$90-$200 All Year

Address: 1723 Le Jeune Blvd **Location:** Jct US 17 and Western Blvd; 2 mi w of Camp Le Jeune main gate. **Facility:** 78 units. 77 one-bedroom standard units, some with efficiencies and/or whirlpools. 1 one-bedroom suite with efficiency and whirlpool. 2 stories (no elevator), interior corridors. **Parking:** on-site. **Amenities:** voice mail, irons, hair dryers. **Pool(s):** heated indoor. **Leisure Activities:** whirlpool, game room. **Guest Services:** valet and coin laundry, wireless Internet. **Business Services:** PC. **Cards:** AX, DC, DS, MC, VI. **Free Special Amenities: continental breakfast and high-speed Internet.**

/ SOME UNITS

QUALITY INN Book at AAA.com **Phone:** (910)347-6111

Hotel
$69-$175 All Year

Address: 701 N Marine Blvd **Location:** Jct SR 24, 0.7 mi n on US 17 business route. **Facility:** 110 units. 105 one-bedroom standard units. 5 one-bedroom suites. 4 stories, exterior corridors. *Bath:* combo or shower only. **Parking:** on-site. **Amenities:** irons, hair dryers. **Pool(s):** outdoor. **Leisure Activities:** exercise room. **Guest Services:** wireless Internet. **Business Services:** meeting rooms, business center. **Cards:** AX, DS, MC, VI.

ASK / SOME UNITS

RAMADA INN Book great rates at AAA.com **Phone:** (910)455-4100

Hotel
$70-$100 All Year

Address: 603 N Marine Blvd **Location:** Jct Western Blvd, 1.8 mi s on US 17 business route. **Facility:** 121 units. 120 one-bedroom standard units. 1 one-bedroom suite with kitchen and whirlpool. 2 stories (no elevator), exterior corridors. **Parking:** on-site. **Amenities:** voice mail, irons, hair dryers. **Pool(s):** outdoor. **Leisure Activities:** exercise room, horseshoes. **Guest Services:** valet laundry, airport transportation-Albert J. Ellis Airport, area transportation-local military bases, wireless Internet. **Cards:** AX, CB, DC, DS, MC, VI. **Free Special Amenities: expanded continental breakfast and high-speed Internet.**

/ SOME UNITS

SLEEP INN & SUITES Book at AAA.com **Phone:** 910/478-0099

Hotel
Rates not provided

Address: 129 Circuit Ln **Location:** Jct US 17, 0.4 mi w on Western Blvd, then just s. **Facility:** 62 one-bedroom standard units, some with whirlpools. 3 stories, interior corridors. *Bath:* combo or shower only. **Parking:** on-site. **Amenities:** voice mail, irons, hair dryers. **Pool(s):** outdoor. **Leisure Activities:** exercise room. **Guest Services:** valet and coin laundry, wireless Internet. **Business Services:** meeting rooms, business center.

/ SOME UNITS

WHERE TO DINE

MAI TAI RESTAURANT **Phone:** 910/346-5382

Chinese
$5-$10

The long-time popular eatery sets up daily lunch and dinner buffets with a wide variety of Chinese and American cuisine. Take-out service is another option. Casual dress. **Bar:** Full bar. **Hours:** 11 am-2:30 & 4:30-10 pm, Fri & Sat-10:30 pm, Sun 11 am-9:30 pm. **Address:** 109 Henderson Dr **Location:** Jct Western Blvd, 1.8 mi s on US 17 business route, then just w. **Parking:** on-site. **Cards:** AX, DC, DS, MC, VI.

MI CABANA MEXICAN RESTAURANT **Phone:** 910/346-8457

Mexican
$4-$12

The colorful cantina presents a lengthy menu of enchiladas, fajitas and other traditional Mexican favorites, along with a list of combination platters. Casual dress. **Bar:** Full bar. **Hours:** 11 am-2:30 & 5-10 pm, Sat 11 am-11 pm, Sun 11 am-9 pm. Closed: 11/26, 12/25. **Address:** 1153 Western Blvd **Location:** Jct US 17, just w. **Parking:** on-site. **Cards:** AX, MC, VI.

RAGAZZI'S | **Phone:** 910/577-2782

Italian
$5-$12

Italian favorites—including lasagna, manicotti, fettuccine Alfredo and pizza—are the focus at the casual eatery. Homemade salad dressing is delicious, and the breadsticks are plentiful. Casual dress. **Bar:** Full bar. **Hours:** 11 am-10 pm, Sun-9 pm. Closed: 11/26, 12/25. **Address:** 1439 Le Jeune Blvd **Location:** Jct US 17, 1 mi e on SR 24. **Parking:** on-site. **Cards:** MC, VI.

TEXAS STEAKHOUSE & SALOON | **Phone:** 910/938-1032

Steak
$6-$25

The typical Texas-style roadhouse focuses on freshly cut steaks, including the popular Duke entree with fries. Southwestern decor and arrows stuck in the walls get diners' minds wandering back to the old days. The popular draft beer is the microbrewed Red Oak lager. Casual dress. **Bar:** Full bar. **Hours:** 11 am-10 pm, Fri & Sat-11 pm. Closed: 11/26, 12/24, 12/25. **Address:** 101 Parkwood Dr **Location:** Jct Western Blvd, just n on US 17. **Parking:** on-site. **Cards:** AX, DS, MC, VI.

JEFFERSON pop. 1,422—*See also WEST JEFFERSON.*

WHERE TO STAY

BEST WESTERN ELDRETH INN AT MOUNT JEFFERSON *Book great rates at AAA.com* | **Phone:** (336)246-8845

AAA SAVE

Motel
$84-$96 All Year

Address: 829 E Main St **Location:** On US 221 and SR 88. Located in a rural mountain area. **Facility:** 48 one-bedroom standard units. 1-2 stories (no elevator), exterior corridors. **Parking:** on-site. **Amenities:** irons, hair dryers. **Leisure Activities:** sauna, exercise room. **Guest Services:** wireless Internet. **Cards:** AX, DC, DS, MC, VI.

/ SOME UNITS

AAA Benefit:
Members save up to 20%, plus 10% bonus points with rewards program.

JEFFERSON LANDING CLUB | **Phone:** 336/982-4653

Motel
Rates not provided

Address: 193 E Landing Dr (Hwy 16/88) **Location:** Jct US 211, 1.5 mi se. **Facility:** Smoke free premises. 18 one-bedroom standard units, some with kitchens. 2 stories (no elevator), exterior corridors. *Bath:* combo or shower only. **Parking:** on-site. **Terms:** check-in 4 pm. **Amenities:** voice mail, irons, hair dryers. *Some:* DVD players. **Pool(s):** heated outdoor. **Leisure Activities:** rental canoes, fishing, 2 tennis courts, hiking trails, playground, exercise room. *Fee:* golf-18 holes. **Guest Services:** wireless Internet. **Business Services:** meeting rooms.

JONESVILLE pop. 1,464

WHERE TO STAY

COMFORT INN *Book great rates at AAA.com* | **Phone:** (336)835-9400

AAA SAVE

Motel
$79-$150 3/1-11/30
$79-$99 12/1-2/28

Address: 1633 Winston Rd **Location:** I-77, exit 82, just w. **Facility:** 79 one-bedroom standard units. 2 stories (no elevator), exterior corridors. **Parking:** on-site. **Amenities:** high-speed Internet, safes (fee), irons, hair dryers. **Pool(s):** heated indoor. **Leisure Activities:** whirlpool, sun deck. **Guest Services:** wireless Internet. **Business Services:** meeting rooms, business center. **Cards:** AX, CB, DC, DS, JC, MC, VI. **Free Special Amenities: expanded continental breakfast and high-speed Internet.**

CALL / SOME UNITS FEE

DAYS INN JONESVILLE-ELKIN *Book great rates at AAA.com* | **Phone:** (336)526-6777

AAA SAVE

Motel
$69-$109 All Year

Address: 1540 NC 67 Hwy **Location:** I-77, exit 82, 0.3 mi w. **Facility:** 50 one-bedroom standard units. 2 stories (no elevator), exterior corridors. **Parking:** on-site. **Terms:** 2-3 night minimum stay - seasonal. **Amenities:** safes, hair dryers. **Pool(s):** outdoor. **Guest Services:** wireless Internet. **Business Services:** PC. **Cards:** AX, DS, MC, VI. **Free Special Amenities: expanded continental breakfast and room upgrade (subject to availability with advance reservations).**

/ SOME UNITS FEE

HAMPTON INN *Book great rates at AAA.com* | **Phone:** (336)835-1994

AAA SAVE

Hotel
$89-$129 All Year

Address: 1632 SR 67 **Location:** I-77, exit 82, just w. **Facility:** 64 one-bedroom standard units. 3 stories, interior corridors. **Parking:** on-site. **Terms:** 7 day cancellation notice. **Amenities:** voice mail, irons, hair dryers. **Pool(s):** outdoor. **Leisure Activities:** exercise room. **Guest Services:** wireless Internet. **Business Services:** PC. **Cards:** AX, CB, DC, DS, MC, VI. **Free Special Amenities: expanded continental breakfast.**

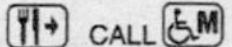    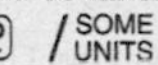 / SOME UNITS

AAA Benefit:
Members save up to 10% everyday!

HOLIDAY INN EXPRESS *Book at AAA.com* **Phone:** (336)835-6000

Hotel

$79-$99 All Year

Address: 1713 NC 67 Hwy **Location:** I-77, exit 82, just e. **Facility:** 105 one-bedroom standard units, some with whirlpools. 2 stories (no elevator), interior corridors. *Bath:* combo or shower only. **Parking:** on-site. **Amenities:** voice mail, irons, hair dryers. **Pool(s):** outdoor. **Leisure Activities:** exercise room. **Guest Services:** valet and coin laundry, wireless Internet. **Business Services:** conference facilities, PC. **Cards:** AX, CB, DC, DS, MC, VI.

ASK CALL / SOME UNITS FEE VCR

WHERE TO DINE

THEO'S **Phone:** 336/526-5888

Italian

$5-$11

The open dining rooms can be bustling at times, and there may be a waiting line for dinner seating on weekends. The restaurant specializes in pizza, oven-baked submarine sandwiches and a wide variety of traditional Italian favorites. Large hand-painted murals are decor highlights. There is a daily all-you-can-eat pizza and salad bar at lunch. Casual dress. **Hours:** 11 am-10 pm. Closed: 1/1, 11/26, 12/25; also Mon. **Address:** 233 Winston Rd **Location:** I-77, exit 82, 1 mi w; in Starmount Crossing Shopping Center. **Parking:** on-site. **Cards:** AX, DS, MC, VI.

CALL

KANNAPOLIS pop. 36,910

WHERE TO STAY

FAIRFIELD INN BY MARRIOTT-KANNAPOLIS *Book great rates at AAA.com* **Phone:** (704)795-4888

Hotel

$108-$116 All Year

Address: 3033 Cloverleaf Pkwy **Location:** I-85, exit 58, just n on US 29, just e on Cloverleaf Plaza, then just s. **Facility:** Smoke free premises. 84 one-bedroom standard units, some with whirlpools. 4 stories, interior corridors. *Bath:* combo or shower only. **Parking:** on-site. **Terms:** cancellation fee imposed. **Amenities:** high-speed Internet, irons, hair dryers. **Pool(s):** outdoor. **Leisure Activities:** exercise room. **Guest Services:** valet laundry, wireless Internet. **Business Services:** meeting rooms. **Cards:** AX, CB, DC, DS, JC, MC, VI.

CALL / SOME UNITS

AAA Benefit:

Members save a minimum 5% off the best available rate.

HOLIDAY INN EXPRESS HOTEL & SUITES *Book at AAA.com* **Phone:** (704)743-1080

Hotel

$95-$299 All Year

Address: 2491 Wonder Dr **Location:** I-85, exit 60 northbound, just w, just s on Roxie St, then just e; exit 60 southbound, just s on Roxie St, then just e. **Facility:** 81 one-bedroom standard units, some with whirlpools. 4 stories, interior corridors. *Bath:* combo or shower only. **Parking:** on-site. **Terms:** cancellation fee imposed. **Amenities:** high-speed Internet, dual phone lines, voice mail, irons, hair dryers. **Pool(s):** heated indoor. **Leisure Activities:** exercise room. **Guest Services:** valet and coin laundry, wireless Internet. **Business Services:** meeting rooms, business center. **Cards:** AX, DC, DS, JC, MC, VI.

ASK CALL / SOME UNITS

WHERE TO DINE

EL AMIGO MEXICAN RESTAURANT **Phone:** 704/938-1111

Mexican

$4-$11

In a small shopping center, the restaurant serves well-prepared traditional Mexican selections. The use of quality ingredients is evident in the good flavors of the food. Mexican background music helps set the relaxed and informal mood. The decor is reminiscent of a hacienda, with a hand-painted mural and accents. Casual dress. **Bar:** Full bar. **Hours:** 11 am-10 pm, Fri-10:30 pm, Sat noon-10:30 pm, Sun noon-10 pm. Closed major holidays. **Address:** 1776 S Cannon Blvd **Location:** I-85, exit 58, 1 mi w; in Market Square Shopping Center. **Parking:** on-site. **Cards:** AX, DS, MC, VI.

LOS ARCOS MEXICAN RESTAURANT **Phone:** 704/932-3550

Mexican

$4-$18

Guests can savor the taste of traditionally prepared cuisine amid a setting filled with Mexican memorabilia. Casual dress. **Bar:** Full bar. **Hours:** 11 am-10 pm, Fri & Sat-10:30 pm. Closed: 1/1, 12/25. **Address:** 1021 S Cannon Blvd **Location:** I-85, exit 58, 2 mi w. **Parking:** on-site. **Cards:** AX, DC, DS, MC, VI.

KENLY pop. 1,569

WHERE TO STAY

ECONO LODGE *Book at AAA.com* **Phone:** (919)284-1000

Motel

$45-$150 6/1-11/30

$39-$150 12/1-5/31

Address: 405 S Church St **Location:** I-95, exit 107, just e. **Facility:** 60 one-bedroom standard units. 2 stories (no elevator), exterior corridors. **Parking:** on-site. **Terms:** cancellation fee imposed. **Amenities:** hair dryers. **Pool(s):** outdoor. **Guest Services:** wireless Internet. **Business Services:** PC. **Cards:** AX, DC, DS, MC, VI.

ASK / SOME UNITS

SUPER 8 *Book at AAA.com* **Phone:** 919/284-3800

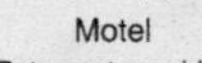

Motel

Rates not provided

Address: 843 Johnston Pkwy **Location:** I-95, exit 106, just w, then just s. **Facility:** 80 one-bedroom standard units. 2 stories (no elevator), exterior corridors. **Parking:** on-site. **Amenities:** hair dryers. **Pool(s):** outdoor. **Guest Services:** wireless Internet.

CALL / SOME UNITS FEE

KERNERSVILLE pop. 17,126

WHERE TO STAY

SLEEP INN *Book at AAA.com* **Phone:** (336)993-6800

Hotel
$75-$150 All Year

Address: 1406 Heartland Dr **Location:** I-40, exit 203, just n on SR 66, then just e. **Facility:** 104 one-bedroom standard units. 2 stories (no elevator), interior corridors. *Bath:* combo or shower only. **Parking:** on-site. **Terms:** 3 day cancellation notice. **Amenities:** high-speed Internet, voice mail. *Some:* irons, hair dryers. **Guest Services:** wireless Internet. **Cards:** AX, CB, DC, DS, JC, MC, VI.

ASK CALL / SOME UNITS

WHERE TO DINE

SAGEBRUSH STEAKHOUSE **Phone:** 336/992-0973

American
$5-$19

Born from the spirit of Texas cattle drives, the restaurant presents a menu of hearty steaks, prime rib, chicken, seafood and baby back ribs. Yummy desserts merit a splurge. Guests can call ahead to facilitate seating. Casual dress. **Bar:** Full bar. **Hours:** 11 am-10 pm, Fri & Sat-11 pm. Closed: 12/25. **Address:** 566 Arbor Hill Rd **Location:** US 40 business route, exit S Main St, just sw to Century Blvd, then just s to Arbor Hill Rd. **Parking:** on-site. **Cards:** AX, DC, DS, MC, VI.

CALL

KILL DEVIL HILLS —*See Outer Banks p. 776.*

KINGS MOUNTAIN pop. 9,693

WHERE TO STAY

HOLIDAY INN EXPRESS HOTEL & SUITES *Book great rates at AAA.com* **Phone:** (704)734-0014

AAA SAVE

Hotel
$70-$150 All Year

Address: 100 Woodlake Pkwy **Location:** I-85, exit 8, just s on SR 161. **Facility:** 74 one-bedroom standard units, some with whirlpools. 3 stories, interior corridors. *Bath:* combo or shower only. **Parking:** on-site. **Terms:** 14 day cancellation notice-fee imposed. **Amenities:** high-speed Internet, dual phone lines, voice mail, irons, hair dryers. **Pool(s):** outdoor. **Leisure Activities:** sauna, exercise room. **Guest Services:** coin laundry, wireless Internet. **Business Services:** meeting rooms, PC. **Cards:** AX, DC, DS, MC, VI. **Free Special Amenities: expanded continental breakfast and high-speed Internet.**

CALL / SOME UNITS

WHERE TO DINE

MOUNTAIN VIEW RESTAURANT **Phone:** 704/734-1265

American
$3-$14

The menu at this family-run eatery includes down-home classics such as roast beef with gravy and fried pork chops, as well as Italian favorites along the lines of spaghetti and lasagna. Service is straight-forward and friendly. Casual dress. **Hours:** 6:30 am-9 pm, Fri & Sat-9:30 pm, Sun 11 am-4 pm. Closed: 4/12, 11/26, 12/24, 12/25; also Greek Orthodox Easter. **Address:** 100 W King St **Location:** I-85, exit 8, 1 mi n on SR 161, then 0.6 mi w on US 74 business route. **Parking:** on-site. **Cards:** AX, MC, VI.

KINSTON pop. 23,688

WHERE TO STAY

HAMPTON INN *Book great rates at AAA.com* **Phone:** (252)523-1400

Hotel
$84-$94 All Year

Address: 1382 Hwy 258 S **Location:** Jct US 70 Bypass and US 258 S. **Facility:** 122 one-bedroom standard units. 4 stories, interior corridors. **Parking:** on-site. **Terms:** 1-30 night minimum stay, cancellation fee imposed. **Amenities:** dual phone lines, voice mail, irons, hair dryers. **Pool(s):** outdoor. **Leisure Activities:** exercise room. **Guest Services:** valet laundry, wireless Internet. **Business Services:** conference facilities, business center. **Cards:** AX, CB, DC, DS, JC, MC, VI.

CALL / SOME UNITS

AAA Benefit:
Members save up to 10% everyday!

WHERE TO DINE

ABBOTT'S COUNTRY BUFFET **Phone:** 252/527-5613

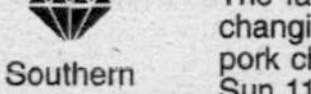

Southern
$8-$14

The family-run restaurant is a longtime favorite rest stop for travelers on their way to the beach. The daily changing buffet lines up food prepared with a Southern flair, such as fried chicken, chicken and dumplings, pork chops, vegetables and cold salads. Casual dress. **Hours:** 11 am-2 & 4:30-8:30 pm, Sat from 4:30 pm, Sun 11 am-3 pm. Closed: 12/25; also Mon. **Address:** 3700 W Vernon Ave (US 70) **Location:** Jct US 258 N, just e on US 70. **Parking:** on-site.

KING'S RESTAURANT

Phone: 252/527-2101

Regional American
$6-$13

Since 1936, the family-run restaurant has served eastern North Carolina pulled-pork barbecue, fried chicken and the original "pig in a puppy," barbecue served on a giant hushpuppy. Casual dress. **Bar:** Full bar. **Reservations:** accepted. **Hours:** 10:30 am-9 pm, Sat & Sun from 7 am. Closed: 12/25. **Address:** 405 E New Bern Rd **Location:** US 70 Bypass, 0.5 mi e of US 258. **Parking:** on-site. **Cards:** DS, MC, VI.

KITTY HAWK —*See Outer Banks p. 780.*

KURE BEACH pop. 1,507

WHERE TO STAY

DARLINGS BY THE SEA-OCEANFRONT WHIRLPOOL SUITES

Phone: 910/458-1429

Bed & Breakfast
$179-$279 All Year

Address: 329 Atlantic Ave **Location:** Oceanfront. US 421, just e on M St, then n; 0.4 mi n of fishing pier. **Facility:** Oceanfront rooms with large, private terraces and whirlpool tubs in nicely-appointed bathrooms are standard at the small inn. Designated smoking area. 5 one-bedroom standard units with whirlpools. 2 stories (no elevator), exterior corridors. **Parking:** on-site. **Terms:** office hours 10 am-10 pm, 2 night minimum stay - seasonal and/or weekends, age restrictions may apply, 7 day cancellation notice. **Amenities:** DVD players, dual phone lines, voice mail, irons, hair dryers. **Leisure Activities:** bicycles, exercise room. **Guest Services:** wireless Internet. **Cards:** AX, DS, MC, VI.

LAKE LURE pop. 1,027

WHERE TO STAY

GAESTEHAUS SALZBURG   Book at AAA.com

Phone: (828)625-0093

Country Inn
$85-$165 2/1-11/30
$79-$165 12/1-1/1

Address: 1491 Memorial Hwy (US 64/74A) **Location:** 2 mi e on US 64/74A. **Facility:** On six acres of wooded hillside with flowering plants and trees, this Alpine-style inn has country-elegant rooms in the main building and in an annex. Smoke free premises. 10 units. 8 one-bedroom standard units, some with efficiencies and/or whirlpools. 2 cabins. 1-2 stories (no elevator), interior/exterior corridors. *Bath:* combo or shower only. **Parking:** on-site. **Terms:** open 12/1-1/1 & 2/1-11/30, 14 day cancellation notice-fee imposed. **Amenities:** video library, irons, hair dryers. *Some:* DVD players, CD players. **Pool(s):** outdoor. **Leisure Activities:** sauna, whirlpool, hiking trails. **Guest Services:** wireless Internet. **Business Services:** meeting rooms, PC. **Cards:** MC, VI.

ASK VCR / SOME UNITS

WHERE TO DINE

HAPPY OURS

Phone: 828/625-0210

American
$5-$12

The casual restaurant across from the marina is great after a day of sun and swimming; kids can find some of their favorites including burgers, chicken tenders and wings, nachos and quesadillas, and of course barbecue is on the menu, too. Casual dress. **Bar:** Full bar. **Hours:** 11 am-9 pm, Fri & Sat-10 pm; hours vary in winter. Closed: 11/26, 12/25. **Address:** 10 Arcade Blvd **Location:** US 64/74A; across from Lake Lure Marina. **Parking:** on-site. **Cards:** MC, VI.

LARKIN'S ON THE LAKE AND THE BAY FRONT BAR & GRILL

Phone: 828/625-4075

Regional American
$8-$32

On Lake Lure, the informal dining room with a bar and grill affords beautiful lake and mountain views and offers regional variations of steak and seafood. The selection of wines is good. Casual dress. **Bar:** Full bar. **Reservations:** suggested. **Hours:** 11:30 am-9:30 pm, Fri & Sat-10 pm; seasonal hours vary. Closed: 11/26, 12/24, 12/25. **Address:** 1020 Memorial Hwy (64/74A) **Location:** 3.3 mi e. **Parking:** on-site. **Cards:** AX, CB, DS, MC, VI.

LA STRADA AT LAKE LURE

Phone: 828/625-1118

Italian
$7-$26

Diners can keep an eye on the activity from this hillside restaurant overlooking Lake Lure. Menu items include pizza, pasta and sandwiches. Casual dress. **Bar:** Full bar. **Hours:** 11 am-10 pm; seasonal hours vary. Closed: 11/26, 12/25. **Address:** 2693 Memorial Hwy (Hwy 9/64) **Location:** Across from Lake Lure Marina. **Parking:** on-site. **Cards:** AX, DS, MC, VI.

POINT OF VIEW RESTAURANT

Phone: 828/625-4380

Regional American
$14-$30

Scenic mountain views are beautiful from the dark, cozy log cabin, which overlooks Lake Lure. Casual dress. **Bar:** Full bar. **Reservations:** suggested. **Hours:** 11 am-9 pm; hours vary in winter. Closed: 4/12, 11/26, 12/24, 12/25. **Address:** 454 Memorial Hwy **Location:** On US 64/74, 4.3 mi e. **Parking:** on-site. **Cards:** AX, DC, DS, MC, VI.

LAKE TOXAWAY

WHERE TO STAY

GREYSTONE INN — **Phone:** (828)966-4700

AAA SAVE

Historic Country Inn

$360-$640 5/1-11/30
$290-$490 12/1-4/30

Address: 220 Greystone Ln **Location:** 3.5 mi n of gate on US 64, follow signs. **Facility:** The handsomely restored 1915 mansion includes an annex section with modern suites overlooking a scenic lake. Winter hours are limited, open weekends only December-March. 33 units. 31 one-bedroom standard units with whirlpools. 2 one-bedroom suites with whirlpools. 2-4 stories (no elevator), interior/exterior corridors. **Parking:** on-site. **Terms:** 2 night minimum stay - weekends, 15 day cancellation notice-fee imposed. **Amenities:** CD players, voice mail, irons, hair dryers. *Some:* DVD players. **Pool(s):** outdoor. **Leisure Activities:** boating, canoeing, marina, waterskiing, fishing, golf-18 holes, recreation programs, bicycles, hiking trails, jogging, playground, exercise room, spa. **Guest Services:** valet laundry, airport transportation (fee)-Asheville Regional Airport, wireless Internet. **Business Services:** meeting rooms, PC. **Cards:** MC, VI. **Free Special Amenities: full breakfast and high-speed Internet.**

FEE VCR / SOME UNITS

LAUREL SPRINGS

WHERE TO STAY

BLUFF'S LODGE — **Phone:** 336/372-4499

AAA SAVE

Motel

$105-$115 10/1-11/2
$95-$105 4/25-9/30

Address: 45356 Blue Ridge Pkwy **Location:** At milepost 241; 7 mi n on Blue Ridge Pkwy from jct SR 18. **Facility:** 24 one-bedroom standard units. 2 stories (no elevator), exterior corridors. **Parking:** on-site. **Terms:** open 4/25-11/2, check-in 4 pm, 14 day cancellation notice-fee imposed. **Amenities:** hair dryers. **Leisure Activities:** outdoor fireplace, hiking trails. **Cards:** AX, MC, VI.

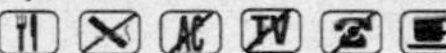

LAURINBURG pop. 15,874

WHERE TO STAY

COMFORT INN — Book at AAA.com — **Phone:** (910)277-7788

Hotel

$97-$130 All Year

Address: 1705 Hwy 401 Bypass S **Location:** Jct US 74 Bypass, just s on US 15/401 Bypass; on service road. **Facility:** 80 one-bedroom standard units, some with whirlpools. 3 stories, interior corridors. *Bath:* combo or shower only. **Parking:** on-site. **Amenities:** high-speed Internet, voice mail, safes (fee), irons, hair dryers. **Pool(s):** outdoor. **Leisure Activities:** exercise room. **Guest Services:** valet laundry, wireless Internet. **Business Services:** meeting rooms, PC. **Cards:** AX, DC, DS, JC, MC, VI.

ASK / SOME UNITS FEE VCR

JAMESON INN — Book at AAA.com — **Phone:** (910)277-0080

Motel

$73-$78 All Year

Address: 14 Jameson Inn Ct **Location:** Jct US 74 Bypass, just n on US 15/401 Bypass, just e. **Facility:** 42 one-bedroom standard units, some with whirlpools. 2 stories (no elevator), exterior corridors. **Parking:** on-site. **Terms:** cancellation fee imposed. **Amenities:** irons, hair dryers. **Pool(s):** outdoor. **Leisure Activities:** exercise room. **Guest Services:** wireless Internet. **Business Services:** PC. **Cards:** AX, DC, DS, MC, VI.

ASK / SOME UNITS FEE

THOMAS WALTON MANOR — **Phone:** 910/276-0551

AAA SAVE

Bed & Breakfast

$175-$275 All Year

Address: 400 W Church St **Location:** Jct US 15/501/401, 0.6 mi e on US 74 business route. **Facility:** The lovely Georgian Colonial home is set on elaborate grounds and offer handsomely-appointed guest rooms. Smoke free premises. 6 units. 5 one- and 1 two-bedroom standard units, some with kitchens and/or whirlpools. 3 stories (no elevator), interior corridors. **Parking:** on-site and street. **Terms:** 2 night minimum stay - seasonal and/or weekends, cancellation fee imposed. **Amenities:** video library, DVD players, irons, hair dryers. **Pool(s):** outdoor. **Leisure Activities:** limited exercise equipment. **Guest Services:** wireless Internet. **Business Services:** PC. **Cards:** AX, MC, VI. **Free Special Amenities: full breakfast and high-speed Internet.**

VCR / SOME UNITS

WHERE TO DINE

WOOLY MCDUFF'S NEIGHBORHOOD GRILLE — **Phone:** 910/276-6632

American

$9-$18

Sports fans appreciate the comfortable, informal grill, which carries out a Scottish golf theme complete with bagpipes and golf memorabilia. Well-prepared, reasonably priced dishes exhibit good flavor and nice presentation. Casual dress. **Bar:** Full bar. **Reservations:** accepted. **Hours:** 5 pm-10 pm. Closed: 7/4, 11/26, 12/25; also Sun. **Address:** 1709 Hwy 401 Bypass S **Location:** US 74 Bypass, just s on US 15/401 Bypass, on service road. **Parking:** on-site. **Cards:** AX, DC, DS, MC, VI.

LAWSONVILLE

WHERE TO STAY

SOUTHWYCK FARM B & B **Phone:** (336)593-8006

Bed & Breakfast
$90-$125 All Year

Address: 1070 Southwyck Farm Rd **Location:** Jct SR 8, 3 mi w on SR 704, then just n. Located in a quiet area. **Facility:** Smoke free premises. 6 one-bedroom standard units, some with whirlpools. 2 stories (no elevator), interior corridors. *Bath:* some shared or private, combo or shower only. **Parking:** on-site. **Terms:** check-in 4 pm, 7 day cancellation notice. **Amenities:** *Some:* hair dryers. **Leisure Activities:** whirlpool, fishing, hiking trails. **Guest Services:** TV in common area. **Cards:** DS, MC, VI.

LELAND pop. 1,938

WHERE TO DINE

EDDIE ROMANELLI'S **Phone:** 910/383-1885

Italian
$6-$21

Menu offering at the casual restaurant include traditional Italian favorites like pizza, lasagna and spaghetti. Other dinner options include steak, pork chop, chicken and seafood entrees. Casual dress. **Bar:** Full bar. **Reservations:** accepted. **Hours:** 4 pm-10 pm, Fri & Sat-11 pm, Sun 11 am-10 pm. Closed: 1/1, 11/26, 12/24, 12/25. **Address:** 503 Olde Waterford Way **Location:** Jct US 74, just s on US 17; at Waterford. **Parking:** on-site. **Cards:** AX, MC, VI.

LENOIR pop. 16,793

WHERE TO STAY

DAYS INN Book at AAA.com **Phone:** 828/754-0731

Hotel
Rates not provided

Address: 206 Blowing Rock Blvd **Location:** Jct US 321, just n of SR 18. **Facility:** 73 one-bedroom standard units. 2 stories, exterior corridors. **Parking:** on-site. **Amenities:** high-speed Internet, safes (fee), hair dryers. **Leisure Activities:** exercise room. **Guest Services:** coin laundry, wireless Internet. **Business Services:** fax.

/ SOME UNITS FEE

JAMESON INN Book at AAA.com **Phone:** (828)758-1200

Motel
$61-$71 All Year

Address: 350 Wilkesboro Blvd **Location:** Jct US 321, 0.4 mi ne on SR 18. **Facility:** 39 one-bedroom standard units. 2 stories (no elevator), exterior corridors. **Parking:** on-site. **Amenities:** high-speed Internet, hair dryers. **Pool(s):** outdoor. **Leisure Activities:** exercise room. **Guest Services:** wireless Internet. **Business Services:** fax (fee). **Cards:** AX, DS, MC, VI.

CALL / SOME UNITS

WHERE TO DINE

SAGEBRUSH STEAKHOUSE **Phone:** 828/754-7543

American
$5-$19

Born from the spirit of Texas cattle drives, the restaurant presents a menu of hearty steaks, prime rib, chicken, seafood and baby back ribs. Yummy desserts merit a splurge. Guests can call ahead to facilitate seating. Casual dress. **Bar:** Full bar. **Hours:** 11 am-10 pm, Fri & Sat-11 pm. Closed: 12/25. **Address:** 954 Blowing Rock Blvd **Location:** Jct US 321/321 alternate route, just se on US 321. **Parking:** on-site. **Cards:** AX, DC, DS, MC, VI.

CALL

LEXINGTON pop. 19,953

WHERE TO STAY

COMFORT SUITES OF LEXINGTON Book at AAA.com **Phone:** 336/357-2333

Hotel
Rates not provided

Address: 1620 Cotton Grove Rd **Location:** I-85, exit 91, just s on SR 8, then just ne. **Facility:** Smoke free premises. 120 one-bedroom standard units, some with whirlpools. 2 stories (no elevator), interior/exterior corridors. **Parking:** on-site. **Terms:** check-in 4 pm. **Amenities:** voice mail, irons, hair dryers. *Some:* high-speed Internet. **Pool(s):** outdoor. **Leisure Activities:** exercise room. **Guest Services:** valet and coin laundry, wireless Internet. **Business Services:** meeting rooms.

CALL / SOME UNITS FEE

ECONO LODGE **Phone:** (336)249-0111

Motel
$75-$125 All Year

Address: 418 Piedmont Dr **Location:** I-85, exit 96, 3.9 mi w on US 64. **Facility:** 100 one-bedroom standard units. 2 stories (no elevator), exterior corridors. **Parking:** on-site. **Terms:** cancellation fee imposed. **Amenities:** irons, hair dryers. **Pool(s):** outdoor. **Guest Services:** coin laundry. **Business Services:** meeting rooms. **Cards:** AX, CB, DC, DS, JC, MC, VI. **Free Special Amenities: continental breakfast and high-speed Internet.**

/ SOME UNITS FEE FEE FEE

QUALITY INN Book at AAA.com **Phone:** (336)243-2929

Hotel
$99-$150 All Year

Address: 101 Plaza Pkwy **Location:** I-85, exit 91, just n on SR 8, then 0.4 mi ne. **Facility:** 59 one-bedroom standard units, some with whirlpools. 3 stories, interior corridors. *Bath:* combo or shower only. **Parking:** on-site. **Terms:** 7 day cancellation notice-fee imposed. **Amenities:** high-speed Internet, irons, hair dryers. **Pool(s):** outdoor. **Guest Services:** wireless Internet. **Business Services:** meeting rooms, PC. **Cards:** AX, DC, DS, MC, VI.

ASK CALL / SOME UNITS

WHERE TO DINE

JIMMY'S BARBECUE — Regional American $4-$9 — **Phone:** 336/357-2311

The locally popular restaurant features traditional North Carolina-style barbecue. The atmosphere, as well as the service, is very casual. Casual dress. **Hours:** 6 am-9:30 pm. Closed major holidays; also Tues. **Address:** 1703 Cotton Grove Rd **Location:** I-85, exit 91, just s on SR 8. **Parking:** on-site. **Cards:** MC, VI.

LEXINGTON BARBECUE 1 — Regional American $4-$10 — **Phone:** 336/249-9814

A no-frills, self-seating type of eatery, the 1950s roadside-style diner serves excellent barbecue, coleslaw and french fries. For those who love the down-home style of cooking, this is dining at its finest. Casual dress. **Hours:** 10 am-9:30 pm. Closed major holidays; also Sun. **Address:** 10 Hwy 29-70 S **Location:** I-85, exit 96, 5.8 mi w on US 64. **Parking:** on-site. **Cards:** MC, VI.

SPEEDY'S BARBECUE — Barbecue $3-$11 — **Phone:** 336/248-2410

You can get good and messy digging into the succulent ribs and sauce-drenched chopped meats at this "barbecue country" hot spot. Casual dress. **Hours:** 10:30 am-9 pm. Closed major holidays; also Sun. **Address:** 1317 Winston Rd (SR 8) **Location:** Jct US 64, 0.6 mi n on SR 8. **Parking:** on-site. **Cards:** DS, MC, VI.

LILLINGTON pop. 2,915

WHERE TO STAY

MICROTEL INN & SUITES — Book at AAA.com — Hotel, Rates not provided — **Phone:** 910/893-2626

Address: 300 E Cornelius Harnett Blvd **Location:** Jct US 401/SR 210, just ne on US 421/SR 27. **Facility:** 57 one-bedroom standard units. 3 stories, interior corridors. *Bath:* combo or shower only. **Parking:** on-site. **Amenities:** voice mail, hair dryers. **Leisure Activities:** exercise room. **Guest Services:** coin laundry, wireless Internet. **Business Services:** meeting rooms.

CALL / SOME UNITS

WHERE TO DINE

HOWARD'S BARBECUE & SEAFOOD — Regional American $5-$15 — **Phone:** 910/893-4571

Overlooking Cape Fear River and popular with locals, the barbecue joint offers pulled-pork barbecue and chicken, fried fish, shrimp and other seafood. Traditional sides include coleslaw, Southern green beans and hushpuppies. Casual dress. **Hours:** 10:30 am-8:30 pm. Closed: Sun & Mon. **Address:** 100 S Main St **Location:** On US 401/SR 210; just s of Cape Fear River. **Parking:** on-site. **Cards:** DS, MC, VI.

LINCOLNTON pop. 9,965

WHERE TO STAY

COMFORT INN — Book at AAA.com — Hotel $66-$99 All Year — **Phone:** (704)732-0011

Address: 1550 E Main St **Location:** US 321, exit 24, just w on SR 150. **Facility:** 77 one-bedroom standard units, some with whirlpools. 3 stories, interior/exterior corridors. **Parking:** on-site. **Amenities:** irons, hair dryers. **Pool(s):** outdoor. **Guest Services:** valet and coin laundry, wireless Internet. **Business Services:** meeting rooms. **Cards:** AX, CB, DC, DS, JC, MC, VI.

ASK / SOME UNITS

DAYS INN — Book at AAA.com — Motel $50-$80 All Year — **Phone:** (704)735-8271

Address: 614 Clark Dr **Location:** US 321, exit 24, 1 mi w on SR 150, then just s on US 321 business route. **Facility:** 62 one-bedroom standard units. 2 stories (no elevator), exterior corridors. **Parking:** on-site. **Amenities:** hair dryers. *Some:* dual phone lines, irons. **Pool(s):** outdoor. **Guest Services:** wireless Internet. **Business Services:** meeting rooms, PC. **Cards:** AX, DS, MC, VI.

ASK / SOME UNITS FEE VCR

WHERE TO DINE

SAGEBRUSH STEAKHOUSE — American $5-$19 — **Phone:** 704/735-1455

Born from the spirit of Texas cattle drives, the restaurant presents a menu of hearty steaks, prime rib, chicken, seafood and baby back ribs. Yummy desserts merit a splurge. Guests can call ahead to facilitate seating. Casual dress. **Bar:** Full bar. **Hours:** 11 am-10 pm, Fri & Sat-11 pm. Closed: 12/25. **Address:** 112 N Generals Blvd **Location:** Jct SR 27/155. **Parking:** on-site. **Cards:** AX, DC, DS, MC, VI.

CALL

LINVILLE FALLS

WHERE TO DINE

SPEAR'S SMOKEHOUSE GRILL — American $6-$23 — **Phone:** 828/765-2658

The restaurant is tucked in the mountains just off the Blue Ridge Parkway. This place smokes its own meats, and the baked beans are excellent. Casual dress. Entertainment. **Bar:** Full bar. **Hours:** Open 5/1-11/30; 11 am-9 pm; seasonal hours vary. Closed: 12/25. **Address:** Hwy 221 N & SR 183 **Location:** 1 mi s on US 221 S from Blue Ridge Pkwy, jct SR 183. **Parking:** on-site. **Cards:** AX, DC, DS, MC, VI.

LITTLE SWITZERLAND

WHERE TO STAY

SWITZERLAND INN — Phone: 828/765-2153

Country Inn
$110-$220 4/18-11/11

Address: 86 High Ridge Rd **Location:** Jct SR 226A and Blue Ridge Pkwy, MM 334. **Facility:** On top of a mountain, the inn offers outstanding views; its rustic rooms have many modern amenities. 64 units. 52 one-bedroom standard units, some with whirlpools. 7 one-bedroom suites. 5 cottages. 2 stories (no elevator), interior/exterior corridors. *Bath:* combo or shower only. **Parking:** on-site. **Terms:** open 4/18-11/11, office hours 7 am-11 am, 7 day cancellation notice-fee imposed. **Amenities:** irons, hair dryers. **Pool(s):** heated outdoor. **Leisure Activities:** whirlpools, 2 tennis courts, hiking trails, horseshoes, shuffleboard. **Guest Services:** wireless Internet. **Business Services:** meeting rooms. **Cards:** AX, MC, VI.

/SOME UNITS

LOUISBURG pop. 3,111

WHERE TO STAY

DAYS INN LOUISBURG — *Book at AAA.com* — **Phone:** (919)340-4449

Hotel
$73-$116 All Year

Address: 201 Sandlewood Ave **Location:** Jct SR 581, just s on US 401/SR 39, then just e. **Facility:** 53 units. 52 one-bedroom standard units, some with whirlpools. 1 one-bedroom suite with efficiency. 2 stories (no elevator), interior corridors. *Bath:* combo or shower only. **Parking:** on-site. **Terms:** cancellation fee imposed. **Amenities:** dual phone lines, voice mail, irons, hair dryers. **Pool(s):** outdoor. **Leisure Activities:** limited exercise equipment. **Guest Services:** valet laundry, wireless Internet. **Business Services:** meeting rooms. **Cards:** AX, CB, DC, DS, MC, VI.

ASK CALL /SOME UNITS

WHERE TO DINE

BAXTER'S ALE HOUSE — **Phone:** 919/496-6909

American
$6-$20

Steaks and ribs are the specialty of the house at the casual downtown eatery. Also on the menu are wings, burgers, chicken and a few seafood items. Casual dress. **Bar:** Full bar. **Hours:** Tues 4 pm-10 pm, Wed 11 am-midnight, Thurs 11 am-10 pm, Fri 11 am-2 am, Sat 4 pm-2 am, Sun 1 pm-9 pm. Closed: 11/26, 12/25; also Mon. **Address:** 200 E Nash St **Location:** Jct US 401, just w; downtown. **Parking:** street. **Cards:** AX, MC, VI.

LUMBERTON pop. 20,795

— WHERE TO STAY —

BEST WESTERN INN

Book great rates at AAA.com

Phone: (910)618-9799

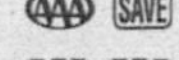

Motel

$79-$149 All Year

Address: 201 Jackson Ct **Location:** I-95, exit 22, just e, then just s. **Facility:** 63 one-bedroom standard units. 2 stories (no elevator), exterior corridors. *Bath:* combo or shower only. **Parking:** on-site. **Amenities:** high-speed Internet, irons, hair dryers. **Pool(s):** outdoor. **Guest Services:** valet laundry, wireless Internet. **Business Services:** meeting rooms. **Cards:** AX, CB, DC, DS, MC, VI. **Free Special Amenities: expanded continental breakfast and local telephone calls.** *(See color ad below)*

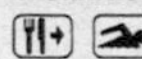  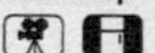   / SOME UNITS FEE 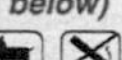 

AAA Benefit:

Members save up to 20%, plus 10% bonus points with rewards program.

COMFORT INN

Phone: (910)739-4800

Motel

$69-$99 All Year

Address: 3070 Roberts Ave **Location:** I-95, exit 20, just w. **Facility:** 62 one-bedroom standard units, some with whirlpools. 2 stories (no elevator), exterior corridors. **Parking:** on-site. **Amenities:** high-speed Internet, irons, hair dryers. **Pool(s):** outdoor. **Leisure Activities:** limited exercise equipment. **Guest Services:** valet laundry. **Cards:** AX, CB, DC, DS, JC, MC, VI.

ASK / SOME UNITS

COUNTRY INN & SUITES BY CARLSON

Book great rates at AAA.com

Phone: (910)738-3838

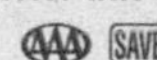

Hotel

$75-$150 All Year

Address: 3010 Roberts Ave **Location:** I-95, exit 20, just w. **Facility:** Smoke free premises. 57 units. 47 one-bedroom standard units. 10 one-bedroom suites. 4 stories, interior corridors. *Bath:* combo or shower only. **Parking:** on-site. **Terms:** cancellation fee imposed. **Amenities:** high-speed Internet, voice mail, irons, hair dryers. **Pool(s):** outdoor. **Leisure Activities:** exercise room. **Guest Services:** complimentary and valet laundry. **Business Services:** PC. **Cards:** AX, DC, DS, MC, VI. **Free Special Amenities: expanded continental breakfast and high-speed Internet.** *(See color ad p 751)*

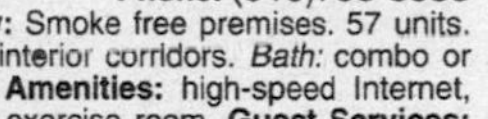

FAIRFIELD INN BY MARRIOTT

Book great rates at AAA.com

Phone: (910)739-8444

Hotel

$98-$106 All Year

Address: 3361 Lackey St **Location:** I-95, exit 20, just w, then 0.5 mi s. **Facility:** Smoke free premises. 104 one-bedroom standard units. 3 stories, interior corridors. *Bath:* combo or shower only. **Parking:** on-site. **Terms:** cancellation fee imposed. **Amenities:** video games (fee), voice mail, irons, hair dryers. **Pool(s):** outdoor. **Leisure Activities:** exercise room. **Guest Services:** valet and coin laundry, wireless Internet. **Business Services:** business center. **Cards:** AX, CB, DC, DS, MC, VI. **Free Special Amenities: expanded continental breakfast and high-speed Internet.**

   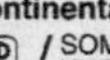   / SOME UNITS

AAA Benefit:

Members save a minimum 5% off the best available rate.

▼ See AAA listing above ▼

HAMPTON INN *Book great rates at AAA.com* **Phone:** (910)738-3332

Hotel
$89-$109 All Year

Address: 201 Wintergreen Dr **Location:** I-95, exit 22, just e, then just n. **Facility:** 68 one-bedroom standard units. 2 stories (no elevator), interior/exterior corridors. **Parking:** on-site. **Terms:** 1-30 night minimum stay, cancellation fee imposed. **Amenities:** voice mail, irons, hair dryers. **Pool(s):** outdoor. **Leisure Activities:** sauna, exercise room. **Guest Services:** valet and coin laundry, wireless Internet. **Business Services:** business center. **Cards:** AX, CB, DC, DS, MC, VI. **Free Special Amenities: expanded continental breakfast and high-speed Internet.** *(See color ad below)*

AAA Benefit:
Members save up to 10% everyday!

CALL / SOME UNITS

HOLIDAY INN *Book great rates at AAA.com* **Phone:** (910)671-1166

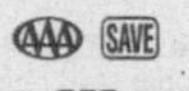

Hotel
$89-$145 All Year

Address: 101 Wintergreen Dr **Location:** I-95, exit 22, just e. **Facility:** 107 one-bedroom standard units. 2 stories (no elevator), interior corridors. **Parking:** on-site. **Amenities:** high-speed Internet, voice mail, irons, hair dryers. **Pool(s):** outdoor. **Leisure Activities:** exercise room. **Guest Services:** valet and coin laundry, wireless Internet. **Business Services:** conference facilities. **Cards:** AX, DC, DS, MC, VI. *(See color ad below)*

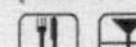

/ SOME UNITS FEE

▼ *See AAA listing above* ▼

▼ *See AAA listing above* ▼

QUALITY INN AND SUITES *Book great rates at AAA.com* **Phone:** (910)738-8261

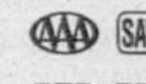

Hotel
$60-$99 All Year

Address: 3608 Kahn Dr **Location:** I-95, exit 20, just e, then just n. **Facility:** 120 units. 94 one-bedroom standard units. 26 one-bedroom suites. 2 stories (no elevator), interior/exterior corridors. **Parking:** on-site. **Amenities:** high-speed Internet, irons, hair dryers. **Pool(s):** outdoor. **Guest Services:** valet laundry, wireless Internet. **Business Services:** meeting rooms. **Cards:** AX, CB, DC, DS, MC, VI. **Free Special Amenities: continental breakfast and high-speed Internet.**

/ SOME UNITS FEE

▼ See AAA listing p 749 ▼

WHERE TO DINE

ABIGAIL'S TEA ROOM **Phone:** 910/272-0660

American
$5-$10

If it's gourmet you seek, look no further. The tiny bistro features homemade soups, salads, quiche and gourmet sandwiches as well as a large selection of gourmet teas and coffees. Casual dress. **Reservations:** accepted. **Hours:** 11 am-3 pm, Fri & Sat also 5 pm-9 pm. Closed major holidays; also Sun. **Address:** 4531 Fayetteville Rd **Location:** I-95, exit 22, 1 mi e; in Sisters Boutique Building. **Parking:** on-site. **Cards:** MC, VI.

BLACK WATER GRILLE *Menu on AAA.com* **Phone:** 910/738-5566

American
$6-$23

In a vintage building downtown, the casual eatery presents a lengthy menu of varied fare. In addition to grilled steaks, salads and burgers, diners will find specialties of Creole chicken, shrimp and grits and chicken parmigiana, as well as pasta, seafood and sandwiches. Casual dress. **Bar:** Full bar. **Hours:** 11 am-11 pm, Fri-2 am, Sat 5 pm-2 am. Closed: 11/26, 12/25; also Sun. **Address:** 111 W 3rd St **Location:** I-95, exit 20, 0.4 mi e on Roberts Ave, 1.6 mi s on Elm St, then just w. **Parking:** on-site. **Cards:** AX, DS, MC, VI.

FULLER'S OLD FASHIONED BAR-B-Q **Phone:** 910/738-8694

American
$6-$9

Enjoy a lunch or dinner buffet at the family-owned restaurant, with selections such as fried chicken, pulled-pork barbecue and lots of vegetables, including corn-on-the-cob and turnip greens. Casual dress. **Hours:** 11 am-9 pm, Sun-4 pm. Closed: 1/1, 5/25, 12/25. **Address:** 3201 Roberts Ave **Location:** I-95, exit 20, 0.4 mi w. **Parking:** on-site. **Cards:** AX, DS, MC, VI.

LUNG WAH CHINESE RESTAURANT **Phone:** 910/739-8888

Chinese
$4-$10

The popular eatery's lunch and dinner buffets line up traditional Chinese fare. Lunch specials and carry-out service are available. Casual dress. **Bar:** Full bar. **Hours:** 11 am-9 pm. Closed: 11/26, 12/25. **Address:** 3417 Lackey St **Location:** I-95, exit 20, just w, then 0.4 mi s. **Parking:** on-site. **Cards:** AX, DS, MC, VI.

PIER 41 SEAFOOD **Phone:** 910/738-8555

Seafood
$5-$10

Locals love the seafood house for the fried and broiled fare that fills its menu. Fish, scallops, shrimp, deviled crab and oysters are offered, as are a salad bar and a few landlubber items. Casual dress. **Hours:** 11 am-9 pm, Sun-8 pm, Wed & Thurs 4 pm-9 pm. Closed: 11/26, 12/25; also Mon & Tues. **Address:** 2401 E Elizabethtown Rd **Location:** I-95, exit 20, 1.5 mi e on Roberts Ave, then just n on SR 41. **Parking:** on-site. **Cards:** MC, VI.

SAN JOSE MEXICAN RESTAURANT **Phone:** 910/671-0866

Mexican
$4-$12

Patrons can snack on tortilla chips and salsa while browsing the lengthy menu of combination platters with all the traditional favorites. Casual dress. **Bar:** Full bar. **Hours:** 11 am-10 pm, Fri-10:30 pm, Sat noon-10:30 pm, Sun noon-9 pm. Closed: 11/26, 12/25. **Address:** 3027 N Roberts Ave **Location:** I-95, exit 20, just w. **Parking:** on-site. **Cards:** AX, DS, MC, VI.

TEXAS STEAKHOUSE & SALOON **Phone:** 910/739-8918

Steak
$6-$25

The typical Texas-style roadhouse focuses on freshly cut steaks, including the popular Duke entree with fries. Southwestern decor and arrows stuck in the walls get diners' minds wandering back to the old days. The popular draft beer is the microbrewed Red Oak lager. Casual dress. **Bar:** Full bar. **Hours:** 11 am-10 pm, Fri & Sat-11 pm. Closed: 11/26, 12/24, 12/25. **Address:** 5093 Fayetteville Rd **Location:** I-95, exit 22, just e. **Parking:** on-site. **Cards:** AX, DS, MC, VI.

VILLAGE STATION RESTAURANT **Phone:** 910/739-0211

American
$5-$14

Since 1976, the train station-themed restaurant has been the locals' favorite for steaks, chicken and pizza. It also offers an extensive salad bar. Casual dress. **Bar:** Beer & wine. **Hours:** 11 am-10 pm, Fri & Sat-10:30 pm, Sun-9 pm. Closed: 11/26, 12/25; also Wed. **Address:** 2725 Roberts Ave **Location:** I-95, exit 20, just e. **Parking:** on-site. **Cards:** MC, VI.

ZENO'S ITALIAN RESTAURANT **Phone:** 910/735-0352

Italian
$5-$15

On the menu are Italian favorites such as pizza, spaghetti, lasagna, stromboli and calzones. Casual dress. **Hours:** 11 am-10 pm, Fri & Sat-11 pm. Closed: 11/26. **Address:** 1925 N Roberts Ave **Location:** I-95, exit 20, 1.5 mi e. **Parking:** on-site. **Cards:** AX, DC, MC, VI.

MAGGIE VALLEY pop. 607

WHERE TO STAY

APPLECOVER INN MOTEL

Phone: 828/926-9100

Motel
Rates not provided

Address: 4077 Soco Rd **Location:** US 19, 4.5 mi w of US 276. Located adjacent to RV park. **Facility:** 20 one-bedroom standard units. 1 story, exterior corridors. *Bath:* combo or shower only. **Parking:** on-site. **Terms:** open 5/1-10/31. **Leisure Activities:** playground. **Guest Services:** coin laundry, wireless Internet.

/ SOME UNITS

BEST WESTERN MOUNTAINBROOK INN

Book great rates at AAA.com

Phone: (828)926-3962

AAA SAVE

Motel
$45-$149 All Year

Address: 3811 Soco Rd **Location:** US 19, 4 mi w of US 276. Located opposite the Carolina Nights Dinner Theater. **Facility:** 50 one-bedroom standard units. 2 stories (no elevator), exterior corridors. *Bath:* combo or shower only. **Parking:** on-site. **Terms:** cancellation fee imposed. **Amenities:** irons, hair dryers. **Pool(s):** heated outdoor. **Leisure Activities:** whirlpool, picnic area with barbecue grills. **Guest Services:** coin laundry, wireless Internet. **Business Services:** PC, fax. **Cards:** AX, CB, DC, DS, JC, MC, VI. **Free Special Amenities: expanded continental breakfast and high-speed Internet.**

CALL / SOME UNITS FEE

AAA Benefit:
Members save up to 20%, plus 10% bonus points with rewards program.

CASTLEWOOD INN

Phone: 828/926-1480

Motel
Rates not provided

Address: 3695 Soco Rd **Location:** US 19, 3.6 mi w of US 276. **Facility:** 34 one-bedroom standard units, some with whirlpools. 2 stories (no elevator), exterior corridors. **Parking:** on-site. **Amenities:** video library, hair dryers. **Pool(s):** heated outdoor. **Leisure Activities:** whirlpool. **Business Services:** fax.

/ SOME UNITS FEE

COMFORT INN

Book great rates at AAA.com

Phone: (828)926-9106

Hotel
$49-$169 All Year

Address: 3282 Soco Rd **Location:** US 19, 3.3 mi w of US 276. **Facility:** 68 units. 67 one-bedroom standard units, some with whirlpools. 1 one-bedroom suite with kitchen and whirlpool. 2 stories (no elevator), interior corridors. **Parking:** on-site. **Terms:** 2 night minimum stay - seasonal, cancellation fee imposed. **Amenities:** voice mail, irons, hair dryers. **Pool(s):** heated indoor. **Leisure Activities:** whirlpool. **Guest Services:** coin laundry, wireless Internet. **Cards:** AX, DS, MC, VI.

/ SOME UNITS

JONATHAN CREEK INN & VILLAS

Phone: (828)926-1232

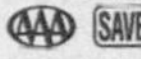

Motel
$65-$150 5/26-11/30
$50-$150 12/1-5/25

Address: 4324 Soco Rd **Location:** US 19, 4.3 mi w of US 276. Located in a quiet setting. **Facility:** 51 units. 44 one-bedroom standard units, some with whirlpools. 7 houses. 2 stories (no elevator), exterior corridors. **Parking:** on-site. **Terms:** 2 night minimum stay - seasonal and/or weekends, 60 day cancellation notice, in villas. **Amenities:** irons, hair dryers. *Some:* DVD players. **Pool(s):** heated indoor. **Leisure Activities:** whirlpool, fishing, hot tubs at vacation homes, playground, basketball. **Guest Services:** coin laundry, wireless Internet. **Business Services:** business center. **Cards:** AX, DS, MC, VI.

/ SOME UNITS

MICROTEL INN & SUITES

Book great rates at AAA.com

Phone: 828/926-8554

Hotel
Rates not provided

Address: 3777 Soco Rd, Hwy 19 **Location:** US 19, 4 mi w of US 276. Located opposite the Carolina Nights Dinner Theater. **Facility:** 57 one-bedroom standard units, some with whirlpools. 2 stories, interior corridors. *Bath:* combo or shower only. **Parking:** on-site. **Amenities:** irons, hair dryers. **Pool(s):** heated indoor. **Leisure Activities:** whirlpool, picnic area with barbecue grills. **Guest Services:** coin laundry, wireless Internet. **Business Services:** meeting rooms, fax (fee). **Free Special Amenities: continental breakfast and local telephone calls.**

CALL / SOME UNITS

PEPPERTREE RESORT VILLAS

Book at AAA.com

Phone: (828)926-3761

Vacation Rental Condominium
$950 5/31-11/30
$850 12/1-5/30

Address: 265 Moody Farm Rd **Location:** US 19, just n; in Maggie Valley Country Club. Located on golf course. **Facility:** Clusters of buildings are set in a beautiful mountain area, with some of the units by a golf course; units are decorated in a mountain rustic style. 40 two-bedroom suites with kitchens and whirlpools. 2 stories (no elevator), exterior corridors. **Parking:** on-site. **Terms:** office hours 9 am-5 pm, check-in 4 pm, 45 day cancellation notice. **Amenities:** video library, irons, hair dryers. *Some:* DVD players. **Pool(s):** heated outdoor. **Leisure Activities:** whirlpool, fishing, golf-18 holes, 2 tennis courts, playground, exercise room. **Guest Services:** complimentary laundry, wireless Internet. **Business Services:** PC.

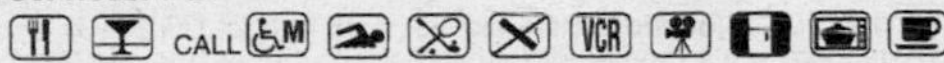

RAMADA LIMITED OF MAGGIE VALLEY *Book great rates at AAA.com* **Phone:** (828)926-7800

Motel

$49-$149 All Year

Address: 4048 Soco Rd **Location:** US 19, 4.3 mi w of US 276. **Facility:** 46 one-bedroom standard units, some with whirlpools. 2 stories (no elevator), interior corridors. *Bath:* combo or shower only. **Parking:** on-site. **Terms:** cancellation fee imposed. **Amenities:** irons, hair dryers. **Pool(s):** heated indoor. **Leisure Activities:** whirlpool. **Guest Services:** coin laundry, wireless Internet. **Business Services:** PC, fax (fee). **Cards:** AX, DC, DS, MC, VI. **Free Special Amenities: expanded continental breakfast and high-speed Internet.**

CALL / SOME UNITS

SCOTTISH INN *Book great rates at AAA.com* **Phone:** (828)926-9137

Motel

$45-$125 5/1-11/30

$35-$70 12/1-4/30

Address: 178 Soco Rd **Location:** US 19, just w of US 276. **Facility:** 21 one-bedroom standard units. 1 story, exterior corridors. **Parking:** on-site, winter plug-ins. **Terms:** 3 day cancellation notice-fee imposed. **Amenities:** high-speed Internet. **Pool(s):** outdoor. **Leisure Activities:** small picnic area with cooking grills. **Cards:** AX, DS, MC, VI. **Free Special Amenities: continental breakfast and local telephone calls.**

/ SOME UNITS

WHERE TO DINE

BEAR'S DEN FAMILY GRILL **Phone:** 828/926-2626

American

$6-$23

After a day of adventure, patrons can opt to take to the porch to eat in the fresh air. The menu lists just about everything you would expect from a grill: burgers, sandwiches, nachos and more. Casual dress. **Bar:** Full bar. **Hours:** 11:30 am-9 pm, Fri & Sat-10 pm, Sun-8 pm. Closed: Tues & Mon-Thurs 10/31-4/1. **Address:** 3434 Soco Rd **Location:** US 19, 3.5 mi w of US 276; across from Market Square. **Parking:** on-site. **Cards:** AX, DC, DS, MC, VI.

GUAYABITOS MEXICAN RESTAURANT **Phone:** 828/926-7777

Mexican

$5-$14

Diners enjoy traditional Mexican fare at the family-owned restaurant on the edge of Maggie Valley. Casual dress. **Bar:** Full bar. **Reservations:** accepted. **Hours:** 11 am-2:30 & 5-10 pm, Sat & Sun noon-10 pm. Closed major holidays. **Address:** 3422 Old Towne Plaza Soco Rd **Location:** US 19, 3.4 mi w of US 276. **Parking:** on-site. **Cards:** AX, DS, MC, VI.

J. ARTHUR'S RESTAURANT **Phone:** 828/926-1817

Steak & Seafood

$13-$28

Prime rib, fresh trout and gorgonzola cheese salad are among modestly prepared specialties served in a two-story, pine-paneled dining room. With fireplaces and a country decor, the cozy and homey atmosphere is just right for dinner with the family. Casual dress. **Bar:** Full bar. **Reservations:** accepted. **Hours:** 4:30 pm-close. Closed: 11/26, 12/25; also Sun-Tues 11/1-5/7. **Address:** 2843 Soco Rd **Location:** US 19, 2.8 mi w of jct US 276. **Parking:** on-site. **Cards:** AX, MC, VI.

CALL

JOEY'S PANCAKE HOUSE **Phone:** 828/926-0212

American

$4-$11

Service is friendly and cheery at the unassuming, breakfast-only restaurant, which is set apart by its delicious specialty pancakes. Slip into the east-facing washrooms to see pretty stained-glass windows. Joey and family have operated this place since 1966. Casual dress. **Reservations:** not accepted. **Hours:** Open 12/1-2/28 & 4/1-11/30; 7 am-noon; hours vary in winter. Closed: 11/26, 12/25; also Thurs. **Address:** 4309 Soco Rd **Location:** US 19, 4.5 mi w of US 276; opposite the post office. **Parking:** on-site. **Cards:** MC, VI.

CALL

SALTY DOG'S SEAFOOD & GRILL **Phone:** 828/926-9105

Seafood

$7-$15

The food is not the only item of enjoyment at the informal, family-operated restaurant. The ceiling is a gallery of kids' artwork, business cards and vacation memorabilia; it's a sight to behold. Seafood, particularly of the fried persuasion, is the forte, but also served is blacken, grilled and broiled seafood and chicken. Casual dress. **Bar:** Full bar. **Hours:** 4 pm-9 pm, Sat & Sun from noon. Closed: 11/26, 12/25. **Address:** 3567 Soco Rd **Location:** US 19, 3.8 mi w of US 276. **Parking:** on-site. **Cards:** MC, VI.

CALL

MANTEO —*See Outer Banks p. 781.*

MARION pop. 4,943

WHERE TO STAY

COMFORT INN *Book at AAA.com* **Phone:** (828)652-4888

Hotel

$70-$150 All Year

Address: 178 Hwy 70 W **Location:** I-40, exit 85, 5 mi n to jct US 221 N Bypass and 70. **Facility:** 56 one-bedroom standard units, some with whirlpools. 2 stories (no elevator), interior corridors. *Bath:* combo or shower only. **Parking:** on-site. **Terms:** cancellation fee imposed. **Amenities:** irons, hair dryers. **Pool(s):** heated indoor. **Leisure Activities:** whirlpool. **Guest Services:** valet and coin laundry, wireless Internet. **Business Services:** meeting rooms, PC. **Cards:** AX, DC, DS, MC, VI.

ASK / SOME UNITS

HAMPTON INN *Book great rates at AAA.com* **Phone:** (828)652-5100

Hotel
$99-$129 All Year

Address: 3560 US 221 S **Location:** I-40, exit 85, just n. **Facility:** 66 one-bedroom standard units, some with whirlpools. 3 stories, interior corridors. *Bath:* combo or shower only. **Parking:** on-site. **Terms:** 1-30 night minimum stay, cancellation fee imposed. **Amenities:** dual phone lines, voice mail, irons, hair dryers. *Some:* high-speed Internet. **Pool(s):** heated indoor. **Leisure Activities:** whirlpool, exercise room. **Guest Services:** coin laundry, wireless Internet. **Business Services:** meeting rooms, PC, fax (fee). **Cards:** AX, CB, DC, DS, MC, VI.

CALL / SOME UNITS

AAA Benefit:
Members save up to 10% everyday!

WHERE TO DINE

CAROLINA CHOCOLATIER **Phone:** 828/652-4496

American
$4-$22

Lunches—such as freshly prepared salads, sandwiches and soups—are tasty, but many patrons rush through them to get to the decadent desserts: tasty homemade baked goods and sinful confections. A buffet is set up Sunday. Casual dress. **Hours:** 9:30 am-3 pm, Thurs-Sat 5 pm-2 am, Sun 11 am-2 pm. Closed: 12/25-1/2. **Address:** 8 N Main St **Location:** Center. **Parking:** street. **Cards:** AX, DS, MC, VI.

MOONDOGGY'S CLASSIC DINER **Phone:** 828/655-1557

American
$5-$14

Patrons can enjoy sandwiches and dinner entrees in the evening while reminiscing to rock 'n' roll oldies. The dining room is decorated with such memorabilia as gas signs and pictures and posters of movie and television personalities of the era. Casual dress. **Reservations:** accepted. **Hours:** 11 am-9 pm. Closed: 11/26, 12/25; also Sun. **Address:** 909 N Main St **Location:** Jct US 70 and 221 Bypass, 1.5 mi n. **Parking:** on-site. **Cards:** MC, VI.

CALL

MARS HILL pop. 1,764

WHERE TO STAY

COMFORT INN *Book at AAA.com* **Phone:** (828)689-9000

Hotel
$89-$159 All Year

Address: 167 J F Robinson Ln **Location:** US 19/23, exit 11. **Facility:** 56 one-bedroom standard units. 4 stories, interior corridors. *Bath:* combo or shower only. **Parking:** on-site. **Terms:** 2 night minimum stay - seasonal and/or weekends. **Amenities:** irons, hair dryers. **Pool(s):** outdoor. **Guest Services:** coin laundry, wireless Internet. **Business Services:** PC, fax. **Cards:** AX, DC, DS, MC, VI.

ASK / SOME UNITS

MATTHEWS —*See Charlotte p. 665.*

MCLEANSVILLE pop. 1,080

WHERE TO STAY

HAMPTON INN-GREENSBORO EAST/MCLEANSVILLE *Book great rates at AAA.com* **Phone:** (336)544-3333

Hotel
$85-$189 All Year

Address: 903 Knox Rd **Location:** I-85/40, exit 132, just n on Mt Hope Church Rd, then just e. **Facility:** 78 one-bedroom standard units, some with whirlpools. 3 stories, interior corridors. *Bath:* combo or shower only. **Parking:** on-site. **Terms:** 1-30 night minimum stay, cancellation fee imposed. **Amenities:** high-speed Internet, dual phone lines, voice mail, irons, hair dryers. **Pool(s):** outdoor. **Leisure Activities:** exercise room. **Guest Services:** coin laundry, wireless Internet. **Business Services:** meeting rooms, business center. **Cards:** AX, CB, DC, DS, MC, VI.

CALL / SOME UNITS

AAA Benefit:
Members save up to 10% everyday!

MEBANE pop. 7,284

WHERE TO STAY

HAMPTON INN *Book great rates at AAA.com* **Phone:** (919)563-5400

Hotel
$94-$160 All Year

Address: 105 Spring Forest Dr **Location:** I-40/85, exit 153, just s, then just e. **Facility:** 63 one-bedroom standard units, some with whirlpools. 3 stories, interior corridors. *Bath:* combo or shower only. **Parking:** on-site. **Terms:** check-in 3:45 pm, 1-30 night minimum stay, cancellation fee imposed. **Amenities:** voice mail, irons, hair dryers. **Pool(s):** outdoor. **Leisure Activities:** exercise room. **Guest Services:** coin laundry, wireless Internet. **Business Services:** meeting rooms, business center. **Cards:** AX, CB, DC, DS, MC, VI.

AAA Benefit:
Members save up to 10% everyday!

HOLIDAY INN EXPRESS HOTEL & SUITES *Book at AAA.com* **Phone:** 919/304-9900

Hotel
Rates not provided

Address: 149 Spring Forest Dr **Location:** I-40/85, exit 153, just s, then just e. **Facility:** 61 one-bedroom standard units, some with whirlpools. 3 stories, interior corridors. *Bath:* combo or shower only. **Parking:** on-site. **Amenities:** high-speed Internet, dual phone lines, voice mail, irons, hair dryers. **Pool(s):** outdoor. **Leisure Activities:** exercise room. **Guest Services:** valet laundry, wireless Internet. **Business Services:** meeting rooms, PC.

CALL / SOME UNITS

MOCKSVILLE pop. 4,178

WHERE TO STAY

COMFORT INN & SUITES *Book great rates at AAA.com* **Phone:** (336)751-5966

AAA SAVE

Hotel
$46-$200 All Year

Address: 629 Madison Rd **Location:** I-40, exit 170, just s on US 601, then just w. **Facility:** 61 one-bedroom standard units, some with whirlpools. 3 stories, interior corridors. *Bath:* combo or shower only. **Parking:** on-site. **Terms:** cancellation fee imposed. **Amenities:** high-speed Internet, dual phone lines, voice mail, irons, hair dryers. **Pool(s):** outdoor. **Leisure Activities:** exercise room. **Guest Services:** coin laundry, wireless Internet. **Business Services:** meeting rooms. **Cards:** AX, DS, MC, VI. **Free Special Amenities: expanded continental breakfast and high-speed Internet.**

CALL / SOME UNITS FEE

QUALITY INN *Book at AAA.com* **Phone:** (336)751-7310

Hotel
$64-$80 All Year

Address: 1500 Yadkinville Rd **Location:** I-40, exit 170, just s on US 601. **Facility:** 50 one-bedroom standard units, some with whirlpools. 2 stories (no elevator), exterior corridors. **Parking:** on-site. **Terms:** cancellation fee imposed. **Amenities:** irons, hair dryers. **Pool(s):** outdoor. **Guest Services:** valet laundry, wireless Internet. **Business Services:** meeting rooms. **Cards:** AX, CB, DC, DS, MC, VI.

ASK / SOME UNITS FEE

MONROE pop. 26,228

WHERE TO STAY

BEST WESTERN INN & SUITES-MONROE *Book great rates at AAA.com* **Phone:** (704)283-4746

AAA SAVE

Hotel
$90-$110 All Year

Address: 2316 Hanover Dr **Location:** Jct US 601, 1.3 mi w on US 74, then just s. **Facility:** 64 one-bedroom standard units, some with whirlpools. 2 stories (no elevator), exterior corridors. *Bath:* combo or shower only. **Parking:** on-site. **Terms:** 14 day cancellation notice. **Amenities:** high-speed Internet, voice mail, irons, hair dryers. **Pool(s):** outdoor. **Leisure Activities:** exercise room. **Guest Services:** valet and coin laundry, wireless Internet. **Business Services:** meeting rooms, PC. **Cards:** AX, CB, DC, DS, MC, VI. **Free Special Amenities: expanded continental breakfast and high-speed Internet.**

CALL / SOME UNITS FEE VCR

AAA Benefit:
Members save up to 20%, plus 10% bonus points with rewards program.

HAMPTON INN *Book great rates at AAA.com* **Phone:** (704)220-2200

Hotel
$105-$124 All Year

Address: 2368 Roland Dr **Location:** Jct US 601, 2 mi w on US 74, then just s. **Facility:** 79 one-bedroom standard units. 3 stories, interior corridors. *Bath:* combo or shower only. **Parking:** on-site. **Terms:** 1-30 night minimum stay, cancellation fee imposed. **Amenities:** dual phone lines, voice mail, irons, hair dryers. *Some:* DVD players. **Pool(s):** outdoor. **Guest Services:** valet laundry, wireless Internet. **Business Services:** meeting rooms, PC. **Cards:** AX, CB, DC, DS, MC, VI.

CALL / SOME UNITS VCR

AAA Benefit:
Members save up to 10% everyday!

HOLIDAY INN EXPRESS *Book at AAA.com* **Phone:** 704/289-1555

Hotel
Rates not provided

Address: 608-E W Roosevelt Blvd **Location:** Jct US 601, 1 mi e on US 74. **Facility:** 81 one-bedroom standard units, some with whirlpools. 2 stories (no elevator), exterior corridors. *Bath:* combo or shower only. **Parking:** on-site. **Amenities:** irons, hair dryers. **Pool(s):** indoor/outdoor. **Guest Services:** valet and coin laundry, wireless Internet. **Business Services:** meeting rooms, PC.

CALL FEE / SOME UNITS

QUALITY INN & SUITES *Book great rates at AAA.com* **Phone:** (704)283-9600

AAA SAVE

Hotel
$58-$110 All Year

Address: 2351 W Roosevelt Blvd **Location:** Jct US 601, 1.3 mi w on US 74. **Facility:** 65 one-bedroom standard units. 2 stories (no elevator), exterior corridors. **Parking:** on-site. **Amenities:** safes (fee), irons, hair dryers. **Pool(s):** outdoor. **Guest Services:** valet and coin laundry, wireless Internet. **Business Services:** meeting rooms, PC. **Cards:** AX, CB, DC, DS, JC, MC, VI. **Free Special Amenities: expanded continental breakfast and high-speed Internet.**

/ SOME UNITS FEE

WHERE TO DINE

CAPITAL CITY BISTRO **Phone:** 704/238-8162

American
$7-$20

Enjoy a friendly atmosphere with casual, comfortable dining. Located within part of a downtown building, the wood floor and brick walls reveal its historic origin. Although limited in number, entrees combine fresh ingredients with special seasonings and sauces, reflecting a hint of upscale cuisine. Casual dress. **Bar:** Full bar. **Hours:** 11 am-2:30 & 5:30-9:30 pm, Fri & Sat-11 pm. Closed: 7/4, 11/26, 12/25; also Sun. **Address:** 100 N Main St **Location:** Jct Windsor St; downtown. **Parking:** street. **Cards:** AX, DC, MC, VI.

CALL

CHINA BUFFET **Phone:** 704/238-8088

Chinese
$4-$12

Beef with broccoli, sesame chicken, spring rolls, dumplings and many other offerings line the expansive buffet. Sushi and some American favorites complement the predominant traditional Chinese fare. Casual dress. **Bar:** Beer & wine. **Hours:** 11 am-10 pm, Fri & Sat-11 pm. **Address:** 2116 W Roosevelt Blvd **Location:** Jct US 601, 1 mi w on US 74. **Parking:** on-site. **Cards:** MC, VI.

EL VALLARTA **Phone:** 704/283-0917

Mexican
$5-$13

The popular spot prepares such traditional Mexican fare as enchiladas, burritos, tacos and fajitas in addition to lunch specials and combination plates. Patio seating is an option. Casual dress. **Bar:** Full bar. **Hours:** 11 am-10 pm, Fri & Sat-11 pm. Closed: 11/26, 12/25. **Address:** 1890 W Roosevelt Blvd **Location:** Jct US 601, just w on US 74. **Parking:** on-site. **Cards:** AX, DS, MC, VI.

NAPOLI **Phone:** 704/292-1440

Italian
$6-$20

The menu lists a variety of Italian specialties, pastas, pizza and hot submarine sandwiches, as well as charcoal-grilled steaks, chicken and seafood. Sauces and dressings are homemade. The dining room resembles a patio, with arbors and covered booths. With the friendly staff, all elements combine for a relaxed, informal experience. Casual dress. **Bar:** Full bar. **Hours:** 11 am-10 pm, Fri & Sat-11 pm. Closed: 11/26, 12/25. **Address:** 2263 W Roosevelt Blvd **Location:** Jct US 601, 1.1 mi w on US 74. **Parking:** on-site. **Cards:** AX, DC, DS, MC, VI.

CALL

SAGEBRUSH STEAKHOUSE **Phone:** 704/289-8157

American
$5-$19

Born from the spirit of Texas cattle drives, the restaurant presents a menu of hearty steaks, prime rib, chicken, seafood and baby back ribs. Yummy desserts merit a splurge. Guests can call ahead to facilitate seating. Casual dress. **Bar:** Full bar. **Hours:** 11 am-10 pm, Fri & Sat-11 pm. Closed: 12/25. **Address:** 608-C W Roosevelt Blvd **Location:** Jct US 74/601/SR 200, just nw on US 74/601 (W Roosevelt Blvd). **Parking:** on-site. **Cards:** AX, DC, DS, MC, VI.

CALL

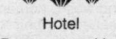

MOORESVILLE pop. 18,823

WHERE TO STAY

FAIRFIELD INN BY MARRIOTT *Book great rates at AAA.com* **Phone:** (704)663-6100

Hotel
$119-$127 All Year

Address: 120 Consumer Square Dr **Location:** I-77, exit 36, just e on SR 150, then just s. **Facility:** Smoke free premises. 97 one-bedroom standard units, some with whirlpools. 3 stories, interior corridors. *Bath:* combo or shower only. **Parking:** on-site. **Terms:** cancellation fee imposed. **Amenities:** high-speed Internet, voice mail, irons, hair dryers. **Pool(s):** outdoor. **Leisure Activities:** whirlpool, exercise room. **Guest Services:** valet and coin laundry, wireless Internet. **Business Services:** meeting rooms, PC. **Cards:** AX, DS, JC, MC, VI.

/ SOME UNITS

AAA Benefit:
Members save a minimum 5% off the best available rate.

HAMPTON INN & SUITES RACE CITY USA *Book great rates at AAA.com* **Phone:** (704)660-7700

Hotel
$129-$189 All Year

Address: 119 Gallery Center Dr **Location:** I-77, exit 36, just w on SR 150, just n on Regency Center Dr, then just e. **Facility:** 105 units. 79 one-bedroom standard units, some with whirlpools. 26 one-bedroom suites with efficiencies. 4 stories, interior corridors. *Bath:* combo or shower only. **Parking:** on-site. **Terms:** cancellation fee imposed. **Amenities:** dual phone lines, voice mail, irons, hair dryers. *Some:* high-speed Internet. **Pool(s):** outdoor. **Leisure Activities:** whirlpool, exercise room. **Guest Services:** valet and coin laundry, wireless Internet. **Business Services:** meeting rooms, business center. **Cards:** AX, CB, DC, DS, MC, VI.

CALL / SOME UNITS

AAA Benefit:
Members save up to 10% everyday!

HOLIDAY INN EXPRESS HOTEL & SUITES *Book at AAA.com* **Phone:** 704/662-6900

Hotel
Rates not provided

Address: 130 Norman Station Blvd **Location:** I-77, exit 36, just e on SR 150, then just s. **Facility:** 74 units. 54 one-bedroom standard units. 20 one-bedroom suites, some with whirlpools. 5 stories, interior corridors. *Bath:* combo or shower only. **Parking:** on-site. **Amenities:** high-speed Internet, dual phone lines, voice mail, irons, hair dryers. **Pool(s):** outdoor. **Leisure Activities:** exercise room. **Guest Services:** valet and coin laundry, wireless Internet. **Business Services:** meeting rooms, business center.

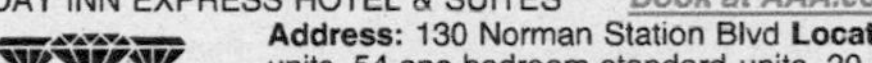

RAMADA LIMITED Book at AAA.com

Hotel
$79-$89 4/1-11/30
$69-$79 12/1-3/31

Phone: (704)664-6556
Address: 138 Norman Station Blvd **Location:** I-77, exit 36, just e on SR 150, then just s. **Facility:** 75 one-bedroom standard units. 2 stories (no elevator), exterior corridors. **Parking:** on-site. **Amenities:** high-speed Internet, voice mail, irons, hair dryers. **Pool(s):** outdoor. **Guest Services:** valet and coin laundry, wireless Internet. **Business Services:** meeting rooms. **Cards:** AX, CB, DC, DS, MC, VI.

SLEEP INN & SUITES Book at AAA.com

Hotel
$79-$229 All Year

Phone: (704)799-7070
Address: 132 Meadow Hill Ct **Location:** I-77, exit 36, just w on SR 150, just s on Rolling Hills Rd, then just e. **Facility:** 71 units. 68 one-bedroom standard units, some with whirlpools. 3 one-bedroom suites with whirlpools. 4 stories, interior corridors. *Bath:* combo or shower only. **Parking:** on-site. **Terms:** cancellation fee imposed. **Amenities:** high-speed Internet, dual phone lines, voice mail, irons, hair dryers. **Pool(s):** heated indoor. **Leisure Activities:** whirlpool, exercise room. **Guest Services:** coin laundry, wireless Internet. **Business Services:** meeting rooms. **Cards:** AX, CB, DC, DS, JC, MC, VI.

SPRINGHILL SUITES BY MARRIOTT Book great rates at AAA.com

Hotel
$147-$158 All Year

Phone: (704)658-0053
Address: 121 Gateway Blvd **Location:** I-77, exit 33, just ne on US 21, then just w. **Facility:** Smoke free premises. 107 one-bedroom standard units, some with whirlpools. 5 stories, interior corridors. *Bath:* combo or shower only. **Parking:** on-site. **Terms:** cancellation fee imposed. **Amenities:** video games (fee), high-speed Internet, voice mail, irons, hair dryers. **Pool(s):** heated indoor. **Leisure Activities:** whirlpool, exercise room. **Guest Services:** valet and coin laundry, wireless Internet. **Business Services:** meeting rooms. **Cards:** AX, DS, MC, VI.

AAA Benefit:
Members save a minimum 5% off the best available rate.

WINGATE BY WYNDHAM Book at AAA.com

Hotel
$129-$199 All Year

Phone: (704)664-4900
Address: 122 Regency Center Dr **Location:** I-77, exit 36, just w on SR 150, then n. **Facility:** 86 units. 83 one-bedroom standard units. 3 one-bedroom suites with whirlpools. 4 stories, interior corridors. *Bath:* combo or shower only. **Parking:** on-site. **Amenities:** video games (fee), high-speed Internet, dual phone lines, voice mail, safes, irons, hair dryers. **Pool(s):** heated indoor. **Leisure Activities:** whirlpool, exercise room. **Guest Services:** valet laundry, wireless Internet. **Business Services:** meeting rooms, business center. **Cards:** AX, CB, DC, DS, JC, MC, VI.

WHERE TO DINE

I BAMBINI

Italian
$5-$17

Phone: 704/799-9522
This locally popular restaurant serves up an extensive menu of well-prepared classic pasta dishes, steaks, chicken, veal, seafood, pizzas and sandwiches. The dining room is casual and comfortable, yet decorated with some upscale treatments. A buffet is offered at lunch Monday through Friday. Casual dress. **Bar:** Full bar. **Hours:** 11 am-10 pm, Fri-10:30 pm, Sat 11:30 am-10:30 pm, Sun 11:30 am-10 pm. Closed: 12/25. **Address:** 2785 Charlotte Hwy **Location:** I-77, exit 36, 1.2 mi e on SR 150, then 0.4 mi s on US 21. **Parking:** on-site. **Cards:** AX, DS, MC, VI.

JEFFREY'S RESTAURANT

American
$5-$27

Phone: 704/799-1110
New American cuisine with a regional flair is offered at the casual eatery. Favorites include Carolina crab cakes and Cajun-style blackened tuna. Other options include grilled steaks and pasta dishes. At lunch, a daily "soul-warming plate" special of hearty comfort foods is featured, with selections like meatloaf, braised beef tips or barbecued pork loin and a choice of vegetable sides. Casual dress. **Bar:** Full bar. **Reservations:** accepted. **Hours:** 11 am-10 pm, Fri-11 pm, Sat 4:30 pm-11 pm. Closed major holidays; also Sun. **Address:** 117 Trade Ct **Location:** I-77, exit 33, just ne on US 21, then just w. **Parking:** on-site. **Cards:** AX, DC, DS, MC, VI.

LANCASTER'S BBQ

Barbecue
$5-$17

Phone: 704/663-5807
A racing car theme prevails at the popular "pit stop" in Race City. Diners should get their engines ready for succulent smoked meats and baked beans. Casual dress. **Bar:** Full bar. **Hours:** 11 am-9:30 pm, Fri & Sat-10 pm. Closed: 11/26, 12/25; also Sun. **Address:** 515 Rhinehart Rd **Location:** I-77, exit 36, 2 mi e on SR 150, then 0.3 mi n. **Parking:** on-site. **Cards:** AX, DS, MC, VI.

SONNY'S REAL PIT BAR-B-Q

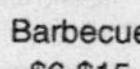

Barbecue
$6-$15

Phone: 704/662-0761
House specialties include pork and chicken grilled over an open pit, barbecue ribs and fresh, homemade pie. The salad bar offers another popular option. Rustic and comfortable, the atmosphere is perfect for family meals. Casual dress. **Bar:** Beer only. **Hours:** 11 am-9:30 pm, Fri & Sat-10 pm. Closed: 11/26, 12/25. **Address:** 328 W Plaza Dr **Location:** I-77, exit 36, just e. **Parking:** on-site. **Cards:** AX, DS, MC, VI.

TEXAS STEAKHOUSE & SALOON **Phone:** 704/664-7557

Steak
$6-$25

The typical Texas-style roadhouse focuses on freshly cut steaks, including the popular Duke entree with fries. Southwestern decor and arrows stuck in the walls get diners' minds wandering back to the old days. The popular draft beer is the microbrewed Red Oak lager. Casual dress. **Bar:** Full bar. **Hours:** 11 am-10 pm, Fri & Sat-11 pm. Closed: 11/26, 12/24, 12/25. **Address:** 140 Regency Center Dr **Location:** I-77, exit 36, just w on SR 150, then just n. **Parking:** on-site. **Cards:** AX, DS, MC, VI.

THAI LANNA **Phone:** 704/663-7004

Thai
$6-$19

Upscale, decorative appointments enhance the dining room, where Thai cuisine is served in a casual setting. The chef prepares every entree himself and uses creative combinations of ingredients and spices to enhance the flavors. Casual dress. **Bar:** Beer & wine. **Hours:** 11:30 am-3:30 & 4:30-9 pm, Fri & Sat 5 pm-10 pm. Closed: 7/4, 11/26, 12/25. **Address:** 335-N W Plaza Dr **Location:** I-77, exit 36, just e; in Consumer Square Shopping Center. **Parking:** on-site. **Cards:** AX, DS, MC, VI.

CALL

MOREHEAD CITY pop. 7,691

— WHERE TO STAY —

ECONO LODGE CRYSTAL COAST *Book great rates at AAA.com* **Phone:** (252)247-2940

Motel
$59-$129 All Year

Address: 3410 Bridges St **Location:** Jct US 70, just n on 35th St. Opposite National Guard Armory and Carteret General Hospital. **Facility:** 56 one-bedroom standard units. 2 stories (no elevator), exterior corridors. **Parking:** on-site. **Terms:** cancellation fee imposed. **Amenities:** safes, hair dryers. **Cards:** AX, DS, MC, VI. **Free Special Amenities: continental breakfast and high-speed Internet.**

/ SOME UNITS

HOLIDAY INN EXPRESS HOTEL & SUITES *Book at AAA.com* **Phone:** 252/247-5001

Hotel
Rates not provided

Address: 5063 Executive Dr **Location:** Jct US 70 and SR 24. **Facility:** 75 one-bedroom standard units, some with whirlpools. 3 stories, interior corridors. *Bath:* combo or shower only. **Parking:** on-site. **Amenities:** dual phone lines, voice mail, irons, hair dryers. **Pool(s):** outdoor. **Leisure Activities:** sauna, exercise room. **Guest Services:** valet and coin laundry, wireless Internet. **Business Services:** meeting rooms, PC.

/ SOME UNITS FEE

— WHERE TO DINE —

MRS. WILLIS' RESTAURANT **Phone:** 252/726-3741

American
$4-$15

Since 1956, the popular establishment has satisfied the appetites of both locals and visitors. On the menu are fresh fish, charcoal steak, vegetables and barbecue. The aromas of homemade soups and desserts are irresistible. Casual dress. **Bar:** Full bar. **Hours:** 11 am-2 & 5-9 pm, Mon & Sat from 5 pm; to 9:30 pm 5/1-10/31. Closed: 12/24-12/31. **Address:** 3114 Bridges St **Location:** Jct US 70, just n on 35th St, then 0.5 mi e. **Parking:** on-site. **Cards:** AX, DS, MC, VI.

RAPS GRILL & BAR **Phone:** 252/240-1213

American
$5-$15

Nestled in a vintage building, the restaurant's menu comprises many steak and seafood entrees at the casual pub-style grill. Lighter selections include sandwiches and such bar staples as wings. Nightly drink and appetizer specials are offered. Casual dress. **Bar:** Full bar. **Hours:** 11:30 am-10 pm, Fri & Sat-10:30 pm, Sun 5 pm-9:30 pm; hours may vary in off season. Closed: 11/26, 12/25. **Address:** 709 Arendell St **Location:** On US 70; between 7th and 8th sts. **Parking:** on-site. **Cards:** AX, DC, DS, MC, VI.

SANITARY FISH MARKET & RESTAURANT **Phone:** 252/247-3111

Seafood
$11-$30

Patrons can peek into the live lobster tank at the family-owned seafood restaurant, an area institution since 1938. "Tar Heel" hush puppies, original recipe coleslaw and homemade lemon pie have put the eatery on the map. Casual dress. **Bar:** Beer & wine. **Reservations:** not accepted. **Hours:** Open 2/2-11/25; 11 am-9 pm. **Address:** 501 Evans St **Location:** Between 5th and S 6th sts; center; on Bogue Sound. **Parking:** on-site and street. **Cards:** DS, MC, VI.

SHEPARD'S POINT **Phone:** 252/727-0815

Steak & Seafood
$15-$28

A romantic atmosphere punctuates the casual spot for fine dining. Steaks, seafood and spirits are at the heart of the menu. Weekly changing specials combine the chef's creativity with seasonal produce and other ingredients. Casual dress. **Bar:** Full bar. **Reservations:** accepted. **Hours:** 5:30 pm-9:30 pm, Fri & Sat-10 pm; Sunday brunch 11 am-2 pm; call for hours in winter. Closed: 1/1, 11/26, 12/25; also Tues & Wed. **Address:** 913 Arendell St **Location:** Jct 10th Ave and US 70. **Parking:** on-site. **Cards:** AX, DS, MC, VI.

TEXAS STEAKHOUSE & SALOON **Phone:** 252/240-2633

Steak
$6-$25

The typical Texas-style roadhouse focuses on freshly cut steaks, including the popular Duke entree with fries. Southwestern decor and arrows stuck in the walls get diners' minds wandering back to the old days. The popular draft beer is the microbrewed Red Oak lager. Casual dress. **Bar:** Full bar. **Hours:** 11 am-10 pm, Fri & Sat-11 pm. Closed: 11/26, 12/24, 12/25. **Address:** 5025 Executive Blvd **Location:** Jct US 70 and SR 24. **Parking:** on-site. **Cards:** AX, DS, MC, VI.

MORGANTON pop. 17,310

WHERE TO STAY

COMFORT INN & SUITES *Book great rates at AAA.com* **Phone:** (828)430-4000

Hotel
$89-$169 4/1-11/30
$79-$169 12/1-3/31

Address: 1273 Burkemont Ave **Location:** I-40, exit 103, just s. **Facility:** 72 one-bedroom standard units, some with whirlpools. 3 stories, interior corridors. *Bath:* combo or shower only. **Parking:** on-site. **Terms:** cancellation fee imposed. **Amenities:** high-speed Internet, dual phone lines, voice mail, safes (fee), irons, hair dryers. **Pool(s):** heated indoor. **Leisure Activities:** whirlpool, exercise room. **Guest Services:** valet and coin laundry, wireless Internet. **Business Services:** meeting rooms, PC. **Cards:** AX, CB, DC, DS, JC, MC, VI. **Free Special Amenities: continental breakfast and high-speed Internet.**

CALL / SOME UNITS FEE

HAMPTON INN *Book great rates at AAA.com* **Phone:** (828)432-2000

Hotel
$90-$99 All Year

Address: 115 Bush Dr **Location:** I-40, exit 105 (SR 18), just n, then just e. **Facility:** 85 one-bedroom standard units, some with whirlpools. 4 stories, interior corridors. *Bath:* combo or shower only. **Parking:** on-site. **Terms:** 1-30 night minimum stay, cancellation fee imposed. **Amenities:** voice mail, irons, hair dryers. **Pool(s):** outdoor. **Leisure Activities:** limited exercise equipment. **Guest Services:** valet laundry, wireless Internet. **Business Services:** meeting rooms, PC. **Cards:** AX, CB, DC, DS, MC, VI.

CALL / SOME UNITS

AAA Benefit:
Members save up to 10% everyday!

HOLIDAY INN-MORGANTON *Book at AAA.com* **Phone:** (828)437-0171

Hotel
$75-$89 All Year

Address: 2400 S Sterling St **Location:** I-40, exit 105 (SR 18), just s. **Facility:** 133 one-bedroom standard units. 2 stories (no elevator), exterior corridors. *Bath:* combo or shower only. **Parking:** on-site. **Amenities:** dual phone lines, voice mail, irons, hair dryers. *Some:* high-speed Internet. **Pool(s):** outdoor. **Leisure Activities:** limited exercise equipment. **Guest Services:** valet laundry, wireless Internet. **Business Services:** meeting rooms, PC. **Cards:** AX, DC, DS, MC, VI.

ASK CALL / SOME UNITS FEE

SLEEP INN *Book at AAA.com* **Phone:** 828/433-9000

Hotel
Rates not provided

Address: 2400A S Sterling St **Location:** I-40, exit 105 (SR 18), just s. **Facility:** 61 one-bedroom standard units. 2 stories (no elevator), interior corridors. *Bath:* combo or shower only. **Parking:** on-site. **Amenities:** irons, hair dryers. **Leisure Activities:** fitness room & pool privileges. **Guest Services:** valet laundry, wireless Internet.

/ SOME UNITS FEE

WHERE TO DINE

HARBOR INN SEAFOOD **Phone:** 828/437-0294

Seafood
$4-$11

The restaurant is known for its broiled and fried seafood. While service is informal and relaxed, staff are attentive to customer needs. The nautically decorated dining room offers a basic, casual setting. Casual dress. **Hours:** 11 am-9 pm, Fri & Sat-10 pm. Closed: 4/12, 11/26, 12/25; also Mon. **Address:** 2006 S Sterling St **Location:** I-40, exit 105 (SR 18), 0.3 mi n. **Parking:** on-site. **Cards:** MC, VI.

CALL

SAGEBRUSH STEAKHOUSE **Phone:** 828/437-2242

American
$5-$19

Born from the spirit of Texas cattle drives, the restaurant presents a menu of hearty steaks, prime rib, chicken, seafood and baby back ribs. Yummy desserts merit a splurge. Guests can call ahead to facilitate seating. Casual dress. **Bar:** Full bar. **Hours:** 11 am-10 pm, Fri & Sat-11 pm. Closed: 12/25. **Address:** 101 Steakhouse Rd **Location:** I-40, exit 105 (SR 18), just se. **Parking:** on-site. **Cards:** AX, DC, DS, MC, VI.

CALL

ZEKO'S VILLAGE III **Phone:** 824/430-6982

Italian
$5-$16

Just off the interstate, the restaurant prepares terrific pizza and other Italian favorites. The friendly staff carries out quick service. Casual dress. **Reservations:** accepted. **Hours:** 11 am-10 pm, Fri & Sat-11 pm. **Address:** 2158 S Sterling St **Location:** I-40, exit 105, just w. **Parking:** on-site.

CALL

MORRISVILLE pop. 5,208 (See map and index starting on p. 790)

WHERE TO STAY

COUNTRY INN & SUITES-RDU AIRPORT *Book at AAA.com* **Phone:** (919)544-1010 60

Hotel
$144 All Year

Address: 201 Airgate Dr **Location:** I-40, exit 284 or 284B, just n, just w on Pleasant Grove Church Rd, then just s. **Facility:** Smoke free premises. 87 units. 41 one-bedroom standard units, some with whirlpools. 46 one-bedroom suites, some with efficiencies. 4 stories, interior corridors. *Bath:* combo or shower only. **Parking:** on-site. **Terms:** 3 day cancellation notice. **Amenities:** high-speed Internet, voice mail, irons, hair dryers. **Pool(s):** heated indoor. **Leisure Activities:** whirlpool, exercise room. **Guest Services:** valet and coin laundry, area transportation, wireless Internet. **Business Services:** meeting rooms, PC. **Cards:** AX, DS, MC, VI.

ASK CALL

(See map and index starting on p. 790)

COURTYARD BY MARRIOTT-AIRPORT Book great rates at AAA.com **Phone:** (919)467-9444 

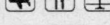

Hotel
$207-$222 All Year

Address: 2001 Hospitality Ct **Location:** I-40, exit 284 or 284A, just s, just e on Aerial Center Pkwy, then just ne. **Facility:** Smoke free premises. 152 units. 140 one-bedroom standard units. 12 one-bedroom suites. 4 stories, interior corridors. *Bath:* combo or shower only. **Parking:** on-site. **Terms:** cancellation fee imposed. **Amenities:** high-speed Internet, dual phone lines, voice mail, irons, hair dryers. **Pool(s):** outdoor. **Leisure Activities:** whirlpool, exercise room. **Guest Services:** valet and coin laundry, airport transportation-Raleigh-Durham International Airport, wireless Internet. **Business Services:** meeting rooms, business center. **Cards:** AX, CB, DC, DS, MC, VI. **Free Special Amenities: local telephone calls and high-speed Internet.**

AAA Benefit: Members save a minimum 5% off the best available rate.

DAYS INN AIRPORT/RTP Book at AAA.com **Phone:** (919)469-8688 69

Hotel
$99-$109 All Year

Address: 1000 Airport Blvd **Location:** I-40, exit 284 or 284A, just s. **Facility:** 111 one-bedroom standard units, some with whirlpools. 3 stories, interior/exterior corridors. **Parking:** on-site. **Terms:** 3 day cancellation notice. **Amenities:** dual phone lines, voice mail, safes (fee), irons, hair dryers. **Pool(s):** outdoor. **Leisure Activities:** exercise room. **Guest Services:** valet and coin laundry, wireless Internet. **Business Services:** meeting rooms, business center. **Cards:** AX, DC, DS, MC, VI.

EXTENDED STAYAMERICA-RDU AIRPORT Book at AAA.com **Phone:** (919)380-1499 63

Motel
$100-$110 All Year

Address: 2700 Slater Rd **Location:** I-40, exit 284 or 284A, 0.4 mi s on Airport Blvd, then just w. **Facility:** 120 one-bedroom standard units with efficiencies. 3 stories, exterior corridors. *Bath:* combo or shower only. **Parking:** on-site. **Terms:** office hours 7 am-11 pm. **Amenities:** voice mail, irons. **Guest Services:** coin laundry, wireless Internet. **Cards:** AX, CB, DC, DS, JC, MC, VI.

FAIRFIELD INN & SUITES BY MARRIOTT-RDU AIRPORT Book great rates at AAA.com **Phone:** (919)468-2660 

Hotel
$177-$190 All Year

Address: 2750 Slater Rd **Location:** I-40, exit 284 or 284A, just s, then just w. **Facility:** Smoke free premises. 112 one-bedroom standard units. 5 stories, interior corridors. *Bath:* combo or shower only. **Parking:** on-site. **Terms:** cancellation fee imposed. **Amenities:** high-speed Internet, voice mail, irons, hair dryers. *Some:* CD players. **Pool(s):** heated indoor. **Leisure Activities:** whirlpool, exercise room. **Guest Services:** valet and coin laundry, airport transportation-Raleigh-Durham International Airport, area transportation-within 1 mi, wireless Internet. **Business Services:** meeting rooms, PC. **Cards:** AX, CB, DC, DS, MC, VI. **Free Special Amenities: expanded continental breakfast and high-speed Internet.**

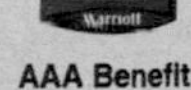

AAA Benefit: Members save a minimum 5% off the best available rate.

HAMPTON INN-RDU Book great rates at AAA.com **Phone:** (919)462-1620 67

Hotel
$123-$149 All Year

Address: 1010 Airport Blvd **Location:** I-40, exit 284 or 284A, just s. **Facility:** 102 one-bedroom standard units. 4 stories, interior corridors. *Bath:* combo or shower only. **Parking:** on-site. **Amenities:** high-speed Internet, voice mail, irons, hair dryers. **Pool(s):** outdoor. **Guest Services:** valet laundry, wireless Internet. **Business Services:** PC. **Cards:** AX, CB, DC, DS, JC, MC, VI.

AAA Benefit: Members save up to 10% everyday!

HILTON GARDEN INN-RALEIGH DURHAM AIRPORT Book great rates at AAA.com **Phone:** (919)840-8088 72

Hotel
$89-$199 All Year

Address: 1500 RDU Center Dr **Location:** I-40, exit 285, just n, then just e. **Facility:** 155 one-bedroom standard units. 6 stories, interior corridors. *Bath:* combo or shower only. **Parking:** on-site. **Terms:** cancellation fee imposed. **Amenities:** dual phone lines, voice mail, irons, hair dryers. **Pool(s):** heated indoor. **Leisure Activities:** whirlpool, exercise room. **Guest Services:** valet and coin laundry, airport transportation-Raleigh-Durham International Airport, area transportation-within 5 mi, wireless Internet. **Business Services:** meeting rooms, business center. **Cards:** AX, DS, JC, MC, VI. **Free Special Amenities: newspaper and high-speed Internet.**

AAA Benefit: Members save 5% or more everyday!

HOLIDAY INN EXPRESS Book at AAA.com **Phone:** (919)653-2260 64

Hotel
$124-$144 All Year

Address: 1014 Airport Blvd **Location:** I-40, exit 284 or 284A, just s. **Facility:** 116 one-bedroom standard units. 4 stories, interior corridors. *Bath:* combo or shower only. **Parking:** on-site. **Terms:** 3 day cancellation notice. **Amenities:** high-speed Internet, dual phone lines, voice mail, irons, hair dryers. **Pool(s):** outdoor. **Leisure Activities:** exercise room. **Guest Services:** valet laundry, wireless Internet. **Business Services:** meeting rooms, PC. **Cards:** AX, CB, DC, DS, JC, MC, VI.

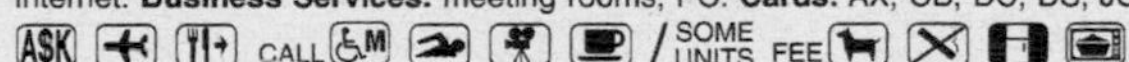

(See map and index starting on p. 790)

HOLIDAY INN - RALEIGH-DURHAM AIRPORT *Book at AAA.com* **Phone:** 919/465-1910 71

Hotel
Rates not provided

Address: 930 Airport Blvd **Location:** I-40, exit 284 or 284A, just s. **Facility:** 143 one-bedroom standard units. 6 stories, interior corridors. *Bath:* combo or shower only. **Parking:** on-site. **Amenities:** high-speed Internet, dual phone lines, voice mail, irons, hair dryers. **Pool(s):** heated indoor. **Leisure Activities:** exercise room. **Guest Services:** valet and coin laundry, area transportation, wireless Internet. **Business Services:** meeting rooms, business center.

CALL / SOME UNITS FEE

HYATT PLACE - RALEIGH-DURHAM AIRPORT *Book great rates at AAA.com* **Phone:** (919)405-2400 

AAA SAVE

Hotel
$89-$209 All Year

Address: 200 Airgate Dr **Location:** I-40, exit 284 or 284B, just n, just w on Pleasant Grove Church Rd, then just s. **Facility:** Smoke free premises. 93 one-bedroom standard units. 5 stories, interior corridors. *Bath:* combo or shower only. **Parking:** on-site. **Terms:** cancellation fee imposed. **Amenities:** high-speed Internet, dual phone lines, voice mail, irons, hair dryers. *Some:* DVD players. **Pool(s):** outdoor. **Leisure Activities:** exercise room. **Guest Services:** valet laundry, airport transportation-Raleigh-Durham International Airport, wireless Internet. **Business Services:** meeting rooms, business center. **Cards:** AX, CB, DC, DS, MC, VI. **Free Special Amenities: continental breakfast and high-speed Internet.**

HYATT PLACE
AAA Benefit:
Ask for the AAA rate and save 10%.

LA QUINTA INN & SUITES - AERIAL CENTER PKWY *Book great rates at AAA.com* **Phone:** (919)481-3600 70

Hotel
$69-$129 All Year

Address: 1001 Aerial Center Pkwy **Location:** I-40, exit 284 or 284A, just s, then just e. Located in Aerial Center Park. **Facility:** 117 one-bedroom standard units. 4 stories, interior corridors. **Parking:** on-site. **Amenities:** video games (fee), voice mail, irons, hair dryers. **Pool(s):** outdoor. **Leisure Activities:** exercise room. **Guest Services:** valet and coin laundry, wireless Internet. **Business Services:** PC. **Cards:** AX, DC, DS, MC, VI.

ASK CALL / SOME UNITS

LA QUINTA INN & SUITES (RALEIGH-DURHAM INT'L AIRPORT) *Book great rates at AAA.com* **Phone:** (919)461-1771 65

Hotel
$69-$149 All Year

Address: 1001 Hospitality Ct **Location:** I-40, exit 284 or 284A, just s, just e on Aerial Center Pkwy, then just ne; in Aerial Center Park. **Facility:** 135 units. 127 one-bedroom standard units. 8 one-bedroom suites. 3-4 stories, interior corridors. *Bath:* combo or shower only. **Parking:** on-site. **Amenities:** video games (fee), high-speed Internet, voice mail, irons, hair dryers. *Some:* dual phone lines. **Pool(s):** outdoor. **Leisure Activities:** whirlpool, exercise room. **Guest Services:** valet and coin laundry, wireless Internet. **Business Services:** meeting rooms, PC. **Cards:** AX, DC, DS, MC, VI.

ASK CALL / SOME UNITS

MICROTEL RDU AIRPORT/RTP *Book great rates at AAA.com* **Phone:** (919)462-0061 62

AAA SAVE

Hotel
$65-$100 All Year

Address: 104 Factory Shops Rd **Location:** I-40, exit 284 or 284A, just s, then just w. Located across from Prime Outlets. **Facility:** 99 one-bedroom standard units. 3 stories, interior corridors. *Bath:* combo or shower only. **Parking:** on-site. **Amenities:** voice mail, safes (fee), irons, hair dryers. **Guest Services:** coin laundry, airport transportation-Raleigh-Durham International Airport, wireless Internet. **Business Services:** PC (fee). **Cards:** AX, DS, MC, VI. **Free Special Amenities: continental breakfast and high-speed Internet.**

CALL / SOME UNITS

STAYBRIDGE SUITES RALEIGH DURHAM AIRPORT *Book at AAA.com* **Phone:** (919)468-0180 66

Hotel
$159-$169 All Year

Address: 1012 Airport Blvd **Location:** I-40, exit 284 or 284A, just s; enter between Hampton Inn and Holiday Inn Express. **Facility:** 88 units. 49 one-bedroom standard units with kitchens. 28 one- and 11 two-bedroom suites with kitchens. 3 stories, interior corridors. *Bath:* combo or shower only. **Parking:** on-site. **Terms:** 3 day cancellation notice. **Amenities:** high-speed Internet, dual phone lines, voice mail, irons, hair dryers. **Leisure Activities:** jogging, exercise room, sports court. **Guest Services:** wireless Internet. **Business Services:** meeting rooms, business center. **Cards:** AX, CB, DC, DS, JC, MC, VI.

ASK CALL / SOME UNITS FEE

WHERE TO DINE

BABYMOON CAFE **Phone:** 919/465-9006 48

Italian
$7-$24

A popular lunch spot for the RTP crowd, the tiny cafe serves pizza, pasta and sandwiches. Patio seating is a favorite option. Casual dress. **Bar:** Full bar. **Reservations:** accepted. **Hours:** 11 am-10 pm, Sat from 4 pm. Closed major holidays; also Sun. **Address:** 100 Jerusalem Dr **Location:** I-40, exit 284 or 284A, 1 mi s on Airport Blvd, then just w. **Parking:** on-site. **Cards:** AX, DC, DS, MC, VI.

(See map and index starting on p. 790)

CAPITAL CITY CHOP HOUSE **Phone:** 919/484-7721 (47)

Steak & Seafood
$8-$36

Popular for its well-prepared, center-cut steaks and fresh seafood, the upscale steakhouse's location makes this a local favorite with the business crowd. Dressy casual. **Bar:** Full bar. **Reservations:** suggested. **Hours:** 11:30 am-10 pm, Sat 4:30 pm-10:30 pm. Closed major holidays; also Sun. **Address:** 151 Airgate Dr **Location:** I-40, exit 284 or 284B, just n, just w on Pleasant Grove Church, then just s. **Parking:** on-site. **Cards:** AX, DC, DS, MC, VI.

LUBRANO'S ITALIAN RESTAURANT **Phone:** 919/678-9030 (49)

Italian
$7-$16

Homemade pasta sauces, delicious garlic knots and New York-style pizza with dozens of toppings are specialties at the cozy, neighborhood bistro. Casual dress. **Bar:** Beer & wine. **Reservations:** accepted. **Hours:** 11 am-10 pm, Fri & Sat 10 am-11 pm. Closed: 4/12, 11/26, 12/25. **Address:** 101 Keybridge Dr, Suite 500 **Location:** I-40, exit 285, 2.5 mi n on Aviation Pkwy, just e on Chapel Hill Rd (SR 54), then just s. **Parking:** on-site. **Cards:** AX, DS, MC, VI.

TEXAS STEAKHOUSE & SALOON **Phone:** 919/468-7194

American
$6-$25

The typical Texas-style roadhouse focuses on freshly cut steaks, including the popular Duke entree with fries. Southwestern decor and arrows stuck in the walls get diners' minds wandering back to the old days. The popular draft beer is the microbrewed Red Oak lager. Casual dress. **Bar:** Full bar. **Hours:** 11 am-10 pm, Fri & Sat-11 pm. Closed: 11/26, 12/24, 12/25. **Address:** 948 Airport Blvd **Location:** I-40, exit 284 or 284A, 0.3 mi s. **Parking:** on-site. **Cards:** AX, DS, MC, VI.

MOUNT AIRY pop. 8,484

WHERE TO STAY

BEST WESTERN BRYSON INN *Book great rates at AAA.com* **Phone:** (336)352-3400

Motel
$70-$124 All Year

Address: 125 Plaza Ln **Location:** I-77, exit 100 (SR 89), just e; I-74, exit 6 (SR 89), 1 mi w. **Facility:** 59 one-bedroom standard units. 2 stories (no elevator), exterior corridors. **Parking:** on-site. **Terms:** 4 day cancellation notice. **Amenities:** voice mail, irons, hair dryers. *Some:* high-speed Internet. **Pool(s):** heated outdoor. **Leisure Activities:** horseshoes. **Guest Services:** wireless Internet. **Cards:** AX, CB, DC, DS, JC, MC, VI. **Free Special Amenities: expanded continental breakfast and high-speed Internet.**

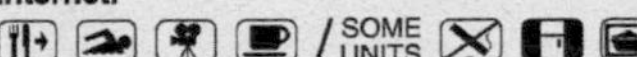

AAA Benefit:
Members save up to 20%, plus 10% bonus points with rewards program.

HAMPTON INN *Book great rates at AAA.com* **Phone:** (336)789-5999

Hotel
$99-$209 All Year

Address: 2029 Rockford St **Location:** Jct US 52, 0.4 mi s on US 601. **Facility:** 125 one-bedroom standard units, some with whirlpools. 3 stories, interior corridors. *Bath:* combo or shower only. **Parking:** on-site. **Amenities:** video games (fee), voice mail, irons, hair dryers. **Pool(s):** heated indoor. **Leisure Activities:** exercise room. **Guest Services:** valet and coin laundry, wireless Internet. **Business Services:** meeting rooms, business center. **Cards:** AX, DC, DS, MC, VI.

  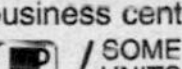  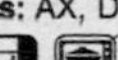

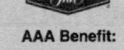

AAA Benefit:
Members save up to 10% everyday!

MAYBERRY MOTOR INN **Phone:** 336/786-4109

Motel
$65-$120 All Year

Address: 501 N Andy Griffith Pkwy **Location:** Jct SR 89, 0.5 mi n on US 52 Bypass. **Facility:** 27 one-bedroom standard units. 1 story, exterior corridors. **Parking:** on-site. **Terms:** cancellation fee imposed. **Amenities:** hair dryers. **Pool(s):** outdoor. **Guest Services:** wireless Internet. **Cards:** AX, CB, DC, DS, MC, VI. **Free Special Amenities: continental breakfast and high-speed Internet.**

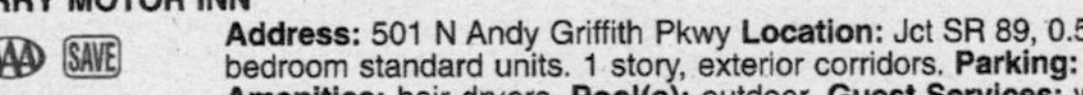

MICROTEL SUITES *Book great rates at AAA.com* **Phone:** (336)789-7660

Hotel
$89-$130 8/1-11/30
$69-$99 12/1-7/31

Address: 1293 Newsome St **Location:** Jct US 601, 0.7 mi s on US 52, then just e. **Facility:** 52 one-bedroom standard units, some with whirlpools. 3 stories, interior corridors. *Bath:* combo or shower only. **Parking:** on-site. **Terms:** cancellation fee imposed. **Amenities:** voice mail, irons, hair dryers. **Pool(s):** heated indoor. **Leisure Activities:** exercise room. *Fee:* game room. **Guest Services:** wireless Internet. **Cards:** AX, CB, DC, DS, MC, VI. **Free Special Amenities: continental breakfast and high-speed Internet.**

QUALITY INN Book at AAA.com

Motel
$69-$140 All Year

Phone: (336)789-2000

Address: 2136 Rockford St **Location:** Jct US 52, 0.6 mi s on US 601. **Facility:** 99 one-bedroom standard units, some with whirlpools. 2 stories (no elevator), exterior corridors. **Parking:** on-site. **Terms:** cancellation fee imposed. **Amenities:** voice mail, irons, hair dryers. **Pool(s):** outdoor. **Guest Services:** valet laundry, wireless Internet. **Business Services:** meeting rooms. **Cards:** AX, DS, MC, VI.

ASK FEE / SOME UNITS FEE

WHERE TO DINE

GOOBER'S 52 INC

American
$6-$15

Phone: 336/786-1845

A colorful, eclectic decor sets the stage for popular lunch offerings of salads and sandwiches while dinner entrees include steak, chicken, pasta, lobster reuben and barbecued salmon sandwich, to name a few. A "food gone wild" theme is behind the menu at this popular eatery that sports a colorful, eclectic decor. Casual dress. **Bar:** Beer & wine. **Hours:** 11 am-10 pm, Fri & Sat-11 pm, Sun noon-8 pm. Closed: 11/26, 12/25. **Address:** 458 N Andy Griffith Pkwy **Location:** Jct SR 89, 0.4 mi n on US 52 Bypass. **Parking:** on-site. **Cards:** AX, DS, MC, VI.

PANDOWDY'S

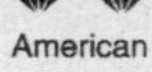

American
$3-$13

Phone: 336/786-1993

Choose from steak and seafood specials as well as burgers, sandwiches, chicken fingers or spaghetti, and top off your meal with the homemade cobbler. Casual dress. **Bar:** Beer & wine. **Hours:** 10:30 am-9 pm. Closed major holidays; also Sun-Tues. **Address:** 243 N Main St **Location:** Center. **Parking:** street.

SAGEBRUSH STEAKHOUSE

American
$5-$19

Phone: 336/786-9717

Born from the spirit of Texas cattle drives, the restaurant presents a menu of hearty steaks, prime rib, chicken, seafood and baby back ribs. Yummy desserts merit a splurge. Guests can call ahead to facilitate seating. Casual dress. **Bar:** Full bar. **Hours:** 11 am-10 pm, Fri & Sat-11 pm. Closed: 12/25. **Address:** 2000 Woodland Dr **Location:** Jct US 52/601, just n to Snowhill Dr, then just n. **Parking:** on-site. **Cards:** AX, DC, DS, MC, VI.

CALL

THAILAND CAFE

Thai
$5-$13

Phone: 336/786-8480

Enjoy traditional Thai cuisine in a pleasantly cozy atmosphere. The menu includes flavorful curries, chicken, seafood, pork, beef and vegetarian dishes, all of which can be spiced to your taste. Casual dress. **Bar:** Beer & wine. **Hours:** 11 am-3 & 5-10 pm, Fri-10:30 pm, Sat 5 pm-10:30 pm, Sun 11 am-10 pm. Closed: 12/25; also Mon. **Address:** 647 W Independence Blvd **Location:** Jct US 52, just e on SR 89; in New Market Crossing Shopping Center. **Parking:** on-site. **Cards:** AX, DS, MC, VI.

MOUNT OLIVE pop. 4,567

WHERE TO STAY

SLEEP INN Book at AAA.com

Hotel
$65-$109 All Year

Phone: (919)658-1002

Address: 710 Henderson St **Location:** Jct US 117, just e on SR 55, then just s. **Facility:** 68 one-bedroom standard units. 2 stories (no elevator), interior corridors. *Bath:* combo or shower only. **Parking:** on-site. **Amenities:** voice mail, irons, hair dryers. **Pool(s):** outdoor. **Guest Services:** wireless Internet. **Business Services:** meeting rooms. **Cards:** AX, CB, DC, DS, JC, MC, VI.

ASK CALL / SOME UNITS

MOUNT PLEASANT pop. 1,259

WHERE TO STAY

CAROLINA COUNTRY INN

AAA SAVE

Motel
$65 All Year

Phone: 704/436-9616

Address: 8514 Hwy 49 **Location:** Jct SR 73, 1 mi n. **Facility:** 26 units. 25 one-bedroom standard units. 1 one-bedroom suite with kitchen. 1-2 stories (no elevator), exterior corridors. **Parking:** on-site. **Cards:** AX, DS, MC, VI. **Free Special Amenities: local telephone calls and preferred room (subject to availability with advance reservations).**

CALL / SOME UNITS

MURPHY pop. 1,568

WHERE TO STAY

BEST WESTERN OF MURPHY Book great rates at AAA.com

AAA SAVE

Hotel
$65-$119 All Year

Phone: (828)837-3060

Address: 1522 Andrews Rd **Location:** US 74, 19 and SR 129, exit Andrews Rd. **Facility:** 54 one-bedroom standard units. 2 stories (no elevator), exterior corridors. **Parking:** on-site. **Terms:** 5 day cancellation notice. **Amenities:** high-speed Internet, voice mail, irons, hair dryers. **Pool(s):** outdoor. **Guest Services:** wireless Internet. **Business Services:** fax (fee). **Cards:** AX, CB, DC, DS, MC, VI. **Free Special Amenities: expanded continental breakfast and high-speed Internet.**

/ SOME UNITS FEE

AAA Benefit:
Members save up to 20%, plus 10% bonus points with rewards program.

DAYS INN *Book great rates at AAA.com* **Phone:** (828)837-0030

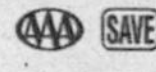

Motel
$79-$99 5/2-11/30
$59-$69 12/1-5/1

Address: 754 Hwy 64 W **Location:** US 64 W/19 S/74 W and 129 S. Located in a commercial area. **Facility:** 55 one-bedroom standard units, some with whirlpools. 2 stories (no elevator), exterior corridors. **Parking:** on-site. **Amenities:** irons, hair dryers. **Pool(s):** indoor. **Guest Services:** wireless Internet. **Business Services:** fax (fee). **Cards:** AX, DC, DS, MC, VI. **Free Special Amenities: continental breakfast and high-speed Internet.**

/ SOME UNITS FEE

HAMPTON INN MURPHY **Phone:** 828/837-1628

fyi
Hotel
$84-$129 All Year

Too new to rate. **Address:** 1500 Andrews Rd **Location:** US 74, 19 and SR 129, exit Andrews Rd. **Amenities:** 58 units, coffeemakers, pool. **Terms:** 1-30 night minimum stay, cancellation fee imposed. **Cards:** AX, CB, DC, DS, MC, VI.

AAA Benefit:
Members save up to 10% everyday!

HOLIDAY INN EXPRESS HOTEL & SUITES *Book at AAA.com* **Phone:** (828)837-1111

Hotel
$90 All Year

Address: 130 Holiday Dr **Location:** US 62 W. **Facility:** 51 one-bedroom standard units, some with whirlpools. 3 stories, interior corridors. *Bath:* combo or shower only. **Parking:** on-site. **Terms:** cancellation fee imposed. **Amenities:** high-speed Internet, voice mail, irons, hair dryers. **Pool(s):** heated indoor. **Leisure Activities:** whirlpool, exercise room. **Guest Services:** coin laundry, wireless Internet. **Business Services:** meeting rooms, business center. **Cards:** AX, DC, DS, MC, VI.

WHERE TO DINE

DOYLE'S CEDAR HILL RESTAURANT **Phone:** 828/837-3400

Continental
$6-$25

Guests can kick back and enjoy the relaxed atmosphere from front-porch rocking chairs or back porch seating that affords a view of the mountains. Local quail and trout contribute to a diversity of entrees. Among favorites are spicy Thai green curry scallops and chopped bison steak with sauteed mushrooms. The restaurant is family-owned. Casual dress. **Bar:** Wine only. **Reservations:** suggested. **Hours:** 11 am-2 & 5-9 pm, Thurs-Sat to 10 pm; Sunday brunch 11 am-3 pm; hours vary in winter. Closed: 12/25. **Address:** 925 Andrews Rd **Location:** US 19/79/129, 0.5 mi w on Bulldog Dr, just n. **Parking:** on-site. **Cards:** AX, DS, MC, VI.

RIB COUNTRY **Phone:** 828/837-4444

Regional Barbecue
$6-$8

At the heart of the menu are succulent racks of ribs, homemade coleslaw or beans and good, smokey-flavored barbecued meats. The restaurant is casual, with picnic tables and a country decor. Casual dress. **Reservations:** not accepted. **Hours:** 11 am-9 pm. Closed: 12/25. **Address:** 2121 US Hwy 64 W **Location:** US 64 W/19 S/74 W and 129 S. **Parking:** on-site. **Cards:** MC, VI.

SHOE BOOTIES CAFE **Phone:** 828/837-4589

American
$10-$25

One example of the good, moderately priced food is the delicious salmon, totally unexpected in this area. Lunch business is brisk. People often gather here on the weekends for the live music. Casual dress. **Bar:** Wine only. **Reservations:** accepted. **Hours:** 11 am-3 & 5-9 pm. Closed major holidays; also Sun & Mon. **Address:** 25 Peachtree St **Location:** Center. **Parking:** on-site. **Cards:** AX, DS, MC, VI.

NAGS HEAD *—See Outer Banks p. 782.*

NEW BERN pop. 23,128

WHERE TO STAY

THE AERIE BED & BREAKFAST **Phone:** 252/636-5553

Bed & Breakfast
$129-$169 All Year

Address: 509 Pollock St **Location:** Downtown; in historic district. **Facility:** Built in the 1880s, the Victorian-style house is situated in the historic district, four blocks from Tryon Palace Historic Site and Gardens. Smoke free premises. 7 one-bedroom standard units, some with whirlpools. 2 stories (no elevator), interior corridors. *Bath:* combo or shower only. **Parking:** on-site. **Terms:** 2 night minimum stay - weekends, 3 day cancellation notice-fee imposed. **Amenities:** video library, DVD players, CD players, high-speed Internet, irons, hair dryers. **Guest Services:** wireless Internet. **Business Services:** meeting rooms. **Cards:** AX, DS, MC, VI.

BRIDGE POINTE HOTEL & MARINA *Book great rates at AAA.com* **Phone:** (252)636-3637

Hotel
$80-$135 All Year

Address: 101 Howell Rd **Location:** US 70 Bypass, exit 417, just w on US 70 business route, then just s. **Facility:** 115 units. 111 one-bedroom standard units. 4 one-bedroom suites with whirlpools. 4 stories, interior corridors. **Parking:** on-site. **Terms:** cancellation fee imposed. **Amenities:** voice mail, irons. **Pool(s):** outdoor. **Leisure Activities:** *Fee:* marina. **Guest Services:** valet laundry, wireless Internet. **Business Services:** meeting rooms, PC. **Cards:** AX, DS, JC, MC, VI. **Free Special Amenities: continental breakfast and high-speed Internet.**

COMFORT SUITES RIVERFRONT PARK Book at AAA.com Phone: (252)636-0022

Hotel
$125-$199 All Year

Address: 218 E Front St **Location:** US 70 Bypass, exit 417 to US 70 W business route, then 0.5 mi w; in historic district. **Facility:** Smoke free premises. 100 units. 98 one-bedroom standard units, some with whirlpools. 2 one-bedroom suites with whirlpools. 4 stories, interior corridors. *Bath:* combo or shower only. **Parking:** on-site. **Amenities:** voice mail, safes (fee), irons, hair dryers. *Some:* high-speed Internet. **Pool(s):** outdoor. **Leisure Activities:** whirlpool, fishing, exercise room. **Guest Services:** valet and coin laundry, wireless Internet. **Business Services:** meeting rooms, PC. **Cards:** AX, CB, DC, DS, MC, VI.

HAMPTON INN Book great rates at AAA.com Phone: (252)637-2111

Hotel
$105-$111 All Year

Address: 200 Hotel Dr **Location:** US 70 Bypass, exit Jacksonville/US 17, just e on US 70 business route, then just s. **Facility:** 101 one-bedroom standard units. 4 stories, interior corridors. *Bath:* combo or shower only. **Parking:** on-site. **Terms:** 1-30 night minimum stay, cancellation fee imposed. **Amenities:** voice mail, irons, hair dryers. **Pool(s):** outdoor. **Leisure Activities:** whirlpool, exercise room. **Guest Services:** valet laundry, wireless Internet. **Business Services:** meeting rooms, PC. **Cards:** AX, CB, DC, DS, MC, VI.

CALL / SOME UNITS

AAA Benefit:
Members save up to 10% everyday!

HARMONY HOUSE INN Phone: (252)636-3810

Bed & Breakfast
$109-$139 All Year

Address: 215 Pollock St **Location:** 0.3 mi e of Tryon Palace; downtown. **Facility:** The 1850 Greek Revival home in the historic district offers unusually spacious rooms; two suites have a heart-shaped Jacuzzi. Smoke free premises. 10 units. 9 one-bedroom standard units, some with whirlpools. 1 one-bedroom suite. 2 stories (no elevator), interior corridors. **Parking:** on-site. **Terms:** 7 day cancellation notice-fee imposed. **Cards:** DS, MC, VI. **Free Special Amenities: full breakfast and high-speed Internet.**

HOLIDAY INN EXPRESS Book at AAA.com Phone: (252)638-8266

Hotel
$125-$145 All Year

Address: 3455 Dr Martin Luther King Jr Blvd **Location:** US 70 Bypass, exit Jacksonville/US 17, 0.5 mi s. **Facility:** Smoke free premises. 60 one-bedroom standard units, some with whirlpools. 2 stories, interior corridors. *Bath:* combo or shower only. **Parking:** on-site. **Amenities:** dual phone lines, voice mail, irons, hair dryers. **Pool(s):** outdoor. **Leisure Activities:** exercise room. **Guest Services:** valet laundry, wireless Internet. **Business Services:** meeting rooms, PC. **Cards:** AX, DC, DS, MC, VI.

ASK CALL / SOME UNITS VCR

HOWARD HOUSE VICTORIAN BED & BREAKFAST Phone: 252/514-6709

Historic Bed & Breakfast
$119-$149 All Year

Address: 207 Pollock St **Location:** 0.3 mi e of Tryon Palace; downtown; in historic district. **Facility:** The 1890 Queen Anne-influenced home is decorated with antiques and family heirlooms; a gourmet breakfast is served each morning in the dining room. Smoke free premises. 6 one-bedroom standard units. 2 stories (no elevator), interior/exterior corridors. *Bath:* combo or shower only. **Parking:** on-site. **Terms:** 7 day cancellation notice. **Amenities:** video library, hair dryers. *Some:* DVD players. **Leisure Activities:** bicycles. **Guest Services:** wireless Internet. **Business Services:** meeting rooms, PC. **Cards:** AX, DS, MC, VI.

ASK / SOME UNITS

MEADOWS INN Phone: 252/634-1776

Bed & Breakfast
$122-$136 All Year

Address: 212 Pollock St **Location:** 0.3 mi e of Tryon Palace; downtown; in historic district. **Facility:** Period furnishings and family mementos are found throughout the restored 1847 Antebellum home. Smoke free premises. 7 units. 6 one-bedroom standard units. 1 two-bedroom suite. 3 stories (no elevator), interior corridors. **Parking:** on-site. **Terms:** 3 day cancellation notice-fee imposed. **Amenities:** video library, hair dryers. **Guest Services:** wireless Internet. **Business Services:** meeting rooms. **Cards:** AX, DS, MC, VI.

ASK VCR

WHERE TO DINE

ANNABELLE'S RESTAURANT Phone: 252/633-6401

American
$5-$15

Offering steaks, chicken, pasta, sandwiches and salads, Annabelle's is the perfect alternative to the fast food joints. Casual dress. **Bar:** Full bar. **Hours:** 11:30 am-10 pm, Fri & Sat-11 pm, Sun-9 pm. Closed: 11/26, 12/25. **Address:** 3100 Martin Luther King Jr Blvd, D-1 **Location:** Jct US 70 Bypass, just s on US 17; in Twin Rivers Mall. **Parking:** on-site. **Cards:** AX, DS, MC, VI.

CAPTAIN RATTY'S SEAFOOD & STEAKHOUSE Phone: 252/633-2088

Seafood
$5-$37

The casual eatery can get crowded as both locals and tourists flock in for steaks, seafood and sandwiches. Crab cakes, lobster tail, steamed shellfish and fried oysters are just a few of the menu highlights. Casual dress. **Bar:** Full bar. **Hours:** 11 am-10 pm, Fri & Sat-11 pm, Sun noon-9 pm. Closed: 11/26, 12/25. **Address:** 202 Middle St **Location:** Corner of S Front and Middle sts; downtown. **Parking:** street. **Cards:** AX, MC, VI.

THE CHELSEA RESTAURANT **Phone:** 252/637-5469

American
$6-$32

In the historic Bradham's Drug Store building, the family-run bistro offers a menu of eclectic American recipes featuring seafood, beef, chicken and pasta. Southern-style fare includes shrimp and grits and black strap pork (marinated in molasses and Dijon mustard). Seafood selections include potato-crusted salmon and sesame-seared tuna. Dressy casual. **Bar:** Full bar. **Hours:** 11 am-9 pm, Fri & Sat-10 pm. Closed major holidays; also 12/24 & Sun. **Address:** 335 Middle St **Location:** Corner of Middle and Broad sts. **Parking:** street. **Cards:** AX, DS, MC, VI. **Historic**

MORGAN'S TAVERN & GRILL **Phone:** 252/636-2430

American
$6-$30

Featuring delicious sandwiches, pasta dishes, steaks and some seafood, the casual eatery—which is housed in a vintage building with ceilings that soar to the rafters—is a popular lunch spot for the locals. Casual dress. **Bar:** Full bar. **Hours:** 11 am-9 pm, Fri & Sat-10 pm. Closed: 11/26, 12/25; also Sun. **Address:** 235 Craven St **Location:** Jct Pollock St, just s; downtown. **Parking:** on-site. **Cards:** AX, DC, DS, MC, VI.

POLLOCK STREET DELICATESSEN & RESTAURANT **Phone:** 252/637-2480

American
$5-$30

Homemade favorites served at the cozy, restored 1880s home include seafood marinara with scallops, shrimp and salmon served over pasta. For dessert, diners can't resist the scrumptious homemade cream cheese brownies. Casual dress. **Bar:** Beer & wine. **Hours:** 7 am-4 pm, Fri also 5 pm-9 pm, Sat 8 am-3 pm, Sun 9 am-3 pm, Mon 8 am-3 pm. Closed: 1/1, 11/26, 12/25. **Address:** 208 Pollock St **Location:** 0.4 mi e of Tryon Palace; downtown; in historic district. **Parking:** on-site and street. **Cards:** AX, MC, VI.

TEXAS STEAKHOUSE & SALOON **Phone:** 252/637-1500

Steak
$6-$25

The typical Texas-style roadhouse focuses on freshly cut steaks, including the popular Duke entree with fries. Southwestern decor and arrows stuck in the walls get diners' minds wandering back to the old days. The popular draft beer is the microbrewed Red Oak lager. Casual dress. **Bar:** Full bar. **Hours:** 11 am-10 pm, Fri & Sat-11 pm. Closed: 11/26, 12/24, 12/25. **Address:** 3231 Dr Martin Luther King Jr Blvd **Location:** US 70 Bypass, exit Jacksonville/US 17, just s. **Parking:** on-site. **Cards:** AX, DS, MC, VI.

NORTH WILKESBORO pop. 4,116—*See WILKESBORO.*

OCEAN ISLE BEACH pop. 426

WHERE TO STAY

THE ISLANDER INN *Book great rates at AAA.com* **Phone:** (910)575-7000

Hotel
$89-$229 All Year

Address: 57 W First St **Location:** Oceanfront. Jct SR 904, just s. **Facility:** 69 one-bedroom standard units. 3 stories, interior corridors. *Bath:* combo or shower only. **Parking:** on-site. **Terms:** check-in 4 pm, 7 day cancellation notice-fee imposed. **Amenities:** high-speed Internet, voice mail, irons, hair dryers. **Pool(s):** outdoor, heated indoor. **Leisure Activities:** whirlpool, exercise room. **Business Services:** meeting rooms. **Cards:** AX, DS, MC, VI. **Free Special Amenities: continental breakfast and high-speed Internet.** *(See color ad p 983)*

  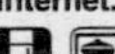 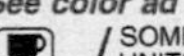 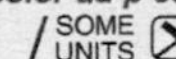 / SOME UNITS

OCEAN ISLE INN *Book great rates at AAA.com* **Phone:** (910)579-0750

Hotel
$79-$199 12/1-9/1
$79-$149 9/2-11/30

Address: 37 W First St **Location:** Oceanfront. Jct SR 904, just s. **Facility:** Smoke free premises. 70 one-bedroom standard units. 3 stories, interior corridors. **Parking:** on-site. **Terms:** 2 night minimum stay - weekends, 7 day cancellation notice-fee imposed. **Amenities:** voice mail, irons, hair dryers. **Pool(s):** outdoor, heated indoor. **Leisure Activities:** whirlpool. **Guest Services:** wireless Internet. **Business Services:** meeting rooms, PC. **Cards:** AX, DS, MC, VI. **Free Special Amenities: expanded continental breakfast and high-speed Internet.** *(See color ad p 984)*

▼ See AAA listing p 768 ▼

THE WINDS RESORT BEACH CLUB *Book great rates at AAA.com* **Phone:** (910)579-6275

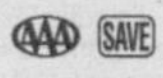

Hotel

$108-$275 6/8-11/30
$67-$234 12/1-6/7

Address: 310 E First St **Location:** Oceanfront. SR 904, 1.6 mi n. **Facility:** Smoke free premises. 86 units. 55 one-bedroom standard units, some with efficiencies. 13 one- and 18 two-bedroom suites with kitchens, some with whirlpools. 3-4 stories, interior/exterior corridors. **Parking:** on-site. **Terms:** check-in 4 pm, 3-7 night minimum stay - seasonal, cancellation fee imposed. **Amenities:** DVD players, voice mail, irons, hair dryers. **Pool(s):** 2 outdoor, heated indoor. **Leisure Activities:** whirlpools, putting green, bocci, table tennis, rental bicycles, exercise room, shuffleboard, volleyball. *Fee:* golf privileges. **Guest Services:** coin laundry, wireless Internet. **Business Services:** meeting rooms. **Cards:** AX, CB, DC, DS, MC, VI. **Free Special Amenities: full breakfast and high-speed Internet.** *(See color ad p 984 & p 767)*

WHERE TO DINE

SUGAR SHACK JAMAICAN RESTAURANT **Phone:** 910/579-3844

Jamaican
$9-$25

Spicy cuisine and friendly service attract both locals and tourists to the small, bright cafe. The menu lists jerk chicken and pork, as well as other traditional Jamaican fare. Casual dress. **Bar:** Beer & wine. **Reservations:** accepted. **Hours:** Open 2/1-11/25; 5 pm-9 pm; Fri & Sat-10 pm in summer. Closed: Sun & Mon. **Address:** 1609 Hale Beach Rd **Location:** SR 904, just s on SR 179, then just e. **Parking:** on-site. **Cards:** AX, DS, MC, VI.

OCRACOKE —*See Outer Banks p. 785.*

ORIENTAL pop. 875

WHERE TO STAY

ORIENTAL MARINA & INN **Phone:** 252/249-1818

Motel
$89-$174 All Year

Address: 103 Wall St **Location:** Jct SR 55 (Broad St), just ne on Hodges St. **Facility:** Smoke free premises. 25 units. 2 one-bedroom standard units. 23 condominiums. 2-3 stories (no elevator), exterior corridors. *Bath:* combo or shower only. **Parking:** on-site. **Terms:** office hours 8 am-10 pm, 2 night minimum stay - seasonal and/or weekends. **Amenities:** DVD players, irons, hair dryers. **Pool(s):** outdoor. **Leisure Activities:** *Fee:* marina. **Guest Services:** coin laundry, wireless Internet. **Business Services:** meeting rooms. **Cards:** AX, DS, MC, VI.

/ SOME UNITS FEE VCR

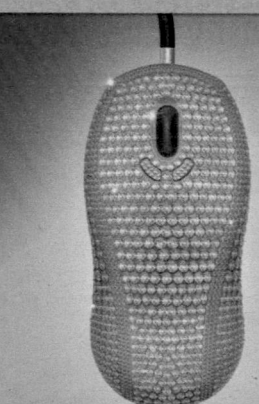

Destination Outer Banks

Lookin' for a place to golf, fish, surf, dive, snorkel, windsurf, jet ski, sail, kayak, parasail, hang glide, watch dolphins and go on an eco-tour? Try The Outer Banks!

And it's a great place to baste in the warm saltwater and then just bake in the sun. When it's time to graze, remember you're in the land of fresh seafood and sumptuous Southern desserts.

© Everett C. Johnson eStock Photo

Pier, Nags Head.
Whether you care to cast a line or simply gaze at the sapphire blue sea, step out onto one of the many piers jutting from the shoreline.

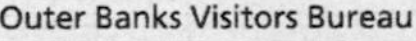

Outer Banks Visitors Bureau

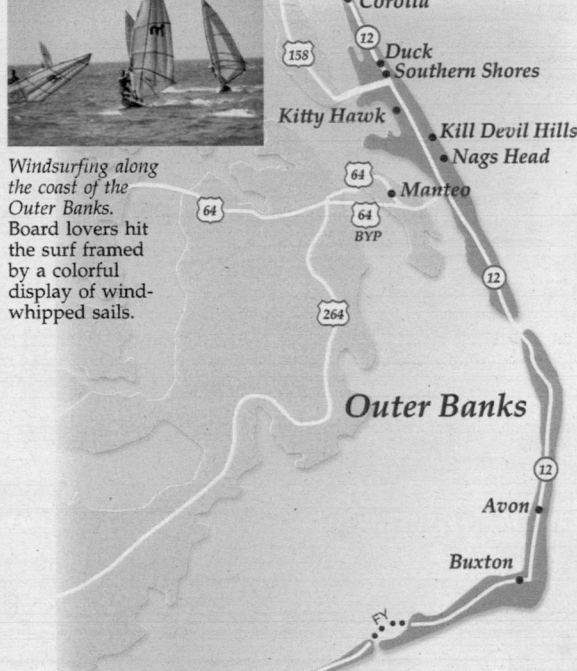

Windsurfing along the coast of the Outer Banks.
Board lovers hit the surf framed by a colorful display of wind-whipped sails.

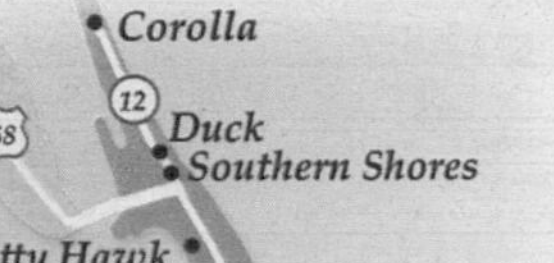

© DK. Khattiya / Alamy

Cape Hatteras Lighthouse, Cape Hatteras National Seashore.
After being moved inland in 1999, this sentinel of the sea resumed its vigil begun in 1870. (See listing page 174)

Shopping, Roanoke Island.
Charming shops with architectural flair and intriguing wares dot the island.

© Roanoke Island Festival Park

Places included in this AAA Destination Area:

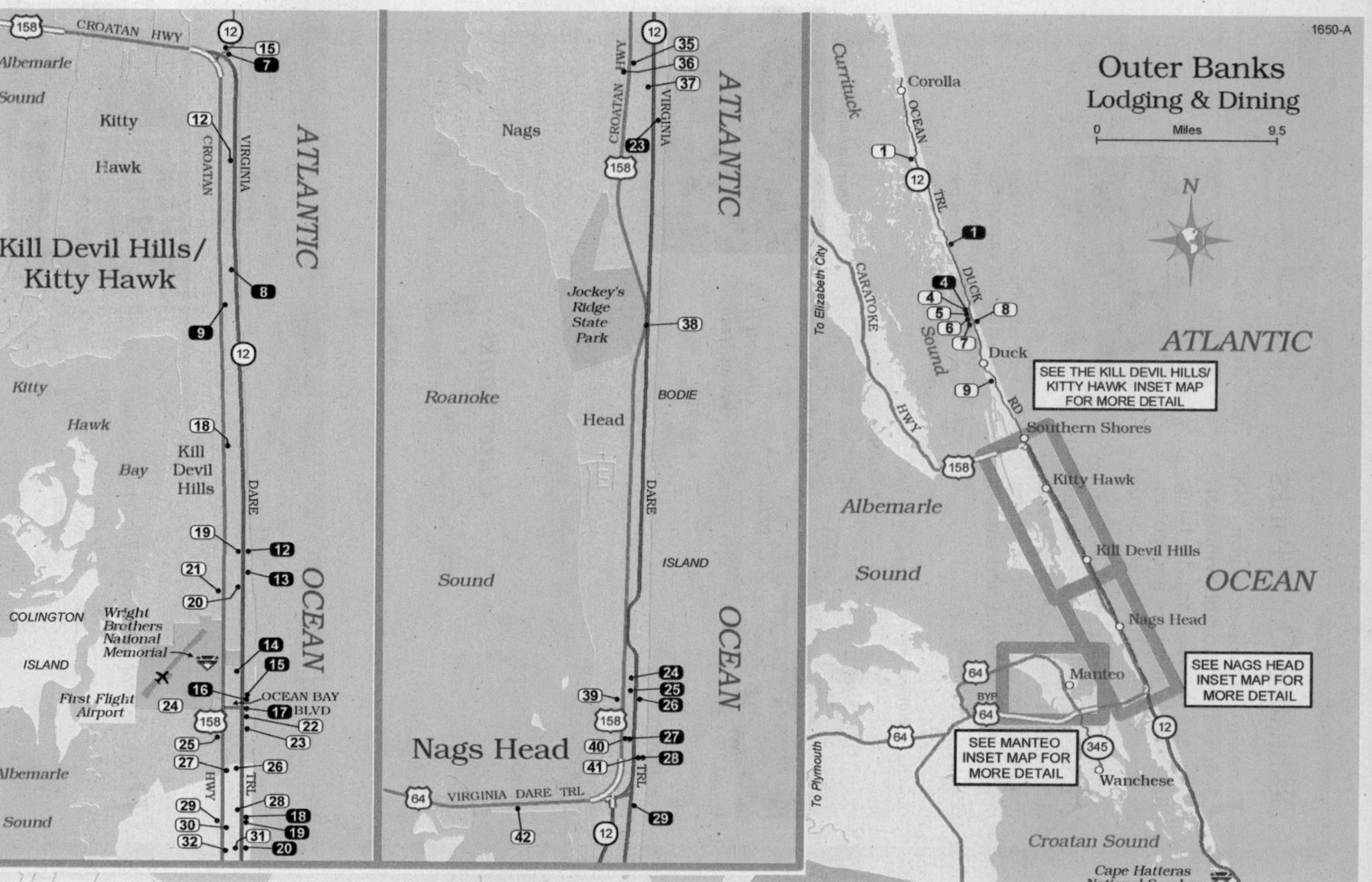
Outer Banks
Lodging & Dining
0
Miles
9.5
N
1650-A
Corolla
OCEAN TRL
DUCK RD
Duck
Currituck
Sound
CARATOKE HWY
To Elizabeth City
ATLANTIC
SEE THE KILL DEVIL HILLS/ KITTY HAWK INSET MAP FOR MORE DETAIL
Southern Shores
Kitty Hawk
Kill Devil Hills
Nags Head
Manteo
Wanchese
OCEAN
SEE NAGS HEAD INSET MAP FOR MORE DETAIL
SEE MANTEO INSET MAP FOR MORE DETAIL
BYP
Albemarle
Sound
To Plymouth
Croatan Sound
Cape Hatteras National Seashore
Nags
CROATAN HWY
VIRGINIA
ATLANTIC
Jockey's Ridge State Park
Roanoke
Head
BODIE
DARE
ISLAND
Sound
OCEAN
Nags Head
VIRGINIA DARE TRL
TRL
CROATAN HWY
Albemarle
Sound
Kitty
Hawk
CROATAN
VIRGINIA
ATLANTIC
Kill Devil Hills/
Kitty Hawk
Kitty
Hawk
Bay
Kill
Devil
Hills
DARE
OCEAN
COLINGTON
ISLAND
Wright Brothers National Memorial
First Flight Airport
OCEAN BAY BLVD
HWY
TRL
Albemarle
Sound

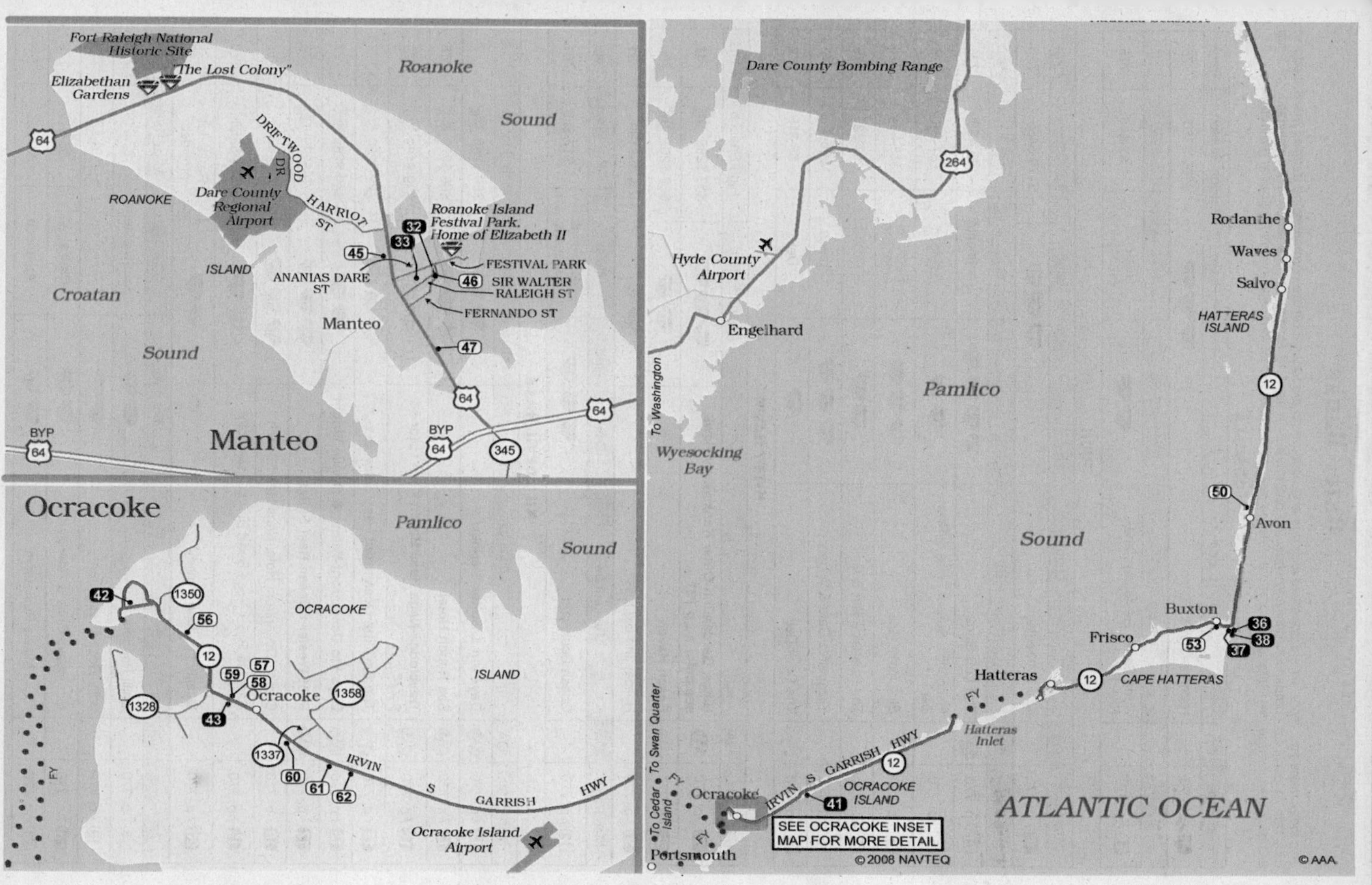
Fort Raleigh National Historic Site
"The Lost Colony"
Elizabethan Gardens
Roanoke
Sound
ROANOKE
ISLAND
Dare County Regional Airport
DRIFTWOOD DR
HARRIOT ST
Roanoke Island Festival Park, Home of Elizabeth II
FESTIVAL PARK
SIR WALTER RALEIGH ST
FERNANDO ST
ANANIAS DARE ST
Manteo
Croatan
Sound
BYP
Manteo
Ocracoke
Pamlico
Sound
OCRACOKE
ISLAND
Ocracoke
IRVIN S GARRISH HWY
Ocracoke Island Airport
FY
Dare County Bombing Range
Hyde County Airport
Engelhard
To Washington
Wyesocking Bay
Pamlico
Sound
Rodanthe
Waves
Salvo
HATTERAS ISLAND
Avon
Buxton
Frisco
CAPE HATTERAS
Hatteras
Hatteras Inlet
To Swan Quarter
To Cedar Island
Ocracoke
Portsmouth
OCRACOKE ISLAND
SEE OCRACOKE INSET MAP FOR MORE DETAIL
© 2008 NAVTEQ
ATLANTIC OCEAN
© AAA

Outer Banks

This index helps you "spot" where approved lodgings and restaurants are located on the corresponding detailed maps. Lodging daily rate range is for comparison only and show the property's high season. Restaurant rate range is a combination of lunch and/or dinner. Turn to the listing page for more detailed rate information and consult display ads for special promotions.

COROLLA

Map Page	OA	Lodging	Diamond Rated	High Season	Page
1 / p. 770		Hampton Inn & Suites	◆◆◆	$100-$350	775

Map Page	OA	Restaurant	Diamond Rated	Cuisine	Meal Range	Page
1 / p. 770		North Banks Restaurant and Raw Bar	◆◆	Regional American	$7-$40	775

DUCK

Map Page	OA	Lodging	Diamond Rated	High Season	Page
4 / p. 770		The Sanderling	◆◆◆	$179-$459	776

Map Page	OA	Restaurants	Diamond Rated	Cuisine	Meal Range	Page
4 / p. 770	AAA	**The Left Bank**	◆◆◆◆	Continental	$69-$99	776
5 / p. 770		Fishbone's Sunset Grille & Raw Bar	◆◆	Seafood	$7-$40	776
6 / p. 770		Blue Point Grill	◆◆◆	Regional American	$8-$34	776
7 / p. 770		The Roadside Bar & Grill	◆◆	Seafood	$6-$30	776
8 / p. 770		Elizabeth's Cafe & Winery	◆◆◆	French	$25-$40	776
9 / p. 770		The Duck Deli	◆	Deli	$5-$15	776

KITTY HAWK

Map Page	OA	Lodgings	Diamond Rated	High Season	Page
7 / p. 770	AAA	**Hilton Garden Inn-Outer Banks/Kitty Hawk** - see color ad p 781	◆◆◆	$89-$289 SAVE	781
8 / p. 770	AAA	**Beach Haven**	◆◆	$68-$205 SAVE	780
9 / p. 770		Holiday Inn Express	◆◆	$79-$169	781

Map Page	OA	Restaurant	Diamond Rated	Cuisine	Meal Range	Page
12 / p. 770		Ocean Boulevard	◆◆◆	Regional American	$17-$29	781

KILL DEVIL HILLS

Map Page	OA	Lodgings	Diamond Rated	High Season	Page
12 / p. 770	AAA	**Days Inn & Suites-Mariner**	◆◆	$59-$289 SAVE	777
13 / p. 770	AAA	**Sea Ranch Hotel**	◆◆◆	$86-$275 SAVE	778
14 / p. 770	AAA	**Travelodge-Nags Head Beach** - see color ad p 778	◆◆	$39-$189 SAVE	779
15 / p. 770	AAA	**The Carolina Oceanfront** - see color ad p 777	◆◆◆	$52-$250 SAVE	777
16 / p. 770	AAA	**Days Inn Oceanfront-Wilbur & Orville Wright**	◆◆	$49-$269 SAVE	777
17 / p. 770	AAA	**Best Western Ocean Reef Suites**	◆◆◆	$79-$279 SAVE	776
18 / p. 770		Clarion Oceanfront Hotel-Nags Head Beach	◆◆◆	$59-$249	777
19 / p. 770		Ramada Plaza Nags Head Beach - see color ad p 778	◆◆	$89-$259	778
20 / p. 770		Quality Inn-John Yancey	◆◆	Rates not provided	778

Map Page	OA	Restaurants	Diamond Rated	Cuisine	Meal Range	Page
18 / p. 770		Chilli Peppers	◆◆	Southwestern	$7-$19	779
19 / p. 770		Jolly Roger Restaurant	◆◆	American	$4-$22	779
20 / p. 770		Goombays Grille & Raw Bar	◆◆	Caribbean	$5-$19	779
21 / p. 770		Mako Mike's Restaurant	◆◆	American	$9-$30	779

Map Page	OA	Restaurants (cont'd)	Diamond Rated	Cuisine	Meal Range	Page
22 / p. 770		Port-O-Call Restaurant and Gift Emporium		Seafood	$14-$25	780
23 / p. 770		Thai Room Restaurant		Thai	$5-$16	780
24 / p. 770		Colington Cafe		Continental	$14-$23	779
25 / p. 770		Outer Banks Brewing Station		American	$5-$29	780
26 / p. 770		Dare Devil's Authentic Pizzeria		Pizza	$6-$14	779
27 / p. 770		JK's Restaurant		Steak & Seafood	$15-$25	779
28 / p. 770		Miller's Seafood & Steak House		Seafood	$12-$23	780
29 / p. 770		Pigman's Bar-B-Que		Barbecue	$7-$19	780
30 / p. 770		Mama Kwan's Grill & Tiki Bar		Island	$6-$20	780
31 / p. 770		Kill Devil Grill		American	$6-$20	779
32 / p. 770		Flying Fish Cafe		American	$19-$26	779

NAGS HEAD

Map Page	OA	Lodgings	Diamond Rated	High Season	Page
23 / p. 770		**Beacon Motor Lodge**		$65-$250 SAVE	782
24 / p. 770		**The Surf Side Hotel**		$55-$284 SAVE	783
25 / p. 770		**First Colony Inn - see color ad p 782**		$79-$309 SAVE	783
26 / p. 770		Blue Heron Motel		$60-$150	782
27 / p. 770		Tar Heel Motel		$55-$110	784
28 / p. 770		**Sea Foam Motel**		$62-$170 SAVE	783
29 / p. 770		Comfort Inn Oceanfront South		Rates not provided	782

Map Page	OA	Restaurants	Diamond Rated	Cuisine	Meal Range	Page
35 / p. 770		New York Pizza Pub		Pizza	$6-$21	784
36 / p. 770		**Kelly's Outer Banks Restaurant & Tavern**		American	$12-$33	784
37 / p. 770		Red Drum Grill & Taphouse		American	$5-$22	784
38 / p. 770		Jockey's Ribs		American	$14-$30	784
39 / p. 770		**Penguin Isle Soundside Restaurant**		Steak & Seafood	$12-$35	784
40 / p. 770		The Dunes Restaurant		American	$6-$20	784
41 / p. 770		**Owens' Restaurant**		Steak & Seafood	$18-$30	784
42 / p. 770		Basnight's Lone Cedar Cafe		Seafood	$7-$30	784

MANTEO

Map Page	OA	Lodgings	Diamond Rated	High Season	Page
32 / p. 770		The Tranquil House Inn		$189-$249	781
33 / p. 770		The White Doe Inn		$195-$325	781

Map Page	OA	Restaurants	Diamond Rated	Cuisine	Meal Range	Page
45 / p. 770		Big Al's Soda Fountain & Grill		American	$4-$14	782
46 / p. 770		1587 Restaurant		Regional American	$20-$30	782
47 / p. 770		Darrell's Seafood Restaurant		Regional American	$3-$21	782

BUXTON

Map Page	OA	Lodgings	Diamond Rated	High Season	Page
36 / p. 770		**Lighthouse View Motel**		$69-$198 SAVE	775

BUXTON (cont'd)

Map Page	OA	Lodgings (cont'd)	Diamond Rated	High Season	Page
37 / p. 770		Comfort Inn	♦♦♦	$119-$179	775
38 / p. 770		Cape Hatteras Bed & Breakfast	♦♦♦	$129-$159	775

Map Page	OA	Restaurant	Diamond Rated	Cuisine	Meal Range	Page
53 / p. 770		Buoy's Beach-n-BBQ Restaurant	♦	Seafood	$4-$28	775

OCRACOKE

Map Page	OA	Lodgings	Diamond Rated	High Season	Page
41 / p. 770	AAA	**Harborside Motel**	♦♦	$70-$105 SAVE	785
42 / p. 770	AAA	**The Anchorage Inn**	♦♦	$99-$299 SAVE	785
43 / p. 770	AAA	**Bluff Shoal Motel**	♦♦	$65-$109 SAVE	785

Map Page	OA	Restaurants	Diamond Rated	Cuisine	Meal Range	Page
56 / p. 770		Pony Island Restaurant	♦	American	$5-$20	786
57 / p. 770		Back Porch Restaurant	♦♦♦	Seafood	$12-$25	785
58 / p. 770		Captain Ben's Restaurant	♦♦	Steak & Seafood	$5-$22	785
59 / p. 770	AAA	**Howard's Pub & Raw Bar Restaurant**	♦♦	American	$6-$25	785
60 / p. 770		The Pelican Restaurant	♦♦	Seafood	$6-$28	785
61 / p. 770		Cafe Atlantic	♦♦	Seafood	$4-$21	785
62 / p. 770		Jason's Restaurant	♦♦	American	$4-$20	785

SOUTHERN SHORES

Map Page	OA	Restaurant	Diamond Rated	Cuisine	Meal Range	Page
15 / p. 770		Meridian 42	♦♦♦	American	$18-$24	786

AVON

Map Page	OA	Restaurant	Diamond Rated	Cuisine	Meal Range	Page
50 / p. 770		The Froggy Dog	♦♦	American	$5-$25	775

AVON (See map and index starting on p. 770)

WHERE TO DINE

THE FROGGY DOG Phone: 252/995-5550 (50)

American
$5-$25

The restaurant started more than 10 years ago with just The Froggy Dog, a hot dog with chili, cheese and onions. Since then, the menu has evolved to include seafood, steaks, chicken, sandwiches and salads. Among favorites are Maryland-style crab cakes and pecan-crusted flounder. Casual dress. **Bar:** Beer & wine. **Hours:** Open 3/15-10/31, 7 am-2:30 & 5-9 pm. **Address:** 40050 Hwy 12 **Location:** SR 12, at MM 54.5. **Parking:** on-site. **Cards:** AX, DS, MC, VI.

BUXTON (See map and index starting on p. 770)

WHERE TO STAY

CAPE HATTERAS BED & BREAKFAST Phone: 252/995-6004 (38)

Bed & Breakfast
$129-$159 4/1-11/30

Address: 46223 Old Lighthouse Rd **Location:** Jct SR 12, just e. **Facility:** Outstanding sunsets may be viewed from the deck of this beach house, which is within walking distance of the beach and near the lighthouse. Smoke free premises. 9 one-bedroom standard units, some with efficiencies. 2 stories (no elevator), exterior corridors. *Bath:* shower only. **Parking:** on-site. **Terms:** open 4/1-11/30, check-in 4 pm, 2 night minimum stay - seasonal, 7 day cancellation notice-fee imposed. **Amenities:** video library, hair dryers. **Leisure Activities:** bicycles. **Guest Services:** wireless Internet. **Cards:** MC, VI.

ASK / SOME UNITS VCR

COMFORT INN *Book at AAA.com* Phone: (252)995-6100 (37)

Motel
$119-$179 4/1-11/30
$79-$99 12/1-3/31

Address: 46745 Hwy 12 **Location:** Jct Old Lighthouse Rd. **Facility:** 60 one-bedroom standard units. 2 stories (no elevator), exterior corridors. **Parking:** on-site. **Terms:** 3 day cancellation notice-fee imposed. **Amenities:** irons, hair dryers. **Pool(s):** outdoor. **Guest Services:** coin laundry. **Cards:** AX, CB, DC, DS, MC, VI.

ASK / SOME UNITS

LIGHTHOUSE VIEW MOTEL Phone: 252/995-5680 (36)

AAA SAVE

Motel
$69-$198 6/7-11/30
$54-$110 12/1-6/6

Address: 46677 Hwy 12 **Location:** Oceanfront. On SR 12; 0.5 mi n of Cape Hatteras Lighthouse. **Facility:** 78 units. 28 one-bedroom standard units. 22 one-, 18 two- and 10 three-bedroom suites, some with efficiencies or kitchens. 2-3 stories (no elevator), exterior corridors. **Parking:** on-site. **Terms:** office hours 7 am-10 pm, 1-7 night minimum stay - seasonal and/or weekends, 30 day cancellation notice. **Amenities:** *Some:* DVD players. **Pool(s):** outdoor. **Leisure Activities:** whirlpool, fishing. **Guest Services:** coin laundry, wireless Internet. **Cards:** AX, DS, MC, VI.

/ SOME UNITS VCR

WHERE TO DINE

BUOY'S BEACH-N-BBQ RESTAURANT Phone: 252/995-6575 (53)

Seafood
$4-$28

Slow-smoked, North Carolina-style barbecue and fresh local seafood as well as fried chicken and barbecue ribs adorn this casual eatery's menu. Casual dress. **Bar:** Beer & wine. **Hours:** Open 12/1-12/15 & 1/16-11/30; 11:30 am-9 pm, Sun 11 am-2 pm; hours may vary off season. Closed: 12/25. **Address:** 47355 NE NC Hwy 12 **Location:** Just n from Old Lighthouse Rd. **Parking:** on-site. **Cards:** AX, DS, MC, VI.

COROLLA (See map and index starting on p. 770)

WHERE TO STAY

HAMPTON INN & SUITES *Book great rates at AAA.com* Phone: (252)453-6565 (1)

Hotel
$100-$350 All Year

Address: 333 Audubon Dr **Location:** Oceanfront. Jct US 158, 12.5 mi n on SR 12, just e. **Facility:** Smoke free premises. 123 one-bedroom standard units, some with whirlpools. 3 stories, interior corridors. *Bath:* combo or shower only. **Parking:** on-site. **Terms:** check-in 4 pm, 2-3 night minimum stay - seasonal and/or weekends, 3 day cancellation notice. **Amenities:** video games (fee), high-speed Internet, dual phone lines, voice mail, safes, irons, hair dryers. **Pool(s):** outdoor, heated indoor. **Leisure Activities:** whirlpool, exercise room. *Fee:* game room. **Guest Services:** coin laundry, wireless Internet. **Business Services:** meeting rooms, PC. **Cards:** AX, CB, DC, DS, JC, MC, VI.

CALL &M

WHERE TO DINE

NORTH BANKS RESTAURANT AND RAW BAR Phone: 252/453-3344 (1)

Regional American
$7-$40

The small casual dining restaurant and raw bar features seating for about 50 diners at stainless-steel-topped tables. Offerings of fresh local seafood include steamed shrimp, chowders, daily fish specials, raw-bar items and live Maine lobsters. Meat-lovers might prefer chops or steaks. Service is friendly and efficient. Casual dress. **Hours:** Open 2/15-11/29; 11:30 am-3:30 & 5-9 pm. Closed: 11/26. **Address:** 794-G Sunset Blvd **Location:** Jct SR 12/US 158, 17 mi n on SR 12, then just w; in Tim Buck II Shopping Village. **Parking:** on-site. **Cards:** AX, DS, MC, VI.

DUCK (See map and index starting on p. 770)

WHERE TO STAY

THE SANDERLING Book at AAA.com **Phone:** (252)261-4111 4

Resort Hotel
$179-$459 4/1-11/30
$119-$229 12/1-3/31

Address: 1461 Duck Rd (SR 12) **Location:** Oceanfront. On SR 12, 5 mi n. **Facility:** This handsome beachfront hotel is in a quiet area and features upscale accommodations and a full-service spa. 93 units. 77 one-bedroom standard units. 11 one-bedroom suites with whirlpools. 5 houses. 2-3 stories, interior corridors. *Bath:* combo or shower only. **Parking:** on-site. **Terms:** check-in 4 pm, 2-4 night minimum stay - seasonal and/or weekends, 7 day cancellation notice-fee imposed. **Amenities:** CD players, voice mail, safes, irons, hair dryers. *Some:* DVD players. **Dining:** The Left Bank, see separate listing. **Pool(s):** outdoor, heated indoor. **Leisure Activities:** whirlpools, steamroom, fishing, 2 tennis courts, rental bicycles, hiking trails, jogging, exercise room, spa. **Guest Services:** valet laundry, wireless Internet. **Business Services:** conference facilities. **Cards:** AX, DC, DS, MC, VI.

ASK / SOME UNITS

WHERE TO DINE

BLUE POINT GRILL **Phone:** 252/261-8090 6

Regional American
$8-$34

Popular for its 1950s diner atmosphere, the grill has won awards for its wine list. The focus of the menu is on fresh ingredients and innovative cuisine prepared with Southern flair. Crab cakes are a signature item. In the summer, outdoor seating is an option. The view of sunsets over Currituck Sound is spectacular. Casual dress. **Bar:** Full bar. **Reservations:** suggested. **Hours:** 11:30 am-2:30 & 5-10 pm, Mon from 5 pm. Closed: 11/26, 12/25; also Mon 1/1-3/31. **Address:** 1240 Duck Rd **Location:** 1 mi n on SR 12; in Waterfront Shops on north end. **Parking:** on-site. **Cards:** AX, MC, VI.

THE DUCK DELI **Phone:** 252/261-3354 9

Deli
$5-$15

The small deli offers sandwiches, salads, fish as well as the house specialty of hickory-smoked barbecue pork, beef and chicken. Seating is limited. Casual dress. **Hours:** 8 am-8 pm. **Address:** 1223 Duck Rd **Location:** On SR 12. **Parking:** on-site. **Cards:** MC, VI.

ELIZABETH'S CAFE & WINERY **Phone:** 252/261-6145 8

French
$25-$40

Wines from the extensive, award-winning list pair with excellent presentations of nouvelle and country-French food. The menu changes daily so check back often. During two nightly seatings, patrons choose between the a la carte menu and six- or seven-course prix fixe wine dinners. A wine bar featuring cheeses and pates opens daily at 2 pm. Casual dress. **Bar:** Full bar. **Reservations:** required. **Hours:** seatings at 6 pm, 6:30 pm, 8:15 pm & 8:45 pm; call for hours off season. Closed: 1/1, 12/25. **Address:** 1177 Duck Rd, Suite 11 **Location:** SR 12, just e on Christopher Ln; center of town; in Scarborough Faire Shoppes. **Parking:** on-site. **Cards:** AX, DC, MC, VI.

FISHBONE'S SUNSET GRILLE & RAW BAR **Phone:** 252/261-3901 5

Seafood
$7-$40

Caribbean jerk cuisine is their specialty at this colorful grill with a large deck overlooking the sound. They catch their own soft-shell crabs when in season. Casual dress. **Bar:** Full bar. **Hours:** 11 am-9 pm; also 8-10 am in summer. Closed: 12/25. **Address:** 1264 Duck Rd **Location:** On SR 12. **Parking:** on-site. **Cards:** AX, DS, MC, VI.

THE LEFT BANK **Phone:** 252/261-4111 4

Continental
$69-$99

The chic, upscale dining room affords spectacular views of Currituck Sound. Guests enjoy superbly prepared French-inspired, contemporary American cuisine. Dishes on the daily changing prix fixe menu feature only the freshest ingredients. The exhibition kitchen provides a view of the chef and his team as they put their superior talents to work in preparing the evening's gastronomic marvels. Examples of fine options include Arctic char, New Zealand venison, duck and foie gras. Dressy casual. **Bar:** Full bar. **Reservations:** required. **Hours:** 5:30 pm-9:30 pm; hours may vary off season. Closed: 12/25; also Sun & Mon. **Address:** 1461 Duck Rd (SR 12) **Location:** On SR 12, 5 mi n; in The Sanderling. **Parking:** on-site. **Cards:** AX, DC, DS, MC, VI.

THE ROADSIDE BAR & GRILL **Phone:** 252/261-5729 7

Seafood
$6-$30

A seasonally changing menu keeps patrons coming back to the casual eatery. The lunch menu includes salads and sandwiches while dinner expands to feature pork chops, lamb, pasta, salmon, and other fare in innovative preparations. When the weather permits, dine al fresco on the outdoor deck. Casual dress. **Bar:** Full bar. **Hours:** 11:30 am-9 pm; to 10 pm in summer. Closed: 11/26, 12/24, 12/25. **Address:** 1193 Duck Rd **Location:** On SR 12. **Parking:** on-site. **Cards:** MC, VI.

KILL DEVIL HILLS pop. 5,897 (See map and index starting on p. 770)

WHERE TO STAY

BEST WESTERN OCEAN REEF SUITES Book great rates at AAA.com **Phone:** (252)441-1611 

Hotel
$79-$279 All Year

Address: 107 S Virginia Dare Tr **Location:** Oceanfront. SR 12, at MM 8.5. **Facility:** 71 one-bedroom suites with kitchens. 5 stories, exterior corridors. **Parking:** on-site. **Terms:** check-in 4 pm, 1-3 night minimum stay - seasonal and/or weekends, 3 day cancellation notice. **Amenities:** high-speed Internet, irons, hair dryers. **Pool(s):** outdoor. **Leisure Activities:** sauna, whirlpool, fishing, exercise room. **Guest Services:** coin laundry, wireless Internet. **Cards:** AX, CB, DC, DS, JC, MC, VI. **Free Special Amenities: continental breakfast and high-speed Internet.**

AAA Benefit:
Members save up to 20%, plus 10% bonus points with rewards program.

(See map and index starting on p. 770)

THE CAROLINA OCEANFRONT — Phone: (252)480-2600 15

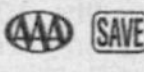

Hotel
$52-$250 All Year

Address: 401 N Virginia Dare Tr **Location:** Oceanfront. SR 12, at MM 8.2. **Facility:** 119 one-bedroom standard units. 3 stories, exterior corridors. **Parking:** on-site. **Terms:** check-in 4 pm. **Amenities:** voice mail, safes, irons, hair dryers. **Pool(s):** outdoor. **Leisure Activities:** fishing. **Guest Services:** coin laundry, wireless Internet. **Business Services:** PC. **Cards:** AX, DC, DS, MC, VI.
(See color ad below)

/ SOME UNITS

CLARION OCEANFRONT HOTEL-NAGS HEAD BEACH *Book at AAA.com* — Phone: (252)441-6333 18

Hotel
$59-$249 All Year

Address: 1601 S Virginia Dare Tr **Location:** Oceanfront. SR 12, at MM 9.5. **Facility:** 105 one-bedroom standard units, some with whirlpools. 4 stories, interior corridors. **Parking:** on-site. **Terms:** check-in 4 pm, 2-3 night minimum stay - seasonal and/or weekends. **Amenities:** voice mail, safes (fee), irons, hair dryers. **Pool(s):** outdoor. **Leisure Activities:** whirlpool, fishing, limited exercise equipment. **Guest Services:** coin laundry, wireless Internet. **Business Services:** meeting rooms, PC. **Cards:** AX, CB, DC, DS, JC, MC, VI.

ASK / SOME UNITS FEE

DAYS INN & SUITES-MARINER *Book great rates at AAA.com* — Phone: (252)441-2021 12

Motel
$59-$289 5/23-11/30
$59-$169 12/1-5/22

Address: 1801 N Virginia Dare Tr **Location:** Oceanfront. SR 12, at MM 7.3. **Facility:** Smoke free premises. 74 units. 36 one-bedroom standard units. 30 one- and 8 two-bedroom suites, some with kitchens. 2-3 stories (no elevator), exterior corridors. *Bath:* combo or shower only. **Parking:** on-site. **Terms:** check-in 4 pm, 2 night minimum stay - seasonal and/or weekends, 3 day cancellation notice-fee imposed. **Amenities:** safes (fee), irons, hair dryers. **Pool(s):** outdoor. **Guest Services:** wireless Internet. **Cards:** AX, DS, MC, VI. **Free Special Amenities: expanded continental breakfast and high-speed Internet.**

DAYS INN OCEANFRONT-WILBUR & ORVILLE WRIGHT *Book great rates at AAA.com* — Phone: (252)441-7211 16

Motel
$49-$269 5/23-11/30
$49-$169 12/1-5/22

Address: 201 N Virginia Dare Tr **Location:** Oceanfront. SR 12, at MM 8.3. **Facility:** Smoke free premises. 54 one-bedroom standard units, some with efficiencies. 2 stories (no elevator), interior/exterior corridors. *Bath:* combo or shower only. **Parking:** on-site. **Terms:** check-in 4 pm, 2 night minimum stay - seasonal and/or weekends, 3 day cancellation notice-fee imposed. **Amenities:** safes (fee), irons, hair dryers. **Pool(s):** outdoor. **Leisure Activities:** fishing. **Guest Services:** coin laundry, wireless Internet. **Business Services:** PC. **Cards:** AX, DS, MC, VI. **Free Special Amenities: expanded continental breakfast and high-speed Internet.**

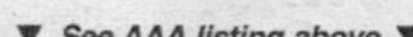

(See map and index starting on p. 770)

QUALITY INN-JOHN YANCEY *Book at AAA.com* **Phone:** 252/441-7141 **20**

Motel

Rates not provided

Address: 2009 S Virginia Dare Tr **Location:** Oceanfront. SR 12, at MM 10.3. **Facility:** 107 one-bedroom standard units. 2-4 stories, interior/exterior corridors. *Bath:* combo or shower only. **Parking:** on-site. **Terms:** check-in 4 pm. **Amenities:** irons, hair dryers. **Pool(s):** outdoor. **Guest Services:** coin laundry, wireless Internet.

/ SOME UNITS FEE

RAMADA PLAZA NAGS HEAD BEACH *Book great rates at AAA.com* **Phone:** (252)441-2151 **19**

Hotel

$89-$259 6/13-11/30

$79-$135 12/1-6/12

Address: 1701 S Virginia Dare Tr **Location:** Oceanfront. SR 12, at MM 9.5. **Facility:** 171 one-bedroom standard units. 5 stories, interior corridors. **Parking:** on-site. **Terms:** check-in 4 pm, 2-3 night minimum stay - seasonal and/or weekends, 3 day cancellation notice. **Amenities:** high-speed Internet, voice mail, safes, irons, hair dryers. **Pool(s):** heated indoor. **Leisure Activities:** whirlpool, exercise room. *Fee:* game room. **Guest Services:** complimentary laundry, wireless Internet. **Business Services:** conference facilities, PC. **Cards:** AX, DS, MC, VI. ***(See color ad below)***

ASK / SOME UNITS FEE

SEA RANCH HOTEL **Phone:** 252/441-7126 **13**

AAA SAVE

Hotel

$86-$275 All Year

Address: 1731 N Virginia Dare Tr **Location:** Oceanfront. SR 12, at MM 7.5. **Facility:** 50 one-bedroom standard units. 2-5 stories, interior/exterior corridors. **Parking:** on-site. **Terms:** check-in 4 pm, 2 night minimum stay - seasonal and/or weekends, cancellation fee imposed. **Amenities:** irons, hair dryers. **Pool(s):** heated indoor. **Leisure Activities:** barbecue grills, picnic tables. **Guest Services:** wireless Internet. **Business Services:** meeting rooms. **Cards:** AX, DS, MC, VI. **Free Special Amenities: full breakfast and high-speed Internet.**

/ SOME UNITS

▼ *See AAA listing above* ▼

▼ *See AAA listing p 779* ▼

(See map and index starting on p. 770)

TRAVELODGE-NAGS HEAD BEACH *Book great rates at AAA.com* **Phone:** (252)441-0411 (14)

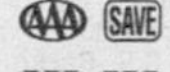

Hotel
$39-$189 All Year

Address: 804 N Virginia Dare Tr **Location:** SR 12, at MM 8.1. **Facility:** 97 one-bedroom standard units. 4 stories, interior/exterior corridors. **Parking:** on-site. **Terms:** check-in 4 pm, 3 day cancellation notice-fee imposed. **Amenities:** safes, irons, hair dryers. **Pool(s):** outdoor. **Guest Services:** wireless Internet. **Cards:** AX, CB, DC, DS, JC, MC, VI. **Free Special Amenities: continental breakfast and high-speed Internet.** *(See color ad p 778)*

/ SOME UNITS FEE

WHERE TO DINE

CHILLI PEPPERS **Phone:** 252/441-8081 (18)

Southwestern
$7-$19

All menu offerings are prepared with a Southwestern flair at the colorful eatery. In addition to quesadillas, burritos and sandwiches, guests can order preparations of salmon, duck, chicken and pork. Casual dress. **Bar:** Full bar. **Hours:** 11 am-10 pm; to 11 pm in season; Sunday brunch 10 am-3 pm. Closed: 11/26, 12/25. **Address:** 3001 N Croatan Hwy **Location:** US 158, at MM 5.5. **Parking:** on-site. **Cards:** AX, DS, MC, VI.

COLINGTON CAFE **Phone:** 252/480-1123 (24)

Continental
$14-$23

Professional staff serve French country-inspired preparations of mostly steak and local seafood at this restored Victorian home. Nightly seafood specials keep diners coming back as do the crab cakes and she-crab soup. Desserts are luscious and homemade. Smoking is permitted outside on the covered gazebo. Casual dress. **Bar:** Beer & wine. **Reservations:** suggested. **Hours:** Open 12/26-1/2 & 3/15-11/30; 5 pm-9:30 pm. Closed: 11/26. **Address:** 1029 Colington Rd **Location:** US 158, at MM 8.3, 1.1 mi w. **Parking:** on-site. **Cards:** DC, DS, MC, VI.

DARE DEVIL'S AUTHENTIC PIZZERIA **Phone:** 252/441-6330 (26)

Pizza
$6-$14

All the usual suspects—freshly made pizza, pasta entrees and huge strombolis overflowing with filling—can be found on the pizzeria's menu. Casual dress. **Bar:** Full bar. **Hours:** noon-10 pm; from 5 pm 11/1-4/14. Closed: 11/26, 12/25. **Address:** 1112 S Virginia Dare Tr **Location:** SR 12, at MM 9. **Parking:** on-site. **Cards:** DS, MC, VI.

FLYING FISH CAFE **Phone:** 252/441-6894 (32)

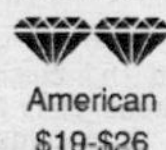

American
$19-$26

The menu includes some Mediterranean entrees, as well as homemade breads, dressings and desserts. One signature item is filet mignon wrapped in bacon and topped with a Gorgonzola crust. The wine list features 40 by-the-glass selections. Patio seating is popular when the weather is pleasant. Dressy casual. **Bar:** Full bar. **Reservations:** suggested. **Hours:** 5 pm-10 pm. Closed: 11/26, 12/25; also Super Bowl Sun. **Address:** 2003 S Croatan Hwy **Location:** US 158, at MM 10. **Parking:** on-site. **Cards:** AX, DS, MC, VI.

GOOMBAYS GRILLE & RAW BAR **Phone:** 252/441-6001 (20)

Caribbean
$5-$19

With its fun food, bright colors and unusual decor that gives diners a sense of being underwater, the popular restaurant appeals to kids of all ages. Caribbean entrees and fresh local seafood are the focus, with curried chicken as the signature entree. Casual dress. **Bar:** Full bar. **Hours:** 11:30 am-2 am. **Address:** 1608 N Virginia Dare Tr **Location:** SR 12, at MM 7. **Parking:** on-site. **Cards:** DS, MC, VI.

JK'S RESTAURANT **Phone:** 252/441-9555 (27)

Steak & Seafood
$15-$25

Specialties include the Colossal Crab Cake and the New York Strip Sanchez marinated in chimichurri sauce. Other menu selections include grilled-to-perfection beef, ribs, poultry and seafood. Casual dress. **Bar:** Full bar. **Hours:** 5 pm-10 pm. Closed: 1/1, 11/26, 12/25; also Sun 11/1-3/15. **Address:** 1106 S Croatan Hwy **Location:** US 158, at MM 9. **Parking:** on-site. **Cards:** AX, DS, MC, VI.

JOLLY ROGER RESTAURANT **Phone:** 252/441-6530 (19)

American
$4-$22

Hearty breakfasts draw a big crowd at the long-time local favorite. Lunch offerings include sandwiches, burgers and salads; dinner features steaks, local seafood and Italian entrees. Casual dress. **Bar:** Full bar. **Hours:** 6 am-2 & 4:30-10 pm. **Address:** 1836 N Virginia Dare Tr **Location:** SR 12, at MM 6.75. **Parking:** on-site. **Cards:** AX, DS, MC, VI.

KILL DEVIL GRILL **Phone:** 252/449-8181 (31)

American
$6-$20

Tabletop jukeboxes and the shiny diner-style exterior add nostalgia to this casual eatery. Classic fare includes meatloaf, spaghetti, chicken pastry and more. Seafood specials are featured daily. Casual dress. **Bar:** Full bar. **Hours:** Open 12/1-12/31 & 1/22-11/30; 11:30 am-10 pm, Fri & Sat-11 pm, Sun 11 am-3 pm; hours may vary off season. Closed: 4/12, 11/26, 12/25; also Mon. **Address:** 2008 S Virginia Dare Tr **Location:** SR 12, at MM 9.5. **Parking:** on-site. **Cards:** MC, VI.

MAKO MIKE'S RESTAURANT **Phone:** 252/480-1919 (21)

American
$9-$30

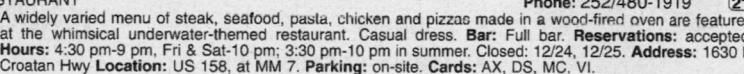

A widely varied menu of steak, seafood, pasta, chicken and pizzas made in a wood-fired oven are featured at the whimsical underwater-themed restaurant. Casual dress. **Bar:** Full bar. **Reservations:** accepted. **Hours:** 4:30 pm-9 pm, Fri & Sat-10 pm; 3:30 pm-10 pm in summer. Closed: 12/24, 12/25. **Address:** 1630 N Croatan Hwy **Location:** US 158, at MM 7. **Parking:** on-site. **Cards:** AX, DS, MC, VI.

(See map and index starting on p. 770)

MAMA KWAN'S GRILL & TIKI BAR Phone: 252/441-7889 (30)

Island
$6-$20

The colorful cafe stays busy at lunchtime. Quick and casual servers deliver an eclectic menu of jerk chicken, fish tacos, crab cakes and other island-themed fare. Casual dress. **Bar:** Full bar. **Hours:** 11:30 am-10 pm. Closed: 11/26, 12/24, 12/25. **Address:** 1701 S Croatan Hwy **Location:** US 158, at MM 9.5. **Parking:** on-site. **Cards:** MC, VI.

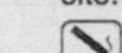

MILLER'S SEAFOOD & STEAK HOUSE Phone: 252/441-7674 (28)

Seafood
$12-$23

For more than 25 years, the family-owned and operated restaurant has served breakfast and dinner to the local and vacationing crowds. Fried, steamed and broiled seafood is the specialty. Casual dress. **Bar:** Full bar. **Hours:** Open 3/1-10/31; 7 am-noon & 5-9 pm. **Address:** 1520 S Virginia Dare Tr **Location:** SR 12, at MM 9.5. **Parking:** on-site. **Cards:** AX, DS, MC, VI.

OUTER BANKS BREWING STATION Phone: 252/449-2739 (25)

American
$5-$29

Desserts are made in-house, as are the beers, just as the name implies. The helpful staff will help you pair your entree with one of their lager varieties. Casual dress. **Bar:** Full bar. **Hours:** 11:30 am-10 pm; hours may vary off season. Closed: 11/26, 12/24, 12/25. **Address:** 600 S Croatan Hwy **Location:** US 158, at MM 8.5. **Parking:** on-site. **Cards:** AX, DC, DS, MC, VI.

PIGMAN'S BAR-B-QUE Phone: 252/441-6803 (29)

Barbecue
$7-$19

Whether you dine in or select take out, this quick-serve eatery offers such favorites as barbecued pork, beef, turkey, tuna and catfish, as well as St. Louis-style ribs and slow-smoked chicken. Casual dress. **Bar:** Beer only. **Hours:** Open 12/1-12/31 & 3/1-11/30; 11 am-9 pm. Closed: 11/26, 12/25. **Address:** 1606 S Croatan Hwy **Location:** US 158, at MM 9.5. **Parking:** on-site. **Cards:** MC, VI.

PORT-O-CALL RESTAURANT AND GIFT EMPORIUM Phone: 252/441-7484 (22)

Seafood
$14-$25

Hospitality and good food abound in a Victorian art gallery setting. Beef, veal, poultry and pasta are well-prepared and served in hearty, tasty portions. Dressy casual. Entertainment. **Bar:** Full bar. **Reservations:** suggested. **Hours:** Open 12/1-1/1 & 3/11-11/30; 4:30 pm-9:30 pm. Closed: 1/1-3/15. **Address:** 504 S Virginia Dare Tr **Location:** SR 12, at MM 8.8. **Parking:** on-site. **Cards:** AX, DS, MC, VI.

THAI ROOM RESTAURANT Phone: 252/441-1180 (23)

Thai
$5-$16

A local favorite for its friendly, knowledge service as well as nice selections of Chinese and Thai cuisine, with some American dishes mixed in as well. A dinner buffet is offered in season. Casual dress. **Bar:** Full bar. **Hours:** Open 12/1-1/15 & 3/1-11/30; 11:30 am-2:30 & 5-9:30 pm, Sun from 5 pm. Closed major holidays; also Mon 9/5-5/31. **Address:** 710 Virginia Dare Tr **Location:** SR 12, at MM 8.9. **Parking:** on-site. **Cards:** AX, MC, VI.

KITTY HAWK pop. 2,991 (See map and index starting on p. 770)

WHERE TO STAY

BEACH HAVEN Phone: (252)261-4785 (8)

AAA SAVE

Motel
$68-$205 4/22-10/12

Address: 4104 Virginia Dare Tr **Location:** SR 12, at MM 3.9. **Facility:** Smoke free premises. 6 one-bedroom standard units. 1 story, exterior corridors. *Bath:* combo or shower only. **Parking:** on-site. **Terms:** open 4/22-10/12, 3 day cancellation notice-fee imposed. **Amenities:** hair dryers. **Leisure Activities:** grill, picnic area. *Fee:* beach equipment. **Cards:** AX, MC, VI. **Free Special Amenities: local telephone calls and early check-in/late check-out.**

(See map and index starting on p. 770)

HILTON GARDEN INN-OUTER BANKS/KITTY HAWK *Book great rates at AAA.com* **Phone:** (252)261-1290 **7**

Hotel
$89-$289 All Year

Address: 5353 N Virginia Dare Tr **Location:** Oceanfront. Jct US 158, just s on SR 12. **Facility:** 180 units. 176 one-bedroom standard units, some with whirlpools. 4 one-bedroom suites. 5 stories, interior corridors. **Parking:** on-site. **Terms:** check-in 4 pm, 1-30 night minimum stay, cancellation fee imposed. **Amenities:** video games (fee), high-speed Internet, voice mail, safes, irons, hair dryers. **Pool(s):** heated outdoor, heated indoor. **Leisure Activities:** whirlpool, exercise room. *Fee:* game room. **Guest Services:** coin laundry, wireless Internet. **Business Services:** meeting rooms, business center. **Cards:** AX, DC, DS, JC, MC, VI. **Free Special Amenities: newspaper and high-speed Internet.** *(See color ad below)*

Hilton Garden Inn

AAA Benefit:
Members save 5% or more everyday!

/ SOME UNITS

HOLIDAY INN EXPRESS *Book at AAA.com* **Phone:** (252)261-4888 **9**

Hotel
$79-$169 All Year

Address: 3919 N Croatan Hwy **Location:** US 158, at MM 4. **Facility:** 98 one-bedroom standard units. 2 stories, interior corridors. **Parking:** on-site. **Terms:** check-in 4 pm, cancellation fee imposed. **Amenities:** dual phone lines, voice mail, irons, hair dryers. **Pool(s):** outdoor. **Guest Services:** wireless Internet. **Cards:** AX, DC, DS, MC, VI.

/ SOME UNITS

WHERE TO DINE

OCEAN BOULEVARD **Phone:** 252/261-2546 **12**

Regional American
$17-$29

Freshness is the goal in homemade breads, sauces and dressings, as well as desserts prepared by the in-house pastry chef. The seasonally changing menu lists quality, regional dishes such as local seafood, wild game and other fare. The open kitchen enhances the cosmopolitan ambience. Relax in the martini bar, and enjoy live music Friday nights. Casual dress. **Bar:** Full bar. **Reservations:** suggested. **Hours:** 5 pm-10 pm. Closed: 12/24, 12/25. **Address:** 4700 Virginia Dare Tr N **Location:** SR 12, at MM 2.5. **Parking:** on-site. **Cards:** AX, MC, VI.

MANTEO pop. 1,052 (See map and index starting on p. 770)

WHERE TO STAY

THE TRANQUIL HOUSE INN **Phone:** (252)473-1404 **32**

Country Inn
$189-$249 5/16-11/30
$149-$179 12/1-5/15

Address: 405 Queen Elizabeth Ave **Location:** Center. Located opposite courthouse and Elizabeth II. **Facility:** This classically styled inn on the downtown waterfront is minutes from beaches and within walking distance of shopping and sightseeing. Smoke free premises. 25 units. 23 one-bedroom standard units. 2 one-bedroom suites. 3 stories (no elevator), interior/exterior corridors. **Parking:** on-site. **Terms:** 2 night minimum stay - weekends, 14 day cancellation notice-fee imposed. **Amenities:** hair dryers. **Dining:** 1587 Restaurant, see separate listing. **Leisure Activities:** bicycles. **Guest Services:** wireless Internet. **Cards:** AX, DS, MC, VI.

ASK

THE WHITE DOE INN **Phone:** 252/473-9851 **33**

Historic Bed & Breakfast
$195-$325 All Year

Address: 319 Sir Walter Raleigh St **Location:** US 64, just nw. Located in the historic district. **Facility:** This 1910 Queen Anne home has antique furnishings and a fireplace in each guest room. Smoke free premises. 8 one-bedroom standard units, some with whirlpools. 3 stories (no elevator), interior/exterior corridors. *Bath:* combo or shower only. **Parking:** on-site. **Terms:** 2 night minimum stay - weekends, age restrictions may apply, 14 day cancellation notice-fee imposed. **Amenities:** video library, DVD players, CD players, hair dryers. **Leisure Activities:** bicycles. **Guest Services:** wireless Internet. **Cards:** MC, VI.

/ SOME UNITS

▼ *See AAA listing above* ▼

(See map and index starting on p. 770)

WHERE TO DINE

1587 RESTAURANT Phone: 252/473-1587 (46)

Regional American
$20-$30

Certified Angus beef, home-grown herbs and a distinct global influence are hallmarks of the casually elegant restaurant. Meals are fresh, flavorful and appealing to the eye. Pleasant servers make for an enjoyable dining experience. Casual dress. **Bar:** Beer & wine. **Reservations:** suggested. **Hours:** 5 pm-10 pm. Closed: 12/25. **Address:** 405 Queen Elizabeth Ave **Location:** Center; in The Tranquil House Inn. **Parking:** on-site. **Cards:** AX, DS, MC, VI.

BIG AL'S SODA FOUNTAIN & GRILL Phone: 252/473-5570 (45)

American
$4-$14

Diners can chill out in the nostalgic diner over a juicy burger and a thick, luscious milkshake while jamming to the jukebox tunes. Casual dress. **Bar:** Beer & wine. **Hours:** Open 3/1-11/30; 11 am-9 pm. **Address:** 716 S Virginia Dare Tr **Location:** 1.2 mi e on US 64 business route. **Parking:** on-site. **Cards:** DS, MC, VI.

DARRELL'S SEAFOOD RESTAURANT Phone: 252/473-5366 (47)

Regional American
$3-$21

Thriving at the location for more than 40 years, the popular family restaurant started out as a simple drive-in but grew into a full-service spot. The multifaceted menu lists traditional Outer Banks seafood, as well as beef and chicken dishes. All items are prepared to order and brought to the table by friendly, down-home servers. Casual dress. **Bar:** Beer & wine. **Hours:** 11 am-8 pm. Closed major holidays; also Sun. **Address:** 521 S Virginia Dare Tr **Location:** Jct US 64 Bypass, just nw on US 64. **Parking:** on-site. **Cards:** AX, DS, MC, VI.

NAGS HEAD pop. 2,700 (See map and index starting on p. 770)

WHERE TO STAY

BEACON MOTOR LODGE Phone: 252/441-5501 (23)

AAA SAVE
Motel
$65-$250 5/22-10/18
$60-$250 3/27-5/21

Address: 2617 S Virginia Dare Tr **Location:** Oceanfront. SR 12 at MM 10.5. **Facility:** 47 units. 42 one- and 2 two-bedroom standard units, some with efficiencies or kitchens. 3 one-bedroom suites with kitchens. 2 stories (no elevator), exterior corridors. *Bath:* combo or shower only. **Parking:** on-site. **Terms:** open 3/27-10/18, office hours 8 am-11 pm, check-in 4 pm, 2-3 night minimum stay - seasonal and/or weekends, 14 day cancellation notice, 60 day for suites & efficiencies-fee imposed. **Amenities:** hair dryers. **Pool(s):** outdoor. **Leisure Activities:** fishing, picnic tables, barbecue grills, playground. **Guest Services:** coin laundry, wireless Internet. **Cards:** AX, DC, DS, MC, VI. **Free Special Amenities: high-speed Internet.**

/ SOME UNITS

BLUE HERON MOTEL Phone: 252/441-7447 (26)

Motel
$60-$150 2/8-11/30
$60-$101 12/1-1/6

Address: 6811 Virginia Dare Tr **Location:** Oceanfront. SR 12, at MM 16. **Facility:** Smoke free premises. 30 one-bedroom standard units, some with efficiencies. 3 stories (no elevator), exterior corridors. **Parking:** on-site. **Terms:** open 12/1-1/6 & 2/8-11/30, office hours 9 am-10 pm, check-in 4 pm, 3-4 night minimum stay - seasonal, 14 day cancellation notice-fee imposed. **Pool(s):** 2 outdoor, heated indoor. **Leisure Activities:** whirlpool, fishing. **Cards:** DS, MC, VI.

COMFORT INN OCEANFRONT SOUTH *Book at AAA.com* Phone: 252/441-6315 (29)

Hotel
Rates not provided

Address: 8031 Old Oregon Inlet Rd **Location:** Oceanfront. SR 12, at MM 17. **Facility:** 105 one-bedroom standard units, some with whirlpools. 7 stories, interior corridors. **Parking:** on-site. **Terms:** check-in 4 pm. **Amenities:** voice mail, safes, irons, hair dryers. **Pool(s):** outdoor. **Leisure Activities:** fishing, limited exercise equipment. **Guest Services:** coin laundry, wireless Internet. **Business Services:** meeting rooms.

/ SOME UNITS FEE

▼ *See AAA listing p 783* ▼

(See map and index starting on p. 770)

FIRST COLONY INN

Phone: 252/441-2343 25

AAA SAVE

Historic Bed & Breakfast

$79-$309 6/15-11/30
$79-$229 12/1-6/14

Address: 6715 S Croatan Hwy **Location:** US 158, at MM 15.7. **Facility:** This weathered, beach-style inn was constructed in 1932 and moved to its present location in 1988; find a variety of room types and sizes. Smoke free premises. 26 one-bedroom standard units, some with efficiencies and/or whirlpools. 3 stories (no elevator), exterior corridors. *Bath:* combo or shower only. **Parking:** on-site. **Terms:** office hours 7 am-11 pm, 7 day cancellation notice. **Amenities:** video library, safes, irons, hair dryers. **Pool(s):** outdoor. **Leisure Activities:** sun deck. **Guest Services:** wireless Internet. **Cards:** AX, MC, VI. *(See color ad p 782)*

SEA FOAM MOTEL

Phone: 252/441-7320 28

AAA SAVE

Historic Motel

$62-$170 All Year

Address: 7111 S Virginia Dare Tr **Location:** Oceanfront. SR 12, at MM 16.5. **Facility:** On the National Register of Historic Places, the oceanfront motel offers rooms and efficiencies, many with a view. 51 units. 49 one-bedroom standard units, some with efficiencies. 2 two-bedroom suites with kitchens. 2 stories (no elevator), exterior corridors. *Bath:* combo or shower only. **Parking:** on-site. **Terms:** office hours 8 am-10 pm, 14 day cancellation notice-fee imposed. **Pool(s):** heated outdoor. **Leisure Activities:** fishing, playground, shuffleboard. **Guest Services:** wireless Internet. **Cards:** AX, MC, VI. **Free Special Amenities: preferred room (subject to availability with advance reservations) and high-speed Internet.**

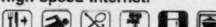

THE SURF SIDE HOTEL

Phone: 252/441-2105 24

AAA SAVE

Hotel

$55-$284 6/9-11/30
$55-$261 12/1-6/8

Address: 6701 S Virginia Dare Tr **Location:** Oceanfront. SR 12, at MM 16. **Facility:** 76 one-bedroom standard units, some with efficiencies and/or whirlpools. 3-5 stories, interior corridors. **Parking:** on-site. **Terms:** office hours 7 am-11 pm, 2-3 night minimum stay - seasonal and/or weekends, 7 day cancellation notice-fee imposed. **Amenities:** irons, hair dryers. **Pool(s):** outdoor, heated indoor. **Leisure Activities:** whirlpool, fishing, exercise room. **Guest Services:** coin laundry, wireless Internet. **Cards:** AX, DS, MC, VI. **Free Special Amenities: expanded continental breakfast and high-speed Internet.**

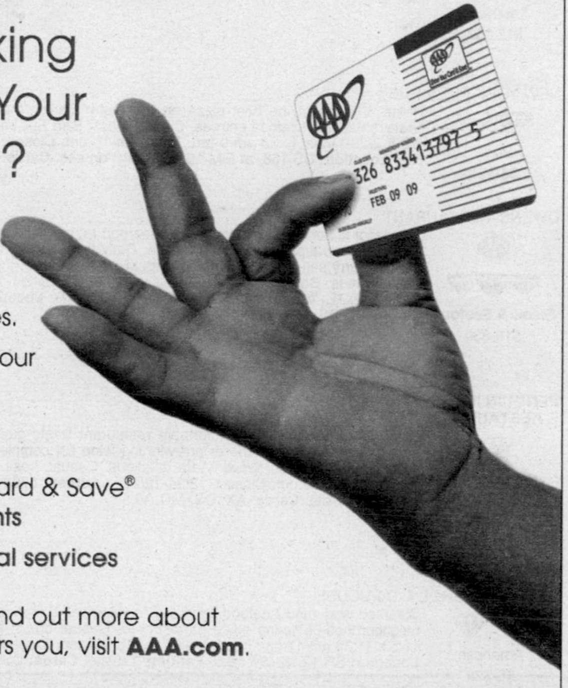

/ SOME UNITS

(See map and index starting on p. 770)

TAR HEEL MOTEL — Phone: 252/441-6150 (27)

Motel
$55-$110 3/15-10/30

Address: 7010 S Virginia Dare Tr **Location:** SR 12, at MM 16. **Facility:** 33 one-bedroom standard units, some with efficiencies. 1 story, exterior corridors. *Bath:* combo or shower only. **Parking:** on-site. **Terms:** open 3/15-10/30, office hours 8 am-10 pm, 2 night minimum stay - seasonal, cancellation fee imposed. **Pool(s):** outdoor. **Guest Services:** wireless Internet. **Cards:** AX, DS, MC, VI.

/ SOME UNITS

WHERE TO DINE

BASNIGHT'S LONE CEDAR CAFE — **Phone:** 252/441-5405 (42)

Seafood
$7-$30

Upon entering, guests are enveloped in the wafting scent of cedar and charmed by the excellent views of Roanoke Sound. Pasta, seafood and Angus beef are the menu's main ingredients, with local soft-shell crab and crab cakes as signature entrees. Casual dress. **Bar:** Full bar. **Hours:** Open 12/1-12/31 & 2/12-11/30; 11:30 am-3 & 4:30-9:30 pm; hours may vary off season. **Address:** 7623 S Virginia Dare Tr **Location:** Jct SR 12 and US 158, 0.8 mi w on US 64. **Parking:** on-site. **Cards:** CB, DC, DS, MC, VI.

THE DUNES RESTAURANT — **Phone:** 252/441-1600 (40)

American
$6-$20

The popular, family-friendly eatery features such classics as steak, chicken and seafood as well as a small salad bar. The Dunes' breakfast usually draws a crowd. Casual dress. **Bar:** Beer & wine. **Hours:** 6:30 am-2 & 4:30-9:30 pm. Closed: 12/25. **Address:** 7013 S Croatan Hwy **Location:** US 158, at MM 16.5. **Parking:** on-site. **Cards:** AX, DS, MC, VI.

JOCKEY'S RIBS — **Phone:** 252/441-1141 (38)

American
$14-$30

Since 1985, the casual eatery has been serving finger-licking ribs, along with steak, seafood and chicken. Casual dress. **Bar:** Full bar. **Hours:** Open 4/15-10/15; 5 pm-9 pm. Closed: Sun-Tues in off season. **Address:** 3948 S Virginia Dare Tr **Location:** SR 12, at MM 13. **Parking:** on-site. **Cards:** AX, DS, MC, VI.

KELLY'S OUTER BANKS RESTAURANT & TAVERN — *Menu on AAA.com* — **Phone:** 252/441-4116 (36)

AAA
American
$12-$33

Many homemade selections adorn the menu, such favorites as the desserts, bread, soups and salad dressing. Fresh, flavorful entrees at the multi-level eatery include local seafood, steak and Iowa prime rib. Casual dress. **Bar:** Full bar. **Reservations:** accepted. **Hours:** 4:30 pm-10 pm. Closed: 12/24, 12/25. **Address:** 2316 S Croatan Hwy **Location:** US 158, at MM 10.5. **Parking:** on-site. **Cards:** AX, DC, DS, MC, VI.

NEW YORK PIZZA PUB — **Phone:** 252/441-2660 (35)

Pizza
$6-$21

Home of some of the best pizza on the Outer Banks, the large, family-friendly restaurant also features pasta, steak and seafood entrees. Casual dress. **Bar:** Full bar. **Reservations:** accepted. **Hours:** Open 12/1-1/2 & 3/20-11/30; 11:30 am-9 pm, Fri & Sat-10 pm. Closed: 4/12, 11/26, 12/25. **Address:** 2217 S Croatan Hwy **Location:** US 158, at MM 10. **Parking:** on-site. **Cards:** AX, DS, MC, VI.

OWENS' RESTAURANT — **Phone:** 252/441-7309 (41)

AAA
Steak & Seafood
$18-$30

The decor is decidedly nautical at the seafood restaurant, which has been family owned and operated since 1946. Service is personal and attentive. Daily fish specials are featured, as is a tray of tempting desserts. Shrimp Surry sausage and cheese grits are a favorite, and jumbo lump crab cakes are the signature dish. Casual dress. **Bar:** Full bar. **Hours:** Open 12/1-1/2 & 3/1-11/30; 5 pm-9 pm; to 10 pm 6/1-9/30. Closed: 12/24, 12/25. **Address:** 7114 S Virginia Dare Tr **Location:** SR 12, at MM 16.5. **Parking:** on-site. **Cards:** AX, DS, MC, VI.

PENGUIN ISLE SOUNDSIDE RESTAURANT — *Menu on AAA.com* — **Phone:** 252/441-2637 (39)

AAA
Steak & Seafood
$12-$35

Spacious and warm, the comfortable restaurant treats guests to postcard-perfect sunsets over Roanoke Sound. Selections from the award-winning wine list complement creative compilations of Angus beef and grilled seafood. Fresh desserts are delicious. Casual dress. **Bar:** Full bar. **Hours:** Open 12/1-12/31 & 3/1-11/30; 5 pm-9:30 pm. Closed: 12/24-12/26. **Address:** 6708 S Croatan Hwy **Location:** US 158, at MM 16. **Parking:** on-site. **Cards:** AX, DS, MC, VI.

RED DRUM GRILL & TAPHOUSE — **Phone:** 252/480-1095 (37)

American
$5-$22

Steamed and fried seafood, burgers, chicken and ribs round out the menu at this eatery that has a neighborhood-gathering place atmosphere. Casual dress. **Bar:** Full bar. **Hours:** Open 12/1-12/31 & 3/1-11/30; 11:30 am-11 pm; hours may vary off season. Closed: 11/26, 12/25. **Address:** 2412 Virginia Dare Tr **Location:** SR 12, at MM 10.5. **Parking:** on-site. **Cards:** DS, MC, VI.

OCRACOKE pop. 769 (See map and index starting on p. 770)

WHERE TO STAY

THE ANCHORAGE INN Phone: (252)928-1101 42

AAA SAVE

Motel

$99-$299 3/15-11/8

Address: 205 Irvin Garrish Hwy (SR 12) **Location:** From Cedar Island Ferry, just n. **Facility:** 35 one-bedroom standard units. 4 stories, exterior corridors. **Parking:** on-site. **Terms:** open 3/15-11/8, 3 day cancellation notice. **Amenities:** hair dryers. **Pool(s):** outdoor. **Leisure Activities:** fishing, charcoal grills, picnic tables, rental bicycles. *Fee:* marina, charter fishing, small power boats, scooters. **Guest Services:** wireless Internet. **Cards:** DS, MC, VI. **Free Special Amenities: continental breakfast and local telephone calls.**

/ SOME UNITS FEE FEE FEE

BLUFF SHOAL MOTEL Phone: 252/928-4301 43

AAA SAVE

Motel

$65-$109 All Year

Address: 306 Irvin Garrish Hwy (SR 12) **Location:** From Cedar Island Ferry, 0.4 mi n. **Facility:** Smoke free premises. 7 one-bedroom standard units. 1 story, exterior corridors. **Parking:** on-site. **Terms:** office hours 8 am-10 pm, 2-3 night minimum stay - seasonal and/or weekends, 3 day cancellation notice-fee imposed. **Leisure Activities:** fishing deck, harbor, bicycles. **Cards:** DS, MC, VI.

HARBORSIDE MOTEL Phone: (252)928-3111 41

AAA SAVE

Motel

$70-$105 4/10-11/15

Address: 244 Irvin Garrish Hwy (SR 12) **Location:** From Cedar Island Ferry, just n. **Facility:** Smoke free premises. 18 one-bedroom standard units, some with efficiencies. 2 stories (no elevator), exterior corridors. **Parking:** on-site. **Terms:** open 4/10-11/15, office hours 8 am-8 pm, 2 night minimum stay - weekends, 3 day cancellation notice-fee imposed. **Leisure Activities:** fishing, outdoor deck. *Fee:* boat dock. **Guest Services:** wireless Internet. **Cards:** AX, DS, MC, VI. **Free Special Amenities: continental breakfast and high-speed Internet.**

/ SOME UNITS

WHERE TO DINE

BACK PORCH RESTAURANT Phone: 252/928-6401 57

Seafood

$12-$25

Guests can relax in the cozy screened porch dining room over a dinner of crab beignets, the signature appetizer, and bourbon pecan chicken. Also on the menu are delicious seafood entrees. Casual dress. **Bar:** Full bar. **Reservations:** not accepted. **Hours:** Open 4/20-11/27; 5 pm-9:30 pm; hours may vary off-season. Closed: 11/26. **Address:** 110 Back Rd **Location:** From Cedar Island Ferry, 0.5 mi n on SR 12, then just w. **Parking:** on-site. **Cards:** MC, VI.

CAFE ATLANTIC Phone: 252/928-4861 61

Seafood

$4-$21

The cafe's lengthy menu features such favorites as fresh seafood, some Italian entrees, crab cakes, veal parmesan and beef tenderloin. Brunch is offered on Sundays, as well as a lunch menu that includes grilled and fried seafood, sandwiches and wraps. Casual dress. **Bar:** Beer & wine. **Hours:** Open 3/1-11/30; 5 pm-9 pm, Sun also 11 am-2 pm; to 9:30 pm in summer. **Address:** 1129 Irvin Garrish Hwy **Location:** From Cedar Island Ferry, 1 mi n on SR 12. **Parking:** on-site. **Cards:** AX, DS, MC, VI.

CAPTAIN BEN'S RESTAURANT Phone: 252/928-4741 58

Steak & Seafood

$5-$22

The family-owned restaurant has been a local favorite for over 35 years, serving such favorites as well-prepared steaks, shrimp scampi, prime rib and Maryland crab cakes. The homemade pumpkin-pie cake is a must-have. Casual dress. **Bar:** Beer & wine. **Reservations:** accepted. **Hours:** Open 4/1-11/30; 11:30 am-9 pm. Closed: Sun. **Address:** 875 Irvin Garrish Hwy (SR 12) **Location:** From Cedar Island Ferry, 0.8 mi n. **Parking:** on-site. **Cards:** AX, DS, MC, VI.

CALL

HOWARD'S PUB & RAW BAR RESTAURANT *Menu on AAA.com* Phone: 252/928-4441 59

AAA

American

$6-$25

Guests can munch on a gourmet hamburger while taking in the ocean view from the upper deck. Seating also is offered on the homey screened porch. More than 200 beer selections can be requested, as can daily fresh fish entrees and fresh pizza. Casual dress. **Bar:** Beer & wine. **Hours:** 11 am-10 pm. **Address:** 1175 Irvin Garrish Hwy (SR 12) **Location:** From Cedar Island Ferry, 1 mi n; north end of village. **Parking:** on-site. **Cards:** DS, MC, VI.

CALL

JASON'S RESTAURANT Phone: 252/928-3434 62

American

$4-$20

The small, family-friendly restaurant specializes in pizza, pasta, submarine sandwiches, salads and seafood. During warm weather, seating on the screened porch is an option. Take-out service is available. Casual dress. **Bar:** Beer & wine. **Hours:** 11:30 am-10 pm. Closed: 11/26; also Sun. **Address:** 1110 Irvin Garrish Hwy (SR 12) **Location:** From Cedar Island Ferry, 0.8 mi n. **Parking:** on-site. **Cards:** MC, VI.

THE PELICAN RESTAURANT Phone: 252/928-7431 60

Seafood

$6-$28

Dine al fresco on the patio, where live music is offered, or in the cozy dining room at the converted home. Enjoy such menu favorites as steak, fresh seafood and pasta. Casual dress. **Bar:** Beer & wine. **Hours:** 8-11 am, 11:30-3 & 5-9 pm; hours vary off season. **Address:** Irvin Garrish Hwy (SR 12) **Location:** From Cedar Island Ferry, 0.4 mi n on SR 12. **Parking:** on-site. **Cards:** DS, MC, VI.

(See map and index starting on p. 770)

PONY ISLAND RESTAURANT **Phone:** 252/928-5701 (56)

American
$5-$20

Specializing for 40 years in casual, family dining, the landmark restaurant has two dining areas. One of them, the Pony Room, is dedicated to the wild ponies that roam Cedar Island. Seafood, steak and pasta dishes make up the bulk of the menu. Casual dress. **Bar:** Beer & wine. **Hours:** Open 4/1-11/30; 7 am-2 pm; also 5 pm-9 pm in summer. Closed: 12/25. **Address:** 51 Ocean View Rd **Location:** From Cedar Island Ferry, 0.7 mi n on SR 12, then just w. **Parking:** on-site. **Cards:** MC, VI.

SOUTHERN SHORES (See map and index starting on p. 770)

WHERE TO DINE

MERIDIAN 42 **Phone:** 252/261-0420 (15)

American
$18-$24

The flavors of the Northern Mediterranean coastline of Spain and Italy inspire creative menu selections. Homemade pastas, gourmet produce, flavorful sauces, specialty meats and the freshest Outer Banks seafood go into the food. Tuscan-style decor and an open kitchen enhance the dining room's warmth. The wine selection is extensive. Casual dress. **Bar:** Full bar. **Reservations:** accepted. **Hours:** 5 pm-9 pm. Closed: 1/1, 11/26, 12/25; also Sun 11/1-3/31 & Wed off season. **Address:** 1 Ocean Blvd **Location:** On SR 12, just e of jct US 158; in Southern Shores Crossing. **Parking:** on-site. **Cards:** AX, DS, MC, VI.

Cape Hatteras Lighthouse, Cape Hatteras National Seashore / Outer Banks Visitors Bureau

This ends listings for the Outer Banks.
The following page resumes the alphabetical listings of cities in North Carolina.

OXFORD pop. 8,338

WHERE TO STAY

BEST WESTERN OXFORD INN & SUITES *Book great rates at AAA.com* **Phone:** (919)692-1000

AAA SAVE
Hotel
$70-$80 All Year

Address: 1000 Linden Ave **Location:** I-85, exit 204, just e. **Facility:** 61 one-bedroom standard units, some with whirlpools. 3 stories, interior corridors. *Bath:* combo or shower only **Parking:** on-site. **Terms:** 3 day cancellation notice. **Amenities:** high-speed Internet, dual phone lines, voice mail, irons, hair dryers. **Pool(s):** outdoor. **Leisure Activities:** exercise room. **Guest Services:** coin laundry, wireless Internet. **Business Services:** meeting rooms. **Cards:** AX, DS, MC, VI. **Free Special Amenities: full breakfast and high-speed Internet.**

/ SOME UNITS

AAA Benefit:
Members save up to 20%, plus 10% bonus points with rewards program.

PILOT MOUNTAIN pop. 1,281

WHERE TO STAY

QUALITY INN & SUITES *Book at AAA.com* **Phone:** (336)368-2237

Motel
$59-$139 All Year

Address: 711 S Key St **Location:** US 52, exit 134, just e on SR 268. **Facility:** 56 units. 46 one-bedroom standard units. 10 one-bedroom suites. 2 stories (no elevator), exterior corridors. **Parking:** on-site. **Amenities:** voice mail, irons, hair dryers. *Some:* high-speed Internet. **Pool(s):** outdoor. **Guest Services:** wireless Internet. **Business Services:** meeting rooms. **Cards:** AX, CB, DC, DS, JC, MC, VI.

ASK CALL / SOME UNITS

WHERE TO DINE

MOUNTAIN VIEW RESTAURANT **Phone:** 336/368-9180

American
$3-$12

A buffet is offered weekdays during lunch and daily for dinner, as well as on weekends for breakfast or Sunday brunch. Typical offerings include fried chicken, meatloaf and varied vegetables. On the menu are seafood plates, sandwiches and Italian fare. Casual dress. **Hours:** 6 am-9 pm, Sun-2 pm. Closed: 11/26, 12/25. **Address:** 701 S Key St **Location:** US 52, exit 134, just e on SR 268. **Parking:** on-site. **Cards:** MC, VI.

PINEHURST pop. 9,706

WHERE TO STAY

THE CAROLINA HOTEL **Phone:** (910)295-6811

AAA SAVE
Classic Historic Hotel
$366-$706 3/8-11/30
$253-$408 12/1-3/7

Address: 80 Carolina Vista Dr **Location:** US 15/501, 1 mi w on SR 2. **Facility:** Built in 1901, this grand hotel exudes the elegance and traditions of times gone by; guest rooms have undergone sweeping renovations in recent years, ensuring the grandeur will continue for years to come. 266 units. 254 one-bedroom standard units. 12 one-bedroom suites. 4 stories, interior corridors. *Bath:* combo or shower only. **Parking:** on-site and valet. **Terms:** check-in 4 pm, 21 day cancellation notice-fee imposed. **Amenities:** voice mail, safes, honor bars, irons, hair dryers. *Fee:* video games, high-speed Internet. *Some:* CD players. **Dining:** Carolina Dining Room, see separate listing, entertainment. **Pool(s):** heated outdoor. **Leisure Activities:** rental boats, rental canoes, rental paddleboats, rental sailboats, marina, fishing, recreation programs, croquet, lawn bowling, bicycles, playground, spa. *Fee:* golf-144 holes, 24 tennis courts (8 lighted), carriage rides. **Guest Services:** valet laundry, airport transportation-Moore County Airport, area transportation within the village, wireless Internet. **Business Services:** conference facilities, business center. **Cards:** AX, DC, DS, MC, VI.

CALL / SOME UNITS

COMFORT INN - PINEHURST *Book at AAA.com* **Phone:** (910)215-5500

Hotel
$79-$279 All Year

Address: 9801 US Hwy 15-501 **Location:** Jct US 1, 2.5 mi n. **Facility:** Smoke free premises. 77 units. 75 one-bedroom standard units. 2 one-bedroom suites. 2 stories, interior corridors. *Bath:* combo or shower only. **Parking:** on-site. **Amenities:** voice mail, irons, hair dryers. **Pool(s):** outdoor. **Leisure Activities:** exercise room. **Guest Services:** valet and coin laundry, wireless Internet. **Business Services:** meeting rooms, PC. **Cards:** AX, DC, DS, MC, VI.

ASK

HOLLY INN *Book great rates at AAA.com* **Phone:** 910/295-6811

AAA SAVE
Historic Hotel
Rates not provided

Address: 155 Cherokee Rd **Location:** Jct US 15/501, 1 mi w on SR 2, follow sign off Midland Rd, then just s. **Facility:** Common areas in this architecturally rich property are accented by an abundance of carved woodwork and upscale appointments that recall a romantic era. 82 units. 75 one-bedroom standard units. 7 one-bedroom suites. 5 stories, interior corridors. *Bath:* combo or shower only. **Parking:** on-site and valet. **Terms:** check-in 4 pm. **Amenities:** voice mail, safes, honor bars, irons, hair dryers. *Fee:* video games, high-speed Internet. *Some:* CD players. **Dining:** 1895 Grille, see separate listing. **Pool(s):** heated outdoor. **Leisure Activities:** pool privileges, croquet, lawn bowling, spa. *Fee:* boating and water activities, golf-144 holes, 24 tennis courts (8 lighted), carriage rides. **Guest Services:** valet laundry, airport transportation-Moore County Airport, area transportation-within the village, wireless Internet. **Business Services:** meeting rooms.

HOMEWOOD SUITES BY HILTON *Book great rates at AAA.com* **Phone:** (910)255-0300

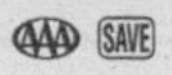

Hotel
$159 All Year

Address: 250 Central Park Ave **Location:** Jct SR 5 and 211; in Olmsted Village. **Facility:** 100 units. 89 one- and 11 two-bedroom suites with efficiencies, some with whirlpools. 4 stories, interior corridors. *Bath:* combo or shower only. **Parking:** on-site. **Terms:** 1-30 night minimum stay, cancellation fee imposed. **Amenities:** video library, video games (fee), high-speed Internet, dual phone lines, voice mail, irons, hair dryers. **Pool(s):** outdoor. **Leisure Activities:** exercise room. *Fee:* tennis privileges. **Guest Services:** valet and coin laundry, airport transportation-Moore County Airport, area transportation-within 5 mi, wireless Internet. **Business Services:** meeting rooms, PC. **Cards:** AX, CB, DC, DS, JC, MC, VI.

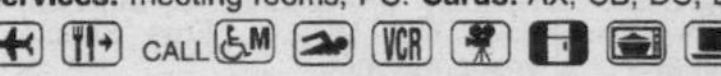

/ SOME UNITS FEE

AAA Benefit:
Members save 5% or more everyday!

THE MANOR INN **Phone:** 910/295-6811

Historic Hotel
Rates not provided

Address: 5 Community Rd **Location:** Jct US 15/501, 0.5 mi w on SR 211, 0.8 mi s on Dundee Rd, then just w. **Facility:** This classically styled inn features attractively decorated accommodations and a variety of room types for the budget-minded traveler. Smoke free premises. 42 units. 27 one- and 12 two-bedroom standard units. 3 one-bedroom suites. 4 stories, interior corridors. **Parking:** on-site. **Terms:** check-in 4 pm. **Amenities:** voice mail, safes, irons, hair dryers. *Fee:* video games, high-speed Internet. **Leisure Activities:** spa. *Fee:* golf-144 holes, 24 tennis courts (8 lighted). **Guest Services:** valet laundry, area transportation.

FEE / SOME UNITS

SPRINGHILL SUITES BY MARRIOTT *Book great rates at AAA.com* **Phone:** (910)695-0234

Address: 10024 US 15/501 **Location:** Jct US 1, 2.3 mi n. **Facility:** Smoke free premises. 107 one-bedroom standard units. 3 stories, interior corridors. *Bath:* combo or shower only. **Parking:** on-site. **Terms:** cancellation fee imposed. **Amenities:** high-speed Internet, dual phone lines, voice mail, irons, hair dryers. **Pool(s):** outdoor. **Leisure Activities:** whirlpool, gas grills, exercise room. **Guest Services:** valet and coin laundry, wireless Internet. **Business Services:** meeting rooms, PC. **Cards:** AX, CB, DC, DS, MC, VI.

Hotel
$97-$112 All Year

CALL

AAA Benefit:
Members save a minimum 5% off the best available rate.

WHERE TO DINE

1895 GRILLE **Phone:** 910/295-6811

Regional American
$18-$52

Set in the center of Holly Inn, the restaurant features upscale Carolina cuisine. Selections change frequently but past menu offerings have included pan-seared Carolina red trout, corn bread-stuffed local quail and pecan-roasted veal tenderloin. Dressy casual. **Bar:** Full bar. **Reservations:** required. **Hours:** 6:30 am-10 & 5:30-9:30 pm, Mon & Tues-10 am. **Address:** 155 Cherokee Rd **Location:** Jct US 15/501, 1 mi w on SR 2, follow sign off Midland Rd, then just s; in Holly Inn. **Parking:** on-site and valet. **Cards:** AX, CB, DC, DS, MC, VI. **Historic**

CALL

CAROLINA DINING ROOM **Phone:** 910/295-6811

American
$12-$52

The mahogany-paneled, chandelier-lit dining room affords a beautiful view of a lovely flower garden. A four-course prix fixe menu changes monthly. The daily lunch buffet and Sunday champagne brunch are popular. Semi-formal attire. Entertainment. **Bar:** Full bar. **Reservations:** required. **Hours:** 6:30 am-10, noon-2 & 6:30-9:30 pm. **Address:** 80 Carolina Vista Dr **Location:** US 15/501, 1 mi w on SR 2; in The Carolina Hotel. **Parking:** on-site and valet. **Cards:** AX, DC, DS, MC, VI.

CALL

NINA'S CLASSIC CUISINE **Phone:** 910/235-4600

Continental
$7-$27

Classic northern Italian cuisine, like chicken saltimbocca and veal Marsala, is served in a small dining room with a casual atmosphere. Casual dress. **Bar:** Full bar. **Hours:** 11:30 am-2 & 5:30-9 pm, Sat from 5:30 pm, Tues 11:30 am-2 pm. Closed major holidays; also Sun & Mon. **Address:** 111 Central Park Ave, Suite L **Location:** Jct SR 5 and 211, just n; in Olmstead Village. **Parking:** on-site. **Cards:** AX, DS, MC, VI.

PINE KNOLL SHORES pop. 1,524

WHERE TO STAY

AMERISUITES ATLANTIC BEACH **Phone:** (252)247-5118

Hotel
$89-$279 All Year

Address: 118 Salter Path Rd **Location:** SR 58, at MM 5. **Facility:** 111 one-bedroom standard units. 4 stories, interior corridors. **Parking:** on-site. **Terms:** 3 day cancellation notice-fee imposed. **Amenities:** video games (fee), dual phone lines, safes, irons, hair dryers. **Pool(s):** heated outdoor. **Leisure Activities:** exercise room. **Guest Services:** coin laundry, wireless Internet. **Business Services:** meeting rooms. **Cards:** AX, CB, DC, DS, JC, MC, VI.

ASK CALL / SOME UNITS FEE

PINEVILLE —*See Charlotte p. 666.*

PLYMOUTH pop. 4,107

WHERE TO STAY

HOLIDAY INN EXPRESS *Book at AAA.com* **Phone:** (252)793-4700

Hotel
$90-$170 All Year

Address: 840 US Hwy 64 W **Location:** Jct SR 32 S, 1 mi w. **Facility:** 60 one-bedroom standard units, some with whirlpools. 2 stories, interior/exterior corridors. *Bath:* combo or shower only. **Parking:** on-site. **Amenities:** dual phone lines, voice mail, irons, hair dryers. **Pool(s):** outdoor. **Leisure Activities:** exercise room. *Fee:* game room. **Guest Services:** valet and coin laundry, wireless Internet. **Business Services:** meeting rooms, PC. **Cards:** AX, CB, DC, DS, MC, VI.

ASK CALL / SOME UNITS FEE

PORT-O PLYMOUTH INN *Book great rates at AAA.com* **Phone:** (252)793-5006

SAVE

Motel
$50-$100 All Year

Address: 510 Hwy 64 E **Location:** On US 64. **Facility:** 58 units. 56 one-bedroom standard units, some with efficiencies (no utensils). 2 one-bedroom suites. 2 stories (no elevator), exterior corridors. *Bath:* combo or shower only. **Parking:** on-site. **Amenities:** *Some:* hair dryers. **Pool(s):** outdoor. **Business Services:** meeting rooms. **Cards:** AX, DS, MC, VI. **Free Special Amenities: continental breakfast and high-speed Internet.**

/ SOME UNITS FEE

WHERE TO DINE

THE BOOK & THE CUP **Phone:** 252/791-0295

Deli
$4-$7

While there's nothing fancy at the downtown coffee and sandwich shop, the sandwiches are made to order and can be toasted or grilled panini-style. Homemade cakes and cookies are a perfect complement to a cup of gourmet coffee. Casual dress. **Hours:** 8 am-5 pm, Sat 9 am-2 pm; 8 am-6 pm, Sat 9 am-3 pm 5/31-9/1. Closed: 12/25; also Sun. **Address:** 111 W Water St **Location:** Jct US 64, n on Washington St, then just s. **Parking:** street. **Cards:** DS, MC, VI.

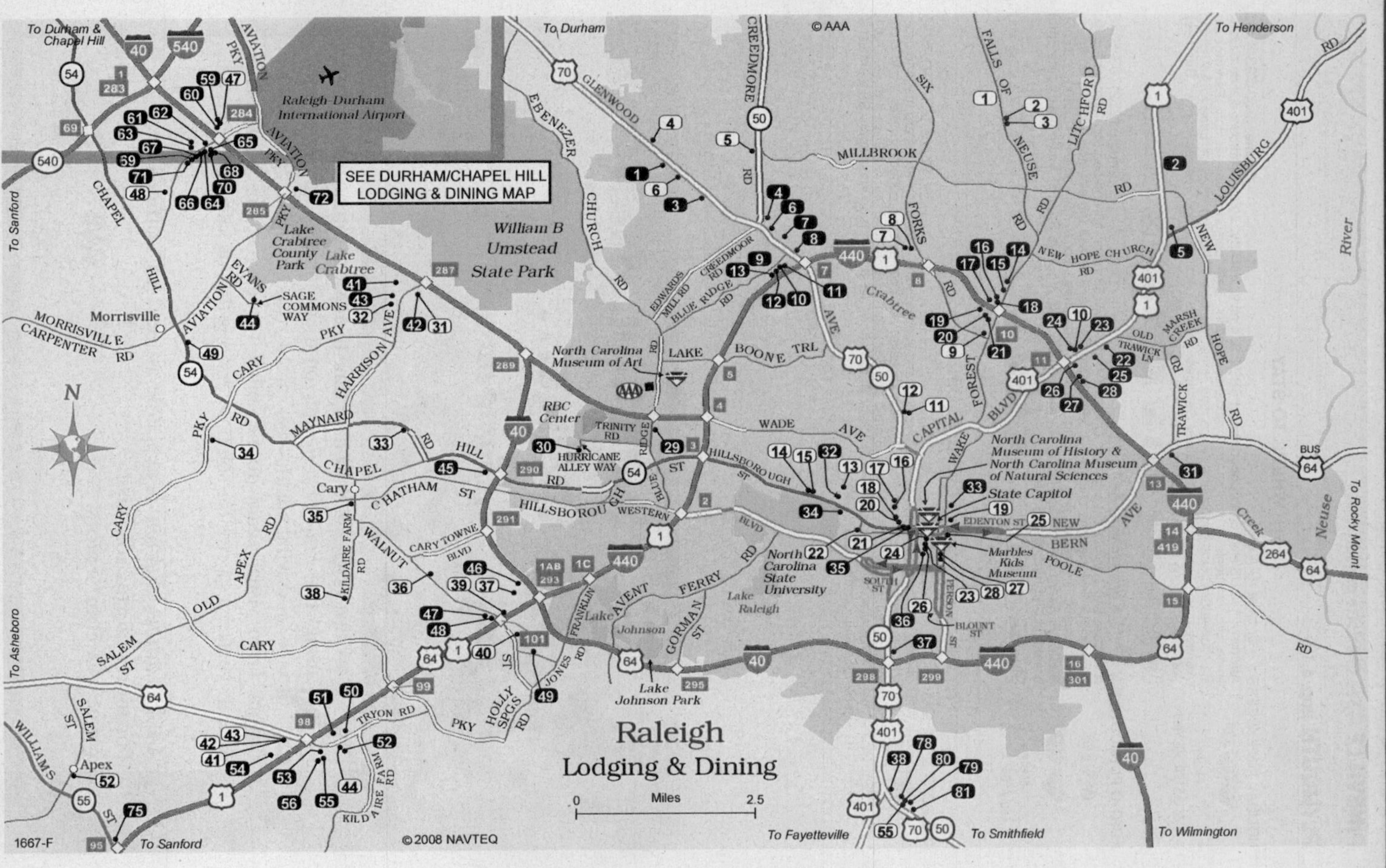
Raleigh
Lodging & Dining
Miles
0
2.5
© AAA
© 2008 NAVTEQ
1667-F
SEE DURHAM/CHAPEL HILL LODGING & DINING MAP
To Durham & Chapel Hill
To Durham
To Henderson
To Sanford
To Asheboro
To Fayetteville
To Smithfield
To Wilmington
To Rocky Mount
Neuse River
Crabtree Creek
Raleigh-Durham International Airport
William B Umstead State Park
Lake Crabtree County Park
Lake Crabtree
North Carolina Museum of Art
RBC Center
North Carolina Museum of History & North Carolina Museum of Natural Sciences
State Capitol
Marbles Kids Museum
North Carolina State University
Lake Raleigh
Lake Johnson
Lake Johnson Park
Cary
Apex
Morrisville
FALLS OF NEUSE RD
LITCHFORD RD
LOUISBURG RD
NEW HOPE RD
NEW HOPE CHURCH RD
MARSH CREEK RD
OLD TRAWICK LN
TRAWICK RD
SIX FORKS RD
MILLBROOK RD
CREEDMORE RD
CREEDMOOR RD
GLENWOOD AVE
EBENEZER CHURCH RD
EDWARDS MILL RD
BLUE RIDGE RD
LAKE BOONE TRL
WADE AVE
HILLSBOROUGH ST
CAPITAL BLVD
WAKE FOREST RD
NEW BERN AVE
POOLE RD
EDENTON ST
PERSON ST
BLOUNT ST
SOUTH ST
TRINITY RD
HURRICANE ALLEY WAY
WESTERN BLVD
GORMAN ST
AVENT FERRY RD
FRANKLIN RD
JONES ST
HOLLY SPGS RD
TRYON RD
KILDAIRE FARM RD
CARY TOWNE BLVD
WALNUT ST
CHATHAM ST
CHAPEL HILL RD
MAYNARD RD
HARRISON AVE
SAGE COMMONS WAY
EVANS RD
AVIATION PKY
CARY PKY
APEX RD
OLD CARY
SALEM ST
WILLIAMS ST
MORRISVILLE CARPENTER RD
CHAPEL HILL
N

Airport Accommodations

Map Page	OA	RALEIGH-DURHAM INTERNATIONAL	Diamond Rated	High Season	Page
34 / p. 681		Comfort Suites Hotel RTP/RDU, 2 mi sw of terminal	◆◆◆	$72-$180	686
29 / p. 681		Extended Stay Deluxe-RTP-Miami Blvd-South, 3 mi w of terminal	◆◆◆	$110-$120	688
32 / p. 681		Hilton-Raleigh-Durham Airport at Research Triangle Park, 2.5 mi sw of terminal	◆◆◆	$99-$249	688
30 / p. 681		Holiday Inn Express Hotel & Suites-RTP, 3 mi w of terminal	◆◆◆	$144-$154	689
31 / p. 681		Homewood Suites by Hilton-Raleigh Durham Airport, 3 mi w of terminal	◆◆◆	$94-$159	689
28 / p. 681		Marriott at Research Triangle Park, 3 mi w of terminal	◆◆◆	$219-$249	690
36 / p. 681	AAA	**Sheraton Imperial Hotel & Convention Center, 2.5 mi sw of terminal**	◆◆◆	$79-$350 SAVE	691
33 / p. 681		Sleep Inn-RDU/RTP, 2 mi w of terminal	◆◆	$79-$149	691
37 / p. 681	AAA	**SpringHill Suites by Marriott-RTP/Airport, 2.5 mi sw of terminal**	◆◆◆	$153-$164 SAVE	691
35 / p. 681		Wingate Inn by Wyndham - RTP/RDU Airport, 2 mi sw of terminal	◆◆◆	Rates not provided	692
27 / p. 681		Wyndham Hotel-Research Triangle Park, 3 mi w of terminal	◆◆◆	Rates not provided	693
60 / p. 790		Country Inn & Suites-RDU Airport, 0.5 mi s of terminal	◆◆◆	$144	760
68 / p. 790	AAA	**Courtyard by Marriott-Airport, 2 mi se of terminal**	◆◆◆	$206-$221 SAVE	761
69 / p. 790		Days Inn Airport/RTP, 2 mi se of terminal	◆◆◆	$99-$109	761
63 / p. 790		Extended StayAmerica-RDU Airport, 2 mi se of terminal	◆◆	$100-$110	761
61 / p. 790	AAA	**Fairfield Inn & Suites by Marriott-RDU Airport, 2 mi se of terminal**	◆◆◆	$177-$190 SAVE	761
67 / p. 790		Hampton Inn-RDU, 2 mi se of terminal	◆◆◆	$123-$149	761
72 / p. 790	AAA	**Hilton Garden Inn-Raleigh Durham Airport, 1 mi se of terminal**	◆◆◆	$89-$199 SAVE	761
64 / p. 790		Holiday Inn Express, 2 mi se of terminal	◆◆◆	$124-$144	761
59 / p. 790	AAA	**Hyatt Place - Raleigh-Durham Airport, 0.5 mi s of terminal**	◆◆◆	$89-$209 SAVE	762
70 / p. 790		La Quinta Inn & Suites - Aerial Center Pkwy, 2 mi se of terminal	◆◆◆	$69-$129	762
65 / p. 790		La Quinta Inn & Suites (Raleigh-Durham Int'l Airport), 2 mi se of terminal	◆◆◆	$69-$149	762
62 / p. 790	AAA	**Microtel RDU Airport/RTP, 2 mi se of terminal**	◆◆	$65-$100 SAVE	762
66 / p. 790		Staybridge Suites Raleigh Durham Airport, 2 mi se of terminal	◆◆◆	$159-$169	762

Raleigh and Vicinity

This index helps you "spot" where approved lodgings and restaurants are located on the corresponding detailed maps. Lodging daily rate range is for comparison only and show the property's high season. Restaurant rate range is a combination of lunch and/or dinner. Turn to the listing page for more detailed rate information and consult display ads for special promotions.

RALEIGH

Map Page	OA	Lodgings	Diamond Rated	High Season	Page
1 / p. 790	AAA	**Hampton Inn Crabtree - see color ad p 798**	◆◆◆	$89-$149 SAVE	798
2 / p. 790		Hampton Inn Capital Blvd North	◆◆◆	$143-$163	797
3 / p. 790		Homestead Studio Suites Hotel-Raleigh/ Crabtree Valley	◆◆	$76-$86	799
4 / p. 790		Embassy Suites Hotel-Raleigh/Crabtree	◆◆◆	$109-$214	796
5 / p. 790	AAA	**Comfort Suites**	◆◆◆	$95-$150 SAVE	795
6 / p. 790		Marriott Hotel-Crabtree Valley	◆◆◆	$227-$243	800

RALEIGH (cont'd)

Map Page	OA	Lodgings (cont'd)	Diamond Rated	High Season	Page
7 / p. 790		Candlewood Suites-Crabtree	◆◆◆	$109	795
8 / p. 790		Holiday Inn Crabtree Valley	◆◆◆	Rates not provided	799
9 / p. 790	AAA	**Homewood Suites by Hilton - see color ad p 800**	◆◆◆	$89-$179 SAVE	799
10 / p. 790	AAA	**Residence Inn by Marriott Crabtree**	◆◆◆	$197-$211 SAVE	801
11 / p. 790	AAA	**Courtyard by Marriott-Crabtree**	◆◆◆	$187-$201 SAVE	796
12 / p. 790	AAA	**Fairfield Inn & Suites by Marriott-Crabtree**	◆◆◆	$157-$169 SAVE	797
13 / p. 790		La Quinta Inn & Suites Raleigh (Crabtree)	◆◆◆	$69-$149	800
14 / p. 790		Homestead Studio Suites Hotel-Raleigh/North Raleigh	◆◆	$76-$86	799
15 / p. 790		Hilton North Raleigh	◆◆◆	$99-$239	798
16 / p. 790	AAA	**Hyatt Place - Raleigh North**	◆◆◆	$69-$209 SAVE	800
17 / p. 790	AAA	**Residence Inn by Marriott-North Raleigh**	◆◆◆	$167-$179 SAVE	801
18 / p. 790		Days Inn	◆◆	$46-$69	796
19 / p. 790		Extended StayAmerica-North Raleigh	◆◆	$76-$86	796
20 / p. 790		Hampton Inn-Raleigh North	◆◆◆	$89-$119	798
21 / p. 790	AAA	**Courtyard by Marriott-North Raleigh**	◆◆◆	$157-$169 SAVE	796
22 / p. 790		Quality Inn-North	◆◆	$63-$72	800
23 / p. 790	AAA	**Holiday Inn Raleigh-North**	◆◆◆	$120-$139 SAVE	799
24 / p. 790	AAA	**Best Western Raleigh North**	◆◆◆	$65-$90 SAVE	795
25 / p. 790	AAA	**Wingate by Wyndham**	◆◆◆	$99-$113 SAVE	802
26 / p. 790	AAA	**Econo Lodge of Raleigh/North**	◆◆	Rates not provided SAVE	796
27 / p. 790		Sleep Inn of Raleigh	◆◆	$70-$125	802
28 / p. 790		Homestead Studio Suites Hotel-Raleigh/ Northeast	◆◆◆	$82-$92	799
29 / p. 790		Ramada - Blue Ridge	◆◆◆	Rates not provided	801
30 / p. 790	AAA	**Comfort Suites Arena**	◆◆◆	$99-$229 SAVE	795
31 / p. 790	AAA	**Best Western Raleigh Inn & Suites**	◆◆◆	$70-$150 SAVE	795
32 / p. 790		Cameron Park Inn	◆◆◆	$139-$199	795
33 / p. 790		The Oakwood Inn Bed & Breakfast	◆◆◆	$154-$254	800
34 / p. 790		Holiday Inn-Brownstone	◆◆◆	$89-$159	798
35 / p. 790		Clarion Hotel State Capital	◆◆◆	Rates not provided	795
36 / p. 790	AAA	**Sheraton Raleigh Hotel**	◆◆◆	Rates not provided SAVE	802
37 / p. 790	AAA	**Red Roof Inn-South**	◆◆	$60-$75 SAVE	801
38 / p. 790	AAA	**Days Inn**	◆◆	$65 SAVE	796

Map Page	OA	Restaurants	Diamond Rated	Cuisine	Meal Range	Page
1 / p. 790		Winston's Grille	◆◆◆	American	$8-$24	805
2 / p. 790	AAA	**Saint Jacques French Cuisine**	◆◆◆	French	$12-$38	804
3 / p. 790		Michael Dean's Seafood Grill & Oyster Bar	◆◆◆	Seafood	$10-$30	804
4 / p. 790		Neo-China Restaurant	◆◆	Chinese	$7-$17	804
5 / p. 790	AAA	**Simpson's Beef & Seafood**	◆◆◆	Steak & Seafood	$14-$40	805
6 / p. 790		Casa Carbone Ristorante	◆◆	Italian	$6-$16	803
7 / p. 790		Vivace	◆◆◆	Italian	$6-$29	805
8 / p. 790		Firebirds Wood Fired Grill	◆◆◆	American	$8-$36	803

Map Page	OA	Restaurants (cont'd)	Diamond Rated	Cuisine	Meal Range	Page
9 / p. 790		Courtney's	◆◆	American	$5-$8	803
10 / p. 790		Carvers Creek	◆◆	Steak	$7-$25	803
11 / p. 790		Bloomsbury Bistro	◆◆◆	New American	$17-$25	802
12 / p. 790		Hayes Barton Cafe & Dessertery	◆◆	American	$5-$20	803
13 / p. 790		Piccola Italia	◆◆	Italian	$7-$18	804
14 / p. 790		Frazier's	◆◆◆	American	$15-$22	803
15 / p. 790		Porter's City Tavern	◆◆◆	American	$4-$20	804
16 / p. 790		Bogart's American Grill	◆◆◆	American	$6-$25	803
17 / p. 790		Sullivan's Steakhouse	◆◆◆	Steak & Seafood	$20-$40	805
18 / p. 790		518 West Italian Cafe	◆◆	Italian	$5-$22	802
19 / p. 790		Side Street Restaurant	◆◆	Deli	$5-$10	804
20 / p. 790		42nd St. Oyster Bar & Seafood Grill	◆◆	Seafood	$6-$20	802
21 / p. 790	AAA	**Second Empire Restaurant & Tavern**	◆◆◆◆	Continental	$24-$40	804
22 / p. 790		Irregardless Cafe	◆◆◆	American	$4-$22	803
23 / p. 790		The Raleigh Times Bar	◆◆	American	$6-$10	804
24 / p. 790		Caffe Luna	◆◆◆	Italian	$6-$16	803
25 / p. 790		Mo's Diner	◆◆◆	American	$14-$26	804
26 / p. 790		Yancy's!	◆◆	Creole	$7-$22	805
27 / p. 790		Vic's Italian Cafe & Restaurant	◆◆	Italian	$5-$19	805
28 / p. 790		Big Ed's City Market Restaurant	◆	American	$5-$10	802

CARY

Map Page	OA	Lodgings	Diamond Rated	High Season	Page
41 / p. 790	AAA	**Embassy Suites-Raleigh-Durham/Research Triangle**	◆◆◆	$119-$259 SAVE	616
42 / p. 790	AAA	**The Umstead Hotel & Spa**	◆◆◆◆◆	$199-$425 SAVE	618
43 / p. 790		StudioPLUS-Harrison Ave	◆◆	$90-$100	618
44 / p. 790	AAA	**TownePlace Suites by Marriott - Raleigh/Cary/Weston Parkway**	◆◆◆	$182-$196 SAVE	618
45 / p. 790		Hampton Inn & Suites	◆◆◆	$119-$139	617
46 / p. 790		Candlewood Suites-Raleigh/Cary	◆◆◆	$95-$100	616
47 / p. 790		Days Inn	◆◆	Rates not provided	616
48 / p. 790	AAA	**Best Western Cary Inn & Extended Stay Suites**	◆◆◆	$60-$130 SAVE	616
49 / p. 790	AAA	**Holiday Inn Hotel & Suites**	◆◆◆	$89-$179 SAVE	617
50 / p. 790	AAA	**Hampton Inn - see color ad p 797**	◆◆◆	$79-$149 SAVE	617
51 / p. 790		Comfort Suites Hotel	◆◆◆	$79-$129	616
52 / p. 790		La Quinta Inn & Suites Raleigh (Cary)	◆◆◆	$79-$129	617
53 / p. 790		Extended StayAmerica-Raleigh/Cary	◆◆	$77-$87	616
54 / p. 790	AAA	**Homewood Suites - see color ad p 797**	◆◆◆	$89-$179 SAVE	617
55 / p. 790		Residence Inn	◆◆◆	$172-$184	618
56 / p. 790		Extended Stay Deluxe Raleigh-Cary-Regency Parkway	◆◆	$92-$102	616

Map Page	OA	Restaurants	Diamond Rated	Cuisine	Meal Range	Page
31 / p. 790	AAA	**Herons Restaurant**	◆◆◆◆	American	$11-$39	619
32 / p. 790		an, new world cuisine	◆◆◆	Asian	$13-$50	618
33 / p. 790		The King and I	◆◆	Thai	$7-$16	619
34 / p. 790		Biaggi's Ristorante Italiano	◆◆◆	Italian	$6-$21	618

Map Page	OA	Restaurants (cont'd)	Diamond Rated	Cuisine	Meal Range	Page
35 / p. 790		Vespa	◆◆◆	Italian	$9-$20	620
36 / p. 790		India Garden	◆◆	Indian	$6-$15	619
37 / p. 790		Kabuki Japanese Steakhouse & Sushi	◆◆	Japanese	$6-$30	619
38 / p. 790		Hibernian Restaurant & Irish Pub	◆◆	American	$5-$20	619
39 / p. 790		Gypsy's Shiny Diner	◆	American	$4-$8	619
40 / p. 790		Bentley's at Crossroads	◆◆◆	American	$6-$29	618
41 / p. 790		Jimmy V's Steakhouse & Tavern	◆◆	Steak	$20-$45	619
42 / p. 790		MacGregor Draft House	◆◆	American	$5-$12	619
43 / p. 790		Tony's Bourbon Street Oyster Bar	◆◆	Seafood	$7-$30	620
44 / p. 790		Lucky 32	◆◆◆	Regional American	$7-$25	619

MORRISVILLE

Map Page	OA	Lodgings	Diamond Rated	High Season	Page
59 / p. 790	AAA	**Hyatt Place - Raleigh-Durham Airport**	◆◆◆	$89-$209 SAVE	762
60 / p. 790		Country Inn & Suites-RDU Airport	◆◆◆	$144	760
61 / p. 790	AAA	**Fairfield Inn & Suites by Marriott-RDU Airport**	◆◆◆	$177-$190 SAVE	761
62 / p. 790	AAA	**Microtel RDU Airport/RTP**	◆◆	$65-$100 SAVE	762
63 / p. 790		Extended StayAmerica-RDU Airport	◆◆	$100-$110	761
64 / p. 790		Holiday Inn Express	◆◆◆	$124-$144	761
65 / p. 790		La Quinta Inn & Suites (Raleigh-Durham Int'l Airport)	◆◆◆	$69-$149	762
66 / p. 790		Staybridge Suites Raleigh Durham Airport	◆◆◆	$159-$169	762
67 / p. 790		Hampton Inn-RDU	◆◆◆	$123-$149	761
68 / p. 790	AAA	**Courtyard by Marriott-Airport**	◆◆◆	$206-$221 SAVE	761
69 / p. 790		Days Inn Airport/RTP	◆◆◆	$99-$109	761
70 / p. 790		La Quinta Inn & Suites - Aerial Center Pkwy	◆◆◆	$69-$129	762
71 / p. 790		Holiday Inn - Raleigh-Durham Airport	◆◆◆	Rates not provided	762
72 / p. 790	AAA	**Hilton Garden Inn-Raleigh Durham Airport**	◆◆◆	$89-$199 SAVE	761

Map Page	OA	Restaurants	Diamond Rated	Cuisine	Meal Range	Page
47 / p. 790		Capital City Chop House	◆◆◆	Steak & Seafood	$8-$36	763
48 / p. 790		Babymoon Cafe	◆◆	Italian	$7-$24	762
49 / p. 790		Lubrano's Italian Restaurant	◆◆	Italian	$7-$16	763

APEX

Map Page	OA	Lodging	Diamond Rated	High Season	Page
75 / p. 790		Holiday Inn Express	◆◆◆	$91	570

Map Page	OA	Restaurant	Diamond Rated	Cuisine	Meal Range	Page
52 / p. 790		The Peak City Grill & Bar	◆◆◆	American	$8-$25	570

GARNER

Map Page	OA	Lodgings	Diamond Rated	High Season	Page
78 / p. 790		Econo Lodge South	◆◆	Rates not provided	708
79 / p. 790		Wingate by Wyndham-Raleigh South	◆◆◆	Rates not provided	708
80 / p. 790		Holiday Inn Express	◆◆	Rates not provided	708
81 / p. 790		Hampton Inn	◆◆◆	$95	708

Map Page	OA	Restaurant	Diamond Rated	Cuisine	Meal Range	Page
55 / p. 790		Ragazzi's	◆◆	Italian	$5-$13	709

RALEIGH pop. 276,093 (See maps and indexes starting on p. 681, 790)

WHERE TO STAY

BEST WESTERN RALEIGH INN & SUITES *Book great rates at AAA.com* **Phone:** (919)256-2800 31

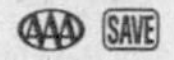

Hotel
$70-$150 All Year

Address: 3018 New Bern Ave **Location:** I-440, exit 13B, just e on US 64 business route. **Facility:** 75 one-bedroom standard units, some with whirlpools. 3 stories, interior corridors. *Bath:* combo or shower only. **Parking:** on-site. **Terms:** 3 day cancellation notice. **Amenities:** high-speed Internet, voice mail, irons, hair dryers. **Pool(s):** heated indoor. **Leisure Activities:** exercise room. **Guest Services:** wireless Internet. **Business Services:** meeting rooms, PC. **Cards:** AX, DC, DS, MC, VI. **Free Special Amenities: continental breakfast and high-speed Internet.**

CALL / SOME UNITS

AAA Benefit:
Members save up to 20%, plus 10% bonus points with rewards program.

BEST WESTERN RALEIGH NORTH *Book great rates at AAA.com* **Phone:** (919)872-5000 24

Hotel
$65-$90 All Year

Address: 2715 Capital Blvd **Location:** I-440, exit 11 or 11B, just n on US 1. **Facility:** 139 units. 121 one-bedroom standard units. 18 one-bedroom suites. 2-3 stories, interior corridors. **Parking:** on-site. **Amenities:** irons, hair dryers. **Pool(s):** outdoor. **Guest Services:** valet and coin laundry, wireless Internet. **Business Services:** meeting rooms, PC. **Cards:** AX, DC, DS, MC, VI. **Free Special Amenities: expanded continental breakfast and high-speed Internet.**

/ SOME UNITS FEE

AAA Benefit:
Members save up to 20%, plus 10% bonus points with rewards program.

CAMERON PARK INN **Phone:** 919/835-2171 32

Bed & Breakfast
$139-$199 All Year

Address: 211 Groveland Ave **Location:** I-440, exit 3, 2.8 mi e on Hillsborough Rd, just n on Oberlin Rd, just e on Park Dr, then just s. **Facility:** The inn's guest rooms are inviting and comfortable. Smoke free premises. 5 units. 2 one-bedroom standard units. 3 one-bedroom suites. 3 stories, interior corridors. *Bath:* combo or shower only. **Parking:** on-site and street. **Terms:** 2 night minimum stay - seasonal, cancellation fee imposed. **Amenities:** video library, DVD players, hair dryers. *Some:* CD players, irons. **Leisure Activities:** bicycles. **Guest Services:** wireless Internet. **Cards:** AX, DS, MC, VI.

ASK / SOME UNITS

CANDLEWOOD SUITES-CRABTREE *Book at AAA.com* **Phone:** (919)789-4840 7

Hotel
$109 All Year

Address: 4433 Lead Mine Rd **Location:** I-440, exit 7 or 7B, just w, then just n. **Facility:** 122 units. 98 one-bedroom standard units with efficiencies. 24 one-bedroom suites with efficiencies. 3 stories, interior corridors. *Bath:* combo or shower only. **Parking:** on-site. **Terms:** office hours 7 am-11 pm, cancellation fee imposed. **Amenities:** video library, DVD players, high-speed Internet, dual phone lines, voice mail, irons, hair dryers. **Leisure Activities:** exercise room. **Guest Services:** complimentary and valet laundry. **Business Services:** business center. **Cards:** AX, DS, MC, VI.

ASK CALL VCR / SOME UNITS FEE

CLARION HOTEL STATE CAPITAL *Book at AAA.com* **Phone:** 919/832-0501 35

Hotel
Rates not provided

Address: 320 Hillsborough St **Location:** Just w; center. **Facility:** Smoke free premises. 202 one-bedroom standard units. 20 stories, interior corridors. *Bath:* combo or shower only. **Parking:** on-site. **Amenities:** high-speed Internet, dual phone lines, voice mail, irons, hair dryers. **Leisure Activities:** limited exercise equipment. **Guest Services:** wireless Internet. **Business Services:** conference facilities, business center.

COMFORT SUITES *Book great rates at AAA.com* **Phone:** (919)876-2211 5

Hotel
$95-$150 All Year

Address: 4400 Capital Blvd **Location:** I-440, exit 11 and 11B, 2.5 mi n on US 1. **Facility:** Smoke free premises. 114 one-bedroom suites. 3 stories, interior corridors. **Parking:** on-site. **Terms:** cancellation fee imposed. **Amenities:** high-speed Internet, voice mail, safes (fee), irons, hair dryers. **Pool(s):** outdoor. **Leisure Activities:** exercise room. **Guest Services:** valet and coin laundry, wireless Internet. **Business Services:** meeting rooms, PC. **Cards:** AX, CB, DC, DS, JC, MC, VI. **Free Special Amenities: early check-in/late check-out and high-speed Internet.**

CALL / SOME UNITS FEE

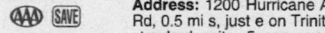

COMFORT SUITES ARENA *Book great rates at AAA.com* **Phone:** (919)854-0502 30

Hotel
$99-$229 All Year

Address: 1200 Hurricane Alley Way **Location:** I-40, exit 289, 1 mi e on Wade Ave, exit Edwards Mill Rd, 0.5 mi s, just e on Trinity Rd, then just s. **Facility:** Smoke free premises. 82 units. 74 one-bedroom standard units. 5 one- and 3 two-bedroom suites with efficiencies (no utensils). 3 stories, interior corridors. *Bath:* combo or shower only. **Parking:** on-site. **Terms:** cancellation fee imposed. **Amenities:** high-speed Internet, dual phone lines, voice mail, safes, irons, hair dryers. *Some:* DVD players. **Pool(s):** outdoor. **Leisure Activities:** exercise room. **Guest Services:** valet and coin laundry, airport transportation-Raleigh-Durham International Airport, area transportation-within 3 mi, wireless Internet. **Business Services:** meeting rooms, PC. **Cards:** AX, DC, DS, JC, MC, VI. **Free Special Amenities: expanded continental breakfast and high-speed Internet.**

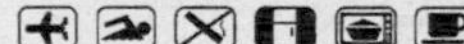

(See maps and indexes starting on p. 681, 790)

COURTYARD BY MARRIOTT-CRABTREE *Book great rates at AAA.com* **Phone:** (919)782-6868  11

AAA SAVE

Hotel

$188-$201 All Year

Address: 3908 Arrow Dr **Location:** I-440, exit 7 or 7B, just w on US 70, just s on Blue Ridge Rd, then just e on Summit Park Ln. **Facility:** Smoke free premises. 84 units. 82 one-bedroom standard units, some with whirlpools. 2 one-bedroom suites with whirlpools. 4 stories, interior corridors. *Bath:* combo or shower only. **Parking:** on-site. **Terms:** cancellation fee imposed. **Amenities:** high-speed Internet, voice mail, irons, hair dryers. **Pool(s):** outdoor. **Leisure Activities:** exercise room. **Guest Services:** valet and coin laundry, area transportation-Crabtree Valley Mall area, wireless Internet. **Business Services:** meeting rooms, PC. **Cards:** AX, DS, MC, VI. **Free Special Amenities: expanded continental breakfast and high-speed Internet.**

CALL / SOME UNITS

AAA Benefit:
Members save a minimum 5% off the best available rate.

COURTYARD BY MARRIOTT-NORTH RALEIGH *Book great rates at AAA.com* **Phone:** (919)821-3400 21

AAA SAVE

Hotel

$158-$169 All Year

Address: 1041 Wake Towne Dr **Location:** I-440, exit 10 (Wake Forest Rd), just s, then just w. **Facility:** Smoke free premises. 153 units. 140 one-bedroom standard units. 13 one-bedroom suites. 2-3 stories, interior corridors. *Bath:* combo or shower only. **Parking:** on-site. **Terms:** cancellation fee imposed. **Amenities:** high-speed Internet, dual phone lines, voice mail, irons, hair dryers. **Pool(s):** outdoor. **Leisure Activities:** whirlpool, exercise room. **Guest Services:** valet and coin laundry, wireless Internet. **Business Services:** meeting rooms, PC. **Cards:** AX, CB, DC, DS, JC, MC, VI. **Free Special Amenities: newspaper and high-speed Internet.**

CALL / SOME UNITS

AAA Benefit:
Members save a minimum 5% off the best available rate.

DAYS INN *Book at AAA.com* **Phone:** (919)878-9310 18

Motel

$46-$69 All Year

Address: 3201 Wake Forest Rd **Location:** I-440, exit 10 (Wake Forest Rd), just n, then just w. **Facility:** 135 one-bedroom standard units. 2 stories (no elevator), exterior corridors. **Parking:** on-site. **Amenities:** safes (fee), irons, hair dryers. **Pool(s):** outdoor. **Guest Services:** coin laundry, wireless Internet. **Business Services:** meeting rooms, PC. **Cards:** AX, DC, DS, MC, VI.

ASK / SOME UNITS FEE

DAYS INN *Book great rates at AAA.com* **Phone:** (919)772-8900 38

AAA SAVE

Motel

$65 All Year

Address: 3901 S Wilmington St **Location:** I-40, exit 298A, 1.9 mi e on US 70. **Facility:** 103 one-bedroom standard units. 3 stories, exterior corridors. **Parking:** on-site. **Terms:** cancellation fee imposed. **Amenities:** hair dryers. **Pool(s):** outdoor. **Guest Services:** wireless Internet. **Cards:** AX, DS, MC, VI. **Free Special Amenities: continental breakfast and high-speed Internet.**

/ SOME UNITS FEE FEE

ECONO LODGE OF RALEIGH/NORTH *Book great rates at AAA.com* **Phone:** 919/856-9800 26

AAA SAVE

Motel

Rates not provided

Address: 2641 Appliance Ct **Location:** I-440, exit 11 or 11B, just n, then 0.3 mi e. **Facility:** 130 one-bedroom standard units. 3 stories, interior/exterior corridors. *Bath:* combo or shower only. **Parking:** on-site. **Amenities:** irons. **Pool(s):** outdoor. **Guest Services:** wireless Internet. **Business Services:** meeting rooms. **Free Special Amenities: continental breakfast and high-speed Internet.**

CALL / SOME UNITS

EMBASSY SUITES HOTEL-RALEIGH/CRABTREE *Book great rates at AAA.com* **Phone:** (919)881-0000 4

Hotel

$109-$214 All Year

Address: 4700 Creedmoor Rd **Location:** I-440, exit 7 or 7B, 0.7 mi w on US 70, then just n. **Facility:** 225 units. 223 one- and 2 two-bedroom suites. 9 stories, interior corridors. *Bath:* combo or shower only. **Parking:** on-site. **Terms:** 1-30 night minimum stay, cancellation fee imposed. **Amenities:** video games (fee), dual phone lines, voice mail, irons, hair dryers. **Pool(s):** heated indoor. **Leisure Activities:** whirlpool, exercise room. **Guest Services:** valet and coin laundry, area transportation, wireless Internet. **Business Services:** conference facilities, business center. **Cards:** AX, CB, DC, DS, JC, MC, VI.

/ SOME UNITS

AAA Benefit:
Members save 5% or more everyday!

EXTENDED STAYAMERICA-NORTH RALEIGH *Book at AAA.com* **Phone:** (919)829-7271 19

Hotel

$76-$86 All Year

Address: 911 Wake Towne Dr **Location:** I-440, exit 10 (Wake Forest Rd), just s, then w. **Facility:** 104 one-bedroom standard units with efficiencies. 3 stories, interior corridors. **Parking:** on-site. **Terms:** office hours 7 am-11 pm. **Amenities:** voice mail, irons. **Leisure Activities:** exercise room privileges. **Guest Services:** coin laundry, wireless Internet. **Cards:** AX, CB, DC, DS, JC, MC, VI.

ASK / SOME UNITS FEE

(See maps and indexes starting on p. 681, 790)

FAIRFIELD INN & SUITES BY MARRIOTT-CRABTREE *Book great rates at AAA.com* **Phone:** (919)881-9800 

Hotel

$158-$169 All Year

Address: 2201 Summit Park Ln **Location:** I-440, exit 7 or 7B, just w on US 70, just s on Blue Ridge Rd, then just e. **Facility:** Smoke free premises. 125 units. 122 one-bedroom standard units, some with whirlpools. 3 one-bedroom suites. 4 stories, interior corridors. **Parking:** on-site. **Terms:** cancellation fee imposed. **Amenities:** voice mail, irons, hair dryers. *Some:* CD players. **Pool(s):** outdoor. **Leisure Activities:** whirlpool, exercise room. **Guest Services:** valet and coin laundry, wireless Internet. **Business Services:** meeting rooms. **Cards:** AX, CB, DC, DS, MC, VI. **Free Special Amenities: expanded continental breakfast and high-speed Internet.**

 CALL  / SOME UNITS FEE 

AAA Benefit: Members save a minimum 5% off the best available rate.

HAMPTON INN CAPITAL BLVD NORTH *Book great rates at AAA.com* **Phone:** (919)872-7111 2

Hotel

$143-$163 All Year

Address: 3621 Spring Forest Rd **Location:** I-440, exit 11 and 11B, 3.5 mi n on US 1, then just e. **Facility:** 131 units. 109 one-bedroom standard units. 22 one-bedroom suites, some with whirlpools. 5 stories, interior corridors. *Bath:* combo or shower only. **Parking:** on-site. **Terms:** cancellation fee imposed. **Amenities:** video games (fee), high-speed Internet, dual phone lines, voice mail, irons, hair dryers. *Some:* DVD players. **Pool(s):** outdoor. **Leisure Activities:** exercise room. **Guest Services:** valet and coin laundry, wireless Internet. **Business Services:** meeting rooms, business center. **Cards:** AX, DC, DS, MC, VI.

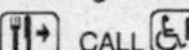 CALL     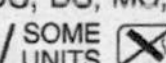 / SOME UNITS

AAA Benefit: Members save up to 10% everyday!

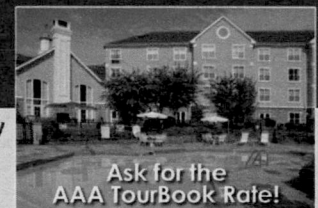

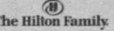

▼ See AAA listing p 617 ▼

▼ See AAA listing p 617 ▼

(See maps and indexes starting on p. 681, 790)

HAMPTON INN CRABTREE *Book great rates at AAA.com* **Phone:** (919)782-1112 **1**

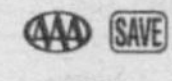

Hotel
$89-$149 All Year

Address: 6209 Glenwood Ave **Location:** I-440, exit 7 or 7B, 2.5 mi w on US 70. **Facility:** 141 units. 132 one-bedroom standard units, some with whirlpools. 9 one-bedroom suites, some with whirlpools. 6 stories, interior corridors. *Bath:* combo or shower only. **Parking:** on-site. **Terms:** cancellation fee imposed. **Amenities:** voice mail, irons, hair dryers. **Pool(s):** outdoor. **Leisure Activities:** sauna, exercise room. **Guest Services:** valet laundry, airport transportation-Raleigh-Durham International Airport, wireless Internet. **Business Services:** meeting rooms, PC. **Cards:** AX, CB, DC, DS, JC, MC, VI. **Free Special Amenities: expanded continental breakfast and high-speed Internet.** *(See color ad below)*

AAA Benefit:
Members save up to 10% everyday!

 CALL   / SOME UNITS FEE 

HAMPTON INN-RALEIGH NORTH *Book great rates at AAA.com* **Phone:** (919)828-1813 **20**

Hotel
$89-$119 All Year

Address: 1001 Wake Towne Dr **Location:** I-440, exit 10 (Wake Forest Rd), just s, then w. **Facility:** 128 one-bedroom standard units. 5 stories, interior corridors. **Parking:** on-site. **Terms:** 1-30 night minimum stay, cancellation fee imposed. **Amenities:** high-speed Internet, voice mail, irons, hair dryers. **Pool(s):** outdoor. **Leisure Activities:** exercise room. **Guest Services:** valet laundry, wireless Internet. **Business Services:** meeting rooms, business center. **Cards:** AX, CB, DC, DS, JC, MC, VI.

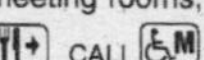 CALL   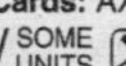 / SOME UNITS 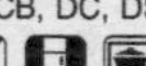

AAA Benefit:
Members save up to 10% everyday!

HILTON NORTH RALEIGH *Book great rates at AAA.com* **Phone:** (919)872-2323 **15**

Hotel
$99-$239 All Year

Address: 3415 Wake Forest Rd **Location:** I-440, exit 10 (Wake Forest Rd), 0.3 mi n. **Facility:** 338 units. 335 one-bedroom standard units. 3 one-bedroom suites. 6 stories, interior corridors. *Bath:* combo or shower only. **Parking:** on-site. **Terms:** 1-30 night minimum stay, cancellation fee imposed. **Amenities:** dual phone lines, voice mail, irons, hair dryers. *Some:* high-speed Internet. **Pool(s):** heated indoor. **Leisure Activities:** whirlpool, exercise room. **Guest Services:** valet laundry, wireless Internet. **Business Services:** conference facilities, business center. **Cards:** AX, CB, DC, DS, JC, MC, VI.

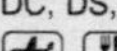  CALL 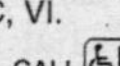   / SOME UNITS  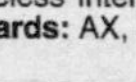

Hilton
AAA Benefit:
Members save 5% or more everyday!

HOLIDAY INN-BROWNSTONE *Book at AAA.com* **Phone:** (919)828-0811 **34**

Hotel
$89-$159 All Year

Address: 1707 Hillsborough St **Location:** I-440, exit 3, 3 mi e. Located adjacent to North Carolina State University. **Facility:** 187 one-bedroom standard units. 9 stories, interior corridors. *Bath:* combo or shower only. **Parking:** on-site. **Terms:** cancellation fee imposed. **Amenities:** high-speed Internet, dual phone lines, voice mail, irons, hair dryers. **Pool(s):** outdoor. **Leisure Activities:** exercise room. **Guest Services:** valet and coin laundry, wireless Internet. **Business Services:** conference facilities, PC. **Cards:** AX, CB, DC, DS, MC, VI.

ASK / SOME UNITS FEE FEE

▼ *See AAA listing above* ▼

(See maps and indexes starting on p. 681, 790)

HOLIDAY INN CRABTREE VALLEY Book at AAA.com Phone: 919/782-8600 8

Hotel
Rates not provided

Address: 4100 Glenwood Ave **Location:** I-440, exit 7 or 7B, just w on US 70. **Facility:** 176 one-bedroom standard units. 12 stories, interior corridors. **Parking:** on-site. **Amenities:** video games (fee), high-speed Internet, dual phone lines, voice mail, irons, hair dryers. **Pool(s):** outdoor. **Leisure Activities:** saunas, exercise room. **Guest Services:** valet laundry, wireless Internet. **Business Services:** conference facilities, business center.

CALL / SOME UNITS FEE

HOLIDAY INN EXPRESS HOTEL & SUITES Book at AAA.com Phone: (919)570-5550

Hotel
$141 All Year

Address: 11400 Common Oaks Dr **Location:** Jct SR 98, 1.2 mi s on US 1, then just w. **Facility:** 94 one-bedroom standard units, some with whirlpools. 3 stories, interior corridors. *Bath:* combo or shower only. **Parking:** on-site. **Amenities:** high-speed Internet, dual phone lines, voice mail, irons, hair dryers. **Pool(s):** outdoor. **Leisure Activities:** limited exercise equipment. **Guest Services:** valet laundry, wireless Internet. **Business Services:** meeting rooms, business center. **Cards:** AX, CB, DC, DS, MC, VI.

ASK CALL / SOME UNITS

HOLIDAY INN RALEIGH-NORTH Book great rates at AAA.com Phone: (919)872-3500 23

AAA SAVE

Hotel
$120-$139 All Year

Address: 2805 Highwoods Blvd **Location:** I-440, exit 11 or 11B, just n on US 1, then just w. **Facility:** 128 one-bedroom standard units. 6 stories, interior corridors. *Bath:* combo or shower only. **Parking:** on-site. **Terms:** cancellation fee imposed. **Amenities:** dual phone lines, voice mail, irons, hair dryers. **Pool(s):** outdoor. **Leisure Activities:** whirlpool, exercise room. **Guest Services:** valet and coin laundry, wireless Internet. **Business Services:** conference facilities, PC. **Cards:** AX, CB, DC, DS, JC, MC, VI. **Free Special Amenities: newspaper and high-speed Internet.**

CALL / SOME UNITS FEE FEE FEE

HOMESTEAD STUDIO SUITES HOTEL-RALEIGH/ CRABTREE VALLEY Book at AAA.com Phone: (919)510-8551 3

Hotel
$76-$86 All Year

Address: 4810 Bluestone Dr **Location:** I-440, exit 7 or 7B, 1.6 mi w on US 70, then just s. **Facility:** 138 one-bedroom standard units with efficiencies. 2 stories (no elevator), exterior corridors. *Bath:* combo or shower only. **Parking:** on-site. **Terms:** office hours 7 am-11 pm. **Amenities:** voice mail, irons. **Guest Services:** valet and coin laundry, wireless Internet. **Cards:** AX, CB, DC, DS, JC, MC, VI.

ASK / SOME UNITS FEE

HOMESTEAD STUDIO SUITES HOTEL-RALEIGH/NORTHEAST Book at AAA.com Phone: (919)807-9970 28

Hotel
$82-$92 All Year

Address: 2601 Appliance Ct **Location:** I-440, exit 11 or 11B, just n on US 1, then just e. **Facility:** 88 units. 64 one-bedroom standard units with efficiencies. 24 one-bedroom suites with efficiencies. 3 stories, interior corridors. *Bath:* combo or shower only. **Parking:** on-site. **Amenities:** dual phone lines, voice mail, irons, hair dryers. **Pool(s):** indoor. **Leisure Activities:** limited exercise equipment. **Guest Services:** coin laundry, wireless Internet. **Cards:** AX, CB, DC, DS, JC, MC, VI.

ASK / SOME UNITS FEE

HOMESTEAD STUDIO SUITES HOTEL-RALEIGH/ NORTH RALEIGH Book at AAA.com Phone: (919)981-7353 14

Motel
$76-$86 All Year

Address: 3531 Wake Forest Rd **Location:** I-440, exit 10 (Wake Forest Rd), 0.5 mi n. **Facility:** 121 one-bedroom standard units with efficiencies. 2 stories (no elevator), exterior corridors. *Bath:* combo or shower only. **Parking:** on-site. **Amenities:** voice mail, irons. **Guest Services:** coin laundry, wireless Internet. **Cards:** AX, CB, DC, DS, JC, MC, VI.

ASK CALL / SOME UNITS FEE

HOMEWOOD SUITES BY HILTON Book great rates at AAA.com Phone: (919)785-1131 9

AAA SAVE

Hotel
$89-$179 All Year

Address: 5400 Homewood Banks Dr **Location:** I-440, exit 7 or 7B, just w on US 70, just s on Blue Ridge Rd, just w on Crabtree Valley, then just s. **Facility:** 137 units. 131 one- and 6 two-bedroom suites with efficiencies. 7 stories, interior corridors. *Bath:* combo or shower only. **Parking:** on-site. **Terms:** cancellation fee imposed. **Amenities:** video games (fee), dual phone lines, voice mail, irons, hair dryers. **Pool(s):** outdoor. **Leisure Activities:** exercise room. **Guest Services:** valet and coin laundry, area transportation-within 3 mi, wireless Internet. **Business Services:** meeting rooms, PC. **Cards:** AX, CB, DC, DS, JC, MC, VI. **Free Special Amenities: full breakfast and high-speed Internet.** *(See color ad p 800)*

CALL / SOME UNITS FEE VCR

(See maps and indexes starting on p. 681, 790)

HYATT PLACE - RALEIGH NORTH Book great rates at AAA.com Phone: (919)877-9997 16

AAA SAVE
Hotel
$69-$209 All Year

Address: 1105 Navaho Dr **Location:** I-440, exit 10 (Wake Forest Rd), just n, then just w. **Facility:** 127 one-bedroom standard units. 6 stories, interior corridors. *Bath:* combo or shower only. **Parking:** on-site. **Terms:** cancellation fee imposed. **Amenities:** video games (fee), dual phone lines, voice mail, irons, hair dryers. *Some:* high-speed Internet. **Pool(s):** heated outdoor. **Leisure Activities:** exercise room. **Guest Services:** valet laundry, wireless Internet. **Business Services:** meeting rooms, business center. **Cards:** AX, CB, DC, DS, JC, MC, VI. **Free Special Amenities: continental breakfast and high-speed Internet.**

CALL / SOME UNITS

LA QUINTA INN & SUITES RALEIGH (CRABTREE) Book great rates at AAA.com Phone: (919)785-0071 13

Hotel
$69-$149 All Year

Address: 2211 Summit Park Ln **Location:** I-440, exit 7 or 7B, just w on US 70, just s on Blue Ridge Rd, then just e. **Facility:** 134 units. 129 one-bedroom standard units. 5 one-bedroom suites. 5 stories, interior corridors. *Bath:* combo or shower only. **Parking:** on-site. **Amenities:** video games (fee), high-speed Internet, dual phone lines, voice mail, irons, hair dryers. **Pool(s):** heated outdoor. **Leisure Activities:** whirlpool, exercise room. **Guest Services:** valet and coin laundry, wireless Internet. **Business Services:** meeting rooms, business center. **Cards:** AX, DC, DS, MC, VI.

ASK CALL / SOME UNITS

MARRIOTT HOTEL-CRABTREE VALLEY Book great rates at AAA.com Phone: (919)781-7000 6

Hotel
$227-$244 All Year

Address: 4500 Marriott Dr **Location:** I-440, exit 7 or 7B, 0.5 mi w on US 70, then just n. Located across from Crabtree Valley Mall. **Facility:** Smoke free premises. 375 units. 374 one-bedroom standard units. 1 one-bedroom suite. 6 stories, interior corridors. *Bath:* combo or shower only. **Parking:** on-site. **Terms:** cancellation fee imposed. **Amenities:** high-speed Internet (fee), voice mail, irons, hair dryers. *Some:* dual phone lines. **Pool(s):** heated indoor/outdoor. **Leisure Activities:** whirlpool, exercise room. **Guest Services:** valet and coin laundry, wireless Internet. **Business Services:** conference facilities, business center. **Cards:** AX, CB, DC, DS, MC, VI.

/ SOME UNITS

THE OAKWOOD INN BED & BREAKFAST Phone: (919)832-9712 33

Historic Bed & Breakfast
$154-$254 All Year

Address: 411 N Bloodworth St **Location:** Ne of center; downtown; in Oakwood Historic District. **Facility:** This 1871 Victorian home with Italian Renaissance Revival influences has antique furniture and gas-log fireplaces in each room. Smoke free premises. 6 one-bedroom standard units. 2 stories (no elevator), interior corridors. *Bath:* combo or shower only. **Parking:** on-site. **Terms:** 4 day cancellation notice-fee imposed. **Amenities:** video library, irons, hair dryers. *Some:* DVD players. **Guest Services:** wireless Internet. **Cards:** AX, CB, DC, DS, JC, MC, VI.

ASK / SOME UNITS VCR

QUALITY INN-NORTH Book at AAA.com Phone: (919)878-9550 22

Hotel
$63-$72 All Year

Address: 2910 Capital Blvd **Location:** I-440, exit 11 or 11B, 0.5 mi n on US 1. **Facility:** 92 one-bedroom standard units. 4 stories, interior corridors. *Bath:* combo or shower only. **Parking:** on-site. **Amenities:** irons, hair dryers. **Pool(s):** outdoor. **Guest Services:** wireless Internet. **Business Services:** meeting rooms. **Cards:** AX, CB, DC, DS, JC, MC, VI.

ASK CALL / SOME UNITS

▼ See AAA listing p 799 ▼

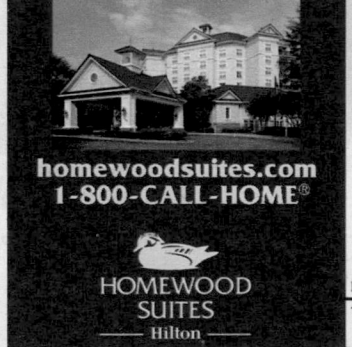

(See maps and indexes starting on p. 681, 790)

RAMADA - BLUE RIDGE Book at AAA.com Phone: 919/832-4100 29

Hotel

Rates not provided

Address: 1520 Blue Ridge Rd **Location:** I-40, exit 289, 2 mi e on Wade Ave, exit Blue Ridge Rd, just s; I-440, exit 4 or 4B, just w on Wade Ave, then just s. **Facility:** Smoke free premises. 123 units. 109 one-bedroom standard units. 14 one-bedroom suites. 2 stories, interior corridors. *Bath:* combo or shower only. **Parking:** on-site. **Amenities:** voice mail, irons, hair dryers. **Pool(s):** outdoor. **Leisure Activities:** exercise room. **Guest Services:** valet and coin laundry, wireless Internet. **Business Services:** meeting rooms, business center.

CALL / SOME UNITS

RED ROOF INN-SOUTH Book great rates at AAA.com **Phone:** (919)833-6005 37

Hotel

$60-$75 All Year

Address: 1813 S Saunders St **Location:** I-40, exit 298B, just n. **Facility:** 133 units. 129 one-bedroom standard units. 4 one-bedroom suites. 4 stories, interior corridors. *Bath:* combo or shower only. **Parking:** on-site. **Amenities:** video games (fee), dual phone lines, voice mail. **Guest Services:** wireless Internet. **Cards:** AX, CB, DC, DS, MC, VI. **Free Special Amenities: local telephone calls.**

CALL / SOME UNITS FEE FEE

RESIDENCE INN BY MARRIOTT CRABTREE Book great rates at AAA.com **Phone:** (919)279-3000 10

Hotel

$197-$212 All Year

Address: 2200 Summit Park Ln **Location:** I-440, exit 7 or 7B, just w on US 70, just s on Blue Ridge Rd, then just e. **Facility:** Smoke free premises. 112 units. 64 one-bedroom standard units with efficiencies. 36 one- and 12 two-bedroom suites with efficiencies, some with whirlpools. 5 stories, interior corridors. *Bath:* combo or shower only. **Parking:** on-site. **Terms:** cancellation fee imposed. **Amenities:** high-speed Internet, dual phone lines, voice mail, irons, hair dryers. *Some:* DVD players (fee). **Pool(s):** outdoor. **Leisure Activities:** whirlpool, putting green, exercise room. **Guest Services:** valet and coin laundry, wireless Internet. **Business Services:** meeting rooms. **Cards:** AX, CB, DC, DS, JC, MC, VI. **Free Special Amenities: full breakfast and high-speed Internet.**

CALL / SOME UNITS FEE

AAA Benefit:

Members save a minimum 5% off the best available rate.

RESIDENCE INN BY MARRIOTT-NORTH RALEIGH Book great rates at AAA.com **Phone:** (919)878-6100 17

Hotel

$168-$180 All Year

Address: 1000 Navaho Dr **Location:** I-440, exit 10 (Wake Forest Rd), just n, then w. **Facility:** Smoke free premises. 144 units. 108 one-bedroom standard units with efficiencies. 18 one- and 18 two-bedroom suites with kitchens. 2 stories (no elevator), exterior corridors. **Parking:** on-site. **Terms:** cancellation fee imposed. **Amenities:** voice mail, irons, hair dryers. **Pool(s):** outdoor. **Leisure Activities:** whirlpool, exercise room, sports court. **Guest Services:** valet and coin laundry, wireless Internet. **Business Services:** meeting rooms, PC. **Cards:** AX, CB, DC, DS, JC, MC, VI. **Free Special Amenities: full breakfast and high-speed Internet.**

CALL / SOME UNITS FEE

Residence Inn Marriott

AAA Benefit:

Members save a minimum 5% off the best available rate.

(See maps and indexes starting on p. 681, 790)

SHERATON RALEIGH HOTEL Book great rates at AAA.com **Phone:** 919/834-9900 36

Hotel
Rates not provided

Address: 421 S Salisbury St **Location:** Just s; downtown. **Facility:** Smoke free premises. 353 units. 349 one-bedroom standard units. 4 one-bedroom suites. 17 stories, interior corridors. *Bath:* combo or shower only. **Parking:** on-site (fee). **Amenities:** high-speed Internet (fee), voice mail, irons, hair dryers. **Pool(s):** heated indoor. **Leisure Activities:** whirlpool, exercise room. **Guest Services:** valet laundry, wireless Internet. **Business Services:** conference facilities, business center. **Free Special Amenities: local telephone calls and newspaper.**

AAA Benefit:
Members get up to 15% off, plus Starwood Preferred Guest® bonuses.

SLEEP INN OF RALEIGH Book at AAA.com **Phone:** (919)755-6005 27

Hotel
$70-$125 All Year

Address: 2617 Appliance Ct **Location:** I-440, exit 11 or 11B, just n on US 1, then 0.4 mi e. **Facility:** 107 one-bedroom standard units. 3 stories, interior corridors. *Bath:* combo or shower only. **Parking:** on-site. **Amenities:** video games (fee), irons, hair dryers. *Some:* high-speed Internet. **Pool(s):** outdoor. **Guest Services:** wireless Internet. **Cards:** AX, DS, MC, VI.

ASK CALL / SOME UNITS

WINGATE BY WYNDHAM Book great rates at AAA.com **Phone:** (919)821-0888 25

Hotel
$99-$113 All Year

Address: 2610 Westinghouse Blvd **Location:** I-440, exit 11 or 11B, 0.5 mi n on US 1, then just e. **Facility:** 85 one-bedroom standard units, some with whirlpools. 4 stories, interior corridors. *Bath:* combo or shower only. **Parking:** on-site. **Terms:** cancellation fee imposed. **Amenities:** video games (fee), high-speed Internet, dual phone lines, voice mail, safes, irons, hair dryers. **Pool(s):** outdoor. **Leisure Activities:** whirlpool, exercise room. **Guest Services:** valet laundry, wireless Internet. **Business Services:** meeting rooms, business center. **Cards:** AX, DC, DS, MC, VI. **Free Special Amenities: continental breakfast and high-speed Internet.**

CALL / SOME UNITS

WHERE TO DINE

42ND ST. OYSTER BAR & SEAFOOD GRILL **Phone:** 919/831-2811 20

Seafood
$6-$20

In a restored 1931 warehouse, the popular and lively restaurant serves fresh oysters, fish and lobster in either fried or steamed platters. Hushpuppies are practically a meal in themselves, and the wine and beer lists are lengthy. Casual dress. **Bar:** Full bar. **Reservations:** suggested, for dinner. **Hours:** 11:30 am-10 pm, Fri-11 pm, Sat 5 pm-11 pm, Sun 5 pm-10 pm. Closed: 1/1, 11/26, 12/24, 12/25; also Super Bowl Sun. **Address:** 508 W Jones St **Location:** From State Capitol, just w on Hillsborough St, then just n on Harrington St. **Parking:** on-site. **Cards:** AX, DC, MC, VI. **Historic**

CALL

518 WEST ITALIAN CAFE **Phone:** 919/829-2518 18

Italian
$5-$22

In a refurbished warehouse in a trendy area of the city, the eatery builds its menu on contemporary Italian cuisine. Guests can savor bread and pizza baked in a wood-burning oven. Standouts include rosemary chicken and pan-seared tuna. Casual dress. **Bar:** Full bar. **Reservations:** accepted. **Hours:** 11:30 am-9:30 pm, Tues-Thurs to 10 pm, Fri & Sat-10:30 pm, Sun 10:30 am-2 & 5-9 pm. Closed: 1/1, 11/26, 12/25. **Address:** 518 W Jones St **Location:** Corner of Glenwood Ave and W Jones St; downtown. **Parking:** on-site. **Cards:** AX, DC, DS, MC, VI.

THE ANGUS BARN **Phone:** 919/787-3505 1

Steak
$30-$60

The rustic atmosphere of a 20th-century barn sustains the Raleigh landmark, where diners sit down to huge portions of perfectly grilled fillets and crisp salads. Rich cheesecake pleases the sweet tooth. Dressy casual. **Bar:** Full bar. **Reservations:** suggested. **Hours:** 5:30 pm-10:30 pm, Sun 5 pm-10 pm. Closed: 1/1, 12/24, 12/25. **Address:** 9401 Glenwood Ave **Location:** I-540, exit 4, just e; US 70, exit 293. **Parking:** on-site. **Cards:** AX, CB, DC, DS, MC, VI.

BIG ED'S CITY MARKET RESTAURANT **Phone:** 919/836-9909 28

American
$5-$10

Guests can get their fill of Southern favorites, such as biscuits with red-eye gravy, chicken and dumplings and turnip greens at the established downtown breakfast and lunch spot. Casual dress. **Hours:** 7 am-2 pm, Sat-noon. Closed major holidays; also 12/24 & Sun. **Address:** 220 Wolfe St **Location:** Jct Fayetteville St, just e on Martin St, just s on Blount St; downtown in City Market. **Parking:** street.

BLOOMSBURY BISTRO **Phone:** 919/834-9011 11

New American
$17-$25

Consistently considered one of the top restaurants in the Triangle, this bistro blends French techniques with ethnic ingredients on a menu that changes seasonally. Artful presentations and polished service combine with a sedate neighborhood atmosphere to create a memorable evening for guests. Dressy casual. **Bar:** Full bar. **Reservations:** suggested. **Hours:** 5:30 pm-10 pm. Closed major holidays; also 12/24 & Sun. **Address:** 509-101 W Whitaker Mill Rd **Location:** I-440, exit 7 or 7A, 2.5 mi e on Glenwood Ave, then just n; in Five Points Village Shopping Center. **Parking:** on-site. **Cards:** AX, CB, DC, MC, VI.

(See maps and indexes starting on p. 681, 790)

BOGART'S AMERICAN GRILL **Phone:** 919/832-1122 (16)

American
$6-$25

The menu at the upscale bistro in the Glenwood South dining district focuses on inventive Southern cuisine and rotisserie-grilled food. Live entertainment is featured several nights a week. Guests can sample an infused vodka creation from the bar or a martini from the lengthy menu. Dressy casual. **Bar:** Full bar. **Reservations:** accepted. **Hours:** 11:30 am-2:30 & 5-10 pm, Fri-11 pm, Sat 5 pm-11 pm, Sun 10 am-3 pm. Closed: 7/4, 11/26, 12/25. **Address:** 510 Glenwood Ave, Suite 109 **Location:** Jct Glenwood and Peace sts, just s; downtown. **Parking:** on-site (fee) and street. **Cards:** AX, DC, DS, MC, VI.

CAFFE LUNA **Phone:** 919/832-6090 (24)

Italian
$6-$16

Since 1996, the downtown eatery infused contemporary Italian cuisine with Tuscan flair. Reasonably priced entrees are served by a friendly staff in casually upscale dining rooms. Casual dress. **Bar:** Full bar. **Reservations:** suggested. **Hours:** 11:30 am-2:30 & 5-10 pm, Sat from 5 pm, Mon & Tues-2:30 pm. Closed major holidays; also Sun. **Address:** 136 E Hargett St **Location:** Corner of Blount and Hargett sts; se of center. **Parking:** street. **Cards:** AX, MC, VI.

CARVERS CREEK **Phone:** 919/872-2300 (10)

Steak
$7-$25

In a hunting and fishing lodge setting complete with fireplace and mounted deer head, the restaurant presents a menu of prime rib, fresh seafood and hand-carved steaks. Many small dining rooms throughout create a cozy, private environment. Casual dress. **Bar:** Full bar. **Reservations:** suggested, weekends. **Hours:** 11:30 am-2 & 5-10 pm, Sat from 5 pm, Sun noon-8 pm. Closed: 12/25. **Address:** 2711 Capital Blvd **Location:** I-440, exit 11 or 11B, just n on US 1. **Parking:** on-site. **Cards:** AX, DC, DS, MC, VI.

CASA CARBONE RISTORANTE **Phone:** 919/781-8750 (6)

Italian
$6-$16

Since 1984, the family-owned-and-operated restaurant has served fine Italian cuisine in a cozy, casually upscale atmosphere. Breads and sauces are made fresh every day. A children's menu ensures the whole family will find something to enjoy. Casual dress. **Bar:** Full bar. **Hours:** 5 pm-10 pm, Sun 4 pm-9 pm. Closed: 4/12, 11/26, 12/25; also Mon. **Address:** 6019-A Glenwood Ave **Location:** I-440, exit 7 or 7B, 2.1 mi w on US 70; in Oak Park Shopping Center. **Parking:** on-site. **Cards:** AX, DC, DS, MC, VI.

COURTNEY'S **Phone:** 919/834-3613 (9)

American
$5-$8

On the menu are omelets, waffles, skillets and other breakfast, brunch and lunch favorites. Service is friendly, and the atmosphere is homelike. Casual dress. **Hours:** 7 am-2:30 pm. Closed: 11/26, 12/25. **Address:** 407 E Six Forks Rd **Location:** I-440, exit 10 (Wake Forest Rd), 0.4 mi s, then just w. **Parking:** on-site. **Cards:** MC, VI.

FIREBIRDS WOOD FIRED GRILL **Phone:** 919/788-8778 (8)

American
$8-$36

The restaurant re-creates the atmosphere of a mountain lodge. Hand-cut steaks and seafood dominate the menu, which also lists a few pork and chicken entrees, as well as elk tenderloin medallions and buffalo meatloaf. The kitchen uses wood grilling, and pizzas bake in a wood-burning oven. Flavorful food, enhanced presentations and a skilled, knowledgeable and attentive staff, together with distinctive physical elements, make this place appealing. Casual dress. **Bar:** Full bar. **Hours:** 11 am-10 pm, Fri & Sat-11 pm. Closed: 1/1, 11/26, 12/25. **Address:** 4350 Lassiter at North Hills Ave **Location:** I-440, exit 8B, just n; in North Hills Mall Complex. **Parking:** on-site. **Cards:** AX, DC, DS, MC, VI.

FRAZIER'S **Phone:** 919/828-6699 (14)

American
$15-$22

The upscale neighborhood bistro presents a seasonally changing menu of flavorful American cuisine. Reservations are recommended, as the cozy dining room fills quickly with guests seeking tasty fare. In addition to the a la carte menu, three- and five-course chef's tasting menus, which can be paired with wines, are offered nightly. Dressy casual. **Bar:** Full bar. **Reservations:** suggested. **Hours:** 5 pm-10 pm, Fri-10:30 pm, Sat 5 pm-10:30 pm. Closed major holidays; also Sun. **Address:** 2418 Hillsborough St **Location:** I-440, exit 3 (Hillsborough St), 2.5 mi e; across from North Carolina State University. **Parking:** street. **Cards:** AX, DS, MC, VI.

HARD TIMES CAFE **Phone:** 919/835-1600

American
$7-$14

The hot and spicy, down-home operation knocks your socks off with an impressive variety of chilies, cooked in styles ranging from Cincinnati to Texas and vegetarian. Casual dress. **Bar:** Full bar. **Hours:** 11 am-1 am. **Address:** 410 Glenwood Ave **Location:** Jct Peace St, just s; downtown. **Parking:** on-site. **Cards:** AX, MC, VI.

HAYES BARTON CAFE & DESSERTERY **Phone:** 919/856-8551 (12)

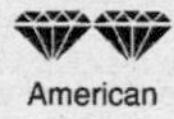

American
$5-$20

The decor at this neighborhood diner evokes the 1940s, and the dinner menu is worded to match, with selections such as the Ava Gardner salad, Marilyn crab cakes and the Bogey burger. Lunch is a relaxed affair, with orders for sandwiches and salads taken at the counter, and cash is the only form of payment. Dinner evolves into a more casually elegant experience, with candlelight and vintage tunes softly playing in the background. Homemade desserts are as gorgeous as they are delicious. Casual dress. **Bar:** Full bar. **Hours:** 11:30 am-2 & 6-9 pm, Tues-2 pm, Fri & Sat-9:30 pm. Closed: 7/4, 11/26, 12/25; also Sun & Mon. **Address:** 2000 Fairview Rd **Location:** I-440, exit 7 or 7A, 2.2 mi e on Glenwood Ave, then just s; in Historic Five Points District. **Parking:** street. **Cards:** MC, VI.

IRREGARDLESS CAFE **Phone:** 919/833-8898 (22)

American
$4-$22

Opened in 1975, the cafe originally was Raleigh's premier vegetarian restaurant. Since then, the menu has expanded to include fresh seafood, chicken and great steaks, but the pride remains the health-conscious fare, including low-fat, non-dairy and vegetarian entrees. Desserts are made fresh daily on site. Dressy casual. Entertainment. **Bar:** Full bar. **Reservations:** suggested. **Hours:** 11:30 am-2:30 & 5:30-10 pm, Sat 5:30 pm-10:30 pm; Sunday brunch 10 am-2 pm. Closed: Mon. **Address:** 901 W Morgan St **Location:** Jct Hillsborough St, just s. **Parking:** on-site and street. **Cards:** AX, DC, DS, MC, VI.

(See maps and indexes starting on p. 681, 790)

MICHAEL DEAN'S SEAFOOD GRILL & OYSTER BAR **Phone:** 919/790-9992 (3)

Seafood
$10-$30

The dining room features sedate, contemporary decor, and a monthly changing menu centers on innovative preparations of fresh seafood as well as chicken, beef, pasta and pizza. Late-night crowds populate the bar for tasty drinks, including the specialty martinis, and live entertainment on weekends. Brunch is served on Sunday. Casual dress. **Bar:** Full bar. **Reservations:** suggested. **Hours:** 11:30 am-2 & 5-10 pm, Thurs & Fri-2 am, Sun 11 am-2 & 5-10 pm. Closed: 11/26, 12/25. **Address:** 6004 Falls of the Neuse Rd **Location:** I-440, exit 10, 3 mi n on Wake Forest Rd to Falls of the Neuse Rd; at North Ridge Shopping Center. **Parking:** on-site. **Cards:** AX, DS, MC, VI.

MO'S DINER **Phone:** 919/856-9938 (25)

American
$14-$26

The truck-stop-styled name belies the casually elegant setting in a quaint purple-tinted bungalow and the simple but delectably prepared classic cuisine. The menu changes frequently, but typical offerings include grilled pork tenderloin in balsamic reduction, sauteed chicken livers and the signature rack of lamb. Dressy casual. **Bar:** Full bar. **Reservations:** suggested. **Hours:** 5:30 pm-9 pm. Closed: 11/26, 12/25; also Sun & Mon. **Address:** 306 E Hargett St **Location:** Jct Person St, just e; downtown. **Parking:** street. **Cards:** AX, DC, DS, MC, VI.

NEO-CHINA RESTAURANT **Phone:** 919/783-8383 (4)

Chinese
$7-$17

Find traditional Hunan and Cantonese cuisine on the lengthy menu at the small, family-owned chain. Savory dishes of beef, poultry, seafood, pork and vegetables line the menu, while original artwork enhances a warm, casual dining room. Courteous, brisk service is the standard. Casual dress. **Bar:** Full bar. **Reservations:** accepted. **Hours:** 11 am-2:30 & 4:30-10 pm, Sat from 4:30 pm, Sun noon-2:30 & 4:30-10 pm. Closed: 11/26. **Address:** 6602-1 Glenwood Ave **Location:** I-440, exit 7 or 7B, 2.6 mi w on US 70; in Townridge Square Shopping Center. **Parking:** on-site. **Cards:** AX, DC, DS, MC, VI.

PICCOLA ITALIA **Phone:** 919/833-6888 (13)

Italian
$7-$18

Family owned and operated for more than 25 years, this casual eatery features Southern Italian fare, with pizza, pasta, chicken and veal dishes taking center stage on the menu. In warm weather, guests enjoy sidewalk seating. Casual dress. **Bar:** Beer & wine. **Hours:** 11 am-2:30 & 5-9:30 pm, Sat noon-9:30 pm. Closed: 1/1, 11/26, 12/24, 12/25; also Sun. **Address:** 423 Woodburn Rd **Location:** I-440, exit 3, 2.2 mi e on Hillsborough St, 0.4 mi n on Oberlin Rd, just e on Clark Ave, then just n; in Cameron Village. **Parking:** on-site. **Cards:** AX, MC, VI.

PORTER'S CITY TAVERN **Phone:** 919/821-2133 (15)

American
$4-$20

Al fresco meals on the tavern's sidewalk patio let patrons unwind over tasty appetizers and entrees. The signature tavern chips, homemade tortillas covered with creative toppings, are just right for sharing. Among popular entrees are steaks, chops, salads, sandwiches and preparations of seafood and pasta. Casual dress. **Bar:** Full bar. **Reservations:** accepted. **Hours:** 11:30 am-10 pm, Fri-11 pm, Sat 5 pm-11 pm, Sun 11:30 am-2:30 & 5-9 pm. Closed major holidays. **Address:** 2412 Hillsborough St **Location:** I-440, exit 3 (Hillsborough St), 2.5 mi e; across from North Carolina State University. **Parking:** street. **Cards:** AX, DC, DS, MC, VI.

THE RALEIGH TIMES BAR **Phone:** 919/833-0999 (23)

American
$6-$10

The menu is limited at this tiny pub, which is popular with the local lunch and after-work crowd. Salads, sandwiches and bar munchies are the only choices, but they're all good. Among favorites are the pimiento cheese wrap and the Reuben with house-cured corned beef. Burgers offer a half-pound of grilled beef. The bar lets patrons choose from a slew of microbrews and imports, and munchies such as chicken-fried pickles and barbecue pork nachos are sized for sharing. Casual dress. **Bar:** Full bar. **Hours:** 11:30 am-2 am, Sun noon-midnight. Closed: 11/26, 12/25. **Address:** 14 E Hargett St **Location:** Jct Fayetteville St, just e; downtown. **Parking:** street. **Cards:** AX, DC, MC, VI.

SAINT JACQUES FRENCH CUISINE **Phone:** 919/862-2770 (2)

French
$12-$38

Gracious, attentive service and delectable French cuisine are hallmarks of this tiny bistro, where the menu changes periodically but typical selections include coq au vin, roasted lamb loin, duck a l'orange and salmon in puff pastry. Dressy casual. **Bar:** Beer & wine. **Reservations:** suggested. **Hours:** 11 am-2 & 5:30-9:30 pm, Fri & Sat-10 pm. Closed: 11/26, 12/25; also Sun & Mon. **Address:** 6112 Falls of the Neuse Rd **Location:** I-440, exit 10, 3 mi n on Wake Forest Rd to Falls of the Neuse Rd; in North Ridge Shopping Center. **Parking:** on-site. **Cards:** AX, DS, MC, VI.

SECOND EMPIRE RESTAURANT & TAVERN ***Menu on AAA.com*** **Phone:** 919/829-3663 (21)

Continental
$24-$40

Patrons dine in grace and style in the elegant dining rooms of Second Empire, which is in the restored 1879 Dodd-Hinsdale house. The monthly changing menu features contemporary American cuisine prepared with fresh, seasonal ingredients. Downstairs in the tavern, guests find a more relaxed atmosphere and casual menu, with year-round patio seating available. Dressy casual. **Bar:** Full bar. **Reservations:** suggested. **Hours:** 5:30 pm-9:30 pm. Closed: 11/26, 12/25; also Sun. **Address:** 330 Hillsborough St **Location:** Downtown; just w of capitol building. **Parking:** on-site. **Cards:** AX, DC, DS, MC, VI. **Historic**

SIDE STREET RESTAURANT **Phone:** 919/828-4927 (19)

Deli
$5-$10

A well-kept secret among downtown government employees, the cozy sandwich shop is the place for a scrumptious lunch or light dinner. From chicken salad with apple chunks and pecans to pimiento cheese, there are almost too many sandwich choices. Casual dress. **Bar:** Beer & wine. **Hours:** 11 am-3 & 5-9 pm, Sat 11 am-3 pm. Closed major holidays; also Sun & for dinner Mon. **Address:** 225 N Bloodworth St **Location:** Corner of Lane and Bloodworth sts; northeast of center. **Parking:** street.

(See maps and indexes starting on p. 601, 790)

SIMPSON'S BEEF & SEAFOOD **Phone:** 919/783-8818 (5)

Steak & Seafood
$14-$40

The classic restaurant welcomes guests to eat aged Western beef and fresh seafood in a candlelit atmosphere. Grilled salmon with Cabernet Sauvignon wine sauce is tasty and authentic. Live piano music adds to the relaxing environment. Dressy casual. **Bar:** Full bar. **Reservations:** suggested. **Hours:** 5 pm-10 pm, Fri & Sat-11 pm. Closed major holidays; also Sun. **Address:** 5625 Creedmoor Rd **Location:** I-440, exit 7, 1 mi w, 0.8 mi w on US 70, then 0.8 mi n; in Creedmoor Crossings. **Parking:** on-site. **Cards:** AX, CB, DC, DS, MC, VI.

SULLIVAN'S STEAKHOUSE **Phone:** 919/833-2888 (17)

Steak & Seafood
$20-$40

Named for John L. Sullivan, heavyweight champion of the world in the 1880s, the upscale steak house prepares a wide selection of steaks, chops and seafood. Decorated with black-and-white photographs of Sullivan, Jack Dempsey and other boxing legends. Dressy casual. **Bar:** Full bar. **Reservations:** suggested. **Hours:** 11 am-1 am. Closed: 12/25. **Address:** 414 Glenwood Ave, Suite 103 **Location:** Jct Peace St, just s. **Parking:** on-site and valet. **Cards:** AX, DC, MC, VI.

VIC'S ITALIAN CAFE & RESTAURANT **Phone:** 919/829-7090 (27)

Italian
$5-$19

The tiny storefront cafe serves both lunch and dinner. On the lengthy menu are pasta dishes, as well as chicken and veal preparations. Pizza, stromboli and calzones are popular. Casual dress. **Bar:** Beer & wine. **Hours:** 11 am-10 pm, Fri & Sat-11 pm. Closed: 1/1, 11/26, 12/25; also Sun. **Address:** 331 Blake St **Location:** 2 blks e, then 2 blks s; downtown; in City Market. **Parking:** on-site (fee) and street. **Cards:** AX, DS, MC, VI.

VIVACE **Phone:** 919/787-7747 (7)

Italian
$6-$29

The casually sophisticated trattoria lets patrons sample tasty Italian food in an intimate atmosphere or on the relaxed sidewalk area. Dishes are tweaked each season to incorporate the freshest ingredients. Freshly made pasta enhances classic dishes, while wood-fired pizza serves as a delicious alternative. Dressy casual. **Bar:** Full bar. **Reservations:** accepted. **Hours:** 11 am-10 pm, Fri & Sat-11 pm, Sun-9 pm. Closed major holidays. **Address:** 4209 Lassiter Mill Rd **Location:** I-440, exit 8B, just n on Six Forks Rd, then just w. **Parking:** on-site. **Cards:** AX, DC, DS, MC, VI.

CALL

WINSTON'S GRILLE **Phone:** 919/790-0700 (1)

American
$8-$24

Abundant artwork contributes to the popular eatery's sharp decor. Innovation marks some dishes, while others, such as the prime rib, stick to the classic preparation style. Servers are competent and attentive. Dressy casual. **Bar:** Full bar. **Reservations:** accepted. **Hours:** 11 am-10 pm, Fri-11 pm, Sat 5 pm-11 pm, Sun 11 am-9:30 pm. Closed: 1/1, 7/4, 12/24, 12/25. **Address:** 6401 Falls of Neuse Rd **Location:** I-440, exit 10 (Wake Forest Rd), 3 mi n. **Parking:** on-site. **Cards:** AX, DC, DS, MC, VI.

YANCY'S! **Phone:** 919/821-7171 (26)

Creole
$7-$22

The lengthy menu features a variety of Creole, Cajun and Southwestern dishes, with choices ranging from gumbo and red beans and rice to pulled pork barbecue and fried catfish. On weekdays, patrons can sample from the lunch buffet, while brunch is an event on Sundays. Musicians perform most nights. Dressy casual. Entertainment. **Bar:** Full bar. **Reservations:** accepted. **Hours:** 11 am-2 am, Sun-10 pm. Closed: 11/26, 12/25. **Address:** 319 Fayetteville St, Suite 105 **Location:** Just s; center. **Parking:** street. **Cards:** AX, DS, MC, VI.

CALL

REIDSVILLE pop. 14,485

WHERE TO STAY

COMFORT INN *Book great rates at AAA.com* **Phone:** (336)634-1275

Motel
$68-$199 All Year

Address: 2203 Barnes St **Location:** US 29, exit 150 (Barnes St), just e. **Facility:** 51 one-bedroom standard units, some with whirlpools. 2 stories (no elevator), exterior corridors. **Parking:** on-site. **Amenities:** irons, hair dryers. *Some:* high-speed Internet. **Pool(s):** outdoor. **Guest Services:** wireless Internet. **Business Services:** PC. **Cards:** AX, CB, DC, DS, MC, VI. **Free Special Amenities: continental breakfast and high-speed Internet.**

CALL / SOME UNITS FEE

DAYS INN *Book great rates at AAA.com* **Phone:** (336)342-2800

Motel
$59-$199 All Year

Address: 2205 Barnes St **Location:** US 29, exit 150 (Barnes St), just e. **Facility:** 34 one-bedroom standard units. 2 stories (no elevator), exterior corridors. **Parking:** on-site. **Terms:** cancellation fee imposed. **Amenities:** hair dryers. **Guest Services:** wireless Internet. **Business Services:** PC. **Cards:** AX, CB, DC, DS, MC, VI. **Free Special Amenities: expanded continental breakfast and high-speed Internet.**

/ SOME UNITS

HOLIDAY INN EXPRESS HOTEL & SUITES *Book at AAA.com* **Phone:** 336/361-4000

Hotel
Rates not provided

Address: 101 Express Dr **Location:** US 29, exit 150 (Barnes St), just e, just s on Rockingham Dr, then just w. **Facility:** 73 one-bedroom standard units, some with whirlpools. 3 stories, interior corridors. *Bath:* combo or shower only. **Parking:** on-site. **Amenities:** dual phone lines, voice mail, irons, hair dryers. *Some:* high-speed Internet. **Pool(s):** outdoor. **Leisure Activities:** exercise room. **Guest Services:** valet laundry, wireless Internet. **Business Services:** meeting rooms, business center.

WHERE TO DINE

CHANEY'S

American
$4-$8

Phone: 336/349-2015

A dinner buffet is offered Thursday and Sunday while a breakfast bar hits the spot Thursday through Sunday mornings. Known for its down-home, family-friendly cuisine, the restaurant's menu features burgers, sandwiches, chopped steak, meatloaf and all-day breakfast entrees. Casual dress. **Hours:** 6:30 am-8:30 pm, Sun-2 pm. Closed: 12/25. **Address:** 1447 Freeway Dr **Location:** US 29, exit 149, 3.2 mi nw on SR 87. **Parking:** on-site. **Cards:** AX, DS, MC, VI.

MONTERREY MEXICAN RESTAURANT

Mexican
$4-$15

Phone: 336/616-0807

Traditional Mexican offerings include enchiladas, quesadillas, burritos and tacos, as well as specialties like arroz con pollo, carne asada, grilled t-bone with ranchero sauce and fajitas. Expect to find a casual, family-friendly atmosphere. Casual dress. **Bar:** Full bar. **Hours:** 10 am-10 pm, Fri & Sat-11 pm, Sun noon-10 pm. Closed: 11/26, 12/25. **Address:** 1537 Freeway Dr, #103 **Location:** US 29, exit 149, 3.7 mi n on SR 87; in Freeway Crossing Shopping Center. **Parking:** on-site. **Cards:** AX, DS, MC, VI.

SAGEBRUSH STEAKHOUSE

American
$5-$19

Phone: 336/349-3303

Born from the spirit of Texas cattle drives, the restaurant presents a menu of hearty steaks, prime rib, chicken, seafood and baby back ribs. Yummy desserts merit a splurge. Guests can call ahead to facilitate seating. Casual dress. **Bar:** Full bar. **Hours:** 11 am-10 pm, Fri & Sat-11 pm. Closed: 12/25. **Address:** 1529 Freeway Dr **Location:** Jct US 158/29 business route, just n on US 29 business route. **Parking:** on-site. **Cards:** AX, DC, DS, MC, VI.

RESEARCH TRIANGLE PARK (See map and index starting on p. 681)

WHERE TO STAY

RADISSON HOTEL IN RESEARCH TRIANGLE PARK *Book at AAA.com* **Phone:** (919)549-8631 51

Hotel
$199-$239 All Year

Address: 150 Park Dr **Location:** I-40, exit 280, just s, then just w. **Facility:** Designated smoking area. 198 units. 196 one-bedroom standard units. 2 one-bedroom suites. 2 stories, interior corridors. **Parking:** on-site. **Amenities:** high-speed Internet, dual phone lines, voice mail, irons, hair dryers. **Dining:** The Galeria, see separate listing. **Pool(s):** outdoor. **Leisure Activities:** 2 lighted tennis courts, jogging, exercise room, basketball, volleyball. **Guest Services:** valet laundry, area transportation. **Business Services:** conference facilities, business center. **Cards:** AX, CB, DC, DS, JC, MC, VI.

ASK / SOME UNITS FEE VCR

WHERE TO DINE

THE GALERIA

American
$8-$21

Phone: 919/549-8631 49

Diners who unwind in the atrium setting—which features subdued lighting, foliage and a skylight—can sample fresh seafood or selections from the popular luncheon buffet. The Research Triangle Park eatery is a favorite among local businesspeople. Smart, casual attire is expected. Dressy casual. **Bar:** Full bar. **Reservations:** suggested, for lunch. **Hours:** 6:30-10:30 am, 11-2 & 5:30-10 pm. Closed: 12/25. **Address:** 150 Park Dr **Location:** I-40, exit 280, just s, then just w; in Radisson Hotel in Research Triangle Park. **Parking:** on-site. **Cards:** AX, CB, DC, DS, JC, MC, VI.

CALL

ROANOKE RAPIDS pop. 16,957

WHERE TO STAY

BEST WESTERN ROANOKE RAPIDS

Book great rates at AAA.com

Phone: (252)537-1011

Motel
$60-$79 All Year

Address: I-95 at NC 46, Exit 176 **Location:** I-95, exit 176, just w. **Facility:** 100 one-bedroom standard units, some with whirlpools. 2 stories (no elevator), exterior corridors. **Parking:** on-site. **Amenities:** irons, hair dryers. **Pool(s):** outdoor. **Guest Services:** wireless Internet. **Cards:** AX, CB, DC, DS, MC, VI. **Free Special Amenities: continental breakfast and high-speed Internet.** *(See color ad below)*

/ SOME UNITS

AAA Benefit: Members save up to 20%, plus 10% bonus points with rewards program.

COMFORT SUITES

Book at AAA.com

Phone: (252)535-3300

Hotel
$80-$250 All Year

Address: 74 Premier Blvd **Location:** I-95, exit 173, just w, then just n. **Facility:** Smoke free premises. 72 one-bedroom standard units, some with whirlpools. 4 stories, interior corridors. *Bath:* combo or shower only. **Parking:** on-site. **Amenities:** high-speed Internet, voice mail, safes, irons, hair dryers. **Pool(s):** outdoor. **Leisure Activities:** exercise room. **Guest Services:** coin laundry, wireless Internet. **Business Services:** meeting rooms, business center. **Cards:** AX, DC, DS, MC, VI.

ASK CALL

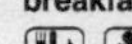

FAIRFAX MOTEL

Phone: 252/537-3567

Motel
$36-$45 All Year

Address: 1135 E 10th St **Location:** I-95, exit 173, 1 mi w on US 158, then 1 mi n. Located in a commercial area. **Facility:** 27 one-bedroom standard units. 1 story, exterior corridors. **Parking:** on-site. **Guest Services:** wireless Internet. **Cards:** AX, DS, MC, VI. **Free Special Amenities: continental breakfast and local telephone calls.**

/ SOME UNITS

HAMPTON INN

Book great rates at AAA.com

Phone: (252)537-7555

Hotel
$99-$119 All Year

Address: 1914 Julian R Allsbrook Hwy **Location:** I-95, exit 173, just w. **Facility:** 60 one-bedroom standard units. 2 stories (no elevator), exterior corridors. **Parking:** on-site. **Terms:** 1-30 night minimum stay, cancellation fee imposed. **Amenities:** video games (fee), voice mail, irons, hair dryers. **Pool(s):** outdoor. **Guest Services:** wireless Internet. **Business Services:** PC. **Cards:** AX, CB, DC, DS, MC, VI.

/ SOME UNITS

AAA Benefit: Members save up to 10% everyday!

▼ See AAA listing above ▼

HILTON GARDEN INN *Book great rates at AAA.com* **Phone:** (252)519-2333

Hotel
$94-$151 All Year

Address: 111 Carolina Crossroads Pkwy **Location:** I-95, exit 171, just s on SR 125, then just n. Adjacent to Carolina Crossroads entertainment complex. **Facility:** Smoke free premises. 147 units. 130 one-bedroom standard units. 17 one-bedroom suites, some with whirlpools. 5 stories, interior corridors. **Parking:** on-site. **Amenities:** high-speed Internet, voice mail, irons, hair dryers. **Pool(s):** heated indoor. **Leisure Activities:** whirlpool, exercise room. **Guest Services:** valet and coin laundry, wireless Internet. **Business Services:** meeting rooms, business center. **Cards:** AX, CB, DC, DS, JC, MC, VI.

CALL

Hilton Garden Inn
AAA Benefit:
Members save 5% or more everyday!

HOLIDAY INN EXPRESS HOTEL & SUITES *Book great rates at AAA.com* **Phone:** (252)536-2300

SAVE

Hotel
$100-$160 5/1-11/30
$90-$150 12/1-4/30

Address: 136 Sheraton Dr **Location:** I-95, exit 171, just n on SR 125, then just e. **Facility:** 80 one-bedroom standard units, some with whirlpools. 2 stories, interior corridors. *Bath:* combo or shower only. **Parking:** on-site. **Terms:** cancellation fee imposed. **Amenities:** high-speed Internet, dual phone lines, voice mail, irons, hair dryers. **Pool(s):** outdoor. **Leisure Activities:** limited exercise equipment. **Guest Services:** wireless Internet. **Business Services:** meeting rooms, business center. **Cards:** AX, CB, DC, DS, JC, MC, VI. **Free Special Amenities: expanded continental breakfast and high-speed Internet.**

CALL    / SOME UNITS

JAMESON INN *Book at AAA.com* **Phone:** (252)533-0022

Motel
$83-$90 All Year

Address: 101 S Old Farm Rd **Location:** I-95, exit 173, 0.5 mi w on US 158, then just s. **Facility:** 41 one-bedroom standard units, some with whirlpools. 2 stories (no elevator), exterior corridors. **Parking:** on-site. **Terms:** cancellation fee imposed. **Amenities:** irons, hair dryers. **Pool(s):** outdoor. **Leisure Activities:** exercise room. **Guest Services:** wireless Internet. **Business Services:** PC. **Cards:** AX, DC, DS, MC, VI.

ASK  / SOME UNITS FEE 

SLEEP INN *Book at AAA.com* **Phone:** 252/537-3141

Hotel
Rates not provided

Address: 101 Sleep Inn Dr **Location:** I-95, exit 173, just w, then just n. Located behind Cracker Barrel Restaurant. **Facility:** 117 one-bedroom standard units. 3 stories, interior corridors. *Bath:* combo or shower only. **Parking:** on-site. **Amenities:** irons, hair dryers. **Pool(s):** heated indoor. **Guest Services:** coin laundry, wireless Internet. **Business Services:** meeting rooms.

CALL / SOME UNITS

WHERE TO DINE

DAVID'S *Menu on AAA.com* **Phone:** 252/537-3262

American
$10-$30

An assortment of beef, chicken and seafood entrees populates the menu at the quiet downtown bistro. Casual dress. **Bar:** Full bar. **Reservations:** accepted. **Hours:** 5 pm-10 pm, Sun 11 am-2:30 pm. Closed: 1/1, 12/25; also Mon. **Address:** 1011 Roanoke Ave **Location:** Jct SR 125, just s on SR 48; downtown. **Parking:** on-site. **Cards:** AX, DC, DS, MC, VI.

TEXAS STEAKHOUSE & SALOON **Phone:** 252/532-8621

Steak
$6-$25

The typical Texas-style roadhouse focuses on freshly cut steaks, including the popular Duke entree with fries. Southwestern decor and arrows stuck in the walls get diners' minds wandering back to the old days. The popular draft beer is the microbrewed Red Oak lager. Casual dress. **Bar:** Full bar. **Hours:** 11 am-10 pm, Fri & Sat-11 pm. Closed: 11/26, 12/24, 12/25. **Address:** 1703 Julian R Allsbrook Hwy **Location:** I-95, exit 173, just w. **Parking:** on-site. **Cards:** AX, DS, MC, VI.

ROBBINSVILLE pop. 747

WHERE TO STAY

BLUE BOAR INN **Phone:** 828/479-8126

Country Inn
$155-$175 3/29-11/7

Address: 1283 Blue Boar Rd **Location:** 1.8 mi n on US 129 and SR 143 W, 9.8 mi w on SR 143, then 1.1 mi on gravel road, follow signs. Located in a remote location. **Facility:** Offering upscale accommodations, the inn is located at the site of a former 1950s hunting lodge; guest units feature a private porch with rockers. Designated smoking area. 8 one-bedroom standard units. 1 story, interior/exterior corridors. **Parking:** on-site. **Terms:** open 3/29-11/7, office hours 7 am-10 pm, 14 day cancellation notice-fee imposed. **Amenities:** CD players, voice mail, hair dryers. **Leisure Activities:** canoeing, boat dock, trout pond, kayaks. *Fee:* boats. **Guest Services:** complimentary laundry, wireless Internet. **Business Services:** PC, fax (fee). **Cards:** AX, DS, MC, VI. **Free Special Amenities: full breakfast and high-speed Internet.**

BLUE WATERS MOUNTAIN LODGE **Phone:** 828/479-8888

Bed & Breakfast
Rates not provided

Address: 292 Pine Ridge Rd **Location:** US 129 N to Ted Jordan Bridge, just left. **Facility:** On a lake; a unique combination of lodge-style accommodations and a relaxed atmosphere provide the setting for a perfect mountain getaway. 9 one-bedroom standard units. 2 stories, interior corridors. *Bath:* combo or shower only. **Parking:** on-site. **Amenities:** high-speed Internet, hair dryers. *Some:* irons. **Leisure Activities:** canoeing, boat dock, fishing, 2 tennis courts, bicycles, hiking trails. **Guest Services:** wireless Internet. **Business Services:** meeting rooms.

/ SOME UNITS

MICROTEL INN & SUITES *Book at AAA.com* **Phone:** (828)479-6772

Hotel
$59-$115 All Year

Address: 111 Rodney Orr Bypass (US 129) **Location:** Center of downtown. **Facility:** 50 units. 49 one-bedroom standard units. 1 one-bedroom suite with whirlpool. 4 stories, interior corridors. *Bath:* combo or shower only. **Parking:** on-site. **Guest Services:** wireless Internet. **Business Services:** meeting rooms, fax (fee). **Cards:** AX, DS, MC, VI.

ASK CALL / SOME UNITS FEE

WHERE TO DINE

The following restaurant has not been evaluated by AAA but is listed for your information only.

BLUE WATERS MOUNTAIN LODGE RESTAURANT **Phone:** 828/479-8888

fyi

Not evaluated. Enjoy beautiful views of the lake while savoring selections from the ever-changing menu like a Low Country boil of shrimp, crab, sausage, potatoes and corn or a pan-seared trout with roasted garlic basil aioli. **Address:** 292 Pine Ridge Rd **Location:** US 129 N to Ted Jordan Bridge, just 1 mi.

ROCKINGHAM pop. 9,672

WHERE TO STAY

COMFORT SUITES *Book great rates at AAA.com* **Phone:** (910)410-0077

Hotel
$100-$130 All Year

Address: 307 Greene St **Location:** US 74, exit 311, 1 mi n on US 1, 1 mi n on US 220, then just w. **Facility:** Smoke free premises. 64 units. 62 one-bedroom standard units, some with whirlpools. 2 one-bedroom suites with whirlpools. 3 stories, interior corridors. *Bath:* combo or shower only. **Parking:** on-site. **Terms:** cancellation fee imposed. **Amenities:** high-speed Internet, dual phone lines, voice mail, irons, hair dryers. **Pool(s):** heated indoor. **Leisure Activities:** sauna, whirlpool, exercise room. **Guest Services:** valet and coin laundry, wireless Internet. **Business Services:** meeting rooms, business center. **Cards:** AX, CB, DC, DS, MC, VI. **Free Special Amenities: expanded continental breakfast and high-speed Internet.**

ROCKY MOUNT pop. 55,893

WHERE TO STAY

BEST WESTERN INN I-95 GOLD ROCK

Phone: (252)985-1450

Motel
$65-$95 All Year

Address: 7095 NC 4 **Location:** I-95, exit 145, just e. **Facility:** 82 one-bedroom standard units. 2 stories (no elevator), exterior corridors. **Parking:** on-site. **Amenities:** high-speed Internet, irons, hair dryers. **Pool(s):** outdoor. **Guest Services:** valet laundry, wireless Internet. **Cards:** AX, CB, DC, DS, JC, MC, VI. **Free Special Amenities: continental breakfast and high-speed Internet.**

/ SOME UNITS FEE

AAA Benefit:
Members save up to 20%, plus 10% bonus points with rewards program.

BEST WESTERN - ROCKY MOUNT INN

Book great rates at AAA.com

Phone: (252)442-8101

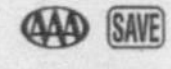

Motel
$60-$80 All Year

Address: 1921 N Wesleyan Blvd **Location:** US 64, exit 468A, 2.2 mi n on US 301 Bypass. **Facility:** 72 one-bedroom standard units. 3 stories (no elevator), exterior corridors. **Parking:** on-site. **Amenities:** irons, hair dryers. *Some:* high-speed Internet. **Pool(s):** outdoor. **Guest Services:** valet and coin laundry, wireless Internet. **Business Services:** meeting rooms. **Cards:** AX, CB, DC, DS, JC, MC, VI. **Free Special Amenities: expanded continental breakfast and high-speed Internet.**

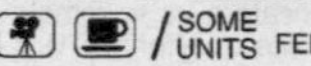

 / SOME UNITS FEE

AAA Benefit:
Members save up to 20%, plus 10% bonus points with rewards program.

COMFORT INN

Book great rates at AAA.com

Phone: (252)937-7765

Hotel
$86-$105 All Year

Address: 200 Gateway Blvd **Location:** I-95, exit 138, 1 mi e on US 64, exit Winstead Ave, then just s. Located adjacent to the Gateway Convention Center. **Facility:** 125 units. 121 one-bedroom standard units. 4 one-bedroom suites. 5 stories, interior corridors. **Parking:** on-site. **Terms:** cancellation fee imposed. **Amenities:** voice mail, irons, hair dryers. **Pool(s):** outdoor. **Leisure Activities:** exercise room. **Guest Services:** valet laundry, wireless Internet. **Business Services:** meeting rooms, business center. **Cards:** AX, CB, DC, DS, JC, MC, VI. **Free Special Amenities: expanded continental breakfast and high-speed Internet.**

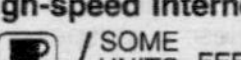

 / SOME UNITS FEE

COURTYARD BY MARRIOTT

Book great rates at AAA.com

Phone: (252)451-4800

Hotel
$128-$137 All Year

Address: 250 Gateway Blvd **Location:** I-95, exit 138, 1 mi e on US 64, exit Winstead Ave, just s, then just e. Located adjacent to Gateway Convention Center. **Facility:** Smoke free premises. 90 units. 87 one-bedroom standard units, some with whirlpools. 3 one-bedroom suites. 3 stories, interior corridors. *Bath:* combo or shower only. **Parking:** on-site. **Terms:** cancellation fee imposed. **Amenities:** video games (fee), dual phone lines, voice mail, irons, hair dryers. **Pool(s):** heated indoor. **Leisure Activities:** whirlpool, exercise room. **Guest Services:** valet and coin laundry, wireless Internet. **Business Services:** meeting rooms, PC. **Cards:** AX, CB, DC, DS, JC, MC, VI. **Free Special Amenities: local telephone calls and high-speed Internet.**

CALL

AAA Benefit:
Members save a minimum 5% off the best available rate.

DOUBLETREE HOTEL ROCKY MOUNT

Phone: (252)937-6888

Hotel
$129-$159 All Year

Address: 651 N Winstead Ave **Location:** I-95, exit 138, 1 mi e on US 64, exit Winstead Ave, then just s. Located adjacent to Gateway Convention Center. **Facility:** 166 units. 159 one-bedroom standard units. 7 one-bedroom suites. 4 stories, interior corridors. **Parking:** on-site. **Amenities:** dual phone lines, voice mail, irons, hair dryers. **Dining:** Texas Steakhouse & Saloon, see separate listing. **Pool(s):** heated outdoor. **Leisure Activities:** exercise room. **Guest Services:** valet laundry, wireless Internet. **Business Services:** conference facilities, PC, fax. **Cards:** AX, CB, DS, MC, VI. **Free Special Amenities: local telephone calls and high-speed Internet.**

/ SOME UNITS FEE FEE

AAA Benefit:
Members save 5% or more everyday!

HAMPTON INN *Book great rates at AAA.com* **Phone:** (252)937-6333

Hotel
$109-$129 All Year

Address: 530 N Winstead Ave **Location:** I-95, exit 138, 1 mi e on US 64, exit Winstead Ave, then just s. **Facility:** 124 one-bedroom standard units, some with whirlpools. 4 stories, interior corridors. *Bath:* combo or shower only. **Parking:** on-site. **Terms:** 1-30 night minimum stay, cancellation fee imposed. **Amenities:** voice mail, irons, hair dryers. **Pool(s):** outdoor. **Leisure Activities:** whirlpool, exercise room, basketball, volleyball. **Guest Services:** valet laundry, wireless Internet. **Business Services:** meeting rooms, PC. **Cards:** AX, CB, DC, DS, MC, VI.

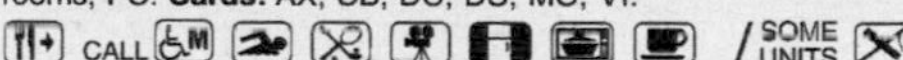

AAA Benefit:
Members save up to 10% everyday!

HOLIDAY INN-ROCKY MOUNT *Book at AAA.com* **Phone:** 252/937-7100

Hotel
Rates not provided

Address: 200 Enterprise Dr **Location:** I-95, exit 138, 1 mi e on US 64, exit Winstead Ave, just n, then just e. **Facility:** 135 units. 127 one-bedroom standard units, some with whirlpools. 8 one-bedroom suites. 6 stories, interior corridors. *Bath:* combo or shower only. **Parking:** on-site. **Terms:** check-in 4 pm. **Amenities:** dual phone lines, voice mail, irons, hair dryers. **Pool(s):** heated indoor. **Leisure Activities:** exercise room. **Guest Services:** valet laundry, wireless Internet. **Business Services:** meeting rooms, business center.

MOTEL 6 #2009 **Phone:** 252/984-0907

Hotel
$42-$48 2/1-11/30
$39-$45 12/1-1/31

Address: 1370 N Weslyan Blvd **Location:** Jct US 64 Bypass, 1.5 mi n on US 301. **Facility:** 124 one-bedroom standard units. 3 stories, interior corridors. *Bath:* combo or shower only. **Parking:** on-site. **Amenities:** dual phone lines, voice mail. **Pool(s):** outdoor. **Cards:** AX, CB, DC, DS, MC, VI.

/ SOME UNITS

QUALITY INN ROCKY MOUNT *Book at AAA.com* **Phone:** (252)972-9400

Hotel
$69-$79 5/1-11/30
$59-$69 12/1-4/30

Address: 1200 Benvenue Rd **Location:** Jct US 301 Bypass, just n on SR 43/48. **Facility:** 100 one-bedroom standard units. 3 stories, interior/exterior corridors. *Bath:* combo or shower only. **Parking:** on-site. **Terms:** cancellation fee imposed. **Amenities:** voice mail, irons, hair dryers. **Pool(s):** outdoor. **Guest Services:** valet and coin laundry, wireless Internet. **Business Services:** meeting rooms, PC. **Cards:** AX, DS, MC, VI.

ASK CALL / SOME UNITS FEE

RESIDENCE INN BY MARRIOTT *Book great rates at AAA.com* **Phone:** (252)451-5600

Hotel
$163-$175 All Year

Address: 230 Gateway Blvd **Location:** I-95, exit 138, 1 mi e on US 64, exit Winstead Ave, just s, then just e. Located adjacent to the Gateway Convention Center. **Facility:** Smoke free premises. 78 units. 51 one-bedroom standard units with efficiencies. 21 one- and 6 two-bedroom suites with efficiencies. 3 stories, interior corridors. *Bath:* combo or shower only. **Parking:** on-site. **Terms:** check-in 4 pm, cancellation fee imposed. **Amenities:** dual phone lines, voice mail, irons, hair dryers. **Pool(s):** heated outdoor. **Leisure Activities:** whirlpool, billiards, gas grill, picnic tables, exercise room, sports court. **Guest Services:** valet and coin laundry, wireless Internet. **Business Services:** PC. **Cards:** AX, CB, DC, DS, MC, VI. **Free Special Amenities: full breakfast and high-speed Internet.**

CALL / SOME UNITS FEE

AAA Benefit:
Members save a minimum 5% off the best available rate.

WHERE TO DINE

CHICO'S MEXICAN RESTAURANT **Phone:** 252/446-8600

Mexican
$6-$17

Dine in a colorful, festive dining room on a large variety of mesquite-grilled items, combination plates and other specialties. **Bar:** Full bar. **Hours:** 11 am-10 pm, Fri & Sat-11 pm. Closed: 11/26, 12/25. **Address:** 1701 Sunset Ave **Location:** Jct US 301 business route, just e; in The Power Plant. **Parking:** on-site. **Cards:** AX, DC, DS, MC, VI.

HIGHWAY DINER **Phone:** 252/451-5270

American
$5-$11

Savor such favorites as cheeseburgers, salads, sandwiches and homemade meatloaf in a classically designed diner. Among fitting accompaniments are onion rings and milkshakes. Casual dress. **Bar:** Beer & wine. **Hours:** 7 am-9 pm. Closed: 11/26, 12/25; also for dinner 12/24. **Address:** 910 N Winstead Ave **Location:** I-95, exit 138, 1 mi e on US 64, exit Winstead Ave, then just n. **Parking:** on-site. **Cards:** AX, DS, MC, VI.

MARIO'S PIZZA & ITALIAN RESTAURANT **Phone:** 252/451-9393

Italian
$6-$16

Select from pizza, pasta and hot and cold submarine sandwiches at the casual eatery. Casual dress. **Bar:** Beer & wine. **Reservations:** accepted. **Hours:** 11 am-10 pm, Fri-11 pm, Sun noon-9 pm. Closed major holidays. **Address:** 3653 Sunset Ave **Location:** I-95, exit 138, 1 mi e on US 64, exit Winstead Ave, 1.5 mi s; in Westridge Shopping Center. **Parking:** on-site. **Cards:** AX, DS, MC, VI.

TEXAS STEAKHOUSE & SALOON **Phone:** 252/443-7396

Steak
$6-$25

The typical Texas-style roadhouse focuses on freshly cut steaks, including the popular Duke entree with fries. Southwestern decor and arrows stuck in the walls get diners' minds wandering back to the old days. The popular draft beer is the microbrewed Red Oak lager. Casual dress. **Bar:** Full bar. **Hours:** 11 am-10 pm, Fri & Sat-11 pm. Closed: 11/26, 12/24, 12/25. **Address:** 651 Winstead Ave **Location:** I-95, exit 138, 1 mi e on US 64, exit Winstead Ave, then just s; in Holiday Inn Gateway Center. **Parking:** on-site. **Cards:** AX, DS, MC, VI.

TEXAS STEAKHOUSE & SALOON **Phone:** 252/443-3888

Steak
$6-$25

The typical Texas-style roadhouse focuses on freshly cut steaks, including the popular Duke entree with fries. Southwestern decor and arrows stuck in the walls get diners' minds wandering back to the old days. The popular draft beer is the microbrewed Red Oak lager. Casual dress. **Bar:** Full bar. **Hours:** 11 am-10 pm, Fri & Sat-11 pm. Closed: 11/26, 12/24, 12/25. **Address:** 711 Sutters Creek Blvd **Location:** US 64, just n on US 301 Bypass, then just w. **Parking:** on-site. **Cards:** AX, DS, MC, VI.

ROXBORO pop. 8,696

WHERE TO STAY

HAMPTON INN *Book great rates at AAA.com* **Phone:** (336)599-8800

Hotel
$103 All Year

Address: 920 Durham Rd **Location:** Jct US 158, n on US 501. **Facility:** 80 units. 77 one-bedroom standard units. 3 one-bedroom suites. 4 stories, interior corridors. *Bath:* combo or shower only. **Parking:** on-site. **Amenities:** voice mail, irons, hair dryers. **Pool(s):** outdoor. **Guest Services:** valet laundry, wireless Internet. **Business Services:** meeting rooms, PC. **Cards:** AX, CB, DC, DS, JC, MC, VI.

  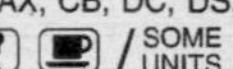 / SOME UNITS  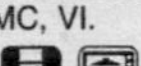

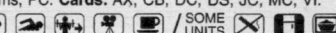

AAA Benefit:
Members save up to 10% everyday!

WHERE TO DINE

CLARKSVILLE STATION **Phone:** 336/599-9153

American
$5-$23

Aptly named, Clarksville Station sports a train depot motif. Steaks and seafood are prominent on the menu. Casual dress. **Bar:** Beer & wine. **Hours:** 11:30 am-2 & 5-9 pm, Fri-10 pm, Sat 5 pm-10 pm, Sun 5:30 pm-9 pm. Closed: 1/1, 11/26, 12/25; also Mon. **Address:** 4080 Durham Rd **Location:** Jct US 158, 2.8 mi s. **Parking:** on-site. **Cards:** AX, DS, MC, VI.

LA COCINA MEXICAN RESTAURANT **Phone:** 336/330-0300

Mexican
$4-$12

The popular spot's traditional Mexican fare ranges from burritos and enchiladas to tacos and fajitas. Lunch specials and combination plates are other choices. Casual dress. **Bar:** Full bar. **Hours:** 11 am-10 pm, Fri & Sat-11 pm, Sun noon-10 pm. Closed: 11/26, 12/25. **Address:** 241 S Madison Ave **Location:** Jct US 158 W, just s on US 501. **Parking:** on-site. **Cards:** AX, DS, MC, VI.

CALL

ST. PAULS pop. 2,137

WHERE TO STAY

DAYS INN *Book at AAA.com* **Phone:** (910)865-1111

Motel
$65-$125 All Year

Address: 931 W Broad St **Location:** I-95, exit 31, just e. **Facility:** 50 one-bedroom standard units, some with whirlpools. 2 stories (no elevator), exterior corridors. *Bath:* combo or shower only. **Parking:** on-site. **Amenities:** hair dryers. **Pool(s):** outdoor. **Guest Services:** wireless Internet. **Cards:** AX, DC, DS, MC, VI.

/ SOME UNITS

SALISBURY pop. 26,462

WHERE TO STAY

COMFORT SUITES *Book at AAA.com* **Phone:** (704)630-0065

Hotel
$109-$189 All Year

Address: 1040 E Innes St **Location:** I-85, exit 76, just w, then n. **Facility:** Smoke free premises. 78 one-bedroom standard units, some with whirlpools. 3 stories, interior corridors. *Bath:* combo or shower only. **Parking:** on-site. **Terms:** 30 day cancellation notice-fee imposed. **Amenities:** high-speed Internet, voice mail, irons, hair dryers. **Pool(s):** outdoor. **Leisure Activities:** exercise room. **Guest Services:** valet and coin laundry, wireless Internet. **Business Services:** meeting rooms. **Cards:** AX, CB, DC, DS, JC, MC, VI.

HAMPTON INN Book great rates at AAA.com

Phone: (704)637-8000

Hotel

$69-$129 All Year

Address: 1001 Klumac Rd **Location:** I-85, exit 75, just n on US 601, then just sw. **Facility:** 119 one-bedroom standard units. 4 stories, interior corridors. **Parking:** on-site. **Terms:** 1-30 night minimum stay, cancellation fee imposed. **Amenities:** voice mail, irons, hair dryers. **Pool(s):** outdoor. **Leisure Activities:** exercise room. **Guest Services:** valet laundry, wireless Internet. **Business Services:** meeting rooms, PC. **Cards:** AX, CB, DC, DS, MC, VI.

AAA Benefit:

Members save up to 10% everyday!

HOLIDAY INN Book at AAA.com

Phone: (704)637-3100

Hotel

$89-$179 4/1-11/30
$89-$139 12/1-3/31

Address: 530 Jake Alexander Blvd S **Location:** I-85, exit 75, 0.5 mi n on US 601. **Facility:** 181 one-bedroom standard units. 2-3 stories, interior/exterior corridors. **Parking:** on-site. **Terms:** 30 day cancellation notice-fee imposed. **Amenities:** dual phone lines, voice mail, irons, hair dryers. **Pool(s):** heated indoor/outdoor. **Leisure Activities:** whirlpool, exercise room, game room. **Guest Services:** valet laundry, wireless Internet. **Business Services:** conference facilities, PC. **Cards:** AX, CB, DC, DS, JC, MC, VI.

ASK CALL SOME UNITS FEE

QUALITY INN

Phone: 704/633-5777

AAA SAVE

Hotel

$90-$129 All Year

Address: 825 Klumac Rd **Location:** I-85, exit 75, just n on US 601, then just ne. **Facility:** 54 one-bedroom standard units, some with whirlpools. 3 stories, interior corridors. *Bath:* combo or shower only. **Parking:** on-site. **Terms:** 3 day cancellation notice. **Amenities:** high-speed Internet, dual phone lines, voice mail, irons, hair dryers. **Pool(s):** outdoor. **Guest Services:** valet laundry, wireless Internet. **Business Services:** meeting rooms. **Cards:** AX, DS, MC, VI. **Free Special Amenities: continental breakfast and high-speed Internet.**

SOME UNITS

ROWAN OAK HOUSE BED & BREAKFAST

Phone: 704/633-2086

Historic Bed & Breakfast

$130-$175 All Year

Address: 208 S Fulton St **Location:** I-85, exit 76, 1.2 mi w on Innes St, then just s. **Facility:** This property's fine china, notable woodwork and manicured English garden with fountains and walkways set a tone of Victorian splendor. Smoke free premises. 4 one-bedroom standard units, some with whirlpools. 2 stories (no elevator), interior corridors. *Bath:* combo or shower only. **Parking:** on-site. **Terms:** check-in 4 pm, 7 day cancellation notice. **Amenities:** video library. **Guest Services:** wireless Internet. **Cards:** DS, MC, VI.

ASK

SUPER 8 Book at AAA.com

Phone: 704/738-8888

Hotel

Rates not provided

Address: 925 Bendix Dr **Location:** I-85, exit 76, just s on US 52, just sw on Faith Rd, then 0.5 mi s. **Facility:** 59 one-bedroom standard units, some with whirlpools. 2 stories (no elevator), interior corridors. *Bath:* combo or shower only. **Parking:** on-site. **Amenities:** high-speed Internet, hair dryers. *Some:* irons. **Pool(s):** heated indoor. **Guest Services:** wireless Internet.

CALL SOME UNITS

WHERE TO DINE

IVAN'S RESTAURANT

Phone: 704/637-2000

AAA

American

$16-$45

Prime cuts of beef and Southern-style seafood are served in a rustic, cozy atmosphere. The setting is reminiscent of a hunting lodge. Casual dress. **Bar:** Full bar. **Hours:** 5 pm-9 pm, Fri & Sat-10 pm. Closed major holidays. **Address:** 2024 Old Mocksville Rd **Location:** I-85, exit 76, 2.4 mi w on W Innes St, 0.7 mi n on Mahaley Ave, then 1.5 mi w on Mocksville Ave. **Parking:** on-site. **Cards:** AX, DS, MC, VI.

CALL

SAGEBRUSH STEAKHOUSE

Phone: 704/637-1811

American

$5-$19

Born from the spirit of Texas cattle drives, the restaurant presents a menu of hearty steaks, prime rib, chicken, seafood and baby back ribs. Yummy desserts merit a splurge. Guests can call ahead to facilitate seating. Casual dress. **Bar:** Full bar. **Hours:** 11 am-10 pm, Fri & Sat-11 pm. Closed: 12/25. **Address:** 428 Jake Alexander Blvd S **Location:** I-85, exit 75, 0.5 mi nw. **Parking:** on-site. **Cards:** AX, DC, DS, MC, VI.

CALL

THE WRENN HOUSE

Phone: 704/633-9978

American

$5-$20

Both the food and the converted home, a historic landmark, are reasons to frequent the popular dining room. The menu focuses on pasta, steak and chicken dishes. Carrot cake is a perennial favorite among the delicious homemade desserts. Casual dress. **Bar:** Full bar. **Reservations:** accepted. **Hours:** 11 am-9 pm, Fri & Sat-11 pm. Closed major holidays; also Sun. **Address:** 115 S Jackson St **Location:** I-85, exit 76, 1 mi w on Innes St, just s on Church St, just w on Fisher St, then just n; downtown. **Parking:** on-site. **Cards:** AX, DS, MC, VI.

SALUDA pop. 575

WHERE TO STAY

THE OAKS BED & BREAKFAST **Phone:** 828/749-2000

Historic Bed & Breakfast

Rates not provided

Address: 339 Greenville St **Location:** I-26, exit 59, 1.1 mi sw, 0.3 mi w on US 176, then cross railway tracks. **Facility:** This turreted 1895 Victorian country home features four varied accommodations with quality period furnishings. Smoke free premises. 6 units. 4 one-bedroom standard units. 2 one-bedroom suites with efficiencies and kitchens. 2 stories (no elevator), interior/exterior corridors. *Bath:* combo or shower only. **Parking:** on-site. **Amenities:** *Some:* CD players, hair dryers.

/ SOME UNITS

SANFORD pop. 23,220

WHERE TO STAY

HAMPTON INN *Book great rates at AAA.com* **Phone:** (919)775-2000

Hotel

$93 All Year

Address: 1904 S Horner Blvd **Location:** Jct US 1, 3.2 mi s on US 421 and SR 87. **Facility:** 86 units. 81 one-bedroom standard units. 5 one-bedroom suites, some with whirlpools. 3 stories, interior corridors. *Bath:* combo or shower only. **Parking:** on-site. **Terms:** 1-30 night minimum stay, cancellation fee imposed. **Amenities:** video games (fee), voice mail, irons, hair dryers. **Pool(s):** outdoor. **Leisure Activities:** exercise room. **Guest Services:** valet and coin laundry, wireless Internet. **Business Services:** meeting rooms, PC. **Cards:** AX, CB, DC, DS, MC, VI.

CALL / SOME UNITS FEE

AAA Benefit:

Members save up to 10% everyday!

HOLIDAY INN EXPRESS HOTEL & SUITES *Book at AAA.com* **Phone:** 919/776-6600

Hotel

Rates not provided

Address: 2110 Dalrymple St **Location:** Jct US 1, 3.5 mi s on US 421 and SR 87, then just w. **Facility:** 69 one-bedroom standard units, some with whirlpools. 3 stories, interior corridors. *Bath:* combo or shower only. **Parking:** on-site. **Amenities:** high-speed Internet, dual phone lines, voice mail, safes, irons, hair dryers. **Pool(s):** heated indoor. **Leisure Activities:** exercise room. *Fee:* game room. **Guest Services:** valet and coin laundry, wireless Internet. **Business Services:** meeting rooms, PC.

CALL / SOME UNITS

JAMESON INN *Book at AAA.com* **Phone:** (919)708-7400

Motel

$83-$90 All Year

Address: 2614 S Horner Blvd **Location:** Jct US 1, 4.1 mi s on US 421 and SR 87. **Facility:** 42 one-bedroom standard units. 2 stories (no elevator), exterior corridors. **Parking:** on-site. **Terms:** cancellation fee imposed. **Amenities:** irons, hair dryers. **Pool(s):** outdoor. **Leisure Activities:** exercise room. **Guest Services:** valet laundry, wireless Internet. **Business Services:** PC. **Cards:** AX, DC, DS, MC, VI.

ASK CALL / SOME UNITS FEE

QUALITY INN *Book at AAA.com* **Phone:** 919/774-6411

Motel

Rates not provided

Address: 1403 N Horner Blvd **Location:** Jct US 1, 0.5 mi n on US 421. **Facility:** 122 units. 120 one-bedroom standard units. 2 one-bedroom suites with whirlpools. 2 stories (no elevator), exterior corridors. **Parking:** on-site. **Amenities:** irons, hair dryers. **Pool(s):** outdoor. **Leisure Activities:** sauna, exercise room. **Guest Services:** valet and coin laundry, wireless Internet. **Business Services:** meeting rooms.

/ SOME UNITS

WHERE TO DINE

CAFE VESUVIO **Phone:** 919/774-9966

Italian

$5-$14

Locals recommend this eatery for the quick lunches and full menu of Italian favorites like spaghetti, manicotti and ravioli, as well as pizza, subs and rotisserie chicken. Casual dress. **Bar:** Beer & wine. **Hours:** 11 am-10 pm, Fri & Sat-11 pm, Sun noon-10 pm. Closed: 4/12, 11/26, 12/25. **Address:** 1945 S Horner Blvd **Location:** 1.5 mi s on US 421 and SR 87; in Sanford Square Shopping Center. **Parking:** on-site. **Cards:** AX, DS, MC, VI.

SAGEBRUSH STEAKHOUSE **Phone:** 919/775-3339

American

$5-$19

Born from the spirit of Texas cattle drives, the restaurant presents a menu of hearty steaks, prime rib, chicken, seafood and baby back ribs. Yummy desserts merit a splurge. Guests can call ahead to facilitate seating. Casual dress. **Bar:** Full bar. **Hours:** 11 am-10 pm, Fri & Sat-11 pm. Closed: 12/25. **Address:** 2100 Dalrymple St **Location:** US 421 and SR 87, 1.5 mi s, just w at light. **Parking:** on-site. **Cards:** AX, DC, DS, MC, VI.

SAPPHIRE

WHERE TO STAY

HAMPTON INN & SUITES-CASHIERS/SAPPHIRE VALLEY *Book great rates at AAA.com*

Phone: (828)743-4545

Hotel
$90-$299 All Year

Address: 3245 Hwy 64 E **Location:** Jct SR 107, 2.6 mi e. **Facility:** Smoke free premises. 60 one-bedroom standard units. 4 stories, interior corridors. *Bath:* combo or shower only. **Parking:** on-site. **Terms:** check-in 4 pm, 2 night minimum stay - seasonal and/or weekends, 7 day cancellation notice-fee imposed. **Amenities:** video games, high-speed Internet, dual phone lines, voice mail, irons, hair dryers. **Pool(s):** heated indoor. **Leisure Activities:** whirlpool, exercise room. **Guest Services:** coin laundry, wireless Internet. **Business Services:** meeting rooms, business center. **Cards:** AX, DC, DS, MC, VI. **Free Special Amenities: expanded continental breakfast and high-speed Internet.**

CALL

AAA Benefit:
Members save up to 10% everyday!

WHERE TO DINE

MICA'S RESTAURANT & O'CONNELL'S PUB

Phone: 828/743-5740

American
$6-$18

Day or night, you're sure to find something to please your taste-buds—from burgers and pizza to veal and trout. Expect to find a friendly, charming atmosphere. Casual dress. **Bar:** Full bar. **Reservations:** suggested. **Hours:** 11:30 am-9 pm; hours may vary in winter. **Address:** 4000 US Hwy 64 E **Location:** Jct SR 107, 3.3 mi e. **Parking:** on-site. **Cards:** AX, DS, MC, VI.

CALL

SCOTLAND NECK pop. 2,362

WHERE TO STAY

BEST WESTERN-SCOTLAND NECK INN *Book great rates at AAA.com*

Phone: (252)826-5141

Motel
$70-$96 All Year

Address: 308 S Main St **Location:** Jct SR 125 S, just s on US 258. **Facility:** 31 one-bedroom standard units, some with efficiencies (no utensils). 1 story, interior corridors. *Bath:* combo or shower only. **Parking:** on-site. **Terms:** cancellation fee imposed. **Amenities:** high-speed Internet, voice mail, irons, hair dryers. **Pool(s):** outdoor. **Guest Services:** coin laundry, wireless Internet. **Business Services:** meeting rooms, PC. **Cards:** AX, DS, MC, VI.

SOME UNITS FEE

AAA Benefit:
Members save up to 20%, plus 10% bonus points with rewards program.

SELMA pop. 5,914

WHERE TO STAY

HAMPTON INN I-95 *Book great rates at AAA.com*

Phone: (919)965-6151

Hotel
$93-$103 All Year

Address: 1695 Industrial Park Dr **Location:** I-95, exit 97, just w, then just s. **Facility:** 77 one-bedroom standard units, some with whirlpools. 4 stories, interior corridors. *Bath:* combo or shower only. **Parking:** on-site. **Terms:** 1-30 night minimum stay, cancellation fee imposed. **Amenities:** voice mail, irons, hair dryers. **Pool(s):** outdoor. **Leisure Activities:** sauna, exercise room. **Guest Services:** valet and coin laundry, wireless Internet. **Business Services:** meeting rooms, business center. **Cards:** AX, CB, DC, DS, JC, MC, VI. ***(See color ad below)***

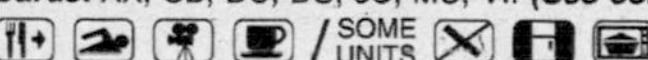
SOME UNITS

AAA Benefit:
Members save up to 10% everyday!

▼ *See AAA listing above* ▼

HOLIDAY INN EXPRESS *Book great rates at AAA.com* **Phone:** (919)965-4000

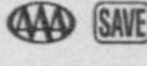

Hotel
$85-$90 All Year

Address: 115 US 70A **Location:** I-95, exit 97, just e, then just n. **Facility:** 60 one-bedroom standard units, some with whirlpools. 2 stories (no elevator), interior corridors. *Bath:* combo or shower only. **Parking:** on-site. **Terms:** 30 day cancellation notice. **Amenities:** high-speed Internet, voice mail, irons, hair dryers. **Pool(s):** outdoor. **Leisure Activities:** exercise room. **Guest Services:** wireless Internet. **Cards:** AX, CB, DC, DS, JC, MC, VI. **Free Special Amenities: expanded continental breakfast and high-speed Internet.**

CALL / SOME UNITS

QUALITY INN *Book great rates at AAA.com* **Phone:** (919)965-5200

Motel
$56-$99 All Year

Address: 1705 Industrial Park Dr **Location:** I-95, exit 97, just w, then just s. **Facility:** 80 one-bedroom standard units, some with whirlpools. 2 stories (no elevator), exterior corridors. **Parking:** on-site. **Amenities:** high-speed Internet, irons, hair dryers. **Pool(s):** outdoor. **Leisure Activities:** limited exercise equipment. **Guest Services:** wireless Internet. **Cards:** AX, DC, DS, MC, VI. **Free Special Amenities: expanded continental breakfast and high-speed Internet.**

/ SOME UNITS FEE FEE FEE

SHALLOTTE pop. 1,381

WHERE TO STAY

COMFORT INN *Book great rates at AAA.com* **Phone:** (910)754-3044

Hotel
$69-$159 All Year

Address: 360 Whiteville Rd **Location:** US 17, exit SR 130, just e, then just s. **Facility:** 58 one-bedroom standard units, some with whirlpools. 3 stories (no elevator), interior corridors. *Bath:* combo or shower only. **Parking:** on-site. **Amenities:** irons, hair dryers. **Pool(s):** outdoor. **Leisure Activities:** limited exercise equipment. **Guest Services:** coin laundry, wireless Internet. **Business Services:** meeting rooms. **Cards:** AX, DC, DS, MC, VI. **Free Special Amenities: expanded continental breakfast and high-speed Internet.**

/ SOME UNITS

HOLIDAY INN EXPRESS *Book great rates at AAA.com* **Phone:** 910/754-3300

Hotel
Rates not provided

Address: 3670 Express Dr **Location:** Jct SR 130, 0.9 mi n on US 17, just w on N Mulberry Dr, then just s. **Facility:** 61 one-bedroom standard units. 2 stories (no elevator), interior corridors. *Bath:* combo or shower only. **Parking:** on-site. **Amenities:** high-speed Internet, voice mail, irons, hair dryers. **Pool(s):** outdoor. **Leisure Activities:** limited exercise equipment. **Guest Services:** coin laundry, wireless Internet. **Business Services:** meeting rooms. **Free Special Amenities: expanded continental breakfast and high-speed Internet.**

/ SOME UNITS

WHERE TO DINE

JEROME'S STEAK & SEAFOOD RESTAURANT **Phone:** 910/754-8680

Steak & Seafood
$6-$16

A favorite of locals, the restaurant serves steaks and fried and broiled seafood in a relaxed, family-friendly atmosphere. Casual dress. **Hours:** 11 am-9 pm. Closed: 1/1, 11/26, 12/24, 12/25. **Address:** 4909 Main St **Location:** Jct SR 130 and 179, just n on US 17 business route. **Parking:** on-site. **Cards:** AX, DS, MC, VI.

ZENG'S GARDEN CHINESE RESTAURANT **Phone:** 910/754-5280

Chinese
$7-$15

The popular, family-friendly restaurant features a daily buffet as well as a la carte and take-out dining. Spicy Szechuan fare is included on the menu of traditional Chinese dishes. Casual dress. **Hours:** 11 am-9:30 pm, Fri & Sat-10 pm. **Address:** 4734 Main St **Location:** US 17, exit SR 130, 1.8 mi e. **Parking:** on-site. **Cards:** AX, MC, VI.

SHELBY pop. 19,477

WHERE TO STAY

ECONO LODGE *Book at AAA.com* **Phone:** (704)482-3821

Motel
$40-$140 All Year

Address: 825 W Dixon Blvd **Location:** Jct SR 18, 0.8 mi w on US 74 Bypass. **Facility:** 55 one-bedroom standard units, some with whirlpools. 1 story, exterior corridors. **Parking:** on-site. **Terms:** cancellation fee imposed. **Amenities:** irons, hair dryers. **Pool(s):** outdoor. **Guest Services:** coin laundry, wireless Internet. **Business Services:** meeting rooms, PC. **Cards:** AX, DC, DS, MC, VI.

ASK / SOME UNITS

HAMPTON INN *Book great rates at AAA.com* **Phone:** (704)482-5666

Hotel
$69-$91 All Year

Address: 2012 E Marion St **Location:** Jct US 74 Bypass E and US 74 business route. Adjacent to Cleveland Mall. **Facility:** 77 one-bedroom standard units. 2 stories, interior corridors. **Parking:** on-site. **Amenities:** voice mail, irons, hair dryers. **Pool(s):** outdoor. **Leisure Activities:** exercise room. **Guest Services:** valet laundry, wireless Internet. **Cards:** AX, CB, DC, DS, JC, MC, VI.

/ SOME UNITS

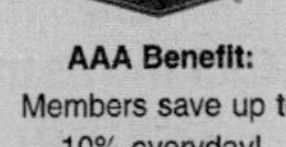

AAA Benefit:
Members save up to 10% everyday!

HOLIDAY INN EXPRESS Book at AAA.com

Phone: (704)480-0881

Hotel

$86-$106 All Year

Address: 2001 E Dixon Blvd **Location:** Jct US 74 business route, 0.4 mi w on US 74 Bypass; use Cleveland Mall entrance. Located adjacent to Cleveland Mall. **Facility:** 58 one-bedroom standard units, some with whirlpools. 2 stories (no elevator), interior corridors. *Bath:* combo or shower only. **Parking:** on-site. **Amenities:** high-speed Internet, dual phone lines, voice mail, irons, hair dryers. **Pool(s):** outdoor. **Leisure Activities:** limited exercise equipment. **Guest Services:** valet laundry, wireless Internet. **Business Services:** meeting rooms, PC. **Cards:** AX, DC, DS, MC, VI.

ASK CALL / SOME UNITS

SUPER 8 Book great rates at AAA.com

Phone: (704)484-2101

Motel

$55-$80 5/21-11/30
$50-$75 12/1-5/20

Address: 1716 E Dixon Blvd **Location:** Jct SR 180, 0.4 mi w on US 74 Bypass. **Facility:** 59 one-bedroom standard units. 2 stories (no elevator), exterior corridors. **Parking:** on-site. **Amenities:** irons, hair dryers. **Guest Services:** coin laundry, wireless Internet. **Business Services:** PC. **Cards:** AX, DC, DS, MC, VI. **Free Special Amenities: expanded continental breakfast and high-speed Internet.**

/ SOME UNITS FEE

WHERE TO DINE

5 EAST RESTAURANT

Phone: 704/487-8266

Continental

$6-$30

The menu changes seasonally at the casually elegant bistro. Examples of flavorful New South-style cuisine include nightly specials, as well as pecan-crusted rainbow trout, pasta primavera in Pinot Grigio-butter sauce and pork tenderloin with black-eyed pea apple relish. Casual dress. **Bar:** Full bar. **Reservations:** accepted. **Hours:** 11 am-9 pm, Fri-10 pm, Sat 4:30 pm-10 pm. Closed: 1/1, 11/26, 12/25; also Sun. **Address:** 5 E Marion St **Location:** Center. **Parking:** on-site. **Cards:** AX, MC, VI.

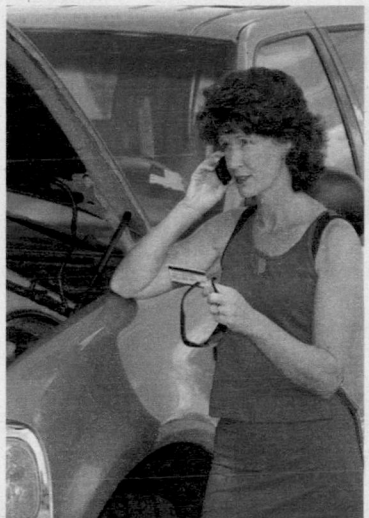

BRIDGES BARBECUE LODGE

Phone: 704/482-8567

Regional Southern

$4-$10

Spicy tomato-based sauce coats chopped pork barbecue, which is served with hushpuppies and slaw in a no-frills atmosphere. Casual dress. **Hours:** 11 am-8 pm. Closed major holidays; also Mon & Tues. **Address:** 2000 E Dixon Blvd **Location:** Jct US 74 W business route, just w on US 74 Bypass. **Parking:** on-site. **Cards:** MC, VI.

CHEN'S RESTAURANT

Phone: 704/484-9669

Chinese

$5-$13

Hunan beef, sweet and sour chicken, grilled steak and Peking-style pork represent several of the traditional choices you'll find at Chen's. On weekdays, avail yourself of the small lunch buffet. Casual dress. **Hours:** 11:30 am-2:30 & 5-9:30 pm, Fri 11 am-2:30 & 5-10 pm, Sat 5 pm-10 pm, Sun 11 am-2:30 & 5-9:30 pm. Closed: 11/26, 12/25. **Address:** 209 W Dixon Blvd **Location:** Jct SR 150, just w on US 74 Bypass. **Parking:** on-site. **Cards:** MC, VI.

SAGEBRUSH STEAKHOUSE

Phone: 704/471-2301

American

$5-$19

Born from the spirit of Texas cattle drives, the restaurant presents a menu of hearty steaks, prime rib, chicken, seafood and baby back ribs. Yummy desserts merit a splurge. Guests can call ahead to facilitate seating. Casual dress. **Bar:** Full bar. **Hours:** 11 am-10 pm, Fri & Sat-11 pm. Closed: 12/25. **Address:** 1237 E Dixon Blvd **Location:** Jct US 74/SR 18, 1.1 mi se. **Parking:** on-site. **Cards:** AX, DC, DS, MC, VI.

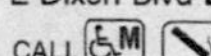

SMITHFIELD pop. 11,510

WHERE TO STAY

BEST WESTERN INN OF SMITHFIELD

Book great rates at AAA.com

Phone: (919)989-4047

AAA SAVE

Hotel

$77-$110 All Year

Address: 145 S Equity Dr **Location:** I-95, exit 95, just w on US 70 business route, just n on Industrial Park Dr, then just w. **Facility:** Smoke free premises. 57 one-bedroom standard units, some with whirlpools. 3 stories, interior corridors. *Bath:* combo or shower only. **Parking:** on-site. **Terms:** 3 day cancellation notice. **Amenities:** high-speed Internet, voice mail, irons, hair dryers. **Pool(s):** heated indoor. **Leisure Activities:** exercise room. **Guest Services:** wireless Internet. **Business Services:** PC. **Cards:** AX, CB, DC, DS, JC, MC, VI. **Free Special Amenities:** **expanded continental breakfast and high-speed Internet.**

CALL / SOME UNITS

AAA Benefit:
Members save up to 20%, plus 10% bonus points with rewards program.

COMFORT INN

Book at AAA.com

Phone: (919)938-4444

Hotel

$89-$119 All Year

Address: 170 S Equity Dr **Location:** I-95, exit 95, just w on US 70 business route, just n on Industrial Park Dr, then just w. **Facility:** 72 one-bedroom standard units, some with whirlpools. 3 stories, interior corridors. *Bath:* combo or shower only. **Parking:** on-site. **Amenities:** high-speed Internet, voice mail, irons, hair dryers. **Pool(s):** outdoor. **Leisure Activities:** exercise room. **Guest Services:** valet and coin laundry, wireless Internet. **Business Services:** meeting rooms, business center. **Cards:** AX, DS, MC, VI.

ASK CALL / SOME UNITS

JAMESON INN

Book at AAA.com

Phone: (919)989-5901

Motel

$78-$85 All Year

Address: 125 S Equity Dr **Location:** I-95, exit 95, just w, just n on Industrial Park Blvd, then just w. **Facility:** 41 one-bedroom standard units, some with whirlpools. 2 stories (no elevator), exterior corridors. **Parking:** on-site. **Terms:** cancellation fee imposed. **Pool(s):** outdoor. **Leisure Activities:** exercise room. **Guest Services:** wireless Internet. **Business Services:** PC. **Cards:** AX, DC, DS, MC, VI.

ASK CALL / SOME UNITS FEE 

LOG CABIN MOTEL

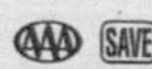

Motel
$45-$52 All Year

Phone: (919)934-1534

Address: 2491 US 70 E (Business Route) **Location:** I-95, exit 95, 0.5 mi e. Located in a quiet area. **Facility:** 60 one-bedroom standard units. 1 story, exterior corridors. **Parking:** on-site. **Pool(s):** outdoor. **Leisure Activities:** fishing. **Guest Services:** coin laundry. **Business Services:** meeting rooms. **Cards:** AX, DC, DS, MC, VI. **Free Special Amenities: continental breakfast and high-speed Internet.**

/ SOME UNITS FEE

SLEEP INN & SUITES

Hotel
$85-$120 All Year

Book great rates at AAA.com

Phone: (919)209-2360

Address: 270 N Equity Dr **Location:** I-95, exit 95, just w, just n on Industrial Park Dr, then just w. **Facility:** 74 one-bedroom standard units, some with whirlpools. 3 stories, interior corridors. *Bath:* combo or shower only. **Parking:** on-site. **Amenities:** high-speed Internet, voice mail, irons, hair dryers. **Pool(s):** outdoor. **Leisure Activities:** exercise room. **Guest Services:** valet and coin laundry, wireless Internet. **Business Services:** meeting rooms, PC. **Cards:** AX, DC, DS, MC, VI. **Free Special Amenities: expanded continental breakfast and high-speed Internet.**

/ SOME UNITS

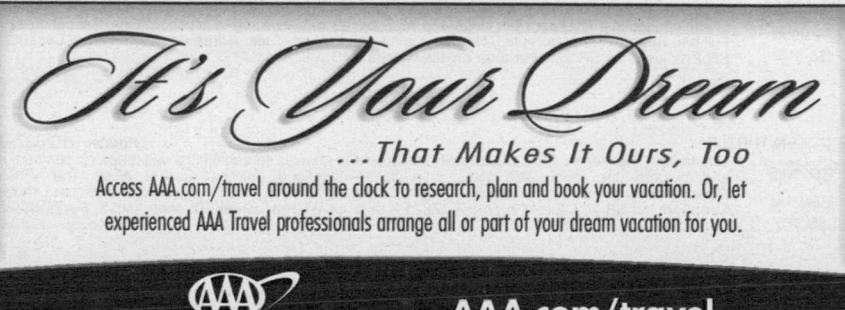

▼ See AAA listing p 820 ▼

SUPER 8 MOTEL *Book great rates at AAA.com* **Phone:** (919)989-8988

Hotel
$75-$120 All Year

Address: 735 Industrial Park Dr **Location:** I-95, exit 95, just w, then just n. Located adjacent to an outlet mall. **Facility:** 80 one-bedroom standard units, some with whirlpools. 2 stories (no elevator), interior corridors. *Bath:* combo or shower only. **Parking:** on-site. **Amenities:** voice mail, irons, hair dryers. **Pool(s):** heated indoor. **Guest Services:** coin laundry, wireless Internet. **Business Services:** PC. **Cards:** AX, DC, DS, MC, VI. **Free Special Amenities: expanded continental breakfast and high-speed Internet.** *(See color ad p 819)*

/ SOME UNITS FEE

WHERE TO DINE

BECKY'S LOG CABIN RESTAURANT *Menu on AAA.com* **Phone:** 919/934-3323

Steak & Seafood
$14-$20

A log cabin atmosphere permeates the dining room, where patrons taste homemade soup, fresh seafood and beef dishes. Broiled flounder with a side of hush puppies is tasty and served with a smile. New York strip, oysters and salad are frequent favorites, too. Casual dress. **Bar:** Full bar. **Hours:** 5 pm-10 pm. Closed: 1/1, 11/26, 12/24, 12/25; also Mon. **Address:** 2491 US 70 E (Business Route) **Location:** I-95, exit 95, 0.5 mi e; adjacent to Log Cabin Motel. **Parking:** on-site. **Cards:** AX, DS, MC, VI.

MARLA'S **Phone:** 919/989-7230

Deli
$4-$8

This downtown sandwich shop is a popular spot for the locals to catch a quick lunch. Wraps and burgers round out the deli menu. Casual dress. **Hours:** 8 am-2:30 pm, Sat from 11 am. Closed: 1/1, 11/26, 12/25; also Sun. **Address:** 135 S Third St **Location:** US 70 business route, just s; downtown. **Parking:** on-site. **Cards:** MC, VI.

TEXAS STEAKHOUSE & SALOON **Phone:** 919/938-3221

Steak
$6-$25

The typical Texas-style roadhouse focuses on freshly cut steaks, including the popular Duke entree with fries. Southwestern decor and arrows stuck in the walls get diners' minds wandering back to the old days. The popular draft beer is the microbrewed Red Oak lager. Casual dress. **Bar:** Full bar. **Hours:** 11 am-10 pm, Fri & Sat-11 pm. Closed: 11/26, 12/24, 12/25. **Address:** 235 Industrial Park Rd **Location:** I-95, exit 95, just w. **Parking:** on-site. **Cards:** AX, DS, MC, VI.

SNEADS FERRY pop. 2,248

WHERE TO STAY

HOLIDAY INN EXPRESS *Book at AAA.com* **Phone:** (910)327-8282

Hotel
$95-$275 4/1-11/30
$95-$155 12/1-3/31

Address: 1565 Hwy 210 **Location:** Jct US 17, 5 mi e. **Facility:** 68 one-bedroom standard units, some with whirlpools. 2 stories, interior corridors. *Bath:* combo or shower only. **Parking:** on-site. **Terms:** cancellation fee imposed. **Amenities:** dual phone lines, voice mail, irons, hair dryers. **Pool(s):** outdoor. **Guest Services:** wireless Internet. **Business Services:** business center. **Cards:** AX, CB, DC, DS, MC, VI.

ASK CALL / SOME UNITS 

WHERE TO DINE

CLAMDIGGER RESTAURANT **Phone:** 910/327-3444

Seafood
$6-$18

Breakfast, lunch and dinner are served at the popular eatery. Buffet-lovers can visit for daily lunch or Friday through Sunday for dinner. In addition to oyster-bar offerings and steamer fare, the menu lists preparations of shrimp, flounder, oysters, clam strips and scallops, as well as some landlubber items. Casual dress. **Bar:** Full bar. **Reservations:** accepted. **Hours:** 7 am-9 pm. Closed: Tues. **Address:** 105 Sugar Ln **Location:** Jct SR 210, just n on SR 172. **Parking:** on-site. **Cards:** MC, VI.

THE GREEN TURTLE **Phone:** 910/327-0262

Seafood
$8-$18

Overlooking the marina, the casual, family restaurant is popular. In addition to well-prepared seafood, steak and burgers, the menu also lists some Italian-influenced entrees. Casual dress. **Bar:** Full bar. **Reservations:** suggested. **Hours:** 5 pm-9 pm. Closed: 1/1, 11/26, 12/25. **Address:** 310 Fulcher Landing Rd **Location:** Jct SR 210, 2.2 mi n on SR 172, 1.2 mi e on Wheeler Creek Rd, then 1 mi n. **Parking:** on-site. **Cards:** AX, DS, MC, VI.

SOUTHERN PINES pop. 10,918

WHERE TO STAY

BEST WESTERN PINEHURST INN *Book great rates at AAA.com* **Phone:** (910)692-0640

Hotel
$69-$119 All Year

Address: 1675 US Hwy 1 S **Location:** Jct US 15/501, 0.5 mi n on US 1. **Facility:** 125 one-bedroom standard units. 2 stories (no elevator), exterior corridors. **Parking:** on-site. **Terms:** 7 day cancellation notice-fee imposed. **Amenities:** video games (fee), voice mail, irons, hair dryers. **Pool(s):** outdoor. **Leisure Activities:** exercise room. **Guest Services:** valet and coin laundry, wireless Internet. **Business Services:** meeting rooms, business center. **Cards:** AX, DS, MC, VI. **Free Special Amenities:** **expanded continental breakfast and high-speed Internet.**

/ SOME UNITS FEE

AAA Benefit: Members save up to 20%, plus 10% bonus points with rewards program.

ECONO LODGE INN & SUITES *Book at AAA.com* **Phone:** (910)692-2063

Hotel
$70-$75 12/1-10/31
$60-$65 11/1-11/30

Address: 408 W Morganton Rd **Location:** US 1, exit Morganton Rd, just w. **Facility:** 38 units. 32 one-bedroom standard units. 6 one-bedroom suites with whirlpools. 2 stories (no elevator), interior corridors. **Parking:** on-site. **Terms:** cancellation fee imposed. **Amenities:** voice mail, irons, hair dryers. **Guest Services:** wireless Internet. **Business Services:** meeting rooms. **Cards:** AX, CB, DC, DS, JC, MC, VI.

ASK / SOME UNITS FEE

MICROTEL INN *Book at AAA.com* **Phone:** (910)693-3737

Hotel
$59-$79 All Year

Address: 205 Windstar Pl **Location:** Jct US 15/501, 0.5 mi n on US 1. **Facility:** 78 one-bedroom standard units. 2 stories (no elevator), interior corridors. *Bath:* combo or shower only. **Parking:** on-site. **Terms:** 7 day cancellation notice. **Guest Services:** valet laundry, wireless Internet. **Cards:** AX, CB, DC, DS, JC, MC, VI.

ASK / SOME UNITS

RESIDENCE INN BY MARRIOTT *Book great rates at AAA.com* **Phone:** (910)693-3400

Extended Stay Hotel
$188-$201 All Year

Address: 105 Brucewood Rd **Location:** Jct US 1, 1.2 mi n on US 15/501, then just e. **Facility:** Select from recently renovated studio units and one- and two-bedroom suites, each sporting a sharp, contemporary decor. Smoke free premises. 80 units. 13 one-bedroom standard units with kitchens. 39 one- and 28 two-bedroom suites with kitchens. 3 stories, interior corridors. *Bath:* combo or shower only. **Parking:** on-site. **Terms:** cancellation fee imposed. **Amenities:** high-speed Internet, dual phone lines, voice mail, irons, hair dryers. **Pool(s):** outdoor. **Leisure Activities:** whirlpool, exercise room, sports court. **Guest Services:** valet and coin laundry, wireless Internet. **Business Services:** PC. **Cards:** AX, CB, DC, DS, JC, MC, VI.

/ SOME UNITS FEE

AAA Benefit: Members save a minimum 5% off the best available rate.

WHERE TO DINE

195 AMERICAN FUSION **Phone:** 910/692-7110

New American
$5-$32

Careful preparations employ organic ingredients and fresh produce. Try blackened salmon and organically-grown vegetables or one of the freshly-made soups, desserts or seafood entrees. Homemade bread and artful salads are memorable. Casual dress. **Bar:** Full bar. **Reservations:** suggested, for dinner. **Hours:** 11 am-3 & 5:30-9:30 pm, Tues-3 pm. Closed: 1/1, 11/26, 12/25; also Sun & Mon. **Address:** 195 Bell Ave **Location:** 0.4 mi s on Old US 1 business route. **Parking:** on-site. **Cards:** DS, MC, VI.

THE JFR BARN **Phone:** 910/692-7700

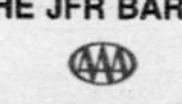

Steak & Seafood
$12-$45

Since 1974, this charmingly rustic steakhouse has been a favorite among locals and golfers for its steaks, fresh seafood, chops and chicken. The extensive wine list has earned many accolades. Service is casual and friendly. Casual dress. **Bar:** Full bar. **Hours:** 5 pm-10 pm. Closed major holidays. **Address:** 305 Rothney Rd **Location:** Jct US 1, exit Morganton Rd, just sw; access via service road on west side of US 1. **Parking:** on-site. **Cards:** AX, MC, VI.

JOHN'S BBQ & SEAFOOD **Phone:** 910/692-9474

Seafood
$5-$27

Expect to find casual, efficient service at the family-friendly eatery. A wide variety of hearty, down-home selections are offered, including fried seafood, grilled steaks and North Carolina-style pork barbecue. Casual dress. **Hours:** 11 am-9 pm. Closed major holidays; also Sun. **Address:** 10985 S US Hwy 15/501 **Location:** Jct US 1, 0.6 mi n. **Parking:** on-site. **Cards:** DS, MC, VI.

THE LOB STEER INN **Phone:** 910/692-3503

Steak & Seafood
$9-$33

Certified Angus beef, fresh seafood and an 80-item buffet that lines up mussels, fresh salad fixings, stuffed mushrooms, homemade desserts and other choice tidbits make the restaurant popular. Breads are particularly tasty. Casual dress. **Bar:** Full bar. **Reservations:** accepted. **Hours:** 5 pm-close. Closed: 11/26, 12/25. **Address:** 625 SE Service Rd, US 1 N **Location:** US 1, exit Morganton Rd; on west side of service road. **Parking:** on-site. **Cards:** AX, MC, VI.

RAGAZZI'S

Italian
$5-$15

Phone: 910/692-4626

Italian favorites—including lasagna, manicotti, fettuccine alfredo and pizza—are the focus at the casual eatery. Homemade salad dressing is delicious and the breadsticks are plentiful. Casual dress. **Bar:** Full bar. **Hours:** 11 am-10 pm. Closed: 11/26, 12/25. **Address:** 1640 US 1 S **Location:** Jct Morganton Rd, just s. **Parking:** on-site. **Cards:** AX, MC, VI.

CALL

THE SQUIRE'S PUB *Menu on AAA.com*

British
$4-$19

Phone: 910/695-1161

In addition to traditional British dishes, such as tasty fish and chips, the casual pub—which has won several local "best of" awards—presents an extensive menu of American fare, including fresh seafood, hand-cut steaks and daily specials. Beer drinkers will have a field day with the 43 imported brews. Casual dress. **Bar:** Full bar. **Hours:** 11 am-10 pm. Closed: 11/26, 12/24, 12/25; also Sun. **Address:** 1720 US 1 S **Location:** On US 1, 1.1 mi s. **Parking:** on-site. **Cards:** AX, DS, MC, VI.

SOUTHERN SHORES —*See Outer Banks p. 786.*

SOUTHPORT pop. 2,351

WHERE TO STAY

COMFORT SUITES *Book great rates at AAA.com*

Hotel
$89-$159 All Year

Phone: (910)454-7444

Address: 4963 Southport Supply Rd (SR 211) **Location:** Jct SR 87, 1.8 mi n. **Facility:** Smoke free premises. 70 one-bedroom standard units, some with whirlpools. 3 stories, interior corridors. *Bath:* combo or shower only. **Parking:** on-site. **Amenities:** voice mail, irons, hair dryers. **Pool(s):** outdoor. **Leisure Activities:** limited exercise equipment. **Guest Services:** valet and coin laundry, wireless Internet. **Business Services:** meeting rooms. **Cards:** AX, CB, DC, DS, JC, MC, VI. **Free Special Amenities: expanded continental breakfast and high-speed Internet.**

/ SOME UNITS FEE

HAMPTON INN *Book great rates at AAA.com*

Hotel
$89-$134 All Year

Phone: (910)454-0016

Address: 5181 Southport Supply Rd SE (SR 211) **Location:** Jct SR 87, 1.3 mi n on SR 211. **Facility:** 80 one-bedroom standard units. 3 stories, interior corridors. *Bath:* combo or shower only. **Parking:** on-site. **Terms:** 1-30 night minimum stay, cancellation fee imposed. **Amenities:** dual phone lines, voice mail, irons, hair dryers. **Pool(s):** outdoor. **Leisure Activities:** exercise room. **Guest Services:** valet laundry, wireless Internet. **Business Services:** meeting rooms, business center. **Cards:** AX, CB, DC, DS, JC, MC, VI.

CALL / SOME UNITS 

AAA Benefit:
Members save up to 10% everyday!

WHERE TO DINE

MR P'S BISTRO

Steak & Seafood
$10-$40

Phone: 910/457-0801

A casually upscale atmosphere sets the mood for a nice evening out. The menu lists preparations of lamb, veal, steak and seafood. Casual dress. **Bar:** Full bar. **Reservations:** accepted. **Hours:** 5 pm-9 pm. Closed: 11/26, 12/25; also Sun. **Address:** 309 N Howe St **Location:** Just n on SR 211 from waterfront. **Parking:** on-site. **Cards:** AX, DS, MC, VI.

SANDFIDDLER SEAFOOD RESTAURANT

Steak & Seafood
$4-$17

Phone: 910/457-6588

Defining the popular restaurant's nautical theme are mounted fish and captain's chairs. A wide variety of steaks, seafood and pasta selections adorn the menu, along with traditional side dishes such as french fries and coleslaw. Casual dress. **Hours:** 11 am-2 & 5-8:30 pm, Sat from 5 pm, Sun noon-2:30 & 5-8:30 pm; hours may vary off season. Closed: 11/26, 12/25. **Address:** 1643 N Howe St **Location:** On SR 211. **Parking:** on-site. **Cards:** MC, VI.

SPRING LAKE pop. 8,098

WHERE TO STAY

HAMPTON INN *Book great rates at AAA.com*

Hotel
$89-$119 All Year

Phone: (910)438-0945

Address: 1050 N Bragg Blvd **Location:** Jct SR 210, 0.8 mi n on SR 87. **Facility:** Smoke free premises. 77 one-bedroom standard units. 4 stories, interior corridors. *Bath:* combo or shower only. **Parking:** on-site. **Terms:** 1-30 night minimum stay, cancellation fee imposed. **Amenities:** high-speed Internet, voice mail, irons, hair dryers. **Pool(s):** outdoor. **Leisure Activities:** exercise room. **Guest Services:** valet and coin laundry, wireless Internet. **Business Services:** meeting rooms, business center. **Cards:** AX, CB, DC, DS, MC, VI.

AAA Benefit:
Members save up to 10% everyday!

HOLIDAY INN EXPRESS HOTEL & SUITES *Book great rates at AAA.com* **Phone:** (910)436-1900

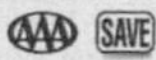

Hotel
$99 All Year

Address: 103 Brook Ln **Location:** Jct SR 210, 0.9 mi nw on SR 24/87. **Facility:** 85 one-bedroom standard units, some with whirlpools. 2 stories, interior corridors. *Bath:* combo or shower only. **Parking:** on-site. **Terms:** cancellation fee imposed. **Amenities:** high-speed Internet, voice mail, irons, hair dryers. **Pool(s):** outdoor. **Leisure Activities:** sauna, putting green, exercise room. **Guest Services:** valet and coin laundry, wireless Internet. **Business Services:** meeting rooms, PC. **Cards:** AX, DC, DS, MC, VI. **Free Special Amenities: expanded continental breakfast and high-speed Internet.**

/ SOME UNITS FEE

SLEEP INN & SUITES *Book at AAA.com* **Phone:** (910)436-6700

Hotel
$95-$135 4/1-11/30
$95-$125 12/1-3/31

Address: 102 Sleepy Dr **Location:** Jct SR 210, 0.8 mi nw on SR 24/87. **Facility:** 92 units. 77 one-bedroom standard units. 15 one-bedroom suites. 2 stories (no elevator), interior corridors. *Bath:* combo or shower only. **Parking:** on-site. **Terms:** cancellation fee imposed. **Amenities:** high-speed Internet, voice mail, safes (fee), irons, hair dryers. **Pool(s):** outdoor. **Leisure Activities:** exercise room. **Guest Services:** valet and coin laundry, wireless Internet. **Business Services:** meeting rooms, PC. **Cards:** AX, DC, DS, MC, VI.

ASK CALL / SOME UNITS

SUPER 8 MOTEL *Book at AAA.com* **Phone:** 910/436-8588

Hotel
Rates not provided

Address: 256 S Main St **Location:** Jct SR 210, just se on SR 24/87, just s. **Facility:** 62 one-bedroom standard units. 3 stories (no elevator), interior corridors. **Parking:** on-site. **Amenities:** hair dryers. **Guest Services:** wireless Internet.

/ SOME UNITS FEE

SPRUCE PINE pop. 2,030

WHERE TO STAY

PINE VALLEY MOTEL & EFFICIENCIES **Phone:** 828/765-6276

Motel
$65-$80 All Year

Address: 11827 Hwy 226 S **Location:** On SR 226 S, 1 mi s. **Facility:** 42 units. 38 one-bedroom standard units. 4 two-bedroom suites with kitchens. 1 story, interior/exterior corridors. *Bath:* combo or shower only. **Parking:** on-site. **Leisure Activities:** small picnic pavilion with barbecue grill. **Guest Services:** coin laundry. **Cards:** AX, DS, MC, VI.

CALL / SOME UNITS

RICHMOND INN **Phone:** (828)765-6993

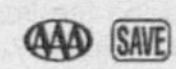

Bed & Breakfast
$85-$135 All Year

Address: 51 Pine Ave **Location:** Exit off US 19 E and 226 to Oak Ave, just n on Walnut Ave, follow signs; center. **Facility:** Dating from 1939, this large, rambling home overlooking the town is shaded by towering pines; guest rooms feature antiques and reproductions. Smoke free premises. 7 one-bedroom standard units, some with whirlpools. 2 stories (no elevator), interior corridors. *Bath:* combo or shower only. **Parking:** on-site. **Terms:** check-in 4 pm, 10 day cancellation notice. **Guest Services:** wireless Internet. **Cards:** MC, VI.

/ SOME UNITS FEE

STATESVILLE pop. 23,320

WHERE TO STAY

BEST WESTERN STATESVILLE INN *Book great rates at AAA.com* **Phone:** (704)881-0111

Hotel
$75-$126 All Year

Address: 1121 Morland Dr **Location:** I-77, exit 49A, just e on US 70 E. **Facility:** 69 one-bedroom standard units, some with whirlpools. 2 stories (no elevator), exterior corridors. *Bath:* combo or shower only. **Parking:** on-site. **Amenities:** irons, hair dryers. **Pool(s):** outdoor. **Leisure Activities:** exercise room. **Guest Services:** wireless Internet. **Business Services:** meeting rooms, PC, fax (fee). **Cards:** AX, DC, DS, MC, VI. **Free Special Amenities: continental breakfast and high-speed Internet.**

AAA Benefit:
Members save up to 20%, plus 10% bonus points with rewards program.

CLICHY INN *Book at AAA.com* **Phone:** (704)929-6458

Bed & Breakfast
$135-$150 5/1-11/30
$128-$140 12/1-4/30

Address: 317 W Front St **Location:** I-77, exit 49B, 1.1 mi w on Salisbury Rd, then 0.6 mi s. **Facility:** In Statesville's downtown historic district, the 1917 Edwardian-style home has been fully renovated and houses an extensive paperweight collection. Smoke free premises. 4 one-bedroom standard units, some with whirlpools. 2 stories (no elevator), interior corridors. *Bath:* combo or tub only. **Parking:** on-site. **Terms:** 7 day cancellation notice-fee imposed. **Amenities:** video library, hair dryers. *Some:* DVD players, CD players. **Guest Services:** wireless Internet. **Cards:** AX, MC, VI.

ASK / SOME UNITS VCR

ECONO LODGE INN & SUITES *Book at AAA.com* **Phone:** (704)872-4101

Motel
$59-$99 All Year

Address: 740 Sullivan Rd **Location:** I-40, exit 151, just s. Located in a commercial area. **Facility:** 129 units. 110 one-bedroom standard units. 19 one-bedroom suites, some with whirlpools. 2 stories (no elevator), exterior corridors. **Parking:** on-site. **Amenities:** video games (fee), voice mail, irons, hair dryers. *Some:* dual phone lines. **Pool(s):** outdoor. **Leisure Activities:** limited exercise equipment. **Guest Services:** valet and coin laundry, wireless Internet. **Business Services:** meeting rooms, business center. **Cards:** AX, DC, DS, MC, VI.

ASK CALL / SOME UNITS FEE FEE FEE

HAMPTON INN *Book great rates at AAA.com* **Phone:** (704)883-8380

Hotel
$109-$189 All Year

Address: 1508 Cinema Dr **Location:** I-77, exit 49B, left at light, left on Folger Dr. **Facility:** 80 one-bedroom standard units. 4 stories, interior corridors. *Bath:* combo or shower only. **Parking:** on-site. **Amenities:** high-speed Internet, voice mail, irons, hair dryers. **Pool(s):** outdoor. **Leisure Activities:** exercise room. **Guest Services:** valet and coin laundry, wireless Internet. **Business Services:** meeting rooms, business center. **Cards:** AX, CB, DC, DS, MC, VI. **Free Special Amenities: expanded continental breakfast and high-speed Internet.** *(See color ad below)*

CALL / SOME UNITS

AAA Benefit:
Members save up to 10% everyday!

HOLIDAY INN STATESVILLE *Book at AAA.com* **Phone:** (704)878-9691

Hotel
$99 All Year

Address: 1215 Garner Bagnal Blvd **Location:** I-77, exit 49B, just e. **Facility:** 134 one-bedroom standard units. 2 stories (no elevator), interior corridors. *Bath:* combo or shower only. **Parking:** on-site. **Amenities:** video games (fee), voice mail, irons, hair dryers. **Pool(s):** outdoor. **Leisure Activities:** exercise room. **Guest Services:** coin laundry, wireless Internet. **Business Services:** conference facilities, business center. **Cards:** AX, DC, DS, MC, VI.

ASK / SOME UNITS

THE KERR HOUSE BED & BREAKFAST **Phone:** 704/881-0957

Historic Bed & Breakfast
$110-$120 All Year

Address: 519 Davie Ave **Location:** 0.5 mi e from town center; in historic district. **Facility:** Common rooms in this restored 1891 house are furnished with antiques, while guest rooms are cozy and individually decorated. Smoke free premises. 4 one-bedroom standard units. 2 stories (no elevator), interior corridors. *Bath:* combo or shower only. **Parking:** on-site. **Terms:** check-in 4 pm, 7 day cancellation notice-fee imposed. **Amenities:** hair dryers. *Some:* DVD players. **Guest Services:** wireless Internet. **Cards:** AX, DS, MC, VI.

ASK

MICROTEL INN & SUITES *Book great rates at AAA.com* **Phone:** (704)881-0353

AAA SAVE

Hotel
$55-$99 All Year

Address: 109 Landson Dr **Location:** I-77, exit 49A, just e. **Facility:** 65 one-bedroom standard units, some with whirlpools. 3 stories, interior corridors. **Parking:** on-site. **Terms:** cancellation fee imposed. **Amenities:** high-speed Internet, voice mail, irons, hair dryers. **Leisure Activities:** limited exercise equipment. **Guest Services:** coin laundry, wireless Internet. **Business Services:** conference facilities, fax (fee). **Cards:** AX, DS, MC, VI. **Free Special Amenities: full breakfast and high-speed Internet.**

CALL / SOME UNITS

QUALITY INN & SUITES *Book at AAA.com* **Phone:** (704)878-2721

Hotel
$70-$130 All Year

Address: 715 Sullivan Rd **Location:** I-40, exit 151, just s. **Facility:** 111 one-bedroom standard units, some with whirlpools. 2 stories (no elevator), exterior corridors. **Parking:** on-site. **Amenities:** voice mail, irons, hair dryers. *Some:* video games (fee). **Pool(s):** outdoor. **Leisure Activities:** exercise room. **Guest Services:** wireless Internet. **Business Services:** meeting rooms, PC, fax. **Cards:** AX, DC, DS, MC, VI.

ASK / SOME UNITS

▼ *See AAA listing above* ▼

SLEEP INN Book great rates at AAA.com

Hotel
$76-$130 All Year

Phone: (704)878-2400

Address: 125 Turnersburg Hwy **Location:** I-40, exit 151, just n on US 21. **Facility:** 70 one-bedroom standard units. 4 stories, interior corridors. *Bath:* combo or shower only. **Parking:** on-site. **Amenities:** voice mail, irons, hair dryers. **Pool(s):** heated indoor. **Leisure Activities:** limited exercise equipment. **Guest Services:** valet laundry, wireless Internet. **Cards:** AX, DS, MC, VI. **Free Special Amenities: expanded continental breakfast and high-speed Internet.**

CALL / SOME UNITS

WHERE TO DINE

CAROLINA BAR-B-Q

Barbecue
$6-$13

Phone: 704/873-5585

The restaurant specializes in pork, beef and chicken barbecue, but also serves a few other meat and seafood items. Another specialty is the daily flavor of freshly baked cobbler. The dining room is basic and casual, and servers are informal and attentive. Casual dress. **Reservations:** accepted. **Hours:** 10:30 am-8 pm, Fri & Sat-9 pm. Closed major holidays; also Sun. **Address:** 213 Salisbury Rd **Location:** I-77, exit 49B, 1.3 mi w. **Parking:** on-site. **Cards:** DS, MC, VI.

CHARANDA MEXICAN GRILL & CANTINA

Mexican
$5-$12

Phone: 704/924-9255

At the end of a large shopping center, the restaurant serves well-prepared traditional Mexican selections. The use of quality ingredients is evident in the good flavors of the food. Bold color accents in the fresh, upbeat dining room help set the mood for relaxed, informal dining. The decor lends to a feeling of dining outdoors, with a hand-painted mural and narrow clay-tile roofs. Casual dress. **Bar:** Full bar. **Hours:** 11 am-10 pm, Fri-10:30 pm, Sat-11 pm. Closed: 11/26, 12/25. **Address:** 1841 E Broad St **Location:** I-77, exit 50, 1 mi e: in The Shoppes at Broad Street Plaza. **Parking:** on-site. **Cards:** AX, DC, DS, MC, VI.

COZUMEL MEXICAN RESTUARANT

Mexican
$4-$10

Phone: 704/878-8930

The casual cantina's menu lists not only traditional Mexican favorites but also several flavorful house specialties. The informal dining room is suited for a casual dining experience. Casual dress. **Bar:** Full bar. **Reservations:** accepted. **Hours:** 11 am-10 pm, Fri-11 pm, Sat noon-11 pm, Sun 11 am-9 pm. Closed: 11/26, 12/25. **Address:** 246 Signal Hill Dr **Location:** I-77, exit 50, 0.3 mi e, then 0.3 mi n; in a small business strip center. **Parking:** on-site. **Cards:** AX, DS, MC, VI.

CALL

MAYO'S RISTORANTE

Italian
$11-$28

Phone: 704/872-5557

Don't let the rustic brick exterior fool you. The restaurant boasts a sophisticated and upscale decor and offers an extensive Italian menu. Included are preparations of pasta, seafood, veal and poultry, as well as an impressive choice of appetizers. The place is popular with the local clientele because of the food, atmosphere and high level of service. Casual dress. **Bar:** Full bar. **Reservations:** suggested. **Hours:** 6 pm-10 pm. Closed major holidays; also Sun & Mon. **Address:** 123 N Center St **Location:** I-40, exit 150, 1.4 mi s on SR 115 (Center St). **Parking:** on-site. **Cards:** AX, DC, DS, MC, VI.

SAGEBRUSH STEAKHOUSE

American
$5-$19

Phone: 704/873-2466

Born from the spirit of Texas cattle drives, the restaurant presents a menu of hearty steaks, prime rib, chicken, seafood and baby back ribs. Yummy desserts merit a splurge. Guests can call ahead to facilitate seating. Casual dress. **Bar:** Full bar. **Hours:** 11 am-10 pm, Fri & Sat-11 pm. Closed: 12/25. **Address:** 117 Turnersburg Rd **Location:** I-40, exit 151, just n. **Parking:** on-site. **Cards:** AX, DC, DS, MC, VI.

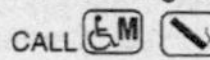

SUNSET BEACH pop. 1,824

WHERE TO STAY

SEA TRAIL GOLF RESORT & CONVENTION CENTER Book great rates at AAA.com

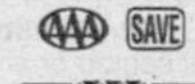

Condominium
$75-$199 All Year

Phone: (910)287-1100

Address: 211 Clubhouse Rd **Location:** US 17, 2.2 mi e on SR 904, then 1.5 mi s on SR 179. **Facility:** Individually owned, this property's villas are each decorated differently and feature screened patios or balconies overlooking the golf course. 600 units. 66 one-bedroom standard units. 534 condominiums. 1-3 stories (no elevator), exterior corridors. **Parking:** on-site. **Terms:** check-in 4 pm, 3 day cancellation notice-fee imposed. **Amenities:** voice mail, irons, hair dryers. *Some:* DVD players, high-speed Internet. **Dining:** 2 restaurants. **Pool(s):** outdoor, heated indoor. **Leisure Activities:** sauna, whirlpools, driving range, recreation programs, rental bicycles. *Fee:* golf-54 holes, golf instruction. **Guest Services:** area transportation-beach, wireless Internet. **Business Services:** conference facilities. **Cards:** AX, DS, MC, VI.

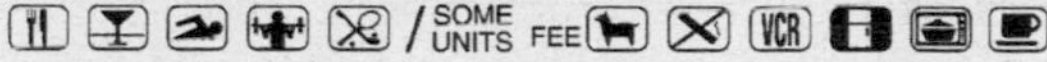

THE SUNSET INN

Bed & Breakfast
$95-$209 12/1-1/1 & 2/1-11/30

Phone: 910/575-1000

Address: 9 N Shore Dr **Location:** Just ne of Sunset Beach Bridge on island, marsh side. **Facility:** Overlooking the saltwater marsh and Intracoastal Waterway, this inn features large rooms with private balconies. Smoke free premises. 14 one-bedroom standard units, some with whirlpools. 3 stories (no elevator), exterior corridors. *Bath:* combo or shower only. **Parking:** on-site. **Terms:** open 12/1-1/1 & 2/1-11/30, office hours 8 am-6 pm, 2 night minimum stay - seasonal and/or weekends, 7 day cancellation notice-fee imposed. **Amenities:** video library, irons, hair dryers. **Guest Services:** wireless Internet. **Cards:** MC, VI.

SWANSBORO pop. 1,426

WHERE TO STAY

BEST WESTERN SILVER CREEK INN *Book great rates at AAA.com* **Phone:** (252)393-9015

AAA SAVE

Hotel

$85-$200 All Year

Address: 801 Cedar Point Blvd **Location:** Jct SR 58, 1 mi w on SR 24. **Facility:** 65 one-bedroom standard units, some with whirlpools. 3 stories, interior corridors. *Bath:* combo or shower only. **Parking:** on-site. **Terms:** 2 night minimum stay - seasonal and/or weekends, 3 day cancellation notice. **Amenities:** high-speed Internet, voice mail, irons, hair dryers. *Some:* dual phone lines. **Pool(s):** outdoor. **Guest Services:** coin laundry. **Business Services:** meeting rooms. **Cards:** AX, DC, DS, MC, VI. **Free Special Amenities: expanded continental breakfast and high-speed Internet.**

CALL / SOME UNITS

Best Western

AAA Benefit:
Members save up to 20%, plus 10% bonus points with rewards program.

WHERE TO DINE

THE GOURMET CAFE **Phone:** 910/326-7114

American

$7-$25

The waterfront restaurant presents a menu of creative pasta, seafood and specialties such as rack of lamb, shrimp and grits, crab Alfredo over angel hair and bourbon-marinated rib-eye. The lunch menu's focus is on salads, sandwiches and fried seafood. Casual dress. **Bar:** Full bar. **Reservations:** suggested. **Hours:** 11 am-3 & 5-9 pm, Fri & Sat-10 pm, Sun 9 am-2 & 5-9 pm. Closed: 11/26, 12/25; also Mon in off season. **Address:** 99 Church St **Location:** Corner of Front and Church sts; downtown. **Parking:** on-site. **Cards:** AX, DS, MC, VI.

WHITE OAK RIVER BISTRO **Phone:** 910/326-1696

Italian

$7-$20

The spacious restaurant presents a menu of veal, beef, seafood and pasta favorites, as well as delicious desserts. A porch for outside dining overlooks the White Oak River. Casual dress. **Bar:** Full bar. **Reservations:** suggested. **Hours:** 11 am-3 & 5-10 pm; to 9 pm off season. Closed: 11/26, 12/25; also Tues off season. **Address:** 206 W Corbett Ave (SR 24) **Location:** On SR 24, just w of White Oak River bridge. **Parking:** on-site. **Cards:** MC, VI.

YANA'S YE OLDE DRUGSTORE RESTAURANT **Phone:** 910/326-5501

American

$4-$8

Guests can hop back to the '50s with signature breakfasts of grits, bacon, omelets and pancakes at the diner, which is decorated with photographs of Marilyn Monroe, James Dean and Elvis. Try homemade pie for dessert or stop at the soda fountain for a float on the way out. **Hours:** 7 am-2 pm, Sat-4 pm. Closed: 11/26, 12/25. **Address:** 119 Front St **Location:** Just s from SR 24; center of town. **Parking:** street. **Cards:** MC, VI.

SYLVA pop. 2,435

WHERE TO DINE

LULU'S ON MAIN **Phone:** 828/586-8989

American

$6-$18

Unusual eclectic fare is the order of the day at this delightful cafe. For lunch, there are varied soup, sandwich and salad. The dinner menu features such temptations as salmon Lulu, tropical pork tenderloins, pecan-encrusted catfish and various pasta dishes. Save room for an excellent homemade dessert. Casual dress. **Bar:** Beer & wine. **Hours:** 11:30 am-8:30 pm, Fri & Sat-9 pm; to 9 pm 5/1-11/30. Closed major holidays; also Sun. **Address:** 612 W Main St **Location:** Center. **Parking:** street. **Cards:** DS, MC, VI.

TARBORO pop. 11,138

WHERE TO STAY

HOLIDAY INN EXPRESS *Book at AAA.com* **Phone:** 252/824-0700

Hotel

Rates not provided

Address: 102 Market Center Dr **Location:** US 64 Bypass, exit 485, just s on US 258. **Facility:** 62 one-bedroom standard units, some with whirlpools. 2 stories, interior corridors. *Bath:* combo or shower only. **Parking:** on-site. **Amenities:** irons, hair dryers. **Pool(s):** outdoor. **Guest Services:** valet laundry, wireless Internet. **Business Services:** meeting rooms, PC.

CALL / SOME UNITS

THOMASVILLE pop. 19,788

WHERE TO STAY

DAYS INN *Book great rates at AAA.com* **Phone:** (336)472-6600

AAA SAVE

Hotel

$50-$70 All Year

Address: 895 Lake Rd **Location:** I-85, exit 102, just w, then just s. **Facility:** 68 one-bedroom standard units. 5 stories, interior corridors. **Parking:** on-site. **Amenities:** irons, hair dryers. **Pool(s):** outdoor. **Guest Services:** coin laundry, wireless Internet. **Business Services:** meeting rooms, PC. **Cards:** AX, DS, MC, VI. **Free Special Amenities: continental breakfast and high-speed Internet.**

MICROTEL INN & SUITES *Book at AAA.com* **Phone:** (336)474-4515

Hotel

$60-$130 All Year

Address: 959 Lake Rd **Location:** I-85, exit 102, just w, then just e. **Facility:** 58 one-bedroom standard units, some with whirlpools. 3 stories, interior corridors. *Bath:* combo or shower only. **Parking:** on-site. **Amenities:** voice mail, irons, hair dryers. **Leisure Activities:** limited exercise equipment. **Guest Services:** coin laundry, wireless Internet. **Cards:** AX, DS, MC, VI.

ASK CALL / SOME UNITS FEE

QUALITY INN & SUITES *Book great rates at AAA.com* **Phone:** (336)472-2310

AAA SAVE

Hotel

$60-$150 All Year

Address: 7 Laura Ln **Location:** I-85, exit 103, just n on SR 109, then just ne. **Facility:** 45 one-bedroom standard units, some with whirlpools. 2 stories, interior corridors. **Parking:** on-site. **Terms:** 3 day cancellation notice. **Amenities:** voice mail, irons, hair dryers. **Pool(s):** outdoor. **Guest Services:** wireless Internet. **Business Services:** meeting rooms. **Cards:** AX, DC, DS, MC, VI. **Free Special Amenities: continental breakfast and newspaper.**

/ SOME UNITS

WHERE TO DINE

ROSA MAE'S CAFE **Phone:** 336/887-3414

American

$3-$14

The cafe prepares home-style cooking along the lines of pork tenderloin, roast beef with gravy and chopped barbecue, all served with a choice of sides from a lengthy list of vegetables. Also on the menu are several Italian favorites, including fettuccine and spaghetti with a variety of sauces. Homemade desserts merit a taste. Casual dress. **Bar:** Beer & wine. **Hours:** 11 am-9 pm, Fri & Sat-10 pm. Closed major holidays; also Sun. **Address:** 1322 National Hwy **Location:** I-85 business route, exit SR 68, 0.5 mi nw. **Parking:** on-site. **Cards:** AX, DS, MC, VI.

TRYON pop. 1,760

WHERE TO STAY

1906 PINE CREST INN & RESTAURANT **Phone:** 828/859-9135

AAA SAVE

Historic Country Inn

$99-$399 All Year

Address: 85 Pine Crest Ln **Location:** I-26, exit 67, 4 mi w on SR 108, just s on New Market Rd, then just e. **Facility:** The inn offers a wide range of accommodations including cottages; lodgings are well appointed and individually decorated. Smoke free premises. 30 units. 18 one-bedroom standard units, some with whirlpools. 6 one- and 1 two-bedroom suites, some with whirlpools. 1 cabin and 4 cottages. 1-2 stories (no elevator), interior/exterior corridors. *Bath:* combo or shower only. **Parking:** on-site. **Terms:** office hours 7 am-11 pm, check-in 4 pm, 14 day cancellation notice-fee imposed. **Amenities:** video library, irons, hair dryers. *Some:* DVD players, CD players, high-speed Internet. **Dining:** restaurant, see separate listing. **Leisure Activities:** table tennis, horseshoes, volleyball. *Fee:* golf privileges. **Guest Services:** valet laundry, wireless Internet. **Business Services:** meeting rooms. **Cards:** AX, DS, MC, VI. **Free Special Amenities: full breakfast and high-speed Internet.**

VCR / SOME UNITS FEE

WHERE TO DINE

1906 PINE CREST INN RESTAURANT **Phone:** 828/859-9135

AAA

Regional American

$13-$31

Nearly flawless service and clearly superb food makes this restaurant a must-dine experience. Your taste buds are titillated from a pre-appetizer to dessert. Relaxing surroundings rich with history. Menu varies daily with local availability. Dressy casual. **Bar:** Full bar. **Reservations:** suggested. **Hours:** 8 am-9:30 & 5-9 pm, Fri-9:30 pm, Sat & Sun 8 am-10 & 6-9:30 pm. **Address:** 85 Pine Crest Ln **Location:** I-26, exit 67, 4 mi w on SR 108, just s on New Market Rd, then just e; in 1906 Pine Crest Inn & Restaurant. **Parking:** on-site. **Cards:** AX, DS, MC, VI.

CALL

WAKE FOREST pop. 12,588

WHERE TO STAY

HAMPTON INN *Book great rates at AAA.com* **Phone:** (919)554-0222

Hotel

$105-$114 All Year

Address: 12318 Wake Union Church Rd **Location:** Jct SR 98, 0.5 mi n on US 1, then 0.5 mi w. Located behind Market Place Shopping Center. **Facility:** 113 units. 109 one-bedroom standard units. 4 one-bedroom suites with whirlpools. 3 stories, interior corridors. *Bath:* combo or shower only. **Parking:** on-site. **Amenities:** dual phone lines, voice mail, irons, hair dryers. **Pool(s):** outdoor. **Leisure Activities:** exercise room. **Guest Services:** valet laundry, wireless Internet. **Business Services:** meeting rooms, PC. **Cards:** AX, CB, DC, DS, JC, MC, VI.

/ SOME UNITS

AAA Benefit:

Members save up to 10% everyday!

SLEEP INN *Book at AAA.com* **Phone:** (919)556-4007

Hotel

$84-$109 4/1-11/30

$79-$104 12/1-3/31

Address: 12401 Wake Union Church Rd **Location:** Jct SR 98, 0.5 mi n on US 1, then just w. **Facility:** 80 one-bedroom standard units, some with whirlpools. 3 stories, interior corridors. *Bath:* combo or shower only. **Parking:** on-site. **Terms:** cancellation fee imposed. **Amenities:** high-speed Internet, dual phone lines, voice mail, irons, hair dryers. **Pool(s):** heated indoor. **Leisure Activities:** whirlpool, limited exercise equipment. **Guest Services:** wireless Internet. **Business Services:** business center. **Cards:** AX, DS, MC, VI.

WHERE TO DINE

OVER THE FALLS DELI — **Phone:** 919/570-8588

Deli
$6-$20

While exploring downtown, browsers can stop in the full-service delicatessen for a salad, pizza or made-to-order sandwich. In warmer weather, deck seating is an option. Casual dress. **Bar:** Beer & wine. **Hours:** 11 am-9 pm. Closed: 11/26, 12/25; also Sun. **Address:** 238 S White St **Location:** Jct SR 98, just s; downtown; in The Cotton Company. **Parking:** on-site. **Cards:** AX, DS, MC, VI.

SHUCKER'S OYSTER BAR — **Phone:** 919/556-7704

Seafood
$9-$34

A lengthy seafood menu brings a bit of the ocean inland, where you can also dine al fresco on the heated, outdoor deck. Casual dress. **Bar:** Full bar. **Hours:** 5 pm-9 pm, Wed-Sat to 10 pm. Closed: 11/26, 12/25; also Mon & Super Bowl Sun. **Address:** 10625 Capital Blvd **Location:** Jct SR 98, 2 mi s on US 1; on service road west of highway. **Parking:** on-site. **Cards:** AX, DC, DS, MC, VI.

TEXAS STEAKHOUSE & SALOON — **Phone:** 919/556-0895

Steak
$6-$25

The typical Texas-style roadhouse focuses on freshly cut steaks, including the popular Duke entree with fries. Southwestern decor and arrows stuck in the walls get diners' minds wandering back to the old days. The popular draft beer is the microbrewed Red Oak lager. Casual dress. **Bar:** Full bar. **Hours:** 11 am-10 pm, Fri & Sat-11 pm. Closed: 11/26, 12/24, 12/25. **Address:** 11735 Retail Dr **Location:** Jct SR 98, just s on US 1, then just w. **Parking:** on-site. **Cards:** AX, DS, MC, VI.

WALLACE pop. 3,344

WHERE TO STAY

HOLIDAY INN EXPRESS HOTEL & SUITES *Book at AAA.com* — **Phone:** 910/285-9200

Hotel
Rates not provided

Address: 131 River Village Pl **Location:** I-40, exit 385, just e on SR 41, then just s. **Facility:** 70 one-bedroom standard units, some with whirlpools. 3 stories, interior corridors. *Bath:* combo or shower only. **Parking:** on-site. **Amenities:** high-speed Internet, dual phone lines, voice mail, irons, hair dryers. **Leisure Activities:** exercise room. **Guest Services:** complimentary and valet laundry, wireless Internet. **Business Services:** meeting rooms, business center.

CALL / SOME UNITS

WHERE TO DINE

MAD BOAR RESTAURANT — **Phone:** 910/285-8888

American
$7-$30

Apple Dijon pork tenderloin, meatloaf, country-fried steak, baby back ribs and fried shrimp represent the hearty choices that await you at Mad Boar. Look to the menu for sandwiches, burgers and preparations of chicken, beef, seafood and pork. Cold salads and fresh ingredients line up on the sprawling salad bar. Visit adjacent Murphy's River Dancer for a sophisticated change of pace. Casual dress. **Bar:** Full bar. **Hours:** 11 am-11 pm, Fri & Sat-midnight. **Address:** 111 River Village Rd **Location:** I-40, exit 385, just e on SR 41, then just s. **Parking:** on-site. **Cards:** AX, DS, MC, VI.

CALL

WARRENTON pop. 811

WHERE TO STAY

IVY BED & BREAKFAST *Book at AAA.com* — **Phone:** (252)257-9300

Bed & Breakfast
$100-$110 All Year

Address: 331 N Main St **Location:** Just n; center. **Facility:** A warm and romantic atmosphere pervades this 1903 Victorian Queen Anne home that is a short walk from the historic downtown shopping district. Smoke free premises. 4 one-bedroom standard units. 2 stories (no elevator), interior corridors. *Bath:* some shared or private, combo or shower only. **Parking:** on-site. **Terms:** 7 day cancellation notice. **Amenities:** video library, hair dryers. *Some:* DVD players. **Guest Services:** complimentary laundry, wireless Internet. **Cards:** AX, DS, MC, VI.

ASK / SOME UNITS VCR

WHERE TO DINE

HARDWARE CAFE — **Phone:** 252/257-2779

Deli
$4-$12

In a former hardware store, the quaint downtown cafe prepares gourmet sandwiches with sport names that recall the location's former occupants. Expect to find friendly service. Casual dress. **Bar:** Beer & wine. **Hours:** 9 am-3 pm, Thurs & Fri-8:30 pm. Closed: Sun. **Address:** 106 S Main St **Location:** Center. **Parking:** street. **Cards:** MC, VI.

WARSAW pop. 3,051

WHERE TO STAY

HOLIDAY INN EXPRESS *Book at AAA.com* — **Phone:** 910/293-2800

Hotel
Rates not provided

Address: 2676 W NC Hwy 24 **Location:** I-40, exit 364, just w. Located behind McDonalds. **Facility:** 61 one-bedroom standard units, some with whirlpools. 2 stories (no elevator), interior corridors. *Bath:* combo or shower only. **Parking:** on-site. **Amenities:** dual phone lines, voice mail, irons, hair dryers. **Pool(s):** outdoor. **Leisure Activities:** limited exercise equipment. **Guest Services:** valet laundry, wireless Internet. **Business Services:** meeting rooms, PC.

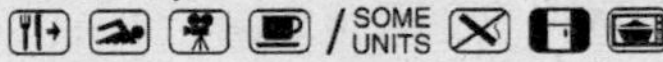

THE SQUIRE'S VINTAGE INN **Phone:** 910/296-1831

Motel

$71-$88 All Year

Address: 748 NC 24 & 50 **Location:** I-40, exit 364, 7.8 mi e on SR 24 business route. **Facility:** 16 one-bedroom standard units. 1-2 stories (no elevator), exterior corridors. *Bath:* combo or shower only. **Parking:** on-site. **Amenities:** high-speed Internet, voice mail, hair dryers. **Dining:** The Country Squire Restaurant & Winery, see separate listing. **Cards:** AX, DC, MC, VI.

ASK / SOME UNITS

WHERE TO DINE

THE COUNTRY SQUIRE RESTAURANT & WINERY **Phone:** 910/296-1727

American

$6-$40

Steaks, seafood, poultry and pork dishes make up the menu at the casually rustic setting, a short drive from the interstate. Casual dress. **Bar:** Full bar. **Reservations:** accepted. **Hours:** 11:30 am-2 & 5:30-10 pm, Fri-11 pm, Sat 5:30 pm-11 pm, Sun noon-2 & 5:30-10 pm. Closed: major holidays; also 12/24. **Address:** 748 NC 24 & 50 **Location:** I-40, exit 364, 7.8 mi e on SR 24 business route; in The Squire's Vintage Inn. **Parking:** on-site. **Cards:** AX, DC, MC, VI.

WASHINGTON pop. 9,583

WHERE TO STAY

COMFORT INN *Book at AAA.com* **Phone:** (252)946-4444

Hotel

$70-$150 All Year

Address: 1636 Carolina Ave **Location:** Jct US 264, 1 mi n on US 17. **Facility:** 56 units. 55 one-bedroom standard units. 1 one-bedroom suite. 2 stories (no elevator), interior corridors. *Bath:* combo or shower only. **Parking:** on-site. **Terms:** 2 night minimum stay - seasonal and/or weekends, cancellation fee imposed. **Amenities:** irons, hair dryers. **Pool(s):** outdoor. **Leisure Activities:** exercise room. **Guest Services:** valet laundry, wireless Internet. **Business Services:** PC. **Cards:** AX, DC, DS, MC, VI.

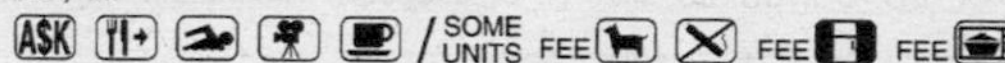

HOLIDAY INN EXPRESS *Book at AAA.com* **Phone:** 252/946-5500

Hotel

Rates not provided

Address: 1031 Carolina Ave **Location:** Jct US 264, 0.5 mi n on US 17. **Facility:** 58 one-bedroom standard units, some with whirlpools. 2 stories (no elevator), interior corridors. *Bath:* combo or shower only. **Parking:** on-site. **Amenities:** dual phone lines, voice mail, irons, hair dryers. **Pool(s):** outdoor. **Leisure Activities:** limited exercise equipment. **Guest Services:** valet laundry, wireless Internet. **Business Services:** meeting rooms, PC.

CALL / SOME UNITS

THE MOSS HOUSE BED & BREAKFAST **Phone:** 252/975-3967

Bed & Breakfast

$110-$135 All Year

Address: 129 Van Norden St **Location:** US 17, just e on W Main St, just n; downtown; in historic district. **Facility:** With high ceilings and heart-of-pine floors, this 1902 Victorian home reflects the easy coastal living-style of the inner banks of North Carolina. Smoke free premises. 4 one-bedroom standard units. 2 stories (no elevator), interior corridors. *Bath:* combo or shower only. **Parking:** on-site. **Terms:** 2 night minimum stay - seasonal and/or weekends, age restrictions may apply, 7 day cancellation notice-fee imposed. **Amenities:** video library, hair dryers. **Guest Services:** wireless Internet. **Cards:** AX, MC, VI.

/ SOME UNITS VCR

WHERE TO DINE

PIA'S OF WASHINGTON **Phone:** 252/940-0600

American

$5-$25

The eclectic eatery is a perfect spot to grab a salad, sandwich, wrap or burger during lunch or, for dinner, a steak, seafood or an Italian dish. Casual dress. **Bar:** Full bar. **Reservations:** accepted. **Hours:** 11 am-10 pm, Sat from 2 pm. Closed: 11/26, 12/25; also Sun. **Address:** 156 W Main St **Location:** Jct US 17, 0.5 mi e. **Parking:** street. **Cards:** AX, DS, MC, VI.

WAYNESVILLE pop. 9,232

WHERE TO STAY

ANDON REID BED AND BREAKFAST INN **Phone:** 828/452-3089

Bed & Breakfast

$129-$189 All Year

Address: 92 Daisey Ave **Location:** US 23/74, exit 102 (US 276) to Main St. Located in a quiet residential area. **Facility:** Situated close to the town center, the inn offers comfortable, inviting guest rooms. Smoke free premises. 5 one-bedroom standard units, some with whirlpools. 3 stories (no elevator), interior corridors. **Parking:** on-site. **Terms:** age restrictions may apply, 14 day cancellation notice-fee imposed. **Amenities:** CD players, irons, hair dryers. **Leisure Activities:** sauna, bicycles, exercise room. *Fee:* massage. **Guest Services:** wireless Internet. **Business Services:** meeting rooms, fax. **Cards:** AX, DS, MC, VI.

ASK / SOME UNITS

BEST WESTERN SMOKY MOUNTAIN INN *Book great rates at AAA.com* **Phone:** (828)456-4402

Motel
$65-$150 All Year

Address: 130 Shiloh Tr **Location:** US 23/74, exit 98. **Facility:** 58 one-bedroom standard units. 2 stories (no elevator), exterior corridors. **Parking:** on-site. **Amenities:** irons, hair dryers. *Some:* DVD players, high-speed Internet, safes. **Pool(s):** outdoor. **Guest Services:** wireless Internet. **Business Services:** meeting rooms. **Cards:** AX, CB, DC, DS, JC, MC, VI. **Free Special Amenities: expanded continental breakfast and high-speed Internet.**

AAA Benefit:
Members save up to 20%, plus 10% bonus points with rewards program.

DAYS INN-WAYNESVILLE *Book at AAA.com* **Phone:** (828)452-9009

Motel
$50-$135 All Year

Address: 232 Phillips Rd **Location:** US 23/74, exit 102, just sw. **Facility:** 39 one-bedroom standard units, some with whirlpools. 3 stories (no elevator), exterior corridors. *Bath:* combo or shower only. **Parking:** on-site. **Amenities:** hair dryers. **Pool(s):** outdoor. **Guest Services:** wireless Internet. **Cards:** AX, DS, MC, VI.

ASK / SOME UNITS

HERREN HOUSE BED & BREAKFAST **Phone:** (828)452-7837

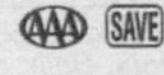

Bed & Breakfast
$115-$160 All Year

Address: 94 East St **Location:** Just e of town offices; center. **Facility:** From 1897 to 1989 the inn operated continuously as a boarding house; subsequently restored, it features charming guest rooms, parlors and gardens. Designated smoking area. 6 one-bedroom standard units. 2 stories (no elevator), interior corridors. *Bath:* combo or shower only. **Parking:** on-site. **Terms:** 2 night minimum stay - seasonal and/or weekends, age restrictions may apply, 3 day cancellation notice-fee imposed. **Amenities:** video library, hair dryers. *Some:* DVD players. **Guest Services:** wireless Internet. **Cards:** AX, CB, DC, DS, JC, MC, VI. **Free Special Amenities: full breakfast and high-speed Internet.**

CALL / SOME UNITS VCR

SUPER 8 *Book at AAA.com* **Phone:** (828)454-9667

Motel
$80-$120 5/1-11/30
$50-$80 12/1-4/30

Address: 79 Liner Cove Rd **Location:** I-40, exit 27, to US 23/74, 3 mi; exit 104 (Liner Cove Rd). **Facility:** 40 one-bedroom standard units. 4 stories, exterior corridors. *Bath:* combo or shower only. **Parking:** on-site. **Amenities:** hair dryers. **Pool(s):** outdoor. **Guest Services:** wireless Internet. **Business Services:** meeting rooms, fax (fee). **Cards:** AX, DS, MC, VI.

ASK / SOME UNITS

THE YELLOW HOUSE ON PLOTT CREEK ROAD **Phone:** 828/452-0991

Bed & Breakfast
$165-$265 All Year

Address: 89 Oakview Dr **Location:** US 23/74, exit 100 eastbound, 1.3 mi nw on Plott Creek Rd; exit 100 westbound, just se, just w on Sulphur Springs Rd, then 1.4 mi nw on Plott Creek Rd. Located in a rural area. **Facility:** On a hill overlooking mountains and fields, this property offers a range of accommodations including a separate, large cottage. Designated smoking area. 10 one-bedroom standard units, some with whirlpools. 2 stories (no elevator), interior/exterior corridors. **Parking:** on-site. **Terms:** age restrictions may apply, 15 day cancellation notice. **Amenities:** irons, hair dryers. *Some:* DVD players, CD players. **Guest Services:** wireless Internet. **Cards:** MC, VI.

ASK / SOME UNITS

WHERE TO DINE

BOGART'S RESTAURANT **Phone:** 828/452-1313

American
$5-$16

Good, moderately priced food is what locals like most about the popular eatery. Attentive servers circulate amid the rustic decor. Casual dress. **Bar:** Beer & wine. **Hours:** 11 am-9 pm, Fri & Sat-10 pm. Closed: 4/12, 11/26, 12/25. **Address:** 303 S Main St **Location:** 0.5 mi s on US 23 business route. **Parking:** on-site. **Cards:** AX, DS, MC, VI.

LOMO GRILL **Phone:** 828/452-5222

American
$17-$30

In a restored downtown building, the chef prepares innovative twists on varied cuisines. Ample portions are creatively presented and served in the casually elegant setting. Save room for one of the delicious desserts. Lunch is in a limited-service setting. Dressy casual. **Bar:** Beer & wine. **Hours:** 4:30 pm-9 pm. Closed major holidays; also Sun & Mon. **Address:** 44 Church St **Location:** Just w; center. **Parking:** on-site. **Cards:** AX, CB, DC, DS, JC, MC, VI.

CALL

PASQUALE'S ITALIAN RESTAURANT **Phone:** 828/454-5002

Italian
$5-$17

Patrons can sample Cuban and Italian entrees in a casually elegant atmosphere. The adjacent tapas bar is more laid-back. Outdoor seating is an option in the warmer months. Casual dress. **Bar:** Beer & wine. **Reservations:** accepted. **Hours:** 11 am-9:30 pm. Closed: 1/1, 12/25; also Sun. **Address:** 1863 S Main St **Location:** 2 mi s on US 23 business route. **Parking:** on-site. **Cards:** AX, DS, MC, VI.

PISGAH INN RESTAURANT Phone: 828/235-8228

Regional American
$6-$30

Patrons of the delightful eatery can relax with a view from the top of Mount Pisgah. On the Blue Ridge Parkway, the restaurant is 30 miles from Waynesville or Asheville. Casual dress. **Bar:** Beer & wine. **Hours:** Open 4/15-10/15; 7:30-10:30 am, 11:30-4 & 5-9 pm. **Location:** Blue Ridge Pkwy at MM 408.6; between jct SR 151 and US 276. **Parking:** on-site. **Cards:** MC, VI.

CALL

SAGEBRUSH STEAKHOUSE Phone: 828/452-5822

American
$5-$19

Born from the spirit of Texas cattle drives, the restaurant presents a menu of hearty steaks, prime rib, chicken, seafood and baby back ribs. Yummy desserts merit a splurge. Guests can call ahead to facilitate seating. Casual dress. **Bar:** Beer & wine. **Hours:** 11 am-10 pm, Fri & Sat-11 pm. Closed: 12/25. **Address:** 895 Russ Ave **Location:** US 23/74, exit 102, just se. **Parking:** on-site. **Cards:** AX, DC, DS, MC, VI.

CALL

WEAVERVILLE pop. 2,416 (See map and index starting on p. 576)

WHERE TO STAY

INN ON MAIN STREET Phone: (828)645-4935 54

Bed & Breakfast
$125-$165 All Year

Address: 88 S Main St **Location:** US 19/23 N, exit 19 (Weaverville/Marshall), ramp toward Weaverville, 0.5 mi, then 0.5 mi s; corner of East St. **Facility:** This pretty, restored Victorian in a quiet setting is outfitted with antiques and heirloom quilts; a rear veranda is perfect for dining al fresco. Smoke free premises. 7 one-bedroom standard units, some with whirlpools. 2 stories (no elevator), interior/exterior corridors. *Bath:* combo or shower only. **Parking:** on-site. **Terms:** check-in 4 pm, 2-3 night minimum stay - seasonal and/or weekends, age restrictions may apply, 14 day cancellation notice-fee imposed. **Amenities:** video library, irons, hair dryers. *Some:* DVD players, CD players. **Guest Services:** wireless Internet. **Cards:** AX, DS, MC, VI.

/ SOME UNITS VCR

WHERE TO DINE

STONEY KNOB CAFE Phone: 828/645-3309 37

American
$7-$28

It's fun and it's funky. Great for weekend brunch, lunch or dinner, this place sustains an eclectic setting with colorful walls and decor. Mediterranean and American cuisine is as fresh and distinctive as the atmosphere. Among menu items are eggs Benedict over crab cakes, paninis, gyros, steaks and pizza. Casual dress. **Bar:** Beer & wine. **Reservations:** accepted. **Hours:** 11 am-9 pm, Sat 8 am-9:30 pm, Sun 9:30 am-3 pm. Closed major holidays; also Mon & 12/25-1/7. **Address:** 337 Merrimon Ave **Location:** US 19/23, exit 21 (New Stock Rd), n at light; just n on Weaverville Hwy (US 19 W). **Parking:** on-site. **Cards:** DS, MC, VI.

SUNNYSIDE CAFE Phone: 828/658-3338 36

American
$6-$10

Inviting features at this historic general store include hardwood floors, antique tables and pressed-tin ceilings. Diners can enjoy house specialties, such as portobello mushroom stack, sauteed lump crab cakes and pan-seared duck breast. Among appetizers are shrimp tempura and roasted oysters. The restaurant remains lively at lunchtime and quietly romantic at night. Try the tasty and creatively presented dessert. Casual dress. **Bar:** Beer & wine. **Hours:** 11:30 am-2:30 & 5:30-9 pm, Mon & Tues-2:30 pm. Closed major holidays; also Sat & Sun. **Address:** 18 N Main St **Location:** Center. **Parking:** street. **Cards:** MC, VI.

WELDON pop. 1,374

WHERE TO STAY

DAYS INN *Book great rates at AAA.com* Phone: (252)536-4867

AAA SAVE

Motel
$55-$75 All Year

Address: 1611 Julian R Allsbrook Hwy **Location:** I-95, exit 173, just e on US 158. **Facility:** 97 units. 93 one-bedroom standard units. 4 one-bedroom suites with whirlpools. 2 stories (no elevator), exterior corridors. **Parking:** on-site. **Amenities:** irons, hair dryers. **Pool(s):** outdoor. **Guest Services:** wireless Internet. **Business Services:** PC. **Cards:** AX, DC, DS, MC, VI. **Free Special Amenities: continental breakfast and high-speed Internet.**

/ SOME UNITS FEE

WHERE TO DINE

RALPH'S BARBECUE Phone: 252/536-2102

Regional Southern
$4-$15

Since 1941, the family-owned restaurant has served vinegar-based pulled pork barbecue and all the trimmings. Buffets are set up weekdays at lunch and dinner. Casual dress. **Reservations:** not accepted. **Hours:** 9 am-8:30 pm. **Address:** 1400 Julian R Allsbrook Hwy **Location:** I-95, exit 173, just e. **Parking:** on-site.

WEST JEFFERSON pop. 1,081—*See also JEFFERSON.*

WHERE TO STAY

NATION'S INN *Book at AAA.com* Phone: 336/246-2080

Motel
Rates not provided

Address: 107 Beaver Creek School Rd **Location:** Jct US 221, just n on SR 194, then just w. **Facility:** 48 one-bedroom standard units. 2 stories (no elevator), exterior corridors. **Parking:** on-site. **Amenities:** irons, hair dryers. **Guest Services:** wireless Internet. **Business Services:** meeting rooms, PC.

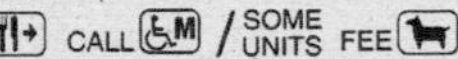
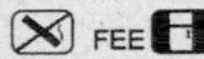
FEE

WHITEVILLE pop. 5,148

WHERE TO STAY

BEST WESTERN PREMIERE INN

Phone: (910)642-2378

Motel
$77-$99 All Year

Address: 503 N J K Powell Blvd **Location:** Jct US 74/76, 1 mi s on US 701 Bypass. Located in a commercial area. **Facility:** 91 one-bedroom standard units, some with whirlpools. 2 stories (no elevator), exterior corridors. **Parking:** on-site. **Terms:** check-in 4 pm, cancellation fee imposed. **Amenities:** voice mail, irons, hair dryers. **Pool(s):** outdoor. **Guest Services:** wireless Internet. **Business Services:** meeting rooms. **Cards:** AX, CB, DC, DS, MC, VI. **Free Special Amenities: newspaper and high-speed Internet.**

/ SOME UNITS FEE

AAA Benefit: Members save up to 20%, plus 10% bonus points with rewards program.

HOLIDAY INN EXPRESS

Phone: 910/641-0644

Hotel
Rates not provided

Address: 1415 N J K Powell Blvd **Location:** Jct US 74/76, just s on US 701 Bypass. **Facility:** 62 one-bedroom standard units, some with whirlpools. 2 stories (no elevator), interior corridors. *Bath:* combo or shower only. **Parking:** on-site. **Amenities:** voice mail, irons, hair dryers. **Pool(s):** outdoor. **Leisure Activities:** exercise room. **Guest Services:** coin laundry, wireless Internet. **Business Services:** meeting rooms.

CALL / SOME UNITS

WHERE TO DINE

DALE'S SEAFOOD OF WHITEVILLE

Phone: 910/642-5770

Seafood
$4-$12

Since 1977, the restaurant has been a favorite for rib-eye steaks and fried seafood, including shrimp, oysters and fish. Lunch specials feature a choice of meat and two vegetables for less than $5. Casual dress. **Hours:** 11 am-9 pm, Fri & Sat-10 pm. Closed major holidays; also Sun. **Address:** 107 S JK Powell Blvd **Location:** On US 701 Bypass. **Parking:** on-site. **Cards:** AX, DS, MC, VI.

WILKESBORO pop. 3,159

WHERE TO STAY

HAMPTON INN

Phone: (336)838-5000

Hotel
$109 All Year

Address: 1300 Collegiate Dr **Location:** US 421, exit SR 268 W, follow signs. **Facility:** 75 one-bedroom standard units, some with whirlpools. 4 stories, interior corridors. *Bath:* combo or shower only. **Parking:** on-site. **Terms:** 1-30 night minimum stay, cancellation fee imposed. **Amenities:** video games (fee), dual phone lines, voice mail, irons, hair dryers. **Pool(s):** outdoor. **Leisure Activities:** sauna, exercise room. **Guest Services:** valet and coin laundry, wireless Internet. **Business Services:** meeting rooms, business center. **Cards:** AX, CB, DC, DS, MC, VI.

CALL / SOME UNITS

AAA Benefit: Members save up to 10% everyday!

HOLIDAY INN EXPRESS

Phone: (336)838-1800

Hotel
$90-$137 All Year

Address: 1700 Winkler St **Location:** 2 mi n on US 421 and SR 16. **Facility:** Smoke free premises. 100 one-bedroom standard units. 4 stories, interior corridors. *Bath:* combo or shower only. **Parking:** on-site. **Terms:** cancellation fee imposed. **Amenities:** voice mail, irons, hair dryers. **Pool(s):** outdoor. **Leisure Activities:** limited exercise equipment, game room. **Guest Services:** valet laundry, wireless Internet. **Business Services:** meeting rooms, business center. **Cards:** AX, CB, DC, DS, JC, MC, VI. **Free Special Amenities: expanded continental breakfast and high-speed Internet.**

CALL / SOME UNITS

WHERE TO DINE

6TH AND MAIN

Phone: 336/903-1166

American
$18-$33

The elegant, converted Victorian house is a local favorite for both its setting and its innovative, well-prepared cuisine. Dressy casual. **Bar:** Full bar. **Reservations:** suggested. **Hours:** 6 pm-10 pm; seasonal hours vary. Closed major holidays; also Sun & Mon. **Address:** 210 6th St **Location:** East side of downtown. **Parking:** on-site. **Cards:** AX, MC, VI.

CALL

SAGEBRUSH STEAKHOUSE

Phone: 336/838-2122

American
$5-$19

Born from the spirit of Texas cattle drives, the restaurant presents a menu of hearty steaks, prime rib, chicken, seafood and baby back ribs. Yummy desserts merit a splurge. Guests can call ahead to facilitate seating. Casual dress. **Bar:** Full bar. **Hours:** 11 am-10 pm, Fri & Sat-11 pm. Closed: 12/25. **Address:** 1302 S Collegiate Dr **Location:** US 421, exit River St, just w, then just s. **Parking:** on-site. **Cards:** AX, DC, DS, MC, VI.

CALL

WILLIAMSTON pop. 5,843

WHERE TO STAY

FAIRFIELD INN & SUITES *Book great rates at AAA.com* **Phone:** (252)799-0100

Hotel
$96-$116 All Year

Address: 1071 Cantle Ct **Location:** US 64, exit 512, just s on SR 125, then just e. **Facility:** Smoke free premises. 101 units. 98 one-bedroom standard units, some with whirlpools. 3 one-bedroom suites. 3 stories, interior corridors. *Bath:* combo or shower only. **Parking:** on-site. **Terms:** cancellation fee imposed. **Amenities:** high-speed Internet, voice mail, irons, hair dryers. *Some:* CD players. **Pool(s):** outdoor. **Leisure Activities:** whirlpool, exercise room. **Guest Services:** coin laundry, wireless Internet. **Business Services:** meeting rooms. **Cards:** AX, CB, DC, DS, MC, VI. **Free Special Amenities: continental breakfast and room upgrade (subject to availability with advance reservations).**

/ SOME UNITS

AAA Benefit: Members save a minimum 5% off the best available rate.

HAMPTON INN *Book great rates at AAA.com* **Phone:** (252)809-1100

Hotel
$69-$89 All Year

Address: 1099 Hampton Ct **Location:** US 64, exit 514, just s on US 17, then just w. **Facility:** 78 one-bedroom standard units, some with whirlpools. 3 stories, interior corridors. *Bath:* combo or shower only. **Parking:** on-site. **Terms:** 1-30 night minimum stay, cancellation fee imposed. **Amenities:** dual phone lines, voice mail, irons, hair dryers. **Pool(s):** outdoor. **Leisure Activities:** exercise room. **Guest Services:** valet and coin laundry, wireless Internet. **Business Services:** meeting rooms, business center. **Cards:** AX, CB, DC, DS, MC, VI.

/ SOME UNITS FEE

AAA Benefit: Members save up to 10% everyday!

HOLIDAY INN *Book at AAA.com* **Phone:** (252)792-3184

Hotel
$89 All Year

Address: 101 East Blvd **Location:** US 64, exit 514, 1.5 mi n on US 17 business route. **Facility:** 110 units. 108 one-bedroom standard units. 2 one-bedroom suites with efficiencies. 2 stories (no elevator), interior/exterior corridors. *Bath:* combo or shower only. **Parking:** on-site. **Amenities:** high-speed Internet, voice mail, irons, hair dryers. **Pool(s):** outdoor. **Leisure Activities:** exercise room. **Guest Services:** valet laundry, wireless Internet. **Business Services:** meeting rooms. **Cards:** AX, CB, DC, DS, JC, MC, VI.

ASK / SOME UNITS

WHERE TO DINE

THE HITCHIN' POST RESTAURANT **Phone:** 252/792-0088

Steak & Seafood
$8-$24

Grilled steaks, seafood, pork chops and chicken are among choices at this casual eatery. Breakfast is offered on weekends, and a lunch buffet is featured every day except Saturday. Casual dress. **Bar:** Full bar. **Hours:** 11:30 am-2 & 5-8:30 pm, Fri-9 pm, Sat 7 am-9 pm, Sun 7 am-10:30 & 11:30-8:30 pm. Closed: 1/1, 11/26, 12/25. **Address:** 1981 Hwy 17 S **Location:** US 64, exit 514, just n on US 17 business route. **Parking:** on-site. **Cards:** AX, DS, MC, VI.

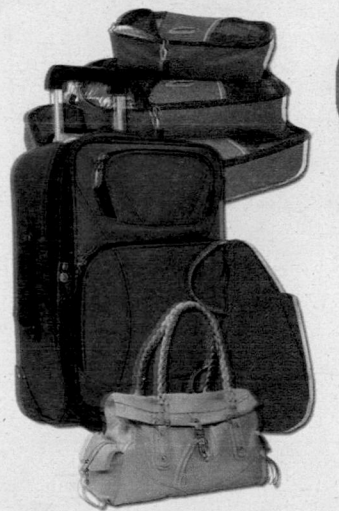

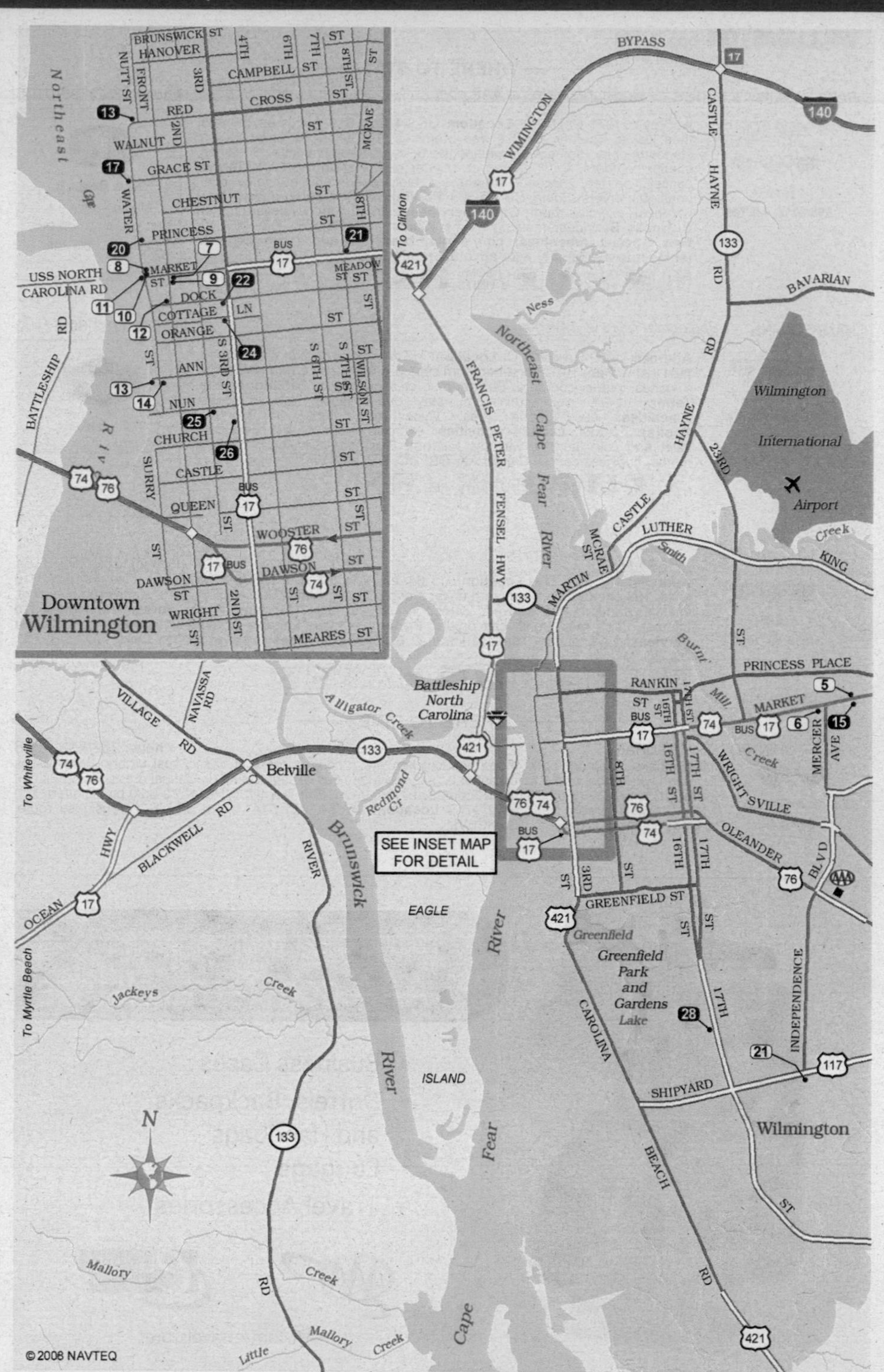

Downtown Wilmington
SEE INSET MAP FOR DETAIL
Battleship North Carolina
Belville
Wilmington International Airport
Greenfield Park and Gardens
Wilmington
EAGLE
ISLAND
To Clinton
To Whiteville
To Myrtle Beach
© 2008 NAVTEQ

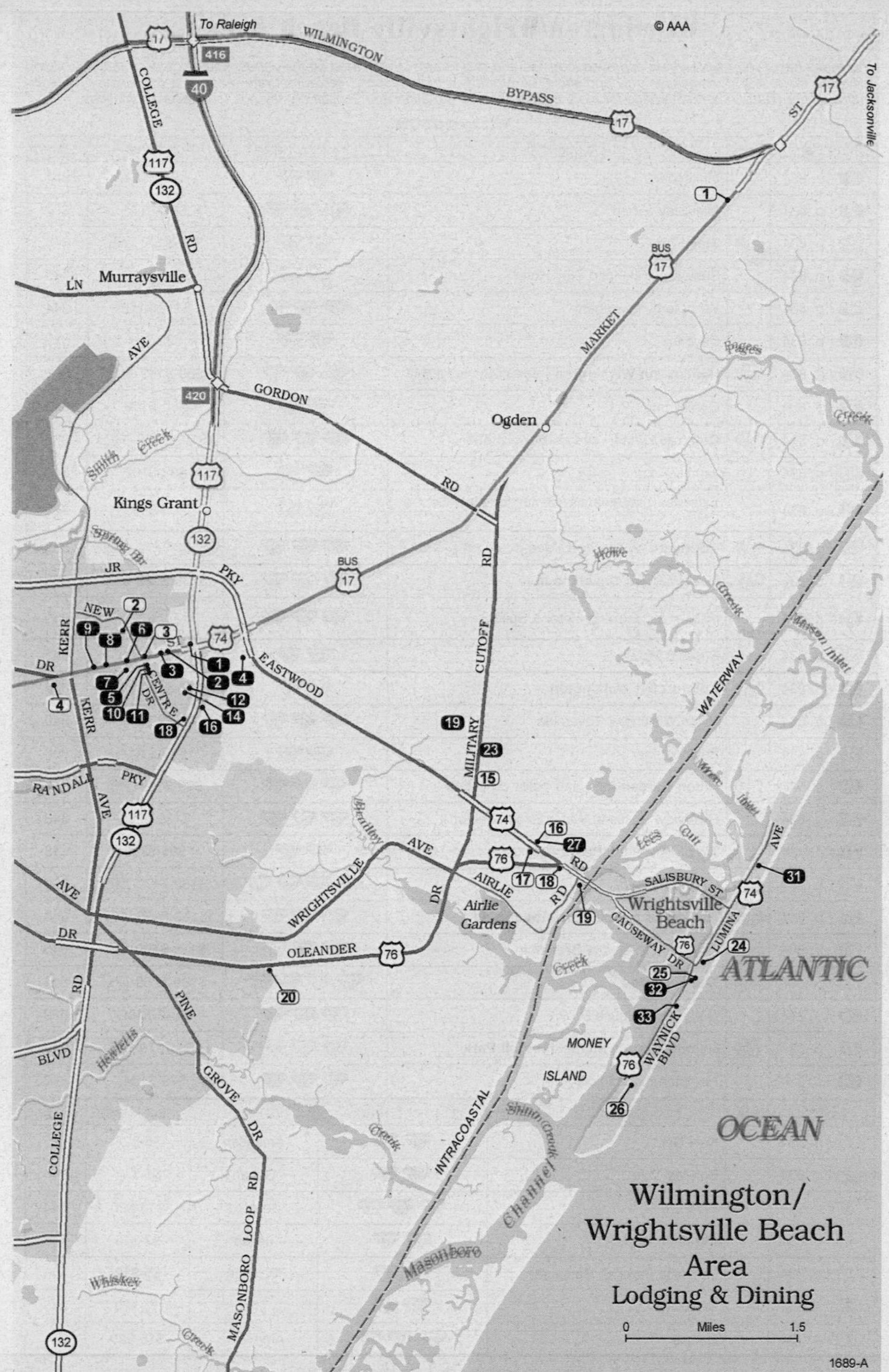

Wilmington/
Wrightsville Beach
Area
Lodging & Dining
© AAA
To Raleigh
To Jacksonville
WILMINGTON
BYPASS
Murraysville
Kings Grant
Ogden
GORDON
RD
MARKET
ST
COLLEGE
RD
EASTWOOD
MILITARY
CUTOFF
WRIGHTSVILLE
AVE
AIRLIE
Airlie
Gardens
OLEANDER
DR
PINE
GROVE
MASONBORO
LOOP
SALISBURY ST
Wrightsville
Beach
CAUSEWAY
LUMINA
WAYNICK
BLVD
MONEY
ISLAND
INTRACOASTAL
WATERWAY
ATLANTIC
OCEAN
Masonboro
Channel
KERR
AVE
RANDALL
PKY
NEW
CENTRE
JR
Miles
0
1.5
1689-A

Wilmington/Wrightsville Beach Area

This index helps you "spot" where approved lodgings and restaurants are located on the corresponding detailed maps. Lodging daily rate range is for comparison only and show the property's high season. Restaurant rate range is a combination of lunch and/or dinner. Turn to the listing page for more detailed rate information and consult display ads for special promotions.

WILMINGTON

Map Page	OA	Lodgings	Diamond Rated	High Season	Page
1 / p. 834		Innkeeper	◆◆	$85-$124	841
2 / p. 834		MainStay Suites	◆◆◆	$89-$350	842
3 / p. 834	AAA	**Sleep Inn**	◆◆	$69-$179 SAVE	843
4 / p. 834		Suburban Extended Stay Hotel	◆◆	$55-$126	843
5 / p. 834		Wingate by Wyndham	◆◆◆	$119-$159	844
6 / p. 834		Days Inn	◆◆	$42-$79	839
7 / p. 834	AAA	**Holiday Inn Wilmington - see color ad p 842**	◆◆◆	$89-$169 SAVE	841
8 / p. 834		Quality Inn	◆◆	$60-$140	842
9 / p. 834	AAA	**Comfort Suites - see color ad p 838**	◆◆◆	$109-$179 SAVE	838
10 / p. 834		Jameson Inn	◆◆	$93-$102	841
11 / p. 834		Extended StayAmerica-Wilmington-New Centre Drive	◆◆	$95-$105	839
12 / p. 834	AAA	**Courtyard by Marriott - see color ad p 839**	◆◆◆	$153-$174 SAVE	839
13 / p. 834	AAA	**Best Western Coastline Inn**	◆◆◆	$139-$189 SAVE	838
14 / p. 834		Holiday Inn Express Hotel & Suites	◆◆◆	Rates not provided	841
15 / p. 834		Super 8 Motel	◆◆	$100-$300	843
16 / p. 834	AAA	**Comfort Inn Wilmington**	◆◆	$70-$159 SAVE	838
17 / p. 834		Hilton Wilmington Riverside	◆◆◆	$129-$249	840
18 / p. 834		Baymont Inn	◆◆	$89-$109	838
19 / p. 834	AAA	**Hilton Garden Inn - see color ad p 840**	◆◆◆	$99-$199 SAVE	840
20 / p. 834		Riverview Suites at Water Street Center	◆◆◆	$129-$250	843
21 / p. 834		Taylor House Inn Bed & Breakfast	◆◆	$95-$250	843
22 / p. 834	AAA	**Graystone Inn**	◆◆◆◆	$169-$379 SAVE	839
23 / p. 834	AAA	**Residence Inn by Marriott-Landfall**	◆◆◆	$159-$179 SAVE	843
24 / p. 834	AAA	**Rosehill Inn Bed & Breakfast**	◆◆◆	$119-$199 SAVE	843
25 / p. 834	AAA	**The Verandas**	◆◆◆◆	$189-$269 SAVE	844
26 / p. 834		C.W. Worth House B & B	◆◆◆	$140-$180	839
27 / p. 834	AAA	**Hampton Inn & Suites-Landfall Park**	◆◆◆	$94-$179 SAVE	840
28 / p. 834		Hampton Inn Medical Park	◆◆◆	$79-$154	840

Map Page	OA	Restaurants	Diamond Rated	Cuisine	Meal Range	Page
1 / p. 834		Kiva Grill	◆◆	American	$5-$28	845
2 / p. 834		Boleros Cafe	◆◆	Cuban	$5-$14	844
3 / p. 834		Bonefish Grill	◆◆◆	Seafood	$13-$20	844
4 / p. 834		Elizabeth's Pizza	◆◆	Italian	$2-$15	845
5 / p. 834		La Costa Mexican Restaurant	◆◆	Mexican	$5-$12	845
6 / p. 834		Indochine	◆◆	Thai	$7-$20	845
7 / p. 834		Deluxe	◆◆◆	American	$15-$29	844

Map Page	OA	Restaurants (cont'd)	Diamond Rated	Cuisine	Meal Range	Page
8 / p. 834		Water Street Restaurant	◆◆	American	$7-$22	846
9 / p. 834		Caffe Phoenix	◆◆◆	Mediterranean	$8-$28	844
10 / p. 834		Caprice Bistro	◆◆◆	Continental	$10-$23	844
11 / p. 834	AAA	**The Riverboat Landing**	◆◆◆	Regional Continental	$6-$29	846
12 / p. 834		The Reel Cafe	◆◆	American	$6-$18	846
13 / p. 834		Elijah's	◆◆	American	$6-$24	845
14 / p. 834		The Pilot House	◆◆	Regional American	$7-$27	845
15 / p. 834		Terrazzo Trattoria	◆◆	Italian	$6-$14	846
16 / p. 834		Port City Chop House	◆◆◆	Steak & Seafood	$8-$35	846
17 / p. 834	AAA	**Port Land Grille**	◆◆◆	Steak & Seafood	$18-$39	846
18 / p. 834		Jerry's Food, Wine, Spirits	◆◆◆	Continental	$18-$28	845
19 / p. 834		Airlie Seafood Company	◆◆	Seafood	$5-$21	844
20 / p. 834		Eddie Romanelli's	◆◆	Italian	$6-$21	845
21 / p. 834		Henry's Restaurant	◆◆◆	American	$6-$25	845

WRIGHTSVILLE BEACH

Map Page	OA	Lodgings	Diamond Rated	High Season	Page
31 / p. 834	AAA	**Holiday Inn SunSpree Resort of Wrightsville Beach**	◆◆◆	$129-$419 SAVE	856
32 / p. 834		Summer Sands Motel	◆◆	Rates not provided	857
33 / p. 834		Blockade Runner Beach Resort	◆◆◆	$139-$419	856

Map Page	OA	Restaurants	Diamond Rated	Cuisine	Meal Range	Page
24 / p. 834		22 North Restaurant	◆◆	Seafood	$7-$19	857
25 / p. 834		South Beach Grill	◆◆	American	$5-$22	858
26 / p. 834		The Oceanic	◆◆	Seafood	$6-$26	857

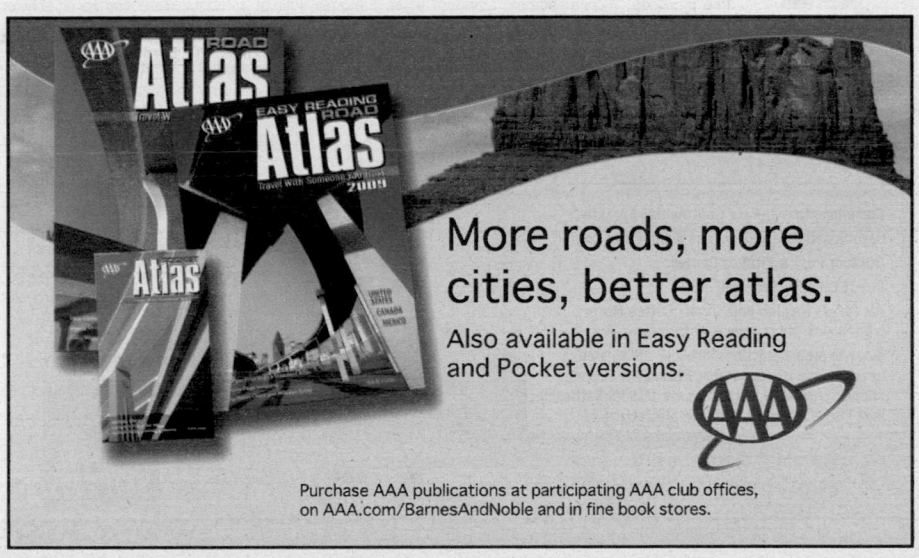

WILMINGTON pop. 75,838 (See map and index starting on p. 834)

WHERE TO STAY

AMERI-STAY INN & SUITES

Book great rates at AAA.com

AAA SAVE

Hotel

$89-$134 All Year

Phone: (910)796-0770

Address: 5600 Carolina Beach Rd **Location:** Jct SR 132, just s on SR 421. **Facility:** 65 one-bedroom standard units, some with whirlpools. 3 stories, interior corridors. *Bath:* combo or shower only. **Parking:** on-site. **Terms:** cancellation fee imposed. **Amenities:** high-speed Internet, voice mail, safes (fee), irons, hair dryers. **Pool(s):** heated indoor. **Leisure Activities:** whirlpool. *Fee:* game room. **Guest Services:** valet and coin laundry, wireless Internet. **Business Services:** meeting rooms. **Cards:** AX, DS, MC, VI.

/ SOME UNITS

BAYMONT INN

Book at AAA.com

Motel

$90-$109 6/1-11/30

$72-$99 12/1-5/31

Phone: (910)392-6767 18

Address: 306 S College Rd **Location:** Jct US 17 business route, just s on SR 132. **Facility:** 134 one-bedroom standard units. 3 stories, interior/exterior corridors. *Bath:* combo or shower only. **Parking:** on-site. **Terms:** 14 day cancellation notice. **Amenities:** irons, hair dryers. **Pool(s):** outdoor. **Guest Services:** wireless Internet. **Business Services:** meeting rooms, business center. **Cards:** AX, CB, DC, DS, MC, VI.

ASK / SOME UNITS FEE 

BEST WESTERN COASTLINE INN

Book great rates at AAA.com

AAA SAVE

Hotel

$139-$189 All Year

Phone: (910)763-2800 13

Address: 503 Nutt St **Location:** Jct Market St, just w on Front St, just s on Red Cross St, then just w. **Facility:** Smoke free premises. 53 units. 47 one-bedroom standard units. 6 one-bedroom suites, some with whirlpools. 4 stories, exterior corridors. *Bath:* combo or shower only. **Parking:** on-site. **Terms:** 2 night minimum stay - seasonal and/or weekends. **Amenities:** voice mail, irons, hair dryers. **Leisure Activities:** exercise room. **Guest Services:** valet laundry, wireless Internet. **Business Services:** meeting rooms, business center. **Cards:** AX, DC, DS, MC, VI. **Free Special Amenities: continental breakfast and high-speed Internet.**

 / SOME UNITS

Best Western

AAA Benefit:

Members save up to 20%, plus 10% bonus points with rewards program.

COMFORT INN WILMINGTON

Book great rates at AAA.com

AAA SAVE

Hotel

$70-$159 All Year

Phone: (910)791-4841 16

Address: 151 S College Rd **Location:** Jct US 17 business route, just s on SR 132. **Facility:** 148 one-bedroom standard units. 6 stories, interior corridors. **Parking:** on-site. **Terms:** cancellation fee imposed. **Amenities:** voice mail, irons, hair dryers. **Pool(s):** outdoor. **Guest Services:** valet and coin laundry, wireless Internet. **Business Services:** meeting rooms, PC. **Cards:** AX, DC, DS, MC, VI. **Free Special Amenities: expanded continental breakfast and high-speed Internet.**

/ SOME UNITS FEE

COMFORT SUITES

Book great rates at AAA.com

AAA SAVE

Hotel

$109-$179 All Year

Phone: (910)793-9300 9

Address: 4721 Market St **Location:** Jct SR 132, 1 mi s on US 17 business route. **Facility:** Smoke free premises. 73 one-bedroom standard units. 3 stories, interior corridors. *Bath:* combo or shower only. **Parking:** on-site. **Terms:** 3 day cancellation notice-fee imposed. **Amenities:** dual phone lines, voice mail, safes (fee), irons, hair dryers. **Pool(s):** outdoor. **Leisure Activities:** exercise room. **Guest Services:** valet and coin laundry, wireless Internet. **Business Services:** PC. **Cards:** AX, CB, DC, DS, JC, MC, VI. **Free Special Amenities: expanded continental breakfast and local telephone calls.** *(See color ad below)*

CALL

▼ See AAA listing above ▼

(See map and index starting on p. 834)

COURTYARD BY MARRIOTT *Book great rates at AAA.com* Phone: (910)395-8224 **12**

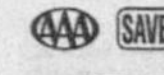

Hotel
$153-$174 All Year

AAA Benefit: Members save a minimum 5% off the best available rate.

Address: 151 Van Campen Blvd **Location:** Jct US 17 business route, 0.3 mi s on SR 132, just se on Imperial Dr, then just w. **Facility:** Smoke free premises. 128 units. 121 one-bedroom standard units, some with whirlpools. 7 one-bedroom suites, some with whirlpools. 2 stories, interior corridors. *Bath:* combo or shower only. **Parking:** on-site. **Terms:** check-in 4 pm, cancellation fee imposed. **Amenities:** voice mail, irons, hair dryers. **Pool(s):** outdoor. **Leisure Activities:** whirlpool, exercise room. **Guest Services:** valet and coin laundry, wireless Internet. **Business Services:** meeting rooms, PC. **Cards:** AX, CB, DC, DS, JC, MC, VI. **Free Special Amenities: newspaper and high-speed Internet.** *(See color ad below)*

CALL / SOME UNITS FEE VCR

C.W. WORTH HOUSE B & B Phone: (910)762-8562 **26**

Historic Bed & Breakfast
$140-$180 All Year

Address: 412 S 3rd St **Location:** Jct Market St, 0.4 mi s. **Facility:** Within walking distance of the downtown historic district and the riverfront, the 1893 Queen Anne-style home features period furnishings. Smoke free premises. 7 one-bedroom standard units, some with whirlpools. 3 stories (no elevator), interior corridors. *Bath:* combo or shower only. **Parking:** on-site and street. **Terms:** check-in 4 pm, 2 night minimum stay - weekends, age restrictions may apply, 3 day cancellation notice. **Amenities:** hair dryers. *Some:* CD players. **Guest Services:** wireless Internet. **Business Services:** PC. **Cards:** DS, MC, VI.

/ SOME UNITS

DAYS INN *Book at AAA.com* Phone: (910)799-6300 **6**

Motel
$42-$79 All Year

Address: 5040 Market St **Location:** Jct SR 132, 0.6 mi s on US 17 business route. **Facility:** 122 one-bedroom standard units. 2 stories (no elevator), exterior corridors. **Parking:** on-site. **Amenities:** irons, hair dryers. **Pool(s):** outdoor. **Guest Services:** valet and coin laundry, wireless Internet. **Business Services:** PC. **Cards:** AX, CB, DC, DS, JC, MC, VI.

ASK / SOME UNITS FEE

EXTENDED STAYAMERICA-WILMINGTON-NEW CENTRE DRIVE *Book at AAA.com* Phone: (910)793-4508 **11**

Extended Stay Hotel
$95-$105 5/1-11/30
$90-$95 12/1-4/30

Address: 4929 New Centre Dr **Location:** Jct SR 132, 0.4 mi s on US 17 business route, just e. **Facility:** Expect to find economy studios with a kitchenette. 104 one-bedroom standard units with efficiencies. 3 stories, interior corridors. *Bath:* combo or shower only. **Parking:** on-site. **Terms:** office hours 7 am-11 pm. **Amenities:** voice mail, irons. **Guest Services:** coin laundry, wireless Internet. **Cards:** AX, CB, DC, DS, JC, MC, VI.

ASK CALL / SOME UNITS FEE

GRAYSTONE INN Phone: (910)763-2000 **22**

AAA SAVE

Classic Historic Bed & Breakfast
$169-$379 All Year

Address: 100 S 3rd St **Location:** Jct Market St, just s. **Facility:** A hand-carved staircase and period furnishings add to the grandeur of this 1906 mansion; some rooms boast champagne baths with glamorous appointments. Smoke free premises. 9 one-bedroom standard units, some with whirlpools. 3 stories (no elevator), interior corridors. *Bath:* combo or shower only. **Parking:** on-site and street. **Terms:** office hours 9 am-9 pm, check-in 4 pm, 2 night minimum stay - weekends, age restrictions may apply, 7 day cancellation notice-fee imposed. **Amenities:** voice mail, irons, hair dryers. *Some:* CD players. **Guest Services:** wireless Internet. **Business Services:** meeting rooms. **Cards:** AX, DS, MC, VI. **Free Special Amenities: full breakfast and high-speed Internet.**

/ SOME UNITS VCR

▼ *See AAA listing above* ▼

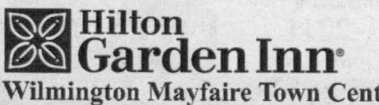

(See map and index starting on p. 834)

HAMPTON INN & SUITES-LANDFALL PARK *Book great rates at AAA.com* **Phone:** (910)256-9600 27

Hotel
$94-$179 All Year

Address: 1989 Eastwood Rd **Location:** Jct US 17 business route, 3 mi e on US 74. **Facility:** 120 units. 90 one-bedroom standard units, some with whirlpools. 30 one-bedroom suites with efficiencies, some with whirlpools. 4 stories, interior corridors. *Bath:* combo or shower only. **Parking:** on-site. **Terms:** 1-30 night minimum stay, cancellation fee imposed. **Amenities:** high-speed Internet, voice mail, irons, hair dryers. *Some:* dual phone lines. **Pool(s):** outdoor. **Leisure Activities:** limited exercise equipment. **Guest Services:** valet and coin laundry, wireless Internet. **Business Services:** meeting rooms, PC. **Cards:** AX, CB, DC, DS, JC, MC, VI. **Free Special Amenities: expanded continental breakfast and high-speed Internet.**

CALL / SOME UNITS

AAA Benefit:
Members save up to 10% everyday!

HAMPTON INN MEDICAL PARK *Book great rates at AAA.com* **Phone:** (910)796-8881 28

Hotel
$79-$154 All Year

Address: 2320 S 17th St **Location:** US 17 business route, 2.5 mi s on 16th St. Located near New Hanover Regional Medical Center. **Facility:** Smoke free premises. 120 one-bedroom standard units, some with whirlpools. 4 stories, interior corridors. *Bath:* combo or shower only. **Parking:** on-site. **Terms:** 1-30 night minimum stay, cancellation fee imposed. **Amenities:** video games (fee), dual phone lines, voice mail, irons, hair dryers. **Pool(s):** outdoor. **Leisure Activities:** exercise room. **Guest Services:** valet laundry, wireless Internet. **Business Services:** meeting rooms, business center. **Cards:** AX, CB, DC, DS, JC, MC, VI.

CALL / SOME UNITS

AAA Benefit:
Members save up to 10% everyday!

HILTON GARDEN INN *Book great rates at AAA.com* **Phone:** (910)509-4046 19

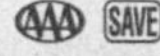

Hotel
$99-$199 All Year

Address: 6745 Rock Spring Rd **Location:** Jct US 17 business route, 2.5 mi e on US 74, then just n; in Mayfaire. **Facility:** 119 units. 117 one-bedroom standard units. 2 one-bedroom suites. 4 stories, interior corridors. *Bath:* combo or shower only. **Parking:** on-site. **Terms:** cancellation fee imposed. **Amenities:** voice mail, irons, hair dryers. **Pool(s):** heated outdoor. **Leisure Activities:** exercise room. **Guest Services:** valet and coin laundry, wireless Internet. **Business Services:** meeting rooms, business center. **Cards:** AX, CB, DC, DS, JC, MC, VI. **Free Special Amenities: newspaper and high-speed Internet.** *(See color ad below)*

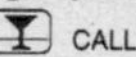

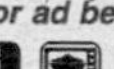

CALL / SOME UNITS

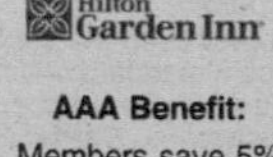

AAA Benefit:
Members save 5% or more everyday!

HILTON WILMINGTON RIVERSIDE *Book great rates at AAA.com* **Phone:** (910)763-5900 17

Hotel
$129-$249 All Year

Address: 301 N Water St **Location:** Jct Market St, 0.4 mi n. Located on Cape Fear River waterfront. **Facility:** Smoke free premises. 272 units. 269 one-bedroom standard units. 3 one-bedroom suites. 9 stories, interior corridors. *Bath:* combo or shower only. **Parking:** on-site and valet. **Terms:** check-in 4 pm, cancellation fee imposed. **Amenities:** high-speed Internet, dual phone lines, voice mail, safes, irons, hair dryers. **Pool(s):** outdoor. **Leisure Activities:** exercise room. **Guest Services:** valet laundry, wireless Internet. **Business Services:** conference facilities, business center. **Cards:** AX, DC, MC, VI.

/ SOME UNITS FEE

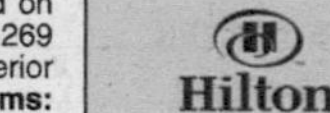

AAA Benefit:
Members save 5% or more everyday!

(See map and index starting on p. 834)

HOLIDAY INN EXPRESS HOTEL & SUITES Book at AAA.com Phone: 910/392-3227 11

Hotel

Rates not provided

Address: 160 Van Campen Blvd **Location:** Jct US 17 business route, 0.3 mi s on SR 132, then just se on Imperial Dr. **Facility:** Smoke free premises. 131 units. 86 one-bedroom standard units. 45 one-bedroom suites, some with whirlpools. 5 stories, interior corridors. *Bath:* combo or shower only. **Parking:** on-site. **Amenities:** video games (fee), high-speed Internet, voice mail, irons, hair dryers. **Pool(s):** outdoor. **Leisure Activities:** exercise room. **Guest Services:** valet and coin laundry, wireless Internet. **Business Services:** meeting rooms, PC.

CALL

HOLIDAY INN WILMINGTON Book great rates at AAA.com **Phone:** (910)392-1101 7

AAA SAVE

Hotel

$89-$169 All Year

Address: 5032 Market St **Location:** Jct SR 132, 0.7 mi s on US 17 business route. **Facility:** 124 units. 123 one-bedroom standard units. 1 one-bedroom suite. 5 stories, interior corridors. *Bath:* combo or shower only. **Parking:** on-site. **Terms:** check-in 4 pm, cancellation fee imposed. **Amenities:** high-speed Internet, dual phone lines, voice mail, irons, hair dryers. **Pool(s):** heated indoor. **Leisure Activities:** whirlpool, limited exercise equipment. **Guest Services:** valet and coin laundry, airport transportation-Wilmington International Airport, wireless Internet. **Business Services:** conference facilities, business center. **Cards:** AX, DS, JC, MC, VI. **Free Special Amenities: local telephone calls and high-speed Internet.** *(See color ad p 842)*

/ SOME UNITS

INNKEEPER Book at AAA.com **Phone:** (910)799-4292 1

Hotel

$85-$124 All Year

Address: 5345 W Market St **Location:** Jct SR 132, just s on US 17 business route. **Facility:** 95 one-bedroom standard units. 4 stories, interior corridors. *Bath:* combo or shower only. **Parking:** on-site. **Terms:** 3 day cancellation notice. **Amenities:** irons, hair dryers. **Pool(s):** outdoor. **Guest Services:** wireless Internet. **Business Services:** meeting rooms, PC. **Cards:** AX, CB, DC, DS, JC, MC, VI.

ASK / SOME UNITS FEE

JAMESON INN Book at AAA.com **Phone:** (910)452-5660 10

Hotel

$93-$102 All Year

Address: 5102 Dunlea Ct **Location:** Jct SR 132, 0.5 mi s on US 17 business route, just w on New Centre Dr. **Facility:** 67 units. 65 one-bedroom standard units. 2 one-bedroom suites. 3 stories, interior corridors. *Bath:* combo or shower only. **Parking:** on-site. **Terms:** cancellation fee imposed. **Amenities:** voice mail, irons, hair dryers. **Pool(s):** outdoor. **Leisure Activities:** exercise room. **Guest Services:** wireless Internet. **Business Services:** meeting rooms, PC. **Cards:** AX, DC, DS, MC, VI.

ASK / SOME UNITS FEE

(See map and index starting on p. 834)

MAINSTAY SUITES Book at AAA.com

Extended Stay Hotel

$89-$350 All Year

Phone: (910)392-1741 **2**

Address: 5229 Market St **Location:** Jct SR 132, just s on US 17 business route. **Facility:** Units are designed for the extended-stay guest, offering spacious and comfortable accommodations. 63 units. 26 one-bedroom standard units with efficiencies. 35 one- and 2 two-bedroom suites with efficiencies. 3 stories, interior corridors. *Bath:* combo or shower only. **Parking:** on-site. **Terms:** 7 day cancellation notice. **Amenities:** high-speed Internet, dual phone lines, voice mail, irons, hair dryers. **Leisure Activities:** exercise room. **Guest Services:** coin laundry, wireless Internet. **Business Services:** business center. **Cards:** AX, CB, DC, DS, JC, MC, VI.

ASK CALL / SOME UNITS FEE

QUALITY INN Book at AAA.com

Motel

$60-$140 All Year

Phone: (910)791-8850 **8**

Address: 4926 Market St **Location:** Jct SR 132, 0.9 mi s on US 17 business route. **Facility:** 119 one-bedroom standard units. 2 stories (no elevator), exterior corridors. **Parking:** on-site. **Terms:** 2 night minimum stay, 3 day cancellation notice-fee imposed. **Amenities:** irons, hair dryers. **Pool(s):** outdoor. **Guest Services:** wireless Internet. **Business Services:** meeting rooms. **Cards:** AX, CB, DC, DS, JC, MC, VI.

ASK / SOME UNITS FEE

(See map and index starting on p. 834)

RESIDENCE INN BY MARRIOTT-LANDFALL *Book great rates at AAA.com* **Phone:** (910)256-0098 

Hotel
$159-$179 All Year

Address: 1200 Culbreth Dr **Location:** Jct US 17 business route, 2.4 mi e on US 74, 0.4 mi n on Military Cutoff Rd, then just e. **Facility:** Smoke free premises. 90 units. 57 one-bedroom standard units with efficiencies. 24 one- and 9 two-bedroom suites, some with efficiencies and/or whirlpools. 3 stories, interior corridors. *Bath:* combo or shower only. **Parking:** on-site. **Terms:** cancellation fee imposed. **Amenities:** high-speed Internet, dual phone lines, voice mail, irons, hair dryers. **Pool(s):** outdoor. **Leisure Activities:** putting green, gas grills, exercise room, sports court. **Guest Services:** valet and coin laundry, wireless Internet. **Business Services:** meeting rooms, PC. **Cards:** AX, CB, DC, DS, JC, MC, VI. **Free Special Amenities: full breakfast and high-speed Internet.**

CALL / SOME UNITS FEE

AAA Benefit:
Members save a minimum 5% off the best available rate.

RIVERVIEW SUITES AT WATER STREET CENTER *Book at AAA.com* **Phone:** (910)772-9988 20

Condominium
$129-$250 All Year

Address: 106 N Water St **Location:** Jct Market St, just n. Located across from Cape Fear River waterfront. **Facility:** Each condo is individually decorated and features a balcony that overlooks Water Street and Cape Fear River. Smoke free premises. 43 one-bedroom suites with efficiencies. 9 stories, exterior corridors. **Parking:** on-site (fee). **Terms:** off-site registration, check-in 4 pm, cancellation fee imposed. **Amenities:** voice mail, irons, hair dryers. **Guest Services:** complimentary laundry, wireless Internet. **Cards:** AX, DC, DS, MC, VI.

ASK

ROSEHILL INN BED & BREAKFAST **Phone:** 910/815-0250 24

Historic Bed & Breakfast
$119-$199 All Year

Address: 114 S 3rd St **Location:** Jct Market St, just s. **Facility:** From a bay-windowed room done in rose, teal and ivory to one with an Oriental theme, the 1848 neoclassical revival home's lodgings have varied decor. Smoke free premises. 6 one-bedroom standard units, some with whirlpools. 2 stories (no elevator), interior corridors. *Bath:* combo or shower only. **Parking:** on-site and street. **Terms:** office hours 8 am-9 pm, check-in 4 pm, 2 night minimum stay - weekends, age restrictions may apply, 3 day cancellation notice. **Amenities:** voice mail, irons, hair dryers. *Some:* DVD players. **Guest Services:** valet laundry, wireless Internet. **Cards:** AX, DS, MC, VI. **Free Special Amenities: full breakfast and high-speed Internet.**

VCR

SLEEP INN *Book great rates at AAA.com* **Phone:** (910)313-6665 3

Hotel
$69-$179 All Year

Address: 5225 Market St **Location:** Jct SR 132, just s on US 17 business route. **Facility:** 104 one-bedroom standard units. 3 stories, interior corridors. *Bath:* combo or shower only. **Parking:** on-site. **Amenities:** high-speed Internet, voice mail, irons, hair dryers. **Pool(s):** outdoor. **Leisure Activities:** exercise room. **Guest Services:** valet laundry, wireless Internet. **Business Services:** meeting rooms. **Cards:** AX, CB, DC, DS, JC, MC, VI. **Free Special Amenities: continental breakfast and high-speed Internet.**

CALL / SOME UNITS

STAYBRIDGE SUITES WILMINGTON **Phone:** 910/202-8500

fyi
Hotel

Under construction, scheduled to open February 2009. **Address:** 5010 New Centre Dr **Location:** Jct SR 132 and US 17 business route. **Amenities:** 93 units, coffeemakers, microwaves, refrigerators, pool. ***(See color ad p 842)***

SUBURBAN EXTENDED STAY HOTEL *Book at AAA.com* **Phone:** (910)793-1920 4

Motel
$55-$126 All Year

Address: 245 Eastwood Rd **Location:** US 17 business route, just e on US 74. **Facility:** 107 one-bedroom standard units with efficiencies. 2 stories (no elevator), exterior corridors. *Bath:* combo or shower only. **Parking:** on-site. **Terms:** office hours 7 am-11 pm. **Amenities:** voice mail, irons, hair dryers. **Pool(s):** outdoor. **Guest Services:** valet and coin laundry, wireless Internet. **Business Services:** meeting rooms, PC. **Cards:** AX, DC, DS, JC, MC, VI.

ASK / SOME UNITS

SUPER 8 MOTEL *Book at AAA.com* **Phone:** (910)343-9778 15

Hotel
$100-$300 4/1-11/30
$60-$150 12/1-3/31

Address: 3604 Market St **Location:** Jct SR 132, 1.8 mi s on US 17 business route. **Facility:** 62 one-bedroom standard units. 3 stories (no elevator), interior corridors. **Parking:** on-site. **Terms:** 2-3 night minimum stay - seasonal and/or weekends, cancellation fee imposed. **Amenities:** safes (fee), hair dryers. **Guest Services:** wireless Internet. **Cards:** AX, CB, DC, DS, JC, MC, VI.

ASK / SOME UNITS

TAYLOR HOUSE INN BED & BREAKFAST **Phone:** (910)763-7581 21

Historic Bed & Breakfast
$95-$250 All Year

Address: 14 N 7th St **Location:** Jct Market St, just n. **Facility:** A candlelit breakfast is served at the restored 1905 neoclassical revival-style home, where rooms sport whimsical names such as Love, Peace and Joy. Smoke free premises. 5 one-bedroom standard units. 2 stories (no elevator), interior corridors. *Bath:* combo or shower only. **Parking:** on-site and street. **Terms:** check-in 4 pm, 7 day cancellation notice. **Leisure Activities:** bicycles. **Cards:** AX, MC, VI.

ASK

(See map and index starting on p. 834)

TOWNPLACE SUITES BY MARRIOTT

Phone: 910/332-3326

fyi

Hotel

$119-$139 All Year

Too new to rate. **Address:** 305 Eastwood Rd **Location:** Jct US 17 business route, just e on US 74. **Amenities:** 111 units, coffeemakers, microwaves, refrigerators, pool. **Terms:** cancellation fee imposed. **Cards:** AX, DS, MC, VI.

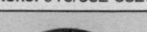

AAA Benefit:

Members save a minimum 5% off the best available rate.

THE VERANDAS

Phone: (910)251-2212 25

Historic Bed & Breakfast

$189-$269 All Year

Address: 202 Nun St **Location:** Jct 2nd St. **Facility:** This elegant Italianate mansion features four verandas as well as an enclosed cupola providing panoramic views from atop the house. Smoke free premises. 8 one-bedroom standard units. 3 stories (no elevator), interior corridors. **Parking:** on-site and street. **Terms:** office hours 7 am-10 pm, 2 night minimum stay - weekends, 7 day cancellation notice. **Amenities:** CD players, irons, hair dryers. *Some:* DVD players. **Guest Services:** wireless Internet. **Cards:** AX, MC, VI. **Free Special Amenities: full breakfast and local telephone calls.**

/ SOME UNITS VCR

WINGATE BY WYNDHAM *Book at AAA.com*

Phone: (910)395-7011 5

Hotel

$119-$159 All Year

Address: 5126 Market St **Location:** Jct SR 132, 0.4 mi s on US 17 business route. **Facility:** Smoke free premises. 100 one-bedroom standard units, some with whirlpools. 4 stories, interior corridors. *Bath:* combo or shower only. **Parking:** on-site. **Amenities:** video games (fee), high-speed Internet, dual phone lines, voice mail, safes, irons, hair dryers. **Pool(s):** outdoor. **Leisure Activities:** whirlpool, exercise room. **Guest Services:** valet laundry, wireless Internet. **Business Services:** meeting rooms, business center. **Cards:** AX, CB, DC, DS, MC, VI.

ASK CALL

WHERE TO DINE

AIRLIE SEAFOOD COMPANY

Phone: 910/256-3693 19

Seafood

$5-$21

A variety of selections are offered, including tuna with a key lime tequila glaze, chili-seared scallops, char-grilled NY strip steak and bourbon-barbecue salmon. For lunch, enjoy salads, sandwiches and a few seafood entrees, like cornmeal-fried oysters or fish-and-chips. Dining options include an outdoor, waterfront deck. Casual dress. **Bar:** Full bar. **Hours:** 11:30 am-9 pm, Fri & Sat-10 pm. Closed: 11/26, 12/25. **Address:** 1410 Airlie Rd **Location:** Jct US 74/76, just s. **Parking:** on-site. **Cards:** AX, MC, VI.

BOLEROS CAFE

Phone: 910/791-5088 2

Cuban

$5-$14

Cuban- and Caribbean-influenced fare contributes to the cafe's menu of multicultural cuisine. Among traditional dishes are picadillo, ropa viejo and arroz con pollo, but guests can expand their horizons with a creative offering, such as baby back ribs in guava-barbecue sauce. Casual dress. **Bar:** Full bar. **Hours:** 11 am-10 pm. Closed: 11/26, 12/25. **Address:** 4724 New Centre Dr **Location:** Jct SR 132, 0.5 mi s on US 17 business route, just w. **Parking:** on-site. **Cards:** AX, MC, VI.

BONEFISH GRILL

Phone: 910/313-1885 3

Seafood

$13-$20

Fish is the house specialty, and the menu and nightly specials offer a variety of choices. Well-prepared food is cooked to perfection. Service is casual in nature, and the staff is skilled and attentive. Casual dress. **Bar:** Full bar. **Reservations:** accepted. **Hours:** 4 pm-close. Closed: 11/26, 12/25. **Address:** 4719 New Centre Dr **Location:** Jct SR 132, 0.4 mi s on US 17. **Parking:** on-site. **Cards:** AX, DC, DS, MC, VI.

CAFFE PHOENIX

Phone: 910/343-1395 9

Mediterranean

$8-$28

In a renovated historic building downtown, the restaurant carries off a classic uptown bistro feel thanks to high ceilings, loft and sidewalk seating and warehouse-size windows. Mediterranean flavors heavily influence the inventive menu selections. Casual dress. **Bar:** Full bar. **Reservations:** suggested. **Hours:** 11:30 am-10 pm, Sun 11 am-4 pm. Closed: 11/26, 12/25. **Address:** 9 S Front St **Location:** Jct Market St, just s; downtown. **Parking:** on-site. **Cards:** AX, DC, DS, MC, VI.

CAPRICE BISTRO

Phone: 910/815-0810 10

Continental

$10-$23

Attentive service and a warm bistro atmosphere lure patrons to the historic district restaurant. A few Belgian dishes share menu space with French-influenced cuisine. Decadent desserts are made on the premises. On weekends, the upstairs sofa lounge serves lighter fare until midnight. Dressy casual. **Bar:** Full bar. **Reservations:** suggested. **Hours:** 5 pm-10 pm, Fri & Sat-midnight. Closed: 12/25. **Address:** 10 Market St **Location:** Just off waterfront; center. **Parking:** street. **Cards:** AX, DC, DS, MC, VI.

DELUXE

Phone: 910/251-0333 7

American

$15-$29

Classic French and Pan-Asian influences are evident in preparations of progressive New American cuisine. Among good appetizers are smoked salmon quesadillas with chevre cheese and vodka creme fraiche and tempura shrimp with cashew dipping sauce. Entrees range from wasabi-grilled salmon to bourbon-cured pork chops to rosemary-seared duck breast. Expanded wine selections match with each dish. Diners can finish a meal with one of the homemade desserts or an espresso, port or cordial. Casual dress. **Bar:** Full bar. **Reservations:** accepted. **Hours:** 5:30 pm-10 pm, Fri & Sat-11 pm; Sunday brunch 10:30 am-2 pm. Closed: 1/1, 11/26, 12/25. **Address:** 114 Market St **Location:** Between 1st and 2nd sts; center. **Parking:** street. **Cards:** AX, DS, MC, VI.

(See map and index starting on p. 834)

EDDIE ROMANELLI'S — Phone: 910/799-7000 (20)

Italian
$6-$21

Traditional favorites are on the menu at the casual and spacious restaurant. Pizza, lasagna and spaghetti and meatballs share menu space with entrees from the grill. Casual dress. **Bar:** Full bar. **Reservations:** accepted. **Hours:** 11 am-1 am, Sun & Mon-11 pm. Closed major holidays. **Address:** 5400 Oleander Dr **Location:** Jct SR 132, 1 mi e. **Parking:** on-site. **Cards:** AX, MC, VI.

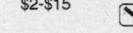

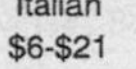

ELIJAH'S — Phone: 910/343-1448 (13)

American
$6-$24

Diners can devour a hearty variety of fresh seafood at this attractive eatery. Begin the meal with a cup of Manhattan or New England clam chowder before the enthusiastic wait staff serves such entrees as broiled shrimp stuffed with crab meat, seasonal soft-shell crab and various catches of the day. Steak, chicken and pasta entrees appeal to landlubbers' palates. Casual dress. **Bar:** Full bar. **Hours:** 11:30 am-3 & 5-10 pm, Fri & Sat-11 pm; to 9 pm, Fri & Sat-10 pm 1/1-3/31. Closed: 1/1, 11/26, 12/25; also for dinner 12/24. **Address:** 2 Ann St **Location:** In Chandler's Wharf; overlooking Cape Fear River. **Parking:** on-site. **Cards:** AX, DC, DS, MC, VI.

ELIZABETH'S PIZZA — Phone: 910/251-1005 (4)

Italian
$2-$15

Visitors can dine in or take out at the busy family restaurant. Stromboli, pizza, New York-style subs and pasta dishes abound. Casual dress. **Bar:** Beer & wine. **Hours:** 10 am-midnight. Closed: 4/12, 11/26, 12/25. **Address:** 4304 Market St **Location:** Jct SR 132, 1.3 mi s on US 17 business route; in North 17 Shopping Center. **Parking:** on-site. **Cards:** AX, MC, VI.

HENRY'S RESTAURANT — Phone: 910/793-2929 (21)

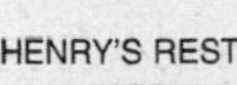

American
$6-$25

Modern American cuisine is served in a comfortable, casually upscale environment. Lunch options include gourmet salads and sandwiches, while dinner features such chicken, beef and seafood choices as slow-roasted prime rib, cashew-sesame-crusted grouper, rotisserie-roasted chicken and the signature crab cakes. Casual dress. **Bar:** Full bar. **Reservations:** accepted. **Hours:** 11 am-11 pm, Sun & Mon-10 pm. Closed: 1/1, 11/26, 12/24, 12/25. **Address:** 2508 Independence Blvd **Location:** Jct SR 132, 1.4 mi s on Shipyard Blvd (US 117); in Barclay Commons. **Parking:** on-site. **Cards:** AX, MC, VI.

CALL

INDOCHINE — Phone: 910/251-9229 (6)

Thai
$7-$20

The lengthy menu comprises such Thai and Vietnamese dishes as cashew chicken, Vietnamese wraps, mahi mahi with mango salsa and Thai curries. The colorful setting is casual inside and more serene in the secluded courtyard garden, which has seating in Thai huts around a lotus pond. Casual dress. **Bar:** Full bar. **Hours:** 11 am-2 & 5-10 pm, Sat noon-3 & 5-10 pm, Sun & Mon from 5 pm. Closed: 11/26, 12/25. **Address:** 7 Wayne Dr **Location:** Jct SR 132, 2.1 mi s on US 17. **Parking:** on-site. **Cards:** AX, DS, MC, VI.

JERRY'S FOOD, WINE, SPIRITS — Phone: 910/256-8847 (18)

Continental
$18-$28

In a small strip mall, the unassuming storefront bistro has earned a strong local following over its long successful run. Chef Jason Godwin's menu includes oysters Rockefeller soup, escargots in Madeira garlic sauce, goat cheese-encrusted grouper and Chateaubriand, among others. Guests also get to enjoy the wonderful aromas from the kitchen, which adds to the ambience. Casual dress. **Bar:** Full bar. **Reservations:** suggested. **Hours:** 6 pm-10 pm. Closed: 7/4, 11/26, 12/25. **Address:** 7220 Wrightsville Ave (US 76) **Location:** From Intracoastal Waterway, just w on US 74/76. **Parking:** on-site. **Cards:** AX, DS, MC, VI.

KIVA GRILL — Phone: 910/686-8211 (1)

American
$5-$28

Mixing the flavors, colors and textures of Southwestern cuisine with a dash of Pacific Rim influences, the grill offers tantalizing favorites like enchiladas del mar, which are tortillas filled with shrimp, scallops and Dungeness crab and topped with a Monterey Jack roasted garlic cream sauce. Casual dress. **Bar:** Full bar. **Reservations:** accepted. **Hours:** 11 am-10 pm, Fri & Sat-10:30 pm. Closed: 11/26, 12/25. **Address:** 8211 Market St, Suite EE **Location:** Jct SR 132, 7.2 mi n on US 17 business route; in Porters Neck Center. **Parking:** on-site. **Cards:** AX, DS, MC, VI.

LA COSTA MEXICAN RESTAURANT — Phone: 910/772-9000 (5)

Mexican
$5-$12

The colorful and casual eatery prepares delicious Mexican cuisine. Burritos, fajitas and enchiladas join such traditional favorites as carne asada and arroz con pollo on the menu of tasty fare. Casual dress. **Bar:** Full bar. **Hours:** 11 am-11 pm. Closed: 11/26, 12/25. **Address:** 3617 Market St **Location:** Jct SR 132, 1.8 mi s on US 17. **Parking:** on-site. **Cards:** AX, DS, MC, VI.

THE PILOT HOUSE — Phone: 910/343-0200 (14)

Regional American
$7-$27

Located in the historic Wharf area overlooking the Cape Fear River. Dine by candlelight on innovative Southern regional cuisine with a focus on seafood. An outdoor patio offers an optional setting. Dressy casual. **Bar:** Full bar. **Reservations:** suggested. **Hours:** 11:30 am-10 pm, Fri & Sat-11 pm. Closed: 1/1, 12/24, 12/25. **Address:** 2 Ann St **Location:** Jct Market St, just s on Water St; at the end of Chandler's Wharf. **Parking:** on-site. **Cards:** AX, DC, DS, MC, VI.

(See map and index starting on p. 834)

PORT CITY CHOP HOUSE

Phone: 910/256-4955 (16)

Steak & Seafood
$8-$35

A tastefully upscale dining room complements the smooth service and well-prepared presentations of beef and seafood. Delicious desserts are sized for sharing. Dressy casual. **Bar:** Full bar. **Reservations:** accepted. **Hours:** 11:30 am-10 pm, Sat 4:30 pm-10:30 pm. Closed major holidays; also 12/24 & Sun. **Address:** 1981 Eastwood Rd **Location:** Jct US 17 business route, 3 mi e on US 74. **Parking:** on-site. **Cards:** AX, DC, DS, MC, VI.

PORT LAND GRILLE

Phone: 910/256-6056 (17)

Steak & Seafood
$18-$39

The award-winning restaurant serves an array of delectable steak and seafood creations in elaborate presentations. Attentive servers navigate the casually upscale dining room. Dressy casual. **Bar:** Full bar. **Reservations:** accepted. **Hours:** 5:30 pm-10:30 pm, Fri & Sat-11 pm. Closed major holidays; also Sun; also Mon 1/1-2/28. **Address:** 1908 Eastwood Rd, Suite 111 **Location:** Jct US 17 business route, 3 mi e on US 74; in Lumina Station. **Parking:** on-site. **Cards:** AX, MC, VI.

THE REEL CAFE

Phone: 910/251-1832 (12)

American
$6-$18

You can sit inside or on the casual waterfront cafe's patio to nosh on sandwiches, pasta or seafood entrees. Casual dress. **Bar:** Full bar. **Hours:** 11:30 am-2 am, Mon from 3 pm. Closed: 11/26, 12/25. **Address:** 100 S Front St **Location:** Jct Dock St; downtown. **Parking:** street. **Cards:** AX, MC, VI.

THE RIVERBOAT LANDING

Phone: 910/763-7227 (11)

Regional Continental
$6-$29

Splendid signature dishes and desserts are made from award-winning recipes, confirmed by the testaments and awards adorning the walls. Located along the waterfront, the restaurant offers a dignified ambience. Casual dress. **Bar:** Full bar. **Reservations:** suggested. **Hours:** 5 pm-10 pm. Closed: 11/26, 12/25. **Address:** 2 Market St **Location:** Jct S Water St; downtown. **Parking:** street. **Cards:** AX, CB, DC, DS, MC, VI. **Historic**

CALL

STICKY FINGERS RIB HOUSE

Phone: 910/452-7427

Barbecue
$7-$26

Diners can put down their silverware and get their fingers ready for classic Carolina sweet ribs, as well as ribs cooked in the Texas and Tennessee styles. Hearty sides of baked beans and coleslaw complement entrees at the friendly cafe. Casual dress. **Bar:** Full bar. **Reservations:** accepted. **Hours:** 11 am-close. Closed: 11/26, 12/25; also for dinner 12/24. **Address:** 5044 Market St **Location:** Jct SR 132, 0.5 mi s on US 17. **Parking:** on-site. **Cards:** AX, DC, DS, MC, VI.

TERRAZZO TRATTORIA

Phone: 910/509-9400 (15)

Italian
$6-$14

Find classic dishes including fettuccine alfredo, lasagna and pasta primavera, along with roasted vegetable ravioli, chicken picatta and marsala-glazed salmon at this cozy bistro. Expect service to be casual yet efficient. Casual dress. **Bar:** Full bar. **Hours:** 11:30 am-9:30 pm, Fri-10 pm, Sat 5 pm-10 pm. Closed major holidays; also Sun. **Address:** 1319 Military Cutoff Rd **Location:** Jct US 74, just n; in Landfall Center Shopping Center. **Parking:** on-site. **Cards:** AX, MC, VI.

WATER STREET RESTAURANT

Phone: 910/343-0042 (8)

American
$7-$22

This former peanut warehouse offers a cozy relaxing atmosphere with sidewalk seating providing a view of the activity on the Cape Fear River. The decor is colorful, rustic and warm. Uniquely prepared soups and salads and entrees ranging from the fresh catch of the day, to steaks, jambalaya, burritos, Greek-style scampi, grilled marinated chicken breast, Cape Fear crab cake and chicken salad tarragon add flair and variety to the entree selections. Casual dress. **Bar:** Full bar. **Reservations:** accepted. **Hours:** 11 am-10 pm, Fri & Sat-11 pm. Closed: 11/26, 12/25. **Address:** 5 S Water St **Location:** Jct Market St; downtown. **Parking:** street. **Cards:** AX, MC, VI.

WILSON pop. 44,405

WHERE TO STAY

BEST WESTERN-WILSON *Book great rates at AAA.com*

Phone: (252)237-8700

Motel
$60-$90 All Year

Address: 817-A Ward Blvd **Location:** US 264, exit 42, 2.6 mi n on Downing St, then just w. **Facility:** 79 one-bedroom standard units, some with whirlpools. 2 stories (no elevator), exterior corridors. **Parking:** on-site. **Amenities:** irons, hair dryers. **Pool(s):** outdoor. **Guest Services:** valet laundry, wireless Internet. **Business Services:** meeting rooms. **Cards:** AX, DS, MC, VI. **Free Special Amenities: continental breakfast and high-speed Internet.**

/ SOME UNITS FEE

AAA Benefit:
Members save up to 20%, plus 10% bonus points with rewards program.

DAYS INN *Book great rates at AAA.com* **Phone:** (252)291-2323

Hotel
$64-$89 All Year

Address: 1801 S Tarboro St **Location:** US 264, exit 40, 3.3 mi e on SR 42. Located across from the Wilson Medical Center. **Facility:** 91 one-bedroom standard units. 2 stories (no elevator), exterior corridors. **Parking:** on-site. **Amenities:** dual phone lines, voice mail, irons, hair dryers. **Pool(s):** outdoor. **Guest Services:** valet laundry, wireless Internet. **Business Services:** meeting rooms. **Cards:** AX, DS, MC, VI. **Free Special Amenities: continental breakfast and high-speed Internet.**

/ SOME UNITS FEE

FAIRFIELD INN & SUITES *Book great rates at AAA.com* **Phone:** (252)265-5660

Hotel
$98-$106 All Year

Address: 4915 Hayes Pl W **Location:** I-95, exit 121, just w, then just s. **Facility:** Smoke free premises. 71 one-bedroom standard units. 3 stories, interior corridors. *Bath:* combo or shower only. **Parking:** on-site. **Terms:** cancellation fee imposed. **Amenities:** high-speed Internet, voice mail, irons, hair dryers. **Pool(s):** heated indoor/outdoor. **Leisure Activities:** whirlpool, exercise room. **Guest Services:** valet and coin laundry, wireless Internet. **Business Services:** business center. **Cards:** AX, CB, DC, DS, JC, MC, VI.

/ SOME UNITS

AAA Benefit:
Members save a minimum 5% off the best available rate.

HAMPTON INN & SUITES *Book great rates at AAA.com* **Phone:** (252)291-0330

Hotel
$109 All Year

Address: 5606 Lamm Rd **Location:** I-95, exit 121, just w, then just n. **Facility:** 71 one-bedroom standard units, some with whirlpools. 4 stories, interior corridors. *Bath:* combo or shower only. **Parking:** on-site. **Terms:** 1-30 night minimum stay, cancellation fee imposed. **Amenities:** high-speed Internet, voice mail, irons, hair dryers. **Pool(s):** outdoor. **Leisure Activities:** exercise room. **Guest Services:** valet laundry, wireless Internet. **Business Services:** meeting rooms, business center. **Cards:** AX, CB, DC, DS, MC, VI.

CALL / SOME UNITS

AAA Benefit:
Members save up to 10% everyday!

HOLIDAY INN EXPRESS & SUITES *Book at AAA.com* **Phone:** (252)246-1588

Hotel
$94 All Year

Address: 2308 Montgomery Dr **Location:** US 264, exit 40, 3.2 mi e on SR 42, then just n. **Facility:** 70 one-bedroom standard units, some with whirlpools. 5 stories, interior corridors. *Bath:* combo or shower only. **Parking:** on-site. **Amenities:** dual phone lines, voice mail, irons, hair dryers. **Pool(s):** outdoor. **Leisure Activities:** exercise room. **Guest Services:** valet laundry, wireless Internet. **Business Services:** meeting rooms, business center. **Cards:** AX, CB, DC, DS, JC, MC, VI.

ASK / SOME UNITS FEE

HOLIDAY INN EXPRESS & SUITES I-95 *Book at AAA.com* **Phone:** (252)234-7900

Hotel
$86-$130 All Year

Address: 5000 Hayes Pl **Location:** I-95, exit 121, just w. **Facility:** 73 one-bedroom standard units, some with whirlpools. 2 stories (no elevator), interior corridors. *Bath:* combo or shower only. **Parking:** on-site. **Terms:** cancellation fee imposed. **Amenities:** high-speed Internet, dual phone lines, voice mail, irons, hair dryers. **Pool(s):** outdoor. **Leisure Activities:** exercise room. **Guest Services:** wireless Internet. **Business Services:** meeting rooms, PC. **Cards:** AX, CB, DC, DS, JC, MC, VI.

/ SOME UNITS

SLEEP INN *Book at AAA.com* **Phone:** (252)234-2900

Hotel
$80-$100 All Year

Address: 5011 Hayes Pl **Location:** I-95, exit 121, just w. **Facility:** 60 one-bedroom standard units, some with whirlpools. 2 stories (no elevator), interior corridors. *Bath:* combo, shower or tub only. **Parking:** on-site. **Amenities:** irons, hair dryers. **Pool(s):** heated indoor. **Leisure Activities:** whirlpool. **Guest Services:** valet laundry, wireless Internet. **Cards:** AX, DC, DS, MC, VI.

ASK / SOME UNITS

WHITEHEAD INN & EXECUTIVE SUITES **Phone:** 252/243-4447

Bed & Breakfast
$90-$149 All Year

Address: 600 Nash St NE **Location:** Jct Tarboro Rd, 0.5 mi n; center. **Facility:** Located in four historic homes on 1.5 acres; all guest rooms feature 12 to 14 foot ceilings, a private bath and lovely antique furnishings. Smoke free premises. 12 one-bedroom standard units. 1-2 stories (no elevator), interior corridors. *Bath:* combo or shower only. **Parking:** on-site. **Terms:** age restrictions may apply, cancellation fee imposed. **Amenities:** irons, hair dryers. *Some:* CD players. **Guest Services:** wireless Internet. **Business Services:** PC. **Cards:** AX, DS, MC, VI.

ASK

WHERE TO DINE

THE CREAMERY FAMILY RESTAURANT **Phone:** 252/243-2934

American
$2-$6

Start your morning with eggs, pancakes and biscuits at this historic landmark. Originally opened in 1946, the burger joint was a favorite hangout for teens. The Creamery's traditional American fare includes burgers, sandwiches and hot dogs. Casual dress. **Hours:** 6 am-9 pm, Sun from 8 am; to 10 pm 3/1-8/31. Closed major holidays. **Address:** 1616 Goldsboro St **Location:** US 264, exit 43, 3 mi n on US 301, then 0.4 mi nw on Ward Blvd. **Parking:** on-site. **Cards:** MC, VI.

GRIFF'S STEAK BARN — Phone: 252/237-5935

American
$5-$20

Since 1971, the casual eatery has been a hometown favorite for lunch and Sunday buffets. Also popular are the salad bar and homemade desserts. Casual dress. **Bar:** Full bar. **Hours:** 11 am-10 pm, Fri-11 pm, Sat 5 pm-11 pm, Sun 11 am-8 pm. Closed: 11/26, 12/24, 12/25. **Address:** 2837 US 301 S **Location:** Jct Forest Hills Rd. **Parking:** on-site. **Cards:** AX, DC, DS, MC, VI.

PARKER'S BARBECUE — Phone: 252/237-0972

Regional American
$5-$8

Grab a seat and belly-up to crispy hush puppies, fresh coleslaw and good ol' North Carolina-style barbecue, served here since 1946. Other menu offerings include pork, chicken and shrimp. **Hours:** 9 am-9 pm. Closed: 11/26, 12/24, 12/25; also week after Father's Day. **Address:** 2514 US Hwy 301 S **Location:** US 264, exit US 301; 1.5 mi n. **Parking:** on-site.

PAUL'S OF NEW YORK — Phone: 252/291-3837

Italian
$6-$14

This casual neighborhood bistro prepares pizza and pasta, as well as chicken and veal dishes. Among entrees are veal Marsala, baked ziti, shrimp scampi and eggplant parmigiana. Casual dress. **Bar:** Full bar. **Hours:** 11 am-2 & 5-10 pm, Sat from 5 pm. Closed major holidays; also Sun. **Address:** 3106 W Nash St **Location:** Jct US 264 alternate route, 1.4 mi ne on Ward Blvd (SR 42), then 1 mi n on SR 58. **Parking:** on-site. **Cards:** DS, MC, VI.

TEXAS STEAKHOUSE & SALOON — Phone: 252/237-2199

Steak
$6-$25

The typical Texas-style roadhouse focuses on freshly cut steaks, including the popular Duke entree with fries. Southwestern decor and arrows stuck in the walls get diners' minds wandering back to the old days. The popular draft beer is the microbrewed Red Oak lager. Casual dress. **Bar:** Full bar. **Hours:** 11 am-10 pm, Fri & Sat-11 pm. Closed: 11/26, 12/24, 12/25. **Address:** 2901 Raleigh Rd **Location:** I-95, exit 121, 3.5 mi e on US 264 alternate route. **Parking:** on-site. **Cards:** AX, DS, MC, VI.

WINDSOR pop. 2,283

WHERE TO STAY

THE INN AT GRAYS LANDING — Phone: 252/794-2255

Bed & Breakfast
$70-$140 All Year

Address: 401 S King St **Location:** US 17, just w on SR 308. **Facility:** Located in a quiet town, within walking distance of Roanoke-Cashie River Center, the 1790 Georgian home features spacious guest rooms. Smoke free premises. 5 units. 3 one-bedroom standard units. 2 one-bedroom suites, some with whirlpools. 2 stories (no elevator), interior corridors. *Bath:* combo or shower only. **Parking:** street. **Terms:** cancellation fee imposed. **Amenities:** video library, CD players, irons, hair dryers. *Some:* DVD players. **Guest Services:** wireless Internet. **Business Services:** meeting rooms. **Cards:** AX, MC, VI.

ASK / SOME UNITS FEE VCR

WINSTON-SALEM pop. 185,776

WHERE TO STAY

AUGUSTUS T ZEVELY INN — Phone: (336)748-9299

AAA SAVE

Historic Bed & Breakfast
$100-$245 All Year

Address: 803 S Main St **Location:** I-40 business route, exit 5D eastbound, 0.5 mi s on Liberty St to Old Salem Rd, just e on Academy St, then just s; exit 5C westbound, just n on Cherry St, just e on 2nd St, 1 mi s on Liberty St to Old Salem Rd, just e on Academy St, then just s. Located in Old Salem Historic District. **Facility:** Built in 1844 as a doctor's house and office, this inn features rustic Colonial charm in its tastefully furnished rooms, some with fireplaces. Smoke free premises. 12 units. 11 one-bedroom standard units, some with whirlpools. 1 one-bedroom suite with whirlpool. 3 stories (no elevator), interior/exterior corridors. *Bath:* combo or shower only. **Parking:** on-site and street. **Terms:** age restrictions may apply, 14 day cancellation notice. **Amenities:** hair dryers. **Cards:** AX, MC, VI. **Free Special Amenities: expanded continental breakfast and early check-in/late check-out.**

/ SOME UNITS FEE

BAYMONT INN & SUITES *Book at AAA.com* — Phone: (336)714-8888

Hotel
$110-$130 All Year

Address: 200 Mercantile Dr **Location:** US 52, exit 115B, just w on University Pkwy, then just n. **Facility:** 90 one-bedroom standard units. 3 stories, interior corridors. *Bath:* combo or shower only. **Parking:** on-site. **Amenities:** voice mail, irons, hair dryers. *Some:* high-speed Internet. **Pool(s):** heated indoor. **Leisure Activities:** whirlpool, exercise room. **Guest Services:** valet laundry, wireless Internet. **Business Services:** meeting rooms. **Cards:** AX, DC, DS, MC, VI.

ASK / SOME UNITS

COMFORT SUITES *Book great rates at AAA.com* — Phone: (336)774-0805

AAA SAVE

Hotel
$89-$159 4/1-11/30
$79-$129 12/1-3/31

Address: 200 Capitol Lodging Ct **Location:** I-40, exit 189 (Stratford Rd), just s, 0.4 mi e on Hanes Mall Blvd to Brookview Hills Blvd. **Facility:** Smoke free premises. 80 units. 76 one-bedroom standard units, some with whirlpools. 4 one-bedroom suites. 5 stories, interior corridors. *Bath:* combo or shower only. **Parking:** on-site. **Terms:** cancellation fee imposed. **Amenities:** voice mail, irons, hair dryers. **Pool(s):** outdoor. **Leisure Activities:** exercise room. **Guest Services:** valet and coin laundry, wireless Internet. **Business Services:** meeting rooms, PC. **Cards:** AX, CB, DC, DS, MC, VI. **Free Special Amenities: expanded continental breakfast and high-speed Internet.**

COURTYARD BY MARRIOTT-HANES MALL *Book great rates at AAA.com* **Phone:** (336)760-5777

Hotel
$123-$133 All Year

Address: 1600 Westbrook Plaza Dr **Location:** I-40, exit 189 (Stratford Rd), 0.5 mi n, just w, then 0.4 mi s. **Facility:** Smoke free premises. 122 units. 118 one-bedroom standard units, some with whirlpools. 4 one-bedroom suites. 4 stories, interior corridors. *Bath:* combo or shower only. **Parking:** on-site. **Terms:** cancellation fee imposed. **Amenities:** high-speed Internet, dual phone lines, voice mail, irons, hair dryers. **Pool(s):** outdoor. **Leisure Activities:** whirlpool, exercise room. **Guest Services:** valet and coin laundry, wireless Internet. **Business Services:** meeting rooms, PC. **Cards:** AX, CB, DC, DS, JC, MC, VI.

AAA Benefit:
Members save a minimum 5% off the best available rate.

COURTYARD BY MARRIOTT-UNIVERSITY *Book great rates at AAA.com* **Phone:** (336)727-1277

Hotel
$128-$137 All Year

Address: 3111 University Pkwy **Location:** I-40 business route, exit 5C (Cherry St), 3 mi n. **Facility:** Smoke free premises. 124 units. 123 one-bedroom standard units. 1 one-bedroom suite with kitchen. 2 stories, interior corridors. **Parking:** on-site. **Terms:** cancellation fee imposed. **Amenities:** high-speed Internet, dual phone lines, voice mail, irons, hair dryers. **Pool(s):** outdoor. **Leisure Activities:** whirlpool, exercise room. **Guest Services:** valet and coin laundry, wireless Internet. **Business Services:** business center. **Cards:** AX, CB, DC, DS, JC, MC, VI. ***(See color ad below)***

CALL / SOME UNITS

AAA Benefit:
Members save a minimum 5% off the best available rate.

CROSSLAND ECONOMY STUDIOS *Book at AAA.com* **Phone:** (336)759-7780

Motel
$60-$70 All Year

Address: 7910 North Point Blvd **Location:** US 52, exit 115B, 2 mi s on University Pkwy, then just e. **Facility:** 133 one-bedroom standard units with efficiencies. 3 stories, exterior corridors. *Bath:* combo or shower only. **Parking:** on-site. **Amenities:** voice mail. **Guest Services:** coin laundry, wireless Internet. **Cards:** AX, CB, DC, DS, JC, MC, VI.

ASK / SOME UNITS FEE

DAYS INN-NORTH *Book great rates at AAA.com* **Phone:** (336)744-5755

SAVE

Motel
$52-$90 All Year

Address: 5218 Germanton Rd **Location:** US 52, exit 114, just n on SR 8. **Facility:** 60 one-bedroom standard units, some with whirlpools. 2 stories (no elevator), exterior corridors. **Parking:** on-site. **Amenities:** hair dryers. **Guest Services:** wireless Internet. **Cards:** AX, DS, MC, VI.

/ SOME UNITS

EMBASSY SUITES-WINSTON-SALEM *Book great rates at AAA.com* **Phone:** (336)724-2300

Hotel
$99-$219 All Year

Address: 460 N Cherry St **Location:** I-40 business route, exit 5C (Cherry St), just n. **Facility:** 146 units. 134 one- and 12 two-bedroom suites. 9 stories, interior corridors. *Bath:* combo or shower only. **Parking:** on-site (fee) and valet. **Terms:** 1-30 night minimum stay, cancellation fee imposed. **Amenities:** video games (fee), high-speed Internet, dual phone lines, voice mail, irons, hair dryers. **Pool(s):** heated indoor. **Leisure Activities:** whirlpool, exercise room. **Guest Services:** valet and coin laundry, area transportation, wireless Internet. **Business Services:** conference facilities, business center. **Cards:** AX, DC, DS, MC, VI.

CALL 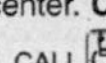     / SOME UNITS

AAA Benefit:
Members save 5% or more everyday!

▼ *See AAA listing above* ▼

EXTENDED STAYAMERICA WINSTON-SALEM-HANES MALL BLVD Book at AAA.com

Phone: (336)768-0075

Motel

$70-$80 All Year

Address: 1995 Hampton Inn Ct **Location:** I-40, exit 189 (Stratford Rd), just s, just e on Hanes Mall Blvd, then just n. **Facility:** 111 one-bedroom standard units with efficiencies. 3 stories (no elevator), exterior corridors. *Bath:* combo or shower only. **Parking:** on-site, winter plug-ins. **Amenities:** voice mail, irons. **Guest Services:** coin laundry, wireless Internet. **Cards:** AX, CB, DC, DS, JC, MC, VI.

ASK / SOME UNITS FEE

FAIRFIELD INN & SUITES Book great rates at AAA.com

Phone: (336)714-3000

Hotel

$94-$149 All Year

Address: 1680 Westbrook Plaza Dr **Location:** I-40, exit 189 (Stratford Rd), 0.5 mi n, just w, then just s. **Facility:** Smoke free premises. 130 units. 106 one-bedroom standard units. 24 one-bedroom suites. 5 stories, interior corridors. *Bath:* combo or shower only. **Parking:** on-site. **Terms:** cancellation fee imposed. **Amenities:** high-speed Internet, voice mail, irons, hair dryers. *Some:* CD players, dual phone lines. **Pool(s):** outdoor. **Leisure Activities:** exercise room. **Guest Services:** valet and coin laundry, wireless Internet. **Business Services:** meeting rooms, PC. **Cards:** AX, DS, MC, VI.

CALL / SOME UNITS

AAA Benefit:

Members save a minimum 5% off the best available rate.

HAMPTON INN-HANES MALL Book great rates at AAA.com

Phone: (336)760-1660

Hotel

$99-$139 All Year

Address: 1990 Hampton Inn Ct **Location:** I-40, exit 189 (Stratford Rd), just s, just e on Hanes Mall Blvd, then just n. **Facility:** 130 one-bedroom standard units, some with whirlpools. 5 stories, interior corridors. *Bath:* combo or shower only. **Parking:** on-site. **Terms:** 1-30 night minimum stay, cancellation fee imposed. **Amenities:** voice mail, irons, hair dryers. *Some:* CD players. **Pool(s):** outdoor. **Leisure Activities:** exercise room. **Guest Services:** valet and coin laundry, wireless Internet. **Business Services:** meeting rooms, PC. **Cards:** AX, CB, DC, DS, MC, VI.

CALL / SOME UNITS

AAA Benefit:

Members save up to 10% everyday!

THE HAWTHORNE INN & CONFERENCE CENTER Book great rates at AAA.com

Phone: (336)777-3000

AAA SAVE

Hotel

$79-$165 All Year

Address: 420 High St **Location:** I-40 business route, exit 5C (Cherry St) eastbound, just e; exit westbound, just w on 1st St, then just s on Marshall St. **Facility:** 143 units. 130 one-bedroom standard units. 13 one-bedroom suites. 7 stories, interior corridors. *Bath:* combo or shower only. **Parking:** on-site. **Terms:** cancellation fee imposed. **Amenities:** voice mail, irons, hair dryers. *Some:* high-speed Internet, safes. **Pool(s):** outdoor. **Leisure Activities:** exercise room. **Guest Services:** valet and coin laundry, area transportation-Wake Forest University Baptist Medical Center, wireless Internet. **Business Services:** conference facilities, PC. **Cards:** AX, DS, MC, VI. **Free Special Amenities: expanded continental breakfast and high-speed Internet.** *(See color ad below)*

CALL / SOME UNITS FEE

▼ See AAA listing above ▼

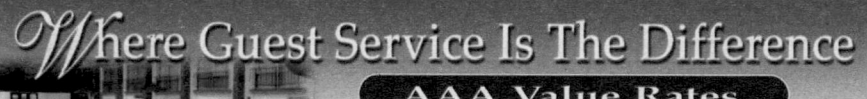

HILTON GARDEN INN WINSTON SALEM **Phone:** 336/765-1298

fyi
Hotel
$79-$179 All Year

Too new to rate, opening scheduled for July 2008. **Address:** 1325 Creekshire Way **Location:** I-40, exit 189 (Stratford Rd). **Amenities:** 112 units, coffeemakers, microwaves, refrigerators, pool. **Terms:** 1-30 night minimum stay, cancellation fee imposed. **Cards:** AX, DC, DS, MC, VI.

HOLIDAY INN EXPRESS *Book great rates at AAA.com* **Phone:** (336)788-1980

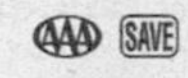
Hotel
$100-$160 All Year

Address: 2520 Peters Creek Pkwy **Location:** I-40, exit 192 (Peters Creek Pkwy), just e on SR 150, make U-turn on Silas Creek Pkwy, then just w. **Facility:** 71 one-bedroom standard units, some with whirlpools. 3 stories, interior corridors. *Bath:* combo or shower only. **Parking:** on-site. **Terms:** cancellation fee imposed. **Amenities:** high-speed Internet, dual phone lines, voice mail, irons, hair dryers. **Pool(s):** outdoor. **Leisure Activities:** limited exercise equipment. **Guest Services:** valet and coin laundry, wireless Internet. **Business Services:** meeting rooms, PC. **Cards:** AX, DC, DS, MC, VI.

CALL / SOME UNITS

HOLIDAY INN EXPRESS **Phone:** (336)721-0220

Hotel
$95-$150 All Year

Address: 110 Miller St **Location:** I-40 business route, exit 4 eastbound; exit 4A westbound, just sw on Cloverdale Ave, then just n. **Facility:** 121 one-bedroom standard units. 5 stories, interior corridors. *Bath:* combo or shower only. **Parking:** on-site. **Terms:** 7 day cancellation notice. **Amenities:** dual phone lines, voice mail, irons, hair dryers. **Leisure Activities:** exercise room. **Guest Services:** valet laundry, area transportation, wireless Internet. **Business Services:** meeting rooms. **Cards:** AX, CB, DC, DS, MC, VI.

ASK / SOME UNITS

HOLIDAY INN SELECT *Book great rates at AAA.com* **Phone:** (336)767-9595

Hotel
$89-$149 All Year

Address: 5790 University Pkwy **Location:** US 52, exit 115B, just s. **Facility:** 150 one-bedroom standard units. 7 stories, interior corridors. *Bath:* combo or shower only. **Parking:** on-site. **Amenities:** video games (fee), dual phone lines, voice mail, irons, hair dryers. **Pool(s):** outdoor. **Leisure Activities:** exercise room. **Guest Services:** valet laundry, wireless Internet. **Business Services:** conference facilities, business center. **Cards:** AX, CB, DC, DS, JC, MC, VI. **Free Special Amenities: newspaper and high-speed Internet.**

CALL / SOME UNITS

INNKEEPER *Book at AAA.com* **Phone:** (336)721-0062

Motel
$52-$60 All Year

Address: 2115 Peters Creek Pkwy **Location:** I-40, exit 192 (Peters Creek Pkwy), just e on SR 150. **Facility:** 126 one-bedroom standard units. 2 stories (no elevator), interior/exterior corridors. **Parking:** on-site. **Terms:** 3 day cancellation notice. **Pool(s):** outdoor. **Guest Services:** wireless Internet. **Cards:** AX, CB, DC, DS, JC, MC, VI.

ASK / SOME UNITS FEE

LA QUINTA INNS & SUITES WINSTON-SALEM *Book great rates at AAA.com* **Phone:** (336)765-8777

Hotel
$69-$139 All Year

Address: 2020 Griffith Rd **Location:** I-40, exit 189 (Stratford Rd), just s, just e on Hanes Mall Blvd, then just s. **Facility:** 131 units. 125 one-bedroom standard units. 6 one-bedroom suites. 6 stories, interior corridors. *Bath:* combo or shower only. **Parking:** on-site. **Amenities:** video games (fee), high-speed Internet, voice mail, irons, hair dryers. *Some:* dual phone lines. **Pool(s):** outdoor. **Leisure Activities:** whirlpool, exercise room. **Guest Services:** valet and coin laundry, wireless Internet. **Business Services:** meeting rooms, PC. **Cards:** AX, DC, DS, MC, VI.

ASK CALL / SOME UNITS

MARRIOTT HOTEL-WINSTON-SALEM *Book great rates at AAA.com* **Phone:** (336)725-3500

Hotel
$177-$190 All Year

Address: 425 N Cherry St **Location:** I-40 business route, exit 5C (Cherry St), just n. **Facility:** Smoke free premises. 315 units. 309 one-bedroom standard units. 6 one-bedroom suites. 17 stories, interior corridors. *Bath:* combo or shower only. **Parking:** on-site (fee) and valet. **Terms:** cancellation fee imposed. **Amenities:** video games (fee), dual phone lines, voice mail, irons, hair dryers. **Pool(s):** heated indoor. **Leisure Activities:** exercise room. **Guest Services:** valet and coin laundry, area transportation, wireless Internet. **Business Services:** conference facilities, business center. **Cards:** AX, CB, DC, DS, JC, MC, VI.

CALL / SOME UNITS

MICROTEL INN Book great rates at AAA.com **Phone:** (336)659-1994

Hotel

$45-$95 All Year

Address: 100 Capitol Lodging Ct **Location:** I-40, exit 189 (Stratford Rd), just s, 0.4 mi e on Hanes Mall Blvd, just s on Brookview Hills Blvd, then just e. **Facility:** 98 one-bedroom standard units. 3 stories, interior corridors. *Bath:* combo or shower only. **Parking:** on-site. **Amenities:** voice mail. **Leisure Activities:** pool privileges. **Guest Services:** coin laundry, wireless Internet. **Business Services:** PC. **Cards:** AX, CB, DC, DS, MC, VI. **Free Special Amenities: continental breakfast and high-speed Internet.**

CALL / SOME UNITS

QUALITY INN & SUITES-HANES MALL Book great rates at AAA.com **Phone:** (336)765-6670

Hotel

$69-$150 All Year

Address: 2008 S Hawthorne Rd **Location:** I-40 business route, exit 2A, 0.5 mi s on Silas Creek Pkwy, then just e. Located across from Forsyth Medical Center. **Facility:** 148 units. 136 one-bedroom standard units. 12 one-bedroom suites. 2-3 stories (no elevator), exterior corridors. *Bath:* combo or shower only. **Parking:** on-site. **Amenities:** video games (fee), high-speed Internet, dual phone lines, voice mail, irons, hair dryers. **Pool(s):** outdoor. **Leisure Activities:** exercise room. **Guest Services:** valet laundry, wireless Internet. **Business Services:** meeting rooms, business center. **Cards:** AX, DS, MC, VI. **Free Special Amenities: continental breakfast and high-speed Internet.**

CALL / SOME UNITS FEE

QUALITY INN-COLISEUM Book great rates at AAA.com **Phone:** (336)767-8240

Hotel

$60-$130 All Year

Address: 531 Akron Dr **Location:** US 52, exit 112, just e. **Facility:** 134 units. 129 one-bedroom standard units. 5 one-bedroom suites, some with whirlpools. 8 stories, interior corridors. **Parking:** on-site. **Terms:** cancellation fee imposed. **Amenities:** voice mail, irons, hair dryers. **Pool(s):** outdoor. **Leisure Activities:** limited exercise equipment. **Guest Services:** valet laundry, wireless Internet. **Business Services:** meeting rooms, PC. **Cards:** AX, CB, DC, DS, JC, MC, VI. **Free Special Amenities: early check-in/late check-out and high-speed Internet.**
(See color ad below)

QUALITY INN UNIVERSITY Book great rates at AAA.com **Phone:** 336/767-9009

Hotel

Rates not provided

Address: 5719 University Pkwy **Location:** US 52, exit 115B, 0.4 mi w. **Facility:** 113 one-bedroom standard units. 2 stories (no elevator), exterior corridors. **Parking:** on-site. **Amenities:** voice mail, safes (fee), irons, hair dryers. **Pool(s):** outdoor. **Leisure Activities:** exercise room. **Guest Services:** valet laundry, wireless Internet. **Business Services:** meeting rooms, PC. **Free Special Amenities: continental breakfast and high-speed Internet.**

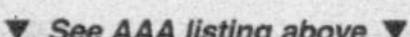

▼ See AAA listing above ▼

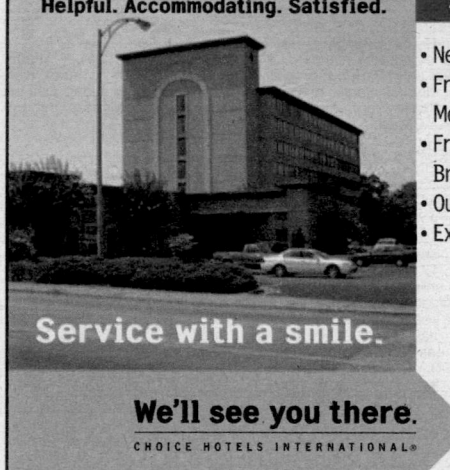

RESIDENCE INN BY MARRIOTT *Book great rates at AAA.com* **Phone:** (336)759-0777

Hotel

$177-$190 All Year

Address: 7835 North Point Blvd **Location:** US 52 N, exit 115B, 2 mi s on University Pkwy, then just e. **Facility:** Smoke free premises. 88 units. 66 one-bedroom standard units with kitchens. 22 two-bedroom suites with kitchens. 2 stories (no elevator), exterior corridors. **Parking:** on-site. **Terms:** cancellation fee imposed. **Amenities:** high-speed Internet, voice mail, irons, hair dryers. **Pool(s):** outdoor. **Leisure Activities:** whirlpool, exercise room, sports court. **Guest Services:** valet and coin laundry, wireless Internet. **Business Services:** meeting rooms, business center. **Cards:** AX, CB, DC, DS, JC, MC, VI.

AAA Benefit: Members save a minimum 5% off the best available rate.

SALEM INN & SUITES *Book at AAA.com* **Phone:** 336/725-8561

Hotel

Rates not provided

Address: 127 S Cherry St **Location:** I-40 business route, exit 5C (Cherry St) eastbound, just e on High St, then just s; exit westbound, just w on 1st St, just s on Marshall St, just e on High St, then just s. **Facility:** 107 units. 85 one-bedroom standard units. 22 one-bedroom suites. 2 stories (no elevator), exterior corridors. **Parking:** on-site. **Amenities:** voice mail, irons, hair dryers. *Some:* high-speed Internet. **Pool(s):** outdoor. **Leisure Activities:** exercise room. **Guest Services:** coin laundry, wireless Internet. **Business Services:** meeting rooms, business center.

/ SOME UNITS FEE

SLEEP INN-HANES MALL *Book at AAA.com* **Phone:** (336)774-8020

Hotel

$80-$95 All Year

Address: 1985 Hampton Inn Ct **Location:** I-40, exit 189 (Stratford Rd), just s, just e on Hanes Mall Blvd, then just n. **Facility:** 73 one-bedroom standard units. 3 stories, interior corridors. *Bath:* combo or shower only. **Parking:** on-site. **Terms:** cancellation fee imposed. **Amenities:** dual phone lines, voice mail, irons, hair dryers. **Guest Services:** valet and coin laundry, wireless Internet. **Business Services:** PC. **Cards:** AX, DS, MC, VI.

CALL / SOME UNITS

SUNDANCE PLAZA HOTEL AND SPA *Book great rates at AAA.com* **Phone:** (336)723-2911

AAA SAVE

Hotel

$60-$150 All Year

Address: 3050 University Pkwy **Location:** I-40 business route, exit 5C (Cherry St), 3 mi n. **Facility:** 194 units. 190 one-bedroom standard units. 4 one-bedroom suites. 4 stories, interior corridors. *Bath:* combo or shower only. **Parking:** on-site. **Amenities:** CD players, voice mail, safes (fee), irons, hair dryers. **Pool(s):** outdoor. **Leisure Activities:** exercise room, spa. **Guest Services:** valet and coin laundry, airport transportation-Piedmont-Triad International & Smith-Reynolds airports, wireless Internet. **Business Services:** conference facilities, PC. **Cards:** AX, CB, DC, DS, MC, VI. **Free Special Amenities: expanded continental breakfast and high-speed Internet.**

/ SOME UNITS FEE

WINGATE BY WYNDHAM *Book at AAA.com* **Phone:** (336)714-2800

Hotel

$99-$149 All Year

Address: 125 S Main St **Location:** I-40 business route, exit 5D, just n. **Facility:** 112 one-bedroom standard units. 5 stories, interior corridors. *Bath:* combo or shower only. **Parking:** on-site and valet. **Amenities:** video games (fee), high-speed Internet, dual phone lines, voice mail, safes, irons, hair dryers. **Leisure Activities:** whirlpool, exercise room. **Guest Services:** valet laundry, wireless Internet. **Business Services:** meeting rooms, business center. **Cards:** AX, CB, DC, DS, JC, MC, VI.

ASK FEE CALL / SOME UNITS

WHERE TO DINE

BERNARDIN'S *Menu on AAA.com* **Phone:** 336/768-9365

American
$7-$27

Contemporary American cuisine is served in a casually elegant atmosphere. The menu lists seafood, veal, lamb, beef, poultry and pasta choices. Dressy casual. **Bar:** Full bar. **Reservations:** accepted. **Hours:** 11:30 am-2 & 5-9 pm, Fri-10 pm, Sat 5 pm-10 pm. Closed: 11/26, 12/25; also Sun. **Address:** 373 Jonestown Rd **Location:** Jct US 421, just ne; in Center Stop Shopping Center. **Parking:** on-site. **Cards:** AX, MC, VI.

BILLY BOB'S SILVER DINER **Phone:** 336/768-0654

American
$6-$13

Step back into the 1950s at the classic-style diner offering burgers, salads and such comfort foods as meatloaf and grilled sirloin tips. For dessert, choose from a list of tasty pies and cakes, or opt for one of the ice cream concoctions. Service is friendly and efficient. Casual dress. **Bar:** Beer & wine. **Hours:** 7 am-10 pm, Fri & Sat-midnight. **Address:** 1650 Hanes Mall Blvd **Location:** US 421, exit Jonestown Rd, just s, then just e. **Parking:** on-site. **Cards:** DS, MC, VI.

BLEU RESTAURANT & BAR **Phone:** 336/760-2026

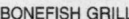

American
$5-$26

Known locally for their tasty fare, daily drink specials and lively atmosphere, the casually upscale eatery offers a seasonally changing menu with such favorites as grilled porkloin in wild mushroom bisque, seared tuna in a chili-soy vinaigrette and grilled salmon with a pecan vinaigrette. Dressy casual. **Bar:** Full bar. **Reservations:** accepted. **Hours:** 11 am-10 pm, Fri & Sat-11 pm, Sun 10:30 am-10 pm. Closed: 1/1, 11/26, 12/25. **Address:** 3425 Frontis St **Location:** I-40, exit 189 (Stratford Rd), just s on Stratford Rd, then just e. **Parking:** on-site. **Cards:** AX, DS, MC, VI.

BONEFISH GRILL **Phone:** 336/724-4518

Seafood
$13-$20

Fish is the house specialty, and the menu and nightly specials offer a variety of choices. Well-prepared food is cooked to perfection. Service is casual in nature, and the staff is skilled and attentive. Casual dress. **Bar:** Full bar. **Reservations:** accepted. **Hours:** 4 pm-close. Closed: 11/26, 12/25. **Address:** 300 S Stratford Rd **Location:** I-40, exit 189 (Stratford Rd), 2.2 mi n. **Parking:** on-site. **Cards:** AX, DC, DS, MC, VI.

BURKE STREET PIZZA **Phone:** 336/721-0011

Pizza
$3-$8

The tiny pizzeria offers pizza with a wide array of toppings as well as chicken pesto, sandwiches, wings in six flavors and the "almost famous" fried ravioli. Dine in, carry out or delivery service available. Casual dress. **Bar:** Beer only. **Hours:** 11 am-10 pm, Thurs-Sat to 3 am. Closed major holidays. **Address:** 1140 Burke St **Location:** I-40 business route, exit 5B, just n on Broad St, 0.4 mi w on W 1st St, then just n. **Parking:** on-site. **Cards:** AX, MC, VI.

CHA DA THAI **Phone:** 336/659-8466

Thai
$5-$14

The bright, cheerful cafe prepares fresh, colorful and well-presented creations. Guests are seated amid traditional Thai artwork on wood-paneled walls. Casual dress. **Bar:** Beer & wine. **Hours:** 11 am-3 & 5-10 pm, Fri-11 pm, Sat 5 pm-11 pm, Sun noon-10 pm. Closed: 7/4, 12/25. **Address:** 420-J Jonestown Rd **Location:** US 421, exit Jonestown Rd, just n; in New Town Shopping Center. **Parking:** on-site. **Cards:** AX, MC, VI.

CITIES GRILL & BAR **Phone:** 336/765-9027

American
$6-$22

A lengthy menu of American favorites and some Greek specialties are offered in a casual, family-friendly setting marked by a sleek cityscape decor. In addition to grilled steaks, options include Southwest-style chicken, grilled salmon and homemade lasagna, among others. Casual dress. **Bar:** Full bar. **Hours:** 11 am-10 pm, Fri-10:30 pm, Sat 3 pm-10:30 pm. Closed major holidays. **Address:** 2438 S Stratford Rd **Location:** I-40, exit 189 (Stratford Rd), 2 mi s. **Parking:** on-site. **Cards:** AX, DS, MC, VI.

CORBIN'S BAR & GRILL **Phone:** 336/768-3301

American
$7-$13

Typical bar munchies, like burgers, wraps, wings, hoagies and sandwiches, are served in a casual setting. Casual dress. **Bar:** Full bar. **Hours:** 11 am-11 pm, Mon-10 pm, Fri & Sat-2 am. Closed: 12/25; also Sun. **Address:** 520 Hanes Mall Blvd **Location:** I-40, exit 189 (Stratford Rd), just s, then just e; in Pavilions Shopping Center. **Parking:** on-site. **Cards:** DS, MC, VI.

DYNASTY BUFFET **Phone:** 336/659-3868

Chinese
$6-$11

At the end of a shopping center, the restaurant specializes in all-you-can-eat Chinese buffets for lunch and dinner. Cooked-to-order stations line up additional selections. Menu service is an option. Casual dress. **Bar:** Beer & wine. **Hours:** 11 am-10 pm, Fri & Sat-11 pm. **Address:** 1086 Hanes Mall Blvd **Location:** I-40, exit 189 (Stratford Rd), just s, then 0.5 mi w; in Hanes Point Shopping Center. **Parking:** on-site. **Cards:** AX, DS, MC, VI.

JIMMY'S SEAFOOD & OYSTER BAR **Phone:** 336/659-1490

Seafood
$9-$25

Although the restaurant specializes in seafood, the menu also lists a few steak, chicken and pasta selections. Well-prepared food is broiled, blackened, deep-fried or grilled. The dining room's nautical theme is associated with harvesting from the ocean. The staff is friendly and helpful. For dessert, try the signature homemade carrot cake. Casual dress. **Bar:** Full bar. **Hours:** 11 am-10 pm, Fri-11 pm, Sat 3 pm-11 pm. Closed: 11/26, 12/25. **Address:** 3440 Frontis St **Location:** I-40, exit 189 (Stratford Rd), just s. **Parking:** on-site. **Cards:** AX, DS, MC, VI.

MARY'S, OF COURSE CAFE **Phone:** 336/725-5764

American
$6-$9

In a shopping center, the eclectic little eatery displays original artwork on the walls and vintage toys as part of its colorful decor. Among homemade lunches are many vegetarian selections. Casual dress. **Hours:** 9:30 am-3 pm, Sat from 10 am, Sun 10 am-2 pm. Closed major holidays; also Mon. **Address:** 301 Brookstown Ave, Suite 100 **Location:** I-40 business route, exit 5C (Cherry St) eastbound, just e on High St, just s on Marshall St, then just e; exit westbound, just w on 1st St, just s on Marshall St, then just e; in Brookstown Centro. **Parking:** on-site. **Cards:** AX, DS, MC, VI.

THE OLD FOURTH STREET FILLING STATION **Phone:** 336/724-7600

American
$6-$23

Occupying a former gas station in the historic West End neighborhood, this family-friendly hangout is known for its tasty, comfort food and patio dining. The menu includes sandwiches, burgers and salads as well as seafood, pasta and chicken entrees. The shrimp and grits is a perennial favorite, as are the crab cakes. Casual dress. **Bar:** Full bar. **Reservations:** accepted. **Hours:** 11 am-10 pm, Fri & Sat-11 pm, Sun 10 am-9 pm. Closed major holidays. **Address:** 871 W Fourth St **Location:** I-40 business route, exit 5B (Basin Bay), 0.5 mi n on Broad St, then just w. **Parking:** on-site. **Cards:** AX, DC, DS, MC, VI.

OYSTER BAY SEAFOOD RESTAURANT **Phone:** 336/659-0388

Seafood
$6-$16

In a shopping center, the casual restaurant specializes in deep-fried and broiled seafood. Dining amid a Key West-themed atmosphere is relaxed and informal. Staffers are pleasant and accommodating. Casual dress. **Bar:** Beer & wine. **Reservations:** accepted. **Hours:** 11 am-9 pm, Fri & Sat-10 pm, Sun 11:30 am-9 pm. Closed: major holidays; also 12/24. **Address:** 576 Hanes Mall Blvd **Location:** I-40, exit 189 (Stratford Rd), just s, then 0.6 mi e; in Pavilions Shopping Center. **Parking:** on-site. **Cards:** AX, MC, VI.

CALL

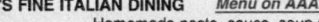

PAUL'S FINE ITALIAN DINING ***Menu on AAA.com*** **Phone:** 336/768-2645

Italian
$6-$24

Homemade pasta, sauce, soup and dessert are served in this popular, but intimate and relaxing, restaurant, where Northern and Southern Italian cuisine makes quite a splash. Tasty lobster ravioli in a creamy sherry sauce is one of the house specials. Casual dress. **Bar:** Full bar. **Reservations:** suggested. **Hours:** 11:30 am-2 & 5-10 pm, Fri-11 pm, Sat 5 pm-11 pm, Sun 4:30 pm-9:30 pm. Closed major holidays; also 12/24. **Address:** 3443-B Robinhood Rd **Location:** I-40 business route, exit 2B, 2.5 mi n on Silas Creek Pkwy N, then 0.8 mi w; in Robinhood Center. **Parking:** on-site. **Cards:** AX, DC, MC, VI.

RESTAURANT J BASUL NOBLE **Phone:** 336/777-8477

Continental
$6-$35

Diners can taste French-Mediterranean flavors in meat and seafood dishes grilled California-style in open oak-hickory, wood-fired ovens. Dressy casual. **Bar:** Full bar. **Reservations:** suggested. **Hours:** 11:30 am-2:30 & 5:30-10 pm, Fri & Sat-11 pm. Closed: major holidays; also 12/24, Sun. **Address:** 380 Knollwood St **Location:** I-40 business route, exit 3A, just s; in Bank of America building. **Parking:** on-site. **Cards:** AX, DC, DS, MC, VI.

RYAN'S RESTAURANT, STEAKS - CHOPS - SEAFOOD **Phone:** 336/724-6132

Steak & Seafood
$18-$35

The popular, rustic and well-established restaurant's comfortable surroundings overlook a wooded stream. Guests pair lobsters from the tank with wines from an extensive list. Knowledgeable staffers provide friendly service. Dressy casual. **Bar:** Full bar. **Reservations:** suggested. **Hours:** 5 pm-10 pm, Fri & Sat-10:30 pm. Closed: major holidays; also 12/24, Sun. **Address:** 719 Coliseum Dr **Location:** I-40 business route, exit 5C (Cherry St), 2.3 mi n on University Pkwy, then just w. **Parking:** on-site. **Cards:** AX, MC, VI.

SAGEBRUSH STEAKHOUSE **Phone:** 336/377-2448

American
$5-$19

Born from the spirit of Texas cattle drives, the restaurant presents a menu of hearty steaks, prime rib, chicken, seafood and baby back ribs. Yummy desserts merit a splurge. Guests can call ahead to facilitate seating. Casual dress. **Bar:** Full bar. **Hours:** 11 am-10 pm, Fri & Sat-11 pm. Closed: 12/25. **Address:** 5920 University Pkwy **Location:** US 52, exit 115A, just e. **Parking:** on-site. **Cards:** AX, DC, DS, MC, VI.

CALL

SALEM TAVERN DINING ROOM **Phone:** 336/748-8585

American
$6-$23

Hearty portions of Continental food and friendly service from period-costumed staff in candlelit Moravian-style dining rooms make the restaurant a good choice. A 15 percent service charge is added to each bill. Casual dress. **Bar:** Full bar. **Reservations:** suggested, for dinner. **Hours:** 11:30 am-2 & 5-9 pm, Fri-9:30 pm, Sat 11:30 am-2:30 & 5-9:30 pm, Sun-2 pm. Closed: 1/1, 12/24, 12/25. **Address:** 736 S Main St **Location:** In Old Salem Historical District. **Parking:** street. **Cards:** AX, MC, VI. **Historic**

SOUTH BY SOUTHWEST **Phone:** 336/727-0800

Southwestern
$12-$21

Mexican guitar music plays in the background of the relaxed and comfortable dining room, which is reminiscent of a hacienda. The chef prepares innovative, upscale Southwestern fare to order using fresh ingredients. Casual dress. **Bar:** Full bar. **Hours:** 5:30 pm-10 pm. Closed major holidays; also Sun & Mon. **Address:** 241 S Marshall St **Location:** I-40 business route, exit 5C (Cherry St) eastbound, just e, then s; exit 5C (Cherry St) westbound, just w on 1st St, then just s. **Parking:** on-site. **Cards:** AX, DS, MC, VI.

SZECHUAN PALACE **Phone:** 336/768-7123

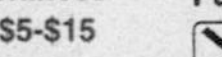

Chinese
$5-$15

The menu puts forth a wide selection of prepared-to-order dishes, with spices adjusted according to the guest's preferences and taste. The staff is knowledgeable about menu preparations and attentive to the guest. The setting is casual. Sunday guests can sample from the lunch buffet. Casual dress. **Bar:** Beer & wine. **Reservations:** accepted. **Hours:** 11 am-9:30 pm, Fri-10 pm, Sat noon-10 pm, Sun noon-9 pm. Closed: 11/26, 12/25. **Address:** 3040 Healy Dr **Location:** I-40, exit 189 (Stratford Rd), 0.7 mi n, then just w. **Parking:** on-site. **Cards:** AX, DC, DS, MC, VI.

TWIN CITY CHOP HOUSE **Phone:** 336/748-8600

Steak
$8-$36

Guests can follow up a well-prepared beef or seafood entree with one of the tasty desserts, which are big enough to share. The staff delivers seamless service in the attractive and sophisticated dining room. Dressy casual. **Bar:** Full bar. **Reservations:** accepted. **Hours:** 11:30 am-10 pm, Sat from 4:30 pm. Closed: major holidays; also 12/24, Sun. **Address:** 115 S Main St **Location:** I-40 business route, exit 5D, just n. **Parking:** on-site. **Cards:** AX, DC, DS, MC, VI.

TWIN CITY DINER **Phone:** 336/724-4203

American
$7-$16

The moderately upscale diner has a varied menu and a good array of homemade desserts. Casual dress. **Bar:** Full bar. **Reservations:** accepted. **Hours:** 11 am-11 pm, Sat from noon. Closed: 7/4, 11/26, 12/25; also Sun. **Address:** 1425 W 1st St, Suite A **Location:** I-40 business route, exit 4B (First St) westbound, just n; exit 4A (Cloverdale Ave) eastbound, just n, then just e; in West End Center. **Parking:** on-site. **Cards:** AX, MC, VI.

VILLAGE TAVERN **Phone:** 336/760-8686

American
$8-$25

Although diners could make a meal of the tasty fried potato chips, doing so would make them miss out on the fresh fish entrees, wood-oven pizza, prime rib, steak, hamburgers, sandwiches and excellent soup and snacks. The service is friendly and attentive. Casual dress. **Bar:** Full bar. **Hours:** 11 am-10 pm, Fri & Sat-11 pm, Sun 10 am-10 pm. Closed: 11/26, 12/25. **Address:** 2000 Griffith Rd **Location:** I-40, exit 189 (Stratford Rd), just s, then just e. **Parking:** on-site. **Cards:** AX, DC, MC, VI.

THE VINEYARDS RESTAURANT **Phone:** 336/748-0269

Continental
$12-$30

Guests can dine in intimate country French surroundings on what was once part of the Reynolds estate, built in 1912. The cuisine is Continental, the pasta homemade and the steak hand-cut. A patio opens for dining in season. Private dining facilities are available. Dressy casual. **Bar:** Full bar. **Reservations:** suggested. **Hours:** 5 pm-10 pm. Closed: 1/1, 11/26, 12/25; also Sun. **Address:** 120 Reynolda Village **Location:** I-40 business route, exit 5C (Cherry St), 2.3 mi n on University Pkwy, 1.2 mi w on Coliseum Dr, then 0.7 mi n on Reynolda Rd; in Reynolda Village. **Parking:** on-site. **Cards:** AX, DC, DS, MC, VI.

ZEVELY HOUSE **Phone:** 336/725-6666

American
$16-$26

In season, patrons are invited to dine in the garden of the restored, early-19th-century historic house. The menu lists preparations of beef, seafood and chicken, and desserts include a tasty assortment of cakes and pies. Service is pleasant and attentive. Casual dress. **Bar:** Full bar. **Reservations:** suggested. **Hours:** 5:30 pm-9 pm, Sun 11 am-2 pm. Closed: 12/25; also Mon. **Address:** 901 W 4th St **Location:** I-40 business route, exit 5B, 0.5 mi n on Broad St, then just w. **Parking:** on-site. **Cards:** AX, DC, DS, MC, VI. **Historic**

WINTERVILLE pop. 2,791

WHERE TO DINE

WIMPIE'S STEAM BAR & CAJUN CAFE **Phone:** 252/355-4220

Seafood
$6-$19

Steamed and fried seafood are house specialties at the casual eatery. Soft-shell crabs, barbecue shrimp, shrimp Creole, jambalaya and steamer buckets are popular choices. A chef's special is featured nightly. Casual dress. **Bar:** Full bar. **Hours:** 5 pm-10 pm, Fri & Sat-midnight. Closed major holidays; also Sun. **Address:** 206 Main St **Location:** Jct SR 11, 0.4 mi e. **Parking:** on-site. **Cards:** AX, MC, VI.

WRIGHTSVILLE BEACH pop. 2,593 (See map and index starting on p. 834)

WHERE TO STAY

BLOCKADE RUNNER BEACH RESORT *Book great rates at AAA.com* **Phone:** (910)256-2251 33

Hotel
$139-$419 3/29-11/30
$99-$219 12/1-3/28

Address: 275 Waynick Blvd **Location:** Oceanfront. 0.5 mi s on US 76. **Facility:** Smoke free premises. 150 one-bedroom standard units, some with whirlpools. 2-7 stories, interior corridors. *Bath:* some combo or shower only. **Parking:** on-site. **Terms:** 2 night minimum stay - weekends, age restrictions may apply, cancellation fee imposed. **Amenities:** voice mail, irons, hair dryers. **Pool(s):** heated outdoor. **Leisure Activities:** sauna, whirlpool, boat dock, fishing, rental bicycles, exercise room, volleyball. *Fee:* charter fishing. **Guest Services:** area transportation, wireless Internet. **Business Services:** conference facilities. **Cards:** AX, DC, DS, MC, VI.

ASK / SOME UNITS FEE VCR

HOLIDAY INN SUNSPREE RESORT OF WRIGHTSVILLE BEACH *Book great rates at AAA.com* **Phone:** (910)256-2231 31

SAVE

Hotel
$129-$419 All Year

Address: 1706 N Lumina Ave **Location:** 1 mi n on US 74. **Facility:** 184 units. 176 one-bedroom standard units, some with whirlpools. 8 one-bedroom suites with whirlpools. 7 stories, interior corridors. *Bath:* combo or shower only. **Parking:** on-site. **Terms:** 3 day cancellation notice. **Amenities:** video games (fee), CD players, voice mail, safes, irons, hair dryers. **Pool(s):** outdoor, heated indoor. **Leisure Activities:** whirlpools, recreation programs in summer, playground, exercise room, horseshoes, volleyball. *Fee:* game room. **Guest Services:** valet and coin laundry, wireless Internet. **Business Services:** conference facilities, business center. **Cards:** AX, CB, DC, DS, JC, MC, VI. **Free Special Amenities: high-speed Internet.**

(See map and index starting on p. 834)

SUMMER SANDS MOTEL Phone: 910/256-4175 32

Motel
Rates not provided

Address: 104 S Lumina Ave **Location:** US 76, just e of causeway. **Facility:** Smoke free premises. 32 one-bedroom standard units with efficiencies. 4 stories, exterior corridors. **Parking:** on-site. **Terms:** office hours 7 am-11 pm. **Amenities:** voice mail, hair dryers. **Pool(s):** outdoor. **Guest Services:** coin laundry.

WHERE TO DINE

22 NORTH RESTAURANT **Phone:** 910/509-0177 24

Seafood
$7-$19

Fresh seafood is prepared with flair at the casual, colorful eatery. Nightly specials join menu regulars of steak, chicken and pasta. Casual dress. **Bar:** Full bar. **Hours:** 5 pm-10 pm. **Address:** 22 N Lumina Ave **Location:** Jct US 76, just n. **Parking:** on-site. **Cards:** AX, DS, MC, VI.

BLUEWATER GRILL **Phone:** 910/256-8500

Seafood
$5-$24

The beach-themed restaurant's waterfront deck is the perfect place to take in a picturesque sunset. Mouthwatering cuisine, including fresh seafood dishes and homemade Key lime pie, has a Caribbean flair. Tasty margaritas are worth a try. Casual dress. **Bar:** Full bar. **Reservations:** accepted. **Hours:** 11:30 am-11 pm; hours vary off season. Closed: 1/1, 12/24, 12/25. **Address:** 4 Marina St **Location:** Jct US 76, just s on Keel St, just w on Causeway St, then just s; on Intracoastal Waterway. **Parking:** on-site. **Cards:** AX, MC, VI.

THE OCEANIC **Phone:** 910/256-5551 26

Seafood
$6-$26

The oceanfront restaurant enables guests to take in panoramic water views while sampling the seafood. When the weather permits, the pier is a preferred seating spot. Casual dress. **Bar:** Full bar. **Hours:** 11:30 am-10 pm, Sun from 10 am; hours may vary off season. Closed: 12/25. **Address:** 703 S Lumina Ave **Location:** US 76, 1.1 mi s on Waynick Blvd, then just e on Nathan St. **Parking:** on-site. **Cards:** AX, MC, VI

(See map and index starting on p. 834)

SOUTH BEACH GRILL **Phone:** 910/256-4646 (25)

American
$5-$22

Guests can enjoy lunch on the patio or dinner in the casual, intimate dining room. The menu lists nightly chef's specials, as well as chicken, beef and fresh seafood preparations. Casual dress. **Bar:** Full bar. **Reservations:** accepted. **Hours:** 11 am-4 & 5-10 pm; hours may vary off season. Closed: 12/24, 12/25; also Mon off season. **Address:** 100 S Lumina Ave **Location:** US 76, just e from causeway. **Parking:** on-site. **Cards:** DS, MC, VI.

YADKINVILLE pop. 2,818

— WHERE TO STAY —

DAYS INN *Book at AAA.com* **Phone:** 336/679-5000

Hotel
Rates not provided

Address: 220 Sharon Dr **Location:** US 421, exit 257, just s on US 601, then just e. **Facility:** 69 one-bedroom standard units, some with whirlpools. 2 stories (no elevator), interior corridors. *Bath:* combo or shower only. **Parking:** on-site. **Amenities:** hair dryers. **Pool(s):** outdoor. **Guest Services:** coin laundry. **Business Services:** meeting rooms.

CALL / SOME UNITS FEE

YANCEYVILLE pop. 2,091

— WHERE TO STAY —

DAYS INN *Book at AAA.com* **Phone:** (336)694-9494

Motel
$65-$170 All Year

Address: 1858 NC Hwy 86 N **Location:** Jct SR 62, 1.6 mi nw on US 158/SR 86. **Facility:** 45 one-bedroom standard units, some with efficiencies (no utensils). 2 stories (no elevator), exterior corridors. *Bath:* combo or shower only. **Parking:** on-site. **Amenities:** hair dryers. **Pool(s):** outdoor. **Guest Services:** coin laundry. **Cards:** AX, CB, DC, DS, MC, VI.

ASK / SOME UNITS FEE  

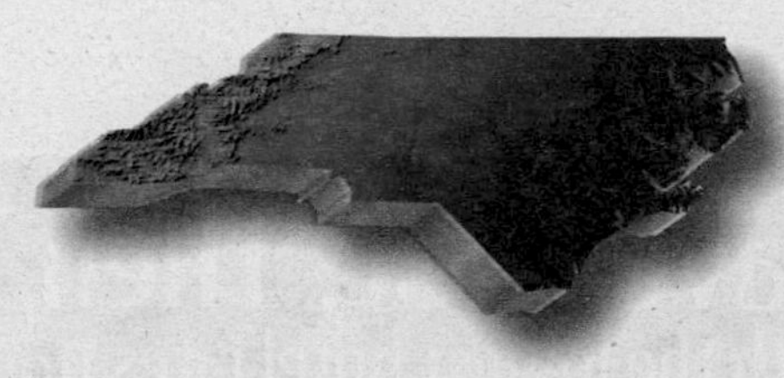

Cypress Gardens,
Moncks Corner

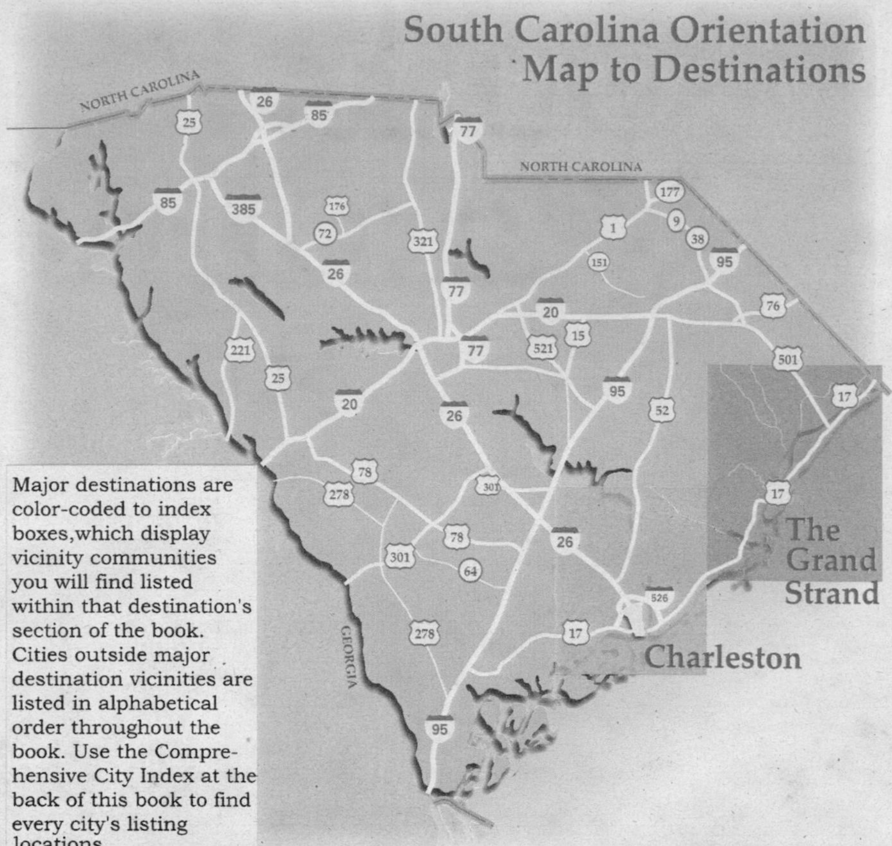
South Carolina Orientation
Map to Destinations
NORTH CAROLINA
NORTH CAROLINA
GEORGIA
The Grand Strand
Charleston
Major destinations are color-coded to index boxes,which display vicinity communities you will find listed within that destination's section of the book. Cities outside major destination vicinities are listed in alphabetical order throughout the book. Use the Comprehensive City Index at the back of this book to find every city's listing locations.

AIKEN pop. 25,337

WHERE TO STAY

COUNTRY INN & SUITES BY CARLSON — *Book at AAA.com* — **Phone:** (803)649-4024

Hotel
$89-$101 All Year

Address: 3270 Whiskey Rd **Location:** Jct US 78/302 and SR 19, 2.7 mi se on SR 19. **Facility:** Smoke free premises. 100 units. 54 one-bedroom standard units, some with whirlpools. 45 one- and 1 two-bedroom suites. 3 stories, interior corridors. *Bath:* combo or shower only. **Parking:** on-site. **Amenities:** high-speed Internet, voice mail, irons, hair dryers. **Pool(s):** outdoor. **Leisure Activities:** limited exercise equipment. **Guest Services:** valet and coin laundry, wireless Internet. **Business Services:** business center. **Cards:** AX, CB, DC, DS, JC, MC, VI.

ASK CALL

FAIRFIELD INN & SUITES — *Book great rates at AAA.com* — **Phone:** (803)648-7808

Hotel
$98-$106 All Year

Address: 185 Colony Pkwy **Location:** Jct US 1/78 and SR 19, 1.8 mi s on SR 19, then just e. **Facility:** Smoke free premises. 84 one-bedroom standard units. 3 stories, interior corridors. *Bath:* combo or shower only. **Parking:** on-site. **Terms:** cancellation fee imposed. **Amenities:** high-speed Internet, voice mail, irons, hair dryers. *Some:* CD players. **Pool(s):** heated indoor. **Leisure Activities:** whirlpool, exercise room. **Guest Services:** valet and coin laundry, wireless Internet. **Business Services:** meeting rooms, business center. **Cards:** AX, CB, DC, DS, JC, MC, VI.

/ SOME UNITS

AAA Benefit:
Members save a minimum 5% off the best available rate.

HAMPTON INN — *Book great rates at AAA.com* — **Phone:** (803)648-2525

Hotel
$79-$279 All Year

Address: 100 Tamil Dr Dr **Location:** Jct US 78 and SR 302/19 (Whiskey Rd), 1.5 mi s on SR 19. **Facility:** 66 one-bedroom standard units, some with whirlpools. 3 stories, interior corridors. *Bath:* combo or shower only. **Parking:** on-site. **Terms:** 1-30 night minimum stay, cancellation fee imposed. **Amenities:** voice mail, irons, hair dryers. **Pool(s):** outdoor. **Guest Services:** valet laundry, wireless Internet. **Business Services:** meeting rooms, business center. **Cards:** AX, CB, DC, DS, MC, VI.

CALL    / SOME UNITS

AAA Benefit:
Members save up to 10% everyday!

HOLIDAY INN EXPRESS — *Book at AAA.com* — **Phone:** (803)648-0999

Motel
$81-$275 All Year

Address: 155 Colony Pkwy/Whiskey Rd **Location:** Jct US 1/78 and SR 19, 1.8 mi s on SR 19. **Facility:** 99 one-bedroom standard units, some with whirlpools. 2 stories (no elevator), exterior corridors. *Bath:* combo or shower only. **Parking:** on-site. **Terms:** check-in 4 pm, cancellation fee imposed. **Amenities:** high-speed Internet, dual phone lines, voice mail, irons, hair dryers. **Pool(s):** outdoor. **Leisure Activities:** whirlpool, exercise room. **Guest Services:** valet and coin laundry, wireless Internet. **Business Services:** meeting rooms, business center. **Cards:** AX, CB, DC, DS, JC, MC, VI.

ASK   / SOME UNITS FEE 

QUALITY INN & SUITES *Book great rates at AAA.com* **Phone:** (803)641-1100

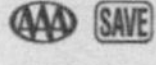

Motel
$55-$80 All Year

Address: 3608 Richland Ave W **Location:** Jct US 1/78 and SR 19, 2.9 mi w on US 1/78. **Facility:** 68 one-bedroom standard units, some with whirlpools. 2 stories (no elevator), exterior corridors. **Parking:** on-site. **Amenities:** safes (fee), irons, hair dryers. **Pool(s):** outdoor. **Leisure Activities:** whirlpool, exercise room. **Guest Services:** coin laundry, wireless Internet. **Business Services:** meeting rooms, fax (fee). **Cards:** AX, DC, DS, MC, VI. **Free Special Amenities: expanded continental breakfast and high-speed Internet.**

/ SOME UNITS FEE

SUPER 8 MOTEL-AIKEN *Book at AAA.com* **Phone:** (803)641-8800

Hotel
$72-$270 All Year

Address: 2577 Whiskey Rd **Location:** Jct US 78 and SR 302/19 (Whiskey Rd), 1.7 mi s on SR 19. **Facility:** 50 one-bedroom standard units, some with whirlpools. 2 stories (no elevator), interior corridors. *Bath:* combo or shower only. **Parking:** on-site. **Amenities:** hair dryers. **Pool(s):** outdoor. **Guest Services:** coin laundry, wireless Internet. **Business Services:** PC, fax (fee). **Cards:** AX, DC, DS, MC, VI.

ASK / SOME UNITS FEE

THE TOWN & COUNTRY INN BED, BREAKFAST AND STABLES **Phone:** 803/642-0270

Bed & Breakfast
Rates not provided

Address: 2340 Sizemore Cir **Location:** Jct US 78 and SR 302/19 (Whiskey Rd), 2.3 mi s on SR 19, then just w. **Facility:** In the heart of horse country, the relaxing inn offers four acres of gardens, koi ponds and paddocks, and its large rooms have contemporary amenities. Smoke free premises. 5 one-bedroom standard units, some with whirlpools. 2 stories (no elevator), interior corridors. **Parking:** on-site. **Terms:** check-in 4 pm, age restrictions may apply. **Amenities:** video library, irons, hair dryers. **Pool(s):** outdoor. **Leisure Activities:** playground. *Fee:* horseback riding. **Guest Services:** wireless Internet. **Business Services:** PC, fax (fee).

VCR

WHERE TO DINE

FATZ CAFE **Phone:** 803/641-4261

American
$8-$18

Friendly staff and appealing country decor help set the tone for a relaxed and enjoyable dining experience. It's not unusual for guests to wait to be seated at the popular spot, which earns raves for its well-prepared variations on chicken, steak, ribs and pasta, as well as salads and sandwiches. The signature Southern-style peach cobbler served with vanilla ice cream and walnuts is scrumptious. Casual dress. **Bar:** Full bar. **Hours:** 11 am-10 pm, Fri & Sat-11 pm, Sun-9 pm. Closed: 11/26, 12/25. **Address:** 996 Pine Log Rd (SR 78) **Location:** Jct Whiskey Rd (SR 19) and Pine Log Rd (SR 78), just w. **Parking:** on-site. **Cards:** AX, DS, MC, VI.

CALL 

MALIA'S RESTAURANT **Phone:** 803/643-3086

American
$6-$30

The skilled kitchen prepares everything from scratch at the sophisticated, downtown restaurant, where the often-changing menu lists steaks, seafood and chops served with complex sauces and creative sides. Dressy casual. **Bar:** Beer & wine. **Reservations:** suggested. **Hours:** 11:30 am-2 pm, Thurs & Fri also 6 pm-9 pm, Sat 6 pm-9 pm. Closed: 11/26, 12/26; also Sun & Mon. **Address:** 120 Laurens St SW **Location:** Between US 1/78 and Hayne Ave SW; in downtown historic district; just w of center. **Parking:** on-site. **Cards:** AX, DS, MC, VI.

RILEY'S WHITBY BULL **Phone:** 803/641-6227

American
$17-$30

Recently renovated, the circa 1880 Second Empire-style house is a charming dining setting. Flavorful dishes are made with quality ingredients. House specialties include Louisiana shrimp and rice, aged black Angus beef and luscious desserts. Casual dress. **Bar:** Full bar. **Reservations:** required. **Hours:** 5 pm-9 pm, Sun 9 am-1 pm. Closed major holidays; also Mon & Tues. **Address:** 801 E Pine Log Rd **Location:** 1.5 mi e of SR 19 (Whiskey Rd), on SR 302. **Parking:** on-site. **Cards:** AX, CB, DC, DS, MC, VI.

WEST SIDE BOWERY RESTAURANT **Phone:** 803/648-2900

American
$5-$22

A family-friendly atmosphere is achieved with deep booths, stained glass and a collection of curios adorning the comfortable dining room. Popular starters include buffalo chicken wings, grilled steak bits and homemade New England clam chowder. The signature blackened ribeye topped with shrimp and melted jack cheese is sure to please, and fresh seafood preparations also are popular. For dessert, the top pick is caramel granny apple pie. Casual dress. **Bar:** Full bar. **Reservations:** suggested. **Hours:** 11:30 am-10 pm. Closed major holidays; also Sun. **Address:** 151 Bee Ln **Location:** Between US 1 and Park Ave; in Aiken's historic "downtown alley area". **Parking:** street. **Cards:** AX, DS, MC, VI.

ANDERSON pop. 25,514

WHERE TO STAY

COMFORT SUITES *Book at AAA.com* **Phone:** (864)622-1200

Hotel
$85-$115 All Year

Address: 118 Interstate Blvd **Location:** I-85, exit 19B, just n, then just se. **Facility:** Smoke free premises. 60 one-bedroom standard units. 4 stories, interior corridors. *Bath:* combo or shower only. **Parking:** on-site. **Terms:** 3 day cancellation notice. **Amenities:** high-speed Internet, dual phone lines, voice mail, irons, hair dryers. **Pool(s):** heated indoor. **Leisure Activities:** whirlpool, limited exercise equipment. **Guest Services:** valet and coin laundry, wireless Internet. **Business Services:** meeting rooms, business center. **Cards:** AX, DC, DS, MC, VI.

ASK

COUNTRY INN & SUITES *Book at AAA.com* **Phone:** (864)622-2200

Hotel

$90-$180 All Year

Address: 116 Interstate Blvd **Location:** I-85, exit 19B, just n, then just se. **Facility:** 55 units. 45 one-bedroom standard units. 9 one- and 1 two-bedroom suites with whirlpools, some with kitchens. 5 stories, interior corridors. *Bath:* combo or shower only. **Parking:** on-site. **Terms:** cancellation fee imposed. **Amenities:** high-speed Internet, voice mail, irons, hair dryers. **Pool(s):** heated indoor. **Leisure Activities:** limited exercise equipment. **Guest Services:** valet and coin laundry, wireless Internet. **Business Services:** fax (fee). **Cards:** AX, DC, DS, MC, VI.

ASK CALL / SOME UNITS FEE

DAYS INN *Book at AAA.com* **Phone:** (864)375-0375

Motel

$63-$150 All Year

Address: 1007 Smith Mill Rd **Location:** I-85, exit 19A, just se. **Facility:** 52 one-bedroom standard units, some with whirlpools. 2 stories (no elevator), exterior corridors. **Parking:** on-site. **Amenities:** irons, hair dryers. **Pool(s):** outdoor. **Guest Services:** valet laundry, wireless Internet. **Business Services:** fax (fee). **Cards:** AX, DS, MC, VI.

ASK CALL / SOME UNITS FEE

FAIRFIELD INN & SUITES *Book great rates at AAA.com* **Phone:** (864)332-9000

Hotel

$94-$100 All Year

Address: 117 Interstate Blvd **Location:** I-85, exit 19B, just n, then just se. **Facility:** Smoke free premises. 79 one-bedroom standard units. 3 stories, interior corridors. *Bath:* combo or shower only. **Parking:** on-site. **Terms:** cancellation fee imposed. **Amenities:** high-speed Internet, dual phone lines, voice mail, irons, hair dryers. *Some:* CD players. **Pool(s):** outdoor. **Leisure Activities:** whirlpool, limited exercise equipment. **Guest Services:** valet and coin laundry, wireless Internet. **Business Services:** business center. **Cards:** AX, DS, MC, VI.

CALL / SOME UNITS

AAA Benefit:

Members save a minimum 5% off the best available rate.

HAMPTON INN *Book great rates at AAA.com* **Phone:** (864)375-1999

Hotel

$99-$145 All Year

Address: 120 Interstate Blvd **Location:** I-85, exit 19B, just n, then just se. **Facility:** 72 units. 70 one-bedroom standard units, some with whirlpools. 2 one-bedroom suites. 3 stories, interior corridors. *Bath:* combo or shower only. **Parking:** on-site. **Terms:** 1-30 night minimum stay, cancellation fee imposed. **Amenities:** voice mail, irons, hair dryers. **Pool(s):** outdoor. **Leisure Activities:** exercise room. **Guest Services:** valet laundry, wireless Internet. **Business Services:** business center. **Cards:** AX, CB, DC, DS, MC, VI.

CALL / SOME UNITS

AAA Benefit:

Members save up to 10% everyday!

HILTON GARDEN INN ANDERSON *Book great rates at AAA.com* **Phone:** (864)964-0100

Contemporary Hotel

$79-$189 All Year

Address: 115 Destination Blvd **Location:** I-85, exit 19A, just s, then just e. **Facility:** Constructed in 2005, the hotel offers spacious, amenity-rich rooms and public areas just minutes from Lake Hartwell and Clemson University. 124 units. 98 one-bedroom standard units. 26 one-bedroom suites with whirlpools. 5 stories, interior corridors. *Bath:* combo or shower only. **Parking:** on-site. **Terms:** 1-30 night minimum stay, cancellation fee imposed. **Amenities:** video games (fee), high-speed Internet, dual phone lines, voice mail, irons, hair dryers. **Pool(s):** indoor. **Leisure Activities:** whirlpool, exercise room. **Guest Services:** coin laundry. **Business Services:** conference facilities, business center. **Cards:** AX, DC, DS, JC, MC, VI.

CALL / SOME UNITS

Hilton Garden Inn

AAA Benefit:

Members save 5% or more everyday!

HOLIDAY INN EXPRESS *Book great rates at AAA.com* **Phone:** (864)231-0231

AAA SAVE

Hotel

$75-$189 All Year

Address: 410 Alliance Pkwy **Location:** I-85, exit 27, just s on SR 81. **Facility:** 64 one-bedroom standard units, some with whirlpools. 3 stories, interior corridors. *Bath:* combo or shower only. **Parking:** on-site. **Terms:** 2 night minimum stay - seasonal and/or weekends, cancellation fee imposed. **Amenities:** voice mail, irons, hair dryers. **Pool(s):** outdoor. **Leisure Activities:** limited exercise equipment. **Guest Services:** coin laundry, wireless Internet. **Business Services:** meeting rooms, business center. **Cards:** AX, CB, DC, DS, JC, MC, VI. **Free Special Amenities: expanded continental breakfast and high-speed Internet.**

CALL / SOME UNITS FEE

HOLIDAY INN EXPRESS HOTEL & SUITES *Book great rates at AAA.com* **Phone:** (864)226-3312

AAA SAVE

Hotel

$94-$194 All Year

Address: 107 Interstate Blvd **Location:** I-85, exit 19B, just n, then just se. **Facility:** 75 one-bedroom standard units, some with whirlpools. 3 stories, interior corridors. *Bath:* combo or shower only. **Parking:** on-site. **Amenities:** high-speed Internet, dual phone lines, voice mail, irons, hair dryers. **Pool(s):** outdoor. **Leisure Activities:** whirlpool, limited exercise equipment. **Guest Services:** valet and coin laundry, wireless Internet. **Business Services:** meeting rooms, business center. **Cards:** AX, CB, DC, DS, JC, MC, VI. **Free Special Amenities: expanded continental breakfast and high-speed Internet.**

CALL / SOME UNITS

JAMESON INN *Book at AAA.com* **Phone:** (864)375-9800

Motel
$78-$85 All Year

Address: 128 Interstate Blvd **Location:** I-85, exit 19B, just n, then just se. **Facility:** 59 one-bedroom standard units, some with whirlpools. 2 stories (no elevator), exterior corridors. *Bath:* combo or shower only. **Parking:** on-site. **Terms:** cancellation fee imposed. **Amenities:** hair dryers. **Pool(s):** outdoor. **Leisure Activities:** exercise room. **Guest Services:** valet laundry, wireless Internet. **Business Services:** meeting rooms, PC, fax (fee). **Cards:** AX, DC, DS, MC, VI.

ASK CALL / SOME UNITS FEE

LA QUINTA INN ANDERSON *Book great rates at AAA.com* **Phone:** (864)225-3721

Motel
$49-$99 All Year

Address: 3430 Clemson Blvd **Location:** I-85, exit 19A, 2.9 mi se on US 76/SR 28; exit 21 southbound, 2.6 mi s on US 178. **Facility:** 100 one-bedroom standard units. 2 stories (no elevator), exterior corridors. *Bath:* combo or shower only. **Parking:** on-site. **Amenities:** video games (fee), voice mail, irons, hair dryers. **Pool(s):** outdoor. **Guest Services:** valet and coin laundry, wireless Internet. **Business Services:** meeting rooms, fax (fee). **Cards:** AX, CB, DC, DS, MC, VI.

ASK / SOME UNITS

MAINSTAY SUITES **Phone:** 864/226-1112

Hotel
Rates not provided

Address: 151 Civic Center Blvd **Location:** I-85, exit 19A, 2.2 mi se on US 76, then 0.6 mi s. Located next to the civic center. **Facility:** 80 units. 54 one-bedroom standard units with efficiencies. 20 one- and 6 two-bedroom suites with efficiencies. 3 stories, interior corridors. **Parking:** on-site. **Terms:** check-in 4 pm. **Amenities:** voice mail, irons, hair dryers. **Pool(s):** outdoor. **Guest Services:** valet and coin laundry, wireless Internet. **Business Services:** business center.

VCR / SOME UNITS FEE

QUALITY INN-ANDERSON *Book at AAA.com* **Phone:** (864)226-1000

Hotel
$66-$140 All Year

Address: 3509 Clemson Blvd **Location:** I-85, exit 19A, 2.7 mi se on US 76/SR 28 (Clemson Blvd); exit 21 southbound, 2.4 mi s on US 178. Located in a commercial area. **Facility:** 121 units. 119 one-bedroom standard units. 2 one-bedroom suites. 4 stories, interior corridors. **Parking:** on-site. **Terms:** 7 day cancellation notice. **Amenities:** voice mail, irons, hair dryers. **Pool(s):** outdoor. **Leisure Activities:** sauna, exercise room. **Guest Services:** valet and coin laundry, wireless Internet. **Business Services:** meeting rooms, business center. **Cards:** AX, DC, DS, MC, VI.

ASK CALL / SOME UNITS

WHERE TO DINE

CARSON'S STEAK WAREHOUSE & SALOON **Phone:** 864/226-9400

Steak
$6-$19

The rustic dining room is decorated with an array of Western pictures and paraphernalia, road signs and neon beer signs. A model train runs around the dining room on a track suspended from the ceiling. Tables are set with buckets of unshelled peanuts for customers to enjoy. The menu emphasis is on steaks, but a few chicken and seafood items also are offered. The setting is casual and service is informal. The staff is knowledgeable, helpful and accommodating. Casual dress. **Bar:** Full bar. **Hours:** 11 am-10 pm, Fri & Sat-11 pm, Sun-9 pm. Closed: 11/26, 12/25. **Address:** 150 W Beltline Blvd **Location:** I-85, exit 19A, 2.7 mi se on US 76/SR 28 (Clemson Blvd), then just s; exit 21 southbound, 2.4 mi s on US 178, then just s. **Parking:** on-site. **Cards:** AX, DC, DS, MC, VI.

CALL

FATZ CAFE **Phone:** 864/965-0055

American
$7-$19

Friendly staff and appealing country decor help set the tone for a relaxed and enjoyable dining experience. It's not unusual for guests to wait to be seated at the popular spot, which earns raves for its well-prepared variations on chicken, steak, ribs and pasta, as well as salads and sandwiches. The signature Southern-style peach cobbler served with vanilla ice cream and walnuts is scrumptious. Casual dress. **Bar:** Full bar. **Hours:** 11 am-10 pm, Fri & Sat-11 pm, Sun-9 pm. Closed: 11/26, 12/25. **Address:** 105 Interstate Blvd **Location:** I-85, exit 19B, just n. **Parking:** on-site. **Cards:** AX, DS, MC, VI.

CALL

THE GALLEY RESTAURANT **Phone:** 864/287-3215

American
$13-$29

A city favorite for many years, the casual restaurant is nestled at the marina on Lake Hartwell. Patrons savor a variety of well-prepared beef, seafood and specialty dishes like tapas prepared in a hearth-oven. For a special treat, request a seat at the chef's table where you can enjoy watching the skilled kitchen staff prepare the entrees. Casual dress. **Bar:** Full bar. **Reservations:** suggested. **Hours:** 5 pm-10 pm. Closed: 1/1, 12/25; also Sun & Mon. **Address:** 1629 Marina Rd **Location:** I-85, exit 14, 1.2 mi s on SR 187, through traffic light, jct SR 24/187, then 0.3 mi s through residential neighborhood; in Portman Marina. **Parking:** on-site. **Cards:** AX, MC, VI.

CALL

NAMI ASIAN BISTRO **Phone:** 864/287-3219

Pacific Rim
$7-$21

Japanese cuisine is creatively and artistically-prepared at the lakefront restaurant. Along with poultry, beef and seafood entrees, offerings include a good selection of sushi. Gracious service and subtle East Asian decor lend to the upscale atmosphere. Casual dress. **Bar:** Full bar. **Reservations:** suggested, weekends. **Hours:** 5:30 pm-10 pm. Closed major holidays; also Sun & Mon. **Address:** 1629 Marina Rd **Location:** I-85, exit 14, 1.2 mi s on SR 187, through traffic light at jct SR 24/187, then 0.3 mi s through residential neighborhood; in Portman Marina. **Parking:** on-site. **Cards:** AX, MC, VI.

CALL

ROMANO'S ITALIAN RESTAURANT Phone: 864/332-0434

Italian
$6-$33

Just south of the interstate, the bright, family-run institution features an array of Italian standards, as well as the chef's creative dishes. Among popular dinner entrees are veggie lasagna, Boursin-stuffed chicken and Maryland-style crab cakes. The lunch menu offers some entree specials but is heavily weighted toward submarine sandwiches, a particularly big draw because of the great-tasting soft bread. A children's menu is available. Casual dress. **Bar:** Beer & wine. **Reservations:** accepted. **Hours:** 11 am-2 & 4-10 pm, Sat from 4 pm. Closed: 11/26, 12/25; also Sun. **Address:** 4126 Clemson Blvd **Location:** I-85, exit 19A, 1.4 mi se on US 76/SR 28 **Parking:** on-site. **Cards:** AX, DS, MC, VI.

SULLIVAN'S METROPOLITAN GRILL ***Menu on AAA.com*** **Phone:** 864/226-8945

Continental
$6-$28

Hand-cut meats and fresh seafood from around the globe are fashioned into "boldly prepared American cuisine with a touch of Mediterranean." The trendy, downtown restaurant resides in the restored historic Sullivan Building. Freshly baked bread with garlic cloves and a drizzle of olive oil and herbs comes with an array of inventive spreads. Service is prompt and knowledgeable, and an extensive wine list is offered. The pastry chef whips up delicious creations. Casual dress. **Bar:** Full bar. **Reservations:** suggested. **Hours:** 11:30 am-2:30 & 5:30-10 pm, Sat from 5:30 pm. Closed major holidays; also Sun. **Address:** 208 S Main St **Location:** Just s; center; next to Courthouse. **Parking:** street. **Cards:** AX, DC, DS, MC, VI.

TUCKER'S **Phone:** 864/226-5474

American
$6-$19

Traditional, well-prepared menu selections are served in an upscale setting where dark woods help define the room's distinctive atmosphere. Casual dress. **Bar:** Full bar. **Hours:** 11 am-10 pm, Fri & Sat-11 pm, Sun 10 am-9 pm. Closed: 11/26, 12/25. **Address:** 3501 Clemson Blvd **Location:** I-85, exit 19A, 2.7 mi se on US 76/SR 28 (Clemson Blvd); exit 21 southbound, 2.4 mi s on US 178. **Parking:** on-site. **Cards:** AX, DC, DS, MC, VI.

CALL

AWENDAW *—See Charleston p. 909.*

BARNWELL pop. 5,035

WHERE TO STAY

DAYS INN *Book at AAA.com* **Phone:** (803)541-5000

Motel
$67-$110 All Year

Address: 10747 Dunbarton Blvd **Location:** Jct US 278/SR 64, 0.6 mi sw on SR 64. Located in a rural area. **Facility:** 31 one-bedroom standard units, some with whirlpools. 2 stories (no elevator), exterior corridors. *Bath:* combo or shower only. **Parking:** on-site. **Terms:** 7 day cancellation notice. **Amenities:** irons, hair dryers. **Pool(s):** outdoor. **Guest Services:** coin laundry, wireless Internet. **Business Services:** business center. **Cards:** AX, CB, DC, DS, MC, VI.

ASK / SOME UNITS

BATESBURG-LEESVILLE pop. 5,517

WHERE TO STAY

THE ABLE HOUSE INN **Phone:** 803/532-2763

Bed & Breakfast
$95-$110 All Year

Address: 244 E Columbia Ave **Location:** Jct US 1/178, 1.6 mi ne on US 1 (E Columbia Ave). **Facility:** The inn features nicely furnished and decorated guest rooms, with telephones available upon request. Smoke free premises. 5 one-bedroom standard units. 2 stories (no elevator), interior corridors. *Bath:* combo or shower only. **Parking:** on-site. **Terms:** check-in 4 pm, age restrictions may apply, 5 day cancellation notice-fee imposed. **Pool(s):** outdoor. **Guest Services:** wireless Internet. **Business Services:** administrative services, fax (fee).

/ SOME UNITS

BEAUFORT pop. 12,950

WHERE TO STAY

THE BEAUFORT INN ***Book great rates at AAA.com*** **Phone:** (843)379-4667

Historic Bed & Breakfast
$165-$425 All Year

Address: 809 Port Republic St **Location:** Between Scott and West sts; downtown; in historic district. **Facility:** Its inviting porches furnished with wicker chairs, this stately, renovated Victorian is imbued with Southern charm. Smoke free premises. 26 units. 21 one-bedroom standard units. 5 one-bedroom suites. 1-3 stories, interior/exterior corridors. *Bath:* combo or shower only. **Parking:** on-site. **Terms:** age restrictions may apply, 7 day cancellation notice-fee imposed. **Amenities:** video library, high-speed Internet, voice mail, irons, hair dryers. *Some:* DVD players, safes. **Guest Services:** valet laundry, wireless Internet. **Business Services:** meeting rooms, fax (fee). **Cards:** AX, DS, MC, VI. **Free Special Amenities: expanded continental breakfast and high-speed Internet.**

CALL VCR / SOME UNITS

BEST WESTERN SEA ISLAND INN *Book great rates at AAA.com* **Phone:** (843)522-2090

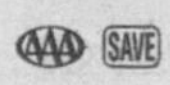

Hotel
$110-$170 All Year

Address: 1015 Bay St **Location:** Jct New Castle St; downtown. **Facility:** Smoke free premises. 43 one-bedroom standard units. 2 stories (no elevator), exterior corridors. **Parking:** on-site. **Terms:** cancellation fee imposed. **Amenities:** high-speed Internet, voice mail, irons, hair dryers. **Pool(s):** outdoor. **Leisure Activities:** jogging, exercise room. **Guest Services:** valet laundry, wireless Internet. **Business Services:** meeting rooms, business center. **Cards:** AX, CB, DC, DS, MC, VI. **Free Special Amenities: newspaper and room upgrade (subject to availability with advance reservations).**

AAA Benefit:
Members save up to 20%, plus 10% bonus points with rewards program.

COMFORT SUITES *Book at AAA.com* **Phone:** (843)379-9400

Hotel
$110-$200 All Year

Address: 131 Big John Rd **Location:** Jct US 21/SR 170, 0.8 mi se on SR 170. **Facility:** Smoke free premises. 70 one-bedroom standard units, some with whirlpools. 3 stories, interior corridors. *Bath:* combo or shower only. **Parking:** on-site. **Amenities:** voice mail, irons, hair dryers. **Pool(s):** heated indoor. **Leisure Activities:** whirlpool, exercise room. **Guest Services:** coin laundry, wireless Internet. **Business Services:** meeting rooms, business center. **Cards:** AX, CB, DC, DS, JC, MC, VI.

COUNTRY INN & SUITES-BEAUFORT WEST *Book great rates at AAA.com* **Phone:** 843/379-4000

Hotel
Rates not provided

Address: 2450 Boundary St **Location:** Jct SR 170, just n on US 21. **Facility:** 77 units. 56 one-bedroom standard units, some with whirlpools. 21 one-bedroom suites. 3 stories, interior corridors. *Bath:* combo or shower only. **Parking:** on-site. **Amenities:** high-speed Internet, voice mail, irons, hair dryers. **Pool(s):** indoor. **Leisure Activities:** whirlpool, limited exercise equipment. **Guest Services:** valet and coin laundry, wireless Internet. **Business Services:** meeting rooms, business center. **Free Special Amenities: expanded continental breakfast and high-speed Internet.**

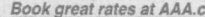

CUTHBERT HOUSE INN **Phone:** (843)521-1315

Historic Bed & Breakfast
$165-$265 All Year

Address: 1203 Bay St **Location:** Jct Church St; downtown. **Facility:** This restored home, built in 1790, overlooks a picturesque bay; porches and tea gardens provide outdoor interest. Smoke free premises. 8 units. 7 one-bedroom standard units, some with whirlpools. 1 one-bedroom suite. 3 stories (no elevator), interior/exterior corridors. *Bath:* combo or shower only. **Parking:** on-site. **Terms:** check-in 3:30 pm, 2 night minimum stay - seasonal and/or weekends, 7 day cancellation notice-fee imposed. **Amenities:** DVD players, CD players, voice mail, irons, hair dryers. **Leisure Activities:** bicycles. **Guest Services:** valet laundry, wireless Internet. **Business Services:** fax (fee). **Cards:** AX, DS, MC, VI.

HAMPTON INN *Book great rates at AAA.com* **Phone:** (843)986-0600

Hotel
$119-$174 All Year

Address: 2342 Boundary St **Location:** Jct SR 170, just s on US 21. **Facility:** 76 one-bedroom standard units. 3 stories, interior corridors. *Bath:* combo or shower only. **Parking:** on-site. **Terms:** cancellation fee imposed. **Amenities:** video games (fee), high-speed Internet, voice mail, irons, hair dryers. **Pool(s):** outdoor. **Leisure Activities:** limited exercise equipment. **Guest Services:** valet laundry, wireless Internet. **Business Services:** business center. **Cards:** AX, DC, DS, MC, VI.

AAA Benefit:
Members save up to 10% everyday!

HILTON GARDEN INN BEAUFORT *Book great rates at AAA.com* **Phone:** (843)379-9800

Contemporary Hotel
$99-$179 All Year

Address: 1500 Queen St **Location:** Jct SR 170/US 21, 0.9 mi e. **Facility:** Opened in 2008, guest rooms at the contemporary property feature a well-appointed decor and comfortable, firmness-adjustable beds. Smoke free premises. 115 units. 106 one-bedroom standard units. 9 one-bedroom suites. 4 stories, interior corridors. *Bath:* combo or shower only. **Parking:** on-site. **Terms:** 30 day cancellation notice. **Amenities:** high-speed Internet, voice mail, irons, hair dryers. **Pool(s):** outdoor. **Leisure Activities:** whirlpool, exercise room. **Guest Services:** valet and coin laundry, wireless Internet. **Business Services:** meeting rooms, business center. **Cards:** AX, CB, DC, DS, MC, VI.

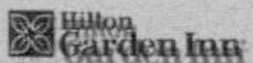

AAA Benefit:
Members save 5% or more everyday!

HOLIDAY INN HOTEL & SUITES *Book at AAA.com* **Phone:** (843)379-3100

Contemporary Hotel
$99-$199 All Year

Address: 2225 Boundary St (US 21) **Location:** Jct SR 170/US 21, just e. **Facility:** Opened in 2008, public areas include a fully-equipped exercise facility and a lounge that affords patrons nice views of the surrounding marshland. Smoke free premises. 97 one-bedroom standard units, some with whirlpools. 4 stories, interior corridors. **Parking:** on-site. **Terms:** check-in 4 pm, cancellation fee imposed. **Amenities:** voice mail, safes, irons, hair dryers. **Pool(s):** indoor. **Leisure Activities:** exercise room. **Guest Services:** valet and coin laundry, wireless Internet. **Business Services:** conference facilities, business center. **Cards:** AX, DS, MC, VI.

THE RHETT HOUSE INN **Phone:** (843)524-9030

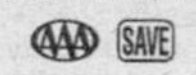

Historic Bed & Breakfast
$195-$350 All Year

Address: 1009 Craven St **Location:** Corner of Craven and New Castle sts; in historic district. **Facility:** This 1820 Greek Revival-style home features a two-tier wraparound porch; guest rooms are furnished with early English and American antiques. Smoke free premises. 17 one-bedroom standard units, some with whirlpools. 2-3 stories (no elevator), interior/exterior corridors. **Parking:** on-site. **Terms:** 2 night minimum stay - weekends, age restrictions may apply, 14 day cancellation notice-fee imposed. **Amenities:** DVD players, CD players, irons, hair dryers. **Leisure Activities:** bicycles. **Guest Services:** valet laundry, wireless Internet. **Business Services:** fax (fee). **Cards:** AX, DS, MC, VI. **Free Special Amenities: early check-in/late check-out and room upgrade (subject to availability with advance reservations).**

/ SOME UNITS

TWOSUNS INN BED & BREAKFAST **Phone:** 843/522-1122

Historic Bed & Breakfast
Rates not provided

Address: 1705 Bay St **Location:** Between Hamar and Adventure sts; downtown. **Facility:** Near shops and restaurants, the 1917 neoclassic revival-style home offers a casual, homelike atmosphere with a wide front porch and bay views. Smoke free premises. 6 one-bedroom standard units. 2 stories (no elevator), interior corridors. *Bath:* combo or shower only. **Parking:** on-site. **Terms:** age restrictions may apply. **Amenities:** video library, hair dryers. **Leisure Activities:** bicycles, horseshoes. **Business Services:** fax (fee).

/ SOME UNITS VCR

WHERE TO DINE

A MATTER OF TASTE **Phone:** 843/521-1700

American
$8-$19

Offering Lowcountry and contemporary cuisine, the restaurant is open for breakfast, lunch and dinner; patio seating is available for al fresco dining. Casual dress. **Bar:** Full bar. **Reservations:** accepted. **Hours:** 11 am-2 & 5:30-9:30 pm, Sat from 8:30 am; Sunday brunch 9 am-2 pm. Closed major holidays; also Mon. **Address:** 1001 Boundry St **Location:** Jct Charlie St. **Parking:** on-site. **Cards:** AX, MC, VI.

EMILY'S RESTAURANT AND TAPAS BAR **Phone:** 843/522-1866

American
$8-$28

Tapas are the house specialty at this cozy, casual eatery with selections ranging from garlic shrimp and crabmeat rangoon to wild boar sausage, alligator ribs and escargot Bourguignon. For more traditional fare, steak and seafood dishes also are available. Chocolate mousse pie is a decadent delight. Casual dress. **Bar:** Full bar. **Reservations:** suggested. **Hours:** 4 pm-10 pm. Closed major holidays; also Sun. **Address:** 906 Port Republic St **Location:** Center. **Parking:** street. **Cards:** AX, DS, MC, VI.

GILLIGAN'S STEAMER & RAW BAR **Phone:** 843/379-2244

Seafood
$7-$21

A casual family oriented neighborhood restaurant, Gilligan's is famous for fresh shrimp right off the boat! Locals flock not only for the shrimp but also for Captain Bookatee's hushpuppies. Not a seafood lover? Come on anyway and enjoy the buffalo wings and chicken fingers. Casual dress. **Bar:** Full bar. **Reservations:** not accepted. **Hours:** 11 am-9 pm, Fri & Sat-10 pm. Closed: 11/26, 12/25. **Address:** 2601 Boundary St **Location:** Jct US 21/SR 280, 0.6 mi e on US 21. **Parking:** on-site. **Cards:** AX, DS, MC, VI.

PLUMS WATERFRONT RESTAURANT **Phone:** 843/525-1946

American
$6-$20

The eclectic, casual cafe features a flavorful menu of gourmet soups, sandwiches, salads, fresh seafood, pasta and choice-cut meats. Wrap up the meal with a bowl of their homemade ice cream. Casual dress. **Bar:** Full bar. **Hours:** 11 am-10 pm. Closed: 11/26, 12/25. **Address:** 904 1/2 Bay St **Location:** Jct Charles St, just ne. **Parking:** street. **Cards:** AX, DC, DS, MC, VI.

SALTUS RIVER GRILL **Phone:** 843/379-3474

Seafood
$16-$29

With a grand view of the Intracoastal Waterway from the Sonoma-style patio or from the expansive full-service bar and dining room, the sizzling, contemporary seafood grill combines the atmosphere of a chic Manhattan eatery with the historic charm found only in the South Carolina's lowcountry. Dressy casual. **Bar:** Full bar. **Reservations:** accepted. **Hours:** 5 pm-10 pm. Closed major holidays. **Address:** 802 Bay St, Suite C **Location:** Jct Scott St; entrance at rear. **Parking:** street. **Cards:** AX, DC, DS, MC, VI.

BENNETTSVILLE pop. 9,425

WHERE TO STAY

BEST WESTERN BENNETTSVILLE ***Book great rates at AAA.com*** **Phone:** (843)479-1700

Motel
$70-$139 All Year

Address: 213 US Hwy 15 & 401 Bypass E **Location:** 0.6 mi s of center, just ne on US 15/401/SR 9. **Facility:** 52 one-bedroom standard units, some with whirlpools. 2 stories (no elevator), exterior corridors. *Bath:* combo or shower only. **Parking:** on-site. **Amenities:** voice mail, irons, hair dryers. **Pool(s):** outdoor. **Guest Services:** valet laundry, wireless Internet. **Business Services:** meeting rooms, fax (fee). **Cards:** AX, DC, DS, JC, MC, VI. **Free Special Amenities: expanded continental breakfast and high-speed Internet.**

   / SOME UNITS FEE 

AAA Benefit:
Members save up to 20%, plus 10% bonus points with rewards program.

BREEDEN INN, COTTAGES & RETREAT ON MAIN
B&B

Historic Bed & Breakfast
$120-$180 All Year

Phone: (843)479-3665

Address: 404 E Main St **Location:** 0.4 mi ne of center, on US 15 business route. **Facility:** The property offers rooms in its 1886 main house, three buildings of similar vintage and an attractive, relaxing garden with tables and walking paths. Smoke free premises. 13 one-bedroom standard units, some with kitchens and/or whirlpools. 2 stories (no elevator), interior corridors. *Bath:* combo or shower only. **Parking:** on-site. **Terms:** check-in 4 pm, age restrictions may apply, 3 day cancellation notice-fee imposed. **Amenities:** video library, high-speed Internet, voice mail, irons, hair dryers. *Some:* DVD players. **Pool(s):** outdoor. **Leisure Activities:** bicycles, volleyball. **Guest Services:** coin laundry, wireless Internet. **Business Services:** meeting rooms, business center. **Cards:** AX, DS, MC, VI.

ASK VCR / SOME UNITS

WHERE TO DINE

LANDMARK RESTAURANT

American
$4-$13

Phone: 843/479-8288

Lining the locally popular buffet are Southern dishes, such as pulled pork barbecue, fried chicken, greens and homemade desserts. Casual dress. **Reservations:** accepted. **Hours:** 11 am-2:30 & 5-8 pm, Sat from 5 pm, Sun 11 am-2:30 pm. Closed: 5/25, 7/4, 12/25. **Address:** 685 Hwy 15/401 E **Location:** Jct SR 9, 1.4 mi ne. **Parking:** on-site. **Cards:** AX, DS, MC, VI.

BLUFFTON pop. 1,275

WHERE TO STAY

HAMPTON INN & SUITES-BLUFFTON *Book great rates at AAA.com*

Hotel
$84-$129 All Year

Phone: (843)705-9000

Address: 29 William Pope Dr **Location:** I-95, exit 8 (US 278), 7.2 mi e, then just s. Located adjacent to Sun City. **Facility:** 100 one-bedroom standard units. 4 stories, interior corridors. *Bath:* combo or shower only. **Parking:** on-site. **Terms:** check-in 4 pm, 1-30 night minimum stay, cancellation fee imposed. **Amenities:** video games (fee), high-speed Internet, dual phone lines, voice mail, irons, hair dryers. **Pool(s):** outdoor. **Leisure Activities:** limited exercise equipment. **Guest Services:** valet and coin laundry, wireless Internet. **Business Services:** meeting rooms, business center. **Cards:** AX, CB, DC, DS, MC, VI.

CALL / SOME UNITS

AAA Benefit:
Members save up to 10% everyday!

HOLIDAY INN EXPRESS HOTEL & SUITES *Book at AAA.com*

Hotel
$99-$139 3/1-11/30
$89-$119 12/1-2/28

Phone: (843)757-2002

Address: 35 Bluffton Rd **Location:** Jct William Hilton Pkwy (US 278/Bluffton Rd US 46), just se. Located in Kittie's Crossing Shopping Center. **Facility:** 112 one-bedroom standard units. 4 stories, interior corridors. *Bath:* combo or shower only. **Parking:** on-site. **Terms:** check-in 4 pm, cancellation fee imposed. **Amenities:** dual phone lines, voice mail, irons, hair dryers. **Pool(s):** outdoor. **Leisure Activities:** limited exercise equipment. **Guest Services:** valet and coin laundry, wireless Internet. **Business Services:** meeting rooms, business center. **Cards:** AX, CB, DC, DS, JC, MC, VI.

ASK CALL / SOME UNITS FEE

THE INN AT PALMETTO BLUFF *Book at AAA.com*

Resort Cottage
Rates not provided

Phone: 843/706-6500

Address: 476 Mount Pelia Rd **Location:** Jct US 278/SR 170, 4.4 mi sw on SR 170 to SR 46, then 2.2 mi e to Palmetto Bluff Rd; check-in at gatehouse. **Facility:** Located on the Bluffton River. 97 units. 47 houses and 50 cottages. 1-3 stories (no elevator), exterior corridors. **Parking:** on-site and valet. **Terms:** check-in 4 pm. **Amenities:** DVD players, CD players, high-speed Internet, dual phone lines, voice mail, safes, irons, hair dryers. **Pool(s):** 5 outdoor. **Leisure Activities:** whirlpool, canoeing, paddleboats, boat dock, fishing, recreation programs, bicycles, hiking trails, jogging, spa. *Fee:* golf-18 holes, 8 lighted tennis courts. **Guest Services:** valet laundry, wireless Internet. **Business Services:** meeting rooms, business center.

24 / SOME UNITS FEE

WHERE TO DINE

AMIGOS BELFAIR

Mexican
$4-$8

Phone: 843/815-8226

It may be small but it's a fun spot to dine, whether dining in, eating at the counter or getting it to go. Mexican standards are creatively prepared but it's the burrito that gets the spotlight due to its size, as large as an adult forearm. Casual dress. **Bar:** Full bar. **Hours:** 11 am-9 pm. Closed major holidays; also Sun. **Address:** 133 Belfair Towne Village **Location:** I-95, exit 8 (US 278), 12.6 mi e; in Belfair Towne Village. **Parking:** on-site. **Cards:** AX, MC, VI.

JIM 'N NICK'S BAR-B-Q

Barbecue
$8-$35

Phone: 843/706-9741

Southern hospitality reigns at Jim 'N Nicks, where you'll get neighborly treatment as you dig into huge portions of tasty lean sausage, fresh chili, juicy smoked beef and pork and sublime homemade pies. Casual dress. **Bar:** Full bar. **Reservations:** not accepted. **Hours:** 10:30 am-9:30 pm, Fri & Sat-10:30 pm. Closed: 11/26, 12/25. **Address:** 842 Fording Island Rd **Location:** Jct SR 46 and US 278, 0.4 mi nw on US 278. **Parking:** on-site. **Cards:** AX, DS, MC, VI.

PEPPER'S PORCH **Phone:** 843/757-2295

Regional American
$7-$30

Follow the oyster shell sidewalk to the homey, fish-camp-style eatery, tucked in the midst of towering, centuries-old oak trees. Indoor and outdoor seating are both attractive and comfortable spots in which to partake of such tasty victuals as jambalaya, fried or steamed seafood, peppered cheesy grits and hush puppies. Casual dress. **Bar:** Full bar. **Reservations:** accepted. **Hours:** 11 am-10 pm. Closed major holidays; also Sun. **Address:** 1255 May River Rd **Location:** SR 46, 0.4 mi w of downtown. **Parking:** on-site. **Cards:** AX, DS, MC, VI.

SIGLER'S ROTISSERIE & SEAFOOD **Phone:** 843/815-5030

American
$15-$35

Adorning the dining room are cookbooks and awards won by the chef's tasty, imaginatively presented dishes. Whether you choose a booth or a bar stool overlooking the open kitchen, you'll find the entrees to be a gastronomic treat. Menu selections include grilled heart of romaine, pan-seared ahi tuna, smoked seafood cakes, rotisserie prime rib and braised lamb. Casual dress. **Bar:** Full bar. **Reservations:** accepted. **Hours:** 4:30 pm-9:30 pm. Closed major holidays; also Sun. **Address:** 12 Sheridan Park Cir **Location:** Jct SR 46 and US 278, 0.4 mi nw on US 278; in Sheridan Park. **Parking:** on-site. **Cards:** AX, DS, MC, VI.

TRUFFLES CAFE ***Menu on AAA.com*** **Phone:** 843/815-5551

American
$8-$26

Diners sit down to steaks, pasta, fresh seafood, homemade soups, salads and sandwiches in a casual, friendly atmosphere. The cafe is known for its chicken pot pie. Casual dress. **Bar:** Full bar. **Reservations:** accepted. **Hours:** 11 am-10 pm. Closed: 11/26, 12/24, 12/25. **Address:** 91 Towne Dr **Location:** I-95, exit 8 (US 278), 12.6 mi e on US 278; in Belfair Towne. **Parking:** on-site. **Cards:** AX, DS, MC, VI.

CALL

BLYTHEWOOD pop. 170

WHERE TO STAY

COMFORT INN *Book at AAA.com* **Phone:** (803)754-1441

Hotel
$90-$139 All Year

Address: 436 McNulty Rd **Location:** I-77, exit 27 (Blythewood Rd), just e. **Facility:** 75 units. 74 one-bedroom standard units, some with whirlpools. 1 one-bedroom suite with whirlpool. 4 stories, interior corridors. *Bath:* combo or shower only. **Parking:** on-site. **Amenities:** high-speed Internet, dual phone lines, voice mail, irons, hair dryers. **Pool(s):** outdoor. **Leisure Activities:** limited exercise equipment. **Guest Services:** coin laundry, wireless Internet. **Business Services:** meeting rooms, business center. **Cards:** AX, DC, DS, MC, VI.

ASK / SOME UNITS

HOLIDAY INN EXPRESS HOTEL & SUITES *Book at AAA.com* **Phone:** (803)333-0315

Contemporary Hotel
$99-$200 All Year

Address: 120 Creech Rd **Location:** I-77, exit 27 (Blythewood Rd), just e, then just s. **Facility:** Convenient to major thoroughfares, this well-appointed hotel offers spacious, upgraded rooms. 88 units. 68 one-bedroom standard units, some with whirlpools. 19 one- and 1 two-bedroom suites, some with kitchens. 4 stories, interior corridors. *Bath:* combo or shower only. **Parking:** on-site. **Terms:** 3 night minimum stay - seasonal. **Amenities:** dual phone lines, voice mail, irons, hair dryers. **Pool(s):** outdoor. **Leisure Activities:** exercise room. **Guest Services:** coin laundry, wireless Internet. **Business Services:** meeting rooms, business center. **Cards:** AX, DS, MC, VI.

ASK CALL / SOME UNITS

BOILING SPRINGS pop. 4,544

WHERE TO DINE

COBY'S STEAK & SEAFOOD **Phone:** 864/599-1779

American
$5-$20

Well-prepared selections are served in a basic, comfortable and casual atmosphere. Entree selections include beef, chicken and seafood. The signature item is deep-fried dill pickles. Casual dress. **Bar:** Full bar. **Hours:** 4 pm-11 pm. Closed major holidays; also Sun. **Address:** 2750 Boiling Springs Rd **Location:** I-85, exit 75 (SR 9), 1.7 mi n. **Parking:** on-site. **Cards:** AX, DS, MC, VI.

COPPER RIVER GRILL **Phone:** 864/814-4701

American
$7-$23

The new regional chain in upstate South Carolina featuring purpose-built facilities reminiscent of an Alaskan mountain lodge. Rustic exteriors, stone fireplaces, plank and rough-hewn timber walls and an open exhibition grill further that end. The menu lists entree salads, stone-fire pizzas, sandwiches, burgers, steaks, ribs, seafood, chicken and table-size desserts for sharing. Signature dishes include slow-roasted prime rib, half-pound burgers and hickory-fired salmon on a smoked hickory plank. Casual dress. **Bar:** Full bar. **Hours:** 11 am-10 pm, Fri & Sat-11 pm. Closed: 11/26, 12/25. **Address:** 2104 Boiling Springs Rd **Location:** I-85, exit 75 (SR 9), 0.7 mi nw. **Parking:** on-site. **Cards:** AX, DS, MC, VI.

CALL

FATZ CAFE **Phone:** 864/599-7909

American
$7-$19

Friendly staff and appealing country decor help set the tone for a relaxed and enjoyable dining experience. It's not unusual for guests to wait to be seated at the popular spot, which earns raves for its well-prepared variations on chicken, steak, ribs and pasta, as well as salads and sandwiches. The signature Southern-style peach cobbler served with vanilla ice cream and walnuts is scrumptious. Casual dress. **Bar:** Full bar. **Hours:** 11 am-10 pm, Fri & Sat-11 pm, Sun-9 pm. Closed: 11/26, 12/25. **Address:** 1925 Boiling Springs Rd **Location:** I-85, exit 75 (SR 9), 0.5 mi n. **Parking:** on-site. **Cards:** AX, DS, MC, VI.

CALL

CAMDEN pop. 6,682

WHERE TO STAY

COLONY INN

Phone: (803)432-5508

Motel
$65-$75 All Year

Address: 2020 W DeKalb St **Location:** Jct US 521/1/601, 1.6 mi w on US 1/601. **Facility:** 72 one-bedroom standard units. 2 stories (no elevator), interior/exterior corridors. *Bath:* combo or shower only. **Parking:** on-site, winter plug-ins. **Amenities:** voice mail, irons, hair dryers. *Some:* high-speed Internet. **Pool(s):** outdoor. **Guest Services:** valet laundry. **Business Services:** fax (fee). **Cards:** AX, CB, DC, DS, MC, VI. ***(See color ad below)***

/ SOME UNITS

COMFORT INN & SUITES

Book at AAA.com

Phone: (803)425-1010

Hotel
$89-$179 All Year

Address: 220 Wall St **Location:** I-20, exit 98 (US 521), just n. **Facility:** Smoke free premises. 66 one-bedroom standard units, some with whirlpools. 3 stories, interior corridors. *Bath:* combo or shower only. **Parking:** on-site. **Amenities:** dual phone lines, voice mail, irons, hair dryers. *Some:* CD players. **Pool(s):** heated outdoor. **Leisure Activities:** whirlpool, exercise room. **Guest Services:** valet and coin laundry, wireless Internet. **Business Services:** business center. **Cards:** AX, DS, MC, VI.

ASK CALL / SOME UNITS

GREENLEAF INN OF CAMDEN

Phone: 803/425-1806

Historic Bed & Breakfast
$109-$159 All Year

Address: 1308 Broad St **Location:** I-20, exit 98 (US 521), 2.5 mi n on Broad St (US 521). **Facility:** The inn offers lodgings in the 1890 Victorian-era McLean House or the 1805 Charleston-style Joshua Reynolds House; each has period furnishings. Smoke free premises. 10 units. 8 one-bedroom standard units. 2 one-bedroom suites. 2 stories (no elevator), interior corridors. **Parking:** on-site. **Terms:** 4 day cancellation notice. **Amenities:** voice mail, irons, hair dryers. *Some:* high-speed Internet. **Guest Services:** wireless Internet. **Business Services:** fax (fee). **Cards:** AX, DS, MC, VI.

ASK

HOLIDAY INN EXPRESS HOTEL & SUITES

Book at AAA.com

Phone: (803)424-5000

Hotel
$99-$189 All Year

Address: 419 Sumter Hwy **Location:** I-20, exit 98 (US 521), just nw. **Facility:** 65 one-bedroom standard units, some with whirlpools. 3 stories, interior corridors. **Parking:** on-site. **Amenities:** high-speed Internet, voice mail, irons, hair dryers. **Pool(s):** outdoor. **Leisure Activities:** limited exercise equipment. **Guest Services:** valet and coin laundry, wireless Internet. **Business Services:** meeting rooms, business center. **Cards:** AX, CB, DC, DS, JC, MC, VI.

ASK CALL / SOME UNITS

WHERE TO DINE

FATZ CAFE

Phone: 803/432-3439

American
$8-$18

Friendly staff and appealing country decor help set the tone for a relaxed and enjoyable dining experience. It's not unusual for guests to wait to be seated at the popular spot, which earns raves for its well-prepared variations on chicken, steak, ribs and pasta, as well as salads and sandwiches. The signature Southern-style peach cobbler served with vanilla ice cream and walnuts is scrumptious. Casual dress. **Bar:** Full bar. **Hours:** 11 am-10 pm, Fri & Sat-11 pm, Sun-9 pm. Closed: 11/26, 12/25. **Address:** 212 Wall St **Location:** I-20, exit 98 (US 521), just n. **Parking:** on-site. **Cards:** AX, DS, MC, VI.

CALL

▼ See AAA listing above ▼

CAYCE pop. 12,150 (See map and index starting on p. 940)

WHERE TO STAY

COUNTRY INN & SUITES BY CARLSON Book great rates at AAA.com **Phone:** (803)794-6200 57

AAA SAVE

Hotel
$100-$200 All Year

Address: 2245 Airport Blvd **Location:** I-26, exit 113, just sw. **Facility:** 64 units. 47 one-bedroom standard units, some with whirlpools. 17 one-bedroom suites. 3 stories, interior corridors. *Bath:* combo or shower only. **Parking:** on-site. **Terms:** cancellation fee imposed. **Amenities:** high-speed Internet, dual phone lines, voice mail, irons, hair dryers. **Pool(s):** heated indoor. **Leisure Activities:** limited exercise equipment. **Guest Services:** coin laundry, airport transportation-Columbia Metropolitan Airport, wireless Internet. **Business Services:** PC, fax (fee). **Cards:** AX, DC, DS, MC, VI. **Free Special Amenities: continental breakfast and high-speed Internet.**

CALL / SOME UNITS

KNIGHTS INN-COLUMBIA, CAYCE AIRPORT Book great rates at AAA.com **Phone:** (803)794-0222 56

AAA SAVE

Motel
$47 All Year

Address: 1987 Airport Blvd **Location:** I-26, exit 113, just ne. **Facility:** 117 one-bedroom standard units, some with kitchens (no utensils) and/or whirlpools. 1 story, exterior corridors. **Parking:** on-site. **Terms:** 14 day cancellation notice. **Pool(s):** outdoor. **Guest Services:** coin laundry, wireless Internet. **Business Services:** fax (fee). **Cards:** AX, DC, DS, MC, VI. **Free Special Amenities: continental breakfast and high-speed Internet.**

/ SOME UNITS

RIVERSIDE INN Book great rates at AAA.com **Phone:** (803)939-4688 55

AAA SAVE

Motel
$62 All Year

Address: 111 Knox Abbott Dr **Location:** US 21, just w of Congaree River Bridge. Located adjacent to the Congaree Riverwalk. **Facility:** 64 one-bedroom standard units. 2 stories (no elevator), exterior corridors. *Bath:* combo or shower only. **Parking:** on-site. **Amenities:** hair dryers. **Pool(s):** outdoor. **Leisure Activities:** putting green, patio with barbecue, hiking trails, jogging. *Fee:* exercise room. **Guest Services:** wireless Internet. **Business Services:** meeting rooms, fax (fee). **Cards:** AX, DS, MC, VI. **Free Special Amenities: expanded continental breakfast and high-speed Internet.**

/ SOME UNITS FEE FEE FEE

WHERE TO DINE

LIZARD'S THICKET **Phone:** 803/791-0314

Regional American
$3-$12

Owned and operated by the same family since 1978, guests can enjoy Southern home cooking at breakfast, lunch, and dinner. Locals love the Calabash style shrimp as well as the fried chicken livers. Be sure and ask about the daily specials which will allow guest a mixing and matching of main course with side dishes. Casual dress. **Hours:** 6 am-9 pm; to 10 pm seasonal. **Address:** 501 Knox Abbott Dr **Location:** Jct US 21/SR 2. **Parking:** on-site. **Cards:** MC, VI.

CALL

CHAPIN pop. 628

WHERE TO DINE

RUSTY ANCHOR RESTAURANT **Phone:** 803/749-1555

Steak & Seafood
$14-$25

Savor such delights as seafood, steak and innovative specials while gazing over Lake Murray and the marina. Expect to find large crowds on Wednesday, Thursday and Sunday for the all-you-can-eat specials. Casual dress. **Bar:** Full bar. **Reservations:** accepted. **Hours:** 5 pm-10 pm. Closed: Mon & Tues, Wed in fall & winter. **Address:** 1925 Johnson Marina Rd **Location:** I-26, exit 101 (US 76), 6.2 mi w to Johnson's Marina Rd, then 2 mi s. **Parking:** on-site. **Cards:** AX, MC, VI.

Destination Charleston

pop. 96,650

Through wars, fires and hurricanes, Charleston has managed to preserve its culture and architecture.

It's evident in the elegant homes. It can be seen on walking tours, or sampled in the Lowcountry cuisine perfected at local restaurants. Charleston is a place where antiques and boutiques coexist, where pride in the past blends with the reality of the present.

SC Dept. of Parks, Recreation & Tourism

Charleston skyline.
The Battery's gracious mansions and tree-lined streets provide a beautiful and dignified welcome.

© Gibson Stock Photography

Lowcountry weavers, Charleston.
Sweetgrass baskets woven by the Gullah people make the perfect Lowcountry souvenir.

© W. Metzen / Robertstock

Nature tours, Charleston vicinity.
The nearby vicinity offers opportunities to observe nature on guided and self-guiding tours.

Moncks Corner
26
52
See Vicinity map page 877
78
Goose Creek
Summerville
Awendaw
17
Ladson
North Charleston
Charleston
526
See Downtown map page 873
Mount Pleasant
Johns Island
Isle of Palms
17
Sullivan's Island
Folly Beach
Kiawah Island

© Joe Sohm Jupiterimages

Southern belles, Charleston.
With their parasols and lace-draped gowns, these ladies exude Southern charm.

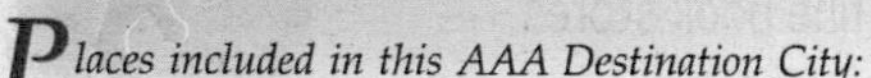

Places included in this AAA Destination City:

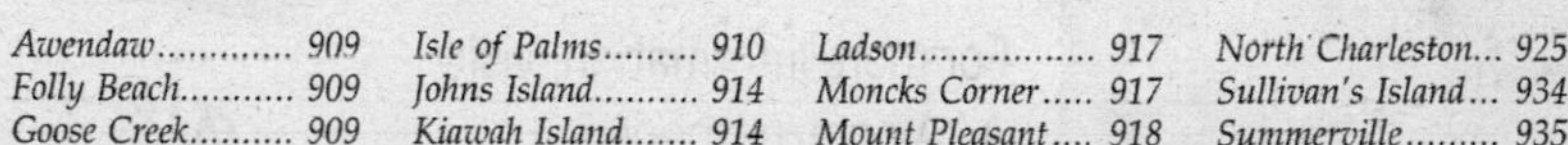

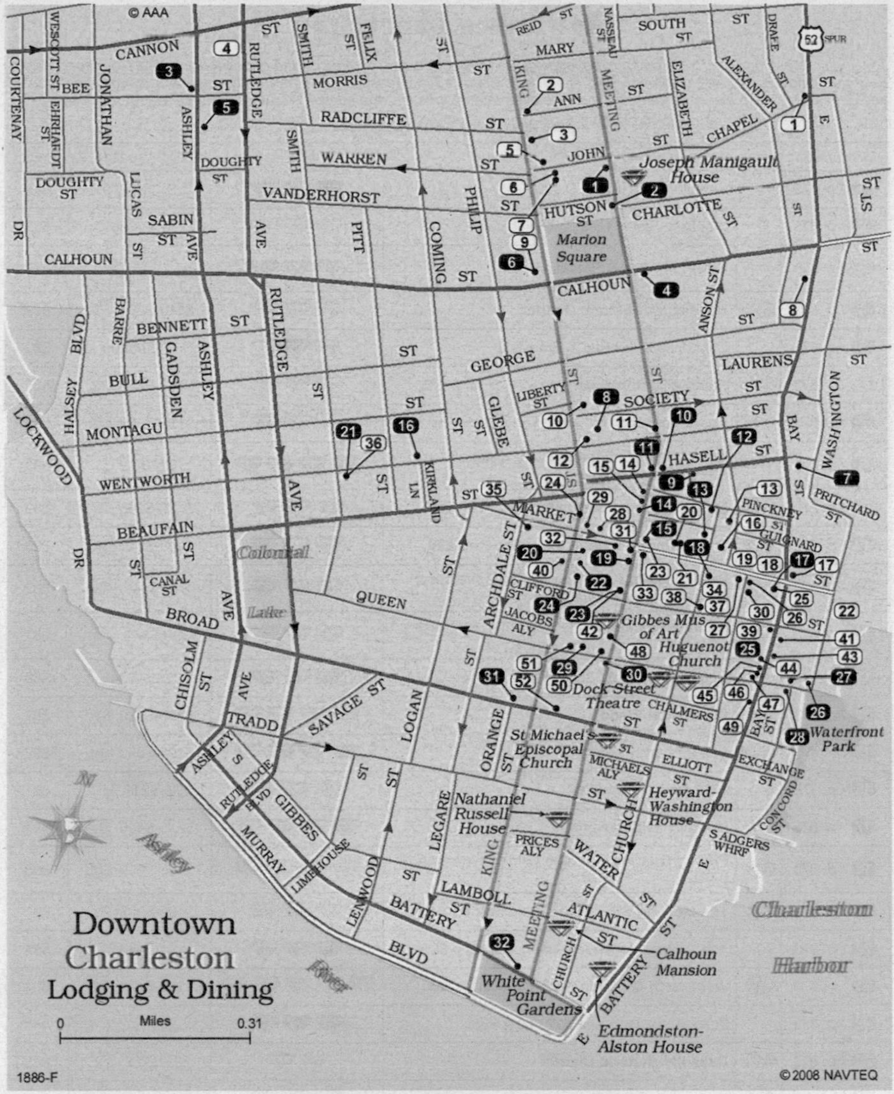

© AAA

Downtown Charleston Lodging & Dining

0 Miles 0.31

1886-F

©2008 NAVTEQ

Downtown Charleston

This index helps you "spot" where approved lodgings and restaurants are located on the corresponding detailed maps. Lodging daily rate range is for comparison only and show the property's high season. Restaurant rate range is a combination of lunch and/or dinner. Turn to the listing page for more detailed rate information and consult display ads for special promotions.

DOWNTOWN CHARLESTON

Map Page	OA	Lodgings	Diamond Rated	High Season	Page
1 / p. 873		Hampton Inn Historic District	◆◆◆	$134-$219	888
2 / p. 873		Embassy Suites Historic Charleston	◆◆◆	$159-$369	883
3 / p. 873		Ashley Inn Bed & Breakfast	◆◆◆	Rates not provided	882
4 / p. 873	AAA	**Holiday Inn Historic District**	◆◆◆	$110-$299 SAVE	889
5 / p. 873		Cannonboro Inn Bed & Breakfast	◆◆◆	$129-$209	882
6 / p. 873	AAA	**Francis Marion Hotel - see color ad p 885**	◆◆◆	$149-$329 SAVE	885
7 / p. 873	AAA	**Ansonborough Inn**	◆◆◆	$159-$359 SAVE	882
8 / p. 873		Renaissance Charleston Hotel Historic District - see color ad p 892	◆◆◆◆	$226-$277	893
9 / p. 873	AAA	**Indigo Inn - see color ad p 890**	◆◆◆	$137-$235 SAVE	889
10 / p. 873	AAA	**The Jasmine House - see color ad p 890**	◆◆◆	$149-$310 SAVE	889
11 / p. 873	AAA	**Best Western King Charles Inn - see color ad starting on p 886**	◆◆◆	$79-$349 SAVE	882
12 / p. 873	AAA	**Andrew Pinckney Inn - see color ad starting on p 886**	◆◆◆	$89-$369 SAVE	881
13 / p. 873		DoubleTree Guest Suites - see color ad p 883	◆◆◆	$129-$349	883
14 / p. 873	AAA	**Charleston Place**	◆◆◆◆	$269-$589 SAVE	882
15 / p. 873	AAA	**Planters Inn - see color ad p 892**	◆◆◆◆	$195-$850 SAVE	892
16 / p. 873	AAA	**1837 Bed & Breakfast**	◆◆◆	$89-$219 SAVE	881
17 / p. 873	AAA	**Market Pavilion Hotel**	◆◆◆◆	$275-$495 SAVE	891
18 / p. 873	AAA	**French Quarter Inn - see color ad starting on p 886**	◆◆◆◆	$169-$419 SAVE	885
19 / p. 873	AAA	**The Meeting Street Inn - see color ad p 890**	◆◆◆	$129-$299 SAVE	891
20 / p. 873		The Victoria House Inn - see color ad p 885	◆◆◆	$159-$260	894
21 / p. 873	AAA	**Wentworth Mansion - see color ad p 885**	◆◆◆◆◆	$300-$470 SAVE	894
22 / p. 873		Fulton Lane Inn - see color ad p 885	◆◆◆	$159-$275	885
23 / p. 873	AAA	**Days Inn Historic District**	◆◆	$89-$269 SAVE	883
24 / p. 873	AAA	**Kings Courtyard Inn - see color ad p 885**	◆◆◆	$159-$260 SAVE	890
25 / p. 873		The Lodge Alley Inn	◆◆◆	$199-$517	891
26 / p. 873	AAA	**HarbourView Inn - see color ad starting on p 886**	◆◆◆◆	$139-$399 SAVE	888
27 / p. 873	AAA	**The Anchorage Inn - see color ad starting on p 886**	◆◆◆	$89-$349 SAVE	881
28 / p. 873	AAA	**Vendue Inn - see color ad p 894**	◆◆◆	$199-$459 SAVE	893
29 / p. 873		The Elliott House Inn	◆◆◆	$119-$349	883
30 / p. 873		Mills House Hotel	◆◆◆	$199-$369	892
31 / p. 873	AAA	**John Rutledge House Inn - see color ad p 885**	◆◆◆◆	$199-$345 SAVE	889
32 / p. 873	AAA	**1843 Battery Carriage House Inn**	◆◆◆	$99-$309 SAVE	881

Map Page	OA	Restaurants	Diamond Rated	Cuisine	Meal Range	Page
1 / p. 873		The Boathouse on East Bay St	◆◆◆	Regional American	$16-$36	896
2 / p. 873		Basil	◆◆◆	Thai	$9-$23	895
3 / p. 873		Fish	◆◆◆	Regional Seafood	$8-$24	896
4 / p. 873		Hominy Grill	◆◆	Regional American	$7-$17	897
5 / p. 873	AAA	**Joe Pasta**	◆◆	Italian	$7-$18	898
6 / p. 873		39 Rue De Jean	◆◆◆	French	$8-$30	895
7 / p. 873		Coast	◆◆◆	Seafood	$15-$30	896
8 / p. 873		Saffron	◆◆	Deli	$8-$14	899
9 / p. 873	AAA	**Swamp Fox Restaurant**	◆◆◆	Regional American	$8-$30	900
10 / p. 873		Sushi Hiro of Kyoto	◆◆	Japanese	$6-$18	900
11 / p. 873		Jestine's Kitchen	◆	Regional American	$5-$16	898
12 / p. 873		Sermet's Corner	◆◆	Mediterranean	$10-$19	899
13 / p. 873		Hank's Seafood Restaurant	◆◆◆	Seafood	$17-$32	897
14 / p. 873	AAA	**Hyman's Seafood**	◆◆	Seafood	$8-$30	897
15 / p. 873	AAA	**Aaron's Deli**	◆◆	Deli	$6-$14	895
16 / p. 873	AAA	**Anson**	◆◆◆	Regional American	$18-$36	895
17 / p. 873		The Noisy Oyster	◆◆	Seafood	$5-$18	898
18 / p. 873		Mad River Bar & Grille	◆◆	American	$8-$20	898
19 / p. 873		Aroma's	◆◆	Thai	$7-$17	895
20 / p. 873		T Bonz Gill & Grill	◆◆	Steak & Seafood	$7-$22	900
21 / p. 873		Kaminsky's	◆	Specialty	$3-$6	898
22 / p. 873	AAA	**Fleet Landing**	◆◆	Regional American	$8-$27	897
23 / p. 873	AAA	**Peninsula Grill**	◆◆◆◆	Regional American	$23-$35	899
24 / p. 873		Old Towne Grill & Seafood	◆◆	Greek	$8-$25	898
25 / p. 873	AAA	**Grill 225**	◆◆◆◆	American	$10-$54	897
26 / p. 873		Charleston Crab House	◆◆◆	Seafood	$15-$22	896
27 / p. 873		Garibaldi	◆◆	Italian	$9-$27	897
28 / p. 873		Palmetto Cafe	◆◆◆◆	American	$17-$26	899
29 / p. 873	AAA	**Charleston Grill**	◆◆◆◆	New American	$26-$39	896
30 / p. 873		A.W. Shucks	◆◆	Regional Seafood	$8-$22	895
31 / p. 873		Cafe Cafe	◆	American	$6-$8	896
32 / p. 873		Sweetwater Cafe	◆	American	$4-$12	900
33 / p. 873		Mistral Restaurant	◆◆◆	Traditional French	$7-$28	898
34 / p. 873		Tommy Condon's Irish Pub	◆◆	Regional American	$7-$20	900
35 / p. 873		Vickery's Bar & Grill	◆◆	American	$6-$20	900
36 / p. 873	AAA	**Circa 1886**	◆◆◆◆	Continental	$24-$36	896

Map Page	OA	Restaurants (cont'd)	Diamond Rated	Cuisine	Meal Range	Page
37 / p. 873	AAA	**Tristan**	◆◆◆◆	New American	$9-$42	900
38 / p. 873		Bocci's Italian Restaurant	◆◆	Italian	$9-$23	896
39 / p. 873		High Cotton	◆◆◆	American	$9-$44	897
40 / p. 873		Fulton Five	◆◆◆	Regional Italian	$16-$36	897
41 / p. 873		Slightly North of Broad	◆◆◆	Regional American	$6-$27	899
42 / p. 873		Diana's	◆◆	American	$6-$18	896
43 / p. 873	AAA	**Robert's of Charleston**	◆◆◆	Continental	$85	899
44 / p. 873		Magnolias Uptown/Down South	◆◆◆	Regional American	$9-$33	898
45 / p. 873		Blossom Cafe	◆◆◆	New American	$8-$24	895
46 / p. 873		Cypress	◆◆◆◆	Regional American	$24-$38	896
47 / p. 873		Southend Brewery & SmokeHouse	◆◆	Regional American	$8-$23	899
48 / p. 873		The Barbadoes Room	◆◆◆	Regional American	$8-$32	895
49 / p. 873	AAA	**McCrady's**	◆◆◆◆	American	$25-$38	898
50 / p. 873	AAA	**Poogan's Porch**	◆◆	Regional American	$8-$28	899
51 / p. 873	AAA	**82 Queen Restaurant**	◆◆◆	Regional American	$10-$28	895
52 / p. 873	AAA	**Gaulart & Maliclet**	◆	New French	$4-$20	897

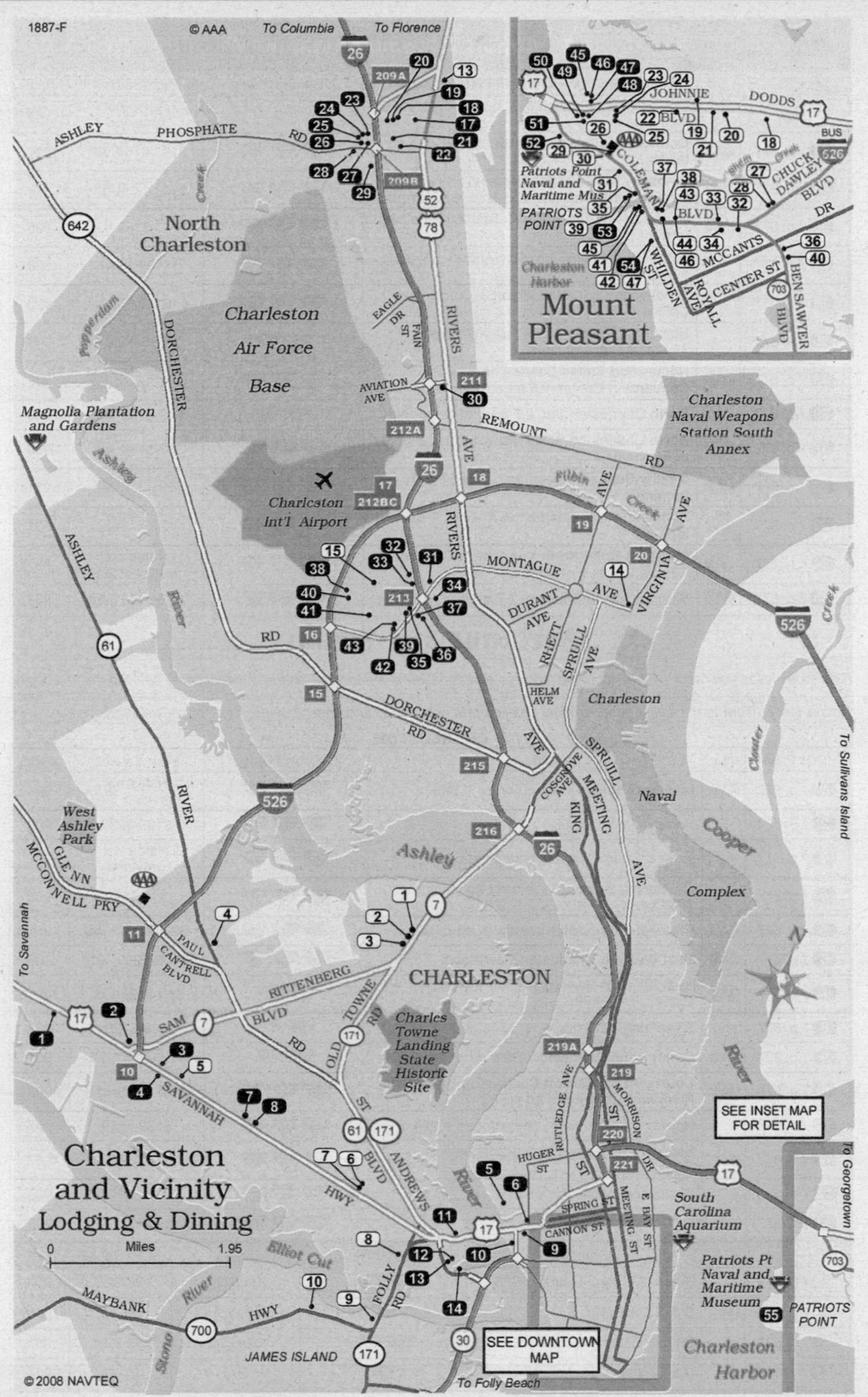

1887-F
© AAA
To Columbia
To Florence
North Charleston
Charleston Air Force Base
Magnolia Plantation and Gardens
Charleston Int'l Airport
Charleston Naval Weapons Station South Annex
West Ashley Park
Charleston Naval Complex
CHARLESTON
Charles Towne Landing State Historic Site
South Carolina Aquarium
Patriots Pt Naval and Maritime Museum
PATRIOTS POINT
Charleston Harbor
JAMES ISLAND
To Savannah
To Sullivans Island
To Georgetown
To Folly Beach
SEE INSET MAP FOR DETAIL
SEE DOWNTOWN MAP
Mount Pleasant
Patriots Point Naval and Maritime Mus
Charleston Harbor
Charleston and Vicinity
Lodging & Dining
Miles
0
1.95
© 2008 NAVTEQ

Airport Accommodations

Map Page	OA	CHARLESTON AFB INTERNATIONAL	Diamond Rated	High Season	Page
N/A		aloft Charleston Airport & Convention Center, 3 mi e of terminal		Rates not provided	925
31 / p. 877	AAA	**Courtyard Charleston North, 3 mi e of terminal**	◆◆◆	$153-$164 SAVE	927
41 / p. 877	AAA	**Embassy Suites Hotel Airport-Convention Center North Charleston, 1.5 mi e of terminal**	◆◆◆	$119-$239 SAVE	927
36 / p. 877	AAA	**Hampton Inn Airport/Coliseum, 2.5 mi e of terminal**	◆◆◆	$114-$169 SAVE	928
40 / p. 877		Hilton Garden Inn-Charleston Airport, 0.9 mi e of terminal	◆◆◆	$109-$199	928
38 / p. 877		Holiday Inn Charleston Airport & Convention Center, 1 mi s of terminal	◆◆◆	$109-$269	928
35 / p. 877		Homestead Studio Suites Hotel-Charleston/ Airport, 2.7 mi e of terminal	◆◆	$95-$110	929
43 / p. 877	AAA	**Homewood Suites Charleston Airport/ Convention Center, 2.5 mi e of terminal**	◆◆◆	$114-$159 SAVE	929
39 / p. 877	AAA	**North Charleston Inn, 2.7 mi e of terminal**	◆◆	$49-$129 SAVE	930
37 / p. 877	AAA	**North Charleston Sleep Inn & Suites, 3 mi e of terminal**	◆◆◆	$80-$120 SAVE	930
32 / p. 877	AAA	**Quality Suites Convention Center, 3.3 mi e of terminal**	◆◆◆	$99-$179 SAVE	931
30 / p. 877	AAA	**Radisson Hotel Charleston Airport, 4 mi e of terminal**	◆◆◆	$169 SAVE	931
34 / p. 877	AAA	**Sheraton Hotel North Charleston Convention Center, 2.5 mi e of terminal**	◆◆◆	Rates not provided SAVE	932
33 / p. 877	AAA	**Wingate Inn Charleston, 2.7 mi e of terminal**	◆◆◆	$99-$179 SAVE	934

Charleston and Vicinity

This index helps you "spot" where approved lodgings and restaurants are located on the corresponding detailed maps. Lodging daily rate range is for comparison only and show the property's high season. Restaurant rate range is a combination of lunch and/or dinner. Turn to the listing page for more detailed rate information and consult display ads for special promotions.

CHARLESTON

Map Page	OA	Lodgings	Diamond Rated	High Season	Page
1 / p. 877	AAA	**Hawthorn Suites - see color ad p 889**	◆◆◆	Rates not provided SAVE	904
2 / p. 877		Hampton Inn & Suites	◆◆◆	$109-$239	903
3 / p. 877		Town & Country Inn & Conference Center	◆◆◆	Rates not provided	907
4 / p. 877		Holiday Inn Express - see color ad starting on p 886	◆◆◆	$79-$199	904
5 / p. 877	AAA	**Charleston Marriott - see color ad p 902**	◆◆◆	$246-$267 SAVE	901
6 / p. 877	AAA	**Best Western Charleston-Downtown**	◆◆◆	$100-$250 SAVE	900
7 / p. 877	AAA	**Best Western Sweetgrass Inn - see color ad starting on p 886**	◆◆	$49-$199 SAVE	901
8 / p. 877		Sleep Inn-Charleston	◆◆	$49-$199	907
9 / p. 877	AAA	**Comfort Inn Charleston - see color ad p 901**	◆◆	$110-$140 SAVE	901
10 / p. 877	AAA	**Courtyard by Marriott Charleston Downtown/ Riverview - see color ad p 903**	◆◆◆	$133-$153 SAVE	903
11 / p. 877		Holiday Inn-Riverview - see color ad p 904	◆◆◆	$139-$269	905
12 / p. 877		SpringHill Suites by Marriott-Charleston Riverview	◆◆◆	$147-$158	907
13 / p. 877		Residence Inn by Marriott	◆◆◆	$147-$158	905
14 / p. 877		La Quinta Inn Riverview	◆◆◆	$69-$159	905

Map Page	OA	Restaurants	Diamond Rated	Cuisine	Meal Range	Page
1 / p. 877		Sunfire Grill and Bistro	◆◆	American	$6-$20	909
2 / p. 877	AAA	**S & S Cafeteria**	◆	American	$4-$8	908
3 / p. 877		Cisco's Cafe	◆◆	Mexican	$7-$20	907
4 / p. 877		Nathan's	◆	Deli	$4-$9	908

Map Page	OA	Restaurants (cont'd)	Diamond Rated	Cuisine	Meal Range	Page
5 / p. 877		Olympik Restaurant & Bakery	♦	Greek	$6-$18	908
6 / p. 877		Al Di La	♦♦♦	Northern Italian	$9-$19	907
7 / p. 877		Triangle Char & Bar	♦♦	American	$7-$20	909
8 / p. 877		Med Bistro	♦	American	$6-$24	908
9 / p. 877		Charleston Crab House	♦♦♦	Seafood	$15-$22	907
10 / p. 877		Locklear's Lowcountry Grill	♦♦	Regional American	$7-$20	908

NORTH CHARLESTON

Map Page	OA	Lodgings	Diamond Rated	High Season	Page
17 / p. 877		Candlewood Suites	♦♦♦	$99-$185	926
18 / p. 877		Holiday Inn Express Hotel & Suites	♦♦♦	$99-$149	929
19 / p. 877		StudioPlus	♦♦	$95-$110	932
20 / p. 877		Residence Inn by Marriott	♦♦♦	$142-$162	931
21 / p. 877	AAA	**Red Roof Inn**	♦♦	$50-$95 SAVE	931
22 / p. 877	AAA	**Country Inn & Suites-Charleston North** - see color ad p 926	♦♦♦	$129-$209 SAVE	926
23 / p. 877		Hampton Inn Charleston North	♦♦♦	$79-$109	928
24 / p. 877	AAA	**Sleep Inn Charleston North**	♦♦	$69-$159 SAVE	932
25 / p. 877	AAA	**Comfort Suites Charleston/N Charleston, SC**	♦♦♦	$89-$169 SAVE	926
26 / p. 877		Quality Inn-Charleston	♦♦	$60-$100	930
27 / p. 877		La Quinta Inn Charleston	♦♦	$49-$139	930
28 / p. 877		Motel 6 #642	♦	$45-$51	930
29 / p. 877	AAA	**Best Western Airport Inn & Suites**	♦♦♦	$89-$139 SAVE	926
30 / p. 877	AAA	**Radisson Hotel Charleston Airport** - see color ad p 893	♦♦♦	$169 SAVE	931
31 / p. 877	AAA	**Courtyard Charleston North**	♦♦♦	$153-$164 SAVE	927
32 / p. 877	AAA	**Quality Suites Convention Center** - see color ad p 905	♦♦♦	$99-$179 SAVE	931
33 / p. 877	AAA	**Wingate Inn Charleston**	♦♦♦	$99-$179 SAVE	934
34 / p. 877	AAA	**Sheraton Hotel North Charleston Convention Center** - see color ad p 932	♦♦♦	Rates not provided SAVE	932
35 / p. 877		Homestead Studio Suites Hotel-Charleston/Airport	♦♦	$95-$110	929
36 / p. 877	AAA	**Hampton Inn Airport/Coliseum** - see color ad p 928	♦♦♦	$114-$169 SAVE	928
37 / p. 877	AAA	**North Charleston Sleep Inn & Suites**	♦♦♦	$80-$120 SAVE	930
38 / p. 877		Holiday Inn Charleston Airport & Convention Center	♦♦♦	$109-$269	928
39 / p. 877	AAA	**North Charleston Inn**	♦♦	$49-$129 SAVE	930
40 / p. 877		Hilton Garden Inn-Charleston Airport	♦♦♦	$109-$199	928
41 / p. 877	AAA	**Embassy Suites Hotel Airport-Convention Center North Charleston**	♦♦♦	$119-$239 SAVE	927
42 / p. 877	AAA	**Residence Inn Charleston Airport**	♦♦♦	$187-$201 SAVE	931
43 / p. 877	AAA	**Homewood Suites Charleston Airport/ Convention Center**	♦♦♦	$114-$159 SAVE	929

Map Page	OA	Restaurants	Diamond Rated	Cuisine	Meal Range	Page
13 / p. 877		The Noisy Oyster	♦♦	Seafood	$7-$20	934
14 / p. 877		Madra Rua	♦♦	Irish	$7-$22	934
15 / p. 877		Centre Pointe Bar & Grill	♦	American	$7-$15	934

MOUNT PLEASANT

Map Page	OA	Lodgings	Diamond Rated	High Season	Page
45 / p. 877	AAA	**Sleep Inn Mt Pleasant** - see color ad p 889	♦♦	$79-$149 SAVE	920

MOUNT PLEASANT (cont'd)

Map Page	OA	Lodgings (cont'd)	Diamond Rated	High Season	Page
46 / p. 877		Extended StayAmerica-Charleston-Mount Pleasant	◆◆	$85-$105	918
47 / p. 877		Inn at River Crossing	◆◆	$60-$120	919
48 / p. 877	AAA	**Red Roof Inn**	◆◆	$56-$140 SAVE	920
49 / p. 877	AAA	**Days Inn Patriots Point**	◆◆	$89-$179 SAVE	918
50 / p. 877		Hampton Inn-Patriots Point	◆◆◆	$84-$134	919
51 / p. 877	AAA	**Best Western Patriots Point**	◆◆	$70-$134 SAVE	918
52 / p. 877		Quality Inn & Suites at Patriots Point	◆◆◆	$79-$209	919
53 / p. 877	AAA	**Shem Creek Inn - see color ad starting on p 886**	◆◆◆	$89-$289 SAVE	920
54 / p. 877		Old Village Post House Inn	◆◆◆	$135-$225	919
55 / p. 877		Charleston Harbor Resort & Marina	◆◆◆	$99-$289	918

Map Page	OA	Restaurants	Diamond Rated	Cuisine	Meal Range	Page
18 / p. 877		La Hacienda	◆◆	Mexican	$4-$15	922
19 / p. 877	AAA	**Langdon's Restaurant and Wine Bar**	◆◆◆◆	Northern American	$12-$35	923
20 / p. 877		Uno Mas	◆◆	Latin American	$7-$17	925
21 / p. 877		Zeus Grill & Seafood	◆◆	Greek	$7-$25	925
22 / p. 877		Yo Burrito	◆	Mexican	$4-$8	925
23 / p. 877		CoCo's Cafe	◆◆◆	French	$7-$23	921
24 / p. 877		Ichiban Restaurant	◆	Japanese	$6-$16	922
25 / p. 877		Alair Bistro	◆◆◆	American	$8-$21	920
26 / p. 877		Bacco	◆◆	Traditional Italian	$8-$15	920
27 / p. 877		The Mustard Seed	◆◆	American	$7-$12	923
28 / p. 877	AAA	**Capriccio**	◆◆◆	Regional Italian	$14-$22	921
29 / p. 877		Pasta Grill	◆◆	Regional Italian	$8-$18	923
30 / p. 877		Locklear's Lowcountry Grill	◆◆	Regional Seafood	$7-$19	923
31 / p. 877		Boulevard Diner	◆◆	American	$5-$13	921
32 / p. 877		Fonduely Yours	◆◆	Fondue	$12-$20	922
33 / p. 877		Page's Okra Grill	◆	Regional American	$6-$15	923
34 / p. 877		Red Drum Gastropub	◆◆◆	American	$16-$32	924
35 / p. 877		Water's Edge	◆◆◆	Regional American	$8-$30	925
36 / p. 877		Giuseppi's Pizza & Pasta	◆◆	Italian	$3-$16	922
37 / p. 877		Shem Creek Bar & Grill	◆◆	Seafood	$6-$30	924
38 / p. 877		Creekside Bar & Grill	◆◆	American	$7-$20	921
39 / p. 877		Vickery's Bar & Grill	◆◆	Regional American	$6-$20	925
40 / p. 877		Barbara Jean's Restaurant & Bar	◆◆	Regional American	$7-$23	921
41 / p. 877		Red's Ice House	◆	Regional Seafood	$6-$16	924
42 / p. 877		Sette	◆◆	Italian	$6-$15	924
43 / p. 877		Senor Tequila	◆◆	Mexican	$5-$13	924
44 / p. 877		Iacafano Deli	◆	Italian	$6-$12	922
45 / p. 877		R. B.'s Seafood Restaurant	◆◆◆	Seafood	$8-$25	924
46 / p. 877		Papa Zuzu's	◆	Greek	$5-$9	923
47 / p. 877		Old Village Post House Restaurant	◆◆◆	Regional American	$10-$25	923

DOWNTOWN CHARLESTON

(See map and index starting on p. 873)

WHERE TO STAY

1837 BED & BREAKFAST

Phone: 843/723-7166 **16**

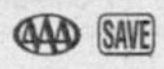

Historic Bed & Breakfast

$89-$219 All Year

Address: 126 Wentworth St **Location:** Between Coming and Pitt sts. **Facility:** The 1837 cotton planter's home offers canopy beds in all its rooms, a comfortable sitting area and a large breakfast serving area next to the kitchen. Smoke free premises. 9 units. 8 one-bedroom standard units. 1 one-bedroom suite. 3 stories (no elevator), exterior corridors. *Bath:* combo or shower only. **Parking:** on-site and street. **Terms:** 2 night minimum stay - weekends, 7 day cancellation notice-fee imposed. **Amenities:** irons, hair dryers. **Guest Services:** wireless Internet. **Cards:** AX, DS, MC, VI. **Free Special Amenities: full breakfast and high-speed Internet.**

1843 BATTERY CARRIAGE HOUSE INN

Book great rates at AAA.com

Phone: (843)727-3100 **32**

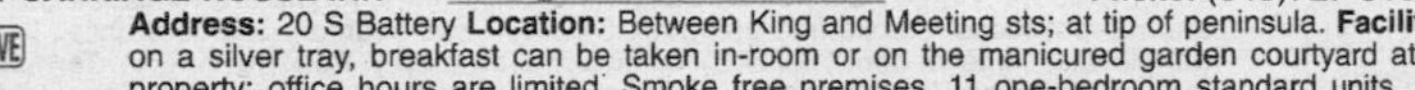

Historic Bed & Breakfast

$99-$309 All Year

Address: 20 S Battery **Location:** Between King and Meeting sts; at tip of peninsula. **Facility:** Served on a silver tray, breakfast can be taken in-room or on the manicured garden courtyard at this 1843 property; office hours are limited. Smoke free premises. 11 one-bedroom standard units, some with whirlpools. 2 stories (no elevator), interior/exterior corridors. *Bath:* combo or shower only. **Parking:** street. **Terms:** office hours 8 am-10 pm, 2 night minimum stay - weekends, age restrictions may apply, 30 day cancellation notice-fee imposed. **Amenities:** voice mail, safes, hair dryers. **Guest Services:** valet laundry, wireless Internet. **Business Services:** fax (fee). **Cards:** AX, DS, MC, VI. **Free Special Amenities: continental breakfast and local telephone calls.**

THE ANCHORAGE INN

Book great rates at AAA.com

Phone: (843)723-8300 **27**

Bed & Breakfast

$89-$349 3/1-11/30

$89-$229 12/1-2/28

Address: 26 Vendue Range **Location:** Off E Bay St. **Facility:** Reproductions of 17th-century English pieces and heavy wood finishes lend an Old World charm to this property located adjacent to the waterfront. There is a public parking lot adjacent to the property. Smoke free premises. 19 units. 18 one-bedroom standard units, some with whirlpools. 1 one-bedroom suite with whirlpool. 2 stories, interior/exterior corridors. **Parking:** street. **Terms:** age restrictions may apply, 3 day cancellation notice-fee imposed. **Amenities:** dual phone lines, voice mail, irons, hair dryers. **Guest Services:** valet laundry, wireless Internet. **Business Services:** meeting rooms, business center. **Cards:** AX, MC, VI. **Free Special Amenities: expanded continental breakfast and high-speed Internet.** *(See color ad starting on p 886)*

ANDREW PINCKNEY INN

Book great rates at AAA.com

Phone: (843)937-8800 **12**

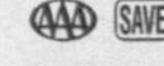

Historic Hotel

$89-$369 3/1-11/30

$89-$249 12/1-2/28

Address: 40 Pinckney St **Location:** Between Pinckney and Market sts. **Facility:** Located near the downtown market and at the horse-drawn carriage pick-up point, the inn's rooms are pleasantly furnished with French country pieces. Smoke free premises. 41 units. 38 one-bedroom standard units, some with whirlpools. 3 one-bedroom suites with whirlpools. 4 stories, interior corridors. *Bath:* combo or shower only. **Parking:** on-site (fee) and street. **Terms:** 3 day cancellation notice-fee imposed. **Amenities:** voice mail, irons, hair dryers. *Some:* CD players, high-speed Internet. **Guest Services:** valet laundry, wireless Internet. **Business Services:** business center. **Cards:** AX, DC, MC, VI. **Free Special Amenities: expanded continental breakfast and high-speed Internet.** *(See color ad starting on p 886)*

 FEE 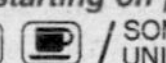  / SOME UNITS

(See map and index starting on p. 873)

ANSONBOROUGH INN Book great rates at AAA.com

Phone: (843)723-1655 7

Historic Hotel

$159-$359 3/1-11/30
$129-$269 12/1-2/28

Address: 21 Hasell St **Location:** Corner of E Bay and Hasell sts. **Facility:** Original heart-pine beams and exposed brick walls give the inn an inviting warmth; a rooftop terrace overlooks the waterfront and adjacent downtown. Smoke free premises. 37 units. 10 one-bedroom standard units. 27 one-bedroom suites. 3 stories, interior corridors. **Parking:** on-site (fee). **Terms:** 3 day cancellation notice-fee imposed. **Amenities:** high-speed Internet, dual phone lines, voice mail, safes, irons, hair dryers. *Some:* CD players. **Leisure Activities:** rooftop terrace. **Guest Services:** valet laundry, wireless Internet. **Business Services:** meeting rooms, business center. **Cards:** AX, DS, MC, VI.

ASHLEY INN BED & BREAKFAST

Phone: 843/723-1848 3

Historic Bed & Breakfast

Rates not provided

Address: 201 Ashley Ave **Location:** Corner of Bee St and Ashley Ave. **Facility:** The inn, dating from 1832, features a large porch overlooking the garden; guest rooms are furnished with period antiques and reproductions. Smoke free premises. 8 units. 7 one-bedroom standard units. 1 cottage. 3 stories (no elevator), interior corridors. *Bath:* combo or shower only. **Parking:** on-site. **Terms:** age restrictions may apply. **Amenities:** hair dryers. **Leisure Activities:** bicycles. **Guest Services:** wireless Internet.

/ SOME UNITS

BEST WESTERN KING CHARLES INN Book great rates at AAA.com

Phone: (843)723-7451 11

Hotel

$79-$349 All Year

Address: 237 Meeting St **Location:** Between Wentworth and Hasell sts. **Facility:** 93 units. 91 one-bedroom standard units. 2 one-bedroom suites with kitchens. 4 stories, interior corridors. *Bath:* combo or shower only. **Parking:** on-site. **Terms:** check-in 4 pm, 3 day cancellation notice-fee imposed. **Amenities:** video games (fee), voice mail, irons, hair dryers. *Some:* high-speed Internet. **Pool(s):** heated outdoor. **Guest Services:** valet laundry, wireless Internet. **Business Services:** business center. **Cards:** AX, DC, DS, MC, VI.
(See color ad starting on p 886)

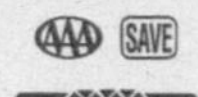

Best Western

AAA Benefit: Members save up to 20%, plus 10% bonus points with rewards program.

/ SOME UNITS FEE FEE

CANNONBORO INN BED & BREAKFAST

Phone: 843/723-8572 5

Historic Bed & Breakfast

$129-$209 All Year

Address: 184 Ashley Ave **Location:** Between Bee and Calhoun sts. **Facility:** Period antiques and reproductions furnish this B&B, which features large piazzas running the length of the first and second floors. Smoke free premises. 6 one-bedroom standard units. 3 stories, interior corridors. *Bath:* combo or shower only. **Parking:** on-site. **Terms:** age restrictions may apply, 7 day cancellation notice-fee imposed. **Amenities:** hair dryers. **Leisure Activities:** bicycles. **Guest Services:** wireless Internet. **Business Services:** fax (fee). **Cards:** AX, DS, MC, VI.

/ SOME UNITS

CHARLESTON PLACE Book great rates at AAA.com

Phone: (843)722-4900 14

Hotel

$269-$589 All Year

Address: 205 Meeting St **Location:** Between King and Meeting sts. **Facility:** European-style spa facilities and a promenade bring a luxurious ambience to this centrally located hotel, which sits atop several upscale shops. 442 units. 430 one-bedroom standard units. 12 one-bedroom suites. 8 stories, interior corridors. **Parking:** on-site (fee) and valet. **Terms:** check-in 4 pm, 3 day cancellation notice-fee imposed. **Amenities:** video library (fee), DVD players, high-speed Internet, voice mail, safes, irons, hair dryers. *Some:* CD players, dual phone lines, fax. **Dining:** Charleston Grill, Palmetto Cafe, see separate listings, entertainment. **Pool(s):** heated indoor. **Leisure Activities:** saunas, whirlpool, steamroom, lighted tennis court, recreation programs, spa. **Guest Services:** valet laundry. **Business Services:** conference facilities, business center. **Cards:** AX, CB, DC, DS, JC, MC, VI. Affiliated with A Preferred Hotel.

24 VCR / SOME UNITS

(See map and index starting on p. 873)

DAYS INN HISTORIC DISTRICT Book great rates at AAA.com Phone: (843)722-8411 23

Motel
$89-$269 All Year

Address: 155 Meeting St **Location:** Between Cumberland and S Market sts. **Facility:** 124 one-bedroom standard units. 2 stories (no elevator), exterior corridors. **Parking:** on-site. **Terms:** 7 day cancellation notice-fee imposed. **Amenities:** voice mail, safes (fee), irons, hair dryers. **Dining:** Diana's, see separate listing. **Pool(s):** outdoor. **Guest Services:** valet laundry, wireless Internet. **Business Services:** meeting rooms, fax (fee). **Cards:** AX, CB, DC, DS, MC, VI. **Free Special Amenities: newspaper and high-speed Internet.**

/ SOME UNITS

DOUBLETREE GUEST SUITES Book great rates at AAA.com Phone: (843)577-2644 13

Hotel
$129-$349 All Year

Address: 181 Church St **Location:** At N Market St. **Facility:** 212 units. 30 one-bedroom standard units. 165 one- and 17 two-bedroom suites. 5 stories, interior corridors. *Bath:* combo or shower only. **Parking:** on-site (fee) and valet. **Terms:** check-in 4 pm, 1-30 night minimum stay, cancellation fee imposed. **Amenities:** dual phone lines, voice mail, irons, hair dryers. *Fee:* video games, high-speed Internet. *Some:* safes. **Leisure Activities:** limited exercise equipment. **Guest Services:** valet and coin laundry, wireless Internet. **Business Services:** conference facilities, business center. **Cards:** AX, CB, DC, DS, JC, MC, VI. ***(See color ad below)***

CALL / SOME UNITS VCR

THE ELLIOTT HOUSE INN Book at AAA.com Phone: (843)723-1855 29

Historic Bed & Breakfast
$119-$349 2/15-11/30
$89-$219 12/1-2/14

Address: 78 Queen St **Location:** Between King and Meeting sts. **Facility:** Built in 1861, this former private residence features canopied beds, oriental rugs and period-style furnishings in its 26 rooms. Smoke free premises. 25 units. 24 one-bedroom standard units. 1 one-bedroom suite. 2-3 stories, exterior corridors. **Parking:** street. **Terms:** age restrictions may apply, 3 day cancellation notice-fee imposed. **Leisure Activities:** whirlpool, bicycles. **Guest Services:** wireless Internet. **Business Services:** fax (fee). **Cards:** AX, DS, MC, VI.

ASK

EMBASSY SUITES HISTORIC CHARLESTON Book great rates at AAA.com Phone: (843)723-6900 2

Historic Hotel
$159-$369 All Year

Address: 337 Meeting St **Location:** At Hutson St; just se of visitor center. Located in historic district, adjacent to Marion Square Park. **Facility:** Built as a fort in 1758, and later serving as the original home of the Citadel Military College, this distinctive hotel features Colonial-style decor. 153 units. 151 one- and 2 two-bedroom suites, some with whirlpools. 5 stories, interior corridors. *Bath:* combo or shower only. **Parking:** on-site (fee) and valet. **Terms:** check-in 4 pm, 1-30 night minimum stay, cancellation fee imposed. **Amenities:** dual phone lines, voice mail, irons, hair dryers. **Pool(s):** outdoor. **Leisure Activities:** whirlpool, exercise room. **Guest Services:** valet and coin laundry, wireless Internet. **Business Services:** meeting rooms, business center. **Cards:** AX, CB, DC, DS, JC, MC, VI.

Embassy Suites Hotels
AAA Benefit:
Members save 5% or more everyday!

/ SOME UNITS

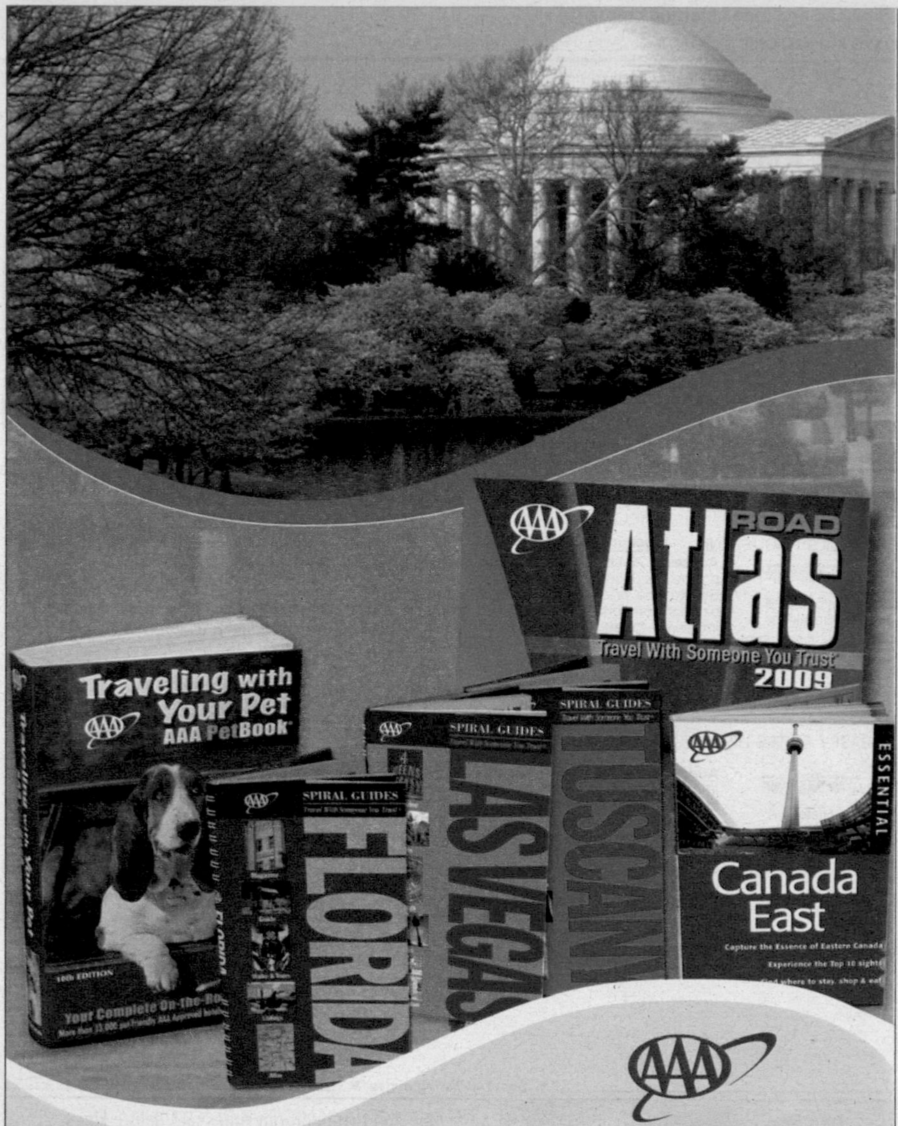
AAA
ROAD
Atlas
Travel With Someone You Trust
2009
Traveling with Your Pet
AAA PetBook
SPIRAL GUIDES
FLORIDA
SPIRAL GUIDES
LAS VEGAS
SPIRAL GUIDES
ESSENTIAL
Canada East
AAA

(See map and index starting on p. 873)

FRANCIS MARION HOTEL Book great rates at AAA.com **Phone:** (843)722-0600 6

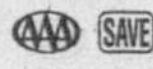

Historic Hotel

$149-$329 All Year

Address: 387 King St **Location:** Corner of Calhoun St; across from Marion Square; in historic district. **Facility:** Combining 1920s style with 21st-century comforts, this hotel offers a variety of room types and an elegant lobby. Smoke free premises. 230 units. 217 one-bedroom standard units. 12 one- and 1 two-bedroom suites. 12 stories, interior corridors. *Bath:* combo or shower only. **Parking:** on-site (fee) and valet. **Terms:** check-in 4 pm, 3 day cancellation notice-fee imposed. **Amenities:** video games (fee), dual phone lines, voice mail, irons, hair dryers. *Some:* CD players. **Dining:** Swamp Fox Restaurant, see separate listing. **Leisure Activities:** exercise room. *Fee:* massage. **Guest Services:** valet laundry, wireless Internet. **Business Services:** conference facilities, business center. **Cards:** AX, DC, DS, MC, VI. **Free Special Amenities: newspaper.** *(See color ad below)*

/ SOME UNITS FEE

FRENCH QUARTER INN Book great rates at AAA.com **Phone:** (843)722-1900 18

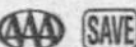

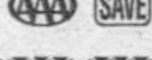

Boutique Hotel

$169-$419 3/1-11/30
$129-$299 12/1-2/28

Address: 166 Church St **Location:** Between Market and Cumberland sts. **Facility:** This property, designed in the European tradition, is an upscale hotel overlooking the market area and many of Charleston's famous steeples. Smoke free premises. 50 units. 46 one-bedroom standard units, some with whirlpools. 4 one-bedroom suites. 4 stories, interior corridors. *Bath:* combo or shower only. **Parking:** on-site (fee) and valet. **Terms:** 3 day cancellation notice-fee imposed. **Amenities:** CD players, high-speed Internet, dual phone lines, voice mail, irons, hair dryers. *Some:* fax. **Leisure Activities:** spa privileges. *Fee:* massage. **Guest Services:** valet laundry. **Business Services:** meeting rooms, business center. **Cards:** AX, DC, DS, MC, VI. **Free Special Amenities: expanded continental breakfast and high speed Internet.** *(See color ad starting on p 886)*

FULTON LANE INN Book great rates at AAA.com **Phone:** (843)720-2600 22

Historic Bed & Breakfast

$159-$275 All Year

Address: 202 King St **Location:** Between Market St and Horlbeck Alley. **Facility:** Berber carpet and pale, painted furniture create an airy ambience in the inn's accommodations; some have whirlpool baths and some have fireplaces. Smoke free premises. 27 units. 23 one-bedroom standard units, some with whirlpools. 4 one-bedroom suites with whirlpools. 3 stories, interior corridors. **Parking:** on-site (fee) and street. **Terms:** 3 day cancellation notice-fee imposed. **Amenities:** irons, hair dryers. **Guest Services:** valet laundry, wireless Internet. **Business Services:** meeting rooms, fax (fee). **Cards:** AX, DC, DS, MC, VI. *(See color ad below)*

ASK CALL / SOME UNITS

(See map and index starting on p. 873)

HAMPTON INN HISTORIC DISTRICT *Book great rates at AAA.com* **Phone:** (843)723-4000 **1**

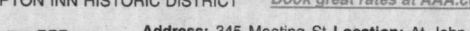

Historic Hotel
$134-$219 All Year

Address: 345 Meeting St **Location:** At John St; just se of visitor center. Located in historic district. **Facility:** An appealing courtyard enhances this Southern-themed hotel. 170 one-bedroom standard units, some with whirlpools. 5 stories, interior corridors. *Bath:* combo or shower only. **Parking:** on-site (fee). **Terms:** check-in 4 pm, 1-30 night minimum stay, cancellation fee imposed. **Amenities:** voice mail, irons, hair dryers. **Pool(s):** outdoor. **Leisure Activities:** limited exercise equipment. **Guest Services:** valet laundry, wireless Internet. **Business Services:** meeting rooms, business center. **Cards:** AX, CB, DC, DS, MC, VI.

AAA Benefit:
Members save up to 10% everyday!

HARBOURVIEW INN *Book great rates at AAA.com* **Phone:** (843)853-8439 **26**

Hotel
$139-$399 3/1-11/30
$129-$299 12/1-2/28

Address: Two Vendue Range **Location:** E Bay St to Vendue Range; corner of Vendue Range and Concord St; in historic district. **Facility:** Overlooking the harbor, this historic-district inn is decorated in a West Indies/Barbados style; late-night cookies and milk snacks are provided. Smoke free premises. 52 units. 51 one-bedroom standard units, some with whirlpools. 1 one-bedroom suite with whirlpool. 4 stories, interior corridors. *Bath:* combo or shower only. **Parking:** on-site (fee) and valet. **Terms:** 3 day cancellation notice-fee imposed. **Amenities:** high-speed Internet, voice mail, safes, irons, hair dryers. **Leisure Activities:** *Fee:* massage. **Guest Services:** valet laundry, wireless Internet. **Business Services:** meeting rooms, fax (fee). **Cards:** AX, DC, DS, MC, VI. **Free Special Amenities: expanded continental breakfast and high-speed Internet.**
(See color ad starting on p 886)

CALL FEE

(See map and index starting on p. 873)

HOLIDAY INN HISTORIC DISTRICT *Book great rates at AAA.com* **Phone:** (843)805-7900 **4**

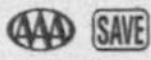

Hotel
$110-$299 All Year

Address: 125 Calhoun St **Location:** Jct Calhoun and Meeting sts. **Facility:** 126 units. 122 one-bedroom standard units. 4 one-bedroom suites. 6 stories, interior corridors. *Bath:* combo or shower only. **Parking:** on-site (fee) and street. **Terms:** check-in 4 pm, 3 day cancellation notice-fee imposed. **Amenities:** high-speed Internet, dual phone lines, voice mail, irons, hair dryers. *Some:* DVD players. **Pool(s):** heated outdoor. **Leisure Activities:** exercise room. **Guest Services:** valet laundry. **Business Services:** meeting rooms, business center. **Cards:** AX, DC, DS, MC, VI. **Free Special Amenities: newspaper and high-speed Internet.**

CALL / SOME UNITS

INDIGO INN *Book great rates at AAA.com* **Phone:** (843)577-5900 **9**

Hotel
$137-$235 All Year

Address: 1 Maiden Ln **Location:** Corner of Meeting and Pinckney sts. **Facility:** Smoke free premises. 40 one-bedroom standard units. 3 stories, exterior corridors. **Parking:** on-site (fee) and street. **Terms:** 2 night minimum stay - weekends, 3 day cancellation notice-fee imposed. **Amenities:** voice mail, hair dryers. **Guest Services:** valet laundry, wireless Internet. **Business Services:** fax (fee). **Cards:** AX, CB, DC, DS, JC, MC, VI. **Free Special Amenities: continental breakfast and high-speed Internet.** *(See color ad p 890)*

THE JASMINE HOUSE **Phone:** (843)577-5900 **10**

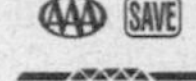

Historic Bed & Breakfast
$149-$310 All Year

Address: 64 Hassell St **Location:** Between Anson and Meeting sts. **Facility:** 1843 Greek Revival mansion located in the Ansonborough area of historic Charleston offers luxurious accommodations and convenient access to shopping. Smoke free premises. 10 units. 8 one-bedroom standard units, some with whirlpools. 2 one-bedroom suites. 3 stories (no elevator), interior/exterior corridors. **Parking:** on-site (fee) and street. **Terms:** off-site registration, 2 night minimum stay - weekends, age restrictions may apply, 3 day cancellation notice-fee imposed. **Amenities:** voice mail, hair dryers. **Guest Services:** valet laundry, wireless Internet. **Business Services:** fax (fee). **Cards:** AX, CB, DC, DS, JC, MC, VI. **Free Special Amenities: continental breakfast and newspaper.** *(See color ad p 890)*

JOHN RUTLEDGE HOUSE INN *Book great rates at AAA.com* **Phone:** (843)723-7999 

Historic Bed & Breakfast
$199-$345 All Year

Address: 116 Broad St **Location:** Corner of King St. **Facility:** A signer of the Constitution is credited with building this 1763 inn featuring elaborate plasterwork, iron balconies and Italian marble fireplaces. Smoke free premises. 19 units. 16 one-bedroom standard units, some with whirlpools. 3 one-bedroom suites, some with whirlpools. 2-4 stories (no elevator), interior corridors. **Parking:** on-site (fee). **Terms:** check-in 4 pm, 3 day cancellation notice-fee imposed. **Amenities:** CD players, voice mail, irons, hair dryers. **Guest Services:** valet laundry, wireless Internet. **Business Services:** meeting rooms, fax (fee). **Cards:** AX, DC, DS, MC, VI. **Free Special Amenities: continental breakfast and local telephone calls.** *(See color ad p 885)*

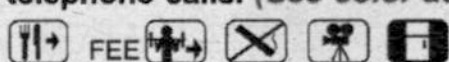
FEE

(See map and index starting on p. 873)

KINGS COURTYARD INN *Book great rates at AAA.com* **Phone:** (843)723-7000 24

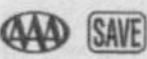

Historic Bed & Breakfast

$159-$260 All Year

Address: 198 King St **Location:** Between Market St and Horlbeck Alley. **Facility:** This renovated 1853 property features three courtyards; each of the inn's rooms has fine 18th-century reproduction furnishings and oriental rugs. 41 one-bedroom standard units. 3 stories, interior/exterior corridors. **Parking:** on-site (fee) and street. **Terms:** 3 day cancellation notice-fee imposed. **Amenities:** irons, hair dryers. **Leisure Activities:** whirlpool. **Guest Services:** valet laundry, wireless Internet. **Business Services:** meeting rooms, fax (fee). **Cards:** AX, DC, DS, MC, VI. **Free Special Amenities: continental breakfast and local telephone calls.** *(See color ad p 885)*

/ SOME UNITS

(See map and index starting on p. 873)

THE LODGE ALLEY INN Book great rates at AAA.com Phone: (843)722-1611 25

Historic Hotel

$199-$517 5/25-11/30
$118-$335 12/1-5/24

Address: 195 E Bay St **Location:** Between Cumberland and Queen sts. **Facility:** In the heart of downtown, the historic buildings comprising this inn offer standard flats and large townhouse-style units with loft bedrooms. 86 units. 79 one- and 7 two-bedroom suites, some with kitchens and/or whirlpools. 3 stories, interior/exterior corridors. **Parking:** valet and street. **Terms:** check-in 4 pm, 2 night minimum stay - seasonal and/or weekends, 3 day cancellation notice-fee imposed. **Amenities:** DVD players, voice mail, irons, hair dryers. **Dining:** High Cotton, see separate listing. **Leisure Activities:** *Fee:* bicycles, massage. **Guest Services:** valet and coin laundry, wireless Internet. **Business Services:** PC, fax (fee). **Cards:** AX, DS, MC, VI.

ASK FEE VCR

MARKET PAVILION HOTEL Book great rates at AAA.com Phone: (843)723-0500 17

AAA SAVE

Boutique Hotel

$275-$495 All Year

Address: 225 E Bay St **Location:** Corner of N Market and E Bay sts. **Facility:** A rooftop lounge offers sweeping views at this luxury downtown hotel near restaurants, shopping and Waterfront Park. Smoke free premises. 70 units. 69 one-bedroom standard units, some with whirlpools. 1 one-bedroom suite with whirlpool. 4 stories, interior corridors. **Parking:** on-site (fee) and valet. **Terms:** cancellation fee imposed. **Amenities:** CD players, high-speed Internet, dual phone lines, voice mail, safes, irons, hair dryers. *Some:* DVD players. **Dining:** Grill 225, see separate listing. **Pool(s):** heated outdoor. **Leisure Activities:** limited exercise equipment. *Fee:* massage. **Guest Services:** valet laundry. **Business Services:** meeting rooms, fax (fee). **Cards:** AX, DC, DS, MC, VI. **Free Special Amenities: newspaper and high-speed Internet.**

/ SOME UNITS VCR

THE MEETING STREET INN Phone: (843)723-1882 19

AAA SAVE

Historic Hotel

$129-$299 All Year

Address: 173 Meeting St **Location:** Between Market and Queen sts. **Facility:** In the heart of the historic district, the 1782 inn has spacious rooms with antiques, and each opens to a sunny piazza overlooking a garden courtyard. Designated smoking area. 56 one-bedroom standard units, some with whirlpools. 4 stories, exterior corridors. **Parking:** on-site (fee) and street. **Terms:** 3 day cancellation notice. **Amenities:** voice mail, safes, irons, hair dryers. **Leisure Activities:** whirlpool. **Guest Services:** valet laundry, wireless Internet. **Business Services:** meeting rooms, business center. **Cards:** AX, DC, DS, MC, VI. **Free Special Amenities: continental breakfast and high-speed Internet.**
(See color ad p 890)

FEE / SOME UNITS

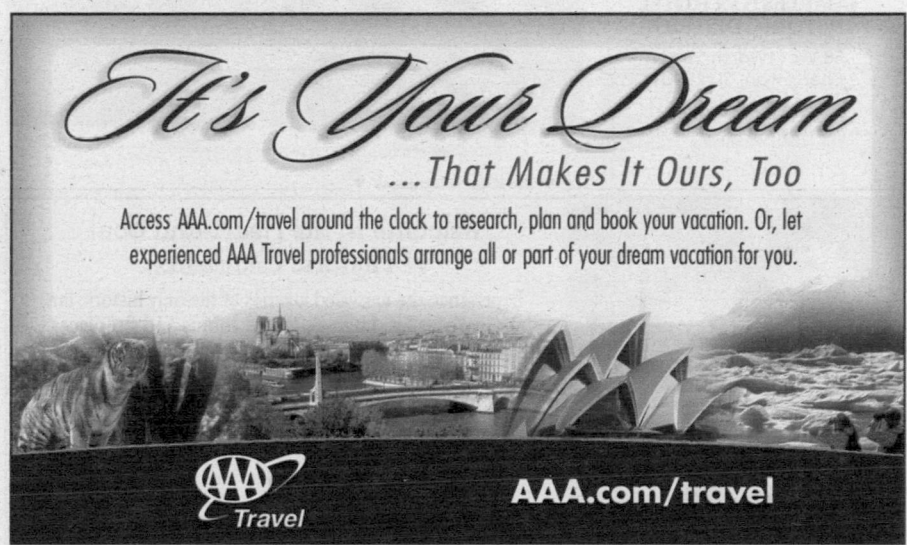

(See map and index starting on p. 873)

MILLS HOUSE HOTEL Book at AAA.com

Historic Hotel

$199-$369 All Year

Phone: (843)577-2400 **30**

Address: 115 Meeting St **Location:** Between Calhoun and Broad sts. **Facility:** This historic hotel offers an attractive courtyard; parking is in a public garage as available. Smoke free premises. 214 units. 210 one-bedroom standard units. 4 one-bedroom suites. 7 stories, interior corridors. **Parking:** valet and street. **Terms:** 2-3 night minimum stay - weekends. **Amenities:** video games (fee), voice mail, irons, hair dryers. **Dining:** The Barbadoes Room, see separate listing. **Pool(s):** outdoor. **Leisure Activities:** exercise room. *Fee:* massage. **Guest Services:** valet laundry, wireless Internet. **Business Services:** conference facilities, business center. **Cards:** AX, CB, DC, DS, JC, MC, VI.

/ SOME UNITS

PLANTERS INN Book great rates at AAA.com

AAA SAVE

Historic Boutique Hotel

$195-$850 All Year

Phone: (843)722-2345 **15**

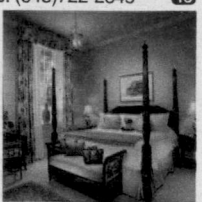

Address: 112 N Market St **Location:** Corner of Meeting St. **Facility:** Orange-spice iced tea is a specialty of this service-oriented inn dating from 1844; furnishings include period reproductions. Smoke free premises. 64 units. 58 one-bedroom standard units, some with whirlpools. 6 one-bedroom suites, some with whirlpools. 4 stories, interior/exterior corridors. **Parking:** on-site (fee) and valet. **Terms:** 2-3 night minimum stay - weekends, 7 day cancellation notice-fee imposed. **Amenities:** CD players, dual phone lines, voice mail, safes, irons, hair dryers. *Some:* DVD players. **Dining:** Peninsula Grill, see separate listing. **Leisure Activities:** *Fee:* massage. **Guest Services:** valet laundry, wireless Internet. **Business Services:** meeting rooms, business center. **Cards:** AX, DC, DS, MC, VI. ***(See color ad below)***

/ SOME UNITS VCR

▼ See AAA listing p 893 ▼

▼ See AAA listing above ▼

(See map and index starting on p. 873)

RENAISSANCE CHARLESTON HOTEL HISTORIC DISTRICT *Book great rates at AAA.com* **Phone:** (843)534-0300 **8**

Hotel
$226-$277 All Year

Address: 68 Wentworth St **Location:** Between Meeting and King sts. **Facility:** The beautifully appointed property features an array of amenities and services that will satisfy business travelers and vacationing families alike. Smoke free premises. 166 units. 162 one-bedroom standard units. 4 one-bedroom suites. 6 stories, interior corridors. *Bath:* combo or shower only. **Parking:** on-site (fee) and valet. **Terms:** 3 day cancellation notice-fee imposed. **Amenities:** video games (fee), high-speed Internet, dual phone lines, voice mail, irons, hair dryers. **Pool(s):** heated outdoor. **Leisure Activities:** exercise room. **Guest Services:** valet laundry. **Business Services:** conference facilities, business center. **Cards:** AX, CB, DC, DS, JC, MC, VI. *(See color ad p 892)*

CALL / SOME UNITS

RENAISSANCE. HOTELS & RESORTS

AAA Benefit:
Members save a minimum 5% off the best available rate.

VENDUE INN *Book great rates at AAA.com* **Phone:** (843)577-7970 **28**

AAA SAVE

Historic Country Inn
$199-$459 All Year

Address: 19 Vendue Range **Location:** Off E Bay St, 1 blk from Waterfront Park; in historic district. **Facility:** This restored 1858 building offering tastefully appointed rooms and the rooftop restaurant offers spectacular harbor views and sunsets. Smoke free premises. 65 units. 60 one-bedroom standard units, some with efficiencies (no utensils) and/or whirlpools. 5 one-bedroom suites with whirlpools. 3 stories, interior corridors. **Parking:** valet and street. **Terms:** 2 night minimum stay - weekends, 3 day cancellation notice-fee imposed. **Amenities:** dual phone lines, voice mail, irons, hair dryers. *Some:* high-speed Internet. **Leisure Activities:** bicycles. **Guest Services:** valet laundry, wireless Internet. **Business Services:** meeting rooms, PC, fax (fee). **Cards:** AX, DC, DS, MC, VI. **Free Special Amenities: full breakfast and high-speed Internet.** *(See color ad p 894)*

FEE / SOME UNITS FEE

▼ *See AAA listing p 931* ▼

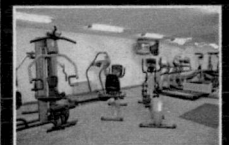

(See map and index starting on p. 873)

THE VICTORIA HOUSE INN Book great rates at AAA.com **Phone:** (843)720-2944 20

Historic Bed & Breakfast

$159-$260 All Year

Address: 208 King St **Location:** Between Market St and Horlbeck Alley; in historic district. **Facility:** 1889 Romanesque style inn, decorated in luxurious Victorian-period furnishings. Located in the famous King Street shopping district. Smoke free premises. 18 one-bedroom standard units, some with whirlpools. 3 stories, interior corridors. **Parking:** on-site (fee) and street. **Terms:** 3 day cancellation notice-fee imposed. **Amenities:** irons, hair dryers. **Guest Services:** valet laundry, wireless Internet. **Business Services:** fax (fee). **Cards:** AX, DC, DS, MC, VI. ***(See color ad p 885)***

WENTWORTH MANSION Book great rates at AAA.com **Phone:** (843)853-1886 21

Classic Historic Country Inn

$300-$470 All Year

Address: 149 Wentworth St **Location:** W of King St at Smith St; in historic district. Located in residential area. **Facility:** This 1886 Second Empire mansion features English tile floors, a marble fireplace and Tiffany stained glass; a rooftop cupola provides panoramic views. Smoke free premises. 21 units. 14 one-bedroom standard units with whirlpools. 7 one-bedroom suites with whirlpools. 4 stories, interior corridors. **Parking:** on-site. **Terms:** check-in 4 pm, 7 day cancellation notice-fee imposed. **Amenities:** DVD players, CD players, dual phone lines, voice mail, safes, irons, hair dryers. **Dining:** Circa 1886, see separate listing. **Leisure Activities:** spa. **Guest Services:** valet laundry, wireless Internet. **Business Services:** meeting rooms. **Cards:** AX, DC, DS, MC, VI. **Free Special Amenities: local telephone calls.** ***(See color ad p 885)***

▼ *See AAA listing p 893* ▼

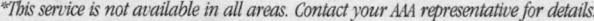

(See map and index starting on p. 873)

WHERE TO DINE

39 RUE DE JEAN — **Phone:** 843/722-8881 (6)

French
$8-$30

French brasserie cuisine, a raw bar, a traditional zinc bar and an extensive wine list are featured in the distinctively decorated, decidedly European restaurant. On the menu are daily changing entrees, such as bouillabaisse and boeuf bourguignon, and fixed items of scallops St. Jacques and duck confit. Meals are great, and the ambience is wonderful. Casual dress. **Bar:** Full bar. **Reservations:** accepted. **Hours:** 11:30 am-1 am, Sat from 5:30 pm, Sun 5:30 pm-11 pm. Closed major holidays. **Address:** 39 John St **Location:** Between King and Meeting sts. **Parking:** street. **Cards:** AX, CB, DC, DS, MC, VI. **Historic**

82 QUEEN RESTAURANT *Menu on AAA.com* — **Phone:** 843/723-7591 (51)

Regional American
$10-$28

Inside a restored Charleston home, with lovely courtyard seating also available. This well established, frequent award winning restaurant serves classic Lowcountry cuisine. Fresh catch of the day, jambalaya and creative steak preparations. The homemade dessert like pecan pie with real whipped cream are a must. Dressy casual. **Bar:** Full bar. **Reservations:** suggested, for dinner. **Hours:** 11:30 am-4 & 5:30-10 pm, Fri & Sat 5:30 pm-10:30 pm, Sun 11:30 am-2:30 & 5:30-10 pm. **Address:** 82 Queen St **Location:** Between Meeting and King sts. **Parking:** street. **Cards:** AX, DC, DS, MC, VI. **Historic**

AARON'S DELI — **Phone:** 843/723-6000 (15)

Deli
$6-$14

Traditional kosher delicatessen items and a variety of fresh seafood dishes line the cafe's menu. The Reuben sandwich is loaded with corned beef. This spot is popular, so expect a wait. Casual dress. **Bar:** Full bar. **Hours:** 11 am-11 pm. Closed: 11/26, 12/25; also Jewish holidays. **Address:** 213 Meeting St **Location:** Between Market and Hasell sts. **Parking:** street. **Cards:** AX, DS, MC, VI. **Historic**

ANDOLINI'S PIZZA — **Phone:** 843/722-7437

Pizza
$4-$18

An old-style pizza parlor in a whimsical, rock 'n' roll setting, it features a no-frills menu including calzones, salad and gigantic pizza with all kinds of toppings. For something different, try the "Almost Greek" pizza, with feta cheese and pineapple. Casual dress. **Bar:** Beer & wine. **Hours:** 11 am-11 pm. Closed major holidays. **Address:** 82 Wentworth St **Location:** Between King and St. Philip sts. **Parking:** street. **Cards:** AX, DS, MC, VI.

ANSON — **Phone:** 843/577-0551 (16)

Regional American
$18-$36

A soft, elegant atmosphere with a casual New Orleans ambience radiates from the eatery, where you'll find regional Charleston seafood entrees like lobster salad and seafood stew as well as creative preparations of fresh pasta and prime meat. Dressy casual. **Bar:** Full bar. **Reservations:** suggested. **Hours:** 5:30 pm-10 pm, Fri & Sat-11 pm. **Address:** 12 Anson St **Location:** Just w of N Market St. **Parking:** street. **Cards:** AX, CB, DC, DS, MC, VI.

AROMA'S — **Phone:** 843/723-9588 (19)

Thai
$7-$17

The extensive menu offerings at the small, late-night bistro include well-prepared Asian and regional American favorites, such as potstickers (an incredible hot and sour soup), pad Thai, kung-po and fried flounder. A children's menu is available. Casual dress. **Bar:** Full bar. **Reservations:** not accepted. **Hours:** 11 am-2 am. Closed: 12/25. **Address:** 50 N Market St **Location:** Between Church and East Bay sts. **Parking:** street. **Cards:** MC, VI.

A.W. SHUCKS — **Phone:** 843/723-1151 (30)

Regional Seafood
$8-$22

Diners peruse a large seafood menu at the boisterous downtown eatery. Choices range from Cajun-inspired fare to creative pasta dishes. It's worth the wait to try the Lowcountry favorite frogmore stew, a seafood boil that includes shrimp, oysters, clams, mussels, fish, sausage, potatoes and corn on the cob. Casual dress. **Bar:** Full bar. **Hours:** 11 am-10 pm, Fri & Sat-11 pm. Closed: 12/25. **Address:** 70 State St **Location:** Between S Market and Cumberland sts; entrances on S Market and State sts. **Parking:** street. **Cards:** AX, DC, DS, MC, VI.

THE BARBADOES ROOM — **Phone:** 843/577-2400 (48)

Regional American
$8-$32

An elegant, formal dining room overlooking a fountain courtyard is the setting for a very pleasant evening out. Efficient, knowledgeable servers bring tasty, well-prepared dishes like black-eyed pea soup and grilled tuna steak with mango fruit relish. Dressy casual. **Bar:** Full bar. **Reservations:** suggested, for holidays. **Hours:** 7 am-2 & 5:30-9 pm. **Address:** 115 Meeting St **Location:** Between Calhoun and Broad sts; in Mills House Hotel. **Parking:** street. **Cards:** AX, CB, DC, DS, JC, MC, VI. **Historic**

CALL

BASIL — **Phone:** 843/724-3490 (2)

Thai
$9-$23

The restaurant is the spot for upscale Thai in downtown Charleston. The wide-ranging, reasonably priced menu provides diners an array of spicy or mild beef, chicken, pork, shrimp and tofu entrees, as well as curry, noodle and fried rice dishes. Red curry crispy duck is the house specialty. Casual dress. **Bar:** Full bar. **Hours:** 11:30 am-2:30 & 5-10:30 pm, Fri-11 pm, Sat 5 pm-11 pm, Sun 5 pm-10 pm. Closed: 12/25. **Address:** 460 King St **Location:** Between Mary and John sts. **Parking:** street. **Cards:** AX, DC, MC, VI.

BLOSSOM CAFE — **Phone:** 843/722-9200 (45)

New American
$8-$24

A bright, bustling atmosphere features innovative, Mediterranean-style cuisine with fresh local seafood and regional produce. The menu also includes fresh pasta and bread, and dessert made in-house. All items are well-done and attractively presented. Dressy casual. **Bar:** Full bar. **Reservations:** suggested. **Hours:** 11:30 am-11 pm, Fri & Sat-midnight, Sun 11 am-2:30 & 4-11 pm. Closed: 1/1, 12/25. **Address:** 171 E Bay St **Location:** Between Cumberland and Queen sts. **Parking:** on-site and street. **Cards:** AX, MC, VI.

(See map and index starting on p. 873)

THE BOATHOUSE ON EAST BAY ST — **Phone:** 843/577-7171 (1)

Regional American
$16-$36

From the wooden boats hanging from the rafters to the menu offerings, you'll have no doubt the specialty here is seafood. Menu offerings include no less than 10 varieties of oysters and grilled fish—such as mahi mahi, black grouper and yellowfin tuna—prepared with flavorful sauces. A sushi bar also offers a wide selection. The homemade desserts are irresistible. Dressy casual. **Bar:** Full bar. **Reservations:** accepted. **Hours:** 5 pm-10 pm, Fri & Sat-11 pm; Sunday brunch 11 am-2 pm. Closed: 1/1, 12/25; also Super Bowl Sun. **Address:** 549 E Bay St **Location:** Corner of E Bay St/US 52 alternate route and Chapel St. **Parking:** on-site. **Cards:** AX, DS, MC, VI. **Historic**

CALL &M

BOCCI'S ITALIAN RESTAURANT — **Phone:** 843/720-2121 (38)

Italian
$9-$23

A series of small rooms, each individually decorated, makes for cozy dining in this restaurant in the city's heart. Start by sharing an amply sized antipasto salad, then savor the exceptional taste of such pasta dishes as baked ziti, lasagna and fettuccine Alfredo. Save room for the flavorful homemade tiramisu or cannoli. Casual dress. **Bar:** Full bar. **Reservations:** suggested. **Hours:** 4:30 pm-10 pm, Fri & Sat-11 pm. Closed: 11/26, 12/25. **Address:** 158 Church St **Location:** Between S Market and Cumberland sts. **Parking:** street. **Cards:** AX, CB, DC, DS, MC, VI. **Historic**

CAFE CAFE — **Phone:** 843/723-3622 (31)

American
$6-$8

Located in the historic district, this restaurant specializes in breakfast and lunch. Homemade soup, sandwiches and wraps are available. Before you order, be sure to visit the dessert display where mouthwatering cakes are displayed. Casual dress. **Hours:** 7 am-5 pm, Fri & Sat-9 pm, Sun-3 pm. **Address:** 177 Meeting St **Location:** Corner of Market and Meeting sts. **Parking:** street. **Cards:** AX, DS, MC, VI.

CHARLESTON CRAB HOUSE — **Phone:** 843/853-2900 (26)

Seafood
$15-$22

The casual, seafood-themed restaurant presents a menu varied enough to please a wide cross-section of patrons. The crab cocktail appetizer is almost a meal in itself, and stuffed mahi mahi and Charleston grouper are house specialties. Also offered is a good selection of steaks, as well as chicken, pasta and grits dishes. Casual dress. **Bar:** Full bar. **Hours:** 11:30 am-10 pm. Closed: 11/26, 12/25; also Super Bowl Sun. **Address:** 41 S Market St **Location:** Corner of State St. **Parking:** street. **Cards:** AX, DS, MC, VI. **Historic**

CHARLESTON GRILL — **Phone:** 843/577-4522 (29)

AAA

New American
$26-$39

This restaurant features traditional Lowcountry cuisine paired with an extensive wine list. Creative, well-prepared dishes include a nice pan-seared pompano in diced lobster sauce over potato-celery puree. A terrific live jazz quartet plays nightly. Dressy casual. Entertainment. **Bar:** Full bar. **Reservations:** suggested. **Hours:** 5 pm-10 pm, Fri & Sat-11 pm. Closed: 1/1; also Super Bowl Sun. **Address:** 224 King St **Location:** Between King and Meeting sts; in Charleston Place. **Parking:** on-site (fee) and valet. **Cards:** AX, CB, DC, DS, MC, VI.

CALL &M

CIRCA 1886 *Menu on AAA.com* — **Phone:** 843/853-7828 (36)

AAA

Continental
$24-$36

This elegant dining spot resides in the carriage house of the Wentworth Mansion. Formerly home to horses, the site was beautifully redone and now is an opulent space with velvet booths, a stone fireplace and romantic candlelight. The chef's fine cuisine is upscale Southern and changes with the season. Representative dishes might include spicy grilled shrimp with fried green tomatoes, crab cake with sassafras cream or grilled beef tenderloin with mushroom and foie gras. Dressy casual. **Bar:** Full bar. **Reservations:** suggested. **Hours:** 5:30 pm-9:30 pm. Closed: 12/25; also Sun. **Address:** 149 Wentworth St **Location:** W of King St at Smith St; in historic district; in Wentworth Mansion. **Parking:** on-site. **Cards:** AX, CB, DC, DS, MC, VI. **Historic**

COAST — **Phone:** 843/722-8838 (7)

Seafood
$15-$30

The menu is so dependent on fresh catches of the day that it's impossible to make specific recommendations without a crystal ball. With more than a dozen wood-grilled, fresh fish offerings daily, a raw bar, seviche five ways and lobster rolls, the diner won't go wrong with any selection at the sophisticated downtown restaurant. Casual dress. **Bar:** Full bar. **Reservations:** accepted. **Hours:** 5:30 pm-10 pm, Fri & Sat-11 pm. Closed major holidays. **Address:** 39-D John St **Location:** Between King and Meeting sts; behind 39 John St, down Hutson Alley. **Parking:** street. **Cards:** AX, DC, DS, MC, VI.

CYPRESS — **Phone:** 843/727-0111 (46)

Regional American
$24-$38

In the historic district, the contemporary restaurant has as its focal point a spectacular three-story glass wine wall displaying 4,000 bottles of global vintages. The decor is decidedly modern, with flying-saucer lighting that changes color and other high-tech features, yet the building's history is not lost on the diner. The menu is as eclectic as the trendy furnishings, with Asian-influenced dishes ranging from tuna tartare and rack of lamb to Chateaubriand and truffled grits with lobster. Dressy casual. **Bar:** Full bar. **Reservations:** suggested. **Hours:** 5:30 pm-10 pm, Fri & Sat-11 pm. Closed: 1/1, 11/26, 12/25. **Address:** 167 E Bay St **Location:** Corner of Queen St. **Parking:** street. **Cards:** AX, DC, MC, VI.

CALL &M

DIANA'S — **Phone:** 843/534-0043 (42)

American
$6-$18

This sister restaurant to Cafe Cafe, also located in the historic district, offers an expanded menu and features an espresso bar. Homemade soup, salad and dessert are the specialty here. Casual dress. **Bar:** Full bar. **Reservations:** accepted. **Hours:** 6:30 am-9 pm, Fri & Sat-10 pm, Sun-3 pm. Closed: 11/26, 12/25. **Address:** 155 Meeting St **Location:** Between Cumberland and S Market sts; in Days Inn Historic District. **Parking:** on-site and street. **Cards:** AX, DS, MC, VI.

FISH — **Phone:** 843/722-3474 (3)

Regional Seafood
$8-$24

In a historic single-family home downtown, the restaurant presents a diverse menu of seasonal seafood. Unpretentious upscale themes prevail, making for a casual fine-dining experience. Dressy casual. **Bar:** Full bar. **Reservations:** suggested. **Hours:** 11:30 am-2 & 5:30-9 pm, Fri-10 pm, Sat 5:30 pm-10 pm. Closed: 1/1, 11/26, 12/24, 12/25; also Sun. **Address:** 442 King St **Location:** Between John and Ann sts. **Parking:** street. **Cards:** AX, MC, VI. **Historic**

(See map and index starting on p. 873)

FIVE LOAVES CAFE — Phone: 843/937-4303

Regional American
$4-$18

Fresh soups and sandwiches are the order of the day. Dishes are prepared to order. The three-cup soup sampler is a great way to try the day's hot offerings. Top it off with a sandwich and a freshly prepared dessert. Casual dress. **Bar:** Beer & wine. **Hours:** 11 am-9 pm, Sat-3:30 pm. Closed: 11/26, 12/25; also Sun. **Address:** 43 Cannon St **Location:** Corner of Coming St. **Parking:** street. **Cards:** AX, MC, VI.

FLEET LANDING *Menu on AAA.com* — **Phone:** 843/722-8100 (22)

Regional American
$8-$27

The waterfront restaurant is distinctive from many perspectives, not the least of which is its fine food. Inside a former Naval debarkation point, with its maritime-chic interior, guests savor a fusion of classic and contemporary Southern seafood in a come-as-you-are atmosphere. The menu is inclusive enough to satisfy any taste, and the view can't be beat. Free on-site parking is limited. Casual dress. **Bar:** Full bar. **Reservations:** accepted. **Hours:** 11 am-10 pm, Fri & Sat-11 pm. Closed: 11/26, 12/25. **Address:** 186 Concord St **Location:** Between S Market and Cumberland sts; on waterfront. **Parking:** on-site and street. **Cards:** AX, DS, MC, VI.

CALL

FULTON FIVE — **Phone:** 843/853-5555 (40)

Regional Italian
$16-$36

Original art blended with an Old World theme creates a visually engaging decor in the cozy, comfortable dining rooms. Mediterranean entrees are prepared to suit any taste and are presented with style. Osso buco—braised veal shank over risotto—and tonno all griglia, which translates to grilled tuna loin with a black olive tapenade, are exceptional. Finish with an old-style soda fountain glass of peach sorbet and a cup of rich coffee. Dressy casual. **Bar:** Full bar. **Reservations:** suggested. **Hours:** 5:30 pm-close. Closed: Sun & 8/27-9/9. **Address:** 5 Fulton St **Location:** Just off King St; in Antique District. **Parking:** on-site (fee). **Cards:** AX, DC, MC, VI. **Historic**

GARIBALDI — **Phone:** 843/723-7153 (27)

Italian
$9-$27

This cozy, softly-lit bistro serves impressive entrees with a northern Italian flair. Start off with the artichoke heart appetizer and make your way into a fresh chicken dish with steamed vegetables. Or try a savory fresh fish entree. Casual dress. **Bar:** Full bar. **Reservations:** accepted. **Hours:** 5:30 pm-10:30 pm. Closed: 11/26, 12/25. **Address:** 49 S Market St **Location:** Between Church and State sts. **Parking:** street. **Cards:** AX, MC, VI. **Historic**

GAULART & MALICLET — **Phone:** 843/577-9797 (52)

New French
$4-$20

Also known as "Fast and French," the attractive, cozy place consists entirely of counters and high stools. Stop in for an unusual salad or delicious snack in the late afternoon. Healthy vegetarian dinners share menu space with such entrees as curried lamb over couscous. Casual dress. **Bar:** Beer & wine. **Hours:** 8:30 am-10 pm, Mon-5 pm, Fri & Sat-11 pm. Closed: 12/25; also Sun. **Address:** 98 Broad St **Location:** Between Meeting and King sts. **Parking:** street. **Cards:** AX, DS, MC, VI.

GRILL 225 — **Phone:** 843/266-4222 (25)

American
$10-$54

This upscale restaurant, appointed with custom furnishings, was designed to provide each table a comfortable, private dining experience. The kitchen has earned the right to boast by priding itself on using only the freshest ingredients. Professional, personalized service perfectly complements the chef's imaginative creations, which are limited only by the diner's personal tastes. This is the perfect reservation for a special occasion. Dressy casual. **Bar:** Full bar. **Reservations:** suggested. **Hours:** 11:30 am-3 & 5:30-10 pm, Fri & Sat-11 pm. **Address:** 225 E Bay St **Location:** Corner of N Market and E Bay sts; in Market Pavilion Hotel. **Parking:** valet and street. **Cards:** AX, CB, DC, DS, MC, VI.

CALL

HANK'S SEAFOOD RESTAURANT — **Phone:** 843/723-3474 (13)

Seafood
$17-$32

In the heart of the historic district, the restaurant overlooks the downtown market area. The menu centers on creative seafood specialties, such as seafood a la Wando, a tasty fish and seafood casserole. An exhibition raw bar is part of the comfortable setting. Casual dress. **Bar:** Full bar. **Reservations:** suggested. **Hours:** 5 pm-10:30 pm, Fri & Sat-11:30 pm. Closed: 12/25. **Address:** 10 Hayne St **Location:** Corner of Church and Hayne sts; just n of Market St. **Parking:** street. **Cards:** AX, CB, DC, DS, MC, VI.

HIGH COTTON — **Phone:** 843/724-3815 (39)

American
$9-$44

Southern gentility and dignified ambience exude from the upscale restaurant. Dishes are prepared from the choicest cuts of lamb, beef, pork and veal and are served with a selection of flavorful sauces ranging from bearnaise to cabernet. Feeling wild? Try venison medallions with juniper reduction. Top off your evening with a made-to-order souffle; a different flavor is featured nightly. Dressy casual. Entertainment. **Bar:** Full bar. **Reservations:** suggested. **Hours:** 5:30 pm-10 pm, Fri-11 pm, Sat 11:30 am-2:30 & 5:30-11 pm; Sunday brunch 10 am-2 pm. Closed: 12/25; also Super Bowl Sun. **Address:** 199 E Bay St **Location:** Between Cumberland and Queen sts; in The Lodge Alley Inn. **Parking:** street. **Cards:** AX, CB, DC, DS, MC, VI.

HOMINY GRILL — **Phone:** 843/965-5588 (4)

Regional American
$7-$17

The favorite home-style haunt serves generous portions of regional Southern cuisine. This place is a hit for breakfast, lunch or dinner. Freshly baked desserts, which can be special ordered, are a big draw. Casual dress. **Bar:** Full bar. **Reservations:** accepted. **Hours:** 7:30 am-8 pm, Sat & Sun 9 am-3 pm. Closed major holidays. **Address:** 207 Rutledge Ave **Location:** Between Cannon and Bee sts. **Parking:** on-site and street. **Cards:** AX, MC, VI. **Historic**

HYMAN'S SEAFOOD — **Phone:** 843/723-6000 (14)

Seafood
$8-$30

Many celebrities have dined at the popular seafood restaurant. Food offerings include many types of fish prepared Cajun, jerk-style, fried or broiled. Hush puppies take the edge off your appetite before the meal. Expect a wait. Casual dress. **Bar:** Full bar. **Hours:** 11 am-11 pm. Closed: 11/26, 12/25; also Jewish holidays. **Address:** 215 Meeting St **Location:** Between Market and Hasell sts. **Parking:** street. **Cards:** AX, DS, MC, VI. **Historic**

(See map and index starting on p. 873)

JESTINE'S KITCHEN **Phone:** 843/722-7224 (11)

Regional American
$5-$16

Enduring Southern recipes with lots of heart and soul, this is home-style cooking in a warm, "juke joint" atmosphere. Listen to blues and jazz while feasting on favorites from meatloaf to shrimp Creole. Top it all off with a terrific coconut cream pie. Casual dress. **Bar:** Beer & wine. **Hours:** 11 am-9:30 pm, Fri & Sat-10 pm, Sun-9 pm. Closed: 11/26, 12/25; also Mon, 1st week of Jan, Yom Kippur & Rosh Hashanah. **Address:** 251 Meeting St **Location:** Corner of Meeting and Wentworth sts. **Parking:** street. **Cards:** MC, VI. **Historic**

CALL

JIM 'N NICK'S BAR-B-Q **Phone:** 843/577-0406

Barbecue
$7-$32

The upscale pig-pickin' palace presents the best of Southern hospitality and cuisine. Hungry diners look to the menu for delicious lean sausage, fresh chili, juicy smoked beef and pork and homemade pies. Portions are huge. Casual dress. **Bar:** Full bar. **Hours:** 10:30 am-9:30 pm, Fri & Sat-10:30 pm. Closed: 11/26, 12/25. **Address:** 288 King St **Location:** Between George and Wentworth sts. **Parking:** street. **Cards:** AX, MC, VI.

CALL

JOE PASTA **Phone:** 843/965-5252 (5)

Italian
$7-$18

Select from several pasta types and pair them with any of several toppings or select from a standard menu of freshly-prepared delights, all prepared tableside by an incredibly friendly chef. Expect to find a relaxed, casual atmosphere. Casual dress. **Bar:** Full bar. **Reservations:** accepted. **Hours:** 11 am-11 pm, Fri & Sat-midnight. Closed: 1/1, 11/26, 12/25. **Address:** 428 King St **Location:** Between Ann and John sts. **Parking:** street. **Cards:** AX, DS, MC, VI.

KAMINSKY'S **Phone:** 843/853-8270 (21)

Specialty
$3-$6

A small and cozy space with an inviting, intimate feel is the perfect setting for decadent desserts and specialty coffee drinks. Satisfy your sweet tooth with an exceptional carrot cake and rich hot chocolate. Some nights feature live acoustical music. Casual dress. **Bar:** Full bar. **Hours:** noon-2 am. Closed: 11/26, 12/25. **Address:** 78 N Market St **Location:** Between Meeting and Church sts. **Parking:** street. **Cards:** AX, MC, VI. **Historic**

MAD RIVER BAR & GRILLE **Phone:** 843/723-0032 (18)

American
$8-$20

Enjoy American pub fare while bopping to live DJ music and catching up on the latest sports action on the numerous high-definition televisions sprinkled throughout the converted church, which still boasts the original stained-glass windows along the front. Casual dress. **Bar:** Full bar. **Hours:** 11 am-10 pm. Closed: 11/26, 12/25. **Address:** 32B N Market St **Location:** Corner of E Bay St. **Parking:** street. **Cards:** AX, MC, VI.

MAGNOLIAS UPTOWN/DOWN SOUTH **Phone:** 843/577-7771 (44)

Regional American
$9-$33

The original circa 1739 Customs House now is home to a stimulating dining atmosphere. Fresh entrees, such as the double-cut, smoked pork chop, are prepared with a Lowcountry flair and served with vintages from the extensive wine list. Dressy casual. **Bar:** Full bar. **Reservations:** suggested. **Hours:** 11:30 am-10 pm, Fri & Sat-11 pm, Sun 11 am-10 pm. Closed: 1/1, 11/26, 12/25. **Address:** 185 E Bay St **Location:** Between Cumberland and Queen sts. **Parking:** on-site and street. **Cards:** AX, DC, MC, VI. **Historic**

MCCRADY'S *Menu on AAA.com* **Phone:** 843/577-0025 (49)

American
$25-$38

The charming, upscale tavern—circa 1778, one of America's oldest—serves well-prepared and artistically presented meat and fresh seafood entrees. Sea bass with leeks, finger potatoes and venison with cherry sauce are examples of excellent and flavorful entrees. Try tomato consume for starters; it's a delight. Dressy casual. **Bar:** Full bar. **Reservations:** suggested. **Hours:** 5:30 pm-10 pm, Fri & Sat-11 pm. Closed major holidays. **Address:** 2 Unity Alley **Location:** Between 149 and 151 E Bay St; in a small alley. **Parking:** street. **Cards:** AX, MC, VI. **Historic**

MISTRAL RESTAURANT **Phone:** 843/722-5708 (33)

Traditional French
$7-$28

Family owned and operated since 1986, the popular restaurant prepares classic country French cuisine that relies heavily on fresh vegetables, especially onions, eggplant, garlic and mushrooms. These combine with delicate yet complex sauces, local seafood, beef and chicken to form the bulk of the long menu. The dense soupe de poisson provencale with baguette is a wonderful prelude to the tasty entrees. Jazz and blues ensembles, featured Monday through Saturday, inspire the restaurant's decor. Casual dress. **Bar:** Full bar. **Reservations:** suggested. **Hours:** 11 am-11 pm. Closed: 12/25. **Address:** 99 S Market St **Location:** Between Meeting and Church sts. **Parking:** street. **Cards:** AX, MC, VI.

THE NOISY OYSTER **Phone:** 843/723-0044 (17)

Seafood
$5-$18

With more than 10 years operating in the area, the popular restaurant has been able to expand to three locations around Charleston. The menu lists only fresh local seafood and aged beef, with a strong emphasis on local oysters and shrimp. There's plenty of diversity for the whole family. Casual dress. **Bar:** Full bar. **Hours:** 11 am-10 pm, Fri & Sat-10:30 pm. Closed: 11/26. **Address:** 24 N Market St **Location:** Corner of E Bay St. **Parking:** street. **Cards:** AX, MC, VI.

OLD TOWNE GRILL & SEAFOOD **Phone:** 843/723-8170 (24)

Greek
$8-$25

The small downtown bistro serves Greek and American standards. Good-size portions and a comfortable atmosphere make this a good choice for a quick bite and a cold beer. Casual dress. **Bar:** Full bar. **Hours:** 11 am-10 pm, Fri & Sat-11 pm, Sun 10 am-10 pm. Closed major holidays. **Address:** 229 King St **Location:** Corner of Market St. **Parking:** street. **Cards:** MC, VI.

(See map and index starting on p. 873)

PALMETTO CAFE **Phone:** 843/722-4000 (28)

American
$17-$26

This upscale breakfast and lunch restaurant provides superior food and service in the naturally lit dining room which overlooks a beautifully landscaped fountain garden; the setting makes a wonderful respite after a morning of shopping or just strolling in the historic district, if only for one of the wonderful desserts. Dressy casual. **Bar:** Full bar. **Reservations:** suggested. **Hours:** 6:30 am-11 & 11:30-3 pm. Closed: 1/1. **Address:** 224 King St **Location:** Between King and Meeting sts; in Charleston Place. **Parking:** valet and street. **Cards:** AX, DC, DS, MC, VI.

CALL

PENINSULA GRILL **Phone:** 843/723-0700 (23)

Regional American
$23-$35

The ambience is a pleasant mix of the contemporary and the traditional. Fabulously creative cuisine using local ingredients and a varied selection of appetizers, seafood, meat and poultry. Dressy casual. **Bar:** Full bar. **Reservations:** suggested. **Hours:** 7 am-10 & 5:30-10:30 pm, Fri-11 pm, Sat 8 am-11 & 5:30-11 pm, Sun 8 am-11 & 5:30-10:30 pm. **Address:** 112 N Market St **Location:** Corner of Meeting St; in Planters Inn. **Parking:** valet and street. **Cards:** AX, CB, DC, DS, MC, VI.

POOGAN'S PORCH **Phone:** 843/577-2337 (50)

Regional American
$8-$28

In the historic Old Charleston district, the lovely bistro occupies a Victorian home. The menu lists spicy items, such as Cajun shrimp and Creole jambalaya, as well as vegetarian dishes. For dessert, try peanut butter pie or bread pudding. Casual dress. **Bar:** Full bar. **Reservations:** suggested. **Hours:** 8-10:30 am, 11-3 & 5-10 pm, Sun 9 am-2:30 & 5-10 pm. **Address:** 72 Queen St **Location:** Between Meeting and King sts. **Parking:** street. **Cards:** AX, MC, VI. **Historic**

ROBERT'S OF CHARLESTON ***Menu on AAA.com*** **Phone:** 843/577-7565 (43)

Continental
$85

A five-course gourmet dinner combined with cabaret music creates a memorable dining experience in itself. Add to this that the owner, a classically trained chef, sings Broadway show tunes between courses and deftly prepares selections from an ever-changing menu when not entertaining. Each course is paired with a wine that complements the flavors. Dressy casual. Entertainment. **Bar:** Beer & wine. **Reservations:** suggested. **Hours:** 7:30 pm seating. Closed major holidays; also Sun-Tues. **Address:** 182 E Bay St **Location:** Between Cumberland and Queen sts. **Parking:** street. **Cards:** MC, VI.

SAFFRON **Phone:** 843/722-5588 (8)

Deli
$8-$14

Known locally for breakfast, the restaurant offers meals with a Middle-East flavor, as well as cheese, meat, freshly baked bread, and take-out items in a deli atmosphere. Breakfast items include frittatas with lox and feta cheese, grits and biscuits. Casual dress. **Bar:** Beer & wine. **Hours:** 7 am-9 pm, Fri & Sat-10 pm, Sun 8 am-8 pm. Closed: 12/25. **Address:** 333 E Bay St **Location:** Just s of Calhoun St. **Parking:** on-site and street. **Cards:** AX, DS, MC, VI.

SERMET'S CORNER **Phone:** 843/853-7775 (12)

Mediterranean
$10-$19

The corner store has plenty of windows for watching the shoppers along King Street. Lending to the bohemian interior are smooth jazz music and the chef's own colorful, original paintings. The menu leans toward creative seafood and vegetarian dishes, but equally well-prepared pork, chicken and beef filets also make an appearance. Cold cucumber soup, baked artichoke torta and pan-seared tuna are delectable. Casual dress. **Bar:** Full bar. **Reservations:** accepted. **Hours:** 11 am-3 & 4-10 pm, Fri & Sat-11 pm. Closed: 11/26, 12/25. **Address:** 276 King St **Location:** Between Wentworth and Society sts. **Parking:** street. **Cards:** AX, MC, VI.

SLIGHTLY NORTH OF BROAD **Phone:** 843/723-3424 (41)

Regional American
$6-$27

Select from unusual yet tasty and unforgettable entrees such as breaded salmon served in a creamy leek sauce at this upscale, Southern kitchen. You'll also want to end the meal with any of the fresh, homemade desserts. Dressy casual. **Bar:** Full bar. **Reservations:** suggested, for dinner. **Hours:** 11:30 am-3 & 5:30-10 pm, Fri-11 pm, Sat 5:30 pm-11 pm, Sun 5:30 pm-10 pm. Closed: 12/25; also Super Bowl Sun. **Address:** 192 E Bay St **Location:** Corner of E Bay and Cumberland sts. **Parking:** on-site (fee) and street. **Cards:** AX, DC, DS, MC, VI. **Historic**

CALL

SOUTHEND BREWERY & SMOKEHOUSE **Phone:** 843/853-4677 (47)

Regional American
$8-$23

Formerly a maritime warehouse, the restaurant features fresh seafood, meat entrees and the signature bouillabaisse. The menu offers enough diversity and unusual plate combinations to set it apart from those at other similar restaurants. Several specialty beers are brewed on the premises. The atmosphere is relaxed and casual. Casual dress. **Bar:** Full bar. **Reservations:** accepted. **Hours:** 11:30 am-10 pm, Fri & Sat-11 pm. Closed: 11/26, 12/25. **Address:** 161 E Bay St **Location:** Corner of E Bay and Queen sts. **Parking:** street. **Cards:** AX, DC, DS, MC, VI. **Historic**

STICKY FINGERS RIB HOUSE **Phone:** 843/853-7427

Barbecue
$7-$26

Diners can put down their silverware and get their fingers ready for classic Carolina sweet ribs, as well as ribs cooked in the Texas and Tennessee styles. Hearty sides of baked beans and coleslaw complement entrees at the friendly cafe. Casual dress. **Bar:** Full bar. **Hours:** 11 am-close. Closed: 11/26, 12/25. **Address:** 235 Meeting St **Location:** Between Market and Hasell sts. **Parking:** street. **Cards:** AX, DC, DS, MC, VI.

(See map and index starting on p. 873)

SUSHI HIRO OF KYOTO — Phone: 843/723-3628 (10)

Japanese
$6-$18

Chopsticks stay busy at the downtown sushi bar, a great site for traditional sushi and tempura. Try the octopus or tuna and salmon dipped in soy sauce. Miso soup and crisp, green salad accompany each dinner. Casual dress. **Bar:** Beer & wine. **Reservations:** accepted, weekends. **Hours:** 11:30 am-2:30 & 5-10 pm, Fri & Sat noon-10:30 pm. Closed: 11/26, 12/25; also Sun. **Address:** 298 King St **Location:** Between Liberty and Society sts. **Parking:** street. **Cards:** AX, MC, VI.

SWAMP FOX RESTAURANT — Phone: 843/724-8888 (9)

Regional American
$8-$30

The well-appointed setting draws patrons for classic regional Southern cuisine. A few of the tasty items on the periodically changing menu are Southern fried chicken, seared jumbo scallops, grilled pork chops, meatloaf, crab cakes and grilled salmon. Casual dress. **Bar:** Full bar. **Reservations:** accepted. **Hours:** 6:30-11 am, 11:30-3 & 5-10 pm. **Address:** 387 King St **Location:** Corner of Calhoun St; across from Marion Square; in historic district; in Francis Marion Hotel. **Parking:** valet and street. **Cards:** AX, CB, DC, DS, JC, MC, VI.

CALL

SWEETWATER CAFE — Phone: 843/723-7121 (32)

American
$4-$12

The downtown '50s-style diner sits in the shadow of upscale hotels and is a good alternative for a tasty meal that's also inexpensive. Large portions come straight off the short-order cook's grill and onto the trays of the hurried wait staff, which deftly tries to keep up with the crowds. Breakfast is served all day, and at lunchtime, the full Lowcountry menu features shrimp and grits, po' boy sandwiches and burgers. Nothing is fancy, but it's still all yummy. Casual dress. **Reservations:** not accepted. **Hours:** 6:30 am-1 pm, Fri & Sat-3 pm. Closed: 11/26, 12/25. **Address:** 137 Market St **Location:** Between Meeting and King sts. **Parking:** on-site. **Cards:** MC, VI.

T BONZ GILL & GRILL — Phone: 843/577-2511 (20)

Steak & Seafood
$7-$22

A leisurely dining experience, the atmosphere is inviting and energetic, with exposed brick walls, ambient lighting and humorous artwork. Excellent servers guide you through a menu that includes choice aged beef, seafood, chicken and vegetarian dishes. Casual dress. **Bar:** Full bar. **Reservations:** not accepted. **Hours:** 11 am-2 am. Closed: 11/26, 12/25. **Address:** 80 N Market St **Location:** Between Meeting and Church sts. **Parking:** street. **Cards:** AX, DS, MC, VI. **Historic**

TOMMY CONDON'S IRISH PUB — Phone: 843/577-3818 (34)

Regional American
$7-$20

Casual dining is the mode in the lively pub-style eatery. The menu features fresh seafood entrees, as well as a few poultry and beef dishes. Specialties include fish 'n' chips and shepherd's pie. Casual dress. **Bar:** Full bar. **Hours:** 11 am-10 pm, Fri & Sat-11 pm. Closed: 12/24, 12/25. **Address:** 160 Church St **Location:** Between S Market and Cumberland sts. **Parking:** street. **Cards:** AX, DC, DS, MC, VI.

TRISTAN — Phone: 843/534-2155 (37)

New American
$9-$42

Impressive food presentations and incomparable tastes are hallmarks of the extraordinary experience at the casual but refined restaurant. The grand piano lends to the relaxing atmosphere, in which diners peruse an extensive menu of French-influenced new flavor combinations and a wine list of more than 400 vintages. Representative of distinctively prepared seafood and grilled specialties are venison osso buco with asiago saute and Block Island swordfish with poached clams in saffron broth. Dressy casual. **Bar:** Full bar. **Reservations:** suggested. **Hours:** 11:30 am-2:30 & 5:30-10 pm, Fri & Sat-11 pm. Closed: 11/26, 12/25. **Address:** 55 S Market St **Location:** Between Church and State sts; in French Quarter Inn. **Parking:** valet and street. **Cards:** AX, DC, DS, MC, VI.

CALL

VICKERY'S BAR & GRILL — Phone: 843/577-5300 (35)

American
$6-$20

Located in a historic building, Vickery's features Lowcountry cuisine with a hint of Cuban spices. The menu lists all types of salads and light fare as well as satisfying entrees like the Cuban pork sandwich with potato salad. Enjoy open-air dining on the patio. Casual dress. **Bar:** Full bar. **Hours:** 11:30 am-1 am. Closed: 11/26, 12/25. **Address:** 15 Beaufain St **Location:** Between Archdale and King sts. **Parking:** on-site. **Cards:** AX, DS, MC, VI.

CHARLESTON pop. 96,650 (See map and index starting on p. 877)

WHERE TO STAY

BEST WESTERN CHARLESTON-DOWNTOWN — *Book great rates at AAA.com* — Phone: (843)722-4000 (6)

Hotel
$100-$250 All Year

Address: 250 Spring St **Location:** I-26, exit 221A (US 17 S), 1.2 mi sw; just e of Ashley River. **Facility:** Smoke free premises. 153 units. 151 one-bedroom standard units. 2 one-bedroom suites. 8 stories, interior corridors. **Parking:** on-site. **Terms:** cancellation fee imposed. **Amenities:** voice mail, safes, irons, hair dryers. **Pool(s):** outdoor. **Leisure Activities:** exercise room. **Guest Services:** valet and coin laundry, wireless Internet. **Business Services:** meeting rooms, business center. **Cards:** AX, DS, MC, VI. **Free Special Amenities: local telephone calls and high-speed Internet.**

AAA Benefit:
Members save up to 20%, plus 10% bonus points with rewards program.

(See map and index starting on p. 877)

BEST WESTERN SWEETGRASS INN *Book great rates at AAA.com* **Phone:** (843)571-6100 7

Hotel
$49-$199 All Year

Address: 1540 Savannah Hwy **Location:** US 17 S, 3.6 mi w of Ashley River Bridge; jct I-526 W (end) and US 17 N, 1.7 mi e. **Facility:** 87 units. 86 one-bedroom standard units. 1 one-bedroom suite. 2 stories (no elevator), exterior corridors. **Parking:** on-site. **Amenities:** video games (fee), irons, hair dryers. *Some:* high-speed Internet. **Pool(s):** outdoor. **Leisure Activities:** exercise room. **Guest Services:** valet and coin laundry, wireless Internet. **Business Services:** business center. **Cards:** AX, CB, DC, DS, MC, VI. *(See color ad starting on p 886)*

/ SOME UNITS FEE 

AAA Benefit: Members save up to 20%, plus 10% bonus points with rewards program.

CHARLESTON MARRIOTT *Book great rates at AAA.com* **Phone:** (843)723-3000 5

Hotel
$246-$267 All Year

Address: 170 Lockwood Blvd **Location:** US 17, just ne of Ashley River Bridge to Lockwood Blvd, then just nw. **Facility:** Smoke free premises. 350 units. 344 one-bedroom standard units, some with kitchens. 6 one-bedroom suites. 13 stories, interior corridors. *Bath:* combo or shower only. **Parking:** on-site. **Terms:** check-in 4 pm, 3 day cancellation notice-fee imposed. **Amenities:** CD players, high-speed Internet (fee), voice mail, safes, irons, hair dryers. **Pool(s):** outdoor. **Leisure Activities:** patio, jogging, exercise room. **Guest Services:** valet and coin laundry, wireless Internet. **Business Services:** conference facilities, fax (fee). **Cards:** AX, CB, DC, DS, JC, MC, VI. *(See color ad p 902)*

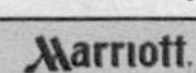

AAA Benefit: Members save a minimum 5% off the best available rate.

COMFORT INN CHARLESTON *Book great rates at AAA.com* **Phone:** (843)577-2224 9

Hotel
$110-$140 3/1-11/30
$81-$110 12/1-2/28

Address: 144 Bee St **Location:** Jct US 17 (Lockwood Blvd), just e, then just e. **Facility:** 129 units. 127 one-bedroom standard units. 2 one-bedroom suites with whirlpools. 7 stories, interior corridors. *Bath:* combo or shower only. **Parking:** on-site. **Terms:** 2 night minimum stay - weekends, cancellation fee imposed. **Amenities:** voice mail, irons, hair dryers. **Pool(s):** outdoor. **Leisure Activities:** exercise room. **Guest Services:** valet and coin laundry, wireless Internet. **Business Services:** meeting rooms, business center. **Cards:** AX, DC, DS, MC, VI. **Free Special Amenities: expanded continental breakfast and high-speed Internet.** *(See color ad below)*

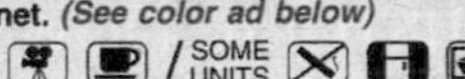

▼ See AAA listing p 901 ▼

(See map and index starting on p. 877)

COURTYARD BY MARRIOTT CHARLESTON DOWNTOWN/RIVERVIEW *Book great rates at AAA.com* **Phone:** (843)722-7229 **10**

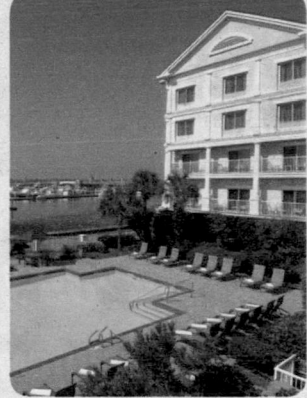

Hotel

$133-$153 All Year

Address: 35 Lockwood Dr **Location:** I-26, exit 221A (US 17 S), 1.2 mi w to Lockwood Blvd, then just s. **Facility:** Smoke free premises. 179 units. 171 one-bedroom standard units, some with whirlpools. 8 one-bedroom suites, some with whirlpools. 4 stories, interior corridors. *Bath:* combo or shower only **Parking:** on site. **Terms:** cancellation fee imposed. **Amenities:** video games (fee), dual phone lines, voice mail, irons, hair dryers. **Pool(s):** outdoor. **Leisure Activities:** whirlpool, exercise room. **Guest Services:** valet and coin laundry, wireless Internet. **Business Services:** meeting rooms, business center. **Cards:** AX, CB, DC, DS, JC, MC, VI. **Free Special Amenities: high-speed Internet.** *(See color ad below)*

 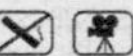 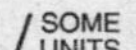 / SOME UNITS 

AAA Benefit:

Members save a minimum 5% off the best available rate.

HAMPTON INN & SUITES *Book great rates at AAA.com* **Phone:** (843)573-1200 

Hotel

$109-$239 All Year

Address: 678 Citadel Haven Dr **Location:** I-526, exit Sam Rittenburg Blvd (SR 7) westbound, just sw, then just w on US 17. **Facility:** 121 units. 93 one-bedroom standard units. 28 one-bedroom suites, some with whirlpools. 4 stories, interior corridors. *Bath:* combo or shower only. **Parking:** on-site. **Amenities:** high-speed Internet, dual phone lines, voice mail, irons, hair dryers. **Pool(s):** outdoor. **Leisure Activities:** limited exercise equipment. **Guest Services:** valet and coin laundry, wireless Internet. **Business Services:** meeting rooms, fax (fee). **Cards:** AX, DC, DS, MC, VI.

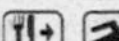   / SOME UNITS 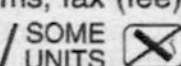  

AAA Benefit:

Members save up to 10% everyday!

▼ *See AAA listing above* ▼

(See map and index starting on p. 877)

HAMPTON INN DANIEL ISLAND Book great rates at AAA.com Phone: (843)216-6555

Hotel
$99-$179 All Year

Address: 160 Fairchild St **Location:** I-526, exit 24 (Daniel Island), just sw. **Facility:** 128 units. 115 one-bedroom standard units. 13 one-bedroom suites. 4 stories, interior corridors. *Bath:* combo or shower only. **Parking:** on-site. **Terms:** 1-30 night minimum stay, cancellation fee imposed. **Amenities:** high-speed Internet, dual phone lines, voice mail, irons, hair dryers. *Some:* DVD players. **Pool(s):** outdoor. **Leisure Activities:** jogging, exercise room. **Guest Services:** valet and coin laundry, wireless Internet. **Business Services:** meeting rooms, business center. **Cards:** AX, CB, DC, DS, MC, VI.

 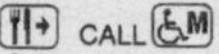  / SOME UNITS  

AAA Benefit:
Members save up to 10% everyday!

HAWTHORN SUITES Book great rates at AAA.com Phone: 843/225-4411 1

Hotel
Rates not provided

Address: 2455 Savannah Hwy **Location:** Jct US 526/SR 7/US 17; 1.3 mi w on US 17 (Savannah Hwy). **Facility:** 77 one-bedroom suites, some with whirlpools. 4 stories, interior corridors. *Bath:* combo or shower only. **Parking:** on-site. **Amenities:** DVD players, voice mail, irons, hair dryers. **Pool(s):** heated indoor. **Leisure Activities:** limited exercise equipment. **Guest Services:** coin laundry, wireless Internet. **Business Services:** meeting rooms, business center. **Free Special Amenities: expanded continental breakfast and high-speed Internet.** *(See color ad p 889)*

CALL / SOME UNITS

HOLIDAY INN EXPRESS Book great rates at AAA.com Phone: (843)402-8300 4

Hotel
$79-$199 All Year

Address: 1943 Savannah Hwy **Location:** US 17, 3.5 mi w of Ashley River Bridge; just n of jct I-526 and US 17. **Facility:** 80 units. 78 one-bedroom standard units. 2 one-bedroom suites, some with whirlpools. 3 stories, interior corridors. *Bath:* combo or shower only. **Parking:** on-site. **Terms:** check-in 4 pm, cancellation fee imposed. **Amenities:** video games (fee), voice mail, irons, hair dryers. *Some:* dual phone lines. **Pool(s):** outdoor. **Leisure Activities:** limited exercise equipment. **Guest Services:** valet and coin laundry, wireless Internet. **Business Services:** business center. **Cards:** AX, DC, DS, MC, VI.
(See color ad starting on p 886)

     / SOME UNITS

▼ See AAA listing p 905 ▼

(See map and index starting on p. 877)

HOLIDAY INN-RIVERVIEW Book great rates at AAA.com **Phone:** (843)556-7100 11

Hotel
$139-$269 2/15-11/30
$119-$209 12/1-2/14

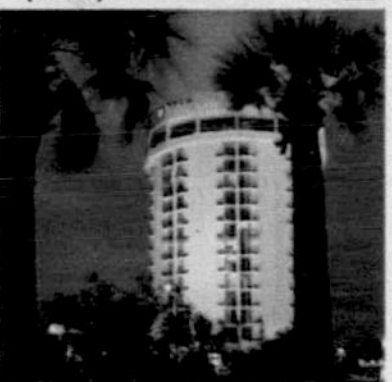

Address: 301 Savannah Hwy **Location:** 1.8 mi w on US 17; sw of Ashley River Bridge. **Facility:** 180 one-bedroom standard units. 14 stories, interior corridors. *Bath:* combo or shower only. **Parking:** on-site. **Terms:** check-in 4 pm, 2-3 night minimum stay - seasonal, cancellation fee imposed. **Amenities:** voice mail, irons, hair dryers. *Some:* dual phone lines. **Pool(s):** outdoor. **Leisure Activities:** limited exercise equipment. **Guest Services:** valet and coin laundry, area transportation, wireless Internet. **Business Services:** meeting rooms, fax (fee). **Cards:** AX, DS, MC, VI. ***(See color ad p 904)***

ASK CALL &M / SOME UNITS

THE INN AT MIDDLETON PLACE Book at AAA.com **Phone:** 843/556-0500

Country Inn
Rates not provided

Address: 4290 Ashley River Rd **Location:** I-526, exit 11 (Ashley River Rd/SR 61), then 10.3 mi on SR 61 N. Located in a quiet area, next to Audubon Park and Cypress Gardens. **Facility:** Overlooking the Ashley River amid live oaks and pines, this inn offers a relaxed, retreat like atmosphere. Smoke free premises. 55 one-bedroom standard units. 2 stories (no elevator), exterior corridors. **Parking:** on-site. **Terms:** check-in 4 pm. **Amenities:** video library, voice mail, irons, hair dryers. *Some:* DVD players (fee). **Pool(s):** outdoor. **Leisure Activities:** recreation programs, hiking trails, jogging, horseback riding. *Fee:* bicycles, massage. **Guest Services:** valet laundry, wireless Internet. **Business Services:** conference facilities, business center.

/ SOME UNITS FEE FEE VCR

LA QUINTA INN RIVERVIEW Book great rates at AAA.com **Phone:** (843)556-5200 14

Hotel
$69-$159 All Year

Address: 11 Ashley Point Dr **Location:** US 17 S, just over Ashley River Bridge to Albermarle Rd, 0.4 mi s to Ashley Pointe Dr. Located at Ripley Light Marina. **Facility:** 175 one-bedroom standard units, some with whirlpools. 3-4 stories, interior/exterior corridors. *Bath:* combo or shower only. **Parking:** on-site. **Amenities:** voice mail, irons, hair dryers. **Pool(s):** outdoor. **Guest Services:** valet and coin laundry, wireless Internet. **Business Services:** meeting rooms, fax (fee). **Cards:** AX, DC, DS, MC, VI.

ASK / SOME UNITS

RESIDENCE INN BY MARRIOTT Book great rates at AAA.com **Phone:** (843)571-7979 13

Hotel
$147-$158 All Year

Address: 90 Ripley Point Dr **Location:** US 17 S, just over Ashley River Bridge to Albermarle Rd, just s. **Facility:** Smoke free premises. 119 units. 96 one- and 23 two-bedroom suites, some with efficiencies or kitchens. 4 stories, interior corridors. *Bath:* combo or shower only. **Parking:** on-site. **Terms:** cancellation fee imposed. **Amenities:** video games (fee), high-speed Internet, dual phone lines, voice mail, irons, hair dryers. **Pool(s):** heated outdoor. **Leisure Activities:** whirlpool, limited exercise equipment, sports court. **Guest Services:** valet and coin laundry, wireless Internet. **Business Services:** meeting rooms, fax (fee). **Cards:** AX, CB, DC, DS, MC, VI.

CALL &M / SOME UNITS FEE

Residence Inn Marriott

AAA Benefit:
Members save a minimum 5% off the best available rate.

▼ See AAA listing p 931 ▼

(See map and index starting on p. 877)

SLEEP INN-CHARLESTON Book at AAA.com Phone: (843)556-6959 8

Hotel
$49-$199 3/1-11/30
$49-$179 12/1-2/28

Address: 1524 Savannah Hwy **Location:** US 17 S, 3.6 mi w of Ashley River Bridge; jct I-526 W (end) and US 17 N, 1.7 mi e. **Facility:** 74 one-bedroom standard units. 4 stories, interior corridors. *Bath:* combo or shower only. **Parking:** on-site. **Amenities:** voice mail, irons, hair dryers. **Pool(s):** outdoor. **Leisure Activities:** exercise room. **Guest Services:** valet laundry, wireless Internet. **Business Services:** business center. **Cards:** AX, CB, DC, DS, JC, MC, VI.

ASK CALL / SOME UNITS

SPRINGHILL SUITES BY MARRIOTT-CHARLESTON RIVERVIEW Book great rates at AAA.com Phone: (843)571-1711 12

Hotel
$147-$158 All Year

Address: 98 Ripley Point Dr **Location:** US 17 S, just over Ashley River Bridge to Albermarle Rd, just s. **Facility:** Smoke free premises. 123 one-bedroom standard units. 5 stories, interior corridors. *Bath:* combo or shower only. **Parking:** on-site. **Terms:** check-in 4 pm, cancellation fee imposed. **Amenities:** dual phone lines, voice mail, irons, hair dryers. **Pool(s):** outdoor. **Leisure Activities:** whirlpool, exercise room. **Guest Services:** valet and coin laundry, wireless Internet. **Business Services:** meeting rooms, business center. **Cards:** AX, CB, DC, DS, JC, MC, VI.

CALL

AAA Benefit:
Members save a minimum 5% off the best available rate.

TOWN & COUNTRY INN & CONFERENCE CENTER Book at AAA.com Phone: 843/571-1000 3

Motel
Rates not provided

Address: 2008 Savannah Hwy **Location:** US 17 S, 3.5 mi nw of Ashley River Bridge; jct I-526 W (end) and US 17 N, just se. Located in a light-commercial area. **Facility:** 124 units. 122 one-bedroom standard units, some with efficiencies and/or whirlpools. 2 one-bedroom suites with kitchens and whirlpools. 2 stories, exterior corridors. **Parking:** on-site. **Amenities:** voice mail, irons, hair dryers. *Some:* dual phone lines. **Pool(s):** outdoor, heated indoor. **Leisure Activities:** saunas, racquetball courts, exercise room. **Guest Services:** valet and coin laundry, wireless Internet. **Business Services:** meeting rooms, fax.

/ SOME UNITS FEE VCR

WHERE TO DINE

AL DI LA Phone: 843/571-2321 6

Northern Italian
$9-$19

Fresh pasta dishes complement Northern Italian preparations of rabbit, pork, chicken and seafood. A good selection of wine accompaniments is available. Local critics have hailed this spot as the best West Ashley restaurant. Casual dress. **Bar:** Beer & wine. **Reservations:** suggested. **Hours:** 6 pm-10 pm. Closed: 1/1, 12/24, 12/25; also Sun & Mon. **Address:** 25 Magnolia Rd **Location:** Jct SR 171/US 17, 0.7 mi w on US 17; in West Ashley. **Parking:** on-site. **Cards:** MC, VI.

CALL

CALIFORNIA DREAMING Phone: 843/766-1644

American
$8-$23

The full-service, fine-dining restaurant appeals to adults, particularly those with an appetite for innovative concepts in food. Revised weekly, the menu consistently incorporates sophisticated, cutting-edge California dishes with Pacific Rim influences throughout. Among house specialties are flatbread appetizers baked in a brick oven, sushi, sashimi and some vegetarian dishes. The wine list focuses primarily on California vintages. Casual dress. **Bar:** Full bar. **Hours:** 11 am-10 pm, Fri & Sat-11 pm. **Address:** 1 Ashley Pointe Dr **Location:** US 17 S, just over Ashley River Bridge to Albermarle Rd, 0.4 mi se, then just e to end of road. **Parking:** on-site. **Cards:** AX, DC, DS, MC, VI.

CHARLESTON CRAB HOUSE Phone: 843/795-1963 9

Seafood
$15-$22

The casual, seafood-themed restaurant presents a menu varied enough to please a wide cross-section of patrons. The crab cocktail appetizer is almost a meal in itself, and stuffed mahi mahi and Charleston grouper are house specialties. Also offered is a good selection of steaks, as well as chicken, pasta and grits dishes. Casual dress. **Bar:** Full bar. **Hours:** 11:30 am-10 pm. Closed: 11/26, 12/25; also Super Bowl Sun. **Address:** 145 Wappoo Creek Dr **Location:** Jct SR 171/700, just w on SR 700 (May Bank Hwy), then just n; on James Island. **Parking:** on-site. **Cards:** AX, DS, MC, VI.

CALL

CISCO'S CAFE Phone: 843/571-6441 3

Mexican
$7-$20

Enormous portions of tamales, enchiladas or sizzling fajitas are standard at the family eatery. Multiple combinations are created from traditional preparations. For something different, try the Mexican egg rolls. Tempting desserts—such as fried ice cream and velvety chocolate mousse—cool the palate. Casual dress. **Bar:** Full bar. **Hours:** 11:30 am-10 pm, Fri & Sat-11 pm. Closed: 7/4, 11/26, 12/25; also Sun. **Address:** 1114 Sam Rittenberg Blvd **Location:** I-26, exit 216A (SR 7), 1.7 mi sw. **Parking:** on-site. **Cards:** AX, DS, MC, VI.

(See map and index starting on p. 877)

DRAGON PALACE

Phone: 843/388-8823

Chinese
$5-$25

Take out is available, but this place is far from typical. The owner imported the restaurant's interior to ensure its authenticity, and it's nothing short of stunning, even breathtaking. Carved solid wood walls, inlaid glass-topped tables and stained-glass backlit ceilings provide an unexpected ambience. The food matches the sophisticated atmosphere. Although diners can feast on traditional standards, the menu also lists a wide selection of upscale fare. Casual dress. **Reservations:** accepted. **Hours:** 11 am-2:30 & 4:30-9:30 pm, Fri & Sat-10:30 pm. Closed: 11/26, 12/25; also Sun. **Address:** 162 Seven Farms Dr, Suite 320 **Location:** I-526, exit 24 (Daniel Island), just w on Seven Farms Dr; in Daniel Island Towne Center. **Parking:** on-site. **Cards:** AX, DS, MC, VI.

CALL &M

LANA'S MEXICAN RESTAURANT

Phone: 843/881-9163

Mexican
$5-$18

On Daniel Island, the simple, family-run restaurant presents a menu of affordably priced, well-prepared and beautifully presented traditional Mexican and Tex-Mex dishes. The dining room is open, the service frenetic and the food outstanding. Patio seating is an option. Casual dress. **Bar:** Full bar. **Hours:** 11 am-10 pm. Closed: 11/26; also Sun. **Address:** 855 Island Park Dr, Unit D **Location:** I-526, exit 24 (Daniel Island), just s. **Parking:** on-site. **Cards:** AX, DS, MC, VI.

LOCKLEAR'S LOWCOUNTRY GRILL

Phone: 843/762-2549 (10)

Regional American
$7-$20

The owners opened this popular local chain in 1980. Professional staffers display their skills from an exhibition kitchen and turn out such delights as the award-winning eggplant tower, she-crab soup, fried seafood and pasta dishes. Special dietary needs are honored. Casual dress. **Bar:** Full bar. **Reservations:** accepted. **Hours:** 11:30 am-9 pm, Fri & Sat-10 pm, Sun 10 am-9 pm. Closed: 9/7, 11/26, 12/25. **Address:** 1970 Maybank Hwy **Location:** Jct SR 171, 0.7 mi w. **Parking:** on-site. **Cards:** AX, DS, MC, VI.

CALL &M

MED BISTRO

Phone: 843/766-0323 (8)

American
$6-$24

Chrome and black accents add to the retro-style feel of the deli, which also is decorated with colorful oil paintings by local artists. A varied selection of tasty entrees can be enjoyed with a choice from the quality wine selection. Recommended is the Monte Carlo, a ham and turkey sandwich with bread dipped in egg batter and grilled with cheese, followed by tasty Snickers pie. Casual dress. **Bar:** Full bar. **Hours:** 11 am-10 pm, Sun 10 am-3 pm. Closed major holidays. **Address:** 90 Folly Rd **Location:** Jct US 17/SR 171, just s on SR 171 (Folly Rd); in South Windermere Shopping Center, West Ashley. **Parking:** on-site. **Cards:** AX, DS, MC, VI.

NATHAN'S

Phone: 843/556-3354 (4)

Deli
$4-$9

The unpretentious, no-frills roadside restaurant prepares New York-style delicatessen sandwiches, which patrons can enjoy inside or on the patio. Casual dress. **Hours:** 6 am-10 pm, Sun-4 pm, Mon-5 pm. Closed major holidays. **Address:** 2004 Ashley River Dr **Location:** I-526, exit Ashley River Rd, just e on Paul Cantrell Blvd to Ashley River Rd (SR 61), then just nw. **Parking:** on-site. **Cards:** MC, VI.

OLYMPIK RESTAURANT & BAKERY

Phone: 843/556-9359 (5)

Greek
$6-$18

Near the mall and hotels in West Ashley, the small restaurant focuses on traditional Greek and Mediterranean dishes and freshly made pastries and cakes. Casual dress. **Bar:** Beer & wine. **Hours:** 11 am-9 pm. Closed: 11/26, 12/25; also Sun. **Address:** 1922 Savannah Hwy **Location:** Jct I-526/US 17, 0.5 mi e on US 17. **Parking:** on-site. **Cards:** MC, VI.

QUEEN ANNE'S REVENGE

Phone: 843/216-6868

American
$7-$26

Named for Blackbeard's infamous ship, the restaurant is fraught with pirate memorabilia, including doubloons, muskets, swords, a ship's brig and portraits of the man himself. The setting is great fun for the entire family. Also a treasure is the food, including beef, chicken, ribs and seafood. Casual dress. **Bar:** Full bar. **Reservations:** suggested. **Hours:** 11:30 am-10 pm, Fri & Sat-11 pm, Sun-9 pm. Closed: 11/26, 12/25. **Address:** 160-B Fairchild St **Location:** I-526, exit 24 (Daniel Island), just w, follow signs. **Parking:** on-site. **Cards:** AX, DC, DS, MC, VI.

CALL &M

S & S CAFETERIA

Phone: 843/556-9420 (2)

AAA

American
$4-$8

A longtime favorite for comfort food, the family-owned cafeteria invites diners to load a plate with traditionally prepared chicken, beef, vegetables, salad and dessert. Casual dress. **Hours:** 11 am-2:15 & 5-8 pm. Closed: 12/25. **Address:** 1104 Sam Rittenberg Blvd **Location:** I-26, exit 216A (SR 7), 1.6 mi sw. **Parking:** on-site. **Cards:** AX, DS, MC, VI.

SIENNA

Phone: 843/881-8820

Regional Italian
$12-$32

Superlative, extraordinary and incredible describes the experience at the casually elegant restaurant. Italian cuisine unlike any other is truly a celebration of food. Each dish is a work of art, a taste sensation and, best of all, affordable. Among extraordinary dishes are carpaccio and Grandma Volpe's Italian wedding soup. The menu changes daily, and two tasting menus are available with or without wine. The floor staff serves meals with skill. Dressy casual. **Bar:** Full bar. **Reservations:** suggested. **Hours:** 11:30 am-2 & 6-9 pm, Fri-10 pm, Sat 6 pm-10 pm. Closed: 11/26, 12/25; also Sun. **Address:** 901 Island Park Dr **Location:** I-526, exit 24 (Daniel Island), just sw. **Parking:** street. **Cards:** AX, MC, VI.

CALL &M

(See map and index starting on p. 877)

SUNFIRE GRILL AND BISTRO **Phone.** 843/766-0223 (T)

American
$6-$20

Independent and eclectic come to mind, but the chef describes the menu as Mediterranean fusion. Regardless, the atmosphere is comfortable, portion sizes are excellent, prices are great, and service is even better. Wide-ranging menu offerings include delights such as hand-made tapenade, pan-fried stuffed chicken, assorted sandwiches and vegetarian dishes. Casual dress. **Bar:** Full bar. **Reservations:** suggested. **Hours:** 11 am-10 pm, Fri & Sat-10:30 pm, Sun 10 am-10 pm. Closed: 7/4, 12/25. **Address:** 1090 Sam Rittenberg Blvd **Location:** I-26, exit 216A (SR 7), 1.6 mi sw. **Parking:** on-site. **Cards:** AX, DS, MC, VI.

CALL

TRIANGLE CHAR & BAR **Phone:** 843/377-1300 (7)

American
$7-$20

In a former service station, the popular restaurant features 15 cuts of meat, a slew of sides and a giant charcoal grill. The New American menu draws on global influences, with selections such as paella, tempura shrimp and penne al fresco, and also lists traditional favorites, including burgers, seafood and baked macaroni and cheese. Daily blue-plate specials also are worth a look. The pace in the small bistro's dining room can be frenetic, but the food is always well prepared and tasty. Casual dress. **Bar:** Full bar. **Reservations:** not accepted. **Hours:** 11 am-2 & 5-10 pm, Fri-11 pm, Sat 5 pm-11 pm, Sun 11 am-3 & 5-10 pm. Closed: 12/24, 12/25. **Address:** 828 Savannah Hwy **Location:** Jct SR 171/US 17, 0.7 mi w on US 17; in West Ashley. **Parking:** on-site. **Cards:** AX, DS, MC, VI.

The Charleston Vicinity

AWENDAW pop. 1,195

WHERE TO DINE

SEE WEE RESTAURANT **Phone:** 843/928-3609

Seafood
$6-$21

Between Georgetown and Charleston, the former 1920s country store is now a formidable country restaurant where wonderful, home-cooked Lowcountry cuisine is served in a no-frills, glad-you're-here manner. Offerings include steaks and a lengthy list of daily specials that keep up with the fresh fish deliveries. Desserts are baked on the premises. Casual dress. **Bar:** Beer & wine. **Hours:** 11 am-9 pm, Fri-10 pm, Sat 8 am-10 pm, Sun 11 am-3 pm. Closed major holidays. **Address:** 4808 N Hwy 17 **Location:** Jct US 17/SR 41, 7.1 mi ne. **Parking:** on-site. **Cards:** CB, DC, DS, MC, VI.

FOLLY BEACH pop. 2,116

WHERE TO STAY

HOLIDAY INN FOLLY BEACH OCEANFRONT *Book great rates at AAA.com* **Phone:** (843)588-6464

AAA SAVE

Hotel
$109-$309 4/1-11/30
$109-$259 12/1-3/31

Address: 1 Center St **Location:** Oceanfront. Terminus of SR 171; center. **Facility:** 132 one-bedroom standard units. 9 stories, exterior corridors. *Bath:* combo or shower only. **Parking:** on-site. **Terms:** check-in 4 pm, 3 day cancellation notice-fee imposed. **Amenities:** voice mail, irons, hair dryers. **Dining:** 2 restaurants. **Pool(s):** heated outdoor. **Leisure Activities:** exercise room. **Guest Services:** valet and coin laundry, wireless Internet. **Business Services:** meeting rooms, business center. **Cards:** AX, DC, DS, MC, VI. **Free Special Amenities: newspaper and high-speed Internet.**

/ SOME UNITS FEE

WATER'S EDGE INN **Phone:** (843)588-9800

Hotel
$199-$279 All Year

Address: 79 W 2nd St **Location:** Jct Center St (SR 171) and W Indian Ave, just sw. **Facility:** Designated smoking area. 10 units. 8 one-bedroom standard units, some with whirlpools. 2 condominiums. 4 stories (no elevator), exterior corridors. **Parking:** on-site. **Terms:** office hours 7:30 am-9 pm, age restrictions may apply, 7 day cancellation notice. **Amenities:** high-speed Internet, voice mail, safes, hair dryers. **Leisure Activities:** whirlpool, bicycles. **Guest Services:** wireless Internet. **Business Services:** fax (fee). **Cards:** AX, MC, VI.

ASK / SOME UNITS

WHERE TO DINE

LOCKLEAR'S BEACH CITY GRILL **Phone:** 843/588-6412

Regional Seafood
$7-$22

At Folly Pier, the oceanside restaurant has a bistro-style dining room and a large, airy covered deck from which diners can experience the salt air. Frozen drinks and cocktails are sipped as surfers catch the waves. The menu centers on well-prepared fresh seafood and pasta dishes. Casual dress. **Bar:** Full bar. **Hours:** 9 am-10 pm; seasonal hours vary. Closed: 1/1, 11/26, 12/25. **Address:** 101 E Artic Ave **Location:** Jct SR 171 (Center St/E Artic Ave), just ne; at Folly Beach Pier. **Parking:** on-site (fee). **Cards:** AX, DS, MC, VI.

GOOSE CREEK pop. 29,208

WHERE TO DINE

GILLIGAN'S STEAMER & RAW BAR **Phone:** 843/818-2244

Seafood
$7-$21

A casual family oriented neighborhood restaurant, Gilligan's is famous for fresh shrimp right off the boat! Locals flock not only for the shrimp but also for Captain Bookatee's hushpuppies. Not a seafood lover? Come on anyway and enjoy the buffalo wings and chicken fingers. Casual dress. **Bar:** Full bar. **Hours:** 11 am-9 pm, Fri & Sat-10 pm. Closed: 11/26, 12/25. **Address:** 219 St James Ave **Location:** Jct US 176/52, 1 mi n on US 176. **Parking:** on-site. **Cards:** AX, DS, MC, VI.

CALL

LOS ARCOS

Mexican
$4-$16

Phone: 843/572-5838

Burritos, Californiano, chori-pollo, Texas fajitas and large bowls of freshly-prepared soups are all excellent choices at the traditional, Mexican-American restaurant. The large menu is loaded with plenty of options for any taste. The bright, welcoming dining room complements the relaxed, friendly atmosphere where wait staff are anxious to assist. Think big because the margaritas are huge as are the meal portions. Casual dress. **Bar:** Full bar. **Hours:** 11 am-10 pm, Fri & Sat-10:30 pm, Sun noon-9 pm. Closed: 11/26, 12/25. **Address:** 214 St. James Ave **Location:** Jct US176/US 52, 1 mi n on US 176; in Shannon Park Shopping Center. **Parking:** on-site. **Cards:** AX, DS, MC, VI.

ISLE OF PALMS pop. 4,583

WHERE TO STAY

THE BOARDWALK INN AT WILD DUNES RESORT *Book great rates at AAA.com* **Phone:** (843)886-6000

AAA SAVE

Boutique Resort Hotel

$125-$1500 All Year

Address: 5757 Palm Blvd **Location:** Isle of Palms connector to jct SR 517 and 703, 3.1 mi ne on SR 703 (Palm Blvd), follow signs. **Facility:** Between the ocean and the Intracoastal Waterway, this resort features casual West Indies decor; live entertainment is provided oceanside in summer. Designated smoking area. 93 units. 85 one-bedroom standard units. 8 one-bedroom suites. 5 stories, interior corridors. *Bath:* combo or shower only. **Parking:** on-site and valet. **Terms:** check-in 4 pm, 7 day cancellation notice-fee imposed. **Amenities:** CD players, high-speed Internet, dual phone lines, voice mail, safes, honor bars, irons, hair dryers. **Dining:** Sea Island Grill & Bar, see separate listing. **Pool(s):** 3 outdoor, heated outdoor. **Leisure Activities:** sauna, steamroom, rental boats, rental canoes, rental sailboards, fishing, recreation programs, resort facilities available, jogging, exercise room, spa, basketball, horseshoes, volleyball. *Fee:* marina, waterskiing, scuba diving, snorkeling, charter fishing, golf-36 holes, 16 tennis courts (5 lighted), rollerblades, bicycles. **Guest Services:** valet laundry, area transportation-Island resort, beauty salon, wireless Internet. **Business Services:** conference facilities, business center. **Cards:** AX, DC, DS, MC, VI. **Free Special Amenities: newspaper and high-speed Internet.**

CALL

THE PALMS HOTEL *Book great rates at AAA.com* **Phone:** (843)886-3003

AAA SAVE

Hotel

$89-$369 3/1-11/30
$79-$199 12/1-2/28

Address: 1126 Ocean Blvd **Location:** Oceanfront. Just s of SR 517 (Isle of Palms connector). **Facility:** 68 one-bedroom standard units. 3 stories, interior corridors. *Bath:* combo or shower only. **Terms:** check-in 4 pm, cancellation fee imposed. **Amenities:** dual phone lines, voice mail, irons, hair dryers. **Pool(s):** outdoor. **Guest Services:** valet and coin laundry, wireless Internet. **Business Services:** fax (fee). **Cards:** AX, DC, DS, MC, VI. **Free Special Amenities: expanded continental breakfast and high-speed Internet.** *(See color ad starting on p 886)*

/ SOME UNITS

SEASIDE INN *Book great rates at AAA.com* **Phone:** (843)886-7000

Motel

$99-$399 4/1-11/30
$65-$259 12/1-3/31

Address: 1004 Ocean Blvd **Location:** Oceanfront. Jct SR 517/703, just se on 14th ave, then just sw. **Facility:** 51 one-bedroom standard units. 3 stories, exterior corridors. *Bath:* shower only. **Parking:** on-site. **Terms:** check-in 4 pm, cancellation fee imposed. **Amenities:** voice mail, irons, hair dryers. **Guest Services:** wireless Internet. **Business Services:** fax (fee). **Cards:** AX, DS, MC, VI. ***(See color ad starting on p 886)***

ASK / SOME UNITS

WILD DUNES RESORT - BEACH CLUB VILLAS **Phone:** 843/886-6000

Vacation Rental Condominium

Rates not provided

Address: 1 Beach Club Villas **Location:** Oceanfront. Main gate, 1 mi e on Palmetto Dr; in Wild Dunes Resort. **Facility:** Three-bedroom, three-bath townhomes are nestled on the ocean; each unit features a private carport and spacious sundeck. Smoke free premises. 17 condominiums. 3 stories (no elevator), exterior corridors. **Parking:** on-site. **Terms:** off-site registration, check-in 4 pm. **Amenities:** voice mail, irons, hair dryers. **Pool(s):** outdoor. **Leisure Activities:** saunas, steamrooms, rental boats, rental canoes, rental sailboards, fishing, recreation programs, jogging, playground, spa, basketball, volleyball. *Fee:* marina, waterskiing, scuba diving, snorkeling, charter fishing, golf-36 holes, 17 tennis courts (5 lighted), bicycles. **Guest Services:** complimentary laundry. **Business Services:** conference facilities, business center.

WILD DUNES RESORT - BOARDWALK VILLAS **Phone:** 843/886-6000

Vacation Rental Condominium

$159-$199 2/14-11/30

Address: 100 Boardwalk Villas **Location:** Main gate, 0.4 mi e on Palmetto Dr, then just s on Grand Pavilion; in Wild Dunes Resort. **Facility:** Upscale three-story townhomes are situated in a quaint neighborhood setting, within easy reach of the resort's activities. Smoke free premises. 10 condominiums. 3 stories (no elevator), exterior corridors. **Parking:** on-site. **Terms:** open 2/14-11/30, off-site registration, check-in 4 pm, 7 day cancellation notice-fee imposed. **Amenities:** voice mail, irons, hair dryers. **Pool(s):** outdoor. **Leisure Activities:** saunas, steamrooms, beach access, rental boats, rental canoes, rental sailboards, fishing, recreation programs, jogging, playground, spa, basketball, volleyball. *Fee:* marina, waterskiing, scuba diving, snorkeling, charter fishing, golf-36 holes, 17 tennis courts (5 lighted), bicycles. **Guest Services:** complimentary laundry. **Business Services:** conference facilities, business center. **Cards:** MC, VI.

WILD DUNES RESORT - LAGOON VILLAS

Phone: 843/886-6000

Vacation Rental Condominium

Rates not provided

Address: 1 Lagoon Rd **Location:** Main gate, 0.7 mi e on Palmetto Dr; in Wild Dunes Resort. **Facility:** Comprised of eleven buildings, the raised, walk-up townhomes feature two bedrooms and two baths; situated near the resort's tennis center. Smoke free premises. 21 condominiums. 3 stories (no elevator), exterior corridors. **Parking:** on-site. **Terms:** off-site registration, check-in 4 pm. **Amenities:** voice mail, irons, hair dryers. **Pool(s):** outdoor. **Leisure Activities:** saunas, steamrooms, beach access, rental boats, rental canoes, rental sailboards, fishing, recreation programs, jogging, playground, spa, basketball, volleyball. *Fee:* marina, waterskiing, scuba diving, snorkeling, charter fishing, golf-36 holes, 17 tennis courts (5 lighted), bicycles. **Guest Services:** complimentary laundry. **Business Services:** conference facilities, business center.

WILD DUNES RESORT - LINKSIDE VILLAS *Book at AAA.com*

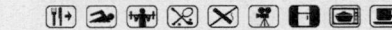

Phone: 843/886-6000

Vacation Rental Condominium

Rates not provided

Address: 1 Linkside Ct **Location:** Main gate, 1.7 mi e on Palmetto Dr; in Wild Dunes Resort. **Facility:** Comprised of 12 three-story buildings located near the 15th and 16th fairways; each two- and three-bedroom townhome includes a whirlpool tub and deck. Smoke free premises. 9 condominiums. 3 stories (no elevator), exterior corridors. **Parking:** on-site. **Terms:** off-site registration, check-in 4 pm. **Amenities:** voice mail, irons, hair dryers. **Pool(s):** outdoor. **Leisure Activities:** saunas, steamrooms, beach access, rental boats, rental canoes, rental sailboards, fishing, recreation programs, jogging, playground, spa, basketball, volleyball. *Fee:* marina, waterskiing, scuba diving, snorkeling, charter fishing, golf-36 holes, 17 tennis courts (5 lighted), bicycles. **Guest Services:** complimentary laundry. **Business Services:** conference facilities, business center.

WILD DUNES RESORT - MARINER'S WALK VILLAS

Phone: 843/886-6000

Vacation Rental Condominium

Rates not provided

Address: 7000 Palmetto Dr **Location:** Oceanfront. Main gate, 1.1 mi e on Palmetto Dr; in Wild Dunes Resort. **Facility:** Comprised of six buildings, the three-story, walk-up complex offers a choice of one-, two- or three-bedroom flats and townhouse-style units. Smoke free premises. 18 condominiums. 3 stories (no elevator), exterior corridors. **Parking:** on-site. **Terms:** off-site registration, check-in 4 pm. **Amenities:** voice mail, irons, hair dryers. **Pool(s):** outdoor. **Leisure Activities:** saunas, steamrooms, rental boats, rental canoes, rental sailboards, snorkeling, fishing, recreation programs, jogging, playground, spa, basketball, volleyball. *Fee:* marina, waterskiing, scuba diving, charter fishing, golf-36 holes, 17 tennis courts (5 lighted), bicycles. **Guest Services:** complimentary laundry. **Business Services:** conference facilities, business center.

WILD DUNES RESORT - OCEAN CLUB VILLAS

Phone: 843/886-6000

Vacation Rental Condominium

Rates not provided

Address: 9510 Palmetto Dr **Location:** Oceanfront. Main gate, 1.6 mi e on Palmetto Dr; in Wild Dunes Resort. **Facility:** Nestled in a six-story, oceanfront building are two-, three- and four-bedroom condo units with a private porch that overlooks the ocean or 18th hole. Smoke free premises. 15 condominiums. 6 stories, exterior corridors. **Parking:** on-site. **Terms:** off-site registration, check-in 4 pm. **Amenities:** voice mail, irons, hair dryers. **Pool(s):** outdoor. **Leisure Activities:** saunas, steamrooms, rental boats, rental canoes, rental sailboards, fishing, recreation programs, jogging, playground, spa, basketball, volleyball. *Fee:* marina, waterskiing, scuba diving, snorkeling, charter fishing, golf-36 holes, 17 tennis courts (5 lighted), bicycles. **Guest Services:** complimentary laundry. **Business Services:** conference facilities, business center. ***(See color ad below)***

▼ *See AAA listing above* ▼

WILD DUNES RESORT - PORT O' CALL VILLAS

Phone: 843/886-6000

Vacation Rental Condominium

Rates not provided

Address: 101A Port O' Call Villas **Location:** Oceanfront. Main gate, 1.5 mi e on Palmetto Dr; in Wild Dunes Resort. **Facility:** Seven three-story, oceanfront buildings surround a central pool area and offer comfortable one-bedroom accommodations. Smoke free premises. 39 condominiums. 3 stories (no elevator), exterior corridors. **Parking:** on-site. **Terms:** off-site registration, check-in 4 pm. **Amenities:** voice mail, irons, hair dryers. **Pool(s):** outdoor. **Leisure Activities:** saunas, steamrooms, rental boats, rental canoes, rental sailboards, fishing, recreation programs, jogging, playground, spa, basketball, volleyball. *Fee:* marina, waterskiing, scuba diving, snorkeling, charter fishing, golf-36 holes, 17 tennis courts (5 lighted), bicycles. **Guest Services:** complimentary laundry. **Business Services:** conference facilities, business center.

WILD DUNES RESORT - RACQUET CLUB VILLAS

Phone: 843/886-6000

Vacation Rental Condominium

Rates not provided

Address: 1 Back Ct **Location:** Main gate, 0.6 mi e on Palmetto Dr; in Wild Dunes Resort. **Facility:** Centered among the 11 three-story, walk-up buildings is the complex's tennis center and pro shop; select from two- and three-bedroom units. Smoke free premises. 19 condominiums. 3 stories (no elevator), exterior corridors. **Parking:** on-site. **Terms:** off-site registration, check-in 4 pm. **Amenities:** voice mail, irons, hair dryers. **Pool(s):** outdoor. **Leisure Activities:** saunas, steamrooms, beach access, rental boats, rental canoes, rental sailboards, fishing, recreation programs, jogging, playground, spa, basketball, volleyball. *Fee:* marina, waterskiing, scuba diving, snorkeling, charter fishing, golf-36 holes, 15 tennis courts (7 lighted), bicycles. **Guest Services:** complimentary laundry. **Business Services:** conference facilities, business center.

WILD DUNES RESORT - SEAGROVE VILLAS

Phone: 843/886-6000

Vacation Rental Condominium

Rates not provided

Address: 1 Seagrove Ln **Location:** Main gate, 0.6 mi e on Palmetto Dr; in Wild Dunes Resort. **Facility:** The three-story buildings contain one-, two- and three-bedroom units with large private decks; some units are located oceanfront. Smoke free premises. 13 condominiums. 3 stories (no elevator), exterior corridors. **Parking:** on-site. **Terms:** off-site registration, check-in 4 pm. **Amenities:** voice mail, irons, hair dryers. **Pool(s):** outdoor. **Leisure Activities:** saunas, steamrooms, beach access, rental boats, rental canoes, rental sailboards, fishing, recreation programs, jogging, playground, spa, basketball, volleyball. *Fee:* marina, waterskiing, scuba diving, snorkeling, charter fishing, golf-36 holes, 17 tennis courts (5 lighted), bicycles. **Guest Services:** complimentary laundry. **Business Services:** conference facilities, business center.

WILD DUNES RESORT - SEASCAPE VILLAS **Phone:** 843/886-6000

Vacation Rental Condominium

Rates not provided

Address: 9002 Palmetto Dr **Location:** Oceanfront. Main gate, 1.5 mi e on Palmetto Dr; in Wild Dunes Resort. **Facility:** Find spacious, individually decorated two- and three-bedroom condo units at the low-rise, oceanfront property; private balconies afford ocean views. Smoke free premises. 13 condominiums. 6 stories, exterior corridors. **Parking:** on-site. **Terms:** off-site registration, check-in 4 pm. **Amenities:** voice mail, irons, hair dryers. **Pool(s):** outdoor. **Leisure Activities:** saunas, steamrooms, rental boats, rental canoes, rental sailboards, fishing, recreation programs, jogging, playground, spa, basketball, volleyball. *Fee:* marina, waterskiing, scuba diving, snorkeling, charter fishing, golf-36 holes, 17 tennis courts (5 lighted), bicycles. **Guest Services:** complimentary laundry. **Business Services:** conference facilities, business center.

WILD DUNES RESORT - SHIPWATCH VILLAS **Phone:** 843/886-6000

Vacation Rental Condominium

Rates not provided

Address: 7600 Palmetto Dr **Location:** Oceanfront. Main gate, 1.3 mi e on Palmetto Dr; in Wild Dunes Resort. **Facility:** Four five-story buildings surround the community pool; select from flats and two- or three-bedroom townhomes, each with a private balcony. Smoke free premises. 31 condominiums. 5 stories, exterior corridors. **Parking:** on-site. **Terms:** off-site registration, check-in 4 pm. **Amenities:** voice mail, irons, hair dryers. **Pool(s):** outdoor. **Leisure Activities:** saunas, steamrooms, rental boats, rental canoes, rental sailboards, fishing, recreation programs, jogging, playground, spa, basketball, volleyball. *Fee:* marina, waterskiing, scuba diving, snorkeling, charter fishing, golf-36 holes, 17 tennis courts (5 lighted), bicycles. **Guest Services:** complimentary laundry. **Business Services:** conference facilities, business center.

WILD DUNES RESORT - SUMMERHOUSE VILLAS **Phone:** 843/886-6000

Vacation Rental Condominium

Rates not provided

Address: 8000 Palmetto Dr **Location:** Oceanfront. Main gate, 1.3 mi e on Palmetto Dr; in Wild Dunes Resort. **Facility:** The spacious two-, three- and four-bedroom units are situated oceanfront. Smoke free premises. 10 condominiums. 6 stories, exterior corridors. **Parking:** on-site. **Terms:** off-site registration, check-in 4 pm. **Amenities:** voice mail, irons, hair dryers. **Pool(s):** outdoor. **Leisure Activities:** saunas, steamrooms, rental boats, rental canoes, rental sailboards, fishing, recreation programs, jogging, playground, spa, basketball, volleyball. *Fee:* marina, waterskiing, scuba diving, snorkeling, charter fishing, golf-36 holes, 17 tennis courts (5 lighted), bicycles. **Guest Services:** complimentary laundry. **Business Services:** conference facilities, business center.

WILD DUNES RESORT - THE VILLAGE AT WILD DUNES RESORT **Phone:** 843/886-6000

fyi

Vacation Rental Condominium

$125-$895 All Year

Too new to rate, opening scheduled for July 2008. **Address:** 5757 Palm Blvd **Location:** Jct SR 517 and 703, 3.1 mi ne on SR 703 (Palm Blvd), follow signs. **Amenities:** 115 units, restaurant, coffeemakers, microwaves, refrigerators, pool, exercise facilities, water sports, golf, tennis. **Terms:** check-in 4 pm, 45 day cancellation notice-fee imposed. **Cards:** AX, DS, MC, VI.

WHERE TO DINE

BAREFOOT BISTRO **Phone:** 843/886-4445

American

$7-$22

With only eight tables, the small storefront restaurant employs friendly servers who guide patrons through a limited but diverse menu centered on lighter choices along the lines of field green salads, quiche of the day, fried green tomatoes and fresh scallops and shrimp with fresh vegetables. Parking can be accessed behind the restaurant. Casual dress. **Bar:** Full bar. **Reservations:** accepted. **Hours:** 11 am-2:30 pm, Wed-Sat 5 pm-9 pm, Sun 10 am-2:30 pm. Closed: 11/24-11/30 & 12/24-1/7. **Address:** 1101 Ocean Blvd **Location:** Jct SR 517 (Isle of Palms connector) and SR 703 (Palm Blvd), just se to Ocean Blvd, then just sw. **Parking:** on-site and street. **Cards:** MC, VI.

THE BOATHOUSE AT BREACH INLET **Phone:** 843/886-8000

Seafood

$18-$37

Guests often have to wait at the popular restaurant, but excellent seafood, crab cakes and steak make it worthwhile. Portions are ample. If the timing is right, request a seat on the covered deck and roof-top bar to catch a view of the spectacular sunset. Casual dress. **Bar:** Full bar. **Reservations:** accepted. **Hours:** 5 pm-10 pm, Fri & Sat-11 pm; Sunday brunch 11 am-2 pm. Closed: 1/1, 12/25. **Address:** 101 Palm Blvd (SR 703) **Location:** On SR 703, at south end of the island; at Breach Inlet Bridge. **Parking:** on-site and valet. **Cards:** AX, DS, MC, VI.

CALL

COCONUT JOE'S **Phone:** 843/886-0046

American

$7-$22

On the beach, the island-themed restaurant offers ocean views from every table, inside and out. Guests can choose from the "zappatizer," "Rasta pastas" and many other selections on a menu that features everything from light fare to full dinners. The staff is friendly and the atmosphere relaxing. Casual dress. **Bar:** Full bar. **Hours:** 11:30 am-10 pm, Fri-11 pm, Sat-Mon 9 am-11 pm. Closed: 11/26, 12/25. **Address:** 1120 Ocean Blvd **Location:** Jct SR 517 (Isle of Palms connector)/SR 703 (Palm Blvd), just se to Ocean Blvd, then just sw; on oceanfront. **Parking:** street. **Cards:** AX, DS, MC, VI.

LONG ISLAND CAFE **Phone:** 843/886-8809

AAA

American

$9-$31

The small storefront restaurant near the beach has been pleasing islanders and visitors alike for over a dozen years; the menu is weighted toward fresh-off-the-dock seafood but beef and chicken dishes are also featured. Casual dress. **Bar:** Full bar. **Reservations:** accepted, for dinner. **Hours:** 11:30 am-2:30 & 5:30-9:30 pm, Fri & Sat-10 pm. Closed: 11/26, 12/24, 12/25. **Address:** 1515A Palm Blvd **Location:** Jct SR 517 (Isle of Palms connector) and 703 (Palm Blvd); in Island Center. **Parking:** on-site. **Cards:** AX, DS, MC, VI.

CALL

MORGAN CREEK GRILL **Phone:** 843/886-8980

Seafood
$16-$24

Everything is offered here: marina views from every seat, live entertainment, alfresco dining and great food. Diners arrive by car or moor at the restaurant's deep water dock. Featured on the eclectic menu are steaks, chops, pasta, seafood and a diverse selection of appetizers. Those who love fish should hold out for the fresh catch of the day. Casual dress. **Bar:** Full bar. **Reservations:** suggested. **Hours:** 5 pm-9 pm, Fri & Sat-10 pm, Sun 10:30 am-2:30 & 5-9 pm. Closed: 1/1, 12/25; also Mon 12/1-2/28. **Address:** 80 41st Ave **Location:** Jct SR 517 (Isle of Palms connector)/SR 703 (Palm Blvd), 1.8 mi ne of SR 703 (Palm Blvd), then just n; in Isle of Palms Marina. **Parking:** on-site. **Cards:** MC, VI.

CALL

SEA BISCUIT CAFE **Phone:** 843/886-4079

American
$5-$11

Tucked away in what looks like a beach house with a small front porch, the eatery offers biscuits, eggs, various breakfast meats and other breakfast fare. The lunch menu lists seafood and burger entrees, but daily specials normally outnumber the listed selections. Casual dress. **Hours:** 6:30 am-2:30 pm, Sat & Sun 7:30 am-1 pm. Closed: 1/1, 12/25; also Mon. **Address:** 21 JC Long Blvd **Location:** Jct SR 517 (Isle of Palms connector)/SR 703 (Palm Blvd), just sw on SR 703, then just s. **Parking:** on-site.

SEA ISLAND GRILL & BAR **Phone:** 843/886-2200

Regional American
$8-$38

The chef promises the freshest seafood available and comes through. On the menu are excellently prepared versions of she crab soup with crab fritter, fresh poached mussels, black grouper, Atlantic salmon, yellowfin tuna and, for landlubbers, black Angus filet and a 22-ounce porterhouse. Dressy casual. **Bar:** Full bar. **Reservations:** suggested. **Hours:** 6:30 am-10 pm. **Address:** 5757 Palm Blvd **Location:** Isle of Palms connector to jct SR 517 and 703, 3.1 mi ne on SR 703 (Palm Blvd), follow signs; in The Boardwalk Inn at Wild Dunes Resort. **Parking:** on-site. **Cards:** AX, CB, DC, DS, MC, VI.

CALL

JOHNS ISLAND

WHERE TO DINE

GILLIGAN'S STEAMER & RAW BAR **Phone:** 843/766-2244

Seafood
$7-$21

A casual family oriented neighborhood restaurant, Gilligan's is famous for fresh shrimp right off the boat! Locals flock not only for the shrimp but also for Captain Bookatee's hushpuppies. Not a seafood lover? Come on anyway and enjoy the buffalo wings and chicken fingers. Casual dress. **Bar:** Full bar. **Hours:** 11 am-9 pm, Fri & Sat-10 pm. Closed: 11/26, 12/25. **Address:** 160 Main Rd **Location:** I-526 to US 17, 4.1 mi s, then 0.3 mi e. **Parking:** on-site. **Cards:** AX, DS, MC, VI.

HEGE'S **Phone:** 843/768-0035

French
$22-$40

The chef/owner has created a comfortable atmosphere with a diverse menu. Select from the cozy, casual dining rooms or dine al fresco on the patio. Combining classic French cooking styles with seasonally fresh, local ingredients results in a menu with Continental panache and Lowcountry sparkle. Offerings include baked, stuffed flounder with lump crabmeat, crispy fried oysters with remoulade sauce and more traditional French items like calves liver with bacon or three-meat stroganoff. Casual dress. **Bar:** Full bar. **Reservations:** suggested. **Hours:** 5:30 pm-10 pm. Closed: 12/25; also Mon. **Address:** 130 Gardners Cir, PMB 108 **Location:** Jct Kiawah Island Pkwy, Seabrook Island Rd and Betsy Kerrison Pkwy; in Freshfields Village. **Parking:** on-site. **Cards:** AX, DS, MC, VI.

CALL

ROSEBANK FARMS CAFE **Phone:** 843/768-1807

Regional American
$8-$25

The country atmosphere celebrates the joys and hardships of life in the South through lovely framed photographs. Southern cooking is modernized to suit contemporary tastes, and dishes use fresh vegetables grown at nearby Rosebank Farms. Casual dress. **Bar:** Full bar. **Reservations:** not accepted. **Hours:** 11 am-2 & 5-9:30 pm. Closed: 11/26, 12/25. **Address:** 1886 Andell Bluff Blvd **Location:** On Seabrook Island; in Bohicket Marina Village. **Parking:** on-site. **Cards:** AX, DC, DS, MC, VI.

KIAWAH ISLAND pop. 1,163

WHERE TO STAY

KIAWAH ISLAND GOLF RESORT - COURTSIDE VILLAS **Phone:** 843/768-2121

Vacation Rental Condominium
Rates not provided

Address: 1401 Shipwatch Rd **Location:** Just e of main gate to Kiawah Beach Dr, then just s; in West Beach Village area. **Facility:** Overlooking the tennis courts of West Beach Tennis Club, these villas are located close to the beach, inn, shops and recreation. 13 condominiums. 2 stories (no elevator), exterior corridors. **Parking:** on-site. **Terms:** off-site registration, check-in 4 pm. **Amenities:** DVD players, CD players, voice mail, safes, irons, hair dryers. **Pool(s):** 4 outdoor, heated outdoor. **Leisure Activities:** rental canoes, sailboats, recreation programs, rental bicycles, jogging, playground, exercise room, sports court, basketball, volleyball. *Fee:* boat ramp, golf-90 holes, 28 tennis courts (8 lighted), massage. **Guest Services:** complimentary laundry, area transportation. **Business Services:** conference facilities, business center.

VCR / SOME UNITS FEE

KIAWAH ISLAND GOLF RESORT - FAIRWAY OAKS VILLAS

Phone: 843/768-2121

Vacation Rental Condominium

Rates not provided

Address: 1301 Kiawah Beach Dr **Location:** Just e of main gate, then just s; in West Beach Village area. **Facility:** The beautiful villas with decks and lush natural landscaping are adjacent to the Cougar Point Golf Course and are a five minute walk from the ocean. 36 condominiums. 2 stories (no elevator), exterior corridors. **Parking:** on-site. **Terms:** off-site registration, check-in 4 pm. **Amenities:** DVD players, CD players, voice mail, safes, irons, hair dryers. **Pool(s):** 4 outdoor, heated outdoor. **Leisure Activities:** rental canoes, sailboats, recreation programs, rental bicycles, jogging, playground, exercise room, sports court, basketball, volleyball. *Fee:* boat ramp, golf-90 holes, 28 tennis courts (8 lighted), massage. **Guest Services:** complimentary laundry, area transportation. **Business Services:** conference facilities, business center.

/ SOME UNITS FEE

KIAWAH ISLAND GOLF RESORT - MARINERS WATCH VILLAS

Phone: 843/768-2121

Vacation Rental Condominium

Rates not provided

Address: 4200 Sea Forest Dr **Location:** Oceanfront. 1.6 mi e of main gate, then just s; in East Beach Village area. **Facility:** The scenic villas are just across from the beach and within a short walk to recreation and Night Heron Park. 44 condominiums. 2 stories (no elevator), exterior corridors. **Parking:** on-site. **Terms:** off-site registration, check-in 4 pm. **Amenities:** DVD players, CD players, voice mail, safes, irons, hair dryers. **Pool(s):** 4 outdoor, heated outdoor. **Leisure Activities:** rental canoes, sailboats, recreation programs, rental bicycles, jogging, playground, exercise room, sports court, basketball, volleyball. *Fee:* boat ramp, golf-90 holes, 28 tennis courts (8 lighted), massage. **Guest Services:** complimentary laundry, area transportation. **Business Services:** conference facilities, business center.

/ SOME UNITS FEE

KIAWAH ISLAND GOLF RESORT - PARKSIDE VILLAS *Book at AAA.com*

Phone: 843/768-2121

Vacation Rental Condominium

Rates not provided

Address: 4501 Park Lake Dr **Location:** 2 mi e of main gate, then just s; in East Beach Village area. **Facility:** Villas and townhomes are conveniently located at Night Heron Park with easy access to the pool and offer a deck, screened porch and fireplace. 40 condominiums. 2 stories (no elevator), exterior corridors. **Parking:** on-site. **Terms:** off-site registration, check-in 4 pm. **Amenities:** DVD players, CD players, voice mail, safes, irons, hair dryers. **Pool(s):** 4 outdoor, heated outdoor. **Leisure Activities:** rental canoes, sailboats, recreation programs, rental bicycles, jogging, playground, exercise room, sports court, basketball, volleyball. *Fee:* boat ramp, golf-90 holes, 28 tennis courts (8 lighted), massage. **Guest Services:** complimentary laundry. **Business Services:** conference facilities, business center.

/ SOME UNITS FEE

KIAWAH ISLAND GOLF RESORT - SEASCAPE VILLAS

Phone: 843/768-2121

Vacation Rental Condominium

Rates not provided

Address: 3510 Shipwatch Rd **Location:** Oceanfront. Just e of main gate, then just s; in West Beach Village area. **Facility:** The scenic villas are located just off the ocean in a quiet wooded area with boardwalks to the beach and are close to tennis, golf and village shops. 41 condominiums. 2 stories (no elevator), exterior corridors. **Parking:** on-site. **Terms:** off-site registration, check-in 4 pm. **Amenities:** DVD players, CD players, voice mail, safes, irons, hair dryers. **Pool(s):** 4 outdoor, heated outdoor. **Leisure Activities:** rental canoes, sailboats, recreation programs, rental bicycles, jogging, playground, exercise room, sports court, basketball, volleyball. *Fee:* boat ramp, golf-90 holes, 28 tennis courts (8 lighted), massage. **Guest Services:** complimentary laundry, area transportation. **Business Services:** conference facilities, business center.

/ SOME UNITS FEE

KIAWAH ISLAND GOLF RESORT - SHIPWATCH VILLAS

Vacation Rental Condominium

Rates not provided

Phone: 843/768-2121

Address: 2200 Shipwatch Rd **Location:** Oceanfront. Just e of main gate, then just s; in West Beach Village area. **Facility:** The resort offers oceanfront and oceanside suites conveniently located adjacent to West Beach Village and all of the conveniences of the shops. 36 condominiums. 4 stories, exterior corridors. **Parking:** on-site. **Terms:** off-site registration, check-in 4 pm. **Amenities:** DVD players, CD players, voice mail, safes, irons, hair dryers. **Pool(s):** 4 outdoor, heated outdoor. **Leisure Activities:** rental canoes, sailboats, recreation programs, rental bicycles, jogging, playground, exercise room, sports court, basketball, volleyball. *Fee:* boat ramp, golf-90 holes, 28 tennis courts (8 lighted), massage. **Guest Services:** complimentary laundry, area transportation. **Business Services:** conference facilities, business center.

/ SOME UNITS FEE

KIAWAH ISLAND GOLF RESORT - TENNIS CLUB VILLAS

Vacation Rental Condominium

Rates not provided

Phone: 843/768-2121

Address: 4659 Tennis Club Ln **Location:** 2.2 mi e of main gate, then just s; at Roy Barth Tennis Center. **Facility:** In a tropical setting, this property offers golf courses, ocean views, pools and recreation areas; many rooms have balconies. 75 condominiums. 2 stories (no elevator), exterior corridors. **Parking:** on-site. **Terms:** off-site registration, check-in 4 pm. **Amenities:** DVD players, CD players, voice mail, safes, irons, hair dryers. **Pool(s):** 4 outdoor, heated outdoor. **Leisure Activities:** rental canoes, sailboats, fishing, recreation programs, rental bicycles, jogging, playground, exercise room, sports court, basketball, volleyball. *Fee:* boat ramp, charter fishing, golf-90 holes, 28 tennis courts (8 lighted), massage. **Guest Services:** complimentary laundry. **Business Services:** conference facilities, business center.

/ SOME UNITS FEE

KIAWAH ISLAND GOLF RESORT - TURTLE COVE VILLAS

Vacation Rental Condominium

Rates not provided

Phone: 843/768-2121

Address: 5501 Green Dolphin Way **Location:** 2.4 mi e of main gate, then just se; at Roy Barth Tennis Center. **Facility:** The villas are close to East Beach Tennis Club, Turtle Point Golf Course, Town Center, and the beach; all villas have screened porches and a wet bar. 49 condominiums. 2 stories (no elevator), exterior corridors. **Parking:** on-site. **Terms:** off-site registration, check-in 4 pm. **Amenities:** DVD players, CD players, voice mail, safes, irons, hair dryers. **Pool(s):** 4 outdoor, heated outdoor. **Leisure Activities:** rental canoes, sailboats, recreation programs, rental bicycles, jogging, playground, exercise room, sports court, basketball, volleyball. *Fee:* boat ramp, golf-90 holes, 28 tennis courts (8 lighted), massage. **Guest Services:** complimentary laundry. **Business Services:** conference facilities, business center.

/ SOME UNITS FEE

KIAWAH ISLAND GOLF RESORT - TURTLE POINT VILLAS

Vacation Rental Condominium

Rates not provided

Phone: 843/768-2121

Address: 4901 Green Dolphin Way **Location:** 2.4 mi e of main gate, then just se; at Roy Barth Tennis Center and Turtle Point Golf Club. **Facility:** Villas are close to East Beach Tennis Club and Turtle Point Golf Course and within walking distance to Night Heron Park and recreation facilities. 60 condominiums. 2 stories (no elevator), exterior corridors. **Parking:** on-site. **Terms:** off-site registration, check-in 4 pm. **Amenities:** DVD players, CD players, voice mail, safes, irons, hair dryers. **Pool(s):** 4 outdoor, heated outdoor. **Leisure Activities:** rental canoes, sailboats, recreation programs, rental bicycles, jogging, playground, exercise room, sports court, basketball, volleyball. *Fee:* boat ramp, golf-90 holes, 28 tennis courts (8 lighted), massage. **Guest Services:** complimentary laundry. **Business Services:** conference facilities, business center.

/ SOME UNITS FEE

KIAWAH ISLAND GOLF RESORT - WINDSWEPT VILLAS

Vacation Rental Condominium

Rates not provided

Phone: 843/768-2121

Address: 4300 Sea Forest Dr **Location:** Oceanfront. 1.6 mi e of main gate, then just s; in East Beach Village area. **Facility:** Large, well-appointed villas, many with stunning views of the ocean, are close to recreation, dining and shopping options. 97 condominiums. 4 stories, exterior corridors. **Parking:** on-site. **Terms:** off-site registration, check-in 4 pm. **Amenities:** DVD players, CD players, voice mail, safes, irons, hair dryers. **Pool(s):** 4 outdoor, heated outdoor. **Leisure Activities:** rental canoes, sailboats, recreation programs, rental bicycles, jogging, playground, exercise room, sports court, basketball, volleyball. *Fee:* boat ramp, golf-90 holes, 28 tennis courts (8 lighted), massage. **Guest Services:** complimentary laundry, area transportation. **Business Services:** conference facilities, business center.

/ SOME UNITS FEE

THE SANCTUARY AT KIAWAH ISLAND GOLF RESORT *Book great rates at AAA.com*

AAA SAVE

Resort Hotel

$286-$4500 All Year

Phone: (843)768-6000

Address: One Sanctuary Beach Dr **Location:** Oceanfront. 1.5 mi ne of security gate, then just s. Located adjacent to West Beach Village. **Facility:** The opulent oceanfront resort and spa is part of a world-class golf complex with beautiful rooms and dining, shopping and sports activities. 255 units. 242 one-bedroom standard units. 11 one- and 2 two-bedroom suites. 4 stories, interior corridors. *Bath:* combo or shower only. **Parking:** on-site. **Terms:** check-in 4 pm, 2 night minimum stay - seasonal and/or weekends, 7 day cancellation notice-fee imposed. **Amenities:** video library, DVD players, CD players, high-speed Internet, dual phone lines, voice mail, safes, honor bars, irons, hair dryers. *Some:* fax. **Dining:** 2 restaurants. **Pool(s):** 2 heated outdoor, indoor. **Leisure Activities:** whirlpools, recreation programs, spa. *Fee:* golf-48 holes, 4 lighted tennis courts. **Guest Services:** valet laundry, area transportation-on island, wireless Internet. **Business Services:** conference facilities, business center. **Cards:** AX, DC, DS, MC, VI. Affiliated with A Preferred Hotel.

CALL / SOME UNITS

WHERE TO DINE

THE OCEAN ROOM AT THE SANCTUARY

New American
$34-$48

Phone: 843/768-6000

A chef's tasting menu is available nightly and can be paired with a comprehensive selection of vintages. The main menu, which changes frequently, offers creative interpretations of antelope, black grouper, Kobe beef and caviar selections. Dressy casual. **Bar:** Full bar. **Reservations:** suggested. **Hours:** 6 pm-10 pm, Fri & Sat from 5:30 pm. Closed: Sun off season. **Address:** One Sanctuary Beach Dr **Location:** 1.5 mi ne of security gate, then just s; in The Sanctuary. **Parking:** on-site. **Cards:** AX, CB, DC, DS, MC, VI.

CALL

SHRIMPERS

American
$9-$22

Phone: 843/768-6075

Diners can eat a leisurely meal in the attractive, casually sophisticated restaurant. Outdoor seating is available on the upper and lower levels. The menu has enough interesting variations to appeal to almost any taste. Casual dress. **Bar:** Full bar. **Reservations:** not accepted. **Hours:** 11 am-10 pm. **Address:** 12 Kiawah Beach Dr **Location:** In West Beach Village; at Straw Market Shops. **Parking:** on-site. **Cards:** AX, DC, DS, MC, VI.

TURTLE POINT SPORTS BAR & GRILL

American
$10-$36

Phone: 843/266-4070

In the middle of the golf course at Turtle Point Clubhouse, the richly appointed dining room affords panoramic views from its many windows. The menu encompasses an array of well-prepared steak and seafood dishes, such as Tabasco lamb T-bones and fettuccine with shrimp. The diner may select from varied specialty sauces to add a twist to the chef's creation. Nightly specials are also a treat. Casual dress. **Bar:** Full bar. **Reservations:** accepted. **Hours:** 7-11 am, 11:30-2:30 & 5-10 pm. Closed: 12/25. **Address:** 12 Kiawah Beach Dr **Location:** In Turtle Point Club House. **Parking:** on-site. **Cards:** AX, DC, DS, MC, VI.

CALL

LADSON pop. 13,264

WHERE TO STAY

BEST WESTERN MAGNOLIA INN & SUITES *Book great rates at AAA.com* **Phone:** (843)553-8888

Hotel
$70-$120 All Year

Address: 747 Treeland Dr **Location:** I-26, exit 203 (College Park Rd), just ne. **Facility:** 61 one-bedroom standard units, some with whirlpools. 3 stories, interior corridors. *Bath:* combo or shower only. **Parking:** on-site. **Terms:** 2 night minimum stay - seasonal and/or weekends. **Amenities:** high-speed Internet, dual phone lines, voice mail, safes (fee), irons, hair dryers. **Pool(s):** outdoor. **Leisure Activities:** limited exercise equipment. **Guest Services:** coin laundry, wireless Internet. **Business Services:** meeting rooms, business center. **Cards:** AX, DC, DS, MC, VI. **Free Special Amenities: continental breakfast and high-speed Internet.**

AAA Benefit:
Members save up to 20%, plus 10% bonus points with rewards program.

WHERE TO DINE

GILLIGAN'S STEAMER & RAW BAR

Seafood
$7-$21

Phone: 843/821-2244

A casual family oriented neighborhood restaurant, Gilligan's is famous for fresh shrimp right off the boat! Locals flock not only for the shrimp but also for Captain Bookatee's hushpuppies. Not a seafood lover? Come on anyway and enjoy the buffalo wings and chicken fingers. Casual dress. **Bar:** Full bar. **Hours:** 11 am-9 pm, Fri & Sat-10 pm. Closed: 11/26, 12/25. **Address:** 3852 Ladson Rd **Location:** I-26, exit 205A (US 78), 2.5 mi nw to Ladson Rd; then 2.5 mi sw. **Parking:** on-site. **Cards:** AX, DS, MC, VI.

CALL

MONCKS CORNER pop. 5,952

WHERE TO DINE

GILLIGAN'S STEAMER & RAW BAR

Seafood
$7-$21

Phone: 843/761-2244

A casual family oriented neighborhood restaurant, Gilligan's is famous for fresh shrimp right off the boat! Locals flock not only for the shrimp but also for Captain Bookatee's hushpuppies. Not a seafood lover? Come on anyway and enjoy the buffalo wings and chicken fingers. Casual dress. **Bar:** Full bar. **Hours:** 11 am-9 pm, Fri & Sat-10 pm. Closed: 11/26, 12/25. **Address:** 582 Dock Rd **Location:** Jct US 52/17A, just ne, then just s; at dock on Cooper River. **Parking:** on-site. **Cards:** AX, DS, MC, VI.

CALL

MOUNT PLEASANT pop. 47,609 (See map and index starting on p. 877)

WHERE TO STAY

BEST WESTERN PATRIOTS POINT
Book great rates at AAA.com
Phone: (843)971-7070 51

Hotel
$70-$134 All Year

Address: 259 McGrath Darby Blvd **Location:** Just e of Cooper River Bridge on US 17 (Johnnie Dodds Blvd), then just s. **Facility:** 70 one-bedroom standard units. 3 stories, interior corridors. *Bath:* combo or shower only. **Parking:** on-site. **Terms:** cancellation fee imposed. **Amenities:** high-speed Internet, irons, hair dryers. **Pool(s):** outdoor. **Guest Services:** wireless Internet. **Business Services:** business center. **Cards:** AX, DS, MC, VI. **Free Special Amenities: expanded continental breakfast and high-speed Internet.**

/ SOME UNITS

Best Western

AAA Benefit:
Members save up to 20%, plus 10% bonus points with rewards program.

CHARLESTON HARBOR RESORT & MARINA
Book at AAA.com
Phone: (843)856-0028 55

Hotel
$99-$289 All Year

Address: 20 Patriots Point Rd **Location:** Base of Cooper River Bridge, 0.6 mi se on Coleman Blvd (SR 703), then 0.8 mi sw; past museum. Located adjacent to Patriots Point Naval Museum. **Facility:** Designated smoking area. 131 units. 125 one-bedroom standard units. 5 one- and 1 two-bedroom suites. 4 stories, interior corridors. *Bath:* combo or shower only. **Parking:** on-site. **Terms:** check-in 4 pm, cancellation fee imposed. **Amenities:** DVD players, dual phone lines, voice mail, safes, honor bars, irons, hair dryers. **Pool(s):** outdoor. **Leisure Activities:** whirlpool, marina, fishing, jogging, horseshoes, volleyball. *Fee:* sailboats, charter fishing, golf-18 holes. **Guest Services:** valet laundry, area transportation, wireless Internet. **Business Services:** conference facilities, business center. **Cards:** AX, DC, DS, MC, VI.

ASK

COMFORT SUITES
Book great rates at AAA.com
Phone: (843)216-0004

Hotel
$119-$229 3/29-11/30
$99-$139 12/1-3/28

Address: 1130 Hungryneck Blvd **Location:** I-526, exit Georgetown/US 17 N, 1.5 mi ne on US 17, then just se on Isle of Palms connector (SR 517). **Facility:** Smoke free premises. 81 units. 79 one-bedroom standard units. 2 one-bedroom suites. 3 stories, interior corridors. *Bath:* combo or shower only. **Parking:** on-site. **Terms:** cancellation fee imposed. **Amenities:** dual phone lines, voice mail, safes (fee), irons, hair dryers. **Pool(s):** outdoor. **Leisure Activities:** exercise room. **Guest Services:** valet and coin laundry, wireless Internet. **Business Services:** meeting rooms, business center. **Cards:** AX, DC, DS, MC, VI. **Free Special Amenities: full breakfast and high-speed Internet.**

CALL

COURTYARD BY MARRIOTT
Book great rates at AAA.com
Phone: (843)284-0900

Hotel
$133-$164 All Year

Address: 1251 Woodland Ave **Location:** I-526, exit Georgetown, jct US 17N, just ne, then just nw. **Facility:** Smoke free premises. 130 units. 125 one-bedroom standard units, some with whirlpools. 5 one-bedroom suites. 3 stories, interior corridors. *Bath:* combo or shower only. **Parking:** on-site. **Terms:** cancellation fee imposed. **Amenities:** voice mail, irons, hair dryers. **Pool(s):** outdoor. **Leisure Activities:** whirlpool, exercise room. **Guest Services:** coin laundry, wireless Internet. **Business Services:** meeting rooms, business center. **Cards:** AX, DS, MC, VI.

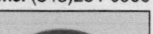

CALL / SOME UNITS

COURTYARD Marriott

AAA Benefit:
Members save a minimum 5% off the best available rate.

DAYS INN PATRIOTS POINT
Book great rates at AAA.com
Phone: (843)881-1800 49

Motel
$89-$179 2/16-11/30
$69-$89 12/1-2/15

Address: 261 Johnnie Dodds Blvd **Location:** Just e of base of Cooper River Bridge. **Facility:** 130 one-bedroom standard units. 3 stories, exterior corridors. **Parking:** on-site. **Terms:** 3 day cancellation notice-fee imposed. **Amenities:** safes (fee), hair dryers. *Some:* irons. **Pool(s):** outdoor. **Guest Services:** coin laundry, wireless Internet. **Business Services:** fax (fee). **Cards:** AX, DC, DS, MC, VI. **Free Special Amenities: local telephone calls and high-speed Internet.**

/ SOME UNITS FEE

EXTENDED STAYAMERICA-CHARLESTON-MOUNT PLEASANT
Book at AAA.com
Phone: (843)884-4453 46

Hotel
$85-$105 All Year

Address: 304 Wingo Way **Location:** Just e of Cooper River Bridge on US 17, then just n. **Facility:** 101 one-bedroom standard units with efficiencies. 3 stories, interior corridors. *Bath:* combo or shower only. **Parking:** on-site. **Terms:** office hours 7 am-11 pm. **Amenities:** voice mail, irons. **Guest Services:** coin laundry, wireless Internet. **Business Services:** fax (fee). **Cards:** AX, CB, DC, DS, JC, MC, VI.

ASK / SOME UNITS FEE

(See map and index starting on p. 877)

HAMPTON INN AND SUITES

Phone: (843)856-3000

Hotel
$109-$229 All Year

Address: 1104 Isle of Palms Connector **Location:** I-526, exit 36 (Georgetown/US 17 N), 1.4 mi ne on US 17 to Isle of Palms connector (SR 517), then just se. **Facility:** 121 units. 81 one-bedroom standard units. 40 one-bedroom suites with efficiencies. 3 stories, interior corridors. *Bath:* combo or shower only. **Parking:** on-site. **Terms:** check-in 4 pm, 1-30 night minimum stay, cancellation fee imposed. **Amenities:** voice mail, irons, hair dryers. *Some:* dual phone lines. **Pool(s):** outdoor. **Leisure Activities:** limited exercise equipment. **Guest Services:** valet and coin laundry, wireless Internet. **Business Services:** meeting rooms, fax (fee). **Cards:** AX, CB, DC, DS, MC, VI.

CALL / SOME UNITS VCR

AAA Benefit:
Members save up to 10% everyday!

HAMPTON INN-PATRIOTS POINT

Phone: (843)881-3300 50

Hotel
$84-$134 All Year

Address: 255 Sessions Way **Location:** Just e of base of Cooper River Bridge, then just e on McGrath-Darby Blvd. **Facility:** 120 one-bedroom standard units. 4 stories, interior corridors. **Parking:** on-site. **Terms:** check-in 4 pm, 1-30 night minimum stay, cancellation fee imposed. **Amenities:** voice mail, irons, hair dryers. **Pool(s):** outdoor. **Guest Services:** valet laundry, wireless Internet. **Business Services:** meeting rooms. **Cards:** AX, CB, DC, DS, MC, VI.

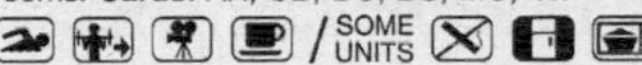

AAA Benefit:
Members save up to 10% everyday!

HOMEWOOD SUITES BY HILTON

Phone: (843)881-6950

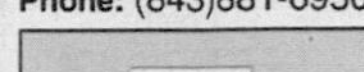

Extended Stay Hotel
$101-$229 All Year

Address: 1998 Riviera Dr **Location:** I-526, exit 32 (Georgetown/US 17 N), 1.4 mi ne on US 17, 1 mi se on Isle of Palms connector (SR 517), then just sw. **Facility:** This amenity-filled lodging offers nicely appointed rooms, spacious public areas and easy access to Atlantic beaches and downtown Charleston. 107 units. 103 one- and 4 two-bedroom suites with efficiencies. 4 stories, interior corridors. *Bath:* combo or shower only. **Parking:** on-site. **Terms:** 1-30 night minimum stay, cancellation fee imposed. **Amenities:** video library (fee), high-speed Internet, dual phone lines, voice mail, irons, hair dryers. **Pool(s):** outdoor. **Leisure Activities:** whirlpool, limited exercise equipment, basketball. **Guest Services:** complimentary laundry, area transportation, wireless Internet. **Business Services:** meeting rooms, business center. **Cards:** AX, CB, DC, DS, MC, VI.

AAA Benefit:
Members save 5% or more everyday!

INN AT RIVER CROSSING

Phone: (843)884-5853 47

Motel
$60-$120 All Year

Address: 310 Hwy 17 (Johnnie Dodds Blvd) **Location:** US 17, 0.7 mi n of Cooper River Bridge. **Facility:** 123 one-bedroom standard units, some with whirlpools. 2 stories (no elevator), exterior corridors. **Parking:** on-site. **Terms:** cancellation fee imposed. **Amenities:** voice mail, irons, hair dryers. **Pool(s):** outdoor. **Guest Services:** valet and coin laundry. **Business Services:** fax (fee). **Cards:** AX, DC, DS, MC, VI.

ASK / SOME UNITS FEE

OLD VILLAGE POST HOUSE INN
Phone: 843/388-8935 54

Historic Bed & Breakfast
$135-$225 All Year

Address: 101 Pitt St **Location:** Corner of Venning St; between King and Hibben sts; in Old Mount Pleasant. **Facility:** The period reproductions furnishing each guest room bring an old-time charm to this inn dating from 1888. Smoke free premises. 6 units. 5 one-bedroom standard units. 1 one-bedroom suite. 3 stories (no elevator), interior corridors. *Bath:* some combo or tub only. **Parking:** street. **Terms:** 2 night minimum stay - weekends, age restrictions may apply, 3 day cancellation notice. **Amenities:** video library, voice mail, irons, hair dryers. *Some:* CD players. **Dining:** restaurant, see separate listing. **Guest Services:** valet laundry. **Business Services:** meeting rooms, fax (fee). **Cards:** AX, DC, DS, MC, VI.

ASK VCR

QUALITY INN & SUITES AT PATRIOTS POINT

Phone: (843)856-8817 52

Hotel
$79-$209 All Year

Address: 196 Patriots Point Rd **Location:** Base of Cooper River Bridge, 0.6 mi se on Coleman Blvd (SR 703), then just sw. Adjacent to Patriots Point Naval Museum and Sports Complex. **Facility:** 103 units. 102 one-bedroom standard units, some with whirlpools. 1 one-bedroom suite with efficiency and whirlpool. 3 stories, interior corridors. *Bath:* combo or shower only. **Parking:** on-site. **Terms:** cancellation fee imposed. **Amenities:** voice mail, irons, hair dryers. **Pool(s):** outdoor. **Leisure Activities:** jogging, limited exercise equipment. **Guest Services:** valet and coin laundry, wireless Internet. **Business Services:** meeting rooms, fax (fee). **Cards:** AX, DC, DS, MC, VI.

ASK CALL / SOME UNITS

(See map and index starting on p. 877)

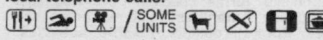

RED ROOF INN Book great rates at AAA.com **Phone:** (843)884-1411 48

Motel

$56-$140 All Year

Address: 301 Johnnie Dodds Blvd **Location:** Just e of base of Cooper River Bridge, on US 17 (Johnnie Dodds Blvd), then just s on McGrath-Darby Blvd. **Facility:** 124 one-bedroom standard units. 2 stories (no elevator), exterior corridors. *Bath:* combo or shower only. **Parking:** on-site. **Amenities:** video games (fee), voice mail. **Pool(s):** outdoor. **Guest Services:** coin laundry, wireless Internet. **Business Services:** fax (fee). **Cards:** AX, CB, DC, DS, MC, VI. **Free Special Amenities: local telephone calls.**

/ SOME UNITS

RESIDENCE INN BY MARRIOTT Book great rates at AAA.com **Phone:** (843)881-1599

Extended Stay Hotel

$159-$239 All Year

Address: 1116 Isle of Palms Connector **Location:** I-526, exit 32 (Georgetown/US 17 N), 1.4 mi ne on US 17 to Isle of Palms connector (SR 517), then just se. **Facility:** The property offers upscale, modern accommodations; rooms have good floor space, and amenities are designed for the extended-stay guest. Smoke free premises. 90 units. 34 one-bedroom standard units, some with efficiencies or kitchens. 35 one- and 21 two-bedroom suites, some with efficiencies or kitchens. 3 stories, interior corridors. *Bath:* combo or shower only. **Parking:** on-site. **Terms:** cancellation fee imposed. **Amenities:** high-speed Internet, dual phone lines, voice mail, irons, hair dryers. **Pool(s):** outdoor. **Leisure Activities:** whirlpool, limited exercise equipment. **Guest Services:** valet and coin laundry, wireless Internet. **Business Services:** meeting rooms, business center. **Cards:** AX, CB, DC, DS, JC, MC, VI.

CALL / SOME UNITS FEE

Residence Inn Marriott

AAA Benefit:

Members save a minimum 5% off the best available rate.

SHEM CREEK INN Book great rates at AAA.com **Phone:** (843)881-1000 53

Hotel

$89-$289 3/1-11/30
$69-$189 12/1-2/28

Address: 1401 Shrimp Boat Ln **Location:** 1.3 mi se on Coleman Blvd (SR 703) from Cooper River Bridge; just s of Shem Creek Bridge. **Facility:** 50 one-bedroom standard units. 3 stories, interior corridors. **Parking:** on-site. **Terms:** 3 day cancellation notice-fee imposed. **Amenities:** voice mail, irons. **Pool(s):** outdoor. **Guest Services:** valet laundry, wireless Internet. **Business Services:** meeting rooms, fax (fee). **Cards:** AX, DC, DS, MC, VI. **Free Special Amenities: continental breakfast and high-speed Internet.** *(See color ad starting on p 886)*

SLEEP INN MT PLEASANT Book great rates at AAA.com **Phone:** (843)856-5000 45

Hotel

$79-$149 All Year

Address: 299 Wingo Way **Location:** Just e of base of Cooper River Bridge, then just n at McGrath-Darby Blvd. **Facility:** 83 one-bedroom standard units, some with whirlpools. 3 stories, interior corridors. *Bath:* combo or shower only. **Parking:** on-site. **Terms:** 14 day cancellation notice-fee imposed. **Amenities:** voice mail, safes (fee), irons, hair dryers. **Pool(s):** outdoor. **Guest Services:** valet and coin laundry, wireless Internet. **Business Services:** PC, fax (fee). **Cards:** AX, DC, DS, MC, VI. **Free Special Amenities: continental breakfast and high-speed Internet.** *(See color ad p 889)*

CALL / SOME UNITS FEE

WHERE TO DINE

ALAIR BISTRO **Phone:** 843/856-9915 25

American

$8-$21

Distinctively prepared dishes all are made from scratch in house at the storefront bistro. Service is professional and attentive. Perfectly prepared beef tenderloin is served over polenta, and desserts merit the indulgence. Casual dress. **Bar:** Full bar. **Reservations:** accepted. **Hours:** 11:30 am-2 & 5:30-9 pm, Fri-10 pm, Sat 5:30 pm-10 pm. Closed: 11/26; also Sun & Mon. **Address:** 920 Houston Northcutt Blvd, #A2 **Location:** 0.7 mi ne of Cooper River Bridge on US 17 (Johnnie Dodds Blvd), then just s; in Village Point Shopping Center. **Parking:** on-site. **Cards:** AX, DS, MC, VI.

ANDOLINI'S PIZZA **Phone:** 843/849-7437

Pizza

$3-$21

Operating continually since 1991, the area favorite has earned awards for its pizza for 13 years in a row. Hand-tossed dough and daily made sauces lend to the outstanding flavor. Other choices on the limited menu include salads, breadsticks, cal"ZONES" and cold beer. Casual dress. **Bar:** Beer & wine. **Hours:** 11 am-10 pm, Fri & Sat-11 pm. Closed major holidays. **Address:** 414 W Coleman Blvd **Location:** 1 mi e of Cooper River Bridge, on SR 703. **Parking:** on-site.

BACCO **Phone:** 843/884-6969 26

Traditional Italian

$8-$15

The cuisine at this storefront restaurant reflects Southern Italian and Sicilian influences, with abundant and skilled use of vegetables, seafood, fresh cheeses and pasta in the menu selections. Among staples are eggplant, roasted peppers, asparagus, capers and tomatoes, which are well mated to fresh fish and shrimp dishes. Shrimp limoncello, swordfish with fennel, mozzarella-wrapped smoked sausage and an outstanding eggplant parmigiana are just a few of the modestly priced selections. Casual dress. **Bar:** Full bar. **Reservations:** accepted. **Hours:** 5:30 pm-10 pm. Closed: 11/26, 12/25; also Sun & Mon. **Address:** 976 Houston Northcutt Blvd, Suite O **Location:** Jct Cooper River Bridge/US 17, 0.7 mi ne to Houston Northcutt Blvd, then 0.5 mi s. **Parking:** on-site. **Cards:** AX, DS, MC, VI.

CALL

(See map and index starting on p. 877)

BARBARA JEAN'S RESTAURANT & BAR **Phone:** 843/884-6655 (40)

Regional American
$7-$23

The homey, family-owned restaurant serves made-from-scratch dishes in hefty portions. Three fresh breads, 15 vegetables and three homemade soups are offered daily along with a menu featuring Eastern Shore-style crab cakes, she-crab soup, pot roast, fried chicken, meatloaf, steaks, catfish and other simply prepared and flavorful choices. Fresh desserts and a children's menu also are available. Casual dress. **Bar:** Full bar. **Reservations:** not accepted. **Hours:** 11 am-9 pm, Fri & Sat-10 pm. Closed: 11/26, 12/25. **Address:** 1440 Ben Sawyer Blvd **Location:** Jct US 17 Business/SR 701/203, just e on SR 703 (Ben Sawyer Blvd); in Bilo Shopping Center. **Parking:** on-site. **Cards:** AX, DS, MC, VI.

CALL

BENITOS BRICKOVEN **Phone:** 843/856-9639

Italian
$6-$20

Pizzas and traditional pasta dishes are prepared with flair at the brightly decorated mall restaurant. Hot dishes are baked in wood-fired brick ovens for added flavor. Several separate dining rooms keep the feeling cozy. Diners who sit in the center dining room can watch food being prepared in the open kitchen. Casual dress. **Bar:** Full bar. **Reservations:** accepted. **Hours:** 11 am-10 pm. Closed: 11/26, 12/25. **Address:** 1244 Belk Dr **Location:** I-526, exit 32 (Georgetown/US 17 N), 1.1 mi ne on US 17, then just e; in Mount Pleasant Towne Center Mall. **Parking:** on-site. **Cards:** AX, CB, DC, DS, MC, VI.

BOULEVARD DINER **Phone:** 843/216-2611 (31)

American
$5-$13

The simple, hugely popular A-frame diner turns out freshly prepared healthy meals with a wide selection of vegetable accompaniments. Service is wonderfully friendly. The menu changes daily. Casual dress. **Bar:** Beer & wine. **Hours:** 7 am-9:30 pm. Closed major holidays; also Sun. **Address:** 409 Coleman Blvd **Location:** 1.8 mi se from base of Cooper River Bridge on SR 703. **Parking:** on-site. **Cards:** AX, MC, VI.

CAPRICCIO ***Menu on AAA.com*** **Phone:** 843/881-5550 (28)

AAA

Regional Italian
$14-$22

Dishes are thoughtfully prepared and served in a warm, inviting atmosphere that mixes Old World charm with local history. The antipasto plate is enough for a main course, and veal parmigiana is served hot with plenty of cheese. Casual dress. **Bar:** Full bar. **Reservations:** accepted. **Hours:** 5 pm-9 pm, Fri & Sat-10 pm. Closed: Sun. **Address:** 1034 Chuck Dawley Blvd **Location:** Jct I-526/17 business route, 1 mi s. **Parking:** on-site. **Cards:** AX, CB, DC, DS, MC, VI.

CHARLESTON CRAB HOUSE **Phone:** 843/884-1617

Seafood
$15-$22

The casual, seafood-themed restaurant presents a menu varied enough to please a wide cross-section of patrons. The crab cocktail appetizer is almost a meal in itself, and stuffed mahi mahi and Charleston grouper are house specialties. Also offered is a good selection of steaks, as well as chicken, pasta and grits dishes. Casual dress. **Bar:** Full bar. **Reservations:** accepted. **Hours:** 11:30 am-10 pm. Closed: 11/26, 12/25. **Address:** 1101 Stockage Storage Ln **Location:** I-526, exit 32 (US 17 N/Georgetown), 2.2 mi ne on US 17 N/SR 701. **Parking:** on-site. **Cards:** AX, DS, MC, VI.

CALL

COCO'S CAFE **Phone:** 843/881-4949 (23)

French
$7-$23

Popular, small and intimate, the restaurant features creative seafood and pasta dishes deliciously crafted by the owner, Chef Ollard, as part of a diverse menu. Flounder Alain is a house specialty, prepared with a special glaze in lemon-butter sauce. Casual dress. **Bar:** Full bar. **Reservations:** suggested. **Hours:** 11:30 am-2 & 5:30-10 pm, Sat from 5:30 pm. Closed: 12/25; also Sun. **Address:** 863 Houston Northcutt Blvd **Location:** 0.7 mi ne of Cooper River Bridge on US 17 (Johnnie Dodds Blvd); in Patriots Plaza. **Parking:** on-site. **Cards:** AX, MC, VI.

CRAVE KITCHEN & COCKTAILS **Phone:** 843/884-1177

New American
$7-$25

With claret-colored walls, original art and a long mahogany bar, this chic American fusion restaurant has raised the stakes in the local food scene. The atmosphere is relaxing, and the food is outstanding. The lengthy menu includes entrees such as Dover sole francese, pesto-encrusted rib-eye and tempura grouper. Each dish is skillfully prepared and professionally delivered by a seasoned staff member. The wine list features numerous world vintages that nicely complement the menu's diversity. Casual dress. **Bar:** Full bar. **Reservations:** accepted. **Hours:** 11 am-2 am, Sun 10 am-midnight. Closed: 11/26, 12/25; also Mon. **Address:** 1968 Riviera Dr, Suite O **Location:** I-526, exit 32 (Georgetown), 1.4 mi ne on US 17 to jct SR 517 (Isle of Palms Connector), then 1 mi se on SR 517; in Seaside Farms. **Parking:** on-site. **Cards:** AX, DS, MC, VI.

CALL

CREEKSIDE BAR & GRILL **Phone:** 843/856-4803 (38)

American
$7-$20

This lively waterfront sport bar features patio seating, several stool bars and high-definition TVs both inside and out. The skilled kitchen staff prepares items from the lengthy menu, including sandwiches, wraps, cooked-to-order burgers and full entrees such as goat cheese- and corn-stuffed chicken breast, herb- and Dijon-encrusted strip steak and adobo-glazed and seared tuna over crispy noodles. Special events and drink specials are offered daily. Casual dress. **Bar:** Full bar. **Hours:** 11 am-2 am. Closed: 12/25. **Address:** 508-B Mill St **Location:** Cooper River Bridge, 1.6 mi se on Coleman Blvd (SR 703), then just ne. **Parking:** on-site. **Cards:** MC, VI.

CALL

THE DOG & DUCK **Phone:** 843/831-3056

American
$5-$11

Fashioned in the vein of an English pub, the restaurant serves light fare—including sandwiches, soups, salads and generous portions of well-prepared fish and chips—with a good selection of draft beers. Casual dress. **Bar:** Full bar. **Hours:** 11 am-midnight, Fri & Sat-1 am. Closed: 11/26, 12/25. **Address:** 624-A Long Point Rd **Location:** I-526, exit Long Point Rd, just ne; in Belle Hall Shopping Center. **Parking:** on-site. **Cards:** AX, DS, MC, VI.

(See map and index starting on p. 877)

FIVE LOAVES CAFE

Phone: 843/849-1043

American
$4-$15

Three fresh soups daily and complex entrees make for a fun dining experience in this small cafe; heavy emphasis is placed on a diverse assemblage of vegetable ingredients in each dish and a soup sampler is offered which features a cup of each of the day's offerings. Casual dress. **Bar:** Beer & wine. **Hours:** 11 am-9 pm. Closed major holidays; also Sun. **Address:** 1055 Johnnie Dodds Blvd, Suite 60 **Location:** Jct I-526/US 17, 0.7 mi w on US 17 (Johnnie Dodds Blvd); in Crickentree Plaza. **Parking:** on-site. **Cards:** MC, VI.

FONDUELY YOURS

Phone: 843/849-6859 (32)

Fondue
$12-$20

Foods cooked fondue-style include vegetables, fruits and a variety of meats and seafood. The casual dining atmosphere evokes a retro '70s feel, in part due to displays of vintage fondue sets and beer bottles collected from around the world. Casual dress. **Bar:** Full bar. **Reservations:** accepted. **Hours:** 5:30 pm-9:30 pm, Fri & Sat-11 pm. Closed major holidays. **Address:** 853 Coleman Blvd **Location:** 2.7 mi se of Cooper River Bridge on Coleman Blvd (SR 703). **Parking:** on-site. **Cards:** AX, DC, DS, MC, VI.

GILLIGAN'S STEAMER & RAW BAR

Phone: 843/849-2244

Seafood
$7-$21

A casual family oriented neighborhood restaurant, Gilligan's is famous for fresh shrimp right off the boat! Locals flock not only for the shrimp but also for Captain Bookatee's hushpuppies. Not a seafood lover? Come on anyway and enjoy the buffalo wings and chicken fingers. Casual dress. **Bar:** Full bar. **Hours:** 11 am-9 pm, Fri & Sat-10 pm. Closed: 11/26, 12/25. **Address:** 1475 Long Grove Dr **Location:** Jct US 17/SR 517 (Isle of Palms connector), 1 mi se on SR 517; in Seaside Farms Shopping Center. **Parking:** on-site. **Cards:** AX, DS, MC, VI.

GIUSEPPI'S PIZZA & PASTA

Phone: 843/856-2525 (36)

Italian
$3-$16

The regional chain prepares New York-style pizza, pasta, baked submarine sandwiches and appetizers. Other than good food, this place also prides itself on prompt, pleasant service and a kid-friendly atmosphere. Casual dress. **Bar:** Full bar. **Hours:** 11 am-10 pm, Fri & Sat-11 pm. Closed: 11/26, 12/25. **Address:** 1440 Ben Sawyer Blvd **Location:** Jct US 17 business/SR 701/SR 703, just e on SR 703 (Ben Sawyer Blvd); in Belo Shopping Center. **Parking:** on-site. **Cards:** AX, DS, MC, VI.

CALL

GULLAH CUISINE

Phone: 843/881-9076

Regional Southern
$7-$15

Lowcountry cuisine is said to be "food that speaks to ya." Among preparations of down-home Southern cooking are hoppin' Johns, Gullah rice and shrimp with hominy. This place is an excellent diversion from the ordinary. Casual dress. **Bar:** Beer & wine. **Reservations:** accepted. **Hours:** 11 am-9:30 pm, Sun-3 pm. Closed major holidays. **Address:** 1717 Hwy 17 N **Location:** I-526, exit 32 (Georgetown/US 17 N), 0.8 mi ne. **Parking:** on-site. **Cards:** DC, DS, MC, VI.

CALL

IACAFANO DELI

Phone: 843/881-2313 (44)

Italian
$6-$12

The sit-down New York-style delicatessen/restaurant serves soups, salads, sandwiches and pizza all day and adds several pasta dishes after 5 pm. Casual dress. **Bar:** Full bar. **Hours:** 11 am-10 pm. Closed: 11/26, 12/25. **Address:** 612 Coleman Blvd **Location:** 1.9 mi se of Cooper River Bridge on SR 701; in Moultrie Plaza. **Parking:** on-site. **Cards:** AX, CB, DC, MC, VI.

CALL

ICHIBAN RESTAURANT

Phone: 843/849-8121 (24)

Japanese
$6-$16

In a strip-mall storefront, the popular restaurant allows patrons to eat in or take out its varied teriyaki dishes, which come with fried or steamed rice. Value-priced meals consist of a bowl of miso soup, dumplings (gyoza) or egg roll, fresh garden salad with ginger dressing and a freshly prepared chicken, beef, fish, shrimp, scallop or vegetable teriyaki dish. Casual dress. **Reservations:** not accepted. **Hours:** 11 am-2 & 5-9 pm, Sat from 5 pm. Closed: 11/26, 12/25. **Address:** 909 Houston Northcutt Blvd **Location:** Just e of Cooper River Bridge on US 17 N, just s; in Patriot's Plaza. **Parking:** on-site. **Cards:** MC, VI.

JACK'S COSMIC DOGS

Phone: 843/884-7677

Deli
$3-$7

Nine toppings can be used to garnish basic and vegetarian dogs. Custard ice cream is another menu favorite. This is a popular stop for beachgoers and day trippers who enjoy the '50s decor, which can be described as The Jetsons meets Happy Days. Casual dress. **Hours:** 11 am-8 pm. Closed major holidays. **Address:** 2805 Hwy 17 N **Location:** Jct SR 41/US 17 N. **Parking:** on-site. **Cards:** MC, VI.

KING STREET GRILLE

Phone: 843/216-7272

New American
$8-$20

The popular downtown sports bar re-creates itself east of the Cooper. Industrial-style decor features 36 wall-mounted plasma and LCD televisions with selectable programming so guests can enjoy their favorite sporting event. Food offerings include many appetizers, sandwiches, pasta dishes, pizzas and beef and seafood entrees. Service is polished, and the food is distinctive and outstanding in presentation and execution. Weekly and daily specials also merit consideration. Casual dress. **Bar:** Full bar. **Hours:** 11:30 am-11 pm, Fri & Sat-2 am. Closed: 11/26, 12/25. **Address:** 1136 A Hungryneck Blvd **Location:** Jct US 17N/SR 517 (Isle of Palms Connector), just se on SR 517 to Hungry Neck Blvd, then just sw; in Irongate Plaza. **Parking:** on-site. **Cards:** AX, DC, MC, VI.

CALL

LA HACIENDA

Phone: 843/856-7223 (18)

Mexican
$4-$15

The chef modifies the extensive array of spicy Mexican food to taste. The restaurant's popularity with the Hispanic community is a good indicator of its ability to prepare authentic cuisine. Casual dress. **Bar:** Full bar. **Hours:** 11 am-10 pm, Fri & Sat-10:30 pm. Closed: 12/25. **Address:** 1035 Johnnie Dodds Blvd (US 17) **Location:** 2.2 mi ne of Cooper River Bridge on US 17 (Johnnie Dodds Blvd); in Fairmount Shopping Center. **Parking:** on-site. **Cards:** AX, DS, MC, VI.

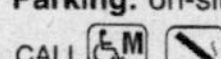

(See map and index starting on p. 877)

LANGDON'S RESTAURANT AND WINE BAR — **Phone:** 843/388-9200 (19)

Northern American
$12-$35

The storefront exterior belies the upscale dining experience inside this gem of a restaurant. Each dish is expertly prepared and presented by a highly skilled staff. The menu changes seasonally so diners enjoy fresh ingredients. Each dish is graced with sauces and reductions, then embellished with fresh garnishes. The professional, knowledgeable wait staff suggests wine pairings from an extensive international cellar to further enhance the meal. Dressy casual. **Bar:** Full bar. **Reservations:** suggested. **Hours:** 11:30 am-2 & 5-9 pm, Fri-11 pm, Sat 5 pm-11 pm. Closed: 11/26, 12/25; also Sun. **Address:** 778 S Shellmore Blvd, Suite 105 **Location:** Cooper River Bridge, 1.4 mi ne on US 17 N, then just n. **Parking:** on-site. **Cards:** AX, DS, MC, VI.

CALL

LOCKLEAR'S LOWCOUNTRY GRILL — **Phone:** 843/884-3346 (30)

Regional Seafood
$7-$19

The award-winning restaurant has been a Mount Pleasant staple since 1980. Fresh, prepared-from-scratch offerings include fried seafood, pastas, salads and a number of low-country favorites. Casual dress. **Bar:** Full bar. **Reservations:** suggested. **Hours:** 11:30 am-2:30 & 5-9:30 pm, Sun noon-9 pm. Closed: 11/26, 12/25. **Address:** 320 W Coleman Blvd (US 701) **Location:** 0.8 mi se of Cooper River Bridge on US 701; in The Shops of Mount Pleasant. **Parking:** on-site. **Cards:** AX, DS, MC, VI.

CALL

LONG POINT GRILL — **Phone:** 843/884-3101

American
$7-$17

The restaurant's location near the shipping terminal might suggest hearty basic fare to some diners, but they'd be wrong. This sibling of the popular Mustard Seed group whips up eclectic American fare from fresh ingredients and complex sauces. The menu lists bourbon- and molasses-marinated pork loin, Gorgonzola- and walnut-stuffed chicken breast, cedar-plank salmon and a luscious selection of cakes fresh from the company bakery. Service is excellent. Casual dress. **Bar:** Beer & wine. **Hours:** 11 am-4 & 5-9:30 pm, Fri & Sat-10 pm. Closed major holidays; also Sun. **Address:** 479 Long Point Rd **Location:** I-526, exit Long Point Rd, just sw. **Parking:** on-site. **Cards:** AX, MC, VI.

LOS ARCOS — **Phone:** 843/971-7838

Mexican
$4-$16

The traditional American-Mexican restaurant serves a wide variety of classic dishes in a bright, welcoming atmosphere. Creative blends of vegetables and meats set many dishes apart. Burrito Californiano and Texas fajitas are both excellent choices, and the margaritas are huge. Casual dress. **Bar:** Full bar. **Hours:** 11 am-10 pm, Fri & Sat-11 pm, Sun from noon. Closed major holidays. **Address:** 1136 Hungryneck Blvd **Location:** Jct US 17/SR 517 (Isle of Palms connector); in Iron Gate Plaza. **Parking:** on-site. **Cards:** AX, DS, MC, VI.

CALL

THE MUSTARD SEED — **Phone:** 843/849-0050 (27)

American
$7-$12

The popular establishment features great service at a frenetic pace. The menu focus is on healthy light cuisine, with an emphasis on seafood, pasta and vegetarian dishes. It's well worth the wait. Casual dress. **Bar:** Beer & wine. **Hours:** 11 am-2:30 & 5-9 pm, Fri-10 pm, Sat 5 pm-10 pm. Closed: 11/26, 12/25; also Sun. **Address:** 1036 Chuck Dawley Blvd **Location:** Jct I-526/US 17 business route, 1 mi s on US 526 business route. **Parking:** on-site. **Cards:** AX, MC, VI.

OLD VILLAGE POST HOUSE RESTAURANT — **Phone:** 843/388-8935 (47)

Regional American
$10-$25

The dining room is in a renovated bed and breakfast in Old Mount Pleasant. The atmosphere is classy but unpretentious, with elegant table settings graced by large wall murals that lampoon notable area locations. The food is exceptional as is the service. Representative of well-executed dishes are such choices as tuna tartare, shrimp and grits, stuffed quail and grilled steaks. Breads and desserts are prepared fresh at Ambrosia Bakery, which is owned by the same restaurateurs. Casual dress. **Bar:** Full bar. **Reservations:** suggested. **Hours:** 11:30 am-3:30 & 5:30-10 pm, Sun 10:30 am-2:30 & 5:30-10 pm. **Address:** 101 Pitt St **Location:** Corner of Venning St; between King and Hibben sts; in Old Mount Pleasant; in Old Village Post House Inn. **Parking:** street. **Cards:** AX, DS, MC, VI.

PAGE'S OKRA GRILL — **Phone:** 843/881-3333 (33)

Regional American
$6-$15

In a freestanding brick building, the family-owned-and-operated restaurant dishes up no-frills Southern comfort food in generous portions. The chalkboard menu lists the day's vegetables, meats and homemade desserts, in addition to blue-plate specials. Burgers can be prepared to any desired temperature. Diners can expect the basics—such as meatloaf, fried and roasted chicken, fried fish, fresh local vegetables and mashed potatoes with gravy—and pleasant, efficient service. Casual dress. **Bar:** Beer & wine. **Hours:** 6 am-3 & 5-8:30 pm, Sun 8 am-1 pm. Closed major holidays. **Address:** 794 Coleman Blvd **Location:** Jct US 701/703/US17 business route; just w on US 701 (Coleman Rd). **Parking:** on-site.

PAPA ZUZU'S — **Phone:** 843/881-9848 (46)

Greek
$5-$9

A sibling of the popular downtown ZuZu, the storefront restaurant provides the same freshly prepared fare: gyro sandwiches and plates, hummus, gazpacho, stuffed pita pockets, grilled pizza, salads and vegetarian dishes. A children's menu is also available, as is patio seating. Although service is fast and friendly, the fare is far from fast food. Casual dress. **Bar:** Beer & wine. **Reservations:** not accepted. **Hours:** 11 am-3 pm, Fri & Sat-9 pm. Closed major holidays. **Address:** 426 Coleman Blvd (SR 703) **Location:** 1 mi e of Cooper River Bridge, on SR 703. **Parking:** on-site. **Cards:** MC, VI.

PASTA GRILL — **Phone:** 843/216-5755 (29)

Regional Italian
$8-$18

After operating a successful Italian restaurant in New York, the owner/chef brought his talents to the South Carolina coast. Befitting this place's name, the menu is rife with well-prepared and reasonably priced homemade pasta dishes but also includes a selection of risotto dishes. The chef's talent shows itself in house sauces, including pesto, vodka sauce and Alfredo. The grilled vegetable tower specialty contains a bit of everything except pasta. Young staff members tend to the service. Casual dress. **Bar:** Beer & wine. **Hours:** 11:30 am-9:30 pm. Closed: 12/25. **Address:** 320 L W Coleman Blvd **Location:** 0.8 mi se of Cooper River Bridge on US 701; in The Shops of Mount Pleasant Shopping Center. **Parking:** on-site. **Cards:** MC, VI.

CALL

(See map and index starting on p. 877)

R. B.'S SEAFOOD RESTAURANT **Phone:** 843/881-0466 (45)

Seafood
$8-$25

Guests can arrive by sea or land at the longtime Shem Creek favorite. Completely rebuilt in 2003, the new building offers the same dockside views and the freshest local seafood and steaks in an upscale nautical decor. Friendly service is particularly impressive. Casual dress. **Bar:** Full bar. **Hours:** 11:30 am-10 pm, Fri & Sat-10:30 pm. Closed major holidays. **Address:** 97 Church St **Location:** 1.6 mi se of Cooper River Bridge on Coleman Blvd (SR 703), just sw. **Parking:** on-site. **Cards:** AX, DS, MC, VI.

CALL

RED DRUM GASTROPUB **Phone:** 843/849-0313 (34)

American
$16-$32

The upscale, well-appointed pub presents an evolving menu with roots in the Southwest. Among tasty and artfully designed seafood dishes are shrimp and crabmeat stack in chipotle ketchup over guacamole and grouper seviche. Beautiful presentations also mark the desserts. Casual dress. **Bar:** Full bar. **Reservations:** suggested, Thurs-Sat weekends. **Hours:** 5:30 pm-10 pm, Fri & Sat-10:30 pm. Closed: 11/26, 12/25; also Sun. **Address:** 803 Coleman Blvd **Location:** 2.6 mi se of Cooper River Bridge on SR 703 (Coleman Blvd). **Parking:** on-site. **Cards:** AX, MC, VI.

CALL

THE RED PEPPER **Phone:** 843/216-6633

Italian
$8-$32

The family-owned restaurant's award-winning chef/owner lords over every dish, leaving the kitchen to ensure quality and consistency. Both the menu and wine list are extensive, and all dishes, including desserts, are made on site. Offerings include many pasta, veal, seafood, pizza and vegetarian dishes, as well as daily specials. The relaxed restaurant lends class and diversity to a night out a la Italiano. Casual dress. **Bar:** Full bar. **Hours:** 11:30 am-10 pm, Fri-11 pm, Sat noon-11 pm, Sun noon-10 pm. Closed: 11/26, 12/25. **Address:** 1960 Riveria Dr **Location:** Jct US 17/SR 517 (Isle of Palms Connector), 1 mi se on SR 517; in Seaside Farms Shopping Center. **Parking:** on-site. **Cards:** AX, MC, VI.

CALL

RED'S ICE HOUSE **Phone:** 843/388-0003 (41)

Regional Seafood
$6-$16

The local watering hole and party bar is complete with tiki torches on the patio, which overlooks the creek. Fresh catches straight off the boat make up the seafood offering. This place is a great destination for a fun night out. Casual dress. **Bar:** Full bar. **Hours:** 11:30 am-11 pm. **Address:** 98 Church St **Location:** 1.6 mi se of Cooper River Bridge on Coleman Blvd (SR 703), just s. **Parking:** on-site. **Cards:** AX, DC, DS, MC, VI.

SENOR TEQUILA **Phone:** 843/856-8998 (43)

Mexican
$5-$13

Offering simple Mexican fare served by a friendly and efficient wait staff, the broad menu features all traditional favorites as well as a wide selection of combination specials. Casual dress. **Bar:** Full bar. **Hours:** 11:30 am-9 pm, Fri & Sat-10 pm. Closed: 11/26, 12/25. **Address:** 612 Coleman Blvd **Location:** 1.9 mi se of Cooper River Bridge, on SR 701; in Moultrie Plaza. **Parking:** on-site. **Cards:** AX, DS, MC, VI.

CALL

SETTE **Phone:** 843/388-8808 (42)

Italian
$6-$15

Near Shem Creek, the small bistro prepares an array of favorites, such as chicken piccata, potato gnocchi and pasta dishes, as well as beef and seafood favorites. The cozy, friendly atmosphere is a treat. Casual dress. **Bar:** Full bar. **Hours:** 11 am-2:30 & 5-9:30 pm, Fri-10 pm, Sat 5 pm-10 pm. Closed major holidays; also Sun. **Address:** 201 Coleman Blvd **Location:** Jct Coleman Blvd (US 703/Shem Creek Bridge), just se. **Parking:** on-site. **Cards:** AX, MC, VI.

SHEM CREEK BAR & GRILL **Phone:** 843/884-8102 (37)

Seafood
$6-$30

On peaceful Shem Creek, the casual eatery offers a splendid view of wildlife rustling through the marsh. Seafood is the focus, but a few beef dishes are available. Casual dress. **Bar:** Full bar. **Reservations:** suggested, weekends. **Hours:** 11:30 am-10 pm, Fri & Sat-10:30 pm. Closed: 11/26, 12/25. **Address:** 508 Mill St **Location:** Cooper River Bridge, 1.6 mi se on Coleman Blvd (SR 703), then just ne. **Parking:** on-site. **Cards:** AX, DC, DS, MC, VI.

CALL

SIX TABLES **Phone:** 843/971-8850

AAA

New American
$75

The adult-oriented dining experience is truly unique and fulfilling. The owner personally greets each guest with a flute of champagne and hors d'ouvres. The chef himself presents the menu tableside, explaining his preparation techniques for each dish. Afterward, a team of professional staff serve each of the six courses on fine china. The menu changes routinely but a few notable courses include pan-seared scallops, butter-poached shrimp, rack of lamb, duck confit and filet of beef served with a creamless creamed-corn. A rich cheese course is served after dinner. The service can be accompanied by well-paired wines or wines-by-the-glass. Dressy casual. **Bar:** Beer & wine. **Reservations:** required. **Hours:** 7:30 pm-close. Closed: Sun & Mon. **Address:** 664 G Long Point Rd **Location:** I-526, exit Long Point Rd, just ne; in Belle Hall Shopping Center. **Parking:** on-site. **Cards:** AX, MC, VI.

SOURI'S ITALIAN BISTRO **Phone:** 843/388-2323

Italian
$9-$26

The chef/owner prepares outstanding Northern Italian cuisine to order. Meat, seafood and pasta dishes are made from scratch. The dining room is comfortable and the atmosphere casual. Casual dress. **Bar:** Full bar. **Reservations:** accepted. **Hours:** 5 pm-9 pm. Closed: 11/26, 12/25; also Sun & Mon. **Address:** 3369 S Morgan Pt Rd **Location:** Jct US 17 N/SR 41, 2 mi ne on US 17 N to National Dr, then just se; in National Crossing Shopping Center. **Parking:** on-site. **Cards:** AX, MC, VI.

CALL

(See map and index starting on p. 877)

STICKY FINGERS RIB HOUSE **Phone:** 843/856-7427

Barbecue
$7-$20

Diners can put down their silverware and get their fingers ready for classic Carolina sweet ribs, as well as ribs cooked in the Texas and Tennessee styles. Hearty sides of baked beans and coleslaw complement entrees at the friendly cafe. Casual dress. **Bar:** Full bar. **Hours:** 11 am-close. Closed: 11/26, 12/25. **Address:** 341 Johnnie Dodds Blvd (US 17) **Location:** Jct Service Rd and Houston Northcutt Blvd, just n of Alair Distro; s of Service Rd. **Parking:** on-site. **Cards:** AX, DC, DS, MC, VI.

UNO MAS **Phone:** 843/856-4868 (20)

Latin American
$7-$17

The latest addition to this dining empire boasts "re-grooved" Mexican fare, including soups, salads, four seviches, new twists on classic dishes and chef's specials. Menu standouts of lime soup, duck marinated in red chile and tequila-flamed shrimp entice. All courses make extensive use of fresh local vegetables, which combine with light but complex house sauces. Best of all, a meal here is affordable. Desserts come from the bakery that also supplies other restaurants in this culinary family. Casual dress. **Bar:** Full bar. **Hours:** 11 am-2:30 & 5-9 pm, Fri-10 pm, Sat 5 pm-10 pm. Closed: 11/26, 12/25; also Sun. **Address:** 880 Allbritton Blvd **Location:** Cooper River Bridge, 1.9 mi e on US 17, then just s. **Parking:** on-site. **Cards:** AX, MC, VI.

VICKERY'S BAR & GRILL **Phone:** 843/884-4440 (39)

Regional American
$6-$20

Friendly service, a diverse menu and nice water views combine to make this dining spot a local favorite. The menu lists a melange of Lowcountry and Cuban dishes, many of which center on fresh seafood. Casual dress. **Bar:** Full bar. **Reservations:** suggested. **Hours:** 11:30 am-1 am. Closed: 11/26, 12/25. **Address:** 1313 Shrimp Boat Ln **Location:** 1.3 mi se of Cooper River Bridge on Coleman Blvd (SR 703), just sw. **Parking:** on-site. **Cards:** AX, DS, MC, VI.

WATER'S EDGE **Phone:** 843/884-4074 (35)

Regional American
$8-$30

On Shem Creek, the restaurant treats most, if not all, diners to an excellent view of the activity on the water. Flights of pelicans, the scent of salt air and the setting sun combine with excellent service and an outstanding menu to make the upscale restaurant a "must dine." The chef personally ensures the perfection of each dish with the liberal application of his skilled and creative talents. There is no single dish to recommend, as they're all great. Casual dress. **Bar:** Full bar. **Reservations:** suggested, Thurs-Sun. **Hours:** 11 am-11 pm. Closed: 12/25. **Address:** 1407 Shrimp Boat Ln **Location:** 1.4 mi se of Cooper River Bridge on Coleman Blvd (SR 703); just nw of Shem Creek Bridge. **Parking:** on-site. **Cards:** AX, DS, MC, VI.

CALL &M

YAMATO SEAFOOD STEAK & SEAFOOD **Phone:** 843/881-1190

Japanese
$10-$29

The "original Japanese Steakhouse of South Carolina", Yamatos tantalizes guest with fresh USDA choice beef, wonderful seafood and fresh vegetables. Families enjoy the casual atmosphere and the show the chefs put on while cooking each individual meal. Casual dress. **Bar:** Full bar. **Reservations:** accepted. **Hours:** 5 pm-9 pm, Fri & Sat-10 pm. Closed: 11/26, 12/25. **Address:** 1993 Riveria Dr **Location:** Jct US 17 N/SR 517 (Isle of Palms connector), 1 mi s on SR 517, then just sw. **Parking:** on-site. **Cards:** AX, DS, MC, VI.

CALL &M

YO BURRITO **Phone:** 843/856-0061 (22)

Mexican
$4-$8

The small regional chain features oversized burritos stuffed with rice, black beans and a choice of steak, chicken, pork, shrimp, mahi mahi or vegetables—alone or in combinations. Also on the menu are tacos, nachos, quesadillas, salads and warm chips with homemade salsa that comes from a self-serve bar offering several options from sweet to hot. Beverage choices include glasses from the "Cheap Beer Hall of Fame" and margaritas served in Mason jars. Casual dress. **Bar:** Full bar. **Hours:** 11 am-9 pm, Fri & Sat-10 pm, Sun noon-9 pm. Closed: 12/25. **Address:** 675 Johnnie Dodds Blvd (US 17) **Location:** Cooper River Bridge, 1.2 mi ne on US 17; on s frontage road. **Parking:** on-site. **Cards:** MC, VI.

ZEUS GRILL & SEAFOOD **Phone:** 843/388-9992 (21)

Greek
$7-$25

A sibling to two other popular area restaurants, the family-owned property adds Greek cuisine to the list of fare available East of the Cooper. With a long selection of Mediterranean standards, diners can find whatever they want, but if everything looks too good, the super special allows for a sampling of just about everything. Also offered are a children's menu and a variety of fresh desserts. Casual dress. **Bar:** Full bar. **Reservations:** accepted. **Hours:** 11 am-10:30 pm, Fri & Sat-11:30 pm, Sun-10 pm. Closed: 11/26, 12/25. **Address:** 725 Johnnie Dodds Blvd (US 17) **Location:** From Cooper River Bridge, 1.4 mi e. **Parking:** on-site. **Cards:** AX, DS, MC, VI.

CALL &M

NORTH CHARLESTON pop. 79,641 (See map and index starting on p. 877)

WHERE TO STAY

ALOFT CHARLESTON AIRPORT & CONVENTION CENTER **Phone:** 843/566-7300

fyi

Contemporary Hotel
Rates not provided

Too new to rate, opening scheduled for September 2008. **Address:** 4875 Tanger Outlet Blvd **Location:** I-26, exit 213A, follow signs to Tanger Outlet Mall. **Amenities:** 136 units, coffeemakers.

(See map and index starting on p. 877)

BEST WESTERN AIRPORT INN & SUITES *Book great rates at AAA.com* **Phone:** (843)574-0911 

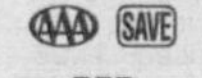

Hotel
$89-$139 All Year

Address: 2470 Prospect St **Location:** I-26, exit 209 (Ashley Phosphate Rd), just w to Mazyck Rd, then just s. **Facility:** 74 units. 68 one-bedroom standard units. 6 one-bedroom suites, some with whirlpools. 4 stories, interior corridors. **Parking:** on-site. **Amenities:** CD players, high-speed Internet, voice mail, irons, hair dryers. **Pool(s):** indoor. **Leisure Activities:** exercise room. **Guest Services:** coin laundry, wireless Internet. **Business Services:** meeting rooms, business center. **Cards:** AX, DS, MC, VI. **Free Special Amenities: expanded continental breakfast and high-speed Internet.**

/ SOME UNITS

AAA Benefit:
Members save up to 20%, plus 10% bonus points with rewards program.

CANDLEWOOD SUITES *Book at AAA.com* **Phone:** (843)797-3535 17

Hotel
$99-$185 3/1-11/30
$99-$175 12/1-2/28

Address: 2177 Northwoods Blvd **Location:** I-26, exit 209 (Ashley Phosphate Rd), just e, then just n. **Facility:** 125 units. 109 one-bedroom standard units with efficiencies. 16 one-bedroom suites with efficiencies. 4 stories, interior corridors. *Bath:* combo or shower only. **Parking:** on-site. **Terms:** office hours 7 am-11 pm, check-in 4 pm. **Amenities:** DVD players, CD players, high-speed Internet, voice mail, irons, hair dryers. **Guest Services:** coin laundry, wireless Internet. **Business Services:** business center. **Cards:** AX, DC, DS, JC, MC, VI.

ASK / SOME UNITS FEE

COMFORT SUITES CHARLESTON/N CHARLESTON, SC *Book great rates at AAA.com* **Phone:** (843)725-5400 25

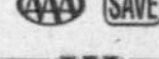

Hotel
$89-$169 All Year

Address: 2520 N Forest Dr **Location:** I-26, exit 209 (Ashley Phosphate Rd), just w of Northside Dr. **Facility:** Smoke free premises. 84 one-bedroom standard units, some with whirlpools. 4 stories, interior corridors. *Bath:* combo or shower only. **Parking:** on-site. **Terms:** cancellation fee imposed. **Amenities:** voice mail, safes (fee), irons, hair dryers. **Pool(s):** outdoor. **Leisure Activities:** limited exercise equipment. **Guest Services:** coin laundry, wireless Internet. **Business Services:** meeting rooms, business center. **Cards:** AX, CB, DC, DS, MC, VI. **Free Special Amenities: full breakfast and high-speed Internet.**

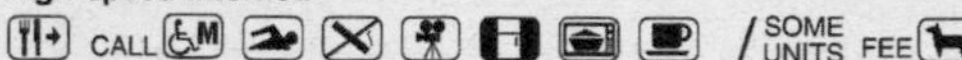
CALL / SOME UNITS FEE

COUNTRY INN & SUITES-CHARLESTON NORTH *Book great rates at AAA.com* **Phone:** (843)572-0083 22

Hotel
$129-$209 All Year

Address: 7429 Stafford Rd **Location:** I-26, exit 209 (Ashley Phosphate Rd), just e. **Facility:** Smoke free premises. 57 units. 46 one-bedroom standard units, some with whirlpools. 11 one-bedroom suites. 4 stories, interior corridors. *Bath:* combo or shower only. **Parking:** on-site. **Terms:** cancellation fee imposed. **Amenities:** high-speed Internet, irons, hair dryers. **Pool(s):** indoor. **Leisure Activities:** limited exercise equipment. **Guest Services:** coin laundry, wireless Internet. **Business Services:** business center. **Cards:** AX, DC, DS, MC, VI. **Free Special Amenities: expanded continental breakfast and high-speed Internet.**
(See color ad below)

CALL

▼ *See AAA listing above* ▼

(See map and index starting on p. 877)

COURTYARD CHARLESTON NORTH *Book great rates at AAA.com* **Phone:** (843)747-9122 31

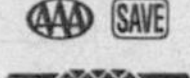

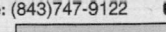

Hotel
$153-$164 All Year

Address: 2415 Mall Dr **Location:** I-26, exit 213 westbound; exit 213B eastbound, just n. **Facility:** Smoke free premises. 123 units. 119 one-bedroom standard units, some with whirlpools. 4 one-bedroom suites. 4 stories, interior corridors. *Bath:* combo or shower only. **Parking:** on-site. **Terms:** cancellation fee imposed. **Amenities:** high-speed Internet, dual phone lines, voice mail, irons, hair dryers. **Pool(s):** outdoor. **Leisure Activities:** whirlpool, limited exercise equipment. **Guest Services:** valet and coin laundry, wireless Internet. **Business Services:** meeting rooms, business center. **Cards:** AX, CB, DC, DS, MC, VI. **Free Special Amenities: newspaper and high-speed Internet.**

CALL / SOME UNITS

AAA Benefit:
Members save a minimum 5% off the best available rate.

EMBASSY SUITES HOTEL AIRPORT-CONVENTION CENTER NORTH CHARLESTON *Book great rates at AAA.com* **Phone:** (843)747-1882

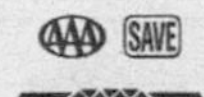

Hotel
$119-$239 All Year

Address: 5055 International Blvd **Location:** I-26, exit 213 westbound; exit 213A eastbound, just s, then w; I-526, exit International Blvd, 0.4 mi e. Located adjoining the performing arts center. **Facility:** 255 one-bedroom suites, some with whirlpools. 9 stories, interior corridors. *Bath:* combo or shower only. **Parking:** on-site. **Terms:** 1-30 night minimum stay, cancellation fee imposed. **Amenities:** video games (fee), dual phone lines, voice mail, irons, hair dryers. **Pool(s):** heated indoor. **Leisure Activities:** sauna, whirlpool, exercise room. **Guest Services:** valet and coin laundry, airport transportation-Charleston AFB International Airport, area transportation (fee)-downtown, wireless Internet. **Business Services:** conference facilities, business center. **Cards:** AX, CB, DC, DS, JC, MC, VI. **Free Special Amenities: full breakfast and newspaper.**

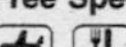  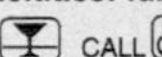  CALL 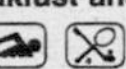   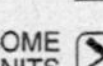 / SOME UNITS

EMBASSY SUITES HOTELS

AAA Benefit:
Members save 5% or more everyday!

FAIRFIELD INN & SUITES - NORTH CHARLESTON *Book great rates at AAA.com* **Phone:** (843)414-2700

Hotel
$128-$137 All Year

Address: 2600 Elm Center Rd **Location:** I-26, exit 205B (US 78), 1.1 mi se; in Elms Plantation. **Facility:** Smoke free premises. 79 one-bedroom standard units. 3 stories, interior corridors. *Bath:* combo or shower only. **Parking:** on-site. **Terms:** cancellation fee imposed. **Amenities:** dual phone lines, voice mail, irons, hair dryers. *Some:* CD players. **Pool(s):** outdoor. **Leisure Activities:** whirlpool, exercise room. **Guest Services:** valet and coin laundry, wireless Internet. **Business Services:** business center. **Cards:** AX, DS, VI.

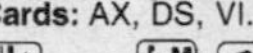 CALL    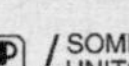  / SOME UNITS

AAA Benefit:
Members save a minimum 5% off the best available rate.

(See map and index starting on p. 877)

HAMPTON INN AIRPORT/COLISEUM 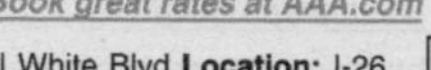 Book great rates at AAA.com **Phone:** (843)554-7154 36

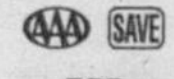

Hotel
$114-$169 All Year

Address: 4701 Saul White Blvd **Location:** I-26, exit 213 westbound; exit 213A eastbound, just s, then e. **Facility:** 124 one-bedroom standard units. 4 stories, interior corridors. **Parking:** on-site. **Terms:** 1-30 night minimum stay, cancellation fee imposed. **Amenities:** video games (fee), voice mail, irons, hair dryers. **Pool(s):** outdoor. **Guest Services:** valet laundry, airport transportation-Charleston AFB International Airport, wireless Internet. **Business Services:** meeting rooms, fax (fee). **Cards:** AX, CB, DC, DS, MC, VI. **Free Special Amenities: expanded continental breakfast and high-speed Internet.** *(See color ad below)*

/ SOME UNITS

AAA Benefit:
Members save up to 10% everyday!

HAMPTON INN CHARLESTON NORTH Book great rates at AAA.com **Phone:** (843)820-2030 23

Hotel
$79-$109 All Year

Address: 7424 Northside Dr **Location:** I-26, exit 209 (Ashley Phosphate Rd), just sw. **Facility:** 102 one-bedroom standard units, some with whirlpools. 4 stories, interior corridors. *Bath:* combo or shower only. **Parking:** on-site. **Terms:** 1-30 night minimum stay, cancellation fee imposed. **Amenities:** dual phone lines, voice mail, irons, hair dryers. **Pool(s):** outdoor. **Leisure Activities:** exercise room. **Guest Services:** valet and coin laundry, wireless Internet. **Business Services:** meeting rooms, business center. **Cards:** AX, CB, DC, DS, MC, VI.

  / SOME UNITS

AAA Benefit:
Members save up to 10% everyday!

HILTON GARDEN INN-CHARLESTON AIRPORT Book great rates at AAA.com **Phone:** (843)308-9330 40

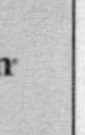

Hotel
$109-$199 All Year

Address: 5265 International Blvd **Location:** I-26, exit 213 westbound; exit 213A eastbound, just s, then w; I-526, exit International Blvd, just e. Located adjacant to Convention Center. **Facility:** Smoke free premises. 168 units. 152 one-bedroom standard units. 16 one-bedroom suites. 5 stories, interior corridors. *Bath:* combo or shower only. **Parking:** on-site. **Terms:** cancellation fee imposed. **Amenities:** video games (fee), high-speed Internet, dual phone lines, voice mail, irons, hair dryers. **Pool(s):** indoor. **Leisure Activities:** whirlpool, limited exercise equipment. **Guest Services:** valet and coin laundry, area transportation, wireless Internet. **Business Services:** conference facilities, business center. **Cards:** AX, CB, DC, DS, JC, MC, VI.

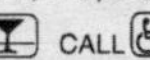    

CALL

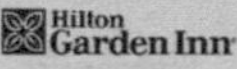

AAA Benefit:
Members save 5% or more everyday!

HOLIDAY INN CHARLESTON AIRPORT & CONVENTION CENTER Book at AAA.com **Phone:** (843)576-0300 38

Hotel
$109-$269 All Year

Address: 5264 International Blvd **Location:** I-26, exit 213 westbound; exit 213A eastbound, just s to International Blvd, then 0.7 mi w; I-526, exit 16 (International Blvd), just e. **Facility:** Smoke free premises. 142 units. 130 one-bedroom standard units. 12 one-bedroom suites. 6 stories, interior corridors. *Bath:* some combo or shower only. **Parking:** on-site. **Terms:** check-in 4 pm, cancellation fee imposed. **Amenities:** video games (fee), high-speed Internet, dual phone lines, voice mail, irons, hair dryers. **Pool(s):** heated outdoor. **Leisure Activities:** whirlpool, exercise room. **Guest Services:** valet and coin laundry, area transportation, wireless Internet. **Business Services:** meeting rooms, business center. **Cards:** AX, DC, DS, MC, VI.

(See map and index starting on p. 877)

HOLIDAY INN EXPRESS HOTEL & SUITES *Book at AAA.com* **Phone:** (843)569-3200

Hotel
$99-$159 All Year

Address: 8975 Elms Center Rd **Location:** I-26, exit 205B (US 78), 1 mi se; in Elms Plantation. **Facility:** Smoke free premises. 86 one-bedroom standard units, some with whirlpools. 4 stories, interior corridors. *Bath:* combo or shower only. **Parking:** on-site. **Terms:** check-in 4 pm, cancellation fee imposed. **Amenities:** high-speed Internet, dual phone lines, voice mail, irons, hair dryers. **Pool(s):** outdoor. **Leisure Activities:** limited exercise equipment. **Guest Services:** valet and coin laundry, wireless Internet. **Business Services:** meeting rooms, business center. **Cards:** AX, CB, DC, DS, JC, MC, VI.

CALL

HOLIDAY INN EXPRESS HOTEL & SUITES *Book at AAA.com* **Phone:** (843)553-1600 18

Hotel
$99-$149 All Year

Address: 7670 Northwoods Blvd **Location:** I-26, exit 209 (Ashley Phosphate Rd), just e, then just n. **Facility:** 98 one-bedroom standard units, some with whirlpools. 4 stories, interior corridors. *Bath:* combo or shower only. **Parking:** on-site. **Amenities:** video games (fee), dual phone lines, voice mail, irons, hair dryers. **Pool(s):** outdoor. **Leisure Activities:** limited exercise equipment. **Guest Services:** valet and coin laundry, wireless Internet. **Business Services:** meeting rooms, business center. **Cards:** AX, CB, DC, DS, JC, MC, VI.

ASK CALL / SOME UNITS

HOMESTEAD STUDIO SUITES HOTEL-CHARLESTON/AIRPORT *Book at AAA.com* **Phone:** (843)740-3440 35

Hotel
$95-$110 All Year

Address: 5045 N Arco Ln **Location:** I-26, exit 213 westbound; exit 213A eastbound; enter through Tanger Outlet access roads. **Facility:** 98 units. 75 one-bedroom standard units with efficiencies. 23 one-bedroom suites with efficiencies. 3 stories, interior corridors. *Bath:* combo or shower only. **Parking:** on-site. **Terms:** office hours 7 am-11 pm. **Amenities:** dual phone lines, voice mail, irons, hair dryers. **Pool(s):** indoor. **Leisure Activities:** exercise room. **Guest Services:** valet and coin laundry, wireless Internet. **Business Services:** fax (fee). **Cards:** AX, CB, DC, DS, JC, MC, VI.

ASK CALL / SOME UNITS FEE

HOMEWOOD SUITES CHARLESTON AIRPORT/ CONVENTION CENTER *Book great rates at AAA.com* **Phone:** (843)735-5000 43

AAA SAVE

Extended Stay Hotel
$114-$159 All Year

Address: 5048 International Blvd **Location:** I-26, exit 213A eastbound, 0.4 mi s, then just w; exit 213 westbound, 0.5 mi s, then just w; I-526, exit 17 to International Blvd, then 0.7 mi e. **Facility:** Opened in 2008, this extended-stay property offers spacious public areas and large guest rooms with a contemporary decor and the latest technology. Smoke free premises. 128 units. 45 one-bedroom standard units with efficiencies. 74 one- and 9 two-bedroom suites with efficiencies. 5 stories, interior corridors. *Bath:* combo or shower only. **Parking:** on-site. **Terms:** check-in 4 pm, 1-30 night minimum stay, cancellation fee imposed. **Amenities:** high-speed Internet, voice mail, irons, hair dryers. **Pool(s):** outdoor. **Leisure Activities:** exercise room. **Guest Services:** coin laundry, airport transportation-Charleston AFB International Airport, area transportation-within 5 mi, wireless Internet. **Business Services:** meeting rooms, business center. **Cards:** AX, CB, DC, DS, MC, VI. **Free Special Amenities: full breakfast and high-speed Internet.**

HOMEWOOD SUITES

AAA Benefit:
Members save 5% or more everyday!

CALL

▼ *See AAA listing p 930* ▼

(See map and index starting on p. 877)

HYATT PLACE NORTH CHARLESTON — **Phone:** 843/735-7100

fyi Hotel

Under construction, scheduled to open April 2009. **Address:** 7329 Mazyck Rd **Location:** I-26, exit 209A (Ashley Phosphate Rd). **Amenities:** 113 units, refrigerators, pool. ***(See color ad p 929)***

HYATT PLACE NORTH CHARLESTON-MONTAGUE — **Phone:** 843/302-8600

fyi Hotel

Under construction, scheduled to open May 2009. **Address:** 3234 W Montague Ave **Location:** I-526, exit 213 (W Montague Ave). **Amenities:** 127 units, refrigerators, pool.

LA QUINTA INN CHARLESTON — *Book great rates at AAA.com* — **Phone:** (843)797-8181 — 27

Hotel
$49-$139 All Year

Address: 2499 La Quinta Ln **Location:** I-26, exit 209 (Ashley Phosphate Rd), just w. **Facility:** 122 units. 120 one-bedroom standard units. 2 one-bedroom suites. 2 stories (no elevator), interior/exterior corridors. **Parking:** on-site. **Amenities:** video games (fee), voice mail, irons, hair dryers. **Pool(s):** heated outdoor. **Guest Services:** wireless Internet. **Business Services:** fax (fee). **Cards:** AX, DC, DS, MC, VI.

ASK / SOME UNITS FEE FEE

MOTEL 6 #642 — *Book at AAA.com* — **Phone:** (843)572-6590 — 28

Motel
$45-$51 3/27-11/30
$39-$45 12/1-3/26

Address: 2551 Ashley Phosphate Rd **Location:** I-26, exit 209 (Ashley Phosphate Rd), just w. **Facility:** 126 one-bedroom standard units. 2 stories (no elevator), exterior corridors. *Bath:* combo or shower only. **Parking:** on-site. **Pool(s):** outdoor. **Guest Services:** coin laundry. **Business Services:** fax (fee). **Cards:** AX, DC, DS, MC, VI.

/ SOME UNITS

NORTH CHARLESTON INN — *Book great rates at AAA.com* — **Phone:** (843)744-8281 — 39

AAA SAVE
Motel
$49-$129 3/1-11/30
$49-$109 12/1-2/28

Address: 2934 W Montague Ave **Location:** I-26, exit 213A eastbound; exit 213 westbound, just s. **Facility:** 149 one-bedroom standard units. 2 stories (no elevator), exterior corridors. **Parking:** on-site. **Amenities:** video games (fee), voice mail, irons, hair dryers. **Pool(s):** outdoor. **Guest Services:** coin laundry, wireless Internet. **Business Services:** meeting rooms, business center. **Cards:** AX, CB, DC, DS, MC, VI.

/ SOME UNITS

NORTH CHARLESTON SLEEP INN & SUITES — *Book great rates at AAA.com* — **Phone:** (843)725-4700 — 37

AAA SAVE
Hotel
$80-$120 All Year

Address: 4715 Saul White Blvd **Location:** I-26, exit 213, just s, then e. **Facility:** Smoke free premises. 61 one-bedroom standard units, some with kitchens. 3 stories, interior corridors. *Bath:* combo or shower only. **Parking:** on-site. **Terms:** 7 day cancellation notice. **Amenities:** voice mail, irons, hair dryers. **Pool(s):** heated indoor/outdoor. **Leisure Activities:** limited exercise equipment. **Guest Services:** coin laundry, wireless Internet. **Business Services:** meeting rooms, business center. **Cards:** AX, DC, DS, MC, VI. **Free Special Amenities: expanded continental breakfast and high-speed Internet.**

QUALITY INN-CHARLESTON — *Book at AAA.com* — **Phone:** (843)572-6677 — 26

Hotel
$60-$100 All Year

Address: 7415 Northside Dr **Location:** I-26, exit 209 (Ashley Phosphate Rd), just w. **Facility:** 118 units. 117 one-bedroom standard units. 1 one-bedroom suite with kitchen. 2 stories (no elevator), exterior corridors. **Parking:** on-site. **Amenities:** voice mail, irons, hair dryers. **Pool(s):** outdoor. **Guest Services:** valet laundry, wireless Internet. **Business Services:** meeting rooms, PC, fax (fee). **Cards:** AX, DS, MC, VI.

ASK / SOME UNITS

(See map and index starting on p. 877)

QUALITY SUITES CONVENTION CENTER Book great rates at AAA.com **Phone:** (843)717-7300 32

AAA SAVE

Hotel
$99-$179 All Year

Address: 5225 N Arco Ln **Location:** I-26, exit 213 westbound; exit 213A eastbound; enter through Tanger Outlet access roads. Located adjacent to Tanger Outlet Mall. **Facility:** 168 one-bedroom suites, some with whirlpools. 5 stories, interior corridors. **Parking:** on-site. **Terms:** 30 day cancellation notice. **Amenities:** video library (fee), voice mail, irons, hair dryers. **Pool(s):** outdoor. **Leisure Activities:** whirlpool, limited exercise equipment. **Guest Services:** valet and coin laundry, airport transportation-Charleston AFB International Airport, wireless Internet. **Business Services:** meeting rooms, fax (fee). **Cards:** AX, CB, DC, DS, JC, MC, VI. **Free Special Amenities: full breakfast and high-speed Internet.** *(See color ad p 905)*

VCR / SOME UNITS FEE

RADISSON HOTEL CHARLESTON AIRPORT Book great rates at AAA.com **Phone:** (843)744-2501 30

AAA SAVE

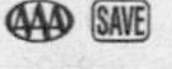

Hotel
$169 3/1-11/30
$129 12/1-2/28

Address: 5991 Rivers Ave **Location:** I-26, exit 211B (Aviation Ave), just ne. **Facility:** 159 one-bedroom standard units. 8 stories, interior corridors. **Parking:** on-site. **Terms:** cancellation fee imposed. **Amenities:** dual phone lines, voice mail, irons, hair dryers. **Pool(s):** heated indoor. **Leisure Activities:** whirlpool, exercise room. **Guest Services:** valet and coin laundry, airport transportation-Charleston AFB International Airport, area transportation-within 5 mi, wireless Internet. **Business Services:** conference facilities, PC, fax (fee). **Cards:** AX, DS, MC, VI. **Free Special Amenities: newspaper and high-speed Internet.** *(See color ad p 893)*

/ SOME UNITS FEE

RED ROOF INN Book great rates at AAA.com **Phone:** (843)572-9100 21

AAA SAVE

Motel
$50-$95 All Year

Address: 7480 Northwoods Blvd **Location:** I-26, exit 209 (Ashley Phosphate Rd), just e, then just n. **Facility:** 109 one-bedroom standard units. 2 stories (no elevator), exterior corridors. *Bath:* combo or shower only. **Parking:** on-site. **Amenities:** video games (fee), voice mail. **Guest Services:** coin laundry, wireless Internet. **Business Services:** fax (fee). **Cards:** AX, CB, DC, DS, MC, VI. **Free Special Amenities: local telephone calls.**

/ SOME UNITS

RESIDENCE INN BY MARRIOTT Book great rates at AAA.com **Phone:** (843)572-5757 20

Extended Stay Hotel
$142-$162 All Year

Address: 7645 Northwoods Blvd **Location:** I-26, exit 209 (Ashley Phosphate Rd), just e, then n. **Facility:** 1- and 2-bedroom units, some with fireplace. Smoke free premises. 96 units. 72 one-bedroom standard units with kitchens. 24 two-bedroom suites with kitchens. 2 stories (no elevator), exterior corridors. **Parking:** on-site. **Terms:** cancellation fee imposed. **Amenities:** high-speed Internet, voice mail, irons, hair dryers. *Some:* dual phone lines. **Pool(s):** outdoor. **Leisure Activities:** whirlpool, sports court. **Guest Services:** valet and coin laundry, wireless Internet. **Business Services:** meeting rooms, PC, fax (fee). **Cards:** AX, CB, DC, DS, JC, MC, VI.

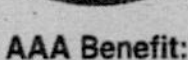

AAA Benefit:
Members save a minimum 5% off the best available rate.

/ SOME UNITS FEE FEE VCR

RESIDENCE INN CHARLESTON AIRPORT Book great rates at AAA.com **Phone:** (843)266-3434 42

AAA SAVE

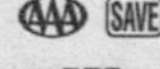

Extended Stay Hotel
$188-$201 All Year

Address: 5035 International Blvd **Location:** I-26, exit 213A eastbound, 0.4 mi s, then just w; exit westbound, 0.4 mi s, then just w; I-526, exit International Blvd, 0.8 mi e. **Facility:** Near a major business park, the airport, an outlet mall and the convention center, the hotel is designed for extended-stay guests. Smoke free premises. 150 units. 38 one-bedroom standard units with efficiencies. 88 one- and 24 two-bedroom suites, some with efficiencies or kitchens. 4 stories, interior corridors. *Bath:* combo or shower only. **Parking:** on-site. **Terms:** cancellation fee imposed. **Amenities:** high-speed Internet, dual phone lines, voice mail, safes, irons, hair dryers. **Pool(s):** outdoor. **Leisure Activities:** whirlpool, exercise room, sports court. **Guest Services:** valet and coin laundry, airport transportation-Charleston AFB International Airport, wireless Internet. **Business Services:** meeting rooms, business center. **Cards:** AX, CB, DC, DS, JC, MC, VI. **Free Special Amenities: expanded continental breakfast and newspaper.**

AAA Benefit:
Members save a minimum 5% off the best available rate.

CALL / SOME UNITS FEE

(See map and index starting on p. 877)

SHERATON HOTEL NORTH CHARLESTON CONVENTION CENTER *Book great rates at AAA.com* **Phone:** 843/747-1900 34

Hotel
Rates not provided

Address: 4770 Goer Dr **Location:** I-26, exit 213 westbound; exit 213B eastbound, just n. **Facility:** 289 units. 281 one-bedroom standard units. 8 one-bedroom suites. 8 stories, interior corridors. **Parking:** on-site. **Amenities:** video games (fee), dual phone lines, voice mail, irons, hair dryers. **Pool(s):** heated indoor/outdoor. **Leisure Activities:** exercise room. **Guest Services:** valet and coin laundry, airport transportation-Charleston AFB International Airport, area transportation (fee)-historic district, wireless Internet. **Business Services:** conference facilities, business center. **Free Special Amenities: high-speed Internet.** *(See color ad below)*

/ SOME UNITS FEE FEE FEE

Sheraton
AAA Benefit:
Members get up to 15% off, plus Starwood Preferred Guest® bonuses.

Sheraton

SLEEP INN CHARLESTON NORTH *Book great rates at AAA.com* **Phone:** (843)572-8400 24

Hotel
$69-$159 All Year

Address: 7435 Northside Dr **Location:** I-26, exit 209 (Ashley Phosphate Rd), just w. **Facility:** 68 one-bedroom standard units. 4 stories, interior corridors. *Bath:* combo or shower only. **Parking:** on-site. **Terms:** cancellation fee imposed. **Amenities:** dual phone lines, voice mail, safes (fee), irons, hair dryers. **Leisure Activities:** exercise room & pool privileges. **Guest Services:** valet and coin laundry, wireless Internet. **Business Services:** business center. **Cards:** AX, CB, DC, DS, MC, VI. **Free Special Amenities: continental breakfast and high-speed Internet.**

FEE / SOME UNITS FEE

STAYBRIDGE SUITES NORTH CHARLESTON **Phone:** 843/377-4600

fyi
Hotel

Under construction, scheduled to open February 2009. **Address:** 7329 Mazyck Rd **Location:** I-26, exit 209A (Ashley Phosphate Rd). **Amenities:** 93 units, coffeemakers, microwaves, refrigerators, pool. *(See color ad p 933)*

STUDIOPLUS *Book at AAA.com* **Phone:** (843)553-0036 19

Hotel
$95-$110 All Year

Address: 7641 Northwoods Blvd **Location:** I-26, exit 209 (Ashley Phosphate Rd), just e, then just n. **Facility:** 72 units. 71 one-bedroom standard units with kitchens. 1 one-bedroom suite with kitchen. 3 stories, interior corridors. *Bath:* combo or shower only. **Parking:** on-site. **Terms:** office hours 7 am-11 pm. **Amenities:** voice mail, irons. *Some:* dual phone lines. **Pool(s):** outdoor. **Leisure Activities:** exercise room. **Guest Services:** coin laundry, wireless Internet. **Business Services:** fax (fee). **Cards:** AX, CB, DC, DS, JC, MC, VI.

ASK / SOME UNITS FEE

▼ See AAA listing above ▼

Sheraton
North Charleston
HOTEL & CONVENTION CENTER
Belong
High Expectations are invited. With eight stories of guestrooms, the area's only indoor/outdoor pool, easy access to championship golf and the beautiful oceanside. High expectations and southern hospitality are delivered at the Sheraton North Charleston Covention Center. Because you don't just stay here. You belong.
Book today at sheraton.com or call 1-866-208-0003 for more information.
STARWOOD PREFERRED GUEST

(See map and index starting on p. 877)

WINGATE BY WYNDHAM

Phone: 843/553-4444

Hotel

Rates not provided

Address: 9280 University Blvd **Location:** I-26, exit 205 eastbound, just e; exit 205A westbound, just e. Located on Charleston Southern University campus. **Facility:** Smoke free premises. 97 one-bedroom standard units. 4 stories, interior corridors. *Bath:* combo or shower only. **Parking:** on-site. **Terms:** check-in 4 pm. **Amenities:** video games (fee), high-speed Internet, voice mail, safes, irons, hair dryers. **Pool(s):** outdoor. **Leisure Activities:** whirlpool, exercise room. **Guest Services:** valet and coin laundry, wireless Internet. **Business Services:** meeting rooms, business center.

CALL 

▼ See AAA listing p 932 ▼

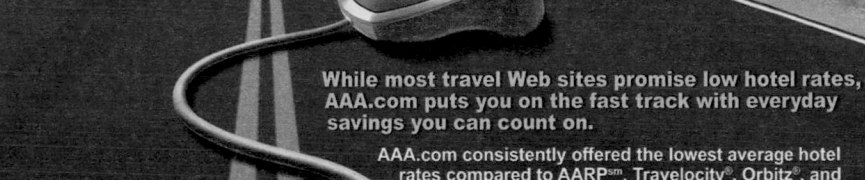

(See map and index starting on p. 877)

WINGATE INN CHARLESTON *Book great rates at AAA.com* **Phone:** (843)308-9666 33

AAA SAVE

Hotel
$99-$179 All Year

Address: 5219 N Arco Ln **Location:** I-26, exit 213 westbound; exit 213A eastbound; enter through Tanger Outlet access roads. Located adjacent to Tanger Outlet Mall. **Facility:** 102 one-bedroom standard units, some with whirlpools. 4 stories, interior corridors. *Bath:* combo or shower only. **Parking:** on-site. **Amenities:** video games (fee), high-speed Internet, dual phone lines, voice mail, safes, irons, hair dryers. **Pool(s):** outdoor. **Leisure Activities:** whirlpool, limited exercise equipment. **Guest Services:** valet and coin laundry, airport transportation-Charleston AFB International Airport, wireless Internet. **Business Services:** meeting rooms, business center. **Cards:** AX, CB, DC, DS, JC, MC, VI. **Free Special Amenities: expanded continental breakfast and high-speed Internet.**

CALL / SOME UNITS

WHERE TO DINE

CENTRE POINTE BAR & GRILL **Phone:** 843/529-9507 15

American
$7-$15

At Tanger Outlet Mall and near several hotels, the large open sports bar features 50-inch wall-mounted and smaller tableside high-definition TVs, a huge bar along one side of the restaurant, a bandstand for Thursday through Saturday live music and nightly drink specials. The menu comprises mostly burgers, steaks, specialty sandwiches, wraps and a long list of finger foods. The atmosphere is energetic and the clientele diverse. Casual dress. **Bar:** Full bar. **Hours:** 11 am-11 pm. Closed: 11/26, 12/25. **Address:** 4950 Centre Pointe Dr, Suite 166 **Location:** I-26, 213 A eastbound; 213 westbound, follow signs to Tanger Outlet Mall, then just nw. **Parking:** on-site. **Cards:** AX, DS, MC, VI.

CALL

FATZ CAFE **Phone:** 843/576-2680

American
$8-$18

Friendly staff and appealing country decor help set the tone for a relaxed and enjoyable dining experience. It's not unusual for guests to wait to be seated at the popular spot, which earns raves for its well-prepared variations on chicken, steak, ribs and pasta, as well as salads and sandwiches. The signature Southern-style peach cobbler served with vanilla ice cream and walnuts is scrumptious. Casual dress. **Bar:** Full bar. **Hours:** 11 am-10 pm, Fri & Sat-11 pm, Sun-9 pm. Closed: 11/26, 12/25. **Address:** 4951 Centre Pointe Dr **Location:** I-526, exit 17 (International Blvd), just e; adjacent to Tanger Outlet Center. **Parking:** on-site. **Cards:** AX, DS, MC, VI.

CALL

MADRA RUA **Phone:** 843/554-2522 14

Irish
$7-$22

Darts, soccer, shepherd's pie, soda bread and good friends come together in a cozy atmosphere. Those who step into Madra Rua (the Red Fox) experience a wee bit of Ireland. Casual dress. **Bar:** Full bar. **Hours:** 11 am-11 pm, Mon-2 pm. **Address:** 1034 E Montague Ave **Location:** I-26, exit 213 westbound; exit 213B eastbound, 2.4 mi e; in The Old Village. **Parking:** street. **Cards:** MC, VI.

THE NOISY OYSTER **Phone:** 843/824-1000 13

Seafood
$7-$20

This rustic fish camp style eatery features a nautical atmosphere of helm wheels, crab traps and portholes with whimsical elements. Fresh seafood and a variety of meat entrees round out a nice menu. Casual dress. **Bar:** Full bar. **Hours:** 11 am-10 pm, Fri & Sat-10:30 pm, Sun-9 pm. Closed: 11/26. **Address:** 7842 Rivers Ave **Location:** I-26, exit 209 (Ashley Phosphate Rd), 0.4 mi e, then 0.8 mi n; in North Rivers Market Shopping Center. **Parking:** on-site. **Cards:** AX, MC, VI.

STICKY FINGERS RIB HOUSE **Phone:** 843/797-7427

Barbecue
$7-$26

Diners can put down their silverware and get their fingers ready for classic Carolina sweet ribs, as well as ribs cooked in the Texas and Tennessee styles. Hearty sides of baked beans and coleslaw complement entrees at the friendly cafe. Casual dress. **Bar:** Full bar. **Hours:** 11 am-close. Closed: 11/26, 12/25. **Address:** 7690 Northwoods Blvd **Location:** I-26, exit 209 (Ashley Phosphate Rd), just n; adjacent to mall. **Parking:** on-site. **Cards:** AX, DC, DS, MC, VI.

CALL

SULLIVAN'S ISLAND pop. 1,911

WHERE TO DINE

OFF THE HOOK **Phone:** 843/883-5030

Regional American
$9-$13

At the beach, the open-air gathering place serves uncomplicated finger foods and pasta in a casual, friendly atmosphere. Casual dress. **Bar:** Full bar. **Hours:** 11:30 am-11 pm. Closed: 12/25. **Address:** 2213-B Middle St **Location:** Center. **Parking:** street. **Cards:** MC, VI.

STATION 22 **Phone:** 843/883-3355

Regional American
$9-$27

The bustling, rustic eatery on this coastal island features Lowcountry cuisine with a smattering of Tex-Mex and Cajun influences. Sample hearty jambalaya with rice or green chilies stuffed with feta cheese and surrounded by black bean salsa, or if something more traditional would fit the bill, go for fish or steak. Casual dress. **Bar:** Full bar. **Hours:** 5:30 pm-9:30 pm, Fri & Sat-10 pm. **Address:** 2205 Middle St **Location:** Just sw of center. **Parking:** on-site. **Cards:** AX, DS, MC, VI.

SULLIVAN'S **Phone:** 843/883-3222

Seafood
$7-$20

Family-run for 20 years, the restaurant on the shore is an area staple. The menu offers a wonderful selection of delicious seafood entrees prepared with Lowcountry flair and care. Fish stew, peel and eat shrimp and any of the house specialties are local favorites. Vegan and beef dishes are prepared with the same expertise. Casual dress. **Bar:** Full bar. **Hours:** 5 pm-9 pm, Fri & Sat-9:30 pm, Sun 11 am-2 & 5-9 pm; hours vary off season. Closed: 11/26, 12/25. **Address:** 2019 Middle St **Location:** Just sw of town center. **Parking:** street. **Cards:** MC, VI.

SUMMERVILLE pop. 27,752

WHERE TO STAY

COUNTRY INN & SUITES Book at AAA.com **Phone:** (843)285-9000

Hotel
$99-$109 All Year

Address: 220 Holiday Dr **Location:** I-26, exit 199A, just w on US 17 alternate route to Holiday Dr, then just n. **Facility:** 85 units. 54 one-bedroom standard units, some with whirlpools. 31 one-bedroom suites. 4 stories, interior corridors. **Parking:** on site. **Amenities:** high-speed Internet, voice mail, irons, hair dryers. **Pool(s):** outdoor. **Leisure Activities:** limited exercise equipment. **Guest Services:** coin laundry, wireless Internet. **Business Services:** meeting rooms, business center. **Cards:** AX, DS, MC, VI.

ASK / SOME UNITS FEE

HAMPTON INN Book great rates at AAA.com **Phone:** (843)871-8300

Hotel
$109-$149 All Year

Address: 1015 Jockey Ct **Location:** I-26, exit 199A, just w, then just s at Rockaway Dr. Located adjacent to shopping mall. **Facility:** 52 one-bedroom standard units. 2 stories (no elevator), interior corridors. **Parking:** on-site. **Terms:** cancellation fee imposed. **Amenities:** voice mail, irons, hair dryers. **Pool(s):** outdoor. **Leisure Activities:** limited exercise equipment. **Guest Services:** valet and coin laundry, wireless Internet. **Business Services:** meeting rooms, business center. **Cards:** AX, DC, DS, MC, VI.

CALL / SOME UNITS

AAA Benefit: Members save up to 10% everyday!

HOLIDAY INN EXPRESS-CHARLESTON/SUMMERVILLE Book great rates at AAA.com **Phone:** (843)875-3300

AAA SAVE

Hotel
$78 All Year

Address: 120 Holiday Dr **Location:** I-26, exit 199A, just w. **Facility:** 123 one-bedroom standard units. 5 stories, interior corridors. *Bath:* combo or shower only. **Parking:** on-site. **Amenities:** voice mail, irons, hair dryers. **Pool(s):** outdoor. **Leisure Activities:** limited exercise equipment. **Guest Services:** valet and coin laundry, wireless Internet. **Business Services:** meeting rooms, business center. **Cards:** AX, DC, DS, MC, VI. **Free Special Amenities: full breakfast and high-speed Internet.** ***(See color ad below)***

CALL / SOME UNITS

SLEEP INN Book at AAA.com **Phone:** 843/851-9595

Hotel
Rates not provided

Address: 115 Holiday Dr **Location:** I-26, exit 199A, just w. **Facility:** 66 one-bedroom standard units. 2 stories (no elevator), interior corridors. *Bath:* combo or shower only. **Parking:** on-site. **Amenities:** voice mail, irons, hair dryers. **Pool(s):** outdoor. **Guest Services:** valet laundry, wireless Internet. **Business Services:** fax (fee).

/ SOME UNITS

SUMMERVILLE ECONO LODGE Book at AAA.com **Phone:** (843)875-3022

Motel
$79-$84 3/2-11/30
$69 12/1-3/1

Address: 110 Holiday Dr **Location:** I-26, exit 199A, just w on US 17A, then just n. **Facility:** 98 one-bedroom standard units. 3 stories, exterior corridors. **Parking:** on-site. **Amenities:** irons, hair dryers. **Guest Services:** wireless Internet. **Cards:** AX, CB, DC, DS, JC, MC, VI.

ASK / SOME UNITS FEE

▼ See AAA listing above ▼

WOODLANDS RESORT & INN *Book great rates at AAA.com* **Phone:** (843)875-2600

AAA SAVE

Resort Country Inn
$325-$890 All Year

Address: 125 Parsons Rd **Location:** I-26, exit 199A, 2 mi s on US 17 alternate route, 1.5 mi w on W Richardson Ave (SR 165), then just s. Located in a quiet wooded area. **Facility:** The 1906 Greek Revival mansion sits on 42 manicured acres and features lavish decor in its large, beautifully appointed guest rooms and public spaces. Smoke free premises. 19 units. 17 one-bedroom standard units, some with whirlpools. 1 one-bedroom suite with whirlpool. 1 cottage. 3 stories, interior corridors. *Bath:* combo or shower only. **Parking:** valet. **Terms:** 7 day cancellation notice-fee imposed. **Amenities:** video library, CD players, high-speed Internet, dual phone lines, voice mail, safes, hair dryers. **Dining:** The Dining Room at Woodlands, see separate listing. **Pool(s):** heated outdoor. **Leisure Activities:** 2 lighted tennis courts, clay tennis court, lawn croquet, bicycles, jogging, spa. **Guest Services:** valet laundry, wireless Internet. **Business Services:** meeting rooms, business center. **Cards:** AX, DC, DS, MC, VI. **Free Special Amenities: newspaper and high-speed Internet.**

VCR / SOME UNITS FEE

WHERE TO DINE

THE CONTINENTAL CORNER **Phone:** 843/871-1160

Greek
$7-$22

Operating continually since 1973, the family-run restaurant prepares a wide selection of traditional Greek cuisine. Guests relax in cozy dining rooms while listening to big band-era music. Casual dress. **Bar:** Beer & wine. **Reservations:** accepted. **Hours:** 11 am-8:30 pm, Fri & Sat-9 pm, Sun-2:30 pm. Closed major holidays. **Address:** 123 W Richardson Ave **Location:** Jct US 17 alternate route, just nw; downtown. **Parking:** on-site. **Cards:** AX, DS, MC, VI.

THE DINING ROOM AT WOODLANDS *Menu on AAA.com* **Phone:** 843/308-2115

AAA

Regional American
$15-$90

Tasty surprises, compliments of the accomplished chef, follow one after another at the elegant, upscale restaurant. Throughout, diners are treated to a creative mix of market-sensitive cuisine that employs fresh, local produce. Presentations are outstanding. Semi-formal attire. **Bar:** Full bar. **Reservations:** suggested, for dinner. **Hours:** 6-10:30 am, 11:30-2 & 6-9 pm. **Address:** 125 Parsons Rd **Location:** I-26, exit 199A, 2 mi s on US 17 alternate route, 1.5 mi w on W Richardson Ave (SR 165), then just s; in Woodlands Resort & Inn. **Parking:** on-site and valet. **Cards:** AX, DC, DS, MC, VI.

CALL M

LAS MARGARITAS **Phone:** 843/871-0078

Mexican
$4-$17

Between downtown and the mall area, the small restaurant presents a large menu of Mexican fare, as well as new interpretations of standards such as fajitas and burritos. Varied soups are a meal in themselves, and fish dishes also merit consideration. Most of the prompt, friendly servers are bilingual. Casual dress. **Bar:** Full bar. **Hours:** 11 am-9 pm, Fri & Sat-10 pm. Closed: 12/25. **Address:** 223 N Main St **Location:** Between 1st and 2nd N sts; just ne of center. **Parking:** on-site. **Cards:** AX, DS, MC, VI.

THE MUSTARD SEED **Phone:** 843/821-7101

American
$7-$12

A sibling to other chain eateries in Mount Pleasant and on James Island, the restaurant is known for its extensive use of fresh vegetables, never-frozen seafood and meats, and herb- and spice-rich sauces. As a result, the list of daily specials tends to be longer than the fixed menu. All of the affordable dishes are prepared to order, and service is efficient and friendly. Though not prepared on site, the popular desserts are baked by the chain's own bakery. A favorite is hummingbird cake. Casual dress. **Bar:** Beer & wine. **Reservations:** not accepted. **Hours:** 11 am-2:30 & 5-9 pm, Fri-10 pm, Sat 5 pm-10 pm. Closed: 11/26, 12/25; also Sun. **Address:** 101 N Main St **Location:** Corner of E Lake Ave; just ne of center. **Parking:** on-site. **Cards:** AX, MC, VI.

THE RED PEPPER **Phone:** 843/873-8600

Italian
$8-$32

The long-experienced chef/owner leaves nothing to chance and personally trains all the staff, each of whom is pleasant and professional. Each authentic Italian dish is prepared to order at the area mainstay. Among selections are bruschetta, fettuccine bianco and saltimbocca alla romana, as well as nightly specials. Patrons can dine al fresco on the covered deck. Casual dress. **Bar:** Full bar. **Hours:** 11:30 am-9 pm, Fri-10 pm, Sat 2 pm-10 pm. Closed: 11/26, 12/25; also Sun. **Address:** 709 N Main St **Location:** I-26, exit 199A, 1.4 mi sw on US 17 alternate route. **Parking:** on-site. **Cards:** AX, MC, VI.

STICKY FINGERS RIB HOUSE **Phone:** 843/871-7427

Barbecue
$7-$26

Diners can put down their silverware and get their fingers ready for classic Carolina sweet ribs, as well as ribs cooked in the Texas and Tennessee styles. Hearty sides of baked beans and coleslaw complement entrees at the friendly cafe. Casual dress. **Bar:** Full bar. **Hours:** 11 am-close. Closed: 11/26, 12/25. **Address:** 1200 N Main St **Location:** I-26, exit 199A, 0.6 mi sw on US 17 alternate route. **Parking:** on-site. **Cards:** AX, DC, DS, MC, VI.

SWEETWATER GRILL & CAFE **Phone:** 843/821-9101

American
$6-$19

Guests can expect a wide selection of home-style delights, such as chicken and dumplings, pot roast and fried green tomatoes. Adding diversity to the mix are seasonal menus with such creative dishes as grilled tilapia over mesclun greens with sweet vinaigrette. Casual dress. **Bar:** Beer & wine. **Reservations:** accepted. **Hours:** 8 am-9 pm, Fri & Sat-10 pm, Sun 8:30 am-3 pm. Closed: 11/26, 12/25. **Address:** 103 S Main St **Location:** Corner of E Doty Ave; center. **Parking:** on-site. **Cards:** AX, DS, MC, VI.

This ends listings for the Charleston Vicinity.
The following page resumes the alphabetical listings of cities in South Carolina.

CHERAW pop. 5,524

WHERE TO STAY

DAYS INN Book at AAA.com Phone: (843)537-5554

Motel
$57-$110 All Year

Address: 820 Market St **Location:** Jct US 52/1/SR 9. **Facility:** 55 one-bedroom standard units. 2 stories (no elevator), exterior corridors. **Parking:** on-site. **Terms:** 2 night minimum stay. **Amenities:** irons, hair dryers. **Pool(s):** outdoor. **Guest Services:** wireless Internet. **Business Services:** *Fee:* PC, fax. **Cards:** AX, DC, DS, MC, VI.

ASK / SOME UNITS FEE

ECONO LODGE Book at AAA.com Phone: 843/537-2101

Motel
Rates not provided

Address: 710 Market St **Location:** Jct SR 9/US 1, just nw on US 1. **Facility:** 72 one-bedroom standard units. 2 stories (no elevator), exterior corridors. **Parking:** on-site. **Amenities:** irons, hair dryers. **Guest Services:** wireless Internet. **Business Services:** PC, fax (fee).

/ SOME UNITS

JAMESON INN Book at AAA.com Phone: (843)537-5625

Motel
$83-$88 All Year

Address: 885 Chesterfield Hwy **Location:** Jct US 1/52/SR 9, 1.6 mi w on SR 9. Located in a commercial area. **Facility:** 59 one-bedroom standard units, some with whirlpools. 2 stories (no elevator), exterior corridors. *Bath:* combo or shower only. **Parking:** on-site. **Terms:** cancellation fee imposed. **Amenities:** irons, hair dryers. **Pool(s):** outdoor. **Leisure Activities:** exercise room. **Guest Services:** wireless Internet. **Business Services:** meeting rooms, PC, fax (fee). **Cards:** AX, DC, DS, MC, VI.

ASK / SOME UNITS FEE

WHERE TO DINE

EL-SHERIF'S HOUSE OF PIZZA Phone: 843/921-0066

Mediterranean
$5-$10

Pizza and stromboli are favorites at the family-friendly downtown eatery. Among other choices are other Italian and Greek dishes. Casual dress. **Bar:** Full bar. **Hours:** 11 am-2:30 & 5-10 pm. Closed major holidays; also Sun. **Address:** 217 Second St **Location:** Center. **Parking:** street. **Cards:** AX, MC, VI.

FATZ CAFE Phone: 843/537-4205

American
$7-$19

Friendly staff and appealing country decor help set the tone for a relaxed and enjoyable dining experience. It's not unusual for guests to wait to be seated at the popular spot, which earns raves for its well-prepared variations on chicken, steak, ribs and pasta, as well as salads and sandwiches. The signature Southern-style peach cobbler served with vanilla ice cream and walnuts is scrumptious. Casual dress. **Bar:** Full bar. **Reservations:** not accepted. **Hours:** 11 am-10 pm, Fri & Sat-11 pm, Sun-9 pm. Closed: 11/26, 12/25. **Address:** 973 Chesterfield Hwy **Location:** Jct US 1/52/SR 9, 1.9 mi w on SR 9. **Parking:** on-site. **Cards:** AX, DS, MC, VI.

CALL

CLEMSON pop. 11,939

WHERE TO STAY

CLEMSON SLEEP INN Book great rates at AAA.com Phone: (864)653-6000

SAVE

Hotel
$70-$300 All Year

Address: 1303 Tiger Blvd **Location:** Jct SR 133 (College Ave) and US 76/123, 0.5 mi e. **Facility:** 57 one-bedroom standard units. 3 stories, interior corridors. *Bath:* combo or shower only. **Parking:** on-site. **Amenities:** irons, hair dryers. **Leisure Activities:** limited exercise equipment. **Guest Services:** valet laundry, wireless Internet. **Business Services:** meeting rooms, business center. **Cards:** AX, DC, DS, MC, VI. **Free Special Amenities: continental breakfast and high-speed Internet.**

CALL / SOME UNITS

COMFORT INN-CLEMSON Book great rates at AAA.com Phone: (864)653-3600

SAVE

Hotel
$85-$175 All Year

Address: 1305 Tiger Blvd **Location:** Jct SR 133 (College Ave) and US 76/123, 0.5 mi e. **Facility:** 122 units. 104 one-bedroom standard units. 18 one-bedroom suites with whirlpools. 4 stories, interior corridors. **Parking:** on-site. **Terms:** check-in 4 pm, cancellation fee imposed. **Amenities:** voice mail, irons, hair dryers. **Pool(s):** outdoor. **Guest Services:** valet and coin laundry, wireless Internet. **Business Services:** meeting rooms, business center. **Cards:** AX, DC, DS, MC, VI. **Free Special Amenities: expanded continental breakfast and high-speed Internet.**

FEE / SOME UNITS FEE

DAYS INN-CLEMSON Book at AAA.com Phone: (864)653-4411

Motel
$79-$250 All Year

Address: 1387 Tiger Blvd **Location:** Jct SR 133 (College Ave) and US 76/123, 0.9 mi e. **Facility:** 44 one-bedroom standard units. 2 stories (no elevator), exterior corridors. **Parking:** on-site. **Terms:** cancellation fee imposed. **Amenities:** irons, hair dryers. *Some:* high-speed Internet. **Guest Services:** wireless Internet. **Business Services:** PC, fax (fee). **Cards:** AX, DS, MC, VI.

ASK FEE / SOME UNITS

HAMPTON INN 

Phone: (864)653-7744

Hotel
$90-$299 All Year

Address: 851 Tiger Blvd (US 76/123) **Location:** Jct SR 133 (College Ave) and US 76/123, 0.8 mi w. **Facility:** 88 one-bedroom standard units, some with whirlpools. 4 stories, interior corridors. *Bath:* combo or shower only. **Parking:** on-site. **Terms:** check-in 4 pm, cancellation fee imposed. **Amenities:** voice mail, irons, hair dryers. **Pool(s):** outdoor. **Leisure Activities:** exercise room. **Guest Services:** valet laundry, wireless Internet. **Business Services:** meeting rooms, business center. **Cards:** AX, CB, DC, DS, JC, MC, VI.

CALL / SOME UNITS

THE JAMES F. MARTIN INN AT CLEMSON UNIVERSITY

Phone: 864/654-9020

SAVE

Hotel
$99-$150 All Year

Address: 120 Madren Center Dr **Location:** Jct US 76/SR 93, just s on US 76 to Perimeter Rd, 1.2 mi w to Cherry Rd, then just s, follow signs to Conference Center & Inn. Located on the golf course, adjacent to Lake Hartwell. **Facility:** 89 units. 62 one-bedroom standard units. 27 one-bedroom suites, some with whirlpools. 4 stories, interior corridors. *Bath:* combo or shower only. **Parking:** on-site. **Amenities:** high-speed Internet, dual phone lines, voice mail, irons, hair dryers. **Pool(s):** outdoor. **Leisure Activities:** 2 lighted tennis courts, hiking trails, limited exercise equipment. *Fee:* golf-18 holes. **Guest Services:** valet laundry, wireless Internet. **Business Services:** conference facilities, business center. **Cards:** AX, DC, DS, MC, VI. **Free Special Amenities: expanded continental breakfast and room upgrade (subject to availability with advance reservations).**

24 CALL / SOME UNITS VCR

WHERE TO DINE

101 KEITH STREET PUB & GRILLE

Phone: 864/654-2274

American
$6-$15

A favorite hangout for the Clemson crowd, the restaurant pairs well-prepared American dishes with numerous selections of beer. This place is definitely crowded on game day. Casual dress. **Bar:** Full bar. **Hours:** 11:15 am-close. Closed major holidays. **Address:** 101 Keith St **Location:** Jct US 76/123 and SR 133 (College Ave), 0.5 mi s on SR 133 (College Ave). **Parking:** on-site and street. **Cards:** AX, DS, MC, VI.

CALL 

CALHOUN CORNERS RESTAURANT

Phone: 864/654-7490

American
$11-$28

Diners can experience the charm and elegance of the South in the restored brick building. The menu lists many well-prepared, traditional American dishes. Dressy casual. **Bar:** Full bar. **Reservations:** suggested, weekends. **Hours:** 5 pm-9:30 pm. Closed major holidays; also Sun. **Address:** 103 Clemson St **Location:** Jct US 76/123 and SR 133 (College Ave), just n on SR 133 (College Ave), then just e on first street after Train Trestle. **Parking:** on-site. **Cards:** AX, DC, DS, MC, VI.

PIXIE & BILL'S

Phone: 864/654-1210

American
$7-$26

A popular spot for the Clemson crowd, the casual restaurant is a good spot for traditionally-prepared dishes. Casual dress. **Bar:** Full bar. **Reservations:** accepted. **Hours:** 11:30 am-1:30 & 5:30-9:30 pm, Sat from 5:30 pm. Closed major holidays; also Sun. **Address:** 1058 Tiger Blvd (Hwy 123) **Location:** Jct US 76/123 and SR 133 (College Ave), just e on US 76/123. **Parking:** on-site. **Cards:** AX, DC, DS, MC, VI.

CLINTON pop. 8,091

WHERE TO STAY

COMFORT INN Book great rates at AAA.com

Phone: (864)833-5558

SAVE

Motel
$69-$99 3/1-11/30
$59-$69 12/1-2/28

Address: 105 Trade St **Location:** I-26, exit 52, just n; behind truck stop. **Facility:** 80 one-bedroom standard units. 2 stories (no elevator), exterior corridors. *Bath:* combo or shower only. **Parking:** on-site. **Terms:** cancellation fee imposed. **Amenities:** safes (fee), irons, hair dryers. **Pool(s):** outdoor. **Leisure Activities:** picnic area with barbecue grill, exercise room. **Guest Services:** valet and coin laundry, wireless Internet. **Business Services:** meeting rooms, business center. **Cards:** AX, CB, DC, DS, JC, MC, VI. **Free Special Amenities: expanded continental breakfast and high-speed Internet.**

/ SOME UNITS FEE

DAYS INN 

Phone: (864)833-6600

SAVE

Motel
$55-$99 All Year

Address: 12374 Hwy 56 N **Location:** I-26, exit 52, just s. **Facility:** 58 units. 57 one-bedroom standard units, some with efficiencies. 1 one-bedroom suite with kitchen. 2 stories (no elevator), exterior corridors. *Bath:* combo or shower only. **Parking:** on-site. **Amenities:** safes (fee), hair dryers. **Pool(s):** outdoor. **Guest Services:** coin laundry, wireless Internet. **Business Services:** fax (fee). **Cards:** AX, CB, DC, DS, JC, MC, VI. **Free Special Amenities: expanded continental breakfast and high-speed Internet.**

/ SOME UNITS FEE

HAMPTON INN & SUITES CLINTON Book great rates at AAA.com Phone: (864)938-1040

Hotel
$109 All Year

Address: 10000 Hwy 72 **Location:** I-26, exit 54, just sw; in East Corporate Center Business Park. **Facility:** 101 one-bedroom standard units, some with whirlpools. 4 stories, interior corridors. *Bath:* combo or shower only. **Parking:** on-site. **Terms:** check-in 4 pm. **Amenities:** DVD players, video games (fee), high-speed Internet, voice mail, irons, hair dryers. **Pool(s):** indoor. **Leisure Activities:** whirlpool, playground, exercise room. **Guest Services:** coin laundry, wireless Internet. **Business Services:** meeting rooms, business center. **Cards:** AX, DC, DS, MC, VI.

Hampton Inn & Suites

AAA Benefit:
Members save up to 10% everyday!

WHERE TO DINE

FATZ CAFE Phone: 864/833-5280

American
$8-$18

Friendly staff and appealing country decor help set the tone for a relaxed and enjoyable dining experience. It's not unusual for guests to wait to be seated at the popular spot, which earns raves for its well-prepared variations on chicken, steak, ribs and pasta, as well as salads and sandwiches. The signature Southern-style peach cobbler served with vanilla ice cream and walnuts is scrumptious. Casual dress. **Bar:** Full bar. **Hours:** 11 am-10 pm, Fri & Sat-11 pm, Sun-9 pm. Closed: 12/24, 12/25. **Address:** 179 E Corporate Center Dr **Location:** I-26, exit 54, just sw, then se. **Parking:** on-site. **Cards:** DS, MC, VI.

CALL

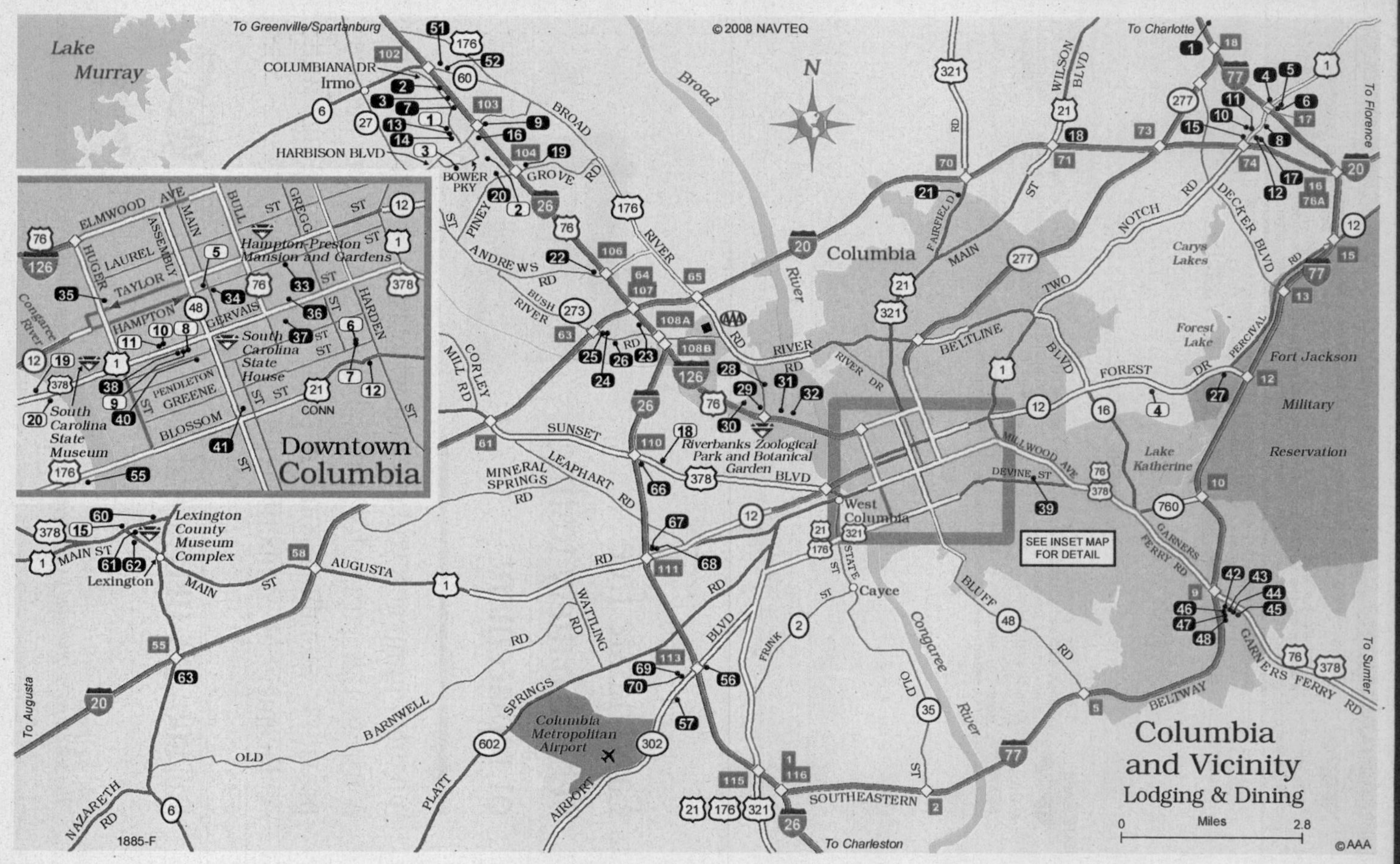
Columbia and Vicinity
Lodging & Dining
Miles
0
2.8
© 2008 NAVTEQ
© AAA
1885-F
Downtown Columbia
SEE INSET MAP FOR DETAIL
To Greenville/Spartanburg
To Charlotte
To Florence
To Sumter
To Charleston
To Augusta
Lake Murray
Broad River
Congaree River
Columbia
West Columbia
Cayce
Irmo
Lexington
Fort Jackson Military Reservation
Forest Lake
Carys Lakes
Lake Katherine
Riverbanks Zoological Park and Botanical Garden
Columbia Metropolitan Airport
Lexington County Museum Complex
Hampton-Preston Mansion and Gardens
South Carolina State House
South Carolina State Museum
COLUMBIANA DR
HARBISON BLVD
BOWER PKY
PINEY GROVE RD
BROAD RIVER RD
ANDREWS RD
BUSH RIVER RD
CORLEY MILL RD
SUNSET BLVD
LEAPHART RD
MINERAL SPRINGS RD
AUGUSTA RD
MAIN ST
WATTLING RD
PLATT SPRINGS RD
AIRPORT BLVD
OLD BARNWELL RD
NAZARETH RD
FRINK ST
STATE ST
OLD ST
SOUTHEASTERN
BLUFF RD
BELTWAY
GARNERS FERRY RD
DEVINE ST
MILLWOOD AVE
FOREST DR
PERCIVAL RD
TWO NOTCH RD
DECKER BLVD
BELTLINE BLVD
RIVER DR
FAIRFIELD RD
WILSON BLVD
ELMWOOD AVE
ASSEMBLY
LAUREL
TAYLOR
HUGER
HAMPTON
GERVAIS
PENDLETON
GREENE
BLOSSOM
BULL ST
GREGG ST
HARDEN ST
CONN

Airport Accommodations

Map Page	OA	COLUMBIA METROPOLITAN	Diamond Rated	High Season	Page
57 / p. 940	AAA	**Country Inn & Suites by Carlson, 1.5 mi e of entrance**	◆◆◆	$100-$200 SAVE	871
56 / p. 940	AAA	**Knights Inn-Columbia, Cayce Airport, 1.9 me ne of entrance**	◆	$47 SAVE	871
69 / p. 940	AAA	**Comfort Inn-Airport, 1.5 mi ne of entrance**	◆◆◆	$89 SAVE	1111
70 / p. 940	AAA	**Sleep Inn-Airport, 1.5 mi ne of entrance**	◆◆	$90-$135 SAVE	1112

Columbia and Vicinity

This index helps you "spot" where approved lodgings and restaurants are located on the corresponding detailed maps. Lodging daily rate range is for comparison only and show the property's high season. Restaurant rate range is a combination of lunch and/or dinner. Turn to the listing page for more detailed rate information and consult display ads for special promotions.

COLUMBIA

Map Page	OA	Lodgings	Diamond Rated	High Season	Page
1 / p. 940		Residence Inn by Marriott	◆◆◆	$137-$147	952
2 / p. 940		Hilton Garden Inn Columbia/Harbison	◆◆◆	$79-$169	948
3 / p. 940		TownePlace Suites by Marriott	◆◆◆	$133-$143	952
4 / p. 940		Holiday Inn Hotel & Suites	◆◆◆	Rates not provided	948
5 / p. 940		Wingate by Wyndham-Northeast	◆◆◆	Rates not provided	953
6 / p. 940		Quality Inn	◆◆◆	$55-$100	950
7 / p. 940		Fairfield Inn Northwest	◆◆◆	$118-$127	946
8 / p. 940	AAA	**Comfort Inn Northeast**	◆◆	$79-$129 SAVE	944
9 / p. 940		Hampton Inn Harbison	◆◆◆	$109-$149	947
10 / p. 940		Hampton Inn Northeast	◆◆◆	$104-$144	947
11 / p. 940	AAA	**Microtel Inn**	◆◆	$59-$90 SAVE	950
12 / p. 940		Jameson Suites	◆◆◆	$103-$113	949
13 / p. 940	AAA	**Wingate Inn Harbison**	◆◆◆	$89-$109 SAVE	953
14 / p. 940		Holiday Inn Express Hotel & Suites Harbison Blvd	◆◆◆	$99-$129	948
15 / p. 940		La Quinta Inn & Suites Columbia NE/Ft. Jackson Area	◆◆	$49-$109	949
16 / p. 940	AAA	**Comfort Suites-Harbison**	◆◆◆	$109-$179 SAVE	945
17 / p. 940		Motel 6 #1291	◆	$47-$53	950
18 / p. 940	AAA	**Days Inn**	◆	$65-$125 SAVE	945
19 / p. 940	AAA	**Quality Inn Harbison Area** - see color ad p 951	◆◆	$79-$119 SAVE	951
20 / p. 940	AAA	**Microtel Inn & Suites Harbison Area**	◆◆	$70-$80 SAVE	950
21 / p. 940	AAA	**Super 8**	◆	$70-$95 SAVE	952
22 / p. 940		Econo Lodge	◆◆	$50-$125	945
23 / p. 940		Courtyard by Marriott-Columbia Northwest	◆◆◆	$133-$143	945
24 / p. 940	AAA	**Columbia Sleep Inn Northwest**	◆◆	$79-$199 SAVE	944
25 / p. 940	AAA	**Radisson Hotel Columbia & Conference Center** - see color ad p 951	◆◆◆	$99-$199 SAVE	951
26 / p. 940	AAA	**Best Western Executive Inn & Suites**	◆◆	$99-$199 SAVE	944
27 / p. 940		Extended StayAmerica Columbia-Fort Jackson	◆◆	$85-$95	946

COLUMBIA (cont'd)

Map Page	OA	Lodgings (cont'd)	Diamond Rated	High Season	Page
28 / p. 940	AAA	**Homewood Suites by Hilton-Columbia, SC**	◆◆◆	$95-$219 SAVE	948
29 / p. 940	AAA	**Embassy Suites Hotel Columbia - Greystone**	◆◆◆	$113-$189 SAVE	946
30 / p. 940		Extended StayAmerica-Columbia-West	◆◆	$65-$75	946
31 / p. 940		Residence Inn by Marriott	◆◆◆	$157-$169	952
32 / p. 940		StudioPLUS Greystone Columbia	◆◆	$75-$85	952
33 / p. 940		Chestnut Cottage Bed & Breakfast	◆◆◆	$159-$229	944
34 / p. 940		Marriott Columbia	◆◆◆	$197-$211	950
35 / p. 940		Comfort Suites-Downtown Vista	◆◆◆	$119-$259	944
36 / p. 940		Clarion Town House Hotel	◆◆◆	Rates not provided	944
37 / p. 940		The Inn at USC	◆◆◆	$149-$349	948
38 / p. 940		Hampton Inn Downtown Historic District	◆◆◆	$149-$259	947
39 / p. 940	AAA	**The Whitney Hotel**	◆◆◆	$159-$179 SAVE	953
40 / p. 940		Hilton Columbia Center	◆◆◆	$149-$259	947
41 / p. 940	AAA	**Courtyard by Marriott Downtown at USC**	◆◆◆	$157-$169 SAVE	945
42 / p. 940		Quality Inn & Suites	◆◆	Rates not provided	950
43 / p. 940		Holiday Inn Express Hotel & Suites	◆◆◆	$125-$229	948
44 / p. 940		La Quinta Inn-Maingate Ft. Jackson	◆◆	$69-$129	949
45 / p. 940		Comfort Inn & Suites-Fort Jackson Main Gate	◆◆◆	$100-$170	944
46 / p. 940		Fort Jackson Inn	◆◆	Rates not provided	946
47 / p. 940		Country Inn & Suites by Carlson	◆◆◆	$99-$225	945
48 / p. 940		Sleep Inn-Fort Jackson	◆◆	Rates not provided	952

Map Page	OA	Restaurants	Diamond Rated	Cuisine	Meal Range	Page
1 / p. 940		Monterrey Mexican Restaurant	◆◆	Mexican	$4-$14	955
2 / p. 940		Bonefish Grill	◆◆◆	Seafood	$13-$30	953
3 / p. 940		Skancheli Mediterranean Classic Cuisine	◆◆	Mediterranean	$6-$28	955
4 / p. 940		Bonefish Grill	◆◆◆	Seafood	$13-$30	953
5 / p. 940		Hampton Street Vineyard	◆◆◆	American	$8-$30	954
6 / p. 940		Mr. Friendly's	◆◆◆	Regional American	$8-$28	955
7 / p. 940		Garibaldi's	◆◆◆	Italian	$13-$29	954
8 / p. 940		Motor Supply Co Bistro	◆◆	American	$8-$25	955
9 / p. 940		Bull Market Restaurant & Taverna	◆◆◆	New Southern	$7-$23	953
10 / p. 940		Ristorante Divino	◆◆◆	Italian	$18-$35	955
11 / p. 940		Blue Marlin Steak & Seafood	◆◆◆	Regional Steak & Seafood	$7-$22	953
12 / p. 940		Yesterdays Restaurant & Tavern	◆◆	American	$6-$12	956

IRMO

Map Page	OA	Lodgings	Diamond Rated	High Season	Page
51 / p. 940	AAA	**Hyatt Place Columbia/Harbison**	◆◆◆	$99-$219 SAVE	1088
52 / p. 940		Extended Stay Deluxe (Columbia-Harbison)	◆◆◆	$95-$105	1088

CAYCE

Map Page	OA	Lodgings	Diamond Rated	High Season	Page
55 / p. 940	AAA	**Riverside Inn**	◆◆	$62 SAVE	871
56 / p. 940	AAA	**Knights Inn-Columbia, Cayce Airport**	◆	$47 SAVE	871
57 / p. 940	AAA	**Country Inn & Suites by Carlson**	◆◆◆	$100-$200 SAVE	871

LEXINGTON

Map Page	OA	Lodgings	Diamond Rated	High Season	Page
60 / p. 940		Hampton Inn	◆◆◆	$89-$129	1090
61 / p. 940		Quality Inn & Suites	◆◆	$79-$159	1090
62 / p. 940		Comfort Suites	◆◆◆	$108	1090
63 / p. 940		Ramada Limited	◆◆	$69-$119	1091

Map Page	OA	Restaurant	Diamond Rated	Cuisine	Meal Range	Page
15 / p. 940		Flight Deck Restaurant & Bakery	◆◆	American	$7-$17	1091

WEST COLUMBIA

Map Page	OA	Lodgings	Diamond Rated	High Season	Page
66 / p. 940	AAA	**Hampton Inn Columbia I-26/Airport - see color ad p 1111**	◆◆◆	$99-$160 SAVE	1111
67 / p. 940		Holiday Inn Airport	◆◆◆	$99-$129	1111
68 / p. 940	AAA	**Quality Inn - see color ad p 949**	◆◆	$59-$99 SAVE	1111
69 / p. 940	AAA	**Comfort Inn-Airport**	◆◆◆	$89 SAVE	1111
70 / p. 940	AAA	**Sleep Inn-Airport**	◆◆	$90-$135 SAVE	1112

Map Page	OA	Restaurants	Diamond Rated	Cuisine	Meal Range	Page
18 / p. 940		Grecian Gardens	◆◆	Mediterranean	$5-$17	1112
19 / p. 940		Al's Upstairs Italian Restaurant	◆◆◆	Italian	$17-$29	1112
20 / p. 940		New Orleans Riverfront Restaurant	◆◆	American	$7-$33	1112

COLUMBIA pop. 116,278 (See map and index starting on p. 940)

WHERE TO STAY

BEST WESTERN EXECUTIVE INN & SUITES *Book great rates at AAA.com* **Phone:** (803)561-9027 26

Hotel
$99-$199 All Year

Address: 1720 Bush River Rd **Location:** I-20, exit 63 (Bush River Rd), just e; I-26, exit 108 (Bush River Rd), 0.5 mi w. **Facility:** 69 one-bedroom standard units, some with whirlpools. 3 stories, interior corridors. *Bath:* combo or shower only. **Parking:** on-site. **Amenities:** high-speed Internet, voice mail, irons, hair dryers. **Pool(s):** outdoor. **Leisure Activities:** exercise room. **Guest Services:** valet laundry, wireless Internet. **Business Services:** meeting rooms, fax (fee). **Cards:** AX, CB, DC, DS, JC, MC, VI. **Free Special Amenities: continental breakfast and high-speed Internet.**

/ SOME UNITS

Best Western
AAA Benefit:
Members save up to 20%, plus 10% bonus points with rewards program.

CHESTNUT COTTAGE BED & BREAKFAST **Phone:** 803/256-1718 33

Historic Bed & Breakfast
$159-$229 All Year

Address: 1718 Hampton St **Location:** SR 12 (Taylor St), just s; between Henderson and Barnwell sts; downtown. **Facility:** The inn, dating from 1850, is said to be where author Mary Chestnut wrote portions of her diary on the Civil War; a new tavern was added in 2007. Smoke free premises. 5 one-bedroom standard units with whirlpools. 2 stories (no elevator), interior corridors. **Parking:** on-site. **Terms:** check-in 4 pm, age restrictions may apply, 15 day cancellation notice-fee imposed. **Amenities:** high-speed Internet, irons, hair dryers. **Guest Services:** wireless Internet. **Business Services:** fax. **Cards:** AX, DS, MC, VI.

ASK / SOME UNITS VCR

CLARION TOWN HOUSE HOTEL *Book at AAA.com* **Phone:** 803/771-8711 36

Hotel
Rates not provided

Address: 1615 Gervais St **Location:** I-26, exit 111 (US 1/Augusta Hwy), 5 mi ne on US 1; between Pickens and Henderson sts; downtown. **Facility:** 163 units. 142 one-bedroom standard units. 21 one-bedroom suites with whirlpools. 2-6 stories, interior/exterior corridors. *Bath:* combo or shower only. **Parking:** on-site. **Amenities:** high-speed Internet, voice mail, irons, hair dryers. **Pool(s):** outdoor. **Leisure Activities:** sauna, exercise room. **Guest Services:** valet laundry, area transportation, wireless Internet. **Business Services:** meeting rooms, fax (fee).

/ SOME UNITS

COLUMBIA SLEEP INN NORTHWEST *Book great rates at AAA.com* **Phone:** (803)731-9999 24

Hotel
$79-$199 All Year

Address: 1901 Rockland Rd **Location:** I-20, exit 63 (Bush River Rd), just e; I-26, exit 108 (Bush River Rd), 0.7 mi w. **Facility:** 78 one-bedroom standard units, some with whirlpools. 4 stories, interior corridors. *Bath:* combo or shower only. **Parking:** on-site. **Terms:** cancellation fee imposed. **Amenities:** voice mail, safes (fee), irons, hair dryers. **Leisure Activities:** limited exercise equipment. **Guest Services:** valet laundry, wireless Internet. **Business Services:** meeting rooms, business center. **Cards:** AX, DC, DS, JC, MC, VI. **Free Special Amenities: continental breakfast and high-speed Internet.**

CALL / SOME UNITS

COMFORT INN & SUITES-FORT JACKSON MAIN GATE *Book at AAA.com* **Phone:** (803)695-5555 45

Hotel
$100-$170 All Year

Address: 7337 Garners Ferry Rd **Location:** I-77, exit 9A, just se. **Facility:** 67 one-bedroom standard units, some with whirlpools. 3 stories, interior corridors. *Bath:* combo or shower only. **Parking:** on-site. **Amenities:** dual phone lines, voice mail, safes (fee), irons, hair dryers. **Pool(s):** heated indoor. **Leisure Activities:** whirlpool, limited exercise equipment. **Guest Services:** valet and coin laundry, wireless Internet. **Business Services:** meeting rooms, fax (fee). **Cards:** AX, CB, DC, DS, JC, MC, VI.

ASK CALL / SOME UNITS

COMFORT INN NORTHEAST *Book great rates at AAA.com* **Phone:** (803)788-5544 8

Hotel
$79-$129 3/1-11/30
$79-$99 12/1-2/28

Address: 7700 Two Notch Rd **Location:** I-20, exit 74 (Two Notch Rd), just n; I-77, exit 17 (Two Notch Rd), 0.5 mi s. Located adjacent to railroad tracks. **Facility:** 96 one-bedroom standard units. 3 stories, interior corridors. **Parking:** on-site. **Amenities:** irons, hair dryers. **Pool(s):** outdoor. **Guest Services:** wireless Internet. **Business Services:** fax (fee). **Cards:** AX, DS, MC, VI. **Free Special Amenities: expanded continental breakfast and high-speed Internet.**

/ SOME UNITS

COMFORT SUITES-DOWNTOWN VISTA *Book at AAA.com* **Phone:** (803)744-4000 35

Hotel
$119-$259 All Year

Address: 501 Taylor St **Location:** I-126, exit 3B (US 21/Huger St), 0.4 mi se. Located adjacent to railroad tracks. **Facility:** Smoke free premises. 81 units. 78 one-bedroom standard units. 3 one-bedroom suites with whirlpools. 4 stories, interior corridors. *Bath:* combo or shower only. **Parking:** on-site. **Amenities:** high-speed Internet, dual phone lines, voice mail, safes, irons, hair dryers. **Pool(s):** outdoor. **Leisure Activities:** limited exercise equipment. **Guest Services:** valet and coin laundry, wireless Internet. **Business Services:** meeting rooms, business center. **Cards:** AX, DS, MC, VI.

ASK CALL

(See map and index starting on p. 940)

COMFORT SUITES-HARBISON *Book great rates at AAA.com* **Phone:** (803)407-4444 16

Hotel
$109-$179 All Year

Address: 750 Saturn Pkwy **Location:** I-26, exit 103 (Harbison Blvd), just sw. **Facility:** Smoke free premises. 82 units. 79 one-bedroom standard units. 3 one-bedroom suites, some with whirlpools. 4 stories, interior corridors. *Bath:* combo or shower only. **Parking:** on-site. **Terms:** cancellation fee imposed. **Amenities:** high-speed Internet, dual phone lines, voice mail, safes (fee), irons, hair dryers. **Pool(s):** heated indoor. **Leisure Activities:** whirlpool, sun deck, limited exercise equipment. **Guest Services:** valet and coin laundry, wireless Internet. **Business Services:** meeting rooms, business center. **Cards:** AX, CB, DC, DS, JC, MC, VI. **Free Special Amenities: full breakfast and early check-in/late check-out.**

CALL

COUNTRY INN & SUITES BY CARLSON *Book at AAA.com* **Phone:** (803)776-6660 47

Hotel
$99-$225 All Year

Address: 220 E Exchange Blvd **Location:** I-77, exit 9A, just se, then s. **Facility:** 78 units. 58 one-bedroom standard units. 20 one-bedroom suites, some with whirlpools. 3 stories, interior corridors. *Bath:* combo or shower only. **Parking:** on-site. **Amenities:** high-speed Internet, dual phone lines, voice mail, safes, irons, hair dryers. **Pool(s):** heated indoor. **Leisure Activities:** whirlpool, exercise room. **Guest Services:** valet and coin laundry, wireless Internet. **Business Services:** fax (fee). **Cards:** AX, DC, DS, MC, VI.

ASK / SOME UNITS

COURTYARD BY MARRIOTT-COLUMBIA NORTHWEST *Book great rates at AAA.com* **Phone:** (803)731-2300 23

Hotel
$133-$143 All Year

Address: 347 Zimalcrest Dr **Location:** I-26, exit 108 (Bush River Rd), just w, then just n; I-20, exit 63 (Bush River Rd), 0.8 mi e, then just n. **Facility:** Smoke free premises. 149 units. 137 one-bedroom standard units. 12 one-bedroom suites. 3 stories, interior corridors. *Bath:* combo or shower only. **Parking:** on-site. **Terms:** cancellation fee imposed. **Amenities:** high-speed Internet, voice mail, irons, hair dryers. **Pool(s):** outdoor. **Leisure Activities:** whirlpool, exercise room. **Guest Services:** valet and coin laundry, wireless Internet. **Business Services:** meeting rooms, business center. **Cards:** AX, CB, DC, DS, JC, MC, VI.

AAA Benefit:
Members save a minimum 5% off the best available rate.

COURTYARD BY MARRIOTT DOWNTOWN AT USC *Book great rates at AAA.com* **Phone:** (803)799-7800 41

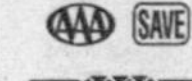

Hotel
$158-$169 All Year

Address: 630 Assembly St **Location:** Jct US 21 connector/SR 48; just s of city center. **Facility:** Smoke free premises. 189 one-bedroom standard units. 9 stories, interior corridors. *Bath:* combo or shower only. **Parking:** on-site (fee) and valet. **Terms:** check-in 4 pm, cancellation fee imposed. **Amenities:** video games (fee), dual phone lines, voice mail, irons, hair dryers. *Some:* high-speed Internet. **Pool(s):** outdoor. **Leisure Activities:** limited exercise equipment. **Guest Services:** valet and coin laundry, airport transportation-Columbia Metropolitan & Owens Downtown airports, area transportation-within 3 mi, wireless Internet. **Business Services:** meeting rooms, business center. **Cards:** AX, CB, DC, DS, JC, MC, VI. **Free Special Amenities: newspaper and high-speed Internet.**

AAA Benefit:
Members save a minimum 5% off the best available rate.

DAYS INN *Book great rates at AAA.com* **Phone:** (803)754-4408 18

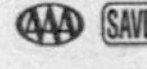

Motel
$65-$125 All Year

Address: 133 Plumbers Rd **Location:** I-20, exit 71 (Wilson Blvd), just n, then just e. Located in an industrial area. **Facility:** 42 one-bedroom standard units. 2 stories (no elevator), exterior corridors. **Parking:** on-site. **Amenities:** irons, hair dryers. **Pool(s):** outdoor. **Guest Services:** wireless Internet. **Business Services:** fax (fee). **Cards:** AX, DS, MC, VI. **Free Special Amenities: local telephone calls and high-speed Internet.**

/ SOME UNITS

ECONO LODGE *Book at AAA.com* **Phone:** (803)772-7275 22

Motel
$50-$125 All Year

Address: 773 St Andrews Rd **Location:** I-26, exit 106A westbound; exit 106 eastbound, just w. **Facility:** 64 one-bedroom standard units, some with whirlpools. 2 stories (no elevator), exterior corridors. **Parking:** on-site. **Terms:** cancellation fee imposed. **Pool(s):** outdoor. **Guest Services:** wireless Internet. **Business Services:** meeting rooms, fax (fee). **Cards:** AX, DS, MC, VI.

ASK / SOME UNITS FEE

(See map and index starting on p. 940)

EMBASSY SUITES HOTEL COLUMBIA - GREYSTONE Book great rates at AAA.com

Phone: (803)252-8700 29

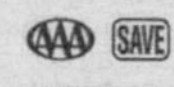

Contemporary Hotel
$113-$189 All Year

Address: 200 Stoneridge Dr **Location:** I-126, exit Greystone Blvd, just n, then just w. **Facility:** The hotel's large atrium lobby features fountains and tropical foliage. 218 units. 4 one-bedroom standard units. 214 one-bedroom suites. 7 stories, interior corridors. *Bath:* combo or shower only. **Parking:** on-site. **Terms:** cancellation fee imposed. **Amenities:** voice mail, irons, hair dryers. *Fee:* video games, high-speed Internet. **Pool(s):** heated indoor. **Leisure Activities:** whirlpool, exercise room. **Guest Services:** valet and coin laundry, airport transportation-Columbia Metropolitan Airport, area transportation-within 5 mi, wireless Internet. **Business Services:** conference facilities, business center. **Cards:** AX, CB, DC, DS, JC, MC, VI. **Free Special Amenities: full breakfast and newspaper.**

/ SOME UNITS

EMBASSY SUITES HOTELS
AAA Benefit:
Members save 5% or more everyday!

EXTENDED STAYAMERICA COLUMBIA-FORT JACKSON Book at AAA.com

Phone: (803)782-2025 27

Extended Stay Motel
$85-$95 All Year

Address: 5430 Forest Dr **Location:** I-77, exit 12, just ne, then just s along service road; behind mall. **Facility:** Find modest, but comfortable and roomy, accommodations behind a mall and just outside the gates of Fort Jackson; recreational facilities are limited. 120 one-bedroom standard units with efficiencies. 3 stories, exterior corridors. *Bath:* combo or shower only. **Parking:** on-site. **Terms:** office hours 7 am-11 pm. **Amenities:** voice mail, irons. **Guest Services:** coin laundry, wireless Internet. **Business Services:** fax (fee). **Cards:** AX, CB, DC, DS, JC, MC, VI.

ASK / SOME UNITS FEE

EXTENDED STAYAMERICA-COLUMBIA-WEST Book at AAA.com

Phone: (803)251-7878 30

Extended Stay Hotel
$65-$75 All Year

Address: 450 Gracern Rd **Location:** I-126, exit Greystone Blvd, just n to Stoneridge Dr, just w to Gracern Rd, then s. **Facility:** Find modest, but comfortable and roomy, accommodations are offered near the Riverbanks Zoo as well as the junction of I-20 and I-26. 120 one-bedroom standard units with efficiencies. 3 stories (no elevator), exterior corridors. *Bath:* combo or shower only. **Parking:** on-site. **Terms:** office hours 7 am-11 pm. **Amenities:** voice mail, irons. **Guest Services:** coin laundry, wireless Internet. **Business Services:** fax (fee). **Cards:** AX, CB, DC, DS, JC, MC, VI.

ASK / SOME UNITS FEE

FAIRFIELD INN & SUITES

Phone: 863/760-1700

fyi

Hotel
$118-$127 All Year

Too new to rate, opening scheduled for October 2008. **Address:** 120 Blarney Dr **Location:** I-77, exit 17, right at exit, then right at 1st light. **Amenities:** 96 units, coffeemakers, microwaves, refrigerators, pool. **Terms:** cancellation fee imposed. **Cards:** AX, CB, DC, DS, JC, MC, VI.

AAA Benefit:
Members save a minimum 5% off the best available rate.

FAIRFIELD INN NORTHWEST Book great rates at AAA.com

Phone: (803)732-4436 

Hotel
$119-$127 All Year

Address: 320 Columbiana Dr **Location:** I-26, exit 103 (Harbison Blvd), just sw, then nw. **Facility:** Smoke free premises. 84 one-bedroom standard units. 4 stories, interior corridors. *Bath:* combo or shower only. **Parking:** on-site. **Terms:** cancellation fee imposed. **Amenities:** high-speed Internet, irons, hair dryers. **Pool(s):** heated indoor. **Leisure Activities:** whirlpool, exercise room. **Guest Services:** valet laundry, wireless Internet. **Business Services:** business center. **Cards:** AX, CB, DC, DS, JC, MC, VI.

 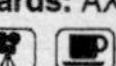  / SOME UNITS

FAIRFIELD INN Marriott
AAA Benefit:
Members save a minimum 5% off the best available rate.

FORT JACKSON INN

Phone: 803/695-0666 46

Hotel
Rates not provided

Address: 240 E Exchange Blvd **Location:** I-77, exit 9A, just se, then just s. **Facility:** 60 one-bedroom standard units, some with whirlpools. 3 stories, interior corridors. *Bath:* combo or shower only. **Parking:** on-site. **Amenities:** irons, hair dryers. **Pool(s):** outdoor. **Guest Services:** wireless Internet. **Business Services:** fax (fee).

CALL / SOME UNITS

(See map and index starting on p. 940)

HAMPTON INN COLUMBIA I-20/CLEMSON ROAD *Book great rates at AAA.com* **Phone:** (803)788-4901

Contemporary Hotel

$125-$141 1/1-11/30
$119-$134 12/1-12/31

Address: 1021 Clemson Frontage Rd **Location:** I-20, exit 80 (Clemson Rd), just n, then e. **Facility:** On the northeast side of the city and convenient to Columbia and Camden. Smoke free premises. 80 one-bedroom standard units. 5 stories, interior corridors. *Bath:* combo or shower only. **Parking:** on-site. **Terms:** cancellation fee imposed. **Amenities:** high-speed Internet, voice mail, irons, hair dryers. **Pool(s):** outdoor. **Leisure Activities:** limited exercise equipment. **Guest Services:** valet and coin laundry, wireless Internet. **Business Services:** meeting rooms, business center. **Cards:** AX, CB, DC, DS, MC, VI. **Free Special Amenities: expanded continental breakfast and high-speed Internet.**

CALL 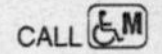    

AAA Benefit: Members save up to 10% everyday!

HAMPTON INN DOWNTOWN HISTORIC DISTRICT *Book great rates at AAA.com* **Phone:** (803)231-2000 

Contemporary Hotel

$149-$259 1/1-11/30
$129-$209 12/1-12/31

Address: 822 Gervais St **Location:** Jct US 1/21, 0.3 mi nw; in downtown Vista area. **Facility:** Centered in Columbia's downtown historic district, the hotel offers many upscale features and personal amenities. 122 one-bedroom standard units, some with whirlpools. 5 stories, interior corridors. *Bath:* combo or shower only. **Parking:** on-site. **Terms:** cancellation fee imposed. **Amenities:** DVD players, video games (fee), high-speed Internet, dual phone lines, voice mail, irons, hair dryers. **Pool(s):** outdoor. **Leisure Activities:** exercise room. **Guest Services:** valet laundry, wireless Internet. **Business Services:** meeting rooms, business center. **Cards:** AX, CB, DC, DS, JC, MC, VI.

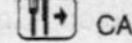 CALL 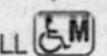  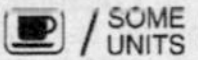 / SOME UNITS  

AAA Benefit: Members save up to 10% everyday!

HAMPTON INN HARBISON *Book great rates at AAA.com* **Phone:** (803)749-6999 

Hotel

$109-$149 All Year

Address: 101 Woodcross Dr **Location:** I-26, exit 103 (Harbison Blvd), just ne, then se. Located on Lake Harbison. **Facility:** 112 units. 107 one-bedroom standard units, some with whirlpools. 5 one-bedroom suites with whirlpools. 6 stories, interior corridors. *Bath:* combo or shower only. **Parking:** on-site. **Terms:** 1-30 night minimum stay, cancellation fee imposed. **Amenities:** voice mail, irons, hair dryers. *Some:* CD players. **Pool(s):** outdoor. **Leisure Activities:** fishing, bicycles, hiking trails, jogging, limited exercise equipment. **Guest Services:** valet and coin laundry, wireless Internet. **Business Services:** meeting rooms, business center. **Cards:** AX, CB, DC, DS, JC, MC, VI.

 CALL     / SOME UNITS

AAA Benefit: Members save up to 10% everyday!

HAMPTON INN NORTHEAST *Book great rates at AAA.com* **Phone:** (803)865-8000 

Hotel

$104-$144 All Year

Address: 1551 Barbara Dr **Location:** I-20, exit 74 (Two Notch Rd), just n; I-77, exit 17 (Two Notch Rd), 0.5 mi s. **Facility:** 111 one-bedroom standard units, some with whirlpools. 5 stories, interior corridors. *Bath:* combo or shower only. **Parking:** on-site. **Terms:** 1-30 night minimum stay, cancellation fee imposed. **Amenities:** voice mail, irons, hair dryers. **Pool(s):** outdoor. **Leisure Activities:** limited exercise equipment. **Guest Services:** valet and coin laundry, wireless Internet. **Business Services:** meeting rooms, business center. **Cards:** AX, CB, DC, DS, MC, VI.

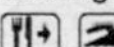  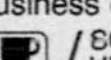 / SOME UNITS 

AAA Benefit: Members save up to 10% everyday!

HILTON COLUMBIA CENTER *Book great rates at AAA.com* **Phone:** (803)744-7800 

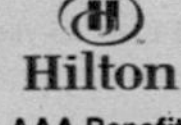

Contemporary Hotel

$149-$259 All Year

Address: 924 Senate St **Location:** Jct US 1/SR 48, just s; downtown. Located in Vista District. **Facility:** Opened in 2007, the full-service hotel is located in the Vista district surrounded by restaurants, government offices and the convention center. Smoke free premises. 222 one-bedroom standard units. 8 stories, interior corridors. *Bath:* combo or shower only. **Parking:** on-site (fee) and valet. **Terms:** check-in 4 pm. **Amenities:** video games, CD players, dual phone lines, voice mail, safes, irons, hair dryers. **Pool(s):** heated outdoor. **Leisure Activities:** exercise room. **Guest Services:** valet laundry, wireless Internet. **Business Services:** conference facilities, business center. **Cards:** AX, DC, DS, MC, VI.

CALL

AAA Benefit: Members save 5% or more everyday!

(See map and index starting on p. 940)

HILTON GARDEN INN COLUMBIA/HARBISON Book great rates at AAA.com Phone: (803)407-6640 2

Hotel
$79-$169 All Year

Address: 434 Columbiana Rd **Location:** I-26, exit 103 (Harbison Blvd), just sw to Columbiana Rd, then 0.8 mi nw. **Facility:** 143 units. 141 one-bedroom standard units, some with whirlpools. 2 one-bedroom suites. 6 stories, interior corridors. *Bath:* combo or shower only. **Parking:** on-site. **Terms:** 1-30 night minimum stay, cancellation fee imposed. **Amenities:** video games (fee), voice mail, irons, hair dryers. **Pool(s):** heated indoor. **Leisure Activities:** whirlpool, exercise room. **Guest Services:** coin laundry, wireless Internet. **Business Services:** meeting rooms, business center. **Cards:** AX, CB, DC, DS, JC, MC, VI.

CALL / SOME UNITS

HOLIDAY INN EXPRESS HOTEL & SUITES Book at AAA.com Phone: (803)695-1111 43

Hotel
$125-$229 All Year

Address: 7329 Garners Ferry Rd **Location:** I-77, exit 9A, just se. **Facility:** Smoke free premises. 100 units. 86 one-bedroom standard units, some with whirlpools. 14 one-bedroom suites. 5 stories, interior corridors. **Parking:** on-site. **Terms:** 7 day cancellation notice-fee imposed. **Amenities:** high-speed Internet, voice mail, irons, hair dryers. **Pool(s):** indoor. **Leisure Activities:** exercise room. **Guest Services:** valet and coin laundry, wireless Internet. **Business Services:** meeting rooms, business center. **Cards:** AX, DC, DS, JC, MC, VI.

ASK

HOLIDAY INN EXPRESS HOTEL & SUITES Book great rates at AAA.com Phone: (803)419-3558

AAA SAVE

Contemporary Hotel
$109 All Year

Address: 1011 Clemson Frontage Rd **Location:** I-20, exit 80 (Clemson Rd), just n. **Facility:** On the northeast side of the city, this property is convenient to Fort Jackson, Columbia Mall, downtown Columbia and the Riverbanks Zoo. 65 one-bedroom standard units, some with whirlpools. 3 stories, interior corridors. *Bath:* combo or shower only. **Parking:** on-site. **Amenities:** high-speed Internet, dual phone lines, voice mail, irons, hair dryers. **Pool(s):** outdoor. **Leisure Activities:** exercise room. **Guest Services:** valet and coin laundry, wireless Internet. **Business Services:** business center. **Cards:** AX, DC, DS, MC, VI. **Free Special Amenities: expanded continental breakfast and high-speed Internet.**

/ SOME UNITS

HOLIDAY INN EXPRESS HOTEL & SUITES HARBISON BLVD Book great rates at AAA.com Phone: (803)732-2229 14

Hotel
$99-$129 All Year

Address: 211 Lanneau Ct **Location:** I-26, exit 103 (Harbison Blvd), just sw to Columbiana Dr, then just nw. **Facility:** 82 one-bedroom standard units. 4 stories, interior corridors. *Bath:* combo or shower only. **Parking:** on-site. **Amenities:** high-speed Internet, dual phone lines, voice mail, irons, hair dryers. **Leisure Activities:** limited exercise equipment. **Guest Services:** valet laundry, wireless Internet. **Business Services:** meeting rooms, business center. **Cards:** AX, DC, DS, MC, VI.

ASK CALL / SOME UNITS

HOLIDAY INN HOTEL & SUITES Book at AAA.com Phone: 803/736-5600 4

Hotel
Rates not provided

Address: 8105 Two Notch Rd **Location:** I-77, exit 17 (Two Notch Rd), just ne. **Facility:** Smoke free premises. 181 units. 158 one-bedroom standard units. 23 one-bedroom suites with whirlpools. 6 stories, interior corridors. *Bath:* combo or shower only. **Parking:** on-site. **Terms:** check-in 4 pm. **Amenities:** voice mail, irons, hair dryers. **Pool(s):** outdoor. **Leisure Activities:** whirlpool, exercise room. **Guest Services:** valet and coin laundry, wireless Internet. **Business Services:** meeting rooms, business center.

CALL

HOMEWOOD SUITES BY HILTON-COLUMBIA, SC Book great rates at AAA.com Phone: (803)239-4663 28

AAA SAVE

Extended Stay Hotel
$95-$219 All Year

Address: 230 Greystone Blvd **Location:** I-126, exit Greystone Blvd, 0.4 mi n. **Facility:** Large rooms with upscale appointments are a features of this extended-stay property convenient to interstates, downtown business district, the Riverbanks Zoo and cinemas. 81 units. 17 one-bedroom standard units with efficiencies, some with whirlpools. 64 one-bedroom suites with efficiencies, some with whirlpools. 5 stories, interior corridors. *Bath:* combo or shower only. **Parking:** on-site. **Terms:** check-in 4 pm, 1-30 night minimum stay, cancellation fee imposed. **Amenities:** DVD players, CD players, high-speed Internet, voice mail, irons, hair dryers. **Pool(s):** heated indoor. **Leisure Activities:** whirlpool, exercise room. **Guest Services:** coin laundry, wireless Internet. **Business Services:** meeting rooms, business center. **Cards:** AX, CB, DC, DS, MC, VI. **Free Special Amenities: full breakfast and high-speed Internet.**

CALL / SOME UNITS

(See map and index starting on p. 940)

THE INN AT USC

Historic Boutique Hotel

$149-$349 All Year

Phone: (803)779-7779 37

Address: 1619 Pendelton St **Location:** Just e of center; between Pendelton and Senate sts; downtown; entrance on Pickens St. **Facility:** This small boutique was thoughtfully designed to complement surrounding historic buildings; public areas are plush, as are amenity-rich rooms. Smoke free premises. 117 units. 88 one-bedroom standard units. 29 one-bedroom suites, some with whirlpools. 3 stories, interior corridors. *Bath:* combo or shower only. **Parking:** on-site. **Amenities:** high-speed Internet, dual phone lines, voice mail, safes, irons, hair dryers. **Leisure Activities:** limited exercise equipment. **Guest Services:** valet and coin laundry, wireless Internet. **Business Services:** meeting rooms, business center. **Cards:** AX, CB, DC, DS, JC, MC, VI.

ASK CALL

JAMESON SUITES

Hotel

$103-$113 All Year

Book at AAA.com

Phone: (803)736-6666 12

Address: 7525 Two Notch Rd **Location:** I-20, exit 74 (Two Notch Rd), just ne; I-77, exit 17 (Two Notch Rd), 0.5 mi sw. **Facility:** 112 one-bedroom standard units. 6 stories, interior corridors. *Bath:* combo or shower only. **Parking:** on-site. **Terms:** cancellation fee imposed. **Amenities:** voice mail, irons, hair dryers. *Some:* high-speed Internet. **Pool(s):** outdoor. **Leisure Activities:** exercise room. **Guest Services:** valet and coin laundry, wireless Internet. **Business Services:** meeting rooms, fax (fee). **Cards:** AX, DC, DS, MC, VI.

ASK / SOME UNITS FEE

LA QUINTA INN & SUITES COLUMBIA NE/FT. JACKSON AREA

Hotel

$49-$109 All Year

Book great rates at AAA.com

Phone: (803)736-6400 15

Address: 1538 Horseshoe Dr **Location:** I-20, exit 74 (Two Notch Rd), just n; I-77, exit 17 (Two Notch Rd), 0.5 mi s. **Facility:** 100 units. 97 one-bedroom standard units. 3 one-bedroom suites. 3 stories, interior corridors. **Parking:** on-site. **Amenities:** video games (fee), voice mail, irons, hair dryers. **Pool(s):** outdoor. **Guest Services:** valet and coin laundry, wireless Internet. **Business Services:** fax (fee). **Cards:** AX, DC, DS, MC, VI.

ASK / SOME UNITS

LA QUINTA INN-MAINGATE FT. JACKSON

Hotel

$69-$129 All Year

Book great rates at AAA.com

Phone: (803)783-5410 44

Address: 7333 Garners Ferry Rd **Location:** I-77, exit 9A, just se. **Facility:** 121 one-bedroom standard units. 5 stories, interior corridors. **Parking:** on-site. **Amenities:** video games (fee), voice mail, irons, hair dryers. **Pool(s):** outdoor. **Guest Services:** valet laundry, wireless Internet. **Business Services:** meeting rooms, PC, fax (fee). **Cards:** AX, DC, DS, MC, VI.

ASK / SOME UNITS

▼ *See AAA listing p 1111* ▼

(See map and index starting on p. 940)

MARRIOTT COLUMBIA Book great rates at AAA.com Phone: (803)771-7000 34

Hotel
$197-$212 All Year

Address: 1200 Hampton St **Location:** 1 blk e of US 21; 1 blk s of SR 12; between Washington and SR 12/Taylor sts; downtown. **Facility:** Smoke free premises. 300 units. 285 one-bedroom standard units. 15 one-bedroom suites. 15 stories, interior corridors. *Bath:* combo or shower only. **Parking:** on-site (fee) and valet. **Terms:** check-in 4 pm, cancellation fee imposed. **Amenities:** video games (fee), voice mail, irons, hair dryers. *Some:* high-speed Internet. **Pool(s):** heated indoor. **Leisure Activities:** whirlpool, exercise room. **Guest Services:** valet and coin laundry, wireless Internet. **Business Services:** conference facilities, business center. **Cards:** AX, CB, DC, DS, MC, VI.

/ SOME UNITS

Marriott HOTELS & RESORTS

AAA Benefit:

Members save a minimum 5% off the best available rate.

MICROTEL INN Book great rates at AAA.com Phone: (803)736-3237 11

SAVE

Hotel
$59-$90 All Year

Address: 1520 Barbara Dr **Location:** I-20, exit 74 (Two Notch Rd), just ne; I-77, exit 17 (Two Notch Rd), 0.5 mi sw. **Facility:** 48 one-bedroom standard units. 2 stories, interior corridors. *Bath:* combo or shower only. **Parking:** on-site. **Amenities:** voice mail. **Guest Services:** coin laundry, wireless Internet. **Business Services:** business center. **Cards:** AX, DC, DS, MC, VI. **Free Special Amenities: early check-in/late check-out and high-speed Internet.**

/ SOME UNITS

MICROTEL INN & SUITES

fyi

Hotel

Under construction, scheduled to open May 2009. **Address:** 7504 Garners Ferry Rd **Location:** I-77, exit 9B. **Amenities:** 64 units, microwaves, refrigerators.

MICROTEL INN & SUITES HARBISON AREA Book great rates at AAA.com Phone: (803)772-1914 20

SAVE

Hotel
$70-$80 All Year

Address: 411 Piney Grove Rd **Location:** I-26, exit 104 (Piney Grove Rd), just sw. **Facility:** 63 one-bedroom standard units. 2 stories, interior corridors. *Bath:* combo or shower only. **Parking:** on-site. **Guest Services:** wireless Internet. **Business Services:** fax (fee). **Cards:** AX, DS, MC, VI.

CALL / SOME UNITS

MOTEL 6 #1291 Book at AAA.com Phone: (803)736-3900 17

Hotel
$47-$53 5/24-11/30
$43-$49 12/1-5/23

Address: 7541 Nates Rd **Location:** I-20, exit 74 (Two Notch Rd), just n, then just e; I-77, exit 17 (Two Notch Rd), 0.5 mi s, then e. **Facility:** 121 one-bedroom standard units. 3 stories, interior corridors. *Bath:* combo or shower only. **Parking:** on-site. **Pool(s):** outdoor. **Guest Services:** coin laundry. **Business Services:** fax (fee). **Cards:** AX, DC, DS, MC, VI.

CALL / SOME UNITS

QUALITY INN Book at AAA.com Phone: (803)736-0822 6

Motel
$55-$100 All Year

Address: 8104 Two Notch Rd **Location:** I-77, exit 17 (Two Notch Rd), just ne. Located near the railroad tracks. **Facility:** 125 one-bedroom standard units. 2 stories (no elevator), exterior corridors. **Parking:** on-site. **Amenities:** video games (fee), irons, hair dryers. **Pool(s):** outdoor. **Leisure Activities:** limited exercise equipment. **Guest Services:** valet laundry, wireless Internet. **Business Services:** meeting rooms, business center. **Cards:** AX, DC, DS, MC, VI.

ASK CALL / SOME UNITS

QUALITY INN Phone: 803/451-2400

fyi

Hotel
Rates not provided

Too new to rate, opening scheduled for October 2008. **Address:** 1335 Garner Ln **Location:** I-20, exit 65 (US 176), just ne. **Amenities:** 86 units, coffeemakers, pool.

QUALITY INN & SUITES Book at AAA.com Phone: 803/776-1700 42

Motel
Rates not provided

Address: 7251 Garners Ferry Rd **Location:** I-77, exit 9A, just se. **Facility:** 66 one-bedroom standard units. 3 stories, exterior corridors. *Bath:* combo or shower only. **Parking:** on-site. **Amenities:** dual phone lines, voice mail, irons, hair dryers. *Some:* DVD players. **Pool(s):** outdoor. **Leisure Activities:** exercise room privileges. **Guest Services:** valet laundry, wireless Internet. **Business Services:** meeting rooms, business center.

/ SOME UNITS FEE

(See map and index starting on p. 940)

QUALITY INN HARBISON AREA *Book great rates at AAA.com* **Phone:** (803)798-0500 19

AAA SAVE

Motel

$79-$119 All Year

Address: 499 Piney Grove Rd **Location:** I-26, exit 104 (Piney Grove Rd), just ne. **Facility:** 86 one-bedroom standard units, some with whirlpools. 2-3 stories, exterior corridors. **Parking:** on-site. **Terms:** cancellation fee imposed. **Amenities:** irons, hair dryers. **Pool(s):** outdoor. **Guest Services:** valet and coin laundry, wireless Internet. **Business Services:** meeting rooms, fax (fee). **Cards:** AX, DS, MC, VI. *(See color ad below)*

/ SOME UNITS

RADISSON HOTEL COLUMBIA & CONFERENCE CENTER *Book great rates at AAA.com* **Phone:** (803)731-0300 25

AAA SAVE

Hotel

$99-$199 12/1-4/30
$89-$189 5/1-11/30

Address: 2100 Bush River Rd **Location:** I-20, exit 63 (Bush River Rd), just e; I-26, exit 108 (Bush River Rd), 0.7 mi w. **Facility:** 238 units. 203 one-bedroom standard units, some with whirlpools. 34 one- and 1 two-bedroom suites, some with whirlpools. 5 stories, interior corridors. *Bath:* combo or shower only. **Parking:** on-site. **Terms:** cancellation fee imposed. **Amenities:** high-speed Internet, dual phone lines, voice mail, safes (fee), irons, hair dryers. **Pool(s):** outdoor. **Leisure Activities:** exercise room. **Guest Services:** valet laundry, airport transportation-Columbia Metropolitan Airport, area transportation-within 2 mi, wireless Internet. **Business Services:** conference facilities, business center. **Cards:** AX, CB, DC, DS, JC, MC, VI. **Free Special Amenities: newspaper and high-speed Internet.** *(See color ad below)*

/ SOME UNITS FEE FEE

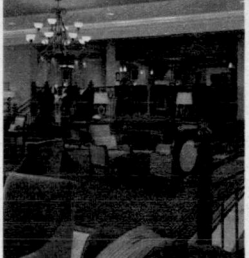

(See map and index starting on p. 940)

RESIDENCE INN BY MARRIOTT *Book great rates at AAA.com* **Phone:** (803)788-8850 1

Extended Stay Hotel
$138-$148 All Year

Address: 2320 Legrand Rd **Location:** I-77, exit 19 southbound, just ne on Farrow Rd to Rabon Rd, then just se; exit 18 northbound. **Facility:** The hotel, built in 2005, is equipped to accommodate extended-stay guests; find ample public spaces and many recreational diversions. Smoke free premises. 113 units. 50 one-bedroom standard units with efficiencies. 45 one- and 18 two-bedroom suites, some with efficiencies or kitchens. 3 stories, interior corridors. *Bath:* combo or shower only. **Parking:** on-site. **Terms:** cancellation fee imposed. **Amenities:** video games (fee), voice mail, irons, hair dryers. **Pool(s):** heated outdoor. **Leisure Activities:** whirlpool, exercise room, sports court. **Guest Services:** valet and coin laundry, wireless Internet. **Business Services:** meeting rooms, business center. **Cards:** AX, DS, MC, VI.

AAA Benefit:
Members save a minimum 5% off the best available rate.

RESIDENCE INN BY MARRIOTT *Book great rates at AAA.com* **Phone:** (803)779-7000 31

Extended Stay Hotel
$158-$169 All Year

Address: 150 Stoneridge Dr **Location:** I-126, exit Greystone Blvd, just n, then just e. **Facility:** The hotel offers accommodations ranging from studios to two-bedrooms, many with fireplaces. Smoke free premises. 128 units. 112 one-bedroom standard units with kitchens. 16 two-bedroom suites with kitchens. 2 stories (no elevator), exterior corridors. *Bath:* combo or shower only. **Parking:** on-site. **Terms:** cancellation fee imposed. **Amenities:** video games (fee), high-speed Internet, voice mail, irons, hair dryers. **Pool(s):** outdoor. **Leisure Activities:** whirlpool, putting green, limited exercise equipment, sports court. **Guest Services:** valet and coin laundry, wireless Internet. **Business Services:** fax (fee). **Cards:** AX, CB, DC, DS, JC, MC, VI.

AAA Benefit:
Members save a minimum 5% off the best available rate.

/ SOME UNITS FEE

SLEEP INN-FORT JACKSON *Book at AAA.com* **Phone:** 803/776-6263 48

Hotel
Rates not provided

Address: 200 E Exchange Blvd **Location:** I-77, exit 9A, just se, then s. **Facility:** 80 one-bedroom standard units, some with whirlpools. 3 stories, interior corridors. *Bath:* combo or shower only. **Parking:** on-site. **Amenities:** irons, hair dryers. **Pool(s):** outdoor. **Leisure Activities:** exercise room. **Guest Services:** valet laundry, wireless Internet. **Business Services:** meeting rooms, fax (fee).

/ SOME UNITS

STAYBRIDGE SUITES COLUMBIA **Phone:** 803/451-5900

fyi
Hotel

Under construction, scheduled to open January 2009. **Address:** 1907 Huger St **Location:** I-26, exit 277. **Amenities:** 93 units, coffeemakers, microwaves, refrigerators, pool.

STUDIOPLUS GREYSTONE COLUMBIA *Book at AAA.com* **Phone:** (803)771-0303 32

Extended Stay Hotel
$75-$85 All Year

Address: 180 Stoneridge Dr **Location:** I-126, exit Greystone Blvd, just n, then just e. **Facility:** These apartment-style lodgings are well suited for extended stays; office hours are limited. 72 units. 71 one-bedroom standard units with kitchens. 1 one-bedroom suite with kitchen. 3 stories (no elevator), interior corridors. *Bath:* combo or shower only. **Parking:** on-site. **Terms:** office hours 7 am-11 pm. **Amenities:** voice mail, irons. **Pool(s):** outdoor. **Guest Services:** valet and coin laundry, wireless Internet. **Business Services:** fax (fee). **Cards:** AX, CB, DC, DS, JC, MC, VI.

ASK / SOME UNITS FEE

SUPER 8 **Phone:** (803)735-0008 21

AAA SAVE

Motel
$70-$95 All Year

Address: 5719 Fairfield Rd **Location:** I-20, exit 70, just s. **Facility:** 43 one-bedroom standard units, some with whirlpools. 2 stories (no elevator), exterior corridors. **Parking:** on-site. **Terms:** cancellation fee imposed. **Guest Services:** coin laundry. **Business Services:** fax (fee). **Cards:** AX, DS, MC, VI. **Free Special Amenities: continental breakfast and local telephone calls.**

/ SOME UNITS FEE

TOWNEPLACE SUITES BY MARRIOTT *Book great rates at AAA.com* **Phone:** (803)781-9391 3

Hotel
$134-$144 All Year

Address: 350 Columbiana Dr **Location:** I-26, exit 103 (Harbison Blvd), just sw to Columbiana Dr, then 0.7 mi nw. **Facility:** Smoke free premises. 89 units. 63 one-bedroom standard units with kitchens. 4 one- and 22 two-bedroom suites with kitchens. 3 stories, interior corridors. *Bath:* combo or shower only. **Parking:** on-site. **Terms:** cancellation fee imposed. **Amenities:** voice mail, irons, hair dryers. **Pool(s):** outdoor. **Leisure Activities:** exercise room. **Guest Services:** valet and coin laundry, wireless Internet. **Business Services:** business center. **Cards:** AX, CB, DC, DS, MC, VI.

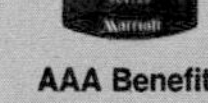

AAA Benefit:
Members save a minimum 5% off the best available rate.

CALL / SOME UNITS FEE VCR

(See map and index starting on p. 940)

THE WHITNEY HOTEL *Book great rates at AAA.com* **Phone:** (803)252-0845 **39**

AAA SAVE

Condominium

$159-$179 All Year

Address: 700 Woodrow St **Location:** Jct Devine and Harden sts, 0.6 mi w on Devine St; between Maple and King sts; in Five Points Section. **Facility:** English and American antique reproductions furnish this traditional-style, service-oriented hotel; it's near the government complex, USC and downtown. 74 units. 17 one- and 57 two-bedroom suites with kitchens, some with whirlpools. 7 stories, interior corridors. **Parking:** on-site. **Terms:** cancellation fee imposed. **Amenities:** video games (fee), high-speed Internet, voice mail, irons, hair dryers. **Pool(s):** outdoor. **Guest Services:** valet and coin laundry, airport transportation-Columbia & Owens Downtown airports, wireless Internet. **Business Services:** meeting rooms, fax (fee). **Cards:** AX, DC, DS, MC, VI. **Free Special Amenities: full breakfast and high-speed Internet.**

/ SOME UNITS

WINGATE BY WYNDHAM-NORTHEAST *Book at AAA.com* **Phone:** 803/699-9333 **5**

Hotel

Rates not provided

Address: 8300 Two Notch Rd **Location:** I-77, exit 17 (Two Notch Rd), just ne. **Facility:** 83 one-bedroom standard units, some with whirlpools. 4 stories, interior corridors. *Bath:* combo or shower only. **Parking:** on-site. **Amenities:** high-speed Internet, dual phone lines, voice mail, safes, irons, hair dryers. **Pool(s):** outdoor. **Leisure Activities:** whirlpool, exercise room. **Guest Services:** valet laundry, wireless Internet. **Business Services:** meeting rooms, business center.

CALL / SOME UNITS

WINGATE INN HARBISON *Book great rates at AAA.com* **Phone:** (803)407-6166 **13**

AAA SAVE

Hotel

$89-$109 All Year

Address: 217 Lanneau Ct **Location:** I-26, exit 103 (Harbison Blvd), just sw to Columbiana Ave, then just nw. Located across from Columbiana Center. **Facility:** 101 units. 98 one-bedroom standard units. 3 one-bedroom suites with whirlpools. 4 stories, interior corridors. *Bath:* combo or shower only. **Parking:** on-site. **Amenities:** high-speed Internet, dual phone lines, voice mail, safes, irons, hair dryers. **Pool(s):** outdoor. **Leisure Activities:** whirlpool, limited exercise equipment. **Guest Services:** valet laundry, wireless Internet. **Business Services:** meeting rooms, business center. **Cards:** AX, CB, DC, DS, MC, VI. **Free Special Amenities: expanded continental breakfast and high-speed Internet.**

CALL / SOME UNITS

WHERE TO DINE

BAILEY'S PUB & GRILLE **Phone:** 803/407-3004

American

$8-$18

Not your typical stuffy Old English Pub, sister restaurants, Bailey's and Fox. Casual dress. **Bar:** Full bar. **Hours:** 11 am-2 am. Closed: 12/25. **Address:** 115 Afton Ct **Location:** I-26, exit 103 (Harbison Blvd), just sw, just nw on Columbiana Dr, then just w. **Parking:** on-site. **Cards:** AX, MC, VI.

BLUE MARLIN STEAK & SEAFOOD **Phone:** 803/799-3838 (11)

Regional Steak & Seafood

$7-$22

Located in a converted train station in the newly refurbished historic district, this nautically themed eatery features Lowcountry cuisine with a focus on seafood dishes. Gumbo and spicy shrimp Creole are terrific washed down with a glass of iced tea. Casual dress. **Bar:** Full bar. **Hours:** 11:30 am-2:30 & 5-10 pm, Fri-11 pm, Sat 4 pm-11 pm, Sun noon-9 pm. Closed: 1/1, 12/24-12/26; also Super Bowl Sun. **Address:** 1200 Lincoln St **Location:** Corner of Gervais and Lincoln sts; in Vista Historic District. **Parking:** on-site. **Cards:** AX, CB, DC, MC, VI.

BONEFISH GRILL **Phone:** 803/407-1599 (2)

Seafood

$13-$30

Fish is the house specialty, and the menu and nightly specials offer a variety of choices. Well-prepared food is cooked to perfection. Service is casual in nature, and the staff is skilled and attentive. Casual dress. **Bar:** Full bar. **Reservations:** accepted. **Hours:** 4 pm-close. Closed: 11/26, 12/25. **Address:** 1260 Bower Pkwy, Suite A-1 **Location:** I-26, exit 103, just sw to Park Terrace Rd, then just se. **Parking:** on-site. **Cards:** AX, DC, DS, MC, VI.

BONEFISH GRILL **Phone:** 803/787-6200 (4)

Seafood

$13-$30

Fish is the house specialty, and the menu and nightly specials offer a variety of choices. Well-prepared food is cooked to perfection. Service is casual in nature, and the staff is skilled and attentive. Casual dress. **Bar:** Full bar. **Reservations:** accepted. **Hours:** 4 pm-close. Closed: 11/26, 12/25. **Address:** 4708 Forest Dr **Location:** I-77, exit 12, 1.5 mi w on SR 12 (Forest Dr). **Parking:** on-site. **Cards:** AX, DC, DS, MC, VI.

BULL MARKET RESTAURANT & TAVERNA **Phone:** 803/343-2855 (9)

New Southern

$7-$23

Situated downtown in a former train station, the restaurant features a broad menu of regional southern entrees with a Mediterranean influence. Specialties include crabcakes with fried, green tomatoes, Niki's shrimp tourkolimano, grilled steaks and seafood. A variety of Greek pastries is a nice way to wrap up the meal. The atmosphere is relaxed and the service is professional and friendly. Casual dress. **Bar:** Full bar. **Reservations:** accepted. **Hours:** 11:30 am-10 pm, Fri & Sat-11 pm. Closed: 11/26, 12/25; also Sun. **Address:** 902 C Gervais St **Location:** Jct US 1/21, 0.3 mi nw; downtown; in Vista area. **Parking:** street. **Cards:** MC, VI.

CALIFORNIA DREAMING **Phone:** 803/254-6767

American

$8-$23

The full-service, fine-dining restaurant appeals to adults, particularly those with an appetite for innovative concepts in food. Revised weekly, the menu consistently incorporates sophisticated, cutting-edge California dishes with Pacific Rim influences throughout. Among house specialties are flatbread appetizers baked in a brick oven, sushi, sashimi and some vegetarian dishes. The wine list focuses primarily on California vintages. Casual dress. **Bar:** Full bar. **Hours:** 11 am-10 pm, Fri & Sat-11 pm. **Address:** 401 S Main St **Location:** 0.3 mi s of Blossom St; center. **Parking:** on-site. **Cards:** AX, DC, DS, MC, VI. **Historic**

(See map and index starting on p. 940)

CAROLINA ALE HOUSE — **Phone:** 803/407-6996

American
$7-$17

The popular sports bar is located at the Columbiana Mall and features signature sandwiches, steak, seafood and ribs. Indulge yourself in sports on any of the high-definition televisions sprinkled throughout the dining room. Find more than 38 beers on tap and even more in ice-cold bottles. Casual dress. **Bar:** Full bar. **Hours:** 11 am-2 am. Closed: 12/25. **Address:** 277 Columbiana Dr **Location:** I-26, exit 103 (Harbison Blvd), just sw to Columbiana Dr, then just nw. **Parking:** on-site. **Cards:** AX, DS, MC, VI.

CALL

FATZ CAFE — **Phone:** 803/782-1183

American
$8-$18

Friendly staff and appealing country decor help set the tone for a relaxed and enjoyable dining experience. It's not unusual for guests to wait to be seated at the popular spot, which earns raves for its well-prepared variations on chicken, steak, ribs and pasta, as well as salads and sandwiches. The signature Southern-style peach cobbler served with vanilla ice cream and walnuts is scrumptious. Casual dress. **Bar:** Full bar. **Hours:** 11 am-10 pm, Fri & Sat-11 pm, Sun-9 pm. Closed: 11/26, 12/25. **Address:** 5590 Forest Dr **Location:** I-77, exit 12, just nw; in East Forest Plaza. **Parking:** on-site. **Cards:** AX, DS, MC, VI.

CALL

GARIBALDI'S — **Phone:** 803/771-8888 (7)

Italian
$13-$29

Set in a lively, Art Deco design, the eatery offers such delectable delights as fresh seafood, veal, poultry and gourmet pizza. Expect to find friendly service. Parking is available behind the building. **Bar:** Full bar. **Reservations:** suggested. **Hours:** 5:30 pm-10:30 pm, Fri & Sat-11 pm. Closed: 12/25. **Address:** 2013 Greene St **Location:** Corner of Greene and Harden sts; in Five Points Section. **Parking:** valet and street. **Cards:** AX, MC, VI.

HAMPTON STREET VINEYARD — **Phone:** 803/252-0850 (5)

American
$8-$30

Serving the downtown area for more than 11 years, the award-winning American bistro's two chef/wine connoisseurs prepare award-winning dishes such as Chilean salmon, confit of duck, braised lamb shank and a host of other delicacies and confections. Casual dress. **Bar:** Full bar. **Reservations:** suggested. **Hours:** 11:30 am-2 & 6-10 pm, Sat from 6 pm. Closed: major holidays; also 12/24, Sun & 1st week in July. **Address:** 1201 Hampton St **Location:** Between Main and Sumter sts; downtown. **Parking:** valet and street. **Cards:** AX, DS, MC, VI.

HARBOR INN SEAFOOD — **Phone:** 803/462-3498

Seafood
$5-$14

Visitors to the bright, open dining room, which carries out a nautical theme, have their choice from a good selection of steamed and fried seafood. Casual dress. **Hours:** 11 am-9 pm, Fri & Sat-10 pm. Closed major holidays; also Mon. **Address:** 9001 Two Notch Rd **Location:** I-77, exit 17 (Two Notch Rd), 1 mi ne. **Parking:** on-site. **Cards:** AX, DS, MC, VI.

CALL

LIZARD'S THICKET — **Phone:** 803/647-0095

Regional American
$3-$12

Owned and operated by the same family since 1978, guests can enjoy Southern home cooking at breakfast, lunch, and dinner. Locals love the Calabash style shrimp as well as the fried chicken livers. Be sure and ask about the daily specials which will allow guest a mixing and matching of main course with side dishes. Casual dress. **Hours:** 6 am-9 pm; to 10 pm seasonal. Closed: 12/25. **Address:** 7938 Garners Ferry Rd **Location:** I-77, exit 9A, 2.3 mi se on US 76/SR 378. **Parking:** on-site. **Cards:** AX, MC, VI.

CALL

LIZARD'S THICKET — **Phone:** 803/779-6407

Regional American
$3-$11

Owned and operated by the same family since 1978, guests can enjoy Southern home cooking at breakfast, lunch, and dinner. Locals love the Calabash style shrimp as well as the fried chicken livers. Be sure and ask about the daily specials which will allow guest a mixing and matching of main course with side dishes. Casual dress. **Hours:** 6 am-9 pm; to 10 pm seasonal. Closed: 12/25. **Address:** 818 Elmwood Ave **Location:** I-126, exit 3A, just ne on SR 76/176/21. **Parking:** on-site. **Cards:** AX, MC, VI.

CALL

LIZARD'S THICKET — **Phone:** 803/738-0006

Regional American
$3-$12

Owned and operated by the same family since 1978, guests can enjoy Southern home cooking at breakfast, lunch, and dinner. Locals love the Calabash style shrimp as well as the fried chicken livers. Be sure and ask about the daily specials which will allow guest a mixing and matching of main course with side dishes. Casual dress. **Hours:** 6 am-9 pm; to 10 pm seasonal. **Address:** 402 Beltline Blvd **Location:** Jct SR 16/US 76/SR 378, just sw on SR 16 (Beltline Blvd). **Parking:** on-site. **Cards:** MC, VI.

CALL

LIZARD'S THICKET — **Phone:** 803/419-5662

Regional American
$3-$12

Owned and operated by the same family since 1978, guests can enjoy Southern home cooking at breakfast, lunch, and dinner. Locals love the Calabash style shrimp as well as the fried chicken livers. Be sure and ask about the daily specials which will allow guest a mixing and matching of main course with side dishes. Casual dress. **Hours:** 6 am-9 pm; to 10 pm seasonal. Closed: 12/25. **Address:** 10170 Two Notch Rd **Location:** I-20, exit 80, 2.6 mi nw on Sparkleberry Ln, then 0.5 mi ne. **Parking:** on-site. **Cards:** AX, MC, VI.

CALL

(See map and index starting on p. 940)

LIZARD'S THICKET **Phone:** 803/787-8781

Regional American
$3-$12

Owned and operated by the same family since 1978, guests can enjoy Southern home cooking at breakfast, lunch, and dinner. Locals love the Calabash style shrimp as well as the fried chicken livers. Be sure and ask about the daily specials which will allow guest a mixing and matching of main course with side dishes. Casual dress. **Hours:** 6 am-9 pm; to 10 pm seasonal. Closed: 12/25. **Address:** 3147 Forest Dr **Location:** Jct US 1/SR 12 (Forest Dr), 1.3 mi e. **Parking:** on-site. **Cards:** AX, MC, VI.

CALL

LIZARD'S THICKET **Phone:** 803/798-6427

Regional American
$3-$12

Owned and operated by the same family since 1978, guests can enjoy Southern home cooking at breakfast, lunch, and dinner. Locals love the Calabash style shrimp as well as the fried chicken livers. Be sure and ask about the daily specials which will allow guest a mixing and matching of main course with side dishes. Casual dress. **Hours:** 6 am-9 pm; to 10 pm seasonal. **Address:** 1824 Broad River Rd **Location:** I-20, exit 65, just se on US 176 (Broad River Rd). **Parking:** on-site. **Cards:** AX, MC, VI.

CALL

LIZARD'S THICKET **Phone:** 803/788-3088

Regional American
$3-$12

Owned and operated by the same family since 1978, guests can enjoy Southern home cooking at breakfast, lunch, and dinner. Locals love the Calabash style shrimp as well as the fried chicken livers. Be sure and ask about the daily specials which will allow guest a mixing and matching of main course with side dishes. Casual dress. **Hours:** 6 am-9 pm; to 10 pm seasonal. **Address:** 7620 Two Notch Rd **Location:** I-20, exit 74 (Two Notch Rd), just ne, then just se; I-77, exit 17 (Two Notch Rd), 0.5 mi sw, then just se. **Parking:** on-site. **Cards:** MC, VI.

CALL

MR. FRIENDLY'S **Phone:** 803/254-7828 (6)

Regional American
$8-$28

The unpretentious, award-winning restaurant has been serving the area since the early '80s. Selections from a 400-bottle wine list and a comprehensive choice of single malts complement offerings of New Southern cuisine. The owner/manager is a demure aficionado who eagerly provides assistance with meal selection. He's a key part of the dining experience. Casual dress. **Bar:** Full bar. **Reservations:** not accepted. **Hours:** 11:30 am-2:30 & 5:30-10 pm, Fri-10:30 pm, Sat 5:30 pm-10:30 pm. Closed: 11/26, 12/25; also Sun. **Address:** 2001-A Greene St **Location:** 1 blk n of US 76; in Five Points area; in The Inn at Claussen's. **Parking:** on-site. **Cards:** AX, DS, MC, VI.

MONTERREY MEXICAN RESTAURANT **Phone:** 803/749-5928 (1)

Mexican
$4-$14

Next to a large mall and near many hotels, the cantina features friendly service and a good selection of traditional Mexican fare. A popular favorite is "a little of everything," a hearty combination plate with a chalupa, chile relleno, beef taco, enchilada, burrito, rice and beans. Casual dress. **Bar:** Full bar. **Hours:** 11:30 am-10 pm, Fri & Sat-10:30 pm. Closed: 12/25. **Address:** 114 Afton Ct **Location:** I-26, exit 103 (Harbison Blvd), just sw to Columbiana Dr, then just nw. **Parking:** on-site. **Cards:** AX, DS, MC, VI.

CALL

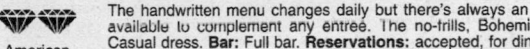

MOTOR SUPPLY CO BISTRO **Phone:** 803/256-6687 (8)

American
$8-$25

The handwritten menu changes daily but there's always an extensive list of vintage or daily wine specials available to complement any entree. The no-frills, Bohemian-style decor defines a relaxed atmosphere. Casual dress. **Bar:** Full bar. **Reservations:** accepted, for dinner. **Hours:** 11:30 am-2:30 & 5:30-9:30 pm, Fri & Sat-10:30 pm, Sun 11 am-3 & 5:30-9 pm; Sunday brunch. Closed major holidays; also Mon. **Address:** 920 Gervais St **Location:** Jct US 21/1, 0.4 mi ne; jct US 76/1, 0.5 mi sw; downtown. **Parking:** on-site and street. **Cards:** AX, DC, DS, MC, VI.

RISTORANTE DIVINO **Phone:** 803/799-4550 (10)

Italian
$18-$35

Freshly prepared entrees with a flair for Northern Italian cuisine. Many dishes feature clams, shrimp, scallops and crab. Additional favorites are the Gnocci, veal marsala, and the tenderloin medallion. A wine list is presented and worthy of perusing before your meal. The chef creates mouthwatering desserts that are worth saving room for. Dressy casual. **Bar:** Full bar. **Reservations:** suggested. **Hours:** 6 pm-10 pm. Closed major holidays; also Sun. **Address:** 803 Gervais St (US 1) **Location:** 0.3 mi s of state capitol building; between Gadsden and Lincoln sts; in Vista Historic District. **Parking:** valet and street. **Cards:** AX, DC, MC, VI.

S & S CAFETERIA **Phone:** 803/782-0545

American
$4-$8

A longtime favorite for comfort food, the family-owned cafeteria invites diners to load a plate with traditionally prepared chicken, beef, vegetables, salad and dessert. Casual dress. **Hours:** 11 am-2:15 & 5-8 pm. Closed: 12/25. **Address:** 3400 Forest Dr, #1088 **Location:** Jct SR 16 (N Beltline Blvd) and 12 (Forest Dr); in Richland Mall. **Parking:** on-site. **Cards:** AX, DS, MC, VI.

SKANCHELI MEDITERRANEAN CLASSIC CUISINE **Phone:** 803/407-3797 (3)

Mediterranean
$6-$28

Authentic, home-style Mediterranean cuisine take center stage at the family-operated, storefront bistro, where you'll find the offerings to focus on healthy vegetarian and traditional lean meat dishes. Lunch selections include hummus, tabouleh, cabbage rolls, baba ganoush and vegetarian stuffed grape leaves, each dish prepared to order and served with flavored yogurt sauces and spices. The dinner menu expands to include grilled marinated lamb and chicken dishes, each accompanied by freshly-prepared vegetable and sauce creations. For the adventurous, special combination platters are provided to offer a variety of the tasty and unique selections. Casual dress. **Bar:** Beer & wine. **Reservations:** accepted. **Hours:** 11 am-2 & 6-9 pm. Closed: 12/25. **Address:** 1150 Bower Pkwy **Location:** I-26, exit 103, just sw to Park Terrace Rd, then just se. **Parking:** on-site. **Cards:** AX, DS, MC, VI.

(See map and index starting on p. 940)

STICKY FINGERS RIB HOUSE **Phone:** 803/781-7427

Barbecue
$7-$26

Diners can put down their silverware and get their fingers ready for classic Carolina sweet ribs, as well as ribs cooked in the Texas and Tennessee styles. Hearty sides of baked beans and coleslaw complement entrees at the friendly cafe. Casual dress. **Bar:** Full bar. **Hours:** 11 am-close. Closed: 11/26, 12/25. **Address:** 380 Columbiana Dr **Location:** I-26, exit 103 (Harbison Blvd), just sw, then 1 mi nw; behind Columbiana Mall. **Parking:** on-site. **Cards:** AX, DC, DS, MC, VI.

CALL

TRAVINIA ITALIAN KITCHEN **Phone:** 803/419-9313

Northern Italian
$9-$19

Professional service and fresh ingredients are keystones at the popular Italian restaurant. Dishes are moderately priced and portions are perfect for an enjoyable meal. The wine list includes 35 Italian and California wines availed by the glass and a hand-picked reserve selection. The chef specializes in distinctive interpretations of veal, chicken, beef, seafood and pasta with interesting sauces. The in-house pastry chef whips up delectable desserts and fresh breads. Casual dress. **Bar:** Full bar. **Hours:** 11:30 am-10 pm, Fri & Sat-11 pm. Closed: 11/26, 12/25. **Address:** 101 Sparkleberry Crossing Rd **Location:** I-20, exit 80, just n on Clemson Rd; in Sparkleberry Crossing Center. **Parking:** on-site.

CALL

YAMATO SEAFOOD STEAK & SEAFOOD **Phone:** 803/407-0033

Japanese
$6-$29

The "original Japanese Steakhouse of South Carolina", Yamatos tantalizes guest with fresh USDA choice beef, wonderful seafood and fresh vegetables. Families enjoy the casual atmosphere and the show the chefs put on while cooking each individual meal. Casual dress. **Bar:** Full bar. **Reservations:** accepted. **Hours:** 5 pm-9:30 pm, Fri & Sat 11:30 am-2 & 5-10:30 pm, Sun 11:30 am-2 pm. Closed: 11/26. **Address:** 360 Columbiana Dr **Location:** I-26, exit 103 (Harbison Blvd), 0.4 mi se to Columbiana Dr, then 0.7 mi n. **Parking:** on-site. **Cards:** AX, DS, MC, VI.

CALL

YESTERDAYS RESTAURANT & TAVERN **Phone:** 803/799-0196 (12)

American
$6-$12

In an eclectic tavern atmosphere, the popular eatery serves spicy cuisine, as well as such tasty dishes as blackened chicken breast with tender black beans and white rice. Tropical fish swim in large tanks that line the walls. Casual dress. **Bar:** Full bar. **Reservations:** accepted. **Hours:** 11:15 am-midnight, Fri & Sat-1 am. Closed: 7/4, 11/26, 12/25. **Address:** 2030 Devine St **Location:** Corner of Devine and Harden sts; in Five Points Section. **Parking:** street. **Cards:** AX, DS, MC, VI.

CONWAY —*See The Grand Strand p. 979.*

DILLON pop. 6,316

WHERE TO STAY

HAMPTON INN *Book great rates at AAA.com* **Phone:** (843)774-0222

Motel
$74-$159 All Year

Address: 817 Radford Blvd **Location:** I-95, exit 193, just s. **Facility:** 50 one-bedroom standard units, some with whirlpools. 2 stories (no elevator), exterior corridors. **Parking:** on-site. **Terms:** 1-30 night minimum stay, cancellation fee imposed. **Amenities:** voice mail, irons, hair dryers. **Pool(s):** outdoor. **Guest Services:** wireless Internet. **Business Services:** fax (fee). **Cards:** AX, CB, DC, DS, MC, VI.

/ SOME UNITS

AAA Benefit:
Members save up to 10% everyday!

DUNCAN pop. 2,870

WHERE TO STAY

HAMPTON INN & SUITES GREENVILLE/DUNCAN *Book great rates at AAA.com* **Phone:** (864)486-8100

Hotel
$73-$129 All Year

Address: 108 Spartangreen Blvd **Location:** I-85, exit 63, just se. **Facility:** 133 units. 100 one-bedroom standard units. 33 one-bedroom suites with efficiencies and whirlpools. 5 stories, interior corridors. *Bath:* combo or shower only. **Parking:** on-site. **Terms:** 1-30 night minimum stay, cancellation fee imposed. **Amenities:** video games (fee), high-speed Internet, dual phone lines, voice mail, irons, hair dryers. *Some:* DVD players. **Pool(s):** outdoor. **Leisure Activities:** playground, exercise room. **Guest Services:** valet and coin laundry. **Business Services:** meeting rooms, business center. **Cards:** AX, CB, DC, DS, MC, VI.

CALL / SOME UNITS

AAA Benefit:
Members save up to 10% everyday!

JAMESON INN *Book at AAA.com* **Phone:** (864)433-8405

Motel
$78-$83 All Year

Address: 1546 E Main St **Location:** I-85, exit 63, 0.4 mi se on SR 290. **Facility:** 42 units. 40 one-bedroom standard units, some with whirlpools. 2 one-bedroom suites. 2 stories (no elevator), exterior corridors. **Parking:** on-site. **Terms:** cancellation fee imposed. **Amenities:** irons, hair dryers. **Pool(s):** outdoor. **Leisure Activities:** exercise room. **Guest Services:** valet laundry, wireless Internet. **Business Services:** PC, fax (fee). **Cards:** AX, DC, DS, MC, VI.

ASK / SOME UNITS FEE

MICROTEL INN — *Book great rates at AAA.com* — **Phone:** (864)433-1000

AAA SAVE

Hotel
$45-$55 All Year

Address: 1534 E Main St **Location:** I-85, exit 63, just se. **Facility:** 61 one-bedroom standard units. 2 stories (no elevator), interior corridors. **Parking:** on-site. **Guest Services:** valet laundry, wireless Internet. **Business Services:** fax (fee). **Cards:** AX, DC, DS, MC, VI. **Free Special Amenities: local telephone calls and high-speed Internet.**

CALL / SOME UNITS

WHERE TO DINE

DEMETRE'S GOURMET GRILLE — **Phone:** 864/433-8788

American
$6-$20

The restaurant's menu incorporates chicken, steak and pasta dishes, including some Italian and Greek choices. The comfortable and relaxed dining room re-creates casual dining under an arbor. Casual dress. **Bar:** Full bar. **Reservations:** accepted. **Hours:** 11 am-10 pm, Fri & Sat-11 pm. Closed major holidays; also Sun except Mother's day. **Address:** 1384 E Main St (SR 290) **Location:** I-85, exit 63, just nw on SR 290. **Parking:** on-site. **Cards:** AX, DS, MC, VI.

CALL

EASLEY pop. 17,754

WHERE TO STAY

COMFORT INN — *Book great rates at AAA.com* — **Phone:** (864)859-7520

AAA SAVE

Motel
$74-$79 All Year

Address: 5539 Calhoun Memorial Hwy **Location:** Jct US 123 and SR 93, just e on US 123. **Facility:** 86 one-bedroom standard units, some with kitchens. 2 stories (no elevator), exterior corridors. **Parking:** on-site. **Amenities:** voice mail, irons, hair dryers. **Pool(s):** outdoor. **Leisure Activities:** picnic area with grill. **Guest Services:** valet laundry, wireless Internet. **Business Services:** meeting rooms, business center. **Cards:** AX, DC, DS, MC, VI.

/ SOME UNITS FEE

HAMPTON INN — *Book great rates at AAA.com* — **Phone:** (864)343-3636

Hotel
$99 All Year

Address: 8 Southern Center Ct **Location:** Jct SR 153/US 123, just w on US 123. **Facility:** 81 one-bedroom standard units. 3 stories, interior corridors. *Bath:* combo or shower only. **Parking:** on-site. **Terms:** 1-30 night minimum stay, cancellation fee imposed. **Amenities:** high-speed Internet, voice mail, safes, irons, hair dryers. **Pool(s):** outdoor. **Leisure Activities:** limited exercise equipment. **Guest Services:** valet laundry, wireless Internet. **Business Services:** meeting rooms, business center. **Cards:** AX, CB, DC, DS, MC, VI.

AAA Benefit:
Members save up to 10% everyday!

JAMESON INN — *Book at AAA.com* — **Phone:** (864)306-9000

Motel
$78-$85 All Year

Address: 211 Dayton School Rd **Location:** Jct US 123 and SR 93, 0.6 mi e on US 123; jct US 123 and SR 153, 1.4 mi w. **Facility:** 58 one-bedroom standard units, some with whirlpools. 2 stories (no elevator), exterior corridors. *Bath:* combo or shower only. **Parking:** on-site. **Terms:** cancellation fee imposed. **Amenities:** hair dryers. *Some:* irons. **Pool(s):** outdoor. **Leisure Activities:** exercise room. **Guest Services:** valet laundry, wireless Internet. **Business Services:** PC, fax (fee). **Cards:** AX, DC, DS, MC, VI.

ASK / SOME UNITS FEE

WHERE TO DINE

FATZ CAFE — **Phone:** 864/859-9832

American
$6-$18

Friendly staff and appealing country decor help set the tone for a relaxed and enjoyable dining experience. It's not unusual for guests to wait to be seated at the popular spot, which earns raves for its well-prepared variations on chicken, steak, ribs and pasta, as well as salads and sandwiches. The signature Southern-style peach cobbler served with vanilla ice cream and walnuts is scrumptious. Casual dress. **Bar:** Full bar. **Hours:** 11 am-10 pm, Fri & Sat-11 pm, Sun-9 pm. Closed: 11/26, 12/25. **Address:** 5051 Calhoun Memorial Pkwy **Location:** Jct US 123/SR 153, 1.5 mi w. **Parking:** on-site. **Cards:** AX, DS, MC, VI.

CALL

FLORENCE pop. 30,248

WHERE TO STAY

BEST WESTERN INN Book great rates at AAA.com **Phone:** (843)678-9292

SAVE

Motel
$69-$79 All Year

Address: 1808 W Lucas St **Location:** I-95, exit 164, just se. Near railroad tracks. **Facility:** 74 one-bedroom standard units, some with whirlpools. 2 stories (no elevator), exterior corridors. **Parking:** on-site. **Terms:** 7 day cancellation notice. **Amenities:** irons, hair dryers. *Some:* high-speed Internet. **Pool(s):** outdoor. **Guest Services:** wireless Internet. **Business Services:** fax (fee). **Cards:** AX, CB, DC, DS, MC, VI. **Free Special Amenities: continental breakfast and high-speed Internet.**

VCR / SOME UNITS

AAA Benefit: Members save up to 20%, plus 10% bonus points with rewards program.

COMFORT INN Book great rates at AAA.com **Phone:** (843)665-4558

SAVE

Motel
$59-$89 All Year

Address: 1916 W Lucas St **Location:** I-95, exit 164, just se. Near railroad tracks. **Facility:** 162 one-bedroom standard units, some with whirlpools. 2 stories (no elevator), interior/exterior corridors. **Parking:** on-site. **Amenities:** voice mail, safes (fee), irons, hair dryers. **Pool(s):** outdoor. **Leisure Activities:** exercise room. **Guest Services:** valet and coin laundry, wireless Internet. **Business Services:** meeting rooms, business center. **Cards:** AX, CB, DC, DS, JC, MC, VI.

/ SOME UNITS FEE

COUNTRY INN & SUITES Book at AAA.com **Phone:** (843)317-6616

Hotel
$81-$250 All Year

Address: 1739 Mandeville Rd **Location:** I-95, exit 164, just nw, then just sw. Near railroad tracks. **Facility:** 80 one-bedroom standard units, some with whirlpools. 3 stories, interior corridors. *Bath:* combo or shower only. **Parking:** on-site. **Terms:** cancellation fee imposed. **Amenities:** high-speed Internet, voice mail, irons, hair dryers. **Pool(s):** outdoor. **Leisure Activities:** exercise room. **Guest Services:** coin laundry, wireless Internet. **Business Services:** meeting rooms, business center. **Cards:** AX, CB, DC, DS, MC, VI.

ASK / SOME UNITS

COURTYARD BY MARRIOTT Book great rates at AAA.com **Phone:** (843)662-7066

Hotel
$119-$127 All Year

Address: 2680 Hospitality Blvd **Location:** I-95, exit 160A, just e, then just s on Radio Dr. Located adjacent to Florence Civic Center. **Facility:** Smoke free premises. 90 units. 87 one-bedroom standard units, some with whirlpools. 3 one-bedroom suites. 3 stories, interior corridors. *Bath:* combo or shower only. **Parking:** on-site. **Terms:** cancellation fee imposed. **Amenities:** high-speed Internet, dual phone lines, voice mail, irons, hair dryers. **Pool(s):** heated indoor. **Leisure Activities:** whirlpool, exercise room. **Guest Services:** valet and coin laundry, wireless Internet. **Business Services:** meeting rooms, business center. **Cards:** AX, CB, DC, DS, JC, MC, VI.

CALL

AAA Benefit: Members save a minimum 5% off the best available rate.

FAIRFIELD INN BY MARRIOTT Book great rates at AAA.com **Phone:** (843)669-1666

Motel
$76-$81 All Year

Address: 140 Dunbarton Dr **Location:** I-95, exit 160A, just e, then just n. Located adjacent to Florence Commons and Magnolia Mall. **Facility:** Smoke free premises. 132 one-bedroom standard units. 3 stories, interior/exterior corridors. *Bath:* combo or shower only. **Parking:** on-site. **Terms:** cancellation fee imposed. **Amenities:** high-speed Internet, irons, hair dryers. **Pool(s):** heated outdoor. **Leisure Activities:** limited exercise equipment. **Guest Services:** valet laundry, wireless Internet. **Business Services:** fax (fee). **Cards:** AX, CB, DC, DS, MC, VI.

CALL / SOME UNITS

AAA Benefit: Members save a minimum 5% off the best available rate.

HAMPTON INN & SUITES **Phone:** 843/413-5115

fyi

Hotel
Rates not provided

Too new to rate, opening scheduled for September 2008. **Address:** 1735 Stokes Rd **Location:** I-95, exit 164 (US 52), just nw. **Amenities:** 136 units, coffeemakers, microwaves, refrigerators.

AAA Benefit: Members save up to 10% everyday!

STOP HERE...ON YOUR WAY THERE!
South Carolina
Smiling Faces Beautiful Places
Rockin' at Darlington Raceway
Fantastic Festivals & Parks
Shopping the Plant & Flower Show
Oudoor Fun & Great Southern Fare
More than 300 Places to Dine and 5,000 Quality Rooms,
Florence is the perfect stop off I-95!
FLORENCE SOUTH CAROLINA
800-325-9005 • www.florencesccvb.com

HAMPTON INN & SUITES *Book great rates at AAA.com* **Phone:** (843)629-9900

Hotel
$79-$225 All Year

Address: 3000 W Radio Dr **Location:** I-95, exit 160A, just e, then just s. Located adjacent to Florence Civic Center. **Facility:** 82 units. 60 one-bedroom standard units. 22 one-bedroom suites with efficiencies. 3 stories, interior corridors. *Bath:* combo or shower only. **Parking:** on-site. **Terms:** 1-30 night minimum stay, cancellation fee imposed. **Amenities:** video games (fee), voice mail, safes, irons, hair dryers. *Some:* dual phone lines. **Pool(s):** outdoor. **Leisure Activities:** whirlpool, limited exercise equipment. **Guest Services:** valet and coin laundry, wireless Internet. **Business Services:** meeting rooms, business center. **Cards:** AX, CB, DC, DS, MC, VI.

Hampton Inn & Suites
AAA Benefit:
Members save up to 10% everyday!

HAMPTON INN-NORTH *Book great rates at AAA.com* **Phone:** (843)662-7000

Motel
$69-$160 All Year

Address: 1826 W Lucas St **Location:** I-95, exit 164, just e on US 52. Near railroad tracks. **Facility:** 122 one-bedroom standard units, some with efficiencies and/or whirlpools. 2 stories (no elevator), exterior corridors. **Parking:** on-site. **Terms:** 1-30 night minimum stay, cancellation fee imposed. **Amenities:** video games (fee), voice mail, safes, irons, hair dryers. **Pool(s):** outdoor. **Guest Services:** valet laundry, wireless Internet. **Business Services:** business center. **Cards:** AX, CB, DC, DS, MC, VI.

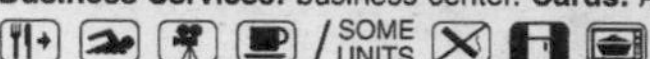

Hampton Inn
AAA Benefit:
Members save up to 10% everyday!

HILTON GARDEN INN *Book great rates at AAA.com* **Phone:** (843)432-3001

Hotel
$99-$169 All Year

Address: 2671 Hospitality Blvd **Location:** I-95, exit 160A, just e, then just s on W Radio Dr. **Facility:** 186 units. 185 one-bedroom standard units, some with whirlpools. 1 one-bedroom suite with whirlpool. 8 stories, interior corridors. *Bath:* combo or shower only. **Parking:** on-site. **Amenities:** video games (fee), high-speed Internet, voice mail, safes, irons, hair dryers. **Pool(s):** heated indoor. **Leisure Activities:** whirlpool, exercise room. **Guest Services:** wireless Internet. **Business Services:** meeting rooms, business center. **Cards:** AX, CB, DC, DS, JC, MC, VI. **Free Special Amenities: newspaper and high-speed Internet.**

CALL / SOME UNITS

Hilton Garden Inn
AAA Benefit:
Members save 5% or more everyday!

HOLIDAY INN EXPRESS CIVIC CENTER *Book great rates at AAA.com* **Phone:** (843)432-1500

Hotel
$99-$134 All Year

Address: 3440 W Radio Dr **Location:** I-95, exit 160A, just e, then just s; adjacent to Civic Center. **Facility:** 87 one-bedroom standard units. 3 stories, interior corridors. *Bath:* combo or shower only. **Parking:** on-site. **Terms:** check-in 4 pm. **Amenities:** high-speed Internet, voice mail, safes, irons, hair dryers. **Pool(s):** heated outdoor. **Leisure Activities:** whirlpool, limited exercise equipment. **Guest Services:** valet laundry, wireless Internet. **Business Services:** meeting rooms, business center. **Cards:** AX, CB, DC, DS, JC, MC, VI. **Free Special Amenities: expanded continental breakfast and high-speed Internet.**

CALL / SOME UNITS

HOLIDAY INN EXPRESS HOTEL & SUITES *Book at AAA.com* **Phone:** (843)629-9779

Hotel
$105-$350 All Year

Address: 2101 Florence Harllee Blvd **Location:** I-95, exit 170, just s. Adjacent to Pee DeeTouchstone Energy Commerce City. **Facility:** 86 one-bedroom standard units, some with whirlpools. 4 stories, interior corridors. *Bath:* combo or shower only. **Parking:** on-site. **Terms:** check-in 4 pm. **Amenities:** high-speed Internet, dual phone lines, voice mail, irons, hair dryers. **Pool(s):** heated indoor. **Leisure Activities:** limited exercise equipment. **Guest Services:** complimentary and valet laundry, wireless Internet. **Business Services:** meeting rooms, business center. **Cards:** AX, CB, DC, DS, JC, MC, VI.

ASK CALL / SOME UNITS

HOLIDAY INN HOTEL & SUITES *Book great rates at AAA.com* **Phone:** (843)665-4555

Hotel
$85-$160 All Year

Address: 1819 W Lucas St **Location:** I-95, exit 164, just se. Near railroad tracks. **Facility:** 202 units. 182 one-bedroom standard units. 20 one-bedroom suites, some with whirlpools. 2 stories (no elevator), exterior corridors. *Bath:* combo or shower only. **Parking:** on-site. **Amenities:** video games (fee), dual phone lines, voice mail, irons, hair dryers. **Pool(s):** outdoor. **Leisure Activities:** limited exercise equipment. **Guest Services:** valet and coin laundry, airport transportation-Florence Municipal Airport, wireless Internet. **Business Services:** conference facilities, fax (fee). **Cards:** AX, DC, DS, MC, VI. **Free Special Amenities: continental breakfast and high-speed Internet.**

CALL / SOME UNITS FEE

HOWARD JOHNSON EXPRESS INN & SUITES *Book great rates at AAA.com* **Phone:** (843)664-9494

Motel
$69 All Year

Address: 3821 Bancroft Rd **Location:** I-95, exit 157, just ne on US 76. **Facility:** 51 one-bedroom standard units, some with whirlpools. 2 stories (no elevator), exterior corridors. *Bath:* combo or shower only. **Parking:** on-site. **Terms:** 4 night minimum stay - seasonal, 60 day cancellation notice. **Amenities:** irons, hair dryers. **Pool(s):** outdoor. **Guest Services:** valet laundry, wireless Internet. **Business Services:** meeting rooms, fax (fee). **Cards:** AX, DC, DS, MC, VI. **Free Special Amenities: expanded continental breakfast and high-speed Internet.**

/ SOME UNITS FEE

MOTEL 6 #1250 *Book at AAA.com* **Phone:** (843)667-6100

Motel

$39-$45 5/2-11/30
$35-$41 12/1-5/1

Address: 1834 W Lucas St **Location:** I-95, exit 164, just sw. Near railroad tracks. **Facility:** 109 one-bedroom standard units. 1 story, exterior corridors. *Bath:* combo or shower only. **Parking:** on-site. **Pool(s):** outdoor. **Guest Services:** coin laundry. **Business Services:** fax (fee). **Cards:** AX, DC, DS, MC, VI.

/ SOME UNITS

QUALITY INN & SUITES *Book great rates at AAA.com* **Phone:** (843)664-2400

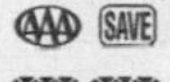

Motel

$59-$100 All Year

Address: 150 Dunbarton Dr **Location:** I-95, exit 160A, just e, then just n. Adjacent to Florence Commons and Magnolia Mall. **Facility:** 80 one-bedroom standard units, some with whirlpools. 2 stories (no elevator), exterior corridors. *Bath:* combo or shower only. **Parking:** on-site. **Amenities:** dual phone lines, voice mail, safes, irons, hair dryers. **Pool(s):** outdoor. **Leisure Activities:** exercise room. **Guest Services:** valet laundry, wireless Internet. **Business Services:** meeting rooms, business center. **Cards:** AX, CB, DC, DS, JC, MC, VI. **Free Special Amenities: full breakfast and high-speed Internet.**
(See color ad below)

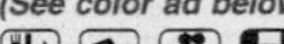
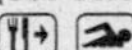
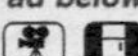

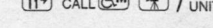

/ SOME UNITS FEE

RED ROOF INN *Book great rates at AAA.com* **Phone:** (843)678-9000

Motel

$45-$125 All Year

Address: 2690 David McLeod Blvd **Location:** I-95, exit 160A, just e on service road. **Facility:** 112 one-bedroom standard units. 2 stories (no elevator), exterior corridors. *Bath:* combo or shower only. **Parking:** on-site. **Amenities:** video games (fee), voice mail. **Guest Services:** valet laundry. **Business Services:** fax (fee). **Cards:** AX, CB, DC, DS, MC, VI. **Free Special Amenities: local telephone calls.**

CALL / SOME UNITS

SLEEP INN *Book great rates at AAA.com* **Phone:** (843)662-8558

Hotel

$70-$250 All Year

Address: 1833 Florence Park Dr **Location:** I-95, exit 164, just nw. Near railroad tracks. **Facility:** 106 one-bedroom standard units. 2 stories (no elevator), interior corridors. *Bath:* combo or shower only. **Parking:** on-site. **Terms:** 3 day cancellation notice-fee imposed. **Amenities:** safes (fee), irons, hair dryers. *Some:* high-speed Internet. **Pool(s):** outdoor. **Leisure Activities:** exercise room. **Guest Services:** valet and coin laundry, wireless Internet. **Business Services:** fax (fee). **Cards:** AX, DC, DS, MC, VI. **Free Special Amenities: expanded continental breakfast and local telephone calls.**

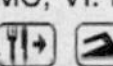

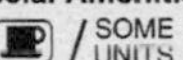

/ SOME UNITS

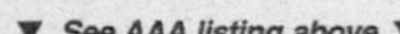
▼ See AAA listing above ▼

SPRINGHILL SUITES BY MARRIOTT *Book great rates at AAA.com* **Phone:** (843)317-9050

Hotel

$119-$127 All Year

Address: 2670 Hospitality Blvd **Location:** I-95, exit 160A, just e, then s. **Facility:** Smoke free premises. 95 one-bedroom standard units. 4 stories, interior corridors. *Bath:* combo or shower only. **Parking:** on-site. **Terms:** cancellation fee imposed. **Amenities:** high-speed Internet, dual phone lines, voice mail, irons, hair dryers. **Pool(s):** heated outdoor. **Leisure Activities:** whirlpool, limited exercise equipment. **Guest Services:** valet and coin laundry, wireless Internet. **Business Services:** business center. **Cards:** AX, DS, MC, VI.

AAA Benefit:

Members save a minimum 5% off the best available rate.

SUBURBAN EXTENDED STAY HOTEL *Book great rates at AAA.com* **Phone:** (843)665-2575

Motel

$49-$59 All Year

Address: 1914 W Lucas St **Location:** I-95, exit 164, just se. Near railroad tracks. **Facility:** 167 one-bedroom standard units, some with efficiencies (no utensils) and/or whirlpools. 2 stories (no elevator), exterior corridors. **Parking:** on-site. **Amenities:** high-speed Internet, voice mail. **Pool(s):** outdoor. **Leisure Activities:** whirlpool, limited exercise equipment. **Guest Services:** wireless Internet. **Cards:** AX, DS, MC, VI. **Free Special Amenities: continental breakfast and high-speed Internet.** ***(See color ad below)***

SUPER 8 MOTEL *Book great rates at AAA.com* **Phone:** (843)661-7267

Motel

$56-$180 All Year

Address: 1832 1/2 W Lucas St **Location:** I-95, exit 164, just se. Near railroad tracks. **Facility:** 67 one-bedroom standard units. 2 stories (no elevator), exterior corridors. **Parking:** on-site. **Terms:** cancellation fee imposed. **Amenities:** hair dryers. **Pool(s):** outdoor. **Guest Services:** wireless Internet. **Business Services:** fax (fee). **Cards:** DS, MC, VI. **Free Special Amenities: continental breakfast and high-speed Internet.**

SOME UNITS FEE

▼ *See AAA listing above* ▼

WINGATE INN Book at AAA.com **Phone:** (843)629-1111

Hotel
$81-$89 All Year

Address: 2123 W Lucas St **Location:** I-95, exit 164, 0.4 mi nw. Near railroad tracks. **Facility:** 84 one-bedroom standard units, some with whirlpools. 3 stories, interior corridors. *Bath:* combo or shower only. **Parking:** on-site. **Amenities:** video games (fee), high-speed Internet, dual phone lines, voice mail, safes, irons, hair dryers. **Pool(s):** outdoor. **Leisure Activities:** whirlpool, exercise room. **Guest Services:** valet laundry, wireless Internet. **Business Services:** meeting rooms, business center. **Cards:** AX, DC, DS, JC, MC, VI.

ASK CALL / SOME UNITS

WHERE TO DINE

ANGELO'S SEAFOOD RESTAURANT **Phone:** 843/665-6132

American
$3-$17

The extremely popular family-operated restaurant serves excellent seafood in a cafeteria-style atmosphere. A drive-through window caters to those in a rush. Casual dress. **Bar:** Beer only. **Hours:** 11 am-10 pm. Closed major holidays; also Sun. **Address:** 1243 W Lucas St (US 52) **Location:** I-95, exit 164, 0.8 mi se. **Parking:** on-site. **Cards:** AX, DS, MC, VI.

CALL

CAFE FLORENTINE **Phone:** 843/669-9621

Continental
$6-$25

In operation since 1991, the restaurant still maintains that it's the best-kept secret in Florence. The small, family-operated bistro features friendly, efficient service and a Northern Italian menu with a Mediterranean flair. Casual dress. **Bar:** Full bar. **Reservations:** accepted. **Hours:** 11 am-2 & 5:30-10 pm, Sat from 5:30 pm. Closed: 12/25; also Sun & Mon. **Address:** 804-C Second Loop Rd **Location:** Jct US 52/Second Loop Rd, just w; in Huntington Plaza. **Parking:** on-site. **Cards:** AX, MC, VI.

FATZ CAFE **Phone:** 843/413-9186

American
$6-$18

Friendly staff and appealing country decor help set the tone for a relaxed and enjoyable dining experience. It's not unusual for guests to wait to be seated at the popular spot, which earns raves for its well-prepared variations on chicken, steak, ribs and pasta, as well as salads and sandwiches. The signature Southern-style peach cobbler served with vanilla ice cream and walnuts is scrumptious. Casual dress. **Bar:** Full bar. **Hours:** 11 am-10 pm, Fri & Sat-11 pm. Closed: 11/26, 12/25. **Address:** 2007 W Lucas St **Location:** I-95, exit 164, just nw. **Parking:** on-site. **Cards:** AX, DS, MC, VI.

CALL

INDIGO JOE'S SPORTS PUB & RESTAURANT **Phone:** 843/667-3888

American
$8-$19

In the growing southwest section of town, the restaurant lines up walls of high-definition TVs, 20 ice-cold draft beers, a wide selection of alcoholic and nonalcoholic specialty drinks and an unusual menu. Accompanying typical bar foods of burgers, sandwiches and fries are healthier alternatives, such as the fresh vegetable basket and fruit and cheese platter. Choosing one of the latter might ease the guilt of those who opt for one of the huge desserts, such as the tripe fudge brownie. Casual dress. **Bar:** Full bar. **Hours:** 11 am-10 pm, Fri & Sat-11 pm. Closed: 11/26, 12/25. **Address:** 3410 S Radio Dr **Location:** I-95, exit 160A, just e, then just s; adjacent to cinema. **Parking:** on-site. **Cards:** AX, DS, MC, VI.

CALL

MICHAEL'S ON THE LOOP **Phone:** 843/669-3771

Italian
$7-$27

Homemade Italian wedding soup, fresh pizza and traditional Italian American standards are featured on the menu at this popular family eatery. Casual dress. **Bar:** Full bar. **Reservations:** accepted. **Hours:** 11:30 am-10 pm. Closed: 1/1, 11/26, 12/25; also Sun & Mon. **Address:** 1937 Second Loop Rd **Location:** Jct US 76/Second Loop Rd, 1.3 mi s; in Sweetbriar Center. **Parking:** on-site. **Cards:** AX, DS, MC, VI.

PERCY & WILLIE'S FOOD AND SPIRITS **Phone:** 843/669-1620

American
$9-$24

Steaks are juicy and tender at the bustling restaurant. The rib-eye is marinated in a blend of fruit juices and seasonings for 72 hours and then grilled to perfection. For dessert, try fresh apple pie topped with ice cream. Casual dress. **Bar:** Full bar. **Hours:** 11 am-10 pm, Fri & Sat-11 pm, Sun-9 pm. Closed: 11/26, 12/25. **Address:** 2401 David McLeod Blvd **Location:** I-95, exit 160A (I-20 business), 1 mi e. **Parking:** on-site. **Cards:** AX, DC, MC, VI.

REDBONE ALLEY RESTAURANT & BAR **Phone:** 843/673-0035

American
$6-$25

Diners seated indoors might feel as though they're at an old-timey sidewalk cafe, complete with a Good Humor truck and painted mural of a back yard. The menu centers on Southern fusion cuisine, with such specialties as Lowcountry shrimp and grits: spicy fried shrimp on creamy cheese grits topped with smoked ham, mushrooms and green onions. Among choices of lighter fare are many entree-size salads. Casual dress. **Bar:** Full bar. **Reservations:** accepted. **Hours:** 11:30 am-10 pm, Fri & Sat-11 pm, Sun-9 pm. Closed major holidays. **Address:** 1903 W Palmetto St **Location:** Jct I-20 business/US 76, just n; in Florence Mall. **Parking:** on-site. **Cards:** AX, DS, MC, VI.

STARFIRE GRILL & SPIRITS **Phone:** 843/661-7827

American
$8-$25

In a commercial area, the restaurant offers pleasant interior surroundings and friendly, efficient service. Meals reflect Greek and Italian influences. Casual dress. **Bar:** Full bar. **Hours:** 10:30 am-10 pm, Fri & Sat-11 pm. Closed major holidays; also Sun & Mon. **Address:** 2130 W Palmetto St **Location:** Jct I-20 business/US 76, just sw. **Parking:** on-site. **Cards:** AX, DS, MC, VI.

STEFANO'S ITALIAN RESTAURANT **Phone:** 843/664-9191

Italian
$4-$16

Guests can order a pizza for take-out or have a seat in the casual dining room. The menu features a lengthy list of pasta dishes, as well as beef, seafood and chicken entrees. Casual dress. **Bar:** Full bar. **Hours:** 11 am-9 pm, Wed & Thurs-10 pm, Fri & Sat-11 pm. Closed: major holidays; also 12/24, Sun & week of 7/4. **Address:** 2600 S Irby St **Location:** 2.6 mi s on US 301 and 52; in South Market Shopping Center. **Parking:** on-site. **Cards:** AX, DS, MC, VI.

VICTOR'S BISTRO & GARDEN ROOM **Phone:** 843/665-0846

Steak & Seafood
$7-$35

Guests can choose from an array of succulent seafood entrees, such as grilled salmon, alligator and lemon-peppered grilled shrimp and scallops with fresh local produce. The romantic bistro offers a fine dining experience. Dressy casual. Entertainment. **Bar:** Full bar. **Reservations:** suggested. **Hours:** 11:30 am-2 & 5-10 pm, Mon from 5 pm. Closed major holidays; also Sun. **Address:** 1247 S Irby St **Location:** Jct SR 51, 0.4 mi n on US 52. **Parking:** on-site. **Cards:** AX, DS, MC, VI.

FOLLY BEACH *—See Charleston p. 909.*

FORT MILL *—See Nearby Nc City Of Charlotte p. 668.*

GAFFNEY pop. 12,968

WHERE TO STAY

HAMPTON INN *Book great rates at AAA.com* **Phone:** (864)206-0011

Hotel
$115-$125 All Year

Address: 115 Nancy Creek Rd **Location:** I-85, exit 90, just nw. **Facility:** 85 one-bedroom standard units, some with whirlpools. 4 stories, interior corridors. *Bath:* combo or shower only. **Parking:** on-site. **Terms:** 1-30 night minimum stay, cancellation fee imposed. **Amenities:** dual phone lines, voice mail, irons, hair dryers. **Pool(s):** outdoor. **Guest Services:** valet laundry, wireless Internet. **Business Services:** meeting rooms, business center. **Cards:** AX, CB, DC, DS, MC, VI.

CALL / SOME UNITS

AAA Benefit:
Members save up to 10% everyday!

JAMESON INN *Book at AAA.com* **Phone:** (864)489-0240

Motel
$78-$85 All Year

Address: 101 Stuard St **Location:** I-85, exit 92, 0.5 mi se on SR 11/W Floyd Baker Blvd. **Facility:** 58 one-bedroom standard units. 2 stories (no elevator), exterior corridors. *Bath:* combo or shower only. **Parking:** on-site. **Terms:** cancellation fee imposed. **Amenities:** irons, hair dryers. **Pool(s):** outdoor. **Leisure Activities:** exercise room. **Guest Services:** valet laundry, wireless Internet. **Business Services:** PC, fax (fee). **Cards:** AX, DC, DS, MC, VI.

ASK / SOME UNITS FEE

SLEEP INN **Phone:** (864)487-5337

Hotel
$84-$90 All Year

Address: 834 Winslow Ave **Location:** I-85, exit 90, just se, then ne on frontage road. **Facility:** 60 one-bedroom standard units. 3 stories, interior corridors. *Bath:* combo or shower only. **Parking:** on-site. **Terms:** cancellation fee imposed. **Amenities:** voice mail, hair dryers. **Pool(s):** outdoor. **Leisure Activities:** limited exercise equipment. **Guest Services:** valet laundry, wireless Internet. **Business Services:** meeting rooms, business center. **Cards:** AX, DS, MC, VI.

ASK CALL / SOME UNITS FEE

SUPER 8 MOTEL *Book great rates at AAA.com* **Phone:** (864)489-1699

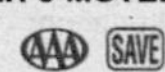

Motel
$54 All Year

Address: 100 Ellis Ferry Ave **Location:** I-85, exit 92, 0.7 mi se on SR 11/W Floyd Baker Blvd. **Facility:** 58 one-bedroom standard units. 2 stories (no elevator), exterior corridors. *Bath:* combo or shower only. **Parking:** on-site. **Terms:** cancellation fee imposed. **Amenities:** irons, hair dryers. **Pool(s):** outdoor. **Leisure Activities:** exercise room. **Guest Services:** valet laundry, wireless Internet. **Business Services:** meeting rooms, fax (fee). **Cards:** AX, CB, DC, DS, JC, MC, VI. **Free Special Amenities: continental breakfast and high-speed Internet.**

/ SOME UNITS FEE

WHERE TO DINE

FATZ CAFE **Phone:** 864/488-0310

American
$7-$19

Friendly staff and appealing country decor help set the tone for a relaxed and enjoyable dining experience. It's not unusual for guests to wait to be seated at the popular spot, which earns raves for its well-prepared variations on chicken, steak, ribs and pasta, as well as salads and sandwiches. The signature Southern-style peach cobbler served with vanilla ice cream and walnuts is scrumptious. Casual dress. **Bar:** Full bar. **Hours:** 11 am-10 pm, Fri & Sat-11 pm, Sun-9 pm. Closed: 11/26, 12/25. **Address:** 294 Peachoid Rd **Location:** I-85, exit 90 northbound, just nw, then 1.8 mi ne; exit 92 southbound, just nw, then 0.5 mi w. **Parking:** on-site. **Cards:** AX, DS, MC, VI.

CALL

SAGEBRUSH STEAKHOUSE **Phone:** 864/487-7350

American
$5-$19

Born from the spirit of Texas cattle drives, the restaurant presents a menu of hearty steaks, prime rib, chicken, seafood and baby back ribs. Yummy desserts merit a splurge. Guests can call ahead to facilitate seating. Casual dress. **Bar:** Full bar. **Hours:** 11 am-10 pm, Fri & Sat-11 pm. Closed: 12/25. **Address:** 1541 W Floyd Baker Blvd **Location:** I-85, exit 92, just se. **Parking:** on-site. **Cards:** AX, DC, DS, MC, VI.

CALL

GARDEN CITY BEACH *—See The Grand Strand p. 1043.*

GEORGETOWN *—See The Grand Strand p. 1043.*

GOOSE CREEK *—See Charleston p. 909.*

Destination The Grand Strand

Although oriented to water-based activities, The Grand Strand also is a golfing paradise. A mild climate and balmy ocean breezes make this stretch of coast popular year-round.

So grab your raft and hit the waves. Or head for the nearest links. If fishing is your thing, drop a line right off a pier or charter a boat for deep-sea action. Maybe hunt for some bargains; there are plenty of shops in which to find that perfect souvenir.

Myrtle Beach Area Chamber of Commerce

Myrtle Beach.
This Atlantic Coast destination offers scenic views and relaxation.

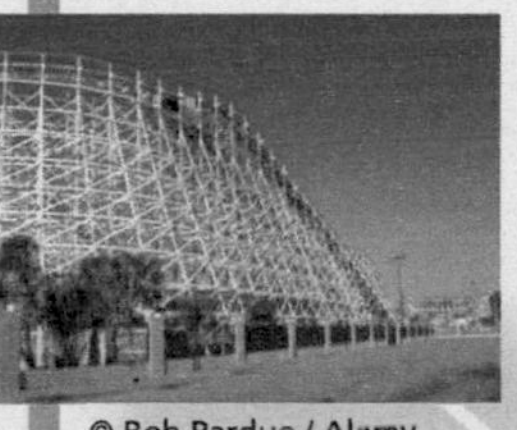

© Bob Pardue / Alamy

Family Kingdom Amusement Park, Myrtle Beach.
This park's carousel, Ferris wheel and wooden roller coaster appeal to visitors looking for the feel of an old-time amusement park. (See listing page 256)

Myrtle Beach Area Chamber of Commerce

Golf course, Myrtle Beach.
Dozens of courses along The Grand Strand lure avid golfers.

The Grand Strand

Loris, Conway, Little River, North Myrtle Beach, Myrtle Beach, Surfside Beach, Garden City Beach, Murrells Inlet, Pawleys Island, Georgetown

See Vicinity map page 970

Myrtle Beach Area Chamber of Commerce

Fishing, Myrtle Beach.
Cast your line and try out the local water.

Places included in this AAA Destination Area:

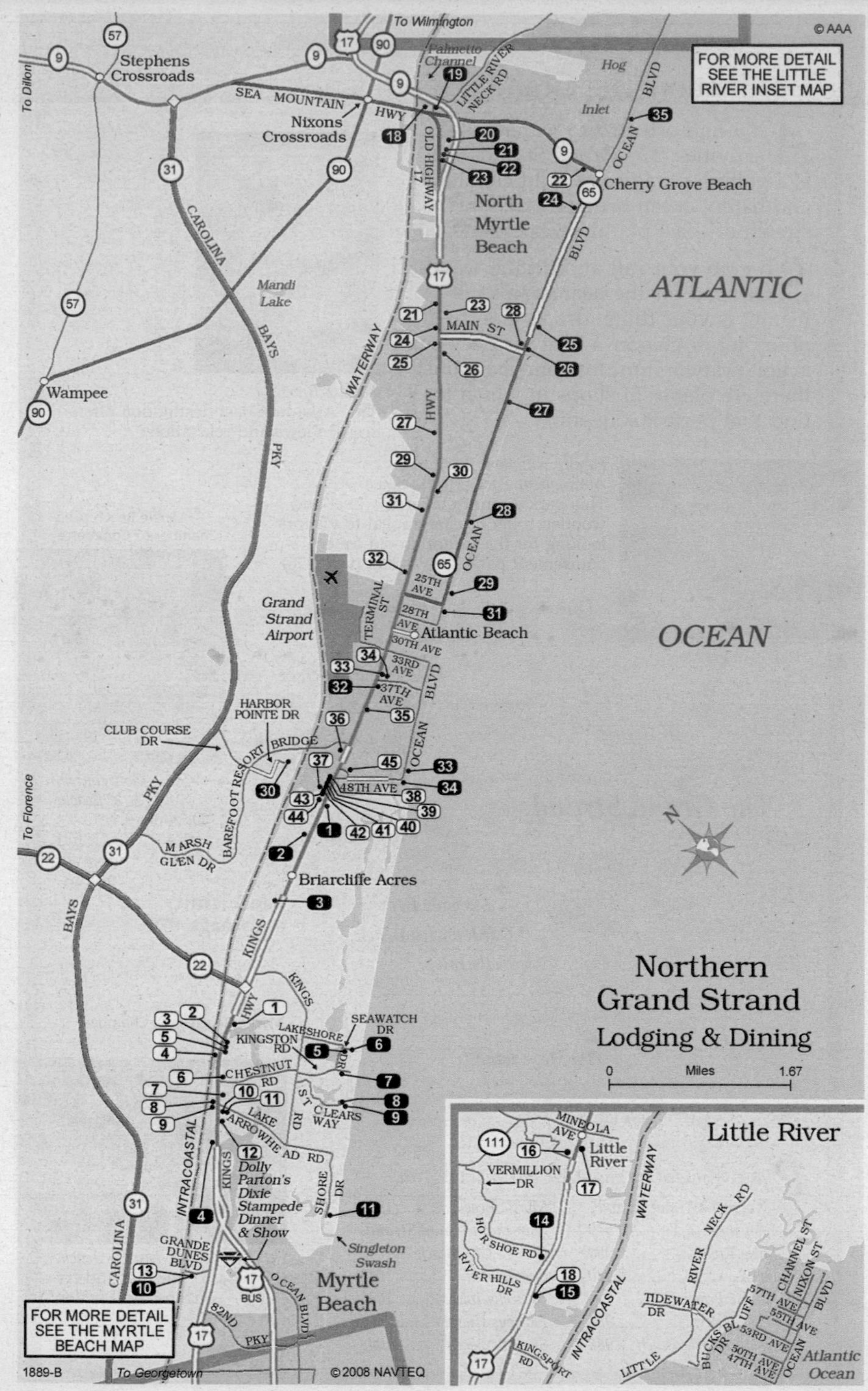

Northern Grand Strand
Lodging & Dining
Little River
FOR MORE DETAIL SEE THE LITTLE RIVER INSET MAP
FOR MORE DETAIL SEE THE MYRTLE BEACH MAP
ATLANTIC OCEAN
Stephens Crossroads
Nixons Crossroads
North Myrtle Beach
Cherry Grove Beach
Atlantic Beach
Grand Strand Airport
Briarcliffe Acres
Wampee
Myrtle Beach
Dolly Parton's Dixie Stampede Dinner & Show
To Wilmington
To Dillon
To Florence
To Georgetown
© AAA
1889-B
©2008 NAVTEQ
Miles 0 1.67

Northern Grand Strand

This index helps you "spot" where approved lodgings and restaurants are located on the corresponding detailed maps. Lodging daily rate range is for comparison only and show the property's high season. Restaurant rate range is a combination of lunch and/or dinner. Turn to the listing page for more detailed rate information and consult display ads for special promotions.

MYRTLE BEACH (NORTHERN)

Map Page	OA	Lodgings	Diamond Rated	High Season	Page
1 / p. 966	AAA	**Ocean Creek Resort - see color ad p 1009**	◆◆◆	$55-$390 SAVE	984
2 / p. 966	AAA	**Courtyard by Marriott Barefoot Landing**	◆◆◆	$99-$159 SAVE	981
3 / p. 966		Fairfield Inn by Marriott Myrtle Beach North	◆◆◆	$71-$143	981
4 / p. 966	AAA	**Holiday Inn Express Restaurant Row**	◆◆◆	$65-$299 SAVE	983
5 / p. 966		Wyndham SeaWatch Plantation	◆◆◆	Rates not provided	985
6 / p. 966	AAA	**Sea Watch Resort - see color ad p 1009**	◆◆◆	$65-$399 SAVE	985
7 / p. 966	AAA	**Hilton Myrtle Beach Resort - see color ad p 982**	◆◆◆	$104-$279 SAVE	983
8 / p. 966	AAA	**Embassy Suites at Kingston Plantation - see color ad p 982**	◆◆◆	$54-$214 SAVE	981
9 / p. 966		Embassy Suites/Kingston Plantation	◆◆◆	$89-$319	981
10 / p. 966	AAA	**Marina Inn at Grande Dunes**	◆◆◆◆	$134-$499 SAVE	983
11 / p. 966		Sands Beach Club Resort	◆◆◆	$69-$299	985

Map Page	OA	Restaurants	Diamond Rated	Cuisine	Meal Range	Page
1 / p. 966		Goober's 52	◆◆	American	$6-$16	986
2 / p. 966		Chestnut Hill	◆◆◆	American	$18-$30	986
3 / p. 966		Chesapeake House	◆◆	Regional American	$11-$40	986
4 / p. 966		Cagney's Old Place	◆◆	Steak & Seafood	$12-$30	986
5 / p. 966	AAA	**Nakato Japanese Steak House**	◆◆	Japanese	$8-$29	987
6 / p. 966		Miyabi Kyoto Japanese Steak & Seafood House	◆◆	Japanese	$11-$30	987
7 / p. 966		Thoroughbreds Chophouse & Seafood Grille	◆◆◆	Continental	$20-$39	987
8 / p. 966		Captain Bennett's Calabash Seafood #2	◆	Seafood	$18-$29	986
9 / p. 966	AAA	**Chuck's Steak House**	◆◆	Steak	$7-$47	986
10 / p. 966		China Buffet	◆	Chinese	$4-$12	986
11 / p. 966	AAA	**Umi Pacific Grille**	◆◆◆◆	Pacific Rim	$18-$60	987
12 / p. 966		Rossi's Italian Restaurant	◆◆◆	Regional Italian	$15-$32	987
13 / p. 966		Waterscapes at the Marina Inn	◆◆◆	American	$9-$38	987

LITTLE RIVER

Map Page	OA	Lodgings	Diamond Rated	High Season	Page
14 / p. 966		Sleep Inn	◆◆	$49-$189	980
15 / p. 966	AAA	**Holiday Inn Hotel & Suites-North Myrtle Beach**	◆◆◆	$49-$229 SAVE	980

Map Page	OA	Restaurants	Diamond Rated	Cuisine	Meal Range	Page
16 / p. 966	AAA	**The Brentwood Restaurant & Wine Bar**	◆◆◆	Continental	$15-$36	980

Map Page	OA	Restaurants (cont'd)	Diamond Rated	Cuisine	Meal Range	Page
17 / p. 966	AAA	**The Parson's Table**	◆◆◆	Continental	$15-$28	980
18 / p. 966		Umberto's at Coquina Harbor	◆◆	Traditional Italian	$14-$35	980

NORTH MYRTLE BEACH

Map Page	OA	Lodgings	Diamond Rated	High Season	Page
18 / p. 966	AAA	**Harbourgate Resort & Marina - see color ad on insert**	◆◆◆	$41-$195 SAVE	989
19 / p. 966		Hampton Inn Harbourgate	◆◆◆	$65-$336	989
20 / p. 966		Comfort Inn - North	◆◆	$60-$189	988
21 / p. 966	AAA	**Quality Inn & Suites**	◆◆◆	$59-$189 SAVE	992
22 / p. 966		La Quinta Inn-North Myrtle Beach	◆◆	$49-$169	989
23 / p. 966	AAA	**Super 8 North Point**	◆◆	$69-$149 SAVE	992
24 / p. 966	AAA	**Tilghman Beach & Golf Resort - see color ad p 993**	◆◆◆	$89-$269 SAVE	993
25 / p. 966	AAA	**Avista Resort - see color ad starting on p 1018**	◆◆◆	$90-$490 SAVE	988
26 / p. 966	AAA	**Ocean Drive Beach & Golf Resort - see color ad p 991**	◆◆◆	$36-$184 SAVE	990
27 / p. 966		Mar Vista Grande - see color ad p 990	◆◆◆	Rates not provided	990
28 / p. 966	AAA	**Best Western Ocean Sands Resort**	◆◆	$70-$396 SAVE	988
29 / p. 966	AAA	**SeaSide - see color ad starting on p 1018**	◆◆◆	$90-$490 SAVE	992
30 / p. 966	AAA	**Yacht Club Villas-Beach Vacations - see color ad on insert**	◆◆◆	$59-$238 SAVE	993
31 / p. 966	AAA	**Bay Watch Resort - see color ad on insert**	◆◆◆	$49-$277 SAVE	988
32 / p. 966		Super 8-Barefoot Landing	◆◆	Rates not provided	992
33 / p. 966	AAA	**Shore Crest Vacation Villas - see color ad p 1010**	◆◆◆	$179-$382 SAVE	992
34 / p. 966	AAA	**Beach Cove Resort - see color ad p 1009**	◆◆◆	$65-$394 SAVE	988
35 / p. 966		Prince Resort at Cherry Grove Pier - see color ad starting on p 1018	◆◆◆	Rates not provided	992

Map Page	OA	Restaurants	Diamond Rated	Cuisine	Meal Range	Page
21 / p. 966	AAA	**SeaBlue Tapas Bar**	◆◆◆	Small Plates	$6-$20	996
22 / p. 966		Duffy Street Seafood Shack	◆	Seafood	$8-$26	994
23 / p. 966		The Grill House	◆◆	American	$6-$24	995
24 / p. 966		Villa Tuscanna	◆◆◆	Regional Italian	$7-$28	996
25 / p. 966		Martini's Casual Dining & Piano Bar	◆◆◆	Continental	$19-$30	995
26 / p. 966		Bonefish Grill	◆◆◆	Steak & Seafood	$13-$20	994
27 / p. 966		Mexico Lindo Mexican Restaurant	◆◆	Mexican	$5-$13	995
28 / p. 966		Duffy Street Seafood Shack	◆	Seafood	$8-$26	994
29 / p. 966		Ocean Garden Restaurant	◆	Chinese	$6-$18	995
30 / p. 966	AAA	**Benny Rappa's Trattoria**	◆◆	Italian	$8-$25	994
31 / p. 966		Benito's Brick Oven Pizza & Pasta	◆◆	Italian	$9-$19	994
32 / p. 966		Dino's House of Pancakes	◆	American	$3-$8	994

Map Page	OA	Restaurants (cont'd)	Diamond Rated	Cuisine	Meal Range	Page
33 / p. 966		Rockefellers Raw Bar	♦♦	Seafood	$7-$60	996
34 / p. 966	AAA	**Horst Gasthaus**	♦♦	German	$13-$19	995
35 / p. 966		Oscar's Food & Spirits	♦♦	American	$6-$11	995
36 / p. 966		House of Blues Restaurant	♦♦♦	Southern American	$9-$26	995
37 / p. 966		"The Original" Umberto's at Barefoot Landing	♦♦	Italian	$16-$30	996
38 / p. 966		Dick's Last Resort	♦♦	American	$7-$18	994
39 / p. 966		TBonz Gill & Grill	♦♦	Steak & Seafood	$6-$21	996
40 / p. 966		River City Cafe	♦	American	$4-$13	995
41 / p. 966		The Crab House	♦♦	Seafood	$8-$40 SAVE	994
42 / p. 966		Ultimate California Pizza	♦	Pizza	$6-$20	996
43 / p. 966		Fire Island Grille	♦♦	American	$9-$35	994
44 / p. 966	AAA	**Greg Norman's Australian Grille**	♦♦♦	Steak & Seafood	$9-$30	995
45 / p. 966		Joe's Bar & Grill	♦♦	Continental	$16-$36	995

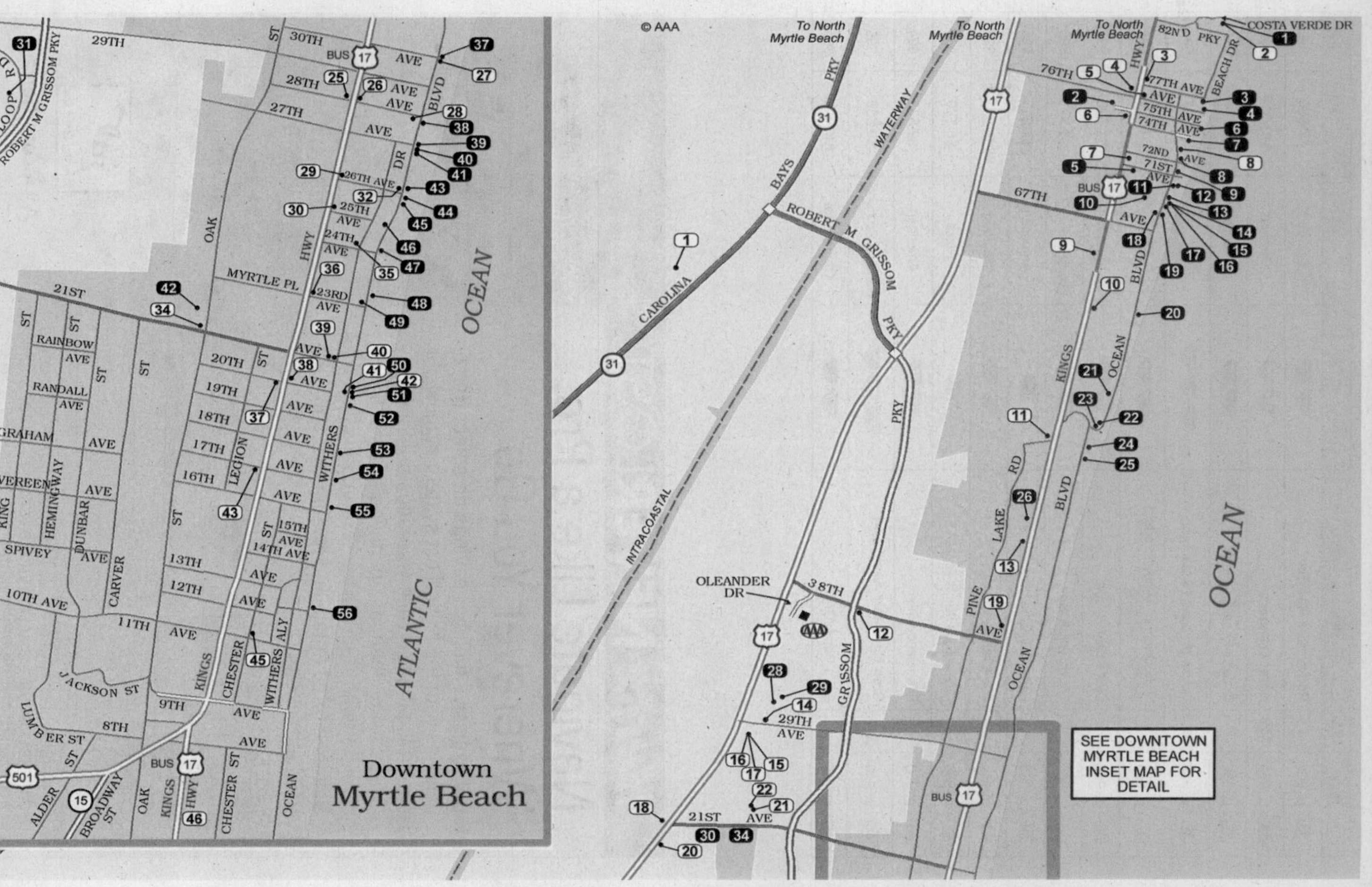
© AAA
To North Myrtle Beach
To North Myrtle Beach
To North Myrtle Beach
COSTA VERDE DR
82ND PKY
BEACH DR
77TH AVE
76TH AVE
75TH AVE
74TH AVE
72ND AVE
71ST AVE
67TH AVE
KINGS HWY
OCEAN BLVD
LAKE RD
PINE AVE
38TH
OLEANDER DR
29TH AVE
21ST AVE
ROBERT M GRISSOM PKY
GRISSOM
CAROLINA BAYS PKY
INTRACOASTAL WATERWAY
OCEAN
SEE DOWNTOWN MYRTLE BEACH INSET MAP FOR DETAIL
Downtown Myrtle Beach
ATLANTIC
OCEAN
29TH
LOOP RD
ROBERT M GRISSOM PKY
30TH AVE
28TH AVE
27TH AVE
26TH AVE
25TH AVE
24TH AVE
23RD AVE
MYRTLE PL
21ST
20TH ST
19TH
18TH
17TH
16TH ST
15TH AVE
14TH AVE
13TH
12TH
11TH AVE
10TH AVE
9TH AVE
8TH AVE
OAK
LEGION
WITHERS DR
WITHERS ALY
CHESTER
RAINBOW AVE
RANDALL AVE
GRAHAM AVE
VEREEN AVE
KING
HEMINGWAY
DUNBAR
SPIVEY AVE
CARVER
JACKSON ST
LUMBER ST
ALDER
BROADWAY ST

Myrtle Beach
Lodging & Dining
0
Miles
0.95
888-B
ATLANTIC
N
Myrtle Beach International Airport
Myrtle Beach State Park
Withers Swash
OCEAN BLVD
KINGS HWY
17TH AVE
HARRELSON BLVD
ROBERT
10TH AVE
SHETLAND LN
OLD SOCASTEE HWY
EMORY RD
FARROW PKY
WATERWAY
INTRACOASTAL
HARBOUR BLVD
OUTLET BLVD
GEORGE BISHOP PKY
FORESTBROOK RD
SOCASTEE BLVD
BUS
To Georgetown
To Conway
© 2008 NAVTEQ

Myrtle Beach

This index helps you "spot" where approved lodgings and restaurants are located on the corresponding detailed maps. Lodging daily rate range is for comparison only and show the property's high season. Restaurant rate range is a combination of lunch and/or dinner. Turn to the listing page for more detailed rate information and consult display ads for special promotions.

MYRTLE BEACH

Map Page	OA	Lodgings	Diamond Rated	High Season	Page
1 / p. 970	AAA	**Myrtle Beach Marriott Resort at Grande Dunes**	◆◆◆◆	$150-$310 SAVE	1027
2 / p. 970		Hampton Inn-Northwood	◆◆◆	$69-$199	1017
3 / p. 970	AAA	**Grande Shores - see color ad starting on p 1018**	◆◆◆	$60-$470 SAVE	1016
4 / p. 970	AAA	**Carolina Winds - see color ad p 1001**	◆◆	$42-$359 SAVE	1011
5 / p. 970		Serendipity Inn	◆◆◆	Rates not provided	1034
6 / p. 970		Ocean Dunes Resort & Villas	◆◆	$59-$209	1027
7 / p. 970		Sand Dunes Resort Hotel	◆◆◆	$59-$249	1032
8 / p. 970	AAA	**The Long Bay Resort - see color ad on insert**	◆◆◆	$36-$531 SAVE	1026
9 / p. 970	AAA	**The Ocean Reef Resort - see color ad on insert**	◆◆◆	$57-$611 SAVE	1028
10 / p. 970		The Caravelle Resort-Sea Mark Towers	◆◆◆	$89-$399	1008
11 / p. 970		The Caravelle Resort-Caravelle Towers	◆◆	$155-$199	1007
12 / p. 970		The Caravelle Resort-St. Clements Tower	◆◆◆	$67-$199	1008
13 / p. 970	AAA	**The Caravelle Resort Hotel - see color ad p 1009**	◆◆◆	$55-$345 SAVE	1008
14 / p. 970		The Caravelle Resort-Drydock Villas	◆◆	$94-$195	1007
15 / p. 970		The Caravelle Resort-Arbor Villas	◆◆	$94-$195	1007
16 / p. 970		The Caravelle Resort-Harborside Villas	◆◆	$94-$195	1008
17 / p. 970		The Caravelle Resort-Carolina Dunes	◆◆◆	$89-$390	1007
18 / p. 970	AAA	**St. John's Inn**	◆◆	$50-$125 SAVE	1031
19 / p. 970	AAA	**Monterey Bay Suites**	◆◆◆	$65-$259 SAVE	1027
20 / p. 970	AAA	**Island Vista - see color ad on insert**	◆◆◆	$68-$615 SAVE	1025
21 / p. 970		Ocean Forest Villas	◆◆	$69-$239	1028
22 / p. 970		Ocean Forest Plaza	◆◆◆	$59-$169	1027
23 / p. 970	AAA	**Forest Dunes Resort - see color ad p 1001**	◆◆	$41-$339 SAVE	1016
24 / p. 970	AAA	**Beach Colony Resort - see color ad p 1000**	◆◆◆	$45-$431 SAVE	998
25 / p. 970	AAA	**Dunes Village Resort - see color ad on insert**	◆◆◆	$41-$597 SAVE	1016
26 / p. 970		La Quinta Inn Myrtle Beach	◆◆◆	$59-$199	1026
27 / p. 970		Country Inn & Suites at Waccamaw	◆◆◆	$59-$259	1011
28 / p. 970	AAA	**Fairfield Inn-Broadway At The Beach**	◆◆◆	$102-$164 SAVE	1016
29 / p. 970	AAA	**Holiday Inn Express-Broadway at the Beach**	◆◆◆	$69-$209 SAVE	1024
30 / p. 970		La Quinta Inn & Suites Myrtle Beach	◆◆◆	$69-$189	1025
31 / p. 970		Hampton Inn Broadway at the Beach	◆◆◆	$139-$339	1017
32 / p. 970		Holiday Inn Hard Rock Parkway	◆◆◆	$79-$189	1024
33 / p. 970		Staybridge Suites-Fantasy Harbour	◆◆◆	$80-$280	1035
34 / p. 970	AAA	**Courtyard by Marriott-Myrtle Beach Broadway**	◆◆◆	$81-$164 SAVE	1014
35 / p. 970	AAA	**Harbour Lights Resort - see color ad p 1010**	◆◆◆	$118-$382 SAVE	1017

MYRTLE BEACH (cont'd)

Map Page	OA	Lodgings (cont'd)	Diamond Rated	High Season	Page
36 / p. 970		Comfort Suites	♦♦♦	$59-$259	1011
37 / p. 970	AAA	**The Caribbean Resort & Villas** - see color ad on insert	♦♦♦	$47-$492 SAVE	1008
38 / p. 970	AAA	**Patricia Grand Resort Hotel** - see color ad on insert	♦♦♦	$48-$210 SAVE	1031
39 / p. 970	AAA	**The Breakers North Tower** - see color ad on insert	♦♦♦	$37-$550 SAVE	1004
40 / p. 970	AAA	**Court Capri** - see color ad p 1014	♦♦	$79-$129 SAVE	1014
41 / p. 970	AAA	**Sea Dip Motel & Condominium Resort** - see color ad p 1014	♦♦	$30-$165 SAVE	1034
42 / p. 970	AAA	**Sheraton Myrtle Beach Convention Center Hotel** - see color ad p 1034	♦♦♦	$99-$249 SAVE	1034
43 / p. 970	AAA	**The Anderson Ocean Club and Spa** - see color ad on insert	♦♦♦	$59-$319 SAVE	996
44 / p. 970	AAA	**Best Western Carolinian Beach Resort** - see color ad on insert	♦♦♦	$46-$415 SAVE	1004
45 / p. 970	AAA	**Palms Resort** - see color ad p 1003	♦♦	$55-$499 SAVE	1031
46 / p. 970	AAA	**Carolina Grande** - see color ad p 1010	♦♦♦	$124-$412 SAVE	1008
47 / p. 970	AAA	**Dayton House Resort** - see color ad p 1015	♦♦♦	$49-$239 SAVE	1015
48 / p. 970	AAA	**Meridian Plaza** - see color ad p 1026	♦♦♦	$43-$201 SAVE	1026
49 / p. 970	AAA	**Boardwalk Beach Resort** - see color ad p 1006	♦♦	$40-$300 SAVE	1004
50 / p. 970	AAA	**The Breakers Resort Hotel** - see color ad on insert	♦♦♦	$44-$430 SAVE	1007
51 / p. 970		The Breakers Paradise Tower - see color ad on insert	♦♦♦	$52-$545	1005
52 / p. 970	AAA	**Camelot by the Sea** - see color ad on insert	♦♦♦	$51-$280 SAVE	1007
53 / p. 970	AAA	**Sandcastle Oceanfront Resort at the Pavilion** - see color ad p 1032	♦♦	$59-$240 SAVE	1032
54 / p. 970	AAA	**Atlantic Coast Resorts** - see color ad p 998	♦♦♦	$30-$250 SAVE	998
55 / p. 970	AAA	**Roxanne Towers**	♦♦♦	$54-$299 SAVE	1031
56 / p. 970	AAA	**Holiday Inn "At The Pavilion"** - see color ad starting on p 1012	♦♦♦	$45-$215 SAVE	1024
57 / p. 970	AAA	**Bay View Resort** - see color ad on insert	♦♦♦	$69-$604 SAVE	998
58 / p. 970	AAA	**The Windsurfer Hotel**	♦♦	$40-$245 SAVE	1036
59 / p. 970	AAA	**Oceans One** - see color ad p 1030	♦♦♦	$47-$419 SAVE	1030
60 / p. 970	AAA	**Westgate Myrtle Beach Oceanfront Resort** - see color ad p 1035	♦♦♦	$49-$299 SAVE	1036
61 / p. 970	AAA	**Hotel Blue** - see color ad p 1002	♦♦	$31-$229 SAVE	1025
62 / p. 970		Atlantic Palms Boutique Resort	♦♦♦	$49-$190	998
63 / p. 970	AAA	**Days Inn Grand Strand**	♦♦	$55-$179 SAVE	1015
64 / p. 970	AAA	**Sea Crest Oceanfront Resort** - see color ad starting on p 1012	♦♦♦	$39-$199 SAVE	1032
65 / p. 970	AAA	**Captain's Quarters Resort** - see color ad p 1002	♦♦	$31-$299 SAVE	1007
66 / p. 970	AAA	**Polynesian Resort** - see color ad p 1029	♦	$48-$199 SAVE	1031
67 / p. 970	AAA	**Ocean Plaza Motel** - see color ad p 1029	♦	$31-$179 SAVE	1028
68 / p. 970	AAA	**Coral Beach Resort** - see color ad starting on p 1012	♦♦♦	$45-$259 SAVE	1011
69 / p. 970	AAA	**Sea Mist Oceanfront Resort** - see color ad p 1033	♦♦	$32-$199 SAVE	1034
70 / p. 970		Waikiki Village	♦♦	$50-$90	1036

MYRTLE BEACH (cont'd)

Map Page	OA	Lodgings (cont'd)	Diamond Rated	High Season	Page
71 / p. 970	AAA	**Landmark Resort - see color ad p 1000**	♦♦♦	$39-$259 SAVE	1025
72 / p. 970	AAA	**The Palace - see color ad p 1003**	♦♦	$41-$255 SAVE	1030
73 / p. 970	AAA	**Hampton Inn & Suites-Oceanfront Resort**	♦♦♦	$209-$269 SAVE	1017
74 / p. 970	AAA	**Best Western Grand Strand Inn & Suites - see color ad p 1005**	♦♦♦	$47-$205 SAVE	1004
75 / p. 970	AAA	**The Oceanfront Viking Motel - see color ad p 1029**	♦	$48-$199 SAVE	1028
76 / p. 970	AAA	**Ocean Park Resort - see color ad on insert**	♦♦	$45-$186 SAVE	1028
77 / p. 970	AAA	**Bluewater Resort**	♦♦	$50-$350 SAVE	1004
78 / p. 970	AAA	**Grand Atlantic Ocean Resort**	♦♦♦	$99-$319 SAVE	1016
79 / p. 970		Mystic Sea Beach & Golf Resort	♦♦	$29-$159	1027
80 / p. 970	AAA	**Paradise Resort**	♦♦♦	$54-$495 SAVE	1031
81 / p. 970	AAA	**Indigo Inn**	♦♦	$50-$260 SAVE	1025
82 / p. 970	AAA	**Sandcastle South Beach**	♦♦	$79-$209 SAVE	1032
83 / p. 970	AAA	**Compass Cove Oceanfront Resort - see color ad on insert**	♦♦♦	$43-$625 SAVE	1011
84 / p. 970	AAA	**M Grand**	♦♦♦	$69-$269 SAVE	1027
85 / p. 970	AAA	**Tropical Seas - see color ad inside front cover**	♦♦	$31-$299 SAVE	1035
86 / p. 970	AAA	**Crown Reef Resort & Conference Center at South Beach Resort - see color ad inside front cover**	♦♦♦	$55-$185 SAVE	1014
87 / p. 970	AAA	**Springmaid Beach Resort & Conference Center - see color ad p 997**	♦♦	$49-$190 SAVE	1035

Map Page	OA	Restaurants	Diamond Rated	Cuisine	Meal Range	Page
1 / p. 970		Villa Mare Restaurant	♦♦	Italian	$10-$22	1042
2 / p. 970		Oceans on 82nd	♦♦♦	American	$10-$36	1040
3 / p. 970		Collectors Cafe	♦♦♦	Mediterranean	$28-$35	1037
4 / p. 970		Liberty Tap Room & Grill	♦♦	American	$7-$21	1039
5 / p. 970	AAA	**City Bar Metropolitian Cuisine**	♦♦♦	American	$7-$30	1037
6 / p. 970		Bonefish Grill	♦♦♦	Seafood	$13-$20	1037
7 / p. 970		Flamingo Grill	♦♦	American	$8-$30	1038
8 / p. 970		River City Cafe	♦	American	$3-$13	1041
9 / p. 970		Akel's Family Restaurant	♦	American	$2-$10	1036
10 / p. 970		Grecian Delight Cafe	♦♦	Greek	$5-$14	1038
11 / p. 970		Aspen Grille	♦♦♦	Steak & Seafood	$17-$36	1036
12 / p. 970		Croissants Bakery & Cafe	♦	Deli	$6-$10	1038
13 / p. 970		Carolina Roadhouse Restaurant	♦♦	American	$6-$25	1037
14 / p. 970		Rioz Brazilian Steakhouse	♦♦♦	Brazilian	$20-$35	1041
15 / p. 970		Landry's Seafood House	♦♦	Regional American	$9-$35 SAVE	1039
16 / p. 970		Amici's Brick Oven & Italian Bistro	♦♦	Italian	$6-$18	1036
17 / p. 970		Key West Grill	♦♦	American	$11-$30	1039
18 / p. 970	AAA	**NASCAR Sports Grille**	♦♦	American	$9-$27	1040
19 / p. 970		East of Chicago Pizza	♦	Pizza	$4-$9	1038

Map Page	OA	Restaurants (cont'd)	Diamond Rated	Cuisine	Meal Range	Page
20 / p. 970		TBonz Gill & Grill	◆◆	Steak & Seafood	$7-$22	1042
21 / p. 970		Liberty Steakhouse & Brewery	◆◆	American	$6-$24	1039
22 / p. 970		The Crab House	◆◆	Seafood	$8-$65 SAVE	1037
23 / p. 970		Fiesta del Burro Loco	◆◆	Mexican	$7-$25	1038
24 / p. 970		The Filling Station	◆	American	$7-$9	1038
25 / p. 970		Chalupa Mexican Restaurant	◆◆	Mexican	$5-$14	1037
26 / p. 970		Omega Pancake and Omelet House	◆	American	$4-$8	1040
27 / p. 970	AAA	**Sea Captain's House**	◆◆	American	$6-$28	1041
28 / p. 970		New York Prime, A Steakhouse	◆◆◆	Steak	$28-$45	1040
29 / p. 970		Spring House Family Restaurant	◆◆	American	$4-$14	1041
30 / p. 970		Ultimate California Pizza	◆	Pizza	$6-$10	1042
31 / p. 970		Dead Dog Saloon North	◆◆	American	$5-$25	1038
32 / p. 970		Magnolia's at 26th - see color ad on insert	◆◆	American	$5-$21	1039
33 / p. 970		Abuelo's The Flavor of Mexico	◆◆◆	Mexican	$7-$18	1036
34 / p. 970		Vidalia's	◆◆	Regional American	$10-$20	1042
35 / p. 970		Uncle John's Family Restaurant	◆◆	American	$4-$11	1042
36 / p. 970		Harry's Breakfast Pancakes	◆	American	$4-$9	1039
37 / p. 970		Ramando's Italian Grill	◆◆	Italian	$10-$30	1041
38 / p. 970		Bagel Factory, Bakery, Deli-Cafe	◆	American	$2-$8	1037
39 / p. 970		Soho Steaks, Seafood & Sushi	◆◆	Continental	$5-$26	1041
40 / p. 970		River City Cafe	◆	American	$4-$15	1041
41 / p. 970		Papa's	◆◆	American	$12-$22	1040
42 / p. 970		Bummz Beach Cafe	◆	American	$7-$24	1037
43 / p. 970	AAA	**Michael's Pizza, Pasta & Grill**	◆◆	Italian	$5-$17	1039
44 / p. 970		Pomodoro's Trattoria & Bar	◆◆	Italian	$9-$28	1040
45 / p. 970		Dagwood's Deli & Bumstead's Pub	◆	Deli	$5-$10	1038
46 / p. 970		Grandma's Kitchen	◆	American	$5-$22	1038
47 / p. 970		Pizza a la Roma III	◆	Italian	$8-$13	1040
48 / p. 970		El Corro Grande	◆◆	Mexican	$6-$14	1038
49 / p. 970		Thorny's Steakhouse & Saloon	◆◆	American	$6-$27	1042
50 / p. 970		Villa Romana	◆◆◆	Traditional Italian	$12-$26	1042
51 / p. 970		International Omelet & Pancake House	◆	Breakfast	$3-$8	1039
52 / p. 970		Pan-American Pancake & Omelet House	◆	American	$3-$9	1040
53 / p. 970		Spring Garden Pancake House	◆	American	$3-$7	1041
54 / p. 970	AAA	**Angelo's Steak & Pasta**	◆◆	Italian	$8-$30	1036
55 / p. 970		J Edward's Great Ribs & More	◆◆	American	$6-$39	1039
56 / p. 970		Toffino's Italian Bakery & Deli	◆	Deli	$3-$8	1042

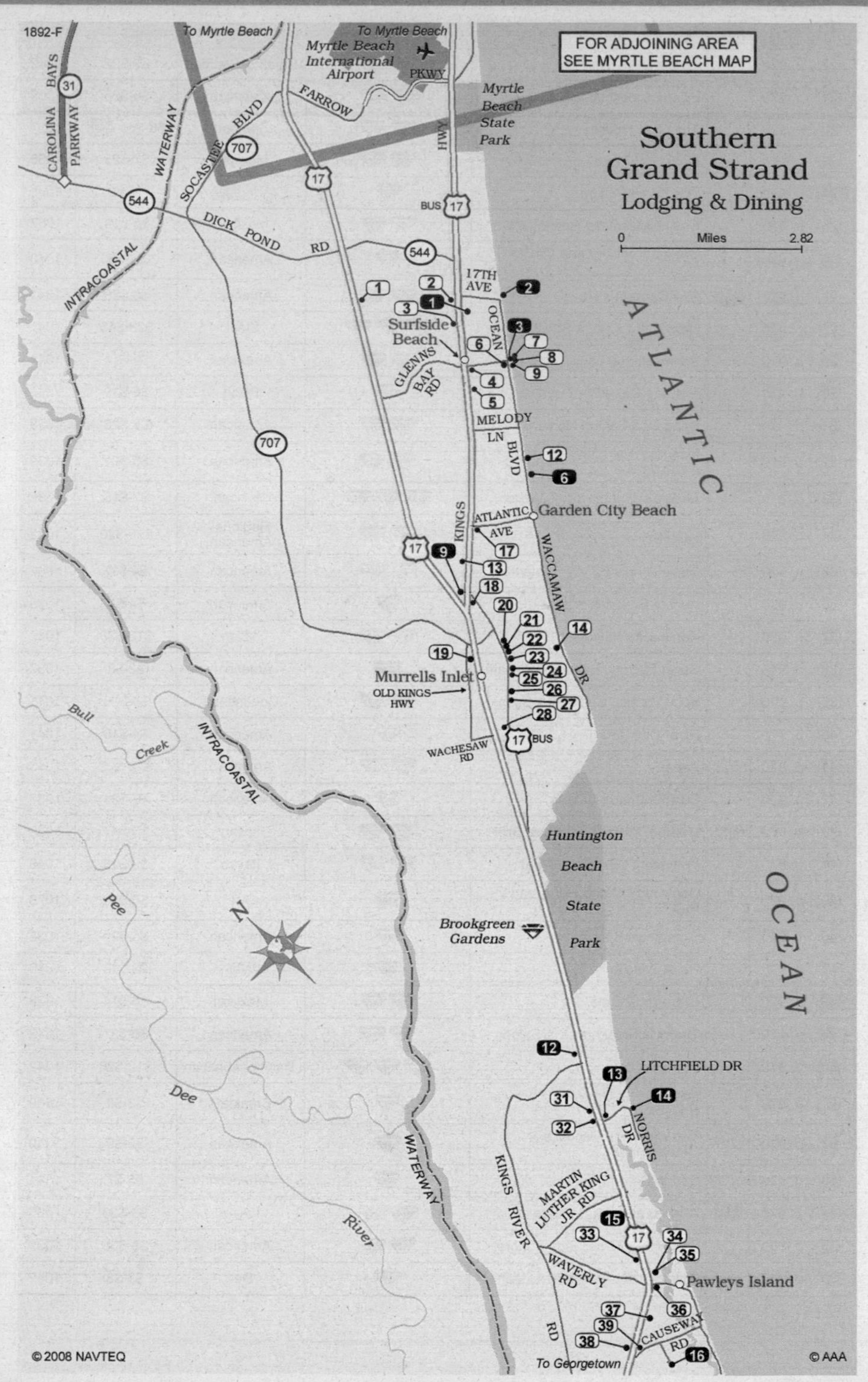

1892-F
FOR ADJOINING AREA SEE MYRTLE BEACH MAP
Southern Grand Strand
Lodging & Dining
0 Miles 2.82
To Myrtle Beach
Myrtle Beach International Airport
Myrtle Beach State Park
ATLANTIC OCEAN
Surfside Beach
Garden City Beach
Murrells Inlet
OLD KINGS HWY
Huntington Beach State Park
Brookgreen Gardens
LITCHFIELD DR
Pawleys Island
To Georgetown
INTRACOASTAL WATERWAY
Bull Creek
Pee Dee River
© 2008 NAVTEQ
© AAA

Southern Grand Strand

This index helps you "spot" where approved lodgings and restaurants are located on the corresponding detailed maps. Lodging daily rate range is for comparison only and show the property's high season. Restaurant rate range is a combination of lunch and/or dinner. Turn to the listing page for more detailed rate information and consult display ads for special promotions.

SURFSIDE BEACH

Map Page	OA	Lodgings	Diamond Rated	High Season	Page
1 / p. 976	AAA	**Comfort Inn**	◆◆	$60-$200 SAVE	1048
2 / p. 976	AAA	**Holiday Inn Oceanfront**	◆◆◆	$69-$229 SAVE	1048
3 / p. 976	AAA	**Days Hotel Surfside Beach Resort**	◆◆	$45-$225 SAVE	1048

Map Page	OA	Restaurants	Diamond Rated	Cuisine	Meal Range	Page
1 / p. 976		Bonefish Grill	◆◆◆	Seafood	$13-$30	1048
2 / p. 976		Ultimate California Pizza	◆	Pizza	$6-$20	1049
3 / p. 976		Dagwood's Deli & Sports Bar	◆	American	$5-$10	1049
4 / p. 976		The Charleston Cafe	◆◆	Regional American	$9-$47	1049
5 / p. 976		Valentino Gourmet Italian Restaurant	◆◆	Italian	$11-$33	1049
6 / p. 976		Bubba's Fish Shack	◆	Seafood	$6-$19	1048
7 / p. 976		River City Cafe	◆	American	$4-$13	1049
8 / p. 976		Latitude 22	◆◆	Caribbean	$12-$28	1049
9 / p. 976	AAA	**Nibil's**	◆	Steak & Seafood	$4-$25	1049

GARDEN CITY BEACH

Map Page	OA	Lodging	Diamond Rated	High Season	Page
6 / p. 976	AAA	**Water's Edge Resort**	◆◆	$92-$310 SAVE	1043

Map Page	OA	Restaurants	Diamond Rated	Cuisine	Meal Range	Page
12 / p. 976		Conch Cafe	◆◆	Seafood	$7-$24	1043
13 / p. 976		Finocchio's Italian Ristorante	◆◆	Italian	$6-$25	1043
14 / p. 976		Gulfstream Cafe	◆◆	Steak & Seafood	$11-$30	1043

MURRELLS INLET

Map Page	OA	Lodging	Diamond Rated	High Season	Page
9 / p. 976	AAA	**Holiday Inn Express Hotel & Suites**	◆◆◆	$69-$999 SAVE	1045

Map Page	OA	Restaurants	Diamond Rated	Cuisine	Meal Range	Page
17 / p. 976		Ultimate California Pizza	◆	Pizza	$6-$20	1046
18 / p. 976		Hoof 'N' Finz Taproom	◆◆	Steak & Seafood	$6-$15	1045
19 / p. 976		Old World Italian Restaurant	◆◆	Italian	$9-$23	1046
20 / p. 976	AAA	**Bovines**	◆◆	Steak & Seafood	$8-$33	1045
21 / p. 976	AAA	**Divine Fish House & Wahoo Raw Bar & Marina**	◆◆◆	Seafood	$19-$35	1045
22 / p. 976		Drunken Jack's Restaurant	◆◆	Steak & Seafood	$8-$42	1045
23 / p. 976	AAA	**Captain Dave's Dockside Restaurant**	◆◆	Seafood	$18-$38	1045
24 / p. 976		Dead Dog Saloon	◆◆	Steak & Seafood	$5-$22	1045
25 / p. 976		Spud's Waterfront Dining	◆◆	Seafood	$8-$29	1046
26 / p. 976		Oliver's Lodge	◆◆	Seafood	$15-$29	1046
27 / p. 976		River City Cafe	◆	American	$4-$14	1046
28 / p. 976	AAA	**Russell's Seafood Grill & Raw Bar**	◆◆	Seafood	$14-$30	1046

PAWLEYS ISLAND

Map Page	OA	Lodgings	Diamond Rated	High Season	Page
12 / p. 976		Hampton Inn Pawleys/Litchfield	♦♦♦	$69-$199	1046
13 / p. 976	AAA	**Litchfield Beach & Golf Resort - see color ad on insert**	♦♦♦	$69-$234 SAVE	1047
14 / p. 976		Litchfield Inn	♦♦	$119-$339	1047
15 / p. 976		Holiday Inn Express	♦♦♦	$89-$159	1046
16 / p. 976	AAA	**Pawleys Plantation Golf Resort**	♦♦♦	$69-$419 SAVE	1047

Map Page	OA	Restaurants	Diamond Rated	Cuisine	Meal Range	Page
31 / p. 976		Rocco's	♦♦♦	Northern Italian	$8-$36	1048
32 / p. 976		The Mayor's House Restaurant & Pub	♦♦♦	Regional American	$13-$28	1048
33 / p. 976		Bistro 217	♦♦	American	$8-$28	1047
34 / p. 976		Louis's at Pawley's	♦♦♦	Seafood	$9-$38	1048
35 / p. 976		Roz's Rice Mill Cafe	♦♦	American	$7-$20	1048
36 / p. 976		Frank's Restaurant & Bar	♦♦♦	Regional American	$20-$30	1047
37 / p. 976		Ocean Dragon	♦	Chinese	$4-$12	1048
38 / p. 976		Landolfi's Italian Pastry Shop & Deli	♦♦	Deli	$7-$10	1047
39 / p. 976		Gator Krawls Restaurant	♦♦	American	$6-$25	1047

Northern Grand Strand

(See map and index starting on p. 966)

CONWAY pop. 11,788

WHERE TO STAY

BEST WESTERN GUEST INN Book great rates at AAA.com **Phone:** 843/234-1678

AAA Benefit: Members save up to 20%, plus 10% bonus points with rewards program.

Motel
Rates not provided

Address: 1004 Waccamaw Dr **Location:** Jct US 701/501, 1.5 mi se on US 501, then just sw; on southeast side of Waccamaw River. **Facility:** 43 one-bedroom standard units, some with efficiencies and/or whirlpools. 2 stories (no elevator), exterior corridors. *Bath:* combo or shower only. **Parking:** on-site. **Amenities:** high-speed Internet, irons, hair dryers. **Pool(s):** outdoor. **Leisure Activities:** basketball. **Guest Services:** coin laundry, wireless Internet. **Business Services:** fax (fee). **Free Special Amenities: continental breakfast and high-speed Internet.**

THE CYPRESS INN **Phone:** (843)248-8199

Bed & Breakfast
$145-$225 12/1-9/30
$135-$190 10/1-11/30

Address: 16 Elm St **Location:** Corner of Elm St and Marina Dr, just s of 1st Ave; center. **Facility:** Close to the Waccamaw River and the river walk, this modern, service-oriented property features individually decorated rooms. Smoke free premises. 11 one-bedroom standard units, some with whirlpools. 3 stories (no elevator), interior corridors. **Parking:** on-site. **Terms:** age restrictions may apply, 5 day cancellation notice-fee imposed. **Amenities:** video library, voice mail, irons, hair dryers. *Some:* CD players. **Leisure Activities:** jogging, exercise room. *Fee:* massage. **Guest Services:** valet laundry, wireless Internet. **Business Services:** meeting rooms, fax (fee). **Cards:** AX, MC, VI.

SLEEP INN Book great rates at AAA.com **Phone:** (843)365-2828

Hotel
$59-$249 5/1-11/30
$59-$119 12/1-4/30

Address: 3345 Church (US 501) St **Location:** Jct US 701/501, 4.1 mi nw on US 501. **Facility:** 54 one-bedroom standard units, some with whirlpools. 2 stories (no elevator), interior corridors. *Bath:* combo or shower only. **Parking:** on-site. **Terms:** cancellation fee imposed. **Amenities:** dual phone lines, voice mail, irons, hair dryers. **Pool(s):** outdoor. **Guest Services:** wireless Internet. **Business Services:** fax (fee). **Cards:** AX, DC, DS, MC, VI. **Free Special Amenities: expanded continental breakfast and high-speed Internet.**

WHERE TO DINE

EL CERRO GRANDE **Phone:** 843/365-4001

Mexican
$5-$14

The meals are large and the service prompt at the friendly, family restaurant. Beef and chicken fajitas come with bell peppers, onions, guacamole and sour cream. The specialty Texanas fajita is a favorite. Servers speak both Spanish and English. Casual dress. **Bar:** Full bar. **Hours:** 11 am-10 pm, Sun-9 pm. Closed major holidays. **Address:** 101 Rivertown Blvd **Location:** Jct US 501/701, 2.6 mi nw on US 501. **Parking:** on-site. **Cards:** DS, MC, VI.

FATZ CAFE **Phone:** 843/369-0591

American
$8-$18

Friendly staff and appealing country decor help set the tone for a relaxed and enjoyable dining experience. It's not unusual for guests to wait to be seated at the popular spot, which earns raves for its well-prepared variations on chicken, steak, ribs and pasta, as well as salads and sandwiches. The signature Southern-style peach cobbler served with vanilla ice cream and walnuts is scrumptious. Casual dress. **Bar:** Full bar. **Hours:** 11 am-10 pm, Fri & Sat-11 pm, Sun-9 pm. Closed: 11/26, 12/25. **Address:** 2495 Church St **Location:** Jct US 501/701, 2.4 mi nw on US 501. **Parking:** on-site. **Cards:** AX, DS, MC, VI.

CALL

SIDEWHEELER RESTAURANT **Phone:** 843/248-7048

American
$9-$26

Traditional American cuisine joins some lowcountry favorites on the menu at this eatery. Enjoy dining on the deck overlooking the Waccamaw River during seasonal weather, and be sure to save room for one of the homemade desserts. Casual dress. **Bar:** Full bar. **Reservations:** accepted. **Hours:** 11 am-2:30 & 5-9 pm, Fri & Sat-9:30 pm. Closed: 11/26, 12/25; also Sun. **Address:** 110 Main St **Location:** Just n of US 501 business route bridge, just e on Kingston, then just s. **Parking:** on-site. **Cards:** AX, DC, DS, MC, VI.

THE TRESTLE BAKERY & CAFE **Phone:** 843/248-9896

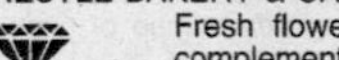

Deli
$4-$8

Fresh flowers grace the tables at the charming cafe, where you'll find a generous serving of bread complements each of the pleasant cuisines, all prepared with a healthy twist. The mixed salad plate combines shrimp, chicken, pasta and fruit salads. Casual dress. **Hours:** 6 am-6 pm, Sat-3 pm. Closed major holidays; also Sun. **Address:** 308 Main St **Location:** Jct US 701/501 business route, just s on US 501. **Parking:** street. **Cards:** AX, DS, MC, VI.

ULTIMATE CALIFORNIA PIZZA — Phone: 843/488-2221

Pizza
$6-$20

One of six locations situated on the Grand Strand, the colorful, downtown cafe prepares a very large variety of pizza heaped with your choice of toppings from a long and exotic list. A few pasta dishes, subs and salads are also featured as well as ice-cold draft beer. Casual dress. **Bar:** Beer & wine. **Reservations:** not accepted. **Hours:** 11 am-1 am. Closed: 12/25. **Address:** 328 Laurel St **Location:** Between 4th (US 701) and 3rd aves; center; at Black Water Market. **Parking:** street. **Cards:** AX, DS, MC, VI.

LITTLE RIVER pop. 7,027 (See map and index starting on p. 966)

WHERE TO STAY

HOLIDAY INN HOTEL & SUITES-NORTH MYRTLE BEACH *Book great rates at AAA.com* — **Phone:** (843)281-9400 15

AAA SAVE

Hotel
$49-$229 All Year

Address: 722 Hwy 17 **Location:** Jct SR 9/US 17, 1 mi e; at Coquina Harbor. Located adjacent to a marina. **Facility:** 79 units. 61 one-bedroom standard units. 15 one- and 3 two-bedroom suites, some with whirlpools. 4 stories, interior corridors. *Bath:* combo or shower only. **Parking:** on-site. **Terms:** cancellation fee imposed. **Amenities:** video games (fee), dual phone lines, voice mail, irons, hair dryers. *Some:* high-speed Internet. **Pool(s):** outdoor. **Leisure Activities:** limited exercise equipment. **Guest Services:** valet and coin laundry, wireless Internet. **Business Services:** meeting rooms, business center. **Cards:** AX, DC, DS, MC, VI. **Free Special Amenities: early check-in/late check-out and high-speed Internet.**

/ SOME UNITS FEE

SLEEP INN *Book at AAA.com* — **Phone:** (843)249-4848 14

Hotel
$49-$189 All Year

Address: 909 US 17 N **Location:** Jct SR 9/US 17, 1.2 mi e. Adjacent to Harbour View Golf Course. **Facility:** 82 one-bedroom standard units, some with whirlpools. 4 stories, interior corridors. *Bath:* combo or shower only. **Parking:** on-site. **Terms:** cancellation fee imposed. **Amenities:** video library (fee), voice mail, irons, hair dryers. **Pool(s):** heated indoor/outdoor. **Leisure Activities:** whirlpool, exercise room. **Guest Services:** coin laundry, wireless Internet. **Business Services:** meeting rooms, fax (fee). **Cards:** AX, CB, DC, DS, JC, MC, VI.

ASK CALL VCR / SOME UNITS

WHERE TO DINE

THE BRENTWOOD RESTAURANT & WINE BAR *Menu on AAA.com* — **Phone:** 843/249-2601 16

AAA

Continental
$15-$36

In a turn-of-the-20th-century Victorian house, the established family-run restaurant serves American fare prepared with a French influence. Among entree choices are escargot, prime rib with poached shrimp and scallops and grilled ostrich, which come with delicate yet rich sauces, in addition to fresh warm bread, a house salad, vegetable and choice of starch. After dinner, guests can retreat to the Upstairs at the Brentwood lounge, where cocktails, coffees and homemade desserts are served. Casual dress. **Bar:** Full bar. **Reservations:** suggested. **Hours:** 5 pm-close; Sunday brunch 10 am-2 pm; Mon in summer. **Address:** 4269 Luck Ave **Location:** 2.1 mi sw of NC/SC border on US 17, then just n. **Parking:** on-site. **Cards:** AX, DS, MC, VI.

CHIANTI SOUTH — **Phone:** 843/249-7888

Northern Italian
$15-$31

Since 1997, the family-operated eatery has served pasta, chicken, veal and seafood dishes, all of which can be enjoyed with a selection from the award-winning wine list. Casual dress. **Bar:** Full bar. **Reservations:** accepted. **Hours:** Open 12/1-12/31 & 2/1-11/30; 5 pm-close. Closed: 11/26, 12/25; also Mon. **Address:** 2109 US 17 N **Location:** 1.1 mi s of NC/SC border. **Parking:** on-site. **Cards:** DS, MC, VI.

THE PARSON'S TABLE *Menu on AAA.com* — **Phone:** 843/249-3702 17

AAA

Continental
$15-$28

Situated in a renovated church with the original stained-glass windows, the historic, award-winning restaurant serves fresh seafood, steaks and other tasty fare. Dressy casual. **Bar:** Full bar. **Reservations:** suggested. **Hours:** Open 12/1-1/1 & 2/1-11/30; 4:30 pm-9 pm; hours vary off season. Closed: Sun. **Address:** 4805 US 17 **Location:** 2.1 mi sw of NC/SC border, just s. **Parking:** on-site. **Cards:** AX, MC, VI.

UMBERTO'S AT COQUINA HARBOR — **Phone:** 843/249-5552 18

Traditional Italian
$14-$35

Situated along the shore with a great view of the marina, the trattoria prepares such dishes as osso buco Milanese, hand-cut chops and steaks, tender veal and a broad selection of market-fresh fish and other seafood. Guest attire ranges from dressy casual to "just off the beach" casual. Casual dress. **Bar:** Full bar. **Reservations:** suggested. **Hours:** 4:30 pm-10 pm. Closed: 11/26, 12/24, 12/25. **Address:** 720 US 17 N, Box 5-A **Location:** Jct SR 9/US 17, 1 mi e; at Coquina Harbor. **Parking:** on-site. **Cards:** AX, MC, VI.

LORIS pop. 2,079

WHERE TO STAY

CAROLINA INN — **Phone:** 843/716-2100

Hotel
Rates not provided

Address: 312 Hwy 701 N **Location:** 4.8 mi s of NC/SC border. **Facility:** 32 one-bedroom standard units, some with whirlpools. 2 stories (no elevator), interior corridors. *Bath:* combo or shower only. **Parking:** on-site. **Amenities:** high-speed Internet, dual phone lines, voice mail, irons, hair dryers. **Guest Services:** coin laundry. **Business Services:** fax (fee).

/ SOME UNITS

MYRTLE BEACH (NORTHERN) (See map and index starting on p. 966)

WHERE TO STAY

COURTYARD BY MARRIOTT BAREFOOT LANDING

Book great rates at AAA.com Phone: (843)361-1730 **2**

Hotel
$99-$159 All Year

Address: 1000 Commons Blvd **Location:** Jct SR 22, 1.7 mi ne on US 17, then just n. **Facility:** Smoke free premises. 157 units. 152 one-bedroom standard units, some with whirlpools. 5 one-bedroom suites. 5 stories, interior corridors. *Bath:* combo or shower only. **Parking:** on-site. **Terms:** cancellation fee imposed. **Amenities:** dual phone lines, voice mail, irons, hair dryers. **Pool(s):** heated indoor. **Leisure Activities:** whirlpool, sun deck, gazebo, exercise room. **Guest Services:** valet and coin laundry, wireless Internet. **Business Services:** meeting rooms, business center. **Cards:** AX, CB, DC, DS, JC, MC, VI. **Free Special Amenities: newspaper.**

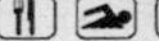   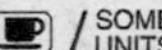 

/ SOME UNITS

AAA Benefit:
Members save a minimum 5% off the best available rate.

EMBASSY SUITES AT KINGSTON PLANTATION

Book great rates at AAA.com Phone: (843)449-0006 

Hotel
$54-$214 All Year

Address: 9800 Queensway Blvd **Location:** Oceanfront. Jct SR 22/Lakeshore Dr and US 17, 0.8 mi se on Lakeshore Dr to Kings Rd, then 0.4 mi sw to Lake Dr, follow signs. Located in Kingston Plantation. **Facility:** 255 one-bedroom suites. 19 stories, interior corridors. **Parking:** on-site and valet. **Terms:** check-in 4 pm, 1-30 night minimum stay, cancellation fee imposed. **Amenities:** video games (fee), high-speed Internet, dual phone lines, voice mail, safes, irons, hair dryers. **Dining:** 2 restaurants. **Pool(s):** 2 outdoor, heated outdoor, heated indoor. **Leisure Activities:** sauna, whirlpools, waterslide, interactive water playground, lazy river, recreation programs, jogging. *Fee:* 9 lighted tennis courts, racquetball courts, massage. **Guest Services:** valet laundry, area transportation-resort & within 2 mi, wireless Internet. **Business Services:** conference facilities, business center. **Cards:** AX, CB, DC, DS, MC, VI. **Free Special Amenities: full breakfast and early check-in/late check-out.** *(See color ad p 982)*

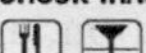   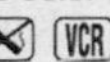  

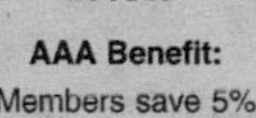

AAA Benefit:
Members save 5% or more everyday!

EMBASSY SUITES/KINGSTON PLANTATION

Book great rates at AAA.com Phone: (843)449-0006 

Vacation Rental Condominium
$89-$319 All Year

Address: 9800 Queensway Blvd **Location:** Oceanfront. Jct SR 22/Lakeshore Dr and US 17, 0.8 mi se on Lakeshore Dr to Kings Rd, then 0.4 mi sw to Lake Dr, follow signs. Located in Kingston Plantation. **Facility:** The complex is comprised of four highrise towers; each unit is individually decorated and provides breathtaking views of the beaches and coastline. 700 condominiums. 2-24 stories, interior/exterior corridors. **Parking:** on-site. **Terms:** off-site registration, check-in 4 pm, 1-30 night minimum stay, cancellation fee imposed. **Amenities:** high-speed Internet, dual phone lines, voice mail, irons, hair dryers. **Pool(s):** 4 outdoor, indoor. **Leisure Activities:** jogging. *Fee:* 9 lighted tennis courts, racquetball courts, massage. **Guest Services:** complimentary laundry, area transportation. **Business Services:** conference facilities. **Cards:** AX, CB, DC, DS, MC, VI.

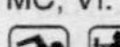    

AAA Benefit:
Members save 5% or more everyday!

FAIRFIELD INN BY MARRIOTT MYRTLE BEACH NORTH

Book great rates at AAA.com Phone: (843)361-8000 

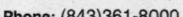

Hotel
$71-$143 All Year

Address: 10231 N Kings Hwy **Location:** Jct SR 22, 0.9 mi ne on US 17. **Facility:** Smoke free premises. 86 one-bedroom standard units. 4 stories, interior corridors. *Bath:* combo or shower only. **Parking:** on-site. **Terms:** cancellation fee imposed. **Amenities:** irons, hair dryers. **Pool(s):** heated indoor. **Leisure Activities:** whirlpool. **Guest Services:** valet and coin laundry. **Business Services:** meeting rooms, fax (fee). **Cards:** AX, CB, DC, DS, JC, MC, VI.

CALL 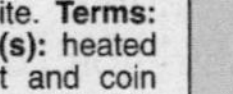 / SOME UNITS

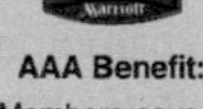

AAA Benefit:
Members save a minimum 5% off the best available rate.

(See map and index starting on p. 966)

HILTON MYRTLE BEACH RESORT *Book great rates at AAA.com* **Phone:** (843)449-5000 **7**

Hotel
$104-$279 All Year

Address: 10000 Beach Club Dr **Location:** Oceanfront. Jct SR 22, just n on US 17, 1.4 mi se on Kings Rd, then just e. **Facility:** 533 units. 377 one-bedroom standard units. 156 condominiums. 15 stories, interior/exterior corridors. *Bath:* combo or shower only. **Parking:** on-site. **Terms:** check-in 4 pm, 1-30 night minimum stay, cancellation fee imposed. **Amenities:** dual phone lines, voice mail, safes, irons, hair dryers. *Fee:* video games, high-speed Internet. **Pool(s):** heated outdoor. **Leisure Activities:** whirlpool, fishing, 4 lighted tennis courts, exercise room. *Fee:* golf-18 holes, game room. **Guest Services:** valet laundry, area transportation-clubhouse, wireless Internet. **Business Services:** conference facilities, business center. **Cards:** AX, CB, DC, DS, JC, MC, VI. **Free Special Amenities: newspaper and early check-in/late check-out.** *(See color ad p 982)*

Hilton
AAA Benefit:
Members save 5% or more everyday!

/ SOME UNITS

HOLIDAY INN EXPRESS RESTAURANT ROW *Book great rates at AAA.com* **Phone:** (843)449-5348 **4**

Hotel
$65-$299 All Year

Address: 9551 Hwy 17 N **Location:** Jct SR 22, 1.4 mi sw on US 17. Located opposite the Galleria Shopping Center. **Facility:** 90 one-bedroom standard units, some with whirlpools. 3 stories, interior corridors. *Bath:* combo or shower only. **Parking:** on-site. **Terms:** cancellation fee imposed. **Amenities:** irons, hair dryers. *Some:* high-speed Internet. **Pool(s):** outdoor. **Guest Services:** valet and coin laundry, wireless Internet. **Business Services:** meeting rooms, PC, fax (fee). **Cards:** AX, CB, DC, DS, JC, MC, VI. **Free Special Amenities: expanded continental breakfast and high-speed Internet.**

/ SOME UNITS

MARINA INN AT GRANDE DUNES *Book great rates at AAA.com* **Phone:** (843)913-1333 **10**

Resort Condominium
$134-$499 All Year

Address: 8121 Amalfi Pl **Location:** Jct US 17 and Grand Dunes Blvd, just nw on Grand Dunes Blvd. **Facility:** On the Intracoastal Waterway, this high-rise, Mediterranean-style resort is comprised of standard hotel units as well as one- to four-bedroom condominiums. Smoke free premises. 197 units. 66 one-bedroom standard units. 131 condominiums. 6-12 stories, interior/exterior corridors. *Bath:* combo or shower only. **Parking:** on-site. **Terms:** check-in 4 pm, 7 day cancellation notice. **Amenities:** video games (fee), CD players, voice mail, safes, irons, hair dryers. **Dining:** 2 restaurants, also, Waterscapes at the Marina Inn, see separate listing. **Pool(s):** outdoor, indoor. **Leisure Activities:** sauna, whirlpools, 8 lighted tennis courts, exercise room. *Fee:* golf-36 holes, massage. **Guest Services:** valet laundry, wireless Internet. **Business Services:** conference facilities, business center. **Cards:** AX, CB, DC, DS, MC, VI.

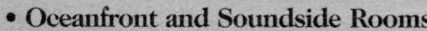

/ SOME UNITS

▼ See AAA listing p 767 ▼

(See map and index starting on p. 966)

OCEAN CREEK RESORT *Book great rates at AAA.com* **Phone:** (843)272-7724 1

Vacation Rental Condominium

$55-$390 5/22-11/30
$55-$235 12/1-5/21

Address: 10600 N Kings Hwy **Location:** Oceanfront. Jct SR 22, 1.9 mi ne on US 17. Located opposite Barefoot Landing. **Facility:** The 57-acre property includes two oceanfront high-rise buildings and a variety of non-oceanfront villa accommodations on lushly landscaped grounds. 350 condominiums. 1-15 stories, exterior corridors. **Parking:** on-site. **Terms:** check-in 4 pm, 14 day cancellation notice-fee imposed. **Amenities:** voice mail, safes, irons, hair dryers. **Pool(s):** 6 outdoor, heated indoor, indoor/outdoor. **Leisure Activities:** whirlpools, putting green, recreation programs in summer, exercise room, horseshoes, volleyball. *Fee:* 8 tennis courts (2 lighted), game room. **Guest Services:** coin laundry, wireless Internet. **Business Services:** conference facilities, fax (fee). **Cards:** AX, DS, MC, VI. ***(See color ad p 1009)***

/ SOME UNITS VCR

(See map and index starting on p. 966)

SANDS BEACH CLUB RESORT *Book great rates at AAA.com* **Phone:** (843)449-1531 11

Vacation Rental Condominium

$69-$299 3/20-11/30
$59-$159 12/1-3/19

Address: 9400 Shore Dr **Location:** Oceanfront. Jct SR 22, 1 mi sw on US 17, 1.1 mi se on Lake Arrowhead Rd, then 0.5 mi sw. Located in Arcadian Shores section. **Facility:** The resort offers a variety of individually decorated guest rooms in two buildings, one of which is oceanfront; all rooms have balconies. 120 condominiums. 5-11 stories, exterior corridors. **Parking:** on-site. **Terms:** 1-5 night minimum stay - seasonal and/or weekends, 4 day cancellation notice-fee imposed. **Amenities:** voice mail, safes, irons, hair dryers. **Pool(s):** outdoor, heated indoor/outdoor. **Leisure Activities:** whirlpool, 4 tennis courts (2 lighted), recreation programs in summer, sports court, basketball, volleyball. **Guest Services:** valet and coin laundry, wireless Internet. **Business Services:** meeting rooms, administrative services (fee), PC. **Cards:** AX, DS, MC, VI.

/ SOME UNITS

SEA WATCH RESORT *Book great rates at AAA.com* **Phone:** (843)918-0000 6

Vacation Rental Condominium

$65-$399 6/1-11/30
$65-$349 12/1-5/31

Address: 161 Sea Watch Dr **Location:** Oceanfront. Jct SR 22/Lakeshore Dr and US 17, 1.2 mi se on Lakeshore Dr. Located in a quiet area; in Arcadian Shores section. **Facility:** This oceanfront resort offers a variety of room types with an attractive, colorful decor and extensive pool facilities. 270 condominiums. 16-20 stories, interior/exterior corridors. **Parking:** on-site. **Terms:** 4-7 night minimum stay - seasonal, age restrictions may apply, 14 day cancellation notice-fee imposed. **Amenities:** voice mail, safes, irons, hair dryers. **Pool(s):** 5 outdoor, 2 heated indoor. **Leisure Activities:** whirlpools, 2 lazy river water rides, recreation programs, exercise room. *Fee:* game room. **Guest Services:** coin laundry, wireless Internet. **Business Services:** meeting rooms, fax (fee). **Cards:** AX, DS, MC, VI.

(See color ad p 1009)

/ SOME UNITS VCR

WYNDHAM SEAWATCH PLANTATION *Book at AAA.com* **Phone:** 843/692-9311 5

Vacation Rental Condominium

Rates not provided

Address: 161 Sea Watch Dr **Location:** Oceanfront. Jct SR 22, just n on US 17, 1 mi se on Kings Rd, then just e on Lakeshore Dr. Located in Arcadian Shores section. **Facility:** This large complex features two oceanfront towers and two low-rise villa buildings; all condos have oceanfront or ocean views. Smoke free premises. 223 condominiums. 4-20 stories, exterior corridors. *Bath:* combo or shower only. **Parking:** on-site. **Terms:** check-in 4 pm. **Amenities:** video library, CD players, voice mail, irons, hair dryers. **Pool(s):** 5 outdoor, 2 heated indoor. **Leisure Activities:** whirlpools, fishing, recreation programs in summer, horseshoes, game room. *Fee:* exercise room, massage. **Guest Services:** complimentary laundry, wireless Internet. **Business Services:** meeting rooms, business center.

VCR

(See map and index starting on p. 966)

WHERE TO DINE

CAGNEY'S OLD PLACE **Phone:** 843/449-3824 (4)

Steak & Seafood
$12-$30

Memorabilia ranging from old movie star photographs to glass gas pumps adorn the walls and floors at the lively eatery. Hearty-size steaks are the popular entree although fresh pasta and seafood entrees, including tender lobster tail, don't disappoint. Casual dress. **Bar:** Full bar. **Hours:** Open 12/1-12/10 & 2/10-11/30; 5 pm-11 pm. Closed: 11/26; also Sun. **Address:** 9911 N Kings Hwy **Location:** Jct SR 22, 0.5 mi sw on US 17; on Restaurant Row. **Parking:** on-site. **Cards:** AX, DS, MC, VI.

CALL

CALIFORNIA DREAMING **Phone:** 843/663-2050

American
$8-$23

The full-service, fine-dining restaurant appeals to adults, particularly those with an appetite for innovative concepts in food. Revised weekly, the menu consistently incorporates sophisticated, cutting-edge California dishes with Pacific Rim influences throughout. Among house specialties are flatbread appetizers baked in a brick oven, sushi, sashimi and some vegetarian dishes. The wine list focuses primarily on California vintages. Casual dress. **Bar:** Full bar. **Hours:** 11 am-10 pm, Fri & Sat-11 pm. **Address:** 10429 N Kings Hwy **Location:** Jct SR 22, 1.7 mi ne on US 17. **Parking:** on-site. **Cards:** AX, DC, DS, MC, VI.

CALL

CAPTAIN BENNETT'S CALABASH SEAFOOD #2 **Phone:** 843/449-7865 (8)

Seafood
$18-$29

Patrons can fill a plate with fresh seafood prepared in a variety of ways at the nautically-appointed buffet. Deviled crab, fried or boiled shrimp, oysters, tender chicken and prime rib are among the 80 choices. A limited, full-service menu offers other alternatives. Children dine at a reduced rate. Casual dress. **Bar:** Full bar. **Hours:** 2:30 pm-10 pm, Sat & Sun from 11 am; to 9 pm off season. **Address:** 9701 N Kings Hwy **Location:** Jct SR 22, 1.1 mi sw on US 17; on Restaurant Row. **Parking:** on-site. **Cards:** AX, MC, VI.

CHESAPEAKE HOUSE **Phone:** 843/449-3231 (3)

Regional American
$11-$40

For more than 33 years, guests have enjoyed dining lakeside at the family-owned restaurant, where original seafood creations are prepared in a casual atmosphere. A cup of fish stew comes complimentary with every entree. The in-house bakery turns out delicious hushpuppies and cinnamon rolls. Casual dress. **Bar:** Full bar. **Reservations:** suggested. **Hours:** 4:30 pm-10 pm, Sun-9 pm; to 9 pm off season. Closed: 11/26. **Address:** 9918 N Kings Hwy **Location:** Jct SR 22, 0.4 mi sw on US 17; on Restaurant Row. **Parking:** on-site. **Cards:** AX, DS, MC, VI.

CHESTNUT HILL **Phone:** 843/449-3984 (2)

American
$18-$30

Overlooking a lake with a beautiful fountain, the restaurant prepares delicious entrees of tender prime rib and seafood. Start with one of the tasty shrimp appetizers and basketfuls of warm, fresh bread and butter. Dressy casual. **Bar:** Full bar. **Reservations:** suggested. **Hours:** 4:30 pm-10 pm, Sun 10 am-1:30 & 4:30-9 pm; Sunday brunch. Closed: 11/26, 12/24, 12/25; also Super Bowl Sun. **Address:** 9922 N Kings Hwy **Location:** Jct SR 22, just sw on US 17; on Restaurant Row. **Parking:** on-site. **Cards:** AX, DC, DS, MC, VI.

CHINA BUFFET **Phone:** 843/692-0238 (10)

Chinese
$4-$12

Patrons at the casual eatery can sample traditional favorites from an extensive buffet. Casual dress. **Bar:** Beer & wine. **Hours:** 11 am-10:30 pm, Fri & Sat-11 pm, Sun noon-10:30 pm. **Address:** 9668 N Kings Hwy **Location:** Jct SR 22, 1 mi sw on US 17; in The Galleria. **Parking:** on-site. **Cards:** AX, DS, MC, VI.

CHUCK'S STEAK HOUSE ***Menu on AAA.com*** **Phone:** 843/449-7611 (9)

AAA

Steak
$7-$47

Since 1979, the restaurant has served thick steaks in a casual atmosphere. Contributing to a feel that is both rustic and elegant are cathedral ceilings, three fireplaces and views of the intracoastal waterway. In addition to steaks, the menu lists seafood and chicken dishes, ribs, salad bar offerings and children's fare. Casual dress. **Bar:** Full bar. **Reservations:** accepted. **Hours:** 4:30 pm-10 pm. Closed: 11/26, 12/25; also Super Bowl Sun. **Address:** 9695 N Kings Hwy **Location:** Jct SR 22, 1.1 mi sw on US 17; on Restaurant Row. **Parking:** on-site. **Cards:** AX, DS, MC, VI.

GOOBER'S 52 **Phone:** 843/839-2295 (1)

American
$6-$16

On the north end of Restaurant Row, the brightly colored eatery features a wide selection of burgers, deli sandwiches and an array of well-prepared entrees, including preparations of pasta, seafood, steak and chicken. Shortly after opening, the restaurant took first place for its peanut butter pie during the "4th Annual Taste of Restaurant Row" competition. Service is professional and friendly. Casual dress. **Bar:** Full bar. **Hours:** 11 am-10 pm, Fri & Sat-11 pm. Closed: 1/1, 11/26, 12/25. **Address:** 9924 N Kings Hwy (US 17) **Location:** Jct US 17 and SR 22 (Conway Bypass), just sw on US 17. **Parking:** on-site. **Cards:** AX, DS, MC, VI.

ISLAMORADA FISH COMPANY **Phone:** 843/361-4700

Steak & Seafood
$8-$46

The 12,000-square-foot restaurant features a large saltwater aquarium, one dining room with numerous hunting trophies on the walls and a separate dining room with scale models of Atlantic fish species suspended from the ceiling, all making for a fascinating and interesting dining experience. Menu items include tropical seafood favorites including Florida lobster, conch and alligator. Casual dress. **Bar:** Full bar. **Hours:** 11 am-10 pm. Closed: 11/26, 12/25. **Address:** 10177 N Kings Hwy **Location:** Jct SR 22 and US 17 (N Kings Hwy), 0.6 mi ne; in Colonial Mall. **Parking:** on-site. **Cards:** AX, DS, MC, VI.

CALL

(See map and index starting on p. 966)

MIYABI KYOTO JAPANESE STEAK & SEAFOOD HOUSE

Phone: 843/449-9294 (6)

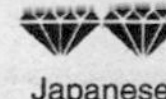

Japanese
$11-$30

Chefs perform traditional hibachi cooking right at the table at the Japanese steakhouse. Try the delicious steak, juicy chicken or tender shrimp with loads of fried rice and vegetables, plus a variety of homemade sauces for dipping. Sushi and tempura also can be had from the full-service sushi bar. The dining room is attractively decorated with traditional Japanese paintings of storks and glass cases filled with Oriental pottery, ceramics and even a samurai warrior's armor. Casual dress. **Bar:** Full bar. **Reservations:** suggested. **Hours:** 5 pm-10 pm, Sat from 4:30 pm, Sun 4:30 pm-9:30 pm. Closed: 11/26, 12/25; also Super Bowl Sun. **Address:** 9732 N Kings Hwy **Location:** Jct SR 22, 0.8 mi sw on US 17; on Restaurant Row. **Parking:** on-site. **Cards:** AX, DS, MC, VI.

NAKATO JAPANESE STEAK HOUSE

Phone: 843/449-3344 (5)

Japanese
$8-$29

In a building reminiscent of traditional Japanese architecture, the restaurant features a sushi bar—where sashimi, tempura and sushi are specialties—and hibachi tables, where the chefs are as entertaining as they are proficient in the Japanese culinary arts. Casual dress. **Bar:** Full bar. **Reservations:** suggested. **Hours:** 4 pm-10 pm. Closed: 12/25. **Address:** 9912 N Kings Hwy **Location:** Jct SR 22, 0.5 mi sw on US 17; on Restaurant Row. **Parking:** on-site. **Cards:** AX, DC, DS, MC, VI.

ROSSI'S ITALIAN RESTAURANT

Phone: 843/449-0481 (12)

Regional Italian
$15-$32

Decorative wood enhancements lend the Italian-themed dining room a moderately upscale appearance. Outstanding menu selections include blackened grouper a la Rossi, a large fillet with crab and scallops in a white wine sauce, and snapper meuniere, a fillet broiled in lemon butter and topped with scallions and lump crabmeat. Diners can extend their evening in the sophisticated environs of Eighty Eights, a piano bar. Casual dress. **Bar:** Full bar. **Reservations:** suggested. **Hours:** 4:30 pm-11 pm; hours may vary in winter. Closed: 11/26, 12/25; also Sun. **Address:** 9636 N Kings Hwy **Location:** Jct SR 22, 1 mi sw on US 17, just s on Arrowhead Rd; in The Galleria. **Parking:** on-site. **Cards:** AX, DS, MC, VI.

CALL

THOROUGHBREDS CHOPHOUSE & SEAFOOD GRILLE

Phone: 843/497-2636 (7)

Continental
$20-$39

Certified Angus beef, seafood and poultry factor heavily into the menu offerings, and some meals come with the added flair of tableside preparation. A good choice for dinner is grouper Nantua, dredged in Japanese bread crumbs with a sauce of shrimp, lobster stock, cream, diced tomatoes and seasoning. Equestrian-themed dining rooms and a climate-controlled covered veranda with a fireplace lend to the upscale setting. The award-winning wine list is extensive. Dressy casual. **Bar:** Full bar. **Reservations:** suggested. **Hours:** 5 pm-10 pm, Fri & Sat-11 pm. Closed: 1/1, 12/24-12/26. **Address:** 9706 N Kings Hwy **Location:** Jct SR 22, 1 mi sw on US 17; on Restaurant Row. **Parking:** on-site. **Cards:** AX, DC, DS, MC, VI.

CALL

UMI PACIFIC GRILLE

Phone: 843/497-6016 (11)

Pacific Rim
$18-$60

The tony establishment almost seems out of place in an area dominated by come-as-you-are spots catering to the beach crowds. Exotic decor emphasizes blue accent lighting and sheer drapes, and a large comfortable gathering area off the lounge provides an inviting destination for an aperitif. The chic exhibition kitchen provides lively entertainment as the extraordinary food is prepared. This is the crown jewel among the Divine Dining Group's numerous local restaurants. The service is exemplary. Dressy casual. **Bar:** Full bar. **Reservations:** suggested. **Hours:** 5 pm-10 pm, Fri & Sat-10:30 pm. Closed: 12/25. **Address:** 959 Lake Arrowhead Rd **Location:** Jct US 17/Lake Arrowhead Rd; in The Galleria. **Parking:** on-site. **Cards:** AX, DS, MC, VI.

CALL

WATERSCAPES AT THE MARINA INN

Phone: 843/913-2845 (13)

American
$9-$38

The award winning chef's well-prepared, beautifully-presented creations complement the lush Mediterranean-style surroundings, over-the-top silver and crystal place settings and marina views. Menu selections may include a pulled duck sandwich, grande lobster club, roasted trigger fish or a 22-ounce "cowboy" rib-eye, each served with its own delicate sauce creation and accompaniment. During preparation, the chef uses the freshest, seasonal ingredients and highest grades of meats and local seafood. Dressy casual. **Bar:** Full bar. **Reservations:** accepted. **Hours:** 6:30 am-4 & 6-10 pm. **Address:** 8121 Amalfi Pl **Location:** Jct US 17 and Grand Dunes Blvd, just nw on Grand Dunes Blvd; in Marina Inn at Grande Dunes. **Parking:** on-site and valet. **Cards:** AX, DC, DS, MC, VI.

CALL

NORTH MYRTLE BEACH pop. 10,974 (See map and index starting on p. 966)

WHERE TO STAY

AVISTA RESORT

Book great rates at AAA.com

Phone: (843)249-2521 25

Vacation Rental Condominium

$90-$490 6/6-11/30
$48-$299 12/1-6/5

Address: 300 N Ocean Blvd **Location:** Oceanfront. Jct 3rd Ave N. **Facility:** The twin-tower, high-rise building features chic public areas, nicely appointed, spacious units, a high-end exercise facility and garage parking. 378 condominiums. 17 stories, interior corridors. *Bath:* combo or shower only. **Parking:** on-site. **Terms:** 3-4 night minimum stay - seasonal, cancellation fee imposed. **Amenities:** high-speed Internet, voice mail, safes, irons, hair dryers. *Some:* DVD players. **Pool(s):** 2 outdoor, heated outdoor, heated indoor/outdoor. **Leisure Activities:** whirlpools, 2 lazy river water rides, recreation programs. *Fee:* massage. **Guest Services:** coin laundry, wireless Internet. **Business Services:** meeting rooms, PC, fax (fee). **Cards:** AX, DC, DS, MC, VI. **Free Special Amenities: newspaper and high-speed Internet.** *(See color ad starting on p 1018)*

  FEE 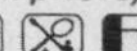  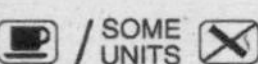  / SOME UNITS

BAY WATCH RESORT

Book great rates at AAA.com

Phone: (843)272-4600 31

Resort Condominium

$49-$277 All Year

Address: 2701 S Ocean Blvd **Location:** Oceanfront. Jct 27th Ave S. **Facility:** Many rooms have balconies at this property, which offers three high-rise towers and a covered parking deck as well as a variety of pools. 414 units. 45 one-bedroom standard units. 369 condominiums. 17 stories, exterior corridors. **Parking:** on-site. **Terms:** 3-4 night minimum stay - seasonal, age restrictions may apply, 7 day cancellation notice-fee imposed. **Amenities:** high-speed Internet, voice mail, safes, irons, hair dryers. **Dining:** 2 restaurants. **Pool(s):** 5 heated outdoor, 3 heated indoor. **Leisure Activities:** whirlpools, indoor & outdoor lazy river water rides, exercise room. *Fee:* golf privileges, massage, game room. **Guest Services:** valet and coin laundry. **Business Services:** conference facilities, business center. **Cards:** AX, DC, DS, MC, VI. **Free Special Amenities: local telephone calls and high-speed Internet.** *(See color ad on insert)*

    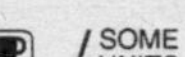 / SOME UNITS 

BEACH COVE RESORT

Phone: (843)918-9000 34

Condominium

$65-$394 All Year

Address: 4800 S Ocean Blvd **Location:** Oceanfront. Jct 48th Ave S. **Facility:** The beachfront property features 800- to 1,500-square-foot units in two high-rise buildings, and numerous recreational facilities are on site. 321 condominiums. 16 stories, exterior corridors. **Parking:** on-site. **Terms:** check-in 4 pm, age restrictions may apply, 14 day cancellation notice-fee imposed. **Amenities:** DVD players, voice mail, safes, irons, hair dryers. **Dining:** 2 restaurants. **Pool(s):** outdoor, 2 heated outdoor, heated indoor. **Leisure Activities:** saunas, whirlpools, fishing, lazy river water ride, racquetball court, recreation programs, movie theater, exercise room. *Fee:* golf privileges, massage, game room. **Guest Services:** valet and coin laundry, airport transportation-Myrtle Beach International Airport, wireless Internet. **Business Services:** conference facilities, administrative services. *Fee:* PC, fax. **Cards:** AX, DS, MC, VI. *(See color ad p 1009)*

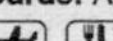     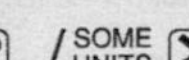 / SOME UNITS

BEST WESTERN OCEAN SANDS RESORT

Book great rates at AAA.com

Phone: (843)272-6101 28

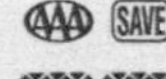

Hotel

$70-$396 All Year

Address: 1525 S Ocean Blvd **Location:** Oceanfront. Jct 16th Ave S. **Facility:** 116 units. 96 one-bedroom standard units, some with efficiencies. 20 one-bedroom suites with efficiencies. 4-10 stories, exterior corridors. *Bath:* combo or shower only. **Parking:** on-site. **Terms:** 2-5 night minimum stay - seasonal and/or weekends, 7 day cancellation notice-fee imposed. **Amenities:** irons, hair dryers. *Some:* high-speed Internet. **Pool(s):** outdoor, heated indoor/outdoor. **Leisure Activities:** whirlpool, lazy river water ride, limited exercise equipment. **Guest Services:** coin laundry. **Business Services:** meeting rooms, fax (fee). **Cards:** AX, DS, MC, VI. **Free Special Amenities: continental breakfast and high-speed Internet.**

AAA Benefit: Members save up to 20%, plus 10% bonus points with rewards program.

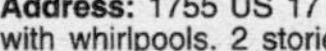 / SOME UNITS

COMFORT INN - NORTH

Book at AAA.com

Phone: (843)249-2490 20

Hotel

$60-$189 3/31-11/30
$60-$80 12/1-3/30

Address: 1755 US 17 N **Location:** Jct SR 9, just s. **Facility:** 60 one-bedroom standard units, some with whirlpools. 2 stories (no elevator), interior corridors. *Bath:* combo or shower only. **Parking:** on-site. **Terms:** 7 day cancellation notice. **Amenities:** irons, hair dryers. **Pool(s):** outdoor. **Guest Services:** wireless Internet. **Business Services:** fax (fee). **Cards:** AX, CB, DC, DS, JC, MC, VI.

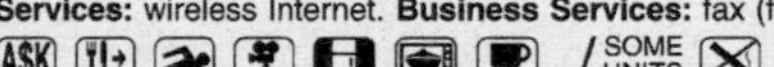

(See map and index starting on p. 966)

HAMPTON INN HARBOURGATE *Book great rates at AAA.com* **Phone:** (843)249-1997 19

Hotel
$65-$336 All Year

Address: 2112 Little River Neck Rd **Location:** US 17, exit Cherry Grove, just w, then just n. **Facility:** 101 units. 94 one-bedroom standard units. 7 one-bedroom suites. 5 stories, interior corridors. *Bath:* combo or shower only. **Parking:** on-site. **Terms:** 2-3 night minimum stay - seasonal, 3 day cancellation notice-fee imposed. **Amenities:** video games (fee), voice mail, irons. **Pool(s):** heated indoor. **Leisure Activities:** exercise room. **Guest Services:** valet and coin laundry, wireless Internet. **Business Services:** meeting rooms, fax (fee). **Cards:** AX, DS, MC, VI.

/ SOME UNITS VCR

AAA Benefit:
Members save up to 10% everyday!

HARBOURGATE RESORT & MARINA *Book great rates at AAA.com* **Phone:** (843)417-1160 18

AAA SAVE

Condominium
$41-$195 All Year

Address: 2100 Sea Mountain Hwy **Location:** US 17, exit Cherry Grove, just w, then just n. **Facility:** Located on the Intracoastal Waterway, select from five different floor plans of one-, two- and three-bedroom condos, all with a kitchen and balcony. Smoke free premises. 69 condominiums. 7 stories, exterior corridors. *Bath:* combo or shower only. **Parking:** on-site. **Terms:** check-in 4 pm, 2-4 night minimum stay - seasonal, 7 day cancellation notice-fee imposed. **Amenities:** voice mail, irons, hair dryers. **Pool(s):** heated outdoor. **Guest Services:** complimentary laundry, wireless Internet. **Business Services:** business center. **Cards:** AX, DS, MC, VI. **Free Special Amenities: local telephone calls and high-speed Internet.** ***(See color ad on insert)***

CALL

LA QUINTA INN-NORTH MYRTLE BEACH *Book at AAA.com* **Phone:** (843)280-4555 22

Hotel
$49-$169 All Year

Address: 1601-B US 17 N **Location:** Jct SR 9, just s. **Facility:** 80 one-bedroom standard units, some with whirlpools. 5 stories, interior corridors. *Bath:* combo or shower only. **Parking:** on-site. **Amenities:** irons, hair dryers. **Pool(s):** outdoor. **Guest Services:** valet laundry, wireless Internet. **Business Services:** fax (fee). **Cards:** AX, DC, DS, MC, VI.

ASK / SOME UNITS

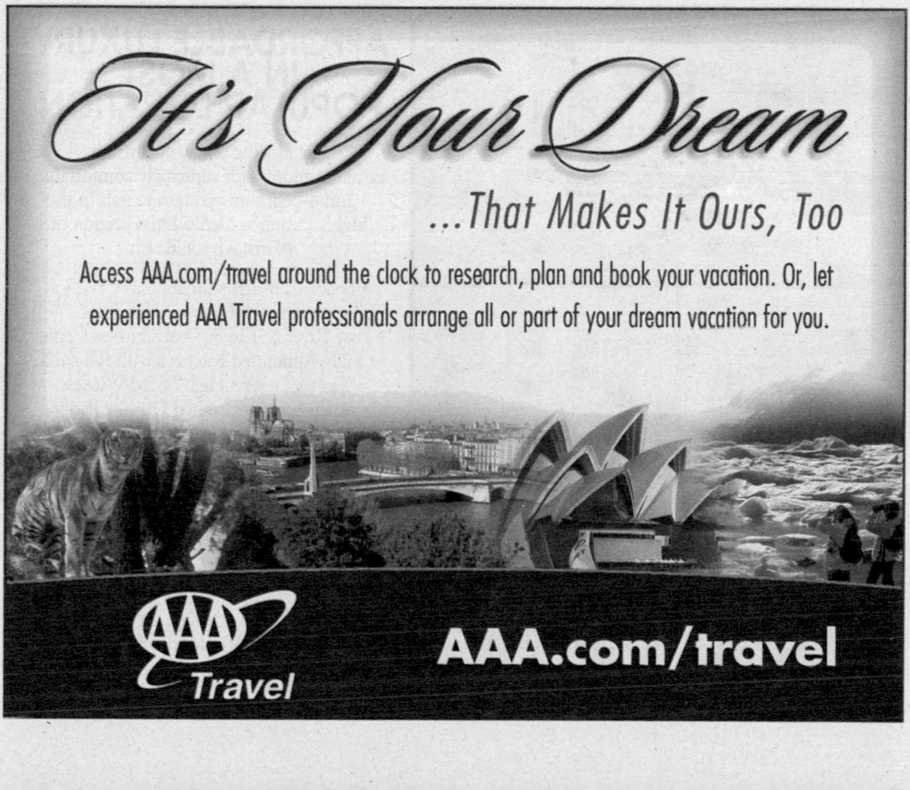

(See map and index starting on p. 966)

MAR VISTA GRANDE — Book great rates at AAA.com — **Phone:** 843/663-1246 — 27

Vacation Rental Condominium

Rates not provided

Address: 603 S Ocean Blvd **Location:** Oceanfront. Jct 6th Ave S. **Facility:** Select from a three- or four-bedroom condo featuring a private balcony and full-size kitchen with granite countertops and stainless steel appliances. 160 condominiums. 14 stories, interior corridors. **Parking:** on-site. **Amenities:** voice mail, safes, irons, hair dryers. **Pool(s):** outdoor, indoor/outdoor. **Leisure Activities:** whirlpools, exercise room. **Guest Services:** complimentary laundry, wireless Internet. **Business Services:** business center. ***(See color ad below)***

CALL 

OCEAN DRIVE BEACH & GOLF RESORT — **Phone:** (843)249-1436 — 26

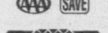

AAA SAVE

Resort Hotel

$36-$184 All Year

Address: 98 N Ocean Blvd **Location:** Oceanfront. Jct Main St, just n. **Facility:** This well-appointed property offers attractive public areas and a choice of accommodation types. 179 units. 80 one-bedroom standard units, some with kitchens. 99 one-bedroom suites, some with kitchens. 12 stories, interior/exterior corridors. *Bath:* combo or shower only. **Parking:** on-site. **Terms:** check-in 4 pm, 2-3 night minimum stay, 7 day cancellation notice-fee imposed. **Amenities:** voice mail, safes, irons, hair dryers. **Dining:** nightclub. **Pool(s):** outdoor, heated indoor. **Leisure Activities:** sauna, whirlpools, lazy river water ride, Shagger's Hall of Fame, exercise room. *Fee:* massage, game room. **Guest Services:** coin laundry, beauty salon, tanning facilities, wireless Internet. **Business Services:** conference facilities, fax (fee). **Cards:** DS, MC, VI. **Free Special Amenities: local telephone calls and high-speed Internet.** ***(See color ad p 991)***

     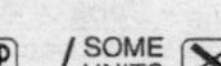 / SOME UNITS

▼ See AAA listing p 990 ▼

• World's Widest Beach • Spacious 1, 2 and 3 Room Suites
• Oceanfront Pools • Indoor Pool • Indoor/Outdoor Whirlpools • Lazy River
• Fitness Center with Sauna • Video Arcade • Gift Shop • Guest Laundry
• Poolside Tiki Hut Snack Bar and Grill • Home of the World Famous Spanish Galleon Night Life
• The O.D. Café Oceanfront Dining • The Beach Club Sports bar & Grill
• Home of the Shaggers Hall of Fame • Golf Packages (Over 80 Courses) • Entertainment Packages Available
• Conveniently Located in the Downtown Area, next to Shopping and OD Pavilion
• Resort Meeting and Conference Facilities for groups up to 400

OCEAN DRIVE
BEACH & GOLF RESORT

98 North Ocean Boulevard • North Myrtle Beach, SC 29582
(843) 249-1436 • Fax: (843) 249-1437
1-800-438-9590
www.oceandriveresort.com

AAA Approved

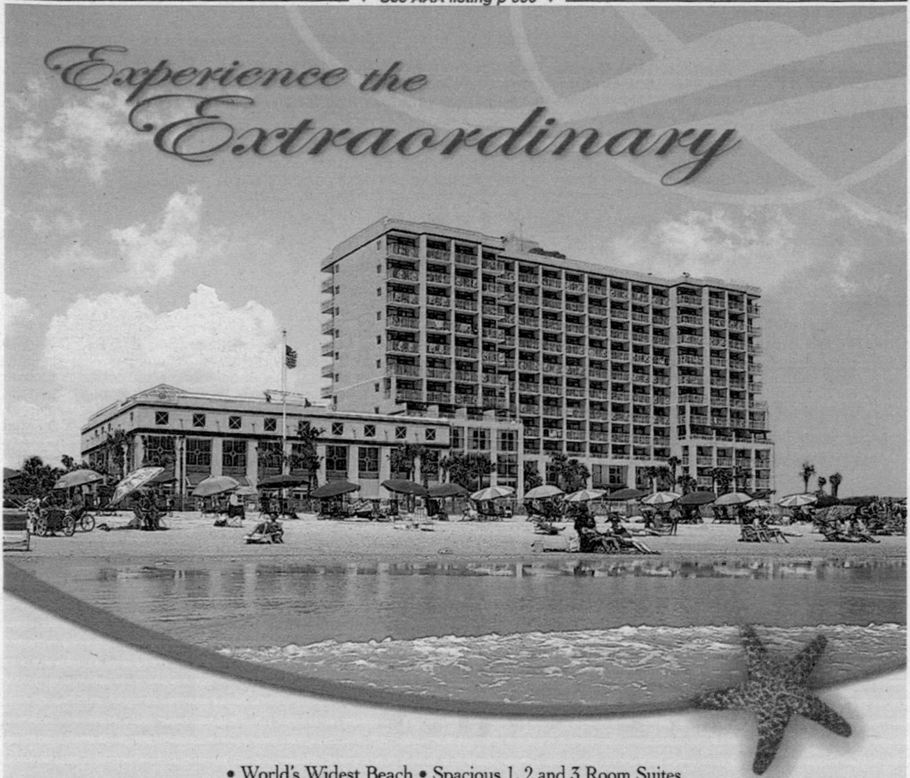

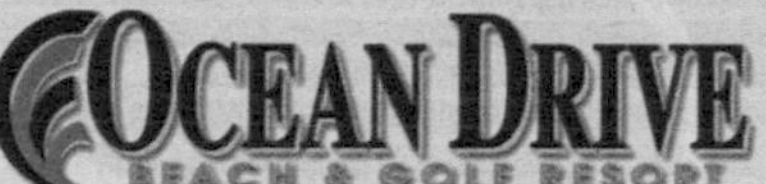

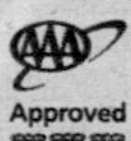

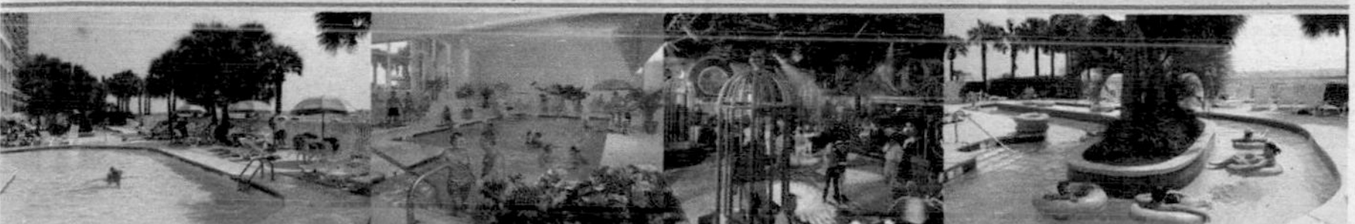

(See map and index starting on p. 966)

PRINCE RESORT AT CHERRY GROVE PIER *Book great rates at AAA.com* **Phone:** 843/417-1300 35

Vacation Rental Condominium

Rates not provided

Address: 3500 N Ocean Blvd **Location:** Oceanfront. Jct 34th Ave N. **Facility:** Located at the Cherry Grove pier, the resort is comprised of three separate high-rise buildings, two of which are directly on the beach. Smoke free premises. 257 condominiums. 18 stories, interior/exterior corridors. **Parking:** on-site. **Amenities:** high-speed Internet, voice mail, safes, irons, hair dryers. **Pool(s):** 2 outdoor. **Leisure Activities:** whirlpools, fishing, exercise room. *Fee:* game room. **Guest Services:** complimentary laundry. **Business Services:** meeting rooms. *Fee:* administrative services, fax. ***(See color ad starting on p 1018)***

QUALITY INN & SUITES *Book great rates at AAA.com* **Phone:** (843)272-6153 21

AAA SAVE

Hotel

$59-$189 All Year

Address: 1601 US 17 N **Location:** Jct SR 9, just s. **Facility:** 75 units. 70 one-bedroom standard units, some with whirlpools. 5 one-bedroom suites. 5 stories, interior corridors. *Bath:* combo or shower only. **Parking:** on-site. **Amenities:** dual phone lines, safes, irons, hair dryers. **Pool(s):** outdoor. **Leisure Activities:** whirlpool, exercise room. **Guest Services:** valet laundry, wireless Internet. **Business Services:** meeting rooms, fax (fee). **Cards:** AX, CB, DC, DS, JC, MC, VI. **Free Special Amenities: continental breakfast and high-speed Internet.**

CALL / SOME UNITS

SEASIDE *Book great rates at AAA.com* **Phone:** (843)272-5166 29

AAA SAVE

Vacation Rental Condominium

$90-$490 6/6-11/30

$55-$309 12/1-6/5

Address: 2301 S Ocean Blvd **Location:** Oceanfront. Jct 23rd Ave S. Located in Crescent Beach section. **Facility:** Each unit, which have been decorated by a professional, features a private balcony with sweeping views of the Atlantic Ocean and Carolina coast. 69 condominiums. 14 stories, interior corridors. **Parking:** on-site. **Terms:** check-in 4 pm, cancellation fee imposed. **Amenities:** voice mail, hair dryers. **Pool(s):** 2 outdoor. **Leisure Activities:** whirlpool, lazy river, exercise room. **Guest Services:** coin laundry. **Business Services:** meeting rooms, PC, fax (fee). **Cards:** AX, DS, MC, VI. **Free Special Amenities: high-speed Internet.** ***(See color ad starting on p 1018)***

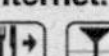     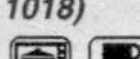

SHORE CREST VACATION VILLAS *Book great rates at AAA.com* **Phone:** (843)361-3600 33

AAA SAVE

Vacation Rental Condominium

$179-$382 5/25-11/30

$124-$318 12/1-5/24

Address: 4709 S Ocean Blvd **Location:** Oceanfront. Jct 48th Ave S, just n. **Facility:** Find bright guest rooms with modern decor in two high-rise towers, one of which is oceanfront; the other is across the street atop a parking garage. 240 condominiums. 12 stories, exterior corridors. **Parking:** on-site. **Terms:** check-in 4 pm, 2 night minimum stay - seasonal and/or weekends, 3 day cancellation notice-fee imposed. **Amenities:** video library (fee), DVD players, CD players, voice mail, irons, hair dryers. **Pool(s):** 2 heated outdoor, heated indoor. **Leisure Activities:** whirlpools, 2 lazy river water rides, recreation programs, rental bicycles, exercise room. *Fee:* game room. **Guest Services:** complimentary laundry. **Business Services:** PC, fax (fee). **Cards:** AX, DS, MC, VI. **Free Special Amenities: local telephone calls.** ***(See color ad p 1010)***

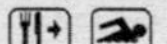

VCR / SOME UNITS

SUPER 8-BAREFOOT LANDING *Book at AAA.com* **Phone:** 843/913-3030 32

Hotel

Rates not provided

Address: 3801 US 17 S **Location:** Jct 38th Ave S. **Facility:** 80 one-bedroom standard units. 3 stories, interior corridors. *Bath:* combo or shower only. **Parking:** on-site. **Amenities:** voice mail, safes, irons, hair dryers. **Pool(s):** outdoor. **Guest Services:** wireless Internet. **Business Services:** meeting rooms, fax (fee).

CALL   / SOME UNITS

SUPER 8 NORTH POINT *Book great rates at AAA.com* **Phone:** (843)249-7339 23

AAA SAVE

Motel

$69-$149 All Year

Address: 1591 US 17 N **Location:** Jct SR 9, just s. **Facility:** 60 one-bedroom standard units, some with whirlpools. 2 stories (no elevator), exterior corridors. *Bath:* combo or shower only. **Parking:** on-site. **Terms:** 3 night minimum stay - seasonal and/or weekends, 4 day cancellation notice-fee imposed. **Amenities:** voice mail, safes (fee), irons, hair dryers. *Some:* high-speed Internet. **Pool(s):** heated indoor. **Leisure Activities:** whirlpool, limited exercise equipment. **Guest Services:** valet and coin laundry, wireless Internet. **Business Services:** meeting rooms, fax (fee). **Cards:** AX, DC, DS, MC, VI.

   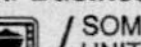 

/ SOME UNITS VCR

(See map and index starting on p. 966)

TILGHMAN BEACH & GOLF RESORT *Book great rates at AAA.com* **Phone:** (843)280-0913 

Vacation Rental Condominium
$89-$269 All Year

Address: 1819 N Ocean Blvd **Location:** Jct SR 9, just sw. **Facility:** Most rooms at the new, high-rise property offer views of the ocean; select from a variety of two- and three-bedroom, contemporary condo units. Smoke free premises. 170 condominiums. 15 stories, interior corridors. **Parking:** on-site. **Terms:** 2 night minimum stay, 30 day cancellation notice-fee imposed. **Amenities:** DVD players, high-speed Internet, voice mail, safes, irons. **Pool(s):** outdoor, heated indoor. **Leisure Activities:** sauna, whirlpools, lazy river, activity pool, exercise room. **Guest Services:** complimentary laundry, wireless Internet. **Business Services:** fax (fee). **Cards:** MC, VI. **Free Special Amenities: local telephone calls and high-speed Internet.** *(See color ad below)*

TOWERS ON THE GROVE **Phone:** 843/497-3024

fyi
Vacation Rental Condominium
Rates not provided

Too new to rate, opening scheduled for November 2008. **Address:** 2100 N Ocean Blvd **Location:** Between 21st and 23rd aves N. **Amenities:** 200 units, coffeemakers, microwaves, refrigerators, pool. ***(See color ad starting on p 1018)***

YACHT CLUB VILLAS-BEACH VACATIONS **Phone:** (843)449-2400 30

Vacation Rental Condominium
$59-$238 All Year

Address: 2151 Bridgeview Ct **Location:** Jct US 17/48 Ave S, just nw on US 17 to Barefoot Resort Bridge Rd, then just nw over bridge. Located in Barefoot Resort. **Facility:** Set in three high-rise buildings, these large condominium units offer upscale furnishings and beautiful views of maritime traffic. 99 condominiums. 7-12 stories, exterior corridors. **Parking:** on-site. **Terms:** office hours 7 am-11 pm, 2-5 night minimum stay - seasonal, 30 day cancellation notice-fee imposed. **Amenities:** DVD players, high-speed Internet, irons, hair dryers. **Pool(s):** outdoor. **Guest Services:** complimentary laundry. **Business Services:** fax (fee). **Cards:** DS, MC, VI. *(See color ad on insert)*

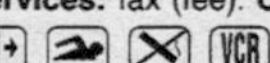   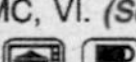

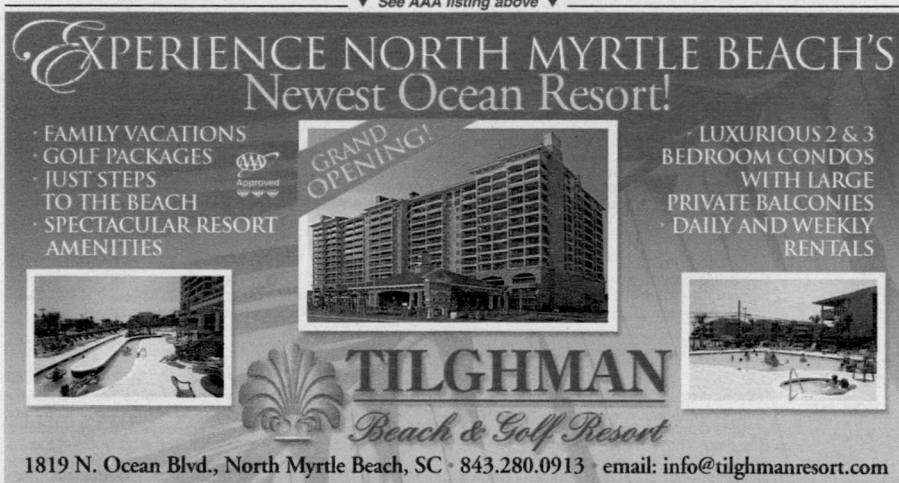

▼ *See AAA listing above* ▼

(See map and index starting on p. 966)

WHERE TO DINE

BENITO'S BRICK OVEN PIZZA & PASTA **Phone:** 843/272-1414 (31)

Italian
$9-$19

The small, casual eatery features a good selection of standard pasta, chicken, veal and seafood dishes, in addition to a long list of original pizza creations, strombolis and calzones prepared in a wood-fired oven. A children's menu is available. Casual dress. **Bar:** Full bar. **Hours:** 4:30 pm-9:30 pm, Fri & Sat-10:30 pm. Closed: 11/26, 12/25; also Sun. **Address:** 1596 Hwy 17 S **Location:** Jct 16th Ave s. **Parking:** on-site. **Cards:** MC, VI.

BENNY RAPPA'S TRATTORIA **Phone:** 843/361-1056 (30)

Italian
$8-$25

The cozy family restaurant combines good food, fine wine and good company. Small candlelit tables and Frank Sinatra background music lend to the trattoria feel. The blackboard menu changes daily, and entrees include preparations of veal, chicken, seafood and steaks. Casual dress. **Bar:** Full bar. **Reservations:** suggested. **Hours:** 5 pm-10 pm, Wed-Fri also 11:30 am-3 pm. Closed: Sun, 12/21-12/25 & Memorial Day weekend. **Address:** 1453 US 17 S **Location:** Jct 14th Ave S. **Parking:** on-site. **Cards:** AX, MC, VI.

BONEFISH GRILL **Phone:** 843/280-6638 (26)

Steak & Seafood
$13-$20

Fish is the house specialty, and the menu and nightly specials offer a variety of choices. Well-prepared food is cooked to perfection. Service is casual in nature, and the staff is skilled and attentive. Casual dress. **Bar:** Full bar. **Hours:** 4 pm-close. Closed: 11/26, 12/25. **Address:** 103 Hwy 17 S **Location:** Jct Main St, just sw. **Parking:** on-site. **Cards:** AX, DC, DS, MC, VI.

CALL

THE CRAB HOUSE **Phone:** 843/272-1062 (41)

SAVE

Seafood
$8-$40

Overlooking Barefoot Landing and the Intracoastal Waterway, the restaurant provides casual dining, beautiful surroundings, wonderful service and great food. The menu offers a cornucopia of fresh shellfish, seafood, pasta, chicken and steaks. The fresh catch can be prepared grilled, broiled or bronzed and served with any of five signature toppings, or left naked. For crab lovers, there's a good selection of the crustacean from all over North America, including Alaskan king crab. Casual dress. **Bar:** Full bar. **Hours:** 11 am-10:15 pm, Fri & Sat-11:15 pm; 11 am-8:15 pm, Fri & Sat-9:15 pm 11/1-2/28. Closed: 12/25. **Address:** 4744 Hwy 17 S **Location:** Jct SR 22, 2.2 mi nw; in Barefoot Landing. **Parking:** on-site. **Cards:** AX, DS, MC, VI.

CALL

DICK'S LAST RESORT **Phone:** 843/272-7794 (38)

American
$7-$18

Not for the faint of heart, this place—in business since 1992—employs a raucous, energetic and sometimes outrageous staff that are as quick to serve a meal as they are mild insults, but it's all in fun. In diner-participation dining experiences, guests will be invited to wear a butcher paper hat with a personalized surly statement written on it. The menu features fresh local seafood selections, cooked-to-order burgers, ice-cold beer and specialty drinks to help patrons swallow their pride. Casual dress. Entertainment. **Bar:** Full bar. **Reservations:** not accepted. **Hours:** 11 am-midnight. Closed: 12/25. **Address:** 4700 Hwy 17 S **Location:** Jct 48th Ave S, just n; in Barefoot Landing. **Parking:** on-site. **Cards:** AX, DS, MC, VI.

DINO'S HOUSE OF PANCAKES **Phone:** 843/272-5411 (32)

American
$3-$8

A lengthy list of breakfast combination plates make up the menu at this pancake house, where breakfast is prepared all day. Lunch offerings include burgers and melts. Casual dress. **Hours:** 6 am-2 pm. Closed: 12/25. **Address:** 2120 US 17 S **Location:** Jct 21st Ave S. **Parking:** on-site. **Cards:** DS, MC, VI.

DUFFY STREET SEAFOOD SHACK **Phone:** 843/249-7902 (22)

Seafood
$8-$26

Family owned and operated since 1992, the rustic corner restaurant provides simple coastal fare of fried seafood, po' boys, burgers and sandwiches, in addition to raw-bar items and ice-cold beer. Casual dress. **Bar:** Full bar. **Reservations:** not accepted. **Hours:** 4 pm-10 pm. Closed: 11/26, 12/24, 12/25. **Address:** 319 Sea Mountain Hwy **Location:** Jct US 17/SR 9, 1.4 mi s on SR 9; in Cherry Grove Area. **Parking:** on-site. **Cards:** DC, DS, MC, VI.

DUFFY STREET SEAFOOD SHACK **Phone:** 843/281-9840 (28)

Seafood
$8-$26

For a laid-back, Lowcountry evening, diners drop into this rustic cafe for a basket of shrimp or bucket of oysters. Casual dress. **Bar:** Full bar. **Hours:** noon-10 pm; hours may vary off season. Closed: 11/26, 12/24, 12/25. **Address:** 202 Main St **Location:** Jct Ocean Blvd, just n. **Parking:** on-site. **Cards:** DS, MC, VI.

FIRE ISLAND GRILLE **Phone:** 843/272-3473 (43)

American
$9-$35

Patrons enter a tropical paradise at the ornately decorated restaurant. Polynesian totems, tiki torches and palm trees adorn the interior of the award-winning nightspot. Seafood, chops, specialty sandwiches and burgers derive flavor from fruit juice marinades, tropical fruit accompaniments, chutneys and remoulades of Key lime. The ultimate specialty, Fire Island grilled skewers, mixes five marinated meats and seafood or strictly vegetables with a pyramid of island rice and five dipping sauces. Casual dress. **Bar:** Full bar. **Reservations:** accepted. **Hours:** 11 am-10 pm, Mon & Tues from 4 pm. Closed: 12/25. **Address:** 4924 Hwy 17 S **Location:** Jct 48th Ave SW, just s; in Barefoot Landing. **Parking:** on-site. **Cards:** AX, DS, MC, VI.

CALL

(See map and index starting on p. 966)

GREG NORMAN'S AUSTRALIAN GRILLE Phone: 843/361-0000 (44)

AAA

Steak & Seafood
$9-$30

This restaurant features attentive service in a large, attractive dining room with a deck overlooking the river. Steaks, chops, and seafood are prepared over a wood grill. Casual dress. **Bar:** Full bar. **Reservations:** suggested. **Hours:** 11 am-3 & 4:30-10 pm, Thurs-Sat to 11 pm, Sun 4:30 pm-10 pm. **Address:** 4030 US 17 S **Location:** Jct 48th Ave S, just n; in Barefoot Landing. **Parking:** on-site. **Cards:** AX, DS, MC, VI.

CALL

THE GRILL HOUSE Phone: 843/249-3033 (23)

American
$6-$24

A cup of soup and two sides come with your choice of entree, which might include steak, seafood or either of two cuts of the popular prime rib. You'll also find chef's specials, burgers and ribs in addition to early-bird specials offered from 11 am to 6 pm. Casual dress. **Bar:** Full bar. **Reservations:** accepted. **Hours:** 11 am-10 pm, Fri & Sat-11 pm. Closed: 11/26, 12/25. **Address:** 228 Hwy 17 N **Location:** Just n; in Surfwood Plaza. **Parking:** on-site. **Cards:** MC, VI.

HORST GASTHAUS Phone: 843/272-3351 (34)

AAA

German
$13-$19

Patrons of the fine Bavarian eatery can participate in the nightly sing-along while digging into fine German fare, such as bratwurst and Wiener schnitzel. An accordion player enhances the lively mood. German flags and cuckoo clocks dress the dark-cedar dining room. Casual dress. Entertainment. **Bar:** Full bar. **Reservations:** suggested, in season. **Hours:** 5 pm-10 pm; to 9 pm 11/1-1/31. Closed: Sun. **Address:** 802 37th Ave S **Location:** Jct US 17 S, just s. **Parking:** on-site. **Cards:** AX, CB, DC, DS, MC, VI.

HOUSE OF BLUES RESTAURANT Phone: 843/272-3000 (36)

Southern American
$9-$26

Also a popular music venue, the restaurant presents a Southern menu heavily influenced by Louisiana and Creole tradition. Among flavorful dishes are seafood jambalaya, Cajun meatloaf and New Orleans seafood gumbo with andouille sausage. The interior is a bona fide American folk art museum with many distractions for guests to explore. Karaoke Thursday gives diners an opportunity to show their talents with a live band and the popular Gospel brunch provides nourishment for body and soul. Casual dress. **Bar:** Full bar. **Hours:** 8 am-10 pm, Fri & Sat-11 pm; 11:30 am-9 pm, Fri-10 pm, Sat 8 am-10 pm 11/1-2/28. Closed: 12/25. **Address:** 4640 Hwy 17 S **Location:** Jct SR 22, 2.2 mi nw; in Barefoot Landing. **Parking:** on-site. **Cards:** AX, DS, MC, VI.

CALL

JOE'S BAR & GRILL Phone: 843/272-4666 (45)

Continental
$16-$36

The interior of the attractive old home, which has a deck overlooking the marsh, resembles a hunting lodge and displays an extensive collection of taxidermy. Well-prepared specialties include shrimp and scallops Alfredo, steak au poivre and scallops meuniere. Casual dress. **Bar:** Full bar. **Reservations:** suggested. **Hours:** 5 pm-10 pm. Closed: 11/26, 12/25. **Address:** 810 Conway St **Location:** Jct 48th Ave S, just n on US 17, then just e. **Parking:** on-site. **Cards:** AX, DS, MC, VI.

MARTINI'S CASUAL DINING & PIANO BAR Phone: 843/249-1134 (25)

Continental
$19-$30

Guests can select a martini from a menu of 30 varieties or choose one of more than 300 wines to enjoy with the music while perusing a menu of fresh seafood, chops and steaks. Dressy casual. Entertainment. **Bar:** Full bar. **Reservations:** suggested. **Hours:** 5 pm-10 pm; hours may vary off season. Closed: 1/1, 12/25; also Mon. **Address:** 98 US 17 S **Location:** Jct Main St, just sw. **Parking:** on-site. **Cards:** AX, MC, VI.

MEXICO LINDO MEXICAN RESTAURANT Phone: 843/361-4667 (27)

Mexican
$5-$13

A good selection of standard Mexican fare is offered on the menu at this brightly colored roadside restaurant, which is family owned and operated. Friendly servers are bilingual. An all-you-can-eat buffet is featured on Sundays. Casual dress. **Bar:** Full bar. **Reservations:** not accepted. **Hours:** 11:30 am-9:30 pm, Fri & Sat-10:30 pm. Closed: 12/24, 12/25. **Address:** 1012 Hwy 17 S **Location:** Jct 11th Ave S. **Parking:** on-site. **Cards:** AX, DC, MC, VI.

OCEAN GARDEN RESTAURANT Phone: 843/361-8788 (29)

Chinese
$6-$18

The casual eatery's menu and buffet both offer Szechuan, Hunan and Cantonese dishes, as well as many seafood selections, including crab legs. A hibachi station allows for the preparation of made-to-order fare. Casual dress. **Bar:** Full bar. **Reservations:** accepted. **Hours:** 11:30 am-3:30 & 4-10 pm. Closed: 11/26, 12/25. **Address:** 1400 US 17 S **Location:** Jct 14th Ave S. **Parking:** on-site. **Cards:** AX, DS, MC, VI.

OSCAR'S FOOD & SPIRITS Phone: 843/272-0707 (35)

American
$6-$11

Guests can nosh on a burger, sandwich or other munchies while watching their favorite team on one of the dozens of TVs. Casual dress. **Bar:** Full bar. **Hours:** 11:30 am-1 am, Sun from noon. Closed: 5/25, 12/25. **Address:** 4101 US 17 S **Location:** Jct 41st Ave S. **Parking:** on-site. **Cards:** DS, MC, VI.

RIVER CITY CAFE Phone: 843/272-7077 (40)

American
$4-$13

In Barefoot Landing, this rustic fish shack-style storefront restaurant prepares an extensive variety of sandwiches that span the taste spectrum from fried bologna on Texas toast to the River City Philly on hoagie. Also on the menu are many seafood platters and 30 signature burgers, including peanut butter or pizza burgers and several with cheese combinations. The casual spot is great for a quick bite and cold beer. A children's menu is available. Casual dress. **Bar:** Full bar. **Reservations:** not accepted. **Hours:** 11 am-9 pm. Closed: 12/25. **Address:** 4742 Hwy 17 S, Suites C & D **Location:** Jct 48th Ave S, just n. **Parking:** on-site. **Cards:** AX, DS, MC, VI.

(See map and index starting on p. 966)

ROCKEFELLERS RAW BAR **Phone:** 843/361-9677 (33)

Seafood
$7-$60

Pay a visit to the nautical-themed bar for steam kettles and seafood, including fresh oysters and shrimp. Televisions around the dining area let you keep up with the sporting action. Casual dress. **Bar:** Full bar. **Hours:** 11:30 am-11 pm. Closed: 5/25, 11/26, 12/25; also 5/27-5/29. **Address:** 3613 US 17 S **Location:** Jct 37th Ave S. **Parking:** on-site. **Cards:** AX, DS, MC, VI.

SEABLUE TAPAS BAR *Menu on AAA.com* **Phone:** 843/249-8800 (21)

AAA

Small Plates
$6-$20

A chic sexy atmosphere, great food and polished service add up to a wonderful dining experience at this upscale tapas restaurant. Casual dress. **Bar:** Full bar. **Reservations:** accepted. **Hours:** Open 12/1-1/1 & 1/15-10/31; 5 pm-10 pm. Closed: 11/26, 12/25; also Mon 5/1-9/30 & Sun. **Address:** 503 Hwy 17 N **Location:** Jct US 17 N/Main St, 0.4 mi ne; in the North Beach Shopping Center. **Parking:** on-site. **Cards:** AX, DS, MC, VI.

CALL

STICKY FINGERS RIB HOUSE **Phone:** 843/663-7675

Barbecue
$7-$26

Diners can put down their silverware and get their fingers ready for classic Carolina sweet ribs, as well as ribs cooked in the Texas and Tennessee styles. Hearty sides of baked beans and coleslaw complement entrees at the friendly cafe. Casual dress. **Bar:** Full bar. **Reservations:** not accepted. **Hours:** 11 am-close. Closed: 11/26, 12/25. **Address:** 4200 Hwy 17 S **Location:** Jct 42nd Ave S. **Parking:** on-site. **Cards:** AX, DC, DS, MC, VI.

TBONZ GILL & GRILL **Phone:** 843/272-7111 (39)

Steak & Seafood
$6-$21

Among specialty shops and amusements in Barefoot Landing, the pleasant setting has high ceilings and whimsical art. On the menu are seafood, Lowcountry dishes, burgers and light snacks. Try the baby back ribs or grilled mahi mahi. Casual dress. **Bar:** Full bar. **Hours:** 11 am-10 pm, Fri & Sat-10:30 pm. Closed: 11/26, 12/25. **Address:** 4732 US 17 S **Location:** Jct SR 22, 2.2 mi ne. **Parking:** on-site. **Cards:** AX, MC, VI.

CALL

"THE ORIGINAL" UMBERTO'S AT BAREFOOT LANDING **Phone:** 843/272-1176 (37)

Italian
$16-$30

Frank Sinatra croons a favorite standard as diners savor the Italian bean soup, salad and angel hair pasta that comes with every meal. Osso buco is the specialty of the house, but the lengthy menu also includes veal, chicken, seafood, steaks and chops entrees, as well as nightly specials. Casual dress. **Bar:** Full bar. **Reservations:** suggested, in season. **Hours:** Open 2/1-11/30; 5 pm-9:30 pm. Closed: 11/26, 12/24, 12/25. **Address:** 4886 US 17 S **Location:** Jct 48th Ave S, just n; in Barefoot Landing. **Parking:** on-site. **Cards:** AX, DS, MC, VI.

ULTIMATE CALIFORNIA PIZZA **Phone:** 843/361-8108 (42)

Pizza
$6-$20

Located in Barefoot Landing, the perennial winner of the "Best of the Beach" award features pizza with over 50 toppings. Also offered are subs, foccacia sandwiches, wraps and wings. Patio dining and takeout is available. Casual dress. **Bar:** Beer & wine. **Reservations:** not accepted. **Hours:** 11 am-1 am. Closed: 12/25. **Address:** 4860 Hwy 17 S **Location:** Jct US 17/48th Ave S, just s on US 17. **Parking:** on-site. **Cards:** AX, DS, MC, VI.

CALL

VILLA TUSCANNA **Phone:** 843/280-2288 (24)

Regional Italian
$7-$28

The casual eatery presents a menu of pasta, chicken, veal and seafood entrees, as well as items off the grill. Casual dress. **Bar:** Full bar. **Reservations:** accepted. **Hours:** 4 pm-10:30 pm; Wed-Fri from 11:30 am. Closed: 11/26, 12/25. **Address:** 97 US 17 N **Location:** Jct Main St, just nw. **Parking:** on-site. **Cards:** AX, DS, MC, VI.

MYRTLE BEACH pop. 22,759 (See map and index starting on p. 970-974)

WHERE TO STAY

THE ANDERSON OCEAN CLUB AND SPA *Book great rates at AAA.com* **Phone:** (843)213-5342 (43)

AAA SAVE

Vacation Rental Condominium
$59-$319 All Year

Address: 2600 N Ocean Blvd **Location:** Oceanfront. Jct 26th Ave N. **Facility:** Opened in November 2007, upscale condos include numerous amenities, cherry cabinetry, flat-panel televisions and granite countertops throughout. Smoke free premises. 304 condominiums. 21 stories, interior corridors. **Parking:** on-site. **Terms:** 3-4 night minimum stay - seasonal, 7 day cancellation notice-fee imposed. **Amenities:** high-speed Internet, safes, irons, hair dryers. **Pool(s):** 2 heated outdoor, heated indoor. **Leisure Activities:** whirlpools, lazy river water ride, exercise room. *Fee:* massage. **Guest Services:** complimentary laundry, wireless Internet. **Business Services:** business center. **Cards:** AX, DC, DS, MC, VI. **Free Special Amenities: local telephone calls and high-speed Internet.** *(See color ad on insert)*

▼ See AAA listing p 1035 ▼

(See map and index starting on p. 970)

ATLANTIC COAST RESORTS **Phone:** (843)448-8327 54

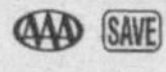

Vacation Rental Condominium

$30-$250 All Year

Address: 1702 N Ocean Blvd **Location:** Oceanfront. Jct 17th Ave N. **Facility:** This property includes two oceanfront high-rise towers with contemporary decor; all guest units have balconies. 137 condominiums. 14 stories, interior corridors. *Bath:* combo or shower only. **Parking:** on-site. **Terms:** off-site registration, cancellation fee imposed. **Amenities:** voice mail, hair dryers. *Some:* irons. **Pool(s):** heated outdoor, heated indoor. **Leisure Activities:** whirlpools, lazy river water ride. **Guest Services:** coin laundry, wireless Internet. **Business Services:** administrative services, fax (fee). **Cards:** DS, MC, VI. *(See color ad below)*

ATLANTIC PALMS BOUTIQUE RESORT **Phone:** (843)448-1616 62

Vacation Rental Condominium

$49-$190 All Year

Address: 703 S Ocean Blvd **Location:** Oceanfront. Jct 7th Ave S. **Facility:** Opened in 2008, the new property offers one-, two- and three-bedroom units with stainless steel appliances, granite counters and triple-sheeted beds. Smoke free premises. 134 condominiums. 9 stories, interior/exterior corridors. **Parking:** on-site. **Terms:** 2-3 night minimum stay - seasonal and/or weekends, 15 day cancellation notice-fee imposed. **Amenities:** DVD players, voice mail, irons, hair dryers. **Pool(s):** outdoor, heated indoor. **Leisure Activities:** whirlpool, exercise room. **Guest Services:** coin laundry, wireless Internet. **Business Services:** meeting rooms, fax (fee). **Cards:** AX, DC, DS, MC, VI.

BAY VIEW RESORT *Book great rates at AAA.com* **Phone:** (843)626-0000 57

Vacation Rental Condominium

$69-$604 All Year

Address: 504 N Ocean Blvd **Location:** Oceanfront. Jct 5th Ave N. **Facility:** High-rise condominiums located on the ocean offering multiple water activities, games on the third floor observation deck and a well-equipped exercise room. Designated smoking area. 183 condominiums. 19 stories, interior corridors. **Parking:** on-site. **Terms:** 14 day cancellation notice-fee imposed. **Amenities:** voice mail, safes, irons, hair dryers. **Pool(s):** outdoor, indoor. **Leisure Activities:** lazy river, exercise room, shuffleboard. **Guest Services:** complimentary laundry, wireless Internet. **Business Services:** fax (fee). **Cards:** AX, DS, MC, VI. **Free Special Amenities: high-speed Internet.** *(See color ad on insert)*

BEACH COLONY RESORT *Book great rates at AAA.com* **Phone:** (843)449-4010 24

Vacation Rental Condominium

$45-$431 All Year

Address: 5308 N Ocean Blvd **Location:** Oceanfront. Jct 52nd Ave N, just n. **Facility:** Waterfront in the Ocean Forest section of Myrtle Beach, the hotel offers one- to four-bedroom units. 214 condominiums. 12-22 stories, exterior corridors. **Parking:** on-site. **Terms:** 2-3 night minimum stay - seasonal, age restrictions may apply, 14 day cancellation notice-fee imposed. **Amenities:** video library, DVD players, voice mail, safes (fee), irons, hair dryers. *Some:* CD players. **Pool(s):** outdoor, 2 heated outdoor, heated indoor. **Leisure Activities:** saunas, whirlpools, lazy river water ride, racquetball court, recreation programs in summer, exercise room. *Fee:* game room. **Guest Services:** coin laundry, wireless Internet. **Business Services:** meeting rooms, PC, fax (fee). **Cards:** AX, DC, DS, MC, VI. **Free Special Amenities: local telephone calls and high-speed Internet.** *(See color ad p 1000)*

/ SOME UNITS

▼ *See AAA listing above* ▼

(See map and index starting on p. 970)

BEST WESTERN CAROLINIAN BEACH RESORT Book great rates at AAA.com **Phone:** (843)448-6861 44

Vacation Rental Condominium
$46-$415 All Year

Address: 2506 N Ocean Blvd **Location:** Oceanfront. Jct 26th Ave N. **Facility:** This property with off-site parking features a selection of standard hotel rooms as well as two-, three- and four-room, condominium-style suites. 220 units. 100 one-bedroom standard units, some with efficiencies. 120 condominiums. 10-22 stories, interior/exterior corridors. **Parking:** on-site. **Terms:** cancellation fee imposed. **Amenities:** voice mail, safes, irons, hair dryers. *Some:* high-speed Internet. **Pool(s):** 2 outdoor. **Leisure Activities:** whirlpool, indoor lazy river water ride, exercise room, game room. **Guest Services:** coin laundry, wireless Internet. **Business Services:** business center. **Cards:** AX, DS, MC, VI. **Free Special Amenities: local telephone calls and high-speed Internet.**
(See color ad on insert)

/ SOME UNITS

AAA Benefit:
Members save up to 20%, plus 10% bonus points with rewards program.

BEST WESTERN GRAND STRAND INN & SUITES Book great rates at AAA.com **Phone:** (843)448-1461 

Motel
$47-$205 All Year

Address: 1804 S Ocean Blvd **Location:** Oceanfront. Jct 18th Ave S. **Facility:** 115 units. 72 one- and 24 two-bedroom standard units, some with efficiencies or kitchens. 16 one-, 1 two- and 2 three-bedroom suites, some with efficiencies, kitchens and/or whirlpools. 3-6 stories, interior/exterior corridors. **Parking:** on-site. **Terms:** 2-5 night minimum stay - seasonal, 14 day cancellation notice-fee imposed. **Amenities:** voice mail, safes, irons, hair dryers. *Some:* DVD players, high-speed Internet. **Pool(s):** outdoor, indoor. **Leisure Activities:** whirlpools, lazy river water ride, sun deck, picnic area with barbecue grills. **Guest Services:** coin laundry, wireless Internet. **Business Services:** *Fee:* administrative services, fax. **Cards:** AX, DC, DS, MC, VI. **Free Special Amenities: continental breakfast and high-speed Internet.** ***(See color ad p 1005)***

AAA Benefit:
Members save up to 20%, plus 10% bonus points with rewards program.

FEE / SOME UNITS VCR

BLUEWATER RESORT **Phone:** (843)626-8345 77

Vacation Rental Condominium
$50-$350 All Year

Address: 2001 S Ocean Blvd **Location:** Oceanfront. Jct 20th Ave S. **Facility:** The resort includes an oceanfront high-rise building and two smaller villas; as each unit is individually decorated, amenities can vary widely. 178 condominiums. 4-15 stories, exterior corridors. *Bath:* combo or shower only. **Parking:** on-site. **Terms:** 4 night minimum stay - seasonal and/or weekends, age restrictions may apply, 7 day cancellation notice-fee imposed. **Amenities:** voice mail, safes, irons, hair dryers. **Pool(s):** 4 outdoor, heated indoor/outdoor. **Leisure Activities:** sauna, whirlpools, lazy river water ride, racquetball court. *Fee:* golf privileges, game room. **Guest Services:** coin laundry, wireless Internet. **Business Services:** meeting rooms. *Fee:* administrative services, fax. **Cards:** AX, DS, MC, VI.

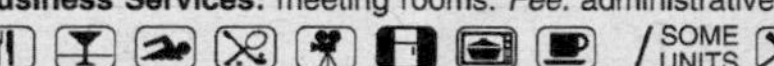

/ SOME UNITS

BOARDWALK BEACH RESORT Book great rates at AAA.com **Phone:** (843)448-8545 

Hotel
$40-$300 5/1-11/30
$40-$175 12/1-4/30

Address: 2301 N Ocean Blvd **Location:** Oceanfront. Jct 23rd Ave N. **Facility:** 353 units. 182 one- and 36 two-bedroom standard units, some with efficiencies and/or whirlpools. 133 one- and 2 three-bedroom suites, some with efficiencies, kitchens and/or whirlpools. 6-14 stories, interior/exterior corridors. *Bath:* combo or shower only. **Parking:** on-site. **Terms:** 14 day cancellation notice-fee imposed. **Amenities:** irons, hair dryers. *Some:* high-speed Internet. **Pool(s):** outdoor, 2 heated outdoor, 3 heated indoor. **Leisure Activities:** sauna, whirlpools, lazy river water ride, exercise room, shuffleboard. *Fee:* golf privileges. **Guest Services:** coin laundry. **Business Services:** meeting rooms. *Fee:* administrative services, fax. **Cards:** AX, DS, MC, VI. **Free Special Amenities: local telephone calls and early check-in/late check-out.**
(See color ad p 1006)

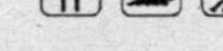

/ SOME UNITS

THE BREAKERS NORTH TOWER **Phone:** (843)444-4444 39

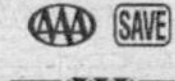

Hotel
$37-$550 All Year

Address: 2700 N Ocean Blvd **Location:** Oceanfront. Jct 27th Ave N. **Facility:** Smoke free premises. 141 units. 78 one-bedroom standard units. 63 condominiums. 19 stories, exterior corridors. *Bath:* combo or shower only. **Parking:** on-site. **Terms:** 14 day cancellation notice-fee imposed. **Amenities:** voice mail, irons, hair dryers. **Pool(s):** heated outdoor. **Leisure Activities:** saunas, whirlpool, exercise room. **Guest Services:** wireless Internet. **Business Services:** fax (fee). **Cards:** AX, DS, MC, VI. **Free Special Amenities: local telephone calls and high-speed Internet.** ***(See color ad on insert)***

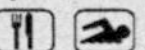

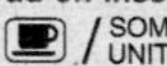

/ SOME UNITS

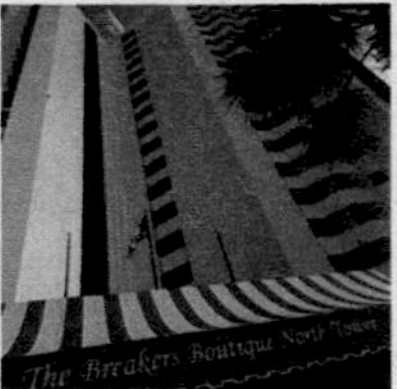

(See map and index starting on p. 970)

THE BREAKERS PARADISE TOWER **Phone:** 843/444-4444 **51**

Vacation Rental Condominium
$52-$545 All Year

Address: 2004 N Ocean Blvd **Location:** Oceanfront. Jct 21st Ave N. **Facility:** The high-rise resort features a variety of room types with a comfortable residential decor; the onsite water park is enclosed during winter months. Smoke free premises. 175 units. 19 one-bedroom standard units. 156 condominiums. 21 stories, interior corridors. **Parking:** on-site. **Terms:** off-site registration, 14 day cancellation notice-fee imposed. **Amenities:** voice mail, irons, hair dryers. **Dining:** Papa's, see separate listing. **Pool(s):** heated indoor/outdoor. **Leisure Activities:** whirlpools. **Guest Services:** coin laundry, wireless Internet. **Business Services:** meeting rooms, fax (fee). **Cards:** AX, DS, MC, VI.
(See color ad on insert)

▼ *See AAA listing p 1004* ▼

▼ See AAA listing p 1004 ▼

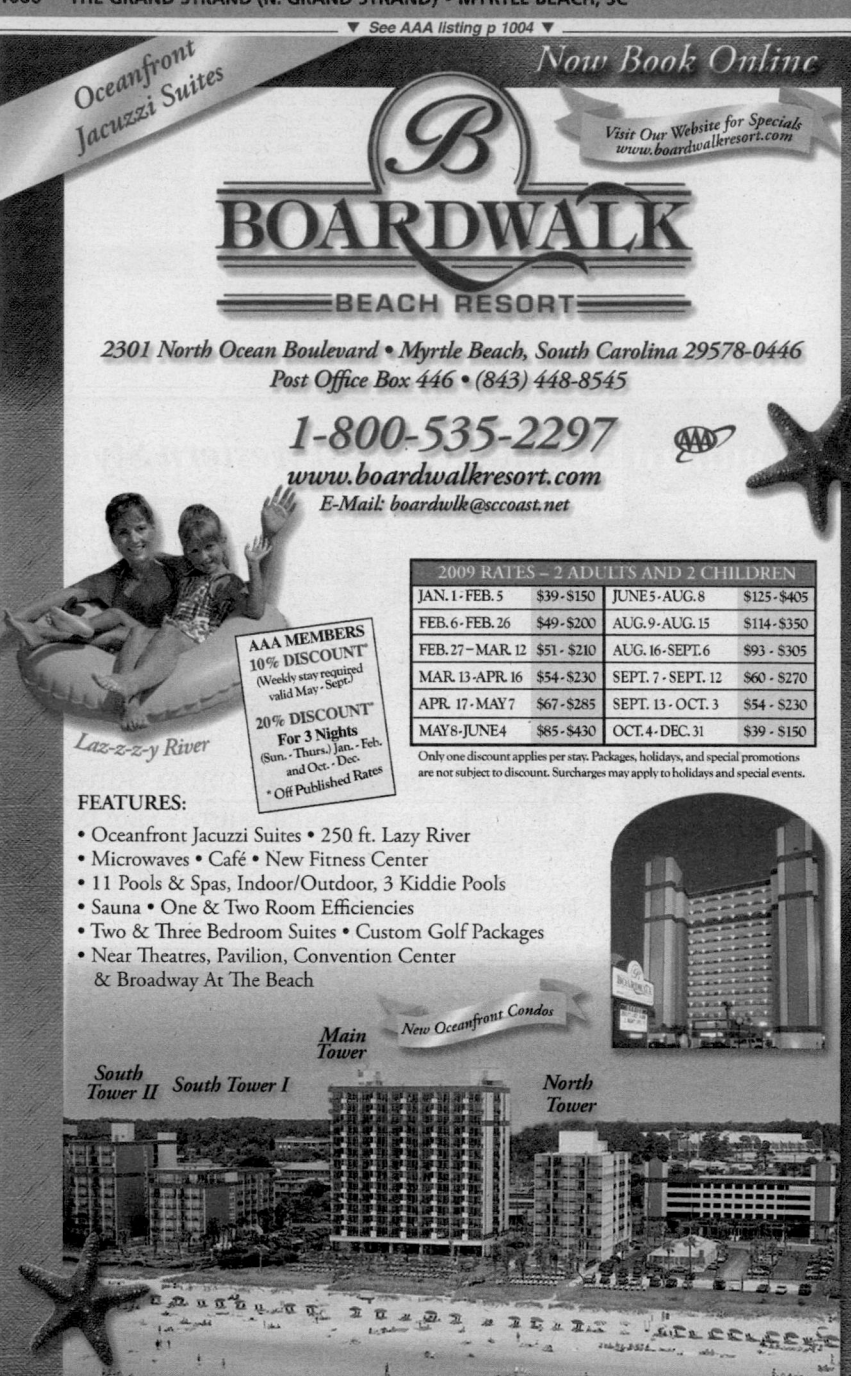

(See map and index starting on p. 970)

THE BREAKERS RESORT HOTEL Phone: (843)444-4444 50

Vacation Rental Condominium
$44-$430 All Year

Address: 2006 N Ocean Blvd **Location:** Oceanfront. Jct 21st Ave N. **Facility:** A variety of room types feature a comfortable, residential decor; the older property is comprised of three separate buildings and a water park. 490 units. 159 one-bedroom standard units, some with efficiencies and/or whirlpools. 331 condominiums. 3-15 stories, interior/exterior corridors. **Parking:** on-site. **Terms:** age restrictions may apply, 14 day cancellation notice-fee imposed. **Amenities:** voice mail, irons, hair dryers. **Dining:** Papa's, see separate listing. **Pool(s):** outdoor, heated indoor/outdoor. **Leisure Activities:** saunas, whirlpools, lazy river water ride, exercise room. *Fee:* golf & tennis privileges, game room. **Guest Services:** coin laundry, wireless Internet. **Business Services:** meeting rooms, administrative services, fax (fee). **Cards:** AX, DS, MC, VI. **Free Special Amenities: local telephone calls and high-speed Internet.** ***(See color ad on insert)***

/ SOME UNITS

CAMELOT BY THE SEA *Book great rates at AAA.com* Phone: (843)916-4700 52

Vacation Rental Condominium
$51-$280 All Year

Address: 2000 N Ocean Blvd **Location:** Oceanfront. Jct 20th Ave N. **Facility:** This oceanfront resort features a medieval theme in the common areas and a crisp, contemporary decor in the guest units. Smoke free premises. 219 condominiums. 18 stories, exterior corridors. **Parking:** on-site. **Terms:** 2-4 night minimum stay - seasonal, 7 day cancellation notice-fee imposed. **Amenities:** voice mail, safes, irons, hair dryers. **Pool(s):** outdoor, heated indoor. **Leisure Activities:** whirlpools, lazy river water ride, exercise room. *Fee:* game room. **Guest Services:** valet and coin laundry, wireless Internet. **Business Services:** business center. **Cards:** AX, DS, MC, VI. **Free Special Amenities: local telephone calls and high-speed Internet.** ***(See color ad on insert)***

CAPTAIN'S QUARTERS RESORT *Book great rates at AAA.com* Phone: (843)448-1404 65

Hotel
$31-$299 All Year

Address: 901 S Ocean Blvd **Location:** Oceanfront. Jct 9th Ave S. **Facility:** 328 units. 130 one- and 56 two-bedroom standard units, some with kitchens. 142 one-bedroom suites with kitchens. 9-15 stories, exterior corridors. *Bath:* combo or shower only. **Parking:** on-site. **Terms:** 2-3 night minimum stay - seasonal, 14 day cancellation notice-fee imposed. **Amenities:** voice mail, safes, irons, hair dryers. **Pool(s):** 2 heated outdoor, heated indoor. **Leisure Activities:** whirlpools, indoor lazy river water ride, kiddie lazy river water ride. *Fee:* bowling alley, game room. **Guest Services:** coin laundry, wireless Internet. **Cards:** AX, MC, VI. ***(See color ad p 1002)***

/ SOME UNITS

THE CARAVELLE RESORT-ARBOR VILLAS Phone: (843)918-8000 15

Vacation Rental Condominium
$94-$195 5/15-11/30
$90-$175 12/1-5/14

Address: 6900 N Ocean Blvd **Location:** Jct 69th Ave N. **Facility:** Located a block and a half from the ocean, the spacious villas are great for families and golfing groups; each private balcony overlooks the pool area. 7 condominiums. 3 stories (no elevator), exterior corridors. **Parking:** on-site. **Terms:** off-site registration, check-in 4 pm, 2-7 night minimum stay - seasonal, age restrictions may apply, 14 day cancellation notice-fee imposed. **Amenities:** voice mail, safes, irons, hair dryers. **Pool(s):** outdoor. **Leisure Activities:** beach access. **Guest Services:** complimentary laundry. **Business Services:** conference facilities, fax (fee). **Cards:** AX, DS, MC, VI.

ASK

THE CARAVELLE RESORT-CARAVELLE TOWERS Phone: (843)918-8000 11

Vacation Rental Condominium
$155-$199 5/15-11/30
$63-$145 12/1-5/14

Address: 6900 N Ocean Blvd **Location:** Jct 69th Ave N. **Facility:** Located on the ocean side of the road, each unit's balcony is positioned so guests can see the ocean; a gift shop is located in the lobby. 49 condominiums. 8 stories, interior corridors. **Parking:** on-site. **Terms:** off-site registration, check-in 4 pm, 2-7 night minimum stay - seasonal, age restrictions may apply, 14 day cancellation notice-fee imposed. **Amenities:** voice mail, safes, irons, hair dryers. **Pool(s):** indoor/outdoor. **Leisure Activities:** beach access. **Guest Services:** valet and coin laundry. **Business Services:** conference facilities, fax (fee). **Cards:** AX, DS, MC, VI.

ASK

THE CARAVELLE RESORT-CAROLINA DUNES Phone: (843)918-8000 17

Vacation Rental Condominium
$89-$390 5/15-11/30
$79-$335 12/1-5/14

Address: 6900 N Ocean Blvd **Location:** Oceanfront. Jct 69th Ave N. **Facility:** These spacious condominiums and penthouses are located directly on the ocean, providing a relaxing breeze. 36 condominiums. 8 stories, interior corridors. **Parking:** on-site. **Terms:** off-site registration, check-in 4 pm, 2-7 night minimum stay - seasonal, age restrictions may apply, 14 day cancellation notice-fee imposed. **Amenities:** voice mail, safes, irons, hair dryers. **Pool(s):** outdoor. **Leisure Activities:** whirlpools. **Guest Services:** complimentary laundry. **Business Services:** conference facilities, fax (fee). **Cards:** AX, DS, MC, VI.

ASK

THE CARAVELLE RESORT-DRYDOCK VILLAS Phone: (843)918-8000 14

Vacation Rental Condominium
$94-$195 5/15-11/30
$90-$175 12/1-5/14

Address: 6900 N Ocean Blvd **Location:** Jct 69th Ave N. **Facility:** Located a block and a half from the ocean, the spacious villas are great for families and golfing groups; each private balcony overlooks the pool area. 9 condominiums. 3 stories (no elevator), exterior corridors. **Parking:** on-site. **Terms:** off-site registration, check-in 4 pm, 2-7 night minimum stay - seasonal, age restrictions may apply, 14 day cancellation notice-fee imposed. **Amenities:** voice mail, safes, irons, hair dryers. **Pool(s):** outdoor. **Leisure Activities:** beach access. **Guest Services:** valet and coin laundry. **Business Services:** conference facilities, fax (fee). **Cards:** AX, DS, MC, VI.

ASK

(See map and index starting on p. 970)

THE CARAVELLE RESORT-HARBORSIDE VILLAS — **Phone:** (843)918-8000 — 16

Vacation Rental Condominium
$94-$195 5/15-11/30
$90-$175 12/1-5/14

Address: 6900 N Ocean Blvd **Location:** Jct 69th Ave N. **Facility:** Located a block and a half from the ocean, the spacious villas are great for families and golfing groups; each private balcony overlooks the pool area. 7 condominiums. 3 stories (no elevator), exterior corridors. **Parking:** on-site. **Terms:** off-site registration, check-in 4 pm, 2-7 night minimum stay - seasonal, age restrictions may apply, 14 day cancellation notice-fee imposed. **Amenities:** voice mail, safes, irons, hair dryers. **Pool(s):** outdoor. **Leisure Activities:** beach access. **Guest Services:** complimentary laundry. **Business Services:** conference facilities, fax (fee). **Cards:** AX, DS, MC, VI.

THE CARAVELLE RESORT HOTEL — *Book great rates at AAA.com* — **Phone:** (843)918-8000 — 13

Vacation Rental Condominium
$55-$345 5/15-11/30
$52-$225 12/1-5/14

Address: 6900 N Ocean Blvd **Location:** Oceanfront. Jct 69th Ave N. **Facility:** Located close to the ocean, the spacious accommodations are great for families and golfing groups; each private balcony overlooks the pool area. 343 condominiums. 15 stories, exterior corridors. *Bath:* combo or shower only. **Parking:** on-site. **Terms:** off-site registration, 2-7 night minimum stay - seasonal, age restrictions may apply, 14 day cancellation notice-fee imposed. **Amenities:** voice mail, safes, irons, hair dryers. **Pool(s):** 2 outdoor, indoor. **Leisure Activities:** whirlpools, fishing, lazy river water ride, children's acitivitiy pool, recreation programs, exercise room, shuffleboard. *Fee:* game room. **Guest Services:** valet and coin laundry, airport transportation-Myrtle Beach International Jetport, wireless Internet. **Business Services:** conference facilities, fax (fee). **Cards:** AX, DS, MC, VI. ***(See color ad p 1009)***

THE CARAVELLE RESORT-SEA MARK TOWERS — **Phone:** (843)918-8000 — 10

Vacation Rental Condominium
$89-$399 5/15-11/30
$79-$285 12/1-5/14

Address: 6900 N Ocean Blvd **Location:** Jct 69th Ave N. **Facility:** Located a block and a half from the beach, the high-rise offers spacious accommodations; unobstructed ocean views are afforded on the upper levels. 28 condominiums. 12 stories, interior corridors. **Parking:** on-site. **Terms:** off-site registration, check-in 4 pm, 2-7 night minimum stay - seasonal, 14 day cancellation notice-fee imposed. **Amenities:** voice mail, safes, irons, hair dryers. **Pool(s):** outdoor. **Leisure Activities:** whirlpool, beach access. **Business Services:** conference facilities, fax (fee). **Cards:** AX, DS, MC, VI.

THE CARAVELLE RESORT-ST. CLEMENTS TOWER — **Phone:** (843)918-8000 — 12

Vacation Rental Condominium
$67-$199 5/15-11/30
$51-$135 12/1-5/14

Address: 6900 N Ocean Blvd **Location:** Jct 69th Ave N. **Facility:** This semicircular building on the ocean offers modest-sized, pie-slice-shaped rooms with great views of the ocean and convenient access to amenities. 60 condominiums. 8 stories, interior corridors. **Parking:** on-site. **Terms:** check-in 4 pm, 2-7 night minimum stay - seasonal, age restrictions may apply, 14 day cancellation notice-fee imposed. **Amenities:** voice mail, safes, irons, hair dryers. **Pool(s):** outdoor. **Leisure Activities:** beach access. **Guest Services:** valet and coin laundry. **Business Services:** conference facilities, fax (fee). **Cards:** AX, DS, MC, VI.

THE CARIBBEAN RESORT & VILLAS — *Book great rates at AAA.com* — **Phone:** (843)448-7181 — 37

Vacation Rental Condominium
$47-$492 All Year

Address: 3000 N Ocean Blvd **Location:** Oceanfront. Jct 30th Ave N. **Facility:** The property offers guest rooms in beachfront towers and in condominium villas across the street. Designated smoking area. 435 units. 42 one-bedroom standard units. 393 condominiums. 3-19 stories, interior/exterior corridors. **Parking:** on-site. **Terms:** 14 day cancellation notice-fee imposed. **Amenities:** voice mail, safes, irons, hair dryers. **Pool(s):** heated outdoor, heated indoor. **Leisure Activities:** whirlpools, lazy river water ride, kids splash deck, recreation programs, exercise room, shuffleboard. *Fee:* game room. **Guest Services:** coin laundry, wireless Internet. **Business Services:** business center. **Cards:** AX, DS, MC, VI. **Free Special Amenities: local telephone calls and high-speed Internet.** ***(See color ad on insert)***

CAROLINA GRANDE — **Phone:** (843)282-8800 — 46

Vacation Rental Condominium
$124-$412 12/1-5/24
$179-$390 5/25-11/30

Address: 2505 N Ocean Blvd **Location:** Jct 25th Ave N. **Facility:** This 2006 condo-hotel across the street from the ocean offers large, well-appointed accommodations with ample, on-site covered parking. 113 condominiums. 20 stories, exterior corridors. **Parking:** on-site. **Terms:** check-in 4 pm, 2 night minimum stay, 3 day cancellation notice-fee imposed. **Amenities:** DVD players, video games (fee), CD players, high-speed Internet, voice mail, irons, hair dryers. **Pool(s):** outdoor. **Leisure Activities:** whirlpool. **Guest Services:** complimentary laundry, wireless Internet. **Business Services:** PC, fax (fee). **Cards:** AX, DS, MC, VI. **Free Special Amenities: local telephone calls.** *(See color ad p 1010)*

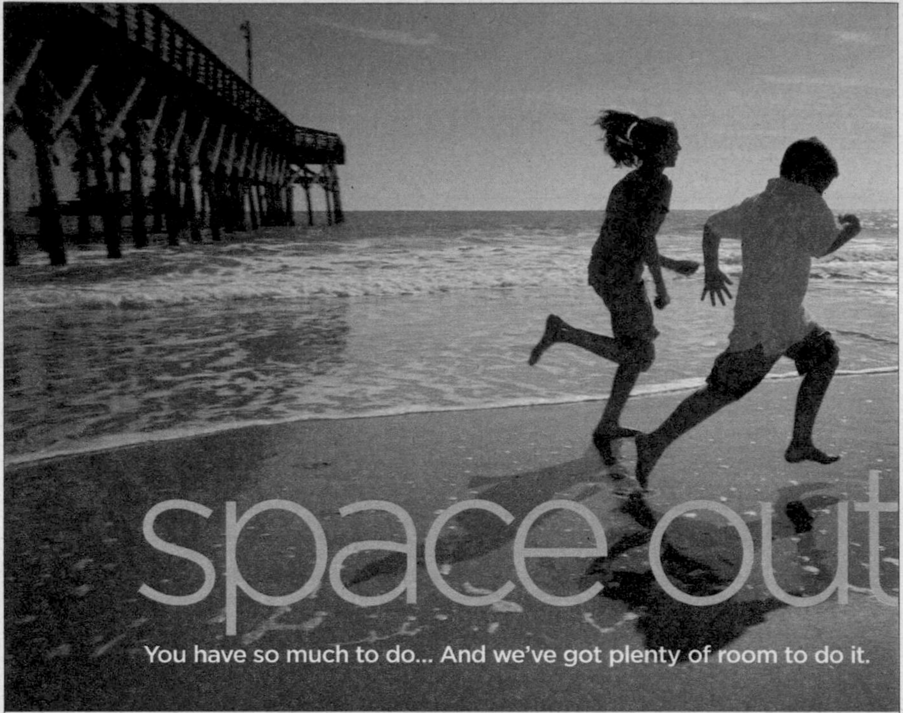
space out
You have so much to do... And we've got plenty of room to do it.

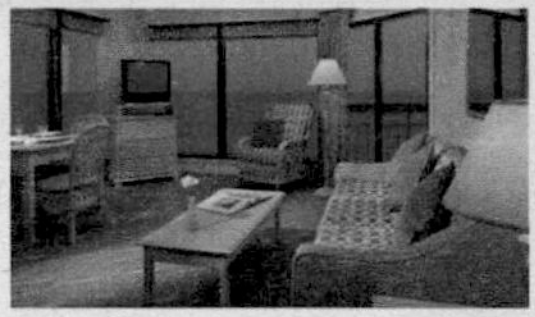

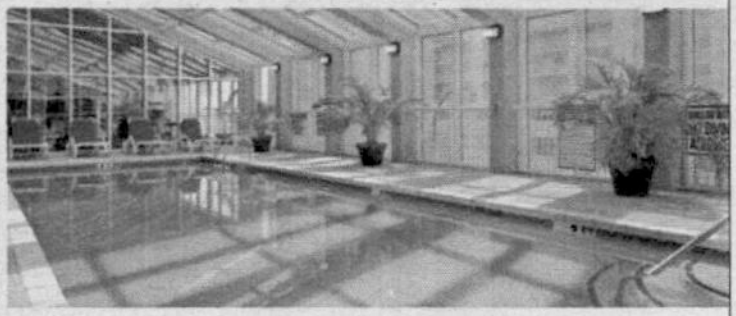

(See map and index starting on p. 970)

CAROLINA WINDS *Book great rates at AAA.com* **Phone:** (843)449-2477 4

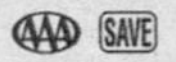

Vacation Rental Condominium
$42-$359 All Year

Address: 200 76th Ave N **Location:** Oceanfront. Jct N Ocean Blvd, just se. **Facility:** This oceanfront high-rise property offers several types of well equipped guest units ranging from 1-, 2- and 3-bedrooms. Guest room decor may vary from more modest and traditional to contemporary. 135 condominiums. 9-12 stories, exterior corridors. **Parking:** on-site. **Terms:** 4-7 night minimum stay - seasonal, age restrictions may apply, 7 day cancellation notice-fee imposed. **Amenities:** high-speed Internet, voice mail, irons, hair dryers. **Pool(s):** heated outdoor, heated indoor. **Leisure Activities:** sauna, whirlpools, lazy river water ride, tennis privileges, limited exercise equipment. *Fee:* game room. **Guest Services:** coin laundry, wireless Internet. **Business Services:** administrative services. *Fee:* PC, fax. **Cards:** AX, DS, MC, VI. **Free Special Amenities: high-speed Internet.**
(See color ad p 1001)

/ SOME UNITS VCR

COMFORT SUITES *Book at AAA.com* **Phone:** (843)448-4884 36

Hotel
$59-$259 All Year

Address: 710 Frontage Rd E **Location:** Jct US 17 Bypass, just se on US 501, then just ne. **Facility:** Smoke free premises. 84 one-bedroom standard units, some with whirlpools. 4 stories, interior corridors. *Bath:* combo or shower only. **Parking:** on-site. **Terms:** cancellation fee imposed. **Amenities:** dual phone lines, voice mail, safes (fee), irons, hair dryers. **Pool(s):** heated outdoor. **Leisure Activities:** limited exercise equipment. **Guest Services:** valet and coin laundry, wireless Internet. **Business Services:** meeting rooms, business center. **Cards:** AX, CB, DC, DS, JC, MC, VI.

ASK

COMPASS COVE OCEANFRONT RESORT *Book great rates at AAA.com* **Phone:** (843)448-8373 83

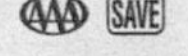

Vacation Rental Condominium
$43-$625 All Year

Address: 2311 S Ocean Blvd **Location:** Oceanfront. Jct 24th Ave S. **Facility:** The property consists of three separate buildings, two of which were renovated in 2006; choose from multiple floor plans, all of which have balconies. 532 units. 57 one-bedroom standard units. 475 condominiums. 5-16 stories, exterior corridors. **Parking:** on-site. **Terms:** 14 day cancellation notice-fee imposed. **Amenities:** voice mail, safes, irons, hair dryers. **Pool(s):** 4 outdoor, 2 heated outdoor, 2 heated indoor. **Leisure Activities:** sauna, whirlpools, three lazy river water rides, recreation programs in summer, exercise room, shuffleboard. *Fee:* game room. **Guest Services:** coin laundry, airport transportation-Myrtle Beach International Airport, wireless Internet. **Business Services:** meeting rooms, administrative services (fee). **Cards:** AX, DS, MC, VI. **Free Special Amenities: local telephone calls and high-speed Internet.**
(See color ad on insert)

CORAL BEACH RESORT *Book great rates at AAA.com* **Phone:** (843)448-8421 

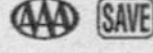

Vacation Rental Condominium
$45-$259 All Year

Address: 1105 S Ocean Blvd **Location:** Oceanfront. Jct 11th Ave S. **Facility:** On expansive grounds, the resort offers many recreational facilities and standard, efficiency and one-bedroom, condo-style rooms, all with balconies. 301 units. 38 one-bedroom standard units. 263 condominiums. 12 stories, exterior corridors. **Parking:** on-site. **Terms:** 15 day cancellation notice-fee imposed. **Amenities:** voice mail, safes, irons, hair dryers. **Dining:** nightclub. **Pool(s):** outdoor, heated outdoor, heated indoor. **Leisure Activities:** saunas, whirlpools, lazy river water ride, bowling alley, indoor play area, exercise room. *Fee:* golf privileges, massage, game room. **Guest Services:** coin laundry, wireless Internet. **Business Services:** conference facilities, administrative services (fee). **Cards:** AX, DS, MC, VI. **Free Special Amenities: local telephone calls and early check-in/late check-out.** *(See color ad starting on p 1012)*

COUNTRY INN & SUITES AT WACCAMAW *Book at AAA.com* **Phone:** (843)236-4500 27

Hotel
$59-$259 4/2-11/30
$59-$129 12/1-4/1

Address: 3516 W US 501 **Location:** Jct US 17 Bypass, 0.7 mi n on US 501, exit River Oaks Rd/George Bishop Pkwy, just e on River Oaks Rd, then just n. **Facility:** 62 units. 42 one-bedroom standard units, some with whirlpools. 20 one-bedroom suites. 3 stories, interior corridors. *Bath:* combo or shower only. **Parking:** on-site. **Terms:** 2-4 night minimum stay - seasonal and/or weekends. **Amenities:** high-speed Internet, voice mail, irons, hair dryers. **Pool(s):** heated indoor. **Leisure Activities:** whirlpool, limited exercise equipment. **Guest Services:** valet and coin laundry, wireless Internet. **Business Services:** PC. *Fee:* administrative services, fax. **Cards:** AX, CB, DC, DS, MC, VI.

(See map and index starting on p. 970)

COURT CAPRI

Phone: (843)448-6119 40

Hotel

$79-$129 12/1-8/12
$49-$89 8/13-11/30

Address: 2610 N Ocean Blvd **Location:** Oceanfront. Jct 26th Ave N. **Facility:** 99 units. 87 one- and 12 two-bedroom standard units, some with efficiencies. 4-10 stories, interior corridors. *Bath:* combo or shower only. **Parking:** on-site. **Terms:** 3 night minimum stay - seasonal and/or weekends, 7 day cancellation notice-fee imposed. **Amenities:** voice mail, irons. **Pool(s):** outdoor, heated indoor. **Leisure Activities:** whirlpools, exercise room. *Fee:* game room. **Guest Services:** coin laundry. **Business Services:** meeting rooms. *Fee:* administrative services, fax. **Cards:** AX, DS, MC, VI. ***(See color ad below)***

COURTYARD BY MARRIOTT-MYRTLE BEACH BROADWAY

Phone: (843)445-6333 34

Hotel

$81-$164 All Year

Address: 1351 21st Ave N **Location:** Jct US 17 Bypass, 0.4 mi se. Located across from Broadway at the Beach. **Facility:** Smoke free premises. 135 units. 126 one-bedroom standard units, some with whirlpools. 9 one-bedroom suites. 4 stories, interior corridors. *Bath:* combo or shower only. **Parking:** on-site. **Terms:** cancellation fee imposed. **Amenities:** video games (fee), dual phone lines, voice mail, irons, hair dryers. **Pool(s):** outdoor. **Leisure Activities:** whirlpool, limited exercise equipment. **Guest Services:** valet and coin laundry, wireless Internet. **Business Services:** meeting rooms, business center. **Cards:** AX, CB, DC, DS, MC, VI. **Free Special Amenities: newspaper and high-speed Internet.**

CALL / SOME UNITS

AAA Benefit:
Members save a minimum 5% off the best available rate.

CROWN REEF RESORT & CONFERENCE CENTER AT SOUTH BEACH RESORT

Phone: (843)626-8077 86

Hotel

$55-$185 All Year

Address: 2913 S Ocean Blvd **Location:** Oceanfront. Jct 29th Ave S. **Facility:** 514 units. 314 one-bedroom standard units, some with efficiencies. 200 one-bedroom suites with kitchens, some with whirlpools. 14 stories, exterior corridors. *Bath:* combo or shower only. **Parking:** on-site. **Terms:** off-site registration, 14 day cancellation notice-fee imposed. **Amenities:** voice mail, safes, irons, hair dryers. *Some:* high-speed Internet. **Dining:** 2 restaurants. **Pool(s):** 2 outdoor, heated indoor, indoor/outdoor. **Leisure Activities:** whirlpools, lazy river water ride, recreation programs, exercise room, shuffleboard. *Fee:* game room. **Guest Services:** valet and coin laundry, airport transportation-Myrtle Beach International Airport, wireless Internet. **Business Services:** conference facilities, business center. **Cards:** AX, DC, DS, MC, VI. **Free Special Amenities: local telephone calls and high-speed Internet.** ***(See color ad inside front cover)***

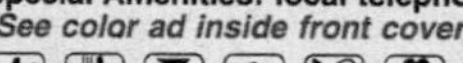
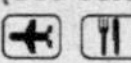

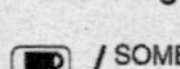

/ SOME UNITS

(See map and index starting on p. 970)

DAYS INN GRAND STRAND *Book great rates at AAA.com* **Phone:** (843)448-8261 63

Motel

$55-$179 3/15-11/30
$29-$69 12/1-3/14

Address: 806 S Ocean Blvd **Location:** Jct 9th Ave S. **Facility:** 57 units. 55 one- and 2 two-bedroom standard units, some with efficiencies (utensil deposit required). 3 stories (no elevator), exterior corridors. *Bath:* combo or shower only. **Parking:** on-site. **Terms:** 2 night minimum stay - weekends, 3 day cancellation notice. **Amenities:** hair dryers. **Pool(s):** outdoor. **Guest Services:** coin laundry, wireless Internet. **Business Services:** administrative services, fax (fee). **Cards:** AX, DS, MC, VI. **Free Special Amenities: continental breakfast and high-speed Internet.**

   / SOME UNITS

DAYTON HOUSE RESORT *Book great rates at AAA.com* **Phone:** (843)448-2441 47

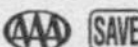

Hotel

$49-$239 All Year

Address: 2400 N Ocean Blvd **Location:** Oceanfront. Jct 24th Ave N. **Facility:** Smoke free premises. 327 units. 231 one-bedroom standard units with efficiencies. 96 one-bedroom suites with efficiencies. 5-16 stories, interior corridors. *Bath:* combo or shower only. **Parking:** on-site. **Terms:** age restrictions may apply, 7 day cancellation notice-fee imposed. **Amenities:** voice mail, safes, irons, hair dryers. **Pool(s):** heated outdoor, heated indoor, heated indoor/outdoor. **Leisure Activities:** saunas, whirlpools, fishing, lazy river water ride, exercise room, shuffleboard. *Fee:* game room. **Guest Services:** coin laundry, wireless Internet. **Business Services:** business center. **Cards:** AX, DS, MC, VI. **Free Special Amenities: local telephone calls and high-speed Internet.** *(See color ad below)*

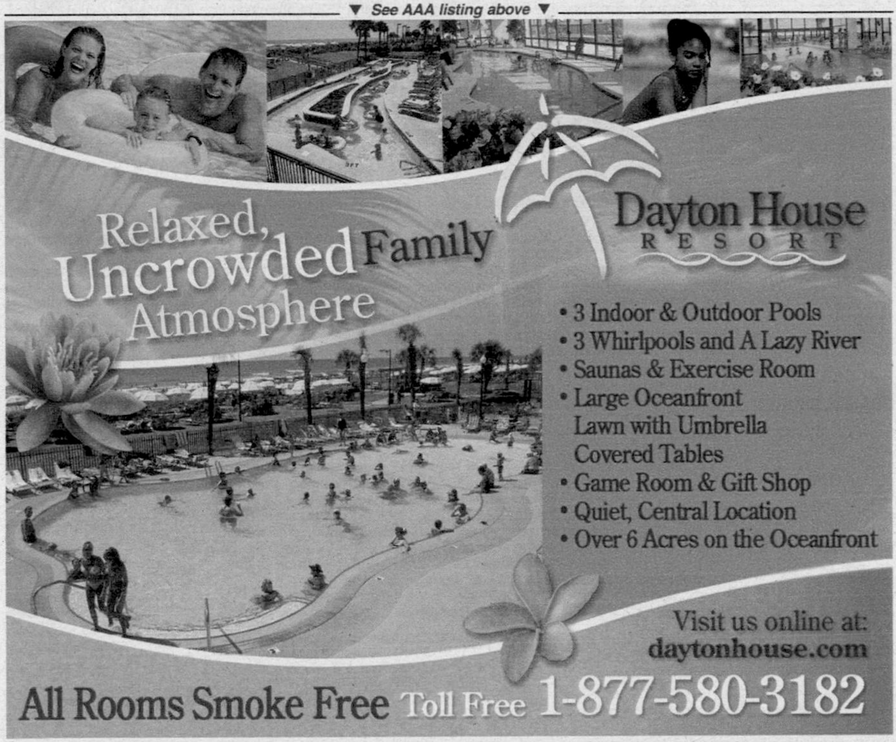

(See map and index starting on p. 970)

DUNES VILLAGE RESORT

Book great rates at AAA.com — **Phone:** (843)449-5275 — 25

Vacation Rental Condominium
$41-$597 All Year

Address: 5300 N Ocean Blvd **Location:** Oceanfront. Jct 52nd Ave N. Located in a quiet residential area. **Facility:** Located in the north-end area of town, the resort features an array of floor plans, ocean views from most rooms and many in-room and onsite amenities. Smoke free premises. 495 condominiums. 14 stories, interior/exterior corridors. **Parking:** on-site. **Terms:** age restrictions may apply, 14 day cancellation notice-fee imposed. **Amenities:** DVD players, high-speed Internet, dual phone lines, voice mail, irons, hair dryers. **Pool(s):** 2 outdoor, 2 heated indoor. **Leisure Activities:** whirlpools, waterslide, lazy river water ride, activity pool, indoor water park, recreation programs in summer, chess game, exercise room, basketball, shuffleboard. *Fee:* game room. **Guest Services:** coin laundry, wireless Internet. **Business Services:** fax (fee). **Cards:** AX, DS, MC, VI. **Free Special Amenities: high-speed Internet.** *(See color ad on insert)*

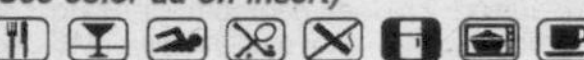

FAIRFIELD INN-BROADWAY AT THE BEACH

Book great rates at AAA.com — **Phone:** (843)444-8097 — 28

Hotel
$102-$164 All Year

Address: 1350 Paradise Cir **Location:** Jct US 17 Bypass/29th Ave N, just se on 29th Ave N, just ne. **Facility:** Smoke free premises. 111 one-bedroom standard units. 4 stories, interior corridors. *Bath:* combo or shower only. **Parking:** on-site. **Terms:** cancellation fee imposed. **Amenities:** voice mail, irons, hair dryers. **Pool(s):** outdoor. **Leisure Activities:** whirlpool. **Guest Services:** valet laundry, wireless Internet. **Business Services:** meeting rooms, business center. **Cards:** AX, CB, DC, DS, JC, MC, VI.

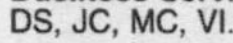 CALL 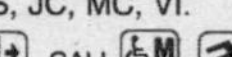    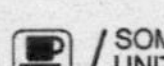 / SOME UNITS 

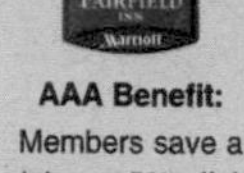

AAA Benefit:
Members save a minimum 5% off the best available rate.

FOREST DUNES RESORT

Phone: 843/449-0864 — 23

Vacation Rental Condominium
$41-$339 All Year

Address: 5511 N Ocean Blvd **Location:** Jct 52nd Ave N, 0.4 mi ne. **Facility:** Individually decorated one- and three-bedroom units provide unobstructed ocean views; ample on-site parking is available in an attached garage. 116 condominiums. 17 stories, exterior corridors. **Parking:** on-site. **Terms:** office hours 7 am-midnight, 2-3 night minimum stay - seasonal, age restrictions may apply, 14 day cancellation notice-fee imposed. **Amenities:** voice mail, irons, hair dryers. **Pool(s):** outdoor, heated indoor. **Leisure Activities:** whirlpool, lazy river water ride, limited exercise equipment. *Fee:* game room. **Guest Services:** coin laundry. **Business Services:** fax (fee). **Cards:** AX, DS, MC, VI. **Free Special Amenities: newspaper.** *(See color ad p 1001)*

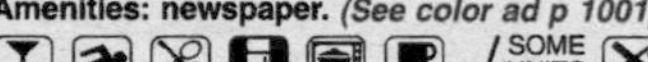 / SOME UNITS

GRAND ATLANTIC OCEAN RESORT

Book great rates at AAA.com — **Phone:** (843)448-7032 — 78

Condominium
$99-$319 6/1-11/30
$99-$280 12/1-5/31

Address: 2007 S Ocean Blvd **Location:** Oceanfront. Jct 20th Ave. **Facility:** Located south of town, the high-rise property offers large, well-appointed units and many amenities; parking is in a garage across the street. 171 units. 38 one-bedroom standard units. 133 condominiums. 20 stories, exterior corridors. **Parking:** on-site. **Terms:** 14 day cancellation notice-fee imposed. **Amenities:** voice mail, safes, irons, hair dryers. **Pool(s):** outdoor, indoor/outdoor. **Leisure Activities:** indoor lazy river, exercise room, shuffleboard. *Fee:* massage. **Guest Services:** complimentary laundry, wireless Internet. **Business Services:** meeting rooms, fax (fee). **Cards:** AX, DS, MC, VI.

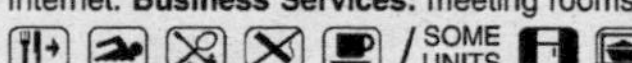 / SOME UNITS

GRANDE SHORES

Book great rates at AAA.com — **Phone:** (843)692-2397 — 3

Hotel
$60-$470 6/6-11/30
$36-$299 12/1-6/5

Address: 201 77th Ave N **Location:** Oceanfront. Jct N Ocean Blvd, just se. **Facility:** 231 units. 51 one-bedroom standard units. 180 condominiums. 6-13 stories, exterior corridors. **Parking:** on-site. **Terms:** 3-4 night minimum stay - seasonal, 14 day cancellation notice-fee imposed. **Amenities:** high-speed Internet, voice mail, irons, hair dryers. **Pool(s):** heated indoor. **Leisure Activities:** whirlpools, 2 lazy river water rides, playground, exercise room. **Guest Services:** coin laundry. **Business Services:** meeting rooms, business center. **Cards:** AX, DS, MC, VI. **Free Special Amenities: early check-in/late check-out and high-speed Internet.** *(See color ad starting on p 1018)*

/ SOME UNITS

(See map and index starting on p. 970)

HAMPTON INN & SUITES-OCEANFRONT RESORT Book great rates at AAA.com **Phone:** (843)946-6400 73

Hotel
$209-$269 5/8-11/30
$109-$169 12/1-5/7

Address: 1803 S Ocean Blvd **Location:** Oceanfront. Jct 18th Ave S. **Facility:** 116 units. 80 one-bedroom standard units, some with whirlpools. 10 one- and 26 two-bedroom suites with efficiencies, some with whirlpools. 14 stories, interior corridors. *Bath:* combo or shower only. **Parking:** on-site. **Terms:** 2-4 night minimum stay - seasonal and/or weekends. **Amenities:** video games (fee), high-speed Internet, dual phone lines, voice mail, irons, hair dryers. *Some:* CD players. **Pool(s):** heated outdoor, heated indoor. **Leisure Activities:** whirlpool, lazy river water ride, recreation programs in summer, limited exercise equipment. **Guest Services:** valet and coin laundry, airport transportation-Myrtle Beach International Airport. **Business Services:** meeting rooms, business center. **Cards:** AX, CB, DC, DS, MC, VI. **Free Special Amenities: expanded continental breakfast and high-speed Internet.**

AAA Benefit:
Members save up to 10% everyday!

HAMPTON INN BROADWAY AT THE BEACH Book great rates at AAA.com **Phone:** (843)916-0600 31

Hotel
$139-$339 All Year

Address: 1140 Celebrity Cir **Location:** Jct US 17 Bypass/29th Ave N, 0.5 mi se on 29th Ave N to Robert Grissom Pkwy, then just sw. Located at Broadway at the Beach Complex. **Facility:** 141 one-bedroom standard units, some with whirlpools. 8 stories, interior corridors. *Bath:* combo or shower only. **Parking:** on-site. **Terms:** 2-3 night minimum stay - weekends. **Amenities:** video games (fee), high-speed Internet, dual phone lines, voice mail, irons, hair dryers. **Pool(s):** heated outdoor, heated indoor. **Leisure Activities:** sauna, whirlpool, exercise room. *Fee:* game room. **Guest Services:** valet and coin laundry, wireless Internet. **Business Services:** meeting rooms, business center. **Cards:** AX, CB, DC, DS, JC, MC, VI.

AAA Benefit:
Members save up to 10% everyday!

HAMPTON INN-NORTHWOOD Book great rates at AAA.com **Phone:** (843)497-0077

Hotel
$69-$199 All Year

Address: 620 75th Ave N **Location:** Jct US 17 business route, just nw. **Facility:** 122 units. 115 one-bedroom standard units. 7 one-bedroom suites, some with whirlpools. 5 stories, interior corridors. *Bath:* combo or shower only. **Parking:** on-site. **Terms:** check-in 4 pm, 1-30 night minimum stay, cancellation fee imposed. **Amenities:** video games (fee), high-speed Internet, voice mail, irons, hair dryers. **Pool(s):** heated indoor. **Leisure Activities:** sauna, whirlpool, exercise room. **Guest Services:** valet and coin laundry, wireless Internet. **Business Services:** meeting rooms, fax (fee). **Cards:** AX, CB, DC, DS, MC, VI.

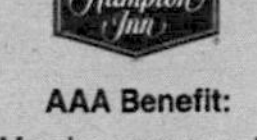

AAA Benefit:
Members save up to 10% everyday!

HAMPTON INN WEST Book great rates at AAA.com **Phone:** (843)236-0045

Hotel
$129-$169 5/2-11/30
$110-$149 12/1-5/1

Address: 4551 US 501 **Location:** Jct SR 31, 1.1 mi n. Located across from Factory Outlet Mall. **Facility:** 80 one-bedroom standard units. 4 stories, interior corridors. *Bath:* combo or shower only. **Parking:** on-site. **Amenities:** dual phone lines, voice mail, irons, hair dryers. **Pool(s):** outdoor. **Leisure Activities:** exercise room. **Guest Services:** valet and coin laundry, wireless Internet. **Business Services:** meeting rooms, business center. **Cards:** AX, CB, DC, DS, MC, VI.

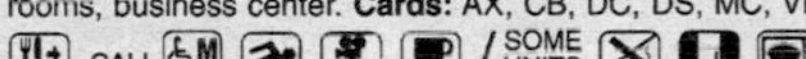

AAA Benefit:
Members save up to 10% everyday!

HARBOUR LIGHTS RESORT Book great rates at AAA.com **Phone:** (843)236-4800 35

Vacation Rental Condominium
$118-$382 5/25-11/30
$118-$230 12/1-5/24

Address: 2690 Harbour Lights Dr **Location:** Jct US 17 Bypass/US 501, 1.2 mi nw on US 501, exit River Oaks Rd/George Bishop Pkwy, just ne on River Oaks Dr, follow signs to Fantasy Harbor. **Facility:** Three-story walk-ups offer large accommodations perfect for an extended vacation; find on-site recreational activities and concierge service. 324 condominiums. 3 stories (no elevator), exterior corridors. **Parking:** on-site. **Terms:** office hours 7 am-10 pm, check-in 4 pm, 2 night minimum stay, 3 day cancellation notice-fee imposed. **Amenities:** DVD players, CD players, voice mail, irons, hair dryers. **Pool(s):** outdoor, indoor. **Leisure Activities:** whirlpool, lazy river water ride, putting green, recreation programs, exercise room. *Fee:* massage, game room. **Guest Services:** complimentary laundry, wireless Internet. **Business Services:** PC. **Cards:** AX, DS, MC, VI. **Free Special Amenities: local telephone calls.** *(See color ad p 1010)*

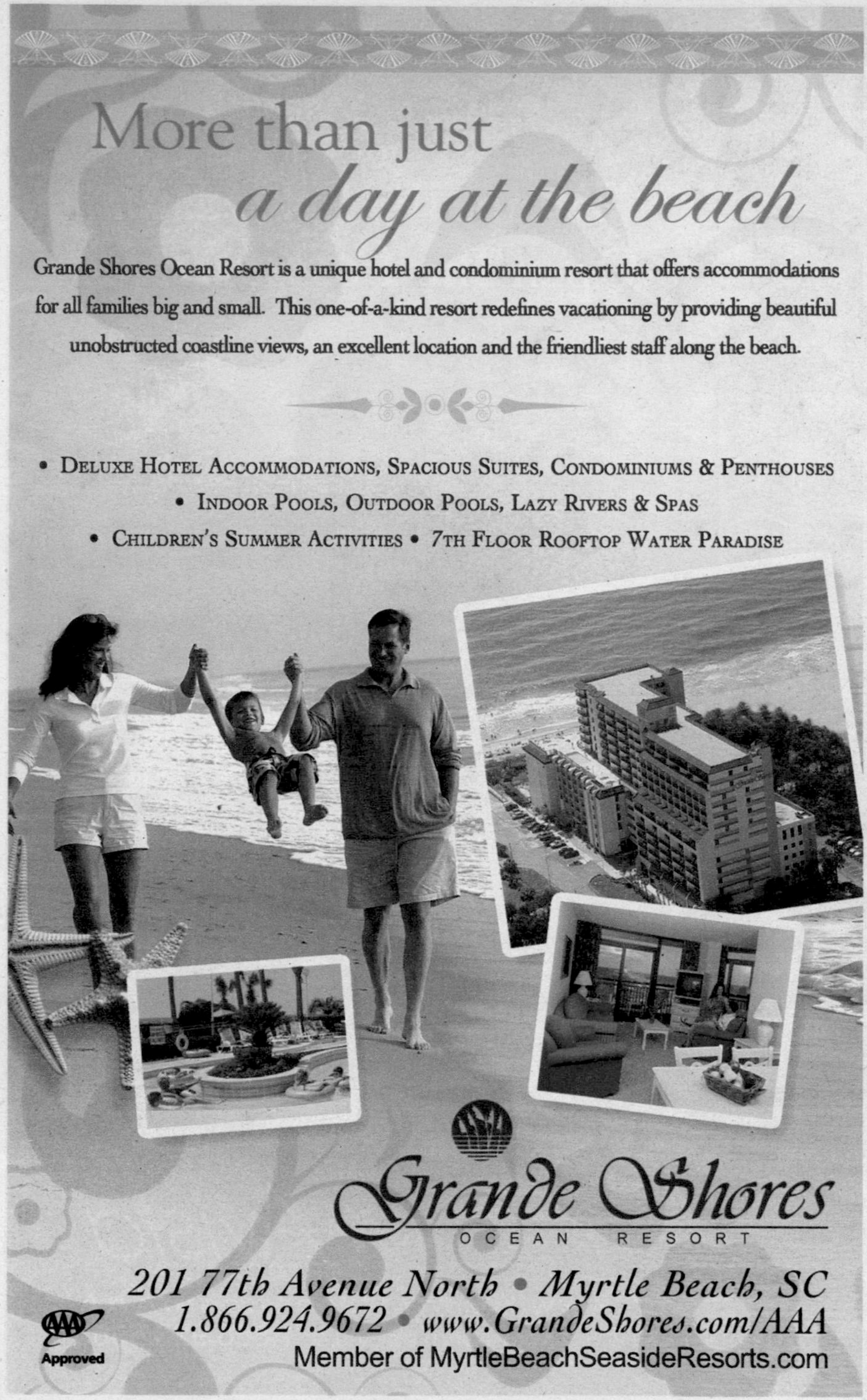
More than just
a day at the beach
Grande Shores Ocean Resort is a unique hotel and condominium resort that offers accommodations for all families big and small. This one-of-a-kind resort redefines vacationing by providing beautiful unobstructed coastline views, an excellent location and the friendliest staff along the beach.
• Deluxe Hotel Accommodations, Spacious Suites, Condominiums & Penthouses
• Indoor Pools, Outdoor Pools, Lazy Rivers & Spas
• Children's Summer Activities • 7th Floor Rooftop Water Paradise
Grande Shores
OCEAN RESORT
201 77th Avenue North • Myrtle Beach, SC
1.866.924.9672 • www.GrandeShores.com/AAA
Member of MyrtleBeachSeasideResorts.com
AAA
Approved

(See map and index starting on p. 970)

HOLIDAY INN "AT THE PAVILION" Book great rates at AAA.com

Phone: (843)913-5805 

Hotel
$45-$215 All Year

Address: 1200 N Ocean Blvd **Location:** Oceanfront. Jct 12th Ave N. **Facility:** 138 units. 93 one-bedroom standard units, some with kitchens. 45 one-bedroom suites with kitchens. 3-10 stories, exterior corridors. *Bath:* combo or shower only. **Parking:** on-site. **Terms:** 15 day cancellation notice-fee imposed. **Amenities:** voice mail, safes, irons, hair dryers. **Pool(s):** heated outdoor, heated indoor. **Leisure Activities:** whirlpool, lazy river water ride, exercise room. **Guest Services:** coin laundry, wireless Internet. **Business Services:** *Fee:* administrative services, fax. **Cards:** AX, DS, MC, VI. **Free Special Amenities: expanded continental breakfast and early check-in/late check-out.**
(See color ad starting on p 1012)

HOLIDAY INN EXPRESS-BROADWAY AT THE BEACH Book great rates at AAA.com

Phone: (843)916-4993 29

Hotel
$69-$209 All Year

Address: 1290 Paradise Cir **Location:** Jct US 17 Bypass/29th Ave N, just se on 29th Ave N, just ne. **Facility:** 114 one-bedroom standard units. 4 stories, interior corridors. *Bath:* combo or shower only. **Parking:** on-site. **Terms:** check-in 4 pm, cancellation fee imposed. **Amenities:** dual phone lines, voice mail, irons, hair dryers. **Pool(s):** heated outdoor. **Leisure Activities:** whirlpool. **Guest Services:** valet and coin laundry, wireless Internet. **Business Services:** meeting rooms, administrative services, fax (fee). **Cards:** AX, CB, DC, DS, JC, MC, VI. **Free Special Amenities: expanded continental breakfast and high-speed Internet.**

/ SOME UNITS

HOLIDAY INN HARD ROCK PARKWAY

Phone: (843)236-1000 32

Hotel
$79-$189 All Year

Address: 101 Hard Rock Pkwy **Location:** Jct US 17 Bypass, 0.7 mi n on US 501, exit River Oaks Rd/George Bishop Pkwy, just w on River Oaks Rd, then 0.7 mi s. Located adjacent to Outlet Mall and Fantasy Harbour. **Facility:** 151 one-bedroom standard units. 6 stories, interior corridors. *Bath:* combo or shower only. **Parking:** on-site. **Terms:** 5 day cancellation notice-fee imposed. **Amenities:** voice mail, irons, hair dryers. **Pool(s):** heated indoor/outdoor. **Leisure Activities:** whirlpool, boat dock, exercise room. **Guest Services:** valet and coin laundry, wireless Internet. **Business Services:** conference facilities, business center. **Cards:** AX, DC, DS, MC, VI.

ASK / SOME UNITS

(See map and index starting on p. 970)

HORIZON OCEAN RESORT — Phone: 843/629-2397

fyi

Vacation Rental Condominium

$50-$319 6/6-11/30
$40-$219 12/1-6/5

Too new to rate, opening scheduled for August 2008. **Address:** 201 77th Ave N **Location:** US 17 Bypass, exit 77th Ave N. **Amenities:** 143 units, coffeemakers, microwaves, refrigerators, pool. **Terms:** 3-4 night minimum stay - seasonal, cancellation fee imposed. **Cards:** AX, MC, VI. *(See color ad starting on p 1018)*

HOTEL BLUE — *Book great rates at AAA.com* — Phone: (843)448-4304 61

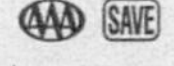

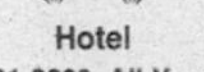

Hotel

$31-$229 All Year

Address: 705 S Ocean Blvd **Location:** Oceanfront. Jct 7th Ave S. **Facility:** 230 units. 140 one-bedroom standard units, some with efficiencies. 90 one-bedroom suites with kitchens. 15 stories, interior/exterior corridors. **Parking:** on-site. **Terms:** office hours 7 am-midnight, 14 day cancellation notice-fee imposed. **Amenities:** voice mail, safes, irons, hair dryers. **Pool(s):** heated outdoor, heated indoor. **Leisure Activities:** whirlpools, lazy river water ride. *Fee:* game room. **Guest Services:** coin laundry. **Business Services:** *Fee:* administrative services, fax. **Cards:** AX, DS, MC, VI. **Free Special Amenities: high-speed Internet.** *(See color ad p 1002)*

INDIGO INN — Phone: 843/448-5101 81

Hotel

$50-$260 All Year

Address: 2209 S Ocean Blvd **Location:** Oceanfront. Jct 23rd Ave S. **Facility:** 53 one-bedroom standard units, some with efficiencies. 9 stories, exterior corridors. **Parking:** on-site. **Terms:** office hours 8 am-10 pm, 3-7 night minimum stay - seasonal and/or weekends, 14 day cancellation notice-fee imposed. **Pool(s):** outdoor. **Leisure Activities:** whirlpool, shuffleboard. **Guest Services:** coin laundry. **Business Services:** administrative services, fax (fee). **Cards:** AX, DS, MC, VI. **Free Special Amenities: local telephone calls and high-speed Internet.**

/ SOME UNITS

ISLAND VISTA — Phone: (843)449-6406 20

Vacation Rental Condominium

$68-$615 All Year

Address: 6000 N Ocean Blvd **Location:** Oceanfront. Jct 60th Ave N. **Facility:** The upscale property features large, one- to four-bedroom units decorated in a tropical motif; all units are oceanfront with private balconies. 149 condominiums. 13 stories, interior corridors. **Parking:** on-site. **Terms:** check-in 4 pm, 2-4 night minimum stay - seasonal and/or weekends, age restrictions may apply, 14 day cancellation notice-fee imposed. **Amenities:** DVD players, voice mail, irons, hair dryers. **Pool(s):** outdoor, heated outdoor. **Leisure Activities:** fishing, lazy river, jogging, exercise room. **Guest Services:** complimentary and valet laundry, wireless Internet. **Business Services:** meeting rooms, fax (fee). **Cards:** AX, DS, MC, VI. **Free Special Amenities: early check-in/late check-out and high-speed Internet.** *(See color ad on insert)*

LANDMARK RESORT — *Book great rates at AAA.com* — Phone: (843)448-9441 71

Hotel

$39-$259 All Year

Address: 1501 S Ocean Blvd **Location:** Oceanfront. Jct 15th Ave S. **Facility:** 566 units. 292 one-bedroom standard units. 274 condominiums. 14 stories, interior/exterior corridors. *Bath:* combo or shower only. **Parking:** on-site. **Terms:** check-in 4 pm, 2-3 night minimum stay - seasonal, 14 day cancellation notice-fee imposed. **Amenities:** voice mail, safes, hair dryers. **Pool(s):** heated outdoor, heated indoor. **Leisure Activities:** sauna, whirlpools, 2 lazy river pools, water park, kiddie lazy river, miniature golf, limited exercise equipment. *Fee:* golf privileges, game room. **Guest Services:** valet and coin laundry, airport transportation-Myrtle Beach International Airport, wireless Internet. **Business Services:** conference facilities, administrative services (fee). **Cards:** AX, DS, MC, VI. **Free Special Amenities: local telephone calls and high-speed Internet.** *(See color ad p 1000)*

/ SOME UNITS

LA QUINTA INN & SUITES MYRTLE BEACH — *Book great rates at AAA.com* — Phone: (843)916-8801 30

Hotel

$69-$189 All Year

Address: 1561 21st Ave N **Location:** Jct US 17 Bypass, just se. Located in a commercial area. **Facility:** 128 units. 120 one-bedroom standard units. 8 one-bedroom suites. 4 stories, interior corridors. *Bath:* combo or shower only. **Parking:** on-site. **Amenities:** video games (fee), high-speed Internet, voice mail, irons, hair dryers. *Some:* dual phone lines. **Pool(s):** outdoor. **Leisure Activities:** whirlpool, exercise room. **Guest Services:** valet and coin laundry, wireless Internet. **Business Services:** meeting rooms, fax (fee). **Cards:** AX, DC, DS, MC, VI.

(See map and index starting on p. 970)

LA QUINTA INN MYRTLE BEACH *Book great rates at AAA.com* **Phone:** (843)449-5231 26

Hotel
$59-$199 All Year

Address: 4709 N Kings Hwy **Location:** Jct 48th Ave N and US 17 business route. **Facility:** 148 one-bedroom standard units. 4 stories, interior corridors. **Parking:** on-site. **Amenities:** video games (fee), voice mail, irons, hair dryers. **Pool(s):** outdoor. **Leisure Activities:** exercise room. **Guest Services:** valet and coin laundry, wireless Internet. **Business Services:** PC, fax (fee). **Cards:** AX, DC, DS, MC, VI.

ASK / SOME UNITS

LEGENDS GOLF RESORT **Phone:** (843)236-9318

Vacation Rental Condominium
$169-$209 All Year

Address: 1500 Legends Dr **Location:** Jct SR 31, 1.1 mi n, then 2.6 mi w. **Facility:** A variety of individually decorated, condominium-style accommodations are offered at this property, along with three golf courses. 244 condominiums. 2 stories (no elevator), exterior corridors. **Parking:** on-site. **Terms:** check-in 4 pm, 3 day cancellation notice-fee imposed. **Amenities:** high-speed Internet, voice mail, irons, hair dryers. *Some:* safes. **Pool(s):** 3 outdoor. **Leisure Activities:** whirlpools, 2 tennis courts. *Fee:* golf-54 holes. **Guest Services:** complimentary and valet laundry. **Business Services:** meeting rooms, administrative services, PC, fax (fee). **Cards:** AX, DS, MC, VI.

ASK / SOME UNITS

THE LONG BAY RESORT *Book great rates at AAA.com* **Phone:** (843)449-3361 8

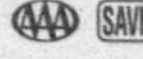

Vacation Rental Condominium
$36-$531 All Year

Address: 7200 N Ocean Blvd **Location:** Oceanfront. Jct 72nd Ave N. **Facility:** A West Indies theme imbues the lobby of this property offering varied lodgings in several buildings. 284 units. 56 one-bedroom standard units. 228 condominiums. 4-15 stories, exterior corridors. *Bath:* combo or shower only. **Parking:** on-site. **Terms:** age restrictions may apply, 14 day cancellation notice-fee imposed. **Amenities:** voice mail, safes, irons, hair dryers. **Dining:** 2 restaurants. **Pool(s):** outdoor, heated indoor. **Leisure Activities:** sauna, whirlpools, indoor lazy river water ride, waterfall mushroom, recreation programs in summer, table tennis, exercise room, shuffleboard. *Fee:* game room. **Guest Services:** coin laundry, wireless Internet. **Business Services:** meeting rooms, fax (fee). **Cards:** AX, DS, MC, VI. **Free Special Amenities: local telephone calls and high-speed Internet.** *(See color ad on insert)*

    / SOME UNITS

MERIDIAN PLAZA **Phone:** (843)626-4734 48

Vacation Rental Condominium
$43-$201 6/9-11/30
$43-$134 12/1-6/8

Address: 2310 N Ocean Blvd **Location:** Oceanfront. Between 23rd and 24th aves N. **Facility:** Each guest unit in this high-rise building is individually owned; the sophistication of the decor and level of amenities varies, but most are upscale. 88 one-bedroom suites with kitchens. 15 stories, interior corridors. **Parking:** on-site. **Terms:** office hours 7 am-11 pm, 14 day cancellation notice-fee imposed. **Amenities:** voice mail. **Pool(s):** outdoor, heated indoor. **Leisure Activities:** whirlpools. **Guest Services:** coin laundry, wireless Internet. **Business Services:** fax (fee). **Cards:** AX, DS, MC, VI. **Free Special Amenities: high-speed Internet.** *(See color ad below)*

/ SOME UNITS

▼ See AAA listing above ▼

(See map and index starting on p. 970)

M GRAND Book great rates at AAA.com Phone: (843)448-2518 84

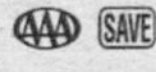

Hotel
$69-$269 All Year

Address: 2701 S Ocean Blvd **Location:** Oceanfront. Jct 27th Ave S. **Facility:** Designated smoking area. 223 units. 214 one-bedroom standard units, some with efficiencies. 9 one-bedroom suites with kitchens. 16 stories, interior corridors. **Parking:** on-site. **Terms:** 14 day cancellation notice-fee imposed. **Amenities:** DVD players, voice mail, safes, irons, hair dryers. **Pool(s):** outdoor, heated indoor. **Leisure Activities:** sauna, whirlpool, exercise room. *Fee:* golf privileges, game room. **Guest Services:** valet and coin laundry, airport transportation-Myrtle Beach International Airport, wireless Internet. **Business Services:** meeting rooms, fax (fee). **Cards:** AX, DC, DS, MC, VI. **Free Special Amenities: local telephone calls and high-speed Internet.**

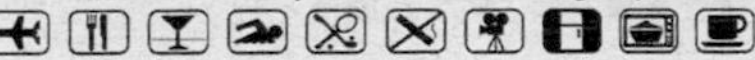

MICROTEL INN & SUITES Book at AAA.com Phone: 843/236-1264

Hotel
Rates not provided

Address: 4360 US 501 **Location:** Jct SR 31, 0.5 mi n. **Facility:** 96 one-bedroom standard units. 3 stories, interior corridors. *Bath:* combo or shower only. **Parking:** on-site. **Amenities:** voice mail, safes. *Some:* irons, hair dryers. **Pool(s):** outdoor. **Guest Services:** coin laundry, wireless Internet. **Business Services:** meeting rooms, fax (fee).

CALL / SOME UNITS

MONTEREY BAY SUITES Phone: (843)449-4833 19

Vacation Rental Condominium
$65-$259 2/22-11/30
$51-$98 12/1-2/21

Address: 6804 N Ocean Blvd **Location:** Oceanfront. Jct 68th Ave N. **Facility:** The all-suite condo/hotel offers a nicely appointed open lobby overlooking the ocean and six different, colorfully decorated room floor plans. 194 condominiums. 16 stories, exterior corridors. *Bath:* combo or shower only. **Parking:** on-site. **Terms:** 3 day cancellation notice-fee imposed. **Amenities:** DVD players, voice mail, safes, irons, hair dryers. **Pool(s):** outdoor, indoor/outdoor. **Leisure Activities:** whirlpools, indoor lazy river water ride. **Guest Services:** coin laundry, wireless Internet. **Business Services:** fax (fee). **Cards:** AX, DS, MC, VI. **Free Special Amenities: expanded continental breakfast.**

/ SOME UNITS

MYRTLE BEACH MARRIOTT RESORT AT GRANDE DUNES Book great rates at AAA.com Phone: (843)449-8880 1

Resort Hotel
$150-$310 All Year

Address: 8400 Costa Verde Dr **Location:** Oceanfront. Jct US 17 business route (N Kings Hwy) and 82nd Pkwy, just se on 82nd Pkwy. **Facility:** The stunning full-service hotel features full resort amenities, beautifully appointed rooms, spacious public areas and golf and tennis facilities. Smoke free premises. 405 units. 397 one-bedroom standard units. 2 one- and 6 two-bedroom suites. 15 stories, interior corridors. *Bath:* combo or shower only. **Parking:** on-site (fee) and valet. **Terms:** check-in 4 pm, age restrictions may apply, 3 day cancellation notice-fee imposed. **Amenities:** high-speed Internet (fee), dual phone lines, voice mail, safes, irons, hair dryers. *Some:* DVD players, CD players. **Dining:** Oceans on 82nd, see separate listing. **Pool(s):** 2 outdoor, heated indoor. **Leisure Activities:** saunas, whirlpools, steamrooms, waterslide, tennis & golf privileges, recreation programs in summer, spa. **Guest Services:** coin laundry, wireless Internet. **Business Services:** conference facilities, business center. **Cards:** AX, CB, DC, DS, JC, MC, VI.

Marriott HOTELS & RESORTS
AAA Benefit:
Members save a minimum 5% off the best available rate.

CALL

MYSTIC SEA BEACH & GOLF RESORT Phone: (843)448-8446 79

Motel
$29-$159 All Year

Address: 2105 S Ocean Blvd **Location:** Oceanfront. Jct 21st Ave S. **Facility:** 60 units. 48 one-bedroom standard units, some with efficiencies. 4 one- and 8 two-bedroom suites with kitchens. 2-3 stories (no elevator), exterior corridors. **Parking:** on-site. **Terms:** office hours 8 am-10 pm, 3-7 night minimum stay - seasonal, 14 day cancellation notice-fee imposed. **Amenities:** safes. **Pool(s):** outdoor. **Leisure Activities:** whirlpool. **Guest Services:** coin laundry. **Business Services:** fax (fee). **Cards:** MC, VI.

ASK / SOME UNITS

OCEAN DUNES RESORT & VILLAS Book great rates at AAA.com Phone: (843)449-7441 6

Vacation Rental Condominium
$59-$209 3/20-11/30
$59-$89 12/1-3/19

Address: 201 75th Ave N **Location:** Oceanfront. Jct N Ocean Blvd, just se. **Facility:** The property is a complex of varied buildings and accommodations. 402 units. 114 one-bedroom standard units. 288 condominiums. 3-15 stories, interior/exterior corridors. **Parking:** on-site. **Terms:** 1-5 night minimum stay - seasonal and/or weekends, 4 day cancellation notice-fee imposed. **Amenities:** voice mail, safes, irons, hair dryers. **Pool(s):** 4 outdoor, heated outdoor, heated indoor. **Leisure Activities:** sauna, whirlpools, steamroom, recreation programs, playground, basketball. *Fee:* massage, game room. **Guest Services:** valet and coin laundry, area transportation, wireless Internet. **Business Services:** conference facilities. **Cards:** AX, DS, MC, VI.

ASK / SOME UNITS

OCEAN FOREST PLAZA Book great rates at AAA.com Phone: (843)497-0044 22

Vacation Rental Condominium

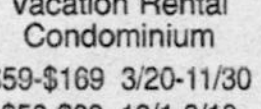

$59-$169 3/20-11/30
$59-$89 12/1-3/19

Address: 5523 N Ocean Blvd **Location:** Jct 52nd Ave N, 0.5 mi ne. **Facility:** Across the street from the ocean, this high-rise condominium-style property offers private balconies with unobstructed ocean views. 90 condominiums. 22 stories, interior/exterior corridors. **Parking:** on-site. **Terms:** 1-5 night minimum stay - seasonal and/or weekends, 4 day cancellation notice-fee imposed. **Amenities:** voice mail, safes, irons, hair dryers. **Pool(s):** outdoor, heated indoor. **Leisure Activities:** sauna, whirlpool, steamroom. **Guest Services:** coin laundry, wireless Internet. **Business Services:** meeting rooms. *Fee:* PC, fax. **Cards:** AX, DS, MC, VI.

ASK / SOME UNITS

(See map and index starting on p. 970)

OCEAN FOREST VILLAS Book great rates at AAA.com **Phone:** (843)449-9661 21

Vacation Rental Condominium

$69-$239 3/20-11/30
$69-$109 12/1-3/19

Address: 5601 N Ocean Blvd **Location:** Jct 52nd Ave N, 0.6 mi ne. **Facility:** Traditional accommodations with varied decor are featured here; office hours are limited. 90 condominiums. 3 stories (no elevator), interior/exterior corridors. **Parking:** on-site. **Terms:** office hours 7 am-11 pm, 1-5 night minimum stay - seasonal and/or weekends, 4 day cancellation notice-fee imposed. **Amenities:** voice mail, safes (fee), irons, hair dryers. **Pool(s):** 2 outdoor. **Leisure Activities:** whirlpools, recreation programs. **Guest Services:** coin laundry. **Business Services:** fax (fee). **Cards:** AX, DS, MC, VI.

ASK / SOME UNITS

THE OCEANFRONT VIKING MOTEL Book great rates at AAA.com **Phone:** (843)448-4355 

Motel

$48-$199 6/6-11/30
$31-$199 12/1-6/5

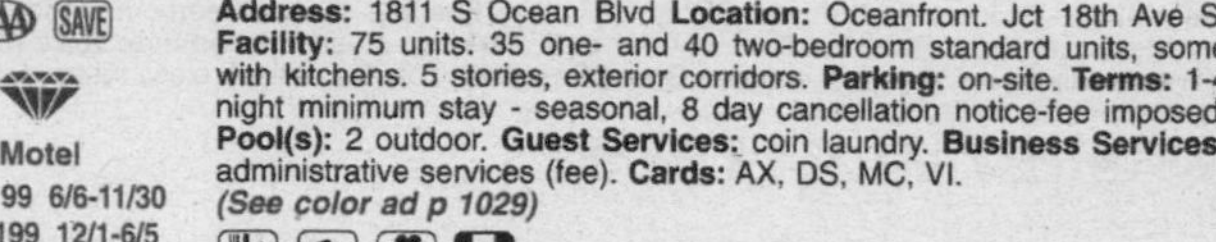

Address: 1811 S Ocean Blvd **Location:** Oceanfront. Jct 18th Ave S. **Facility:** 75 units. 35 one- and 40 two-bedroom standard units, some with kitchens. 5 stories, exterior corridors. **Parking:** on-site. **Terms:** 1-4 night minimum stay - seasonal, 8 day cancellation notice-fee imposed. **Pool(s):** 2 outdoor. **Guest Services:** coin laundry. **Business Services:** administrative services (fee). **Cards:** AX, DS, MC, VI.
(See color ad p 1029)

OCEAN PARK RESORT Book great rates at AAA.com **Phone:** (843)448-1915 76

Vacation Rental Condominium

$45-$186 All Year

Address: 1905 S Ocean Blvd **Location:** Oceanfront. Jct 19th Ave S. **Facility:** Located south of town, the property has numerous floor plans, and unit decor varies based on individual unit owners' tastes. 126 units. 22 one-bedroom standard units. 104 condominiums. 12 stories, interior/exterior corridors. **Parking:** on-site. **Terms:** 2-4 night minimum stay - seasonal, 7 day cancellation notice-fee imposed. **Amenities:** voice mail, safes (fee), irons, hair dryers. **Pool(s):** outdoor, heated indoor. **Leisure Activities:** saunas, whirlpools, exercise room. *Fee:* golf privileges, game room. **Guest Services:** coin laundry, wireless Internet. **Business Services:** business center. **Cards:** AX, DS, MC, VI. **Free Special Amenities: local telephone calls and high-speed Internet.** *(See color ad on insert)*

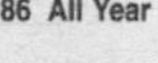

/ SOME UNITS

OCEAN PLAZA MOTEL Book great rates at AAA.com **Phone:** (843)448-7191 67

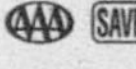

Motel

$31-$179 All Year

Address: 1005 S Ocean Blvd **Location:** Oceanfront, Jct 10th Ave S. **Facility:** 65 units. 59 one- and 6 two-bedroom standard units, some with efficiencies. 7 stories, exterior corridors. *Bath:* combo or shower only. **Parking:** on-site. **Terms:** 8 day cancellation notice-fee imposed. **Pool(s):** outdoor, heated indoor. **Leisure Activities:** whirlpools. **Guest Services:** coin laundry. **Business Services:** fax (fee). **Cards:** AX, DS, MC, VI. **Free Special Amenities: early check-in/late check-out and preferred room (subject to availability with advance reservations).**
(See color ad p 1029)

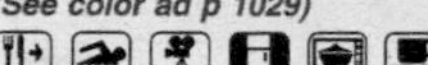

THE OCEAN REEF RESORT Book great rates at AAA.com **Phone:** (843)449-4441 9

Vacation Rental Condominium

$57-$611 All Year

Address: 7100 N Ocean Blvd **Location:** Oceanfront. Jct 71st Ave N. **Facility:** The resort features standard hotel rooms, efficiencies and spacious one- to four-bedroom condo units, all of which have a balcony facing the ocean. 343 units. 106 one-bedroom standard units. 237 condominiums. 15-17 stories, interior/exterior corridors. **Parking:** on-site. **Terms:** age restrictions may apply, 14 day cancellation notice-fee imposed. **Amenities:** voice mail, safes, irons, hair dryers. **Pool(s):** heated outdoor, heated indoor. **Leisure Activities:** saunas, whirlpools, lazy river water ride, activity pool, recreation programs in summer, exercise room. *Fee:* golf & tennis privileges, game room. **Guest Services:** coin laundry, wireless Internet. **Business Services:** conference facilities, fax (fee). **Cards:** AX, DS, MC, VI. **Free Special Amenities: local telephone calls and high-speed Internet.**
(See color ad on insert)

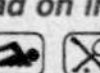

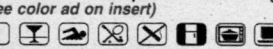

(See map and index starting on p. 970)

OCEANS ONE

Phone: 843/626-2033 59

AAA SAVE

Condominium

$47-$419 6/1-11/30
$47-$250 12/1-5/31

Address: 102 S Ocean Blvd **Location:** Oceanfront. Jct 2nd Ave S. **Facility:** Opened in 2008, the chic Bauhaus-influenced design features floor-to-ceiling windows with breathtaking, panoramic ocean and city views. Smoke free premises. 135 condominiums. 21 stories, interior corridors. **Parking:** on-site. **Terms:** off-site registration, 3 night minimum stay - seasonal, 14 day cancellation notice-fee imposed. **Amenities:** voice mail, irons, hair dryers. **Pool(s):** 2 outdoor, 2 heated indoor. **Leisure Activities:** whirlpools, lazy river. **Guest Services:** complimentary laundry, wireless Internet. **Business Services:** fax (fee). **Cards:** AX, DS, MC, VI. **Free Special Amenities: local telephone calls and high-speed Internet.** *(See color ad below)*

THE PALACE Book great rates at AAA.com

Phone: (843)448-4300 72

AAA SAVE

Vacation Rental Condominium

$41-$255 All Year

Address: 1605 S Ocean Blvd **Location:** Jct 16th Ave S. **Facility:** Most rooms offer ocean views, and all units are decorated by private owners, so each is unique, and in-room amenity levels vary. 225 condominiums. 23 stories, interior corridors. **Parking:** on-site. **Terms:** 2-3 night minimum stay - seasonal, 14 day cancellation notice-fee imposed. **Amenities:** voice mail, irons, hair dryers. **Pool(s):** 2 outdoor, indoor/outdoor, heated indoor/outdoor. **Leisure Activities:** sauna, whirlpools, steamroom, exercise room. *Fee:* game room. **Guest Services:** coin laundry, wireless Internet. **Business Services:** meeting rooms, fax (fee). **Cards:** AX, MC, VI. **Free Special Amenities: newspaper.** *(See color ad p 1003)*

/ SOME UNITS

▼ *See AAA listing above* ▼

(See map and index starting on p. 970)

PALMS RESORT Phone: (843)626-8334 45

Vacation Rental Condominium
$55-$499 All Year

Address: 2500 N Ocean Blvd **Location:** Oceanfront. Between 24th and 26th aves N. **Facility:** On the north side, the hotel's two high-rise units offer shotgun-style efficiency suites with one to four bedrooms; penthouse suites have two floors. 84 condominiums. 16 stories, exterior corridors. **Parking:** on-site. **Terms:** 2-7 night minimum stay - weekends, age restrictions may apply, 14 day cancellation notice-fee imposed. **Amenities:** irons, hair dryers. **Pool(s):** outdoor, heated indoor. **Leisure Activities:** saunas, whirlpools, exercise room. **Guest Services:** coin laundry. **Business Services:** fax (fee). **Cards:** AX, MC, VI. **Free Special Amenities: high-speed Internet.** *(See color ad p 1003)*

SOME UNITS

PARADISE RESORT *Book great rates at AAA.com* Phone: (843)916-9500 80

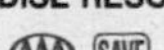

Vacation Rental Condominium
$54-$495 All Year

Address: 2201 S Ocean Blvd **Location:** Oceanfront. Jct 22nd Ave S. **Facility:** Opened in 2007, the property offers a variety of studio units and one- to four-bedroom suites with a balcony overlooking the ocean. Designated smoking area. 174 condominiums. 20 stories, interior corridors. **Parking:** on-site. **Terms:** check-in 4 pm, 2 night minimum stay - seasonal and/or weekends, 15 day cancellation notice-fee imposed. **Amenities:** voice mail, irons. **Pool(s):** heated indoor/outdoor. **Leisure Activities:** whirlpool, lazy river water ride, kiddie pool, sundeck, recreation programs in summer, seasonal band stand, exercise room. **Guest Services:** complimentary laundry, wireless Internet. **Business Services:** business center. **Cards:** AX, DS, MC, VI. **Free Special Amenities: local telephone calls and high-speed Internet.**

CALL

PATRICIA GRAND RESORT HOTEL *Book great rates at AAA.com* Phone: (843)448-8453 38

Hotel
$48-$210 All Year

Address: 2710 N Ocean Blvd **Location:** Oceanfront. Jct 27th Ave N. **Facility:** 308 units. 207 one-bedroom standard units, some with efficiencies. 101 condominiums. 18 stories, exterior corridors. **Parking:** on-site. **Terms:** 2-4 night minimum stay - seasonal, 7 day cancellation notice-fee imposed. **Amenities:** voice mail, safes, irons, hair dryers. **Pool(s):** outdoor, heated indoor. **Leisure Activities:** saunas, whirlpools, indoor lazy river water ride, exercise room. **Guest Services:** coin laundry, wireless Internet. **Business Services:** fax (fee). **Cards:** AX, DS, MC, VI. **Free Special Amenities: local telephone calls and high-speed Internet.** *(See color ad on insert)*

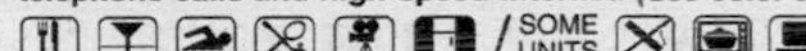

SOME UNITS

POLYNESIAN RESORT *Book great rates at AAA.com* Phone: (843)448-1781 

Hotel
$48-$199 6/6-11/30
$30-$179 12/1-6/5

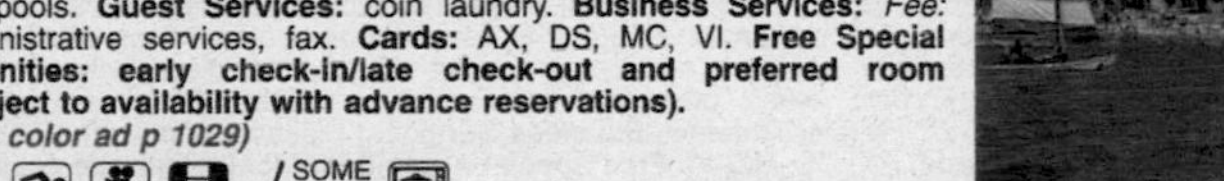

Address: 1001 S Ocean Blvd **Location:** Oceanfront. Jct 10th Ave S. **Facility:** 175 units. 137 one- and 30 two-bedroom standard units, some with efficiencies. 7 one- and 1 two-bedroom suites with efficiencies. 5-9 stories, exterior corridors. **Parking:** on-site. **Terms:** 8 day cancellation notice-fee imposed. **Pool(s):** outdoor, heated indoor. **Leisure Activities:** whirlpools. **Guest Services:** coin laundry. **Business Services:** *Fee:* administrative services, fax. **Cards:** AX, DS, MC, VI. **Free Special Amenities: early check-in/late check-out and preferred room (subject to availability with advance reservations).** *(See color ad p 1029)*

SOME UNITS

ROXANNE TOWERS Phone: 843/448-9486 55

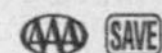

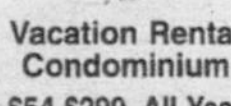

Vacation Rental Condominium
$54-$299 All Year

Address: 1604 N Ocean Blvd **Location:** Oceanfront. Jct 16th Ave N. **Facility:** Part of a popular shopping center featuring restaurants and shops, the property is near outlet malls and several golf courses. 72 units. 2 one-bedroom standard units. 70 condominiums. 14 stories, exterior corridors. **Parking:** on-site. **Terms:** 2-5 night minimum stay - seasonal, age restrictions may apply, 14 day cancellation notice-fee imposed. **Amenities:** high-speed Internet, voice mail, safes, irons, hair dryers. **Pool(s):** outdoor, heated indoor. **Leisure Activities:** whirlpool, lazy river water ride. **Guest Services:** complimentary laundry. **Business Services:** fax (fee). **Cards:** AX, DS, MC, VI. **Free Special Amenities: local telephone calls and high-speed Internet.**

ST. JOHN'S INN Phone: (843)449-5251 18

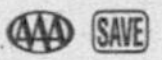

Motel
$50-$125 5/15-11/30
$40-$105 12/1-5/14

Address: 6803 N Ocean Blvd **Location:** Jct 68th Ave N. **Facility:** 50 one-bedroom standard units, some with efficiencies. 3 stories, exterior corridors. **Parking:** on-site. **Terms:** off-site registration, check-in 4 pm, 2-7 night minimum stay - seasonal, 14 day cancellation notice-fee imposed. **Amenities:** safes, irons, hair dryers. **Pool(s):** outdoor. **Leisure Activities:** whirlpool, beach access, resort privileges, shuffleboard. **Guest Services:** coin laundry, airport transportation-Myrtle Beach International Airport. **Business Services:** meeting rooms, administrative services, fax (fee). **Cards:** AX, DS, MC, VI.

SOME UNITS

(See map and index starting on p. 970)

SANDCASTLE OCEANFRONT RESORT AT THE PAVILION Book great rates at AAA.com Phone: (843)448-7101 53

SAVE

Hotel

$59-$240 12/1-6/5
$59-$229 6/6-11/30

Address: 1802 N Ocean Blvd **Location:** Oceanfront. Jct 18th Ave N. **Facility:** 241 units. 189 one-bedroom standard units, some with efficiencies. 52 condominiums. 8-9 stories, interior corridors. *Bath:* combo or shower only. **Parking:** on-site. **Terms:** age restrictions may apply, 14 day cancellation notice-fee imposed. **Amenities:** voice mail. **Pool(s):** outdoor, heated indoor. **Leisure Activities:** whirlpool, lazy river water ride. *Fee:* golf privileges. **Guest Services:** coin laundry. **Business Services:** administrative services, fax (fee). **Cards:** AX, DS, MC, VI. *(See color ad below)*

/ SOME UNITS

SANDCASTLE SOUTH BEACH Book great rates at AAA.com Phone: (843)448-4316 82

SAVE

Hotel

$79-$209 6/6-11/30
$79-$189 12/1-6/5

Address: 2207 S Ocean Blvd **Location:** Oceanfront. Jct 22nd Ave S. **Facility:** 240 units. 144 one-bedroom standard units, some with efficiencies. 96 condominiums. 14 stories, exterior corridors. *Bath:* combo or shower only. **Parking:** on-site. **Terms:** 2-4 night minimum stay - seasonal and/or weekends, age restrictions may apply, 14 day cancellation notice, in season-fee imposed. **Amenities:** voice mail, irons, hair dryers. **Pool(s):** heated outdoor, heated indoor. **Leisure Activities:** whirlpools, lazy river water ride. **Guest Services:** coin laundry, wireless Internet. **Business Services:** *Fee:* administrative services, fax. **Cards:** AX, DS, MC, VI. **Free Special Amenities: high-speed Internet.**

/ SOME UNITS

SAND DUNES RESORT HOTEL Book great rates at AAA.com Phone: (843)449-3313 7

Vacation Rental Condominium

$59-$249 3/20-11/30
$59-$109 12/1-3/19

Address: 201 74th Ave N **Location:** Oceanfront. Jct N Ocean Blvd, just se. **Facility:** The hotel offers extensive recreational facilities; all guest rooms include balconies. 444 units. 152 one-bedroom standard units. 292 condominiums. 14-19 stories, interior/exterior corridors. **Parking:** on-site. **Terms:** 5 night minimum stay - seasonal and/or weekends, 4 day cancellation notice-fee imposed. **Amenities:** high-speed Internet, voice mail, safes, irons, hair dryers. **Pool(s):** outdoor, heated indoor. **Leisure Activities:** sauna, whirlpools. *Fee:* game room. **Guest Services:** valet and coin laundry, area transportation, wireless Internet. **Business Services:** conference facilities, fax (fee). **Cards:** AX, DS, MC, VI.

ASK / SOME UNITS

SEA CREST OCEANFRONT RESORT Book great rates at AAA.com Phone: (843)913-5800 64

SAVE

Condominium

$39-$199 All Year

Address: 803 S Ocean Blvd **Location:** Oceanfront. Jct 8th Ave S. **Facility:** Just south of city center and decorated in a tropical theme, the property offers multiple floor plans and a range of amenities and views. 285 condominiums. 3-15 stories, exterior corridors. **Parking:** on-site. **Terms:** 15 day cancellation notice-fee imposed. **Amenities:** voice mail, safes, irons, hair dryers. **Pool(s):** heated outdoor, heated indoor. **Leisure Activities:** whirlpools, 2 lazy river water rides, children's activity pool, water park, tennis privileges, exercise room. **Guest Services:** coin laundry, wireless Internet. **Business Services:** meeting rooms, fax (fee). **Cards:** AX, DS, MC, VI. **Free Special Amenities: local telephone calls and early check-in/late check-out.** *(See color ad starting on p 1012)*

▼ See AAA listing p 1034 ▼

(See map and index starting on p. 970)

SEA DIP MOTEL & CONDOMINIUM RESORT *Book great rates at AAA.com* **Phone:** (843)448-7971 41

Hotel
$30-$165 All Year

Address: 2608 N Ocean Blvd **Location:** Oceanfront. Jct 26th Ave N. **Facility:** 95 units. 52 one- and 7 two-bedroom standard units with efficiencies. 36 condominiums. 3-12 stories, interior/exterior corridors. **Parking:** on-site. **Terms:** 2-4 night minimum stay - seasonal and/or weekends, 14 day cancellation notice-fee imposed. **Pool(s):** outdoor, heated indoor. **Leisure Activities:** whirlpools, lazy river water ride. **Guest Services:** coin laundry, wireless Internet. **Business Services:** PC, fax (fee). **Cards:** AX, DS, MC, VI. *(See color ad p 1014)*

/ SOME UNITS

SEA MIST OCEANFRONT RESORT *Book great rates at AAA.com* **Phone:** (843)448-1551 

Resort Hotel
$32-$199 All Year

Address: 1200 S Ocean Blvd **Location:** Oceanfront. Jct 12th Ave S. **Facility:** This large complex of varied buildings and room styles includes extensive recreational facilities. 800 units. 639 one-bedroom standard units, some with kitchens. 142 one-, 16 two- and 3 three-bedroom suites with kitchens. 2-16 stories, interior/exterior corridors. *Bath:* combo or shower only. **Parking:** on-site. **Terms:** check-in 4 pm, 14 day cancellation notice-fee imposed. **Amenities:** voice mail, safes. *Some:* irons. **Dining:** 2 restaurants. **Pool(s):** 6 outdoor, heated outdoor, 2 heated indoor, heated indoor/outdoor. **Leisure Activities:** saunas, whirlpools, steamroom, waterslide, recreation programs in summer, cookout areas, playground, exercise room, volleyball. *Fee:* water park, miniature golf, game room. **Guest Services:** coin laundry, wireless Internet. **Business Services:** conference facilities, fax (fee). **Cards:** AX, CB, DC, DS, JC, MC, VI. *(See color ad p 1033)*

   / SOME UNITS FEE 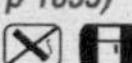

SERENDIPITY INN **Phone:** 843/449-5268 5

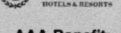

Bed & Breakfast
Rates not provided

Address: 407 71st Ave N **Location:** Jct US 17 business route, just se. Located in a secluded residential area. **Facility:** Fully equipped kitchens are featured in some rooms at this Spanish Mission-style inn, which combines elements of a B&B and a motel. Smoke free premises. 15 units. 13 one-bedroom standard units, some with efficiencies. 2 one-bedroom suites with efficiencies. 2 stories (no elevator), exterior corridors. *Bath:* combo or shower only. **Parking:** on-site. **Amenities:** video library, DVD players, irons, hair dryers. **Pool(s):** outdoor. **Leisure Activities:** whirlpool, bicycles, shuffleboard. **Guest Services:** wireless Internet. **Business Services:** fax (fee).

/ SOME UNITS

SHERATON MYRTLE BEACH CONVENTION CENTER HOTEL *Book great rates at AAA.com* **Phone:** (843)918-5000 42

Hotel
$99-$249 All Year

AAA Benefit:
Members get up to 15% off, plus Starwood Preferred Guest® bonuses.

Address: 2101 N Oak St **Location:** US 17 business route, just w on 21st Ave N. **Facility:** Smoke free premises. 402 units. 392 one-bedroom standard units, some with whirlpools. 9 one- and 1 two-bedroom suites. 12 stories, interior corridors. *Bath:* combo or shower only. **Parking:** on-site (fee) and valet. **Amenities:** video games (fee), CD players, high-speed Internet, dual phone lines, voice mail, safes, irons, hair dryers. **Dining:** Vidalia's, see separate listing. **Pool(s):** heated indoor. **Leisure Activities:** whirlpool, exercise room. *Fee:* golf privileges. **Guest Services:** valet laundry, airport transportation-Myrtle Beach International Airport, area transportation-within 3 mi. **Business Services:** conference facilities, business center. **Cards:** AX, CB, DC, DS, JC, MC, VI. *(See color ad below)*

 CALL   / SOME UNITS 

(See map and index starting on p. 970)

SLEEP INN & SUITES WACCAMAW PINES *Book at AAA.com* **Phone:** 843/236-0102

Hotel
Rates not provided

Address: 108 Waccamaw Pines Dr **Location:** Jct SR 31, 0.7 mi n, then just e. Located across from Factory Outlet Mall. **Facility:** 68 units. 60 one-bedroom standard units. 8 one-bedroom suites with efficiencies. 2 stories, interior corridors. *Bath:* combo or shower only. **Parking:** on-site. **Amenities:** voice mail, safes, irons, hair dryers. **Pool(s):** outdoor. **Leisure Activities:** exercise room. **Guest Services:** coin laundry, wireless Internet. **Business Services:** *Fee:* administrative services, fax.

CALL / SOME UNITS

SPRINGMAID BEACH RESORT & CONFERENCE CENTER *Book great rates at AAA.com* **Phone:** (843)315-7100 87

AAA SAVE
Hotel
$49-$190 All Year

Address: 3200 S Ocean Blvd **Location:** Jct 30th Ave S, 0.4 mi s. **Facility:** 487 units. 464 one-bedroom standard units. 8 one-, 8 two- and 6 three-bedroom suites, some with efficiencies. 1 cottage. 3-6 stories, exterior corridors. *Bath:* combo or shower only. **Parking:** on-site. **Terms:** check-in 4 pm, 2-3 night minimum stay - seasonal and/or weekends, 15 day cancellation notice-fee imposed. **Amenities:** voice mail, safes, irons, hair dryers. **Dining:** 2 restaurants. **Pool(s):** 2 outdoor, heated indoor, heated indoor/outdoor. **Leisure Activities:** 2 lazy river water rides, recreation programs in summer, exercise room, game room. *Fee:* fishing pier, miniature golf. **Guest Services:** coin laundry, wireless Internet. **Business Services:** conference facilities, PC, fax (fee). **Cards:** AX, DC, DS, MC, VI. ***(See color ad p 997)***

/ SOME UNITS

STAYBRIDGE SUITES-FANTASY HARBOUR *Book at AAA.com* **Phone:** (843)903-4000 33

Extended Stay Hotel
$80-$280 All Year

Address: 303 Hard Rock Pkwy **Location:** Jct US 17 Bypass, 0.7 mi n on US 501, exit River Oaks Rd/George Bishop Pkwy, just w on River Oaks Rd, then 0.4 mi s. Located between Outlet Mall and Fantasy Harbour. **Facility:** This newer property offers an upscale great room and a well-equipped exercise room. 119 units. 23 one-bedroom standard units with kitchens. 61 one- and 35 two-bedroom suites with kitchens. 3 stories, interior corridors. *Bath:* combo or shower only. **Parking:** on-site. **Terms:** 2 night minimum stay - seasonal and/or weekends, 7 day cancellation notice-fee imposed. **Amenities:** DVD players, high-speed Internet, dual phone lines, voice mail, irons, hair dryers. **Pool(s):** heated outdoor. **Leisure Activities:** whirlpool, exercise room, sports court. **Guest Services:** complimentary and valet laundry, wireless Internet. **Business Services:** meeting rooms, business center. **Cards:** AX, CB, DC, DS, JC, MC, VI.

ASK VCR / SOME UNITS FEE

TROPICAL SEAS **Phone:** (843)448-1171 85

AAA SAVE
Hotel
$31-$299 All Year

Address: 2807 S Ocean Blvd **Location:** Oceanfront. Jct 28th Ave S. **Facility:** 91 units. 69 one- and 6 two-bedroom standard units, some with kitchens. 16 one-bedroom suites with kitchens. 9 stories, interior corridors. **Parking:** on-site. **Terms:** office hours 7 am-11 pm, 2-3 night minimum stay - seasonal and/or weekends, 14 day cancellation notice-fee imposed. **Pool(s):** outdoor, heated outdoor. **Leisure Activities:** whirlpool. **Guest Services:** coin laundry. **Business Services:** fax (fee). **Cards:** AX, DS, MC, VI. ***(See color ad inside front cover)***

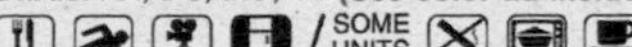

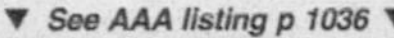

▼ *See AAA listing p 1036* ▼

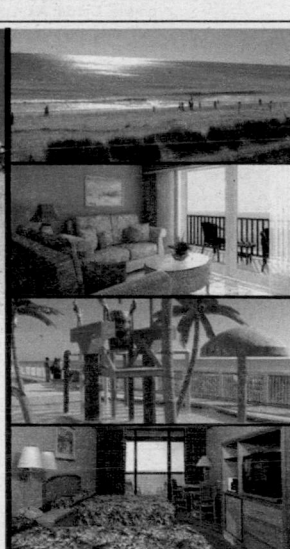

(See map and index starting on p. 970)

WAIKIKI VILLAGE

Motel
$50-$90 6/1-11/30
$30-$60 12/1-5/31

Phone: 843/448-8431 70

Address: 1500 S Ocean Blvd **Location:** Jct 15th Ave S. **Facility:** 43 units. 33 one-bedroom standard units, some with kitchens. 10 one-bedroom suites with kitchens. 2 stories (no elevator), exterior corridors. *Bath:* combo or shower only. **Parking:** on-site. **Terms:** age restrictions may apply, 21 day cancellation notice-fee imposed. **Amenities:** irons. **Pool(s):** outdoor. **Leisure Activities:** whirlpool, putting green, shuffleboard. **Guest Services:** coin laundry, wireless Internet. **Business Services:** *Fee:* administrative services, fax. **Cards:** DS, MC, VI.

/ SOME UNITS

WESTGATE MYRTLE BEACH OCEANFRONT RESORT *Book great rates at AAA.com*

Hotel
$49-$299 All Year

Phone: (843)448-4481 60

Address: 415 S Ocean Blvd **Location:** Oceanfront. Jct 6th Ave S, just ne. **Facility:** 212 one-bedroom standard units. 6-8 stories, interior corridors. **Parking:** on-site. **Terms:** check-in 4 pm, 3 day cancellation notice. **Amenities:** voice mail, safes, irons, hair dryers. **Pool(s):** outdoor, heated indoor. **Leisure Activities:** sauna, whirlpool, exercise room. *Fee:* game room. **Guest Services:** valet and coin laundry, wireless Internet. **Business Services:** conference facilities, business center. **Cards:** AX, DS, MC, VI. **Free Special Amenities: full breakfast and room upgrade (subject to availability with advance reservations).** *(See color ad p 1035)*

/ SOME UNITS

THE WINDSURFER HOTEL

Hotel
$40-$245 All Year

Phone: 843/448-3475 58

Address: 210 N Ocean Blvd **Location:** Oceanfront. Jct 2nd Ave N. **Facility:** 69 units. 46 one-bedroom standard units, some with kitchens and/or whirlpools. 23 one-bedroom suites with kitchens, some with whirlpools. 3-9 stories, exterior corridors. *Bath:* combo or shower only. **Parking:** on-site. **Terms:** 4 night minimum stay - seasonal and/or weekends, 14 day cancellation notice-fee imposed. **Amenities:** voice mail. *Some:* irons. **Pool(s):** outdoor, indoor/outdoor. **Leisure Activities:** whirlpool, picnic tables. **Guest Services:** coin laundry. **Business Services:** administrative services, fax (fee). **Cards:** AX, DS, MC, VI.

/ SOME UNITS

WHERE TO DINE

ABUELO'S THE FLAVOR OF MEXICO

Mexican
$7-$18

Phone: 843/448-5533 33

Look around and you'll think you're dining al fresco in an authentic Mexican courtyard, complete with hand-carved statues, ornate columns, wall murals and lighting that casts over the sky-like ceiling. House specialties include bacon-wrapped fillets, crab-stuffed chicken with shrimp and scallops in a creamy lobster sauce. Vegetarians will find several distinctive dishes. Casual dress. **Bar:** Full bar. **Hours:** 11 am-10 pm, Fri & Sat-11 pm. Closed: 11/26, 12/24, 12/25. **Address:** 740 Coastal Grande Cir **Location:** Jct US 501/17, 0.7 mi sw on US 17; on north side of Coastal Grande Mall. **Parking:** on-site. **Cards:** AX, DS, MC, VI.

CALL

AKEL'S FAMILY RESTAURANT

American
$2-$10

Phone: 843/449-4815 9

The city's first pancake house is known for its flapjacks and huge omelets. On the menu are mainly breakfast items, along with a selection of deli sandwiches, burgers and patty melts. Casual dress. **Reservations:** not accepted. **Hours:** 6:30 am-2 pm, Thurs-Sat from 10 pm; seasonal hours vary. Closed: 11/26, 12/25. **Address:** 6429 N Kings Hwy **Location:** Jct 64th Ave N and US 17 business route. **Parking:** on-site. **Cards:** AX, DS, MC, VI.

AMICI'S BRICK OVEN & ITALIAN BISTRO

Italian
$6-$18

Phone: 843/444-0006 16

The family-friendly eatery's specialty is brick-oven pizzas but patrons may also select from chicken, veal, seafood and pasta entrees. Casual dress. **Bar:** Beer & wine. **Hours:** 11 am-11 pm; to 10:30 pm in summer; hours vary off season. Closed: 11/26, 12/25. **Address:** 1310 Celebrity Cir **Location:** US 17 Bypass, just se on 29th Ave N, then just sw; at Broadway at the Beach. **Parking:** on-site. **Cards:** DS, MC, VI.

ANGELO'S STEAK & PASTA

Italian
$8-$30

Phone: 843/626-2800 54

The casual eatery is known for its perfectly seasoned steaks served on a sizzling skillet, as well as traditionally prepared Italian dishes, such as spaghetti with meatballs and veal parmigiana. The large buffet lines up three kinds of pizza, lasagna, stuffed shells and other good dishes. Hot garlic rolls and crisp salad with the delicious house dressing are good accompaniments. Casual dress. **Bar:** Full bar. **Reservations:** accepted. **Hours:** 4 pm-10 pm; to 9:30 pm off season. Closed: 11/26; also 12/22-12/26 & 1/3-1/9. **Address:** 2011 S Kings Hwy **Location:** Jct 21st Ave S and US 17 business route. **Parking:** on-site. **Cards:** AX, DC, DS, MC, VI.

ASPEN GRILLE

Steak & Seafood
$17-$36

Phone: 843/449-9191 11

The menu at this casually upscale dining room features a wide variety of entrees like lamb, veal, chicken and seafood, all presented with flair. Selections include roasted giant sea scallops with brie spaetzle, spinach and truffle jus, Ed's Famous Crabcakes, and veal osso bucco. Casual dress. **Bar:** Full bar. **Reservations:** suggested. **Hours:** 5 pm-10 pm. Closed: 11/26, 12/25; also Sun. **Address:** 5101 N Kings Hwy **Location:** Jct 51st Ave N and US 17 business route. **Parking:** on-site. **Cards:** AX, DC, DS, MC, VI.

(See map and index starting on p. 970)

BAGEL FACTORY, BAKERY, DELI-CAFE **Phone:** 843/626-6445 (38)

American
$2-$8

At times, a boisterous crowd fills the New York, deli-style cafe, which is open for breakfast and lunch. Freshly baked bread is used for all bagels and made-to-order sandwiches. Casual dress. **Hours:** 6:30 am-3 pm, Sat-2 pm, Sun 7 am-2 pm. Closed: 11/26, 12/25. **Address:** 2012 N Kings Hwy **Location:** Jct 21st Ave N and US 17 business route; in Studebaker's Plaza. **Parking:** on-site. **Cards:** MC, VI.

BONEFISH GRILL **Phone:** 843/497-5294 (6)

Seafood
$13-$20

Fish is the house specialty, and the menu and nightly specials offer a variety of choices. Well-prepared food is cooked to perfection. Service is casual in nature, and the staff is skilled and attentive. Casual dress. **Bar:** Full bar. **Hours:** 4 pm-close. Closed: 11/26, 12/25. **Address:** 7401 N Kings Hwy **Location:** Jct US 17 business route and 75th Ave N. **Parking:** on-site. **Cards:** AX, DC, DS, MC, VI.

BUMMZ BEACH CAFE **Phone:** 843/916-9111 (42)

American
$7-$24

The small 1930s-era oceanfront beach house is wedged between two high-rise hotels in a popular area of the Strand. It features a large bar and dining room on the interior and covered and garden dining areas with ocean views. The menu lists finger foods, fried and grilled seafood, sandwiches and burgers. The atmosphere is necessarily relaxed and friendly and has been known to get lively in the evening as guests let their hair down during karaoke nights or while listening to live entertainment. Casual dress. **Bar:** Full bar. **Reservations:** not accepted. **Hours:** 11:30 am-11 pm. Closed: 12/25. **Address:** 2003 N Ocean Blvd **Location:** Jct 20th Ave N. **Parking:** street. **Cards:** AX, DS, MC, VI.

CAPTAIN GEORGE'S SEAFOOD RESTAURANT **Phone:** 843/916-2278

Eastern Seafood
$13-$25

An extensive, all-you-can-eat seafood buffet—which includes everything from Alaskan crab legs and shrimp to prime rib and dessert—satisfies even the heartiest of appetites. Nautical accents such as ropes and fish nets convey the oceanic feel. Casual dress. **Bar:** Full bar. **Hours:** 3 pm-10 pm, Sun from noon; 4 pm-9 pm, Fri & Sat-10 pm, Sun noon-9 pm 5/26-9/1. Closed: 12/25. **Address:** 1401 29th Ave N **Location:** Jct US 17 Bypass, just nw; across from Broadway at the Beach. **Parking:** on-site. **Cards:** AX, DC, MC, VI.

CALL

CAROLINA ROADHOUSE RESTAURANT **Phone:** 843/497-9911 (13)

American
$6-$25

High ceilings with wood beams lend spaciousness to the traditional, roadhouse-style restaurant. Candle lanterns and pewter plates add to the ambiance. Diners can select from a menu of hearty foods, such as ribs, fresh seafood and sandwiches, including the locally popular po'boy. Casual dress. **Bar:** Full bar. **Reservations:** accepted. **Hours:** 11 am-10 pm, Fri & Sat-11 pm. **Address:** 4617 N Kings Hwy **Location:** Jct 46th Ave N and US 17 business route. **Parking:** on-site. **Cards:** AX, DC, DS, MC, VI.

CHALUPA MEXICAN RESTAURANT **Phone:** 843/626-4566 (25)

Mexican
$5-$14

Traditional Mexican fare is on the menu at the cantina. Chicken, beef, pork and seafood entrees make an appearance, as do combination plates. Casual dress. **Bar:** Full bar. **Reservations:** accepted. **Hours:** 11 am-10 pm. Closed: 12/25. **Address:** 2801 N Kings Hwy **Location:** Jct 28th Ave N and US 17 business route. **Parking:** on-site. **Cards:** AX, CB, DC, DS, JC, MC, VI.

CITY BAR METROPOLITAN CUISINE **Phone:** 843/449-7013 (5)

AAA

American
$7-$30

Two prix fixe menus are available featuring three or four courses. A lengthy tapas menu is also offered a la carte or as a 90-minute culinary journey where guests get to select eight different plates that are sequenced over the period so everyone at the table can sample the kitchen's creations. Tapas selections include Chinatown crab wontons, lime grilled tuna tacos, Louisiana stuffed shrimp Rockefeller and artisan cheese plate. Over 40 martinis and a variety of vintage wines are available. Casual dress. **Bar:** Full bar. **Reservations:** accepted. **Hours:** 5 pm-midnight, Fri & Sat-2 am. Closed: 12/25. **Address:** 7604 N Kings Hwy **Location:** Jct US 17/77th Ave N. **Parking:** on-site. **Cards:** AX, DS, MC, VI.

CALL

COLLECTORS CAFE **Phone:** 843/449-9370 (3)

Mediterranean
$28-$35

Original artwork adorns the walls of the Mediterranean bistro, a hot spot for meat, pasta and fresh seafood creations. An example is the scallop cake, pan-sauteed in a tomato, scallion, garlic and butter sauce with grilled fresh vegetables. Diners can end their gastronomic affairs with the award-winning tiramisu and a specialty coffee. Live jazz or acoustic music is provided most Fridays. Dressy casual. **Bar:** Full bar. **Reservations:** suggested. **Hours:** 6 pm-10 pm, Fri & Sat-10:30 pm. Closed: 1/1, 11/26, 12/24, 12/25; also Sun. **Address:** 7726 N Kings Hwy **Location:** Jct 77th Ave N and US 17 business route; in Professional Mall. **Parking:** on-site. **Cards:** AX, DC, DS, MC, VI.

THE CRAB HOUSE **Phone:** 843/444-2717 (22)

SAVE

Seafood
$8-$65

A huge hit at the lively bistro is the daily, fresh catch as well as crabs, prepared every way imaginable. The trademark blue crabs are prepared South Florida-style with garlic and butter. Casual dress. **Bar:** Full bar. **Hours:** 11:30 am-10:15 pm; hours may vary off season. Closed: 12/25. **Address:** 1313 Celebrity Cir **Location:** US 17 Bypass, just se on 21st Ave N, then just ne; at Broadway at the Beach. **Parking:** on-site. **Cards:** AX, DC, DS, JC, MC, VI.

CALL

(See map and index starting on p. 970)

CROISSANTS BAKERY & CAFE **Phone:** 843/448-2253 (12)

Deli
$6-$10

Patrons of the tiny cafe can pop in for a quick breakfast or lunch or linger over coffee and one of the many sweets on display at the counter. The made-to-order salads, wraps and sandwiches can also be requested for takeout. Casual dress. **Hours:** 7 am-8 pm, Sat 8 am-4 pm. Closed major holidays; also Sun. **Address:** 3751 Robert M Grissom Pkwy **Location:** Jct 38th Ave N (Robert M Grissom Pkwy); in The Beach First Center. **Parking:** on-site. **Cards:** AX, MC, VI.

DAGWOOD'S DELI & BUMSTEAD'S PUB **Phone:** 843/448-0100 (45)

Deli
$5-$10

A few blocks off the beach, the delicatessen serves salads, cheese steaks, burgers and giant sandwiches. Takeout and delivery service also are available. Casual dress. **Bar:** Full bar. **Hours:** 11 am-midnight, Sun from 4 pm. Closed: 1/1, 11/26, 12/25. **Address:** 400 Mr. Joe White Ave (11th Ave N) **Location:** US 17 business route, just e. **Parking:** on-site and street. **Cards:** AX, MC, VI.

DEAD DOG SALOON NORTH **Phone:** 843/839-9144 (31)

American
$5-$25

The legend of Dudley is alive and well at the Dead Dog. The casual dining restaurant features a large bar, huge menu and nightly live entertainment. Guests can choose from sandwiches and burgers, a wide appetizer selection, pasta, fresh seafood, steak, ribs, chicken and salads. All entrees come with a Dog House salad, vegetable of the day, starch of your choice and, of course, fresh hush puppies. Casual dress. Entertainment. **Bar:** Full bar. **Hours:** 11 am-11 pm, Fri & Sat-midnight. Closed: 11/26. **Address:** 760 Coastal Grande Cir **Location:** Jct US 50/17, 0.7 mi sw on US 17; on north side of Coastal Grande Mall. **Parking:** on-site. **Cards:** AX, MC, VI.

CALL

EAST OF CHICAGO PIZZA **Phone:** 843/448-3335 (19)

Pizza
$4-$9

A fun, family-friendly setting adorns the self-service, all-you-can-eat restaurant. Buffet offerings include thin crust pizzas including several different topping combinations, pasta and sauces, salads and pizza desserts. The bright, open dining room is surrounded by an arcade featuring the latest electronic games and games of chance. Casual dress. **Bar:** Beer only. **Reservations:** not accepted. **Hours:** 11 am-9 pm; hours vary off season. Closed: 12/25. **Address:** 3901 N Kings Hwy **Location:** Jct 39th Ave N. **Parking:** on-site. **Cards:** AX, DS, MC, VI.

EL CERRO GRANDE **Phone:** 843/946-9562 (48)

Mexican
$6-$14

Enhanced only by colorful murals of Mexican scenery and wall-mounted serapes and sombreros, the simple decor and no-frills atmosphere eliminates any distraction from the delicious food. Hearty portions of tortilla chips and salsa, spicy beef enchiladas and other popular selections combine with prompt service for an enjoyable experience. Casual dress. **Bar:** Full bar. **Hours:** 11 am-10 pm, Sat 11:30 am-10:30 pm, Sun 11:30 am-9 pm. Closed major holidays. **Address:** 108 S Kings Hwy **Location:** Jct 2nd Ave S and US 17 business route. **Parking:** on-site. **Cards:** AX, DS, MC, VI.

FIESTA DEL BURRO LOCO **Phone:** 843/626-1756 (23)

Mexican
$7-$25

Near the action of Broadway at the Beach, the airy, festively-decorated restaurant serves a variety of burritos and fajitas. Among specialties are shrimp enchiladas and barbecue ribs. Casual dress. **Bar:** Full bar. **Hours:** 11 am-10 pm. Closed: 11/26, 12/25. **Address:** 960 Jason Blvd **Location:** Jct 10th Ave N and US 17 Bypass, just n. **Parking:** on-site. **Cards:** AX, DC, DS, MC, VI.

CALL

THE FILLING STATION **Phone:** 843/626-9435 (24)

American
$7-$9

Guests can order burgers, hot dogs and other sandwiches from the grill or join the crowd at the pizza buffet. Among other buffet offerings are a soup and salad bar, spaghetti bar and a build-your-own-sandwich station. Casual dress. **Bar:** Beer only. **Hours:** 11 am-9 pm. Closed major holidays. **Address:** 1913 10th Ave N **Location:** US 17 Bypass, just se. **Parking:** on-site. **Cards:** MC, VI.

FLAMINGO GRILL **Phone:** 843/449-5388 (7)

American
$8-$30

The impressive Art Deco interior includes pink and black marble floors at the lively seafood grill. Among creative entrees are the popular grouper Oscar topped with crabmeat, asparagus and creamy bearnaise sauce. Casual dress. **Bar:** Full bar. **Hours:** 4:30 pm-10 pm. Closed: 11/26, 12/24-12/26; also Sun. **Address:** 7050 N Kings Hwy **Location:** Jct US 17 business route and 71st Ave N. **Parking:** on-site. **Cards:** AX, DS, MC, VI.

CALL

GRANDMA'S KITCHEN **Phone:** 843/448-2126 (46)

American
$5-$22

Country cookin' makes up the menu at the family-friendly restaurant. In addition to the menu, lunch and dinner buffets line up such hearty fare as fried chicken and pork chops, as well as vegetables and an array of desserts. A breakfast buffet also is set up. Casual dress. **Hours:** 7 am-9 pm. Closed: Memorial Day weekend. **Address:** 610 N Kings Hwy **Location:** Jct 7th Ave N and US 17 business route. **Parking:** on-site. **Cards:** DS, MC, VI.

GRECIAN DELIGHT CAFE **Phone:** 843/497-8882 (10)

Greek
$5-$14

The small, family-operated storefront restaurant offers a wide variety of Mediterranean fare and popular Greek favorites such as gyros, spanakopita, lemon soup and stuffed grape leaves. All courses are prepared to order and served by a friendly staff or the owner herself, who is a most gracious hostess. Diners should take a look in the deli case loaded with desserts before they order so they don't fill up too much on the entree. Casual dress. **Bar:** Beer & wine. **Reservations:** accepted. **Hours:** 11 am-9 pm, Fri & Sat-10 pm. Closed: 11/26, 12/24, 12/25; also Sun. **Address:** 5900 N Kings Hwy, Suite G (US 17) **Location:** Jct US 17/Sunset Tr. **Parking:** on-site. **Cards:** MC, VI.

(See map and index starting on p. 970)

HARRY'S BREAKFAST PANCAKES — **Phone:** 843/448-8013 (36)

American
$4-$9

This diner-style operation serves a variety of breakfast favorites, including a number of Belgian waffle concoctions. Mediterranean fare is also available during lunch. Casual dress. **Reservations:** not accepted. **Hours:** 5:30 am-2 pm. **Address:** 2306 N Kings Hwy **Location:** Jct 23rd Ave N. **Parking:** on-site. **Cards:** MC, VI.

INTERNATIONAL OMELET & PANCAKE HOUSE — **Phone:** 843/448-2652 (51)

Breakfast
$3-$8

A breakfast menu of 30 different omelets, as well as waffles and pancakes, is made available day and night at this no-frills grill. A small lunch menu is available after 11 am and features burgers and sandwiches. Casual dress. **Reservations:** not accepted. **Hours:** 6 am-2 pm. **Address:** 1201 S Kings Hwy **Location:** Jct 12th Ave S. **Parking:** on-site. **Cards:** MC, VI.

J EDWARD'S GREAT RIBS & MORE — **Phone:** 843/626-9986 (55)

American
$6-$39

Perfect for rib lovers, the casual bistro presents an array of barbecue ribs, prime rib, steak, chicken, pork and seafood. Casual dress. **Bar:** Full bar. **Reservations:** suggested. **Hours:** 3 pm-10 pm; hours vary off season. Closed: 12/24. **Address:** 2300 S Kings Hwy **Location:** Jct 23rd Ave S and US 17 business route. **Parking:** on-site. **Cards:** AX, DS, MC, VI.

JIMMY BUFFET'S MARGARITAVILLE — **Phone:** 843/448-5455

American
$9-$20

A mecca for parrotheads, tourists and locals, the huge, animated restaurant offers great food, wonderful music and the perfect atmosphere to change your latitude. On the menu are Caribbean-themed seafood, chicken and beef, as well as the signature cheeseburger in paradise. Casual dress. **Bar:** Full bar. **Hours:** 11:30 am-10 pm. Closed: 11/26, 12/25. **Address:** 1114 Celebrity Cir **Location:** Jct US 17 Bypass/29th Ave N, just se, then just sw; in Broadway at the Beach. **Parking:** on-site. **Cards:** AX, DS, MC, VI.

CALL

KEY WEST GRILL — **Phone:** 843/444-3663 (17)

American
$11-$30

Spicy food reflects Cuban, Spanish and Calusa Indian influences. Perfectly seasoned seafood dishes include crispy conch fritters, fried calamari and the catch of the day, an example of which is citrus-marinated mahi mahi served with star fruit and black bean papaya salsa. With imitation palm trees and a ceiling painted to look like a tropical sky, the casual dining room is designed to appear like a courtyard cafe in a Key West hotel. Casual dress. **Bar:** Full bar. **Reservations:** accepted. **Hours:** 11 am-10 pm, Fri & Sat-11 pm; hours vary off season. Closed: 11/26, 12/25. **Address:** 1214 Celebrity Cir **Location:** US 17 Bypass, just se on 29th Ave N, then just sw; at Broadway at the Beach. **Parking:** on-site. **Cards:** AX, DC, DS, MC, VI.

CALL

LANDRY'S SEAFOOD HOUSE — **Phone:** 843/444-1010 (15)

SAVE

Regional American
$9-$35

An ideal spot for healthy seafood dinners and special occasions, the restaurant produces a wonderful clam chowder. Menu selections come from all the world's oceans. Casual dress. **Bar:** Full bar. **Hours:** 11 am-10 pm; Mon-Fri to 9 pm in winter. Closed: 12/25. **Address:** 1312 Celebrity Cir **Location:** Jct US 17 Bypass and 29th Ave N, just se on 29th Ave N, then just sw; at Broadway at the Beach. **Parking:** on-site. **Cards:** AX, DC, DS, MC, VI.

CALL

LIBERTY STEAKHOUSE & BREWERY — **Phone:** 843/626-4677 (21)

American
$6-$24

Eight flavors of beers are brewed on the premises and also used as ingredients in many recipes. Food choices range from fish 'n' chips to pizza to steak. Try the prime rib sandwich, a monster cut of beef cooked to order and served with steak fries. Casual dress. **Bar:** Full bar. **Reservations:** not accepted. **Hours:** 11 am-11 pm. Closed: 11/26, 12/25. **Address:** 1321 Celebrity Cir **Location:** US 17 Bypass, just se on 21st Ave N, then just ne; at Broadway at the Beach. **Parking:** on-site. **Cards:** AX, DS, MC, VI.

LIBERTY TAP ROOM & GRILL — **Phone:** 843/839-4677 (4)

American
$7-$21

This brewpub features four handcrafted beers daily and a wide selection of domestic and imported ales, lagers and stouts; the menu complements the variety of beers with enough steak, burger, pasta, chicken, seafood and pizza options to please the diner. Casual dress. **Bar:** Full bar. **Hours:** 11 am-midnight. Closed: 11/26, 12/25. **Address:** 7651 N Kings Hwy **Location:** Between 78th and 79th aves N on US 17 business route; in Northwood Shopping Center. **Parking:** on-site. **Cards:** AX, DC, DS, MC, VI.

CALL

MAGNOLIA'S AT 26TH — **Phone:** 843/839-3993 (32)

American
$5-$21

The friendly, professional staff serves simple home-style American fare. Casual dress. **Bar:** Beer & wine. **Hours:** 6:30 am-2:30 & 5-9 pm. Closed: 12/25. **Address:** 2605 N Ocean Blvd **Location:** Jct 26th Ave N. **Parking:** on-site. **Cards:** MC, VI. ***(See color ad on insert)***

CALL

MICHAEL'S PIZZA, PASTA & GRILL — **Phone:** 843/448-0344 (43)

AAA

Italian
$5-$17

Menu offerings at the cozy grill include pizza, strombolis and pasta dishes, which are available for eat-in or take-out. Casual dress. **Bar:** Beer & wine. **Hours:** Open 12/1-12/14 & 1/8-11/30; 11 am-10 pm; to 11 pm 3/1-10/31. Closed major holidays; also Sun. **Address:** 1701 N Kings Hwy **Location:** Jct 17th Ave N and US 17 business route. **Parking:** on-site. **Cards:** AX, DS, MC, VI.

(See map and index starting on p. 970)

NASCAR SPORTS GRILLE — **Phone:** 843/946-7223 (18)

American
$9-$27

Racing fans can sit in booths set up like pit areas in a racetrack infield. Loads of memorabilia—including autographed drivers' suits, complete race cars and a small hall of fame—contribute to the NASCAR theme. The distinctly Southern menu is built around down-home dishes, such as farm-raised catfish, which is cut into strips, lightly dusted in seasoned cornmeal and fried golden brown. Casual dress. **Bar:** Full bar. **Reservations:** accepted. **Hours:** 11 am-10 pm, Sun-9 pm; Fri & Sat-11 pm in summer. Closed: 12/25. **Address:** 1808 21st Ave N **Location:** Jct US 17 Bypass, just w; across from Broadway at the Beach. **Parking:** on-site. **Cards:** AX, DC, DS, MC, VI.

CALL

NEW YORK PRIME, A STEAKHOUSE — **Phone:** 843/448-8081 (28)

Steak
$28-$45

Behind the rustic facade, patrons discover a classic steakhouse with gracious service and an extensive wine list. Quality USDA prime steak selections, perfectly prepared as ordered, are the mainstay of a menu that also features lobster and a fresh catch of the day. Side dish portions are big enough for two. Casual dress. **Bar:** Full bar. **Reservations:** suggested. **Hours:** 5 pm-11 pm. Closed: 11/26, 12/25. **Address:** 405 28th Ave N **Location:** Jct US 17 business route, just se. **Parking:** on-site. **Cards:** AX, DC, DS, MC, VI.

OCEANS ON 82ND — **Phone:** 843/449-8880 (2)

American
$10-$36

The oceanside full-service restaurant offers a diverse menu of fine cuisine sure to please any of the resort's guests; the presentation of each entree is extraordinary. Casual dress. **Bar:** Full bar. **Hours:** 6-11 am, 11:30-2:30 & 5-10 pm. **Address:** 8400 Costa Verde Dr **Location:** Jct US 17 business (N Kings Hwy) and 82nd Pkwy, just se on 82nd Pkwy; in Myrtle Beach Marriott Resort at Grande Dunes. **Parking:** on-site. **Cards:** AX, CB, DC, DS, JC, MC, VI.

CALL

OMEGA PANCAKE AND OMELET HOUSE — **Phone:** 843/626-9949 (26)

American
$4-$8

Refuel after a round of golf at the casual eatery, which is located near area golf course and on the main strip. Dig in to large stacks of waffles, pancakes, specialty omelets and cooked-to-order eggs. Casual dress. **Hours:** 10 pm-2 pm. Closed: 12/24, 12/25. **Address:** 2800 N Kings Hwy **Location:** Jct 28th Ave N and US 17 business route. **Parking:** on-site. **Cards:** MC, VI.

CALL

PAN-AMERICAN PANCAKE & OMELET HOUSE — **Phone:** 843/448-3629 (52)

American
$3-$9

The pancake house closes after the lunch rush and reopens at 10 pm, so those who crave an omelet in the middle of the night are in luck. All the usual breakfast favorites are offered, as are sandwiches for lunch. Casual dress. **Hours:** 10 pm-2 pm. Closed: 12/25. **Address:** 1305 S Kings Hwy **Location:** Jct 13th Ave S and US 17 business route. **Parking:** on-site. **Cards:** MC, VI.

PAPA'S — **Phone:** 843/626-4700 (41)

American
$12-$22

The menu at the casually upscale eatery focuses on steak, chops, seafood and pasta. Many items, including Caribbean quesadillas and jambalaya, are prepared with Caribbean flair. Casual dress. **Bar:** Full bar. **Reservations:** accepted. **Hours:** 6 am-10 & 5-10 pm; to 9 pm 11/1-2/28. **Address:** 2005 N Ocean Blvd **Location:** Jct 21st Ave N; in The Breakers Paradise Tower & The Breakers Resort Hotel. **Parking:** on-site. **Cards:** AX, DS, MC, VI.

PHILLIPS CRAB HOUSE — **Phone:** 843/626-2722

Seafood
$15-$30

Since 1956, the small chain—which originated in Ocean City, Maryland—has used family recipes to create delicious Maryland-style crab, shrimp, fish, scallops, oysters and lobster dishes as well as some landlubber fare. Casual dress. **Bar:** Full bar. **Reservations:** accepted. **Hours:** 4 pm-10 pm; hours may vary off season. Closed: 11/26, 12/25. **Address:** 1807 21st Ave N **Location:** US 17 Bypass, just w; across from Broadway at the Beach. **Parking:** on-site. **Cards:** AX, DS, MC, VI.

CALL

PIZZA A LA ROMA III — **Phone:** 843/448-7203 (47)

Italian
$8-$13

Near the city center, the small family-owned-and-operated restaurant has been a popular dining spot for more than 20 years. The menu is dominated by Greek and Italian dishes, including the signature calzones, hot oven subs, hand-tossed pizza, pasta entrees and gyros. An all-you-can-eat lunch buffet is offered, in season, Monday through Saturday. Corn dogs and pita pizza are among offerings on the children's menu. Casual dress. **Bar:** Beer & wine. **Hours:** 11 am-11 pm, Sun 4 pm-10 pm. Closed: 11/26, 12/25. **Address:** 412 N Kings Hwy **Location:** Jct 4th Ave N. **Parking:** on-site. **Cards:** AX, DS, MC, VI.

POMODORO'S TRATTORIA & BAR — **Phone:** 843/626-3161 (44)

Italian
$9-$28

Near the Jetport, the family-run restaurant features traditional Italian and Tuscan fare that's both well-prepared and nicely presented. Inside the brick building, Roman arches connect several dining rooms and the open lounge. Pasta, chicken and veal are featured along with char-grilled selections and the chef's own creations, such as jambalaya di Napoli with shrimp, chicken and Italian sausage over pasta. Servers are efficient, friendly and eager to help patrons navigate the menu or wine list. Casual dress. **Bar:** Full bar. **Reservations:** accepted. **Hours:** 5 pm-10 pm; from 4 pm 5/1-9/30. Closed: 11/26, 12/25. **Address:** 364 Robert M Grissom Pkwy **Location:** Jct US 501, 0.5 mi w. **Parking:** on-site. **Cards:** AX, DS, MC, VI.

CALL

(See map and index starting on p. 970)

RAMANDO'S ITALIAN GRILL — **Phone:** 843/626-7060 (37)

Italian
$10-$30

In addition to large portions of Italian standards, patrons can sample specialty chicken, veal and seafood dishes made with distinctive house sauces. Char-grilled steaks and brick-oven pizzas also pique interest. Children can order from the kids' menu. Casual dress. **Bar:** Full bar. **Reservations:** accepted. **Hours:** 3:30 pm-9:30 pm. Closed: 12/25. **Address:** 2001 N Kings Hwy **Location:** Jct 20th Ave N and US 17 business route. **Parking:** on-site. **Cards:** AX, MC, VI.

HIOZ BRAZILIAN STEAKHOUSE — **Phone:** 843/839-0777 (14)

Brazilian
$20-$35

Guests are treated to continual tableside service, as roving gauchos entice with pieces of 15 cuts of marinated beef, pork, lamb, poultry and fish. The traditional Brazilian cocktail—the Caipirinha—is prepared tableside with fresh limes, sugar and Brazilian rum. Also part of the meal, the salad bar lines up nearly three dozen items. Every table gets a dish of cheese-topped mashed potatoes, fried bananas, polenta and cheese bread. Last is the roving dessert cart loaded with delicacies. Casual dress. **Bar:** Full bar. **Reservations:** accepted. **Hours:** 4 pm-10 pm. Closed: 12/25. **Address:** 2920 Hollywood Dr **Location:** Jct US 17 Bypass/29th Ave N, just se; adjacent to Broadway at the Beach. **Parking:** on-site. **Cards:** AX, DS, MC, VI.

CALL

RIVER CITY CAFE — **Phone:** 843/449-8877 (8)

American
$3-$13

Near several resorts in the north end, the casual restaurant is notable for its numerous interpretations of the hamburger and complimentary baskets of roasted peanuts. Many other sandwiches and finger foods are available, and flying cows and license plates cover the walls. Casual dress. **Bar:** Full bar. **Hours:** 11 am-10 pm. Closed: 11/26, 12/25. **Address:** 208 73rd Ave N **Location:** Jct N Ocean Blvd. **Parking:** on-site. **Cards:** MC, VI.

RIVER CITY CAFE — **Phone:** 843/448-1990 (40)

American
$4-$15

Just a block from the beach, the restaurant is the ultimate in "casual." Guests can toss peanut shells on the floor and autograph the walls if they find any remaining space among the license plates and signatures of the multitudes who came before. Befitting the casual nature of the restaurant, the wait staff don shorts and logoed T-shirts. Casual dress. **Bar:** Full bar. **Hours:** 11 am-10 pm. Closed: 11/26, 12/25. **Address:** 404 21st Ave N **Location:** Jct US 17 business route, just se. **Parking:** on-site. **Cards:** DS, MC, VI.

SEA CAPTAIN'S HOUSE ***Menu on AAA.com*** — **Phone:** 843/448-8082 (27)

AAA

American
$6-$28

Constructed in 1930 as a family beach cottage and operating as a restaurant since 1962, the casual eatery boasts scenic views of the ocean, sand dunes and sea oats swaying in the breeze. The enclosed rear porch offers the best vistas. The menu comprises preparations of fresh seafood, beef and chicken. Reservations aren't accepted, but the comfortably furnished sitting room makes the wait easier. Casual dress. **Bar:** Full bar. **Hours:** 6-10:30 am, 11:30-2:30 & 5-10 pm. Closed: 11/26, 12/24-12/26. **Address:** 3002 N Ocean Blvd **Location:** Jct 30th Ave N. **Parking:** on-site. **Cards:** AX, DS, MC, VI.

SENOR FROG'S — **Phone:** 843/444-5506

International
$7-$16

Part of the chain of Mexican restaurants that also includes Carlos 'n Charlie's, the fun and festive eatery is a great place to eat with the family or rendezvous with friends. The menu is lined with Tex-Mex, American and Mexican favorites, such as Buffalo wings, quesadillas, fajitas and burritos. After hours, a bar atmosphere prevails. Casual dress. **Bar:** Full bar. **Hours:** 11 am-10:30 pm; hours vary off season. **Address:** 1304 Celebrity Cir, Broadway at Beach **Location:** At Broadway at the Beach. **Parking:** on-site. **Cards:** AX, DS, MC, VI.

SOHO STEAKS, SEAFOOD & SUSHI — **Phone:** 843/443-9441 (39)

Continental
$5-$26

The intimate cafe presents an eclectic menu of foods that reflect Pan-Asian and Italian influences. Guests can also partake in the sushi bar. Casual dress. **Bar:** Full bar. **Reservations:** accepted. **Hours:** 11:30 am-1 am; hours vary off season. Closed: 12/25. **Address:** 406 21st Ave N **Location:** Jct US 17 business route, just se. **Parking:** on-site. **Cards:** AX, DS, MC, VI.

SPRING GARDEN PANCAKE HOUSE — **Phone:** 843/448-4270 (53)

American
$3-$7

On your way in, take a few seconds to greet the live parrots that greet everyone. Located among oceanfront hotels on the Southside, Spring Gardens is a favorite spot for breakfast or lunch. Casual dress. **Hours:** Open 12/1-12/15 & 1/15-11/30; 6:30 am-2 pm; to 1 pm 11/1-12/15 & 1/15-3/31. Closed: 12/25. **Address:** 1702 Ocean Blvd **Location:** Jct 17th Ave S. **Parking:** on-site. **Cards:** MC, VI.

CALL

SPRING HOUSE FAMILY RESTAURANT — **Phone:** 843/626-5941 (29)

American
$4-$14

The busy, family-friendly eatery offers an array of comfort foods, including roast beef, pot roast, liver and onions, meatloaf, sandwiches and a large assortment of cakes and pies. Breakfast is available all day. Casual dress. **Bar:** Beer & wine. **Hours:** 6 am-10 pm; hours vary off season. Closed: 12/25. **Address:** 2600 N Kings Hwy **Location:** Jct 26th Ave N and US 17 business route. **Parking:** on-site. **Cards:** AX, DS, MC, VI.

STICKY FINGERS RIB HOUSE — **Phone:** 843/839-7427

Barbecue
$7-$26

Diners can put down their silverware and get their fingers ready for classic Carolina sweet ribs, as well as ribs cooked in the Texas and Tennessee styles. Hearty sides of baked beans and coleslaw complement entrees at the friendly cafe. Casual dress. **Bar:** Full bar. **Hours:** 11 am-close. Closed: 11/26, 12/25. **Address:** 2461 Coastal Grand Cir **Location:** Jct US 17/501, 0.7 mi sw on US 17; on west side of Coastal Grand Mall. **Parking:** on-site. **Cards:** AX, DC, DS, MC, VI.

CALL

(See map and index starting on p. 970)

TBONZ GILL & GRILL **Phone:** 843/946-7111 (20)

Steak & Seafood
$7-$22

The restaurant features high ceilings and a rustic decor package that includes a mix of uncovered tables and booths. Large humorous paintings, including one of many celebrities dining and drinking together, enhance the pleasant, casual atmosphere. Basic preparations of fresh seafood, Low Country dishes, burgers and light snacks are served with a selection of microbrewed beers. Casual dress. **Bar:** Full bar. **Hours:** 11 am-10 pm, Fri & Sat-10:30 pm. Closed: 11/26, 12/25. **Address:** 1169 Seaboard St **Location:** US 17 Bypass, just se on 21st Ave N; across from Broadway, at Beach in Seaboard Commons. **Parking:** on-site. **Cards:** AX, DS, MC, VI.

THORNY'S STEAKHOUSE & SALOON **Phone:** 843/448-2333 (49)

American
$6-$27

The family-operated and family-oriented steak and seafood restaurant offers complete adult and child menus, as well as an arcade. The entree selection is broad, steaks are hand-cut, and most entrees are served with freshly baked yeast rolls. Early-bird specials are nightly options. Casual dress. **Bar:** Full bar. **Hours:** 11 am-10 pm, Fri & Sat-11 pm. Closed: 1/1, 12/25; also 1/02-1/07. **Address:** 600 S Kings Hwy **Location:** Jct 6th Ave S. **Parking:** on-site. **Cards:** AX, DS, MC, VI.

TOFFINO'S ITALIAN BAKERY & DELI **Phone:** 843/477-1598 (56)

Deli
$3-$8

Kitchen staffers at the old-style delicatessen and pastry shop make their own bread, pizza and Italian ices. Many recipes are more than 100 years old. For a quick lunch, grab soup with a hot or cold sandwich, and finish off the meal with a European dessert. Casual dress. **Hours:** 8 am-9 pm. Closed: 4/12, 12/25; also Sun. **Address:** 880 Farrow Pkwy **Location:** Jct US 17 business route and Howard Pkwy, 0.9 mi nw; in South Park Village, on west side of jetport. **Parking:** on-site. **Cards:** DS, MC, VI.

TRIPPS **Phone:** 843/626-6455

Steak & Seafood
$6-$21

Located in the Broadway at the Beach complex, the lively eatery serves traditional cuisine in a comfortable dining area. Casual dress. **Bar:** Full bar. **Hours:** 11 am-10 pm, Fri & Sat-11 pm. Closed: 11/26, 12/25. **Address:** 1311 Celebrity Cir **Location:** US 17 Bypass, just se on 21st Ave N, then just ne; at Broadway at the Beach. **Parking:** on-site. **Cards:** AX, DS, MC, VI.

CALL

ULTIMATE CALIFORNIA PIZZA **Phone:** 843/626-8900 (30)

Pizza
$6-$10

The colorful cafe is one of six locations on the Grand Strand. Select from a variety of pizzas heaped with a choice of toppings from a long and exotic list. A few pasta dishes, subs and salads also share the menu. Casual dress. **Bar:** Full bar. **Hours:** 11 am-11 pm, Fri & Sat-midnight; hours vary off season. Closed: 12/25. **Address:** 2500 N Kings Hwy **Location:** Jct 25th Ave N and US 17 business route. **Parking:** on-site. **Cards:** DS, MC, VI.

CALL

UNCLE JOHN'S FAMILY RESTAURANT **Phone:** 843/626-2016 (35)

American
$4-$11

Breakfast is served all day at the family eatery, which is just steps from the beach. Among other offerings are sandwiches and traditional American fare. Casual dress. **Hours:** 5:30 am-2:30 pm. Closed: 12/25. **Address:** 402 24th Ave N **Location:** Jct US 17 business route, just se. **Parking:** on-site. **Cards:** MC, VI.

VIDALIA'S **Phone:** 843/918-5000 (34)

Regional American
$10-$20

Upscale southern cuisine and friendly, polished service are on the menu at this tastefully decorated dining room. Dressy casual. **Bar:** Full bar. **Reservations:** accepted. **Hours:** 6:30 am-2:30 & 5-10 pm, Sat & Sun from 7 am. **Address:** 2101 N Oak St **Location:** US 17 business route, just w on 21st Ave N; in Sheraton Myrtle Beach Convention Center Hotel. **Parking:** on-site and valet. **Cards:** AX, CB, DC, DS, JC, MC, VI.

CALL

VILLA MARE RESTAURANT **Phone:** 843/903-8654 (1)

Italian
$10-$22

Pictures of Italian scenes decorate the walls of the casual, storefront restaurant. The cafe-style spot is noted for its friendly service and large portions. Made-to-order specialties include chicken Florentine, veal Milanese and many pasta dishes. Those with less of an appetite might opt for a calzone or pizza. Casual dress. **Bar:** Full bar. **Reservations:** accepted. **Hours:** 4 pm-10 pm. Closed major holidays; also Sun. **Address:** 4999 Carolina Forest Blvd, Unit 4 **Location:** Jct SR 31 (International Dr), 0.6 mi n to River Oaks Dr, then 0.7 mi sw; in Forest Crossings Plaza. **Parking:** on-site. **Cards:** DS, MC, VI.

VILLA ROMANA **Phone:** 843/448-4990 (50)

Traditional Italian
$12-$26

This award-winner serves high-quality Italian cuisine in a dining room decorated with Roman villa accents. Guests won't find pizza. Instead, each dish is skillfully prepared to order and delivered by professional waiters. The menu emphasizes veal dishes, some standard and some original, such as veal Absolut. Innovative chicken, seafood and pasta dishes also tempt. Entrees come with fresh bread and complimentary soup, bruschetta and salad. Live accordion music adds to the festive experience. Casual dress. Entertainment. **Bar:** Full bar. **Reservations:** suggested. **Hours:** 4:30 pm-10 pm. Closed: 11/26, 12/25. **Address:** 707 S Kings Hwy **Location:** Jct 8th Ave S and US 17 business route. **Parking:** on-site. **Cards:** AX, DS, MC, VI.

YAMATO SEAFOOD STEAK & SEAFOOD **Phone:** 843/448-1959

Japanese
$10-$32

The "original Japanese Steakhouse of South Carolina", Yamatos tantalizes guest with fresh USDA choice beef, wonderful seafood and fresh vegetables. Families enjoy the casual atmosphere and the show the chefs put on while cooking each individual meal. Casual dress. **Bar:** Full bar. **Reservations:** suggested. **Hours:** 4:30 pm-10 pm; to 9 pm 11/1-3/15. Closed: 12/25; also Super Bowl Sun. **Address:** 1213 Celebrity Cir, R-5 **Location:** US 17 Bypass, just se on 21st Ave N, then just ne; at Broadway at the Beach. **Parking:** on-site. **Cards:** AX, DC, DS, MC, VI.

Southern Grand Strand

(See map and index p. 976-977)

GARDEN CITY BEACH (See map and index starting on p. 976)

WHERE TO STAY

WATER'S EDGE RESORT *Book great rates at AAA.com* **Phone:** (843)651-0002 6

AAA SAVE

Vacation Rental Condominium

$92-$310 All Year

Address: 1012 N Waccamaw Dr **Location:** Oceanfront. US 17 business route, 1 mi e on Atlantic Ave, 0.6 mi n. **Facility:** Units at this property are individually owned, so furnishings and decor vary widely; the resort's on-site exercise facility is extensive and modern. 102 condominiums. 15 stories, exterior corridors. **Parking:** on-site. **Terms:** check-in 4 pm, 14 day cancellation notice-fee imposed. **Amenities:** voice mail. *Some:* irons. **Pool(s):** heated indoor/outdoor. **Leisure Activities:** whirlpools, exercise room. **Guest Services:** complimentary laundry. **Business Services:** *Fee:* administrative services, fax. **Cards:** AX, DC, DS, MC, VI. **Free Special Amenities: high-speed Internet.**

/ SOME UNITS

WHERE TO DINE

CONCH CAFE **Phone:** 843/651-6556 12

Seafood

$7-$24

A tropical, nautical decor punctuates the restaurant, which pleases diners with oceanfront views and al fresco tables. Fresh catches are prepared Oscar-style, topped with crabmeat, shrimp, scallops, asparagus and hollandaise or Neptune-style, with shrimp, artichokes, roma tomatoes and Parmesan cheese. Homemade key lime pie is a tangy treat. Casual dress. **Bar:** Full bar. **Hours:** Open 2/15-10/31; 11 am-10 pm. Closed: Sun off season. **Address:** 1870 N Waccamaw Dr **Location:** Jct US 17 business route and Woodland Dr, 0.8 mi se on Woodland Dr, then just ne. **Parking:** on-site. **Cards:** AX, DS, MC, VI.

FINOCCHIO'S ITALIAN RISTORANTE **Phone:** 843/651-2110 13

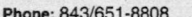

Italian

$6-$25

The storefront bistro's owner/chef satisfies with good-size portions of nicely presented Italian fare. Flavors in prepared-to-order dishes are divine, in everything from simple minestrone with a heartily spiced tomato base to sauteed veal with wild mushrooms to pancetta-wrapped jumbo shrimp in garlic balsamic reduction. The menu includes chicken, fish, pasta, veal, soups, salads and appetizers, in addition to early-bird options. Pizza is nowhere to be found. Casual dress. **Bar:** Full bar. **Reservations:** accepted. **Hours:** 11:30 am-2 & 5-10 pm, Tues & Sat from 5 pm. Closed: 11/26, 12/25; also Sun & Mon. **Address:** 3100 Hwy 17 Business **Location:** Jct US 17 and US 17 business route, 0.9 mi n on US 17 business route; in South Beach Exchange Mall. **Parking:** on-site. **Cards:** AX, DS, MC, VI.

GULFSTREAM CAFE **Phone:** 843/651-8808 14

Steak & Seafood

$11-$30

Every table at the casual restaurant offers a beautiful view of the Atlantic Ocean and Murrell's Inlet. Among seafood dishes are deep-fried shrimp stuffed with crabmeat and wrapped in bacon. Casual dress. **Bar:** Full bar. **Reservations:** suggested. **Hours:** 4 pm-close. Closed: 12/24, 12/25. **Address:** 1536 S Waccamaw Dr **Location:** Jct Atlantic Ave, 2.2 mi sw; at Marlin Quay Marina. **Parking:** on-site. **Cards:** AX, DC, DS, MC, VI.

GEORGETOWN pop. 8,950

WHERE TO STAY

GEORGETOWN QUALITY INN & SUITES AND CONFERENCE CENTER *Book great rates at AAA.com* **Phone:** (843)546-5656

AAA SAVE

Motel

$80-$199 All Year

Address: 210 Church St **Location:** Jct US 17/17 alternate route/701, 1.2 mi se on US 17; just w of ICW Bridge at Georgetown Landing. **Facility:** 97 units. 80 one-bedroom standard units. 17 one-bedroom suites. 2 stories (no elevator), exterior corridors. *Bath:* combo or shower only. **Parking:** on-site. **Terms:** cancellation fee imposed. **Amenities:** voice mail, irons, hair dryers. **Pool(s):** outdoor. **Leisure Activities:** limited exercise equipment. **Guest Services:** valet and coin laundry, wireless Internet. **Business Services:** meeting rooms, business center. **Cards:** AX, DS, MC, VI. **Free Special Amenities: expanded continental breakfast and high-speed Internet.**

/ SOME UNITS

HAMPTON INN GEORGETOWN MARINA *Book great rates at AAA.com* **Phone:** (843)545-5000

Hotel

$99-$119 All Year

Address: 420 Marina Dr **Location:** Jct US 17/17 alternate route/701, 1.2 mi se on US 17; just w of ICW Bridge at Georgetown Landing. **Facility:** 98 units. 92 one-bedroom standard units. 6 one-bedroom suites with whirlpools. 4 stories, interior corridors. *Bath:* combo or shower only. **Parking:** on-site. **Terms:** 1-30 night minimum stay, cancellation fee imposed. **Amenities:** voice mail, irons, hair dryers. **Pool(s):** outdoor. **Leisure Activities:** marina, fishing, limited exercise equipment. **Guest Services:** valet laundry, wireless Internet. **Business Services:** meeting rooms, business center. **Cards:** AX, CB, DC, DS, MC, VI.

CALL / SOME UNITS

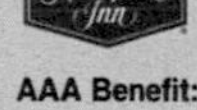

AAA Benefit:

Members save up to 10% everyday!

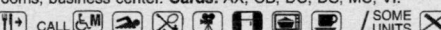

HARBOR HOUSE BED & BREAKFAST **Phone:** 843/546-6532

Historic Bed & Breakfast
$159-$199 2/14-11/30

Address: 15 Cannon St **Location:** Jct US 17/Front St, 0.8 mi se on Front St; between St James and Queen sts; downtown. **Facility:** The parlor, dining room, light-filled guest rooms and rocking chair front porch of this converted 1765 warehouse offer tranquil harbor views. Smoke free premises. 4 one-bedroom standard units, some with whirlpools. 3 stories (no elevator), interior corridors. *Bath:* combo, shower or tub only. **Parking:** on-site. **Terms:** open 2/14-11/30, office hours 8 am-8 pm, age restrictions may apply, 7 day cancellation notice-fee imposed. **Amenities:** video library, irons, hair dryers. **Leisure Activities:** bicycles. **Cards:** MC, VI.

JAMESON INN GEORGETOWN *Book at AAA.com* **Phone:** (843)546-6090

Motel
$78-$95 All Year

Address: 120 Church St **Location:** Jct US 17/17 alternate route/701, 1.2 mi se on US 17; just w of ICW Bridge at Georgetown Landing. **Facility:** 61 one-bedroom standard units, some with whirlpools. 2 stories (no elevator), exterior corridors. *Bath:* combo or shower only. **Parking:** on-site. **Terms:** cancellation fee imposed. **Amenities:** hair dryers. *Some:* irons. **Pool(s):** outdoor. **Leisure Activities:** exercise room. **Guest Services:** wireless Internet. **Business Services:** meeting rooms, PC, fax (fee). **Cards:** AX, DC, DS, MC, VI.

ASK / SOME UNITS FEE VCR

THE SHAW HOUSE **Phone:** (843)546-9663

Bed & Breakfast
$100 All Year

Address: 613 Cypress St **Location:** Jct US 17/701, 0.4 mi se to Willow Bank Rd, just ne to Palmetto St, then just se. **Facility:** This Colonial Revival-style home's parlor has a fireplace, piano, library, board games and large windows overlooking an adjacent marsh habitat. Smoke free premises. 3 one-bedroom standard units. 2 stories (no elevator), interior corridors. **Parking:** on-site. **Terms:** cancellation fee imposed. **Amenities:** irons, hair dryers. **Leisure Activities:** bicycles. **Cards:** MC, VI.

ASK

WHERE TO DINE

LANDS END RESTAURANT **Phone:** 843/527-1376

American
$6-$27

Along the Intracoastal Waterway, the popular marina restaurant has plenty of windows for watching sunsets and marina activity. On the menu is a wide selection of seafood dishes prepared with locally caught fish, as wells as burgers and steaks. Casual dress. **Bar:** Full bar. **Reservations:** accepted. **Hours:** 11 am-2:30 & 4-10 pm, Sun-2:30 pm. Closed: 12/25. **Address:** 444 Marina Dr **Location:** Jct US 17/17 alternate route/701, 1.2 mi se on US 17; just w of ICW Bridge at Georgetown Landing. **Parking:** on-site. **Cards:** AX, DS, MC, VI.

LA ROCCA **Phone:** 843/545-7777

Italian
$4-$21

On the waterfront in historic downtown, the restaurant serves authentic Italian fare, including some of the owner's family recipes. Popular choices include stuffed mushrooms a la Rocca, eggplant parmigiana and veal Milanese di Ciro, in addition to steaks and local seafood favorites. Guests can enjoy views of the marina from the main dining room and from the covered seasonal patio. Service is friendly and casual. Casual dress. **Bar:** Beer & wine. **Reservations:** accepted. **Hours:** 11 am-10 pm. Closed: 11/26, 12/24, 12/25; also Sun. **Address:** 713 Front St **Location:** Between Broad and Screven sts. **Parking:** street. **Cards:** AX, DS, MC, VI.

OLD FISH HOUSE RESTAURANT **Phone:** 843/546-1045

Seafood
$7-$16

Patrons can eat and have a cold beer with local denizens of the waterfront community. The menu is limited to burgers and a few specials of the day. The restaurant is on the riverfront. Casual dress. **Bar:** Full bar. **Hours:** noon-midnight, Sat from 10 am. **Address:** 807 Front St **Location:** Jct US 17/Front St, 0.5 mi se; on waterfront. **Parking:** street. **Cards:** MC, VI.

RICE PADDY RESTAURANT **Phone:** 843/546-2021

Regional American
$8-$28

Located in the center of the downtown historic district, the restaurant features upscale Lowcountry cuisine including an excellent domestic rack of lamb, many fresh local seafood entrees and nightly specials, but it is the famous crab cakes that keep guests coming back. Casual dress. **Bar:** Full bar. **Reservations:** suggested. **Hours:** 11 am-2:30 & 6-10 pm. Closed major holidays; also Sun. **Address:** 732 Front St **Location:** Between Broad and Screven sts; downtown. **Parking:** street. **Cards:** AX, DS, MC, VI.

RIVER ROOM RESTAURANT **Phone:** 843/527-4110

Regional Seafood
$6-$22

In the downtown historic district, the casual waterfront restaurant is right on the boardwalk. Fresh fish comes daily directly from the docks. Popular menu items include the famous River Room shrimp and grits and McClellanville lump crab cake, as well as great Creole, pasta, chicken and steak dishes. Casual dress. **Bar:** Full bar. **Reservations:** not accepted. **Hours:** 11 am-2:30 & 5-10 pm. Closed: 12/24, 12/25; also Sun & 1/1-1/10. **Address:** 801 Front St **Location:** Jct Broad and Front sts; on waterfront adjacent to Frances Marion Park. **Parking:** street. **Cards:** AX, MC, VI.

CALL

MURRELLS INLET pop. 5,519 (See map and index starting on p. 976)

WHERE TO STAY

HOLIDAY INN EXPRESS HOTEL & SUITES *Book great rates at AAA.com* **Phone:** (843)357-0100 9

AAA SAVE

Hotel
$69-$999 All Year

Address: 1303-A Tadlock Dr **Location:** Jct US 17 Bypass and US 17 S business route. Located adjacent to Inlet Square Mall. **Facility:** 71 units. 56 one-bedroom standard units, some with whirlpools. 2 one- and 13 two-bedroom suites with whirlpools. 5 stories, interior corridors. *Bath:* combo or shower only. **Parking:** on-site. **Terms:** check-in 4 pm, 3 day cancellation notice-fee imposed. **Amenities:** video library, dual phone lines, voice mail, safes, irons, hair dryers. *Some:* video games, CD players. **Pool(s):** heated indoor. **Leisure Activities:** limited exercise equipment. **Guest Services:** coin laundry, wireless Internet. **Business Services:** administrative services, fax (fee). **Cards:** AX, CB, DC, DS, JC, MC, VI. **Free Special Amenities: expanded continental breakfast and high-speed Internet.**

/ SOME UNITS VCR

WHERE TO DINE

BOVINES **Phone:** 843/651-2888 20

AAA

Steak & Seafood
$8-$33

Nestled waterfront, the Western-theme eatery is a popular spot for mouthwatering steaks, ribs and seafood prepared on an open-flame grill. Corn custard pudding, prepared from an original recipe, is yummy. Casual dress. **Bar:** Full bar. **Reservations:** accepted. **Hours:** 4:30 pm-10 pm. Closed: 12/23-12/25. **Address:** 3979 US 17 Business Route **Location:** 0.8 mi ne of center. **Parking:** on-site. **Cards:** AX, DS, MC, VI.

CALL M

CAPTAIN DAVE'S DOCKSIDE RESTAURANT **Phone:** 843/651-5850 23

AAA

Seafood
$18-$38

Along the shore of Murrells Inlet, the casual, nautical-themed restaurant presents a menu of savory seafood selections. Among delicious entrees is pan-crusted grouper topped with Dijon shrimp and a light cream sauce. Tables on a large deck overlook the water. Casual dress. **Bar:** Full bar. **Reservations:** accepted. **Hours:** 11:30 am-2:30 & 4:30-10 pm, Mon from 4:30 pm; Sunday brunch 11 am-2 pm; hours vary off season. Closed: 12/24, 12/25; also 12/31. **Address:** 4037A US 17 Business Route **Location:** 0.7 mi ne of center. **Parking:** on-site. **Cards:** AX, MC, VI.

DEAD DOG SALOON **Phone:** 843/651-0664 24

Steak & Seafood
$5-$22

Featuring live music most nights, the casual eatery offers a widely varied menu with such local favorites as she-crab soup and crab cakes. A large deck overlooking the tidal marsh provides seasonal outdoor seating. Casual dress. **Bar:** Full bar. **Reservations:** accepted. **Hours:** 11:30 am-midnight. Closed: 11/26, 12/25. **Address:** 4079 US 17 Business Route **Location:** 0.6 mi ne of center. **Parking:** on-site. **Cards:** AX, MC, VI.

DIVINE FISH HOUSE & WAHOO RAW BAR & MARINA **Phone:** 843/651-5800 21

AAA

Seafood
$19-$35

Patrons of the colorful restaurant overlooking the waterfront will discover classic and innovative seafood in artful presentations. In addition to salmon, flounder, mahi mahi and sea bass, the menu lists prime rib, duck and other meats. The adjacent outdoors Wahoo's Raw Bar features a full menu and occasional live entertainment. Casual dress. **Bar:** Full bar. **Reservations:** accepted. **Hours:** 5 pm-10 pm, Fri & Sat-10:30 pm. Closed: 12/25. **Address:** 3993 US 17 Business Route **Location:** 0.8 mi ne of center. **Parking:** on-site. **Cards:** AX, DS, MC, VI.

DRUNKEN JACK'S RESTAURANT **Phone:** 843/651-2044 22

Steak & Seafood
$8-$42

A tribute to Jack the Drunken pirate, the entertaining restaurant offers a wide selection of fresh seafood, including local favorites such as tasty crab legs and a luscious lobster tail. For a change of fare, take a leap of faith and order the frog legs. Casual dress. **Bar:** Full bar. **Hours:** 11:30 am-2:30 & 4:30-10 pm, Mon from 4:30 pm; hours vary off season. Closed: 11/26, 12/25. **Address:** 4031 US 17 Business Route **Location:** 0.8 mi ne of center. **Parking:** on-site. **Cards:** AX, DC, DS, MC, VI.

HOOF 'N' FINZ TAPROOM **Phone:** 843/357-3616 18

Steak & Seafood
$6-$15

Whether you want a casual, bar setting or an upscale dining experience, you'll find it here. Chef Braddock, an award-winning chef, prepares such tasty dishes as marinated flat-iron steak and andouille-encrusted sea scallops. Sandwiches and a kids' menu are available, and weekends feature live entertainment. Casual dress. **Bar:** Full bar. **Reservations:** accepted. **Hours:** Open 12/1-2/9 & 4/2-11/30; 4 pm-10 pm, Fri & Sat-11 pm, Sun 10:30 am-4 pm. Closed: 11/26, 12/25. **Address:** 3415 US 17 Business **Location:** Jct US 17/US 17 business route; on north end of town. **Parking:** on-site. **Cards:** AX, DS, MC, VI.

CALL M

(See map and index starting on p. 976)

OLD WORLD ITALIAN RESTAURANT **Phone:** 843/357-3494 (19)

Italian
$9-$23

The locals' choice for Italian cuisine, the busy, family-run restaurant specializes in veal and homemade desserts, including delicious tiramisu. Casual dress. **Bar:** Beer & wine. **Reservations:** suggested. **Hours:** 4:30 pm-9 pm. Closed: 1/1, 11/26, 12/25; also Sun & Mon. **Address:** 3850 US 17 Bypass S **Location:** Jct US 17 Bypass/SR 707, just sw. **Parking:** on-site. **Cards:** AX, DS, MC, VI.

OLIVER'S LODGE **Phone:** 843/651-9523 (26)

Seafood
$15-$29

Tucked on the shores of the marsh, the 1860 plantation house served family-style meals from 1910 until World War II. Later, it adopted the menu that has evolved into the one used today. At its heart are seafood and steak entrees, as well as Lowcountry and creative American fare. Casual dress. **Bar:** Full bar. **Reservations:** accepted. **Hours:** 4:30 pm-close; Sunday brunch 11 am-2 pm. Closed: 1/1, 12/25; also Mon. **Address:** 4204 Business Hwy 17 **Location:** Jct US 17, 1.6 mi s. **Parking:** on-site. **Cards:** AX, MC, VI.

RIVER CITY CAFE **Phone:** 843/651-1004 (27)

American
$4-$14

On the waterfront, this rustic fish shack-style storefront restaurant prepares an extensive variety of sandwiches that span the taste spectrum from fried bologna on Texas toast to the River City Philly on hoagie. Also on the menu are many seafood platters and 30 signature burgers, including peanut butter or pizza burgers and several with cheese combinations. The casual spot is great for a quick bite and cold beer. A children's menu is available. Casual dress. **Bar:** Full bar. **Reservations:** not accepted. **Hours:** 11 am-10 pm. Closed: 11/26, 12/25. **Address:** 4393 Hwy 17 Business **Location:** Center. **Parking:** on-site. **Cards:** AX, DS, MC, VI.

RUSSELL'S SEAFOOD GRILL & RAW BAR **Phone:** 843/651-0553 (28)

AAA

Seafood
$14-$30

This no-frills staple has been providing freshly-cooked seafood to locals for years, boasting the best she-crab soup on the Strand. Guests can also enjoy fresh, salty oysters and clams from the raw bar, huge grouper sandwiches and fresh key lime pie. Casual dress. **Bar:** Full bar. **Hours:** Open 12/1-12/31 & 2/1-10/31; 4 pm-10 pm. Closed: 11/26, 12/24, 12/25; also Sun. **Address:** 4609 Hwy 17 Business **Location:** 1 mi sw of center. **Parking:** on-site. **Cards:** AX, DS, MC, VI.

SPUD'S WATERFRONT DINING **Phone:** 843/651-9987 (25)

Seafood
$8-$29

Grab a seat on the covered patio and enjoy pelicans and sea gulls hovering over the inlet as you dig into well-prepared fresh seafood, steak, pasta and shellfish entrees. The lunch menu offers a lighter fare of fresh sandwiches and a raw bar. Attractive indoor dining is also available as well as a gift shop. Service is friendly and the atmosphere is always relaxing. Casual dress. **Bar:** Full bar. **Reservations:** not accepted. **Hours:** 11 am-10 pm, Fri & Sat-11 pm. Closed: 11/26, 12/25. **Address:** 4123 Hwy 17 Business S **Location:** Jct US 17, 1.5 mi s; at Capt Dick's Marina. **Parking:** on-site. **Cards:** AX, DS, MC, VI.

ULTIMATE CALIFORNIA PIZZA **Phone:** 843/357-2297 (17)

Pizza
$6-$20

One of six locations on the Grand Strand, the colorful cafe offers dozens of pizzas heaped with your choice of toppings from a long and exotic list. A few pasta dishes, subs and salads are also featured. To wash it all down, a cold draft beer will do the job. Casual dress. **Bar:** Beer & wine. **Reservations:** not accepted. **Hours:** 11 am-1 am. Closed: 12/25. **Address:** 2751 Hwy 17 Business Rt **Location:** Jct US 17 business route/Atlantic Ave, just ne. **Parking:** on-site. **Cards:** AX, DS, MC, VI.

PAWLEYS ISLAND pop. 138 (See map and index starting on p. 976)

WHERE TO STAY

HAMPTON INN PAWLEYS/LITCHFIELD *Book great rates at AAA.com* **Phone:** (843)235-2000 (12)

Hotel
$69-$199 All Year

Address: 150 Willbrook Blvd **Location:** US 17, just w; across from Litchfield Market Village. **Facility:** 66 units. 60 one-bedroom standard units. 6 one-bedroom suites with whirlpools. 3 stories, interior corridors. *Bath:* combo or shower only. **Parking:** on-site. **Terms:** 1-30 night minimum stay, cancellation fee imposed. **Amenities:** dual phone lines, voice mail, irons, hair dryers. **Pool(s):** outdoor. **Leisure Activities:** limited exercise equipment. **Guest Services:** valet laundry, wireless Internet. **Business Services:** meeting rooms, business center. **Cards:** AX, CB, DC, DS, MC, VI.

Hampton Inn

AAA Benefit:
Members save up to 10% everyday!

HOLIDAY INN EXPRESS *Book at AAA.com* **Phone:** (843)235-0808 (15)

Hotel
$89-$159 All Year

Address: 11445 Ocean Hwy **Location:** 1 mi n on US 17. **Facility:** 63 one-bedroom standard units. 2 stories, interior corridors. *Bath:* combo or shower only. **Parking:** on-site. **Terms:** cancellation fee imposed. **Amenities:** irons, hair dryers. *Some:* high-speed Internet. **Pool(s):** outdoor. **Leisure Activities:** limited exercise equipment. **Guest Services:** valet and coin laundry, wireless Internet. **Business Services:** meeting rooms, business center. **Cards:** AX, DS, MC, VI.

(See map and index starting on p. 976)

LITCHFIELD BEACH & GOLF RESORT *Book great rates at AAA.com* **Phone:** (843)237-3000 13

Vacation Rental Condominium

$69-$234 4/3-11/30
$59-$159 12/1-4/2

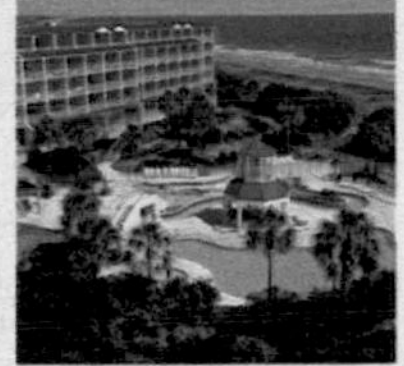

Address: 14276 Ocean Hwy **Location:** Oceanfront. In Litchfield Beach; on US 17. Located opposite Litchfield Exchange. **Facility:** Salt marshes, beaches and a golf course provide ample recreational diversions at this resort hotel close to shopping and dining. Smoke free premises. 546 condominiums. 1-5 stories, exterior corridors. *Bath:* combo or shower only. **Parking:** on-site. **Terms:** off-site registration, check-in 4 pm, 2-7 night minimum stay - seasonal, age restrictions may apply, 14 day cancellation notice-fee imposed. **Amenities:** voice mail. *Some:* DVD players, irons, hair dryers. **Dining:** 2 restaurants. **Pool(s):** 10 outdoor, 2 heated indoor. **Leisure Activities:** sauna, whirlpools, fishing, lazy river water rides, tennis instruction, recreation programs, bike paths, rental bicycles, jogging, basketball, horseshoes, volleyball. *Fee:* golf-54 holes, golf instruction, 17 tennis courts (3 lighted), racquetball court, massage. **Guest Services:** coin laundry, airport transportation (fee)-Myrtle Beach International Airport, area transportation-beach shuttle, wireless Internet. **Business Services:** conference facilities, business center. **Cards:** AX, DS, MC, VI. ***(See color ad on insert)***

FEE / SOME UNITS

LITCHFIELD INN *Book at AAA.com* **Phone:** (843)237-4211 14

Motel

$119-$339 All Year

Address: 1 Norris Dr **Location:** Oceanfront. Jct US 17/ Litchfield Dr, 0.4 mi e, then just se. **Facility:** 141 units. 125 one-bedroom standard units, some with efficiencies. 16 two-bedroom suites with efficiencies. 2-7 stories, exterior corridors. **Parking:** on-site. **Terms:** check-in 4 pm, cancellation fee imposed. **Amenities:** voice mail. *Some:* irons, hair dryers. **Pool(s):** outdoor. **Leisure Activities:** jogging. **Guest Services:** coin laundry, wireless Internet. **Business Services:** meeting rooms, fax (fee). **Cards:** DS, MC, VI.

/ SOME UNITS

PAWLEYS PLANTATION GOLF RESORT *Book great rates at AAA.com* **Phone:** (843)237-6000 16

Vacation Rental Condominium

$69-$419 All Year

Address: 70 Tanglewood Dr **Location:** 2 mi sw on US 17. **Facility:** On a golf course designed by Jack Nicklaus, the resort's variety of villas are convenient to the beach and many shopping and dining outlets. 100 condominiums. 1-2 stories, exterior corridors. **Parking:** on-site. **Terms:** office hours 6 am-11 pm, 4 day cancellation notice-fee imposed. **Amenities:** voice mail, irons, hair dryers. *Some:* high-speed Internet. **Dining:** 2 restaurants. **Pool(s):** 2 outdoor. **Leisure Activities:** 2 lighted tennis courts, exercise room. *Fee:* golf-18 holes, golf instruction. **Guest Services:** complimentary laundry, wireless Internet. **Business Services:** conference facilities, business center. **Cards:** AX, DS, MC, VI. **Free Special Amenities: preferred room (subject to availability with advance reservations) and high-speed Internet.**

/ SOME UNITS VCR

VISTA INN & SUITES *Book at AAA.com* **Phone:** (843)237-4261

Motel

$59-$129 All Year

Address: 7903 Ocean Hwy **Location:** 2.6 mi sw on US 17. **Facility:** 90 units. 82 one-bedroom standard units. 8 one-bedroom suites. 2 stories (no elevator), exterior corridors. *Bath:* combo or shower only. **Parking:** on-site. **Amenities:** voice mail, irons, hair dryers. **Pool(s):** outdoor. **Guest Services:** wireless Internet. **Business Services:** administrative services, fax (fee). **Cards:** AX, CB, DC, DS, MC, VI.

ASK / SOME UNITS FEE

WHERE TO DINE

BISTRO 217 **Phone:** 843/235-8217 33

American

$8-$28

Upscale touches mark the casual courtyard dining spot in the heart of Pawleys Island. The menu features a good selection of seafood, steaks and pasta, with a tempting list of homemade specialty desserts. Popular entrees include hoisin-seared duck, herb-roasted chicken and pan-seared lobster, shrimp and scallops over linguine. Service is professional and skilled at pairing a perfect glass or bottle of wine from the well-crafted list of uncommon vintages. Casual dress. **Bar:** Full bar. **Reservations:** accepted. **Hours:** 11 am-4 & 5-10 pm. Closed: 12/25; also Sun. **Address:** 10707 Ocean Hwy (US 17) **Location:** Just ne of center; on US 17. **Parking:** on-site. **Cards:** AX, DS, VI.

FRANK'S RESTAURANT & BAR **Phone:** 843/237-3030 36

Regional American

$20-$30

An open kitchen with a chef's counter enables diners to watch the cooking action while savoring their own gourmet seafood and Lowcountry cuisine. Traditional entrees are prepared in unusual and exciting ways, like the New Zealand lamb chops and crab cakes. A rustic design evokes the spirit of old South Carolina. Dressy casual. **Bar:** Full bar. **Reservations:** suggested. **Hours:** 5:30 pm-10 pm. Closed: 1/1, 11/26, 12/24, 12/25; also Sun. **Address:** 10434 Ocean Hwy **Location:** Just s on US 17. **Parking:** on-site. **Cards:** AX, DS, MC, VI.

GATOR KRAWLS RESTAURANT **Phone:** 843/235-8228 39

American

$6-$25

Opened in 2007, the tidy and bright family-run restaurant just south of downtown employs a young, energetic staff that carries out friendly service. The menu centers on local seafood, sandwiches, burgers, wraps and pasta. The presentation of the food is as thoughtful as the preparation, and the atmosphere is light and relaxed. Casual dress. **Bar:** Full bar. **Hours:** 9 am-9 pm, Fri & Sat-10 pm. Closed: 11/26, 12/25; also Tues. **Address:** 9448 Ocean Hwy (US 17) **Location:** 1.0 mi SW on US 17; center. **Parking:** on-site. **Cards:** MC, VI.

CALL M

LANDOLFI'S ITALIAN PASTRY SHOP & DELI **Phone:** 843/237-7900 38

Deli

$7-$10

This family deli-bakery is now in its fourth generation. The delicious desserts are too many to mention, and the cafe menu covers sandwiches, paninis, and pizzas from an authentic wood-fired brick oven. Casual dress. **Bar:** Beer & wine. **Hours:** 10 am-9 pm, Tues & Wed-5 pm. Closed: 11/26, 12/25; also Sun & Mon. **Address:** 9305 Ocean Hwy **Location:** 1.2 mi se on US 17. **Parking:** on-site. **Cards:** MC, VI.

(See map and index starting on p. 976)

LOUIS'S AT PAWLEY'S — Phone: 843/237-8757 (34)

Seafood
$9-$38

Chef and owner Louis Osteen is renowned for his innovations in Lowcountry cuisine—traditional South Carolina dishes using fresh, local ingredients and prepared with flair. Shrimp and grits is a must-try. Save room for one of the homemade desserts. Casual dress. **Bar:** Full bar. **Reservations:** suggested. **Hours:** 11 am-3 & 5:30-10 pm. Closed: 12/25. **Address:** 10880 Ocean Hwy (US 17) **Location:** Just n on US 17; in The Hammock Shops. **Parking:** on-site. **Cards:** AX, DS, MC, VI.

THE MAYOR'S HOUSE RESTAURANT & PUB — Phone: 843/237-9082 (32)

Regional American
$13-$28

The bistro overlooks a serene pond, adding to the intimate ambiance. Fresh fish is prepared in a creative fashion. Other favorite menu offerings include veal Oscar and rack of lamb. Flambeed desserts are an after-meal highlight. Casual dress. **Bar:** Full bar. **Reservations:** accepted. **Hours:** 5 pm-10 pm. **Address:** 13089 Ocean Hwy **Location:** 2.6 mi n on US 17. **Parking:** on-site. **Cards:** AX, CB, DC, DS, MC, VI.

OCEAN DRAGON — Phone: 843/237-9988 (37)

Chinese
$4-$12

The traditional Chinese eatery serves everything from crispy egg rolls and breaded sweet and sour chicken to luscious lo mein and fried rice. Try the tasty boneless spare ribs with sauteed peppers and onions in a creamy brown gravy. Casual dress. **Hours:** 11 am-10 pm, Thurs-Sat to 10:30 pm, Sun noon-10 pm. Closed: 1/1, 11/26, 12/25. **Address:** 9380 Ocean Hwy (US 17) **Location:** 1.1 mi s on US 17; in Food Lion Shopping Center. **Parking:** on-site. **Cards:** MC, VI.

ROCCO'S — Phone: 843/235-3674 (31)

Northern Italian
$8-$36

Featuring well-prepared, beautifully presented Northern Italian fare, the storefront bistro features two nicely-decorated dining rooms and a professional wait staff. The menu is lengthy and includes a number of veal dishes, seafood, wild boar chops and a few pasta dishes. There is also a long list of appetizers to accompany dinner or to enjoy at the bar with a glass of wine or cocktail. Dressy casual. **Bar:** Full bar. **Reservations:** accepted. **Hours:** 11:30 am-10 pm. Closed: 1/1, 11/26, 12/25; also Sun. **Address:** 13313 Ocean Hwy **Location:** 1.5 mi ne of center on US 17. **Parking:** on-site. **Cards:** AX, DS, MC, VI.

CALL

ROZ'S RICE MILL CAFE — Phone: 843/235-0196 (35)

American
$7-$20

Delicious lunches are built from offerings of homemade soup, gourmet sandwiches and fresh salads at the rustic cafe. Casual dress. **Bar:** Beer & wine. **Hours:** 11 am-2:30 & 5:30-9:30 pm, Mon-2:30 pm. Closed major holidays; also Sun. **Address:** 10880 Ocean Hwy (US 17) **Location:** Just n on US 17; in The Hammock Shops. **Parking:** on-site. **Cards:** AX, DS, MC, VI.

SURFSIDE BEACH pop. 4,425 (See map and index starting on p. 976)

WHERE TO STAY

COMFORT INN — *Book great rates at AAA.com* — **Phone:** (843)233-8585 (1)

AAA SAVE
Hotel
$60-$200 All Year

Address: 1201 US 17 N **Location:** Jct SR 544, 0.8 mi sw. **Facility:** 68 one-bedroom standard units, some with whirlpools. 2 stories (no elevator), interior corridors. *Bath:* combo or shower only. **Parking:** on-site. **Terms:** 3 day cancellation notice-fee imposed. **Amenities:** high-speed Internet, irons, hair dryers. **Pool(s):** outdoor. **Leisure Activities:** sun deck. **Guest Services:** coin laundry, wireless Internet. **Business Services:** fax (fee). **Cards:** AX, DS, MC, VI. **Free Special Amenities: continental breakfast and high-speed Internet.**

/ SOME UNITS

DAYS HOTEL SURFSIDE BEACH RESORT — *Book great rates at AAA.com* — **Phone:** (843)238-4444 (3)

AAA SAVE
Hotel
$45-$225 6/1-11/30
$35-$195 12/1-5/31

Address: 15 S Ocean Blvd **Location:** Jct Surfside Dr and S Ocean Blvd, just s. **Facility:** 157 one-bedroom standard units. 8 stories, interior corridors. **Parking:** on-site. **Terms:** 3 day cancellation notice. **Amenities:** voice mail, safes (fee), hair dryers. *Some:* irons. **Pool(s):** outdoor. **Leisure Activities:** whirlpool. **Guest Services:** valet laundry, wireless Internet. **Business Services:** meeting rooms, administrative services, fax (fee). **Cards:** AX, CB, DC, DS, MC, VI.

/ SOME UNITS

HOLIDAY INN OCEANFRONT — *Book great rates at AAA.com* — **Phone:** (843)238-5601 (2)

AAA SAVE
Hotel
$69-$229 All Year

Address: 1601 N Ocean Blvd **Location:** Oceanfront. Jct 16th Ave N and N Ocean Blvd. **Facility:** 133 one-bedroom standard units. 6 stories, interior corridors. *Bath:* combo or shower only. **Parking:** on-site. **Terms:** check-in 4 pm, 2-5 night minimum stay - seasonal, 3 day cancellation notice-fee imposed. **Amenities:** voice mail, safes, irons, hair dryers. **Pool(s):** heated outdoor. **Leisure Activities:** whirlpool, recreation programs in summer, barbecue grills, picnic area, limited exercise equipment. *Fee:* game room. **Guest Services:** valet and coin laundry, wireless Internet. **Business Services:** meeting rooms, administrative services, fax (fee). **Cards:** AX, CB, DC, DS, MC, VI.

/ SOME UNITS FEE

WHERE TO DINE

BONEFISH GRILL — Phone: 843/215-4374 (1)

Seafood
$13-$30

Fish is the house specialty, and the menu and nightly specials offer a variety of choices. Well-prepared food is cooked to perfection. Service is casual in nature, and the staff is skilled and attentive. Casual dress. **Bar:** Full bar. **Reservations:** accepted. **Hours:** 4 pm-close. Closed: 11/26, 12/25. **Address:** 8703 US 17 Bypass **Location:** Jct US 17 Bypass and SR 544, 1.0 mi s. **Parking:** on-site. **Cards:** AX, DC, DS, MC, VI.

(See map and index starting on p. 976)

BUBBA'S FISH SHACK **Phone:** 843/232-9798 (6)

Seafood $6-$19

Steamed shrimp and clams as well as fried seafood platters are served in a rustic, nautical setting. Casual dress. **Bar:** Full bar. **Hours:** 11 am-10 pm. Closed: 11/26, 12/25. **Address:** 16 S Ocean Blvd **Location:** Surfside Dr and S Ocean Blvd, just s. **Parking:** on-site. **Cards:** AX, DS, MC, VI.

CALIFORNIA DREAMING **Phone:** 843/215-5255

American $8-$23

The full-service, fine-dining restaurant appeals to adults, particularly those with an appetite for innovative concepts in food. Revised weekly, the menu consistently incorporates sophisticated, cutting-edge California dishes with Pacific Rim influences throughout. Among house specialties are flatbread appetizers baked in a brick oven, sushi, sashimi and some vegetarian dishes. The wine list focuses primarily on California vintages. Casual dress. **Bar:** Full bar. **Hours:** 11 am-10 pm, Fri & Sat-11 pm. **Address:** 2657 Beaver Run Blvd **Location:** Jct US 17 Bypass/SR 544, just se on SR 544, then just s. **Parking:** on-site. **Cards:** AX, DC, DS, MC, VI.

CALL

THE CHARLESTON CAFE **Phone:** 843/238-2200 (4)

Regional American $9-$47

Located near the beach in a charming shopping area, the intimate eatery treats diners to certified Angus beef entrees and a lengthy wine-by-the-glass menu. Piano music lends to the dinner atmosphere on Tuesday and Thursday. Casual dress. **Bar:** Full bar. **Reservations:** suggested. **Hours:** 11:30 am-2 & 5:30-9 pm. Closed: 1/1, 11/26, 12/24; also Sun & Mon. **Address:** 815 Surfside Dr **Location:** Jct SR 544/US 17, 1.6 mi sw on US 17 business route, then just se. **Parking:** on-site. **Cards:** AX, CB, DC, DS, MC, VI.

DAGWOOD'S DELI & SPORTS BAR **Phone:** 843/828-4600 (3)

American $5-$10

This new edition of the popular downtown Myrtle Beach mainstay, which has been in business since 1988, is a lot bigger and a bit more sophisticated, but the award-winning menu is the same. The menu lists a large selection of finger foods and a huge selection of signature sandwiches, which can be ordered with extra meat on a wide variety of available breads. Service is friendly and prompt, and the prices seem like they're from the original 1988 menu. Casual dress. **Bar:** Full bar. **Reservations:** not accepted. **Hours:** 11 am-10 pm. Closed: 11/26, 12/24, 12/25. **Address:** 600 Hwy 17 N **Location:** Jct 10th Ave N. **Parking:** on-site. **Cards:** AX, DS, MC, VI.

LATITUDE 22 **Phone:** 843/232-9796 (8)

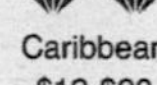

Caribbean $12-$28

Decorated in a tropical theme, the third-floor restaurant occupies an oceanfront setting. Such selections as mango tuna and jerk chicken egg rolls reflect a Caribbean influence. Casual dress. **Bar:** Full bar. **Reservations:** accepted. **Hours:** 4 pm-10 pm; hours vary off season. Closed: 11/26, 12/24, 12/25. **Address:** 11 N Seaside Dr **Location:** Jct Surfside Dr and S Ocean Blvd, just n. **Parking:** on-site. **Cards:** AX, DS, MC, VI.

NIBIL'S **Phone:** 843/238-5080 (9)

Steak & Seafood **$4-$25**

Situated near the pier, diners can enjoy great ocean and beach views while noshing on fresh seafood dinners, sandwiches and surf and turf. Thursday night is Irish night, with corned beef and cabbage the specialty. Casual dress. **Bar:** Beer & wine. **Reservations:** accepted, for dinner. **Hours:** Open 2/15-11/30; 6:30 am-8:30 pm, Sun-2 pm; hours and days vary off season. **Address:** 11 S Ocean Blvd **Location:** Oceanfront at Surfside Dr; on Surfside Pier. **Parking:** on-site. **Cards:** DS, MC, VI.

RIVER CITY CAFE **Phone:** 843/232-9797 (7)

American $4-$13

Situated oceanfront, the restaurant offers a casual, kid-friendly atmosphere with inside or deck seating. Snack on peanuts while perusing the menu, where you'll find tasty finger foods, over 25 signature burgers, seafood, salads and sandwiches. Don't forget to autograph the wall if you can find space among the license plates and signatures of the multitudes who came before. Casual dress. **Bar:** Full bar. **Reservations:** not accepted. **Hours:** 11 am-9 pm, Fri & Sat-10 pm. Closed: 12/25. **Address:** 11 N Seaside Dr **Location:** End of Surfside Dr; center. **Parking:** on-site. **Cards:** AX, DS, MC, VI.

ULTIMATE CALIFORNIA PIZZA **Phone:** 843/477-8282 (2)

Pizza $6-$20

The perennial winner of the "Best of the Beach" award features pizza with over 50 toppings, subs, foccacia sandwiches, wraps and wings. Patio dining and takeout is available. Casual dress. **Bar:** Beer & wine. **Reservations:** not accepted. **Hours:** 11 am-1 am. Closed: 12/25. **Address:** 1502 Hwy 17 N **Location:** Jct 15th Ave N/US 17 business route. **Parking:** on-site. **Cards:** AX, DS, MC, VI.

CALL

VALENTINO GOURMET ITALIAN RESTAURANT **Phone:** 843/828-4488 (5)

Italian $11-$33

Sharing menu space with other pasta, veal, chicken and seafood entrees are traditional favorites like chicken parmigiana and veal piccata. Casual dress. **Bar:** Full bar. **Reservations:** accepted. **Hours:** 3 pm-9 pm, Fri & Sat-10 pm. Closed: 11/26, 12/25. **Address:** 637 US 17 Business Route **Location:** Jct SR 544, 2 mi s. **Parking:** on-site. **Cards:** AX, MC, VI.

This ends listings for the Grand Strand.

The following page resumes the alphabetical listings of cities in South Carolina.

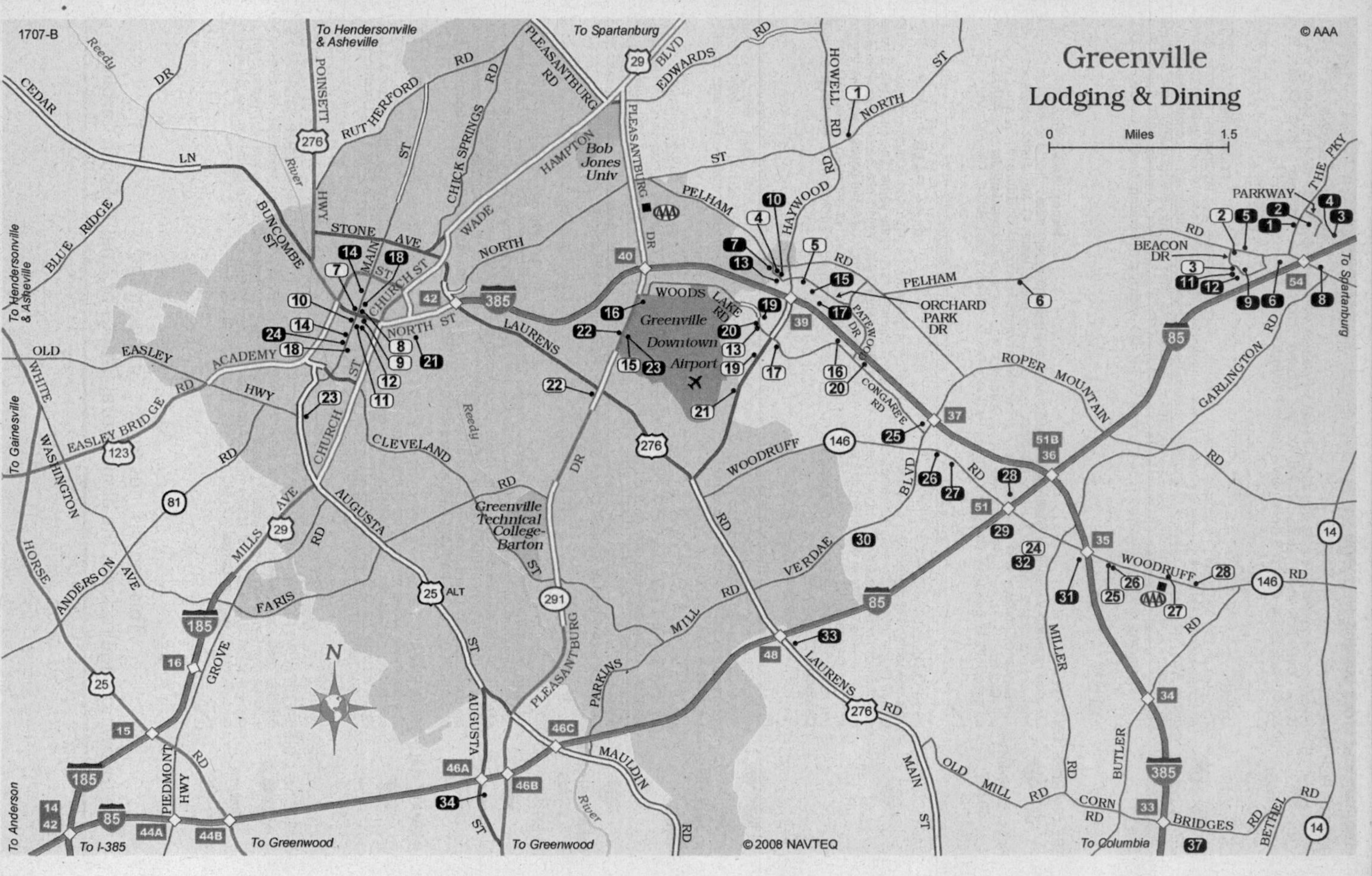
Greenville
Lodging & Dining
Miles
0
1.5
© AAA
© 2008 NAVTEQ
1707-B
To Spartanburg
To Columbia
To Greenwood
To Anderson
To I-385
To Gainesville
To Hendersonville & Asheville
Greenville Downtown Airport
Bob Jones Univ
Greenville Technical College-Barton
PLEASANTBURG DR
WOODRUFF RD
LAURENS RD
HAYWOOD RD
PELHAM RD
ROPER MOUNTAIN RD
GARLINGTON RD
AUGUSTA ST
MILLS AVE
CHURCH ST
MAIN ST
NORTH ST
STONE AVE
BUNCOMBE ST
POINSETT HWY
WADE HAMPTON BLVD
VERDAE BLVD
MAULDIN RD
WHITE HORSE RD
ANDERSON RD
CLEVELAND ST
ACADEMY ST
MILLER RD
BUTLER RD
Reedy River

Airport Accommodations

Map Page	OA	GREENVILLE-SPARTANBURG	Diamond Rated	High Season	Page
1 / p. 1050		Courtyard Greenville/Spartanburg Airport, 3.2 mi sw of airport	◆◆◆	$153-$164	1054
5 / p. 1050		Extended StayAmerica-Greenville Airport, 3 mi w of terminal	◆◆	$81-$91	1055
12 / p. 1050	AAA	**Hampton Inn I-85 at Pelham Road/Airport, 4.2 mi sw of airport**	◆◆◆	$114-$129 SAVE	1056
4 / p. 1050		Holiday Inn Express Hotel & Suites, 3 mi sw of terminal	◆◆◆	$99-$155	1056
3 / p. 1050		MainStay Suites-Greenville, 3 mi sw of terminal	◆◆	$80-$126	1058
2 / p. 1050	AAA	**Marriott Hotel Greenville/Spartanburg Airport, 4.8 mi sw of airport**	◆◆◆	$206-$221 SAVE	1058
6 / p. 1050		Microtel Inn Greenville, 2.7 mi sw of terminal	◆◆	$50-$70	1059
9 / p. 1050		Wingate by Wyndham, 4.2 mi sw of airport	◆◆◆	Rates not provided	1060

Map Page	OA	GREENVILLE DOWNTOWN AIRPORT	Diamond Rated	High Season	Page
23 / p. 1050		The Phoenix Greenville's Inn, just e of airport	◆◆◆	$89-$295	1059
16 / p. 1050	AAA	**Quality Inn Executive Center, 0.7 mi n of airport**	◆◆	$66-$86 SAVE	1059
22 / p. 1050	AAA	**Sleep Inn Palmetto Expo Center, 0.4 mi e of airport**	◆◆	$59-$109 SAVE	1060

Greenville

This index helps you "spot" where approved lodgings and restaurants are located on the corresponding detailed maps. Lodging daily rate range is for comparison only and show the property's high season. Restaurant rate range is a combination of lunch and/or dinner. Turn to the listing page for more detailed rate information and consult display ads for special promotions.

GREENVILLE

Map Page	OA	Lodgings	Diamond Rated	High Season	Page
1 / p. 1050		Courtyard Greenville/Spartanburg Airport	◆◆◆	$153-$164	1054
2 / p. 1050	AAA	**Marriott Hotel Greenville/Spartanburg Airport - see color ad p 1058**	◆◆◆	$206-$221 SAVE	1058
3 / p. 1050		MainStay Suites-Greenville	◆◆	$80-$126	1058
4 / p. 1050		Holiday Inn Express Hotel & Suites	◆◆◆	$99-$155	1056
5 / p. 1050		Extended StayAmerica-Greenville Airport	◆◆	$81-$91	1055
6 / p. 1050		Microtel Inn Greenville	◆◆	$50-$70	1059
7 / p. 1050		La Quinta Inn & Suites Greenville (Haywood)	◆◆◆	$69-$109	1057
8 / p. 1050	AAA	**Best Western Greenville Airport Inn**	◆◆	$63-$72 SAVE	1054
9 / p. 1050		Wingate by Wyndham	◆◆◆	Rates not provided	1060
10 / p. 1050	AAA	**Hyatt Place Greenville/Haywood**	◆◆◆	$99-$299 SAVE	1057
11 / p. 1050		Fairfield Inn by Marriott	◆◆◆	$108-$115	1055
12 / p. 1050	AAA	**Hampton Inn I-85 at Pelham Road/Airport**	◆◆◆	$114-$129 SAVE	1056
13 / p. 1050	AAA	**Hilton Greenville**	◆◆◆	$100-$240 SAVE	1056
14 / p. 1050		Holiday Inn Express Hotel & Suites Downtown	◆◆◆	$129-$199	1056
15 / p. 1050		Hawthorn Suites	◆◆◆	Rates not provided	1056
16 / p. 1050	AAA	**Quality Inn Executive Center - see color ad p 1059**	◆◆	$66-$86 SAVE	1059

GREENVILLE (cont'd)

Map Page	OA	Lodgings (cont'd)	Diamond Rated	High Season	Page
17 / p. 1050	AAA	**Courtyard by Marriott-Greenville Haywood Mall**	◆◆◆	$147-$158 SAVE	1054
18 / p. 1050	AAA	**Hyatt Regency Greenville**	◆◆◆	$79-$269 SAVE	1057
19 / p. 1050	AAA	**Hampton Inn**	◆◆◆	$119-$129 SAVE	1055
20 / p. 1050		StudioPLUS-Greenville-Haywwod Mall	◆◆	$80-$90	1060
21 / p. 1050		Pettigru Place Bed & Breakfast	◆◆◆	$115-$195	1059
22 / p. 1050	AAA	**Sleep Inn Palmetto Expo Center**	◆◆	$59-$109 SAVE	1060
23 / p. 1050		The Phoenix Greenville's Inn	◆◆◆	$89-$295	1059
24 / p. 1050	AAA	**The Westin Poinsett - see color ad p 1060**	◆◆◆◆	Rates not provided SAVE	1060
25 / p. 1050		Crowne Plaza Hotel and Resort Greenville	◆◆◆	$138-$179	1054
26 / p. 1050		Microtel Inn & Suites	◆◆	$56-$79	1058
27 / p. 1050		Holiday Inn Express Hotel & Suites-I-85/385	◆◆◆	$104-$209	1057
28 / p. 1050		La Quinta Inn Greenville (Woodruff Rd)	◆◆	$49-$99	1057
29 / p. 1050		Drury Inn & Suites-Greenville	◆◆◆	$90-$175	1054
30 / p. 1050	AAA	**Embassy Suites Golf Resort Hotel**	◆◆◆	$99-$169 SAVE	1055
31 / p. 1050	AAA	**Hampton Inn Greenville I-385 at Woodruff Rd**	◆◆◆	$114-$139 SAVE	1056
32 / p. 1050		Staybridge Suites Greenville/Spartanburg	◆◆◆	$86-$180	1060
33 / p. 1050	AAA	**Red Roof Inn**	◆◆	$50-$100 SAVE	1059
34 / p. 1050		Holiday Inn I-85/Augusta Rd	◆◆◆	$86-$119	1057

Map Page	OA	Restaurants	Diamond Rated	Cuisine	Meal Range	Page
1 / p. 1050		Portofino's Italian Restaurant	◆◆	Italian	$9-$16	1063
2 / p. 1050		The Original Acropolis	◆◆	Mediterranean	$6-$17	1063
3 / p. 1050		Chophouse '47	◆◆◆	American	$19-$40	1062
4 / p. 1050		Stax's Omega Diner	◆◆	American	$6-$16	1064
5 / p. 1050		Stax's Peppermill	◆◆◆	Continental	$14-$40	1064
6 / p. 1050		Bangkok Thai	◆◆	Thai	$6-$20	1061
7 / p. 1050		Bistro Europa	◆◆◆	New American	$7-$22	1061
8 / p. 1050		Bertolo's Pizza	◆	Pizza	$3-$9	1061
9 / p. 1050		Tsunami	◆◆	Japanese	$3-$22	1064
10 / p. 1050		Sassafras Southern Bistro	◆◆◆	Regional American	$18-$31	1063
11 / p. 1050		Lemongrass Thai Cuisine	◆◆◆	Thai	$9-$21	1062
12 / p. 1050		Ristorante Bergamo	◆◆◆	New Italian	$10-$30	1063
13 / p. 1050		Italian Market & Grill	◆◆	Italian	$8-$25	1062
14 / p. 1050	AAA	**The Cazbah**	◆◆	Small Plates	$6-$9	1062
15 / p. 1050		The Palms	◆◆◆	Continental	$9-$30	1063
16 / p. 1050		Monterrey by the Mall, Restaurante Mexicano	◆◆	Mexican	$5-$15	1063
17 / p. 1050		Stax Grill	◆◆	American	$7-$52	1064

Map Page	OA	Restaurants (cont'd)	Diamond Rated	Cuisine	Meal Range	Page
(18) / p. 1050		Soby's	◆◆◆	New Southern	$17-$27	1064
(19) / p. 1050		City Range Steakhouse Grill	◆◆◆	American	$8-$26	1062
(20) / p. 1050		John Paul's Armadillo Oil Company	◆◆	American	$6-$28	1062
(21) / p. 1050		Saskatoon Steaks, Fish & Wild Game	◆◆◆	Wild Game	$15-$27	1063
(22) / p. 1050		33 Liberty Restaurant & Catering	◆◆◆	Regional American	$20-$50	1061
(23) / p. 1050		Brick Street Cafe	◆◆	American	$6-$27	1061
(24) / p. 1050		Azia	◆◆◆	Fusion	$25-$80	1061
(25) / p. 1050		Boston Pizzeria	◆◆	Mediterranean	$4-$16	1061
(26) / p. 1050		Arizona Steakhouse	◆◆	American	$8-$22	1061
(27) / p. 1050		Bonefish Grill	◆◆◆	Seafood	$13-$30	1061
(28) / p. 1050		Travinia Italian Kitchen	◆◆◆	Italian	$9-$21	1064

SIMPSONVILLE

Map Page	OA	Lodging	Diamond Rated	High Season	Page
(37) / p. 1050		Ryan Nicholas Inn	◆◆◆◆	$155	1103

GREENVILLE pop. 56,002 (See map and index starting on p. 1050)

WHERE TO STAY

BEST WESTERN GREENVILLE AIRPORT INN

Book great rates at AAA.com

Phone: (864)676-1167 **8**

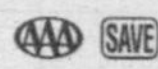

Motel

$63-$72 All Year

Address: 5009 Pelham Rd **Location:** I-85, exit 54 (Pelham Rd), just se. **Facility:** 141 one-bedroom standard units, some with efficiencies. 2 stories (no elevator), exterior corridors. **Parking:** on-site. **Amenities:** voice mail, safes, irons, hair dryers. **Pool(s):** outdoor. **Leisure Activities:** exercise room. **Guest Services:** coin laundry, airport transportation-Greenville-Spartanburg International Airport, wireless Internet. **Business Services:** meeting rooms, administrative services, fax (fee). **Cards:** AX, DC, DS, MC, VI. **Free Special Amenities: expanded continental breakfast and high-speed Internet.**

AAA Benefit:
Members save up to 20%, plus 10% bonus points with rewards program.

COURTYARD BY MARRIOTT-GREENVILLE HAYWOOD MALL

Book great rates at AAA.com

Phone: (864)234-0300 **17**

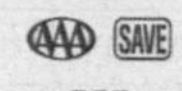

Hotel

$147-$158 All Year

Address: 70 Orchard Park Dr **Location:** I-385, exit 39 (Haywood Rd), just n, then e. **Facility:** Smoke free premises. 146 units. 134 one-bedroom standard units. 12 one-bedroom suites. 3 stories, interior corridors. *Bath:* combo or shower only. **Parking:** on-site. **Terms:** cancellation fee imposed. **Amenities:** high-speed Internet, voice mail, irons, hair dryers. **Pool(s):** outdoor. **Leisure Activities:** whirlpool, gazebo in courtyard, exercise room. **Guest Services:** valet and coin laundry, wireless Internet. **Business Services:** meeting rooms, business center. **Cards:** AX, CB, DC, DS, MC, VI. **Free Special Amenities: early check-in/late check-out and high-speed Internet.**

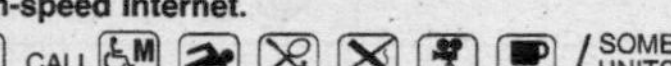

AAA Benefit:
Members save a minimum 5% off the best available rate.

COURTYARD GREENVILLE/SPARTANBURG AIRPORT

Book great rates at AAA.com

Phone: (864)213-9009 **1**

Hotel

$153-$164 All Year

Address: 115 The Parkway **Location:** I-85, exit 54 (Pelham Rd), just w to The Parkway, then just n. **Facility:** Smoke free premises. 136 units. 132 one-bedroom standard units, some with whirlpools. 4 one-bedroom suites with whirlpools. 5 stories, interior corridors. **Parking:** on-site. **Terms:** cancellation fee imposed. **Amenities:** video games (fee), high-speed Internet, dual phone lines, voice mail, irons, hair dryers. **Pool(s):** heated indoor. **Leisure Activities:** whirlpool, exercise room. **Guest Services:** valet and coin laundry, wireless Internet. **Business Services:** meeting rooms, business center. **Cards:** AX, CB, DC, DS, JC, MC, VI.

/ SOME UNITS

AAA Benefit:
Members save a minimum 5% off the best available rate.

CROWNE PLAZA HOTEL AND RESORT GREENVILLE

Book at AAA.com

Phone: (864)297-6300 **25**

Hotel

$138-$179 All Year

Address: 851 Congaree Rd **Location:** I-385, exit 37, just s, then just nw. **Facility:** 205 one-bedroom standard units. 6 stories, interior corridors. *Bath:* combo or shower only. **Parking:** on-site. **Amenities:** CD players, voice mail, irons, hair dryers. *Some:* dual phone lines. **Pool(s):** heated indoor. **Leisure Activities:** whirlpool, exercise room. **Guest Services:** valet and coin laundry, area transportation, wireless Internet. **Business Services:** conference facilities, business center. **Cards:** AX, CB, DC, DS, MC, VI.

ASK CALL / SOME UNITS FEE FEE

DRURY INN & SUITES-GREENVILLE

Book at AAA.com

Phone: (864)288-4401 **29**

Hotel

$90-$175 All Year

Address: 10 Carolina Point Pkwy **Location:** I-85, exit 51A, just se; I-385, exit 35, 0.6 mi nw. **Facility:** 180 units. 144 one-bedroom standard units, some with whirlpools. 36 one-bedroom suites. 7 stories, interior corridors. *Bath:* combo or shower only. **Parking:** on-site. **Amenities:** voice mail, irons, hair dryers. **Pool(s):** heated indoor/outdoor. **Leisure Activities:** whirlpool, exercise room. **Guest Services:** valet and coin laundry, wireless Internet. **Business Services:** meeting rooms, business center. **Cards:** AX, DC, DS, MC, VI.

ASK / SOME UNITS

(See map and index starting on p. 1050)

EMBASSY SUITES GOLF RESORT HOTEL Book great rates at AAA.com Phone: (864)676-9090 30

Hotel
$99-$169 All Year

Address: 670 Verdae Blvd **Location:** I-85, exit 48B, 0.4 mi n, then 1.1 mi ne. Located in a quiet area. **Facility:** 268 one-bedroom suites. 9 stories, interior corridors. *Bath:* some combo or shower only. **Parking:** on-site. **Terms:** cancellation fee imposed. **Amenities:** dual phone lines, voice mail, irons, hair dryers. *Some:* high-speed Internet (fee). **Pool(s):** heated outdoor, heated indoor. **Leisure Activities:** sauna, whirlpool, exercise room. *Fee:* golf-18 holes, 4 lighted tennis courts. **Guest Services:** valet and coin laundry, airport transportation-Greenville-Spartanburg International Airport, area transportation-within 3 mi, wireless Internet. **Business Services:** conference facilities, business center. **Cards:** AX, CB, DC, DS, MC, VI. **Free Special Amenities: full breakfast and newspaper.**

CALL / SOME UNITS

AAA Benefit: Members save 5% or more everyday!

EXTENDED STAYAMERICA-GREENVILLE AIRPORT Book at AAA.com Phone: (864)213-9698 5

Extended Stay Hotel
$81-$91 All Year

Address: 3715 Pelham Rd **Location:** I-85, exit 54 (Pelham Rd), 0.5 mi w. **Facility:** Modest, but comfortable, accommodations are near a mall and the air force base; the property has limited public areas and recreational facilities. 109 one-bedroom standard units with efficiencies. 3 stories, interior corridors. *Bath:* combo or shower only. **Parking:** on-site. **Terms:** office hours 7 am-11 pm. **Amenities:** voice mail, irons. *Some:* DVD players (fee). **Guest Services:** coin laundry, wireless Internet. **Business Services:** fax (fee). **Cards:** AX, CB, DC, DS, JC, MC, VI.

ASK / SOME UNITS FEE

FAIRFIELD INN BY MARRIOTT Book great rates at AAA.com Phone: (864)234-9916 11

Hotel
$108-$116 All Year

Address: 48 Fisherman Ln **Location:** I-85, exit 54 (Pelham Rd), 0.6 mi w to Beacon Dr, then just s. **Facility:** Smoke free premises. 94 one-bedroom standard units, some with whirlpools. 4 stories, interior corridors. *Bath:* combo or shower only. **Parking:** on-site. **Terms:** cancellation fee imposed. **Amenities:** high-speed Internet, dual phone lines, voice mail, irons, hair dryers. **Pool(s):** outdoor. **Leisure Activities:** whirlpool, exercise room. **Guest Services:** coin laundry. **Business Services:** meeting rooms, business center. **Cards:** AX, CB, DC, DS, JC, MC, VI.

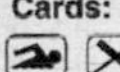  

CALL

AAA Benefit: Members save a minimum 5% off the best available rate.

HAMPTON INN Book great rates at AAA.com Phone: (864)288-1200 19

Hotel
$119-$129 All Year

Address: 246 Congaree Rd **Location:** I-385, exit 39 (Haywood Rd), just s, then nw. Located in a quiet area. **Facility:** 123 one-bedroom standard units. 4 stories, interior corridors. **Parking:** on-site. **Terms:** 1-30 night minimum stay, cancellation fee imposed. **Amenities:** video games (fee), voice mail, irons, hair dryers. **Pool(s):** outdoor. **Guest Services:** valet laundry, wireless Internet. **Business Services:** meeting rooms, business center. **Cards:** AX, DC, DS, MC, VI. **Free Special Amenities: expanded continental breakfast and high-speed Internet.**

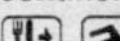    / SOME UNITS  

AAA Benefit: Members save up to 10% everyday!

(See map and index starting on p. 1050)

HAMPTON INN GREENVILLE I-385 AT WOODRUFF RD *Book great rates at AAA.com* **Phone:** (864)213-8200 31

Hotel
$114-$139 All Year

Address: 15 Park Woodruff Dr **Location:** I-385, exit 35, just w on SR 146, then s. **Facility:** 115 one-bedroom standard units, some with whirlpools. 5 stories, interior corridors. *Bath:* combo or shower only. **Parking:** on-site. **Terms:** 1-30 night minimum stay, cancellation fee imposed. **Amenities:** video games (fee), high-speed Internet, dual phone lines, voice mail, irons, hair dryers. **Pool(s):** outdoor. **Leisure Activities:** exercise room. **Guest Services:** valet laundry, wireless Internet. **Business Services:** meeting rooms, business center. **Cards:** AX, DC, DS, MC, VI. **Free Special Amenities: expanded continental breakfast and high-speed Internet.**

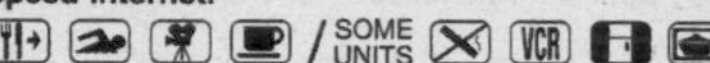

AAA Benefit:
Members save up to 10% everyday!

HAMPTON INN I-85 AT PELHAM ROAD/AIRPORT *Book great rates at AAA.com* **Phone:** (864)288-3500 12

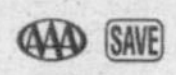

Hotel
$114-$129 All Year

Address: 47 Fisherman Ln **Location:** I-85, exit 54 (Pelham Rd), 0.6 mi w to Beacon Dr, then just s. **Facility:** 140 units. 136 one-bedroom standard units. 4 one-bedroom suites, some with whirlpools. 3-6 stories, interior corridors. *Bath:* combo or shower only. **Parking:** on-site. **Terms:** 1-30 night minimum stay, cancellation fee imposed. **Amenities:** video games (fee), voice mail, irons, hair dryers. *Some:* DVD players. **Pool(s):** outdoor. **Leisure Activities:** exercise room. **Guest Services:** valet laundry, airport transportation-Greenville-Spartanburg International Airport, wireless Internet. **Business Services:** meeting rooms, fax (fee). **Cards:** AX, CB, DC, DS, MC, VI. **Free Special Amenities: expanded continental breakfast and high-speed Internet.**

AAA Benefit:
Members save up to 10% everyday!

HAWTHORN SUITES *Book at AAA.com* **Phone:** 864/297-0099 15

Extended Stay Hotel
Rates not provided

Address: 48 McPrice Ct **Location:** I-385, exit 39 (Haywood Rd), just n, just e on Orchard Park Rd, then just s. **Facility:** Studios and two-bedroom loft units, many with fireplaces, are offered here. 72 one-bedroom standard units with kitchens. 2 stories (no elevator), exterior corridors. **Parking:** on-site. **Amenities:** voice mail, irons, hair dryers. **Pool(s):** outdoor. **Leisure Activities:** whirlpool, exercise room, sports court. **Guest Services:** valet and coin laundry, wireless Internet. **Business Services:** meeting rooms, business center.

/ SOME UNITS FEE FEE

HILTON GREENVILLE *Book great rates at AAA.com* **Phone:** (864)232-4747 

Hotel
$100-$240 All Year

Address: 45 W Orchard Park Dr **Location:** I-385, exit 39 (Haywood Rd), just n, then w. **Facility:** Smoke free premises. 256 units. 250 one-bedroom standard units. 6 one-bedroom suites, some with whirlpools. 9 stories, interior corridors. **Parking:** on-site. **Terms:** 1-30 night minimum stay, cancellation fee imposed. **Amenities:** video games (fee), dual phone lines, voice mail, irons, hair dryers. **Pool(s):** heated indoor. **Leisure Activities:** saunas, whirlpool, exercise room. **Guest Services:** valet laundry, airport transportation-Greenville-Spartanburg International Airport, area transportation-within 10 mi, wireless Internet. **Business Services:** conference facilities, business center. **Cards:** AX, CB, DC, DS, JC, MC, VI. **Free Special Amenities: newspaper and high-speed Internet.**

CALL / SOME UNITS

AAA Benefit:
Members save 5% or more everyday!

HOLIDAY INN EXPRESS HOTEL & SUITES *Book at AAA.com* **Phone:** (864)213-9331 4

Hotel
$99-$155 All Year

Address: 2681 Dry Pocket Rd **Location:** I-85, exit 54 (Pelham Rd), just w to The Parkway, just n to Parkway E, then just se. **Facility:** 82 units. 80 one-bedroom standard units. 2 one-bedroom suites with whirlpools. 3 stories, interior corridors. *Bath:* combo or shower only. **Parking:** on-site. **Amenities:** video games (fee), high-speed Internet, irons, hair dryers. **Pool(s):** heated indoor. **Leisure Activities:** whirlpool, limited exercise equipment. **Guest Services:** valet and coin laundry, wireless Internet. **Business Services:** business center. **Cards:** AX, CB, DC, DS, JC, MC, VI.

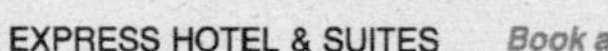

HOLIDAY INN EXPRESS HOTEL & SUITES DOWNTOWN *Book at AAA.com* **Phone:** (864)678-8000 14

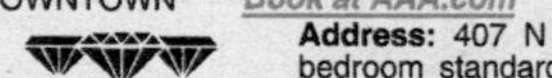

Hotel
$129-$199 All Year

Address: 407 N Main St **Location:** Jct Elford St; just n of center; downtown. **Facility:** 80 one-bedroom standard units, some with whirlpools. 5 stories, interior corridors. *Bath:* combo or shower only. **Parking:** on-site. **Terms:** check-in 4 pm. **Amenities:** dual phone lines, voice mail, irons, hair dryers. **Pool(s):** outdoor. **Leisure Activities:** limited exercise equipment. **Guest Services:** valet and coin laundry, wireless Internet. **Business Services:** meeting rooms, business center. **Cards:** AX, DC, DS, MC, VI.

(See map and index starting on p. 1050)

HOLIDAY INN EXPRESS HOTEL & SUITES-I-85/385 Book at AAA.com **Phone:** (864)678-5555 27

Contemporary Hotel
$104-$209 All Year

Address: 1036 Woodruff Rd **Location:** I-85, exit 51A, 0.5 mi nw; I-385, exit 37, just sw on Roper Mountain Rd, then just se. **Facility:** West of the city near a science center, shopping malls and golf courses, the hotel has inviting public areas and large rooms with plenty of amenities. 155 units. 149 one-bedroom standard units, some with whirlpools. 6 one-bedroom suites. 4 stories, interior corridors. *Bath:* combo or shower only. **Parking:** on-site. **Amenities:** high-speed Internet, dual phone lines, voice mail, irons, hair dryers. **Pool(s):** outdoor, heated indoor. **Leisure Activities:** limited exercise equipment. **Guest Services:** valet and coin laundry, wireless Internet. **Business Services:** meeting rooms, business center. **Cards:** AX, DC, DS, MC, VI.

ASK CALL / SOME UNITS

HOLIDAY INN I-85/AUGUSTA RD Book great rates at AAA.com **Phone:** (864)277-8921 34

Hotel
$86-$119 All Year

Address: 4295 Augusta Rd **Location:** I-85, exit 46A, just s. **Facility:** 152 one-bedroom standard units. 5 stories, interior corridors. *Bath:* combo or shower only. **Parking:** on-site. **Amenities:** voice mail, irons, hair dryers. **Pool(s):** outdoor. **Leisure Activities:** limited exercise equipment. **Guest Services:** valet and coin laundry, area transportation, wireless Internet. **Business Services:** meeting rooms, fax (fee). **Cards:** AX, DC, DS, JC, MC, VI.

ASK CALL / SOME UNITS FEE

HYATT PLACE GREENVILLE/HAYWOOD Book great rates at AAA.com **Phone:** (864)232-3000 10

Contemporary Hotel
$99-$299 All Year

Address: 40 W Orchard Park Dr **Location:** I-385, exit 39 (Haywood Rd), just n, then w. **Facility:** Suited for both the business and leisure traveler, the hotel features large rooms with divided sleeping and sitting areas to afford semi-privacy. 126 one-bedroom standard units. 6 stories, interior corridors. *Bath:* combo or shower only. **Parking:** on-site. **Terms:** cancellation fee imposed. **Amenities:** voice mail, irons, hair dryers. *Some:* dual phone lines. **Pool(s):** outdoor. **Leisure Activities:** limited exercise equipment. **Guest Services:** valet and coin laundry, wireless Internet. **Business Services:** meeting rooms, business center. **Cards:** AX, CB, DC, DS, JC, MC, VI. **Free Special Amenities: continental breakfast and high-speed Internet.**

CALL / SOME UNITS

HYATT PLACE
AAA Benefit:
Ask for the AAA rate and save 10%.

HYATT REGENCY GREENVILLE  Book great rates at AAA.com **Phone:** (864)235-1234 18

Hotel
$79-$269 All Year

Address: 220 N Main St **Location:** Just n; center. **Facility:** 328 one-bedroom standard units. 8 stories, interior corridors. *Bath:* combo or shower only. **Parking:** on-site (fee) and valet. **Terms:** cancellation fee imposed. **Amenities:** video games (fee), voice mail, irons, hair dryers. **Pool(s):** outdoor. **Leisure Activities:** exercise room. *Fee:* massage. **Guest Services:** valet laundry, airport transportation-Greenville-Spartanburg International Airport, area transportation-within 5 mi, wireless Internet. **Business Services:** conference facilities, business center. **Cards:** AX, CB, DC, DS, JC, MC, VI.

/ SOME UNITS

HYATT HOTELS & RESORTS
AAA Benefit:
Ask for the AAA rate and save 10%.

LA QUINTA INN & SUITES GREENVILLE (HAYWOOD) Book great rates at AAA.com **Phone:** (864)233-8018 7

Hotel
$69-$109 All Year

Address: 65 W Orchard Park Dr **Location:** I-385, exit 39 (Haywood Rd), just n, then w. **Facility:** 125 units. 118 one-bedroom standard units. 7 one-bedroom suites. 7 stories, interior corridors. *Bath:* combo or shower only. **Parking:** on-site. **Amenities:** video games (fee), high-speed Internet, voice mail, irons, hair dryers. *Some:* dual phone lines. **Pool(s):** heated outdoor. **Leisure Activities:** whirlpool, exercise room. **Guest Services:** valet and coin laundry, area transportation, wireless Internet. **Business Services:** meeting rooms, business center. **Cards:** AX, DC, DS, MC, VI.

ASK VCR / SOME UNITS

LA QUINTA INN GREENVILLE (WOODRUFF RD) Book great rates at AAA.com **Phone:** (864)297-3500 28

Motel
$49-$99 All Year

Address: 31 Old Country Rd **Location:** I-85, exit 51A, just nw on SR 146; I-385, exit 37, just sw on Roper Mountain Rd, then 0.9 mi se. **Facility:** 123 units. 121 one-bedroom standard units. 2 one-bedroom suites. 2 stories (no elevator), interior/exterior corridors. **Parking:** on-site. **Amenities:** video games (fee), voice mail, irons, hair dryers. *Some:* high-speed Internet, dual phone lines. **Pool(s):** outdoor. **Guest Services:** coin laundry, wireless Internet. **Business Services:** fax (fee). **Cards:** AX, DC, DS, MC, VI.

ASK / SOME UNITS

(See map and index starting on p. 1050)

MAINSTAY SUITES-GREENVILLE *Book at AAA.com* **Phone:** (864)987-5566 3

Extended Stay Hotel
$80-$126 All Year

Address: 2671 Dry Pocket Rd **Location:** I-85, exit 54 (Pelham Rd), just w to The Parkway, just n to Parkway E, then just se. **Facility:** This hotel offers after-hours check-in through an automated system. 100 units. 85 one-bedroom standard units. 15 one-bedroom suites. 3 stories, interior corridors. *Bath:* combo or shower only. **Parking:** on-site. **Terms:** cancellation fee imposed. **Amenities:** video games (fee), high-speed Internet, dual phone lines, voice mail, irons, hair dryers. **Pool(s):** outdoor. **Leisure Activities:** limited exercise equipment. **Guest Services:** valet and coin laundry, wireless Internet. **Business Services:** business center. **Cards:** AX, DC, DS, JC, MC, VI.

ASK / SOME UNITS FEE VCR

MARRIOTT HOTEL GREENVILLE/SPARTANBURG AIRPORT *Book great rates at AAA.com* **Phone:** (864)297-0300 2

AAA SAVE
Hotel
$207-$222 All Year

Address: 1 Parkway E **Location:** I-85, exit 54 (Pelham Rd), just w to The Parkway, just n, then just e. **Facility:** Smoke free premises. 203 units. 199 one-bedroom standard units, some with whirlpools. 4 one-bedroom suites. 7 stories, interior corridors. *Bath:* combo or shower only. **Parking:** on-site. **Terms:** cancellation fee imposed. **Amenities:** dual phone lines, voice mail, safes, irons, hair dryers. *Some:* DVD players. **Pool(s):** heated outdoor, heated indoor. **Leisure Activities:** sauna, whirlpool, exercise room. *Fee:* massage. **Guest Services:** valet laundry, airport transportation-Greenville-Spartanburg International Airport, wireless Internet. **Business Services:** conference facilities, business center. **Cards:** AX, CB, DC, DS, JC, MC, VI. *(See color ad below)*

Marriott HOTELS & RESORTS

AAA Benefit:
Members save a minimum 5% off the best available rate.

CALL / SOME UNITS FEE VCR

MICROTEL INN & SUITES *Book at AAA.com* **Phone:** (864)297-3811 26

Hotel
$56-$79 All Year

Address: 1024 Woodruff Rd **Location:** I-85, exit 51A, 0.5 mi nw; I-385, exit 37, just nw on Roper Mountain Rd, then just se. **Facility:** 98 one-bedroom standard units. 3 stories, interior corridors. *Bath:* combo or shower only. **Parking:** on-site. **Terms:** 7 day cancellation notice-fee imposed. **Amenities:** irons, hair dryers. **Leisure Activities:** exercise room. **Guest Services:** coin laundry, wireless Internet. **Business Services:** business center. **Cards:** AX, DC, DS, MC, VI.

ASK / SOME UNITS FEE

▼ *See AAA listing above* ▼

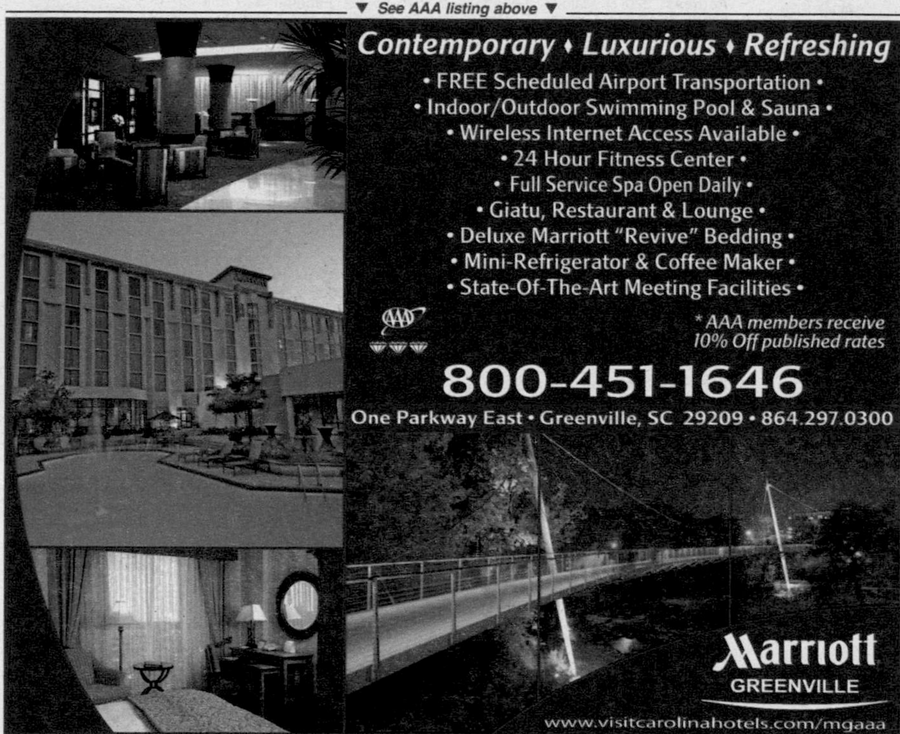

(See map and index starting on p. 1050)

MICROTEL INN GREENVILLE *Book at AAA.com* **Phone:** (864)297-7866 **6**

Hotel
$50-$70 All Year

Address: 20 Interstate Ct **Location:** I-85, exit 54 (Pelham Rd), just w, then s. **Facility:** 122 one-bedroom standard units. 3 stories, interior corridors. *Bath:* combo or shower only. **Parking:** on-site. **Amenities:** video games (fee), safes. **Guest Services:** valet and coin laundry, wireless Internet. **Business Services:** fax (fee). **Cards:** AX, DC, DS, MC, VI.

ASK / SOME UNITS FEE FEE

PETTIGRU PLACE BED & BREAKFAST *Book at AAA.com* **Phone:** (864)242-4529 **21**

Historic Bed & Breakfast
$115-$195 All Year

Address: 302 Pettigru St **Location:** 0.4 mi e on Washington St, then just ne; center. **Facility:** Near the scenic downtown historic district, this B&B offers a convivial atmosphere and tastefully decorated rooms with many amenities. Smoke free premises. 5 one-bedroom standard units, some with whirlpools. 2 stories (no elevator), interior corridors. *Bath:* combo or shower only. **Parking:** on-site. **Terms:** check-in 4 pm, age restrictions may apply, 4 day cancellation notice-fee imposed. **Amenities:** hair dryers. **Guest Services:** wireless Internet. **Business Services:** fax (fee). **Cards:** AX, DS, MC, VI.

/ SOME UNITS VCR

THE PHOENIX GREENVILLE'S INN *Book at AAA.com* **Phone:** (864)233-4651 **23**

Boutique Hotel
$89-$295 All Year

Address: 246 N Pleasantburg Dr **Location:** I-385, exit 40B, 0.6 mi s on SR 291. **Facility:** This hillside property has the ambience of a Colonial country estate. 184 units. 181 one-bedroom standard units. 2 one- and 1 two-bedroom suites. 2 stories (no elevator), exterior corridors. *Bath:* combo or shower only. **Parking:** on-site. **Terms:** 3 day cancellation notice. **Amenities:** voice mail, irons, hair dryers. **Dining:** The Palms, see separate listing. **Pool(s):** outdoor. **Guest Services:** valet laundry, area transportation, wireless Internet. **Business Services:** meeting rooms, PC, fax (fee). **Cards:** AX, DC, DS, MC, VI.

ASK / SOME UNITS FEE FEE FEE

QUALITY INN EXECUTIVE CENTER *Book great rates at AAA.com* **Phone:** (864)271-0060 **16**

AAA SAVE

Motel
$66-$86 All Year

Address: 540 N Pleasantburg Dr **Location:** I-385, exit 40B, just s. **Facility:** 184 one-bedroom standard units. 2 stories (no elevator), exterior corridors. **Parking:** on-site. **Terms:** cancellation fee imposed. **Amenities:** video games (fee), voice mail, irons, hair dryers. **Pool(s):** outdoor. **Guest Services:** coin laundry, wireless Internet. **Business Services:** meeting rooms, business center. **Cards:** AX, DC, DS, MC, VI. **Free Special Amenities: full breakfast and high-speed Internet.** *(See color ad below)*

/ SOME UNITS FEE

RED ROOF INN *Book great rates at AAA.com* **Phone:** (864)297-4458 **33**

AAA SAVE

Motel
$50-$100 All Year

Address: 2801 Laurens Rd **Location:** I-85, exit 48A, just se to frontage road, then just e to end. Located in a quiet area. **Facility:** 108 one-bedroom standard units. 2 stories (no elevator), exterior corridors. *Bath:* combo or shower only. **Parking:** on-site. **Terms:** 14 day cancellation notice. **Amenities:** voice mail. **Business Services:** fax (fee). **Cards:** AX, CB, DC, DS, MC, VI. **Free Special Amenities: local telephone calls.**

CALL / SOME UNITS

▼ *See AAA listing above* ▼

(See map and index starting on p. 1050)

SLEEP INN PALMETTO EXPO CENTER *Book great rates at AAA.com* **Phone:** (864)240-2006 22

AAA SAVE

Hotel

$59-$109 All Year

Address: 231 N Pleasantburg Dr (SR 291) **Location:** I-385, exit 40B, 0.6 mi s on SR 291. **Facility:** 63 one-bedroom standard units. 3 stories, interior corridors. *Bath:* combo or shower only. **Parking:** on-site. **Terms:** 3 day cancellation notice-fee imposed. **Amenities:** irons, hair dryers. **Guest Services:** valet laundry, wireless Internet. **Business Services:** business center. **Cards:** AX, CB, DC, DS, JC, MC, VI. **Free Special Amenities: expanded continental breakfast and high-speed Internet.**

CALL / SOME UNITS FEE

STAYBRIDGE SUITES GREENVILLE/SPARTANBURG *Book at AAA.com* **Phone:** (864)288-4448 32

Extended Stay Hotel

$86-$180 All Year

Address: 31 Market Point Dr **Location:** I-85, exit 51A (Woodruff Rd), 0.5 mi se to Miller Rd, 0.5 mi s to S Oak Forest Dr, then just nw; I-385, exit 35, nw to Miller Rd, 0.5 mi s to S Oak Forest Dr, then just nw. **Facility:** Featuring spacious rooms with the latest comforts and technology, the property is centrally located near shops, area universities and businesses. 96 units. 49 one-bedroom standard units with efficiencies. 30 one- and 17 two-bedroom suites with efficiencies. 3 stories, interior corridors. *Bath:* combo or shower only. **Parking:** on-site. **Amenities:** DVD players, high-speed Internet, voice mail, irons, hair dryers. **Pool(s):** outdoor. **Leisure Activities:** exercise room. **Guest Services:** valet and coin laundry, wireless Internet. **Business Services:** meeting rooms, business center. **Cards:** AX, CB, DC, DS, JC, MC, VI.

ASK / SOME UNITS FEE

STUDIOPLUS-GREENVILLE-HAYWWOD MALL *Book at AAA.com* **Phone:** (864)288-4300 20

Extended Stay Hotel

$80-$90 All Year

Address: 530 Woods Lake Rd **Location:** I-385, exit 39, just s, then just w. **Facility:** Modest, but comfortable and roomy, accommodations near a mall and the air force base include very limited public areas and recreational facilities. 72 units. 71 one-bedroom standard units with kitchens. 1 one-bedroom suite with kitchen. 3 stories (no elevator), interior corridors. **Parking:** on-site. **Terms:** office hours 7 am-11 pm. **Amenities:** voice mail, irons. **Pool(s):** outdoor. **Leisure Activities:** exercise room. **Guest Services:** coin laundry, wireless Internet. **Business Services:** fax (fee). **Cards:** AX, CB, DC, DS, JC, MC, VI.

ASK / SOME UNITS FEE

THE WESTIN POINSETT *Book great rates at AAA.com* **Phone:** 864/421-9700 24

AAA SAVE

Historic Hotel

Rates not provided

Address: 120 S Main St **Location:** Just s; center. **Facility:** Original woodwork and a lobby floor of black and white marble are among the restored features beautifying this newly renovated historic hotel. Smoke free premises. 200 units. 191 one-bedroom standard units. 9 one-bedroom suites. 11 stories, interior corridors. **Parking:** on-site (fee) and valet. **Amenities:** dual phone lines, voice mail, safes, irons, hair dryers. *Fee:* video games, high-speed Internet. **Leisure Activities:** exercise room. *Fee:* golf privileges, massage. **Guest Services:** valet laundry, airport transportation-Greenville-Spartanburg International Airport, wireless Internet. **Business Services:** conference facilities, business center. **Free Special Amenities: early check-in/late check-out and room upgrade (subject to availability with advance reservations).** *(See color ad below)*

WESTIN HOTELS & RESORTS

AAA Benefit:

Enjoy up to 15% off your next stay, plus Starwood Preferred Guest® bonuses.

/ SOME UNITS FEE VCR

WINGATE BY WYNDHAM *Book at AAA.com* **Phone:** 864/281-1281 9

Contemporary Hotel

Rates not provided

Address: 33 Beacon Dr **Location:** I-85, exit 54 (Pelham Rd), 0.6 mi w, then just s. **Facility:** The hotel offers spacious, well-appointed rooms with many amenities. 120 one-bedroom standard units, some with whirlpools. 4 stories, interior corridors. *Bath:* combo or shower only. **Parking:** on-site. **Amenities:** video games (fee), high-speed Internet, dual phone lines, voice mail, safes, irons, hair dryers. **Pool(s):** outdoor. **Leisure Activities:** whirlpool, exercise room. **Guest Services:** valet laundry, wireless Internet. **Business Services:** meeting rooms, business center.

/ SOME UNITS VCR

(See map and index starting on p. 1050)

WHERE TO DINE

33 LIBERTY RESTAURANT & CATERING — **Phone:** 864/370-4888 (22)

Regional American
$20-$50

With only six tables, the tiny, off-the-beaten-path bistro operates as a laboratory for the owner's successful catering business. Guests never know what surprises are on the limited menu, which changes each day. Ingredients are fresh from the market and of the finest quality. The prix fixe menu lists exquisitely-prepared foods served in moderate portions. The chef presides over every aspect of dinner, graciously explaining techniques used during preparation. Dressy casual. **Bar:** Wine only. **Reservations:** suggested. **Hours:** 6 pm-9 pm. Closed major holidays; also Sun & Mon. **Address:** 33 Liberty Ln **Location:** I-385, exit 40 (SR 291), 1.2 mi s, under US 276, then just nw. **Parking:** on-site. **Cards:** AX, MC, VI.

ARIZONA STEAKHOUSE — **Phone:** 864/281-7777 (26)

American
$8-$22

The Southwestern-themed restaurant presents a menu of grain-fed Choice beef and slow-roasted chicken preparations. The house specialty oven-roasted prime rib is available only after 5:30 pm daily. Casual dress. **Bar:** Full bar. **Hours:** 11:30 am-10 pm, Fri & Sat-11 pm, Sun noon-9 pm. Closed: 1/1, 11/26, 12/25. **Address:** 1298 Woodruff Rd **Location:** I-385, exit 35, 0.3 mi se; in The Shops at Merovan. **Parking:** on-site. **Cards:** AX, DS, MC, VI.

AZIA — **Phone:** 864/297-0788 (24)

Fusion
$25-$80

A "global fuzion" best describes the Azia experience, considering the range of fresh ingredients imported from around the world and skillfully intermingled to present eye-pleasing, palate pleasers. While absorbing the chic surroundings and light electronica in the background, guests are presented with a menu where dishes such as krunchy tempura shrimp Thai tacos, chevre and lump crab crusted mahi, char-su grilled rack of lamb and the showcase Kobe beef and lobster can be found. Casual dress. **Bar:** Full bar. **Reservations:** accepted. **Hours:** 5 pm-10 pm, Fri & Sat-11 pm. Closed: 12/25. **Address:** 15 Market Point Dr **Location:** I-385, exit 35 (Woodruff Rd), 0.4 mi w, then just s; I-85, exit 51 (Woodruff Rd), just se, then just s. **Parking:** on-site. **Cards:** AX, DS, MC, VI.

CALL

BAILEY'S PUB & GRILLE — **Phone:** 864/281-9347

American
$8-$18

Not your typical stuffy Old English Pub, sister restaurants, Bailey's and Fox. Casual dress. **Bar:** Full bar. **Hours:** 11 am-2 am. Closed: 12/25. **Address:** 2409 Laurens Rd **Location:** I-385, exit 39 (Haywood Rd), 1.7 mi s on Haywood Rd, then just se. **Parking:** on-site. **Cards:** AX, MC, VI.

BANGKOK THAI — **Phone:** 864/458-7866 (6)

Thai
$6-$20

At the end of a business and shopping center, the restaurant sustains a relaxed atmosphere. The decor is pleasant and subdued. Noodle, yum, seafood, curry and other selections are well prepared and made on the premises from fresh ingredients. The presentations of some items are enhanced with such flourishes as carved carrot swans. Casual dress. **Bar:** Beer & wine. **Hours:** 11 am-2 & 5-10 pm, Sat from 5 pm; seasonal hours may vary. Closed: Sun. **Address:** 1440 Pelham Rd **Location:** I-85, exit 54 (Pelham Rd), 2.4 mi w; in Pelham Oaks Plaza. **Parking:** on-site. **Cards:** AX, DC, DS, MC, VI.

BERTOLO'S PIZZA — **Phone:** 864/467-9555 (8)

Pizza
$3-$9

The scents of garlic and oregano waft out the door of the popular Main Street restaurant. Amid the downtown hustle and bustle, this city institution is a must for a family-size pizza with the works. Popular demand prompted this place to expand to another location outside of town. Uninhibited, kid-friendly decor is inviting, luring patrons to linger amid the aromas of freshly baked dough and tomato sauce. Casual dress. **Bar:** Beer & wine. **Hours:** 10:30 am-2:30 pm, Tues-Thurs to 9 pm, Fri-10:30 pm, Sat 11 am-10:30 pm. Closed major holidays; also Sun. **Address:** 200 N Main St, Suite 103 **Location:** Between E North St and Beattie Pl; center of downtown. **Parking:** street. **Cards:** AX, DC, DS, MC, VI.

BISTRO EUROPA — **Phone:** 864/467-9975 (7)

New American
$7-$22

The convenient restaurant on Main Street prepares something for everyone: great sandwiches, fresh pasta, homegrown vegetables and judiciously spiced creations. Sandwich plates for lunch are the specialty. This place offers excellent value for families or just about anyone who wants a good meal, lunch or dinner. The terrace is nice for alfresco dining. The experienced chef constantly brings new ideas to the table. The wine list is award-winning. Dressy casual. **Bar:** Full bar. **Reservations:** accepted. **Hours:** 11:30 am-2:30 & 5-10 pm. Closed major holidays; also Sun & Mon. **Address:** 219 N Main St **Location:** Corner of North St; center. **Parking:** street. **Cards:** AX, DS, MC, VI.

BONEFISH GRILL — **Phone:** 864/297-5142 (27)

Seafood
$13-$30

Fish is the house specialty, and the menu and nightly specials offer a variety of choices. Well-prepared food is cooked to perfection. Service is casual in nature, and the staff is skilled and attentive. Casual dress. **Bar:** Full bar. **Reservations:** accepted. **Hours:** 4 pm-close. Closed: 11/26, 12/25. **Address:** 1515 Woodruff Rd **Location:** I-385, exit 35 (Woodruff Rd), 0.9 mi e. **Parking:** on-site. **Cards:** AX, DC, DS, MC, VI.

BOSTON PIZZERIA — **Phone:** 864/329-1999 (25)

Mediterranean
$4-$16

The family-run restaurant's friendly staff serves New England-style pizza and submarine sandwiches, plus Greek fare and Italian dinners. Food is prepared fresh daily and includes such traditional dishes as manicotti, spaghetti, lasagna and hoagies. Casual dress. **Bar:** Beer & wine. **Reservations:** not accepted. **Hours:** 11 am-10 pm. Closed major holidays; also Sun. **Address:** 1262 Woodruff Rd **Location:** I-385, exit 35, just se; in The Shops at Merovan. **Parking:** on-site. **Cards:** AX, MC, VI.

BRICK STREET CAFE — **Phone:** 864/421-0111 (23)

American
$6-$27

Lunchtime can be hectic at the casual eatery, as locals gather to enjoy tasty soups, salads and sandwiches. Chicken salad with chopped walnuts and bits of cheddar cheese is popular, as are the many homemade cakes and pies. Casual dress. **Bar:** Beer & wine. **Hours:** 11 am-3 pm, Thurs-Sat also 5:30 pm-9:30 pm. Closed: 11/26, 12/25; also Sun. **Address:** 315 Augusta St (US 25) **Location:** Jct US 29/25, 0.6 mi n on US 25. **Parking:** on-site. **Cards:** AX, DS, MC, VI.

(See map and index starting on p. 1050)

CALIFORNIA DREAMING

Phone: 864/234-9000

American
$8-$23

The full-service, fine-dining restaurant appeals to adults, particularly those with an appetite for innovative concepts in food. Revised weekly, the menu consistently incorporates sophisticated, cutting-edge California dishes with Pacific Rim influences throughout. Among house specialties are flatbread appetizers baked in a brick oven, sushi, sashimi and some vegetarian dishes. The wine list focuses primarily on California vintages. Casual dress. **Bar:** Full bar. **Hours:** 11 am-10 pm, Fri & Sat-11 pm. **Address:** 40 Beacon Dr **Location:** I-85, exit 54 (Pelham Rd), just w, then just s. **Parking:** on-site. **Cards:** AX, DC, DS, MC, VI.

THE CAZBAH

Phone: 864/241-9909 (14)

Small Plates
$6-$9

Nurturing a new concept that's trendy and delicious at the same time, the tapas restaurant specializes in eclectic regional and international bites prepared by a great and innovative kitchen. Guests can watch the show unfold from intimate banquette perches loaded with comfortable pillows. Food and drink take center stage at the popular gathering place. Casual dress. **Bar:** Full bar. **Reservations:** accepted. **Hours:** 5 pm-11 pm, Fri-1 am, Sat 6 pm-1 am, Sun 6 pm-11 pm. Closed major holidays. **Address:** 16 W McBee Ave **Location:** Corner of Main St; center. **Parking:** street. **Cards:** AX, DS, MC, VI.

CHOPHOUSE '47

Phone: 864/286-8700 (3)

American
$19-$40

Reminiscent of a men's club with lots of dark woods and low lighting, the upscale restaurant is a model for other aspiring steakhouses. Efficient, professional staff serve such favorites as aged meats, fresh seafood and other top-notch items. An extensive wine list is available. Dressy casual. **Bar:** Full bar. **Reservations:** suggested. **Hours:** 5 pm-10 pm, Fri & Sat-11 pm. Closed: 11/26, 12/25; also Sun. **Address:** 36 Beacon Dr **Location:** I-85, exit 54 (Pelham Rd), just w, then just s. **Parking:** on-site. **Cards:** AX, DC, DS, MC, VI.

CALL

CITY RANGE STEAKHOUSE GRILL

Phone: 864/286-9018 (19)

American
$8-$26

Home of hearty American cuisine and kindred spirits, the well-established contemporary upscale restaurant prepares hand-cut beef and fresh seafood. Professional staffers contribute to a relaxing dining experience. Casual dress. **Bar:** Full bar. **Reservations:** accepted. **Hours:** 11 am-10 pm, Fri-11 pm, Sat noon-11 pm, Sun 11:30 am-9 pm. Closed: 7/4, 11/26, 12/25. **Address:** 615 Haywood Rd **Location:** I-385, exit 39 (Haywood Rd), 0.4 mi s. **Parking:** on-site. **Cards:** AX, CB, DC, DS, JC, MC, VI.

CALL

FATZ CAFE

Phone: 864/627-9077

American
$8-$18

Friendly staff and appealing country decor help set the tone for a relaxed and enjoyable dining experience. It's not unusual for guests to wait to be seated at the popular spot, which earns raves for its well-prepared variations on chicken, steak, ribs and pasta, as well as salads and sandwiches. The signature Southern-style peach cobbler served with vanilla ice cream and walnuts is scrumptious. Casual dress. **Bar:** Full bar. **Hours:** 11 am-10 pm, Fri & Sat-11 pm, Sun-9 pm. Closed: 11/26, 12/25. **Address:** 1145 Woodruff Rd **Location:** I-85, exit 50, just se; US 385, exit 35, just nw. **Parking:** on-site. **Cards:** AX, DS, MC, VI.

CALL

ITALIAN MARKET & GRILL

Phone: 864/234-8464 (13)

Italian
$8-$25

Dining rooms are designed and decorated for a comfortable, yet upscale, residential-like appeal. The kitchen puts out an array of tempting pasta dishes, as well as other classic and innovative choices. Pleasant, knowledgeable servers are accommodating and attentive. All the elements come together for an enjoyable dining experience. Casual dress. **Bar:** Full bar. **Hours:** 11 am-10 pm, Fri & Sat-11 pm, Sun 10 am-10 pm; Sunday brunch. Closed: 7/4, 12/25. **Address:** 534 Woods Lake Rd **Location:** I-385, exit 39 (Haywood Rd), just s, then just w. **Parking:** on-site. **Cards:** AX, DC, DS, MC, VI.

CALL

JOHN PAUL'S ARMADILLO OIL COMPANY

Phone: 864/288-8607 (20)

American
$6-$28

The restaurant fills up guests with ample portions of hand-cut steak and Danish baby back ribs, as well as chops, chicken and pasta dishes. The owner's mounted hunting trophies surround the dining room. Casual dress. **Bar:** Full bar. **Hours:** 4 pm-10 pm, Fri & Sat-11 pm. Closed: 1/1, 11/26; also Sun. **Address:** 637 Congaree Rd **Location:** I-385, exit 39 (Haywood Rd), just s to Gongaree Rd, then 0.8 mi se. **Parking:** on-site. **Cards:** AX, DC, MC, VI.

LEMONGRASS THAI CUISINE

Phone: 864/241-9988 (11)

Thai
$9-$21

Thai food with a twist! From this convenient location on Main Street, this oasis of serenity offers a tasty respite. Selections offered vary from vegetables to seafood and chicken, and all dishes include fresh herbs. Traditional as well as modern versions of Thai classics provide scrumptious and exotic tastes. Light and modern Asian decor with bamboo walls and gleaming wooden floors help make for a great casual lunch or a more dressy dinner. Casual dress. **Bar:** Full bar. **Reservations:** accepted. **Hours:** 11:30 am-2:30 & 5:30-10 pm, Fri-10:30 pm, Sat 5:30 pm-10:30 pm. Closed major holidays; also Sun. **Address:** 106 N Main St **Location:** Center; near corner of North St. **Parking:** street. **Cards:** AX, DS, MC, VI.

MR. GATTI'S

Phone: 864/234-0910

Pizza
$6-$8

Diners find great value for the dollar at the casual eatery, where the extensive salad and pizza bar includes a variety of dessert pizzas. Casual dress. **Reservations:** accepted. **Hours:** 11 am-9 pm, Fri & Sat-10 pm. Closed: 11/26, 12/25; also 12/31. **Address:** 1040 Woodruff Rd, Suite A **Location:** I-85, exit 51A (Woodruff Rd), 0.5 mi nw; I-385, exit 37, just sw on Roper Mountain Rd, then just se. **Parking:** on-site. **Cards:** AX, DC, DS, MC, VI.

(See map and index starting on p. 1050)

MONTERREY BY THE MALL, RESTAURANTE MEXICANO — Phone: 864/284-6554 (16)

Mexican $5-$15

Patrons of the casual cantina can savor traditional Mexican favorites, such as enchiladas and burritos, as well as several flavorful specialties of the house. Casual dress. **Bar:** Full bar. **Hours:** 11 am-10:30 pm, Fri & Sat-11 pm, Sun-10 pm. Closed: 7/4, 11/26, 12/24, 12/25. **Address:** 501 Congaree Rd **Location:** I-385, exit 37, just s, then 1 mi nw. **Parking:** on-site. **Cards:** MC, VI.

THE ORIGINAL ACROPOLIS — Phone: 864/458-8900 (2)

Mediterranean $6-$17

Guests might feel like they have stepped into Greece when they enter The Acropolis. Statues and ivy-strewn walls set the stage for the authentic meal to follow. Start with hummus on warm pita bread, then move on to a large serving of moussaka. Don't leave without a flavorful piece of baklava. In addition to Greek foods, there is a nice selection of Italian entrees, including pizza. Casual dress. **Bar:** Full bar. **Hours:** 11 am-10 pm, Fri & Sat-11 pm. Closed major holidays; also Sun. **Address:** 3620 Pelham Rd **Location:** I-85, exit 54 (Pelham Rd), 0.5 mi w; in Earth Fare Plaza. **Parking:** on-site. **Cards:** MC, VI.

THE PALMS — Phone: 864/370-9181 (15)

Continental $9-$30

Expect fine dining in a setting of refined country elegance. A selection of creative, artistic meat and seafood dishes incorporate French and regional American influences, including such fare as smoked salmon in ginger mushroom sauce on couscous. Dressy casual. **Bar:** Full bar. **Reservations:** suggested. **Hours:** 6-10:30 am, 11-2 & 6-10 pm, Sat & Sun 7 am-11 & 6-10 pm. Closed: 12/24, 12/25. **Address:** 246 N Pleasantburg Dr **Location:** I-385, exit 40B, 0.6 mi s on SR 291; in The Phoenix Greenville's Inn. **Parking:** on-site. **Cards:** AX, CB, DC, DS, MC, VI.

PORTOFINO'S ITALIAN RESTAURANT — Phone: 864/268-9432 (1)

Italian $9-$16

Homemade pasta dishes are highlights on a menu of traditional Italian entrees and other items. The casual restaurant's cordial and knowledgeable staff is attentive to customer needs. Casual dress. **Bar:** Beer & wine. **Hours:** 5:30 pm-9:30 pm, Fri & Sat-10:30 pm. Closed: 11/26, 12/25; also Sun. **Address:** 3795 E North St **Location:** I-385, exit 39 (Haywood Rd), 1.4 mi n on Haywood/Howell, then just ne; in Patchwork Plaza. **Parking:** on-site. **Cards:** AX, DS, MC, VI.

CALL M

RAFFERTY'S RESTAURANT & BAR — Phone: 864/297-0004

American $9-$20

For quick bites or full meals, the menu lines up plenty of pleasing variations on American standards. Favorites include the ultimate club sandwich and the black and blue strip. Casual dress. **Bar:** Full bar. **Hours:** 11 am-10 pm, Fri & Sat-11 pm. Closed: 12/25. **Address:** 600 Congaree Rd **Location:** I-385, exit 39 southbound, just s, then 0.8 mi se; exit 37, just sw, then 0.8 mi ne. **Parking:** on-site. **Cards:** MC, VI.

RISTORANTE BERGAMO — Phone: 864/271-8667 (12)

New Italian $10-$30

A bright, open and contemporary dining room sets the stage for pasta and seafood specialties prepared with a new Italian/American flair. Casual dress. **Bar:** Full bar. **Reservations:** suggested. **Hours:** 6 pm-9:30 pm. Closed major holidays; also Sun & Mon. **Address:** 100 N Main St **Location:** Corner of E Coffee St; center of downtown. **Parking:** street. **Cards:** AX, DS, MC, VI.

S & S CAFETERIA — Phone: 864/233-3339

American $4-$8

A longtime favorite for comfort food, the family-owned cafeteria invites diners to load a plate with traditionally prepared chicken, beef, vegetables, salad and dessert. Casual dress. **Hours:** 11 am-2:15 & 5-8 pm. Closed: 12/25. **Address:** 1037 N Pleasantburg Dr (SR 291) **Location:** I-385, exit 40A, 0.5 mi n on SR 291 N, then w. **Parking:** on-site. **Cards:** AX, DS, MC, VI.

SASKATOON STEAKS, FISH & WILD GAME — Phone: 864/297-7244 (21)

Wild Game $15-$27

Warmly inviting, a rustic Northwoods lodge-style decor and ambience compliment and set the mood for the house specialties such as hickory grilled emu, roasted rack of kangaroo loin with a forest mushroom sauce or the hickory grilled venison with cherry peppercorn sauce. A variety of fish from lakes, streams and oceans are offered. Save room for the mammoth-size chocolate moose pie! Casual dress. **Bar:** Full bar. **Reservations:** required. **Hours:** 5 pm-10 pm, Fri & Sat-11 pm, Sun-9 pm. Closed major holidays. **Address:** 477 Haywood Rd **Location:** I-385, exit 39 (Haywood Rd), 0.8 mi s; in Regency Square. **Parking:** on-site. **Cards:** AX, DC, DS, MC, VI.

SASSAFRAS SOUTHERN BISTRO — Phone: 864/235-5670 (10)

Regional American $18-$31

The casual bistro serves Low Country fare, such as shrimp and grits and Southern-fried chicken livers served with goat cheese mashed potatoes, collard greens and topped with caramelized Vidalia onions. Also on the menu are steaks, seafood and pasta dishes. Casual dress. **Bar:** Full bar. **Reservations:** suggested. **Hours:** 5 pm-9 pm, Fri & Sat-10 pm. Closed major holidays; also Sun & Mon. **Address:** 12 Piazza Plaza, Suite A **Location:** Between W North and W Washington sts; downtown; in Bergamo Courtyard. **Parking:** street. **Cards:** AX, DC, DS, MC, VI.

(See map and index starting on p. 1050)

SOBY'S

Phone: 864/232-7007 (18)

New Southern
$17-$27

A varied, creative menu is complemented by an extensive wine list. Set in historic downtown, the building has been lovingly restored with wood floors, brick walls and an open kitchen. Casual dress. **Bar:** Full bar. **Reservations:** suggested. **Hours:** 5:30 pm-10 pm, Fri & Sat-11 pm. Closed major holidays. **Address:** 207 S Main St **Location:** Corner of E Court St; downtown. **Parking:** street. **Cards:** AX, CB, DC, DS, JC, MC, VI.

CALL

SONNY'S REAL PIT BAR-B-Q

Phone: 864/220-6482

Barbecue
$6-$15

House specialties include pork and chicken grilled over an open pit, barbecue ribs and fresh, homemade pie. The salad bar offers another popular option. Rustic and comfortable, the atmosphere is perfect for family meals. Casual dress. **Bar:** Beer only. **Hours:** 11 am-9:30 pm, Fri & Sat-10 pm. Closed: 11/26, 12/25. **Address:** 3528 Earl E Morris Jr Hwy **Location:** I-85, exit 40, 1.6 mi nw on SR 153. **Parking:** on-site. **Cards:** AX, DS, MC, VI.

STAX GRILL

Phone: 864/288-5546 (17)

American
$7-$52

Rich dark woods and upscale decor elements give a distinctive look to the dining room. The atmosphere is relaxed and casual and service informal and accommodating. The restaurant emphasizes seafood but also prepares other high-quality food. Casual dress. **Bar:** Full bar. **Reservations:** accepted. **Hours:** 11 am-2 & 5-9 pm, Fri-10 pm, Sat 5 pm-10 pm. Closed major holidays; also Sun. **Address:** 850 Woods Crossing Rd **Location:** I-385, exit 39A (Haywood Rd), just s, then just se; at far end of CrossPointe Shopping Center. **Parking:** on-site. **Cards:** AX, DC, DS, MC, VI.

CALL

STAX'S OMEGA DINER

Phone: 864/297-6639 (4)

American
$6-$16

Sustaining the casual atmosphere of a diner, the restaurant serves a large breakfast menu all day and late into the night. On the extensive lunch and dinner menu are American, Greek and Italian favorites, as well as sandwiches and salads. Portions are large and service is friendly and efficient. Prominent at the entry, a large dessert display showcases numerous tempting confections, which are prepared fresh in the bakery next door. Cakes and pies are offered by the slice or in their entirety. Casual dress. **Bar:** Beer & wine. **Hours:** 6:30 am-midnight, Fri & Sat-3 am. Closed: 12/25. **Address:** 72 Orchard Park Dr **Location:** I-385, exit 39 (Haywood Rd), just n, then just e; in The Shops at Orchard Park. **Parking:** on-site. **Cards:** AX, CB, DC, DS, MC, VI.

CALL

STAX'S PEPPERMILL

Phone: 864/288-9320 (5)

Continental
$14-$40

Specializing in fish and shellfish—all prepared to your liking or with an interesting interpretation of classic dishes—the menu also shares space with landlubber favorites. You'll find the dining room to be inviting and cozy. Dressy casual. Entertainment. **Bar:** Full bar. **Reservations:** suggested. **Hours:** 11:30 am-2 & 5:30-10 pm, Sat from 5:30 pm. Closed major holidays; also Sun. **Address:** 30 Orchard Park Dr **Location:** I-385, exit 39, just n, then e; in Haywood Plaza. **Parking:** on-site. **Cards:** AX, CB, DC, DS, MC, VI.

CALL

STICKY FINGERS RIB HOUSE

Phone: 864/331-7427

Barbecue
$7-$26

Diners can put down their silverware and get their fingers ready for classic Carolina sweet ribs, as well as ribs cooked in the Texas and Tennessee styles. Hearty sides of baked beans and coleslaw complement entrees at the friendly cafe. Casual dress. **Bar:** Full bar. **Reservations:** not accepted. **Hours:** 11 am-close. Closed: 11/26, 12/25. **Address:** 1 S Main St **Location:** Jct Washington St; downtown. **Parking:** on-site. **Cards:** AX, DC, DS, MC, VI.

CALL

STICKY FINGERS RIB HOUSE

Phone: 864/458-7427

Barbecue
$7-$26

Diners can put down their silverware and get their fingers ready for classic Carolina sweet ribs, as well as ribs cooked in the Texas and Tennessee styles. Hearty sides of baked beans and coleslaw complement entrees at the friendly cafe. Casual dress. **Bar:** Full bar. **Reservations:** not accepted. **Hours:** 11 am-close. Closed: 11/26, 12/25. **Address:** 3 Market Point Dr **Location:** I-85, exit 50 (SR 146), just se; I-385, exit 35, just nw. **Parking:** on-site. **Cards:** AX, DC, DS, MC, VI.

CALL

TRAVINIA ITALIAN KITCHEN

Phone: 864/458-8188 (28)

Italian
$9-$21

Professional service and fresh ingredients are keystones at the popular Italian restaurant. Dishes are moderately priced and portions are perfect for an enjoyable meal. The wine list includes 35 Italian and California wines availed by the glass and a hand-picked reserve selection. The chef specializes in distinctive interpretations of veal, chicken, beef, seafood and pasta with interesting sauces. The in-house pastry chef whips up delectable desserts and fresh breads. Casual dress. **Bar:** Full bar. **Hours:** 11:30 am-10 pm, Fri & Sat-11 pm. Closed: 1/1, 11/26, 12/25; also Sun. **Address:** 1625 Woodruff Rd **Location:** I-385, exit 35, 0.9 mi e. **Parking:** on-site. **Cards:** AX, DS, MC, VI.

CALL

TSUNAMI

Phone: 864/467-1055 (9)

Japanese
$3-$22

Patrons can opt for tatami mat floor seating or take a seat near the bar to watch native Japanese chefs prepare dinner. Informal, quick and economical, the little bistro is a popular destination for the college crowd. The fish is always fresh and the tastes vibrant. Casual dress. **Bar:** Full bar. **Reservations:** accepted. **Hours:** 11:30 am-2:30 & 5-midnight, Thurs & Fri 5 pm-2 am, Sat 5 pm-midnight, Sun 5 pm-10 pm. Closed: 7/4, 11/26, 12/25. **Address:** 106 E North St **Location:** Just se of center; between N Brown and N Spring sts; downtown. **Parking:** street. **Cards:** AX, DC, DS, MC, VI.

GREENWOOD pop. 22,071

WHERE TO STAY

DAYS INN Book at AAA.com Phone: (864)223-1818

Motel
$55-$65 All Year

Address: 230 Birchtree Dr **Location:** Jct US 25/US 25 Bypass (SR 72 NE), just ne on US 25 Bypass (SR 72 NE), then just s. **Facility:** 60 one-bedroom standard units. 3 stories (no elevator), interior corridors. **Parking:** on-site. **Amenities:** hair dryers. **Guest Services:** wireless Internet. **Business Services:** fax (fee). **Cards:** AX, DS, MC, VI.

ASK / SOME UNITS FEE

FAIRFIELD INN & SUITES Book great rates at AAA.com Phone: (864)330-3300

Hotel
$91-$97 All Year

Address: 527 Bypass 72 NW **Location:** Jct US 25/US 25 Bypass (SR 72 NW), 1 mi sw on US 25 Bypass (SR 72 NW). **Facility:** Smoke free premises. 76 one-bedroom standard units. 3 stories, interior corridors. *Bath:* combo or shower only. **Parking:** on-site. **Terms:** cancellation fee imposed. **Amenities:** high-speed Internet, dual phone lines, voice mail, irons, hair dryers. *Some:* CD players. **Pool(s):** heated indoor. **Leisure Activities:** whirlpool, limited exercise equipment. **Guest Services:** valet and coin laundry, wireless Internet. **Business Services:** business center. **Cards:** AX, DS, MC, VI.

CALL / SOME UNITS

AAA Benefit:
Members save a minimum 5% off the best available rate.

HAMPTON INN GREENWOOD Book great rates at AAA.com Phone: (864)388-9595

Hotel
$65-$99 All Year

Address: 1624 Bypass SR 72 NE **Location:** Between SR 254 and US 221/SR 72. Located in a commercial area. **Facility:** 75 units. 73 one-bedroom standard units. 2 one-bedroom suites. 3 stories, interior corridors. *Bath:* combo or shower only. **Parking:** on-site. **Terms:** 1-30 night minimum stay, cancellation fee imposed. **Amenities:** high-speed Internet, voice mail, irons, hair dryers. **Pool(s):** outdoor. **Leisure Activities:** exercise room. **Guest Services:** valet laundry, wireless Internet. **Business Services:** meeting rooms, business center. **Cards:** AX, CB, DC, DS, MC, VI.

CALL   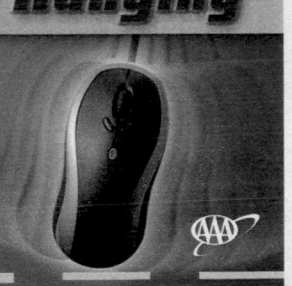 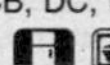 / SOME UNITS

AAA Benefit:
Members save up to 10% everyday!

HOLIDAY INN EXPRESS HOTEL & SUITES Book at AAA.com Phone: (864)223-2296

Hotel
$95-$150 All Year

Address: 110 Birchtree Dr **Location:** Jct US 25 Bypass/US 25 business route, just se on US 25 business route, then just ne. **Facility:** 70 one-bedroom standard units, some with whirlpools. 2 stories, interior corridors. *Bath:* combo or shower only. **Parking:** on-site. **Terms:** cancellation fee imposed. **Amenities:** high-speed Internet, dual phone lines, voice mail, irons, hair dryers. **Pool(s):** outdoor. **Leisure Activities:** exercise room. **Guest Services:** valet and coin laundry, wireless Internet. **Business Services:** meeting rooms, business center. **Cards:** AX, DC, DS, MC, VI.

/ SOME UNITS

INN ON THE SQUARE, A CLARION COLLECTION Book great rates at AAA.com Phone: (864)330-1010

AAA SAVE

Boutique Hotel
$95-$125 All Year

Address: 104 E Court Ave **Location:** Jct Main St, just s of center; downtown. **Facility:** A charming inn in revitalized uptown district. Rooms with solid mahogany period reproductions. 48 one-bedroom standard units. 3 stories, interior corridors. **Parking:** on-site. **Amenities:** high-speed Internet, voice mail, irons, hair dryers. **Pool(s):** outdoor. **Guest Services:** valet laundry, wireless Internet. **Business Services:** meeting rooms, business center. **Cards:** AX, DS, MC, VI. **Free Special Amenities: full breakfast and high-speed Internet.**

/ SOME UNITS

WHERE TO DINE

CAPRI'S ITALIAN RESTAURANT **Phone:** 864/223-0367

Italian
$6-$22

Originally established in 1944 to satisfy the dietary desires of Italian-American servicemen stationed in the South, the family-owned regional chain serves Italian standards as well as steak and seafood. Specialties are served with a complimentary glass of house wine, fresh bread and salad. The atmosphere is inviting and mellow. Casual dress. **Bar:** Full bar. **Hours:** 11:30 am-2 & 5-10 pm, Sat from 5 pm. Closed: 11/26, 12/25; also Sun. **Address:** 1704 Bypass SR 72 NE **Location:** Jct SR 254/US 25 Bypass (SR 72 NE), 0.5 mi e on US 25 Bypass (SR 72 NE). **Parking:** on-site. **Cards:** AX, DS, MC, VI.

FATZ CAFE **Phone:** 864/229-3711

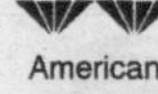

American
$8-$18

Friendly staff and appealing country decor help set the tone for a relaxed and enjoyable dining experience. It's not unusual for guests to wait to be seated at the popular spot, which earns raves for its well-prepared variations on chicken, steak, ribs and pasta, as well as salads and sandwiches. The signature Southern-style peach cobbler served with vanilla ice cream and walnuts is scrumptious. Casual dress. **Bar:** Full bar. **Hours:** 11 am-10 pm, Fri & Sat-11 pm, Sun-9 pm. Closed: 11/26, 12/25. **Address:** 1302 Montague Ave **Location:** Jct US 25 Bypass/US 25, just nw on US 25. **Parking:** on-site. **Cards:** AX, DS, MC, VI.

PASCAL'S CAFE & GRILL **Phone:** 864/223-2329

Continental
$12-$28

This converted house has an eclectic, upscale bistro look, enhanced by tapestry chair seat upholstery, framed posters and hand-painted murals. The chef's innovative flair is evident in the varied combinations of ingredients and seasonings used to create the flavorful cuisine. Entrees include steaks, seafood, chicken, duck and lamb. Dressy casual. **Bar:** Full bar. **Reservations:** suggested. **Hours:** 5:30 pm-10 pm. Closed major holidays; also Sun. **Address:** 307 W Cambridge Ave **Location:** Jct US 25/SR 178, just w. **Parking:** on-site. **Cards:** AX, DS, MC, VI.

GREER pop. 16,843

WHERE TO STAY

CANDLEBERRY INN B&B DAY SPA & HAIR SALON **Phone:** (864)201-1411

Bed & Breakfast
$110-$160 All Year

Address: 105 Marshland Ln **Location:** I-85, exit 56, just n to Johns Rd, just sw to W Phillips Rd, 0.7 mi nw to Gibb Shoals Rd, 0.7 mi to Chartwell Estates, then just e to Marshland Ln. **Facility:** The large, Cape-style house has almost 2 acres of manicured lawns; inside, find huge, thoughtfully decorated bedrooms with large, attached baths. Smoke free premises. 4 units. 3 one- and 1 two-bedroom standard units, some with whirlpools. 2 stories (no elevator), interior corridors. *Bath:* some shared or private. **Parking:** on-site. **Terms:** age restrictions may apply, 14 day cancellation notice-fee imposed. **Amenities:** video library, DVD players, irons, hair dryers. **Leisure Activities:** whirlpool, spa. **Guest Services:** complimentary laundry, beauty salon, wireless Internet. **Business Services:** meeting rooms, business center. **Cards:** AX, DC, DS, MC, VI.

ASK VCR

HOLIDAY INN EXPRESS *Book at AAA.com* **Phone:** (864)877-0076

Hotel
$95-$105 All Year

Address: 1315 W Wade Hampton Blvd **Location:** Jct SR 101 and 290, 0.4 mi se on US 29. **Facility:** 63 units. 62 one-bedroom standard units, some with whirlpools. 1 one-bedroom suite with whirlpool. 3 stories, interior corridors. *Bath:* combo or shower only. **Parking:** on-site. **Amenities:** high-speed Internet, dual phone lines, voice mail, irons, hair dryers. **Pool(s):** outdoor. **Leisure Activities:** limited exercise equipment. **Guest Services:** valet and coin laundry, wireless Internet. **Business Services:** meeting rooms, business center. **Cards:** AX, DS, MC, VI.

ASK CALL / SOME UNITS

SUPER 8 MOTEL *Book at AAA.com* **Phone:** (864)848-1626

Hotel
$60-$70 All Year

Address: 1515 Hwy 101 S **Location:** I-85, exit 60, just nw. **Facility:** 59 one-bedroom standard units, some with whirlpools. 2 stories (no elevator), interior corridors. *Bath:* combo or shower only. **Parking:** on-site. **Terms:** 7 day cancellation notice. **Amenities:** *Some:* irons, hair dryers. **Pool(s):** outdoor. **Guest Services:** coin laundry, wireless Internet. **Business Services:** fax (fee). **Cards:** AX, DC, DS, MC, VI.

ASK CALL / SOME UNITS FEE

WHERE TO DINE

THE DRAGON DEN **Phone:** 864/292-2828

Chinese
$5-$16

Situated in a shopping center, the casual, relaxed dining room makes room for extensive choices of Oriental dishes served in a traditional setting. Casual dress. **Bar:** Beer & wine. **Hours:** 11:30 am-10 pm. Closed: 11/26, 12/25. **Address:** 2420 Hudson Rd, Unit #13 **Location:** Jct Old Spartanburg Rd; in Brushy Creek Crossing Shopping Center. **Parking:** on-site. **Cards:** AX, DS, MC, VI.

FATZ CAFE **Phone:** 864/801-9782

American
$8-$19

Friendly staff and appealing country decor help set the tone for a relaxed and enjoyable dining experience. It's not unusual for guests to wait to be seated at the popular spot, which earns raves for its well-prepared variations on chicken, steak, ribs and pasta, as well as salads and sandwiches. The signature Southern-style peach cobbler served with vanilla ice cream and walnuts is scrumptious. Casual dress. **Bar:** Full bar. **Hours:** 11 am-10 pm, Fri & Sat-11 pm, Sun-9 pm. Closed: 11/26, 12/25. **Address:** 1361 Wade Hampton Blvd, Suite A **Location:** Jct SR 101 and 290, 0.6 mi sw on US 29; in Dill Creek Commons Shopping Center. **Parking:** on-site. **Cards:** AX, DC, DS, MC, VI.

HARDEEVILLE pop. 1,793

WHERE TO STAY

SLEEP INN HARDEEVILLE *Book great rates at AAA.com* **Phone:** (843)784-7181

AAA SAVE

Hotel
$59-$149 All Year

Address: 16553 Whyte Hardee Blvd **Location:** I-95, exit 5 (US 17), just se. **Facility:** 74 one-bedroom standard units. 3 stories, interior corridors. *Bath:* combo or shower only. **Parking:** on-site. **Terms:** 7 day cancellation notice. **Amenities:** irons, hair dryers. **Pool(s):** outdoor. **Guest Services:** wireless Internet. **Business Services:** fax (fee). **Cards:** AX, DC, DS, MC, VI. **Free Special Amenities: full breakfast and high-speed Internet.**

CALL / SOME UNITS FEE

HARTSVILLE pop. 7,556

WHERE TO STAY

FAIRFIELD INN BY MARRIOTT *Book great rates at AAA.com* **Phone:** (843)332-9898

Hotel
$108-$116 All Year

Address: 200 S 4th St **Location:** Just e of center. **Facility:** Smoke free premises. 74 one-bedroom standard units, some with whirlpools. 3 stories, interior corridors. *Bath:* combo or shower only. **Parking:** on-site. **Terms:** cancellation fee imposed. **Amenities:** high-speed Internet, voice mail, irons, hair dryers. **Pool(s):** outdoor. **Leisure Activities:** limited exercise equipment. **Guest Services:** valet laundry, wireless Internet. **Business Services:** meeting rooms, business center. **Cards:** AX, CB, DC, DS, MC, VI.

CALL     / SOME UNITS

AAA Benefit:
Members save a minimum 5% off the best available rate.

WHERE TO DINE

BIZZELL'S FOOD & SPIRIT **Phone:** 843/857-9080

American
$5-$20

The charming downtown eatery serves soups, salads and sandwiches to the lunchtime crowds. Among entree favorites are crab cakes, shrimp and grits and chicken piccata. Guests should save room for one of the signature desserts, including CJ's 10-layer caramel cake and chocolate cobbler. Casual dress. **Bar:** Full bar. **Reservations:** accepted. **Hours:** 11 am-2 & 5-9 pm, Fri-10 pm, Sat 5 pm-10 pm. Closed major holidays; also Sun. **Address:** 137 E Carolina Ave **Location:** Jct US 15 and 151 business routes, just e. **Parking:** on-site. **Cards:** AX, MC, VI.

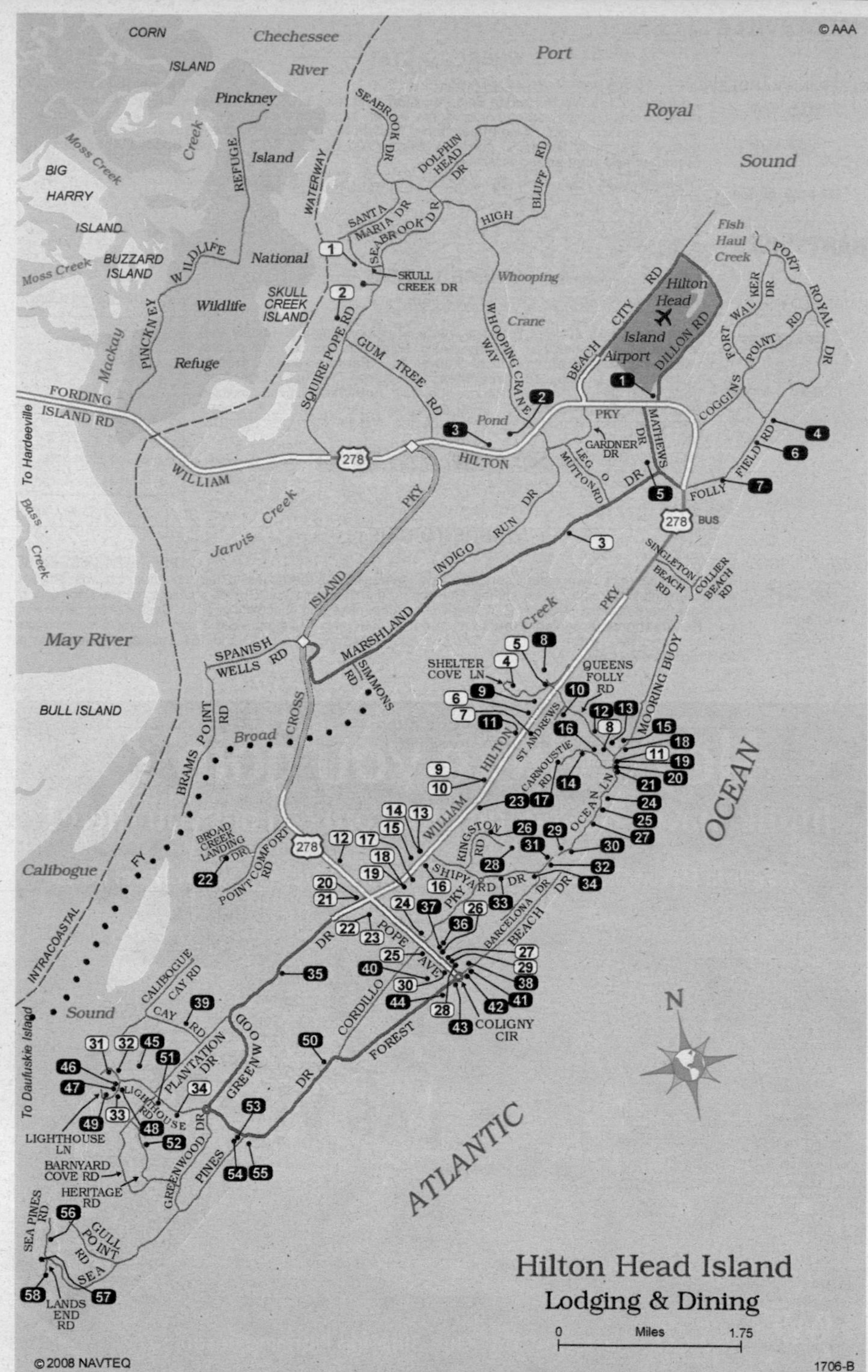
Hilton Head Island
Lodging & Dining
0 Miles 1.75
© AAA
© 2008 NAVTEQ
1706-B
Port Royal Sound
ATLANTIC OCEAN
Calibogue Sound
May River
Hilton Head Island Airport
Pinckney Island National Wildlife Refuge
To Hardeeville
To Daufuskie Island

Hilton Head Island

This index helps you "spot" where approved lodgings and restaurants are located on the corresponding detailed maps. Lodging daily rate range is for comparison only and show the property's high season. Restaurant rate range is a combination of lunch and/or dinner. Turn to the listing page for more detailed rate information and consult display ads for special promotions.

HILTON HEAD ISLAND

Map Page	OA	Lodgings	Diamond Rated	High Season	Page
1 / p. 1068		Hampton Inn	◆◆◆	$89-$142	1076
2 / p. 1068		Main Street Inn & Spa	◆◆◆	$159-$299	1080
3 / p. 1068		Quality Inn & Suites of Hilton Head Island	◆◆	$59-$139	1081
4 / p. 1068	AAA	**Westin Hilton Head Island Resort & Spa -** see color ad p 1083	◆◆◆◆	$119-$489 SAVE	1083
5 / p. 1068	AAA	**The Greens-Coastal Home and Hilton Head Vacation Rentals**	◆◆◆	$92-$208 SAVE	1076
6 / p. 1068	AAA	**The Island Club-Coastal Home and Hilton Head Vacation Rentals -** see color ad p 1079	◆◆◆	$82-$365 SAVE	1079
7 / p. 1068		Hilton Head Island Beach & Tennis Resort	◆◆		1077
8 / p. 1068	AAA	**Disney's Hilton Head Island Resort**	◆◆◆	$110-$457	1075
9 / p. 1068		Days Inn	◆◆◆	$69-$129	1075
10 / p. 1068		St. Andrews Common Villas	◆◆◆		1081
11 / p. 1068	AAA	**Red Roof Inn-Hilton Head**	◆◆	$50-$105 SAVE	1081
12 / p. 1068		Queens Grant Villas	◆◆◆		1081
13 / p. 1068	AAA	**The Village at Palmetto Dunes-Hilton Head Accommodations**	◆◆◆	$89-$220 SAVE	1083
14 / p. 1068		Fazio Villas-ResortQuest Hilton Head	◆◆◆	Rates not provided	1076
15 / p. 1068	AAA	**Ocean Cove Club Villas-Hilton Head Accommodations**	◆◆◆	$99-$219 SAVE	1080
16 / p. 1068		Centrecourt Villas-ResortQuest Hilton Head	◆◆◆	Rates not provided	1074
17 / p. 1068	AAA	**Inverness Villas-Coastal Home and Hilton Head Vacation Rentals**	◆◆◆	$104-$162 SAVE	1079
18 / p. 1068		Moorings Villas-ResortQuest Hilton Head	◆◆◆	$925-$1725	1080
19 / p. 1068	AAA	**Hilton Head Marriott Resort & Spa**	◆◆◆◆	$149-$329 SAVE	1077
20 / p. 1068		Villamare Villas	◆◆◆		1083
21 / p. 1068		Captain's Walk Villas-ResortQuest Hilton Head	◆◆◆	$1275-$2975	1073
22 / p. 1068	AAA	**Forest Beach Villas-Coastal Home and Hilton Head Vacation Rentals**	◆◆	$84-$200 SAVE	1076
23 / p. 1068	AAA	**Park Lane Hotel & Suites -** see color ad p 1081	◆◆◆	$89-$179 SAVE	1080
24 / p. 1068	AAA	**Hilton Oceanfront Resort Hilton Head Island**	◆◆◆◆	$139-$339 SAVE	1078
25 / p. 1068		Windsor Court Villas-ResortQuest Hilton Head	◆◆◆	Rates not provided	1084
26 / p. 1068	AAA	**Southwind II Villas-Hilton Head Accommodations**	◆◆◆	$109-$220 SAVE	1082
27 / p. 1068		Hampton Place Villas-ResortQuest Hilton Head	◆◆◆	$1150-$3925	1076
28 / p. 1068	AAA	**Colonade Club Villas-Coastal Home and Hilton Head Vacation Rentals**	◆◆◆	$105-$162 SAVE	1074
29 / p. 1068		Huntington Villas-ResortQuest Hilton Head	◆◆◆	$925-$2525	1078
30 / p. 1068		Barrington Court Villas-ResortQuest Hilton Head	◆◆◆	$1075-$2275	1072
31 / p. 1068	AAA	**Beachwalk Villas-Coastal Home and Hilton Head Vacation Rentals**	◆◆◆	$98-$236 SAVE	1073
32 / p. 1068	AAA	**Crowne Plaza Hilton Head Island Beach Resort -** see color ad p 1075	◆◆◆◆	$134-$299 SAVE	1075
33 / p. 1068		Evian Villas	◆◆◆		1076

HILTON HEAD ISLAND (cont'd)

Map Page	OA	Lodgings (cont'd)	Diamond Rated	High Season	Page
34 / p. 1068	AAA	**Spinnaker Villas-Hilton Head Accommodations**	◆◆◆	$109-$220 SAVE	1082
35 / p. 1068		Carolina Place Villas-ResortQuest Hilton Head	◆◆◆	$775-$1325	1074
36 / p. 1068		Waterside by Spinnaker	◆◆◆	Rates not provided	1083
37 / p. 1068	AAA	**Beachwalk Hotel & Condominiums - see color ad p 1072**	◆◆◆	$59-$149 SAVE	1072
38 / p. 1068	AAA	**North Shore Place-The Sea Pines Resort**	◆◆◆	$150-$360 SAVE	1080
39 / p. 1068		Calibogue Club Villas-ResortQuest Hilton Head	◆◆◆	$925-$1625	1073
40 / p. 1068	AAA	**Comfort Inn - see color ad p 1074**	◆◆	$49-$199 SAVE	1074
41 / p. 1068		SeaCrest Villas	◆◆◆		1082
42 / p. 1068		The Breakers	◆◆		1073
43 / p. 1068	AAA	**Holiday Inn Oceanfront Resort**	◆◆◆	$79-$299 SAVE	1078
44 / p. 1068		Shorewood Villas	◆◆◆		1082
45 / p. 1068	AAA	**Stoney Creek Villas - The Sea Pines Resort**	◆◆◆	$140-$270 SAVE	1082
46 / p. 1068	AAA	**Ketch Court Villas-The Sea Pines Resort**	◆◆◆	$120-$330 SAVE	1079
47 / p. 1068	AAA	**Cutter Court Villas-The Sea Pines Resort**	◆◆◆	$120-$330 SAVE	1075
48 / p. 1068	AAA	**The Inn at Harbour Town**	◆◆◆◆	$149-$369 SAVE	1078
49 / p. 1068	AAA	**Caravel Court Villas-The Sea Pines Resort**	◆◆◆	$120-$330 SAVE	1073
50 / p. 1068	AAA	**Night Heron Villas-Coastal Home and Hilton Head Vacation Rentals**	◆◆	$94-$175 SAVE	1080
51 / p. 1068	AAA	**Lighthouse Tennis Villas-The Sea Pines Resort**	◆◆◆	$110-$250 SAVE	1079
52 / p. 1068	AAA	**Heritage Villas-The Sea Pines Resort**	◆◆◆	$140-$315 SAVE	1077
53 / p. 1068		Plantation Club Villas	◆◆◆		1081
54 / p. 1068		Ocean Course Villas-ResortQuest Hilton Head	◆◆◆	$1025-$1525	1080
55 / p. 1068		Turtle Lane Club Villas-ResortQuest Hilton Head	◆◆◆	$1575-$3475	1082
56 / p. 1068		Bluff Villas-ResortQuest Hilton Head	◆◆◆	$625-$1275	1073
57 / p. 1068		South Beach Club Villas-ResortQuest Hilton Head	◆◆◆	$1225-$2375	1082
58 / p. 1068		Beachside Tennis Villas	◆◆◆		1072

Map Page	OA	Restaurants	Diamond Rated	Cuisine	Meal Range	Page
1 / p. 1068	AAA	**Old Fort Pub**	◆◆◆◆	Continental	$14-$35	1086
2 / p. 1068		Charley's Crab Hilton Head	◆◆◆	Seafood	$8-$40	1084
3 / p. 1068	AAA	**The Old Oyster Factory**	◆◆◆	Seafood	$17-$30	1086
4 / p. 1068	AAA	**Ocean Grille**	◆◆◆	American	$18-$27	1086
5 / p. 1068		Kingfisher Seafood Restaurant	◆◆	Steak & Seafood	$8-$26	1086
6 / p. 1068		Hilton Head Diner	◆◆	American	$5-$17	1086
7 / p. 1068	AAA	**Flora's Italian Cafe**	◆◆◆	Italian	$17-$28	1085
8 / p. 1068	AAA	**Alexander's**	◆◆◆	Steak & Seafood	$14-$49	1084
9 / p. 1068		Bonefish Grill	◆◆◆	Seafood	$13-$20	1084
10 / p. 1068		Del Vecchio's Restaurant & Pizzeria	◆◆	Italian	$11-$18	1085
11 / p. 1068		Conroy's	◆◆◆	American	$17-$36	1085
12 / p. 1068	AAA	**Red Fish Restaurant**	◆◆◆	Cuban	$9-$32	1087

Map Page	OA	Restaurants (cont'd)	Diamond Rated	Cuisine	Meal Range	Page
13 / p. 1068		Hugo's at Wexford	2 diamonds	Regional American	$6-$33	1086
14 / p. 1068	AAA	**The Jazz Corner**	3 diamonds	American	$22-$36	1086
15 / p. 1068	AAA	**Antonio's**	4 diamonds	Italian	$17-$38	1084
16 / p. 1068		Charlie's L'Etoile Verte	3 diamonds	French	$9-$39	1086
17 / p. 1068	AAA	**Crane's Tavern & Steakhouse Restaurant**	3 diamonds	Steak & Seafood	$20-$46	1085
18 / p. 1068		Catch 22	3 diamonds	Steak & Seafood	$12-$42	1084
19 / p. 1068	AAA	**Michael Anthony's Cucina Italiana**	3 diamonds	Regional Italian	$18-$36	1086
20 / p. 1068		Trinity Restaurant & Bar	3 diamonds	Regional American	$10-$28	1087
21 / p. 1068		Juleps	3 diamonds	Regional American	$8-$31	1086
22 / p. 1068		Alligator Grille Seafood Restaurant and Sushi Bar	3 diamonds	New American	$17-$34	1084
23 / p. 1068		Two Eleven Park Wine Bar & Bistro	3 diamonds	Regional American	$13-$30	1088
24 / p. 1068		The Studio	3 diamonds	Continental	$20-$34	1087
25 / p. 1068		Amigos Cafe 'y Cantina	1 diamond	Mexican	$4-$8	1084
26 / p. 1068		Aunt Chiladas "Easy Street Cafe"	2 diamonds	American	$8-$27	1084
27 / p. 1068		Flavors	3 diamonds	New American	$18-$32	1085
28 / p. 1068		Sage Room	3 diamonds	New American	$20-$38	1087
29 / p. 1068	AAA	**Plantation Cafe and Deli**	1 diamond	American	$6-$9	1087
30 / p. 1068		The Smokehouse	1 diamond	American	$6-$21	1087
31 / p. 1068		Topside at the Quarterdeck	3 diamonds	American	$9-$32	1087
32 / p. 1068	AAA	**C Q's Restaurant**	3 diamonds	American	$19-$30	1085
33 / p. 1068	AAA	**The Harbour Town Grill**	3 diamonds	American	$11-$45	1085
34 / p. 1068	AAA	**Truffles Cafe**	2 diamonds	American	$8-$26	1087

HILTON HEAD ISLAND pop. 33,862 (See map and index starting on p. 1068)

WHERE TO STAY

BARRINGTON COURT VILLAS-RESORTQUEST HILTON HEAD

Vacation Rental Condominium

$1075-$2275 All Year

Phone: (843)842-3006 30

Address: 101 Barrington Ct **Location:** Oceanfront. Jct US 278 business route/Queens Folly Rd, 0.9 mi s on Queens Folly Rd to Ocean Ln, then 0.9 mi sw; in Palmetto Dunes. **Facility:** Each unit is uniquely decorated in contemporary furnishings and offer ocean and courtyard views; a beachside pavilion and bike trails are available. 30 condominiums. 5 stories, exterior corridors. **Parking:** on-site. **Terms:** office hours 9 am-5 pm, off-site registration, check-in 4 pm, 3-7 night minimum stay - seasonal, cancellation fee imposed. **Amenities:** voice mail, irons. **Pool(s):** outdoor. **Leisure Activities:** whirlpool. **Guest Services:** complimentary laundry. **Business Services:** PC (fee). **Cards:** AX, DS, MC, VI.

ASK CALL

BEACHSIDE TENNIS VILLAS

Vacation Rental Condominium

For rates and additional information, visit AAA.com 58

Location: Coligny Plaza, 5.2 mi sw on S Forest Beach Dr/Sea Pines Dr. **Overview:** Located next to South Beach Marina Village's many shops and restaurants, the resort offers a beachfront pool and guestrooms with ocean and sound views. 37 units.

SAVE **The Sea Pines Resort:** 32 Greenwood Dr, Hilton Head Island. 843/785-3333

ResortQuest Hilton Head: 21 Pope Ave Executive Park Rd, Hilton Head Island. 843/842-3006

BEACHWALK HOTEL & CONDOMINIUMS

Book great rates at AAA.com

Phone: (843)842-8888 37

SAVE

Hotel

$59-$149 All Year

Address: 40 Waterside Dr **Location:** Sea Pines Cir, 0.7 mi se on Pope Rd, just e. **Facility:** 91 one-bedroom standard units, some with efficiencies. 3 stories, exterior corridors. *Bath:* combo or shower only. **Parking:** on-site. **Terms:** check-in 4 pm, cancellation fee imposed. **Amenities:** dual phone lines, voice mail, irons, hair dryers. **Pool(s):** outdoor. **Leisure Activities:** putting green. **Guest Services:** coin laundry, wireless Internet. **Business Services:** fax (fee). **Cards:** AX, CB, DC, DS, JC, MC, VI. **Free Special Amenities: expanded continental breakfast and high-speed Internet.**
(See color ad below)

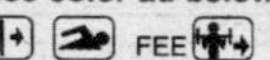  FEE  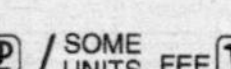 / SOME UNITS FEE 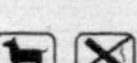

▼ See AAA listing above ▼

(See map and index starting on p. 1068)

BEACHWALK VILLAS COASTAL HOME AND HILTON HEAD VACATION RENTALS

Phone: (843)689-3010 **31**

Vacation Rental Condominium

$98-$236 All Year

Address: 106 Beachwalk Villas **Location:** Jct US 278 business route/Shipyard Dr, 1.3 mi se, then just n; in Shipyard Plantation. **Facility:** Located directly across from the Shipyard Beach Club, the proeprty offers an easy walk to the beach and tennis. 14 condominiums. 2 stories (no elevator), exterior corridors. **Parking:** on-site. **Terms:** office hours 9 am-6 pm, off-site registration, check-in 4 pm, check-out 9:30 am, 3-7 night minimum stay - seasonal, 45 day cancellation notice-fee imposed. **Amenities:** irons. **Pool(s):** outdoor. **Guest Services:** complimentary laundry. **Business Services:** fax (fee). **Cards:** DS, MC, VI. **Free Special Amenities: local telephone calls.**

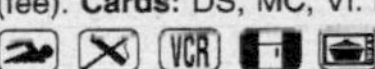

BLUFF VILLAS-RESORTQUEST HILTON HEAD

Phone: (843)842-3006 **56**

Vacation Rental Condominium

$625-$1275 All Year

Address: 1650 Bluff Villas **Location:** Coligny Plaza, 5.3 mi sw along S Forest Beach/Sea Pines drs. Located in South Beach Marina Village. **Facility:** The resort is a short walk from the beach; some guest units offer views of Braddock Cove and the sound. 24 condominiums. 3 stories (no elevator), exterior corridors. **Parking:** on-site. **Terms:** office hours 9 am-5 pm, off-site registration, check-in 4 pm, 5-7 night minimum stay - seasonal, cancellation fee imposed. **Amenities:** irons. **Pool(s):** outdoor. **Guest Services:** complimentary laundry. **Business Services:** fax (fee). **Cards:** AX, DS, MC, VI.

THE BREAKERS

Vacation Rental Condominium

For rates and additional information, visit AAA.com **42**

Location: At Coligny Plaza; in Forest Beach area. **Overview:** Small oceanfront villas in three-story walk-up. Adjacent to many shops, restaurants and activities in the popular Coligny Plaza area. 24 units.

Coastal Home and Hilton Head Vacation Rentals: 430 William Hilton Pkwy, Suite 504, Hilton Head Island. 843/689-3010

ResortQuest Hilton Head: 21 Pope Ave Executive Park Rd, Hilton Head Island. 843/842-3006

CALIBOGUE CLUB VILLAS-RESORTQUEST HILTON HEAD

Phone: (843)842-3006 **39**

Vacation Rental Condominium

$925-$1625 All Year

Address: 2601 Calibogue Club **Location:** Sea Pines Cir, 2.2 mi sw on Greenwood Dr to Calibogue Cay Rd, then just nw; in Sea Pines Plantation. **Facility:** Offering large living areas, vaulted ceilings and nicely decorated interiors, every villa also has a large wooden deck and some include a sun porch. 5 condominiums. 1 story, exterior corridors. **Parking:** on-site. **Terms:** office hours 9 am-5 pm, off-site registration, check-in 4 pm, 3-7 night minimum stay - seasonal, cancellation fee imposed. **Amenities:** irons. **Pool(s):** outdoor. **Leisure Activities:** 4 tennis courts. **Guest Services:** complimentary laundry. **Business Services:** fax (fee). **Cards:** AX, DS, MC, VI.

CALL

CAPTAIN'S WALK VILLAS-RESORTQUEST HILTON HEAD

Phone: (843)842-3006 **21**

Vacation Rental Condominium

$1275-$2975 All Year

Address: 401 Captain's Walk **Location:** Oceanfront. Jct US 278 business route/Queens Folly Rd, 0.9 mi on Queens Folly Rd to Ocean Ln, then just s; in Palmetto Dunes. **Facility:** These oceanfront villas offer sensational views of the Atlantic Ocean from the master bedroom, living area and a wide balcony in every unit. 16 condominiums. 3 stories (no elevator), exterior corridors. **Parking:** on-site. **Terms:** office hours 9 am-5 pm, off-site registration, check-in 4 pm, 5-7 night minimum stay - seasonal, cancellation fee imposed. **Amenities:** irons. **Pool(s):** outdoor. **Guest Services:** complimentary laundry. **Business Services:** fax (fee). **Cards:** AX, DS, MC, VI.

CALL

CARAVEL COURT VILLAS-THE SEA PINES RESORT

Phone: (843)785-3333 **49**

Vacation Rental Condominium

$120-$330 All Year

Address: 1023 Caravel Ct **Location:** Sea Pines Cir, 2.8 mi sw on Greenwood/Plantation drs to Lighthouse Rd, 0.4 mi nw to Lighthouse Ln, then just sw. **Facility:** Located in Sea Pines Resort at Harbour Town and convenient to shops and boutiques, villas offer relaxing views of the waterfront from private patios. 20 condominiums. 4 stories, interior corridors. **Parking:** on-site. **Terms:** office hours 6:30 am-10 pm, off-site registration, check-in 4 pm, 2 night minimum stay - weekends, 21 day cancellation notice-fee imposed. **Amenities:** voice mail, irons. **Pool(s):** outdoor. **Leisure Activities:** beach access, rental boats, rental sailboards, recreation programs, hay rides, eco tours, hiking trails, jogging, spa. *Fee:* sailboats, marina, waterskiing, fishing, charter fishing, kayaking, parasailing, golf-54 holes, 23 lighted tennis courts, bicycles, horseback riding. **Guest Services:** complimentary laundry. **Business Services:** administrative services, fax (fee). **Cards:** AX, DC, DS, MC, VI.

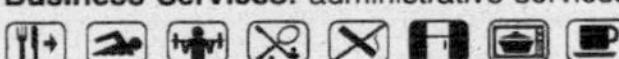

(See map and index starting on p. 1068)

CAROLINA PLACE VILLAS-RESORTQUEST HILTON HEAD

Vacation Rental Condominium
$775-$1325 All Year

Phone: (843)842-3006 35

Address: 3401 Carolina Place Villas **Location:** Sea Pines Cir, 1 mi sw on Greenwood Dr, then just s; in Sea Pines Plantation. **Facility:** All units are nicely decorated and have peaceful lagoon views; Harbour Town and Sea Pines Beach Club are only a short bicycle ride away. 5 condominiums. 1 story, exterior corridors. **Parking:** on-site. **Terms:** office hours 9 am-5 pm, off-site registration, check-in 4 pm, 3-7 night minimum stay - seasonal, cancellation fee imposed. **Amenities:** irons. **Pool(s):** outdoor. **Leisure Activities:** whirlpool, 4 tennis courts. **Guest Services:** complimentary laundry. **Business Services:** fax (fee). **Cards:** AX, DS, MC, VI.

ASK CALL VCR

CENTRECOURT VILLAS-RESORTQUEST HILTON HEAD

Vacation Rental Condominium
Rates not provided

Phone: 843/842-3006 16

Address: 7801 Centre Ct **Location:** Jct US 278 business route/Queens Folly Rd, 0.9 mi s on Queens Folly Rd to Carnoustie Rd, then just n; in Palmetto Dunes. **Facility:** Adjacent to a golf course and tennis courts, the resort offers two-story walk-ups in connected quads in a quiet, lush location. 17 condominiums. 2 stories (no elevator), exterior corridors. **Parking:** on-site. **Terms:** office hours 9 am-5 pm, off-site registration, check-in 4 pm. **Amenities:** irons. **Pool(s):** outdoor. **Guest Services:** complimentary laundry. **Business Services:** meeting rooms, fax (fee).

COLONADE CLUB VILLAS-COASTAL HOME AND HILTON HEAD VACATION RENTALS

AAA SAVE

Vacation Rental Condominium
$105-$162 All Year

Phone: (843)689-3010 28

Address: 137 Collonade Club Villas **Location:** Jct US 278 business route/Shipyard Dr, 0.4 mi se on Shipyard Dr, then 0.7 mi ne on Kingston Rd; in Shipyard Plantation. **Facility:** Most units have golf and lagoon views from the living room, master bedroom and balcony; walk or bike to the beach club and the Shipyard Racquet Club. 6 condominiums. 2 stories (no elevator), exterior corridors. **Parking:** on-site. **Terms:** office hours 9 am-6 pm, off-site registration, check-in 4 pm, check-out 9:30 am, 3-7 night minimum stay - seasonal, 45 day cancellation notice-fee imposed. **Amenities:** irons. **Pool(s):** outdoor. **Leisure Activities:** whirlpool, 4 tennis courts. **Guest Services:** complimentary laundry. **Business Services:** fax (fee). **Cards:** DS, MC, VI. **Free Special Amenities: local telephone calls.**

VCR

COMFORT INN *Book great rates at AAA.com*

AAA SAVE

Hotel
$49-$199 All Year

Phone: (843)842-6662 40

Address: 2 Tanglewood Dr **Location:** Sea Pines Cir, 1.1 mi se on Pope Ave, just sw; at Coligny Plaza. **Facility:** 153 one-bedroom standard units. 5 stories, interior corridors. **Parking:** on-site. **Terms:** off-site registration, check-in 4 pm, cancellation fee imposed. **Amenities:** high-speed Internet, voice mail, safes, irons, hair dryers. **Pool(s):** outdoor. **Leisure Activities:** *Fee:* bicycles. **Guest Services:** coin laundry, area transportation-beach, wireless Internet. **Business Services:** meeting rooms, fax (fee). **Cards:** AX, CB, DC, DS, JC, MC, VI. **Free Special Amenities: high-speed Internet.**
(See color ad below)

/ SOME UNITS FEE

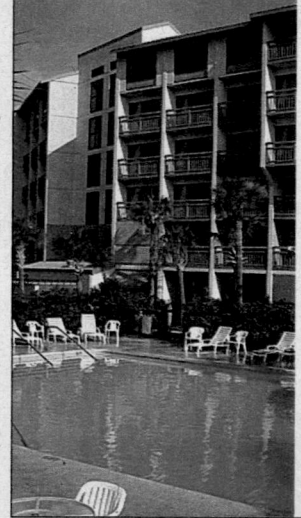

(See map and index starting on p. 1068)

CROWNE PLAZA HILTON HEAD ISLAND BEACH RESORT *Book great rates at AAA.com* **Phone:** (843)842-2400 32

AAA SAVE

Resort Hotel

$134-$299 All Year

Address: 130 Shipyard Dr **Location:** Oceanfront. Jct US 278 business route/Shipyard Dr, 1.3 mi se; in Shipyard Plantation. **Facility:** Featuring upgraded, residential-style amenities, the property offers rooms overlooking the pool or a lagoon. 340 units. 335 one-bedroom standard units. 5 one-bedroom suites, some with whirlpools. 5 stories, interior corridors. *Bath:* combo or shower only. **Parking:** on-site. **Terms:** check-in 4 pm, 5 day cancellation notice-fee imposed. **Amenities:** CD players, high-speed Internet, dual phone lines, voice mail, safes, honor bars, irons, hair dryers. **Dining:** 2 restaurants. **Pool(s):** outdoor, heated indoor. **Leisure Activities:** saunas, whirlpools, fishing, recreation programs, jogging, playground, spa. *Fee:* paddleboats, sailboats, golf-27 holes, 8 tennis courts (3 indoor, 8 lighted), bicycles. **Guest Services:** valet and coin laundry, area transportation-golf course & Shipyard Plantation, wireless Internet. **Business Services:** conference facilities, business center. **Cards:** AX, CB, DC, DS, JC, MC, VI. ***(See color ad below)***

SOME UNITS FEE

CUTTER COURT VILLAS-THE SEA PINES RESORT **Phone:** (843)785-3333 47

AAA SAVE

Vacation Rental Condominium

$120-$330 All Year

Address: 901 Cutter Ct **Location:** Sea Pines Cir, 2.8 mi sw on Greenwood/Plantation drs to Lighthouse Rd, 0.4 mi nw to Lighthouse Ln, then just sw; in Sea Pines resort, near Harbour Town. **Facility:** Near shops and boutiques, privately-owned and -decorated villas offer views of the golf course and marina from private patios. 27 condominiums. 2-4 stories, exterior corridors. **Parking:** on-site. **Terms:** office hours 6:30 am-10 pm, off-site registration, check-in 4 pm, 2 night minimum stay - weekends, 21 day cancellation notice-fee imposed. **Amenities:** voice mail, irons. **Pool(s):** outdoor. **Leisure Activities:** beach access, rental boats, rental sailboards, 23 tennis courts (Fee: 23 lighted), recreation programs, hay rides, eco tours, hiking trails, jogging, spa. *Fee:* sailboats, marina, waterskiing, fishing, charter fishing, kayaking, parasailing, golf-54 holes, bicycles, horseback riding. **Guest Services:** complimentary laundry. **Business Services:** administrative services, fax (fee). **Cards:** AX, DC, DS, MC, VI.

DAYS INN *Book at AAA.com* **Phone:** (843)842-4800 9

Motel

$69-$129 All Year

Address: 9 Marina Side Dr **Location:** 11.9 mi from J Wilton Graves Bridge on US 278 business route. Located adjacent to Shelter Cove Mall. **Facility:** 119 units. 105 one-bedroom standard units. 14 one-bedroom suites. 3 stories, interior/exterior corridors. *Bath:* combo or shower only. **Parking:** on-site. **Amenities:** irons, hair dryers. *Some:* dual phone lines. **Pool(s):** heated outdoor. **Leisure Activities:** limited exercise equipment. *Fee:* miniature golf. **Guest Services:** valet and coin laundry, wireless Internet. **Business Services:** fax (fee). **Cards:** AX, DS, MC, VI.

ASK FEE / SOME UNITS

DISNEY'S HILTON HEAD ISLAND RESORT *Book great rates at AAA.com* **Phone:** (843)341-4100 8

AAA

Resort Hotel

$110-$457 12/1-8/22
$110-$277 8/23-11/30

Address: 22 Harbourside Ln **Location:** 8.5 mi from J Wilton Graves Bridge on US 278 business route, just nw in Shelter Cove. **Facility:** Decorated in a rustic lodge theme, the resort's spacious rooms all have private balconies and most have washer/dryers. Smoke free premises. 123 units. 21 one-bedroom standard units with efficiencies. 21 one-, 76 two- and 5 three-bedroom suites with kitchens and whirlpools. 3 stories, exterior corridors. **Parking:** on-site. **Terms:** check-in 4 pm, 6 day cancellation notice-fee imposed. **Amenities:** video library (fee), DVD players, voice mail, safes, irons, hair dryers. *Some:* CD players. **Dining:** 2 restaurants. **Pool(s):** 2 heated outdoor. **Leisure Activities:** whirlpool, waterslide, fishing, recreation programs, picnic areas with grills, playground, horseshoes, shuffleboard, volleyball, game room. *Fee:* charter fishing, golf & tennis privileges, bicycles. **Guest Services:** complimentary laundry, area transportation-Disney Beach House, Palmetto Dunes, wireless Internet. **Business Services:** fax (fee). **Cards:** AX, DC, DS, JC, MC, VI.

FEE

▼ See AAA listing above ▼

(See map and index starting on p. 1068)

EVIAN VILLAS

Vacation Rental Condominium

For rates and additional information, visit AAA.com 33

Location: Jct US 278 business route/Shipyard Dr, 0.7 mi se on Shipyard Dr; in Shipyard Plantation. **Overview:** The two-story townhouses offer lake and golf course views as well as spacious living and dining areas. 21 units.

Coastal Home and Hilton Head Vacation Rentals: 430 William Hilton Pkwy, Suite 504, Hilton Head Island. 843/689-3010

ResortQuest Hilton Head: 21 Pope Ave Executive Park Rd, Hilton Head Island. 843/842-3006

FAZIO VILLAS-RESORTQUEST HILTON HEAD **Phone:** 843/842-3006 14

Vacation Rental Condominium

Rates not provided

Address: 1 Fazio Villas **Location:** Jct US 278 business route/Queens Folly Rd, 0.9 mi s on Queens Folly Rd to Carnoustie Rd, then just n; in Palmeto Dunes. **Facility:** The two-story villas offer golf and lagoon views, open floor plans and kitchens with breakfast bar and are a short walk to the beach. 15 condominiums. 2 stories (no elevator), exterior corridors. **Parking:** on-site. **Terms:** office hours 9 am-5 pm, off-site registration, check-in 4 pm. **Amenities:** irons. **Pool(s):** 2 outdoor. **Leisure Activities:** 4 tennis courts. **Guest Services:** complimentary laundry. **Business Services:** fax (fee).

FOREST BEACH VILLAS-COASTAL HOME AND HILTON HEAD VACATION RENTALS **Phone:** (843)689-3010 22

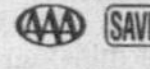

Vacation Rental Condominium

$84-$200 All Year

Address: 110 Forest Beach Villas **Location:** Jct Coligny Plaza/S Forest Beach Dr, just s; at South Forest Beach. **Facility:** Outside of plantation communities, the property offers natural surroundings, recreational activities and large units across the street from the ocean. 5 units. 1 one-, 3 two- and 1 three-bedroom suites with kitchens. 4 stories, exterior corridors. **Parking:** on-site. **Terms:** office hours 9 am-6 pm, off-site registration, check-in 4 pm, check-out 9:30 am, 3-7 night minimum stay - seasonal, 45 day cancellation notice-fee imposed. **Amenities:** irons. **Pool(s):** outdoor. **Leisure Activities:** 2 tennis courts, nature walk. **Guest Services:** complimentary laundry. **Business Services:** fax (fee). **Cards:** DS, MC, VI. **Free Special Amenities: local telephone calls.**

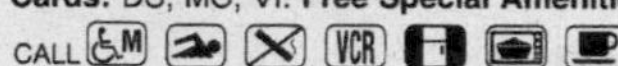

THE GREENS-COASTAL HOME AND HILTON HEAD VACATION RENTALS **Phone:** (843)689-3010 5

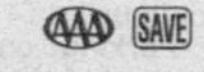

Vacation Rental Condominium

$92-$208 All Year

Address: 101 The Greens **Location:** Jct US 278 business route/Shipyard Dr, 1.2 mi se on Shipyard Dr; in Shipyard Plantation. **Facility:** The two-story, walk-up townhouse has individually decorated units with private patios and golf course and lagoon views; each bedroom has its own bath. 8 units. 2 one-, 5 two- and 1 three-bedroom suites with kitchens. 2 stories (no elevator), exterior corridors. **Parking:** on-site. **Terms:** office hours 8 am-6 pm, off-site registration, check-in 4 pm, check-out 9:30 am, 3-7 night minimum stay - seasonal, 45 day cancellation notice-fee imposed. **Amenities:** irons, hair dryers. **Pool(s):** outdoor. **Guest Services:** complimentary laundry. **Business Services:** fax (fee). **Cards:** DS, MC, VI. **Free Special Amenities: local telephone calls.**

HAMPTON INN *Book great rates at AAA.com* **Phone:** (843)681-7900 1

Hotel

$89-$142 All Year

Address: One Dillon Rd **Location:** 5 mi e of J Wilton Graves Bridge on US 278 business route. **Facility:** 115 units. 107 one-bedroom standard units. 8 one-bedroom suites. 2 stories, interior corridors. *Bath:* combo or shower only. **Parking:** on-site. **Terms:** check-in 4 pm, 1-30 night minimum stay, cancellation fee imposed. **Amenities:** high-speed Internet, voice mail, irons, hair dryers. *Some:* DVD players. **Pool(s):** outdoor. **Leisure Activities:** limited exercise equipment. **Guest Services:** coin laundry, wireless Internet. **Business Services:** meeting rooms, business center. **Cards:** AX, CB, DC, DS, JC, MC, VI.

/ SOME UNITS

AAA Benefit:

Members save up to 10% everyday!

HAMPTON PLACE VILLAS-RESORTQUEST HILTON HEAD **Phone:** (843)842-3006 27

Vacation Rental Condominium

$1150-$3925 All Year

Address: 5101 Hampton Pl **Location:** Oceanfront. Jct US 278 business route/Queens Folly Rd, 0.9 mi s on Queens Folly Rd to Ocean Ln, then 0.6 mi sw; in Palmetto Dunes. **Facility:** The spacious, well-appointed villas on the ocean offer covered parking and a community barbecue area. 36 condominiums. 5 stories, exterior corridors. **Parking:** on-site. **Terms:** office hours 9 am-5 pm, off-site registration, check-in 4 pm, 3-7 night minimum stay - seasonal, cancellation fee imposed. **Amenities:** irons. **Pool(s):** outdoor. **Leisure Activities:** whirlpool. **Guest Services:** complimentary laundry. **Business Services:** fax (fee). **Cards:** AX, DS, MC, VI.

(See map and index starting on p. 1068)

HERITAGE VILLAS THE SEA PINES RESORT Phone: (843)785-3333 52

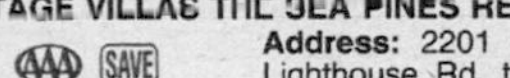

Vacation Rental Condominium
$140-$315 All Year

Address: 2201 Heritage **Location:** Sea Pines Cir, 2.8 mi sw on Greenwood/Plantation drs to Lighthouse Rd, then just nw; in center of Sea Pines Resort. **Facility:** South of Harbour Town, a racquet club and golf course, these townhouse villas have golf and lagoon views; each unit is privately owned and decorated. 41 condominiums. 2 stories (no elevator), exterior corridors. **Parking:** on-site. **Terms:** office hours 6:30 am-10 pm, off-site registration, check-in 4 pm, 2 night minimum stay - weekends, 21 day cancellation notice-fee imposed. **Amenities:** voice mail, irons. **Pool(s):** outdoor. **Leisure Activities:** beach access, rental boats, recreation programs, hay rides, hiking trails, jogging, spa. *Fee:* sailboats, marina, waterskiing, fishing, charter fishing, kayaking, eco tours, parasailing, golf-54 holes, 23 lighted tennis courts, bicycles, horseback riding. **Guest Services:** complimentary laundry. **Business Services:** administrative services, fax (fee). **Cards:** AX, DC, DS, MC, VI.

HILTON GARDEN INN HILTON HEAD *Book great rates at AAA.com* **Phone:** (843)837-8111

Hotel
$70-$180 All Year

Address: 1575 Fording Island Rd **Location:** US 278, on mainland just w of J Wilton Graves Bridge. **Facility:** 104 units. 64 one-bedroom standard units, some with whirlpools. 40 one-bedroom suites. 3 stories, interior corridors. *Bath:* combo or shower only. **Parking:** on-site. **Terms:** 1-30 night minimum stay, cancellation fee imposed. **Amenities:** high-speed Internet, dual phone lines, voice mail, irons, hair dryers. **Pool(s):** outdoor. **Leisure Activities:** whirlpool, exercise room. **Guest Services:** valet and coin laundry, wireless Internet. **Business Services:** meeting rooms, business center. **Cards:** AX, CB, DC, DS, JC, MC, VI.

CALL      / SOME UNITS

Hilton Garden Inn
AAA Benefit:
Members save 5% or more everyday!

HILTON HEAD ISLAND BEACH & TENNIS RESORT

Vacation Rental Condominium

For rates and additional information, visit AAA.com 7

Location: 6.2 mi from J Wilton Graves Bridge via US 278 business route to Folly Field Rd, then just e.

Hilton Head Island Beach & Tennis Resort: 40 Folly Field Rd, Hilton Head Island. 843/842-4402
(See color ad below)

Coastal Home and Hilton Head Vacation Rentals: 430 William Hilton Pkwy, Suite 504, Hilton Head Island. 843/689-3010

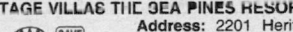

(See map and index starting on p. 1068)

HILTON HEAD MARRIOTT RESORT & SPA Book great rates at AAA.com **Phone:** (843)686-8400 

Resort Hotel

$149-$329 All Year

Address: One Hotel Cir **Location:** Oceanfront. 8.5 mi e from J Wilton Graves Bridge on US 278 business route, then 1.2 mi se on Queens Folly Rd; in Palmetto Dunes. **Facility:** An upscale ocean resort with plush seaside or island-view rooms, the property offers numerous activities as well as large areas for lounging. Smoke free premises. 513 units. 486 one-bedroom standard units. 27 one-bedroom suites. 10 stories, interior corridors. *Bath:* combo or shower only. **Parking:** on-site and valet. **Terms:** check-in 4 pm, 3 day cancellation notice-fee imposed. **Amenities:** dual phone lines, voice mail, safes, irons, hair dryers. **Dining:** 2 restaurants, also, Conroy's, see separate listing. **Pool(s):** 2 outdoor, indoor. **Leisure Activities:** saunas, whirlpools, banana boats, kayaking, parasailing, water trikes, recreation programs, hiking trails, jogging, spa, basketball. *Fee:* windsurfing, waterskiing, fishing, charter fishing, golf-18 holes, 48 tennis courts (8 lighted), bicycles, horseback riding, game room. **Guest Services:** valet and coin laundry, wireless Internet. **Business Services:** conference facilities, business center. **Cards:** AX, CB, DC, DS, JC, MC, VI.

CALL

HILTON OCEANFRONT RESORT HILTON HEAD ISLAND Book great rates at AAA.com **Phone:** (843)842-8000 24

Resort Hotel

$139-$339 All Year

Address: 23 Ocean Ln **Location:** Oceanfront. Jct US 278 business route/Queens Folly Rd, 0.9 mi se to Ocean Ln, then just sw; in Palmetto Dunes Plantation. **Facility:** The resort offers large accommodations with luxury appointments, and each room features a balcony or patio. 323 units. 295 one-bedroom standard units. 28 one-bedroom suites. 5 stories, interior/exterior corridors. *Bath:* combo or shower only. **Parking:** on-site and valet. **Terms:** check-in 4 pm, 1-30 night minimum stay, cancellation fee imposed. **Amenities:** voice mail, safes, irons, hair dryers. *Some:* CD players. **Pool(s):** 2 heated outdoor. **Leisure Activities:** saunas, whirlpools, recreation programs, shoreside pavilion, rental bicycles, playground, exercise room, spa, volleyball. **Guest Services:** valet and coin laundry, area transportation-Palmetto Dunes area. **Business Services:** meeting rooms, business center. **Cards:** AX, CB, DC, DS, JC, MC, VI.

CALL / SOME UNITS

HOLIDAY INN OCEANFRONT RESORT Book great rates at AAA.com **Phone:** (843)785-5126 43

Hotel

$79-$299 All Year

Address: 1 S Forest Beach Dr **Location:** Oceanfront. Sea Pine Cir, 1.1 mi se on Pope Ave, just sw at Coligny Cir. **Facility:** 202 one-bedroom standard units. 5 stories, interior corridors. *Bath:* combo or shower only. **Parking:** on-site. **Terms:** check-in 4 pm. **Amenities:** voice mail, irons, hair dryers. **Pool(s):** outdoor. **Leisure Activities:** recreation programs, playground, limited exercise equipment, volleyball. *Fee:* golf & tennis privileges. **Guest Services:** valet and coin laundry, wireless Internet. **Business Services:** meeting rooms, business center. **Cards:** AX, CB, DC, DS, MC, VI.

CALL / SOME UNITS FEE

HUNTINGTON VILLAS-RESORTQUEST HILTON HEAD **Phone:** (843)842-3006 29

Vacation Rental Condominium

$925-$2525 All Year

Address: 7601 Huntington Villas **Location:** Jct US 278 business route/Queens Folly Rd, 0.9 mi se on Queens Folly Rd to Ocean Ln, then 1 mi sw; in Palmetto Dunes. **Facility:** The resort offers attractive villas with fireplaces and screened porches, most with lagoon views, and are a short walk to the beach. 30 condominiums. 5 stories, exterior corridors. **Parking:** on-site. **Terms:** office hours 9 am-5 pm, off-site registration, check-in 4 pm, 3-7 night minimum stay - seasonal, cancellation fee imposed. **Amenities:** irons. **Pool(s):** outdoor. **Leisure Activities:** playground. **Guest Services:** complimentary laundry. **Business Services:** fax (fee). **Cards:** AX, DS, MC, VI.

ASK CALL VCR

THE INN AT HARBOUR TOWN Book great rates at AAA.com **Phone:** (843)363-8100 48

Boutique Hotel

$149-$369 3/1-11/30

$129-$199 12/1-2/28

Address: 7 Lighthouse Ln **Location:** 2.8 mi sw of Sea Pines Cir via Greenwood and Plantation drs, just nw. **Facility:** Bordered by a major golf course and a large racquet club, this is an upscale, full-service hotel with a luxurious ambience. Smoke free premises. 60 one-bedroom standard units. 3 stories, interior corridors. *Bath:* combo or shower only. **Parking:** on-site and valet. **Terms:** check-in 4 pm, 7 day cancellation notice-fee imposed. **Amenities:** CD players, high-speed Internet, dual phone lines, voice mail, safes, irons, hair dryers. *Some:* DVD players. **Dining:** The Harbour Town Grill, see separate listing. **Pool(s):** outdoor. **Leisure Activities:** beach access, rental boats, rental sailboards, recreation programs, eco tours, hay rides, bicycles, hiking trails, jogging, spa. *Fee:* sailboats, marina, waterskiing, kayaks, parasailing, golf-36 holes, 23 lighted tennis courts, horseback riding. **Guest Services:** valet laundry, wireless Internet. **Business Services:** conference facilities, business center. **Cards:** AX, DC, DS, MC, VI. **Free Special Amenities: newspaper and high-speed Internet.**

(See map and index starting on p. 1068)

INVERNESS VILLAS-COASTAL HOME AND HILTON HEAD VACATION RENTALS

Phone: (843)689-3010 17

Vacation Rental Condominium

$104-$162 All Year

Address: 900 Inverness Villas **Location:** Jct US 278 business route/Queens Folly Rd, 0.9 mi se on Queens Folly Rd to Carnoustie Rd, then 0.6 mi nw; in Palmetto Dunes. **Facility:** Townhouse villas have a private screened porch from which to enjoy golf course and lagoon views. 5 two-bedroom suites with kitchens. 2 stories (no elevator), exterior corridors. **Parking:** on-site. **Terms:** office hours 8 am-6 pm, off-site registration, 3-7 night minimum stay - seasonal, 45 day cancellation notice-fee imposed. **Amenities:** irons. **Pool(s):** outdoor. **Leisure Activities:** 6 tennis courts. **Guest Services:** complimentary laundry. **Business Services:** fax (fee). **Cards:** DS, MC, VI. **Free Special Amenities: local telephone calls.**

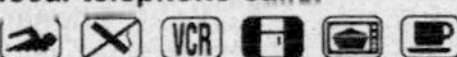

THE ISLAND CLUB-COASTAL HOME AND HILTON HEAD VACATION RENTALS *Book great rates at AAA.com*

Phone: (843)689-3010 6

Vacation Rental Condominium

$82-$365 All Year

Address: 85 Folly Field Rd **Location:** Oceanfront. 6.2 mi from J Wilton Graves Bridge via US 278 business route to Folly Field Rd, then 0.8 mi e. **Facility:** The modest condos and stand-alone homes offered by this agency contain as many as six bedrooms; some are oceanfront. 80 units. 14 one-, 59 two- and 7 three-bedroom suites with kitchens, some with whirlpools. 2-5 stories, exterior corridors. **Parking:** on-site. **Terms:** office hours 9 am-6 pm, off-site registration, check-in 4 pm, check-out 9:30 am, 3-7 night minimum stay - seasonal, 45 day cancellation notice-fee imposed. **Amenities:** voice mail, irons. *Some:* DVD players, hair dryers. **Pool(s):** outdoor. **Leisure Activities:** tennis instructor, recreation programs, picnic area with grill, playground, exercise room, basketball. *Fee:* bicycles. **Guest Services:** complimentary laundry. **Business Services:** meeting rooms, fax (fee). **Cards:** DS, MC, VI. **Free Special Amenities: local telephone calls and high-speed Internet.** *(See color ad below)*

KETCH COURT VILLAS-THE SEA PINES RESORT

Phone: (843)785-3333 46

Vacation Rental Condominium

$120-$330 All Year

Address: 818 Ketch Ct **Location:** Sea Pines Cir, 2.8 mi sw on Greenwood Dr/Plantation drs to Lighthouse Rd, 0.4 mi nw to Lighthouse Ln, then just sw. Located in Sea Pines Resort, near Harbour Town. **Facility:** Near shops and boutiques, privately-owned and -decorated villas offer relaxing views of the marina from private patios. 39 condominiums. 4 stories, interior/exterior corridors. **Parking:** on-site. **Terms:** office hours 6:30 am-10 pm, off-site registration, check-in 4 pm, 2 night minimum stay - weekends, 21 day cancellation notice-fee imposed. **Amenities:** voice mail, irons. **Pool(s):** outdoor. **Leisure Activities:** beach access, rental boats, rental sailboards, pool privileges, parasailing, recreation programs, hay rides, eco tours, hiking trails, jogging, spa. *Fee:* sailboats, marina, waterskiing, fishing, charter fishing, kayaking, golf-54 holes, 23 lighted tennis courts, bicycles, horseback riding. **Guest Services:** complimentary laundry. **Business Services:** administrative services, fax (fee). **Cards:** AX, DC, DS, MC, VI.

LIGHTHOUSE TENNIS VILLAS-THE SEA PINES RESORT

Phone: (843)785-3333 51

Vacation Rental Condominium

$110-$250 All Year

Address: 2370 Lighthouse Tennis **Location:** Sea Pines Cir, 2.8 mi sw on Greenwood/Plantation drs to Lighthouse Rd, then just se. **Facility:** Located in the Harbour Town area; each one- and two-bedroom walk-up flat offers a private balcony with views of the lagoon and pool. 15 condominiums. 3 stories (no elevator), exterior corridors. **Parking:** on-site. **Terms:** office hours 6:30 am-10 pm, off-site registration, check-in 4 pm, 2 night minimum stay - weekends, age restrictions may apply, 21 day cancellation notice-fee imposed. **Amenities:** voice mail, irons. **Pool(s):** outdoor. **Leisure Activities:** rental boats, rental sailboards, recreation programs, hiking trails, jogging, spa. *Fee:* sailboats, marina, waterskiing, fishing, charter fishing, kayaking, parasailing, golf-54 holes, 23 lighted tennis courts, hay rides, eco tours, bicycles, horseback riding. **Guest Services:** complimentary laundry. **Business Services:** administrative services, fax (fee). **Cards:** AX, DC, DS, MC, VI.

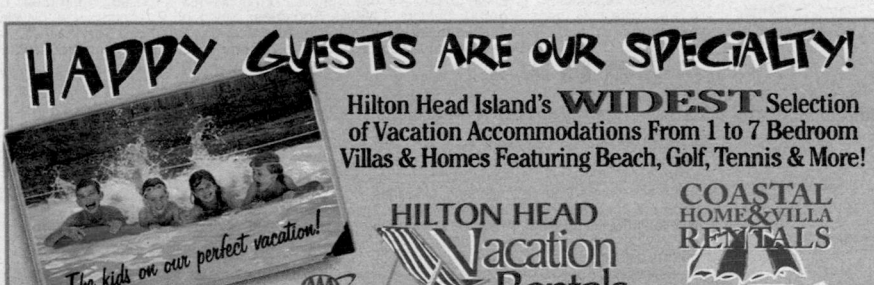

(See map and index starting on p. 1068)

MAIN STREET INN & SPA *Book at AAA.com* **Phone:** (843)681-3001 **2**

Hotel

$159-$299 4/1-11/30
$109-$259 12/1-3/31

Address: 2200 Main St **Location:** 3.5 mi of J Wilton Graves Bridge on US 278 business route, just n. **Facility:** Smoke free premises. 33 one-bedroom standard units, some with whirlpools. 3 stories, exterior corridors. **Parking:** on-site. **Terms:** check-in 4 pm, 3 day cancellation notice-fee imposed. **Amenities:** irons, hair dryers. **Leisure Activities:** whirlpool. *Fee:* massage. **Guest Services:** valet laundry, wireless Internet. **Business Services:** meeting rooms, business center. **Cards:** AX, DC, DS, MC, VI.

MOORINGS VILLAS-RESORTQUEST HILTON HEAD **Phone:** (843)842-3006 **18**

Vacation Rental Condominium

$925-$1725 All Year

Address: 1 Moorings Villas **Location:** Jct US 278 business route/Queens Folly Rd, 0.9 mi s to Mooring Buoy, then just ne; in Palmetto Dunes. **Facility:** The three-story walk-ups feature oversized private decks and are within walking distance of the ocean. 24 condominiums. 3 stories (no elevator), exterior corridors. **Parking:** on-site. **Terms:** office hours 9 am-5 pm, off-site registration, check-in 4 pm, 3-7 night minimum stay - seasonal, cancellation fee imposed. **Amenities:** irons. **Pool(s):** outdoor. **Guest Services:** complimentary laundry. **Business Services:** fax (fee). **Cards:** AX, DS, MC, VI.

NIGHT HERON VILLAS-COASTAL HOME AND HILTON HEAD VACATION RENTALS **Phone:** (843)689-3010 **50**

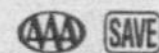

Vacation Rental Condominium

$94-$175 All Year

Address: 1 Night Heron Villas **Location:** Jct Coligny Plaza/S Forest Beach Blvd, 1.5 mi sw; in Sea Pines Resort Oceangate. **Facility:** The stand-alone units offer marsh views of the forest preserve; some units are octagonal in shape. 4 cottages. 1 story, exterior corridors. **Parking:** on-site. **Terms:** office hours 8 am-6 pm, off-site registration, check-in 4 pm, check-out 9:30 am, 3-7 night minimum stay - seasonal, 45 day cancellation notice-fee imposed. **Amenities:** irons. **Business Services:** fax (fee). **Cards:** DS, MC, VI. **Free Special Amenities: local telephone calls.**

NORTH SHORE PLACE-THE SEA PINES RESORT **Phone:** (843)785-3333 **38**

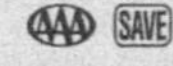

Vacation Rental Condominium

$150-$360 All Year

Address: 3 N Forest Beach Dr **Location:** Coligny Plaza, just ne; in Forest Beach area. **Facility:** A gated, five-story condominium complex is just a block from the beach and near many popular nightspots; find undercover parking and a rooftop pool. 10 condominiums. 6 stories, exterior corridors. **Parking:** on-site. **Terms:** office hours 6:30 am-10 pm, check-in 4 pm, 2 night minimum stay - weekends, 21 day cancellation notice-fee imposed. **Amenities:** voice mail, irons. **Pool(s):** outdoor. **Leisure Activities:** *Fee:* resort privileges. **Guest Services:** complimentary laundry. **Business Services:** administrative services, fax (fee). **Cards:** AX, DC, DS, MC, VI.

OCEAN COURSE VILLAS-RESORTQUEST HILTON HEAD **Phone:** (843)842-3006 **54**

Vacation Rental Condominium

$1025-$1525 All Year

Address: 547 Ocean Course **Location:** Coligny Plaza, 2.9 mi sw on S Forest Beach/Sea Pines drs, then just n; in Sea Pines Resort. **Facility:** The resort offers attractively furnished units with screened porches, sunny lagoon and fairway views and a short walk to the ocean. 10 condominiums. 3 stories (no elevator), exterior corridors. **Parking:** on-site. **Terms:** office hours 9 am-5 pm, off-site registration, check-in 4 pm, 3-7 night minimum stay - seasonal, cancellation fee imposed. **Amenities:** irons. **Pool(s):** outdoor. **Guest Services:** complimentary laundry. **Business Services:** fax (fee). **Cards:** CB, DS, MC, VI.

OCEAN COVE CLUB VILLAS-HILTON HEAD ACCOMMODATIONS **Phone:** (843)686-6662 **15**

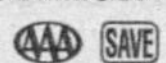

Vacation Rental Condominium

$99-$219 All Year

Address: 801 Ocean Cove Club **Location:** Jct US 278 business route/Queens Folly Rd, 0.9 mi se on Queens Folly Rd to Mooring Buoy, then just ne; in Palmetto Dunes. **Facility:** These villas offer private balconies overlooking lagoon or forest views and are convenient to Shelter Cove Marina Village. 12 condominiums. 2 stories (no elevator), exterior corridors. **Parking:** on-site. **Terms:** office hours 9 am-5 pm, off-site registration, check-in 5 pm, 45 day cancellation notice-fee imposed. **Amenities:** CD players, voice mail, irons. **Pool(s):** outdoor. **Leisure Activities:** whirlpool, 2 tennis courts, bicycles, playground. *Fee:* golf-27 holes. **Guest Services:** complimentary laundry. **Business Services:** PC, fax (fee). **Cards:** DS, MC, VI. **Free Special Amenities: local telephone calls and high-speed Internet.**

PARK LANE HOTEL & SUITES *Book great rates at AAA.com* **Phone:** (843)686-5700 **23**

Hotel

$89-$179 All Year

Address: 12 Park Ln **Location:** 10 mi of J Wilton Graves Bridge on US 278 business route. Located in Central Park Complex. **Facility:** Smoke free premises. 156 units. 112 one-bedroom standard units with kitchens. 44 one-bedroom suites with kitchens. 3 stories, interior corridors. *Bath:* combo or shower only. **Parking:** on-site. **Terms:** check-in 4 pm, cancellation fee imposed. **Amenities:** video games (fee), dual phone lines, voice mail, irons, hair dryers. *Some:* high-speed Internet. **Pool(s):** outdoor. **Leisure Activities:** whirlpool, putting green, 2 lighted tennis courts, barbecue grill, picnic tables, playground, limited exercise equipment, basketball. *Fee:* bicycles. **Guest Services:** valet and coin laundry, wireless Internet. **Business Services:** meeting rooms, business center. **Cards:** AX, DC, DS, MC, VI. *(See color ad p 1081)*

/ SOME UNITS FEE

(See map and index starting on p. 1068)

PLANTATION CLUB VILLAS

Vacation Rental Condominium

For rates and additional information, visit AAA.com 53

Location: Jct Greenwood Dr/Lighthouse Rd, just se on Greenwood dr; in Sea Pines Resort. **Overview:** Most units have fairway and lagoon views and all are a five to seven minute walk to the ocean. The three bedroom units are two-level townhomes. 33 units.

AAA SAVE **The Sea Pines Resort:** 32 Greenwood Dr, Hilton Head Island. 843/785-3333
ResortQuest Hilton Head: 21 Pope Ave Executive Park Rd, Hilton Head Island 843/842-3006

QUALITY INN & SUITES OF HILTON HEAD ISLAND *Book at AAA.com* **Phone:** (843)681-3655 3

Hotel
$59-$139 All Year

Address: 200 Museum St **Location:** 3.3 mi e of J Wilton Graves Bridge on US 278 business route. **Facility:** 127 units. 113 one-bedroom standard units. 14 one-bedroom suites with efficiencies. 3 stories, exterior corridors. **Parking:** on-site. **Terms:** check-in 4 pm, cancellation fee imposed. **Amenities:** safes, irons, hair dryers. **Pool(s):** outdoor. **Leisure Activities:** putting green, bicycles. **Guest Services:** valet and coin laundry, wireless Internet. **Business Services:** meeting rooms, business center. **Cards:** AX, CB, DC, DS, JC, MC, VI.

ASK / SOME UNITS FEE

QUEENS GRANT VILLAS

Vacation Rental Condominium

For rates and additional information, visit AAA.com 12

Location: Jct US 278 business route/Queens Folly Rd, just se on Queens Folly Rd; in Palmetto Dunes Resort. **Overview:** The quaintly clustered villas offer either fairway, pool or natural views. The units have spacious floor plans with private patios and decks. 28 units.

AAA SAVE **Coastal Home and Hilton Head Vacation Rentals:** 430 William Hilton Pkwy, Suite 504, Hilton Head Island. 843/689-3010
ResortQuest Hilton Head: 21 Pope Ave Executive Park Rd, Hilton Head Island. 843/842-3006

RED ROOF INN-HILTON HEAD *Book great rates at AAA.com* **Phone:** (843)686-6808 11

AAA SAVE

Motel
$50-$105 All Year

Address: 5 Regency Pkwy **Location:** Over bridge, 9 mi e on US 278 business route; between Shipyard Plantation and Palmetto Dunes. **Facility:** 111 units. 107 one-bedroom standard units. 4 one-bedroom suites. 2 stories (no elevator), exterior corridors. **Parking:** on-site. **Amenities:** video games (fee), voice mail. *Some:* irons. **Pool(s):** outdoor. **Guest Services:** wireless Internet. **Business Services:** fax (fee). **Cards:** AX, CB, DC, DS, MC, VI. **Free Special Amenities: local telephone calls.**

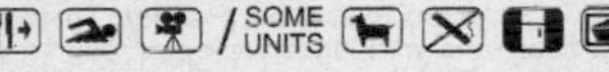

ST. ANDREWS COMMON VILLAS

Vacation Rental Condominium

For rates and additional information, visit AAA.com 10

Location: Jct US 278 business route/Queens Folly Rd, just se on Queens Folly Rd; in Palmetto Dunes Resort. **Overview:** The contemporary low-rise villas on lushly landscaped grounds overlook a golf course. French doors open to a wraparound deck. 29 units.

AAA SAVE **Coastal Home and Hilton Head Vacation Rentals:** 430 William Hilton Pkwy, Suite 504, Hilton Head Island. 843/689-3010
ResortQuest Hilton Head: 21 Pope Ave Executive Park Rd, Hilton Head Island. 843/842-3006

▼ *See AAA listing p 1080* ▼

(See map and index starting on p. 1068)

SEACREST VILLAS

Vacation Rental Condominium

For rates and additional information, visit AAA.com 41

Location: Jct Coligny Plaza/Forest Beach Dr, just n; in Forest Beach area. **Overview:** This beautifully landscaped oceanfront units offer covered parking and an interior promenade. Baths feature garden tubs with separate stand-up showers. 38 units.

AAA SAVE **Coastal Home and Hilton Head Vacation Rentals:** 430 William Hilton Pkwy, Suite 504, Hilton Head Island. 843/689-3010

AAA SAVE **The Sea Pines Resort:** 32 Greenwood Dr, Hilton Head Island. 843/785-3333

ResortQuest Hilton Head: 21 Pope Ave Executive Park Rd, Hilton Head Island. 843/842-3006

SHOREWOOD VILLAS

Vacation Rental Condominium

For rates and additional information, visit AAA.com 44

Location: Jct Coligny Plaza/Forest Beach Dr, just s. **Overview:** The oceanfront complex is in a private gated community offering covered and open parking and lushly landscaped grounds. All units are individually decorated and offer large balconies. 35 units.

AAA SAVE **Coastal Home and Hilton Head Vacation Rentals:** 430 William Hilton Pkwy, Suite 504, Hilton Head Island. 843/689-3010

ResortQuest Hilton Head: 21 Pope Ave Executive Park Rd, Hilton Head Island. 843/842-3006

SOUTH BEACH CLUB VILLAS-RESORTQUEST HILTON HEAD

Phone: (843)842-3006 57

Vacation Rental Condominium

$1225-$2375 All Year

Address: 1905 S Beach Club Villas **Location:** Coligny Plaza, 5.3 mi sw on S Forest Beach/Sea Pines drs; in South Beach area of Sea Pines Resort on Calipogue Sound. **Facility:** Located on the sound, each unit offers lush natural landscaping, whirlpool in the master bath and seasonal access to the beachfront pool. 10 condominiums. 4 stories, exterior corridors. **Parking:** on-site. **Terms:** office hours 9 am-5 pm, off-site registration, check-in 4 pm, 3-7 night minimum stay - seasonal, cancellation fee imposed. **Amenities:** irons. **Pool(s):** outdoor. **Guest Services:** complimentary laundry. **Business Services:** fax (fee). **Cards:** AX, DS, MC, VI.

ASK CALL VCR

SOUTHWIND II VILLAS-HILTON HEAD ACCOMMODATIONS

Phone: (843)686-6662 26

AAA SAVE

Vacation Rental Condominium

$109-$220 All Year

Address: 2001 Southwind II **Location:** Jct US 278 business route/Shipyard Dr, 0.4 mi se on Shipyard Dr, then 0.7 mi ne on Kingston Rd; in Shipyard Plantation. **Facility:** These individually decorated villas and townhomes offer a variety of floorplans with lagoon and golf course views. 24 condominiums. 2 stories (no elevator), exterior corridors. **Parking:** on-site. **Terms:** office hours 9 am-5 pm, off-site registration, check-in 5 pm, 45 day cancellation notice-fee imposed. **Amenities:** CD players, voice mail, irons. **Pool(s):** outdoor. **Leisure Activities:** whirlpool, 2 tennis courts, bicycles, playground. *Fee:* golf-27 holes. **Guest Services:** complimentary laundry. **Business Services:** PC, fax (fee). **Cards:** DS, MC, VI. **Free Special Amenities: local telephone calls and high-speed Internet.**

VCR

SPINNAKER VILLAS-HILTON HEAD ACCOMMODATIONS

Phone: (843)686-6662 34

AAA SAVE

Vacation Rental Condominium

$109-$220 All Year

Address: 101 Spinnaker Villas **Location:** Jct US 278 business route/Shipyard Dr, 1.1 mi se to Barcelona Dr, then just sw; in Shipyard Plantation. **Facility:** These award-winning, professionally designed villas offer golf course views from their large private decks. 48 condominiums. 2 stories (no elevator), exterior corridors. **Parking:** on-site. **Terms:** office hours 9 am-5 pm, off-site registration, check-in 5 pm, 45 day cancellation notice-fee imposed. **Amenities:** CD players, voice mail, irons. **Pool(s):** outdoor. **Leisure Activities:** whirlpool, 2 tennis courts, bicycles, playground. *Fee:* golf-27 holes. **Guest Services:** complimentary laundry. **Business Services:** PC, fax (fee). **Cards:** DS, MC. **Free Special Amenities: local telephone calls and high-speed Internet.**

VCR

STONEY CREEK VILLAS - THE SEA PINES RESORT

Phone: (843)785-3333 45

AAA SAVE

Vacation Rental Condominium

$140-$270 All Year

Address: 238 Stoney Creek **Location:** Sea Pines Cir, 2.8 mi sw on Greenwood/Plantation drs to Lighthouse Rd, then just nw; in Sea Pine Resort, near Harbour Town. **Facility:** Start and end your day by relaxing on the private balcony found in each of the one- and two-bedroom walk-up condominiums. 26 condominiums. 3 stories (no elevator), exterior corridors. **Parking:** on-site. **Terms:** office hours 6:30 am-10 pm, off-site registration, check-in 4 pm, 2 night minimum stay - weekends, 21 day cancellation notice-fee imposed. **Amenities:** voice mail, irons. **Pool(s):** outdoor. **Leisure Activities:** rental boats, recreation programs, hiking trails, jogging, spa. *Fee:* sailboats, marina, waterskiing, fishing, charter fishing, kayaking, parasailing, golf-54 holes, 23 lighted tennis courts, hay rides, eco tours, bicycles, horseback riding. **Guest Services:** complimentary laundry. **Business Services:** administrative services, fax (fee). **Cards:** AX, DC, DS, MC, VI.

TURTLE LANE CLUB VILLAS-RESORTQUEST HILTON HEAD

Phone: (843)842-3006 55

Vacation Rental Condominium

$1575-$3475 All Year

Address: 1 Turtle Ln **Location:** Oceanfront. Coligny Plaza, 2.5 mi sw on S Forest Beach/Sea Pines drs; in Sea Pines Resort. **Facility:** The townhouse-style villas are set on a lagoon amid lush landscaping; all offer a center atrium, large living rooms and a deck overlooking the lagoon. 21 condominiums. 2 stories (no elevator), exterior corridors. **Parking:** on-site. **Terms:** office hours 9 am-5 pm, off-site registration, check-in 4 pm, 5-7 night minimum stay - seasonal, cancellation fee imposed. **Amenities:** irons. **Pool(s):** 2 outdoor. **Guest Services:** complimentary laundry. **Business Services:** fax (fee). **Cards:** AX, DS, MC, VI.

(See map and index starting on p. 1068)

THE VILLAGE AT PALMETTO DUNES-HILTON HEAD ACCOMMODATIONS *Book great rates at AAA.com* **Phone:** (843)842-4649 **13**

Vacation Rental Condominium

$89-$220 All Year

Address: 10 Trent Jones Ln **Location:** Jct US 278 business route/Queens Folly Rd, 0.7 mi se on Queens Folly Rd; in Palmetto Dunes Plantation; adjacent Trent Jones Tennis and Golf Center. **Facility:** Studio to three-bedroom cottages are nestled near golf and tennis facilities. 62 condominiums. 1-3 stories (no elevator), exterior corridors. **Parking:** on-site. **Terms:** office hours 9 am-5 pm, check-in 5 pm, 45 day cancellation notice-fee imposed. **Amenities:** DVD players, voice mail, irons, hair dryers. **Pool(s):** outdoor. **Leisure Activities:** whirlpool, golf & tennis privileges. **Guest Services:** complimentary laundry, wireless Internet. **Business Services:** fax (fee). **Cards:** DS, MC, VI. **Free Special Amenities: local telephone calls and high-speed Internet.**

VILLAMARE VILLAS

Vacation Rental Condominium

For rates and additional information, visit AAA.com **20**

Location: Jct US 278 business route/Queens Folly Rd, 0.9 mi se to Ocean Ln, then just s; in Palmetto Dunes Plantation. **Overview:** Three towers offer ocean views and an oceanfront pool, while paved walkways meander through flowering gardens and over lagoons. All units provide private balconies. 42 units.

Coastal Home and Hilton Head Vacation Rentals: 430 William Hilton Pkwy, Suite 504, Hilton Head Island. 843/689-3010

ResortQuest Hilton Head: 21 Pope Ave Executive Park Rd, Hilton Head Island. 843/842-3006

WATERSIDE BY SPINNAKER *Book at AAA.com* **Phone:** 843/341-8850 **36**

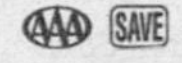

Vacation Rental Condominium

Rates not provided

Address: 45 Waterside Dr **Location:** Jct Sea Pines Cir/Pope Ave, 0.9 mi se on Pope Ave, then just ne. **Facility:** The semi-private complex is located between the restaurant section of the island and the ocean; units offer a contemporary decor and plenty of room. 198 condominiums. 2-5 stories, exterior corridors. *Bath:* combo or shower only. **Parking:** on-site. **Terms:** office hours 8:30 am-10 pm, check-in 4 pm. **Amenities:** DVD players, voice mail, irons, hair dryers. **Pool(s):** outdoor. **Leisure Activities:** whirlpool, recreation programs, game room. **Guest Services:** complimentary laundry, wireless Internet. **Business Services:** fax (fee).

/ SOME UNITS VCR

WESTIN HILTON HEAD ISLAND RESORT & SPA *Book great rates at AAA.com* **Phone:** (843)681-4000 **4**

Resort Hotel

$119-$489 All Year

Address: Two Grass Lawn Ave **Location:** 5.6 mi from J Wilton Graves Bridge on US 278 business route to Coggins Point Rd, then just e, follow signs. Located in Port Royal Plantation. **Facility:** Sculptured gardens, a swan pond and ocean views add interest to this property; of special note is the ornately decorated rotunda sitting room. Smoke free premises. 412 units. 405 one-bedroom standard units. 7 one-bedroom suites, some with kitchens and/or whirlpools. 5 stories, interior corridors. *Bath:* combo or shower only. **Parking:** on-site and valet. **Terms:** check-in 4 pm. **Amenities:** high-speed Internet, dual phone lines, voice mail, safes, honor bars, irons, hair dryers. *Some:* DVD players (fee), CD players. **Pool(s):** 2 outdoor, heated indoor. **Leisure Activities:** saunas, whirlpool, steamrooms, recreation programs in summer, rental bicycles, jogging, playground, spa, volleyball. *Fee:* sailboats, windsurfing, charter fishing, aqua aerobics, kayaking, golf-54 holes, 16 tennis courts (6 lighted), kids night out, kids camp, yoga. **Guest Services:** valet laundry, area transportation-tennis, golf, shopping, wireless Internet. **Business Services:** conference facilities, business center. **Cards:** AX, CB, DC, DS, JC, MC, VI. ***(See color ad below)***

WESTIN HOTELS & RESORTS

AAA Benefit:

Enjoy up to 15% off your next stay, plus Starwood Preferred Guest® bonuses.

24 / SOME UNITS FEE VCR

▼ See AAA listing above ▼

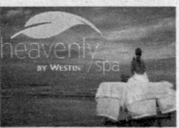

(See map and index starting on p. 1068)

WINDSOR COURT VILLAS-RESORTQUEST HILTON HEAD

Vacation Rental Condominium

Rates not provided

Phone: 843/842-3006 (25)

Address: 4101 Windsor Ct **Location:** Oceanfront. Jct US 278 business route/Queens Folly Rd, 0.9 mi s on Queens Folly Rd to Ocean Ln, then 0.7 mi sw; in Palmetto Dunes. **Facility:** Oceanfront villas offer barbecue and entertainment area, covered parking, winding walkways and ocean views from private balconies. 50 condominiums. 5 stories, exterior corridors. **Parking:** on-site. **Terms:** office hours 9 am-5 pm, off-site registration, check-in 4 pm. **Pool(s):** outdoor. **Leisure Activities:** whirlpool, playground. **Guest Services:** complimentary laundry. **Business Services:** fax (fee).

CALL VCR

WHERE TO DINE

ALEXANDER'S *Menu on AAA.com*

AAA

Steak & Seafood

$14-$49

Phone: 843/785-4999 (8)

Distinctively decorated with glistening vintage Harley-Davidsons, the casual tiered restaurant on the water provides legendary service. Award-winning wines are paired with superior cuisine from a well-rounded menu. Representative of professionally prepared and exquisitely presented dishes are Neptune's seafood platter, Wiener schnitzel, rack of lamb and roasted duck. The island mainstay has treated patrons to relaxed evenings out since 1977. Casual dress. **Bar:** Full bar. **Reservations:** suggested. **Hours:** 5 pm-10 pm. Closed: 11/26, 12/24, 12/25. **Address:** 76 Queens Folly Rd **Location:** J Wilton Graves Bridge, 8.5 mi e, 0.8 mi s on Queens Folly Rd; in Palmetto Dunes. **Parking:** on-site. **Cards:** AX, DC, DS, MC, VI.

ALLIGATOR GRILLE SEAFOOD RESTAURANT AND SUSHI BAR

New American

$17-$34

Phone: 843/842-4888 (22)

The mode here: "an eclectic mood with sophisticated food." Included among upscale dishes are preparations of seafood, vegetarian dishes, steaks, chops and, of course, alligator. You can watch your choice being prepared at the chef's bar or relax over offerings of sushi. Folks seek out this place for casually refined dining. Casual dress. **Bar:** Full bar. **Reservations:** suggested. **Hours:** Open 12/15-1/1 & 1/14-11/30; 4:45 pm-10 pm, Fri & Sat-11 pm. Closed: 1/1. **Address:** 33 Office Park Rd, Suite #229 **Location:** Jct Sea Pines Cir/Greenwood Dr, just w on Greenwood Dr to Office Park Rd, then just s; in Park Plaza Shopping Center. **Parking:** on-site. **Cards:** AX, DC, DS, MC, VI.

CALL

AMIGOS CAFE 'Y CANTINA

Mexican

$4-$8

Phone: 843/785-8226 (25)

This small, cozy cantina takes an informal approach, serving authentic dishes from the Coast of Baja on paper plates and plastic utensils. Feast on huge portions in a colorful whirl of sombreros, Mexican blankets, bullfight posters and Baja beach scenes. Casual dress. **Bar:** Full bar. **Hours:** 11 am-9 pm. Closed: 11/26. **Address:** 70 Pope Ave **Location:** Sea Pines Cir, 0.8 mi se; in The Circle Center. **Parking:** on-site. **Cards:** MC, VI.

ANTONIO'S *Menu on AAA.com*

AAA

Italian

$17-$38

Phone: 843/842-5505 (15)

This small Italian eatery is nestled among many shops in the Wexford Plaza. Large selections of wine are displayed behind glass. Dark mahogany accents and upscale decor create a wonderful dining ambience. The food presentation is imaginative and fun. Entrees from different regions of Italy are featured monthly as well as Mediterranean dishes. Dressy casual. Entertainment. **Bar:** Full bar. **Reservations:** suggested. **Hours:** 5:30 pm-10 pm; 5 pm-9:30 pm 12/1-2/29. Closed: 12/25. **Address:** Village of Wexford, G-2 **Location:** Sea Pines Cir, 0.5 mi e on US 278 business route. **Parking:** on-site. **Cards:** AX, DC, DS, MC, VI.

AUNT CHILADAS "EASY STREET CAFE"

American

$8-$27

Phone: 843/785-7700 (26)

Talk about diversity. The laid-back restaurant's menu features Southwestern, American, Italian and Mexican favorites, with everything from meatball subs and lasagna to Alaskan snow crab and chimichangas. The large bar is a favorite haunt for the beach crowd. Casual dress. **Bar:** Full bar. **Reservations:** accepted. **Hours:** 11:30 am-11 pm, Fri & Sat-midnight. Closed: 11/26, 12/24, 12/25. **Address:** 69 Pope Ave **Location:** Jct Coligny Cir/Pope Ave, just nw. **Parking:** on-site. **Cards:** AX, CB, DS, MC, VI.

BONEFISH GRILL

Seafood

$13-$20

Phone: 843/341-3772 (9)

Fish is the house specialty, and the menu and nightly specials offer a variety of choices. Well-prepared food is cooked to perfection. Service is casual in nature, and the staff is skilled and attentive. Casual dress. **Bar:** Full bar. **Hours:** 4 pm-close. Closed: 11/26, 12/25. **Address:** 890 William Hilton Pkwy, Suite 74 **Location:** 9.8 mi e of J Wilton Graves Bridge on US 278 business route; in Fresh Market Shoppes. **Parking:** on-site. **Cards:** AX, DC, DS, MC, VI.

CALL

CATCH 22

Steak & Seafood

$12-$42

Phone: 843/785-6261 (18)

Menu offerings at the casual restaurant include fresh seafood, USDA prime beef, chops and pasta as well as low-carbohydrate selections. A diverse wine list is available with selections from Europe, Australia and California. Casual dress. **Bar:** Full bar. **Reservations:** accepted. **Hours:** 5 pm-10 pm. Closed: 12/25; also Super Bowl Sun. **Address:** 37 New Orleans Rd, Suite K **Location:** Sea Pines Cir, just se on Pope Ave to New Orleans Rd; in Orleans Plaza. **Parking:** on-site. **Cards:** AX, MC, VI.

CHARLEY'S CRAB HILTON HEAD

Seafood

$8-$40

Phone: 843/342-9066 (2)

From the beautifully landscaped exterior to the well-appointed interior, this spot just over the bridge from Bluffton affords waterway views from both indoors and out. The lengthy seasonal menu features fresh local seafood, including shrimp from the dock behind the restaurant; vegetables purchased from local farms; aged beef; and homemade pastas. The delicious Charley's chowder—a Mediterranean-style tomato-based fish chowder—is a nice departure from cream-based soups. Casual dress. **Bar:** Full bar. **Reservations:** suggested, in season. **Hours:** 11 am-9:30 pm, Sun-9 pm. **Address:** Two Hudson Rd **Location:** J Wilton Graves Bridge, 1.8 mi e on US 278 business route to Squire Pope Rd, then 1.4 mi n. **Parking:** on-site. **Cards:** AX, DC, DS, MC, VI.

CALL

(See map and index starting on p. 1068)

CHARLIE'S L'ETOILE VERTE — **Phone:** 843/785-9277 (16)

French
$9-$39

Interesting and exciting flavors and ingredient combinations make for an intriguing daily changing menu of mostly seafood and lamb specialties. Representative of the fare are such dishes as salmon au citron and filet mignon bousin au poire beurre. Eclectic decor recalls the French country style. Casual dress. **Bar:** Full bar. **Reservations:** suggested. **Hours:** 11:30 am-2 & 6-9:30 pm, Mon from 6 pm. Closed major holidays; also Sun. **Address:** 8 New Orleans Rd **Location:** 0.6 mi ne of Sea Pines Cir on US 278 business route, just se. **Parking:** on-site. **Cards:** AX, DS, MC, VI.

CONROY'S — **Phone:** 843/686-8499 (11)

American
$17-$36

Overlooking the ocean, the restaurant treats guests to original steak and seafood creations prepared in the exhibition kitchen. The wine list is lengthy. Oak-smoked pork chops in lingonberry jus and flourless chocolate cake are favorites. Dressy casual. **Bar:** Full bar. **Reservations:** suggested. **Hours:** 5:30 pm-10:30 pm, Sun also 10 am-2 pm. **Address:** One Hotel Cir **Location:** 8.5 mi e from J Wilton Graves Bridge on US 278 business route, then 1.2 mi se on Queens Folly Rd; in Palmetto Dunes; in Hilton Head Marriott Resort & Spa. **Parking:** on-site and valet. **Cards:** AX, CB, DC, DS, JC, MC, VI.

CALL

C Q'S RESTAURANT *Menu on AAA.com* — **Phone:** 843/671-2779 (32)

American
$19-$30

Diners enjoy a memorable experience at this charming restaurant, which brims with memorabilia of a bygone era. The menu offers mostly traditional selections, such as Australian rack of lamb. However, more adventurous palates may appreciate the smattering of progressive preparations, including the delicious venison in leek shallot Madeira reduction. Also offered are an extensive wine and martini list and tempting desserts. Dressy casual. **Bar:** Full bar. **Reservations:** suggested. **Hours:** 5:30 pm-10 pm; 5 pm-9:30 pm 10/1-2/28. Closed: Super Bowl Sun. **Address:** 140 Lighthouse Rd **Location:** At Harbour Town; in Sea Pines Plantation. **Parking:** on-site. **Cards:** AX, DC, DS, MC, VI.

CRANE'S TAVERN & STEAKHOUSE RESTAURANT *Menu on AAA.com* — **Phone:** 843/341-2333 (17)

Steak & Seafood
$20-$46

The Crane family brings a 70-year tradition to the island. The cozy, English-style pub and open, Colonial-style dining room give the restaurant an Old Philadelphia atmosphere. All dishes are prepared in house and there is a full selection of steak cuts for every appetite. Prime rib is the local favorite but seafood lovers won't be disappointed. Service is friendly and professional. Dressy casual. **Bar:** Full bar. **Reservations:** suggested. **Hours:** 5 pm-10 pm. Closed: 11/26, 12/25. **Address:** 26 New Orleans Rd **Location:** Sea Pines Cir, just s on Pope Ave, then 0.4 mi ne. **Parking:** on-site. **Cards:** AX, MC, VI.

DEL VECCHIO'S RESTAURANT & PIZZERIA — **Phone:** 843/842-8700 (10)

Italian
$11-$18

Homemade Italian cuisine is served in the strip-mall pizzeria, which also boasts serving the largest pizzas on the island. Casual dress. **Hours:** 11:30 am-3 & 5-close. Closed major holidays; also Sun. **Address:** 890 William Hilton Pkwy, Suite 1 **Location:** 9.8 mi e of J Wilton Graves Bridge on US 278 business route; in Fresh Market Shoppes. **Parking:** on-site. **Cards:** MC, VI.

FLAVORS — **Phone:** 843/785-3115 (27)

New American
$18-$32

The chef/owner has trained and cooked in world-class restaurants around the globe and has brought his finely tuned talents to the beach. The chef's adept range is reflected in such distinctive culinary delights as churrasco Argentino, Yucatan-style red snapper, paella, saku tuna and many others. Each dish is expertly prepared and then presented by a talented floor staff. Casual dress. **Bar:** Full bar. **Reservations:** suggested. **Hours:** 5 pm-10 pm, Fri & Sat-11 pm. Closed: 1/1, 11/26, 12/25. **Address:** 81 Pope Ave **Location:** Jct Coligny Cir and Pope Ave, just nw; in Heritage Plaza. **Parking:** on-site. **Cards:** AX, DS, MC, VI.

CALL

FLORA'S ITALIAN CAFE *Menu on AAA.com* — **Phone:** 843/842-8200 (7)

Italian
$17-$28

On the family-run restaurant's menu are Italian veal, pasta and seafood dishes prepared with a Continental flair, as well as award-winning desserts made daily by pastry chef and cafe namesake Flora. Casual dress. **Bar:** Full bar. **Reservations:** accepted. **Hours:** 5 pm-10 pm. Closed: Sun. **Address:** 841 William Hilton Pkwy **Location:** 9.1 mi e of J Wilton Graves Bridge on US 278 business route; in South Island Square. **Parking:** on-site. **Cards:** AX, MC, VI.

CALL

THE HARBOUR TOWN GRILL — **Phone:** 843/363-8380 (33)

American
$11-$45

In the Harbour Town Club House, the small, upscale restaurant overlooks the fairways of the famous Heritage Classic. Dinner presentation, preparation and taste are outstanding, and views from the abundant windows make for a relaxing experience. The diverse menu has offerings for all tastes, including pinwheel of Atlantic salmon, roast rack of Australian lamb and chateaubriand. Casual dress. **Bar:** Full bar. **Reservations:** suggested. **Hours:** 7 am-3 & 5-9 pm. **Address:** 11 Lighthouse Ln **Location:** 2.8 mi sw of Sea Pines Cir via Greenwood and Plantation drs, just nw; in The Inn at Harbour Town. **Parking:** on-site and valet. **Cards:** AX, CB, DC, DS, JC, MC, VI.

CALL

(See map and index starting on p. 1068)

HILTON HEAD DINER
Phone: 843/686-2400 (6)

American
$5-$17

Take a trip back in time at this popular, traditional diner, where a mini juke box is the centerpiece of each booth. Offering an extensive breakfast, lunch and dinner menu, you'll find yourself indecisive as you scan over 750 selections. Around-the-clock offerings include homemade soups, fresh seafood, gourmet Italian cuisine and steak. Casual dress. **Bar:** Full bar. **Hours:** 24 hours. **Address:** 6 Marina Side Dr **Location:** 10.4 mi e of J Wilton Graves Bridge on US 278 business route. **Parking:** on-site. **Cards:** AX, DS, MC, VI.

CALL

HUGO'S AT WEXFORD
Phone: 843/785-4846 (13)

Regional American
$6-$33

The owner personally greets each guest and provides personalized service to ensure a pleasurable experience. The menu is bursting with local favorites and specials like steak Hugo, rack of lamb, Debbie's crabcakes, chateaubriand for two and fresh-off-the-dock seafood. A long, fresh dessert menu with many tableside flambeed selections is available as is a children's menu. Takeout is offered for most menu items. Casual dress. **Bar:** Full bar. **Reservations:** accepted. **Hours:** 11:30 am-4 & 4:30-10 pm. Closed: 11/26, 12/25. **Address:** 1000 William Hilton Pkwy, Suite J6 **Location:** Jct Sea Pines Cir/US 278 business route, 0.5 mi ne on US 278 business route; in The Village of Wexford. **Parking:** on-site. **Cards:** AX, DS, MC, VI.

THE JAZZ CORNER *Menu on AAA.com*
Phone: 843/842-8620 (14)

American
$22-$36

Arrive early and plan on staying late. The Jazz Corner is a one-seating restaurant since patrons tend to dine then stay for the evening's musical talent. Seatings start at 5 pm, 6 pm during the off-season, and the music typically starts around 7:30 pm. The menu is diverse enough to offer Thai curry seafood, crispy flounder, wiener schnitzel and egg rolls. There is a one entree or two appetizer minimum per patron, which is very little given the quality of the entertainment and food. Casual dress. **Bar:** Full bar. **Reservations:** suggested. **Hours:** 6 pm-11 pm. Closed: 12/25. **Address:** 1000 William Hilton Pkwy, Suite C1 **Location:** Jct Sea Pines Cir/US 278 business route, 0.5 mi ne on US 278 business route; in The Village of Wexford. **Parking:** on-site. **Cards:** MC, VI.

JULEPS
Phone: 843/842-5857 (21)

Regional American
$8-$31

The upscale restaurant boasts a Southern menu of fine, well-prepared selections including Dixie cornmeal flounder, trout N'awlins, duck with peach-ginger sauce and Deep South derby pie. Expect to find gracious hospitality with a Southern flair. Dressy casual. **Bar:** Full bar. **Reservations:** suggested. **Hours:** 11:30 am-2 & 5:30-10 pm, Sat & Sun from 5:30 pm. Closed: 12/25. **Address:** 14 Greenwood Dr, Suite 104 **Location:** Sea Pines Cir, just e; in The Gallery of Shops. **Parking:** on-site. **Cards:** AX, MC, VI.

CALL

KINGFISHER SEAFOOD RESTAURANT
Phone: 843/785-4442 (5)

Steak & Seafood
$8-$26

If you time it right, you'll enjoy a splendid sunset over Shelter Cove Harbor as you savor such seafood favorites as a succulent lobster tail served with steamed vegetables and a baked potato. Casual dress. Entertainment. **Bar:** Full bar. **Reservations:** accepted. **Hours:** 5 pm-10 pm. Closed: 12/24, 12/25. **Address:** 18 Harbourside Ln **Location:** Off US 278, opposite Palmetto Dunes; in Shelter Cove Harbour. **Parking:** on-site. **Cards:** AX, DS, MC, VI.

MICHAEL ANTHONY'S CUCINA ITALIANA
Phone: 843/785-6272 (19)

Regional Italian
$18-$36

Classic and creative regional Italian dishes prepared with a contemporary touch set this cozy restaurant apart. An extensive wine selection complements nightly choices of homemade gnocchi, succulent veal, traditional pasta dishes and fresh fish. Creativity extends to the freshly made desserts, which provide a perfect finish to a great dining experience. Casual dress. **Bar:** Full bar. **Reservations:** suggested. **Hours:** 5:30 pm-10 pm. Closed major holidays; also Sun. **Address:** 37 New Orleans Rd, Suite L **Location:** Sea Pines Cir, just se on Pope Ave to Orleans Rd, just ne; in Orleans Plaza. **Parking:** on-site. **Cards:** AX, MC, VI.

OCEAN GRILLE
Phone: 843/785-3030 (4)

American
$18-$27

Nestled along the shore, splendid views can be enjoyed from all three dining levels. Featuring seafood entrees as well as a variety of meat and pasta, the menu offers New Zealand rack of lamb and oven-baked grouper as house specialties. Dressy casual. **Bar:** Full bar. **Reservations:** required. **Hours:** 5 pm-10 pm. Closed: 12/25. **Address:** 1 Shelter Cove Ln **Location:** Off US 278 across from Palmetto Dunes; on harbor; in Shelter Cove. **Parking:** on-site. **Cards:** AX, DC, DS, MC, VI.

OLD FORT PUB *Menu on AAA.com*
Phone: 843/681-2386 (1)

Continental
$14-$35

Carolina crab cakes, she-crab soup and artistically displayed courses such as crispy tender roasted duck confit, seared sea scallops with beurre blanc, caviar and sun-dried tomato cream and snow pea stack are just a sampling of the contemporary signature creations offered. The freshest possible ingredients are used in classic American dishes that show a Southern flair and Continental influences. Sinful homemade desserts, such as chocolate pecan pie, end a perfect evening. Dressy casual. **Bar:** Full bar. **Reservations:** suggested. **Hours:** 5 pm-10 pm; Sunday brunch 11 am-2 pm; hours vary off season. **Address:** 65 Skull Creek Dr **Location:** J Wilton Graves Bridge, 1.8 mi e on US 278 to Squire Pope Rd, then 2.2 mi n; in Hilton Head Plantation. **Parking:** on-site. **Cards:** AX, DC, DS, MC, VI.

THE OLD OYSTER FACTORY *Menu on AAA.com*
Phone: 843/681-6040 (3)

Seafood
$17-$30

As the name implies, the restaurant is located in a former oyster factory. The location affords diners views of the area's best sunsets over Broad Creek. Well-trained staff serve perfectly prepared entrees such as almond-crusted or peppered mahi mahi, whole Maine lobster or a juicy steak. Oyster lovers will appreciate an outstanding selection of tasty bivalves harvested as far away as Prince Edward Island and the Florida Gulf Coast. Casual dress. **Bar:** Full bar. **Hours:** 5 pm-10 pm; to 9 pm 12/1-1/31. Closed: 11/26, 12/25. **Address:** 101 Marshland Rd **Location:** 5 mi e of J Wilton Graves Bridge on US 278 business route to Matthews Rd, 0.6 mi s on Matthews Rd to Marshland Rd, then 1.1 mi w. **Parking:** on-site. **Cards:** AX, DC, DS, MC, VI.

CALL

(See map and index starting on p. 1068)

PLANTATION CAFE AND DELI **Phone:** 843/785-9020 (29)

American
$6-$9

Start your day with a hearty breakfast, especially any of the cafe's country-style, blue-plate specials. Service is efficient at the family-friendly diner. Casual dress. **Bar:** Full bar. **Hours:** 6:30 am-3 pm, Sun 7:30 am-close. Closed: 11/26, 12/25. **Address:** 81 Pope Ave, Suite 14A **Location:** Sea Pines Cir, 0.9 mi se on Pope Ave; in Heritage Plaza. **Parking:** on-site. **Cards:** AX, DS, MC, VI.

RED FISH RESTAURANT *Menu on AAA.com* **Phone:** 843/686-3388 (12)

Cuban
$9-$32

As you enter through the retail wine shop, purchase a bottle and have it served with your dinner. Menu selections include swordfish steak with avocado mango salsa, sweet guava chicken and scallops with mango and jalapeno. For pickier eaters, entrees can be ordered naked—grilled with only extra virgin olive oil. The casually, elegant dining room is airy and comfortable. Dressy casual. **Bar:** Full bar. **Reservations:** suggested. **Hours:** 11:30 am-2 & 5-10 pm, Sun from 5 pm; hours vary off season. Closed: 12/25; also Super Bowl Sun. **Address:** 8 Archer Rd **Location:** Sea Pines Cir, 0.4 mi nw on US 278. **Parking:** on-site. **Cards:** AX, DS, MC, VI.

CALL

SAGE ROOM **Phone:** 843/785-5352 (28)

New American
$20-$38

Steaks, chops and seafood, in addition to a wide variety of nightly chef's specials, draw on influences from around the world. You'll appreciate not only the great flavors but also the striking presentations. Encrusted tuna or grouper, coconut mahi mahi, rack of lamb and roasted pork tenderloin give you an idea of the specialties, and the scrumptious made-from-scratch desserts taste great with a dessert wine or single malt. Casual dress. **Bar:** Full bar. **Reservations:** suggested. **Hours:** 6 pm-10 pm. Closed: 1/1, 11/26, 12/24, 12/25; also Sun. **Address:** 13 Heritage Plaza **Location:** Jct Coligny Cir and Pope Ave, just nw; in Heritage Plaza. **Parking:** on-site. **Cards:** AX, MC, VI.

CALL

THE SMOKEHOUSE **Phone:** 843/842-4227 (30)

American
$6-$21

House-smoked barbecue ribs, Texas-style beef brisket, strip steaks and burgers tempt you at this rustic bar and restaurant, located across from the beach. Come casual and you'll be right at home. Casual dress. **Bar:** Full bar. **Reservations:** not accepted. **Hours:** 11:30 am-10 pm. Closed: 11/26, 12/25. **Address:** 102 Pope Ave **Location:** Jct Coligny Cir and Pope Ave, just nw. **Parking:** on-site. **Cards:** AX, MC, VI.

STICKY FINGERS RIB HOUSE **Phone:** 843/686-7427

Barbecue
$7-$26

Diners can put down their silverware and get their fingers ready for classic Carolina sweet ribs, as well as ribs cooked in the Texas and Tennessee styles. Hearty sides of baked beans and coleslaw complement entrees at the friendly cafe. Casual dress. **Bar:** Full bar. **Hours:** 11 am-close. Closed: 11/26, 12/25. **Address:** 34 Palmetto Bay Rd **Location:** Sea Pines Cir, just nw. **Parking:** on-site. **Cards:** AX, DC, DS, MC, VI.

CALL

THE STUDIO **Phone:** 843/785-6000 (24)

Continental
$20-$34

The hostess, a professional artist, takes time out during lulls to display her skills as a painter and sculptor. Completed pieces adorn the walls and shelves of the two dining rooms. Menu offerings include flounder and shrimp pad Thai, duck breast with prosciutto, venison chops and a bone-in "cowboy" ribeye. Specials are offered each evening and shouldn't be overlooked since that's where the chef's creative and experimental side shines. An early bird special is offered 5:30 pm to 6 pm. Casual dress. Entertainment. **Bar:** Full bar. **Reservations:** suggested. **Hours:** 5:30 pm-10 pm. Closed: 11/26, 12/25; also Sun & Mon. **Address:** 20 Executive Park Rd **Location:** Jct Sea Pines Cir/Pope Ave, 0.6 mi se on Pope Ave to Executive Park Rd, then just ne. **Parking:** on-site. **Cards:** MC, VI.

TOPSIDE AT THE QUARTERDECK **Phone:** 843/842-1999 (31)

American
$9-$32

The laid-back second-floor restaurant is directly beneath the Harbour Town Lighthouse and affords great views of Calibogue Sound. Although the menu focuses on creatively prepared seafood, the skilled staff can steer guests toward a few steak and pasta dishes. Particularly worthy of consideration are sauteed flounder, shrimp and grits and cracked pepper scallops. A children's menu is available. Casual dress. **Bar:** Full bar. **Reservations:** accepted. **Hours:** 5 pm-10 pm. Closed: 12/1-1/31. **Address:** 149 N Lighthouse Rd **Location:** In Sea Pines Resort, at Harbour Town Lighthouse. **Parking:** on-site. **Cards:** AX, DS, MC, VI.

TRINITY RESTAURANT & BAR **Phone:** 843/785-5070 (20)

Regional American
$10-$28

To cater to the bar crowd, there is a long list of interesting finger foods and tapas. For the serious diner, the menu features American, Italian and French influences. Entree selections include a 20-ounce porterhouse, penne a la vodka, roast duck, osso bucco, braised grouper and many others—all of which are accompanied by tasty and delicate sauces prepared by the professionally trained chef. Casual dress. **Bar:** Full bar. **Reservations:** accepted. **Hours:** 11 am-2 & 5-10 pm, Sat & Sun from 5 pm. Closed: 11/26, 12/25. **Address:** 14 Greenwood Dr, Suite 102 **Location:** Jct Sea Pines Cir/Greenwood Dr, just sw; in The Gallery of Shops. **Parking:** on-site. **Cards:** AX, DS, MC, VI.

TRUFFLES CAFE *Menu on AAA.com* **Phone:** 843/671-6136 (34)

American
$8-$26

The bustling restaurant serves seafood, pasta and homemade soups and bread. Try the salmon covered with barbecue and onion salsa served over a bed of couscous and pine nuts. Casual dress. **Bar:** Full bar. **Hours:** 11 am-10 pm. Closed: 11/26, 12/25. **Address:** 71 Lighthouse Rd, Sea Pines Center **Location:** 2.8 mi w of Sea Pines Cir, then just s; in Sea Pines Center. **Parking:** on-site. **Cards:** AX, DS, MC, VI.

CALL

(See map and index starting on p. 1068)

TWO ELEVEN PARK WINE BAR & BISTRO Phone: 843/686-5212 (23)

Regional American
$13-$30

Blending American, Southern and Italian influences, the restaurant's menu choices include boutique pizza and preparations of fresh seafood, pasta and meat. An extensive wine list of more than 75 selections is available, many are served by the glass. Casual dress. **Bar:** Full bar. **Reservations:** accepted. **Hours:** 5:30 pm-10 pm. Closed major holidays; also Sun. **Address:** 33 Office Park Rd, Suite 211 **Location:** Just se of Sea Pines Cir on Pope Ave; in Park Plaza Shopping Center. **Parking:** on-site. **Cards:** AX, DS, MC, VI.

CALL

IRMO pop. 11,039 (See map and index starting on p. 940)

WHERE TO STAY

EXTENDED STAY DELUXE (COLUMBIA-HARBISON) Book at AAA.com Phone: (803)781-8590 (52)

Extended Stay Hotel
$95-$105 All Year

Address: 1170 Kinley Rd **Location:** I-26, exit 102B, just e, then n. **Facility:** This contemporary property is geared toward the extended-stay traveler. 87 units. 75 one-bedroom standard units with efficiencies. 6 one- and 6 two-bedroom suites with efficiencies. 4 stories, interior corridors. *Bath:* combo or shower only. **Parking:** on-site. **Amenities:** DVD players, dual phone lines, voice mail, irons, hair dryers. **Pool(s):** outdoor. **Leisure Activities:** exercise room. **Guest Services:** valet and coin laundry, wireless Internet. **Business Services:** fax (fee). **Cards:** AX, CB, DC, DS, JC, MC, VI.

ASK CALL / SOME UNITS FEE

HYATT PLACE COLUMBIA/HARBISON Book great rates at AAA.com Phone: (803)407-1560 (51)

AAA SAVE

Hotel
$99-$219 All Year

Address: 1130 Kinley Rd **Location:** I-26, exit 102B, just e, then n. **Facility:** Smoke free premises. 127 one-bedroom standard units. 6 stories, interior corridors. *Bath:* combo or shower only. **Parking:** on-site. **Terms:** cancellation fee imposed. **Amenities:** voice mail, irons, hair dryers. *Some:* high-speed Internet, dual phone lines. **Pool(s):** outdoor. **Leisure Activities:** exercise room. **Guest Services:** valet and coin laundry, wireless Internet. **Business Services:** meeting rooms, business center. **Cards:** AX, CB, DC, DS, JC, MC, VI. **Free Special Amenities: continental breakfast and high-speed Internet.**

CALL

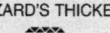

AAA Benefit:
Ask for the AAA rate and save 10%.

WHERE TO DINE

FATZ CAFE Phone: 803/781-5036

American
$8-$18

Friendly staff and appealing country decor help set the tone for a relaxed and enjoyable dining experience. It's not unusual for guests to wait to be seated at the popular spot, which earns raves for its well-prepared variations on chicken, steak, ribs and pasta, as well as salads and sandwiches. The signature Southern-style peach cobbler served with vanilla ice cream and walnuts is scrumptious. Casual dress. **Bar:** Full bar. **Hours:** 11 am-10 pm, Fri & Sat-11 pm, Sun-9 pm. Closed: 11/26, 12/25. **Address:** 7420 Broad River Rd **Location:** I-26, exit 101 (US 176), 0.4 mi e. **Parking:** on-site. **Cards:** AX, DS, MC, VI.

CALL

LIZARD'S THICKET Phone: 803/732-1225

Regional American
$3-$12

Owned and operated by the same family since 1978, guests can enjoy Southern home cooking at breakfast, lunch, and dinner. Locals love the Calabash style shrimp as well as the fried chicken livers. Be sure and ask about the daily specials which will allow guest a mixing and matching of main course with side dishes. Casual dress. **Hours:** 6 am-9 pm; to 10 pm seasonal. **Address:** 7569 St. Andrews Rd **Location:** I-26, exit 102A, 1.1 mi sw on SR 60, then just nw. **Parking:** on-site. **Cards:** MC, VI.

CALL

ISLE OF PALMS —See Charleston p. 910.

JOHNS ISLAND —See Charleston p. 914.

KIAWAH ISLAND —See Charleston p. 914.

KINGSTREE pop. 3,496

WHERE TO STAY

BEST WESTERN KINGSTREE Book great rates at AAA.com Phone: (843)355-5888

AAA SAVE

Motel
$68 All Year

Address: 1610 N Longstreet St **Location:** 1.6 mi n of center on US 52. **Facility:** 46 one-bedroom standard units, some with efficiencies and/or whirlpools. 2 stories (no elevator), interior corridors. *Bath:* combo or shower only. **Parking:** on-site. **Amenities:** irons, hair dryers. **Pool(s):** outdoor. **Leisure Activities:** grill and picnic area. *Fee:* game room. **Guest Services:** coin laundry, wireless Internet. **Business Services:** fax (fee). **Cards:** AX, CB, DC, DS, MC, VI. **Free Special Amenities: continental breakfast and high-speed Internet.**

/ SOME UNITS

AAA Benefit:
Members save up to 20%, plus 10% bonus points with rewards program.

LADSON —*See Charleston p. 917.*

LANCASTER pop. 8,177

WHERE TO STAY

BEST WESTERN-LANCASTER *Book great rates at AAA.com* **Phone:** (803)283-1200

Motel
$72-$77 All Year

Address: 1201 Hwy 9 Bypass **Location:** Jct SR 9 Bypass and US 521, 1.3 mi w on SR 9. **Facility:** 60 one-bedroom standard units, some with whirlpools. 2 stories (no elevator), exterior corridors. **Parking:** on-site. **Terms:** 3 day cancellation notice. **Amenities:** irons, hair dryers. **Pool(s):** outdoor. **Guest Services:** coin laundry, wireless Internet. **Business Services:** PC, fax (fee). **Cards:** AX, DC, DS, MC, VI. **Free Special Amenities: continental breakfast and high-speed Internet.**

/ SOME UNITS

AAA Benefit:
Members save up to 20%, plus 10% bonus points with rewards program.

JAMESON INN *Book at AAA.com* **Phone:** (803)283-1188

Motel
$73-$78 All Year

Address: 114 Commerce Blvd **Location:** Jct SR 9 Bypass and US 521, 1.3 mi w on SR 9 Bypass. **Facility:** 61 one-bedroom standard units, some with whirlpools. 2 stories (no elevator), exterior corridors. *Bath:* combo or shower only. **Parking:** on-site. **Amenities:** hair dryers. *Some:* irons. **Pool(s):** outdoor. **Leisure Activities:** exercise room. **Guest Services:** valet laundry, wireless Internet. **Business Services:** PC, fax (fee). **Cards:** AX, DC, DS, MC, VI.

CALL / SOME UNITS FEE

WHERE TO DINE

MARIACHI'S MEXICAN RESTAURANT **Phone:** 803/286-9488

Mexican
$6-$19

Near hotels, the brightly colored restaurant features an extensive menu of well-prepared Mexican standards and Mexican dishes modified to American tastes, with huge portions and baked cheese toppings. Flavorful soups are a meal in themselves. Service is efficient and friendly. Casual dress. **Bar:** Full bar. **Hours:** 11 am-10 pm, Fri & Sat-11 pm. **Address:** 1217 Hwy 9 Bypass **Location:** Jct SR 9 Bypass and US 521, 1.3 mi w on SR 9. **Parking:** on-site. **Cards:** AX, DS, MC, VI.

LANDRUM pop. 2,472

WHERE TO STAY

THE RED HORSE INN **Phone:** 864/895-4968

Bed & Breakfast
$175-$400 All Year

Address: 45 Winstons Chase Ct **Location:** Jct SR 14/414, 1.5 mi w on SR 414 to Campbell Rd, then 0.7 mi n. **Facility:** The 100-acre property offers hilltop cottages with mountain views and a romantic B&B where rooms feature fireplaces, whirlpools and upscale amenities. Smoke free premises. 6 one-bedroom standard units with whirlpools. 2 stories (no elevator), interior corridors. **Parking:** on-site. **Terms:** check-in 4 pm, 2 night minimum stay - weekends, cancellation fee imposed. **Amenities:** DVD players, voice mail, irons, hair dryers. **Leisure Activities:** fishing, hiking trails. *Fee:* massage. **Guest Services:** wireless Internet. **Business Services:** fax (fee). **Cards:** DS, MC, VI. **Free Special Amenities: expanded continental breakfast and high-speed Internet.**

THE RED HORSE INN COTTAGES **Phone:** 864/895-4968

Cottage
$210-$400 All Year

Address: 45 Winstons Chase Ct **Location:** Jct SR 14/414, 1.5 mi w on SR 414 to Campbell Rd, then 0.7 mi n. **Facility:** Six cottages sit adjacent to the main inn atop a grassy hill in the foothills of the Blue Ridge Mountains, surrounded by horse farms. Smoke free premises. 6 cottages. 2 stories (no elevator), exterior corridors. **Parking:** on-site. **Terms:** check-in 4 pm, 2 night minimum stay - weekends, cancellation fee imposed. **Amenities:** DVD players, voice mail, irons, hair dryers. **Leisure Activities:** fishing, hiking trails. *Fee:* massage. **Guest Services:** wireless Internet. **Business Services:** fax (fee). **Cards:** DS, MC, VI.

/ SOME UNITS FEE

LATTA pop. 1,410—*See also FLORENCE.*

WHERE TO STAY

ABINGDON MANOR **Phone:** 843/752-5090

Classic Historic Country Inn
$170-$205 All Year

Address: 307 Church St **Location:** I-95, exit 181, 0.9 mi s on SR 38, 5.2 mi e on SR 917, just n on Marion St, then just ne. **Facility:** In a quaint historic village, the striking Greek Revival building is situated on 3 manicured acres reminiscent of an English country estate. Smoke free premises. 7 one-bedroom standard units. 2 stories (no elevator), interior corridors. *Bath:* combo or shower only. **Parking:** on-site. **Terms:** age restrictions may apply. **Amenities:** video library, irons, hair dryers. *Some:* DVD players, CD players. **Dining:** The Dining Room at Abingdon Manor, see separate listing. **Leisure Activities:** bird & historic tours, cooking school. *Fee:* golf privileges. **Guest Services:** valet laundry, wireless Internet. **Business Services:** meeting rooms, fax (fee). **Cards:** AX, DS, JC, MC, VI. **Free Special Amenities: full breakfast and high-speed Internet.**

/ SOME UNITS

BEST WESTERN EXECUTIVE INN *Book great rates at AAA.com*

Phone: (843)752-5060

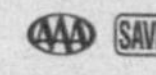

Hotel

$79-$165 All Year

Address: 1534 Hwy 38 W **Location:** I-95, exit 181B, just nw. **Facility:** 52 one-bedroom standard units, some with whirlpools. 3 stories, interior corridors. *Bath:* combo or shower only. **Parking:** on-site. **Terms:** 7 day cancellation notice. **Amenities:** voice mail, irons, hair dryers. *Some:* high-speed Internet. **Pool(s):** heated indoor. **Leisure Activities:** limited exercise equipment. **Guest Services:** valet laundry, wireless Internet. **Business Services:** business center. **Cards:** AX, CB, DC, DS, MC, VI. **Free Special Amenities: continental breakfast and high-speed Internet.**

  / SOME UNITS  

AAA Benefit:

Members save up to 20%, plus 10% bonus points with rewards program.

WHERE TO DINE

THE DINING ROOM AT ABINGDON MANOR

Phone: 843/752-5090

American

$50

Diners can sip a glass of wine in the parlor while chatting with other guests before moving into the intimate, comfortably elegant dining room. Selections from the nightly changing four-course menu are fresh and exquisite. Dressy casual. **Bar:** Full bar. **Reservations:** required, 24 hrs in advance. **Hours:** 7:30 pm seating. Closed: 12/24, 12/25. **Address:** 307 Church St **Location:** I-95, exit 181, 0.9 mi s on SR 38, 5.2 mi e on SR 917, just n on Marion St, then just ne; in Abingdon Manor. **Parking:** on-site. **Cards:** AX, DS, MC, VI.

LEXINGTON pop. 9,793 (See map and index starting on p. 940)

WHERE TO STAY

COMFORT SUITES *Book at AAA.com*

Phone: (803)996-2000 62

Contemporary Hotel

$108 All Year

Address: 325 W Main St **Location:** I-20, exit 58 (US 1), 3.5 mi w. **Facility:** Spacious guest rooms feature a comfortable seating area, a 32-inch television and plush beds partially hidden behind a Japanese-inspired screen. Smoke free premises. 82 one-bedroom standard units, some with whirlpools. 3 stories, interior corridors. *Bath:* combo or shower only. **Parking:** on-site. **Amenities:** DVD players, high-speed Internet, voice mail, safes, irons, hair dryers. **Pool(s):** heated indoor. **Leisure Activities:** exercise room. **Guest Services:** coin laundry, wireless Internet. **Business Services:** meeting rooms, business center. **Cards:** AX, CB, DC, DS, MC, VI.

HAMPTON INN *Book great rates at AAA.com*

Phone: (803)356-8300 60

Hotel

$89-$129 All Year

Address: 601 Columbia Ave **Location:** On US 378, just w of jct SR 6. **Facility:** 71 one-bedroom standard units, some with whirlpools. 4 stories, interior corridors. *Bath:* combo or shower only. **Parking:** on-site. **Amenities:** dual phone lines, voice mail, irons, hair dryers. **Pool(s):** outdoor. **Guest Services:** valet laundry, wireless Internet. **Business Services:** meeting rooms, business center. **Cards:** AX, DC, DS, MC, VI.

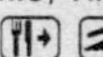    / SOME UNITS 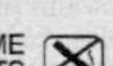 

AAA Benefit:

Members save up to 10% everyday!

HILTON GARDEN INN COLUMBIA-LEXINGTON

Phone: 803/520-9400

fyi

Hotel

Under construction, scheduled to open October 2009. **Address:** 4336 Sunset Blvd **Location:** I-20, exit 378. **Amenities:** 122 units, restaurant, coffeemakers, microwaves, refrigerators.

AAA Benefit:

Members save 5% or more everyday!

QUALITY INN & SUITES *Book at AAA.com*

Phone: (803)359-3099 61

Motel

$79-$159 All Year

Address: 328 W Main St **Location:** I-20, exit 58 (US 1), 3.5 mi w. Located in a rural area. **Facility:** 59 units. 53 one-bedroom standard units, some with whirlpools. 6 one-bedroom suites, some with efficiencies or kitchens (no utensils). 2 stories (no elevator), exterior corridors. **Parking:** on-site, winter plug-ins. **Amenities:** high-speed Internet, voice mail, irons, hair dryers. **Pool(s):** outdoor. **Guest Services:** coin laundry, wireless Internet. **Business Services:** meeting rooms, fax (fee). **Cards:** AX, CB, DC, DS, JC, MC, VI.

ASK / SOME UNITS

(See map and index starting on p. 940)

RAMADA LIMITED *Book at AAA.com* **Phone:** (803)356-6533 63

Motel
$69-$119 All Year

Address: 1015 S Lake Dr **Location:** I-20, exit 55 (SR 6), just s. **Facility:** 46 one-bedroom standard units, some with whirlpools. 2 stories (no elevator), exterior corridors. *Bath:* combo or shower only. **Parking:** on-site. **Amenities:** high-speed Internet, voice mail, irons, hair dryers. **Pool(s):** outdoor. **Guest Services:** coin laundry. **Business Services:** fax (fee). **Cards:** AX, DC, DS, MC, VI.

ASK / SOME UNITS

WHERE TO DINE

FATZ CAFE **Phone:** 803/808-1905

American
$8-$18

Friendly staff and appealing country decor help set the tone for a relaxed and enjoyable dining experience. It's not unusual for guests to wait to be seated at the popular spot, which earns raves for its well-prepared variations on chicken, steak, ribs and pasta, as well as salads and sandwiches. The signature Southern-style peach cobbler served with vanilla ice cream and walnuts is scrumptious. Casual dress. **Hours:** 11 am-10 pm, Fri & Sat-11 pm, Sun-9 pm. Closed: 11/26, 12/25. **Address:** 5462 Augusta Rd **Location:** I-20, exit 58, 1.6 mi w on US 1. **Parking:** on-site. **Cards:** AX, DS, MC, VI.

CALL

FLIGHT DECK RESTAURANT & BAKERY **Phone:** 803/957-5990 15

American
$7-$17

The numerous model airplanes, flight instruments and signed aviation-theme photos adorning the dining room will certainly spark conversation as you wait for your American, Italian, Mexican and Greek entrees. A bakery and gift shop are also on site. Casual dress. **Bar:** Beer & wine. **Hours:** 11 am-9 pm, Fri & Sat-10 pm. Closed major holidays; also Sun. **Address:** 109 A Old Chapin Rd **Location:** Jct US 1/378, just nw of center; in Shoppes of Flight Deck. **Parking:** on-site. **Cards:** AX, DS, MC, VI.

CALL

GILLIGAN'S STEAMER & RAW BAR **Phone:** 803/808-2244

Seafood
$7-$21

A casual family oriented neighborhood restaurant, Gilligan's is famous for fresh shrimp right off the boat! Locals flock not only for the shrimp but also for Captain Bookatee's hushpuppies. Not a seafood lover? Come on anyway and enjoy the buffalo wings and chicken fingers. Casual dress. **Bar:** Full bar. **Hours:** 11 am-9 pm, Fri & Sat-10 pm. Closed: 11/26, 12/25. **Address:** 938 N Lake Dr **Location:** Jct US 378/SR 6, just n on SR 6; at Lexington Towne Center. **Parking:** on-site. **Cards:** AX, DS, MC, VI.

CALL

LIZARD'S THICKET **Phone:** 803/951-3555

Regional American
$3-$12

Owned and operated by the same family since 1978, guests can enjoy Southern home cooking at breakfast, lunch, and dinner. Locals love the Calabash style shrimp as well as the fried chicken livers. Be sure and ask about the daily specials which will allow guest a mixing and matching of main course with side dishes. Casual dress. **Hours:** 6 am-9 pm, to 10 pm seasonal. Closed: 12/25. **Address:** 621 W Main St **Location:** Jct US 378/1, just sw on US 378. **Parking:** on-site. **Cards:** MC, VI.

CALL

LITTLE RIVER —*See The Grand Strand p. 980.*

LORIS —*See The Grand Strand p. 980.*

LUGOFF pop. 6,278

WHERE TO STAY

RAMADA LIMITED *Book at AAA.com* **Phone:** (803)438-1807

Motel
$65 All Year

Address: 542 Hwy 601 S **Location:** I-20, exit 92 (US 601), just n. **Facility:** 40 one-bedroom standard units, some with whirlpools. 2 stories (no elevator), exterior corridors. **Parking:** on-site, winter plug-ins. **Amenities:** high-speed Internet, voice mail, irons, hair dryers. **Pool(s):** outdoor. **Business Services:** meeting rooms, fax (fee). **Cards:** AX, DS, MC, VI.

/ SOME UNITS FEE

MANNING pop. 4,025

WHERE TO STAY

BEST WESTERN PALMETTO INN *Book great rates at AAA.com* **Phone:** (803)473-4021

Motel
$63-$90 All Year

Address: 2825 Paxville Hwy **Location:** I-95, exit 119 (SR 261), just se. **Facility:** 57 one-bedroom standard units. 2 stories (no elevator), exterior corridors. **Parking:** on-site. **Amenities:** irons, hair dryers. *Some:* high-speed Internet. **Pool(s):** outdoor. **Guest Services:** wireless Internet. **Business Services:** fax (fee). **Cards:** AX, CB, DC, DS, MC, VI. **Free Special Amenities: expanded continental breakfast and high-speed Internet.**

AAA Benefit:
Members save up to 20%, plus 10% bonus points with rewards program.

HAMPTON INN *Book great rates at AAA.com* **Phone:** (803)505-4800

Hotel
$95-$140 All Year

Address: 2822 Paxville Hwy **Location:** I-95, exit 119 (SR 261), just se. **Facility:** 73 one-bedroom standard units. 3 stories, interior corridors. *Bath:* combo or shower only. **Parking:** on-site. **Amenities:** voice mail, irons, hair dryers. **Pool(s):** outdoor. **Leisure Activities:** limited exercise equipment. **Guest Services:** valet laundry, wireless Internet. **Business Services:** business center. **Cards:** AX, DS, MC, VI.

CALL / SOME UNITS

AAA Benefit:
Members save up to 10% everyday!

HOLIDAY INN EXPRESS *Book great rates at AAA.com* **Phone:** (803)473-5334

AAA SAVE

Motel
$79 All Year

Address: 2284 Raccoon Rd **Location:** I-95, exit 119 (SR 261), just se, then s. **Facility:** 51 one-bedroom standard units, some with whirlpools. 2 stories (no elevator), exterior corridors. *Bath:* combo or shower only. **Parking:** on-site. **Amenities:** voice mail, irons, hair dryers. **Pool(s):** outdoor. **Guest Services:** coin laundry, wireless Internet. **Business Services:** business center. **Cards:** AX, DC, DS, MC, VI. **Free Special Amenities: continental breakfast and high-speed Internet.**

/ SOME UNITS

RAMADA INN *Book at AAA.com* **Phone:** 803/473-5135

Motel
Rates not provided

Address: 2816 Paxville Hwy **Location:** I-95, exit 119 (SR 261), just se. **Facility:** 41 one-bedroom standard units, some with whirlpools. 2 stories (no elevator), exterior corridors. **Parking:** on-site. **Amenities:** voice mail, safes (fee), irons, hair dryers. **Pool(s):** heated outdoor. **Leisure Activities:** whirlpool. **Guest Services:** valet and coin laundry, wireless Internet. **Business Services:** PC, fax (fee).

/ SOME UNITS FEE

MAULDIN pop. 15,224

WHERE TO STAY

SUPER 8 MOTEL *Book great rates at AAA.com* **Phone:** (864)751-0003

AAA SAVE

Hotel
$75 All Year

Address: 310 W Butler Rd **Location:** I-85, exit 46C, 3.8 mi s on Old Mauldin Rd (which becomes W Butler Rd). **Facility:** 49 one-bedroom standard units, some with whirlpools. 2 stories (no elevator), interior corridors. *Bath:* combo or shower only. **Parking:** on-site. **Amenities:** irons, hair dryers. *Some:* high-speed Internet. **Pool(s):** outdoor. **Leisure Activities:** limited exercise equipment. **Guest Services:** coin laundry, wireless Internet. **Business Services:** fax (fee). **Cards:** AX, DS, MC, VI.

CALL / SOME UNITS FEE VCR

MONCKS CORNER —*See Charleston p. 917.*

MONTMORENCI

WHERE TO STAY

ANNIE'S INN BED & BREAKFAST **Phone:** 803/649-6836

Historic Bed & Breakfast
$90-$135 All Year

Address: 3083 Charleston Hwy **Location:** Jct US 1/78, 5.7 mi se on US 78. **Facility:** Set in the horse country just outside Aiken, this property offers a casual ambience and well-appointed rooms. Smoke free premises. 11 units. 5 one-bedroom standard units. 6 cottages. 2 stories (no elevator), interior/exterior corridors. *Bath:* combo or shower only. **Parking:** on-site. **Terms:** 3 day cancellation notice. **Amenities:** irons. **Pool(s):** outdoor. **Guest Services:** complimentary laundry, wireless Internet. **Business Services:** fax (fee). **Cards:** AX, MC, VI.

/ SOME UNITS

MOUNT PLEASANT —*See Charleston p. 918.*

MULLINS pop. 5,029

WHERE TO STAY

COMFORT INN *Book at AAA.com* **Phone:** 843/423-0516

Hotel
Rates not provided

Address: 2693 E Hwy 76 **Location:** Jct US 501 Bypass/US 76, just e. **Facility:** 55 one-bedroom standard units. 2 stories (no elevator), interior corridors. **Parking:** on-site. **Amenities:** irons, hair dryers. *Some:* high-speed Internet. **Pool(s):** outdoor. **Guest Services:** wireless Internet. **Business Services:** meeting rooms, fax (fee).

/ SOME UNITS

MURRELLS INLET —*See The Grand Strand p. 1045.*

MYRTLE BEACH —*See The Grand Strand p. 996.*

NEWBERRY pop. 10,580

WHERE TO STAY

AMERICA'S BEST VALUE INN — **Phone:** (803)276-5850

Motel
$65-$75 All Year

Address: 11701 S Carolina Hwy 34 **Location:** I-26, exit 74 (SR 34), just ne. **Facility:** 113 one-bedroom standard units. 1-2 stories (no elevator), exterior corridors. **Parking:** on-site. **Amenities:** voice mail, irons, hair dryers. **Pool(s):** outdoor. **Guest Services:** valet laundry. **Business Services:** meeting rooms, fax (fee). **Cards:** AX, DC, DS, MC, VI. **Free Special Amenities: expanded continental breakfast and high-speed Internet.**

SOME UNITS FEE

WHERE TO DINE

THE CABANA CAFE & STORM CELLAR PUB — **Phone:** 803/405-0030

American
$7-$42

Convenient to the Opera House, the steak-and-seafood house is home to the famous cabana soups, which are prepared daily. The menu centers on grilled steaks, seafood and sandwich specialties. Casual dress. **Bar:** Full bar. **Hours:** 11 am-10 pm, Fri-11 pm, Sat 5 pm-11 pm; hours vary in winter. Closed major holidays; also Sun & Mon. **Address:** 1215 Boyce St **Location:** Between College and Caldwell sts; downtown. **Parking:** street. **Cards:** AX, MC, VI.

DELAMATER'S — **Phone:** 803/276-3555

Regional American
$6-$22

The diverse menu centers on well-prepared regional dishes, with a focus on chicken, beef and pasta. Burgers and sandwiches also are available during dinner. Start with the French onion soup dome, a treat for the eyes and palate. The restaurant is located near the opera house. Casual dress. **Bar:** Beer & wine. **Reservations:** accepted. **Hours:** 11:30 am-2:30 & 5-9 pm, Fri & Sat-10 pm. Closed major holidays; also Sun. **Address:** 1117 Boyce St **Location:** Between Caldwell and McKibben sts; downtown. **Parking:** street. **Cards:** AX, MC, VI.

STEVEN W'S DOWNTOWN BISTRO — **Phone:** 803/276-7700

Mediterranean
$9-$26

Diners appreciate excellent service at the Italian bistro, which is convenient to the opera house. The menu lists a good selection of standards, such as veal piccata and fettuccine alfredo. Dressy casual. **Bar:** Full bar. **Reservations:** suggested. **Hours:** 5:30 pm-close; later hours during Opera House events. Closed major holidays; also Sun & Mon. **Address:** 1100 Main St **Location:** Between Caldwell and McKibben sts; downtown. **Parking:** street. **Cards:** AX, DS, MC, VI.

CALL

NORTH AUGUSTA pop. 17,574

WHERE TO DINE

S & S CAFETERIA — **Phone:** 803/279-7882

American
$4-$8

A longtime favorite for comfort food, the family-owned cafeteria invites diners to load a plate with traditionally prepared chicken, beef, vegetables, salad and dessert. Casual dress. **Reservations:** not accepted. **Hours:** 11 am-2:15 & 5-8 pm. Closed: 12/25. **Address:** 352 E Martintown Rd **Location:** Jct US 25 business route/SR 230 (Martintown Rd), 0.4 mi se on SR 230. **Parking:** on-site. **Cards:** AX, DS, MC, VI.

NORTH CHARLESTON —*See Charleston p. 925.*

NORTH MYRTLE BEACH —*See The Grand Strand p. 988.*

ORANGEBURG pop. 12,765

WHERE TO STAY

BEST WESTERN ORANGEBURG INN & SUITES *Book great rates at AAA.com* — **Phone:** (803)515-9700

Contemporary Hotel
$90 All Year

Address: 746 Citadel Rd **Location:** I-26, exit 145A (US 601), just s. **Facility:** Opened in 2008, guest rooms feature a spacious desk with an ergonomic chair, a pull-out sofa and a 32-inch, high-definition television. Smoke free premises. 69 one-bedroom standard units. 3 stories, interior corridors. *Bath:* combo or shower only. **Parking:** on-site. **Terms:** 7 day cancellation notice. **Amenities:** high-speed Internet, voice mail, irons, hair dryers. **Pool(s):** indoor. **Leisure Activities:** exercise room. **Guest Services:** coin laundry, wireless Internet. **Business Services:** meeting rooms, business center. **Cards:** AX, CB, DC, DS, JC, MC, VI. **Free Special Amenities: continental breakfast and high-speed Internet.** *(See color ad p 1095)*

Best Western

AAA Benefit:
Members save up to 20%, plus 10% bonus points with rewards program.

CALL

COUNTRY INN & SUITES *Book at AAA.com* **Phone:** (803)928-5300

Hotel
$105-$190 All Year

Address: 731 Citadel Rd **Location:** I-26, exit 145B, just s. **Facility:** 81 units. 48 one-bedroom standard units. 33 one-bedroom suites. 4 stories, interior corridors. *Bath:* combo or shower only. **Parking:** on-site. **Terms:** cancellation fee imposed. **Amenities:** high-speed Internet, voice mail, irons, hair dryers. **Pool(s):** heated indoor. **Leisure Activities:** whirlpool, exercise room. **Guest Services:** coin laundry, wireless Internet. **Business Services:** meeting rooms, business center. **Cards:** AX, DS, MC, VI.

ASK CALL / SOME UNITS FEE

FAIRFIELD INN BY MARRIOTT *Book great rates at AAA.com* **Phone:** (803)533-0014

Hotel
$89-$95 All Year

Address: 663 Citadel Rd **Location:** I-26, exit 145A (US 601), just sw, then just e. **Facility:** Smoke free premises. 65 one-bedroom standard units, some with whirlpools. 3 stories, interior corridors. **Parking:** on-site. **Terms:** cancellation fee imposed. **Amenities:** high-speed Internet, voice mail, irons, hair dryers. **Pool(s):** outdoor. **Leisure Activities:** whirlpool. **Guest Services:** valet laundry, wireless Internet. **Business Services:** meeting rooms, fax (fee). **Cards:** AX, CB, DC, DS, JC, MC, VI. *(See color ad p 1095)*

  / SOME UNITS 

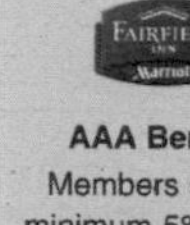

AAA Benefit:
Members save a minimum 5% off the best available rate.

HAMPTON INN ORANGEBURG *Book great rates at AAA.com* **Phone:** (803)531-6400

Motel
$79-$109 All Year

Address: 3583 St Matthews Rd **Location:** I-26, exit 145A (US 601), 0.5 mi sw. **Facility:** 69 one-bedroom standard units, some with whirlpools. 2 stories (no elevator), exterior corridors. *Bath:* combo or shower only. **Parking:** on-site. **Amenities:** voice mail, irons, hair dryers. **Pool(s):** outdoor. **Guest Services:** valet laundry, wireless Internet. **Business Services:** fax (fee). **Cards:** AX, DC, DS, MC, VI. **Free Special Amenities: expanded continental breakfast and high-speed Internet.** *(See color ad below)*

  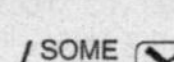 / SOME UNITS

AAA Benefit:
Members save up to 10% everyday!

HOLIDAY INN EXPRESS HOTEL AND SUITES *Book great rates at AAA.com* **Phone:** (803)539-2900

Hotel
$109-$169 All Year

Address: 118 Sleep Inn Rd **Location:** I-26, exit 145A (US 601), just sw. **Facility:** 78 units. 66 one-bedroom standard units, some with whirlpools. 12 one-bedroom suites. 3 stories, interior corridors. *Bath:* combo or shower only. **Parking:** on-site. **Terms:** cancellation fee imposed. **Amenities:** high-speed Internet, dual phone lines, voice mail, irons, hair dryers. *Some:* safes. **Pool(s):** heated indoor. **Leisure Activities:** limited exercise equipment. **Guest Services:** coin laundry, wireless Internet. **Business Services:** meeting rooms, business center. **Cards:** AX, CB, DC, DS, MC, VI. *(See color ad p 1095)*

CALL / SOME UNITS

▼ See AAA listing above ▼

Great Values In Orangeburg, I-26, Exit 145-A

By Choice Hotels

AAA

* All Interior Corridors
* Complimentary Continental Breakfast
* HBO w/ Full Cable
* Free Local Calls
* Guest Laundry
* Outdoor Pool
* Free High Speed Internet

I-26, Exit 145A • 803-531-7200 • 800-396- 8378

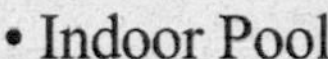

- Indoor Pool
- Exercise Room
- Large Modern Rooms
- Complimentary Continental Breakfast
- Free Local Calls
- Free High Speed Internet

Approved

I-26, Exit 145-A • 803-539-2900 • 800-HOLIDAY

Approved

- Complimentary Continental Breakfast
- Large Outdoor Pool & Whirpool
- Free Local Calls
- Free High Speed Internet

I-26 • Exit 145-A • 803-533-0014 • 800-228-2800

Approved

- Complimentary Continental Breakfast
- Indoor Pool • Excercise Room
- Free High Speed Internet
- Free Local Calls

Orangeburg Inn & Suites

BRAND NEW

I-26, Exit 145-A • 803-515-9700 • 800-710-0778

JAMESON INN ORANGEBURG *Book at AAA.com* **Phone:** (803)534-1611

Motel

$78-$85 All Year

Address: 2350 Chestnut St NE **Location:** I-26, exit 145A (US 601), 3.9 mi sw to jct US 601 and 21/178 Bypass, then 2 mi nw. Located adjacent to the Prince of Orange Mall. **Facility:** 58 one-bedroom standard units, some with whirlpools. 2 stories (no elevator), exterior corridors. *Bath:* combo or shower only. **Parking:** on-site. **Terms:** cancellation fee imposed. **Amenities:** hair dryers. *Some:* irons. **Pool(s):** outdoor. **Leisure Activities:** exercise room. **Guest Services:** valet laundry, wireless Internet. **Business Services:** PC, fax (fee). **Cards:** AX, DC, DS, MC, VI.

ASK / SOME UNITS FEE

SLEEP INN ORANGEBURG *Book great rates at AAA.com* **Phone:** (803)531-7200

Hotel

$68-$98 All Year

Address: 3689 St Matthews Rd **Location:** I-26, exit 145A (US 601), just sw. **Facility:** 69 one-bedroom standard units. 4 stories, interior corridors. *Bath:* combo or shower only. **Parking:** on-site. **Amenities:** high-speed Internet, voice mail, irons, hair dryers. **Pool(s):** outdoor. **Guest Services:** coin laundry, wireless Internet. **Business Services:** meeting rooms, fax (fee). **Cards:** AX, DC, DS, MC, VI. ***(See color ad p 1095)***

/ SOME UNITS

TRAVELER'S INN *Book great rates at AAA.com* **Phone:** (803)531-2590

Motel

$55-$150 All Year

Address: 3691 St Matthews Rd **Location:** I-26, exit 145A (US 601), just sw. **Facility:** 76 one-bedroom standard units, some with whirlpools. 2 stories (no elevator), exterior corridors. **Parking:** on-site. **Amenities:** hair dryers. **Pool(s):** outdoor. **Guest Services:** wireless Internet. **Business Services:** fax (fee). **Cards:** AX, DC, DS, MC, VI. **Free Special Amenities: expanded continental breakfast and high-speed Internet.**

/ SOME UNITS FEE

WHERE TO DINE

CHESTNUT GRILL **Phone:** 803/531-1747

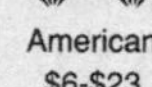

American

$6-$23

Family owned and operated for more than 20 years, the restaurant consistently offers friendly service, well-prepared and reasonably priced meals and a comfortable unhurried atmosphere. The menu lists many chicken, steak and seafood dishes, but the draw here is prime rib. House specialties include mixed grill of chicken and ribs, rack of lamb and grilled pork chops. Entrees come with soup or salad, a choice from many sides and honey croissants. Casual dress. **Bar:** Full bar. **Reservations:** accepted. **Hours:** 11 am-9:30 pm, Fri & Sat-10 pm. Closed: 12/25; also Sun. **Address:** 1455 Chestnut St **Location:** 1.4 mi e of center on US 301, then just s on US 21. **Parking:** on-site. **Cards:** AX, DS, MC, VI.

CALL

FATZ CAFE **Phone:** 803/534-8000

American

$8-$18

Friendly staff and appealing country decor help set the tone for a relaxed and enjoyable dining experience. It's not unusual for guests to wait to be seated at the popular spot, which earns raves for its well-prepared variations on chicken, steak, ribs and pasta, as well as salads and sandwiches. The signature Southern-style peach cobbler served with vanilla ice cream and walnuts is scrumptious. Casual dress. **Bar:** Full bar. **Hours:** 11 am-10 pm, Fri & Sat-11 pm, Sun-9 pm. Closed: 11/26. **Address:** 3575 St Matthews Rd **Location:** I-26, exit 145A (US 601), 0.6 mi sw. **Parking:** on-site. **Cards:** AX, DS, MC, VI.

CALL

MEDITERRANEAN GRILL & SPIRITS *Menu on AAA.com* **Phone:** 803/539-9912

Continental

$6-$23

Near area hotels, the restaurant prepares a wide selection of Greek and Italian standards and sets out a steam-line buffet at lunch. Casual dress. **Bar:** Full bar. **Hours:** 11:30 am-9 pm, Fri & Sat-10 pm. Closed major holidays; also Sun. **Address:** 3667 St Matthews Rd **Location:** I-26, exit 145A (US 601), just sw. **Parking:** on-site. **Cards:** MC, VI.

PAWLEYS ISLAND

—See The Grand Strand p. 1046.

PICKENS pop. 3,012

WHERE TO STAY

THE INN AT TABLE ROCK **Phone:** (864)878-0078

Bed & Breakfast

$129-$229 All Year

Address: 117 Hiawatha Tr **Location:** Jct US 178/SR 11, 4.6 mi ne on SR 11, then just se; on southeast side of Table Rock State Park. **Facility:** This B&B's guest rooms all have ceiling fans and are furnished with Victorian and late-19th-century antiques. Smoke free premises. 6 one-bedroom standard units, some with whirlpools. 2 stories (no elevator), interior corridors. **Parking:** on-site. **Terms:** 7 day cancellation notice-fee imposed. **Amenities:** video library, high-speed Internet, hair dryers. *Some:* DVD players. **Pool(s):** outdoor. **Business Services:** meeting rooms, fax (fee). **Cards:** DS, MC, VI.

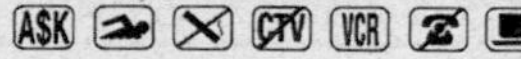

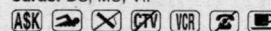

LAUREL MOUNTAIN INN

Motel
$75-$105 All Year

Phone: (864)878-8500
Address: 129 Hiawatha Tr **Location:** Jct US 178/SR 11, 4.6 mi ne on SR 11, then just se; on southeast side of Table Rock State Park. **Facility:** Smoke free premises. 5 one-bedroom standard units. 1 story, exterior corridors. **Parking:** on-site. **Terms:** 7 day cancellation notice-fee imposed. **Amenities:** video library, hair dryers. **Leisure Activities:** hiking trails. **Guest Services:** wireless Internet. **Business Services:** fax (fee). **Cards:** DS, MC, VI.

/ SOME UNITS VCR

RICHBURG pop. 332

WHERE TO STAY

COMFORT INN *Book at AAA.com*

Hotel
Rates not provided

Phone: 803/789-7100
Address: 3041 Lancaster Hwy **Location:** I-77, exit 65, just w on SR 9. **Facility:** 64 one-bedroom standard units, some with whirlpools. 2 stories (no elevator), interior corridors. *Bath:* combo or shower only. **Parking:** on-site. **Amenities:** voice mail, irons, hair dryers. **Pool(s):** outdoor. **Leisure Activities:** whirlpool, exercise room. **Guest Services:** coin laundry, wireless Internet. **Business Services:** meeting rooms, PC, fax (fee).

/ SOME UNITS

RODEWAY INN & SUITES *Book at AAA.com*

Hotel
Rates not provided

Phone: 803/789-7770
Address: 2912 Parkway Blvd **Location:** I-77, exit 65, just w on SR 9. **Facility:** 61 one-bedroom standard units, some with whirlpools. 2 stories, interior corridors. *Bath:* combo or shower only. **Parking:** on-site. **Amenities:** high-speed Internet, voice mail, irons, hair dryers. **Leisure Activities:** exercise room. **Guest Services:** coin laundry, wireless Internet. **Business Services:** fax (fee).

/ SOME UNITS

SUPER 8 MOTEL *Book great rates at AAA.com*

AAA SAVE

Motel
$59-$89 All Year

Phone: (803)789-7888
Address: 3085 Lancaster Hwy **Location:** I-77, exit 65, just w on SR 9. **Facility:** 58 one-bedroom standard units. 2 stories (no elevator), exterior corridors. **Parking:** on-site. **Terms:** 7 day cancellation notice. **Amenities:** hair dryers. **Pool(s):** outdoor. **Guest Services:** coin laundry, wireless Internet. **Business Services:** fax (fee). **Cards:** AX, CB, DC, DS, JC, MC, VI.

/ SOME UNITS FEE

WHERE TO DINE

COUNTRY OMELET

American
$4-$14

Phone: 803/789-5840
Simple breakfast fare is prepared 24 hours a day, and at lunch and through most of the evening, a whiteboard lists daily specials, mostly Southern comfort staples centered on meat, potatoes and vegetables. Near listed hotels, the basic roadside diner employs a NASCAR motif, and you can dine in or take out. A bevy of friendly and patient waitresses provides service. Casual dress. **Reservations:** not accepted. **Hours:** 24 hours. Closed: 12/25. **Address:** 3038 Lancaster Hwy **Location:** I-77, exit 65, just w. **Parking:** on-site. **Cards:** AX, DS, MC, VI.

THE FRONT PORCH RESTAURANT

American
$4-$11

Phone: 803/789-5029
In a clapboard-sided building replete with front porch, rocking chairs and displays of Americana, the home-like restaurant prepares a wide selection of comfort foods. The daily changing menu is listed only on strategically placed chalkboards. Patrons can expect to find steak, chicken and fish, in addition to a slew of freshly prepared vegetables and potatoes or rice. Friendly staffers promptly make guests feel at home. Casual dress. **Reservations:** not accepted. **Hours:** 11 am-9 pm. Closed major holidays. **Address:** 3072 Lancaster Hwy **Location:** I-77, exit 65, just w. **Parking:** on-site. **Cards:** MC, VI.

RIDGELAND pop. 2,518

WHERE TO STAY

COMFORT INN *Book great rates at AAA.com*

AAA SAVE

Hotel
$79-$109 All Year

Phone: (843)726-2121
Address: Hwy 336 & I-95 **Location:** I-95, exit 21 (US 336), just nw. **Facility:** 101 one-bedroom standard units, some with whirlpools. 2 stories (no elevator), interior/exterior corridors. **Parking:** on-site. **Terms:** cancellation fee imposed. **Amenities:** irons, hair dryers. **Pool(s):** outdoor, heated indoor. **Leisure Activities:** limited exercise equipment. **Guest Services:** coin laundry, wireless Internet. **Business Services:** fax (fee). **Cards:** AX, CB, DC, DS, JC, MC, VI. **Free Special Amenities: expanded continental breakfast and high-speed Internet.**

/ SOME UNITS FEE

WHERE TO DINE

JASPER'S PORCH LAKEFRONT DINING *Menu on AAA.com*

AAA

American
$7-$24

Phone: 843/726-9521
Located just a block away from the interstate, this family-run full service restaurant offers relaxing and casual dining right on Blue Heron Lake. The menu includes a good selecion of seafood, chicken, beef and pasta dishes. Diners can enjoy alligators sunning themselves, and can walk off the hearty meal with a casual stroll down the Blue Heron Nature Trail afterwards. A wonderful respite after a long day of driving. Casual dress. **Bar:** Full bar. **Reservations:** accepted. **Hours:** 8 am-9 pm, Sun 11 am-3 pm. Closed: 12/24, 12/25. **Address:** 100 James Taylor Dr **Location:** I-95, exit 21 (US 336), just w to W Frontage Rd, then just n. **Parking:** on-site. **Cards:** MC, VI.

ROCK HILL *—See Nearby NC City Of Charlotte p. 668.*

ST. GEORGE pop. 2,092

WHERE TO STAY

COMFORT INN Book great rates at AAA.com **Phone:** (843)563-4180

Motel
$54-$110 All Year

Address: 139 Motel Dr **Location:** I-95, exit 77 (US 78), just e. Located in a small RV park with back-in parking. **Facility:** 104 one-bedroom standard units, some with whirlpools. 2 stories (no elevator), exterior corridors. **Parking:** on-site. **Amenities:** irons, hair dryers. **Pool(s):** outdoor. **Guest Services:** coin laundry, wireless Internet. **Business Services:** fax (fee). **Cards:** AX, DS, MC, VI.

/ SOME UNITS FEE

ECONO LODGE Book great rates at AAA.com **Phone:** (843)563-4195

Motel
$55-$80 All Year

Address: 5971 W Jim Bilton Blvd **Location:** I-95, exit 77 (US 78), just e. **Facility:** 67 one-bedroom standard units. 2 stories (no elevator), exterior corridors. **Parking:** on-site. **Pool(s):** outdoor. **Guest Services:** wireless Internet. **Business Services:** fax (fee). **Cards:** AX, CB, DC, DS, MC, VI. **Free Special Amenities: continental breakfast and high-speed Internet.**

/ SOME UNITS FEE

QUALITY INN- ST GEORGE Book great rates at AAA.com **Phone:** (843)563-4581

Motel
$54-$100 All Year

Address: 6014 W Jim Bilton Blvd **Location:** I-95, exit 77 (US 78), just e. **Facility:** 115 one-bedroom standard units. 2 stories (no elevator), exterior corridors. *Bath:* combo or shower only. **Parking:** on-site. **Amenities:** irons, hair dryers. **Pool(s):** outdoor. **Guest Services:** wireless Internet. **Business Services:** meeting rooms, PC, fax (fee). **Cards:** AX, DC, DS, MC, VI.

CALL / SOME UNITS FEE

WHERE TO DINE

GEORGIO'S **Phone:** 843/563-9030

Mediterranean
$6-$19

A broad menu of Mediterranean dishes, Italian standards and a sprinkling of American fare make this experience well worth the stop. There's something for everyone, including vegetarians. Casual dress. **Bar:** Beer & wine. **Hours:** 11 am-10 pm, Fri & Sat-11 pm. Closed major holidays. **Address:** 5945 W Jim Bilton Blvd **Location:** I-95, exit 77 (US 78), 0.4 mi e. **Parking:** on-site. **Cards:** AX, DS, MC, VI.

SANTEE pop. 740

—— WHERE TO STAY ——

BAYMONT INN & SUITES *Book great rates at AAA.com* **Phone:** (803)854-3221

AAA SAVE

Motel

$45-$75 All Year

Address: 249 Britain St **Location:** I-95, exit 98 (SR 6), just nw, then just s. **Facility:** 62 one-bedroom standard units, some with whirlpools. 2 stories (no elevator), exterior corridors. *Bath:* combo or shower only. **Parking:** on-site. **Terms:** 3 day cancellation notice. **Amenities:** irons, hair dryers. *Some:* safes. **Pool(s):** outdoor. **Leisure Activities:** limited exercise equipment. **Guest Services:** coin laundry, wireless Internet. **Business Services:** PC, fax (fee). **Cards:** AX, DS, MC, VI. **Free Special Amenities: continental breakfast and high-speed Internet.**

/ SOME UNITS

BEST WESTERN SANTEE INN *Book great rates at AAA.com* **Phone:** (803)854-3089

AAA SAVE

Motel

$80-$90 All Year

Address: Hwy 6 **Location:** I-95, exit 98 (SR 6), just se. **Facility:** 106 one-bedroom standard units, some with whirlpools. 1 story, exterior corridors. **Parking:** on-site. **Amenities:** irons, hair dryers. **Dining:** Captain's Quarters Restaurant, see separate listing. **Pool(s):** heated outdoor. **Leisure Activities:** exercise room. **Guest Services:** wireless Internet. **Business Services:** meeting rooms, business center. **Cards:** AX, DC, DS, MC, VI. **Free Special Amenities: expanded continental breakfast and high-speed Internet.** *(See color ad below)*

/ SOME UNITS

AAA Benefit:

Members save up to 20%, plus 10% bonus points with rewards program.

CLARK'S INN **Phone:** 803/854-2141

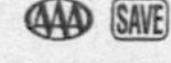

Motel

$82-$125 All Year

Address: 114 Bradford Blvd **Location:** I-95, exit 98 (SR 6), just nw. **Facility:** Smoke free premises. 74 units. 66 one-bedroom standard units. 8 one-bedroom suites, some with kitchens. 2 stories (no elevator), exterior corridors. **Parking:** on-site. **Terms:** cancellation fee imposed. **Amenities:** voice mail, hair dryers. **Dining:** restaurant, see separate listing. **Pool(s):** outdoor. **Guest Services:** coin laundry, wireless Internet. **Business Services:** meeting rooms, PC, fax (fee). **Cards:** AX, DS, MC, VI. **Free Special Amenities: preferred room (subject to availability with advance reservations) and high-speed Internet.** *(See color ad p 1100)*

/ SOME UNITS

▼ *See AAA listing above* ▼

COUNTRY INN & SUITES SANTEE *Book great rates at AAA.com* **Phone:** (803)854-4104

AAA SAVE

Hotel
$87-$111 All Year

Address: 221 Britain St **Location:** I-95, exit 98 (SR 6), just nw, then just s. **Facility:** 61 units. 45 one-bedroom standard units. 16 one-bedroom suites, some with whirlpools. 3 stories, interior corridors. *Bath:* combo or shower only. **Parking:** on-site, winter plug-ins. **Amenities:** irons, hair dryers. **Pool(s):** outdoor. **Leisure Activities:** limited exercise equipment. **Guest Services:** coin laundry, wireless Internet. **Business Services:** business center. **Cards:** AX, DC, DS, JC, MC, VI. **Free Special Amenities: expanded continental breakfast and high-speed Internet.**

/ SOME UNITS

HAMPTON INN *Book great rates at AAA.com* **Phone:** (803)854-2444

AAA SAVE

Hotel
$77-$80 All Year

Address: 9060 Old Hwy 6 **Location:** I-95, exit 98 (SR 6), just se. **Facility:** 81 one-bedroom standard units, some with whirlpools. 3 stories, interior corridors. *Bath:* combo or shower only. **Parking:** on-site. **Terms:** 1-30 night minimum stay, cancellation fee imposed. **Amenities:** video games (fee), dual phone lines, voice mail, irons, hair dryers. **Pool(s):** outdoor. **Leisure Activities:** whirlpool, exercise room. **Guest Services:** coin laundry, wireless Internet. **Business Services:** meeting rooms, business center. **Cards:** AX, CB, DC, DS, MC, VI. **Free Special Amenities: expanded continental breakfast and high-speed Internet.**
(See color ad p 1101)

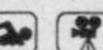  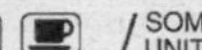 / SOME UNITS

Hampton Inn

AAA Benefit:
Members save up to 10% everyday!

HOLIDAY INN SANTEE *Book great rates at AAA.com* **Phone:** (803)854-9800

AAA SAVE

Hotel
$62-$135 All Year

Address: 139 Bradford Blvd **Location:** I-95, exit 98 (SR 6), just nw, then just sw. **Facility:** 84 units. 83 one-bedroom standard units, some with whirlpools. 1 one-bedroom suite with whirlpool. 4 stories, interior corridors. *Bath:* combo or shower only. **Parking:** on-site. **Terms:** check-in 4 pm. **Amenities:** high-speed Internet, dual phone lines, voice mail, safes, irons, hair dryers. **Pool(s):** heated indoor. **Leisure Activities:** whirlpool, exercise room. **Guest Services:** complimentary laundry, wireless Internet. **Business Services:** meeting rooms, business center. **Cards:** AX, CB, DC, DS, JC, MC, VI. **Free Special Amenities: local telephone calls and high-speed Internet.**

CALL / SOME UNITS FEE

HOWARD JOHNSON EXPRESS INN Book great rates at AAA.com **Phone:** (803)854-3870

Motel
$58-$63 All Year

Address: 9112 Old Hwy 6 **Location:** I-95, exit 98 (SR 6), 0.4 mi se. **Facility:** 77 one-bedroom standard units. 1 story, exterior corridors. **Parking:** on-site. **Amenities:** voice mail, irons, hair dryers. **Pool(s):** outdoor. **Guest Services:** wireless Internet. **Business Services:** meeting rooms. **Cards:** AX, DS, MC, VI. **Free Special Amenities: continental breakfast and high-speed Internet.**

/ SOME UNITS FEE

QUALITY INN & SUITES SANTEE Book great rates at AAA.com **Phone:** (803)854-2121

Hotel
$81-$123 All Year

Address: 8020 Old Number 6 Hwy **Location:** I-95, exit 98 (SR 6), just nw. **Facility:** 153 units. 136 one-bedroom standard units. 17 one-bedroom suites. 2 stories (no elevator), exterior corridors. *Bath:* combo or shower only. **Parking:** on-site. **Terms:** cancellation fee imposed. **Amenities:** voice mail, irons, hair dryers. **Pool(s):** outdoor. **Leisure Activities:** whirlpool, putting green, limited exercise equipment, shuffleboard. **Guest Services:** coin laundry, wireless Internet. **Business Services:** meeting rooms, business center. **Cards:** AX, CB, DC, DS, MC, VI. **Free Special Amenities: full breakfast and high-speed Internet.** *(See color ad p 1100)*

/ SOME UNITS FEE

SUPER 8 MOTEL Book great rates at AAA.com **Phone:** (803)854-3456

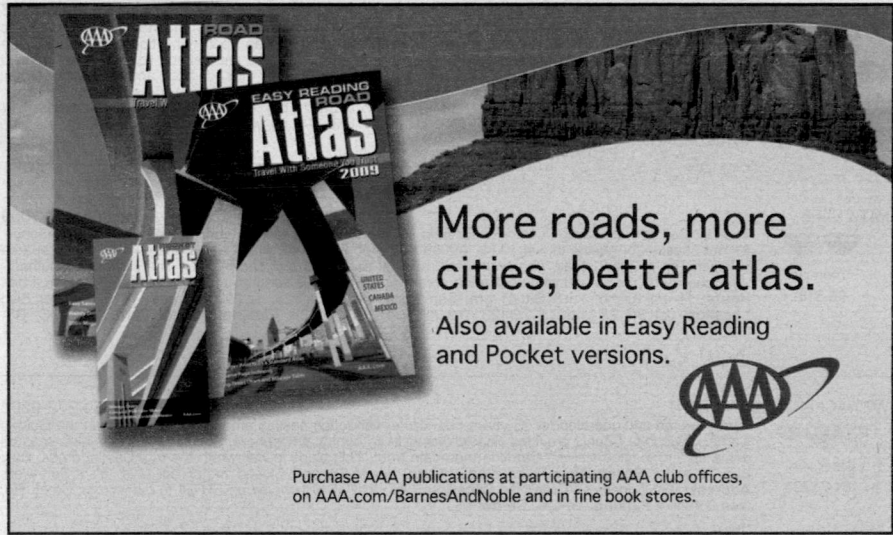

Motel
$65-$75 All Year

Address: 9125 Old Hwy 6 **Location:** I-95, exit 98 (SR 6), 0.4 mi se. **Facility:** 41 one-bedroom standard units, some with whirlpools. 1 story, exterior corridors. **Parking:** on-site. **Terms:** cancellation fee imposed. **Amenities:** hair dryers. **Pool(s):** outdoor. **Guest Services:** coin laundry, wireless Internet. **Business Services:** PC, fax (fee). **Cards:** AX, CB, DC, DS, MC, VI. **Free Special Amenities: continental breakfast and high-speed Internet.**

/ SOME UNITS FEE

▼ See AAA listing p 1100 ▼

WHERE TO DINE

CAPTAIN'S QUARTERS RESTAURANT — **Phone:** 803/854-4695

Steak & Seafood
$11-$22

Convenient to the interstate, the homey, Southern-style restaurant has a wrap-around porch with rocking chairs. On the menu are broiled or fried scallops, shrimp and flounder served with salad or the usual sides. Crispy, flour-dredged fried oysters are a good choice. Service is rushed but focused. Casual dress. **Bar:** Full bar. **Reservations:** suggested. **Hours:** 5 pm-9 pm. Closed: 12/25. **Address:** Rt 6 & I-95 **Location:** I-95, exit 98 (SR 6), just se; adjacent to Best Western Santee Inn. **Parking:** on-site. **Cards:** AX, MC, VI.

CLARK'S RESTAURANT — **Phone:** 803/854-2101

American
$7-$26

A hunting and fishing motif weaves through the rustic, country-lodge atmosphere. Diners who relax in the former old home are inundated with choices from the lengthy menu. The view from the windows overlooking the courtyard is a treat. Casual dress. **Bar:** Full bar. **Hours:** 6 am-9 pm, Fri & Sat-10 pm. Closed: 12/25. **Address:** 8920 Old Hwy 6 **Location:** I-95, exit 98 (SR 6), just nw; in Clark's Inn. **Parking:** on-site. **Cards:** AX, CB, DC, DS, MC, VI.

SENECA pop. 7,652

WHERE TO STAY

BEST WESTERN EXECUTIVE INN *Book great rates at AAA.com* — **Phone:** (864)886-9646

Hotel
$76-$175 All Year

Address: 511 Hwy 123 Bypass **Location:** Jct SR 130 and US 78/123, 0.8 mi w on US 78/123. **Facility:** 58 one-bedroom standard units, some with whirlpools. 3 stories, interior corridors. *Bath:* combo or shower only. **Parking:** on-site. **Terms:** 7 day cancellation notice. **Amenities:** high-speed Internet, voice mail, irons, hair dryers. **Pool(s):** outdoor. **Guest Services:** wireless Internet. **Business Services:** PC, fax (fee). **Cards:** AX, DC, DS, MC, VI.

AAA Benefit:
Members save up to 20%, plus 10% bonus points with rewards program.

JAMESON INN *Book at AAA.com* — **Phone:** (864)888-8300

Motel
$83-$90 All Year

Address: 226 Hi-Tech Rd **Location:** Jct SR 28 and US 76/123, 0.9 mi w on US 76/123, just se. **Facility:** 62 one-bedroom standard units, some with whirlpools. 2 stories (no elevator), exterior corridors. *Bath:* combo or shower only. **Parking:** on-site. **Terms:** cancellation fee imposed. **Amenities:** hair dryers. *Some:* irons. **Pool(s):** outdoor. **Leisure Activities:** exercise room. **Guest Services:** valet laundry, wireless Internet. **Business Services:** PC, fax (fee). **Cards:** AX, DC, DS, MC, VI.

ASK CALL / SOME UNITS FEE

WHERE TO DINE

COPPER RIVER GRILL — **Phone:** 864/888-8788

American
$7-$23

The new upstate chain features purpose-built facilities reminiscent of an Alaskan mountain lodge, with rustic exteriors, stone fireplaces, plank and rough-hewn timber walls and an open exhibition grill. Portions are huge in signature dishes of slow-roasted prime rib, half-pound burgers and salmon roasted on a smoked hickory plank. Also on the menu are entree salads, stone-fire pizzas, ribs, chicken and children's dishes. Desserts are meant for sharing. Service is casual and attentive. Casual dress. **Bar:** Full bar. **Reservations:** not accepted. **Hours:** 11 am-10 pm, Fri & Sat-11 pm. Closed: 11/26, 12/25. **Address:** 514 Hwy 123 Bypass **Location:** Jct SR 130 and US/76/123, 0.9 mi w on US 76/123. **Parking:** on-site. **Cards:** MC, VI.

CALL

FATZ CAFE — **Phone:** 864/888-1009

American
$6-$18

Friendly staff and appealing country decor help set the tone for a relaxed and enjoyable dining experience. It's not unusual for guests to wait to be seated at the popular spot, which earns raves for its well-prepared variations on chicken, steak, ribs and pasta, as well as salads and sandwiches. The signature Southern-style peach cobbler served with vanilla ice cream and walnuts is scrumptious. Casual dress. **Bar:** Full bar. **Hours:** 11 am-10 pm, Fri & Sat-11 pm, Sun-9 pm. Closed: 11/26, 12/25. **Address:** 1615 Sandifer Blvd **Location:** Jct SR 28 and US 76/123, 0.9 mi w on US 76/123. **Parking:** on-site. **Cards:** AX, DC, DS, MC, VI.

WEINACKER'S RESTAURANT — **Phone:** 864/972-9302

American
$14-$22

Family owned and operated for 35 years, the former fish lodge nestled among the rolling hills in the Golden Corner of Oconee County provides classic dishes in a country atmosphere. Specialties include slow-roasted prime rib and toasted almond Carolina mountain trout. This place is well worth the trip. Casual dress. **Bar:** Beer & wine. **Reservations:** accepted. **Hours:** 5 pm-10 pm. Closed major holidays; also Sun-Wed. **Address:** 930 Conecross Creek Rd **Location:** I-85, exit 11, 6.1 mi nw on SR 24 to Conecross Creek Rd, then 0.9 mi n. **Parking:** on-site. **Cards:** MC, VI.

SIMPSONVILLE pop. 14,352 (See map and index starting on p. 1050)

WHERE TO STAY

DAYS INN Book at AAA.com **Phone:** 864/963-7701

Motel
Rates not provided

Address: 45 Ray E Talley Ct **Location:** I-385, exit 27, just s, then just e. **Facility:** 40 one-bedroom standard units, some with whirlpools. 2 stories, exterior corridors. **Parking:** on-site. **Amenities:** high-speed Internet, irons, hair dryers. *Some:* DVD players (fee). **Pool(s):** outdoor. **Leisure Activities:** exercise room. **Guest Services:** valet laundry, wireless Internet. **Business Services:** PC, fax (fee).

/ SOME UNITS FEE FEE VCR

HAMPTON INN-SIMPSONVILLE Book great rates at AAA.com **Phone:** (864)963-9292

Hotel
$99-$119 All Year

Address: 3934 Grandview Dr **Location:** I-385, exit 27, just s on Fairview Rd, then just se along Service Rd. **Facility:** 83 units. 74 one-bedroom standard units, some with whirlpools. 9 one-bedroom suites, some with whirlpools. 4 stories, interior corridors. *Bath:* combo or shower only. **Parking:** on-site. **Terms:** 1-30 night minimum stay, cancellation fee imposed. **Amenities:** dual phone lines, voice mail, irons, hair dryers. **Pool(s):** outdoor. **Leisure Activities:** exercise room. **Guest Services:** valet laundry, wireless Internet. **Business Services:** meeting rooms, business center. **Cards:** AX, CB, DC, DS, MC, VI.

CALL / SOME UNITS

HOLIDAY INN EXPRESS-SIMPSONVILLE Book at AAA.com **Phone:** 864/962-8500

Hotel
Rates not provided

Address: 3821 Grandview Dr **Location:** I-385, exit 27, just s. **Facility:** 87 one-bedroom standard units, some with whirlpools. 4 stories, interior corridors. *Bath:* combo or shower only. **Parking:** on-site. **Amenities:** high-speed Internet, dual phone lines, voice mail, irons, hair dryers. **Pool(s):** outdoor. **Leisure Activities:** exercise room. **Guest Services:** coin laundry, wireless Internet. **Business Services:** meeting rooms, business center.

/ SOME UNITS

MOTEL 6 #4266 Book at AAA.com **Phone:** (864)962-8484

Hotel
$45-$55 All Year

Address: 3706 Grandview Dr **Location:** I-385, exit 27, just s, then just w. **Facility:** 50 one-bedroom standard units. 2 stories (no elevator), interior corridors. *Bath:* combo or shower only. **Parking:** on-site. **Amenities:** safes. **Guest Services:** coin laundry, wireless Internet. **Business Services:** PC, fax (fee). **Cards:** AX, DC, DS, MC, VI.

ASK CALL / SOME UNITS FEE

QUALITY INN Book great rates at AAA.com **Phone:** (864)963-2777

AAA SAVE

Motel
$69-$89 3/1-11/30
$59-$79 12/1-2/28

Address: 3755 Grandview Dr **Location:** I-385, exit 27, just s. **Facility:** 82 one-bedroom standard units, some with whirlpools. 2 stories (no elevator), exterior corridors. **Parking:** on-site. **Terms:** cancellation fee imposed. **Amenities:** voice mail, safes, irons, hair dryers. **Pool(s):** outdoor. **Leisure Activities:** whirlpool, exercise room. **Guest Services:** coin laundry, wireless Internet. **Business Services:** meeting rooms, business center. **Cards:** AX, DS, MC, VI. **Free Special Amenities: expanded continental breakfast and high-speed Internet.**

/ SOME UNITS FEE

RYAN NICHOLAS INN **Phone:** (864)286-6000 37

Bed & Breakfast
$155 All Year

Address: 815 Holland Rd **Location:** I-385, exit 33, just e on Bridges Rd. **Facility:** Normally booked for weddings on most weekends of the year, this upscale B&B offers a pleasant weekday stay for those seeking a memorable experience. Smoke free premises. 4 units. 3 one-bedroom standard units, some with whirlpools. 1 one-bedroom suite with whirlpool. 2 stories, interior corridors. *Bath:* combo or shower only. **Parking:** on-site. **Terms:** cancellation fee imposed. **Amenities:** video library, irons, hair dryers. *Some:* CD players. **Business Services:** meeting rooms, fax. **Cards:** AX, CB, DC, DS, JC, MC, VI.

ASK VCR

WHERE TO DINE

DRAGON DEN RESTAURANT **Phone:** 864/967-9717

Chinese
$4-$16

Located in a shopping center, patrons can select from an extensive list of Oriental foods, served in a traditional, casual setting. Casual dress. **Bar:** Full bar. **Hours:** 11:30 am-2:30 & 4:30-10 pm. Closed: 11/26, 12/25. **Address:** 621-A Fairview Station Shopping Center **Location:** I-26, exit 27, just se; at south end of Fairview Station. **Parking:** on-site. **Cards:** AX, MC, VI.

CALL

EL TEJANO MEXICAN RESTAURANT **Phone:** 864/962-8657

Mexican
$4-$16

The popular restaurant's menu lines up an array of traditional, well-prepared selections and combination plates. When busy, the dining rooms bustle; a wait for a table can be expected. Casual dress. **Bar:** Full bar. **Hours:** 11 am-10 pm, Fri-9:30 pm, Sat noon-10:30 pm, Sun 11:30 am-9:30 pm. Closed: 1/1, 11/26, 12/25. **Address:** 38 Ray E Talley Ct **Location:** I-26, exit 27, 0.4 mi s on Fairview Rd, then just e; in Talley Station. **Parking:** on-site. **Cards:** AX, MC, VI.

CALL

SPARTANBURG pop. 39,673

WHERE TO STAY

BEST WESTERN *Book great rates at AAA.com* **Phone:** (864)699-0000

Hotel
$66-$76 All Year

Address: 125 Sloane Garden Rd **Location:** I-85, exit 75, just s. **Facility:** Smoke free premises. 69 one-bedroom standard units, some with whirlpools. 6 stories, interior corridors. *Bath:* combo or shower only. **Parking:** on-site. **Terms:** cancellation fee imposed. **Amenities:** high-speed Internet, irons, hair dryers. **Pool(s):** outdoor. **Leisure Activities:** whirlpool, exercise room. **Guest Services:** valet and coin laundry, wireless Internet. **Business Services:** meeting rooms, business center. **Cards:** AX, DC, DS, MC, VI. **Free Special Amenities: continental breakfast and high-speed Internet.**

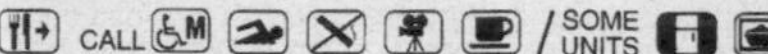

AAA Benefit: Members save up to 20%, plus 10% bonus points with rewards program.

COURTYARD BY MARRIOTT *Book great rates at AAA.com* **Phone:** (864)585-2400

Hotel
$98-$106 All Year

Address: 110 Mobile Dr **Location:** I-85 business route, exit 4 (SR 56), just ne. **Facility:** Smoke free premises. 108 units. 102 one-bedroom standard units. 6 one-bedroom suites. 3 stories, interior corridors. *Bath:* combo or shower only. **Parking:** on-site. **Terms:** cancellation fee imposed. **Amenities:** high-speed Internet, voice mail, irons, hair dryers. **Pool(s):** outdoor. **Leisure Activities:** whirlpool, exercise room. **Guest Services:** valet and coin laundry, wireless Internet. **Business Services:** meeting rooms, business center. **Cards:** AX, CB, DC, DS, MC, VI.

AAA Benefit: Members save a minimum 5% off the best available rate.

EXTENDED STAYAMERICA-SPARTANBURG-ASHEVILLE HWY *Book at AAA.com* **Phone:** (864)573-5949

Extended Stay Motel
$70-$80 All Year

Address: 130 Mobile Dr **Location:** I-85 business route, exit 4/4B, just se, then just ne on service road. **Facility:** Near the junctions of interstates 26, 85 and 585, the motel offers modest, comfortable rooms; public areas and recreational facilities are limited. 126 one-bedroom standard units with efficiencies. 2 stories (no elevator), exterior corridors. *Bath:* combo or shower only. **Parking:** on-site. **Terms:** office hours 7 am-11 pm. **Amenities:** voice mail, irons. **Guest Services:** coin laundry, wireless Internet. **Business Services:** fax (fee). **Cards:** AX, CB, DC, DS, JC, MC, VI.

FAIRFIELD INN SPARTANBURG *Book great rates at AAA.com* **Phone:** (864)542-0333

Hotel
$78-$84 All Year

Address: 160 Simuel Rd **Location:** I-85 business route, exit 4 (SR 56), just nw. **Facility:** Smoke free premises. 92 one-bedroom standard units, some with whirlpools. 4 stories, interior corridors. *Bath:* combo or shower only. **Parking:** on-site. **Terms:** cancellation fee imposed. **Amenities:** irons, hair dryers. **Pool(s):** outdoor. **Leisure Activities:** whirlpool, limited exercise equipment. **Guest Services:** coin laundry, wireless Internet. **Business Services:** meeting rooms, PC, fax (fee). **Cards:** AX, CB, DC, DS, JC, MC, VI.

AAA Benefit: Members save a minimum 5% off the best available rate.

HAMPTON INN & SUITES SPARTANBURG/I-26 *Book great rates at AAA.com* **Phone:** (864)699-2222

Hotel
$118-$128 All Year

Address: 801 Spartan Blvd **Location:** I-26, exit 21B (US 29), just e to Blackstock Rd, 0.7 mi n, then just w. Adjacent to Westgate Mall. **Facility:** 126 one-bedroom standard units. 5 stories, interior corridors. *Bath:* combo or shower only. **Parking:** on-site. **Terms:** cancellation fee imposed. **Amenities:** high-speed Internet, dual phone lines, voice mail, irons, hair dryers. **Pool(s):** indoor. **Leisure Activities:** limited exercise equipment. **Guest Services:** area transportation, wireless Internet. **Business Services:** conference facilities, business center. **Cards:** AX, CB, DC, DS, JC, MC, VI.

AAA Benefit: Members save up to 10% everyday!

HOLIDAY INN EXPRESS HOTEL & SUITES *Book at AAA.com* **Phone:** 864/699-7777

Hotel
Rates not provided

Address: 895 Spartan Blvd **Location:** I-26, exit 21B (US 29), just e to Blackstock Rd, then 0.7 mi n; adjacent to Westgate Mall. **Facility:** 88 one-bedroom standard units, some with whirlpools. 4 stories, interior corridors. *Bath:* combo or shower only. **Parking:** on-site. **Amenities:** high-speed Internet, dual phone lines, voice mail, irons, hair dryers. **Pool(s):** heated indoor. **Leisure Activities:** exercise room. **Guest Services:** valet and coin laundry, area transportation, wireless Internet. **Business Services:** meeting rooms, business center.

HOWARD JOHNSON INN *Book at AAA.com* **Phone:** (864)576-0042

Hotel
$54-$69 All Year

Address: 6690 Pottery Rd **Location:** I-26, exit 17, just w. **Facility:** 52 one-bedroom standard units. 3 stories, interior corridors. *Bath:* combo or shower only. **Parking:** on-site. **Amenities:** voice mail, irons, hair dryers. **Guest Services:** wireless Internet. **Business Services:** fax (fee). **Cards:** AX, DC, DS, MC, VI.

ASK / SOME UNITS

RADISSON HOTEL & SUITES *Book great rates at AAA.com* **Phone:** (864)574-2111

AAA SAVE

Hotel
$89-$105 All Year

Address: 9027 Fairforest Rd **Location:** I-85 business route, exit 2C, just e, then just s. **Facility:** 200 units. 100 one-bedroom standard units. 100 one-bedroom suites, some with whirlpools. 5 stories, interior corridors. **Parking:** on-site. **Amenities:** voice mail, irons, hair dryers. *Some:* high-speed Internet. **Pool(s):** heated indoor. **Leisure Activities:** exercise room. **Guest Services:** valet and coin laundry, airport transportation-Greenville-Spartanburg Airport, wireless Internet. **Business Services:** conference facilities, PC, fax (fee). **Cards:** AX, DC, DS, JC, MC, VI. **Free Special Amenities: local telephone calls and high-speed Internet.**

/ SOME UNITS

SLEEP INN *Book great rates at AAA.com* **Phone:** (864)595-4040

AAA SAVE

Hotel
$65-$79 4/1-11/30
$62-$72 12/1-3/31

Address: 501 S Blackstock Rd **Location:** I-26, exit 22 (SR 296), just w. **Facility:** 63 one-bedroom standard units. 3 stories, interior corridors. *Bath:* combo or shower only. **Parking:** on-site. **Terms:** cancellation fee imposed. **Amenities:** irons, hair dryers. **Guest Services:** valet laundry, wireless Internet. **Business Services:** fax (fee). **Cards:** AX, DC, DS, JC, MC, VI. **Free Special Amenities: expanded continental breakfast and high-speed Internet.**

CALL / SOME UNITS

SPARTANBURG MARRIOTT AT RENAISSANCE PARK *Book great rates at AAA.com* **Phone:** (864)596-1211

Hotel
$138-$148 All Year

Address: 299 N Church St **Location:** Jct US 29/SR 56/US 221, just n on SR 56/US 221; downtown. **Facility:** Smoke free premises. 247 units. 240 one-bedroom standard units. 7 one-bedroom suites, some with whirlpools. 9 stories, interior corridors. *Bath:* combo or shower only. **Parking:** on-site (fee) and valet. **Terms:** cancellation fee imposed. **Amenities:** high-speed Internet (fee), dual phone lines, voice mail, safes, irons, hair dryers. **Pool(s):** heated outdoor. **Leisure Activities:** saunas, whirlpool. *Fee:* massage. **Guest Services:** valet laundry, wireless Internet. **Business Services:** conference facilities, business center. **Cards:** AX, DS, MC, VI.

/ SOME UNITS

WHERE TO DINE

CAPRI'S ITALIAN RESTAURANT **Phone:** 864/576-4152

Italian
$7-$17

Italian fare is prepared from secret recipes at the family-owned-and-operated restaurant. American selections also make menu appearances. Casual dress. **Bar:** Beer & wine. **Hours:** 4:30 pm-9:30 pm, Fri & Sat-10 pm. Closed: 1/1, 11/26, 12/24, 12/25; also Super Bowl Sun. **Address:** 1600 John B White Sr Blvd, Suite 1007 **Location:** I-26, exit 22 (SR 296), 0.6 mi e; in Camelot Center. **Parking:** on-site. **Cards:** AX, DS, MC, VI.

CALL

FATZ CAFE **Phone:** 864/574-4814

American
$7-$19

Friendly staff and appealing country decor help set the tone for a relaxed and enjoyable dining experience. It's not unusual for guests to wait to be seated at the popular spot, which earns raves for its well-prepared variations on chicken, steak, ribs and pasta, as well as salads and sandwiches. The signature Southern-style peach cobbler served with vanilla ice cream and walnuts is scrumptious. Casual dress. **Bar:** Full bar. **Hours:** 11 am-10 pm, Fri & Sat-11 pm, Sun-9 pm. Closed: 11/26, 12/25. **Address:** 6750 Pottery Rd **Location:** I-26, exit 17, just w, then just s. **Parking:** on-site. **Cards:** AX, DS, MC, VI.

CALL

FATZ CAFE **Phone:** 864/576-6228

American
$7-$19

Friendly staff and appealing country decor help set the tone for a relaxed and enjoyable dining experience. It's not unusual for guests to wait to be seated at the popular spot, which earns raves for its well-prepared variations on chicken, steak, ribs and pasta, as well as salads and sandwiches. The signature Southern-style peach cobbler served with vanilla ice cream and walnuts is scrumptious. Casual dress. **Hours:** 11 am-10 pm, Fri & Sat-11 pm, Sun-9 pm. Closed: 11/26, 12/25. **Address:** 100 Southport Rd **Location:** I-26, exit 22, 1 mi e on SR 295/296 (John B White Sr Blvd), then just s. **Parking:** on-site. **Cards:** AX, DS, MC, VI.

GERHARD'S CAFE **Phone:** 864/591-1920

German
$12-$27

Expertly-prepared, traditional German fare is served in an elegant, inviting setting. Dressy casual. **Bar:** Full bar. **Reservations:** accepted. **Hours:** 5:30 pm-10 pm, Fri & Sat-10:30 pm. Closed: 1/1, 12/25; also Sun. **Address:** 1200 E Main St **Location:** 2 mi e on US 29; in Converse Plaza. **Parking:** on-site. **Cards:** AX, DC, DS, MC, VI.

MR. GATTI'S

Pizza
$6-$8

Phone: 864/585-8897

Diners find great value for the dollar at the casual eatery, where the extensive salad and pizza bar includes a variety of dessert pizzas. Casual dress. **Reservations:** accepted. **Hours:** 11 am-9 pm, Fri & Sat-10 pm. Closed: 11/26, 12/25. **Address:** 100 McMillan Dr **Location:** Jct US 221/176, just se on US 176 to McCravy Dr, just ne. **Parking:** on-site. **Cards:** AX, DC, DS, MC, VI.

THAI TASTE

Thai
$6-$21

Phone: 864/595-6040

Said to have the best Thai cuisine in town, locals flock to the restaurant for dishes prepared with the freshest herbs. While the decor is modest, the food is anything but. Casual dress. **Bar:** Beer & wine. **Reservations:** accepted. **Hours:** 11 am-9:30 pm, Fri-10 pm, Sat noon-10 pm. Closed major holidays; also Sun. **Address:** 145 Southport Rd **Location:** I-26, exit 22 (SR 296), 1 mi e to Southport Rd/SR 295, then 0.6 mi s. **Parking:** on-site. **Cards:** AX, DS, MC, VI.

SULLIVAN'S ISLAND —*See Charleston p. 934.*

SUMMERTON pop. 1,061

WHERE TO STAY

DAYS INN OF SUMMERTON *Book great rates at AAA.com*

AAA SAVE

Motel
$34-$65 All Year

Phone: (803)485-2865

Address: 400 Bluff Blvd **Location:** I-95, exit 108, just n. **Facility:** 54 one-bedroom standard units, some with whirlpools. 2 stories (no elevator), exterior corridors. **Parking:** on-site. **Amenities:** hair dryers. **Pool(s):** outdoor. **Guest Services:** wireless Internet. **Business Services:** fax (fee). **Cards:** AX, DC, DS, MC, VI. **Free Special Amenities: expanded continental breakfast and high-speed Internet.**

/ SOME UNITS FEE

SUMMERVILLE —*See Charleston p. 935.*

SUMTER pop. 39,643

WHERE TO STAY

BEST WESTERN SUMTER INN *Book great rates at AAA.com*

AAA SAVE

Motel
$65-$68 All Year

Phone: (803)773-8110

Address: 1050 Broad St **Location:** On US 76/521, 0.7 mi s of jct US 76/378/521. **Facility:** 47 one-bedroom standard units, some with whirlpools. 1 story, exterior corridors. **Parking:** on-site. **Amenities:** irons, hair dryers. **Pool(s):** outdoor. **Guest Services:** wireless Internet. **Business Services:** fax (fee). **Cards:** AX, DC, DS, MC, VI. **Free Special Amenities: continental breakfast and high-speed Internet.**

  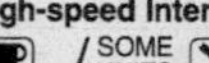 / SOME UNITS

AAA Benefit:
Members save up to 20%, plus 10% bonus points with rewards program.

COMFORT SUITES *Book at AAA.com*

Hotel
Rates not provided

Phone: 803/469-0200

Address: 2500 Broad St Ext **Location:** On US 76/378, 1 mi w of jct US 76/378/521. **Facility:** Smoke free premises. 65 one-bedroom standard units, some with whirlpools. 3 stories, interior corridors. *Bath:* combo or shower only. **Parking:** on-site. **Amenities:** DVD players, high-speed Internet, dual phone lines, voice mail, safes (fee), irons, hair dryers. *Some:* fax. **Pool(s):** outdoor, heated indoor. **Leisure Activities:** sauna, whirlpool, exercise room privileges. **Guest Services:** valet and coin laundry, wireless Internet. **Business Services:** meeting rooms, business center.

CALL

COUNTRY INN & SUITES SUMTER

fyi

Hotel
$104 All Year

Phone: 803/469-6666

Too new to rate. **Address:** 2491 Broad St **Location:** On US 378. **Amenities:** 65 units, coffeemakers, microwaves, refrigerators. **Cards:** AX, DS, MC, VI.

DAYS INN & SUITES *Book at AAA.com*

Motel
$66-$76 All Year

Phone: (803)469-8400

Address: 2430 Broad St Ext **Location:** On US 76/378, 1 mi w of jct US 76/378/521. **Facility:** 48 one-bedroom standard units, some with whirlpools. 1 story, exterior corridors. **Parking:** on-site. **Amenities:** irons, hair dryers. **Pool(s):** outdoor. **Guest Services:** wireless Internet. **Business Services:** fax (fee). **Cards:** AX, DC, DS, MC, VI.

ASK / SOME UNITS

HOLIDAY INN EXPRESS HOTEL & SUITES *Book at AAA.com*

Hotel
$110-$200 All Year

Phone: (803)469-4444

Address: 2490 Broad St **Location:** On US 76/378, 1 mi w of jct US 76/378/521. **Facility:** 79 one-bedroom standard units, some with whirlpools. 3 stories, interior corridors. *Bath:* combo or shower only. **Parking:** on-site. **Amenities:** high-speed Internet, dual phone lines, voice mail, irons, hair dryers. **Pool(s):** heated indoor. **Leisure Activities:** limited exercise equipment. **Guest Services:** coin laundry, wireless Internet. **Business Services:** meeting rooms, business center. **Cards:** AX, CB, DC, DS, JC, MC, VI.

RAMADA INN *Book at AAA.com* **Phone:** (803)775-2323

Motel
$69-$73 All Year

Address: 226 N Washington St **Location:** US 76 business route/521, just n. **Facility:** 125 one bedroom standard units, some with kitchens. 2-3 stories, exterior corridors. **Parking:** on-site. **Amenities:** voice mail, irons, hair dryers. **Pool(s):** outdoor. **Leisure Activities:** whirlpool, putting green. **Guest Services:** coin laundry, wireless Internet. **Business Services:** meeting rooms, fax (fee). **Cards:** AX, CB, DC, DS, MC, VI.

ASK / SOME UNITS FEE

SLEEP INN-SUMTER *Book at AAA.com* **Phone:** 803/469-0500

Hotel
Rates not provided

Address: 2510 Broad St Ext **Location:** On US 76/378, 1 mi w of jct US 76/378/521. **Facility:** 60 one-bedroom standard units, some with efficiencies. 3 stories, interior corridors. *Bath:* combo or shower only. **Parking:** on-site. **Amenities:** high-speed Internet, dual phone lines, voice mail, irons, hair dryers. **Pool(s):** outdoor. **Leisure Activities:** putting green, exercise room. **Guest Services:** valet laundry. **Business Services:** business center.

VCR / SOME UNITS

TRAVELERS INN & SUITES **Phone:** (803)469-9210

Motel
$59-$89 All Year

Address: 1210 Camden Rd **Location:** Jct US 521/US 76. **Facility:** 103 one-bedroom standard units, some with whirlpools. 2 stories (no elevator), exterior corridors. **Parking:** on-site. **Amenities:** *Some:* irons, hair dryers. **Pool(s):** outdoor. **Guest Services:** coin laundry, wireless Internet. **Business Services:** meeting rooms, fax (fee). **Cards:** AX, DS, MC, VI. **Free Special Amenities: continental breakfast and high-speed Internet.**

/ SOME UNITS FEE

WHERE TO DINE

REDBONE ALLEY RESTAURANT & BAR **Phone:** 803/905-7750

American
$7-$21

The interior brings the outside in, with a "sidewalk cafe" feel permeating a room that looks as if its set amid storefronts in downtown Charleston. Birds perched on flower boxes and umbrellas over tables lend to an atmosphere that's as close to al fresco as indoor dining can get. The menu includes hand-cut steaks and seafood and many specialty salads and sandwiches. Among popular entrees are smothered pork chops, Redbone rubbed St. Louis ribs, quail, and grits and gravy. Casual dress. **Bar:** Full bar. **Reservations:** accepted. **Hours:** 11:30 am-10 pm, Fri & Sat-11 pm, Sun-9 pm. Closed: 11/26, 12/25. **Address:** 1342 Broad St **Location:** On US 76/378, 0.6 mi n of jct US 76/378/521. **Parking:** on-site. **Cards:** AX, DS, MC, VI.

SURFSIDE BEACH —*See The Grand Strand p. 1048.*

TIMMONSVILLE pop. 2,315

WHERE TO STAY

ECONO LODGE *Book at AAA.com* **Phone:** (843)346-9696

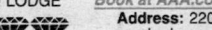

Motel
$59-$150 All Year

Address: 2200 Cale Yarborough Hwy (SR 403) **Location:** I-95, exit 150 (SR 403), just s. **Facility:** 37 one-bedroom standard units. 2 stories (no elevator), exterior corridors. *Bath:* combo or shower only. **Parking:** on-site. **Terms:** 7 day cancellation notice. **Amenities:** hair dryers. **Guest Services:** wireless Internet. **Business Services:** fax (fee). **Cards:** AX, DS, MC, VI.

ASK CALL / SOME UNITS VCR

TRAVELERS REST pop. 4,099

WHERE TO STAY

HAMPTON INN TRAVELERS REST *Book great rates at AAA.com* **Phone:** (864)834-5550

Hotel
$94-$99 All Year

Address: 593 Roe Center Ct **Location:** Jct US 25 and 276, just n on US 276. **Facility:** 62 one-bedroom standard units, some with whirlpools. 4 stories, interior corridors. *Bath:* combo or shower only. **Parking:** on-site. **Terms:** 1-30 night minimum stay, cancellation fee imposed. **Amenities:** dual phone lines, voice mail, irons, hair dryers. **Pool(s):** outdoor. **Leisure Activities:** limited exercise equipment. **Guest Services:** valet laundry, wireless Internet. **Business Services:** meeting rooms, fax (fee). **Cards:** AX, CB, DC, DS, MC, VI.

CALL / SOME UNITS

AAA Benefit:
Members save up to 10% everyday!

SLEEP INN *Book at AAA.com* **Phone:** 864/834-7040

Hotel
Rates not provided

Address: 110 Hawkins Rd **Location:** US 25, exit Hawkins Rd. **Facility:** 62 one-bedroom standard units, some with whirlpools. 3 stories, interior corridors. *Bath:* combo or shower only. **Parking:** on-site. **Amenities:** safes (fee), irons, hair dryers. **Pool(s):** outdoor. **Guest Services:** wireless Internet. **Business Services:** meeting rooms, fax (fee).

CALL / SOME UNITS FEE

WALHALLA pop. 3,801

— WHERE TO DINE —

DAKOTA GRILL

Regional American
$6-$18

Phone: 864/718-0553

Menu selections at the family-operated, family-friendly restaurant feature steaks, chops and some seafood dishes. The grill is located near the scenic foothills, just outside Sumter National Forest. Casual dress. **Bar:** Beer & wine. **Hours:** 5 pm-9 pm. Closed: 11/26, 12/25; also Sun & Mon. **Address:** 2911 Highlands Hwy **Location:** 4.2 mi nw of jct SR 183/28 on SR 28. **Parking:** on-site. **Cards:** AX, DS, MC, VI.

WALTERBORO pop. 5,153

— WHERE TO STAY —

BEST WESTERN OF WALTERBORO *Book great rates at AAA.com* **Phone:** (843)538-3600

AAA SAVE

Hotel
$69-$99 All Year

Address: 1428 Sniders Hwy **Location:** I-95, exit 53 (SR 63), just e. **Facility:** 106 units. 99 one-bedroom standard units. 7 one-bedroom suites, some with whirlpools. 2 stories, exterior corridors. **Parking:** on-site. **Terms:** 3 day cancellation notice. **Amenities:** voice mail, irons, hair dryers. *Some:* DVD players. **Pool(s):** outdoor. **Guest Services:** wireless Internet. **Business Services:** meeting rooms, fax (fee). **Cards:** AX, CB, DC, DS, JC, MC, VI. **Free Special Amenities: expanded continental breakfast and high-speed Internet.**

/ SOME UNITS FEE

AAA Benefit:
Members save up to 20%, plus 10% bonus points with rewards program.

COMFORT INN & SUITES *Book great rates at AAA.com* **Phone:** (843)538-5911

AAA SAVE

Hotel
$69-$129 All Year

Address: 97 Downs Ln **Location:** I-95, exit 53 (SR 63), just e, then sw. **Facility:** 96 one-bedroom standard units, some with whirlpools. 2 stories, interior corridors. *Bath:* combo or shower only. **Parking:** on-site. **Terms:** 7 day cancellation notice. **Amenities:** voice mail, irons, hair dryers. *Some:* high-speed Internet. **Pool(s):** outdoor. **Leisure Activities:** limited exercise equipment. **Guest Services:** wireless Internet. **Business Services:** business center. **Cards:** AX, CB, DC, DS, JC, MC, VI. **Free Special Amenities: expanded continental breakfast and high-speed Internet.**

DAYS INN Book at AAA.com Phone: (843)538-2933

Motel
$57-$65 All Year

Address: 1787 Sniders Hwy **Location:** I-95, exit 53 (SR 63), just w. **Facility:** 61 one-bedroom standard units, some with whirlpools. 2 stories (no elevator), exterior corridors. **Parking:** on-site. **Amenities:** hair dryers. **Pool(s):** outdoor. **Leisure Activities:** sauna, limited exercise equipment. **Guest Services:** wireless Internet. **Business Services:** PC, fax (fee). **Cards:** AX, DC, DS, MC, VI.

ASK / SOME UNITS

ECONO LODGE Book great rates at AAA.com Phone: (843)538-3830

AAA SAVE
Motel
$49-$99 All Year

Address: 1145 Sniders Hwy **Location:** I-95, exit 53 (SR 63), just e. **Facility:** 95 one-bedroom standard units. 2 stories (no elevator), exterior corridors. **Parking:** on-site. **Guest Services:** wireless Internet. **Business Services:** fax (fee). **Cards:** AX, DC, DS, MC, VI. **Free Special Amenities: continental breakfast and high-speed Internet.**

/ SOME UNITS FEE

HAMPTON INN Book great rates at AAA.com Phone: (843)538-2300

Motel
$79-$109 All Year

Address: 1835 Sniders Hwy **Location:** I-95, exit 53 (SR 63), just w. **Facility:** 78 one-bedroom standard units. 2 stories, exterior corridors. *Bath:* combo or shower only. **Parking:** on-site. **Amenities:** voice mail, irons, hair dryers. **Pool(s):** outdoor. **Leisure Activities:** exercise room privileges. **Guest Services:** valet laundry, wireless Internet. **Business Services:** fax (fee). **Cards:** AX, DC, DS, MC, VI. ***(See color ad p 1108)***

CALL / SOME UNITS

AAA Benefit:
Members save up to 10% everyday!

HOLIDAY INN EXPRESS HOTEL & SUITES Book at AAA.com Phone: (843)538-2700

Hotel
$89-$109 All Year

Address: 1834 Sniders Hwy **Location:** I-95, exit 53 (SR 63), just w. **Facility:** 81 one-bedroom standard units. 3 stories, interior corridors. *Bath:* combo or shower only. **Parking:** on-site. **Amenities:** high-speed Internet, voice mail, irons, hair dryers. **Leisure Activities:** limited exercise equipment. **Guest Services:** valet and coin laundry, wireless Internet. **Business Services:** meeting rooms, business center. **Cards:** AX, DC, DS, MC, VI. ***(See color ad p 1108)***

ASK CALL / SOME UNITS

MICROTEL INN AND SUITES Book great rates at AAA.com Phone: (843)539-5656

AAA SAVE
Hotel
$59-$69 All Year

Address: 130 Cane Branch Rd **Location:** I-95, exit 53 (SR 63), just w, then just s. **Facility:** 70 one-bedroom standard units. 3 stories, interior corridors. *Bath:* combo or shower only. **Parking:** on-site. **Terms:** 10 day cancellation notice. **Amenities:** voice mail, hair dryers. *Some:* irons. **Pool(s):** outdoor. **Guest Services:** wireless Internet. **Business Services:** fax (fee). **Cards:** AX, DC, DS, MC, VI. **Free Special Amenities: expanded continental breakfast and high-speed Internet.**

CALL / SOME UNITS FEE

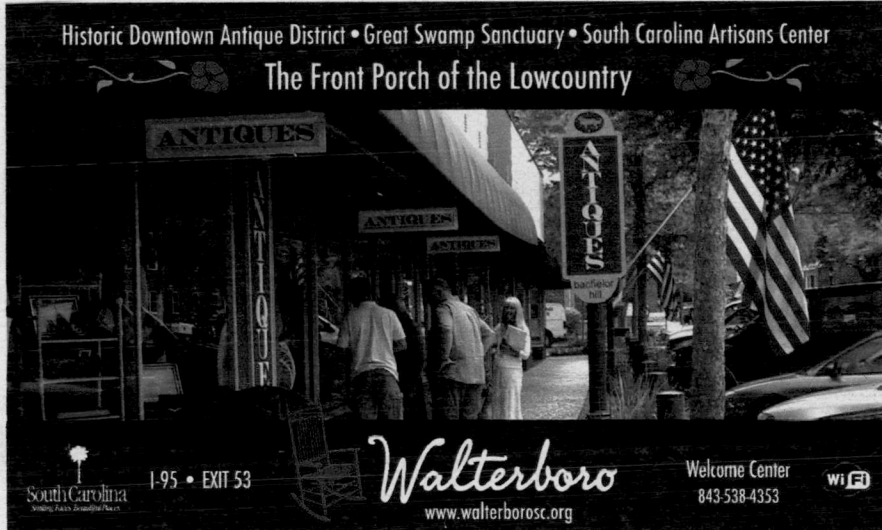

QUALITY INN & SUITES *Book at AAA.com*

Motel
$59-$89 All Year

Phone: (843)538-5473
Address: 1286 Sniders Hwy **Location:** I-95, exit 53 (SR 63), just e. **Facility:** 85 units. 75 one-bedroom standard units. 10 one-bedroom suites. 2 stories (no elevator), exterior corridors. **Parking:** on-site. **Amenities:** voice mail, irons, hair dryers. **Pool(s):** outdoor. **Leisure Activities:** exercise room. **Guest Services:** wireless Internet. **Business Services:** meeting rooms, fax (fee). **Cards:** AX, DS, MC, VI.

ASK / SOME UNITS FEE

RAMADA INN OF WALTERBORO *Book at AAA.com*

Hotel
$65 All Year

Phone: (843)538-5403
Address: 1245 Sniders Hwy **Location:** I-95, exit 53 (SR 63), just e. **Facility:** 100 units. 99 one-bedroom standard units, some with whirlpools. 1 one-bedroom suite with whirlpool. 2 stories (no elevator), exterior corridors. **Parking:** on-site. **Amenities:** voice mail, irons, hair dryers. **Pool(s):** outdoor. **Guest Services:** wireless Internet. **Business Services:** meeting rooms, fax (fee). **Cards:** AX, CB, DC, DS, MC, VI.

ASK / SOME UNITS FEE

RICE PLANTERS INN

AAA SAVE

Motel
$44 All Year

Phone: 843/538-8964
Address: 97 Ladson Ln **Location:** I-95, exit 53 (SR 63), just e. **Facility:** 76 one-bedroom standard units. 1-2 stories (no elevator), exterior corridors. *Bath:* combo or shower only. **Parking:** on-site. **Pool(s):** outdoor. **Business Services:** fax (fee). **Cards:** AX, DS, MC, VI. **Free Special Amenities: full breakfast and local telephone calls.**

/ SOME UNITS FEE

SLEEP INN OF WALTERBORO *Book great rates at AAA.com*

AAA SAVE

Hotel
$69-$89 3/1-11/30
$69 12/1-2/28

Phone: (843)539-1199
Address: 3043 Hiers Corner Rd **Location:** I-95, exit 57 (SR 64), just se. **Facility:** 56 one-bedroom standard units. 3 stories, interior corridors. *Bath:* combo or shower only. **Parking:** on-site. **Amenities:** high-speed Internet, irons, hair dryers. **Pool(s):** outdoor. **Guest Services:** wireless Internet. **Business Services:** fax (fee). **Cards:** AX, CB, DC, DS, JC, MC, VI. **Free Special Amenities: continental breakfast and high-speed Internet.**

CALL M / SOME UNITS FEE FEE

SUPER 8 MOTEL *Book great rates at AAA.com*

AAA SAVE

Motel
$46-$61 All Year

Phone: 843/538-5383
Address: 1972 Bells Hwy **Location:** I-95, exit 57 (SR 64), just nw. **Facility:** 45 one-bedroom standard units. 1-2 stories (no elevator), exterior corridors. **Parking:** on-site. **Terms:** 7 day cancellation notice. **Amenities:** hair dryers. **Pool(s):** outdoor. **Guest Services:** wireless Internet. **Business Services:** fax (fee). **Cards:** AX, DS, MC, VI. **Free Special Amenities: continental breakfast and high-speed Internet.**

/ SOME UNITS FEE

WHERE TO DINE

DIMITRIO'S HOUSE OF PIZZA ITALIAN RESTAURANT

Mediterranean
$6-$12

Phone: 843/549-5597
Just north of the city center, the popular storefront eatery presents a broad menu of Greek and Italian selections, such as lemon soup, spanikopita, pasta and manicotti. Casual dress. **Bar:** Beer & wine. **Reservations:** not accepted. **Hours:** 11 am-9 pm, Sat from 5 pm. Closed major holidays; also Sun. **Address:** 656 Bells Hwy **Location:** I-95, exit 57 (SR 64), 1 mi s on SR 64. **Parking:** on-site. **Cards:** MC, VI.

DUKE'S BAR-B-QUE

Barbecue
$9

Phone: 843/549-1446
This popular all-you-can-eat buffet restaurant features home-style cooking: hickory-smoked pulled pork and ribs, fried chicken, a wide selection of freshly cooked vegetables, rice and hash. Everything's simple but good. Casual dress. **Reservations:** not accepted. **Hours:** 11 am-8 pm, Fri & Sat-9 pm, Sun-2 pm. Closed: 4/12, 11/26, 12/25; also Mon & Tues. **Address:** 949 Robertson Blvd **Location:** I-95, exit 57, 1 mi se on Bells Hwy (SR 64), to Robertson Blvd, then 1 mi e. **Parking:** on-site. **Cards:** MC, VI.

GLASS HOUSE SEAFOOD RESTAURANT

Steak & Seafood
$9-$19

Phone: 843/538-6544
Near hotels and right off the interstate, the popular restaurant serves steaks, seafood and salads. A full-time chef is eager to make your experience memorable. Casual dress. **Bar:** Full bar. **Reservations:** accepted. **Hours:** 4 pm-10 pm, Fri & Sat-10:30 pm. Closed major holidays; also Sun. **Address:** 69 Downs Ln **Location:** I-95, exit 53 (SR 63), just e. **Parking:** on-site. **Cards:** AX, DS, MC, VI.

LONGHORN STEAKHOUSE

American
$7-$18

Phone: 843/538-2921
Not to be confused with the chain of a similar name, this family-run business features a no-frills buffet of meats, seafood and vegetables, as well as a dessert selection of iced sheet cakes. Casual dress. **Bar:** Full bar. **Reservations:** accepted. **Hours:** 11 am-10 pm, Fri & Sat-11 pm. Closed major holidays. **Address:** 98 Ladson St **Location:** I-95, exit 53 (SR 63), just e. **Parking:** on-site. **Cards:** AX, DS, MC, VI.

WEST COLUMBIA pop. 13,064 (See map and index starting on p. 940)

— WHERE TO STAY —

COMFORT INN-AIRPORT *Book great rates at AAA.com* **Phone:** (803)796-0044 69

AAA SAVE

Motel
$89 All Year

Address: 110 Branch Rd **Location:** I-26, exit 113 (Airport Blvd), just sw. **Facility:** 61 units. 60 one-bedroom standard units, some with whirlpools. 1 one-bedroom suite with whirlpool. 2 stories (no elevator), exterior corridors. *Bath:* combo or shower only. **Parking:** on-site. **Terms:** 7 day cancellation notice. **Amenities:** high-speed Internet, voice mail, irons, hair dryers. **Pool(s):** outdoor. **Leisure Activities:** limited exercise equipment. **Guest Services:** valet and coin laundry, airport transportation-Columbia Metropolitan Airport, wireless Internet. **Business Services:** meeting rooms, business center. **Cards:** AX, CB, DC, DS, MC, VI. **Free Special Amenities: expanded continental breakfast and high-speed Internet.**

CALL / SOME UNITS

HAMPTON INN COLUMBIA I-26/AIRPORT *Book great rates at AAA.com* **Phone:** (803)791-8940 66

AAA SAVE

Hotel
$99-$160 All Year

Address: 1094 Chris Dr **Location:** I-26, exit 110 (US 378), just se to Oakwood Dr, then just sw. **Facility:** 120 one-bedroom standard units. 4 stories, interior corridors. **Parking:** on-site. **Terms:** 1-30 night minimum stay, cancellation fee imposed. **Amenities:** video games (fee), voice mail, irons, hair dryers. **Pool(s):** outdoor. **Guest Services:** valet laundry, airport transportation-Columbia Metropolitan Airport, area transportation-within 5 mi, wireless Internet. **Business Services:** meeting rooms, business center. **Cards:** AX, DC, DS, MC, VI. **Free Special Amenities: expanded continental breakfast and high-speed Internet.** *(See color ad below)*

Hampton Inn
AAA Benefit:
Members save up to 10% everyday!

/ SOME UNITS

HOLIDAY INN AIRPORT *Book at AAA.com* **Phone:** (803)794-9440 67

Hotel
$99-$129 All Year

Address: 500 Chris Dr **Location:** I-26, exit 111B (US 1 N), just ne, then just n. **Facility:** 144 units. 141 one-bedroom standard units. 3 one-bedroom suites with whirlpools. 2 stories (no elevator), exterior corridors. *Bath:* combo or shower only. **Parking:** on-site. **Amenities:** dual phone lines, voice mail, irons, hair dryers. **Pool(s):** outdoor. **Leisure Activities:** limited exercise equipment. **Guest Services:** valet and coin laundry, area transportation, wireless Internet. **Business Services:** meeting rooms, business center. **Cards:** AX, CB, DC, DS, JC, MC, VI.

ASK / SOME UNITS

QUALITY INN *Book great rates at AAA.com* **Phone:** (803)791-5160 68

AAA SAVE

Hotel
$59-$99 All Year

Address: 2516 Augusta Rd **Location:** I-26, exit 111B (US 1 N), just e. **Facility:** 82 one-bedroom standard units. 2 stories (no elevator), interior/exterior corridors. **Parking:** on-site. **Amenities:** irons, hair dryers. **Pool(s):** outdoor. **Guest Services:** wireless Internet. **Business Services:** meeting rooms, business center. **Cards:** AX, DC, DS, JC, MC, VI. **Free Special Amenities: continental breakfast and high-speed Internet.** *(See color ad p 949)*

/ SOME UNITS FEE

(See map and index starting on p. 940)

SLEEP INN-AIRPORT *Book great rates at AAA.com* **Phone:** (803)926-9260 70

Hotel
$90-$135 All Year

Address: 2208-A Edmond Hwy **Location:** I-26, exit 113 (Airport Blvd), just sw. **Facility:** 69 one-bedroom standard units, some with whirlpools. 5 stories, interior corridors. *Bath:* combo or shower only. **Parking:** on-site. **Amenities:** high-speed Internet, voice mail, irons, hair dryers. **Pool(s):** outdoor. **Leisure Activities:** exercise room. **Guest Services:** valet and coin laundry, airport transportation-Columbia Metropolitan Airport, wireless Internet. **Business Services:** meeting rooms, business center. **Cards:** AX, CB, DC, DS, JC, MC, VI. **Free Special Amenities: continental breakfast and high-speed Internet.**

/ SOME UNITS

WHERE TO DINE

AL'S UPSTAIRS ITALIAN RESTAURANT **Phone:** 803/794-7404 19

Italian
$17-$29

Intimate second-floor dining rooms feature original art, light jazz background music and beautiful views of the city skyline, especially at sunset. Carefully crafted veal, seafood and steak dishes are served with starch and vegetable accompaniments. Featured selections include veal saltimbocca, rack of lamb, chicken Charleston and lobster fra diavolo. Desserts are prepared in house, and an extensive wine list completes the dining experience. Dressy casual. **Bar:** Full bar. **Reservations:** suggested. **Hours:** 5 pm-10 pm. Closed: 12/25; also Sun. **Address:** 304 Meeting St **Location:** Jct US 1 and 378; just w of Gervais St Bridge. **Parking:** on-site. **Cards:** AX, DC, DS, MC, VI.

GRECIAN GARDENS **Phone:** 803/794-7552 18

Mediterranean
$5-$17

The family-run restaurant offers a menu of Greek, Italian, American and Mediterranean fare along with grilled steaks, chops and Greek pizza. Signature courses include the Greek salad, lemon chicken soup, pistachio-stuffed flounder and a selection of Italian pasta dinners. All entrees are served with their popular fresh bread, a cup of soup or a dinner salad, a vegetable and a starch. A kid-friendly menu is also available. Casual dress. **Bar:** Full bar. **Hours:** 11 am-9 pm. Closed: 12/25. **Address:** 2312 Sunset Blvd **Location:** I-26, exit 110 (US 378), just e. **Parking:** on-site. **Cards:** AX, DS, MC, VI.

LIZARD'S THICKET **Phone:** 803/796-7820

Regional American
$3-$12

Owned and operated by the same family since 1978, guests can enjoy Southern home cooking at breakfast, lunch, and dinner. Locals love the Calabash style shrimp as well as the fried chicken livers. Be sure and ask about the daily specials which will allow guest a mixing and matching of main course with side dishes. Casual dress. **Hours:** 6 am-9 pm; to 10 pm seasonal. Closed: 12/25. **Address:** 2240 Airport Blvd **Location:** I-26, exit 113 (Airport Blvd), 0.5 mi sw. **Parking:** on-site. **Cards:** MC, VI.

CALL

LIZARD'S THICKET **Phone:** 803/794-0923

Regional American
$3-$12

Owned and operated by the same family since 1978, guests can enjoy Southern home cooking at breakfast, lunch, and dinner. Locals love the Calabash style shrimp as well as the fried chicken livers. Be sure and ask about the daily specials which will allow guest a mixing and matching of main course with side dishes. Casual dress. **Hours:** 6 am-9 pm; to 10 pm seasonal. **Address:** 2234 Sunset Blvd **Location:** I-26, exit 110 (US 378), 0.5 mi e. **Parking:** on-site. **Cards:** MC, VI.

CALL

NEW ORLEANS RIVERFRONT RESTAURANT **Phone:** 803/794-5112 20

American
$7-$33

Overlooking the Congaree River just outside downtown, the Cajun-inspired restaurant combines great views with a huge menu. As might be expected, steaks, seafood and jambalaya dominate the menu, but what's unexpected is the addition of the chef's own 22-spice Cajun seasoning, which adds zest to each dish without overwhelming the taste of the ingredients. Sunset dining is a treat. Casual dress. **Bar:** Full bar. **Hours:** 11 am-10 pm. Closed major holidays; also Sun. **Address:** 121 Alexander St **Location:** Just s of US 1; on west bank of Congaree River. **Parking:** on-site. **Cards:** AX, DC, DS, MC, VI.

WINNSBORO pop. 3,599

WHERE TO STAY

DAYS INN *Book at AAA.com* **Phone:** (803)635-1447

Motel
$55 All Year

Address: 1894 US Hwy 321 Bypass **Location:** I-77, exit 34 (SR 34), 6.5 mi w; jct US 321/SR 34/213. Located in a quiet rural area. **Facility:** 45 one-bedroom standard units. 2 stories (no elevator), exterior corridors. **Parking:** on-site. **Amenities:** hair dryers. **Pool(s):** outdoor. **Guest Services:** coin laundry, wireless Internet. **Business Services:** meeting rooms, fax (fee). **Cards:** AX, DC, DS, MC, VI.

ASK / SOME UNITS FEE

FAIRFIELD MOTEL **Phone:** (803)635-3458

Motel
$50-$65 All Year

Address: 56 US 321 Bypass S **Location:** Jct SR 213/US 321 Bypass S, 1.8 mi n. **Facility:** 60 units. 59 one-bedroom standard units. 1 one-bedroom suite. 1-2 stories (no elevator), exterior corridors. **Parking:** on-site. **Amenities:** voice mail, hair dryers. **Pool(s):** outdoor. **Business Services:** meeting rooms, fax (fee). **Cards:** AX, DS, MC, VI. **Free Special Amenities: expanded continental breakfast and high-speed Internet.**

/ SOME UNITS FEE

YEMASSEE pop. 807

WHERE TO STAY

BEST WESTERN POINT SOUTH

Phone: 843/726-8101

AAA SAVE

Motel

$70-$90 12/1-8/20
$60-$80 8/21-11/30

Address: 3536 Point South Dr **Location:** I-95, exit 33 (US17), just ne. **Facility:** 110 one-bedroom standard units, some with whirlpools. 2 stories (no elevator), exterior corridors. **Parking:** on-site. **Amenities:** irons, hair dryers. **Pool(s):** heated outdoor. **Guest Services:** coin laundry, wireless Internet. **Business Services:** PC, fax (fee). **Cards:** AX, CB, DC, DS, JC, MC, VI. **Free Special Amenities: local telephone calls and high-speed Internet.**
(See color ad below)

/ SOME UNITS FEE

AAA Benefit:
Members save up to 20%, plus 10% bonus points with rewards program.

HAMPTON INN POINT SOUTH/YEMASSEE

Book great rates at AAA.com

Phone: (843)726-9222

Hotel

$99 All Year

Address: 139 Frampton Dr **Location:** I-95, exit 33 (US 17), just ne, then n. **Facility:** 80 one-bedroom standard units. 4 stories, interior corridors. *Bath:* combo or shower only. **Parking:** on-site. **Terms:** 1-30 night minimum stay, cancellation fee imposed. **Amenities:** high-speed Internet, dual phone lines, voice mail, irons, hair dryers. **Pool(s):** outdoor. **Leisure Activities:** limited exercise equipment. **Guest Services:** valet and coin laundry, wireless Internet. **Business Services:** meeting rooms, business center. **Cards:** AX, CB, DC, DS, MC, VI.

CALL    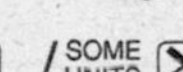 / SOME UNITS

AAA Benefit:
Members save up to 10% everyday!

HOLIDAY INN EXPRESS POINT SOUTH/YEMASSEE

Book at AAA.com

Phone: (843)726-9400

Hotel

$69-$139 All Year

Address: 138 Frampton Dr **Location:** I-95, exit 33 (US 17), just ne. **Facility:** 53 one-bedroom standard units. 2 stories (no elevator), interior corridors. *Bath:* combo or shower only. **Parking:** on-site. **Amenities:** high-speed Internet, voice mail, irons, hair dryers. **Pool(s):** outdoor. **Guest Services:** valet laundry, wireless Internet. **Business Services:** business center. **Cards:** AX, CB, DC, DS, JC, MC, VI.

ASK CALL / SOME UNITS FEE

Offices

Cities with main offices are listed in **BOLD TYPE** and toll-free member service numbers in *ITALIC TYPE.*
All are closed Saturdays, Sundays and holidays unless otherwise indicated.
The addresses, phone numbers and hours for any AAA/CAA office are subject to change.
The type of service provided is designated below the name of the city where the office is located:

- ✚ Auto travel services, including books and maps, and on-demand TripTik® routings.
- ● Auto travel services, including selected books and maps, and on-demand TripTik® routings.
- ■ Books/maps only, no marked maps or on-demand TripTik® routings.
- ▲ Travel Agency Services, cruise, tour, air, car and rail reservations; domestic and international hotel reservations; passport photo services; international and domestic travel guides and maps; travel money products; and International Driving Permits. In addition, assistance with travel related insurance products including trip cancellation, travel accident, lost luggage, trip delay and assistance products.
- ✪ Insurance services provided.
- ✖ Car Care Plus Facility provides car care services.

AAA NATIONAL OFFICE: 1000 AAA DRIVE, HEATHROW, FLORIDA 32746-5063, (407) 444-7000

GEORGIA

ATLANTA—AAA AUTO CLUB SOUTH, 4540B ROSWELL RD, 30342. MON/WED/FRI 8:30-5:30, TUE/THU 10:00-7:00. (404) 843-4500. ✚ ▲ ✪

AUGUSTA—AAA AUTO CLUB SOUTH, 3601 WALTON WAY EXT, 30909. MON/WED/FRI 8:30-5:30, TUE/THU 10:00-7:00. (706) 738-6611. ✚ ▲ ✪

COLUMBUS—AAA AUTO CLUB SOUTH, 2449 AIRPORT THRUWAY, 31904. MON/WED/FRI 8:30-5:30, TUE/THU 10:00-7:00. (706) 324-7121. ✚ ▲ ✪

MACON—AAA AUTO CLUB SOUTH, 175 TOM HILL SR BLVD #E, 31210. MON/WED/FRI 8:30-5:30, TUE/THU 10:00-7:00. (478) 471-0800. ✚ ▲ ✪

MARIETTA—AAA AUTO CLUB SOUTH, 4101 ROSWELL RD NE #301, 30062. MON/WED/FRI 8:30-5:30, TUE/THU 10:00-7:00. (770) 565-5700. ✚ ▲ ✪

MORROW—AAA AUTO CLUB SOUTH, 1500 MT ZION RD STE 205, 30260. MON/WED/FRI 8:30-5:30, TUE/THU 10:00-7:00. (770) 961-8085. ✚ ▲ ✪

NORCROSS—AAA AUTO CLUB SOUTH, 5450 PEACHTREE PKY STE 1F, 30092. MON/WED/FRI 8:30-5:30, TUE/THU 10:00-7:00. (770) 448-7024. ✚ ▲ ✪

SAVANNAH—AAA AUTO CLUB SOUTH, 712 MALL BLVD, 31406. MON/WED/FRI 8:30-5:30, TUE/THU 10:00-7:00. (912) 352-8222. ✚ ▲ ✪

TUCKER—AAA AUTO CLUB SOUTH, 2200 NORTHLAKE PKY #129, 30084. MON/WED/FRI 8:30-5:30, TUE/THU 10:00-7:00. (770) 939-7520. ✚ ▲ ✪

NORTH CAROLINA

ASHEVILLE—AAA CAROLINAS, 1000 MERRIMON AVE STE B, 28804. WEEKDAYS (M-F) 8:30-5:30, SAT 10:00-2:00. (828) 253-5376, *(800) 477-4222.* ✚ ▲ ✪

CHARLOTTE—AAA CAROLINAS, 6600 AAA DR, 28212. WEEKDAYS (M-F) 8:30-5:30. (704) 569-3600. ✚ ▲ ✪

CHARLOTTE—AAA CAROLINAS, 1408-A EAST BLVD, 28203. WEEKDAYS (M-F) 8:30-5:30, SAT 10:00-2:00. (704) 319-4222, *(800) 477-4222.* ✚ ▲ ✪

CHARLOTTE—AAA CAROLINAS, 8662 JW CLAY BLVD #3, 28262. WEEKDAYS (M-F) 8:30-5:30, SAT 10:00-2:00. (704) 548-1334, *(800) 477-4222.* ✚ ▲ ✪

DURHAM—AAA CAROLINAS, 3909 UNIVERSITY DR, 27707. WEEKDAYS (M-F) 8:30-5:30, SAT 10:00-2:00. (919) 489-3306, *(800) 477-4222.* ✚ ▲ ✪

FAYETTEVILLE—AAA CAROLINAS, 181 GLENSFORD DR, 28314. WEEKDAYS (M-F) 8:30-5:30, SAT 10:00-2:00. (910) 864-3115, *(800) 477-4222.* ✚ ▲ ✪

GASTONIA—AAA CAROLINAS, 3750 E FRANKLIN BLVD, 28056. WEEKDAYS (M-F) 8:30-5:30, SAT 10:00-2:00. (704) 824-2088, *(800) 477-4222.* ✚ ▲ ✪

GREENSBORO—AAA CAROLINAS, 306 PISGAH CHURCH RD, 27455. WEEKDAYS (M-F) 8:30-6:00, SAT 10:00-4:00. (336) 544-0841. ✚ ▲

GREENSBORO—AAA CAROLINAS, 5404 SAPP RD, 27409. WEEKDAYS (M-F) 8:30-6:00, SAT 10:00-4:00. (336) 852-0506, *(800) 477-4222.* ✚ ▲ ✪

HENDERSONVILLE—AAA CAROLINAS, 136 S KING ST STE D, 28792. WEEKDAYS (M-F) 8:30-5:30, SAT 10:00-2:00. (828) 697-8778, *(800) 477-4222.* ✚ ▲

MATTHEWS—AAA CAROLINAS, 9404 E INDEPENDENCE BLVD, 28106. WEEKDAYS (M-F) 7:30-6:00, SAT 8:00-4:00. (704) 815-0570. ✚ ▲ ✪

PINEVILLE—AAA CAROLINAS, 9433-A PINEVILLE MATTHEWS, 28134. WEEKDAYS (M-F) 8:30-5:30, SAT 10:00-2:00. (704) 541-7409, *(800) 477-4222.* ✚ ▲ ✪

RALEIGH—AAA CAROLINAS, 2301 BLUE RIDGE RD, 27607. WEEKDAYS (M-F) 8:30-5:30, SAT 10:00-2:00. (919) 832-0543, *(800) 477-4222.* ✚ ▲ ✪

ROCKY MOUNT—AAA CAROLINAS, 3607 SUNSET AVE, 27804. WEEKDAYS (M-F) 8:30-5:30, SAT 10:00-2:00. (252) 443-7117, *(800) 765-7117.* ✚ ▲ ✪

SOUTHERN PINES—AAA CAROLINAS, 171 BEVERLY LN, 28387. WEEKDAYS (M-F) 8:30-5:30, SAT 10:00-2:00. (910) 693-0335, *(800) 477-4222.* ✚ ▲ ✪

WILMINGTON—AAA CAROLINAS, 3501 OLEANDER DR #3, 28403. WEEKDAYS (M-F) 8:30-5:30, SAT 10:00-2:00. (910) 763-8446, *(800) 477-4222.* ✚ ▲ ✪

WINSTON-SALEM—AAA CAROLINAS, 606-A S STRATFORD RD, 27103. WEEKDAYS (M-F) 8:30-6:00, SAT 10:00-4:00. (336) 774-1200, *(800) 477-4222.* ✚ ▲ ✪

SOUTH CAROLINA

AIKEN—AAA CAROLINAS, 1543 WHISKEY RD, 29803. WEEKDAYS (M-F) 8:30-5:30, SAT 10:00-2:00. (803) 642-0142, *(800) 477-4222.* ✚ ▲ ✪

BLUFFTON—AAA CAROLINAS, 25 BLUFFTON RD STE 606, 29910. WEEKDAYS (M-F) 8:30-5:30, SAT 10:00-2:00. (843) 815-3775, *(800) 477-4222.* ✚ ▲ ✪

CHARLESTON—AAA CAROLINAS, 1975-K MAGWOOD RD, 29414. WEEKDAYS (M-F) 8:30-5:30, SAT 10:00-2:00. (843) 766-2394, *(800) 477-4222.* ✚ ▲ ✪

COLUMBIA—AAA CAROLINAS, 4558 FOREST DR, 29206. WEEKDAYS (M-F) 7:30-6:00, SAT 8:00-4:00. (803) 798-9205. ✚ ▲ ✪

COLUMBIA—AAA CAROLINAS, 130 FORUM DR STE 13, 29229. WEEKDAYS (M-F) 8:30-6:00, SAT 10:00-4:00. (803) 727-1520. ✚ ▲

COLUMBIA—AAA CAROLINAS, 810 DUTCH SQUARE BLVD, 29210. WEEKDAYS (M-F) 8:30-5:30, SAT 10:00-2:00. (803) 798-9205, *(800) 477-4222.* ✚ ▲

GREENVILLE—AAA CAROLINAS, 924 N PLEASANTBURG DR, 29607. WEEKDAYS (M-F) 8:30-6:00 (AUTO REPAIR HOURS 7:30-6:00), SAT 10:00-4:00 (AUTO REPAIR HOURS 8:00-4:00). (864) 404-4220, *(800) 477-4222.* ✚ ▲ ✪

GREENVILLE—AAA CAROLINAS, 2 TANNER RD, 29607. WEEKDAYS (M-F) 8:30-6:00, SAT 10:00-4:00. (864) 404-4240. ✚ ▲

IRMO—AAA CAROLINAS, 929 LAKE MURRAY BLVD, 29063. WEEKDAYS (M-F) 8:30-6:00, SAT 10:00-4:00. (803) 678-4000. ✚ ▲ ✪

MOUNT PLEASANT—AAA CAROLINAS, 320-A W COLEMAN BLVD, 29464. WEEKDAYS (M-F) 8:30-5:30, SAT 10:00-2:00. (843) 856-4607, *(800) 477-4222.* ✚ ▲ ✪

MYRTLE BEACH—AAA CAROLINAS, 3733 OLEANDER DR, 29577. WEEKDAYS (M-F) 8:30-5:30, SAT 10:00-2:00. (843) 692-9601, *(800) 477-4222.* ✚ ▲ ✪

Metric Equivalents Chart

TEMPERATURE

To convert Fahrenheit to Celsius, subtract 32 from the Fahrenheit temperature, multiply by 5 and divide by 9. To convert Celsius to Fahrenheit, multipy by 9, divide by 5 and add 32.

Celsius °		Fahrenheit °
100	**BOILING**	**212**
37		100
35		95
32		90
29		85
27		80
24		75
21		70
18		65
16		60
13		55
10		50
7		45
4		40
2		35
0	**FREEZING**	**32**
-4		25
-7		20
-9		15
-12		10
-15		5
-18		0
-21		-5
-24		-10
-27		-15

ACRES

1 acre = 0.4 hectare (ha)   1 hectare = 2.47 acres

MILES AND KILOMETRES

Note: A kilometre is approximately 5/8 or 0.6 of a mile.
To convert kilometres to miles multiply by 0.6.

Miles	Kilometres	Kilometres	Miles
15	24.1	30	18.6
20	32.2	35	21.7
25	40.2	40	24.8
30	48.3	45	27.9
35	56.3	50	31.0
40	64.4	55	34.1
45	72.4	60	37.2
50	80.5	65	40.3
55	88.5	70	43.4
60	96.6	75	46.6
65	104.6	80	49.7
70	112.7	85	52.8
75	120.7	90	55.9
80	128.7	95	59.0
85	136.8	100	62.1
90	144.8	105	65.2
95	152.9	110	68.3
100	160.9	115	71.4

LINEAR MEASURE

Customary	Metric
1 inch = 2.54 centimetres	1 centimetre = 0.4 inches
1 foot = 30 centimetres	1 metre = 3.3 feet
1 yard = 0.91 metres	1 metre = 1.09 yards
1 mile = 1.6 kilometres	1 kilometre = .62 miles

LIQUID MEASURE

Customary	Metric
1 fluid ounce = 30 millilitres	1 millilitre = .03 fluid ounces
1 cup = .24 litres	1 litre = 2.1 pints
1 pint = .47 litres	1 litre = 1.06 quarts
1 quart = .95 litres	1 litre = .26 gallons
1 gallon = 3.8 litres	

WEIGHT

If You Know:	Multiply By:	To Find:
Ounces	28.000	Grams
Pounds	0.450	Kilograms
Grams	0.035	Ounces
Kilograms	2.200	Pounds

PRESSURE

Air pressure in automobile tires is expressed in kilopascals. Multiply pound-force per square inch (psi) by 6.89 to find kilopascals (kPa).

24 psi = 165 kPa   28 psi = 193 kPa
26 psi = 179 kPa   30 psi = 207 kPa

GALLON AND LITRES

Gallons	Litres	Gallons	Litres	Litres	Gallons	Litres	Gallons
5	19.0	12	45.6	10	2.6	40	10.4
6	22.8	14	53.2	15	3.9	50	13.0
7	26.6	16	60.8	20	5.2	60	15.6
8	30.4	18	68.4	25	6.5	70	18.2
9	34.2	20	76.0	30	7.8	80	20.8
10	38.0	25	95.0	35	9.1	90	23.4

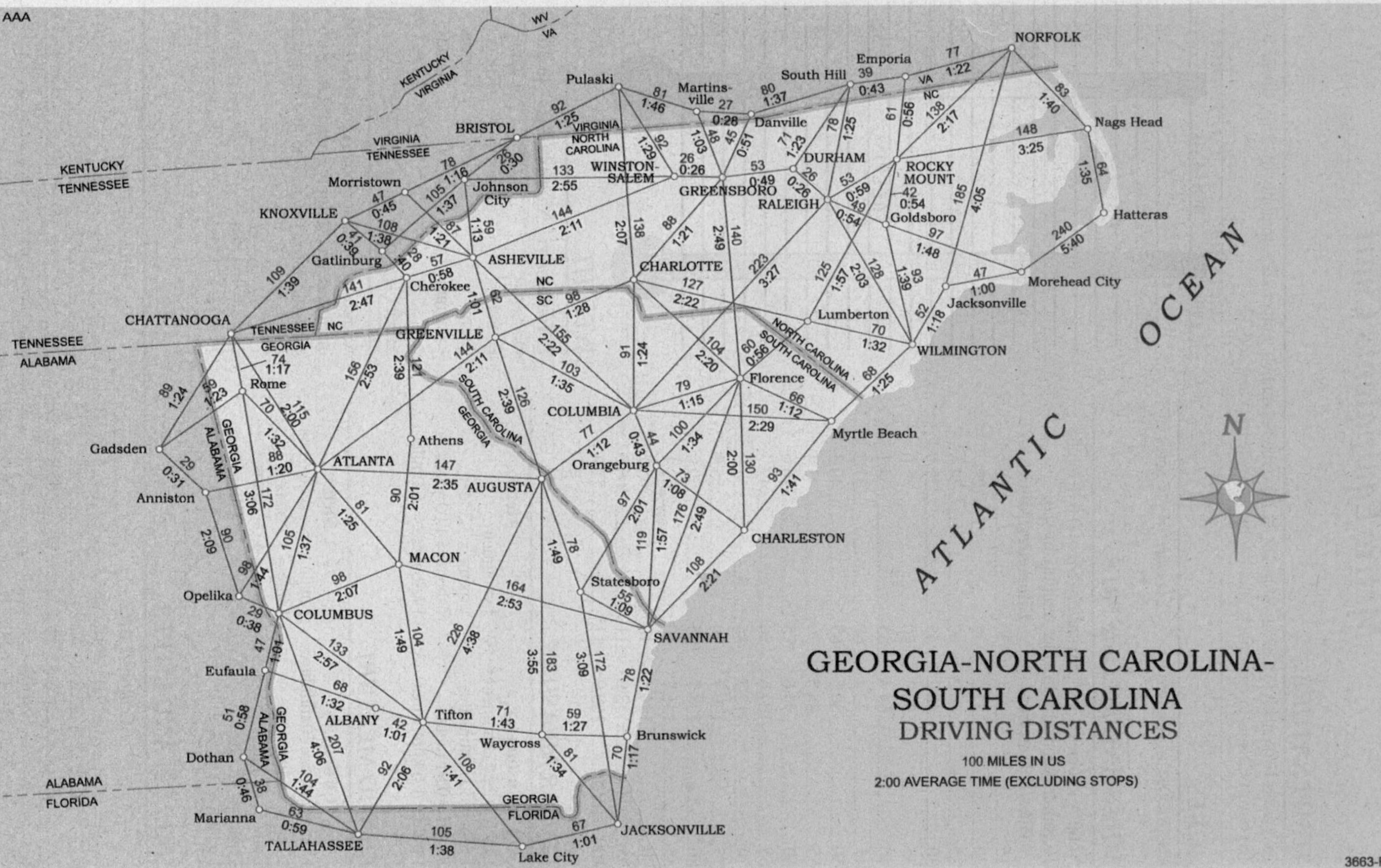

GEORGIA-NORTH CAROLINA-
SOUTH CAROLINA
DRIVING DISTANCES
100 MILES IN US
2:00 AVERAGE TIME (EXCLUDING STOPS)
ATLANTIC
OCEAN
N
NORFOLK
Nags Head
Hatteras
Morehead City
Jacksonville
WILMINGTON
ROCKY MOUNT
Goldsboro
Emporia
South Hill
DURHAM
RALEIGH
Lumberton
Myrtle Beach
Danville
Martins-ville
GREENSBORO
WINSTON-SALEM
CHARLOTTE
Florence
CHARLESTON
Pulaski
COLUMBIA
Orangeburg
SAVANNAH
Statesboro
Brunswick
JACKSONVILLE
BRISTOL
Johnson City
ASHEVILLE
GREENVILLE
AUGUSTA
Waycross
Lake City
Morristown
KNOXVILLE
Gatlinburg
Cherokee
Athens
ATLANTA
MACON
Tifton
ALBANY
TALLAHASSEE
COLUMBUS
Rome
CHATTANOOGA
Gadsden
Anniston
Opelika
Eufaula
Dothan
Marianna
NORTH CAROLINA
SOUTH CAROLINA
GEORGIA
ALABAMA
FLORIDA
VIRGINIA
TENNESSEE
KENTUCKY
WV
VA
NC
SC
© AAA
3663-F

Points of Interest Index

Index Legend

NB	national battlefield	NR	national river
NBP	national battlefield park	NS	national seashore
NC	national cemetery	NWR	national wildlife refuge
NF	national forest	PHP	provincial historic(al) park
NHM	national historic(al) monument	PHS	provincial historic(al) site
NHP	national historic(al) park	PP	provincial park
NHS	national historic(al) site	SF	state forest
NL	national lakeshore	SHM	state historic(al) monument
NME	national memorial	SHP	state historic(al) park
NMO	national monument	SHS	state historic(al) site
NMP	national military park	SME	state memorial
NP	national park	SP	state park
NRA	national recreation area	SRA	state recreation area

GEM: Points of Interest Offering a *Great Experience for Members*®

ARTS & CRAFTS

ATOMIC ENERGY INSTALLATIONS & NUCLEAR PLANTS

AUDITORIUMS

BATTLEFIELDS

BATTLE RE-ENACTMENTS

BEACHES

BIRTHPLACES & CHILDHOOD HOMES

BOARDWALKS

BRIDGES

BRIDGES, COVERED

BUILDINGS, MASONIC

BUILDINGS, OFFICE

BUILDINGS, PUBLIC; CAPITOL; CITY HALL

BUTTERFLY HOUSES

CANALS

CANYONS

CARILLONS

CAROUSELS

CAVE & ROCK DRAWINGS, PAINTING

CAVES

CEMETERIES

CHILDREN'S ATTRACTIONS

CHURCHES, CATHEDRALS & BASILICAS

EXHIBITS & COLLECTIONS-CLOCKS

EXHIBITS & COLLECTIONS-COINS

EXHIBITS & COLLECTIONS-DOLLS & TOYS

EXHIBITS & COLLECTIONS-HISTORICAL

EXHIBITS & COLLECTIONS-INDIAN

EXHIBITS & COLLECTIONS-MUSIC

EXHIBITS & COLLECTIONS-RELIGIOUS ITEMS

EXHIBITS & COLLECTIONS-REVOLUTIONARY WAR

EXHIBITS & COLLECTIONS-SCIENCE

EXHIBITS & COLLECTIONS-SPORTS

EXHIBITS & COLLECTIONS-VEHICLES

EXHIBITS & COLLECTIONS-WARS

EXHIBITS & COLLECTIONS-WEAPONS

FARMS

FERRY SERVICES—BOATS & AIRCRAFT

FISH HATCHERIES

FORESTS

FORESTS, NATIONAL; STATE

FORTS & MILITARY INSTALLATIONS

FOSSILS

FOUNTAINS

GAMBLING ESTABLISHMENTS

GAPS & PASSES

GARDENS

GENEALOGICAL INFORMATION

GEOLOGICAL FORMATIONS

GHOST TOWNS

GRAVES & TOMBS

HALLS OF FAME

HISTORIC BUILDINGS & HOUSES

HISTORIC DOCUMENTS, MANUSCRIPTS & RARE BOOKS

HISTORIC SITES

MUSIC HALLS & OPERA HOUSES

NATURAL PHENOMENA

NATURE CENTERS

NATURE TRAILS

OBSERVATORIES

PAINTINGS

PARKS, CITY; STATE; PROVINCIAL

PARKS, NATIONAL

PERFORMING ARTS ORGANIZATIONS

PLANETARIUMS

RACETRACKS-AUTO

RACETRACKS-HORSE

RADIO & TV STATIONS

RAILROADS

RAILROADS-LOCOMOTIVES & CARS

RAILROADS & SKI LIFTS, CABLE; COG; INCLINE; NARROW GAUGE

RANCHES

RECREATION-SUMMER ACTIVITIES

RECREATION-WINTER ACTIVITIES

RESEARCH ORGANIZATIONS

RESORTS

RESTORED VILLAGES & SETTLEMENTS

RIVERS

ROCKS

RUINS

SCENIC DRIVES

SCHOOL BUILDINGS

SCHOOLS

SCHOOLS-COLLEGES & UNIVERSITIES

SCHOOLS-INSTITUTES

SELF-GUIDING TOURS

SHIPS & BOATS

SHOPS, FIRMS & STORES

SIGHTSEEING-AIRCRAFT RIDES & TOURS

SIGHTSEEING TOURS

SIGHTSEEING TOURS-ARCHITECTURAL

SIGHTSEEING TOURS-BOATS

VIEWS

VISITOR CENTERS

VISITOR INFORMATION

WALKING TOURS

WATERFALLS

WATER PARKS

WILDERNESS AREAS

WILDLIFE SANCTUARIES

WINERIES

ZIPLINES

ZOOLOGICAL PARKS & EXHIBITS

ZOOLOGICAL PARKS & EXHIBITS-CHILDREN'S ZOOS

SAVE Attraction Admission Discount Index

GEORGIA

NORTH CAROLINA

SOUTH CAROLINA

Bed & Breakfast Lodgings Index

Some bed and breakfasts listed below might have historical significance.
Those properties are also referenced in the Historical index.

GEORGIA

ACCOMMODATIONS

NORTH CAROLINA

ACCOMMODATIONS

SOUTH CAROLINA

ACCOMMODATIONS

Country Inns Index

Some of the following country inns can also be considered as bed-and-breakfast operations.

GEORGIA

ACCOMMODATIONS

NORTH CAROLINA

ACCOMMODATIONS

SOUTH CAROLINA

ACCOMMODATIONS

Historical Lodgings & Restaurants Index

Some of the following historical lodgings can also be considered as bed-and-breakfast operations.

GEORGIA

ACCOMMODATIONS

RESTAURANTS

NORTH CAROLINA

ACCOMMODATIONS

RESTAURANTS

SOUTH CAROLINA

ACCOMMODATIONS

Historical Lodgings & Restaurants (cont'd)

RESTAURANTS

Resorts Index

Many establishments are located in resort areas; however, the following places have extensive on-premises recreational facilities:

GEORGIA

ACCOMMODATIONS

NORTH CAROLINA

ACCOMMODATIONS

SOUTH CAROLINA

ACCOMMODATIONS

Comprehensive City Index

Here is an alphabetical list of all cities appearing in this TourBook® guide. Cities are presented by state/province. Page numbers under the POI column indicate where points of interest text begins. Page numbers under the L&R column indicate where lodging and restaurant listings begin.

Comprehensive City Index (cont'd)

Comprehensive City Index (cont'd)

Comprehensive City Index (cont'd)